TENTH EDITION

SCHROEDER'S

ANTIQUES

PRICE GUIDE

Edited by Sharon & Bob Huxford

COLLECTOR BOOKS

A Division of Schroeder Publishing Co., Inc.

The current values in this book should be used only as a guide. They are not intended to set prices, which vary from one section of the country to another. Auction prices as well as dealer prices vary greatly and are affected by condition as well as demand. Neither the Editors nor the Publisher assumes responsibility for any losses that might be incurred as a result of consulting this guide.

On the cover, clockwise from left:

Marble top commode washstand, 30"w, 20" deep, 3-pc. walnut bedroom set including bedstead, dressing case and washstand, $7,500.00. Courtesy of *Collector's Encyclopedia of American Furniture, Volume I* by Robert W. & Harriet Swedberg.

1908 Coca-Cola™ Calendar, $950.00. Courtesy of *Goldstein's Coca-Cola™ Collectibles*.

Covered jug, Imperial Hunt Scene, $200.00-250.00. Photo courtesy of Gene Florence.

Condiment set, solid hand applied gold with elaborate heavy enamelled blue flowers, shakers 3⅜", $375.00-400.00. Courtesy of *The World of Salt Shakers, 2nd Edition* by Mildred & Ralph Lechner.

Dopey and Happy Bookends, $110.00. Courtesy of *Stern's Guide to Disney Collectibles* by Michael Stern.

Introduction

It's been ten years since the first edition of *Schroeder's* was published. As its editors and staff, our steadfast goal has been to compile the most useful, comprehensive, and accurate background and pricing information possible. In order to realize our goal, we have been assisted by many top authors, appraisers, researchers, national collectors' clubs, dealers, and other authorities. We constantly try to enlarge our advisory board, until over the years we have more than doubled its original size — this year more than three hundred people have worked with us on more than seven hundred categories, carefully editing the printouts we compile from auction results, trade paper ads, dealer lists, etc. At our request they go over our listings line by line, deleting those that are misleading or too vague to be of merit; they often send background information and photos. We appreciate their assistance very much — only through their expertise and experience in their special fields are we able to offer with confidence what we feel are useful, accurate evaluations that provide a sound understanding of the dealings in the market place today. Correspondence with so large an advisory panel adds months of extra work to an already monumental task, but we feel that to a very large extent this is the foundation that makes *Schroeder's* the success that it has become.

Our Directory, which you will find in the back of the book, lists each contributor by state. These are people who have allowed us to photograph various examples of merchandise from their show booths, sent us pricing information, or in any way have contributed to this year's book. Feel free to contact them; many will be glad to ship you the merchandise you need. If you happen to be traveling, consult the Directory for shops along your way. We also list clubs who have worked with us and auction houses who have agreed to permit us the use of photographs from their catalogs. Our Advisory Board lists only names and home states, so check the Directory for addresses and telephone numbers should you want to correspond with one of our experts. Remember that when you do, if you expect an answer from either an advisor or a contributor, please send a SASE (stamped, self-addressed envelope).

To be used to your best advantage, this guide should be regarded as a basic tool, a rule of thumb, only one source of the information you need to digest in order to become a knowledgeable dealer or collector. Antique shows, trade papers, collectors' books, and association with others sharing the same interests all contribute toward making you more keenly aware of market trends and thus educate you toward becoming a wise and confident buyer.

We have organized our topics alphabetically, following the most simple logic, usually either by manufacturer or by type of product. If you have difficulty in locating your subject, consult the index. Our guide is unique in that much more space has been allotted to background information than any other publication of this type, and it is easier to read due to the larger-than-average print. Our readers tell us that these are features they enjoy. To be able to do this, we have adopted a format of one-line listings wherein we describe the items to the fullest extent possible by using several common-sense abbreviations; they will be easy to read and understand if you will first take the time to quickly scan through them.

The Editors

Listing of Standard Abbreviations

The following is a list of abbreviations that have been used throughout this book in order to provide you with the most detailed descriptions possible in the limited space available. No periods are used after initials or abbreviations. When two dimensions are given, height is noted first. If only one dimension is listed, it will be height, except in the case of bowls, dishes, plates, or platters, when it will be diameter. The standard two-letter state abbreviations apply.

For glassware, if no color is noted, the glass is clear. Hyphenated colors, for example blue-green, olive-amber, etc., describe a single color tone; colors divided by a slash mark indicate two or more colors, i.e. blue/white. A number following the last comma in a listing indicates how many items are included in the lot price. Teapots, sugar bowls, and butter dishes are assumed to be 'with cover.' Condition is extremely important in determining market value. This year, in order to conserve space, the condition line has been left out of the narrative, except when our advisors requested that it remain, or when the category contained items of such a varied nature that we felt it advantageous to leave the line in to avoid confusion. Common sense suggests that art pottery, china, and glassware values would be given for examples in pristine, mint condition, while suggested prices for utility wares such as Redware, Mocha, and Blue and White Stoneware, for example, reflect the probability that since such items were subjected to everyday use in the home they may show minor wear (which is acceptable) but no notable damage. Values for other categories reflect the best average condition in which the particular collectible is apt to be offered for sale without the dealer feeling it necessary to mention wear or damage. For instance, advertising items are assumed to be in excellent condition since mint items are scarce enough that when one is offered for sale the dealer will most likely make mention of that fact. The same holds true for Toys, Banks, Coin-Operated Machines, and the like. Paper ephemera is evaluated as if in very good to excellent condition unless otherwise noted. A basic rule of thumb is that an item listed as VG (very good) will bring 40% to 60% of its mint price (a first-hand, personal evaluation will enable you to make the final judgment); EX (excellent) is a condition midway between mint and very good, and values would correspond.

Am .... American	drw .... drawer	mahog .... mahogany	rpr .... repaired
appl .... applied	ea .... each	mk .... mark	rpl .... replaced
att .... attributed to	emb .... embossed, embossing	MIG .... Made in Germany	rstr .... restored
bk .... back	embr .... embroidered	M .... mint	rtcl .... reticulated
bsk .... bisque	eng .... engraved, engraving	MIB .... mint in box	rvpt .... reverse painted
b3m .... blown 3-mold	EX .... excellent	MOP .... mother-of-pearl	rnd .... rnd
bl .... blue	ext .... exterior	mt, mtd .... mount, mounted	s&p .... salt and pepper
brn .... brown	ft, ftd .... foot, feet, footed	mc .... multicolor	sgn .... signed
bulb .... bulbous	fr .... frame, framed	NE .... New England	SP .... silverplated
cb .... cardboard	Fr .... French	NM .... near mint	sz .... size
CI .... cast iron	G .... good	NP .... nickel plated	sm .... small
C .... century	grad .... graduated	opal .... opalescent	sq .... square
ca .... circa	grpt .... grain painted	orig .... original	std .... standard
compo .... composition	gr .... green	o/l .... overlay	str .... straight
c .... copyright	HP .... hand painted	o/w .... otherwise	trn .... turned, turning
cr/sug .... creamer and sugar	hdl, hdld .... handle, handled	pnt .... paint	turq .... turquoise
X, Xd .... cross, crossed	imp .... impressed	pr .... pair	uphl .... upholstered
c/s .... cup and saucer	ind .... individual	Pat .... patented	VG .... very good
cvd .... carved	int .... interior	ped .... pedestal	Vict .... Victorian
cvg .... carving	irid .... iridescent	pc .... piece	wht .... white
dk .... dark	Invt T'print .... Inverted Thumbprint	pk .... pink	W .... width
dtd .... dated	lg .... large	pt .... pint	w/ .... with
decor .... decoration	lav .... lavender	prof .... professional	w/o .... without
dia .... diameter	ldgl .... leaded glass	porc .... porcelain	yel .... yellow
Dia Quilt .... Diamond Quilted	L .... length	rfn .... refinished	
dbl .... double	lt .... light	re .... regarding	
dvtl .... dovetail	litho .... lithograph	rpt .... repainted	

A B C Plates

Children's plates featuring the alphabet as part of the design were popular from as early as 1820 until after the turn of the century. The earliest English creamware plates were decorated with embossed letters and prim moralistic verses; but the later Staffordshire products were conducive to a more relaxed mealtime atmosphere — often depicting playful animals and riddles or scenes of pleasant leisure-time activities. They were made around the turn of the century by American potters as well. All featured transfer prints, but color was sometimes brushed on by hand to add interest to the design. Braille plates were made for the blind, but these are rather scarce and therefore usually more valuable. You may also find an occasional bowl or mug.

Ceramic

Am Sports, Baseball, Caught on the Fly, brn transfer, 7" 250.00
Baker, worker places loaves in brick oven, Staffordshire, 7" 135.00
Blinn Girl, mc, English, 6" 95.00
Blk men raise glasses, Rule of Three, Staffordshire, 8" 195.00
Bowl, girl & boy play doctor, ABCs at scalloped rim, 8½" 70.00
Boy Scouts (ca WWI) in woods 125.00
Boys & banjos, bl transfer, England..95.00
Conundrum (or riddle), Blks fishing, answer on bk, mc, 6⅛" 295.00
Daniel in Lion's Den, mc transfer 165.00
Deaf & Dumb (sign language), pk Dutch children transfer, 6¼" .195.00
Elephant, fishing, Staffordshire..120.00
F Is for Frank Who a Sailor Would Be, Staffordshire, 7¾" 175.00
Flowers That Never Fade..., Staffordshire, 7", EX 130.00
General McClellan, bl transfer, 7", EX 225.00
It Is Hard for...Bag To Stand Upright, Staffordshire, 7" 135.00

Man and child on donkey, no mark, 7½", $125.00.

Miss Muffet, bl transfer, England 75.00
Mug, Nightingale transfer 175.00
Nations of the World, polychrome, Brownhill Pottery, 6½" 175.00
Niagara From Edge of American Falls, Staffordshire, 7¼" 145.00
Now I Have a Cow, Franklin Maxim, 5⅛" 175.00
Seal hunters, Elsmore, 7" 150.00
Sioux Indian Chief, brn transfer, Allerton, England, 6¾" 120.00
View of Quebec & Boston State House, sepia transfer/mc, 7¾" ..275.00

Why Is This...Fishing?, Blks in boat, Staffordshire, 6⅛" 165.00
Wm Penn (portrait), sepia transfer, Staffordshire, 7¾" 275.00

Glass

ABC rim, souvenir Greenville OH, milk glass 125.00
Clock, ABC rim, 7" 95.00
Garfield, ABC rim 95.00
Mug, twig hdl 75.00
Quilted center, ABCs & numbers on stippled ground 95.00
Stork, clear/frosted, ABC rim, 6" 95.00

Tin

Girl on swing, 6¼" 65.00
Hey Diddle Diddle, 8" 55.00
Jumbo, elephant emb in center, 6¼" 110.00
Mary Had a Little Lamb, 8" 125.00
Washington, bust in center, 5⅝" 195.00
Who Killed Cock Robin?, 8" 85.00

Abingdon

From 1934 until 1950, the Abingdon Pottery Co. of Abingdon, Ill., made a line of art pottery with a white vitrified body decorated with various types of glazes in many lovely colors. Novelties, cookie jars, utility ware, and lamps were made in addition to several lines of simple yet striking art ware. Fern Leaf, introduced in 1937, featured molded vertical feathering. La Fleur, in 1939, consisted of flowerpots and flower-arranger bowls with rows of vertical ribbing. Classic, 1939-40, was a line of vases, many with evidence of Chinese influence. Several marks were used, most of which employed the company name. In 1950 the company reverted to the manufacture of sanitary ware that had been their mainstay before the Art Ware Division was formed.

Highly decorated examples and those with black, bronze, or red glaze usually command at least 25% higher prices.

Chess piece, bronze, black, 5", $235.00.

#109, vase, Alpha, wht matt, 5" 18.00
#110, vase, Beta, lt bl, 6" 30.00

#126, candlestick, Classic, wht, pr 32.00
#142, vase, Classic, bl, mini, 5" 28.00
#266D, vase, pk, scalloped, decor, 8" 35.00
#302L, lamp base, Lunge, wht, brass fittings......................175.00
#305, bookend, sea gull, pk, pr 50.00
#310, vase, Chang, copper brn, 1934-36, rare.....................275.00
#312, vase, Han, ftd, Regency gr, older style 40.00
#314, vase, Swedish, lt gr, 1934-36, 8".............................135.00
#315, vase, Athenia Classic, wht, 1934-36, 9"......................32.00
#375, wall pocket, dbl morning-glory, deep red....................55.00
#375, wall pocket, dbl morning-glory, wht 40.00
#377, wall pocket, morning-glory, pk, 1937-50 ....15.00
#383, bowl, sunflower, turq matt, 1936-38, 9½" 75.00
#3905b, chessman, bishop, bronze/blk, 1937, rare 235.00
#3906, shepherdess & fawn, yel w/gold traces......................95.00
#395, flower ring, wht, 2-pc, 1936-38, 11½" dia 75.00
#402, vase, box form, wht, 1937-38, 5½" 65.00
#412, vase, Volute, wht, 1937-40, lg 125.00
#416, peacock, turq gloss 40.00
#416, peacock, wht, 1937-38 & 1942 ....35.00
#427, bud vase, Fern Leaf, lt gr, 1937-38, 5½" 70.00
#432, bowl, Fern Leaf, red matt, 15" 40.00
#441, bookend, horse head, wht, pr 50.00
#442, vase, Laurel, red, 1938-39, 5½" 45.00
#442, vase, Laurel, turq matt, 1938-39, 5½" 33.00
#468, vase, sea gull, decor, wht & bl, 1946-47 ....35.00
#483D, bud vase, Petit, decor 30.00
#487, floor vase, egret, chartreuse 85.00
#488, ash tray, box form, turq, 1936-38 ....42.00
#491, vase, wht, fan form w/built-in flower holder, 5x7"......22.00
#492, vase, bowl form, gr, 1940, sm 20.00
#493, wall pocket, dbl, turq, 1940, 8" 65.00
#496, vase, hollyhock, decor, 1940 & 1946-47 ....36.00
#504, vase/planter, shell, wht, 7"...15.00
#509, ash tray, elephant, wht, scarce 95.00
#510, ash tray, donkey, blk, scarce 95.00
#511, vase, Ionic, wht, bowl form 25.00
#517, vase, Arden, gr, 1940-50 ....20.00
#527, bowl, hibiscus, pk, 1941-48, sm 28.00
#528, bowl, hibiscus, yel, 1941-49, lg 45.00
#565, cornucopia, blk, 1942-47 ....25.00
#568, compote, pk, ftd, 1942-47...24.00
#569, cornucopia, bl 20.00
#569, cornucopia, decor...25.00
#571, goose, wht 25.00
#572D, pelican, decor, scarce 40.00
#587, wall shelf, cherub face, yel, 8x4x4½".........................30.00
#593D, cache pot, bl, decor 25.00
#604D, vase, tulip, wht, decor...48.00
#648, wall pocket, acanthus, wht, rare 55.00
#660, ash tray, leaf, blk & yel, 5" dia...................................35.00
#661, swan, chartreuse 35.00
#666, jam jar, cherry top, bl 9.00
#698, vase, Chinese Terrace, yel, 6" 25.00
#705, vase, Modern, bl gloss 25.00
#711, wall pocket, carriage, chartreuse.................................35.00
Cookie jar, #471, Old Lady, Blk, decor................................190.00
Cookie jar, #471, Old Lady, decor 100.00
Cookie jar, #471, Old Lady, no decor 70.00
Cookie jar, #495, Fat Boy, beige..90.00
Cookie jar, #549, Hippo, no decor, 8" 80.00
Cookie jar, #561, Baby 110.00
Cookie jar, #588, Money Sack 50.00
Cookie jar, #6021, Hobby Horse...100.00

Cookie jar, Little Miss Muffett, #662, $115.00.

Cookie jar, #611, Jack-in-the-Box, 11"................................130.00
Cookie jar, #651, Locomotive 70.00
Cookie jar, #653, Clock...60.00
Cookie jar, #662, Little Miss Muffet 115.00
Cookie jar, #663, Humpty Dumpty, decor.............................120.00
Cookie jar, #664, Pineapple, decor...45.00
Cookie jar, #665, Wigwam 200.00
Cookie jar, #674, Pumpkin 140.00
Cookie jar, #677D, Daisy..42.00
Cookie jar, #678, Windmill...100.00
Cookie jar, #692, Witch 150.00
Cookie jar, #693, Little Girl 52.00
Cookie jar, #694, Little Bo Peep 130.00
Cookie jar, #695, Mother Goose, bl ruffles, goose by side ...175.00
Cookie jar, #696, Three Bears 55.00
Vase, what not (A); bl & wht, sm hdl, 3½" 75.00
Vase, what not (B); bl & wht, hdld, rare 85.00
Vase, what not (C); wht, medallion in center, 4½"................85.00

Adams

    Wm. Adams, whose potting skills were developed under the tutelage of Josiah Wedgwood, founded the Greengates Pottery at Tunstall, England, in 1769. Many types of wares including basalt, ironstone, parian, and jasper were produced; and various impressed or printed marks were employed. Until 1800 'Adams Co.' or 'Adams' impressed in block letters identified the company's earthenwares and a fine type of jasper similar in color and decoration to Wedgwood's. The latter mark was used again from 1845 to 1864 on parian figures. Most examples of their product found on today's market are transfer-printed dinnerwares with ornate backstamps which often include the pattern name and the initials 'W.A. & S.' This type of product was made from 1820 until about 1920. After 1890 the word 'England' was included in the mark; 'Tunstall' was added after 1896. From 1914 through 1940, a printed crown with 'Adams, Estbd 1657, England' identified their products. From 1900 to 1965, they produced souvenir plates with transfers of American scenes, many of which were marketed in this country by Roth Importers of Peoria, Illinois. In 1965 the company affiliated with Wedgwood. Although there were other Adams potteries in Staffordshire, their marks incorporate either the first name initial or a partner's name and so are easily distinguished from those of this company. See also Spatter; Staffordshire; Adam's Rose.

Bowl, Cries of London, Dr. Syntax Reading His Tour, 9", $50.00.

Bowl, Dr Syntax Stopt by Highwaymen, 10¼" 65.00
Bowl, vegetable; Columbus Discovers Am, gr transfer, 11" L 150.00
Butter chip, Cries of London 18.00
Candlestick, Cries of London, 3½", pr 70.00
Cup & saucer, cottage w/3 people, dk bl transfer, NM................170.00
Cup & saucer, handleless; stick spatter w/gaudy floral, EX............45.00
Cup plate, group of sheep, dk bl transfer, 3⅞", NM 275.00
Jug, drunken Silenus, boys w/goat, wht stoneware, 9½" 350.00
Jug, 4 panels (Seasons), jasper, bl/wht, metal lid, 10"..................450.00
Muffineer, Jasper, bl 195.00
Plate, Andalusia, man & lady on horses, pk transfer, 8"..............35.00
Plate, Columbia, red transfer, mk, 10¾" 30.00
Plate, Currier & Ives, Husking, 10½"....................................25.00
Plate, fishing/cottage scene, dk bl transfer, 7¾" 65.00
Plate, My Old KY Home, dk bl transfer 35.00
Plate, Seasons (Winter), pk transfer, 9½" 55.00
Platter, bl feather edge, 15", EX 75.00
Platter, 2 stags/3 does, bl transfer, 1850s, 16" 275.00
Soup plate, fishing/cottage scene, dk bl transfer, 10", NM 75.00
Urn, cobalt w/wht coat of arms, miniature, 2½" 75.00
Vase, Cupid/Venus/Apollo, jasper, bl/wht, hdls, 9"....................225.00

Adams Rose, Early and Late

In the second quarter of the nineteenth century, the Adams and Son Pottery produced a line of hand-painted dinnerware decorated in large, red brush-stroke roses with green leaves on whiteware, which collectors call Adams' Rose. Later, G. Jones and Son (and possibly others) made a similar ware with less brilliant colors on a gray-white surface.

Bowl, early, rare sz, 9", M 750.00
Bowl, vegetable; late, 10¾", M 125.00
Creamer, early, 5¾", M 285.00
Pitcher, early, stains/minor flakes, 7" 205.00
Pitcher, late, 6¾", M 175.00
Plate, early, emb scalloped rim, 10½", NM................................125.00
Plate, early, 9", M 190.00
Plate, late, 8¾", EX..110.00
Plate, late, 9½", EX..110.00
Platter, late, 12", EX..125.00

Soup plate, early, wear/minor stains/glaze flakes, 9" 80.00
Sugar bowl, w/lid, early, M...350.00
Sugar bowl, w/lid, late, M..175.00
Tea bowl & saucer, early, M...195.00
Tea bowl & saucer, late, M..125.00
Teapot, early, dome lid, rpr, 11½" 750.00
Teapot, late, M 300.00

Advertising

The advertising world has always been a fiercely competitive field. In an effort to present their product to the customer, every imaginable gimmick was put into play. Colorful and artfully decorated signs and posters, thermometers, tape measures, fans, hand mirrors, and attractive tin containers — all with catchy slogans, familiar logos, and often-bogus claims — are only a few of the many examples of early advertising memorabilia that are of interest to today's collectors.

Porcelain signs were made as early as 1890 and are highly prized for their artistic portrayal of life as it was then . . . often allowing amusing insights into the tastes, humor, and way of life of a bygone era. As a general rule, older signs are made from a heavier gauge metal. Those with three or more fired-on colors are especially desirable.

Tin containers were used to package consumer goods ranging from crackers and coffee to tobacco and talcum. After 1880 can companies began to decorate their containers by the method of lithography. Though colors were still subdued, intricate designs were used to attract the eye of the consumer. False labeling and unfounded claims were curtailed by the Pure Food and Drug Administration in 1906, and the name of the manufacturer as well as the brand name of the product had to be printed on the label. By 1910 color was rampant with more than a dozen hues printed on the tin or on paper labels. The tins themselves were often designed with a second use in mind — as canisters, lunch boxes, even toy trains. As a general rule, tobacco-related tins are the most desirable, though personal preference may direct the interest of the collector to peanut butter pails with illustrations of children, or talcum tins with irresistible babies or beautiful ladies. Coffee tins are popular, as are those made to contain a particularly successful or well-known product.

Perhaps the most visual of the early advertising gimmicks were the character logos — the Fairbank Company's Gold Dust Twins, the goose trademark of the Red Goose Shoe Company, Nabisco's ZuZu Clown and Uneeda Kid, the Campbell Kids, the RCA dog Nipper, and Mr. Peanut, to name only a few. Any example of these brings high prices on the market today.

Our listings are alphabetized by company name or, in lieu of that information, by word content or other pertinent description. When no condition is indicated, the items listed below are assumed to be in excellent condition, except glass and ceramic items, which are assumed mint. Remember that condition greatly effects value. For instance, a sign in excellent or mint condition may bring twice as much as the same one in only very good condition.

We have several advertising advisors; Allen Smith specializes in Buster Brown, Pepsi-Cola, Planters Peanuts, and Red Goose Shoes. He is listed in the Directory under Texas. Our Dr. Pepper advisor is Bill Rickets, listed under North Carolina. Nearly all of the remaining topics and the general listings are under the advisement of Dennis O'Brien and George Goehring of Dennis and George Collectibles; they are listed in the Directory under Maryland.

See also Advertising Dolls; Advertising Cards; Coca-Cola; Banks; Calendars; Cookbooks; Paperweights; Posters; Sewing Items.

Key:
cb — cardboard   ps — porcelain sign

cl — celluloid
lcs — litho on canvas
pp — pre-prohibition

sf — self-framed
tc — tin container
ts — tin sign

ABC Beer, die-cut tin sign, eagle/cherubs, 13½x9½", EX........ **2,000.00**
ABC Bohemian Beer, cl sign w/metal corners, 6½x9", EX **210.00**
AC Huff Organs & Pianos, tip tray, elk, 4¼", EX.............................**25.00**
Adam's Yel Kid Chewing Gum, gum card, 1896, NM...................**88.00**
Adams Honey Chewing Gum, tc, peacocks, flat, 1x9x5½", G.......**50.00**
Adams Pepsin Gum, tin display, 1920s, 3½x16x12" **400.00**
Adams Pure Chewing Gum, glass jar, ca 1915-20, 12", NM **160.00**
Adams Tutti-Frutti Gum, cb display, 10x5x1¼", EX.....................**100.00**
Admiration Cigars, felt banner, moon-man smokes, 12x19", EX...**75.00**
Admiration Cigars, glass change tray, lady, oval, 6x7", EX **55.00**

Admiration Cigars, tin sign, easel back, 20", $895.00.

Akro Agates, cb sign, children playing marbles, 15x13", NM **800.00**
Akron Sewer Pipes, letter folder, tin litho, 1890s, 12", VG **275.00**
All Nations Tobacco, display bin, tin, hinged, 8x11x7½", EX **250.00**
Allyn & Blanchard, match holder, tin litho diecut, 7x4", EX **150.00**
Alta Ginger Ale, sf ts, Queen of Mineral..., 20x14", NM **2,100.00**
Amaco, porc sign, Authorized...Station, 2-sided, 17x20", VG.....**375.00**
Amazon Insurance, letter folder, tin litho, 1890s, 12x3", VG......**150.00**
American Eagle Tobacco, cb fan, bucket shape, EX....................**125.00**
American Express, tin sign, ca 1913, 27x19½", EX **400.00**
American Express, 2-sided porc sign, 1910, 13x17", VG **165.00**
American Family Soap, cb sign, red, 32x24" **550.00**
American Family Soap, die-cut ts, eagle/soap, 20x19", EX....... **5,500.00**
Anheuser-Busch, knife, German silver hdl, 3", VG......................**60.00**
Anheuser-Busch, tin tray, factory, oval, 15½x18½", EX **350.00**
Anheuser-Busch Budweiser, sf ts, girl, 1905-10, 38x26", VG.......**550.00**
Arden Hard Candies, tc, Christmas scene, 5-lb, EX **25.00**
Artie Cigars, ts, Artie atop bridge, 1905-10, 10x14", EX **450.00**
Atkins Silver Steel Saw, ts, saw, 1900s, 8½x18", EX...................**200.00**
Austin's Gun Powder, ts, orig marbleized fr, 12x24", VG........ **1,000.00**
Ayer's Hair Vigor, ts, girl w/bottle, 1880s, 16x12", EX **2,200.00**
Ayer's Sarsaparilla, ts, nurse scene, 1880s, 20x14", NM **10,500.00**
Bagley's Mayflower Tobacco, ledger marker, 1920s, 12", EX .. **1,000.00**
Bagley's Old Colony Mixture, pocket tin, lady, 4½x3x1", EX **150.00**
Bagley's Old Colony Mixture, pocket tin, sample sz.....................**200.00**
Baker's Extract, oak case, glass front, 24x24x15", NM **650.00**
Baldwin Dry Air Refrigerator, ts, animals, 1885, 3x10", VG **425.00**
Ballard's Obelisk Flour, pocket mirror, Egyptian scenes, 1¾" **25.00**
Baltimore Dairy Lunch, mug, JA Whitcomb, 3¼", VG.................**55.00**
Bambino Tobacco, pocket tin, Babe Ruth, rare **1,500.00**

Bardahl Oil, tin dispenser, hanging, 12x3", VG **22.00**
Bartel's Beer, sf ts, mug/meal/man, 1905-10, 24x20", EX **450.00**
Bartholomay Brewery, tin sign, elegant lady, 20x16", EX........ **1,400.00**
Batchelor Bros Cigars, tin sign, bumble bee, 28x20", EX **85.00**
Batchelor's Bigger Peas, tin can display, '20s, 14", EX **80.00**
Bayonne Motors, key chain, w/tube to hold license, 1940s **16.00**
Beech-Nut Chewing Gum, display box, tin litho, 14", NM.........**300.00**
Beech-Nut Gum, display rack **300.00**
Beech-Nut Mints, tin display box, 9½x8½", EX..........................**150.00**
Benedict English Peas, tin can display, '20s, 14x8½", EX **100.00**
Bernard Fischer Whiskey, tin tray, Shonk, 1910s, 12", EX **200.00**
Betsy Ross Bread, stick fan, boy eating, mc, EX **25.00**
Better Yet Peanuts, tc, Blk boys w/peanuts, 5-lb, NM **800.00**
BF Gravely Tobacco, pocket tin, upright, rare **1,200.00**
BF Gravely's Cut Plug, tc, man smoking pipe, 4½x3½", VG **30.00**
Bigger Hair Tobacco, cb canister, Blk lady, 1-lb, EX...................**115.00**
Binghamton Ice Cream, tray, tin litho, 16x13", NM **800.00**

Biscuit Tins

Golf bag, McCormick's Biscuits, London and Canada, 8", $1,200.00.

Gray Dunn & Co, Concertina, 1903 ....**185.00**
Huntley & Palmer, Arabian, natives on side & bottom...............**185.00**
Huntley & Palmer, athletes running/etc, triangular, 1892 ....**225.00**
Huntley & Palmer, Book, 1930..**100.00**
Huntley & Palmer, Bookstand, dtd 1905 ....**150.00**
Huntley & Palmer, Chinese Vase, 1928 ....**50.00**
Huntley & Palmer, florals w/gold on red, 1½x7x10" **145.00**
Huntley & Palmer, Geo V & Mary, Silver Jubilee 1935 ....**235.00**
Huntley & Palmer, golf scene on lid, Paris Exposition **95.00**
Huntley & Palmer, Inkstand, w/porc inkwell, 1928 ....**185.00**
Huntley & Palmer, Locket, 1912 ....**150.00**
Huntley & Palmer, marble pillar form, VG **225.00**
Huntley & Palmer, Nanking bls/wht/blk, 7", NM **85.00**
Huntley & Palmer, Nautical, Xmas tin, 1895.............................**225.00**

Huntley & Palmer, Olympian, Greek & Roman figures, 1892.....**145.00**
Huntley & Palmer, Princess Mary, emb brass, Xmas 1914, sm **60.00**
Huntley & Palmer, Queen Victoria, military heroes **65.00**
Huntley & Palmer, Queen Victoria's Golden Jubilee, 1887.........**165.00**
Huntley & Palmer, Robinson Crusoe, ca 1890............................**100.00**
Huntley & Palmer, Seaside, children at beach, 1890 ....**45.00**
Huntley & Palmer, twilight nature scene......................................**45.00**
McFarlane, Lang, & Co, Trunk, 1913...**50.00**
McFarlane, Lang, & Co, Yule Log, w/hatchet hdl, 1910.............**135.00**
Preek, Frean, & Co, Castle, 1923...**160.00**
W&R Jacobs & Co, Coronation Coach, w/orig box, 1936 ....**250.00**
W&R Jacobs & Co, Houseboat, Waterwitch, ca 1923.................**300.00**
Wm Crawford & Sons, Globe, 1938 ....**50.00**

Black Label Whiskey, tin on cb sign, mc on blk, 19x13", VG **250.00**
Blackhawks Blood & Body Tonic, tc, paper label, 4½x2", EX **28.00**
Bliss Native Herbs, match holder, tin litho, Capital bldg, EX **175.00**
Blue Ribbon, blotter, 3½x5", NM **5.00**
Bluebird Ice Cream, 2-sided porc sign, 1915, 28x20", EX........ **2,800.00**
Bluebird Marshmallows, tc, campfire, 3-sided, 6½x8", EX **90.00**
Bohemian Brewing, tip tray, lady w/glass, 4½" **200.00**
Bohemian Brewing, tray, lady w/glass, 13" dia, G........................**150.00**
Boone Cola, cb sign, Daniel Boone on bottle, 15x5", EX.............**35.00**
Borden's, Elsie motorized figure, rubber, 37x22x27", EX..............**500.00**
Borden's Condensed Milk, cb sign, girl/cats, 1893, 15x11", G.....**450.00**
Borden's Milk, jar, nickel-over-brass lid, 6½", NM **195.00**
Born Steel Range, match holder, tin litho, 4⅞x3⅜", G **225.00**
Boschee's German Syrup, mirror, ornate gesso fr, 21x21", EX **220.00**
Boston Belting, glass paperweight, 2¾", G....................................**10.00**
Boston Belting, paper sign, factory, fr, 25x21", VG......................**250.00**
Boston Cigars, mirror, fancy etching, kite shape, 24", EX **325.00**
Boston Herald, tip tray, newsboy w/papers, '05, 3½", NM.............**85.00**
Brako Coffee, tc, Drake ea side, 1920, 1-lb, VG **85.00**
Brickmore Gall Cure, cb tri-fold display, 51x34", NM.................**140.00**
Brotherhood Tobacco, cb sign, 18x26" **150.00**
Brotherhood Tobacco, paper on cb sign, fr, 43x33", EX **1,500.00**
Brown's Hungarian Flour, pocket mirror, 2", G **30.00**
Brunswick Bowling Balls, wood/metal stand, 1915, G.................**110.00**
Buffalo Brand Peanut Butter, tc, buffalo on red, 1-lb, EX **45.00**
Buffalo Brand Peanuts, dispenser, w/jar, 21½", NM **550.00**
Buffalo Brand Peanuts, jar, emb buffalo, tin base, 10", EX **210.00**
Buffalo Salted Peanuts, tc, charging buffalo, 10-lb, EX **150.00**
Buick Valve in Head, porc sign, 20" dia, M...................................**300.00**
Bull Durham, cb sign, Blk father/son hunt, fr, 26x18", G **500.00**
Bunnies Salted Peanuts, rabbit on 2 sides, 10-lb, 11", EX **295.00**
Burkhardt's Lager Beer, tin sign, mug, early, 17x14", NM **800.00**

Buster Brown

Buster Brown was the creation of cartoonist Richard Felton; his comic strip first appeared in the *New York Herald* on May 4, 1902. Since then Buster and his dog Tige (short for Tiger) have adorned sundry commercial products but are probably best known as the trademark for the Brown Shoe Company established early in this century. Today hundreds of Buster Brown premiums, store articles, and advertising items bring substantial prices from many serious collectors.

Bank, BB & Tige w/horse & Good Luck, CI, EX pnt, Arcade.....**200.00**
Bank, plastic, red w/BB & Tige, EX **25.00**
Bowl, cereal; porc, BB transfer, 2x4" **40.00**
Camping set, 5-pc, ea w/logo on bottom, EX.................................**85.00**
Coat hook, orig...**35.00**

Comic book, 1908, VG...**65.00**
Comic strip book, Happy Days, 1911, lg **55.00**
Cup, ceramic, MIG, 1900s, 4" **95.00**
Dictionary, 1927, pocket sz..**20.00**
Figurine, BB & Tige, bsk, Germany, 5" **55.00**
Fork, SP, 1904 ....**20.00**
Fountain pen, 14k point **28.00**
Gun, cb, EX **10.00**
Hatchet, BB logo, 13" **40.00**
Hobby horse, EX orig..**225.00**
Mannequin, BB, plastic, 41" **100.00**
Mask, BB Shoes, cb, NM **25.00**
Match safe, tin litho, BB Bread **400.00**
Paper doll sheet, BB Hosiery, uncut **15.00**
Patch, felt, 1950s, EX **5.00**
Pencil case, pencil form, 1930s, EX...**65.00**
Pencil clip **15.00**
Periscope **23.00**
Pin-bk button, cl, EX color, 1½", EX **32.00**
Play Money, $5, $1, 50¢, set for **10.00**
Playing cards, mini, complete **60.00**
Pocket mirror, brass, sm hdl **150.00**
Poker chip, Tige, red/wht or bl, set of 200 ....**140.00**
Post card, BB Shoes, illus, ca 1930, EX **15.00**
Post card, Outcault illustration, 1908, EX...................................**20.00**
Poster, linen, w/Tige, Outcault illustration, Selchow, 17x24" **40.00**
Rocking horse, wood fr w/springs front & bk, 34x34x17", EX **135.00**
Shoe box, w/cutouts of Andy's Gang **75.00**
Shoe stretcher **35.00**
Sign, BB Bread, tin litho, BB/Tige/wheat, '20s, 23x31", VG **350.00**
Sign, Brown's Bread, die-cut tin, 1920s, 12x14", NM **100.00**
Sign, standup figure, tin diecut, BB & Tige, 32½", VG, pr...... **3,500.00**
Sign, 2-pc tin cutout: dog pulls BB in shoe, 25x40", NM **13,000.00**
Socks, orig labels, pr..**25.00**
Waffle iron, BB & Tige on bk, sm...**75.00**
Whistle, wood, paper label **20.00**

Trade card, $35.00.

C.D. Kenny

C.D. Kenny was determined to be a successful man, and he was. Between 1890 and 1934, he owned seventy-five groceries in fifteen states. He realized his success in two ways: fair business dealings and premium giveaways. These ranged from trade cards and advertising mirrors to tin commemorative plates and kitchen items. There were banks and toys, clocks and tins. Today's collectors are finding scores of these items, all carrying Kenny's name.

Coffee bag 5.00
Figurine, Indian in canoe, ceramic 15.00
Funnel 20.00
Match holder, elephant figural, gr, common.....................5.00
Plaque, George Washington, rnd, 1920s, sm, NM 50.00
Plaque, girls at tea party, tin litho 225.00
Plate, Santa & sleeping child, tin, 9½", M 175.00
Pocket mirror, folding, metal case 35.00
Salt shaker, Geisha Girl...12.00
Strainer 45.00
Tape measure, retractable 15.00
Tip tray, Victorian lady, seated, 4".............................100.00
Tip tray, 3 monkeys, See No Evil..., EX..........................80.00

Cadillac Service, neon clock, 8-sided, EX 900.00
Canadian Club, pocket tin, 8", NM 450.00
Capudine Liquid, tray, cherubs, 9¾" dia, NM 525.00
Carlings Ale, ts, 9 Pints of the Law, Bobbies, 12x9", NM 95.00
Carnation Gum, sf ts, girl w/flowers, sq, 14", VG 600.00
Carter's Ink, ts, bookkeeper, ca 1900, 25x19", EX 1,350.00
Cascade Beer, tray, Uncle Sam at party, 12¼x17¼", G 550.00
Case Bros Razors, display razor, 14", NM 1,250.00
Castle's Ice Cream, cb sign, fr, 14x11", EX 120.00
Central Brewing, tray, factory, 13⅝x16⅝", EX 1,300.00
Central Union Tobacco, cb litho sign, fr, 10½x13½", VG 150.00
Central Union Tobacco, lunch box, 7x5", EX.................65.00
Central Union Tobacco, pocket tin 200.00
Ceresota Flour, ts, boy cuts bread, 28½x22", VG 1,000.00
Chero Cola, paper sign, bottle, Drink..., fr, 24x15", EX 600.00
Cheroots, paper sign, girl w/fan, 9x7", NM 35.00
Cherry Phosphate, cb sign, lady, orig fr, 22½x15", VG 310.00
Chevrolet Sales & Service, porc sign, dbl-sided, 28x40", NM 750.00

Chief Watta Pop, chalkware, holes for suckers, 9½", $135.00.

Clark's Peanut Butter, pail, moose hunt, Canada, '15, 1-lb, EX...170.00
Cleveland & Buffalo Line, paperweight mirror, EX, 3½" dia 100.00

Cleveland-Akron Bus Co, cl sign, early bus, 12x7", EX 115.00
Club Manhattan Cocktails, tin sign, man, 1894, 16x12", EX 900.00
Club Manhattan Cocktails, ts, gold fr, 1894, 15x22", EX 375.00
Clysmic Table Water, tray, tin litho, Meek, 13¼x10½", VG 325.00
Clysmic Water, tip tray, sexy lady & stag, oval, 6", EX 75.00
Coldan's Taffy-Tolu Gum, jar, figural face on lid, 11", EX..........120.00
Columbia Batteries, flanged/2-sided ts, 1910s, 14x18", NM 800.00
Columbia Brewing Tacoma WA, tray, allegorical, 9¾" dia, EX ..550.00
Columbia Brewing Tacoma WA, tray, lady in long gown, 12" 700.00
Columbia Grafonola, tin sign, 1920s couple, 18x24", EX 275.00
Columbian Beer, tin sign w/chain, bottle, mc, 14x10", EX...........300.00
Congress Beer, match holder, tin litho, Haberle, 4⅝x5⅜", G......150.00
Consumer's Brewing, rvpt sign, 1890s, 25x35", G 500.00
Cortez Cigars, cb die-cut sign, For Men of Brains, 12x17", G 225.00
CP Boss & Son Biscuits, wooden box, 1920, 5x21x10", G..........60.00
Crane & Byron, letter folder, dbl-sided, 1890s, 12x3", G...........100.00
Cream of Wheat, note reminder, leather, VG 25.00
Crescent Club Mixture, tc, 2¼x4⅜x3¼", EX 25.00
Crossett Shoes, brass sign, Makes Life's..., 20x14", NM 170.00
Crown Diamond, flanged porc sign, 5-color, 16x17", EX 125.00
Cyclist Touring Club, porc sign, early, 16x16", NM............... 1,275.00
Cyrus Noble Whiskey, cb sign, Strowbridge, early, 14x11", G.....225.00
Daniel Webster Flour, tin sign, red/blk on yel, 14x48", EX..........130.00
Davis Maryland Rye, tray, cherub w/maiden, 14x17", NM 225.00
Deer Run Whiskey, rvpt sign, stag, 24x34" 1,000.00
Deer Run Whiskey, tin sign, stag, Baetzhold, 12" dia, NM..........250.00
DeLaval Separators, oak cabinet, tin front, 25x18x11", EX 375.00
DeLaval Separators, tin sign, girl & cows, fr, 41x20", NM 3,200.00
DeLaval Separators, tip tray, farm scene, 4", EX......................100.00
DeLaval Separators, tip tray, lady & son, 1905, 4⅜" 150.00
Delco Batteries, glass sign, lights up, 9x18", M 800.00
Detroit-Bohemian Beer, match holder, tin, Brownies, 5½", G ...100.00
Dexter Cigars, porc sign, 3-color, 3x18", G 35.00
Diamond Chewing Tobacco, ts, crown, early, fr, 20x14", G 350.00
Diamond Dyes, book, hard bound, 16-pg, 5x9", EX....................16.00
Diamond Dyes, cabinet, Ages of Women, 24x15x9", VG.............650.00
Diamond Dyes, cabinet, balloon, Am Art, 1912, 25x16x9", EX..575.00
Diamond Dyes, cabinet, court jester, 27x21x10", NM................650.00
Diamond Dyes, cabinet, Cycle of Life, 7x2x2", EX 400.00
Diamond Dyes, cabinet, fairy scene, 31x24x10", EX 1,000.00
Diamond Dyes, cabinet, governess, 30x23x10", EX 500.00
Diamond Dyes, cabinet, jump rope scene, 25x15x9", EX............975.00
Diamond Dyes, cabinet, little girl, 20x17x9", VG.....................950.00
Diamond Dyes, cabinet, mansion, 1910s, 25x16x9", EX.............500.00
Diamond Dyes, cabinet, maypole scene, 1906, 30x23x9", EX......750.00
Diamond Dyes, cabinet, washer woman scene, 30x23x10", VG ..800.00
Diamond Dyes, sign, die-cut parrot, hanging, 9x13", EX 700.00
Ditto Cigars, cl sign, Indian, Whitehead-Hoag, 12x8", EX..........425.00
Dixie Salted Peanuts, tc, Blk boy w/watermelon, 10-lb, EX 250.00
Doane's Pills, wood thermometer, worn pnt, 21x4", VG..............60.00
Dr Baxter's Mandrake Bitters, ts, 1880s, 20x14", EX 1,600.00
Dr Daniel's Veterinary Medicines, cabinet, w/4 bottles, 29" ... 1,200.00
Dr Daniel's...Medicines, cb sign, cat & dog remedies, 10x18" 100.00
Dr Hess' Louse Killer, mc tin container, 6x3", EX 30.00
Dr Lesure's Famous Remedies, wood cabinet, 27x21x7", EX........800.00

Dr Pepper

A young pharmacist, Charles C. Alderton, was hired by W.B. Morrison, owner of Morrison's Old Corner Drug Store in Waco, Texas, around 1884. Alderton, an observant sort, noticed that the drugstore's patrons could never quite make up their minds as to which flavor of extract to order. He concocted a formula that combined many flavors, and Dr. Pepper was born. The name was chosen by Morrison in honor of a beautiful young girl with whom he had once been in love. The girl's father, a Virginia doctor by the name of Pepper, had discouraged the relationship due to their youth, but Morrison had never forgotten her. On December 1, 1885, a U.S. patent was issued to the creators of Dr. Pepper.

Bottle, clear, AM&B Co, circle A, EX............................25.00
Bottle, seltzer; Cheerio-Memphis..................................150.00
Calendar, 1938, lady in yel gown, NM 250.00
Calendar, 1949, complete, NM 50.00
Clock, brick wall effect, blk on beige, lt gr fr, rnd, 15"......100.00
Dispenser, Phos-Ferrates, sq ceramic, marble base, 21"......7,500.00
Door pull, metal, bottle form, VG 45.00
Fan, cb, 6-pack, gr/red, VG..50.00
Plate, roses, Vienna Art...175.00
Post card, 10¢ coupon, M 5.00
Sign, tin, cut-out cap, 28", NM.......................................50.00
Thermometer, tin, bottle shape, early, 26", NM...........150.00
Watch fob, St Louis World's Fair, silvered brass, 1904......125.00

Dr Shoop's Restorative, ts, lists cures, ca 1904, 10x7", EX......675.00
Dr Swett's Root Beer, tin on cb sign, EX color, 6x9", VG......200.00
Dr Swett's Root Beer, tin sign, HD Beach, fr, 9x24", EX......550.00
Drink Burchola, tin sign, 3-color, 10x28", EX 35.00
Drink Squeeze, ts, 3-color, ca 1920s, 4x19½", EX..........40.00
Duffy Malt Whiskey, bottle, 10¼", VG...........................20.00
Duke's Mixture, cb poster, comical, mc, fr, 27x21", VG......600.00
DuPont Sporting Powders, envelope, bird, 3½x6½", G......30.00
Durham Duplex Safe Razor, tin sign, easel bk, 6x27", VG......325.00
Durham Smoking Tobacco, cb sign, comic, Wald, 14x11", VG..600.00
Durham Smoking Tobacco, pocket tin, very rare 3,300.00
Dutchess Trousers, tin sign, $2 to $5, 24x20", NM 95.00
Dwinell Wright Coffee, bin, 4-color, 20x14x19", G 230.00
Dybalas Spring Soda, cb hanging sign, red/wht, 9x24", EX......25.00
Eberhard Faber, cb sign, mc erasers, 11½x15½", EX.......210.00
Edelweiss Beer, tray, lady, Schoenhofen, 1913, 13½" dia, EX......175.00
Eden Tobacco, pocket tin, yel leaf on red, 3¾", EX 400.00
Educator Crackers, tc, Noah's Ark, Shonk, 4x11x5", EX......1,600.00
Ehret's Beer, tray, deep dish type, blk/red/gold, 12", NM......165.00
El Paterno Cigars, sf tin sign, man's portrait, 26x18", VG......700.00
Electrolier Co Can, Deco floor ash tray, 24", NM.........460.00
Elgin Watches, wood sign, boy w/watch, 1910s, 22x15", VG......300.00
Entertainer Tobacco, wooden pail, paper litho, 11x13", EX......400.00
ER Johnson's Educator Crackers, tin container, 6", EX......25.00
Essolube Motor Oil, dbl-sided porc sign, 30" dia, VG......345.00
Esterbrook's Oval Pen, cl on cb sign, hanging, 8x12", VG......275.00
Eveready, razor blade tin, brn/gold, 1x2x2", EX.........12.50
Eveready Flashlights, tin die-cut sign, 11x4", VG......375.00
Ex-Lax, porc thermometer, 5-color, 36x8", NM 130.00
Excelsior Life Ins, tin ledger marker, 1890s, 12½", NM......25.00
F&M Schaefer Brewing, tray, Est 1842, Shonk, 13¾x16¾", EX..325.00
Fairy Soap, tip tray, angelic girl on soap, 4", NM.........60.00
Family Tea, canister, stag & teacup, pre 1900, 9", NM......140.00
Farm House Peanut Products, tc, Am Can, 13x12½" dia, VG......250.00
Fatima Cigarettes, sf ts, veiled lady, ca 1905, 19" dia, EX......700.00
Fatima Cigarettes, ts, Turkish girl, 16x12", VG.............65.00
Faultless Wonder Nipples, bottle, w/glass nipple, 13", NM......1,500.00
FC Wagner Shoes, tip tray, blonde girl, 6", VG 110.00
Fehr's Malt Tonic, match holder, tin diecut, 6¼x2¼", G......225.00
Ferris Waists, sf ts, sepia, oval, 23x16½", NM 4,500.00
Ferris Waists, sf ts, sepia, 1900, 22x16", VG 800.00
Fidelity & Casualty, letter folder, calendar bk, 1891, VG......120.00
Five Roses, porc thermometer, red/wht, 39x8", EX 125.00

Fleishmann's Yeast, tin sign, cherubs, 14x20", EX 1,700.00
Fordson Tractors, tin sign, mc pnt, 12x36", EX............425.00
Forest & Stream Tobacco, pocket tin, fisherman, Canadian, 5"....65.00
Forest & Stream Tobacco, pocket tin, men in canoe, Canadian .400.00
Foss & Deering, mustard pail, cup shape, ¼-lb, NM......155.00
Foster Hose Supporters, cl on paper over cb sign, 17x9", NM......400.00
Foster Hose Supporters, cl over cb sign, lady, 9x17", NM......180.00
Fostoria Undermuslin, tip tray, lady, 1908, 4¼", NM......105.00
Four Roses Tobacco, cb sign, roses, fr, 12x16", EX......325.00
Four Roses Tobacco, pocket tin, flip top......................50.00
Fra-Bac Tobacco, pocket tin, unopened, 9½", M............1,500.00
Frank Jones Homestead Ale, tip tray, NM, 5" 35.00
Franklin Caro Gum, jar, emb lid, 12", EX....................90.00
Franklin Cigars, horse blanket, cloth, 72x55", VG 150.00
Fredericksburg Beer, tin die-cut standup display, 6x10", G......325.00
Fredericksburg Lager Beer, tin sign, girl w/hood, 13½" dia......500.00
Frostee Root Beer, bottle-cap ts, Stout, 1950s, 37", EX......75.00
Gail & Ax Navy Tobacco, tc, sailor, kidney shape, 8¼x7"......3,000.00
Gail & Ax Navy Tobacco, tin sign, sailor, 20x14", VG......1,400.00
Garfield Headache powder, packet, portrait, EX 10.00
Gayrock Clothing, tin sign, Kohn Bros, fr, 39x27", NM......1,300.00
General Arthur Cigars, tin sign, dbl-sided, 7¾" dia, EX......160.00
Gillies Crushed Coffee, tin bin, 1915, 19x13x13½", G......85.00
Girard Cigars, tin on cb sign, Am Artworks, 19x13", VG......325.00
Glendora Coffee, tin sign, gold/bl/wht, 14x9", NM........80.00
GMC Trucks, clock, neon lights, EX orig.....................650.00
GMC Trucks, dbl-sided porc sign, 30" dia, VG.............650.00
GO Blake Whiskey, tray, aristocrat w/pipe, 1910s, 12", NM......150.00
Goebel Beer, tray, man drinking, 12" dia, G................175.00
Gold Coin Stoves, ts, Wells & Hope, 1880s, 6x7", EX......170.00
Gold Dust Tobacco, pocket tin, Canadian, rare 2,000.00
Gold Dust Washing Powder, paper sign, twins, fr, 26x13", EX. 5,500.00
Golden Orangeade, cb sign, oranges, orig fr, 22½x15½", VG......325.00
Golden Wedding Whiskey, tin/cb sign, Am Art, 19x13", EX......175.00
Golden West Brewing, tray, factory scene, 12" dia, EX 375.00
Goodwill Shoes, knife, Holliston MA, Germany, 2¾", G......75.00
Grand Rapids Brewing, tray, Silver Foam, Shonk, 12" dia, EX....425.00
Greyhound Lines, porc sign, dog, 2-sided oval, 21x36", VG......525.00

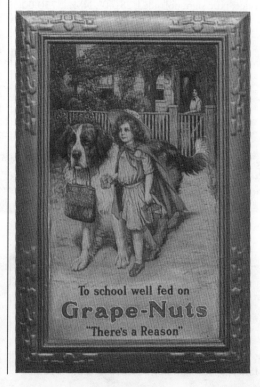

Grape Nuts, self-framed lithographed tin, light scratches, 20" x 30", $1,000.00.

Grossvander Old German Lager, tray, couple, 10x13", EX 175.00
Gussard Corsets, pocket mirror, 2¾", VG 80.00
H&R Arms, tin sign, emb mc letters, 10x14", EX 625.00
Hambone 5¢ Cigar, blkboard, early, 20x13", VG 50.00
Hamm's Beer, radio, can shape, EX 22.50
Hanleg's Peerless Ale, tray, bulldog, 12", VG 45.00
Happy Thought Plug Tobacco, cb sign, sailor, fr, 39x28", EX . 2,000.00
Harrison's Town & Country Paints, ts, lady, fr, 14x20", EX 750.00
Hartford Fire Ins, tin sign, stag, yel/blk, 20x9", NM 32.00
Harvard Brewing, tray, brunette by table, 13" dia, VG 275.00
Harvard Cigars, tin sign, youth's portrait, 37x25", EX 600.00
Harvard Cigars, wind-up cutter, boy, 7x9", VG 120.00
Heinz Apple Butter, crock, 2 labels, 4¼x8", EX 225.00
Heinz Catsup, Burger Blaster radio, bottle form, EX....................35.00
Heinz Peanut Butter, tc, 1930s, 10-lb, EX 75.00
Heinz Pickles, plastic pickle pin, 1½", M 3.00
Heinz Sweet Pickles, wooden bucket, worn label, 13x13", G 90.00
Hi Ho Tobacco, pocket tin, man watches boat race, rare 2,000.00
High Grade Cigarettes, cb sign, 2 women, fr, 14x8", VG..............250.00
High Grade Tobacco, pocket tin, Ilsley & Co, late 1800s 1,200.00
Hinckel's Lager Beer, tray, elk scene, 12" dia, EX 160.00
Hire Tire, die-cut ts, uniformed man, 1910s, 36x10", EX 1,100.00

Hires

Charles E. Hires, a drugstore owner in Philadelphia, became interested in natural teas. He began experimenting with roots and herbs and soon developed his own special formula. Hires introduced his product to his own patrons and soon began selling concentrated syrup to other soda fountains and grocery stores. Samples of his 'root beer' were offered for the public's approval at the 1876 Philadelphia Centennial. Today's collectors are often able to date their advertising items by observing the Hires boy on the logo. From 1891 to 1906 he wore a dress; until 1914 he was shown in a bathrobe. From 1915 until 1926, he was depicted in a dinner jacket. The apostrophe may or may not appear in the Hires name; this seems to have no bearing on dating an item.

Buckle, belt; Drink Hires Root Beer... 5.00
Diecut, bottle, 5", NM...175.00
Dispenser, porc, hourglass shape w/orig pump, 1910-20, NM 475.00
Glass, soda; Enjoy Nature's..., syrup line, NM............................45.00
Mug, ceramic, boy lifts mug, Mettlach, EX 150.00
Mug, stoneware, hourglass, boy decal on hdl, Doulton, 4½", EX ...75.00
Opener, over-the-top, NM..12.00
Pocket mirror, Put Roses in Your Cheeks, NM............................175.00
Sign, cl on metal, Drink Hires, girl, 10x7", EX............................375.00
Sign, lady in low-cut gown w/glass, 1930s, fr, 39x24", EX 500.00
Sign, paper, German peasant/Colonial man, 1890s, 18x21" 475.00
Sign, paper, pop-eyed soda jerk, 5x13"..125.00
Sign, tin, boy points, ...to Your Health, 28x20", NM 7,500.00
Sign, tin, Brunch, Lunch, Munch, VG...70.00
Sign, tin, emb lettering, bl/red/wht, 1940s, 20x27½", EX 60.00
Sign, tin, It's High Time for..., 1930s, 42x14", NM......................65.00
Straw dispenser 750.00
Tire cover, canvas, for spare, 29" dia, EX 200.00
Trade card, boy & dog, 1892, EX 25.00
Tray, Haskel Coffin girl, oval, 10x13", EX...................................190.00
Tray, Just What the Doctor..., 1914, EX......................................400.00

Hoffman House Bouquet Cigars, sign, paper litho, 36x26" 700.00
Hoffman House Pure Rye, ts, topless scene, 27x20", VG......... 4,500.00
Hold Fast Cut Plug, cb sign, Blk children w/sled, 23x11", VG 550.00
Home Insurance, letter folder, 1890s, 12x3", VG.........................120.00

H.O. Wilbur & Sons Cocoa and Chocolate, paper sign, 20", $695.00.

Honest Scrap, tin display store bin, 14x18x12", EX................. 1,600.00
Honeymoon Tobacco, pocket tin, man on the moon.....................75.00
Honeymoon Tobacco, pocket tin, 2 men on moon........................550.00
Honeymoon Tobacco, trolley car sign, canoe, fr, 11x21", EX......325.00
Hood Tires, blkboard-type ts, Hood Tire man, 11x17", VG 85.00
Hood's Sarsaparilla, flag card game, EX......................................28.00
Horse Shoe Cut Plug, tin sign, battleship, 24x36", VG 6,500.00
Horseshoe Brand Clothes Wringer, display rack, 56x15", EX 220.00
HP Hood & Sons Milk, porc sign, cow, 28" dia, EX.....................295.00
Hunham's Cocoanut, brass thermometer, 1888, VG....................250.00
Hunkel's Seeds, paper sign, girl/produce, 1925, 31x23", EX.........425.00
Hunter Baltimore Rye, ts, First Over..., 1910s, 24x18", NM ... 1,400.00
Hupmobile Service, porc sign, dbl-sided, 18x30", VG 575.00
HW Clark Biscuits, wood box, paper label, '20, 11x21x14", G 40.00
IC Baking Powder, pocket mirror, 1¾", VG 25.00
Ideal Slipover Goggles, display card, w/goggles, 13½x11" 300.00
IL Springfield Watches, tin/cb sign, trainman, 19x13", EX 600.00
Imperial Cube Cut Tobacco, glass humidor, emb logo, 8", M 85.00
Independent Locks, die-cut 2-sided ts, key, '20s, 14x32", EX.......200.00
Index Brand...Cocoa, tc, Am Can, Montgomery Ward, 5-lb, G ...45.00
Inland Pride Beer, tray, bottle & glass, 12" dia, VG 225.00
Internat'l Tailoring, pocket mirror, bead game, 2", VG 15.00
Iroquois Brewery, tip tray, Indian..150.00
Iroquois Brewery, tray, Minnie-Ha-Ha in canoe, 12" dia, G 375.00
Ithaca Guns, ts, dbl-barrel & shells, 1895, 6½x13½", G 450.00
Iver Johnson Revolvers, die-cut tin sign, 2-sided, 12x15", VG ...700.00
J Leisey Brewing, tray, factory, 1890s, 14x17", NM 2,000.00
J&P Coats Spool Cotton, paper sign, fishing, 18x23", G 275.00
J&P Coats Spool Cotton, wood display box, w/contents, 12½" ..260.00
Jap Rose Soap, die-cut easel-bk tin sign, 13x19", EX 800.00
Jap Rose Soap, hinged box, 32x8x14", VG 60.00
JI Case Threshing Machines, ts, fr, 1880s, 14x20", EX 2,000.00
Johnson's Log Cabin Coffee, bin, cabin form, 25x24x18", EX . 3,000.00
Jumbo Spark Plugs, tin display box, 14x11x6", EX.....................300.00
Just Suits Tobacco, porc sign, ...Wise One, 8x12", VG 110.00
Keeley Brewing, ts, men drink, hanging, ca 1911, 14x14", EX.....650.00
Keely Stoves, match holder, tin litho diecut, 5½x3¾", VG.........125.00

Kendall Motor Oils, curved porc sign, can shape, 30x20", M.. **1,850.00**
Kendall Motor Oils, dbl-sided porc sign, 24" dia, VG **145.00**
Keystone Watch Cases, paper sign, men at tree, 20x28", G **1,200.00**
Kikkoman Soy Sauce, bamboo stick fan, 1940s, EX **15.00**
King Edward Tobacco, pocket tin, Canadian, 8", NM **700.00**
King George Tobacco, pocket tin **250.00**
King's Pure Malt, change tray, Panama Pacific Expo, oval, 6" **50.00**
King's Pure Malt, tip tray, maid, oval, '15, 6x4½", EX **40.00**
Klondike Paint, die-cut tin sign, Baer Bros, 13x19", VG **2,500.00**
Korbel Champagne, tin sign, Am Art, 13x19", VG **275.00**
Kryptok Eyeglasses, rvpt sign, Master Lens, oval, 9x12", EX........**325.00**
Kuntz Brewery, tray, lady serving beer, 13⅛" dia, EX **400.00**
Kyanize Varnish, pocket mirror, 2-faced man, blk/wht, EX............**27.50**
La Palina Cigars, tin on cb sign, Am Artworks, 19x13", G..........**200.00**
Las Amantes Cigars, cb sign, 3 for 25¢, 7x15", EX **27.50**
Lembeck & Betz, tray, zeppelin, sq, 13¼", EX **1,700.00**
Lenox Chocolates, tin over cb sign, open box, 9x14", EX **600.00**
Life Savers, tin box, 5 flavors shown, 15¾x9⅛x4½", NM **1,700.00**
Linser's American Maid Beer, tray, lady, 10½x13¼", EX.............**450.00**
Lion Brand Shirts, mirror, CI lions at top of fr, 16x13", G............**55.00**
Lion Coffee, wooden slant-top bin, 32x22", EX **350.00**
Lipton Tea, cb sign, lady w/tea set, fr, 23x17", NM **1,000.00**
Lipton Tea, tin sign, 1910, wood fr, EX **45.00**

Log Cabin Syrup

Log Cabin Syrup tins have been made since the 1890s in variations of design that can be attributed to specific years of production. Until about 1914, they were made with paper labels. These are quite rare and highly prized by today's collectors. Tins with colored lithographed designs were made after 1914. When General Foods purchased the Towle Company in 1927, the letters 'GF' were added.

A cartoon series, illustrated with a mother flipping pancakes in the cabin window and various children and animals declaring their appreciation of the syrup in voice balloons, was introduced in the 1930s. A Frontier Village series followed in the late 1940s. A schoolhouse, jail, trading post, doctor's office, blacksmith shop, inn, and private homes were also available. Examples of either series today often command prices of $75.00 to $200.00 and up.

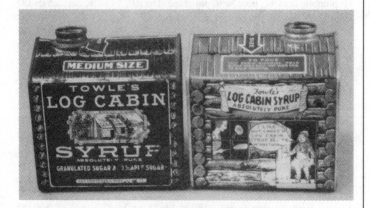

Log Cabin Syrup tins, left: $65.00; right: $110.00.

Bank, glass cabin figural, EX **32.00**
Can opener, Towle's, metal **12.00**
Syrup tin, bear in door, cartoon ends, Towle's, 5-lb **140.00**
Syrup tin, blacksmith, 33-oz..**135.00**
Syrup tin, boy w/lasso, 1-lb...**110.00**
Syrup tin, cartoon all sides, sm..**110.00**
Syrup tin, children, man by pump, Towle's, 33-oz.......................**150.00**
Syrup tin, children playing, Towle's, 33-oz, NM **135.00**

Syrup tin, Dr RU Well, cartoon style, rare **250.00**
Syrup tin, Express Office, coach, Towle's, 33-oz...........................**150.00**
Syrup tin, Frontier Inn, cowboys & horse, 5-lb **220.00**
Syrup tin, Frontier Jail, 12-oz **150.00**
Syrup tin, hand w/finger pointing on top, Towle's, med **165.00**
Syrup tin, Home Sweet Home, 12-oz **150.00**
Syrup tin, paper label, sample sz, 2x1½", rare **300.00**
Syrup tin, red, 5-lb **50.00**
Syrup tin, Stockade School, Towle's, 33-oz.................................**150.00**
Syrup tin, Wigwam, 1-lb, very rare, 4x3¼x3½" **500.00**
Syrup tin (bank), woman & girl in door, 1-lb, EX **45.00**
Teaspoon...**17.50**

Log Cabin Mustard, milk glass container, 4", VG **15.00**
London & Lancashire, rvpt sign, oak fr, 27x23", EX **100.00**
Longley Hats, lamp, milk glass globe w/brass base, 18", EX..........**475.00**
Lucky Strike, cb sign, bathing beauties, fr, 21x10", EX **120.00**
Lucky Strike, cb sign, Gracie Allen, fr, 21x14", EX **120.00**
Lucky Strike, clock, printed dial, rvpt panel, 24" **1,100.00**
Lucky Strike, pocket tin, wht, upright **350.00**
Luden's Cough Drops, die-cut tin sign, box, 6½x8¼", G **250.00**
Luden's Cough Drops, tc, letters 1 side, early, 4x8x6", VG **50.00**
Luden's Menthol Cough Drops, cb sign, child/box, 10x7", EX **500.00**
Madison Cigars, cb sign, Indian maid, 1906, 30x15", EX............**450.00**

Mail Pouch Tobacco, cardboard-under-glass sign, rare, 15" x 20", $1,600.00.

Malachrino Cigarettes, 4-fold tin display, Arabs, 13x20", EX......**325.00**
Maltex Cereal, paper sign, kids at table, 1950s, 16x21", EX...........**20.00**
Mandalay Punch, cb sign, 2-tone, 8x22", EX................................**25.00**
Marathon Products, dbl-sided porc sign, runner, 30" dia, NM.. **1,300.00**
Mason & Hamlin Pianos, tin sign, piano, fr, 24x32", G **150.00**
Master Mason Tobacco, cb sign, man w/pipe, fr, 22x15", EX **900.00**
Master Mason Tobacco, pocket tin, man w/plugs, Canadian.......**200.00**
Masury House Paints, ts, train, EX color, 28x20", VG............. **5,500.00**
Masury's Pure Colors, ts, Acknowledged..., 18x24", EX **2,000.00**
Matoaka Tobacco, pocket tin, Pocahontas, EX............................ **1,500.00**

Mayo's, creamer pail, paper label, 10", EX 125.00
Mayo's Cut Plug, cb sign, 6 men in car, 1915, 12x19", NM 275.00
McAvoy's Malt Marrow, tray, Shonk, 1899, 12" dia, EX 500.00
McCullogh's Leap Rye Whiskey, tray, 1890s, 12", EX 250.00
Mecca Cigarettes, cb sign, Christy girl, fr, 20x11", VG.............350.00
Mennen's Borated Talcum, trolley car sign, 11x21", VG 650.00
Mentholatum, die-cut ts, girl w/injured boy, 19x15", EX............185.00
Meredith's Diamond Club Pure Rye, china jug, 5½", G.................15.00
Michigan Stoves, match holder, NP iron, 8x4½", EX.................130.00
Milburn Wagons, paper sign, M'randa There..., 21x27", EX ... 2,600.00
Miller Beer, tray, girl in moon, 13", EX 100.00
Milward's Helix Needles, walnut case, 2-drw, 8x13", NM 300.00
Modox, tip tray, tin litho, Indian chief diecut, 4⅜x4½", G 325.00
Moerlein Beer, tray, gold on tan, 12" dia, NM.....................165.00
Monarch Teenie Weenie Peanut Butter, tc, '26, 12½" dia 400.00
Moose Herbs, cb & paper container, EX 20.00
Morrison's English Remedies, cabinet, glass door, 28", NM 800.00
Morton Salt, cl pencil clip, EX 5.00
Mother's Oats, cb sign, fr, 1920s, 19x13", VG 50.00

Moxie

The Moxie Company was organized in 1884 by George Archer of Boston, Massachusetts. It was at first touted as a 'nerve food' to improve the appetite, promote restful sleep, and in general to make one 'feel better!' Emphasis was soon shifted, however, to the good taste of the brew, and extensive advertising campaigns rivaling those of such giant competitors as Hires and Coca-Cola resulted in successful marketing through the 1930s. Today the term Moxie has become synonymous with courage and audacity, traits displayed by the company who dared compete with such well-established rivals. For more information we recommend *The Book of Moxie* by Frank N. Potter, available at your local bookstore or from Collector Books.

Box, Catarrh Cure, w/2 bottles, 3", NM 205.00
Candy tin, Moxiemobile, scarce....................................150.00
Diecut, cb, Moxie boy, Moxie-teers, 1928, EX 695.00
Diecut, tin, Moxie boy, ca 1908-11, 6¾x4½", EX 290.00
Display, tin, Frank Archer diecut, 2-sided, 6x6", NM 550.00
Fan, cb, Frances Prichard w/glass, 8x10", EX.......................55.00
Fan, cb, girl & soda jerk, sm 37.00
Gravy boat, girl's face w/banner, swag border, 8", EX 85.00
Post card, Moxie Horsemobile......................................20.00
Sign, cb, Moxie boy w/feather, Learn To Drink..., 37x20"..........600.00
Sign, cb, 1700s girl, easel bk, ca 1900, 6¼x5", NM 400.00
Sign, cb diecut, Moxieland, Home of Moxie, 29x38", EX 225.00
Sign, tin, Eclipse, 1930s, 54x19", VG 400.00
Sign, tin, Learn To Drink, ca 1905, 20x14", VG 500.00
Sign, tin, Moxiemobile, man on horse, 12x36", EX..................975.00
Sign, tin diecut, lady w/glass & bottle, 7x6", EX 700.00
Thermometer, metal, Moxie man pointing, 26x20", EX 125.00
Thermometer sign, tin, It's Always a Pleasure..., '40s, 24x9" 90.00
Tip tray, tin, blonde woman on bl, ca 1907, 6", NM................275.00
Tip tray, tin, dbl-trail logo, cream/gold/maroon, 3½", M 450.00
Tip tray, tin, girl & violets, ca 1900-10, 5", EX 200.00
Tip tray, tin, girl drinking, ca 1905, 5", EX 200.00
Tip tray, tin, girl on gr, ca 1900, 6", NM 225.00
Tray, glass over metal, lady w/glass, 1910, 10", EX...............300.00
Tray, glass over metal, Moxie boy, ca 1910, 10", EX...............250.00
Tumbler, glass, Licensed Only for Serving, 4", NM 40.00

Muehlebach's Pilsner Beer, tip tray, medallion, 5", NM.............50.00
Munsing Union Suits, tin & wood display, 1¾x8¼x3¼", VG.....375.00

Munsingwear, sf ts, sm girl in long underwear, 1910, 26x38"....700.00
Murine, cb sign, lady w/dropper, fr, 28x17½", EX................. 2,300.00
Nat'l Biscuits, glass jar, w/lid, 12", EX 105.00
Nat'l Biscuits, oak display rack, 4 shelves, 47x56x15", EX........600.00
Nat'l Biscuits, tin container, Favorite assortment, EX.............35.00
Nat'l Brewing, tray, St Louis factory, 1890s, 10¼x13¾", EX........400.00
Nat'l Lead, paperweight mirror, Dutch boy, 4", VG 40.00
Nat'l Life Insurance, letter folder, 1890s, 12x3", G 130.00
Nat'l Mazda Electric Lamps, display stand, 12½x27½", VG 425.00
Navarre Steel Cut Golden Sun Coffee, tin spoon, 4", G 60.00
New Home Sewing Machines, stick fan, portrait, 1860s, EX 75.00
New Home Sewing Machines, tip tray, granny, 1900s, 4⅛", EX .155.00
New Process Gas Ranges, match holder, tin litho, 3¼x2", EX 100.00
Newton's Horse Remedy, tc, horses, sq lid, 7½", NM 110.00
Newtone Handphone, tip tray, lady/flowers, '10, 4¼", NM 170.00
Nonesuch Mince Meat, ts, Old Sleepy Eye, 1890s, 28x20" 1,800.00
North Pole Cut Plug Tobacco, tc, polar bears, 4x6", M 150.00
Nu-Grape Soda, tin thermometer, bl/gr/yel, 16", EX................35.00
Oh-Boy Gum, tin sign, elf & boy, 7½x15½", NM 120.00
Ohio Blue Tip Matches, paperweight mirror, 3½" dia 70.00
Ohio Blue Tip Matches, pocket mirror, 3½", VG.....................40.00
Ohio Farmers Ins, compo sign, farmer on fence, 24x18", EX 225.00
Old Barbee Whiskey, tray, College Widow, '13, 12½x16", G........90.00
Old Guckenheimer Rye, cb sign, oversz bottle, 11x15", EX.........250.00
Old Judson, match holder, tin, family by fire, 5x3½", NM..........130.00
Old McGregor Bourbon, tin sign, early, fr, 12x16", VG 750.00
Old Squire Tobacco, pocket tin, bl, Canadian, 8½", NM........ 1,500.00
Old Squire Tobacco, pocket tin, orange, Canadian 100.00
Old VA Cheroots, cb sign, Uncle Sam, 1900, 24x15", VG 900.00
Oldsmobile Service, porc sign, 2-sided, 60" dia, NM 1,395.00
Oliver Chilled Plows, ts, 2 men/horse, 1890s, 33x24", VG 6,000.00
Oliver Plows, mirror, portrait on cl, 3", NM 70.00
Omar Gasoline, porc sign, dbl-sided, 30" dia, M 950.00
Opera Beauties Cigars, tc, opera lady, 4½x3½", EX...............150.00
Orange Crush, London Toy, windup, decals, VG 60.00
Orange Crush, paper sign, 1926, 12x16", EX 22.50
Orange Crush, tin flanged sign, 18x18", VG 45.00
Orange Crush, tin sign, Ask for a Crush, 3¼x26½", EX 30.00
Orange Crush, tin thermometer, bottle figural, 29", EX............45.00
Oswald General Merchandise, cb/canvas sign, fr, 15x20", EX 300.00
Oswego Bridge Co, ts, sepia bridge scene, 13½x19", EX 375.00
Ozone Soap, tin sign, yel on bl, 1930s, 17½x36", VG 130.00
P Lorillard Tobacco, display rack, dk wood, 33x40x3", EX 600.00
Pabst Blue Ribbon, electric light-up sign, 1950s, 19x14" 35.00
Pabst Blue Ribbon, sf tin sign, Am Art, 1924, 10x13", EX 220.00
Pabst Blue Ribbon Beer, porc sign, bl/wht, 30x42", NM 110.00
Paris Garters, cb display sign, 6 ladies' legs, 44x29", VG 45.00
Parker Pens, electric clock, wood case, 19x19", NM 330.00
Patriotic Fireworks, flyer, boy & dog/Uncle Sam, 9½x7", EX 50.00
Patterson Tobacco, tin sign, 2-sided pipe form, 9x19", EX 1,500.00
Paul Jones Tobacco, pocket tin, bl, 7", NM.......................950.00
Paul Jones Tobacco, pocket tin, red, rare, 8", NM 2,500.00
Pearl Lustre Dye, cabinet, wood & tin, mc pnt, 22", NM 850.00
Peerless Dye, cabinet, gypsy, ca 1888, 26x19x10", VG 2,300.00

Pepsi-Cola

Pepsi-Cola was first served in the early 1890s to customers of Caleb D. Bradham, a young pharmacist who touted his concoction to be medicinal as well as delicious. It was first called 'Brad's Drink,' but was renamed Pepsi-Cola in 1898.

Bottle, clear w/paper label, 1930s, 12-oz, M.......................32.00
Bottle, gr w/paper label, 1930s, 12-oz, M 55.00

Calendar, 1944, lady in rocker, 2 men, EX **60.00**
Carrier, cb, Bigger-Better, 1930s, EX **35.00**
Clock, glass front light-up, 1950s, 15" dia, EX.........................**50.00**
Clock, plastic & metal, light-up, 16" dia, EX **160.00**
Clock, plastic counter style, 1970s, 6x14", NM........................**22.50**
Cooler, metal, bl, 1950s, EX..**50.00**
Door push, tin, ...on Lips of Millions, 1930s, 10x3", NM.............**100.00**
Menu board, tin, 1940s, 30x20", EX.......................................**90.00**
Napkin holder, plastic, 1960s, 3x9", M...................................**12.00**
Pencil, mechanical, ca 1950s, EX...**30.00**
Push bar, porc, diamond grillwork, 3x30", NM.........................**48.00**

**Pepsi-Cola serving tray, minor scrapes and rust, 13½",
$1,150.00.**

Shakers, ceramic, Pepsi logo, 1930s, pr...**165.00**
Sign, cb, On the Lips of Millions, 1930s, 11x28", EX **225.00**
Sign, cb cutout, Pepsi & Pete, beach girl, 12x8½", EX................**175.00**
Sign, cl/tin, Blk girl w/bottle, oval, 1960s, 8x12", EX..................**55.00**
Sign, cl/tin, bottle cap, 1940s, 9" dia, NM.............................**75.00**
Sign, sf cb, lady in wide hat, 1930s, 34x25", EX.....................**165.00**
Sign, tin, Drink..., red/wht/bl, fr, 16x17", NM **250.00**
Sign, tin, Enjoy 5¢, red/wht/bl, 1940s, 10x26", NM **135.00**
Sign, tin, Tops, streaming caps, 1940s, 12x36", NM **120.00**
Sign, tin on cb, Say..., cap & bottle, 1960, 9x11", EX **20.00**
Tap knob, plastic w/tin insert, 1930s, 2½x1¾", M...................**75.00**
Thermometer, tin, yel, 1960s, 27x7", M **22.50**
Tip tray, tin litho, girl drinks w/straw, 6⅛x4⅜", VG...................**300.00**
Tip tray, tin litho, girl w/flowers, 6⅛x4⅜", VG........................**325.00**
Tip tray, tin litho, girl w/glass, ca 1908, 6⅛x4⅜", EX................**400.00**
Tray, bottle cap, red/wht/bl/yel, 1950s, 13x13", NM..................**40.00**
Tray, lady w/hand to face, 1900s, 14x11", EX **1,000.00**
Tray, Quality...Quantity, bottle cap, 1940s, 14x10", EX.............**250.00**
Trolley card, 1941, cartoon by Whitney Darrow **65.00**
Watch fob, New Bern NC...**90.00**
Whistle, plastic, 1950s, 3", EX..**30.00**

Perfect Patent Flour, paper sign, Bridal Veil, 30x13", VG **300.00**
Perfection Cigarettes, sf ts, hand w/pack, 1915, 17x12", EX........**400.00**

Perfection Dyes, cabinet, wood/tin litho, 1885, 14x10", NM **500.00**
Peter Doelger Bottled Beer, tip tray, eagle, 4", NM....................**100.00**
Peter Schulyer 10¢ Cigars, sf ts, portrait, 28x22", EX.................**475.00**
Peters Cartridges, cb tri-fold sign, man & 2 boys, 28x35", EX **55.00**
Peters' Weatherbird Shoes, paper sign, Uncle Sam, 21x30", EX. **1,000.00**
PH Mayo & Brother, dbl-sided cb sign, factory, 13x20", NM **650.00**
Pheasant Pure Lard, can, pheasants, 13" cylinder, G...................**140.00**
Phillip Morris Cigarettes, ts, Johnny, raised rim, 16" dia, G **300.00**
Phoenix Brewery, tray, phoenix bird, oval, 15¼x18¼", EX **230.00**
Phoenix Collar Buttons, oak box, 6-compartment, 4x7", NM **95.00**
Phoenix Horse Shoes, paper sign, 1909, fr, 23x15" **140.00**
Pickaninny Peanuts, butter pail **175.00**
Pickaninny Peanuts, tc, Blk girl & doll, 10-lb, EX **280.00**
Piedmont Cigarettes, cb fan, baseball, EX **135.00**
Pillsbury Flour, wooden ruler, old, 15", EX **12.50**

Planters Peanuts

Mr. Peanut, the dashing peanut man with the top hat, spats, monocle, and cane, has represented the Planters Peanut Company from 1916 to 1961 when the company was purchased by Standard Brands. He promoted the company's product by appearing on premium giveaways, store displays, jars, scales, and in special promotional events. Among the favored treasures of collectors today are the glass display jars. They come in a variety of styles — They are square, some hexagonal, some barrel-shaped, and others are round. The earliest, issued in 1926, was octagonal and is usually referred to as the 'pennant' jar. Although later reproduced, these are marked 'Made in Italy' on the bottom. The original is embossed on the back panel 'Sold Only in Printed Planters Red Pennant Bags.' In a second octagonal style, this embossed message was replaced with a paper label.

In 1930 a 'fishbowl' jar was introduced, and in 1932 a 'four-corner peanut' jar was issued. The rarest jar of all, the 'football' jar, was also used during the early 1930s. The Planters' square jar followed in the 1930s and was replaced by the 'barrel' jar. The six-sided jar with Mr. Peanut decals and the 'pickle' jar were later. All in all, more than fifteen different styles were developed.

In the late 1930s, premiums such as glass and metal figural paperweights, pens, and pencils were distributed. Post-war items were often made of plastic — Mr. Peanut salt and pepper shakers, mugs, and banks were popular. Today's collectors find a treasure trove of advertising memorabilia depicting that debonair gentleman, Mr. Peanut.

Box, Mixed Nuts, 1-lb **15.00**
Buckle, gold-tone metal, Mr Peanut figural, M **10.00**
Coloring book, American Ecology, Mr Peanut, 1972, unused........**12.00**
Cuff links, gold-tone metal, Mr Peanut, pr **75.00**
Dart board, Mr Peanut, unused, M..**125.00**
Diecut/standup, Mr Peanut, 48" **18.00**
Jar, Barrel, running Mr Peanut, paper label **275.00**
Jar, chocolate-covered cashews, paper label, 1944, 4½-oz **25.00**
Jar, Clipper, orig lid **75.00**
Jar, Fish Bowl, rectangular label **150.00**
Jar, Fish Bowl, sq paper label **150.00**
Jar, Football, peanut finial..**300.00**
Jar, frosted label, big knob, rnd...**45.00**
Jar, Leap Year, orig lid...**50.00**
Jar, mixed nuts, paper label, orig lid, 1950s, 4½-oz **15.00**
Jar, octagon, Pennant 5¢, 7 sides emb **250.00**
Jar, octagon, Pennant 5¢, 8 sides emb **300.00**
Jar, peanut butter, early Mr Peanut on tin lid, scarce **25.00**
Jar, Pennant 5¢, paper label **175.00**
Jar, sq, peanut finial, Planters emb ea side **150.00**
Jar, Streamline, tin lid **65.00**

Jar, 4-corner, lg blown-out peanut ea corner, M......................300.00
Jar, 6-sided, printed sq label...60.00

Jar, fish bowl with rectangular label, 13", $150.00.

Luggage tag, yel & bl, Mr Peanut..15.00
Lunch box, vinyl, Mr Peanut, 8½x11x5", M.........................20.00
Mug, Mr Peanut, bl plastic, 1950s, M in mailer....................25.00
Mug, tan plastic, Mr Peanut, 3¾".. 9.00
Nut dish, gold metal, Mr Peanut figural...............................35.00
Paint book, US Presidents, Washington to Eisenhower, VG.........28.00
Peanut, papier-mache, lg...45.00
Peanut, plastic, lg...18.00
Pencil, mechanical...20.00
Pin-bk button, celluloid, Mr Peanut, old, EX.......................15.00
Plate, pewter, Super Bowl XIII, lg......................................75.00
Poster, History of Winter Olympics, 1980, 18x26", M 7.00
Punchboard, early, EX 50.00
Punchboard, 600-hole, M..35.00
Radio, Cocktail Peanuts can, Mr Peanut, MIB......................45.00
Radio, Mr Peanut figural, MIB 75.00
Refrigerator magnet, Mr Peanut...12.00
Shakers, Mr Peanut, plastic, gr, 3", pr................................. 8.00
Shakers, Mr Peanut, plastic, pk or red, pr............................ 7.00
Shakers, Mr Peanut, plastic, yel, pr.................................... 5.00
Spoon, gold-tone metal w/enamel Mr Peanut, demitasse 22.00
Statue, Mr Peanut, metal, 2 peanuts at base, 8", EX...............350.00
Tin container, red diamonds on gr, 10-lb, VG 395.00
Tin container, Salted Mixed Nuts, 7-oz................................16.00
Tray, dk gr plastic, Mr Peanut..35.00
Wax paper, Mr Peanut, 10 sheets..12.00

Plow Boy Tobacco, canister, plow boy label, 5-lb, EX...................35.00
Plow Boy Tobacco, store bin, tin litho, 9½x8½x10½", VG..... 1,100.00
Polarine Oil, porc sign, dbl-sided flange, 14x24", VG 900.00
Poll Parrot Shoes, cb die-cut sign, fr, 12½x20", EX....................450.00
Poll Parrot Shoes, paper sign, Harlequin boy, 20x13", VG 325.00
Portsmouth Ales, tray, Frank Jones, 1930s, 13", VG 48.00
Post Toasties, cb sign, girl & dog, 17x24", EX...........................200.00
Potosi Brewing, sf ts, picnic scene, ca 1905, 34x33", EX.......... 1,200.00
Powwow Peanuts, tc, Indian on gr, 10-lb, NM 500.00
Pozzoni's Medicated Complexion Powder, cb sign, 16x16", VG..175.00
Prairie Tea, tin container, mc, Canadian, rare, 9x7x5", EX.........150.00

Pratt's Veterinary Remedies, cabinet, tin door, 33x17x7", EX.....950.00
Precision Hoodolites, paper sign, 1915, 30x23", NM 165.00
Prince Albert, sf tin sign, 4-color, 13x39", NM 250.00
Prosperity Whiskey, paper sign, Blk wedding, fr, 15x19", VG........65.00
Providence Salad Oil Dressing, tc, early, 9½", 7½-lb, EX..............70.00
Prudential Life Ins, metal letter opener, 1910, 10", EX 24.00
Pulver's Cocoa, tip tray, lady, 4½", VG 310.00
Quaker Denatured...Anti-Freeze, linen sign, 35x56", G 295.00
Quaker Oats, die-cut tin display, ca 1920s, 25x19x7", EX 950.00
Quaker Rolled White Oats, china bowl, 7½", VG 40.00
Quaker State...Oil, porc sign, 2-sided, early, 6x25", NM 300.00
Queen Bee Chop Tea, roll-top store bin, 21x10x13", G 185.00
Queen of VA Smoking Tobacco, paper sign, Russell, 10x7", EX...45.00
Queen Quality Shoe Dressing, tin on cb sign, box, 9x13", VG....165.00
Queen Quality Shoes, rvpt sign, queen in oval, 15x42", EX 150.00
Quick Meal Ranges, match holder, tin litho, 5x3½", G...............150.00

RCA Victor

Nipper, the RCA Victor trademark, was the creation of Francis Barraud, an English artist. His pet's intent fascination with the music of the phonograph seemed to him a worthy subject for his canvas. Although he failed to find a publishing house who would buy his work, the Gramaphone Co. saw its potential and adopted Nipper to advertise their product. The company eventually became the Victor Talking Machine Co. and was purchased by RCA in 1929. Nipper's image appeared on packaged accessories, in ads and brochures. If you are very lucky you may find a life-size statue of him — but all are not old, they have been reproduced! Except for the years between 1971 and 1981, Nipper has seen active duty; and, with his image spruced up only a bit for the present day, the ageless symbol for RCA still listens intently to 'His Master's Voice.'

Ash tray, ceramic, card suit shapes, old, NM, 4 for......................50.00
Doll, RCA Majorette, wooden, jtd, 1920s, EX 650.00
Figure, Nipper, chalk, 4½" 35.00
Figure, Nipper, papier-mache, rare, 41" 1,350.00
Needle tin, Nipper, yel/gold/blk, NM 27.50
Post card, hold-to-light, 1907...10.00
Poster, Popular Artists..., dog, 35x25", EX..............................525.00
Puzzle, opera scene, record shape, early, dtd 1908.....................75.00
Record brush, Nipper...30.00
Shakers, Nipper, Lenox, 3½", ea..35.00
Sign, wooden, phonograph & dog..185.00
Snow dome, Nipper 50.00
Stick pin, Nipper 60.00

R&T Whalen Tobacco, ts, ca 1880, 20x14", VG.........................275.00
Ranier Beer, tray, Evelyn Nesbitt, 1901, 13¼" dia, EX 450.00
Reading Brewing, tin sign, factory, fr, 28x40", EX 3,500.00
Recruit Little Cigars, cb sign, 1909, fr, 15x20", EX 275.00
Red Crest Tobacco, leather lunch box, rooster, 8x4x5", EX 150.00

Red Goose Shoes

Realizing that his last name was difficult to pronounce, Herman Giesecke, a shoe company owner, determined to give the public a modified, shortened version that would be better suited to the business world. The results suggested the use of the goose trademark, with the last two letters, 'ke,' represented by the key that this early goose held in his mouth. Upon observing an employee casually coloring in the goose trademark with a red pencil, Giesecke saw new advertising potential and renamed the company Red Goose Shoes. Although the company has changed hands down through the years, the Red Goose emblem has remained. Collectors of this desirable fowl increase in number yearly, as do prices. Beware of reproductions — new chalkware figures are prevalent.

Address book, EX	6.00
Bank, goose, CI/red pnt, Red Goose School Shoes, 3¾"	225.00
Bank, goose, plastic, NM	25.00
Bank, Save w/Shoes...Kid, tin, worn pnt, M-1585, 5⅝"	45.00
Bank, tin, gr w/paper label, rnd, old, 2½", EX	125.00
Bell, Ring for Red Goose Shoes	25.00
Bill spindle, old	15.00
Clicker, yel, Red Goose logo, 1950s, M	12.00
Clock, papier-mache, Germany, 23", EX	1,200.00
Figure, goose, chalk, red on gr base, 12", EX	55.00
Figure, goose, papier-mache, nodder, rpr, 24"	75.00
Figure, goose, red vinyl, atop wood box, gives free eggs	150.00
Helmet, cloth hat w/straps, child's	45.00
Hood ornament, CI Arcade goose bank mtd on cap, 6", NM	600.00
Horn, paper, 6", EX	2.50
Marbles, early logo, cb box of 5, EX	50.00
Mirror, floor; shoe store, sm decal, 15½x23"	150.00
Pencil box, wood, sliding top, old, 2x9", EX	85.00
Pencil holder, pencil shape, early, EX	50.00
Puzzle, cb, chain, ca 1925, 3½x6¼", EX	35.00
Shoe bench, seats 3	650.00
Shoe holder, wood, 18"	200.00
Shoehorn, metal	12.00
Sign, diecut, boy holds goose by neck, ca 1910, EX	275.00
Sign, diecut, porc/neon/red pnt, 24", EX	1,400.00
Sign, display; cb, 9x12"	25.00
String holder, CI, goose figural, EX pnt	1,400.00
Tablet, school; Red Goose Rodeo, ca 1935, VG	12.50
Watch fob, metal, oval, emb Red Goose, rare, 2"	145.00
Whistle, tin, red/bl/yel	15.00

Red Indian Cut Plug, tc, slip-open top, Ginna, 6½x5", EX	700.00
Red Indian Tobacco, tc, Indian on bl, 7", EX	225.00
Red Jacket Tobacco, pocket tin, horse & rider, 4½", NM	25.00
Red Man Cigars, paper sign, lady in wht, fr, 9½x6", VG	40.00
Red Man Tobacco, store box, 5-color, held 36, EX	185.00
Red Raven Splits, tip tray, It's a Dream, mc, G	75.00
Remington UMC, roll-down poster, hunters/mtn, 26x28", NM	500.00
Remington UMC Firearms, die-cut cb standup, 20x14", EX	375.00
Rexall Dye, wooden cabinet, stenciled front, 35x15", NM	425.00
Richmond Cigarettes, cb sign, lady in pk, fr, 9x16", EX	210.00
Richmond Straight Cut Cigarettes, ts, man, 19" dia, VG	650.00
Richmond Union Suits, paperweight mirror, 3½" dia	90.00
Rising Sun Stove Polish, paper sign, factory, 28x18", EX	1,200.00
Rising Sun Stove Polish, roll-down sign, 35x19", EX	195.00
Robert Smith's Misty Ale, ceramic cup, 4", EX	25.00
Robin Hood Flour, push bar, 3x20", NM	50.00
Robinson Crusoe Glue, trolley car sign, Crusoe, 11x21", EX	155.00
Robinson's Sons, tray, Blk man serves group in rowboat, 12"	450.00
Robinson's Sons, tray, factory, Shonk, deep rim, 12" dia, EX	350.00
Rochester Brewery, paper sign, Liberty, 1890s, 32x22", NM	1,500.00
Rockford Oats, ironstone bowl, Staffordshire, 5½", VG	50.00

Roly Poly

The Roly Poly tobacco tins were patented on November 5, 1912,

by Washington Tuttle and produced by Tindeco of Baltimore, Maryland. There were six characters in all — Satisfied Customer, Storekeeper, Mammy, Dutchman, Singing Waiter, and Inspector. Four brands of tobacco were packaged in selected characters; some tins carry a printed tobacco box on the back to identify their contents. Mayo and Dixie Queen Tobacco were packed in all six; Red Indian and U.S. Marine Tobacco in only Mammy, Singing Waiter, and Storekeeper. Of the set, the Inspector is considered the rarest and in mint condition may fetch as much as $1,000 on today's market.

Dutchman, Mayo, EX	400.00
Dutchman, Mayo, NM	550.00
Inspector from Scotland Yard, Mayo, NM	1,000.00
Mammy, Mayo, EX	600.00
Singing Waiter, Mayo, EX	500.00
Singing Waiter, US Marine, VG	400.00
Storekeeper, Mayo, NM	650.00

Royal Blend Coffee, pocket mirror, 2¾", VG	100.00
Royal Shield Tea, tc, mc on bl, Canadian, 9x9x5", VG	40.00
Royal Tailors, glass light-up sign, 1925-30, 17x12x9", EX	425.00
Ruhstaller's Gilt Edge Beer, tray, auto scene, 13¼", EX	425.00
Rumsey's Blackville Fire Brigade, paper sign, fr, 18x25", EX	1,400.00
Runkel Bros Cocoa & Chocolates, sf ts, ca 1904, 29x22", EX	950.00
S&H Green Stamps, tip tray, Nouveau lady, 4", EX	55.00
Salada Tea, porc sign, purple/yel/blk, 3x15", NM	100.00
Salada Tea, porc sign, red letters, early, 5½x12", NM	130.00
Sambo Axle Grease, tin pail, smiling Blk boy, 7x9", EX	135.00
Sanford's Ink & Mucilage, tin sign, mc bottles, 14x20", G	950.00
Sapolin Enamel, shadow-box sign, 1911, 19x20x4", EX	1,025.00
Sapolin Enamel, tin-over-cb sign, hanging, 10x13", VG	325.00
Schepps Coconut, tin container, monkey, 1890s, 5", G	100.00
Schrafft's Candy, candy dish, cut glass, etched base, 4x7"	60.00
Scott's Emulsion, tri-fold cb display, 33x49", EX	120.00
Seattle Brewing & Malting, tray, lady at table, 12" dia, VG	525.00
Sen-Sen, emb die-cut tin sign, We Sell..., 4⅜x6⅛", EX	300.00
Seneca Cameras, ts, Indian girl, 2-sided flange, 14x14", EX	2,000.00
Sharples, match holder, tin, farm scene, 6½x2½", EX	150.00
Shaw Pianos, cb diecut sign, girl/cat, '05, 13x9½", EX	165.00
Sheboygan Mineral Water..., tray, tin litho, 12" dia, VG	500.00
Shell Oil, porc sign, dbl-sided shell form, 25x25", VG	550.00
Sherwin Williams, porc sign, mc, 4x8x1", VG	22.50
Sherwin Williams, 2-sided porc sign, 4-color, 9x21", EX	100.00
Shinola, shoehorn, mc brushes & product, 5", EX	35.00
Shredded Wheat, display box, falls/factory, 15x12x8", EX	150.00
Shredded Whole Wheat, wood crate/cb inserts, 21x33x17", EX	25.00
Singer Sewing Machines, bird cards, set of 16, NM	28.00
Skelly Aromax Gasoline, porc sign, 2-sided, 30" dia, NM	950.00
Skelly Tagolene Motor Oil, porc sign, 2-sided, 30" dia, NM	950.00
Sky Chief, porc pump sign, 4-color, 12x18", EX	40.00
Slippery Elm Lozenges, tc w/glass front, early, 5x8x7", EX	80.00
Smith Bros Cough Drops, cb sign, 2-sided, hanging, 7x10", EX	350.00
Snider's Catsup, die-cut tin sign, mc, 7x10", EX	575.00
Solarine Metal Polish, match holder, tin, 5x3½", NM	75.00
Songster, needle tin, yel/wht/red, 2x1", EX	12.50
Southern Girl Shoes, sf tin sign, lady/flowers, 19x13", EX	1,100.00
Spanish Segaros, paper sign, Collins Cigars, 22x17", EX	110.00
Spencer-Tracy Suits, man in brown, 1911, 48", EX	675.00
Spencer-Tracy Suits, man in gray, 1911, 48", EX	500.00
Spitt Spark Plug, ts, Am Art, 1930s, 11½x18¼", G	35.00
Springfield Insurance, letter folder, tin litho, 12x3", EX	140.00
Springfield Watches, tin sign, Columbia, 23½x11½", G	600.00
Squirrel Brand Salted Almonds, tc, yel, 5-lb, 8½", NM	150.00

Standard Bottling, cl sign, lady in red, 1900s, 6" dia, NM..............**95.00**
Standard Brewing, pocket mirror, 1¾", G.. **5.00**
Standard Brewing, sf ts, Sioux execution, '10s, 18x26", EX.........**900.00**
Standard Brewing, tray, 1862 Indian execution, 12" dia, VG.....**350.00**
Star Cars, porc sign, gr/wht/bl, dbl-sided, 24x36", EX.................**285.00**
Star Plug Tobacco, die-cut cb sign, dbl-sided, fr, 20" dia......... **1,600.00**
Star Weekly, porc push bar, 3x30", NM **35.00**
Stegmaier Brewing, tray, lady, Am Art, ca 1904, 13½", EX.........**160.00**
Sterling Beer, tin sign, Tops Them All, 1938, 27x21", EX **450.00**
Sterling Oils, porc sign, dbl-sided, 21" dia, VG **425.00**
Stetson Hats, porc sign, yel & blk, 8x30", EX **255.00**
Stillson Wrench, die-cut figural tin sign, 2-sided, 12x16", G **275.00**
Stonewall Jackson Cigars, die-cut tin standup, 10x11x3", G **275.00**
Studebaker Service Station, dbl-sided porc sign, 14x30", VG **650.00**
Sunny Brook Whiskey, match holder, tin litho, 5x3½", VG **110.00**
Sunshine Crackers, tin sign, box/hands/product, 10x28", NM **375.00**
Sure Shot Tobacco, tin display bin, 10x15x7", EX.......................**475.00**
Sweet Caporal, canvas banner, red/wht/gr/blk, 36x60", EX **18.00**
Sweet Cuba Tobacco, cb container, Am Can, 1913, lg, EX.........**120.00**
Sweet Violet Tobacco, pocket tin, M.. **1,250.00**
Taka-Cola, tray, tin litho, ...Every Hour, 13¼" dia, VG **250.00**
Texaco Kerosene, pnt tin, 12x20", EX...**75.00**
Theo Geir Vineyards, ts, family scene, 1870s, 14x14", EX **1,300.00**
Thomas Inks, tin sign, blk cat/brn puppy, fr, 18x11", VG **5,000.00**
Thomson Bros, change tray, Romanesque lady, 4", NM **140.00**
Three Bee Blacking, cb sign, Blk boy, 1880s, 12x17", EX........ **2,400.00**
Three Bee Blacking, ts, shoeshine scene, 19x14", VG............. **4,000.00**
Tiger Chewing Tobacco, cb sign, tiger, 1890s, 31x25", EX..........**350.00**
Tiger Chewing Tobacco, pocket tin **150.00**
Tiger Chewing Tobacco, tc, tiger, 6x8", EX **45.00**
Tirador Havana Cigars, sf ts, mc portrait, fr, 28x23", NM **1,250.00**
Tivoli Hofbrau Beer, match holder, tin diecut, 6½x2½", VG......**450.00**
Toiletine, die-cut cb sign, bandaged man, 6x9", EX **35.00**
Tuckett's Marguerite Cigars, sf ts, 1910s, 28x22", VG **750.00**
Turkish Cross-Cut Cigarettes, brunette, fr, 21x9", EX **450.00**
Tuxedo Pure White Pepper, spice tin, EX **100.07**
Tuxedo Tobacco, trolley car sign, Cohan portrait, 11x21", NM..**700.00**
Tuxedo Tobacco, trolley car sign, H Fisher, 11x21", EX..............**325.00**
Tuxedo Tobacco, trolley car sign, TA Dorgan, 11x21", EX.........**125.00**
Two Orphans Cigars, box, 2 children on front, 5½x5", EX............**25.00**
Uniform Cut Plug Tobacco, tc, sailor, 6x4", G **1,000.00**
Union Jack 5¢ Cigar, tin-on-cb sign, Am Artworks, 19x13", G ..**200.00**
Union Leader Tobacco, tc, Uncle Sam w/pipe, 6x5¼", EX............**70.00**
United Brand Robes..., ts, men in night wear, 18x12", NM **4,500.00**
United States 5¢ Cigars, tin sign, eagle/flag, 13x9", G..............**625.00**
Universal Stoves..., match holder, tin litho, 5x3½", EX..................**75.00**
US Tires, clock, litho on wood, brass hands, 18", EX **4,000.00**
US Tires, tri-fold cb display, car/tires/driver, 36x49", EX............**260.00**
USG Harnass Oil, clock, oak & brass, ca 1890, 25x17x5", EX **700.00**
Utah Brau, Standard Brewery, tray, eagle, 12" dia, VG **225.00**
Van Houten's Cocoa, cb sign, lady, oak fr, 30x25", G.................**350.00**
Van Houten's Cocoa, wooden box, paper label, 5x14x10", G........**75.00**
Van's Special Tobacco, cb container, 11x6¼x8⅛", EX................**500.00**
Vaseline, tin & cl display case, EX color, 7x13x6", EX **120.00**
Victory Tobacco, paper sign, ladies, fr, 14x19", EX......................**350.00**
Virginia Dare Wines, ts, couple in woods, '10s, 46x36", EX **1,100.00**
Walter Baker Breakfast Cocoa, tin sign, lady, 20x14", VG **700.00**
Ward's Orange Crush, rvpt clock, oak case, '10, 36", NM **850.00**
Warner's Safe Cure Medicines, pamphlet, 1888, EX **16.00**
Washington's Coffee, wood & glass case, '20s, 15x15x11", NM ..**300.00**
Waterman's Pens, thermometer, tin diecut, mc, 19½x4", VG **900.00**
Watson's Imperial Cough Drops, tc, 1900s, 7x7x4¾", G...............**55.00**
Wayne Brewing, tray, Mad Anthony Wayne..., 12" dia, VG.......**110.00**
Weed Tire Chains, mechanical sign, 1926, 23x17", EX **1,450.00**

Weed Tire Chains, mechanical sign, 1930, 23x17", EX..............**475.00**
Weir Plows, tin sign, factory, 1890s, 20x28", EX **9,000.00**
Welcome Soap, paper sign, coastal scene, fr, 26x17", NM...........**150.00**
Welsbach Lighting, tip tray, mom/daughter, 1910s, 4⅛", NM....**120.00**
Westinghouse Mazda Lamps, dbl-sided cb sign, 26x19", VG... **1,295.00**
Weyman's...Snuff, cb sign, Am Litho, 1890s, 20x16", EX...........**250.00**
White Rock, beer opener, steel, girl logo, 3", EX **7.50**
White Rock Table Water, pocket mirror, wht, 1⅞", G.................**15.00**
White Rock Table Water, tip tray, girl, 4⅜", VG.......................**100.00**
Winner Tobacco, lunch box, car scene, wire bail, 8x5", G..........**100.00**
Wm Peter Brewing, tray, Peter Brau, 13¾x16¾", EX..................**325.00**
Wm Tell Flour, match holder, tin, knights on horsebk, 5", EX......**75.00**
Yellowstone Whiskey, tray, waterfall, 13¼x10½", VG..................**65.00**
Yosemite Lager, tray, lady w/roses, 1905, 13¼" dia, EX **475.00**
7-Up, tin sign, EX color, 6x25", NM...**20.00**
7-Up, tin sign, 1930s, 28x11", EX **25.00**

Yankee Boy Cut Plug, pocket tin, EX, $625.00.

Advertising Cards

Advertising trade cards enjoyed a heyday during the last quarter of the nineteenth century when the printing process known as chromolithography was refined and put into popular use. The purpose of the trade card was to acquaint the public with a place of business, a product, or a service. Most trade cards range in size from 2" x 3" to 3" x 5"; however, some are found in both smaller and larger sizes. Four categories of particular interest to collectors are:

Mechanical — those which achieve movement through the use of a pull tab, fold-out side, or rotating disk.

Metamorphic — cards that transform a person or a thing from a 'before' to an 'after' condition, which of course represents a marked improvement immediately upon use of the featured product.

Hold-to-light — cards that reveal their design only when viewed before a strong light.

Diecuts — cards in figural forms such as the Heinz pickle series. Diecuts are usually in the shape of the advertised product or a theme-related object.

For a more thorough study of the subject, we recommend *The Advertising Trade Card* by Kit Barry; his address can be found in the Directory under Vermont. When no condition is indicated, the items listed below are assumed to be in near-mint condition.

A&P, A Light, Please?, 4-card set **15.00**
American Puzzle Card, basket of fruit **5.00**
American Puzzle Card, HMS Pinafore **10.00**
Ariosa Coffee, In the Managerie **6.00**
Ariosa Coffee, set of state cards w/map, ea.................................. **3.00**
Ariosa Coffee, set of state cards w/scenes, ea **3.00**
Barry & Fay's Comedy Co, Muldoon's Picnic **6.00**

Bay State Fertilizer, Potato Man facing right 8.00
Bensdorp Cocoa, John Milton 5.00
Bensdorp Cocoa, Richelieu 5.00
Borden's Milk, girl drinking, pug dog lower right 8.00
Bradley's Fertilizer, Indian w/spear, cornstalks 10.00
Buckeye Force Pump, baby crying at pump, rabbit............. 8.00
Buckeye Force Pump, girl w/pump, house to left................15.00
Bugbee & Brownell Spices, Ginger 6.00
Bugbee & Brownell Spices, Pimento 6.00
Charter Oak Lawn Mower, girl mowing, woman seated 12.00
Clarks ONT Thread, 2 boys flying kite 4.00
Domestic Sewing Machine, 3 Chinamen in tree 8.00
Doring's Reliable Shoe Store, 2 men shooting pool 12.00
Dueber Watch Case, factory scenes, statue 12.00
Dueber Watch Case, 3 men leaving watch store..................... 8.00
Eagle Pencil, castle upper left, pencil center 8.00
Ferry Seeds, Phlox 8.00
Ferry Seeds, Verbena... 8.00
Fords Hotel, Richmond VA, hotel......................................12.00
Gilt Edge Leather Dressing, Peep-Bo 5.00
Gold Coin Stoves, girl reaching to Christmas tree 6.00
Hampden Watches, girl w/watch by woman who knits.........12.00
Home Insurance Co, girl standing by tree......................... 4.00
Home Insurance Co, girl w/ribbon 4.00
Inman Line, City of Rome steamship.................................35.00
Ivers & Pond Piano, 2 girls skating, 1 pushing other 4.00
Kazine Washing Compound, Jumbo.................................. 4.00
Kazine Washing Compound, Raphael................................ 3.00
Kineo Stoves, skating scene w/boy falling down 5.00
King's Irish Oatmeal, Irishman dancing, piano 8.00
La Confiance Insurance Co, 18th-C veranda scene 9.00
McGibney Family, portrait w/instruments 15.00
McLaughlin's Coffee, girl playing teacher 5.00
McLaughlin's Coffee, The Skipping Rope 8.00
Merchants Gargling Oil, Hero of Home Run, baseball..............15.00
Merrick Thread, In Search of the North Pole.................... 5.00
Merrick Thread, tight rope walker, US flag 6.00
Michigan Central & Great Western Railroad, Niagara Falls 10.00
Milwaukee Harvester, woman holding branches 8.00

Newman Organs, 4¾" x 3⅛", $6.00.

Niagara Starch, 2 girls on swing, boy holding swing........................ 4.00
People's Church, donation to building, pictures brick 6.00
Philadelphia Lawn Mower, Horticulture Hall & boy 15.00

Prudential Insurance Co, girl w/umbrella & ducks 6.00
Prudential Insurance Co, I'll Take Care of You................................ 6.00
Prudential Insurance Co, salesman at door 8.00
Putnam Nail Co, cowboy shooting Indian 5.00
Putnam Nail Co, Those Horrid Boys 3.00
Pyle's Perline, Stolen Kiss 4.00
Quaker Bread, Santa in window, 2 children reading 10.00
Red Star Line, boy asleep on bed.. 6.00
Reid's Seeds. high-wheeled bicycles, seed store 8.00
Reynold's Shoes, 2 puppies w/shoe 4.00
Rice's Seeds, A Corned Indian 10.00
Ridges' Food, girl w/rattle, baby in crib 5.00
Salisbury's Troubador Turtle, turtle diecut................................ 8.00
Sanford's Ginger, Blk girl, baby in watermelon 12.00
Schaff Piano, boy in piano-crate cart, 2 goats 8.00
Shomer Piano, girl & baby at piano, flowers............................. 8.00
Sing Fat Co, San Francisco, dragon... 5.00
Soapine Soap, whale w/sailor diecut, 4½" 6.00
Soapine Soap, whale w/sailor diecut, 6¼" 8.00
Spencerian Pen, 5 schoolboys, 1 w/head on desk....................10.00
Stickney & Poor, boy pushing sled w/girl................................. 5.00
Stickney & Poor, girl falling down stairs 5.00
Syracuse Plow, man & woman fishing 15.00
Thurber Spices, 2 camels, desert scene 5.00
Tulip Soap, 2 girls playing in sand... 5.00
Universal Fashion Co, girl & boy w/sailboat............................. 4.00
Waterbury Watch, man w/2 women on ea arm......................... 6.00
Waterbury Watch, woman pours tea for man 6.00
White Sewing Machine, Don't Cry, Jonnie 5.00
Wilcox & White Organs, 2 girls w/dolls 3.00
Wilson's Corned Beef, Moriarity & Mary Ann.......................... 8.00
Wilsons Corned Beef, 2 sailors on ship 6.00

Advertising Dolls

Whether your interest in ad dolls is fueled by nostalgia or strictly because of their amusing, often clever advertising impact, there are several points that should be considered before making your purchases. Condition is of utmost importance; never pay book price for dolls in poor condition, whether they are cloth or of another material. Restoring fabric dolls is usually unsatisfactory and involves a good deal of work — seams must be opened, stuffing removed, the doll washed and dried, and then reassembled. Washing old fabrics may prove to be disastrous — colors may fade or run, and most stains are totally resistant to washing. It's usually best to leave the fabric doll as it is.

Watch for new dolls as they become available. Save related advertising literature, extra coupons, etc., and keep these along with the doll to further enhance your collection. Old dolls with no marks are sometimes challenging to identify. While some products may use the same familiar trademark figures for a number of years — the Jolly Green Giant, Pillsbury's Poppin' Fresh, and the Keebler Elf, for example — others appear on the market for a short time only and may be difficult to trace. Most libraries have reference books with trademarks and logos that might provide a clue in tracking down your doll's identity. Children see advertising figures on Saturday morning cartoons that are often unfamiliar to adults, or other ad doll collectors may have the information you seek.

Advertising dolls are still easy to find and relatively inexpensive, ranging in cost from $1.00 to $100.00, with the average price at about $10.00. They are popular with children as well as adults. For a more thorough study of the subject, we recommend *Advertising Dolls*, by Joleen Robison and Kay Sellers. Joleen is our advisor; she is listed in the Directory under Kansas.

Kellogg's cat and alligator, 10", $65.00 each.

A&W Restaurant, teddy bear, 1975, 13" **10.00**
Anahist, Hello Dolly, extra gown, 1966, 12" **15.00**
Armour & Co, International Dolls, plastic, unmk, 8" **5.00**
Aunt Jemima, Diana, cloth, ca 1905, 15" **130.00**
Aunty Drudge, Fels-Naptha Soap, uncut cloth, 1933 ....**150.00**
Babbit Cleanser, Babbit Boy, compo/cloth, 1916, 15".......**250.00**
Baggie Food Storage Bags, alligator, inflatable, gr, 1974 .... **7.50**
Bazooka Bubble Gum, Bazooka Joe, stuffed cotton, 1973 ....**15.00**
Beaver Enterprises, beaver, felt/plastic/cloth, 12" **15.00**
Birds-Eye Frozen Food, Merry, Minx, & Mike; cloth, '53, 11", ea..**30.00**
Blue Bonnet Margarine, Bl Bonnet Sue, plastic, bl dress, 8" **8.00**
Blue Ribbon Malt Extract, Lena, uncut cloth, 1930, 14" **175.00**
Breck Hair Products, Bonnie Breck, vinyl, 1971, 9" **25.00**
Bumble Bee Tuna, Yum Yum Bumble Bee, inflatable plastic, 24"... **5.00**
Buster Brown Shoes, Buster Brown, cloth, 1902, 13" **150.00**
Campbell's, cheerleader, vinyl, 1957-61, 9½", M **20.00**
Carnation Milk, Cry Baby, jointed vinyl, 1962, 18" **35.00**
Chesty Potato Chip Co, Chesty Boy, bosomy chest, 1950, 8" **25.00**
Chicken of the Sea, mermaid, fabric, Mattel, 1974, 15".................**30.00**
Chore Girl, fabric, 1970, 16" **20.00**
Clairol, Clairol Bears, plush w/plastic face, 1958, 15" **12.00**
Coast-to-Coast Hardwares, Elfy doll, inflatable, 20".......... **7.00**
Coca-Cola, Rushton Santa Claus, 1958...........................**85.00**
Collingbourne Cotton, Happy Family, cutout...............**135.00**
Cookie Crisp, Cookie Crook & Cop, plush, pr.................**40.00**
Coronet Brandy, figural, compo, 19".............................**30.00**
Country Kitchen Restaurants, Country Boy, cloth, 1975, 24" **15.00**
Cracker Jack, sailor by Vogue, 1974, 15" **25.00**
Cricket Lighters, Cricket, gr, inflatable, 1972, 24" **7.50**
Dak Meat Co, Thor, inflatable, 1974, 28"....................... **7.50**
Derby Oil Co, Derby Man, cloth, 1960s, 17".................**15.00**
Domino Sugar, Domino Bear, plush, 1975, 15" **7.50**
Dunkin Donuts, Munchkin, inflatable, 1976, 24" **7.50**
Eskimo Pie Corp, Eskimo Pie Boy, cloth, 1963 .... **7.50**
Esskay Meats, Baron Von Esskay, cloth, 11" **12.00**
Fab Detergent, Americana Doll, plastic, 1957, 7¾"..........**20.00**
Farmer's Sweet Corn, barefoot farm boy in bibs & hat, cloth **90.00**
Flintstones Vitamins, Fred Flintstone, inflatable, mk, 1971 .... **7.00**
General Mills, Betty Crocker doll, cloth, 13" **25.00**
General Mills, Boo Boo Ghost, 1975, 7½".....................**10.00**
General Mills, Count Chocula, 1975................................**10.00**
Gerber, Blk baby, vinyl, flirty eyes, anniversary, MIB **40.00**
Green Giant Co, Sprout, inflatable vinyl, 1976, 24" **7.50**

Hostess Bakery, Happy Ho Ho, inflatable, 1970s, 48" **8.00**
Hotpoint, man in red suit, pnt/jtd wood, H on hat, 15", NM **350.00**
John Deere Farm Machinery, stuffed gr deer, VG..........**20.00**
Keebler, elf, vinyl, 1964, 6½" **8.00**
Kellogg's, Dig 'Em Frog, fabric, 1973, 16" **12.00**
Kellogg's, Pop, hard vinyl, 1975, 8".............................**12.00**
Kelly Girl, Knickerbocker, 1978, M.............................**25.00**
Kentucky Fried Chicken, Colonel, nodder, mk, 7"........**18.00**
Lingerie Sue, vinyl, gr crepe dress, mk, 6" **25.00**
Long John Silvers, boy pirate & parrot, fabric, 1974, 13", pr **20.00**
Maypo, Marky Mapo, vinyl, 10" **20.00**
MD Bathroom Tissue, Cheshire Cat, cloth litho, unmk, 11".......**20.00**
Mr Salty Pretzels, cloth..**15.00**
Munsingwear, penguin, vinyl **20.00**
Nestles, rabbit, brn/tan plush, vinyl eyes/teeth, 1976 .....**10.00**
Peters' Weatherbird Shoes, compo, cloth body, 1920, 22"..........**150.00**
Post Cereal, Sugar Crisp Bear, plush, 1972, 12"............**12.00**
Procter & Gamble, Cheer dolls, vinyl, 1960s, 10" **5.00**
Quaker Oats, Crackels, uncut cloth, 1930 ....**135.00**
Scott Paper, Scottie dogs, blk & wht, 1976, 7½", pr.......**16.00**
Sweets Candy, Peppermint Pattie, bean bag, 1973, 10" **15.00**
Vlasic Pickles, Vlasic Stork, inflatable, 1977, 53" **10.00**

African Art

These artifacts of the African nation are a unique form of folk art, of interest not only in relation to the craftsmanship evident in their making but because of the culture they represent.

Basket, Masai, Kenya, bamboo reeds & leather, 10½x17½".........**105.00**
Bronze, Bobo, female figure, conical breasts, 7¼" **25.00**
Cvg, Chi Wara antelope, Banbara, Mali, cowrie trim, late, 31" **20.00**
Doll, ceremonial; Cameroon, Namdji, typical form, 10" **2,200.00**
Doll, Zulu, articulated limbs, feather inserts, beads, 9" **655.00**
Door lock, Bambara, stylized reptile, EX patina, 17" **455.00**
Fetish, Songye, Zaire, female, tacks/shells/horn trim, 46" **125.00**
Figure, ancestral; Baule, Ivory Coast, male, EX cvg, 23½" **150.00**
Figure, Mali, human figure, terra cotta, 1200s, 10" **1,250.00**
Flute, Mossi, abstract human form, cvd wood, old, 8½" **295.00**
Flute, Yaka, Zaire, Janus faces cvd in wood, 3", EX **188.00**
Headdress, ceremonial; Bamun, Tunggunga, deep-set eyes, 19"...**950.00**
Heddle pulley, Baga, mask feature at top, EX cvg/patina, 6¾" **275.00**
Heddle pulley, Senufo, stylized bird form, EX patina, 7¼" **395.00**

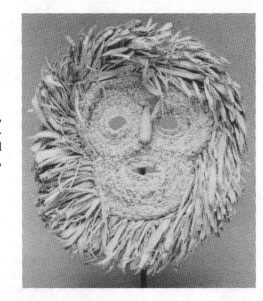

Mali, Dogon, Tellem male figure, encrusted brown patina, 11", $325.00.

Marionette, Ibibio, E Nigeria, wood cvg w/jtd arms, old, 14".......**500.00**
Mask, cvd wood, mc beaded face, cowrie shells, 13"......................**85.00**
Mask, Dan, stylized form w/scarification, 1920s, 10"...................**350.00**
Mask, Dan, typical stylized form, glassy patina, 1800s, 8½".....**1,350.00**
Mask, dbl-faced; Ibibio, 2 females, EX patina/cvg, old, 12".....**1,150.00**
Mask, Guronsi, Bukina, Faso, mc w/chicken feathers, worn, 32"..**85.00**
Pipe, East Africa, colonial style, metal-lined bowl, 12"................**125.00**
Robe, Hausa, Nigeria, cotton, dk colors w/wht embr, EX..............**85.00**
Slave anklet, Dan, Liberia, 5" dia, EX..**185.00**
Spear, iron, primitive, w/cvd wooden shaft, 51"............................**25.00**
Spoon, ceremonial; Dan, cvd bone, w/mask hdl, old, 7¼".........**225.00**
Staff, Luba chief's; cvd head finial, 1800s, 20", EX.....................**375.00**
Sword, ritual; Yoruba Ogboni Society, flared iron blade, 24"..**1,800.00**
Thumb piano, Baluba, Zair, hollow cvd box, inset panel, 11"......**120.00**
Walking stick, Maori, spiralling geometrics, 1880s, 36"..............**885.00**

Agata

Agata is New England peachblow (the factory called it 'Wild Rose') with an applied metallic stain which produces gold tracery and dark blue mottling. The stain is subject to wear, and the amount of remaining stain greatly affects the value. It is especially valuable (and rare) when found on peachblow of intense color. Caution — be sure to use only gentle cleaning methods.

Currently rare types of art glass have been realizing erratic prices at auction; until they stablize, we can only suggest an average range of values. In the listings that follow, examples are glossy unless noted otherwise. See also Green Opaque.

Creamer...**1,200.00**
Finger bowl, ruffled, VG mottling, 2¾x5½"................................**475.00**
Punch cup, appl hdl, deep color, 2¾x3"....................................**650.00**
Spittoon, lady's, 2¾x5"...**600.00**
Sugar bowl, EX gold & mottling, 4"..**1,250.00**
Toothpick holder, bulbous, ruffled rim, VG mottling..................**375.00**
Toothpick holder, sq top, EX color & mottling...........................**675.00**
Toothpick holder, tricorn, EX mottling, 2¼"..............................**575.00**
Tumbler, lemonade; tapered, curlicue hdl, 5"...........................**1,000.00**
Tumbler, VG color & mottling, 3¾"..**600.00**
Vase, lily; VG color & mottling, 5¾"...**900.00**
Vase, ovoid w/sqd rim, hdls, 4"...**750.00**

Agate Ware

Clays of various natural or artificially-dyed colors were combined to produce agate ware, a procedure similar to the methods used by Niloak in potting their Mission Ware. It was made by many Staffordshire potteries from about 1740 until about 1825.

Cat, seated, blk/wht w/bl, solid, Wheildon type, rpr, 4"...............**800.00**
Cream pitcher, 3 lion mask & paw ft, bl/brn clay, rpr, 4½".........**925.00**
Porringer, lg hdls, allover mottle, 1750s, rprs, 10" W..............**1,500.00**
Stag, recumbent, on oval base, 1745, rpr, 3" H.....................**3,300.00**
Teapot, brn/cream, sq w/short ft, foo dog finial, rpr, 5¼"........**6,300.00**

Akro Agate

The Akro Agate Co. founded in 1914 primarily as a marble maker, operated in Clarksburg, West Virginia, until 1951. Their popular wares included children's dishes, powder jars, flowerpots, and novelty items along with the famous 'Akro Aggies.' Much of their glass was produced in the distinctive marbleized colors they called Red Onyx, Blue Onyx,

etc.; solid opaque and transparent colors were also produced. Most of the wares are marked with their trademark, a crow flying through the letter 'A' holding an Aggie in its beak and one in each claw. Other marks include 'J.P.' on children's pieces, 'J.V. Co., Inc,' 'Braun & Corwin,' 'N.Y.C. Vogue Merc Co. U.S.A.,' 'Hamilton Match Co.,' and 'Mexicali Pickwick Cosmetic Corp.' on novelty items. In 1936 Akro obtained the moulds from the Balmer-Westite Co. of Weston, West Virginia. Westite produced a similar line of products for several years. Their ware is drab in color when compared to Akro and is generally unmarked. The embossed Westite logo does appear occasionally on the bottom of some pieces. Westite is commonly accepted as a companion collectible of Akro.

For more information we recommend *Children's Dishes*, by Margaret and Kenn Whitmyer, available at your local bookstore. Our advisor for miscellaneous Akro Agate is Albert Morin; he is listed in the Directory under Massachusetts.

Chiquita

Creamer, baked-on colors, 1½"... **8.00**
Creamer, opaque gr, 1½"... **5.00**
Creamer, opaque turq, lav, or caramel, 1½".........................**12.00**
Creamer, transparent cobalt, 1½".......................................**10.00**
Cup, opaque gr, 1½".. **4.00**
Cup, opaque turq, lav, or caramel, 1½"...............................**15.00**
Cup, transparent cobalt, 1½".. **6.00**
Plate, baked-on colors, 3¾".. **4.00**
Plate, transparent cobalt, 3¾".. **5.00**
Saucer, baked-on colors, 3⅛"... **1.50**
Saucer, gr opaque, 3⅛"... **1.00**
Saucer, opaque lav, caramel, or yel, 3¼".............................. **5.00**
Saucer, transparent cobalt, 3⅛".. **1.50**
Set, 16-pc, baked-on colors...**70.00**
Set, 16-pc, opaque colors other than gr...............................**125.00**
Set, 16-pc, opaque gr...**47.00**
Set, 16-pc, transparent cobalt...**105.00**
Sugar bowl, baked-on colors, open, 1½"............................... **8.00**
Sugar bowl, opaque turq, lav, or caramel, open, 1½".............**12.00**
Sugar bowl, transparent cobalt, open, 1½"...........................**10.00**
Teapot, baked-on colors, w/lid, 3".......................................**15.00**
Teapot, opaque gr, w/lid, 3"... **9.00**
Teapot, opaque turq or lav, w/lid, 3"...................................**35.00**
Teapot, transparent cobalt, w/lid, 3"...................................**25.00**

Concentric Rib

Creamer, opaque colors other than gr or wht, 1¼"................. **7.50**
Creamer, opaque gr or wht, 1¼".. **5.00**
Cup, opaque colors other than gr or wht, 1¼"....................... **5.00**
Cup, opaque gr or wht, 1¼".. **3.00**
Plate, opaque colors other than gr or wht, 3¼"..................... **3.00**
Plate, opaque gr or wht, 3¼".. **2.00**
Saucer, opaque gr or wht, 2¾".. **1.50**
Sugar bowl, opaque colors other than gr or wht, 1¼"............. **7.50**
Sugar bowl, opaque gr or wht, 1¼"...................................... **4.50**
Teapot, opaque colors other than gr or wht, w/lid, 3⅜".........**10.00**
Teapot, opaque gr or wht, w/lid, 3½"................................... **9.00**

Concentric Ring

Cereal, lg, solid opaque colors, 3⅜".....................................**18.00**
Cereal, lg, transparent cobalt, 3⅜"......................................**30.00**
Creamer, lg, marbleized bl, 1⅜"..**45.00**
Creamer, lg, transparent cobalt, 1⅜"...................................**30.00**
Creamer, sm, marbleized bl, 1¼"...**35.00**

Creamer, sm, solid opaque colors, 1¼" 14.00
Cup, lg, opaque lav or yel, 1⅜" 30.00
Cup, lg, opaque marbleized colors 30.00
Cup, lg, opaque pumpkin, 1⅜" 20.00
Cup, sm, transparent cobalt, 1¼" 24.00
Plate, lg, solid opaque colors, 4¼" 6.00
Plate, lg, transparent cobalt, 4¼" 12.00
Plate, sm, solid opaque colors, 3¼" 6.00
Plate, sm, transparent cobalt, 3¼" 12.00
Saucer, lg, solid opaque colors, 3⅛" 4.00
Saucer, lg, transparent cobalt, 3⅛" 5.00
Saucer, sm, solid opaque colors, 2¾" 3.00
Set, 16-pc, solid opaque colors, sm 105.00
Set, 21-pc, marbleized bl, lg 460.00
Sugar bowl, lg, solid opaque colors, w/lid, 1⅞" 25.00
Sugar bowl, lg, transparent cobalt, w/lid, 1⅞" 45.00
Teapot, lg, marbleized bl, w/lid, 3¾" 80.00
Teapot, lg, solid opaque colors, w/lid, 3¾" 35.00

Interior Panel

Cereal, lg, azure bl or yel, 3⅜" 18.00
Cereal, lg, marbleized gr/wht, 3⅜" 25.00
Creamer, lg, marbleized bl/wht, 1⅜" 20.00
Creamer, lg, pk or gr lustre, 1⅜" 14.00
Creamer, sm, azure bl or yel, 1¼" 27.00
Creamer, sm, pk or gr lustre, 1¼" 22.00
Cup, lg, marbleized red/wht, 1⅜" 25.00
Cup, sm, marbleized red/wht, 1¼" 22.00
Cup, sm, pk or gr lustre, 1¼" 8.00
Cup, sm, pumpkin, 1¼" 20.00
Pitcher, sm, transparent gr or topaz, 2⅞" 14.00
Plate, lg, azure bl or yel, 4¼" 12.00
Plate, sm, marbleized bl/wht, 3¾" 7.00
Plate, sm, pk or gr lustre, 3¾" 5.00
Saucer, sm, azure bl or yel, 2⅜" 5.50
Saucer, sm, marbleized red/wht, 2⅜" 5.00
Set, lg, 21-pc, marbleized bl/wht 325.00
Set, lg, 21-pc, pk or gr lustre 225.00
Set, sm, 16-pc, marbleized red/wht, MIB 220.00
Set, sm, 16-pc, pk or gr lustre, MIB 125.00
Set, sm, 8-pc, marbleized bl/wht, MIB 105.00
Set, sm, 8-pc, transparent gr or topaz 40.00
Sugar bowl, lg, lemonade/oxblood, w/lid, 1⅞" 50.00
Sugar bowl, lg, transparent gr or topaz, w/lid, 1⅞" ...25.00
Sugar bowl, sm, azure bl or yel, 1¼" 27.00
Sugar bowl, sm, marbleized bl/wht, 1¼" 25.00

Interior Panel tea set, blue marbled, 16-piece set, $220.00.

Teapot, lg, lemonade/oxblood, w/lid, 3¾" 50.00
Teapot, sm, azure bl or yel, w/lid, 3⅜" 40.00
Teapot, sm, marbleized bl/wht, w/lid, 3⅜" 40.00
Tumbler, sm, opaque, 2" 40.00
Tumbler, sm, transparent gr or topaz, 2" 8.00

J.P. (Made for J. Pressman Company)

Cup, baked-on colors, 1½" 4.00
Cup, transparent cobalt w/ribs, 1½" 6.00
Cup, transparent gr, 1½" 25.00
Cup, transparent red or brn, 1½" 35.00
Plate, transparent gr, 4¼" 8.50
Plate, transparent red or brn, 1½" 30.00
Saucer, baked-on colors, 3¼" 1.50
Saucer, transparent cobalt w/ribs, 3¼" 4.00
Set, 17-pc, transparent gr 185.00
Set, 21-pc, baked-on colors 105.00
Sugar bowl, baked-on colors, w/lid, 1½" 10.00
Sugar bowl, transparent gr, w/lid, 1½" 25.00
Teapot, baked-on colors, w/lid, 1½" 15.00
Teapot, transparent gr, w/lid, 1½" 45.00

Miss America

Creamer, forest gr or marbleized orange/wht 42.00
Creamer, wht 35.00
Cup, forest gr or marbleized orange/wht 32.00
Cup, wht 27.00
Plate, forest gr or marbleized orange/wht 20.00
Plate, wht 15.00
Saucer, forest gr or marbleized orange/wht 11.00
Saucer, wht 10.00
Sugar bowl, forest gr or marbleized orange/wht, w/lid ...60.00
Teapot, forest gr or marbleized orange/wht, w/lid 90.00

Octagonal

Cereal, lg, dk gr, bl, or wht, 3⅜" 6.00
Cereal, lg, lemonade/oxblood, 3⅜" 20.00
Cereal, lg, pk, other opaques, 3⅜" 6.00
Creamer, lg, beige, pumpkin, or lt bl, closed hdl, 1½" ...14.00
Creamer, lg, dk gr, bl, or wht, closed hdl, 1½" 9.00
Creamer, sm, dk gr, bl, or wht, 1¼" 12.00
Plate, sm, dk gr, bl, or wht, 3⅜" 4.00
Saucer, sm, yel or lime gr, 3⅜" 5.00
Set, lg, 21-pc, dk gr, bl, or wht 90.00
Set, lg, 21-pc, lemonade/oxblood, closed hdls, MIB ...300.00
Sugar bowl, sm, dk gr, bl, or wht, 1¼" 8.00
Teapot, lg, bl or gr 16.00
Tumbler, sm, pumpkin, yel, or lime gr, 2" 14.00

Raised Daisy

Creamer, yel, 1¾" 45.00
Cup, bl, 1¾" 35.00
Cup, gr, 1¾" 18.00
Plate, bl, 3" 8.00
Saucer, beige, 2½" 6.00
Sugar bowl, yel, 1¾" 45.00
Teapot, bl, 2⅜" 57.00
Teapot, yel, 2⅜" 40.00
Tumbler, bl (no embossed pattern), 2" 55.00
Tumbler, yel or beige, 2" 18.00

Stacked Disc

Creamer, opaque colors other than gr or wht, 1¼"	7.50
Creamer, pumpkin, 1¼"	14.00
Cup, opaque gr or wht, 1¼"	5.00
Pitcher, opaque colors other than gr or wht, 2⅞"	12.00
Pitcher, opaque gr, 2⅞"	8.00
Plate, opaque bl, 3¼"	4.00
Set, 21-pc, opaque colors other than gr or wht	90.00
Set, 21-pc, opaque gr or wht	60.00
Sugar bowl, opaque colors other than gr or wht, 1¼"	7.50
Sugar bowl, pumpkin, 1¼"	14.00
Teapot, opaque colors other than gr or wht, 3⅜"	12.00
Teapot, opaque gr or wht, 3⅜"	9.00
Teapot, pumpkin, 3⅜"	20.00
Tumbler, opaque gr or wht, 2"	5.00
Tumbler, pumpkin, 2"	25.00

Stacked Disc and Interior Panel

Cereal, lg, marbleized bl, 3⅜"	35.00
Cereal, lg, transparent gr, 3⅜"	17.00
Creamer, lg, opaque solid colors, 1⅜"	18.00
Creamer, lg, transparent gr or cobalt, 1⅜"	25.00
Creamer, sm, opaque solid colors, 1¼"	13.00
Cup, lg, transparent cobalt, 1⅜"	20.00
Cup, sm, marbleized bl, 1¼"	22.00
Pitcher, sm, transparent gr, 2⅞"	12.00
Plate, lg, opaque solid colors, 4¾"	7.00
Set, lg, 21-pc, opaque solid colors, MIB	225.00
Set, lg, 21-pc, transparent cobalt, MIB	350.00
Set, sm, 8-pc, opaque solid colors, MIB	65.00
Set, sm, 8-pc, transparent cobalt, MIB	115.00
Sugar bowl, lg, marbleized bl, w/lid, 1⅞"	45.00
Sugar bowl, sm, transparent gr, open, 1¼"	20.00
Teapot, lg, transparent gr, w/lid, 3¾"	35.00
Teapot, sm, transparent gr, w/lid, 2"	17.00
Tumbler, sm, opaque solid colors, 2"	20.00
Tumbler, sm, transparent cobalt, 2"	9.00

Stippled Band

Creamer, lg, transparent gr, 1½"	15.00
Creamer, sm, transparent amber, 1¼"	18.00
Cup, lg, transparent azure, 1½"	18.00
Cup, sm, transparent amber, 1¼"	5.00
Pitcher, sm, transparent amber, 2⅞"	10.00
Plate, lg, transparent amber, 4¼"	7.00
Plate, lg, transparent azure, 4¼"	10.00
Plate, sm, transparent gr, 3¼"	4.00
Saucer, lg, transparent gr, 3¼"	2.00
Set, lg, 17-pc, transparent amber	150.00
Set, sm, 8-pc, transparent gr, MIB	35.00
Sugar bowl, lg, transparent amber, w/lid, 1⅞"	18.00
Sugar bowl, sm, transparent amber, open, 1¼"	18.00
Tumbler, sm, transparent amber, 1¾"	6.00
Tumbler, sm, transparent gr, 1¾"	7.00

Miscellaneous

Ash tray, blk, 3" sq	12.00
Ash tray, gr, Hotel Edison	24.00
Ash tray, hexagonal, emb Atlantic Foundry Co	85.00
Bell, crystal, fine rib	30.00

Bell, yel	85.00
Bowl, bl, Stacked Disc	18.00
Bowl, gr, ftd fruit	100.00
Bowl, marbleized gr/wht, Stacked Disc	45.00
Candlestick, blk, 3¼", pr	200.00
Candlestick, pumpkin, 3¼", pr	160.00
Flowerpot, blk, ribbed top, #300F	12.00
Flowerpot, cobalt, mk Made in USA, #1308	75.00
Flowerpot, custard, Graduated Dart Fluted, 4"	65.00
Flowerpot, marbleized bl/wht, #294	24.00
Flowerpot, marbleized gr/wht, Ribs & Flutes, #307	28.00
Flowerpot, marbleized orange/wht, Ribs & Flutes, #305	14.00
Flowerpot, orange & wht, Ribbed Top w/Darts, #295	125.00
Flowerpot, pumpkin, mk Made in USA, #1310	65.00
Flowerpot, yel, Banded Dart, 3¼"	24.00
Flowerpot, yel, Graduated Dart, 3"	20.00
J Vivaudou, apothecary jar, pk	65.00
J Vivaudou, apothecary jar, wht	15.00
J Vivaudou, mortar & pestle, blk	12.00
J Vivaudou, powder box, floral, wht	20.00
J Vivaudou, shaving/coffee mug, blk	35.00
Jardiniere, bl, Ribs & Flutes, #306	24.00
Knife, Grid, crystal, Kitchen Novelty CO NJ, orig box	65.00
Knife, Grid, transparent pk	85.00
Lamp, boudoir; gr w/metal base	60.00
Lamp, marbleized orange/wht w/ or w/o shade	165.00
Planter, bl, rectangular, #656, 6"	4.00
Planter, orange/wht marbleized, lilies, #657	6.00
Powder jar, Colonial Lady, bl	58.00

Colonial Lady powder jar, in pumpkin (rare color), $1,000.00.

Powder jar, Mexicali, bl/wht	30.00
Powder jar, Ribbed, orange/ wht marbleized	34.00
Powder jar, Scotty dog, gr	85.00
Tire/pen holder, Goodrich Tires, marbleized bl/wht	65.00
Westite, flowerpot, marbleized brn/wht, Graduated Dart	10.00
Westite, sugar bowl, marbleized gr/wht	14.00
Westite, vase, marbleized brn/wht, 8¾"	18.00

Alexandrite

Alexandrite is a type of art glass introduced around the turn of the century by Thomas Webb and Sons of England. It is recognized by its characteristic shading— pale yellow to rose and blue. Although it was also produced by other companies, only examples made by Webb command premium prices. Prices for Alexandrite (as well as many other types of fine art glass) have been erratic for several months; values suggested below are average.

Bowl, Honeycomb, ruffled, +5¾" ruffled plate..............................775.00
Finger bowl, EX color, 5¼"..850.00
Finger bowl, ruffled, 4", +5" ruffled plate 700.00
Toothpick holder, Honeycomb, str rim, Webb, 2⅛" 495.00
Vase, 8-petal top, 8-panel amber std & base, Webb, 6½" 985.00

Alhambra China

A line of dinnerware made in Vienna during this century, the Alhambra pattern is strongly geometric with bold colors and gold trim. It is marked with the line name and the country of origin.

Aluminum, though being the most abundant metal in the earth's crust, always occurs in combination with other elements. Before a practical method for its refinement was developed in the late nineteenth century, articles made of aluminum were very expensive. After the process for commercial smelting was perfected in 1916, it became profitable to adapt the ductile, non-tarnishing material to many uses.

Box, 2½" dia...65.00
Compote, sm...85.00
Creamer & sugar bowl, w/lid, 2½", 4¾" 150.00
Cup & saucer 65.00
Cup & saucer, bouillon; dbl hdls...70.00
Demitasse pot 185.00
Jam jar, hdls, w/lid & underplate 110.00
Pitcher, 8½x4¾" 150.00
Plate, 6" 25.00
Plate, 8" 40.00
Teapot, openwork, scalloped top, 4½" 150.00
Tray, rnd, integral hdls 75.00

Almanacs

The earliest evidence indicates that almanacs were used as long ago as Ancient Egypt. Throughout the Dark Ages they were circulated in great volume and were referred to by more people than any other book except the Bible. *The Old Farmer's Almanac* first appeared in 1793 and has been issued annually since that time. Usually more of a pamphlet than a book (only a few have hard covers), the almanac provided planting and harvesting information to farmers, weather forecasts for seamen, medical advice, household hints, mathematical tutoring, postal rates, railroad schedules, weights and measures, 'receipts,' and jokes. Before 1800 the information was unscientific and based entirely on astrology and folklore. The first almanac in America was printed in 1639 by William Pierce Mariner; it contained data of this nature. One of the best-known editions, *Ben Franklin's Poor Richard's Almanac,* was introduced in 1732 and continued to be printed for twenty-five years.

By the nineteenth century, merchants saw the advertising potential in a publication so widely distributed, and the advertising almanac evolved. These were distributed free of charge by drug stores and mercantiles and were usually somewhat lacking in information, containing simply a calendar, a few jokes, and a variety of ads for quick remedies and quack cures.

Today their concept and informative, often amusing text make almanacs popular collectibles that may usually be had at reasonable prices. Because they were printed in such large numbers and often saved from year to year, their prices are still low — most fall within a range of $4 to $15. Those printed before 1860 are especially collectible.

Quite rare and highly prized are the Kate Greenaway 'Almanacks,' printed in London from 1883 to 1897. These are illustrated with her drawings of children, one for each calendar month.

1744, Almanack for Year of Our Lord Christ, N Ames, VG........120.00
1795, Bickerstaff's Genuine New England, EX 12.00
1808, Middlebrook's, printed on laid paper, twine ties................. 8.00
1810, Beer's, laid paper, VG 6.00
1811, Middlebrook's, hand-sewn edges, EX 6.00
1814, Beer's, EX 8.00
1815, printed on hand press, EX 6.00
1855, Farmer's Almanac, wear...15.00
1859, Dr Jayne's Family Medicines, wear 20.00
1874, Farmer's & Mechanic's Almanac, EX 18.00
1886, Merchant's Gargling Oil, EX 15.00
1890, Morse's Indian Root Pills, Indian/horse, 6½x6"...................18.00
1891, Public Ledger, Phila, 73-pg, EX 5.00

Drake's Plantation Bitters, 'Morning, Noon, Night Almanac,' multicolored cover, 1891 or 1892, rare, NM, $50.00 each.

1897, The Household Almanac, NM...10.00
1907, Ayer's American, EX 5.00
1908, Dobbs (Medical Co), EX 7.50
1916, Armour's Maid on Farm...15.00
1917, VA Fire & Marine Ins, Confederate cover, VG 28.00
1917, Watkins Almanac, Home Doctor & Cookbook, EX 12.00
1920-25, John Baer's Agricultural, ea 8.50
1928, Dr Miles' Weather Almanac, color, EX 10.00
1958, Herbilist Almanac... 8.00
1959, World, 588-pg, M 25.00

Aluminum

By the late thirties, novelties, trays, pitchers, and many other tableware items were being produced. They were often hand-crafted with elaborate decoration. Russel Wright designed a line of lovely pieces such as lamps, vases, and desk accessories that are becoming very collectible. Many who crafted the ware marked it with their company logo, and these signed pieces are attracting the most interest. Wendell August Forge (Grove City, PA) is a mark to watch for; this firm produced some particularly nice examples and upwardly mobile market values reflect their popularity with today's collectors. In general, 'spun' aluminum is from the thirties or early forties, and 'hammered' aluminum is from the fifties. See also Russel Wright.

Our advisor for this category is Ted Haun; he is listed in the Directory under Indiana.

Ash tray, 6 incised flowers, Buenilum, 6½" dia 5.00
Basket, acorns, scalloped rim, 6x11¾" dia.....................................12.50
Bowl, console; ruffled, hammered, hdls 8.00
Bowl, grapes, Hammerkraft, 11½" 7.50
Butter dish, bamboo, clear glass insert, Everlast, ¼-lb 7.50
Cake saver, spun, acorn finial, West Bend 10.00
Candlestick, acanthus leaf base, Continental, 7⅝", pr 22.50
Candy server, roses, coiled hdl, Thames.....................................10.00
Coaster, roses, Everlast, 4 for 4.00
Ice bucket, insulated, Hammerkraft 12.00
Lazy susan, daffodils, glass insert, 18" 15.00
Relish, sectioned, glass inserts, Continental 30.00
Server, bamboo, 2-tier, Everlast 10.00
Silent butler, pine cones & needles, Everlast 9.00
Syrup server, w/lid.. 9.00
Teakettle, hammered, Italian..15.00

Left: #142, 6", in white matt, $125.00, in bright blue gloss, $140.00; Right: #149, 6", in white matt, $135.00, in bright blue gloss, $150.00.

Vase, #S2, yel-gr matt, 3½" 35.00
Vase, #22, gr matt, sm hdls, 6" 35.00
Vase, #25, bl/gr glossy drip, w/hdls, 8x9" 145.00
Vase, #4, tan/brn speckled, glossy, 4¾" 30.00
Vase, #42, ivory matt w/bl & red highlights, bulbous, 7" 135.00
Vase, #50, gr/red gloss, high sq hdls, 7¾" 95.00
Vase, #75, yel matt, stick form, 5"...45.00
Vase, #98, tan gloss, 6" 125.00

Tray, embossed bronco rider, hand hammered, 15", $25.00.

Tray, bread; grape clusters, 13½" 7.50
Tray, bread; ornate stamped motif 7.50
Tray, flying geese, cattails, Wendell August Forge, 14x9" 17.50
Tray, pierced & emb motif, twisted hdls 15.00
Tray, poinsettia, crimped, loop hdls 9.00
Tray, strawberries, rnd 7.50
Tray, tulips, Kent, 14"...22.50
Tray, wildlife, 4¼x7¼".. 5.00

AMACO, American Art Clay Co.

AMACO is the logo of the American Art Clay Co. Inc., founded in Indianapolis, Indiana, in 1919, by Ted O. Philpot. They produced a line of art pottery from 1931 through 1938 that is today beginning to interest collectors. The company is still in business but now produces only supplies, implements, and tools for the ceramic trade.

Values for AMACO have risen sharply, especially those for figurals, items with Art Deco styling, and pieces with uncommon shapes.

Our advisor for this category is Virginia Heiss; she is listed in the Directory under Indiana.

Figural head, #515, dk yel matt, Deco, 5" 110.00

Amberina

Amberina, one of the earliest types of art glass, was developed in 1883 by Joseph Locke, of the New England Glass Company. The trademark was registered by W.L. Libbey, who often signed his name in script within the pontil.

Amberina was made by adding gold powder to the batch, which produced glass in the basic amber hue. Part of the item, usually the top, was simply reheated to develop the characteristic deep red or fuchsia shading. Early amberina was mold-blown, but cut and pressed amberina was also produced. The rarest type is plated amberina, made by New England for a short time after 1886. It has been estimated that less than 2,000 pieces were ever produced. Other companies, among them Hobbs and Brockunier, Mt. Washington Glass Company, and Sowerby's Ellison Glassworks of England, made their own versions, being careful to change the name of their product to avoid infringing on Libbey's patent. Prices have been erratic at auction for several months; values given below are in the average range. See also Libbey.

Bowl, Daisy & Button, sq, flint, 5½"....................................125.00
Bowl, lt ribbing, EX color, Mt WA, 1½x5x4½" 400.00
Bowl, lt ribbing, flared/ruffled, NE Glass, 3x5½" 375.00
Bowl, lt ribbing, 3-cornered, Mt WA, 2½x5" 275.00
Butter dish, Invt T'print, amber knob, ruffled base, 7" 800.00
Butter pat, Daisy & Button, Hobbs & Brockunier.........................110.00
Candlestick, twisted ribs, bobeche, 5½", pr 975.00
Celery vase, Invt T'print, sq top, NE Glass, 6½" 500.00
Celery vase, Venetian Dmn, ground pontil, NE Glass, 7½".........475.00
Celery vase, Venetian Dmn, sq top, NE Glass, 6½" 435.00

Celery vase, 12-scallop top, #52½ S, Mt WA, 6½" 550.00
Creamer, reeded loop hdl, 3-corner, NE Glass by Locke, 4" 465.00
Creamer & sugar, Invt T'print, reeded hdls, NE Glass, sm...........500.00
Cruet, Invt T'print, ball form, orig stopper, 3" 195.00
Cruet, Invt T'print, NE Glass 595.00
Cruet, Invt T'print, wht florals, sq base, flared rim, 8¼" 450.00
Finger bowl, scalloped, NE Glass, 5½" 200.00
Finger bowl, T'print, reverse color w/mc flowers, +plate.............565.00
Ice cream dish, blown-out ribs, scalloped rim, 3x9¼x6½" 295.00
Pitcher, Invt T'print, amber hdl, tankard form, 5¾" 155.00
Pitcher, Invt T'print, amber hdl, 7⅜x5⅛" 175.00
Pitcher, Invt T'print, clear hdl, blown, 9" 185.00
Pitcher, water; HP florals...400.00
Punch cup, Venetian Dmn, reeded hdl, bbl form, NE Glass 125.00
Rose bowl, 5-crimp top, amber ft, 3½x4¼" 125.00
Shade, Dia Quilt, ruffled, Mt WA, 2" opening, 4x5" 575.00
Spooner, Daisy & Button, 5"..150.00
Spooner, Venetian Dmn, sq top, NE Glass, 4½" 425.00
Toothpick holder, Daisy & Button 385.00
Toothpick holder, Venetian Dmn, sq mouth 225.00
Tumbler, Invt T'print, 3¾" 125.00
Tumbler, Swirl, flint, ground pontil, NE Glass, 4" 125.00
Tumbler, Venetian Dmn, EX fuchsia coloring, 4" 135.00
Tumbler, Venetian Dmn, NE Glass, 6" 165.00
Vase, bbl form, Mt WA, 4x4" 400.00
Vase, Herringbone, 6" 525.00
Vase, lily; lt ribbing, EX color, 12½" 550.00
Vase, lily; NE Glass, 7" 450.00
Vase, swirled ribs, scalloped, 12x6½" 350.00
Vase, swirled ribs, slim w/bulbous base, amber rim, 10"...............300.00
Whiskey taster, Venetian Dmn, bbl form, NE Glass, 2½"............185.00
Wine, bbl form, att NE Glass 385.00

Plated Amberina

Cruet, 6¾", $2,500.00.

Bowl, ribbed, incurvate pinched top, 7½" **4,750.00**
Butter dish, ribbed, SP base w/unicorn in center, 4¾" **3,400.00**
Condiment, ribbed, 4" shakers in SP fr mk Toronto **2,000.00**
Cruet, EX ribbing, amber hdl, tricorn, rnd stopper, 7"............ **2,500.00**
Mug, ribbed, fine color, amber hdl.. **2,100.00**
Pitcher, ribbed, amber hdl, 6¾" **5,500.00**
Pitcher, ribbed, EX color, amber hdl, tricorn, 4½" **4,750.00**
Punch cup, ribbed, amber pigtail hdl, fine color, 2¾" **2,250.00**

Punch cup, slightly ribbed top, amber hdl, EX color, 3¾" **1,800.00**
Rose bowl, ribbed, 5½" **1,800.00**
Shaker, salt; distinct ribbing, fine color **900.00**
Tumbler, EX ribbing & color... **1,500.00**
Underplate, ribbed, ruffled, 6⅜" **1,150.00**

American Encaustic Tiling Co.

A.E. Tile was organized in 1879 in Zanesville, Ohio. Until its closing in 1935, they produced beautiful ornamental and architectural tile equal to the best European imports. They also made vases, figurines, and novelty items with exceptionally fine modeling and glazes.

Bookends, cupid w/rabbit, mk, 1926, 5x5", pr 125.00
Paperweight, ram figural 65.00
Tile, bird, HP, wood fr, 10½x6¼", pr.......................................350.00

Tile, embossed stylized deer, black on bronze, $125.00.

Tile, fish in waves, 4-color, 2x4" 65.00
Tile, floral, bl, 6" 25.00
Tile, floral, mc on tan, fr, 6" 45.00
Vase, lt gr, buttress-style arms, 8"..145.00

American Indian Art

That time when the American Indian was free to practice the crafts and culture that was his heritage has always held a fascination for many. They were a people who appreciated beauty of design and colorful decoration in their furnishings and clothing; and because instruction in their crafts was a routine part of their rearing, they were well accomplished. Several tribes developed areas in which they excelled. The Navajo were weavers and silversmiths; the Zuni, lapidaries. Examples of their craftsmanship are very valuable. Today even the work of contemporary Indian artists — weavers, silversmiths, carvers, and others — is highly collectible. For a more thorough study we recommend *North American Indian Artifacts* by our advisor, Lar Hothem; you will find his address in the Directory under Ohio.

Key:
bw — beadwork   NE — Northeastern
dmn — diamond   S — Southern
E — Eastern   W — Western

Apparel and Accessories

Before the white traders brought the Indian women cloth from which to sew their garments and beads to use for decorating them, clothing was made from skins sewn together with sinew, usually made of buffalo tendon. Porcupine quills were dyed bright colors and woven into bags and armbands and used to decorate clothing and moccasins. Examples of early quillwork are scarce today and highly collectible.

Early in the nineteenth century, beads were being transported via pony pack trains. These 'pony' beads were irregular shapes of opaque glass imported from Venice. Nearly always blue or white, they were twice as large as the later 'seed' beads. By 1870 translucent beads in many sizes and colors had been made available, and Indian beadwork had become commercialized. Each tribe developed its own distinctive methods and preferred decorations, making it possible for collectors today to determine the origin of many items. Soon after the turn of the century, the craft of beadworking began to diminish.

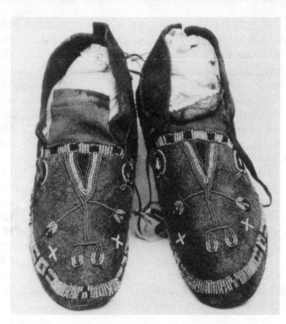

Moccasins, Eastern Sioux, sinew sewn, hard soled, multicolored beadwork, 10½", $650.00.

Arm bands, Plateau, full bw, brass-bead florals, 1900, 2" **250.00**
Arm bands, Sioux, fully quilled hide w/fringe, 1900, 10x1½" **200.00**
Belt, Cheyenne, full bw geometrics, gr/yel, 1920, 35x2" **150.00**
Belt, Cheyenne, leather w/full geometric bw, 1910, 38x3½" **200.00**
Belt, Crow, 4" leather w/brass tacks & bw, 1890, 43"..................**700.00**
Breastplate, Blackfoot, hairbone, shell/ribbon drops, 22" **750.00**
Breastplate, Cheyenne, bone/brass beads, orig, 1870, 18x14".. **2,200.00**
Breastplate, Crow, hairpipe/crow & bone beads, 1910, 11x8" **300.00**
Clout, Nez Perce, corn husk w/buckskin trim, fringe, 1890 ....**300.00**
Clout, Sioux, bl trade cloth, quillwork front, 1890, 50x12"..... **1,300.00**
Cuffs, dance; Blackfoot, full bw, 1965, 5½x5" **125.00**
Cuffs, Sioux, hide w/floral & star bw, fringe, 1920, 7x4½" **175.00**
Dance yoke, Blackfoot, bugle heads/brass thimbles, 1890, 50" . **1,000.00**
Dance yoke, Blackfoot, full bw, bead fringe, 1940, 20x13" **350.00**
Dance yoke, Nez Perce lady's, bw/suspensions/etc on velvet........**300.00**
Dress, buckskin w/bead & feather trim, 1-shoulder, modern **50.00**
Dress, Cheyenne, cowrie shells on trade cloth, fringe, 1920 ....**225.00**
Dress, Cheyenne girl's, wht buckskin w/bw & fringe, 1920..........**200.00**
Dress, Chippewa, 2-pc trade cloth 'jingler' w/tin cones, '20 ....**500.00**
Dress, Kiowa, buckskin w/EX bw, fringe, tin cones, 1935, lg........**800.00**
Dress, Navajo, handspun wool, red stripes on blk, 50x65"....... **6,250.00**
Dress, Nez Perce, wht buckskin, glass seed beads, 1900, 48" **450.00**
Dress, Sioux, Sitting Bull's daughter's, wool/cowrie shells....... **1,700.00**
Dress, Wakima, buckskin w/bw, long fringe, 1935.......................**500.00**
Gauntlets, Flathead, contour bw, calico lined, fringe, 1900........**350.00**
Gauntlets, Plateau, bw cuff w/florals on bl, fringe, 16".................**150.00**
Gauntlets, Plateau, bw horse on bk of hand, ornamental style **275.00**
Gauntlets, Plateau, 4-color floral bw, 14" **100.00**
Headdress, Sioux, deer/porcupine hair roach, 1940, 12x3" **200.00**
Jacket, Cree, buckskin, fringe, bw bib/pockets/cuffs, 1900 ....**600.00**
Jacket, Kiowa, buffalo tunic, bw/fringe/floral embr, 1880 .... **1,500.00**
Legging strips, Chippewa, full floral bw, 1920, 29x3½", pr **300.00**
Leggings, Arapaho, hide, yel dyed, geometric bw, 1890, 10x6"...**600.00**
Leggings, Blackfoot, trade wool blanket w/bw, 1900, 31x24"......**750.00**
Leggings, Cheyenne lady's, elk w/geometric bw lines, 1910 ....**350.00**
Leggings, Crow, buffalo head bw on navy stroud, 1880, 32" **600.00**
Leggings, Kiowa, trade cloth, ribbonwork along edge, 1920 ....**150.00**
Leggings, Kiowa lady's, hide w/geometric bw, 1900, 18x7" **500.00**
Leggings, Sioux, bw panels on bl cloth, sequins, 1920, 24" **550.00**
Moccasins, Blackfoot, full geometric bw, 1940, 12" **275.00**
Moccasins, Blood, buffalo w/intricate bw top, 1900, 11".............**400.00**
Moccasins, Cheyenne, full bw on pk, sinew sewn, 1890, 11" . **1,000.00**
Moccasins, Crow, full bw geometrics, buffalo hide, 1890, 9" **600.00**
Moccasins, Crow, sinew-sewn buffalo w/mc geometric bw, 1910.**350.00**
Moccasins, Crow, very elaborate full bw on hide, 1890, 10" ... **1,900.00**
Moccasins, Iroquois, pony beads/floral bw, 1880, 9"....................**300.00**
Moccasins, Plain's ritual, full bw top/soles, 10" **1,000.00**
Moccasins, Sioux, buffalo hide w/full bw, sinew sewn, 1890........**650.00**
Moccasins, Sioux, quillwork: wht/red on purple, 1930, 11" **150.00**

Moccasins, Tlingit, ceremonial, bw eagle/foliage, 1890, 9"..........**500.00**
Pants, Crow, ochred buckskin w/floral bw, 1930, med **300.00**
Robe, Sioux, hide w/EX story painting, 1870, 58x40" **2,700.00**
Robe, Sioux, pnt cow hide w/sunbursts, 1870, 78x60" **2,500.00**
Sash, assumption; Hudson Bay, finger woven/fringe, 1880, 96" ...**300.00**
Sash, Chippewa, loom bw floral, hand-woven fringe, 1920, 57" ...**250.00**
Sash, Great Lakes, pony/seed beads woven in, 1890, 82x8".........**350.00**
Sash, Potowatamie, finger woven, bw/drops/wool braids, 1900.. **2,200.00**
Shirt/leggings/clout, Blackfoot, hide/loom bw strips, '20s **800.00**
Vest, Blackfoot, buffalo hide, full bw geometrics, 1900, lg...........**650.00**
Vest, Blackfoot, trade cloth w/lg bugle bead florals, 1910 ....**400.00**
Vest, Flathead, lg/complex floral bw w/bl bkground, 1920...........**950.00**
Vest, Nez Perce, floral bw panels, rpl leather, 1920, lg.................**800.00**
Vest, Nez Perce, hide w/yel pnt & floral bw front/bk, 1910 ....**400.00**
Vest, Otto, bw on red wool stroud ea side, 1875, lg......................**800.00**
Vest, Santee Sioux, bw on hide ea side w/embr horses, 1920.......**300.00**
Vest, Sioux, full bw geometrics/bear tracks/Xs, 1890, 21" **4,250.00**
Vest, Sioux, full geometric bw on wht bkground, 1920 .... **1,100.00**
Vest, Sioux child's, full bw geometrics, 1900, 14x11" **1,100.00**

Arrowheads and Points

Relics of this type usually display characteristics of a general area, time period, or a particular location. With study, those made by the Plains Indians are easily discerned from those of the West Coast. Because modern man has imitated the art of the Indian by reproducing these artifacts through modern means, use caution before investing your money in 'too good to be authentic' specimens.

Agate Basin, MO, gray, 3½" **35.00**
Angostura, TN, tan/wine, classic, 2¾" **55.00**
Breckenridge Dalton, dk gray, classic, well made, 3" **45.00**
Bulverde, TX, gray, 1¾"...**80.00**
Clovis, AR, off-wht, 2¾"...**120.00**
Clovis, beige, 4 ....**290.00**
Clovis, off-wht, classic, 3" **115.00**
Dalton, AR, off-wht, well made, 3½"..**75.00**
Dalton, AR, off-wht, 2" **22.00**
Dalton, AR, tan, deeply serrated, 2¾" **36.00**
Dalton, MO, gray/tan, 2¼"...**20.00**

Hardin, MO, rose/wht, 3⅜" 75.00
Hemphill, MO, off-wht, 1⅞" 12.00
Hopewell-Snyder, IL, off-wht, classic, 3¼" 135.00
Hopewell-Snyder, IL, pk/red, 3" 85.00
Keota, AR, tan, classic, 1" 12.00
Meserve Point, AL, off-wht, shallow flutes, classic, 3¼" 90.00
Nebo Hill, tan, 4⅜" 48.00
Noland, TX, lt brn, 2¾" 48.00
Palmillas, TX, off-wht, 2¼" 6.00
Pedernales, TX, gray, 5" 95.00
Perdiz, brn, 1" 12.00
Scottsbluff, TX, gray, classic, 4¼" 235.00
Table Rock, AR, off-wht, 1¾", VG 8.00
Thebes Point, OH, gray, classic, 3" 175.00
Washita, AR, off-wht translucent agate, classic, 1¼" 12.00
Wells, TX, dk gray, 2" 16.00

Arts and Crafts

Cvg, Haida, argillite, woman w/baby on bk, 1910, 5½x2" 150.00
Painting, Hopi, Pueblo Dancer, Waldo Mootzka, 1955................450.00
Painting, Kachina dancer, sgn Polineymatewa, 1972, 27x17" 75.00
Painting, Kachina dancer, sgn Raymond Naha, 1965, 18x12" 800.00
Painting, Navajo girl/sheep, sgn Raymond Naha, 1965, 19x23" ..250.00
Sandpainting, Yei-Bi-Chai, Harry Begay, 1975, 36x24"...............450.00
Tapestry, Navajo, 4-color train, 1890, 16x17", EX 725.00
Weaving, Navajo, birds in tree, Fredie Tisi, 1988, 28x34" 500.00
Weaving, Navajo, cornstalks on dk gold, hand spun, 32x33" 125.00
Weaving, Navajo, sandpnt rug by H Klah's niece, 56x52" 1,600.00
Weaving, Navajo, 3-color on red, hand spun, 1900, 33x22".........425.00
Weaving, Transitional, red/wht geometrics, 1910, 74x47" 300.00
Weaving, 4-figure rainbow yei, Lakachukai, 1960, 38x57" 800.00

Bags and Cases

The Indians used bags for many purposes, and most display excellent form and workmanship. Of the types listed below, many collectors consider the pipe bag to be the most desirable form. Pipe bags were long, narrow, leather and bead or quillwork creations made to hold tobacco in a compartment at the bottom and the pipe, with the bowl removed from the stem, in the top. Long buckskin fringe was used as trim and complemented the quilled and beaded design to make the bag a masterpiece of Indian Art.

Apache, pony-beaded hide pouch, tin cone suspensions, ca 1850s, 6", $3,800.00.

Apache, medicine, made from tanned deer's head, 1880, 12x9" ..250.00
Blackfoot, knife case, hide w/cutout, tacks & bw, 1910, 14"........450.00
Blackfoot, pipe, full bw, ermine/hairlock drops, 1860, 25" 2,500.00
Blackfoot, pipe, hide w/floral bw & fringe, 1890, 20x7"...............550.00
Blackfoot, saddlebags, floral bw on red stroud, 1800s, 49".........850.00
Cheyenne, pipe, full bw bands/Xs/etc, fringe, 15x6" 1,150.00
Cree, pouch, buckskin w/silk embr, fringe, 1890, 8x3½".............225.00
Crow, parfleche, EX pnt motif, folded, 1880, 28x16" 900.00
Crow, parfleche 'suitcase,' pnt traces, 1880, 25x10" 250.00
Crow, pipe, antelope, ochre/bw/quilling/fringe, 1870, 34" 1,600.00
Crow, possible, buffalo, bw stripes/tin cones, 1880, 25x15" ... 1,000.00
Crow, possible, buffalo, bw/quilling/tin cones, 1890, 26x6"...... 3,000.00
Crow, possible, full bw geometric front/ends, 1890, 16x12" ... 1,500.00
Crow, strike-a-lite, hide w/quillwork & tin cones, 1940, 5".........300.00
Flathead, bag, full bw w/mc florals, 1935, 12x10" 150.00
Flathead, parfleche war bonnet case, pnt/buffalo fringe, 15"........800.00
Iroquois, trade cloth w/bw floral ea side, 1880, 7x7" 175.00
Kiowa, strike-a-lite, bw/tin cones on buffalo, 1890, 5x3½" 800.00
Menomenee, bandolier, intricate full bw, 1880, 39x8" 1,950.00
N Plains, whole unborn buffalo hide, bw ft, 1860, 22x6".........2,500.00
Nez Perce, bag, full contour floral bw, 1875, 15x12"............... 1,200.00
Nez Perce, bag, woven yarn forms banded pattern, 11x10"..........200.00
Nez Perce, corn husk, twined geometrics, choice, 1880, 18".......900.00
Nez Perce, throw-over saddlebags, elk/full bw, 1880, 14" W ... 3,000.00
Nez Perce, twined corn husk, geometric/hearts/Xs, 1900, 10"......400.00
Nez Perce, twined corn husk w/geometrics, 1880, 21x4"............450.00
Ojibway, pouch, cloth, floral bw, bead trim/fringe, 1890, 7".......175.00
Plateau, bag, bw deer & eagle, 1930, 16x13" 300.00
Plateau, bag, geometric bw, 1920, 12x11"..................................250.00
Plateau, belt pouch, full bw w/EX eagle & arrows, 1900, 6" 1,100.00
Plateau, heart-shaped, full bw w/Indian lady, 1920, 16x12".........450.00
Plateau, semi-contour full bw, Fr velvet bk, 1900, 9x11" 300.00
S Plains, knife case, 4-color bw, worn feathers, 1880, 10"...........475.00
Sioux, dr's bag shape, mc bw geometrics, 1935, 11x7x5" 300.00
Sioux, dr's bag shape w/full bw geometrics, 1890, 7x13".......... 1,600.00
Sioux, knife case, hide, sinew-sewn geometric bw, 1910, 10" 600.00
Sioux, lady's handbag, full bw geometrics, 1960, 10x7" 200.00
Sioux, pipe, bw horse/rider ea side, quilled fringe, 28x8".........3,000.00
Sioux, pipe, sinew sewn/bw, quilled fringe, 1890, 32x8" 1,750.00
Sioux, possible, buffalo, completely quilled, 1890, 21x14" 2,750.00
Sioux, sinew sewn, geometric bw/ochre/tin cones, 1900, 6x3".....200.00
Sioux, sinew-sewn buffalo w/ribbon quillwork, 1880, 9x8".........350.00
Sioux, tobacco, bw birds/florals, 1870, 8x4" 300.00
Ute, tobacco, sinew-sewn bw on ochred antelope, hawk bells.....800.00
Wasco, bag, row of birds all around, 1880, 6x3"..........................150.00
Wasco, sally bag, deer/mtn sheep/etc, 1890, 5x8" 2,500.00
Wasco, sally bag, horses/deer ea side, 1860, 8x6", VG 1,300.00
Winnebago, bandolier, full bw geometrics/florals, 13x37" 1,250.00
Yakima, bag, bw depicting Mary & Baby Jesus, 1980, 21x12".....500.00
Yurok, purse, elk antler section w/cvd geometrics, 20th C 250.00

Baskets

In the following listings, examples are basket form and coiled unless noted otherwise. The given dimension is diameter for bowls and round trays; for rectangular items, length is given.

Apache, bowl, central star/geometrics, 1930, 12" 700.00
Apache, bowl, lightning/humans, finely coiled, 1920, 13" 1,300.00
Apache, bowl, red/blk dmns, tightly coiled, 1910, 11" 1,300.00
Apache, bowl, red/gr dmns, tightly coiled, 1900, 5x17"..............400.00
Apache, bowl, repeating star designs, very fine, 2½x11".............650.00
Apache, burden type, mc, well crafted, 17x14", EX 325.00
Apache, olla, checked lines form dmns, ea w/dog or X, 7½" ... 2,400.00
Apache, olla, triangles/men/dogs all around, 1920, 7x7" 1,600.00

Apache trays, left: black devil's claw woven in radiating rosettes, 16" diameter, $2,400.00; right: willow and dark brown devil's claw woven in a spoked pattern, 16" diameter, $1,500.00.

Apache, olla, Xs in stepped dmn grid, 11x8", NM **1,475.00**
Apache, olla, 2-color humans/animals in dmns, 13x11", EX ... **1,450.00**
Apache, stepped terraces/dogs, 5½" **425.00**
Apache, tray, 12-point star, fine weave, 1900, 10" dia **450.00**
Chemeuvi, bowl, rattlesnake band, 1930, 2½x8½" **575.00**
Chemeuvi, bowl, stepped terraces, sm hole, 3x12" **1,400.00**
Hopi, bowl, 3-color on natural, Orabi from 3rd Mesa, 15"...........**225.00**
Hopi, Kachina design in earth tones, 2nd Mesa, 4x6½"...............**115.00**
Hopi, plaque, blk thunderbird on faded gr, Orabi, 12" **115.00**
Hupa, bowl, twined, blk geometrics, 1910, 4½x6½" **500.00**
Hupa, bowl, twined, blk stylized stars, 1920, 3x6" **250.00**
Hupa, bowl, twined, parallelograms, 1920, 3½x5" **150.00**
Hupa, bowl, 3 lines of meandering stairsteps, 1910, 7x5"............**500.00**
Hupa, lady's cap, blk geometrics, twined, 1900, 7x4" **500.00**
Hupa, lady's cap, red/blk geometrics, 1910, 6½x3" **500.00**
Hupa, mush bowl, parallelograms, by F Silverheels, 3½x6½"........**130.00**
Hupa, storage, twined, Xs/geometrics, w/lid, 1910, 14x12" **2,750.00**
Hupa, twined, 3 openwork bands+3 of geometrics, 1920, 10x9"..**175.00**
Karok, bowl, outstanding blk geometrics, 1920, 4½x3"................**250.00**
Karok, bowl, twined, blk geometrics, 1910, oval, 5" L **750.00**
Klamath, bowl, twined, brn stars w/yel quillwork, 1900, 8" **150.00**
Klamath, gambling tray, twined, geometrics, 1900, 20" dia **400.00**
Klamath, gambling tray, twined/quilled, 1890, 15" dia **700.00**
Klamath, twined, yel chevron quillwork, 1900, 9x11"..................**425.00**
Maidu, bowl, geometrics in redbud, 1910, 4x8" **300.00**
Maidu, bowl, quail topknot motif, 1910, 5x8½" **350.00**
Maidu, bowl, red connecting triangles, 1920, 3½x10" **700.00**
Maidu, bowl, red flames, fine weave, 1920, 2½x4" **120.00**
Mission, jar, hourglass motif, 1910, 8x4" **500.00**
Mono, bowl, unusual dmn design, 1920, 3½x6½" **275.00**
Mono, bowl, 2 bands of hourglasses, str/flaring, 2½x9" **550.00**
Mono, bowl, 2 bands of rattlesnakes, 1910, 2x10½"....................**350.00**
Mono, bowl, 4 groups of geometrics, 1900, 5x12" **650.00**
Panamint, bowl, ascending stairsteps, rim ticking, 1910, 10" .. **1,300.00**
Papago, olla, bands of gila monsters/humans, 13x13"....................**550.00**
Papago, olla, stepped 'Ls,' 12½x11".......................................**200.00**
Piaute, burden, twined; conical w/geometrics, 1910, 19x14" **550.00**
Piaute, burden, twined, 3 linear bands, conical, 1920, 10"...........**150.00**
Pima, bowl, 2 bands of human figures on side, 7x16".............. **1,600.00**
Pima, bowl, 5-petal squash blossom motif, 1930, 1x6" **800.00**
Pima, fret motif, 3x12" **325.00**
Pima, geometrics/arrowheads, 1925, 5x10" **275.00**
Pima, overall hooked geometrics, str/flaring sides, 7x12" **575.00**
Pima, tray, horsehair w/blk squash blossoms, 1985, 5" dia **375.00**
Pit River, bowl, stairsteps/stars/etc, 1910, 6x8" **360.00**

Pit River, storage, twined, parallel chevrons, 1900, 9x8" **450.00**
Pomo, bowl, feathered, w/quail topknots, 1920, 2¼x1¼"............**550.00**
Pomo, bowl, lightning designs all around, 1900, 3x12" **350.00**
Pomo, feathered/quail topknots, 1920, 6x2¾"................. **1,850.00**
Pomo, meal basket, twined, Bam Tush, 1900, 3x8"................**275.00**
Pomo, storage, twined, 3 design bands, Bam Tush, 1910, 14"......**700.00**
Pomo, tray, twined, 2 bands of designs, Bam Tush, 1910, 12"......**700.00**
Pomo, treasure basket, feathers/shells/drops, McKay, 4x1" **500.00**
Puma, bowl, blk X & line motif, 1930, 3x5" **250.00**
Salish, storage trunk, imbricated, w/lid & hdls, 1920, 19" **400.00**
Salish, storage trunk, imbricated geometrics, 1880, 24" **350.00**
Salish, 4 'S' designs on cylinder form, 7½x6½"..........................**220.00**
Thompson River, fully imbricated/zigzags, w/lid, 8½x9x19" **325.00**
Tlingit, twined, human face ea side, 1910, 5x3" **300.00**
Tlingit, twined, rattle top, 2-color geometrics, 1910, 7x5" **1,800.00**
Tlingit, twined, 3 bands of design, 1900, 9x7" **600.00**
Tulare, olla, 1 band ea: rattlesnakes/centipedes, 1930, 6"........ **1,050.00**
Walapai, storage, twined, 3 bands of line design, 1900, 17".........**250.00**
Washo, bowl, blk/red stars, 1925, 5x10" **400.00**
Washo, bowl, geometrics, tightly coiled, 1920, 2x6" **275.00**
Washo, bowl, strong 'V' designs, 1920, 4x9" **600.00**
Woodland, red/blk checkerbrd, w/lid, 15x21" **825.00**
Woodland, 3-color splint, bentwood hdl, 17" L **175.00**
Yavapai, plate, humans/animals all around, 1975, 24" **400.00**
Yokuts, bowl, vertical dmn bands/human figures, 6½x13" **800.00**
Yurok, bowl, twined, red/blk zigzags, superfine, 1900, 6x5".........**900.00**
Yurok, bowl, twined, red/blk/yel quillwork, 1920, 5x15".............**600.00**
Yurok, tobacco basket, twined, w/lid, 1910, 4x4" **250.00**

Blankets, Navajo

Pueblo Indians first made blankets centuries ago, but today most are made by Navajo Indians. Blankets were still made into the 1800s, when Pendleton and Hudson's Bay blankets became widely available. Around the turn of the century, rugs were developed because tourists were more likely to buy them as floor coverings and wall-hangings. Rugs or blankets are made in various regional styles; an expert can usually identify the area where it was made — sometimes even the individual who made it. The colors of wool are natural (gray-white, brown-black), vegetal (from plant dyes), or artificial (aniline, from synthetic chemicals.) Value factors include size, tightness of weave, artistry of design, and condition. Examples by artists whose names are well known command the higher prices.

Navajo woman's wearing blanket/rug in red, blue, white, and black, 75" x 46", $2,900.00.

Bands w/stepped dmns, 3-color on red, Germantown, 55x36".. **5,500.00**
Central sawtooth designs, wedge weave homespun, 1890........ **3,700.00**

Classic Revival, bl/blk/wht stripes, 1910, 82x71" **1,200.00**
Saddle, dbl weave, central lozenge, 1920, 64x38" **300.00**
Saddle, star/feathers motif, 1930, 30x28" **300.00**
Wearing type, lady's, rows of sqs or dmns, 4-color, 75x46" **2,900.00**
Wearing type, lady's, 9-point stepped dmns, 4-color, 54x40".......**550.00**
3rd Phase Chief's, classic designs, 1985, 58x58" **600.00**
3rd Phase Chief's, Revival Period, 1910, 66x57" **1,000.00**

Ceremonial Items

Bells, Chippewa, Jingle Dance, tin can rattles, 1935, 2 for **150.00**
Bird stone, Mound Builder, pop-eyed, mottled gray stone, 3½" ...**125.00**
Blanket, Kwakiutl, 'sun' in copper buttons/shells, '80, 54x51".....**600.00**
Bonnet, Sioux, horns, beaded brow band, 20th C, 20".................**250.00**
Bowl, Klamath, full geometric bw, 1920, 43x2½" **800.00**
Dance stick, cvd as pipe tomahawk, mc, 27" **1,500.00**
Drum, Blackfoot, hide coverd, pnt medicine birds, 1900, 14"......**250.00**
Drum, Blackfoot, rawhide, pnt heart-line buffalo, 1980, 15".........**90.00**
Drum, Kwakiutl, pnt eagle/fish, 1935, 22" dia **225.00**
Drum, N Plains, Ghost Dance motif, HP, 1800s, 17" dia **350.00**
Fetish, Cheyenne, umbilical turtle w/bw Am flag, 1880, 7x4" **300.00**
Fetish, S Plains, umbilical cord, 4-color bw on leather, 5" **100.00**
Fetish, Sioux, umbilical lizard, quilled/tin cones, 6x2¼" **475.00**
Fetish, Sioux, umbilical turtle, bw/quilled, 1890, 6x4" **900.00**
Fetish, Zuni, blk jet bear, bead/arrowhead wrap, 1940, 4x2" **120.00**
Fetish, Zuni, serpentine bear w/turq eyes, shell mouth, 8" **100.00**
Headdress, Blackfoot, horned weasel, Sun Dance lodge type **700.00**
Headdress, Plains, buffalo hide & horns/bw/hair dangles......... **1,000.00**
Headdress, Sioux, deer/porcupine roach, hair base, '40, 18" **600.00**
Idol, Mound Builder, pottery, excavated in 1910, 5x2" **100.00**
Mask, False Face Society, w/hair & copper eyes, 1910, 12x6½"...**500.00**
Mask, Iroquois, False Face Society, twined corn husk, 1910 ....**350.00**
Mask, Kwakiutl, Bukwas, cvd/pnt, 1940, 13x9" **350.00**
Mask, Kwakiutl, cvd cedar, human hair, labret, 20th C, 9x7" **400.00**
Mask, Kwakiutl, cvd/pnt, hatch mks, labret, 20th C, 12x8" **400.00**
Mask, Onondaga Iroquois, Bushy-Head, red pnt/corn husk, 10"..**450.00**
Mask, Tlingit, cvd wood, labret, 1930, 9x6" **200.00**
Mask, Wolf Dance; Kwakiutl, cvd/pnt cedar, movable jaw, 16" ..**650.00**
Mask, Woodland, Cayuga Husk Face Society, braided, 16" **475.00**
Mortar, Wasco, Columbia River, stone, rattlesnake form, 10".....**400.00**
Paint dish, NW Coast, frog cvg w/cup on bk, 7" L **600.00**
Rattle, Blackfoot, pnt moose hoof, 1870, 10x3" **250.00**
Rattle, Iroquois, False Face Society, turtle shell, 1880 ....**375.00**
Rattle, Kwakiutl, human face w/wrinkles, EX cvg, 10x4"...........**450.00**
Sash, Great Lakes, finely woven, 1890, 74x5" **200.00**
Snake, Hopi, cvd wood Snake Dance pc, w/stand, 1935 ....**400.00**
Spoon, Crow, mtn sheep horn, bw hdl, 1860, 15" **800.00**
Spoon, Tlingit, copper w/totemic eng, cvd antler hdl, 1900 ....**250.00**
Spoon, Tlingit, mtn goat/sheep horn, shell inlay, 1900, 7" **500.00**
Tabletta, Apache, Devil Dancer, mask & wands, 1930, 35x35" ..**450.00**
Talking sticks, Makah, cvd eagles/dew claw suspensions, '75.......**350.00**
Totem pole, cedar, 3-figure, cvd/pnt, 17" **900.00**
Totem pole, Haida, argillite 4-figure, eagle atop, '50, 12" **475.00**
Totem pole, Kwakiutl, cvd/pnt by Charlie James, 1920, 16x9"...**600.00**
Wand, Sioux, buffalo horn, long fully beaded hdl, 20th C...........**200.00**
War bonnet, Plains style, flannel cap, maribou/bw/feathers...........**45.00**

Dolls

Kachina, Bird, crouching, elaborate costume, 1920, 9x8" **950.00**
Kachina, Kiva, cylindrical w/pnt features, 1945, 14" **250.00**
Kachina, Kiva, simply cvd, bold facial features, 1900, 9" ... **1,500.00**
Kachina, Kiva, simply cvd/pnt, 1900, 10" **250.00**
Kachina, Maiden, EX cvg/pnt, 1902, 10x4" **2,200.00**

Kachina, Mongwa (Great Horned Owl), pnt wood, 1940, 9" **325.00**
Kachina, Pahi-Ala, old style, w/headdress, 20th C, 15x6" **350.00**
Kachina, Shooting Star, in action, H Shelton, 1980, 21" **600.00**
Kachina, Snow Kachina Girl, EX pnt/cvg, Colton #133, 11" **250.00**
N Plains, male, bw war shirt/leggings, human hair, '30, 9"..........**200.00**
NW Coast, Wolf Dancer, full costume, Erla Graham, 29" **800.00**

Plains beaded and fringed hide doll, quillwork belt, 1880s, 14", $1,600.00.

Plains, buckskin lady, bw clothing human hair, 1920, 9" **150.00**
Plains, buffalo fur stuffing, EX bw/fringed hide dress, 14" **1,100.00**
Plains, buffalo fur-stuffed muslin, EX hide w/bw dress, 15" **375.00**
Plains, cotton, hide dress & mocs w/bw & fringe, 10" **250.00**
Plains, cvd wood, male in full bw costume, E Graham, 13".........**250.00**
Plains, muslin, bw/fringed clothing, horsehair hair, 12" **550.00**
Sioux, buckskin, bw outfit w/Am flag, 20th C, 16" **900.00**
Sioux, bw vest/mocs/leggings, horsehair braid, 1880, 12" **800.00**
Skookum, couple, compo heads/elaborate outfits, 38", 20"...... **1,000.00**
Skookum, female w/baby on bk, 1915, 14" **125.00**
Skookum, male w/blanket, orig sticker, 1920, 19", M **225.00**

Domestics

Bkrest, Santee Sioux, willow/trade cloth, floral bw, 1920 .... **1,700.00**
Blanket, Pendleton, geometric stripes, 1925, 56x64" **150.00**
Cradle, Apache, willow w/sunshade, hide sides, 1935 ....**400.00**
Cradle, Cheyenne, full bw, orig tacked brds, 1920, 24x13" **4,000.00**
Cradle, Cheyenne (?), mc bw/yel stain on hide, 38x16", EX .. **1,450.00**
Cradle, Flathead, floral beaded top & apron, 1900, 24x10" **1,000.00**
Cradle, Hupa, basketry 'Pickkenagon,' 1900, 28x6x14" **400.00**
Cradle, NW Coast, relief-cvd animals, Charlie Mickey, 34" **500.00**
Cradle, Paiute, basketry, buckskin sunshade w/bw, 1910, 36" . **1,300.00**
Spoon, Haida, bent mtn goat horn, 1870, 5x2" **125.00**
Toy cradle, Shoshone, bw, w/buckskin doll, 1890, 14" **350.00**
Toy cradle, Sioux, full bw geometrics on buffalo, 1900, 14".........**600.00**
Toy cradle, Sioux, full bw Xs/flags/geometrics, 20th C, 15" **950.00**

Toy cradle, Sioux, tacks, full bw Am flag, 1900, 27x8".......... **1,600.00**

Jewelry

As early as 500 A.D., Indians in the Southwest drilled turquoise nuggets and strung them on cords made of sinew or braided hair. The Spanish introduced them to coral, and it became a popular item of jewelry; abalone and clam shells were favored by the Coastal Indians. Not until the last half of the nineteenth century did the Indians learn to work with silver. Each tribe developed its own distinctive style and preferred design, which until about 1920 made it possible to determine tribal origin with some degree of accuracy. Since that time, because of modern means of communication and travel, motifs have become less distinct.

Quality Indian silver jewelry may be antique or contemporary—age, though certainly to be considered, is not as important a factor as fine workmanship and good stones. Pre-1910 silver will show evidence of hammer marks, and designs are usually simple. Beads have sometimes been shaped from coins. Stones tend to be small; when silver wire was used, it is usually square. To insure your investment, choose a reputable dealer.

Belt, US Army issue w/added 1920s coin conchos & bear claws....**65.00**
Bola, inlaid chief dancer, by Eddie Bayuka, 1975, 6x3"................**300.00**
Bola, Navajo, silver Eagle Dancer w/turq, sgn HI, '65, 4x4" **300.00**
Bola, Navajo, w/huge Bl Gem turq, silver tips, 1940, 5" **300.00**
Bola, Zuni, Indian on horse hunts buffalo, inlay, 1940, 4" **250.00**
Bola, Zuni, inlaid bird in center, sgn Latoma, 1950, 5x3" **300.00**
Bola, Zuni, inlaid eagle carrying snake, 1975, 5x5½" **350.00**
Bola, Zuni, inlaid zoomorphic heart line figure, 1920, 4x3" **1,700.00**
Bracelet, Navajo, coin silver w/huge oval turq, 1904 ....**175.00**
Bracelet, Navajo, hammered silver w/stampwork, 1935, 6x2" ...**100.00**
Bracelet, Navajo, hand-hammered ingot silver+gr turq, 3" W.....**175.00**
Bracelet, Navajo, turq/coral/bear claw, M Thomas, 3" W **300.00**
Bracelet, Navajo, 2 lg Bl Gem turq, silver leaves, 3" W **200.00**
Bracelet, Navajo, 3" cluster w/54 gem quality turq, 1930.............**275.00**
Bracelet, watch; Navajo man's, coin silver+4 lg turq, sgn AC.....**200.00**
Bracelet, Zuni, 3" cluster w/Lone Mtn turq, EX work/quality **300.00**
Choker, Crow, bone/brass beads w/4 lg bear claws, 1890 ....**950.00**
Concho belt, Navajo, old pawn, conchos/butterflies, 39x3" .. **1,150.00**
Concho belt, Navajo, stamped conchos/butterflies, '35, 52".......**600.00**
Concho belt, Navajo, 5 conchos+6 butterflies w/turq, 43x5" **650.00**
Concho belt, Navajo, 7 plaques+buckle, ea w/3 Lone Mtn turq..**500.00**
Concho belt, Zuni, inlay Knife Wing Dancer, 1930, 32x3"..... **2,500.00**

Squash blossom, Lone Mountain turquoise, 1930s, $3,000.00.

Necklace, Crow, 12 buffalo teeth on cobalt trade beads, 26".......**450.00**
Necklace, hand-cut natural Sleeping Beauty turq beads, 16".........**50.00**

Necklace, Navajo, grad turq plaques on 3-strand beads, naja.......**900.00**
Necklace, Navajo, silver/turq needlepoint, sgn Begay, 22" **200.00**
Necklace, Navajo, 1 strand hand-wrought silver beads, 1910......**600.00**
Necklace, Plains, horse's teeth strung w/sm trade beads, 21" **225.00**
Necklace, Pueblo, silver beads+15 handmade crosses, 19th C.. **1,800.00**
Necklace, silver w/untreated lapis, Anne Forbes, 1975 ....**200.00**
Necklace, squash blossom; Navajo, ea w/2 turq, cluster naja **300.00**
Necklace, squash blossom; Navajo, inlaid heads, 1970, 18" **950.00**
Necklace, squash blossom; Navajo, stamped naja, 1925, 15" **300.00**
Necklace, squash blossom; Zuni, channel inlay, 2-row, '50 ......**650.00**
Necklace, squash blossom; 8 Morgan dollars+Mercury dimes.. **1,100.00**
Necklace, untreated hand-cut rnd turq beads, 1970, 30" **200.00**
Pendant, shaman's; Tlingit, cvd bone/inlay killer whale.............**900.00**
Pendant, Zuni, inlay Kachina, 1930, 4x1" **600.00**
Pin, Navajo, w/lg natural Bl Gem turq, sgn RD, 1935, 3x2" **100.00**
Pin, Navajo, whirling log design, stampwork/1 turq, 2¼"..............**25.00**
Trade beads, amber, grad szs, 1890, 20"....................................**70.00**
Trade beads, cobalt Peking glass beads, 1890, 31" **150.00**
Trade beads, mc Venetian glass, 1870, very lg **100.00**

Knives and Chipped Blades

The knife was an indispensable tool to the Indian whether he was in battle, hunting game, or doing chores at the campsite. Before the white man's metal blades, all were made of copper, obsidian, flint, or chert. Knife cases, fashioned of leather with intricate decorations of quilling or beadwork, were sometimes suspended from the neck, or they were attached to the belt.

Blade, Archaic, Woodlands, pk, bevel on right, 2¼x1¼" **35.00**
Blade, Pedernales, Edwards Plateau flint, hafted, TX, 4¾".........**400.00**
Corner-tang, NE, beige, classic, 4¾"...**265.00**
Corner-tang, TX, gray/tan, 4¼" **190.00**
Crooked, E Woodlands, bird effigy hdl, 1900, 11x1½" **45.00**
Gray stone, TX, flaked, 4¾x2⅜"..**10.00**
Woodland, crooked, scrolled wood hdl w/cvd heart, 11" **300.00**

Pipes

Pipe bowls were usually carved from soft stone, such as catlinite or pipestone, an argilaceous sedimentary rock composed mainly of clay. Granite was also used. Some ceremonial pipes were simply styled, while others were intricately designed naturalistic figurals, sometimes in bird or frog forms called effigies. Their stems, made of wood and often covered with leather, were sometimes nearly a yard in length.

Blackfoot, catlinite T-bowl, fur/feather trim, 1965, 28x2" **85.00**
Cheyenne, flop knob, hide covered, bw hdl, 20th C, 25x2" **110.00**
Chippewa, catlinite, lady's head bowl, +human/animal, '20 ....**250.00**
Chippewa, gr stone 'ram's head' pipe bowl, 1880, 3½x3" **150.00**
Chumash, cloud blower, stone w/bone bead inlay, 1700, 8x2" **300.00**
Mound Builder, gray stone bird effigy, pre-historic, 10x4" **550.00**
N Plains, inlay blk stone T-bowl/bw puzzle stem, 20th C, 25" **700.00**
Pipe tomahawk, CI head, hide on wood hdl, 20th C, 16x6" **100.00**
Pipe tomahawk, Fr CI head/brass-trim wood stem, 1800, 17x7" ..**600.00**
Pipe tomahawk, iron, long tacked wood stem, 24x6" **500.00**
Pipe tomahawk, iron w/pnt & inlaid twist stem, 1870, 26x7"......**200.00**
Plains, blk stone w/drilled holes, bw/tacked stem, 23x4" **1,900.00**
Plains, blk T-bowl, pewter/pipestone inlay, bw stem, 34x4" **600.00**
Plains, catlinite T-bowl, tacked wood stem, 1870, 15x3"...........**550.00**
Plains, inlaid blk stone 4" T-bowl, cut-out puzzle stem **600.00**
Prehistoric, gr-gray stone skeleton face form, 3x3" **450.00**
Red catlinite T-bowl cvd as striking snake, modern, 9" **300.00**
Sioux, catlinite T-bowl, bw stem, 1880, 24x3" **150.00**

Sioux, red catlinite T-bowl/cvd catlinite stem, 1890, 24x5" **350.00**
Southeastern, cvd stone seated human effigy, 7" **500.00**
Woodlands, catlinite/wood, bowl: snake & frog, mc pnt, 29".. **3,100.00**

Pottery

Indian pottery is nearly always decorated in such a manner as to indicate the tribe that produced it or the pueblo in which it was made. For instance, the designs of Cochiti potters were usually scattered forms from nature or sacred symbols. The Zuni preferred an ornate repetitive decoration of a closer configuration. They often used stylized deer and bird forms, sometimes in dimensional applications.

Acoma, canteen, pictorial w/bird, woven strap, 1920, 9x11" **750.00**
Acoma, jar, mc parrot/etc, 1930, 9x7" **475.00**
Acoma, jar, umber motif on cream, twist hdls, wear, 8" **75.00**
Acoma, jar, umber/orange motif on wht slip, 1920, 6x8" **225.00**
Acoma, pot, pnt bird motif, 1920, 11x10"................................. **1,200.00**
Acoma, pot, scrolls/sqs/etc, brn/cream, sgn NM, 1930s, 7x9" **300.00**
Acoma, storage jar, geometrics/curvilinears, 1920, 11x8" **550.00**
Acoma, vase, geometrics/florals/lines, hdld olla form, 13" **2,200.00**
Acoma, wedding vase, polychrome foliage, 1902, 11x8" **850.00**
Anasazi, bowl, blk geometrics/curvilinears on wht, 6x12" **350.00**
Casas Grandes, animal effigy w/rust & blk, prehistoric, 9" **250.00**
Casas Grandes, olla, thin walled, geometrics, A Silveria **250.00**
Chaco, pitcher, blk angled lines on wht, prehistoric, 7½" **450.00**
Cochiti, candle holder, lg pnt Indian face, 1920, 5", pr **350.00**
Cochiti, olla, curvilinears, blk on buff, 1940, 18x13" **850.00**
Cochiti, olla, leaves/curvilinears, blk on buff, 1890, 8x8" **300.00**
Cochiti, ram figure, att Helen Cordero, 1940, 13x8" **400.00**
Hopi, bowl, extensions/hdls ea end, sgn Flower Woman, 12" **250.00**
Hopi, canteen, stylized rain clouds, 1940, 10x8" **600.00**
Hopi, jar, geometrics/curvilinears, Nellie Nampeyo, 3x3"..............**80.00**
Hopi, jar, stylized birds, 3 rim hdls, 1920, 7x5" **175.00**
Hopi, jar, stylized motif, by orig Nampeyo, 1900, 10x5" **500.00**
Hopi, jar, w/butterfly maid, 2-color on orange, rstr, 11" **400.00**
Hopi, seed jar, tan/brn, cvd figures, Nampeyo, 1980, 7x5½" **550.00**
Hopi, vase, stylized birds, by orig Nampeyo, 1910, 9x5".............**350.00**
Hopi, vase, stylized birds, 1935, 14x5" **350.00**
Jemez, storyteller, 12 babies, sgn Judy Toya, 1970, 9"...............**250.00**
Kayenta, canteen, blk on wht, 2 lugs, 8½x7" **900.00**
Laguna, bowl, early classic design, 1910, 4x8" **175.00**
Maricopa, bowl, blk on red w/imp design, 1900, 4x5½" **125.00**
Mojave, frog figure, Annie Fields, 1966, 6x4" **500.00**
Navajo, wedding vase, Mary Saxon, 1982, 13x9" **175.00**
Santa Clara, basket, cvd blkware w/snake, R Naranjo, 7x6" **250.00**
Santa Clara, bowl, blk, cvd feathers, Camelio Tafoya, 5x10" **350.00**
Santa Clara, bowl, blk/blk, sgn Lela Tapia, 1965, 4x10" **300.00**
Santa Clara, bowl, cvd red/sienna, 2 dancers, C Tafoya, 4" **300.00**
Santa Clara, bowl, geometrics/etc, Margaret Tafoya, 9".............**225.00**
Santa Clara, olla, bear paw motif, M Naranjo, 1945, 18x14".......**650.00**
Santa Clara, olla, blk, bear paw, att M Tafoya, 1940, 24" **1,700.00**
Santa Clara, plate, blk, emb bear paw, M Tafoya, 1955, 5" **450.00**
Santa Clara, wedding vase, blk, florals/foliage, 1902, 9x8" **125.00**
Santo Domingo, dough bowl, blk on gray, sgn M Lavato, 3x8" ...**175.00**
Santo Domingo, jar, blk geometrics on cream, 1930, 9½x9" **350.00**
Santo Domingo, olla, blk foliage on cream, 1880, 16x15"....... **5,500.00**
Santo Domingo, olla, blk leaves/ovals on cream, 1910, 8x7".......**400.00**
Santo Domingo, pitcher, 2-spout, foliage/florals, 1920, 12" **350.00**
Shipibo, bowl, face effigy, mc geometrics, 1940, 6x16" **200.00**
Wallace Youvella, bowl, lg eagle on branch/geometrics, 9" **450.00**
Zia, dough bowl, mc motif, 1880, 4½x13" **650.00**
Zia, olla, deer smelling flowers, 1965, 8x7½" **200.00**
Zuni, candlestick, sacred frog hdl, rpr, 7"..................................**125.00**

Zuni canteen, red and dark brown devices on white, 1800s, native repair, 16" x 12", **$3,250.00.**

Zuni, owl figure, brn on wht, sgn Josephine N, 1905, 8", NM........**90.00**
Zuni, pot, terraced rim, pnt polliwogs/insects, 1935, 4x8"...........**375.00**

Pottery, San Ildefonso

The pottery of the San Ildefonso pueblo is especially sought after by collectors today. Under the leadership of Maria Martinez and her husband Julian, experiments began about 1918 which led to the development of the 'black-on-black' design achieved through exacting methods of firing the ware. They discovered that by smothering the fire at a specified temperature, the carbon in the smoke that ensued caused the pottery to blacken. Maria signed her work from the late teens to the 1960s; she died in 1980. Today a piece with her signature may bring prices in the $500 to $3,500 range.

Acoma, jar, cream slip on orange w/umber geometrics, 7x10" **475.00**
Bowl, blk/blk, abstract leaves, Maria & Santana, 5½", NM.........**300.00**
Bowl, blk/blk, geometrics/scallops, Maria & Julian, 5x13" **3,200.00**
Bowl, blk/red motif on pk-cream slip, Maria Poveka, 9", NM......**150.00**
Bowl, polished blkware, Lucy (Martinez), 1940, 3x5" **60.00**
Bowl, redware w/geometrics, Marie, 6½x10½" **1,650.00**
Bowl vase, blk/blk, abstract feathers, Maria, 11½" dia, NM **1,800.00**
Bowl vase, redware, cvd snake band, Maria & Julian, 5x7" **3,400.00**
Box, blk/blk, feathers, hdl atop, Juanita, 3½x7x4", NM **350.00**
Box, blk/blk, geometrics, hdl atop, Marie, 5x4¾x4" **1,300.00**
Charger, blk/blk, feathers, Marie & Santana, 14", NM **1,300.00**
Jar, blk/blk, bear paw motif, bulbous, Maria & Julian, 4¾" ... **1,800.00**
Jar, blk/blk, bear paw motif, Maria & Julian, 3x4".....................**400.00**
Jar, blk/blk, cvd shoulder band, Rose Gonzales, 4x6½" **375.00**
Jar, blk/blk, feathered neck band, Marie & Santana, 4x3½" **550.00**
Jar, blk/blk, feathered shoulder band, Marie & Santana, 6" **1,100.00**
Jar, blk/blk, feathers, bulbous, Marie & Julian, 7" **2,900.00**
Jar, blk/blk, geometrics/curvilinears, Santana, 3¼x4½" **175.00**
Jar, blk/blk, serpent motif, sgn Tonita, 1935, 4½x5" **200.00**
Jar, blk/blk, terraces/wings, Maria & Julian, 3x5" **425.00**
Jar, blk/blk, wave band at shoulder, Maria & Julian, 3x4¾" **475.00**
Jar, feathers, buff on red, Albert & Josephine, 1965, 4x3"............**55.00**
Jar, red, cvd buffalo, Tsepe & Dora, 1975, 5x7" **500.00**
Jar, stylized wing shoulder band, Maria & Julian, 3x4"................**800.00**
Plate, blk/blk, abstract motif, Maria & Popovi, 5½"....................**800.00**
Plate, blk/blk, feather motif, Maria & Julian, 13", NM............ **2,100.00**
Plate, blk/blk, stylized parrots/ducks, Marie & Julian, 12" **4,800.00**
Plate, highly polished blk, Blue Corn, 1965, 11" **125.00**
Vase, blkware, polished, incurvate, Maria Poveka, 1965, 4" **900.00**
Vase, blkware, polished, incurvate, Maria Poveka, 1965, 6" **1,300.00**

Rugs, Navajo

Bk-to-bk triangles w/in dmn forms, 1944, 156x72" **3,500.00**
Centipede motif, tan/yel/red/blk on gray-brn, 85x46" **550.00**
Concentric Xd bands, 1963, 165x78" **3,000.00**
Concentric Xs, stepped terraces, 4-color, 148x73" **1,100.00**
Crossing stair steps, interlocking 'Ss,' 1950, 130x100" **3,750.00**
Crystal w/banded pattern of serrated motifs, vegetal, 68x37" **140.00**
Elongated stepped dmn, castellated borders, 3-color, 74x45" **650.00**
Eye-dazzler, 5-color on red, 76x55" **950.00**
Feather/geometric devices, natural, 4-color, 102x54" **800.00**
Ganado, rows of serrated dmns, 1943, 145x72" **2,500.00**
Ganado Red, geometrics, 1964, 115x80" **3,700.00**
Geometric motif, JB Moore, 1925, 78x48" **400.00**
Geometrics, stepped border, 5-color, 66x31" **360.00**
Geometrics, 4-color on brn, fine weave, 84x54" **1,000.00**
Lg concentric lozenge w/in meander border, 4-color, 88x55" **600.00**
Lozenge motif, natural wool, 1963, 130x85" **3,000.00**
Mc opposing diagonals, 1967, 150x84" **3,000.00**
Optical pattern of stair steps, 1964, 86x70" **1,500.00**
Pine Springs area, intricate geometrics, 1965, 65x44" **550.00**
Serrated border & lines, triangles, 1943, 140x84" **2,500.00**
Serrated dmn/Maltese Xs, sawtooth border, 82x59", EX **700.00**
Serrated dmns, natural/analine, 6-color on red, 91x62" **5,000.00**
Serrated X on field of stars/feathers, 5-color, 71x45", EX **400.00**
Stepped dmns, wht/brn on taupe, brn border, 1900s, 60x35" .. **3,250.00**
Storm, Xs & swastikas, 1930, 78x50" **1,400.00**
Teec Nos Pos, central lozenge, 1965, 58x37" **400.00**
Zigzag dmns, red/ochre/brn, wool, 1930, 42x43" **350.00**
2 Gray Hills, concentric/stepped geometrics, 4-color, 74x47" **375.00**
2 Gray Hills, geometrics, natural wool, 1930, 81x58" **400.00**
2 Gray Hills, pictorial w/stars in corners, natural, 59x34" **350.00**
3rd Phase Chief's, natural/analine homespun, 1895, 120x75" . **2,500.00**

Tools

Awl, AR, bone, cave find **6.00**
Awl, Crow, cvd bone, in well-used buckskin case, 1890 .... **150.00**
Axe, Hohokam, gray stone, fully grooved, prehistoric, 7" **50.00**
Axe, red stone, ¾-grooved, from WI, prehistoric, 7x3" **90.00**
Celt, IL, gray, chipped/polished, 6½" **135.00**
Celt, Mississippian, dk gray, 7¾x2½" **110.00**
Celt, OH, gray stone, ground, 5¾x2½" **45.00**
Celt, OH, gray stone, 2½" **125.00**
Celt, OH, hardstone, 3½", EX **60.00**
Drill, AR, off-wht, 1⅛" **10.00**
Drill, AR, oval base, gray, 1½" **6.00**
Drill, AR, sq bk, tan, 1¾", VG **6.00**
Drill, Etley, MO, shades of tan, 4¼" **75.00**
Maul, Plains, rawhide-covered hdl & stone head, 8½" **185.00**
Pounder, NW Coast, detailed wolf's head cvg, 3x7" **1,500.00**
Scraper, Sioux, elk antler w/iron blade, 1860, 11x4" **150.00**

Weapons

Axe, Cheyenne, full bw hdl, 1880, rare sz, 13x3" **150.00**
Bow, N CA, pnt w/geometrics, 48x2¼" **250.00**
Bow, N CA, pnt w/overall 3-color stars, 50x3" **1,000.00**
Club, Crow, horn, bw hdl, quill suspensions, 1880, 22x7" **450.00**
Club, metal blade, smoking on hdl, 17x5" **75.00**
Club, Plains, fixed stone head, buffalo hide drops/bw, 28" **450.00**
Club, Plains, full bw hdl, red pnt head, 20x4" **200.00**
Club, Plains, stone head, bw hide-wrap hdl, 1900, 17x4" **65.00**
Club, Sioux, rawhide-wrapped stone, horse tail drops, 31x2" **400.00**

Club, wooden ball & spike, 1860 .... **125.00**
Skull cracker, Plains, sinew sewn, w/hdl attachments, 36" **675.00**
Spear point, mahog obsidian, well notched, 11½x1⅜" **90.00**
Spear point, Texas, prehistoric, 8" **30.00**
Tomahawk, wood w/wrought iron trade head, Fr/Indian war **450.00**

Miscellaneous

Ash tray, Tlingit, wood stand w/totem cvg & abalone inlay **350.00**
Blanket, Chimayo, mc lozenge on bl, 1935, 80x49" **250.00**
Blanket, Pendleton, lines of swastika on gray, 1920, 60x54" **500.00**
Blanket, Saltillo, tight weave, mc, dragonfly center, 1940 ....**500.00**
Box, birch bark, scraped floral/stars/etc, w/lid, 8½x6½" **320.00**
Bridle, finely braided horsehide headstall, 1920, lg **900.00**
Bridle, horsehair, red/wht/bl/yel, 1920 .... **2,200.00**
Bridle, Navajo, silver headstall, silver-mtd bit, 1920, 23" **1,200.00**
Bridle, Sioux, hide w/geometrics, Spanish bit, 1910 ....**250.00**
Buffalo skull, from Flathead Reservation in MT, 1900, 27" **200.00**
Canoe paddle, Woodlands, many pnt fish, 67" **600.00**
Canteen, Navajo, hammered/stamped silver, 20th C, 5½" **250.00**
Canteen, tobacco; Zuni, silver w/allover inlay, 1940, 6" **600.00**
Flute, Sioux, cvd of juniper wood, 1935, 23x2" **100.00**
Gamestone, discoidal, AR, mini..**12.00**
Horse's headstall, full bw on red velvet, mirror trim, 22" **75.00**
Ketoh, Navajo, silver bow guard w/stamped leather, 1920, 3½" ..**350.00**
Ketoh, Navajo, silver w/4 turq, rpl leather, choice, 1940 ....**275.00**
Ledger drawing, Sioux, Indians in ceremonial dress, 4 for **550.00**
Powder horn, Haida, cvd, brass trim, 1880, 8x3" **900.00**
Powder horn, NW Coast, cvd sea monster, 1880, 11x3" **1,200.00**
Saddle, Crow, buffalo hide, sinew sewn, 1890, 18x11" **550.00**
Saddle, Crown lady's, bw/stroud cloth/Hawk bells, EX **450.00**
Saddle, Plains lady's, rawhide on wood, tacks/fringe, 21" **2,000.00**

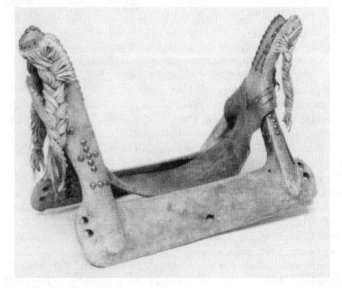

Comanche tacked and fringed woman's saddle, sinew sewn rawhide on wood frame, yellow pigment on braided fringe, brass tacks, 1890, 14", EX, $1,200.00.

Stirrups, Crow, sinew-sewn hide, bw/pnt/tacks, 1890, 7x5" **400.00**
Treaty, names 3 Bears chief of Agallalla Sioux, 1878...................**200.00**
Treaty medal, silver, 4" oval, +book showing same, 1795........ **1,800.00**

Amphora

The Amphora Porcelain Works in the Teplitz-Turn area of

Bohemia, produced Art Nouveau-styled vases and figurines during the latter part of the 1800s through the first few decades of the twentieth century. They marked their wares with various stamps, some incorporating the name and location of the pottery with a crown or a shield. Because Bohemia was part of the Austro-Hungarian empire prior to WWI, some examples are marked Austria; items marked with the Czechoslovakia designation were made after the war.

Our advisor for this category is Jack Gunsaulus; he is listed in the Directory under Michigan.

Ewer, water lilies HP on gold sponged ground, 1905 mk, 13".. **1,500.00**
Figurine, girl on rock w/baskets, mk, ca 1905, 8½x19x9" **675.00**
Jar, goose in reserve, fox finial, 10½" **350.00**
Jardiniere, lg vining florals, blk trim, 6½" **150.00**
Planter, boy in short pants w/basket figural, 12½x11" **595.00**
Planter, Deco band, blk rim, ram's head hdl, 4-ftd, 3¾"..............**150.00**
Vase, Arts & Crafts trees & flowers, open loops at rim, 18".........**750.00**
Vase, bronze coloring w/appl wolfhound, mk, 11½" **695.00**
Vase, Egyptian figures on mottled brn, 13¾"..............................**350.00**
Vase, floral, salamander hdls, 2 mks, ca 1840s, 10x8" **350.00**
Vase, floral band w/bl decor & rim, 6⅞" **145.00**
Vase, floral basket w/gold, salamander hdls, mk, 10½" **350.00**
Vase, florals in relief, pk on gr, hdls, mk, 10¾", pr **175.00**
Vase, HP florals, cobalt rim, Deco style, mk, 9x6¼"...................**175.00**
Vase, jeweled/rtcl flowerheads, cylinder base w/4 hdls, 12".........**275.00**
Vase, lg blown-out grapes w/appl leaves, 1880s, 21"....................**950.00**
Vase, long-tail rooster sits on side, branches at top, 16" **2,400.00**
Vase, low-relief leaves ea side, branching stem hdls, 8¾"............**495.00**
Vase, low-relief lotus on trumpet form, 4 base hdls, 8½".............**600.00**
Vase, mc jewels & gold spider webs, butterflies below, 6" **800.00**
Vase, molded vintage rim, 2 lg 3-D children, mk/#d, 17x10".......**800.00**

**Vase, incised parrots,
12½", $295.00.**

Vase, poppies, wht on pk/silver/gold, lobed bulb base, 15"...........**385.00**
Vase, rtcl/glass bosses, 3-D lady on low shoulder, 26", EX **2,750.00**
Vase, seated Egyptian figure in reserve, 13⅜" **350.00**
Vase, spider webs w/jewels & moths on teal & blk, 12" **950.00**
Vase, trees, lav/purple on ivory w/gold, rim hdls, 22" **700.00**
Vase, water lilies emb at incurvate rim, pk/olive, 11½"................**750.00**
Vase, 3 high-relief birds on shouldered bottom, jewels, 13".....**4,000.00**

Wall pocket, basketweave w/bl band & florals, 9"........................**110.00**

Animal Dishes with Covers

Covered animal dishes have been produced for nearly two centuries and are as varied as their manufacturers. They were made in many types of glass — slag, colored, clear, and milk glass — as well as china and pottery. On bases of nests and baskets, you will find animals and birds of every sort. The most common was the hen.

Some of the smaller versions made by McKee, Indiana Tumbler and Goblet Company, and Westmoreland Glass of Pittsburgh, Pennsylvania, were sold to food-processing companies who filled them with prepared mustard, baking powder, etc. Occasionally one will be found with the paper label identifying the product and processing company still intact.

Many of the glass versions produced during the latter part of the nineteenth century have been recently reproduced. As late as the 1960s, the Kemple Glass Company made the rooster, fox, lion, cat, lamb, hen, horse, turkey, duck, dove, and rabbit on split-ribbed or basketweave bases. They were made in amethyst, blue, amber, and milk glass, as well as a variegated slag. It is sometimes necessary to compare items in question to verified examples of older glass in order to recognize reproductions.

For more information, we recommend *Covered Animal Dishes* by our advisor, Everett Grist, whose address is in the Directory under Illinois. In the listings below, when only one dimension is given, it is length. See also Greentown.

Bird on rnd basket, milk glass, mk Vallerysthal **85.00**
Camel, resting, bl opaque, Westmoreland Specialty, 6¼" **155.00**
Cat on ribbed base, bl w/wht head, Westmoreland Specialty **95.00**
Chick on eggs, lacy base, milk glass, Atterbury, dtd, 7x7"...........**165.00**
Chicken egg on sleigh, milk glass, Westmoreland, 5½" **65.00**
Deer on fallen tree base, milk glass, Flaccus **250.00**
Dog, recumbent, milk glass, mk McKee, 5½" **350.00**
Duck, Atterbury; any color, Wright repro.....................................**75.00**
Duck, milk glass w/amethyst head, Atterbury, 11" **500.00**
Duck, Pintail; milk glass, Westmoreland Specialty, 5½" **55.00**
Duck, swimming, milk glass, Vallerysthal, 5"...............................**65.00**
Duck on cattail base, milk glass, 5½" **85.00**
Eagle Mother, milk glass, Westmoreland, mk WG **75.00**
Elephant w/rider, bl, Vallerysthal, 7"..**125.00**
Fish, Entwined; compote base, milk glass..................................**275.00**
Fish, milk glass, Challinor, Taylor, & Co, lg **185.00**
Fish on ribbed base, gr, Fostoria, 8½" **35.00**
Fox, lacy base, milk glass, dtd...**175.00**
Fox on lacy base, milk glass, Atterbury, dtd, 6¼" **150.00**
Frog, milk glass, umk McKee...**550.00**
Hand & Dove, milk glass, undtd...**85.00**
Hen, milk glass, 2 McKee mks, 5½" **350.00**
Hen (str head), clear, Indiana Glass, lg or sm **10.00**
Hen (str head) on basketweave, amberina, Indiana Glass.............**25.00**
Hen on basketweave, bl, Westmoreland Specialty **85.00**
Hen on basketweave, Challinor, Taylor, & Co, 8".....................**110.00**
Hen on basketweave, milk glass, Westmoreland, 3" **10.00**
Hen on basketweave, Vallerysthal, 2" **35.00**
Hen on cattails, milk glass, 5½" **65.00**
Hen on lacy base, bl opaque head, Atterbury, rare **175.00**
Irish Setter on sq base, gr, att Flaccus **195.00**
Lamb on split-rib base, amber **15.00**
Lion on lacy base, milk glass, Atterbury, 6¼" **135.00**
Lion on picket base, bl, Westmoreland **85.00**
Lion on sq scroll base, milk glass, 5½".......................................**65.00**

Lion on lid, marked Imperial, amber, 6", $65.00.

Owl head, milk glass, mk McKee, 5½" 875.00
Quail on scroll base, milk glass 65.00
Rabbit, bl, Atterbury, 9" 375.00
Rabbit, Mule Eared; picket base, bl, Westmoreland 85.00
Rabbit on egg, Vallerysthal, sm 225.00
Rabbit on split-rib base, milk glass, dome lid, 5½" 75.00
Rat on egg, pk, Vallerysthal 175.00
Rooster, standing, clear, Westmoreland Specialty 55.00
Rooster on basketweave, bl opaque, Westmoreland 65.00
Rooster on basketweave, clear, pnt, Challinor, Taylor, 8" 95.00
Rooster on Vallerysthal-type base, amberina, Wright repro 10.00
Snail on strawberry, milk glass, Vallerysthal, sm 85.00
Steer head on ribbed base, milk glass, 9½" 2,200.00
Swan, Block; clear/frosted, Challinor, Taylor, & Co, 7" 135.00
Swan, head down, milk glass, unmk McKee, 5½" 185.00
Swan (open neck) on basketweave, amber, Belmont Glass, 7" ...165.00
Swan (raised wings) on lacy base, Atterbury 165.00
Turkey, clear/frosted, Cambridge 55.00
Turtle, amber, lg 125.00

Antiquities

The ancient Egyptians, Romans, and the early craftsmen of India and China have left us with exquisite treasures bearing mute witness of their esthetic convictions that even a water carrier, a knife, or a rug should be created a thing of beauty. Though time and the elements have taken their toll on the more fragile works of these ancient artisans, it is incredible that many remain intact to this day. The thin-walled tear and scent bottles blown by Roman artisans from the last century A.D., and examples of the red or black predynastic potteries of Egypt — though understandably quite rare — can yet occasionally be found on the market today. Jewelry, often interred with the dead, has survived the centuries well; figurines of marble and terra cotta, ceremonial masks, earthenware vessels, and other relics such as these offer us of the twentieth century the only tangible link possible to the ancient world.

Bronze

Bowl, Seljuk, 1200 AD, Islamic designs, ftd, 6", 7", pr 200.00

Fibula, Etruscan, 400 BC, boat shape, lineation, 3" 50.00
Sword, Luristan, 1200-800 BC, gr patina, w/stand, 18" 250.00

Hardstones

Bust, Rome, 100 BC, Greek man, marble, molded base, 19½" . **3,200.00**
Cvg, Egyptian style, Nile carp, limestone, EX detail, 5¼" 200.00
Figure, Central India, goddess in dhoti, sandstone, 14" **1,100.00**
Figure, India, 1100 AD, female deity, buff sandstone, 18" **400.00**
Figure, Rome, 100 AD, bust of Herm, wood base, 6" **1,900.00**
Fragment, India, 1100 AD, attendants, standstone, 17½" **200.00**
Fragment, India, 1100 AD, attendants & equestrian, 16" **200.00**
Fragment, India, 1100 BC, Vishnu, sandstone, 14" **400.00**
Plaque, Egypt, Late, limestone, hieroglyphics, 19" **6,000.00**

Pottery

Alabastron, Corinth, 500 BC, teardrop shape, 4½" 150.00
Shroud, mummy's head; Egypt, 900-300 BC, faience, 14" 150.00
Skyphos, Southern Italy, 300 BC, Red Figure, 6½" **1,200.00**
Ushabti, Egypt, 26th Dynasty, faience, molded, 6½" 200.00

Terra Cotta

Figure, Phoenicia, 300 BC, Mother Goddess, 7½" 785.00
Figure, Rome, 100 AD, bull charging, legs missing, 5" 350.00
Lamp, oil; Roman, 200 AD, erotic scene, gadrooned rim, 4" 200.00

Miscellaneous

Barge, funerary; Egypt, Late Period, polychromed wood, 19" .. **2,000.00**
Bowl, Egypt, alabaster, rnd w/4 protruding turtle heads, 8" 150.00
Fragment, sarcophagus, Egypt, Ptolemaic, pnt wood, 12" 250.00
Mask, mummy; Egypt, 300 BC, gesso traces/blk pigment, 10" 150.00
Plaque, Egypt, Late Period, cvd female, gesso/pigment, 16" 850.00
Sarcophagus mask, Egyptian 700-800 BC, 8½x7" 250.00

Appliances, Electric

Electric appliances have been very collectible for quite some time with almost every type being sought ater. Even larger appliances such as early washing machines and refrigerators add a finishing touch to remodeled period rooms. Smaller appliances such as toasters, coffee makers, waffle irons, fans, and other table-top items should be in working order. Check for safety before using.

Prices listed below are for appliances in very good to excellent condition and in working order. Our advisor for this category is Jim Barker; he is listed in the Directory under Pennsylvania.

Bathroom heater, Markel #82, Deco styling, sm 35.00
Blender, Knapp Monarch Liquidizer, Deco style, 1940s, EX 45.00
Fan, Emerson Trojan, all brass, EX..165.00
Fan, General Electric, coin operated, EX.....................................250.00
Fan, General Electric, oscillating, desk type, 1938, lg, NM..........125.00
Fan, Knapp type, battery operated, 6" blades, EX 400.00
Fan, 1888 Fly Fan, orig instructions on base 600.00
Hot plate/toaster, Breakfaster T-2, 1930s, NM 45.00
Iron, Am Beauty, red hdl, EX...50.00
Iron, Proctor, Never Lift, EX 55.00
Iron, Toastmaster, EX 35.00
Refrigerator, General Electric, rnd motor on top, 1930s, 64".......350.00
Toaster, Am Electrical #5825-G, EX 45.00
Toaster, Edison, chrome & Bakelite, #129-T-31 ....125.00

'Flip Flop' toaster, Rutenber Electric, EX, $55.00.

Toaster, Hotpoint #115-T-9, EX	45.00
Toaster, Kenmore #3076322, Deco style, EX	35.00
Toaster, L&H Electrics #204, EX	50.00
Toaster, Merit-Made Model Z, EX	45.00
Toaster, Toast Queen, EX	45.00
Toaster, Toast-O-Lator, 'conveyor' works, 1940s, EX	125.00
Toaster, Toastmaster #1-A-2, EX	40.00
Toaster, Torrid, flip-out, EX	15.00
Toaster, Torrid Sidewinder, EX	65.00
Toaster, Universal #E-9412, EX	50.00
Toaster, Universal #E-945, EX	50.00
Toaster, Universal #E-946, EX	45.00
Toaster, Westinghouse #TT-23, EX	45.00
Waffle iron, L&H #315, EX	45.00
Waffle iron, Porcelier, EX	75.00
Waffle iron, Sampson United, chrome, gr hdls, EX	35.00
Waffle iron, Westinghouse #WD-4	35.00

Arequipa

The Arequipa Pottery operated from 1911 until 1918 at a sanitorium near Fairfax, California. Its purpose was two-fold — therapy for the patients and financial support for the insitution. Frederick H. Rhead was the originator and director. The ware, made from local clays, was often hand thrown, simply styled and decorated. Marks were varied but always incorporated the name of the pottery and the state. A circular arrangement encompassing the negative image of a vase beside a tree is most common.

Bowl, stylized floral panels on tan, ftd, sgn R/dtd '12, 6"	500.00
Vase, cvd iris on chocolate, bulbous, sgn BR, 5x4"	400.00
Vase, dk gr matt, 4 thick angled rim-to-base hdls, GCR, 5"	225.00
Vase, gray-plum, sq rim, vertically fluted corners, 8", EX	600.00
Vase, stylized spikey leaves cvd on pk semigloss, rpr, 8x5"	275.00
Vase, tree branch cvg, shades of bl, sgn, 6", EX	900.00

Argy-Rousseau, G.

Gabriel Argy-Rousseau produced both fine art glass and quality commercial ware in Paris, France, in 1918. He favored Art Nouveau as well as Art Deco and in the twenties produced a line of vases in the

Egyptian manner, made popular by the discovery of King Tut's tomb. One of the most important types of glass he made was pate-de-verre. Most of his work is signed. Items listed below are pate-de-verre unless noted otherwise.

Bottle, scent; forsythia frieze on earth tone, no top, 5"	1,900.00
Bowl vase, acanthus leaf cvg, purple/bl-gray on gray, 3" H	3,000.00
Bowl vase, spiders in webs/branches, natural colors, 4¼" H	9,000.00
Vase, berries in roundels at rim, U-form, 6¾"	4,800.00

Vase, floral panels in blue, purple, and green on almond with gray bands, signed, 9", $3,800.00.

Vase, lg gr lizard, front ft on rim of paneled form, 11"	55,000.00
Vase, stylized floral band, bl/turq/blk on gray, 4"	2,000.00
Vase, stylized flowering/leafy vines on rose & purple, 5½"	3,000.00
Vase, stylized leaves at base of conical top, 6"	4,000.00
Vase, trailing vines in teardrop panels, 6¾"	5,000.00

Art Deco

To the uninformed observer, 'Art Deco' evokes images of chrome and glass, streamlined curves and aerodynamic shapes, mirrored prints of pink flamingos, and statues of slender nudes and greyhound dogs. Though the Deco movement began in 1925 at the Paris International Exposition and lasted to some extent into the 1950s, within that period of time the evolution of fashion and taste continued as it always has, resulting in subtle variations.

The French Deco look was one of opulence — exotic inlaid woods, rich material, lush fur and leather. Lines tended toward symmetrical curves. American designers adapted the concept to cover every aspect of fashion and home furnishings from small inexpensive picture frames, cigarette lighters, and costume jewelry to high-fashion designer clothing and exquisite massive furniture with squared or circular lines. Vinyl was a popular covering, and chrome-plated brass was used for chairs, cocktail shakers, lamps, and tables. Dinnerware, glassware, theaters, and train stations were designed to reflect the new 'Modernism.'

The Deco movement made itself apparent into the fifties in wrought iron lamps with stepped pink plastic shades and Venetian blinds. The sheer volume of production during those twenty-five years provides collectors today with fine examples of the period that can be bought for as little as $10 or $20 up to the thousands. Chrome items signed 'Chase' are prized by collectors, and blue glass radios and tables with blue glass tops are high on the list of desirability in many areas.

Those interested in learning more about this subject will want to read *Collector's Guide to Art Deco* by our advisor, Mary Frank Gaston. She is listed in the Directory under Texas. See also Bronzes; Chase; Frankart; Furniture; Jewelry; Lalique; Radios; etc.

Ash tray, blk glass, geometric style, unmk, lg.................................12.00
Ash tray, ceramic, Snufferette, 4" dia...25.00
Ash tray, nude on pillar, Nuart..125.00
Ash tray, standing nude holds tray, Nuart 95.00
Bar accessory, jigger & stirrer combination, SP, 9"..........................12.00
Bookends, dancing nudes, bronze, gr patina, Schroedin, 5", pr 95.00
Bookends, nude w/arched bk holds tambourine, bronze, '27, pr...275.00
Bookends, nude w/man at ft, Bronzmet, c 1923, dtd 1924, pr......100.00
Bookends, Scottie dogs, pearl finish, Nuart, pr 75.00
Bottle, scent; silver lattice border on blk glass, French 75.00
Box, jewel; nickel silver, blk velvet lined, 2½x6½" 25.00
Box, jewel; red/blk geometrics pnt on brass, 8x5" 55.00
Box, nudes/foliage enameled on glass, M Goupy, 5½" L 3,800.00
Box, powder; ceramic, abstract florals, blk trim, Czech 75.00
Box, powder; ceramic, nude w/drape finial, Germany 75.00
Box, silver metal, stylized horse form, Hagenauer, 4¾" H............700.00
Box, silver/gold, eng geometrics, Aprey London, 9" L............11,000.00
Chandelier, chrome, center shade+4 arms w/frosted plates..........900.00
Cigarette holder, celluloid, 5"..12.00
Cigarette holder, plastic, bl w/silver trim, 2".................................14.00
Cigarette holder, tortoise shell, 4"..12.00
Cigarette lighter, tortoise shell, Ronson, Pat Nov 19-23................40.00
Clock, boudoir; peach glass, mirrored base, Am, 7x6" dia..........150.00
Clock, mantel; mahog & walnut w/inlay, Germany, 8¼x14½" ...400.00
Clock, marble, shape-on-shape form, Fr, 13", +2 side panels.......300.00
Cocktail, red glass, chrome stem, Stainless Chrome, 3" 12.00
Compact, Egyptian figures on yel w/blk trim, French....................80.00
Compact, enamel florals on blk, heavy sterling 65.00
Compact, geometric decor, JV Pilcher, 3½"...................................25.00
Compact, lt gr Bakelite, EX...25.00
Compact, silver w/allover blk enamel, gold medallion, France 140.00
Curling iron, electric, gr Bakelite hdl, M in Deco box 20.00
Door knocker, Egyptian styling, brass, 6½" 30.00
Figurine, cat, brass/wood base, Hagenauer, 16"...........................800.00
Figurine, semi-nude figure w/bowl, Kent Art Ware, 11" 175.00
Flower frog, draped nude, ceramic, Coronet, 13½".........................85.00
Ice bucket, chrome w/cobalt glass insert, Hazel Atlas, 11x8".........50.00
Inkwell, hammered copper/cast brass, hinged lid, glass insert 95.00

Lamp, dancer, spelter & ivorine, on alabaster globe, 15" 300.00
Lamp, kneeling nudes ea side jeweled globe, bronze, 16" L 700.00
Lamp, lady supports glass sphere, porc, Argilor Paris, 19½"..... 1,800.00
Lamp, nude w/dog, mercury glass shade, Nuart.............................275.00
Lamp, reclining nude, bronze w/clock, M Tarmler, EX 450.00
Lamp base, flamingo, pk on blk base, ceramic, pr........................275.00
Lighter, nude, left breast lights, Electro, 8"....................................65.00
Match holder, brass, bowl form w/attached tray, 4"........................60.00
Newspaper holder, copper-finished metal, 11¼x8½"......................35.00
Stem, nude supports pk glass bowl, unmk, 5".................................45.00
Table lighter, nude lady, Parker 35.00
Table lighter, pillar (chrome) w/red Bakelite ball...........................55.00
Tumbler, gr glass, 6 on tray w/chrome hdls & holders, Am...........80.00
Vase, deer in forest enameled on mottled glass, Goupy, 7x6" .. 6,000.00
Watch pendant, gr/blk enamel w/silver trim, pentagon, Borel.....225.00

Art Glass Baskets

A popular novelty and gift item during the Victorian era, these one-of-a-kind works of art were produced in just about any type of art glass in use at that time. They were never marked, since these were not true production pieces but 'whimsies' made by glassworkers to relieve the tedium of the long work day. Some were made as special gifts. The more decorative and imaginative the design, the more valuable the basket.

Amber w/appl apple front & bk, amber thorn hdl, 6x6½x5" 750.00
Aqua/brn spatter, swirled ribs, ruffled, clear hdl, 6½x5"..............245.00
Bl spangle, frosted braided hdl, ruffled, 6¾x5".............................145.00
Bl spangle overlay, ruffled, clear hdl, 6¾x6x4½" 125.00
Bl/wht spangle, clear twist hdl, 7½x10½" 275.00
Cranberry, clear ft & ruffle, reeded hdl, 8¼x5½" 245.00
Cranberry opal, sq form, wafer ft, clear hdl, 6¾x5¾" 195.00
Cream opaque, appl spatter flower, amber hdl, 7x4⅜" 165.00
Optic Panels, vaseline, HP garlands/gold flowers, 7x6" 115.00
Orange spangle, 8-crimp top, clear thorn hdl, 7½x4¼"................195.00
Peach to pk opal w/appl clear vines, int ribs, ped ft, 9" 265.00
Pk opal, Dia Quilt, w/appl vaseline rim, 7x6¾x5" 265.00
Pk satin, appl ft, fluted edge, frosted hdl, 7½x4¾" 225.00
Pk/wht spatter, thorn hdl, 11x9"...250.00
Rainbow spatter/opal cased, Coin Spot, 7½x4½".........................425.00
Rainbow Stripe spangle, bl/pk, wht lining, 8½x7x5" 850.00
Rose overlay w/mica, clear ruffled rim, thorn hdl, 8x4½" 175.00
Vaseline opal, snakeskin hdl, appl rigaree, 7½x6½" 385.00
Wht opal w/gr ruffle, Swirl, clear hdl, 6x5⅞" 145.00
Yel opaque, Dia Quilt, clear hdl, 4¾x3¾"......................................88.00
Yel to opal stripes, melon-rib base, clear hdl, 5x12x9" 275.00
Yel/wht spatter, emb basketweave, ruffled, 5¾x4⅜" 95.00

Art Nouveau

From the famous 'L'Art Nouveau' shop in the rue de Provence in Paris, 'New Art' spread across the continent and belatedly arrived in America in time to add its curvilineal elements and asymmetrical ornamentation to the ostentatious remains of the Rococo revival of the 1880s. Nouveau manifested itself in every facet of decorative art. In glassware Tiffany turned the concept into a commercial success that lasted well into the second decade of this century and created a style that inspired other American glassmakers for decades. Furniture, lamps, bronzes, jewelry, and automobiles were designed within the realm of its dictates. Today's market abounds with lovely examples of Art Nouveau, allowing the collector to choose one or several areas that hold a special

Table lamp, patinated metal and glass on marble plinth, modeled by Fayral, 20" long, $1,500.00.

interest. See also Bronzes; Jewelry; Tiffany; Silver; specific manufacturers; etc.

Bowl, silver, maid's face ea side, Korschann, 6½" L.....................600.00
Box, silver, rtcl, emb maid w/mirror, Liberty, 2⅜" H, EX.............450.00
Bust, gold wash, lady w/wht rose in hair, Wahliss, 10" 750.00
Candlestick, pewter, maiden raises 3 cups, Bonnefond, 14" 600.00

Silverplated candlestick by WMF, 10½", $1,000.00.

Clock, cvd mahog w/water lilies, cage-like uprights, 16" 3,000.00
Ewer, bronze, Neptune mask spout, nude to side, Ledru, 24".... 3,800.00
Figurine, compo, Egyptian girl w/2 baskets, mc/gilt, 22" 225.00
Mirror, brn-tone metal maid holds oval mirror aloft, 17".............150.00
Mirror, cvd gilt-wood shaped rectangle w/oval glass, 43x30".... 2,500.00
Painting on ivory, maid/trees, gilt-metal fr, B Minot, 5x9"...... 2,000.00
Pen tray, bronze, shaped end w/head of lady, Gurnscher, 11".. 1,500.00
Plaque, gilt/silvered metal, bust of maid, H Gradl, 20" dia 1,000.00
Spectacle case, sterling, eng orchids/monogram, silk lining 75.00
Tray, sterling, emb iris/naiad busts, Birmingham mks, 9x12".......600.00
Vase, SP pewter, 3-D maid/water nymph/frog/etc, 22" 1,700.00

Arts and Crafts

The Arts and Crafts movement began in England during the last quarter of the 19th century, and its influence was soon felt in this country. Among its proponents in America were Elbert Hubbard (see Roycroft) and Gustav Stickley (see Stickley.) They rebelled against the mechanized mass production of the Industrial Revolution and against the cumulative influence of hundreds of years of man's changing taste. They subscribed to the theory of purification of the styles — that designs be geared strictly to necessity. At the same time they sought to elevate these basic ideals to the level of accepted 'art.' Simplicity was their virtue; to their critics it was a fault.

The type of furniture they promoted was squarely built of heavy oak, and so simple was its appearance that as a result many began to copy the style which became known as 'Mission.' Soon factories had geared production toward making cheap copies of their designs. In 1915 Stickley's own operation failed, forced into bankruptcy by the machinery he so despised. Hubbard lost his life that same year on the ill-fated *Lusitania*. Within the decade the style had lost its popularity.

Metal ware was produced by numerous crafts people, from experts such as Dirk Van Erp and Albert Berry to unknown novices. Prices for Arts and Crafts accessories rose dramatically in 1988 but by the begin-

ning of 1991 appeared to have leveled off and (in some cases) were dropping. Metal items or hardware should not be scrubbed or scoured; to do so could remove or damage the rich, dark patina typical of this period. See also Furniture, Roycroft, Silver, Stickley, and specific manufacturers. Our advisor for this category is Bruce Austin; he is listed in the Directory under New York.

Andirons, brass, sq finials on tapered std, unsgn, 36" 400.00
Andirons, brass washed, stippled w/lobed pods, unsgn, 17" 100.00
Andirons, hammered iron, spade-shape fr, appl rings, 27" 375.00
Andirons, Prairie-style, iron balls on sq columns, 18"..................225.00
Ash tray, A Berry, copper bowl w/in 4-point antlers, 6" 400.00
Basket, sterling, rnd/8-sided, strap hdl, glass int, 6x4" 100.00
Bookends, Jarvie, hammered copper, rnd w/tulip border, sgn........750.00
Bowl, Kalo, hammered silver, flower shape, 2x9½" 700.00
Bowl, Kalo, hammered silver, rolled rim, ftd, monogram, 10"......300.00
Bowl, Porter Blanchard, sterling, flared, 3½x8" 225.00
Bowl, Randahl, hammered silver, trefoil, folded lip, 10" 325.00
Box, C Rholfs, oak, half-rnd, eng S, sgn R/1900, 10" L...............500.00
Box, hammered copper, floral decor, ball ft, hdls, 5x10x7" 175.00
Box, Taxco, sterling, ball/ribbon finial, #925, 4½" L...................250.00
Candle holder, Heintz, bronze, appl silver leaves, 10", pr 500.00
Candle holder, Jarvie, brass, trumpet form w/cup bobeche, 6" 475.00
Candlestick, att Jarvie, bronze, wide std/rnd base, 14", VG..... 1,100.00
Candlestick, brass, bulbous socket, unsgn, 11½", pr 350.00
Candlestick, bronze, ringed neck/disk base, unsgn, 9", pr 150.00
Candlestick, C Rholfs, oak w/copper bobeches, h-form, 21" 600.00
Candlestick, Jarvie, brass, pencil stem, disk base, 14"..................700.00
Candlestick, Jarvie, brass, sgn, 11", pr 1,200.00
Candlestick, Jarvie, brass, sgn/I, EX orig patina, 14", pr 10,000.00
Candlestick, Jarvie, brass, slim std, 1 sgn, 11½", pr 550.00
Candlestick, Jarvie, bronze, sgn/B, 12x6", pr 6,500.00
Candlestick, Jarvie, disk ft, emb poppy bud on std, 13¾" 2,400.00
Candlestick, Jessie Preston, brass, slim std, 14", pr 825.00
Candlestick, Onondaga, hammered pewter, 2 lg hdls, 9x3½" 70.00

Oak and copper candlesticks by Charles Rohlfs, 14", $1,200.00 for the pair.

Carpet, India Drugget, honeycomb motif, 108x144", EX.............850.00
Clock, mantel; hammered copper, floriform finial, 13x9" 275.00
Clock, shelf; Tempus, oak w/slag glass, brass face, 15x11" 500.00
Console set, Cellini Shop, pewter, 14" bowl+13" candelabra 250.00
Dish, serving; A Stone, sterling, shallow, 5-lobe, sgn HAT.........350.00
Dish, Stone Assn, sterling, scalloped, logo/sgn C, 8x5", NM.......250.00

Fire screen, oak w/embr panels, rnd knobs on fr, English 200.00
Fork, A Stone, sterling, eng/rtcl thistles, sgn B, 8½" 325.00
Fork, fish-serving; Stone Assn, sterling, antique style, 9".............180.00
Lamp, att Benedict, copper, 4-panel 26" shade w/mica, 20" ... 2,000.00
Lamp, att Benedict, copper w/mica panels, 32x20½".............. 3,000.00
Lamp, copper, scenic silhouette overlay on slag glass, 21"............550.00
Lamp, D Van Erp, baluster w/16½" mica shade, 8" 15,400.00
Lamp, D Van Erp, bronze w/4 mica panels in 16" shade, 22" .. 9,000.00
Lamp, D Van Erp, copper ball form w/16" mica shade, 15½" .46,200.00
Lamp, Heintz, bronze w/silver decor, openwork shade, 10x8"......700.00
Lamp, Heintz, bronze w/silver-overlay 9½" unsgn shade.........750.00
Lamp, U-form oak base w/ash tray under slag shade, 20x15" 275.00
Lamp, 6-panel gr slag glass 15" shade; sq oak std, 23" 375.00
Lantern, brass, hipped roof over slag glass box, 18x12" 225.00
Loving cup, hammered copper, riveted decor/scroll hdls, 12" 175.00
Mirror, Lifetime, #510, 5 dbl hooks, label, 20x48", M 850.00
Pen tray, A Stone, sterling, appl/chased lines, 8" L 600.00
Pen tray/inkwell, Forest Craft, brass, coral finial, 12" 125.00
Pitcher, A Stone, sterling, angle shoulder, sgn HAT, 8¾" 1,600.00
Pitcher, Wise & Son, copper w/appl silver decor, 8x9¾" 650.00
Plate, Kalo, hammered silver, inscribed/1920, 14" 275.00
Plate, Shreve & Co, chrome on silver, riveted band, 15".............300.00
Print, Sisters, Ed Penfield, commercial litho, fr, 7x7" 200.00
Sconce, brass sheet w/acid-cut floral, 12x5½"..........................100.00
Shelf, Mission Oak, 3-tier, shaped gallery, 28x24" 300.00
Spoon, condiment; A Stone, shield hdl, rtcl grapes on stem 200.00
Spoon, condiment; A Stone, sterling, Onslow pattern, 4½".........200.00
Spoon, martini; Gorham, silver, rtcl thistles, sgn ONC, 13".......100.00
Textile, linen runner, flowers, gold/yel on brn, 23x50", NM 225.00
Textile, linen w/water lilies & gr pads, fringed, 27" dia 375.00
Tongs, Kalo, sterling, pierced fork ends, appl 'BH,' 8" 350.00
Tray, Att Metcalf Co, copper w/silver strapwork, 8¾" 225.00
Tray, KF Leinonen, sterling, wide rim, monogram: EMK, 12½" .350.00
Tray, Shreve & Co, sterling strapwork rim on oak, rfn, 11".........300.00
Umbrella stand, att Benedict, riveted sides/ft, hdls, 25" 600.00
Vase, A Stone, sterling, eng floral, trumpet form, 5¼" 350.00
Vase, bud; Shreve & Co, sterling, strapwork border, 7" 225.00
Vase, Chicago Art Silver Shop, conical w/4-lobe rim, 7" 475.00
Vase, D Van Erp, copper w/lt brn patina, 6x4½" 600.00
Vase, Heintz, bronze w/silver floral, dk patina, 12x5" 200.00
Wastebasket, Van Ar Co None Better Made, 9-slat sides, 15".....140.00

Aurene

Aurene, developed in 1904 by Frederick Carder of the Steuben Glass Works, is a metallic iridescent glassware similar to some of Tiffany's. Usually a rich lustrous gold or blue, green and red may also be found on rare occasion. It was used alone and in combination with calcite, a cream-colored glass with a calcium base also developed by Carder. Decorated examples are very rare. It is usually marked Aurene or Steuben, sometimes with the factory number added, etched into the glass by hand. Paper labels were also used. See also Steuben.

Basket, gold, ornate ormolu fr & hdl, 14" 2,600.00
Bottle, scent; bl, steeple stopper, sgn/#1414, 7¾" 785.00
Bottle, scent; gold, bulbous/4-lobed body, 4½" 475.00
Bowl, bl, flaring, sgn, 4¾x11½" 600.00
Bowl, bl, flaring, sgn/#2851, 10" 475.00
Bowl, bl, inverted rim, #2687, 3½" 350.00
Bowl, bl, stretched flaring rim, sgn/#178, 1¾x6" 400.00
Bowl, bl, 3 appl ft, incurvate, sgn/#2586, 6¾", NM 375.00
Bowl, salad; gold, flared/stretched rim, sgn/#3059, 8" dia.............200.00
Bowl vase, gold, ruffled/stretched rim, sgn/#171, 3¾x7" 250.00

Candlesticks, gold, #3100, 8", $700.00 for the pair.

Compote, gold, tall std, sgn/#2642, 8x6" 500.00
Decanter, gold, dimpled, undulating rim, peaked stopper, 10"....650.00
Desk lamp, sm gold teardrop hangs from scroll arm, 16" 400.00
Dish, gold, 6-ruffle flared rim, 4 leaf ft, #139, 2x4" 400.00
Goblet, gold, sgn, 6½" 175.00
Pitcher, tankard; gold, sgn Haviland & Co, Aurene, 10x8" 1,750.00
Plate, gold w/pk highlights, 6" 100.00
Rose jar, gold, 3 holes in lid, Haviland label/#2812, 5½" 1,200.00
Shade, gold, ribbed, 4¾x5", pr 265.00
Shade, gold, ribbed, 4⅝x2⅜", pr 250.00
Sherbet, bl, sgn/#2680, +6" saucer 500.00
Tumbler, gold, ftd, 1870s-80s Haviland mk, 3½" 300.00
Vase, bl, baluster, 6½" 900.00
Vase, bl, dbl gourd, sgn/#1647, 2½" 600.00
Vase, bl, floriform, knop stem, 14" 1,000.00
Vase, bl, gold zigzag-band cuff rim, vines at shoulder, 10" 13,000.00
Vase, bl, ribbed & flared, sgn, 5½" 675.00
Vase, bl, shade shape, lt ribbing, 5" 595.00
Vase, bl-cut-to-cobalt vintage frieze, sgn/#2683, 10x10" 4,000.00
Vase, bud; gold, slim ftd tube, sgn/#2556, 10" 325.00
Vase, gold, gr free-form lily pads/pulled decor, sgn, 7¾" 2,200.00
Vase, gold, ruffled rim, #1143, 6" 525.00
Vase, gold, slim form w/bun ft, sgn/#2418, 14" 700.00
Vase, gold, 10-rib flared U-form, sgn, 5¾" 500.00
Vase, gold, 12-rib body, elongated ovoid, sgn, 13" 750.00
Vase, gold w/pk & bl highlights, swirled top, #6034, 12" 950.00

Austrian Glass

Many examples of fine art glass were produced in Austria during the time of Loetz and Moser that cannot be attributed to any glasshouse in particular, though much of it bears striking similarities to the products of both artists.

Bowl, purple, appl trailings/2 pk & wht floriforms, 4¾" H...........200.00
Centerpiece, yel irid shell pulled by bronze cherub, 8x11" 1,000.00
Rose bowl, gr irid w/threading, ped ft, incurvate, 8" 200.00
Rose bowl, lt gr irid w/bronze & copper nuts & leaves, 5x6" 150.00
Vase, bl w/gold vines & 'jewel' butterflies, spherical, 3"............450.00
Vase, bronze o/l oak branches & acorns on mc mottle, 6" 400.00
Vase, citron w/orange dappling at base, inverted rim, 10" 400.00
Vase, floriform in silver w/gr spots on tall slim std, 7" 1,600.00
Vase, gr w/bulbous red top, allover irid, 3-fold rim, 13½".............225.00
Vase, irid lt gr w/silver rim, appl snake, bulbous, 6½"..................200.00
Vase, lt yel w/gold waves, bulbous shoulder, 12" 400.00
Vase, purple & gold irid w/appl snake, twisted, 8½".....................300.00

Vase, silver o/l curvilinears on streaky purple irid, 10" **700.00**
Vase, silver o/l swirling leaves on irid, dimpled ovoid, 3½".........**450.00**

Austrian Ware

From the late 1800s until the beginning of WWI, several companies were located in the area known at the turn of the century as Bohemia. They produced hard-paste porcelain dinnerware and decorative items primarily for the American trade. Today examples bearing the marks of these firms are usually referred to by collectors as Austrian ware, indicating simply the country of their origin. Of those various companies, these marks are best known: M.Z. Austria; Victoria, Carlsbad, Austria (Schmidt and Company); and O. & E.G. (Royal) Austria.

Though most of the decorations were transfer designs which were sometimes signed by the original artist, pieces marked Royal Austria were often hand painted and so indicated alongside the backstamp.

Of these three companies, Victoria, Carlsbad, Austria, is the most highly valued. Collectors should note that in our listings transfer decorations showing 'signatures' (sgn), such as 'Wagner,' 'Kauffmann,' 'LeBrun,' etc., were not actually painted by those artists but were merely based on their original paintings.

Cake plate, rose decal, rtcl hdls, 11" **35.00**
Chamberstick, roses, pk on gr, gold hdl, ball ft, 3⅛x3¼"................**65.00**
Charger, violets & roses w/gold, Imperial mk, 13" **65.00**
Chocolate pot, apples on gr branches, pear shape, mk, 9" **75.00**
Cup & saucer, mythological scene, Kauffmann, gold hdl **150.00**
Cup & saucer, 4 ladies w/pitcher & fruit w/gold, Carlsbad **45.00**

Ewer, romantic transfer, signed Kauffman, 7½", $225.00.

Humidor, lady's head figural, flowers in hair **175.00**
Plaque, Charmante, woodland scene, sgn Burer, fr, 10x15½" .. **2,000.00**
Plate, dog's portrait, Rococo edge, 13" **225.00**
Plate, ladies in French garden, dk bl border, 10" **100.00**
Plate, Niagara Falls souvenir, gr w/gold, 6" **28.00**
Shakers, pk rose & bud, gr leaves, mk, 2⅝", pr **25.00**
Urn, portrait transfer on cobalt, hdls, metal ft, 19½" **375.00**
Vase, cupid, curved/split top, snake hdl, Carlsbad, 8x5" **175.00**
Vase, fuchsias in heavy enamel, cobalt hdls, 14½" **355.00**
Vase, pk & wht florals, rtcl top, Alexandria Turn, 6" **75.00**

Autographs

Autograph collecting, also known as 'philography' or 'love of writing,' used to be a hobby shared by a few thousand dedicated collectors.

But in recent years, autograph collecting has become a serious pursuit for more than 2,000,000 collectors worldwide. And in the past decade, more investors are adding rare and valuable autograph portfolios to their traditional investments. One reason for this sudden interest in autograph investing relates to the simple economic law of supply and demand. Rare autographs have a 'fixed' supply, meaning that unlike diamonds, gold, silver, stock certificates, etc., no more are being produced. There are only so many Abraham Lincoln, Marilyn Monroe, and Charles Lindbergh autographs available. In the meantime, it's estimated that more than 20,000 new collectors enter the market each year, thus creating an ever-increasing demand. Hence, the rare autographs generally rise steadily in value each year. Because of this scarcity, a serious collector will pay over $10,000 for a photograph signed by both Wilbur and Orville Wright, or as much as $25,000 for a handwritten letter of George Washington.

But by far, the majority of autograph collectors in the country do it for the love of the hobby. A polite letter and self-addressed, stamped envelope sent to a famous person will often bring the desired result. And occasionally one receives not only an autograph but a nice handwritten letter thanking the fan as well!

In terms of value, there are five general types of autographs: 1) mere signatures on an album page or card; 2) signed photographs; 3) signed documents; 4) typed letters signed; and 5) handwritten letters. The signatures are the least valuable, and handwritten letters the most valuable. The reasoning here is simple: with a handwritten letter, not only do you get an autograph but the handwritten message of the person as well. And this content can sometimes increase the value many times over. A handwritten letter of Babe Ruth thanking a fan for a gift might fetch a few thousand dollars. But if the letter were to mention Ruth's feelings on the day he retired, it could sell for $10,000 or more.

There are several major autograph collector organizations where members can exchange celebrity addresses or buy, sell, and trade their autographed wares. Philography can be a fun and rewarding hobby. And who knows — in 10 or 20 years, those autographs you got for free could be worth a small fortune!

In the listings below, photos are assumed black and white unless noted color. Our advisor for autographs is Tim Anderson; he is listed in the Directory under Utah.

Key:
ADS — handwritten document signed	ins — inscription
ALS — handwritten letter signed	ISP — inscribed signed photo
ANS — handwritten note signed	LH — letterhead
AQS — autograph quotation signed	LS — signed letter, typed or written by someone else
CS — counter signed	PLH — personal letterhead
DS — document signed	sig — signature
	SP — signed photo

Achard, Marcel; ISP, 4x6" **20.00**
Adams, John; ADS, ship's paper, 1797, 1-pg, VG................... **1,200.00**
Alda, Alan; color SP, scarce..**35.00**
Alda, Robert; blk & wht SP, 1940s, 5x7" **40.00**
Alexander, Jane; SP, 8x10" **10.00**
Ali, Muhammad; blk & wht SP, action shot, 8x10" **30.00**
Allen, Fred; SP, 8x10"...**75.00**
Allen, Rex; color SP, 8x10"...**30.00**
Allen, Steve; ISP, 1954, 8x10" **20.00**
Allen, Woody; SP, 8x10"..**20.00**
Allyson, June; SP, 8x10"..**10.00**
Anderson, Loni; color SP, 8x10"..**15.00**
Anton, Susan; ISP, 8x10".. **7.00**
Armstrong, Neil; sig on card, 3x5"...**30.00**

Arness, James; SP, w/cast 25.00
Astaire, Fred; SP w/Helen Hayes, 8x10" 75.00
Atkins, Homer M; LS, 1963 ....30.00
Bacall, Lauren; SP, early, 8x10" 20.00
Baez, Joan; blk & wht SP, 3x4" 5.00
Baily, Pearl; SP, 8x10" 12.00
Barnum, PT; ALS, arrangements/speeches, 3-pg, VG 250.00
Baxter, Alan; blk & wht SP, 1940s, 8x10" 20.00
Benjamin, Lincoln; ALS, military orders, 1779, 2-pg, EX 500.00
Benny, Jack; sig on picture post card, 1930s, EX.........................75.00
Bertinelli, Valerie; color SP, 8x10" 15.00
Blanc, Mel; color SP, w/characters, 4x6" 20.00
Boone, Daniel; ADS, receipt for land, 1780, 1-pg...................**4,200.00**
Boone, Pat; ISP, early, 8x10" 20.00
Borge, Victor; ALS, lg bold sig, 1950s..20.00
Brandt, Willy; SP, Chancellor of W Germany, 3½x5½" 20.00
Brenner, Yul; sig on still from King & I 55.00
Bridges, Lloyd; color SP, 8x10" 15.00
Bronson, Charles; sig on still from Death Hunt............................12.00
Bryant, Wm Cullen; poem re: war, 1864, 1-pg, +eng portrait......300.00
Buchanan, James; free frank, cover only, postmark: WA DC 170.00
Cher, sig on color cover of Parade..25.00
Clemens, Samuel; ANS, PLH, +CDV by Gurney & Son, EX 450.00
Connery, Sean; SP, as James Bond 25.00
Connors, Chuck; ISP, early, 8x10" 10.00
Coolidge, Calvin; sig on card, w/date & place 150.00
Cooper, James Fenimore; ALS, re: payment owed, 1844, VG......200.00
Crosby, Bing; ANS, 6 lines 40.00
Curtis, Jamie Lee; color SP 15.00
Curtis, Ken; SP, as Festus, 8x10" 25.00
Curtis, Tony; ISP, early, 7x9" 15.00
Dali, Salvador; sgn print, dbl mat, 10x8", M 175.00
De Carlo, Yvonne; SP, 1953, 8x10" 10.00
DeLuise, Dom; color SP, 4x6" 10.00
DeMille, Cecil B; sgn check, Apr 26, 1957 ....165.00
Dempsey, Jack, sig on picture post card..50.00
DeQuincey, Thomas; ALS, complains of illness, 1843, EX..........300.00
Dickinson, Angie; sig on 4x6" card 5.00
Domino, Fats; color SP, 8x10" 30.00
Dunbar, Bonnie; color ISP, 8x10" 20.00
Eisenhower, Dwight D; White House LH, March 25, 1958.........685.00
Elm, Jack; blk & wht SP 75.00
Fairbanks, Douglas, Jr; ISP, scene, 5x7" 10.00
Fillmore, Millard; ADS, military appointment, 1-pg, EX 350.00
Fillmore, Millard; free frank, as member of Congress 190.00
Forsythe, John; blk & wht ISP, 5x7" 12.50
French, Victor; ISP, 8x10", w/John Wayne 30.00
Garner, James; color still from Hour of the Gun 15.00
Gibson, Mel; SP, scarce 45.00
Gleason, Jackie; blk & wht ISP, w/Steve McQueen......................65.00
Gobel, George; ISP, 8x10" 10.00
Goldberg, Whoopie; sgn program cover from Color Purple 30.00
Goldwater, Barry; ISP, 8x10" 10.00
Goulet, Robert; blk & wht ISP 15.00
Grant, Ulysses S; DS, appointing officer, 1872, 16x18" 525.00
Grant, US; ALS, thanks for books, 1877, 1-pg, VG....................500.00
Harrison, Benjamin; ADS on vellum, miltary appointment, EX .280.00
Hart, John; sgn Colonial currency, 18 pence, 1776, EX 160.00
Hayes, Rutherford B; ADS on vellum, military appointment 250.00
Henry, Clay; ALS, miscellaneous context, 1844, 1-pg................200.00
Hooker, Joseph; ALS as General, re: Civil War, 1864, 3½-pg 500.00
Hoover, Herbert; LS, Sept 7, 1939, M 150.00
Hull Isaac; ALS, naval dispatch, 1824, 1½-pg, EX......................220.00
Jackson, Andrew; land grant in OH on vellum, 1830, 10x15" 550.00

Katherine Hepburn, photograph inscribed and signed five times, $1,750.00.

Jackson 5, SP, dtd 1971 ....200.00
Jimmy the Greek, SP, 8x10"...20.00
Kennedy, John F; & Johnson, Lyndon; sgn paperboard, 3x3½" ...750.00
Kissinger, Henry; blk & wht SP, 8x10" 20.00
Ladd, Alan; ISP, sepia, 1930s, 2x3"...50.00
Lee, Peggy; ISP, 8x10" 7.50
Lemmon, Jack; color SP, Fr uniform, 4x6" 10.00
Leverett, Sir John; ADS, re: iron works as Gov of MA, 1-pg.......450.00
Lincoln, A; free franked envelope, rpr, VG.............................2,800.00
Lindbergh, Charles; & Orteig, SP, hands joined, 1927, 8x10" **1,000.00**
Lindbergh, Charles; clipped sig, full & bold, EX..........................300.00
Loren, Sophia; sgn still from It Started in Naples.........................30.00
Madison, James; ADS on vellum, military appointment, EX 700.00
Manson, Charles; ALS, w/2 aka's, 14 very full pgs 250.00
Massena, Andre; ALS as Gen of Napoleon's army, 1-pg, EX 160.00
Mattlack, Timothy; ALS, military protocol, 1779, 1-pg 160.00
McKinley, William; DS, officer's commission, bold sig, 1899......375.00
McKinley, William; SP as President, 1900, 9x6" 850.00
McKinley, William; SP w/ins, formal pose by Parker, EX 550.00
Moreno, Rita; ISP, early, 8x10"...12.00
O'Brien, Hugh; SP, as Wyatt Earp 15.00
O'Conner, Donald; sig on 3x5" card 12.50
O'Hara, Maureen; ISP, 1950s, 8x10" 30.00
Owens, Jessie; blk & wht ISP, 8x10"..110.00
Pearl, Minnie; Christmas card 15.00
Queen Victoria, DS..250.00
Remick, Lee; SP, 8x10" 10.00
Reynolds, Debbie; DS, 1951, release form....................................20.00
Ride, Sally; color SP, trying helmet, 8x10" 45.00
Rogers, Roy; color SP, 8x10" 20.00
Roosevelt, Theodore; ADS on vellum, military appointment 500.00
Roosevelt, Theodore; DS, military commission, 1905, EX..........350.00
Roosevelt, Theodore; his book w/sgn 'rough rider' photo, EX......380.00

Russell, Jane; ALS, re Fuzzy Pk Nightgown, 1957............................30.00
Savalas, Telly; sgn still from Town Called Hell, 1971 ....15.00
Schultz, Charles; blk & wht cartoon, sig on 8x10" card 20.00
Scobee, Dick; SP, w/Challenger crew, 1 sig only.........................150.00
Scott, George C; sgn blk & wht still from Patton.........................75.00
Scott, Sir Walter; ALS, invitation to dinner, 1816, EX.................250.00
Sheen, Martin; SP, family portrait, 8x10".....................................25.00
Smith, William; ALS, Sec of Legislation, trade habits, 1792.......500.00
Stallone, Sylvester; sgn still from Rocky 20.00
Stone, Andrew; LS, 20th Century Fox, 1953 ....25.00
Streisand, Barbara; color SP, 4½x6"...25.00
Suess, Dr; ISP, 4x5"...12.00
Temple, Shirley; ISP, blk & wht glossy, ca 1930s, 8x10" 27.50
Van Buren, Martin; ANS...200.00
Warden, Jack; ISP, 1956...10.00

Washington and Jefferson, handwritten signed
document (ship's papers), dated 1793, paper
and wax seals, EX, $11,000.00.

Warhol, Andy; color SP, 8½x11" 150.00
Welch, Raquel; color SP, 4x6" 10.00
Wilson, Woodrow; ALS, campaign appreciation, 1912, EX 150.00
Zadora, Pia; blk & wht ISP..10.00

Automobilia

While some automobilia buffs are primarily concerned with restoring vintage cars, others concentrate on only one area of collecting. For instance, hood ornaments were often quite spectacular. Made of chrome or nickel plate on brass or bronze, they were designed to represent the 'winged maiden' Victory, flying bats, sleek greyhounds, soaring eagles, and a host of other creatures. Today they bring prices in the $75 to $200 range. R. Lalique glass ornaments go much higher!

Horns, radios, clocks, gear shift knobs, and key chains with company emblems are other areas of interest. Generally, items pertaining to the classics of the thirties are most in demand. Paper advertising material, manuals, and catalogs in excellent condition are also collectible.

License plate collectors search for the early porcelain-on-cast-iron examples. First year plates — e.g., Massachusetts, 1903; Wisconsin, 1905; Indiana, 1913 — are especially valuable. The last of the states to issue regulation plates were South Carolina and Texas in 1917, and Florida in 1918. While many northeastern states had registered hundreds of thousands of vehicles by the 1920s making these plates relatively common, those from the southern and western states of that period are considered rare. Naturally, condition is important. While a pair in mint condition might sell for as much as $100 to $125, a pair with chipped or otherwise damaged porcelain may sometimes be had for as little as $25 to $30. See also Gas Globes and Panels. Our advisors for this category are Dennis O'Brien and George Goehring of Dennis and George Collectibles; they are listed in the Directory under Maryland.

Ash tray, General Tire, rubber tire, glass insert, M........................35.00

Banner, Studebaker showroom, 1943, 52x38", EX 85.00
Booklet, Auto Mechanics Service, 1929, 95-pg, EX......................15.00
Booklet, Boston Motorist, Triple A, 1933, 15-pg, EX 12.50
Booklet, Packard, color/blk & wht illus, 1939, 38-pg, EX 40.00
Booklet, Studebaker Is King of Vehicles, 1890, 95-pg................25.00
Brochure, Hudson dealer's, 1950, EX 25.00
Carton, oil; Phillips 66, 1-qt..15.00
Catalog, Midget Motors Directory, OH, 1952, VG 18.00
Clock, dashboard; Cadillac Jaeger, 1930-31 ....150.00
Clock, dashboard; Elgin, 8-day movement, 3¾" dia, VG 60.00
Clock, dashboard; Westclox, luminous, from '32 Ford, 2½"..........22.00
Folder, Chevrolet for 1925, opens to 15½x19", EX 15.00
Folder, Oldsmobile 1949 Futurama, mc, opens to 24x30"............20.00
Frost shield, Cler-Vue, amber non-glare type, '40s, EX, pr 25.00
Gear shift knob, orange swirl 35.00
Generator, brass, carbide gas, lever action, 12", EX.....................275.00
Generator, brass, carbide gas, wing-nut opening system, 12" 300.00
Generator, carbide gas, Solar, Badger Brass, 1915, VG 60.00
Gloves, driving; leather, lg gauntlets, pr, EX..................................15.00
Hat, It's Ford for '40, canvas, red/wht/bl, EX 17.50
Hood ornament, biplane, aluminum/tin, LVA 1917, 7" W, EX...175.00

Lucas King of the Road brass headlamps, #W082, very rare, 13",
$3,000.00 for the pair.

Hood ornament, Deco phantom, SP brass, 6¼", EX 375.00
Hood ornament, Mack bulldog, diecast, Pat #, 5¾", EX...............50.00
Hood ornament, policeman whirligig, cast aluminum, 6¼", EX .425.00
Hood ornament, Pontiac Indian, chrome, 17", EX.........................25.00
Hood ornament, witch, brass on brass cap, rare, 5", EX 375.00
Horn, brass, w/aluminum bracket, 11" L, EX................................100.00
Horn, old Claxon-type 'ooga,' EX..55.00
Key chain, Chevrolet 50th Anniversary, brass, 1¼", VG...............22.50
Lamp, side; beveled glass lens, Gray & Davis, 13", EX, pr 350.00
Lamp, side; brass, carbide/kerosene, w/chimney, 12", pr 550.00
Lamp kit, Mazda, metal oval hinged case, EX color, 5" 35.00
Lap robe, brn & bl wool, embr Packard, 72x108", EX.................400.00
License plate, Idaho, 1932, EX..22.00
License plate, Kentucky, rpt, 1918..42.50
License plate, New Hampshire, 1919, EX.......................................18.00
License plate, New York, 1915, 6x16", M.......................................75.00
License plate, Pennsylvania, porc on steel, 1909, NM 200.00
License plate, South Dakota, 1916, EX...62.50
License plate, Wisconsin, 1924, VG 6.00
Manual, Oldsmobile, 1935, 36-pg, VG 65.00
Mirror, Auburn See Right, orig leather strap, 9", pr 60.00
Mirror, side; tire mtd, Deco style, EA Laboratories, 6½", pr.........200.00
Moto-meter, Boyce, radiator gauge, brass, Pat Aug 13, 1910 ....18.00
Pamphlet, Presenting...Dodge, 1950, EX..20.00

Paperweight, Auto Mutual Indemnity Co, 1920s, 4¼x2¾" **25.00**
Post card, Overland Model 83 touring car, NM................**12.00**
Poster, Dodge, cars shown in color, ca 1948, EX **30.00**
Promo car, Ford Fairlane, 1964, VG................**30.00**
Radiator cap, Lincoln greyhound, ca 1930, EX................**125.00**
Radiator cap, Model T Ford................**45.00**
Repair kit, Phillips, inner tube, blk & orange **20.00**
Searchlight, brass, Saxon Lamps, w/bracket, 8½" dia, VG **275.00**
Searchlight, Rushmore Dynamo Works...NJ, 8" dia, VG............**160.00**
Steering wheel, aluminum/wood, Guardian Lock, 17" dia, EX **400.00**
Tire, Jiffi-No-Jac Spare, aluminum & rubber, 29", EX **275.00**
Tire stand, Mobil, 1950s................**30.00**
Trunk, car accessory w/metal corner braces, 18x36x15½", VG ...**100.00**
Vase, bud; bl, fluted, w/bracket, 8¼", pr **160.00**
Vase, bud; gr pearlescent glass, Benzer, w/bracket, 7½", pr **150.00**
Vase, marigold carnival glass **50.00**
Windscreen, brass w/plexiglas lens, 15" dia, EX **180.00**

Autumn Leaf

In 1933 the Hall China Company designed a line of dinnerware for the Jewel Tea Company, who offered it to their customers as premiums. Although you may hear the ware referred to as 'Jewel Tea,' it was officially named 'Autumn Leaf' in the 1940s. In addition to the dinnerware, frosted Libbey glass tumblers, stemware, and a melmac service with the orange and gold bittersweet pod were available over the years, as were tablecloths, plastic covers for bowls and mixers, and metal items such as cake safes, hot pads, coasters, waste baskets, and canisters. Even shelf paper and playing cards were made to coordinate. In 1958 the International Silver Company designed silverplated flatware in a pattern called 'Autumn' which was to be used with dishes in the Autumn Leaf pattern. A year later, a line of stainless flatware was introduced. These accessory lines are prized by collectors today.

One of the most fascinating aspects of collecting the Autumn Leaf pattern has been the wonderful discoveries of previously unlisted pieces. Among these items are two different bud-ray lid one-pound butter dishes; most recently a one-pound butter dish in the 'Zephyr' or 'Bingo' style; a miniature set of the 'Casper' salt and pepper shakers; coffee, tea, and sugar canisters; a pair of candlesticks; an experimental condiment jar; and a covered candy dish. All of these china pieces are attributed to the Hall China Company. Other unusual items have turned up in the accessory lines as well and include a Libbey frosted tumbler in a pilsner shape, a wooden serving bowl, and an apron made from the oilcloth (plastic) material that was used in the 1950s tablecloth. These latter items appear to be professionally done, and we can only speculate as to their origin. Collectors believe that the Hall items were sample pieces that were never meant to be distributed.

Hall discontinued the Autumn Leaf line in 1978. At that time the date was added to the backstamp to mark ware still in stock in the Jewel warehouse. A special promotion by Jewel saw the reintroduction of basic dinnerware and serving pieces with the 1978 backstamp. These pieces have made their way into many collections. Additionally, in 1979 Jewel released a line of enamel-clad cookware and a Vellux blanket made by Martex which were decorated with the Autumn Leaf pattern. They continued to offer these items for a few years only, then all distribution of Autumn Leaf items was discontinued.

It should be noted that the Hall China Company has produced several limited edition items for the National Autumn Leaf Collectors Club (NALCC): a New York-style teapot (1984); a vase (1987 — different than the original shape); candlesticks (1988); a Philadelphia-style teapot, creamer and sugar set (1990); a sugar packet holder (1990); and a tea-for-two set (1991). Other items are scheduled for production. All of these are plainly marked as having been made for the NALCC and are appropriately dated.

Baker, oval, Fort Pitt **75.00**
Batter bowl, Saf-Hdl **1,500.00**
Bean pot, 1-hdl **300.00**
Bean pot, 2-hdl, 2¼-qt **85.00**
Bowl, cereal; 6" **8.00**
Bowl, coupe soup **10.00**
Bowl, cream soup; 2-hdl **18.00**
Bowl, fruit; 5½" **3.00**
Bowl, metal, enamelware, set of 3 ....**100.00**
Bowl, mixing; set of 3: 6¼", 7½", 9" **55.00**
Bowl, Royal Glas-Bake, set of 4 ....**45.00**
Bowl, salad **14.00**
Bowl, stackette; set of 3: 18-oz, 24-oz, 34-oz, w/lid **70.00**
Bowl, vegetable; divided, 10½" **75.00**
Bowl, vegetable; oval, w/lid, 10" **35.00**
Bowl, vegetable; oval, 10½" **12.00**
Bowl, vegetable; rnd, 9" **75.00**
Bowl cover set, plastic, 8-pc: 7 assorted covers in pouch **50.00**
Bread box, metal **150.00**
Butter dish, 1-lb **225.00**
Butter dish, ¼-lb **125.00**
Butter dish, ¼-lb, Square Top **400.00**
Butter dish, ¼-lb, Wings **500.00**
Cake plate, 9½" **12.00**

Butter dish, 1-lb., $225.00.

Cake safe, metal, motif on top & sides, 5" **35.00**
Cake safe, metal, side decor only, 4½x10½" **30.00**
Cake stand, metal base, orig box **125.00**
Candy dish **325.00**
Canister, metal, rnd, w/coppertone lid, set of 4 ....**175.00**
Canister, metal, rnd, w/ivory plastic lid **10.00**
Canister, metal, rnd, w/matching lid, 6" **15.00**
Canister, metal, rnd, w/matching lid, 7" **25.00**
Canister, metal, rnd, w/matching lid, 8¼" **35.00**
Canister, metal, sq, set of 4: 8½" & 4½" **115.00**
Casserole, Royal Glas-Bake, deep, w/clear glass lid **25.00**
Casserole, Royal Glas-Bake, shallow, w/clear glass lid **20.00**
Casserole, Tootsie-hdl, w/lid **22.00**
Casserole/souffle, swirl, 3-pt **15.00**
Casserole/souffle, 10-oz **10.00**
Casserole/souffle, 2-pt **65.00**
Cleanser can, metal, sq, 6" **250.00**
Clock, orig works **350.00**
Coaster, metal, 3⅛" **4.00**
Coffee dispenser/canister, metal, wall type, 10½x19" dia **125.00**
Coffee maker, 5-cup, all china, w/china insert **200.00**

Coffee maker, 9-cup, w/metal dripper, 8" 35.00
Coffee percolator, electric, all china 225.00
Coffee percolator/carafe, Douglas, w/warmer base, MIB 250.00
Cookie jar, Tootsie 125.00
Creamer, New Style 8.00
Creamer, Old Style, 4¼" 15.00
Cup & saucer 8.00
Cup & saucer, St Denis 18.00
Custard cup 4.00
Flatware, silverplate, ea 15.00
Flatware, stainless, ea 10.00
Fruit cake tin, metal 10.00
Golden Ray base, to use w/candy dish or cake plate, pr 50.00
Gravy boat 15.00
Hot pad, metal, red or gr felt-like bking, rnd 12.00
Hot pad, oval 10.00
Hurricane lamp, Douglas, w/metal base, pr 400.00
Kitchen utility chair, metal 450.00
Marmalade jar, 3-pc 45.00
Mixer cover, Mary Dunbar, plastic 25.00
Mug, beverage 45.00
Mug, Irish coffee 85.00
Mustard jar, 3½" 45.00
Napkin, ecru muslin 25.00
Pickle dish or gravy liner, oval, 9" 18.00
Picnic thermos, metal 250.00
Pie baker, 9½" 18.00
Pitcher, utility; 2½-pt, 6" 15.00
Place mat, paper, scalloped 25.00
Place mat, set of 8, M in orig package 195.00
Plate, 10" 10.00
Plate, 6" or 7", ea 4.00
Plate, 8" 8.00
Plate, 9" 7.00
Platter, 11½" 14.00
Platter, 13½" 16.00
Playing cards, regular or Pinochle 125.00
Range set, shakers & covered drippings jar 35.00
Sauce dish, serving; Douglas, Bakelite hdl 125.00
Shakers, Casper, pr 18.00
Shakers, range, hdl, pr 18.00
Sugar bowl, New Style 12.00
Sugar bowl, Old Style, 3½" 18.00
Tablecloth, cotton sailcloth w/gold stripe, 54x54" 75.00
Tablecloth, cotton sailcloth w/gold stripe, 54x72" 85.00
Tablecloth, ecru muslin, 56x81" 150.00
Tablecloth, plastic 150.00
Teakettle, metal enamelware 150.00
Teapot, Aladdin 38.00
Teapot, long spout, 7" 45.00
Teapot, Newport 115.00
Teapot, Newport, dtd 1978 ....90.00
Toaster cover, plastic, fits 2-slice toaster 25.00
Towel, dish; pattern & clock motif 45.00
Towel, tea; cotton, 16x33" 35.00
Trash can, metal, red 65.00
Tray, glass, wood hdl, 19½x11¼" 95.00
Tray, metal, oval 55.00
Tray, red w/allover red & yel design, red border 65.00
Tray, tidbit; 2-tier 35.00
Tray, tidbit; 3-tier 45.00
Tumbler, Brockway, 13-oz 18.00
Tumbler, Brockway, 16-oz 20.00
Tumbler, Brockway, 9-oz 16.00

Tumbler, frosted, 14-oz, 5½" 12.00
Tumbler, frosted, 9-oz, 3¾" 18.00
Tumbler, gold frost etched, flat, 10-oz 30.00
Tumbler, gold frost etched, flat, 15-oz 45.00
Tumbler, gold frost etched, ftd, 10-oz 45.00
Tumbler, gold frost etched, ftd, 6½-oz 45.00
Vase, bud; 6" 150.00
Warmer base, oval 125.00
Warmer base, rnd 100.00
Warmer base, rnd, w/4 orig candles, orig mk box 110.00

Aviation

Aviation buffs are interested in any phase of flying — from early developments with gliders, balloons, airships and flying machines to more modern innovations. Books, catalogs, photos, patents, lithographs, ad cards, and posters are among the paper ephemera they treasure alongside models of unlikely flying contraptions, propellers and rudders, insignia and equipment from WWI and WWII, and memorabilia from the flights of the Wright Brothers, Lindbergh, Earhart, and the Zeppelins. See also Militaria. Our advisor for this category is John R. Joiner; he is listed in the Directory under Georgia.

Blanket, Continental Airlines, wool, Pendleton 45.00
Book, Fighting the Flying Circus, sgn by Rickenbacker, NM 55.00
Book, Lone Eagle, story of Lindbergh's flight, 1928, VG 20.00
Book, We, Charles Lindbergh, 48 illus, NY, 1927, EX 50.00
Book, Who's Who in Aviation, 1942-43, EX 27.50
Book, Why Has America No Rigid Airships, 1945, EX 15.00
Booklet, Braniff, Portraits of Progress, 1948, 5½x8½" 6.00
Booklet, United, Vacationland, 1949 ....6.00
Bowl, brass, 25th Anniversary Flying Tiger Line, 6½" 45.00
Envelope, Hindenburg stamps, dtd 1936, EX 32.00
Fan, Pan-Am Airlines, routes/birds, bamboo hdl, 1940s, 14" 45.00
Letter opener, United Airlines, stainless steel, 9½" 4.00
Photograph, Lindbergh by early plane, orig fr, 16x13" 165.00
Pin, Am Airlines, Jr Pilot, brass, VG 12.00
Pin, Am Legion, Lindy's plane form, 1930s, EX 15.00
Pin-bk, Amelia Earhart in aviator's helmet, 1¼", EX 42.50
Pin-bk, Welcome Lindy, portrait 16.00
Pinball game, Air Ways, 1930s, EX 55.00
Playing cards, Ozark Air Lines, 1984 World's Fair, sealed 3.00

Ford tri-motor plane by Schieble, 28" long, EX, $850.00.

Post card, Airship Hindenburg, 1936, EX 45.00
Post card, John Polando & Russel Boardman, 1932, EX 35.00
Poster, Have You Seen This Girl?, Kern, early, 15x20", VG 280.00
Schedule, TWA, 1947, NM 15.00

Schedule, TWA, 1947, NM	15.00
Sign, TWA, mc stand-up type, 1938, 12x9", EX	20.00
Timetable, Eastern, 1948	10.00
Timetable, Lufthansa, summer of 1956, EX	8.00
Tumbler, Pan Am, 1960s	10.00
Wings, Delta, plastic	1.00
Wings, Eastern, plastic	1.00
Wings, Pan Am Junior Clipper Pilot, metal	8.00

Avon

The California Perfume Company, the parent of the Avon Co., was founded in 1886. Although an 'Avon' line was introduced by the company in the mid-twenties, not until 1939 did it become known as Avon Products, Inc. Collectible Avon items include not only figural bottles and jars but jewelry, awards, product samples, magazine ads, and catalogs as well. For more information concerning the Avon Collectors Club, see the Clubs, Newsletters, and Catalogs section of the Directory. See also California Perfume Company.

In the listings that follow, unless noted MIB, prices are for bottles only.

Apple Blossom Complexion Soap, 1925, 3 bars, MIB	80.00
Attention Toilet Water, 1934-46, gold or plastic cap, 2-oz, M	28.00
Baby Powder, 1954-56, wht & pk can, 2-oz	24.00
Bath Classic, 1962-63, glass w/gold design, no box, M	12.00
Bay Rum, 1930-36, glass bottle, blk cap, 8-oz, M	44.00
Bay Rum Soap, 1964-65, gr box, 2 bars, MIB	25.00
Bird of Paradise Perfume Glace Ring, 1970-72, MIB	10.00
Blue Blazer Soap & Sponge Set, 1966-67, MIB	25.00
Brocade Soap, 1968, brn & wht wrapper, M	5.00
Charisma Tray, 1968-70, red plastic w/gold trim, M	10.00
Chateau of Flowers Book, gr, story of Lily of the Valley	3.00
Cotillion Beauty Dust, 1959-61, pk & wht plastic, MIB	15.00
Crystal Cologne, 1966-70, 4-oz, 5½" bottle	4.00
Cute As a Button Set, 1961-63, nail polish & lipstick, MIB	20.00
Forever Spring Body Powder, 1956-59, frosted jar, no box	15.00
Gentlemen's Choice, 1969-70, 5-bottle set, no box	5.00
Gift Atomizer Perfume, 1931-34, red glass bottle, 1-oz	80.00

Gift Bows Soaps, 1962-64, MIB, $25.00.

Hair Tonic Eau De Quinne, 1931-36, ribbed bottle, no box	43.00
Lily of The Valley Scented Pillow, 1979, gr & wht, 10x10", MIB	10.00
Nail Clippers, 1960s, rare	7.50
Nail White, 1924-29, sm gold & blk can, M	20.00
Nearness Beauty Dust, 1959-61, turq w/pearl lid, MIB	15.00
Nearness Sea Shell Necklace, 1956 only	21.00
Oily Polish Remover, 1946-50, bottle w/turq cap, MIB	13.00
Overnighter, 1965-66, brn zipper bag, MIB	25.00
Persian Wood Beauty Dust, 1960-66, wht w/red design, M	10.00
Soap & Sponge, 1967-70, pk soap, 9" sponge, MIB	10.00

Sweet Sixteen Face Powder, 1916, yel, pk, & gr box, M	47.00
To a Wild Rose Soap, 1957-68, 3 bars, M in lg box	28.00
Wild Country Pendant, 1978, bull's head on chain, MIB	5.00
Wild Roses Set, 1964, multi-flowered pk box, 2-oz, MIB	21.00
Young Hearts Beauty Dust, 1954-55, M in mc box	27.00

Baccarat

The Baccarat Glass company was founded in 1765 near Luneville, France, and continues to this day to produce quality crystal tableware, vases, perfume bottles, and figurines. The firm became famous for the high-quality millefiori and caned paperweights produced there from 1845 until about 1860. Examples of these range from $300 to as much as several thousand. Since 1953 they have resumed the production of paperweights on a limited edition basis. See also Paperweights.

Bottle, scent; frosted florals, pine cone stopper, 6"	150.00
Bottle, scent; paneled/bulbous, hollow stopper, sgn, 4½"	125.00
Bottle, scent; Rose Tiente Swirl, 6⅛x2⅜"	65.00
Box, Rose Tiente Swirl, knob finial, 5x3⅝" dia	88.00
Box, Rose Tiente Swirl, oval, mk, 2⅜x4⅞x3¼"	95.00
Chandelier, cut glass, 4-branch, baluster column, 25x32"	800.00
Compote, Rose Tiente Swirl, gold rim, low ft, 3½x7", pr	220.00

Decanters, Lagny, 13", $300.00 for the pair.

Goblet, cameo floral, red on gr w/gold, dbl-knob std, 6½"	325.00
Lamp, fairy; Rose Tiente Swirl, emb Sunburst pattern, 4"	235.00
Lamp, perfume; Rose Tiente Swirl, metal lid, 5x5⅝"	118.00
Obelisk, sgn, 17"	800.00
Old Fashioned, honeycomb, set of 12	700.00
Pitcher, tankard; Rose Tiente Swirl, appl hdl, 9⅞"	225.00
Toothpick holder, cameo cut, cranberry to wht frost, 2¼"	175.00
Vase, bamboo branch form w/bug & snake, rocky base, 8½"	400.00
Vase, triangular free-form, stick neck, 9"	120.00

Badges

The breast badge came into general usage in this country about 1840. Since most are not marked and styles have changed very little to the present day, they are often difficult to date. The most reliable clue is the pin and catch. One of the earliest types, used primarily before the turn of the century, involved a 't-pin' and a 'shell' catch. In a second style, the pin was hinged with a small square of sheet metal, and the clasp was cylindrical. From the late 1800s until about 1940, the pin and clasp were made from one continuous piece of thin metal wire. The same type, with the addition of a flat back plate, was used a little later. There are exceptions to these findings, and other types of clasps were also used. Hallmarks and inscriptions may also help pinpoint an approximate age.

Badges have been made from a variety of materials, usually brass or nickel silver; but even solid silver and gold were used for special orders. They are found in many basic shapes and variations — stars with five to seven points, shields, disks, ovals, and octagonals being most often encountered. Of prime importance to collectors, however, is that the title and/or location appear on the badge. Those with designations of positions no longer existing (City Constable, for example) and names of early western states and towns are most valuable.

Badges are among the most commonly-reproduced (and faked) types of antiques on the market. At any flea market, ten fakes can be found for every authentic example. Genuine law badges start at $30.00 to $40.00 for recent examples (1950-1970); earlier pieces (1910-1930) usually bring $50.00 to $90.00. Pre-1900 badges often sell for more than $100.00. Authentic gold badges are usually priced at a minimum of scrap value (karat, weight, spot price for gold); fine gold badges from before 1900 can sell for $400.00 to $800.00, and a few will bring even more. A fire badge is usually valued at about half the price of a law badge from the same circa and material.

Our advisor for this category is Gene Matzke; he is listed in the Directory under Wisconsin.

Auxiliary Police, silvered metal, shield/eagle, 2¾" 20.00
Chief, Thorp WI, eagle/shield 35.00
Chief Quarterman Packer, VA, nickeled brass, shield/eagle 18.00
Deputy Sheriff, Monroe County WI, eagle/shield...........................35.00
Deputy Sheriff, NY, brass, eagle over circular form, NM................50.00
Deputy Sheriff, Tooele County UT, silver-color circle star............55.00
Deputy Sheriff, Wayne County, bronze tone, ca 1900, 2½" 45.00
Deputy US Marshall, NM, brass, hallmk, 1910, 2" 65.00
Deputy US Marshall, sterling, 6-point star, 1900 ....250.00
Naval Police, Seabees emblem, 1940s...80.00
Patrol Driver, Chicago, 6-point star, 1910....................................200.00
Patrolman, Chicago, silver color, 5-point star 75.00

14k yellow gold, Philadelphia Fire Insurance Patrol, 1860s, $400.00.

Police Sergeant, TN Hwy Patrol, 1930s 85.00
Policeman, Carroll NY, SP, shield/eagle, 3" 25.00
Policeman, MI Hwy Patrol, gold w/blk enamel, wallet clip............55.00
Policeman, VA, silver color, eagle atop, 1½".................................20.00

Salt Lake City UT, nickeled, shield..100.00
Set, Buffalo NY, custom die 175.00
Set, Rochester NY, lug bk, custom die 250.00
Sheriff, Bowie County, gold color/blk enamel, 5-point star...........30.00
Special Deputy Sheriff, gold color, ca 1914, EX............................40.00
Special Police, silver color, octagonal, early 30.00
Veterans Administrative Police, old shield....................................45.00

Banks

Collectors of mechanical and still banks have seen considerable change in the pricing picture in the past few years. An increasing number of banks are appearing in general auctions, and some auctions are now devoted entirely to banks and toys. Often the prices realized at auction varies greatly from advertised prices. This can sometimes be attributed to 'auction fever,' but it may also represent buyers with specific knowledge concerning the banks they are bidding on. Condition has become an important price-determining factor. A pristine bank will frequently sell for two to four times the price realized by the same bank in only 'good' condition. Always look for examples in the best-possible condition. They will cost more, but they will be the best investment for you. Banks should always be complete with all parts present, original, and in good working condition (if it is a mechanical). Replaced parts or retouched paint lessen a bank's value. Rarity is also an important factor in pricing banks — almost as important as condition.

Still banks are found in nearly every shape and size, and many types of material have been used in their making. Exactly how many styles were made is unknown; but about three thousand have been identified, and there are thousands more that are unlisted in any book. Cast iron examples are the most popular, but there is an increasing interest in the early tin and pottery banks made in the United States.

The category of mechanical banks is unique. Along with cast iron bell toys, they are among the most outstanding products of the Industrial Revolution and are recognized as some of the most successful of the mass-produced products of the nineteenth century. The earliest mechanicals were made of wood or lead; but when John Hall introduced Hall's Excelsior, a cast iron mechanical bank, it was an immediate success. J. and E. Stevens produced the bank for Hall and soon began to make their own designs. Several companies followed suit, most of which were already in the hardware business. They used newly-developed iron-molding techniques to produce these novelty savings devices for the emerging toy market. Mechanical banks reflect the social and political attitudes of the times, racial prejudices, the excitement of the circus, and humorous everyday events. Their designers made the most of simple mechanics to produce banks with captivating actions that served not only to amuse but to promote the concept of thrift to the children. The quality of detail in the castings are truly fine examples of industrial art. The most collectible examples were made during the period of 1870 to 1900; however, they continued to be made until the early days of World War II. J. and E. Stevens, Shepard Hardware, and Kyser and Rex are some of the more well-known manufacturers — most made still banks as well.

While the cast iron banks dominate the market, there are examples made from many other materials. Combinations of tin and cardboard and banks made from tin alone are very collectible. Some of the European tin banks are quite rare; England made some fine cast iron mechanicals and many aluminum examples. The popularity of old mechanicals has created a market for reproductions and fakes. Reproductions may have minor value as such, but not as true collectibles. A few of the fakes have attained collectible status but are still not regarded as true mechanical banks.

The increase in auction activity has made a great impact on mechanical bank prices. The prices realized clearly show the premium buyers are paying for condition. The spread between a bank in Good condition and an Excellent bank continually increases. In comparing prices realized and estimates, over 60% of the banks brought more than their estimates. Only 14% fell below the estimate and the balance were within the range suggested in the auction catalog. This year some major still bank auctions are planned, and they will certainly affect the market.

As both value and interest continue on the increase, it becomes even more important to educate one's self to the fullest extent possible. We recommend these books for your library: *The Dictionary of Still Banks* by Long and Pitman, *The Penny Bank Book* by Moore, and *The Bank Book* by Norman. If you are primarily interested in mechanicals, *Penny Lane,* a new book by Davidson, is considered the most complete reference available. It contains a cross-reference listing of numbers from all other publications on mechanical banks.

In the listings that follow, banks are identified by L for Long, G for Griffith, M for Moore, N for Norman, D for Davidson, and W for Whiting.

Key:
CI — cast iron   NPCI — nickel-plated cast iron
EPCI — electroplated cast iron

Boy Robbing Bird's Nest, painted cast iron, 7½", EX, $7,200.00.

Advertising

AC Spark Plug, horse in tub, cast metal, rubber wheels, EX........**135.00**
Bank on Republic Pig Iron, M-331, CI, no pnt, modern, 7"...........**25.00**
Bokar Coffee, tin, EX...**12.00**
Cincy Stove, CI, lt bl porc enamel, nickel grill, 3½"....................**45.00**
Cities Service, cb...**20.00**
Coors Beer, aluminum can form, M...**5.00**
Fidelity Trust Vaults, M-903, CI, old rpt, 6½"............................**175.00**
Howard Johnson's Restaurant, CI, dk patina, modern, 4¾" L........**45.00**
Majestic Ice Box, M-1332, CI & sheet metal...............................**250.00**
Old Dutch Cleanser, tin, NM..**35.00**
Phillips 66, piggy bank, old-style logo, EX..................................**20.00**
Radiation Stoves, tin, 5¼", VG...**110.00**
RL Berry's Piano, M-840, sheet steel, bronze pnt, 5⅛", VG.........**100.00**
Rochester Trust & Save, CI, 5", EX..**100.00**
Roper Stove, M-1342, CI, gr pnt, Arcade decal, 4", EX.............**300.00**
Somerset Savings Bank, metal, Add-O-Matic, worn pnt, 4x4½" ..**37.50**
Tang Robot, plastic...**5.00**
Tony the Tiger, plastic..**10.00**
Union 76, metal...**12.50**
Universal Stoves & Ranges, tin, revolving globe.........................**235.00**
Wolf Head Motor Oil, CI...**15.00**
Worcester Salt, M-451, elephant, wht metal, gr patina, 4¼" **35.00**

Mechanical

Acrobat, D-1, J&E Stevens, CI, worn pnt, 5", EX **3,850.00**
Always Did 'Spise a Mule, Book of Knowledge repro, 9⅜" **55.00**
Always Did 'Spise a Mule, N-2940-A, bench, Stevens, 10" L, G.**375.00**
Always Did 'Spise a Mule, N-2950-A, jockey, 10⅛" L, VG **650.00**
Artillery, D-11, J&E Stevens, Confederate, pnt CI, 7" **1,760.00**
Artillery, N-1060-D, J&E Stevens, pnt CI, lt rust **275.00**
Bad Accident, D-20, J&E Stevens, pnt CI, rpr bushes, EX...... **3,520.00**
Bad Accident, N-1050-A, upside-down letters, Stevens, EX... **2,300.00**
Bill E Grin, D-33, J&E Stevens, CI, worn pnt, no trap, 4½" **600.00**
Boy Scout Camp, D-52, J&E Stevens, pnt CI, 9⅞" L, EX **4,700.00**
Bulldog, N-1430-A, JH Bowen, Stevens, eyes missing, VG..... **1,500.00**
Cabin, D-93, J&E Stevens, CI, worn pnt, VG.............................**425.00**
Calumet, N-1650, tin, cb, & printed paper, 5½", EX **115.00**
Cat & Mouse, D-104, J&E Stevens, pnt CI, EX **9,500.00**

Chief Big Moon, N-1740-C, J&E Stevens, pnt CI, 10" L, EX . **3,000.00**
Clown, N-1870, Chein, tin, 5" **45.00**
Clown on Globe, N-1930-A, J&E Stevens, pnt CI, 9", G....... **1,200.00**
Confectionary, D-131, J&E Stevens, pnt CI, orig tray, 8½" ...**14,000.00**
Creedmore, N-2000-B, J&E Stevens, pnt CI, 8", EX **400.00**
Darktown Battery, N-2080-A, Stevens, pnt CI, broken bat.... **1,400.00**
Dentist, D-152, J&E Stevens, CI, 9½", G **4,180.00**
Dinah, D-153, J Harper, pnt CI, short sleeves, 7", VG **330.00**
Eagle & Eaglettes, D-165, J&E Stevens, pnt CI, 6¾", EX **770.00**
Elephant, D-173, man pops out, Enterprise, pnt CI, 6", EX **1,650.00**
Elephant, D-183, 3 stars, CI, 9" L, EX.................................... **1,320.00**
Elephant, N-2300-A, pull tail, Hubley, pnt CI, 5½", EX **170.00**
Elephant, Royal Trick; D-420, European, CI, 7" L, G **1,100.00**
Frog on Rnd Base, D-204, J&E Stevens, pnt CI, 4½", EX...........**400.00**
Frogs, 2; D-200, J&E Stevens, eye missing, G **1,100.00**
Gem Bank, N-2570-A, CI, no pnt, rpl spring, G **150.00**
Girl in Victorian Chair, D-216, WS Reed, CI, VG pnt, 4½" .. **3,960.00**
Hall's Excelsior, D-228, J&E Stevens, 6", EX............................**275.00**
Hall's Excelsior, N-2710-D, yel variant, 5¾", VG......................**190.00**
Hall's Lilliput, D-229, J&E Stevens, CI, EX pnt, rpl trap **1,045.00**
Home Bank, D-244, Morrison, tin litho, lt rust, 5½", G **120.00**
Home Bank w/Dormers, D-242, J&E Stevens, VG pnt, 5½" ... **1,760.00**
Humpty Dumpty, D-248, Shepard Hardware, pnt CI, 5" L, VG ..**770.00**
Indian & Bear, D-257, Stevens, wht bear, pnt CI, 11", EX **1,980.00**
Initiating Bank, 1st Degree; N-3000-A, CI, worn pnt/lt rust... **8,500.00**
Jolly Nigger, D-276, John Harper, CI, G pnt, 7" **350.00**
Jolly Nigger, N-3130, high hat, Harper, CI, worn pnt, 8", G **300.00**
Jolly Nigger, N-3270, aluminum, worn mc pnt, 6" **85.00**
Jolly Nigger, N-3370, J&E Stevens, pnt CI, G **160.00**
Jonah & Whale, Book of Knowledge repro, 10" **75.00**
Jonah & Whale, N-2490, Shepard Hardware, pnt CI, EX....... **1,800.00**
Jumbo Savings Bank, England, tin, 5", EX................................**85.00**
Lion & Monkeys, D-300, Keyser-Rex, 1 peanut, EX pnt, 9½" .. **2,420.00**
Lion Hunter, D-301, J&E Stevens, pnt CI, 7½", EX............... **8,800.00**
Magic Bank, D-311, J&E Stevens, CI, 4", EX **1,045.00**
Mammy & Child, N-3790, Keyser-Rex, pnt CI, VG **2,400.00**
Mason, D-321, Shepard Hardware, pnt CI, 7⅜" L, EX **8,250.00**
Memorial Bank (Liberty Bell), D-322, pnt CI, 6½", EX **1,320.00**
Milking Cow, Book of Knowledge repro, 9⅝"............................**65.00**
Monkey, N-3990, Chein, tin, 5", VG **50.00**
Monkey w/Tray, D-337, European, tin, 6½", G **495.00**

Mule Entering Barn, D-342, J&E Stevens, pnt CI, VG **1,540.00**
Mule Entering Barn, N-4030-B, Stevens, lt gr pnt, VG **250.00**
Novelty Bank, D-361, J&E Stevens, CI, worn pnt, 7½" **935.00**
Organ Bank, D-368, boy & girl, Keyser-Rex, CI, rpt, 8" **265.00**
Organ Bank, D-369, cat & dog, Keyser-Rex, CI, G pnt, 8"..........**155.00**
Organ Bank, D-371, medium, Keyser-Rex, CI, EX pnt, 6" **495.00**
Owl, D-373, slot in book, Kilgore, pnt CI, 5½", EX **880.00**
Owl, D-374, slot in head, Kilgore, pnt CI, 5½", EX **715.00**
Owl, N-4380-C, turns head, Stevens, CI, worn pnt, rpl eyes.......**160.00**
Paddy & the Pig, D-376, J&E Stevens, EX pnt, 7⅛" L **4,500.00**
Panorama, D-377, pnt CI, roof crack, 6½" **5,280.00**
Pay Phone, M-4470-B, J&E Stevens, pnt CI, 7", EX **1,650.00**
Pelican, N-4510, Mammy version, pnt CI, rpl bill, VG **950.00**
Penny Pineapple, Imswiler & Saylor, modern, 8½", MIB..............**85.00**
Professor Pug Frogs...Feat, D-400, pnt CI, 8", EX **6,050.00**
Punch & Judy, D-404, Shepard Hardware, pnt CI, 6⅛" L, EX... **1,980.00**
Record Money Box, D-411, weighs English pennies, CI, G **800.00**
Rooster, D-419, Keyser-Rex, CI, G pnt, orig lever, 6½" **825.00**
Speaking Dog, D-447, Shepard Hardware, EX pnt, 7⅛" L........ **4,400.00**
Speaking Dog, N-5170-A, Shepard Hardware, pnt CI, EX **700.00**
Springing Cat, N-5190-A, Bailey, pnt lead alloy/wood base .**17,000.00**
Stump Speaker, N-5370-B, Shepard, pnt CI, 9½", VG **500.00**
Tammany, D-455, CI, brn pants/bl coat, EX pnt, 6" **400.00**
Tammany, D-455, J&E Stevens, brn coat, lt rust, 5", G **165.00**
Tammany, N-5420-A, CI, Stevens, gray/blk pnt, 6½", EX **250.00**
Teddy & Bear, D-459, J&E Stevens, pnt CI, 9", EX **2,860.00**
Thrifty Scotchman, N-5500, wooden, orig mc pnt, 8¼"...............**65.00**
Trick Dog, D-481, Shepard Hardware, CI, EX pnt, 8¾" L...........**500.00**
Trick Pony, D-484, Shepard Hardware, worn pnt, 7" L........... **1,430.00**
Uncle Sam, Book of Knowledge repro, 11" **75.00**
Uncle Sam, D-493, Shepard Hardware, pnt CI, 11½", NM **5,280.00**
Uncle Sam, N-5740, CI, worn pnt, VG....................................**450.00**
Uncle Tom, Star, D-497, Keyser-Rex, CI, worn pnt, 6" **285.00**
Uncle Wiggily, Chein, 5", EX **75.00**
William Tell, N-5940, J&E Stevens, pnt CI, 6¾", EX **700.00**
Wireless Bank, N-5980, J Hugo, tin/CI/wood, battery op, VG.......**80.00**
World's Fair, N-6040-B, J&E Stevens, pnt CI, EX **850.00**
You Pay, I Play, N-4080 variant, velvet fr, 8", VG **4,180.00**

Mama Katzenjammer, painted cast iron, by Kenton, ca 1910, paint good, trap replaced, 6", $4,900.00.

Registering

B&R Mfg, NY, 10¢ register 12.00
Bed Post, M-1305, 5¢ register 70.00
Book of Knowledge 12.00
Bucket, CI, 1¢ register, Japan, Pat Appl, 2¾" 90.00
Daily Dime Clown 17.50
Donald Duck, 10¢ register, Disney, tin, 1930s, NM 90.00
Dopey, 10¢ register, Disney, 1938, EX 60.00
Elves Rolling Coins 50.00
Keep 'Em Smiling, 10¢ register, battleship litho, EX 100.00
Popeye, 10¢ register, NM..45.00
Radio, English, tin litho, rnd, 5", VG 25.00
Rockford Nat'l Bank, 10¢ register 28.00
Snow White..185.00
Spinning Wheel, W Germany, tin litho w/2 scenes, sq, 4½" 25.00
TV Bank, W Germany, tin litho, various denominations, 4".........15.00
Wee Folks Money Box, England, tin litho, sq, 5" 50.00
World Scope 32.00

Still

Air Mail, M-848, pnt CI, minor wear, 6⅜" 350.00
Andy Gump, pnt die-cast metal, 5½", EX 235.00
Apple, pottery, orig yel & red pnt, 3" 175.00
Arabian Safe, M-882, CI, gold pnt traces, 4½" 80.00
Atlas, L-631, world on shoulders, pot metal, 4½", EX..................245.00
Aunt Jemima, M-175, w/basket, pnt wht metal, 5¼", EX 65.00
Aunt Jemima, M-256, pnt CI, minor wear, modern, 8¼"...............25.00
Auto, M-1487, CI, worn mc pnt, 6¾" 350.00
Baby, C-535, emerging from eggshell, EX 45.00
Bank Building, L-419, CI, bronze finish traces, 3⅜" 115.00
Barrel, M-916, Puzzle...#3, NPCI, worn, 5⅛" 85.00
Basset Hound, M-380, CI, worn gold pnt, 3⅛" 785.00
Battle of Gettysburg, M-1194, CI, mc pnt, modern, 4⅝" 450.00
Battleship Maine, L-1581, CI, 4½", EX 325.00
Battleship Oregon, L-1017 (M-1349), EX 310.00
Bear, Grisly; M-703, lead, bright copper pnt, 2¾" 35.00
Bear Stealing Honey, M-1308, CI, japanning w/gold, 7", EX 175.00
Bear Stealing Pig, W-246 ....975.00
Beehive bank/string holder, M-684, CI, NP brass finial, 5½" 450.00
Billiken, M-74, Good Luck, CI, gold pnt w/red, 4", VG 125.00
Billiken on Throne, L-649, Good Luck, pnt CI, EX....................140.00
Billy Can, M-79, CI, gold/bl/red pnt, 5", G 650.00
Black Boy, M-83, 2-faced, CI, mc pnt, minor wear, 4⅛".............150.00
Black Boy, M-84, 2-faced, CI, worn blk & gold pnt, 3⅛" 65.00
Boy Scout, L-654, CI, 8" 500.00
Buffalo, M-556, Amherst Stones, CI, blk pnt, 8"........................320.00
Bull, M-537, on base, CI, mc pnt, minor pitting, 5" L 125.00
Bull, M-555, aluminum, blk pnt, minor wear, 7⅜".....................110.00
Bungalow, M-993, CI, gold pnt, red roof, worn, 3" 60.00
Bungalow, M-999, CI, mc pnt, partition missing, worn, 3⅜".......105.00
Camel, L-30 (M767), lg, VG..450.00
Camel, M-768, CI, 4¾", EX 185.00
Camel, Oriental; M-769, on rockers, CI, rpt, 4" 425.00
Campbell Kids, L-669, CI, worn gold pnt, 3¼" 195.00
Carpet Bag, C-352, bronze, 3½", EX 45.00
Castle, M-1114, 2 towers, CI, brn japanning, minor wear, 7"......400.00
Castle, M-954, CI, brn japanning w/gold, 3", EX 280.00
Cat, L-44, on tub, CI, gold pnt, 4", VG 165.00
Cat, M-352, w/ball, CI, gray & gold pnt, minor wear, 5⅝" L 150.00
Cat, M-366, seated, CI, worn mc pnt, 4⅛" 145.00
Charlie Chaplin, M-299, pnt pressed glass, tin lid, 4⅛" 225.00
Charlie McCarthy, M-209, papier-mache, minor wear, 9¼" 85.00

Chest, Pirate; M-936, lead, bronze pnt, 2⅝", VG 12.50
Chest, Treasure; M-928, CI, worn red & gold pnt, 2¾" 165.00
Chick Bank '84, aluminum, mc pnt, modern, 4⅛", NM........25.00
Clock, Hall; M-1540, w/pendulum, CI, 3¾", VG...........485.00
Clock, Mantel; M-1550, lead, bronze pnt, brass trim, 7", VG 35.00
Clown, M-212, brass, wht pnt, foundry pattern, 6" 215.00
Clown, M-217, CI, gold pnt w/red trim, minor wear, 6" 85.00
Colonial House, M-992, CI, silver pnt, bl roof, 4"...........40.00
Columbia Bank, M-1070, NPCI, Kenton, 6"...........235.00
Columbia Bank, M-906, CI, worn metallic pnt, 4⅞"...........165.00
County Bank, M-1110, brass, 4¼"...........115.00
Cow, M-540, NP steel, mc pnt, 7" L, EX 195.00
Cow, M-553, CI, worn gold pnt, 5⅜" L...........135.00
Cross, M-1628, Faith/Hope/Charity, CI, worn blk pnt, 9⅜" 975.00
Cupola Bank, M-1145, CI, 5½", EX...........140.00
Cupola Bank, M-1146, CI, red pnt w/mc trim, minor wear, 4" 115.00
Cupola Bank, M-1147, CI, worn mc pnt, lt rust, 3¼" 125.00
Derby, Pass 'Round the Hat, CI, worn brn pnt, 3⅛" 135.00
Devil, L-695, 2-faced, CI, mc pnt, 4¼" 500.00
Doc Yak, L-692, CI, 4⅝"...........220.00
Dog, Fala, L-124 (M-430), VG 145.00
Dog on Tub, L-93 (M-437), G 135.00
Dolphin, M-33, CI, pnt traces, 4½" 325.00
Dome Bank, M-1177, CI, gold pnt, lt rust, 4¼"...........55.00
Dome Bank, M-1183, CI, silver & gold pnt, lt wear, 4¾" 50.00
Donkey, M-498, hinged saddle & padlock, CI, worn pnt, 3½" 45.00
Donkey, M-500, CI, mc pnt, minor wear, 7"...........215.00
Donkey, M-502, on base, CI, worn mc pnt, 7½" 425.00
Duck, M-624, CI, mc pnt, minor wear, 5"...........150.00
Elephant, Circus; M-462, CI, EX mc pnt, 3⅞"...........115.00
Elephant, M-446, w/howdah, wheels, CI, EX gold pnt, 4"...........225.00
Elephant, M-449, CI, EX bl pnt, 4"...........90.00
Elephant, M-455, swivel trunk, CI, blk & gold pnt, 3½", EX 225.00
Elephant, M-457, w/howdah, CI, gold pnt, 2⅜", EX 55.00
Elephant, M-461, wht metal, worn blk pnt, 5" 20.00
Elephant, M-476, w/howdah, CI, gray/gold/silver pnt, 6⅝" L 75.00
Elephant, M-477, w/howdah, CI, worn mc pnt, 5⅛"...........40.00
Elephant, M-479, missing chariot, CI, worn pnt, 6⅞"...........95.00
Elephant, M-483, on tub, CI, gold pnt, 5½", EX 170.00
Empire Bank, M-1320, CI, brn japanning w/gold, 6¾", EX 135.00
Fidelity Safe, M-864, CI, dk brn japanning w/gold, 3", EX 95.00
Fido, M-417, CI, blk pnt w/mc trim, 5", M 115.00
Flat-Iron Building, M-1160, CI, silver pnt, no trap, 5¾"...........65.00
Foxy Grandpa, M-320, CI, worn pnt, 5½"...........325.00
Frog, M-692, Iron Art, CI, gr pnt, 7" L...........55.00
Garage, M-1009, 1-car, CI, worn gold & red pnt, 2½"...........65.00
Gen Butler, M-54, CI, worn mc pnt, 6½"...........950.00
Gen Pershing, M-150-B, CI, EX...........65.00
Gen Pershing, M-151, CI, bronze finish, 7¾", EX...........225.00
General Sheridan, L-730 (M-50), VG...........750.00
German Helmet, M-1405, tin, worn olive-drab pnt, 4⅞"...........175.00
German Shepherd, bronze foundry pattern, 7¼" L...........200.00
Give Me a Penny, L-733, Wing Mfg, CI, 5¾"...........175.00
Globe, M-791, paper-covered steel, wooden base, 4⅜", EX...........25.00
Globe, M-812, CI, worn striped bronze finish, 5⅜"...........115.00
Globe on Wire Arc, L-924, Arcade, CI, worn pnt, 4⅝"...........165.00
Good Luck, M-508, CI bell form, blk & gold pnt, 4¼", EX 100.00
Goose, M-614, CI, pnt traces, 3¾"...........180.00
Graf Zeppelin, L-1539, CI, aluminum & gr pnt, 6¾"...........240.00
Gun Boat, M-1462, CI, bl/wht/brn pnt, 8½", EX 850.00
Harleysville Bank, M-1017, CI, mc pnt, modern, 5¼" L...........30.00
Hen, M-549, CI, mc pnt, lt wear, 6"...........45.00
Hippopotamus, M-721, CI, worn gold pnt, 5" L...........200.00
Horse, M-506, prancing, CI, gold pnt, minor wear, 4¾"...........185.00

Horse, M-508, Good Luck, Arcade, CI, blk & gold pnt, 4" 110.00
Horse, M-509, on drum, CI, mc pnt, minor wear, 5½" 110.00
Horse, M-513, prancing, oval base, CI, gold rpt, 5".................35.00
Horse, M-520, prancing, CI, old gold rpt, 7¼", EX.................85.00
Horse, M-533, CI, worn bronze finish, 4⅞" L.................35.00
House, M-1002, CI, gold pnt, lt wear, 3".................50.00
Independence Hall, M-1242, CI, 10⅛", EX.................565.00
Indian, M-237, arms Xd, CI, mc pnt, 4⅛", EX.................80.00
Kewpie, M-292, papier-mache, worn mc pnt, no trap, 5" 35.00
Keyless Safety Deposit, CI, metal finish/nickel dials, 5⅞" 50.00
Labrador, M-412, CI, blk & gold pnt, minor wear, 4⅝".................245.00
Liberty Bell, M-793, steel w/wood yoke, orig finish, 3¾" 15.00
Lindbergh Bust, L-779, aluminum, 6¼".................50.00
Lion, M-754, CI, bl pnt, 5", VG.................65.00
Lion, M-757, CI, gold pnt, minor wear, 4½" L.................35.00
Lion, M-760, on wheels, CI, worn silver rpt, 4¾".................65.00
Log Cabin, M-1021, ...Lincoln Was Born..., ceramic, 3¾" L 12.50
Lost Dog, M-407, CI, no pnt, 5⅜".................575.00
Main Street Trolly, M-1469, CI, gold pnt, 6⅝" L, EX.................375.00
Mammy w/Hands on Hips, M-176-A, CI, EX orig pnt.................95.00
Mary & Lamb, M-164, CI, worn mc pnt, 4⅜".................325.00
Mickey Mouse w/Mandolin, M-203, wht metal, worn pnt, 4⅝" ..145.00
Middy, M-36, CI, worn metallic pnt, 5⅛".................95.00
Minute Man Soldier, L-864 (M-44), VG.................475.00
Monkey, M-744, wht metal, mc pnt, minor wear, rpl trap, 4¼" 75.00
Mosque, M-1177, CI, 4¼", VG.................95.00
Mourner's Purse, L-1481, lead, 1902, 5".................50.00
Mulligan the Cop, L-802 (M-177), w/advertising, EX 185.00
Mutt & Jeff, M-157, CI, gold pnt, minor wear, 5⅛".................140.00
New Deal, M-148, Roosevelt bust, bronze, minor wear, 4¾" 225.00
North Pole, M-1372, brass, foundry pattern, 4¼".................375.00
Organ Grinder, M-216, CI, steel base, worn pnt, 6½".................150.00
Our Kitchener, M-1313, CI, 6½" 145.00
Owl, M-598, Be Wise, Save Money, CI, EX mc pnt, 5".................165.00
Pagoda, M-1153, CI, silver w/worn gold overpnt, 5".................265.00
Pig, M-579, grin on face, lead, bronze pnt, 4¼" L.................25.00
Pig, M-606, on haunches, CI, worn pnt w/gold traces, 5⅛".................95.00
Pig, M-607, CI, no pnt, modern, 4⅜", NM.................12.50
Pig, M-621, chalkware, old rpt, leg rpr, 7⅛" L, VG 45.00
Pig, Wise; M-609, partial rpt, 6¾".................55.00
Polar Bear, standing, CI.................115.00
Policeman, L-820, Arcade, CI, worn pnt, 5⅝".................325.00
Presto, M-1167, CI, silver w/gold dome, minor wear, 4⅛" 65.00
Professor Pug Frog, M-311, CI, metallic gr & gold pnt, 5¼" 450.00
Pug dog, seated, L-110 (M-405), G 50.00
Punch & Judy, M-1299, tin, 4⅜", EX.................70.00
Quilted Lion, M-758, CI, worn gold & red pnt, 5".................225.00
Rabbit, M-567, w/carrot, CI, wht w/mc details, 3⅜", EX 85.00
Rabbit, M-568, CI, rpt traces, 3¾".................65.00
Radio, Crosley; L-982 (M-819), EX 385.00
Radio, M-821, CI, bl pnt w/gold trim, 3¼", EX.................100.00
Recording Bank, M-1062, worn NPCI, 6⅝".................170.00
Roof Bank, M-1124, CI, bronze finish, lt wear & rust, 5¼".................125.00
Safe, Jewel; M-896, NPCI, sm crack, 5½".................100.00
Safe, M-807, NPCI, worn, rtcl florals, 3⅜".................35.00
Santa, L-843, standing w/tree, Hubley, CI, 6", EX 145.00
Santa, M-104, at chimney, lead, mc pnt, 4½", EX.................125.00
Save & Smile Money Bank, M-24, pnt CI, minor wear, 4⅛".................365.00
Save Your Pennies..., M-1545, CI, gold pnt, minor wear, 3½".....125.00
Save...To Make Dollars, M-1545, eagle clock, CI, 3½".................165.00
Scottie, M-430, CI, blk pnt, 2⅞", EX.................60.00
Shell Out, L-1178, CI, 2½".................350.00
Sidewheeler, M-1459, CI, bl & red pnt, 7½" L, EX.................170.00
Soldier, M-45, CI, gold & red pnt, minor wear, 6" 145.00

Space Heater w/Bird, M-1087, CI, dk bronze finish, 6½" **65.00**
Spitz, M-409, CI, gold pnt traces, lt rust, 4" **175.00**
St Bernard, M-429, w/pack, pnt traces on CI, 5⅝" **35.00**
St Bernard, M-437, w/pack, CI, gold rpt, 7¾"................**25.00**
Stag, M-737, NPCI, worn pnt, 9½", EX................**65.00**
State Bank, M-1085, CI, metallic japanning/bronze trim, 3⅛" **95.00**
State Bank, M-1663, CI, worn brn japanning/gold trim, 5½" **115.00**
Statue of Liberty, M-1164, CI, worn gold pnt, 6" **115.00**
Sun Bonnet Sue, M-257, CI, mc pnt, minor wear, modern, 7⅜" ..**75.00**
Tank, M-1437, USA, CI, gold pnt, minor wear, 4⅜" L **115.00**
Teddy Roosevelt, L-831 (M-120), EX.................**320.00**
Time Around the World, L-1500 (M-1539), EX.................**425.00**
Top Hat, M-1391, tin, blk pnt, College on band, 4¼", EX **200.00**
Traders Bank of Canada, L-613, EX **675.00**
Turkey, M-587, CI, old blk rpt, 3½" **40.00**
US Mail, M-835, CI, silver & red pnt, 4¾", VG **60.00**
US Mail, M-838, CI, silver & red pnt, minor wear, 3⅜" **30.00**
US Mail, M-855, CI, worn NP finish, 4¼" **30.00**
US Mail, M-856, CI, red pnt traces, 5¼" **22.50**
Villa, M-959, 1882, CI, dk brn japanning w/gold, 5½" **175.00**
Von Hindenburg, M-152, lead, dk brn pnt, 9¼", EX...................**350.00**
Washington Monument, M-1048, CI, EX gold pnt, 6⅛" **125.00**
Whippet, M-362, on base, conversion, CI, gold pnt, 5" L, EX.....**135.00**
Wire-haired Terrier, M-422B, pnt CI, VG **75.00**
Wireless Bank, N-5980, CI, lt rust & wear, 6⅝" **75.00**

Wise Pig Savings Bank, worn paint, VG, $75.00.

Woolworth Building, M-1041, CI, gold pnt, minor wear, 8"..........**95.00**
Yel Cab, L-1570, CI, 4", VG.................**400.00**
3 Monkeys, M-743, See No..., CI, bronze & gold pnt, 3¼", EX...**335.00**
4 Tower, M-1121, CI, brn japanning w/gold, 5¾", EX **185.00**

Barber Shop Collectibles

Even for the stranger in town, the local barber shop was easy to find, its location vividly marked with the traditional red and white striped barber pole that for centuries identified such establishments. As far back as the twelfth century, the barber has had a place in recorded history. At one time he not only groomed the beards and cut the hair of his gentlemen clients but was known as the 'blood-letter' as well — hence the red stripe for blood and the white for the bandages. Many early barbers even pulled teeth! Later, laws were enacted that divided the practices of barbering and surgery.

The Victorian barber shop reflected the charm of that era with fancy barber chairs upholstered in rich wine-colored velvet; rows of

bottles made from colored art glass held hair tonics and shaving lotion. Backbars of richly carved oak with beveled mirrors lined the wall behind the barber's station. During the late nineteenth century, the barber pole with a blue stripe added to the standard red and white as a patriotic gesture came into vogue.

Today the barber shop has all but disappeared from the American scene, replaced by modern unisex salons. Collectors search for the barber poles, the fancy chairs, and the tonic bottles of an era gone but not forgotten. See also Bottles; Razors; Shaving Mugs.

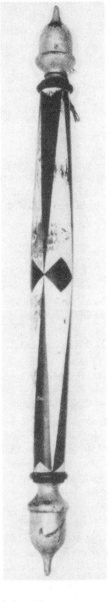

Barber pole, wooden with black and white geometric paint tapering to silver acorns on either end, 1800s, paint loss, minor age cracks, 34" long, $1,100.00.

Blade bank, Dandy Dan, celluloid w/metal clips, 7" **30.00**
Blade bank, donkey figural, Listerine Shaving Cream, 3½"............**27.50**
Blade bank, frog figural, ceramic, Listerine advertising **15.00**
Blade bank, pole form, ceramic, red/wht, 6½", EX **20.00**
Blade bank, safe form, w/combination, tin, Gem, EX....................**27.50**
Blade holder, shaving brush form, ceramic, 5", NM **65.00**
Brush, shaving lather; ornate SP hdl....................**25.00**
Chair, child's, fluted column, horse's head, Koken, rstr...........**2,200.00**
Chair, cvd oak, Archer, ca 1880, EX....................**500.00**
Chair, oak w/velvet upholstery, Koch, rstr...................**900.00**
Chair, rnd bk, tufted leather, Koch, rstr **2,950.00**
Clippers, Andis, ca 1940s, NM **28.00**
Curling iron, Marcel/Repose Acier, insulated hdls, 10½", EX........ **6.00**

Headrest, for chair, padded, Koken, dtd 1909 ....30.00
Hone, Bracher Jr Mfg, 1920s, EX...5.00
Mirror, Gillette advertising, NM.......................................22.50
Mug rack, wood w/appl moulding, holds 24 mugs, 40" H 425.00
Neck duster, cherry wood hdl, EX.......................................22.50
Neck duster, sterling scroll hdl, soft bristles, 7½".................35.00
Pole, art glass, floor model, Koken, EX 3,200.00
Pole, electric, metal & glass, revolves, 3-color, 1930s, 26"..........265.00
Pole, leaded glass, porc top & base, 5-color, rstr, 33" 850.00
Pole, leaded glass, 3-color, w/orig wall mt bracket, 13" 350.00
Pole, porc, floor model, Paidar, rstr 1,900.00
Pole, porc, sidewalk type, rstr.. 2,000.00
Pole, wood, blk & wht pnt, silver ends, 1850s, 34", G 1,100.00
Pole, wood, HP, primitive, early, 36", EX............................150.00
Pole, wood, w/3-color rpt, 77", EX......................................500.00
Razor, hair trimming; metal, Playtex, NM in box......................12.00
Razor case, oak veneer, brass trim, holds 24 razors, NM.............28.00
Razor gauge, steel, Alexis Witte, NY, Pat Feb 4, 1902, EX 45.00
Scissors, Sheffield England, EX 10.00
Showcase, cvd wood, 2-shelf, fancy door pull, 25x12x7½"............95.00
Showcase, wood & glass, Universal Cutlery, 15" 85.00
Sterilizer, brass plated, red cross on glass, w/key, EX..................25.00
Sterilizer, glass cabinet w/metal door, 10", NM 32.00
Strop, leather, Victorian SP, ornate, NM 48.00
Strop, leather, wood hdl w/sheath, 4-sided, Lamont, 14", EX 45.00
Strop, wood & leather, retractable, extends to 17", EX.................25.00
Stropping tool, Safety Auto Stropper, EX................................12.50
Thinning shears, Marks, Solingen Germany, NM 8.00
Token, Gillette giveaway..27.50
Towel steamer, NP copper, Ideal Metal Works, 61", EX..............400.00

Barometers

Barometers are instruments designed to measure the weight or pressure of the atmosphere in order to anticipate approaching weather changes. Those made around the turn of the century — earlier in England and on the continent — were beautifully housed in period cases of mahogany, rosewood, walnut, or cherry, often with brass trim. These quality pieces bring high prices on today's market.

Chas Wilder, mahog, Pat 1860, 38" 2,600.00
Chas Wilder, rosewood grpt case, 1860s, rpr, 38", VG 500.00
Compensated #1157 Cary & Pall...London, aneroid, 2⅞" dia........80.00
E&GW Blunt, rosewood w/floral abalone inlay, 1850s, 41" 2,600.00
F Giobbi, mahog veneer Hplwht w/inlay, pediment, 40", EX 400.00
Gauge & Instrument Mfr Co 12/35, aneroid, 9½" 200.00
Jenry Frodsham, spiral-cvd mahog, leaf-cvd pendant, 38"............700.00
US Life Saving Service, aneroid, mtd on orig housing, VG 200.00
Wm Lambrecht, brass w/silvered scale, EX 80.00
Woodruff's Pat June 5, 1860, rosewood veneer, 38" 400.00

Basalt

Basalt is a type of unglazed black pottery developed by Josiah Wedgwood and copied by many other companies during the late eighteenth and early nineteenth centuries. It was also called 'Egyptian Black.' See also Wedgwood.

Bust of Admiral Duncan, military dress/war trophies, 7¾"..........425.00
Coffeepot, emb motif, dome lid w/widow Warburton, 10", VG ..300.00
Figurine, seated nude & frog on rocky base, Hasselberg, mk........165.00
Jug, swags/ribbons, engine-trn bands, att Yates, 1790, 5" 180.00
Spill vase, emb cherubs, copper lustre int, 4¾"..........................200.00

Baskets

Basket weaving is a craft as old as ancient history. Baskets have been used to harvest crops, for domestic chores, and to contain the catch of fishermen. Materials at hand were utilized, and baskets from a specific region are often distinguishable simply by analyzing the natural fibers used in their construction. Early Indian baskets were made of corn husks or woven grasses. Willow splint, straw, rope, and paper are only a few of the materials that have been used. Until the invention of the veneering machine in the late 1800s, splint was made by water-soaking a split log until the fibers were softened and flexible. Long strips were pulled out by hand and, while still wet and pliable, woven into baskets in either a cross-hatch or hexagonal weave.

Most handcrafted baskets on the market today were made between 1860 and the early 1900s. Factory baskets with a thick, wide splint cut by machine are of little interest to collectors. The more popular baskets are those designed for a specific purpose, rather than the more commonly-found utility baskets that had multiple uses. Among the most costly forms are the Nantucket Lighthouse baskets, which were basically copied from those made there for centuries by aboriginal Indians. They were designed in the style of whale oil barrels and named for the South Shoal Nantucket Lightship where many were made during the last half of the nineteenth century. Cheese baskets (used to separate curds from whey), herb-gathering baskets, and finely woven Shaker miniatures are other highly-prized examples of the basket weaver's art.

In the listings that follow, assume that each has a center bentwood handle (unless handles of another type are noted) that is not included in the height. Unless another type of material is indicated, assume that each is made of splint. See also American Indian; Eskimo; Sewing; Shaker.

Ash splint, cat's ear points on rnded-out sq bottom, 15" dia..........95.00
Buttocks, EX age & color, minor wear/damage, 10x17x18" 145.00

Buttocks basket, 12" across, $140.00.

Buttocks, half-rnd, 6x8x10" 180.00
Buttocks, mini, 4¼" 120.00
Buttocks, orig red, mini, 4x5" 155.00
Buttocks, orig red, splayed-out form, 1850s, 11x12x10" 265.00
Buttocks, reed/cane, 1-egg sz, comtemporary, sgn/dtd, 5" 60.00
Buttocks, well made, 13x14" 175.00

Cheese, rnd rim, str sides, hexagonal base, 1825, 22" **265.00**
Clam-gathering, wire base/splint top, 1850s, 16x14"...................**345.00**
Egg, checkered pattern, oval, 8x9x9", NM **75.00**
Egg, Eye-of-God hdl, radiating ribs, worn pnt, 13" L, EX............**150.00**
Egg, gr pnt, hexagonal openweave, 1800s, 6x4" **385.00**
Egg, oak splint, 1890s, 10x10x14", VG...**65.00**
Egg & berry, potato stamped, att NY State Indians, 4" dia **300.00**
Flower, oval top/oblong bottom, 1900s, 6x6¼x10"......................**75.00**
Garden, oak splint, 2-color, cvd oak hdl, 1900, 4½x15x10" **85.00**
Half bushel, 11x15", EX...**55.00**
Laundry, bentwood rim hdls, wood runner ft, 28", EX **110.00**
Laundry, scrubbed gray finish, rim hdls, 11x22x32" **210.00**
Laundry, wide splint, bentwood rim hdls, 21½" dia.....................**120.00**
Laundry, wide splint, rim hdls, 12x25x38", EX **135.00**
Laundry, woven vines w/dk patina, Zoar OH, 10x19" **145.00**
Lunch, wide splint, 2 bentwood hdls, domed lid, sm **55.00**

Lunch basket, woven splint, green and white, 15" long, $200.00.

Market, gr pnt, ca 1910, 11x12x18", EX..**50.00**
Market, oak splint, 1890s, 14x14x14", NM **80.00**
Melon rib, Eye-of-God hdl, minor wear/damage, 6x12" dia **225.00**
Melon rib, oval, 6x12x12½", NM **145.00**
Nantucket, ca 1900, 10" dia...**600.00**
Nantucket, swing hdl, oval trn base, 5x8x10", EX **1,100.00**
Nantucket, swing hdl, wood ears, 1850s, 8x11½", NM **1,000.00**
Potato field, heavy wire, bail hdl..**20.00**
Potato print, 3-color, w/lid, 8½x11x14½" **115.00**
Rye straw, bowl form, 2¾x12¾" **45.00**
Rye straw, oval, w/lid, 17x21" **125.00**
Splint, attached lid slides up bentwood hdl, 12" dia, EX..............**140.00**
Splint, bentwood rim hdls, ca 1900, 18x13" **185.00**
Splint, bentwood rim hdls, wear/minor damage, mini, 6½" dia......**75.00**
Splint, Eye-of-God hdl, radiating ribs, early, 7x7", EX................**275.00**
Splint, fine weave, EX age/color, 12x13" dia, NM **285.00**
Splint, orig yel, oval, 1800s, 14x10½" at rim **195.00**
Splint, oval rim, rectangular base, mini, 2¾x3" **95.00**
Splint, red/bl/natural, w/lid, 7x9x12", EX....................................**295.00**
Splint, sgn/dtd 1904, no hdls, sq, 4¼x13½x13½" **165.00**
Splint, swing hdl, dk finish, 8x14", EX **135.00**
Splint, swing hdl, worn red pnt, 1800s, 6x11" L, EX...................**245.00**
Splint, well made, EX age/color, 15½" dia **185.00**
Splint, 4 rim hdls, old pnt, 5½x12", EX...**115.00**

Willow, picnic style, ash hdls/lid, brass hinges, 15x20x15"...........**75.00**

Batchelder

Ernest A. Batchelder was a leading exponent of the Arts and Crafts movement in the United States. His influential book, *Design in Theory and Practice,* was originally published in 1910. He is best known, however, for his artistic tiles which he first produced in Pasedena, California, from 1909 to 1916. In 1906 the business was relocated to Los Angeles where it continued until 1932, closing because of the Depression.

In 1938 Batchelder resumed production in Pasedena under the name of 'Kinneola Kiln.' Output of the new pottery consisted of delicately cast bowls and vases in an Oriental style. This business closed in 1951. Tiles carry a die-stamped mark; vases and bowls are hand incised.

Bookend, 2¾" tiles set in Potter Studio brass mts, pr **250.00**
Bowl, Pasadena mk, dk teal, rose int, 3x7"....................................**65.00**
Bowl, Pasadena mk, rose, oval, 4x12x7" **135.00**
Bowl, Pasadena mk, flared, #217, 8"...**75.00**
Tile, architectural, grapes, bl wash, 7x12".....................................**95.00**
Tile, castle, matt, 6x6"...**85.00**
Tile, fruit, bl, 4" **60.00**
Tile, Northwind face, spigot mouth, 12x10x5" **165.00**
Tile, peacocks in high relief, bl wash, mk, 12"..............................**200.00**
Tile, stylized ivy, tan & bl, 7", VG..**145.00**
Tile, 2 birds over spigot fountain, 17x12x4" **265.00**

Battersea

Battersea is a term that refers to enameling on copper or other metal. Though originally produced at Battersea, England, in the mid-eighteenth century, the craft was later practiced throughout the Staffordshire district. Boxes are the most common examples — some are figurals, and many bear an inscription. Values are given for examples with only minimal damage, which is normal.

Bonbonniere, floral scrolls/relief parrot on lt yel, 1⅝" **650.00**
Bonbonniere, florals/ptd-on 'hdls,' basketweave ground, 2" L.....**650.00**
Bonbonniere, pug's head form, goldstone lid, 2" **3,000.00**

Bonbonnieres, rabbit form, brown and green paint, 3" long, $4,000.00; pug dog form, 2" long, $1,760.00.

Bonbonniere, recumbent cow form, lid w/scenic, 1⅞" L........... **1,750.00**
Bonbonniere, seated rabbit form, lid w/courting scene, 3" L ... **4,000.00**
Box, 2 figures in 18th-C landscape on lid, 1800s, 7" L............. **1,100.00**
Etui case, 2 portraits on pk gingham ground, 2-part int, 2¼"... **1,100.00**
Needle case, elaborate floral sprays on wht, 4½" L **650.00**
Needle case, floral/insects on yel, rstr, 4¾" L.............................**550.00**
Needle case, gold floral/pastoral scene on pk, 4½" L **425.00**
Nutmeg grater, floral on pk, gilt grater, ovoid, rstr, 2" **495.00**
Patch box, birds medallion on wht lid, pk base, 1¾x1½" **265.00**
Patch box, bluebird on foliage on wht lid, bl base, 1⅝x1½"..........**275.00**

Patch box, floral on wht lid, gr base, 1⅛" dia 375.00
Patch box, foliage/urn/motto, wht beaded border, oval, 1¾" L 450.00
Patch box, seated dog form, lid w/floral, mirror w/in, VG 2,000.00
Patch box, spotted calf form, lid w/floral, mirror w/in, 1⅝" L . 2,400.00
Snuff box, floral/relief scrolls on bl, portrait w/in, 3" L............ 1,750.00
Snuff box, French/English naval battle, 2" L 750.00

Bauer

Originally founded in Paducah, Kentucky, in 1885, the J.A. Bauer Company moved to Los Angeles where it was re-established in 1909. Until the 1920s, their major products were terra cotta gardenware, flowerpots, and stoneware and yellowware bowls. During prohibition they produced crocks for home use. A more artful form of product began to develop with the addition of designer Louis Ipsen to the staff in 1915. Some of his work — a line of molded vases, flowerpots, bowls, etc. — was awarded a bronze medal at the Pacific International Exposition the following year.

In 1930 the first of many dinnerware lines was tested on the market. Their initial pattern, Plain Ware, was well accepted and led the way to the introduction of the most popular dinnerware in their history and with today's collectors — Ring Ware. It was produced from 1932 into the early 1960s in solid colors of jade green, royal blue, Chinese yellow, light blue, orange-red, and (in very limited quantities) black or white. Its simple pattern was a design of closely-spaced concentric ribs, either convex or concave. Over the years, more than one hundred shapes were available. Some were made in limited quantities, resulting in rare items to whet the appetites of Bauer buffs today. Other patterns were La Linda, produced during the 1940s and 1950s, and Monterey Moderne, introduced in 1948 and remaining popular into the 1950s (made in pink, black, gray, brown, and green.)

After WWII a flood of foreign imports drastically curtailed their sales, and the pottery began a steady decline that ended in failure in 1962. Prices listed below reflect the California market. For more information, we recommend *The Complete Collector's Guide to Bauer Pottery* by Jack Chipman, our advisor for this category, and Judy Stangler. Mr Chipman's address may be found in the Directory under California.

Monterey, see listings for specific values.

Ash tray, Mexican hat, all colors but blk 90.00
Bean pot, plain, blk, 3-qt...120.00

Bowl, cereal; Monterey Moderne, all colors but blk, 6"...............10.00
Bowl, dessert; Al Fresco, speckled, gr, or gray, 5".......................... 3.75
Bowl, dessert; Contempo, any color, decals, 5".............................. 4.00
Bowl, fruit; Monterey, all colors but wht, 8"................................27.50
Bowl, ramekin; Ring, yel, gr, or turq, 4" 15.00
Bowl, Ring, red-brn, lt bl, or yel, #36, 1-pt 15.00
Bowl, salad; El Fresco, coffee brn or Dubonnet, 13" 22.50
Bowl, salad; Ring, chartreuse, olive, or gray, 9" 40.00
Bowl, salad/flower; plain, all colors but blk, 8½" 50.00
Bowl, vegetable; Al Fresco, speckled, gr, or gray, 9¼" 12.00
Bowl, vegetable; La Linda, all matt colors, oval, 8" 18.00
Bowl, vegetable; Ring, blk, oval, 8" 70.00
Butter dish, Contempo, any color, decals, oval 20.00
Butter dish, La Linda, burgundy or dk brn, oblong 60.00
Butter dish, Monterey, wht, oblong 60.00
Butter dish, Ring, orange-red, dk bl, or ivory, rnd 70.00
Candle holder, Monterey, all colors but wht 27.50
Candlestick, plain, blk, handmade 100.00
Canister, spice; Al Fresco, coffee brn or Dubonnet...................... 7.50
Casserole, Ring, chartreuse, lt bl, or jade gr, 7½".......................45.00
Coffee server, plain, blk 80.00
Cup, punch; Ring, blk 60.00
Cup & saucer, Al Fresco, speckled, gr, or gray............................ 7.50
Cup & saucer, Contempo, any color, decals 8.00
Cup & saucer, demitasse; Ring, burgundy or wht, 3-oz................45.00
Cup & saucer, El Chico, any color 45.00
Cup & saucer, La Linda, gray, ivory, or lt brn............................15.00
Cup & saucer, Monterey, all colors but wht................................26.00
Cup & saucer, Monterey Moderne, blk, tall 15.00
Cup & saucer, plain, all colors but blk 40.00
Flowerpot, Ring, Ruffle-Italian, all colors but blk, 4" 15.00
Goblet, plain, all colors but blk 70.00
Honey jar, Ring, lt bl or yel 250.00
Ice bowl holder, metal, for #30 mixing bowl...............................25.00
Jardiniere, plain, blk, 5" 25.00
Jardiniere, Ring, burgundy or ivory, 8" 45.00
Lug soup, Ring, dk bl, ivory, or wht, 6" 30.00
Mug, Contempo, any color, decals, 12-oz.................................... 8.00
Pickle dish, Ring, blk...30.00
Pitcher, Al Fresco, speckled, gr, or gray, ice lip, 2-qt..................11.50
Pitcher, beer; Ring, all colors but blk, cylindrical......................150.00
Pitcher, blk, tall Dutch style, handmade, 3-qt...........................100.00
Pitcher, La Linda, turq, pk, or gray, 1½-pt................................18.00
Pitcher, Monterey Moderne, all colors but blk, 2-qt...................30.00
Pitcher, Ring, blk, 1-qt 60.00
Plate, Al Fresco, coffee brn or Dubonnet, 11½" 9.00
Plate, bread & butter; Monterey Moderne, blk, 6½" 9.00
Plate, Contempo, any color, decals, 7".. 4.00
Plate, El Chico, any color, 9" 25.00
Plate, grill; Monterey Monterne, all colors but blk, rnd 15.00
Plate, Monterey Moderne, blk, 10½" 36.00
Plate, plain, blk, 10½" 80.00
Plate, Ring, yel, lt bl, olive, or gray, 10½"..................................30.00
Platter, Contempo, any color, decals, 10½" 6.50
Platter, La Linda, burgundy or dk brn, oval, 10" 16.00
Platter, Monterey, all colors but wht, oval, 12" 20.00
Platter, Monterey, wht, oval, 12" 27.00
Platter, Ring, dk bl or ivory, oval, 9"...20.00
Punch bowl, Ring, yel, jade gr, olive, or gray, 14" 185.00
Shakers, Contempo, any color, decals, pr.................................... 5.00
Shakers, Ring, blk, barrel form, pr...40.00
Stein, Ring, yel, jade gr, lt bl, or chartreuse, 5"..........................40.00
Sugar bowl, La Linda, gr, yel, or turq, new shape 15.00
Sugar bowl, Monterey, midget, wht 20.00

Sugar bowl, plain, blk **50.00**
Sugar shaker, Ring, orange-red, dk bl, or wht, 5" **100.00**
Teapot, Al Fresco, coffee brn or Dubonnet, 6-cup..........................**22.50**
Teapot, Contempo, any color, decals, 6-cup................................**16.00**
Teapot, La Linda, burgundy or dk brn, 6-cup..............................**45.00**
Teapot, Monterey, all colors but wht, new shape, 6-cup **45.00**
Teapot, Ring, blk, wood hdl, 6-cup......................................**150.00**
Tray, Monterey, all colors but wht, oval, for midget cr/sug **35.00**
Tumbler, La Linda, burgundy or dk brn, 8-oz.............................**16.00**
Tumbler, Ring, burgundy, wht, or ivory, 12-oz **30.00**
Vase, bud; Ring, all colors but blk, 5".................................**37.50**
Vase, Ruffle, all colors but blk, cylindrical, 8" **37.50**

Bavaria

Bavaria, Germany, was long the center of that country's pottery industry; in the 1800s, many firms operated in and around the area. Chinaware vases, novelties, and table accessories were decorated with transfer prints as well as by hand by artists who sometimes signed their work. The examples here are marked with 'Bavaria' and the logos of some of the various companies which were located there.

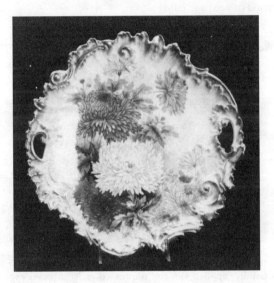

Bowl, gold Rococo border, mums in center, artist signed, 12" diameter, $150.00.

Box, classical scene on lt bl, 3½" **80.00**
Box, floral on gr, gold trim, 4½" dia **90.00**
Box, lady w/rose bouquet figural, 9" **110.00**
Chocolate pot, roses, artist sgn, +cr/sug **185.00**
Cookie jar, roses, pk on gr shaded w/gold, mk, 7½x5½" **100.00**
Mug, floral, lizard hdl, 6¼" **75.00**
Pitcher, Grecian ladies, gold tracing, mk, 6x4"....................**95.00**
Pitcher, tankard; grapes w/gold, Guillaume, 11¼"..................**110.00**
Plate, Siamese cat's head, gold rim, sgn/mk, 8"...................**45.00**
Plate, stencil reserve w/maiden, rose border, scalloped, 9" **65.00**
Shelf sitter, boy fishing, gr hat, orange pants **45.00**
Teapot, alternating panels w/gold, +6 c/s **175.00**
Teapot, pk roses w/gold, ribbed, ZS&Co, +1 c/s....................**80.00**
Vase, birds & florals, HP, dtd 1912, 5¼".........................**25.00**

Beer Cans

When the flat-top can was first introduced in 1934, it came with printed instructions on how to use the triangular punch opener. Cone-top cans, which are rare today, were patented in 1935 by the Continental Can Company. By the 1960s, aluminum cans with pull tabs had made both types obsolete.

The hobby of collecting beer cans has been rapidly gaining momentum over the past ten years. Series types, such as South African Brewery, Lion, and the Cities Series by Schmit and Tucker, are especially popular.

Condition is an important consideration when evaluating market price. Grade 1 must be in like-new condition with no rust. However, the triangular punch hole is acceptable. Grade 2 cans may have slight scratches or dimples but must be free of rust. For Grade 3, light rust, minor scratching, and some fading may be acceptable. When these defects are more pronounced, a can is defaulted to Grade 4. Those in less-than-excellent condition devaluate sharply. In the listings that follow, cans are arranged alphabetically by brand name, not by brewery. Unless noted otherwise, values are for cans in Grade 1 condition.

Our advisor for this category is Lowell Owens; he is listed in the Directory under New York.

Wooden Shoe Lager Beer, EX, $100.00.

Amber Brau, pull top, blk & wht, 12-oz............................ **5.00**
Aspen Gold, pull top, bl label w/gold band, 10-oz **2.00**
Becker's Unita Club, cone top, silver w/red & bl label, 12-oz **140.00**
Blatz, flat top, blk & wht label on bl, 11-oz **30.00**
Blatz, pull top, brn on lt brn, 11-oz **2.00**
Blatz, pull top, lt brn w/dk brn label, 16-oz **4.00**
Brau Haus, pull top, shield label on wht, 12-oz **15.00**
Buckeye Sparkling Dry, cone top, silver w/red & wht label, 12-oz.**45.00**
Budweiser, flat top, red, wht, & bl, 12-oz **10.00**
Budweiser, pull top, red, wht, & bl on wht, 10-oz **3.00**
Cardinal, flat top, red w/cardinal on wht label, 12-oz...........**75.00**
Coors, flat top, gold can w/blk bottom band, 12-oz **90.00**
Dawson's Ale, cone top, brn w/blk & red lettering, 12-oz **55.00**
Dis-Go Beer, pull top, man w/guitar on wht, 11-oz **10.00**
Esslinger, flat top, blk & red label on wht, 12-oz **70.00**
Fox DeLuxe, flat top, wht label w/gold lettering, 11-oz **20.00**
Goebel Luxury, flat top, red, blk, & gold, 12-oz.................**10.00**
Goebel Private Stock 22, flat top, red, blk, & gold, 11-oz **15.00**
Golden Crown, flat top, gold label, red & wht lettering, 11-oz....... **8.00**
Great Falls Select, pull top, wht label on gray w/red bands **11.00**
Harvard, flat top, gold w/red bands & blk lettering, 11-oz............**40.00**
Hauenstein, cone top, red w/wht label, 12-oz **24.00**
Heidelberg, pull top, gold w/wht label, 15-oz **5.00**

Iron City, pull top, 1972 Christmas can, gr wreath, 16-oz **25.00**
Krueger, pull top, wht w/red label, 12-oz 8.00
Lone Star, pull top, wht w/red label w/gold star, 11-oz 5.00
Michelob, pull top, gold w/emb lettering, 11-oz.............................. 2.00
Miller Malt Liquor, pull top, red w/wht Miller, 15-oz 5.00
Milwaukee's Best, flat top, wht w/red & gold label, 12-oz **15.00**
Oertel's 92, cone top, silver w/silver 92 on blk, 12-oz...................**20.00**
Old Dutch Brand, flat top, wht w/red O & D, 11-oz....................**15.00**
Old Milwaukee Draft, flat top, 1966, wht w/red label, 11-oz.......... 3.00
Old Reading, flat top, wht w/bl heart-shape label, 12-oz...............**90.00**
Ortileb's Lager, cone top, silver w/red label, 12-oz.......................**90.00**
Pabst, flat top, silver, bl bottom band, red Pabst, 11-oz 7.00
Pabst, pull top, red, wht, & bl on silver, 7-oz 1.50
Pearl, flat top, red label on tan, 12-oz...**25.00**
Point, flat top, dk bl w/red label, 11-oz 5.00
Regal Amber, flat top, red w/wht lettering & band, 11-oz **325.00**
Reisch Gold Top, cone top, gold w/wht label, 12-oz **35.00**
Schiltz, flat top, silver & wht w/bl bull, 16-oz............................... 8.00
Schmidt's Tiger Brand Ale, cone top, bl tiger, 12-oz....................**30.00**
Whale's White Ale, pull top, blk w/wht whale, 15-oz...................**20.00**

Belleek, American

From 1883 until 1930, several American potteries located in New Jersey and Ohio manufactured a type of china similar to the famous Irish Belleek soft-paste porcelain. The American manufacturers identified their porcelain by using 'Belleek' in their marks. American Belleek is considered the highest achievement of the American porcelain industry. Production centered around artistic cabinet pieces and luxury tablewares. Many examples emulated Irish shapes and decor with marine themes and other naturalistic styles. While all are highly collectible, some companies ' products are rarer than others. The best-known manufacturers are Ott and Brewer, Willets, The Ceramic Art Company (CAC), and Lenox. You will find more detailed information in those specific categories. For a more thorough study of the subject, we recommend you refer to *American Belleek* by our advisor Mary Frank Gaston; you will find her address in the Directory under Texas.

Key:
AAC — American Art China   CAP — Columbian Art Pottery
                                                              Works

Bowl, florals, pk on wht w/in & w/out, AAC, 2½x5"..................**275.00**
Creamer, floral border, sponged gold, ornate hdl, AAC, 4" **235.00**
Cup & saucer, demitasse; Tridacna, gold trim, CAP **110.00**
Cup & saucer, floral reserves in red border, Morgan **220.00**
Ewer, roses, mc on tan shaded, branch hdl, Beleek (sic) mk........**550.00**
Plate, floral border w/in wide yel rim, Coxon, 10½"....................**220.00**
Plate, peacocks & mixed florals w/gold, Gordon, 7".......................**55.00**
Salt cellar, sponged gold, scalloped rim, pk int, AAC, 2½" **135.00**
Soup, floral reserves w/in red border, Morgan **220.00**
Teapot, dragon form, gold paste leaves, CAP, 7½x9" **1,100.00**
Vase, florals on wht, gold emb hdls, AAC, 12", pr **1,550.00**

Belleek, Irish

Belleek is a very thin translucent porcelain that takes its name from the village in Ireland where it originated in 1857. The glaze is a creamy ivory color with a pearl-like lustre. Tablewares, baskets, figurines, and vases have been produced; Shamrock, Tridacna, Echinus, and Lotus are but a few of the many patterns.

It is possible to date an example to within twenty to thirty years of

manufacture by the mark. Pieces with an early stamp often bring prices nearly triple that of a similar but current item. With some variation, the marks have always incorporated the wolfhound, round tower, harp, and shamrock. The first three marks (usually in black) were used from 1863 to 1946. A series of green marks has been in use since 1946; the most current mark is gold, which was introduced on April, 1980. In the listings below, numbers designated with the prefix 'D' relate to the book *Belleek — The Complete Collector's Guide and Illustrated Reference*. Portfolio Press, 170 Fifth Avenue, New York, NY 10010. Our advisor for Belleek is Richard K. Degenhardt; he is listed in the Directory under North Carolina.

Key:
A — pearl/plain   I — 1863-1890
B — cob lustre   II — 1891-1926
C — hand tinted   III — 1926-1946
D — hand painted   IV — 1946-1955
E — hand painted shamrocks   V — 1955-1965
F — hand gilted   VI — 1965–3/31/1980
G — hand tinted and gilted   VII — 4/1/1980–current
H — hand painted shamrocks
     and gilted
I — hand painted and gilted

Aberdeen, vase, floral, D58-IV, D, med sz **240.00**
Artichoke Tea Ware, creamer, D719-I, F, 4½"...........................**250.00**
Basket, oval, floral, D1270, 4-strand, D, 6¾"............................**500.00**
Basket, oval, w/lid, D113, 4-strand, D, lg **6,450.00**

Oval uncovered 4-strand basket, rim with applied flowers and stem handle, applied Belleek impressed pads on base, registry mark, D118, large, 12" long, $1,200.00.

Bird's Nest, tree stump vase, D57-VI, D.................................. **1,500.00**
Bust of Lord James Butler, D1128-I, A, 11"............................ **2,500.00**
Celtic Tea Ware, plate, D1435-III, I, 6½" **60.00**
Chinese, tea urn, D482-I, D, lg.. **9,000.00**
Cleary, creamer, D249(CR)-IV, B **20.00**
Cleary, spill, D193-VI, A **25.00**
Diamond, flowerpot, VI, A, 3½" **40.00**
Double Shell, creamer & sugar bowl, D288-VI/D1301-VI, B.........**50.00**
Echinus, bowl, ftd, D1521-VI, A, 8¼" **450.00**
Echinus Tea Ware, mustache cup, D664(C)-I, F, 2½" **325.00**
Egg frame & cups (6), D621-VI, G **300.00**
Erne Tea Ware, creamer, D447-II, B, 2¾".................................**125.00**
Feather, vase, D155-V, B, sm **35.00**
Figurine, boy & girl basket bearers, D17-VI/D19-VI, A, pr **750.00**
Figurine, leprechaun, D1142-III, A, 5½" **250.00**
Figurine, pig, D231-II, B, lg..**200.00**
Fish, spill, D184-I, B, 7" **600.00**
Florence, jug, D1288-VII, G, sm **75.00**
Flowerpot, floral, D47-II, A, sm **175.00**
Grass Tea Ware, honey pot on stand, D755-I, I, 6½", EX **700.00**

Shamrock Ware, teapot, D367-III, E, med 225.00
Shamrock Ware, teapot, D384-III, E, lg 275.00
Shell Tea Ware, creamer, D590-II, B...125.00
Sycamore, plate, D641-V, B, 4½" 21.00
Sydenham, twig basket, D108, 3-strand, A, 11¼" 3,200.00
Toy Shell, creamer, D250(CR)-II, D, 3¾" 75.00
Tridacna Tea Ware, coffee cup & saucer, D462-II, B...................90.00
Tridacna Tea Ware, mustard, D1348-III, B, 2½" 50.00
Tridacna Tea Ware, plate, D464-VI, F, 6" 25.00
Tridacna Tea Ware, teacup & saucer, D454-I, E 155.00
Tridacna Tea Ware, teacup & saucer, D454-IV, B 40.00
Undine, creamer, D305-VI, B, 5" dia...38.00

Bells

　　The earliest form of bell, the crotal or closed-mouth, is most familiar to us today as the sleigh bell. Rattles, hollow forms containing stones or seed pods, are also of this type of construction. Gongs, most often associated with the Orient, have no clapper and must be struck to sound. The more common forms of bells are made with a flaring shape and a freely-moving interior clapper that causes the bell to ring as it is swung. Bells come in many shapes and serve many uses. They have been used throughout history to sound an alarm, call a congregation, announce dinnertime, or signal a victory. School bells called children in from recess, and cow bells made the herd easier to locate. Bells have been made in brass, glass, china, bronze, and cast iron; in simple as well as elaborately embossed forms; and in amusing figurals. See also Schoolhouse Collectibles.

Brass, braided cord clapper, oval base, 7x6" 110.00
Brass, knight figural hdl, Hemony, 6⅞x3⅜" 125.00
Brass, Lucy Locket, fancy clothes & hat, 4¾x2⅛" 65.00
Brass, Napoleon figural hdl, 7x3⅜" 70.00
Brass, Red Riding Hood figural..45.00
Brass, St Peter's cross atop, 7x4⅛"..150.00
Brass, warrior's head emb ea side, 4" 45.00

Figure of Meditation, D20-VII, gold mark (7th mark), 15", $520.00.

Figural brass bell, 3¾", $55.00.

Harp Shamrock Tea Ware, teapot, D525-VI, E, 4½" 165.00
Heart, plate, No 3, D636-V, B, 6¼" 35.00
Henshall, spill, D61-V, A, 5½", EX 175.00
Hexagon Tea Ware, dejeuner tray, D395-II, C 1,000.00
Hexagon Tea Ware, teapot, D392-I, C..550.00
Institute Tea Ware, plate, D724-I, A, 6 for 600.00
Island, vase, D88-VI, E, 8"...80.00
Ivy Tea Ware, plate, D1413-III, B, 7" 65.00
Lattice, ash tray, D1581-VI, B, 4" dia 20.00
Lily, creamer, D235(CR)-I, A, 3¼" 150.00
Limpet Tea Ware, plate, D1372-III, A, 8" 65.00
Limpet Tea Ware, teacup, D549(C)-II, A, 3¾"..............................65.00
Limpet Tea Ware, teapot, D565-III, B..275.00
Lithophane, Girl w/Goat, D1537-III, A, 8½x6¾" 1,000.00
Lyre, wall bracket, D1546-I, A, 8½"..700.00
Mask, creamer, tall shape, D1484-III, A, sm...................................60.00
Nautilus, creamer, D270-II, A, 4"...225.00
Neptune Tea Ware, plate, D422-II, A, 6"...70.00
Neptune Tea Ware, teapot, D415-II, C, 5" 350.00
New Shell Tea Ware, biscuit jar, D599-VI, B, 7"............................90.00
Primrose, butter plate, D1554-III, G, 4¾".......................................75.00
Rathmore, basket, oval, D117, 4-strand, D 6,500.00
Rathmore, vase, D1219-VI, B, 7½"...70.00
Ribbon, creamer & sugar bowl, D243-IV, B...................................60.00
Rose Isle, vase, D1222-VI, D..950.00
Scroll Tea Ware, teacup & saucer, D502-II, G...............................200.00
Shamrock Ware, box, oval, D604-II, E, 3¾" 175.00
Shamrock Ware, cereal bowl, D380-III, E, 2½x4½" 70.00
Shamrock Ware, coffeepot, D1319-III, E, 7" 325.00
Shamrock Ware, creamer & sugar, D369-III/D368-III, E, sm 145.00
Shamrock Ware, egg cup, D389-II, E, 2¼" 50.00
Shamrock Ware, kettle, D387-II, E, sm 425.00
Shamrock Ware, name mug, D215-II, E, 2¾"..................................85.00
Shamrock Ware, plate, D378-III, E, 8" 75.00
Shamrock Ware, teacup & saucer, D366-II, E...............................125.00

Bronze, Northwood Lucky Bell, 2½-lb, 4½x2¾x3¾".......................55.00
China, lady figural, gold lustre, Germany 35.00
Cow bell, copper, lg, EX 12.00
Door type, spring turns w/wht porc doorknob, Taylor, 1860 ....95.00
Farm type, CI, upright, Crystal Metal #2 ....100.00

Glass, cranberry, wht opaque edge, clear hdl, 15" 200.00
Glass, custard, smocking pattern, orig clapper 145.00
Gong, brass, on stand w/wood striker, 7"...12.00
Harness, brass, 13 on straps (3 sections) 55.00
Hotel desk, acorn clapper 80.00
Silver, cherub figural, hallmk..145.00
Sleigh, brass, 1¼" dia, 23 on orig leather strap, EX......................165.00
Sleigh, brass, 4 on arched metal strap..40.00
Tap, NP brass, in yoke on std, dtd 1882, 6" 50.00

Bennett, John

Bringing with him the knowledge and experience he had gained at the Doulton (Lambeth) Pottery in England, John Bennett opened a studio in New York City around 1877, where he continued his methods of decorating faience under the glaze. Early wares utilized imported English biscuit, though subsequently local clays (both white and cream-colored) were also used. His first kiln was on Lexington Avenue; he built another on East Twenty-Fourth Street. Pieces are usually signed 'J. Bennett, N.Y.,' often with the street address and date. Later examples may be marked 'West Orange, N.J.,' where he retired. The pottery was in operation approximately six years in New York. Pieces signed with other initials are usually worth less. Our advisor for this category is Robert Tuggle; he is listed in the Directory under New York.

Charger, calla lily on cobalt, sgn/1877, 17¾" 6,750.00
Charger, floral branch/5 insects on apple gr, sgn/1878, 14½" .. 4,620.00
Vase, crab apple blossoms on cobalt mottle, sgn/ 1880s, 10" ... 5,280.00
Vase, hibiscus, urn form, top missing, sgn/1879............................990.00

Vase, pink and red peonies on mottled cobalt ground, signed and dated 1882, 26", $22,000.00.

Bennington

Although the term has become a generic one for the mottled brown ware produced there, Bennington is not a type of pottery, but rather a town in Vermont where two important potteries were located. The Norton Company, founded in 1793, produced mainly redware and salt-glazed stoneware; only during a brief partnership with Fenton (1845-47) was any Rockingham attempted. The Norton Company endured until 1894, operated by succeeding generations of the Norton family. Fenton organized his own pottery in 1847. There he manufactured not only redware and stoneware, but more artistic types as well — graniteware, scroddled ware, flint enamel, a fine parian, and vast amounts of their famous Rockingham. Though from an aesthetic standpoint his work rated highly among the country's finest ceramic achievements, he was economically unsuccessful. His pottery closed in 1858.

It is estimated that only one in five Fenton pieces were marked; and although it has become a common practice to link any fine piece of Rockingham to this area, careful study is vital in order to be able to distinguish Bennington's from the similar wares of many other American and Staffordshire potteries. Although the practice was without the permission of the proprietor, it was nevertheless a common occurrence for a potter to take his molds with him when moving from one pottery to the next, so particularly well-received designs were often reproduced at several locations. Of eight known Fenton marks, four are variations of the '1849' impressed stamp — 'Lyman Fenton Co., Fenton's Enamel Patented 1849, Bennington, Vermont.' These are generally found on examples of Rockingham and flint enamel. A raised, rectangular scroll with 'Fenton's Works, Bennington, Vermont,' was used on early examples of porcelain. From 1852 to 1858, the company operated under the title of the United States Pottery Company. Three marks — the ribbon mark with the initials USP, the oval with a scrollwork border and the name in full, and the plain oval with the name in full — were used during that period.

Among the more sought-after examples are the bird and animal figurines, novelty pitchers, figural bottles, and all of the more finely-modeled items. Recumbent deer, cows, standing lions with one forepaw on a ball, and opposing pairs of poodles with baskets in their mouths and 'coleslaw' fur were made in Rockingham, flint enamel, and occasionally in parian. Numbers in the listings below refer to the book *Bennington Pottery and Porcelain* by Barret. Our advisors for Bennington (except for parian and stoneware) are Barbara and Charles Adams; they are listed in the Directory under Massachusetts.

Key: c/s — cobalt on salt glaze

Book flask, Bennington Companion, flint enamel, 2-qt, M.........950.00
Book flask, Departed Spirits, flint enamel, sm rpr, 5½" 475.00
Book flask, Hermit's Companion, flint enamel, mk, pt, EX.........950.00
Bowl, vegetable; flint enamel, 1849 mk, oval, 11", EX 500.00
Candlestick, flint enamel, B 198, 6½" 600.00
Candlestick, flint enamel, B 198, 8" 700.00
Candlestick, Rockingham, B 197-C, 8", M....................................500.00
Candlestick, Rockingham, B 198, 8" 500.00
Candlestick, Rockingham, B 198-D, 9½" 500.00
Chamber pot, flint enamel, 1849 mk, 8¾" dia, EX......................250.00
Coachman, Rockingham, 1849 mk, B 419-B, M 695.00
Coffeepot, flint enamel, Scalloped Rib, base crack, 12" 850.00
Creamer, seated toby, flint enamel, grapevine hdl, mk, rpr.........550.00
Cuspidor, scroddled, bl, 8" dia, EX..550.00
Cuspidor, Shell, 2 side vents, 8½" 150.00
Figurine, Scotsman & goat, lady & lamb, parian, 8", pr..............550.00
Foot bath, flint enamel, Creased Rib, 1849 mk, 20" 1,500.00
Foot warmer, flint enamel, B 183-2, spout rpr, 11"......................400.00
Goblet, Rockingham, w/hdl, 4½", M 475.00
Nameplate, Rockingham fr w/parian letters, 3½x8", M 400.00
Picture fr, Rockingham, B 8-F, oval, 9½x8½" 550.00
Pipkin, Rockingham, Alternate Rib, 7½", EX 1,200.00

Pitcher, flint enamel, Lyman Fenton & Co., 8¾", EX, $875.00; Frame with mirror, flint enamel, 12" x 11", $850.00; Toby pitcher, Rockingham, Lyman & Fenton, impressed mark, 6½", $675.00.

Pitcher, flint enamel, paneled, 1849 mk, B IX-A, 12½" 900.00
Pitcher, flint enamel, Tulip & Heart, 1849 mk, 6½", EX 550.00
Pitcher, Rockingham, emb floral panels, N&F mk, B 23-C, 9" ...675.00
Plate, flint enamel, 9½" 135.00
Snuff jar, toby, non-flint, 4½" 850.00
Sugar bowl, flint enamel, spherical body, B 126-C, 5¾", EX 850.00
Tile, flint enamel, lattice design, 1849 mk, 8½x7", EX 250.00
Tile, flint enamel, sq w/diagonal gridwork, mk, 7", EX 300.00
Vase, flint enamel, Heron 575.00
Vase, parian, boy w/sheaf of wheat figural, 7", NM 100.00
Vase, tulip; flint enamel, 10", NM..600.00
Wash bowl, flint enamel, paneled, B 167, 13½", EX.....................350.00
Wash bowl, flint enamel, 1849 mk, B IX-A, mfg flaw, 13½" 800.00

Stoneware

Churn, floral spray (elaborate), c/s, E Norton, 5-gal 1,000.00
Crock, chicken pecking corn, c/s, J Norton, 2-gal 800.00
Crock, floral, c/s, J&E Norton, 10", NM 290.00
Crock, floral (bold/dotted), c/s, E&LP, 6-gal, EX 350.00

Crock, pair of pheasants in cobalt, marked J. Norton & Co., Bennington VT, 12", EX, $1,600.00

Jug, bird on dotted leafy branch, c/s, E&LP, 4-gal, M 1,500.00
Jug, bird on stump looks bk, c/s, J&E, mfg flaw, 15"................. 2,200.00
Jug, floral, brushed, c/s, L Norton, ovoid, 18", EX 420.00
Jug, floral, c/s, E&LP, sm flakes/hairlines, 15½" 400.00

Jug, floral, c/s, LP Norton, 2-gal 150.00
Jug, floral (3-loop), c/s, Julius Norton, ribbed hdls, 16"...............650.00
Jug, floral/foliage, brushed in brn, L Norton, ovoid, 12" 500.00
Jug, parrot on branch, c/s, J Norton & Co, 10¾", EX..................590.00
Jug, parrot on branch, c/s, J Norton & Co, 12"...........................925.00
Pitcher, Albany slip, E&LP, 1½-gal 300.00

Beswick

In the early 1890s, James Wright Beswick operated a pottery in Longston, England, where he produced fine dinnerware as well as ornamental ceramics. Today's collectors are most interested in the figurines made since 1936 by a later generation Beswick firm, John Beswick, Ltd. They specialize in reproducing accurately detailed bone china models of authentic breeds of animals. Their Fireside Series includes dogs, cats, elephants, horses, the Huntsman, and an Indian figure, which measure up to 14" in height. The Connoisseur line is modeled after the likenesses of famous racing horses. Beatrix Potter's characters and some of Walt Disney's are charmingly recreated and appeal to children and adults alike. Other items, such as character Tobys, have also been produced. The Beswick name is stamped on each piece. The firm was absorbed by the Doulton group in 1973.

Ash tray, 5 puppies, #869, 6" 18.00
Jug, Little Nell's Grandfather 75.00
Shakers, Laurel & Hardy, pr, +tray 90.00
Teapot, Peggotty, M 65.00

Tray, bird on berried branch in relief, #1832, 7½", $35.00.

Big Little Books

The first Big Little Book was published in 1933 and copyrighted in 1932 by the Whitman Publishing Company of Racine, Wisconsin. Its hero was Dick Tracy. The concept was so well accepted that others soon followed Whitman's example; and, though the 'Big Little Book' phrase became a trademark of the Whitman Company, the formats of his competitors — Saalfield, Goldsmith, Van Wiseman, Lynn, and World Syndicate — were exact copies. Today's Big Little Book buffs collect them all.

These hand-sized sagas of adventure were illustrated with full-page cartoons on the right-hand page and the story narration on the left.

Colorful cardboard covers contained hundreds of pages, usually totaling over an inch in thickness. Big Little Books originally sold for 10¢ at the dime store; as late as the mid-1950s when the popularity of comic books caused sales to decline signaling an end to production, their price had risen to a mere 20¢. Their appeal was directed toward the pre-teens who bought, traded, and hoarded Big Little Books. Because so many were stored in attics and closets, many have survived. Among the super heroes are G-Men, Flash Gordon, Tarzan, the Lone Ranger, and Red Ryder; in a lighter vein, you'll find such lovable characters as Blondie and Dagwood, Mickey Mouse, Little Orphan Annie, and Felix the Cat.

In the early to mid-'30s, Whitman published several Big Little Books as advertising premiums for the Coco Malt Company, who packed them in boxes of their cereal. These are highly prized by today's collectors, as are Disney stories and super-hero adventures.

Our advisor for this category is Ron Donnelly; he is listed in the Directory under Florida.

Alley Oop & Dinny, 1935, EX	45.00
Andy Panda, Presto the Pup, EX	20.00
Bambi, Better Little Book, 1942, VG	60.00
Bambi's Children, 1943, M	55.00

Big Chief Wahoo, Whitman, 1938, VG, $25.00; Tom Mix, Better Little Book, 1940, VG, $25.00.

Billy the Kid, 1935	30.00
Blondie, Count Cookie In Too, EX	25.00
Blondie, Who's Boss, 1942, EX	35.00
Brer Rabbit, Song of the South, 1945-47, EX	50.00
Buck Rogers, Depth Men of Jupiter, 1935, VG	50.00
Buck Rogers, Fiend of Space, VG	50.00
Buck Rogers, War w/Planet Venus, 1938, VG	50.00
Bugs Bunny, Masked Marvel, 1949, EX	25.00
Capt Frank Hawks, Air Ace & League of 12, 1938, EX	25.00
Capt Midnight, Sheik Jomak Khan, 1946, EX	40.00
Charlie McCarthy, 1938, VG	25.00
Chester Gump at Silver Creek Ranch, 1933, EX	40.00
Cinderella & the Magic Wand, 1950, VG	25.00
Coach Bernie Bierman's Brick Barton & the Winning Eleven, G	10.00
Dan Dunn, Underworld Gorillas, 1941, G	15.00
David Copperfield, 1934, VG	35.00
Dick Tracy, Adventures of; 1st Big Little Book, 1933, rare, NM	125.00
Dick Tracy, Adventures of; 1st Big Little Book, 1933, VG	100.00
Dick Tracy, Boris Arson Gang, 1935, EX	55.00
Dick Tracy, Phantom Ship, 1940, VG	40.00
Dick Tracy, Racketeer Gang, 1936, VG	40.00
Dickie Moore, Little Red Schoolhouse, 1936, EX	40.00
Don O'Dare Finds War, 1940, EX	25.00

Donald Duck, Ghost Morgan's Treasure, 1946, EX	70.00
Donald Duck, Headed for Trouble, flip pages, 1942, EX	50.00
Donald Duck, Hunting for Trouble, 1938, VG	30.00
Donald Duck, Off the Beam, 1943, EX	50.00
Donald Duck Sees the Stars, 1941, NM	50.00
Ellery Queen & Adventures of The Last Man Club, 1940, EX	30.00
Erik Noble & the Forty Niners, 1934, EX	35.00
Flash Gordon, Fiery Desert Mongo, 1948, EX	45.00
Flash Gordon, Power Men of Mongo, 1943, EX	50.00
Flash Gordon, Witch Queen of Mongo, EX	60.00
Freckles & Lost Diamond Mine, 1937, NM	32.00
G-Man & The Radio Bank Robberies, 1937, EX	30.00
G-Man Vs the 5th Column, 1941, VG	30.00
Gene Autry, Land Grab Mystery, 1948, EX	30.00
Gene Autry, Law of the Range, 1939, NM	40.00
Gene Autry, Mystery of Paint Rock, 1947, NM	35.00
Gene Autry, Raiders of the Range, 1946, NM	35.00
Gene Autry, The Hawk of the Hills, 1942, VG	30.00
Gun Justice, Featuring Ken Maynard, 1934, NM	45.00
Huckleberry Finn, Adventures of; 1948, VG	24.00
Inspector Wade, Red Aces, 1937, VG	20.00
Jackie Cooper Star of Skippy, 1933, VG	35.00
Jim Craig State Trooper, Kidnapped Governor, 1938, VG	25.00
Jungle Jim, Vampire Woman, 1937, EX	50.00
Keep 'Em Flying USA, 1943, EX	35.00
King of the Royal Mounted Gets His Man, Z Grey, 1938, VG	30.00
Li'l Abner Among the Millionaires, 1939, EX	50.00
Little Orphan Annie, $1,000,000, 1936, NM	45.00
Little Orphan Annie & Chizzler, 1933, VG	50.00
Little Orphan Annie & Sandy, #716, 1933, VG	60.00
Little Orphan Annie & the Goonyville Mystery, 1937, NM	40.00
Little Orphan Annie & the Haunted Mansion, 1941, VG	40.00
Little Orphan Annie in the Movies, 1937, VG	38.00
Lone Ranger & Blk Shirt Highwayman, Whitman, '39, EX	45.00
Lone Ranger & His Horse Silver, 1935, NM	55.00
Lone Ranger & the Renegades, 1939, VG	40.00
Lone Ranger & the Silver Bullets, 1946, NM	45.00
Lone Ranger Follows Through, 1941, NM	45.00
Mandrake the Magician, Mighty Solver of Mysteries, 1941, EX	48.00
Mickey Mouse, Bell Boy Detective, 1945, VG	45.00
Mickey Mouse, Dude Ranch Bandit, 1943, VG	45.00
Mickey Mouse, Lazy Day Mystery, 1947, EX	45.00
Mickey Mouse, Mail Pilot, 1933, NM	55.00
Mickey Mouse & Bobo the Elephant, 1935, NM	65.00
Mickey Mouse & Pluto the Racer, 1936, VG	60.00
Mickey Mouse & the Bat Bandit, 1935, VG	60.00
Mickey Mouse & the Sacred Jewel, 1936, VG	55.00
Mickey Mouse in Blaggard Castle, 1934, VG	60.00
Mickey Mouse Presents a Disney Silly Symphony, 1934, VG	65.00
Mickey Mouse Runs His Own Newspaper, 1937, NM	45.00
Mickey Mouse Sails for Treasure Island, 1933, NM	70.00
Mickey Mouse the Detective, 1934, NM	65.00
Mickey Rooney, Judy Garland, 1941, VG	40.00
Phantom, Desert Justice, 1941, EX	50.00
Pluto the Pup, 1938, NM	50.00
Powder Smoke Range, 1935, VG	25.00
Radio Patrol, 1935, EX	35.00
Red Ryder, Hoofs of Thunder, 1939, EX	40.00
Red Ryder, War on the Range, 1945, VG	30.00
Red Ryder & Circus Luck, 1947, NM	30.00
Red Ryder & the Secret Canyon, 1948, NM	30.00
Red Ryder & the Squawtooth Rustlers, 1946, VG	30.00
Red Ryder the Fighting Westerner, 1940, NM	40.00
Roy Rogers, King of the Cowboys, 1943, EX	30.00

Roy Rogers, Range Detective, 1950, EX 20.00
Roy Rogers at Crossed Feather Ranch, 1945, EX 35.00
Shooting Sheriffs, Wild West, 1936, VG.......................................20.00
Snow White & the 7 Dwarfs, 1938, NM.......................................75.00
Son of Mystery, 1939, NM 18.00
Speed Douglas & the Mole Gang, 1941, NM 30.00
Sybil Jason in Little Big Shot, 1935, EX 35.00
Tarzan, Fearless, 1934, EX 50.00
Tarzan, Twins, 1934, rare, NM 175.00
Terry & the Pirates, Mountain Stronghold, 1941, VG.................35.00
Terry & the Pirates, War in the Jungle, 1946, NM 40.00
Tim McCoy on Tomahawk Trail, 1937, VG 30.00
Tim McCoy the Westerner, 1936, NM 45.00
Tom Beatty, Ace of Service, 1934...25.00
Tom Mix & the Hoard of Montezuma, 1937, NM 45.00
Treasure Island, 1934, EX 35.00
Vick Sands of the US Flying Fortress, 1944, NM 35.00
Walt Disney's Dumbo of the Circus, 1941, NM 60.00
Will Rogers, The Story of; 1935..30.00

Bing and Grondahl

In 1853 brothers M.H. and J.H. Bing formed a partnership with Frederick Vilhelm Grondahl in Copenhagen, Denmark. Their early wares were porcelain plaques and figurines designed by the noted sculptor Thorvaldsen of Denmark. Dinnerware production began in 1863, and by 1889 their underglaze color 'Copenhagen Blue' had earned them worldwide acclaim. They are perhaps most famous today for their Christmas plates, the first of which was made in 1895. See also Limited Edition Plates.

Coffeepot, sea gull, w/gold, lg...150.00
Creamer, sea gull, w/gold 40.00
Cup & saucer, sea gull w/gold 40.00
Figurine, bird on branch, head turned right, 6" 95.00
Figurine, bullfinch, #1909, bl/tan on lt gr rock, 4¾" 100.00
Figurine, children playing, #1568 ....135.00
Figurine, Colonial man playing cello, #2032 ....255.00
Figurine, Dancing School, #1845 ....285.00
Figurine, girl talking to doll, #2191 ....155.00
Figurine, Goose Girl, #2254 ....275.00
Figurine, Little Match Girl, #1655 ....175.00
Figurine, mermaid 620.00
Figurine, nude man asleep on mule, #4026, 9¼" 660.00
Figurine, Old Gray Goose, #1902 ....48.00
Figurine, polar bear, 12" 165.00
Figurine, Siamese cat, #2464, wht, 5½" 88.00
Figurine, woodpecker, #1717, 4¾" 210.00
Gravy boat, sea gull, w/gold, attached tray 150.00
Plate, bread & butter; sea gull, w/gold..................................20.00
Plate, sea gull w/gold, 9⅝" 40.00
Platter, sea gull, w/gold, 16x11" 175.00
Soup, rim; sea gull, w/gold 40.00
Sugar bowl, sea gull, w/gold, w/lid...75.00

Bisque

Bisque is a term referring to unglazed earthenware or porcelain that has been fired only once. During the Victorian era, bisque figurines became very popular. Most were highly decorated in pastels and gilt and demonstrated a fine degree of workmanship in the quality of their modeling. Few were marked. See also Heubach; Nodders; Dolls; Piano Babies.

Baby in carriage, floral spokes, facing pr, 8½" L.....................450.00
Baby in straw trunk w/appl flowers, mk Depose, 6x7½", EX 500.00
Boy & girl hold umbrella, 7½" 100.00
Bust, blonde girl w/yel bonnet, on floral ped, #327, 8¾" 95.00
Bust, Spring & Autumn allegories, sgn L Kley, 10", pr 325.00
Edwardian couple, flowing dress, long coat, Fr, 21", pr 1,150.00
Girl holds kittens in skirt, dog aside, cat at ft, 6" 275.00
Girl in ermine robe, star in hair, gold/mc, 13¾" 600.00
Girl in wht blouse & bl dress holds cat, 1920, German, 15" 250.00
Girl w/doll, bl coat w/pk trim, 6½x2¼" 75.00
Girl winking, I Do Like Kissing, 7x2½" 120.00
Hen on nest, mc features on head, tan base, French, 8" L.............175.00
Man, bl tricorner hat, lav coat, standing, 13½" 150.00
Man, hand to chin, leans on thresher, 1800s, 36" 2,500.00
Man, 18th-century attire, by tree, arm out, 6¾" 38.00
Night light, cat w/glass eyes, gray w/bl ribbon, 3¾x3" 195.00
Shoe w/mouse atop, baby mouse emerging, 3½x5" 60.00

Black Americana

Black memorabilia is without a doubt a field that encompasses the most widely-exploited ethnic group in our history. But within this field there are many levels of interest — arts and achievements such as folk music and literature, caricatures in advertising, souvenirs, toys, fine art, and legitimate research into the days of their enslavement and enduring struggle for equality. The list is endless.

In the listings below are some with a derogatory connotation. Thankfully, these are from a bygone era and represent the mores of a culture that existed nearly a century ago. They are included only to convey the fact that they are a part of this growing area of collecting interest.

Our advisor for this category is Linda Rothe; she is listed in the Directory under Washington. Black Americana catalogs featuring a wide variety of items for sale are available; see the Directory under Clubs, Newsletters, and Catalogs for more information. See also Post Cards, Posters, Sheet Music.

Apron, Mammy w/pie, child at side, 30x19", M 45.00
Ash tray, alligator w/Blk head in mouth, ceramic, souvenir...........35.00
Ash tray, baby at clothesline, Who Left This Behind? 8.50
Ash tray, boy w/card, ceramic 25.00
Ash tray, Coon Chicken Inn, glass, sq 40.00
Ash tray, fishing boy hooks alligator, ceramic, 4¾x4" 35.00
Bank, farmer, CI, EX orig pnt 85.00
Bank, Mammy w/laundry basket, pot metal, EX 110.00
Book, Here They Are Amos 'N Andy, Correll & Gosden, '31, EX ..40.00
Book, Little Brown KoKo Has Fun, hardbk, 1945, 96-pg, EX 40.00
Book, Slave Power, leather bound, 1877, 3-volume set................150.00
Book, Story of Little Blk Sambo, 1937, 10-pg, EX....................30.00
Book, Teenie Weenies in the Wildwood, Donahey, 1923, EX.......25.00
Book, Uncle Tom's Cabin, condensed version, Owen, 1918, EX...20.00
Book, Who's Who in Colored America, NY, 1930-32, EX 75.00
Booklet, Negro Songs, 1924, EX 35.00
Bottle, Jungle Juice, man on front, ceramic 65.00
Bottle stopper, head figural..15.00
Brush, Mammy figural, bristles form skirt, pre-1940, M...........25.00
Clock, Li'l Hannibal graphics on face, metal body, Westclox......400.00
Clothespin bag, Mammy wooden die-cut head, cloth body, 14" 22.50
Cookbook, Aunt Caroline's Dixieland Recipes, 1922, EX 22.00
Cookie jar, Chef, Japan 250.00
Cookie jar, Mammy, basket hdl, Mauhon Ware HP Japan 195.00
Cookie jar, Mammy, Luzianne repro, unmk................................75.00
Cookie jar, Mammy, Memories of Mama, McCoy Mammy repro ..42.00

Cookie jar, F&F Mold & Die Works, Dayton OH, red plastic, 12", $200.00.

Cookie jar, Mandy, c Omnibus Japan 55.00
Cracker jar, Mammy's head, red scarf, ceramic, wicker hdl, M 450.00
Creamer & sugar bowl, Aunt Jemima & Uncle Mose, gr, F&F...165.00
Creamer & sugar bowl, Aunt Jemima & Uncle Mose, yel, F&F....85.00
Doll, stocking; embr features, button eyes, 1930s, 14", EX.............30.00
Doll, Topsee, rubber, braids, Japan, M in sealed pkg......................15.00
Doll, Uncle Moses, vinyl, Aunt Jemima Pancake premium, M......40.00
Figure, jockey, pnt wood, 1950s, 48", EX..145.00
Figure, man w/horse, chalkware, Green River ad pc, 9x18" 265.00

Chalkware figure, marked J Nardi of Boston, 1898, 11", $350.00.

Figurine, baby asleep, sucking thumb, chalkware 25.00
Figurine, boy w/bk to monkey behind tree, bsk, Germany, 3¼"...145.00
Figurine, girl w/basket, bl & wht dress, Occupied Japan, 5" 35.00
Figurine, Mammy sitting in rocker, compo, lg, NM 150.00
Figurine, native scratching head, ceramic, 5" 25.00
Figurine, native w/grass skirt & drum, ceramic, 1950s, 6" 25.00
Figurine, One Moment Please, figure in outhouse 12.50
Fishing plug, naughty Blk Sambo, 1950, MIB.................................25.00
Game, Alabama Coon, ball toss, EX in box...................................195.00
Hotpad holder, Mammy & Chef, chalkware, pr 35.00
Humidor, Mammy figural head, ceramic, M 275.00
Incense burner, boy on pot, mouth wide, pot metal, NM, 6¼" 65.00
Mammy, cloth doll, holds 2 wht babies w/plastic faces, sm 55.00
Mask, grotesque exaggerated Blk features, rubber, EX....................25.00

Measuring spoon holder, Mammy figural, chalkware, old 45.00
Memo pad holder, Mammy, compo, Hampton novelty, +pencil ...65.00
Mug, beer; ceramic, Muscle Moe, EX...65.00
Noisemaker, Blk figure w/big eyes, tin, US Metal Toys 8.00
Ornament, nude baby, wax over papier-mache, Occupied Japan...30.00
Paper towel holder, Mammy stands at side, wooden.....................115.00
Paperweight, Mammy in snow scene..75.00
Pincushion, half doll, bsk 95.00
Pincushion, Mammy figural, litho on wood, skirt cushion, 4½".....35.00
Planter, girl by stump w/melon, Interco, 5"....................................45.00
Planter, Mammy on washer, ceramic 50.00
Plaque, Sambo, chalkware 25.00
Plate, Coon Chicken Inn, Inca Ware, dinner sz 175.00
Plate, Coon Chicken Inn, Inca Ware, 5¾"....................................125.00
Platter, Coon Chicken Inn, Inca Ware, 11" 200.00
Post card, Coon Chicken Inn, mc, unused, NM..............................30.00
Post card, It's Pleasant To Be Pushed, porter pushes lady, EX 25.00
Potholder caddy, boy & girl under umbrellas, chalkware, pr..........60.00
Potholder hanger, boy w/watermelon, chalkware, 1949 ....30.00
Print, Ten Little Niggers, McLoughlin, fr, EX 150.00
Puppet, hand; compo head, cloth body, old, EX 27.50
Recipe box, Jemima, yel hard plastic, orig folder & cards 125.00
Record, Little Blk Sambo, Paul Wing, RCA....................................30.00
Saucer, Coon Chicken Inn...60.00
Scouring pad holder, Mammy, ceramic, wall hanging 85.00
Shakers, Aunt Jemima & Uncle Mose, red, F&F, lg, pr 55.00
Shakers, Aunt Jemima & Uncle Mose, red, F&F, sm, pr...............25.00
Shakers, blk w/wht aprons & red ladles, gold label, 4", pr 24.00
Shakers, boy w/banjo rides hippo, ceramic, pr 65.00
Shakers, lady w/nodding head holds melon slice, ceramic, pr 100.00
Shakers, Mammy & Chef, Brayton, pr...35.00
Shakers, native heads, gold bangle chokers, ceramic, pr.................25.00
Shakers, natives, wood, pearl earrings, 2½", pr 12.00
Shakers, Salty & Peppy, ceramic, 22k gold trim, 7¼", pr 85.00
Shelf sitter, boy w/red pants, yel hat, wht shirt, unmk, 4½" 25.00
Shoe horn, man's head at tip of long hdl 30.00
Shot glass, Here's Looking at You, figures under palms 6.00
Shot glass, man ready to cook wht lady, 22k gold trim 6.00
Sign, Coon Chicken Inn, reserves table..12.00
Soap dish, Mammy w/basket on head, CI, EX pnt 165.00
Spice set, 6 glass containers w/pnt caricatures on wood rack..........65.00
Spoon rest, Chef, brn w/yel tie & wht hat, M..................................90.00
Spoon rest, Mammy's head, wht scarf w/red dots, M 90.00
Sprinkler, Sprinkling Sambo, wood, jtd arm holds hose, 30" 185.00
String holder, Mammy, Nat'l Silver..110.00
String holder, Mammy's head, plaster, EX.....................................195.00
Syrup, Aunt Jemima, F&F...35.00
Syrup, Little Blk Sambo scenes, chrome top, 5¼" 65.00
Tablecloth, figures eating watermelon, 48x48", EX 95.00
Tablecloth, Mammy & family at chores, lg, EX...............................85.00
Target game, Blk Sambo, tin, lg, EX 95.00
Teapot, clown's head, ceramic 45.00
Toaster doll, Mammy, cotton-stuffed body, 1940s, 18", EX............25.00
Token, slave auctioneer, brass, dtd 1846, EX 55.00
Toothpick holder, Coon Chicken Inn...195.00
Towel, Mammy embr, week days, cross-stitch, unused, 7 for 65.00
Towel, Mammy w/little boy, unused 35.00
Tumbler, Coon Chicken Inn, 4" 45.00

Black Cats

The main producer of the 'Black Cats' collectibles was the Shafford Company, although occasionally pieces will be found bearing the marks of other firms. Wood and Sons, Ltd., in Burslem, England, produced an 8" figural teapot as part of a novelty line marketed in this country by Fondeville of New York. Other items have been found marked 'Wales,' 'Empress,' and 'Napco Ceramics, Japan.' Black Cat collectors usually prefer to limit their 'litter' to those kittens with a shiny black glaze and styling similar to the Shafford cats.

Ash tray, head only, open mouth, Shafford label, 3"	18.00
Bookends, cat on book, fluffy hair, 5½"	30.00
Condiment set, 2 heads, bow finials, gr eyes, 4"	30.00
Cookie jar, head only, red bows/ears, gr eyes, 5"	75.00
Creamer, seated, paw spout, red bow, yel eyes, 6"	15.00
Cruet, seated, tail hdl, red bow tie, 7½"	16.50
Decanter, seated, red polka dots, head stopper, 7", +6 cups	55.00
Figurine, arched bk, on book by vase, yel eyes/red ears, 3"	12.00
Figurine, reclining kitten, wht eyes, red ears, 1¼"	6.00
Letter holder, recumbent, w/wire holder in bk, 3¼x6½"	12.00
Pincushion, crouches, cushion on bk, tongue measure, 2x4¼"	22.50
Planter, seated, gr emerald eyes, Alco-Japan label, 6"	12.00
Shakers, seated, voice box in base, Japan label, 5", pr	20.00
Shakers, voice box in base, Souvenir of..., 3⅛", pr	14.00
Spice set, cat's face on 3" sq jar, Shafford, 6 w/rack	75.00
Sugar bowl, full figure, seated, red bow, gr eyes, 4⅞"	18.00

Utensil rack, 8" long, $40.00.

Teapot, crouched, scarf/gold disk, spout through mouth, 3¾"	20.00
Teapot, paw spout, 8½"	35.00
Wall pocket, gr eyes, red bow, sq pocket at bk, 5½"	45.00

Black Glass

Black glass is a type of colored glass that when held to strong light usually appears deep purple — though since each glasshouse had its own formula, tones may vary. It was sometimes etched or given a satin finish; and occasionally it was decorated with silver, gold, enamel, coralene, or any of these in combination. The decoration was done either by the glasshouse or by firms that specialized in decorating glassware. Crystal, jade, colored glass, or milk glass was sometimes used with the black as an accent. Black glass has been made by many companies since the seventeenth century. Contemporary glasshouses produced black glass during the Depression, seldom signing their product. It is still being made today.

To learn more about the subject, we recommend *A Collector's Guide to Black Glass*, written by our advisor, Marlena Toohey; she is listed in the Directory under Arkansas. Look for a newly updated value guide. See also Tiffin and specific manufacturers.

Ash tray, Deco chrome skater on top, 5x5½"	75.00
Ash tray, dog stands in center, Greensburg, 1920s-30s, 6¼"	19.00
Bottle, shoe form, screw cap, unmk, ca 1880-1910, 3½x5¼"	50.00

Bowl, cupped, ftd, shallow, ca 1921, 9¼"	27.50
Bowl, shell form w/gold rim, unmk, 5¾"	16.50
Bowl, 6-scallop rim w/gilt, ftd, unknown mfg, 1920s-30s, lg	70.00
Box, wht florals & bird, hinged, ftd, 4½x7"	325.00
Candlestick, molded to imitate crackle glass, 1926-30s, 7"	50.00
Candlestick, Pompeian, United States Glass, ca 1926	100.00
Celery tray, clear swan hdl, Viking, #951/1S, 1940-60	70.00
Comport, att Co-Operative Flint Glass, ca 1924, 6½"	38.00
Comport, Chatham openwork rim, United States Glass, 8½"	82.50
Creamer, Cloverleaf, Hazel-Atlas, early to mid-1930s	13.50
Creamer & sugar bowl, Greensburg, #5029, 1925-30, pr	38.50
Match holder, Half Scroll, unmk, ca 1900-10	27.50
Relish, 3-compartment, ornate metal fr, ca 1925-35	33.00
Sauce boat, wide panels, att Dmn Glass-Ware, ca 1926-31, 5¾"	44.00
Shakers, red plastic tops, att Hazel-Atlas, 3", pr	15.00
Sherbet, clear bowl, blk stem & ft, unknown mfg, 1930s	10.00
Tumbler, clear bowl w/blk domed foot, ca 1929-35, 12-oz	13.50
Vase, bulbous, scalloped, Greensburg, #1018, 1925-35, 6"	17.50
Vase, classic form, unknown mfg, 9"	50.00
Vase, HP floral, ringed neck, ped ft, 15", pr	175.00
Vase, wht enamel florals, unmk, ca 1915-35, 3"	17.50

Vase, frieze band with figures, 6½", $40.00.

Blown Glass

Blown glass is rather difficult to date; eighteenth and nineteenth century examples vary little as to technique or style — it ranges from the primitive to the sophisticated. But the metallic content of very early glass caused tiny imperfections that are obvious upon examination, and these are often indicative of age.

In America, Stiegel introduced the English technique of using a patterned, part-size mold, a practice which was generally followed by many glasshouses after the Revolution. From 1820 to about 1850, glass was blown into full-size 3-part molds. In the listings below, glass is assumed clear unless color is mentioned. Numbers refer to a standard reference book, *American Glass* by Helen McKearin. See also Bottles and specific manufacturers.

Our advisor for this category is Mark Vuono; he is listed in the Directory under Connecticut.

Key: ps — pontil scar

Bowl, amethyst, pontil, 5x7"	50.00

Bowl, aqua, bubbly, tall sides, early form, 4½x7" 175.00
Bowl, aqua, folded rim, appl ft, pontil scar, 3¾x6" 550.00
Bowl, aqua, high base kick-up, pontil, 4½x10", NM 140.00
Bowl, aqua, wide flaring folded-under lip, 1850s, 1½x8½" 225.00
Bowl, cobalt, ftd, 3¾" H 60.00
Bowl, dk sapphire, str/slightly flaring sides, 4½x7½" 300.00
Bowl, folded inner lip, pontil, Am, 2¼x5¾" 60.00
Bowl, gr-aqua, wide flared lip, thick, 1¾x7" 150.00
Bowl, grass gr, appl lip rim, crude/bubbly, very early, 5x6" 1,300.00
Bowl, lt gr, folded lip, crude, early, 6x10" 325.00
Bowl, lt gr, folded rim, pontil, thin, Am, 1½x3⅝" 300.00
Bowl, med smoky bl, 24 dmn, appl ft, pontil, English, 3" H........320.00
Bull's eye, amethyst, folded rim, 6" dia...25.00
Compote, cobalt w/wht rim on lip & ft edge, 1800s, 3⅝x5" 425.00
Creamer, aqua, appl ft & hdl (w/crimping), 4" 300.00
Creamer, dk bl-purple, flaring top, solid hdl w/curl, 3" 475.00
Creamer, med amethyst, flared lip, ftd, hdl w/crimping, 4" 650.00
Creamer, 14 str ribs, appl ft, hdl w/crimping, non-lead, 5" 75.00
Cuspidor, powder bl translucent, 8⅝" dia 225.00
Flip, blown w/molded ribs in base, primitive rim eng, 6".............250.00
Fly catcher, removable cover, non-lead, 1800s, 7" 250.00
Hat whimsey, aqua, thin, pontil, 2⅝"...40.00
Jar, aqua, Marcelin David on seal, thin, folded lip, 9½" 225.00
Jar, dk gr, folded lip, minor burst bubble, 1860s, 11½" 100.00
Jar, dk olive, cylindrical w/corseted neck, NE, 1830s, 12"............155.00
Jar, olive, ovoid body w/flared lip, crude, 1800, 5⅜" 1,200.00
Lamp filler, appl spout/hdl, 5⅝", EX..70.00
Milk pan, aqua, folded lip, pontil, early, 4x16"............................200.00
Milk pan, aqua-lt gr, pouring spout, folded-under rim, 4½" 425.00
Pitcher, aqua, flared rim on long neck, appl ft, 5" 400.00
Pitcher, dk olive, threading at lip, solid ft, ear hdl, 2½" 1,300.00
Pitcher, flaring lip, appl ft, hdl w/medial rib, lead, 2¼" 100.00
Pitcher, molded loop panels in bulbous base, 8½" 250.00
Rolling pin, aqua, 6"...40.00
Salt, master; 16-rib, 20 swirled ribs, appl bl rim..........................100.00
Vase, cobalt, rolled-out lip, NE, 1850s, 8", EX 550.00
Vase, dk bl, raised rim, tooled lip, minor stain, 7" 150.00
Vase, dk orange-amber, appl ft, pontil, 9½" 1,100.00
Vase, fiery opal, trumpet top, dome ft w/2 rings, 5¾" 100.00

Large vessel blown in medium green bubbly glass, applied ring at base, folded-over lip, 17", $110.00.

Wine, air twist stem w/knop, lead glass, pontil, 6" 300.00
Wine, baluster stem, 4"..45.00

Wine, cotton stem, eng vintage/birds, English, 5" 175.00
Wine, ogee bowl, long stem w/knop-like widening, 1730s, 6" 150.00
Wine, 2 wht spirals/mesh, ogee bowl, English, 6"........................175.00
Wine, 4 wht bands/gauze spiral stem, European, 5", NM 50.00

Blown Three-Mold Glass

A popular collectible in the 1920s, '30s, and '40s, blown three-mold glass has again gained the attention of many. Produced from approximately 1815 to 1840 in various New York, New England, and Midwestern glasshouses, it was a cheaper alternative to the expensive imported Irish cut glass.

Distinguishing features of blown three-mold glass are the three distinct mold marks and the concave-convex appearance of the glass. For every indentation on the inner surface of the ware, there will be a corresponding protuberance on the outside. Blown three-mold glass is most often clear with the exception of inkwells and a few known decanters. Any colored three-mold glass commands a premium price.

The numbers in the listings that follow refer to the book *American Glass*, by George and Helen McKearin.

Our advisor for this category is Mark Vuono; he is listed in the Directory under Connecticut.

Bottle, GIII-16, olive gr, 1-pt 350.00
Bottle, vinegar; GI-7, sapphire bl, 6¾" 250.00
Creamer, GII-18, tooled lip w/pour spout, 2⅞" 190.00
Decanter, GII-2, type 1, blk-olive, Mt Vernon NY, qt 4,500.00

Decanter, GIII-16, olive-amber, open pontil, tooled flared lip, 7", $250.00.

Dish, GIII-25, folded lip, pontil, 1¾x5½" 125.00
Flip, GII-18, clear w/gray tint, pontil, NE, 4½" 130.00
Flip, GII-18, clear w/gray tint, pontil, NE, 5¾" 175.00
Flip, GII-18, pontil, NE, 1830s, 5¾" 150.00
Flip, GII-25, clear w/gray tint, pontil, 5½" 150.00
Hat whimsey, similar to G111-6, cobalt 750.00
Pitcher, GIII-12, mini, 2½" 175.00
Pitcher, GV-17, hdl check, 8½" 400.00
Salt cellar, GIII-21, solid ft, wide onion-form bowl, 2¼" 200.00
Tumbler, GI-24, clear w/bl rim, pontil, NE, 1830s, 3" 1,800.00

Tumbler, GII-18, bbl form, tooled lip, 1¾" 150.00
Tumbler, GII-18, pontil, NE, 1830s, 3¾" 130.00
Tumbler, 30-honeycomb over 30 flutes, non-lead, 5" 75.00

Blue and White Stoneware

Blue and white stoneware, much of which was decorated with such in-mold designs as grazing cows and Dutch children, was made by practically every American pottery from the turn of the century until the mid-1930s. Crocks, pitchers, wash sets, rolling pins, and canisters are only a few of the items that may be found in this type of 'country' pottery that has become one of today's popular collectibles.

Roseville, Brush-McCoy, Uhl Co., and Burley Winter were among those who produced it; but very few pieces were ever signed. Naturally, condition must be a prime consideration, especially if one is buying for resale; pieces with good, strong color and fully-molded patterns bring premium prices. Normal wear and signs of age are to be expected since this was utility ware and received heavy use in busy households. In the listings that follow, crocks and jars are assumed without lids unless noted otherwise. See also specific manufacturers.

Bean pot, Boston Baked Beans, Flemish, w/lid 290.00
Bowl, Apricot, 9½" 85.00
Bowl, Daisy on Waffle, 10¾" 95.00
Bowl, Daisy on Waffle, 9½" 90.00
Bowl, dough; dk bl, scalloped rim, lg 85.00
Bowl, mixing; Feathers, 10½" 125.00
Bowl, plain, 11" 70.00
Bowl, Wedding Ring, 10" 125.00
Butter crock, Apple Blossom, orig lid & bail 155.00
Butter crock, Apricot, orig lid & bail 200.00
Butter crock, Apricots w/Honeycomb, orig lid & bail 225.00
Butter crock, Butterfly, orig lid & bail, 6½" 120.00
Butter crock, Cow, stenciled, orig lid & bail 120.00
Butter crock, Cows & Columns, orig lid & bail 250.00
Butter crock, Daisy & Trellis, orig lid & bail, 4½" 175.00
Butter crock, Diffused Bl, orig lid & bail, 1-lb, 4x4½" 95.00
Butter crock, Dutch Couple, orig lid & bail, lg 155.00
Butter crock, Eagle, orig lid & bail 450.00
Butter crock, Indian Good Luck Sign, orig lid & bail 125.00
Butter crock, Wildflower, orig lid & bail 150.00
Canister, Basketweave, Coffee, orig lid 195.00
Canister, Basketweave, Raisins, orig lid 225.00
Canister, Diffused Bl, Tea, orig lid 125.00
Canister, Snowflake, Rice, orig lid 110.00
Canister, Wildflower, Crackers, orig lid 175.00
Coffeepot, devil on body, emb Blanke's Coffeepot on lid, 9½" 350.00
Cookie jar, Basketweave, Put Your Fist In, orig lid, 7½" 350.00
Cookie jar, Brickers, orig lid 245.00
Cookie jar, Flying Birds, orig lid 350.00
Cup & saucer, Flowerpot, deep, ca 1820 ....125.00
Humidor, stippled w/bird dog on side, flower finial, w/lid 150.00
Mug, advertising 150.00
Mug, Basketweave 95.00
Mug, Cattails 125.00
Mug, Diffused Bl 75.00
Mug, Flying Bird 175.00
Mug, golfer, bl/gray, Robinson Clay Products 150.00
Mug, plain 65.00
Mug, Windy City (Fannie Flagg), Robinson Clay Products 150.00
Pickle crock, Bl Bands, advertising, bail hdl, 5-gal 150.00
Pie plate, Star Mfg 145.00
Pitcher, Acorns 115.00

Pitcher, American Beauty Rose, 10" 175.00
Pitcher, Apricot, 8" 150.00
Pitcher, Barrel, +6 mugs 395.00
Pitcher, Basketweave & Flowers 175.00
Pitcher, Bl Band, plain 80.00
Pitcher, Bl Band Scroll 160.00
Pitcher, Bl Sawtooth, Wht Hall 95.00
Pitcher, Bow Tie 135.00
Pitcher, Butterfly, 4¾" 245.00
Pitcher, Butterfly, 9x7" 250.00
Pitcher, Castle & Fishscale, 8" 195.00
Pitcher, Cattails, 7½" 160.00
Pitcher, Cattails, 9" 155.00
Pitcher, Cattails & Butterfly 150.00
Pitcher, Cherry Cluster 225.00
Pitcher, Cosmos 195.00
Pitcher, Cow 175.00

Pitchers, Diffused Blue, 8¾", $100.00; American Beauty Rose, 9", $175.00.

Pitcher, Doe & Fawn 250.00
Pitcher, Dutch Boy & Girl 160.00
Pitcher, Dutch Landscape, stenciled, tall 150.00
Pitcher, Eagle 450.00
Pitcher, Eagle w/Shield & Arrows, rare 495.00
Pitcher, Edelweiss, flower on gray bkground, M 90.00
Pitcher, Edelweiss, no flower 175.00
Pitcher, Fishscale & Wild Rose, sm 95.00
Pitcher, flat iron bldg/girl, Robinson Clay Products, 8½" 185.00
Pitcher, Flowers, stenciled 100.00
Pitcher, Flying Bird 495.00
Pitcher, Grape Cluster on Trellis, 8½" 155.00
Pitcher, Grapes on Waffle 165.00
Pitcher, Grapes w/Rickrack, 8" 150.00
Pitcher, Hunting Scene, rare 300.00
Pitcher, Indian Boy & Girl 225.00
Pitcher, Indian Head in War Bonnet, waffled body, 8", EX 250.00
Pitcher, Leaping Deer 225.00
Pitcher, Lincoln w/Log Cabin 450.00
Pitcher, Lovebird, arc bands, deep color, 8½" 325.00
Pitcher, Lovebird, pale color, 8½" 175.00
Pitcher, Morning-Glory 150.00
Pitcher, Poinsettia, 6½" 250.00
Pitcher, Rose & Fishscale, 6" 165.00
Pitcher, Scroll & Leaf, advertising 250.00
Pitcher, Stag & Pine Trees, 9" 295.00

Pitcher, Swan, long beak, arched neck, deep color, 8½" 250.00
Pitcher, Swirl..155.00
Pitcher, tavern scene, Flemish Jugs...Kinney & Levan, 9" 165.00
Pitcher, Tulip...225.00
Pitcher, Wild Rose..275.00
Pitcher, Wildflower, stenciled...185.00
Pitcher, Windmill & Bush, 7"..165.00
Pitcher, 2 old men w/canes, dog's-head spout, Germany, 11" 200.00
Potty, Beaded Rose 110.00
Rolling pin, lg swirl 475.00
Rolling pin, Wildflower...200.00
Salt crock, Apricot, orig lid 135.00
Salt crock, Blackberry, orig lid 145.00
Salt crock, Butterfly, orig lid 185.00
Salt crock, Daisy on Snowflakes, orig lid 220.00
Salt crock, Eagle w/Arrow, orig lid......................................325.00
Salt crock, Flying Bird, orig lid 350.00
Salt crock, Grape on Basketweave, orig lid.............................150.00
Salt crock, Oak Leaf, orig lid 125.00
Salt crock, Peacock, orig lid 350.00
Salt crock, Wildflower, orig lid 250.00
Slop jar, Bow Tie 125.00
Slop jar, Fishscale & Wild Rose...150.00
Soap dish, Beaded Panels w/Open Rose.................................125.00
Soap dish, Beaded Rose 120.00
Soap dish, Fishscale w/Wild Rose...95.00
Soap dish, Indian in War Bonnet..195.00
Spittoon, Peacock & Fountain...245.00
Toothbrush holder, Bow Tie, stenciled flower............................50.00
Toothbrush holder, Fishscale & Wild Rose 70.00
Umbrella stand, oak leaves/animals emb, 21", NM.....................350.00
Vase, Swirl, cone shape 300.00
Wash set, Bow Tie, 2-pc...350.00
Wash set, Fishscale & Wild Rose, 5-pc 600.00
Wash set, Rose on Trellis, 2-pc 300.00
Water cooler, Apple Blossom...500.00
Water cooler, Bl Band, orig lid..150.00
Water cooler, Cupid, orig lid 600.00
Water cooler, Polar Bear, orig lid...500.00
Water cooler, Rachel at the Well, orig lid................................500.00

Blue Ridge

Blue Ridge dinnerware was produced by Southern Potteries of Erwin, Tennessee, from the late 1930s until 1956 in eight basic styles and eight hundred different patterns, all of which were hand decorated under the glaze. Vivid colors lit up floral arrangements of seemingly endless variation, fruit of every sort from simple clusters to lush assortments, barnyard fowl, peasant figures, and unpretentious textured patterns. Although it is these dinnerware lines for which they are best known, collectors prize the artist-signed plates from the forties and the limited line of character jugs made during the fifties most highly. Examples of the French Peasant pattern are valued at double the prices listed below; very simple patterns will bring 25% to 50% less.

Our advisors, Betty and Bill Newbound, have compiled a lovely book, *Blue Ridge Dinnerware*, Revised Third Edition, with beautiful color illustrations and current market values. They are listed in the Directory under Michigan. For information concerning the National Blue Ridge Newsletter, see the Clubs, Newsletters, and Catalogs section of the Directory.

Ash tray, advertising, w/rest 55.00
Ash tray, individual 13.00

Bonbon, divided, center hdls, china.......................................85.00
Bowl, cereal/soup; 6" 9.00
Bowl, divided, 8"...17.00
Bowl, fruit; 5"...4.00
Bowl, mixing; 8½"...28.00
Bowl, rnd, 8"..13.00
Bowl, salad; 10½"..45.00
Bowl, salad; 11½"..45.00
Bowl, soup; flat, 8"..10.00
Bowl, vegetable; divided, oval, 9"..22.50
Bowl, vegetable; oval, 9"...20.00
Box, candy; rnd w/lid..95.00
Box, cigarette..65.00
Box, cigarette; w/4 trays...110.00
Box, Mallard..300.00
Box, raised or sculptured designs 82.50
Box, Sherman Lily...450.00
Breakfast set..330.00
Butter dish, ¼-lb, w/lid...40.00
Butter pat/coaster..17.00
Cake lifter..22.50

Candy dish in the French Peasant pattern, 6" diameter, $170.00.

Carafe, w/lid..60.00
Casserole, w/lid..40.00
Celery, leaf shape, china 32.50
Celery, Skyline shape...28.00
Child's cereal bowl..28.00
Child's feeding dish, deep...30.00
Child's feeding dish, divided 28.00
Child's mug..17.00
Child's plate 28.00
Child's play set...240.00
Chocolate pot, pedestal, china...135.00
Coffeepot..100.00
Creamer, china...45.00
Creamer, demitasse..50.00
Creamer, regular...11.00
Cup & saucer, demitasse; china...30.00
Cup & saucer, regular 13.00
Dish, baking; 13x8"...27.50
Egg cup, dbl..20.00
Egg dish, deviled..32.50
Gravy boat 20.00
Gravy tray 17.00
Jug, batter; w/lid...65.00
Jug, character; china 475.00
Jug, syrup; w/lid...80.00

Lamp, china	110.00
Pie baker	25.00
Pitcher, fancy, china	95.00
Plate, aluminum edge, 12"	19.00
Plate, artist sgn, china	465.00
Plate, cake; 10½"	28.00
Plate, Christmas or Turkey	60.00
Plate, dinner; 10"	17.00
Plate, dinner; 9½"	10.00
Plate, party; w/cup well & cup	22.50
Plate, salad; bird decor, 8½"	50.00
Plate, snack; 3-compartment	17.00
Plate, sq, 7½"	9.00
Plate, 11½"	28.00
Plate, 6"	3.00
Platter, artist sgn, 17½"	770.00
Platter, Thanksgiving Turkey	195.00
Platter, Turkey w/Acorns	195.00
Platter, 11"	11.00
Platter, 12½"	17.00
Platter, 13"	17.00
Platter, 15"	22.00
Ramekin, w/lid, 5"	22.00
Ramekin, w/lid, 7½"	32.50
Relish, deep shell, china	50.00
Relish, heart shape, sm	35.00
Relish, loop hdl, china	65.00
Relish, Maple Leaf, china	45.00
Relish, Martha, 3-compartment, china	80.00
Relish, T-hdl, china	40.00
Salad fork	28.00
Salad spoon	28.00
Server, center hdl	28.00
Shakers, Apple, pr	11.00
Shakers, Blossom Top, pr	32.50
Shakers, Bud Top, pr	32.50
Shakers, Chickens, pr	90.00
Shakers, mallards, pr	150.00
Shakers, Moderne, pr	28.00
Shakers, Range, pr	32.50
Shakers, regular, short, pr	20.00
Sugar bowl, demitasse	28.00
Sugar bowl, ped or flare, china	45.00
Sugar bowl, regular, w/lid	13.00
Tea tile, rnd or sq	32.50
Teapot, china	80.00
Teapot, demitasse	80.00
Teapot, earthenware	70.00
Tidbit, 2-tier	30.00
Tidbit, 3-tier	32.50
Toast, covered	90.00
Tray, chocolate pot; china	385.00
Tray, flat shell, china	55.00
Vase, boot, 8"	70.00
Vase, bud	85.00
Vase, rnd, china, 5½"	60.00
Vase, ruffled top, 9¼"	80.00
Vase, tapered	85.00

Bluebird China

Made from 1910 to 1934, Bluebird china is lovely ware decorated with bluebirds flying among pink flowering branches. It was inexpen-sive dinnerware and reached the height of its popularity in the second decade of this century. Several potteries produced it; shapes differ from one manufacturer to another, but the decal remains basically the same. Among the backstamps you'll find W.S. George, Cleveland, Carrolton, Homer Laughlin, Limoges China of Sebring, Ohio; and there are others.

Bowl, fruit; Deerwood, 5½"	12.50
Bowl, fruit; Hopewell China, 5"	10.00
Bowl, gravy; w/saucer, Hopewell China	50.00
Bowl, sauce; SP Co, 4½"	10.00
Bowl, soup; PMC Co, 8"	25.00
Butter dish, 4½" holder w/in 7" dia dish, Steubenville	85.00
Casserole, w/lid, Ostro China, 10½" dia	95.00
Casserole, w/lid, SP Clinchfield, 8½" dia	85.00

Footed chocolate cup, 3½", $35.00.

Creamer & sugar bowl, w/lid, Homer Laughlin	45.00
Cup, coffee; unmk, 3½"	25.00
Plate, dessert; Limoges, 6"	8.00
Plate, Homer Laughlin, 8½"	10.00
Plate, National China, 8"	10.00
Plate, rtcl, sq, unmk, 9"	35.00
Platter, Homer Laughlin, 15½x10½"	75.00
Platter, Hopewell China, 17½x13"	95.00
Platter, Steubenville, 12¾x9½"	55.00
Platter, unmk, 9x7"	35.00
Sauce ladle, gold scrolling	25.00
Teapot, ELP Co, 8½x8½"	125.00

Boch Freres

Founded in the early 1840s in La Louviere, Boch Freres Keramos became the foremost producer of art pottery in Belgium. Though primarily they served a localized market, in 1844 they earned worldwide recognition for some of their sculptural works on display at the International Exposition in Paris.

In 1907 Charles Catteau of France was appointed head of the art department. Before that time, the firm had concentrated on developing glazes and perfecting elegant forms. The style they pursued was traditional, favoring the re-creation of established eighteenth-century ceramics. Catteau brought with him to Boch Freres the New Wave (or Art Nouveau) influence in form and decoration. His designs won him international acclaim at the Exhibition d'Art Decoratif in Paris in 1925, and it is for his work that Boch Freres is so highly regarded today. He occasionally signed his work as well as that of others who under his direct supervision carried out his preconceived designs. He was associated with the company until 1950 and lived the remainder of his life in Nice, France, where he died in 1966. The Boch Freres Keramis factory continues to operate today, producing bathroom fixtures and other utilitarian wares. A variety of marks have been used, all incorporating some combination of 'Boch Freres,' 'Keramis,' 'BFK,' or 'Ch Catteau.'

Vase, Delft, bl floral reserves, foo dog finial, 1930s, 16" 250.00
Vase, mc flowers on blk/yel panels, high hdls, 14" 285.00
Vase, mc flowers on crazed cream, C Catteau, ovoid, 10½" 300.00
Vase, mc stylized flowers on wht, bulbous, 6" 145.00
Vase, wide band of stylized cranes, C Catteau, ovoid, 36" 12,000.00

Vase, two stags and a doe, blue and black on crazed cream, designed by Catteau, 12½", $900.00.

Boehm

Boehm sculptures were the creation of Edward Marshall Boehm, a ceramic artist who coupled his love of the art with his love of nature to produce figurines of birds, animals, and flowers in lovely background settings accurate to the smallest detail. Sculptures of historical figures and those representing the fine arts were also made and along with many of the bird figurines, have established secondary-market values many times their original prices. His first pieces were made in the very early 1950s in Trenton, New Jersey, under the name of Osso Ceramics. Mr. Boehm died in 1969, and the firm has since been managed by his wife. Today known as Edward Marshall Boehm, Inc., the private family-held corporation produces not only porcelain sculptures but collector plates as well. Both limited and non-limited editions of their works have been issued. Examples are marked with various backstamps, all of which have incorporated the Boehm name since 1951. 'Osso Ceramics' in upper case lettering was used in 1950 and 1951.

Alec's Red Rose, #300-39 .... 1,250.00
American Redstarts, #40138.................................... 1,800.00
Black Rhinoceros 10,000.00
Blue Grosbeak w/Fall Foliage, 11" 1,300.00
Blue Nile Rose, #300-80 .... 1,450.00
Bobolink 1,400.00
Brown Thrasher 1,600.00
Cardinals, #415 .... 3,400.00
Cheetah.. 2,750.00

Common Tern 6,000.00
Downy Woodpeckers, #427 .... 1,500.00
Fallow Deer 7,200.00
Fledgling Canada Warbler, #491 .... 1,900.00
Golden-Crowned Kinglets, #419 .... 2,100.00
Hooded Warbler... 3,000.00
Hunter... 1,250.00

Kildeer Plover with Bluebells, 1964, 10", $1,500.00 at auction.

Lady Helen Rose, #30070 .... 1,500.00
Lapwing... 2,850.00
Magnolia Grandiflora, #300-12 .... 1,200.00
Mountain Bluebirds, #470..................................... 6,100.00
Mute Swans, sm, pr 7,800.00
Northern Water Thrush, #490.................................. 1,500.00
Orchard Orioles.. 2,000.00
Ptarmigans, #463, pr.. 3,200.00
Red Squirrels 2,650.00
Ring Neck Pheasants, #409, pr 1,500.00
Roy Hartley Begonia, #300-41................................. 1,500.00
Snow Buntings 2,800.00
Tiger Lilies, #30077 ....850.00
Towhee.. 2,500.00
Winter Robin... 1,350.00

Bohemian Glass

The term 'Bohemian glass' has come to refer to a type of glass developed in Bohemia in the late sixth century at the Imperial Court of Rudolf II, the Hapsburg Emperor. The popular artistic pursuit of the day was stone carving, and it naturally followed to transfer familiar procedures to the glassmaking industry. During the next century, a formula was discovered that produced a glass with a fine crystal appearance which lent itself well to deep, intricate engraving, and the art was further advanced.

Although many other types of art glass were made there, collectors today use the term 'Bohemian glass' to most often indicate clear glass overlaid with color through which a design is cut or etched. Red on crystal is common, but other colors may also be found. Another type of Bohemian glass involves cutting through and exposing three layers of color in patterns that are often very intricate. Items such as these are sometimes further decorated with enamel work.

Bowl, ruby, naturalistic scenes, 5x6" 100.00
Compote, lav, castle, deer & birds, 5¾" 75.00
Cruet, red, deer...100.00
Cruet, red, grapes, 5½" 75.00
Decanter, amber, deer & castle, 15" 95.00
Decanter, red, birds & monkeys, 11" 120.00
Decanter, red, deer & birds, 11" 100.00
Goblet, red, stags in forest, cut panels, 6½"................45.00
Jar, red, vintage/dmn & oval cuts, dome lid, 1800s, 16".....225.00
Jug, armorial; lt gr, opaque enameling, Egermann, 10¼" 1,850.00
Pokal, gr, HP horse & rider, jeweled, steeple stopper, 26"..600.00
Powder dish, red, bird in branches w/gold 65.00
Tumbler, bridal; olive-gr, coats-of-arms enameling, 7½", pr....1,000.00
Tumbler, red, florals & stripes, 3⅝"..........................58.00
Tumbler, ruby, draped flower bands 65.00
Urn, amber, nature scene, tall knob std w/eng base, 20" 1,200.00

Vases, ruby with etched stag in forest, 9½", $495.00 for the pair.

Vase, amber, vintage & mitres, bulbous, 6" 85.00
Vase, red, deer & forest, 10-panel petal top, ftd, 10".......135.00
Vase, red, triple dmn, scalloped, 10" 75.00
Vase, wht opaque cut to gr, HP florals w/gold, 9½" 225.00

Bookends

Though a few were produced before 1880, bookends became a necessary library accessory and a popular commodity after the printing industry was revolutionized by Mergenthaler's invention, the linotype. Books became abundantly available at such affordable prices that almost every home suddenly had need for bookends. They were carved from wood, cast in iron, bronze, or brass, or cut from stone. Today's collectors may find such designs as ships, animals, flowers, and children. Patriotic themes, art reproductions, and those with Art Nouveau and Art Deco styling provide a basis for a diverse and interesting collection.

Abe Lincoln, profile, bronze, 1880s-1900, 14-lb, pr 125.00
Amish couple seated, CI, 4½", pr..............................35.00
Blacksmith, bronze-plated iron, gilt traces, pr...............32.00
Boston Bulldog pup, iron, Hubley #409, 6x4½", pr.............100.00
Buccaneer, chalkware, sgn Herzel, pr.........................265.00
Cockatoo, cvd marble, glass eyes, pr.........................275.00
Dancer, Deco style, bronze, heavy, 7½", pr 150.00

Dutch boy and girl, Frankart, 5", $125.00.

Dante & Beatrice busts, mc pnt, Armor Bronze 68.00
End of Trail, bronzed metal, dtd 1930 ....42.00
Eve, nude, copper over CI, Verona, pr 95.00
Farmer & wife pray in field, wheelbarrow/pitchfork, bronze, pr....55.00
Football players, bronze over iron, ca 1920, 4x6", pr 75.00
Hartford Fire Insurance, solid bronze, dtd 1935, pr 100.00
Horse, bronze, after Rose Bonhear, pr 55.00
Horse, bronze over plaster, 8x8", pr..........................65.00
Horse, Frankart, pr...80.00
Horse's head, cvd alabaster, pr...............................85.00
Lady's head, bronze finish, Frankart, pr.....................155.00
Lincoln giving Gettysburg Address, bronzed metal, pr 45.00
Nude man wrestling lion, bronzed iron, Deco style, 6", pr 40.00
Nude on rearing horse, glass, 6", pr..........................65.00
Old Ironsides, copper-plated CI, heavy, 5", pr................60.00
Oriental man & lady in ornate dress, bronze, pr...............55.00
Owl, buff & brn pnt CI, pr....................................65.00
Parrots, copper clad, heavy, 5½x6¼", pr 55.00
Race car w/goggled driver, brass plated, pr...................69.00
Roman soldier w/horse, CI, Deco style, pr 30.00
Scottie dog, CI, orig blk pnt, pr 65.00
Scottie dog, Frankart, pr....................................150.00
Scottie dog, spelter, pr......................................35.00
Ship, Viking w/Spirit of St Louis overhead, bronze, 4½", pr....95.00
Spanish galleon in full sail, CI, EX mc pnt, 4½", pr 40.00
Teddy Roosevelt, bronze, sgn Gregory Allen, pr 375.00
Teddy Roosevelt, copper-plated CI, pr.........................65.00
Terrier, Frankart, pr 125.00
Terrier, seated, gilt pnt iron, pr...........................22.50
Wire-haired terrier, CI, mc pnt, 6x6½x2¼", pr 70.00

Bootjacks and Bootscrapers

Bootjacks were made from metal or wood — some were fancy figural shapes, others strictly business! Their purpose was to facilitate the otherwise awkward process of removing one's boots. Bootscrapers were handy gadgets that provided an effective way to clean the soles of mud and such.

Bootjacks

Beetle-shaped jaws, CI, no pnt, ca 1880 ....38.00
Boss emb on shaft, lacy CI, 15" L 135.00
Cricket, CI, 12"..35.00

Fish (stylized), cvd wood, worn finish, 22" L 115.00
Hickory, bentwood hdl, hinged/folds, use w/out bending over.......75.00
Lever action, wood/CI, EX 130.00
Musselman's Boot-Jack Plug Tobacco, CI, sunflower decor 150.00
Naughty Nellie, mc pnt, 10", EX 205.00
Naughty Nellie, pnt traces, 1890s, 9x4x2½" 85.00
V-shape, ornate CI, VG...45.00
Wood, simple form, orig red pnt, EX..40.00

Bootscrapers

Aunt Jemima figure atop, CI, rpt, 14½" 250.00
Baroque scrollwork, CI, set in marble block, 14" 80.00
Cat walking, CI, open heart-shaped eye, tail up, 1800s, 10x10" ..395.00
Dachshund, CI, old worn wht pnt, 1900s, 22x7x5".....................225.00
Pig silhouette, cut-out eye, CI, 8½x12" 195.00
Salem witch on broom, worn orig pnt, 1800s 375.00
Scottie dog, CI, orig pnt, EX 65.00
Wrought iron, simple uprights w/scooped blade set in stone........125.00
2 quail ea end, CI, rectangular pan, pnt traces, 7x16" 275.00

Boru, Sorcha

Sorcha Boru was the professional name used by California ceramist Claire Stewart. She was a founding member of the Allied Arts Guild of Menlo Park (California) where she maintained a studio from 1932 to 1938. From 1938 until 1955, she operated Sorcha Boru Ceramics, a production studio in San Carlos. Her highly-acclaimed output consisted of colorful, slip-decorated figurines, salt and pepper shakers, vases, wall pockets, and flower bowls. Most production work was incised 'S.B.C.' by hand.

Figurine, angel with Christmas tree, 6", $75.00.

Figurine, Blue Jay, bl, 6½" 165.00
Figurine, Penelope, recumbent fawn, 6"..50.00
Pitcher, pk lustre florals w/gold centers, beading, 6½"....................65.00
Shakers, fat king & queen, 1940s, 5", pr 75.00
Shakers, fawns, turq, sm, pr 45.00

Bottle Openers

Around the turn of the century, manufacturers began to seal bottles with a metal cap that required a new type of bottle opener. Now the screw cap and the flip top have made bottle openers nearly obsolete. There are many variations, some in combination with other tools. Many openers were used as means of advertising a product. Various materials were used including silver and brass.

A figural bottle opener is defined as a figure designed for the sole purpose of lifting a bottle cap. The actual opener must be an integral part of the figure itself. The major producers of iron figurals were Wilton Products, John Wright Inc., Gadzik Sales, and L & L Favors. Openers may be free-standing and three-dimensional, wall hung, or flat. They can be made of cast iron (often painted), brass, bronze, or aluminum.

Those seeking additional information concerning figural bottle openers are encouraged to contact the Figural Bottle Opener Collectors, whose address can be found in the Directory under Clubs, Newsletters, and Catalogs.

Alligator, open mouth, CI, worn mc pnt, 6" L...............................50.00
Alligator w/head up, CI, EX pnt...95.00
Beer drinker, Iron Art, wall mt, EX..35.00
Blk boy & alligator, CI, Wilton 140.00
Blk man, CI, EX pnt, wall hanging, Wilton 100.00
Bottle figural, Pabst Blue Ribbon advertising, old 20.00
Boy winking, toothy grin, CI, wall mt 650.00
Bull's head, curved tail hdl, CI, 5"..30.00
Cockatoo, CI, VG orig pnt 155.00
Cow, CI w/wood hdl, worn pnt 65.00
Cowboy at signpost, CI, NM..120.00
Donkey, wide ears, CI, EX pnt 35.00
Drunk, wall mt, Wilton, MIB..50.00
Drunk on palm tree, CI, EX pnt, John Wright Co............................50.00
Fish, CI, worn pnt..75.00
Flamingo, CI, EX pnt..90.00
Foundryman, aluminum..15.00
Foundryman, CI..90.00
Goat, brass..40.00
Goat, horns are opener, CI, EX pnt, 4½" 55.00
Horse's head, metal..15.00
Lady's leg, aluminum, Italy 18.00
Lady's leg, Emporia Bottling Works, flat steel................................27.50
Lobster, CI, EX orig red pnt, 3½" L..35.00
Mallard duck, CI, EX pnt 60.00
Mr Snifter, mechanical, EX...95.00
Nude, arms above head, 4" 30.00
Nude, Fink Brewing, Harrisburg PA 12.00
Palm tree, brass..25.00
Parrot, chrome, w/corkscrew, 5"...65.00
Parrot, CI, EX pnt, w/can punch 85.00
Pelican, CI, EX pnt, 3½" 50.00

Figural pheasant head, cast metal painted in natural colors, opener in base, 2½", $85.00.

Ram, CI, 4" 22.00
Sea horse, brass 25.00
Siamese dancing man, brass.....................................22.00
Squirrel on log, CI w/EX pnt, 2"..............................75.00
Teeth, full set, pnt CI, wall mt 69.00
Tennis racquet, brass 20.00
Truck shape, Grimm Bros Auto Glass........................20.00
4-Eyed man, CI, G pnt, Wilton 50.00
4-Eyed man, CI, worn pnt, John Wright Co, EX...........50.00

Bottles and Flasks

As far back as the first century B.C., the Romans preferred blown glass containers for their pills and potions. Though you're not apt to find many of those, you will find bottles of every size, shape, and color made to hold perfume, ink, medicine, soda, spirits, vinegar, and many other liquids. American business firms preferred glass bottles in which to package their commercial products and used them extensively from the late eighteenth century on. Bitters bottles contained 'medicine' (actually herb-flavored alcohol); and, judging from the number of these found today, their contents found favor with many! Because of a heavy tax imposed on the sale of liquor in seventeenth-century England by King George, who hoped to curtail alcohol abuse among his subjects, bottlers simply added 'curative' herbs to their brew and thus avoided taxation. Since gin was taxed in America as well, the practice continued in this country. Scores of brands were sold; among the most popular were Dr. H.S. Flint & Co. Quaker Bitters, Dr. Kaufman's Anti-Cholera Bitters, and Dr. J. Hostetter's Stomach Bitters. Most bitters bottles were made in shades of amber, brown, and aquamarine. Clear glass was used to a lesser extent, as were green tones. Blue, amethyst, red-brown, and milk glass examples are rare.

Perfume or scent bottles were produced abroad by companies all over Europe from the late sixteenth century on. Perfume making became such a prolific trade that as a result, beautifully decorated bottles were fashionable. In America they were produced in great quantities by Stiegel in 1770 and by Boston and Sandwich in the early nineteenth century. Cologne bottles were first made in about 1830 and toilet-water bottles in the 1880s. Rene Lalique produced fine scent bottles from as early as the turn of the century. The earliest were one-of-a-kind creations with silver casings. He later designed bottles for the Coty Perfume Company with a different style for each Coty fragrance. Prices for commercial perfumes vary according to condition, whether it is sealed and full, and has the original label and most of the original packaging or box. Deluxe versions bring premium prices. Example: blue flat Dans La Nuit cologne by Rene Lalique, value 6" size, $250.00. Dans La Nuit, enameled with stars by Rene Lalique, 3" round ball, $900.00.

Spirit flasks from the nineteenth century were blown in specially designed molds with varied motifs including political subjects, railroad trains, and symbolic devices. The most commonly-used colors were amber, dark brown, and green.

From the twentieth century, early pop and beer bottles are very collectible, as is nearly every extinct commercial container.

Bottles may be dated by the methods used in their production. For instance, a rough pontil indicates a date before 1845. The iron pontil, used from then until about 1860, left a metallic residue on the base of the bottle, which is evident upon examination. A seam that reaches from base to lip marks a machine-made bottle from after 1903, while an applied or hand-finished lip points to an early mold-blown bottle. The Industrial Revolution saw keen competition between manufacturers; and, as a result, scores of patents were issued. Many concentrated on various types of closures; the crown bottle cap, for instance, was patented in 1892. If a manufacturer's name is present, consulting a book on marks may help you date your bottle.

Among our advisors for this category are Madeleine France (see the Directory under Florida), Mark Vuono (Connecticut), and Steve Ketcham (Minnesota). In the listings that follow (most of which have been taken from auction catalogs), glass is assumed to be clear unless color is indicated. Numbers refer to a standard reference book, *American Glass*, by George and Helen McKearin. See also Advertising, various companies; Avon; Barber Shop Collectibles; Blown Glass; Blown Three-Mold Glass; California Perfume Company; Czechoslovakia; De Vilbiss; Fire Fighting; Lalique; Medical Collectibles; Steuben.

Key:
am — applied mouth	GW — Glass Works
bbl — barrel	ip — iron pontil
bt — blob top	ps — pontil scar
b3m — blown 3-mold	rm — rolled mouth
cm — collared mouth	sb — smooth base
fm — flared mouth	sl — sloping
gm — ground mouth	sm — sheared mouth
gp — graphite pontil	tm — tooled mouth

Barber Bottles

Amethyst, mc florals, 7¾" 160.00
Bay Rum on mc under-glass label on milk glass, 10" 275.00
Bl opaque w/HP bird & flowers, 8¾" 425.00
Coin Spot, cranberry opal, 7¼" 140.00
Cranberry, 8 cut panels, silver cap, lg 150.00
CS Fay on blk & gold under-glass label on milk glass, 6½" 140.00
Hobnail, cranberry w/clear rigaree, 7" 175.00
Honey amber, cut flutes & circles, sheared lip 110.00
Honey amber satin, T Noonan...Boston Mass 110.00
Invt T'print, amber w/enameling, 8" 160.00
JV Rice Tonic label under glass, pretty girl, orig cap, 8" 475.00
Lav cut o/l, pewter top, 5½", M...................................60.00
M Snell Bay Rum/HP floral on milk glass, orig cap, 10" 325.00
Milk glass w/HP cherubs & flowers, am/ps, tooled lip, 8"..............350.00
Sapphire bl, HP flowers & leaves w/gold, bbl shape 195.00
Seaweed, bl opal, lg 185.00
Wht opal reversed raised swirls, rolled lip.....................125.00

Bitters Bottles

African Stomach, amber, am/sb, minor wear/haze, 9½" 30.00
Bourbon Whiskey, med puce, am/sb, stain/wear, 9" 160.00
Bourbon Whiskey, med strawberry-puce, am/sb, 9⅜" 235.00
Brn's Celebrated Indian Herb Pat 1868, yel-amber, 12", NM 350.00
Brn's Iron, Brn Chemical Co, amber, am/sb, 8⅝" 30.00
California Fig, CA Extract of Fig Co, amber, tm/sb, 9¾" 25.00
Canton, med amber, emb star, am/sb, 12" 325.00
Carmeliter for All Kidney & Liver Complaints, amber, 10" 40.00
Celebrated Crown, F Chevalier & Co, amber, am/sb, 8⅞" 180.00
David Andrews Vegetable Jaundice, aqua, crude collar, 8"..........460.00
DeWitt's Stomach, Chicago, amber, tm/sb, 9¼".............................25.00
Doyles Hop, 1872, amber, emb hop berries, 10"..............................30.00
Dr Blake's Aromatic, NY, aqua, am/ps, 7⅜" 300.00
Dr Harter's Wild Cherry, Dayton O, amber, tm/sb, 8" 65.00
Dr Harter's Wild Cherry, St Louis, amber, am/sb, 7½" 25.00
Dr J Hostetter's Stomach, dk olive, am/sb, 9½" 95.00
Dr J Hostetter's Stomach, yel-amber, am/sb, lt stain, 9" 40.00
Dr LG Bertram's Long Life Aromatic & Stomach, amber, 9½" ...250.00
Dr Manly Hardy Genuine Jaundice, Bangor ME, aqua, am/ps, 7" ..175.00
ER Clarke's Sarsaparilla, Sharon MA, aqua, am/ps, 7½".............225.00
Fish, WH Ware Pat 1866, amber, rm/sb, 12" 135.00
German Tonic, Boggs Cottman & Co, aqua, am/ip, 9¾" 625.00

Greeley's Bourbon, med olive-gr, am/sb, 9" 575.00
Greeley's Bourbon Whiskey, med puce, am/sb, stain, 9½" 275.00

Greer's Eclipse Bitters, Louisville KY, yellow-amber, smooth base, applied mouth, $140.00; Hall's Bitters, E. E. Hall, New Haven, Established 1842, yellow-amber, smooth base, applied mouth, light inside stain, $120.00.

Hall's, EE Hall New Haven Estb 1842, orange-amber, 9" 170.00
Holtzermann's Patent Stomach, amber, tm/sb, 9¾" 180.00
Hutchings Dyspepsia, NY, aqua, am/ip, 8½" 275.00
Johnson's Indian Dyspeptic, aqua, am/ps, 6¾" 350.00
Kimball's Jaundice, Troy NH, olive-amber, am/ip, 7" 325.00
King Solomon's, Seattle WA, amber, tm/sb, 8¼" 80.00
Marshall's, Best Laxative & Blood Purifier, amber, tm, 9" 50.00
National, amber, am/sb, seedy glass, 12" 190.00
Only 75 Cts Clarke's Vegetable Sherry Wine, aqua, 11", EX 150.00
Oswego, 25 Cents, amber, tm/sb, 7" 75.00
Peruvian, KW (in shield monogram), amber, am/ps, seedy, 9".......75.00
Pineapple, W & Co, amber, pineapple form, stain, 8½" 300.00
Prune Stomach & Liver, Best Cathartic..., amber, tm/sb, 9" 70.00
Red Jacket, Bennett Pieters & Co, amber, am/sb, lt haze, 9"..........55.00
ST Drake's Plant'n X 1862, amber, 6-log, lt stain, 10" 45.00
ST Drake's Plant'n X 1862, med amber, 4-log, 10".......................50.00
ST Drake's Plant'n X 1862, med puce, 6-log, 9¾" 95.00
ST Drake's Plant'n X 1862, puce, 6-log, 10" 80.00
ST Drake's Plant'n X 1862, yel-amber, 6-log, am, 10", NM...........80.00

Blown Glass Bottles and Flasks

Beehive flask, aqua, swirl to right, am/ps, lt wear, 9" 130.00
Chestnut bottle, dk olive, am/ps, NE, 1800s, 5½" 160.00
Chestnut bottle, olive-amber, sl cm/ps, 10" 150.00
Chestnut flask, olive-gr, crude lip, ps, NE, 5" 140.00
Chestnut flask, red-amber, 24 broken rib left swirl, 4⅝" 450.00
Chestnut flask, yel-amber, 18 rib right swirl, sm/ps, 6½" 325.00
Chestnut flask, yel-olive, 24 vertical ribs, sm/ps, 5" 850.00
Decanter, GII-18, b3m, type-2 stopper, lt int haze, qt....................100.00
Decanter, GIII-2, b3m, flaring lip, NE, qt....................................175.00
Decanter, GIII-5, type-2 stopper, ps, NE, qt 150.00

Decanter, GIII-6, flaring lip, ps, pt 150.00
Decanter, GV-9, b3m, ps, lt stain, qt 100.00
Flask, med olive-gr, 20 vertical melon ribs, sm/ps, pt 145.00
Globular, aqua, 18-rib left swirl, am/ps, mfg flaw, 7⅜" 160.00
Globular, lt olive, appl ring below lip, ps, lt stain, 3⅞" 225.00
Globular, olive-amber, crudely appl ring lip, 11x9"......................275.00
Ludlow, med yel-amber w/dk swirled striations, am/ps, 9"...........240.00
Pitkin flask, apple gr, broken swirl, sm/ps, pt 1,600.00
Pitkin flask, aqua-gr, 32-rib broken swirl, sm/ps, pt....................400.00
Pitkin flask, forest gr, 16-rib broken swirl, lt stain, pt...................375.00
Pitkin flask, lt gr, 32 broken rib left swirl, 6¾" 375.00
Pitkin flask, med gr, broken left swirl, sm/ps, pt..........................350.00
Pitkin flask, olive, broken right swirl, sm crack, ½-pt 175.00

Cologne, Perfume, and Toilet Water Bottles

Amethyst, 16-rib right swirl, 2-pc mold, sm/ps, 2⅞" 175.00
Bl, clear ft/4 vertical bands of rigaree, 1820, 2¾", NM.................425.00

Blue cut overlay colognes, 9", NM, $200.00; 7", M, $300.00.

Canary yel, McKearin 241-28, NM...125.00
Cobalt, tam-o'-shanter stopper, Sandwich type, lt stain, 6½" 200.00
Cobalt, 6-petal inverted flower form base, emb CB, 4" 90.00
Cranberry, eng floral band w/gold, cut stopper, 4x2¾"................125.00
Cut Dmn Panel, ruby overshot w/gold & mica, sterling lid, 3" 225.00
Gr, mc coat of arms & florals, gr ball stopper, 2x1½" 60.00
Gr satin w/florals & gold, lay-down, sterling cap, 4¾" 385.00
Med bl-gray, molded, 12-panel, rm/ps, MA, 1840, 4¼"...............175.00
Milk glass, beaded rib pattern, Am, 1880s, 10" 85.00
Monument, milk glass, tm/sb, 12" 110.00
Powder horn, ruby, grooved pattern, sterling cap ea end, 4" 125.00
Rubena, cut panels & stopper, 6⅞x2¼" 85.00
Sapphire bl w/HP florals & dots, bl ball stopper, 6½x2" 125.00
Sapphire bl w/opal swirls, concave side, pewter top, 2⅝" 250.00
Sea horse, opaque wht, ribbed, 2¾", NM 50.00
St Louis, cvd floral, red on lt gr, faceted neck, 7" 600.00
Sunburst, dk bl-purple, 12 beads on edges/12 rays, 2¾" 300.00
Teal, 12-sided, sloped shoulders, att Sandwich, 5" 210.00
Teal, 26 vertical ribs, sm/polished pontil, Am, 1880s, 2" 65.00

Figural Bottles

Bear, seated, milk glass, 11" 70.00

Boot, Saratoga Dressing, aqua, tm, 4½" 20.00
Broom, ceramic, Dust Remover emb, wht/bl/brn, 6" 50.00
Bunker Hill Monument, cologne, Am, 1880s, 12" 25.00
Coachman, Van Dunck's Genever Trade Mark, dk amber, 8½" ..125.00
Elk's bust w/clock in antlers, EX orig pnt, 12" 75.00
Elk's tooth, wht porc, brn clock face/elk/BPOE, 4½" 45.00
Fireman (or policeman), gm/sb, 8½" 65.00
Hessian soldier, Am, 1900, 7" 40.00
Kummer Bear, milk glass, am/sb, 11" 75.00
Pig, lt amethyst, Drink While It Lasts, whiskey, Am, 6¾" 175.00

Figural bottle of Prizefighter Bob Fitzsimmons, flesh-colored opaque glass upper body on clear frosted lower torso, painted features, smooth base, ground lip, 15", $1,150.00.

Seeing Eye, bk: Eye Opener, milk glass w/mc pnt, 5" 160.00
Skull, cobalt, Xd bones on base, Poison, 4", NM 1,300.00

Flasks

Baltimore GW/Sheaf of Grain, GXIII-48, aqua, ip, qt 125.00
Baltimore Monument/Fells Point, GI-20, aqua, sm/ps, pt 90.00
Baltimore Monument/Fells Point, GVI-2, very lt aqua, ½-pt.......275.00
Baltimore Monument/Liberty Union, GVI-3, aqua, sm/ps, pt 275.00
Benjamin Franklin/TW Dyott, GI-94, lt aqua, sm/ps, pt 120.00
Clasped Hands/Eagle, GXII-18, aqua, am/sb, pt, EX 30.00
Columbia-Kensington/Eagle-Union, GI-118, lt yel-gr, ½-pt ... 2,150.00
Columbia/Eagle (portrait), aqua, EX impression, sm/ps, pt 260.00
Cornucopia & Lancaster GW/Urn, GIII-16, teal, pt, NM...........275.00
Cornucopia/Urn, GIII-4, teal-gr, sm/ps, Coventry, pt.................225.00
Cornucopia/Urn, GIII-7, dk olive-gr, am/sb, ½-pt.....................160.00
Dbl Eagle, GII-24, bright med gr, sm/ps (w/chip), pt................900.00
Dbl Eagle, GII-24, sapphire, sm/ps, att KY GW, pt 2,500.00
Dbl Eagle, GII-26, ice bl, sm/ip, att KY GW, qt 300.00
Dbl Eagle, GII-70, olive-amber, sm/ps, pt 225.00
Dbl Eagle, GII-86, dk olive-amber, sm/ps, ½-pt.........................75.00
Dbl Eagle, GII-87, olive, bubbly, sm/ps, ½-pt.........................150.00
Eagle, GII-65, olive-amber, narrow rnd collar, sb, ½-pt 150.00
Eagle & Pittsburgh PA/Eagle, GII-106, olive-amber, pt 140.00
Eagle-Furled Flag/For Our Country, GII-52, aqua, sm/ps, pt 65.00
Eagle/Cornucopia, GII-11, aqua, sm/ps, ½-pt 140.00
Eagle/Cornucopia, GII-11A, lt yel-gr, sm/ps, ½-pt 750.00

Eagle/Cornucopia, GII-58, med yel-olive, rare, ½-pt **4,150.00**
Eagle/Eagle, GII-26, gray-clambroth, sm/ps, qt............................**650.00**
Eagle/Liberty & Oak Tree, GII-60, amber, very lt wear, ½-pt ... **1,000.00**
Eagle/Liberty & Oak Tree, GII-60, aqua, sm/ps, ½-pt **400.00**
Eagle/Oak Tree, GII-60, dk gold-amber, sm/ps, ½-pt..............**1,600.00**
Flora Temple, GXIII-24, puce, crudely am/sb, lt stain, pt **200.00**
For Pike's Peak & Prospector/bk plain, GXI-2, aqua, pt **35.00**
Gen WA/Eagle (portrait), GI-1, lt bl-gr, sm/ps, pt.....................**500.00**
Gen WA/WA & Eagle, GI-1, dk aqua, sm/ps, lt wear, pt **325.00**
Gen WA/WA & Eagle, GI-15, aqua, sm/ps, lt wear, pt **130.00**
Gen'l Taylor/Fells Point, GI-73, dk amethyst, pt, NM **3,000.00**
Hunter/Fisherman, GXIII-4, apricot, am/ip, calabash, NM..........**230.00**
Jenny Lind/Glass Factory, GI-104, bl-aqua, am/ip, calabash **95.00**
Jenny Lind/Glass Factory, GI-104, sapphire, ip, calabash........ **1,250.00**
Kossuth (portrait), BI-113, olive-yel, ps, qt calabash....................**265.00**
Lafayette Coventry CT/Liberty Cap, GI-85, olive-yel, pt............**400.00**
Lafayette/DeWitt Clinton, GI-80, olive, sm/ps, pt, EX **400.00**
Masonic/Eagle, GII-7, med gr-aqua, heavy cm/ps, pt.................**475.00**
Masonic/Eagle, GIV-18, olive-amber, sm/ps, Keene, pt **160.00**
Masonic/Eagle, GIV-19, gold-amber, sm/ps, Keene, pt **120.00**

Masonic-Eagle flask, GIV-7, medium olive-green, tooled lip, pontil scar, pint, NM, $550.00.

Masonic/Zanesville, Eagle & J Shepard, GIV-32, gr-aqua, pt **210.00**
Monument, Balto/Fells Point & Sailboat, GVI-2, olive, ½-pt .. **2,900.00**
Sailboat/Star, GX-9, med gr-aqua, sm/ps, ½-pt, NM...................**225.00**
Scroll, GIX-10, dk olive, sm/ps, pt...**350.00**
Scroll, GIX-2, cobalt, EX color, sm/ps, qt.............................. **1,650.00**
Success to the RR, GII-5, gold-amber, sm/ps, int haze, pt **150.00**
Success to the RR, GII-6, dk olive-amber, sm/ps, pt **200.00**
Success to the RR, GV-1, ice bl, sm/ps, pt.................................**300.00**
Success to the RR, GV-5, amber, pt **160.00**
Success to the RR, GV-5, dk forest gr, sm/ps, NY, pt.................**400.00**
Summer Tree/Summer Tree, GX-17, bright yel, am/sb, pt **950.00**
Summer Tree/Winter Tree, GX-16, aqua, beveled collar, ½-pt **50.00**
Summer Tree/Winter Tree, GX-19, yel to topaz, qt.....................**975.00**
Sunburst, GVIII-10, olive-amber, sm/ps, Keene NH, ½-pt **220.00**
Sunburst, GVIII-11, med gr w/yel, ½-pt **1,250.00**
Sunburst, GVIII-14, med gr w/bl tint, Keene, sm/ps, ½-pt...........**850.00**
Sunburst, GVIII-16, olive, sm/ps, Coventry GW, ½-pt **400.00**
Sunburst, GVIII-26, aqua, thin, EX impression, sm/ps, pt...........**310.00**
Sunburst, GVIII-3, olive, sm w/flared lip, ps, pt **275.00**

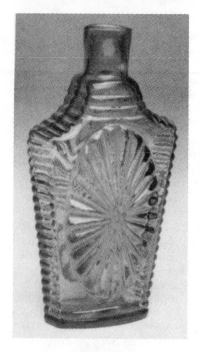

Sunburst flask, GVIII-2, sheared lip, pontil scar, pint, NM, $300.00.

Sunburst, GVIII-5A, lt olive, sm/ps, att Pitkin GW, pt........... 1,000.00
Sunburst, GVIII-8, olive-amber, sm/ps, Keene, pt, NM 300.00
Sunburst-P&W/Sunburst-Keene, GVIII-9, aqua, rare, ½-pt........775.00
Union & Clasped Hands/Eagle, GXII-34, aqua, am/sb, ½-pt 50.00
Washington/Taylor, GI-39, med pk-amethyst, qt 2,700.00
Washington/Taylor, GI-42, aqua, dbl cm/ps, qt 80.00
Washington/Taylor, GI-43, smoky mauve, sm/ps, qt 1,200.00
Washington/Taylor, GI-51, med bl-gr, dbl cm, qt.......................210.00
Washington/Taylor, GI-54, lt to med teal-bl, am/ps, qt...............200.00
Westford Glass Co/Sheaf of Wheat, GXIII-36, red-amber, pt 150.00

Food Bottles and Jars

B&D, aqua, emb, str-sided bbl form, ps, 5¼" 170.00
Mustard, GIII-23, b3m, ps, 5½", NM 175.00
Peppersauce, aqua, cathedral, emb cross/tassel, sq, 9½".................70.00

Pickle jars, Wm. Underwood Co., Boston, medium blue-green, open pontil, rolled lip, 11", NM, $375.00; Cathedral panels, aqua, smooth base, rolled lip, 11½", $75.00.

Pickle, aqua, cathedral w/embossing over arches, 9" 70.00
Pickle, aqua, 4 arch panels/emb floral sprig, tm/ps, 13" 190.00

Ink Bottles

B3m, GII-18, yel-amber, 1¾x2⅝" dia 275.00
Carter's, cobalt, cathedral, EX labels & cap................................135.00
Cottage, aqua, emb doors/windows/X-hatched roof, 2½", EX 45.00
David's, med amber, dome (turtle) top, sm/sb, 1⅞" 325.00
House form, aqua, sq w/rnded shoulders, Am, 1880s, 6½" 650.00
Locomotive, aqua, ground lip, 2" 500.00
Olive, b3m, Keene, 1⅜x2¼" 125.00
Olive-amber, cylindrical, am/ps, crude, Am, 1830s, 6" 65.00
Teakettle, amethyst, 8-sided, sb, no cap, 2" 400.00
Teakettle, clear, pointed domed top, tooled/sm, 2¼" 230.00
Teakettle, cobalt, ground lip, sb, minor lip chipping, 2" 425.00
Teakettle, sapphire, ground sm/sb, 2" 425.00

Teakettle ink, yellow-amber, original cap, 2¼", M, $500.00.

Umbrella, aqua, 8-sided, James S Mason, rm/ps, 2½" 150.00
Umbrella, bl-gr, 8-sided, 80% label: Steel Pen Ink, 2½"................90.00
Umbrella, lt-med emerald, 6-sided, 2½" 90.00
Umbrella, orange-amber, 8-sided, sm/ps, 2½x2¼" 160.00
WE Bonney, aqua, bbl form, tm/sb, orig label, 2⅝" 95.00

Medicine Bottles

American Cough Drops, thick flared rm/ps, 5¼" 160.00
B Denton Healing Balsam, aqua, 8-sided, am/ps, 4" 35.00
Bach's American Compound Auburn, aqua, am/ip, 7⅜"..................80.00
Baker's Celery Kola Phil Blumauer Portland Ore, amber, 10"......65.00
Bonpland's Fever & Ague Remedy NY, aqua, am/ps, 5"..................30.00
Bowman's Vegetable Compound New Castle PA, dk aqua, 8" 230.00
Brant's Purifying Extract MT Wallace, aqua, am/ps, 10".............100.00
Bromo Seltzer, cobalt, measuring cap, 5" 9.00
C Mathewson's Remedy, aqua, rectangular, am/ps, 7" 75.00
Clarke's/Lincoln/World Famed Blood Mixture, gray-bl, 7" 30.00
Clemens Indian Tonic Prepared by Geo W House, aqua, 5⅝" 350.00
CS Thurber Arnold's Vital Fluid, aqua, am/ps, 7" 120.00
Dr Carter's Compound, aqua, flared lip, ps, 5"..............................50.00
Dr Gordak's Iceland Jelly, aqua, wide rm/ps, 6¾" 120.00
Dr H Swayne's Compound Syrup of Wild Cherry, aqua, 6" 100.00
Dr Ham's Aromatic Invigorating Spirit NY, aqua, am/ip, 8½" 100.00
Dr J M'Clintock's Family Medicines, am/ps, NM label, 5" 75.00
Dr J M'Clintock's Family Medicines, am/ps, 8½" 55.00
Dr Pinkham's Emmenagogue, dk aqua, am/ps, 6", NM...................60.00
Dr Throop's Syrup of Blood Root Scranton PA, aqua, 6½" 275.00
Dr Tobias Venetian Horse Liniment NY, aqua, am/ps, 8" 45.00
Dr Wistar's Balsam of Wild Cherry Sanford & Park, aqua, 6".......55.00
Fry's Great Rheumatic Cure Allegheny PA, full/in box, 8½" 150.00
HH Warner & Co Tippecanoe Pat Nov 20, '83, amber, 9"............65.00
Hub Punch Registered, amber, EX label, neck crack, 9" 65.00
Hurd's Cough Balsam, aqua, rm/ps, 4½" 85.00
JB Wheatley's Compound Syrup Dallasburgh KY, dk aqua, 6" 110.00
Jelly of Pomegranate Preparate by Dr Gordak Only, aqua, 7" 80.00

John G Baker Co Cod Liver Oil Philadelphia, aqua, 9" 130.00
JS Francher Grecian Fancheronian Drops NY, aqua, am/ps, 8" ...120.00
Kickapoo Sage Hair Tonic, cobalt, 4½" 95.00
Lediard's Morning Call, olive, seedy, am/sb, lt stain, 10" 65.00
Lilly Syrup J Fish Rochester NY, aqua, am/ps, 5⅝" 525.00
Log Cabin Hops & Buchu Remedy, amber, 6-sided, 10" 180.00
LQC Wishart's Trade Mark Pine Tree Tar Cordial, 9¾", EX.........65.00
Maria H Mellen Cough Syrup Spafford NY, aqua, bubbly, 5½" ...350.00
Mendenhall's Cough Remedy, aqua, rm/ps, 4⅜"..............................90.00
Mexican Mustang Liniment, dk aqua, am/ip, 7½" 140.00
Morse's Celebrated Syrup Providence, med gr, pontil, 9½"..........500.00
Owl Drug Co San Francisco, bright gr, sm/tm, 9⅝" 65.00
Prof JR Tilton Great Hair Producer SF Cal, med sapphire, 7" 125.00
Pure Family Nectar, am/ps, 9" 70.00
Queru's Cod Liver Oil Jelly, aqua, wide rm/ps, 5½" 95.00
Reed Cutler Co Vegetable Pulmonary Balsam, aqua, am/ps, 7" 85.00
Rohrer's Wild Cherry Tonic Expectoral, amber, pyramidal, 11"..375.00
Rohrer's Wild Cherry Tonic Expectoral, bright yel, 10½" 400.00
Sanderson's Blood Renovator Milton VT, aqua, am/ps, 8½" 425.00
Sanford's Radical Cure, cobalt, lt stain, 7½"..................................30.00
Shecut's Southern Balm Coughs, Colds, Consumption, aqua, 6"..160.00
Taylor's Indian Ointment, aqua, 6-sided, rm/ps, 3" 205.00
Taylor's Opocura, aqua, rm/ps, 3" 75.00

Warner's Safe Cure, amber, smooth base, applied mouth, small potstone, light inside stain, rare, 11", $240.00.

Warner's Safe Nervine Rochester NY, amber, tm/sb, 7", NM........35.00
Warranted Pure Cod Liver Oil HW&Co NY, aqua, am/ps, 10" 85.00
WC Sweet HCB&L Rochester NY, aqua, am/ps, 6"........................30.00
Winans Bros Indian Cure/Blood Purifier, aqua, w/box, 9" 425.00
Zoeller's Kidney Remedy Pittsburgh, amber, NM labels, 9" 250.00

Milk Bottles

AG Smalley, This Bottle To Be Washed, metal lid/hdl, qt............75.00
Alta Crest Farms, bl pyro, crown top, Pat 1929 on base, qt............70.00
Alta Crest Farms, gr, lt wear, qt 700.00
Big Elm Dairy Co, gr, pt 175.00
Brook Farms, emb baby's face, 1-qt, M 70.00
Brookfield, emb baby's face, sq, qt..50.00
Brookfield, emb baby's face, 1-pt, 5½", M..30.00
Deluxe Cream Separator in red pyro, cream top, rare, qt 350.00
EF Mayer, amber, qt...50.00
Emb measuring lines, Climax Pat 1898, sq, tin top, pt 80.00
FERG Co-34, amber, 'wash & return' on side, pre-1920s, qt 30.00
Flanders, emb baby's face, 1-qt, M..65.00

Milk bottles, Big Elm Dairy Co., green, quart, $250.00; E.F. Mayer, amber, quart, $50.00; F.E.R.G. Co. - 34 on base, 'wash and return' on side, pre-1920s, by Reed Glass Co., $30.00; Alta Crest Farms, green, quart, $700.00; Werckerle, green, quart, $150.00.

Lang Creamery, Buffalo NY, gr, qt 300.00
Roger Williams, emb face, 1-qt, M 95.00
Thatcher's, emb Absolutely Pure, man/cow, qt 275.00
This Bottle To Be Washed..., domed tin cap, qt............................300.00
VM&IC Co's (in circle), amber, ½-pt 148.00
Wanzer's Kazol 32 E 30th St (in circle), amber, 6-oz 148.00
Weckerle (circles jar twice), gr, qt 338.00

Mineral Water and Soda Bottles

Adirondack Spring Whitehall NY, emerald, am/sb, 8", EX............60.00
Deep Rock Spring Oswego NY, aqua, am/sb, pt, 7⅞" 135.00
Deep Rock Spring Oswego NY, med bl-gr, am/sb, 7¾" 235.00
Dr Wieber's European, med bl-gr, sm int lip bruise, ½-pt.............100.00
Eureka Spring Co, aqua, smooth rnd bottom, am, 8⅞" 220.00
Magnetic Spring Hennicker NH, amber, am/sb, 9", NM 185.00
Missisquoi Springs, med gr, emb A, am, 9⅝" 50.00
Oak Orchard Acid Springs Alabama, med bl-gr, am/sb, 8¾" 300.00
Oak Orchard Acid Springs Lockport, emerald, am/sb, 9" 70.00
Poland Water, amber, Moses figural, sl collar/sb, haze, 11" 500.00
Saratoga Spring, amber, emb star, am/sb, 7½" 160.00
Spa Phila THD Congress Water, yel-amber, am/sb, 7½"..............120.00
Vichy Water Patterson & Brazeau NY, olive-yel, am/sb, 8" 210.00

Poison Bottles

Dmn pattern, cobalt, flared tm/sb, no stopper, 11" 700.00
Dmn pattern, cobalt, HB Co, flared tm, Poison stopper, 7" 95.00
Poison, amber, skull/X-bones between stars, EX label, 4½"..........725.00
Poison, olive gr, emb on diagonal, ribs, clear stopper, 14"............210.00
Poison CLC Co Pat Appl For, bright gr, tm/sb, 5"..........................75.00
Poison ea side skull & X-bones, cobalt, 6-sided, 2¾"......................85.00
Poison w/1-winged owl on mortar, cobalt, sm/tm, 6" 140.00
Poison/protrusions, amber, coffin form, tm/sb, 3⅜" 275.00

Spirits Bottles

Back bar, amber w/S Whiskey under-glass label, Walton, 12" 150.00
Beiser & Fisher, amber, pig figural, ft crack/haze, 9½"..................200.00

Bininger's Old Dominion Wheat Tonic...NY, olive-gr, 10".........**175.00**
Bininger's Regulator, honey amber, clock form, 6", NM **200.00**
Case gin, dk olive, crude am/sb, sq, 12½" **175.00**
Case gin, olive-amber, sqd cylinder, sm, Netherlands, 9½".........**120.00**
Caspers Whiskey...Honest North Carolina People, cobalt, 12"...**300.00**
Chestnut Grove Whiskey CW, red-amber, am, appl hdl, 9"........**210.00**
EG Booz's Old Cabin Whiskey, CVII-3, honey amber, 7¾" **900.00**
I Alsop 1763 on seal, dk olive, sm w/bevel, 12", NM **700.00**
Phoenix Old Bourbon, Naber Alfs & Brune..., amber, 6½" **145.00**
Pineapple, W&Co, amber, pineapple form, dbl cm, stain, 8½" ..**200.00**
RB Cutter Louisville, amber, whittled, w/hdl, blob top, 8½".......**125.00**
RB Cutter's Pure Bourbon, red-amber, am, appl hdl, 8", EX **85.00**
Royal Imperial Gin London, med cobalt, 9¾", NM **110.00**
Star Whiskey NY WB Crowell Jr, yel-amber, am/ps, 8", EX **550.00**
TC Pearsall on seal, high kick-up, str sides, ps, 11" **425.00**
Wharton's Whiskey 1850 Chestnut Grove, yel-amber, 10", EX .**245.00**

Miscellaneous

Ammonia, SF Gaslight Co, aqua, tm/sb, seedy, 9"..........................**85.00**
Ammonia, SF Gaslight Co, citron (rare color), tm/sb, 9" **200.00**
Hair restorer, Martha Washington, labels/wrapper, 7" **160.00**
Lavender Salts, Goetting & Co, see California Perfume Co
Merry Christmas/Happy New Year w/elf, recessed-label flask **725.00**
Pocket flask, label under glass w/girl reading book, 6"..................**600.00**
Pocket flask, recessed label under glass w/girl, 6"..........................**400.00**
Pomade, bear figural, bl opaque, J Hauel & Co, 3¾", EX **700.00**
Robert Gibson & Sons, Lozenge Makers, aqua, English, 13"..........**30.00**
Snuff, Lorilards Maccoby, olive, sm/ps, lt stain, 4½" **75.00**
Soda, Crystal Palace Premium, dk bl-gr, blob top, 7", EX **475.00**
Soda, J&A Dearborn NY, cobalt, blob top, rare, 7" **450.00**
Soda, Lancaster GW NY, med sapphire-bl, blob top, rare............**150.00**
Sweet 16, Goetting & Co, see California Perfume Co

Bow Porcelains

Bow porcelain originated in West Ham, England, on the Essex side of Bow Bridge in the early 1740s. This fine soft paste was produced by the firm of Alderman Arnold & Co. Early wares were simple, heavy, and often unmarked. Most decoration was blue underglaze. Later examples were lighter in weight and more chalky. The decoration evolved to ornate florals and raised scrollwork bases. These later pieces are often marked with a red anchor and dagger. The company closed sometime in the 1700s.

Basket, partridge, Kakiemon pattern, rtcl, 1765, 6" dia **2,800.00**
Bowl, grapevines on shaped rim, bl/wht, soft paste, 8", pr............**650.00**
Figurine, Blackamoor boy carries goblet on tray, 1760, 6¾" **475.00**
Figurine, boy (girl), Turkish attire on mound, 1765, 6", pr..........**450.00**
Figurine, fire allegorical, lad holds brazier in arms, 8" **300.00**
Figurine, maid faces right, basket of flowers in arm, 6".................**300.00**
Figurine, man in wine tricorn hat/jacket, floral tunic, 8" **600.00**
Figurine, Mars, in plumed helmet, w/flag & bush, 12", EX **475.00**
Figurine, shepherd w/dog, companion w/sheep, rstr, 6", pr **1,500.00**
Pickle dish, fruiting vine, bl on wht, leaf form, 4"........................**225.00**
Sauce boat, panel w/Oriental boating figure, fluted, 6", EX........**220.00**

Boxes

Boxes have been used by civilized man since ancient Egypt and Rome. Down through the centuries, specifically designed containers have been made from every conceivable material. Precious metals, papier-mache, battersea, Oriental lacquer, and wood have held riches from the treasuries of kings, snuff for the fashionable set of the last century, China tea, and countless other commodities. See also Toleware; specific manufacturers.

Ash/poplar, Christmas tree-like crest, red rpt, 12x9" **275.00**
Bentwood, copper tacks, old patina, oval, 4" **85.00**
Bentwood, old red finish, handwritten label, oval, 5" **225.00**
Bentwood, old wht pnt, 7¾" dia **200.00**
Bentwood, unusual 3-sided shape, floral/stripes on red, 7"....... **1,300.00**
Bentwood, varnished, 9¾x15½"..**175.00**
Bentwood, 1-finger construction w/copper tacks, natural, 5½"....**150.00**
Blackball, cherry/pine, dvtl, sliding lid, 4x8"+hdl **135.00**
Blanket, poplar, red w/lyre stencil & name, w/history, mini **325.00**
Book form, snake pops out when lid is slid open, 6" **250.00**
Candle, pine, sq nails, EX patina, 3½x12¼x4¼"...........................**125.00**
Candle, sliding lid, table model, 5½x6x14" **350.00**
Candle, tin, cylindrical, hinged lid, 13x4¼" dia **235.00**
Candle, wood, gr pnt, leather hinges, 1820s, 7x9x12"..................**395.00**
Chip cvd, fine allover designs, ivory escutcheon, 7", VG **250.00**
Comb, pine, chip cvd, cvd sunbursts, hanging, 4x8x8½".............**250.00**
Document, leather covered, brass fittings, 1820s, 8x12x6" **55.00**
Document, leather covered, brass tacks, pre-1800 hdl, 10" **65.00**
Document, pnt pine, mitered corners, dvtl, ca 1800, 12"...............**225.00**
Document, wood w/tooled leather, wrought lock, 8", VG **275.00**
Dough, poplar w/orig red grpt, sq nails, 8½", EX **225.00**
Egg, pine, tin bands, wire loop hinges, 14½x14½x13" **75.00**
Egg, wood, old bl pnt w/blk lettering, bail hdl, EX **85.00**
Game, inlaid cribbage brd top/bottom, unfolds for play, 5".........**100.00**
Handkerchief, burntwood, brass fittings, sq, 1910, 6" **15.00**
Jewel, cranberry glass w/medallions, metal filigree, 4½".............**540.00**
Jewel, sapphire bl glass w/floral, hinged, 3x7".............................**275.00**
Kindling, poplar w/worn gr pnt, primitive, 12x28x30", VG.........**250.00**
Knife, bird's-eye walnut, dvtl, 9x15" **800.00**
Knife, cherry/pine, chip-cvd hdl w/trn acorns & open heart........**155.00**
Leather covered, dome top, brass fittings, 1800s, 7x11x5" **85.00**
Mahog, dvtl, brass bail & lock, 9½"...**75.00**
Pantry, wood, natural finish, 1-finger lid, 9x15" **130.00**

Pantry box, dark green, yellow, and black with carved pinwheels, flowerheads, and stars, inscribed J.P., early 1800s, 5x10" diameter, $1,900.00.

Patch, papier-mache, Joys of Angling reserve, English, 3" **200.00**
Pine, dvtl, dome top, sq nails, red pnt, 1860s, 4x15x10"..............**130.00**
Pine w/orig brn grpt, brass hasp, minor wear, 5x12x15"..............**140.00**
Pine w/walnut & pine trim, chip-cvd fans, dvtl, 6x21x31"..........**140.00**
Pnt beech w/orig mc florals, etc, wooden hinges, 12" **1,000.00**
Pnt pine/poplar dome-top w/EX sponging & florals, 31" **6,100.00**
Pnt w/house in rolling landscape, 1825, 9"................................ **1,600.00**
Salt, pine, mustard yel pnt, hinged lid, 1800s, 10x7x7"................**85.00**
Spice, bentwood w/7 int canisters, pnt labels, 8" dia **165.00**
Spice, cherry, 9 dvtl drw w/trn pulls & labels, 12x14x8".............**550.00**
Spice, pine w/red pnt, 3-part int, shaped slide lid, 10" **195.00**

Spice, poplar w/worn finish, dvtl, slant-top lid, 12x15" **325.00**
Wallpaper on cb, castles/etc, AR Vallee label, 8" **300.00**
Wallpaper on cb, lined w/1857 newspaper, minor wear, 12" L **300.00**
Walnut, cvd Am eagle, shield w/E Pluribus..., 1-pc, 8" **175.00**
Workman's, soft pine, ca 1900, rfn, 14x26x14", EX **165.00**
Writing, poplar, brn grpt/pnt scene (2 more w/in), 18" L **3,200.00**

Bradley and Hubbard

The Bradley and Hubbard Mfg. Company was a firm which produced metal accessories for the home. They operated from about 1860 until the early part of this century, and their products reflected both the Arts and Crafts and Art Nouveau influence. Their logo was a device with a triangular arrangement of the company name containing a smaller triangle and an Aladdin lamp.

Our advisor for this category is Daniel Batchelor; he is listed in the Directory under New York.

Lamps

Banquet, HP globe w/flowers, cast base, sgn, 37"..........................**425.00**
Banquet, wireware shade/std/base; rpl glass shade, 24" **400.00**
Piano, brass/wrought iron, frosted beaded drape 10" shade **550.00**
Table, rvpt 22" 8-panel tulip shallow dome shade; 3-leg std **900.00**

Miscellaneous

Andirons, wrought iron, inverted Y-form w/ball finial, 16" **300.00**
Candlestick, brass, std flares to wide base, mk, 12x6", pr **650.00**
Desk set, Deco style, 5-pc...**150.00**

Brass

Brass is an alloy consisting essentially of copper and zinc in variable proportions. It is a medium that has been used for both utilitarian items and objects of artistic merit. Today, with the inflated price of copper and the popular use of plastics, almost anything made of brass is collectible. Our advisor, Mary Frank Gaston, has compiled a lovely book, *Antique Brass*, with full-color photos; you will find her address in the Directory under Texas. See also Candlesticks.

Mail box, Cutler Mfg., 1920s, $140.00.

Ash tray, owl, deeply feathered, English, 5½x3½".........................**27.50**
Ash tray, plain, hammered, 4" dia **5.00**
Ash tray, scuttle form, eng leaf, China, 4x3½" **8.00**
Ash tray, University of MO, 1926..**10.00**

Button, acorn & leaf pattern, 14 for...**10.00**
Button, boar's head relief, old..**10.00**
Button, uniform; Chicago Motor Coach, 1" dia............................. **7.00**
Candlestick, saucer base, side push-up, 8", VG **115.00**
Candlestick, sq base, short stem, 3¾"...**100.00**
Candlestick, 3-branch, Art Deco, 15", pr **135.00**
Door slot, 'Mail' **15.00**
Flagpole top, eagle, 7" wingspan, EX...**25.00**
Incense burner, open-mouthed chick, 2¼x2½" **15.00**
Jardiniere, eng dragons & geometrics, China, 9½" **60.00**
Kettle, cast, wrought iron bail hdl, 10" dia....................................**55.00**
Kettle, cast, 2 rim spouts, wrought iron bail hdl, 7" dia **75.00**
Kettle, copper bottom, iron ears w/bail hdl, primitive..................**100.00**
Kettle, spun sheet brass, wrought iron bail hdl, 13" dia **70.00**
Letter clip, cast owl form, orig red pnt, ca 1900, 4¼" **55.00**
Music stand, crown/acanthus page support, sq std, 13" **200.00**
Pail, iron bail hdl, mk Hayden's Pat, 6x9½" **65.00**
Plaque, 3-masted ship, England, 11¾" dia......................................**20.00**
Plate, hammered, 5½"... **5.00**
Rack, towel; dolphin shape, solid, pr...**25.00**
Stencil, rooster w/'HA&Co 56 Boston,' 13½" sq, VG **210.00**
Sundial, Menant, pocket style, leather case, 1750s, 3" **500.00**
Tea strainer, sm... **8.00**
Teapot, tin lined, copper rivets, gooseneck spout, 8¼" **150.00**
Toothpick holder, eng flowering tree, China, 1⅜x1¾" **12.00**
Tray, tooled geometrics, heavy, 19¾" dia.......................................**40.00**
Vase, bud; eng florals, scalloped rim, China, 5" **9.00**
Vase, urn shape, cast, heavy, 2¼"..**12.50**

Brastoff, Sascha

The son of immigrant parents, Sascha Brastoff was encouraged to develop his artistic talents to the fullest — encouragement that was well taken, as his achievements aptly attest. Though at various times he has been a dancer, sculptor, Hollywood costume designer, jeweler, and painter, it is his ceramics that are today becoming highly-regarded collectibles.

Sascha began his career in the United States in the late 1940s. In a beautiful studio built for him by his friend and mentor, Winthrop Rockefeller, he designed innovative wares that even then were among the most expensive on the market. All designing was done personally by Brastoff; he also supervised the staff which at the height of production numbered approximately 150. Wares signed with his full signature (not merely backstamped 'Sascha Brastoff') were personally crafted by him and are valued much more highly than those signed 'Sascha B.,' indicating work done under his supervision. Sascha Brastoff still resides in Los Angeles, California, at present producing 'Sascha Holograms,' which are distributed by the Hummelwerk Company.

Another medium he used in his work was resin, and such pieces are also very collectible, though extremely scarce. In the listings below, all items are signed 'Sascha B.' unless otherwise indicated (full signature).

Ash tray, abstract enameling, bl, 6" **45.00**
Ash tray, Alaska, rnd, 8" **40.00**
Ash tray, hooded, allover gold decor..**30.00**
Ash tray, mosaic decor...**30.00**
Ash tray, Rooftops line...**28.00**
Bowl, dandelions, free-form, 10" **40.00**
Bowl, mc abstract, matt, 10"..**45.00**
Bowl, shallow, 3 geometric legs, 7¼"..**28.00**
Figure, hippo, resin, violet..**165.00**
Figure, stylized horse, mc on wht...**150.00**

Lighter, enamelware 28.00
Plate, ceramic, stylized lion, blk, full signature, 10".............175.00

Server, 12", and small 6" plate, fish form, signed Sascha B., $75.00 for the set.

Table lighter, ceramic, abstract flowers, full signature.................135.00
Tray, mc abstract matt, 17" dia 65.00
Tray, Surf Ballet, 10" 33.00
Vase, striped, ftd egg shape, 7" 45.00

Brayton, Laguna

Durlin E. Brayton made hand-crafted vases, lamps, and dinnerware in a small kiln at his Laguna Beach, California, home in 1927. He soon married; and, with his wife, Ellen Webster Grieve, as his partner, the small business became a successful commercial venture. They are most famous for their amusing, well-detailed figurines, some of which were commissioned by Walt Disney Studios. Though very successful even through the Depression years, with the influx of imported novelties that deluged the country after WWII, business began to decline. By 1968 the pottery was closed.

Cookie jar, Grandma, arms folded, floral border on skirt.............145.00
Cookie jar, Mammy, gr skirt, wht apron, hands on sides, 13" 275.00
Cookie jar, Matilda, fat, wears kerchief 175.00
Cookie jar, Swedish Lady, floral apron, wears bonnet.................145.00

Bar singers (Gay 90s Series), 9" x 8½", $85.00.

Figurine, cow, purple, 8" 50.00
Figurine, Dutch girl...27.50
Figurine, peasant lady w/open baskets, 8" 45.00
Figurine, penguin, lg & sm, pr 95.00
Figurine, Sally, flower holder....................................25.00
Figurine, seal, turq crackle 40.00
Planter, duck 20.00
Planter, Mandy, girl with open basket, ink stamp.................40.00
Shakers, Chef & Jemima, wht chef's hat & apron, pr...................45.00
Shakers, clown & dog, stamped mk, pr.............................25.00

Bread Plates and Trays

Bread plates and trays have been produced not only in many types of glass but in metal and pottery as well. Those considered most collectible were made during the last quarter of the nineteenth century from pressed glass with well-detailed embossed designs, many of them portraying a particularly significant historical event. A great number of these plates were sold at the 1876 Philadelphia Centennial Exposition by various glass manufacturers who exhibited their wares on the grounds. Among the themes depicted are the Declaration of Independence, the Constitution, McKinley's memorial 'It Is God's Way,' Rememberance of Three Presidents, the Purchase of Alaska, and various presidential campaigns, to mention only a few.

'L' numbers correspond with a reference book by Lindsey; 'S' refers to a book by Stuart.

Our advisor for this category is Darlene Yohe; she is listed in the Directory under Arkansas.

Actress, Miss Nelson, 13x9" 90.00
Baltimore Pear, hdls..28.00
Bates, L-375 ....65.00
Beaded Oval Windows, 13½x8½" 60.00
Beehive, Be Industrious, deer border..............................75.00
Bible, L-200 ....55.00
Bunker Hill, L-44, 13¼x9" 100.00
Canadian Seal 45.00
Chain & Shield 24.00
Classic, Cleveland, L-310 ....175.00
Columbus, L-4 ....45.00
Constitution, L-43 ....55.00
Continental Hall, hand-form hdls, 1776-1876, 12¾" L.................75.00
Crying Baby 50.00
Cupid & Venus, amber, 10½" dia 100.00
Cupid & Venus, 10½" dia...45.00
Dewdrop w/Sheaf of Wheat, Give Us This Day, S-7, 11" 35.00
Diagonal Band 28.00
Egyptian (Cleopatra), 13" L 50.00
Elk center BPOE, clock, Cervus Alces, floral border.................125.00
Eureka, w/motto, L-103 ....45.00
Faith, Hope, & Charity, plain center, Pat Nov 23, 1875.............45.00
Flamingo Sword, L-209 ....95.00
Frosted Stork, floral & deer border...............................55.00
GAR, L-505, 11" L 90.00
Garden of Eden, Give Us This Day, 12½x9" 35.00
Garfield Drape, L-303, 11"...42.00
Garfield Memorial, We Mourn Our Nation's Loss, L-302, 10" L...65.00
Garfield Star, frosted bust, L-299 ....45.00
Gen US Grant, Patriot & Soldier 32.00
Give Us This Day, sheaf of wheat, rnd 75.00
Golden Rule, L-221 ....65.00
Grant, sq, L-291 ....60.00
Grant, vaseline, L-291, 10" 115.00

Horseshoe, single hdl, 13" L 50.00
Horseshoe (Good Luck), 10" 65.00
Independence Hall, oval...................................95.00
Ionia 25.00
It Is Pleasant To Labor for Those We Love, 12½" 55.00
Kansas, motto 48.00
Knights of Labor, bl, ca 1889 ....200.00
Liberty & Freedom, w/eagle, 12" L 75.00
Liberty Bell, Signers, 1776-1876 ....85.00
Lion...100.00
Lord's Prayer 40.00
Lord's Supper, goofus, L-235 ....35.00
McKinley, Forget Me Not, L-344 ....30.00
McKinley, It Is God's Way, L-356, 10½" L 60.00
Minerva (Mars)...60.00
Mormon Temple, w/eye & beehive........................300.00
Nelly Bly, 11"...185.00
Niagara Falls, L-489 ....95.00
Old State House Philadelphia, bl, L-32 ....110.00
Old State House Philadelphia, 12½" dia 55.00
Panelled Dewdrop, Daily Bread, fancy rim............55.00
Peabody, L-272 ....45.00
Polar Bear, ship, frosted, L-486, 16" 150.00

Prescott Stark, Heroes of Bunker Hill, 13" long, $100.00.

Railroad w/Engine, L-134, 9x12" 110.00
Rock of Ages, L-236 ....85.00
Rock of Ages, milk glass, oval 165.00
Royal Lady, pale vaseline 135.00
Scroll w/Flowers, 12" dia 30.00
Shell & Tassel, oval 55.00
Stippled Cherry, Our Daily Bread, 9½" 25.00
Swan w/Flowers...35.00
Teddy Roosevelt, dancing bears, L-357, 10" L......140.00
Texas Centennial, Alamo center 85.00
Thousand Eye, bl, folded corners 35.00
Union Pacific Railroad 80.00
US Coin 1892...275.00
US Grant, Let...Peace, amber, leaf border, L-289, 10½" dia 90.00
Washington, 13-star border, L-258 ....50.00
Washington Centennial 1876, frosted, L-27 ....130.00
Wheat & Barley, milk glass 60.00
Wildflower, sq 28.00
3 Graces, Pat & dtd 1875 ....45.00
3 Presidents, In Remembrance, L-249...................75.00

Bride's Baskets and Bowls

Victorian brides were showered with gifts, as brides have always been; one of the most popular gift items was the bride's basket. Art glass inserts from both European and American glasshouses, some in lovely transparent hues with dainty enameled florals, others of Peachblow, Vasa Murrhina, satin or cased glass were cradled in complementary silverplated holders. While many of these holders were simply engraved or delicately embossed, others such as those from Pairpoint and Wilcox were wonderfully ornate, often with figurals of cherubs or animals. The bride's basket was no longer in fashion after the turn of the century.

Watch for 'marriages' of bowls and frames. To warrant the best price, the two pieces should be the original pairing. If you can't be certain of this, at least check to see that the bowl fits snuggly into the frame. Beware of later-made bowls (such as Fenton's) in Victorian holders.

In the listings that follow, if no frame is described, the price is for a bowl only.

Amberina Coin Spot, Mt WA; ornate Pairpoint stand, 12x9" 875.00
Amberina Invt T'print; Rogers SP fr, 8½" 500.00
Bl shaded, yel decor; twisted bail, ftd SHM fr, 10" 350.00
Bl w/HP florals; Webster Bros fr, worn SP, 14½"..........275.00
Cranberry, HP florals/butterflies; ftd/trimmed, 11", EX SP 500.00
Cranberry satin, HP florals, gold leaves; ornate SP fr, 12½".........350.00
Cream to bl, jewels/flowers, sq; orig SP fr, 10x10x12" 435.00
Crown Milano w/mc & gold pansies; sgn/#d Pairpoint fr, 12" . 2,000.00
Dia Quilt, amberina cased satin, HP roses; Barbour fr, 8x11".. 1,000.00
Dia Quilt bl MOP, 3-corner; SP stand, 10½x9½" 750.00

Enameled wild roses with gold stems and leaves on peach; silverplated frame with sea motif and engraved lobster, 11", $1,600.00.

Gr shaded satin overlay, emb lattice rim, 3¾x11½" 225.00
Lt gr satin, pk roses w/gold; lg cherubs on Wilcox stand.......... 2,500.00
Pk, amber rim, wht int; ornate ftd Wilcox fr, EX SP......................425.00
Pk, ruffled, ftd stand w/dolphin, sgn Meriden, VG SP, 10" 195.00
Pk cased, heavy gilt/pnt; hummingbirds on ftd Wilcox fr, EX......450.00
Pk cased, ruffled rim; low ftd fr; sm 85.00
Pk overlay, mc florals, scalloped, 3½x11" 175.00
Pk shaded, HP plums w/gold; ornate fr w/dbl hdl, 14x12"............375.00
Purple shaded w/wht rim, ruffled; SP pewter fr, 11¼" 250.00
Sapphire w/Mary Gregory girl on 4¾" disk; NM sgn fr 1,000.00
Yel opaque w/mc floral, sgn Webb; ornate fr, 9½" dia 185.00

Bristol Glass

Bristol is a type of semi-opaque opaline glass whose name was derived from the area in England where it was first produced. Similar glass was made in France, Germany, and Italy. In this country, it was made by the New England Glass Company and to a lesser extent by its contemporaries. During the eighteenth and nineteenth centuries, Bristol glass was imported in large amounts and sold cheaply, thereby contributing to the demise of the earlier glasshouses here in America. It is very difficult to distinguish the English Bristol from other opaline types. Style, design, and decoration serve as clues to its origin; but often only those well versed in the field can spot these subtle variations.

Biscuit jar, gray, ostrich & stork, 7x4¼" 160.00
Bottle, robin's egg bl, HP lilies w/gold, cone stopper, 9"................**95.00**
Bowl, bl, HP florals, ruffled, sm 65.00
Box, wht, cherubs in floral/scroll border, 4" dia 60.00
Lustre, bl, wht scalloped rim, gilt florals, prisms, 10", pr 300.00
Pitcher, azure bl w/mc acorns & leaves, 5¾".......................................80.00
Pitcher, turq w/gold florals, bands & scrolls, mini, 2x2" 45.00
Shade, wht, for library lamp, 14" dia, EX 48.00
Sweetmeat, bl w/ducks & cranes, SP cow finial, 4" 350.00

Vase, blue with birds, insects, and flowers, four gold feet, 11", $550.00.

Vase, bl, gold leaves, red flowers, 11⅜", pr 265.00
Vase, bl w/lav ruffled rim, mc butterfly/floral, 11" 175.00
Vase, bl w/wht flowers, cone form in SP Webster holder, 15" 275.00
Vase, custard, HP florals, goat's head hdls, 8½" 60.00
Vase, gr, birds/apple blossoms, bulbous, 14"..................................250.00
Vase, gr, lady's portrait, 2 at 15", 1 w/lid at 22"....................... 1,000.00
Vase, gray, sparrows & cornflowers w/gold, blk hdls, 12" 175.00
Vase, ivory, mc cherubs, 7", pr...150.00

British Royalty Commemoratives

While most modern-day commemorative collectors start their collections with souvenirs issued during Queen Victoria's reign, interest in royal commemorative collecting has been evident for centuries. A commemorative medal was issued for Edward VI's 1547 coronation. Ceramics are the most popular type of commemoratives. Food tins are gaining in popularity — so are glass, paper, and metal souvenirs. Since commemoratives have always been a commercial endeavor, nearly any item

with room for a portrait and an inscription has been manufactured as a souvenir; thus a wide variety is available in all price ranges. Since royal events are an ongoing state of affairs, it is possible to choose almost any time in British history as a commemorative starting point. Even present-day souvenirs make a good, inexpensive beginning collection. Today's events will be tomorrow's history!

For further study we recommend *British Royal Commemoratives*, by our advisor for this category, Audrey Zeder; she is listed in the Directory under California.

Key:
anniv — anniversary	jub — jubilee
chr — christening	LE — limited edition
com — commemorative	mem — memorial
cor — coronation	wed — wedding

Bank, Charles/Diana wed, bl portrait/design, ceramic 30.00
Bank, Charles/Diana wed, red mailbox shape 20.00
Bank, Elizabeth, red mailbox shape, tin 20.00
Bank, Geo VI cor, red mailbox shape, tin 25.00
Beaker, Charles/Diana wed, sepia portraits, Doulton 100.00
Beaker, Elizabeth 1959 Canada visit, bl decor on glass.................25.00
Bell, Andrew/Sarah wed, mc portrait, wooden hdl 40.00
Bell, Charles/Diana, pk dress/red jacket, 5" 25.00
Bell, Charles/Diana wed, mc portrait, wooden hdl 40.00
Bell, Elizabeth, reverse: Charles/Diana/William/Henry, 3½" 25.00
Bust, Victoria, amber celluloid on blk base, 5½" 195.00
Cup & saucer, Charles/Diana wed, blk/wht portrait, mc design.....40.00
Cup & saucer, Edward VI cor, sepia portrait, enameling..............150.00
Cup & saucer, Elizabeth cor, blk/wht portrait: Charles/Anne......150.00
Cup & saucer, Elizabeth cor, mc portrait on lt gr, Aynsley 60.00
Cup & saucer, Geo V cor, blk/wht portrait, w/color & lustre 150.00
Cup & saucer, Queen Mother 90th birthday, mc portrait 40.00
Cup & saucer, Victoria 1897 jub, sepia portrait/castles...............175.00
Ephemera, Charles/Diana wed, box of 50 matchbooks 30.00
Ephemera, Edward VIII Prince of Wales, candy box 45.00
Ephemera, Geo V jub, cigarette card, set of 60 ....35.00
Ephemera, Geo V jub, cigarette card album, filled 45.00
Ephemera, Geo VI cor, cigarette card, set of 60.............................35.00
Ephemera, Royal Family, sticker album w/190 pictures 30.00
Ephemera, Victoria & relatives on advertising card 35.00
Ephemera, Victoria Christmas card, portrait & Windsor 35.00
Ephemera, Victoria cor, Festival Proclamation 175.00
Ephemera, Victoria 1887 jub, procession program.........................50.00
Figural, Victoria, removable lid, Staffordshire, 1854 ....495.00
Loving cup, Charles/Diana wed, LE, Royal Doulton 100.00
Loving cup, Charles/Diana wed, mc portrait, LE Paragon...........950.00
Loving cup, Prince Philip 60th birthday, Royal Crown Derby.....100.00
Medal, Charles/Diana wed, Elizabeth on bk 10.00
Medal, Edward VII cor, gold/purple ribbon, 1⅝" 25.00
Medal, Edward VII student attendance award, 1900-10, 1½" 25.00
Medal, Edward/Alexandra wed 1863, orig box, 1½" 60.00
Medal, Elizabeth II jub, Queen on horsebk, 1½" 10.00
Medal, Geo VI/Elizabeth, relief profile, red/wht/bl ribbon 20.00
Medal, Victorial mem, blk ribbon, 1½"...25.00
Miniature, Charles/Diana molded plastic figures, 4½".................25.00
Miniature, Charles/Diana plate, mc portrait in wed clothes..........20.00
Miniature, Charles/Diana wed, photo album w/pictures................20.00
Miniature, Elizabeth photo album w/pictures, 1½x1" 20.00
Mug, 3 royal August ladies' birthdays, Cider 35.00
Mug, Edward VII cor, sepia portraits/design, Doulton 150.00
Mug, Edward VIII cor, mc crest, lion hdl, Paragon 75.00
Mug, Geo V jug, relief portrait, hammered bk, pewter 65.00
Mug, Princess Beatrice birth, wht/gold, Wedgwood 60.00

Mug, Queen Mother 90th birthday, mc portrait, gold rim	30.00
Mug, Victoria 1897 centenary of golden jub, Caverswall	75.00
Mug, Victoria 1897 jub, bl portrait/design, JC&N	175.00
Novelty, Charles/Diana, 'Splitting Image' key ring, pr	10.00
Novelty, Charles/Diana wed, coaster set, leather, 4 in box	10.00
Novelty, Charles/Diana wed, plastic ruler, 12"	5.00
Novelty, Charles/Diana wed, puzzle, 11x15", in box	25.00
Novelty, Charles/Diana/William/Henry, key ring	5.00
Novelty, Charles/Diana/William/Henry, nail clipper key ring	6.00
Novelty, Elizabeth, 'Splitting Image' key chain	5.00
Novelty, Elizabeth cor, braided hatpin	25.00
Novelty, Elizabeth 1977 jub, sterling charm	15.00
Novelty, Elizabeth/Philip, watch, leather band, quartz	60.00
Novelty, Geo VI cor, pin-bk w/light, orig box	25.00
Novelty, Victoria 1887 jub, woven pincushion	325.00
Novelty, Victoria 1897, buckle clasp	30.00
Pitcher, Elizabeth cor, sepia portrait, gold trim, 2½"	70.00
Pitcher, Geo V/Queen Mary, mc portraits, lustre, 3"	100.00
Pitcher, Victoria 1887 jub, Goss, 3¼"	195.00
Pitcher, Victoria 1897 jub, tan/brn portrait, Doulton, 7½"	275.00
Plate, Charles/Diana wed, Branscombe design for Minton	200.00
Plate, Charles/Diana wed, enameling, LE, Paragon, 10"	150.00
Plate, Charles/Diana wed, Faulkner design for Doulton	175.00
Plate, Edward VII mem, mc portrait, blk wreath, 4"	75.00
Plate, Elizabeth w/young Charles & Anne, china, 4½"	55.00
Plate, Elizabeth 60th birthday, mc portrait, Coalport, 4¼"	20.00
Plate, Geo V jub, Art Deco style, Doulton, 3x2"	75.00
Plate, Prince Henry birthday, LE, Royal Doulton, 8"	100.00
Plate, Prince William chr, LE, Royal Crown Derby, 8"	100.00
Plate, Queen Mother 90th birthday, mc portrait, 3"	15.00
Plate, Queen Mother 90th birthday, mc portrait, 8"	30.00
Plate, Victoria 1887 jub, pressed glass w/cut glass edge	250.00
Plate, Victoria 1897 jub, relief portrait/design, Spode	275.00
Plate, 3 royal ladies' August birthdays, bl rim, 12"	55.00
Plate, 3 royal ladies' August birthdays, bl rim, 8"	30.00
Post card, Charles/Diana wed, Norfolk Railway ticket	5.00
Post card, Diana at Nottingham in 1985	2.50
Post card, Diana at Worcestershire in 1986	2.50
Post card, Diana paper doll	3.00

Post card, Duke/Duchess of York in Australia 1988, LE	5.50
Post card, Elizabeth opening '88 Australian Expo	3.00
Post card, Geo V & allied military leaders, blk/wht, unused	30.00
Post card, Geo V & family on crown bkground, unused	15.00
Post card, Prince Charles/Princess Anne, blk/wht, Tuck, unused	10.00
Post card, Prince William going to school, Dec 1988	2.50
Post card, Princes Bea chr, blk/wht	2.50
Post card, Princess Elizabeth w/Queen Elizabeth, sepia, unused	15.00
Post card, Princess Eugenie birth, Mar 1990	5.00
Post card, Queen Mother 90th birthday, yel dress	3.00
Post card, Queen/Queen Mother studying racing form	2.50
Post card, Victoria mem, blk/wht portrait, unused	30.00
Post card set, Charles/Diana wed, set of 12	30.00
Post card set, Queen Mother 90th birthday, silk picture, 8	35.00
Spoon, Andrew/Sarah wed, in wed clothes	10.00
Spoon, Andrew/Sarah/baby Beatrice, SP	10.00
Spoon, Diana in blk dress, SP	10.00
Spoon, Diana in crown, off-shoulder dress, SP	10.00
Spoon, Edward VII, relief portraits, red enamel, sterling	75.00
Spoon, Elizabeth cor, relief portrait, inscription	20.00
Spoon, Geo VI cor, relief portrait, sterling, Birks	50.00
Spoon, Princess Anne wearing wht, SP	10.00
Spoon, Queen Mary, relief portrait, enamel fr & crown	50.00
Spoon, Victoria 1897 jub, relief portrait in bowl	50.00
Stamp album, Charles/Diana wed, w/650 stamps	950.00
Stamp album, Diana 21st birthday, w/320 stamps	350.00
Teapot, Edward VII, mc portrait, pk lustre, 2-cup	255.00
Teapot, Geo V jub, mc portraits/design, 4-cup	150.00
Teapot, Queen Mother 90th birthday, mc portrait, 2-cup	50.00
Tin, Charles/Diana wed, portraits on plaid	30.00
Tin, Charles/Diana wed/mc portraits w/relief design	30.00
Tin, Edward VII, 3 generations, octagonal	175.00
Tin, Edward VII cor, portrait in military uniform	50.00
Tin, Edward VIII accession to the throne, hinged	75.00
Tin, Elizabeth, Trooping of the Colors, Edward Sharp Co	30.00
Tin, Elizabeth cor, mc portrait, octagonal, MacFarlane Lang	45.00
Tin, Elizabeth cor, portrait & relief decor	35.00
Tin, Elizabeth cor, portraits/castles, octagonal, Tetley Tea	30.00
Tin, Elizabeth cor, surrounded by previous queens	45.00
Tin, Elizabeth Silver jub, portrait on purple	25.00
Tin, Elizabeth Silver jub, portraits, unopened	30.00
Tin, Geo V cor, Cadbury, 3½x2⅜"	60.00
Tin, Geo V jub, mc portraits, ornate design	45.00
Tin, Geo VI, mc portrait, rnd, Mackintosh	50.00
Tin, Geo VI cor, king/queen/daughters portraits	45.00
Tin, Geo VI cor, portraits, octagonal	40.00
Tin, Prince of Wales (future Edward VII) 1929 Exhibition	55.00
Tin, Princess Elizabeth/Margaret, sepia, rnd	50.00
Tin, Princess Mary, gift to troops, brass, 1914	100.00
Tin, Princess Mary 1922 wed, portraits, hinged	85.00
Tin, Queen Mother 90th birthday, elaborate, Walkers	35.00
Tin, Victoria, gift to S Africa conflict troops, 1900	100.00
Tin, Victorial, young/old portraits, octagonal	175.00
Tray, Charles/Diana wed, mc portrait in wedding clothes, 12"	35.00
Tray, Elizabeth jub, mc portrait w/Philip, tin, 12x16"	25.00
Trivet, Edward VII, cor, dk gr portrait/commonwealth, Minton	225.00
Trivet, Elizabeth jub, relief portrait, chrome	30.00
Vase, Queen Mary, mc portrait, gr dress, 2"	45.00
Vase, Victoria 1897 jub, 4 generations, pk lustre	195.00

Double-handled vase, Elizabeth II Coronation, Royal Doulton limited edition, 10¾", $950.00.

Broadmoor

In the Spring of 1933, the Broadmoor Art Pottery was formed and space rented at 217 East Pikes Peak Avenue, Colorado Springs, Colorado. Most of the pottery produced would not be considered elaborate, and only a handful was decorated. Many pieces were signed by P.H. Genter, J.B. Hunt, Eric Hellmann, and Cecil Jones. It is reported that this plant closed in 1936, and Genter moved his operations to Denver.

Broadmoor pottery is marked in several ways: a Greek or Egyptian-type label depicting two potters (one at the wheel and one at a tile-pressing machine) and the word Broadmoor; an ink-stamped 'Broadmoor Pottery, Colorado Springs (or Denver), Colorado'; and an incised version of the latter.

The bottoms of all pieces are always white and can be either glazed or unglazed. Glaze colors are turquoise, green, yellow, cobalt blue, light blue, white, pink, pink with blue, maroon red, black, and a copper lustre. Both matt and high gloss finishes were used.

The company produced many advertising tiles, novelty items, coasters, ash trays, and vases for local establishments around Denver and as far away as Wyoming. An Indian head device was incised into many of the advertising items, which also often bear a company or a product name. A series of small animals — horses, dogs, elephants, squirrels, a toucan bird, and a hippo — each about 2" high, are easily recognized by the style of their modeling and glaze treatments, though all are unmarked. Our advisors for this category are Carol and Jim Carlton; they are listed in the Directory under Colorado.

Candle holder, 3 tulip cups, branching metal base, 14" 100.00
Cigarette urn, wht tulip cup on 5" turq leafy pad, 5" 25.00
Lamp, gr, 17x22" dia...125.00
Paperweight, beetle...35.00
Tile, wht squirrel atop 5" turq disk..25.00
Vase, blk gloss, bulbous, orig label, 7½" 35.00
Vase, candy apple red, bulbous w/rnd shoulder, label, 5¾"............25.00
Vase, cobalt, ovoid w/vertical ribbing, orig label, 16" 150.00
Vase, med gr, hdld urn form, 7"...35.00
Vase, turq, shouldered cylinder, 7" 25.00

Broadsides

Webster defines a broadside as simply a large sheet of paper printed on one side. During the 1880s, they were the most practical means of mass-communication. By the middle of the century they had become elaborate and lengthy with information, illustrations, portraits, and fancy border designs.

Last Rally! At Kennett Square, Scott and Graham Club, plus six additional lines, ca 1852, minor folding, 13" x 10", $400.00.

Administratrix Sale at Auction, dairy cows, 1890, VG.................45.00
Beggar's Opera, Boston theatre, 1843, 15x5½", EX.......................37.50
Dr McHenry's Syrup, Bitters, etc, 1870s, 11x14", EX....................18.50
Exhibition & Fair, 1842, 9x11½", VG 55.00
General Fast, Thos Hutchinson, printed by Draper, 1770, EX.....280.00
Kessely's Wonderful Marionettes, 1880s, 8½x6", VG...................42.50
La Femme de Lavone, theatre ad, 1836, 10x7¼", VG 48.00
Regimental orders for NH Militia, 1841, EX.................................55.00
Report on US Representatives, Phila, 1830, EX 330.00
Theatre Royal, School of Reform, 1811, 12x7½", EX 75.00

Bronzes

Thomas Ball, George Bessell, and Leonard Volk were some of the earliest American sculptors who produced figures in bronze for home decor during the 1840s. Pieces of historical significance were the most popular, but by the 1880s a more fanciful type of artwork took hold. Some of the fine sculptors of the day were Daniel Chester French, Augustus St. Gaudens, and John Quincy Adams Ward. Bronzes reached the height of their popularity at the turn of the century. The American West was portrayed to its fullest by Remington, Russell, James Frazier, Hermon MacNeil, and Solon Borglum. Animals of every species were modeled by A.P. Proctor, Paul Bartlett, and Albert Laellele, to name but a few.

Art Nouveau and Art Deco influenced the medium during the twenties, evidenced by the works of Allen Clark, Harriet Frismuth, E.F. Sanford, and Bessie P. Vonnoh.

Be aware that recasts abound. While often aesthetically satisfactory, they are not original and should be priced accordingly. In much the same manner as prints are evaluated, the original castings made under the direction of the artist are the most valuable. Later castings from the original mold are worth less. A recast is not made from the original mold. Instead, a rubber-like substance is applied to the bronze, peeled away, and filled with wax. Then, using the same 'lost wax' procedure as the artist uses on completion of his original wax model, a clay-like substance is formed around the wax figure and the whole fired to vitrify the clay. The wax, of course, melts away — hence the term 'lost wax.' Recast bronzes lose detail and are somewhat smaller than the original due to the shrinkage of the clay mold. For further study we recommend *Huxford's Fine Art Value Guide*, available at your bookstore.

Adnet, Jean & Jacques; female dancer, walnut base, 13" 2,420.00
Alliot, Lucien; nude on 1 knee, brn patina, wood plinth, 15" . 1,100.00
Arman, Statue of Liberty, gr patina, sgn, 30x8x9" 16,500.00

Austrian bronze, cats and dogs before doghouse, M, $650.00.

Austria, hound dog, howling, tail between legs, pnt, 7" **600.00**
Barye, Alfred; Joan of Arc, on horse, brn patina, 34" **6,834.00**
Barye, Alfred; pointer & rabbit, gilt, sgn, 6x8" **660.00**
Barye, Antoine; Gen Bonaparte, on horse, brn patina, 14" **8,800.00**
Bastide, P; Napoleon, blk patina, sgn, 41" **2,750.00**
Bennes, J; jockey on horsebk, golden-brn patina, 18x19" **2,640.00**
Biegas, Boleslas; figure w/serpents, blk patina, sgn, 34" ...**13,200.00**
Bitter, Ary; 2 nymphs & satyr, marble base, 29" L **2,600.00**
Bock, Richard; Indian w/pipe, blk patina, sgn/dtd 94, 13" L.... **7,150.00**
Campbell, Abraham Lincoln, bust, brn patina, sgn, 6" **418.00**
Carpeaux, J Baptiste; Anna Foucard, bust, brn patina, 20" **3,850.00**
Carvin, Louis A; stalking leopard, Etling, Paris, 12x25" **3,000.00**
Chalon, Louis; L'Orchidee, nude as flower stem, lamp, 29" **7,000.00**
Chemin, Victor; horse & jockey, Belgian marble base, 10" **1,100.00**
Collet, Edouard-Louis; Nocturne, nude in flight, 38" **2,700.00**
Constant, Maurice; Le Travail, man w/hammer, anvil, 30" **950.00**
Coysevox, A (after); female riding Pegasus, gilt, sgn, 19" **1,760.00**
D'aste, J; standing lady, w/gilt & ivory, stone ped, 11" **1,100.00**
D'Illiers, Gaston; horse jumping fence, blk patina, sgn, 14" **2,200.00**
Dallin, Cyrus; Indian on horsebk, brn patina, sgn, 23" **11,000.00**
de Bologne, Jean; Fortune, nude, emb bacchanalian base, 30"... **2,100.00**
De Monard, L; rearing stallion & groom, brn patina, sgn, 23". **3,520.00**
Descomps, Joe; nude holds garland aloft, stone base, 16" **800.00**
Despiau, Charles; seated nude, blk patina, sgn/dtd 1923, 14".. **9,350.00**
Epple, Emil; standing nude, red marble base, 25" **2,200.00**
Fromet, E; Napoleon III, in plumed hat, on base, 14½" **1,600.00**
Gaudez, Art Nouveau woman, gr-brn patina, sgn, 23" **600.00**
Gechter, reclining spaniel, gr-brn patina, sgn, 6x10" **1,100.00**
Gennaretti, Amadeo; Pilot, man in chariot+others, 33" L **4,000.00**
Gilioli, Emile; Angel, polished bronze, sgn, 32" **8,250.00**
Greene, Saya; Isadora Duncan dancing, gr-brn patina, 19"..........**950.00**
Gross, Chaim; head of a girl, brn patina, sgn/dtd 1947, 7"....... **1,045.00**
Hischinger, 4 birds on a branch, gr patina, sgn, 13" **715.00**
Huntington, A; yawning tiger, gr-brn patina, sgn, 14" L **2,200.00**
Jungbluth, Alfred; elegant lady, sgn, ca 1900, 15" **495.00**
Kanuth, bust of young man, brn patina, sgn, ca 1900, 10" **150.00**
Korschann, Charles; lady w/flowers, golden patina, sgn, 13".......**800.00**
Lambeaux, bust, Art Nouveau woman, ped base, sgn, 24" **418.00**
Laporte, Emile (after); bust of young lady, ca 1900, 10" **250.00**
Le Faguays, Pierre; Minaret, semi-nude, w/ivory, 19" **1,650.00**
Lenoir, Pierre; girl sits/arms bk of head, marble base, 21"............**400.00**
Leonard, Agathon (after); lady w/tambourine, gilt, 22" **4,000.00**
Lipchitz, Jacques; Hagar & the Angel, golden patina, 14"......**11,000.00**
Lorin, Georges; woman dancing, brn patina, sgn, 16" **3,850.00**
Manship, Paul H; Madonna & Child, brn patina, 1914, 12".. **3,575.00**
Martins, Maria; nude in grass skirt, sgn, ca 1942, 61" **11,550.00**
Mene, Pierre Jules; Arab stallion, brn patina, sgn, 8" **1,870.00**
Mene, Pierre Jules; bull, brn patina, sgn, 9x14" **2,640.00**
Moigniez, Jules; cow & bull, golden-brn patina, sgn, 18" L **2,640.00**
Moore, Henry (after); reclining female, gr marble base, 13" **2,500.00**
Nakian, Reuben; Leda & the Swan, lt brn patina, 19" **2,200.00**
Norton, Elizabeth; sleeping lioness, gr-brn patina, 4" **2,700.00**
Patigian, Haig; Ancient History, female allegorical, 38" **9,000.00**
Pautrot, Ferdinand; rooster & lizard, red-brn patina, 9x9"....... **2,420.00**
Picault, Emile L; Bonaparte, bust, brn patina, sgn, 9" **528.00**
Piel, Paul; nude & snake, marble base eng Medusa, 10½" **1,700.00**
Preiss, F; ballerina en pointe, polychrome/ivory, 9" **3,300.00**
Rucki, Jean Lambert; couple embracing, brn patina, 19" **6,600.00**
Schwatenberg, S (after); standing male nude, brn patina, 12" **300.00**
Silvestre, seated fawn, 9" **742.00**
Szekessy, Zolton; flute player, dk brn patina, 7" L **330.00**
Turcan, Jean; peasant girl walking w/jar, brn patina, 30" **2,900.00**
Valton, Charles; attacking dog, sgn, 24x29" **440.00**
Van Biesbroeck, male figure, blk patina, sgn, 20" **1,430.00**

Van Wouw, Anton; man panning for gold, sgn, 7" **5,500.00**
Villanis, E; bust of young woman, gr-brn patina, 23" **1,400.00**
Volti, Antoniucci; reclining nude, brn patina, sgn, 6x10" **7,700.00**
Vonnoh, Bessie P; nymph riding dolphin, sgn, 17" **15,000.00**
Weinman, Adolph; Chief Blackbird, brn patina, sgn, 16" **20,000.00**
Wieghorst, Olaf; Indian by campfire, brn patina, sgn, 4" **1,760.00**
Zach, Bruno; ballerina, blk patina, gr marble base, 19" **2,640.00**
Zach, Bruno; dancing couple, gr patina, marble base, 17" **1,980.00**
Zorach, William; mother & child, blk patina, sgn, 8" L **2,640.00**

Brouwer

Theophlis A. Brouwer, an accomplished artist even before his interests turned to the medium of pottery, started a small one-man operation in 1894 in East Hampton, New York. Two years later he relocated in Westhampton, where he perfected the technique of fire-painting, learning to control the effects of the kiln to produce the best-possible results. In 1925 he founded the Ceramic Flame Company in New York, but it is for his earlier work that he is best known. Brouwer died in 1932.

Vase, irid brn/gr-gold gloss, bulbous w/long neck, mk, 9" **1,600.00**
Vase, irid yel/brn/orange, cupped rim, mk Flame, 7¾x6" **2,700.00**
Vase, irid yel/orange, mk Flame, rim chip, 3½x4¼" **375.00**
Vase, orange/gold/gr, bulbous w/flare neck, 7½x11" **1,000.00**

Brownies by Palmer Cox

Created by Palmer Cox in 1883, the Brownies charmed children through the pages of books and magazines, as dolls on their dinnerware, in advertising material, and on souvenirs. Each had his own personality — among them The Bellhop, The London Bobby, The Chairman, and Uncle Sam. But the oversized, triangular face with the startled expression, the protruding tummy, and the spindlelegs were characteristics of them all. They were inspired by the Scottish legends related to Cox as a child by his parents, who were of English descent. His introduction of the Brownies to the world was accomplished by a poem called *The Brownies Ride*. Books followed in rapid succession — thirteen in the series, all written as well as illustrated by Palmer Cox.

By the late 1890s, the Brownies were active in advertising. They promoted such products as games, coffee, toys, patent medicines, and rubber boots. 'Greenies' were the Brownies' first cousins, created by Cox to charm and to woo through the pages of the advertising almanacs of the G.G. Green Company of New Jersey. Perhaps the best-known endorsement in the Brownies' career was for the Kodak Brownie, which became so popular and sold in such volume that their name became synonymous with this type of camera.

Almanac, G Green Woodbury, Palmer Cox illus, 1890 ....**20.00**
Ash tray, RS Germany, 1913..**45.00**
Book, Bomba the Merry Old King, 1903, EX...................................**30.00**
Book, Brownies in Fairyland, Century Co.......................................**35.00**
Book, Brownies Through the Union, Palmer Cox illus, 1895 ....**65.00**
Book, Brownies' Kind Deed, WB Conkey, Chicago, 1903, VG **25.00**
Book, Busy Brownies, Brownie Series Weekly Vol 1, #1 ....**25.00**
Book, Famous Adventures by the Brownies, Cox illus, c 1900.......**15.00**
Book, Monk's Victory, 1911, EX...**25.00**
Book, Queer People, Palmer Cox illus, 1894, EX **45.00**
Bottle, soda; emb Brownies, M **30.00**
Box, Log Cabin Brownies, cabin form, Nat'l Biscuit Co, '20s **125.00**
Candlestick, Uncle Sam & Brownies, majolica................................**175.00**
Comic sheet, 1907, lg, EX **25.00**

Brownie Blocks, set of twenty cubes, six pictures of Brownies at work and play, original booklet and box, 14" x 11", VG, $500.00.

Creamer, Little Boy Blue verse & 4 Brownies w/gold	75.00
Cup & saucer, china	50.00
Cup & saucer, SP	100.00
Dish, child's, SP, 19 brownies, 8½"	125.00
Dolls, uncut cloth, dtd 1892, set of 4	450.00
Game, Auto Race, tin board	38.00
Game, Horseshoe, orig box	50.00
Game, Jump-Up, EX in box	50.00
Humidor, Brownie Sailor's head figural, Fr majolica, EX	150.00
Match holder, Brownie on striker, majolica	155.00
Napkin ring, SP, Brownie climbs up side	165.00
Package of needles, Brownie policeman, 1893 Columbian Expo	45.00
Paper dolls, from 1895 paper supplement, 1-sheet	25.00
Paperweight, Brownie figural, SP	110.00
Picture frame, paper on wood, 8x10"	32.00
Pitcher, china, 2 Brownies on front, 3 on bk, 4½"	65.00
Plate, china, lobster chasing Brownies	55.00
Plate, SP, Brownies on rim, 8½"	45.00
Puzzle, Brownies skating, 20-pc, early, fr, 10½x12½"	95.00
Sign, emb Brownies on tin, Howell's Root Beer, EX	150.00
Stamps, wood & rubber, orig pad & box, set of 6	25.00

Brush

George Brush began his career in the pottery industry in 1901 working for the J.B. Owens Pottery Co. in Zanesville, Ohio. He left the company in 1907 to go into business for himself, only to have fire completely destroy his pottery less than one year after it was founded. Brush became associated with J.W. McCoy in 1909 and for many years served in capacities ranging from General Manager to President. (From 1911 until 1925, the firm was known as The Brush-McCoy Pottery Co.; see that section for information.) After McCoy died, the family withdrew their interests, and in 1925 the name of the firm was changed to The Brush Pottery. The era of hand-decorated art pottery had passed for the most part and would soon be completely replaced by the production of commercial lines. Of all the wares bearing the later Brush script mark, their figural cookie jars are the most collectible. See also Brush-McCoy.

Cookie Jars

Antique Touring Car	125.00
Boy w/Balloons	250.00
Chick in Nest	115.00
Cinderella Pumpkin	95.00
Circus Horse	175.00
Clown, yel pants	95.00
Clown Bust	95.00
Cookie House	65.00

Covered Wagon	175.00
Cow, w/cat on bk, brn	65.00
Cow, w/cat on bk, purple	300.00
Davy Crockett, gold trim	175.00
Davy Crockett, no gold	125.00
Dog w/Basket	85.00
Donkey & Cart	120.00
Elephant, w/monkey on bk	250.00
Elephant w/Baby Bonnet	125.00
Fish	120.00
Formal Pig	95.00
Granny	85.00
Happy Bunny	85.00
Hen on Basket	75.00
Hillbilly Frog	300.00
Hobby Horse	225.00
Humpty Dumpty, w/beanie & bow tie	95.00
Humpty Dumpty, w/peaked hat	85.00
Lantern, brn/cream, mk K1	65.00
Laughing Hippo	150.00
Little Angel	225.00
Little Boy Blue, gold trim, sm	175.00
Little Boy Blue, no gold, sm	140.00
Little Boy Blue. lg	150.00
Little Girl, #017	95.00
Little Red Riding Hood, basket in arm, mk K24	135.00
Nite Owl	75.00
Old Clock	75.00
Old Shoe	75.00
Panda	95.00
Peter Pan	125.00
Peter Pan, gold trim	230.00
Peter Peter Pumpkin Eater, boy/girl/pumpkin, mk W24	75.00
Puppy Police	225.00
Raggedy Ann	95.00
Sitting Hippo	115.00
Sitting Pig	115.00
Smiling Bear	165.00
Squirrel on Log	55.00
Squirrel w/Top Hat	85.00
Stylized Owl	75.00
Stylized Siamese	85.00
Teddy Bear, feet apart	80.00
Teddy Bear, feet together	85.00
Treasure Chest	75.00

Miscellaneous

Basket, emb leaves, yel, ftd bowl form, #658, 9½"	27.50
Hanging basket, Stardust, flying saucer form, 1957	45.00
Lamp, Wise Birds, owl figural, 8"	150.00
Planter, free-form, emb gazelle's head, maroon/gray, 11" L	18.00
Planter, seated bear figural, wht w/pk, 1941, sm	9.00
Shakers, cloverleaf, red/gr on wht, 1955, pr	9.00
Vase, rust/gray mottled gloss, horizontal ribs at waist, 8"	14.00
Vase, Southern Belle before fan-shaped receptacle, #218	30.00
Wall pocket, boxer dog form, #542, 1956	30.00
Window box, dusty rose, vertical ribs, #156, 8" L	6.00

Brush-McCoy

The Brush-McCoy Pottery was formed in 1911 in Zanesville, Ohio, an alliance between George Brush and J.W. McCoy. Brush's original pottery had been destroyed by fire in 1907; McCoy had operated his own business there since 1899. After the merger, the company expanded and produced not only their staple commercial wares, but also fine artware. Lines such as Navarre, Venetian, Persian, Oriental, and Sylvan were of fine quality equal to that of their larger competitors. Because very little of the ware was marked, it is often mistaken for Weller, Roseville, or Peters and Reed.

In the twenties, after a fire in Zanesville had destroyed the manufacturing portion of that plant, all production was contained in their Roseville (Ohio) plant #2. A stoneware type of clay was used there; and, as a result, the artware lines of Jewell, Zuniart, King Tut, Florastone, and Panel-Art are so distinctive that they are more easily recognizable. Examples of these lines are unique and very beautiful — also quite rare and highly prized!

The Brush-McCoy Pottery operated under that name until after J.W. McCoy's death when it became the Brush Pottery. The Brush-Barnett family retained their interest in the pottery until 1981 when it was purchased by the Dearborn Company. See also Brush.

Bowl, Navarre, gr w/wht Nouveau lady, 4½x8" 150.00
Bowl, Panelart, 7½" 350.00
Candlestick, Zuniart, 10¼", pr 325.00
Ferner, Zuniart, w/liner, 5" 150.00
Jar, Nurock, emb peacocks, w/lid, sm flake, 5x6½" 95.00
Jardiniere & ped, Woodland, sgn A Cusick, 28" 550.00
Jug, Pastel Kitchenware, 7" 95.00
Lamp, Kolor Kraft, 5½" sphere 150.00
Umbrella stand, Onyx, #74, 22½" 250.00

Bud vase, Zuniart, 8½",
$175.00.

Vase, Chrome Art, road & trees, 8½" 200.00
Vase, Cleo, 10" 375.00
Vase, Jetwood, baluster, 10½" 450.00
Vase, Navarre, gr w/wht Nouveau lady, w/hdls, 8½" 275.00
Vase, Onyx, baluster, 8" 35.00
Vase, Sylvan, dk gr gloss, trees, bulbous top, 10" 75.00
Vase, Vestal, cameo, 6" 75.00

Buffalo Pottery

The founding of the Buffalo Pottery in Buffalo, New York, in 1901, was a direct result of the success achieved by John Larkin through his innovative methods of marketing 'Sweet Home Soap.' Choosing to omit 'middle-man' profits, Larkin preferred to deal directly with the consumer and offered premiums as an enticement for sales. The pottery soon proved a success in its own right and began producing advertising and commemorative items for other companies, as well as commercial tableware. In 1905 they introduced their Blue Willow line after extensive experimentation resulted in the development of the first successful underglaze cobalt achieved by an American company. Between 1905 and 1909, a line of pitchers and jugs were hand decorated in historical, literary, floral, and outdoor themes. Twenty-nine styles are known to have been made. These have been found in a wide array of color variations.

Their most famous line was Deldare Ware, the bulk of which was made from 1908 to 1909. It was hand decorated after illustrations by Cecil Aldin. Views of English life were portrayed in detail through unusual use of color against the natural olive-green cast of the body. Today the 'Fallowfield Hunt' scenes are more difficult to locate than 'Scenes of Village Life in Ye Olden Days.' A Deldare calendar plate was made in 1910. These are very rare and are highly valued by collectors. The line was revived in 1923 and dropped again in 1925. Every piece was marked 'Made at Ye Buffalo Pottery — Deldare Ware Underglaze.' Most are dated, though date has no bearing on the value. Emerald Deldare, made with the same olive body and on standard Deldare Ware shapes, featured historical scenes and Art Nouveau decorations. Most pieces are found with a 1911 date stamp. Production was very limited due to the intricate, time-consuming detail. Needless to say, it is very rare and extremely desirable.

Abino Ware, most of which was made in 1912, also used standard Deldare shapes, but its colors were earthy and the decorations more delicately applied. Sailboats, windmills, and country scenes were favored motifs. These designs were achieved by overpainting transfer prints and were often signed by the artist. The ware is marked 'Abino' in handprinted block letters. Production was limited; and as a result, examples of this line are scarce today. Prices only slightly trail those of Emerald Deldare Ware.

The many uncataloged items that have been found over the years indicate that Buffalo Pottery decorators were free to use their own ideas and talents to create many beautiful one-of-a-kind pieces.

Our advisors for this category are Ruth and Dale Van Kuren; they are listed in the Directory under New York. Assistance was also provided by Shrader's Antiques; see California. See also Willow Ware.

Abino

Bowl, fruit; windmills & pond, 9" 825.00
Matchbox holder/ash tray, 3¾" 800.00
Plaque, The Waning Day, 13½" 1,525.00
Plate, Portland ME, Portland Head Light, 8½" 525.00
Tankard, sailing scene, 6½" 775.00
Tankard, Toward the Harbor, 10½" 1,150.00
Teapot, sailing scene, 1913 ....950.00
Tray, millpond & boat scene, 12½x9" 1,125.00

Deldare

Ash tray/matchbox holder, Emerald, scenic 760.00
Bowl, fruit; Ye Village Tavern, 9" 450.00
Bowl, punch; untitled Fallowfield Hunt scenes, 15" 3,825.00
Bowl, sauce; Fallowfield Hunt, Breaking Cover, 5" 160.00
Bowl, soup; Fallowfield Hunt, 9" 265.00
Bowl, Ye Olden Days, 6½" 150.00
Candle holder/match holder combination, untitled....................475.00
Candlestick, Emerald, untitled, 9" 950.00
Candlestick, Fallowfield Hunt, untitled, 9" 425.00

Candlestick, Village Scenes, untitled, 9", pr 695.00
Creamer, Fallowfield Hunt, Breaking Cover 225.00
Creamer & sugar bowl, Ye Olden Days, w/lid...........................375.00
Cup, punch; untitled 195.00
Cup & saucer, demitasse; Ye Olden Days 350.00
Cup & saucer, Fallowfield Hunt 250.00
Egg cup, untitled 225.00
Hair receiver, Ye Village Street 325.00
Humidor, Emerald, Dr Syntax scenes, 7" 625.00
Humidor, Emerald, There Was an Old Sailor..., 8" 800.00
Humidor, Fallowfield Hunt scenes, 7" 735.00
Humidor, Ye Lion Inn, 7"...........................525.00
Inkwell, Emerald, Art Nouveau decor, lid missing 950.00
Jar, powder; village scenes, w/lid 350.00
Mug, Emerald, Dr Syntax, Dr Syntax Made Free, 4¼" 450.00
Mug, Emerald, Dr Syntax, I Give the Law..., 2¼" 450.00
Mug, Fallowfield Hunt, At the Three Pigeons, 3½" 310.00
Mug, Fallowfield Hunt, The Fallowfield Hunt, 3½" 310.00
Mug, Fallowfield Hunt, untitled, 2½" 350.00

Mug, Fallowfield Hunt, 4½", $450.00.

Mug, Scenes of Village Life, 2½" 295.00
Mug, Ye Lion Inn, 3½" 245.00
Pin tray, Ye Olden Days, 6¼x3½" 300.00
Pitcher, Emerald, Dr Syntax Setting Out..., 8¾" 940.00
Pitcher, Emerald, Noble Hunting Party (Dr Syntax), 10" 1,200.00
Pitcher, Fallowfield Hunt, The Return, 8" 500.00
Pitcher, Their Manner of Telling Stories, 6" 400.00
Pitcher, W/a Cane Superior Air..., 9" 550.00
Plaque, Emerald, Dr Syntax Sketching..., 12" 1,075.00
Plaque, Fallowfield Hunt, Breakfast at Three Pigeons, 12" 540.00
Plaque, Ye Lion Inn, 12" 485.00
Plate, An Evening at Ye Lion Inn, 14" 525.00
Plate, At Ye Lion Inn, 6¼" 90.00
Plate, Calendar, 9½" 1,300.00
Plate, Fallowfield Hunt, Breaking Cover, 8"...........................165.00
Plate, Fallowfield Hunt, The Start, 14" 600.00
Plate, Fallowfield Hunt, The Start, 9¼" 200.00
Plate, salesman's sample, 7" 900.00
Plate, Ye Olden Times, 9½" 175.00
Plate, Ye Town Crier, 8¼" 155.00
Plate, Ye Village Street, 7¼" 125.00
Platter, Ye Olden Times, 8½x6½" 375.00
Relish dish, The Fallowfield Hunt, 12x6½"...........................450.00

Sugar bowl, Fallowfield Hunt scene, 6-sided...........................285.00
Tankard, Fallowfield Hunt, Hunt Supper, 12½"...........................855.00
Tea tile, Emerald, Taking Possession..., 6"...........................490.00
Tea tile, The Fallowfield Hunt, 6" 300.00
Tea tile, Traveling in Ye Olden Days, 6"...........................295.00
Teapot, Emerald, Art Nouveau decor, 4¾"...........................750.00
Teapot, Fallowfield Hunt, Breaking Cover, 3¾"...........................365.00
Teapot, Scenes of Village Life, 5¾"...........................395.00
Tray, calling card; The Fallowfield Hunt, 7¼"...........................350.00
Tray, calling card; Village Scenes, 7¼"...........................300.00
Tray, dresser; Dancing Ye Minuet, 9x12"...........................575.00
Tray, Emerald, Thus Syntax Ate..., 13½x10¼" 1,000.00
Tray, tea; Heirlooms, 12x10½"...........................675.00
Vase, untitled, fashionable man & woman, 8" 850.00
Vase, untitled, village scenes, 9" 325.00
Vase, Ye Village Parson, 8½"...........................750.00

Miscellaneous

Ash tray, Sea Cave, Multifleure Lamelle, 4" dia...........................35.00
Bowl, punch; Tom & Jerry, 11½" 85.00
Canister, Coffee, w/lid, 7"...........................65.00
Canister, Nutmeg, w/lid, 3"...........................35.00
Creamer, Baby Bunting, 2¾" 45.00
Creamer, Roosevelt Bears, 3" 110.00
Cup & saucer, Bl Willow...........................25.00
Cup & saucer, Bluebird...........................25.00
Cup & saucer, Pk Rose 15.00
Dish, child's feeding; Campbell Kids, 7½"...........................75.00
Dish, child's feeding; Roosevelt Bears, 7½"...........................110.00
Egg cup, dbl, Bl Willow...........................45.00
Fish set, RK Beck, platter+6 9" plates...........................450.00
Mug, Expectation, 4½"...........................95.00
Mug, Fallowfield Hunt scenes on Colorido body, 4½" 250.00
Mug, Tom & Jerry, 3½"...........................25.00
Pitcher, Bl Willow, 7"...........................175.00
Pitcher, Cinderella, 6"...........................450.00
Pitcher, Gaudy Willow, 7½"...........................300.00
Pitcher, George Washington, w/gold, 7½"...........................550.00
Pitcher, Geranium, bl-gr, 4"...........................150.00
Pitcher, Geranium, mc...........................265.00
Pitcher, Gloriana, bl, 9¼"...........................440.00
Pitcher, Holland (scenes of Dutch children), 6"...........................340.00
Pitcher, John Paul Jones, 9¼"...........................450.00
Pitcher, Pilgrim, 9"...........................590.00
Pitcher, Robin Hood, 8¼"...........................400.00
Pitcher, Roosevelt Bears, 5"...........................160.00
Pitcher, Sailor, 9¼"...........................600.00
Plate, Bl Willow, 10½"...........................49.00
Plate, Bl Willow, 9"...........................35.00
Plate, Caribou Deer, 9"...........................50.00
Plate, Christmas, 1950-60, 9½", ea...........................50.00
Plate, commemorative, B&M Smelter, Montana, 7½"...........................125.00
Plate, commemorative, Modern Woodmen of America, 7½"...........................85.00
Plate, commemorative, WCTU, 1908, 9"...........................165.00
Plate, Gaudy Willow, 9½"...........................125.00
Plate, historical, Fauneuil Hall, Boston, 10½" 65.00
Plate, Sea Cave Restaurant, Multifleure Lamelle, 9½"...........................75.00
Teapot, Bl Willow, 6-cup...........................165.00
Teapot, Gaudy Willow, 4½"...........................235.00
Vase, Geranium, mc, 3¾"...........................125.00
Vase, HP roses, 7"...........................75.00
Vase, Multifleure Lamelle, 4"...........................35.00
Vase, Natural Wood decor, 4"...........................35.00

Burmese

Burmese glass was patented in 1885 by the Mount Washington Glass Co. It is typically shaded from canary yellow to a rosy salmon color. The yellow is produced by the addition of uranium oxide to the mix. The salmon color comes from the addition of gold salts and is achieved by reheating the object (partially) in the furnace. It is thus called 'heat sensitive' glass. Thomas Webb of England was licensed to produce Burmese and often added more gold, giving an almost fuchsia tinge to the salmon in some cases. They called their glass 'Queen's Burmese,' and this is sometimes etched on the base of the object. This is not to be confused with Mount Washington's 'Queen's Design,' which refers to the design painted on the object. Both companies added decoration to many pieces. Mount Washington-Pairpoint produced some Burmese in the late 1920s and Gunderson and Bryden in the '50s and '70s, but the color and shapes are different.

Our advisors for this category are Dolli and Wilfred Cohen; they are listed in the Directory under California.

Bell, clear hdl, 9¾"	585.00
Bottle, oil; ribbed cylinder, faceted stopper, Mt WA, 5½"	300.00
Bottle, scent; berries & leaves, lay-down, screw cap, 4⅞"	1,250.00
Bottle, scent; purple flowers, sterling lid, Webb, 3½"	695.00
Bottle, scent; Queen's, lay-down, sterling mk top, 5"	1,250.00
Bowl, Dia Quilt, Mt WA, 2¼x4½"	285.00
Bowl, EX color, thin, rectangular top, Mt WA, 2x4½x5"	435.00
Bowl, florals, appl rim, mk Webb, 3¾x5¼"	1,110.00
Bowl, shiny, Webb, 2½x5", in SP holder	685.00
Bowl, 3 shell ft, ruffled, berry pontil, Mt WA, 6x7"	1,500.00
Celery vase, in sgn Rogers SP base, 8½"	800.00
Charger, blackberries/autumn leaves/gilt, 14" dia	1,285.00
Creamer, ovoid w/long spout, Mt WA, 3¾"	400.00
Creamer & sugar bowl, open, Queen's, Mt WA, ftd, 4"	4,100.00
Cruet, melon ribs, +pr cylindrical s&p in Pairpoint fr	1,485.00
Cruet, melon ribs, mushroom stopper, Mt WA, 6½"	1,050.00
Cruet, shiny, ribbed, hollow stopper, loop hdl, Mt WA	950.00
Cruets (2) ribbed, w/lapidary stoppers, s&p, Mt WA, SP fr	2,250.00
Hat, Dia Quilt, Gunderson, 4" brim, 3"	365.00
Mustard, ribbed bbl form, metal collar/lid #1134, Mt WA	285.00
Pitcher, crimped rim, Mt WA, 5½"	650.00
Pitcher, Hobnail, yel hdl, Mt WA, 5½x3"	900.00
Pitcher, petticoat form, loop hdl, Mt WA, 5x3"	850.00
Pitcher, shiny, tankard form, Mt WA, 10"	785.00
Pitcher, Should Auld Acquaintance..., grapes, 8x6"	3,450.00
Pitcher, squatty w/long cylinder neck, 7½"	665.00
Plate, EX color, Gunderson, 9"	350.00
Plate, EX color, very thin, Mt WA, 9¾"	375.00
Rose bowl, florals, 8-crimp top, Webb, 2⅜x3½"	295.00
Rose bowl, pk to yel, 8-crimp, att Webb, 3¼x3⅜"	195.00
Rose jar, Persian, mc 'jewels'/gold, Burmese lid, Mt WA, 5"	995.00
Saucer, shiny, Mt WA, 5"	175.00
Shakers, ribbed, SP tops, Mt WA, 4", pr	295.00
Sweetmeat, vintage w/gold, SP trim, Webb, 3¼x4¾"	695.00
Toothpick holder, Dia Quilt, Mt WA, 2¾"	385.00
Toothpick holder, lav pansies, sq mouth	425.00
Toothpick holder, pansies, red rim, bulbous w/sq top, Mt WA	525.00
Toothpick holder, tricorner	285.00
Tumbler, bl forget-me-nots, Mt WA, 3¾"	650.00
Tumbler, rose buds/swags, thin walled, Mt WA, 3¾"	650.00
Vase, acorns & leaves, gr & gold, Webb, 4¼x3"	325.00
Vase, asters allover (att Steffin), gourd form, Mt WA, 12"	1,850.00
Vase, bulbous w/flared rim, Mt WA, 5½"	550.00
Vase, EX color, gourd form, Mt WA, 10x6"	775.00

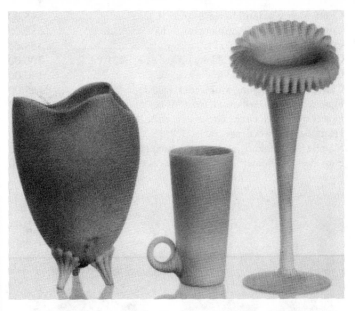

Vase, footed, berry pontil, 7", $800.00; Lemonade glass, 5", $350.00; Jack-in-the-Pulpit vase, 9¾", $650.00.

Vase, ferns/mc leaves, w/gold, petticoat shape, Mt WA, 7"	1,250.00
Vase, florals, ruffled rim, Webb, 4¼x2½"	325.00
Vase, folded star top, unmk Webb, 3½x2¾"	195.00
Vase, jack-in-pulpit; scalloped, appl base, Pairpoint, 8x7"	650.00
Vase, jack-in-pulpit; uncrimped top, Mt WA, 10x4"	700.00
Vase, lily; EX color, Mt WA, 8x3¾"	585.00
Vase, lily; Gunderson, 9½"	375.00
Vase, lily; ruffled, Mt WA, 9¾x4½"	625.00
Vase, long slim neck, trefoil top, Mt WA, 12½"	685.00
Vase, oak leaves/bl dots, stick neck, Mt WA, 10"	1,250.00
Vase, pear shape w/stick neck, Mt WA, 12"	750.00
Vase, prunus, wht dots at top, dbl gourd, Mt WA, 8½x5"	950.00
Vase, Queen's, w/gold, dbl gourd, Mt WA, 8½"	3,250.00
Vase, shiny, bulbous, 6"	350.00
Vase, shiny, ruffled top, bulbous bottom, Pairpoint, 6x7"	525.00
Vase, shiny, trumpet form w/scalloped top, Pairpoint, 10"	625.00
Vase, 4 birds, dbl gourd, Mt WA, 8x5"	1,200.00
Water set, Egyptian-style pitcher w/sq hdl, Mt WA, 5-pc	2,250.00
Whiskey, Optic Dia Quilt, Mt WA, 2¾"	275.00

Butter Molds and Stamps

The art of decorating butter began in Europe during the reign of Charles II. This practice was continued in America by the farmer's wife who sold her homemade butter at the weekly market to earn extra money during hard times. A mold or stamp with a special design, hand carved either by her husband or a local craftsman, not only made her product more attractive but also helped identify it as hers. The pattern became the trademark of Mrs. Smith, and all who saw it knew that this was her butter. It was usually the rule that no two farms used the same mold within a certain area, thus the many variations and patterns available to the collector today. The most valuable are those which have animals, birds, or odd shapes. The most sought-after motifs are the eagle, cow, fish, and rooster. These works of early folk art are quickly disappearing from the market.

Molds

Acorn, 1 in ea of 2 sqs, trn hdl, 4x7"	135.00

Cherries, twig w/3, rpr hinge, 4¼x8½" L 45.00
Cow, EX cvg, ca 1820, w/plunger, 5" dia 350.00
Cow, EX details, 1700s, 2x2½"......................................385.00
Cow, fluted sides, rnd in oblong hinged case, rpr, 10" L..............300.00
Cow, minor age cracks, 3¼" dia 180.00
Cow, primitive, oblong w/hinged fr, nailed rpr, 11" L 165.00
Flower, primitive, self-cased, 6½x9" L 85.00
Flower in serrated circle, circles in corner, 1800s, 8½" L 95.00
Heart, delicately cvd, age cracks, 3¾" dia 180.00
Maltese Cross, folding, w/4 pattern stamps & binder hoop..........250.00
Star, glass, mk Bomer 50.00

Butter mold, rare double strawberry design, dovetailed, 7¾" long, $225.00.

Swan, EX cvg, maple, ca 1830, 4" dia 220.00
Swan, primitive, 4⅛" dia 95.00
4 sqs ea w/sheaf, ear of corn, etc, 4x13" 175.00
8 sqs w/cvd leaves, acorns, sheaf of wheat, etc, ftd, 5½x11".........225.00

Stamps

Acorn & leaves, EX cvg, old 90.00
Cow & floral roller, wood yoke, early, 5¾" L, EX.............375.00
Cow & keg, 1-pc w/trn hdl, age cracks, 3¼" dia 95.00
Cow w/standing grain, chip-cvd edge, trn hdl, 2½x4¾"..............200.00
Cow w/tree, 1-pc w/trn hdl, 3⅜" dia 175.00
Eagle, simple cvg, 1-pc trn hdl, 3⅛" dia.......................200.00
Eagle (stylized) w/foliage & star, 1-pc, 4⅝" dia............450.00
Eagle w/shield & stars, hdl missing, 4½" dia 200.00
Eagle w/X-hatching, scratch-cvd 'EDC, 1841,' no hdl, 4½" dia ...695.00
Fish, simple design, lollipop form, 7" 100.00
Floral, on roller wheel, sgn, 7¾"..................................200.00
Floral (dbl) & leaves, 1-pc trn hdl, age cracks, 3¾" dia............100.00
Floral (stylized), inserted trn hdl, semicircular, 3½x7".........185.00
Floral (stylized) w/paisley, hdl gone, edge damage, 4" dia..............65.00
Floral (stylized) w/tulip, 1-pc knob hdl, 4½"...................200.00
Floral (stylized) w/tulip & heart, hdl missing, 3⅞" dia 165.00
Flower & 4 birds, primitive, 1-pc flat hdl (chip), 4¾" dia 225.00
Flowering pomegranate, 1-pc trn hdl, 4¼" dia............................100.00
Foliage, rayed rim, 1-pc trn hdl, 3½" dia......................100.00
Foliage (stylized), oblong, 4x6½"................................150.00
Fruit (stylized), 1-pc trn hdl, 3⅞" dia..........................75.00
Geometric 'shield,' 4¼" dia 75.00
Heart w/foliage & X-hatching, EX cvg, trn hdl, 4⅜" dia 300.00
House w/tree, tab hdl, sq knob, ca 1830s, 4x5", EX..............175.00
Pineapple, EX cvg, 1850s, 4¼" dia 125.00

Pineapple, 1-pc w/trn hdl, 3⅛" dia 45.00
Pineapple, 1-pc w/trn hdl, 4⅝" dia 65.00
Pineapple & leaves, X-hatching, EX details, 1-pc, 3"..................120.00
Pinwheel, deeply cvd, 3¾" dia......................................115.00
Sheaf of wheat, 1-pc w/trn hdl, 4½" dia..........................125.00
Sheaf of wheat (dbl), EX cvg, rectangular, 1830s, 2x4", EX....185.00
Star, hewn & cvd, EX details, 1800s, 2¾" 150.00
Starflower, bk: same, minor edge damage, 5½" dia..............175.00
Starflower ea side, lollipop hdl to side, wear, 8½"..............500.00
Strawberries & leaves, detailed cvg, knob hdl, 2½" dia 175.00
Sunburst, 'Haughton & Southington' cvd around rim, oval, 5"...325.00
Sunflower w/2 leaves, trn hdl, 4¼" dia 430.00
Swan...85.00
Thistle & leaves, long hdl, 1-pc, 1830s, 5" dia 350.00

Butter Pats

Butter pats were most commonly used during the Victorian era, although both earlier and later examples are known to exist, including some commercial pats still in use in the 1970s. They are sometimes called by different names such as butter chips, butters, butter plates, and even butter dishes; however, 'butter pat' is the most popular colloquial name and was the term favored by manufacturers. These small plates, used at each place setting for individual 'pats' of butter, were mentioned in published material as far back as the 1850s. Their small size, availability, and affordability contribute to their collector appeal. They can be found in sterling, silverplate, pewter, glass (including pattern glass), ironstone, vitrified china, fine china, and porcelain.

There are two basic types: 1) commercial pats — used by hotels, railroads, steamships, etc. These are usually of vitrified china, but may be found in metals and fine china as well. Designs incorporating the company on the front or top side are most sought after and often have historical interest. And 2) domestic pats — those used in the household. These range from basic to ornate styles and were made in a wide variety of materials including ironstone, sterling, and fine porcelain. They were made by nearly all major manufacturers both here and abroad.

Some collectors concentrate on a particular country, producer, material, or design. Many are unmarked; but comparisons with larger, marked pieces of dinnerware patterns are often helpful in identification. Because butter pats are widely available, avoid worn or damaged examples; and don't confuse them with small plates intended for other uses such as nut and sauce dishes, salt dips, coasters, or children's toy dishes.

In the listings below, pats are assumed round unless noted otherwise. Those interested in learning more about butter pats may wish to subscribe to *Butter Pat Collectors' Notebook*; the address is listed in the Directory under Clubs, Newsletters, and Catalogs. Our advisor for this category is Marjorie Geddes; she is listed in the Directory under Oregon.

Key:
BS — backstamp   VC — vitrified china
TM — top mark

Commercial

Clipper Line logo TM, VC, Rorstrand, 3⅝".........................7.50
Crindley, VC, Dundee for Mitchell Woodbury BS, 3¼" 3.50
Grindley, Hotel Ware, gr & orange bands, 3¼".........................3.00
Meakin, Waldorf, ironstone, 3¼".......................................2.50
Royal Worcester, Boston for Jones McDuffee & Stratton BS..........7.50
San Diego Hotel, VC, logo TM, 3¼".................................7.50

UPRR, Harriman Bl, VC **20.00**

Domestic, Ceramic

Bl Willow, Made in Japan, 3" **10.00**
Bl Willow, Myott, Son & Co, England, 3" **15.00**
Bl Willow, Occupied Japan, 3" **15.00**
China, emb waffle pattern, folded napkin center, 3¼" **5.00**
Copeland Spode, Old Salem, bl & wht, 3" **12.00**
Flow Bl, Aldine, Grindley **12.50**
Flow Bl, Argyle, Grindley **22.50**
Flow Bl, Bl Danube, Johnson Bros................................**22.50**
Flow Bl, Scinde, Alcock **25.00**
Flow Bl, Virginia **18.00**
GDA Limoges, pk roses, emb chain border, 3⅝" **7.50**
Haviland, blk/yel Greek key border on cream lustre **7.00**
Haviland, wild flowers, scalloped rim, 2⅝" **12.00**
Heubach, lady's portrait, fan shape, impressed mk **20.00**
Heubach, shell shape, sailing ship transfer, HP details **12.00**
Ironstone, Anglais, brn transfer of Holyrood Palace, 3" **12.00**
Ironstone, Argosy, gr floral transfer **5.00**
Ironstone, brn floral transfer, 2½" sq **6.50**
Ironstone, brn scenic transfer, unmk, 2½" sq **10.00**
Ironstone, floral, emb scroll rim, Grindley, 3" **5.00**
Majolica, begonia leaf, 3" **20.00**
Majolica, Pansy, Etruscan, 3" **37.50**
Nippon, HP leaf & stem border, M in wreath mk **7.50**
Nippon, HP pine cones, M in wreath mk, 3¾" **8.50**
Nippon, HP roses, rising sun mk, 3½" **6.50**
O&EG Royal Austria, pk roses, 3½" **7.00**
Rosenthal, Carmen, HP forget-me-nots, 3⅝" **7.50**
Rosenthal, Tilly, yel & wht daisies **9.00**
Royal Bayreuth, bird & foliage, US Zone Germany...........**8.00**
Shelley, Bridal Rose, 6 flutes **22.50**
Shelley, Heraldic, 6 flutes **18.50**
Williamsburg repro of Wedgwood Husk......................**7.50**

Domestic, Glass

Early Am pattern glass, Daisy & Button, amber **12.50**
Early Am pattern glass, Daisy & Button, crystal, sq..........**7.50**
Early Am pattern glass, Hobbs Daisy & Button, amber daisies.......**32.00**
Early Am pattern glass, Tree of Life, bl **27.50**
Glass, clear, lady etched in border & center, gold rim...........**4.00**
Heisey, Ipswich, Sahara, 2⅜" sq **17.50**
Heisey, Narrow Flute, pk, 3"..**15.00**

Domestic, Metal

Pewter, plain, beaded edge, 3" **6.00**
Pewter w/china inset, raised cornflower center, 2¾" **18.00**
SP, Webster, emb floral/shell border, woman/churn center **12.50**
Sterling, Gorham, emb rose border, monogram center, 3¼" sq **22.50**

Buttonhooks

Buttonhooks were made from around the mid-1800s when high-button shoes made of stiff leather became fashionable and continued to be used to some extent until 1935. They were made of bone, brass, iron, or silver — simple utilitarian no-nonsense styles, fold-up styles with jeweled gold handles, and combination styles with built-in gadgets — all designed to ease the struggle of buttoning high-top shoes, long kid gloves, and stiffly starched collars. While most do have a hook end,

some were made with a wire loop instead. Study the construction; quality workmanship is an important worth-assesing factor in addition to the more obvious elements of material and design.

Brass, bird figural hdl **45.00**
Brass, repousse, folding type, 2 hooks........................**27.00**
Celluloid, gr w/marble overlay, 7" **9.00**
Ivory hdl, 2½" **25.00**
Lead, lady's-leg hdl, 7" **40.00**
Mother-of-pearl hdl, 2¼" **7.50**
Mother-of-pearl hdl, 3½" **18.00**
Plique-a-jour, HP floral, gold on silver, Shiebler, 3¼" **165.00**
SP, repousse, hollow hdl, 7¼" **26.00**
Sterling, Nouveau lady's head, flowing hair forms hdl, 6½" **65.00**
Sterling, orange/dk gr stones, Scotland, 1900, 2½" **65.00**
Sterling, repousse scrolls..**35.00**

Bybee

The Bybee Pottery was founded in 1809 in the small town of Bybee, Kentucky. Their earliest wares were primarily stoneware churns and jars. Today the work is carried on by sixth generation Cornelison potters who still use the same facilities and production methods to make a more diversified line of pottery. From a fine white clay mined only a few miles from the potting shed itself, the shop produces vases, jugs, dinnerware, and banks in a variety of colors, some of which are shipped to the larger cities to be sold in department stores and specialty shops. The bulk of their wares, however, is sold to the thousands of tourists who are attracted to the pottery each year.

Candle holder, bl gloss, saucer base, hdl **35.00**
Candlestick, gr mottle, spiral mold, 6x3", pr **42.00**
Jar, burgundy, mk, 1-gal..**175.00**
Lamp, gr mottle, triple hdl, 7" **55.00**
Mug, olive gloss...**14.00**
Vase, bl-gray semi-matt, wide shoulder w/flower holes, 4x5" **27.00**
Vase, dusty rose semi-matt, thrown, pinched, 4x3¼" **22.00**
Vase, gr variegated matt, ftd, hdls, 5x5" **36.00**
Vase, grasses relief, matt gr, flared rim, 11"................**200.00**

Calendar Plates

Calendar plates were advertising give-aways most popular from about 1906 until the late twenties. They were decorated with colorful underglaze decals of lovely ladies, flowers, animals, birds — and, of course, the twelve months of the year of their issue. During the late thirties they came into vogue again, but never to the extent they were originally. Those with exceptional detailing, or those with scenes of a particular activity are most desirable — so are any from before 1906.

1907, Christmas scene & holly **75.00**
1908, dog, 8½" **45.00**
1908, roses, 8" **40.00**
1909, fruit & flowers, 7" **25.00**
1909, Gibson Girl, 8½" **30.00**
1909, horse's head, gold trim **30.00**
1909, scenic, 8½" **25.00**
1910, Betsy Ross, Jersey City **38.00**
1910, irises, 8" **28.00**
1910, Niagara Falls, NY City...**25.00**
1911, harbor scene, MA **35.00**
1911, Old Acquaintance **25.00**

1910, Indian chief's portrait, Imperial China, 8", $25.00.

1912, airplanes, Peterson Bros, Hawley MN 25.00
1914, deer at stream, 7"...35.00
1915, Panama Canal, Am flag, gilt rim, 6" 30.00
1916, birds, Family Liquor Store, Steelton PA 38.00
1920, Victory, Sawtelle CA...35.00
1924, Happy New Year, Asbury Park 35.00
1928, deer scene, 8¾"..40.00
1930, Dutch boy & dog, 9" 50.00

Calendars

Calendars are collected for their colorful prints, often attributed to a well-recognized artist of the period. Advertising calendars from the turn of the century often have a double appeal when representing a company whose products are themselves collectible. See also Parrish, Maxwell; Rockwell, Norman.

1810-1920, DeLaval Cream Separators, perpetual, 5½x6½", VG .265.00
1876, Metropolitan, nymphs/cherubs, 15x11", NM 125.00
1888, Hood's Sarsaparilla, face diecut, fr, 18x11", EX.................325.00
1890, Aetna Insurance, mc cb, fr, 26x19", EX..............................290.00
1890, Hood's Sarsaparilla, children, cb, fr, 16½x10", EX 350.00
1890, NY Life Ins, EX 10.00
1893, Hood's Sarsaparilla, children, EX 25.00
1894, Hood's Sarsaparilla, young lady, VG 18.00
1894-95, Hood's Sarsaparilla, Sweet Sixteen, fr, 11x9", VG..........65.00
1896-97, Hood's Sarsaparilla, girl w/scarf, fr, 11x9", EX 425.00
1897, Winchester, 2 scenes by Frost, 26x14", VG.........................750.00
1900, Fairbanks Fairy Soap, girl w/flag, 10x12", EX......................20.00
1900, Montgomery Ward, building in Chicago, fr, 23x16", EX ...325.00
1900, Winchester, 2 hunting scenes, 26x14", EX..........................800.00
1902, Harrington/Richardson Arms, gun maker, fr, 20x11", EX..450.00
1904, DeLaval Cream Separators, children/corn, 18x12", VG ...250.00
1904, Tabor Prang litho, sunbonnet-type illus, 4-pg, EX...............55.00
1905, hunting dog, Bemis Bag Co, EX..250.00
1906, Armour's, lovely ladies, 1-pg missing, 15x10" 25.00
1906, Rice Seeds, girl's portrait, fr, 18x12", VG 40.00
1906, Youth Companion, Revolutionary militia, 24x13", EX........50.00
1908, McCormick, Harry Roseland illus, EX 250.00
1909, DeLaval Cream Separators, lady in pk, 20x13", EX............200.00

De Laval Cream Separators, 1908, $250.00.

1910, Comfort, mother & child, Gannett, fr, 8¾x5¼", EX..........45.00
1910, DeLaval Cream Separators, w/pad, 21½x13", EX 350.00
1911, Sharples Separators, people/cow/separator, 14x7", EX 140.00
1913, Deering, baseball scene, Hayes Litho, 19½x13", EX...........425.00
1913, Garden Calendar, 4-pg, 14x11", VG....................................15.00
1913, Henry Rogler, emb diecut, girl w/dove, fr, 18x12", EX.......125.00
1915, Magic Yeast, paper litho, Ketterlinus, 18x10", VG 225.00
1916, City Bank of Wheeling, girls, 16x10½", NM......................75.00
1916, Weed Tire Chains, ladies, fr, 30x10", VG 250.00
1917, DeLaval Cream Separators, w/pad, 24x12", EX 275.00
1919, American Art Works, fr, 28x16¾", VG...............................175.00
1920, lady golfer, Watkins, full pad, NM 20.00
1923, Old Chum Tobacco, complete, 32x18", EX.........................60.00
1928, DeLaval Cream Separators, children/goat, 22x12", EX 170.00
1928, Harrisburg Pilot, Not a Newspaper, 45x22", EX 90.00
1929, Star Brand Shoes, lady at window, fr, 26x10½", EX...........140.00
1930, DeLaval, Story of John & Mary, N Price, M in mailer 150.00
1936, Conewago Dairy, milking scene, complete, 17x11", EX 60.00
1937, Fruit Wine, Currier & Ives, 12-pg, EX 23.00
1938, Disney Silly Symphony, NM..115.00
1939, Mobilgas, 12-pg, 23x13", EX 25.00
1942, Texaco, pin-up girls, full sz, EX 38.00
1946, Vargas girls, complete pad, 12x8"...65.00

Caliente

Caliente was a line of colored dinnerware made by the Paden City Pottery Company in Paden City, West Virginia. It was produced during the 1930s and 1940s in tangerine, yellow, blue, green, and cobalt blue.

Bowl, orange, 9"...12.50
Bowl, salad; orange, 10" 12.50
Bowl, yel, 6"..6.00
Candle holder, red 9.00
Cup & saucer, aqua...6.00
Cup & saucer, cobalt 8.00
Plate, cobalt, 9"..5.00
Plate, red, 9"...5.00
Platter, yel, 14" 14.00

California Faience

California Faience was the trade name used by William V. Bragdon and Chauncy R. Thomas on vases, bowls, and other artware produced at their pottery known as 'The Tile Shop' in Berkeley, California, from 1920 to 1930. Faience tile was the principal product of the business during these years and is the favorite with today's collectors. Items in a glossy glaze are rare and therefore more valuable. Tiles were marked 'California Faience' with a die stamp.

Bookends, bear, reddish-brn, 4x4½x6", pr **300.00**
Bowl, bl, shell form, 12x15" **125.00**
Bowl, dk bl gloss, bl int, multi-sided, 2½x6" **85.00**
Candle holder, bl gloss, 5", pr...**175.00**
Flower holder, Oriental lady washing clothes........................**100.00**
Ginger jar, robin's egg bl gloss, mk, 10½x4½"......................**500.00**
Pitcher, gr, 8½"...**225.00**
Tile, flower, red w/gr leaves on sky bl, mk, 5½" dia..............**250.00**
Tile, mc fruit, 5" **240.00**
Tile, stylized bluebirds, turq/bl, 3¾" **165.00**
Vase, bl alligatored matt, 5" **170.00**
Vase, red gloss, stylized leaves, 6½" **175.00**
Vase, red matt, 3¼" **95.00**
Vase, 2-color, 3x5" **155.00**

California Perfume Company

D.H. McConnell, Sr., founded the California Perfume Company (C.P. Company; C.P.C.) in 1886 in New York City. He had previously been a salesman for a book company, which he later purchased. His door-to-door sales usually involved the lady of the house, to whom he presented a complimentary bottle of inexpensive perfume. Upon determining his perfume to be more popular than his books, he decided that the manufacture of perfume might be more lucrative. He bottled toiletries under the name 'California Perfume Company' and a line of household products called 'Perfection' until 1929, when 'Avon Products, Inc.' appeared on the label. In 1939 the C.P.C. name was entirely removed from the product. The success of the company is attributed to the door-to-door sales approach and 'money back' guarantee offered by his first 'Depot Agent,' Mrs. P.F.E. Albee, known today as the 'Avon Lady.'

The company's containers are quite collectible today, especially the older, hard-to-find items. Advanced collectors seek bottles and other items labeled Goetting & Co., New York; Goetting's; or Savoi Et Cie, Paris. Such examples date from 1871 to 1896. The Goetting Company was at one time owned by D.H. McConnell; Savoi Et Cie was a line which they imported to sell through department stores. Also of special interest are packaging and advertising with the Ambrosia or Hinze Ambrosia Company label. This was a subsidiary company whose objective seems to have been to produce a line of face creams, etc., for sale through drugstores and other such commercial outlets. They operated in New York from about 1875 until 1954. Because very little is known about these companies and since only a few examples of their product containers and advertising material have been found, market values for such items have not yet been established. Other examples of rare items sought by the collector include products marked Gertrude Recordon; Marvel Electric Silver Cleaner; Easy Day Automatic Clothes Washer; pre-1930 catalogs; and California Perfume Company 1909 and 1910 calendars.

There are hundreds of local Avon Collector Clubs throughout the world that also have C.P.C. collectors in their membership. If you are interested in joining, locating, or starting a new club, contact the National Association of Avon Collectors, Inc., listed in the Directory under Clubs, Newsletters, and Catalogs. Those wanting a National Newsletter Club or price guides may contact Avon Times or Avon Collectors' Club Western World listed in the same section. Inquiries concerning California Perfume Company items should be directed toward our advisor, Dick Pardini, whose address is given under California. (Please send SASE, not interested in Avon or Anniversary Keepsakes.)

American Ideal Lipstick, 1929, CPC on tube, M **40.00**
American Ideal Perfume, wood box, introductory sz, 1910, M.....**225.00**
American Ideal Perfume, 1929, gr satin box, 1-oz, MIB **140.00**
Ariel Perfume, 1930, glass stopper, 1-oz, MIB...........................**125.00**
Ariel Toilet Water, 1930-1935, 2-oz, M....................................**105.00**
Baby Set, 3-pc, w/box, 1916, MIB...**350.00**
Bandoline Hair Dressing, 1923, 4-oz, M...................................**65.00**
Bay Rum, 4-oz, 1908, M..**120.00**
Boudoir Manicure Set, 4-pc, w/booklet, 1929, M......................**125.00**
California Tooth Tablet, metal lid, glass bottom, ca 1900, M........**80.00**
Catalog, color, w/tabs, 1920s, M..**90.00**
CPC Sample Case, basketweave w/label, 1915, M **100.00**
Cut Glass Perfume, 1915, 2-oz, MIB...**225.00**
Daphne Bath Salts, 1925, glass jar w/gold label, 10-oz, MIB **70.00**
Daphne Talcum Powder, tin container, gr can, 1923, 4-oz, M.......**65.00**
Depilatory, 1915, 1-oz, M **100.00**
Easy Day/Simplex Auto Clothes Washer, '18, zinc, 11x9", MIB..**100.00**
Eau De Quinine, 1923, 6-oz, M **90.00**
Elite Powder, Perfect Foot Powder, oval can, 1923, sm, M.............**35.00**
Elite Powder, Perfect Foot Powder, tin can, 1923, 1-lb, M **75.00**
Gentleman's Shaving Set, 7-pc, w/box, 1917, MIB.....................**400.00**
Gertrude Recordon's Introductory Facial Treatment Set, MIB....**300.00**
Juvenile Set, 1915, MIB **435.00**
Lavender Salts, gr glass, 1910, MIB..**225.00**
Lemonal Cleansing Cream, jar, 1926, M **65.00**
Lilac Vegetal, ribbed glass, 1925, 2-oz, M **65.00**
Liquid Shampoo, 1923, 6-oz, M **85.00**
Little Folks Set, 4 bottles, 1937, MIB **175.00**
Lotus Cream, 1917, 12-oz, MIB..**160.00**
Lotus Cream, 1925, 4-oz, MIB..**90.00**
Marvel Electric Silver Cleaner, 1918, Pat Jan 11, 1910, MIB......**100.00**
Massage Cream, jar, 1916, M..**125.00**
Mission Garden Dbl Compact, brass, 1922, M **45.00**
Nail Cream, tin container, 1924, M...**10.00**
Narcissus Perfume, 1925, 1-oz, M..**120.00**
Narcissus Perfume, 1929-30, mc box, 1-oz, MIB **160.00**
Natoma Rose Perfume, 1914-15, glass bottle w/stopper, ½-oz, M .**160.00**
Natoma Rose Perfume, 1916, ½-oz, M......................................**150.00**
Natoma Rose Talcum, Indian woman, triangular, tin, '14, 4-oz, M..**110.00**
Natoma Rose Talcum Powder, tin container, 1911, 3½-oz, MIB .**160.00**
Perfection, Auto Lustre, can, 1930, 1-pt, M **80.00**
Perfection, Baking Powder, can, 1931, 1-lb, MIB......................**20.00**
Perfection, Coloring, bottle, 1934, ½-oz, M **15.00**
Perfection, Coloring Set, 5 bottles in wood box, 1920, MIB........**200.00**
Perfection, Furniture Polish, can, 1916, 12-oz, M **70.00**
Perfection, Kwick Cleaning Polish, can, 1922, 8-oz, M **50.00**
Perfection, Laundry Crystals, in box, 1931, MIB.......................**40.00**
Perfection, Liquid Shoe White, sample, 1935, ½-oz, M **30.00**
Perfection, Liquid Shoe White, 1931, 4-oz, M...........................**20.00**
Perfection, Liquid Spots Out, 1925, 4-oz, M.............................**45.00**
Perfection, Mending Cement, tube, 1933, MIB..........................**15.00**
Perfection, Mothicide, can, 1925, ½-lb, M **40.00**
Perfection, Olive Oil, can, 1931, 1-pt, M **40.00**
Perfection, Powdered Cleaner, can, ca 1934, 19-oz, M...............**12.00**
Perfection, Prepared Starch, can, 1931, 6-oz, M **20.00**
Perfection, Savoury Coloring, 1941, 4-oz, M.............................**12.00**
Perfection, Silver Cream Polish, can, 1931, ½-lb, M **20.00**
Perfume Sample Set, 1931, MIB **200.00**
Powder Sachet, bottle, ca 1915, M **50.00**

Powder Sachets, 1890s, M 90.00
Powder tin, 2 nude babies play w/giant rose ea side, 1912, M 100.00
Radiant Nail Powder, tin container, 1923, M.................................30.00
Rose Pomade, jar, milk glass, 1914, M 65.00
Shampoo Cream, milk glass, 1908, 4-oz, M 75.00
Sweet Sixteen Face Powder, paper container, 1916, M..................50.00
Tooth Tablet, aluminum lid, clear or milk wht bottom, '20s, M ...50.00
Tooth Wash, emb bottle w/label, 1915, M 105.00
Trailing Arbutus Face Powder, paper container, 1925, MIB 40.00
Trailing Arbutus Talcum, tin container, 1914, sample sz, M 85.00
Trailing Arbutus Talcum, tin container, 1925, 1-lb, M 70.00
Verna Talc, 1928, mc container, 4-oz, MIB 95.00
Vernafleur Face Powder, tin container, 1925, M 20.00
Vernafleur Perfume, 1923, 1-oz, MIB...140.00
Vernafleur Toilet Soap, 3 bars in paper box, 1936, MIB 60.00
Violet Almond Meal, tin container, 1923, 4-oz, M 45.00
Witch Hazel Cream, 1904, 2-oz tube, MIB...................................50.00

Calling Cards, Cases, and Receivers

The practice of announcing one's arrival with a calling card borne by the maid to the mistress of the house was a social grace of the Victorian era. Different messages — condolences, a personal visit, or a good-by — were related by turning down one corner or another. The custom was forgotten by WWI. Fashionable ladies and gents carried their personally engraved cards in elaborate cases made of such materials as embossed silver, mother-of-pearl with intricate inlay, tortoise shell, and ivory. Card receivers held cards left by visitors who called while the mistress was out or 'not receiving.' Calling cards with fringe, die-cut flaps that cover the name, or an unusual decoration are worth about $3.00 to $4.00, while plain cards usually sell for around $1.00.

Cases

Filigree, appl butterflies/florals/beads, unmk, 3¾x2⅝".................110.00
Gold, 14k, Art Nouveau style 650.00
Porc, lady's portrait HP on MOP, hinged lid, 2½x3¾" 195.00
Silver, eng foliage scrolls & scene of Whitley Court, 4"..............145.00
SP, children emb 135.00
Tortoise shell, ivory mts, English, 1800s 75.00

Receivers

CI, cupped hands w/grapes at wrist, 1865.......................................55.00

Bird on perch above scalloped, engraved tray, Pairpoint, 9", $245.00.

Pewter-like metal, lady w/flowing hair, 4½x7".................................78.00
Pk Dia Quilt MOP, HP florals/butterflies, metal fr, 9½" H 925.00
SP, Greenaway girl & dog atop rnd tray, Derby, EX 195.00
SP, 2 owls on branch by tray, Tufts...235.00
SP, 2 owls on oak branch support, inscription, Derby, 7".............450.00
Sterling, repousse floral border, claw ft, Dominick & Haff..........300.00
Sterling, woodland courtship scene, Nouveau style 250.00

Camark

The Camden Art and Tile Company of Camden, Arkansas, was organized in 1926. John Lessell and his wife were associated with the company only briefly before he died that same year. After his death, his wife stayed on and continued to decorate wares very similar to those he had made for Weller. Le-Camark closely resembled Weller LaSa; Lessell was almost a duplication of Marengo. Perhaps the most outstanding was a mirror black line with lustre decoration. Naturally, examples of these lines are very rare. The company eventually became known as Camark and began to produce commercial ware of the type listed below.

In 1986 the pottery was purchased and reopened, but according to the new owners the old molds will not be used.

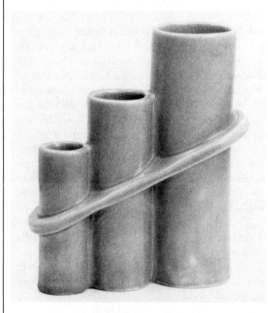

Three-cylinder yellow vase, 8", $20.00.

Basket, dbl; maroon, #138, 4½x5½" 12.00
Basket, flowers emb on cream, 5x3" 12.00
Basket, gr, flared, 2 hdls, 4½x5" 10.00
Bowl, angular, ribbing, bl, Deco, 6"...14.00
Bowl, console; Iris..11.00
Bowl, fruit; cream w/appl cherries, leaf hdls, 13" 18.00
Bowl, gr, leaf form w/turned-up end, 12" L 9.00
Bowl, gr, ribbed, scalloped, #624, 5x9¼"......................................15.00
Bowl, turq, ribbed, scalloped, 3x9½" 7.50
Candle holder, triple; wht, leaf motif...12.00
Cornucopia, ivory, horizontal ribs, 8x9"..9.50
Counter sign...50.00
Jardiniere, aqua, 9½"...25.00
Pitcher, bl w/parrot hdl, gold mk, 6" 40.00
Pitcher, Colonial man, chocolate, 5½" 20.00
Pitcher, maroon, Aladdin lamp style, #791, 8" L...........................12.00
Pitcher, wht, #139B, 4¼" 5.00
Pitcher, yel, #791 ....12.00
Pitcher & bowl, apple gr, emb scrolls, 3¼" pitcher 9.50

Planter, dbl swan, wht w/HP beak & eyes, 7x7" 12.00
Shakers, S&P shapes, pr 8.00
Teapot & warmer, swirled, 8"...18.50
Vase, blk, #288, 10x12" 12.50
Vase, geometrics at flared top & base, gr matt, #406, 7"................12.00
Vase, roses, #807 ....16.00
Vase, yel, leaf form, flared/split top, ftd, #827, 5" 7.50
Wall pocket, window box form, #218... 7.50

Cambridge Glass

The Cambridge Glass Company began operations in 1901 in Cambridge, Ohio. Primarily they made primarily crystal dinnerware and well-designed accessory pieces until the 1920s when they introduced the concept of color that was to become so popular on the American dinnerware market. Always maintaining high standards of quality and elegance, they produced many lines that became best-sellers; through the twenties and thirties they were recognized as the largest manufacturer of this type of glassware in the world.

Of the various marks the company used, the 'C in triangle' is the most familiar. Production stopped in 1958. For a more thorough study of the subject, we recommend *Colors in Cambridge Glass*, by the National Cambridge Collectors, Inc.; their address may be found in the Directory under Clubs. See also Carnival Glass.

Animals and Birds

Bluejay, flower holder...125.00
Bluejay, peg base 100.00
Eagle, bookend, ea 80.00
Eagle on ball 135.00
Heron, lg, 12"..125.00
Heron, sm, 9" 75.00
Lion, bookend, ea 95.00
Pouter pigeon, bookend, ea 40.00
Scottie, bookend, pr 150.00
Scottie, frosted, ea..75.00
Sea gull, flower frog...45.00
Swan, candlestick, milk glass, 4½" 175.00
Swan, carmen, 3½" 75.00
Swan, carmen, 6½"...200.00
Swan, carmen, 8½"...250.00
Swan, Crown Tuscan, 3½"..35.00
Swan, Crown Tuscan, 8½"..95.00
Swan, ebony, 10½"..300.00
Swan, ebony, 12½"..350.00
Swan, ebony, 3½"..60.00
Swan, ebony, 6½"...100.00
Swan, ebony, 8½"...125.00
Swan, emerald, 3½"...35.00
Swan, emerald, 6½"...85.00
Swan, emerald, 8½"...125.00
Swan, milk glass, 3½"..60.00
Swan, milk glass, 4½"..75.00
Swan, milk glass, 6½"..125.00
Swan, milk glass, 8½"..300.00
Turkey, amber, w/lid..450.00
Turkey, bl, w/lid 500.00
Turkey, gr, w/lid 450.00
Turkey, pk, w/lid 400.00

Apple Blossom, colors; bowl, low ftd, 11" 42.00

Apple Blossom, colors; bowl, 4-ftd, 12"..50.00
Apple Blossom, colors; candelabrum, 3-lite, keyhole 37.50
Apple Blossom, colors; candlestick, 2-lite, keyhole 32.50
Apple Blossom, colors; cup..22.50
Apple Blossom, colors; pitcher, #3130, 64-oz..............................200.00
Apple Blossom, colors; plate, salad; sq..16.00
Apple Blossom, colors; plate, sandwich; hdls, 12½" 38.00
Apple Blossom, colors; plate, tea; 7½".. 12.00
Apple Blossom, colors; tumbler, #3025, 10-oz...............................26.00
Apple Blossom, colors; tumbler, #3135, ftd, 12-oz.........................30.00
Apple Blossom, colors; tumbler, #3135, ftd, 5-oz...........................18.00
Apple Blossom, colors; tumbler, #3400, ftd, 9-oz...........................20.00
Apple Blossom, colors; vase, 2 styles, 8", ea 55.00
Apple Blossom, crystal; bowl, baker, 10".......................................20.00
Apple Blossom, crystal; bowl, cereal; 6" 10.00
Apple Blossom, crystal; bowl, flat, 12"...28.00
Apple Blossom, crystal; bowl, pickle; 9" 11.00
Apple Blossom, crystal; bowl, 13" 20.00
Apple Blossom, crystal; candlestick, 1-lite, keyhole 12.00
Apple Blossom, crystal; comport, fruit cocktail; 4" 12.50
Apple Blossom, crystal; creamer, ftd 11.00
Apple Blossom, crystal; pitcher, #3025, 64-oz..............................100.00
Apple Blossom, crystal; pitcher, ball, 80-oz..................................110.00
Apple Blossom, crystal; pitcher, ftd, 50-oz.....................................85.00
Apple Blossom, crystal; plate, dinner; sq 35.00
Apple Blossom, crystal; tumbler, #3130, ftd, 8-oz 12.00
Apple Blossom, crystal; vase, 5" 22.00
Caprice, blue; bonbon, #154, sq, hdls 300.00
Caprice, blue; bowl, #65, oval, hdls, 4-ftd, 11" 600.00
Caprice, blue; bowl, jelly; #151, hdls, 5" 27.50
Caprice, blue; bowl, relish; #124, 8" 32.50
Caprice, blue; cake plate, #36, ftd, 13" 250.00
Caprice, blue; candlestick, keyhole; #647, 5" 35.00
Caprice, blue; cigarette box, #207, w/lid, 3½x2¼".........................27.50
Caprice, blue; cigarette holder, #204, triangular, 3x3" 40.00
Caprice, blue; comport, #136, 7"..70.00
Caprice, blue; mayonnaise, #106, 3-pc set, 8"................................67.50
Caprice, blue; plate, #30, 16" 65.00
Caprice, blue; plate, cabaret; #32, 4-ftd, 11" 40.00
Caprice, blue; plate, cabaret; #33, 4-ftd, 14" 42.50
Caprice, blue; plate, lemon; #152, hdl, 6½" 20.00
Caprice, blue; salad dressing, #112, ftd, hdld, 3-pc 325.00
Caprice, blue; shakers, #92, ind, flat, pr 200.00
Caprice, blue; tumbler, #10, ftd, 10-oz 33.00
Caprice, blue; tumbler, #310, flat, 10-oz 40.00
Caprice, blue; tumbler, #9, ftd, 12-oz 40.00
Caprice, blue; tumbler, juice; #300, ftd, 5-oz 36.00
Caprice, blue; vase, #254, 6" 100.00
Caprice, blue; vase, #342, 6" 85.00
Caprice, colors; bowl, relish; #124, 3-part, 8".................................32.50
Caprice, crystal; ash tray, #215, 4" 7.00
Caprice, crystal; bottle, #186, 7-oz...65.00
Caprice, crystal; bowl, #58, sq, 4-ftd, 10" 30.00
Caprice, crystal; bowl, #62, belled, 4-ftd, 12½"..............................30.00
Caprice, crystal; candle reflector..125.00
Caprice, crystal; candy dish, #168, w/lid, 6" 50.00
Caprice, crystal; creamer, #40, ind 12.00
Caprice, crystal; decanter, #187, w/stopper, 35-oz.........................100.00
Caprice, crystal; mustard, #87, w/lid, 2-oz......................................40.00
Caprice, crystal; oil, #100, w/stopper, 5-oz.....................................65.00
Caprice, crystal; plate, #22, 8½"..14.00
Caprice, crystal; plate, bread & butter; #21, 6½" 10.00
Caprice, crystal; shakers, #90, ball, ind, pr 30.00
Caprice, crystal; tumbler, #12, ftd, 3-oz 18.00

Caprice, crystal; tumbler, #15, str sided, 12-oz................35.00
Caprice, crystal; tumbler, #300, 10-oz..............................18.00
Caprice, crystal; tumbler, #310, flat, 10-oz......................15.00
Caprice, crystal; tumbler, juice; #301, blown, 5-oz.........13.00
Caprice, crystal; tumbler, tea; #301, blown, 12-oz..........17.00
Caprice, crystal; vase, ivy bowl; #232.............................40.00

Caprice vase, cobalt, 9", $275.00.

Centennial, blk; candlestick, #627, ca 1927-36..............45.00
Chantilly, crystal; bowl, celery or relish; 3-part, 12"........30.00
Chantilly, crystal; bowl, celery or relish; 5-part, 12"........30.00
Chantilly, crystal; bowl, relish or pickle; 7" 18.00
Chantilly, crystal; bowl, tab hdls, 11" 27.00
Chantilly, crystal; bowl, 4-ftd, flared, 12".......................30.00
Chantilly, crystal; candlestick, 2-lite, fleur-de-lis, 6" 26.00
Chantilly, crystal; candlestick, 5"...................................17.50
Chantilly, crystal; candy box, rnd, w/lid 52.50
Chantilly, crystal; comport, 5½" 30.00
Chantilly, crystal; creamer..14.50
Chantilly, crystal; lamp, hurricane; candlestick base 75.00
Chantilly, crystal; mayonnaise, w/liner, 2 ladles 38.00
Chantilly, crystal; pitcher, Doulton 190.00
Chantilly, crystal; pitcher, upright.................................155.00
Chantilly, crystal; plate, salad; 8".....................................12.50
Chantilly, crystal; plate, service; 4-ftd, 12".....................23.00
Chantilly, crystal; shakers, pr 27.50
Chantilly, crystal; tumbler, juice; #3600, ftd, 5-oz...........14.00
Chantilly, crystal; tumbler, tea; #3779, ftd, 12-oz...........18.00
Chantilly, crystal; tumbler, water; #3625, ftd, 10-oz........15.00
Chantilly, crystal; tumbler, water; #3775, ftd, 10-oz........15.00
Chantilly, crystal; vase, bud; 10"....................................25.00
Chantilly, crystal; vase, flower; ftd, 13".............................45.00
Chantilly, crystal; vase, flower; high ftd, 8" 22.00
Chantilly, crystal; vase, globe; 5" 27.00
Cleo, all colors; bowl, comport; 4-ftd, 6"..........................35.00
Cleo, all colors; bowl, console; miniature, 8"....................90.00
Cleo, all colors; bowl, oval, 11" 35.00
Cleo, all colors; bowl, pickle; Decagon, 9".......................25.00
Cleo, all colors; bowl, relish; 2-part..................................20.00
Cleo, all colors; bowl, vegetable; w/lid, 9".......................100.00
Cleo, all colors; candy box..65.00
Cleo, all colors; humidor 250.00
Cleo, all colors; pitcher, #804, w/lid, 60-oz....................210.00
Cleo, all colors; pitcher, w/lid, 22-oz...............................125.00

Cleo, all colors; plate, hdls, Decagon, 11"......................24.00
Cleo, all colors; plate, hdls, Decagon, 7".........................14.00
Cleo, all colors; plate, 15"..55.00
Cleo, all colors; plate, 7"..11.50
Cleo, all colors; platter, w/lid...150.00
Cleo, all colors; platter, 15"...55.00
Cleo, all colors; tumbler, #3077, ftd, 10-oz.....................22.50
Cleo, all colors; tumbler, #3077, ftd, 2 ½-oz....................20.00
Cleo, all colors; tumbler, #3115, ftd, 12-oz.....................27.00
Cleo, all colors; tumbler, #3115, ftd, 5-oz.......................20.00
Cleo, all colors; tumbler, #3115, ftd, 8-oz.......................22.00
Cleo, all colors; vase, 11"...100.00

Crown Tuscan ball jug, rare, $3,400.00.

Crown Tuscan, bowl, flying nude, #3011/40 ....195.00
Crown Tuscan, bowl, seashell, #18, 3-toed, 10" 75.00
Crown Tuscan, candlestick, dolphin, shell, ftd, 4", pr........100.00
Crown Tuscan, candy dish, #3500/57, 3-part, w/lid 65.00
Crown Tuscan, compote, nude stem, gold trim w/roses, 7" 150.00
Crown Tuscan, compote, nude stem, 7" 100.00
Crown Tuscan, compote, seashell, floral decor, 7" 125.00
Crown Tuscan, dish, shell, 3-ftd, 11" 75.00
Crown Tuscan, flower holder, seashell 58.00
Crown Tuscan, vase, centerpiece; shell, ftd, 8"................88.00
Crown Tuscan, vase, cornucopia; #3900/575, 10"...........55.00
Decagon, blk; bowl, #984, hdls, 10"................................65.00
Decagon, blk; cup, #865, ca 1928-31............................... 8.00
Decagon, blk; tray (for sugar bowl & creamer), #1095 ....22.00
Decagon, pastels; bowl, almond; ftd, 6".............................20.00
Decagon, pastels; bowl, vegetable; rnd, 9" 14.00
Decagon, pastels; comport, tall, 7" 20.00
Decagon, pastels; plate, service; 10" 8.50
Decagon, pastels; sauce boat, w/underplate.....................45.00
Decagon, pastels; stem, cordial...25.00
Decagon, pastels; stem, sherbet; 6-oz............................... 9.00
Decagon, pastels; sugar bowl, lightning-bolt hdls 7.00
Decagon, pastels; tray, pickle; 9"....................................10.00
Decagon, pastels; tray, service; oval, 12"..........................10.00
Decagon, pastels; tumbler, ftd, 10-oz..............................12.00
Decagon, pastels; tumbler, ftd, 8-oz................................10.00
Decagon, red or bl; bowl, berry; 10" 20.00
Decagon, red or bl; bowl, bouillon; w/liner 12.50
Decagon, red or bl; bowl, cereal; belled, 6" 12.50
Decagon, red or bl; bowl, cereal; flat rim, 6" 12.00
Decagon, red or bl; bowl, cream soup; w/liner 22.00
Decagon, red or bl; bowl, relish; 2-part, 11" 17.50

Decagon, red or bl; bowl, relish; 2-part, 9"................15.00
Decagon, red or bl; creamer, lightning-bolt hdls................12.00
Decagon, red or bl; gravy boat, hdls, w/liner................85.00
Decagon, red or bl; gravy boat, w/hdld liner................85.00
Decagon, red or bl; mayonnaise, hdls, w/hdld liner & ladle..........40.00
Decagon, red or bl; mayonnaise, w/liner & ladle................30.00
Decagon, red or bl; plate, grill; 10"................14.00
Decagon, red or bl; plate, hdls, 7"................15.00
Decagon, red or bl; stem, cordial; 10-oz................20.00
Decagon, red or bl; stem, water; 9-oz................30.00
Decagon, red or bl; sugar bowl, tall, ftd, lg................18.00
Decagon, red or bl; tray, service; hdls, 13"................30.00
Decagon, red or bl; tray, service; oval, 11"................15.00
Decagon, red or bl; tumbler, ftd, 5-oz................15.00
Diane, crystal; bowl, berry; 5"................20.00
Diane, crystal; bowl, celery or relish; 3-part, 12"................32.50
Diane, crystal; bowl, celery or relish; 3-part, 9"................30.00
Diane, crystal; bowl, hdls, 11"................35.00
Diane, crystal; bowl, relish or pickle; 7"................22.00
Diane, crystal; bowl, relish; 2-part, 6"................18.00
Diane, crystal; bowl, water; #3106, w/liner................25.00
Diane, crystal; cabinet flask................150.00
Diane, crystal; candelbrum, 2-lite................22.50
Diane, crystal; candlestick, 5"................17.50
Diane, crystal; cigarette urn................35.00
Diane, crystal; cocktail shaker, glass top................100.00
Diane, crystal; creamer, #3400, scroll hdls................14.00
Diane, crystal; lamp, hurricane; candlestick base................90.00
Diane, crystal; pitcher, Doulton................200.00
Diane, crystal; plate, bonbon; hdls, ftd, 8"................11.00
Diane, crystal; plate, hdls, 6"................7.00
Diane, crystal; plate, torte; 4-ftd, 13"................35.00
Diane, crystal; shakers, ftd, glass tops, pr................32.00
Diane, crystal; stem, cocktail; #1066, 3-oz................16.00
Diane, crystal; stem, oyster/cocktail; #1066, 5-oz................12.00
Diane, crystal; stem, sherbet; #3122, 7-oz................11.00
Diane, crystal; tumbler, sham bottom, 12-oz................30.00
Diane, crystal; tumbler, sham bottom, 14-oz................35.00
Diane, crystal; tumbler, sham bottom, 5-oz................27.00
Diane, crystal; tumbler, water; #3106, ftd, 9-oz................11.00
Diane, crystal; vase, flower; high ftd, 8"................28.00
Diane, crystal; vase, keyhole base, 12"................45.00
Elaine, crystal; bowl, pickle or relish; 7"................18.00
Elaine, crystal; bowl, 4-ftd, flared, 12"................30.00
Elaine, crystal; cake plate, tab hdld, 13½"................30.00
Elaine, crystal; candlestick, 3-lite, 6"................32.00
Elaine, crystal; creamer................11.00
Elaine, crystal; lamp, hurricane; candlestick base................75.00
Elaine, crystal; pitcher, upright................145.00
Elaine, crystal; plate, salad; 8"................12.50
Elaine, crystal; shakers, pr................27.50
Elaine, crystal; stem, cordial; #3121, 1-oz................47.50
Elaine, crystal; stem, sherbet; #1402, tall................15.00
Elaine, crystal; stem, water; #3121, 10-oz................21.00
Elaine, crystal; stem, wine; #3121, 3½-oz................27.50
Elaine, crystal; stem, wine; #3500, 2½-oz................25.00
Elaine, crystal; sugar bowl................10.00
Elaine, crystal; tumbler, juice; #3500, ftd, 5-oz................17.00
Elaine, crystal; tumbler, tea; #1402, ftd, tall, 12-oz................20.00
Elaine, crystal; vase, ftd, 6"................22.00
Elaine, crystal; vase, ftd, 8"................82.00
Flower frog, Bashful Charlotte, amber, 13"................180.00
Flower frog, Bashful Charlotte, crystal, 11"................150.00
Flower frog, Bashful Charlotte, crystal, 6½"................75.00

Flower frog, Bashful Charlotte, gr, 11"................250.00
Flower frog, Bashful Charlotte, gr, 6½"................145.00
Flower frog, Bashful Charlotte, lt amber, 11"................250.00
Flower frog, Bashful Charlotte, lt gr, 11"................250.00
Flower frog, Bashful Charlotte, midnight bl, 11"................550.00
Flower frog, Bashful Charlotte, pk, 6½"................125.00
Flower frog, Bashful Charlotte, pk frost, 11"................200.00
Flower frog, Buddha, amber................350.00
Flower frog, Draped Lady, amber, 8½"................175.00
Flower frog, Draped Lady, bl, 8½"................280.00
Flower frog, Draped Lady, crystal, 12½"................150.00
Flower frog, Draped Lady, crystal, 8½"................95.00
Flower frog, Draped Lady, crystal frost, 13"................250.00
Flower frog, Draped Lady, dk amber, 13"................325.00
Flower frog, Draped Lady, dk amber, 8½"................195.00
Flower frog, Draped Lady, gr, 13"................225.00
Flower frog, Draped Lady, gr, 8½"................125.00
Flower frog, Draped Lady, gr frost, 13"................225.00
Flower frog, Draped Lady, gr frost, 8½"................125.00
Flower frog, Draped Lady, lt emerald, #513, 13"................250.00
Flower frog, Draped Lady, mandarin gold, #518, 8½"................200.00
Flower frog, Draped Lady, moonlight bl frost, 8½"................325.00
Flower frog, Draped Lady, pk, 13"................250.00
Flower frog, Draped Lady, pk, 8½"................100.00
Flower frog, Draped Lady, pk frost, 8½"................125.00
Flower frog, Draped Lady, yel, 8½"................230.00
Flower frog, Geisha Girl, crystal, w/base................300.00
Flower frog, Geisha Girl, pk, w/base................450.00
Flower frog, Mandolin Lady, crystal................150.00
Flower frog, Mandolin Lady, gr, bent bk, 9"................370.00
Flower frog, Mandolin Lady, lt gr................225.00
Flower frog, Mandolin Lady, pk................225.00
Flower frog, Melon Boy, gr................400.00
Flower frog, Melon Boy, pk................400.00
Flower frog, Rose Lady, amber, 8½"................200.00
Flower frog, Rose Lady, crystal, low base................190.00
Flower frog, Rose Lady, crystal, tall base................125.00
Flower frog, Rose Lady, crystal satin, tall base................225.00
Flower frog, Rose Lady, dk amber satin, tall base................250.00
Flower frog, Rose Lady, gr frost................230.00
Flower frog, Rose Lady, lt amber................265.00
Flower frog, Rose Lady, lt gr................165.00
Flower frog, Rose Lady, pk................200.00
Flower frog, 2 Kids, crystal................150.00
Flower frog, 2 Kids, gr frost................225.00
Flower frog, 2 Kids, mocha, 9"................250.00
Gloria, colors; bowl, bonbon; ftd, 5½"................19.00
Gloria, colors; bowl, cranberry; 4-ftd, 3½"................32.00
Gloria, colors; bowl, fruit; hdls, 11"................55.00
Gloria, colors; bowl, relish; 3-hdld, 3-part, 8"................34.00
Gloria, colors; comport, tall, 7"................65.00
Gloria, colors; cup, sq, 4-ftd................10.00
Gloria, colors; plate, hdls, 11"................25.00
Gloria, colors; plate, salad; sq................12.00
Gloria, colors; stem, cocktail; #3035, 3-oz................28.00
Gloria, colors; stem, cordial; #3120, 1-oz................75.00
Gloria, colors; stem, water; #3130, 8-oz................25.00
Gloria, colors; tray, sandwich; center hdl, 11"................30.00
Gloria, colors; tumbler, #3035, high ftd, 12-oz................23.00
Gloria, colors; tumbler, #3120, ftd, 10-oz................20.00
Gloria, colors; tumbler, #3130, ftd, 12-oz................21.00
Gloria, colors; vase, 11"................80.00
Gloria, crystal; bowl, bonbon; hdls, 5½"................14.00
Gloria, crystal; bowl, relish; hdls, 2-part, 8"................15.00

Gloria, crystal; bowl, vegetable; hdls, 9½" 55.00
Gloria, crystal; bowl, 4-ftd, oval, 12" 30.00
Gloria, crystal; creamer, ftd 11.00
Gloria, crystal; pitcher, w/lid, 64-oz 95.00
Gloria, crystal; plate, chop or salad; 14" 35.00
Gloria, crystal; shakers, tall, glass tops, pr 27.50
Gloria, crystal; stem, sherbet; #3035, tall, 6-oz 11.00
Gloria, crystal; stem, sherbet; #3120, tall, 6-oz 11.00
Gloria, crystal; sugar bowl, ftd, tall 11.00
Gloria, crystal; tray, pickle; tab hdld, 9" 15.00
Gloria, crystal; tumbler, #3115, ftd, 8-oz 12.00
Gloria, crystal; tumbler, #3130, ftd, 5-oz 12.00
Gloria, crystal; vase, neck indent, 11" 42.50
Gloria, crystal; vase, 4 indents, oval, 9" 45.00
Imperial Hunt Scene, colors; bowl, 3-part, 8½" 40.00
Imperial Hunt Scene, colors; bowl, 8" 37.50
Imperial Hunt Scene, colors; ice tub 55.00
Imperial Hunt Scene, colors; mayonnaise, w/liner 50.00
Imperial Hunt Scene, colors; pitcher, #3077, w/lid, 63-oz 195.00
Imperial Hunt Scene, colors; plate, 8" 22.00
Imperial Hunt Scene, colors; stem, cocktail; #1402, 3-oz 30.00
Imperial Hunt Scene, colors; stem, tomato; #1402, 6-oz 20.00
Imperial Hunt Scene, colors; tumbler, #1402, tall, 10-oz 22.50
Imperial Hunt Scene, colors; tumbler, #3077, ftd, 15-oz 18.00
Mt Vernon, amber; ash tray, #68, 4" 11.00
Mt Vernon, amber; bowl, #121, flared, 12½" 32.00
Mt Vernon, amber; bowl, #43, deep, 10½" 25.00
Mt Vernon, amber; bowl, #61, shallow, cupped, 11½" 25.00
Mt Vernon, amber; bowl, fruit; #6, 5¼" 10.00
Mt Vernon, amber; box, #15, rnd, ftd, w/lid, 4½" 30.00
Mt Vernon, amber; candelabrum, #38, 13½" 40.00
Mt Vernon, amber; candlestick, #110, 2-lite, 5" 15.00
Mt Vernon, amber; celery, #79, 12" 20.00
Mt Vernon, amber; cigarette holder, #66 ....15.00
Mt Vernon, amber; comport, #11, 7½" 25.00
Mt Vernon, amber; comport, #77, hdls, 5½" 15.00
Mt Vernon, amber; creamer, #4, ind 10.00
Mt Vernon, amber; decanter, #47, 11-oz 40.00
Mt Vernon, amber; honey jar, #74, w/lid 25.00
Mt Vernon, amber; lamp, hurricane; #1607, 9" 60.00
Mt Vernon, amber; pickle, #78, 1-hdl, 6" 12.00
Mt Vernon, crystal; bowl, bonbon; #10, ftd, 7" 12.50
Mt Vernon, crystal; bowl, finger; #23 ....10.00
Mt Vernon, crystal; pitcher, #95, ball, 80-oz 90.00
Mt Vernon, crystal; plate, bread & butter; #19, 6⅜" 4.00
Mt Vernon, crystal; plate, dinner; #40, 10½" 20.00
Mt Vernon, crystal; relish, #101, hdls, 2-part, 8" 17.50
Mt Vernon, crystal; relish, #103, 3-hdl, 3-part, 8" 20.00
Mt Vernon, crystal; shakers, #28, pr 22.50
Mt Vernon, crystal; shakers, #88, short, pr 20.00
Mt Vernon, crystal; stem, claret; #25, 4½" 12.50
Mt Vernon, crystal; stem, cocktail; #26, 3½" 9.00
Mt Vernon, crystal; stem, water; #1, 10-oz 12.50
Mt Vernon, crystal; sugar bowl, #44, ind 10.00
Mt Vernon, crystal; tumbler, old fashioned; #57, 7-oz 14.00
Mt Vernon, crystal; tumbler, tea; #20, ftd, 12-oz 16.00
Mt Vernon, crystal; tumbler, whiskey; #55, 2-oz 10.00
Mt Vernon, crystal; vase, #107, wide, 6½" 27.50
Mt Vernon, crystal; vase, #42, 5" 15.00
Mt Vernon, crystal; vase, #54, ftd, 7" 35.00
Nude stem, amber; brandy 100.00
Nude stem, amber; cocktail 90.00
Nude stem, amethyst; ash tray 200.00
Nude stem, amethyst; claret 100.00

Nude stem, amethyst; cocktail 90.00
Nude stem, amethyst; comport, flared 125.00
Nude stem, amethyst; goblet, water 115.00
Nude stem, carmen; brandy 120.00
Nude stem, carmen; champagne 135.00
Nude stem, carmen; claret 125.00
Nude stem, carmen; comport, cupped 125.00
Nude stem, carmen; goblet, water 120.00
Nude stem, carmen; ivy ball 200.00
Nude stem, cobalt; brandy 90.00
Nude stem, cobalt; goblet water 140.00
Nude stem, Crown Tuscan; ash tray 250.00
Nude stem, Crown Tuscan; bowl; flying nude, gold trim 225.00
Nude stem, Crown Tuscan; candlestick 110.00
Nude stem, Crown Tuscan; compote, SS-11, 7¾" 155.00
Nude stem, Crown Tuscan; ivy ball 225.00
Nude stem, crystal; comport, cupped 125.00
Nude stem, crystal; goblet, water 115.00
Nude stem, dk gr; brandy 100.00
Nude stem, dk gr; claret 100.00
Nude stem, dk gr; cocktail 90.00
Nude stem, dk gr; comport, cupped 120.00
Nude stem, dk gr; goblet, water 125.00
Nude stem, dk gr; ivy ball 200.00
Nude stem, emerald gr; brandy 125.00
Nude stem, Gold Krystol; brandy 110.00
Nude stem, Gold Krystol; cocktail 100.00
Nude stem, Gold Krystol; cocktail, w/Crown Tuscan stem & ft ..115.00
Nude stem, pistachio; cocktail 95.00
Nude stem, pk & Tahoe bl; cocktail 150.00
Nude stem, royal bl; claret 125.00
Nude stem, royal bl; goblet, water 145.00
Nude stem, topaz; sauterne 500.00
Nude stem, Windsor bl; bowl 750.00
Nude stem, Windsor bl; compote, SS-11, 7¾" 450.00
Portia, crystal; bowl, relish or pickle; 7" 18.00
Portia, crystal; bowl, relish; 2-part, 6" 16.00
Portia, crystal; candlestick, 5" 17.50
Portia, crystal; candy box, rnd, w/lid 60.00
Portia, crystal; comport, 5½" 27.50
Portia, crystal; creamer, hdls, ball 15.00
Portia, crystal; mayonnaise, w/liner & ladle 30.00
Portia, crystal; pitcher, ball 100.00
Portia, crystal; plate, salad; 8" 12.50
Portia, crystal; plate, torte; 4 ftd, 13" 30.00
Portia, crystal; shakers, pr 25.00
Portia, crystal; stem, oyster cocktail; #3121, 4½" 15.00
Portia, crystal; stem, sherbet; #3121, low, 6-oz 13.50
Portia, crystal; stem, sherbet; #3126, tall, 7-oz 15.00
Portia, crystal; stem, wine; #3121, 2½" 22.50
Portia, crystal; sugar bowl, ind 11.50
Portia, crystal; tumbler, bar; #3121, 2½-oz 20.00
Portia, crystal; tumbler, juice; #3126, 5-oz 14.00
Portia, crystal; tumbler, water; #3121, ftd, 10-oz 16.50
Portia, crystal; vase, bud; 10" 30.00
Portia, crystal; vase, ftd, 8" 40.00
Rosalie, colors; bowl, basket; hdls, 7" 225.00
Rosalie, colors; bowl, bonbon; hdls, 5½" 15.00
Rosalie, colors; bowl, console; oval, 15" 35.00
Rosalie, colors; bowl, finger; w/liner 25.00
Rosalie, colors; bowl, oval, 15½" 45.00
Rosalie, colors; candlestick, 3-lite, keyhole, 6" 400.00
Rosalie, colors; celery, 11" 22.50
Rosalie, colors; comport, hdls, 5½" 20.00

Rosalie, colors; comport, low ftd, 6½" 30.00
Rosalie, colors; creamer, ftd, tall.................................20.00
Rosalie, colors; nut, ftd, 2½" 35.00
Rosalie, colors; plate, bread & butter; 6¾" 5.50
Rosalie, colors; plate, hdls, 11" 22.50
Rosalie, colors; plate, hdls, 8⅜" 13.50
Rosalie, colors; relish, 2-part, 9" 17.50
Rosalie, colors; stem, cordial; #3077, 1-oz..................50.00
Rosalie, colors; tray, center hdl, 11" 30.00
Rosalie, colors; tray for sugar shaker & creamer 25.00
Rosalie, colors; tumbler, #3077, ftd, 5-oz 16.00
Rosalie, colors; vase, 6" 40.00
Rose Point, crystal; ash tray, #3500/124, 3¼" 30.00
Rose Point, crystal; bowl, #3400/168, flared, 10½" 60.00
Rose Point, crystal; bowl, #3500/49, hdld, 5" 42.50
Rose Point, crystal; bowl, #3900/62, 4-ftd, flared, 12" 65.00
Rose Point, crystal; bowl, cereal; #3500/11, 6" 40.00
Rose Point, crystal; bowl, relish; #3400/91, 3-part, 8" 40.00
Rose Point, crystal; candlestick, #3900/67, 5" 50.00
Rose Point, crystal; candy box, #103, rnd, w/lid, 7" 125.00
Rose Point, crystal; cheese & cracker plate, #3900/135, 13" 100.00
Rose Point, crystal; cigarette box, #615, w/lid 90.00
Rose Point, crystal; comport, #3400/74, 4-ftd, 5" 35.00
Rose Point, crystal; creamer, #3900/41, ftd.................22.50
Rose Point, crystal; decanter, #3400/119, w/stopper, 12-oz..........165.00
Rose Point, crystal; lamp, hurricane; #1603, keyhole base 225.00
Rose Point, crystal; mayonnaise, #3900/111, w/liner & ladle........80.00
Rose Point, crystal; pitcher, #3900/115, 76-oz............155.00
Rose Point, crystal; pitcher, #3900/118, 32-oz............180.00
Rose Point, crystal; plate, #1397, rolled edge, 13½" 75.00
Rose Point, crystal; plate, luncheon; #3400/63, 9½" 32.50
Rose Point, crystal; plate, salad; #3900/115, 76-oz 155.00
Rose Point, crystal; plate, service; #3900/26, 4-ftd 65.00
Rose Point, crystal; plate, torte; #3400/65.................77.50

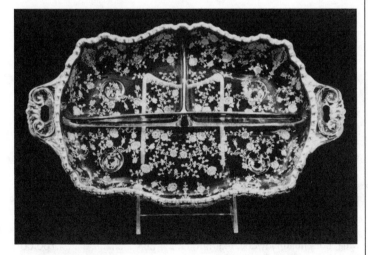

Rose Point three-part relish tray, 12", $55.00.

Rose Point, crystal; relish, #3500/65, 4-part, 10" 60.00
Rose Point, crystal; shakers, #3400/77, ftd, w/chrome tops, pr 50.00
Rose Point, crystal; stem, claret; #3121, 4½-oz 55.00
Rose Point, crystal; tumbler, #3900, 5-oz 40.00
Rose Point, crystal; tumbler, water; #3500, low ftd, 10-oz.............20.00
Rose Point, crystal; urn, #3500/41, 10" 200.00
Rose Point, crystal; vase, #1238, ftd, keyhole, 12".......125.00
Rose Point, crystal; vase, bud; #1528, 10" 75.00
Valencia, crystal; ash tray, #3500/126, rnd, 4".............12.00
Valencia, crystal; bowl, #3500/115, hdls, ftd, 9½" 35.00

Valencia, crystal; bowl, finger; #3500, ftd 27.50
Valencia, crystal; celery, #1402/94, 12" 30.00
Valencia, crystal; cigarette holder, #1066, ftd..............35.00
Valencia, crystal; comport, #3500/36, 6" 27.50
Valencia, crystal; creamer, #3500/15, ind 15.00
Valencia, crystal; cup, #3500/1....................................17.50
Valencia, crystal; decanter, #4300/119, ball, 12-oz........55.00
Valencia, crystal; nut dish, #3400/71, 4-ftd, 3" 30.00
Valencia, crystal; plate, breakfast; #3500/5, 8½"...........12.00
Valencia, crystal; plate, sandwich; #1402, hdld, 11½".....22.50
Valencia, crystal; plate, torte; #3500/38, 13" 25.00
Valencia, crystal; relish, #1402/91, 3-part, 8" 25.00
Valencia, crystal; shakers, #3400/18.............................45.00
Valencia, crystal; stem, goblet; #1402 ....20.00
Valencia, crystal; stem, wine; #1402 ....30.00
Valencia, crystal; tumbler, #3400/115, 14-oz................20.00
Valencia, crystal; tumbler, #3500, ftd, 13-oz 16.00
Wildflower, crystal; bowl, bonbon; hdls, ftd, 6" 17.50
Wildflower, crystal; bowl, pickle; ftd, 9½" 22.00
Wildflower, crystal; bowl, 4-ftd, flared, 12" 29.50
Wildflower, crystal; candlestick, 5" 25.00
Wildflower, crystal; comport, 5½"................................30.00

Wildflower shakers, flat: $20.00, footed, $25.00; Individual creamer and sugar bowl, $35.00 for the set.

Wildflower, crystal; lamp, hurricane; candlestick base.................100.00
Wildflower, crystal; pitcher, ball 95.00
Wildflower, crystal; plate, bonbon; hdls, 8" 17.50
Wildflower, crystal; plate, salad; 8" 11.00
Wildflower, crystal; plate, service; 4-ftd, 12" 30.00
Wildflower, crystal; plate, torte; 14"...........................35.00
Wildflower, crystal; stem, cocktail; #3121, 3-oz............22.50
Wildflower, crystal; stem, water; #3121, 10-oz..............20.00
Wildflower, crystal; tumbler, water; #3121, 10-oz 15.00
Wildflower, crystal; tumbler, 13-oz.............................20.00
Wildflower, crystal; vase, bud; 10" 30.00
Wildflower, crystal; vase, flower; ftd, 11" 42.00
Wildflower, crystal; vase, flower; ftd, 8" 35.00

Cambridge Pottery

The Cambridge Art Pottery operated in Cambridge, Ohio, from 1900 until 1909. During that time several lines of artware were developed under the direction of C.B. Upjohn, an established ceramic artist of the period. Their standard brown-glazed line was Terrhea, examples of which are often found bearing the signature of the artist responsible for the underglaze decoration. Oakwood was a second brown-glazed line, without the slip painting. Other lines were Acorn, introduced in 1904; and Otoe, a matt green ware (introduced in 1907) that utilized already existing shapes from earlier lines. However, their most successful product was a line of cookware called Gurnsey, made from a red-brown clay with a white-glazed interior. Sales proved to be so profitable that by 1908 all artware was discontinued in favor of its exclusive production. By the following year, the firm elected to change the name of their pottery to the Gurnsey Earthenware Company. Marks varied, but all incorporate a device comprised of the letters 'CAP,' with the co-joined 'AP' most often contained within a larger scale 'C.'

Bank, pig form, brn mottle, 3¼x6" 75.00
Teapot, Gurnsey Cooking Ware, glossy terra cotta, wht int 35.00
Tile, high-relief floral, majolica-type glaze, 6x6", pr......................28.00
Vase, bud; Oakwood, emb flowers, streaky brn, 7x5".....................65.00
Vase, Terrhea, floral, sgn S, #228, 6x5" 100.00

Cameo

The technique of glass carving was perfected 2,000 years ago in ancient Rome and Greece. The most famous ancient example of cameo glass is the Portland Vase, made in Rome around 100 A.D. After glass blowing was developed, glassmakers devised a method of casing several layers of colored glass together, often with a light color over a darker base, to enhance the design. Skilled carvers meticulously worked the fragile glass to produce incredibly detailed classic scenes. In the eighteenth and nineteenth centuries Oriental and Near-Eastern artisans used the technique more extensively. European glassmakers revived the art during the last quarter of the nineteenth century. In France, Galle and Daum produced some of the finest examples of modern times, using as many as five layers of glass to develop their designs, usually scenics or subjects from nature. Hand carving was supplemented by the use of a copper engraving wheel, and acid was used to cut away the layers more quickly.

In England, Thomas Webb and Sons used modern machinery and technology to eliminate many of the problems that plagued early glass carvers. One of Webb's best-known carvers, George Woodall, is credited with producing over four hundred pieces. Woodall was trained in the art by John Northwood, famous for reproducing the Portland Vase in 1876. Cameo glass became very popular during the late 1800s, resulting in a market that demanded more than could be produced, due to the tedious procedures involved. In an effort to produce greater volume, less elaborate pieces with simple floral or geometric designs were made, often entirely acid etched with little or no hand carving. While very little cameo glass was made in this country, a few pieces were produced by James Gillender, Tiffany, and the Libbey Glass Company. Though some continued to be made on a limited scale into the 1900s, for the most part, inferior products caused a marked reduction in its manufacture by the turn of the century. See also specific manufacturers.

Our advisor for this category is Don Williams; he is listed in the Directory under Missouri.

English

Perfume, lay down; floral, wht on citron, mk top, 5" 1,325.00
Rose bowl, floral/berries, butterfly on bk, wht on citron 1,400.00
Vase, clematis branch, wht on bl, ornate rim, 7½x5¼" 3,750.00
Vase, floral branch, wht on red frost, cylinder, unmk, 6" 895.00
Vase, florals, red frost on clear, unmk, 5½x2½" 800.00
Vase, florals, wht on bl, unmk, 5x4" 950.00
Vase, florals, wht on citron frost, unmk, 3⅞x3"...........................850.00

French

Lamp, floral shade & base, red to purple on yel, Degue, 19".... 2,400.00

Vase, bands/triangles, red on blk matt, ovoid, Degue, 14½" ... 2,000.00
Vase, carnations, red on yel mottle, Pantin, 14½" 1,600.00
Vase, farm scene, brn to tan, Arsall, 6x3"...................................835.00
Vase, floral vines at rim, orange/brn on yel, Degue, 8" 1,800.00
Vase, house/mtns/lake/etc on pk frost, 3 cuts, Arsall, 6" 795.00
Vase, irises, amber on lt bl, trumpet form, sgn Sevres, 13" 400.00
Vase, landscape/house, brn on tan, Arsall, 6" 750.00
Vase, sailboat/lighthouse, 3-color, Michel, 10" 1,220.00
Vase, stylized floral, brn to orange on yel, Degue, 17" 3,100.00
Vase, trees, lapis bl & blk on lt bl, bun ft, Degue, 19" 2,400.00
Vase, zigzags, purple on clear, ftd baluster, Degue, 11" 500.00

Vase, green over white opal with stylized floral, signed Editions D'Art des Cristalleries de Nancy, 13", $800.00.

Canary Lustre

Canary lustre was produced from the late 1700s until about the mid-nineteenth century in the Staffordshire district of England. The body of the ware was of yellow clay with a yellow overglaze; more often than not, copper or silver lustre trim was added. Decorations were usually black-printed transfers, though occasionally hand-painted polychrome designs were also used.

Cup & saucer, handleless; Cupid/Psyche, red transfer, mini 200.00
Flowerpot, mc floral, emb lion's heads, prof rpr, 3¾" 300.00
Jug, satyr face, mc/blk feather-like bkground, 6", EX 325.00
Mug, emb frowning & smiling faces, prof rpr, rim flakes, 2½"......100.00
Mug, horse/man/lady/dog, red transfer, 2½", EX 100.00
Mug, Mary, blk transfer, emb leaf hdl, minor stains, 2½"............425.00
Mug, Nightingale for Eliza, red transfer, minor flakes, 2⅝"..........350.00
Mug, Trifle for James, brn transfer, silver lustre rim, 2⅛"............400.00
Pitcher, A Free-born Englishman..., hunters/dog, 5", EX............525.00
Pitcher, Liberty/Sir Francis Bindell Bar, emb motif, 6", EX 425.00
Pitcher, mc floral band, leaf band at top, 5⅝" 275.00
Pitcher, silver lustre/resist & red pnt designs, 5¾", EX................400.00
Pitcher, silver-resist floral, prof rpr, worn, 4½" 100.00
Plate, blk transfer scene, floral border, 8½", EX............................55.00
Plate, blk transfer: Puss & Boots, titled, French, 8½", NM 100.00
Plate, castle/stripes, blk transfer, P&H Choisy, Fr, 4⅜"................150.00
Plate, red scrolling foliage, pattern-rtcl rim, 8½", EX..................400.00

Plate, tan landscape transfer, floral border, mk, 8", NM...............**175.00**
Platter, scalloped/openweave border, red/silver lines, 10"........ **1,400.00**
Salt cellar, emb design, prof rpr, 1¾" **110.00**

Candle Holders

The earliest type of candlestick, called a pricket, was constructed with a sharp point on which the candle was impaled. The socket type, first used in the sixteenth century, consisted of the socket and a short stem with a wide drip pan and base. These were made from sheets of silver or other metal; not until late in the seventeenth century were candlesticks made by casting. By the 1700s, styles began to vary from the traditional fluted column or baluster form and became more elaborate. A Rococo style with scrolls, shellwork, and naturalistic leaves and flowers came into vogue that afforded the individual silversmith the opportunity to exhibit his skill and artistry. The last half of the eighteenth century brought a return to fluted columns with neoclassic motifs. Because they were made of thin sheet silver, weighted bases were used to add stability. The Rococo styles of the Regency period were heavily encrusted with applied figures and flowers. Candelabra with six to nine branches became popular. By the Victorian era when lamps came into general use, there was less innovation and more adaptation of the earlier styles. See also Silver; specific manufacturers.

Key: QA — Queen Anne

Bell metal, sq base, baluster stem, Spanish, 1700, 5" **250.00**
Bell metal, stepped rnd base, Flemish/Scandinavia, 1650, 5".......**900.00**
Brass, bell-shape base, drip pan, S Europe, ca 1600, 5½"..............**400.00**
Brass, bl & wht latticinio swirl shade, 5" **340.00**
Brass, butterfly base, trn stem, China, 5" **17.50**

Venetian brass and silver inlaid candlestick, late 15th century, 4¾", $7,500.00.

Brass, chamberstick, ejector style, early, pr **160.00**
Brass, chamberstick, w/push-up, 3¾" **105.00**
Brass, cobra form, tail forms 7x8" base, 8¼".....................................**60.00**
Brass, octagonal baluster, 5" dia base, 10", pr................................**125.00**
Brass, octagonal base, early, 5½" **275.00**
Brass, openwork flat stem forms Oriental emblem, 4-ftd, 6"..........**12.50**
Brass, QA, rpr std w/metal inset, 7" **250.00**
Brass, QA style (not period), 8" **75.00**
Brass, rnd base, central drip pan, Heemserk, 1580s, 8" **850.00**
Brass, saucer base, side push-up, battering/rim splits, 8" **65.00**

Brass, sconce, removable S-scroll arms, polished, 8½", pr........ **3,100.00**
Brass, sq base, early, 5½"..**125.00**
Brass, stepped hexagonal base, Anglo-French, 1700s, 9", pr **385.00**
Brass, taperstick, stepped 6-sided base, English, 1700s, 5" **325.00**
Brass, triangular base, plain stem, Spanish, 1650s, 5", pr **1,100.00**
Brass, triangular base w/3 paw ft, Continental, 1680s, 12"..........**600.00**
Brass, trumpet base, plain stem, English, 1680s, 5" **700.00**
Brass, twist stem, saucer base, China, 6½", pr **55.00**
Brass, w/push-up, Victorian, 11", EX **120.00**
Cut glass, dmns/ribs, Anglo-Irish, ca 1900, 7½", pr.....................**600.00**
Glass, canary yel, flint, hexagonal, 9", pr.......................................**600.00**
Iron, hogscraper, w/push-up, worn tin plate,7" **100.00**
Iron, hogscraper, w/push-up & lip hanger, 4", EX.........................**125.00**
Iron, hogscraper, w/push-up & lip hanger, 5½", VG **100.00**
Iron, hogscraper, w/push-up mk Shaw, 7", EX...............................**140.00**
Pewter, w/push-up, 8", pr..**230.00**
Steel, hogscraper, brass wedding band, sgn, 6½"...........................**395.00**
Steel, hogscraper, Pat 1863 on tab, 4"..**135.00**
Steel, hogscraper, wedding band, Shaw, 1700s, 6½" **440.00**
Steel, hogscraper, 13", EX...**350.00**
Tin, push-up tab, side ring hdl, 4x5¼" **80.00**

Candlewick

Candlewick crystal was made by the Imperial Glass Corporation, a division of Lenox Inc., Bellaire, Ohio. It was introduced in 1936; and, though never marked except for paper labels, it is easily recognized by the beaded crystal rims, stems, and handles inspired by the tufted needlework called candlewicking, practiced by our pioneer women. During its production, more than 741 items were designed and produced. In September 1982 when Imperial closed its doors, thirty-four pieces were still being made.

Identification numbers and mold numbers used by the company help collectors recognize the various styles and shapes. Most of the pieces are from the #400 series, though other series numbers were also used. Stemware was made in eight styles — five from the #400 series made from 1941 to 1962, one from #3400 series made in 1937, another from #3800 series made in 1941, and the eighth style from the #4000 series made in 1947. In the listings that follow, some #400 items lack the mold number because that information was not found in the company files.

A few pieces have been made in color or with a gold wash. At least two lines, Valley Lily and Floral, utilized Candlewick with floral patterns cut into the crystal. These are scarce today. Other rare items include gifts such as the desk calendar made by the company for its employees and customers; the dresser set comprised of a mirror, clock, puff jar, and cologne; and the chip and dip set.

Ash tray, heart form, 4½" **9.00**
Ash tray, oblong, 4½" **6.00**
Ash tray, rnd, 2¾" **4.50**
Ash tray, rnd, 5" **8.00**
Ash tray, sq, 5¾" **15.00**
Ash tray set, sq, nesting, 3-pc...**36.00**
Basket, hdl, 6½" **27.50**
Bell, 4" **32.00**
Bottle, bitters; w/tube, 4-oz **40.00**
Bowl, belled, 14" **85.00**
Bowl, hdld, 12" **35.00**
Bowl, heart form, 9"...**85.00**
Bowl, jelly; w/lid, 5½" **45.00**
Bowl, oval, 11" **125.00**
Bowl, pickle/celery; 7½" **15.00**

Bowl, relish; oblong, 4-compartment, 12"	50.00
Bowl, relish; oval, hdls, 10"	22.50
Bowl, relish; 2-part, 8"	17.50
Bowl, relish; 7"	20.00
Bowl, rnd, hdls, 4¾"	10.00
Bowl, rnd, 12"	27.50
Butter, w/lid, rnd, 5½"	27.50
Butter & jam set, 5-pc	200.00
Cake stand, high ftd, 11"	55.00
Cake stand, low ftd, 10"	45.00
Candle holder, flat, 3½"	20.00
Candle holder, flower form, sq, 6½"	25.00
Candle holder, flower form, 2-bead stem, 4"	37.50
Candle holder, flower form, 5"	20.00
Candle holder, 3-bead stem, 5½"	60.00
Candle holder, 3-toed, 4½"	37.50
Candy box, rnd, w/lid, 3-compartment, 7"	125.00
Cigarette box, w/lid	25.00
Clock, rnd, 4"	100.00
Compote, bead stem, 8"	65.00
Compote, 2-bead stem, 8"	65.00
Compote, 4-bead stem, 5½"	18.00
Creamer, bridge; ind	5.00
Creamer, plain ft	6.00
Cruet, oil; bead base, 4-oz	35.00
Cruet, oil; bulbous bottom, 4-oz	35.00
Decanter, w/stopper, 26-oz	210.00
Fork & spoon set	22.00
Hurricane lamp, candle base, 2-part	70.00
Ice tub, deep, 5½x8" dia	75.00
Jar tower, 3-compartment	150.00
Knife, butter	150.00
Ladle, marmalade; 3-bead stem	6.00
Marmalade set: jar, lid, & spoon, +liner saucer	35.00
Mirror, rnd, standing, 4½"	75.00
Pitcher, plain, 20-oz	30.00
Pitcher, plain, 80-oz	35.00
Pitcher, short rnd, 14-oz	65.00
Plate, hdls, 10"	15.00
Plate, hdls, 5½"	6.50
Plate, luncheon; 9"	12.50
Plate, salad; 7"	8.00
Plate, service; cupped edge, 13½"	35.00
Plate, service; 12"	25.00
Platter, 16"	125.00
Punch set, family; bowl, 8 demitasse cups, ladle, & lid	400.00
Salt cellar, 2¼"	6.50
Shakers, bead ft, str sided, chrome top, pr	16.00
Shakers, ftd bead base, pr	25.00
Shakers, ind, pr	10.00
Sherbet, low, 5-oz	10.00
Sherbet, tall, 5-oz	14.50
Stem, brandy; #3800	20.00
Stem, claret; #3800	30.00
Stem, cocktail; +plate w/indent	25.00
Stem, tea; #4000, 12-oz	20.00
Stem, wine; #4000, 5-oz	28.00
Sugar bowl, beaded hdls, 6-oz	6.50
Sugar bowl, ind bridge	6.00
Tray, condiment; 5¼x9¼"	40.00
Tray, party; center hdl, 11½"	30.00
Tray, relish; 5-compartment, 13"	45.00
Tray, 6½"	15.00
Tumbler, #3400, ftd, 9-oz	14.00

Tumbler, juice; 5-oz	10.00
Tumbler, tea; 12-oz	40.00
Vase, bead ft, neck ball, sm, 4"	40.00
Vase, bud; bead ftd, 8½"	60.00
Vase, rose bowl, ftd, 7½"	125.00
Vase, 6" dia	160.00

Smoker's set with etched flying ducks motif: tray, cigarette urn, and four individual ash trays, $265.00.

Candy Containers

Figural glass candy containers have been made in many different styles since 1876 when the Liberty Bell and Independence Hall were created for our country's centennial celebration. The production of these glass toys launched an industry that lasted until the mid-1960s.

Candy containers include automobiles, animals, doll furniture, telephones and other household items, comic characters, guns, and hundreds of other intriguing designs. The oldest containers (prior to 1920) were usually hand painted and often contained extra metal parts in addition to the metal strip or screw closures. During the 1950s, these metal parts were replaced with plastic, a practice that continued until candy containers met their demise in the 1960s. While predominately clear, nearly all colors of glass can be found including milk glass, green, amber, pink, emerald, cobalt, ruby flashed, and light blue. Usually the color was intentional, but leftover glass was often used resulting in unplanned colors — light blue, for instance. Various examples are found in light or ice blue, and new finds are always being discovered. Production of the glass portion of candy containers was centered around the western Pennsylvania city of Jeannette. Major producers include Westmoreland Glass, West Bros., Victory Glass, J.H. Millstein, J.C. Crosetti, L.E. Smith, Jack Stough, and T.H. Stough. While 90% of all glass candies were made in the Jeannette area, other companies such as Eagle Glass, Play Toy, and Geo. Borgfeldt Co. have a few to their credit as well.

Buyer beware! Many candy containers have been reproduced. Some, for instance the Rabbit Pushing Wheelbarrow, come already painted from distributors. The following list should alert you to possible reproductions:

#12 — Chicken on Nest
#24 — Dog (clear and cobalt)
#38 — Mule and Waterwagon (original marked Jeanette, PA)
#47 — Rabbit Pushing Wheelbarrow (eggs are speckled on the repro; solid on the original)

#55 — Peter Rabbit
 #58 — Rocking Horse (original in clear only)
 #76 — Independence Hall (original is rectangular; repro has offset base with red felt-lined closure)
 #89 — Happifats on Drum (no notches on repro for closure to hook into)
 #90 — Jackie Coogan (marked inside 'B')
 #91 — Kewpie (must have Geo. Borgfeldt on base to be original)
 #94 — Naked Child
 #103 — Santa (original has plastic head; repro is all glass and opens at bottom)
 #114 — Mantel Clock
 #144 — Amber Pistol (first sold full in the 1970s)
 #168 — Uncle Sam's Hat
 #233 — Santa's Boot
 #238 — Camera (original must say Pat Appld For; repro says B Shakman or could be ground off)
 #254 — Mailbox
 #255 — Drum Mug
 #268 — Safe
 #289 — Piano (original in only clear and milk glass, both painted)
 #352 — Auto
 #377 — Auto
 #378 — Station Wagon
 #386 — Fire Engine
 Others are possible.

Those who desire further information on candy containers may contact Candy Collectors of Americas Club listed in our Directory under Clubs, Newsletters, and Catalogs. A bimonthly newsletter offers insight on new finds, reproductions, updates, and articles from over three hundred collectors and members, including all authors of books on candy containers.

Numbers used in this category refer to a standard reference series, *An Album of Candy Containers*, Vols 1 and 2, by Jennie Long. Values are given for undamaged examples with original paint and metal parts when applicable or unless noted otherwise. Repaired pieces (often repainted) are worth only a small fraction of one that is perfect. The symbol (+) at the end of some of the following lines was used to indicate items that have been reproduced.

Airplane, P-38; cb closure, #326 ....125.00
Airplane, Stough's, musical, #331, #332, or #333, ea 25.00

Spirit of Goodwill, 5" long, $100.00.

Amos & Andy, #77, G pnt 425.00
Barney Google on Pedestal, w/pnt, #78 ....190.00
Basket, flower design, #224 ....35.00
Battleship on Waves, #335 ....165.00

Bear in Auto, #2 ....175.00
Bear on Circus Tub, orig blades, #1 ....300.00
Bell, Hand; wood hdl, #494 ....150.00
Bell, Liberty; #1, pewter top, paper label, #227 ....75.00
Bird on Mound, w/whistle 550.00
Black Cat for Luck, #4 ....700.00
Black Cat Sitting, #5 ....750.00
Boat, w/photograph, #594 ....100.00
Bottle, Apothecary; #62 or #63 ....10.00
Bottle, Rnd Nurser; #70 ....20.00
Bottle, Waisted Nurser; complete w/contents, #71 ....15.00
Bugle or Megaphone, #278 ....22.00
Bulldog, closure, #15 ....55.00
Bus, Jitney; closure, #340 ....350.00
Bus, Rapid Transit; no pnt 400.00
Camera, #238 ....250.00
Candelabrum, #202 ....25.00
Cane, penny toy, #241 ....110.00
Cannon, cobalt bbl, orig carriage, #534 ....450.00
Cannon, Quick Firer; orig carriage, #537 ....1,000.00
Cannon, sm bbl, orig carriage, #535 ....475.00
Car, Electric Coupe #2; closure, #356 (+) 50.00
Car, Ribbed-Top Sedan; closure, #376 ....25.00
Charlie Chaplin by Barrel, Borgfeldt, closure, orig pnt, #83 ....125.00
Chick in Egg Shell Auto, closure, orig pnt, #7 ....275.00
Chicken, fancy closure, #9 ....550.00
Clock, Alarm; #11, #549 ....100.00
Clock, Mantel; rnd top, #113 ....200.00
Clock, Oval; pnt milk glass, closure, #114 ....155.00
Coal Car, Overland Limited; #600 ....550.00
Coal Car on Tender, #402 ....200.00
Coal Car on Tender, orig wheels, #396 ....200.00
Coupe, Long Hood #3; #359 ....110.00
Dog, Mutt; #11, #476 ....25.00
Dog by Barrel, closure, orig pnt, #13 ....200.00
Dog w/Top Hat, #480 ....25.00
Drum, milk glass w/emb cannon & flag, orig lid, 2⅞" dia 425.00
Fire Engine, bl glass, #381 ....100.00
Fire Engine, Stough's 1914, closure, orig wheels, #379-A 100.00
Flatiron, orig pnt, closure, #249 ....375.00
Gas Pump, #316 ....200.00
Gun, metal, #157 ....75.00
Gun, Victory Glass, #541, tiny 45.00
Happifats on Drum, orig pnt, #89 (+) 200.00
Helicopter, single blade 110.00
Hot Doggie, clear w/pnt, #14 ....375.00
House, closure, orig pnt, #75 ....150.00
Jack-O'-Lantern, open top, #552 ....125.00
Kettle, orig closure/hdl, #251 ....30.00
Kiddie Kar, #253 ....225.00
Kiddies' Breakfast Bell, #18 ....25.00
Lamp, Hurricane; mini, #211 ....100.00
Lamp, Novelty, complete, #205 ....500.00
Lamp, Valentine; #556, all orig 350.00
Lantern, beveled glass globe, gilt/ruby-flashed, #175 ....75.00
Lantern, brass cap, #184 ....15.00
Lantern, fancy trim, #190 ....20.00
Lantern, glass reflector, #185 ....18.00
Lantern, Little Ball; Signal, bl-gr globe, #181 ....25.00
Lantern, Stough's #3, lg, #196 ....12.00
Lantern, Victory Glass #1, #191 (+Avon) 10.00
Limousine, Westmoreland Specialty, #351 ....175.00
Locomotive, dbl rectangle windows, litho closure, #413 ....75.00
Locomotive, no wheels, #395 ....50.00

Locomotive, Stough's #5, w/whistle, #428 ....25.00
Lynn Doll Nurser, #72 ....25.00
Mailbox, silver pnt, #254 (+) 115.00
Mounted Policeman, closure, orig pnt, #551 .... 1,300.00
Mr Rabbit w/Hat, #39, no pnt 1,100.00
Mr Rabbit w/Hat, #39, orig pnt 1,250.00
Naked Child, kewpie type, #93 ....85.00
Naked Child w/Derby, #95 ....45.00
Owl, closure, glass eyes, #37 ....100.00
Parlor Stove, pewter top/base, #644 ....85.00
Piano, #289, w/pnt (+) 175.00
Play Nursing Set, complete, #259 ....130.00
Pumpkin Head Witch, #265 ....550.00
Rabbit, Basket on Arm, #49 ....75.00
Rabbit, Stough's, closure, #54 (+) 20.00
Rabbit Family, orig pnt, #43 ....675.00
Rabbit Nibbling Carrot, #53 ....35.00
Rabbit Pushing Cart, G pnt, #44 ....325.00
Rabbit w/Collar, #51 ....75.00
Rabbit w/Paws Together, #52 ....55.00
Racer or Convertible, #433 ....45.00
Rainbow Condiment Set, #503 ....125.00
Rocking Horse #1, #58 (+) 300.00
Rooster Crowing, orig pnt, #56, EX 175.00
Rubber Boot, #234 ....85.00
Santa Claus, sq chimney, #99 ....275.00
Scotty Dog, #17 ....12.00
Sedan, 4-door, orig tin wheels, no pnt, #370 ....75.00
Sedan, 4-door, orig tin wheels, w/pnt, #370 ....90.00
Seltzer Bottle, #505 ....350.00
Soldier by Tent, #108 .... 2,500.00
Spark Plug, no pnt, #109 ....85.00
Spark Plug, w/pnt, #109 ....90.00
Suitcase, clear, #217 ....30.00
Swan, #492 ....125.00
Swan Boat, orig pnt, #60 ....750.00
Telephone, Stough's #3, #308 ....40.00
Telescope, #270 ....600.00
Telescope, magnifying lens, #632 ....125.00
Train, Overland Limited; #394, 4-pc, EX 900.00
Trunk, milk glass, no pnt 110.00
Village Buildings, no glass inserts, #76, ea 20.00
Volkswagon, #373 ....35.00
Wheelbarrow, tin, #611 ....75.00
Windmill, pewter top, #443 ....400.00
Windmill, shaker top, #445 ....150.00

Papier-Mache, Composition

Bird, feather wings & tail, worn pnt, 7½" L, VG 125.00
Bug-eyed chick, head removes, Germany, 5", EX 165.00
Cat, appl eyes, pnt compo, 4½", G 95.00
Collie, appl eyes, worn pnt, 6½", VG 165.00
Dog & slipper, appl eyes, worn pnt, minor cracks, 4", VG 185.00
Elephant, pnt compo, missing tusks, soiled, 7", G 95.00
Elf emerging from egg, Germany, EX 125.00
Football player, jtd limbs, wood base, lt wear, 8½" 450.00
Man in Moon, pnt flakes, 6", G 100.00
Man in shoe, pop-up spring action, worn, 6", VG 275.00
Mrs Duck, worn pnt, Germany, 5", VG 65.00
Pig, appl eyes, covered compo, mended leg, 5½" L, G 200.00
Policeman on chick, worn pnt, 5", VG 250.00
Rabbit, appl eyes, Germany, 7¾", G 250.00
Rabbit, glass eyes, Germany, 1900s, sm rpr, 16" 195.00

Black cat, glass eyes, 8" long, $395.00.

Rabbit, glass eyes, well dressed, head removes, Germany, 5" 125.00
Rabbit hunter, jtd arms, wood base, 11", VG 850.00
Sailor boy rabbit in grass atop box, Germany 145.00
Turkey, pnt compo, 7" H, EX 150.00
Washington & cherry tree, appl fruit/etc, Germany, 7½", VG ...195.00
Washington on horse, worn pnt, 6", G 85.00
Youth on rabbit, worn pnt, rpr, 6", VG 165.00

Canes

Fancy canes and walking sticks were once the mark of a gentleman. Hand-carved examples are collected and admired as folk art from the past. The glass canes that never could have been practical are unique whimseys of the glass-blower's profession. Gadget and container sticks, which were produced in a wide variety, are highly desirable. Character, political, and novelty types are also sought after as are those with handles made of precious metals.

Our advisor for this category is Bruce Thalburg.

Canes

Gadget type, parade, 36-star flag inside 275.00
Gadget type, 1939 World's Fair, map inside 200.00

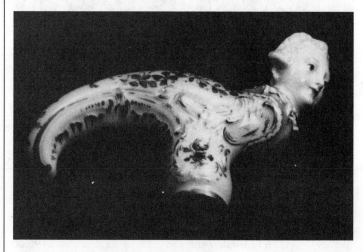

China ware handle with hand-painted lady's face, attributed to Meissen, 4½" long, $250.00.

Glass, aquamarine w/gold mica, baton tip, 52" **195.00**
Glass, bl, blk spiral twist, mushroom knob, baton style, 42" **400.00**
Glass, cranberry cased w/clear, swirled int ribbing, 32" **150.00**
Glass, gold-amber, hollow, twisted shank, Am, 1860s, 39" **125.00**
Glass, honey amber spirals, rope swirls at base, 33" **145.00**
Glass, lt aquamarine & clear ribbed swirl, 32" **135.00**
Rhinocerous hide, shaped/varnished, solid w/bent hdl, 35" **115.00**
Rosewood w/gold-filled bands, horn tip & hdl, 36" **125.00**
Whalebone, ebony separator, trn ivory knob hdl, 36", EX...........**300.00**
Whalebone, serpent hdl cvd from whale tooth, 1850s, 31".........**475.00**
Whalebone, trn whale ivory knob, 34", EX **225.00**
Wood, cvd bone dog's head hdl, 1900, 36" **200.00**
Wood, cvd hinged Death's Head atop, container type, 1900, 35" .**250.00**
Wood, cvd mustachioed man's head, 1895, 36" **165.00**
Wood, ivory L-hdl w/ebony & ivory separators, 32" **100.00**
Wood, rope cvd shaft, turk's head knot hdl, 36", EX...................**165.00**

Walking Sticks

Bamboo, pnt fan pattern, stained bands at root end, 35"...............**75.00**
Bamboo w/cvd alligator hdl, sterling ferrule, 34" **88.00**
Blackthorne, wrapped in vines, root end hdl, 37".........................**70.00**
Bronze, cast Blk man's head, rosewood shaft **450.00**
Celluloid, molded Blk man's head, wood shaft **200.00**
Ebony, cvd ivory hdl: smiling man's head, Japan, 36" **450.00**
Ebony shaft, agate hdl, gold ferrule, France, 34½" **245.00**
Ebony shaft w/horn tip & 8" horn hdl, 37" **135.00**
Gadget type, drinking (flask & glass inside) **200.00**
Hickory, cvd snake entwines shaft, inlaid pearl eyes, 36" **110.00**
Horn, cvd Blk man's head, glass eyes, wood shaft........................**350.00**
Ivory cvd hdl & shaft, ornate Oriental motif................................**800.00**
Ivory cvd hdl: Art Deco Egyptian lady's head..............................**400.00**
Ivory cvd hdl: 3 horses' heads, 1 head on bk................................**650.00**
Malacca, cast metal McKinley bust, eagle base, 33" **250.00**
Malacca, cvd lady's leg hdl, 35"...**85.00**
Nut, Blk boy's head, tinted, glass eyes, wood shaft **300.00**
Papier-mache, Blk clown's head, glass eyes, carnival type **275.00**
Polychromed, cvd parrot's head hdl, Brazil, 36"...........................**75.00**
Tiger maple, silver repousse flashlight hdl, Austria, 35" **180.00**
Tiger maple w/orange varnish, octagonal shaft, 1840s, 35" **125.00**
Wood, covered w/rattlesnake skin, 33½" **135.00**
Wood, cvd Blk butler's head (lg), 1-pc...**550.00**
Wood, cvd Blk dandy's head, buttermilk pnt, glass eyes..............**450.00**
Wood, cvd Blk head, glass eyes/ivory teeth/sterling trim **650.00**
Wood, cvd bulldog, glass eyes, silver overlay trim, 38"................**275.00**
Wood, cvd miller w/grain sack at top, mid 1800s, 83".................**450.00**
Wood, dog's head w/glass eyes, metal collar, lady's, 35½" **125.00**
Wood, snakes in relief, clenched fist hdl, 42"..............................**235.00**
Wood, 2 spiraling cvd snakes, worn mc pnt decor, 37" **155.00**

Canton

From the last part of the eighteenth century until the early 1900s, porcelain was made in and around Canton, China, expressly for western export. This pattern, whose name was borrowed from the city of its manufacture, is decorated in blue on a white ground with a scene containing a bridge, willow trees, birds, and a teahouse, all within a rain and cloud border. The popularity of Canton (porcelain) prompted potteries in England and the U.S. to adapt the pattern to earthenware dinner services which are referred to as Willow Ware today.

Bidet, Rain Cloud border, med bl-gray, 1850s, 24", EX **2,200.00**
Bowl, fruit; Rain Cloud border, rtcl, 1850s, 9", +tray, EX.........**1200.00**

Bowl, Rain Cloud border, med bl, 1850s, w/lid, 9" L, NM **350.00**
Bowl, Rain Cloud border, scalloped, set: 8", 9", 10", EX.......... **1,400.00**
Bowl, Rain Cloud border, scalloped, 1840s, prof rpr, 9¼" **300.00**
Bowl, Rain Cloud border, w/lid, 11x9", EX **550.00**
Bowl, Rain Cloud border, 1840s, 11x9" **450.00**
Bowl, salad; Rain Cloud border, med bl, 1850s, 9½", EX **900.00**
Bowl, salad; Rain Cloud border, med bl, 1850s, 9½", NM **1,200.00**
Bowl, sauce; Rain Cloud border, med bl, 1850s, 6", NM **200.00**
Butter chip, Str Line border, med bl, 1800s, 3" dia, NM **40.00**
Butter dish, Rain Cloud border, med bl, w/strainer, 7", NM.... **1,700.00**
Coffeepot, Rain Cloud border, med bl, 1850s, 8¾", NM **1,250.00**
Creamer, helmet shape, 5" **300.00**
Dish, tobacco leaf form, 1800s, 7"...**350.00**
Egg cup, Criss-Cross border, med to dk bl, 1850s, 2½", pr............**300.00**
Ginger jar, Str Line border, med gray-bl, 1800s, 5¾" **225.00**
Hot water plate, 9" **250.00**
Mug, Rain Cloud border, med/dk bl, twist hdl, 1850s, 4", EX......**475.00**
Pie plate, Rain Cloud border, med bl, 1850s, 8", NM **350.00**
Pitcher, Rain Cloud border, med bl, bulbous, 1850s, 7", NM **850.00**
Pitcher, Rain Cloud border, med bl, helmet form, 4", EX **475.00**
Plate, chop; Rain Cloud border, 1850s, mfg flaw, 16" **1,300.00**
Plate, Rain Cloud border, med bl, 1800s, 10", set of 6 .... **1,200.00**
Plate, Rain Cloud border, 1860s, 7"..**60.00**
Plate, Rain Cloud border, 1860s, 8½", EX **95.00**
Platter, Rain Cloud border, dk bl, 1850s, 8-sided, 17½".............**650.00**
Platter, Rain Cloud border, med bl, 1850s, 13½" **500.00**
Platter, Rain Cloud border, 1840s, 16x14", EX **750.00**
Saucer, str line border, 1880s, 5½" **30.00**
Saucer, str line border, 1880s, 6" **35.00**
Sugar bowl, Rain Cloud border, med bl, dbl-twist hdls, 4" **375.00**
Tazza, Str Line border, med bl, 1880s, 8", NM **500.00**
Tea caddy, med/dk bl, 1800s, rpl lid, 13", EX, pr **4,500.00**

Tea caddies, 1850s, 6", EX, $5,750.00 for the pair; Chop plate, 1800s, 15" diameter, $950.00; Tea canister, 1800s, 6", NM, $2,100.00.

Tea tile, Criss-Cross border, med/dk bl, 1850s, 8-sided, NM **550.00**
Tray, Rain Cloud border, 1840s, 6x8"..**300.00**
Tureen, Rain Cloud border, med bl, boar's-head hdls, 13" **2,500.00**
Tureen, sauce; Rain Cloud border, 1850s, 7".............................**700.00**
Water bottle, med bl-gray, 1850s, 8¾"...**425.00**

Capo-Di-Monte

Established in 1743 near Naples and sponsored by Charles II, who was King of Naples at that time, Capo-Di-Monte produced soft-paste porcelain figurines and dinnerware usually marked with a 'crown over N' device, though a fleur-de-lis was used on occasion. The factory was closed throughout the 1760s but reopened in 1771 in the city of Naples. There both hard- and soft-paste porcelains were made, sometimes decorated with applied florals in high relief. Their technique as well as their marks were blatantly copied. As a result, this type of encrusted decoration is often referred to today as Capo-Di-Monte. The original factory closed in 1821. Some of their molds were purchased by the Docceia Porcelain factory in Florence which continues to operate to the present time. Most examples on the market today are of fairly recent manufacture. Capo-Di-Monte type wares have been made in Hungary and Germany, as well as France and Italy. Many of these pieces continue to bear the 'crown over N' gold stamp. As more collectors recognize and appreciate the quality of the older ware, buyer demand drives prices higher.

Box, brn/ivory, rose bouquet inside, 4 curved ft, 8x9" 80.00
Box, centaurs abduct Deidameia, shaped sides, 10" L 1,500.00
Box, children/trees relief, fruit finial, 3 paw ft, 7" dia 75.00
Figurine, African Crowned Crane, 1 ft raised, G Armani, 14"......175.00
Figurine, boy on stump w/fishing pole in hand, 6x4½" 95.00
Figurine, buccaneer on rocky base draws sword, A Colle, 12" 175.00
Figurine, chestnut vendor, old woman & urchin by stove, 10" 250.00
Figurine, dandy in long coat/floral vest holds flowers, 8" 160.00
Figurine, fisherman w/pipe holds torn net, G Armani, 11" 225.00
Figurine, girl by tree w/dog (w/roses & parasol), 10", pr 250.00
Figurine, girl in wide hat holds roses, basket at ft, 10" 150.00
Figurine, Pan, seated on sq bat-emb pyramid base, 8½" 325.00
Figurine, Pan seated on sq plinth, gold trim, 8½" 295.00
Figurine, pearl fisherman holds bag, Bonalberti, 10x8" 185.00
Figurine, young boy photographs girl on brick wall, 10x9" 150.00
Shoe, high-heeled pump w/cherubs relief, 5x6" 45.00
Urn, cherubs, gold hdls, cherub w/wreath finial, ftd, 20½" 550.00

Triptych, depicting the coronation of Charles the Great in cathedral-like setting, wood frame forms box when closed, 17" x 20" overall, $1,200.00.

Urn, cherubs & grapes emb, Bacchus hdls, w/lid, 15", pr 375.00
Urn, nymphs/cherubs in dolphin boat, cherub hdls, lid, 20" 650.00
Urn, warrior slays man, man/lady watch, swan/mask hdls, 25" 950.00

Vase, semi-nudes/grapes/jugs, gold hdls, urn form, 14" 250.00

Carlton

Carlton Ware was the product of Wiltshaw and Robinson, who operated in the Staffordshire district of England from about 1890. During the 1920s, they produced ornamental ware with enameled and gilded decorations such as flowers and birds, often on a black background. In 1958 the firm was renamed Carlton Ware Ltd. Their trademark was a crown over a circular stamp with 'W & R, Stoke on Trent' surrounding a swallow. 'Carlton Ware' was sometimes added by hand.

Biscuit jar, mc florals on cream w/cobalt trim, 9½" 110.00
Jar, mahog w/gold trim, HP flowers, bulbous, mk, 5" 65.00
Leaf dish, yel, 5" 25.00
Salad set, floral w/SP trim, 9¾" bowl+11½" spoon/fork 385.00
Vase, Rouge Royal, 11½" 175.00
Vase, water scene, mc on bl w/gold trim, mk, 10¼", pr 225.00

Carnival Collectibles

Carnival items from the early part of this century represent the lighter side of an America that was alternately prospering and sophisticated or devastated by war and domestic conflict. But whatever the country's condition, the carnival's thrilling rides and shooting galleries were a sure way of letting it all go by — at least for an evening.

For further information on chalkware figures, we recommend *The Carnival Chalk Prize* by Thomas G. Morris, who is listed in the Directory under Oregon. Our advisors for shooting gallery targets are Richard and Valerie Tucker; their address is listed in the Directory under Texas.

Chalkware figure, Beach Flirt, mohair wig, 1919, 9½" 75.00
Chalkware figure, Betty Boop, Fleisher, 1930s, 14½" 195.00
Chalkware figure, boy & horse, unmk, ca 1935-45, 11½" 15.00
Chalkware figure, Charley McCarthy, sitting, 7½" 15.00
Chalkware figure, circus horse, unmk, 1935-45, 11" 22.00
Chalkware figure, Donald's nephew on snowball, 6½" 15.00
Chalkware figure, eagle, God Bless America, 12" 35.00
Chalkware figure, Friends, lady w/horse, 1930s, 8½x9¾" 45.00
Chalkware figure, hula girl, 1940s, 12½" 30.00
Chalkware figure, Indian boy, arms Xd, 1935-45, 8½" 15.00
Chalkware figure, kitten bank, ca 1935-50, 7" 10.00
Chalkware figure, lion, unmk, 9¼x12" 10.00

Chalkware figure, Lone Ranger, 16", $40.00.

Chalkware figure, Lone Ranger on Silver, LR, 10½", NM **32.00**
Chalkware figure, Majorette, El Segundo, 1949, 12" **25.00**
Chalkware figure, Pinocchio, unmk, ca 1940, 10" **20.00**
Chalkware figure, Scottie dog, unmk, ca 1935-45, 3½" **5.00**
Chalkware figure, service man, 1930s, 15" **20.00**
Chalkware figure, Shirley Temple, 1930s, 10" **45.00**
Shooting gallery target, bird, brass, worn wht pnt, 5x5x½" **85.00**
Shooting gallery target, bird, CI, self standing, 4x2¼x1½" **45.00**
Shooting gallery target, cow, pine w/leather ears, 46x47" **350.00**
Shooting gallery target, duck, CI, worn red pnt, 7x5½" **60.00**
Shooting gallery target, jumping lion, CI, 1900s, 11x7"...............**185.00**
Shooting gallery target, owl, old red & wht pnt, 1900s, 11" **265.00**
Shooting gallery target, squirrel, HC Evans, wht pnt, 7¾"...........**65.00**
Shooting gallery target, wheel w/7 hinged figures, 36" dia **225.00**
Shooting gallery target, WWI soldier w/rifle, wht pnt, 7½" **120.00**
Shooting gallery target, 3 dbl-spinner targets on tube, CI............**150.00**

Carnival Glass

Carnival glass is pressed glass that has been coated with a sodium solution and fired to give it an exterior lustre. First made in America in 1905, it was produced until the late 1920s and had great popularity in the average American household; for unlike the costly art glass produced by Tiffany, carnival glass could be mass-produced at a small cost. Colors most found are marigold, green, blue, and purple; but others exist in lesser quantities and include white, clear, red, aqua opalescent, peach opalescent, ice blue, ice green, amber, lavender, and smoke.

Companies mainly responsible for its production in America include the Fenton Art Glass Company, Williamstown, West Virginia; the Northwood Glass Company, Wheeling, West Virginia; the Imperial Glass Company, Bellaire, Ohio; the Millersburg Glass Company, Millersburg, Ohio; and the Dugan Glass Company (Diamond Glass), Indiana, Pennsylvania. In addition to these major manufacturers, lesser producers included the U.S. Glass Company, the Cambridge Glass Company, the Westmoreland Glass Company, and the McKee Glass Company.

Carnival glass has been highly collectible since the 1950s and has been reproduced for the last twenty-five years. Several national and state collectors' organizations exist, and many fine books are available on old carnival glass, including *The Standard Encyclopedia of Carnival Glass* by Bill Edwards.

A Dozen Roses (Imperial), bowl, gr, rare, ftd, 10" **495.00**
Acanthus (Imperial), plate, marigold, 10" **155.00**
Acorn (Millerburg), compote, amethyst, rare **1,800.00**
Acorn & File, compote, pastel, rare, ftd **1,000.00**
Acorn Burrs (Northwood), bowl, gr, flat, 10" **160.00**
Acorn Burrs (Northwood), pitcher, water; gr **750.00**
Acorn Burrs (Northwood), tumbler, marigold...............................**60.00**
Age Herald (Fenton), bowl, amethyst, scarce, 9¼" **985.00**
Age Herald (Fenton), plate, amethyst, scarce, 10" **1500.00**
Amaryillis (Northwood), compote, pastel, sm...............................**240.00**
American (Fostoria), tumbler, marigold, rare **500.00**
Ancanthus (Imperial), bowl, gr, 8" **110.00**
Apple Blossom Twigs (Dugan), plate, bl.......................................**225.00**
Apple Blossoms (Dugan), plate, peach opal, 8¼" **165.00**
Apple Panels (English), creamer, marigold **30.00**
Apple Panels (English), sugar, gr, open..**36.00**
Apple Tree (Fenton), tumbler, bl..**52.00**
April Showers (Fenton), vase, amethyst **55.00**
Arcadia Baskets, plate, marigold, 8" **50.00**
Arched Panels, tumbler, marigold...**50.00**
Arcs (Imperial), bowl, gr, 8½"...**45.00**
Arcs (Imperial), compote, amethyst..**50.00**

Art Deco (English), bowl, marigold, 4"...**32.00**
Asters, bowl, marigold, 6"...**58.00**
Astral, shade, marigold **45.00**
August Flowers, shade, marigold **36.00**
Aurora, bowl, amethyst, decorated, 8½" **150.00**
Australian Swan (Crystal), bowl, amethyst, 5" **50.00**
Autumn Acorns (Fenton), bowl, amethyst, 8¾" **45.00**
Autumn Acorns (Fenton), plate, gr, rare......................................**750.00**
Aztec (McKee), pitcher, marigold, rare **1300.00**
Aztec (McKee), tumbler, marigold, rare **500.00**
Baby Bathtub (US Glass), miniature, pastel **75.00**
Baby's Bouquet, child's plate, marigold, scarce **90.00**
Baker's Rosette, ornament, amethyst **80.00**
Ball & Swirl, mug, marigold **90.00**
Balloons (Imperial), cake plate, marigold **60.00**
Balloons (Imperial), compote, marigold..**55.00**
Banded Diamonds (Crystal), bowl, marigold, 5"............................**50.00**
Banded Diamonds (Crystal), tumbler, amethyst, rare **350.00**
Banded Grape & Leaf (English), pitcher, water; marigold **500.00**
Banded Panels (Crystal), sugar bowl, amethyst, open....................**45.00**
Banded Portland (US Glass), puff jar, marigold.............................**60.00**
Banded Rib, pitcher, marigold **120.00**

Banded Rib, tumbler, marigold **20.00**
Basketweave (Fenton), vase whimsey, bl, rare.............................**625.00**
Beaded, hatpin, amethyst **24.00**
Beaded Acanthus (Imperial), pitcher, milk; gr **210.00**
Beaded Band & Octagon, lamp, kerosene; marigold.......................**85.00**
Beaded Cable (Northwood), rose bowl, aqua opal........................**400.00**
Beaded Hearts (Northwood), bowl, gr **60.00**
Beaded Panels (Imperial), bowl, marigold, 5"................................**22.00**
Beaded Panels (Imperial), powder jar, marigold, w/lid..................**50.00**
Beaded Shell (Dugan), bowl, amethyst, ftd, 5"..............................**38.00**
Beaded Shell (Dugan), pitcher, water; marigold..........................**360.00**
Beaded Shell (Dugan), tumbler, bl..**150.00**
Beaded Spears (Crystal), pitcher, marigold, rare **175.00**
Beaded Stars, banana boat, marigold, 8¾" **90.00**
Beaded Stars (Fenton), bowl, marigold **35.00**
Beaded Swirl (English), pitcher, milk; bl **70.00**
Beads (Northwood), bowl, gr, 8½"..**60.00**
Bellaire Souvenir (Imperial), bowl, marigold, scarce **85.00**
Bells & Beads (Dugan), bowl, peach opal, 7½"..............................**60.00**
Bells & Beads (Dugan), compote, marigold **40.00**
Bells & Beads (Dugan), nappy, amethyst.......................................**65.00**
Bells & Beads (Dugan), plate, amethyst, 8"..................................**120.00**
Big Fish (Millersburg), bowl, marigold, tricorner **1,000.00**
Big Fish (Millersburg), bowl, pastel, sq, very rare....................**5,500.00**
Bird & Cherries (Fenton), bonbon, bl **60.00**
Bird w/Grapes (Cockatoo), wall vase, marigold **65.00**
Birds & Cherries (Fenton), compote, amethyst..............................**60.00**
Black Bottom (Fenton), bowl, marigold, ftd, 9".............................**47.00**

Blackberry (Fenton), plate, bl, rare 375.00
Blackberry Block (Fenton), pitcher, gr............................12.00
Blackberry Bramble (Fenton), bowl, bl 50.00
Blackberry Miniature (Fenton), compote, marigold, sm..............75.00
Blackberry Spray (Fenton), compote, bl 45.00
Blackberry Wreath (Millersburg), bowl, gr, 5"..................65.00
Blackberry Wreath (Millersburg), plate, marigold, rare, 10".... 4,000.00
Blossoms & Band (Imperial), bowl, marigold, 5" 20.00
Blossoms & Band (Imperial), wall vase, marigold, complete 42.00
Blossomtime (Northwood), compote, gr............................250.00
Bo Peep (Westmoreland), ABC plate, marigold, rare 450.00
Border Plants (Dugan), bowl, peach opal, flat, 8½" 170.00
Bouquet (Fenton), pitcher, pastel 595.00
Brocaded Summer Gardens, bonbon, pastel............................62.00
Brocaded Summer Gardens, cake plate, pastel, center hdl 95.00
Brocaded Summer Gardens, rose bowl, pastel........................90.00
Brocaded Summer Gardens, tray, cake; pastel 90.00
Brocaded Summer Gardens, vase, pastel 90.00
Brocker's (Northwood), advertising plate, gr......................350.00
Broken Arches (Imperial), punch bowl & base, amethyst 475.00
Brooklyn Bridge (Dugan), bowl, marigold, unlettered, rare 750.00
Bubble Perry, shade, pastel 60.00
Bubbles, hatpin, amethyst 36.00
Bull's Eye (US Glass), oil lamp, marigold 185.00
Bull's Eye & Loop (Millersburg), vase, gr, rare, 7"..................300.00
Bull's Eye & Spearhead, wine, marigold......................48.00
Bumblebees, hatpin, amethyst......................26.00
Bunny, bank, marigold 30.00
Butterflies (Fenton), bonbon, pastel 70.00
Butterflies & Waratah (Crystal), compote, amethyst, lg..............250.00
Butterfly (Fenton), ornament, gr, rare 200.00
Butterfly (Northwood), bonbon, amethyst, ribbed ext................260.00
Butterfly (US Glass), tumbler, marigold, rare 5,500.00
Butterfly & Berry (Fenton), bowl, bl, ftd, 5" 40.00
Butterfly & Berry (Fenton), plate, bl, ftd 1,350.00
Butterfly & Berry (Fenton), sugar bowl, amethyst......................170.00
Butterfly & Berry (Fenton), tumbler, bl......................60.00
Butterfly & Fern (Fenton), pitcher, bl......................500.00
Butterfly Bower (Crystal), cake plate, amethyst, stemmed..........175.00
Butterfly Bush (Crystal), compote, amethyst, lg..................150.00
Button & Fan, hatpin, amethyst......................55.00
Buttress (US Glass), pitcher, marigold, rare 300.00
Buzz Saw, shade, marigold 40.00
Cane (Imperial), wine, marigold 50.00
Cane & Scroll (Sea Thistle) (English), creamer, bl 70.00
Cannonball Vt, tumbler, marigold......................60.00
Capitol (Westmoreland), bowl, bl, ftd, sm......................65.00
Captive Rose (Fenton), bonbon, gr......................60.00
Captive Rose (Fenton), bowl, gr, 10"......................48.00
Captive Rose (Fenton), compote, amethyst......................60.00
Captive Rose (Fenton), plate, amethyst, 7"......................110.00
Carnival Honeycomb (Imperial), bonbon, gr......................45.00
Carnival Honeycomb (Imperial), bowl, marigold, hdld, 6"..........30.00
Carnival Honeycomb (Imperial), creamer, marigold..................28.00
Carolina Dogwood (Westmoreland), plate, peach opal, rare 290.00
Caroline (Dugan), banana boat, peach opal 300.00
Cartwheel #411 (Heisey), compote, marigold 40.00
Cathedral (Sweden), bowl, marigold, 10"......................40.00
Cathedral (Sweden), flower holder, marigold......................60.00
Cathedral (Sweden), pitcher, bl, rare 2,500.00
Cathedral Arches (English), punch bowl, marigold, 1-pc..........250.00
Cattails, hatpin, amethyst......................26.00
Chatelaine (Imperial), tumbler, amethyst, rare 460.00
Chatham (US Glass), candlestisk, marigold, pr 75.00

Checkerboard (Westmoreland), goblet, amethyst, rare..............295.00
Checkerboard (Westmoreland), punch cup, marigold..................75.00
Checkerboard (Westmoreland), tumbler, amethyst, rare 450.00
Checkerboard (Westmoreland), wine, marigold, rare 250.00
Checkerboard Bouquet, plate, amethyst, 8"......................50.00
Checkers, bowl, marigold, 4"......................18.00
Checkers, plate, marigold, 7"......................50.00
Cherry (Dugan), bowl, amethyst, ftd, 8½"......................275.00

Cherry (Dugan), bowl, marigold, flat, 8" 50.00
Cherry (Millersburg), banana compote, amethyst, rare 2,000.00
Cherry (Millersburg), bowl, gr, rare, 7"......................75.00
Cherry (Millersburg), compote, gr, rare, lg 1,000.00
Cherry (Millersburg), creamer, gr 90.00
Cherry (Millersburg), pitcher, marigold, scarce......................750.00
Cherry (Millersburg), pitcher, milk; gr, rare......................625.00
Cherry (Millersburg), plate, gr, rare, 10"......................3,350.00
Cherry (Millersburg), sugar bowl, gr, w/lid......................100.00
Cherry (Millersburg), tumbler, gr, 2 variations......................250.00
Cherry & Cable (Northwood), bowl, marigold, scarce, 5"..........45.00
Cherry & Cable (Northwood), bowl, marigold, scarce, 9"............95.00
Cherry & Cable (Northwood), tumbler, marigold, rare..............400.00
Cherry & Cable Intaglio (Northwood), bowl, marigold, 5".........50.00
Cherry Blossoms, tumbler, bl......................28.00
Cherry Chain (Fenton), bowl, gr, 10"......................70.00
Cherry Circles (Fenton), bowl, amethyst, 8" 60.00
Cherry Circles (Fenton), compote, bl......................60.00
Cherry Circles (Fenton), plate, bl, rare......................120.00
Cherry Smash (US Glass), bowl, marigold, 8"......................50.00
Cherry Smash (US Glass), tumbler, marigold 135.00
Chippendale Souvenir, creamer, amethyst 80.00
Christmas Compote, compote, amethyst, rare, lg......................2,600.00
Chrysanthemum (Fenton), bowl, bl, flat, 9"......................75.00
Circle Scroll (Dugan), bowl, amethyst, 5" 45.00
Circle Scroll (Dugan), creamer, amethyst......................200.00
Circle Scroll (Dugan), sugar bowl, amethyst......................350.00
Classic Arts (Czech), vase, marigold, Egyptian, 7"......................245.00
Classic Arts (Czech), vase, marigold, rare, 10"......................300.00
Cobblestones (Dugan), bowl, marigold, 9" 55.00
Cobblestones (Dugan-Imperial), plate, amethyst, rare............ 1,000.00
Cobblestones (Imperial), bowl, amethyst, 8½"......................70.00
Coin Dot (Fenton), bowl, amethyst, 6" 50.00
Coin Dot (Fenton), rose bowl, bl......................70.00
Coin Dot Vt (Westmoreland), rose bowl, amethyst......................75.00
Coin Spot (Dugan), compote, marigold......................40.00
Colonial (Imperial), candlestick, marigold, pr......................185.00
Colonial (Imperial), goblet, lemonade; marigold......................60.00
Columbia (Imperial), compote, gr......................57.00
Columbia (Imperial), vase, amethyst 48.00
Concave Diamonds (Dugan), pitcher, pastel, w/lid......................550.00
Concave Diamonds (Dugan), tumbler, gr 400.00
Concave Flute (Westmoreland), rose bowl, gr......................65.00

Concord (Fenton), plate, amethyst, rare, 10" 700.00
Connie (Northwood), tumbler, pastel..............90.00
Coral (Fenton), plate, bl, rare, 9½" 850.00
Cornucopia (Fenton), candle holder, pastel, 6½" 100.00
Cornucopia (Fenton), candlestick, marigold, 5", pr 75.00
Cosmos & Cane, compote, marigold, tall, rare 300.00
Cosmos & Cane, creamer, marigold............125.00
Cosmos & Cane, tumbler, marigold, rare..........85.00
Cosmos Vt (Fenton), bowl, bl, 9"............80.00
Cosmos Vt (Fenton), plate, amethyst, rare, 10" 110.00
Country Kitchen (Millersburg), creamer, amethyst........325.00
Crab Claw (Imperial), bowl, fruit; marigold, w/base........90.00
Crab Claw (Imperial), bowl, marigold, 10"..........45.00
Crab Claw (Imperial), tumbler, marigold, scarce........95.00
Crackle (Imperial), pitcher, amethyst, dome base 140.00
Crackle (Imperial), plate, marigold..........30.00
Crackle (Imperial), tumbler, gr, dome base..........26.00
Crackle (Imperial), window planter, marigold, rare..........95.00
Crucifix (Imperial), candlestick, marigold, rare, ea 400.00
Cut Arcs (Fenton), bowl, marigold, 10"............32.00
Cut Arcs (Fenton), compote, bl............45.00
Cut Cosmos (Millersburg), tumbler, marigold, rare 295.00
Cut Crystal (US Glass), bottle, water; marigold........165.00
Cut Crystal (US Glass), compote, marigold, 5½" 90.00
Cut Ovals (Fenton), candlestick, marigold, pr..........65.00
Dahlia (Dugan), bowl, amethyst, ftd, 5"..........50.00
Dahlia (Dugan), creamer, marigold 75.00
Daisy & Cane (English), spittoon, bl, rare..........185.00
Daisy & Plume (Northwood), candy dish, gr 60.00
Daisy & Plume (Northwood), compote, amethyst..........60.00
Daisy Chain, shade, marigold 45.00
Daisy in Oval Panels (US Glass), creamer, marigold..........50.00
Daisy Squares, compote, pastel, rare 500.00
Daisy Squares, goblet, pastel, rare 350.00
Dandelion (Northwood), tumbler, bl..........90.00
Deep Grape (Millersburg), compote, amethyst, ruffled, rare.....1,850.50
Deep Grape (Millersburg), rose bowl, gr, stemmed 1,950.00
Diamond & Daisy (US Glass), compote, amethyst 60.00
Diamond & File, bowl, marigold, 9"..........35.00
Diamond & Rib (Fenton), vase, funeral; amethyst, 17" 850.00
Diamond & Rib (Fenton), vase, gr, 7" 32.00
Diamond & Sunburst (Imperial), decanter, gr..........150.00
Diamond & Sunburst (Imperial), oil cruet, gr, rare 800.00
Diamond Band (Crystal), sugar bowl, amethyst, open..........45.00
Diamond Band & Fan (English), cordial set, marigold, rare 750.00
Diamond Checkerboard, bowl, marigold, 5"..........25.00
Diamond Flutes (US Glass), creamer, marigold..........35.00
Diamond Lace (Imperial), pitcher, amethyst..........285.00
Diamond Lace (Imperial), tumbler, marigold 75.00
Diamond Ovals (English), compote, marigold, open..........35.00
Diamond Point Columns (Imperial), creamer, marigold 40.00
Diamond Point Columns (Imperial), plate, marigold, 7" 35.00
Diamond Point Columns (Imperial), powder jar, marigold..........50.00
Diamond Point Columns (Imperial), vase, gr..........40.00
Diamond Ring (Imperial), bowl, amethyst, 5"............28.00
Diamond Top (English), creamer, marigold..........32.00
Diamonds (Millersburg), tumbler, marigold 40.00
Diving Dolphins (English), bowl, bl, ftd, 7"..........160.00
Dogwood Sprays (Dugan), compote, bl..........160.00
Dotted Daisies, plate, marigold, 8" 65.00
Double Dolphins (Fenton), cake plate, pastel, center hdl 70.00
Double Dolphins (Fenton), candy dish, pastel, stemmed 75.00
Double Fan (English), tumbler, marigold, rare 100.00
Double Loop (Northwood), creamer, bl..........100.00

Double Star (Cambridge), pitcher, gr, scarce..........395.00
Double Star (Cambridge), tumbler, amethyst, scarce 110.00
Double Stem Rose (Dugan), bowl, peach opal, dome base, 8½" .125.00
Dragon & Lotus (Fenton), bowl, peach opal, ftd, scarce, 9" 680.00
Dragon & Strawberry (Fenton), bowl, gr, ftd, scarce, 9" 350.00
Dragonfly, shade, pastel..........48.00
Drapery Vt (Fenton), tumbler, marigold, scarce 70.00
Dreibus Parfait Sweets (Northwood), plate, amethyst, 6" 175.00
Dugan Fan (Dugan), gravy boat, peach opal, ftd 145.00
Dutch Mill, ash tray, marigold..........35.00
Dutch Twins, ash tray, marigold..........45.00
Embroidered Mums (Northwood), bowl, bl, 9"..........60.00
Embroidered Mums (Northwood), plate, pastel..........875.00
English Button Band (English), creamer, marigold..........38.00
Engraved Floral (Fenton), tumbler, gr 85.00
Engraved Grapes (Fenton), tumbler, juice; marigold..........20.00
Estate (Westmoreland), vase, bud; marigold, 6"..........40.00
Exchange Bank (Northwood), plate, amethyst, 6" 200.00
Fanciful (Dugan), bowl, peach opal, 8½"..........275.00
Fancy Cut (English), miniature pitcher, marigold, rare..........125.00
Fantail (Fenton), bowl, marigold, ftd, 9" 60.00
Fantail (Fenton), compote, bl 160.00
Fashion (Imperial), creamer, amethyst 110.00
Fashion (Imperial), pitcher, pastel 500.00
Fashion (Imperial), punch cup, amethyst..........35.00
Feather & Heart (Millersburg), pitcher, gr, scarce 675.00
Feather Swirl (US Glass), vase, marigold..........50.00
Fentonia Fruit (Fenton), pitcher, bl, rare..........670.00
Fern (Fenton), bowl, bl, rare, 9"..........800.00
Field Flower (Imperial), pitcher, gr, scarce 365.00
Field Flower (Imperial), pitcher, milk; gr, rare..........185.00
Field Thistle (US Glass), tumbler, marigold, scarce..........38.00
Field Thistle (US Glass), vase, marigold..........60.00
File (Imperial & English), bowl, amethyst, 7"..........50.00
File (Imperial & English), creamer, marigold 100.00
Fine Cut & Roses (Northwood), candy dish, aqua opal, ftd........760.00
Fine Cut Rings (English), bowl, marigold, rnd 35.00
Fine Cut Rings (English), jam jar, marigold, w/lid..........50.00

Fine Cut Rings (English), sugar bowl, marigold, stemmed 45.00
Fine Rib (Northwood & Fenton), compote, bl..........150.00
Five Hearts (Dugan), bowl, amethyst, dome base 52.00
Flannel Flower (Crystal), compote, amethyst, lg..........140.00
Floral & Grape (Dugan), pitcher, bl 170.00
Floral & Grape Vt (Fenton), pitcher, gr, 2 variations, ea 190.00
Floral & Grape Vt (Fenton), tumbler, bl..........30.00
Floral & Optic (Imperial), cake plate, pastel, ftd..........50.00
Floral & Wheat (US Glass), bonbon, bl, stemmed..........42.00
Floral Fan, etched vase, marigold 42.00
Florentine (Fenton), candlestick, bl, pr 115.00
Flowering Vine (Millersburg), compote, gr, tall, very rare........2,000.00
Flute (British), sherbet, marigold, mk British 45.00

Flute (Millersburg), bowl, amethyst, variant, 4" 40.00
Flute (Millersburg), bowl, amethyst, 5" 30.00
Flute (Millersburg), punch bowl & base, amethyst, rare 225.00
Flute (Northwood), creamer, gr...90.00
Flute (Northwood), ring tree, marigold, rare 175.00
Flute & Cane (Imperial), pitcher, marigold, stemmed, rare 385.00

Flute & Cane (Imperial), wine, marigold......................................40.00
Flute #3 (Imperial), bowl, amethyst, 5" 65.00
Flute #3 (Imperial), punch bowl & base, gr 495.00
Folding Fan (Dugan), compote, bl 75.00
Footed Prism Panels (English), vase, gr......................................75.00
Footed Rib (Northwood), vase, bl, advertising 70.00
Forty-niner (Imperial), decanter, marigold..................................125.00
Forty-niner (Imperial), pitcher, marigold, squat...........................250.00
Fostorial #1299 (Fostoria), tumbler, marigold..............................75.00
Fountain Lamp, marigold, complete, scarce 265.00
Four Flowers (Finland), plate, gr, 6½" 75.00
Four Flowers Vt (Westmoreland), bowl, gr, ftd, 8½" 75.00
Four Flowers Vt (Westmoreland), plate, gr, rare 650.00
Frosted Block (Imperial), compote, marigold................................85.00
Frosted Block (Imperial), plate, pastel, 9".....................................65.00
Frosted Ribbon, tumbler, marigold 27.00
Fruit & Flowers (Northwood), bowl, gr, 5" 32.00
Fruit & Flowers (Northwood), plate, bl, 7"...................................140.00
Fruit Basket (Millersburg), compote, amethyst, hdld, rare 1,200.00
Fruit Salad (Westmoreland), cup, peach opal, rare 40.00
Garden Path (Dugan), bowl, peach opal, 5" 47.00
Garden Path (Dugan), compote, amethyst, rare...........................300.00
Garden Path Vt (Dugan), bowl, fruit; peach opal, 10"..................395.00
Gay 90s (Millersburg), tumbler, amethyst, rare........................ 1,150.00
God & Home (Dugan), tumbler, bl, rare 135.00
Goddess of Harvest (Fenton), plate, amethyst, very rare..............67.00
Golden Cupids (Crystal), bowl, pastel, rare, 5" 95.00
Golden Grapes (Dugan), bowl, gr, 7"...45.00
Golden Harvest (US Glass), decanter, amethyst, w/stopper 230.00
Golden Honeycomb (Imperial), compote, marigold.......................47.00
Golden Honeycomb (Imperial), creamer, marigold.......................32.00
Good Luck Vt (Northwood), bowl, gr, 8¾".................................275.00
Gooseberry Spray, bowl, amethyst, 10" 85.00
Gooseberry Spray, bowl, amethyst, 5"...110.00
Gooseberry Spray, compote, amethyst, rare 210.00
Graceful (Northwood), vase, amethyst 70.00
Grape, Heavy (Dugan), bowl, peach opal, 10".............................500.00
Grape, Heavy (Imperial), bowl, bl, 9" 56.00
Grape, heavy (Imperial), plate, gr, 6"..65.00
Grape (Fenton's Grape & Cable), bowl, bl, flat, 8" 48.00
Grape (Imperial), bowl, fruit; gr, 8¾" 48.00
Grape (Imperial), cup & saucer, gr..85.00
Grape (Imperial), punch bowl & base, gr 275.00
Grape (Imperial), tray, marigold, center hdl.................................38.00
Grape (Imperial), wine, pastel..30.00

Grape (Northwood's Grape & Cable), bonbon, peach opal 295.00
Grape (Northwood's Grape & Cable), bowl, gr, flat, 5½" 40.00
Grape (Northwood's Grape & Cable), cologne, gr, w/stopper 195.00
Grape (Northwood's Grape & Cable), cookie jar, amethyst 265.00
Grape (Northwood's Grape & Cable), cup, gr................................195.00
Grape (Northwood's Grape & Cable), decanter, amethyst 800.00
Grape (Northwood's Grape & Cable), plate, gr, ftd 115.00
Grape & Gothic Arches (Northwood), bowl, bl, 10" 60.00
Grape & Gothic Arches (Northwood), creamer, bl 80.00
Grape Wreath (Millersburg), bowl, bl, 9"....................................400.00
Grapevine Lattice (Fenton), tumbler, bl, rare 90.00
Hammered Bell Chandelier, shade, pastel 95.00
Hattie (Imperial), plate, gr, rare..430.00
Hawaiian Lei (Higbee), creamer, marigold 65.00
Headress, bowl, marigold, 2 variations, 9", ea............................36.00
Heart & Horsrshoe (Fenton), plate, marigold, rare, 9"................900.00
Heart & Vine (Fenton), advertising plate, marigold...................400.00
Heart Band Souvenir, mug, gr, sm..95.00
Hearts & Flowers (Northwood), compote, peach opal 625.00
Heavy Diamond (Imperial), compote, gr 50.00
Heavy Diamond (Imperial), creamer, marigold 28.00
Heavy Diamond (Imperial), sugar bowl, marigold.......................28.00
Heavy Shell (Fenton), candle holder, pastel, ea..........................92.00
Heavy Vine, lamp, marigold..162.00
Heisey, breakfast set, pastel 185.00
Heisey Cartwheel, compote, pastel 65.00
Heisey Floral Spray, candy dish, pastel, stemmed, 11" 70.00
Heisey Set, creamer & tray, marigold..75.00
Hexagon & Cane (Imperial), sugar bowl, marigold, w/lid............65.00
Hobnail (Millersburg), creamer, bl, rare.....................................500.00
Hobnail (Millersburg), pitcher, bl, rare 1,600.00
Hobnail (Millersburg), spittoon, amethyst, rare 600.00
Hobstar & Cut Triangles (English), bowl, gr...............................58.00
Hobstar & Feather (Millersburg), bowl, marigold, heart form 300.00
Hobstar & Feather (Millersburg), compote, marigold, rare, 6". 1,500.00
Hobstar & Feather (Millersburg), creamer, gr, rare 800.00
Hobstar & Feather (Millersburg), dessert, marigold, stemmed.....650.00
Hobstar & Feather (Millersburg), punch cup, bl, scarce................80.00
Hobstar & File, tumbler, marigold, rare......................................170.00
Hobstar & Fruit (Westmoreland), bowl, peach opal, rare, 10" 125.00
Hobstar Band (Imperial), bowl, marigold, rare 70.00
Hobstar Flower (Northwood), compote, bl, scarce 75.00
Hobstar Panels (English), creamer, marigold 45.00
Hobstar Panels (English), sugar bowl, marigold, stemmed 45.00
Holiday (Northwood), tray, marigold, rare, 11" 250.00
Holly, Panelled (Northwood), bonbon, gr, ftd.............................57.00
Holly (Fenton), goblet, marigold...30.00
Holly & Berry (Dugan), bowl, peach opal, 7" 60.00
Holly Sprig or Whirl (Millersburg), bowl, gr, tricorner, 7" 185.00
Holly Sprig or Whirl (Millersburg), compote, amethyst, rare 325.00
Holly Sprig Vt (Millersburg), bowl, gr, scarce 145.00
Honeycomb & Clover (Imperial-Fenton), compote, bl 48.00
Horn, Powder (Cambridge), candy holder, marigold...................185.00
Horses Heads (Fenton), bowl, bl, ftd, 8" 85.00
Horses Heads (Fenton), plate, gr, 6½" 110.00
Hourglass, vase, bud; marigold..46.00
Humpty-Dumpty, mustard jar, marigold 75.00
Ice Crystals, candlestick, pastel, pr..160.00
Illinois Daisy (English), cookie jar, marigold, w/lid 55.00
Illusion (Fenton), bowl, bl...90.00
Imperial #5 (Imperial), vase, marigold, rare................................90.00
Imperial Grape (Imperial), shade, marigold.................................65.00
Imperial Paperweight (Imperial), advertising, amethyst, rare 900.00
Indiana Statehouse (Fenton), plate, bl, rare................................ 3,350.00

Intaglio Daisy (English), bowl, marigold, 4½" 26.00
Intaglio Ovals (US Glass), bowl, pastel, 7" 65.00
Interior Panels, mug, marigold 75.00
Interior Poinsettia (Northwood), tumbler, marigold, rare............465.00
Interior Rays (Westmoreland), creamer, marigold......................40.00
Inverted Coin Dot (Northwood-Fenton), tumbler, bl 85.00
Inverted Feather (Cambridge), creamer, amethyst, rare 320.00
Inverted Feather (Cambridge), pitcher, marigold, squat, rare......900.00
Inverted Feather (Cambridge), pitcher, marigold, tall, rare..... 3,700.00
Inverted Strawberry, candlestick, gr, rare, pr 300.00
Inverted Strawberry, powder jar, gr, rare 130.00
Inverted Thistle (Cambridge), box, bl, w/lid, rare..................350.00
Inverted Thistle (Cambridge), creamer, amethyst, rare 380.00
Iris (Fenton), goblet, buttermilk; gr, scarce 65.00
Isaac Benesch, bowl, amethyst, w/advertising, 6½" 350.00
Jackman, whiskey bottle, marigold 30.00
Jacobean Ranger (Czech & English), tumbler, juice; marigold 70.00
Jacobean Ranger (Czech & English), wine, marigold 28.00
Jelly Jar, complete, marigold, rare...................................65.00
Jewel Box, inkwell, marigold 75.00
Jewelled Heart (Dugan), bowl, peach opal, 10" 135.00
Jewelled Heart (Dugan), tumbler, marigold, rare...................100.00
Jewels (Imperial), candlestick, amethyst, pr 140.00
Jewels (Imperial), creamer, amethyst 70.00
Jockey Club (Northwood), bowl, amethyst, 7"......................145.00
Kangaroo (Australian), bowl, marigold, 5" 47.00
Kingfisher & Vt (Australian), bowl, amethyst, 9½" 90.00
Kittens (Fenton), bowl, cereal; bl, scarce..........................165.00
Kiwi (Australian), bowl, marigold, rare, 10".......................350.00
Knight Templar (Northwood), mug, advertising; marigold, rare .700.00
Knotted Beads (Fenton), vase, bl, 4".................................37.00
Kokomo (English), rose bowl, bl, ftd................................50.00
Kookaburra & Vts (Australian), bowl, amethyst, 5" 48.00
Kookaburra & Vts (Australian), bowl, marigold, 10" 80.00
Lacy Dewdrop (Westmoreland), bowl, pastel, w/lid 240.00
Lacy Dewdrop (Westmoreland), compote, pastel, w/lid.............285.00
Lacy Dewdrop (Westmoreland), creamer, pastel 90.00
Lacy Dewdrop (Westmoreland), goblet, pastel......................150.00
Lacy Dewdrop (Westmoreland), sugar bowl, pastel 90.00
Large Kangaroo (Australian), bowl, marigold, 5" 40.00
Lattice & Daisy (Dugan), pitcher, marigold 135.00
Lattice & Grape (Fenton), pitcher, gr 385.00
Lattice & Grape (Fenton), tumbler, bl 40.00
Lattice & Points (Dugan), vase, pastel...............................55.00
Lattice & Sprays, vase, marigold, 10½" 40.00
Lattice Heart (English), bowl, marigold, 5".........................30.00
Lattice Heart (English), compote, bl.................................85.00
Laurel & Grape, vase, marigold, 6" 110.00
Laurel Band, tumbler, marigold......................................42.00
Laurel Leaves (Imperial), plate, amethyst 55.00
Leaf & Beads (Northwood-Dugan), bowl, nut; peach opal, rare ..550.00
Leaf & Beads (Northwood-Dugan), candy dish, gr, ftd 52.00
Leaf & Beads (Northwood-Dugan), plate whimsey, marigold......200.00
Leaf Chain (Fenton), plate, bl, 7½" 90.00
Leaf Tiers (Fenton), creamer/spooner, marigold, ftd 82.00
Leaf Tiers (Fenton), pitcher, gr, ftd, rare...........................630.00
Lily of the Valley, pitcher, bl, rare 4,500.00
Lined Lattice (Dugan), vase, gr, 7"..................................45.00
Lion (Fenton), plate, marigold, rare, 7½" 500.00
Little Beads, compote, marigold, sm.................................26.00
Little Daisies (Fenton), bowl, bl, rare, 8"..........................245.00
Little Daisy, lamp, pastel, complete, 8"............................395.00
Little Fishes (Fenton), bowl, gr, flat or ftd, 10"....................90.00
Little Flowers (Fenton), plate, marigold, rare, 7".................185.00

Little Stars (Millersburg), bowl, amethyst, rare, 9"................550.00
Little Stars (Millersburg), plate, gr, rare, 7⅝" 475.00
Long Hobstar, bowl, marigold, 8½" 45.00
Long Horn, wine, marigold 35.00
Long Thumbprint (Dugan), creamer, marigold 38.00
Lotus & Grape (Fenton), bowl, gr, flat, 7"...........................50.00
Louisa (Westmoreland), candy dish, gr, ftd 65.00
Louisa (Westmoreland), plate, amethyst, ftd, rare, 8" 150.00
Lustre & Clear (Imperial), creamer, amethyst 65.00
Lustre & Clear (Imperial), shakers, marigold, pr 70.00

Lustre & Clear (Imperial), tray, celery; marigold, 8" 35.00
Lustre & Clear (Imperial), tumbler, marigold.......................40.00
Lustre Flute (Northwood), bonbon, gr 55.00
Lustre Flute (Northwood), compote, amethyst 48.00
Lustre Flute (Northwood), cup, marigold............................15.00
Lustre Rose (Imperial), bowl, gr, 9"..................................58.00
Lustre Rose (Imperial), plate, amethyst, 6".........................70.00
Lustre Rose (Imperial), sugar bowl, marigold 45.00
Lustre Rose (Imperial), tumbler, amethyst 30.00
Magnolia Drape, tumbler, marigold 50.00
Malaga (Dugan), plate, amethyst, rare, 10" 250.00
Many Fruits (Dugan), cup, bl 40.00
Many Stars (Millersburg), bowl, amethyst, tricorner 1,500.00
Maple Leaf (Dugan), creamer, amethyst 65.00
Marilyn (Millersburg), tumbler, gr, rare............................400.00
Mary Ann (Dugan), vase, amethyst, 2 variations, 7", ea 80.00
Massachusetts (US Glass), vase, marigold 150.00
Mayflower, bowl, amethyst, 7½" 40.00
Mayflower, compote, amethyst.......................................50.00
Melon Rib (Imperial), powder jar, marigold, w/lid 35.00
Melon Rib (Imperial), shakers, marigold, pr 50.00
Memphis (Northwood), bowl, gr, 5" 50.00
Memphis (Northwood), creamer, amethyst 50.00
Memphis (Northwood), cup, gr..42.00
Memphis (Northwood), punch bowl, gr, w/base.....................550.00
Milady (Fenton), pitcher, bl..500.00
Mitered Ovals (Millersburg), vase, gr, rare 2,200.00
Miniature Shell, candle holder, pastel, ea............................75.00
Mirrored Lotus (Fenton), bonbon, marigold 50.00
Mirrored Lotus (Fenton), bowl, gr, 7"................................58.00
Mirrored Peacocks, tumbler, marigold, rare........................150.00
Moonprint (English), candlestick, marigold, rare, ea 50.00
Moonprint (English), cheese keeper, marigold, rare................135.00
Moonprint (English), creamer, marigold.............................45.00
Moonprint (English), pitcher, milk; marigold, scarce...............100.00
Moonprint (English), sugar bowl, marigold, stemmed...............50.00
Morning Glory (Millersburg), tumbler, gr, rare.................. 1,000.00
Moxie, bottle, pastel, rare 78.00
Multi-Fruit & Flowers (Millersburg), punch bowl & base, gr .. 1,600.00
My Lady, powder jar, marigold, w/lid 87.00
Mystic (Cambridge), vase, marigold, ftd, rare 120.00

Napoleon, bottle, pastel..............................70.00
Near Cut Souvenir (Cambridge), mug, marigold, rare 175.00
Nell (Higbee), mug, marigold.............................65.00
Nesting Swan (Millersburg), bowl, gr, tricorner, rare 1,100.00
New Orleans Shrine (US Glass), champagne, pastel.....................90.00
Night Stars (Millersburg), bonbon, gr, rare 580.00
Night Stars (Millersburg), nappy, amethyst, tricorner, rare..... 1,800.00
Night Stars (Millersburg), tray, card; amethyst, rare 700.00
Nippon (Northwood), plate, gr, 9"..............................375.00
Northern Star (Fenton), bowl, marigold, 6"..............................28.00
Northwood's Nearcut, goblet, amethyst, rare 145.00
Northwood's Nearcut, pitcher, marigold, rare 1,500.00
Northwood's Poppy, tray, amethyst, oval, rare 180.00
Octagon (Imperial), bowl, gr, 4½"..............................28.00
Octagon (Imperial), decanter, amethyst, complete 250.00
Octagon (Imperial), pitcher, milk; gr, scarce 170.00
Octagon (Imperial), shakers, amethyst, old only, pr.................150.00
Octagon (Imperial), sugar bowl, gr..............................76.00
Octagon (Imperial), tumbler, gr, ...44.00
Ohio Star (Millersburg), compote, marigold, rare 950.00
Oklahoma (Mexican), pitcher, marigold, rare 495.00
Oklahoma (Mexican), tumbler, marigold, rare..........................450.00
Open Rose (Imperial), bowl, amethyst, flat, 9"..............................40.00
Open Rose (Imperial), plate, gr, 9"..............................185.00
Optic & Buttons (Imperial), plate, marigold, 10½"..............................70.00
Optic #66 (Fostoria), goblet, marigold..............................45.00
Optic Flute (Imperial), bowl, marigold, 10"..............................40.00
Orange Peel (Westmoreland), cup, amethyst 32.00
Orange Peel (Westmoreland), dessert, gr, stemmed, scarce.....................70.00
Orange Peel (Westmoreland), punch bowl & base, marigold......125.00
Orange Tree (Fenton), bowl, bl, ftd, 5½"..............................32.00
Orange Tree (Fenton), bowl, centerpiece; bl, rare 1,600.00
Orange Tree (Fenton), compote, gr, sm..............................50.00
Orange Tree (Fenton), powder jar, pastel, w/lid..........................120.00
Orange Tree (Fenton), tumbler, bl..............................42.00
Orange Tree (Fenton), wine, peach opal 60.00
Orange Tree & Scroll (Fenton), pitcher, gr..............................425.00
Orange Tree Orchard (Fenton), pitcher, gr 425.00
Oriental Poppy (Northwood), tumbler, bl..............................265.00
Ostrich (Australian), compote, amethyst, rare, lg 265.00
Oval & Round (Imperial), bowl, amethyst, 7"..............................30.00
Oval & Round (Imperial), plate, gr, 10"..............................74.00
Owl Bank, marigold..............................38.00
Owl Bottle, pastel 65.00
Painted Castle, shade, marigold..............................55.00
Palm Beach (US Glass), banana bowl, amethyst.....................220.00
Palm Beach (US Glass), bowl, marigold, 9" 50.00
Palm Beach (US Glass), sugar bowl, marigold, ea 75.00
Panelled Dandelion (Fenton), candle lamp whimsey, bl, rare . 3,000.00
Panelled Dandelion (Fenton), pitcher, gr..............................625.00
Panelled Hobnail (Dugan), vase, gr, 5"..............................70.00
Panelled Prism, jam jar, marigold, w/lid..............................48.00
Panelled Thistle (Higbee), tumbler, marigold 95.00
Panels & Ball (Fenton), bowl, marigold, 11"..............................48.00
Pansy (Imperial), bowl, gr, 8¾"..............................45.00
Pansy (Imperial), nappy, marigold, old only 18.00
Pansy (Imperial), plate, gr, ruffled, rare..............................85.00
Pansy (Imperial), tray, dresser; gr..............................85.00
Panther (Fenton), bowl, bl, ftd, 5"..............................80.00
Paperweight, flower-shaped, pastel, rare 195.00
Parlor Panels, vase, amethyst 75.00
Pastel Panels (Imperial), creamer, marigold..............................160.00
Pastel Panels (Imperial), pitcher, pastel 320.00
Pastel Panels (Imperial), tumbler, pastel 95.00

Peach Blossom, bowl, amethyst, 7½" 70.00
Peacock, Fluffy (Fenton), pitcher, bl..............................750.00
Peacock (Millersburg), bowl, banana; pastel, rare 2,700.00
Peacock (Millersburg), bowl, gr, rare, 7½"..............................375.00
Peacock (Millersburg), bowl, ice cream; gr, rare, 10" .. 1,000.00
Peacock & Dahlia (Fenton), plate, bl, rare, 8½"..............................210.00
Peacock & Urn (Fenton), compote, bl 42.00
Peacock & Urn (Fenton), goblet, bl, rare 75.00
Peacock & Urn (Northwood), bowl, marigold, 5"..............................42.00
Peacock at the Fountain (Northwood), bowl, gr, 5" 42.00
Peacock at the Fountain (Northwood), compote, amethyst 225.00
Peacock Tail (Fenton), bonbon, bl..............................38.00
Peacock Tail (Fenton), plate, bl, 6"..............................70.00
Peacock Tail & Daisy, bowl, amethyst, very rare 1,100.00
Peacocks on Fence (Northwood), plate, bl, 9"..............................725.00
Pearl #37 (Northwood), shade, pastel..............................60.00
Penny, match holder, amethyst, rare..............................245.00
Perfection (Millersburg), pitcher, gr, rare..............................4,000.00
Persian Garden (Dugan), bowl, berry; amethyst, 10" 150.00
Persian Garden (Dugan), bowl, fruit; amethyst, w/base 270.00
Persian Garden (Dugan), plate, marigold, rare, 6"..............................90.00
Persian Medallion (Fenton), bowl, gr, 5"..............................36.00
Persian Medallion (Fenton), compote, bl 68.00
Persian Medallion (Fenton), plate, amethyst, 9½"..............................148.00
Persian Medallion (Fenton), plate, bl, 7"..............................75.00
Petal & Fan (Dugan), bowl, peach opal, 5" 50.00
Petal & Fan (Dugan), plate, amethyst, ruffled, 6" 95.00
Petals (Dugan), banana bowl, peach opal..............................110.00
Petals (Dugan), bowl, bl, 8¾"..............................110.00
Peter Rabbit (Fenton), bowl, gr, rare, 9"..............................850.00
Peter Rabbit (Fenton), plate, bl, rare, 10" 2,000.00
Pigeon, paperweight, marigold 80.00
Pillow & Sunburst (Westmoreland), bowl, pastel, 9" 62.00
Pine Cone (Fenton), bowl, bl, 6"..............................40.00
Pine Cone (Fenton), plate, gr, rare, 8"..............................96.00
Pineapple (English), bowl, amethyst, 7"..............................56.00
Pineapple (English), creamer, marigold 40.00
Pinwheel (Dugan), bowl, marigold, 6"..............................38.00

Pinwheel (English), vase, amethyst, 6½"..............................85.00
Plain Buttermilk (Fenton), goblet, bl 60.00
Plain Petals (Northwood) nappy, gr, scarce 90.00
Plume Panels, vase, bl, 7"..............................45.00
Poinsettia (Northwood), bowl, bl, flat or ftd, 8½" 290.00
Pond Lily (Fenton), bonbon, bl..............................52.00
Poppy (Millersburg), compote, gr, scarce..............................400.00
Poppy Show (Northwood), plate, bl, rare, 9"..............................500.00
Potpourri (Millersburg), pitcher, milk; marigold, rare..............1,150.00
Premium (Imperial) bowl, pastel, 12"..............................100.00
Pretty Panels (Fenton), tumbler, marigold, hdld..............................52.00
Pretty Panels (Northwood), pitcher, gr..............................160.00
Primrose (Millersburg), bowl, bl, ruffled, 8¾"..............................3,500.00

Primrose & Fishnet (Imperial), vase, red, rare, 6" 400.00
Prism, shakers, marigold, pr......60.00
Prism & Daisy Band (Imperial), compote, marigold......35.00
Propeller (Imperial), vase, marigold, stemmed, rare......75.00
Quartered Block, creamer, marigold......50.00
Question Marks (Dugan), bonbon, peach opal......70.00
Question Marks (Dugan), compote, amethyst......52.00
Quill (Dugan), pitcher, amethyst......2,350.00
Ragged Robin (Fenton), bowl, bl, scarce, 8¾"......60.00
Raindrops (Dugan), bowl, amethyst, 9"......60.00
Ranger (Mexican), creamer, marigold......40.00
Ranger (Mexican), sugar bowl, marigold......140.00
Rasberry (Northwood), compote, gr......58.00
Rasberry (Northwood), tumbler, marigold......36.00
Rays & Ribbons (Millersburg), plate, amethyst, rare......1,100.00
Regal Swirl, candlestick, marigold, ea......55.00
Ribbed Swirl, tumbler, gr......70.00
Ribbon & Leaves, sugar bowl, marigold, sm......48.00
Ribbon Tie (Fenton), plate, bl, flat, 9½"......285.00
Ribbon Tie (Fenton), plate, bl, ruffled, 9"......140.00
Rising Sun (US Glass), creamer, marigold......75.00
Rising Sun (US Glass), pitcher, bl, 2 shapes, rare......1,850.00
Rising Sun (US Glass), tray, bl, rare......400.00
Robin (Imperial), pitcher, marigold, old only, scarce......275.00
Robin (Imperial), tumbler, marigold, old only, scarce......50.00
Roll, pitcher, pastel, rare......275.00
Roll, shaker, marigold, rare, ea......40.00
Roman Rosette (US Glass), goblet, pastel, rare, 6"......90.00
Rosalind (Millersburg), compote, marigold, ruffled, rare, 8"......850.00
Rose, bottle, pastel......120.00
Rose Garden (Sweden), vase, marigold, rnd, 9"......200.00
Rose Show Vt (Northwood), plate, aqua opal, 9"......1,000.00
Roses & Fruit (Millersburg), bonbon, gr, ftd, rare......700.00
Rosettes (Northwood), bowl, amethyst, dome base......85.00
Round-up (Dugan), plate, peach opal, rare, 9"......360.00
Royalty (Imperial), punch bowl & base, marigold......125.00
Ruffles & Rings (Northwood), bowl, peach opal, very rare......700.00
S-Repeat (Dugan), creamer, amethyst, sm......60.00
S-Repeat (Dugan), cup, amethyst, rare......110.00
S-Repeat (Dugan), punch bowl & base, amethyst, rare......1,700.00
Sailboats (Fenton), compote, marigold......37.00
Sailboats (Fenton), plate, pastel......295.00
Sailboats (Fenton), wine, bl......210.00
Saint (English), candlestick, marigold, ea......275.00
Scales (Westmoreland), plate, amethyst, 6"......58.00
Scottie, powder jar, marigold, w/lid......25.00
Scroll Embossed Vt (English), ash tray, amethyst, hdld, 5"......60.00
Seaweed (Millersburg), plate, gr, rare, 10"......900.00
Serrated Ribs, shaker, marigold, ea......50.00
Shell (Imperial), plate, amethyst, 8½"......145.00
Sheraton (US Glass), tumbler, pastel......48.00
Silver & Gold, pitcher, marigold......100.00
Singing Birds (Northwood), creamer, marigold......80.00
Singing Birds (Northwood), pitcher, amethyst......365.00
Singing Birds (Northwood), tumbler, amethyst......54.00
Ski-Star (Dugan), bowl, marigold, 8"......58.00
Small Rib (Dugan), compote, gr......40.00
Smooth Panels (Imperial), bowl, pastel, 6½"......35.00
Smooth Panels (Imperial), pitcher, gr......170.00
Smooth Rays (Northwood-Dugan), bowl, marigold, 9"......44.00
Smooth Rays (Northwood-Dugan), plate, peach opal, 8"......80.00
Southern Ivy, wine, marigold, 2 szs, ea......38.00
Spiderweb (Northwood-Dugan), vase, marigold, 8"......45.00
Spiral (Imperial), candlestick, gr, ea......75.00

Split Diamond (English), creamer, marigold, sm......36.00
Spring Opening (Millersburg), plate, amethyst, rare, 6½"......400.00
Springtime (Northwood), bowl, gr, 5"......56.00
Springtime (Northwood), tumbler, amethyst, rare......110.00
Stag & Holly (Fenton), plate, marigold, ftd, 13"......900.00
Star & File (Imperial), bowl, marigold, 7"......30.00
Star & File (Imperial), plate, marigold, 6"......65.00
Star & File (Imperial), tumbler, marigold......140.00
Star Center (Imperial), plate, amethyst, 9"......65.00
Star Medallion (Imperial), goblet, marigold......45.00
Star Medallion (Imperial), tray, celery; marigold......42.00
Star Spray (Imperial), plate, marigold, scarce, 7½"......50.00
Starfish (Dugan), compote, gr......55.00
Stippled Acorns, candy dish, bl, ftd, w/lid......90.00
Stippled Rays (Fenton), compote, bl......40.00
Stork (Jenkins), vase, marigold......48.00
Stork & Rushes (Dugan), creamer, amethyst, rare......100.00
Taffeta Lustre (Fostoria), perfume, amethyst, w/stopper......75.00
Ten Mums (Fenton), bowl, bl, 8"......95.00
Texas Headdress (Westmoreland), punch cup, marigold......40.00
Thin Rib (Fenton), candlestick, marigold, pr......60.00
Thistle (Fenton), banana boat, bl, scarce......375.00
Thistle (Fenton), plate, gr, rare, 9"......1,800.00
Thistle & Thorn (English), bowl, marigold, ftd, 6"......46.00
Three Flowers (Imperial), tray, marigold, center hdl, 12"......47.00
Three Fruits (Northwood), amethyst, dome base, 8⅝"......75.00
Three Fruits Medallion (Northwood), bowl, bl, ftd, rare......275.00
Three-in-One (Imperial), plate, marigold, 6½"......55.00
Tiger Lily (Imperial), tumbler, gr......38.00
Tobacco Leaf (US Glass), champagne, pastel......140.00
Top O' the Walk, hatpin, amethyst......60.00
Tornado (Northwood), vase, bl, ribbed, 2 szs......190.00
Tracery (Millersburg), bonbon, gr, rare......600.00
Tree Bark (Imperial), candlestick, marigold, 7", pr......60.00
Tree of Life (Imperial), bowl, marigold, 5½"......27.00

Tree of Life (Imperial), pitcher, marigold......60.00
Tree Trunk (Northwood), vase, aqua opal, 7"......985.00
Triands (English), celery vase, marigold......55.00
Tropicana (English), vase, marigold, rare......1,200.00
Tulip & Cane (Imperial), goblet, marigold, rare, 8-oz......62.00
Two Flowers (Fenton), bowl, amethyst, 8"......47.00
Two Flowers (Fenton), bowl, bl, 5"......42.00
Two Flowers (Fenton), plate, marigold, rare, 13"......695.00
Umbrella Prisms, hatpin, amethyst, sm......26.00
US Diamond Block, (US Glass), shakers, marigold, pr......60.00
Vintage (Fenton), bowl, gr, 10"......60.00
Vintage (Fenton), compote, gr......46.00
Vintage (Fenton), plate, amethyst, 7¾"......175.00
Vintage Banded (Dugan), tumbler, marigold, rare......450.00
Virginia Blackberry (US Glass), pitcher, bl, rare, sm......225.00
Waffle Block (Imperial), bowl, marigold, 7"......36.00

Waffle Block (Imperial), creamer, marigold..60.00
Water Lily (Fenton), bonbon, marigold 35.00
Water Lily & Cattails (Fenton), sugar bowl, marigold 90.00
Water Lily & Cattails (Fenton), tumbler, marigold 95.00
Weeping Cherry (Dugan), bowl, amethyst, flat base 75.00
Weeping Cherry (Dugan), bowl, marigold, dome base 45.00
Whirling Hobstar (US Glass), pitcher, marigold........................150.00
Whirling Leaves (Millersburg), bowl, gr, rnd or ruffled, 9" 95.00
Whirling Leaves (Millersburg), bowl, gr, tricorner, 10" 335.00
Whirling Star (Imperial), punch bowl & base, marigold 135.00
Wickerwork (English), candy, amethyst, w/lid 42.00
Wild Blackberry (Fenton), bowl, gr, scarce, 8½" 58.00
Wild Loganberry (Westmoreland), creamer, pastel, rare 150.00
Wild Rose (Northwood), bowl, gr, open edge, ftd, 6" 42.00
Wild Strawberry (Dugan), bowl, amethyst, 9" 135.00
Wild Strawberry (Dugan), plate, amethyst, rare, 7" 385.00
Wildflower (Millersburg), compote, jelly; amethyst, rare 1,600.00
Windflower (Dugan), bowl, bl, 8½" 47.00
Windmill (Imperial), bowl, gr, 5" 24.00
Winken, lamp, marigold 95.00
Wishbone (Northwood), bowl, bl, flat, 8" 95.00
Wishbone (Northwood), plate, amethyst, ftd, rare, 9" 375.00
Wisteria (Northwood), tumbler, pastel, rare...........................900.00
Woodpecker & Ivy, vase, gr, rare...................................... 1,000.00
Wreath of Roses (Fenton), compote, bl 42.00
Wreathed Cherry (Dugan), pitcher, amethyst...........................420.00
Wreathed Cherry (Dugan), tumbler, pastel 160.00
Zig Zag (Fenton), pitcher, marigold, decorated, rare 180.00
Zig Zag (Millersburg), bowl, gr, tricorner, 10" 500.00
Zipper Vt (English), sugar bowl, marigold, w/lid..........................47.00
474 (Imperial), creamer, amethyst 110.00
474 (Imperial), cup, amethyst 40.00

474 (Imperial), vase, gr, rare, 14" 1,200.00
474 (Imperial), wine, marigold, rare....................................75.00

Carousel Figures

Who can forget the dazzle of the merry-go-round — lights blinking, animals prancing proudly by to the waltzes that bellowed from the band organ . . .

Gustav Dentzel, a German woodworker, created one of the first carousels in America in 1867. By the turn of the century, his animals had evolved from horses with a military bearing to fanciful creatures in various postures with garlands of flowers, exotic saddles, and other adornment. Dentzel was followed in the business by his son William, and both are noted for the exacting perfection of their carving and painting. The Philadelphia Toboggan Company, established in 1903, is famous today for its superior chariot designs. In 1901 Marcus Charles Illions formed his company, M.C. Illions and Sons. Illions' carvings

became more intricate with the growth of his company, and those from the twenties are generally valued more highly than those from between 1901 and 1910. The largest carousels were produced by the Artistic Carousel Manufacturers of Brooklyn, Harry Goldstein and Solomon Stein. Charles Carmel and Daniel Muller are both exquisite carvers whose work is today very highly regarded. Other builders whose works are also very valuable (though much less intricate) are The Herschell — Spillman Company; American Merry-Go-Round and Novelty Company; Charles Dare of the New York Carousel Manufacturing Company; and Charles Parker.

Until the 1930s, carousels were found in nearly every fair and amusement park in the country. One by one, as they fell into disrepair, many have been dismantled and junked or sold at auction. Today these hand-carved creatures are respected examples of American folk art and often bring prices well into the thousands. Price is based on a number of factors, the most important of which are: carver (with Dentzel, Looff, PTC, Carmel, Illions, and Muller the most valued), type of animal (some species are rarely encountered), and intricacy of carving. Also to be considered are size, wood and paint condition, where the figure was located on the carousel, whether it stands or jumps, and in some cases its age. Because there are so many factors to consider and since no two figures are identical, exact pricing is difficult. All of these prices are from public auctions; and, where applicable, the 10% buyers premium is included. All animals listed were in good condition. Price list furnished by *The Carousel News & Trader*; for subscription information see the Directory under Clubs, Newsletters, and Catalogs.

Key:
IR — inside row   OR — outside row
MR — middle row   PTC — Philadelphia Toboggan Co.

Allan Herschell, half & half (wood & aluminum), (4-90) 2,200.00
Allan Herschell, wood, (4-90) 3,700.00
Allan Herschell jumper, blanket, (2-90) 2,310.00
Allan Herschell Trojan jumper horse, rstr, (2-90) 5,280.00
Anderson dbl-seater galloper (English), (3-90)....................... 4,400.00
Anderson dragon (English), (3-90) 11,000.00
Armitage Herschell, (8-90).. 2,750.00
Armitage Herschell jumper, rstr, (2-90) 4,730.00
Armitage Herschell jumper, track machine, (3-90)................. 6,600.00
Bayol donkey (French), (3-90) 16,500.00
Bayol goat (French), (3-90) 5,500.00
Bayol rabbit (French), (3-90) 4,950.00
Carmel jumper, (11-90)..10,450.00
Carmel stander, IR, (12-89)......................................12,100.00
Carmel stander, OR, (12-89)......................................28,600.00
Carmel stander, OR, (12-89)......................................42,900.00
Dare horse, (4-90).. 5,200.00
Dentzel cat, fish in mouth, fiberglass coating, (12-89)............28,600.00
Dentzel deer, jumper, (8-90).....................................19,500.00
Dentzel jumper, (2-90)... 7,150.00
Dentzel jumper, (8-90)... 8,000.00
Dentzel ostrich, stripped, (12-89)...............................24,200.00
Dentzel pig, w/acorn, (8-90).....................................13,000.00
Dentzel prancer, (4-90)...14,000.00
Dentzel rounding board, hen & rooster picture, (8-90) 4,000.00
Dentzel rounding board, moose picture, (8-90) 1,500.00
Dentzel shield, (8-90).. 1,000.00
Dentzel stander, 'Dandy' horse, (8-90)...........................52,000.00
Dentzel stander, roached mane, (8-90) 29,500.00
Dentzel tiger, (8-90) 57,500.00
Herschell-Spillman jumper, (11-90)............................... 5,280.00
Herschell-Spillman jumper, rstr, (2-90) 8,800.00
Herschell-Spillman mule, (11-90)................................10,450.00

Heyn jumper (German), (9-30)	5,775.00
Illions deer, w/eagle, OR, (2-90)	34,000.00
Illions jumper, IR, (2-90)	9,000.00
Illions jumper, MR, roached mane, (2-90)	12,000.00
Illions jumper, OR, (12-89)	25,300.00
Illions jumper, OR, w/bedroll, (2-90)	17,000.00
Illions rounding board, (2-90)	1,000.00
Looff camel, (3-90)	13,200.00
Looff deer, OR, (12-89)	15,400.00
Looff giraffe, (3-90)	13,200.00
Looff goat, (11-90)	12,300.00
Looff goat, prancer, (12-89)	9,900.00
Looff jumper, early, (2-90)	7,480.00
Looff prancer, (12-89)	9,900.00
Looff stander, IR, (12-89)	6,050.00
Muller pig, (11-90)	4,840.00

Muller jumper, simple trappings, ca 1910, 48" long, $6,000.00 to $7,000.00.

Muller stander, OR, rstr, (12-90)	42,900.00
Parker jumper, armored, (5-90)	12,500.00
Parker jumper, early track machine, (11-90)	10,780.00
Parker jumper, Indian head, MR, (5-90)	5,000.00
Parker jumper, IR, (11-90)	3,850.00
Parker jumper, stargazer, w/bearskin & feathers, (11-90)	28,600.00
PTC, western-style/military, Niagara Falls carousel	36,000.00
PTC jumper, IR, (8-90)	5,000.00
PTC jumper, MR, (3-90)	7,700.00
PTC stander, w/knotted tail, OR, (8-90)	22,000.00
Savage cockerel (English), (2-90)	5,720.00
Savage ostrich (English), (11-90)	5,390.00
Spooner rooster (English), (3-90)	5,225.00
Stein & Goldstein jumper, IR, (4-90)	7,200.00
Stein & Goldstein jumper, MR, (8-90)	15,000.00
Stein & Goldstein stander, MR, (4-90)	10,500.00
Stein & Goldstein stander, OR, rstr, (2-90)	21,670.00

Carpet Balls

Carpet balls are glazed china spheres decorated with intersecting lines or other simple designs that were used for indoor games in the British Isles during the early 1800s. Mint condition examples are rare.

Allover sm wht dots w/bl centers on bl, 3½", M	145.00
Blk & bl circles around bull's eye on wht, 3", VG	50.00
Blk w/blk dots w/in wht frilly circles, 3⅜", NM	80.00
Dk gr, emb Henselite Indoor, NM	35.00
Gr & blk stripes wrap around 3 ways on wht, 2⅝", VG	100.00
Gr w/gr shamrock w/in wht splash, 3", NM	120.00
Pk w/pk dots w/in wht circles, frilled rim, 3½", M	135.00
Purple w/wht polka dots, 3", NM	95.00
Wht w/purple stripes, 3¼", NM	100.00
Yel w/yel dots w/in wht circles, frilled rim, 3", NM	100.00
3 bands of pk stripes wrap around 3 ways on wht, 3¼", VG	50.00

Cartoon Art

Collectors of cartoon art are interested in many forms of original art — animation cels, sports, political or editorial cartoons, syndicated comic strip panels, and caricature. To produce even a short animated cartoon strip, hundreds of original drawings are required, each showing the characters in slightly advancing positions. Called 'cels' because those made prior to the 1950s were made from a celluloid material, collectors often pay hundreds of dollars for a frame from a favorite movie. Prices of Disney cels with backgrounds vary widely. Background paintings, model sheets, storyboards, and preliminary sketches are also collectible — so are comic book drawings executed in India ink and signed by the artist. Daily 'funnies' originals, especially the earlier ones portraying super heroes, and Sunday comic strips, the early as well as the later ones, are collected. Cartoon art has become recognized and valued as a novel yet valid form of contemporary art.

Animation Cel, Full Color

Alice in Wonderland, Wht Rabbit, Disney, 1951, 5x4"	1,150.00
Aristocats, Frou Frou, close-up, 1970, 9½x6"	165.00
Bambi, wobbly legs, w/mother, Courvoisier ground, '42, 7x8"	4,500.00
Bugs Bunny, portrait of early orig Bugs, Clampett, 10x7"	245.00
Cinderella, w/Prince, 1950, 1 of 500, '87, 11½x15½ "	775.00

Donald Duck as a pirate, gouache on celluloid applied to photographic background, 8½" x 11", $850.00.

Fox & Hound, Copper, as pup w/butterfly, 1981, 7½x10½ " **345.00**
Jungle Book, Kaa, slinky slithery pose, full cell **385.00**
Peter Pan, Nana in nightcap, Disney, 1953, 5½x5" **975.00**
Rescuers, Bernard, close-up, Disney, 1977, 7x7" **385.00**
Rescuers, Bianca, about to climb rope, 1977, 9½x4¼" **345.00**
Rescuers, Medusa talking to Crock, full cell **325.00**
Robin Hood, Prince John, smiling, 1973, 8x6¾" **235.00**
Secret of Nimh, Jeremy Crow tied up, Bluth, 1982, 8x9".............**265.00**
Sleeping Beauty, Briar Rose, Disney, 1959, 9½x12" **1,500.00**
Sword in Stone, Merlin & Archimedes in cottage, '63, 9x10"... **1,550.00**
Tom & Jerry, Tom laughing, 1965, 6x4½" **285.00**
1001 Rabbit Tales, Bugs Bunny w/book, sgn Freleng, 6x4½" **545.00**
101 Dalmations, Colonel, barn beyond, Disney, 1961, 8x10" **565.00**

Animation Drawing

Bambi, froliking in flowers, pencil, lg...**465.00**
Bugs Bunny, concept of Bugs in old attire, McKimson.................**285.00**
Dude Duck, Donald Duck, pencils, 1951, 5x4" **300.00**
Dumbo, Jim Crow, full figure, pencils, 1941, 5½x4" **365.00**
Goofy on bike w/torch, pen & ink, for poster, fr, 13x18".............**220.00**
Inky, w/lion, full figure, pencils, EX color, lg..............................**450.00**
Lonesome Ghost, angry Donald Duck, pencils, 1937, 7x10" **165.00**
Lonesome Ghost, Donald Duck excited, pencil, '37, 3¼x2¾" **450.00**
Mickey Mouse bathing in tub, pencils, oval mat **145.00**
Mother Goose Goes Hollywood, Freddy Bartholomew, '38, 5x9".**385.00**
Peter Pan, Captain Hook, head only, sgn Thomas, '53, 10x6".....**535.00**
Puppy Love, smiling Mickey & Minnie, 1933, 4½x3½"...............**995.00**
Sleeping Beauty, Prince Phillip, pencils, 1959, 7x3" **250.00**
Snow White & 7 Dwarfs, Sleepy, pencils, 1937, 4½x3¼"............**435.00**
3 Little Pigs, Fiddler & Fifer Pig, pencil, 1930s, 4x6" **265.00**

Snow White and the Seven Dwarfs, 1937, graphite and red pencil, 7" x 10", $700.00.

Model Sheets

Donald Duck & Mickey Mouse, action poses, '30s, 11x14" **500.00**
Jungle Book, Bagheera, preliminary study, 1967, 12x15" **100.00**
Jungle Book, Mowgli, varied poses, 1967, 12½x15" **135.00**
Little Hiawatha, boy w/deer & raccoon, varied, 1937, 12x15" **185.00**
Pinocchio, Jiminy Cricket, varied poses, dtd 1939, 11x14" **445.00**
Popeye & Olive Oyl, varied poses, pencils, Waldman, 10x13" **265.00**
Raggedy Andy & Camel, varied poses, sgn Oriolo, 8½x11" **80.00**
Sea Scouts, sea gulls, notations, 1939, 11x14" **55.00**
Superman, Clark in varied poses, detailed, 1941, 15x20".............**400.00**

Storyboard

Common Cold, Goofy w/cold, 1949, 3-pg, overall: 14x17".........**135.00**

Fantasia, Pegasus family, on paper, 1940, 11x14" **400.00**
Little Audrey, pencils, Waldman, '40s, 2-pg, overall: 10x7" **300.00**
You Can't Win, Goofy gambling, 3-pg, overall: 14x17".............**325.00**
101 Dalmations, Cruella buys pups, 2-pg, overall: 8½x6½".......**345.00**

Sunday Newspaper Comics

Brick Bradford, fights pirates, May 10, 1941, 11x16".....................**15.00**
Dick Tracy, w/Gravel Gertie/Sparkle/BO Plenty, 1947, ½-pg........**18.00**
Flash Gordon, w/Dale & Ming, Mar 1941, ½-pg **18.00**
Mandrake the Magician, w/Narda, magic panels, Dec 1945...........**15.00**
Orphan Annie, w/lost infant child, Dec 4, 1927, ½-pg, EX **12.00**
Peter Rabbit, Oct 15, 1944, ½-pg, EX **8.00**
Pogo, Xmas theme, bear as Santa, 1953, 10½x14" **15.00**
Prince Valiant, w/Aleta & maidens, Dec 1941, EX **15.00**
Superman, w/Clark & Lois, Aug 9, 1942 ....**15.00**
Tarzan, Heart of the Mountain, Hogarth, Dec 1942, 11x16".........**12.00**
Tarzan, Soldiers of the Jungle, July 1937, 11x16" **10.00**

Cartoon Books

'Books of cartoons' were printed during the first decade of the twentieth century and remained popular until the advent of the modern comic book in the late thirties. Cartoon books, printed in both color and black and white, were merely reprints of current newspaper comic strips. The books, ranging from thirty to seventy pages and in sizes from 3½" x 8" up to 11" x 17", were usually bound with cardboard covers and were often distributed as premiums in exchange for coupons saved from the daily paper. One of the largest of the companies who printed these books was Cupples and Leon, producer of nearly half of the two hundred titles on record. Among the most popular sellers were Mutt and Jeff, Bringing Up Father, and Little Orphan Annie.

Bringing Up Father, 1st Series, McManus, 3-color cover, EX **70.00**
Bringing Up Father, 11th Series, some illus hand tinted, NM **60.00**
Bringing Up Father, 2nd Series, McManus, 3-color cover, VG......**50.00**
Bringing Up Father, 5th Series, hand-tinted covers, VG **50.00**
Bringing Up Father, 6th Series, McManus, VG.............................**35.00**
Bringing Up Father, 7th Series, McManus, 3-color cover, VG **35.00**
Buster Brown, c 1908 by NY Herald, covers missing, VG **35.00**
Buster Brown & His Pets, Cupples & Leon, '13, cover missing......**35.00**
Buster Brown on His Travels, 1909, Cupples & Leon, EX **60.00**
Charlie Chaplin, c 1917, 16x9¾", EX...**55.00**

Charlie Chaplin's Funny Stunts, c 1917, M.A. Donohue, some wear, $65.00; Buster Brown on His Travels, c 1909, Cupples and Leon, G, $60.00.

Gumps, Sidney Smith, Cupples & Leon, 3-color covers, VG **50.00**
Keeping Up w/Joneses, 2nd Series, Cupples & Leon, EX **35.00**

Moon Mullins, by Willard, Cupples & Leon, VG 70.00
Tillie the Toiler Book 2, Cupples & Leon, 3-color cover, EX........25.00

Cash Registers

Cash registers are being restored, rebuilt, and used as they were originally intended, in businesses ranging from eating establishments to antique stores. Their brass and marble construction has made them almost impervious to aging, and with just a bit of polish and shine they bring a bit of the grand Victorian era into modern times.

Antique cash registers are categorized as either restored or unrestored. A restored register is one where the cabinet has been stripped, polished, and lacquered; indicators are free of dust, dirt, and visible signs of wear; key arms are rust-free, plated or painted; and key checks and rings are new, used, or originals. The drawer has been stripped and revarnished, and the rails are in good condition. All mechanisms are completely reworked; broken parts are replaced, oiled, and working perfectly. Prices for registers in unrestored condition vary greatly. Unrestored registers are classed as either working or non-working. Values for those with missing major parts are much lower. In the listings that follow, M condition refers to fully-restored cash registers; VG condition is for registers in original unrestored working condition. For further information we recommend the highly-informative books, *Antique Cash Registers 1880 - 1920,* by Bartsch and Sanchez (Mr. Bartsch's address may be found in our Directory under Oregon); and *The Incorruptible Cashier Vol. I,* which is currently available from our advisor, John Apple, who is listed in the Directory under Wisconsin.

Hopkins & Robinson #188, wood cabinet, early, 20x14x8", VG.500.00
Michigan #2, candy store, scrollwork...375.00

National Cash Register Co., brass and oak on marble slab, 4-drawer, 24" x 31", $900.00.

NCR #11, candy store, early, VG 850.00
NCR #130, barber shop, sm, VG...800.00
NCR #216, VG...800.00
NCR #225, VG...650.00
NCR #250, VG...850.00
NCR #313, barber shop, brass, all orig, 10" W, VG 750.00
NCR #317, M.. 1,200.00

NCR #323, marble on 3 sides, extended base, sm, M 1,750.00
NCR #327, VG...950.00
NCR #332, brass, VG...400.00
NCR #47, mahog w/inlay, up to $5, 18x18x16", VG............... 1,950.00
NCR #50, brass, w/front plate, 16½x16x10", VG.......................850.00
NCR #51, Renaissance design, candy store, VG 950.00
NCR #542-5E, oak base, bronze case, floor model, VG 2,000.00
NCR #7, scroll design, VG 750.00
NCR #8, VG...650.00

Cast Iron

In the mid-1800s, the cast iron industry was raging in the United States. It was recognized as a medium extremely adaptable for uses ranging from ornamental architectural filigree to actual building construction. It could be cast from a mold into any conceivable design that could be reproduced over and over at a relatively small cost. It could be painted to give an entirely versatile appearance. Furniture with open-work designs of grapevines and leaves and intricate lacy scrollwork was cast for gardens as well as inside use. Figural doorstops of every sort, bootjacks, trivets, and a host of other useful and decorative items were made before the 'ferromania' had run its course. See also Kitchen, Cast Iron Bakers and Kettles; and other specific categories.

Bridge plate sign, Built By...1890, 20x16x1" 85.00
Buggy steps, pr..20.00
Chair, swivel; oval bk w/3 feathers, 3-leg base, Motta Pat 375.00
Cookie mold, flower basket & grape clusters, ca 1800, 5½x6" 265.00
Cup & saucer, old gilt surface, 1-pc, 3½ ", 5½" dia......................220.00
Dipper, 14"...30.00
Flower holder, funerary; tulip shaped, dk gr pnt, 9x5½" 65.00
Footstool, pierced apron, cabriole legs, needlepoint uphl 350.00
Garden figure, standing stag, Whitman Foundry, pnt, 64" 4,250.00
Hall stand, scrolled/pierced, sm mirror/umbrella stand, 72" 350.00
Herb grinder, crescent mortar, roller pestle, 18" L......................475.00

Hall tree, mirror, six scrolled hooks, marked Jon. W. Moore, N.Y. #8, 75", $550.00.

Hitching post, tree stump w/2 looped branches at top, 64" 300.00
Hitching post finial, horse head, harness/wire ring, 13" 700.00
Kettle, gypsy; 9½x12" dia 85.00
Lamp, ornate wall bracket style, w/reflector....................................70.00
Lawn sprinkler, alligator form, orig pnt, ca 1910 ....170.00
Mop wringer, Pat 1902, EX 27.50
Nut dish, leaf shape w/figural fly inside, 8½" 35.00
Paperweight, floppy-eared dog, old...20.00
Paperweight, turtle, Hoosier advertising, 2½"...............................55.00
Par marker, flat rnd shape w/stake at base, pnt, old, EX 85.00
Porringer, pierced hdl, Kenrich & Co, ½-pt, 4¾" 90.00
Settee, 3-chair bk w/scrolls, arms, J McLean/1890, 35".............400.00
Shelf, candle; star in circle design, old pnt, 1850s, 5x8½"..........240.00
Shoeshine footrest, camel form, chrome plated, 8x8x3½" 85.00
Stove plate, Dance of Death inscription, 1750s, 22x24".............500.00
Urn, fluted lower body, sq plinth, pnt, 12", pr..........................280.00
Wall plaque, pig face in relief, scalloped, hdls, 9½".....................465.00

Castor Sets

Castor sets became popular during the early years of the eigh-teenth century and continued to be used through the late Victorian era. Their purpose was to hold various condiments for table use. The most common type was a circular arrangement with a center handle on a revolving pedestal base that held three, four, five, or six bottles. Some had extras; a few were equipped with a bell for calling the servant. Frames were made of silverplate, glass, or pewter. Though most bottles were of pressed glass, some of the designs were cut; and occasionally colored glass with enameled decorations was used. To maintain authen-ticity and value, castor sets should have matching bottles. Prices listed below are for those with matching bottles and in frames with plating that is in excellent condition (unless noted otherwise).

Watch for new frames and bottles in both clear and colored glass — these have recently been appearing on the market.

Silverplated stand with figure of Liberty with shield and flag, four cut and etched amberina shakers, mustard jar, vinegar bottle, 16", EX, $1,800.00.

3-bottle, Gothic Arch, blown; orig stoppers, pewter fr 95.00
4-bottle, Alabama, gr; orig SP fr 365.00
4-bottle, Am Shield; plated wht metal fr w/eagle, mini, 8½" 165.00
4-bottle, cranberry, orig stoppers; pressed glass holder 225.00

4-bottle, Daisy & Button; glass base...125.00
4-bottle, King's Crown; glass fr w/metal hdl................................150.00
4-bottle, Log & Star, amber; orig ped-base fr 135.00
5-bottle, Button Band; orig SP fr 175.00
5-bottle, cut glass; rstr Simpson-Hall-Miller fr, 18" 275.00
5-bottle, etched; Japanese-motif SP fr, bird at top.......................225.00
5-bottle, Honeycomb; ornate Wilcox fr 285.00
5-bottle, opaque, HP floral, att Mt WA; rstr Middleton fr 395.00
6-bottle, cut glass; rstr Simpson-Hall-Miller fr, 18" 275.00
6-bottle, eng; tiered Simpson-Hall-Miller fr revolves 165.00
6-bottle, etched; Rogers rstr SP fr revolves, 19" 295.00
6-bottle, etched; rstr ornate fr w/call bell, sgn Meriden 395.00
6-bottle, plain; SP fr w/eng skirt, bird hdl, 18" 265.00
6-bottle, wreath cut; 19" ftd ornate fr revolves 295.00
7-bottle, cut crystal; gadrooned/shell-border Geo III fr 465.00

Catalina Island

Catalina Island pottery was made on the island of the same name, which is about twenty-six miles off the coast of Los Angeles. The pot-tery was started in 1927 at Pebbly Beach, by Wm. Wrigley, Jr., who was instrumental in developing and using the native clays. Its principal products were brick and tile to be used for the construction on the island. Garden pieces were first produced, then vases, bookends, lamps, ash trays, novelty items, and finally dinnerware. The ware became very popular and was soon being shipped to the mainland as well.

Some of the pottery was hand thrown; some was made in molds. Most pieces are marked Catalina Island or Catalina with a printed incised stamp, or handwritten with a pointed tool. Cast items were sometimes marked in the mold; a few have an ink stamp, and a paper label was also used.

The color of the clay can help to identify approximately when a piece was made: 1927 to 1932 — brown to red clay; 1931 to 1932 — an experimental period with various colors; 1932 to 1937 — mainly white clay, but tan to brown were also used on occasion.

Items marked Catalina Pottery are listed in Gladding McBean.

Dinnerware

Catalina Island, bowl, berry...18.00
Catalina Island, candle holder, low...55.00
Catalina Island, carafe, yel gloss..65.00
Catalina Island, cup & saucer 35.00
Catalina Island, custard cup...20.00
Catalina Island, plate, bread & butter; rimmed, 6½" 15.00
Catalina Island, plate, dinner; 11" 25.00
Catalina Island, plate, luncheon; 8" 15.00
Catalina Island, sugar bowl..20.00
Catalina Island, tumbler, lg 18.00
Catalina Island, wine cup, hdld 13.00
Rope Edge, cup...20.00
Rope Edge, plate, bread & butter 10.00
Rope Edge, plate, chop; 12" 60.00
Rope Edge, plate, dinner...20.00
Rope Edge, saucer 10.00

Miscellaneous

Bowl, flower or fruit; 3½x10"...95.00
Bowl, ruffled rim, ink stamp, 2½x9" 25.00
Box, cigarette; horse's head..150.00
Candelabrum, 3-hole, half-circle...95.00
Candelabrum, 3-hole, straight 150.00

Charger, swordfish, HP on lt bl, 14" **195.00**
Flowerpot, Ring style **55.00**
Humidor, treasure chest..**165.00**
Plate, Spanish galleon, mc, mk Catalina, 12"..................**375.00**
Shakers, cactus, pr..**50.00**
Shakers, tulip, pr..**65.00**
Vase, bright sky bl, hdls, incised mk, 11"..................**85.00**
Vase, bud; 5"..**45.00**
Vase, flared top, 7½ "..**85.00**
Vase, gr drip, 8"..**55.00**
Vase, Monterey Brn, flowerpot form, old mk, 5½"........**38.00**

Catalogs

Catalogs are not only intriguing to collect on their own merit, but for the collector with a specific interest, they are often the only remaining source of background information available, and as such they offer a wealth of otherwise unrecorded data. The mail-order industry can be traced as far back as the mid-1800s. Even before Aaron Montgomery Ward began his career in 1872, Laacke and Joys of Wisconsin and the Orvis Company of Vermont, both dealers in sporting goods, had been well established for many years. The E.C. Allen Company sold household necessities and novelties by mail on a broad scale in the 1870s. By the end of the Civil War, sewing machines, garden seed, musical instruments — even medicine — were available from catalogs. In the 1880s, Macy's of New York issued a 127-page catalog; Sears and Spiegel followed suit in about 1890. Craft and art supply catalogs were first available about 1880 and covered such varied fields as china painting, stenciling, wood burning, brass embossing, hair weaving, and shellcraft. Today, some collectors confine their interests not only to craft catalogs in general, but often to one subject only. Examples may range from $1 to as much as $50 and up for the larger, color-illustrated versions.

Allied Radios, Chicago, 1930, EX..................................**24.00**
Arthur Honen, dolls & toys, 1950, 172-pg, EX..................**35.00**
Bailey & Farrell, bathroom fixtures, 1921, 400-pg, EX **75.00**
Brown & Sharpe Tools, 1920, 609-pg, 4x6", EX..................**20.00**
Buckeye Sports Supply, 1969, NM **15.00**
Converse Footwear, 1955, EX **25.00**
Crane, valves & fittings, 1929, 428-pg, EX..................**50.00**
DeLong Fraternal Building Furniture, 1928, 28-pg........**7.50**
DT Bohon Carriages, Harrodsburg KY, 1925, 50-pg, 9x12", VG..**50.00**
Endicott Johnson Shoes, color, 1913, 79-pg, EX..................**35.00**
Estrey Organs, 1884, EX..**35.00**
F Haslam, surgical instruments, hard bk, 1917, EX..................**50.00**
Farmer's Seed Nursery, 1924, EX..................................**9.00**
Flanagan, school supplies & equipment, 1941, 111-pg, EX **40.00**
Hepburn Boat & Oar Co, 1895, 72-pg, VG..................**40.00**
Herter's, guns & fishing equipment, 1969, EX..................**16.00**
Hodges Kitchen Specialties, 1929, 107-pg, 7x10" **25.00**
Hotpoint Appliances, 1928, 62-pg, 8½x10", EX..................**25.00**
Hub Cycles, 1919, 68-pg..**55.00**
J Kelly, fire equipment, color, 1925, 38-pg, 6½x10", EX **65.00**
Jenkins Band Instruments, 1912, 196-pg, EX..................**90.00**
John Plain, jewelry & toys, 1963, 770-pg..................**24.00**
Kalamazoo Stoves, 1928-29, 90-pg, VG..................**10.00**
Kimball, player pianos, 1910s, 16-pg, EX..................**30.00**
Laurel Gas Ranges, 1917-18, 16-pg..................................**25.00**
Lyon Healy Band Instruments & Uniforms, 1909, 168-pg, EX **190.00**
Lyons Ejector Cigarette Cases, 1930s, 3-pg..................**8.00**
Marble & Shattuck Chairs, 1930, EX **25.00**
Marlin Arms, 1914, EX **115.00**
Metropolitan, watches & jewelry, 1930, 72-pg, EX..................**40.00**

Mideke Supply, farm tools, etc, hardbk, 1947, 886-pg..................**25.00**
Mueller, fire hydrants, etc, 1938, 48-pg, EX..................**40.00**
Myers Pump & Water Systems, 1932, EX..................**12.00**
Nat'l Cloak & Suits, Christy cover, 1909-10, EX..................**35.00**
Nat'l Electric, trolly car equipment, illus, 1903, 57-pg..................**32.00**
Newcomb-Macklin, picture frames, mouldings, early, 50-pg..........**15.00**
Noonan, barber supplies, color illus, ca 1925, 176-pg, EX **45.00**
Oklahoma City Hardware, 1938, 810-pg, EX..................**60.00**
Orgill Bros, many early toys, ca 1956, 310-pg, 9x11", EX **200.00**
Oshkosh Trunks & Luggage, 1941, 55-pg, VG **8.00**
Richardson & Boynton Kitchen Ranges, 1922, 31-pg, EX **25.00**
Ringen Stoves, steel & iron ranges, 1905, 56-pg, EX..................**25.00**
Rochester Can, metalware, color, '20s, 50-pg, 8x11", EX..................**45.00**
Rockford Standard Furniture, all oak, 1917, 67-pg, EX..................**75.00**
Sears Roebuck & Co, #112, 1902, G **35.00**
Sears Roebuck Stoves, 1915, EX **45.00**
Sedgwick Machines, dumbwaiters, elevators, 1926, 32-pg **20.00**
Shelbyville Desks, 1938, EX..**20.00**
Siekert & Baum, office supplies, 1929, EX **40.00**
Simmons Gun Specialties, 1968, NM **20.00**
Snap-On Tools, 1934, EX..**40.00**
Spiegel, clothing, Spring & Summer, 1950..................**22.00**
Starrett Tools, 1938, 282-pg, EX **7.50**
Sunray Gas Stoves, 1915, 48-pg, 7x10", EX..................**25.00**
Sutcliffe, KY, uniforms/sports equipment, Cobb cover, EX...........**55.00**
Thayer & Chandler, wht china, 1909, 64-pg, EX **50.00**
Thompson Boats, 1937, 32-pg, EX..................................**45.00**
United Merchandise, carnival items, 1926, 64-pg, EX..................**40.00**
Universal Stoves & Ranges, 1927, 86-pg, EX..................**45.00**
Ward's Wallpaper, 1933, 92-pg, VG **10.00**
Wards Airline Radios, 1940, 22-pg..................................**11.00**
Weis Office Supply, 1929, EX..**22.00**
Williams Hardware, 1940, 532-pg, EX..................................**30.00**
Wright & Wilhelmy, general hdw, 1938, 1324-pg, EX **500.00**

Caughley Ware

The Caughley Coalport Porcelain Manufactory operated from about 1775 until 1799 in Caughley, near Salop, Shropshire, in England. The owner was Thomas Turner, who gained his potting experience from his association with the Worcester Pottery Company. The wares he manufactured in Caughley are referred to as 'Salopian.' He is most famous for his blue-printed earthenwares, particularly the Blue Willow pattern, designed for him by Thomas Minton. For a more detailed history, see Coalport.

Bowl, floral/fruit clusters, bl transfer, 1790, 6"..................**225.00**
Bowl, junket; bl floral fruit transfers, emb shells, 10" **650.00**
Jug, Cabbage Leaf, mask spout, chinoiserie transfer, 8½"..................**750.00**
Jug, flowers/'JB,' mask spout, ovoid, 7"..................**225.00**
Jug, fruit/flowers, bl transfer, ovoid, 1785, 4½" W..................**300.00**
Mug, floral/fruit clusters, bl transfer, 1790, 5¾"..................**300.00**
Pickle dish, fisherman scene, bl transfer, mk, 1785, 4", pr..........**225.00**
Teapot, fruit clusters, bl transfer, bulbous, 1790, 4½"..................**475.00**

Ceramic Art Company

Jonathan Coxon, Sr., and Walter Scott Lenox established the Ceramic Art Company in 1889 in Trenton, New Jersey, where they produced fine belleek porcelain. Both were experienced in its production, having previously worked for Ott and Brewer. They hired artists to hand paint their wares with portraits, scenes, and lovely florals.

Today, artist-signed examples bring the highest prices. Several marks were used, three of which contain the 'CAC' monogram. A green wreath surrounding the company name in full was used on special-order wares, but these are not often encountered. Coxon eventually left the company, and it was later reorganized under the Lenox name. See also Lenox.

Our advisor for this category is Mary Frank Gaston; she is listed in the Directory under Texas.

Bell, tulip shaped, silver decor on wht, unmk	135.00
Buttonhook, mc florals w/gold, factory decor, unmk, 7¾"	250.00
Chocolate pot, marine life, mermaid spout/hdl, mk, 12"	1,100.00
Cup, chocolate; bl beading & gold on ivory, ped ft	45.00
Cup, demitasse; floral, gold on wht, Engagement shape, mk, 2"	60.00
Decanter, brn to gr, sterling hdls, silver script letters, lg	145.00
Loving cup, florals w/gold, heads atop hdls (3), mk, 8½"	550.00
Mug, berries & leaves, mk, 5½ "	135.00
Mug, mc pomegranates, 1890 palette mk, 5½"	165.00
Mug, stylized florals HP on blk, gr mk, 5½"	140.00

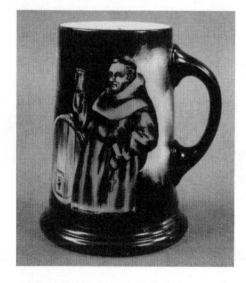

Mug, black transfer of monk, 5½ ", $250.00.

Pitcher, cider; 3-color grapes, beaded hdl, lg	130.00
Pitcher, dbl-spouted, florals w/gold, mk, 3"	165.00
Pitcher, tankard; Indian corn, 14"	395.00
Pitcher, tankard; mc grapes, palette mk, 14"	280.00
Pitcher, tankard; pines & full moon on dk gr, gr mk	225.00
Pitcher, tankard; winter scene & holly, gold trim, 13"	295.00
Pitcher, tankard; yel roses, sgn, scalloped, ornate hdl	225.00
Salt cellar, swan figural, gold trim, mk, 1¾"	55.00
Stein, HP golfing scene, mk, ca 1900, 5¾"	2,350.00
Vase, portrait medallion w/gold on brn, sgn, mk, 15"	1,325.00
Vase, purple lustre on body, bulbous, gr mk, 3¾"	110.00
Vase, 3 heron reserves, iris on blk at neck, mk, 22"	500.00

Ceramic Arts Studio, Madison

The Ceramic Arts Studio Company began operations sometime prior to the 1940s; but it was about then that Betty Harrington started marketing her goods through this company. Betty Harrington is the designer primarily responsible for creating the line of figurines and knick-knacks that have recently become so popular with collectors. There were two others — Ulli Rebus, who designed several of the animals; and Ruth Planter, who worked there for only a short time. About 65% of these items are marked, but even unmarked items become easily recognizable after only a brief study of their distinctive styling and glaze

colors. Those that are marked carry either the black ink stamp or the incised mark: 'Ceramic Arts Studio, Madison, Wisc.'; a paper sticker was also used.

After the 1955 demise of the company in Madison, the owner (Ruben Sand) went to Japan where he continued production under the same name using many of the same molds. After a short time, the old molds were retired and new and quite different items were produced. Most of the Japan pieces can be found with a Ceramic Arts Studio backstamp. The Japan identification was on a paper label and is often missing. Japan pieces are never marked Madison, Wisc., but not all Madison pieces are either. Red or blue backstamps are exclusively Japanese.

Another company that also produced figurines operated at about the same time as the Madison studio. It was called Ceramic Art (no 's') Studio; do not confuse the two.

A second and larger building in the C.A.S. complex in Madison was for the exclusive production of metal accessories. The creator and designer of this related line was Zona Liberace, Liberace's stepmother, who was Art Director for the line of figurines as well. These pieces are rising fast in value and because they weren't marked can sometimes be found at bargain prices. They were so popular that other ceramic companies bought them to complement their lines as well, so they may also be found with ceramic figures other than C.A.S.'s.

For those seeking additional information, video tapes (Series 1 and 2) are available from the author, BA Wellman, whose address can be found under Massachusetts. Mr. Wellman will also send a series of articles written for *The Daze* to those who will include a legal-size SASE and four stamps with their requests.

Ash tray, hippo, 3½"	38.00
Bank, Skunky, 4"	48.00
Bell, Winter Belle, 5¼"	48.00
Bowl, Bonita	30.00
Bowl, rectangular, shallow, 2¼"	22.00
Candle holder, Bedtime Boy (Bedtime Girl), 4¾", pr	48.00
Figurine, angel, praying on knees, 4½"	25.00
Figurine, angel, singing, 3½"	25.00
Figurine, angel, standing w/star, 5½"	25.00
Figurine, Annie Elephant, 3¼"	28.00
Figurine, baby monkey, 3"	22.00
Figurine, Bali Lao, topless, 8½"	65.00
Figurine, Balinese dance couple, 9½", pr	85.00
Figurine, Bass Viol Boy, 4¾"	28.00
Figurine, bride & groom, 4¾", 5", pr	55.00
Figurine, Burmese man, 5"	20.00
Figurine, child w/towel, 5"	35.00
Figurine, Chinese lantern couple, 6", pr	38.00
Figurine, Cupid, 5"	40.00
Figurine, Egyptian man & woman, pr	135.00
Figurine, Flute Lady, standing	65.00
Figurine, fox, modern	35.00
Figurine, Hansel & Gretel, 1-pc, 4½"	28.00
Figurine, Harmonica boy, 4"	25.00
Figurine, Hiawatha, 3½"	48.00
Figurine, Indian girl, 3¼"	20.00
Figurine, Isaac, 12"	75.00
Figurine, kitten, washing paw, 2"	17.50
Figurine, leopards, fighting, rare, 8½" L, 6½" H, pr	95.00
Figurine, Little Miss Muffett, 4½"	28.00
Figurine, Madonna, gold halo, 9½"	65.00
Figurine, Mr & Mrs Skunk, Inky, & Dinky, set of 4	75.00
Figurine, Pansie, standing ballerina, 5¾"	35.00
Figurine, Pensive & Blythe, pr	95.00
Figurine, Peter Rabbit, 3¾"	25.00

Figurine, Piper Boy, running, 3½" 28.00
Figurine, Praise & Blessing angels, 6", 5¾", pr 37.50
Figurine, Red Devil Imp, standing, rare 65.00
Figurine, Smi-li & Mo-Pi, yel, pr 38.00
Figurine, Southern Gentleman, Colonel Jackson 35.00
Figurine, St George on Charger, 8½" 95.00
Figurine, Sultan, 4½" 35.00
Figurine, Temple Dancers, 6¾", pr 125.00
Figurine, toadstool, 3" 20.00
Figurine, Toby, horse, 2¾" 22.00
Figurine, Willing, 4¾" 25.00
Figurine, Winter Willy, 4" 28.00
Figurine, zebra, 5" 32.00
Jug, Aladdin, 2" 22.50
Jug, Diana the Huntress, 3" 20.00
Jug, Toby, 3½" 22.50
Lamp, Chinese lantern figure 125.00
Lamp, Flutist, on base 165.00
Lamp, Zorina, on base 85.00
Planter, African man & lady, 8", pr 145.00
Planter, Lorelei on seashell, 6" 45.00
Planter, Manchu, 7½" 45.00
Planter, Mei-ling head, 5" 35.00

Wall planter, African woman, black and Terra Cotta, 7½", $150.00.

Plaque, Attitude & Arabesque, 9½", pr 55.00
Plaque, Dutch boy & girl, red trim, 8", pr 65.00
Plaque, fish, striped, lg & sm, pr 65.00
Plaque, Harlequin & Columbine, 8", pr 125.00
Plaque, mermaid, 6" 40.00
Plaque, Shadow Dancers, pr 65.00
Plaque, Water Sprite, fish w/head down, 4¼" 20.00
Shakers, bunnies, kissing, 4", 2½", pr 28.00
Shakers, Chinese boy & girl, 4¼", 4", pr 17.50
Shakers, dog & doghouse, pr 25.00
Shakers, elf & mushroom, 2½", 3", pr 20.00
Shakers, Eskimo boy & girl, pr 25.00
Shakers, fox & goose, 3¼", 2¼", pr 30.00
Shakers, French couple, 3", pr 25.00
Shakers, Indian boy & girl, 3", pr 30.00
Shakers, Scottish couple, 3", pr 28.00
Shakers, snuggle cow & calf, 5¼", pr 35.00

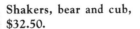
Shakers, bear and cub, $32.50.

Shakers, snuggle Suzette on pillow, 3", pr 30.00
Shakers, Sootie & Taffy, dogs, 3", pr 28.00
Shakers, Swedish boy & girl, 3¼", pr 20.00
Shelf sitter, boy w/dog, girl w/cat, 4¼", pr 35.00
Shelf sitter, Nip & Tuck, 4", pr 38.00
Shelf sitter, spaniel, lying, 1¾", pr 45.00
Shelf sitter, Sun-Li & Sun-Lin, 5¼", pr 35.00
Vase, bud; bamboo, no figure, 6" 20.00
Vase, textured, sq, 2" 14.00

Metal Accessories

Arched window, for Madonna w/child 32.00
Artist palette, left & right, 12", pr 38.00
Artist palette w/shelves, left & right, 12", pr 42.00
Beanstalk for Jack, rare 45.00
Birdcage w/perch, 14" 30.00
Diamond shadow box, for Attitude & Arabesque 22.00
Frame w/shelf 25.00
Free-form, left & right, pr 38.00
Free-form w/shelf, left & right, pr 48.00
Pyramid shelves, ea 35.00
Shadow box, w/wood, sq, 13" 28.00
Sofa, for Maurice & Michele 32.00
Star, for angel trio, 9" 15.00
Triple ring shelves, ea 28.00

Chalkware

Chalkware figures were a popular commodity from approximately 1860 until 1890. They were made from gypsum or plaster of Paris formed in a mold and then hand painted in oils or watercolors. Items such as animals and birds, figures, banks, toys, and religious ornaments modeled after more expensive Staffordshire wares were often sold door to door. Their origin is attributed to Italian immigrants. Today regarded as a form of folk art, nineteenth century American pieces bring prices in the hundreds of dollars. Carnival chalkware from this century is also collectible, especially figures that are personality related. For those, see Carnival Collectibles.

Bank, dove, worn orig mc pnt, bottom has 2 open holes, 11" 350.00
Bird on plinth, worn mc pnt, chips/damage to head, 6" 150.00

Cat, ball between front paws, worn mc pnt, solid, 9" 100.00
Cat, seated, EX modeling, mc pnt, minor edge chips, 5⅜" 425.00
Cat, seated, EX orig pnt, 5" 610.00
Cat, seated, pipe in mouth, worn mc pnt, 10" 235.00
Cat, seated, worn orig mc pnt, base chips, 5¾" 225.00
Cat on high oval pillow base, mouse in mouth, worn pnt, 4" 650.00

Cat, red, yellow, and black watercolor, 1850s, 10½", $2,090.00.

Horse, standing, worn brn/gr pnt, minor wear, 10½" 550.00
Madonna & Child, orig mc pnt, 10" 400.00
Parrot on plinth, worn mc pnt, 8" 350.00
Poodle, sitting, EX 3-color pnt, 5¼", EX 375.00
Rooster, mc rpt, rpr, 5½" 95.00
Spaniel, seated, smoke decor, gilt finish, 8½", EX 500.00
Squirrel, acorn in mouth, worn mc pnt, rprs, 6" 300.00

Champleve

Champleve, enameling on brass, differs from cloisonne in that the design is depressed or incised into the metal, rather than being built up with wire dividers as in the cloisonne procedure. The cells, or depressions, are filled in with color, and the piece is then fired.

Vase, stylized floral bands, figural handles, Japan, 1890, 13", $300.00.

Ash stand, knobbed shaft, Oriental, 29" 300.00
Box, arabesque decor, florals, ca 1900, 6" dia 550.00

Candlestick, stylized florals, baluster form, 1900, 9¾", pr 175.00
Centerpc, etched trumpet vase on base w/2 cupids, Fr, 17" 300.00
Clock, bronze w/faux dmns & enamel dial, French, 6½" 600.00
Figure of Guan Yin, on bk of lion, Chinese, rpr, 20x22".......... 1,400.00
Frame, w/mirror, mk France, 7x9" 185.00
Inkwell, in form of Louis XVI bureau, ormolu mts, 6" 800.00
Jardiniere, dragons in geometric panels, 11½" 400.00
Lamp, sq baluster, demon mask, ring hdls, Chinese, 1900, 15" 475.00
Teapot, dragon form w/3 monkey ft, monkey finial, rpr, 12" 400.00
Umbrella stand, 2 reserves w/phoenix birds, Chinese, 23" 400.00
Urn, bronze w/2 flower & leaf bands, foo dog hdls, 12x7½"........350.00
Urn, geometrics/florals, alabaster base, French, 6" 200.00
Vase, floral/lappet bands/birds, dragon hdls, 12" 300.00
Vase, porc w/HP cherub, champleve socle, onyx base, 8", pr.......700.00
Vase, Tao mask, bronze, imp Oriental M King, 4¾", pr 125.00

Chase Brass & Copper Company

Americans were shocked in 1923 when an invitation to stage an exhibit at the first major post-war fair, *The 1925 Exposition des Arts Decoratifs et Industriels*, was declined by the American government because the U.S. could not comply with the exposition's requirement that only original work would be exhibited. Even though American industry produced a vast quantity of varied goods, there was very little 'original American' to show, since most design ideas were being brought in from Europe.

This blow to American prestige and the uproar that resulted prompted a dispatch of designers (among them Donald Deskey, Walter Dorwin Teague, and Russel Wright) to the Paris exhibition. They were to determine what steps would be necessary in order for U.S. designs to compete with European standards. They returned championing the new modernist style. By the mid-1930s, products were being designed and marketed that were attractive to the reluctant consumer insistent upon buying a streamline style that was uniquely American. During the decade of the thirties, the Chase Brass & Copper Company offered lamps, smoking acessories, and housewares similar to those Americans were seeing on the Hollywood screen at prices the average buyer could afford. These products are highly valued today not only because of their superior quality but also because of those who created them — Walter von Nessen, Gerth & Gerth, Rockwell Kent, Russel Wright, Laurelle Guild, and Dr. A. Reimann were some of Chases' well-known designers. Emily Post, who served as spokesperson for Chase, promoted a trend away from expensive silver and toward chromium serving pieces.

Besides chromium, Chase manufactured many products in brass, copper, nickel plate, or a combination of these metals; all are equally collectible. Some items had glass inserts which collectors also seek.

Nearly all Chase products were marked, either on the item itself or on a screw or rivet. On sets containing several pieces, the trademark may appear on only one. Be cautious — check unmarked items to make sure they measure up to Chase's standard of quality. Lamps and lighting fixtures that are unmarked may be compared with pictures of verified examples. For safety's sake, replace both cords and internal wiring before attempting to use any electrical product. Not only will you be protected against possible loss from fire, but you will enhance the value of your collectible as well.

For more thorough study we recommend *Art Deco Chrome, The Chase Era*, and *Art Deco Chrome, Book 2, A Collector's Guide, Industrial Design in the Chase Era*. Both are authored by our advisor, Richard J. Kilbride; he is listed in the Directory under Connecticut. In the listings that follow, examples are polished unless noted satin.

Ash receiver, chrome, copper, or bronze, flip top, #871, 3¼".........40.00
Ash tray, Whirligig, brass & plastic, #884, 1¼x5½" dia 42.00

Bank, nickel, barrel form, #405005, 2¼x2¼" **47.00**
Bar caddy, chrome & metal, multiple tool, #90141, 6⅛" **42.00**
Bell, chrome/copper or brass, plastic hdl, #13008, 3¾" **39.00**
Bookends, brass or bronze, crescents, #90137, pr........................**175.00**
Bookends, brass/walnut/plastic, ship's wheel, #90138, pr **95.00**
Bowl, berry; chrome, 10", #90083, w/13" plastic-hdld spoon **73.00**
Bowl, glass ball shape on chrome or copper base, #90098, 5⅛"......**48.00**
Box, chrome or copper, 3-tray, #17015, 6¾x4¾" dia...................**75.00**
Box, cigarette; Plaza, plastic w/bronze or chrome, #880, 9" **42.00**
Box, powder; chrome w/Bakelite & ebony hearts on lid.................**75.00**
Butter dish, chrome, plastic knob, #17067, 2⅝x6" **75.00**
Can, water; Rain Beau, brass & copper, #5006, 6¼x9" **225.00**
Candelabrum, chrome, brass or satin silver, #17114, 13½" **95.00**
Candle snuffer, brass or silver w/plastic, #90151, 15½" **22.00**
Candlestick, Deerfield, brass or bronze, #24011, 10½" **45.00**
Coaster, Danube, chrome or copper, #17072, 3¾" dia, 4 for **52.00**
Cocktail set, Target, #90129, chrome shaker & tray+6 stems......**225.00**
Coffee set, chrome w/plastic, #90073, 3 stacking pcs, ind **150.00**
Coffee set, Continental, chrome, #17054, 9⅜" pot+cr/sug **275.00**
Creamer & sugar bowl, Kent, chrome, #17089, 3½", 4½" **75.00**

Creamer, sugar bowl, and tray, Savoy #26008, $125.00.

Cruets, clear ribbed glass, 2 in chrome fr, #26009, 8" **95.00**
Cup, cocktail; chrome, #26002, 2x2¾" **15.00**
Cup, iced drink; chrome, plastic leaf decor, #90085, 5¼"...............**25.00**
Dish cover, chrome, plastic knob, #17099, 4½x8⅝"......................**38.00**
Flowerpot, brass, copper, or bronze, #04007, 4¾x6⅛" **32.00**
Fork & spoon, chrome, plastic hdls, #90076, 10⅛", pr **48.00**
Hot plate, chrome, electric, #90109, 5⅜" dia **75.00**
Jar, jam; Jubilee, chrome/glass, #26005, 4", +plate & spoon...........**35.00**
Lamp, Alden, brass w/bronze, plastic shade, #6166, 14½" **95.00**
Lamp, Brewster, brass or bronze, #6179, 17¼" **75.00**
Lamp, Chancellor, English bronze/plastic, #6189, 17" **175.00**
Lamp, Glow, chrome or copper, metal shade, #01001, 8¼" **125.00**
Lamp, hurricane; brass, cut chimney, #6307, 7¼" **42.00**
Lamp, Parthenon, brass or bronze, plastic shade, #6318, 18¼".......**95.00**
Lamp, student; Adam, bronze, #6196, 19½" **75.00**
Lantern, masthead; brass, clear/red or gr globe, #25008, 8⅝".........**42.00**
Lighter, plastic w/chrome or brass top, #872, 3⅝x1¼" **43.00**
Nutcracker, chrome or brass, #90150, 5⅞".....................................**25.00**
Pitcher, Stir-It, chrome, #17091, 8⅝"...**125.00**
Pitcher, water; Arcadia, chrome or copper, #90123, 7¼" **135.00**
Rack, newspaper; silver, bronze, or brass & copper, #27027...........**95.00**
Relish, Savory, chrome/glass, 5-compartment, #90054, 12" dia **42.00**
Saucer, Olympia, chrome, #90072, 6¾" dia **45.00**
Shakers, chrome, #28004, 1¾" dia, 1⅛" dia, pr **150.00**
Stand, smoking; Lazy Boy, bronze or chromium, #17031, 22" **650.00**
Table chef, chrome, electric, #17087, 6¼x10" **225.00**
Tea ball, chrome, plastic hdl, #90118, 5" L..................................**58.00**
Tea set, chrome, electric kettle, #90119, 4-pc **425.00**
Tray, cheese & cracker; chrome or walnut, #09016, 15⅞x5⅜" **38.00**
Tray, Diplomat, copper or blk, #17030, 10" dia...........................**150.00**
Tray, Savoy, chrome or copper, #09024, 11⅜x5" **22.00**

Trowel, cake & sandwich; chrome, plastic knob, #17060, 8¼" **85.00**
Wall bracket, brass, copper or bronze, #90029, 9½" **21.00**
Whisk broom, bronze, brass, or chrome, #90133, 8⅛" **20.00**

Chelsea

The Chelsea Porcelain Works operated in London from the middle of the eighteenth century, making porcelain of the finest quality. In 1770 it was purchased by the owner of the Derby Pottery and for about twenty years operated as a decorating shop. Production periods are indicated by trademarks: 1745-1750 — incised triangle, sometimes with 'Chelsea' and the year added; early 1750s — raised anchor mark on oval pad; 1752-1756 — small painted red anchor, only rarely found in blue underglaze; 1756-1769 — gold anchor; 1769-84 — Chelsea Derby mark with the script 'D' containing a horizontal anchor. Many reproductions have been made; be suspicious of any anchor mark larger than ¼".

Bowl, floral sprays, fluted/shaped oval, 1760, 13¾" L..................**450.00**

'Aesop's Fables' candlesticks, each titled, minor losses, 10½", $2,500.00 for the pair.

Dish, floral sprays/scattered flowers, brn rim, 6", pr......................**375.00**
Figurine, boy w/sheaf of wheat, beehive at ft, 6¾", EX **175.00**
Figurine, girl w/flower & fruit basket, flowered shirt, 7"...............**200.00**
Figurine, he w/basket of flowers, she w/apron full, 11", pr...........**500.00**
Figurine, she w/flower basket, he w/rabbit & goose, 7", pr **400.00**
Figurine, shepherd w/dog, lady w/sheep, 1760s, rstr, 6", pr..........**600.00**
Plate, exotic birds, butterflies in feather-emb rim, 8½" **350.00**
Plate, floral sprays/scattered flowers, scroll rim, 11".....................**900.00**
Soup plate, exotic birds/prunus, Kakiemon palette, 1775, 9½" **180.00**
Vase, birds on branches, appl flowers, rtcl rim, hdls, 7½" **600.00**

Chelsea Dinnerware

Made from about 1830 to 1880 in the Staffordshire district of England, this white dinnerware is decorated with lustre embossings in the grape, thistle, sprig, or fruit and cornucopia patterns. The relief designs vary from lavender to blue, and the body of the ware may be porcelain, ironstone, or earthenware. Because it was not produced in Chelsea as the name would suggest, dealers often prefer to call it 'Grandmother's Ware.'

Grape, bowl, sauce; 6"... **8.00**

Grape, bowl, 8"	30.00
Grape, coffee cup	22.50
Grape, coffeepot, 2-cup, stick hdl, 7"	60.00
Grape, creamer	30.00
Grape, egg cup	25.00
Grape, pitcher, milk; 40-oz	42.00
Grape, plate, 6"	12.00
Grape, plate, 7"	18.00
Grape, plate, 8"	20.00
Grape, sauce boat	30.00
Grape, sugar bowl, w/lid	32.00
Grape, teacup	22.00
Grape, teapot, 2-cup	60.00
Sprig, plate, cake; 9"	35.00
Sprig, plate, dinner	25.00
Sprig, plate, 7"	18.00
Thistle, cup & saucer	25.00
Thistle, plate, 7"	15.00

Chelsea Keramic Art Works

Established in 1872 in Chelsea, Massachusetts, by several members of the Robertson family who later formed the Dedham Pottery, this firm is most noted for its experiments in attempting to re-create the ancient Oriental oxblood-red glaze. They succeeded in this in 1885 and also developed several other outstanding glazes as a result of their perseverance. One was their Oriental crackle glaze which they ultimately used in the manufacture of the very successful Dedham dinnerware. Though their very early artware utilized a redware body, by the late 1870s it was replaced with yellow- or buff-burning clay. A line called Bourgla-Reine (underglaze slip-decorated ware with primarily blue and green backgrounds) was produced, though not to any great extent. Other pieces were designed in imitation of metalware, even to the extent that surfaces were 'hammered' to further enhance the effect. Occasionally live flora were pressed into the damp vessel walls to leave a decorative impression. The pottery closed in 1889. Early wares were not marked; those made from 1875 to 1880 were marked with either two or three lines containing 'Chelsea Keramic Art Works, Robertson and Son,' the 'C-KA-W' cipher, or 'CPUS' in a 4-leaf clover. These were used up to 1889. A paper label was used for a short time on the crackleware. See also Dedham.

Pillow vase, with lion handles, blue-green gloss, marked CKW, Robertson & Sons, 12½", $550.00.

Bowl, brn streaks on bl gloss, scalloped, CKAW, 3¾x7", EX	100.00
Bowl, brn streaks on gr, ruffled/bulbous, 3¾" H, EX	150.00
Flask, striated gr/brn, flat rnd body, 4 ball ft, 9", EX	375.00

Jar, olive gloss, urn form w/lid, cut-out ft, CKAW, rpr, 6"	200.00
Pitcher, brn/bl striated gloss, 3-pinch rim, 6¾"	250.00
Pitcher, gr gloss, bulbous, mk CKAW, 5¾"	200.00
Plate, Chestnut, mk CPUS in cloverleaf, 10"	325.00
Plate, emb dolphins & young, sgn Mills, CPUS, 8½ "	1,400.00
Shoe, curled toe/sq heel, emb clovers, yel gloss, mk, 6"	300.00
Vase, bird/thistle branch relief, bsk, pillow form, 6", EX	350.00
Vase, brn matt, bottle form w/tube-like neck, #80/Sc/0, 6"	750.00
Vase, crackleware, swollen form w/narrow neck, CKAW, 7", EX	250.00
Vase, honeycombed w/floral stippling, bl-gr, CKAW, 12"	550.00
Vase, oxblood, long neck on slender ovoid, CKAW, 8"	950.00
Vase, oxblood, orange peel texture, baluster, no mk, 8"	1,200.00
Vase, oxblood, orange peel texture, mk CKAW, 8"	1,400.00

Children's Books

Children's books, especially those from the Victorian era, are charming collectibles. Colorful lithographic illustrations that once delighted little boys in long curls and tiny girls in long stockings and lots of ribbons and lace have lost none of their appeal. Some collectors limit themselves to a specific subject, while others may be far more interested in the illustrations. First editions are more valuable than later issues, and condition and rarity are very important factors to consider before making your purchase.

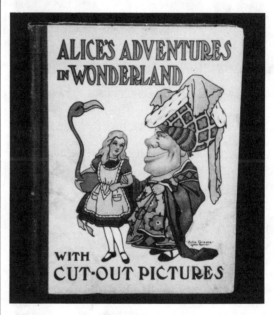

Alice's Adventures in Wonderland, illustrated by Julia Greene after Tenniel, London (no date), 9¾" x 7¾", $65.00.

Arabian Nights, Lang, Longmans Green, 1st ed, 1946, VG	15.00
Arrogance, Couperus, Farrar & Rhinehart, 1st ed, 1930	35.00
Bible Boys & Girls, Wilson & Reeves, Lothrop, 1896, G	4.00
Bobbsey Twins in the Land of Cotton, 1st ed, 1942, EX	5.00
Book of Pirates, Pyle, NY, dust jacket, 1921	35.00
Buddy & the Secret Cave, Caris, Cupples & Leon, 1934	4.00
Buddy Jim, Gordon, Wise-Parslow, color, 1935	15.00
Calico Bush, Field, MacMillan, 1st ed, 1931, EX	15.00
Canterbury Tales, Chaucer, Fox, Duffield, 1st ed, '04, EX	40.00
Count of Monte Cristo, Dumas, Dodd Mead, 1st ed, VG	25.00
Donkey of God, Untermeyer, Harcourt Brace, blk/wht, '32, VG	20.00
Eagle in the Wind, Carmer, Aladdin, blk/wht & color, 1948	25.00
Frost King, Alcott, Whitman, color text heading, '20s, EX	20.00
Invisible Scarlet O'Neil, Stamm, 1943, G	5.00
Ivanhoe, Scott, Houghton Mifflin, color, 1913	30.00
Jack in the Jungle, PT Barnum, 1908, VG	10.00
James & the Giant Peach, Daul, Burkert, 1st ed, 1961	17.50

Jolly Stories, linen, McLoughlin, ca 1900, NM **28.00**
King Arthur & His Knights, Pitz, blk/wht, 1915 ....**22.50**
Knock at the Door, Coatsworth, MacMillan, 1st ed, 1931 ....**35.00**
Last of the Mohicans, Cooper, Scribner, 1933, VG...................**30.00**
Legends of Paul Bunyan, Felton, Knof, blk/wht & color, '50 ....**15.00**
Little House in the Big Woods, Wilder, Harper & Bros, 1953, VG... **6.00**
Mammy Cottontail & Her Bunnies, Chaffee, McLoughlin, '34, G.. **4.00**
Mr Revere & I, Lawson, Little Brown, 1st ed, 1953, VG **25.00**
Omnibus Boners, Suess, Blue Ribbon, 1st ed, 1931, VG **350.00**
Peter Pan, Grosset & Dunlap, blk/wht & color, 1942 .... **9.50**
Ragman of Paris & His Ragamuffins, Jones, Oxford U, 1937 ....**17.50**
Robin Hood, Rhead, New York, blk/wht, 1912 ....**16.00**
Robinson Crusoe, Defoe, Rand McNally, 1st ed, color, 1914 ....**45.00**
Robinson Crusoe, McLoughlin, ca 1890, VG...........................**30.00**
Tales of the Alhambra, Irving, Tuck & McKay, VG.....................**35.00**
Tanglewood Tales, Hawthorne, Hampton, 1921 ....**50.00**
Tarzan & the Forbidden City, Burroughs, 1952 .... **7.00**
Thief in the Attic, Weise, Viking, 1st ed, 1965, EX.....................**12.00**
Wagon Train, Nesbit, TV ed, 1959, G... **4.50**
Water Babies, Kingsley, Lippincott, 1917, VG............................**25.00**
Water Babies, Kingsley, W Foulman & Co, G **4.00**
500 Hats of Bartholomew Cubbins, Suess, 1st ed, 1938, EX **100.00**

Children's Things

Nearly every item devised for adult furnishings has been reduced to child's size — furniture, dishes, sporting goods, even some tools. All are very collectible. During the late seventeenth and early eighteenth centuries, miniature china dinnerware sets were made both in China and in England. They were not intended primarily as children's play-things, however, but instead were made to furnish miniature rooms and cabinets that provided a popular diversion for the adults of that period. By the nineteenth century, the emphasis had shifted, and most of the small-scaled dinnerware and tea sets were made for children's play.

Late in the nineteenth century and well into the twentieth, toy pressed glass dishes were made, many in the same pattern as full-scale glassware. Today these toy dishes often fetch prices in the same range as those for the 'grown-ups'!

Authorities Margaret and Kenn Whitmyer have compiled a lovely book, *Children's Dishes*, with full-color photos and current market values; you will find their address in the Directory under Ohio. We also recommend *Children's Glass Dishes, China, and Furniture*, by Doris Anderson Lechler, available at your local bookstore or public library. See also A B C Plates; Canary Lustre; Willow Ware.

Key:
Emp — Empire   Vict — Victorian

China

Bowl, cereal; Tom Tom the Piper's Son **30.00**
Bowl, Tommy Tucker, Shenango...**20.00**
Dinner set, Fishers, brn & wht, Malkin, 19-pc, EX **365.00**
Mug, A Mothers Affection, girl on swing, bl on wht, 2⅝" **95.00**
Mug, band w/horse, canary lustre, int lustre band, 2", NM **275.00**
Mug, bird, blk transfer on gray w/bl, 2⅜" **70.00**
Mug, blacksmith scene, Staffordshire..**110.00**
Mug, Blind Man's Bluff, mc transfer, Staffordshire, 2½"................**80.00**
Mug, boy & dog, blk & wht transfer, 2⅜" **70.00**
Mug, cat in bonnet w/glasses, 2⅜" **70.00**
Mug, cats at play, mc transfer, 2¾"...**60.00**
Mug, child w/caged bird, cobalt transfer, Staffordshire, 2¼" **60.00**
Mug, children fishing, bird whistle hdl, Germany, 1900s...............**45.00**

Wash set, Germany, 3½" pitcher, 7-piece, $175.00.

Mug, Cornwallis Resigning His Sword, pk lustre rim, 2"..............**450.00**
Mug, Dr Franklin's Poor Richard: Miners Handle Your..., 2⅛"....**165.00**
Mug, Goddess of War, purple transfer, Staffordshire, 2½".............**95.00**
Mug, hunters, mulberry transfer, Edge Malkin, 3" **90.00**
Mug, Indian chief transfer, bbl shape, 2" **25.00**
Mug, Newfoundland Dog for Robert, canary yel, NM..................**275.00**
Mug, Peg in the Ring, girls play game, mc transfer, 2¾"...............**75.00**
Mug, pig feeding, pigs, house, fence, 2¾"....................................**80.00**
Mug, pk lustre floral, orange flowers, 2⅝" **155.00**
Mug, Prosper Freedom, eagle ea side hdl, brn transfer, 2½ " **65.00**
Mug, Shave for a Penny, blk transfer/pk lustre rim, 2¼" **180.00**
Mug, Well House Coresbrook Castle, rose transfer, 2¾" **55.00**
Plate, Docteur-Doctor, 3 children, 6⅜" **90.00**
Plate, Franklin Maxim: It Is Hard for an Empty Bag, 6½" **65.00**
Plate, Little Tom Tucker, Royal Doulton, 9"..................................**48.00**
Plate, pk & bl floral rim on wht, Nippon, 5"................................. **5.00**
Tea set, bl lustre, blk trim, 15-pc..**100.00**
Tea set, Blue Willow, Japan, 23-pc, MIB.....................................**275.00**
Tea set, Blue Willow, 15-pc, MIB...**350.00**
Tea set, Bower, blk & wht, Edge Malkin, 16-pc **475.00**
Tea set, Chintz, bl & wht, Ridgway, 16-pc **325.00**
Tea set, Circus Tricks, luster on porc, Germany, serves 4 ....**150.00**
Tea set, copper lustre, 21-pc **60.00**
Tea set, Kittens, Bavaria, 19-pc...**300.00**
Tea set, Moss Rose, Japan, 26-pc **160.00**
Tea set, Paris scene HP on porc, France, 1890-1910, serves 4......**175.00**
Tea set, Teaberry, English ironstone, 15-pc **3,100.00**
Tea set, wht w/gold trim, Noritake, 17-pc **145.00**
Tea set, Wind Flower, England, ca 1830, serves 4......................**900.00**
Teapot, Cat's Thanksgiving, Germany, +cr/sug **200.00**
Teapot, Nursery Scenes, Germany, 4½".......................................**35.00**

Furniture

Examples with no dimensions given are child's size unless noted doll size.

Armchair, Arts & Crafts oak, floral-cvd splat, 28" **175.00**
Armchair, red/blk grpt w/yel striping, seat cut for potty **65.00**
Armchair, wing-bk, pine w/pnt traces, branded Lovel, 18" **150.00**
Bed, Adirondack, varnished, 1910, 13" L **150.00**
Bed, bl enameled metal, ds, 26"...**65.00**
Bed, Gothic Revival style, CI, 1890s, 19x11", EX.........................**55.00**
Bed, pine w/red grpt, mortised/pinned, trn posts, 14" L...............**375.00**
Bed, rope, orig old red pnt, ds, 10½x16x25½", EX.....................**495.00**
Bed, walnut, rondel crests, spindle sides, SP Hovely, 32" **200.00**

Buggy, wicker, 1900s, ds, EX	350.00
Carriage, willow, velvet lined, wood wheels, ds, 25x13x31", G	300.00
Chair, hickory & pine, orig hide seat, 20"	350.00
Chair, ladder-bk, splint seat, primitive, ds	125.00
Chest of drw, birch Emp w/red finish, cvd pilasters, 29"	2,600.00
Chest w/mirror, 3-drw, CI, pnt traces, 1890s, 10¼"	165.00
Cradle, pine w/orig bl pnt, 16" L	120.00
Cradle, poplar w/EX detail, heart cutouts, old red, 24", EX	195.00
Cradle, poplar w/re-grpt, scalloped hood, rpr/cracks, 36"	250.00
Cupboard, grain pnt, ca 1860, 32x15"	450.00
Doll bed, CI, old gr pnt, Victorian, 20" L, EX	185.00
Dry sink, walnut, 1-drw, 2-door, 24x14x34"	400.00
Highchair, captain's style, worn grpt w/floral, VG	125.00
Highchair, primitive, pencil-post legs, simple, 33"	500.00
Highchair, wood, Strombecker, ds, 8"	12.50
Ice box, walnut, metal lined, 1-door, 19"	165.00
Lap desk, suitcase style w/pens & bottles, 8" W	275.00
Pie safe, pine, bottom drw, 2-door, 20x27"	400.00
Rocker, wood litho, cane seat, 17x9", VG	95.00
Settee & rocker, bentwood, cane seats, labels, 1940s, ds	200.00
Stand, library; oak, 2-shelf, ca 1920, 19x11x11"	155.00
Table, oak, ped base, 22x29" dia, +4 oak pressed-bk chairs	550.00
Table, walnut, trn legs, 1 dvtl drw w/porc pull, 16x12x15"	400.00

Glassware

Acorn, butter dish, 4"	185.00
Acorn, sugar bowl, w/lid, 4¾"	145.00
Acorn, table set, 4-pc	535.00
Amazon, sugar bowl, w/lid	60.00
Arched Panel, pitcher, amber	85.00
Austrian, butter dish, chocolate, 2¼"	750.00
Austrian, sugar bowl, canary, w/lid, 3¾"	325.00
Beautiful Lady, cake stand	32.00
Braided Belt, sugar bowl, floral on milk glass	185.00
Bucket (Wooden Pail), butter dish	250.00
Bucket (Wooden Pail), sugar bowl, w/lid	200.00
Button Panel, spooner, gold flashed	80.00
Button Panel, sugar bowl, w/lid, 4⅝"	85.00
Clear & Diamond Panels, creamer, bl, 2¾"	40.00
Clear & Diamond Panels, spooner, gr	40.00
Colonial, creamer, gr	30.00
Colonial, pitcher, 3¼"	22.00
Colonial, punch bowl, 3¼"	45.00
D&M #42, creamer, 2⅝"	55.00
D&M #42, honey jug, 2⅜"	60.00
D&M #42, sugar bowl, w/lid	85.00
Dewdrop, creamer, clear, 2¾"	60.00
Dewdrop, spooner, bl, 2¾"	110.00
Dewdrop, table set (butter dish, spooner, cr/sug)	335.00
Diamond Ridge, butter dish	175.00
Diamond Ridge, creamer	70.00
Doyle's #500, butter dish, bl, 2¼"	110.00
Doyle's #500, creamer, bl	55.00
Doyle's #500, tray, 6⅝"	45.00
Drum, butter dish	120.00
Drum, sugar bowl, w/lid, 3½"	115.00
Dutch Kinder, candlestick, bl opaque, 3"	135.00
Dutch Kinder, pitcher, milk glass, 2¼"	110.00
English Hobnail, cruet	18.00
Fancy Cut, butter dish	32.00
Fancy Cut, butter dish, teal	195.00
Fancy Cut, punch cup	25.00
Fancy Cut, spooner, 2¼"	28.00

Fancy Cut, table set	150.00
Finecut Star & Fan, cake stand	32.00
Flute, bowl, berry; gold flashed, master	60.00
Frances Ware, pitcher, amber or bl stain, 4¾"	115.00
Frances Ware, tumbler, frosted w/amber or red stain, 2¼"	65.00
Galloway, pitcher, gold trim, 3⅞"	32.00
Galloway, tumbler, blush	20.00
Grape Vine w/Ovals, spooner, 1⅞"	45.00
Hawaiian Lei, creamer	25.00
Heron & Peacock, mug, milk glass, old	45.00
Hobnail, salt cellar, milk glass	12.00
Hobnail w/T'print, creamer	35.00
Hobnail w/T'print, creamer, bl	55.00
Hobnail w/T'print, spooner, bl	70.00
Hobnail w/T'print, tray, amber	50.00
Hobnail w/T'print, tray, 7⅜"	55.00
Hook, creamer	25.00
Hook, mug	16.00
Horizontal Threads, butter dish, red flashed, 1⅞"	85.00
Invt Strawberry, punch bowl, 3¾"	60.00
Kittens, banana dish, marigold	135.00
Kittens, cup & saucer, bl	200.00
Lamb, butter dish, milk glass, 3⅛"	185.00
Large Block, spooner	8.00
Liberty Bell, butter dish	180.00
Liberty Bell, spooner	225.00
Lion, butter dish, frosted, 4¼"	165.00
Lion, cup & saucer, 1¾", 3¼"	60.00
Lion, sugar bowl, frosted heads, w/lid	145.00
Little Jo, pitcher	30.00
Little Ladders, banana stand	45.00
Martyrs, mug	65.00
Menagerie, creamer, amber, 3¾"	145.00
Menagerie, spooner, bl, 2⅝"	135.00
Michigan, sweetmeat	35.00
Mirror & Fan, decanter, gold flashed	60.00
Mug, jester riding pig bkwards	45.00
Mug, Two Dogs Standing, amethyst	45.00
Nursery Rhyme, butter dish, 2⅜"	85.00
Nursery Rhyme, mug, Humpty Dumpty, amber, 3½"	35.00
Nursery Rhyme, punch cup, bl opaque, 1⅜"	45.00

Nursery Rhyme table set, $225.00.

Oval Star, pitcher, +6 tumblers	150.00
Oval Star, pitcher, water	85.00
Oval Star, tray, 7¼"	85.00
Oval Star, tumbler	10.00
Pennsylvania, butter dish, gr, 3½"	195.00
Pennsylvania, sugar bowl, gr w/gold, w/lid, 4"	190.00

Pert, butter dish, 2¾" 125.00
Petite Hobnail, pitcher, color...............................235.00
Petite Hobnail, tray 145.00
Plain #13, butter dish, cobalt 165.00
Plain #13, sugar bowl, clear w/frosted panels, w/lid, 3¼" 80.00
Planet, cruet 35.00
Plate, boy w/dog on steps, Gillinder, 6"............40.00
Punch set, Nursery Rhymes, milk glass, 7-pc ...245.00
Rexford, butter dish 30.00
Rooster, creamer 135.00
Rooster, sugar bowl, clear or milk glass, w/lid 165.00
Sandwich Ivy, sugar bowl, amethyst.....................125.00
Sawtooth, creamer 35.00
Sawtooth, spooner 40.00
Sawtooth, sugar bowl, w/lid...................................45.00
Sawtooth Band #1225, creamer, red flashed, 2½" 85.00
Standing Lamb, sugar bowl, frosted, w/lid, 5⅛" 450.00
Steigel (type), tumbler...20.00
Stippled Dewdrop & Raindrop, spooner 60.00
Stippled Diamond, sugar bowl, bl or amber, w/lid, 3⅛" 145.00
Stippled Vines & Beads, butter dish, sapphire bl, 2⅜" 135.00
Stippled Vines & Beads, spooner, 2⅛".................75.00
Stippled Vines & Beads, sugar bowl, w/lid 95.00
Style (Arrowhead-in-Ovals), butter dish, clear 30.00
Sultan, creamer...45.00
Sultan, sugar bowl, gr frosted, w/lid, 4½" 185.00
Sunbeam, butter dish 145.00
Tulip & Honeycomb, bowl, oval, 1¾".....................65.00
Twist, butter dish..22.50
Twist, butter dish, bl opal.....................................165.00
Twist, butter dish, frosted 70.00
Two Band, spooner 40.00
Wee Branches, butter dish 135.00
Wheat Sheaf, bowl, berry 10.00
Wild Rose, creamer, milk glass, 1¾" 55.00
Wild Rose, punch bowl 85.00
Wild Rose, punch cup, bl opaque, 1¼" 35.00

Miscellaneous

Alphabet board, Pat Feb '86, 13½" L, VG 90.00
Baby buggy, fringed leather surrey top, gold decor, 43", VG 500.00
Bowl, Uncle Wiggily, Farberware, 1924 ....175.00
Buggy, Pram Storkline, blk leather & chrome, 1940s, full sz........150.00
Buggy seat, wooden, red pnt, 4½x9¼x16", EX.....................85.00
Flute, tin w/wood mouthpc, 2-color, 1950s, 12" 4.00
Handkerchief, Wild Beasts printed in red, 12x14", EX 25.00
Horn, celluloid, emb birds on branch, 5¾" 35.00
Kaleidoscope, mc cb, 1950s, 3½x1".........................5.00
Kaleidoscope, tin, Indian bead pattern, 1830s, 7", EX 225.00
Kit, fishing; Jr Ace, NY Toy & Game, complete 125.00

Muff, celluloid doll's face and wool mohair, ca 1920s, 10", $68.00.

Mug, tin w/old bl japanning, yel florals & name, 2x3¾" 50.00
Paint set, wood box & palettes, pnts, etc, Schwartz, 1925, VG 55.00
Rattle, celluloid, HP pk & gr florals, 1870s, EX.........35.00
Rattle, celluloid, turtle figural 20.00
Rattle, telephone, Plakie, MIB.............................22.50
Rattle, wooden, red varnish, long hdl, 8¾" 75.00
Rubber boots, Goodyear India Rubber, ca 1915, MIB 40.00
Sewing card set, w/needle & thimble, Germany, EX in box..........30.00
Sled, Paris, wood, stenciled horse head, 32x13", EX 400.00
Sled, Paris #82, peaked runner, daisies on red, 32", EX 325.00
Sled, pnt wood w/stenciled horse & border, 32", VG.................525.00

Cast iron teakettle, marked Wagner, 3½", $140.00.

Table, graniteware top w/Noah's Ark & ABCs, NM, +2 chairs .295.00
Wagon, stenciled/Express on side, brass horn, 1880s, 36" L.........350.00

Chocolate Glass

Jacob Rosenthal developed chocolate glass, a rich shaded opaque brown sometimes referred to as caramel slag, in 1900 at the Indiana Tumbler and Goblet Company of Greentown, Indiana. Later, other companies produced similar ware. Only the latter is listed here. See also Greentown. Our advisors for this category are Jerry and Sandi Garrett; they are listed in the Directory under Indiana.

Bottle, Venetian, w/stopper..500.00
Collar box, 3¼" H 400.00
Compote, Melrose, 8½ "..325.00
Creamer, Geneva..200.00
Pitcher, Wild Rose w/Bow Knot 500.00
Plate, Serenade, 8¼"...200.00
Shaker, Beaded Triangle 375.00
Tumbler, Chrysanthemum Leaf 450.00
Tumbler, Geneva..125.00

Christmas Collectibles

Christmas past . . . lovely mementos from long ago attest to the ostentatious Victorian celebrations of the season.

St. Nicholas, better known as Santa, has changed much since 300 A.D. when the good Bishop Nicholas showered needy children with gifts and kindnesses. During the early eighteenth century, Santa was portrayed as the kind gift-giver to well-behaved children and the stern switch-bearing disciplinarian to those who were bad. In 1822 Clement Clark Moore, a New York poet, wrote his famous *Night Before Christmas*, and the Santa he described was jolly and jovial — a lovable old elf who was stern with no one. Early Santas wore robes of yellow, brown, blue, green, red, or even purple. But Thomas Nast, who worked as an illustrator for Harper's Weekly, was the first to depict Santa in a red suit instead of the traditional robe, and to locate him the entire year at the North Pole headquarters.

Today's collectors prize early Santa figures, especially those in robes of fur or mohair or those dressed in an unusual color. Some early examples of Christmas memorabilia are the pre-1870 ornaments from Dresden, Germany. These cardboard figures — angels, gondolas, umbrellas, dirigibles, and countless others — sparkled with gold and silver trim. Late in the 1870s, blown glass ornaments were imported from Germany. There were over 6,000 recorded designs — all painted inside with silvery colors. From 1890 through 1910, blown glass spheres were often decorated with beads, tassels, and tinsel rope.

Christmas lights, made by Sandwich and some of their contemporaries, were either pressed or mold-blown glass shaped into a form similar to a water tumbler. They were filled with water and then hung from the tree by a wire handle; oil floating on the surface of the water served as fuel for the lighted wick.

Kugels are glass ornaments that were made as early as 1820 and as late as 1890. Ball-shaped examples are more common than the fruit and vegetable forms and have been found in sizes ranging from 1" to 14" in diameter. They were made of thick glass with heavy brass caps, in cobalt, green, gold, silver, and occasionally in amethyst.

Although experiments involving the use of electric lightbulbs for the Christmas tree occured before 1900, it was 1903 before the first manufactured socket set was marketed. These were very expensive and often proved a safety hazard. In 1921 safety regulations were established, and products were guaranteed safety approved. The early bulbs were smaller replicas of Edison's household bulb. By 1910 G.E. bulbs were rounded with a pointed end, and until 1919 all bulbs were hand blown. The first figural bulbs were made around 1910 in Austria. Japan soon followed, but their product was never of the high quality of Austrian wares. American manufacturers produced their first machine-made figurals after 1919. Today, figural bulbs — especially character-related examples — are very popular collectibles. Bubble lights were popular from about 1945 to 1960 when miniature lights were introduced. These tiny lamps dampened the public's enthusiasm for the bubblers, and manufacturers stopped providing replacement bulbs.

Feather trees were made from 1850 to 1950 — all are collectible. Watch for newly-manufactured feather trees that have lately been reintroduced.

Bulbs

Acorn, mc pnt, clear, VG	20.00
Angel, mc pnt, molded wings, clear, Japan	42.50
Ape w/rifle sits on mound, mc pnt, milk glass, rare	125.00
Bird, clear, Japan	35.00
Bird, milk glass, red/yel plumage, working	22.50
Boy in hip boots, worn pnt, milk glass	32.00
Bunny, sitting, mc pnt, milk glass, NM	70.00
Bunny sits in basket, mc pnt, celluloid, NM	135.00
Cat, mc pnt, milk glass, 4"	35.00
Cat & fiddle, mc pnt, milk glass, Japan	42.50
Chick in egg, yel & pk pnt, milk glass, 2¾", NM	125.00
Clown head, dbl-faced, pointed cap, mc pnt, milk glass, EX	50.00

Clown on ball, mc pnt, milk glass, 3"	75.00
Cross, pk, milk glass, 3"	30.00
Dick Tracy, EX mc pnt, milk glass, 3"	140.00
Dog in basket, worn pnt, milk glass, VG	45.00
Dog w/bandage, mc pnt, milk glass	55.00
Drummer boy, mc pnt, milk glass, EX	55.00
Father Christmas, mc pnt, milk glass, European, NM	200.00
Fruit basket, mc pnt, milk glass, lg, NM	40.00
Girl, mc pnt, milk glass, EX	25.00
Girl w/toothache, mc pnt, milk glass, VG	65.00
Hayseed Farmer, EX pnt	95.00
Indian's head, mc pnt, blown	110.00
Keystone Cop, mc pnt, milk glass, EX	85.00
Lantern, mc pnt, milk glass, Japan, sm	25.00
Little Orphan Annie, EX pnt, mk c 1935, 3⅛"	65.00
Lucky Lindy, mc w/gold plane, milk glass, EX	50.00
Mickey Mouse, EX pnt, milk glass	70.00
Moon Mullins, EX pnt, milk glass	125.00
Rose, open, EX red pnt, milk glass	42.50
Santa, full figure w/pack, mc pnt, milk glass, 4"	45.00
Santa, mc pnt, milk glass, 9", EX	120.00
Santa on chimney, milk glass, EX	65.00
Santa on oval, mc pnt, milk glass, 3¾", NM	65.00
Smitty, milk glass, VG	85.00
Snowman, EX mc pnt, milk glass, European	65.00
Snowman holding club, EX pnt, sm	35.00
Snowman w/shovel, red hat, yel scarf, milk glass, VG	30.00
Teddy bear, EX pnt, milk glass	70.00
Tom the Piper's Son, mc pnt, EX	245.00
Tulip, pk w/gr leaves, milk glass, EX	35.00
Turkey, EX mc pnt, milk glass	80.00
World globe, EX pnt, milk glass	95.00

Candy Containers

Banjo, Dresden, 3-D, silver/gold/brn/red, 3½x1½", EX	165.00
Barrel, Dresden, brn & tan, 3-D, 2¼"	150.00
Basket, Dresden, corrugated pattern, EX	145.00
Candle, pressed paper, red w/wick & ribbon, 5½", EX	45.00
Cornucopia, crepe paper w/paper diecuts, EX	85.00
Elf, compo, stands, detailed face, Germany, 8¼", EX	350.00
Father Christmas, compo/spun cotton, 9", VG	250.00
Father Christmas, pnt compo, Germany, 12"	500.00
Irish heart, Dresden, gr w/opal stone, 2"	115.00

Papier-mache Santa, felt costume, movable arms, 17", VG, $450.00.

Santa, Belsnickle, ca 1880, 8" 575.00
Santa, plastic, Irwin, early, 5" 55.00
Santa in basket, plaster hands, Japan, 5" 110.00
Santa in boot, compo/paper, Japan, 7½", G 145.00
Santa in car, compo, wooden wheels, 6" 275.00
Santa in sled, papier-mache, celluloid face, 5x5½" 195.00
Santa in sleigh, papier-mache, EX pnt, lg 195.00
Santa in wagon pulled by deer, plastic, 4x8" 195.00
Santa in zeppelin, papier-mache, EX 225.00
Santa on skis, plastic, red/gr 65.00
Santa on snowshoes, plastic, Rosbro, 5" 65.00
Santa w/tree, papier-mache, orange robe, 4½", EX...........500.00
Santa w/tree, papier-mache, wht robe w/yel trim, 12", EX...........785.00
Santa w/tree, pnt compo & cotton, 4½", VG 185.00
Santa's head, bsk, Germany, 1900s, 8" 550.00
Slipper, Dresden, pk crepe w/gold, 8" 255.00
Snow White & 7 Dwarfs, cb, Germany, 8-pc set..............450.00
Snowball, celluloid, 2" 55.00
Snowman, papier-mache w/cb hat, comic, 7½" 85.00
Star medallion, Dresden, cb/glitter, 3" 110.00
Top hat, Dresden, red silk w/silver rosettes, 2", EX 245.00
Turtle, Dresden, mc pnt, EX 395.00
Violin case w/wood violin, Dresden, 3", EX 220.00
Wreath, Dresden, 4½", EX 185.00

Ornaments

Airplane, blown, spun glass wings, tin wheels, 1920s..................165.00
Airplane, Sebnitz, silver w/wax figure, 5½" 325.00
Airship, blown, mc pnt, scrap & tinsel trim, 5¼", G 145.00
Alligator, blown, pearly wht/pk/bl/red, 10" 450.00
Angel, Dresden, die-cut face, gold stars & wings, 5½" 165.00
Angel, Dresden, die-cut face, silver starburst, flat 185.00
Apple, blown, pk frost, 2½" 50.00
Apple, pressed cotton, mc pnt, 2¼", EX 35.00
Baboon, blown, mc pnt, 3" 165.00
Balloon, wire wrapped, die-cut Santa w/in, 1900s, 3½" 35.00
Balloon, wire wrapped, scrap angel w/Am flag w/in, 1910, 6" 75.00
Basket, blown, unsilvered, scrap angel w/in, lg 75.00
Bear, blown, annealed legs, EX silvering, 1920s, 3¾" 325.00
Bear, blown, gr w/blk, 2½ " 165.00
Bear w/stick, blown, EX pnt, ca 1910, 2¼" 65.00
Bee, Dresden, mc w/fabric wings, delicate legs, NM...........325.00
Beetle, molded, pearly wht, red wings, 2½", NM 65.00
Bell w/clapper, blown, silver w/holly decor, 1900, 2½" 45.00
Berry, molded, gold w/gr, ca 1910, 2" 25.00
Billiken, blown, pearly wht/red/brn, 1920s, EX 150.00
Birdcage, Dresden, mc w/gold, flat, 5" 145.00
Birds on swing, compo w/wire loop, 2¾x3¾", EX............55.00
Boot, Sebnitz, cotton-covered wire fr, metal overlay, 1800s 150.00
Boy clown head, molded milk glass, 3", G 65.00
Boy w/letter, molded, worn mc pnt, ca 1920, 3½" 80.00
Camel, Dresden, mc pnt, flat, EX.................................85.00
Camel, Dresden, 1-hump, w/Blk rider, 3¼x3½", EX 395.00
Candy cane, red-striped mercury glass, 6" 25.00
Carousel horse, wht cotton, red paper trim, stands, EX..............195.00
Cart, Sebnitz w/Dresden wheels, wax figure w/in, EX 225.00
Cat, Dresden, gold w/red & gr, flat 195.00
Cat in Shoe, molded, gr w/wht trim, ca 1930, 3" 135.00
Cat w/fiddle, blown, wht w/gold fiddle, 1920s, 3¼" 145.00
Champagne bottle, Dresden, foil top, French label, early 125.00
Child's face on grapes, molded, flesh face w/gr & gold, 3½"..........375.00
Cigar, brn w/wht frosted tip, paper band, ca 1910, 3¾" 185.00
Clam shell, Dresden, gold 135.00

Clown, molded, mc pnt, 3½ ", VG 85.00
Clown on ball, molded, mc w/silver, ca 1910, 3½" 135.00
Clown on moon, molded, mc w/silver, ca 1910s, 3", EX 185.00
Clown playing fiddle, molded, pk/gold/silver, '50s, 4" 65.00
Cock Robin, molded milk glass, worn pnt, on clip, 4", VG 145.00
Comic car, blown, mc pnt w/gold, 1920s, 2x2¾"...........185.00
Corn, molded, pk w/gr & gold leaves, 1920s, 3" 55.00
Crescent moon, M pnt, recent repro 20.00
Dancer, cotton, paper clothes, compo face, 5", EX 500.00
Deer head, Dresden, silver w/pk bag, 4" 385.00
Devil, blown, pearly wht w/red, 2½" 195.00
Dog, Dresden, gold, flat, 4½ x5½" 285.00
Dog blowing horn, blown, mc w/silver, ca 1910, 3¼", EX 350.00
Doll head, molded, glass eyes, mc pnt, ca 1910, 2½", EX 135.00
Donkey pulls sleigh, Dresden, 4" 525.00
Dwarf, blown, silver, 4" 95.00
Eagle, Dresden, glass eyes, natural colors, 5¼", EX 495.00
Elephant, molded glass, mc pnt, 4", G 195.00
Elephant, pressed cotton, glass eyes, wire tusks, 3x6", EX 195.00
Elk, Dresden, 3-D, lg 350.00
Fat man w/accordion, blown, mc w/gold, ca 1910, 3¼".........165.00
Fish, blown, mc pnt, paper tail, ca 1900, 6½", VG 115.00
Fish, molded, pearly wht w/gold & red, 4" 45.00
Flower girl, flesh face, gold hair, mc flowers, 4" 145.00
Flowers in pot, molded, red & gold, 4½"........................95.00
Foxy Grandpa, molded, pearly face, pk hat, 5½"............350.00
Girl in bag, molded, pearly wht/pk/bl, ca 1920, 3", VG 135.00
Girl in basket, molded, mc pnt w/gold, ca 1920, 2" 135.00
Girl in long coat, mc pnt, milk glass, ca 1910, 3½" 125.00
Girl in sweater, molded, yel hair, pk sweater, 3" 155.00

Ornaments, Girl on ribbed ball, 3½", $65.00; Owl, 3¼", $55.00.

Girl's head, blown, mc pnt, glass eyes, w/hanger, 1920s, 2¼".........85.00
Gladiator w/spear & shield, Dresden, mc pnt, flat, EX 195.00
Goat, Dresden, long haired, gold & gr, flat, 2¾x4½", EX 195.00
Goldilock's head, blown, mc pnt, ca 1910, 3x2½ ", EX.............215.00
Hedge hog, molded, pearlescent pnt, lg 195.00
Horn, wire wrapped, pk w/fancy hdl, ca 1900, 4¾", EX 110.00
Horse, Dresden, gold w/mc trim, flat, EX.......................250.00
House, molded, golden satin, early, 3" 85.00
Icicle, blown, annealed hanger, 5½" 15.00
Icicle, cotton-wrapped w/ridges, EX 45.00
Indian, blown, pearly gold/red/yel, on clip, 3¼" 275.00
Indian on pine cone, blown, mc pnt, 4" 385.00
Jester's hat, Dresden, soldier boy diecut, mc pnt, EX 325.00

Keystone Cop, blown, EX mc pnt, on clip, 3½" 255.00
Kugel, ball, bl, w/orig MIG label, rpr brass hanger, 5¾" 275.00
Kugel, ball, cobalt, Baroque cap, 2½" 110.00
Kugel, ball, cobalt, ribbed, common hanger, 1⅝" 250.00
Kugel, ball, cobalt, swirl leaf-end brass hanger, 4" 165.00
Kugel, ball, cobalt, 8-petal hanger, 1½" 110.00
Kugel, ball, gold, mercury lined, orig hanger, 8" 165.00
Kugel, ball, gr, brass fastener, Made in France, 7½" 475.00
Kugel, ball, med gr, 2½" 110.00
Kugel, ball, red, Baroque hanger, 2" 185.00
Kugel, ball, red, brass fastener, 4¼" 450.00
Kugel, ball, red, brass hanger, 7" 600.00
Kugel, ball, red/silver/wht stripes, brass cap, 1890s, 2¾" 350.00
Kugel, ball, smoky bl, emb brass cap, French, 2½" 145.00
Kugel, grapes, bl, 6", EX 350.00
Kugel, grapes, cobalt, brass hanger, 4" 250.00
Kugel, grapes, silver, brass clip, 5" 250.00
Kugel, grapes, silver, emb brass hanger, 7" 285.00
Kugel, grapes, silver w/gr, 8-petal cap, ca 1890, 4" 235.00
Kugel, pear, emerald gr, Baroque brass hanger, 3¾" 250.00
Kugel, pear, silver, brass hanger, 9½" 250.00
Kugel, teardrop, silver, Baroque hanger, 2¼" 185.00
Kugel, teardrop, silver, Baroque hanger, 3½" 225.00
Kugel, turnip, silver, metal holder, lg 250.00
Lady w/feather tree, Dresden, cotton w/compo face, 4½" 450.00
Lamb, Dresden, gold w/mc flowers, flat, 3x4¾" 250.00
Lemon, pressed cotton, bright colors, 3" 40.00
Lion, Dresden, EX molding, mc pnt, 2½" 350.00
Llama, Dresden, silver, EX molding, 2½" 175.00
Lord Fauntleroy, blown, pearly wht w/red tie, 3" 365.00
Man in barrel, mc pnt, bl chenille limbs, 5", EX 325.00
Man's face on pear, molded, pearly wht w/blk, 1910s, 3" 175.00
Man's head, blown, bl face & red hair, ca 1910, 2¼", EX 145.00
Man's head, molded, pearly wht, EX detail, 1910s, 2¼" 225.00
Mary Pickford, blown, annealed legs, VG pnt, 4¼" 365.00
Mary Pickford, molded, gold hair, wht dress, 5" 425.00
Miss Liberty, paper litho diecut on cotton w/tinsel, 12", G 195.00
Miss Muffett, molded, pearly wht, pnt features, 1910s, 4" 135.00
Mouse, blown, pearly wht & yel, Italy, 5" 85.00
Mrs Claus, molded, pearly wht & red, 4½" 275.00
Native boy, blown, Rogers, 1900s, 4½", EX 325.00
Nude on bell, gold curls, red bell, 1910s, 3" 235.00
Orange, molded, pebbly surface, unsilvered, 1910s, 2", EX 35.00
Peacock, blown, mc pnt, in metal ring w/gr spun glass tail 50.00
Pig, Dresden, gold, curly tail, EX molding, 2½" 265.00
Pine cone, blown, bl w/wht frosting, 2½", EX 35.00
Pinocchio, molded, pearly wht/yel/pk/bl/red, 4½", EX 165.00
Policeman, blown, silvered, chenille limbs, 6½", EX 350.00
Popcorn head, molded, frosty wht w/blk & red, 4½" 425.00
Prince's head on spike, molded, mc pnt, '15, 6¼", EX 145.00
Prussian helmet, wire wrapped, gold spike, tinsel, 9", EX 525.00
Rabbit & carrot, molded glass, EX pnt, 3½" 145.00
Reindeer, Dresden, mc w/gold, flat, 3½ x4⅞", EX 135.00
Roman chariot w/2 horses, Dresden, 3½", EX 325.00
Rooster, Dresden, mc irid pnt, silk bag at bk, EX 275.00
Santa, blown, pearly red & wht, on clip, 5", VG 95.00
Santa, chromo diecut w/spun glass, 9", VG 75.00
Santa, molded, mc pnt, chenille legs, 4½" 145.00
Santa head, molded, pearly silver/blk/pk/gold, 1910s, 3¼" 110.00
Santa in car, celluloid, red/wht/gr, 3x4½" 185.00
Santa in sleigh, celluloid, red/wht/gr, 2½ x4½" 65.00
Santa on leaf, molded, silver w/pk shading, Am, 2¾" 55.00
Santa w/deer, celluloid, red/wht/gr, mechanical, 3½ x6" 110.00
Santa w/lantern, celluloid, red w/silver, 2" 65.00

Santa's head, molded, mc pnt, 3½" 65.00
Saxaphone, molded, pearly pk, 1920s, 4½" 40.00
Scotty, blown, mc pnt, 3¾" 75.00
Shoe, Dresden, dk silver, orange silk bag, 3" 145.00
Sled, Dresden, cb w/Father Christmas diecut, 3¾" 195.00
Snow child, molded, pearly gold w/pnt features, 1920s, 3¾" 80.00
Star, dbl-sided, Dresden, silver, 4" 85.00
Starburst, wire center, 14 points w/silver balls, 1900s, 3¼" 65.00
Sun, dbl-faced, pearly wht/pk/yel, 2½", EX 115.00
Swan, free blown, mc pnt, '40s, 5¼" w/8" tinsel tail, EX 135.00
Teddy bear, blown, gold pnt, 3½" 110.00
Teddy bear, blown, pk w/gold & bl clothes, 4½" 150.00
Train engine & coach, rubber, Japanese, early, pr 30.00
Tree w/candles, Dresden, gold w/gr & red, flat, 6½", VG 80.00
Tree-top angel, Dresden, bl skirt w/gold, 5½" 150.00
Twins in a blanket, molded, worn mc pnt 85.00
Umbrella, wire wrapped, pk w/gold stem, ca 1900, 7½" 85.00
Windmill, molded, unsilverd wht, Dresden paper blades, 2½" 65.00
Woodpecker on tree trunk, molded, EX pnt, glass tail, 3¼" 175.00
Wreath, Dresden, gold/red berries, w/Father Christmas, 4" 88.00

Miscellaneous

Angel, wax over compo, spun glass wings, red skirt, lg, EX 95.00
Bells, Noma, red cellophane, 2 on string 15.00
Blocks, Christmas ABCs, McLoughlin Bros, 1897, set of 9, M. **1,150.00**
Book, Christmas on Stage, pop-up, 1950s, VG 45.00
Bubble light, Noma, red & gr 4.00
Bubble light, Royal, red 3.00
Bulb cover, Fairy Tales set, celluloid, Noma, 1929, 15 for 265.00
Candle holder, corn, blown, pk & wht, 3½" 115.00
Candle holder, tin litho angel w/trumpet, dbl sided, 3¼" 165.00
Candlelight, Santa, mc pnt on ivory plastic, NM in box 15.00
Candlelight, tree w/snow & balls on wood base, 8½" 15.00
Candolier, Timco, 5-light, NM in box 35.00
Candolier, 7 cb tubes on wood base, M 25.00
Church, plastic, wht w/glitter, rpl tree, Japan 25.00
Cow, papier-mache, rope tail, EX pnt, Germany, 5¾" 150.00
Cow, Putz, brn, 2½ x3½" 55.00
Cup & saucer, Father Christmas w/toys, bsk, Germany 65.00
Diecut, Santa w/bag of toys, standup, dtd 1951, 72", EX 20.00
Donkey, compo, w/saddle & reins, Germany, sm 65.00
Donkey, papier-mache, worn pnt, Germany, 4¼" 65.00
Father Christmas, compo, molded bag over arm, Germany, 2¼" ..60.00
Father Christmas, cotton & crepe, die-cut trim, 19", VG 145.00
Father Christmas, papier-mache nodder, Germany, 10", VG 425.00
Father Christmas, Tuck, die-cut bust, Dresden rosettes, 11" 175.00
Fence, CI, gate, ball finials, fan crests, 24" sq, EX 295.00
Fence, plastic, w/gate, ca 1950, EX in orig box 38.00
Fence, twig style w/gate, Germany, lg, EX 145.00
Fence, wood, orig red & gr pnt, 4-pc, 16" sq, M in box 165.00
Fence, wood, red & gr pickets, red gate, 18" sq, EX 165.00
Garland, bl & silver beads, 96", EX 65.00
Garland, mc blown glass beads, 1900s, 132", EX 85.00
Garland, mc glass beads, 2 free-blown stars, 140", EX 95.00
Horse, fabric over wood, fur tail, glass eyes, 5¼ x4¾" 195.00
House, bsk, w/Santa & dog, Japan, 3¾" on 6½x4" base 65.00
House, plastic, mc, Japan, lg, +lg tree & bl fence, EX 45.00
Icicles, Double Glo, lead, EX in M box 25.00
Lamb, compo head & body, wood legs, wool covered, 5½" 150.00
Lamb, papier-mache, EX pnt, Italy, 2¾" 25.00
Light, Dmn Point, amethyst glass, 3¾" 42.50
Light, Dmn Point, gr glass, 3¾" 40.00
Light, Expanded Dmn, fiery opal glass, M 250.00

Lights, Detect-O-Lites, set of 8, EX................................65.00
Lights, Noma, Mazda, string of 15, EX 35.00
Lights, Noma, 15 flame-shaped lights on string, EX 35.00
Lights, Real Lite, Mazda, MIB 25.00
Lights, strawberries, strand of 20, EX 45.00
Madonna & Child, molded glass, 3", VG 75.00
Manger set, heavy cb, complete, 1930s, unassembled, NM...........65.00
Mug, Santa in brn robe cuts tree, ceramic, early, 2½" 88.00
Night light, Santa, plastic, hole in bk for bulb, 17" 15.00
Pin, Santa, Merry Christmas, ad on bk, 1¼", EX 55.00
Ram, compo w/metal horns, wool covering, 3½"................60.00
Reindeer, celluloid, glass eyes, Japan, 5¼", EX 20.00
Reindeer, lead, mother & fawn, Germany, 1⅝", 1½", pr.........75.00
Roly poly, monkey, gr & silver w/pk collar & mouth, 3"................50.00
Roly poly, Santa, celluloid, mc, Japan, 5", EX 110.00
Rudolf, tin, Japan, 6" 12.00
Santa, Belsnickel, brn coat w/gold, 5½"..........................465.00
Santa, Belsnickel, gr robe, w/feather tree, Germany, 9½" 800.00
Santa, Belsnickel, lav robe, rare, 7" 675.00
Santa, Belsnickel, red robe, 9½"....................................600.00
Santa, cb diecut, 8"..60.00
Santa, celluloid, bright colors, 6", EX in orig box 75.00
Santa, compo face & boots, felt clothes, Japan, '30s, 5", VG.........75.00
Santa, compo face/boots/hands, Occupied Japan, 5", EX 85.00
Santa, nodder, pnt compo & cb w/wood fr, 11", VG................195.00
Santa, plastic, red & wht, Irving, 4" 65.00
Santa, plastic, red & wht w/gr, lights up, lg, EX 65.00

Santa, plaster of Paris, electrified, 14" diameter, VG, $150.00.

Santa & reindeer, nodder, compo, clockwork, 40x18", EX 1,100.00
Sheep dog, bsk face, wooly body, Germany, 2¼"................78.00
Snowman, plastic, w/top hat & scarf, 3".........................10.00
Spinning wheel, Sebnitz, foil over wire fr, Dresden wheel 115.00
Stocking, tan suede & red plastic, Santa, 11" 20.00
Swan, celluloid, Germany, sm...20.00
Tree, cellophane, gr, 1950s, 55"......................................90.00
Tree, cellophane, wht, 1950s, 29", EX 45.00
Tree, feather; gr, candle clips, wood base, 22" 195.00
Tree, feather; gr, wht bsk base, red crepe flowers, 6¾", EX 150.00
Tree, feather; gr, 5-tier, 5 candle holders, Germany, 35" 365.00
Tree, feather; gr w/red berries, German base, 24", EX 285.00

Tree stand, CI, musical, windup, w/orig key 465.00
Tree stand, Echardt, musical, key wind, Pat 1878, EX 550.00
Tree top angel, wax, molded wings & tiara, wire spring base, 7" .325.00
Tree top star, Paramount, EX in box................................35.00
Wreath, pressed cb, 10½", VG 35.00
Wreath, red chenille, red & silver poinsettia, 10½" dia 35.00

Chrysanthemum Sprig, Blue

This is the blue opaque version of Northwood's popular pattern, Chrysanthemum Sprig. Though collectors often refer to it as 'blue custard,' in the strictest sense it is not. It was made at the turn of the century and is today very rare, as its values indicate.

Master fruit bowl, 10½" wide, $550.00.

Bowl, berry; sm 300.00
Butter dish 800.00
Compote, jelly 475.00
Condiment tray, rare, VG gold 750.00
Creamer 350.00
Cruet 775.00
Pitcher, water...900.00
Shakers, pr 450.00
Spooner..250.00
Sugar bowl, open 300.00
Sugar bowl, w/lid 425.00
Toothpick holder..450.00
Tumbler 200.00

Circus Collectibles

The 1890s — the Golden Age of the circus. Barnum and Bailey's parades transformed mundane city streets into an exotic never-never land inhabited by trumpeting elephants with jeweled gold headgear strutting by to the strains of the calliope that issued from a fine red- and gilt-painted wagon extravagantly decorated with carved wooden animals of every description. It was an exciting experience — is it any wonder that collectors today treasure the mementos of that golden era?

See also Posters.

Key:
B&B — Barnum & Bailey   RB — Ringling Bros.

Cvg, Medusa head, from circus wagon, worn rpt, 19"..................550.00

Magazine, RB B&B, Coles Bros, 1947, EX......................25.00
Menu, RB, color litho, 1907, 16-pg..........................95.00
Program, B&B color cover, 1911, NM 85.00
Program, RB, 1947, EX 17.50
Program, RB B&B, 1955, EX 25.00

Clarice Cliff

Between 1928 and 1935, in Burslem, England, as the director and part owner of Wilkinson and Newport Pottery Companies, Clarice Cliff and her 'paintresses' created a body of hand-painted pottery whose influence is felt to the present time.

The name for the oevre was Bizarre Ware, and the predominant sensibility, style, and appearance was Deco. Almost all pieces are signed and include the pattern names. There were over 160 patterns and more than 400 shapes, all of which are illustrated in *A Bizarre Affair — the Life and Work of Clarice Cliff*, published by Harry N. Abrams, Inc., written by Len Griffen and our advisors, Susan and Louis Meisel, whose address is listed in the Directory under New York.

Clarice Cliff died in 1972, shortly after the Victoria and Albert Museum showed her work in retrospect, and collectors (primarily in England) began seeking and admiring her work. In September of 1982, the Metropolitan Museum of Art in New York acquired and placed on view a selection of six pieces.

Biscuit Barrel, Geometric, 8" 1,400.00
Biscuit Barrel, Honolulu, 8" 1,700.00
Bowl, Autumn, 10" 1,200.00
Bowl, Umbrellas, 10"................................. 900.00
Charger, Latona Floral, 18" 15,000.00
Charger, Sunray, 18" 12,000.00
Charger, Umbrellas, 18" 9,000.00
Coffee set, Lugano, 3-pc.......................... 4,000.00
Conical sugar sifter, Blue Chintz 650.00
Conical sugar sifter, Crocus.......................300.00
Conical sugar sifter, Gibralter.................. 1,200.00
Honey pot, Stripes, Beehive........................300.00
Honey pot, Windbells, Beehive 500.00
Isis jug, Geometric, 10" 3,000.00
Isis jug, Inspiration, 10"......................... 2,400.00
Jam pot, Melon, cylindrical........................400.00
Jam pot, Trees & House, cylindrical 600.00
Lotus jug, Blue W, 12" 7,500.00
Lotus jug, Farmhouse, 12" 5,000.00

Geometric Lotus jug, ca 1929, 12", $4,500.00.

Plate, Blue Firs, rectangular, 9" 1,100.00
Plate, Citrus Delicia, 10" 300.00
Plate, Honolulu, octagonal, 8½" 800.00
Plate, Secrets, 10" 475.00
Plate, Windmill, 9" 6,800.00
Vase, Baluster, Gardenia, 9" 1,600.00
Vase, Cylinder, Geometric, 7" 1,000.00
Vase, Globe, Geometric, 4" 3,200.00
Vase, Triangle, Oranges, 8" 1,200.00

Cleminson

A hobby turned to enterprise, Cleminson is one of several California potteries whose clever hand-decorated wares are attracting the attention of today's collectors. The Cleminsons started their business at their El Monte home in 1941 and were so successful that eventually they expanded to a modern plant that employed more than 150 workers. They produced not only dinnerware and kitchen items such as cookie jars, canisters, and accessories, but novelty wall vases, small trays, plaques, etc., as well. Though nearly always marked, Cleminson wares are easy to spot as you become familiar with their distinctive glaze colors. Their grayed-down blue and green, berry red, and dusty pink say 'Cleminson' as clearly as their trademark. Unable to compete with foreign imports, the pottery closed in 1963.

Ash tray, boat shape, for 6 cigarettes, mk.........18.00
Bowl, Distlefink, 4½x12½x6½"........................25.00
Butter dish, lady figural 35.00
Canister, tree branches w/apples, red/gr on wht....22.00
Cookie jar, potbellied stove.......................75.00
Creamer & sugar bowl, Distlefink 22.00
Gravy boat, Distlefink, w/ladle....................22.00
Hair receiver, girl w/hands folded, 2-pc...........25.00

Pitcher, Gala Gray, 7", $22.50.

Plaque, Let's Pay Off the Mortgage 12.00
Plate, Deco fruit, red on ivory, wall hanging 14.00
Server, Distlefink.................................24.00
Shakers, Distlefink, lg, pr........................15.00
Sprinkler, Chinese boy 17.50
Tray, sandwich; Deco fruit, center hdl, mk.........25.00
Wall pocket, coffeepot.............................15.00
Wall pocket, mortgage bank.........................12.00

Clewell

Charles Walter Clewell was a metal worker who perfected the technique of plating an entire ceramic vessel with a thin layer of copper or bronze treated with an oxidizing agent to produce a natural deterioration of the surface. Through trial and error, he was able to control the degree of patina achieved. In the early stages, the metal darkened and, if allowed to develop further, formed a natural turquoise-blue or green corrosion. He worked alone in his small Akron, Ohio, studio from about 1906, buying undecorated pottery from several Ohio firms, among them Weller, Owens, and Cambridge. His work is usually marked. Clewell died in 1965, having never revealed his secret process to others.

Candlestick, dk metallic w/gr on base, #4115-2-6, 10", pr 475.00
Mug, orig patina, 4½"..150.00
Vase, bronze o/l w/free-form motif in patina, slim, 19" 1,500.00
Vase, bronze w/bl patina, long flared neck, mk, 13" 900.00
Vase, copper o/l w/cut-out church & trees, 7" 325.00
Vase, copper w/orange & gr patina, sm rim/wide base, 12x5" 900.00
Vase, EX patina, slim form, 4½"...225.00
Vase, grapes emb, flask form, no mk, 7¾x5" 200.00

Vase, green patina, 7", $350.00.

Clews

Brothers Ralph and James Clews were potters who operated in Cobridge in the Staffordshire district from 1817 to 1835. They are best known for their blue and white transfer-printed earthenwares, which included American Views, Moral Maxims, Picturesque Views, and English Views. A series called *Three Tours of Dr. Syntax* contained nearly eighty different scenes with each piece bearing a descriptive title. Two other popular series were *Don Quixote* with twenty prints and *Pictures of Sir David Wilkie* with twelve. Both printed and impressed-marks were used, often incorporating the pattern name as well as the pottery. See also Staffordshire, Historical. Our advisor for this category is Richard Marden; he is listed in the Directory under New Hampshire.

Cup & saucer, Christmas Eve, dk bl transfer, Wilkie series, EX...165.00
Cup plate, Dr Syntax Drawing After Nature, partial view, 4"......310.00
Plate, Christmas Eve, bl transfer, 9" 165.00

Plate, Don Quixote, Curious Impertinent..., dk bl, 5½" 165.00
Plate, Dr Syntax & the Bees, bl transfer, 10" 275.00
Plate, Dr Syntax Mistakes a Gent's House..., 10", NM 150.00
Plate, Dr Syntax Painting a Portrait, bl transfer, 10"...................275.00
Plate, Dr Syntax Presenting a Floral Offering, 6¾" 250.00
Plate, Dr Syntax Star Gazing, dk bl transfer, 9", NM 210.00
Plate, Dr Syntax Turned Nurse, bl transfer, 7" 200.00
Plate, Escape of the Mouse, dk bl transfer, 10" 165.00
Plate, Mambrino's Helmet, Don Quixote, bl transfer, 10" 175.00
Plate, Sancho, the Priest & Barber, dk bl transfer, 7⅝"..............145.00
Platter, Sancho Panza & the Duchess, ca 1820, 18½" 650.00
Soup plate, English Cathedral, dk bl transfer, 10", NM 100.00

Clifton

Clifton Art Pottery of Clifton, New Jersey, was organized ca 1903. Until 1911 when they turned to the production of wall and floor tile, they made artware of several varieties. The founders were Fred Tschirner and William A. Long. Long had developed the method for underglaze slip painting that had been used at the Lonhuda Pottery in Steubenville, Ohio, in the 1890s. Crystal Patina, the first artware made by the small company, utilized a fine white body and flowing, blended colors, the earliest a green crystalline. Indian Ware, copied from the pottery of the American Indians, was decorated in black geometric designs on red clay. Robin's Egg Blue, pale blue on the white body, and Tirrube, a slip-decorated matt ware, were also produced.

Humidor, Indian Ware, geometrics, blk on terra cotta bsk.............95.00
Teapot, Crystal Patina, 5½" 100.00
Teapot, imp motif on yel lustre, gold trim, 7½" 55.00

Indian Ware vase with handle, signed/#246, 4" x 7½", $175.00.

Vase, Indian Ware, blk/wht on red, Middle MS Valley, 13x10"..350.00
Vase, Indian Ware, geometrics, pnt/cvd, Homolobi, squat, 8".....325.00
Vase, Indian Ware, geometrics, red/blk, cylinder neck, 8" 325.00
Vase, Indian Ware, scalloped medial band, red/tan/blk, 3½" 50.00
Vase, Tirrube, stork & foliage, #257, 12x7"................................325.00

Clocks

In the early days of our country's history, clock makers were influenced by styles imported from Europe and Germany. They copied their cabinets and re-constructed their movements. But needed materials were in short supply; modifications had to be made. Of necessity was born mainspring motive power and spring clocks. Wooden movements were made on a mass-production basis as early as 1808. Before the middle of the century, metal movements had been developed.

Today's collectors prefer clocks from the eighteenth and nineteenth centuries with pendulum-regulated movements. Bracket clocks made during this period utilized the shorter pendulum improvised in 1658 by Fromentiel, a prominent English clock maker. These smaller square-face clocks usually were made with a dome top fitted with a handle or a decorative finial. The case was usually walnut or ebony and was sometimes decorated with pierced brass mountings. Brackets were often mounted on the wall to accommodate the clock, hence the name. The banjo clock was patented in 1802 by Simon Willard. It derived its descriptive name from its banjo-like shape. A similar but more elaborate style was called the lyre clock.

Prices have been stable for several years. Unless noted otherwise, values are given for clocks in mint, original condition. Clocks that have been altered, damaged, or have had parts replaced are worth considerably less.

Our advisor is Bruce A. Austin; he is listed in the Directory under New York. Our novelty clock advisors are DLK Nostalgia and Collectibles; their address is given under Pennsylvania.

Key:
br — brass	T&S — time and strike
dl — dial	wt — weight
esc — escapement	vrn — veneer
mvt — movement	2nds — seconds
pnd — pendulum	8d — 8-day
reg — regulator	30h — 30-hour
rswd — rosewood	

Banjo Clocks

H Tifft, mahog/vnr, 2 blk & gold tablets, orig wt, 34", EX **600.00**
Howard-Davis, grpt poplar, 2 blk & gold tablets, 32", EX **800.00**
Little-Eastman, mahog, br mts/bezel/eagle, 2 rvpt, 32" **500.00**
New Haven, mahog, brass #s/pnt dl, ¼-hr strike, rpl, 26" **150.00**
New Haven, 2 rvpt, 8d T&S, ½-hr strike, 36", EX **125.00**
New Haven, 2 rvpt (Mt Vernon), 3-train mvt/chimes, 25", NM.**250.00**
R Whiting, presentation, gilt, 8d T/step train/wt, 41", EX **1,500.00**
Sessions, gr-pnt case, rvpt, 8d lever time mvt, 1900, 22" **40.00**
Sessions, Revere, eng dl, 2 fine rvpt, hr strike, 32", EX **120.00**
Unknown, gold stenciled fr, 2 rvpt, iron dl, eagle, 35", EX...... **2,700.00**
Unknown, walnut, 2 blk/gold tablets, zinc dl, 8d, 29", EX **500.00**
Waltham, mahog w/cvd bracket, 2 fine rvpt, jewel lever, 21" **550.00**
Waltham, presentation, mahog, 2 rvpt (G WA/etc), 41", EX . **1,050.00**

Beehive Clocks

Brewster-Ingraham, rswd vnr, 8d T&S/pnd, 19", EX **280.00**
C Boardman, rswd vnr, etch tablet, pnt zinc dl, fusee, 19" **500.00**
Jerome, rswd vnr, rvpt, 8d T&S/pnd, 19", EX **210.00**
Seth Thomas, mahog, porc dl, 8d lever mvt, 1920, 5½" **40.00**
Smith & Bro, mahog vnr, M rvpt, pnt wood dl, rstr, 21" **1,100.00**
Terry-Andrews, pnt metal dl, bl lyre 8d T&S, rstr, 19" **285.00**
Terry-Andrews, rswd vnr, mirror, paper label, lyre mvt, 19" **300.00**

Calendar Clocks

Ithaca, #10 Farmer's, walnut, paper/zinc dl, 8d T, 26", EX **600.00**
Ithaca, #3½ Parlor, walnut w/pressed compo decor, 21" **2,250.00**
Ithaca, #9 shelf cottage, walnut, Welch 8d T&S, rstr, 22" **400.00**
Ithaca, Farmer, walnut, Welch 15d dbl wind T mvt, 21", EX **450.00**
Ithaca, Kildare, hanging, Welch mvt, repro case, 33", EX **850.00**
Ithaca, shelf steeple, walnut, trn finial, Pat 1866, 24", EX **500.00**

Seth Thomas, Office #3, rswd vnr, pnt zinc dl, 33", EX **500.00**
Waterbury, Oswego, pressed oak, Pat 1889, 29", EX **350.00**
Welch, Italian Type, rswd vnr, BB Lewis calendar, 20", EX **375.00**
Welch Spring, Wagner model, walnut, 2-dial, rfn/rpl, 31" **500.00**

Carriage Clocks

France, br, free-standing columns, porc dl, alarm, 1875, 7" **1,300.00**
France, oval, br, bevel glass, porc dl, jewel lever mvt, 7" **650.00**
France, serpentine br w/bevel glass, Tiffany mk porc dl, 6" **200.00**
H&H France, br w/wht enamel face, key, 4⅜" **375.00**
Waterbury, br w/bevel glass, porc dl, 30h, 1910, hdl up: 3" **60.00**
Waterbury, Midge, gun-metal color, bevel glass, porc dl, 3½" **60.00**

China Clocks

Ansonia, gr case w/florals mk Rainbow, 8d T&S, 11", EX **235.00**
Connecticut, bl w/florals, paper dl, 8d T&S, 1880, 13", EX **235.00**
Forestville Hdw, shelf, ftd scrolled case/zinc dl, 11", VG **150.00**
France, elaborate, man/lady/horse atop, 8d T&S, 26", EX **1,600.00**
France, man/lady atop, 8d T&S, Parie dl, 1880, 17", EX **385.00**
Germany, porc dl, wag-on-wall, 30h T&S/alarm, 1875, 10" **175.00**
Royal Bonn, bl Rococo case w/florals, Ansonia mvt, 13", NM **375.00**
Royal Bonn, La Orne, florals, Ansonia mvt, 8d T&S, 11", NM ..**300.00**
Winnebago, Rococo case w/gilt & florals, Ansonia mvt, 12" **175.00**

Cottage Clocks

Daniel Pratt & Son, mahog vnr, decal tablet, 11", EX **75.00**
H Sperry, pnt case, EX rvpt, sgn zinc dl, 30h/pnd, 12" **250.00**
Henry Sperry, grpt, rvpt, sgn zinc dl, 30h, rpl pnd, 12" **300.00**
Ingraham, rswd vnr, rvpt, paper-on-zinc dl, 8d T&S, 13" **160.00**
Jerome, mahog, blk/gold rvpt, 30h T/alarm, zinc dl, 9", EX **150.00**
SB Terry, zinc dl, 30h Time Ladder mvt/alarm/pnd bob, 11" **650.00**
Seth Thomas, rswd, mirror, pnt zinc dl, 30h T/alarm, 9", EX **175.00**

Crystal Regulators

Ansonia, br, bevel glass, porc dl, 8d T&S/mercury pnd, 11" **260.00**
France, br, bevel glass, porc dl w/florals, mercury pnd, 11" **325.00**
France, oval br w/bevel glass, floral porc dl, 11", EX **300.00**
Seth Thomas, elliptic front, br w/Corinthian capitals, 9" **350.00**
Seth Thomas, fancy cast br w/bevel glass, 1900, 14", EX **375.00**
Seth Thomas (Shreve-Crump-Low), br/bevel glass, porc dl, 10" .**325.00**
Waterbury, gr onyx top/base, porc dl, 8d T&S, 11", NM **385.00**
Wm Gilbert, br, bevel glass, porc dl, visible esc, 10", EX **120.00**
Wm Gilbert, br/br-plated, bevel glass, porc dl, pnd, 10" **150.00**

Kitchen Clocks

Ansonia, Hampden, pressed/cvd oak, rpl glass, 22", EX **125.00**
Ansonia, Parisian, walnut dome top, trn finial/drops, 24" **300.00**
Ansonia, Triumph, br, 8d T&S, 25" **350.00**
Ansonia, walnut, silvered glass, zinc dl, pnd, 18", EX **170.00**
F Kroeber, walnut, paper-on-zinc dl, 8d T&S/alarm, 18", NM **200.00**
F Kroeber, walnut, pnt tablet, pnd w/regulating gauge, 18" **250.00**
Gilbert, Calypso, spider/web on tablet, alarm missing, 20" **200.00**
Waterbury, Belmont, pressed oak, cathedral gong, 22", NM **150.00**
Wm Gilbert, Regal #78, cvd oak, paper dl, 8d T&S, 21" **150.00**

Mantel Clocks

Ansonia, Vivian, cvd oak, porc dl, 8d T&S, rfn, 17" **180.00**
Austria, blk w/marble columns, rvpt over porc dl, 20", EX **300.00**

Austria, blk w/ormolu, porc dl, 3-train mvt/calendar, 16", EX **350.00**
Austria, blk w/ormolu, porc dl, 30h/calendar, 16", VG **350.00**
Europe, blk/ormolu, eng br/gilt dl, musical mvt/pnd, 18" **1,400.00**

French Neoclassical bronze mantel clock, late 19th century, 21", $1,200.00.

France, cast br, porc dl, 8d T&S/thread suspension, 16", EX **450.00**
France, marble, appl florals, cast br dl, 30h fusee, 16" **275.00**
France, porc w/Oriental motif, br dl, 8d T&S, 16", EX **270.00**
France, quality mahog, porc dl mk Tiffany, 8d T&S/pnd, 11" **170.00**
France, vnr w/inlay, eng dl, 8d T&S/pnd, 1830, 8½" **450.00**
Ingraham, maple w/blk finials, paper-on-zinc dl, 19", EX.............**275.00**
Junghans, mahog tambour, silvered dl w/appl #s, chimes, 9"........**100.00**
Kroeber, walnut Victorian, fancy glass pnd, porc dl, 20" **225.00**
New Haven, mahog, silvered br dl, chimes, 1900, 14", EX **125.00**
Raingo Feres, marble, porc dl, 8d T&S/pnd, minor loss, 9" **225.00**
Seth Thomas, beehive, inlaid mahog, porc dl, T&S/pnd, 12" **110.00**
US, mahog, porc dl, 8d T&S/pnd, 1920, 9½", EX **60.00**

Novelty Clocks

Art Nouveau, digital, NM **125.00**
Barbie, 3", NM..**100.00**
Batman Talking Clock, NM..**125.00**
Bird Song, bird on top, alarm **30.00**
Blessing, duck w/rocking butterfly, sm letters **40.00**
Blessing, paddle boat, paddle turns, late 1960s **45.00**
Bradley-Hubbard, Geo Washington figure, pnt CI, 17" **1,200.00**
Bugs Bunny, talking figural, M **125.00**
Chicken pecks at ground, ceramic, 1970s....................................**140.00**
Deer, eye moves, ceramic...**45.00**
Diamond, dragon, head rocks, Shanghai, China............................**45.00**
GE, dog w/ball on nose, ball rolls to top of nose **160.00**
German, blksmith elf, arm w/hammer lifts, 1920s **300.00**
German, windmill, beveled glass, pre-WWII, 1920s **280.00**
God Bless America, animated flags, 1940s.................................**100.00**
Indian head, Iroquois Beer & Ale **125.00**
Ingraham, Roy Rogers **100.00**
Ives, Blk man w/banjo (dial), rolling eyes, pnt CI, 16" **1,200.00**
Jerger, men's arms strike alarm bells, 1960s.................................**45.00**
Keebler, bulldog w/kitten, EX **50.00**
Keebler, Martha & Geo Washington, kissing bird **100.00**
Keebler, quail cuckoo, 8-day mvt, 8x7½" **250.00**
Lux, Blk man organ grinder, VG...**150.00**
Lux, clown w/seals, animated, NM **260.00**
Lux, cottage shape, VG **40.00**
Lux, dog w/wagging tongue **87.50**

Lux, Lindbergh, airplane shape, NM.......................................**55.00**
Lux, mechanical bell, digital, G **35.00**
Lux, organ grinder w/monkey, arm turns, 1930s **200.00**
Lux, showboat, paddle turns, 1950 ....**90.00**
Lux, train, steam engine, 1970 ....**50.00**
Lux, Village Mill, figural, alarm, 1920, EX................................**75.00**
Master Crafters, church figural, animated/electric, 12", EX **20.00**
Mouse & bird, bird pecks, ceramic **45.00**
Musical alarm w/ballerina, animated, NM................................**90.00**
Powder box, musical, metal, WWI..**150.00**
Raggedy Ann, talking clock **20.00**
Roosevelt, Spirit of USA, w/Johnson & Perkins, 10"...................**135.00**
Smith, boxing dog & bear, arms move, 1960s **105.00**
Smith, rooster pecks ground, sq case, late 1950s.........................**210.00**
Smurf, talking figural, alarm, NM **25.00**
Tiempo, horse race, horse rocks, Brazil......................................**60.00**
Tiempo, police, police car rocks, Brazil.....................................**60.00**
UEC, Bartender, arm moves, 1933...**125.00**
UEC, Roosevelt Band Leader, 1934 ....**90.00**
UEC, Spirit of 76 Drummer **100.00**
Windmill, animated, alarm, 5" sq celluloid face **30.00**
Woodcutter, cuckoo, people saw & chop wood, music box, M **125.00**

Ogee Clocks

Atkins-Porter, mahog vnr, EX rvpt, pnt zinc dl, 26", EX **190.00**
Elisha Manross, mahog/rswd vnr, EX rvpt, pnt zinc dl, 26" **175.00**
Forestville Mfg, rswd/mahog vnr, M rvpt w/bldg, rfn, 29" **300.00**
Geo Marsh, mahog/rswd vnd, rvpt US Hotel Saratoga, 25", NM .**250.00**
H Welton, mahog/rswd vnr, rvpt bldg, pnt wood dl, 26", VG **175.00**
Levi Smith, mahog vnr, compass wheel rvpt, wood dl, 25", EX ...**225.00**
Wm Johnson, mahog vnr w/mirror, wood dl, iron wts, 26", EX ...**200.00**
Wm Johnson, mahog X-banding/bird's eye maple vnr, 28", VG .**200.00**

Pillar and Scroll Clocks

E Terry & Sons, mahog, trn columns, scroll crest, 32", VG **750.00**
Eli & Samuel Terry, mahog, 3 br finials, 1830, rstr, 32" **1,000.00**
Eli Terry, 3 br finials, EX orig rvpt, 1830, rpr, 32" **1,400.00**

Elmer Stennes custom mahogany cased pillar and scroll clock, brass time and strike movement, 20th century, 30½", $900.00.

France, rswd vnr w/EX inlay, br mts, rope columns, 18", EX........**500.00**
Mark Leavenworth, mahog bonnet, VG rvpt, 30h, 30", EX ... **1,000.00**
Seth Thomas, mahog, rvpt, wood dl, 30h T&S/pnd, rstr, 31" . **1,200.00**
Seth Thomas, mahog vnr, rvpt, 8d T&S, wood dl, 29", VG........**500.00**
Unknown, shelf, mahog, trn ft/finials, 8d T&S, 48", EX......... **4,250.00**

Regulators

Chelsea, #2, walnut, pnt zinc dl w/2nds, 8d/pnd, 38", EX........ **1,000.00**
E Howard, #41, walnut, pnt iron dl, high quality, 42", EX **1,500.00**
E Howard, #70, oak, sgn zinc dl, pnt glass, wt/pnd, 32"...............**900.00**
Gustave Becker, fruitwood, Ionic columns/EX cvgs, 52", NM . **1,100.00**
New Haven, #2, oak, paper-on-zinc dl, 8d T/pnd, 35", EX..........**575.00**
New Haven, Bank, long drop, pressed case, rfn, 36".....................**385.00**
New Haven, Bank, long drop, pressed trim, 34", EX.....................**250.00**
New Haven, long drop, walnut, pnt dl, spring mvt, 33", EX **325.00**
Sessions, poplar, orig tablets, tin dl, calendar, 32", EX.................**200.00**
Seth Thomas, #2, EX oak, pnt zinc dl w/2nds, br pnd, 36" **700.00**
Seth Thomas, #2, oak, zinc dl w/2nds, 8d/br weight/pnd, 37"......**700.00**
Seth Thomas, #3, oak, pnt zinc dl w/2nds, 42", EX **800.00**
Seth Thomas, golden oak, zinc dl, 8d T/pnd/brass wt, 36"....... **1,000.00**
Silas Terry, mahog vnr, zinc dl, solid plate 8d, 33", EX................**550.00**
Unknown, oak, 2 decor tablets, paper dl, 8d T/pnd, 38", EX **150.00**
Vienna, lg cvd leaves, porc dl/pnd, 8d T&S, 1900, 29", EX **475.00**
Vienna, walnut vnr/blk trim, porc dl, pnd/br weights, 50".........**600.00**
Vienna, walnut vnr/blk trim, trn finials/columns, 33", EX **200.00**
Waterbury, cvd oak, pnt zinc dl, 8d T/pnd, 1890, 31", EX...........**260.00**
Waterbury, oak, long drop, Regulator tablet, pnd, 32", EX **375.00**
Wm Gilbert, Observatory, pressed oak, zinc dl, 37", EX **225.00**

Schoolhouse Clocks

Ansonia, drop octagon 'B,' oak, paper-on-zinc dl, rfn, 26"...........**275.00**
Ansonia, mahog, octagonal, short sq drop, br mvt, 24", EX **175.00**
Ansonia, octagon-top ash, long drop, 8d br mvt, 1880, 32" **350.00**
E Ingraham, Dew Drop, rnd fr w/short drop, spring mvt, 24".......**185.00**
Sessions, octagon-top pressed oak, short drop/calendar, 27" **285.00**
Seth Thomas, octagon-top oak, extra long drop, 1880, 54"..... **1,400.00**
Seth Thomas, octagonal w/short drop, rpl dl, 21" **225.00**

Shelf Clocks

Am Clock, iron front, blk w/gilt, paper dl, 8d T&S, rpl, 19" **175.00**
Ansonia, iron front, gold/MOP, brass dial, lyre mvt, 14", EX **300.00**
Barnes-Bartholomew, 3-deck mahog vnr, rpl eagle, 41", EX........**300.00**
Birge-Fuller, figured mahog & vnr sleigh front, 2 rvpt, 33"..........**400.00**
Boardman-Wells, mahog & vnr, stencils, lithograph, 32", EX.....**125.00**
Brewster Mfg, blk/MOP/gilt, EX zinc dl, 8d T&S/pnd, 17", EX...**160.00**
Bristol Brass-Clock, grpt CI, 2 pnt scenes, 8d T&S/pnd, 20".......**220.00**
C Boardman, stenciled columns/splat, 30h T&S/pnd, 35", EX ...**160.00**
Europe, ornately cvd/gilded, br dl, 8d T&S/pnd, 1900, 27" **300.00**
Ingraham, rnd top, rswd vnr/gilt columns, zinc dl, rpl, 16" **175.00**
Ingraham, Venetian, rswd vnr/maple figure-8 door, 18", NM **150.00**
JC Brn, blk w/gilt & MOP, 2 rvpt, 8d T&S/pnd, rpl mvt, 18" **225.00**
Jerome, blk w/MOP & gilt, zinc dl, 30h fusee/pnd, 13", EX **150.00**
Jerome, mahog vnr w/grpt & gilt columns, iron wts, 25", EX.......**150.00**
Jerome & Co, walnut vnr, 2 rvpt, 8d T&S/pnd, EX pnt, 16".......**175.00**
Jerome & Darrow, mahog w/eagle, EX dial/rvpt, rstr/rpl, 27".......**325.00**
Jerome-Darrow, mahog vnr, cvd ft, wood dl, pnd, 33", EX...........**250.00**
Lucius Bradley, mahog, rvpt, 2nds, 8d T&S/pnd/wts, 34", EX. **2,400.00**
Seth Thomas, burl walnut vnr, zinc dl, 8d T&S/pnd, 16", EX......**325.00**
Seth Thomas, mahog, stenciled columns, eagle splat, 34", EX.....**350.00**
Seth Thomas, sleigh front, rswd vnr w/gilt & grpt, 33", EX.........**275.00**
Silas Hoadley, mahog vnr, stencil columns, mirror, 30", EX.........**500.00**

Spencer Hotchkiss shelf clock, mahogany veneer, 8-day time and strike weight-driven Salem Bridge movement with iron weights and pendulum, veneer repair, restored, 34", $475.00.

Smith-Goodrich, rswd vnr, rvpt, 30h T&S fusee/pnd, 16", EX....**300.00**
Unknown, iron front, gold/MOP, pnt dl, 8d T&S/pnd, 21", EX..**250.00**
Unknown, papier-mache w/gilt & MOP, 8d T&S/pnd, 21", EX..**260.00**
Waterbury, mahog vnr/gilt columns, 30h/alarm/pnd, rstr, 17".....**250.00**
Wm Johnson, rippled rswd vnr, rvpt, solid wheels, 16", EX **475.00**

Ship Clocks

Chelsea, br, eng br dl w/2nds, jewel lever T, 20, 13" **500.00**
Chelsea, cast br on mahog stand, eng dl sgn Wise, 8", EX **550.00**
Seth Thomas, NP br, br dial, 2nds, 30h, bell strike, 7", EX..........**150.00**
Seth Thomas, outside bell, br case/dl, 2nds, 30h, 11", EX **350.00**
Waterbury, heavy cast bronzed br, jewel lever mvt, '20, 9" **300.00**

Skeleton Clocks

England, Gothic plates, eng br dl, fusee, br ball ft, 10" **1,200.00**
England, Gothic plates, 2 gilt lions, br dl, fusee/pnd, 15".............**650.00**
England, scroll plates, pnt dl, fusee/pnd, 1860, 16", EX...............**700.00**
England, scroll plates/trn pillars, fusee, 1860, 14", EX **1,100.00**
France, for exhibit in Hyde Park, 1851, 8d, porc dl, 11" **325.00**
France, 8d T/bell alarm in base on pull cord, 1850, 11", EX **450.00**
Terry, Parlour model, iron base w/orig decor, rpl dome, 9" **550.00**

Statue Clocks

Ansonia, Crystal Palace, hunter/fisherman, 17", EX **350.00**
Ansonia, Olympia atop ornate ftd base, lever esc, 25", NM **900.00**
Ansonia, siren figure, visible esc, porc dl, 1906 ....**450.00**
Ansonia, Wm Shakespeare, seated, porc dl, blk base, 18" L **300.00**
France, angel sits atop blk marble base w/porc dl, 22", EX...........**250.00**
France, wht metal lady holds clock aloft, for garden, 60" **2,100.00**
Germany, Lady Diana swinger, 30h pnd mvt, porc dl, 14", EX....**325.00**
Japan, wht metal elephant, 30h pnd mvt, pnt dl, 1970, 12"........**100.00**
Kroeber Saxonia, CI gladiator, gargoyle sides, 20" **450.00**
New Haven, cherubs flank porc dl, lever esc, 1880, 8" **125.00**
New Haven, semi-nude supports scrollwork w/silvered dl, 22" **150.00**
USA, wht metal w/patriots & symbols, 1890, rpt, 11"...................**75.00**

Steeple Clocks

Ansonia, rswd vnr, rvpt eagle, paper-on-zinc dl, 20", EX.............**150.00**

Brewster-Ingraham, mahog vnr, cut glass, 8d T&S/pnd, 20" **350.00**
C Boardman, figured mahog, frosted tablet, T&S fusee, 20" **300.00**
EN Welch, rswd vnr, rvpt, zinc dl, 30h T&S/alarm, 20", VG **125.00**
Gilbert, rswd w/frosted glass, 30h, rpl, 20", EX **125.00**
JC Brn, rswd vnr, rvpt eagle, 8d T&S/pnd, 20", EX **325.00**
Jerome, rswd vnr, rvpt, zinc dl, T&S/alarm/pnd, 16", EX............**250.00**
Jerome & Co, rswd vnr, rvpt, 30h T&S/pnd, rpt dl, 16" **125.00**
Pomeroy-Parket, mahog vnr, orig tablet, zinc dl, 20", EX **250.00**
Sessions, mahog, pnt dl, stenciled glass, pnd, 192016" **125.00**

Tall Case Clocks

Bigelow Kennard, mahog, moon phase/2nds, 101", EX **3,000.00**
Europe, mahog scroll top, iron dl, br mvt/iron wts, 83", EX.........**900.00**
Geo Tyler, oak, eng brass dl, 2nds/calendar apertures, 88" **1,150.00**
Gideon Roberts, slim pine case, cut-out base, wood mvt, 84" . **2,250.00**
Herschedes, mahog w/cvd crest & columns, 1930s, 98", NM.. **3,100.00**
R Whiting, cherry, broken-arch pediment, 1820s, 91", NM.... **2,400.00**
Silas Hoadley, arched cornice, glass door, 1820, rstr, 81" **1,200.00**
Unknown, inlaid oak bonnet top, trn columns, 1825, 83", EX.. **1,300.00**
Wm Cuff, cvd oak, eng br dl, 3-train musical mvt, 93", EX **1,000.00**

Wag-on-the-Wall Clocks

European, pnt iron dl on shaped bkplate, ca 1700, 11", EX **1,450.00**
Gray-Vulliamy, arch-top eng br, alarm indicator, 8", EX......... **1,500.00**
T Lovejoy, trn bezel, pk porc dl, 30h T/alarm, wt drive, 11".......**150.00**

Wall Clocks

Ansonia, oak octagon, paper dl w/2nds, rfn, 1880, 11" **200.00**
Ansonia, Queen Elizabeth, mahog, paper dl, 8d T&S, 37" **350.00**
E Howard, #70, oak, red/gold rpt rvpt, pnt zinc dl, 8d, 31" **1,100.00**
E Ingraham, Ionic, poplar, rpt blk/gold tablet, 8d, 22" **450.00**
E Ingraham, octagonal oak, paper dl, 8d T, label, 15", EX **125.00**
France, ebonized w/pnt panel around glass dl, 1880, 15" sq **175.00**
Germany, porc, 30h T, wood plates/br gears, 1880, 6", EX **325.00**
Junghans, softwood, silvered br dl, 8s T&S, '26, 18", EX **125.00**
Mignon, Germany; softwood, 3-pc bevel glass door, '20, 31".......**150.00**
Seth Thomas, oak, pediment top/cvd bracket, 2nds, 40", EX **700.00**
Seth Thomas, Queen Anne, walnut, fine trn, 8d T, 36", NM **500.00**
Waltham, rnd mahog bezel, dl mk Tiffany, lever esc, '20, 13" **275.00**

Cloisonne

Cloisonne is a method of decorating metal with enameling. Fine metal wires are soldered onto the metal body following the lines of a predetermined design. The resulting channels are filled in with enamels of various colors, and the item is fired. The final step is a smoothing process that assures even exposure of the wire pattern. The art is predominately Oriental and has been practiced continuously, except during war years, since the sixteenth century. The most excellent examples date from 1865 until the turn of the century. The early twentieth century export variety is usually lightweight and the workmanship inferior. Modern wares are of good quality and are produced in Taiwan as well as China.

Several variations of the basic art include plique-a-jour, achieved by removing the metal body after firing, leaving only the transparent enamel work; foil cloisonne, using transparent or semi-translucent enameling over a layer of embossed silver covering the metal body of the vessel; wireless cloisonne, made by removing the wire dividers prior to firing; and cloisonne executed on ceramic, wood, or lacquer rather than metal.

Our advisor for this category is Donald Penrose; he is listed in the Directory under Ohio.

Apple box, clouds/peonies on bl, 3½x4" **80.00**
Bottle, peaches on yel fretwork, globular, mk, 10½", pr **650.00**
Bowl, cloud scrolls/peonies on wht, short ped ft, 3½x10" **250.00**
Censer, floral, 3-leg, gourd finial, China, 1800s, 14½" **1,295.00**
Charger, crane w/fish on speckled blk, 1880s, 12" **275.00**
Charger, flowers/crane on dk bl, 1880s, 18", NM **325.00**
Chocolate pot, phoenix/butterflies on blk floral, 1910, 7" **180.00**
Crane, on rocks/branch in beak, dragons on dk bl, 26", pr **2,600.00**
Incense burner, arabesques on yel, lion head ft, 13", EX **500.00**
Incense pot, peonies on bl, cauldron type, 4" **45.00**
Jar, butterflies/rosettes on blk simulated aventurine, 3" **120.00**
Jar, floral medallions on blk, long concave neck, 1910, 7" **200.00**
Pencil pot, mc floral on bl, cylindrical, 6½", pr **130.00**
Plate, peony tree/butterfly on turq, floral border, 12", NM **200.00**
Teapot, butterflies/flowers on blk, squat form, 1910, 5" **120.00**
Teapot, butterfly panels in red/gr on melon form, 1910, 6"..........**150.00**
Teapot, floral on bl, 3½x5" **80.00**
Teapot, 2 pr Buddhist lions on bl, peach finial, 1800s, 13" **900.00**
Vase, alternate panels of birds & lotus on yel, 1930s, 11" **75.00**
Vase, birds/mums, silver cloisons on brn mottle, 1880s, 6" **300.00**
Vase, butterflies/flowers on blk aventurine, long neck, 6"............**160.00**
Vase, butterflies/flowers on dk bl, shouldered, 1910, 14" **250.00**
Vase, dragon/phoenix on brn, buff shoulder/neck bands, 7" **100.00**
Vase, floral/birds on bl, hu-form, ring hdls, 1800s, 14" **275.00**
Vase, mc panels of dragons & jewels, Japan, 10" **650.00**

Vase, mythical beasts and floral bands, 15", $500.00; Vase, lobed form with peonies and scrolling tendrils amidst red Shou characters on white, 15", $550.00.

Vase, phoenix/floral upright panels, ribbed, 1900, 12", pr **600.00**
Vase, symbols on turq, trumpet form w/4-part knob, 13", pr........**600.00**
Vase on stand, marine animals, 1850s, 18", EX **150.00**

Clothing and Accessories

'Second-hand'or 'vintage'? It's all a matter of opinion. But these days it's considered good taste — downright fashionable — to wear clothing from Victorian to styles from the sixties. Jackets with padded shoulders from the thirties are 'trendy.' Jewelry from the Art Deco era is just as beautiful and often less expensive than current copies. Victorian blouses on models with Gibson Girl hair styles are pictured in leading fashion magazines — but why settle for new when the genuine article can be bought for the same price with exquisite lace that no reproduction can rival! When once the 'style' of the day was so strictly obeyed, today — in New York and the larger cities of California and Texas, in particular — nothing well-designed and constructed is 'out of style.' And though in recent days costumes by such designers as Chanel, Fortuny, and Lanvin may bring four-figure prices at fine auction houses, as a general rule, prices are very modest considering the wonderful fabrics one may find in vintage clothing, many of which are no longer available. Cashmere coats, elegant furs, and sequined or beaded gowns can be bought for only a small fraction of today's retail. Though some are strictly collectors, many do buy their clothes to wear. Care must be given to alterations, and gentle cleaning methods employed to avoid damage that would detract from their value.

Our advisor for this category is Ruth Osborne; she is listed in the Directory under Ohio.

Key:
cap/s — cap sleeves	n/s — no sleeves
embr — embroidery	plt — pleated
hs — handsewn	s/p — shoulder pads
lgth — length	s/s — shortsleeves
l/s — long sleeves	/s — sleeves
ms — machine sewn	

Lace dress and jacket ensemble, Irish lace trim, 1910, $700.00; Battenburg lace coat with crocheted buttons, 1910, $500.00; White lawn summer dress, Irish lace insertions, 1910, $265.00.

Blouse, blk silk, tucked lace, l/s, 1900s, EX 35.00
Blouse, middy; wht poplin, 1910s, EX...24.00
Blouse, print on satin, s/s, cowel neck, 1950s............................14.00
Blouse, sheer nylon, lace yoke, glass buttons, l/s, '40s............15.00
Blouse, silk crepe, lace collar, l/s, 1930s, EX.............................35.00
Blouse, wht dmn embr voile, n/s, V neck, peplum, 1930s.............20.00
Bonnet, child's, gr chiffon w/ruffles, EX...................................35.00
Bonnet, child's, leghorn w/braided trim, 1830s, EX.....................60.00
Bonnet, ecru, ruffled/tatted brim, neck cover, M.......................24.00
Bonnet, leghorn w/braided trim, 1830s, EX 85.00
Bonnet, polka dots on navy, ruffled brim, neck cover, NM............15.00
Bustle, 2-tiered wire mesh, adjustable, EX..............................100.00
Camisole, wht linen, drawstring neck, button sides, EX................35.00
Cape, opera; red velvet, wht satin lined, NM............................125.00
Coat, blk plush, fishtail bk, 1910s, EX 85.00
Coat, cutaway, blk velvet, Victorian, EX.................................250.00
Coat, evening; velvet, magenta, l/s, 1920s, EX...........................75.00
Coat, red cashmere w/silver fox collar, full lgth, 1940s.............60.00
Coat, vinyl w/simulated gray Persian collar & cuffs, EX.............15.00
Corset, bust flattener, pk, embr, bl/pk trim, ca 1890-1910, M 100.00
Dress, blk satin, padded shoulders, swag at waist, '40s, EX.............80.00
Dress, calico, prairie style, 1900s, EX 75.00
Dress, child's, red calico, Cluny lace insert, tucked hem, EX 25.00
Dress, child's, w/pinafore & cap, Amish style, EX 40.00
Dress, child's, wht cotton, rickrack/rosette, s/s, 1920s 27.50
Dress, christening; wht cotton, rows of tucks, handmade, NM 75.00
Dress, ecru satin, shirring/ruffles, bustle bk, 2-pc, 1890s..........250.00
Dress, evening; blk lace, deep V neck, full skirt, '30s, EX............90.00
Dress, evening; lace top/crepe skirt, V neck, l/s, '40s, M 45.00
Dress, evening; organza w/rhinestones, long skirt, 1940s............50.00
Dress, evening; silver embr/beads on linen, n/s, long, 1920s........250.00
Dress, lace inserts on satin, l/s, long, Victorian, EX.................350.00
Dress, rayon floral, sweetheart neck, s/s, 1940s, EX 32.00
Dress, silk chiffon, cording, drop waist, s/s, 1920s........................85.00
Dress, wht batiste w/lace, high neck, full skirt, l/s, 1900 ....250.00
Fur bolero, leopard, full sleeves, 18", EX.................................250.00
Fur coat, blk seal, puffed shoulders, ¾-lgth, 1940s, EX 75.00

Fur coat, lynx paw, full length, sm, EX 400.00
Fur coat, monkey, 1930s, 36" L, EX 300.00
Fur coat, mouton, turn-bk cuffs, shirred bk, dbl-breasted, EX 50.00
Fur coat, Persian lamb, fur collar, full length, EX 150.00
Fur hat, autumn haze mink, designer label, EX..............................35.00
Fur hat, blk Alaskan seal, cloche style, silk lined, EX....................45.00
Fur jacket, ocelot, EX...295.00
Fur muff, blk seal, lined, 1920s, 10x12", EX...................................32.00
Fur muff, mink, many hanging tails, 1940s, EX.............................120.00
Gloves, blk Chantilly lace, elbow lgth, pr...................................12.00
Gloves, wht kid, buttons at wrist, full lgth, 1950s, EX....................18.00
Gown, wedding; ivory lace net, l/s & train, 1950s, EX.....................75.00
Gown, wedding; ivory satin w/lace, l/s, full skirt, '50s, EX.............65.00
Hat, blk silk, ruching, bows/ribbons/feathers, lg brim, EX.............65.00
Hat, lilac plush, knit band, rhinestone buckle, EX.........................18.00
Hat, pill box, simulated Persian lamb, red lined, EX.......................3.00
Hat, Stetson, dk tan, feather band, MIB..32.00
Hat, top; silk/beaver, NM in leather box 125.00
Jacket, Battenburg lace over silk, EX 75.00
Jacket, wht wool, bolero style, l/s, EX...15.00
Nightgown, embr lace w/ribbons, Edwardian style 95.00
Nightgown, peach silk, much lace, long, NM.................................25.00
Nightgown, rayon, ecru lace bodice, ties, M.................................22.50
Pajamas, silk, ribbon rosettes/crochet trim, 1920s, NM...............100.00
Pantaloons, tucked, drawstring waist, eyelet trim, long, NM.........35.00
Parasol, blk brocade w/fringe, ornate wood hdl, 1880s, EX 125.00
Parasol, blk satin, scalloped pinked edge, 1860s, EX....................125.00
Parasol, blk silk w/wht embr, ebony hdl, 1890s, EX......................125.00
Parasol, Chantilly lace, branch-cvd ivory hdl w/red coral 300.00
Parasol, Duchesse lace, repousse silver hdl, 21".........................300.00
Parasol, flowered silk, crooked ivory hdl, 25"............................150.00
Parasol, gr/rose brocade, ivory finial, folding, 1820s, VG.............125.00
Parasol, lace covered w/cvd ivory hdl, EX....................................125.00
Parasol, red silk, MOP inlaid folding hdl, 1850s, EX....................125.00
Shawl, intricate blk lace, 1920s, 66x12", EX 65.00
Shawl, silk, embr florals on blk, lg, EX..78.00
Shirt, wht cotton, l/s, French cuff, no collar, 1920s, NM 24.00
Shoes, baby's, high button, Victorian, pr, EX 45.00

Shoes, lady's pumps, pointed toe, squatty heel, 1930s, pr **20.00**
Shoes, Oxfords, navy suede w/mesh inserts, 1930s, EX...................**18.00**
Shoes, Patinos, blk velvet w/mc feathers, chunky heel, EX **12.00**
Shoes, pumps, satin, 1920s, EX...**22.00**
Shoes, pumps, silver T-strap, 1920s, pr, EX................................**15.00**
Shoes, pumps, tan leather w/leopard vamp & heel, 1940s...............**7.50**
Shoes, Schiaparelli pumps, sling-bk, 1940s, pr, EX........................**30.00**
Shoes, slipper style w/satin flower & fringe, EX **50.00**
Skirt, wire & tape elliptical hoop style, all orig, 1860s **150.00**
Stockings, cream silk, pr **10.00**
Sweater, wht rabbit fur trim w/beadwork **38.00**
Swim suit, wool, blk, 1920s **30.00**
Waist, wht, l/s, Victorian..**50.00**

Cluthra

The name Cluthra is derived from the Scottish word 'clutha,' meaning cloudy. Glassware by this name was first produced by J. Couper and Sons, England. Frederick Carder developed Cluthra while at the Steuben Glass Works, and similar types of glassware were also made by Durand and Kimball. It is found in both solid and shaded colors and is characterized by a spotty appearance resulting from small air pockets trapped between its two layers.

Bowl, bl to wht to clear, shouldered, Steuben, 4x12" **550.00**
Bowl, blk to clear to wht, heavy, conical, Steuben, 8x15" **800.00**
Bowl, gr/clear/wht swirl, ftd U-form, Steuben, 5¾x7½" **600.00**

Vases, white to pomona green, Fleur-de-lis mark, signed Steuben, 12", $650.00; white shaded to black, unsigned Steuben, 12", $700.00.

Vase, gr, clear cased, thick, unmk Steuben, 11", pr **2,000.00**
Vase, orange/gray, polished pontil, Kimball, 1910-6, 7x5" **625.00**
Vase, pk w/rose & wht streaks, shouldered, Steuben, 11x10" **950.00**
Vase, rose/pk/clear, flared cylinder, 14½" **375.00**
Vase, wht to gr, clear cased, V-form, unmk Steuben, 6" **475.00**

Coalport

In 1745 in Caughley, England, Squire Brown began a modest business fashioning crude pots and jugs from clay mined in his own fields. Tom Turner, a young potter who had apprenticed his trade at Worcester, was hired in 1772 to plan and oversee the construction of a 'proper' factory. Three years later he bought the business, which he named Caughley Coalport Porcelain Manufactory. Though the dinnerware he produced was meant to be only everyday china, the hand-painted florals, birds, and landscapes used to decorate the ware were done in exquisite detail and in a wide range of colors. In 1780 Turner introduced the Willow pattern which he produced using a newly-perfected method of transfer printing. (Wares from the period between 1775 and 1799 are termed 'Caughley' or 'Salopian' — see section on Caughley.) John Rose purchased the Caughley factory from Thomas Turner in 1799, adding that holding to his own pottery which he had built two years before in Coalport. (It is from this point in the pottery's history that the wares are termed 'Coalport.') The porcelain produced there before 1814 was unmarked with very few exceptions. After 1820 some examples were marked with a '2' with an oversize top loop. The term 'Coalbrookdale' refers to a fine type of porcelain decorated in floral bas relief, similar to the work of Dresden.

After 1835 highly-decorated ware with rich ground colors imitated the work of Sevres and Chelsea, even going so far as to copy their marks. From about 1895 until the 1920s, the mark in use was 'Coalport' over a crown with 'England, A.D. 1750' indicating the date claimed as the founding, not the date of manufacture. From the 1920s until 1945, 'Made in England' over a crown and 'Coalport' below was used. Later, the mark was 'Coalport' over a smaller crown with 'Made in England' in a curve below. In 1926 the Coalport Company moved to Shelton in Staffordshire and today belongs to a group headed by the Wedgwood Company. See also Indian Tree.

Dish, floral/fruit on buff w/gilt, shell shape, 1825, 9"...................**500.00**
Dish, Japan-style vase/flowers, shell shape w/hdl, 1815, 9" **125.00**
Flask, Japanese floral on bl, molded 3-lobe hdls, 1880s, 7"..........**250.00**
Plate, floral reserve center on lt bl w/emb gold, 1900, 10½"...........**45.00**
Tea bowl & saucer, Willow ware, underglaze bl, gilt rims **40.00**
Teapot, flowers on 'marble,' dog spout, bird hdl, rpr, 8" **150.00**
Teapot, Willow ware, fluted/rectangular, CB Dale mk, 10" W **185.00**

Coalbrookdale vases, white with turquoise and heavy gilt, 1850s, 15", EX, $700.00 for the pair.

Vase, appl florals, flower/bird reserve, leaf hdls, 12" **500.00**
Vase, appl florals on cobalt, hdls, ftd, pr at 7", 1 at 8"....................**300.00**
Vase, ovals w/flowers on apple gr, scroll hdls, 14", pr....................**450.00**
Vase, pate-sur-pate w/flowers on pk, urn form, 8" **750.00**
Vase, shaped floral reserves, ftd gourd form w/lid, 12", pr **600.00**

Cobalt Glass

Cobalt glass is characterized by its deep transparent blue color obtained by mixing cobalt oxide and alumina to the batch. It may be found in free-blown, mold-blown, and pressed glassware. See Blown Glass.

Bowl, much gold decor, flared rim, 4¼x8⅛"	175.00
Butter dish, Criss-Cross	75.00
Ewer, allover mc decor w/gold, ftd, clear hdl, 5½"	70.00
Pitcher, mc florals, 3¾x2¾"	85.00
Pitcher, water; enamel decor w/gold, +6 tumblers	225.00
Rose bowl, gold decor/pk/bl florals, 8-crimp, 3-ftd, 4½"	135.00
Urn, ftd sphere, stepped lid w/wht-pnt finial, blown, 12"	300.00
Vase, pk florals w/gold, ewer form, 5¼"	75.00
Vase, silver overlay leaves & vines, sgn Boda, 4½"	105.00
Vase, wht daisies & sanded gold, 5x2¾"	55.00

Coca-Cola

J.S. Pemberton, creator of Coca-Cola, originated his world-famous drink in 1886. From its inception the Coca-Cola Company began an incredible advertising campaign which has proven to be one of the most successful promotions in history. The quantity and diversity of advertising material put out by Coca-Cola in the last one hundred years is literally mind-boggling. From the beginning, the company has projected an image of wholesomeness and Americana. Beautiful women in Victorian costumes, teenagers and schoolchildren, blue- and white-collar workers, the men and women of the Armed Forces — even Santa Claus — have appeared in advertisements with a Coke in their hands. Some of the earliest collectibles include trays, syrup dispensers, gum jars, pocket mirrors, and calendars. Many of these items fetch prices in the thousands of dollars. Later examples include radios, signs, lighters, thermometers, playing cards, clocks, and toys — particularly toy trucks.

In 1970 the Coca-Cola Company initialed a multi-million dollar 'image refurbishing campaign,' which introduced the new 'Dynamic Countour' logo, a twisting white ribbon under the Coca-Cola and Coke trademarks. The new logo often serves as a cut-off point to the purist collector. Newer and very ardent collectors, however, relish the myriad of items marketed since that date, as they often cannot afford the high prices that the vintage pieces command. For more information we recommend *Petretti's Coca-Cola Collectibles Price Guide*; you may order a copy from Nostalgia Publications, Inc., whose address is listed in under Auction Houses in the Directory.

Beware of reproductions — prices are given for the genuine original articles, but the symbol (+) at the end of some of the following lines indicate items that have been reproduced. Watch for frauds:genuinely old celluloid items ranging from combs, mirrors, knives and forks to doorknobs that have been recently etched with a new double-lined trademark. Still another area of concern deals with reproduction and fantasy items. A fantasy item is a novelty made to appear authentic with inscriptions such as 'Tiffany Studios,' 'Trans Pan Expo,' 'World's Fair,' etc. In reality, these items never existed as originals. For instance, don't be fooled by a Coca-Cola cash register — no originals are known to exist! Large mirrors for bars are being reproduced and are often selling for $10.00 to $50.00.

Reproductions and Fantasies

The following items have been reproduced and are among the most deceptive of all:

Pocket mirrors from 1905, 1906, 1908, 1909, 1910, 1911, 1916, and 1920.

Trays from 1899, 1910, 1913, 1914, 1917, 1920, 1923, 1925, 1926, 1934, and 1937.

Tip trays from 1907, 1909, 1910, 1913, 1914, 1917, and 1920.

Knives: many versions of the German brass model.

Cartons: wood versions, yellow with logo.

Belt buckle, no originals thought to exist (F), up to	5.00
Bottle, dk amber, w/arrows, heavy, narrow spout (R)	10.00
Bottle carrier, wood, yel w/red logo, holds 6 bottles (R)	10.00
Clock, mantel; brass, battery-op, Ridgway Anniv, '80, 6x9" (R)	100.00
Cooler, Glascock Jr, made by Coca-Cola USA (R)	200.00
Doorknob, glass w/etched trademark (F)	3.00
Knife, bottle shape, 1970s (F)	5.00
Knife, fork, or spoon w/celluloid hdl, newly-etched TM (F)	5.00
Knife, pocket; yel & red, 1933 World's Fair (F)	2.00
Letter opener, stamped metal, Coca-Cola 5¢ (F)	3.00
Sign, cb, lady w/fur, dtd 1911, 9x11" (F)	3.00
Sign, oval, girl w/fur, 1970s (R)	10.00
Soda fountain glass holder, word 'Drink' not on orig (R)	5.00
Thermometer, bottle figural, DONASCO, 17" (R)	5.00
Trade card, copy of 1905 'Bathtub' foldout, emb 1978 (R)	3.00
Vanity pc (mirror/brush/etc), celluloid, newly-etched TM (F)	5.00
Watch, pocket; often old watch w/new face (R)	10.00

Centennial Items

1986 was the year for the Coca-Cola Company to celebrate her 100th birthday; and amidst all the fanfare comes many new collectible items, all sporting the 100th anniversary logo. These items are destined to become an important part of the total Coca-Cola Collectible spectrum. The following pieces are among the most popular centennial items. These items are currently being marketed:

Brass button, 18", Taiwan (R)

Brass thermometer, bottle shape, 24", Taiwan

Cast iron toys (none ever made)

Cast iron door pull, bottle shape, made to look old

Poster, Yes Girl (R)

Button sign, 12", has 1 round hole while original has 4 slots (R)

Bullet trash receptacles (old cans with decals)

Paperweight, rectangular, with Pepsin Gum insert

1949 cooler radio(new)

Countless trays

Bottle, gold dipped, in velvet sleeve, 6½-oz	50.00
Bottle, Hutch, amber, Root Co, 6½-oz, 3 in case	150.00
Bottle, International, set of 9 in plexiglas case	175.00
Bottle, leaded crystal, 100th logo, 6½-oz, MIB	100.00
Medallion, bronze, w/box, 3" dia	50.00
Pin set, wood fr, 101 pins	250.00
Scarf, silk, 30x30"	35.00
Thermometer, glass cover, 14" dia, M	22.00

Coca-Cola Originals

Ad, 1915, Confederate reunion, from newspaper, 9x13", M	75.00
Ad, 1920, Collier's, July 10, mat & fr, EX	20.00
Blotter, 1927, couple leans on open icebox, NM	40.00
Blotter, 1931, Tune In, NM	85.00
Blotter, 1935, A Home Run..., NM	40.00
Blotter, 1940, clown, NM	50.00
Blotter, 1950, scout, NM	7.50
Blotter, 1956, Friendliest Drink, NM	5.00
Bookmark, 1903-04, Hilda Clark, 6x2", EX	350.00
Bottle, Cadada misprint, aqua, EX	20.00
Bottle, Canada, Property of..., script, aqua, str sides, EX	10.00
Bottle, display; Pat D, w/cap, 20", NM	250.00
Bottle, Indiana PA, lt amber, EX	40.00

Bottle, Morgantown WV, med amber, logo at top/str sides, NM ...25.00
Bottle, seltzer; Norwich Coca-Cola Bottling Co, NM..................125.00
Bottle, seltzer; 1930-40, Royal Palm, NM..................80.00
Bottle, syrup; 1900s, label under glass, w/cap, NM 450.00
Bottle, syrup; 1910s, wreath, w/cap, minor wear, NM 350.00
Bottle, 1920s, Christmas display, w/cap, 20", M..................250.00
Bottle, 1930s, 2½", set of 12 in wood case 65.00
Bottle cap set, 1950s, Tour the World, NM..................65.00
Bottle carrier, 1930s, cb, Serve Ice Cold, NM..................42.50
Bottle carrier, 1950s, plastic, 12-bottle, NM..................15.00
Bottle opener, 1910-30, lion head style, NM..................100.00
Bottle opener, 1930s, shoehorn style, EX..................125.00
Bottle opener, 1930s, wire w/faux bone hdl, NM..................22.50
Bowl, pretzel; 1930s, aluminum, NM..................125.00
Bowl, 1930s, gr opaque glass, Drink...Ice Cold, NM..................175.00
Calculator, pocket; Coke Is It, NM..................12.00
Calendar, 1902, lady holds glass, full pad, 14½x7½", NM 2,500.00
Calendar, 1904, Lillian Nordica, 1-pg, 15¼x7¾", EX............ 2,000.00
Calendar, 1916, girl w/rose basket, complete, EX+ 600.00
Calendar, 1917, Constance w/bottle, complete, EX......750.00
Calendar, 1917, Constance w/glass, complete, fr, 32x13", EX...900.00
Calendar, 1927, girl w/glass & bottle, EX 350.00
Calendar, 1937, boy fishing/dog, Wyeth illus, full pad, NM 450.00
Calendar, 1941, Canadian, complete, 6-pg, NM..................125.00
Calendar, 1945, lady in scarf, complete, NM..................100.00
Calendar, 1951, girl & confetti, complete, NM 80.00
Calendar, 1955, Santa, ...for Your Home, M..................10.00
Calendar, 1963, lady at mirror, 6-pg, 14x14", NM..................28.00
Can, 1980 Russian Olympics, opened, EX..................35.00
Case, 1920s, wood, EX pnt & logo..................35.00
Case, 1950s, wood, EX pnt & logo..................20.00
Chalkboard, 1950s, porc, Canadian, red/yel/wht, 26x18", EX........75.00
Clock, 1910, leather bottle-shape case, 8x3", EX 550.00
Clock, 1916, regulator, Gilbert, ...in Bottles, EX..................850.00
Clock, 1939, Coca-Cola in Bottles, wood fr, 16x16", EX............220.00
Clock, 1942, neon, w/bottle, 16x16", NM (+) 400.00
Clock, 1950s, sq face, lights up, NM..................125.00
Clock, 1950s, w/bottle, lights up, 14" dia, NM..................275.00
Clock, 1951, maroon, 17½" dia, EX..................50.00
Clock, 1960s, plastic, lights up, fishtail, EX..................75.00
Clock, 1972, plastic, schoolhouse style, NM..................40.00
Clock, 1974, plastic, Betty, M..................35.00
Clock, 1987, mini regulator, battery op, wood case, 27x13", NM.100.00
Coaster, 1950, foil, sq, M..................5.00
Coaster, 1950s, children join in circle, Germany, EX..................5.00
Cooler, 1929, table top, Glascock, w/faucet, no legs..................750.00
Coupon, 1928, Rockwell art, free bottle, EX 10.00
Cup holder, wood, Drink Coca-Cola Iced, for 2 stacks, NM..........75.00
Dart board, 1940s, silhouettes, EX..................35.00
Decal, 1950s, Fountain Service, 10x10", M..................25.00
Decal, 1950s, Please Pay Cashier, NM..................5.00
Dictionary, 1925, Webster's Little Gem, EX..................30.00
Dispenser, 1930s, stainless w/enamel plates, dbl sz, EX 500.00
Dispenser, 1950s, rnd 'outboard motor' style, NM..................325.00
Display, 1957, Santa in rocket ship, 3-D, 33x13", EX..................100.00
Doll, 1950, Santa Claus, blk vinyl boots, NM 100.00
Fan, 1911, cb, H-O-T-T Isn't It, Chinese, NM 125.00
Fan, 1912-14, Chew Coca-Cola Gum, children on front, EX.. 1,000.00
Fan, 1920s, child picks flowers, paddle shape, NM 30.00
Fly swatter, 1920s, advertising ea side of hdl, EX..................50.00
Glass, 1900s, Moriarty & Neil, flared, rare 525.00
Glass, 1941, fountain, 'trademark' under logo, 6-oz..................12.50
Ice pick, 1960s, rnd wood hdl, EX 4.00
Jar, 1916-24, Coca-Cola Chewing Gum, paper label, NM (+). 1,000.00

Kite, 1930s, paper, American Flyer, EX..................200.00
Knife, 1930s, Compliments of..., stainless steel, Germany, NM 50.00
Lighter, butane, new logo, M..................5.00
Match striker, 1939, porc, Drink..., 4-color, 4½" sq, NM............175.00
Matchbook, 50th Anniversary, NM..................15.00
Menu board, 1929, tin, Specials To-Day, EX..................100.00
Menu board, 1939, tin, silhouette girl, EX..................75.00
Menu board, 1960s, tin, fishtail, NM..................50.00
Mug, 1920, ceramic, emb Coca-Cola, very rare, no chips..........500.00
Napkin, 1911, paper, lady in chair, NM..................50.00
Necktie, 1950, Sprite boy..................65.00
Opener, 1950s, curved bottle shape, Germany, EX 10.00
Pencil, mechanical; Have a Coke, M..................20.00
Plate, sandwich; 1930s, china, rare sz, 8¼", NM..................450.00
Plate, sandwich; 1930s, china, 7¼", NM 125.00
Playing cards, 1943, airplane spotter, NM in box..................65.00
Playing cards, 1959, girl in water, Sign of..., MIB..................50.00
Playing cards, 1961, girl w/score pad, MIB..................45.00
Playing cards, 1971, Boy Scouts Jamboree, EX in box..................60.00
Playing cards, 1976, Enjoy Coca-Cola, red & wht, NM in box....... 5.00
Pocket mirror, 1910, H King/JB Caroll, oval, NM (+)..................225.00
Pocket mirror, 1911, H King/Whitehead-Hoag, oval, NM (+)....200.00
Pocket mirror, 1916, Elaine, Whitehead-Hoag, NM (+) 250.00
Post card, Coke billboard & clock, Danville VA, M 3.50
Post card, Pause That Refreshes, M..................6.00
Post card, 1935, IH truck, color, NM..................15.00
Pushbar, 1930s, porc w/wrought end pcs, NM..................225.00
Pushbar, 1950s, porc, Iced Coca-Cola Here, EX 60.00
Radio, can figural, EX (+)..................15.00
Radio, 1930s, Bakelite, bottle figural, 30", NM..................1,850.00
Record, 1965, Petula Clark, 33⅓ rpm, NM..................15.00
Ruler, Work Refreshed/Play Refreshed, NM..................3.50
Scorekeeper, 1907, baseball, NM..................50.00
Sheet music, 1944, Rum & Coca-Cola, Fr version, 10½x13"..........38.00
Sheet music, 1970s, Look Up America, NM..................5.00

Self-framed tin sign, Passaic Metal Co., 30" x 20", NM, $3,900.00.

Sign, 1907, self-fr tin, Relieves Fatigue, 27x18½", EX (+) 4,000.00
Sign, 1910-14, tin, str-sided bottle, 19x27", EX 600.00
Sign, 1920s, tin, Drink Coca-Cola, 12x36", NM 425.00
Sign, 1926, cb cutout, 7 Million Drinks, 32x18", EX............ 1,250.00
Sign, 1930s, cb, Our CC Is Below 40(degrees), 9x12", EX..........400.00

Sign, 1930s, neon, Deco style w/chrome, 15x24", EX 1,800.00
Sign, 1931, cb, girl w/arm up, Niagara Litho, 38x21", EX 450.00
Sign, 1931, tin, hand holds bottle, 9x12", NM 275.00
Sign, 1932, glass, stand-up fan style, 24", NM 1,200.00
Sign, 1933, tin bottle diecut, 5-color, 36", NM 425.00
Sign, 1934, cb, Joan Crawford, 24x14", EX 500.00
Sign, 1934, porc, Fountain Service, 14x27", EX 325.00
Sign, 1936, cb, girl by water, It Cools You, 30x14", EX 400.00
Sign, 1937, cb, lady, boy & dog, Wilbur, 43x22", NM 275.00
Sign, 1937, cb, running girl, 30x14", NM 375.00
Sign, 1940s, celluloid, Delicious & Refreshing, 9" dia, EX 75.00
Sign, 1941, wood & masonite, silhouette girl, 14x36", EX 250.00
Sign, 1946, cb, skater girl, Right Off the Ice, 27x16", M 150.00
Sign, 1948, tin, bottle, 40x16", EX 100.00
Sign, 1948, tin, 6 bottles in carrier, 2-pc, 40x16", NM 175.00
Sign, 1950, glass & plastic, Please Pay Cashier, 12x20", NM 325.00
Sign, 1950, plastic front, Have a Coke, lights up, 10x17", NM ..125.00
Sign, 1950s, plastic, emb letters, aluminum ring, 67" dia 325.00
Sign, 1950s, porc, Fountain Service, 12x28", M 275.00
Sign, 1950s, tin, emb bottle diecut, 36", EX 325.00
Sign, 1960s, cb, couple leaves boat, aluminum fr, 20x38", EX 60.00
Sign, 1960s, plastic, Sno-ee Frozen Drink, 18x18", NM 45.00
Sign, 1960s, porc, Kosher Delicatessen, 28x28", EX 125.00
Sign, 1963, tin, fishtail, 22x28", NM 75.00
Thermometer, 1915, wood, 21x5", NM 350.00
Thermometer, 1930s, tin, bottle shape, Pat 1923, 17", EX 125.00
Thermometer, 1939, porc, Thirst Knows..., 4-color, 18", NM 275.00

Thermometers, bottle shaped, tin, ca 1940s, 16½", $100.00; embossed silhouette girl, tin, ca 1940, 16", $125.00.

Thermometer, 1950s, glass front, bottle, Drink, 12" dia, NM 150.00
Thermometer, 1956, gold bottle, 7½x2¼", NM 12.00
Thermometer, 1960s, plastic, Sprite, NM 12.50
Tip tray, 1903, Hilda Clark, Shonk litho, 6" dia, NM 1,800.00
Tip tray, 1903, Hilda Clark, Shonk litho, 6" dia, VG 500.00
Tip tray, 1906, Juanita, Wolf litho, 4" dia, EX 450.00
Tip tray, 1907, Relieves Fatigue, Shonk litho, 6x4½", VG 390.00
Tip tray, 1909, St Louis Fair, 4¼x6", NM 225.00
Tip tray, 1910, Hamilton King girl, Am Art, 6x4½", NM 475.00
Tip tray, 1914, Betty, Passic litho, 4½x6", NM 250.00
Toy shopping basket, 1950s, cb/metal, EX 125.00
Toy train, 1950, tin windup, 4-pc, 14", EX 225.00
Toy truck, 1940s, Sprite boy, yel, 21" L, EX 150.00
Toy truck, 1950s, Buddy L, empty shelves, EX 75.00
Toy truck, 1950s, metal, Marx, no bottles or cases, G 75.00
Toy truck, 1950s, plastic w/cb inserts, no doors, Marx, MIB........ 325.00

Toy truck, 1950s, tin, Marx, #12, 12½", MIB 325.00
Toy truck, 1950s, tin, Marx, #21, +cases/bottles, 13", EX 175.00
Toy truck, 1960, pickup w/cb insert, NM 450.00
Toy truck, 1970s, Jumbo Trailer, Japan, 16", MIB 125.00
Toy van, 1970, plastic, Mexico, 4", EX 55.00
Tray, TV; 1958, serving cart, 13½x18¾", EX 25.00
Tray, TV; 1963, Mexican food, 13½x18¾", NM 48.00
Tray, 1909, St Louis Fair girl, oval, 16½x13½", NM 1,650.00
Tray, 1913, Hamilton King girl, oval, 12½x15¼", EX 500.00
Tray, 1914, Betty, oval, 12½x15¼", EX 380.00
Tray, 1914, Betty, 10½x13¼", EX 275.00
Tray, 1914, Betty, 10½x13¼", NM 475.00
Tray, 1917, Elaine w/Coke, 8½x19", NM 275.00
Tray, 1920, garden girl, 10½x13¼", EX 325.00
Tray, 1920, garden girl, 10½x13¼", NM 475.00
Tray, 1921, autumn girl, 10½x13¼", EX 300.00
Tray, 1921, autumn girl, 10½x13¼", NM 450.00
Tray, 1922, summer girl, 10½x13¼", NM 525.00
Tray, 1922, summer girl, 10½x13¼", VG 375.00
Tray, 1923, flapper girl, 10½x13¼", EX 150.00
Tray, 1923, flapper girl, 10½x13¼", NM 325.00
Tray, 1924, smiling girl, 10½x13¼", EX 200.00
Tray, 1924, smiling girl, 10½x13¼", NM 375.00
Tray, 1925, girl w/fur, 10½x13¼", NM (+) 375.00
Tray, 1926, golfers, 10½x13¼", NM 450.00
Tray, 1927, bobbed-hair girl, 10½x13¼", EX 250.00
Tray, 1927, curb-side survice, 10½x13¼", M 525.00

Tray, 1928, soda jerk, 10" x 13", M, $500.00 to $600.00.

Tray, 1929, lady sitting w/bottle, 10½x13¼", EX 165.00
Tray, 1930, bathing beauty, 10½x13¼", EX 175.00
Tray, 1930, bathing beauty, 10½x13¼", NM 375.00
Tray, 1930, telephone girl, 10½x13¼", EX 125.00
Tray, 1931, Rockwell boy w/sandwich & dog, 10½x13¼", NM ..525.00
Tray, 1932, girl in yel swimsuit, 10½x13¼", EX 275.00
Tray, 1933, Francis Dee, 10½x13¼", EX 250.00
Tray, 1934, Weismuller & O'Sullivan, 10½x13¼", EX (+) 350.00
Tray, 1935, Madge Evans, 10½x13¼", NM 225.00
Tray, 1936, Hostess, 10½x13¼", NM 185.00
Tray, 1937, running girl, 10½x13¼", EX (+) 125.00
Tray, 1938, girl in afternoon, 10½x13¼", NM 125.00
Tray, 1939, springboard girl, 10½x13¼", EX 80.00
Tray, 1940, sailor girl, 10½x13¼", EX 65.00
Tray, 1941, skater girl, 10½x13¼", NM 140.00
Tray, 1948, girl w/wind in hair, 10½x13¼", NM 45.00
Tray, 1948, girl w/wind in hair, 10½x13¼", VG 35.00

Tray, 1950, menu girl, 10½x13¼", EX	15.00
Tray, 1957, birdhouse, 10½x13¼", M	85.00
Tray, 1957, rooster, 10½x13¼", EX	50.00
Tray, 1957, umbrella girl, 10½x13¼", NM	225.00
Tray, 1957, 6 sandwiches/6 Cokes, 10½x13¼", NM	60.00
Tray, 1958, picnic basket, 10½x13¼", NM	25.00
Tray, 1960, fishtail, Drive In for Coke, rare, NM	225.00
Tray, 1961, pansy garden, 10½x13¼", NM	18.00
Tray, 1970, Santa (not Long John Silver), 10½x13¼", NM	10.00
Tray, 1972, girl in duster, NM	10.00
Tray, 1976, Canadian Olympics, NM	10.00
Tray, 1978, Capt Cook, 10½x13¼", NM	8.00
Tray, 1982, Nashville Fair, rnd, M	5.00
Uniform patch, 1950s, Drink Coca-Cola in Bottles, lg, M	5.00
Visor brim, 1950s, Have a Coke, VG	6.00
Watch fob, 1920s, Coke bulldogs, 1½x1", EX	100.00
Wrapper, 1913-16, Coca-Cola Gum, peppermint pepsin, NM	200.00

Vendors

Interest in Coca-Cola machines of the 1949 — 1959 era has risen dramatically. The major manufacturers of these curved top, 5¢ and 10¢ machines were Vendo (V), Vendorlator (VMC), Cavalier (C or CS), and Jacobs. Market forecasters forsee tremendous investment potential over the next five years. In the following listings, 'VG' values are for machines in clean, original condition.

Cavalier, model #CS72, M rstr	3,500.00
Cavalier, model #CS72, VG	450.00
Cavalier, model #C27, M rstr	3,000.00
Cavalier, model #C27, VG	350.00
Cavalier, model #C51, M rstr	2,500.00
Cavalier, model #C51, VG	350.00
Jacobs, model #26, M rstr	4,500.00
Jacobs, model #26, VG	750.00
Vendo, model #23, M rstr	2,000.00
Vendo, model #23, VG	350.00
Vendo, model #39, M rstr	2,500.00
Vendo, model #39, VG	500.00
Vendo, model #44, M rstr	5,000.00
Vendo, model #44, VG	1,250.00
Vendo, model #56, M rstr	4,500.00
Vendo, model #56, VG	650.00
Vendo, model #80, M rstr	2,250.00
Vendo, model #80, VG	250.00
Vendo, model #81, M rstr	4,500.00
Vendo, model #81, VG	750.00
Vendorlator, model #27, M rstr	3,000.00
Vendorlator, model #27, VG	500.00
Vendorlator, model #27A, M rstr	3,500.00
Vendorlator, model #27A, VG	500.00
Vendorlator, model #33, M rstr	3,500.00
Vendorlator, model #33, VG	500.00
Vendorlator, model #44, M rstr	5,000.00
Vendorlator, model #44, VG	1,000.00
Vendorlator, model #72, M rstr	3,500.00
Vendorlator, model #72, VG	500.00

Coffee Grinders

The serious collector of kitchenwares and country store items rank coffee mills high on the list of desirable examples. A trend is developing toward preferring items whose manufacturers are easily identifiable. Names to look for include Adams, Arcade, Baldwin Bros., Daisy, Elgin National, Elma, Enterprise, Lane Bros., Parker, Regal, and Sun Mfg. Co.; there are many others. Any of these marks found on coffee mills represent companies who were in business at or before the turn of the century.

Side mills usually have a brass tag located on the tin hopper. If the hopper was made of cast iron, the name was usually cast into the metal. Some of the less expensive versions had no identification. Decals were often used on the front of lap mills and table styles, though sometimes you will find these decals on the inside of the drawer. Because decals are prone to flaking off and fading, and since they are often destroyed when the mill is being refinished, lap and table mills are the most difficult types to attribute to a specific manufacturer. Canister mills had names and patent dates molded into the cast iron housing or on the canister itself. Commercial mills used in country and general stores were made of cast iron. Important information such as manufacture and patent dates were usually cast into the wheels, housing, or base of the mill. Such identification helps determine date of manufacture and contributes considerably toward value.

Good examples of early coffee mills are rapidly becoming difficult to find. Beware of the many imported imposters that are on the market today.

Key: adj — adjustment

A Kendrick & Sons No 1, lap, CI w/brass hopper	95.00
American Beauty, canister, w/orig cup & papers	45.00
Arcade, Crystal No 3, canister, CI w/glass hopper, ca 1910	65.00
Arcade, Favorite, lap, fancy CI top & hopper	95.00
Arcade, Favorite, lap, wood box, CI works, red label	65.00
Arcade, Favorite No 27, side, CI, orig CI lid	65.00
Arcade, Favorite No 7, side, CI, grind adj front	65.00
Arcade, Imperial, lap, wood & CI, 11"	75.00
Arcade, Imperial, table, 2-lb, wood & CI, 13"	75.00
Arcade, Imperial No 200, lap, oak, CI eagle, Pat 1888-89	95.00
Arcade, IXL, table, fancy CI top, wood box, crank hdl, 10½"	135.00
Arcade, Jewel, canister, rectangular w/glass hopper	75.00
Arcade, Sunbeam, canister, CI w/glass hopper, tin lid	75.00
Arcade, table, 1-lb, w/decal, Pat 6/5/1884, 7x7x12½"	90.00
Arcade Crystal No 44, CI w/glass hopper, orig lid & glass	75.00
Arcade No 147, lap, fancy CI closed top, wood box	85.00
Arcade No 700, lap, w/dust cover, Sears, ca 1908	90.00
Blacksmith made, wall, funnel hopper, ca 1790	180.00
Brighton, Wrights Hdwe, table, 1-lb, 8"	75.00
Bronson Walton, canister, tin & CI, Pat 1911	75.00
C Ibach stamped on hdl, dvtl walnut, iron hopper	145.00
Canister, boy & girl decal, miniature, 5½x1½"	85.00
Caravan, canister, CI works, tin hopper, ca 1910	60.00
Chas Parker No 350, side, CI, Pat 4/1876	65.00
Chas Parker No 5005, counter, CI, 12½" wheels, 17"	475.00
Clevis Walton, canister, orig cup, Pat 7/9/1901	60.00
Coffee bean roaster, tin cylinder & holder, CI/wood hdl	125.00
Coles Mfg No 7, counter, CI, Pat 1887, 16" wheels, 27"	475.00
Common unmk, lap, decals, box joints, CI hopper, 8x6½x6½"	65.00
Common unmk, 1-lb, wood & CI	65.00
DeVe, Holland, lap, 1950s, 4¾x5⅛x8⅛"	45.00
Elgin National No 40, counter, CI, 2 wheels	325.00
Elgin National No 44, orig CI w/eagle, 15" wheels, 24"	395.00
Elgin National No 48, 2 wheels w/eagle, orig lily decal	425.00
Elma, counter, CI w/wooden drw, 10¾" single wheel, 17"	85.00
Enterprise, counter, CI, eagle on hopper, 2 wheels, Pat 1873	475.00
Enterprise, counter, closed hopper, blk hdl, Pat 1873, 12"	180.00
Enterprise, floor, eagle at top, Pat 1873, 39" wheels, 72"	3,500.00
Enterprise, table, CI, brass hopper, Pat 1873, 6" wheels	395.00

Enterprise, table, CI w/CI cup, orig gold decal.............................50.00
Enterprise No 1, counter, open hopper, Pat 1873, 11" hdl...........180.00
Enterprise No 12, counter, 2 lg wheels w/eagle, Pat 1898............625.00
Enterprise No 216, floor, CI hopper, decals, Pat 1898 .... 2,600.00
Enterprise No 7, counter, CI, 17" wheels w/eagle.......................475.00
Enterprise No 9, CI, brass eagle, Pat 1898, 19" wheels, 28".........525.00
Euclid No 4, counter, CI w/aluminum hopper, 2 10" wheels 385.00
Fairbanks Morse, floor, CI, brass hopper, 72" 1,300.00
Golden Rule, canister, CI w/glass front, wood box 235.00
Grand Union Tea, canister, red, orig writing, Pat 1910 ....85.00
Grand Union Tea, table, CI, sq base, rnd hopper..........................95.00
J Fisher, Warranted, lap, dvtl mahog, pewter hopper 145.00
J Fisher, Warranted, lap, dvtl walnut, brass hopper 150.00
K&M, lap, maple clips on drw, aluminum hopper 45.00
KM Geschmiedeetes und Gefrates Mahlwerk, brass hopper 55.00
L&S, side, CI, mtd on orig board 65.00
L'il Tot, orig drw, miniature, 4x2¾x2¾" 80.00
Landers, Frary & Clark, canister, tin & CI, Pat 1905....................65.00
Landers, Frary & Clark, counter, CI, #50 drw, 12" wheels...........425.00
Landers, Frary & Clark, lap, fancy CI top, wood box 95.00
Landers, Frary & Clark, Regal No 44, canister, tin & CI 80.00
Landers, Frary & Clark, table, CI, Pat Feb 14, 1905.....................60.00
Landers, Frary & Clark, Universal No 14, table, Pat 1905 ....60.00
Lap, CI, octagon shape, open hopper, 4x4x4" 75.00
Lees, canister, CI works, rnd glass hopper....................................65.00
Lightning, canister, CI works, tin hopper 70.00
Logan & Strobridge, Franco American, lap, CI & wood................90.00
National, coffee & spice, counter, 12" wheels, 25"......................425.00
National, coffee & spice, counter, 17" wheels, 28"......................425.00
National No 5, CI body & drw, 12" wheels 395.00
National Specialty Mfg, Philadelphia PA, CI, 25" wheels 575.00
New Home, table, 1-lb, CI top, enclosed hopper, wood box 75.00
New Model, lap, CI w/CI drw, 5½x4½x5½"..................................75.00
None Such, Bronson Co, Cleveland OH, table, tin 50.00
Parker, side, CI, grind adj on front, Pat 1876..............................60.00
Parker Eagle No 144, canister, tin hopper 65.00
Parker No 2, counter, CI w/orig decals, 9" wheels 375.00
Parker No 449, canister, CI works, rnd w/glass hopper 75.00
Parker No 5000, counter, CI, Pat 1897, 12" wheels, 17"..............275.00
Parker No 555, Challenge, table, fast grind, 1-lb 75.00
Parker No 60, side, eagle on tin hopper, Parker lid......................60.00
Persepolis, table, CI & brass 155.00
Peugeot Freres, lap, wood box, tin-covered hopper 40.00
Primitive, lap, brass/iron/dvtl walnut, handmade 160.00
Primitive, lap, dvtl cherry, brass hopper, 4x4" 155.00
Primitive, lap, red buttermilk pnt, pewter hopper, ca 1850..........150.00
PS&W No 3500, side, CI 65.00
PSW & Co No 6, side, CI 60.00
Putz stamped on hdl, lap, walnut, brass hopper 150.00
Queen, child's miniature, wood w/CI hopper & drw front 80.00
Rock Hard, Garant-Sewaarborge, lap, 4¾x4¾x5½" 40.00
Royal, side, CI w/CI cup, open hopper, Pat Apr 15, 1890.............65.00
RR Kreiterr, Lewisberry, York County PA, dvtl, pewter hopper ..155.00
Russer, canister, porc top...55.00
S&H, counter, CI w/drw, 19" wheels, 21" 450.00
Star, canister, tin w/CI works, Pat 1910......................................65.00
Star, floor, CI, lg wheels, 72"...975.00
Sun Mfg, rnd table, 1-lb, wood, 13" 195.00
Sun Mfg, table, 1-lb, orig decal, screw lid, 12" 75.00
Sun Mft No 1080, Challenge Fast Grind, Columbus OH, 1-lb......75.00
Swift, side, CI, Pat 1845, Pat Aug 16, 1859 ....75.00
Swift No 13, orig metal drw, Pat 1885, 12" wheels, 19" 350.00
Swift No 15, CI, orig decals, Pat 1875, 19" wheels......................875.00
Telephone, canister, wood w/no CI, ca 1900-10 ....65.00

Round table mill, 1-lb capacity, 13" x 7½" diameter, $175.00.

Turkish, brass cylinder, folding hdl, old 55.00
Turkish, table, primitive, 13x7½" sq box on 28" board 155.00
W Cross & Sons, lap, CI w/orig CI drw, brass hopper 75.00
WW Weaver, lap, primitive, dvtl walnut, pewter hopper 155.00
X-Ray, canister, glass front, wood hopper, 1908 ....70.00

Coin-Operated Machines

Coin-operated machines may be the fastest-growing area of collector interest in today's market. Many machines are bought, restored, and used for home entertainment. Older examples from the turn of the century and those with especially elaborate decoration and innovative accessories are most desirable, often bringing prices in excess of $7,000.00.

Vending machines sold a product or a service. They were already in common usage by 1900 selling gum, cigars, matches, and a host of other commodities. Peanut and gumball machines are especially popular today. The most valuable are those with their original finish and decals. Older machines made of cast iron are especially desirable, while those with plastic globes have little or no collector value. When buying unrestored peanut machines, beware of salt damage.

The coin-operated phonograph of the early 1900s paved the way for the jukeboxes of the twenties. Seeburg was first on the market with an automatic 8-tune phonograph. By the 1930s, Wurlitzer was the top name in the industry with dealerships all over the country. As a result of the growing ranks of competitors, the forties produced the most beautiful machines made. Wurlitzers from this era are probably the most popularly sought-after models on the market today. The model 1015 of 1946 is considered the all-time classic, and often brings prices in excess of $6,000.

Coin-Op Newsletter; *Jukebox Collectors' Newsletter*; *Chicagoland Antique Advertising, Slot Machine, and Jukebox Gazette*; and *Loose Change Magazine* are all excellent publications for those interested in coin-operated machines; see the Clubs, Newsletters, and Catalogs section of the Directory for publishing information.

Jackie and Ken Durham are our advisors (for all but Jukeboxes); they are listed in the Directory under the District of Columbia.

Arcade Machines

Advance 1¢ Electric Shock Machine, 1940s, EX orig 325.00

Advance 1¢ Vista Scope, stereo card viewer, EX orig 495.00
Atlas 5¢ Tilt Test, formica case, flat-top game, EX 295.00
Big Game Hunter 1¢ Pistol Shoot, 1925, EX orig 525.00
Booze Barometer 5¢, countertop, EX 195.00
Caille Uncle Sam, grip tester, EX orig.................................. 3,500.00
Challenger 1¢ Target Pistol Shoot, VG 295.00
Duck 1¢ Pistol Shoot, duck marquee, EX orig 225.00
Exhibit 1¢ Five Ball Shooter, rstr...800.00
Exhibit 1¢ Lucky Horseshoe Fortune Teller, EX orig 550.00
Exhibit 1¢ Photoscope, 5 sets of stereo views, EX 385.00
Exhibit 5¢ Oracle Fortune Teller, EX orig 425.00
Holly Grip Strength Tester, countertop, 13x9x8", EX orig..........145.00
Keep 'Em Bombing, 1¢ Smak a Jap, penny drop, EX orig.............625.00
Kicker Catcher 1¢, full kicker, early version, EX 595.00
Little Whirl Wind 1¢, flip ball game, countertop, sm, VG 425.00
Madame Zita, EX orig 6,000.00
Mercury 1¢ Grip Test, rstr...225.00
Mexican 1¢ Baseball, 2-player, metal case, EX orig 395.00
Mills 1¢ Wizard Fortune Teller, ornate casting, EX orig.......... 1,495.00
Mills 1¢ Wizard Fortune Teller, wooden case, 1920s, EX orig 350.00
Mutoscope Indian Front, ca 1900, NM 4,500.00
Pikes Peak 1¢, balls on moving ramps, rpt, EX 525.00
Play Basketball 1¢, 2-player, 1930s, rpt..................................450.00
Play Poker 1¢, flip game, EX orig 365.00
Safe Driver 5¢ Reaction Meter, rpt, EX 285.00
Seeburg Chicken Sam, ca 1931, EX orig 750.00
Skill Thrill 1¢ Penny Pistol Shoot, WWII graphics, EX 395.00
Steeplechase 1¢ Skill Game, balls on ramps, horse motif, EX......495.00
Stephens 1¢ Babe Ruth Baseball, ca 1935, EX orig 500.00
Watling 1¢ Scultoscope, countertop, rstr...............................345.00
Wee Gee 1¢ Fortune Teller, penny drop, metal w/cast front, EX .325.00
What Kind of Person Are You?, countertop, 11x9x18", EX.........395.00
Whiz Ball 1¢, flip game, rstr 345.00

Jukeboxes

AMI A, EX orig... 3,000.00
AMI New Yorker, 1968, NM 550.00
Mills Carousel, 12-selection, ca 1934, NM 850.00
Mills Empress, ca 1939, EX orig...................................... 2,000.00
Mills Throne of Music, ca 1939, EX orig............................ 1,500.00
Peacock, M rstr...19,000.00
Rockola #1422, Magic Glo series, EX rstr 3,600.00
Rockola #1428, EX orig 3,000.00
Rockola #429, EX orig 450.00
Rockola Monarch, ca 1938, NM 1,500.00
Rockola Nite Club, ca 1936, EX orig.................................. 1,000.00
Rockola Premier, ca 1942, EX orig 3,500.00
Seeburg, trash can type, EX rstr....................................... 2,000.00
Seeburg #100C, ca 1950, EX rstr 2,500.00
Seeburg #8800, EX orig 1,200.00
Seeburg Classic, ca 1940, EX orig 1,000.00
Seeburg E, gilded harp, EX orig....................................... 4,000.00
Seeburg E, oak, w/xylophone, rstr 8,500.00
Victory, M rstr... 9,500.00
Wurlitzer #1015, M rstr...11,000.00
Wurlitzer #1015, 1946, EX 7,500.00
Wurlitzer #1017, M 2,000.00
Wurlitzer #1080, EX rstr.. 8,500.00
Wurlitzer #1100, EX rstr.. 6,500.00
Wurlitzer #1800, EX orig 2,000.00
Wurlitzer #2200, ca 1958, NM 1,400.00
Wurlitzer #24, VG orig 1,600.00
Wurlitzer #500, ca 1938, EX orig..................................... 2,000.00

Wurlitzer Countertop jukebox, plays twelve 78 rpm selections, complete, unrestored, 22½", $2,100.00.

Wurlitzer #61, countertop, NM rstr..................................... 3,000.00
Wurlitzer #700, ca 1940, EX orig....................................... 2,700.00
Wurlitzer #716 Simplex, ca 1936, VG 900.00
Wurlitzer #750, EX rstr 8,500.00
Wurlitzer #780, EX rstr 5,500.00
Wurlitzer #81, countertop, NM 5,500.00
Wurlitzer P-12, 1930s, NM rstr.. 1,600.00

Slot Machines

AC 5¢ Multi-Bell, EX orig 2,400.00
Bally 25¢ Reliance Dice, gr finish, 16x18x11", EX 3,200.00
Bally 5¢ Spark Plug Horse Race, metal front, 14x16x11", EX . 2,500.00
Bally 5-25¢ Dbl Bell, EX orig 3,000.00
Buckley Bones, countertop, ca 1936, EX orig........................ 3,500.00
Buckley 5¢, Criss Cross Bell, ca 1947, EX orig 1,125.00
Caille Big Six, ca 1940, VG... 8,500.00
Caille Superior Bell, nude on hdl, ca 1926, EX 2,900.00
Caille Victor, ca 1902, EX orig 1,250.00
Caille 1¢ Ben Hur, G orig 4,500.00
Caille 5¢ Cadet Bell, ca 1936, EX orig 1,000.00
Caille 5¢ New Century Detroit Upright w/Music, EX 12,000.00
Field 3 Jacks, countertop, ca 1929, EX orig...........................800.00
Jennings 1¢ Little Duke, oak case, single jackpot, '33, EX....... 2,500.00
Jennings 5¢ Baseball, 3-reel, w/gumball vendor, EX orig 3,000.00
Jennings 5¢ Dixie Bell, ca 1937, EX 1,200.00
Jennings 5¢ Export Chief, EX orig 1,500.00
Jennings 5¢ New Victoria, ca 1931, EX orig 1,400.00
Jennings 5¢ Operator Bell, CI, ca 1920, rstr.......................... 1,950.00
Jennings 5¢ Silver Moon, console, ca 1940, EX orig............... 1,050.00
Jennings 5¢ Sportsman Bell, ca 1938, VG............................ 1,200.00
Jennings 5¢ Standard Chief, EX orig 1,500.00
Jennings 5¢ 4-Star Chief, Indian scenes, rstr 1,550.00
Keeney Track Time, console model, ca 1937, NM 1,500.00
Keeney Twin Bonus Super Bell, 2-player, EX orig 3,500.00
Mills 1¢ Cricket, upright, ca 1904, EX orig 9,500.00
Mills 1¢ Judge, upright, ca 1899, VG 8,500.00
Mills 1¢ Mystery Bell Castle Front, ca 1933, VG................... 1,900.00
Mills 1¢ QT Firebird Bell, ca 1934, EX orig 1,700.00
Mills 10¢ Golden Falls, EX orig... 1,800.00
Mills 10¢ Hi-Top, EX orig 2,000.00
Mills 25¢ Anniversary, oak case, 1936, VG 2,100.00
Mills 25¢ Bursting Cherry, orig red pnt, EX......................... 1,500.00
Mills 25¢ Bursting Cherry, 1941, VG orig............................ 2,000.00

Mills 25¢ Extra Bell, ca 1946, EX orig.................................... 1,500.00
Mills 25¢ Gooseneck Silent Bell, skyscraper front, 1930s, VG. 1,500.00
Mills 25¢ Poinsettia Front, EX orig 1,500.00
Mills 25¢ War Eagle, ca 1931, NM................................... 3,000.00
Mills 5¢ Aikens Front, EX orig 1,850.00
Mills 5¢ Bursting Cherry, metal, on wood table base, VG....... 1,500.00
Mills 5¢ Bursting Cherry, 1940s, EX orig 1,500.00
Mills 5¢ Chicago, upright, ca 1900, EX orig.......................... 9,000.00
Mills 5¢ Chrome Bell Diamond Front, EX orig..................... 1,200.00
Mills 5¢ Dewey Jackpot, upright, oak case, decals, EX 8,000.00
Mills 5¢ Horsehead Bonus, EX orig 2,500.00
Mills 5¢ Jackpot Bell Torch Front, ca 1928, VG.................... 1,500.00
Mills 5¢ Lion Front, EX orig 1,750.00
Mills 5¢ Operator Bell, CI, EX orig 5,995.00
Mills 5¢ QT, twin jackpot, oak case, 12x18x14", EX............... 1,400.00
Mills 5¢ Silent Front OK, EX orig 2,200.00
Mills 5¢ Vest Pocket, metal case, ca 1935, 7x9x8", EX 395.00
Mills 5¢ War Eagle, EX orig... 2,500.00
Mills 50¢ Castle Front, EX orig 1,850.00
Pace 5¢ Chrome Comet Deluxe, ca 1939, VG........................ 1,200.00

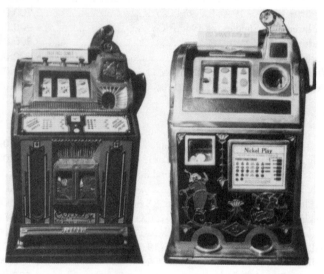

Pace Comet, 1934, EX orignial, $1,800.00; Jennings Dutch Boy, 5¢, EX original, $2,000.00.

Watling 10¢ Rola-A-Top, bird & coin cast front, 1935, EX ... 3,800.00
Watling 25¢ Bl Seal, EX orig... 1,750.00
Watling 5¢ Big Six, upright, raised panel oak case, 66", EX.... 8,500.00
Watling 5¢ Treasury, eagle & coins on front, rare, VG 4,500.00

Trade Stimulators

Ad Lee 1¢ Bluebird Dice, sq shape, decals, rstr.........................345.00
Ad Lee 1¢ Try It, dice game, decals, rstr 365.00
Baby Grand 10¢ Black Jack, punchboard type, EX orig..............115.00
Baker's 1¢ Pick-A-Pack, dice game, rstr.................................585.00
Bally 1¢ Baby, 5-reel, ca 1936, EX orig.................................350.00
Bluebird 1¢, coin drop, metal case, gumball dispenser, EX 355.00
Bomb Hitler 1¢, coin drop, EX orig....................................795.00
Brunhoff, spinning top under glass dome, cigar vending, EX... 4,500.00
Buckley Cent-A-Pak, cigarette reels, ca 1935, EX orig 395.00
Burlesque Girl 1¢, coin drop, pk wood case, 16x10x8", EX...........65.00
Caille 1¢ Banker, 5-reel, ca 1906, VG 4,000.00
Caille 1¢ Baseball, 1-reel, ca 1911, EX orig........................... 4,000.00
Caille 1¢ Quintette, 5-reel, ca 1901, EX orig 8,000.00
Daval 1¢ American Eagle, 3-reel, good luck symbols, EX orig.....250.00
Daval 1¢ Penny Pack, 3-reel, ca 1939, 9x11x9", EX 375.00

Daval 1¢ Tri-O-Pak, rpl mechanism, rpt case, EX....................350.00
Daval 5¢ Derby, horse race game, ca 1937, NM.......................550.00
Daval 5¢ Puritan Baby, 3-reel, w/vendor, ca 1931, VG..............395.00
Daval 5¢ 21, blackjack w/draw windows, rstr..........................365.00
Exhibit 1¢ Play Ball, coin drop, rstr 1,295.00
Five Jacks 1¢, coin drop, cast aluminum, 19x20", NM 1,295.00
Groetchen 1¢ Gold Rush, rstr..425.00
Groetchen 1¢ Penny Smoke, ca 1936, EX orig.........................400.00
Groetchen 1¢ Sparks, 3-reel, rstr 265.00
Groetchen 5¢ Dixie Dominoes, 5-reel, EX orig........................375.00
Groetchen 5¢ Klix 21, 5-reel, w/gum vendor, EX.....................395.00

Hazard Three of a Kind National Coin Exchange, 1930s, $185.00.

High Stakes 1¢, horse race on reel strips, EX 695.00
Jennings 1¢ Favorite, coin drop, gum vendor, 14x20x13", EX.. 1,495.00
Jennings 1¢ Target Indian Front, coin drop, EX orig....................575.00
Jennings 5¢ Puritan Girl, 3-reel, EX orig 595.00
Joker's Wild 10¢, playing cards motif, EX orig...........................225.00
Keeney's 1¢ Magic Clock, numbers on reel, EX orig 395.00
Keeney's 5¢ Spinner Winner, coin drop, EX glass........................495.00
Line 'Em Up 1¢, coin drop, comic caricatures, rstr......................425.00
Little Dream 1¢, coin drop, oak case, EX orig 395.00
Maley 5¢ Stoneburner Eclipse, oak, US Novelty, 1893, EX 2,850.00
Mills 1¢ Draw Poker, 5-reel, ca 1900, VG............................. 1,450.00
Mills 1¢ New Target Practice, coin drop, EX orig 595.00
Mills 5¢ Perfection, 5-reel, urpight, ca 1901, VG 750.00
Mills 5¢ Tickette, punch card w/puncher, w/cards, 1930s, EX.....200.00
Puritan Baby, pay-out in front, 11x10x12", NM........................695.00
Puritan 1¢ Confection, Chicago Mint Co, EX orig......................525.00
Rockola 1¢ Official Sweepstakes Horse Race, rstr 1,495.00
Rockola 1¢/5¢ Hold & Draw, Art Deco, EX orig.......................625.00
Spin It 1¢, horse reel, candy dispenser, EX orig.........................225.00
Star 5¢ Sparky Poker, flat top, EX orig 175.00
Steeplechase 1¢ Marble, horse race game, 14x9x18", EX 600.00
Stephens 1¢ Draw Poker, reels spin, rpt, EX.............................435.00
Three Jacks 1¢, metal case, EX orig 725.00
Trip-L-Jax 1¢, coin drop, cast aluminum front, oak case, EX.......750.00

Vendors

Acorn 1¢, gum, multiple columns, orig decals, 7x16x7", EX 90.00

Ad-Lee Ever-Ready 1¢, bulk vendor, 4-compartment, ca 1937 ..150.00
Advance, gumball, football glove, 1923, rstr 175.00
Advance, Hershey 1¢ Chocolate Bars, EX...................................225.00
Advance, Kotex, 1920s, M orig...60.00
Advance Bigmouth, peanuts, 1923, rstr 225.00
Asco 5¢, nuts, w/Dixie Cup dispenser, EX orig 225.00
Atlas Bantam 5¢, peanuts, Deco style, w/key, EX orig 150.00
Atlas 1-Match Box, ca 1915, 17", EX 750.00
Atlas 10¢, gumball, glass top, rstr...60.00
Atlas 5¢ Bantam, peanuts, Deco style, EX orig 150.00
Baker Man 1¢, gumball, rstr.. 2,500.00
Columbus A, gumball, flat coin entry, 1946, EX.........................300.00
Columbus M, gumball, porc on CI, EX orig.................................225.00
Columbus 5¢ Bimore, aluminum, orig decals, EX orig.................585.00
Dixie Cup 1¢, wall mt, NM..425.00
E-Z, gumball, aluminum base, 18", EX.......................................595.00
Exhibit 1¢ Post Office, oak cabinet, EX 1,800.00
Fleer's 1¢, gum, oak/brass/tin, ca 1898, 15x10x4", G 1,250.00
Ford, gumball, ca 1950, M 65.00
Ford, gumball, Pat 1919, EX...150.00
Hawkeye, peanuts, 1940s, EX...80.00
Holli-Ware 1¢ Sugar Bowl, candy, 3-column, 11x19x7", EX.......145.00
Jaw Tester 1¢, bubble gum, countertop w/metal base, EX 25.00
Jennings in the Bag, ca 1934, EX orig 595.00
Jergens Lotion 1¢, Deco style, rpt..450.00
Kelly 1¢ Matchbox, 1920-30, 14¼x10½x8", EX 375.00
Mansfield 5¢ Automatic Clerk, Pepsin gum, NM 825.00
Masters, fantail, EX 1,200.00
Mills 1¢, Tab gum, used in subways, EX orig 225.00
Mills 1¢ Postage Stamps, oak/CI/metal, ca 1915, 22", EX 1,700.00
Nat'l 1¢ Sweet Chocolate, tin, ca 1917, 17", M 500.00
Northwestern #22, peanuts, frosted globe, orig locks, rstr 350.00
Northwestern #33, peanuts, frosted globe, red porc, rstr 350.00
Northwestern #60, peanuts, EX orig...60.00
Northwestern 5¢ 49er, peanuts, EX 65.00
Oak Vista 25¢, peanuts, MIB 60.00
Pencil Imprinter 5¢, select letters, minor rstr.............................595.00
Perfection 1¢, gum, Appleton Novelty, orig marquee, '27, EX 625.00
Pulver, clown figure, yel, clockworks, M 650.00
Pulver, cop directing traffic, red porc, rstr 850.00
Rocket Ship 1¢, coin drop, w/penny return, EX orig...................145.00
Scripto 25¢, pens, oak cabinet, countertop, 20¼", MIB 65.00
Shipman, stamps, bl porc, EX orig 75.00
Shipman 5¢ Select-A-Bar, candy, EX orig....................................175.00
Silver Comet 1¢, stick gum, EX orig 185.00
Silver King, gumball, EX 65.00
Silver King, hot nuts, EX orig 125.00
Star, popcorn, floor model, EX orig...750.00
Stollwerk 5¢ Chocolate, wood/metal/glass, ca 1900, rstr..............600.00
Stoner 1¢ Fresh Gum, w/orig paper card dtd 1953, EX.................85.00
Topper 1¢, gumball, EX 95.00
Triple Challenger, glass-side cup dispenser on stand....................575.00
Victor Baby Grand, gumball, 1950s, EX orig 45.00
Victor Baby Grand Deluxe, gumball, golden oak, 1951, EX..........75.00
Victor Super V, gumball, ca 1954, EX orig 75.00
Victor 1¢ V, peanuts, EX orig 65.00
Victor 10¢, coin drop, w/gumball vendor, EX orig 100.00
Victor 15¢ Vendorama, toys, oak, 1940, 24", EX 100.00
Victor 5¢ Selectomat, gumball, ca 1940s, EX orig 75.00
Zeno 1¢, gum, wood/CI, clockworks, 17x10x9", EX....................800.00

Miscellaneous

Caille Aristocrat Deluxe 1¢ Scale, lollipop style, 72", EX...........850.00

Caille Geo Washington Scale, rstr 5,500.00
Watling 1¢ Scale, cast aluminum, EX orig................................395.00

Comic Books

Public acceptance of the cartoon book as an enjoyable form of entertainment caused printing companies to experiment with size and format; by the early 1930s, the comic book as we know it today had evolved — 7" x 9" paper-back books stapled together and selling for 10¢. Each unfolded a new saga of adventure as experienced by detective extraordinaire Dick Tracy; super-heroes like Batman and Robin, Superman and Wonderwoman, Tarzan and The Lone Ranger; or the science fictional characters, Flash Gordon and Captain Midnight.

Today first issues in excellent condition may bring prices as high as $300 or over. Though values on the majority of comic books are still modest, Marvel Comics #1, published in 1938, has sold for the astounding price of $35,000. Rarity, age, and quality of artwork are prime factors in determining comic book values. Condition is also important — prices below reflect examples in fine condition unless otherwise noted.

Our advisor for this category is Steve Fishler; he is listed in the Directory under New York.

Ace Comics, #1, G 180.00
Ace Comics, #63, G+ 10.00
Action Comics, #112, G 30.00
Action Comics, #19, G 80.00
Action Comics, #28, VG 135.00
Action Comics, #79, EX 86.00
Adventure Comics, #245, G 12.00
Adventure Comics, #246, G 13.00
Amazing Spiderman, #149, NM 9.75
Amazing Spiderman, #16, VG/EX 48.00
Amazing Spiderman, #30, VG+ 29.00
Amazing Spiderman, #38, VG 18.00
Archie's Madhouse, #1, G/VG 24.00
Archie's Pal, Jughead, #32, VG+ 4.00
Astonishing, #16, VG 12.75
Atom, The; #9, EX/NM...40.00
Batman, #122, G/VG 18.50
Batman, #150, VG 13.50
Batman, #426, M 25.00
Beware the Creeper, #2, NM/M 20.00
Black Hood Comics, #19, G/VG 21.00
Brave & Bold, #53, EX- 9.00
Bulletman, #5, G...42.00
Buzzy, #54, G/VG 2.00
Calling All Boys, #2, EX..11.00
Captain America Comics, #55, NM 320.00
Captain Marvel Adventures, #10, EX..118.00
Captain Marvel Adventures, #31, G/VG..24.00
Challengers of the Unknown, #38, EX... 6.00
Crown Comics, #1, VG 30.00
Dale Evans Comics, #16, VG 13.75
Daredevil, #37, VG.. 4.50
Detective Comics, #371, NM...10.50
Fantastic Four, #71, NM..13.00
Flash, The; #139, VG 9.00
Flash, The; #147, VG+ 4.25
Four Color, 2nd series, #1025, EX 24.00
Four Color, 2nd series, #1077, VG++ 16.00
Four Color, 2nd series, #1169, EX 32.00
Four Color, 2nd series, #1237, EX 30.00
Four Color, 2nd series, #951, EX/NM 56.00

Frankenstein, #1, G/VG 48.00
Frankie Comics, #14, VG/EX 4.75
Frontline Combat, #1, VG 59.00
Frontline Combat, #2, G 23.00
Frontline Combat, #5, VG/EX 35.00
House of Mystery, #143, VG+ 12.50
House of Mystery, #145, VG 4.00
House of Mystery, #154, EX 6.50
House of Secrets, #1, G 39.00
House of Secrets, #44, VG+ 3.50
I Spy, #3, EX/NM 16.75
Journey Into Mystery, #111, EX 9.25
Journey Into Mystery, #84, M 20.00
Jughead's Fantasy, #3, G 6.50
Jungle Jim, #12, VG+ 3.25
Justice League of America, #36, EX 4.25
Justice League of America, #5, G 20.00
Kerry Drake Detective Cases, #12, EX/NM 20.00
Kerry Drake Detective Cases, #24, VG+ 6.00
Key Ring Comics, #1, EX 10.00
Kid Komics, #1, G/VG 180.00
King Comics, #140, EX 20.00
Konga, #14, NM 27.00
Krazy Komics, #1, EX 62.00
Leading Comics, #7, G+ 42.00
Little Lulu, #188, NM 9.00
Little Lulu & Tubby Annual, #1, VG+ 43.00
Marvel Mystery, #68, VG 82.00
Marvel Tales, 2nd series, #2, EX 29.00
Master Comics, #44, VG+ 38.00
Maverick, #14, EX- 11.00
Menace, #1, EX 70.00
Mickey Mouse Four Color, #248, VG+ 23.00
Mickey Mouse Four Color, #296, G/VG 12.75
Mighty Mouse Comics, 2nd series, #39, G 7.00
My Greatest Adventure, #50, VG- 3.00
National Comics, #48, VG 17.00
New Gods, #2, EX/NM 3.75
Parole Breakers, #1, VG 33.00
Pep Comics, #1, VG 345.00
Phantom Lady, 1st series, #21, VG+ 115.00
Planet Comics, #12, VG+ 250.00
Planet Comics, #52, VG 59.00
Popular Comics, #82, EX 45.00
Ringo Kid Western, #21, VG 4.00
Silver Surfer, #5, VG/EX 12.00
Space Busters, #1, VG/EX 85.00
Space Detective, #1, VG+ 132.00
Sparky Watts, #1, G- 13.00
Special Edition Comics, #1, EX 750.00
Spellbound, #12, VG 9.00
Strange Adventures, #118, EX- 13.50
Strange Adventures, #197, VG/EX 1.75
Strange Tales, #155, EX/NM 11.00
Strange Tales, #75, G 7.00
Strange Tales Annual, #1, G 27.00
Superboy, #52, G 6.75
Superboy, #62, G- 4.75
Superboy, #95, EX 5.75
Superman, #238, NM 6.50
Superman, #52, G- 29.00
Tales of Suspense, #49, G- 7.00
Tales To Astonish, #42, EX 35.00
Tales To Astonish, #57, G- 6.00

Tarzan, #71, G/VG 4.25
Teen Titans, #26, VG+ 2.50
Thunder Agents, #7, EX 5.75
Unknown Worlds, #29, VG 1.50
USA Comics, #1, VG- 585.00
Whiz Comics, #2, G 3,000.00
Wings Comics, #3, VG- 45.00
Wings Comics, #46, VG 18.00
Wings Comics, #62, VG 16.00
World's Finest Comics, #36, G- 35.00
X-Men, #159, NM+ 3.75
X-Men, #26, G/VG 7.25
Young Allies, #19, VG 62.00
Young Allies, #5, VG 87.00
Young Eagle, #2, G- 3.50

Compasses

Creach-Osborn Marching Compass...Brooklyn NY, 2½" dia 38.00
Negus NY Ritchie Boston, brass on wood stand, 5¼" dia 50.00
Ritchie & Sons, chrome/brass, lights from beneath, 10" dia 250.00
Unmk, brass w/brass lid, ca 1840s, 2½" dia, EX 55.00

Consolidated Lamp and Glass

The Consolidated Lamp and Glass Company of Coraopolis, Pennsylvania, was incorporated in 1894. For many years their primary business was the manufacture of lighting glass such as oil lamps and shades for both gas and electric lighting. The popular 'Cosmos' line of lamps and tableware was produced from 1894 to 1915. (See also Cosmos.) In 1926 Consolidated introduced their Martele line, a type of 'sculptured' ware closely resembling Lalique glassware of France. (Compare Consolidated's 'Lovebirds' vase with the Lalique 'Perruches' vase.) It is this line of vases, lamps, and tableware which is often mistaken for a very similar type of glassware produced by the Phoenix Glass Company, located nearby in Monaca, Pennsylvania. For example, the so-called Phoenix 'Grasshopper' vases are actually Consolidated's 'Katydid' vases.

Items in the Martele line were produced in blue, pink, green, crystal, white, or custard glass decorated with various fired-on color treatments or a satin finish. For the most part, their colors were distinctively different from those used by Phoenix. Although not foolproof, one of the ways of distinguishing Consolidated's wares from those of Phoenix is that most of the time Consolidated applied color to the raised portion of the design, leaving the background plain, while Phoenix usually applied color to the background leaving the raised surfaces undecorated. This is particularly true of those pieces in white or custard glass.

Consolidated closed its doors for good in 1964. Subsequently a few of the molds passed into the hands of other glass companies that later reproduced certain patterns; one such re-issue is the 'Chickadee' vase, found in avocado green, satin finish custard, or milk glass.

Key: mg — milk glass

Bird of Paradise, fan vase, amber on crystal, 10" 150.00
Bird of Paradise, plate, gr stain on crystal, 12" 60.00
Catalonian, bowl, salad; emerald, str-sided, 9" 50.00
Catalonian, candle holder, honey stain, wide bobeche, #1131 ......40.00
Catalonian, cigarette box, Spanish rose, w/2 ash trays 65.00
Catalonian, creamer & sugar bowl, amethyst on crystal, open 25.00
Catalonian, Spanish Knobs, pinch vase, amethyst stain, 7" 65.00
Catalonian, violet vase, ruby stain on crystal 70.00
Chickadee, vase, amethyst birds, brn/gr floral on custard 140.00

Chrysanthemum, vase, red glass, 12" 300.00
Dancing Girl, vase, 7 women/Pan, gr on wht satin, 11½" 350.00
Dancing Nymphs, plate, teal bl, 8" 60.00
Dancing Nymphs, plate, wht bkground, crystal figures, 17" 400.00
Dancing Nymphs, tumbler, pk, ftd, 5½" 60.00
Dogwood, vase, turq on wht satin, 10" 125.00
Dogwood, vase, 24k gold on glossy wht, 10" 130.00
Dragonfly, vase, gr cased, 6" 165.00
Fish, comport, honey stain on crystal, ftd, 6" 50.00
Fish, tray, water lily border, amethyst stain on crystal 150.00
Five Fruits, goblet, amethyst stain on crystal 30.00
Five Fruits, plate, brn (sepia) stain on crystal, 14" 95.00
Five Fruits, sundae w/snack tray, gr stain on crystal 35.00
Floral, vase, ruby on crystal, 9" 125.00
Florentine, vase, gr, oblong, #2201, 6½" 170.00
Flower & Leaf, mayonnaise bowl, amethyst stain, ftd 40.00
Flower & Leaf, tumbler, pk stain on crystal, ftd 35.00
Foxglove, vase, bl flowers, gr leaves on wht satin, 10" 115.00
Goldfish, vase, coral fish, bl bkground on mg, oblong, 9" 150.00
Hummingbird, vase, brn birds/coral/turq on custard 100.00
Hummingbird & Roses, puff box, honey stain on crystal, 7" 80.00
Jonquil, vase, pk flowers, gr leaves on wht satin, 6¼" 75.00
Katydids, tumbler vase, gr stain on crystal, 9" 130.00
Katydids, vase, coral on wht satin, ovoid, 7" 145.00
LeFleur/Poppy, vase, bl glass, satin finish, 10½" 220.00
Lovebirds, puff box, pk stain on crystal, 4" 50.00
Lovebirds, vase, amethyst birds/coral/brn on wht, 10½" 220.00
Mermaid, bowl, amethyst stain on crystal, 9" 150.00
Nuthatch, window box, red birds/brn/gr on custard 200.00
Olive, bowl, salad; honey stain on crystal, deep 70.00
Olive, plate, gr stain on crystal, 8" 35.00
Olive, window box, amethyst fruit, gr leaves, 8" 110.00
Owls, vase, yel cased, 6" 225.00
Pine Cone, vase, gold on wht gloss, 7" 120.00
Ruba Rombic, cigarette box, smoky topaz 340.00
Ruba Rombic, sherbet, sunshine 65.00
Ruba Rombic, vase, cased gr opal, 9½" 2,400.00
Ruba Rombic, vase, jungle gr, 6½" 170.00

Ruba Rombic vase, sunshine, 9½", $350.00.

Santa Maria, cigar jar, ship finial, crystal 200.00
Santa Maria, cigarette box, orchid on crystal 140.00
Sea gulls, vase, wht birds w/blk accents, bl bkground, 11" 225.00
Swallows, bowl, lt bl on crystal, low, flared, 9" 125.00
Vine/Line 700, plate, French crystal, 8" 35.00
Vine/Line 700, sundae, lt gr stain on crystal 20.00
Vine/Line 700, vase, bl stain on crystal, 10" 250.00

Vine/Line 700, vase, gold on wht satin, 6½" 95.00

Cookbooks

Cookbooks from the nineteenth century, though often hard to find, are a delight to today's collectors both for their quaint formats and printing methods as well as for their outmoded, often humorous views on nutrition. Recipes required a 'pinch' of salt, butter 'the size of an egg' or a 'walnut,' or a 'handful' of flour. Collectors sometimes specialize in cookbooks issued as advertising premiums. Especially desirable are the figurals that were shaped like a jar, a slice of bread, or some other form relative to the product. Others with unique features such as illustrations by well-known artists or references to famous people or places are priced in accordance. Cookbooks written earlier than 1874 are the most valuable and when found command prices as high as $200; figurals usually sell in the $10 to $15 range.

Key: CB — Cookbook

Baker's Chocolate Recipes, color illus, 1932, EX 13.00
Casseroles by Hulse, 1914 ....16.00
CI Hood & Co, Lowell MA, 1877, 62-pg, EX 12.50
Enterprising Housekeeper, by Enterprise Mfg, 1897, EX 40.00
Gold CB by Master Chef Louis P deGouy, 1960 ....18.00
Hood's Practical CB, 1897, 349-pg, EX 20.00

The Jell-O Girl Entertains, Rose O'Neill illustration, contains advertisement of ice cream powder, 5" x 7", $50.00.

Karo Kookery, 1942, EX 9.00
Liberace Cooks, 1970, M in dust jacket 20.00
Lippencott's Housewifery, 1921, 353-pg, EX 15.00
Little Daisy Salad Book, 1923, EX 10.00
Master Cake Baker, Calumet, 1927, 107-pg, EX 15.00
Metropolitan CB, 1918 .... 5.00
Nature Cure CB, 1918 ....36.00
One Hundred Prize Dinners, 1900, 780-pg, EX 20.00
Pennsylvania Dutch CB, 1936 ....15.00
Pillsbury's Country American #33, 1983 .... 9.00
Pillsbury's 6th Grand National, 1954 ....16.00
Recipes from the Old South, 1961, EX 9.00
Saturday Evening Post Family CB, J Eisenhour editor, 1975 .... 9.00
Sheraton World CB, 1982 ....12.00
Waring CB, 14-speed blender, 1970, EX 4.00
White House CB, 1887, G 60.00

100...World's Greatest...by J Beard, Benson & Hedges, 1976.........**13.00**

Cookie Cutters

Early hand-fashioned cookie cutters have recently been commanding stiff prices at country auctions, and the ranks of interested collectors are growing steadily. Especially valuable are the figural cutters; and the more complicated the design, the higher the price. A follow-up of the carved wooden cookie boards, the first cutters were probably made by itinerant tinkers from left-over or recycled pieces of tin. Though most of the eighteenth-century examples are now in museums or collections, it is still possible to find some good cutters from the late 1800s when changes in the manufacture of tin resulted in a thinner, less expensive material. The width of the cutting strip is often a good indicator of age — the wider the strip, the older the cutter. While the very early cutters were 1" to 1½" deep, by the twenties and thirties, many were less than ½" deep. Crude, spotty soldering indicates an older cutter, while a thin line of solder usually tends to suggest a much later manufacture. The shape of the backplate is another clue. Later cutters will have oval, round, or rectangular backs, while on the earlier type the back was cut to follow the lines of the design. Cookie cutters usually vary from 2" to 4" in size, but gingerbread men were often made as tall as 12". Birds, fish, hearts, and tulips are common; simple versions can be purchased for as little as $12.00 to $15.00. The larger figurals, especially those with more imaginative details, often bring $75.00 and up.

Ax, 4"	**6.50**
Bird, aluminum, 4¾"	**3.00**
Bird, 4"	**20.00**
Buxom lady w/arms akimbo, strap hdl, early, 8"	**495.00**
Camel, aluminum, strap hdl	**3.00**
Chick, 3¾"	**15.00**
Chicken, aluminum, 4"	**3.00**
Cornucopia, strap hdl, rolled edges, 4" L	**45.00**
Country lady, 7"	**50.00**
Diamond, 3"	**12.00**
Dog, EX detail, 4½" L	**45.00**
Dog, sm	**15.00**
Duck, star perforation	**20.00**
Duck, 3½" L	**18.00**
Fish, fluted fins, strap hdl, 1830s, 3x7½"	**260.00**
Fish, solid bk w/air hole, no hdl, 1800s, 4"	**36.00**
Fish, wide strap hdl, 3x7", EX	**200.00**
Girl Scout, aluminum	**5.00**
Goose, 4x4½"	**25.00**
Hatchet, 2¼"	**5.00**
Heart, lg	**30.00**
Horse, EX detail, 6"	**130.00**
Horse, 8½"	**200.00**
Lady w/hair piled high, full figure, 8x2½x1", EX	**150.00**
Lamb, 4"	**18.00**
Lion, 4"	**20.00**
Man, stylized figure, 8½"	**85.00**
Pig, 1890s, ¾x3x6½"	**35.00**
Rabbit, aluminum, 4"	**3.00**
Rabbit, running, 4"	**20.00**
Rooster, EX detail, 6"	**85.00**
Rooster, tin, 1890s, ½x3¼x3½"	**18.00**
Shaker man	**38.00**
Shamrock, 3½"	**12.50**
Spade, 3"	**12.00**
Star, 3"	**15.00**

Rabbit, 4" x 5½", $30.00.

Cookie Jars

The appeal of the cookie jar is universal; folks of all ages, both male and female, love to collect 'em! The early thirties' heavy stoneware jars of a rather nondescript nature quickly gave way to figurals of every type imaginable. Those from the mid to late thirties were often decorated over the glaze with 'cold paint,' but by the early forties underglaze decorating resulted in cheerful, bright, permanent colors and cookie jars that still have a new look forty years later.

Unmarked jars, unless properly identified and rare, bring the lowest prices, while cookie jars trimmed in gold are usually highly valued. The examples listed below were made by companies other than those found elsewhere in this book; see also specific manufacturers.

Our advisor for this catgory is Barry Thomsen; he is listed in the Directory under Ilinois. For further study, we recommend *An Illustrated Guide to Cookie Jars* by Ermagene Westfall, and *The Collector's Encyclopedia of Cookie Jars*, by Fred and Joyce Roerig.

See specific manufactures such as Brush, Metlox, and McCoy.

After School Cookies, mk 741 USA, American Bisque	**27.00**
Albert Apple, PD Co, 1942	**100.00**
Alice's Adventures in Wonderland, outside of house, Japan	**195.00**
Angel, Treasure Craft	**50.00**
Animal Crackers, American Bisque	**22.00**
Atlantic Owl	**10.00**
Baby Bear, Treasure Craft	**38.00**
Balloon Lady, Pottery Guild, NM	**88.00**
Bear, visor hat, American Bisque	**85.00**
Bear on Stump w/Sucker, Twin Winton	**30.00**
Bear Police Chief, Twin Winton	**45.00**
Bell, Ring for Cookies, mk USA, American Bisque	**30.00**
Betsy Ross, Napco	**100.00**
Blk Little Girl, gr dress, patch heart, Treasure Craft	**88.00**
Blk Little Girl, w/cookie, pk or wht dress, Sears	**500.00**
Blk Mammy, bl & wht check dress, red bandana	**400.00**
Blk Mammy, yel/red dots, hands on chest, no mark	**800.00**
Blkboard Little Girl, mk USA, American Bisque	**80.00**
Bo Peep, Napco	**90.00**
Boots, mk USA, American Bisque	**100.00**
Bow Bear, eyes closed, American Bisque	**35.00**
Campbell Kid, nodding head, mk DA-AR in oval w/V	**350.00**
Canister, Treasure Craft	**20.00**
Canister w/Flowers, Robinson Ransbottom	**25.00**

Carousel, Treasure Craft, MIB 50.00
Casper, Harvey Productions 700.00
Cat, brn/yel, pk bow, unmk American Bisque 20.00
Cat, sitting, flat bk, early 25.00
Cat in Basket, unknown mfg 20.00
Cheerleaders, #802 USA Corner Cookie Jar, American Bisque ...90.00
Chef, Robinson Ransbottom 80.00
Chianti Wine Bottle, Doranne of CA 65.00
Chick w/Tam, American Bisque 45.00
Chicken, Twin Winton 20.00
Chimpanzee, Japan 22.50
Churn, red flowers, 24k gold trim, American Bisque 20.00
Cinderella, Napco 85.00
Climbing Bear, Japan 25.00
Clown, finger in mouth, CA Originals 50.00
Clown, raised arms, American Bisque 38.00
Clown on Stage, flasher, American Bisque 70.00
Coffeepot, Treasure Craft 50.00
Collegiate Owl, cap w/tassel, mk USA, American Bisque 40.00
Cookie Boy, LA Potteries 45.00
Cookie Catcher Wagon, Twin Winton 45.00
Cookie Club Mushroom, Treasure Craft 50.00
Cookie Pot, Twin Winton 45.00
Cottage, Twin Winton CA USA 40.00
Cow Jumped Over the Moon, Robinson Ransbottom 70.00
Cow Jumped Over the Moon, yel, Doranne of CA 175.00
Davy Crockett w/Bear, Sierra Vista 600.00
Davy Crockett w/Rifle, American Bisque 180.00
Donald Duck, w/hand in jar, Disney 90.00
Donald Duck w/Pumpkin, CA Originals 275.00
Donkey w/Milk Wagon, American Bisque 70.00
Drum Major, Japan 65.00
Dutch Boy, Pottery Guild 65.00
Elephant, brn, wht sailor hat, Twin Winton 25.00
Elf Head, various colors, unmk 55.00
Elsie the Cow, Pottery Guild 155.00
Elves & Schoolhouse, CA Originals 25.00
Ernie, Keebler Elf, F&F 50.00
Flintstone Rubbles House, American Bisque, M 450.00
Flowers & Dots on brn, Mar-Crest Oven Proof Stoneware USA ..30.00
French Poodle, American Bisque 40.00
Garage, #306, Cardinal 40.00
Garbage Can, Doranne of CA 40.00
German Man's Head, West Germany 225.00
Goldilocks, Regal China 150.00
Granny, American Bisque 95.00
Gumball Machine, CA Originals 65.00
Hen w/Chick on Bk, Fredricksburg 25.00

Hobo Clown, Treasure Craft 55.00
Hootie Owl, Robinson Ransbottom 40.00
Hopalong Cassidy, decal, shirt style, scarce 300.00
Horse Doctor, Japan 25.00
Hound Dog, Market Square, made for JC Penney 22.50
Hubert the Lion, Regal China 375.00
Ice Cream Sundae w/Cherry, Doranne of CA 50.00
Jack-in-the-Box, American Bisque 45.00
Jukebox, 1946 Bubbler, Treasure Craft 55.00
Keystone Cop, CA Originals 50.00
Keystone Cop, mk GK1 USA 35.00
Kitten on Beehive, American Bisque 32.00
Kookie Lamb, unmk 48.00
Kraft Marshmallow Bear, Regal China, lg 155.00
Lady Pig, American Bisque 75.00
Lady w/Muffler, gray coat, hands in muffler, old, EX 90.00
Lamb, Twin Winton 45.00
Lamb w/Flowers, American Bisque 60.00
Lion, K-02 USA, Doranne of CA 40.00
Little Girl, #301, Cardinal 50.00
Little Sprout, Pillsbury 45.00
Majorette, gold trim, Regal China 110.00
Majorette, unmk, American Bisque 70.00
Merry-Go-Round, mk USA 40.00
Mexican, Treasure Craft 40.00
Modern Rooster, split tail, cold pnt, American Bisque 55.00
Monk, Thou Shalt Not Steal, Twin Winton 32.00
Monk, Treasure Craft 25.00
Monkey, arms over head, unmk 45.00
Mouse Face, tail in bk, early '80s, Treasure Craft 44.00
Noah's Ark, Treasure Craft 40.00
Old King Cole, Robinson Ransbottom 250.00
Old Time Victrola Phonograph, CA Originals 65.00
Olive Oyl, American Bisque 1,200.00
Oreo Cookies, Market Square, made for JC Penney 22.00
Oscar the Grouch, CA Originals 45.00
Panda Bear, unmk 45.00
Peter Peter Pumpkin Eater, Robinson Ransbottom 80.00
Pig, boy or girl, unmk American Bisque 40.00
Pig, little pig finial, Japan 15.00
Pig in a Polk, American Bisque 50.00
Pillsbury Doughboy, American Bisque 35.00
Pine Cone Coffeepot, mk USA, American Bisque 25.00
Popeye, American Bisque 900.00
Porky Pig, Warner Bros. 30.00
Puppy, on yel pot, unmk American Bisque, 1958 ....35.00
Quaker Oats, oatmeal box form, Regal China, M 110.00
Rabbit, Gillinder 60.00
Rabbit in Brn Coat, CA Originals 60.00
Rabbit w/Baseball Bat, tie around neck 30.00
Racoon, Twin Winton 35.00
Raggedy Ann, Japan 20.00
Red Riding Hood, Pottery Guild 85.00
Rocking Horse, Treasure Craft 50.00
R2D2, orig movie jar, bl & wht, M 90.00
Sailor Mouse, Twin Winton 45.00
Sandman Cookies, kids watch TV, #801, American Bisque 70.00
Santa, American Bisque 90.00
Santa in Rocker, Lefton China 85.00
Sheriff Pig, Robinson Ransbottom 85.00
Sheriff w/Hole in Hat, CA Originals 50.00
Smart Cookie, #303, Cardinal 45.00
Smiley Pig, Terrace Ceramics 28.00
Snacks, teapot shape, mk USA, American Bisque 15.00

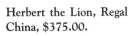
Herbert the Lion, Regal China, $375.00.

Soldier, #312, Cardinal..50.00
Soldier Boy, CA Originals 235.00
Space Ship, American Bisque 100.00
Stagecoach, plastic windows, scarce, Sierra Vista 275.00
Sugar Dairy, Twin Winton...25.00
Sweet Pea, crawling..710.00
Tat-L-Tale, w/voice box in lid, NM............................350.00
Telephone, #311, Cardinal 30.00
Tigger Tiger, Disney, EX 145.00
Tom & Jerry, MGM, 1981 ....160.00
Tony Tiger, Kellogg, plastic...35.00
Train, Pfaltzgraff 65.00
Train, Twin Winton...35.00
Transformer Robot, Japan 60.00
Trolley Car, Treasure Craft 55.00
Tugboat, Treasure Craft...55.00
Tugboat, Twin Winton...45.00
Umbrella Kids, American Bisque.................................100.00
Victorian House, Treasure Craft 45.00
Walrus, Doranne of CA..50.00
Winking Farmer Pig, Robinson Ransbottom 40.00
Winnie the Pooh, Disney, dk yel & red 90.00
Witch, stirs brew, unmk...85.00
Wooden Soldier, American Bisque 30.00

Yogi Bear, Hanna Barbera, $275.00.

Yarn Doll, aqua, unmk American Bisque 55.00
Ye Olde Cookie Jar, San Juan Capistrano, dtd '59........................15.00
Zoo, animals in relief on gr, Ace Hardware...................................40.00

Cooper, Susie

A twentieth-century ceramic designer whose works are now attracting the attention of collectors, Susie Cooper was first affiliated with the A.E. Gray Pottery in Henley, England in 1922 where she designed in lustres and painted items with her own ideas as well. (Examples of Gray's lustreware is rare and costly.) By 1930 she and her brother-in-law, Jack Beeson, had established a family business. Her pottery soon became a success and she was subsequently offered space at Crown Works, Burslem. In 1940 she received the honorary title of

Royal Designer for Industry, the only such distinction ever awarded by the Royal Society of Arts solely for pottery design. Miss Cooper received the Order of the British Empire in the New Year's Honors List of 1979. She was the chief designer for the Wedgwood group from 1966 until she resigned in 1972. Since 1980 she has worked on a free-lance basis.

Bowl, Cubist pattern, Grays 250.00
Coffee set, Beechwood, Rex shape, 7¾" pot, 3-pc 150.00
Coffeepot, Sea Anemone, bl-gr buds & spots w/pk wash, 7¾" 75.00
Cup & saucer, blk decor on wht matt, 2¼"..................35.00
Cup & saucer, demitasse; bl bands on beige, sgn 20.00
Jug, olive gr, emb tulips, 6½" 250.00
Plaque, Gray Leaf, brn wash border, 14" 275.00
Plaque, heart-shaped leaf, maroon border, 11" 200.00
Plate, Pear in Pompadour, gr/blk/red/yel, 6"................20.00
Plate, sgraffito pineapple, turq, 9" 65.00
Sauce boat, Chinese Fern, 6" 40.00
Sweet dish, Dresden Spray, yel wash border, 7½" dia 40.00
Teacup, chartreuse & metallic gold, 2¼" 40.00

Vases: S 103-B, white ribbed, $350.00; S 102-C, ochre with tulips, $300.00; S 112, hand painted, $250.00.

Vase, pk, appl buttons, 7½"..350.00
Wall charger/plaque, flowers (bold) on lt bl, mk, 13" 400.00

Coors

The firm that became known as Coors Porcelain Company in 1920 was founded in 1908 by John J. Herold, originally of the Roseville Pottery in Zanesville, Ohio. Though still in business today, they are best known for their artware vases and Rosebud dinnerware produced before 1939.

Coors vases produced before the late thirties were made in a matt finish; by the latter years of the decade, high-gloss glazes were also being used. Nearly fifty shapes were in production, and some of the more common forms were made in three sizes. Typical colors in matt are white, orange, blue, green, yellow, and tan. Yellow, blue, maroon, pink, and green are found in high gloss. All vases are marked with a triangular arrangement of the words 'Coors Colorado Pottery' enclosing the word 'Golden.' You may find vases (usually 6"– 6½") marked with the Colorado State Fair stamp and dated 1939. For such a vase, add $10.00 to the suggested values given below.

Our advisor for this category is Jo Ellen Winther. Advice for miscellaneous listings was provided by Jim and Carol Carlton; all are listed in the directory under Colorado.

Apple baker, Rosebud, 4¾" dia	20.00
Ash tray, Rosebud, 3½"	75.00
Baking pan, Rosebud, rectangular, 2x12x8"	30.00
Bowl, cereal; Rosebud, 6"	15.00
Bowl, fruit; Rosebud, 5"	8.00
Bowl, mixing; Rosebud, 6"	12.50
Bowl, pudding; Rosebud, 3-pt, sm	14.00
Casserole, Rosebud, w/lid, 14-cup	38.00
Creamer, Rosebud, 3"	15.00
Cup, custard; Rosebud, 4"	8.00
Egg cup, Rosebud, 6-oz	25.00
Honey pot, Rosebud, w/lid & ladle	75.00
Muffin set, Rosebud, 8" plate w/5½" dome lid	65.00
Pitcher, Rosebud, open, 4-pt	35.00
Plate, Rosebud, 7¼"	7.50
Plate, Rosebud, 9"	10.00
Platter, Rosebud, 12x9"	15.00
Saucer, Rosebud, 5½"	6.00
Teapot, Rosebud, 2-cup	45.00
Tumbler, Rosebud, ftd, no hdl, 12-oz	30.00
Tumbler, Rosebud, hdl, 8½-oz	25.00
Underplate, Rosebud, 7"	8.00
Water server, Rosebud, corked stopper, 6-cup	40.00

Miscellaneous

Ash tray, 'Beer, Butter, Malted Milk,' rnd, flat	45.00
Ash tray, ivory, common	3.00
Bank, clown, hanging	45.00
Bank, clown, sitting	45.00
Bowl vase, scroll hdls extend above wide collar neck, 6"	40.00
Bowl vase, scroll hdls extend above wide collar neck, 7¼"	75.00
Bud vase, bulbous w/long trumpet neck, 9"	40.00
Coffee maker, porc, 4-part	75.00
Crock, malted milk; porc, w/lid	75.00
Figurine, Monks, laughing/crying, pr	175.00
Lamp, cvd leaves & berries, bulbous, 7", +shade	150.00
Mug, w/Colorado State Fair, 1934	45.00
Mug, w/lion decal	18.00
Shaker, bottle form	15.00
Shaker, keg form	15.00
Vase, bulbous urn form w/hdls, 12"	100.00
Vase, bulbous urn form w/hdls, 7¼"	40.00
Vase, bulbous urn form w/hdls, 9"	75.00
Vase, bulbous w/collar neck, rope hdls, 9½"	60.00
Vase, cvd leaves & berries, bulbous, 6½"	35.00
Vase, Empire State Bldg, sq w/stepped buttresses, 9"	75.00
Vase, ftd bowl form w/akimbo rim-to-shoulder hdls, #7, 6½"	40.00
Vase, ftd bowl form w/akimbo rim-to-shoulder hdls, #7, 8"	75.00
Vase, horizontal ribbing, molded ring hdls, 5"	40.00
Vase, ½-circle rim-to-base hdls, Deco shape, 5¾"	25.00
Vase, ½-circle rim-to-base hdls, Deco shape, 6¼"	35.00
Vase, ½-circle rim-to-base hdls, Deco shape, 8¼"	75.00

Coper, Hans

Hans Coper was born in Germany in 1920. He fled to England from Nazi Germany in 1939 and took up ceramics in 1946 when Lucie Rie hired him as a helper to make buttons for the clothing industry.

Coper had a keen interest in ceramics and learned to throw on the potter's wheel within days. He left Lucie Rie's studio in 1958 and set up his own. Even though he was married and had children, he lived and worked alone until his death in 1981. He was probably the most successful twentieth-century potter.

Coper's pieces are mostly vases characterized by marble- and basalt-like surfaces. they are impressed with a seal mark on the bottom using the initials 'HC,' but turned 90 degrees so as to resemble a bowl on a potter's wheel.

Vase, buff clay, heavy-combed blk matt, ftd/dbl-lobed, 7"	**5,800.00**
Vase, wht w/exposed blk clay rim, emb mid-band, ovoid, 5"	**1,300.00**
Vase, 2-lobed U-form on can ft, combed blk on buff, 7"	**6,000.00**

Copper

Hand-crafted copper was made in America from early in the eighteenth century until about 1850, with the center of its production in Pennsylvania. Examples have been found signed by such notable coppersmiths as Kidd, Buchanan, Babb, Bently, and Harbeson. Of the many utilitarian items made, teakettles are the most desirable. Early examples from the eighteenth century were made with a dovetailed joint which was hammered and smoothed to a uniform thickness. Pots from the nineteenth century were seamed. Coffeepots were made in many shapes and sizes and along with mugs, kettles, warming pans, and measures are easiest to find. Stills ranging in sizes of up to fifty-gallon are popular with collectors today.

Our advisor, Mary Frank Gaston, has compiled a lovely book, *Antique Copper*, with many full-color photos and current market values; you will find her address in the Directory under Texas.

Bowl, antelope/elephant/floral/camel medallions, hammered, 15"	55.00
Bowl, fruit; rtcl, ped ft, Manning Bowman, 4x7½"	27.50
Coal bucket, emb knight/dragon/2 eagles	190.00
Coffee server, brass fittings/finial, blk wood stick hdl	25.00
Fish poacher, oval w/rolled rim, swing hdl, lid, 21" L	330.00
Fish slice, pierced 3x4" pad, flat hdl, early, 10½"	85.00
Funnel, 12½" dia	40.00
Kettle, tapered cylinder, rolled rim, swing hdl, 21x32"	250.00
Lamp, egg form on slim std, saucer base, no burner, 5"	300.00
Measure, haystack form, dvtl, battered/soldered rpr, 8"	95.00
Measure, haystack form, dvtl, mk Gallon, 12"	115.00
Measure, weighted, false brass bottom, English, qt, 6", VG	250.00
Pail, milking; wire bail, ca 1865, mini, 4½x5"	40.00
Pan, iron hdls ea side, dvtl, stamped name, w/lid, 7x10"	85.00

Pan, wrought iron and brass handles, 1850s, 12", 32" length, $350.00; Milk pan, double handles, rolled rim, dovetailed, early 1900s, 19" diameter, $400.00.

Pot, dvtl, ear hdls, battered, 4½"	65.00
Pot, dvtl, w/iron bail & hook, 9¼"	165.00

Pot, dvtl, wrought hdl, Middle Eastern, 9"..**65.00**
Saucepan, iron hdl, dvtl, Carmichael Wilks mk, rpr, 7x9"............**65.00**
Saucepan, iron hdl, 8¾x11", VG **65.00**
Skillet, iron hdl, mk NN, 12", 10½" hdl..............................**75.00**
Teakettle, dvtl, mk J Ebert, Hamilton, rpr, 8½" **550.00**
Teakettle, dvtl, rpr hdl, rpl finial, 3¾" **95.00**
Teakettle, W Heiss #213 North St Phila, 1820s, 7", EX **375.00**
Teapot, gooseneck spout, loop finial, tin lined, 4½x8¼" **150.00**

Copper Lustre

Copper lustre is a term referring to a type of pottery made in Staffordshire after the turn of the nineteenth century. It is finished in a metallic rusty-brown glaze resembling true copper. Pitchers are found in abundance, ranging from simple styles with dull bands of color to those with fancy handles and bands of embossed, polychromed flowers. Bowls are common; goblets, mugs, teapots, and sugar bowls much less so. It's easy to find, but not in good condition. Pieces with hand-painted decoration and those with historical transfers are the most valuable.

Our advisor for this category is Richard Marden; he is listed in the Directory under New Hampshire.

Bowl, floral on orange band, ftd, w/dome lid, 6x6¾"...................**200.00**
Bust, Plato, 8½" **75.00**
Candlestick, cherub on scroll support, Czech, late, 6", pr **20.00**
Creamer, Success to Queen..., blk w/emb wht busts, 3½" **225.00**
Figurine, dbl pulpit w/clerics, wear/rpr, 9½" **625.00**
Figurine, dog, seated, 7½" **175.00**
Figurine, whippet, seated, free-standing front legs, 7½", pr..........**360.00**
Flowerpot, emb wht scenes, pk lustre trim, 3½", +saucer **365.00**
Flowerpot, gray band w/emb birds, lion head/ring hdls, 6" **200.00**
Goblet, Faith & Hope, pk transfer on wht, 4½" **95.00**
Mug, pk lustre band w/3-color floral, 4⅞" **200.00**
Mug, tan band w/emb wht busts, mc/purple lustre floral, 3" **85.00**
Mug, wht sanded bands, w/lid, 5½" **100.00**
Mug, wide gr band, 6 yel bands, child's, 2¾x4" **65.00**
Pitcher, badminton scene transfer on canary band, 8", NM.........**125.00**
Pitcher, bl band, emb stag/dog, mc/pk lustre, lion hdl, 6" **150.00**
Pitcher, bl bands w/mc emb florals, ftd, 9" **325.00**
Pitcher, florals, mc on wide gr band, prof rpr, 8½" **200.00**
Pitcher, florals on bl band, hairlines in hdl, 9½" **150.00**
Pitcher, Gen Jackson, Hero..., blk transfer on bl, 8½", EX **1,375.00**

Pitcher, continuous band of houses, 6", $75.00.

Pitcher, Lafayette & Cornwallis reserves on canary band, 7".......**700.00**
Pitcher, Masonic transfer on bl, J&S Jones, 1819, 9", EX **375.00**
Pitcher, wht band w/copper lustre warriors, 7½" **135.00**
Spill vase, canary band, mother/child in reserves, rpr, 4½".........**135.00**
Teapot, mc florals, gooseneck spout, dome lid, 7½" **175.00**
Tumbler, wht band w/mc florals, wear, 2⅝".................................**65.00**
Vase, bl bands/mc florals, lid-like flower frog, 5¾"....................**150.00**
Vase, cherubs, wht on bl band, urn form, 4⅝", NM **100.00**
Vase, emb floral on orange, scroll hdls, 5½", pr, VG..................**125.00**
Vase, Faith/clock, purple transfer on wht disk, hdls, 7⅜" **65.00**
Vase, floral, mc on wht band, pk lustre, ftd, 6", NM, pr..............**270.00**
Vase, John Wesley & clock on wht medallions, hdld/ftd, 5¾" **200.00**

Coralene Glass

Coralene is a unique type of art glass easily recognized by the tiny grains of glass that form its decoration. Lacy allover patterns of seaweed, geometrics, and florals were used, as well as solid forms such as fish, plants, and single blossoms. It was made by several glasshouses both here and abroad. Values are based to a considerable extent on the amount of beading that remains.

Our advisors for this category are Betty and Clarence Maier; they are listed in the Directory under Pennsylvania.

Bowl, Herringbone, bl MOP w/pk seaweed motif, 3½x5½" **615.00**

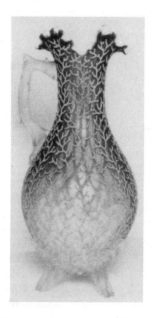

Ewer, blue Diamond Quilt Mother-of-Pearl with orange seaweed coralene, frosted feet and thorn handle, 15", $495.00.

Tumbler, bl shaded overlay, overall yel motif, 3¾x2¾" **235.00**
Vase, amberina w/lg flower & bird in branch, gold top, 4" **250.00**
Vase, pk MOP w/seaweed decor, ruffled, 10¾x5" **465.00**
Vase, pk MOP w/seaweed motif, 6-crimp, amber ft, 10x5½"........**695.00**
Vase, pk satin w/coral motif, egg form on 3 amber ft, 10" **695.00**
Vase, Snowflake, pk MOP w/wheat motif, can neck, 5½x4" **500.00**

Coralene, Oriental

Ceramics decorated in the same manner as coralene glass was produced in Japan during the early 1900s. Many items are marked 'Patent Pending' or with a specific patent date.

Ewer, fruit w/gr & gold trim, 4x3½"..**200.00**
Plate, florals, pk on gr bsk, much gold, 7¾" **85.00**

Vase, iris, pk/lav on gr, cobalt & gold trim, 9x3½" **455.00**
Vase, nasturtiums, pk on brn, cylindrical, sm hdls, 8¼" **410.00**

Vase, pink roses with gold on blue ground, 4", $425.00.

Cordey

The Cordey China Company was founded in 1942 in Trenton, New Jersey, by Boleslaw Cybis. The operation was small with less than a dozen workers. They produced figurines, vases, lamps, and similar wares, much of which was marketed through gift shops both nationwide and abroad. Though the earlier wares were made of plaster, Cybis soon developed his own formula for a porcelain composition which he called 'Papka.' Cordey figurines and busts were characterized by old-world charm, Rococo scrolls, delicate floral appliques, ruffles, and real lace which was dipped in liquified clay to add dimension to the work.

Although on rare occasions some items were not numbered or signed, the 'basic' figure was cast both with numbers and the Cordey signature. The molded pieces were then individually decorated and each marked with its own impressed identification number as well as a mark to indicate the artist-decorator. Their numbering system began with 200 and in later years progressed into the 8000s. As can best be established, Cordey continued production until sometime in the mid-1950s. Boleslaw Cybis died in 1957, his wife in 1958.

Key: ff — full figure

Ash tray, #6035, Versailles Group, 5½" **18.00**
Bird, #2037, perched on stump, 8½" **115.00**
Box, florals & gold, Rococo, ftd, 4½x7x4½" **50.00**
Bust, #5010, lady, 6½" **60.00**
Bust, #5014, Junior Prom, ringlets, 7" **48.00**
Bust, #5038, Napoleon, 8" **45.00**
Candle holder, triple; #8013, scrolled, gold highlights, pr.............**80.00**
Clock, mantel; #914, Rococo, Lanshire Electric, 9½" **175.00**
Clock frame, #912, cherubs, Rococo, 11" **225.00**
Lady, #302, ff, lav & navy clothes, 16½" **225.00**
Lady, #4073, ff, much lace, 13" **185.00**
Lady, #5054, ff, flowers in hair, bustle, 9¼" **110.00**
Lady, #5060, 9" **90.00**
Lady, #5082, ringlets, lace kerchief, 10½" **110.00**
Lady, #5084, ff, upswept hair, much lace, scroll base, 11¾" **125.00**
Lady, #5089, ff, lace trim, 10¾" **110.00**
Lady, #8039, 15" **200.00**
Lamb, #6025, Bambi, scroll base, scarce **135.00**

Lamp, #31386, lady w/much lace, Rococo base **250.00**
Lamp, #5041/#5084, man & lady, 13", pr **250.00**
Lamp, #5084, lady, upswept gray hair, lace, bustle, 11½" **110.00**
Lamp, Madame DuBarry bust, much lace, 15" **250.00**
Man, #303, ff, holds hat in left hand, 16½" **195.00**
Man, #305, ff, grape harvester, 16" **200.00**
Man, #4072, lg base w/tree stump & flowers, 14" **150.00**
Man, #4074, ff, 13" **165.00**
Man, #4153, ff, much lace, 14" **185.00**
Man, #5042, ff, much lace, scroll base, 10½" **110.00**
Man & Lady, #300/#301, ff, 15½", pr **225.00**
Man & Lady, #4129-A, man w/violin, seated lady, 11"...............**300.00**
Neopolitan Boy, #5046, 9½" **110.00**
Shelf, #7028, corncuopia form w/flowers, 8¼" **95.00**
Tray, leaf form, 13" **65.00**
Vase, #7036, 5½" **45.00**
Wall bracket, #861, Victorian style, 7½", pr................................**100.00**
Wall masque, #902, lady's face, 10" **200.00**
Wall vase, figural lady w/wide brim hat **150.00**
Yorkshire Girl, #5047, ff, grapes in dress folds, 10" **110.00**

Couple under floral tree, 12", $175.00.

Corkscrews

The history of the corkscrew dates back to the mid-1600s, when wine makers concluded that the best-aged wine was that stored in smaller containers, either stoneware or glass. Since plugs left unsealed were often damaged by rodents, corks were cut off flush with the bottle top and sealed with wax or a metal cover. Removing the cork cleanly with none left to grasp became a problem. The task was found to be relatively simple using the worm on the end of a flintlock gun rod — and the corkscrew evolved. Endless patents have been issued for mechanized models. Handles range from carved wood, ivory, and bone to porcelain and repousse silver. Celluloid lady's legs are popular.

Our advisor for this category is Roger Baker; he is listed in the Directory under California.

Anheuser-Busch, bottle shape, EX **45.00**
Belgiu, Challenge type, ca 1850, EX **22.00**
Boar's tusk hdl w/3" cvg, sterling end cap, ca 1900....................**170.00**
CJ Johnson Sheffield, horn hdl, steel blade, ca 1880, EX.............**75.00**
Clough 1910 Pat, cap lifter at end of wood sleeve, EX **30.00**

Dartmouth Pixie, brass, 1927 ....38.00
English, bone hdl, sq shaft, ca 1870, EX 75.00
English, brass shaft, Henshall-type button, wood hdl, EX 115.00
English, hippo tusk hdl, silver end cap, ca 1890 ....150.00
Farrow & Jackson Ltd London, sq shaft, wire helix, ca 1885 ....56.00
French, wooden dbl hdl w/figure cvg, rnd fr, NM 37.50
German, Christian Brothers, open fr, spring-covered shaft 12.50
German, spring action, open fr, Archimedean worm, EX 50.00
German, spring bbl w/pin-type lock, wood hdl, EX 70.00
German, unmk Hercules, common type, EX 40.00
Haff Patent, mk brass ring, Pat Apr & May 1885, EX 85.00
Italian, barman figural, dbl-lever, toasts on bk, 10½" 47.50
James Heeley & Sons A1 Dbl Lever, copper finish, EX 135.00
JH Perille L'Excelsior, ebonized hdl, EX 335.00
Lund Patentee London, rack & pinion, Pat 1855, EX 285.00
Man w/straw-hat figural, dbl-lever, modern, 8½" 17.50
Ram's horn hdl (7"), plain helix worm, EX 22.50
Stag horn hdl (forked, 13"), silver cap, ca 1900, EX 175.00
Surprise, English, registry #1884, EX 48.00
Thomason, appl bronze crest tablet, bone hdl, Pat 1802, EX 425.00
Three Wise Monkeys, brass 45.00
US, stag horn hdl, silver end caps, ca 1900, 8" 120.00
US Clough Pat of 1904, crown cap lifter, advertising 30.00
Walrus tusk hdl w/sterling ends, SP worm/lifter, Pat 1906 ....155.00
Wm Bennet, wood hdl, Pat 1883 ....195.00

Cosmos

Cosmos, sometimes called Stemless Daisy, is a patterned glass tableware produced from 1894 through 1915 by Consolidated Lamp and Glass Company. Relief-molded flowers on a fine cross-cut background were painted in soft colors of pink, blue, and yellow. Though nearly all were made of milk glass, a few items may be found in clear glass with the designs painted on. In addition to the tableware, lamps were also made.

Bottle, cologne; orig stopper, rare 150.00
Butter dish, 7½" dia 235.00
Condiment set, 3-pc in fr 350.00
Creamer 150.00
Lamp, banquet; kerosene, 24" 475.00
Lamp, banquet; slender base, rnd globe, all orig, 16" 525.00
Lamp, 10" 400.00
Pickle castor, dbl, mk SP fr 500.00
Pickle castor, single, ftd SP fr 350.00

Syrup pitcher, 6",
$200.00.

Pitcher, milk; 5" 170.00
Pitcher, 8¾" 250.00
Shakers, tall, orig lids, pr 135.00
Spooner 125.00
Sugar bowl, open 150.00
Sugar bowl, w/lid 185.00
Tumbler, 3¾" 65.00

Cottageware

You'll find a varied assortment of novelty dinnerware items — all styled as cozy little English cottages or huts with cone-shaped roofs; some may have a waterwheel or a windmill. Marks will vary. English-made Price Brothers or Beswick pieces are valued in the same range as those marked Occupied Japan, while items marked simply Japan are considered slightly less pricey.

Our advisor for this category is Grace Klender; she is listed in the Directory under Ohio.

Chocolate pot, English, $110.00.

Condiment set, pr shakers+mustard on tray, English 35.00
Cookie jar, Japan, sm 40.00
Cookie jar, Japan, 7" 45.00
Creamer & sugar bowl, English, 2½", 4½" 30.00
Cup & saucer, English 40.00
Egg cup, 1¾" 10.00
Pitcher, water; English 125.00
Sugar box, for cubes, English, 5¾" 45.00
Teapot, English or Occupied Japan, 6½" 55.00
Teapot, Japan, 6½" 40.00
Tumbler, Japan, 3½", set of 6 ....60.00

Coverlets

The Jacquard attachment for hand looms represented a culmination of weaving developments made in France. Introduced to America by the early 1820s, it gave professional weavers the ability to easily create complex patterns with curved lines. Those who could afford the new loom adaptation could now use hole-punched pasteboard cards to weave floral patterns that before could only be achieved with intense labor on a draw-loom.

Before the Jacquard mechanism, most weavers made their coverlets in geometric patterns. Use of indigo-blue and brightly-colored wools often livened the twills and overshot patterns available to the small-loom home weaver. Those who had larger multiple-harness looms could produced warm double-woven, twill-block, or summer-and-winter designs.

While the new floral and pictorial patterns' popularity had displaced the geometrics in urban areas, the mid-Atlantic, and the Midwest by the 1840s, even factory production of the Jacquard coverlets was disrupted by cotton and wool shortages during the Civil War. A revived production in the 1870s saw a style change to a center-medallion motif, but a new fad — for white 'Marseilles' spreads — soon halted sales of Jacquard-woven coverlets. Production of Jacquard carpets continued to the turn of the century.

Rural and frontier weavers continued to make geometric-design coverlets through the nineteenth century, and local craft revivals have continued this tradition through this century. All-cotton overshots were factory-produced in Kentucky from the 1940s, and factories and professional weavers made cotton-and-wool overshots during the past decade.

Many Jacquard-woven coverlets have dates and names of places and people (often the intended owner — not the weaver) woven into corners or borders.

In the listings that follow, examples are blue and white unless noted otherwise.

Jacquard

Centennial, Memorial Hall, lg bldg, 5-color, 70x72", EX **450.00**
Centennial, Memorial Hall, 1776-1876, red/wht, 1-pc single......**600.00**
Christian/Heathen border, birds feeding young, 2-pc dbl.............**850.00**
Christian/Heathen border, birds/etc, 3-color, 2-pc dbl, EX..........**500.00**
Christian/Heathen border, corners sgn/dtd 1867, 86x74" **550.00**
Eagle/WA on horse/United We Stand, red/wht, dtd 1840, EX....**800.00**
Floral, bird border, corners sgn/dtd 1844, OH, 2-pc single...........**800.00**
Floral, corners: Knox Co OH 1844, 4-color, 68x80", EX **450.00**
Floral, eagle/star border, corners sgn/dtd 1842, 4-color **750.00**
Floral medallion, bird border, red/wht, 1-pc single, MN **400.00**
Floral medallions, floral border, 4-color, sgn/1848, 2-pc **450.00**
Geometric florals, intricate border w/stars, 4-color, 1-pc **450.00**

Red and white jacquard weave coverlet with figure of Liberty above Memorial Hall flanked by spreadwing eagle and shields, floral border inscribed 'Memorial Hall 1786-1876,' 78" x 78", $600.00.

Geometrics, foliage border, red/bl/wht, 86x94" **250.00**
Star medallions, dbl-peacock border, 2-pc, NM **500.00**
Star/floral medallion, eagles/Virtue, Liberty..., 6-color, NM **600.00**
Star/floral medallion, floral borders, sgn Hausman/1852, EX......**600.00**
Starflower, floral border, 4-color, 1-pc single, 84x88" **350.00**
Stars/medallions, bird border, 3-color, wear/rebound, 66x88"......**325.00**
Summer/Winter, 4-pointed stars, NM **450.00**
Sunflower/snowflake, grapevine border, D Ingham/1868, NM. **1,150.00**
Turkey/peacock/tree medallions alternate w/florals, 2-pc............**700.00**
4 lg floral medallions, urn/vintage borders, 3-color, 1846 ....**600.00**
4 rose medallions/vintage border, corners sgn/dtd 1860 ....**400.00**

Overshot

Optical pattern, red/bl/gr, 2-pc, overall wear, 76x88" **350.00**
Optical pattern, red/navy, 2-pc, wear/sm holes, 76x90" **300.00**
Plaid w/lines & dk bands, 4-color, 84x92" **195.00**
Sqs/bars, red & natural wht, sewn-on fringe, 64x86"....................**195.00**
X-hatched sqs, dk lines w/bars, 3-color, minor wear, 88x64" **250.00**

Cowan

Guy Cowan opened a small pottery near Cleveland, Ohio, ca 1912, where he made tile and artware on a small scale from the natural red clay available there. He developed distinctive glazes — necessary, he felt, to cover the dark red body. After the war and a temporary halt in production, Cowan moved his pottery to Rocky River, where he made a commercial line of artware utilizing a highly-fired white porcelain. Although he acquiesced to the necessity of mass-production, every effort was made to insure a product of highest quality. Fine artists, among them Waylande Gregory, Thelma Frazier Winter, and Viktor Schreckengost, molded figurines which were often produced in limited editions, some of which sell today for prices in the thousands. Most of the ware was marked 'Cowan' or 'Lakewood Ware,' not to be confused with the name of the 1927 mass-produced line called 'Lakeware.' Falling under the crunch of the Great Depression, the pottery closed in 1931.

Bookend, horse, turq, 9½" **375.00**
Bottle, burnt orange, ribbed, w/stopper, 10½" **125.00**
Bowl, console; bl/gr mottled sea horse ea side, 17" **110.00**
Bowl, copper lustre, flared top, 4x8" **40.00**
Bowl, cream, apple gr int, scalloped, ftd, 4x9¼" **35.00**
Candle holder, leaping gazelle, caramel gloss, 5¾" **135.00**
Candle holder, nude, ivory, 12½", pr..**600.00**
Candle holder, sea horse, gr, 4", pr **35.00**
Candlestick, Rowfant Club, ground hog, gr, ltd ed, 9½" **800.00**
Cigarette holder, Delft bl, sea horse base **30.00**
Comport, ivory, sea horses support, oval, 6" **25.00**
Compote, pk on ivory, #C838..**35.00**
Decanter, King from Alice in Wonderland, ca 1929, 12" **475.00**
Decanter, rose, narrow paneled shape, 12" **225.00**
Figurine, pueblo mother & child, FL Mora, 14" **1,100.00**
Figurine, Spanish dancer, male & female, mc, pr **750.00**
Flower frog, nude, ivory, #698, 6½" **135.00**
Hot plate, ivory, fish decor **165.00**
Jar, ginger; purple lustre, w/lid, 5½" **150.00**
Lamp, pk lustre, candlestick shape, #L31, early, 8", pr **250.00**
Lamp, russet, allover star-shaped flowers, ovoid, 21" **110.00**
Plate, turq, reef w/starfish & coral, fish in rim, 11½"...................**250.00**
Punch bowl, Jazz, bl/blk, sgn Schreckengost, 8" H **15,000.00**
Tea set, yel, melon rib, 3-pc, ea w/lid..**225.00**
Trivet, fish, bl, imp mk, 5½" **150.00**

Russian Peasant, terra cotta crackle, signed A. Blazys, #78, 8½", $395.00.

Trivet, floral relief, 5-color, 6-sided, mks 325.00
Urn, ram's-head decor, ivory w/gold trim, hdls, V-88..................175.00
Vase, apple gr, ribbed, trumpet form, w/frog, 5¾x7½"...................42.00
Vase, blk satin, ftd, V-form, 6½" 70.00
Vase, brn crystalline, paneled fan form, 8" 60.00
Vase, bud; pk, sea horse base, fluted oval form, 7" 42.00
Vase, chartreuse flambe/brn, flat flaring U-form, ftd, 5x8" 50.00
Vase, lav irid over beige, ribbed, trumpet form, 9½".......................90.00
Vase, orange matt, bulbous, flared lip, 8" 90.00
Vase, Oriental red, cylindrical, 10" 185.00
Vase, Oriental red, mk, 5½" 110.00
Vase, turq/gr, sea horse base, unmk, sm..35.00

Cracker Jack

Kids have been buying Cracker Jack since it was first introduced in the 1890s. By 1912 it was packaged with a free toy inside. Before the first kernel was crunched, eager fingers had retrieved the surprise from the depth of the box — actually no easy task, considering the care required to keep the contents so swiftly displaced from spilling over the side! Though a little older, perhaps, many of those same kids still are looking — just as eagerly — for the Cracker Jack prizes. Point of sale, company collectibles, and the prizes as well have over the years reflected America's changing culture. Grocer sales and incentives from around the turn of the century — paper dolls, post cards and song books — were often marked Rueckheim Brothers (the inventors of Cracker Jack) or Reliable Confections. The first loose-packed prizes were toys made of wood, clay, tin, metal, and lithographed paper. Plastic toys were introduced in 1946. Paper wrapped for safety purposes in 1948, subjects echo the 'hype' of the day — Yo-Yos, tops, whistles, and sports cards in the simple, peaceful days of our country, propaganda and war toys in the forties, games in the fifties, and space toys in the sixties. Few of the estimated 15 billion prizes were marked. Advertising items from Angelus Marshmallow and Checkers Confections (cousins of the Cracker Jack family) are also collectible. When no condition is indicated, the items listed below are assumed to be in excellent condition. 'CJ' indicates that the item is marked.

Our advisor for this category is Wes Johnson; he is listed in the Directory under Kentucky.

Cast Metal Prizes

Badge, shield, CJ Jr Detective, silver, 1931, 1¼" 35.00
Badge, 6-point star, mk CJ Police, silver, 1931, 1¼".......................35.00
Button, stud bk, Me for Cracker Jack, boy & dog 18.00
Button, stud bk, Xd bats & ball, CJ pitcher/etc series, 1928...........78.00
Chair, T (Tootsie), 3 different sectional pcs, pnt, mini, ea 12.00
Dollhouse items: lantern, mug, candlestick, etc; no mk, ea............ 6.50
Horse & wagon, CJ, 3-D, silver or gold, early, 2½", ea 250.00
Pistol, soft lead, inked, CJ on barrel, early, rare, 2⅛" 180.00
Ring, alphabet letter setting (series), unmk, ea.............................. 3.00
Rocking horse, no rider, 3-D, inked, early, 1⅛" 9.00
Rocking horse w/boy, 3-D, inked, early, 1½" 22.00
Tootsie Toy series: boats, cars, animals; '31, ¾"-1½", ea 7.00

Dealer Incentives

Cart w/2 movable wheels, wood dowel tongue, CJ 33.00
Corkscrew/opener, metal plated, CJ/Angelus, 3" 65.00
Corkscrew/opener, metal plated, CJ/Angelus, 3¾" tube case 65.00
Jigsaw puzzle, CJ or Checkers, 1 of 4, 7x10", in envelope 35.00
Magic puzzle, metal, CJ/Angelus, 1 of 15, 1934, ea.........................14.00
Mask, Halloween; paper, CJ, 10" or 12", ea 15.00
Match holder, hinged, eng gold-tone case, CJ, 2½x1⅞" 650.00
Palm puzzle, mirror bk, CJ, mk Germany/RWB, 1910-14, 1½"....110.00
Pencil top clip, metal/celluloid, oval boy & dog logo..................125.00
Pencil top clip, metal/celluloid, tube shape w/package..................75.00
Post card, bear, 1 of 16, CJ, 1907..22.00

Packaging

Box, popcorn; red scroll border, CJ, ca 1920..................................85.00
Box, popcorn; store display, CJ, 1923, no contents 65.00
Canister, tin, CJ Candy Corn Crisp, 10-oz 75.00
Canister, tin, CJ Coconut Corn Crisp, 1-lb 55.00
Canister, tin, CJ Coconut Corn Crisp, 10-oz 65.00
Crate, shipping; wood, CJ, early, lg 150.00

Paper Prizes

Baseball CJ score counter, 3⅜" L..85.00
Book, Animals (or Birds), to color, Makatoy, CJ, 1949, mini 35.00
Book, Bess & Bill on CJ Hill, series of 12, 1937, mini.....................75.00
Book, Birds We Know, CJ, 1928, mini..45.00
Book, drawing w/tracing paper, CJ, 1920s, mini...........................110.00
Book, Twigg & Sprigg, CJ, 1930, mini..75.00
Booklet, stickers/wise cracks/riddles, Borden, CJ, 1965 on 1.00
Decal, cartoon or nursery rhyme figure, 1947-49, CJ 26.00
Disguise, ears, red (punch out from carrier), 1950, pr......................20.00
Disguise, glasses, hinged, cellophane lenses, CJ, 1933 ....65.00
Disguise, glasses, hinged, w/eyeballs, 1933 .... 6.00
Disguise, mustache, blk/brn, in carrier, CJ, 1949 ....45.00

Fortune Telling Wheels, tin (left), $43.00, paper (right), $48.00.

Game, Midget Auto Race, wheel spins, CJ, 1949, 3⅜" H **25.00**
Game spinner, ...baseball at home, rectangle, CJ, 2¾" W **125.00**
Game spinner, ...baseball at home, unmk, 1946, 1½" dia **40.00**
Hat, fold out, More You Eat/More You Want, CJ, early................**70.00**
Magic game book, erasable slate, series of 13, 1946, ea.................**27.00**
Movie, boy at blkboard, turn wheel: draws/erases, CJ, '31, 2" **95.00**
Movie, Goofy Zoo, turn wheel(s): change animals, 1939 ....**12.00**
Movie, pull tab for 2nd picture, series, CJ, 1943, 1¼", ea **55.00**
Movie, pull tab for 2nd picture, yel, early, 3", in envelope...........**115.00**
Palm puzzle, ball(s) roll into holes, plastic dome, from 1966 .... **1.00**
Riddle card, 2 series of 20, in pkg/from factory, CJ, ea **7.00**
Sand picture, sand pours for action, series of 14, 1967, ea **9.00**
Top, golf game, wood stick center, CJ, 1933..........................**35.00**
Transfer, iron on, sport figure or patriotic, CJ, 1939, ea **26.00**
Whistle, Razz Zooka, C Carey Cloud design, CJ, 1949..................**32.00**

Plastic Prizes

Animals, standup, letter on bk, series of 26, Nosco, 1953, ea **3.50**
Animals, standup on base, assorted, Nosco or CJ, 1947 on, ea........ **1.00**
Badge, pin-bk, celluloid, pretty lady, CJ label, 1¼" **65.00**
Baseball players, 3-D, bl or gray team, 1958, 1½", ea.................. **8.00**
Disc, emb comic character, series of 12, 1954, 1½" dia **12.00**
Disc, emb fish plaque, oval, series of 10, 1956, ea......................... **9.00**
Dog, 3-D, hollow base, series of 10, CJCO, 1954, ea **4.50**
Figure, circus; stands on base, 1 of 12, Nosco, 1951-54................. **1.75**
Figure on rocking base, semi-flat, 1 of 9, cloud design, '56 .... **3.00**
Fob, alphabet letter w/loop on top, 1 of 26, 1954, 1½" **2.25**
Magnifying glass, many designs/shapes, from 1961, ea................... **1.00**
Pinball game, lever shoots ball/score in holes, 1964 to recent........ **2.00**
Signs, road; Stop, Caution, etc, yel, series of 10, 1954-60, ea......... **3.00**
Spinner, varied colors, 10 designs, from 1948, ea **1.50**
Toys, take apart/assemble, variety, from '62, assembled, ea **1.00**
Toys, take apart/assemble, variety, from '62, unassembled, ea **2.25**
Whistle, tube w/animals on top, CJ, 1 of 6, 1950-53, 1⅜".............. **8.50**

Premiums

Bat, baseball; wood, Hillerich & Bradsby, CJ, full sz **125.00**
Book, pocket; jester on cover, CJ **42.00**
Book, pocket; riddle/sailor boy/dog on cover, RWB, CJ **35.00**
Harmonica, full scale, emb CJ, early, rare, 5⅛" **385.00**
Recipe book, Angelus, 1930s...**22.00**
Wings, air corps type, silver or blk, stud-bk, CJ, '30s, 3", ea..........**42.00**

Tin Prizes

Badge, emb/plated CJ officer, 2⅜" or 1⅝", early, ea **85.00**
Bank, 3-D book form, red/gr/or blk, CJ Bank, early, 2" **95.00**
Boy & dog, diecut, complete w/bend over tab, CJ.......................**110.00**
Boy & dog, diecut, w/o tab at top **85.00**
Boy & dog, stand-up litho rectangle, est 1916, lg or sm, ea.............**145.00**
Brooch or pin, various design on card, CJ/logo, early, ea **100.00**
Cash register, litho, More You Eat, CJ, early, 1⅞" **400.00**
Clicker, 'Noisy CJ Snapper,' pear shape, aluminum, 1949 ....**25.00**
Doll dishes, tin plated, CJ, '31, 1¾", 1⅞", & 2⅛" dia, ea..............**32.00**
Helicopter, yel propellor, wood stick, unmk, 1937, 2⅝" **18.00**
Horse & wagon, litho diecut, CJ & Angelus, 2⅛" **41.00**
Horse & wagon, litho diecut, gray/red mks, CJ, 1914-23, 3⅛"....**275.00**
Model T Ford, License: NY 1915 #999, blk/wht, CJ, rare, 2".......**350.00**
Oval standup, Am flag, 1 of 4, unmk, 1936-46 ....**11.00**
Oval standup, comic character, 1 of 10, CJ, 1936-46 ....**65.00**
Pocket watch, silver of gold, CJ as numerals, 1931, 1½".................**35.00**
Sled, tin plated, CJ, 1931, 2" L..**20.00**

Soldier, litho, die-cut standup, officer/private/etc, unmk, ea..........**17.00**
Tall box shape: Frozen Foods locker freezer, '47, unmk, 1¾"..........**65.00**
Tall box shape: grandfather clock, unmk, 1947, 1¾" **50.00**
Tall box shape: radio, Tune in w/CJ, brn/yel, 1939, 1¾" **115.00**
Tall box shape: Refrigerator Car, CJ 2006, 1947, 1¾" L **85.00**
Train, litho coach only, red, 1941, rare...................................**22.00**
Train, litho engine only, red, 1941, unmk **17.00**
Tray, emb, litho w/early pkg, smaller version **115.00**
Tray, emb, litho w/early pkg, 2¼x1¾"................................**95.00**
Wagon shape: Caterpillar tractor, unmk, 1931, 1¾" L **31.00**
Wagon shape: CJ Shows, circus wagon, series of 5, ea.................**95.00**
Wagon shape: Playtime Trailer (auto trailer), unmk, 1947.............**35.00**
Wagon shape: tank, orange/red/gr camouflage, unmk..................**65.00**
Wagon shape: Tank Corps No 57, gr & blk, 1941 ....**30.00**
Wheelbarrow, tin plated, bk leg in place, 1931, 2½" L.................**22.00**

Miscellaneous

Ad, comic book, CJ, ea **9.00**
Ad, Saturday Evening Post, mc, CJ, 1919, 11x14" **18.00**
Hat, ball park vendor cap, CJ, 1930s....................................**30.00**
Medal, CJ salesman award, brass, 1939, scarce **165.00**
Sign, bathing beauty, 5-color cb, CJ, early, 17x22" **185.00**
Sign, boy or girl w/box of CJ, 5-color cb, early, 17x22", ea **185.00**
Sign, Jack & Bingo, die-cut litho, easel standup, CJ, early.............**145.00**
Sign, Santa & prizes, mc cb, Angelus, early, lg.........................**95.00**
Sign, Santa & prizes, mc cb, CJ, early, lg...............................**165.00**

Crackle Glass

Crackle glass (or craquelle) was made during the 1800s in America as well as abroad. The name is derived from the texture of the ware, achieved by first plunging the hot glass into cold water, then reheating and reblowing the vessel, thereby producing ware with a crackled appearance.

Cruet, cranberry, appl hdl, faceted stopper **155.00**
Pitcher, cranberry, rnd mouth, bulbous, 7¼x5½" **175.00**
Rose bowl, cranberry to clear, crimped top, 3½x4½" **100.00**
Tumbler, ruby w/HP floral, 4" **40.00**
Vase, amberina, clear ruffled top, appl leaves, 6⅛"......................**395.00**

Cranberry

Cranberry glass is named for its resemblance to the color of cranberry juice. It was made by many companies both here and abroad, becoming popular in America soon after the Civil War. It was made in free-blown ware as well as mold-blown. Today, cranberry glass is being reproduced, and it is sometimes difficult to distinguish the old from the new. Ask a reputable dealer if you are unsure. See also Cruets; Salts; Sugar Shakers; Syrups.

Bell, clear twist at hdl end, no clapper, 1870s, 14" **350.00**
Biscuit jar, ribs, clear ruffled trim, vaseline collar, 8" **545.00**
Bottle, scent; Gothic arches, cased, self stopper, 5½" **435.00**
Bowl, appl crystal ribbons, 3½x4½" **250.00**
Bowl, mc florals w/gold, clear appl finial, 5½x6" **195.00**
Bowl, 3 rows of appl crystal leaves, 3 scroll ft, 5¾" **350.00**
Creamer, Invt T'print, amber thorn hdl w/appl leaves, 5" **335.00**
Creamer, pressed or mold blown, 7 sm clear ft, 3¾" **110.00**
Cruet, cherry blossoms, mc bird on gold branch........................**210.00**
Cruet, gold florals & scrolls, faceted bubble stopper, 10½" **165.00**

Decanter, clear hdl, clear cut faceted stopper, 11¼" 195.00
Decanter, clear spun rope hdl, bulbous, faceted stopper, 9" 165.00
Jar, mc florals w/gold, crystal trim & ft, 4¾" dia 425.00
Jar, powder; mc florals on frost, brass ft, 3" dia 195.00
Muffineer, 12-sided, metal top, 5¼" 150.00
Pitcher, enameling w/gold, long high spout, clear hdl, 9" 275.00
Pitcher, florals w/gold, long neck, amber hdl, 10" 310.00
Pitcher, Invt T'print, sq mouth, clear hdl, 7½" 150.00
Pitcher, Optic, clear hdl, 13x6⅜" 265.00
Rose bowl, interior melon ribs, 3½" H 125.00
Tumble up, ribbed, bottle: 6½", tumbler: 2½" 140.00
Tumbler, juice; conical shape on clear base, 4-oz 160.00
Vase, allover sanded gold leaves, ftd pear form, 11" 245.00
Vase, bud; Mary Gregory-type boy, brass mts, 6¾" 300.00
Vase, gold hearts & swags, bulbous, crimped rim, 6x7¼" 225.00
Vase, HP partridge among florals, 10¾", pr 460.00
Vase, mc florals, 7½" 68.00
Vase, mc florals w/gold, twisted ribbed neck, 7½" 150.00
Vase, mold blown, sq top, long neck, 6¾" 170.00
Vase, sanded wht Roman Key motif, ormolu base, 6x3", pr 265.00
Vase, swirled, clear ft & rim, trumpet form, 12⅛x4⅝" 145.00
Vase, wht enameling, 3-petal top, 7x4" 125.00
Wine, gilt metal stem & base, 5½" 125.00

Creamware

Creamware was a type of earthenware developed by Wedgwood in the 1760s and produced by many other Staffordshire potteries, including Leeds. Since it could be potted cheaply and was light in weight, it became popular abroad as well as in England, due to the lower freight charges involved in its export. It was revived at Leeds in the late nineteenth century, and the type most often reproduced was heavily reticulated or molded in high relief. These later wares are easily distinguished from the originals since they are thicker and tend to craze heavily. See also Leeds.

Bowl, mc floral sprays/scattered flowers, 4" 300.00
Creamer, King of Prussia, blk transfer, bk: angel, 4" 200.00
Jug, people & boats/Courtship & Matrimony, blk transfer, 7" 300.00
Mug, emb panels w/bands of yel w/bl lines, leaf hdl, 6", EX 200.00
Mug, red transfer: Success to the Blacksmith, 5" 300.00

Oyster stand, bird perched among five shell-shaped dishes, ca 1785, 8½", $1,200.00.

Plate, blk transfer initials/garlands, rtcl, 9", EX 75.00
Plate, ship in center, grisaille birds on rim, 1790, 10" 250.00
Plate, Triumph of Cupid, blk transfer, mc flowers, 8" 225.00
Shaker, bl-gr stripes, brn foliage bands, 4¾", EX 150.00
Tea caddy, HP florals/geometrics, early, 4x4½", EX 80.00
Teapot, birds/fruits in blk/mc, rnd body, 1770, rstr, 3½" 500.00
Teapot, scattered mc flowers, entwined hdls, rnd, 6" W 450.00

Crown Ducal

Earthenware marked 'Crown Ducal' and decorated by Charlotte Rhead is becoming quite collectible. This is the mark of A.G. Richardson & Co., Ltd., located in Tunstall and Ferrybridge in the Staffordshire district of England.

Ewer, Arabesque, sgn Charlotte Rhead, 15" 255.00
Pitcher, Byzantine, florals, sgn Charlotte Rhead, 7x4¾" 165.00
Pitcher, hydrangeas, sgn Charlotte Rhead, mk, 7¾" 255.00
Pitcher, Manchu, gr dragon on gr, sgn Charlotte Rhead, 8" 195.00
Plaque, florals, mc w/gold on cream, sgn C Rhead, 12¼" 225.00
Plaque, geometrics, mc w/metallics, sgn Charlotte Rhead, 13" 225.00
Vase, brn decor on lt rust-brn mottle, sgn C Rhead, 8½" 195.00
Vase, florals, mc on gray to tan, sgn Charlotte Rhead, 8⅝" 195.00
Vase, florals, mc on lt gr, dk gr band, sgn C Rhead, 7" 165.00
Vase, florals, mc on tan, octagonal, sgn C Rhead, 8½" 175.00
Vase, florals, mc on tan, sgn Charlotte Rhead, 7x4¾" 150.00
Vase, geometrics, mc on tan, sgn Charlotte Rhead, 5¼x6¾" 165.00
Vase, Manchu, dragon in gold, sgn Charlotte Rhead, 10½" 195.00

Crown Milano

Crown Milano was introduced in 1884 by the Mt. Washington Glass Company. When the company merged with Pairpoint in 1894, it continued to be one of their best sellers. It is an opaque, highly-decorated ware with gold or colored enamels in intricate designs on pale backgrounds. Many pieces were marked 'CM' with a crown. Since it is nearly always found in a satin finish, in the listings that follow, satin is assumed unless glossy is indicated.

Our advisors for this category are Betty and Clarence Maier; they are listed in the Directory under Pennsylvania.

Biscuit jar, apple blossoms on yel to wht, emb lid, 6x5½" 685.00
Biscuit jar, bamboo, gr/gold/brn on pnt Burmese, SP mts, 6"... 1,100.00
Biscuit jar, fall foliage/berries/traceries, sgn SP lid 1,100.00
Biscuit jar, floral, 16-panel cylinder w/emb scrolls........................635.00
Biscuit jar, florals/gold scrolls, floral-emb lid, 7½" dia 950.00
Biscuit jar, pansies, cylindrical, butterfly finial, 5x4" 945.00
Bowl, bride's; pnt Burmese w/floral medallions, scrolls, 10" 875.00
Bowl, emb ornamentation, mc florals, folded top, 11" 475.00
Creamer & sugar, floral transfers, ribbed, sgn metal mts.......... 1,000.00
Creamer & sugar, violets w/gold, 3½", 4¼" 915.00
Cup & saucer, shiny w/mc florals & gilt, ribbed, ornate hdl 750.00
Dish, trinket; floral, mc w/gold on beige, 5" dia 225.00
Ewer, florals/geometrics/mc dots on wht w/gilt, 12" 1,750.00
Ewer, gold chrysanthemums & scrolls, 12" 875.00
Planter, mums, maroon/purple on pk & gray detailing, 6x9" .. 1,250.00
Sugar shaker, daisies on bl to wht, vertical ribs, 6x2½" 435.00
Sweetmeat, blown-out pearlized cactus flowers, mk, 4" 650.00
Sweetmeat, pansies on unfired Burmese w/star-shaped bosses . 1,250.00
Sweetmeat, swirled w/jewels, turtle on lid, 4½" 900.00
Syrup pitcher, acorns/oak leaves, mc/gold, melon form, 5½" 950.00
Syrup pitcher, 6 floral panels on wht w/in ribbed columns 485.00

Sweetmeat, florals and gold on melon ribs, 3¾", $800.00.

Vase, colonial children/flowers, grey on wht, 8½" 1,350.00
Vase, floral on wht opaque, gold rim, mk, 4x5½" 295.00
Vase, mc dots & orange florals, bulbous, 12½" 935.00
Vase, mc pansies w/gold, triangular, 3 leaf hdls, 8" 1,875.00
Vase, thistles, gold-traced/mc on cream, bulbous, 9½" 1,475.00
Vase, wild roses, bl on lt bl, ruffled cylinder, 6" 395.00

Cruets

Cruets, containers made to hold oil or vinegar, are usually bulbous with tall narrow throats and a stopper. During the nineteenth century and for several years after, they were produced in abundance in virtually every type of glassware available. Those listed below are assumed to be with stopper and mint unless noted otherwise.

Alaska, bl opal, rpl stopper, 6½" 200.00
Arched Fleur-de-Lis, ruby stain, Higbee 475.00
Bag Wear, gr 135.00
Bag Wear, vaseline 185.00
Beaded Grape (California) 75.00
Beaded Loop (Oregon) 55.00
Beaded Swag, Heisey 65.00
Beaded Swirl & Lens, ruby stain 135.00
Block & Lattice (Big Button) 50.00
Broken Column 65.00
Bubble Lattice, clear satin opal 165.00
Buckingham 48.00
Bull's Eye w/Point (Reverse Torpedo) 75.00
Butterfly & Daisy, Pairpoint, 7" 145.00
Champion, amber stain 145.00
Chrysanthemum Base Lg Swirl, bl speckled, scarce 365.00
Chrysanthemum Sprig, custard 295.00
Circled Scroll, clear opal 195.00
Coin Spot, amberina opal, very rare 625.00
Coin Spot, cranberry opal, jug shape 350.00
Cone, pk satin w/frosted hdl, faceted stopper, 5¼" 295.00
Coreopsis, HP florals 295.00
Croesus, gr w/EX gold, lg 295.00
Croesus, gr w/EX gold, sm 195.00
Cut Log, lg 45.00
Cut Log, sm 35.00
Daisy & Fern, Apple Blossom mold, bl opal 210.00
Daisy & Fern, cranberry opal.......................................500.00
Daisy & Fern, wht opal, faceted stopper 110.00
Dbl Circle, bl 185.00
Delaware Rose, EX gold, very rare 395.00

Dia Quilt, reversed amberina, faceted stopper, 6½" 350.00
Empress 75.00
Esther, gr w/gold, lg 255.00
Feather 55.00
Feather, gr 325.00
Fine Cut, dk amber 115.00
Forget-Me-Not, butterscotch, rare 295.00
Galloway 75.00
Geneva, custard, EX gr stain & gold 400.00
Gr opaque, w/decor, Mt WA 1,150.00
Herringbone, bl opal, teardrop stopper, 7x3⅝" 450.00
Herringbone, pk MOP, frosted hdl & stopper 450.00
Herringbone Buttress, emerald gr 385.00
Hobnail, amber 225.00
Hobnail, rubena verde 475.00
Hobnail, vaseline, Hobbs & Brockunier, 7¾" 335.00
Intaglio, clear opal 110.00
Invt T'print, amberina, EX color, EX 325.00
Invt T'print, amberina, orig amber stopper, Mt WA 350.00
Invt T'print, bl w/HP florals, bl reeded hdl, 7½" 145.00
Invt T'print, rubena, funnel shape 195.00
Invt T'print, rubena verde, faceted stopper, att Hobbs, 6¾" 395.00
Invt T'print, rubena verde, funnel shape 275.00
Jacob's Ladder, orig Maltese Cross stopper.........................125.00
Keystone...30.00
Lacy Daisy 35.00
Ladder w/Diamond (Fine Cut & Ribbed Bars) 30.00
Late Butterfly (Mikado)..65.00
Manhattan, lg 75.00
Massachusetts 45.00
Medallion Sprig, gr, scarce 295.00
Medallion Sprig, rubena, scarce 350.00
Millefiori..120.00
Moon & Star..95.00
New Hampshire (Bent Buckle), orig Teasel stopper....................40.00
New Jersey 45.00
Orinda...40.00
Panelled Daisy & Button, amber stain...............................245.00
Panelled Diamond Block...50.00
Panelled Sprig w/Lattice design, clear opal........................120.00
Panelled Thistle 55.00
Plantation, Heisey...50.00
Rib Optic (Utopia Optic, Tiny Optic), gr w/HP decor 135.00
Rose opaline 135.00
Sapphire bl, amber hdl & amber teardrop stopper, 7" 125.00
Sapphire bl, HP lily of the valley, amber stopper 135.00
Shoshone 50.00
Snail, ruby stain, very rare..475.00
Spangle, bl w/wht mottle & silver mica, Hobbs & Brockunier ...295.00
Swag w/Brackets, bl opal 435.00
Swag w/Brackets, vaseline opal......................................435.00
Thousand Eye, amber, Richard & Hartley variant 185.00
Thousand Eye, amber, 3-knob...135.00
Tokyo, bl opal..265.00
Wild Rose & Bow Knot, chocolate.....................................385.00
Windows, cranberry opal, oval, scarce, 6½" 385.00

Cup Plates, Glass

Before the middle 1850s, it was socially acceptable to pour hot tea into a deep saucer to cool. The tea was sipped from the saucer rather than the cup, which frequently was handleless and too hot to hold. The cup plate served as a coaster for the cup. It is generally agreed that the first examples of pressed glass cup plates were made about 1826 at the Boston and Sandwich Glass Co. in Sandwich, Cape Cod, Massachusetts. Other glassworks in three major areas — New England, Philadelphia, and the Midwest (especially Pittsburgh) — quickly followed suit.

Antique glass cup plates range in size from 2⅝" up to 4¼" in diameter. The earliest plates had simple designs inspired by cut glass patterns, but by 1829 they had become more complex. The span from then until about 1845 is known as the 'Lacy Period,' when cup plate designs and pressing techniques were at their peak. To cover pressing imperfections, the backgrounds of the plates were often covered with fine stippling which endowed them with a glittering brilliance called 'laciness.' They were made in a multitude of designs — some purely decorative, others commemorative. Subjects include the American eagle, hearts, sunbursts, log cabins, ships, George Washington, the political candidates Clay and Harrison, plows, beehives, etc. Of all the patterns, the round George Washington plate is the rarest and most valuable — only three are known to exist today.

Authenticity is most important. Collectors must be aware that contemporary plates which have no antique counterparts and fakes modeled after antique patterns have had wide distribution. Condition is also important, though it is the exceptional plate that does not have some rim roughness. More important considerations are scarcity of design and color.

Our advisor for this category is John Bilane; he is listed in the Directory under New Jersey. The book *American Glass* by George and Helen McKearin has a section on glass cup plates. A more definitive book is *American Glass Cup Plates,* by Ruth Webb Lee and James H. Rose. Numbers in the listings that follow (computer sorted) refer to the latter. When no condition is indicated, the examples listed below are assumed to have only minor rim roughness as is normal. See also Staffordshire; Pairpoint.

R-101, G 40.00
R-107A, scarce, VG...51.00
R-11, G 31.00
R-124A, VG 35.00
R-13C, G 28.00
R-130, extremely rare, VG 170.00
R-136A, rare, VG 75.00
R-146, scarce, G...38.00
R-148, VG 31.00
R-149, VG 29.00
R-151, G 18.00
R-151A, G 18.00
R-151V1, VG 32.00
R-166B, rare..65.00
R-172A, VG 33.00
R-172B, VG 33.00
R-177, EX 45.00
R-180A, G 28.00
R-191D, G 19.00
R-20, G 22.00
R-203, VG 45.00
R-216, VG 65.00
R-217, G 68.00
R-22, VG 28.00
R-229B, scarce, VG 44.00
R-232, scarce, G..50.00
R-235, G 20.00
R-246, VG 36.00
R-247, EX 32.00
R-255, G 18.00
R-258, clambroth, EX...70.00

R-264X2, G...30.00
R-269, VG 30.00
R-271A, VG 32.00
R-272, G 28.00
R-275, VG 32.00
R-277, scarce, VG 48.00
R-279, olive gr, EX 90.00
R-28, G 19.00

R-285, opalescent, attributed to Sandwich, minimal rim roughage, $110.00.

R-285V1, VG 42.00
R-29X1, VG 30.00
R-291, med bl, EX 200.00
R-313, VG 19.00
R-322, VG 19.00
R-323, VG 18.00
R-324, G 27.00
R-332A, VG 20.00
R-339, G 12.00
R-343B, scarce, VG 36.00
R-365, G 11.00
R-376, VG 15.00
R-385, VG 18.00
R-389, G 11.00
R-39, G 21.00
R-390A, G 11.00
R-391, EX 14.00
R-396, EX 15.00
R-402, VG 14.00
R-41A, eagle, NM 190.00
R-43, rare, VG 85.00
R-439, VG 25.00
R-440B, cobalt, hearts, EX 150.00
R-440B, scarce, VG 75.00
R-444, EX 41.00
R-447, VG 28.00
R-457A, VG 24.00
R-459E, G 16.00
R-459F, G 14.00
R-465F, G 16.00
R-465N, G 16.00
R-465RV1, scarce, EX 32.00
R-465S, scarce, VG...29.00
R-467B, G 15.00
R-47, G 18.00
R-477, G 16.00
R-479, G 15.00
R-501, G 11.00
R-510, peacock bl, EX 200.00
R-522, G 21.00
R-537, G 12.00
R-538, scarce, VG 28.00
R-56, scarce, EX..60.00
R-563, G 22.00

R-565, G	26.00
R-565B, G	28.00
R-565B, sapphire bl, Henry Clay, EX	70.00
R-566B, rare, VG	60.00
R-568X1, VG	98.00
R-569, G	39.00
R-576, G	24.00
R-593, scarce, G	36.00
R-596, VG	45.00
R-605A, scarce, VG	135.00
R-610C, VG	39.00
R-619, G	38.00
R-619, M	55.00
R-62A, scarce, EX	60.00
R-628, scarce, VG	65.00
R-634, med gr, Maid of Mist, EX	650.00
R-641, G	14.00
R-641A, G	15.00
R-643, G	19.00
R-654A, G	18.00
R-654A, very rare, EX	300.00
R-662, G	31.00
R-666, G	30.00
R-666A, scarce, G	40.00
R-670A, VG	38.00
R-671, very rare, VG	110.00
R-672, scarce, VG	50.00
R-679, VG	30.00
R-680, VG	30.00
R-680B, VG	35.00
R-691, scarce, VG	87.00
R-78, scarce, EX	63.00
R-79, VG	41.00
R-82, opal, rare, EX	400.00
R-890, EX	14.00
R-95, VG	36.00
R-99, rare, VG	68.00

Custard

As early as the 1880s, custard glass was produced in England. Migrating glassmakers brought the formula for the creamy ivory ware to America. One of them was Harry Northwood, who in 1898 founded his company in Indiana, Pennsylvania, and introduced the glassware to the American market. Soon other companies were producing custard, among them Heisey, Tarentum, Fenton, and McKee. Not only dinnerware patterns but souvenir items were made. Today, custard is the most expensive of the colored pressed glassware patterns. The formula for producing the luminous glass contains uranium salts which imparts the cream color to the batch and causes it to glow when it is examined under a black light.

Argonaut Shell, bowl, master berry; gold & decor, 10½" L	225.00
Argonaut Shell, butter dish, no gold	245.00
Argonaut Shell, compote, jelly; gold & decor, scarce	135.00
Argonaut Shell, creamer	110.00
Argonaut Shell, creamer, gold & decor	125.00
Argonaut Shell, cruet, gold & decor	450.00
Argonaut Shell, pitcher, water; gold & decor	335.00
Argonaut Shell, sauce, ftd, gold & decor	65.00
Argonaut Shell, spooner, gold & decor	115.00
Argonaut Shell, sugar bowl, w/lid, gold & decor	160.00
Argonaut Shell, tumbler, gold & decor	95.00

Argonaut Shell, butter dish, gold trim, $350.00.

Bead Swag, goblet, floral & gold	60.00
Bead Swag, sauce, floral & gold	45.00
Bead Swag, tray, pickle; floral & gold, rare	260.00
Bead Swag, wine, floral & gold	58.00
Beaded Circle, bowl, master berry; floral & gold	225.00
Beaded Circle, butter dish, floral & gold	325.00
Beaded Circle, creamer, floral & gold	135.00
Beaded Circle, cruet, floral & gold, rare	800.00
Beaded Circle, pitcher, water; floral & gold	550.00
Beaded Circle, shakers, floral & gold, pr	450.00
Beaded Circle, spooner, floral & gold	135.00
Beaded Circle, sugar bowl, w/lid, floral & gold	200.00
Beaded Circle, tumbler, floral & gold, very rare	100.00
Cane Insert, berry set, 7-pc	365.00
Cane Insert, table set, 4-pc	425.00
Cherry & Scales, bowl, master berry; nutmeg stain	130.00
Cherry & Scales, butter dish, nutmeg stain	225.00
Cherry & Scales, creamer, nutmeg stain	115.00
Cherry & Scales, pitcher, water; nutmeg stain, scarce	325.00
Cherry & Scales, spooner, nutmeg stain, scarce	85.00
Cherry & Scales, sugar bowl, w/lid, nutmeg stain, scarce	125.00
Cherry & Scales, tumbler, nutmeg stain, scarce	50.00
Chrysanthemum Sprig, bowl, master berry; gold & decor	235.00
Chrysanthemum Sprig, bowl, master berry; no gold	175.00
Chrysanthemum Sprig, butter dish, gold & decor	250.00
Chrysanthemum Sprig, celery vase, gold & decor, rare	1,000.00
Chrysanthemum Sprig, compote, jelly; gold & decor	115.00
Chrysanthemum Sprig, compote, jelly; no decor	75.00
Chrysanthemum Sprig, creamer, gold & decor	105.00
Chrysanthemum Sprig, cruet, gold & decor, 6¾"	290.00
Chrysanthemum Sprig, pitcher, water; gold & decor	425.00
Chrysanthemum Sprig, sauce, ftd, gold & decor	50.00
Chrysanthemum Sprig, shakers, gold & decor, pr	250.00
Chrysanthemum Sprig, spooner, gold & decor	105.00
Chrysanthemum Sprig, spooner, no gold	70.00
Chrysanthemum Sprig, toothpick holder, gold & decor	275.00
Chrysanthemum Sprig, toothpick holder, no decor	165.00
Chrysanthemum Sprig, tumbler, gold & decor	55.00
Dandelion, mug, nutmeg stain	165.00
Delaware, creamer, breakfast; pk stain	70.00
Delaware, sauce, pk stain	65.00
Delaware, tray, pin; gr stain	75.00
Delaware, tumbler, pk stain	55.00
Diamond w/Peg, bowl, master berry; roses & gold	215.00
Diamond w/Peg, butter dish, roses & gold	200.00
Diamond w/Peg, creamer, ind; no decor	30.00

Diamond w/Peg, creamer, ind; souvenir 45.00
Diamond w/Peg, creamer, roses & gold 75.00
Diamond w/Peg, mug, souvenir 50.00
Diamond w/Peg, napkin ring, roses & gold, rare 150.00
Diamond w/Peg, pitcher, roses & gold, 5½" 175.00
Diamond w/Peg, sauce, roses & gold 40.00
Diamond w/Peg, shakers, souvenir, pr 155.00
Diamond w/Peg, sugar bowl, w/lid, roses & gold 160.00
Diamond w/Peg, toothpick holder, roses & gold 90.00
Diamond w/Peg, tumbler, roses & gold 55.00
Diamond w/Peg, water set, souvenir, 7-pc 600.00
Diamond w/Peg, wine, roses & gold 55.00
Diamond w/Peg, wine, souvenir 40.00
Everglades, bowl, master berry; gold & decor 215.00
Everglades, butter dish, gold & decor 365.00
Everglades, creamer, gold & decor 145.00
Everglades, sauce, gold & decor 60.00
Everglades, shakers, gold & decor, pr 325.00
Everglades, spooner, gold & decor 130.00
Everglades, sugar bowl, w/lid, gold & decor 175.00
Everglades, tumbler, gold & decor 100.00
Fan, bowl, master berry; good gold 185.00
Fan, butter dish, good gold 210.00
Fan, creamer, good gold 110.00
Fan, ice cream set, good gold, 7-pc 500.00
Fan, pitcher, water; good gold 275.00
Fan, sauce, good gold 55.00
Fan, spooner, good gold 95.00
Fan, sugar bowl, w/lid, good gold 135.00
Fan, tumbler, good gold 75.00
Fan, water set, good gold, 7-pc 700.00
Fine Cut & Roses, rose bowl, fancy int, nutmeg stain 100.00
Fine Cut & Roses, rose bowl, plain int. 85.00
Geneva, bowl, master berry; floral decor, ftd, oval, 9" L 90.00
Geneva, bowl, master berry; floral decor, rnd, 9" 120.00
Geneva, butter dish, floral decor 175.00
Geneva, butter dish, no decor 125.00
Geneva, compote, jelly; floral decor 85.00
Geneva, creamer, floral decor 90.00
Geneva, cruet, floral decor 325.00
Geneva, pitcher, water; floral decor 225.00
Geneva, sauce, floral decor, oval 45.00
Geneva, sauce, floral decor, rnd 45.00
Geneva, shakers, floral decor, pr 200.00
Geneva, spooner, floral decor 90.00
Geneva, sugar bowl, open, floral decor 85.00
Geneva, sugar bowl, w/lid, floral decor 150.00
Geneva, syrup, floral decor 350.00
Geneva, toothpick holder, floral w/M gold 200.00
Geneva, tumbler, floral decor 50.00
Georgia Gem, bowl, master berry; good gold 115.00
Georgia Gem, bowl, master berry; gr opaque 90.00
Georgia Gem, butter dish, good gold 190.00
Georgia Gem, celery vase, good gold 145.00
Georgia Gem, creamer, good gold 75.00
Georgia Gem, creamer, no gold 50.00
Georgia Gem, mug, good gold 45.00
Georgia Gem, powder jar, w/lid, good gold 60.00
Georgia Gem, shakers, good gold, pr 95.00
Georgia Gem, spooner, souvenir 55.00
Georgia Gem, sugar bowl, w/lid, no gold 60.00
Grape (& Cable), bottle, scent; orig stopper, nutmeg stain 525.00
Grape (& Cable), bowl, master berry; nutmeg stain, ftd, 11".......265.00
Grape (& Cable), bowl, nutmeg stain, 7½" 50.00

Grape (& Cable), butter dish, nutmeg stain 235.00
Grape (& Cable), compote, jelly; open, nutmeg stain 95.00
Grape (& Cable), compote, nutmeg stain, 4½x8" 250.00
Grape (& Cable), cracker jar, nutmeg stain 600.00
Grape (& Cable), creamer, breakfast; nutmeg stain 75.00
Grape (& Cable), humidor, bl stain, rare 600.00
Grape (& Cable), humidor, nutmeg stain, rare 650.00
Grape (& Cable), nappy, nutmeg stain, rare 45.00
Grape (& Cable), pitcher, water; nutmeg stain 375.00
Grape (& Cable), plate, nutmeg stain, 7" 45.00
Grape (& Cable), plate, nutmeg stain, 8" 55.00
Grape (& Cable), powder jar, nutmeg stain 300.00
Grape (& Cable), punch bowl, w/base, nutmeg stain 1,150.00
Grape (& Cable), sauce, nutmeg stain, ftd 45.00
Grape (& Cable), spooner, nutmeg stain 110.00
Grape (& Cable), sugar, breakfast; open, nutmeg stain 75.00
Grape (& Cable), sugar bowl, w/lid, nutmeg stain 165.00
Grape (& Cable), tray, dresser; nutmeg stain, scarce, lg.....325.00
Grape (& Cable), tray, pin; nutmeg stain 125.00
Grape (& Cable), tumbler, nutmeg stain 75.00
Grape & Gothic Arches, bowl, master berry; pearl w/gold...........200.00
Grape & Gothic Arches, butter dish, pearl w/gold 200.00
Grape & Gothic Arches, creamer, pearl w/gold, rare 90.00
Grape & Gothic Arches, favor vase, nutmeg stain 80.00
Grape & Gothic Arches, goblet, pearl w/gold 60.00
Grape & Gothic Arches, pitcher, water; pearl w/gold.........275.00
Grape & Gothic Arches, sauce, pearl w/gold, rare...............80.00
Grape & Gothic Arches, spooner, pearl w/gold 80.00
Grape & Gothic Arches, sugar bowl, w/lid, pearl w/gold 125.00
Grape & Gothic Arches, tumbler, pearl w/gold....................65.00
Grape Arbor, vase, hat form 90.00
Heart w/T'print, creamer 80.00
Heart w/T'print, lamp, good pnt, scarce, 8" 325.00
Heart w/T'print, sugar bowl, ind. 75.00
Honeycomb, wine 65.00
Horse Medallion, bowl, gr stain, 7" 70.00
Intaglio, bowl, master berry; gold & decor, ftd, 9" 250.00
Intaglio, butter dish, gold & decor, scarce 300.00
Intaglio, compote, jelly; gold & decor 125.00
Intaglio, creamer, gold & decor 110.00
Intaglio, cruet, gold & decor 350.00
Intaglio, pitcher, water; gold & decor 345.00
Intaglio, sauce, gold & decor 48.00
Intaglio, shakers, gold & decor, pr 200.00
Intaglio, spooner, gold & decor 115.00
Intaglio, sugar bowl, w/lid, gold & decor 145.00
Intaglio, tumbler, gold & decor 75.00

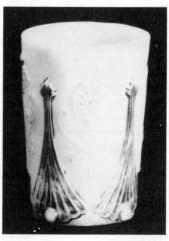

Inverted Fan and Feather, tumbler, gold and decoration, 4", $85.00.

Inverted Fan & Feather, bowl, master berry; gold & decor 215.00
Inverted Fan & Feather, butter dish, gold & decor 295.00
Inverted Fan & Feather, compote, jelly; gold & decor, rare........435.00
Inverted Fan & Feather, creamer, gold & decor 130.00
Inverted Fan & Feather, cruet, gold & decor, scarce, 6½" 725.00
Inverted Fan & Feather, pitcher, water; gold & decor 450.00
Inverted Fan & Feather, punch cup, gold & decor.......................250.00
Inverted Fan & Feather, sauce, gold & decor 65.00
Inverted Fan & Feather, shakers, gold & decor, pr 450.00
Inverted Fan & Feather, spooner, gold & decor 130.00
Inverted Fan & Feather, sugar bowl, w/lid, gold & decor.............185.00
Jackson, bowl, master berry; good gold, ftd................................125.00
Jackson, creamer, good gold..85.00
Jackson, pitcher, water; good gold..250.00
Jackson, pitcher, water; no decor 150.00
Jackson, sauce, good gold 45.00
Jackson, shakers, good gold, pr...135.00
Jackson, tumbler, good gold 45.00
Louis XV, berry set, w/nutmeg, 7-pc 375.00
Louis XV, bowl, master berry; good gold.....................................165.00
Louis XV, butter dish, good gold 200.00
Louis XV, creamer, good gold...80.00
Louis XV, cruet, good gold 250.00
Louis XV, pitcher, water; good gold 225.00
Louis XV, sauce, good gold, ftd..47.00
Louis XV, spooner, good gold..80.00
Louis XV, sugar bowl, w/lid, good gold 150.00
Louis XV, tumbler, good gold 65.00
Maple Leaf, bowl, master berry; gold & decor, scarce.................300.00
Maple Leaf, butter dish, gold & decor 255.00
Maple Leaf, compote, jelly; gold & decor, rare 455.00
Maple Leaf, creamer, gold & decor 135.00
Maple Leaf, cruet, gold & decor, rare 1,750.00
Maple Leaf, pitcher, water; gold & decor......................................345.00
Maple Leaf, sauce, gold & decor, scarce..95.00
Maple Leaf, shakers, gold & decor, pr 550.00
Maple Leaf, spooner, gold & decor 115.00
Maple Leaf, sugar bowl, w/lid, gold & decor 175.00
Maple Leaf, tumbler, gold & decor 85.00
Panelled Poppy, lamp shade, nutmeg stain, scarce 800.00
Peacock & Urn, bowl, ice cream; nutmeg stain, sm......................80.00
Peacock & Urn, bowl, ice cream; nutmeg stain, 10" 310.00
Punty Band, shakers, pr 130.00
Punty Band, spooner, floral decor 60.00
Punty Band, tumbler, floral decor, souvenir...................................65.00
Ribbed Drape, butter dish, scalloped, roses & gold.....................280.00
Ribbed Drape, compote, jelly; roses & gold, rare.........................200.00
Ribbed Drape, creamer, roses & gold, scarce 125.00
Ribbed Drape, cruet, roses & gold, scarce 425.00
Ribbed Drape, pitcher, water; roses & gold, rare 345.00
Ribbed Drape, sauce, roses & gold 40.00
Ribbed Drape, shakers, roses & gold, rare, pr 235.00
Ribbed Drape, spooner, roses & gold 115.00
Ribbed Drape, toothpick holder, roses & gold.............................235.00
Ribbed Drape, tumbler, roses & gold 65.00
Ribbed Thumbprint, wine, floral decor 75.00
Ring Band, bowl, master berry; roses & gold...............................135.00
Ring Band, butter dish, roses & gold..200.00
Ring Band, compote, jelly; roses & gold, scarce 165.00
Ring Band, creamer, roses & gold 90.00
Ring Band, cruet, roses & gold..300.00
Ring Band, pitcher, roses & gold, 7½"...250.00
Ring Band, sauce, roses & gold 40.00
Ring Band, shakers, roses & gold, pr..115.00

Ring Band, spooner, roses & gold..95.00
Ring Band, syrup, roses & gold...335.00
Ring Band, toothpick holder, roses & gold 110.00
Ring Band, tray, condiment; roses & gold 175.00
Singing Birds, mug, nutmeg stain...85.00
Tarentum's Victoria, bowl, master berry; gold & decor 200.00
Tarentum's Victoria, butter dish, gold & decor, rare....................275.00
Tarentum's Victoria, celery vase, gold & decor, rare....................225.00
Tarentum's Victoria, creamer, gold & decor, scarce.....................115.00
Tarentum's Victoria, pitcher, water; gold & decor, rare................365.00
Tarentum's Victoria, spooner, gold & decor..................................115.00
Tarentum's Victoria, sugar bowl, w/lid, gold & decor 160.00
Tarentum's Victoria, tumbler, gold & decor....................................70.00
Vermont, butter dish, bl decor...185.00
Vermont, toothpick holder, bl decor 135.00
Vermont, vase, floral decor, jeweled...75.00
Wide Band, bell, roses 175.00
Wild Bouquet, butter dish, gold & decor, rare 475.00
Wild Bouquet, creamer, no gold 145.00
Wild Bouquet, cruet, no decor, w/clear stopper...........................300.00
Wild Bouquet, sauce, gold & decor 60.00
Wild Bouquet, spooner, gold & decor 145.00
Wild Bouquet, tumbler, no decor 75.00
Winged Scroll, bowl, master berry; gold & decor, 11" L 140.00
Winged Scroll, butter dish, good gold...185.00
Winged Scroll, butter dish, no decor...150.00
Winged Scroll, celery vase, good gold, rare...................................400.00
Winged Scroll, cigarette jar, scarce 155.00
Winged Scroll, compote, ruffled, rare, 6¾x10¾"..........................495.00
Winged Scroll, hair receiver, good gold 120.00
Winged Scroll, pitcher, water; bulbous, good gold 300.00
Winged Scroll, sauce, good gold..35.00
Winged Scroll, shakers, bulbous, good gold, rare, pr 350.00
Winged Scroll, shakers, str sides, good gold, pr...........................165.00
Winged Scroll, sugar bowl, w/lid, good gold 150.00
Winged Scroll, syrup, good gold..365.00
Winged Scroll, tumbler, good gold 75.00

Cut Glass

The earliest documented evidence of commercial glass cutting in the United States was in 1810; the producers were Bakewell and Page of Pittsburgh. These first efforts resulted in simple patterns with only a moderate amount of cutting. By the middle of the century, glass cutters began experimenting with a thicker glass which enabled them to use deeper cuttings, though patterns remained much the same. This period is usually referred to as Rich Cut. Using three types of wheels — a flat edge, a mitered edge, and a convex edge — facets, miters, and depressions were combined to produce various designs. In the late 1870s, a curved miter was developed which greatly expanded design potential. Patterns became more elaborate, often covering the entire surface. The Brilliant Period of cut glass covered a span from about 1880 until 1915. Because of the pressure necessary to achieve the deeply cut patterns, only glass containing a high grade of metal could withstand the process. For this reason and the amount of handwork involved, cut glass has always been expensive.

Bowls cut with pinwheels may be either foreign or of a newer vintage, beware! Identifiable patterns and signed pieces that are well cut and in excellent condition bring the higher prices on today's market.

Key:
dmn — diamonds
strw — strawberry

X-cut — cross-cut
X-hatch — crosshatch

Basket, allover checkerboard fans, triple-knotched hdl, 7½" 165.00
Basket, dmns/stars/mitres, 6x6" 125.00
Biscuit jar, dmn cutting, dome lid w/ball finial, 8½" 300.00
Bottle, scent; hobstars/fans/dmn point, gr to clear, 7" 275.00
Bowl, buzz stars/hobstar rosettes, sawtooth rim, 3x8" 125.00
Bowl, chrysanthemum/cane/dmns, shaped/serrated rim, 9".........275.00
Bowl, chrysanthemum/pineapple blossom, 3 scroll legs, 8" 100.00
Bowl, daisies/dmns/hobstars, Harvard, scalloped, 7⅜x2¼" 135.00
Bowl, Golden Rod, ftd, Bergen, 8x8" 425.00
Bowl, hobstars/X-hatched triangles/fans, 8" 175.00
Bowl, ice cream; chrysanthemum/dmn, serrated rim, 12" 275.00
Bowl, Jubilee, smooth vesicas/hobstars, 9" 500.00
Bowl, pinwheels/hobstars/fans, 8½" 150.00
Bowl, Rex Variant, 9" 750.00
Bowl, star rosettes/oval panels/stars, cobalt to clear, 4x9" 350.00
Bowl, strw dmn, sgn Hoare, 4½x12" 550.00
Box, cigarette; top becomes ash tray, buzz stars, 3x4" 45.00
Box, collar; intaglio fruit, cut sides, 5x9" 595.00
Butter dish, buzz stars, rayed base, dome lid, 4x5" dia.............125.00
Candlestick, flutes/notches, sgn Hoare, 8½"........................175.00
Candy dish, Daisy & Button, scalloped, hdls, 8", EX..................75.00
Caviar, hobstars/minor intaglio, 5½".................................225.00
Celery, Block, ped ft, 10½"...325.00
Celery vase, Hunts Royal, 11" 250.00
Champagne cooler, chrysanthemum/dmns, tapered cylinder, 7" .600.00
Cheese dish, strw/dmn w/fan, dome lid, faceted knob, 9" dia.......450.00
Compote, Florentine Star, hobstar base, tricorner, 4½" 150.00
Compote, fruit; Buffalo, heavy, 8⅝x8".................................350.00
Compote, hobstars/fans, flute-cut stem w/teardrop, 8x6" 175.00
Compote, jelly; dmns/fams, etched roses & leaves, 6x6" 60.00
Creamer, stars/fans/dmns, rayed base, 4½x3½" 40.00
Creamer & sugar bowl, Hunt's Royal.................................200.00
Cruet, hobstars/X-hatching, tricorner lip, appl hdl, heavy 85.00
Decanter, buzz star/dmn blocks/fans, gr to clear, 15½" 150.00
Decanter, cordial; Harvard, 10" 175.00
Decanter, Harvard, high ped, bulbous, faceted stopper, 13" 2,950.00
Decanter, hobstars/fans, notched hdl, 11" 250.00
Decanter, Monarch, Hoare, 12" 250.00
Decanter, pinwheel, 12", pr...350.00
Decanter, Punty & Flutes, gr to clear, hexagonal, 10½" 325.00
Horseradish jar, Pinwheel & T'print, orig stopper 135.00
Humidor, hobstars/fans, hobstar lid, 8-sided, ½-lb...................285.00
Humidor, strw/dmn/fans, 6" 325.00
Knife rest, zipper cut center, dmns/fans, dumbell form..................25.00
Lamp, table; hobstars, w/32 prisms, 17" 1,550.00
Loving cup, Hawkes-like floral & vine cuttings, 3-hdl, 10" 450.00
Mayonnaise jar, zipper/dmns, faceted finial, w/spoon, 4½"............45.00
Pitcher, buzz stars/fans, bulbous, 8x7½" 150.00
Pitcher, chrysanthemum & Harvard, 9½" 300.00
Pitcher, chrysanthemum/dmns, scalloped, strap hdl, 6½" 225.00
Pitcher, dmns/fans, etched rose/leaf panels, 7"........................75.00
Pitcher, hobstars, bulbous, 9" 275.00
Pitcher, pineapple/fans, very heavy, 8½" 250.00
Pitcher, Russian, t'print strap hdl, scalloped rim, 11"..................725.00
Pitcher, Shooting Star & Cross Dmn, cobalt to clear, 11½" 150.00
Pitcher, strw/dmn/fan, triple-notch stem, bulbous, 7½" 300.00
Pitcher, sunburst, +6 tumblers..350.00
Pitcher, tankard; allover cut, sgn Hoare, 9½" 185.00
Pitcher, tankard; flower & Harvard, 14½", +6 tumblers...............325.00
Pitcher, tankard; hobstars/cane/dmns, Hoare, 11"....................250.00
Pitcher, tankard; notched prisms, silver top, 10" 175.00
Pitcher, tankard; paneled hobstars/dmn fan, t'print hdl, 11" 250.00
Pitcher, tankard; stars/circles, vintage silver mts, 12"................800.00
Pitcher, vertical mitres w/cuts between, star base, 11" 250.00

Pitcher, water; Alloy, heavy, att Bergen 325.00

Punch bowl on stand, cut rose with butterflies pattern, 12" x 9", NM $400.00; Candy dish, Daisy and Button, 8½" diameter, NM, $125.00.

Rose bowl, hobstars, strw dmns, fans, heavy, 5" 185.00
Rose bowl, Russian, 6x7"...300.00
Spooner, strw/fan 175.00
Syrup, pinwheels/mitres/X-hatching, ball shape, 5½" 135.00
Toothpick holder, stars, notching 28.00
Tray, hobstar clusters, oval, 14" 375.00
Tray, ice cream; hobstars/mitre cuts/fans, sgn Straus, 18" 650.00
Tumbler, pineapples, 4"..25.00
Urn, hobstars/pinwheels, 10"...325.00
Vase, chrysanthemum, lacy rim, rnd ped, ray base, 12" 150.00
Vase, Harvard, bulbous tapering form w/short rim, 6".................125.00
Vase, hobstars/canes, 14½"...550.00
Vase, hobstars/stars, flared, 8½".......................................225.00
Vase, 3 panels ea: florals/X-hatch, marble/bronze base, 14" 90.00
Wine, hobstars/fans...38.00
Wine, Meriden, 4½", set of 6 ....165.00
Wine, strw dmn/fan, cranberry to clear, 4 for 700.00

Cut Overlay Glass

Glassware with one or more overlying colors through which a design has been cut is called 'Cut Overlay.' It was made both here and abroad.

Mantel lustre, white cut to green with gold enameling, ten prisms, 10", $125.00; Vase, purple cut to white to clear, 10", $125.00; Candlestick, dark blue cut to white to clear, Baccarat, 9¾", $150.00.

Bottle, scent; clear w/bl ribs, petticoat form, 7" 300.00
Jar, wht over red to clear, criss-cross/star cuts, 5x6" 175.00
Newel post finial, wht to cranberry w/stars & circles, 6½" 600.00
Vase, cobalt/clear, roses/vertical ribs/stars, 10½" 225.00
Vase, wht on gr, portrait/floral medallions, gilt, 12", pr 1,200.00

Cut Velvet

Cut Velvet glassware was made during the late 1800s. It is characterized by the effect achieved through the application of relief-molded patterns, often ribbing or diamond quilting, which allows its white inner casing to show through the outer pastel layer.

Bowl, pk, appl clear trim, ftd, 4¼x6" 255.00
Rose bowl, Dia Quilt, bl, 3-crimp, egg form, 4⅜x3½" 135.00
Rose bowl, Dia Quilt, bl, 4-petal top, 6x3¾" 165.00
Rose bowl, Dia Quilt, rose pk, 4-crimp top, 4⅛x3" 165.00

Vase, Diamond Quilted, deep blue, 7", $150.00.

Vase, Dia Quilt, bl, bottle form, 9½" 225.00
Vase, Dia Quilt, bl, bulbous, 4½" 160.00
Vase, Dia Quilt, bl, pinched rim, 4x2½" 135.00
Vase, Dia Quilt, bl, ruffled top, 6x3" 175.00
Vase, Dia Quilt, bl, sq top, 6¼x3¼" 165.00
Vase, Ribbed, bl, ruffled top, 7x3¼" 145.00
Vase, Ribbed, dk pk, sq w/rnd top, 7¾x3¼" 145.00
Vase, Ribbed, pk, bottle form, 8¾" 150.00

Cybis

Boleslaw Cybis was a graduate of the Academy of Fine Arts in Warsaw, Poland, and was well recognized as a fine artist by the time he was commissioned by his government to paint murals in the Polish Pavillion's Hall of Honor at the 1939 World's Fair. Finding themselves stranded in America at the outbreak of WWII, the Cybises founded an artists' studio, first in Astoria, New York, and later in Trenton, New Jersey, where they made fine figurines and plaques with exacting artistry and craftsmanship entailing extensive handwork. The studio still operates today producing exquisite porcelains on a limited edition basis.

Beatrice 875.00
Bl Headed Vireo w/Lilac, pr 2,000.00
Carousel Horse..............................775.00
Crow Dancer 4,200.00
Dahlia 675.00

Elephant 4,500.00
Flight Into Egypt 2,800.00
Great Thunder 3,900.00
Guinevere 625.00
Horse 1,650.00
Iris..............................2,950.00
Lady Macbeth..............................865.00
Pegasus..............................1,400.00
Queen Esther 950.00
Scarlett 1,200.00
Skylarks, pr 1,500.00
Unicorn 1,250.00

Czechoslovakian Collectibles

Czechoslovakia came into being as a country in 1918. Located in the heart of Europe, it was a land with the natural resources necessary to support a glass industry that dates back to the mid-fourteenth century. This ware has recently captured the attention of today's collectors, and for good reason. There are beautiful vases — cased, ruffled, applied with rigaree or silver overlay — fine enough to rival those of the best glasshouses. Czechoslovakian art glass baskets are quite as attractive as Victorian America's, and the elegant cut glass perfumes made in colors as well as crystal are unrivaled. There are also pressed glass perfumes, molded in lovely Deco shapes, of various types of art glass. Some are overlaid with gold filigree set with 'jewels.' Jewelry, lamps, porcelains and fine art pottery are also included in the field.

More than thirty-five marks have been recorded, including those in the mold, ink stamped, acid etched, or on a small metal name plate. The newer marks are incised, stamped 'Royal Dux made in Czechoslovakia' (see Royal Dux), or simply a paper label which reads 'Bohemian Glass made in Czechoslovakia.' For a more thorough study of the subject, we recommend you refer to the book *Made in Czechoslovakia*, by Ruth A. Forsythe; she is listed in the Directory under Ohio. In the listings that follow when one dimension is given, it refers to height; decoration is enamel unless noted otherwise.

Perfume bottles, Crystal with overall cuttings, 7", $110.00; Tango Dancers, 6", $550.00.

Candy Baskets

Gr varicolored stripes, lt gr hdl, flared rim, 8" 85.00
Gr varicolored w/red overlay at base, flared rim, 8½" 110.00

Mc mottle, crystal flat-top hdl, slender/incurvate, 8½" 85.00
Mc mottle, flat-top crystal thorn hdl, 6½" 110.00
Solid color, blk petal rim, crystal hdl, 6½" 110.00
Varicolored, wide ruffled rim, squat, str Hobnail sides, 5½".........145.00

Cased Art Glass

Bowl, red, wide flared rim, 12" 55.00
Candy jar, yel, appl florals, lid missing, 3¾" 35.00
Candy jar, yel, appl florals, w/lid, 3¾" 95.00
Decanter, orange, silver-deposit bird, 12" 95.00
Pitcher, brn & yel mottle, bl hdl, 9½" 95.00
Vase, bl, ruffled rim, clear hdls, long neck, 8¼" 75.00
Vase, bl, 3 blk buttress ft, 9" 95.00
Vase, bl pull-ups on bl, flared cylinder, 7" 65.00
Vase, blk, silver-deposit ships, bulbous, 7¼" 75.00
Vase, bud; orange, silver-deposit florals, 6¼" 30.00
Vase, dbl cased, varicolored swirl, bulbous w/can neck, 5½" 65.00
Vase, deep yel w/blk at rim & base, stick form, 10½" 35.00
Vase, jack-in-the-pulpit; yel w/mottled base, 7½" 55.00
Vase, mottled, ruffled rim, appl serpentine decor, 9⅝" 95.00
Vase, orange, silver & blk Greek figure, classic form, 12" 145.00
Vase, pk, canes, red overlay veins, hdls, 7" 350.00
Vase, red w/gr aventurine, fan form, 7½" 125.00
Vase, varicolored, blk mottle on yel, dbl-gourd form, 8" 85.00
Vase, varicolored, bulbous, flared rim, 11½" 180.00
Vase, varicolored w/mottled base, bulbous, 4½" 65.00
Vase, wht, emb decor, clear ruffled rim, 6½" 45.00
Vase, yel, appl blk serpentine decor, shouldered form, 7¼" 85.00
Vase, yel, slim w/ruffled blk rim, 8½" 38.00
Vase, yel satin, mc desert scene, flared cylinder, 8½" 145.00
Vase, yel satin, mc pastoral scene, flared cylinder, 9½" 180.00
Wine, yel, tall blk stem & base, 7½" 25.00

Cut Glass Perfume Bottles

Amber, tall slim form, crystal faceted stopper, 6⅛" 145.00
Amber, 4 scrolling ft, frosted floral teardrop stopper, 7⅞".........450.00
Amethyst, diagonal cuttings, rnd crystal stopper, 4⅜"..................95.00
Amethyst, shouldered form, frosted floral stopper, 4¾" 145.00
Bl, pyramidal, frosted florals in rectangular stopper, 6½" 125.00
Bl, sq shoulders, bl prism stopper, 5⅝" 75.00
Blk opaque, stepped Deco form, crystal stopper, 4⅝" 110.00
Crystal, overall cuttings, frosted butterfly stopper, 5½" 185.00
Crystal, overall cuttings, tall slim red stopper, 4⅛" 65.00
Crystal, stepped sides, bl shield-form stopper, 6½" 60.00
Crystal, tall crystal rectangular stopper, 5⅞" 80.00
Crystal, wide base, frosted lady stopper, 5⅝" 250.00
Crystal, wide base, yel prism stopper, 4" 65.00
Crystal, wide shoulders, blk opaque stopper, 4½" 65.00
Crystal w/bl ped base, 2-pc, bl frosted floral stopper, 5¾" 185.00
Gr, flared base, gr prism stopper, 5¼" 155.00
Gr, gold jewels, gr frosted stopper, 4¾" 145.00
Gr, sq base w/angled shoulders, slim crystal stopper, 6¼".............125.00
Gr, wide shoulders, frosted florals in stopper, 6½" 125.00
Pk, stepped base, crystal triangular stopper, 5⅝" 120.00
Pk w/frosted figure, angle shoulders, pk stopper, 4⅛" 365.00
Red, shouldered form, crystal cut stopper, 5⅞" 400.00
Topaz, bulbous, crystal triangular stopper, 5⅛"............................110.00

Lamps

Art Deco geometrics, spherical, matching Deco cone shade, 9" ..210.00
Basket, bl beaded, beaded fruit, emb metal trim, 8"......................400.00

Basket, crystal beads, glass fruit, metal trim, 10"........................500.00
Deco-style dancer beside crystal bubble sphere on ped, 9" 450.00
Desk, acid-cut counterbalance shade, slim/trn std, 10" 160.00
Goebel girl in glass flower dress, 10¼" 585.00
Milk glass, pk & gold pnt, kerosene, 12¾".....................................110.00
Mottled satin base & shade, 12½"...180.00
Peacock figural, brass w/beaded tail, blk onyx base, 12¼" 550.00
Student, acid-cut shade, pnt metal quatrefoil base, 12"...............350.00
Table, dk bl lustre, classic form, rpl shade, 13¼" 85.00
Wall sconce, 2-arm, prisms, 14½"...145.00

Mold Blown and Pressed Bottles

Bl, nude & butterfly, bl stopper, scarce, 5¼".................................385.00
Bl, sloped shoulders, atomizer, 3" 65.00
Cranberry opalescent Hobnail, wht opal stopper, 5½" 85.00
Crystal, squat, floral ornaments on stopper, 1¾"............................35.00
Gr, w/wht veins, low-shouldered base, orange stopper, 7⅛" 40.00
Mottle cased, slim neck, puff-box base, blk stopper, 6⅜" 135.00
Orange cased, blk base & stopper, 6¼" 55.00

Opaque, Crystal, Colored Transparent Glass

Decanter, amber, floral cuttings, cylindrical, 8" 55.00
Pitcher, amber, yel overlay pull-ups, quilted, 11½" 165.00
Pitcher, bl bubbly glass, squat, tall stopper, 8⅝" 85.00
Pitcher, orange & gr, stacked cone form, clear hdl, 12½"...............85.00
Tumbler, bl, HP exotic bird, 5½" 38.00
Tumbler, gr bubbly glass, HP coach scene, 5¾" 60.00
Vase, blk w/orange spiraling stripes, cylindrical, 6½" 65.00
Vase, crystal, red spiral threading, ftd cylinder, 8¼" 65.00
Vase, dk bl cut to clear, florals, 10¼" 150.00
Vase, frosted, emb wild horses, spherical, 7" 45.00
Vase, mauve, acid etched, ruffled rim w/blk trim, 5⅝" 110.00
Vase, mottled w/canes, red overlay veins, hdls, 7"........................300.00
Vase, pk lustre w/threading at top, ftd cylinder, 9⅜"....................200.00
Vase, red/yel/bl mottle, slim neck, 8⅛" 55.00
Vase, robin's egg bl w/appl yel threading, fan form, 9½"..............165.00
Wine, gr bubbly glass, HP riding scene, 4¼" 40.00

Pottery, Porcelain, Semi-Porcelain

Bowl, mc Deco floral band on blk, wht int, str sides, 3x7" 55.00
Candlestick, mc Deco florals on blk w/gold, wall mt, 9⅛" 65.00
Creamer, chicken figural, 4" 30.00
Creamer, cow figural, tail forms hdl, 6¼" 48.00
Creamer, parrot figural, 4½" 25.00
Cup & saucer, floral swags & medallions on wht, 2¼" 15.00
Figurine, Deco lady, wht, 9¾" 85.00
Figurine, hound dog, brn & wht, 5" 35.00
Flower holder, bird on stump form, 5⅜" 22.00
Flower holder, bird perched at side of open log, 3½" 25.00
Jar, Egyptian decor, gold trim, hdls, 8½"......................................350.00
Shakers, Mexican couple figurals, red/wht/yel, 2¾", pr 18.00
Teapot, Peasant Art, Deco, sgn Mrazck, 8" 125.00
Teapot, pk lustre, bulbous, 6⅛" 30.00
Vase, Egyptian figures in wide band, 9⅛" 300.00
Wall pocket, bird at edge of wishing well form, 6" 25.00

D'Argental

D'Argental cameo glass was produced in France from the 1870s until about 1920 in the Art Nouveau style. Browns and tans were favored colors used to complement florals and scenic designs developed through acid cuttings.

Our advisor for this category is Don Williams; he is listed in the Directory under Missouri.

Cameo

Bottle, scent; columbines, lt/dk wine on gr, metal top, 5"	1,100.00
Box, roses, mauve on yel, compressed sphere, 7" dia	1,100.00
Perfume burner, floral, rust/brn on opal, bell form, 6"	1,600.00
Vase, lake/mtns fr by trees, amber & brn on yel-orange, 12"	2,500.00
Vase, mums, brn on amber frost, baluster, 14"	3,000.00
Vase, palm trees/river, brn on tan & amber frost, 10"	1,100.00
Vase, poppies, salmon on lemon & gray mottle, ovoid, 8"	1,200.00
Vase, sea plants/creatures, amber/brn on yel, 8"	3,000.00
Vase, storks/village, purple on wht, shouldered, 10"	2,500.00
Vase, vines/tendrils, dk brn on yel, 5½"	500.00
Vase, wildflowers, rosy orange on lemon, elongated/ftd, 13"	1,600.00

Daum Nancy

Daum was an important producer of French cameo glass, operating from the late 1800s until after the turn of the century. They used various techniques — acid cutting, wheel engraving, and handwork — to create beautiful scenic designs and nature subjects in the Art Nouveau manner. Virtually all examples are signed.

Our advisor for this category is Don Williams; he is listed in the Directory under Missouri.

Cameo

Bowl vase, mums/gilt on wht opal mottle, silver ft, 5"	2,000.00
Box, floral cut/pnt on yel to purple, dome lid, 3½" H	2,000.00
Box, flowers/vines, amber on yel-gr frost, 6¾" dia	2,800.00
Box, fuchsia cut/pnt on wht mottle to purple, 2½" H	1,000.00
Box, mistletoe limbs cut/pnt on pk frost, rnd, 2½" H	1,000.00
Cruet, berry branches cut/pnt, gold detail, SP holder, 7"	1,600.00
Ewer, lilies, emerald gr on frost, ornate silver o/l, 13"	4,500.00
Ewer, thistles/leaves on bl, blk enamel w/gold, slim, 18"	13,000.00
Lamp, trees/lake, brn on mottle, on 7½" shade/base, 15"	15,000.00
Lamp, trees/river, red on yel, on 12" dome shade/slim base	18,000.00
Toothpick holder, rose sprig, gilt on cranberry, 2"	485.00
Vase, bellflowers, brn on red mottle, slim/ftd, 14"	4,900.00

Vase, polished berry branches, green on green, yellow, and orange mottle, signed, 12", $4,500.00.

Vase, cherry blossoms, red on yel mottle, ftd, 11½"	5,000.00
Vase, clematis cut/pnt on gr & yel mottle, 3¼"	1,700.00
Vase, columbine cut/pnt on purple mottle, cylindrical, 5"	2,000.00
Vase, daisies, bl on yel-to-bl frost, 9"	3,600.00
Vase, elephant-ear leaves, gr to rust on striated wht, 25"	3,300.00
Vase, floral cut/pnt, gr on clear frost, silver o/l, 8"	4,000.00
Vase, floral cut/pnt on wht & yel to dk base, 4½x4"	1,600.00
Vase, floral w/gold on cranberry frost, 14x5"	935.00
Vase, floral/leaves, bl/gr on cobalt mottle to wht, 12"	4,000.00
Vase, flowering vine cut/pnt on lav mottle to orange, 4¾"	1,700.00
Vase, foxglove, red on ginger frost, slim/ftd, 21"	12,000.00
Vase, freesia cut/pnt on yel mottle to purple, slim/ftd, 9"	2,400.00
Vase, girl/geese cut/pnt on wht opal mottle, 3"	2,600.00
Vase, hazelnut limbs, tan on yel/orange mottle, 13x6"	4,900.00
Vase, hyacinths cut/pnt on bl to cobalt, flattened, 4x5"	3,000.00
Vase, irises cut/pnt on rose-to-gr frost, angle hdls, 4¾"	3,400.00
Vase, magnolias, red on pastel mottle, 11x8"	15,000.00
Vase, morning-glories cut/pnt on yel/amber, slim, 10"	4,000.00
Vase, mushrooms cut/pnt on yel & orange mottle, sqd, 4½"	7,500.00
Vase, mushrooms/pine cones cut/pnt on yel mottle, 16"	20,000.00
Vase, persimmon branches cut/pnt on gr to orange, ftd, 7½"	3,000.00
Vase, pines/sailboats, red on yel/red mottle, slim, 24"	9,000.00
Vase, quince branches, pk & gr on wht mottle, 17½"	5,700.00
Vase, river scene/mtns, dbl o/l, cylinder w/bun ft, 8"	3,000.00
Vase, sailboats, brn on mottle, ftd ovoid, 11½"	4,000.00
Vase, sailboats cut/pnt on orange mottle, baluster, 8"	4,900.00
Vase, sailboats/windmill in gray enamel, mini, 1⅛"	800.00
Vase, snow scene cut/pnt on ginger & yel mottle, slim, 22"	14,000.00
Vase, swan/trees cut/pnt on lt bl, sq rim/oval body, 4½"	7,000.00
Vase, thistles cut/pnt on striated amber & pk, 4¾"	800.00
Vase, thorny vines, gr-brn on opal, 3 snail hdls, 7½"	10,000.00
Vase, tiger lilies, purple on lav/amber mottle, 13x10"	9,000.00
Vase, tiger lilies, purple on wht/amber mottle, 12x9"	7,500.00
Vase, tree limbs, brn on yel/brn mottle, bun ft, 23"	5,200.00
Vase, tree limbs, olive on lt mottle to purple, hdls, 17"	4,000.00
Vase, trees in meadow cut/pnt on opal, pillow form, 4½"	1,600.00
Vase, vines, appl jeweled insects, wide base, 23"	11,000.00
Vase, violets cut/pnt on purple, 5 appl base hdls, 5x5"	31,000.00
Vase, wildflowers cut/pnt on wht/yel to purple, ftd, 5x4"	2,400.00

Miscellaneous

Bowl, etched ribs on gr, ftd w/flaring rim, 5½x11¾"	1,700.00
Bowl, gr/brn mottle w/foil inclusions, flattened oval, 5½"	1,400.00
Bowl, silver vine o/l on mottle, triangular/ftd, 5"	5,500.00
Bowl, turq w/cobalt & gold foil inclusions, 3½x9"	1,500.00
Lamp, wrought iron 3-arm base; mottled shade, 17"	1,200.00
Lamp, pk/purple w/foil, 9½" dome shade/wide-ftd base, 18"	8,000.00
Lamp, wrought iron 3-strap base w/leafy ft; 14" shade, 25"	4,600.00
Paperweight, pate-de-verre, mouse on rock, gr tones, 2½"	2,000.00
Salt cellar, windmill/sailboats on wht frost, 1¾"	800.00
Sconce, wrought iron mt w/grapes, mottled 6" bell shade	500.00
Tray, pate-de-verre, fish w/in waves, 7½" L	6,800.00
Vase, airtraps, 2 crystal 'ropes,' flowerpot form, 6x8"	2,000.00
Vase, etched fan-like geometrics on amber, spherical, 9"	3,500.00
Vase, etched fan-like geometrics on smoke, spherical, 9"	3,500.00
Vase, etched fine ribs on turq, spherical, 13½"	8,000.00
Vase, etched geometric motif on dk topaz, stacked ft, 13"	9,000.00
Vase, etched irregular stripes on icy bl, pear form, 7½"	2,900.00
Vase, etched stripes on pk & gray flecked, slim, 7"	600.00
Vase, etched stylized floral on blk-flecked clear, 8x12"	3,000.00
Vase, etched stylized floral on orange mottle, 10"	3,000.00
Vase, etched trapezoid key motif on gr mottle, ftd, 18"	4,000.00

Vase, mtns/trees on wht frost, flattened oval, 4¾" 3,500.00
Vase, rust w/dk brn splotches, sgn, 8" 250.00

Davenport

W. Davenport and Company were Staffordshire potters operating in that area from 1793 to 1887, producing earthenware, creamware, porcelain, and ironstone. Many different stamps, all with 'Davenport,' were used to mark the various types of ware. See also Mulberry; Flow Blue.

Jug, Japan pattern, serpent hdls, diaper border, 1820s, 4"............200.00
Plate, cattle & thatch hut, med-lt bl transfer, 10" 65.00
Plate, Many a little makes..., Franklin's, dk bl on wht, 9" 195.00
Tazza, Imari pattern, 9½" dia...120.00
Tureen, sauce; Flute Player, bl transfer, anchor mk, EX.................95.00

Davis, Lowell

Figurines, plates, bells, and ornaments painted by Lowell Davis and produced by Border Fine Arts, Schmid Sculptured Porcelain, capture the heritage of rural America.

Lowell Davis, known better as Mr. Lowell to his farm animals, is described by many as 'just a country farmer from Missouri' fulfilling his dreams of preserving rural America as he knew it in the 1930s. Mr. Lowell rebuilt Red Oak II, a 1930 village, from actual buildings he spent hours in as a child. You can visit this unique town refurbished with antiques and 'supplies' in Grandpa's General Store in Carthage, Missouri.

A Secondary Market Price Guide is published by Rosie Wells Enterprises for his collectibles. She is listed in the Directory under Clubs, Newsletters, and Catalogs. Items below are assumed to be in mint condition with box.

Blossom, #225-032, retired.. 1,600.00
Brer Coyote, #225-255, retired.......................................510.00
Bride, #221-001, 1st Club pc..250.00
Broken Dreams, #225-035, retired............................... 1,200.00
Chow Time, #221-003, Club pc..120.00
Critics, #223-600, ltd ed 1200 .... 1,350.00
Fowl Play, #225-033, retired..425.00
From a Friend to a Friend, #223-602, ltd ed 1200 .... 1,200.00
General Store, Red Oak II Series, ltd ed 300 pc...................... 1,000.00
Good Clean Fun, #225-020, retired 80.00
His Master's Dog, #225-244, retired................................155.00
Mail Order Bride, #225-263, Fox Fire Farm on mailbox 350.00
Right Church, Wrong Pew, #225-204, ltd ed 4000 ....395.00
Surprise in the Cellar, #225-200, ltd ed 2500 .... 1,200.00
Thirsty, #892-050, Club pc from 1985 ....85.00
Waiting for His Master, #225-281, locked door, retired..............300.00
1983 Country Xmas, #223-550, Hooker at Mailbox, ltd ed 785.00

De Vez

De Vez was a type of acid-cut French cameo glass produced by Cristallerie de Pantin in Paris around the turn of the century.

Our advisor for this category is Don Williams; he is listed in the Directory under Missouri.

Cameo

Atomizer, flower & insect, blk on pk, 9" 850.00

Box, butterflies/sm flowers, bl on irid frost, 3x3½" dia 575.00
Lamp, boudoir; island scene, gr/coral/yel, 3 cuts, 6¾" 1,800.00
Vase, bridge/buildings/mtns, gr on lt bl, slim neck, 14" 1,600.00
Vase, castle on mtn/lake & trees in bl, 9" 1,250.00
Vase, house on tree-lined lake, dbl o/l, baluster, 4¾" 750.00
Vase, lg bird on floral branch, orange/yel/bl on opal, 8" 1,600.00

Vase, woodland scene with deer, orange and blue on yellow mottle, signed, 11", $1,800.00.

De Vilbiss

Perfume bottles, atomizers, and dresser accessories marketed by the De Vilbiss Company are appreciated by collectors today for the various types of lovely glassware used in their manufacture, as well as for their pleasing shapes. Various companies provided the glass, while De Vilbiss made only the metal tops. They marketed their merchandise not only here but in Paris, England, Canada, and Havana as well. Their marks were acid stamped, ink stamped, in gold script, molded in, or on paper labels. One is no more significant than another. For more information we recommend *Bedroom and Bathroom Glassware of the Depression Years* by Margaret and Kenn Whitmyer; their address is listed in the Directory under Ohio.

Atomizer, blk Deco decor on pk opaque, mesh cord & bulb........185.00
Atomizer, blk enamel on frosted crystal, octagonal, 4⅛"...............50.00

Atomizer, clear opal swirl, 4", $68.00.

Atomizer, deer, bl on clear, bl mesh bulb, 6½" 235.00
Atomizer, dk bl & blk enamel, ivory cord & bulb, 5¼".................60.00
Atomizer, gold decor on smoked glass, orig label, +cologne...........75.00

Atomizer, gold on crystal w/gold draped lady stem, 7¼" 255.00
Atomizer, lav enamel, orig cord & netted bulb, 6¼" 70.00
Atomizer, orange & clear w/blk & gold enamel, 7" 245.00
Atomizer, pk, gold caryatid stem, orig bulb, 7¼" 275.00
Atomizer, tangerine, orig cord & bulb, 6⅜" 90.00
Atomizer, topaz opal, ball form, by Fenton 35.00
Atomizer, yel & blk enamel stripes on crystal 40.00
Bottle, scent; pebbled amethyst, rpl bulb, w/label, 4" 95.00
Lamp, perfume; exotic bird on glass insert, sq, 8½" 135.00
Lamp, perfume; nude figure on glass insert, rnd, 12" 235.00
Lamp, perfume; nude figure on glass insert, rnd, 7" 185.00
Set, lav cased satin perfume & atomizer, all orig 295.00
Vanity set, lt bl & crystal frost, 4-pc, rare 70.00

Decanters

Ceramic whiskey decanters were brought into prominence in 1955 by the James Beam Distilling Company. Few other companies besides Beam produced these decanters during the next ten years or so; however, other companies did eventually follow suit. At its peak in 1975, at least twenty prominent companies and several on a lesser scale made these decanters.

We have tried to list those brands that are the most popular with collectors. Likewise, individual decanters listed are the ones (or representative of the ones) most commonly found. These are a small fraction of the several thousand different decanters that have been produced. These decanters come from all over the world. While Jim Beam owns its own china factory in the U.S., some of the others import from Mexico, Taiwan, Japan and elsewhere. They vary in size from miniatures (approximately 2 oz.) to gallons. Values range from a few dollars to more than $3,000 per decanter. A mint condition decanter is one with no chips or cracks and all labels intact. Whether a decanter is full or not has no bearing on the value, nor does a missing federal tax stamp. It is advisable to empty the contents of a ceramic decanter, otherwise the thin inner glaze could crack, allowing the contents to seep through the porous body, thus ruining the decanter. An (m) behind a listing indicates a miniature. All others are fifth or 750 ml unless noted otherwise.

Our advisor for this category is Roy Willis; he is listed in the Directory under Kentucky.

Animals, Domestic

Beam, Cats, Burmese, Siamese, or Tabby, ea 10.00
Beam, Dog, Great Dane 10.00
Beam, Dog, Poodle, gray or wht 10.00
Beam, Dog, St Bernard 30.00
Beam, Horse, Apaloosa 10.00
Beam, Horse, Mare & Foal 50.00
Beam, Horse, Stallion, rearing, blk/brn/or gray, '61 or '62, ea 18.00
Hoffman, Cat, 6 different, ea 12.00
Hoffman, Dog, mini set #2 ....15.00
Hoffman, Horse, 6 different, (m), ea 12.00
Old Bardstown, Dog, Bulldog 85.00
Old Bardstown, Horse, Citation 150.00
Old Commonwealth, Dog, Golden Retriever 35.00
Old Commonwealth, Horse, Tennessee Walking 35.00
Ski Country, Dog, Bassett Hound 60.00
Ski Country, Dog, Labrador w/pheasant 75.00

Animals, Wild

Beam, Doe 20.00
Brooks, Fox, Redtail..40.00

Brooks, Lion, African 25.00
Brooks, Raccoon...35.00
Brooks, Tiger, Bengal 30.00
Cyrus Noble, Elk, Bull 45.00
Cyrus Noble, Walrus 45.00
Famous Firsts, Panda..65.00
Hoffman, Doe & Fawn 30.00
Old Bardstown, Tiger..20.00
Old Bardstown, Wildcat #1 ....60.00
Ski Country, Bobcat & Chipmunk 65.00
Ski Country, Deer, Wht Tail 125.00
Ski Country, Fox & Butterfly 75.00
Ski Country, Raccoons (wall plaque).................................60.00
Ski Country, Sheep, Rocky Mountain 75.00
Ski Country, Sheep, Stone 80.00
Ski Country, Skunk Family 50.00
Ski Country, Squirrels (wall plaque)................................110.00

Automotive

ASI, Cadillac, 1903, bl or wht......................................45.00
ASI, Chevrolet, 1914 ....50.00
ASI, Oldsmobile...75.00

Beam's Grant Locomotive, $80.00.

Beam, Chevy, 1953 Corvette, wht.....................................125.00
Beam, Chevy, 1957 Bel Air, Hot Rod Yel 75.00
Beam, Chevy, 1957 Bel Air, turq.....................................60.00
Beam, Chevy, 1963 Corvette, silver or red 65.00
Beam, Chevy, 1969 Camaro, bl or orange..............................60.00
Beam, Chevy, 1969 Camaro, Convertible Pacecar 75.00
Beam, Chevy, 1978 Corvette, blk 150.00
Beam, Chevy, 1978 Corvette, red, yel, or wht 60.00
Beam, Chevy, 1978 Corvette Indy Pacecar 150.00
Beam, Chevy, 1984 Corvette, blk 85.00
Beam, Chevy, 1984 Corvette, red or wht 65.00
Beam, Chevy, 1986 Corvette, Pacecar, yel 75.00
Beam, Duesenberg, Convertible Coupe, 1935 ....160.00
Beam, Duesenberg, 1934, lt or dk bl 110.00
Beam, Fire Engine, 1867 Mississippi Pumper..........................100.00
Beam, Ford, Woodie Station Wagon 50.00
Beam, Ford, 1903 Model A, blk or red................................40.00
Beam, Ford, 1913 Model T, blk or gr 45.00
Beam, Ford, 1928 Fire Chief's Car 125.00
Beam, Ford, 1928 Model A..75.00
Beam, Ford, 1929 Phaeton..50.00
Beam, Ford, 1929 Police Car 90.00

Beam, Ford, 1930 Fire Truck, Model A 140.00
Beam, Ford, 1964 Mustang, blk 125.00
Beam, Ford, 1964 Mustang, wht 55.00
Beam, Jewel Tea Wagon 80.00
Beam, Mack, 1917 Fire Truck 125.00
Beam, Mercedes, bl or red 40.00
Beam, Oldsmobile, 1904 ....40.00
Beam, Racecar, Unser Olsonite Eagle 60.00
Beam, Stutz Bearcat, 1914, gray or yel 50.00
Beam, Thomas Flyer, 1907, bl or cream 70.00
Beam, Volkswagen, red or bl 40.00
McCormick, Packard, 1937, blk or cream 40.00
Pacesetter, Fire Truck #1, LaFrance 45.00
Pacesetter, Fire Truck #2, Pirsch 50.00
Pacesetter, Fire Truck #3, Ahrens Fox 110.00
Pacesetter, Tractor #1, John Deere 150.00
Pacesetter, Tractor #2, Green Machine 75.00
Pacesetter, Tractor #4, Ford 70.00

Birds and Waterfowl

Beam, Blue Jay 9.00
Beam, Cardinal, female..12.00
Beam, Cardinal, male 25.00
Beam, Ducks Unlimited #1, Mallard 45.00
Beam, Ducks Unlimited #2, Wood Duck..........................45.00
Beam, Ducks Unlimited #3, Mallard Hen 40.00
Beam, Ducks Unlimited #4, Mallard Head 35.00
Beam, Owl, red or gray 18.00
Beam, Pheasant..10.00
Brooks, Baltimore Oriole 30.00
Brooks, Duck, Canadian Loon..25.00
Brooks, Macaw 45.00
Brooks, Owl #1, 'Ol Ez 30.00
Brooks, Snow Egret 25.00
Cyrus Noble, Penguin Family 45.00
Lionstone, Duck, Canvasback 40.00
Lionstone, Goose, Canadian 50.00
Lionstone, Goose, Snow..65.00
Lionstone, Pheasant..50.00
Ski Country, Dove 60.00
Ski Country, Duck, King Eider 55.00
Ski Country, Duck, Mallard, 1980 ....50.00
Ski Country, Duck, Pintail 85.00
Ski Country, Duck, Widgeon 45.00
Ski Country, Eagle, Harpy 125.00
Ski Country, Eagle on Water 100.00
Ski Country, Falcon, Gyrafalcon..65.00
Ski Country, Falcon, Wht 85.00
Ski Country, Gamecocks, Fighting 125.00
Ski Country, Grouse, Ruffed 50.00
Ski Country, Hawk, Redtail 90.00
Ski Country, Owl, Barn..70.00
Ski Country, Owl, Horned 85.00
Ski Country, Owl, Saw-whet..60.00
Ski Country, Pheasant, Fighting 90.00
Ski Country, Pheasant in Corn 55.00
Wild Turkey, Series I, #1 ....275.00
Wild Turkey, Series I, #2 ....175.00
Wild Turkey, Series I, #3 ....70.00
Wild Turkey, Series I, #4 ....70.00
Wild Turkey, Series I, #5 ....30.00
Wild Turkey, Series I, #6 ....20.00
Wild Turkey, Series I, #7 ....20.00

Wild Turkey, Series I, #8 ....35.00

People

McCormick, Elvis, Gold..195.00
McCormick, Elvis, Karate 125.00
McCormick, Elvis, Karate, (m) 50.00
McCormick, Elvis, Sergeant..225.00
McCormick, Elvis, Sergeant, (m) 45.00
McCormick, Elvis, Silver 125.00
McCormick, Elvis #1 ....80.00
McCormick, Elvis #1, (m) 40.00
McCormick, Elvis #2 ....55.00
McCormick, Elvis #2, (m) 30.00
McCormick, Elvis #3 ....60.00
McCormick, Elvis #3, (m) 30.00
McCormick, Hank Williams, Jr...95.00
McCormick, Hank Williams, Sr..50.00

Vocations — Coalminers

Old Bardstown, Surface Miner 20.00
Old Commonwealth, Miner #1, (m) 20.00
Old Commonwealth, Miner #1, w/Shovel........................100.00
Old Commonwealth, Miner #2, (m) 20.00
Old Commonwealth, Miner #2, w/Pick..............................50.00
Old Commonwealth, Miner #3, (m) 25.00
Old Commonwealth, Miner #3, w/Lump of Coal 35.00
Old Commonwealth, Miner #4, (m) 20.00
Old Commonwealth, Miner #4, Lunch Time......................35.00
Old Commonwealth, Miner #5, (m) 20.00
Old Commonwealth, Miner #5, Coal Shooter 35.00

Vocations — Firefighters

Lionstone, #1, w/Hose 110.00
Lionstone, #2, w/Child..100.00
Lionstone, #3, Down Pole 80.00
Lionstone, #6, Hydrant..60.00
Lionstone, #7, Helmet 75.00
Lionstone, #8, Alarm Box 65.00
Lionstone, #9, Fire Extinguisher..55.00
Old Commonwealth, Professional #1, Modern Hero..........35.00
Old Commonwealth, Professional #2, Nozzleman 40.00
Old Commonwealth, Professional #3, On Call..................45.00
Old Commonwealth, Professional #4, Fallen Comrade 45.00
Old Commonwealth, Professional #5, Harmony 45.00
Old Commonwealth, Volunteer #2, Volunteer 50.00
Old Commonwealth, Volunteer #3, Valiant Volunteer 50.00
Old Commonwealth, Volunteer #4, Heroic Volunteer 55.00
Old Commonwealth, Volunteer #5, Lifesaver 45.00
Old Commonwealth, Volunteer #6, Breaking Through 45.00

Vocations — Railroad

Beam, Train, Baggage Car 55.00
Beam, Train, Boxcar, yel or brn 50.00
Beam, Train, Caboose, red 65.00
Beam, Train, Caboose, yel or gray 55.00
Beam, Train, Casey Jones Engine w/Tender 75.00
Beam, Train, Coal Tender..25.00
Beam, Train, Combination Car..65.00
Beam, Train, Dining Car..85.00
Beam, Train, General Locomotive......................................85.00

Beam, Train, Grant Locomotive 80.00
Beam, Train, JB Turner Locomotive 125.00
Beam, Train, Log Car 60.00
Beam, Train, Lumber Car 30.00
Beam, Train, Observation Car 35.00
Beam, Train, Passenger Car 50.00
Beam, Train, Tank Car 30.00
Beam, Train, Wood Tender, for General Locomotive....................60.00
Beam, Train, Wood Tender, for JB Turner Locomotive.............35.00

Decoys

American colonists learned the craft of decoy making from the Indians who used them to lure birds out of the sky as an important food source. Early models were carved from wood such as pine, cedar, balsa, etc., and a few were made of canvas or papier-mache. There are two basic types of decoys: water floaters and shorebirds (also called 'stick-ups'). Within each type are many different species, ducks being the most plentiful since they migrated along all four of America's great waterways. Market hunting became big business around 1880, resulting in large-scale commercial production of decoys which continued until about 1910 when such hunting was outlawed by the Migratory Bird Treaty.

Today, decoys are one of the most collectible types of American folk art. The most valuable are those carved by such artists as Laing, Crowell, Ward, and Wheeler, to name only a few. Each area, such as Massachusetts, Connecticut, Maine, the Illinois River, and the Delaware River, produces decoys with distinctive regional characteristics. Examples of commercial decoys produced by well-known factories — among them Mason, Stevens, and Dodge — are also prized by collectors. Though mass-produced, these nevertheless required a certain amount of hand carving and decorating. Well-carved examples, especially those of rare species, are appreciating rapidly, and those with original paint are more desirable. Writer Carl F. Luckey has compiled a fully-illustrated identification and value guide, *Collecting Antique Bird Decoys*; you will find his address in the Directory under Alabama. *The Collector's Guide to Decoys* by Sharon and Bob Huxford contains hundreds of photos (many in color) and gives values realized at auction during the past two years. Available from your local bookstore or Collector Books.

In the listings that follow, all decoys are solid-bodied unless noted hollow.

Key:
OP — original paint   RP — repaint
ORP — old repaint   WOP — worn original paint
OWP — original working paint   WRP — working repaint

Barrows Goldeneye, Fred Wrightmore, mk WFR, NM OP, NM .150.00
Blk Duck, Charles Jester, NM OP, NM..................................1,300.00
Blk Duck, Crowell, sleeping, stamp, M blended pnt, NM 13,000.00
Blk Duck, H Conklin brand, sleeping, NM OP..........................325.00
Blk Duck, Ira Hudson, unusual breast cvg, scratch pnt, EX 1,550.00
Blk Duck, Madison Mitchell, hairline, NM OP 400.00
Blk Duck, Ward Bros, trn head, '30s, RP bill o/w EX OP, EX . 1,700.00
Blk Mallard, Chris Smith, EX feathering, 1920, OP, EX 550.00
Blk-Breasted Plover, Mason's, rpl bill/hairline/pnt traces.............275.00
Bluebill drake, Dodge Co, 1884, some RP, VG structure 475.00
Bluebill drake, Evans Co, hollow, stamp, EX OP/chip 500.00
Bluebill drake, Evans' Standard, hollow, all orig, NM 400.00
Bluebill drake, Jim Currier, rpr crack, NM OP w/touchup...........100.00
Bluebill drake, Peterson, slope breast, EX 550.00
Bluebill drake, Pratt Co, hairline, ORP 70.00

Decorative preening Yellowlegs by A. Elmer Crowell, raised wing and carved wing and tail feather details, stamped and signed, wing requires reattachment, 14", $8,500.00.

Bluebill drake, St Clair Flats, hollow, trn head, RP/rpr, EX.........150.00
Bluebill hen, Frank Combs, 2 hairlines, OP.............................1,200.00
Bluebill hen, Lee & Lem Dudley, LD brand, VG.....................2,500.00
Bluebill pr, Mr X, mk Pat Appl For, 1898, EX.........................4,000.00
Brant, Chauncey Wheeler, Mackey mk, early, rpr/EX OP, EX. 1,050.00
Brant, Ira Hudson, age splits/sm neck cracks, EX OP................1,150.00
Brant, Jim Pierce, swimming, M..145.00
Brant, Ward Bros, trn head, EX feathering, sgn/dtd '71, NM .. 1,500.00
Brant, Wildfowler Co, several sm body dents, NM OP 275.00
Brant pr, Capt H Jones, NM OP, NM 300.00
Canada Goose, Crowell, brand, mini, tiny chip, o/w M...........1,000.00
Canvas Pintail pr, Burley Russell, EX OP 275.00
Canvasbk drake, Mason's Premier, snakey head, rpr/RP, sm.........775.00
Canvasbk drake, Wildfowler Co, balsa, inlet cedar head, NM.....275.00
Canvasbk hen, Evans' Standard, hollow, '24, EX rpr & OP.........400.00
Canvasbk hen, Mason's Standard #3, glass eye, rstr/OP, EX 475.00
Canvasbk hen, Pratt Co #1, hollow, 3 shot scars, EX OP 575.00
Canvasbk pr, Joe Anderlik, decorative, full sz, sgn, OP, M 675.00
Canvasbk pr, Pratt Co #2, w/labels, EX filler/OP 475.00
Coot, Mason's Challenge Special, head trn/wing mks, EX OP .. 1,150.00
Crow, Delaware River, raised wing tips, NM OP, EX 100.00
Crow, Pratt Co, NM OP & construction......................................375.00
Dove, Hurley Conklin, HC brand, NM OP, EX 225.00
Eider hen, G Levy, Nova Scotia, w/weight, no eyes, ORP...........485.00
Goldeneye drake, Tom Savage, raised wing cvg, sgn, M 275.00
Goldeneye pr, H Conklin brand, trn heads, NM OP, EX.............850.00
Greenwing Teal drake, Paul Arness, OP, NM 225.00
Greenwing Teal drake, Wm Groene, VG OP, EX........................195.00
Hudsonian Godwit, Eddie Wozny, raised cvd wings, sgn, M........150.00
Mallard drake, Dodge Co, rpl eyes, worn RP, EX structure 285.00
Mallard drake, Mason's Premier, rstr by Schalk, M pnt, EX 375.00
Mallard hen, Armstrong Co, canvas, partial RP, o/w EX OP.........45.00
Mallard hen, Dodge #2, tack eye, 1882, filler gone/crack.............650.00
Mallard hen, Mason's Standard, pnt eyes, filler gone, WOP 80.00
Mallard hen, Pratt Co, #1 OP w/flaking, body cracks....................65.00
Mallard pr, Animal Trap Co, tack eye (1 gone), VG 150.00
Mallard pr, Evans' Standard, hollow, no mk, OP, VG 425.00
Mallard pr, Harry Jobes, swimming, OP 325.00
Old Squaw drake, metal tail, CW brand, tiny chip, EX OP.........110.00
Pintail drake, Lloyd Tyler, pnt by Lem Ward, NM OP, EX 450.00
Pintail drake, Scott Co, 1930s, NM OP, NM 100.00
Pintail drake, Tom Savage, raised wing cvg, tucked head 370.00
Pintail drake, Wm Enright, balsa, weighted, 1940s, OP, EX 375.00
Pintail hen, Art Ladehoff, EX detail, M.....................................150.00
Pintail hen, Featherlite Co, canvas, EX OP, VG 55.00
Pintail pr, Heck Whittington, decorative, sgn/1978, M 1,500.00
Redhead drake, Ben Schmidt, w/weight, NM OP 1,000.00

Redhead drake, Cecil Johns, EX cvg, VG rpt, 13½" **95.00**
Redhead drake, Mason's Challenge, snakey, hollow, EX RP........**950.00**
Redhead drake, Mr X, head to left, hollow, rpl eyes, OP **1,150.00**
Redhead pr, Marv Bernet, pnt by Donald Soderland, sgn, M.......**250.00**
Ruddy Trnstone, Mark McNair, raised wing tips, sgn, NM OP ..**375.00**
Snow Goose, Wildfowler Co, Quogue stamp, sm dents, NM OP.**450.00**
Widgeon hen, Mason's Standard, EX structure/pnt.....................**975.00**

Dedham Art Pottery

In 1895 the Chelsea Pottery moved to Dedham, changing its name to indicate the new locality and to avoid confusion with the Chelsea companies of England. Though their primary product was the blue-printed crackle-glazed dinnerware, two types of artware were also produced: crackle glaze and flambe. Their notable volcanic ware was a type of the latter. The mark is incised and often accompanies the cipher of Hugh Robertson. See also Chelsea Keramic Art Works.

Vase, brn/gr flambe, bulbous w/cylinder neck, HCR, 8", NM **250.00**
Vase, crackleware, butterfly/flowers in bl, HCR, rpr, 9" **1,700.00**
Vase, crackleware, stylized plants/florals in bl, 1900s, 6" **2,300.00**
Vase, dk gr gloss, broad/bulbous, sgn HCR/BW, 8½x6" **800.00**
Vase, gr gloss top, acid-etched base, experimental, 5".................**100.00**
Vase, gr/brn mottle, experimental, sgn DPGD, 7½", NM **225.00**
Vase, heavy dk gr/turq/wht volcanic, HCR, baluster, 7¾"....... **4,100.00**
Vase, mauve dripped gloss, baluster, HCR monogram, 6" **1,700.00**

Vases, Sang de Boeuf, signed and numbered, hairline, $6,750.00; Oxblood, deep iridescent red, initialed DP 88G, paper label, 6½", $2,500.00.

Vase, oxblood, short neck on squat bulbous form, DP97E, 6" . **1,600.00**
Vase, volcanic umber/khaki/turq flambe, sgn HR, 9x6"........... **1,200.00**

Dedham Dinnerware

Originally founded in Morrisville, Pennsylvania, as the Chelsea Keramic Works, the name was changed to Dedham Pottery in 1895 after the firm relocated in Dedham, near Boston, Massachusetts. The move was effected to make use of the native clay deemed more suitable for the production of the popular dinnerware designed by Hugh Robinson, founder of the company. The ware utilized a gray stoneware body with a crackle glaze and simple cobalt border designs of flowers, birds, and animals. Decorations were brushed on by hand using an ancient Chinese method which suspended the cobalt within the overall glaze. There were thirteen standard patterns, among them Magnolia, Iris, Butterfly, Duck, Polar Bear, and the Rabbit, the latter of which was

chosen to represent the company on their logo. On the very early pieces the rabbits face left; decorators soon found the reverse position easier to paint, and the rabbits were turned to the right. In addition to the standard patterns, other designs were produced for special orders. These and artist signed pieces are highly valued by collectors today.

The firm was operated by succeeding generations of the Robertson family until it closed in 1943. See also Chelsea Keramic Works.

Snowtree cup and saucer, $225.00; Moth plate, 6", NM, $275.00; Rabbit marmalade jar, 4½", $375.00; Clover plate, 10", NM, $650.00; Rabbit celery dish, 10" long, $325.00.

Ash tray, Dutch boy on shallow oval, no mk, rstr, 4¾" **600.00**
Ash tray, Elephant, stamped, 4"...**350.00**
Ash tray, Magnolia, stamped registered, 4" dia............................**200.00**
Bouillon cup, Duck, stamped, w/6" dia plate **400.00**
Bowl, Rabbit, flared rim, stamped, 7½" **300.00**
Bowl, Rabbit, shallow, imp/stamped 9½" **425.00**
Bowl, Rabbit, stamped, 8¾" **400.00**
Bowl, Rabbit, stamped registered, 7"..**350.00**
Bowl, vegetable; Rabbit, stamped, 11" **475.00**
Bowl, whipped cream; Rabbit, flared, no mk, 5" dia....................**175.00**
Brochure, introduction by JM Robertson, 1938, EX....................**225.00**
Candlestick, Rabbit, stamped registered, 1½x3½", pr **575.00**
Creamer, Rabbit, angle hdl, heat check in hdl, 4½" **250.00**
Creamer, Rabbit, cylindrical, stamped, rim rpr, 3" **140.00**
Creamer, Rabbit, cylindrical, stamped registered, 5"....................**425.00**
Cup & saucer, Rabbit, stamped, dtd 1931, 4" **325.00**
Dish, Rabbit, 5-sided, stamped registered, 7" **475.00**
Egg cup, dbl; Elephant, stamped, glaze flaws, 2¾" **300.00**
Egg cup, dbl; Polar Bear, stamped, glaze flaws, 2¾x3" **325.00**
Egg cup, single; Rabbit, unmk, 1½" **275.00**
Flower frog, Turtle, no mk, 3¼" L **400.00**
Knife rest, Rabbit, no mk, 3¼" **425.00**
Knife rest, Rabbit, stamped, 3¾" L **375.00**
Marmalade, Rabbit, spherical, stamped, dtd 1932, 5"..................**375.00**
Mug, Rabbit, stamped, heat check in side, 3½" **225.00**
Paperweight, rabbit figural, stamped, 2½" L **425.00**
Pitcher, Rabbit, pear shape w/angle hdl, stamped, 7"..................**500.00**
Pitcher, tankard; Rabbit, registered/dtd 1931, sm crack, 6⅞".......**350.00**
Plate, Azalea, imp/stamped, minor nick, 10" **200.00**
Plate, Azalea, imp/stamped, 6" **175.00**
Plate, Azalea, sgn Hugh Robertson, 10".......................................**600.00**
Plate, Bird in Potted Orange Tree, imp, 6".................................**475.00**
Plate, Bird in Potted Orange Tree, stamped, 10".........................**500.00**
Plate, Butterfly, sgn Maude Davenport, imp/stamped, 10" **1,800.00**
Plate, Chestnut, imp, 6"..**175.00**
Plate, Chestnut, sgn Maude Davenport, imp/stamped, 9¾" **275.00**
Plate, Clover, imp/stamped, 6"...**500.00**

Plate, Clover, imp/stamped, 8½", NM 400.00
Plate, Clover, stamped, 9¾", EX 500.00
Plate, Crab, imp/stamped, 6¼" 450.00
Plate, Crab, imp/stamped, 8" 650.00
Plate, Crab, repeating seaweed border, imp/stamped, 6" 450.00
Plate, Crab, stamped registered, dtd 1931, 8" 650.00
Plate, Crab, w/star & waves, imp/stamped, 6" 550.00
Plate, Dolphin, imp/stamped, nick/roughness, 8½" 200.00
Plate, Dolphin, imp/stamped, 8½", NM......................................550.00
Plate, Dolphin, imp/stamped registered, 7½" 650.00
Plate, Duck, sgn Maude Davenport, imp/stamped, 6" 300.00
Plate, Duck, stamped, 8½" 350.00
Plate, Elephant, imp rabbit mk, 8½" 500.00
Plate, Elephant, imp/stamped, 6" 475.00
Plate, Grape, stamped, 8½" 275.00
Plate, Grapes, grapes in border, imp/stamped, 8½" 325.00
Plate, Horse Chestnut, imp/stamped, 6" 200.00
Plate, Iris, sgn Maude Davenport, imp/stamped, 9¾", NM 250.00
Plate, Lobster, imp, stamped w/1931 mk, 8½" 650.00
Plate, Lobster, imp/stamped, 8" 650.00
Plate, Magnolia, imp/stamped, 10" 275.00
Plate, Magnolia, stamped, 7" 175.00
Plate, Moth, imp/stamped, 10", EX 450.00
Plate, Moth, sgn HCR, exhibition label, imp/stamped, 10" 475.00
Plate, Moth, stamped, 8½" 375.00

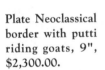

Plate Neoclassical border with putti riding goats, 9", $2,300.00.

Plate, Owl, imp/stamped, 8½", EX 600.00
Plate, Polar Bear, imp/stamped, rim rpr, 10" 425.00
Plate, Polar Bear, stamped, 10" 950.00
Plate, Pond Lily, imp, 10" 275.00
Plate, Rabbit, imp/stamped, minor roughness, 12" 275.00
Plate, Snow Tree, imp/stamped, 6" 195.00
Plate, Snow Tree, sgn Davenport, imp/stamped, 6" 225.00
Plate, Swan, imp/stamped, 7½" 350.00
Plate, Tapestry Lion, imp/stamped, glaze imperfections, 8½".......450.00
Plate, Tufted Duck, w/lily pads, imp mk, 10" 800.00
Plate, Turkey, sgn Maude Davenport, imp/stamped, 10".............475.00
Plate, Turkey, stamped, minor nick, 8½" 275.00
Plate, Turkey, stamped, 8" 350.00
Plate, Turkey, stamped, 9¾" 400.00
Plate, Turtle, 5 prs at rim, dtd 2/17/16, imp/stamped, 8½" 950.00
Shakers, Rabbit, unsgn, 2¾", pr 400.00
Shakers, Rabbit, 3½", EX, pr 400.00
Sugar bowl, Rabbit, squat/bulbous, 3x4¾" 275.00
Tea tile, Rabbit, stamped, dtd 1931, 4⅝" 300.00
Tray, bacon; Rabbit, stamped, 10" L 275.00

Tray, pin; Rabbit, bunny medallion in center, stamped, 4" 275.00
Tray, Rabbit, stamped, 8x13" 425.00

Degenhart

The Crystal Art Glass factory in Cambridge, Ohio, opened in 1947 under the private ownership of John and Elizabeth Degenhart. John had previously worked for the Cambridge Glass Company and was well known for his superior paperweights. After his death in 1964, Elizabeth took over management of the factory, hiring several workers from the defunct Cambridge Company, including Zack Boyd. Boyd was responsible for many unique colors, some of which were named for him. From 1964 to 1974, more than twenty-seven different moulds were created, most of them resulting from Elizabeth Degenhart's work and creativity, and over 145 official colors were developed. Elizabeth died in 1978, requesting that the ten moulds she had built while operating the factory were to be turned over to the Degenhart Museum. The remaining moulds were to be held by the Island Mould and Machine Company, who (complying with her request) removed the familiar 'D in heart' trademark. The factory was eventually bought by Zack's son, Bernard Boyd. He also acquired the remaining Degenhart moulds, to which he added his own logo.

In general, slags, jades, and opaques should be valued 15% to 20% higher than crystals in color.

Basket Toothpick, Cobalt...20.00
Beaded Oval Toothpick, Fawn...18.00
Bicentennial Bell, Canary 15.00
Bicentennial Bell, Ebony 5.00
Bird Salt & Pepper, Opalescent...35.00
Colonial Drape & Heart Toothpick, Sapphire 15.00
Creamer, Texas; Crystal...11.00
Creamer, Texas; Green 15.00
Daisy & Button Salt, Cobalt 22.00
Daisy & Button Toothpick, Milk Blue..22.00
Forget-Me-Not Toothpick, Bluebell 14.00
Forget-Me-Not Toothpick, Canary 18.00
Forget-Me-Not Toothpick, Peach Opaque 22.00
Forget-Me-Not Toothpick, Sapphire 10.00
Gypsy Pot Toothpick, Cobalt...22.50
Gypsy Pot Toothpick, Crystal..10.00
Gypsy Pot Toothpick, Tomato...30.00
Hand, Crown Tuscan..18.00
Hat, Vaseline, unsgn..20.00
Heart & Lyre Cup Plate, Crown Tuscan...28.00
Heart Box, Elizabeth Blue..37.50
Heart Box, Light Chocolate Creme 35.00
Heart Box, Sapphire 20.00
Heart Toothpick, Caramel..42.00
Heart Toothpick, Crystal..12.00
Heart Toothpick, Daffodil 15.00
Hen, Caramel Custard, 3" 45.00
Hen, Sapphire, 3" 25.00
Hobo Shoe, Blue & White Slag 25.00
Owl, Amberina 50.00
Owl, Charteruse 40.00
Owl, Dark Crown Tuscan...40.00
Owl, Dark Elizabeth Lime Ice..55.00
Owl, Dark Frosted Jade..50.00
Owl, Heatherbloom...50.00
Owl, Pink Lady 34.00
Owl, Sunset 28.00
Pooch, Blue Marble Slag...22.00

Hen on basketweave bottom, Tomato, $80.00.

Pooch, Caramel Slag...26.00
Pooch, Charcoal 20.00
Pooch, Cobalt 25.00
Pooch, Crystal...12.50
Pooch, Daffodil 15.00
Pooch, Fawn..22.50
Pooch, Gray Marble 22.50
Pooch, Green Caramel 32.00
Pooch, Green Opalescent 20.00
Pooch, Gun Metal 24.00
Pooch, Henry Blue 15.00
Pooch, Ivory Slag 25.00
Pooch, Jade 22.50
Pooch, Milk White 18.00
Pooch, Periwinkle 15.00
Priscilla, Blue & White...90.00
Priscilla, Green Lavender Slag 78.50
Priscilla, Jade Green 110.00
Robin Covered Dish, Fawn.....................................55.00
Skate Shoe, Green, unsgn, decal............................30.00
Star & Dewdrop Salt, Opalescent 18.00
Texas Boot, Amethyst...18.00
Texas Boot, Baby Green..20.00
Texas Boot, Peach Blo 15.00
Tomahawk, Amber..18.00
Tomahawk, Carnival Blue.......................................42.50
Tomahawk, Cobalt..24.00
Turkey Covered Dish, Amberina 55.00
Turkey Covered Dish, Gray Slag............................80.00
Turkey Covered Dish, Milk Blue, unsgn 70.00
Wildflower Candy Dish, Twilight Blue....................38.00

Delatte

Delatte was a manufacturer of French cameo glass. Founded in 1921, their style reflected the influence of the Art Deco era with strong color contrasts and bold design.

Our advisor for this category is Don Williams; he is listed in the Directory under Missouri.

Cameo

Vase, floral, purple on wht, 2 cuts, 5⅝x3⅞" 600.00
Vase, irises, bl/purple on wht, narrow neck, 8"..........................1,200.00
Vase, roses, purple on pk, pear form, 8" 1,200.00
Vase, trees at river, pk/mauve, 2 cuts, mk, 7½x4⅜" 1,200.00
Vase, wisteria, bl tones on frost & bl, 10"...................................1,250.00

Miscellaneous

Vase, nudes dance/play harp, HP on yel, clear cased, 8½"........ 1,200.00
Vase, wht w/hot pk flecks & foil inclusions, spherical, 11" 500.00

Delft

Old Delftware, made as early as the sixteenth century, was originally a low-fired earthenware coated in a thin opaque tin glaze with painted-on polychrome designs. It was not until the last half of the 19th century, however, that the ware became commonly referred to as Delft, acquiring the name from the Dutch village that had become the major center of its production. English, German, and French potters also produced Delft, though with noticeable differences both in shape and decorative theme.

In the early part of the 18th century, the German potter, Bottger, developed a formula for porcelain; in England, Wedgwood began producing creamware — both of which were much more durable. Unable to compete, one by one the Delft potteries failed. Soon only one remained. In 1876 De Porcelyne Fles reintroduced Delftware on a hard white body with blue and white decorative themes reflecting the Dutch countryside, windmills by the sea, and Dutch children. This manufacturer is the most well known of several operating today. Their products are now produced under the Royal Delft label. Examples listed here are blue on white unless noted otherwise. See also specific manufacturers.

Bonbon, floral, 1942, 6" dia..80.00
Bowl, Dutch, floral, mc, conical on rnd ft, 1820s, 10".................250.00
Bowl, Dutch, floral panels, bl/gr/rust, 1700s, 3", EX 400.00
Bowl, Dutch, floral panels, 3-color, 1700s, 9", EX 1,200.00
Bowl, Dutch or German, Oriental lady/panels, 1700s, 12", VG...225.00
Bowl, English, fruit basket reserve, shallow, 1825, 8" 225.00
Bowl, Lambeth, bird among flowers, ruffled, 1725, 9"................600.00
Bowl, meandering floral, floral int rim, 1700s, 8½", EX 265.00
Charger, Dutch, floral center/rim panels, sgn HB, 14", EX 250.00
Charger, Dutch, lady & flowers, floral border, 3-color, 14".........700.00

Charger, Dutch, early 18th century, 13½", EX, $800.00.

Charger, English, bamboo & garden w/bldg, 1760, 14"...............500.00
Charger, English, feathers in center, florals, 1740, 12".................275.00
Charger, English, flower garden, floral rim, 1750s, 14", EX..........400.00
Charger, Lambeth, Oriental garden w/fence, yel rim, 13", EX.....350.00
Flower brick, English, floral, rnd/sq holes, 5½", EX....................300.00
Lavabo, Dutch, Halls of Justice, lion spout, rstr, 15½"............. 1,100.00
Plate, boat, floral border, 20th C, 10" 125.00
Plate, boat, floral border, 20th C, 5½" 49.00
Plate, Dutch, floral, geometric border, 1700s, 9", EX 200.00

Plate, English, bamboo/floral reserve, 1760, 9", set of 4 ....500.00
Plate, flower & bird motif, mc, 20th C, 9".................................129.00
Plate, Lambeth, floral/parrot, mc, 9", EX...............................275.00
Plate, 350th Mayflower commemorative, floral border, 7".............75.00
Tile, att Bristol, sheep scene in manganese, 1760, 5".................325.00
Tile, Dutch, farming scene/poem, mc, 12 in fr: 18x23", VG.......350.00
Tile, sailing ship, 20th C, 6"..16.00
Tobacco jar, Dutch, St Vincent in cartouch, floral vine, 10"..1,000.00
Vase, Dutch, figures on bridge/flowers, paneled, 1780s, 10".........275.00
Vase, English, chinoiserie birds/flowers, 1820s, 11".....................275.00
Vase, English, floral, lobed ovoid, 1750s, 8½".............................400.00
Vase, mill at sea front, bulbous, 20th C, 6¾"..............................125.00
Wall pocket, European, mc heads/scrolls emb on fan form, 8".....650.00

Depression Glass

Other than coins and stamps, colored glassware produced during the Depression era is probably the most sought-after collectible in the field today. There are literally thousands of collectors in the United States and Canada buying, selling, and trading 'Depression Glass' on today's market.

Depression Glass is defined by Gene Florence, author of several best-selling books on the subject, as 'the inexpensive glassware made primarily during the Depression era in the colors of amber, green, pink, blue, red, yellow, white, and crystal.' This glass was mass produced, sold through five-and-dime stores and mail-order catalogs, and given away as premiums with gas and food products.

The listings in this book are far from being complete. If you want a more thorough presentation of this fascinating glassware, we recommend *The Collector's Encyclopedia of Depression Glass*, *Pocket Guide to Depression Glass*, and *Very Rare Depression Glass, Vol. II*, by Gene Florence, whose address is listed in the Directory under Kentucky.

Key: PAT — pattern around top

Adam, ash tray, gr, 4½"..18.00
Adam, bowl, cereal; gr, 5¾"...30.00
Adam, bowl, dessert; gr, 4¾"..10.00
Adam, bowl, gr, w/lid, 9"...70.00
Adam, bowl, pk, oval, 10"...17.50
Adam, bowl, pk, 7¾"..16.50
Adam, butter dish, gr, w/lid..260.00
Adam, candlesticks, gr, 4", pr..80.00
Adam, creamer, gr...16.00
Adam, creamer, pk...14.00
Adam, pitcher, pk, 32-oz, 8"..30.00
Adam, plate, dinner; gr, sq, 9"...17.00
Adam, plate, grill; pk, 9"..14.00
Adam, plate, salad; gr, sq, 7¾"...9.00
Adam, platter, gr, 11¾"..16.00
Adam, saucer, gr, sq, 6"...5.00
Adam, shakers, gr, 4", pr...85.00
Adam, sherbet, pk, 3"..20.00
Adam, tumbler, iced tea; gr, 5½"..35.00
Adam, tumbler, pk, 4½"..20.00
Adam, vase, pk, 7½"..190.00
American Pioneer, bowl, console; pk, 10⅜".................................42.50
American Pioneer, bowl, gr, hdls, 5"..15.00
American Pioneer, bowl, pk, w/lid, 8¾".....................................80.00
American Pioneer, candlesticks, gr, 6½", pr................................75.00
American Pioneer, candy jar, gr, w/lid, 1-lb................................85.00
American Pioneer, cheese/cracker set, gr, platter/compote...........50.00
American Pioneer, coaster, pk, 3½"...20.00

American Pioneer, creamer, gr, 3½"...19.00
American Pioneer, creamer, pk, 2¾"..15.00
American Pioneer, goblet, water; gr, 8-oz, 6"..............................35.00
American Pioneer, goblet, wine; pk, 3-oz, 4"...............................30.00
American Pioneer, ice bucket, gr, 6"..45.00
American Pioneer, lamp, gr, 8½"...95.00
American Pioneer, mayonnaise, pk, 4¼"......................................50.00
American Pioneer, pitcher, gr, w/lid, 5".....................................145.00
American Pioneer, pitcher, pk, w/lid, 7".....................................135.00
American Pioneer, plate, gr, hdls, 11½".......................................15.00
American Pioneer, plate, gr, 6"..12.00
American Pioneer, plate, gr, 8"..7.00
American Pioneer, plate, pk, hdls, 6"...10.00
American Pioneer, saucer, gr..4.00
American Pioneer, sherbet, gr, 4¾"..30.00
American Pioneer, sherbet, pk, 3½"..12.00
American Pioneer, sugar bowl, pk, 2¾"...15.00
American Pioneer, tumbler, juice; gr, 5-oz....................................25.00
American Pioneer, tumbler, pk, 12-oz, 5".......................................30.00
American Pioneer, vase, gr, crimped edge, 7".................................85.00
American Pioneer, vase, pk, str, 7"...65.00
American Sweetheart, bowl, berry; pk, flat, 3¾".............................27.50
American Sweetheart, bowl, berry; pk, rnd, 9"...............................25.00
American Sweetheart, bowl, cereal; monax, 6"..................................9.00
American Sweetheart, bowl, vegetable; monax, oval, 11"..................48.00
American Sweetheart, creamer, pk, ftd...8.00
American Sweetheart, cup, monax..8.00
American Sweetheart, pitcher, pk, 60-oz, 7½".................................425.00
American Sweetheart, plate, salad; pk, 8"...7.00
American Sweetheart, plate, salver; monax, 12"...............................11.00
American Sweetheart, platter, monax, oval, 13"................................42.00
American Sweetheart, shakers, pk, ftd, pr.......................................285.00
American Sweetheart, sherbet, pk, ftd, 3¾".....................................13.00
American Sweetheart, tumbler, pk, 10-oz, 4¾".................................60.00
Anniversary, bowl, fruit; crystal, 9"..7.00
Anniversary, bowl, soup; pk, 7⅜"..10.00
Anniversary, butter dish, pk, w/lid...47.50
Anniversary, cake plate, crystal, w/lid...12.00

Anniversary, compote, pk, ftd...8.00
Anniversary, creamer, pk, ftd..7.50
Anniversary, relish dish, pk, 8"...8.00
Anniversary, sherbet, pk, ftd..6.00
Anniversary, sugar bowl, crystal..2.00
Anniversary, vase, crystal, 6½"...9.00
Anniversary, wine glass, pk, 2½-oz...11.00
Aunt Polly, bowl, berry; bl, 4⅜"...10.00
Aunt Polly, bowl, bl, oval, 8⅜"...50.00
Aunt Polly, bowl, pickle; bl, oval, hdls, 7¼"....................................20.00
Aunt Polly, butter dish, gr, w/lid..200.00
Aunt Polly, creamer, bl...35.00
Aunt Polly, plate, luncheon; bl, 8"..15.00

Aunt Polly, plate, sherbet; bl, 6" 9.00
Aunt Polly, shakers, bl, pr 175.00
Aunt Polly, sugar bowl, gr.................................20.00
Aunt Polly, tumbler, bl, 8-oz, 3⅝".........................20.00
Aunt Polly, vase, gr, ftd, 6½".............................25.00
Aurora, bowl, cobalt, 4½"..................................22.50
Aurora, bowl, cobalt, 5⅜".................................11.00
Aurora, creamer, cobalt, 4½"..............................12.00
Aurora, cup, cobalt 7.00
Aurora, plate, cobalt, 6½" 7.50
Aurora, saucer, cobalt 3.00
Aurora, tumbler, cobalt, 4¾"..............................15.00
Avocado, bowl, gr, oval, hdls, 8".........................23.00
Avocado, bowl, pk, hdls, 5¼"..............................20.00
Avocado, bowl, preserve; gr, hdl, 7"......................23.00
Avocado, bowl, relish; gr, ftd, 6".........................23.00
Avocado, bowl, salad; pk, 7½".............................27.50
Avocado, creamer, gr, ftd.................................27.50
Avocado, pitcher, gr, 64-oz..............................750.00
Avocado, plate, luncheon; gr, 8¼".........................16.00
Avocado, plate, sherbet; pk, 6¾"..........................11.00
Avocado, saucer, gr.......................................20.00
Avocado, sugar bowl, pk, ftd..............................25.00
Avocado, tumbler, gr.....................................150.00
Beaded Block, bowl, gr, sq, 5½"........................... 6.00
Beaded Block, bowl, jelly; opal, hdls, 4½" 14.00
Beaded Block, bowl, opal, rnd, flared, 7¼"................16.00
Beaded Block, bowl, pickle; opal, hdls, 6½"...............15.00
Beaded Block, creamer, opal...............................22.00
Beaded Block, pitcher, gr, 5¼" 85.00
Beaded Block, plate, opal, sq, 7¾"........................ 9.00
Beaded Block, sugar bowl, gr..............................12.50
Beaded Block, vase, gr, 6"................................10.00
Block Optic, bowl, berry; gr, lg, 8½".....................18.00
Block Optic, bowl, berry; pk, 4¼".......................... 5.00
Block Optic, bowl, salad; gr, 7¼".........................17.00
Block Optic, butter dish, gr, w/lid, 3x5".................37.50
Block Optic, candy jar, gr, w/lid, 2¼"....................35.00
Block Optic, creamer, pk, ftd............................. 9.50
Block Optic, goblet, cocktail; pk, 4" 28.00
Block Optic, goblet, wine; pk, 4½".........................28.00
Block Optic, ice bucket, gr...............................30.00
Block Optic, ice/butter tub, pk, open 75.00
Block Optic, pitcher, gr, 68-oz, 7⅝".......................60.00
Block Optic, pitcher, pk, 80-oz, 8".......................50.00
Block Optic, sandwich server, gr, center hdl..............45.00
Block Optic, shakers, gr, squatty, pr 60.00
Block Optic, sherbet, pk, 6-oz, 4¾"........................ 9.00
Block Optic, tumbler, gr, flat, 9-oz......................12.00
Block Optic, tumbler, pk, flat, 5-oz, 3½".................14.00
Block Optic, vase, gr, blown, 5¾".........................175.00
Block Optic, whiskey, gr, 2-oz, 2¼".......................18.00
Bowknot, bowl, berry; gr, 4½".............................10.00
Bowknot, bowl, cereal; gr, 5½" 14.00
Bowknot, cup, gr.. 5.00
Bowknot, plate, salad; gr, 7"............................. 7.50
Bowknot, sherbet, gr, low ftd 10.00
Bowknot, tumbler, gr, ftd, 10-oz, 5"......................14.00
Bowknot, tumbler, gr, 10-oz, 5"...........................14.00
Bubble, bowl, berry; bl, 4"...............................10.00
Bubble, bowl, fruit; bl, 4½".............................. 8.00
Bubble, bowl, soup; bl, flat, 7¾".........................10.00
Bubble, creamer, crystal.................................. 3.50
Bubble, cup, crystal 2.00

Bubble, pitcher, red, ice lip, 64-oz......................45.00
Bubble, plate, bread & butter; bl, 6¾" 3.00

Bubble, plate, grill; bl, 9⅜" 14.00
Bubble, platter, bl, oval, 12"............................12.00
Bubble, saucer, bl 1.00
Bubble, tumbler, juice; red, 6-oz 8.00
Bubble, tumbler, lemonade; red, 16-oz 15.00
Cameo, bowl, cereal; yel, 5½"............................26.00
Cameo, bowl, cream soup; gr, 4¾"..........................48.00
Cameo, bowl, soup; gr, rimmed, 9".........................33.00
Cameo, butter dish, yel, w/lid 1,250.00
Cameo, cake plate, gr, 3-leg, 10".........................16.00
Cameo, candlestick, gr, 4", pr............................85.00
Cameo, candy jar, gr, w/lid, 6½"..........................100.00
Cameo, cookie jar, gr, w/lid..............................40.00
Cameo, decanter, gr, w/stopper, 10".......................115.00
Cameo, goblet, wine; gr, 3½"..............................450.00
Cameo, pitcher, juice; gr, 36-oz, 6"......................45.00
Cameo, plate, sandwich; gr, 10"...........................10.00
Cameo, plate, yel, sq, 8½"................................125.00
Cameo, relish, yel, 3-part, ftd, 7½"......................125.00
Cameo, sherbet, gr, 3⅛"...................................10.00
Cameo, sherbet, yel, 4⅞"..................................30.00
Cameo, tumbler, juice; gr, 5-oz, 3¾"......................22.00
Cameo, tumbler, water; gr, 9-oz, 4".......................20.00
Cameo, vase, gr, 5¾".....................................140.00
Cherry Blossom, bowl, berry; pk, 4¾"......................10.00
Cherry Blossom, bowl, berry; pk, 8½"......................35.00
Cherry Blossom, bowl, vegetable; gr, oval, 9".............28.00
Cherry Blossom, cake plate, pk, 3-leg, 10¼"...............20.00
Cherry Blossom, creamer, pk..............................15.00
Cherry Blossom, creamer, pk, child's......................30.00
Cherry Blossom, cup, pk, child's..........................25.00
Cherry Blossom, mug, gr, 7-oz............................145.00
Cherry Blossom, pitcher, pk, PAT, flat, 42-oz, 8" 35.00
Cherry Blossom, plate, salad; gr, 7".....................16.00
Cherry Blossom, platter, pk, oval, 9"....................700.00
Cherry Blossom, shakers, pk, scalloped bottom, pr 1,100.00
Cherry Blossom, sugar bowl, gr...........................11.00
Cherry Blossom, tray, sandwich; gr, hdls, 10½" 18.00
Cherryberry, bowl, berry; pk or gr, 4".................... 7.00
Cherryberry, butter dish, pk or gr, w/lid................130.00
Cherryberry, creamer, pk or gr, lg, 4⅝"...................25.00
Cherryberry, pickle dish, pk or gr........................10.00
Cherryberry, pitcher, pk or gr, 7¾".......................135.00
Cherryberry, plate, salad; pk or gr, 7½"..................11.00
Cherryberry, tumbler, pk or gr, 9-oz, 3⅝".................25.00
Chinex Classic, bowl, salad; decor, 7"....................17.00
Chinex Classic, bowl, soup; ivory, flat, 7¾"..............11.00
Chinex Classic, butter dish, ivory 50.00
Chinex Classic, plate, sherbet; decor, 6¼" 2.50

Chinex Classic, sherbet, decor, low ftd 9.00
Chinex Classic, sugar bowl, ivory 4.00
Christmas Candy, bowl, soup; crystal, 7⅜" 5.00
Christmas Candy, creamer, teal.................................15.00
Christmas Candy, cup, teal..14.00
Christmas Candy, plate, luncheon; teal, 8¼" 14.00
Christmas Candy, saucer, crystal 1.50
Christmas Candy, sugar bowl, crystal 7.50
Circle, bowl, gr or pk, flared, 5½" 5.00
Circle, creamer, gr or pk 5.00
Circle, goblet, wine; gr or pk, 4½" 12.00
Circle, pitcher, gr or pk, 80-oz..................................25.00
Circle, plate, luncheon; gr or pk, 8¼" 3.50
Circle, sherbet, gr or pk, 4¾" 5.00
Circle, tumbler, gr or pk, 15-oz.................................20.00
Cloverleaf, ash tray, blk, match holder in center, 4" 57.50
Cloverleaf, bowl, gr, 8" 45.00
Cloverleaf, bowl, salad; yel, 7" 40.00
Cloverleaf, candy dish, yel, w/lid...............................90.00
Cloverleaf, cup, yel 8.00
Cloverleaf, plate, grill; gr, 10¼" 15.00
Cloverleaf, plate, sherbet, 6" 5.00
Cloverleaf, shakers, yel, pr 85.00
Cloverleaf, sugar bowl, yel, ftd, 3⅝" 13.00
Cloverleaf, tumbler, gr, flat, 9-oz, 3¾" 32.00
Cloverleaf, tumbler, gr, ftd, 10-oz, 5¾" 18.00
Colonial, bowl, berry; gr, lg, 9" 22.00
Colonial, bowl, pk, 3¾" 35.00
Colonial, butter dish, pk, w/lid................................500.00
Colonial, goblet, cordial; gr, 1-oz, 3¾" 25.00
Colonial, goblet, water; gr, 8½-oz, 5¾" 25.00
Colonial, mug, pk, 12-oz, 4½" 400.00
Colonial, plate, grill; gr, 10" 20.00
Colonial, platter, gr, oval, 12" 18.00
Colonial, shakers, gr, pr 115.00
Colonial, sherbet, gr 11.00

Colonial, spoon or celery holder, pk 95.00
Colonial, sugar bowl, pk, 5" 18.00
Colonial, tumbler, gr, 10-oz......................................35.00
Colonial, tumbler, ice tea; pk, 12-oz..........................37.00
Colonial, tumbler, lemonade; gr, 15-oz 60.00
Colonial, whiskey, gr, 1½-oz, 2½" 10.00
Colonial Block, bowl, gr or pk, 7" 14.00
Colonial Block, butter tub, gr or pk 30.00
Colonial Block, candy dish, gr or pk, w/lid, 8½" 30.00
Colonial Block, sugar bowl, gr or pk........................... 9.00
Colonial Fluted, bowl, berry; gr, lg, 7½" 12.00
Colonial Fluted, bowl, berry; gr, 4"............................. 4.00
Colonial Fluted, creamer, gr 4.50
Colonial Fluted, saucer, gr 1.00
Colonial Fluted, sherbet, gr 5.00

Columbia, bowl, crystal, ruffled edge, 10½" 15.00
Columbia, bowl, salad; crystal, 8½"............................13.00
Columbia, bowl, soup; crystal, low, 8" 13.00
Columbia, butter dish, crystal, w/lid 15.00
Columbia, plate, bread & butter, pk, 6" 8.00
Columbia, plate, chop; crystal, 11¾" 7.00
Columbia, plate, snack; crystal 30.00
Columbia, tumbler, crystal, 9-oz................................17.00
Coronation, bowl, nappy; red, 6½"............................. 9.00
Coronation, pitcher, pk, 68-oz, 7¾" 195.00
Coronation, plate, luncheon; pk, 8½" 3.50
Coronation, saucer, pk... 1.50
Coronation, sherbet, pk 3.50
Coronation, tumbler, pk, ftd, 10-oz, 5" 15.00
Cremax, bowl, cereal; ivory w/decor, 5¾" 6.00
Cremax, creamer, ivory w/decor.................................. 6.00
Cremax, plate, sandwich; ivory, 11½" 4.00
Cremax, saucer, ivory 1.50
Cremax, sugar bowl, ivory w/decor.............................. 6.00
Cube, bowl, dessert; gr, 4½" 5.00
Cube, bowl, pk, deep, 4½" 5.00
Cube, butter dish, pk, w/lid.......................................45.00
Cube, candy jar, gr, w/lid, 6½" 25.00
Cube, coaster, gr, 3¼" 5.00
Cube, pitcher, gr, 45-oz, 8¾" 175.00
Cube, powder jar, gr, 3-leg, w/lid...............................17.50
Cube, shakers, gr, pr 27.50
Cube, sugar bowl, gr, 3" 6.00
Cube, tumbler, gr, 9-oz, 4" 45.00
Daisy, bowl, berry; amber, 4½" 7.00
Daisy, bowl, vegetable; amber, oval, 10" 13.00
Daisy, cup, crystal... 2.50
Daisy, plate, grill; amber, 10⅜" 9.50
Daisy, plate, sherbet; crystal, 6" 1.00
Daisy, platter, amber, 10¾" 11.00
Daisy, relish dish, crystal, 3-part, 8⅜" 10.00
Daisy, sherbet, crystal, ftd 4.00
Daisy, sugar bowl, crystal, ftd..................................... 4.00
Daisy, tumbler, amber, ftd, 12-oz 30.00
Diamond Quilted, bowl, bl, crimped edge, 7" 12.00
Diamond Quilted, bowl, cream soup; gr, 4¾" 6.50
Diamond Quilted, cake plate, gr, tall, 10" dia..............45.00
Diamond Quilted, candy jar, gr, ftd, w/lid...................50.00
Diamond Quilted, compote, gr, w/lid, 11½" 60.00
Diamond Quilted, creamer, gr 6.00
Diamond Quilted, cup, bl 12.00
Diamond Quilted, goblet, cordial; gr, 1-oz 8.00
Diamond Quilted, plate, salad; bl, 7" 6.50
Diamond Quilted, sandwich server, bl, center hdl........40.00
Diamond Quilted, tumbler, gr, ftd, 12-oz....................12.50
Diamond Quilted, tumbler, iced tea; gr, 12-oz.............. 8.00
Diana, bowl, amber, scalloped edge, 12" 8.00
Diana, bowl, cereal; pk, 5" 4.50
Diana, bowl, cream soup; amber, 5½" 9.00
Diana, candy jar, pk, w/lid, rnd..................................22.00
Diana, creamer, pk, oval... 4.50
Diana, plate, sandwich; pk, 11¾" 6.00
Diana, platter, pk, oval, 12" 9.00
Diana, shakers, amber, pr 85.00
Diana, tumbler, pk, 9-oz, 4⅛"......................................20.00
Dogwood, bowl, fruit; gr, 10¼" 125.00
Dogwood, cake plate, pk, heavy solid ft, 13" 75.00
Dogwood, plate, luncheon; pk, 8" 5.00
Dogwood, platter, pk, oval, rare, 12" 290.00

Dogwood, saucer, pk 4.50
Dogwood, sherbet, pk, low ftd 22.00
Dogwood, sugar bowl, pk, thick, 3¼" 12.00
Doric, butter dish, pk, w/lid 55.00
Doric, candy dish, pk, w/lid, 8" 25.00
Doric, creamer, gr, 4" 8.50
Doric, pitcher, pk, flat, 36-oz, 6" 25.00

Doric, plate, grill; gr, 9" 14.00
Doric, plate, salad; gr, 7" 14.00
Doric, relish tray, pk, 4x4" 5.00
Doric, shakers, gr, pr 27.50
Doric, tray, pk, hdld, 10" 8.00
Doric, tray, serving; gr, 8x8" 13.00
Doric, tumbler, gr, ftd, 12-oz, 5" 80.00
Doric, tumbler, pk, flat, 9-oz, 4½" 35.00
Doric & Pansy, bowl, ultramarine, hdls, 9" 25.00
Doric & Pansy, creamer, ultramarine 105.00
Doric & Pansy, cup, ultramarine 15.00
Doric & Pansy, plate, dinner; ultramarine, 9" 20.00
Doric & Pansy, plate, salad; ultramarine, 7" 25.00
Doric & Pansy, sugar bowl, ultramarine 100.00
Doric & Pansy, tumbler, ultramarine, 9-oz, 4½" 45.00
English Hobnail, ash tray, pk or gr, several shapes.................18.50
English Hobnail, bowl, nappy; pk or gr, 11" & 12", ea 37.50
English Hobnail, bowl, relish; pk or gr, oval, 8" & 9", ea 17.50
English Hobnail, candlestick, pk or gr, 3½", pr.....................30.00
English Hobnail, candy dish, pk or gr, cone shaped, ½-lb 45.00
English Hobnail, cigarette box, pk or gr 25.00
English Hobnail, cologne bottle, pk or gr 25.00
English Hobnail, decanter, pk or gr, w/stopper, 20-oz 95.00
English Hobnail, goblet, claret; pk or gr, 5-oz.......................18.00
English Hobnail, goblet, wine; pk or gr, 2-oz.........................20.00
English Hobnail, lamp, pk or gr, 9¼" 90.00
English Hobnail, marmalade, pk or gr, w/lid 35.00
English Hobnail, pitcher, pk or gr, 39-oz 165.00
English Hobnail, plate, dinner; pk or gr, 10" 20.00
English Hobnail, tumbler, pk or gr, ftd, 12½-oz....................22.00
English Hobnail, tumbler, pk or gr, ftd, 9-oz.........................15.00
English Hobnail, whiskey, pk or gr, 1½ & 3-oz......................23.00
Fire-King Alice, cup, jadite..2.00
Fire-King Alice, plate, jadite 11.00
Fire-King Alice, saucer, jadite...50
Fire-King Jane Ray, bowl, dessert; jadite, 4⅞" 2.00
Fire-King Jane Ray, bowl, soup; jadite, 7⅝" 5.00
Fire-King Jane Ray, cup, demi; jadite 11.00
Fire-King Jane Ray, plate, salad; jadite, 7¾" 2.00
Fire-King Jane Ray, platter, jadite, 12"................................... 9.00
Fire-King Oven Glass, baker, bl, 1½-qt 9.00
Fire-King Oven Glass, cake pan, bl, deep, 8¾" 16.00
Fire-King Oven Glass, casserole, bl, knob hdl, w/lid, 1-qt............10.00
Fire-King Oven Glass, coffee mug, bl, 7-oz 18.00

Fire-King Oven Glass, loaf pan, bl, deep, 9⅛" 20.00
Fire-King Oven Glass, plate, pie; bl, 9" 9.00
Fire-King Oven Glass, utility pan, bl, 8⅛x12½" 17.50
Fire-King Philbe, bowl, cereal; all colors, 5½" 35.00
Fire-King Philbe, bowl, salad; all colors, 7¼" 45.00
Fire-King Philbe, cookie jar, all colors, w/lid 600.00
Fire-King Philbe, creamer, all colors, ftd, 3¼" 75.00
Fire-King Philbe, pitcher, all colors, 54-oz, 8½" 700.00
Fire-King Philbe, plate, grill; all colors, 10½" 30.00
Fire-King Philbe, plate, luncheon; all colors, 8" 25.00
Fire-King Philbe, tumbler, all colors, ftd, 10-oz, 5¼" 50.00
Fire-King Square, bowl, salad; all colors, 7⅜" 6.00
Fire-King Square, plate, dinner; all colors, 9¼" 5.00
Fire-King Square, plate, luncheon; all colors, 8⅜" 3.00
Fire-King Swirl, bowl, berry; jadite, 4⅞" 2.25
Fire-King Swirl, platter, jadite, 12" 9.00
Fire-King Turquoise Blue, bowl, berry; 4½" 4.50
Fire-King Turquoise Blue, bowl, vegetable; 8" 11.00
Fire-King Turquoise Blue, creamer 4.50
Fire-King Turquoise Blue, mug, 8-oz 7.00
Fire-King Turquoise Blue, plate, w/cup indent, 9" 4.00
Fire-King Turquoise Blue, plate, 7" 6.00
Fire-King Turquoise Blue, relish, 3-part 8.00
Fire-King Turquoise Blue, sugar bowl.................................... 4.00
Floragold, bowl, cereal; irid, rnd, 5½" 25.00
Floragold, bowl, irid, ruffled, 9½" 7.50
Floragold, bowl, irid, sq, 4½" 4.50
Floragold, butter dish, irid, w/lid, rnd...................................35.00
Floragold, pitcher, irid, 64-oz..30.00
Floragold, plate, dinner; irid, 8½" 25.00
Floragold, shakers, irid, plastic tops......................................40.00
Floragold, sugar bowl, irid 5.00
Floragold, tumbler, irid, ftd, 11-oz..12.50
Floragold, tumbler, irid, ftd, 15-oz..60.00
Floragold, vase or celery, irid...295.00
Floral, bowl, berry; gr, 4"...13.00
Floral, bowl, cream soup; pk, 5½" 650.00
Floral, butter dish, pk, w/lid 72.50
Floral, candy jar, gr, w/lid 33.00
Floral, compote, pk, 9" 600.00
Floral, lamp, gr...245.00
Floral, pitcher, lemonade; gr, 48-oz, 10¼" 200.00
Floral, plate, salad; pk, 8"... 7.00
Floral, refrigerator dish, gr, w/lid, sq, 5"..............................55.00
Floral, tumbler, juice; pk, ftd, 5-oz, 4" 13.00
Floral, vase, gr, 3-leg, flared...400.00
Floral & Diamond Band, bowl, berry; gr, lg, 8" 11.00
Floral & Diamond Band, bowl, nappy; gr, hdls, 5¾".............. 8.00
Floral & Diamond Band, butter dish, pk, w/lid 115.00
Floral & Diamond Band, compote, gr, tall, 5½" 12.50
Floral & Diamond Band, creamer, gr, 4¾" 16.00
Floral & Diamond Band, pitcher, pk, 42-oz, 8" 75.00
Floral & Diamond Band, plate, luncheon; gr, 8" 25.00
Floral & Diamond Band, sugar bowl, pk, 5¼" 10.00
Floral & Diamond Band, tumbler, iced tea; pk, 5"................25.00
Florentine No 1, ash tray, yel, 5½" 25.00
Florentine No 1, bowl, berry; yel, lg, 8½" 22.00
Florentine No 1, butter dish, gr, w/lid.................................100.00
Florentine No 1, creamer, gr, ruffled 30.00
Florentine No 1, pitcher, yel, ftd, 36-oz, 6½" 40.00
Florentine No 1, plate, grill; yel, 10"....................................11.00
Florentine No 1, platter, yel, oval, 11½"...............................17.00
Florentine No 1, shakers, gr, ftd, pr 33.00
Florentine No 1, sugar bowl, gr, ruffled................................25.00

Florentine No 1, tumbler, iced tea; gr, ftd, 12-oz, 5¼" 22.50
Florentine No 1, tumbler, juice; yel, ftd, 5-oz, 3¾" 18.00
Florentine No 2, bowl, yel, 5¼" 30.00
Florentine No 2, candlestick, yel, 2¾", pr 50.00
Florentine No 2, candy dish, yel, w/lid 135.00
Florentine No 2, coaster, gr, 3¼" 10.00
Florentine No 2, custard cup or jello, gr 50.00
Florentine No 2, pitcher, yel, 76-oz, 8" 300.00
Florentine No 2, plate, grill; yel, 10¼" 8.00
Florentine No 2, platter, gr, oval, 11" 12.00
Florentine No 2, shakers, gr, pr 37.50
Florentine No 2, tumbler, gr, ftd, 9-oz, 4½" 20.00
Florentine No 2, vase or parfait, gr, 6" 28.00
Flower Garden w/Butterflies, candlestick, any color, 4", pr...........50.00
Flower Garden w/Butterflies, candy dish, any color, 6" 25.00
Flower Garden w/Butterflies, creamer, any color 65.00
Flower Garden w/Butterflies, plate, dinner; any color, 10" 40.00
Flower Garden w/Butterflies, powder jar, any color, ftd................85.00
Flower Garden w/Butterflies, vase, any color, 10" 125.00
Flower Garden w/Butterflies, vase, blk, 7" 125.00
Forest Green, bowl, soup; dk gr, 6" 12.00
Forest Green, creamer, dk gr, flat 4.50
Forest Green, pitcher, dk gr, rnd, 3-qt...22.00
Forest Green, platter, dk gr, rectangular 22.00
Forest Green, tumbler, dk gr, 10-oz 4.00
Forest Green, vase, dk gr, 9" 5.00
Fortune, bowl, pk, rolled edge, 5¼" 5.00
Fortune, candy dish, pk, flat, w/lid 17.50
Fortune, tumbler, juice; pk, 5-oz, 3½" 5.00
Fruits, bowl, berry; gr, 8" 43.00
Fruits, plate, luncheon; gr, 8" 4.00
Fruits, saucer, gr 3.00
Fruits, sherbet, gr 6.00
Fruits, tumbler, pk, 12-oz, 5" 55.00
Georgian, bowl, cereal; gr, 5¾" 16.00
Georgian, bowl, vegetable; gr, oval, 9" 52.50
Georgian, butter dish, gr, w/lid..72.50
Georgian, creamer, gr, ftd, 4" 12.00
Georgian, hot plate, gr, center design, 5" 37.50
Georgian, plate, dinner; gr, 9¼" 22.00
Georgian, sugar bowl, gr, ftd, 4" 8.50
Georgian, tumbler, gr, flat, 12-oz, 5¼" 77.50
Harp, ash tray or coaster, crystal... 3.50
Harp, saucer, crystal 2.50
Harp, tray, crystal, rectangular 25.00
Harp, vase, crystal, 6" 12.50
Heritage, bowl, berry; crystal, lg, 8½" 25.00
Heritage, bowl, fruit; crystal, 10½" 12.00
Heritage, creamer, crystal, ftd 19.00
Heritage, plate, sandwich; crystal, 12" 9.50
Heritage, sugar bowl, crystal, ftd 13.00
Hex Optic, bowl, berry; pk or gr, ruffled, 4¼" 4.00
Hex Optic, bucket reamer, pk or gr..45.00
Hex Optic, ice bucket, pk or gr, metal hdl....................................15.00
Hex Optic, platter, pk or gr, rnd, 11" 10.00
Hex Optic, shakers, pk or gr, pr 22.00
Hex Optic, sugar shaker, pk or gr 125.00
Hex Optic, tumbler, pk or gr, 9-oz, 3¾" 4.00
Hobnail, decanter, crystal, w/stopper, 32-oz.................................22.50
Hobnail, pitcher, milk; crystal, 18-oz 16.00
Hobnail, tumbler, cordial; crystal, ftd, 5-oz 6.00
Hobnail, tumbler, juice; crystal, 5-oz... 3.00
Holiday, bowl, berry; pk, lg, 8½" 15.00
Holiday, bowl, console; pk, 10¾" 77.50

Holiday, butter dish, pk, w/lid 32.50
Holiday, creamer, pk, ftd 6.50
Holiday, pitcher, milk; pk, 16-oz, 4¾" 48.00
Holiday, plate, cake; pk, 3-leg, 10½" 75.00
Holiday, plate, chop; pk, 13¾" 72.50
Holiday, tumbler, pk, flat, 10-oz, 4" 16.00
Holiday, tumbler, pk, ftd, 6" 80.00
Homespun, bowl, pk, closed hdls, 4½" 5.00
Homespun, butter dish, pk, w/lid...45.00
Homespun, creamer, pk, ftd 7.00
Homespun, cup, pk, child's sz 22.50
Homespun, teapot, pk, child's sz...30.00
Homespun, tumbler, water; pk, 9-oz, 4" 13.00
Indiana Custard, bowl, cereal; ivory, 5¾" 15.00
Indiana Custard, bowl, soup; ivory, flat, 7½" 26.00
Indiana Custard, butter dish, ivory, w/lid.......................................55.00
Indiana Custard, creamer, ivory 12.50
Indiana Custard, plate, bread & butter; ivory, 5¾" 5.00
Indiana Custard, plate, luncheon; ivory, 8⅞" 10.00
Indiana Custard, platter, ivory, oval, 11½" 26.00
Indiana Custard, sherbet, ivory 80.00
Indiana Custard, sugar bowl, ivory 9.00
Iris, bowl, berry; crystal, beaded, 4½" 30.00
Iris, bowl, fruit; crystal, ruffled, 11" 8.50
Iris, bowl, sauce; irid, 5" 17.50
Iris, butter dish, irid, w/lid 35.00
Iris, candy jar, crystal, w/lid 80.00

Iris, creamer, irid, ftd.. 9.00
Iris, cup, demi; irid 95.00
Iris, goblet, irid, 8-oz, 5¾" 100.00
Iris, goblet, wine; crystal, 4½" 15.00
Iris, pitcher, crystal, ftd, 9½" 30.00
Iris, plate, dinner; irid, 9" 32.00
Iris, plate, luncheon; crystal, 8" 40.00
Iris, sherbet, crystal, ftd, 2½" 19.00
Iris, tumbler, crystal, flat, 4" 60.00
Iris, tumbler, irid, ftd, 6" 12.00
Iris, vase, crystal, 9"...22.00
Jubilee, bowl, fruit; topaz, hdld, 9" 100.00
Jubilee, cheese & cracker set, topaz..125.00
Jubilee, creamer, topaz 18.50
Jubilee, goblet, topaz, 12½-oz, 6⅛" 90.00
Jubilee, goblet, topaz, 6-oz, 5" 55.00
Jubilee, mayonnaise, topaz, w/plate & ladle.................................195.00
Jubilee, plate, sandwich; topaz, 13" 40.00
Jubilee, sugar bowl, topaz 17.50
Jubilee, tray, sandwich; topaz, center hdl.....................................100.00
Lace Edge, bowl, cereal; pk, 6⅜" 13.50
Lace Edge, bowl, pk, 3-leg, 10½" 150.00
Lace Edge, candy jar, pk, w/lid, ribbed 37.50
Lace Edge, compote, pk, 7"..17.50

Lace Edge, creamer, pk 17.00
Lace Edge, cup, pk 18.00
Lace Edge, plate, grill; pk, 10½" 14.00
Lace Edge, plate, luncheon; pk, 8¾" 14.00
Lace Edge, platter, pk, 12¾" 20.00
Lace Edge, platter, pk, 5-part, 12¾" 20.00
Lace Edge, sherbet, pk, ftd 65.00
Lace Edge, sugar bowl, pk 16.00
Lace Edge, tumbler, pk, ftd, 10½-oz, 5" 52.50
Laced Edge, bowl, bl or gr, oval, 11" 65.00
Laced Edge, bowl, soup; bl or gr, 7" 27.50
Laced Edge, cup, bl or gr 22.00
Laced Edge, mayonnaise, bl or gr, 3-pc 85.00
Laced Edge, plate, bread & butter; bl or gr, 6½" 12.00
Laced Edge, platter, bl or gr, 13" 75.00
Laced Edge, saucer, bl or gr 9.00
Laced Edge, sugar bowl, bl or gr............................26.00
Laced Edge, tumbler, bl or gr, 9-oz 37.50
Laced Edge, vase, bl or gr, 5½" 42.00
Lake Como, bowl, soup; wht w/bl decor, flat 75.00
Lake Como, creamer, wht w/bl decor, ftd 16.00
Lake Como, plate, salad; wht w/bl decor, 7¼" 11.50
Lake Como, saucer, wht w/bl decor 7.00
Lake Como, shakers, wht w/bl decor, pr 32.00
Lake Como, sugar bowl, wht w/bl decor, ftd 15.00
Laurel, bowl, berry; ivory, 5" 6.00
Laurel, bowl, gr, 3-leg, 6" 11.00
Laurel, cheese dish, ivory, w/lid 50.00
Laurel, creamer, ivory, tall.....................................11.00
Laurel, plate, dinner; gr, 9⅛" 10.00
Laurel, platter, ivory, oval, 10¾" 22.50
Laurel, sherbet, gr... 8.00
Laurel, sugar bowl, ivory, tall.................................11.00
Laurel, tumbler, ivory, flat, 12-oz, 5" 37.50
Lincoln Inn, ash tray, bl or red 16.00
Lincoln Inn, bonbon, bl or red, hdld, oval..............14.00
Lincoln Inn, bowl, blk, crimped, 6" 7.00
Lincoln Inn, candy dish, bl or red, ftd, oval 18.00
Lincoln Inn, goblet, wine; pk 15.00
Lincoln Inn, nut dish, jade, ftd..............................10.00
Lincoln Inn, pitcher, bl or red, 46-oz, 7¼"..............750.00
Lincoln Inn, tumbler, bl or red, ftd, 7-oz................15.00
Lorain, bowl, berry; gr, deep, 8" 70.00
Lorain, bowl, salad; yel, 7¼" 50.00
Lorain, creamer, yel, ftd 18.00
Lorain, plate, sherbet; yel, 5½" 8.00
Lorain, relish, yel, 4-part, 8" 25.00
Lorain, sherbet, gr, ftd..15.00
Lorain, tumbler, yel, ftd, 9-oz, 4¾" 23.00
Madrid, ash tray, gr, sq, 6" 125.00
Madrid, bowl, cream soup; amber, 4¾" 12.00
Madrid, butter dish, gr, w/lid 72.00
Madrid, candlestick, amber, 2¼", pr.......................18.00
Madrid, cookie jar, amber, w/lid 35.00
Madrid, gravy boat & platter, amber 1,000.00
Madrid, hot dish coaster, amber 32.50
Madrid, jello mold, amber, 2⅛" 10.00
Madrid, pitcher, gr, sq, 60-oz, 8" 125.00
Madrid, plate, cake; amber, rnd, 11½" 12.00
Madrid, plate, grill; gr, 10½" 14.00
Madrid, tumbler, gr, 9-oz, 4¼" 20.00
Manhattan, ash tray, crystal, sq, 4½".......................18.00
Manhattan, bowl, pk, closed hdls, 8" 20.00
Manhattan, candy dish, crystal, w/lid 35.00

Manhattan, candy dish, pk, 3-leg...................... 8.50
Manhattan, coaster, crystal, 3½" 10.00
Manhattan, creamer, crystal, oval 8.00

Manhattan, pitcher, crystal, tilted, 80-oz...............30.00
Manhattan, plate, dinner; pk, 10¼" 75.00
Manhattan, plate, sandwich; crystal, 14" 15.00
Manhattan, relish tray, pk, 4-part, 14" 15.00
Manhattan, sugar bowl, crystal, oval 8.00
Manhattan, tumbler, crystal, ftd, 10-oz 13.00
Manhattan, vase, crystal, 8" 15.00
Mayfair, bowl, cream soup; pk, 5" 36.00
Mayfair, bowl, fruit; scalloped, deep, 12" 60.00
Mayfair, bowl, vegetable; pk, 7" 18.00
Mayfair, butter or vegetable dish, bl, w/lid, 7" 242.50
Mayfair, candy dish, pk, w/lid 40.00
Mayfair, celery dish, pk, divided, 10" 155.00
Mayfair, celery dish, pk, 10" 27.50
Mayfair, cookie jar, bl, w/lid 185.00
Mayfair, cup, pk 15.00
Mayfair, goblet, cocktail; pk, 3½-oz, 4" 62.00
Mayfair, goblet, water; bl, 9-oz, 5¾" 50.00
Mayfair, goblet, wine; pk, 3-oz, 4½" 62.00
Mayfair, pitcher, bl, 37-oz, 6" 97.00
Mayfair, pitcher, bl, 60-oz, 8" 120.00
Mayfair, plate, cake; bl, ftd 45.00
Mayfair, plate, cake; bl, hdls, 12" 45.00
Mayfair, plate, dinner; bl, 9½" 50.00
Mayfair, plate, luncheon; bl, 8½" 30.00
Mayfair, platter, pk, open hdls, oval, 12" 18.00
Mayfair, sandwich server, bl, center hdl.................50.00
Mayfair, shakers, pk, flat, pr.................................45.00
Mayfair, sherbet, bl, flat, 2¼" 75.00
Mayfair, sherbet, pk, ftd, 4¾" 60.00
Mayfair, sugar bowl, bl, ftd...................................50.00
Mayfair, tumbler, iced tea; bl, ftd, 15-oz, 6½" 120.00
Mayfair, tumbler, juice; bl, 5-oz, 3½" 75.00
Mayfair, tumbler, water; pk, 11-oz, 4¾" 115.00
Mayfair, whiskey, pk, 1½-oz, 2¼" 50.00
Mayfair Federal, bowl, cream soup; amber, 5" 16.00
Mayfair Federal, bowl, sauce; gr, 5" 8.00
Mayfair Federal, creamer, gr, ftd 13.00
Mayfair Federal, plate, salad; gr, 6¾" 7.00
Mayfair Federal, saucer, amber 2.50
Mayfair Federal, sugar bowl, gr, ftd.......................12.50
Mayfair Federal, tumbler, amber, 9-oz, 4½" 18.50
Miss America, bowl, vegetable; pk, oval, 10"...........20.00
Miss America, butter dish, crystal, w/lid 190.00
Miss America, candy jar, pk, w/lid, 11½"................100.00
Miss America, celery dish, pk, oblong, 10½" 18.00
Miss America, coaster, crystal, 5¾" 12.50
Miss America, goblet, juice; pk, 5-oz, 4¾" 70.00

Miss America, goblet, wine; pk, 3-oz, 3¾" 55.00
Miss America, pitcher, pk, 65-oz, 8" 95.00
Miss America, plate, grill; pk, 10¼" 17.00
Miss America, plate, sherbet; pk, 5¾" 6.00
Miss America, platter, pk, oval, 12" 19.00
Miss America, relish, crystal, 4-part, 8¾" 8.00
Miss America, shakers, crystal, pr 25.00
Miss America, sugar bowl, pk 14.00
Miss America, tumbler, water; pk, 10-oz, 4½" 22.00
Moderntone, bowl, berry; cobalt, 5" 17.50
Moderntone, bowl, cream soup; cobalt, ruffled, 5" 27.50
Moderntone, cheese dish, cobalt, w/metal lid, 7" 250.00
Moderntone, creamer, amethyst 7.00
Moderntone, cup, custard; cobalt, no hdl 12.00
Moderntone, plate, luncheon; cobalt, 7¾" 7.50
Moderntone, plate, sandwich; amethyst, 10½" 30.00
Moderntone, platter, cobalt, oval, 11" 30.00
Moderntone, saucer, cobalt 3.00
Moderntone, shakers, amethyst, pr 30.00
Moderntone, sherbet, amethyst 8.00
Moderntone, sugar bowl, cobalt 8.00
Moderntone, tumbler, cobalt, 5-oz 27.50
Moderntone, tumbler, cobalt, 9-oz 22.00
Moderntone, whiskey, cobalt, 1½-oz 20.00
Moondrops, ash tray, cobalt 16.00
Moondrops, bowl, berry; red or bl, 5¼" 10.00
Moondrops, bowl, celery; pk, boat shaped, 11½" 22.00
Moondrops, bowl, red or bl, ftd, concave top, 8⅜" 30.00
Moondrops, bowl, red or bl, 3-leg, ruffled, 9½" 35.00
Moondrops, bowl, soup; dk gr, 6¾" 10.00
Moondrops, bowl, vegetable; red or bl, oval, 9¾" 28.00
Moondrops, butter dish, red or bl, w/lid 385.00
Moondrops, candy dish, red or bl, ruffled, 8" 30.00
Moondrops, compote, red or bl, 4" 19.00
Moondrops, creamer, red or bl, mini, 2¾" 15.00
Moondrops, cup, red or bl 12.00
Moondrops, decanter, red or bl, lg, 11¼" 75.00
Moondrops, goblet, liquor; blk, ¾-oz, 2⅞" 20.00
Moondrops, goblet, wine; red or bl, metal stem, 5⅛" 13.50
Moondrops, mug, red or bl, 12-oz, 5⅛" 32.00
Moondrops, perfume bottle, pk, rocket style 135.00
Moondrops, pitcher, red or bl, w/lip, lg, 50-oz, 8" 175.00
Moondrops, plate, bread & butter; gr, 5⅞" 6.00
Moondrops, plate, luncheon; gr, 8½" 10.00
Moondrops, plate, sandwich; red or bl, rnd, 14" 30.00
Moondrops, platter, pk, oval, 12" 15.00
Moondrops, sherbet, red or bl, 4½" 22.00
Moondrops, tumbler, red or bl, hdld, 9-oz, 4⅞" 25.00
Moondrops, tumbler, red or bl, 5-oz, 3⅝" 11.00
Moondrops, vase, gr, flat, ruffled top, 7¾" 35.00
Moondrops, vase, red or bl, rocket style, 9¼" 165.00
Moonstone, bowl, dessert; opal, crimped, 5½" 6.50
Moonstone, candle holder, opal, pr 15.00
Moonstone, candy jar, opal, w/lid, 6" 20.00
Moonstone, cigarette jar, opal, w/lid 17.50
Moonstone, plate, sandwich; opal, 10" 18.00
Moonstone, puff box, opal, rnd, w/lid, 4¾" 18.00
Moonstone, saucer, opal 3.50
Moonstone, sugar bowl, opal, ftd 6.00
Moonstone, vase, bud; opal, 5½" 9.00
Moroccan Amethyst, bowl, fruit; 4¾" 4.50
Moroccan Amethyst, cocktail shaker, 32-oz 20.00
Moroccan Amethyst, plate, salad; 7¼" 4.50
Moroccan Amethyst, tumbler, juice; 4-oz, 2½" 6.00

Moroccan Amethyst, vase, ruffled, 9" 32.50
Mt Pleasant, bowl, blk, rolled out edge, 3-ftd, 7" 17.50
Mt Pleasant, bowl, fruit; cobalt, scalloped, 10" 32.00
Mt Pleasant, creamer, blk amethyst 15.00
Mt Pleasant, mayonnaise, cobalt, 3-ftd, 5½" 20.00
Mt Pleasant, sandwich server, cobalt, center hdl 33.00
Mt Pleasant, sugar bowl, blk amethyst 14.00
Mt Pleasant, vase, cobalt, 7¼" 25.00
New Century, ash tray or coaster, gr, 5⅜" 25.00
New Century, bowl, casserole; gr, w/lid, 9" 47.50
New Century, bowl, cream soup; gr, 4¾" 11.00
New Century, butter dish, gr, w/lid 50.00
New Century, creamer, gr 6.00
New Century, goblet, cocktail; gr, 3¼-oz 16.00
New Century, pitcher, gr, w/ice lip, 80-oz, 8" 32.00
New Century, plate, breakfast; gr, 7⅛" 6.50
New Century, plate, grill; gr, 10" 8.00
New Century, shakers, gr, pr 30.00
New Century, tumbler, gr, ftd, 9-oz, 4⅞" 15.00
New Century, tumbler, gr, 9-oz, 4⅛" 12.00
New Century, whiskey, gr, 1½-oz, 2½" 12.00
Newport, bowl, cereal; cobalt, 5¼" 26.00
Newport, bowl, cream soup; cobalt, 4¾" 14.00
Newport, cup, cobalt 8.50

Newport, plate, sandwich; amethyst, 11½" 25.00
Newport, plate, sherbet; amethyst, 6" 3.50
Newport, platter, cobalt, oval, 11¾" 32.50
Newport, shakers, cobalt, pr 40.00
Newport, sherbet, cobalt 10.00
Newport, sugar bowl, amethyst 11.00
No 610 Pyramid, bowl, berry; yel, 4¾" 28.00
No 610 Pyramid, bowl, pickle; yel, 9½" 48.00
No 610 Pyramid, ice tub, yel, w/lid 600.00
No 610 Pyramid, pitcher, yel 400.00
No 610 Pyramid, relish tray, yel, hdld, 4-part 50.00
No 610 Pyramid, tumbler, yel, ftd, 8-oz 45.00
No 612 Horseshoe, bowl, berry; yel, 4½" 17.00
No 612 Horseshoe, bowl, cereal; gr, 6½" 18.00
No 612 Horseshoe, butter dish, gr, w/lid 550.00
No 612 Horseshoe, creamer, yel, ftd 12.50
No 612 Horseshoe, cup, gr 8.50
No 612 Horseshoe, pitcher, yel, 64-oz, 8½" 245.00
No 612 Horseshoe, plate, dinner; gr, 10⅜" 16.00
No 612 Horseshoe, plate, grill; gr, 10⅜" 50.00
No 612 Horseshoe, plate, luncheon; yel, 9⅜" 11.00
No 612 Horseshoe, platter, yel, oval, 10¾" 19.00
No 612 Horseshoe, relish, yel, ftd, 3-part 30.00
No 612 Horseshoe, sherbet, gr 12.00
No 612 Horseshoe, tumbler, gr, 12-oz, 4¾" 110.00
No 612 Horseshoe, tumbler, gr, 9-oz, 4¼" 80.00
No 612 Horseshoe, tumbler, yel, ftd, 9-oz 17.00

No 616 Vernon, creamer, yel, ftd 19.00
No 616 Vernon, cup, yel 13.00
No 616 Vernon, plate, sandwich; gr, 11" 22.00
No 616 Vernon, saucer, gr 4.50
No 616 Vernon, sugar bowl, gr, ftd 21.50
No 616 Vernon, tumbler, yel, ftd, 5" 27.50
No 618 Pineapple & Floral, ash tray, crystal, 4½" 15.00
No 618 Pineapple & Floral, bowl, cereal; amber, 6" 17.50
No 618 Pineapple & Floral, bowl, salad; amber, 7" 8.50
No 618 Pineapple & Floral, creamer, crystal, dmn shaped 6.50
No 618 Pineapple & Floral, cup, crystal 7.50
No 618 Pineapple & Floral, plate, salad; amber, 8⅜" 6.00
No 618 Pineapple & Floral, plate, sandwich; amber, 11½" ...13.50
No 618 Pineapple & Floral, platter, amber, closed hdls, 11" ...15.00
No 618 Pineapple & Floral, sherbet, crystal, ftd 16.00
No 618 Pineapple & Floral, tumbler, crystal, 12-oz, 5" 35.00
No 618 Pineapple & Floral, tumbler, crystal, 8-oz, 4¼" 30.00
No 618 Pineapple & Floral, vase, crystal, cone shaped, lg 35.00
No 622 Pretzel, bowl, olive; crystal, leaf shaped, 7" 3.00
No 622 Pretzel, creamer, crystal 4.50
No 622 Pretzel, pitcher, crystal, 39-oz 135.00
No 622 Pretzel, plate, bread & butter; crystal, 6" 2.00
No 622 Pretzel, plate, dinner; crystal, 9⅜" 5.00
No 622 Pretzel, plate, sandwich; crystal, 11½" 8.00
No 622 Pretzel, sugar bowl, crystal 4.00
No 622 Pretzel, tumbler, crystal, 12-oz 25.00
No 622 Pretzel, tumbler, juice; crystal, 5-oz 17.50
Normandie, bowl, cereal; pk, 6½" 15.00
Normandie, bowl, vegetable; pk, oval, 10" 26.00
Normandie, plate, dinner; pk, 11" 75.00
Normandie, plate, grill; amber, 11" 12.00
Normandie, shakers, amber, pr 40.00
Normandie, tumbler, iced tea; pk, 12-oz, 5" 50.00
Normandie, tumbler, juice; amber, 5-oz, 4" 15.00
Old Cafe, bowl, cereal; pk, 5½" 5.00
Old Cafe, bowl, red, closed hdls, 9" 11.50
Old Cafe, candy dish, red, low, 8" 10.00
Old Cafe, lamp, pk 15.00
Old Cafe, plate, dinner; pk, 10" 22.00
Old Cafe, sherbet, pk, low ftd 5.00
Old Cafe, tumbler, juice; pk, 3" 8.50
Old Cafe, vase, pk, 7¼" 10.00
Old English, bowl, any color, flat, 9½" 26.00
Old English, bowl, berry; any color, 4" 14.00
Old English, candlestick, any color, 4", pr 25.00
Old English, candy jar, any color, w/lid, ftd 45.00
Old English, fruit stand, any color, ftd, 11" 35.00

Old English, vase, any color, fan form, 7" 40.00
Old English, vase, any color, ftd, 12" 45.00
Ovide, bowl, berry; blk, lg, 8" 14.00
Ovide, bowl, cereal; blk, 5½" 7.00
Ovide, candy dish, gr, w/lid 18.00
Ovide, cup, blk 5.00
Ovide, plate, luncheon; blk, 8" 6.00
Ovide, saucer, blk 2.00
Ovide, shakers, blk, pr 22.50
Ovide, sugar bowl, blk, open 5.00
Oyster & Pearl, bowl, red, deep, hdls, 6½" 15.00
Oyster & Pearl, candle holder, pk, 3½", pr 17.50
Oyster & Pearl, plate, sandwich; pk, 13½" 12.50
Oyster & Pearl, relish dish, pk, oblong, 10¼" 8.00
Parrot, bowl, soup; gr, 7" 30.00
Parrot, bowl, vegetable; amber, oval, 10" 50.00
Parrot, butter dish, amber, w/lid 1,000.00
Parrot, creamer, amber, ftd 35.00
Parrot, cup, gr 25.00
Parrot, hot plate, gr, 5" 600.00
Parrot, pitcher, gr, 80-oz, 8½" 1,250.00
Parrot, plate, grill; gr, rnd, 10½" 22.00
Parrot, plate, salad; gr, 7½" 25.00
Parrot, platter, amber, oblong, 11¼" 50.00
Parrot, shakers, gr, pr 195.00
Parrot, sherbet, amber, cone shaped, ftd 16.00
Parrot, sugar bowl, amber 25.00
Parrot, tumbler, gr, 12-oz, 5½" 115.00
Patrician, bowl, cereal; gr, 6" 20.00
Patrician, bowl, vegetable; amber, oval, 10" 25.00
Patrician, butter dish, gr, w/lid 95.00
Patrician, cookie jar, gr, w/lid 325.00
Patrician, pitcher, amber, 75-oz, 8" 95.00
Patrician, pitcher, gr, 75-oz, 8¼" 115.00
Patrician, plate, dinner; gr, 10½" 27.50
Patrician, plate, grill; amber, 10½" 10.00
Patrician, plate, luncheon; gr, 9" 8.00
Patrician, platter, amber, oval, 11½" 25.00
Patrician, shakers, gr, pr 50.00
Patrician, sherbet, amber 10.00
Patrician, sugar bowl, amber 7.00
Patrician, tumbler, amber, 9-oz, 4½" 22.00
Patrician, tumbler, gr, 5-oz, 4" 26.00
Patrick, bowl, fruit; yel or pk, 9" 35.00
Patrick, candlestick, yel or pk, pr 42.00
Patrick, candy dish, yel or pk, 3-ftd 45.00
Patrick, cheese & cracker set, yel or pk 47.50
Patrick, goblet, juice; yel or pk, 6-oz, 4¾" 25.00
Patrick, plate, salad; yel or pk, 7½" 8.50
Patrick, saucer, yel or pk 3.00
Patrick, sherbet, yel or pk, 4¾" 22.50
Patrick, tray, yel or pk, center hdl, 11" 32.50
Petalware, bowl, berry; monax, lg, 8¾" 13.00
Petalware, lamp shade, monax, any size 7.50
Petalware, plate, dinner; pk, 9" 6.00
Petalware, plate, salad; monax, 8" 3.00
Petalware, platter, pk, oval, 13" 12.00
Petalware, sherbet, monax, low, ftd 4.50
Petalware, sugar bowl, pk, ftd 3.50
Primo, bowl, yel or gr, 7¾" 15.00
Primo, creamer, yel or gr 8.00
Primo, plate, cake; yel or gr, 3-ftd, 10" 16.00
Primo, plate, dinner; yel or gr, 10" 12.00
Primo, plate, grill; yel or gr, 10" 7.50

Old English, pitcher, any color 55.00
Old English, pitcher, any color, w/lid 95.00
Old English, sandwich server, any color, center hdl 45.00
Old English, tumbler, any color, ftd, 4½" 17.50

Primo, plate, yel or gr, 7½" 5.00
Primo, sherbet, yel or gr 8.00
Primo, sugar bowl, yel or gr 8.00
Primo, tumbler, yel or gr, 9-oz, 5¾" 14.00
Princess, ash tray, gr, 4½" 62.00
Princess, bowl, berry; gr, 4½" 19.00
Princess, bowl, gr, hat shaped, 9½" 33.00
Princess, bowl, salad; pk, octagonal, 9" 20.00
Princess, butter dish, pk, w/lid 75.00
Princess, cake stand, pk, 10" 15.00
Princess, candy dish, gr, w/lid 40.00
Princess, coaster, pk 55.00
Princess, cookie jar, pk, w/lid 42.50
Princess, creamer, gr, oval 11.00
Princess, pitcher, gr, ftd, 24-oz, 7⅜" 500.00
Princess, pitcher, gr, 37-oz, 6" 38.00
Princess, plate, salad; gr, 8" 10.00
Princess, plate, sandwich; pk, hdld, 11½" 7.50
Princess, platter, gr, closed hdls, 12" 13.50
Princess, relish, gr, plain, 7½" 70.00
Princess, shakers, pk, 4½", pr 35.00
Princess, tumbler, juice; pk, 5-oz, 3" 17.00
Princess, vase, gr, 8" 26.00
Queen Mary, butter dish or preserve, pk, w/lid 90.00
Queen Mary, candy dish, crystal, w/lid 15.00
Queen Mary, celery or pickle dish, pk, 5x10" 17.50
Queen Mary, cigarette jar, crystal, oval, 2x3" 4.00
Queen Mary, creamer, crystal, oval 4.00
Queen Mary, plate, salad; crystal, 8½" 3.50
Queen Mary, plate, sandwich; pk, 12" 10.00
Queen Mary, relish tray, pk, 3-part, 12" 10.00
Queen Mary, serving tray, pk, 14" 15.00
Queen Mary, shakers, crystal, pr 17.50
Queen Mary, sherbet, pk, ftd 4.00
Queen Mary, sugar bowl, crystal, oval 4.00
Queen Mary, tumbler, pk, ftd, 10-oz, 5" 33.00
Queen Mary, tumbler, water; pk, 9-oz, 4" 9.00
Radiance, bonbon, red or bl, 6" 12.00
Radiance, bowl, amber, 2-part, 7" 10.00
Radiance, bowl, celery; red or bl, 10" 17.50
Radiance, bowl, crystal, flared, 12" 20.00
Radiance, bowl, nut; red or bl, hdld, 5" 14.00
Radiance, butter dish, amber 150.00
Radiance, comport, red or bl, 5" 20.00
Radiance, cruet, red or bl, ind 47.50
Radiance, decanter, red or bl, hdld, w/stopper 130.00
Radiance, lamp, red or bl, 12" 85.00
Radiance, mayonnaise, crystal, 3-pc 20.00
Radiance, pitcher, red or bl, 64-oz 175.00
Radiance, plate, cheese & cracker; crystal, 11" 22.00
Radiance, plate, luncheon; amber, 8" 8.00
Radiance, punch bowl, red or bl 150.00
Radiance, shakers, amber, pr 40.00
Radiance, tray, red or bl, oval 25.00
Radiance, tumbler, red or bl, 9-oz 22.00
Radiance, vase, red or bl, crimped, 12" 65.00
Raindrops, bowl, berry; gr, 7½" 30.00
Raindrops, cup, gr 4.50
Raindrops, plate, luncheon; gr, 8" 4.00
Raindrops, plate, sherbet; gr, 6" 2.00
Raindrops, saucer, gr 1.00
Raindrops, shakers, gr, pr 150.00
Raindrops, tumbler, gr, 4-oz, 3" 3.50
Raindrops, whiskey, gr, 1⅞" 5.00

Ribbon, bowl, berry; gr, lg, 8" 20.00
Ribbon, candy dish, gr, w/lid 30.00
Ribbon, creamer, gr, ftd 10.00
Ribbon, saucer, gr 1.00

Ribbon, shakers, gr, pr 22.50
Ribbon, sugar bowl, gr, ftd 9.00
Ribbon, tumbler, gr, 13-oz, 6½" 17.50
Ring, bowl, soup; gr, 7" 10.00
Ring, cocktail shaker, crystal 15.00
Ring, creamer, gr, ftd 5.00
Ring, ice tub, crystal 12.00
Ring, pitcher, crystal, 60-oz, 8" 13.00
Ring, sandwich server, gr, center hdl 22.00
Ring, shakers, crystal, 3", pr 15.00
Ring, sherbet, gr, ftd, 4¾" 7.50
Ring, tumbler, cocktail; crystal, ftd, 3½" 5.00
Ring, tumbler, gr, 12-oz, 5⅛" 7.00
Ring, tumbler, gr, 5-oz, 3½" 5.00
Ring, vase, crystal, 8" 12.50
Ring, whiskey, crystal, 1½-oz, 2" 3.50
Rock Crystal, bonbon, red, scalloped edge, 7½" 45.00
Rock Crystal, bowl, fruit; red, scalloped edge, 5" 20.00
Rock Crystal, bowl, salad; red, scalloped edge, 7" 45.00
Rock Crystal, candelabra, crystal, 2-light, pr 35.00
Rock Crystal, candlestick, crystal, low, 5½", pr 27.50
Rock Crystal, candy jar, red, w/lid, rnd 135.00
Rock Crystal, compote, crystal, 7" 27.50
Rock Crystal, creamer, red, ftd, 9-oz 55.00
Rock Crystal, goblet, red, low ftd, 8-oz, 7½" 45.00
Rock Crystal, jelly, red, scalloped edge, ftd, 5" 40.00
Rock Crystal, lamp, red, electric 380.00
Rock Crystal, plate, bread & butter; scalloped edge, 6" 12.50
Rock Crystal, sandwich server, red, center hdl 85.00
Rock Crystal, saucer, crystal 5.00
Rock Crystal, sugar bowl, crystal, flat, 10-oz 17.50
Rock Crystal, sugar bowl, red, ftd, w/lid, 10-oz 90.00
Rock Crystal, sundae, red, low ftd, 6-oz 28.00
Rock Crystal, tumbler, whiskey; crystal, 2½-oz 13.50
Rock Crystal, vase, red, ftd, 11" 125.00
Rose Cameo, bowl, cereal; gr, 5" 9.00
Rose Cameo, bowl, gr, str side, 6" 13.00
Rose Cameo, plate, salad; gr, 7" 6.00
Rose Cameo, sherbet, gr 8.00
Rosemary, bowl, berry; gr, 5" 6.00
Rosemary, bowl, cream soup; amber, 5" 10.00
Rosemary, bowl, vegetable; gr, oval, 10" 22.00
Rosemary, creamer, amber, ftd 7.00
Rosemary, plate, dinner; amber 7.00
Rosemary, plate, grill; gr 10.00
Rosemary, platter, gr, oval, 12" 17.00
Rosemary, saucer, amber 2.00

Rosemary, sugar bowl, gr, ftd 10.00
Rosemary, tumbler, amber, 9-oz, 4¼" 22.50
Roulette, cup, gr 4.50
Roulette, pitcher, gr, 64-oz, 8" 25.00
Roulette, plate, sandwich; gr, 12" 9.00
Roulette, saucer, gr... 2.25
Roulette, tumbler, iced tea; pk, 12-oz, 5⅛" 15.00
Roulette, tumbler, water; gr, 9-oz, 4⅛"..............16.00
Roulette, whiskey, gr, 1½-oz, 2½" 13.00
Round Robin, domino tray, gr............................27.50
Round Robin, plate, luncheon; irid, 8" 3.00
Round Robin, plate, sherbet; irid, 6" 1.50
Round Robin, saucer, irid 1.50
Round Robin, sherbet, irid 5.00
Round Robin, sugar bowl, gr.............................. 5.00
Roxana, bowl, cereal; yel, 6" 8.00
Roxana, bowl, yel, 4½x2⅜"................................ 6.00
Roxana, saucer, yel 3.00
Roxana, sherbet, yel, ftd 5.00
Roxana, tumbler, yel, 9-oz, 4" 12.00
Royal Lace, bowl, berry; bl, rnd, 10" 45.00
Royal Lace, bowl, berry; pk, 5" 22.00
Royal Lace, bowl, bl, str edge, 3-leg, 10" 45.00
Royal Lace, bowl, cream soup; bl, 4¾" 26.00
Royal Lace, candlestick, bl, rolled edge, pr 125.00
Royal Lace, cookie jar, bl, w/lid 275.00
Royal Lace, creamer, pk, ftd 14.00
Royal Lace, pitcher, bl, str sides, 48-oz 90.00
Royal Lace, pitcher, pk, 96-oz, 8½"....................67.00
Royal Lace, plate, dinner; bl, 10" 30.00
Royal Lace, plate, luncheon; pk, 8½" 10.00
Royal Lace, platter, pk, oval, 13"........................20.00
Royal Lace, shakers, bl, pr 210.00
Royal Lace, sherbet, pk, ftd 12.00
Royal Lace, tumbler, bl, 5-oz, 3½" 35.00
Royal Lace, tumbler, pk, 10-oz, 4⅞"...................32.00
Royal Ruby, bowl, red, 5¼" 10.00
Royal Ruby, bowl, salad; red, 11½" 25.00
Royal Ruby, bowl, soup; red, 7½" 10.00
Royal Ruby, bowl, vegetable; red, oval, 8" 32.50
Royal Ruby, card holder, red 45.00
Royal Ruby, creamer, red, ftd 7.50
Royal Ruby, goblet, red, ball stem 8.50
Royal Ruby, pitcher, red, tilted, 3-qt..................30.00
Royal Ruby, plate, dinner; red, 9".......................8.50
Royal Ruby, plate, sherbet; red, 6½" 2.00
Royal Ruby, punch bowl, red, w/stand 57.50
Royal Ruby, punch cup, red................................ 2.50
Royal Ruby, tumbler, wine; red, ftd, 2½" 11.00
Royal Ruby, vase, red, ball shaped, 4" 4.50
Sandwich, bowl, cereal; crystal, 6" 22.50
Sandwich, bowl, console; pk, 10" 18.00
Sandwich, bowl, pk, 6-sided, 6" 3.50
Sandwich, bowl, pk, 8¼" 10.00
Sandwich, bowl, salad; crystal, 7" 6.50
Sandwich, butter dish, crystal, low.....................35.00
Sandwich, butter dish, pk, w/lid, dome 160.00
Sandwich, candlestick, crystal, 7", pr 38.00
Sandwich, creamer, crystal 6.50
Sandwich, decanter, crystal, w/stopper................40.00
Sedwich, goblet, crystal, 9-oz 11.00
Sandwich, pitcher, gr, ice lip, ½-gal...................200.00
Sandwich, pitcher, juice; gr, 6"...........................97.50
Sandwich, plate, bread & butter; pk, 7" 3.00

Sandwich, plate, dessert; crystal, 7" 8.00
Sandwich, plate, luncheon; pk, 8⅜" 4.00
Sandwich, plate, sandwich; pk, 13" 10.00
Sandwich, plate, sherbet; pk, 6" 2.50
Sandwich, sandwich server, crystal, center hdl....20.00
Sandwich, saucer, pk 2.00
Sandwich, sugar bowl, gr 20.00
Sandwich, sugar bowl, pk 6.00
Sandwich, tumbler, iced tea; crystal, ftd, 12-oz...12.00
Sandwich, tumbler, water; crystal, ftd, 8-oz 10.00
Sandwich, wine, crystal, 4-oz, 3" 17.00
Sharon, bowl, cream soup; pk, 5" 33.00
Sharon, bowl, fruit; amber, 10½" 19.00
Sharon, bowl, vegetable; amber, oval, 9½" 13.00
Sharon, butter dish, pk, w/lid 40.00
Sharon, candy jar, amber, w/lid 37.50
Sharon, cheese dish, pk, w/lid...........................700.00
Sharon, creamer, amber, ftd 11.00
Sharon, cup, pk 10.00
Sharon, jam dish, amber, 7½" 30.00
Sharon, plate, bread & butter; pk, 6" 4.00
Sharon, plate, cake; pk, ftd, 11½" 28.00
Sharon, plate, dinner; amber, 9½".......................9.50
Sharon, platter, pk, oval, 12½"...........................15.00
Sharon, saucer, amber 4.00
Sharon, shakers, amber, pr................................35.00
Sharon, sherbet, pk, ftd....................................11.00
Sharon, sugar bowl, pk 9.50
Sharon, tumbler, amber, thick or thin, 12-oz, 5¼" .40.00
Sharon, tumbler, pk, ftd, 15-oz, 6½" 35.00
Sierra, bowl, berry; gr, lg, 8½" 20.00
Sierra, bowl, vegetable; gr, oval, 9½" 75.00
Sierra, butter dish, pk, w/lid.............................50.00
Sierra, creamer, gr 16.00
Sierra, cup, gr...10.00

Sierra, pitcher, pk, 32-oz, 6½" 55.00
Sierra, serving tray, gr, hdls 14.00
Sierra, shakers, pk, pr......................................30.00
Sierra, tumbler, gr, ftd, 9-oz, 4½".......................60.00
Spiral, bowl, mixing; gr, 7" 7.50
Spiral, creamer, gr, flat or ftd 6.00
Spiral, ice or butter tub, gr 20.00
Spiral, platter, gr...17.50
Spiral, preserve, gr, w/lid..................................25.00
Spiral, sandwich server, gr, center hdl................20.00
Spiral, tumbler, juice; gr, 5-oz, 3" 3.00
Starlight, bowl, cereal; crystal, 5½" 5.00
Starlight, cup, crystal 3.00
Starlight, plate, bread & butter; crystal, 6" 2.00
Starlight, plate, dinner; crystal, 9" 5.00
Starlight, plate, luncheon; crystal, 8½"................ 2.50

Starlight, relish dish, crystal 10.00
Starlight, sherbet, crystal 10.00
Starlight, sugar bowl, crystal, oval 4.00
Strawberry, bowl, berry; pk or gr, deep, 7½" 16.00
Strawberry, bowl, pk or gr, 2" deep, 6¼" 55.00
Strawberry, butter dish, pk or gr, w/lid 130.00
Strawberry, compote, pk or gr, 5¾" 15.00
Strawberry, creamer, pk or gr, sm 12.50
Strawberry, olive dish, pk or gr, 1-hdl, 5" 10.00
Strawberry, pitcher, pk or gr, 7¾" 135.00
Sunflower, creamer, gr 15.00
Sunflower, plate, cake; pk, 3-leg, 10" 10.00
Sunflower, plate, dinner; pk, 9" 10.00
Sunflower, sugar bowl, pk 12.00
Sunflower, trivet, gr, 3-leg, turned-up edge, 7" 225.00
Swirl, bowl, console; pk, ftd, 10½" 14.00
Swirl, bowl, salad; ultramarine, 9" 16.00
Swirl, butter dish, ultramarine, w/lid 210.00
Swirl, candy dish, pk, w/lid 65.00
Swirl, pitcher, ultramarine, ftd, 48-oz 1,250.00
Swirl, plate, dinner; ultramarine, 9¼" 12.00
Swirl, plate, sandwich; ultramarine, 12½" 16.00
Swirl, plate, ultramarine, 7¼" 8.00
Swirl, shakers, ultramarine, pr 30.00
Swirl, sherbet, pk, low ftd 7.00
Swirl, tumbler, pk, 13-oz, 5⅛" 25.00
Swirl, tumbler, pk, 9-oz, 4" 8.00
Swirl, vase, pk, ftd, 6½" 11.50
Tea Room, bowl, banana split; pk, 7½" 70.00
Tea Room, bowl, finger; gr 42.00
Tea Room, candlestick, gr, low, pr 40.00
Tea Room, cup, gr 40.00
Tea Room, ice bucket, pk 40.00
Tea Room, lamp, gr, electric 40.00
Tea Room, pitcher, gr, 64-oz 110.00
Tea Room, plate, luncheon; pk, 8¼" 23.00
Tea Room, saucer, gr 22.00
Tea Room, shakers, gr, pr 45.00
Tea Room, sundae, pk, ruffled, ftd 60.00
Tea Room, vase, pk, ruffled or str edge, 11" 75.00
Thistle, bowl, cereal; pk, 5½" 15.00
Thistle, bowl, fruit; pk, lg, 10¼" 200.00
Thistle, plate, grill; gr, 10¼" 16.00
Thistle, plate, luncheon; gr, 8" 12.50
Thistle, saucer, pk 7.50
Twisted Optic, bowl, soup; pk or gr, 7" 7.00
Twisted Optic, candlestick, pk or gr, 3", pr 12.00
Twisted Optic, candy jar, pk or gr, w/lid 22.50
Twisted Optic, pitcher, pk or gr, 64-oz 25.00
Twisted Optic, plate, luncheon; pk or gr, 8" 2.00
Twisted Optic, plate, salad; pk or gr, 7" 2.00
Twisted Optic, sandwich server, pk or gr, center hdl 17.50
Twisted Optic, sherbet, pk or gr 5.00
Twisted Optic, tumbler, pk or gr, 12-oz, 5¼" 7.00
US Swirl, bowl, berry; gr, lg, 7⅛" 12.00
US Swirl, bowl, berry; pk, 4⅜" 5.00
US Swirl, bowl, pk, oval, 8¼" 22.00
US Swirl, butter dish, pk, w/lid 70.00
US Swirl, candy dish, pk, w/lid, hdld 25.00
US Swirl, creamer, pk 12.00
US Swirl, pitcher, 48-oz, 8" 35.00
US Swirl, plate, salad; pk, 7⅞" 5.00
US Swirl, plate, sherbet; pk, 6⅛" 1.75
US Swirl, shakers, gr, pr 35.00

US Swirl, sugar bowl, gr, w/lid 25.00
US Swirl, tumbler, pk, 12-oz, 4⅝" 10.00
US Swirl, vase, pk, 6½" 15.00
Victory, bowl, pk, rolled edge, 11" 22.00
Victory, bowl, soup; bl, flat, 8½" 32.00
Victory, candlestick, bl, 3", pr 75.00
Victory, cup, bl 25.00
Victory, gravy boat & platter, pk 135.00
Victory, plate, dinner; bl, 9" 30.00
Victory, plate, salad; bl, 7" 12.00
Victory, sandwich server, pk, center hdl 22.00
Victory, saucer, bl 7.00
Victory, sugar bowl, bl 35.00
Vitrock, bowl, berry; wht, 4" 3.50
Vitrock, bowl, cream soup; wht, 5½" 12.00
Vitrock, creamer, wht, oval 3.50
Vitrock, plate, salad; wht, 7¼" 1.50
Vitrock, plate, soup; wht, 9" 9.00
Vitrock, platter, wht, 11½" 22.00
Waterford, bowl, berry; pk, lg, 8¼" 12.50
Waterford, butter dish, pk, w/lid 185.00
Waterford, creamer, pk, oval 7.50
Waterford, goblet, crystal, 5¼" 12.00
Waterford, pitcher, pk, w/ice lip, tilted, 80-oz 110.00
Waterford, plate, dinner; pk, 9⅝" 13.00

Waterford, plate, sandwich; pk, 13¾" 20.00
Waterford, plate, sherbet; pk, 6" 3.50
Waterford, sherbet, pk, ftd 9.50
Waterford, sugar bowl, crystal 3.00
Waterford, tumbler, pk, ftd, 10-oz, 4⅞" 15.00
Waterford, vase, crystal, 6¾" 8.50
Windsor, ash tray, pk, 5¾" 30.00
Windsor, bowl, cream soup; crystal, 5" 5.00
Windsor, bowl, pk, 3-leg, 7⅛" 20.00
Windsor, butter dish, pk, w/lid 40.00
Windsor, candlestick, pk, 3", pr 65.00
Windsor, candy jar, pk, w/lid 25.00
Windsor, coaster, pk, 3¼" 8.00
Windsor, compote, crystal 3.50
Windsor, cup, pk 7.00
Windsor, pitcher, pk, 16-oz, 4½" 95.00
Windsor, pitcher, pk, 52-oz, 6¾" 18.50
Windsor, plate, cake; crystal, thick, 13½" 6.50
Windsor, plate, dinner; pk, 9" 10.00
Windsor, plate, salad; crystal, 7" 3.00
Windsor, platter, pk, oval, 11½" 15.00
Windsor, relish platter, pk, divided, 11½" 175.00
Windsor, shakers, crystal, pr 12.50
Windsor, tray, pk, sq, 4" 7.00
Windsor, tumbler, pk, 9-oz, 4" 15.00

Derby

William Duesbury operated in Derby, England, from about 1755, purchasing a second establishment, The Chelsea Works, in 1769. During this period fine porcelains were produced which so impressed the King that in 1773 he issued the company the Crown Derby patent. In 1810, several years after Duesbury's death, the factory was bought by Robert Bloor. The quality of the ware suffered under the new management, and the main Derby pottery closed in 1848. Within a short time, the work was revived by a dedicated number of former employees who established their own works on King Street in Derby.

The earliest-known Derby mark was the crown over a script 'D'; however this mark is rarely found today. Soon after 1782, that mark was augmented with a device of crossed batons and six dots, usually applied in underglaze blue. During the Bloor period, the crown was centered within a ring containing the words 'Bloor' above and 'Derby' below the crown, or with a red printed stamp — the crowned Gothic 'D.' The King Street plant produced figurines that may be distinguished from their earlier counterparts by the presence of an 'S' and 'H' on either side of the crown and crossed batons.

In 1876 a new pottery was constructed in Derby, and the owners revived the earlier company's former standard of excellence. The Queen bestowed the firm the title Royal Crown Derby in 1890; it still operates under that name today. See also Royal Crown Derby.

Bottle, scent; florals w/in gilt ovals on dk bl, 1820, 4½" 125.00
Can, gilt vines/bands, ribbed banding, 1825, 4½" 325.00

Candle holder group modeled as two rabbits by a flowering bush, ca 1868, restorations, 7", $450.00.

Candlestick, as boy (or girl)/flowering bush, 1768, 7", pr.............500.00
Candlestick, Captivity, female/floral bocage/sheep, 12", VG.......450.00
Cup, head of nymph mold, fruiting vines in hair, 1815, 3¾" 300.00
Dish, bird's nest/eggs among dense flowers, gilt border, 11".........475.00
Dish, bouquets, fruiting vine border, shaped oval, 9" 450.00
Figurine, Autumn & Winter, 1830s, rstr/losses, 6½", pr 400.00
Figurine, cow/recumbent calf by flowering tree, 1800, 4½"..........210.00
Figurine, Falstaff, shield on left arm, scroll base, 14"................ 1,000.00
Figurine, he w/tambourine, she w/triangle, 1768, 7", pr 225.00
Figurine, huntress holds bird, gun by right side, 1770, 5¾" 150.00
Figurine, lady w/basket & flowers, seated, 1830, 5", EX 240.00
Figurine, Minerva by bush in turq & red, owl/books, 12".............300.00
Figurine, musician/sm animal in bocage, 1768, rstr, 8", pr....... 1,000.00
Figurine, ram, head right, brn-tinged coat, 1768, 4" L, VG 180.00
Figurine, recumbent cat, wht w/gold collar, 1820, 2¼" L.............300.00
Figurine, Shakespeare (or Milton), by column, 1810, 10", pr 600.00

Figurine, shepherd on tree stump, recumbent ewe, bsk, 11" 225.00
Figurine, Vicar (from Tythe Pig group), wht, 1820, 7" 180.00
Flowerpot, flowers/leaves, 1810, rstr/losses, 8", +stand.................160.00
Plate, alternate panels of Buddhistic lions & flowers, 8¾" 180.00
Teapot, flower sprays & scattered flowers, globular, 7"..................300.00
Teapot, scattered flowers w/in pk scroll borders, lobed, 9" 225.00
Tray, mc floral rim w/gilt, red crown mk, 11" 65.00
Vase, floral panels, ftd shield shape w/hdls, 1820, 9", VG............220.00
Vase, flowers w/in vine reserve, gilt on salmon, 7½" 275.00

Desert Sands

As early as the 1850s, the Evans family living in the Ozark Mountains of Missouri produced domestic clay products. Their small pot shop was passed on from one generation to the next. In the 1920s it was moved to North Las Vegas, Nevada, where the name Desert Sands was adopted. Succeeding generations of the family continued to relocate, taking the business with them. From 1937 to 1962 it operated in Boulder City, Nevada; then it was moved to Barstow where it remained until it closed in the late 1970s.

Desert Sands pottery is similar to Mission Ware by Niloak. Various mineral oxides were blended to mimic the naturally occuring sand formations of the American West. A high-gloss glaze was applied to add intensity to the colorful striations that characterize the ware. Not all examples are marked, making it sometimes difficult to attribute. Marked items carry an ink stamp with the Desert Sands designation. Paper labels were also used.

Bowl, swirled colors, 4½" 10.00
Mug, swirled colors, mk 25.00
Tumbler, swirled colors...10.00
Vase, swirled colors, cactus ink mk, 7"..28.00
Vase, swirled colors, 3½x3" 15.00

Vase, 5", $20.00; Salt and pepper shakers, $10.00 for the pair.

Dickota

The Dickota Pottery, a name coined from Dickinson, North Dakota, where it was founded as a brickyard, began operations in the early 1930s. In 1934 potters formerly associated with the North Dakota School of Mines and Charles Hyten from Niloak began their own operation there. Hyten developed a line of swirled ware which was marked 'Dickota Badlands.' Vases, bowls, and ash trays in a mottled glaze were also made. A variety of marks were used, all of which contain the Dickota name. The company closed in the late 1930s.

Ash tray, cowboy hat, advertising 45.00
Bookends, ram form, pr...90.00

Pitcher, lime to aqua, 7", $90.00.

Vase, mauve, flat fan shape w/scallops, 4½" 33.00
Vase, mc swirls, sgn Howard Lewis, 6¾" 250.00
Vase, Niloak type swirl, 6½" 65.00

Documents

Although the word 'document' is defined in the general sense as 'anything printed or written, etc., relied upon to record or prove something. . .,' in the collectible market, the term is more diversified with broadsides, billheads, checks, invoices, letters and letterheads, land grants, receipts, and waybills some of the most sought after. Some documents in demand are those related to a specific subject such as advertising, mining, railroads, military, politics, banking, slavery, nautical, or legal (deeds, mortgages, etc.). Other collectors look for examples representing a specific period of time such as colonial documents, Revolutionary, or Civil War documents, early western documents or those from a specific region, state, or city.

Aside from supply and demand, there are five major factors which determine the collector-value of a document. These are:

1) Age — Documents from the eastern half of the country can be found that date back to the 1700s or earlier. Most documents sought by collectors usually date from 1800 to 1900. Those with twentieth century dates are still abundant and not in demand unless of special significance or beauty.

2) Region of origin — Depending on age, documents from rural and less-populated areas are harder to find than those from major cities and heavily populated states. The colonization of the West and Mid-West did not begin until after 1850, so while an 1870s billhead from New York or Chicago is common, one from Albuquerque or Phoenix is not, since most of the Southwest was still unsettled.

3) Attractiveness — Some documents are plain and unadorned, but collectors prefer colorful, profusely illustrated pieces. Additional artwork and engravings add to the value.

4) Historical content — Unusual or interesting content, such as a letter written by a Civil War soldier giving an eyewitness account of the Battle of Gettysburg or a western territorial billhead listing numerous animal hides purchased from a trapper, will sell for more than one with mundane information.

5) Condition — Through neglect or environmental conditions, over many decades paper articles can become stained, torn, or deteriorated. Heavily damaged or stained documents are generally avoided altogether while those with minor problems are more acceptable,

although their value will decrease anywhere from 20% to 50% depending upon the extent of damage. Avoid attempting to repair tears with scotch tape — sell 'as is' so that the collector can take proper steps toward restoration.

Foreign documents are plentiful; and, though some are very attractive, resale may be difficult. The listings that follow are generalized; prices are variable depending entirely upon the five points noted above. Values here are based upon examples with no major damage.

Our advisor for this category is Warren Anderson; he is listed in the Directory under Utah.

Key: illus — illustrated   vgn — vignette

Apprentice bond, 12-year old's indenture until 21, 1829, EX 28.00
Assay report, ID Territory, printed, 1889, 5x8" 20.00
Bank draft, CO, Indian vgn, 1904, 4x9", EX 25.00
Bill of sale, manuscript, slave sale, 1838, 4-pg, 8x11", EX 35.00
Bill of sale, ship Mercator medical supplies, 1810, VG...................25.00
Booklet, Why Millions Are Lost in Oil, dtd 1921, 12-pg, VG 25.00
Certificate, CT, service & pay of soldier, 1782, 12x7", VG 85.00
Certificate, fraternal membership/beneficiary, 1911, 9x14" 15.00
Certificate, Royal Lifesaving Society, vgns, 1900s, EX..................45.00
Check, Bank of Gays, IL, dtd 1909, 3x8", EX...............................15.00
Check, Marine Bank, New Bedford MA, whaling vgn, 1862, G....20.00
Check, NM Territory, mining company, vgn, 1900, EX 20.00
Check, Office of VA Fire & Marine Ins, Richmond, 1873 ....15.00
Check, Washoe Smelter stack vgn, Anaconda MT, 1926, EX........ 4.00
Check, WY Territory, Fort Bridger, 1886, 4x9", EX 85.00
Commission, to military officer, vellum, dtd 1750, EX 30.00
Company orders, handwritten, need for drill/etc, 1813, 8x12".......18.00
Confederate exemption, VA, deaf man, 1862, EX 23.00
Contract, MS Territory, transporting mails, 1817, 12-pg, EX 15.00
Criminal complaint, MT, men fighting, dtd 1889, 8x14" 30.00
Deed, AZ ranch, printed, dtd 1888, 2-pg 25.00
Deed, CO, printed, filled out, not sgn, 1880, 11x17" 25.00
Deed, Norfolk NY, handwritten, 1852, 10x16", EX 10.00
Deed, quit claim; NY, handwritten, 1859, VG 8.00
Envelope, UT, Wells Fargo Express, 1880s, EX 25.00
Express way bill, GA, shipping stove to AL, 1861, EX....................24.00
Extradition papers, WV, custody of murderer, 1899, EX 21.00
Field note, Hopkins Co, boundaries, 1888, 3-pg, EX 15.00
Field orders, TN Army, looting criticism, 1864, 1½-pg..................40.00
General orders, re court martials, 1864, 4½x7", EX 15.00
Indenture papers, Colonial VA, handwritten, 1698, 12x14", EX..110.00
Indenture papers, England, 2 seals, dtd 1724, 31x23", VG............65.00
Indenture papers, printed, 8-year old orphan, 1807, 8x12" 28.00
Insurance policy, NY, $335 on house, etc, 1863, G 8.00
Inventory report, weapons of 9th NY near Petersburg, EX.............10.00
Invoice, CA, quartermaster funds, handwritten, 1873, 8x10" 45.00
Invoice, IN, cattle sales, vgn, 9x12", EX 15.00
Land claim, MT Territory, stag vgn, 1866, EX 45.00
Land grant, PA, vellum, sgn by governor, 1852, 12x17", EX 20.00
Ledger sheet, NV, gold dust/Orientals, ca 1880, EX.....................30.00
Letter, CA, San Francisco news/mining mentioned, 1906, 3-pg....15.00
Letter, CA, typed, mining info, colorful, 1905, 7-pg 15.00
Letter, IA, cavalry soldier's news, 1863, 2-pg, VG........................30.00
Letter, ID Territory, business, Express letterhead, 2-pg 30.00
Letter, MT, First Nat'l Bank letterhead, 1876, 1-pg......................25.00
Letter, MT, printed, vining letterhead, 1887, 2½-pg......................20.00
Letter, OK, Sheriff's letterhead, to Smith & Wesson, 1927 ....10.00
Letter, Union Soldier news from near Atlanta, 1862, 4-pg.............30.00
Letter to Congress, Sec of War lists officers, 1866, 6-pg 10.00
License, liquor store, dtd 1863, EX... 9.00
List of supplies, Continental Army needs, 1777, EX 25.00

Memorandum, NV, lists silver bars/coinage at mint, 1886.............20.00
Military pass, LA, to attend drill, 1862, EX 28.50
Muster roll, NJ, lists men & supplies, 1816, 11x18", EX 24.00
Muster roll, 53rd Colored Infantry, X mks, dtd 1864, EX..............22.00
Order, ID Territory, Fort Laramie, hay for beds, 1864 ....45.00
Ordinance, ME, firearms for volunteers, 1862 ....25.00
Pay voucher, TN, Gen JA Maltby, sgn twice, 1864, G.................45.00
Payroll, NV, gold miners' wages, w/voucher, 1907, 8x14".............20.00
Prospectus, Goldfield Mascot Mining, 1907, 15-pg, EX 25.00
Prospectus, NM, Sierra Gold Mining Co, 1904, 40-pg, 6x9" 30.00
Receipt, American Express, NY, 1869, 4x8", EX 20.00
Receipt, Civil War shipment of arms, 1862, 5x8", VG 32.00
Receipt, NM Territory, handwritten, forage, 1868, 6x8" 25.00
Receipt, NV, payment for labor in silver mine, 1865, 4x8" 35.00
Receipt, NY, $1000 of shale oil, 1919, 2½x8", VG 10.00
Receipt, NY, freight from steamer Croton, 1845, VG....................15.00
Receipt, Paducah KY Quartermaster Stores, lumber/etc, 1865.......15.00
Receipt, Providence Assoc of Fireman, aid for injured, 1859.........18.00
Receipt, San Francisco, Wells Fargo, 1886, 4x7" 20.00
Receipt, VA, Civil War supplies, dtd 1864, 10x16", VG 24.00
Sheriff's writ, AL, bond on Negro man, 1844, 5x8", EX 22.00
Slave order, Richmond, assigned work for Confederacy, 1862.......28.00
Statement, exchange of prisoners, NY, 1780, EX 65.00
Statement, KS, military payment lost, 1868, 1-pg 25.00
Taxing of slave estate, VA, lists property, 1815, EX....................21.00
Voucher, salary of Walla Walla chief, 1870, EX..........................60.00

Dollhouses and Furnishings

Dollhouses were introduced commercially in this country late in the 1700s by Dutch craftsmen who settled in the East. By the mid-1800s, they had become meticulously detailed, divided into separate rooms, and lavishly furnished to reflect the opulence of the day. Originally intended for the amusement of adults of the household, by the latter 1800s their status had changed to that of a child's toy. Though many early dollhouses were lovingly hand-fashioned for a special little girl, those made commercially by such companies as Bliss and Schoenhut are highly valued.

Furniture and furnishings in the Biedermeier style featuring stenciled Victorian decorations often sell for several hundred dollars each. Other early pieces made of pewter, porcelain, or papier-mache are also quite valuable. Certainly less expensive but very collectible, nonetheless, is the quality, hallmarked plastic furniture produced during the forties by Renwal and Acme and the 1960s Petite Princess line produced by Ideal. In the listings that follow, dollhouses are litho paper on wood, unless otherwise noted. When no manufacturer or country of origin is noted, examples are German, turn of the century.

Our advisor for this category is Barbara Rosen; she is listed in the Directory under New Jersey. See also Miniatures.

Furniture

Andirons, Petite Princess, pr 5.00
Armchair, satin, Petite Princess, EX 15.00
Bed, brass, fancy, 1950s, for lg doll, VG 125.00
Bed, brn w/molded spread, Renwal, twin sz 5.00
Bed, ormolu brass, 3x5", VG..250.00
Bed, tubular brass, scrollwork, 1900s, 14x27x15", EX.........195.00
Chair, dining; Biedermeier 40.00
Chair, parlor; uphl, Biedermeier.......................................185.00
Chair, red w/yel seat, Renwal 4.00
Chair, rocker; Tootsie Toy, 1935, NM.................................22.50
Chair, wing bk, brocade, Petite Princess, M........................16.00

Fretwork bedroom furniture, oak; settee, bed, and armoire, 12½", EX, $450.00 for three pieces.

Chaise lounge, Little Hostess 12.00
Chandelier, brass w/3 glass globes, VG 350.00
Clock, grandfather; w/door, Little Hostess..........................9.50
Dining room set, Tootsie Toy, 1928, 8-pc, EX in box.............120.00
End table, CI, Arcade, ca 1925...88.00
Fireplace, Little Hostess 12.50
Fireplace, Petite Princess 20.00
Fireplace, unmk/unidentified, nickeled, 7½x7½x2½" 50.00
Grand piano, CI, Arcade, 1920s, VG 55.00
Grand piano, w/bench, Tootsie Toy, NM 40.00
Ice box, CI, Arcade, 1920s..100.00
Kitchen sink, CI, Arcade, ca 1925 ....100.00
Lamp, table; gr shade, Petite Princess...............................8.00
Log holder, brass, w/logs, Petite Princess...........................5.50
Play pen, pk, Renwal 12.50
Porch swing, CI, Arcade...35.00
Secretary desk, CI, Arcade, ca 1925..................................95.00
Sideboard, Biedermeier, 6" H...400.00
Slide, CI, Arcade...35.00
Sofa, cream & gold, Petite Princess, EX 25.00
Sofa & chair, CI, Arcade, ca 1925 ....195.00
Stepladder, CI, Arcade..35.00
Stove, tin, alcohol burning, brass accessories, 14" L, VG 400.00
Sweeper, Sally Ann, Arcade..65.00
Table, dining; w/2 chairs, Petite Princess..........................48.00
Table, drop leaf; gateleg style, w/2 drws, Little Hostess 14.00
Table, kitchen; ivory, plastic, Renwal................................7.00
Table, library; Tootsie Toy, 1925, EX 15.00
Table, rnd, ped ft, Renwall...7.00
Table, tilt-top; rnd, ped ft, Petite Princess 12.00
Table & 4 chairs, wood, Strombecker.................................35.00
Tea cart, metal, Tootsie Toy, 1920s, M...............................30.00
Tea cart w/mirror, metal, Germany, ca 1900, EX 50.00
Tub, pk & bl, Renwal 6.00
Vase, gold metal w/pearl flowers, Petite Princess 2.50

Houses

Bliss, 2-story/2-room, balcony/porch/stairs, 18x8½x10", EX 825.00
Bliss, 2-story/2-room, paper on wood, 1890s, 11x8x5", EX 600.00
Bliss type, 2-story/3-room, balcony/porch, rpt, 18x8x12" 385.00
English Tudor, 2-story/6-room, paper/wood, 22x39x13", EX.......325.00
Germany, bathroom, pnt int pcs, 13½" L, VG 500.00
Germany, kitchen, paper/pnt wood, pnt tin pcs, 13", EX...........325.00
Germany, kitchen, pnt wood, tin/wood pcs, 14x28x12", EX .. 1,100.00

Bliss, bright cream-colored 'clapboard' with yellow, red, and blue details; small balcony marked 'B'; simulated stained glass window, 17" x 11", EX, $700.00.

Germany, stable, litho on pnt wood, w/horses & cart, 9", VG.....**200.00**
Germany, Telegraph Station, pnt wood, hinged, 14½", VG **250.00**
Germany, Tudor, 2-story/4-room, pnt wood, 18½" L, VG....... **1,000.00**
Germany, 3-story/3-room, Victorian, 13" L, G............................**600.00**
Handmade, clapboard farmhouse, 2-story/4-room, 23x35x35".....**100.00**
McLoughlin Bros, folding, 4-room, Pat 1894, 12x12", EX **425.00**
Schoenhut, Colonial, 2-story/4-room, staircase, 24x25x17", EX ..**650.00**
Schoenhut, Colonial, 2-story/4-room, 16x17x11", VG...............**525.00**
Tootsie Toy #13, 2-story/5-room, completely furnished, NM . **1,400.00**
Unknown, stable, litho on pnt wood, w/2 horses, 8½", G **165.00**

Dolls

Collecting dolls of any sort is one of the most rewarding hobbies in the United States. The rewards are in the fun, the search, and the finds — plus there is a built-in factor of investment. No hobby, be it dolls, glass, or anything else, should be based completely on investment; but any collector should ask: 'Can I get my money back out of this item if I should ever have to sell it?' Many times we buy on impulse rather than with logic, which is understandable; but by asking this question we can save ourselves a lot of 'buyer's remorse' which we have all experienced at one time or another.

Since we want to learn to invest our money wisely while we are having fun, we must become aware of defects which may devaluate a doll. In bisque, watch for eye chips, hairline cracks and chips, or breaks on any part of the head. Composition should be clean, not crazed or cracked. Vinyl and plastic should be clean with no pen or crayon marks. Though a quality replacement wig is acceptable for bisque dolls, composition and hard plastics should have their originals in uncut condition. Original clothing is a must except in bisque dolls, since it is unusual to find one in its original costume.

A price guide is only that — a guide. It suggests the average price for each doll. Bargains can be found for less-than-suggested values, and 'unplayed-with' dolls in their original boxes may cost more. Dealers must become aware of condition so that they do not over-pay and therefore over-price their dolls — a common occurrence across the country. Quantity does not replace quality, as most find out in time. A faster turnover of sales with a smaller margin of profit is far better than being stuck with an item that does not sell because it is over-priced. It is important to remember that prices are based on condition and rarity. When no condition is noted, dolls are assumed to be in excellent condition with the exceptions of Armand Marseille, Madame Alexander, and Effanbee dolls, which are priced in mint condition. In relation to bisque dolls, excellent means having no cracks, chips, or hairlines,

being nicely dressed, shoed, wigged, and ready to to be placed into a collection. For a more thorough study of the subject, we recommend you refer to the many lovely doll books written by authority Pat Smith, available at your favorite bookstore or public library.

Key:
bjtd — ball-jointed
blb — bent limb body
bsk — bisque
c/m — closed mouth
hh — human hair
hp — hard plastic
jtd — jointed
MIG — Made In Germany
NC — no clothes
o/c — open closed

OC — original clothes
p/e — pierced ears
pnt — painted
pwt — paperweight eyes
RpC — replaced clothes
ShHd — shoulder head
ShPl — shoulder plate
SkHd — socket head
str — straight
trn — turned

Armand Marseille

Alma, ShHd, 12" **185.00**
Alma, ShHd, 15" **250.00**
Alma, ShHd, 26" **550.00**
AM, baby, flange neck, 1907, 16" **525.00**
AM, Darling Baby, 1906, 12" **325.00**
AM, Floradora, ShHd, 20" **395.00**
AM, Floradora, ShHd, 21½" **400.00**
AM, Floradora, ShHd, 23" **425.00**
AM, Floradora, ShHd, 24" **475.00**
AM, Floradora, SkHd, 12" **185.00**
AM, Floradora, SkHd, 15" **300.00**
AM, Floradora, SkHd, 17" **325.00**
AM, Floradora, SkHd, 27" **775.00**
AM, Floradora 1374, ShHd, fur eyebrows, 21" **475.00**
AM, Floradora 3748, ShHd, 21" **475.00**
AM, Indian, SkHd, o/c, 1890s, 8" **400.00**
AM, Kiddiejoy, ShHd, cloth body, c/m, girl, 20" **1,900.00**
AM, Kiddiejoy, ShHd, 9" **200.00**
AM, lady, SkHd, c/m, mk MH (Max Handwerck), 1913, 10" **950.00**
AM, My Dearie, SkHd, 1908, 14" **325.00**
AM, My Playmate (body), closed dome & c/m, 18" **1,400.00**
AM, Rosebud, ShHd, 1902, 15" **325.00**
AM, Roseland, 1910, 18" **400.00**
AM, ShHd, boy, 14" **300.00**
AM, SkHd, c/m, 14" **700.00**
AM, SkHd, CM Bergmann, 24" **565.00**
AM, SkHd, o/c eyes, 7" **125.00**
AM, SkHd, o/m, blk, 12" **475.00**
AM, SkHd, 16" **225.00**
AM, SkHd, 17" **295.00**
AM, SkHd, 26" **575.00**
AM, SkHd, 8" **165.00**
AM, Sunshine, ShHd, 1910, 24" **500.00**
AM, trn ShHd, talks, 16" **450.00**
AM 1894, ShPl, 26" **525.00**
AM 1894, SkHd, blk, 12" **475.00**
AM 1894, SkHd, wht, 12" **250.00**
AM 1894, SkHd, wht, 16½" **325.00**
AM 1894, SkHd, 14" **250.00**
AM 200, SkHd, googly eyes, 11½" **2,800.00**
AM 210, SkHd, googly eyes, 6" **1,800.00**
AM 231, Fany, baby, c/m, 1913, 25" **9,800.00**
AM 248, mk GB (G Borgfeldt), o/m, 1912, 10" **185.00**
AM 250, mk GB (G Borgfeldt), SkHd, c/m, molded hair, 10½"..**375.00**

AM 252, SkHd, googly eyes, 10" 800.00
AM 252, SkHd, googly eyes, 1915, 9½" 800.00
AM 253, SkHd, googly eyes, 1915, 16" 2,800.00
AM 253, SkHd, googly eyes, 6½" 750.00
AM 253, SkHd, googly eyes, 8" 900.00
AM 254, SkHd, googly eyes, molded hair, 8" 950.00
AM 255, SkHd, intaglio eyes, 7½" 425.00
AM 257, baby, SkHd, 1914, 22" 550.00
AM 300n, adult, SkHd, 15½" 600.00
AM 315, Queen Louise, SkHd, 27" 850.00
AM 320, SkHd, c/m, googly eyes, 6½" 650.00
AM 3200, ShHd, some trn, 15" 350.00
AM 3200, ShHd, some trn, 1898, 14" 285.00
AM 3200, ShHd, some trn, 1898, 16" 375.00
AM 3200, ShHd, some trn, 22" 500.00
AM 3200, ShHd, some trn, 26" 600.00
AM 323, SkHd, googly eyes, 11" 1,200.00
AM 323, SkHd, googly eyes, 7½" 850.00
AM 324, googly eyes, 7" 465.00
AM 327, SkHd, baby, fur hair, 1914, 12" 325.00
AM 327, SkHd, 1914, 12" 185.00
AM 327, SkHd, 1914, 20" 525.00
AM 328, baby, SkHd, closed dome, 1922, 14" 365.00
AM 329, girl, SkHd, 9" 250.00
AM 341, My Dream Baby, flange, c/m, wht, 8" 250.00
AM 341, My Dream Baby, flange, c/m, 15" 525.00
AM 341, My Dream Baby, flange, c/m, 18" 675.00
AM 341, My Dream Baby, flange, c/m, 1924, 7" 185.00
AM 341, My Dream Baby, flange, c/m, 21" 700.00
AM 341, My Dream Baby, SkHd, c/m, 16" 600.00
AM 347, SkHd, 1909, 16" 475.00
AM 3500, ShHd, 17" 400.00
AM 351, My Dream Baby, flange, o/m, wht, 22" 850.00
AM 351, My Dream Baby, flange, o/m, 26" 1,200.00
AM 351, My Dream Baby, flange, o/m, 6" 145.00
AM 351, Wee One, rubber body, 1922, 7" 165.00
AM 352, Baby Love, flange, 1914, 19" 625.00
AM 3524, Baby Gloria, flange neck, 18" 1,000.00
AM 362, Teenie Weenie, baby, closed dome, wht, 15" 400.00
AM 370, fur eyebrows, 22½" 425.00
AM 370, 12" 175.00
AM 370, 15" 250.00
AM 370, 15½" 250.00
AM 370, 16½" 300.00
AM 370, 19½" 325.00
AM 370n, 12" 175.00
AM 372, Kiddiejoy, ShHd, molded hair, 1926, 9" 350.00
AM 375, Kiddiejoy, girl, SkHd, c/m, molded hair, 20" 2,600.00
AM 390, My Dearie, SkHd, 1908-22, 18½" 425.00
AM 390, My Dearie, 23" 485.00
AM 390, o/m, 7½" 150.00
AM 390, pnt bsk, 9" 145.00
AM 390, walks, 22" 525.00
AM 390, 16" 365.00
AM 390, 18" 400.00
AM 390, 21" 450.00
AM 390, 22" 485.00
AM 390, 24" 525.00
AM 390, 9½" 225.00
AM 390n, Louisa, 1915, 27" 625.00
AM 390n, Patrice, 18" 650.00
AM 390n, 1915, 11" 275.00
AM 395, Heidi, SkHd, 1920, 9" 225.00
AM 402, SkHd, pnt bsk, 14" 250.00

AM 450, SkHd, c/m, provincial attire, 19" 1,000.00
AM 500, Infant Berry, molded hair, 1908, 10" 500.00
AM 500, Infant Berry, molded hair, 1908, 5" 250.00
AM 500, Infant Berry, molded hair, 1908, 8" 300.00
AM 550, SkHd, c/m, 16" 2,400.00
AM 560a, Dorothy, 1912, 15" 550.00
AM 590, Hoopla Girl, o/c eyes & mouth, 16" 1,600.00
AM 600, SkHd, flange, c/m, 1910, 10" 1,200.00
AM 800, Baby Sunshine, 'Mama' talker in head, 1925, 16" 2,100.00
AM 917, Mobi, baby, Germany, Skhd, 1921, 16" 450.00
AM 95, trn ShHd, 20" 425.00
AM 966, baby, SkHd, flirty eyes, 14" 450.00
AM 970, Ladie Marie, Otto Gans, 1916, 20" 650.00
AM 975, Sadie, baby, Otto Gans, 1914, 17" 525.00
AM 975, Sadie, baby, SkHd, 1914, 24" 700.00
AM 975, Sadie, baby, SkHd, 1914, 9" 200.00
AM 980, baby, SkHd, 14" 350.00
AM 985, baby, SkHd, 13½" 400.00
AM 990, Happy Tot, baby, SkHd, 13" 400.00
AM 990, Happy Tot, baby, SkHd, 1910, 16" 450.00
AM 990, Happy Tot, baby, SkHd, 1910, 21" 675.00
AM 990, Happy Tot, baby, SkHd, 8" 185.00
AM 991, Kiddiejoy, baby, SkHd, 14" 400.00
AM 992, baby, SkHd, 1914, 22" 750.00
AM 995, baby, SkHd, 12" 300.00
AM 996, baby, SkHd, 15" 425.00
AM 997, Kiddiejoy, baby, SkHd, 14" 400.00
Columbia, ShHd, 1904, 24" 550.00
Lily, ShHd, 1913, 17" 300.00
Mabel, ShHd, 1898, 15" 250.00
Mabel, ShHd, 1898, 17" 300.00
Queen Louise, SkHd, 1910, 22" 450.00
Queen Louise, 100, Germany, SkHd, 1910, 12" 250.00
Queen Louise, 100, SkHd, 1910, 18½" 425.00
Wonderful Alice, SkHd, fur eyebrows, 26" 650.00

Barbie Dolls and Related Dolls

Though the face has changed three times since 1959, Barbie is still as popular today as she was when she was first introduced. Named after the young daughter of the first owner of the Mattel Company, the original Barbie had a white iris but no eye color. These dolls are nearly impossible to find, but there is a myriad of her successors and related collectibles just waiting to be found. When no condition is indicated, the dolls listed below are assumed to be nude and in excellent condition unless otherwise specified. For further information, we recommend *An Illustrated Price Guide to Collectible Barbie Dolls* by Paris, Susan, and Carol Manos; and *The Collector's Encyclopedia of Barbie Dolls and Collectibles* by Sibyl DeWein and Joan Ashabraner.

Barbie, 1959, #1, blond, swimsuit, holes in feet, MIB 2,500.00
Barbie, 1960, #3, bl eyes, curved brows, ivory skin, MIB..............350.00
Barbie, 1960, #4, vinyl plastic, tan skin 250.00
Barbie, 1961, #5, hollow body, curly bangs, MIB....................200.00
Barbie, 1961, Bubble Cut, MIB 150.00
Barbie, 1963, Fashion Queen, w/3 wigs, swimsuit, MIB 250.00
Barbie, 1964, Ponytail Swirl, no curly bangs...............250.00
Barbie, 1965, Dutch boy hairstyle, bendable legs, MIB 165.00
Barbie, 1967, Twist 'N Turn, MIB 85.00
Barbie, 1968, Spanish Talking, MIB 185.00
Barbie, 1971, Dramatic New Living, MIB.......................75.00
Barbie, 1972, Busy, long blond hair..............................85.00
Barbie, 1972, Walk Lively Miss America, Kellogg, MIB 75.00
Barbie, 1973, Quick Curl, blond, bendable knees..........85.00

Barbie, 1974, Sun Valley, w/ski accessories, MIB 80.00
Barbie, 1974, Sweet Sixteen, Barbie's birthday, MIB 85.00
Barbie, 1975, Free Moving, blond, MIB 70.00
Barbie, 1975, Hawaiian, str hair, grass skirt, MIB 75.00
Barbie, 1976, Ballerina, blond ponytail, wht tutu, MIB................40.00
Barbie, 1976, Beautiful Bride, bendable knees, w/gown, MIB 85.00
Barbie, 1976, Plus 3, in package, M..75.00
Barbie, 1978, Beautiful Bride, MIB 40.00
Barbie, 1978, Fashion Photo, remote control play camera, MIB....60.00
Barbie, 1978, Super Star, In the Spotlight, w/3 outfits, MIB.........85.00
Barbie, 1979, Kissing, w/2 gowns, lipstick, & stand, MIB..............65.00
Barbie, 1980, Beauty Secrets, MIB 30.00
Barbie, 1981, Western, MIB..25.00
Barbie, 1983, Twirly Curls..25.00
Brad, 1970, Talking, Black, pnt hair, MIB 125.00
Brad, 1971, bendable legs, MIB 85.00
Cara, 1975, Free Moving, Black, long hair w/bows, MIB 70.00
Cara, 1976, Ballerina, Black, swivel head & arms, blk hair...........60.00
Carla, 1965, Black, blk ponytail w/wht ribbon, MIB 45.00
Casey, 1967, blond or brunette, MIB...125.00
Casey, 1975, Baggie, blond, str legs, swimsuit, MIB......................50.00
Christie, 1969, Talking, Black..95.00
Christie, 1976, Super Star, MIB...55.00
Christie, 1979, Kissing, w/lipstick, MIB..45.00
Christie, 1980, Golden Dream, 2nd issue, MIB.............................40.00
Curtis, 1976, Free Moving, MIB..60.00
Francie, 1966, str legs, pnt lashes, swimsuit 100.00
Francie, 1967, Black, 1st issue, brn eyes/red oxidized hair............400.00
Francie, 1970, Growin' Pretty Hair, MIB......................................90.00
Francie, 1970, Hair Happenin's, 4 blond hairpieces, MIB............165.00
Francie, 1978, Malibu, MIB...35.00
Guardian Goddess, Sun Spell, MIB 165.00
Julia, 1969, Twist 'N Turn, 2-pc nurse's uniform, MIB 185.00
Ken, 1961, Flocked Hair, movable head, arms, & legs 125.00
Ken, 1969, Talking, bendable knees, jacket & shorts, MIB 150.00
Ken, 1970, Spanish Talking, bl & orange outfit, MIB..................175.00
Ken, 1972, Walk Lively, pnt hair, MIB 95.00
Ken, 1973, Mod Hair, MIB..30.00
Ken, 1974, Ward's Dressed, bl & blk tuxedo, mod hair, MIB 165.00
Ken, 1976, Funtime, bl trunks, MIB..50.00
Ken, 1976, Gold Medal Skier, w/skis & ski poles, MIB.................60.00
Ken, 1976, Now Look, MIB 35.00
Ken, 1977, Super Star, w/free gift, MIB 75.00
Ken, 1981, Western, MIB...30.00
Ken, 1982, All Star, MIB..35.00
Kitty O'Neil, MIB 45.00
Kristie McNichol, MIB..40.00
Midge, 1965, bendable legs, bouffant hair 150.00
Miss America, 1972, Kellogg's Walk Lively, wht gown, MIB 250.00
Miss America, 1974, Kellogg's Blond Quick Curl, MIB...............100.00
PJ, 1971, Live Action PJ on Stage 95.00
PJ, 1975, Gold Medal Gymnast, w/balance beam 50.00
PJ, 1976, Deluxe Quick Curl, MIB 40.00
PJ, 1976, Free Moving, MIB..45.00
Ricky, 1965, red hair, str legs, freckles 100.00
Skipper, 1967, Funtime, blond, bendable knees 80.00
Skipper, 1970, Pose 'N Play, MIB..60.00
Skipper, 1976, Growing Up, MIB..45.00
Skipper, 1979, Super Teen, MIB..30.00
Skipper, 1981, Western, MIB...30.00
Skooter, 1964, str legs, MIB...85.00
Skooter, 1965, str legs, pigtails & freckles.....................................40.00
Stacey, 1968, Talking, British accent, w/plastic box 125.00
Stacey, 1968, Twist 'N Turn, MIB 90.00

Steffie, 1972, Busy Talking, blond 145.00
Tiff, 1972, Pose 'N Play, swing-free arms 65.00
Truly Scrumptious, 1969, Talking, bendable legs.........................250.00
Twiggy, 1967, blond, bendable knees, mini dress, MIB................145.00

Barbie Gift Sets and Related Accessories

When no condition is indicated, the items listed below are assumed to be mint and in the original box.

Barbie, Sun Shower Play Set, M in pkg 80.00
Barbie & Ken Dune Buggy, Irwin..80.00
Barbie & PJ Olympic Gymnast Set, MIB.......................................35.00
Barbie Autograph Book, 1962, M...20.00
Barbie Baby-Sitting Room, Canada, MIB 95.00
Barbie Ballerina Fashion, Princess Aurora, MIB............................40.00
Barbie Ballerina Fashion, Snow Fairy, MIB 35.00
Barbie Ballerina Fashion, Sugar Plum Fairy, MIB.........................45.00
Barbie Ballerina Stage, MIB...20.00
Barbie Diary, 1963, M 25.00
Barbie Fur Collection Gift, MIB...95.00
Barbie Make-Up Case, 1963, M..20.00
Barbie Malibu Beach Party Play Set, w/doll, M in case 65.00
Barbie Motor Roller, w/Funtime Barbie, MIB...............................100.00
Barbie Olympic Ski Village, MIB..40.00
Barbie Photo Album, 1963, lg, M..35.00
Barbie Playhouse, Europe, MIB..75.00
Barbie Record Tote, 1961, M..18.00

Barbie Round the Clock Gift Set #1013, 1964 booklet, MIB, $600.00.

Barbie Sew-Free Fashion Fun...20.00
Barbie Silver Vette, MIB...35.00
Barbie Star Cycle, MIB...20.00
Barbie Superstar Photo Studio, Canada, MIB.................................60.00
Barbie Superstar Stage, MIB...30.00
Barbie Sweet 16 Necklace, promotional, M....................................10.00
Barbie Travelin' Trailer, MIB..45.00
Barbie Wrist Watch, sm dial..50.00
Clothes, Arabian Nights, #0874 (1963 booklet) 45.00
Clothes, Barbie Bicentennial Dress, M in pkg.................................35.00
Clothes, Barbie Dress Collection, MIB, ea......................................50.00
Clothes, Barbie McDonald outfit, M in pkg.....................................30.00
Clothes, Chill Chaser #1926 (1965 booklet)....................................45.00
Clothes, Evening Gala, #1660 (1965 booklet) 55.00
Clothes, Fur & Leather Collection, Germany, ea..............................60.00

Clothes, Heavenly Holidays, Series 1, MIB 30.00
Clothes, Icebreaker, #942 (1962 booklet)................................35.00
Clothes, Ken Casual Clothes, MIB, ea...................................70.00
Clothes, Ken Dress Suit, MIB, ea 75.00
Clothes, Ken in Mexico, #0820 (1963 booklet) 65.00
Clothes, Ken Suit Collection, MIB, ea 45.00
Clothes, Oscar De La Renta, Series 4-5, MIB, ea 20.00
Clothes, Princess Aurora, 1976-86, MIB................................35.00
Clothes, Roman Holiday, #964 (#1 1958 booklet).......................185.00
Clothes, Silver Sensation, Series 3, MIB..............................35.00
Clothes, Skipper Bicentennial Set, M in pkg...........................40.00
Clothes, Snow Fairy, 1976-86, MIB 30.00
Clothes, Springtime Magic, Series 2, MIB..............................25.00
Clothes, Sugar Plum Fairy, 1976-86, MIB...............................25.00
Dallas, Barbie's horse, jointed legs, Germany, MIB 95.00
Dancer, Barbie's horse, w/Barbie, Canada, MIB 95.00
Honey, Skipper's horse, MIB...25.00
Midnight, Barbie's stallion, MIB 20.00
Skipper 'N Skooter Double Bunk Beds & Ladder 55.00

Belton

Concave head, 2 or 3 hole, EX bsk, o/c or c/m w/wig, 10" 1,500.00
Concave head, 2 or 3 hole, EX bsk, o/c or c/m w/wig, 13" 1,900.00
Concave head, 2 or 3 hole, EX bsk, o/c or c/m w/wig, 15" 2,200.00
Concave head, 2 or 3 hole, EX bsk, o/c or c/m w/wig, 16" 2,300.00
Concave head, 2 or 3 hole, EX bsk, o/c or c/m w/wig, 17" 2,400.00
Concave head, 2 or 3 hole, EX bsk, o/c or c/m w/wig, 20" 3,000.00
Concave head, 2 or 3 hole, EX bsk, o/c or c/m w/wig, 22" 3,200.00
Concave head, 2 or 3 hole, EX bsk, o/c or c/m w/wig, 23" 3,300.00
Concave head, 2 or 3 hole, EX bsk, o/c or c/m w/wig, 26" 3,800.00
Concave head, 2 or 3 hole, EX bsk, o/c or c/m w/wig, 8" 975.00

Bru

Closed mouth, all kid body, bsk lower arms; Bru, 16" 9,000.00
Closed mouth, all kid body, bsk lower arms; Bru, 18" 12,000.00
Closed mouth, all kid body, bsk lower arms; Bru, 21" 18,000.00
Closed mouth, all kid body, bsk lower arms; Bru, 26" 24,000.00
Closed mouth, kid/wood body, bsk lower arms; Bru Jne, 12" .20,000.00
Closed mouth, kid/wood body, bsk lower arms; Bru Jne, 14" .18,000.00
Closed mouth, kid/wood body, bsk lower arms; Bru Jne, 16" .20,000.00
Closed mouth, kid/wood body, bsk lower arms; Bru Jne, 20" .24,000.00
Closed mouth, kid/wood body, bsk lower arms; Bru Jne, 25" .30,000.00
Closed mouth, kid/wood body, bsk lower arms; Bru Jne, 28" .36,000.00
Closed mouth, kid/wood body, bsk lower arms; Bru Jne, 32" .42,000.00
Closed mouth, mk Bru, circle dot, 16" 22,000.00
Closed mouth, mk Bru, circle dot, 19" 25,000.00
Closed mouth, mk Bru, circle dot, 23" 29,000.00
Closed mouth, mk Bru, circle dot, 26" 32,000.00
Open mouth, comp walker's body, throws kisses, 18" 5,600.00
Open mouth, comp walker's body, throws kisses, 22" 6,400.00
Open mouth, comp walker's body, throws kisses, 26" 7,300.00
Open mouth, nursing (Bebe), high color, late SFBJ, 12" 1,900.00
Open mouth, nursing (Bebe), high color, late SFBJ, 15" 2,800.00
Open mouth, nursing (Bebe), high color, late SFBJ, 18" 3,400.00
Open mouth, nursing Bru (Bebe), early, EX bsk, 12"............. 5,600.00
Open mouth, nursing Bru (Bebe), early, EX bsk, 15" 7,800.00
Open mouth, nursing Bru (Bebe), early, EX bsk, 18" 9,700.00
Open mouth, socket head, compo body; Bru, R, 14", EX bsk .. 4,800.00
Open mouth, socket head, compo body; Bru, R, 17", EX bsk .. 6,000.00
Open mouth, socket head, compo body; Bru, R, 22", EX bsk .. 8,200.00
Open mouth, socket head, compo body; Bru, R, 25", EX bsk .. 8,200.00

Bru, 26" swivel-head with cork pate, paperweight eyes, pierced ears, kid body, bisque lower arms, carved wood lower legs, $24,000.00.

Open mouth, socket head, compo body; Bru, R, 28", EX bsk .. 9,000.00

Bye-Lo

#1269, compo body, bsk SkHd, K&W, 14" 1,600.00
#1360/30, compo, jtd, o/c eyes, Grace S Putnam, RpC, 11".........475.00
Bl sleep eyes, mk head & body, christening gown, 16" 1,000.00
Bsk, pnt eyes, molded hair, jtd hips/shoulders, 8" 625.00
Bsk/cloth, o/c eyes, cm, c Grace Putnam, MIG, RpC, 11" 550.00
Cloth w/celluloid hands, o/c eyes, c/m, 1923, Putnam, 14" 950.00
Cloth w/celluloid hands, 15" bsk head, o/c eyes, OC, 18" 1,600.00
Compo hands, christening gown & hat, 21" 1,900.00
Frozen bsk, lying on bk, arms/legs raised, 3½" 350.00
Molded bl shoes, molded hair, glass eyes, OC, carriage, 5"..........625.00
O/c eyes, cloth w/compo hands, str legs, 1923, Putnam, 12".........575.00
Vinyl/cloth, pnt eyes, molded hair, Grace Storey Putnam, 16"....300.00

China, Unmarked

Adelina Patti, center part, curls at temples, 1860s, 14" 350.00
Adelina Patti, center part, curls at temples, 1860s, 18" 500.00
Adelina Patti, center part, curls at temples, 1860s, 22" 675.00
Biedermeier or Bald Head, takes wig, RpC, 14" 975.00
Biedermeier or Bald Head, takes wig, RpC, 20" 1,500.00
Brown Eyes (pnt), any hairstyle or date, 16"................................950.00
Brown Eyes (pnt), any hairstyle or date, 20" 1,400.00
Common Hairdo, blond or blk hair, RpC, after 1905, 12" 145.00
Common Hairdo, blond or blk hair, RpC, after 1905, 23" 200.00
Common Hairdo, blond or blk hair, RpC, after 1905, 8" 85.00
Covered Wagon Style, sausage curls, RpC, 1840s-70s, 12" 425.00
Covered Wagon Style, sausage curls, RpC, 1840s-70s, 24" 850.00
Curly Top, loose ringlet curls, RpC, 1845-60s, 16" 625.00
Curly Top, loose ringlet curls, RpC, 1845-60s, 20" 750.00
Dolly Madison, modeled ribbon & bow, RpC, 1870-80s, 14" 275.00
Dolly Madison, modeled ribbon & bow, RpC, 1870-80s, 18" 485.00
Dolly Madison, modeled ribbon & bow, RpC, 1870-80s, 21" 550.00
Flat Top, blk hair, mid-part/short curls, RpC, ca 1860, 17" 285.00
Flat Top, blk hair, mid-part/short curls, RpC, ca 1860, 20" 325.00
Glass Eyes, various hairstyles, RpC, 1840s-70s, 14" 2,000.00
Glass Eyes, various hairstyles, RpC, 1840s-70s, 22" 3,000.00
Japanese, blk or blond hair, mk or unmk, RpC, 1910-20s, 14"....145.00
Japanese, blk or blond hair, mk or unmk, RpC, 1910-20s, 17".....185.00
Man or Boy, glass eyes, side part, RpC, 14" 1,600.00
Man or Boy, pnt eyes, side part, RpC, 14", EX 1,200.00
Man or Boy, pnt eyes, side part, RpC, 16" 1,400.00
Man or Boy, pnt eyes, side part, RpC, 21½" 3,400.00

Peg Wood Body, early hairdo, 16", EX **3,800.00**
Pet Name, molded shirtwaist w/name on front, RpC, 1905, 19"..**350.00**
Pet Name, molded shirtwaist w/name on front, RpC, 1905, 8"....**125.00**
Pierced Ears, various hairstyles, RpC, 14" **600.00**
Pierced Ears, various hairstyles, RpC, 18" **850.00**
Snood/Combs, any appl hair decor, RpC, 14" **600.00**
Snood/Combs, any appl hair decor, RpC, 17" **850.00**
Spill Curls, w/or w/out head band, RpC, 14" **450.00**
Spill Curls, w/or w/out head band, RpC, 22" **775.00**
Wood Body, articulated/slim hips, RpC, 1840s-50s, 12" **1,500.00**
Wood Body, articulated/slim hips, RpC, 1840s-50s, 17" **4,600.00**
Wood Body, jtd hips, covered-wagon hairdo, 1840s-50s, 12" **950.00**
Wood Body, jtd hips, covered-wagon hairdo, 1840s-50s, 15" . **1,900.00**

Cloth

Amish, plain face, bl dress/wht apron, rag stuffed, 13" **100.00**
Blk boy, embr features, button eyes, OC, 1910s, 15" **250.00**
Chase, stockinette, ca 1900, jtd limbs, 16", EX.......................**1,000.00**
Drayton, Chocolate Drop, pnt face, label, 11" **400.00**
Jack & Jill, litho on cloth, Arbuckle Coffee, EX, pr **100.00**

Little Lulu, painted features on cloth, black yarn hair, 1920s, 15", $400.00; Orphan Annie, painted features on cloth, red mohair, original clothes, offered by *Saturday Evening Post* **as premium ca 1920, 18", $600.00.**

Merry Marie, American Litho, ca 1900, 24", M **300.00**
Red Riding Hood, litho on cloth, 1890s, EX **165.00**
Silk face, yarn hair, handmade, 1920s, OC, 12", EX **45.00**

Effanbee

Bernard Fleischaker and Hugo Baum became business partners in 1910; and, after two difficult years of finding toys to buy and a retail market to sell them in, they decided to manufacture dolls of their own. Their lovely dolls were a decided success largely because of their dedication to their work and the mutual trust and respect they held for each other. This is reflected in the Effanbee trademark — Eff stands for Fleischaker and bee for Baum. The company still exists today.

Bedtime Story Collection, 1972, ea **55.00**
Button Nose, compo, OC, 9" **175.00**
Candy Kid, compo, jtd, o/c eyes, molded hair, OC, 13" **300.00**
Colonial Prosperity, Historical Series, pnt eyes, OC, 14" **1,200.00**
Currier & Ives Collection, 1978-80, ea..**65.00**
Happy Boy, 1959-65, 11"...**70.00**
Lee, compo/cloth, OC, 18" **125.00**
Little Lady, compo/rubber w/pnt, o/c eyes, yarn hair, 27" **800.00**
Lovems, compo, o/c eyes, o/m w/teeth, molded hair, 18" **300.00**
Noma Electronic Talker, 1949-51, 30" **175.00**
Patsy Baby, compo, celluloid over tin o/c eyes, c/m, 10" **285.00**
Patsy Ruth, compo, jtd, glass eyes, heart bracelet, RpC, 26" **725.00**

Regal Heirloom Collection, 1976-78, ea..**95.00**
Strolling in the Park, 1982-83 ....**55.00**
Sweetie Pie, compo, strung limbs/head, o/c eyes, wig, 16" **200.00**
Twinkie, vinyl (thin), o/c eyes, o/m nurser, 1980, OC, 16" **35.00**

Half Dolls

Half dolls, lovely porcelain figures awaiting attachment to secure bases, were never meant to be objects of play. Most of these lovely ladies were firmly sewn into pincushion bases that were beautifully decorated and served as the skirt of their gown. Other skirts were actually covers for items on milady's dressing table. Some were used for parasol or brush handles or for tops to candy containers or perfume bottles. Most popular from 1900 to about 1930, they will most often be found marked with the country of their origin — Bavaria, Germany, France, and Japan. You may also find some fine quality pieces marked Goebel, Dressel and Kester, and Heubach.

For further information we recommend *The Collector's Encyclopedia of Half Dolls* by Frieda Marion and Norma Werner, available at your local bookstore or from Collector Books.

Arms & hands away from body, china or bsk, 12" **900.00**
Arms & hands away from body, china or bsk, 5" **300.00**
Arms & hands away from body, china or bsk, 8" **425.00**
Arms & hands to body, china, 3"..**25.00**
Arms & hands to body, china, 5"..**35.00**
Arms & hands to body, china, 8"..**50.00**
Arms & hands to body, papier-mache or compo, 3" **15.00**
Arms & hands to body, papier-mache or compo, 5" **22.00**
Arms away, hands to body, china or bsk, 3" **60.00**
Arms away, hands to body, china or bsk, 5" **70.00**
Arms away, hands to body, china or bsk, 8" **95.00**
Child or man, jtd shoulders, 3"..**40.00**
Child or man, jtd shoulders, 5"..**65.00**
Child or man, jtd shoulders, 7"..**95.00**
Japan, mk, 3" **15.00**
Japan, mk, 5" **28.00**
Japan, mk, 7" **45.00**
Jtd shoulders, wax over papier-mache, 4" **38.00**
Jtd shoulders, wax over papier-mache, 7" **90.00**

German half doll, lady holding teacup, no mark, 4½", $195.00.

Handwerck

#10, compo, jtd, p/c eyes, p/e, 18" **525.00**
#109-13¾, o/c eyes, o/m/teeth, p/e, curly wig, jtd, 25" **950.00**

#119-13, o/c eyes, o/m, jtd compo, RpC, 28", VG 1,000.00
#69 12x, o/m, o/c eyes, p/e, jtd, RpC, 24", VG 650.00
#69-12, bl o/c eyes, o/m/teeth, braided wig, RpC, 23½" 600.00
#99, o/c eyes, o/m, p/e, jtd compo, 1900s, RpC, 21" 550.00
Child, bsk, bjtd, glass eyes, o/m, wig, after 1885, RpC, 18" 475.00

Heubach

#1000-0, o/c eyes, o/m, jtd, RpC, 16½", EX 500.00
#10633, Dainty Dorothy, o/m, glass eyes, RpC, 16" 525.00

Heubach boy, all bisque, jointed, 9", $900.00.

#3/0, bsk ShHd, intaglio eyes, c/m, flocked hair, RpC, 10" 400.00
#5730, Santa, child body, o/c eyes, jtd, 20" 2,800.00
#7604, laughing child, compo, glass eyes, 15" 1,400.00
#7634, crying baby, o/c eyes, RpC, 15" 1,300.00
#7977, Baby Stuart, bsk bonnet, glass eyes, RpC, 12" 1,600.00
#8774, Whistling Jim, eyes to side, puckered mouth, 16" 1,000.00
#9373, bsk, googly eyes, c/m, 5-pc body, RpC, 7" 750.00
Character boy, bsk SkHd, intaglio eyes, crying face, 11" 650.00

Horsman

Blink, compo w/cloth body closed eyes, RpC, 13" 275.00

Pair of composition Campbell Kids by Horsman, molded hair, painted eyes, original costumes and tags, ca 1948, 12½", $450.00 for the pair.

Dimples Toddler, RpC, 15" 175.00
Ella Cinders, compo/cloth, pnt eyes, molded hair, RpC, 18" 575.00
Pippi Longstocking, 1972, MIB 35.00
Pram Baby, vinyl, glass o/c eyes, c/m, trns head/coos, 19" 65.00
Ruthie, vinyl, glass o/c eyes, c/m, jtd, walks/talks, 16" 25.00
Tynie Baby, bsk head, o/c eyes, molded hair, RpC, 12" 675.00

Ideal

Baby Jane, compo, o/c eyes, o/m w/teeth, orig wig, RpC, 18" 250.00
Betsy Wetsy, compo w/rubber body, molded hair, 14" 120.00
Betty Jane, compo, o/c eyes, o/m w/teeth, OC, 18" 300.00
Deanna Durbin, compo, o/c eyes, o/m w/teeth, OC, 14" 450.00
Jiminy Cricket, compo & wood, 9" 265.00
Miss Revlon, hp/plastic, rooted hair, o/c eyes, c/m, OC, 17" 200.00
Pinocchio, compo & wood, molded head, pnt features, 10½" 265.00
Princess Mary, plastic/vinyl, ballgown/wrist tags, 1952, 21" 200.00
Sara Ann, hp, o/c eyes, c/m, jtd, OC, 14" 250.00
Saralee, vinyl/cloth, o/c eyes, o/c mouth, RpC, 18" 185.00
Toni, Red Cross Nurse, hp, o/c eyes, orig wig, OC, 15" 300.00

Jumeau

Emile Jumeau took over his father's doll company sometime in the 1870s. He brought many new innovations and ideas to the business. One fascination Jumeau had concerned dolls' eyes and led to the patents for eyelids that dropped over the eye itself; a second type allowed the doll to 'sleep.' Jumeau's distaste for German dolls is apparent in the booklets that were packaged with his dolls. These booklets referred to the German dolls as cheap and ugly and and as having 'stupid' faces. In reality, these less-expensive dolls were the downfall of the French doll manufacturers, and in 1899 the Jumeau company had to combine with several others in an effort to save the French doll industry from the German competition.

Closed mouth, mk EJ (incised) Jumeau, 10" 5,200.00
Closed mouth, mk EJ (incised) Jumeau, 14" 5,700.00
Closed mouth, mk EJ (incised) Jumeau, 16" 6,200.00
Closed mouth, mk EJ (incised) Jumeau, 19" 6,600.00
Closed mouth, mk EJ (incised) Jumeau, 21" 7,200.00
Closed mouth, mk Tete Jumeau, 10" 3,600.00
Closed mouth, mk Tete Jumeau, 14" 3,300.00
Closed mouth, mk Tete Jumeau, 16" 3,800.00
Closed mouth, mk Tete Jumeau, 19" 4,200.00
Closed mouth, mk Tete Jumeau, 21" 4,800.00
Closed mouth, mk Tete Jumeau, 23" 5,300.00
Closed mouth, mk Tete Jumeau, 25" 5,500.00
Closed mouth, mk Tete Jumeau, 28" 6,400.00
Closed mouth, mk Tete Jumeau, 30" 7,000.00
Depose/Tete Jumeau, swivel head, p/e, long curls, 18" 6,200.00
Depose/Tete Jumeau, swivel head, p/e, long curls, 28" 9,200.00
E 6 J/Jumeau, swivel head, inset eyes, kid body, 16" 5,800.00
E 6 J/Jumeau, swivel head, inset eyes, kid body, 20" 6,600.00
EJ/Depose Brevete, swivel head, inset eyes, 'mama/papa,' 16" . 5,800.00
Jumeau 1907, SkHd, appl ears, o/m, 18" 2,400.00
Jumeau 1907, swivel head, o/m, o/c eyes, p/e, 18" 2,400.00
Jumeau 1907, swivel head, o/m, o/c eyes, p/e, 23" 2,800.00
Jumeau 1909, swivel head, o/m, inset eyes, p/e, 21" 2,600.00
Long face, c/m, 21" 23,000.00
Long face, c/m, 30" 26,000.00
Mechanical/musical, cm, p/e, pwt eyes, hh, 12" on 4" box 3,800.00
Open mouth, mk Tete Jumeau, 10" 995.00
Open mouth, mk Tete Jumeau, 14" 1,400.00
Open mouth, mk Tete Jumeau, 16" 1,600.00
Open mouth, mk Tete Jumeau, 19" 1,900.00
Open mouth, mk Tete Jumeau, 21" 2,400.00
Open mouth, mk Tete Jumeau, 23" 2,800.00
Open mouth, mk Tete Jumeau, 25" 4,000.00
Open mouth, mk Tete Jumeau, 28" 4,800.00
Open mouth, mk Tete Jumeau, 30" 5,200.00
Open mouth, mk 1907 Jumeau, 14" 1,400.00

Open mouth, mk 1907 Jumeau, 17"	1,700.00
Open mouth, mk 1907 Jumeau, 20"	2,000.00
Open mouth, mk 1907 Jumeau, 25"	2,500.00
Open mouth, mk 1907 Jumeau, 28"	3,000.00
Open mouth, mk 1907 Jumeau, 32"	3,400.00
Phonograph in body, o/m, 20"	3,400.00
Phonograph in body, o/m, 25"	4,800.00
Portrait Jumeau, c/m, 16"	5,800.00
Portrait Jumeau, c/m, 20"	7,400.00

Kammer and Reinhardt

#101, boy or girl w/glass eyes, 12"	2,000.00
#101, boy or girl w/glass eyes, 16"	4,800.00
#101, boy or girl w/glass eyes, 20"	6,500.00
#101, boy or girl w/glass eyes, 9"	1,500.00
#101, boy or girl w/pnt eyes, 12"	1,400.00
#101, boy or girl w/pnt eyes, 16"	2,800.00
#101, boy or girl w/pnt eyes, 20"	3,600.00
#101, boy or girl w/pnt eyes, 9"	1,200.00
#109, rare, w/glass eyes, 15"	15,000.00
#109, rare, w/glass eyes, 18"	24,000.00
#109, rare, w/pnt eyes, 15"	9,000.00
#109, rare, w/pnt eyes, 18"	16,000.00
#112, rare, w/glass eyes, 15"	16,000.00
#112, rare, w/glass eyes, 18"	19,000.00
#112, rare, w/pnt eyes, 15"	9,800.00
#112, rare, w/pnt eyes, 18"	15,000.00
#114, rare, w/glass eyes, 15"	6,500.00
#114, rare, w/glass eyes, 18"	7,500.00
#114, rare, w/pnt eyes, 15"	5,800.00
#114, rare, w/pnt eyes, 18"	5,600.00
#115 or #115a, closed mouth, 15"	3,400.00
#115 or #115a, closed mouth, 18"	4,600.00
#115 or #115a, closed mouth, 22"	5,200.00
#115 or #115a, open mouth, 15"	1,600.00
#115 or #115a, open mouth, 18"	2,600.00
#115 or #115a, open mouth, 22"	2,500.00
#116 or #116a, closed mouth, 15"	2,500.00
#116 or #116a, closed mouth, 18"	3,300.00
#116 or #116a, closed mouth, 22"	4,200.00
#116 or #116a, open mouth, 15"	1,600.00
#116 or #116a, open mouth, 18"	2,000.00
#116 or #116a, open mouth, 22"	2,400.00
#117, closed mouth, 18"	4,600.00
#117, closed mouth, 24"	6,400.00
#117, closed mouth, 30"	7,400.00
#117a, closed mouth, 18"	4,900.00
#117a, closed mouth, 24"	7,500.00
#117a, closed mouth, 30"	9,000.00
Dolly face, open mouth, mold #400-403-109, etc, 16"	600.00
Dolly face, open mouth, mold #400-403-109, etc, 20"	725.00
Dolly face, open mouth, mold #400-403-109, etc, 24"	850.00
Dolly face, open mouth, mold #400-403-109, etc, 28"	1,000.00
Dolly face, open mouth, mold #400-403-109, etc, 38"	2,500.00
Dolly face, open mouth, mold #400-403-109, etc, 40"	2,700.00

Kestner

Johannes D. Kestner made buttons at a lathe in a Waltershausen factory in the early 1800s. When this line of work failed, he used the same lathe to turn doll bodies. Thus the Kestner company began. It was one of the few German manufacturers to make the complete doll. By 1860 with the purchase of a porcelain factory, Kestner made doll heads

of china and bisque as well as wax, worked-in-leather, celluloid, and cardboard. In 1895 the Kestner trademark of a crown with streamers was registered in the U.S. and a year later in Germany. Kestner felt the mark was appropriate since he referred to himself as the 'king of German dollmakers.'

A, ShHd, o/m, MIG/Kestner, 19"	700.00
A/5, ShHd, o/c mouth, 23"	2,600.00
B/6, ShHd, kid w/bsk ½-arms, o/m w/teeth, o/c eyes, 19"	700.00
B/6, SkHd, jtd compo, o/m w/2 teeth, set eyes, 22"	850.00
Bergmann, SkHd, made for CM Bergmann, o/m, JDK/CM, 14"	450.00
Bergmann, SkHd, made for CM Bergmann, o/m, JDK/CM, 17"	525.00
Bergmann, SkHd, made for CM Bergmann, o/m, JDK/CM, 20"	675.00
Century Doll Co, flanged closed dome, c/m, 15"	650.00

Character doll, swivel head, sleep eyes, original wig and label, 7", $575.00.

D/8, SkHd & ShHd, kid w/bsk ½-arms, c/m, 15"	1,100.00
E/9, ShHd, o/m, MIG, 26"	1,300.00
E/9, SkHd, o/m, 1892, 26"	1,500.00
G/11, SkHd, brn, o/m, 16"	700.00
G/8, trn ShHd, o/m, MI/JDK, 19"	600.00
Grace Putnam, bsk, 1-pc, pnt eyes, 10/10/COPR, 6"	650.00
Grace Putnam, bsk, 1-pc body & head, 1/COPR, 1923, 6"	650.00
Grace Putnam, Bye-Lo baby, 6 12/COPR, 1927, 16"	800.00
H1/2, ShHd, o/m, 23"	650.00
H/12, SkHd, o/c mouth, JDK, 1892, 23"	2,800.00
Handwerck, SkHd, made for Handwerck, o/m, JDK/H/12, 23"	625.00
Handwerck, SkHd, made for Handwerck, o/m, JDK/H/12, 27"	750.00
I/13, SkHd, o/m, JDK, 1892, 16"	475.00
I/13, SkHd, o/m, JDK, 1892, 26"	1,300.00
J/13, SkHd, o/m, 1896, 27"	1,400.00
JDK, bsk head on celluloid, R Gummi Co, turtle mk, 18"	650.00
K/12, ShHd, made for Century, o/c mouth, molded hair, 21"	2,200.00
Kewpie, bsk, Rose O'Neill/10 945G, 1913, 8"	350.00
KK/14 1/2d, o/m, 1896, 26"	850.00
L1/2/15 ½, SkHd, c/m, 14"	1,800.00
L/15, SkHd, bsk ShPl, c/m, 21"	2,200.00
L/15, SkHd, c/m, 21"	2,300.00
L/3, ShHd, o/c mouth w/molded teeth, 23"	2,600.00
N/17, SkHd, o/m, 1892, 17"	525.00
SkHd, Oriental, o/m, JDK/Kestner, 14"	4,600.00
SkHd, pnt eyes, JDK/3 4/0, 8"	500.00
Trn ShHd, Kidoline w/bsk ½-arms, o/c eyes, G/MIG, 16"	700.00
10, SkHd, bsk ShPl, c/m, 21"	2,200.00
10, SkHd, o/c mouth w/2 teeth, JDK/MIG, 12"	650.00

10/G, SkHd, c/m, JDK, 1912, 12" **600.00**

1070, SkHd, o/m, G11/237 15/JDK Jr 1914 HILDA/GES, 16".. **3,600.00**

11, SkHd, o/c mouth, pnt eyes to side, JDK/MIG, 11" **600.00**

12, SkHd, 5-pc baby, o/c eyes, o/m/2 teeth, JDK/MIG, 15" **650.00**

13, SkHd, o/m, JDK/MIG, 18" **800.00**

143, ShHd, kid w/bsk ½-arms, o/m, 17" **850.00**

143, ShHd, kid w/bsk ½-arms, o/m/teeth, 12" **495.00**

145, ShHd, kid w/bsk ½-arms, o/c mouth, 15" **1,400.00**

145, SkHd, c/m, MI/O/G/18, 14" **1,200.00**

145, SkHd, c/m, 143/4/0/JDK, 11" **700.00**

146, SkHd, swivel, on ShPl, o/m, JDK, 18" **650.00**

147, trn ShHd, o/m, JDK, 25" **800.00**

148, ShHd, kid w/bsk ½-arms, o/m, 7 1/2, 18" **700.00**

148, ShHd, kid w/bsk ½-arms, o/m, 7 1/2, 21" **800.00**

150.1, bsk, Kestner seal on body, 8" **350.00**

151, SkHd, 5-pc baby, intaglio eyes, o/m/teeth, MIG/5, 12" **425.00**

151, SkHd, 5-pc baby, intaglio eyes, o/m/teeth, MIG/5, 16" **575.00**

151, SkHd, 5-pc baby, intaglio eyes, o/m/teeth, MIG/5, 20" **675.00**

152, SkHd, made for Wolf, o/m, LW & CO 12, 1916, 20" **750.00**

154, SkHd/ShHd, kid w/bsk ½-arms, o/m/teeth, DEP, 14"..........**500.00**

154, SkHd/ShHd, kid w/bsk ½-arms, o/m/teeth, DEP, 17"..........**700.00**

154, SkHd/ShHd, kid w/bsk ½-arms, o/m/teeth, DEP, 20"..........**800.00**

154, SkHd/ShHd, kid w/bsk ½-arms, o/m/teeth, DEP, 26" **1,000.00**

16, SkHd, o/m, JDK/MIG, 21" **625.00**

16/GES#1, ShHd, o/c mouth, molded boy's hair, 16" **2,200.00**

167, SkHd, jtd compo, o/m, p/e, F 1/2/MI6 1/2/G, 16"...............**500.00**

167, SkHd, jtd compo, o/m, p/e, F 1/2/MI6 1/2/G, 20"...............**600.00**

168, SkHd, o/m, MID/G7, 26" **850.00**

169, SkHd, jtd compo, c/m, o/c eyes, B 1/2/BI6 1/2G, 16" **2,000.00**

169, SkHd, jtd compo, c/m, o/c eyes, B 1/2/BI6 1/2G, 18" **2,500.00**

171, SkHd, jtd compo, o/m, o/c eyes, 'Daisy,' F/M110, 15" **465.00**

171, SkHd, jtd compo, o/m, o/c eyes, 'Daisy,' F/M110, 18" **625.00**

171, SkHd, jtd compo, o/m, o/c eyes, 'Daisy,' F/M110, 22" **750.00**

180 12/Ox/Crown seal, SkHd, o/m, 16" **465.00**

201, ShHd, celluloid on kid, o/m, set eyes/lashes, JDK, 19" **500.00**

211, SkHd, 5-pc baby, o/c mouth, o/c eyes, MI10/G/JDK, 12".....**550.00**

211, SkHd, 5-pc baby, o/c mouth, o/c eyes, MI10/G/JDK, 15".....**725.00**

215, SkHd, jtd compo, fur eyebrows, o/m, MI9/GJDK, 21"..........**800.00**

217A/Kestner, bsk, c/m smile, googly pnt eyes, 12" **2,400.00**

221/GES/GESCH, SkHd, c/m smile, googly eyes, G/JDK, 21" .. **8,200.00**

235, toddler, kid body, 16" **725.00**

245, SkHd, 5-pc baby, G/MIG/11/JDK Jr/1914 Hilda, 14" **2,700.00**

245, SkHd, 5-pc baby, G/MIG/11/JDK Jr/1914 Hilda, 17" **3,600.00**

257, SkHd, 5-pc baby, o/m, G/JDK, 10" **450.00**

257, SkHd, 5-pc baby, o/m, G/JDK, 16" **675.00**

257, SkHd, 5-pc baby, o/m, G/JDK, 20" **850.00**

257, SkHd, 5-pc baby, o/m, G/JDK, 24" **1,400.00**

26, K&Co/JDK/MIG/81, 16"..................................**465.00**

270, SkHd, o/m, made for Carl Trautman, CP/39, 38" **2,400.00**

639, trn ShHd, closed dome, c/m, G/6, 18" **1,800.00**

7 1/2/B, ShHd, kid w/bsk ½-arms, o/m w/teeth, o/c eyes, 14" **425.00**

Lenci

Eleanora Scavani, separated from her husband who was in the service of Italy during WWI, found herself painfully alone after the death of her baby. With her brother as her partner, this talented artist began designing lovely felt-covered dolls with beautiful hand-painted features. These dolls became her children, and she regarded them as a tribute to her lost daughter.

Following the war, her husband returned and joined the firm as a partner. The Lenci firm (a name he used as a term of endearment for his wife) soon became well-known in the doll-making industry. Great care was taken in every detail. Characteristics of Lenci dolls include seamless, steam-molded felt heads, quality clothing, childishly plump bodies, and painted eyes that glance to the side. Fine mohair wigs were used, and the middle and fourth fingers were sewn together. Look for the factory stamp on the foot, though paper labels were also used. Dolls under 10" are known as mascots and usually sell for $125.00 to $150.00. The Lenci factory continues today, producing dolls of the same high quality.

Baby, jtd w/bent limbs, organdy dress/bonnet, 16", M **1,400.00**

Chinaman, w/opium pipe, 1920s, 12½", M **1,650.00**

Girl, blond curls, organdy dress & bonnet, 21" **1,300.00**

Girl, brn braids, felt dress & shoes, 20½" **1,300.00**

Girl toddler, red wig, OC, 17" **1,000.00**

Glass eyes, braided bun, canvas-type body/limbs, 18" **2,600.00**

Old woman, gray mohair wig, opens in bk for sewing goods.... **1,200.00**

Peasant girl, swivel neck/jtd body, all orig, 16", EX **975.00**

Romana, swivel head, w/labels, ca 1920s, 28", NM.................. **1,800.00**

Madame Alexander

Beatrice Alexander founded the Alexander Doll company in 1923 using a lovely doll that was designed after her daughter Mildred. With the help of her three sisters, the company prospered; and by the late 1950s there were three factories with over six hundred employees making Madame Alexander dolls. The company still produces these lovely dolls today.

Alice in Wonderland, cloth, 1933-33, 16" **600.00**

Amanda, hp, Wendy Ann, 1961 Americana Group, 8" **1,550.00**

American Child, compo, Tiny Betty, 1938, 7" **200.00**

Amish Boy, hp, bend knee, Wendy Ann, 1966-69, 8" **475.00**

Amish Girl, hp, bend knee, Wendy Ann, 1966-69, 8" **475.00**

Anastasia, Cissette, 1988 to date, 10" **65.00**

Anthony, Mark, 1980-85, 12" **70.00**

Babs Skater, compo, Margaret, 18" **500.00**

Baby Ellen, Black Sweet Tears, 1965-72, 14" **145.00**

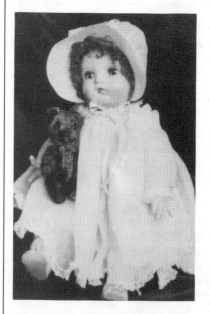

Madame Alexander 'Baby McGuffey,' composition head and limbs, 1940s, $250.00.

Baby Precious, cloth/vinyl, 1975 only, 14" **125.00**

Barbara Jane, cloth/vinyl, 1952, 29" **400.00**

Barbary Coast, hp, Cissette, 1962-63, 11" **1,400.00**

Belle of the Ball, Cissette, 10" **70.00**

Binnie, hp, Cissy, 14" **400.00**

Birthday Dolls, compo, Tiny Betty, 7" **175.00**

Bo Peep, hp, bend knees, Wendy Ann, 1965-72, 8".....................150.00
Brenda Starr, hp, 1964, 12".....................265.00
Bud, cloth/vinyl, 1952, 16".....................145.00
Bunny, plastic/vinyl, Melinda, 1962, 18".....................465.00
Carmen, compo, Wendy Ann, 21" 1,600.00
Cherry Twins, hp, Wendy Ann, 1954, 8".....................750.00
China, hp, bend knees, Wendy Ann, 1972, 8".....................125.00
Christening Baby, cloth/vinyl, 1951-54, 11".....................125.00
Cissette, hp, Beauty Queen w/trophy, 1961, 10".....................265.00
Civil War, hp, Wendy Ann, 1953-54 ....950.00
Coco, plastic/vinyl, in various clothes, 1966, 21" 2,500.00
Colonial, compo, Tiny Betty, 1937-38, 7".....................175.00
Country Cousins, Marybel, 1958, 16½".....................300.00
Cousin Marie & Mary, hp, Wendy Ann, 1963, 8" 700.00
Cynthia, hp, Black Margaret, 1952, 15".....................700.00
David Copperfield, compo, Tiny Betty, 7".....................175.00
Davy Crockett Girl, hp, Wendy Ann, 1955, 8" 1,100.00
Degas Girl, plastic/ vinyl, Mary Ann, 1967-87, 14".....................100.00
Denmark, hp, Cissette, 1962, 11" 1,000.00
Ding Dong Dell, compo, Tiny Betty, 1937, 7".....................175.00
Egyptian, compo, Tiny Betty, 1936, 7" 150.00
Emily Dickinson, 1987 to date, 14".....................90.00
Gibson Girl, hp, Cissette, eyeshadow, 1962, 10" 1,300.00
Gigi, 1986-87,14".....................85.00
Ginger Rogers, compo, Wendy Ann, 1940-45, 14".....................650.00
Goldilocks, plastic/vinyl, Mary Ann, 1978-84, 14".....................80.00
Good Fairy, hp, Margaret, 14".....................550.00
Graduation, hp, Wendy Ann, 1957, 8".....................1,000.00
Greek Boy, hp, bend knee walker, Wendy Ann, 1965-68, 8" 500.00
Guardian Angel, hp, Wendy Ann, 1954, 8".....................950.00
Hansel, compo, Tiny Betty, 1937, 7".....................175.00
Hiawatha, hp, Wendy Ann, 1967-69, 8".....................550.00
Huckleberry Finn, hp, Wendy Ann, 1989 to date, 8" 45.00
Indian Boy, hp, bend knee, Wendy Ann, pre-1966, 8".....................550.00
Ingres, plastic/vinyl, 1987 only, 14" 65.00
Jamaica, str legs, 1986-89, 8".....................60.00
Janie, ballerina, 1965 only.....................385.00
Juliet, compo, Wendy Ann, 21" 1,600.00
June Bride, compo, 21" 1,600.00
Kathy, hp, Maggie, 1951, 15".....................500.00
King, compo, 1942-46, 21".....................1,800.00
Klondike Kate, hp, Cissette, 1963, 11".....................1,400.00
Lady Bird, 1988 to date, 8".....................50.00
Lady in Waiting, hp, Wendy Ann, 1955, 8".....................1,600.00
Leslie, vinyl, Black Polly, 1965-71, 17".....................400.00
Lincoln, Mary Todd, 3rd set, 1982-84 ....150.00
Little Boy Blue, compo, Tiny Betty, 1937, 7".....................175.00
Little Jack Horner, compo, Tiny Betty, 1937, 7".....................175.00
Little Southern Boy/Girl, latex/vinyl, 1951, 10".....................145.00
Little Women (Meg, Jo, Amy, Beth), 1933, 16", ea.....................600.00
Madame Pompadour, hp/vinyl arms, Jacqueline, 1970, 21".....1,200.00
Maid of Honor, compo, Wendy Ann, 18" 750.00
Marie Antoinette, 1987-89, 21".....................365.00
Mary Cassatt Baby, cloth/vinyl, 1969-70, 14".....................145.00
Miss America, compo, holds flag, 1940, 14".....................650.00
Mother Goose, 1988 to date, 8" 50.00
Napoleon, 1980, 12".....................65.00
Nurse, compo, Tiny Betty, 7".....................175.00
Orphan Annie, plastic/vinyl, Mary Ann, 1965, 14".....................500.00
Patty Pigtails, hp, 1949, 14".....................625.00
Peter Pan, hp, 1953, Wendy Ann, 8".....................1,100.00
Pierrot Clown, hp,1956, Margaret, 18".....................1,200.00
Pocahantas, hp, bend knee, Wendy Ann, 1967-70, 8".....................550.00
Pollyanna, rigid vinyl, 1960 (mk 1959), 16".....................425.00

Poodles, standing or sitting, 14".....................300.00
Prince Charming, compo, Margaret, 1947, 16".....................725.00
Princess Doll, compo, 13".....................400.00
Princess Elizabeth, compo, Tiny Betty, 7" 200.00
Pussy Cat, cloth/vinyl, 1965 to date, 14".....................95.00
Queen of Hearts, 1987 to date, 8".....................55.00
Queen Scarlet, 1955, velvet robe.....................900.00
Rebecca, compo, Wendy Ann, 1940, 14".....................500.00
Renoir, hp, Cissette, 1968, 11".....................600.00
Renoir Child, plastic/vinyl, Nancy Drew, 1967, 12" 200.00
Rhet, 1981-85, 12".....................65.00
Robin Hood, 1988 to date, 8".....................55.00
Romeo, hp, Wendy Ann, 1955, 8".....................950.00
Rosette, Cissette, 1987 to date, 10".....................60.00
Royal Evening, hp, Margaret, 1953, 18".....................950.00
Russian, compo, Tiny Betty, 1935-36, 7".....................150.00
Sailorette, hp, Cissette, 1988 only, 10".....................90.00
Scarlett O'Hara, compo, Wendy Ann, 1945, 21" 1,600.00
Scottish, hp, bend knee walker, Wendy Ann, 1964-65, 8" 275.00
Sir Winston Churchill, hp, Margaret, 1953, 18".....................800.00
Sleeping Beauty, hp, Cissette, 1960, 10".....................600.00
Smiley, cloth/vinyl, Happy, 1971 only, 20" 350.00
Snow White, hp, Margaret, 1952, 15".....................650.00
Soldier, compo, Wendy Ann, 17".....................350.00
Sound of Music, full set of 7 dolls, 1965-70 ....1,500.00
Sound of Music, lg set, Louisa, 14".....................350.00
Southern Belle, hp, Lissy, 1963, 12".....................1,400.00
Spanish Boy, hp, bend knee walker, 1964-68, 8".....................500.00
Spanish Girl, hp, bend knee walker, Wendy Ann, 1961-65, 8"...275.00
Story Princess, hp, Magaret, 1954-56, 15".....................500.00
Stuffy (Boy), hp, Margaret, 1952.....................900.00
Sugar Darlin', cloth/vinyl, 1964 only, 14".....................100.00
Sunbeam, newborn infant, 1951, 11".....................95.00
Sunbonnet Sue, compo, Little Betty, 1937, 9".....................200.00
Sweet Baby, cloth/latex, 1948, 20".....................85.00
Sweet Tears, 1965-82, 14" 85.00
Teeny Twinkle, cloth, flirty eyes 600.00
Tiny Tim, compo, Wendy Ann, 1938, 14" 650.00
Tom Sawyer, hp, Maggie Mixup, 1989 to date, 8".....................55.00
Treena Ballerina, hp, 1952, 15".....................500.00
Tyler, Julia, 1979-81, 2nd set 140.00
Wendy Angel, hp, Wendy Ann, 1954, 8".....................1,000.00
Wendy Ann, compo, 17".....................600.00
Wilson, Ellen, 1988, 5th set.....................150.00
Yolanda, Brenda Starr, 1965, 12".....................350.00
Zorina Ballerina, compo, Wendy Ann, 1937, 17" 1,000.00
3 Little Pigs & Wolf, compo, 1938, ea 500.00

Papier-Mache

Braided hair, pnt eyes, kid body, fancy clothes, 11½".....................650.00
Man, molded/pnt head, cloth w/wood arms, suit/hat, 10"...........600.00
Molded hair, cloth w/kid hands, prof rpr, 1850s, RpC, 28".....................350.00
Molded hair, fixed glass eyes, o/m/teeth, jtd limbs, Fr, 33" 1,800.00
Molded hair, glass eyes, o/m/teeth, cloth/kid, RpC, 31" 1,700.00
Molded hair, pnt eyes, cloth w/kid arms, Germany, RpC, 13" 250.00
Molded hair, pnt eyes, cloth w/kid arms, Greiner, 26" 1,500.00
Molded hair, pnt eyes, cloth w/kid arms, Greiner, 29" 1,850.00
Molded hair, pnt eyes, cloth w/kid arms, RpC, 23" 550.00
Molded long curls, ShHd, kid body, wood limbs, 13" 1,500.00
Motschmann type, pnt overlay, muslin body, glass eyes, 5" 145.00
ShHd, cloth body, #1858 label, RpC, Greiner, 30", EX...........1,900.00
ShHd, pnt hair, glass eyes, o/m, kid body, 26".....................1,400.00
ShPl, cloth body, #1858 label, Greiner, 30", VG 1,550.00

ShPl, compo arms, cloth body, RpC, 18", G 450.00
Stationary glass eyes w/no pupils, o/m, 4 bamboo teeth, 28" ... 2,700.00

Parian

Blond molded hair, cloth w/leather arms, OC, 18" 500.00
Blond molded hair/kid hands, cloth body/legs, Germany, 14" 450.00
Cafe-au-lait hair w/snood, 10½" 485.00
Greiner type, center part, cloth body, OC, 15" 550.00
Man, blond molded hair, cloth body, OC, 17½" 600.00
Molded braid wrapped around head, p/e, pnt eyes, 18" 850.00
Sh/Hd, molded hair, cloth, pk/silver accents, bsk limbs, 9" 850.00

Schoenhut

Albert Schoenhut left Germany in 1866 to go to Pennsylvania to work as a repairman for toy pianos. He eventually applied his skills to wooden toys and later designed an all-wood doll which he patented on January 17, 1911. These uniquely jointed dolls were painted with enamels and came with a metal stand. Some of the later dolls had stuffed bodies, voice boxes, and hollow heads; some were made with heads of imitation bisque. These innovations influenced the development of the popular Bye-Lo Baby which was introduced in 1924. Due to the changing economy and fierce competition, the company closed in the mid-1930s.

Baby head, o/c eyes, o/m w/teeth, jtd, OC, 14" 625.00
Baby head, pnt hair & eyes, o/c mouth, jtd, 16" 700.00
Baby head, SkHd, pnt eyes, bent limbs, 1913, RpC, 15" 600.00
Character girl, cvd hair w/bow, intaglio eyes, jtd, OC, 14"...... 2,000.00
Compo, molded hair, pnt eyes, c/m, jtd neck, 1924, RpC, 13" 425.00
Dolly face, decal eyes/pnt teeth/jtd/mohair wig/OC, 21", EX 875.00
Dolly face, o/ or c/m, pnt eyes/spring jtd/wig, OC, 17", EX..........675.00
Dolly face boy, o/m w/teeth, decal eyes, RpC, 20", VG 600.00
Dolly face girl, o/m/teeth, pnt eyes, rpl wig, RpC, 21", VG..........650.00
Girl, brn o/c eyes, OC, 19", M 1,300.00
Girl, cvd brn hair w/pk ribbon, RpC, orig shoes, wear, 16" 2,600.00
Girl, cvd hair w/comb mks, intaglio brn eyes, RpC, 19" 2,500.00
Girl, cvd hair w/comb mks/etc, c/m, spring jtd, OC, 16" 2,300.00
Girl, cvd hair w/ribbon, pnt eyes, jtd, RpC, 15", EX................. 2,600.00
Girl, smiling o/m w/teeth, brn hair, Pat Jan 17, '11, 18" 750.00
Girl, wooden SkHd, spring jtd, pnt eyes, Pat Jan 17, 16" 650.00
Girl, wooden SkHd, spring jtd, pnt eyes, 1911, 19"......................750.00
Pouty, orig paper label, 1919, 11½" 550.00
Pouty boy, bl eyes, jtd body, #1913, 1910, 11", EX......................550.00
Pouty boy, pnt eyes, rpl wig, RpC, 15", EX.................................650.00
Pouty child, intaglio eyes, no wig, RpC, 14"................................300.00
Sailor boy, spring jtd, OC, 15", VG..550.00
Walker, bl pnt eyes, c/m, mohair wig, mk head/body, 16½" 1,000.00
Walker, pnt eyes, o/c mouth, OC, 17".................................... 1,000.00

SFBJ

By 1895 Germany was producing dolls of good quality at much lower prices than the French dollmakers because of lower wages in German factories. This was a serious threat to the French companies; and, in a supreme effort to save the doll industry, several leading French manufacturers united to form one large company in the hope they could combine their strengths to save the French market. Bru, Raberry and Delphieu, Pintel and Godshaux, Fleischman and Bodel, and Jumeau united to form the company today known as SFBJ. Their dolls did well while Germany was otherwise occupied with WWII, but after the war German doll production proved to be too strongly competitive, and SFBJ closed in 1958.

Bebe Parisiana, bsk head, c/m, inset eyes, 1902, 16" 2,600.00
Celestine, bsk SkHd on papier-mache, o/m, inset eyes, 18" 950.00
SkHd, jtd papier-mache/wood body, o/m, o/c eyes, 30" 2,500.00
Tete Jumeau, p/e, o/m, o/c eyes/lashes, 18" 1,400.00
20, molded ptd shoes & eyes, 5-pc body, Paris/12, 10" 350.00
203, 1900 bsk head on compo, o/c mouth, inset eyes, 20" 2,800.00
215, bsk swivel on compo, c/m, inset eyes, 15" 2,000.00
223, bsk, closed dome, o/m w/8 teeth, molded hair, 17" 2,000.00
227, brn swivel closed dome head, animal skin wig, 15" 2,400.00
227, brn swivel closed dome head, animal skin wig, 18" 2,000.00
227, closed dome, o/m, inset eyes, pnt hair, 15" 1,800.00
228, toddler, papier-mache body, c/m, inset eyes, 16" 2,000.00
229, compo w/swivel head, o/c mouth, inset eyes, 18" 3,500.00
229, wood walker, o/c mouth, inset eyes, 18" 3,600.00
230, compo walker, p/e, o/m, inset eyes, 16" 1,500.00
230, SkHd, p/e, o/m, o/c eyes, 23" 2,400.00
235, closed dome, molded hair, o/c mouth & eyes, 16" 2,300.00
235, closed dome, molded hair, o/c mouth & eyes, 8" 750.00
236, laughing Jumeau, o/m, o/c eyes, dbl chin, 12" 1,600.00
236, laughing Jumeau, o/m, o/c eyes, dbl chin, 20" 2,400.00
238, compo w/swivel head, o/m, inset eyes, Paris 6, 15" 3,000.00
239, Poulbot, c/m, street urchin, red wig, 14" 16,000.00
239, Poulbot, c/m, street urchin, red wig, 17" 19,000.00
245, boy, o/c mouth, lg glass eyes, googly, pnt shoes, 12" 2,800.00
245, boy, o/c mouth, lg glass eyes, googly, pnt shoes, 8" 1,000.00
247, toddler, o/c mouth/2 inset teeth, 16" 2,600.00
247, toddler, o/c mouth/2 inset teeth, 20" 2,900.00
247, toddler, o/c mouth/2 inset teeth, 24" 3,400.00
247, Twirp, SkHd, o/c mouth & eyes/2 teeth, 21" 2,800.00
251, toddler, 25" 2,900.00
251, 1099 character baby, o/c mouth, eyes, hair lashes, 16" 1,700.00
251, 1099 character baby, o/c mouth, eyes, hair lashes, 18" 2,000.00
252, pouty, c/m, inset eyes, papier-mache body, 18" 6,200.00
252, pouty, c/m, inset eyes, papier-mache body, 22" 7,900.00
257, 1900 toddler, o/c mouth, inset eyes, 16" 2,500.00
266, character, bsk head, closed dome, o/c mouth, 20" 3,800.00
301, bsk SkHd on compo, o/m, inset eyes, 16" 725.00
301, bsk SkHd on compo, o/m, inset eyes, 22" 1,200.00
301, bsk SkHd on compo, o/m, inset eyes, 30" 2,000.00
60, French WWI nurse, 5-pc body, SFBJ/13/0, 8½" 400.00
60, kiss-blower, cryer/walker, 22"... 1,900.00
60, SkHd, compo w/str legs, o/m, curved arms, 15" 650.00
60, SkHd, papier-mache/compo, plunger cryer, o/m, 1-pc, 11"....450.00

Shirley Temple

Bsk, Japan, 7½"...285.00
Compo, 11", cowboy outfit, orig pin, EX 725.00
Compo, 11", in trunk, EX..850.00
Compo, 13", tagged bl/wht dress w/pin, 1930s, all orig 625.00
Compo, 15", OC, Ideal..600.00
Compo, 16", o/c eyes, o/m, handmade clothes, 1936, EX 225.00
Compo, 16", red dotted dress, velvet coat/hat, all orig................650.00
Compo, 18", Ideal, all orig, VG...685.00
Compo, 18", Ideal, o/c eyes, o/m, jtd, mohair wig, '30s 685.00
Compo, 18", OC, EX...685.00
Compo, 20", Ideal 750.00
Compo, 20", OC, NM 750.00
Compo, 20", tagged clothes, all orig, orig box 900.00
Compo, 22", OC, rpl wig..450.00
Compo, 22", teeth, orig bl dress w/daisies, Ideal, 1934, NM 750.00
Compo, 25", sailor suit, EX..900.00
Compo, 27", flirty eyes, orig, EX 1,100.00
Vinyl, 12", complete w/4 outfits, Ideal, 1957, MIB 285.00

Shirley Temple by Ideal, composition with mohair wig, sleep eyes, in original dress, 25", VG, $550.00; Cowgirl, jointed composition body, sleep eyes with hair eyelashes, mohair wig, original clothes, 18", EX, $850.00.

194a 75%

Vinyl, 12", gr/wht dress, slip, complete, Ideal, 1957, MIB...........200.00
Vinyl, 14", flirty eyes, orig clothes, 1952, M..................................300.00
Vinyl, 14", Montgomery Ward's, 1972, MIB.................................200.00
Vinyl, 15", Heidi outfit, w/pin & tag, 1957 ....300.00
Vinyl, 15", RpC, Ideal...245.00
Vinyl, 16", Ideal, 1973, MIB..200.00
Vinyl, 16", Rebecca, Ideal, 1972...200.00
Vinyl, 16", red dotted dress/Captain Jan outfit, 1973, MIB.........200.00
Vinyl, 16", red polka-dot dress, Ideal, 1972................................200.00
Vinyl, 16", Stand Up & Cheer dress, 1973, MIB 200.00
Vinyl, 17", Heidi outfit, w/pin, MIB 400.00
Vinyl, 19", flirty eyes, all orig, 1957...450.00
Vinyl, 19", Heidi, 1957, MIB +2 extra orig outfits 500.00
Vinyl, 36", OC, EX 1,800.00
Vinyl, 36", pk pleated dress, EX... 1,800.00
Vinyl, 8", Stowaway, Ideal, 1982..45.00

Simon and Halbig

Simon and Halbig was a large German doll firm that operated from ca 1870 until the 1930s. They were a popular supplier of bisque heads to French dollmakers of the 1870s and '80s. This company made dolls for such famous companies as Gimbel Bros., Jumeau, Kammer and Reinhardt, as well as many others. Halbig became the sole owner of the company in 1895 but did not register 'S&H' as his trademark until ten years later.

AW, SkHd, o/m, SH/13, 21" 675.00
Baby Blanche, SkHd, o/m baby, S&H, 16"................................800.00
Baby Blanche, SkHd, o/m baby, S&H, 21"................................950.00
CM Bergmann, SkHd, o/m, Simon & Halbig, 3 1/2, 18" 575.00
CM Bergmann, SkHd, o/m, 1895, Halbig/S&H5, 30" 1,300.00
CM Bergmann, SkHd, o/m, 1897, S&H6, 12" 350.00
Elenore, SkHd, o/m, CMB/Simon & Halbig, 18" 600.00
G68, SkHd, flirty eyes, 1908, S&H/K*R, 16" 550.00
Handwerck, SkHd, o/m, G/Halbig, 4, 26"................................850.00
Handwerck, SkHd, o/m, 1893, 16"...450.00
Handwerck, SkHd, o/m, 1895, G/S&H/1, 16"...........................450.00
S&H3, all bsk, c/m, inset eyes, molded-on shoes, 6" 285.00
10, SkHd, o/m, G/Halbig/S&H, 16"..475.00
10, SkHd, o/m, G/Halbig/S&H, 19"..575.00
10, SkHd, o/m, G/Halbig/S&H, 22"..675.00
10 1/2, SkHd, o/m, flirty o/c eyes, S&H, 18".............................625.00
100, SkHd, o/m, Simon & Halbig/S&C/G, 15" 475.00

100, SkHd, o/m, Simon & Halbig/S&C/G, 22" 675.00
101, SkHd, c/m, Simon & Halbig/K*R, 16"........................... 4,800.00
1039, SkHd, o/m w/teeth, p/e, jtd arms/wrists, hh, 22" 725.00
109, SkHd, o/m, 1895, Handwerck/G/Halbig, 23" 675.00
114, SkHd, c/m, glass eyes, Simon & Halbig K*R/L, 14" 6,300.00
114, SkHd, c/m, glass eyes, Simon Halbig K*R/L, 20" 7,900.00
114, SkHd, c/m, Simon & Halbig K*R/L, 9" 1,200.00
115, SkHd, c/m, 1912, K*R/Simon & Halbig, 16" 3,400.00
115a, SkHd, c/m pouty, K*R/Simon & Halbig, 15" 3,400.00
1159, SkHd, adult, 1905, G/Simon & Halbig/S&H7, 14"....... 1,200.00
1159, SkHd, adult, 1905, G/Simon & Halbig/S&H7, 18"....... 1,800.00
1159, SkHd, adult, 1905, G/Simon & Halbig/S&H7, 24"....... 2,700.00
1159, SkHd, swivel on ShPl, wood w/kid fashion, o/m, 19" 2,000.00
116a, SkHd, c/m, K*R/Simon & Halbig, 17" 3,200.00
116a-38, SkHd, 2 teeth, tongue, K*R/Simon & Halbig, 17" ... 2,000.00
117, SkHd, c/m, 1919, Simon & Halbig/K*R, 16" 4,000.00
117, SkHd, c/m, 1919, Simon & Halbig/K*R, 20" 4,700.00
117a, SkHd, c/m, K*R/Simon & Halbig, 16" 4,400.00
117a, SkHd, c/m, K*R/Simon & Halbig, 20" 5,000.00
117n, SkHd, o/m, Simon & Halbig/K*R, 20" 2,000.00
119, SkHd, o/m, 13/Handwerck 5/Halbig, 16" 575.00
121, SkHd, o/c mouth/teeth, flirty o/c eyes, 1920, K*R, 16" ... 1,400.00
121, SkHd, o/c toddler, 16" 1,200.00
121, SkHd, o/m, 1920, K*R/Simon & Halbig, 14" 1,000.00
121, SkHd, o/m, 1920, K*R/Simon & Halbig, 19" 1,500.00
122, SkHd, 1920, K*R/Simon & Halbig, 14".............................850.00
126, SkHd, o/c mouth, SH, 23" 950.00
126, SkHd, o/m, Simon & Halbig/K*R, 14" 500.00
126, SkHd, o/m, Simon & Halbig/K*R, 19" 800.00
127, SkHd, o/m, K*R/Simon & Halbig, 18" 675.00
128, SkHd, o/m, K*R/Simon & Halbig, 14" 800.00
128, SkHd, o/m, K*R/Simon & Halbig, 19" 1,300.00
1296, SkHd, 1911, FS&Co/Simon & Halbig, 14" 475.00
1329, SkHd, o/m, olive, G/Simon & Halbig/SH, 14" 2,200.00
151, SkHd, o/c mouth, pnt eyes, S&H/1, 16" 9,000.00
156, SkHd, 1925, S&H, 18" 625.00
156, SkHd, 1925, S&H, 22" 725.00
159, SkHd, o/m, Simon & Halbig, 16" 550.00
179, SkHd, o/m, Simon & Halbig S11H DEP, 20" 700.00
1848, SkHd, o/m, Jutta Simon & Halbig, 16"..............................525.00
191, SkHd, o/m, Bergmann/CB, 18" 625.00
1923, SkHd, o/m, SH Sp 5 3/4/G, 14" 500.00
1923, SkHd, o/m, SH Sp 5 3/4/G, 21" 700.00
1923, SkHd, o/m, SH Sp 5 3/4/G, 26" 950.00
246, SkHd, o/m, 1900, K*R/Simon & Halbig, 18" 650.00
282, SkHd, o/m, SH, 14"...500.00
282, SkHd, o/m, SH, 18"...650.00
282, SkHd, o/m, SH, 22"...725.00
383, SkHd, flapper body, SH, 14" 1,200.00
402, SkHd, o/m, K*R SH, 16" 625.00
403, SkHd, o/c mouth, K*R, Simon & Halbig, 20" 2,800.00
403, SkHd, o/m, walker, K*R SH, 21" 1,400.00
409, SkHd, o/m, S&H, 24"..685.00
409, SkHd, o/m, S&H, 26"..850.00
409, SkHd, o/m, S&H, 30"... 1,400.00
48m SkHd, o/m, 1905, Simon & Halbig/K*R, 27" 1,000.00
50, SkHd, c/m, Simon & Halbig, 16" 1,800.00
50, SkHd, o/m, 1900, K*R/Simon & Halbig, 14".......................500.00
53, SkHd, c/m, brn bsk, Simon & Halbig/K*R, 16" 1,800.00
530, SkHd, o/m, G/Simon & Halbig, 21" 675.00
540, SkHd, o/m, G/Halbig/S&H, 16" 750.00
540, SkHd, swivel on bsk ShPl, o/m, S&H, G, 16"......................750.00
550, SkHd, o/m, Simon & Halbig/S&H, 16" 525.00
570, SkHd, o/m, Halbig S&H/G, 18" 700.00

570, SkHd, o/m, walking, head turns, G/Halbig S&H, 18".........750.00
576, SkHd, o/m, Simon & Halbig, 16"...........................575.00
612, SkHd, o/m, MIG/S&H/CM Bergmann, 16"....................550.00
670, SkHd, o/m, Simon & Halbig, 16"...........................575.00
70, SkHd, o/m, 1896, Halbig/K*R, 26".........................850.00
719, SkHd, c/m, S&H DEP, 16"............................... 2,400.00
719, SkHd, swivel, ShPl, c/m, S&H, DEP, 20".............. 3,000.00
739, SkHd, c/m, brn, S 5 H DEP, 14"...................... 1,800.00
739, SkHd, c/m, brn, S 5 H DEP, 18"...................... 2,400.00
759, SkHd, o/m, brn, S 10 H DEP, 20".......................800.00
769, SkHd, c/m, S&H DEP, 17"............................... 2,300.00
905, SkHd, swivel on ShPl, c/m, SH, 21".................. 3,000.00
908, SkHd, swivel on ShPl, c/m, SH, 16".................. 2,600.00
929, SkHd, c/m, S&H, DEP, 20"............................. 2,800.00
929, SkHd, c/m, S&H, DEP, 25"............................. 3,200.00
939, SkHd, c/m, S 11H DEP, 17"........................... 2,600.00
939, SkHd, c/m, S 11H DEP, 23"........................... 3,000.00
939, SkHd, o/c eyes, o/m, S16H, 30"...................... 3,600.00
940, SkHd, closed dome, o/c mouth, S 2 H, 26"........... 3,600.00
940, SkHd, swivel on ShPl, o/c mouth, S 2 H, 14"........ 2,000.00
945, SkHd, c/m, S 2 H DEP, 16"........................... 2,000.00
99, SkHd, o/m, 1899, 11 1/2 Handwerck/Halbig, 16".......525.00

Steiner

Jules Nicholas Steiner established one of the earliest French doll manufactories in 1855. Having been a clockmaker, he began with mechanical dolls and his patents grew to include walking and talking dolls. In 1880 he registered a patent for a doll with moving eyes. This doll could be put to sleep by turning a rod that operated a wire attached to its eyes. Though these new innovations brought much acclaim to the Steiner company, it closed around 1910 because it could not compete with the less-expensive German dolls that were flooding the market at that time.

A Series, wire eyes, c/m, jtd, RpC, 16"....................... 4,800.00
A Series child, c/m, o/c eyes, jtd, cb pate, RpC, 12"............. 3,200.00
A Series child, c/m, o/c eyes, jtd, cb pate, RpC, 16"............. 4,000.00
A Series child, c/m, o/c eyes, jtd, cb pate, RpC, 20"............. 5,500.00
A Series child, c/m, o/c eyes, jtd, cb pate, RpC, 25"............. 6,800.00
B Series, jtd, wire-eyed, o/m teeth, p/e, crier, 20½"............. 6,000.00

Steiner bisque-headed Bebe, sleep eyes operated by wire mechanism, open mouth with two rows of teeth, inoperative cryer, 23", $4,000.00.

Bourgoin, c/m, pwt eyes, 1870s, RpC, 16"................ 4,800.00
Bourgoin, c/m, pwt eyes, 1870s, RpC, 20"................ 6,200.00
Bourgoin, c/m, pwt eyes, 1870s, RpC, 25"................ 7,500.00

C Series, bl eyes, c/m, p/e, jtd body, RpC, 12"........... 2,600.00
C Series, wire eyes, c/m, RpC, 16"....................... 4,900.00
C Series child, c/m, rnd face, pwt eyes, RpC, 16"........ 4,700.00
C Series child, c/m, rnd face, pwt eyes, RpC, 20"........ 6,200.00
Le Parisien, A Series, 1892, 16"........................ 4,000.00
Mechanical, key wind, kicks/cries, RpC, 20", EX......... 2,600.00
Mechanical, key wind, kicks/cries, teeth, RpC, 18"...... 2,200.00
Motschmann style, bsk, RpC, 18"........................ 5,500.00
Unmk, early wht bsk, o/m w/teeth, jtd, RpC, 18"........ 5,900.00
Unmk, early wht bsk, rnd face, o/m w/teeth, jtd, RpC, 14".... 4,200.00

Vogue

Baby Dear, vinyl/cloth, pnt eyes, rooted hair, 1964, 12", M..........60.00
Brickette, vinyl, o/c eyes, curly hair, 1978, OC, 16".....................65.00
Ginny, Bo Peep, hp, o/c eyes, pnt lashes, '52, OC, 8", M.............300.00
Ginny, Ginger, hp, orig red velvet dress, 8"............................300.00
Ginny, Toddles, compo, OC, 7½", M....................................285.00
Ginny Crib Crowd, bent-leg baby, lamb's wool wig, NM.................650.00
Ginny Hawaiian, hp, brn skin tones, OC, 16"........................ 1,500.00
Little Imp Country Cousin, hp, o/c eyes, freckles, OC, 10½".........75.00
Littlest Angel, plastic/vinyl, o/c eyes, OC, 1965, 15"..................65.00
Miss 1920, hp, orig taffeta dress/hat/shoes, 1950, 8", EX.............500.00
Wee Imp, vinyl, red wig, OC, 8"..450.00

Wax, Poured Wax

Motschmann type, over compo, cloth body, glass eyes, 14", G....475.00
Over compo, c/m, glass eyes, cloth body, wig, RpC, 29".............500.00
Over compo, o/c eyes, c/m, mohair wig, 1890s, 22", EX.............425.00
Over compo, ShHd, cloth body, kid hands, RpC, 33", VG.........450.00
Over compo, ShHd, o/c eyes, auburn hair, orig dress, 18"...........400.00
Over compo, ShHd, set eyes, molded hair, cloth body, 15".........350.00
Over compo, ShHd, swivel neck, Holz-Masse, 21", EX..............750.00
Over compo, ShHd, talker, 1890s, 19½", EX.........................875.00
Over compo, ShHd, wire-eyed (blk glass), wig, kid arms, 26"......800.00
Over compo, slit head, blk eyes, cloth body, 14".....................700.00
Over papier-mache, jtd wooden body, wire-eyed, all orig, 11".....550.00
Poured, bl pwt eyes, England, OC, 24"............................ 3,000.00
Poured, cloth body, glass eyes, inset hair, England, 21", VG ... 1,400.00
Poured, cloth body, glass eyes, p/e, Marsh, 22", VG................ 1,000.00
Poured, cloth body, glass eyes, set-in hair, 19".................... 1,600.00
Poured, cloth body, rpl hands, English type, 22", G................ 1,000.00
Poured, inset wig & lashes, EX pnt, RpC, 22", EX.................. 1,500.00

Door Knockers

Door knockers, those charming precursors of the door bell, come in an intriguing array of shapes and styles. The very rare ones come from England. Cast iron examples made in this country were often produced in forms similar to the more familiar doorstop figures.

Amish man, CI, eyes open & close 35.00
Basket of flowers, CI, EX orig pnt................................65.00
Couple kissing against roses, brass, 5½"........................85.00
Cupid, CI, oval base, EX orig pnt 175.00
Devil's head, brass, old...60.00
Jenny Jones, brass...75.00
Kewpie, metal, full-length figural, 3" 120.00
Oliver Twist, brass..20.00
Parrot, CI, EX orig pnt...75.00
Sea horse & shell, brass, EX.....................................80.00
Spider hanging from web w/bee, CI, lt pnt wear, 3½" 125.00

Lady's head form in brass, foliate back plate, 10", $200.00.

Doorstops

Although introduced in England in the mid-1800s, cast iron doorstops were not made to any great extent in this country until after the Civil War. Once called 'door porters,' their function was to keep doors open to provide better ventilation. They have been produced in many shapes and sizes, both dimensional and flat backed, and in the past few years have become a popular, yet affordable collectible. While cast iron examples are the most common, brass, wood, and chalk were also used. An average price is in the $40 to $50 range, though some are valued at more than $200. Doorstops retained their usefulness and appeal well into the thirties.

The prices below reflect market values in the east where doorstops are now at a premium. For other areas of the country, it may be necessary to adjust prices down about 25%. In the listings below, items are assumed flat backed unless noted full figured and cast iron unless noted otherwise.

Key: ff — full figured

Ann Hathaway's Cottage, Hubley, EX pnt, 6⅜x8⅜"	225.00
Apple Blossoms, in basket, Hubley #329, VG pnt, 7⅝x5⅜"	85.00
Aunt Jemima, arms akimbo, no pnt, 10½x6½"	300.00
Basket of Tulips, woven-look basket, Hubley, VG pnt, 13x9"	225.00
Bear w/Honey, stands, ff, worn pnt, 15x6½"	500.00
Boston Terrier, faces left, VG pnt, 9⅞x8¼"	65.00
Boston Terrier, faces right, Hubley, ff, EX pnt, 10x10"	100.00
Boxer, faces right, Hubley, ff, worn pnt, 8½x9"	225.00
Boy w/Fruit Basket, tall hat, EX orig pnt, 9¼x3⅞"	325.00
Bulldog, Porcelainized; ff, 5¾x8½", NM	125.00
Butler, arms akimbo, EX orig pnt, 12½x6"	350.00
Butler, Colonial clothes, EX orig pnt, 10⅛x3¼"	400.00
Cape Cod, cottage, Albany Foundry, EX pnt, 5¾x8¾"	125.00
Carpenter, hands on knees, #665, ff, EX pnt, 5½x2¾"	185.00
Castle, winding road to top, EX pnt, 8x5¼"	250.00
Cat, rubber, dry cracked pnt, 8¾x4⅜"	120.00
Cat, Sculptured Metal Studios, worn pnt, 10¾x7½"	350.00
Cat, slim seated figure, Hubley, ff, EX pnt, 10x3⅛"	125.00
Clown, seated, legs crossed, EX pnt, 8x3½"	425.00
Cockatoo, perched on limb, ff, EX orig pnt, 14x4½"	200.00
Cocker Spaniel, faces front, Metalcrafters, wedge, 9x7", EX	110.00
Conestoga Wagon, faces left, #100, EX pnt, 8x11"	100.00
Cosmos Vase, Hubley #455, EX pnt, 17¾x10¼"	275.00
Cottage, simple style, AA Richardson, EX pnt, 5⅛x8"	125.00
Cottage w/Fence, Nat'l Foundry #32, VG pnt, 5¼x8"	115.00

Daisy Bowl, Hubley #232, EX orig pnt, 7x5"	85.00
Daisy Bowl, Hubley #452, EX orig pnt, 7½x5⅞"	100.00
Dancing Girl, Nat'l Foundry, EX pnt, 9½x6¾"	275.00
Deco Woman, arms up, EX orig pnt, 17x6½"	350.00
Dolly Dimple, lg bonnet, Hubley, ff, worn pnt, 7¾x3¾"	225.00
Donald Duck, w/Stop sign, W Disney 1971, 8⅜x5¼", NM	195.00
Drum Major, marching pose, ff, EX pnt, 13½x6½"	325.00
Duck w/Top Hat, faces left, EX pnt, 7½x4¼"	200.00
Dutch Girl w/Big Shoes, VG pnt, 9¾x9¼"	285.00
Fisherman at Wheel, hand to eyes, worn pnt, 6¼x6"	100.00
Flowered Doorway, floral archway at door, EX pnt, 7⅝x7½"	250.00
Frog w/Blk Boy, boy on bk, ff, pnt traces, 5½x6½"	150.00
Geisha, kneels w/instrument, Hubley, ff, EX pnt, 7x6"	185.00
German Shepherd, Hubley, ff, EX pnt, 9¾x13"	135.00
Giraffe, stands, faces right, Hubley, EX pnt, 12½x9"	500.00
Gladiolus, in hdld vase, Hubley #489, EX pnt, 10x8"	125.00
Gnome w/Barrel, pours from shoulder, ff, EX pnt, 14½x6½"	425.00
Goldenrods, Hubley #268, Made in USA, EX pnt, 7⅛x5½"	155.00
Graf Zepplin, pnt traces, 8¼x13"	485.00
Halloween Girl, holds pumpkin, worn pnt, 13¾x9¾"	500.00
Highland Lighthouse, Cape Cod, EX orig pnt, 9x7¾"	275.00
Hoop Skirt Flapper, EX pnt, 9¼x6¼"	325.00
Horse on Base, dog beneath hooves, EX pnt, 7¼x8½"	150.00
Hunchbk Cat, tail up, Hubley, ff, EX pnt, 10⅝x7½"	125.00
Jungle Boy, boy on knee, head to left, EX pnt, 12¾x12"	500.00
Lambs Under Tree, 2 beneath willow, EX pnt, 7¼x6⅜"	235.00
Lighthouse, rocky base, #1290, worn pnt, 7¾x5"	150.00
Lighthouse of Gloucester Mass, Greenblatt, EX pnt, 11½x9"	250.00
Little Colonial Woman, ff, worn pnt, 4⅜x3¼"	100.00
Little Girl by Wall, Albany Foundry, ff, EX pnt, 5¼x3¼"	165.00
Little Southern Bell, Nat'l Foundry, ff, 5¼x3⅜", NM	95.00
Man w/Top Hat, hands to bk, ff, pnt traces, 9⅜x3⅝"	200.00
Mary Quite Contrary, flowers & tools, #1292, EX pnt, 15x8"	350.00
Monkey on Barrel, Taylor Cook #3, 1930, worn pnt, 8⅜x4⅞"	275.00
Olive Picker, man & donkey, CI, EX pnt, 7¾x8¾"	465.00
Organ Grinder, monkey at ft, faces left, EX pnt, 9⅞x5¾"	285.00
Owl, realistic details, B&H #7707, EX pnt, 15½x5"	500.00
Patrol, man w/lantern, titled base, ff, EX pnt, 8¾x3¾"	195.00
Peasant Girl, basket on head, Hubley, worn pnt, 8¾x5"	165.00
Persian Cat, looks left, Hubley, ff, EX pnt, 8½x6½"	125.00
Peter Rabbit, faces right, Hubley, #96, EX pnt, 9½x4¾"	365.00
Pinocchio, lead, ff, NM orig pnt, 9½x2¾"	500.00
Pirate w/Sack, faces left, EX pnt, 11⅞x9⅝"	435.00
Puppies in Basket, C 1932 M Rosenstein, EX pnt, 7x7⅜"	325.00
Rabbit, faces left, wedge, EX orig pnt, 11½x8¾"	365.00
Rooster, faces left, foliate base, EX pnt, 10x6"	250.00
Rose Vase, Nat'l Foundry #145, EX pnt, 10½x7"	135.00

Sailor, repainted cast iron, 11⅜", $365.00.

Senorita, Spanish lady w/flower basket, VG pnt, 11¼x7" 225.00
Sitting Figure, nude w/head to right, Hubley, EX pnt, 8x3¼" 165.00
Sleeping Cat, Nat'l Foundry, ff, EX pnt, 3⅜x9⅝" 200.00
Sophia Smith House, 2-story, EX pnt, 8¼x5½" 225.00
Southern Belle, Nat'l Foundry, worn orig pnt, 11¼x6" 85.00
Spanish Guitarist, long waist sash, ff, EX orig pnt, 11x3⅜" 500.00
Squirrel, on stump w/nut, EX orig pnt, 9x6⅜" 155.00
St Bernard, recumbent, Hubley, ff, EX pnt, 3½x10½" 285.00
Sunbonnet Girl, faces right, EX orig pnt, 9⅞x5½" 350.00
Swan, arched neck, Nat'l Foundry, ff, EX pnt, 5¾x4½" 185.00
Swan, preening, EX pnt, 15¼x6¾" 225.00
Terrier Pup, seated, ff, EX pnt, 8¼x7½" 200.00
Tiger Lilies, Hubley #472, worn pnt, 10½x6" 150.00
Tropical Woman, lady w/tray on head, EX pnt, 13x6¼" 200.00
Tulip Vase, Hubley, #3443, VG orig pnt, 10x8" 95.00
Tulips, in basket w/lg bow, EX pnt, 12¾x6⅞" 225.00
Tulips in Pot, LA-CS #770, EX orig pnt, 10½x5⅞" 200.00
Twin Cats, well dressed, Nat'l Foundry, EX pnt, 7x5¼" 275.00
Twin Penguins, heads turned away, EX pnt, 7¼x7½" 165.00
Whippet, faces left, EX pnt, 6¾x7½" 110.00
Whistling Boy, hands in pockets, ff, #429-B, EX pnt, 10x5½" 225.00
White Caddie, man w/long golf bag, EX orig pnt, 8x6" 500.00
Windmill, Nat'l Foundry, VG orig pnt, 6¾x6⅞" 75.00
Wirehaired Fox Terrier, Hubley, #467, EX pnt, 10½x12¾" 400.00
Wolfhound, seated/head up, Spencer, wedge, 6½x3½", NM........175.00
Woman Curtsying, skirt held wide, G pnt, #12, 9¼x6⅞" 150.00
Woman Holding Flower Baskets, #1270, 8x4¾" 185.00
Woman Holding Hat, left hand to face, ff, 6⅜x4⅛" 165.00
Woman w/Muff, ff, EX orig pnt, 9¼x5" 195.00
Yawning Dog, ff, worn orig pnt, 7x5" 175.00

Dorflinger

C. Dorflinger was born in Alsace, France, and came to this country when he was ten years old. When still very young, he obtained a job in a glass factory in New Jersey. As a young man, he started his own glassworks in Brooklyn, New York, opening new factories as profits permitted. During that time he made cut glass articles for many famous people including President and Mrs. Lincoln, for whom he produced a complete service of tableware with the United States Coat of Arms. In 1863 he sold the New York factories because of ill health and moved to his farm near White Mills, Pennsylvania. His health returned, and he started a plant near his home. It was there that he did much of his best work, making use of only the very finest materials. Christian died in 1915, and the plant was closed in 1921 by consent of the family.

Dorflinger glass is rare and often hard to identify. Very few pieces were marked — many only carried a small paper label which was quickly discarded.

Bowl, nut; Cross Cut Diamond & Fan, 4" 125.00
Cordial, Royal, stemmed 110.00
Cruet, Marlboro, paper label, 11" 145.00
Decanter, gr to clear, #1150, cut stopper 1,900.00
Humidor, Colonial, 9½x6" 1,200.00
Plate, sandwich; #1170..600.00
Vase, Kalana Poppy, flared, 6"...275.00

Dragon Ware

An undulating moriage dragon with a fierce expression decorates shaded gray bisque backgrounds in this type of ware that was very popular as gift-shop items during the forties and fifties. It was produced in

Japan and may sometimes be found with the Nippon mark.

Cup, demitasse 9.00
Demitasse set, lithophane, 15-pc..150.00
Pitcher, mini, 1¾" 12.50
Tea set, Nippon, 12-pc..200.00

Dresden

The term Dresden is used today to indicate the porcelains that were produced in Meissen and Dresden, Germany, from the very early eighteenth century well into the next. John Bottger, a young alchemist, discovered the formula for the first true porcelain in 1708 while being held a virtual prisoner at the palace in Dresden because of the King's determination to produce a superior ware. Two years later a factory was erected in nearby Meissen with Bottger as director. There fine tableware, elaborate centerpieces, and exquisite figurines with applied details were produced. In 1731, to distinguish their product from the wares of such potters as Sevres, Worcester, Chelsea, and Derby, Meissen adopted their famous crossed swords trademark. During the next century, several potteries were producing porcelain in the 'Meissen style' in Dresden itself. Their wares were marked with their own logo and the Dresden indication. Those listed here are from that era. See the Meissen section for examples with the crossed swords marking.

Basket, rtcl w/appl flowers, 4 Baroque ft, floral hdl, 5x7" 150.00
Bowl, fruit; appl flowers, rtcl sides, ftd, 7x9½" 225.00
Bowl, HP & appl flowers, boat shape, ftd, 7½x17" 325.00
Bowl, HP florals, rtcl sides, gold trim, 1860 mk, 7½x10½".........250.00
Compote, flowers, mc/gold, lattice bowl, crown mk, 5x9" 350.00
Figurine, Amour Tete-a-Tete, girl, boy, & lamb, 7x9" 450.00
Figurine, ballerina in wht lace dress w/appl flowers, 6½".............250.00
Figurine, ballerina w/pk lace skirt, rnd base, 6" 175.00
Figurine, Dame de la Cour de Francois I, C Thieme, 8" 350.00
Figurine, dancing pr, she in lace w/appl flowers, MZ, 6" 350.00

Three figures in 18th-century French costumes with courtier by coach, lacy details, 7", $1,200.00.

Figurine, gypsy lady, goat resting ft on her leg, 11" 450.00
Figurine, lady w/music book on couch, man w/violin, 10"....... 1,050.00
Figurine, Little Sister, wht w/gold & much lace 250.00
Figurine, man/lady at chess table, appl flowers, 5½x6½" 450.00
Figurine, tea party, 2 ladies/man, lace/appl roses, 8x12" 950.00
Figurine, 2 ladies, seated, 1 w/book, 1 w/flowers, 12x10" 950.00
Figurine, 2 men w/violins (1 sits), lady at piano, 10x11" 1,050.00
Figurine, 3 girls dance in circle, lace/appl flowers, 9x7" 450.00
Ice cream set, courting couples, sgn R Klemm, 1890s, 9-pc 775.00
Lamp, 4 lithophanes (1 nude), florals & cherubs, porc, 18" 1,895.00
Plaque, lady/2 cupids at 'Love' (or 'Bacchus') shrine, 8x4", pr 650.00

Tea set, roses, emb masks, C Thieme, 15-pc..................850.00
Urn, dancing nymph medallion, gold hdls, w/lid, AR mk, 24½" .650.00
Urn, 2 panels w/lovers on red w/florals, R Klemm, 12x7" 550.00
Urn, 3 nymphs & cherubs on maroon, gold branch hdls, 25" 650.00
Vase, Victorian lovers medallion w/gold on cobalt, 8" 295.00

Dresser Accessories

Dresser sets, ring trees, figural or satin pincushions, manicure sets — all those lovely items that graced milady's dressing table — were at the same time decorative as well as functional. Today they appeal to collectors for many reasons. The Victorian era is well represented by repousse silver-backed mirrors and brushes and pincushions that were used to display ornamental pins for the hair, hats, and scarves. The hair receiver — similar to a powder jar but with an opening in the lid — was used to hold the lovely strands of hair retrieved from the comb or brush. These were wound around the finger and tucked in the opening to be used later for hair jewelry and pictures, many of which survive to the present day. (See Hair Weaving.)

Celluloid dresser sets were popular during the late 1800s and early 1900s. Some included manicure tools, pill boxes, and buttonhooks, as well as the basic items. Because celluloid tends to break rather easily, a whole set may be hard to find today. (See also Plastics.) With the current interest in anything Art Deco, sets from the thirties and forties are especially collectible. These may be made of crystal, Bakelite, or silver, and the original boxes just as lavishly appointed as their contents.

Dresser set, Lucite mother-of-pearl box and jar lid, pink satin jar with embossed nudes, $58.00 for the pair.

Box, English Hobnail, cobalt glass 40.00
Box, satin glass w/HP floral, bell shape, hinged, 5½x8½".............250.00
Clothes brush, sterling, Nouveau lady emb 50.00
Hair receiver, china, allover violets w/gr leaves, 4x3" 45.00
Mirror, beveled, fr pivots on ftd stand, 15x11", EX 130.00
Set, celluloid/pearlized ivory/amber, 5-pc+tray........................35.00
Set, French ivory, 10-pc on 11x7½" tray.................................75.00
Set, French ivory, 5-pc on 5¾x9¾" tray..................................50.00
Set, Milady, canary glass, puff box+2 scent bottles........................95.00
Set, Paneled Grape, gold on milk glass, Westmoreland, 4-pc.........95.00
Tray, brass 2" rtcl fr, mirrored, 11x16"..............................18.00
Tray, gold-tone openwork w/mirror base, 20x14", NM 16.00
Tray, mirrored w/MOP fr, 1930s, 12x20" 40.00

Duncan and Miller

The firm that became known as the Duncan and Miller Glass Company in 1900 was organized in 1874 in Pittsburgh, Pennsylvania, a partnership between George Duncan, his sons Harry and James, and his son-in-law Augustus Heisey. John Ernest Miller was hired as their designer. He is credited with creating the most famous of all Duncan's glassware lines, Three Face. (See Pattern Glass.) The George Duncan and Sons Glass Company, as it was titled, was only one of eighteen companies that merged in 1891 with U.S. Glass. Soon after the Pittsburgh factory burned in 1892, the association was dissolved, and Heisey left the firm to set up his own factory in Newark, Ohio. Duncan built his new plant in Washington, Pennsylvania, where he continued to make pressed glassware in such notable patterns as Bagware, Amberette, Duncan Flute, Button Arches, and Zippered Slash. The firm was eventually sold to U.S. Glass in Tiffin, Ohio, and unofficially closed in August, 1955.

In addition to the early pressed dinnerware patterns, today's Duncan and Miller collectors enjoy searching for opalescent vases in many patterns and colors, frosted 'Satin Tone' glassware, acid-etched designs, and lovely stemware such as the Rock Crystal cuttings. Milk glass was made in limited quantity and is considered a good investment. Ruby glass, Ebony (a lovely opaque black glass popular during the twenties and thirties), and, of course, the glass animal and bird figurines are all highly valued examples of the art of Duncan and Miller.

Expect to pay at least 25% more than values listed for 'color' for ruby and cobalt and as much as 50% more in the Georgian, Pall Mall and Sandwich lines. Pink, green, and amber Sandwich is worth approximately 30% more than the same items in crystal. Milk glass examples of American Way are valued up to 30% higher than color, 50% higher in Pall Mall. Add approximately 40% to listed prices for opalescent items. Etchings, cuttings, and other decorations will increase values by about 50%. For further study, we recommend *The Encyclopedia of Duncan Glass*, by Gail Krause; she is listed in the Directory under Pennsylvania.

Animals and Birds

Bird of Paradise 475.00
Donkey, cart & peon 475.00
Goose, fat, 6x6" 245.00
Heron, 7" 95.00
Leaf Swan, bl or pk, 6½" 85.00
Leaf Swan, vaseline opal, 6½" 185.00
Ruffled Grouse 500.00
Swan, bl opal, W&F, spreadwing, 10x12½"..............225.00
Swan, crystal w/gray cut, 10½" 95.00
Swan, gr opal, W&F, spreadwing, 10x12½"..............200.00
Swan, solid, 3" 25.00
Swan, solid, 5" 20.00
Swan, solid, 7" 35.00
Swordfish 145.00
Swordfish, bl opal, rare 395.00

Astaire, color; goblet, champagne 12.00
Astaire, crystal; goblet, cocktail...............................6.00
Canterbury, color; bowl, berry; 5¼" 9.00
Canterbury, color; goblet, water; 8-oz 16.00
Canterbury, color; goblet, wine 15.00
Canterbury, color; plate, 8" 10.00
Canterbury, color; relish, divided 20.00
Canterbury, color; sherbet 12.00
Canterbury, color; torte plate, 15"............................20.00
Canterbury, crystal; bonbon, heart form 18.00
Canterbury, crystal; bowl, flared, 10½" 25.00
Canterbury, crystal; bowl, oval, 9" 25.00
Canterbury, crystal; cake plate, plain ped, 13"............70.00

Canterbury, crystal; candlestick, 4¼", pr......................20.00
Canterbury, crystal; champagne, 5-oz.........................10.00
Canterbury, crystal; cigarette box, SP lid....................45.00
Canterbury, crystal; cocktail 8.00
Canterbury, crystal; cocktail, seafood........................ 9.00
Canterbury, crystal; compote, high ft 20.00
Canterbury, crystal; creamer, 5-oz 8.00
Canterbury, crystal; creamer, 9-oz 10.00
Canterbury, crystal; cruet, pr+tray............................60.00
Canterbury, crystal; goblet, water.............................10.00
Canterbury, crystal; pickle dish, 6"............................ 7.00
Canterbury, crystal; plate, 12".................................35.00
Canterbury, crystal; relish, gold overlay, 3-part 22.00
Canterbury, crystal; relish, 3-part, hdl, 5½"...............15.00
Canterbury, crystal; relish, 3-part, rnd......................14.00
Canterbury, crystal; relish, 3-part, 3-hdl....................15.00
Canterbury, crystal; relish, 4-part 15.00
Canterbury, crystal; sherbet/champagne, tall 10.00
Canterbury, crystal; sugar bowl, 9-oz 10.00
Canterbury, crystal; torte plate, cupped, 14" 45.00
Canterbury, crystal; tray, oval, 8" 14.00
Canterbury, crystal; tray, 6" 12.50
Canterbury, crystal; tumbler, water; flat 10.00
Canterbury, crystal; wine, 3-oz 12.00
Caribbean, crystal; plate, 6" 4.00
Caribbean, crystal; plate, 8½" 8.00
Caribbean, crystal; punch bowl 75.00
Caribbean, crystal; punch cup, ruby hdl 6.00
Caribbean, crystal; relish, 5-part, 12½".....................45.00

Caribbean, water pitcher, $350.00.

Cretan, crystal; goblet, water; cut decor 9.00
Cretan, crystal; goblet, wine; cut decor...................... 9.00
First Love, crystal; bowl, fruit; hdls, 5½" 27.50
First Love, crystal; candlestick, 2-lite, pr..................85.00
First Love, crystal; candy box, 3-part, #115, 7".........35.00
First Love, crystal; flower bowl, flared, #6, 12" 70.00
First Love, crystal; goblet, champagne......................14.00
First Love, crystal; mayonnaise set, 4-pc 75.00
First Love, crystal; plate, 8½" 20.00
First Love, crystal; relish, 4-part, hdls, 9" 50.00
First Love, crystal; sandwich plate, 13" 40.00
First Love, crystal; sugar bowl, hdls, 7-oz.................24.00
First Love, crystal; urn, sq hdl, 7".............................60.00
First Love, crystal; vase, cornucopia; 8" 75.00
Georgian, crystal; mug, appl red hdl..........................25.00
Hobnail, bl opal; candy dish, 1-lb, 9½".......................65.00
Hobnail, bl opal; compote, ruffled top 28.00

Hobnail, crystal; plate, 8½" 20.00
Hobnail, crystal; sherbet, 5-oz 10.00
Hobnail, pk opal; goblet, water 18.00
Language of Flowers, crystal; bowl, 11½" 35.00
Language of Flowers, crystal; candlestick, 3", pr 35.00
Language of Flowers, crystal; mayonnaise, ftd 25.00
Laurel Wreath, crystal; goblet, champagne; cut decor .. 6.00
Mardi Gras, crystal; cake plate, ftd, 10" 65.00
Mardi Gras, crystal; punch cup..................................8.00
Mardi Gras, crystal; salt cellar, ind 9.00
Mardi Gras, crystal; sherry decanter, 12-oz, +6 ftd cordials........185.00
Murano, pk opal; bowl, crimped, 11½".......................85.00
Nautical, crystal; anchor & rope bookends 295.00
Pall Mall, color; swan, 10½"....................................80.00
Pall Mall, color; swan, 7"..50.00
Pall Mall, crystal; swan, silver overlay, 7" 35.00
Pall Mall, crystal; swan, 3½"....................................25.00
Pall Mall, crystal; swan bowl, 10½"...........................45.00
Plaza Punties, crystal; shakers, pr.............................30.00
Remembrance, crystal; goblet, champagne 14.00
Remembrance, crystal; tumbler, iced tea....................18.00
Sandwich, color; compote, 5-oz................................18.00
Sandwich, color; deviled egg plate, 12".....................48.00
Sandwich, color; goblet, water 16.00
Sandwich, crystal; basket, 5½"..................................65.00
Sandwich, crystal; bowl, cereal; 6".............................13.00
Sandwich, crystal; bowl, crimped, 11½"......................50.00
Sandwich, crystal; bowl, flared, 12"...........................50.00
Sandwich, crystal; bowl, fruit; 5" 9.00
Sandwich, crystal; bowl, ring hdls, 5".........................15.00
Sandwich, crystal; bowl, salad; deep, 10" 65.00
Sandwich, crystal; cake plate, ftd, 13"........................60.00
Sandwich, crystal; candlestick, 1-lite, pr....................50.00
Sandwich, crystal; candlestick, 4", pr 6.00
Sandwich, crystal; candy dish, flat, w/lid, sq, 6" 135.00
Sandwich, crystal; candy dish, ftd, 8½".......................47.00
Sandwich, crystal; celery dish, 4-part, 10½"................35.00
Sandwich, crystal; cheese compote 15.00
Sandwich, crystal; cheese dish, dome lid....................97.00
Sandwich, crystal; coaster, 5" 8.00
Sandwich, crystal; creamer & sugar bowl.....................21.00
Sandwich, crystal; cruet...32.00
Sandwich, crystal; cup & saucer................................15.00
Sandwich, crystal; epergne, fruit & flower decor, ftd, 14" 210.00
Sandwich, crystal; epergne, 3-pc 155.00
Sandwich, crystal; finger bowl, 4"............................. 6.00
Sandwich, crystal; goblet, cocktail; 4½".....................10.00
Sandwich, crystal; goblet, ice cream; 5-oz.................. 8.00
Sandwich, crystal; goblet, wine 15.00
Sandwich, crystal; goblet, 9-oz, 6".............................13.00
Sandwich, crystal; mayonnaise, 2-pc..........................35.00
Sandwich, crystal; mint plate, ring hdls, 7".................27.00
Sandwich, crystal; nappy, ring hdls, 6"........................19.00
Sandwich, crystal; pitcher, water 65.00
Sandwich, crystal; plate, 7"......................................11.00
Sandwich, crystal; plate, 8"......................................10.00
Sandwich, crystal; relish, 2-part, oval, 7" 35.00
Sandwich, crystal; relish, 3-part, oval, 10" 32.00
Sandwich, crystal; sundae comport, flared 15.00
Sandwich, crystal; syrup, metal lid 55.00
Sandwich, crystal; tumbler, ftd, 9-oz 12.00
Sandwich, crystal; tumbler, juice; ftd, 5-oz.................10.00
Sanibel, bl opal; relish, 2-part, 8¾".............................35.00
Spiral Flutes, color; bowl, 4¼" 5.00

Spiral Flutes, color; cigarette holder, cut decor 20.00
Spiral Flutes, color; compote 12.00
Spiral Flutes, color; compote, tall...28.00
Spiral Flutes, color; creamer & sugar bowl....................................25.00
Spiral Flutes, color; cup & saucer, demi.......................................25.00
Spiral Flutes, color; goblet, water; 6½".......................................12.00
Spiral Flutes, color; goblet, water; 8-oz.......................................17.50
Spiral Flutes, color; oyster plate, 3-flange....................................12.00
Spiral Flutes, color; plate, 7½"... 8.00
Spiral Flutes, color; plate, 8½"... 6.00
Spiral Flutes, color; sherbet, 5-oz..10.00
Spiral Flutes, color; sugar bowl...10.00
Spiral Flutes, crystal; soup.. 8.00
Spiral Flutes, crystal; sugar bowl, low...22.00
Spiral Flutes, crystal; tumbler, juice; ftd...................................... 5.00
Sylvan, crystal; plate, 7¼".. 7.50
Tavern, crystal; compote, ftd, 5"...12.00
Tavern, crystal; cruet, 6-oz...16.00
Teardrop, crystal; ash tray, 3" dia... 6.00
Teardrop, crystal; bonbon, 4-hdl, 6"..20.00
Teardrop, crystal; bowl, hdls, 6½"..10.00
Teardrop, crystal; bowl, hdls, 9" sq..29.00
Teardrop, crystal; butter dish, SP lid, ¼-lb...................................18.00
Teardrop, crystal; candlestick, 2-lite, pr......................................40.00
Teardrop, crystal; cheese compote...20.00
Teardrop, crystal; cheese stand...10.00
Teardrop, crystal; claret...14.00
Teardrop, crystal; compote, 4".. 8.00
Teardrop, crystal; cordial, 4"..24.00
Teardrop, crystal; goblet, wine; 4⅞"..20.00
Teardrop, crystal; goblet, 7½"..15.00
Teardrop, crystal; ice bucket, w/monogram, 6"..................................30.00
Teardrop, crystal; lemon dish, 4-hdl, 7"..10.00
Teardrop, crystal; marmalade, 4"..35.00
Teardrop, crystal; mayonnaise, ftd, w/ladle.....................................28.00
Teardrop, crystal; mayonnaise, hdls, 3x4".......................................18.00
Teardrop, crystal; mustard..30.00
Teardrop, crystal; nut dish, 2-part, 6"...10.00
Teardrop, crystal; olive dish, 2-part, 6"....................................... 7.00
Teardrop, crystal; pickle relish, 6"..15.00
Teardrop, crystal; plate, 10½"..22.00
Teardrop, crystal; saucer... 3.00
Teardrop, crystal; stem, 5¾"..10.00
Teardrop, crystal; tumbler, iced tea; flat, 12-oz...............................12.00
Teardrop, crystal; tumbler; iced tea; ftd, 5½"..................................14.00
Terrace, color; ash tray, ind...25.00
Terrace, color; cup & saucer..65.00
Terrace, color; plate, hdls, 6¾"..18.00
Terrace, color; tumbler, juice; flat..32.00
Terrace, color; urn, w/lid...310.00
Terrace, crystal; relish, 5-part, w/lid, 10½"...................................35.00
Touraine, crystal; goblet, water.. 8.00
Williamsburg, crystal; candle holder, pr..28.00

Durand

Durand Art Glass was a division of Vineland Glass Works in Vineland, New Jersey. Created in 1924, it was geared specifically toward the manufacture of fine handcrafted artware. Iridescent, opalescent, and cased glass was used to create such patterns as King Tut, reminiscent of Tiffany and Steuben. Production halted in 1931 after the death of Victor Durand. Very few examples are signed, and unmarked pieces are often mistaken for Steuben or Quezal. Unmarked items are often hard to sell, sometimes bringing only about half the price of a similar but signed piece.

Ash tray, bl w/irid 'waves,' match holder center, 5".....................750.00
Candlestick, bl irid, baluster on rnd ft, att, 11", pr......................900.00
Candlestick, King Tut, bl on red irid, gold ft, set of 3............. 1,325.00
Compote, bl w/wht feathers, lime stem/ft, 8" dia........................725.00
Lamp base, bright bl w/random threading, 13", NM.......................795.00
Lamp base, cobalt irid w/random threading, baluster, 11"...........575.00
Luncheon set, bl w/wht feathers, plate+sherbet+c/s..................975.00
Plate, pulled feather floral, wht on cobalt, Larsen, 6".................125.00
Spill vase, bl irid, flared rim, sgn, 7½"..................................450.00
Vase, amber cased to opal w/bl heart leaves, gold int, 6"............600.00
Vase, amber w/3 bl swirls, eng floral, incurvate, 5½"..................300.00
Vase, bl irid, bl-gr shading at top, spherical, #1995, 6"...............600.00
Vase, bl irid, long slim neck, bulbous body, sgn/#d, 19".......... 2,000.00
Vase, bl irid, long trumpet neck on bun body, #1990-8, 8".........500.00
Vase, bl irid, orange int, tapered form, ftd, sgn, 10".................700.00
Vase, bl irid, tapered cylinder, #170-8, 8".............................650.00
Vase, bl irid w/wht leaves & vines, ovoid, #1968, 6".................750.00
Vase, cobalt w/wht & silver hearts & vines, baluster, 6½"..........950.00
Vase, cobalt w/wht leaves & vines, ovoid, 9½"........................750.00

Bowl, feather pattern in ruby, opaque, and clear, signed/1995-8", 7", $700.00; Vase, feather pattern in ruby, opaque, and clear, signed/20120-12", 11½", $600.00.

Vase, gold, flat base, sgn/#20120-16, 15"..............................850.00
Vase, gr, ribbed/paneled, att, 5½x3".....................................300.00
Vase, gr irid swirls, cobalt int, pontil, ruffled rim, 5"............. 1,200.00
Vase, King Tut, gr cased to opal, orange int, #1968-8, 8½".... 1,200.00
Vase, King Tut, lt gr w/gold swirls, sgn, 7"............................700.00
Vase, King Tut, opal w/gr, gold int, slim ftd U-form, 14"....... 1,200.00
Vase, orange cased to opal w/gr leaves & vines, rnd, 7x8"...... 1,400.00
Vase, random threads on bl irid, bowl form, #1995-4, 4"...........500.00

Durant Kilns

The Durant Pottery Company operated in Bedford Village, New York, in the early 1900s. Its founder was Mrs. Clarence Rice; she was aided by L. Volkmar to whom she assigned the task of technical direction. (See also Volkmar.) The artware and tableware they produced was simple in form and decoration. The creative aspects of the work were carried on almost entirely by Volkmar himself, with only minimal crew to help with production. After Mrs. Rice's death in 1919, the pottery was purchased by Volkmar, who chose to drop the Durant name by 1930. Prior to 1919 the ware was marked simply 'Durant' and dated. After that time a stylized 'V' was added.

Bowl, concentric wedges, floral rim, bl on turq, V mk, 11"..........500.00
Bowl, raspberry/chocolate, ftd, sgn/1926, 3½x6" 225.00
Candlestick, gold/turq crackle, dtd 1915, 4x13", pr.....................395.00
Vase, cobalt, exposed ft, flanged U-form, 1917, 6x7½" 275.00

Easter

Eggs, bunnies, chicks, and baskets have all become basic elements of our Easter celebrations; and the older, more interesting examples are being collected, often for nostalgic reasons, and displayed during the holidays to make the festivities brighter.

Candy container, bunny in fire truck, papier-mache, 6", NM........60.00
Candy container, chicken, papier-mache, mc pnt, 4", EX.............95.00
Candy container, egg, papier-mache, 5", NM................................40.00
Candy container, rabbit, papier-mache, glass eyes, mc, 10" 165.00
Candy container, rabbit, papier-mache, 9", EX 25.00
Candy tin, ducks & bunnies litho, w/hdl 20.00
Decoration, rabbit w/carrot, compo, Germany, 4" 45.00
Diecut, chicks w/goblet & violets, 6x9¾" 15.00
Diecut, children around chick in shell, floral border, 8½" 12.50
Diecut, egg chariot driven by rabbit, pansy border, 9½x7".............22.00
Diecut, 4 chicks in basket, apple blossoms, 7½x7"........................12.50
Egg, HP florals on blown milk glass...20.00
Egg, Victorian ladies in park, papier-mache, sgn, lg 75.00

Elfinware

Made in Germany from about 1920 until the 1940s, these miniature vases, boxes, salt cellars, and miscellaneous novelty items are characterized by the tiny applied flowers that often cover their entire surface. Pieces with animals and birds are the most valuable, followed by the more interesting examples such as diminutive grand pianos, candle holders, etc. See also Salts, Open.

Basket, 2 hdls, 2½x2½" 30.00
Basket, 2½x3" 38.00
Bowl, oval, 4" 65.00
Box, appl forget-me-nots, orange lustre, 2½" 40.00
Box, appl roses, heart shape, 2" 45.00
Dutch shoe, 4" 75.00
Pitcher, 2" 55.00
Place card holder, appl roses on fan shape, Germany 25.00
Shoe, baby's, 3" 35.00

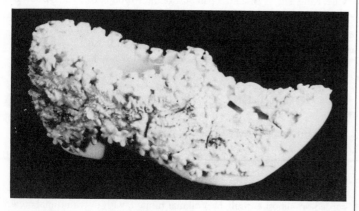

Shoe, 4" long, $75.00.

Slipper, appl rose, Germany, 3" 45.00
Swan, 2¼" 55.00

Teapot, appl forget-me-nots & roses, 2½"...................................55.00
Vase, hdls, 2½"...50.00
Watering can 45.00

English Stoneware Relief-Molded Jugs

Early relief-molded pitchers (ca 1830s-1840s) were made in two-piece molds into which sheets of clay were pressed. The relief decoration was deep and well defined, usually of animal or human subjects. Most of these pitchers were designed with a flaring lip and substantial footing. Gradually styles changed, and by the 1860s the rim had become flatter and the foot less pronounced. The relief decoration was not as deep, and foliage became a common design. By the turn of the century, many other types of pitchers had been introduced, and the market for these early styles began to wane.

Watch for recent reproductions; these have been made by the slip-casting method. Unlike relief-molded ware which is relatively smooth inside, slip-cast pitchers will have interior indentations that follow the irregularities of the relief decoration.

Anti-slavery jug with scenes of a slave auction, green glaze, Ridgway and Abington, ca 1835, 7¾", $595.00.

Apostle, wht, Meigh, 1842, 9⅞" 495.00
Bacchanalian Dance, wht, Meigh, 1844, 7⅝"..............................295.00
Eglinton Tournament, buff, Ridgway, 1840, 7¼" 275.00
Gipsy, lav on parian, Alcock, 1842, 4¾" 195.00
Julius Caesar, gray, appl laurel wreath, Meigh, 1839, 8¼"...........595.00
Naomi & Daughter-in-Law, lav on parian, Alcock, 1847, 8¾" ...275.00
Pan (w/lid), buff, Wm Ridgway, 1830s, 7¼" 350.00
Silenus, gr, Minton, 1845, 9" 250.00
Tam O'Shanter, glazed bl, Ridgway, 1835, 8¼"............................295.00
Tulip, bl & wht, Dudson, 1860, 7" 75.00
Two Drivers, gray, Minton, ca 1849, 7⅞" 750.00

Epergnes

Popular during the Victorian era, epergnes were fancy centerpieces often consisting of several tiers of vases (called lilies), candle holders, or dishes, or a combination of components. They were made in all types of art glass, and some were set in ornate plated frames.

Bl int w/HP florals, single trumpet vase in SP fr, 16x11" 350.00
Bl opal, HP florals w/gold, 1-lily, 13½x8½" 275.00
Burmese fairy lamp on gilt std on clear base w/2 vases, 17".........685.00
Clambroth, gold florals, appl ribbon edge, 1-lily, 3¾x2½" 125.00
Clear floriform vases, 10 in tiered SP holder, 1900, 12x14"........150.00
Cranberry w/appl ribbons, 3-lily, +2 clear 'canes,' 21" 1,150.00
Cranberry w/Mary Gregory putti, 1-lily; ornate ormolu base 685.00
Cranberry w/opal edge, 4 lilies in petaled/ftd bowl, 20" 450.00

Gr to clear overshot, metal base w/butterfly lady, 21x10" 375.00
Pk/wht satin, 1 lily in ftd bowl, ruffles/rigaree, 12" 350.00
Red to pk cased satin, frosted rigaree, 1-lily/bowl, 12x9" 975.00
Vaseline opal, 4-lily, appl rigaree, 20" 895.00

Lime opalescent lily and two baskets with rigaree in Meriden stand with cherubs, 26", $600.00.

Erickson

Carl Erickson of Bremen, Ohio, produced hand-formed glassware from 1943 until 1960 in artistic shapes, no two of which were identical. One of the characteristics of his work was the air bubbles that were captured within the glass. Though most examples are clear, colored items were also made. Rather than to risk compromising his high standards by selling the factory, when Erickson retired, the plant was dismantled and sold.

Bottle, scent; emerald gr, bubble stopper 95.00
Bowl, smoke, controlled bubbles, paperweight, 13½" 95.00
Candlestick, gr, controlled bubbles, paperweight, tall, pr.............125.00
Compote, smoke & gr, bubble-ball base, #3805, sm, pr................90.00
Decanter, cranberry, w/stopper, unsgn 95.00
Vase, crystal & flamed amethyst, 10x7" 75.00
Vase, smoke, clear paperweight base w/bubbles, 6½" 40.00
Vase, smoke w/sq crystal base, 14" 165.00

Erphila

Ebeling and Ruess, an importing company in Philadelphia, began operations in 1886. The acronym 'Erphila' was frequently substituted for the manufacturer's mark, a practice that evidently continued into the early 1950s; since then, 'E and R' has been used. The company imported from factories such as Furstenberg, W. Gobel, Villeroy and Boch, Heinrich, Keramos, and Schumann, to name a few. Figurines, art pottery, and some utilitarian items can be found bearing the Erphila mark. Examples are hard to find. Early German marks (those prior to 1900) often contain the word 'Fayence' in black ink. After the turn of the century a rectangular mark in green ink was used. Following WWI (1918 to the late 1930s), porcelain items imported from Czechoslovakia sometimes carried gold and silver labels. In the thirties the mark was 'Philadelphia' encircled by the sweeping front leg of an R. 'INC.' was added in the late 1930s and was used into the forties; these may also appear as paper labels. 'Bavaria,' 'Black Forest,' and 'Italy' are sometimes found in combination with 'Erphila.'

Biscuit jar, yel, red berries w/leaves on lid 48.00

Bottle, wht porc, bulbous, w/gold stopper, MIG 28.50
Box, fruit in relief on lid, basket form w/hdls, mk, 6¼" 300.00
Candlestick, child on base, mk, MIG.....................................32.00
Coffeepot, blk poodle sits on hind legs, MIG, 8½" 115.00
Creamer, cow standing, mc spots, 4½" 38.00
Creamer, duck shape, bl/wht, head as lid, 5½" 95.00
Creamer, horse & wagon scene, blk/tan, w/lid, 5½" 85.00
Creamer, wht w/blk cat hdl, 3" 35.00
Figurine, cat, wht w/gold ball, #1360, MIG, 8½" L.................65.00
Figurine, dog, blk/wht, hunting pose, MIG, 10" L...................45.00
Figurine, fox, crouching, brn, MIG, 8½" L...........................95.00
Figurine, horse, wht, gold label, 3¾" 24.00
Figurine, lion, tan, MIG, 3" L..10.00
Figurine, rooster, wht, silver label, 11¾" 40.00
Figurine, terrier, sitting, mk US Zone, MIG, 4½" 30.00
Figurine, 2 parrots on tree stump, gr/bl, MIG, 6½" 52.00
Figurine, 2 pheasants on oval base, MIG, 5½" 40.00

Inkwell, modeled as a lady, marked 'Erphila, Ink Girls, Germany #6003,' 4½", $87.50.

Mug, coach scene, mc, ½-liter, 4¼" 35.00
Mug, Toby type, red, 4¼" 35.00
Pitcher, men in cavalier costume on brn, w/3 mugs, 9" 210.00
Pitcher, troll head, #1038, yel w/blk & red..............................130.00
Plate, grapes on majolica, Blk Forest, MIG, 9" 160.00
Shakers, Dutch man & woman, pr..18.00
Sprinkling can, poppies, orange on wht, porc, 5½" 45.00

Eskimo Artifacts

While ivory carvings made from walrus tusks or whale teeth have been the most emphasized articles of Eskimo art, basketry and woodworking are other areas in which these Alaskan Indians excell. Their designs are effected through the application of simple yet dramatic lines and almost stark decorative devices. Though not pursued to the extent of American Indian art, the unique work of this northern tribe is beginning to attract the serious attention of today's collectors.

Basket, baleen, baleen-inlay ivory seal surmount, 1x3", EX 475.00
Basket, baleen, cvd ivory surmount, sgn Sikvayugak/1965, 6". 1,200.00
Basket, coiled baleen, ivory seal on lid, 3¾x4" 800.00
Belt, lady's, hide panels w/row of caribou incisors, 49".................500.00
Bola, throwing; hide-covered, beaded decor, 1870, 24" 300.00
Bowl, horn/ivory, w/sinew string wrap, 1880, 38x1½".................550.00
Box, wood, cvd as a bowhead whale, red-stained cvd mouth, 9"..650.00
Cribbage brd, ivory, cvd hunting scenes, Alaska map, 21"...........600.00
Cribbage brd, ivory, cvd w/whale scene, 1960, 5x2" 50.00
Cribbage brd, men/animals cvd & pnt on tusk, att Happy Jack ...900.00

Cvg, gray soapstone, Eskimo lady holding animal, 1940, 11".......150.00
Cvg, gray soapstone, Eskimo woman, 1950, 14" 100.00
Cvg, ivory, goose, 1920, 2½x2" 70.00
Cvg, ivory, kayak w/man & 2 seals, 1930, 2x7" 185.00
Cvg, ivory, walking polar bear, 1940, 3x1" 80.00
Cvg, ivory/baleen, polar bear, arms open at elbow, 5" 550.00
Doll, half-torso, cvd head, red stain/scaring, beads, 2½" 400.00
Doll's head, Bering Sea Culture, cvd ivory, dk patina, 2¼" .. 1,250.00
Earrings, cvd ivory w/3 drops of baleen & trade beads, 3" 1,400.00
Game ball, pitch on wood, baleen dot-inlay ivory disks, 4" 200.00
Game drag hdl, looped hide w/3 baleen-inlay cvd ivory seals.. 2,000.00
Goggles, snow; wood, cvd lines/red & blk pigment, visor, 5".......550.00
Hairpin, bone, serrated/polished, Alaska, 300-200 BC, 8½" 135.00
Harpoon point, Bering Sea Culture, ivory, EX patina, 2¼" 165.00
Harpoon rest, ivory, eng whales/etc, bead eyes, Y-form, 8" 450.00
Hatchet, cvd bone blade & hdl, 1900, 10x5"................................65.00
Hatchet, cvd/polished bone, 1900, 10x14" 125.00
Hide scraper, ivory, Alaska, 400-300 BC 35.00
Kayak model, EX detail, ivory attachments, 23"...........................225.00
Kayak model, hide/wood/ivory, w/cloth-covered Eskimo, 33" 210.00
Kayak model, sealskin on wood fr, ivory mts, 25" L....................300.00
Mask, ceremonial; Loon, 13 appendages, 1940s, 20x18"..............400.00

Polychrome wood mask representing a seal. Inserted animal whiskers; green, black, natural and red paint; bentwood framing; sinew bound. Mask only: 8¾", $1,200.00.

Mask, forehead; wood, depicts animal w/exposed bkbone, 16" 200.00
Mask, human face, fish/animal/hand appendages, 20th C, 15" 250.00
Mask, stylized features, fur coiffure, bone teeth, 1920, 9" 700.00
Mural, inlaid sealskin, drummer & 2 dancers, 1920, 31x24" 300.00
Needlecase, ivory, well-cvd thimble guard, trade beads, 5" 500.00
Pipe, ivory, dogs/wolves//etc, baleen inlay/pigment, 12".......... 1,000.00
Pipe, ivory, eng circles/dots in red & blk, sq shaft, 9"...................425.00
Pipe, ivory, sea mammals/kayak surmount, blk pigment, 8" 600.00
Pouch, sealskin w/hide embr, mc wood fastener, bone clasp 450.00
Shaman's wand, ivory, detailed bust of man as finial, 8" 900.00
Spear, bird; wood w/3 bone barbs & bone point, 65" 475.00
Tusk, cvd as sled & dog team, 1940, 18x4" 500.00
Tusk, walrus; no decor, natural patina, 26" L 450.00
Wand, Oosik, whalebone, animal on baleen plaque ea end, 21" .425.00

Fabris Porcelain

Similar in quality, workmanship, and design, fine Fabris porcelain sculptures might easily be confused with Meissen and Dresden pieces; only the red-iron anchor mark denotes the difference.

The French sculptor, Jean-Pierre Varion, formerly of the Vincennes factory, settled in Este, Italy, during the 1750s. He died soon after developing his own formula for porcelain. His wife, Fiorina, and a partner, Antonio Costa, formed a business and manufactured the first Fabris sculptures at Bassano del Grappa in 1875. Many of the figurines and groupings were after paintings by 18th-century artists such as Fragonard, the Rococo decorator; Longhi; and the playwright, Carlo Goldoni. Most of the figures and groups were of a limited production; strict attention was given to detail.

The Museum Collection, a 1980-1982 re-issue, utilized the very early molds. A gold anchor mark was used on this limited line only; after this period, they reverted back to the red-iron anchor. Items listed here bear the red mark unless noted otherwise. Our advisor for this category is Donald Penrose; he is listed in the Directory under Ohio.

Aunt, aunt on sofa chaperoning 2 lovers, 9x16" 2,000.00
Beauties, 2 ladies on flowered balcony, 8½x10" 650.00
Cecilia, girl w/wht skirt, 2 flower baskets, 4½x5¼" 300.00
Coppersmith, man sits/mends copper pot, tricorn hat, 5½x8" 350.00
Flamenco Dancer, girl in red bodice & lace dress, 13½" 950.00
Gertrude, flowered dress, knitting bag, 6x7"..............................425.00
Girl in pk lace skirt, holding basket of flowers, 5x8½" 550.00
Harlequin's Love, girl & clown in costume, seated, 11x15" 2,700.00
Lady Beatrice, wht skirt, fashion magazine in lap, 7½x7½"..........550.00
Lovers, lady w/man resting head on her lap, 9x7" 750.00
Margarita, girl w/ft on bl pillow, wht skirt, 6x6"........................350.00
Melon Vendor, brn pants, wht apron, & melons, 5½x10½" 350.00
Musical, 2 figures: man at piano, woman singing, 6½x8½" 550.00

Rug Vendor, 10", $550.00.

Swing, girl on swing in floral & leaf arbor, 10x11½" 1,500.00
2-Faced Woman, young girl on 1 side, old hag on other, 9" 450.00

Fairings

Fairings, small chinaware figural groups that portray amusing (if not risque) scenes of courting couples, marital woes, and family feuds, were popular purchases and prizes at 19th-century English fairs. From 1840 through the 1850s, their bases were embossed with marks that identified the manufacturer as well as the artist who applied the polychrome enameling. From 1860 until 1870, they were no longer marked and became smaller in size. During the 1870s, they retained their smaller size but once again were marked in relief, indicating manufacturer and artisan. Through the 1880s, all marks were omitted; but the bases were much more shallow than those from the 1860s. About 1890, the Staffordshire potters sold the molds to German manufacturers who marked their product with the name of their country until about 1900. Examples from this period are most commonly encountered. Fairings made in Germany in the early 20th century often have two holes in their bases.

Generally, the more complex groups and those that are marked bring the higher prices. Earlier examples from the sixties and seventies are of better quality. Similiar items such as small boxes and match holders with much the same type of theme and figural decoration are also listed here.

Bank, pk cottage w/Present From Scarborough in gold, 4" W 150.00
Ben Franklin, blk hair, red vest, grassy base, 3" 65.00
Box, cat w/frog, English, 3"..90.00
Box, child at table, 3"...90.00
Box, child in bed w/kitten, Elbogen mk, 4½" 100.00
Box, child on bed pulls on pajama bottoms, Elbogen mk, 4" 120.00
Box, child overlooks duck in pond, English, 4½" 90.00

Box, dresser with musical instruments on lid, 3¾", $95.00.

Box, girl w/puppy, Elbogen mk, 4½" 100.00
Box, reclining child w/basket of flowers, English, 3½" 90.00
Box, Token of Friendship, English, 4½" 100.00
Box, tree stump w/bird on lid, wings spread 80.00
Box, 2 children w/picture book, English, 4"..................................90.00
Cat stands on gr base, 2½x3"...130.00
Come Where Love Lies Dreaming, lady in bed, Germany 155.00
Did You Ring Sir?, man in tub & maid, early 135.00
Five O'Clock Tea, kittens/saucers of milk, Elbogen style, 6".........30.00
Grandma & Grandpa, w/flower basket & cane, pr 285.00
Happy Father, What 2?..., couple/twins, 1880s, 3½" 110.00
I Am Off w/Him, lady w/dog & basket...175.00
I Am Starting for a Long Journey, man w/satchel & book 175.00
Last in Bed To Put Out the Light, 3½"..225.00
Lor, Three Legs! I'll Charge..., 3-legged man & boy....................255.00
Merry Widow, lady cat w/roses at ft 250.00
Oysters Sir, lady at bench, w/match striker...................................255.00
Sheep, wht on gr grass base, Staffordshire, ca 1800, 2x2" 130.00
Twelve Months After Marriage, unmk, 3½x3½"..........................250.00
Uncle Sam figure on sm dish, Germany...200.00
Union Forever, soldier leading charge, w/match striker 325.00
Welsh Tea Party, mk Germany...275.00
Who Said Rats?, cat in bed, mouse on table, early 135.00

Fans

The Japanese are said to have invented the fan. From there it went to China, and Portuguese traders took the idea to Europe. Though usually considered milady's accessory, even the gentlemen in 17th-century England carried fans! More fashionable than practical, some were of feathers and lovely hand-painted silks with carved ivory or tortoise sticks. Some French fans had peepholes. There are mourning fans, calendar fans, and those with advertising.

Fine antique fans (pre-1900) of ivory or mother of pearl have recently escalated in value. Those from before 1800 often sell for upwards of $1,000.00. Examples with mother of pearl sticks are most desirable; least desirable are those with sticks of celluloid. Our advisor for this category is Vicki Flanigan; she is listed in the Directory under Virginia.

Boy & girl under palm leaf on island HP on silk, MOP sticks......**300.00**
Brise, pierced horn, sticks: gilt/jewels/enamel, 1800s, 7" **550.00**
Chantilly lace, plain tortoise-shell sticks, 1880s, 12" **160.00**
Chantilly lace w/flowers, tortoise-shell sticks, 1910, 14".............**150.00**
Chinese figures, HP, well-cvd MOP sticks, Canton, 1880, 10"....**325.00**
Floral spray HP on silk, plain MOP sticks, 9½" **150.00**
Italian scene printed/HP ea side, rtcl MOP sticks, 1850, 11".......**450.00**
Lace/sequin bird on net, tortoise sticks w/steel pique, 1890 ....**300.00**

Lace and hand-painted tulle, tortoise shell sticks, French, 26" wide, NM with box, $150.00.

Lady & gardener, chromolitho on silk, MOP sticks, 11" **135.00**
Military officers & king/Marquis de Lafayette, printed, 11" **900.00**
Needlepoint lace w/people, rtcl celluloid sticks, 1900, 14" **300.00**
Pastoral scene, printed paper, cvd ornate MOP sticks, 1850........**495.00**
Pheasant feathers, tortoise-shell sticks, 1910, 9" **100.00**
Point plat de venise lace, bone sticks, 1860, 10" **220.00**
Rosepoint lace: scrolls/florals, celluloid sticks, 1900, 14" **275.00**
Scene on paper, cvd/rtcl/silvered MOP sticks, Fr, 1850 ....**400.00**
Scene printed ea side on paper, cvd MOP sticks, 1850, 11" **400.00**
Scene printed/HP on paper, rtcl MOP sticks, Europe, 1850.........**400.00**
Silk, gauze leaves/sequins/embr, cvd MOP sticks, 1850, 11" **400.00**
Wedding party HP, MOP/gilt-floral sticks, sgn/Madrid, '05, 12" .**250.00**

Farm Collectibles

Country living in the 19th century entailed plowing, planting, and harvesting; gathering eggs and milking; making soap from lard rendered on butchering day; and numerous other tasks performed with primitive tools of which we in the 20th century have had little first-hand knowledge. For more information on this subject, we recommend *Collecting Farm Antiques*, an identification and value guide by our advisor for this category, Lar Hothem; his address is listed in the Directory under Ohio. See also Cast Iron; Woodenware; Wrought Iron.

Bean sorter, wood, slatted bottom, 1870s, 3½x19x18¼" 225.00
Blinder, mule; tin & leather, ca 1900, 19x12x10", EX 70.00
Book, Dr Hess' Stock book, illus, 1901, EX....................................15.00
Book, Farm Implement News Buyer's Buide, 1913, VG 6.50
Corn dryer, braided/twisted wire, 50-prong, 31", EX 35.00
Corn husker, brass, A&O, 1862, EX 25.00
Corn sheller, wood block w/hollow center, handmade, 13½" L 65.00
Hay fork, wood, 3-tine, old varnish, 1-pc, 59" 140.00
Implement seat, CI, Bradley's Mower 100.00

Implement seat, CI, Buckeye, Akron, 1900s, 16x15x3½" 80.00	Aqua Crest, vase, bowl form...22.00
Implement seat, CI, heart form, openwork, ca 1900, 18x14" 50.00	Aqua Crest, vase, dbl-crimped, #4517, 6½" 34.00
Implement seat, CI, Jenkins 55.00	Aqua Crest, vase, dbl-crimped, 4" 20.00
Implement seat, CI, KPCO 45.00	Aqua Crest, vase, ruffled, 6" 35.00
Implement seat, CI, Walter A Wood 40.00	Aqua Crest, vase, tulip; 4" 30.00
Manual, McCormick-Deering Farmall F-14, 1936, EX.............25.00	Aqua Crest, vase, tulip; 5" 35.00
Manual, Stock Raisers, pamphlet type, EX 9.00	Beaded Melon, bottle, cologne; gr overlay, low, w/stopper 50.00
Pamphlet, Minneapolis-Moline Universal Tractor, 1937, 23-pg....10.00	Beaded Melon, creamer, milk glass, 4".........................22.00
	Beaded Melon, jug, gold overlay, hdl, 6"......................45.00
	Beaded Melon, rose bowl, bl overlay, 3½".....................20.00
	Beaded Melon, rose bowl, dk gr overlay, 3½".................40.00
	Beaded Melon, vase, gr overlay, #2711, mini.................17.50
	Beaded Melon, vase, gr overlay, #711, 8".....................42.00
	Beaded Melon, vase, gr overlay, decor, 4"....................35.00
	Beaded Melon, vase, gr overlay, 4"...........................22.50
	Beaded Melon/Peach Crest, basket, 7".........................80.00
	Beaded Melon/Peach Crest, bowl, 7"...........................56.00
	Beaded Melon/Peach Crest, vase, 5"...........................48.00
	Beaded Melon/Silver Crest, vase, 6"...........................15.00
	Big Cookies, basket, ruby 100.00
	Big Cookies, cookie jar, amber, #1681 ....90.00
	Big Cookies, macaroon jar, ebony, #1681, 7".................115.00
	Black Crest, bonbon, hdld, #7333............................45.00
	Black Rose, vase, hand form, #5155, 10½"...................195.00
	Black Rose, vase, tulip; 8" 145.00

Pulley block, cypress with iron fixtures, used to anchor the rope in order to pull hay up into the barn loft, $40.00.

Seed grader, wood fr, tin bottom, red pnt, 2½x11½x20" 60.00	Block & Star, candlestick, turq, pr..............................28.00
Shovel, maple, hewn, open-D hdl, 1800s, EX patina, 36"...........225.00	Blue Overlay, basket, #1924, 7"...............................65.00
Shovel, scoop style w/D-hdl, wear/age splits, EX 150.00	Blue Overlay, jug, hdl, #192, 8½"............................55.00
Stool, milking; iron, 3-legged, sm...................................20.00	Bubble Optic, vase, honey amber, 11½"......................125.00
Stool, milking; wood, stick legs pegged through sq top, 10" 45.00	Burmese, boot, glossy 35.00
Yoke, oxen; wood, orig red pnt, crude, 1800s, 45x6½x4½" 85.00	Burmese, vase, tulip; 11" 75.00
Yoke, oxen; wood, well shaped, 45" 150.00	Butterfly Net, finger bowl, French opal, w/underplate 225.00
Yoke, shoulder; cvd wood, dk gr pnt, ca 1820, 37" L 85.00	Cameo, bowl, cameo opal, #857, 11½" 30.00
	Celeste Blue, vase, fan form, #203, 9½".....................50.00
	Chinese Yellow, bowl, cupped, #846, on ebony base, 6" H.........125.00
	Chinese Yellow, bowl, oval, #1663, 13".....................150.00
	Chinese Yellow, candlestick, #315, 3½" 50.00
	Coin Dot, atomizer, French opal 33.00
	Coin Dot, basket, bl opal, 4½" 35.00
	Coin Dot, basket, cranberry opal, 7".........................110.00
	Coin Dot, bowl, bl opal, 10"..................................80.00

Fenton

Frank and John Fenton were brothers who founded the Fenton Art Glass Company in 1906 in Martin's Ferry, Ohio. The venture, at first only a decorating shop, began operations in July of 1905 using blanks purchased from other companies. This operation soon proved unsatisfactory, and by 1907 they had constructed their own glass factory in Williamstown, West Virginia. John left the company in 1909 and organized his own firm in Millersburg, Ohio.

The Fenton Company produced over 130 patterns of carnival glass. They also made custard, chocolate, opalescent, and stretch glass. This company has always been noted for its various colors of glass and has continually changed its production to stay attune with current tastes in decorating. In 1925 they produced a line of 'handmade' items that incorporated the techniques of threading and mosaic work. Because the process proved to be unprofitable, the line was discontinued by 1927. Even their glassware made in the past twenty-five years is already regarded as collectible. Various paper labels have been used since the 1920s; only since 1970 has the logo been stamped into the glass.

For information concerning Fenton Art Glass Collectors of America, Inc., see the Clubs, Newsletters, and Catalogs section of the Directory. See also Carnival Glass; Custard Glass; Stretch Glass.

Apple Tree, vase, topaz opal, ruffled rim, rare, 12" 185.00	Coin Dot, bowl, topaz opal, crimped, 6½" 45.00
Aqua Crest, bonbon, dbl-crimped, 6" 12.00	Coin Dot, candlestick, cranberry opal, #1524, 5¾", pr.........65.00
Aqua Crest, bowl, 8½"...37.00	Coin Dot, creamer, French opal, 4" 28.00
Aqua Crest, candle holder, cornucopia form, 6", pr 45.00	Coin Dot, cruet, French opal, #208, 7" 75.00
Aqua Crest, plate, 12" 35.00	Coin Dot, decanter, cranberry opal, #894, 12" 140.00
Aqua Crest, sherbet 25.00	Coin Dot, pitcher, lime opal, lg 150.00
Aqua Crest, tidbit tray, 3-tier...65.00	Coin Dot, top hat, bl opal 30.00
	Coin Dot, vase, cranberry opal, dbl-crimped, #203, 4x4¾" 48.00
	Coin Dot, vase, cranberry opal, tricorner, 7" 60.00
	Coin Dot, vase, cranberry opal, 4½".........................30.00
	Coin Dot, vase, cranberry opal, 7½"........................105.00
	Coin Dot, vase, cranberry opal, 8¾".......................120.00
	Coin Dot, vase, French opal, dbl-crimped, #1925, 6"..........45.00
	Coin Dot, vase, tulip; lime opal, 10½" 125.00
	Crystal Crest, bowl, crimped, rare, 7".......................50.00
	Crystal Crest, plate, 8½"....................................50.00
	Crystal Crest, vase, tricorner, 4"............................47.00
	Daisy & Button, bonbon, milk glass, 5½"....................12.00
	Daisy & Button, candlestick, milk glass, pr..................22.50
	Daisy & Button, console set, milk glass, #1904, 3-pc.........40.00
	Daisy & Button, creamer, Colonial bl........................17.50
	Daisy & Button, vanity set, rose, #957, 3-pc on fan tray.............160.00
	Dancing Ladies, vase, Mongolian Gr, #901, 8½"...............185.00

Dancing Ladies, vase, Moonstone, #901	195.00
Diamond Lace, cake plate, bl opal, ped ft, #1948	55.00
Diamond Lace, candle holder, French opal, pr	25.00
Diamond Lace, epergne, bl opal, 3-lily, apartment sz	95.00
Diamond Lace, epergne, French opal, 11"	145.00
Diamond Optic, basket, ruby overlay, 7"	60.00
Diamond Optic, bowl, bl opal, rolled rim, #1502, 14"	25.00
Diamond Optic, ice bucket, ruby	70.00
Diamond Optic, vase, bl opal, flared, 8½"	48.00
Diamond Optic, vase, lime gr overlay, 9½"	70.00
Diamond Optic, vase, swung; lt gr opal, 12"	25.00
Dolphin, bonbon, jade gr, hdls, 6"	22.00
Dolphin, bowl, jade gr, ftd, oval, #1608	95.00
Dolphin, bowl, royal bl, etched, sq, #1621-E, 9½"	48.00
Dolphin, candlestick, ruby, 3½"	25.00
Dolphin, compote, orchid, ftd, 7½"	55.00
Dolphin, compote, ruby, ftd, 7½"	55.00
Dolphin, vase, jade gr, hdls, 5½"	30.00
Dolphin, vase, pk, cut decor, fan form, 6"	65.00
Dot Optic, pitcher, bl opal, 9"	125.00
Dot Optic, pitcher, cranberry opal, cream sz	75.00
Dot Optic, pitcher, gr opal, 9"	125.00
Dot Optic, pitcher, lemonade; ruby, +6 tumblers	325.00
Dot Optic, sugar shaker, cranberry opal, #2293, 4½"	125.00
Dot Optic, tumbler, cranberry opal, flat, #1353, 4"	25.00
Ebony, bowl, cupped, #607, 8"	60.00
Ebony, bowl, oval, 10½"	65.00
Ebony, candlestick, #449, 8½", pr	85.00
Ebony, vase, fan form, 7¼"	48.00
Emerald Crest, bowl, heart shape	40.00
Emerald Crest, cake plate, 13"	80.00
Emerald Crest, cake tray, metal hdl	55.00
Emerald Crest, compote, 6"	30.00
Emerald Crest, compote, 7"	22.50
Emerald Crest, cup & saucer	40.00
Emerald Crest, flowerpot	40.00
Emerald Crest, flowerpot, decor, 1-pc	75.00
Emerald Crest, saucer	15.00
Emerald Crest, sherbet	25.00
Emerald Crest, vase, #298, 6"	26.00
Emerald Crest, vase, fan form, 4"	18.00
Figurine, cat, carnival, 11"	55.00
Flame, bowl, #847, 7½"	75.00
Georgian, claret, ruby, #1611, 4½-oz	18.00
Georgian, creamer & sugar bowl, ruby, #1611	35.00
Georgian, cup & saucer, ruby, #1611	18.00
Georgian, shakers, ruby, #1611, 4½", ea	60.00
Georgian, sherbet, ruby, 8"	6.00
Georgian, tumbler, ruby, 2½-oz	8.00
Gold Crest, bowl, decor, 11"	50.00
Gold Crest, vase, dbl-crimped, #1924, 4"	40.00
Hobnail, ash tray, bl opal, fan shape, 5½"	28.00
Hobnail, banana boat, milk glass	42.50
Hobnail, basket, bl opal, 4"	42.50
Hobnail, basket, bl opal, 7"	65.00
Hobnail, basket, cranberry opal, 10"	145.00
Hobnail, basket, French opal, shallow, 10"	110.00
Hobnail, basket, French opal, 4"	40.00
Hobnail, basket, French opal, 7½"	55.00
Hobnail, basket, peachblow, shallow, 5½"	42.50
Hobnail, basket, ruby overlay, 7"	75.00
Hobnail, basket, yel opal, 4"	55.00
Hobnail, bonbon, French opal, 5½"	20.00
Hobnail, bottle, cologne; cranberry opal, 4"	50.00

Hobnail, bowl, bl opal, 10"	65.00
Hobnail, bowl, French opal, dbl-crimped, ftd, 11"	85.00
Hobnail, bowl, fruit; milk glass, oval, 12"	20.00
Hobnail, bowl, nappy, cranberry opal, dbl-crimped, 6½"	22.00
Hobnail, bowl, plum opal, 6-sided, crimped, ftd, 8½"	75.00
Hobnail, butter dish, French opal, rnd lid	95.00
Hobnail, cake plate, topaz opal, ftd, 13"	125.00
Hobnail, candle holder, bl opal, cornucopia form, 6", pr	37.50
Hobnail, candle holder, French opal, cornucopia form, 6", pr	25.00
Hobnail, candlestick, French opal, #3870, pr	32.00
Hobnail, candlestick, topaz opal, squat	22.00
Hobnail, candy dish, French opal, ftd	45.00
Hobnail, compote, gr pastel, tall, w/lid	50.00
Hobnail, compote, turq, tall w/lid	40.00
Hobnail, creamer & sugar bowl, bl opal, 3"	20.00
Hobnail, creamer & sugar bowl, topaz opal, ind, 2"	36.00
Hobnail, cruet, bl opal, 4"	25.00
Hobnail, cruet, cranberry opal, 4"	75.00
Hobnail, cruet, cranberry opal, 6"	68.00
Hobnail, cruet; French opal, 4"	22.00
Hobnail, epergne, bl opal, 3-lily, apartment sz	90.00
Hobnail, jug, milk glass, 80-oz	65.00
Hobnail, lamp, hurricane; peachblow, #3998	95.00
Hobnail, marmalade, bl opal, 4-pc	90.00
Hobnail, mustard set, bl opal, 3-pc	27.50
Hobnail, pitcher, cranberry opal, sq top, 5½"	80.00

Hobnail pitcher, cranberry opal, water size, $200.00.

Hobnail, pitcher, topaz opal, #285, 5½"	38.00
Hobnail, planter, milk glass, sq, 4"	7.00
Hobnail, shakers, bl opal, flat, pr	55.00
Hobnail, shakers, cranberry opal, flat, pr	65.00
Hobnail, shakers, cranberry opal, ftd, pr	50.00
Hobnail, shakers, French opal, flat, pr	35.00
Hobnail, sugar bowl, bl opal, ind, 2"	10.00
Hobnail, top hat, bl opal, 2¾"	22.50
Hobnail, top hat, bl opal, 3½"	35.00
Hobnail, tumbler, topaz opal, bbl form, 12-oz	37.00
Hobnail, tumbler, topaz opal, flat, 9-oz, 4½"	25.00
Hobnail, vase, bl opal, crimped, 4"	15.00
Hobnail, vase, bl opal, fan form, 3¾"	24.00
Hobnail, vase, bud; topaz opal, ftd, 8"	30.00
Hobnail, vase, cranberry opal, cupped, flared, 5"	60.00
Hobnail, vase, cranberry opal, tricorner, 4"	37.00
Hobnail, vase, cranberry opal, 8"	95.00
Hobnail, vase, gr opal, dbl-crimped, 3"	38.00
Hobnail, vase, gr opal, 4"	18.00

Hobnail, vase, plum opal, pitcher form, #3760	185.00
Hobnail, vase, swung; bl opal, ftd, 15"	75.00
Hobnail, vase, swung; plum opal, 14"	60.00
Hobnail, vase, topaz opal, dbl-crimped, 4¾"	42.00
Hobnail, vase, topaz opal, tricorner, 4"	30.00
Hobnail, vase, topaz opal, tricorner, 8½"	145.00
Ivory Crest, cornucopia candlesticks, #1522, pr	50.00
Ivory Crest, vase, #186, 8"	45.00
Jade Green, bowl, oval, hdls, #1563, 17"	95.00
Jade Green, candelabrum, #2318, 6"	50.00
Jade Green, vase, fan form, #551, 8½"	28.00
Jade Green, vase, fan form, 7¼x10½"	40.00
Jade Green, vase, flip; 9"	62.50
Lilac, biscuit jar, cased, w/lid, rare	260.00
Lilac, shell bowl, cased, #9020, 10"	110.00
Lincoln Inn, comport, dk gr	85.00
Lincoln Inn, cup & saucer, pk	22.50
Lincoln Inn, goblet, water; crystal, 5⅞"	14.00
Lincoln Inn, plate, ruby, 6"	28.00
Lincoln Inn, plate, ruby, 7"	10.00
Lincoln Inn, saucer, fruit; pk, 5"	45.00
Lincoln Inn, shakers, blk, pr	250.00
Lincoln Inn, sherbet, cobalt, 4¾"	25.00
Lincoln Inn, sherbet, ruby, 4¾"	25.00
Lincoln Inn, tumbler, amber, ftd, rare, 7-oz	30.00
Lincoln Inn, tumbler, bl, ftd, 6"	28.00
Lincoln Inn, vase, jade gr, 10"	175.00
Lincoln Inn, wine, jade gr, ca 1931, 4"	32.50
Macaroon, cookie jar, jade gr, #1681	110.00
Mandarin Red, bowl, #950, 11"	100.00
Mandarin Red, vase, crimped, 6½"	65.00
Melon Rib, bottle, scent; bl overlay, w/stopper, 9"	35.00
Melon Rib, bottle, scent; mulberry, low, w/stopper, 9"	95.00
Melon Rib, bottle, scent; rose overlay, w/stopper, 5½"	30.00
Melon Rib/Gold Crest, candlestick, 5", pr	30.00
Melon Rib/Gold Crest, vase, 6"	30.00
Melon Rib/Silver Crest, bottle, scent; w/stopper, 7"	32.00
Ming, cornucopia candlestick, rose pastel, #950, 5½", pr	55.00
Ming, cornucopia centerpc, rose pastel, +2 candlesticks	125.00
Ming, pitcher, gr, 10"	95.00
Ming, vase, rose, #621, 6½"	38.00
Mongolian Green, basket, reeded hdl	100.00
Mongolian Green, vase, #847, 5" dia	70.00
Moonstone, candlestick, ebony base, #346, 8"	58.00
Peach Crest, basket, crystal hdl, #203, 7"	75.00
Peach Crest, bowl, dbl-crimped, 10"	80.00
Peach Crest, bowl, salad; 10"	65.00
Peach Crest, candlestick, #1523, 5", pr	55.00
Peach Crest, jug, hdl, #192	75.00
Peach Crest, vase, dbl-crimped, 6¼"	20.00
Peach Crest, vase, hat form, #75, 3"	28.00
Peach Crest, vase, tulip; 9"	50.00
Peach Crest, vase, 6"	30.00
Pekin Blue, bowl, oval, #1663, 12½"	80.00
Pekin Blue, candlestick, 8½", pr	125.00
Pekin Blue, vase, #621, 6"	45.00
Periwinkle Blue, bowl, crimped, #847, 8½"	60.00
Periwinkle Blue, vase, crimped, #847, 6½"	62.50
Periwinkle Blue, vase, fan form, #847, 9"	75.00
Pineapple, goblet, bl opal, ftd	9.00
Plymouth, champagne, ruby	12.50
Plymouth, goblet, water; ruby	17.50
Plymouth, highball, amber, #1620, 8-oz	18.00
Plymouth, tumbler, juice; ruby	15.00
Polka Dot, rose bowl, cranberry opal, 5"	110.00
Polka Dot, shakers, cranberry opal, 3", pr	65.00
Polka Dot, vase, cranberry opal, #3160, 6"	95.00
Rib Optic, finger lamp, ruby overlay, appl amber hdl	88.00
Rib Optic, pitcher, lemonade; ruby overlay, +6 tumblers	325.00
Rib Optic, wine decanter, cranberry opal	110.00
Rosalene, bell	45.00
Rosalene, bud vase	25.00
Rose Crest, bowl, 3½x7"	25.00
Rose Crest, jug, hdl, #192A, 9"	48.00
Rose Crest, plate, 10"	55.00
Rose Overlay, basket, #1924, 5"	50.00
Rose Overlay, puff jar & lid	28.00
Rose Pastel, basket, #1924	75.00
Ruby, ash tray, 3-ftd, #848	27.50
Ruby, plate, hdls, sq, #1639, 12"	65.00
Ruby Overlay, basket, 5"	65.00
Ruby Overlay, ivy ball, ftd, #1021	60.00
Ruby Overlay, vase, tricorner, 6"	37.50
San Toy, cornucopia centerpc, rose, #950, 11"	85.00
San Toy, vase, rose, etched, #898, 11½"	65.00
Sheffield, bowl, bl, ruffled, 12½"	25.00
Sheffield, tumbler, ruby, #1800, 4¼"	20.00
Sheffield, vase, wht stretch, unusual shape, 7¼"	125.00
Silver Crest, basket, divided, rare, 9"	95.00
Silver Crest, basket, shallow, 8"	20.00
Silver Crest, bell	32.50
Silver Crest, bonbon, ruffled, metal center hdl, 8"	10.00
Silver Crest, bowl, flat, 6"	10.00
Silver Crest, cake plate, low, ftd, 13"	32.50
Silver Crest, compote, 7"	12.00
Silver Crest, cornucopia candlestick, 6", pr	30.00
Silver Crest, dish, heart shape w/hdl	10.00
Silver Crest, epergne, 12"	125.00
Silver Crest, fruit stand, tall, 11"	20.00
Silver Crest, nut dish, ftd	18.00
Silver Crest, plate, 15"	38.00
Silver Crest, plate, 8"	10.00
Silver Crest, sandwich server, hdls	25.00
Silver Crest, shakers, pr	40.00
Silver Crest, tidbit tray, 2-tier, lg	45.00
Silver Crest, tidbit tray, 2-tier, sm	22.50
Silver Crest, tidbit tray, 3-tier	45.00
Silver Crest, tumbler, ftd, 6"	25.00
Silver Crest, vase, tricorner, 2¼"	22.50
Silver Crest, vase, violet decor, #186, 8"	30.00
Silver Crest, vase, 4½"	15.00
Silver Crest, vase, 6"	20.00
Silver Crest, vase, 8"	25.00
Silvertone, bowl, amber, flared, #1002, 9"	28.00
Silvertone, pitcher, iced tea; crystal, #1352	70.00
Silvertone, plate, amethyst, 3-ftd, #1009, 7½"	27.50
Snow Crest, bowl, gr, dbl-crimped, 6"	20.00
Snow Crest, bowl, ruby, heart shape	30.00
Sophisticated Ladies, vase, blk, ball shape, 8"	115.00
Sophisticated Ladies, vase, blk, 10½"	115.00
Spiral, rose bowl, French opal, 4½"	18.00
Spiral, vase, cranberry opal, #3253, 6"	57.00
Spiral/Blue Ridge, vase, triangular, #894, 10½"	68.00
Stars & Stripes, tumbler, cranberry opal, 3¾"	125.00
Stretch, bonbon, Florentine gr, #643	35.00
Stretch, candy dish, aquamarine, #531	35.00
Stretch, lemon dish, yel, 5"	32.00
Swirled Feather, bottle, scent; cranberry opal satin, #2005	50.00

Swirled Feather, lamp, fairy; cranberry opal satin, #2092 ....80.00
Thumbprint, compote, pk..15.00
Vasa Murrhina, basket, gr/bl aventurine, 11"................................78.00
Vasa Murrhina, basket, gr/bl aventurine, 11¼" 100.00
Vasa Murrhina, basket, red/gr, 11"...145.00
Vasa Murrhina, pitcher, Autumn Orange, sm 66.00
Vasa Murrhina, vase, gr/bl aventurine, 4" 50.00
Vasa Murrhina, vase, gr/bl aventurine, 7½" 60.00
Velva Rose, epergne, pk stretch, lg, 5-pc.....................................225.00
Venetian Red, candlestick, #449, 8¾", pr....................................150.00
Venetian Red, cornucopia centerpc, #950...................................165.00
Violets in Snow, bowl, 8"...42.50
Violets in Snow, compote, 7"...24.00
Water Lily, candy dish, rosalene, w/lid.......................................100.00
Water Lily & Cattail, bowl, purple opal, 9" 68.00
Wistaria, basket, wht satin, #1684..60.00
Wistaria, vase, crystal, #184, 11½" 40.00

Fiesta

Fiesta is a line of dinnerware produced by the Homer Laughlin China Company of Newell, West Virginia, from 1936 until 1973. It was made in eleven different solid colors with over fifty pieces in the assortment. The pattern was developed by Frederic Rhead, an English Stoke-on-Trent potter who was an important contributor to the art-pottery movement in this country during the early part of the century. The design was carried out through the use of a simple band-of-rings device near the rim. Fiesta Red, a strong red-orange glaze color, was made with depleted uranium oxide. It was more expensive to produce than the other colors and sold at higher prices. Today's collectors still pay premium prices for Fiesta Red pieces. During the fifties the color assortment was gray, rose, chartreuse, and dark green. These colors are relatively harder to find and along with Fiesta Red and medium green (new in 1959) command the higher prices.

Fiesta Kitchen Kraft was introduced in 1939; it consisted of seventeen pieces of kitchenware such as pie plates, refrigerator sets, mixing bowls, and covered jars in four popular Fiesta colors.

As a final attempt to adapt production to modern-day techniques and methods, Fiesta was restyled in 1969. Of the original colors, only Fiesta Red remained. This line, called Fiesta Ironstone, was discontinued in 1973.

Two types of marks were used: an ink stamp on machine-jiggered pieces and an indented mark molded into the hollowware pieces.

In 1986 HLC reintroduced a line of Fiesta dinnerware in five colors: black, white, pink, apricot, and cobalt (darker and denser than the original shade). Yellow was added in 1989 and turquoise and blue in 1990. However, collectors feel the new ware will pose no threat to their investment.

In the listings below, 'original colors' indicates only four of the original six — ivory, light green, turquoise, and yellow. Red and cobalt values are listed separately. For more information we recommend *The Collector's Encyclopedia of Fiesta, Harlequin, and Riviera* by Sharon and Bob Huxford, now in its seventh edition. Available at your local bookstore or from Collector Books.

Dinnerware and Accessories

Ash tray, '50s colors 50.00
Ash tray, orig colors 32.00
Ash tray, red or cobalt 40.00
Bowl, covered onion soup; cobalt & ivory..................................275.00
Bowl, covered onion soup; red 300.00
Bowl, covered onion soup; turq 1,200.00

Bowl, covered onion soup; yel or lt gr.......................................225.00
Bowl, cream soup; '50s colors 40.00
Bowl, cream soup; med gr..1,200.00
Bowl, cream soup; orig colors 25.00
Bowl, cream soup; red or cobalt..35.00
Bowl, dessert; '50s colors, 6" 35.00
Bowl, dessert; med gr, 6" 190.00
Bowl, dessert; orig colors, 6" 25.00
Bowl, dessert; red or cobalt, 6" 30.00
Bowl, fruit; '50s colors, 4¾" 22.00
Bowl, fruit; '50s colors, 5½" 26.00
Bowl, fruit; med gr, 4¾" 180.00
Bowl, fruit; med gr, 5½" 50.00
Bowl, fruit; orig colors, 11¾" 105.00
Bowl, fruit; orig colors, 4¾" 18.00
Bowl, fruit; orig colors, 5½" 18.00
Bowl, fruit; red or cobalt, 11¾" 140.00
Bowl, fruit; red or cobalt, 4¾" 22.00
Bowl, fruit; red or cobalt, 5½" 22.00
Bowl, ftd salad; orig colors..160.00
Bowl, ftd salad; red or cobalt 190.00
Bowl, ind salad; med gr, 7½" 62.00
Bowl, ind salad; red, turq, & yel, 7½" 50.00
Bowl, nappy; '50s colors, 8½" 36.00
Bowl, nappy; med gr, 8½" 60.00
Bowl, nappy; orig colors, 8½" 25.00
Bowl, nappy; orig colors, 9½" 30.00
Bowl, nappy; red or cobalt, 8½"...35.00
Bowl, nappy; red or cobalt, 9½"...40.00
Bowl, Tom & Jerry, ivory w/gold letters......................................120.00
Bowl, unlisted; red, cobalt, or ivory 175.00
Bowl, unlisted; yel..55.00
Candle holder, bulb; orig colors, pr...52.00
Candle holder, bulb; red or cobalt, pr 65.00
Candle holder, tripod; orig colors, pr...200.00
Candle holder, tripod; red, cobalt, or ivory, pr............................245.00
Carafe, orig colors..115.00
Carafe, red or cobalt 135.00
Casserole, '50s colors..165.00
Casserole, French; standard colors other than yel 300.00
Casserole, French; yel...160.00
Casserole, med gr 240.00
Casserole, orig colors 75.00
Casserole, red or cobalt...115.00
Coffeepot, '50s colors..150.00
Coffeepot, demi; orig colors..135.00
Coffeepot, demi; red, cobalt, or ivory...165.00
Coffeepot, orig colors 95.00
Coffeepot, red or cobalt..120.00
Compote, orig colors, 12" 75.00
Compote, red or cobalt, 12" 95.00
Compote, sweets; orig colors 34.00
Compote, sweets; red or cobalt..42.00
Creamer, '50s colors...20.00
Creamer, ind; red 105.00
Creamer, ind; turq 165.00
Creamer, ind; yel 42.00
Creamer, med gr..35.00
Creamer, orig colors...14.00
Creamer, red or cobalt..16.00
Creamer, stick hdld, orig colors...22.00
Creamer, stick hdld, red or cobalt 25.00
Cup, demi; '50s colors..120.00
Cup, demi; orig colors...35.00

Cup, demi; red or cobalt 40.00
Egg cup, '50s colors 85.00
Egg cup, orig colors 32.00
Egg cup, red, cobalt, or ivory 40.00
Lid, for mixing bowl #1-#3, any color 275.00
Lid, for mixing bowl #4, any color 300.00
Marmalade, orig colors 100.00
Marmalade, red or cobalt 135.00
Mixing bowl, #1, orig colors 55.00
Mixing bowl, #1, red, cobalt, or ivory 78.00
Mixing bowl, #2, orig colors 40.00
Mixing bowl, #2, red or cobalt 52.00
Mixing bowl, #3, orig colors 45.00
Mixing bowl, #3, red or cobalt 55.00
Mixing bowl, #4, orig colors 50.00
Mixing bowl, #4, red or cobalt 58.00
Mixing bowl, #5, orig colors 58.00
Mixing bowl, #5, red or cobalt 62.00
Mixing bowl, #6, orig colors 75.00
Mixing bowl, #6, red, cobalt, or ivory 82.00
Mixing bowl, #7, orig colors 128.00
Mixing bowl, #7, red, cobalt, or ivory 145.00
Mug, Tom & Jerry; '50s colors 60.00
Mug, Tom & Jerry; ivory w/gold letters..............................45.00
Mug, Tom & Jerry; orig colors 36.00

Tom and Jerry Mug, cobalt, $52.00.

Mustard, orig colors 95.00
Mustard, red or cobalt...130.00
Pitcher, disk juice; gray 600.00
Pitcher, disk juice; red 165.00
Pitcher, disk juice; yel 30.00
Pitcher, disk water; '50s colors 150.00
Pitcher, disk water; med gr 340.00
Pitcher, disk water; orig colors...60.00
Pitcher, disk water; red or cobalt 85.00
Pitcher, ice; orig colors 60.00
Pitcher, ice; red or cobalt..75.00
Pitcher, jug, 2-pt; '50s colors 70.00
Pitcher, jug, 2-pt; orig colors 38.00
Pitcher, jug, 2-pt; red, cobalt, or ivory 48.00
Plate, '50s colors, 10" 34.00
Plate, '50s colors, 6" 6.00
Plate, '50s colors, 7" 9.50
Plate, '50s colors, 9" 15.00
Plate, cake; lt gr or yellow 300.00
Plate, cake; red or cobalt 365.00
Plate, calendar; 1954 or 1955, 10" 30.00
Plate, calendar; 1955, 9" 35.00
Plate, chop; '50s colors, 13" 40.00
Plate, chop; '50s colors, 15" 45.00

Plate, chop; med gr, 13" 65.00
Plate, chop; orig colors, 13" 22.00
Plate, chop; orig colors, 15" 25.00
Plate, chop; red or cobalt, 13" 25.00
Plate, chop; red or cobalt, 15" 32.00
Plate, compartment; '50s colors, 10½" 30.00
Plate, compartment; orig colors, 10½" 20.00
Plate, compartment; orig colors, 12" 30.00
Plate, compartment; red or cobalt, 10½"............................24.00
Plate, compartment; red or cobalt, 12" 28.00
Plate, deep; '50s colors 35.00
Plate, deep; med gr..58.00
Plate, deep; orig colors 24.00
Plate, deep; red or cobalt 34.00
Plate, med gr, 10" 55.00
Plate, med gr, 6" 10.00
Plate, med gr, 7" 15.00
Plate, med gr, 9" 30.00
Plate, orig colors, 10" 22.00
Plate, orig colors, 6" 3.00
Plate, orig colors, 7" 6.00
Plate, orig colors, 9" 7.50
Plate, red or cobalt, 10" 28.00
Plate, red or cobalt, 6" 5.00
Plate, red or cobalt, 7" 8.00
Plate, red or cobalt, 9" 14.00
Platter, '50s colors...32.00
Platter, med gr...60.00
Platter, orig colors...20.00
Platter, red or cobalt..28.00
Sauce boat, '50s colors 40.00
Sauce boat, med gr...60.00
Sauce boat, orig colors 28.00
Sauce boat, red or cobalt 40.00
Saucer, '50s colors 4.50
Saucer, demi; '50s colors 34.00
Saucer, demi; orig colors 10.00
Saucer, demi; red or cobalt 12.00
Saucer, med gr...7.50
Saucer, orig colors 2.50
Saucer, red or cobalt 3.50
Shakers, '50s colors, pr...28.00
Shakers, med gr, pr...48.00
Shakers, orig colors, pr...15.00
Shakers, red or cobalt, pr 20.00
Sugar bowl, ind; turq 160.00
Sugar bowl, ind; yel...65.00
Sugar bowl, w/lid, '50s colors, 3¼x3½" 36.00
Sugar bowl, w/lid, med gr, 3¼x3½" 55.00
Sugar bowl, w/lid, orig colors, 3¼x3½" 22.00
Sugar bowl, w/lid, red or cobalt, 3¼x3½"............................30.00

Sweets comport, yellow, $34.00.

Syrup, orig colors 165.00
Syrup, red or cobalt..190.00
Teacup, '50s colors..28.00
Teacup, med gr..32.00
Teacup, orig colors...20.00
Teacup, red or cobalt 25.00
Teapot, lg; orig colors 80.00
Teapot, lg; red or cobalt 95.00
Teapot, med; '50s colors....................................155.00
Teapot, med; med gr...260.00
Teapot, med; orig colors 70.00
Teapot, med; red or cobalt..................................92.00
Tray, figure-8; cobalt...45.00
Tray, figure-8; turq...135.00
Tray, figure-8; yel..150.00
Tray, relish; mixed colors, no red........................130.00
Tray, utility; orig colors 22.00
Tray, utility; red or cobalt...................................28.00
Tumbler, juice; chartreuse, Harlequin yel or dk gr 160.00
Tumbler, juice; orig colors 20.00
Tumbler, juice; red or cobalt 28.00
Tumbler, juice; rose..30.00
Tumbler, water; orig colors.................................36.00
Tumbler, water; red or cobalt 40.00
Vase, bud; orig colors...38.00
Vase, bud; red or cobalt 50.00
Vase, orig colors, 10" 350.00
Vase, orig colors, 12" 425.00
Vase, orig colors, 8" 265.00
Vase, red or cobalt, 10".....................................425.00
Vase, red or cobalt, 12".....................................535.00
Vase, red or cobalt, 8"......................................350.00

Kitchen Kraft

Bowl, mixing; lt gr or yel, 10" 60.00
Bowl, mixing; lt gr or yel, 6" 32.00
Bowl, mixing; lt gr or yel, 8" 50.00
Bowl, mixing; red or cobalt, 10" 70.00
Bowl, mixing; red or cobalt, 6" 38.00
Bowl, mixing; red or cobalt, 8" 60.00
Cake plate, lt gr or yel...35.00
Cake plate, red or cobalt 40.00
Cake server, lt gr or yel 55.00
Cake server, red or cobalt 65.00
Casserole, ind; lt gr or yel 90.00
Casserole, ind; red or cobalt 100.00
Casserole, lt gr or yel, 7½" 65.00
Casserole, lt gr or yel, 8½" 70.00
Casserole, red or cobalt, 7½" 70.00
Casserole, red or cobalt, 8½" 75.00
Covered jar, lg; lt gr or yel 160.00
Covered jar, lg; red or cobalt..............................180.00
Covered jar, med; lt gr or yel..............................150.00
Covered jar, med; red or cobalt...........................165.00
Covered jar, sm; lt gr or yel 145.00
Covered jar, sm; red or cobalt.............................160.00
Covered jug, lt gr or yel.....................................140.00
Covered jug, red or cobalt..................................160.00
Fork, lt gr or yel...45.00
Fork, red or cobalt..50.00
Metal frame for platter..20.00
Pie plate, lt gr or yel, 10" 35.00
Pie plate, lt gr or yel, 9" 30.00

Pie plate, red or cobalt, 10" 40.00
Pie plate, red or cobalt, 9" 35.00
Shakers, lt gr or yel, pr 60.00
Shakers, red or cobalt, pr....................................70.00
Spoon, lt gr or yel...48.00
Spoon, red or cobalt..52.00
Stacking refrigerator lid, lt gr or yel......................40.00
Stacking refrigerator lid, red or cobalt....................45.00
Stacking refrigerator unit, lt gr or yel 25.00
Stacking refrigerator unit, red or cobalt 30.00

Finch, Kay

Kay Finch and her husband, Braden, operated a small pottery in Corona Del Mar, California, from 1939 to 1963. The company remained small, employing from twenty to forty local residents who Kay trained in all but the most requiring tasks, which she herself performed. The company produced animal and bird figurines, most notably dogs, Kay's favorites. Figures of 'Godey' type couples were also made, as were tableware (consisting of breakfast sets) and other artware. Most pieces were marked.

Ash tray, shell, pk lustre/wht................................12.00
Bank, panda figural, 9".......................................35.00
Bank, pig, florals, 6¾"..35.00
Camel, mc, 5"...45.00

Cat, Ambrosia, salmon pink details on oatmeal, 11", $150.00.

Cookie jar, Pup, mc, 12¾"..................................125.00
Duck, 3¼" 75.00
Owl, Hoot, mc, 8¾"..65.00
Peasant couple, boy & girl, mc, 6¾"......................50.00
Penguin, Pete, bow tie, 7½".................................50.00
Planter, non-figural, pk/bl, 4x5¾" 12.00
Rabbit, HP details, ink mk, 2½x4".........................35.00
Rooster Hen set, yel/brn, 8¼"...............................28.00
Seahorse, pk, wall hanging, 16"............................65.00
Shakers, turkey, brn gloss w/gold & red, 3¼x3¾" 25.00

Findlay Onyx and Floradine

Findlay, Ohio, was the location of the Dalzell, Gilmore, and Leighton Glass Company, one of at least sixteen companies that flourished there between 1886 and 1901. Their most famous ware, Onyx, is very rare. It was produced for only a short time beginning in 1889 due to the heavy losses incurred in the manufacturing process.

Onyx is layered glass, usually found in creamy white with a dainty floral pattern accented with metallic lustre that has been trapped between the two layers. Other colors found on rare occasions include a light amber (with either no lustre or with gilt flowers), light amethyst (or lavender), and rose. Although old tradepaper articles indicate the company originally intended to produce the line in three distinct colors, long-time Onyx collectors report that aside from the white, production was very limited. Other colors of Onyx are very rare, and the few examples that are found tend to support the theory that production of colored Onyx ware remained for the most part in the experimental stage. Even three-layered items have been found (they are extremely rare) decorated with three-color flowers. As a rule of thumb, using white Onyx prices as a basis for evaluation, expect to pay two to three times more for colored examples.

Floradine is a separate line that was made with the Onyx molds. A single-layer rose satin glassware with white opal flowers, it is usually priced in the general range of colored Onyx.

Chipping around the rims is very common, and price is determined to a great extent by condition. Our advisors for this category are Betty and Clarence Maier; they are listed in the Directory under Pennsylvania.

Floradine

Box, dresser; 5½" dia.	700.00
Creamer	945.00
Mustard	850.00
Spooner, 4¼"	925.00
Sugar bowl, w/lid, 3¾x4½"	950.00
Sugar shaker	1,250.00
Toothpick holder	1,100.00
Tumbler, 3¾", NM	550.00

Onyx

Bowl, master berry	400.00
Box, wht w/silver decor, 5½" dia	600.00
Butter dish, wht w/silver decor	1,250.00
Celery vase, wht w/silver decor, 6½"	425.00
Creamer, wht w/silver decor, 4½"	450.00
Jam jar, wht w/silver decor	450.00
Pitcher, wht w/silver decor, 8"	1,200.00
Shakers, wht w/silver decor, 3", pr	600.00
Spooner, wht w/silver decor, 4¼"	245.00
Sugar bowl, wht w/silver decor, 5½"	500.00

Sugar shaker, white with platinum flowers, $475.00.

Syrup, wht w/silver decor, 7"	750.00
Toothpick holder, wht w/silver decor, 2½"	375.00

Fire Fighting Collectibles

Fire fighting antiques from the nineteenth century reflect the feeling of pride the men had in their companies and in their role as volunteer fire fighters. Fancy dress uniforms, helmets, and silver trumpets full of flowers recall the charisma of the 'Laddies' on parade. Leather buckets, bed keys, muffin bells, rattles, torches, lanterns, and riveted leather hose all serve as reminders of that era, long past.

In the 1860s the old volunteer units begrudgingly gave way to the 'paid municipal firefighter.' The politically astute and sometimes physically aggressive volunteer organizations many times went down hard and maintained group integrity many years after paid forces were in place.

With the inception of 'disciplined,' paid forces, the ascension to more sophisticated fire alarms and fire supression equipment was accelerated. Hand and horse-drawn equipment predominated until about WWI when apparatus motorization really took hold and for the most part was the dominating factor by 1920. Suspicious of the new machines, many northern fire departments kept horse-drawn sleighs in reserve well into the late 1920s.

Today there is a large, active group of collectors for fire department antiques (items over 100 years old) and an even larger group seeking related collectibles (those less than 100 years old). Note: In the extinguishers listed below, the term 'apparatus type' refers to that which is carried on or by fire apparatus; 'building type' are those found hanging on walls of buildings. S+A indicates 'soda and acid'; CCL4, 'carbon tetrachloride.'

Axe, parade; wooden representation, 20th century	35.00
Axe, pick head, wood hdl, 6-lb	20.00
Axe, pick head, wooden hdl, ¾-sz	17.50
Axe, Viking style, serpentine wood hdl	210.00
Badge, East Syracuse, Maltese cross, NP	20.00
Badge, Engineer #5, self-propelled steamer, NP	95.00
Badge, retirement; ...Engine #1, Active 1895-1927, gold tone	55.00
Baton, marching; wood shaft, nickel/brass top, dtd 1890, 52"	150.00
Bed key, iron, 19th century, EX	140.00
Bed key, 3-way wrench type	110.00
Bell, Ahrens-Fox, apparatus type, complete, NP, 12"	575.00
Bell, Am LaFrance, apparatus type, NP, w/eagle, early, 12"	575.00
Bell, apparatus, locomotive style, NP/brass, complete, 10"	375.00
Bell, apparatus, locomotive style, NP/brass, complete, 12"	435.00
Bell, rotary apparatus type, nickel/brass, foot operated	350.00
Bell, Seagrave, apparatus type, NP, complete, 12"	475.00
Bell, Simpson Electric, Canton MA, 110 volts, 10" dia	75.00
Belt, H&L #1 SFD, brass buckle, red & wht leather, EX	95.00
Belt, spanner type, leather, 20th century	17.50
Book, Automatic Fire Alarm Signals, NY City FD, 1885	24.00
Book, Enjine-Enjine, paperbk, ca 1939	60.00
Book, Footprints of Assurance, Bolan	45.00
Book, Reminiscences of...Depts of NY & Brooklyn, 1885, EX	85.00
Bucket, leather, D Hayward's Pat 1854, VG	210.00
Bucket, leather, First Church Chancy Place 1821, rpt, EX	125.00
Bucket, leather, orig gr pnt, w/hdl, EX	210.00
Bucket, leather w/mc pnt: joined hands/name/1807, 11", EX	1,900.00
Clamp, hose; Akron, all metal, modern	30.00
Clamp, hose; Akron, wooden hdls, 20th century	175.00
Clamp, hose; LaFrance, all metal, modern	65.00
Clamp, hose; Peerless, all metal	50.00
Clamp, hose; Pirsch, wooden hdls, 20th century	230.00

Extinguisher, Acme Dry Chemical, tin, 22", EX 27.50
Extinguisher, Alaskan, Gen Fire Truck Corp, 2½-gal 35.00
Extinguisher, Buffalo, copper, building type, 2½-gal 35.00
Extinguisher, Elkhart, Elk logo, copper, s+a, 2½-gal 95.00
Extinguisher, Excelsior, Fire Appliance Co, canister......................30.00
Extinguisher, Fireen Fire Equipment, dry chemical 20.00
Extinguisher, Hanks, dry chemical, 13", EX 25.00
Extinguisher, Pyrene, brass, pump type w/bracket, CCL4, 1-qt......30.00
Extinguisher, Pyrene, brass, vehicle type, CCL4, 1½-qt 35.00
Extinguisher, Pyrene, brass, w/mounting bracket, 1-pt, EX 25.00
Extinguisher, Pyrene, copper w/gauge, pressure type, 1-gal 35.00
Extinguisher, Stop Fire, Foamite-Childs, CCL4, brass, 1-qt..........45.00
Gauge, compound to 600 psi; ALF, brass, panel mt, 5" 55.00
Gauge, compound to 600 psi; Seagrave, panel mount, 3" 50.00
Gong, Gamewell, brass, turtle style, center wind, 10" 200.00
Gong, Gamewell, chain wind, 10" 175.00
Gong, Gamewell, fancy oak case, 18", EX............................3,500.00
Gong, Gamewell, oak case, 6", EX.......................................650.00
Gong, Holtzer-Cabot, brass, 11"...165.00
Gong, Star Electric, Binghamton NY, fancy oak case, 16" ...1,800.00
Gong, US Fire & Police Telegraph Co, maple case, 15".........1,500.00

Grenade, Diamond Fire Ext'r Pat'd June 29th 1869, amber, tooled lip, inside stain, rare, 6", $1,000.00 at auction.

Grenade, Firex, cobalt, unemb, sealed in orig box, 3¾" 65.00
Grenade, Harden's, turq, full w/paper label, 6¾" 65.00
Grenade, Harden's Star, bl, rnd, full 75.00
Grenade, Harden's Star, cobalt, full, 6½" 100.00
Grenade, Hayward #407 Broadway, cobalt, H Pat on base, 6" 220.00
Grenade, HSN (Nutting), yel-amber, 7", EX 200.00
Grenade, Red Comet, w/contents, bracket, & orig carton 15.00
Helmet, aluminum, high eagle, Dover FD 145.00
Helmet, leather, high eagle, Wilson fancy frontpc, VG 265.00
Helmet, leather, high eagle w/fancy frontpc, early 4-comb 325.00
Helmet, leather, high eagle w/frontpc, Cairns, EX 235.00
Helmet, leather, low New Yorker, w/Boston frontpc 145.00
Helmet, leather, low New Yorker, w/phony frontpc....................145.00
Helmet, leather, low New Yorker, w/Saugus #27, EX 95.00
Invitation, 1st Annual Ball, Reliance Hose Co, 1887, EX 10.00
Lantern, Adams-Westlake Queen, nickel/brass.........................275.00
Lantern, Am LaFrance, battery/hand type w/mount bracket..........95.00
Lantern, Dietz, tin, mill lantern, wire cage 35.00
Lantern, Dietz Queen, brass, EX 650.00
Lantern, Eclipse, bl over clear globe, EX 1,000.00
Lantern, Ham's Chief, brass, EX 235.00
Nozzle, ALFCO, complete playpipe w/hard rubber hdls..............150.00
Nozzle, cellar; brass, Am Fire Equipment, 7", EX 195.00

Nozzle, cellar; Bresnan (distributor), brass............................165.00
Nozzle, Elkheart, shut-off & tip only 50.00
Nozzle, Fairy, garden hose threads......................................10.00
Nozzle, Fog Nozzle Co, booster sz 25.00
Nozzle, Fog Nozzle Co, brass, sz 1½....................................35.00
Nozzle, LaFrance, complete playpipe w/leather hdls..................200.00
Nozzle, playpipe; Underwriters, string wrapped 95.00
Nozzle, Rockwood, brass, booster sz....................................25.00
Nozzle, Rockwood, brass, sz 1½ 35.00
Nozzle, Rockwood, brass, sz 2½ 35.00
Photo, horse-drawn ladder truck w/firemen, 4½x7", EX..............10.00
Pin, 1903 Fireman's Assn, enameling on metal 10.00
Plaque, bronze, Hamnanimous Support, NY, 1917, 11½x10½" ..165.00
Reel, for punch register, w/clockwork, brass housing, 8", EX 150.00
Register, Gamewell, brass, ½" rnd hole type, EX 325.00
Ribbon, convention, MA State Assoc Sept 29-Oct 1, 1915, EX ...10.00
Ribbon, convention; common variety, post-1900 ....12.00
Ribbon, convention; fancy metal attachments, early 35.00
Strainer, Am LaFrance, chrome, w/mounting bracket, 4½", EX ...65.00
Strainer, Powhatan, brass/nickel, 4½"...................................35.00
Tank, brass, Indian bk-pack style, complete, EX 35.00
Ticket, 5th Annual Ball, Washington Fire Co #1, 1891 ....10.00
Torch, parade; nickel/brass, wooden hdl..............................160.00
Trumpet, nickel/brass, working...325.00

Fire Marks

During the early eighteenth century, insurance companies used fire marks — signs of insurance — to indicate to the volunteer fire fighters which homes were covered by their company. Handsome rewards were promised to the brigade that successfully extinguished the blaze, so competition was fierce between rivals and sometimes resulted in an altercation at the scene to settle the matter of which brigade would be the one to fight the fire! Fire marks were originally made of cast iron or lead; later examples were sometimes tin or zinc. They were used abroad as well as in this country, and those from England tended to be much more elaborate. When municipal fire departments were organized in the mid- to late 1860s, volunteer departments and fire marks became obsolete.

Eagle, emb on CI, 8½x11" 90.00
FA w/hydrant & hose, CI, gr pnt, oval, EX 570.00
Fire Assoc of Phila, oval, gold-colored hose, 10¾x7½", G 85.00
Germantown 1843 Mutual Fire, CI, 8x11¼".............................40.00
Guardian Assurance Co of London, copper.............................125.00
Masonic, CI, early..200.00
Mutual Assurance Co, Philadelphia, CI, oval, ca 1827................700.00
Mutual Insurance, angel flies over Charleston, 9½x7½" 65.00
Protector, copper, fireman w/hose, burning building, 1825 ....190.00
Securitas Anterpen, Belgium, tin, oval, M 135.00
UF, pumper relief, CI, oval, 12" L......................................125.00
4 clasped hands/No 906 on CI plaque, 10½x7" 300.00

Fireglow

Fireglow is a type of art glass that first appears to be an opaque cafe au lait, but glows with rich red 'fire' when held to a strong source of light.

Biscuit jar, alternate ribs, pk/wht flowers, SP hdl, 6x8½" 375.00
Creamer & sugar bowl, florals, 3" 150.00
Epergne, 1-lily, HP flowers, crimped, ornate silver fr, 19"............275.00

Ewer, birds on tree branches, 7" 165.00
Garniture, 2 10" vases+13" urn, exotic florals, Sandwich 650.00
Rose bowl, bl daisies, 4½" dia 125.00
Rose bowl, mc florals, egg shape, 6-crimp top, appl ft 165.00
Tumbler, narrow ribs, M...110.00

Vase, multicolored stylized flowers, six relief green rings, 12½", $295.00.

Vase, asters/ferns in bl & brn, mk Durand-Kimberly, 16" 225.00
Vase, flowers/leaves in bl, corset waist, 4¼" 125.00
Vase, gold-traced mauve flowers & leaves, mk PK, 11".................250.00
Vase, mc flowers, ornate brass holder, 7½" 150.00
Vase, mc wild roses, bulbous, 5½" 150.00
Vase, stick neck, 7½"...110.00

Fireplace Implements

In the colonial days of our country, fireplaces provided heat in the winter and were used year round to cook food in the kitchen. The implements that were a necessary part of these functions were varied and have become treasured collectibles, many put to new use in modern homes as decorative accessories. Gypsy pots may hold magazines; copper and brass kettles, newly polished and gleaming, contain dried flowers or green plants. Firebacks, highly ornamental iron panels that once reflected heat and protected masonry walls, are now sometimes used as wall decorations.

By Victorian times, the cookstove had replaced the kitchen fireplace, and many of these early utensils were already obsolete. But as a source of heat and comfort, the fireplace continued to be used for several more decades. See also Wrought Iron.

Andirons, brass, ball atop cylinder, arch legs, 1780s, 12" 1,000.00

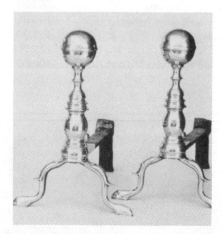

Andirons, brass, ball tops, signed Hunneman #417, early 1800s, $400.00.

Andirons, brass, beehive design, w/log stops, 1880, 20" 2,000.00
Andirons, brass, late Fed, trn std, arched/spurred legs, 6" 1,000.00
Andirons, bronze, recumbent greyhound on draped base, 8" 600.00
Andirons, CI, heart amid 2 branching legs, 1850s, 13", pr 175.00
Andirons, Hessian soldier, CI w/blk pnt, ca 1900, 19", pr 235.00
Andirons, wrought iron, penny ft, faceted finials, 20"...................225.00
Andirons, wrought iron, penny ft, scroll finials, 19" 250.00
Bellows, dk smoked pnt w/stencil & freehand fruit, 18", VG.......175.00
Bellows, dome top, brass mts, orig leather, VG pnt......................165.00
Bellows, orig fruit & floral pnt decor, worn leather, sm...............165.00
Bellows, stenciled fruit/etc on smoked wht, rstr, 17" 265.00
Bellows, wood/leather/tole spout, 1870s, 17", EX..........................45.00
Bellows, yel pnt w/stencil & freehand floral, rstr, 19" 275.00
Bird spit, cabriole legs, snake ft, English, 1700s, 32" 600.00
Broiler, wrought iron, revolves, ftd, rattail hdl, 1840, EX 235.00
Fender, iron w/wire grill, brass top rail, 20x21x12" 275.00
Fender, wire grill w/brass trim, paw ft, 42" 190.00
Fender, wrought fr w/wire grill & brass rail w/3 finials 725.00
Fire screen, wire w/brass base & top w/3 acorns, 1870s, 43".........750.00
Fireback, CI, manger scene, angels in border, 1700s, 40" 1,400.00
Fork, dbl prong, wrought, long flat hdl, 1830s, 21".........................35.00
Fork, wrought, twisted rods form ornate hdl, 1800s, 19" 55.00
Jamb hook, 2-tier brass mushroom hooks on iron jamb, 7" 65.00
Kettle, brass, w/stationary iron hdl, 1850s, 15x15" 125.00
Kettle lifter, wrought iron w/2 pivoting ends, 15"............................50.00
Kettle shelf, wrought horseshoe w/sm brass heart, 13" L 150.00
Lid lifter, twisted wrought iron, rattail hook, 1700s, 3½" 95.00
Mantle, poplar, simple design, 47x51" 160.00
Peel, wrought iron, ram's head curl hdl, 1700s, 46"......................220.00
Peel, wrought iron, ram's horn hdl, 40½" 125.00
Shovel, wrought iron, open heart figural hdl, 1700s, 30" 150.00
Spider, CI, rnd, ftd, rattail hdl, 4½x5¾"...125.00
Toaster, star shape, wire w/wood hdl, 1900, EX...............................40.00
Toaster, wire w/Maltese cross design, long wood hdl......................40.00
Tongs, ember; wrought iron, scissors style, 1700s, 11½"...............150.00
Tongs, scissors style, serrated ends, iron, 9"....................................35.00
Tongs, wrought iron, ca 1820s, 15½" 25.00
Tongs, wrought iron, lathe-trn hdl w/brass finial, 21" 85.00

Fishing Collectibles

Collecting old fishing tackle is becoming more popular every year. Though at first most interest was geared toward old lures and some reels, rods, advertising, and miscellaneous items are quickly gaining ground. Values are given for examples in excellent or better condition and should be used only as a guide. For more information contact our advisor Randy Hilst, an appraiser and collector whose address and phone number are listed in the Directory under Illinois.

Catalog, Heddon, 1946 ....65.00
Catalog, Paw Paw, 1947...25.00
Catalog, South Bend, 1932 ....20.00
Lure, Al Foss Oriental Wiggler, glass eyes, plastic 12.00
Lure, Arbogast Jitterbug, pnt eyes, wood..20.00
Lure, Creek Chub Champ Spoon, pnt eyes, metal 20.00
Lure, Creek Chub Ding Bat, glass eyes, wood 20.00
Lure, Creek Chub Dive Bomber, pnt eyes, wood 15.00
Lure, Creek Chub Pikie, glass eyes, wood 10.00
Lure, Creek Chub Plunking Dinger, glass eyes, wood.....................20.00
Lure, Creek Chub River Rustler, glass eyes, wood 70.00
Lure, Creek Chub Seven Thousand, bead eyes, wood 25.00
Lure, Creek Chub Wee Dee, glass eyes, wood 225.00
Lure, Creek Chub Wiggle Fish, glass eyes, wood 35.00

Lure, Garland Cork Head Minnow, tack eyes, wood.....................125.00
Lure, Heddon #1600 Deep Diving Wiggler, no eyes, wood 75.00
Lure, Heddon #1700 Near Surface Wiggler, glass eyes, wood 80.00
Lure, Heddon Crazy Crawler, pnt eyes, wood 15.00
Lure, Heddon Game Fisher, no eyes, wood......................................20.00
Lure, Heddon Luny Frog, pnt eyes, plastic, frog color 45.00
Lure, Heddon Meadow Mouse, bead eyes, wood...........................25.00
Lure, Heddon Vamp, glass eyes, wood..25.00
Lure, Heddon Wiggle King, no eyes, wood.....................................40.00
Lure, Heddon Zig Wag, glass eyes, wood..20.00
Lure, Paw Paw #50 Minnie Mouse, tack eyes, wood.....................25.00
Lure, Paw Paw Trout Caster, tack eyes, wood................................30.00
Lure, Paw Paw Watta Frog, tack eyes, wood 25.00
Lure, Paw Paw Wobbler, tack eyes, wood 10.00
Lure, Pflueger Globe, no eyes, wood..15.00
Lure, Pflueger Kent Frog, glass eyes, wood 300.00
Lure, Pflueger Palomine, glass eyes, wood 15.00
Lure, Pflueger Scoop, glass eyes, wood 25.00

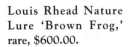

Louis Rhead Nature Lure 'Brown Frog,' rare, $600.00.

Lure, Roberts Mud Puppy, glass eyes, wood 20.00
Lure, Shakespeare Grumpy, cvd eyes, wood.................................... 5.00
Lure, Shakespeare Padler, cvd eyes, wood......................................50.00
Lure, Shakespeare Revolution, no eyes, metal..............................150.00
Lure, Shakespeare River Pup, cvd eyes, wood 5.00
Lure, Shakespeare Swimming Mouse, glass eyes, wood...................15.00
Lure, Shakespeare Tantalizer, glass eyes, wood 65.00
Lure, South Bend Min Oreno, tack eyes, wood 20.00
Lure, South Bend Surf Oreno, glass eyes, wood 25.00
Lure, South Bend Whirl Oreno, no eyes, wood 75.00
Lure, South Bend 5-Hook Underwater Minnow, glass eyes, wood.50.00
Lure, Wilson Cupped Wobbler, no eyes, wood.............................100.00
Lure, Winchester, 2-hook model, glass eyes, wood.......................200.00
Lure, Winchester, 3-hook model, glass eyes, wood.......................350.00
Lure, Winchester, 5-hook model, glass eyes, wood.......................350.00
Reel, Heddon 3-15, non-level wind 100.00
Reel, JA Coxe, 25C, German silver, level wind 60.00
Reel, Langley Lure Cast, level wind 7.00
Reel, Meisselbach, Tripart, non-level wind 25.00
Reel, Pflueger Akron, level wind...10.00
Reel, Pflueger Skilcast, level wind...12.00
Reel, Pflueger Summit, level wind 15.00
Reel, Pflueger Supreme, level wind...25.00
Reel, Shakespeare Marhoff, level wind 15.00
Reel, Shakespeare True Blue, level wind 7.00
Reel, Shakespeare Wonderreel, level wind 7.00
Reel, South Bend, direct drive, level wind...................................... 8.00
Rod, Heddon Blk Beauty, bamboo, fly rod......................................75.00
Rod, South Bend, bamboo, fly rod...25.00

Flags of the United States

The brevity and imprecise language of the first Flag Act of 1777 allowed great artistic license for our early flag makers. As a result, vast and varied interpretations were produced until 1912 when stringent design standards were established for the new 48-star flag. Early patterns ranged from 'scatter' arrangements to elaborate wreaths and 'Great Stars.' Most surviving vintage flags are of the 'generic' variety, devoid of any special pedigree or proven history. Nevertheless, these cherished artifacts continue to be avidly collected on the basis of age, scarcity, configuration, craftsmanship, and aesthetic merit.

Pre-Civil War flags of 33 stars or less are very scarce and usually surface as 'big ticket' items. In those relatively uncharted waters, the terms of any given transaction are always subject to the influence of personal predisposition as well as the give-and-take of the negotiating process itself. There has also been a surging interest in Civil War-era flags of 34 and 35 stars as more Americans begin to focus on that epic period of U.S. history. That, in combination with the demands of a large and well-entrenched fraternity of Civil War collectors, has dramatically stimulated pricing into what is now clearly a seller's market.

Since 36 star flags are more likely to be post-Civil War flags, they, along with 37 star flags, have less broad-based appeal. Nevertheless, both vintages can fetch very respectable prices. Flags of 38 stars and the unofficial vintages of 39, 40, and 42 stars provide a popular, moderately-priced marketplace for journeyman flag buffs and collectors of Americana, while the elusive 43 star flag is sought by nearly everyone. Flags of 44, 45, and 46 stars are production line items. Nevertheless, they are not without collecting merit and are usually available at comparatively modest prices. Ordinary 48 star flags flood the flea markets and are of little interest to most collectors, but the scarcer 49 star flag can generate occasional attention. 13 star flags, produced over a period of 200 years, surface in all forms and must be judged on a case-by-case basis. Many flag buffs favor flag sizes that are manageable for wall display, and most will make allowances for normal wear and tear. With rare exception, modern-day repros of historical flags have little or no collector appeal.

The dollar value of a flag is by no means based on age alone. The wide price swings in the listings that follow are the result of a variety of special considerations and features. Mass-printed flags, for instance, are generally not the equal of hand-crafted flags, nor do unions with conventional rows of stars compare to the remarkable 'Great Star' and wreath patterns of the past. In fact, almost any special feature that stands out as unusual or distinctive is a potential asset. Imprinted flags and inscribed flags; 8-pointed stars, gold stars, and added stars; extra stripes, missing stripes, tri-color stripes, and war stripes are all part of the pricing equation. And while political and military flags may rank above all others in terms of prestige and price, any flag with a significant and well-documented historical connection has 'star' potential (pardon the pun).

Our advisor for this category is Robert Banks; he is listed in the Directory under Maryland.

13 stars, Betsy Ross flag, by grandaughter, 1903, 8x12".................**500.00**
13 stars, Civil War boat ensign, USS Wabash, 44x64"............ **1,200.00**
13 stars, in semi-wreath, hand sewn, 1870s, 54x102"...................**140.00**
13 stars, printed, w/advertisement, 1880s, 4x7".............................**30.00**
13 stars, US Navy boat ensign, dtd Sept 1904, 44x78".................**75.00**
13 stars, 3-2 pattern, machine sewn, 1880s, 24x48"......................**75.00**
13 stars, 3rd MD pattern, hand sewn, 1840s, 32x45"...................**445.00**
19 stars, 16 orig+3, sewn scrap fabric, 39x66"............................**960.00**
23 stars, Civil War related, home-sewn muslin, 48x96" **200.00**
25 stars, stenciled burlap on 24" wood tripod pole, 5x7".............**170.00**
26 stars, Great Star, embr on sewn silk, 30x43"............................**630.00**

31 stars, Great Star, Lincoln related, printed, 11x14" 145.00
31 stars, Great Star, 14 stripes, hand sewn, 39x69" 550.00
32 stars, dbl wreath of inset stars, hand sewn, 36x48" 435.00
33 stars, hand-/machine-sewn wool bunting, 66x92" 375.00
33 stars, wreath pattern, printed glazed muslin, 16x22" 85.00
33 stars, wreath w/10 stripes, hand sewn, 77x127" 380.00
34 stars, dbl-wreath pattern, hand-sewn bunting, 24x36" 500.00
34 stars, dbl-wreath pattern, printed silk, 18x28" 120.00
34 stars, Great Star, mixed fabrics, sewn, 91x154" 460.00
34 stars, Great Star, mixed fabrics, sewn, 92x125" 427.00
34 stars, pattern variation, stitched cotton, 76x136" 360.00
34 stars, printed, added Garfield campaign legend, 24x48" 325.00
34 stars form shield, all hand sewn, worn, 51x66" 600.00
35 stars, hand/machine sewn, 96x180" 300.00
35 stars, recruiting flag, sewn bunting, 50x116" 345.00
36 stars, Civil War, 8-pointed sewn wreath, 78x90" 720.00
36 stars, hand-sewn wool bunting, 68x85" 200.00
36 stars, printed silk handkerchief, 19x19" 50.00
36 stars, 11 tricolor stripes, hand sewn, 51x99" 230.00
37 stars, hand/machine-sewn wool bunting, 48x69" 195.00
37 stars, printed silk, 32x40" 40.00
37 stars, row pattern, stitched bunting, 30x48" 150.00
37 stars, wreath pattern, hand-sewn cotton, 72x106" 290.00
38 stars, Blaine campaign, printed cotton, 17x27" 275.00
38 stars, Centennial 1886, printed cotton, 15x24" 48.00

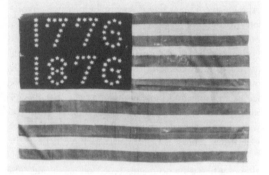

38 Star Centennial flag, printed linen, 28" x 46", $250.00.

38 stars, dbl-wreath pattern, sewn muslin, 87x128" 160.00
38 stars, Great Star, printed silk, gold fringe, 12x17" 40.00
38 stars, pattern variation, hand sewn, 96x164" 80.00
38 stars, pattern variation, hand/machine-sewn, 48x95" 66.00
38 stars, printed glazed muslin pattern variation, 30x48" 50.00
38 stars, triple-wreath pattern, sewn bunting, 76x136" 240.00
38 stars, Union on red war stripe, homemade, 44x84" 75.00
38 stars, 1776-1876 pattern, printed linen, 27½x46" 250.00
39 stars, clamp-dye printed wool bunting, 56x117" 95.00
39 stars, originally 34 Great Star, sewn, 69x129" 310.00
39 stars, row pattern variation, printed silk, 12x24" 45.00
39 stars, scatter pattern, hand sewn, 78x120" 170.00
39 stars, triple wreath, hand-sewn bunting, 60x108" 250.00
39 stars, unofficial silk flag, printed, 12x16" 32.00
40 stars, printed heavy-gauge bunting, 43x64" 55.00
40 stars, unofficial, hand/machine sewn, 61x115" 90.00
40 stars, wreath-in-box pattern, hand sewn, 43x82" 140.00
40 stars backed by 39, hand sewn, unique, 72x114" 250.00
41 stars, unofficial, printed, rare, some damage, 16x24" 100.00
42 stars, minor pattern variation, sewn bunting, 96x138" 68.00
42 stars, printed cotton, unhemmed, 18x24" 22.00
42 stars, Union scatter pattern, hand sewn, 48x72" 134.00
43 stars, machine-sewn bunting, extremely rare, 29x70" 382.00
43 stars (1 side only), 98989 pattern, homemade, 38x48" 150.00
44 stars, family flag w/history, machine sewn, 84x156" 75.00

44 stars, hand-sewn bunting, 70x144", EX 85.00
44 stars, machine-sewn cotton bunting, 53x82" 45.00
45 stars, machine-sewn cotton bunting, 80x108" 24.00
45 stars, modified 38-star, hand sewn, 120x192" 110.00
45 stars, triple-wreath GAR flag, printed muslin, 11x16" 40.00
45 stars, Union, hand-sewn wool bunting, 92x135" 30.00
45 stars, Union Jack, machine-sewn bunting, 50x76" 37.00
45 stars, 878787 row pattern, all machine sewn, 60x108" 42.00
46 stars, machine-sewn cotton bunting, 96x142" 28.00
46 stars, machine-sewn wool bunting, 72x138" 35.00
46 stars, printed silk, in baton-type carrying tube, 12x17" 17.00
46 stars, random pattern, machine sewn, 40x100" 55.00
47 stars, unofficial, sewn bunting, 108x137" 140.00
48 stars, machine-sewn cotton bunting, 60x96" 12.00
48 stars, modified 44-star flag, hand sewn, 60x90" 60.00
48 stars, sewn canton resting on red war stripe, 41x61" 35.00
48 stars, staggered rows (early), printed muslin, 13x23" 10.00
48 stars, Whipple Peace Flag, printed silk, 14x24" 160.00
48 stars, 10-9 pattern, printed bunting, rare, 39x61" 55.00
49 stars, embr w/sewn stripes, cotton bunting, 24x36" 8.00
49 stars, embr w/sewn stripes, gold fringe, 48x72" 30.00
49 stars, machine-sewn cotton bunting, 36x60" 15.00
49 stars, Navy Jack, machine-sewn nylon, 32x48" 12.00
50 stars, Carter campaign, printed plastic, 12x18" 15.00
50 stars, flew over the capitol memento, new, 60x96" 20.00
52 stars, Spanish Am war era, home sewn, rare, 44x84" 185.00
56 stars, printed crepe paper, Oriental, 1920s, 9x9" 18.00

Florence Ceramics

Figurines marked 'Florence Ceramics' were produced in the forties and fifties in Pasadena, California. The quality of the ware and the attention given to detail are prompting a growing interest among today's collectors. The names of these lovely ladies, gents, and figural groups are nearly always incised into their bases. The company name is ink-stamped. Because this is a relatively new area of collecting and the rarity of many items has yet to be determined, examples are evaluated by size and the intricacy of design.

Ava 100.00
Ballerina, 7" 75.00
Betsy, wht w/gold, 7½" 75.00
Brooch, lady's bust 45.00
Camille, 8½" 100.00
Charmaine, 8½" 100.00
Chinese boy & girl, 7¾", pr 90.00
Clock, Sessions, cherub atop, 11" 150.00
Delia, dusty rose gown, 8" 95.00
Diana, 8½" 120.00
Diane, 7¾" 80.00
Douglas, 8¼" 80.00

Elizabeth seated on couch, 7", $200.00.

Eve, 8½"	115.00
Frame, appl florals, pk/cream/gold, 4½x6½"	45.00
Irene, 5½"	65.00
Jim, bl coat, wht vest & pants, leans on ped, 6¼"	80.00
Kay, pk, 5¾"	65.00
Lamp, TV; Dear Ruth, seated on ped bench	200.00
Louis XVI & Marie Antoinette, 10", pr	300.00
Louise, gray & gold, 7½"	65.00
Marcie	60.00
Martin, 10½"	150.00
Matilda, 8½"	80.00
Melanie, 7½"	65.00
Musette, purple gown & hat, much lace	135.00
Nancy, gray, 7"	60.00
Nita, 8"	85.00
Our Lady of Grace Madonna, 9¾"	75.00
Pinkie & Blue Boy, 12", pr	300.00
Rebecca, seated, 7½"	100.00
Rhett, 9"	100.00
Scarlett, pk & gold, 9"	100.00
Victoria, seated	200.00
Vivian, gr dress w/umbrella, 9¾"	135.00

Florentine Cameo

Although its appearance may look much like English cameo, the decoration on this type of glass is not wheel cut or acid etched. Instead, a type of heavy paste — usually a frosty white — is applied to the surface to create a look very similar to true cameo. It was produced in France as well as England; it is sometimes marked 'Florentine.'

Cruet, peach w/wht decor, frosted hdl & stopper, 5¾"	30.00
Pitcher, bl satin w/yel chinoiserie, basketweave cut, 8"	195.00
Tumbler, orange w/wht flowers, 3½"	65.00
Tumbler, red w/wht flowers, 3¾"	100.00
Vase, apricot w/wht flowers, mk, 7"	90.00
Vase, aqua w/wht bird & foliage, mk, 8"	170.00
Vase, citron w/wht bird & foliage, 5"	45.00
Vase, pk w/wht morning-glories, 4-loop ribbon hdls, 12", pr	995.00

Flow Blue

Flow Blue ware was produced by many Staffordshire potters; among the most familiar were Meigh, Podmore and Walker, Samuel Alcock, Ridgway, John Wedge Wood (who often signed his work Wedgwood), and Davenport. It was popular from about 1825 through 1860 and again from 1880 until the turn of the century. The name describes the blurred or flowing affect of the cobalt decoration, achieved through the introduction of a chemical vapor into the kiln. The body of the ware is ironstone, and Oriental motifs were favored. Later issues were on a lighter body and often decorated with gilt.

Our advisor, Mary Frank Gaston, has compiled a lovely book, *The Collector's Encyclopedia of Flow Blue China*, with full-color illustrations and current market values; you will find her address in the Directory under Texas.

Abbey, cup & saucer, Geo Jones	65.00
Abbey, plate, Geo Jones, 6"	20.00
Abby, plate, deep, P Regout, 8"	40.00
Alaska, bowl, vegetable; w/lid, Grindley	195.00
Alaska, butter pat, Grindley	32.50
Alaska, gravy boat, Grindley	80.00
Alaska, plate, Grindley, 10"	60.00

Alaska, plate, Grindley, 6"	25.00
Alaska, plate, Grindley, 7¾"	35.00
Alaska, platter, Grindley, 16"	195.00
Alaska, soup, rimmed, Grindley, 9"	45.00
Albany, butter dish	235.00
Albany, gravy boat, Grindley	75.00
Albany, plate, Johnson Bros, 7½"	29.00
Albany, saucer, 5¼"	14.00
Aldine, gravy boat, Grindley	65.00
Alice, platter, med	80.00
Amerillia, sauce tureen, w/undertray, Podmore Walker	735.00
Amoy, cup plate, Davenport	85.00
Amoy, plate, Davenport, 10½"	110.00
Amoy, plate, Davenport, 9½"	90.00
Amoy, plate, dessert; Davenport	55.00
Amoy, sauce dish, Davenport	65.00
Arabesque, cup plate, Mayer	95.00
Arabic, plate, Grindley, 8"	17.50
Argyle, bowl, vegetable; hdls, w/lid, EX gold, Grindley	235.00
Argyle, butter pat, Grindley	30.00
Argyle, platter, Grindley, 17½x12"	195.00
Argyle, sauce dish, Grindley	30.00
Argyle, soup, Grindley, 7½"	55.00
Ashburton, gravy boat, w/undertray, Grindley	125.00
Ashburton, soup ladle, Grindley	275.00
Atlanta, bowl, vegetable; lg	80.00
Avon, plate, Booth's, 10"	75.00
Baltic, plate, Grindley, 10"	70.00
Beaufort, bowl, vegetable; Grindley, lg	80.00
Beauties of China, plate, MV & Co, 8½"	75.00
Belford, gravy boat	65.00
Bleeding Heart, sauce ladle	275.00
Blue Danube, cup & saucer	55.00
Bluebell, toothbrush holder, w/lid	350.00
Blyswood, platter, 14"	145.00
Bohemia, platter, Dimmock, 20"	475.00
Brampton, bowl, vegetable; w/lid	160.00
Brunswick, plate, Wood & Son, 9"	45.00
Brunswick, saucer, Wood & Son	12.00
Brussel, platter, lg	130.00
Brussel, platter, med	80.00
Burlington, waste bowl, Wedgwood	80.00
Burma, pitcher, tankard; Ford, 8"	275.00
Camellia, charger, Wedgwood, 12½"	395.00
Camellia, platter, Wedgwood, 18½"	475.00
Candia, chocolate pot, Cauldon	450.00
Candia, pitcher, melon ribs, Cauldon, cream sz	165.00
Candia, plate, Cauldon, 10½"	95.00
Candia, plate, Cauldon, 7"	48.00
Canton, bowl, potato; Edwards, 10"	265.00
Carlton, bowl, vegetable; rose finial, Alcock	395.00
Carlton, cup plate, Alcock	75.00
Carlton, gravy boat, w/underplate, Alcock	135.00
Carlton, plate, Alcock, 10¼"	125.00
Carlton, platter, Alcock, 13½"	195.00
Cashmere, cup & saucer, handleless; Ridgway & Morley	125.00
Cashmere, plate, Ridgway & Morley, 10⅝"	130.00
Catherine Mermet, bowl, Grindley, 10"	95.00
Celtic, gravy boat	65.00
Chang, soup, 8½"	45.00
Chapoo, platter, Wedge Wood, 13½x10½"	350.00
Chapoo, saucer, Wedge Wood	21.00
Chapoo, teapot, Wedge Wood	475.00
Chen-Si, plate, Meir, 1935, 8¾"	80.00

Chinese, bowl, vegetable; lg 80.00
Chinese, plate, Dimmock, 9" 85.00
Chinese, platter, Dimmock, 15½" 295.00
Ching, sauce dish, Davenport 50.00
Chusan, drainer, Wedgwood, 12¼" dia 450.00
Chusan, pitcher, Wedgwood, 7½" 325.00
Chusan, plate, Royal Doulton, 10¼" 125.00
Chusan, teapot, Fell 400.00
Circassia, soup, 10½" 45.00
Claremont, plate, Johnson Bros, 10" 50.00
Clarence, sugar bowl, w/lid, Johnson Bros 150.00
Clayton, platter, Johnson Bros, 11½" 75.00
Clifton, bowl, vegetable; lg 80.00
Clifton, platter, lg 130.00
Clover, bowl, vegetable; Grindley, 11" 250.00
Clover, cup & saucer, Grindley 60.00
Clover, plate, Grindley, 5¾" 30.00
Clover, plate, Grindley, 9" 45.00
Clover, platter, Grindley, 14¼" 150.00
Clover, relish, 7½" 65.00
Clover, soup, Grindley, 7¾" 40.00
Coburg, pitcher & bowl, Edwards 1,750.00
Coburg, platter, Edwards, 17x12" 450.00
Colonial, plate, Meakin, 9" 40.00
Colonial, relish, Meakin, ca 1891 ....60.00
Colonial, sugar bowl, Meakin 45.00
Conway, bowl, New Wharf Pottery, 9" 80.00
Conway, cup & saucer, New Wharf Pottery 65.00
Conway, soup, New Wharf Pottery, 9" 55.00
Coral, plate, Johnson Bros, 9" 48.00
Countess, gravy boat 65.00
Cows, plate, deep, Wedgwood, 10" 90.00
Crossed Bands, dish, heart shape, hdl, Ridgway, 11x8" 225.00
Crumlin, gravy boat, Myott 65.00
Cyprus, cake plate, ped ft, Ridgway, 12" 395.00
Dahlia, cup & saucer, brushstroke w/lustre, Upper Hanley 95.00
Dainty, egg cup, Maddock & Son 95.00
Dainty, plate, Maddock & Son, 7" 16.00
Dainty, saucer, Maddock & Son 10.00
Daisy, gravy boat 65.00
Davenport, creamer, Wood & Sons 85.00
Davenport, teapot, Longport 450.00
Del Monte, bowl, vegetable; VG gold, Johnson Bros, 9½" 55.00
Del Monte, creamer, Johnson Bros..................................85.00
Delft, plate, Minton, 8½" 50.00
Delph, bowl, Wood & Sons, 10½" 90.00
Devon, bowl, vegetable; w/lid, Fell 195.00
Devon, platter, Grindley, 10" 50.00
Diana, butter pat, Meakin 27.50
Dog Rose, jardiniere, much gold, Ridgway, 12½" 350.00
Doreen, toothbrush holder, ca 1891-1914 ....145.00
Douglas, gravy boat, Ford & Sons 85.00
Dover, plate, Grindley, 13" 65.00
Dresden, plate, Johnson Bros, 7" 20.00
Dudley, sauce tureen, w/ladle & tray, Ford & Sons 375.00
Dundee, sauce dish, Ridgway 30.00
Eastern Vines, soup tureen, w/undertray, Meigh 395.00
Empress, plate, 10½" 90.00
Excelsior, plate, Fell, 10½" 115.00
Fairy Villas, butter pat, Adams 28.00
Fairy Villas, cup & saucer, Adams 60.00
Fairy Villas, plate, Adams, 11" 100.00
Fairy Villas II, bowl, Adams, 10¼" 175.00
Farm, plate, Ford, 10" 58.00

Fenton, bowl, J Kent, 10" 85.00
Fleur-de-Lis, sauce tureen, w/undertray & lid 245.00
Floral, gravy boat, scalloped, Johnson Bros, 8¼" 70.00
Florence, soup, flanged, Geo Jones, 9¼" 95.00
Florida, bowl, Grindley, 7½" 55.00
Florida, plate, Grindley, 10" 60.00
Florida, plate, Johnson Bros, 10" 60.00
Florida, plate, Johnson Bros, 8⅞" 48.00
Florida, soup, Johnson Bros, 7½" 50.00
Formosa, compote, octagonal, hdls, Ridgway, 9" 950.00
Formosa, plate, Mayer, 9¾" 115.00
Formosa, platter, Mayer, 13¼" 295.00
Gainsborough, bowl, Ridgway, 9½" 145.00
Gainsborough, chamber pot, bl hdls, Ridgeway, 5½x9½" 275.00
Geisha, bowl, Upper Hanley, 9¾" 175.00
Geisha, creamer, Upper Hanley 100.00
Geisha, cup & saucer, Ford & Sons 90.00
Gem, plate, Hammersley, 9¾" 165.00
Gem, soup, Johnson Bros 40.00
Georgia, bowl, berry; Johnson Bros, ind 30.00
Georgia, plate, Johnson Bros, 10" 55.00
Gironde, bowl, vegetable; w/lid, Grindley 185.00
Gironde, pitcher, Grindley, 1-qt 175.00
Gladys, plate, scalloped, New Wharf Pottery, 9¾" 45.00
Glenmore, bowl, vegetable; oval, Grindley, 8¾" 55.00
Glenmore, bowl, vegetable; oval, w/lid, Grindley 160.00
Glenmore, creamer & sugar bowl, Grindley 185.00
Glenmore, cup & saucer, Grindley 50.00
Glenmore, gravy boat, Grindley 75.00
Glenmore, plate, Grindley, 8" 30.00
Glenmore, platter, Grindley, 10¼" 55.00
Glenmore, platter, Grindley, 12" 85.00
Glenmore, sauce dish, Grindley 20.00
Glentine, bowl, berry; Grindley, sm 55.00
Glentine, creamer & sugar bowl, Grindley 175.00
Glentine, cup & saucer, Grindley 55.00
Glentine, gravy boat, Grindley 85.00
Glentine, plate, Grindley, 6" 25.00
Glentine, plate, Grindley, 8" 30.00
Glentine, plate, Grindley, 9" 40.00
Glentine, soup, Grindley, 7¾" 40.00
Glenwood, chamber pot, Wood, 8½" 170.00
Glenwood, vegetable tureen, w/lid, Johnson 225.00
Grace, bowl, vegetable; Grindley, lg 80.00
Grace, butter pat, Grindley 28.00
Grace, egg cup, Grindley 60.00
Grace, plate, Grindley, 10" 68.00
Grace, platter, Grindley, 21" 345.00
Grecian Statue, bowl, vegetable; w/lid, lg 250.00
Haddon, gravy boat 65.00
Hague, tureen, w/lid & underplate, Johnson Bros, 6½x8x6½" 245.00
Hamilton, sauce ladle, Maddock & Son 85.00
Heath's Flower, platter, 13½" 350.00
Heuman, platter, med 80.00
Hindustan, cup plate, John Maddock 95.00
Holland, bowl, vegetable; w/lid, Meakin 150.00
Holland, platter, Johnson Bros, 14" 145.00
Hollyhock, bowl, salad; Wedgwood, +SP trimmed fork/spoon 295.00
Honc, bowl, 10" 75.00
Honc, cup & saucer, Petrus Regout 50.00
Honc, plate, 6" 25.00
Hong Kong, bowl, vegetable; w/lid, Meigh 275.00
Hong Kong, pitcher, water; Meigh 360.00
Hong Kong, plate, Meigh, 10¼" 125.00

Hong Kong, platter, Meigh, 18x12" 650.00
Hops, cup & saucer, Royal Bonn.................................25.00
Horticultural, chestnut basket, w/tray, Wedgwood.....................695.00
Horticultural, compote, ped ft, Wedgwood, 4x11¾x8" 395.00
Horticultural, sauce ladle, Wedgwood 100.00
Idris, bone dish, Grindley.....................................55.00
Idris, butter pat, Grindley.....................................20.00
Idris, platter, Grindley, 11½x8½".............................65.00
Indian, cup & saucer, Pratt....................................100.00
Indian, cup plate, Pratt.......................................65.00
Indian, soup, Pratt, 10½"....................................110.00
Indian Bridge, plate, red accents, 9½".......................100.00
Indian Jar, bowl, vegetable; oval, 8-sided, w/lid, Furnival 595.00
Indian Jar, plate, Furnival, 10¼" 100.00
Indian Jar, platter, Furnival, 14" 400.00
Indian Jar, platter, 22"..................................... 1,150.00
Iris, gravy boat, Grindley 85.00
Iris, plate, Royal Pottery, 10" 22.50
Ivanhoe, plate, Wedgwood, 10¼" 85.00
Janette, bowl, vegetable; Grindley, lg.........................80.00
Janette, plate, Grindley, 8" 60.00
Jeddo, relish, Adams, 5x7½"..................................60.00
Kaolin, plate, Podmore Walker, ca 1845, 7½" 45.00
Kenworth, bowl, oval, Johnson Bros, 8¾".......................75.00
Khan, bowl, vegetable; w/lid 160.00
Knox, pitcher, New Wharf Pottery, 6"..........................155.00
Knox, platter, New Wharf Pottery, 10½".......................100.00
Kyber, bowl, vegetable; 8-sided, w/lid, Adams 350.00
Kyber, cup & saucer, handleless; Adams........................135.00
Kyber, plate, Adams, 10" 110.00
Kyber, plate, Adams, 8".......................................75.00
Kyber, plate, Adams, 9".......................................90.00
Kyber, platter, hexagonal, Adams, 14½x11".....................235.00
La Belle, bowl, fruit; scalloped, Wheeling.....................175.00
La Belle, bowl, vegetable; w/lid, Wheeling, 10¼" 250.00
La Belle, bowl, vegetable; Wheeling, 10".......................95.00
La Belle, bowl, vegetable; Wheeling, 6½x9" 75.00
La Belle, celery tray, Wheeling, 13x6¼".......................175.00
La Belle, chop plate, Wheeling, 11½"..........................122.50
La Belle, creamer & sugar bowl, Wheeling......................350.00
La Belle, cup & saucer, Wheeling 55.00
La Belle, oyster bowl, rnd, Wheeling, 9".......................360.00
La Belle, pitcher, Wheeling, 1½-qt 175.00
La Belle, pitcher, Wheeling, 2½-qt 275.00
La Belle, plate, Wheeling, 7".................................27.50
La Belle, plate, Wheeling, 9".................................55.00
La Belle, platter, Wheeling, 11½x8".............................105.00
La Belle, platter, Wheeling, 12¾"..............................110.00
La Belle, relish, Wheeling, 11x4".............................110.00
La Belle, soup, Wheeling, 7½"..................................35.00
La Belle, syrup, pewter lid, Wheeling 250.00
La Belle, waste bowl, Wheeling, 6" 50.00
La Francais, bowl, 8½" 20.00
La Francais, cup & saucer 15.00
La Francais, platter, 12½x9½"..................................60.00
La Francais, platter, 15" 100.00
Lahore, creamer, Philips & Son 185.00
Lahore, platter, 16x12"..350.00
Lahore, soup, flanged 58.00
Lakewood, cup & saucer, Wood...................................55.00
Lakewood, platter, Wood, 12½"..................................95.00
Lancaster, cup & saucer, New Wharf Pottery.....................65.00
Lancaster, plate, Bishop & Stonier, 9".........................35.00
Lancaster, plate, New Wharf Pottery, 9".........................50.00

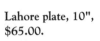

Lahore plate, 10",
$65.00.

Lancaster, platter, New Wharf Pottery, 1890s, 12½" 95.00
Lancaster, sauce dish 30.00
Lawrence, butter pat, Bishop & Stonier........................32.00
Le Pavot, bone dish, Grindley 20.00
Le Pavot, pitcher, milk; Grindley 265.00
Lonsdale, platter, Samuel Ford, ca 1898-1939, 10x8"...................85.00
Lorne, bowl, vegetable; open, Grindley 90.00
Lorne, bowl, vegetable; w/lid, Grindley 250.00
Lorne, gravy boat, Grindley...................................80.00
Lorne, gravy boat, w/undertray, Grindley 130.00
Lorne, plate, Grindley, 10"...................................55.00
Lorne, platter, Grindley, 14x10"..............................98.00
Lotus, bone dish, Grindley....................................20.00
Lotus, gravy boat 95.00
Lozere, cup plate, Challinor..................................50.00
Lynton, wash basin, oval, Ceramic Art, 17½"...................225.00
Madras, gravy boat, Doulton 80.00
Madras, pitcher, Doulton, 5"..................................110.00
Madras, pitcher, Doulton, 8"..................................365.00
Madras, plate, dinner; Doulton................................85.00
Madras, sauce dish, Doulton...................................28.00
Mandarin, pitcher, water; Pountney 395.00
Mandarin, plate, Pountney, 10"................................70.00
Mandarin, platter, Pountney, 12¾x9½"..........................90.00
Manhattan, butter pat, Alcock, 3⅝" 28.00
Manhattan, cup & saucer, Alcock 50.00
Manhattan, soup, flanged, Alcock 68.00
Manilla, pitcher, water; Podmore Walker.......................475.00
Manilla, plate, Podmore Walker, 8"............................90.00
Manilla, platter, Podmore Walker, ca 1845, 16" 350.00
Manilla, teapot 625.00
Marble Variant, slop jar, w/lid...............................900.00
Marechal Niel, creamer, Grindley..............................145.00
Marechal Niel, platter, Grindley, 12½x9".......................90.00
Marechal Niel, sauce tureen, w/ladle, Grindley................295.00
Marechal Niel, soup, Grindley, 7¾"............................60.00
Marguerite, platter, Grindley, 18"............................160.00
Marie, bowl, salad; Grindley, 8"..............................20.00
Marie, bowl, vegetable; oval, w/lid, Grindley, 11x8"...........245.00
Marie, bowl, vegetable; rnd, w/lid, Grindley..................160.00
Marie, butter pat, Grindley...................................25.00
Marie, gravy boat, Grindley...................................70.00
Marie, plate, 9"..45.00
Marie, platter, Grindley, 16" 200.00
Marie, soup tureen 450.00
Marquis, cup & saucer, Grindley...............................55.00
Martha, bone dish 25.00

Martha Washington, cup & saucer	40.00
Medieval, plate, 9½"	95.00
Meissen, sauce tureen, Minton	295.00
Melbourne, butter pat, Grindley, 3¼"	27.50
Melbourne, cup & saucer, Grindley	50.00
Melbourne, platter, Grindley, 16"	185.00
Mentone, gravy boat	65.00
Mercer, bowl, vegetable; w/lid	160.00
Milan, butter pat, Grindley	18.00
Milan, butter pat, Grindley, 4 for	70.00
Mongolia, bowl, Johnson Bros, 3x8½"	70.00
Mongolia, platter, Johnson Bros, 12"	145.00
Navy, cup & saucer, Till	55.00
Navy, plate, Till, 7"	30.00
Navy, plate, Till, 9"	40.00
Navy, relish, Till, 8¾"	65.00
Navy, sauce dish, Till	30.00
Neapolitan, bowl, vegetable; w/lid	160.00
Nelson, bowl, Upper Hanley, 10"	40.00
Neopolitan, butter pat	26.00
Non Pareil, bowl, vegetable; w/lid, Burgess & Leigh	225.00
Non Pareil, charger, Burgess & Leigh, 13¼"	325.00
Non Pareil, plate, Burgess & Leigh, 8¾"	85.00
Non Pareil, soup, flanged, Burgess & Leigh	75.00
Norbury, bowl, Royal Doulton, 16½"	225.00
Normandy, bowl, cereal; Johnson	25.00
Normandy, butter pat, Johnson	28.00
Normandy, plate, Johnson, 10"	55.00
Normandy, platter, Johnson, 16x12"	175.00
Olympia, bowl, vegetable; Grindley, lg	80.00
Olympia, bowl, vegetable; oval, w/lid, Grindley	145.00
Olympia, butter dish, Grindley	105.00
Olympia, gravy boat, w/underplate, Grindley	85.00
Olympia, sugar bowl, w/lid, Grindley	90.00
Orchid, teapot, Maddock	325.00
Oregon, plate, Mayer, 9½"	115.00
Oregon, platter, Mayer, 10½"	225.00
Oregon, teapot, Mayer	595.00
Oriental, plate, Ridgway, 5¾"	28.00
Osborne, gravy boat, Ridgway	65.00
Osborne, soup tureen, Ridgeway	400.00
Oxford, butter dish, Johnson, 3-pc	165.00
Paris, plate, Johnson Bros, 10"	55.00
Peking, bowl, 2x9½"	80.00
Percy, plate, Morley, 9½"	90.00
Persian, platter, 18½x13½"	375.00
Poppea, dessert stand	165.00
Poppy, bowl, Bennett, 8½"	50.00
Poppy, gravy boat, Grindley	90.00
Poppy, plate, Grindley, 9"	35.00
Portman, butter pat	26.00
Priscilla, butter pat	20.00
Raleigh, cup & saucer, Burgess & Leigh	50.00
Raleigh, plate, Burgess & Leigh, 9½"	45.00
Rhine, cup plate	85.00
Rhoda Gardens, saucer	40.00
Richmond, butter dish, Johnson Bros	98.00
Richmond, plate, Johnson Bros, 10"	45.00
Richmond, platter, Johnson Bros, lg	150.00
Rock, plate, Challinor, 7½"	60.00
Rose, platter, lg	150.00
Rose Festoon, platter, Alcock, 16½"	395.00
Royston, plate, 10"	40.00
Savoy, gravy boat, Stoke	100.00
Savoy, sugar bowl, w/lid	115.00
Scinde, bowl, vegetable; w/lid, 10½"	390.00
Scinde, creamer, Walker	325.00
Scinde, gravy boat, Alcock	275.00
Scinde, plate, Alcock, 8½"	95.00
Scinde, plate, Walker, 9"	110.00
Scinde, plate, 12-sided, Alcock, 7"	85.00
Scinde, platter, Walker, 17¾"	495.00
Scinde, sauce tureen, w/ladle & underplate, Alcock	1,195.00
Sefton, gravy boat	65.00
Seville, gravy boat, Wood & Sons	95.00
Shanghae, plate, Furnival, 10¼"	125.00
Shanghai, bowl, vegetable; oval, Grindley	95.00
Shanghai, platter, Grindley, 14x10"	255.00
Shell, pitcher & bowl	1,150.00
Shell, plate, Challinor, 8½"	70.00
Shell, plate, Challinor, 9¾"	90.00
Sloe Blossom, mug, Ridgway, lg	295.00
Sloe Blossom, toothbrush holder, w/lid, Ridgway	250.00
Sobraon, platter, 16"	425.00
Spinach, bowl, Regout, 4¼"	65.00
St Louis, platter, 16"	245.00
Sydney, gravy boat	65.00
Sylph, plate, 10"	85.00
Temple, cup & saucer, handleless; Podmore Walker	135.00
Temple, plate, Podmore Walker, 8⅝"	90.00
Temple, plate, Podmore Walker, 9¾"	125.00
Timor, bowl, 3x6"	20.00
Tivoli, gravy boat	160.00
Tivoli, platter, 10"	110.00
Tivoli, soup tureen	1,950.00
Tivoli, teapot	625.00
Togo, butter pat, Winkle	24.00
Togo, gravy boat, Winkle	65.00
Togo, platter, Colonial Pottery, 12"	125.00
Togo, platter, 10"	110.00
Tonquin, plate, Heath, 10½"	135.00
Tonquin, plate, Heath, 7½"	65.00
Touraine, bone dish, Stanley	45.00
Touraine, bowl, berry; Stanley, sm	45.00
Touraine, bowl, oval, Stanley, 9"	100.00
Touraine, bowl, vegetable; w/lid, Stanley	295.00
Touraine, butter pat	34.00
Touraine, creamer & sugar bowl, Alcock	300.00
Touraine, cup & saucer, Stanley	75.00
Touraine, gravy boat	65.00
Touraine, plate, Alcock, 7¾"	35.00
Touraine, plate, Alcock, 8¾"	45.00
Touraine, plate, Stanley, 10"	80.00
Touraine, plate, Stanley, 6½"	30.00
Touraine, platter, Alcock, 10"	85.00
Touraine, platter, Stanley, 12½"	150.00
Touraine, platter, Stanley, 14⅝"	265.00
Touraine, soup, rimmed, Stanley, 8¾"	65.00
Touraine, teapot	325.00
Tower, soup, Rowland Marcus, 8½"	90.00
Trellis, platter, Grindley, 12½"	75.00
Trilby, cake plate, advertising, 10½"	55.00
Troy, teapot	695.00
Turin, platter, Johnson Bros, 16x12"	150.00
Venice, toothbrush jar, Grimwade's	80.00
Venus, gravy boat	65.00
Vermont, gravy boat, w/underliner	125.00
Vermont, sauce, Burgess & Leigh, 5"	22.00

Vermont, sauce ladle 100.00
Vermont, soup, 9" 40.00
Verona, butter pat, Meakin 25.00
Verona, pickle dish, Ridgway, 5x8½" 50.00

Verona platter, 16½", $195.00.

Victoria, bowl, Wood & Son, 10" 75.00
Vine, plate, Wedgwood, 8" 35.00
Virginia, platter, Maddock, 18x15" 325.00
Virginia, soup tureen, Maddock & Sons 575.00
Wagon Wheel, mug, child's sz...135.00
Wagon Wheel, tea set, child's, complete 900.00
Waldorf, bowl, vegetable; New Wharf Pottery, lg 80.00
Waldorf, plate, New Wharf Pottery, 9" 50.00
Watteau, beaker, Doulton 65.00
Watteau, bowl, Doulton, 7" 45.00
Watteau, bowl, Doulton, 9¾" 80.00
Watteau, bowl, flanged, Doulton, 12½" 125.00
Watteau, bowl, New Wharf Pottery, 10½" 170.00
Watteau, bowl, vegetable; Doulton, 8¼" 75.00
Watteau, bowl, vegetable; Doulton, 9¼" 85.00
Watteau, chamberpot, Doulton, 8½" 175.00
Watteau, compote, fruit; hdls, ped ft, Doulton, 4¾x9¾".............300.00
Watteau, cup & saucer, Doulton...65.00
Watteau, meat server, well & tree, dome lid, Doulton, 12¾" 550.00
Watteau, plate, Doulton, 10½" 100.00
Watteau, plate, Doulton, 6½" 35.00
Watteau, plate, Doulton, 8½" 65.00
Watteau, plate, Doulton, 9½" 80.00
Watteau, plate, scalloped, Doulton, 8"....................................65.00
Watteau, platter, Doulton, 13¼x11" 295.00
Watteau, platter, scalloped, Doulton, 12¼" 225.00
Watteau, soup, flanged, gold rim, Doulton, 10¼" 85.00
Weir, platter, Ford & Sons, 12x9" 85.00
Whampoa, mug, lg..275.00
Windsor, gravy boat..65.00
Windsor Scroll, creamer...295.00

Flue Covers

When spring house cleaning started and the heating stove was taken down for the warm weather season, the unsightly hole where the stovepipe joined the chimney was hidden with an attractive flue cover. They were made with a colorful litho print behind glass with a chain for hanging. Although scarce today, some scenes were actually reverse painted on the glass itself. The most popular motifs were florals, children, and lovely ladies. Square, rectangular, or diamond shapes are more valuable than oval or round covers, especially when Victorian ladies or children are pictured. Occasionally flue covers were made in sets of three — one served a functional purpose, while the other two were added to provide a more attractive wall arrangement. They range in size from 7"-8" to 13"-14", but 9" is the average.

**Ballerinas, 10",
$50.00.**

Brn japanning, Electric Pat Jan 7, 1890, 14"...................................55.00
Fox hunters meet people in early auto, glass covered, oval, 9".....135.00
Ladies in early gr Renault, Germany, 6¾", EX 200.00
Little girl w/flowers, under glass..32.00
Roman lady's profile, gold emb paper...24.00
Victorian interior scene, under glass, 9" 45.00
Victorian lady in lg hat, under glass, 9½" 34.00
Victorian maid, gold glitter trim, 12"...75.00
Winter country scene, brass fr, sgn..24.00

Folk Art

That the creative energies of the mind ever spark innovations in functional utilitarian channels as well as toward playful frivolity is well documented in the study of American folk art. While the average early settler rarely had free time to pursue art for its own sake, his creative energy exemplified itself in fashioning useful objects carved or otherwise ornamented beyond the scope of pure practicality. After the advent of the Industrial Revolution, the pace of everyday living became more leisurely, and country folk found they had extra time. Not accustomed to sitting idle, many turned to carving, painting, or weaving. Whirligigs, imaginative toys for the children, and whimsies of all types resulted. Though often rather crude, this type of early art represents a segment of our heritage and as such has become valued by collectors. See also Baskets; Decoys; Frakturs; Samplers; Trade Signs; Weathervanes; Wood Carvings.

Articulated figure, Blk caricature, 1930s, 9½", EX 65.00
Ash tray, moose's hoof w/metal tray at top, ca 1900, 11x6x4" 85.00
Cutout, dbl landscape, delicate/intricate, bl ground, 6x6½" 525.00
Cutout, folded/cut in rnd, blk w/color, fr, 8x8"............................200.00
Cutout, foliage/houses/trees/people/tombstones, fr, 10x10" 1,250.00
Cutout, harp w/flowers & foliage, mtd, 15x11" 65.00
Cutout, heart-in-heart w/in foliage wreath w/birds, 14x17" 2,100.00
Cutout, tree w/birds/squirrel/cat, S Linsey, 1849, 9x11"...............400.00
Cvg, anchor & chain, from 1-pc of wood 155.00
Cvg, bird on branch, wire legs, burned pattern, '20s, 7x6x2" 55.00
Cvg, cat, recumbent, limestone, worn pnt, late 1800s, 9"............165.00

Cvg, dog w/bushy tail, wood, pnt eyes/nose, 1900s, 5x5x2" **45.00**
Cvg, Indian brave bust, braided hair, 7x4x3½", EX.....................**125.00**
Cvg, man w/hat, wood, jtd arms, pnt clothes, 1920s, 6" **68.00**
Cvg, moose jumping over log, pnt/varnished wood, 12x10x3" ..**240.00**
Cvg, old couple, wood, mc pnt, EX detail, 5", pr **60.00**

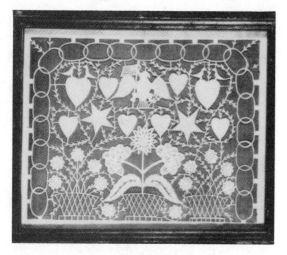

Cutwork, unsigned, early 1800s, mounted on blue cloth, 12½" x 16", $2,500.00.

Doll, Blk girl, cloth, embr features/button eyes, 1930s, 18" **85.00**
Doll, cloth, pnt features, print dress, 1900s, 18½" **175.00**
Drawing, Washington's House..., pencil, 1852, 16x13"................**225.00**
Fish decoy, yel perch, metal fins, tack eyes, Blanchard, 6" **200.00**
Hat stand, wooden sunflower on wire stem, EX pnt, 12x4x4" **40.00**
Incense burner, cvd log cabin, metal base, 1900s, 8x6x6".............**125.00**
Lamp base, cvd wood cactus, branching arms, EX pnt, '50s, 13" ...**75.00**
Lawn ornament, log house model, many windows, 1900s, 26".....**150.00**
Mirror, cvd walnut fr w/trn ½-columns, 16x21" **850.00**
Painting in oil, horse's head, EX details, 1880s, 26x20" **240.00**
Painting on canvas, Indian on horse in mtns, fr, 1910s, EX.........**165.00**
Painting on glass, girl w/basket in winter, 1880s, fr, 17x15" **165.00**
Pastel on paper, cherries falling from basket, 29x24", EX **135.00**
Plant stand, Adirondac, 10-pot, 58" **250.00**
Tattoo design, patriotic, allegory w/ship, drawing, 9x7"..............**300.00**
Theorem on paper, watercolor, fruit compote/flowers, 25x24". **1,200.00**
Theorem on paper w/stencils, deer/horse/bldgs/etc, 10x5" **800.00**
Theorem on velvet, flower basket, butterfly, 20x22".....................**450.00**
Theorem on velvet, vase of flowers, gilt fr, 20x15".......................**450.00**
Wall pocket, stylized owl, wood & metal w/marble eyes, 11".......**100.00**
Whirligig, birdhouse, mc pnt, 1900s, 11x12"..............................**60.00**
Whirligig, Blk lady washing, mc pnt, ca 1920, 18" L, EX.............**200.00**
Whirligig, flying mallard duck, mc pnt, 1920s, 25x12x4" **235.00**
Whirligig, Indian w/paddle vanes, mc pnt, 15" **850.00**
Whirligig, lady churns butter, pnt wood, 1920s, 18x13x13" **125.00**
Whirligig, Mammy washing, tub & washboard, 1930s, 16x11x2".**110.00**
Whirligig, old man saws log, old pnt, 27x14", EX **200.00**
Whirligig, sailor, arms w/paddles pivot, cvd/pnt, 1700s, 8" **285.00**
Whirligig, WWII twin-engine plane, pnt wood, '40s, 23x17x6"..**185.00**
Whistle, cvd from branch, cvd bird on top, mc pnt, 1900s, 4" **35.00**
Yard ornament, Boston Terrier, sheet tin, orig pnt, 1920s, 24"......**85.00**

Fostoria

The Fostoria Glass Company was built in 1887 at Fostoria, Ohio, but by 1891 it had moved to Moundsville, West Virginia. During the next two decades, they produced many lines of pressed patterned table-ware and lamps. Their most famous pattern, American, was introduced in 1915 and was produced continuously from that time until the company's closing in well over two hundred different pieces. From 1920 to 1925, top artists designed tablewares in colored glass — canary (vaseline), amber, blue, orchid, green, and ebony — in pressed patterns as well as etched designs. By the late thirties, Fostoria was recognized as the largest producer of handmade glassware in the world. The company ceased operations in Moundsville in 1986.

Watch for reproductions of Coin Glass by Lancaster Colony; they are also making a copy of the American cookie jar that retails for about $40.00. Our advisor for this category is Michael Baker; he is listed in the Directory under West Virginia. We are assisted in our listings by the Fostoria Glass Society of America, Inc., whose mailing address may be found in the Directory under Clubs, Newsletters, and Catalogs.

Animals and Birds

Colts, sitting..**35.00**
Colts, sitting, bl...**30.00**
Deer, sitting or standing **40.00**
Deer, sitting or standing, milk glass **35.00**
Deer, sitting or standing, silver mist...............................**40.00**
Dog's head, ash tray, frosted **40.00**
Duck w/3 ducklings, amber, set **50.00**
Eagle, bookend..**90.00**
Elephant, bookends, blk, pr **75.00**
Frog..**85.00**
Goldfish, tail up **95.00**
Horse, bookends, blk, pr **75.00**
Horse, bookends, pr **45.00**
Mermaid, 10"...**100.00**
Owl, bookend...**175.00**
Pelican **50.00**
Penguin **75.00**
Polar bear **75.00**
Polar bear, amber...**200.00**
Pony, bl **20.00**
Ram's head, ash tray, frosted **40.00**
Sea horse, bookend **75.00**
Seal..**85.00**
Seal, frosted **60.00**
Seal, wisteria **85.00**
Squirrel..**20.00**
Squirrel, frosted **20.00**
Whale **20.00**

American, ash tray, oval, 3⅞" **9.00**
American, ash tray, sq, 5"...**27.50**

American basket, rattan handle, 9" wide, $100.00.

American, bell 65.00
American, bottle, bitters; w/tube, 4½-oz, 5¾".....55.00
American, bottle, cologne; w/stopper, 8-oz, 7¼" ...52.50
American, bottle, condiment or catsup; w/stopper.....80.00
American, bottle, cordial; w/stopper, 9-oz, 7¼".....75.00
American, bottle, water; 44-oz, 9¼".................375.00
American, bowl, almond; oval, 3¾"...................12.50
American, bowl, banana split; 9x3½".................200.00
American, bowl, cream soup; hdls, 5".................45.00
American, bowl, fruit; flared, 4¾"....................15.00
American, bowl, jelly; 4¼x4¼".........................15.00
American, bowl, lemon; w/lid, 5½"....................32.50
American, bowl, nappy; 4½".............................10.00
American, bowl, rose; 3½"...............................16.00
American, bowl, shrimp; 12¼"..........................310.00
American, box, jewel; w/lid, 5¼x2¼"................125.00
American, box, puff; w/lid, 3⅛x2¾"..................115.00
American, butter, w/lid, ¼-lb............................15.00
American, candlestick, octagon ft, 6"..................20.00
American, candy, ped ft, w/lid..........................27.50
American, cigarette box, w/lid, 4¾"...................30.00
American, comport, jelly; flared, 5"...................12.00
American, creamer, 9½-oz................................10.50
American, cup, flat.. 5.00
American, cup, punch; flared rim.......................10.00
American, decanter, w/stopper, 24-oz, 9¼".........85.00
American, goblet, claret; #2056, 7-oz, 4⅞".........35.00
American, goblet, wine; #2056, hex ft, 2½-oz, 4⅜".....12.00
American, hair receiver, 3x3"...........................175.00
American, hat, tall, 4"....................................40.00
American, hat, western style............................125.00
American, ice bucket, w/tongs..........................50.00
American, ice cream saucer, 2 styles...................60.00
American, ice tub, w/liner, 5⅝".........................47.50
American, jar, pickle; w/pointed lid, 6"...............225.00
American, mayonnaise, divided 7.50
American, mug, beer; 12-oz, 4½"......................40.00
American, mustard, w/lid................................27.50
American, oil, 5-oz..27.50
American, picture frame 5.50
American, pitcher, flat, 1-qt.............................20.00
American, plate, dinner; 9½"...........................18.00
American, plate, sandwich; sm center, 9"............14.00
American, platter, oval, 10½"..........................37.50
American, ring holder 110.00
American, shaker, 3¼", ea.............................. 9.50
American, spooner, 3¾" 32.50
American, strawholder, 10".............................230.00
American, sugar bowl, hdls, w/lid 17.50
American, tray, appetizer; w/6 inserts, 10½".......210.00
American, tray, ice cream; oval, 13½".................52.50
American, tray, oval, hdld, 6"..........................35.00
American, tray, pin; oval, 5½x4½".....................45.00
American, tray, rectangular, 5x2½" 65.00
American, tumbler, iced tea; hdld 165.00
American, urn, sq, ped ft, 6"............................25.00
American, vase, bud; ftd, 6"............................10.00
American, vase, flared, 8"...............................77.50
Baroque, bl; bowl, celery; 11".........................30.00
Baroque, bl; bowl, cream soup 60.00
Baroque, bl; bowl, jelly; w/lid, 7½"...................75.00
Baroque, bl; candelabrum, 3-lite, 24-lustre, 9½".....95.00
Baroque, bl; candy, 3-part, w/lid 95.00
Baroque, bl; comport, 6½"..............................32.00

Baroque, bl; ice bucket.................................65.00
Baroque, bl; pitcher, w/ice lip, 7"....................600.00
Baroque, bl; plate, 7"................................... 9.00
Baroque, bl; plate, 9"...................................45.00
Baroque, bl; saucer..................................... 5.00
Baroque, bl; shakers, pr...............................130.00
Baroque, bl; sugar bowl, ind, 3".......................22.00
Baroque, bl; tray, oval, 11"............................25.00
Baroque, bl; tumbler, iced tea; ftd, 12-oz, 6"........30.00
Baroque, bl; vase, 7"....................................50.00
Baroque, crystal; bowl, flared, 12"....................21.50
Baroque, crystal; bowl, punch; ftd.....................295.00
Baroque, crystal; bowl, 3-ftd, 7".......................12.50
Baroque, crystal; cup, punch; 6-oz.................... 8.00
Baroque, crystal; mustard, w/lid.......................22.00
Baroque, crystal; oil, w/stopper, 5½"..................45.00
Baroque, crystal; plate, sandwich; center hdl, 11"....15.00
Baroque, crystal; shakers, ind, pr......................50.00
Baroque, crystal; stem, water; 9-oz, 6¾"..............12.50
Baroque, crystal; vase, 6½".............................15.00
Baroque, yel; ash tray...................................13.00
Baroque, yel; bowl, pickle; 8"..........................20.00
Baroque, yel; candlestick, 2-lite, 4½".................20.00
Baroque, yel; creamer, ftd, 3¾".........................12.00
Baroque, yel; mayonnaise, w/liner, 5½"...............35.00
Baroque, yel; platter, oval, 12".........................35.00

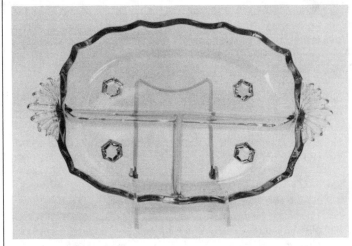

Baroque divided relish, yellow, 10", $25.00.

Baroque, yel; sweetmeat, w/lid, 9"....................125.00
Baroque, yel; tumbler, water; 9-oz, 4¼"..............21.00
Century, bowl, serving; hdls, 9½"......................25.00
Century, bowl, snack; ftd, 6¼" 12.50
Century, candlestick, dbl, 7"...........................25.00
Century, candy, w/lid, 7" 27.50
Century, comport, 4⅜"..................................13.50
Century, ice bucket......................................45.00
Century, mustard, w/spoon & lid 25.00
Century, pitcher, 48-oz, 7⅛"...........................85.00
Century, relish, 3-part, 11⅛"..........................20.00
Century, stem, wine; 3½-oz, 4½"......................24.00
Century, vase, bud; 6"..................................17.50
Chintz, bowl, #2496, tricornered, 4⅝".................15.00
Chintz, bowl, vegetable; #2496, 9½"...................60.00
Chintz, candlestick, #2496, 4".........................12.00
Chintz, candy, #2496, w/lid, 3-part....................90.00
Chintz, celery, #2496, 11"..............................27.50

Chintz, pickle, #2496, 8" 27.50
Chintz, pitcher, #5000, ftd, 48-oz...................295.00
Chintz, platter, 12" 75.00
Chintz, sauce boat, oval.................................65.00
Chintz, vase, #4143, ftd, 7½".........................95.00
Coin, amber; ash tray, 5" 14.00
Coin, amber; ash tray, 7½"..............................22.00
Coin, amber; bowl, oval, 9"..............................45.00
Coin, amber; candlestick, 4½", pr.....................35.00
Coin, amber; candy box..................................35.00
Coin, amber; candy jar, w/lid...........................32.00
Coin, amber; cigarette urn, ftd.........................32.00
Coin, amber; compote, ftd, 8½".........................40.00
Coin, amber; compote, 4½"..............................20.00
Coin, amber; compote, 8½"..............................40.00
Coin, amber; creamer.....................................20.00
Coin, amber; finger lamp, #310.......................110.00
Coin, amber; match holder..............................15.00
Coin, amber; nappy, hdls, 5"............................18.00
Coin, amber; pitcher, 1-qt...............................65.00
Coin, amber; shakers, pr.................................35.00
Coin, amber; sugar bowl, w/lid.........................32.50
Coin, amber; vase, bud; 8"..............................25.00
Coin, bl; ash tray, 7"......................................18.00
Coin, bl; bowl, oval, 8¾".................................65.00
Coin, bl; candlestick, 4½", pr...........................42.50
Coin, bl; pitcher, water..................................140.00
Coin, bl; sugar bowl, w/lid..............................38.00
Coin, bl; vase, bud; #799................................50.00
Coin, crystal; ash tray, raised center, 7"..............27.50
Coin, crystal; ash tray, 7½".............................20.00
Coin, crystal; bowl, oval, 9".............................27.50
Coin, crystal; bowl, wedding; w/lid....................60.00
Coin, crystal; bowl, 8"...................................22.50
Coin, crystal; candlesticks, 4½", pr....................30.00
Coin, crystal; candy dish................................28.00
Coin, crystal; compote, jelly............................15.00
Coin, crystal; cruet......................................75.00
Coin, crystal; pitcher, water............................75.00
Coin, crystal; shakers, pr...............................32.00
Coin, crystal; vase, bud; 8".............................20.00
Coin, emerald gr; candy urn, w/lid, 13" 150.00
Coin, olive gr; ash tray, raised center, 10"...........45.00
Coin, olive gr; bowl, fruit; ftd..........................50.00
Coin, olive gr; bowl, oval, 9"...........................40.00
Coin, olive gr; bowl, wedding; #162...................60.00
Coin, olive gr; candlestick, 4½", pr....................35.00
Coin, olive gr; candy dish, #347.......................37.00
Coin, olive gr; candy urn, 13"..........................45.00
Coin, olive gr; compote, 8½"............................30.00
Coin, olive gr; condiment tray..........................15.00
Coin, olive gr; creamer..................................25.00
Coin, olive gr; jelly dish, #448.........................22.50
Coin, olive gr; nappy, hdls..............................18.00
Coin, olive gr; pitcher, water...........................55.00
Coin, olive gr; shakers, #652, pr.......................45.00
Coin, olive gr; sugar bowl, w/lid.......................30.00
Coin, red; ash tray, #199, 7"............................40.00
Coin, red; ash tray, 8"...................................50.00
Coin, red; bowl, #179....................................55.00
Coin, red; bowl, oval, #189.............................60.00
Coin, red; bowl, wedding; #162.........................95.00
Coin, red; candy box, low 45.00
Coin, red; nappy, hdls, 5¼".............................20.00

Coin Glass candy jar, red, $65.00.

Coin, red; vase, bud; 8"..................................45.00
Coin, red; wine goblet..................................100.00
Colony, ash tray, rnd, 4½"..............................12.50
Colony, bowl, almond; ftd, 2¾"........................13.00
Colony, bowl, bonbon; 5"................................ 9.00
Colony, bowl, console; rolled edge, 9"................30.00
Colony, bowl, cream soup; 5"...........................37.50
Colony, butter dish, ¼-lb...............................30.00
Colony, candlestick, 9".................................25.00
Colony, candy, w/lid, ftd, ½-lb.........................55.00
Colony, cheese & cracker...............................45.00
Colony, cup, punch......................................10.00
Colony, ice bucket, plain edge.........................80.00
Colony, oil, w/stopper, 4½-oz..........................35.00
Colony, pitcher, milk; 16-oz...........................65.00
Colony, pitcher, w/ice lip, 48-oz.....................175.00
Colony, plate, bread & butter; 6"....................... 4.00
Colony, plate, cake; hdls, 10"..........................20.00
Colony, shakers, 3⅝", pr...............................12.50
Colony, stem, wine; 3¼-oz, 4¼".......................20.00
Colony, sugar bowl, ind, 2¾"........................... 5.50
Colony, tumbler, water; 9-oz, 3⅞"....................12.00
Colony, vase, flared, 7½"...............................35.00
Fairfax, amber; bottle, salad dressing.................60.00
Fairfax, amber; bowl, soup;, 7".........................12.00
Fairfax, amber; butter dish, w/lid......................80.00
Fairfax, amber; comport, 5".............................15.00
Fairfax, amber; creamer, ftd............................. 7.00
Fairfax, amber; ice bucket..............................30.00
Fairfax, amber; mayonnaise ladle......................20.00
Fairfax, amber; plate, cake; 10".........................13.00
Fairfax, amber; plate, canape..........................10.00
Fairfax, amber; platter, oval, 12".......................20.00
Fairfax, amber; sauce boat..............................20.00
Fairfax, amber; shakers, ftd, ind, pr...................20.00
Fairfax, amber; sugar bowl, flat........................10.00
Fairfax, amber; tray, center hdl, 11"...................12.00
Fairfax, amber; vase, 2 styles, 8".......................35.00
Fairfax, bl; bowl, fruit; 5"...............................12.00
Fairfax, bl; candlestick, flattened top.................15.00
Fairfax, bl; mayonnaise.................................15.00
Fairfax, bl; plate, whipped cream 11.00
Fairfax, bl; relish, 11½"..................................15.00
Fairfax, bl; sugar pail...................................40.00
Fairfax, blk; lemon dish, #2375, 7"+hdls.............18.00
Fairfax, gr; baker, oval, 9"..............................20.00

Fairfax, gr; candlestick, 3"....................................10.00
Fairfax, gr; creamer, flat....................................12.00
Fairfax, gr; cup, after dinner....................................12.50
Fairfax, gr; nut cup, blown....................................20.00
Fairfax, gr; pickle, 8½"....................................9.00
Fairfax, gr; plate, salad; 7½"....................................3.50
Fairfax, gr; platter, oval, 15"....................................32.00
Fairfax, gr; saucer, after dinner....................................5.00
Fairfax, gr; tumbler, ftd, 2½-oz....................................12.00
Fairfax, gr; whipped cream pail....................................28.00
Fairfax, orchid; ash tray, 2½"....................................15.00
Fairfax, orchid; bowl, centerpiece; 12"....................................25.00
Fairfax, orchid; cheese & cracker set, 2 styles....................................35.00
Fairfax, orchid; ice bowl....................................15.00
Fairfax, orchid; plate, bread; oval, 12"....................................40.00
Fairfax, orchid; stem, cocktail; 3-oz, 5¼"....................................24.00
Fairfax, rose; bouillon, ftd....................................11.00
Fairfax, rose; grapefruit....................................25.00
Fairfax, rose; pitcher, #5000....................................175.00
Fairfax, rose; platter, oval, 10½"....................................30.00
Fairfax, rose; shakers, ftd, pr....................................55.00
Fairfax, rose; tumbler, ftd, 12-oz, 6"....................................25.00
Fairfax, topaz; bowl, nappy, rnd, 8"....................................14.00
Fairfax, topaz; comport, 7"....................................12.00
Fairfax, topaz; plate, grill; 10¼"....................................20.00
Fairfax, topaz; stem, cordial; ¾-oz, 4"....................................35.00
Fairfax, topaz; sugar bowl, ftd....................................8.00
June, bl; bowl, finger; w/liner....................................45.00
June, bl; bowl, soup; 7"....................................75.00
June, bl; candlestick, 3"....................................25.00
June, bl; candy, w/lid, 3-pt....................................225.00
June, bl; creamer, ftd....................................25.00
June, bl; goblet, cocktail; 3-oz, 5¼"....................................40.00
June, bl; plate, bread & butter; 6"....................................12.00
June, bl; plate, canape....................................18.00
June, bl; plate, grill; 10"....................................75.00
June, bl; sauce boat....................................275.00
June, bl; tumbler, ftd, 12-oz, 6"....................................45.00
June, crystal; bowl, bouillon; ftd....................................12.00
June, crystal; bowl, cereal; 6"....................................15.00
June, crystal; candlestick, 5"....................................15.00
June, crystal; celery, 11½"....................................25.00
June, crystal; cream soup, ftd....................................12.00
June, crystal; cup, ftd....................................15.00
June, crystal; goblet, claret; 4-oz, 6"....................................30.00
June, crystal; goblet, water; 10-oz, 8¼"....................................21.00
June, crystal; ice bucket....................................47.50
June, crystal; mayonnaise, w/liner....................................22.50
June, crystal; pail, whipped cream....................................65.00
June, crystal; pitcher....................................195.00
June, rose; ash tray....................................45.00
June, rose; bowl, centerpiece; 11"....................................60.00
June, rose; comport, #2400, 5"....................................40.00
June, rose; goblet, wine; 3-oz, 5½"....................................80.00
June, rose; plate, dinner; sm, 9½"....................................20.00
June, rose; sugar pail....................................195.00
June, topaz; bowl, baker; oval, 9"....................................65.00
June, topaz; bowl, mint; 3-ftd, 4½"....................................15.00
June, topaz; bowl dessert; hdls, lg....................................45.00
June, topaz; candlestick, 2"....................................20.00
June, topaz; comport, #2375, 7"....................................35.00
June, topaz; creamer, tea....................................37.50
June, topaz; decanter....................................400.00
June, topaz; goblet, cordial; ¾-oz, 4"....................................65.00

June, topaz; grapefruit....................................60.00
June, topaz; ice dish....................................37.50
June, topaz; parfait, 5¼"....................................50.00
June, topaz; plate, cream soup; 7½"....................................7.50
June, topaz; tray, center hdl, 11"....................................35.00
Kashmir, bl; ash tray....................................30.00
Kashmir, bl; bowl, cream soup....................................25.00
Kashmir, bl; bowl, pickle; 8½"....................................25.00
Kashmir, bl; candlestick, 3"....................................25.00
Kashmir, bl; candlestick, 9½"....................................50.00
Kashmir, bl; cheese & cracker set....................................85.00
Kashmir, bl; cup....................................20.00
Kashmir, bl; cup, after dinner; ftd....................................35.00
Kashmir, bl; pitcher, ftd....................................350.00
Kashmir, bl; plate, dinner; 10"....................................45.00
Kashmir, bl; plate, grill; 10"....................................50.00
Kashmir, bl; plate, salad; 8"....................................10.00
Kashmir, bl; shakers, pr....................................125.00
Kashmir, bl; stem, claret; 4-oz....................................40.00
Kashmir, bl; stem, cordial; ¾-oz....................................100.00
Kashmir, bl; stem, water; 9-oz....................................35.00
Kashmir, bl; vase, 8"....................................100.00
Kashmir, gr; bowl, finger....................................15.00
Kashmir, gr; candlestick, 2"....................................15.00
Kashmir, gr; candy, w/lid....................................75.00
Kashmir, gr; comport, 6"....................................35.00
Kashmir, gr; ice bucket....................................65.00
Kashmir, gr; plate, luncheon; 9"....................................9.00
Kashmir, gr; stem, ftd, 2½-oz....................................25.00
Kashmir, gr; stem, 11-oz....................................22.50
Kashmir, yel; bowl, soup; 7"....................................25.00
Kashmir, yel; candlestick, 5"....................................22.50
Kashmir, yel; grapefruit....................................40.00
Kashmir, yel; plate, cake; 10"....................................35.00
Kashmir, yel; plate, salad; sq, 7"....................................6.00
Kashmir, yel; stem, parfait; 5½-oz....................................30.00
Kashmir, yel; sugar bowl, ftd....................................15.00
Lotus, blk; candlestick, clear bowl, low, #318....................................15.00
Navarre, bell, dinner....................................30.00
Navarre, bowl, #2496, flared, 12"....................................55.00
Navarre, bowl, bonbon; #2496, ftd, 7⅜"....................................25.00
Navarre, candlestick, #2496, 5½"....................................25.00
Navarre, celery, #2440, 9"....................................25.00
Navarre, comport, cheese; #2496, 3¼"....................................25.00
Navarre, mayonnaise, #2375, 3-pc....................................65.00
Navarre, pickle, #2440, 8½"....................................27.50
Navarre, plate, dinner; #2440, 9½"....................................35.00
Navarre, relish, #2496, 4-part, 10"....................................50.00
Navarre, saucer, #2440....................................3.50
Navarre, shakers, #2375, ftd, 3½", pr....................................85.00
Navarre, stem, wine; #6106, 3¼-oz, 5½"....................................30.00
Navarre, vase, #2470, ftd, 10"....................................125.00
Royal, amber; bowl, bouillon; #2350½, ftd....................................12.50
Royal, amber; candy, w/lid, ftd, ½-lb....................................125.00
Royal, amber; celery, #2350, 11"....................................25.00
Royal, amber; cologne, #2322, tall....................................30.00
Royal, amber; creamer, #2350½, ftd....................................13.00
Royal, amber; cup, demi; #2350....................................22.50
Royal, amber; grapefruit, w/insert....................................65.00
Royal, amber; pitcher, #5000, 48-oz....................................250.00
Royal, amber; plate, chop; #2350, 13"....................................27.50
Royal, amber; platter, #2350, 12"....................................40.00
Royal, amber; saucer, demi; #2350....................................5.00
Royal, amber; stem, wine; #869, 2¾-oz....................................27.50

Royal, amber; vase, #2292, flared 85.00
Royal, gr; bowl, #2267, ftd, 7" 30.00
Royal, gr; bowl, cream soup; #2350½, ftd...............15.00
Royal, gr; candlestick, #2324, 9" 40.00
Royal, gr; cologne, #2323, short 25.00
Royal, gr; comport, #2327, 7" 28.00
Royal, gr; cup, #2350½, ftd 13.00
Royal, gr; egg cup, #2350 ....22.50
Royal, gr; pickle, #2350, 8" 20.00
Royal, gr; plate, luncheon; #2350, 8½" 8.00
Royal, gr; platter, #2350, 10½" 30.00
Royal, gr; server, #2287, center hdl, 11" 25.00
Royal, gr; shakers, #5100, pr 55.00
Royal, gr; stem, water; #869, 9-oz 20.00
Royal, gr; tumbler, #5000, ftd, 9-oz 16.00
Royal, gr; tumbler, #859, flat, 9-oz 25.00
Seville, amber; bowl, baker; #2350, oval, 9" 25.00
Seville, amber; bowl, soup; #2350, 7¾" 17.50
Seville, amber; butter dish, #2350, w/lid, rnd 150.00
Seville, amber; comport, #2327, twisted stem, 7½" ...20.00
Seville, amber; creamer, #2350½, ftd 12.50
Seville, amber; cup, #2350, flat 10.00
Seville, amber; ice bucket, #2378 ....50.00
Seville, amber; plate, luncheon; #2350, 8½" 6.00
Seville, amber; platter, #2350, 10½" 22.50
Seville, amber; shakers, #5100, pr 60.00
Seville, amber; stem, cordial; #870 ....60.00
Seville, amber; tray, #2287, center hdl, 11" 27.50
Seville, amber; urn, #2324, sm 65.00
Seville, gr; ash tray, #2350, 4" 22.50
Seville, gr; bowl, bouillon; #2350, flat.....................15.00
Seville, gr; bowl, vegetable; #2350 ....25.00
Seville, gr; candlestick, #2324, 4" 15.00
Seville, gr; celery, #2350, 11" 17.50
Seville, gr; comport, #2350, 8" 32.50
Seville, gr; cup, after dinner; #2350 ....30.00
Seville, gr; egg cup, #2350 ....35.00
Seville, gr; grapefruit, #2315, molded......................25.00
Seville, gr; pickle, #2350, 8" 15.00
Seville, gr; pitcher, #5084, ftd 225.00
Seville, gr; plate, dinner; #2350, 10½" 35.00
Seville, gr; platter, #2350, 15" 75.00
Seville, gr; sauce boat, #2350..................................60.00
Seville, gr; saucer, after dinner; #2350 .... 5.00
Seville, gr; stem, parfait; #870 ....30.00
Seville, gr; sugar bowl, #2350½, ftd.........................13.50
Seville, gr; vase, #2292, 8" 60.00
Trojan, rose; bottle, salad dressing; #2983 ....400.00
Trojan, rose; bowl, #2354, 3-ftd, 6" 30.00
Trojan, rose; bowl, centerpiece; #2394, ftd, 12".......45.00
Trojan, rose; bowl, whipped cream; #2375...............15.00
Trojan, rose; candlestick, #2394, 2" 18.00
Trojan, rose; celery, #2375, 11½" 35.00
Trojan, rose; comport, #5299/2400, 6" 35.00
Trojan, rose; goblet, claret; #5099, 4-oz, 6" 85.00
Trojan, rose; goblet, water; #5299, 10-oz, 8¼" 37.50
Trojan, rose; grapefruit, #5282½ 50.00
Trojan, rose; mayonnaise, #2375, w/liner.................60.00
Trojan, rose; mayonnaise ladle.................................30.00
Trojan, rose; plate, #2375, rnd, 14" 50.00
Trojan, rose; plate, cake; #2375, hdls, 10" 35.00
Trojan, rose; plate, chop; #2375, 13" 50.00
Trojan, rose; plate, dinner; #2375, sm, 9½" 20.00
Trojan, rose; plate, dinner; #2375, 10¼" 65.00

Trojan, rose; plate, grill; #2375, rare, 10¼" 65.00
Trojan, rose; platter, #2375, 15" 125.00
Trojan, rose; relish, #2350, rnd, 3-part, 8¾" 45.00
Trojan, rose; saucer, after dinner; #2375 ....10.00
Trojan, rose; sugar bowl, #2375½, ftd......................22.50
Trojan, rose; tray, #2375, center hdl, 11" 35.00
Trojan, rose; tumbler, #5099, ftd, 2½-oz 50.00
Trojan, rose; tumbler, #5099, ftd, 5-oz, 4½" 30.00
Trojan, rose; vase, #4105, 8" 195.00
Trojan, topaz; ash tray, #2350, lg............................40.00
Trojan, topaz; bowl, cereal; #2375, 6½" 25.00
Trojan, topaz; bowl, lemon; #2375 ....16.00
Trojan, topaz; candlestick, #2375, flared, 3" 18.00
Trojan, topaz; candlestick, #2395½, scroll, 5" 55.00
Trojan, topaz; cheese & cracker set, #2375/2368.......60.00
Trojan, topaz; comport, #2375, 7" 40.00
Trojan, topaz; creamer, tea; #2375½ 45.00
Trojan, topaz; decanter, #2439, 9" 750.00
Trojan, topaz; goblet, cocktail; #5099, 3-oz, 5¼" 27.50
Trojan, topaz; goblet, cordial; #5099, ¾-oz, 4" 70.00
Trojan, topaz; grapefruit liner, #945½ 40.00
Trojan, topaz; ice dish, #2451/2455..........................35.00
Trojan, topaz; oil, #2375, ftd 235.00
Trojan, topaz; pail, whipped cream; #2378 ....110.00
Trojan, topaz; parfait, #5099 ....45.00
Trojan, topaz; pitcher, #5000 ....275.00
Trojan, topaz; plate, luncheon; #2375, 8¾" 15.00
Trojan, topaz; relish, #2375, 8½"..............................15.00
Trojan, topaz; sauce boat, #2375 ....90.00
Trojan, topaz; shakers, #2375, ftd, pr 75.00
Trojan, topaz; sugar pail, #2378...............................110.00
Trojan, topaz; tumbler, #5099, ftd, 12-oz, 6" 27.50
Trojan, topaz; vase, #2369, 9" 195.00
Versailles, bl; ash tray, #2350 ....30.00
Versailles, bl; bowl, #2394, ftd, 12" 50.00
Versailles, bl; bowl, cream soup; #2375, ftd.............27.50
Versailles, bl; bowl, finger; #869/2283, w/6" liner......40.00
Versailles, bl; bowl, whipped cream; #2375 ....18.00
Versailles, bl; candy, #2331, w/lid, 3-part 165.00
Versailles, bl; mayonnaise, #2375, w/liner................50.00
Versailles, bl; oil, #2375, ftd...................................450.00
Versailles, bl; pitcher, #5000 ....395.00
Versailles, bl; plate, bread & butter; #2375, 6" 5.00
Versailles, bl; plate, dinner; #2375, sm, 9½" 30.00
Versailles, bl; platter, #2375, 12"..............................75.00
Versailles, bl; sauce boat, #2375 ....100.00
Versailles, bl; saucer, #2375 .... 6.00
Versailles, bl; sugar pail, #2378 ....195.00
Versailles, gr; bowl, mint; 3-ftd, 4½" 25.00
Versailles, gr; bowl, soup; #2375, 7" 35.00
Versailles, gr; celery, #2375, 11½" 35.00
Versailles, gr; comport, #5098, 3" 25.00
Versailles, gr; creamer, tea; #2375½ 42.50
Versailles, gr; grapefruit, #5082½ 40.00
Versailles, gr; ice dish liner, #2451 ....20.00
Versailles, gr; mayonnaise ladle...............................30.00
Versailles, gr; plate, chop; #2375, 13" 45.00
Versailles, gr; plate, luncheon; #2375, 8¾" 8.00
Versailles, gr; saucer, after dinner; #2375 .... 4.00
Versailles, gr; tray, service & lemon 275.00
Versailles, pk; bowl, baker; #2375, 9" 50.00
Versailles, pk; bowl, cereal; #2375, 6½" 22.50
Versailles, pk; candlestick, #2395½, scroll, 5" 25.00
Versailles, pk; comport, #2400, 8" 65.00

Versailles, pk; grapefruit liner, #945½ 35.00
Versailles, pk; sugar bowl, #2375½, ftd 15.00
Versailles, pk; vase, #4100, 8" 125.00
Versailles, yel; bowl, fruit; #2375, 5" 20.00
Versailles, yel; candlestick, #2394, 2" 17.50
Versailles, yel; comport, #5099/2400, 6" 30.00
Versailles, yel; decanter, #2439, 9" 575.00
Versailles, yel; ice dish, #2451 ....30.00
Versailles, yel; pail, whipped cream; #2378 ....100.00
Versailles, yel; plate, dinner; #2375, 10¼" 55.00
Versailles, yel; plate, sauce boat; #2375 ....20.00
Versailles, yel; platter, #2375, 15" 90.00
Versailles, yel; shakers, #2375, ftd, pr 85.00
Versailles, yel; vase, #2417, 8" 135.00
Vesper, amber; bowl, #2329, rolled edge, 15" 45.00
Vesper, amber; bowl, #2371, oval, 13" 37.50
Vesper, amber; bowl, fruit; #2350, 5½" 12.50
Vesper, amber; bowl, soup; deep, 8¼" 25.00
Vesper, amber; butter dish, #2350 ....750.00
Vesper, amber; celery, #2350 ....22.00
Vesper, amber; cheese, #2368, ftd 20.00
Vesper, amber; comport, 8" 45.00
Vesper, amber; creamer, #2350½, ftd 16.00
Vesper, amber; cup, after dinner; #2350 ....25.00
Vesper, amber; egg cup, #2350 ....35.00
Vesper, amber; plate, chop; 13¾" 37.50
Vesper, amber; sauce boat, #2350, w/liner 110.00
Vesper, amber; shakers, #5100, pr 75.00
Vesper, amber; stem, water goblet; #5093 ....27.50
Vesper, amber; stem, wine; #5093, 2¾-oz 35.00
Vesper, amber; tumbler, #5100, ftd, 9-oz 18.00
Vesper, amber; urn, lg 70.00
Vesper, amber; vase, #2292, 8" 75.00
Vesper, bl; bowl, baker; #2350, oval, 9" 50.00
Vesper, bl; bowl, bouillon; #2350, ftd 20.00
Vesper, bl; candlestick, #2394, 9" 50.00
Vesper, bl; creamer, #2315½, fat, ftd 25.00
Vesper, bl; plate, bread & butter; #2350, 6" 10.00
Vesper, bl; plate, dinner; #2350, sm, 9½" 20.00
Vesper, bl; platter, #2350, 15" 95.00
Vesper, bl; stem, cocktail; #5093, 3-oz 30.00
Vesper, bl; stem, sherbet; #5093, low 22.00
Vesper, gr; bowl, #2329, rolled edge, 13" 35.00
Vesper, gr; bowl, #2375, 3-ftd, 12½" 35.00
Vesper, gr; bowl, baker; #2350, oval, 10½" 60.00
Vesper, gr; bowl, cream soup; #2350, ftd 20.00
Vesper, gr; candlestick, #2394, 3" 15.00
Vesper, gr; candy jar, #2331, w/lid, 3-part 85.00
Vesper, gr; comport, #2327, twisted stem, 7½" 27.50
Vesper, gr; cup, #2350 ....14.00
Vesper, gr; grapefruit, #5082½, blown 40.00
Vesper, gr; pickle, #2350 ....20.00
Vesper, gr; plate, #2287, center hdl, 11" 22.50
Vesper, gr; platter, #2350, 10½" 30.00
Vesper, gr; stem, cordial; #5093, ¾-oz 70.00
Vesper, gr; stem, sherbet; #5093, high 16.00
Vesper, gr; sugar bowl, #2315, ftd 18.00
Vesper, gr; tumbler, #5100, ftd, 2-oz 30.00

Fraktur

Fraktur is a German style of black letter text type. To collectors the fraktur is a type of hand-lettered document used by the people of

German descent who settled in the areas of Pennsylvania, New Jersey, Maryland, Virginia, North and South Carolina, Ohio, Kentucky, and Ontario. These documents recorded births and baptisms and were used as bookplates and as certificates of honor. They were elaborately decorated with colorful folk-art borders of hearts, birds, angels, and flowers. Examples by recognized artists and those with an unusual decorative motif bring prices well into the thousands of dollars. Frakturs made in the late 1700s after the invention of the printing press provided the writer with a prepared text that he needed only to fill in at his own discretion. The next step in the evolution of machine-printed frakturs combined woodblock-printed decorations along with the text which the 'artist' sometimes enhanced with color. By the mid-1800s, even the coloring was done by machine. The vorschrift was a handwritten example prepared by a fraktur teacher to demonstrate his skill in lettering and decorating. These are often considered to be the finest of frakturs. Those dated before 1820 are most valuable.

The practice of fraktur art began to diminish after 1830 but hung on even to the early years of this century among the Pennsylvania Germans ingrained with such customs.

Our advisor for this category is Rev. Frederick S. Weiser; he is listed in the Directory under Pennsylvania.

Key:
brd — board
lp — laid paper
pr — printed
p/i — pen and ink
wc — watercolored
wp — wove paper

Birth Record

P/i/wc/lp, birds/angels, flying angel artist, 12x16", VG **3,000.00**
P/i/wc/lp, data/1808, by flying angel artist, 15x17" **2,650.00**
P/i/wc/lp, pr lions/crown, data in lg circle, 14x17", VG **3,000.00**
P/i/wc/wp, floral/lg letters, 5-color, sgn/no date, 8x8" **450.00**
P/i/wc/wp, flowers/hearts, att Brechall, 1830, 8x13", VG **1,100.00**
Pr/wc, stylized foliage/3 hearts, F Krebs/1797, 13x15" **650.00**
Pr/wc, Taufschein, by S Baumann, Ephrata, 15x18", EX **400.00**
Pr/wc, 1831 birth, printed by John Ritter, 20x17", VG **150.00**

Miscellaneous

P/i/wc, birds/floral, verse/1829 on bk, flame mahog fr, 7x6" **650.00**
P/i/wc, drawing, parrot in cherry tree, 8x8", EX **700.00**

Ehre Vater artist, religious text, 4-hue watercolor on laid paper, early 19th century, 15½" x 12½", $3,000.00.

P/i/wc/lp, certificate, baptism; tulips/birds, 1815, 10x15" **700.00**

P/i/wc/lp, vorchrift, lg letters 179(?), 8x13", EX 400.00
P/i/wc/wp, birds/flowers/1793, 4-color, 8x12", VG 425.00
P/i/wc/wp, certificate, interlaced foil/ribbon, 8x12", VG 260.00
Pr/wc, house blessing, hearts/zigzag border, stains, 16x19" 325.00

Frames

Styles in picture frames have changed with the fashion of the day, but those that especially interest today's collectors are the deep shadow boxes made of fine woods such as walnut or cherry, those with Art Nouveau influence, and the oak frames decorated with molded gesso and gilt from the Victorian era.

Brass, ornate border, metal bk, 6x4¾" 30.00
Brass, plain border, metal bk, 3½x2¾" 10.00
CI w/gilt, rtcl leaves, metal bk, desk type, 11½x8¼" 55.00
Curly maple, 15x19" 150.00

Gold-washed metal, Patented 1897, 8", $65.00.

Laminated mahog/pine, shaped perimeter w/appl bosses, 9x13" 35.00
Silver, girl/geese emb, Nouveau form, Birmingham mks, 8" 1,300.00
Silver, lily pads/humming birds emb, Nouveau, English, 12"... 1,900.00
Walnut criss-cross, heart corners, PA, 1860s, 8x10" 160.00

Frances Ware

Frances Ware, produced in the 1880s by Hobbs, Brockunier and Company of Wheeling, West Virginia, is a clear or frosted tableware with amber-stained rim bands. The most often found pattern is Hobnail, but Swirl was also made.

Hobnail, clear; bowl, 7½" 65.00
Hobnail, clear; butter dish 95.00
Hobnail, clear; creamer..60.00
Hobnail, clear; finger bowl, 4" 35.00
Hobnail, clear; pitcher, 8½" 125.00
Hobnail, clear; spooner 40.00
Hobnail, frosted; bowl, ftd, berry pontil, 6x10" 150.00
Hobnail, frosted; bowl, oblong, 8" 70.00
Hobnail, frosted; bowl, sq, 7½" 70.00
Hobnail, frosted; bowl, 2½x5½" 40.00
Hobnail, frosted; bowl, 4½" 30.00
Hobnail, frosted; bowl, 8" 75.00
Hobnail, frosted; bowl, 9" 85.00
Hobnail, frosted; butter dish 120.00

Frosted Hobnail creamer, $75.00.

Hobnail, frosted; celery vase 75.00
Hobnail, frosted; finger bowl, 4" 35.00
Hobnail, frosted; marmalade 125.00
Hobnail, frosted; pitcher, milk 150.00
Hobnail, frosted; pitcher, water; sq top 175.00
Hobnail, frosted; plate, sq, 5¾" 25.00
Hobnail, frosted; sauce dish, sq, 4" 28.00
Hobnail, frosted; shakers, pr 75.00
Hobnail, frosted; spooner 70.00
Hobnail, frosted; sugar bowl, w/lid 80.00
Hobnail, frosted; syrup, pewter lid..165.00
Hobnail, frosted; toothpick holder 60.00
Hobnail, frosted; tray, cloverleaf, 12" 125.00
Hobnail, frosted; tray, oblong, 14" 150.00
Hobnail, frosted; tumbler, water...45.00
Swirl, clear; shakers, pr 55.00
Swirl, clear; syrup...90.00
Swirl, frosted; bowl, 3¾" H...40.00
Swirl, frosted; cruet 175.00
Swirl, frosted; cruet, orig stopper, miniature 260.00
Swirl, frosted; mustard jar...140.00
Swirl, frosted; shakers, pr 75.00
Swirl, frosted; sugar shaker, orig lid...125.00
Swirl, frosted; syrup, Pat dtd..145.00
Swirl, frosted; toothpick holder...110.00
Swirl, frosted; tumbler...35.00

Franciscan

Franciscan is a trade name used by Gladding McBean and Co., founded in northern California in 1875. In 1923 they purchased the Tropico plant in Glendale where they produced sewer pipe, gardenware, and tile. By 1934 the first of their dinnerware lines, El Patio, was produced. It was a plain design made in bright, attractive colors. El Patio Nouveau followed in 1935, glazed in two colors — one tone on the inside, a contrasting hue on the outside. Coronado, a favorite of today's collectors, was introduced in 1936. It was styled with a wide, swirled border and was made in pastels in both a satin and glossy finish. Before 1940 fifteen patterns had been produced. The first hand-decorated lines were introduced in 1937, the ever-popular Apple pattern in 1940, Desert Rose in 1941, and Ivy in 1948. Many other hand-decorated and decaled patterns were produced there from 1934 to 1984.

Dinnerware marks before 1940 include 'GMcB' in an oval, 'F'

within a square, or 'Franciscan' with 'Pottery' underneath (which was later changed to 'Ware.') A circular arrangement of 'Franciscan' with 'Made in California USA' in the center was used from 1940 until 1949. At least forty marks were used before 1975; several more were introduced after that. At one time, paper labels were used.

The company merged with Lock Joint Pipe Company in 1963, becoming part of the Interpace Corporation. In July of 1979, Franciscan was purchased by Wedgwood Limited of England, and the Glendale plant closed in October, 1984.

Our advisor, authority Delleen Enge, has compiled an informative book, *Franciscan Ware*, with current values. You will find her address in the Directory under California. See also Gladding McBean.

Coronado

Bowl, cereal	10.50
Bowl, cream soup	13.00
Bowl, vegetable; serving, oval	25.00
Bowl, vegetable; serving, rnd	13.00
Candlesticks, pr	25.00
Candy dish, rnd, w/lid	45.00
Casserole, w/lid	25.00
Cigarette box	35.00
Coffeepot, demitasse	45.00
Creamer & sugar bowl, w/lid	28.00
Cup & saucer	10.00
Cup & saucer, demitasse	20.00
Gravy boat, w/attached plate	25.00
Nut cup, ftd	14.00
Plate, chop; 12"	20.00
Plate, chop; 14"	30.00
Plate, 6½"	7.00
Plate, 7½"	8.50
Plate, 8½"	9.50
Platter, 11½"	20.00
Platter, 15½"	30.00
Saucer, cream soup	5.50
Shakers, pr	13.00
Sherbet	9.00
Teapot	35.00

El Patio

Bowl, cereal	10.00
Bowl, fruit	9.00
Bowl, salad; 3-qt	22.00
Bowl, vegetable; oval	28.00
Butter dish	28.00
Creamer	8.00
Cup	8.00
Cup, jumbo	16.00
Gravy boat, w/attached underplate	24.00
Plate, bread & butter	6.00
Plate, 10½"	12.00
Plate, 8½"	10.00
Saucer	3.00
Saucer, jumbo	6.00
Sherbet	9.00
Sugar bowl, w/lid	15.00
Teapot, w/lid, 6-cup	35.00

Franciscan Fine China

The main line of fine china was called Masterpiece. There were at least four marks used during its production from 1941 to 1977. Almost every piece is clearly marked. This china is true porcelain, the body having been fired at a very high temperature. Many years of research and experimentation went into this china before it was marketed. Production was temporarily suspended during the war years. More than 170 patterns and many varying shapes were produced. All are valued about the same with the exception of the Renaissance group, which is 25% higher.

Bowl, vegetable; serving, oval	45.00
Cup	15.00
Plate, bread & butter	15.00
Plate, dinner	25.00
Plate, salad	18.00
Saucer	10.00

Hand-Painted Embossed Earthenware

Values listed here apply to these patterns: Apple, Desert Rose, Ivy, Meadow Rose, Forget-Me-Not, October, Strawberry, Fresh Fruit, and other hand-painted lines.

Ash tray, ind	10.00
Bowl, batter	45.00
Bowl, lug hdl, sm	14.00
Bowl, soup; flat	14.00
Bowl, vegetable; sm	12.00
Bowl, vegetable; w/lid	45.00
Bowl, 7½"	25.00
Bowl, 8¼"	35.00
Casserole, stick hdls, 12-oz	20.00
Coaster, 3¾"	15.00
Coffeepot	65.00
Compote, lg	35.00
Creamer, lg	14.00
Cup & saucer, demitasse, ea	20.00
Cup & saucer, jumbo	25.00
Egg cup	14.00
Goblet	22.00
Mug, lg	18.00
Pickle dish, 10¼"	28.00
Pitcher, 1-pt	22.00

Desert Rose water pitcher, $75.00.

Plate, chop; 14"	50.00
Plate, grill; 10¾"	30.00
Plate, 10½"	15.00

Plate, 6½"	6.00
Plate, 8½"	12.00
Plate, 9½"	14.00
Platter, 12½"	30.00
Platter, 19½"	95.00
Relish, 3-part, 11"	30.00
Shakers, Rosebud, pr	18.00
Shakers, tall, pr	30.00
Sugar bowl, open, sm	25.00
Sugar bowl, w/lid, lg	28.00
Tray, 3-tier	35.00
Tumbler, 5⅛"	15.00

Frankart

During the 1920s, Frankart, Inc., of New York City, produced a line of accessories that included figural nude lamps, bookends, ash trays, etc. These white metal composition items were offered in several finishes including verde green, jap black, and gun-metal gray. The company also produced a line of caricatured animals, but the stylized nude figurals have proven to be the most collectible today. With few exceptions, all pieces were marked 'Frankart, Inc.' with a patent number or 'pat. appl. for.' All pieces listed are in very good original condition unless otherwise indicated.

Our advisor for this category is Walter Glenn; he is listed in the Directory under Georgia.

Aquarium, 3 kneeling nudes encircle 10" aqua bowl, 10½"	650.00
Ash tray, ballet girl in center of 8" rnd onyx tray, 10"	435.00
Ash tray, stylized duck holds tray in outstretched wings, 5"	225.00

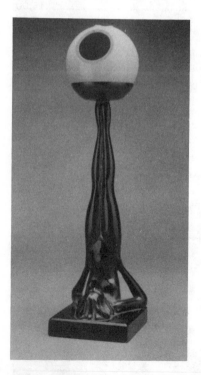

Inverted nude balances ash-ball on toes, 12", $385.00.

Bookends, Roman-inspired masks, 7½", pr	345.00
Bookends, stylized (chip-cvd) seated polar bears, 6½", pr	145.00
Bookends, stylized dolphins, 6½", pr	125.00
Bowl, fruit; 2 bk to bk kneeling nudes hold 8" dish, 6"	675.00
Clock, 2 nudes kneel & hold 10" dia glass clock, 12½"	1,350.00
Incense burner, standing nude holds tray for incense, 10"	375.00
Lamp, kneeling nude gazes into 5" dia amber globe, 7"	585.00

Lamp, 2 bk to bk dancing nudes hold sq glass cylinder, 13"	725.00
Lamp, 2 kneeling nudes embrace 8" crackle glass globe, 9"	685.00
Lamp, 2 standing bk-to-bk nudes hold skyscraper globe, 21"	675.00
Lamp, 4 standing nudes surround sq glass cylinder, 13"	850.00
Plaque, Diana the Huntress, 8" sq, pr	525.00
Smoke set, seated nude, tray in ea arm, box on base, 9"	475.00
Smoke stand, monkey holds tray overhead w/tail, 26"	665.00
Smoke stand, nude stands atop ball, holds tray aloft, 25"	475.00
Vase, dancing nude holds 10" vase to side, 12½"	650.00
Vase, 2 bk-to-bk standing nudes hold 7" glass vase, 13"	525.00

Frankoma

The Frank Pottery, founded in Oklahoma in 1933 by John Frank, became known as Frankoma in 1934. The company produced decorative figurals, vases, and such, marking their ware from 1936-38 with a pacing leopard 'Frankoma' mark. These pieces are highly sought. The entire operation was destroyed by fire in 1938, and new molds were cast — some from surviving pieces — and a similar line of production was pursued. The body of the ware was changed in 1954 from a honey tan to a red brick clay, and this, along with the color of the glazes (over forty have been used), helps determine the period of production. A Southwestern theme has always been favored in design as well as in color selection.

In 1965 they began to produce a limited-edition series of Christmas plates, followed by a bottle vase series in 1969. Considered very collectible are their political mugs, bicentennial plates, Teenagers of the Bible plates, and the Wildfire series. Their ceramic Christmas cards are also very popular items with today's collectors.

Frankoma celebrated their 50th Anniversary in 1983. On September 26 of that same year, Frankoma was again destroyed by fire. Because of a fire-proof wall, master molds of all 1983 production items were saved, allowing plans for rebuilding to begin immediately. 'Grand Opening' was celebrated in July, 1984.

Cash flow problems resulting from the fire and poor management were too much for Joniece Frank to overcome and a Chapter 11 was filed in April of 1990. Maryland entrepreneur Richard Bernstein purchased Frankoma Pottery in March of 1991, completing the company's bankruptcy reorganization. Production of the pottery continues with plans for improvements and expansions to worldwide distribution.

For a more thorough study of the subject, we recommend that you refer to *Frankoma Treasures* by Phyllis and Tom Bess, our advisors; you will find their address in the Directory under Oklahoma.

Ash tray, Arrow Head, gr & brn	10.00
Ash tray, elephant, #459, 1951-52, 6½"	75.00
Ash tray, fish, #T-8, 1962-76, 7"	20.00

Collie bookend, Flame Red, 7½", $75.00.

Bookend, female figure, seated, w/Taylor name, #425, 5½" 350.00
Bookend, Irish Setter, Ada clay, blk, pr 200.00
Bookend, Mountain Girl, Ada clay, #425, 5¾" 125.00
Bookend, Ocelot, Ada clay, #422, 1934-38, 7¼" 100.00
Bookend, Rearing Clydesdale, #431, pr 250.00
Bookend, Walking Ocelot, w/Taylor name, #424 ....350.00
Bowl, ball form, ped ft, #42, 6½" 25.00
Bowl, ped ft, #101-P, 6" 14.00
Bowl, 4-leaf clover, Clay Bl, #223 .... 8.00
Button, non-production item, rare 15.00
Candelabrum, #306, 11¾" 55.00
Candle holder, Ada clay, #304, pr 25.00
Candle holder, Ada clay, pacing leopard mk, #300, pr 65.00
Candle holder, blk onyx high gloss, dbl, #304, pr 20.00
Candle holder, Dusty Rose, Ada clay, dbl, #304, pr 30.00
Candle holder, Monks, #308, pr 225.00
Candle holder, Oral Roberts 10.00
Candy dish, clam shell, Prairie Gr 8.00
Carafe, w/lid, all colors 20.00
Casserole, #946, 1948-54, ind 25.00
Christmas card, 1947-48 ....75.00
Christmas card, 1950-51 ....70.00
Christmas card, 1952, Donna Frank 85.00
Christmas card, 1953-54 ....75.00
Christmas card, 1955-56 ....70.00
Christmas card, 1958 ....60.00
Christmas card, 1960 ....60.00
Christmas card, 1967-68 ....40.00
Christmas card, 1972 ....20.00
Christmas card, 1973-74 ....25.00
Christmas card, 1975, bird in hand, Grace Lee, rare 100.00
Christmas plate, 1966 ....75.00
Christmas plate, 1968 ....35.00
Christmas plate, 1971-73 ....22.50
Christmas plate, 1977-80 ....20.00
Compote, shell form, #214, 1942-50, 6" 8.00
Cornucopia, Wht Sand, Ada clay, #57, 9½" 45.00
Decanter, Fingerprint, #84, 1942-49, 1-qt, 7" 35.00
Donkey mug, 1975, Autumn Yel 25.00
Donkey mug, 1976, Centennial Red 25.00
Donkey mug, 1978, Woodland Moss 20.00
Donkey mug, 1980, Terra Cotta 20.00
Elephant mug, 1968, Wht Sand 85.00
Elephant mug, 1969, Nixon/Agnew, Flame 85.00
Elephant mug, 1970, bl 55.00
Elephant mug, 1972, Prairie Gr 40.00
Flower holder, boot, stars on sides, Ada clay, #507, 3½" 10.00
Flower holder, boots on thong, Ada clay, #507-S, mini, 3½" 15.00
Flower holder, duck, #184, 3¾" 135.00
Flowerabrum, Wht Sand, Ada clay 65.00
Grease jar, w/lid, #46, 1938, 3¾" 20.00
Honey jar, Beehive, Ada clay, #803, 12-oz 22.00
Jug, Golda's Corn, brn, dtd 1951 ....20.00
Lamp base, from #28 vase 45.00
Lamp base, from Wagon Wheel sugar bowl 45.00
Lazy susan, Wagon Wheel, Desert Gold 75.00
Medallion, woman's profile, oval, 1⅞" 85.00
Mug, War God, #T-3, 1962-63, 12-oz 12.00
Pitcher, Autumn Yel, 2-qt 10.00
Pitcher, Fireside, #77-A 65.00
Pitcher, Guernsey, Prairie Gr, lg 25.00
Pitcher, jug form, #554, 1942, 2¾" 15.00
Pitcher, jug form, w/stopper, 1934-35, 3-cup, 5" 50.00
Pitcher, Wagon Wheel, brn & cream, #94-D, 2-qt..................25.00

Syrup jug, embossed Eastern Star Lodge logo on turquoise, $90.00.

Pitcher, Westwind, brn, 2-qt 12.00
Planter, Madonna of Grace, #231-B, 6" 50.00
Planter, Oblong Cactus, #206, 1949-52, 10½" 30.00
Planter, swan, turq, Ada clay, middle sz 60.00
Plaque, Will Rogers, w/border, Prairie Gr, Ada clay................32.50
Plate, Bicentennial of Methodism 1776-1976, Wht Sand............20.00
Plate, Bob White Quail, 1972 ....75.00
Plate, Buffalo, 1979 ....50.00
Plate, Conestoga Wagon, Special Bl, #689 ....50.00
Plate, Easter, wht, 7½" 15.00
Plate, Rural Letter Carrier 75.00
Plate, White-tail Deer, 1973 ....60.00
Plate, Wild Turkey, 1978..50.00
Sculpture, Amazon Woman, mk Taylor, 6¼x8" 350.00
Sculpture, Blk Man w/His Donkey, Gun-Metal Gray, 8" 250.00
Sculpture, Bucking Bronco, no stepped base, #423, 5" 165.00
Sculpture, Charger Horse, Ada clay......................................100.00
Sculpture, Circus Horse, Cherokee Red, #138, 4½" 85.00
Sculpture, Circus Horse, Desert Gold, #138 ....50.00
Sculpture, Dreamer Girl, Sorghum 125.00
Sculpture, English Setter, #163, 2⅞" 40.00
Sculpture, Fan Dancer, Ada clay, #113, 13½" 225.00
Sculpture, Gardener Boy, Prairie Gr, belted, #702 ....100.00
Sculpture, Greyhound, 6 petals on bk base, 1983 repro, 14" 50.00
Sculpture, Harlem Hoofer, #127, 13" 600.00
Sculpture, Indian Chief, Ada clay, #142 ....90.00
Sculpture, Indian Mask, The Chief, Ada clay, #131 ....38.00
Sculpture, Indian Mask, The Maiden, ivory, Ada clay, #138 ....38.00
Sculpture, Peter Pan, SAI on bk, #100, 6" 45.00
Sculpture, Prancing Colt, #117, 8" 485.00
Sculpture, Prancing Percheron, #108, 4¾" 200.00
Sculpture, Seated Puma, Ada clay, #114, 1934-63, 7½" 85.00
Sculpture, Squirrel, #105, 6" 5.00
Sculpture, Swan, Desert Gold, #168, mini 35.00
Sculpture, Torch Singer, #126, ca 1934, 13½" 600.00
Sculpture, Trojan Horse, #162, 2½" 35.00
Sculpture, Walking Elephant, #169, 1¾" 75.00
Shakers, Bull, #166, 2", pr 55.00
Shakers, Snail, Desert Gold, Ada clay, #558-H, pr 10.00
Shakers, Teepee, Ada clay, pr 10.00
Sign, Frankoma Pottery, late 1940s-60 ....65.00
Sugar bowl, w/lid, Ada clay 10.00
Trade token, 1" dia 35.00
Tray, Mayan, Desert Gold, 9" 4.00
Tray, oval, #36, 1955-64, 12" 25.00

Tray, Palm Leaf, #T-11, 1962-67, 17" 35.00
Trivet, Cherokee, brn, 5" 5.00
Trivet, Zodiac, #Z-TR, 1971-76 ....10.00
Tumbler, juice; #90-C, 1938-65, 3-oz, 2½" 3.00
Vase, #505, 1950-51, 2¾" 15.00
Vase, bird hdls, pacing leopard mk, #85 ....50.00
Vase, bottle form, Chinese Red, #14, 9½" 200.00
Vase, bottle form, Peach Glow, 9" 25.00
Vase, bud; Blk Onyx, high gloss 20.00
Vase, Cactus, Red Bud 30.00
Vase, collector; V-1, Prairie Gr, 1969, 15" 70.00
Vase, collector; V-10, Morning-Glory Bl, wht int, 11½" 35.00
Vase, collector; V-11, Morning-Glory Bl, 1979, 11½" 35.00
Vase, collector; V-12, 1980 ....40.00
Vase, collector; V-13, blk & Terra Cotta, 1981, 13" 40.00
Vase, collector; V-14, Flame Red & blk, 1982 ....55.00
Vase, collector; V-2, turq, 1970, 12" 55.00
Vase, collector; V-3, red & blk, 1971, 12" 70.00
Vase, collector; V-4, blk & Terra Cotta, 1972 ....65.00
Vase, collector; V-5, Flame Red, 1973, 13" 70.00
Vase, collector; V-8, Freedom Red & wht, 1976 ....60.00
Vase, Flying Goose, #60-B, 6" 20.00
Vase, leaf hdls, early glaze, #71, 1942, 10" 60.00
Vase, pacing leopard mk, #502, 3" 60.00
Vase, Ring, turq, #500, 1951-52 ....20.00
Vase, scalloped top, #79, 1934-38, 7" 125.00
Vase, Snail, #31, 6" 10.00
Vase, Wagon Wheel, #94, 1942-61, 7" 25.00
Wall pocket, boot, gr, Ada clay, 7" 15.00
Wall pocket, Negro, late 1930s, 2½" 110.00
Wall pocket, Phoebe, bsk, HP features & hair............125.00
Wall pocket, Phoebe, Prairie Gr, Ada clay, #730 ....75.00
Wall pocket, Wagon Wheel, #94-Y, 1949-53, 7" 35.00

Fraternal Organizations

Fraternal memorabilia is a vast and varied field. Emblems representing the various organizations have been used to decorate cups, shaving mugs, plates, and glassware. Medals, swords, documents, and other ceremonial paraphernalia from the 1800s and early 1900s are especially prized.

Masons

Apron, leather w/gilt symbols, worn, 15"....................185.00
Chocolate pot, lodge & officers, ceramic w/platinum, '10............145.00

Plate, 64th Annual Conclave, Toledo, 1906, Masonic emblems in border, marked K&K, 8", $75.00.

Cookie mold, CI, 4⅞"..25.00
Cup, horn eng w/symbols in reserves, 1830s, 3¾", EX.................300.00
Goblet, eng design, tooled lip/polished pontil, England, 6" 140.00
Letter opener, symbols on metal.................................20.00
Mold, ice cream; emblem form, pewter, 5½" 15.00
Mug, Rising Star Lodge, china, 1903 ....40.00
Pendant, brass/paper/MOP, symbol form, 3¼" dia 90.00
Penny, Bristol VT, 1872, hole for wearing, EX 15.00
Plaque, cvd wood, shield shape, ca 1900, 8¼"............. 5.00
Straight razor, H Boker, emblems etched on blade, 1890s.............75.00
Tankard, bottomless, 1893 Chicago, 10" 200.00
Trivet, brass, symbols 35.00
Trivet, symbols & Comfort, cast brass, 7¼x9½" 35.00
Watercolor on paper, symbolism w/EX color, ca 1821, 7x7" 75.00

Shrine

Champagne, 4 tobacco leaves on base, 2 scimitars, 1909 ....65.00
Cup & saucer, glass, Los Angeles, 1906 ....70.00
Goblet, clear, St Paul, 1908..65.00
Goblet, ruby, silver/gold symbols, St Paul, 1908 ....50.00
Goblet, ruby flashed, Pittsburgh PA, 1908 ....65.00
Mug, ceramic, Indian, Saratoga, 1903 ....65.00
Mug, ceramic, Syria Temple, Pittsburgh, 1895, EX gold 110.00
Mug, glass, Atlantic City, silver fish hdl, 1904 ....65.00
Mug, glass, Indian's head/feathers emb, scimitar hdl, 1903 ....65.00
Plate, ceramic, man w/bandaged face.........................25.00
Tumbler, milk glass, Minneapolis 1717, sq 55.00
Tumbler, milk glass, Pittsburgh 1918, rnd 50.00
Watch fob, 1920s, 4-pc, EX 35.00
Wine, Buffalo 1899 ....50.00

Miscellaneous

Elks, elk's tooth, gold fittings, 1930s 28.00
Elks, note pad & pencil, Ladies Night, 1916, EX.........35.00
Knights of Pythias, lectures of 1920 ....10.00
Odd Fellows, banner, symbols on bl, gold braid, 30x18", EX.........85.00
Odd Fellows, emblem, horseshoe w/dove atop, pnt CI, 7½x6x1"...65.00
Odd Fellows, paperbk souvenir book, 1922 Convention................25.00

Fruit Jars

As early as 1829, canning jars were being manufactured for use in the home preservation of foodstuffs. For the past twenty-five years, they have been sought as popular collectibles. At the last estimate, over four thousand fruit jars and variations were known to exist. Some are very rare, perhaps one-of-a-kind examples known to have survived to the present day. Among the most valuable are the black glass jars, the amber Van Vliet, and the cobalt Millville. These often bring prices in excess of $3,000.00 when they can be found. Aside from condition, values are based on age, rarity, color, and special features.

Our advisor for this category is John Hathaway; he is listed in the Directory under Maine.

A&DH Chambers Union Fruit Jar Pittsburgh PA base, bl, qt 99.00
Acme (on shield w/stars & stripes), clear, ½-gal............................ 9.00
Agnew & Co Pittsburgh Pat Appl for 1887, b3m, clear, qt............78.00
American (NAGCO) Porcelain Lined, aqua, qt 23.00
Atlas (clover) Good Luck, clear, pt................................ 3.00
Atlas (HA in circle) Mason, clear, ½-gal.......................... 4.00
Atlas E-Z Seal, aqua, 58-oz 43.00
Atlas E-Z Seal, gr, aqua lid, qt 5.00

Atlas Mason, clear, ½-pt.. 3.00
Atlas Strong Shoulder Mason, aqua, pt 3.00
Ball (3 L loop) Mason, gr, qt 35.00
Ball Ideal, bl, sq, pt 6.00
Ball Ideal, reverse: Bicentennial medallion, bl, qt 3.00
Ball Perfect Mason, clear, ribbed, ½-pt 3.00
Ball Perfect Mason, deep olive gr, ½-gal 63.00
Ball Perfect Mason (italic & block letters), clear, qt 8.00
Ball Refrigerator & Freezer Jar, clear, freezer cap, 16-oz .. 2.00
Ball Sure Seal, bl, ½-gal 7.00
Beaver (emb beaver), aqua, midget 85.00
Best, clear, qt..28.00
Brockway Sur-Grip Mason, clear, qt 3.00
Calcutt's Pat's Apr 11th Nov 7th 1893 (on lid), clear, qt 38.00
Canadian Jewell Made in Canada, clear, pt 2.00
Canton Domestic Fruit Jar, clear, repro wire, pt...........135.00
Canton Manufacturing Co Boston (on base), amber, pt ... 6.00
CF Spencer's Pat Rochester NY, aqua, ½-gal..................98.00
Clark's Peerless, cornflower bl, pt...................................23.00
Cohansey (written in arch), aqua, qt 18.00
Columbia, clear, pt..18.00
Crown Cordial & Extract Co NY, clear, ½-gal 7.00
Crown Crown (ring crown), aqua, qt................................12.00
Darling Imperial (below monogram), aqua, midget.........215.00
Dexter (circled by fruits & vegetables), aqua, qt..............58.00
Dexter Improved (around circle of fruit), aqua, ½-gal 58.00
DG CO (lg intertwined monogram), aqua, unemb insert, ½-gal....48.00
Dolittle (in script), clear, pt 43.00
Double Safety, clear, narrow mouth, ½-gal 7.00
Drey Improved Everseal, clear, ½-gal 5.00
DSGCo, aqua, ½-gal...33.00
Eagle, aqua, ½-gal..125.00
Electric (world globe) Fruit Jar, aqua, qt.........................78.00
Empire (in stippled cross), clear, pt................................. 4.00
Erie Lightning, aqua, qt...48.00
Excelsior Improved, aqua, ½-gal 48.00
Franklin Dexter No 2 Fruit Jar, aqua, qt..........................38.00
Franklin No 1 Fruit Jar, aqua, no lid, qt 55.00
Gem Rutherford & Co, aqua, qt 15.00
Genuine Boyds Mason, aqua, ½-gal 8.00
Geo Brown & Co, aqua, pt..49.00
Glassboro TM Improved, aqua, qt....................................18.00
Haine's Improved March 1st 1870, aqua, repro wire, qt 88.00
Hansee's Place Home Jar, clear, qt...................................68.00
Haserot Company Cleveland Mason Pat, aqua, qt 9.00
Hazel Atlas E-Z Seal, aqua, qt 9.00
Hero, aqua, screw-band glass insert, qt............................14.00
Hero (over cross), aqua, qt...48.00
Hero Improved, aqua, ½-gal...23.00
Herr 'Self Sealing' Trade Mark Reg Mason, clear, ½-pt 3.00
HW Pettit Westville NJ (on base), aqua, pt.......................10.00
Ideal Imperial, aqua, qt...23.00
Improved Corina Jar Made in Canada, clear, pt 3.00
Improved Everlasting Jar (in oval), clear, qt 18.00
Improved Gem Made in Canada, clear, pt 2.50
Jewell Jar Made in Canada, clear, pt 5.00
Jos Middleby, Jr Inc (vertically), clear, ½-gal 5.00
Kerr 'Self Sealing' Mason, amber, qt...............................18.00
Knowlton Vacuum (star) Fruit Jar, aqua, pt.....................33.00
Lafayette (in script), aqua, qt..88.00
Lamb Mason, clear, zinc lid, qt 2.00
Lockport Mason Improved, clear, ½-gal...........................10.00
Longlife (in script) Wide Mouth, amber, qt.....................10.00
Lynchburg Standard Mason, aqua, qt...............................18.00

Lyon & Bossard's Jar Stroudsburg PA, aqua, qt 448.00
Manufactured for JT Kinney Trenton NJ, aqua, qt..........173.00
Mason Fruit Jar (3 lines), aqua, pt...................................10.00
Mason Improved Pat'd, aqua, qt....................................... 5.00
Mason's (cross) Improved, aqua, pt..................................10.00
Mason's (keystone in circle) Pat Nov 30th 1858, aqua, qt 8.00
Mason's (Keystone) Pat Nov 30th 1858, aqua, midget......18.00
Mason's BCCo Improved, aqua, qt....................................58.00
Mason's CFJ Improved, aqua, ½-gal 4.00
Mason's CFJCo Pat Nov 20th 1858, aqua, midget 18.00
Mason's Cross Pat Nov 30th 1858, aqua, pt 4.00
Mason's Crystal Jar, clear, qt...28.00
Mason's LGW Improved, clear, qt....................................20.00
Mason's Pat Nov 30th 1858, aqua, Ball Bros insert, midget 65.00
Mason's Pat Nov 30th 58, aqua, midget...........................58.00
Metro E-Z Pack Mason, clear, zinc lid, pt 2.00
Millville Atmospheric Fruit Jar, aqua, qt.........................28.00
Mission (bell) TM Mason Jar Made in CA, aqua, pt 9.00
Monarch (lion's head) Finer Foods, clear, qt.................... 3.00
N in star on base, aqua, wax sealer, qt.............................15.00
Pat July 11 1793 VJC Co (on base), lt aqua, qt................13.00
Patd Aug 5 1862 WW Lyman 7, aqua, qt...........................33.00
Presto Glass Top (bk: Mfg by Illinois Glass), clear, ½-pt ... 5.00
Princess (in shield & fr), clear, qt...................................23.00
Protector (recessed panels), aqua, qt 53.00
Putnam Glass Works Zanesville O (on base), aqua, qt.......33.00
Queen (circled by Pat dates), ½-gal 28.00
Quick Seal (in circle), bl, qt.. 2.50
Reliable Home Canning Mason, clear, qt.......................... 4.00
Safety Seal Made in Canada, clear, ½-gal........................ 5.00
Safety Valve Pat May 21 1895 (on base), aqua, ¾-qt........10.00
Security Seal (in triangles), clear, qt............................... 5.00
Silicon (in circle), aqua, qt...12.00
Silicon Glass Co Pittsburgh Penna (in circle), aqua, pt 15.00
Simplex (in dmn on lid), clear, ½-pt.................................. 5.00

Smalley Full Measure (AGS monogram) Quart, amber, original aluminum lid, smooth base, ground lip, M, $45.00.

Standard (reverse: erased mastadon) & W McC&Co, aqua, qt 18.00
Standard (shepherd's crook), aqua, wax sealer, qt 28.00
Star (below stippled star), clear, qt..................................48.00
Star (emblem), aqua, tin lid, qt..28.00
Sterling (in script) Mason, clear, qt................................. 3.00
Sunshine Brand Coffee (lion & sun), clear, zinc lid, qt....... 4.00
Sure Seal (in circle), bl, qt.. 3.00
Sure Seal Made for L Bamberger & Co, bl, qt 12.00

Swayzee's Improved Mason, aqua, qt..................8.00
TM Lightning Reg US Pat Office, aqua, ½-gal 8.00
Trade Mark Lightning, amber, ½-gal..................53.00
Trade Mark The Dandy, amber, qt..................98.00
Trademark Climax Registered, bl, pt..................5.00
Trademark Climax Registered, bl, qt..................5.00
Trademark Keystone Registered, clear, pt..................7.00
Veteran (bust of veteran), clear, qt..................18.00
Victory Reg'd 1925 (on lid), 2 side clamps, clear, ½-pt..................10.00
Wan-Eta Cocoa Boston, aqua, qt..................5.00
Wears (on banner below crown), clear, 2 side clamps, qt..................14.00
Weideman (boy w/platter), clear, pt..................6.00
Wm L Haller Carlisle PA, aqua, pt..................448.00
Woodbury, aqua, qt..................28.00

Fry

Henry Fry established his glassworks in 1901 in Rochester, Pennsylvania. There, until 1933 when it was sold to the Libbey Company, he produced glassware of the finest quality. In the early years, they produced beautiful cut glass; and when it began to wane in popularity, Fry turned to the manufacture of occasional pieces and oven glassware. He is perhaps most famous for the opalescent pearl glass called 'Foval.' It was made in combination with crystal or colored trim; because it was in production for only a short time in 1926 and 1927, it is hard to find.

Collectors of depression-era glassware look for the opalescent reamers and opaque green kitchenware made during the early thirties.

Our advisor for this category is Ron Damaska; he is listed in the Directory under Pennsylvania. See also Kitchen Collectibles.

Aquarium, amber, polished pontil, 7½x12" dia..................165.00
Bowl, centerpc; amber, rolled rim, polished pontil, 3½x12"..................125.00
Bowl, fruit; Foval, bl trim, ftd, 12" dia..................575.00
Compote, gr w/clear swirled connector & petal ft, 4½x10"..................325.00
Compote, royal bl, clear swirled connector/petal ft, 3x7"..................265.00
Compote, royal bl, polished pontil, 4x6"..................130.00
Compote, wht opal w/bl stem, flared rim, 7x6" dia..................275.00
Creamer & sugar, Foval, Delft bl trim/hdls, ftd, 3½", 2½"..................325.00
Cup & saucer, Foval, lt gr opal w/gr hdl..................85.00
Goblet, clear crackle w/appl gr base..................120.00
Hat, wht w/red trim, 2"..................65.00
Liquor glass, clear w/blk ft, optic ribs, swirl connector..................40.00
Plate, Foval, gr rim, 8½", set of 8..................695.00

Foval tea set, green jade accents, pot: 6½", $400.00

Tumbler, acid-etched floral, w/hdls..................145.00
Tumbler, iced tea; Sheraton etch..................95.00
Tumbler, juice; De Chicken, ftd, 3¼"..................185.00
Vase, jack-in-pulpit; Foval, bl trim, 10½x3½"..................250.00

Wine, rose etch, optic ribs, 6¼"..................95.00

Fulper

The Fulper Pottery was founded in 1899, after nearly a century of producing utilitarian stoneware under various titles and managements. Not until 1909 did Fulper venture into the art pottery field. Vasekraft, their first art line, utilized the same heavy clay body used for their utility ware. Although shapes were unadorned and simple, the glazes they developed were used with such flair and imagination (alone and in unexpected combined harmony) that each piece was truly a work of art. Graceful Oriental shapes were produced to compliment the important 'famille rose' glaze developed by W.H. Fulper, Jr. Other shapes and glazes were developed in line with the Arts and Crafts movement of the same period.

During WWI, doll's heads and Kewpies were made to meet the demand for hard-to-find imports. Figural perfume lamps and powder boxes were made both in bisque and glazed ware. Examples prized most highly by collectors today are those made before a devastating fire destroyed the plant in 1929, resulting in an operations takeover by Martin Stangl later that same year.

Several marks were used: a vertical 'Fulper' in a line reserve, a horizontal mark, a Vasekraft paper label, 'Rafco,' 'Prang,' and 'Flemington.'

Fulper values are to a major degree determined by the desirability of the glazes and forms. And, of course, larger examples command higher prices as well. Lamps with colored glass inserts are rare and highly prized.

Bowl, bl flambe, accordion folded hdls, ftd, 6½"..................175.00
Bowl, bl tones, ink mk, 13"..................350.00
Bowl, bl/khaki flambe, bl crystalline int, emb, 14", NM..................250.00
Bowl, effigy; bl/gold/brn flambe on mustard, gray/yel int..................600.00
Bowl, gold/bl matt w/gr flambe int, 3 lg ibis supports, 12"..................500.00
Bowl, gr-bl on gold matt, bl/yel flambe int, notch rim, 9"..................200.00
Bowl, gr/olive crystalline, loop hdls, 3x7x12"..................275.00
Bowl, mirror blk, hammered, 3 lg scroll supports, rpr, 10"..................450.00
Bowl, sky-bl flambe, squat/closed, 3x5"..................125.00
Candlestick, blk matt/gr crystalline, lily pad form, 5" dia..................75.00
Cider set, mustard matt, cylindrical 12" pitcher+6 mugs..................900.00
Coffeepot, gr crystalline/brn, w/lappets, 7", +cr/sug..................500.00
Figurine, goose, #876, 5x9"..................350.00
Lamp, cylindrical, cone shade w/inset glass, #106, 14"..................4,100.00
Lamp, gold matt/gr flambe, 2¾x6"..................100.00
Lamp, lt brn crystalline 16" shade w/24 pcs ldgl, '10, NM..................11,000.00
Lamp, mushroom form, colored glass inset in 17" shade, 22"..................16,500.00
Lamp base, blk/gr flambe over mauve, baluster, 21"..................375.00
Lamp base, copper dust/celadon, angle hdls, low width, 20"..................475.00
Mirror, blk humidor, with lid, rare, 6½"..................600.00
Vase, apple gr matt crystalline, collar neck w/hdls, 11x6"..................250.00
Vase, aqua crystalline to gr, beehive form w/hdls, 9½"..................350.00
Vase, bl, rose in high relief, gr-tinged petals, 6½x6"..................250.00
Vase, bl crystalline/brn, collared, 4 sm shoulder hdls, 14"..................550.00
Vase, bl drip over olive, classic form, molded mk, 15"..................1,300.00
Vase, bl matt, bulbous w/hdls, ink mk, 8½x7½"..................325.00
Vase, bl w/brn & blk drip at shoulder, baluster, 12"..................3,800.00
Vase, bl-gr flambe, bulbous, 8x10"..................450.00
Vase, bl/gr drip over buff, baluster, ink mk, 16"..................1,800.00
Vase, blk drip over gr irid, baluster, relief mk, 17"..................2,000.00
Vase, blk/brn cat's eye glaze, ogee sides, 13x6"..................550.00
Vase, blk/gold crystalline flambe, urn form, ½-hdls, 15"..................800.00
Vase, brn matt, ovoid w/2 appl ring hdls, 13"..................400.00
Vase, brn matt, wide mouth on squat bulb, angle hdls, 8x10"..................325.00
Vase, brn/blk drip over bl-gr, doughnut neck, 12x10"..................3,000.00

Vase, bud; bl-gr flambe, sq form w/4 projecting ft, 8" **150.00**
Vase, Chinese bl over blk/brn flambe, mirror gloss, 12x9" **750.00**
Vase, copper crystalline, emb design at angle shoulder, 11" **4,600.00**
Vase, copper dust, akimbo hdls, angle shoulder, 5x6" **175.00**
Vase, copper dust w/blk drip glaze, teardrop form, 12" **1,400.00**
Vase, cream/brn/bl flambe, bulbous w/hdls, #517, 12"..................**550.00**
Vase, cucumber mottle w/hammered surface, hdls, 12x11" **425.00**
Vase, dk brn crystalline to striated tan, ring hdls, 12" **600.00**
Vase, dk gr flambe, ogee sides, 7x6" **175.00**
Vase, foamy bl-gr drip on periwinkle, upright hdls, 9x7½" **750.00**
Vase, foamy oatmeal/mahog/bl-gr drip over brn & blk, 14x6". **1,500.00**
Vase, gold copper dust, bulbous w/tall loop hdl, 12x8", NM........**600.00**
Vase, gold crystalline/bl flambe, basket hdl, unmk, 5½"..............**125.00**
Vase, gr to rose flambe, 3 rim-to-shoulder hdls, ink mk, 7"..........**250.00**
Vase, gr/bl flame over bl matt, sqd upright hdls, 10x8" **800.00**

Vase, green with heavy crystals, 9½", $950.00.

Vase, gray/pk streaky to mixed gr matts, mk Prang, 8x5" **375.00**
Vase, gun metal/gray-gr, sq w/rtcl band, ftd, 4x3½".......................**250.00**
Vase, lav/bl/gr streaky, gourd w/ring at flaring neck, 14" **1,200.00**
Vase, lt bl-gr crystalline, ovoid w/2 ear hdls, 12" **400.00**
Vase, lt bl/olive, cylindrical w/angle hdls, mk MP, 12" **310.00**
Vase, lt/cobalt bl, scroll-hdld urn form, 11x6", NM **200.00**
Vase, mocha matt, triangular cutouts, 4 buttresses, 13½" **2,200.00**
Vase, mustard w/ivory & tan 'draped' top half, 12" **1,900.00**
Vase, mustard/lt bl flambe over gold-brn, septagonal, 10" **500.00**
Vase, perwinkle w/gray metallic drips, cylindrical, 13½"..............**265.00**
Vase, turq flambe w/crystals over bl/gr/rose matt, hdls, 9"............**650.00**
Vase, turq-to-brn dripping flambe, bulbous, 5x6" **225.00**

Furniture

From the cabinetmaker's shop of the early 1800s with apprentices and journeymen who learned every phase of the craft at the side of the master carpenter, the trade had evolved by the mid-century to one with steam-powered saws and turning lathes and workers who specialized in only one operation. By 1870 the Industrial Revolution was in progress, and large factories in the East and Midwest turned out increasingly elaborate styles, ornately machine carved and heavily inlaid. Rococo, Egyptian, and Renaissance Revival furniture adapted well to factory production. Eastlake offered a welcome respite from Victorian frumpery and a return to quality handcrafting. All of these styles remained popular until the turn of the century.

As early as 1880, factories began using oak; early mail-order catalogs offered oak furniture, simply styled and lighter in weight, since long-distance shipping was often a factor. Mission, or Craftsman, a style introduced around 1890, was simple to the extreme. Stickley and Hubbard were two of its leading designers. Other popular Victorian styles were Colonial Revival, Cottage, Bentwood, and Windsor. Prices are as variable as the styles.

To learn more about furniture, we recommend *The Collectors Encyclopedia of American Furniture* by Robert and Harriet Swedberg.

Key:
Am — American	G — good
brd — board	Geo — Georgian
Chpndl — Chippendale	grpt — grainpainted
Co — Country	hdbd — headboard
cvd — carved	hdw — hardware
cvg — carving	Hplwht — Hepplewhite
c&b — claw and ball	NE — New England
do — door	QA — Queen Anne
drw — drawer	trn — turning
Emp — Empire	Vict — Victorian
Fed — Federal	W/M — William and Mary
Fr — French	: — over (example: 1 do:2 drw —
ftbd — footboard	1 door over 2 drawers)

Bed

Bentwood, arched/scrolled hd/ft brd w/pressed frieze, 1800s **500.00**

Cherrywood turned post four-poster bed 90" high, $3,000.00.

Day, curly maple/cherry, scrolled posts w/trn spindles.................**975.00**
Day, Limbert, #651, flat sides w/heart cutout, label, EX..............**450.00**
Day, Mission oak, worn leather pad, stepped-finial posts **500.00**
Hired man's, poplar, trn posts, converted from rope bed..............**200.00**
Mahog late Fed, acanthus-cvd 78" posts, scroll hdbd............... **2,800.00**
Rope, cherry, EX trn posts w/acorn finials & scroll hdbd......... **1,850.00**
Rope, cherry/poplar Co Empire, scroll hd/ftbd, trn finials............**400.00**
Rope, red rpt, trn posts & finials, high legs, str hdbd....................**225.00**
Rope trundle, hardwood w/pine hdbd, rnd posts, pnt, 60" **350.00**
Tiger maple, ring-trn tall posts, w/tester, rfn/rpl, 65" **1,200.00**
Walnut Vict, cartouch-cvd hdbd, urn finials, 83" **1,200.00**

Bench

Kneeling, pine w/worn gr pnt, 30" **150.00**
Kneeling, pine w/worn orig gray pnt, primitive, 4x40" **175.00**
Mahog classic, uphl w/scrollwork base, 1835, 17x42x16" **5,000.00**
Mammy's, decor Co Sheraton, removable guard, 60" **1,500.00**

Mission oak, solid bk/box seat, rnded arms, unsgn, 52" 225.00
Pine, shaped sides, allover red, PA, 1820s, 62" bk, 58" 1,600.00
Pine PA w/wood box seat, red rpt w/compass stars, 74" 1,400.00
Poplar w/oak edge, metal liner, cut-out apron/ft, late, 73" 425.00
Settle, arrow bk, rpr/rfn, 78" 525.00
Settle, arrow-bk, blk rpt w/gold striping, 72" 400.00
Soft wood Co w/dk gr pnt, bootjack ends, crack in top, 87"...........85.00
Walnut Co, bk w/dbl row of spindles, 2 hinged seats, 59" 2,100.00
Water, oak Co, bootjack ft, gallery top:shelf, rpt, 29x43" 400.00
Water, poplar Co, brn rpt, 1 shelf, top w/well, damage, 40".........350.00
Water, poplar Co, cut-out arched ft, sq nails, 2-tier, 48".............500.00
Window, Limbert, #243, 4 cutouts ea end, VG leather seat 4,500.00
Windsor, spindle bk/simple crest/knuckle arms, rpt/rpr, 88" 3,000.00
Windsor, 31-spindle bk w/scroll arms, 8-leg, ca 1800, 70" 12,500.00

Blanket Chest

Cherry, sq posts/trn ft, till w/secret compartment, 20x32" 725.00
Curly maple Chpndl, 2-drw, lift top, rpl base/hdw, 39" L.............250.00
Oak Co w/red traces, primitive, mfg label, damage/rpr, 47" 100.00

Decorated dower chest, hand-painted tulips on dark green, 1700s, repainted, feet added, 54" long, $800.00.

Pine Co English w/worn red flame grpt, 1-drw, 38" 250.00
Pine PA Co Hplwht, red pnt w/traces of grpt, 50" 2,200.00
Pine QA, 2 false drw:2, EX orig pnt/hdw, 1750s, 42x35"........ 2,250.00
Pine w/brn grpt, trn ft, dvtl, lid very worn, 24x38".......................225.00
Pine/poplar, brn grpt on yel w/stencil 'MH,' trn ft, 49" 950.00
Pine/poplar, orig bl pnt/lg yel initials, rpl ft, rpr, 51" 900.00
Poplar w/orig brn grpt in bold stripes, minor wear, 46" 1,200.00
Poplar w/orig red pnt, blk trim/yel stripes, PA, dtd 1878 .... 3,400.00
Walnut Co Sheraton, trn high ft, losses, 46" 400.00

Bookcase

Fed walnut w/inlay 3-part breakfront, drws, 1800, 87x76"....... 7,000.00
Lifetime, 3 8-pane do, through tenons, metal tag, 62", EX 4,000.00
Oak, sectional, 4-unit, 1920s, rstr/rfn..500.00
Oak, 1-do, simple styling, 4-shelf, rfn/rstr 300.00
Onandaga, #228½, 2-do, gallery/exposed tenons, 57x49" 4,750.00
Rosewood classical, 2 glass do w/urn-form overlay:desk, 90" ..14,000.00
Shop of Crafters, 2 glaze do ea w/3 glass inserts, 58x28" 1,200.00

Bureau, See Chest

Cabinet

China, att Lifetime, oak w/2 glass do & sides, 57x43" 650.00

China, oak, ldgl sides/do, mirror bk, 1900s 900.00
Corner china, oak, beveled mirror bk/ldgl do, 3-leg, paw ft..... 1,200.00
Curio, bird's eye maple, 3-shelf, dbl glass do, 35x52" 700.00
Kitchen, oak, 2 glass do:step bk shelf:2 drw:2 do, 1920s........500.00
Oak A/C, 6-pane do:shelf, unsgn, 29x30x18"........................900.00
On chest, walnut Fed, 2 recessed panel do:base w/5 drw, 89" .. 9,000.00

Candlestand

Birch Hplwht, trn ped, spider legs, rfn 900.00
Cherry Co, tripod w/trn column, dished 1-brd 19" dia top..........400.00
Cherry Co, tripod w/trn column & chip-cvg, 17" dia top 450.00
Cherry Co Chpndl style, trn std w/tripod, lg 4-brd tilt top 350.00
Cherry Co Hplwht, trn column, tripod, 1-brd tilt top 525.00
Cherry Co w/red rpt on base, trn column/tripod, 2-brd top 400.00
Cherry Hplwht, tripod w/spider legs, oval 15x19" top................800.00
Hardwood w/blk grpt on brn, trn column/tripod, 13" dia top.......300.00
Mahog Chpndl, tripod base w/snake ft, bird cage, tilt top 4,200.00
Maple w/red stain, Pilgrim style, shoe ft, octagonal top 800.00
Oak Co, whittled legs, 1-brd 18" octagonal top, early 650.00

Chair

Arm, A/C oak, 5-slat bk/4-slat sides, spring seat, 44x30" 700.00
Arm, Harden, oak, bk adjusts, 5-slat sides, label 850.00
Arm, Harden, oak, 5-slat bk/slat sides, spring seat, label.............500.00
Arm, mahog, cvd crest/eagle slat, new leather seat 600.00
Bannister bk side, maple/etc, spliced rpr, rush seats, pr 2,400.00
Belter, rosewood, cvd floral crest/solid bk, no arms, 35" 1,200.00
Corner, Co hardwood w/blk rpt, splint seat 450.00
Corner, ebonized Aesthetic, decorative panels/trn in rail 3,000.00
Corner, maple/etc Co, bold trn/well-shaped arm rail, rpt...........600.00
Ladderbk arm, maple/hickory (some curl), rockers added 300.00
Ladderbk side, Co, 3 curved slats, trn finals, old red pnt............225.00
Ladderbk side, maple, 5 arched splats/EX trn, rpl seats, pr 1,100.00
Ladderbk side, 3 arched slats/trn finials, paper rush seat 250.00
Limbert, #79, 'bicycle' seat, unmk, new leather bk, 42" 500.00
Lolling, cherry-fr Chpndl, re-uphl/rfn 1,300.00
Moose/deer horn fr, suede uphl seat/bk, nailhead trim 1,400.00
Morris, Limbert, 4-slat bk/5-slat bent arm, decal, EX 2,800.00
Morris, Young & Co, att; 5-slat bk/4-slat side, web seat 1,300.00
Parlor, burl walnut Vict, trn legs, uphl bk/seat, 1800s, pr.............250.00
Parlor, giltwood Eastlake, rtcl floral bk, 1885 ....175.00
Rocker, walnut Vict spindle-side bbl bk, molded splat, late.........150.00
Rocker arm, Salem-style arrow bk, red pnt, rpr/rpl, 42" 300.00
Sewing rocker, Limbert, 5-slat bk, cushion seat, label, 28" 120.00
Side, burl walnut Vict, cvd rondels, uphl, pr 300.00
Side, Cherry Co Chpndl, starflower in pierced splat, rstr 325.00
Side, Hitchcock Sheraton w/gilt eagle on blk, rpt, rpl seat 425.00
Side, mahog Co Chpndl, molded crest w/scrolled ears 750.00
Side, mahog Fed, cvd slat w/cornucopias, sabre legs.................500.00
Side, mahog Hplwht, urn bk, Am, 1780s, EX............................825.00
Side, mahog Hplwht, 3 bk slats ea w/oval cvd patera 625.00
Side, maple Co Chpndl, pierced splat, crest w/cvd ears, EX 1,050.00
Side, maple Co QA, EX trn legs/Spanish ft, rpl rush seat............750.00
Side, Moravian, well-cvd scrolling bk, dtd 1830, EX...................115.00
Side, walnut English QA, EX detail, trn H-stretcher, VG.......1,850.00
Side, walnut Vict, shell crest, cvd splat, caned seat, pr 150.00
Windsor, bamboo side, rpr seat/bk, rfn......................................300.00
Windsor, bow-bk side, worn blk/gold pnt, shaped seat, pr....... 1,100.00
Windsor, bow-bk side, 7-spindle, saddle seat, gray pnt 1,250.00
Windsor, continuous arm, saddle seat, bulbous trn, rpt, EX..... 6,500.00
Windsor, fan-bk arm, 1780s, rpt, pr.. 3,500.00
Windsor, fan-bk side, earred crest, saddle seat, rfn 400.00

Windsor fan-back side chair, old black paint, $700.00.

Chippendale mahogany block-front chest, ca 1780, refinished, replaced base and brasses, 30" x 33", $14,000.00.

Wingbk, cherry fr Chpndl, H stretcher, 1775, EX **3,500.00**
Wingbk, mahog QA style, uphl, cabriole legs w/pad ft................**325.00**
Wingbk, mahog w/inlay fr Hplwht, stripped, 1780s................. **3,750.00**
Wingbk, mahog-fr Chpndl, sq legs & H stretcher, stripped..... **1,900.00**

Chair Set

Dining, mahog Geo III, pierced vase splat, 2 arm+6 side......... **3,500.00**
Dining, mahog Hplwht, pierced bk splats, 1 arm+5 side **1,150.00**
Side, faux rosewood w/brass inlay Regency, 1825, 6 for........... **2,500.00**
Side, grpt/fruit stencils, rush seat, NE, 1820s, EX, 10 for......... **1,600.00**
Side, ladderbk, trn stiles, rpl rush seat, NE, 1700s, 4 for............**425.00**
Side, Limbert, #911, 1 bk slat, mk, rpl leather, 6 for............... **1,200.00**
Side, mahog classical, scrolled str crest, NY 1820, 6 for **4,000.00**
Side, mahog Fed, cvd fan surmounts on spindles, 6 for **9,500.00**
Side, red-stain maple QA, solid splat, 1730s, pr.....................**11,000.00**
Side, spindle bk/plank seat, yel on 2-color grpt, EX, 6 for........ **1,350.00**
Side, walnut Vict Emp style, curve bk/Ionic capitals, 8 for...... **1,500.00**
Windsor, bamboo side, red/blk grpt w/yel stripes, 4 for........... **1,700.00**

Chest

Cherry Chpndl, c/b ft, fluted/chamfered corners, 7-drw, 45"... **1,650.00**
Cherry Co, 4-drw, trn ft, paneled ends, rpl ft, 42x41" **275.00**
Cherry Co Chpndl, 6 dvtl cockbeaded drw, rpl hdw, 58x36".. **3,500.00**
Cherry Fed w/mahog veneer X-bands & line inlay, D-front **1,350.00**
Cherry Hplwht, inlay escutcheons, scalloped apron, 37x40".. **1,000.00**
Cherry w/burl trim Emp, free trn pilasters, 46x42" **450.00**
Cherry w/curly maple drw fronts Co Sheraton bow front, 40" **900.00**
Cherry w/PA decor, red w/gold floral/name/1863, 48", EX...... **1,100.00**
Crotch walnut Vict, pk marble top, leaf pulls, 5-drw **400.00**
Curly maple, 5-drw, orig hdw, RI, 1750s, 51x38".................... **5,750.00**
Curly maple Chpndl, bracket base, rfn/rpl, 1775, 50x38"........ **4,000.00**
Curly maple/birch Hplwht, orig hdw, rfn, 33x36"....................**3,400.00**
Eldred Wheeler, chest-on chest, flame grpt, 63" **1,100.00**
Mahog Chndl, oxbow front, 1780s, rpl hdw/rpr, 33x38" **2,100.00**
Mahog Chpndl bow front, c/b ft, rpl hdw/ft, 35x40" **800.00**
Mahog Fed, bow front, veneer crossbanding, 1815, orig hdw . **1,500.00**
Maple Chpndl, bracket base, orig hdw, rfn/rpl, 44x38" **2,250.00**
Maple/mahog veneer Fed, bow front, orig hdw/finish, 36x40".. **2,600.00**
Mule, maple w/red rpt Co QA, scroll bracket ft, 40x36" **2,450.00**
Mule, pine w/red flame grpt, lift lid w/til, 2-drw, 43x44" **2,250.00**
On chest, maple, orig hdw, 1790s, rfn, 76x38" **9,000.00**

Pine Co, red stain, 3 dvtl drw, simple, rpl pulls, 36x38" **200.00**
Pine/poplar Co Emp w/brn-on-yel grpt, scroll crest, 38" **2,000.00**
Poplar Co Chpndl w/orig red-brn pnt, 5-drw, orig hdw, 50" .. **6,500.00**
Tiger maple Chpndl, high ogee bracket base, rfn/rpl, 36x39".. **9,750.00**
Walnut Co Hplwht, 4-drw, scrolled Fr ft, 44x40" **1,400.00**

Commode

Mahog w/ormolu mts Emp, canister ft, 4-drw, rpl top, 50" **2,200.00**
Oak Louis XVI Provincial, 3-drw, fluted pilasters, 35" **1,700.00**

Burl walnut commode, English style, early 1700s, 42" wide, $1,200.00.

Walnut, X-band breakfront top:2 drw, German, 1800s, 30x35" ..**900.00**
Walnut Italian Neoclassic, inlaid ivory maids/florals, 52" **7,500.00**
Walnut Vict, 3-drw, splash bk, blk teardrop pulls, 34x30" **200.00**
Walnut w/inlay hunting scenes & florals, Italian, 1850s, pr.... **7,000.00**

Cupboard

Corner, butternut Co, panel do/beaded edge, 1856, 79x41".... **1,200.00**
Corner, Co cherry, panel do, cut-out ft, rprs, 76x40" **4,100.00**
Corner, pine w/VG bl pnt (some overpnt), 1-pc, 82x39" **6,400.00**
Corner, pine/poplar 2-pc architectural, raised panel do, 95" ... **3,500.00**
Corner, poplar Co, 1-pc, EX cornice, 2 8-pane do:2, 87".........**1,800.00**
Corner, walnut, raised panel do, EX cornice, rpl/rpr, 90" **4,000.00**
Corner, walnut Chpndl, rosette-cvd scroll top, flame finial **8,000.00**
Grpt Fed step-bk, 3 open shelves:2 cupboard do, 1820s, 87" ..**40,000.00**

Hanging, cherry, dvtl, base/cornice moldings, rpl, 30", EX 375.00
Hanging, cherry Co, simple cornice:6-pane do, losses, 33" 450.00
Hanging, oak w/curly maple grpt, cvd arch in do, rpl, 38x28" 575.00
Hanging, pine, wide cornice, panel do w/cvd arch, 39x33"..........400.00
Hanging, pine w/red stain, 2 glazed do, wide cornice, 36x27"......325.00
Hanging, pine w/rpt, raised panel do, 22x13" 300.00
Hanging, pine w/yel over earlier pnt, brd/batten do, 42x31" 350.00
Hanging, poplar Co w/orig old red, 1 panel do, 37x28x8"............775.00
Jelly, walnut, dvtl, cut-out ft/raised panel do, 54x39" 4,900.00
Pewter, pine, bent-bk, rfn, PA, 1800s, 82x45" 1,000.00
Pewter, pine Co down to mustard pnt, brd/batten do, 77x36". 1,500.00
Pewter, pine/poplar Co, 1 drw in base:2 panel do, 75x40" 600.00
Pine Co, step-bk, 1-brd ends, panel do:2 drw:do, 36" W 1,600.00
Pine Scandinavian, 3 floral-pnt panels in do, 1800, 74x39" 300.00
Poplar w/orig brn flame grpt, 2 8-pane do:2 drw:2 do, 84" 2,700.00
Walnut, EX detail, 2 raised panel do:3 drw:2 do, 84x28"........ 6,250.00
Walnut Co, red traces, scalloped apron, 1-brd do top/base 1,950.00
Walnut Co, 2 6-pane do:step-bk:drw:2 panel do, 1-pc, 64x35".. 1,000.00

Desk

A/C dropfront w/drw, step-bk upper case, 46x35x18" 250.00
Cherry Chpndl, slant lid, bracket ft, fitted int, 46x38"............ 6,000.00
Cherry Chpndl, slant lid, fitted int, 1 ft rpl, 39" 3,500.00
Cherry Co plantation, bookcase top is marriage, slant lid 1,600.00
Cherry w/band inlay Co Hplwht, slant lid, fitted, 41x41" 2,100.00

Curly maple slant-lid desk, American, late 1700s, restored and refinished, 30" x 34", $2,200.00.

Figured walnut Chpndl, slant lid/ogee ft, totally rstr, 45" 2,800.00
Kimble & Cabus, Aesthetic, superstructure w/many trns, 64" . 3,500.00
Lap-top, poplar w/worn red pnt & stenciled eagle, 23" 250.00
Limbert, 2 shelves:drop-front:shelf/side cutouts, unmk, 51" 5,000.00
Mahog Chpndl block front, slant lid, rope cvg, c/b ft 11,000.00
Quaint, #6187-2810, bookcase sides, brand/decal, 30x40x26".....350.00
Schoolmaster's, pine, lift top, tapered legs, 1800s........................250.00
Tiger maple Chpndl, slant lid, orig hdw, 1780s, 42x37" 7,500.00

Dresser

Henderon, mahog Vict, serpentine, easel mirror, cvgs, 72" 800.00
Mahog Vict, oval easel mirror w/cvd harp supports, 76x44" 500.00
Oak, curved facade, swivel mirror, press/cvd decor......................450.00
Walnut Renaissance Revival/Eastlake, marble top......................850.00
Walnut Vict, marble top, 2 drw+2 sm drw, mirror, 75x40"..........300.00

Highboy

Cherry QA flat top w/2 cvd fans, scalloped apron, 1750, 73".18,000.00

Figured Chpndl flat top w/fan cvg, fancy apron, att Dunlap...22,000.00
Mahog Chpndl flame/urn-finial scroll top, c/b ft, 1760, 93"...55,000.00
Maple QA, bonnet top, ball/spire finials & drops, 80" 26,000.00
Tiger maple QA, flat top, NE, 1740s, 72x39" 13,000.00
Walnut, bird/fan inlay bonnet top, finials/drops, 1770, 90"....30,000.00

Lowboy

Figured maple QA, heart-pierced apron, Spanish ft, 29x40" .41,000.00
Mahog QA, fan cvg, 4-drw, orig hdw, 1740, 31x34"...............66,000.00
Walnut w/inlay QA, paw ft, acorn drops, 1740, 31x33".........20,000.00

Rack

Drying, pine, 10 19" slats, folding, 22x5", EX 50.00
Drying, pine, 2-section, shoe ft, mortised/pinned, 48x54" 175.00
Drying, pine w/gray rpt, folding, ea part: 27x32" 300.00
Plate, pine, brn sponged/combing, 3-tier, scroll sides, 36"............750.00

Secretary

Corner, primitive, 2 glazed arched do, red pnt, rpl, 86x54"..........700.00
Lady's, Fed, shaped top:2 glaze do w/dmn overlay, 65x31" 2,600.00
Mahog Fed 2-part: bookcase w/Gothic-glazed do:4-drw, 86..... 5,500.00
Mahog/inlay Fed, brass ball/spire finials, arched panes, 80 .....11,000.00
Pnt/gilt Venetian Rococo style, serpentine, bonnet top, 99"... 9,500.00

Settee

Harden, oak, 12-slat bk, even arms, spring seat, 80" 1,500.00
Joseph Hoffman, bentwood, scrolled bk/armrests, cane seat 600.00
Pail Bros, bbl form w/narrow rail-to-floor slats, 46" 2,600.00
Rosewood Vict, 3-shield bk, fruit crest, open arms, 60" 1,800.00
Sheraton w/wht rpt & stenciling, EX detail, rush seat, 37"...... 2,300.00
Walnut Vict, cvd floral crest, uphl, 60" 1,200.00
Window, cvd mahog classical, acanthus armrests/legs, 53"...... 3,500.00
Windsor, cage-bk:15 bamboo stiles, bamboo legs, 38" 8,000.00

Shelf

Folk art, 3-tier, widens toward top, chip-cvd, 22x20" 230.00
Pine, blk/red grpt & floral, whale ends, 4-tier, 38x26"............ 1,150.00
Pine Co, floor standing, 3-shelf, cut-out ft, 47x34" 800.00
Poplar, 3-tier, scalloped ends, late wire nails, 29x22"..................260.00
Poplar, 4-tier, closed bk, bootjack ft, 72x38" 900.00

Sideboard

Cherry Co Sheraton w/bird's-eye veneer drw fronts, 35x35" .. 1,600.00

Victorian marble-top sideboard, carved with fish and ducks, 72", $1,000.00.

J Ramson & Sons, mahog/figured maple inlay Fed, 1805, 58" ... **9,000.00**
Mahog classical w/marble top & pilasters, 1820, 72" **12,000.00**
Mahog Geo w/ebony & box wood inlays, bow front, 61"......... **1,800.00**
Mahog veneer classic, hairy paw ft, acanthus cvg, 61", EX **6,000.00**
Mahog w/chevron & string inlay Fed, serpentine, 73"............**24,000.00**
Mahog w/inlay Fed, serpentine front, bottle drw, rpr, 72" **1,000.00**
Mahog w/inlay Geo III, w/cellarette drw, rpr, 71" **2,700.00**
Oak Vict, open & glass-do shelves, mirror, leaf/mask cvg............**800.00**

Sofa

Mahog Emp, EX cvg w/flower basket finials, rfn/uphl, 83" **1,500.00**
Mahog Emp, leaf-cvd fr w/scroll arms, ormolu mts, 1820, 85". **7,700.00**
Mahog Emp, scroll crest rail:shaped bk, acanthus ft, 98".............**475.00**

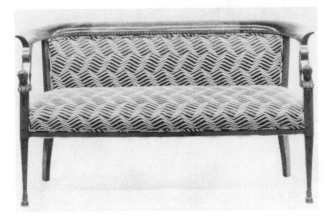

Continental neoclassical style bronze-mounted marquetry mahogany sofa, late 1800s, 58" long, $2,700.00.

Mahog Fed, open trn on front of arms, 6-leg, rprs, 78" **1,500.00**
Mahog Fed, serpentine bk, uphl scroll arms, 1800, 91" **17,600.00**
Mahog Sheraton, reeded crest, spindle sides, 66" **1,450.00**
Mahog Vict, lg paw ft, 1890, 80"...**300.00**
Rosewood Rococo Revival, 3-part bk, fruit crest, 66" **1,800.00**

Stand

Cherry, trn legs, 1 dvtl drw, 1-brd 18x18" top, rfn **350.00**
Cherry Co Hplwht, 1-drw, rpr/cracked 19x21" top **550.00**
Cherry Fed, scrolled front legs/trn bk legs, rpl 19" sq top **200.00**
Cherry/curly maple Co Sheraton, 1-drw, rfn 19" 2-brd top..........**550.00**
Cherry/poplar w/red finish, EX trn, 1-drw, 20" 1-brd top **350.00**
Curly maple, 1-drw, trn legs, 1-brd 10" sq top, rfn.......................**750.00**
Hardwood/mahog veneer Emp, trn/rope-cvd legs, 2-drw.............**225.00**
Mahog/poplar Co Hplwht, 1-brd top, rpr/re-worked **450.00**
Oak/birch Co Hplwht, 1 brd top (rpl?) w/4 breadbrd ends...........**250.00**
Pine Hplwht w/grpt, drw on all 4 sides, pegged, OH, 1840...... **1,450.00**
Poplar Co Hplwht, sq legs w/severe taper, rpl drw **500.00**
Poplar w/orig red flame grpt, compass stars, some wear............ **1,100.00**
Walnut, drop leaf, 2 dvtl drw, trn legs, 1-brd 16x21" top **450.00**
Walnut Co Hplwht, splayed base, sq legs, rpl 17" sq top..............**225.00**
Walnut Co w/blk pnt compass star in top, mortised/pinned **350.00**
Walnut/birch/cherry, trn legs, 15" sq top has crack, 21" H **200.00**

Stool

Footstool, cvd mahog classical, scroll ends w/trn balusters............**500.00**
Footstool, oak Eastlake, leather top, drw, 15x15" **50.00**
Footstool, pencil post legs, primitive, VG....................................**95.00**
Footstool, walnut, Vict, uphol top, 18x17" **1,300.00**

Footstool, walnut Eastlake, leather uphl, drw, 16" **75.00**
Mahog Chpndl style, uphl seat, scroll cvg/c&b ft, 19x24" **275.00**
Mahog classic, uphl, dbl-scroll/trn-stretcher base, 15x20" **1,800.00**
Piano, mahog classical, trn legs/X-stretcher, 1800, 14" dia **700.00**
Piano, walnut Aesthetic, cvd ped w/2 scroll ft....................................**375.00**
Poplar w/orig florals & stripes on gr, 9x8x10", M **500.00**

Table

Banquet, pine, expanding, 8 trn legs, folding top+4 leaves...... **1,500.00**
Bedside, FL Wright/Herendon Co, teak w/Greek Key border **500.00**
Card, mahog Emp, hinged top, cvd/reeded legs, 37" **475.00**
Card, mahog w/inlay Sheraton, reeded legs, wheat cvg, sgn ... **2,000.00**
Card, walnut w/figure Chpndl-to-Hplwht, orig hdw...............**2,700.00**
Coffee, mahog w/boullework border in legs, 20x37" **500.00**
Demilune, pine Co w/worn rpt on base, sq tapered legs, 36".........**300.00**
Dining, Hickory Co, branch supports, 48" dia, +4 chairs......... **1,300.00**
Dining, Limbert, #1480, w/leaves, unmk, 48" dia, EX **2,500.00**
Dressing, mahog English Hplwht, sq tapered legs, 3-drw.............**350.00**
Dressing, mixed wood Co Sheraton w/curly maple grpt, 34".........**450.00**
Dressing, pine w/stenciled vintage on gr, scroll crest, 32" **500.00**
Drop leaf, birch w/curly maple top Co Sheraton, 13" leaves.........**750.00**
Drop leaf, bird's eye/curly maple Co Sheraton, open: 44x44" **800.00**
Drop leaf, pine Co Hplwht, mortised apron w/cutouts, 17x36" ...**200.00**
Drop leaf, pine Co Hplwht, VG red pnt, 20x36"+8" leaves..... **1,500.00**
Drop leaf, QA, pad ft, 1700s, 48" L **3,900.00**
Drop leaf, walnut Chpndl, swing leg, rpl, 19x31"+16" leaves.. **1,400.00**
Eldred Wheeler, banquet, maple QA style, extends to 124".... **1,600.00**
End, bamboo fr w/pnt top, medial shelf, 1800s, 27x21" **150.00**
Game, pine/maple Co Chpndl, 36x16" shaped top, 1 drw, rfn **600.00**
Hutch, maple w/comb grpt, hinged seat, 51x54" **1,300.00**
Hutch, pine, 1825, sq 47x37" top...**475.00**
Library, Limbert, 8-sided, cutouts, tenon/key mortised, 40" **1,100.00**
Limbert, #118, 36" dia leather top, X-stretchers, mk, 30" **1,000.00**
Limbert, #158, oval top/base shelf, 4-leg support, 48", M **6,250.00**
Majorelle, floral inlay 38" L top, relief-cvd apron, sgn............**12,000.00**
Majorelle, 2-tier w/fruit inlay, 3-leg, 15" W **5,000.00**
Mixing, curly maple Co Sheraton stand w/20" marble top **1,000.00**
Occasional, faux bamboo curly maple, medial shelf, 28x23" .. **1,000.00**
Occasional, Limbert, #158, 2-tier oval, branded, EX **3,750.00**
Onondaga Shops, att; chestnut, arched X-stretchers, #7786 .. **1,400.00**
Parlor, walnut Vict, 28" oval marble top, 4 leg, acorn drop **600.00**
Pembroke, figured maple/cherry Fed, twist-cvd legs, 42x40" ... **3,800.00**
Pembroke, mahog (highly figured) Hplwht, 1-drw, 18x26" **900.00**
Pembroke, walnut Chpndl, Marlboro ft, open: 44x30" **9,000.00**
Pier, rosewood classical, marble top, giltwood leafy legs **7,700.00**
Sewing, cherry Hplwht, Am 1800..**800.00**
Sewing, maple/curly maple Sheraton, splay legs, drop leaves.......**400.00**
Sewing, pine/maple, splay legs, 1800s, 25x13x15"......................**500.00**
Side, mahog Vict, cartouch shape, drw, 27x18" **100.00**
Side, Majorelle, mahog, floral-cvd apron, 26x22" top.............. **6,000.00**
Side, Majorelle, mahog w/gilt-bronze leaf & flower mts **15,000.00**
Tabouret, Limbert, #240, rnded 18" top, boxed base, unmk.... **1,000.00**
Tavern, hardwood/pine Co QA, rpl 1-brd 26x40" top **2,100.00**
Tea, mahog Chpndl, tripod/snake ft, 1-brd 30" dia tilt top..........**600.00**
Work, cherry, 1850s, rfn/rpl knobs, 29" H **200.00**
Work, mahog classical, trn/reeded legs, rpl bag, 18x10"...............**500.00**
Work, mahog Emp, 2-drw w/lacy glass knobs, rope-trn legs.........**800.00**
Work, mahog Fed, ped base, 2-drw, orig hdw, 1825 ....**425.00**
Work, mahog/bird's-eye maple veneer, brass paw ft, 15x19" .. **1,150.00**
Work, pine Co Hplwht w/old red pnt, 2-brd 30x43" top **275.00**
Work, poplar/pine, 2 drw, 3-brd 36x63" top is rpl, PA **925.00**
Work, Southern pine Co Hplwht, cleaned to old bl, 51", VG **350.00**
Work, walnut Co QA, 3-drw/orig hdw, 33" 3-brd top **8,300.00**

Washstand

Birch/pine Co Sheraton, red traces, shelf w/scalloped sides 300.00
Burl walnut Am Eastlake, marble top w/bksplash+2 sm shelves ..500.00
Faux bamboo maple, marble top:2 short+2 long drw, 72x40" 700.00
Mahog w/inlay Fed corner, fitted top, medial shelf w/drw 2,500.00
Oak, towel bar in harp fr, serpentine drw: 2 sm drw+sm do 250.00
Walnut Vict, marble top, finish wear, 31½" 550.00

Miscellaneous

Bench, organ; walnut Vict, spindle gallery, uphl, 1900s...............125.00
Duncan Phyfe, cellarette, figured mahog, paw ft, 1820, 25" ...13,000.00
Etagere, mahog Vict, trn/beaded gallery:4 shelves, 41x18" 300.00
Hall tree, walnut Vict w/marble, rtcl crest, mirror, 86"............ 1,500.00
Kas, pine, 1 panel do, molded cornice, rprs, 65x36"................ 1,600.00
Linen press, cherry/mahog Fed, rpl hdw, rfn, 1800, 84x46" ... 4,000.00
Linen press, walnut Hplwht 2-pc w/inlay, broken arch crest ... 5,250.00
Pedestal, Eastlake, rtcl dahlia apron, shelf, 39x16" sq 200.00
Pedestal, walnut Eastlake, cvd, 11" dia marble top, 30" 100.00
Sink, dry; pine w/red pnt, dvtl drw:2 base drw.........................650.00

Galle

Emile Galle was one of the most important producers of cameo glass in France. His firm, founded in Nancy in 1874, produced beautiful cameo in the Art Nouveau style during the 1890s, using a variety of techniques. He also produced glassware with enameled decoration, as well as some fine pottery — animal figurines, table services, vases, and other objects d' art. In the mid-1880s, he became interested in the various colors and textures of natural woods and as a result began to create furniture which he used as yet another medium for expression of his artistic talent. Marquetry was the primary method Galle used in decorating his furniture, preferring landscapes, Nouveau floral and fruit arrangements, butterflies, squirrels, and other forms from nature. It is for his furniture and his cameo glass that he is best known today. All Galle is signed.

Our advisor for this category is Don Williams; he is listed in the Directory under Missouri.

Cameo

Bottle, hydrangeas, gr/lav on frost to peach, sqd body, 4½" 3,000.00
Bowl, berries/vines, gr/red/wht enamel on lt gr-yel, 7½" 1,000.00
Lamp, mums, bl/purple on yel 9" dome shade/bulbous base....41,000.00
Lamp, roses, red on yel/wht frost, on 10" dome shade/base 55,000.00
Lamp base, mtn lake/trees, purple/bl on frost, slim, 13½" 3,800.00
Vase, astors, rust/dk brn on wht & yel frost, slender, 6½" 5,000.00
Vase, bamboo shoots, red on yel frost, oviform, 3".................. 2,000.00
Vase, blown-out berry branches, tan on wht frost, 12" 24,000.00
Vase, blown-out clematis, brn/yel on yel frost, 10x8" 13,000.00
Vase, blown-out hyacinths, bl/olive on yel frost, 12" 24,000.00
Vase, buttercups, lav on amber, tapered cylinder, 5"................ 1,500.00
Vase, carnations, red on amber, slim body/wide bun ft, 8½" ... 3,500.00
Vase, cherry blossoms, red on yel frost, slim form, 8" 3,500.00
Vase, clematis, bl/purple on caramel frost, ftd U-form, 13" 9,000.00
Vase, clematis, purple on salmon frost, polished, 4"................ 1,500.00
Vase, crabapple limbs, orange on tangerine, flat sided, 9" 3,500.00
Vase, floral, gray/brn on yel, baluster, 6" 1,500.00
Vase, floral, lav on lemon yel, ovoid, 4¼" 1,200.00
Vase, floral, lav on yel, ovoid on ped ft, 9" 3,500.00
Vase, floral, red on yel & wht frost, shouldered, 11" 7,000.00
Vase, floral, red on yel frost, baluster, 27" 19,000.00

Vase, floral in green and brown, carved and hammered background, signed, 24", $4,100.00.

Vase, floral vine, purple on yel frost, ftd baluster, 12" 4,900.00
Vase, flowers/butterflies, navy/purple on wht, tapered, 6" 2,500.00
Vase, fronds, celery on pk to frost, banjo form, 6⅞"................ 1,600.00
Vase, fruit blossom/foliage, dbl overlay, slim, 7½" 3,000.00
Vase, fuchsias, wine on yel frost, spherical, 5½"..................... 2,900.00
Vase, gladioli blossoms, triple overlay, slim form, 29".............27,000.00
Vase, honeysuckle, amber/gr on bl, incurvate cylinder, 9" ... 3,500.00
Vase, hyacinths, dbl overlay, appl petals/scarab, 7½".............16,000.00
Vase, hydrangeas, brn on yel, slim pear form, 6½" 2,500.00
Vase, hydrangeas, purple/pk on lt pk, banjo form, 6½" 1,600.00
Vase, hydrangeas, red/burgundy on lt yel, baluster, 16" 17,600.00
Vase, iris, lt bl/purple on yel to wht, slim form, 17" 8,000.00
Vase, iris, purple on fire-polished gray, 5x6½" 2,400.00
Vase, iris/leaves, triple overlay, baluster, 20".........................18,000.00
Vase, ivy, gr-yel on rose w/red enamel, bottle form, 6¾" 1,800.00
Vase, lake/trees/boats, gr/brn on frost, ped ft, 14" 6,000.00
Vase, leaves/berries, amber on yel frost, bottle form, 15½" 3,500.00
Vase, leaves/berries, gr/brn on pk, cylinder w/bun ft, 13" 3,000.00
Vase, lilac clusters, red on yel frost, ftd baluster, 20" 12,000.00
Vase, lilies, garnet on yel frost, baluster, 9½" 8,000.00
Vase, maple leaves/pods, triple overlay, banjo form, 6½"......... 2,000.00
Vase, morning-glories, purple on gray, tapered cylinder, 4" 900.00
Vase, morning-glories, purple on sea gr, bottle form, 24" 8,000.00
Vase, morning-glories, purple on yel frost, baluster, 11" 5,000.00
Vase, mtns/trees/peacock, dk bl on yel frost to wht, 14x10"...55,000.00
Vase, mums, bl on yel frost, full body, 5½"............................. 4,000.00
Vase, mumshroom/snail/spider web, pk/ginger on clear, 12" .15,000.00
Vase, nasturtiums, lav on apricot to frost, 6⅞"........................ 4,500.00
Vase, nasturtiums, orange on frost, 2½".................................800.00
Vase, oak limbs/acorns, gr/brn on lt pk, trumpet neck, 5¾" 2,500.00
Vase, vines, purple on frost, squat baluster, 2¾", pr 1,000.00
Vase, vines/flowers, burgundy on lemon yel frost, 20" 7,500.00
Vase, violets, purple on dusky rose, ftd baluster, 3½" 1,200.00
Vase, wisteria, purple on frost, candlestick form, 3" 500.00
Vase, wisteria, red on frost, slim form, 10" 5,000.00
Vase, wisteria branches, lav/gr on pk cased in clear, 4½"......... 1,000.00
Vase, wooded river scene, brn/olive on pk & wht frost, 26" ...22,000.00
Vase, wooded river scene, yel-to-gr on frost, 11½" 3,500.00

Enameled Glass

Bowl vase, thistles, mc on emerald, swirl mold, 8" dia 2,400.00
Cruet, wildflowers, wht red/gr on clear, bulbous, 5½" 3,000.00
Cup & saucer, thistles/X Lorraine on lt amber w/gilt............... 1,000.00
Decanter, bow-tied festoons/dragonflies, 8", +7" underbowl ... 4,000.00
Dish, lady bugs/dragonfly on leafy twigs, scroll hdl, 6½" 2,300.00

Dish, wildflowers/dragonfly on lt amber, 1 side uptrn, 12" **3,500.00**
Ewer, wildflower sprays on lt amber w/gilt inclusions, 8" **2,200.00**
Pitcher, walled city/floral sprigs on clear, 4½" **2,300.00**
Rose bowl, wildflowers/intaglio flowers on gray opal, 4¾" **1,800.00**
Vase, chrysanthemums/dragonfly on clear, 7" **1,800.00**
Vase, grasshopper/branches on lt topaz, floriform, 9" **2,700.00**

Vase, florals and insects on light topaz, applied shell ornaments each side, 3⅝", $3,300.00.

Vase, tulips, gr & gr foil inclusions, bun base, 12¾" **5,000.00**

Marquetry, Wood

Table, game; 2-part 20x18" top, sweetpeas/hearts/stars/etc...... **5,000.00**
Table, sewing; floral 24" L top, branch-cvd apron & Xd legs .. **3,000.00**
Table, 2-tier, poppies/leaves, pod legs, sgn, 30x17x29"............ **5,000.00**

Octagonal tray with owl's mask handles, 24" wide, $3,000.00.

Tray, pine cones/limbs, galleried, oval, 16" **2,000.00**
Tray, 2 shepherds ride camels in desert, hdls, 19" L................. **3,000.00**
Umbrella stand, exotic leafage, spade ft, hexagonal, 28" **4,900.00**

Pottery

Bowl, lowland 'Delft' scenes in bl, ftd, w/lid, 7x10" dia **1,800.00**
Candlestick, Baroque, umber/gray scrolls, 8½", pr **1,200.00**
Candlestick, upright lion form, bl on wht, 16", pr **3,500.00**
Cat, smiling, head trn aside, dog in her locket, 13" **4,000.00**
Centerpc, frog steers shell supported by 2 catfish, 13½" **3,500.00**
Clock, open scrollwork fr, 16" **2,600.00**
Inkwell, Oriental couple pulls fabric between them, 18" L **2,000.00**
Tray, turtle shell w/head as hdl, HP insects, 12" L **900.00**
Vase, bugs/floral branches, blossom hdls, 15", VG, pr **2,000.00**

Gambling Memorabilia

Bingo cage, wood/Bakelite, 13", w/balls & 50+ cards 68.00
Book, Tricks w/Cards, London, 1923, EX 22.00
Cards, Faro, Samuel Hart & Co, EX, no box 130.00
Cheating device, card clip, ca 1888, EX 125.00
Cheating device, clip w/needle to stick under table, ivory hdl.....625.00
Cheating device, holds deck between knees to make switch ... **1,250.00**
Cheating device, placed on forearm to release card, EX..............455.00
Chip, Buster Brown's Dog Tige, red/wht/or bl, set of 200 ....140.00
Chip, clay, emb decor, 12 for 20.00
Chip, clay, emb sailing ship, 110 in sq wood holder 45.00
Chip, compo, early plane emb, complete set of 100, MIB 70.00
Chip, ivory, fleur-de-lis scrimshaw decor, tan dye, pr, EX 25.00
Chip, ivory, horse in horseshoe, red/wht/bl 12.00
Chip, ivory, ornate scrimshaw decor, lg, pr, EX 45.00
Chip, ivory, scrimshaw rose, gr border, lg....................................20.00
Dice, bone, ⅝", pr 7.50
Dice, celluloid, mk RC, pr 4.00
Dice, redware w/yel dots, 1¼x1½", pr 140.00
Dice cage, cast base & pole, sm, EX..200.00
Dice cage, nickel over brass, felt lined, 11", +5 dice...................135.00
Dice cage, NP brass, dbl-posted, 16½", +3 dice 235.00
Dice cage, NP wire on stand, single hdl, relined, 11x4½" 25.00
Dice cup, leather, Brandy, Gran Reserva, San Marcos 22.00
Dice drop, wood, rnd sleeve type w/internal bezels, EX...............215.00
Faro case keeper, Harris & Co, NY, w/compo markers, EX..........675.00
Faro layout, WM Ellis, Providence RI, VG...................................565.00
Pool scorekeeper, wooden disks strung on wire, EX 37.50
Rack, oak, contains 100 inlaid red & gr chips 45.00
Roulette ball, ivory, 1"..35.00
Score card, Faro, HC Evans & Co, Chicago IL, EX.......................15.00
Wheel, Hazzard; HC Evans & Co, Chicago, full sz, G............. **2,250.00**
Wheel, pnt wood w/alphabet, metal pins, rare, 35", EX 185.00
Wheel, roulette; traveling type, 1900s, EX 195.00
Wheel, wood, cut-out posts, HP florals, early, 36", EX................125.00
Wheel, wood, dbl-sided, metal center, Slack Chicago, EX............85.00
Wheel, wood, HP, early, 19½", EX 75.00
Wheel, wood, HP decor, panda decals, 30", EX.........................100.00
Wheel of fortune, wood, bird decals, 24", EX 55.00
Wheel of fortune, wood, HP, 50 numbers, 24" dia, EX 115.00

Game Calls

Those interested in hunting and fishing collectibles are beginning to take notice of the finer specimens of game calls available on today's market. Our advisor for this category is Randy Hilst; he is listed in the Directory under Illinois.

Crow, cedar, Charles Perdew...100.00
Crow, hard rubber, PS Olt Co..15.00
Dove, wood, Herter's 15.00
Duck, cedar, 2 silver bands, Charles Perdew.......................300.00
Duck, cedar, 3 silver bands, Charles Perdew.......................700.00
Duck, hard rubber, rnd hole stopper, PS Olt Co....................50.00
Duck, wood, Emil Stegmaier 300.00
Duck, wood, hard rubber stopper, Al Sonderman 125.00
Duck, wood, Irvin Redshaw 100.00
Duck, wood, metal stopper, Charles Ditto 75.00
Duck, wood, metal stopper, Fred Allen 50.00
Goose, hard rubber, mk A-5 Perfect Goose Call, PS Olt Co..........40.00
Goose, metal, wood stopper, David Fuller 100.00

Goose, wood, Irving Lohman 10.00
Predator, wood, Faulk's Call Co 10.00

Gameboards

The bold designs and vivid primary colors of the handmade game-boards from the 18th and 19th centuries make them highly collectible. Folk art and Americana devotees value these 'playthings,' and great examples go for thousands of dollars. Even the more routine designs can be expensive. Unfortunately, many 'new' gameboards have found their way into the market. Collectors should take the time to study the field before beginning their collections.

Checkers, border: sqs of stars/etc ea sgn by maker, ca 1900 ..... **2,000.00**
Checkers, incised sqs, sq nails, orig pnt, 1900s, 12" 175.00
Checkers, pnt on bk of pine/plywood sorting brd, pnt, worn..........**15.00**
Checkers, poplar w/orig red & blk grpt, mc stripes, 20x20" **350.00**
Checkers, rvpt glass, 20", VG **95.00**
Checkers/Bkgammon, folding, pine w/orig 3-color pnt, 8x16".....**425.00**
Checkers/Bkgammon, molded edges, 1800s, 19x19" **400.00**
Oilcloth, intricate mc designs on blk, 26x26", VG **250.00**

Red, yellow, and black Parcheesi gameboard, hand-painted castle and marine scenes, 17" x 17", $2,800.00.

Games and Puzzles

Interest in game collecting has increased over the past few years. People who appreciate early lithography are drawn to the 19th-century examples. The work of the lithographers of that period is unmatched by modern techniques. In addition, they provide insight into the social and historical life of the era. Some may choose to collect by manufacturers such as W.B. Ives, McLoughlin, and J.H. Singer; each has a distinct style of artwork and lithography. Many designs were executed by well-known artists. Collectors may look for sports, track, or educational subject matter. Any of the makers of the 1840-1900 period are worthy of consideration if you are interested in antique games.

20th-century games are also collectible, though most do not have the graphic quality of the early products. Personalities are featured in a large number of games of the 1920s and '30s. In the thirties, famous names from radio became popular subjects, and they were soon joined by TV heroes.

Puzzles were first made in the mid-1850s. Early examples featured subjects that helped educate the young and gave them a look at the world around them. Originally 'jig-saw' types were handcrafted from wood. These early scroll-type puzzles with good lithography have values that are consistent with board games of the same period. By the 1890s, jig-saw puzzles became a major form of home entertainment. In the thirties, they became as popular as the new game of Monopoly. Cube puzzles were often made by the same manufacturers as games, and their litho quality is just as appealing. All subjects are collectible. Some, such as Santa blocks, command prices which may exceed board games.

Antique American Games by Lee Dennis provides an excellent overview of games from 1840-1940. *The Games People Played* (Collectors Showcase, January/February) by Earnest and Ida Long is an excellent review of 19th-century games and historical material on games in general. This magazine has recently featured several other informative articles on games as well as puzzles.

Games

Across the Continent, Parker Bros, 1952, NM 55.00
Aerial Contest, Spear Works, EX in 15½" box 80.00
All Star Baseball, Cadaco, 1968, complete, EX 32.00
Ally-Oop, Royal Toys, 1937, EX...135.00
Apollo, spacecraft game, battery op, NM in box 35.00
As the World Turns..25.00
Authors, Milton Bradley, bust of Bryant on lid............................18.00
Babes in Toyland, Whitman, Disney, 1961, EX in box 25.00
Banana Splits, Hasbro, 1969, MIB 18.00
Barney Miller, Parker Bros, 1977, EX in box 18.00
Battle at Sea, Post's Magic Slate, EX 5.00
Bradley's Circus, Milton Bradley, 1882, EX in box 150.00
Charlie's Angels, Milton Bradley, 1977, EX................................20.00
Check & Double Check, cards, Milton Bradley, 1930, EX 12.50
Congo Bongo, pinball marbles, Wolverine, 11½x20", EX.............38.00
County Fair, board game, Parker Bros, EX 85.00
Crazy Clock, Ideal, 1964, EX...65.00
Crazy Traveler, board game, ca 1892, EX 165.00
Crossword Letter Game, cards, Russell Mfg, 1938, complete 40.00
Dark Shadows, Whitman, 1968, NM..35.00
Department Store, McLoughlin Bros, 1898, 14½x20½", EX........335.00

The Errand Boy, McLoughlin Bros., 1891, EX, $425.00.

Fantastic Voyage, Milton Bradley, 1968, M 15.00
Finance & Fortune, Parker Bros, 1936, complete, EX 27.50
Fire Extinguishers, fire truck on box, Milton Bradley 45.00

Flight to Paris, Milton Bradley, 1920s, EX 85.00
Flying Nun, EX 15.00
Game About the United Nations, Payton, 1961, MIB.................35.00
Game of Letters, Parker, 1890s, VG 50.00
Game of Travel, board game, 1890s, VG 100.00
Gengalee, Game of the East, board game, 1945, EX in box.........15.00
Godzilla, Mattel, 1978, EX 25.00
Good Old Game of Proverbs, Parker Bros, 1890s, EX in box 85.00
Have Gun Will Travel, Parker Bros, 1959, VG 35.00
Jan Murray's TV Word Game, MIB 35.00
Kentucky Derby, spinner-type racing, 1960s, NM in box 17.50
Magnetic Jack Straws, Milton Bradley, 1920s, EX in box..............12.50
McHale's Navy, board game, 1962, VG 27.50
Menageria, board game, 1895, VG in orig box 200.00
Milkman, 4" truck & playing pcs, Hasbro, EX 25.00
Monopoly, Jr edition, wood markers, 1936, VG 30.00
Monopoly, metal markers, no board, 1936, EX 30.00
My First Game, Disney, 1955, EX 37.50
Naval War, McLoughlin Bros, 1898, EX 165.00
North Pole, cb, 1914, VG in box 75.00
O'Grady's Goat, Milton bradley, 1906, EX in colorful box 32.00
Peanuts, 1959, EX 20.00
Perils of Pauline, Marx, 1963, EX 135.00
Peter Coddle's Trip to NY, Milton Bradley, EX in orig box 15.00
Pirates of the Caribbean, Parker Bros, 1965, EX.......................17.50
Pit Bull & Bear Edition, cards, Parker Bros, EX in box................20.00
Pop-Up Store, 3-D board game, Milton Bradley, EX 35.00
Scripture Cards, Improved, McLoughlin, 1888, VG 80.00
Snakey Eyes, Jr Edition, EX 45.00
Squashville County Fair, reading, Parker Bros, 1905, EX 25.00
Student Survival, board game, Gamemasters, 1968, M 38.00
Tale of Wells Fargo, board game, 1959, MIB............................30.00
Taxi, board game, wood pcs, Selchow & Righter, EX in box 25.00
Tip the Bell Boy, 1925, NM in box 85.00
To the North Pole by Air Ship, McLoughlin Bros, EX 200.00
Tomorrowland, Parker Bros, Disney, EX 28.00
United States Postman, 1914, EX in 10x20" box 185.00
Venetian Fortune Teller, cards, Parker Bros, 1942, VG in box......18.00
Voyage of Fear, Whitman, 1979, M 7.50
Walt Disney Tiddley Winks, Whitman, 1963, NM.....................27.50
War at Sea, McLoughlin Bros, 1898, EX 225.00
Welcome Back Kotter, cards, Milton Bradley, 1976, MIB 12.00
Wonder Game of Oz, Parker Bros, 1921, EX in 19" sq box 125.00
World's Fair, board game, Parker Bros, 1890s, EX 265.00

Puzzles

Be Sociable, Gutmann, EX in orig box 35.00
Beach scene, wood, 250-pc, complete, VG 35.00
Bird Strip, paper litho, fr, 1890s, 22x30" 70.00
Boy clown w/fiddle & dog, ca 1900, EX 7.50
Chew Lotties Puzzle Tobacco, boy working puzzle, 10x10½".......145.00
City of Worcester, paper on cb, paddle wheeler, 11x36", EX.....275.00
Continental Automobiles, dbl jigsaw, 10x14", EX 20.00
Couple listen to Victrola, dtd 1922, 8x9" 125.00
Dissecting US Map, McLoughlin 65.00
Dockyard & Ship, All Stages, litho wood, London, 1800s, EX....130.00
Farm scene, wood, made in Holland, rnd, 1940s, complete, NM...30.00
Flying Puzzle, 14 mk wood pcs, put plane in Paris, EX 12.50
Hood's hot air balloon, 1891, fr, 10x14¾", EX 275.00
Hopkins & Allen Arms Co, prairie girl, fr, 21½x10", EX 1,700.00
Horse, McLoughlin, dtd 1898, EX in orig litho box 135.00
Interlocking Alphabet, Gibson Art Co, EX in box........................32.00
Lady & the Tramp, orig...15.00

Little Miss Dixie & Spot, advertising, 1930s, 18x16", NM 65.00
Locomotive Picture Puzzle, McLoughlin Bros, 24½", VG............400.00
Pears Soap, Blk mother w/screaming child, ca 1910, EX 1,500.00
Problem Puzzles, Gilbert, 1930s, set of 6 in box, EX 55.00
Puzzle Parties Game, Gilbert, 1920, EX 25.00
RCA Victor, couple listening to Victrola, 1922, rare, M 150.00
Shasta Through the Pines, wood, 300-pc, VG..............................35.00
Singer, Indians using sewing machine, fr, 7x10", EX.................130.00
Singer, logo on carriage pulled by buffalo, fr, 7x10", EX 75.00
Space Patrol, frame tray 45.00
Sputnick, litho on wood, Japan, 1958, NM 15.00

Tally Ho Puzzle, Seymour Lyman, 1878, box lid only, VG, $550.00.

Total Warfare, War Bonds Minuteman on box, EX 18.00
Victor Talking Machines, record shape, dtd 1908.......................98.00
Wash Day, Milton Bradley 65.00
Wild Bill Hickok, Built Rite, 6¾x10¾", EX 22.50
Wild West, McLoughlin, 1890, 8x12", EX 32.00
World's Columbian Expo, McLoughlin 85.00

G. A. R. Memorabilia

'The Grand Army of the Republic' was first conceived by Chaplain W.J. Rutledge and Major B.J. Stephenson early in 1864 when they were tent-mates during our own Civil War. These men vowed to each other that if they were spared they would establish an organization that would preserve friendships and memories formed during this time. Shortly after the war ended, Rutledge and Stephenson made their desires a reality. The first National Convention of the Grand Army of the Republic was held in Indianapolis, Indiana, on November 20, 1866. The purpose of the organization was to provide aid and assistance to the widows and orphans of the fallen Union dead and to care for the hospitalized veterans as needed. The last comrade of the G.A.R. died in 1949.

Many items are surfacing from the early encampments which were held on both state and national levels, resulting in a wide variety of souvenir items having been made.

Badge, membership; cannon bronze, eagle/flag/star, 2nd issue 40.00
Badge, membership; cannon bronze, eagle/flag/star, 3rd issue 25.00
Book, History of GAR, 1889, EX 75.00
Button, brass, lg or sm, ea 2.00
Cane, Washington, Grant's bust at top, 1892, EX........................50.00
Casket, jewel; eng 1884, Pittsburgh...70.00
Cup, tin, souvenir, printed in red & bl.......................................25.00
Flask, canteen; china, Grant & Lee, 5½x4½" 200.00
Flask, canteen; china, mk Gettysburgh PA, July 1863, 1913 ......150.00
Flask, clear w/label: Encampment Sept 1895, KY, no lid, 6"........450.00

Flask, stoneware, Martyred Presidents decals, 1902......................**145.00**
Goblet, pressed glass, souvenir..**45.00**
Hat, CI, souvenir, blk & gold **25.00**
Match safe, CI, lg wall type, w/logo & all corps insignia **200.00**
Medal, made from captured cannon..**30.00**
Membership application, information completed, 1890s, EX........**10.00**
Pin, bi-metal, Grant Monument, frayed ribbon, Chicago, 1900 ....**35.00**
Pin, brass, Ladies of the GAR, Toledo OH, 1908........................**20.00**
Pin, Excelsior Brewing Co, w/suspended metal, 1897, EX.............**27.50**
Pin-bk button, brass, bl & gold enameling, old, EX....................**15.00**
Post card, 1907...**4.00**
Ribbon, memorial to Gen Grant, 1800s....................................**35.00**
Sword, ceremonial, w/scabbard, clean.....................................**150.00**
Teaspoon, rifle figural hdl, SP, 1894, EX **30.00**

Gas Globes and Panels

Gas globes and panels, once a common sight, have vanished from the countryside but are being sought by collectors as a unique form of advertising memorabilia. Early globes from the 1920s, now referred to as 'one-piece globes,' were made of molded milk glass and were globular in shape. The gas company name was etched or painted on the glass. Few of these were ever produced, and this type is valued very highly by collectors today.

A new type of pump was introduced in the early 1930s; the old 'visible' pumps were replaced by 'electric' models. Globes were changing at the same time. By the mid-thirties, a five-piece globe consisting of a pair of inserts, two retaining rings, and a metal body was being produced in both 15" and 16½" sizes. Collectors prefer to call globes that are not one-piece or plastic 'three-piece glass' (Type 2) or 'metal body, glass inserts' (Type 3). Though metal body globes (Type 3) were popular in the 1930s, they were common in the 1920s, and some were actually made as early as 1915. Though rare in numbers, their use spans many years. In the 1930s, Type 2 and Type 3 globes became the replacements of the one-piece globe. The most recently manufactured gas globes, used since the late 1940s, are made with a plastic body that contains two 13½" glass lenses.

Note: Standard Crowns with raised letters are one-piece globes that were made in the 1920s; those made in the 1950s (no raised letters), though one-piece, are not regarded as such by today's collectors. Both variations are listed below.

Our advisor for this category is Scott Benjamin; he is listed in the Directory under California.

Type 1, Plastic Body, Glass Inserts—1931-1950s

Ashland Diesel...**125.00**
Champlin...**125.00**
D-X Marine, rare...**325.00**
Deeprock...**125.00**
Dixie, plastic band..**125.00**
DX Ethyl..**125.00**
DX Lubricating Gasoline, tan body **150.00**
Falcon..**300.00**
Frontier Gas, Rarin' To Go, w/horse.......................................**225.00**
Marathon, no runner **90.00**
Marine, sea horse, EX color...**325.00**
Never Nox Ethyl..**150.00**
Shamrock, oval body...**150.00**
Shamrock, w/clover...**150.00**
Spur..**125.00**
Texaco Sky Chief...**100.00**
Viking, pictures Viking ship..**200.00**

Wood River..**125.00**
66 Flite Fuel, Phillips, shield shape **175.00**

Type 2, Glass Frame, Glass Inserts—1926-1940s

American..**200.00**
Atlantic Hi-Arc, glass gill body..**225.00**
Coltex Service Gasoline, unused **250.00**
Crown, crown figural w/red traces, 16", EX **185.00**
Derby...**225.00**
Esso..**150.00**
Frontier Gas, no horse...**175.00**
Gulf..**250.00**

Guyler Brand, three-piece globe with milk glass frame and two colorful glass lenses, 18", $600.00.

Indian Gas, Red Dot..**275.00**
Koolmotor, clover shape..**400.00**
Mobil Gas **225.00**
Pure..**200.00**
Shell, milk glass, clam shape **350.00**
Shell, shell shape, red letters...**325.00**
Sinclair Dino, milk glass, EX...**175.00**
Sinclair H-C, narrow glass body, Red Dot **200.00**
Sinclair Pennant...**325.00**
Skelly Anomarx w/Ethyl...**250.00**
Skelly Powermax..**200.00**
Spartan...**210.00**
Standard Crown, bl, gr, & orange **450.00**
Standard Crown, wht, red, & gold **300.00**
Texaco Diesel Chief..**250.00**
Texaco Ethyl..**325.00**
Texaco Star, blk outline on 'T' **225.00**
Trophy, Our Premium Gasoline...**200.00**
White Flash, gill body...**200.00**
White Rose, glass body, 13½"..**375.00**
WNAX..**400.00**

Type 3, Metal Frame, Glass Inserts—1915-1930s

Atlantic Ethyl, 16½"...**350.00**
Atlantic White Flash, 16½"...**350.00**
Cities Services Oils, 15" metal fr, 1929....................................**350.00**
Essolene, 16" **250.00**
Happy Gas, metal band, 16½" **325.00**
Mobil Gas, winged horse, metal fr, NM **400.00**
Mobilfuel Diesel, lg horse, high profile, metal band........................**425.00**
Multipower (Marathon), 15" **1,000.00**
Pure, porc body, 15"...**400.00**

Purol Gasoline, w/arrow, porc body 650.00
Purol Pep, porc body..450.00
Red Crown Ethyl 425.00
Richfield 375.00
Rocor, w/eagle, metal fr 450.00
Signal, rstr metal fr, 19", VG 1,500.00
Socony, milk glass inserts 650.00
Sunland Ethyl, 15"..350.00
Sunoco, 15", pr 300.00
Texaco Leaded, glass panels, in fr, pr....................... 1,800.00
Tidex, 16" 350.00
Tydol, cast faces, 15" 500.00
Tydol, 16½"..350.00
White Star, rfn metal fr, General Ethyl face on bk, 19", EX 400.00

Type 4, One-Piece Glass Globes, No Inserts, Co. Name Etched, Raised or Enameled—1914-1931

Atlantic, chimney cap 2,200.00
Champlin Gasoline 850.00
Diamond 550.00
Dixie, etched, 1-pc...900.00
Gasoline, emb on dk gr ground, 14", NM 375.00
Iowa Gas 850.00
Mobil Oil Gargoyle, emb, red & blk details, 12", EX.............. 1,000.00
Musgo 2,000.00
Pierce Pennant, etched 1,600.00
Red Crown, rnd, etched 1,800.00
Republic, English Globe, 1-pc 300.00
Shell, rnd, etched 450.00
Sinclair, etched, milk glass 650.00
Sinclair Aircraft, etched 2,200.00
Sinclair Aircraft, pnt 1,600.00
Sinclair H-C, pnt 600.00
Skelly 600.00
Standard Red Crown Ethyl, emb letters 600.00
Super Shell, clam shape 750.00
Super Shell, rnd, etched.. 1,400.00
Texaco, milk glass, emb letters, brass collar 500.00
Texaco Ethyl...650.00
That Good Gulf..., emb, orange & blk letters, 16", EX 700.00
White Eagle, eagle shape, blunt nose............................800.00
White Rose, pnt 1,700.00

Gaudy Dutch

Inspired by Oriental Imari wares, Gaudy Dutch was made in England from 1800 to 1820. It was hand decorated on a soft-paste body with rich underglaze blues accented in orange, red, pink, green, and yellow. It differs from Gaudy Welsh in that there is no lustre (except on Water Lily). There are seventeen patterns, some of which are: War Bonnet, Grape, Dahlia, Oyster, Urn, Butterfly, Carnation, Single Rose, Double Rose, and Water Lily.

Butterfly, creamer 850.00
Butterfly, cup plate 675.00
Butterfly, pitcher, milk; 4", M 800.00
Butterfly, plate, 6½", M 650.00
Butterfly, plate, 9¾", M 950.00
Butterfly, sugar bowl, M 1,200.00
Butterfly, tea bowl & saucer, EX 650.00
Butterfly, teapot, squat baluster form, 5", M 1,800.00
Butterfly, waste bowl 900.00

Zinnia, 8¼" plate, marked Riley, NM, $900.00.

Carnation, bowl, 8¼", NM...600.00
Carnation, plate, 8", EX..550.00
Carnation, plate, 9¾", EX..700.00
Carnation, soup plate, 9", M.......................................800.00
Carnation, sugar bowl, EX..650.00
Carnation, tea bowl & saucer, M....................................475.00
Carnation, tea bowl & saucer, rstr.................................265.00
Dahlia, sugar bowl...950.00
Dahlia, tea bowl & saucer 750.00
Double Rose, creamer, M..500.00
Double Rose, plate, 10"..800.00
Double Rose, plate, 7", M..425.00
Double Rose, soup plate, 9", M.....................................600.00
Double Rose, tea bowl & saucer, M 475.00
Double Rose, teapot, NM... 1,300.00
Double Rose, waste bowl, 3x5½", EX.................................475.00
Dove, plate, 10", M..900.00
Dove, plate, 8", M...500.00
Dove, sugar bowl, w/lid..750.00
Dove, tea bowl & saucer, M...550.00
Dove, waste bowl, M..650.00
Grape, creamer 600.00
Grape, plate, pnt flaking, 9¾"......................................250.00
Grape, plate, toddy, 5", NM..425.00
Grape, plate, wear/sm rpr, 8"......................................300.00
Grape, plate, 7", M..475.00
Grape, plate, 9¾", M...600.00
Grape, tea bowl & saucer, EX.......................................350.00
Grape, teapot, hairlines/lt stains, 6½"............................500.00
Grape, teapot, imperfections, 6½", NM..............................600.00
Oyster, ceramer, M...600.00
Oyster, plate, minor wear, 9¼".....................................475.00
Oyster, soup plate, 8½", EX..450.00
Oyster, tea bowl & saucer, M.......................................550.00
Single Rose, coffeepot, dbl gourd form, 10¾", M................ 1,800.00
Single Rose, plate, minor wear, 9¾"................................425.00
Single Rose, plate, 7", M..475.00
Single Rose, plate, 8", M..475.00
Single Rose, sugar bowl, w/lid, M..................................650.00
Single Rose, tea bowl & saucer, M..................................450.00
Strawflower, creamer, M..800.00
Strawflower, plate, 8", M..650.00
Strawflower, soup plate, EX..800.00
Strawflower, tea bowl & saucer, M..................................650.00
Urn, creamer...600.00
Urn, plate, sectional border, 7"...................................550.00

Urn, plate, 5", M	500.00
War Bonnet, creamer, M	700.00
War Bonnet, plate, M	650.00
War Bonnet, plate, minor flaking, 8"	450.00
War Bonnet, plate, toddy; M	475.00
War Bonnet, tea bowl & saucer, NM	525.00
War Bonnet, teapot	1,500.00
War Bonnet, teapot, prof rpr, crow's ft/wear, 5⅞"	750.00
Water Lily, tea bowl & saucer, EX	500.00

Gaudy Ironstone

Gaudy Ironstone was produced in the mid-1800s in Staffordshire, England. Some of the ware was decorated in much the same colors and designs as Gaudy Welsh, while other pieces were painted in pink, orange, and red with black and light blue accents. Lustre was used on some designs, omitted on others. The heavy ironstone body is its most distinguishing feature.

Key:
pc — polychrome   ug bl — underglaze blue

Cup & saucer, handleless; floral w/urn	150.00
Pitcher, floral, dragon hdl, octagonal, 6", pr	350.00
Plate, deep, Flow Blue, 9¼"	120.00
Plate, urn pattern, minor wear, 8¾", pr	300.00
Platter, rose, 4-color, mk England, 13"	175.00
Teapot, floral, w/luster, fruit final, mk Walley, 9½", VG	235.00

Gaudy Welsh

Gaudy Welsh was an inexpensive hand-decorated ware made in both England and Wales from 1820 until 1860. It is characterized by its colors — principally underglaze blue, orange-rust, and copper lustre — and by its uninhibited patterns. Accent colors may be yellow and green. (Pink lustre may be present, since lustre applied to the white areas appears pink. A copper tone develops from painting lustre onto the dark colors.) The body of the ware may be heavy ironstone, creamware, earthenware, or porcelain; even style and shapes vary considerably. Patterns, while usually floral, are also sometimes geometric and may have trees and birds. Beware — the Wagon Wheel pattern has been reproduced!

Asian, cup & saucer	95.00
Carnation, cup & saucer	75.00
Cherry Tree, creamer, 5½"	175.00
Cherry Tree, cup & saucer	100.00
Cherry Tree, plate, 7"	150.00
Cherry Tree, teapot	525.00
Columbine, cup & saucer	50.00
Columbine, plate, 7½"	50.00
Columbine, plate, 8"	85.00
Columbine, waste bowl, 6½"	55.00
Daisy & Chain, creamer	150.00
Daisy & Chain, cup & saucer	75.00
Daisy & Chain, sugar bowl, w/lid	150.00
Daisy & Chain, teapot	325.00
Feather, cake plate	60.00
Flower Basket, bowl, 10½"	195.00
Flower Basket, cup & saucer	65.00
Flower Basket, plate, 12-sided, purple lustre trim, 8⅞"	80.00
Flower Basket, sugar bowl, w/lustre, lion's-head hdls, lid	145.00

Flower Basket, teapot, underglaze bl/mc/pk lustre, 7", VG	325.00
Grape, creamer, 4"	110.00
Grape, cup & saucer	80.00
Grape, mug, cobalt leaves/rust-colored vine, 2¼x2¼"	70.00
Grape II, mug, cobalt floral, orange petals, 2⅜x2⅛"	75.00
Grape VII, pitcher & bowl set, mini, 4"	295.00
Morning-Glory, bowl, red/gr berries, octagonal, 8⅝", NM	110.00
Morning-Glory, bowl, shell form, 7½" L, EX	90.00
Morning-Glory, creamer, 5", EX	100.00
Morning-Glory, cup & saucer, 5", EX	75.00
Morning-Glory, pitcher, underglaze bl w/purple lustre, 8"	195.00
Morning-Glory, plate, toddy; 4⅜", EX	65.00
Morning-Glory, plate, 8", NM	60.00
Morning-Glory, sugar bowl, w/lid	95.00

Oyster, bowl, 4" x 8", $75.00.

Oyster, creamer, 1820s, 3¾", M	80.00
Oyster, cup & saucer	60.00
Oyster, jug, hot water	100.00
Oyster, pitcher, 4½x4½"	90.00
Pagoda, cup & saucer	100.00
Pagoda, pitcher, 8"	295.00
Pagoda, plate, 7"	135.00
Peacock, pitcher, 8"	495.00
Peppermint, cup & saucer	115.00
Poppy, cup & saucer	70.00
Pot de Fleurs II, vase, 4½"	325.00
Rhoda, cup & saucer	85.00
Sahara, cup & saucer	125.00
Shanghai, creamer	120.00
Shanghai, plate, 5½"	85.00
Shanghai, sugar bowl, w/lid	110.00
Sunflower, creamer, 5"	200.00
Sunflower, cup & saucer	95.00
Sunflower, pitcher, 7½"	275.00
Trumpet, cup & saucer	95.00
Trumpet, pitcher, 8"	325.00
Tulip, creamer	90.00
Tulip, mug, mini, 1⅞"	25.00
Tulip, plate, 6"	45.00
Tulip, sugar bowl, 6¾"	140.00
Tulip, teapot, ca 1840	180.00
Tulip, wine, 2½"	275.00
Venus, cup & saucer	120.00
Village, creamer, 5"	175.00
Village, cup & saucer	110.00
Village, plate, 7½"	135.00

Geisha Girl

Upon the discovery of tea in China some four thousand years ago, civilization was beset with a small problem — what to use in serving this special beverage. One solution came in the form of 'Geisha Girl' porcelain. At the end of the 19th century, this lovely type of Japanese tea service found its way to the west. Produced in more than sixty-five patterns, this fine porcelain features geishas going about the everyday activities of Japanese life. Mt. Fuji is very often included in the background along with a wide variety of flora and fauna. Though some items were entirely hand painted and others were hand decorated over decals, most were made by the raised stencil method. Tea sets, snack sets, children's items, salt and pepper shakers, and even such items as mustache cups may be found. Pieces were bordered in one of many bright colors — red, yellow, blue, green, or brown. (Colors mentioned in the descriptions that follow refer to border colors.) As interest continues to climb, so will the values. For further information, we recommend *The Collector's Encyclopedia of Geisha Girl Porcelain* by Elyce Litts, available at your local bookstore or from Collector Books.

```
Key:
#2 — Torii                    #20 — Made in Japan
#4 — T in Cherry Blossom      #35 — Plum Blossom
#19 — Japan                   #J16 — Kutani
```

Bowl, Boat Festival, lt cobalt, #35, 8"	25.00
Bowl, Feeding the Carp, red w/gold, 6"	18.00
Bowl, Flower Gathering, pine gr, #19, 9"	25.00
Bowl, master berry; Thousand Geisha, cobalt w/gold	35.00
Bowl, master nut; Porch, cobalt	25.00
Bowl, Tea Time, lobed, red w/gold, 7½"	23.00
Butter pat, Duck Watching B, red, 4¼"	8.00
Cake plate, Meeting C, hdls, waves in red-orange, 11"	28.00
Candy jar, Sm Sounds of Summer, red w/gold	75.00
Celery dish, Battledore, apple gr w/gold	38.00
Celery dish, Vantine's Bl, floriated edge, 6-lobed	34.00
Compote, Duck Watching, ftd, enameled, 7½"	95.00
Creamer, Basket B, ftd, dk apple gr	20.00
Creamer, Garden, ribbed, bl-gr w/gold, 4"	15.00
Creamer, Pointing A, red, #20, 2½"	14.00
Creamer, River's Edge, red-orange, stenciled	10.00
Creamer, Samurai & Geisha, bulbous	12.00
Creamer & sugar bowl, Child Reaching for Butterfly, pine gr	26.00
Creamer & sugar bowl, Flute & Koto, red w/gold buds	22.00
Creamer & sugar bowl, Garden Beach L, maroon w/gold	35.00
Creamer & sugar bowl, Lesson, bl w/gold	25.00
Creamer & sugar bowl, Waterboy, pine gr	15.00
Cup & saucer, Bamboo Trellis, dk gr	18.00
Cup & saucer, Cloud A, red-orange w/yel	10.00
Cup & saucer, cocoa; Fan B, red w/gold	18.00
Cup & saucer, tea; Flower Gathering B, maroon	10.00
Cup & saucer, tea; Lady in Rickshaw B, red	13.00
Hatpin holder, Prayer Ribbon, swirl fluted, red	45.00
Hatpin holder, Temple A, mc	45.00
Mustard jar, Daikoku, red w/gold lacing	25.00
Pitcher, Rokkasen, red w/yel, 3"	12.00
Plate, Bamboo Tree, 6"	5.00
Plate, Dragonboat, cobalt w/gold, #J16, 8"	45.00
Plate, Dressing, red, 7"	12.00
Plate, Feather Fan, plain rnd	10.00
Plate, Garden Beach D, swirl fluted, waves in red-orange, 6"	10.00
Plate, Gardening, bl w/gold, #2, 7"	20.00
Plate, Rendevous, cobalt w/gold, J16, 7"	20.00

Plate, Servant w/Sacks, scalloped, red-orange w/gold, 6½"	10.00
Plate, Temple B, red w/gold buds, 7"	12.00
Powder jar, Footbridge A	32.00
Saucer, Picnic C, cobalt bl	7.00
Shakers, Basket A, sea gr, pr	16.00
Shakers, Bouncing Ball, bl-gr, pr	22.00
Shakers, Torii & Parasol B, red-orange, pr	10.00
Teapot, Geisha in Sampan A, gold, decal, #20	15.00
Tray, dresser; Parasol E, diamond-shaped, red	29.00

German Porcelain

Unless otherwise noted, the porcelain listed in this section is marked simply 'Germany.' Products of other German manufactures are listed in specific categories. See also Bisque; Pink Pigs; Elfinware.

Biscuit jar, cobalt bl w/mc floral panels, 6x7½"	180.00
Bottle, scent; gallant w/pug dog under his arm, 1880s, 3½"	150.00
Bowl, trunk std w/putti & vines, rtcl, HP flowers, 17", EX	350.00
Box, gr lustre w/gold, emb reserve w/classical female, 3"	100.00
Brooch, cherub embraces maid amongst clouds, gilt fr, 2½"	225.00
Centerpiece, girl between 2 shell bowls w/cupids, 9x17"	395.00
Chocolate pot, lovers in garden, Kauffman, Selesia, 10"	225.00
Dish, Victorian lady, 4" dia, set of 6	75.00
Figurine, courting couple, he bends over her hand, 7"	125.00
Figurine, girl w/kitten, bl & pk, ca 1920, 14½"	250.00
Figurine, lady in chair w/mending, pastels, 8¾x5x2¾"	225.00
Figurine, lady in toga cvg bust of man w/chisel, 8"	275.00
Figurine, peasant girl plays harmonica, Fisher, 10"	45.00

Jar, Cupid in reserve on 'snow baby'-textured background with gold dots, 5", $110.00.

Pipe bowl, head of man in jeweled turban, metal mts, 1800s	**1,500.00**
Pitcher, floral sprigs, gilt border, ovoid, 1800s, 12"	150.00
Plaque, 3 boys play dice, dog/basket of fruit, 1880s, 7½"	450.00
Plate, floral, wide raspberry border, 10½", set of 12	600.00
Tureen, blanc de chine, 4 cupid supports, appl flowers, 10"	250.00
Vase, appl fruit/twigs/birds, floral finial, 1880s, 18"	225.00
Vase, florals, putti at hdls, ped ft, w/lid, 7", pr	275.00

Gladding McBean and Company

This company was established in 1875 in Lincoln, California. They first produced only clay drainage pipes, but in 1883 architectural terra cotta was introduced, which has been used extensively in the

United States as well as abroad. Sometime later a line of garden pottery was added. They soon became the leading producers of tile in the country. In 1923 they purchased the Tropico Pottery in Glendale, California, where in addition to tile they also produced huge garden vases. Their line was expanded in 1934 to included artware and dinnerware.

At least fifteen lines of art pottery were developed between 1934 and 1942. For a short time they stamped their wares with the Tropico Pottery mark; but the majority was signed 'GMcB' in an oval. Later the mark was changed to 'Franciscan' with several variations. After 1937 'Catalina Pottery' was used on some lines. (All items marked 'Catalina Pottery' were made in Glendale.)

Bowl, Coronado Art Ware, ivory satin, low, 13" 30.00
Candle holder, Capistrano Art Ware, ivory/celadon, sq, pr 28.00
Coffeepot, demitasse; Ruby Art Ware...68.00
Compote, Avalon Art Ware, turq/ivory, 8" 18.00
Flower bowl, Tropico Art Ware 20.00
Jardiniere, Tropico Art Ware, turq...17.50
Lamp base, Ox Blood Art Ware, detached underplate 60.00
Tile, angel fish, 6x6"...50.00
Vase, Bamboo, ivory/gr, cylindrical, 8" 45.00
Vase, bud; Encanto Art Ware, celadon..10.00

Vase, periwinkle/blue texture, marked Catalina Pottery USA, 6", $95.00.

Vase, Catalina Art Ware, coral satin, ribbed, 7¾"...........................27.50
Vase, Coronado Art Ware, ivory satin, bulbous base, 8½" 28.00
Vase, Coronado Art Ware, turq satin, 10½"....................................25.00
Vase, Garden Ware, bl-gr, bead relief at neck, 35"......................500.00
Vase, Ox Blood Art Ware, 11"...175.00

Glidden

Genius designer Glidden Parker established Glidden Pottery in 1940 in Alfred, New York, having been schooled at the unrivaled New York State College of Ceramics at Alfred University. Glidden pottery is characterized by a fine stoneware body, innovative forms, outstanding hand-milled glazes, and hand decoration which make the pieces individual works of art. Production consisted of casual dinnerware, accessories, and artware that was distributed internationally.

In 1949 Glidden Pottery became the second ceramic plant in the country to utilize the revolutionary Ram pressing machine. This allowed for increased production and for the most part eliminated the previously used slip-casting method. However Glidden stoneware continued to reflect the same superb quality of craftsmanship until the factory closed in 1957. Although the majority of form and decorative patterns were Mr. Parker's personal designs, Fong Chow and Sergio Dello Strologo also designed award-winning lines.

Glidden will be found marked on the unglazed underside with a signature that is hand incised, mold impressed, or ink stamped. Interest in this unique stoneware is growing as collectors discover that it embodies the very finest of Mid-Century High Style. Our advisor is David Pierce; he is listed in the Directory under Ohio.

In the Ric Rac pattern (yellow): Cup, #141, 2¾" x 5¼", $10.00; Saucer, #142, 6" square, $5.00; Teapot, #140, 9", $30.00; Sugar bowl, #144, with lid, 6", $20.00.

Ash tray, leaves (Fred Press), #274, 5½" sq.................................15.00
Bottle, dressing; Alfred Stoneware, Saffron, #812, 5½x5½"..........40.00
Bowl, cobalt, #15, 4x7x5¼"..15.00
Bowl, High Tide, #17, 4¼x8"...20.00
Bowl, Plaid, #27, 1¼x5¾x5¾"...15.00
Bowl, Turq Matrix, #26, 1¼x6½x5" 8.00
Canister, Garden, #601, w/lid, 5x5½"...30.00
Casserole, Sage & Sand, #167, w/lid, 4¼x5¼" 8.00
Casserole, Will o' the Wisp, #165, w/lid, 5½x8½".........................20.00
Coaster, Mexican Cock, #19, 4" sq 6.00
Creamer, Boston Spice, #1430, 3½x6x3½"......................................25.00
Cup, Pear, #141, 2¾x5¼"..12.00
Lug soup, Viridian, #467, 3½x7½x6"...15.00
Pitcher, Boston Spice, #614, 1½-pt 35.00
Planter, Turq Matrix, #122, 2x6"..15.00
Plate, canape; Chi-Chi Poodle, #35, 5½" sq 6.00
Plate, canape; Weathervane, #35, 5½" sq.......................................25.00
Plate, chop; Feather, wht englobe, #608, 17"................................35.00
Plate, Feather, wht englobe, #31, 10¼" sq 8.00
Plate, Handsome Fish, Viridian, 3410, 8x7¼"..................................25.00
Plate, Marine Fantasia, Lucent Gr, #431, 11½x10¼" 40.00
Tumbler, Menagerie, Hippo, #1127, 5½"..20.00
Tumbler, striped, bl, #1127, 5¼x3¼"...10.00
Vase, early pk, pillow form, #128, 4½x5¼x2½" 10.00
Vase, Loop Artware, purple, #945, 10½x6" 200.00
Vase, Yellowstone, ball form, #49, 6½x6" 35.00

Goebel

F.W. Goebel founded the Hummelwork Porcelain Manufactory in 1871, located in Rodental, West Germany. They produced porcelain figurines, plates, and novelties, the most famous of which are the Hummel figurines (these are listed in a separate section). There were many other series produced by Goebel — Disney characters, birds, animals, Art Deco figurines, and the Friar Tuck Monks that are especially popular.

Ash tray, Friar Tuck Monks, 3-line mk 75.00

Creamer, Cardinal, 4½" 85.00
Creamer, Friar Tuck Monk, stylized bee mk, 2½" 30.00
Decanter, Friar Tuck Monks, bee mk............................165.00
Egg cup, Friar Tuck Monks, stylized bee mk 30.00
Figurine, boxer dog sitting, crown mk, 4½x6" 65.00
Figurine, donkey, brn, full bee mk, 1x2½x3" 85.00
Figurine, girl holds cat, 1958, 6" 50.00
Figurine, Madonna, ¾-figure, crown mk, 3½" 60.00
Figurine, Mary, Joseph, & Christ Child, 5" 40.00
Figurine, peacock, blk/tan/yel/gr, 1984, 11x16" 90.00

Dancer, floral dress, signed Latour, 8", $400.00.

Poodle, 7" x 8", $68.00.

Figurine, shepherd boy, full bee mk, #200, 6" 75.00
Humidor, Friar Tuck Monks, stylized bee mk 220.00
Mug, Friar Tuck Monks, stylized bee mk, 5" 65.00
Mustard jar, Cardinal, stylized bee mk 145.00
Mustard jar, Friar Tuck Monks, bee mk 70.00
Nativity set, #HX-257, ca 1959, 11-pc 325.00
Night light, jester/devil/owl, Deco style, 1925, 10" 200.00
Shakers, Friar Tuck Monks, stylized bee mk, 2⅜" 35.00
Shakers, Friar Tuck Musicians, pr 30.00
Sugar bowl, Friar Tuck Monks, stylized bee mk 37.50

Goldscheider

The Goldscheider family operated a pottery in Vienna for many generations before seeking refuge in the United States following Hitler's invasion of their country. They settled in Trenton, New Jersey, in the early 1940s where they established a new corporation and began producing objects of art and tableware items. In 1946 Marcel Goldscheider established a pottery in Staffordshire where he manufactured bone china figures, earthenware, etc., marked with a stamp of his signature. Larger artist-signed examples from either location are very valuable.

Figurine, butterfly girl, Lorenzl, rstr, 18½" 2,300.00
Figurine, Chinese princess, Lindloff, #8950, 12" 150.00
Figurine, dancer in full yel dress, Latour, 8¾" 400.00
Figurine, lady, White Christmas, 6½" 75.00
Figurine, lady holding skirt of blk & wht lace dress, 7½" 150.00
Figurine, lady in bl floral dress walks forward, Dakon, 19".......1,400.00
Figurine, lady in pk gown holds fan, 12" 195.00
Figurine, lady w/flower basket, USA, 7½" 75.00
Figurine, lady w/umbrella, 11½" 95.00
Figurine, Madonna, 3-quarter length, 5" 60.00
Figurine, Madonna bust, wooden base, 9½" 85.00
Figurine, Yankee Doodle Dandy, 7" 80.00

Gonder

Lawton Gonder grew up a ceramist. By the time he opened his own pottery in December, 1941, he had a solid background in both production and management. Gonder Ceramic Arts, Inc., purchased the old Peters and Reed — Zane Pottery in South Zanesville, Ohio. There they turned out quality commercial ware with graceful shapes in both Oriental and contemporary designs. Their greatest achievements were the development of their superior glazes: flambe; 24k gold crackle; and Chinese crackle glazes in celadon, ming yellow, and blue. Most of the ware is marked with 'Gonder' impressed in script and a mold number.

Basket, pk/bl, L-019, 12x9" 25.00
Basket, yel/br, pk int, H-39, 8x6¾" 10.00
Bowl, yel, ribbing, E-12, 6½" 6.00
Candle holder, fish, #561, 5", pr 18.00
Cornucopia, bl/pk, #521, 12" L 20.00
Ewer, knuckle hdl, E-65, 6¼" 7.00
Ewer, tan/gray mottle, pk int, bulbous bottom, H-73, 7½" 10.00

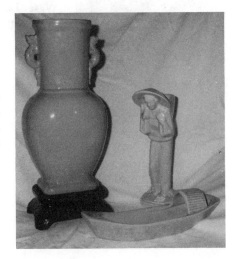

Oriental vase with base, #535, 14", $35.00; Coolie, #519, 9", $15.00; Sampan, #550, 9½", $8.50.

Pitcher, gr/tan mottle, pk int, J-69, 9⅜" 9.00
Planter, Madonna, bl, pk int, E-303, 5¾" 15.00

Planter, swan, J-31, 6x7" 12.00
Planter, swan, yel w/pk mottle, E-44, 5".................... 8.00
Vase, Nordic style w/horns, gold crackle, H-604, 9¼" 25.00
Vase, twisted body w/3 fish at base, H-85, 8½" 11.00

Goofus Glass

Goofus was an inexpensive type of lustre-painted pressed glassware made by many companies during the first two decades of the 20th century. Bowls and trays are most common, and red and gold combinations are found more often than blues and greens.

Bottle, scent; pk tulips, orig pnt & stopper, 3½", EX 20.00
Bowl, belle rose, orig pnt, sq, 5½", EX........................40.00
Bowl, butterfly, hexagonal, orig pnt, 8", EX................45.00
Bowl, dahlias, orig pnt, 10", EX..................................35.00
Bowl, grapes on amethyst, scalloped, sq, orig pnt, 10", EX 75.00
Bowl, pine cones & roses, 8-sided, orig pnt, 9½", EX 45.00
Bowl, roses, 5-sided, rpt, 9" 75.00
Cake plate, carnations, rpt, 12" 30.00
Cake plate, morning-glory, rpt, 12"...........................35.00
Candy dish, figure-8 design, serrated rim, orig pnt, 8½" 55.00
Card holder, poppies, gold w/red, orig pnt, 4x7", NM 20.00
Coaster, flowers, orig pnt, rare, 3" dia, EX, set of 4 ......40.00
Compote, cherry, ruffled, orig pnt, 10", EX.................100.00
Compote, Grape & Cable, rpt, 4" 35.00
Lamp, oil; cabbage roses on amethyst, orig pnt, 15", M 100.00
Lamp, Roses in Snow, glass base, w/chimney, orig pnt, 15" 95.00
Plate, Easter Greetings, chick hatching, orig pnt, 7½" 30.00
Plate, monk drinking, rose edge, orig pnt, rare, 7", EX 35.00
Plate, poppy, gr, mkd N, 7"......................................30.00
Powder box, puffy roses, orig pnt, 3x5" 45.00
Tray, dresser; cabbage rose, orig pnt, 6", EX 30.00
Vase, cabbage rose, baluster, orig silver pnt, 12", EX 40.00

Vase, Dogwood Blossoms and Hearts, 15", $50.00.

Vase, grape cluster on crackle, cylindrical, rpt, 14" 60.00
Vase, grape clusters, thick glass, baluster, rpt, 10" 25.00
Vase, peacock, bulbous, rpt, rare, 10½"....................100.00
Vase, peacock in tree, baluster, orig pnt, 15", EX 100.00
Vase, Roses in Snow, classic form, rpt, 10" 20.00

Goss

William Henry Goss received his early education at the Govern-

ment School of Design and as a result of his merit was introduced to Alderman William Copeland, who owned a large pottery firm. Under the influence of Copeland, Goss quickly learned the trade and soon became their chief designer. Little is known about this brief association, and in 1858 Goss left to begin his own business. After a short-lived partnership with a Mr. Peake, Goss opened a pottery on John Street, Stoke-on-Trent, but by 1870 he had moved to his business to a location near London Road. This pottery became the famous Falcon Works.

Many of the early pieces made by Goss were left unmarked and are difficult to discern from products made by the Copeland factory, but after he had been in business for about fifteen years, all of his wares were marked. Today, unmarked items do not command the prices of the later marked wares.

Adulphus William Henry Goss joined his father's firm in the 1880s. He introduced cheaper lines, though the more expensive lines continued in production. Shortly after his father's death in 1906, Adulphus retired and left the business to his two younger brothers. The business suffered from problems created by a war economy, and in 1936 Goss assets were held by Cauldron Potteries Ltd. These were eventually taken over by the Coalport Group, who retained the right to use the Goss trademark. Messrs. Ridgeway Potteries bought all the assets in 1954, as well as the right to use the Goss trademark and name. Now it remains to be seen if Goss ware will ever be produced again.

Abbots cup, Fountains Abbey 25.00
Beer barrel, Burton, Kingston on Hull 30.00
Beer bowl, dragon 25.00
Bottle, Sunderland, Sir William Wallace......................32.00
Bowl, Glastonbury, Dawlish 18.00
Bowl, Scarlett, #38660...35.00
Cup, Fountain's Abby, Gloucester Modern 32.00
Cup, St George, Wiltshire, Calne, 3-hdl.......................25.00
Ewer, Japan, Windsor crest......................................37.50
Flask, Caerleon Tear, Ilfracombe................................24.00
Font, Bexhill-N-Sea 185.00
Huer's House...200.00
Irish Mather, Hastings...20.00
Jug, Dorchester, Arms of Australia............................24.00
Jug, Kendall, Assyrian Armour 25.00
Jug, Litchfield, St Alban's Abbey 30.00
Jug, Newcastle Roman, Falmouth..............................32.00
Jug, Reading, Frinton on Sea....................................25.00
Jug, Spanish, Eddystone, Hastings 37.50
Jug, St George 25.00
Kettle, Hastings, Colchester.....................................27.50
Look Out House 140.00
Manx Cottage..105.00
Milk can, Welsh, St Helena 25.00
Pipkin, Southampton, Blairgowrie.............................32.00
Pitcher, Devon Oak, Ipwich.....................................30.00
Porridge pot, Guy's, Waswick...................................42.00
Pot, Roman, Painswick, Arundel................................18.00
Pot, Roman, Painswick, London Hospital 24.00
Rufus Stone...40.00
Shaker, Scarborough, early mk 32.00
Shakespeare's House..100.00
St Nicholas Chapel...200.00
Urn, Leek British, Fareham 24.00
Urn, Mullelburg, Norway, Kirkpark 25.00
Urn, Seaford, Sir Thomas Lucy of Charlelot 36.00
Vase, bud; St Andrews University, sm 28.00
Vase, Exeter, Brighton..28.00
Vase, Exeter, Sheffield..22.50
Wall pocket, Christ Church, lg...................................32.00

Water jug, Egyptian, Wickford 32.00
Yorick's Skull..135.00
1st & Last House 135.00

Gouda

Since the 18th century the main center of the pottery industry in Holland was in Gouda. One of its earliest industries, the manufacture of clay pipes, continues to the present day. The artware so easily recognized by collectors today was first produced about 1885. It was decorated in the Art Nouveau manner. Stylized florals, birds, and geometrics were favored motifs; only rarely is the scene naturalistic. The Nouveau influence was strong until about 1915. Art Deco was attempted but with less success. Though most of the ware is finished in a matt glaze, glossy pieces in both pastels and dark colors are found on occasion and command higher prices. Decoration on the glossy ware is usually very well executed. Most of the workshops failed during the depression, though earthenware is still being made in Gouda and carries the Gouda mark. Until very recently, Regina was still making a limited amount of the old Gouda-style pottery in a matt finish. Watch for the Gouda name, which is usually a part of the backstamp of the various manufacturers.

Ash tray, Dutch shoe form, mc, mk, 2¼x5¼" 55.00
Bowl, floral, w/lid, Anjer house mk, #3888, 6" 70.00

**Bowl, marked Koninkiyk #4816/30, Delores, Royal Crown, 11½",
$195.00.**

Candlestick, mc Nouveau motif, self saucer, mk Candis, 3¾" 50.00
Decanter, mc florals on blk, ped ft, Nadra, 10½x3¼" 150.00
Ewer, Kabor, floral, crown mk, 1925, 8"................................30.00
Lantern, canister w/cone top, loop atop, rpl font, 9" 250.00
Pitcher, tulip on gr to gray, house mk, 7½"............................60.00
Plate, mc florals w/blk, Nadra, 12" 110.00
Rose bowl, Anjer, naturalistic florals, house mk, 4" 35.00
Vase, blk matt w/bl & mustard trim, house mk, 7½"..................65.00
Vase, floral, mc on blk high gloss, Regina, 10" 125.00
Vase, high glaze, sq, 4-hdl, Zuid Holland, 9x4x4" 250.00
Vase, lg stylized orchids, mc, house mk, sgn AR, 17" 650.00
Vase, Padua, florals on blk, Arnhem Holland, 8" 45.00
Vase, repeating leaf & band motif, mc, mk/#d, 6x6" 70.00
Vase, stylized tulips on blk/dk bl, bowl form, mk, 1918, 13" 625.00
Vase, Uni, high-gloss floral on bl, Regina mk, #226, 7" 60.00
Vase, Zenith, geometrics/advertising, mk, 3" 25.00
Wall pocket, mc Nouveau motif on blk, house mk, 11½"............110.00

Grand Feu

The Grand Feu Art Pottery operated from 1912 until about 1918 in Los Angeles, California. It was owned and operated by Cornelius Brauckman, who developed a method of producing remarkably artistic glaze effects achieved through extremely high temperatures during the firing process. The body of the ware, as a result of the intense heat (2500 degrees), was vitrified as the glaze matured. Brauckman signed his ware, either with his name or 'Grand Feu Pottery, L.A. California'. His work is regarded today as being among the finest art pottery ever produced in the United States. Examples are rare and command high prices on today's market.

Bowl, lt mustard & terra cotta, bulbous, imp mk, 4"........................85.00
Vase, brn flambe drip, long trumpet neck, stamped mk, 8" 900.00
Vase, gr matt w/bl crystals, str sides, 8x3"................................ 1,600.00
Vase, silver bl irid, mk, 6½" 1,400.00

Graniteware

Graniteware, made of a variety of metals with enamel coatings, derives its name from its appearance. The speckled, swirled, or mottled effect of the vari-colored enamels may look like granite — but there the resemblance stops. It wasn't especially durable! Expect at least minor chipping if you plan to collect.

Graniteware was featured in 1876 at Phily's Expo. It was mass-produced in quantity, and enough of it has survived to make at least the common items easily affordable. Color is an important consideration in evaluating an item; cobalt blue and white, green and white, brown and white, and old red and white swirled items are unusual, thus more expensive. Pieces of heavier weight, seam constructed, and those with wooden handles and tin lids are usually older.

For further study, we recommend *The Collector's Encyclopedia of Graniteware — Colors, Shapes, and Values* by our advisor, Helen Greguire. She is listed in the Directory under New York. For the address of the National Graniteware Society, see the section on Clubs, Newsletters, and Catalogs.

**Covered chamber pot, brown and white large swirl, 7½"
high, $235.00.**

Baking pan, cream & gr, oval, EX 35.00
Bedpan, bl & wht fine mottled w/wht top & cobalt trim, NM 85.00
Boiler, gray, iron hdl, hangs in fireplace, L&G Mfg, EX 125.00
Boston cream can, sky bl 135.00

Bowl, cereal; cream & gr, 5", VG 12.50
Bowl, cream & gr, 10¾", EX 15.00
Bowl, Emerald Ware, gr & wht lg swirl, 8", EX 185.00
Bowl, mixing; bl mottled, med sz, VG......................48.00
Bowl, mixing; old red & wht lg swirl, sm, EX..........225.00
Bowl, mixing; robin's egg bl mottled, 8", NM...........38.00
Bread box, gr & wht speckled, 11½", EX 55.00
Butter dish, red solid, EX......................................105.00
Cake pan, bl & wht swirl, 10", EX 55.00
Candle holder, wht, mini, 1¼", NM.......................125.00
Chamber pot, bl & wht mottled, w/lid, EX...............75.00
Chamber pot, gray & wht mottled, child's.................20.00
Chamber pot, wht w/blk trim, M.............................12.00
Churn, bl & wht lg swirl, dasher type, floor model, EX 2,500.00
Coaster, Blue Belle Ware, bl shaded, 3⅞", EX..........65.00
Coffee biggin, bl & wht fine mottle, squatty, 3-pc, M 550.00
Coffee biggin, wht w/blk trim, 2-cup, EX 65.00
Coffee boiler, bl & wht lg swirl, EX 225.00
Coffee boiler, cobalt & wht speckled, 2-gal, VG 65.00
Coffee boiler, Columbian lg swirl, EX 395.00
Coffee boiler, gray, tin lid, VG 55.00
Coffee boiler, turq & wht swirl, 1½-gal, VG............135.00
Coffee urn, gray solid, EX 155.00
Coffeepot, bird on wht, pewter spout/hdl/top, lg 265.00
Coffeepot, bl, lg, EX...65.00
Coffeepot, bl & wht lg swirl, 10", EX 125.00
Coffeepot, bright yel, gooseneck, M.........................40.00
Coffeepot, Emerald Ware, gr & wht lg swirl, 10", NM..........425.00
Coffeepot, med bl speckled, rpl hinge, 6-cup 40.00
Coffeepot, roses on wht, porc hdl, pewter trim, 11½"..........235.00
Coffeepot, sky bl, w/self lid, 4-cup, M...................110.00
Coffeepot, wht, Foval dome, ftd, EX.......................40.00
Colander, brn & wht mottled, EX............................35.00
Colander, robin's egg bl lg swirl, EX 150.00
Cream can, gray, tin lid, 6¼"................................125.00
Creamer, bl solid, EX..125.00
Creamer, wht, EX 25.00
Creamer & sugar bowl, red & wht swirl, ftd, 1950s, sm, EX 190.00
Cup, gr & wht swirl, 3½", EX 42.00
Cup, med teal bl, 2x4½", NM 95.00
Cuspidor, brn solid, 2-pc, EX 40.00
Cuspidor, gr solid w/blk trim, M.............................45.00
Custard cup, lt bl & wht lg swirl, blk trim, wht int, NM..........95.00
Custard cup, wht w/cobalt trim, Sweden, VG............15.00
Dipper, gray solid, EX...15.00
Dish pan, lt bl & wht swirl, blk trim, wire hdls, 13" 75.00
Dish pan, lt gray w/bl trim, 2x5", VG......................30.00
Double boiler, bl & wht swirl, 3-pc, EX..................155.00
Double boiler, cream & gr, EX 95.00
Double boiler, dk gr & wht lg swirl, NM.................345.00
Dough riser, bl & wht mottled, lg, NM...................260.00
Dust pan, gray, EX..395.00
Dust pan, gray mottled, VG..................................365.00
Dutch oven, bl swirl, NM.......................................75.00
Dutch oven, lt bl & wht lg swirl, EX.......................45.00
Egg plate, wht w/dk bl rim & hdls, 4¾", EX.............38.00
Flask, powder; cobalt, EX......................................65.00
Funnel, bl & wht mottled, lg, EX.............................65.00
Funnel, canning; gray, NM.....................................45.00
Funnel, gray, elliptical, lg, M.................................55.00
Funnel, wht w/bl trim, side hdl, 3", M......................20.00
Gas heater, blk & wht w/clipper ship, 15x10", EX 48.00
Grater, cheese; gray mottled, rotary style 95.00
Grater, cobalt solid, lg, NM...................................120.00

Grater, red, EX..75.00
Grater, sky bl, EX...80.00
Kettle, Berlin; bl & wht swirl, w/lid, EX.................115.00
Kettle, cream & gr, bail hdl, w/lid, lg......................30.00
Kettle, gray swirl, w/lid, from Domestic Science set, mini............95.00
Kettle, Lava Ware, bl & wht lg swirl, EX................165.00
Kettle, robin's egg bl speckled, lg, EX.....................40.00
Ladle, bl & wht swirl, wht int, EX...........................85.00
Ladle, gray solid, EX...20.00
Ladle, wht w/bl hdl, lg, M......................................30.00
Lady finger pan, gray mottled, NM.........................295.00
Lunch pail, cobalt, 4-pc, EX..................................120.00
Measure, gray mottled, 1-cup, EX............................55.00
Meat grinder, gr mottled, Harper England, EX........120.00
Milk can, blk & wht speckled, strap hdl, 1-qt, VG 40.00
Milk pan, bl & wht lg swirl, EX...............................65.00
Mold, strawberry, gray, NM..................................350.00
Mold, turk's head, gray, EX....................................75.00
Muffin pan, bl & wht mottled, 6-cup, EX.................225.00
Muffin pan, cobalt & wht lg swirl, 8-cup, M............395.00
Muffin pan, dk bl & wht lg swirl, 6-cup, NM............425.00
Muffin pan, gray solid, 6-cup, EX............................35.00
Muffin pan, mottled gray, 12-cup, EX.......................48.00
Mug, blk & wht speckled, mini, EX..........................45.00
Mug, royal bl, wht band, gold trim, EX.....................30.00

In gray granite: Mug, 2", $165.00; Measuring cup with rings, 2¾", $125.00.

Onion keeper, sky bl, VG.......................................65.00
Pail, berry; bl & wht lg swirl, EX...........................145.00
Pail, bl & wht speckled, dk bl ears & rim, wire hdl, 3¼" 75.00
Pan, dk bl & wht swirl, blk trim, wht int, 10¼"........45.00
Pan, lt bl & wht swirl w/blk trim, 5¾", EX................35.00
Pan, robin's egg bl, 3½x11¾", NM...........................35.00
Pan, 5-eyed egg; gray mottled, hdl, EX...................195.00
Pie pan, gray mottle, 10" 40.00
Pie pan, gray mottled, mini, 3½", VG.......................45.00
Pie pan, lt gray w/bl rim, mini, 4¾", VG...................45.00
Pie pan, teal gr & wht swirl, 9"...............................45.00
Pitcher, molasses; mottled gray 225.00
Pitcher, water; bl solid, VG....................................75.00
Pitcher & bowl, gray solid, VG..............................115.00
Plate, bl & wht speckled, mini, 2", EX......................45.00
Plate, cream & gr, 8½", EX....................................12.00
Plate, gray lg mottle, lg, M....................................40.00
Plate, turq & wht lg swirl, divided, ca 1970, M..........25.00
Platter, bacon; bl & wht swirl, NM.........................125.00
Platter, bl & wht swirl, oval, 14", EX......................195.00
Platter, bl-gray, blk rim, 16x12½", EX 55.00
Platter, gr & wht speckled, EX................................30.00

Platter, turq speckled, oval, EX 85.00
Rack, utensil; Delft bl & wht, w/matching utensils 195.00
Refrigerator dish, bl & wht swirl, ca 1950, 5x8" 100.00
Refrigerator dish, wht w/blk trim, w/lid, EX..............................20.00
Roaster, bl & wht speckled, 13x6½", EX 45.00
Roaster, Emerald Ware, rectangular, lid vent, 17" 325.00
Roaster, gray & wht swirl, bl trim, EX...................................45.00
Roaster, gray mottled, w/lid, 15", EX 40.00
Roasting pan, lt gr w/bl rim, mini, 1x4½x3", EX......................55.00
Salt box, gray mottled, NM..395.00
Sauce pan, bl & wht lg swirl, VG...65.00
Sauce pan, gray & wht, aluminum lid, 3-pc set 135.00
Scoup, grocer's, gray lg mottle, open end hdl, rivets, EX 135.00
Sink strainer, cream & gr, triangular, EX................................30.00
Sink strainer, gray, triangular, EX.......................................65.00
Skimmer, bl & wht fine swirl, 11" blk hdl, EX 70.00
Skimmer, cobalt wht lg swirl 195.00
Soap dish, brn & wht lg swirl, w/insert, hanging, NM 235.00
Soap dish, med bl & wht swirl, hanging, NM...........................125.00
Spatula, gray & wht mottled 65.00
Spoon, basting; wht w/cobalt hdl, EX 45.00
Spoon, cream & gr, 11¾", EX 15.00
Sugar bowl, gray, tin lid, mk L&G, NM 325.00
Sugar bowl, wht, w/matching lid, EX.....................................85.00
Tea pot, brn & wht relish w/pewter, cr/sug/tray 1,700.00
Tea set, bl & wht speckled, child's, ca 1900, 9-pc, EX 455.00
Tea set, red w/bl & wht panel, child's, ca 1900, 11-pc, EX 495.00
Tea steeper, shaded bl Thistle, matching lid, NM.....................135.00
Tea strainer, gray mottled, VG...45.00
Tea strainer, gray solid, EX 45.00
Tea strainer, red solid, EX..65.00
Tea strainer, sky bl, EX...55.00
Teakettle, lt gray on CI, Wrought Iron Range Co, EX...............110.00
Teapot, bl & wht mottled, gooseneck spout, sm, VG 190.00
Teapot, bl & wht mottled, 2-cup, NM.................................475.00
Teapot, crystolite, gooseneck, EX 250.00
Teapot, red & wht swirl, gooseneck, ca 1960, EX 125.00
Tray, bl & wht mottled, NM...100.00
Trivet, robin's egg bl, triangular, EX 55.00
Wash basin, bl & wht swirl, salesman sample, 3¼" 75.00
Wash basin, cream & gr, EX..20.00
Wash basin, lt bl, NM...45.00
Washboard, cobalt, no advertising, EX 50.00

Green and Ivory

Green and ivory are the colors of a type of country pottery decorated with in-mold designs very similar to those of the more familiar blue and white wares. It is unmarked and was produced from about 1910 to 1935 by many manufacturers as part of their staple line of kitchenwares.

Bowl, Apricot, 9½" 75.00
Bowl, Daisy & Waffle, 10" 65.00
Butter crock, Apricots & Honeycomb, w/lid & bail.....................95.00
Butter crock, Daisy & Waffle, w/lid 115.00
Compote, Scroll, 6-sided 185.00
Compote, Waffle, sm rim flake 145.00
Mug, Grape 45.00
Pitcher, Basketweave & Morning-Glory, rope hdl, 9" 150.00
Pitcher, Grape...115.00
Pitcher, Indian Head in War bonnet, waffle body, 8½", NM.......165.00
Pitcher, Pine Cone, 9" 145.00

Pitcher, Cows, 7",
$150.00.

Spittoon, Cosmos, 6" 75.00
Toothpick holder, Swan 30.00
Umbrella stand, Irises, 20"...325.00

Green Opaque

Introduced in 1887 by the New England Glass Company, this ware is very scarce due to the fact that it was produced for less than one year. It is characterized by its soft green color and a wavy band of gold reserving a mottled blue metallic stain. It is usually found in satin; examples with a shiny finish are extremely rare.

Bowl, deep, 4" dia 495.00
Bowl vase, NM gold & mottling, 3x4¼".............................850.00
Cruet, tricorn, 6" 1,150.00
Shakers, squat form, EX mottling, 2¾", pr............................475.00
Spooner, M gold & mottling, 3¾x4" 850.00
Toothpick holder, 2"... 1,150.00
Tumbler, lemonade; w/hdl, 5" 900.00
Tumbler, M gold & mottling, thin walls...............................585.00
Vase, flared mouth, M gold & mottling, 6" 900.00

Greenaway, Kate

Kate Greenaway was an English artist who lived from 1846 to 1901. She gained worldwide fame as an illustrator of children's books, drawing children clothed in the styles worn by proper English and American boys and girls of the very early 1800s. Her book, *Under the Willow Tree*, published in 1878, was the first of many. Her sketches appeared in leading magazines, and her greeting cards were in great demand. Manufacturers of china, pottery, and metal products copied her characters to decorate children's dishes, tiles, and salt and pepper shakers as well as many other items. See also Almanacs; Napkin Rings.

Biscuit jar, ceramic, boy w/tinted features, w/lid........................150.00
Book, Almanack for 1927, London, VG 50.00
Book, Birthday Book for Children, ca 1800, 4x4", NM................95.00
Book, Day in a Child's Life, London, 1st edition, 1881, VG.........85.00
Book, Greenaway's Birthday Book, color illus, Warne, VG 45.00
Book, Kate Greenaway Biography, 1905, EX..........................225.00
Book, Mother Goose, London, Routledge, 1st ed, 1881, VG........95.00
Book, Under the Window, London, 1st ed, VG.......................125.00
Bowl, Daisy & Button, amber, girl/dog on Reed & Barton fr 525.00
Butter pat, china, children playing.......................................35.00

Cup & saucer, pk lustre 125.00
Engraving, Harper's Bazaar, Jan 1879, full-pg 25.00
Figurine, rope jumpers, mk on 1, 9½", pr.....................600.00
Match holder, china, boy holds rabbit, w/striker 65.00
Match safe, SP, emb children, sm...................................48.00

Milk pitcher, no mark,
6½", $165.00.

Plate, ABC, girl in lg hat, Staffordshire, 7" 85.00
Plate, children at play, fruit, birds & flowers, 9" 100.00
Tea set, semi-porc, floral motif, 3-pc...............................60.00
Thimble holder, bsk, girl sits on stump, basket on bk 40.00
Toothpick holder, glass, 2 girls sit beside basket...........85.00
Toothpick holder, SP, standing girl, ornate, Tufts 175.00
Vase, bud; ornate Tufts holder w/4" girl, glass insert 145.00
Vase, majolica figural, 6" 175.00
Wall pocket, ceramic, 6 girls on open book form, 6x9x3"............110.00

Greentown Glass

Greentown glass is a term refering to the product of the the Indiana Tumbler and Goblet Company of Greentown, Indiana, ca 1894 to 1903. Their earlier pressed glass patterns were #11, a pseudo-cut glass design; #137, Pleat Band; and #200, Austrian. Another line, Dewey, was designed in 1898. Many lovely colors were produced in addition to crystal. Jacob Rosenthal, who was later affiliated with Fenton, developed his famous chocolate glass in 1900. The rich shaded opaque brown glass was an overnight success. Two new patterns, Leaf Bracket and Cactus, were designed to display the glass to its best advantage, but previously existing molds were also used. In only three years, Rosenthal developed yet another important color formula, golden agate. The Holly Amber pattern was designed especially for its production. The Dolphin covered dish with a fish finial is perhaps the most common and easily-recognized piece ever produced. Other animal dishes were also made; all are highly collectible. There have been many repros — not all are marked!

Our advisors for this category are Jerry and Sandi Garrett; they are listed in the Directory under Indiana. See the Pattern Glass section for clear pressed glass, only colored items are listed here.

Animal dish, bird w/berry, chocolate 650.00
Animal dish, bird w/berry, teal bl.................................250.00
Animal dish, cat on hamper, amber, tall.......................250.00
Animal dish, cat on hamper, clear, low 250.00
Animal dish, cat on hamper, emerald gr, tall.................225.00
Animal dish, cat on hamper, teal bl, tall 450.00
Animal dish, dolphin, beaded, amber 300.00
Animal dish, dolphin, beaded, chocolate 225.00

Animal dish, dolphin, beaded, Nile gr 1,500.00
Animal dish, dolphin, sawtooth, clear 200.00
Animal dish, dolphin, sawtooth, cobalt.........................425.00
Animal dish, dolphin, smooth, chocolate.......................300.00
Animal dish, hen, canary 240.00
Animal dish, hen, chocolate 450.00
Animal dish, hen, emerald gr 140.00
Animal dish, hen, teal bl 150.00
Animal dish, hen, wht opaque 125.00
Animal dish, rabbit, amber (reproduced).......................135.00
Animal dish, rabbit, cobalt...300.00
Animal dish, rabbit, teal bl...135.00
Austrian, bowl, rectangular, canary, 8" L 145.00
Austrian, compote, canary, 4½" dia..............................175.00
Austrian, creamer, chocolate, 4¼" 150.00
Austrian, spooner, canary 150.00
Austrian, tumbler, canary 125.00
Brazen Shield, bowl, bl, 7½" dia....................................85.00
Brazen Shield, relish tray, bl..75.00
Brazen Shield, sauce dish, bl, 4⅜" 35.00
Brazen Shield, tumbler, bl 65.00
Brazen Shield, water set, bl, 7-pc 500.00
Cactus, bowl, chocolate, 9½" 175.00
Cactus, butter dish, chocolate 175.00
Cactus, butter dish, ped ft, chocolate.............................625.00
Cactus, compote, chocolate, 5¼" dia 150.00
Cactus, compote, chocolate, 7¼" dia 210.00
Cactus, cracker jar, chocolate 260.00
Cactus, cracker jar, red agate..275.00
Cactus, mug, chocolate...75.00
Cactus, nappy, chocolate, hdls 150.00
Cactus, spooner, chocolate 100.00
Cactus, sweetmeat, chocolate, rare 625.00
Cactus, syrup, chocolate 175.00
Cactus, toothpick holder, chocolate 80.00
Cactus, tumbler, chocolate 60.00
Cord Drapery, butter dish, emerald gr, 4¾" 225.00
Cord Drapery, creamer, emerald gr, 4¾" 150.00
Cord Drapery, pickle dish, amber.................................125.00
Cord Drapery, pitcher, water; emerald gr......................235.00
Cord Drapery, spooner, cobalt 125.00
Cord Drapery, syrup, chocolate 190.00
Cord Drapery, toothpick holder, amber 325.00
Cord Drapery, tumbler, cobalt 125.00
Cupid, butter dish, Nile gr..400.00
Cupid, creamer, chocolate 350.00
Cupid, sugar bowl, w/lid, wht opaque............................100.00

Dewey, mug, green, 3½",
$65.00.

Dewey, butter dish, canary, lg, 5" 110.00	Leaf Bracket, tumbler, chocolate............................60.00
Dewey, butter dish, chocolate, 4" dia 150.00	Novelty, Dewey bust, amber, w/base.....................175.00
Dewey, creamer, amber, 5".......................................70.00	Novelty, hairbrush, clear 65.00
Dewey, cruet, amber..150.00	Novelty, Indian head creamer, clear, w/lid...........200.00
Dewey, cruet, canary..165.00	Novelty, skillet, Nile gr 400.00
Dewey, pitcher, water; canary 150.00	Novelty, trunk, wht opaque....................................200.00
Dewey, pitcher, water; emerald gr 140.00	Novelty, wheelbarrow, amber.................................140.00
Dewey, shakers, amber, pr 110.00	Novelty, wheelbarrow, teal bl 150.00
Dewey, sugar bowl, chocolate, 2¼" dia 100.00	Pitcher, Heron, chocolate 500.00
Dewey, tray, serpentine, amber, lg..........................75.00	Pitcher, Ruffled Eye, amber....................................150.00
Dewey, tumbler, amber 55.00	Pitcher, Squirrel, chocolate....................................475.00
Diamond Prisms, tumbler, chocolate, rare 450.00	Scalloped Flange, vase, chocolate 80.00
Early Diamond, pitcher, emerald gr 185.00	Scalloped Flange, vase, Nile gr...............................275.00
Fleur-de-lis, butter dish, chocolate........................500.00	Shuttle, butter dish, chocolate, rare 900.00
Fleur-de-lis, creamer, chocolate.............................175.00	Shuttle, creamer, chocolate....................................500.00
Fleur-de-lis, spooner, chocolate.............................175.00	Shuttle, nappy, chocolate 200.00
Fleur-de-lis, tumbler, chocolate.............................100.00	Shuttle, punch cup, chocolate................................100.00
Greentown Daisy, butter dish, chocolate...............250.00	Shuttle, sugar bowl, w/lid, chocolate.....................600.00
Greentown Daisy, sugar bowl, open, chocolate 100.00	Shuttle, tumbler, chocolate....................................100.00
Herringbone Buttress, bowl, emerald gr, 7¼" dia........180.00	Stein, dog & child, Nile gr......................................320.00
Herringbone Buttress, cruet, emerald gr................350.00	Stein, indoor drinking scene, chocolate, 5" 175.00
Herringbone Buttress, goblet, emerald gr..............225.00	Stein, indoor drinking scene, Nile gr, 5¾" 125.00
Herringbone Buttress, wine, emerald gr.................185.00	Stein, outdoor drinking scene, Nile gr...................120.00
Holly Amber, bowl, rectangular, 4x10" 1,000.00	Teardrop & Tassel, butter dish, wht opaque...........125.00
Holly Amber, bowl, 8½"..600.00	Teardrop & Tassel, compote, w/lid, Nile gr, 4⅝" dia....325.00
Holly Amber, cake stand 2,400.00	Teardrop & Tassel, goblet, emerald gr 235.00
Holly Amber, compote, w/lid, 4½" 1,200.00	Teardrop & Tassel, sauce dish, chocolate, 4½".......200.00
Holly Amber, compote, w/lid, 8¼" dia 2,200.00	Teardrop & Tassel, spooner, cobalt...........................90.00
Holly Amber, creamer..600.00	Teardrop & Tassel, sugar bowl, w/lid, chocolate 470.00
Holly Amber, cruet, 6½".................................... 1,850.00	Teardrop & Tassel, tumbler, Nile gr........................275.00
Holly Amber, plate, 7¼"...750.00	Toothpick holder, dog's head, Nile gr....................150.00
Holly Amber, relish, hdls 350.00	Toothpick holder, picture frame, teal bl.................275.00
Holly Amber, sauce dish, 4½" dia...........................270.00	Toothpick holder, sheaf of wheat, amber...............175.00
Holly Amber, spooner, 4".......................................650.00	Toothpick holder, witch's head, Nile gr.................125.00
Holly Amber, sugar bowl, w/lid..............................850.00	Tumbler, Uneeda Milk Biscuit, chocolate..............125.00
Holly Amber, syrup, SP hinged lid, 5¾" 900.00	
Holly Amber, toothpick holder, lg 495.00	
Holly Amber, tumbler, plain rim.............................450.00	
Holly Amber, vase, 6"...650.00	
Leaf Bracket, berry set, chocolate, 7-pc 300.00	
Leaf Bracket, butter dish, chocolate......................145.00	
Leaf Bracket, celery tray, chocolate, 11" 100.00	
Leaf Bracket, creamer, chocolate.............................90.00	
Leaf Bracket, cruet, chocolate...............................185.00	
Leaf Bracket, nappy, chocolate................................65.00	
Leaf Bracket, pitcher, chocolate............................400.00	
Leaf Bracket, relish, oval, chocolate, 7" 85.00	
Leaf Bracket, salt shaker, chocolate 125.00	
Leaf Bracket, spooner, chocolate.............................85.00	
Leaf Bracket, sugar bowl, chocolate, w/lid 150.00	

Grueby

William Henry Grueby joined the firm of the Low Art Tile Works at the age of fifteen; and in 1894, after several years of experience in the production of architectural tiles, founded his own plant, the Grueby Faience Company, in Boston, Massachusetts. Grueby began experimenting with the idea of producing art pottery and had soon perfected a fine glaze — soft and without gloss — in shades of blue, gray, yellow, brown, and his most successful, cucumber green. In 1900 his exhibit at the Paris Exposition Universelle won three gold medals.

Grueby pottery was hand thrown and hand decorated in the Arts and Crafts style. Vertically-thrust stylized leaves and flowers in relief were the most common decorative devices. Tiles continued to be an important product — unique (due to the matt glaze decoration) as well as durable. Grueby tiles were often a full inch thick. Obviously incompatible with the Art Nouveau style, the artware was discontinued soon after 1910. The ware is marked in one of several ways: 'Grueby Pottery, Boston, USA'; 'Grueby, Boston, Mass.'; or 'Grueby Faience.' The artware is often artist signed.

Bowl, curdled brn matt, gr gloss int, ridged, 2½x9" 375.00	
Bowl, gr, repeating leaves, sq pinched rim, sgn RE, 6", NM.........475.00	
Paperweight, scarab, gr mk, 4" L, EX 325.00	
Tile, abstract floral, gr/lav/cream/ochre, rpr, no mk, 6" 50.00	
Tile, armoured knight on horse, gold matt on bl, mk, 6" 200.00	
Tile, candlestick, yel/gr on curdled gr, no mk, 6", EX 750.00	
Tile, cherub & cornucopia, beige on bl, artist sgn, 6" 140.00	

Leaf Bracket, toothpick holder, chocolate, $285.00.

Tile, cherub & cornucopia, gold/cream on gr, sgn EM, 6" dia......225.00
Tile, Eros, tan & rust 165.00
Tile, gulls & waves, 4-color, cloisonne style, sgn KY, 4" 500.00
Tile, monk plays cello, bl on gold, no mk, 6" 175.00
Tile, polar bear, wht on dk bl, no mk, 5½x7" 425.00
Tile, St Geo & dragon, gr/bl, unsgn, minor chips, 8" dia 800.00
Tile, stylized figure, yel on red, no mk, 6", NM 135.00
Tile (2/continuous), lg bird/gulls/bouy, 4-color, sgn, 4x8" 950.00
Tile frieze, 4 cows graze, trees/river, 2-pc, 12" L, EX 6,000.00
Vase, bl, 5 vertical lines, swollen cylinder, 5", NM 550.00
Vase, brn, vertical lines, canister neck/bulb bottom, 7x4" 700.00
Vase, bud; lt bl, cylindrical, 4" 275.00
Vase, dk cucumber w/tooled ribbing, flared, mk, 6x7" 1,300.00
Vase, dk gr, 3 lg upright leaves, by Lingley, mk/#233, 8x4" 1,700.00
Vase, feathered dk gr w/exposed wht, tooled/appl leaves, 8" ...1,850.00
Vase, feathered gr, tooled leaves/buds, W Post, 12" 6,000.00
Vase, feathered gr w/ribs, faience mk, sgn, rim rpr, 5x8" 750.00
Vase, gr, broad leaves alternate w/buds, 4½"................................475.00
Vase, gr, bulbous base w/cvd realistic leaves, 11¾" 2,500.00
Vase, gr, cvd vertical ribbing suggests broad leaves, 22" 16,500.00
Vase, gr, cylinder neck on spherical base, mk, 8" 700.00

Vase, leathery green glaze, four wide leaves alternate with four having curled tips, 10" x 8", $3,200.00.

Vase, gr, ringed neck on squat base, 3½x6" 425.00
Vase, gr, short neck, bulbous base, mk, 3¼x5½", EX....................525.00
Vase, gr, spherical, filled base chip, 4½" 475.00
Vase, gr, trefoils at rim, leaves at bulbous base, WP, 9" 3,000.00
Vase, gr, vertical stems, rolled rim, 7¾", NM 900.00
Vase, gr, 3 wide leaves, scroll rim hdl between ea, 10", EX......1,900.00
Vase, gr, 7 upright leaves, JE monogram, 12", NM 2,400.00
Vase, gr impasto w/3 groups of wht jonquils, sgn WP, 11½"...30,000.00
Vase, gr w/upright yel buds between wide leaves, sgn RE, 11". 5,200.00
Vase, gr w/yel trefoils, cvd leaves at bulbous base, 12" 4,900.00
Vase, gr w/3-color daffodils, rim rpr, 11" 1,800.00
Vase, lav, tooled/appl leaves, 4 scroll hdls, 10", EX 6,750.00
Vase, lt bl mottle, tooled leaves, sgn Erikson, dtd '07, 9".........1,100.00
Vase, mustard impasto w/wht trefoils, cvd leaves, 4¾x5" 2,200.00
Vase, navy bl, squat gourd form w/4 buttresses at rim, 6½" 1,900.00
Vase, thick bl, cylindrical w/bulbous base, #32, 12¾"..............2,200.00
Vase, thick gr w/vertical ribs, baluster, RE monogram, 7½" ...2,500.00
Wall pocket, gr, tooled lapets, hemispherical, no mk, 7x5½" 800.00

Gutta Percha

Gutta Percha is the plastic substance from the latex of several types of Malaysian trees. It resembles rubber but contains more resin. A patent for the use of this material in manufacturing an early type of

plastic was issued in the 1850s, and it was used extensively for daguerreotype cases and picture frames. Numbers in the following listings refer to *American Miniature Case Art* by Rinhart, an excellent reference that is now out of print. When found, copies of this book usually sell for $100.00 to $150.00.

Case, Accented Oval, Rinhart #205 variant, 4th-plate, VG..........35.00
Case, angel & couple w/water jugs, 5-compartment, 1856, 6x4" .195.00
Case, Apple Picker, Rinhart #22, ca 1858, 6th-plate, EX 100.00
Case, Beehive w/grain border, Rinhart #20, 6th-plate, VG............50.00
Case, Blind Beggar, 9th-plate, EX 50.00
Case, Chess Players, Rinhart #42 variant, 9th-plate, EX 50.00
Case, Church Window, Rinhart #52, ca 1857, 9th-plate 30.00
Case, crucifix, w/SP mts, 1860s, 3"..40.00
Case, Faithful Hound, Rinhart #40, 6th-plate, NM 110.00
Case, floral cluster design, w/ambro, 6th-case, EX 50.00
Case, floral scallops, 8-sided, 3¾x3¼", NM 100.00
Case, florals w/EX gold, oval, 3x1¼" 75.00
Case, girl & pigs at fence, EX gold, oval, 16th-plate, EX 125.00

Case, Habana, fourth-plate, $150.00.

Case, Huntress & Falcon, Rinhart #44, 6th-plate, VG 75.00
Case, Indian profile in relief, gold decor, 16th-plate, NM............165.00
Case, leafy rosette fr in inverted oval, 9th-plate, VG 45.00
Case, nesting birds w/roses, oval, w/tintype, 9th-plate, EX............40.00
Case, Profile of a Patriarch, Rinhart #38, EX 75.00
Case, scroll motif, w/daguerreotype, 6th-plate, VG......................60.00
Case, Wheat Sheaves, Rinhart #14, 6th-plate, EX 75.00
Case, wreath design, octagonal, w/daguerreotype, 6th-plate 35.00
Case, 8-pointed mariner's rosette, w/daguerreotype, 9th-plate 45.00
Cup, Nile's Drinking Cup, collapsible, dtd 1860, EX 85.00
Hand mirror, Victorian lady & florals, ca 1860 ....50.00

Hair Weaving

A rather unusual craft became popular during the mid-1800s. Human hair was used to make jewelry (rings, bracelets, lockets, etc.) by braiding and interlacing fine strands of hair into hollow forms with pearls and beads added for effect. Hair wreaths were also made, often using hair from deceased family members as well as the living. They were displayed in deep satin-lined frames along with mementoes of the weaver or her departed kin. The fad was abandoned before the turn of the century.

Our advisor for this category is Steve DeGenaro; he is listed in the Directory under Ohio. See also Mourning Collectibles.

**Brooch, blond and brown plaits, gold mounts, 4½",
$195.00.**

Brooch, glass over braid, 32 seed pearls in gold fr, 1⅛" 60.00
Charm, cross form, woven over solid core, gold mts, 1870s, 1" 85.00
Ring, woven heart set in top of 14k gold band, 1860s 175.00
Wreath, elaborate florals, 4-color hair, 27" fr, EX 135.00

Hall

The Hall China Company of East Liverpool, Ohio, was established in 1903. Their earliest product was whiteware toilet seats, mugs, jugs, etc. By 1920 their restaurant-type dinnerware and cookingware had become so successful that Hall was assured of a solid future. They continue today to be one of the country's largest manufacturers of this type of product.

Hall introduced the first of their famous teapots in 1920; new shapes and colors were added each year until about 1948, making them the largest teapot manufacturer in the world. These and the dinnerware lines of the thirties through the fifties have become popular collectibles. For more thorough study of the subject, we recommend *Hall China* by Margaret and Kenn Whitmyer; their address may be found in the Directory under Ohio.

Acacia, bowl, Radiance, 9" 14.00
Acacia, shakers, hdld, pr 18.00
Acacia, teapot, Radiance 95.00
Blue Blossom, batter jug, Sundial 150.00
Blue Blossom, casserole, #77, rnd, hdld 35.00
Blue Blossom, casserole, Thick Rim 45.00
Blue Blossom, cookie jar, Five Band 150.00
Blue Blossom, creamer, morning 30.00
Blue Blossom, drip jar, #1188, open 35.00
Blue Blossom, jug, #3, ball form 50.00
Blue Blossom, shakers, Five Band, pr 35.00
Blue Blossom, sugar bowl, w/lid, New York 30.00
Blue Blossom, teapot, Sundial 165.00
Blue Bouquet, baker, French fluted 18.00
Blue Bouquet, bowl, salad; 9" 16.00
Blue Bouquet, bowl, soup; flat, 8½" 12.00
Blue Bouquet, bowl, Thick Rim, 6" 10.00
Blue Bouquet, cake plate 16.00
Blue Bouquet, coffeepot, Five Band 50.00
Blue Bouquet, creamer, Boston 10.00
Blue Bouquet, jug, #3, Medallion 18.00
Blue Bouquet, plate, 6" 3.00
Blue Bouquet, shakers, hdld, pr 18.00
Blue Bouquet, sugar bowl, w/lid, Boston 12.00
Blue Bouquet, teapot, Boston 60.00

Blue Garden, cookie jar, Sundial 175.00
Blue Garden, sugar bowl, w/lid, New York 25.00
Blue Garden, teapot, Streamline 175.00
Blue Willow, teapot, 2-cup, Boston 75.00
Cactus, bowl, Five Band, 6" 12.00
Cactus, casserole, Five Band 35.00
Cactus, cookie jar, Five Band 95.00
Cactus, shakers, Five Band, pr 30.00
Cactus, sugar bowl, w/lid, Viking 15.00
Cameo Rose, bowl, fruit; 5¼" 3.50
Cameo Rose, bowl, oval, 10½" 14.00
Cameo Rose, bowl, vegetable; w/lid 30.00
Cameo Rose, creamer 8.00
Cameo Rose, plate, 10" 7.00
Cameo Rose, plate, 8" 5.00
Cameo Rose, platter, oval, 15½" 20.00
Cameo Rose, sugar bowl, w/lid 14.00
Clover, bowl, Radiance, 9" 16.00
Clover, casserole, #65, #68, #70, ea 30.00
Clover, shakers, hdld, pr 30.00
Crocus, bowl, salad; 9" 16.00
Crocus, cake plate 20.00
Crocus, coffeepot, Meltdown 50.00
Crocus, creamer, Art Deco 15.00
Crocus, creamer, Meltdown 18.00
Crocus, cup 7.00
Crocus, drip jar, #1188, open 30.00
Crocus, jug, #3, ball form 35.00
Crocus, mug, tankard style 28.00
Crocus, plate, 9" 9.00
Crocus, shakers, hdld, pr 16.00
Crocus, sugar bowl, w/lid, Medallion 14.00
Crocus, sugar bowl, w/lid, New York 14.00
Crocus, teapot, Boston 65.00
Crocus, water bottle, Zephyr 150.00
Fantasy, teapot, Streamline 200.00

Gold Dot coffeepot, $35.00.

Heather Rose, bowl, Flare, 8¾" 11.00
Heather Rose, bowl, fruit; 5¼" 3.00
Heather Rose, cookie jar, Flare 35.00
Heather Rose, mug, Irish coffee 25.00
Heather Rose, platter, oval, 13¼" 12.00
Heather Rose, sugar bowl, w/lid 10.00
Heather Rose, teapot, Flare 25.00
Heather Rose, teapot, London 20.00

Morning Glory, bowl, str-sided, 9" 16.00
Mt Vernon, bowl, cereal; 6¼" 4.50
Mt Vernon, bowl, vegetable; w/lid 30.00
Mt Vernon, pickle dish, 9" 8.00
Mt Vernon, plate, 8" 5.00
Mt Vernon, platter, oval, 15½" 14.00
Mt Vernon, sugar bowl, w/lid 8.00
Mums, bowl, Radiance, 9" 12.00
Mums, coffeepot, Terrace 40.00
Mums, creamer, Medallion 10.00
Mums, plate, 9" 8.00
Mums, platter, oval, 13¼" 16.00
Orange Poppy, bowl, Radiance, 6" 10.00
Orange Poppy, bowl, Radiance, 9" 16.00
Orange Poppy, casserole, oval, 8" 25.00
Orange Poppy, coffeepot, Great American 40.00
Orange Poppy, creamer, Great American 12.00
Orange Poppy, drip jar, w/lid, Radiance 18.00
Orange Poppy, jug, #3, ball form 32.00
Orange Poppy, jug, #5, Radiance 16.00
Orange Poppy, mustard, w/liner 20.00
Orange Poppy, plate, 7¾" 6.00
Orange Poppy, pretzel jar 75.00
Orange Poppy, saucer 2.00
Orange Poppy, shakers, hdld, pr 18.00
Orange Poppy, sugar bowl, w/lid, Great American 11.00
Orange Poppy, teapot, donut 150.00
Orange Poppy, teapot, Streamline 85.00
Pastel Morning Glory, bowl, Radiance, 6" 8.00
Pastel Morning Glory, bowl, soup; flat, 8½" 12.00
Pastel Morning Glory, coffeepot, Terrace 45.00
Pastel Morning Glory, jug, donut 85.00
Pastel Morning Glory, plate, 9" 8.00
Pastel Morning Glory, shakers, hdld, pr 18.00
Pastel Morning Glory, sugar bowl, w/lid, New York 12.00
Pastel Morning Glory, teapot, Aladdin 65.00
Red Poppy, baker, French fluted 16.00
Red Poppy, bowl, cereal; 6" 8.00
Red Poppy, bowl, Radiance, 6" 10.00
Red Poppy, bowl, salad; 9" 16.00
Red Poppy, clock, teapot shape, metal 45.00
Red Poppy, clock, teapot shape, plastic 40.00
Red Poppy, coffepot, Daniel 32.00
Red Poppy, creamer, modern 10.00
Red Poppy, cutting board, wooden 30.00
Red Poppy, drip jar, #1188, open 27.00
Red Poppy, jug, milk or syrup; Daniel, 4" 25.00
Red Poppy, pie baker 18.00
Red Poppy, plate, 8¼" 6.00
Red Poppy, plate, 9" 8.00
Red Poppy, recipe box, metal 22.00
Red Poppy, shakers, hdld, pr 20.00
Red Poppy, soap dispenser, metal 30.00
Red Poppy, sugar bowl, w/lid, modern 12.00
Red Poppy, teapot, New York 45.00
Red Poppy, tray, rnd, metal 18.00
Red Poppy, tumbler, clear glass 18.00
Red Poppy, tumbler, frosted glass, 2 styles 12.00
Red Poppy, waste can, rnd, metal 27.00
Richmond, bowl, soup; flat, 8" 6.00
Richmond, pickle dish, 9" 5.00
Richmond, platter, oval, 13¼" 12.00
Rose Parade, bowl, str-sided, 6" 10.00
Rose Parade, bowl, str-sided, 9" 16.00

Rose Parade, shakers, Pert, pr 20.00
Rose Parade, sugar bowl, Pert 12.00
Rose Parade, teapot, 6-cup, Pert 35.00
Rose White, bowl, str-sided, 9" 12.00
Rose White, casserole, hdld 18.00
Rose White, shakers, Pert, pr 18.00
Rose White, sugar bowl, Pert 12.00
Royal Rose, bowl, salad; 9" 20.00
Royal Rose, bowl, str-sided, 9" 18.00
Royal Rose, bowl, Thick Rim, 8½" 16.00
Royal Rose, shakers, hdld, pr 18.00
Serenade, bowl, fruit; 5½" 3.00
Serenade, bowl, Radiance, 6" 6.00
Serenade, bowl, rnd, 9¼" 14.00
Serenade, creamer, modern 8.00
Serenade, drip jar, w/lid, Radiance 14.00
Serenade, jug, #3, ball form 22.00
Serenade, plate, 6" 3.00
Serenade, platter, 13¼" 14.00
Serenade, sugar bowl, w/lid, modern 10.00
Shaggy Tulip, canister, Radiance 95.00
Shaggy Tulip, teapot, Radiance 95.00
Silhouette, bowl, flared, 3⅝" 10.00
Silhouette, bowl, Medallion, 8½" 16.00
Silhouette, bowl, salad; 9" 14.00
Silhouette, bowl, vegetable; rnd, 9¼" 16.00
Silhouette, cake safe 45.00
Silhouette, coaster 4.00
Silhouette, coffeepot, Medallion 35.00
Silhouette, creamer, modern 10.00
Silhouette, drip jar, w/lid, Medallion 18.00
Silhouette, jug, Simplicity 75.00
Silhouette, pitcher, clear glass, Federal 95.00
Silhouette, plate, 6" 5.00
Silhouette, pretzel jar 75.00
Silhouette, shakers, Five Band, pr 16.00
Silhouette, shakers, Medallion, pr 35.00
Silhouette, soap dispenser 35.00
Silhouette, sugar bowl, w/lid, Medallion 12.00
Silhouette, teapot, Five Band 35.00
Silhouette, tray, oval, metal 32.00
Silhouette, tray, rectangular, metal 32.00
Silhouette, waffle iron 75.00
Springtime, bowl, cereal; 6" 8.00
Springtime, bowl, Thick Rim, 6" 10.00
Springtime, cake plate 12.00
Springtime, plate, 9" 7.00
Springtime, platter, oval, 13¼" 14.00
Springtime, shakers, hdld, pr 18.00
Teapot, Adele, maroon 65.00
Teapot, Airflow, cobalt w/gold floral 35.00
Teapot, Aladdin, Chinese red, w/insert 50.00
Teapot, Automobile, maroon w/silver 350.00
Teapot, Baltimore, gold decor 35.00
Teapot, Basketball, Chinese red 375.00
Teapot, Cleveland, warm yel w/gold 32.00
Teapot, Connie, celadon gr 30.00
Teapot, Donut, cobalt w/gold 200.00
Teapot, Football, emerald gr w/gold 350.00
Teapot, Globe, maroon w/gold 65.00
Teapot, Hollywood, emerald gr w/gold, 6-cup 32.00
Teapot, Melody, Chinese red 95.00
Teapot, Murphy, turq bl, 1940s 35.00
Teapot, New York, cobalt w/gold, 6-cup 30.00

Teapot, New York, delphinium bl w/gold, 2-cup	22.00
Teapot, New York, wheat/poppy pattern, 6-cup	65.00
Teapot, Star, cobalt w/gold	75.00
Teapot, Surfside, yel w/gold	65.00
Teapot, World s Fair	275.00
Tulip, bowl, cereal; 6"	10.00
Tulip, bowl, oval	15.00
Tulip, bowl, Radiance, 9"	14.00
Tulip, bowl, Thick Rim, 6"	10.00
Tulip, casserole, Radiance	30.00
Tulip, creamer, modern	8.00
Tulip, plate, 6"	6.00
Tulip, plate, 9"	8.00
Tulip, shakers, hdld, pr	22.00
Wild Poppy, bowl, Radiance, 9"	20.00
Wild Poppy, casserole, #4, Sundial	45.00
Wild Poppy, coffeepot, drip; sm, Terrace	125.00
Wild Poppy, cookie jar, Five Band	150.00
Wild Poppy, creamer, Hollywood	20.00
Wild Poppy, shakers, Novelty Radiance, pr	50.00
Wild Poppy, sugar bowl, w/lid, Hollywood	25.00
Wildfire, bowl, cereal; 6"	8.00
Wildfire, bowl, oval	14.00
Wildfire, bowl, str-sided, 6"	12.00
Wildfire, bowl, Thick Rim, 6"	12.00
Wildfire, cake plate	16.00
Wildfire, casserole, Thick Rim	22.00
Wildfire, drip jar, w/lid, Thick Rim	18.00
Wildfire, plate, 7"	6.00
Wildfire, platter, 11¼"	15.00
Wildfire, shakers, hdld, pr	18.00
Wildfire, sugar bowl, w/lid, modern	12.00
Wildfire, teapot, Boston	75.00
Yellow Rose, bowl, cereal; 6"	8.00
Yellow Rose, bowl, Radiance, 6"	8.00
Yellow Rose, casserole, Radiance	25.00
Yellow Rose, coffeepot, Dome	35.00
Yellow Rose, plate, 6"	4.00
Yellow Rose, plate, 9"	7.00
Yellow Rose, shakers, hdld, pr	18.00
Yellow Rose, sugar bowl, w/lid, Norse	12.00

Hallmark

Hallmark introduced a line of artplas (molded plastic) ornaments in 1973 that has quickly become popular with collectors. Also of growing interest to collectors are the small artplas party-type favors now known as Merry Miniatures. A magazine edited by Rosie Wells, our advisor for this category, is available if you want more information. Rosie also publishes a yearly official Secondary Price Guide on Hallmark ornaments. Her address is listed in the Directory under Clubs, Newsletters, and Catalogs, and again under Illinois. Items listed below are assumed to be in mint condition with the original box.

1975, Raggedy Ann, QX121-I, yarn ornament, rare	38.00
1977, Betsey Clark, QX264-2, 5th in series, glass ornament	360.00
1979, Here Comes Santa, QX155-9, Santa's Motorcar	300.00
1980, Frosty Friends, QX137-4, 2st in series, Cool Yule	500.00
1982, Tin Locomotive, QX460-3, 1st in series	450.00
1985, Chris Mouse, QLX703-2, 1st in series, lighted	50.00
1986, Mr & Mrs Claus, QX402-6, Merry Mistletoe Time	65.00
1989, Crayola, QX435-2, 1st in series, Bright Journey	20.00
1990, Mom-to-Be, QX491-6	35.00

1990, Rocking Horse, QX464-6, 10th in series	37.50
1990, Santa's Ho-Ho-Hoedown, QLX 725-6	45.00

Halloween

The origin of Halloween can be traced back to the ancient practices of the Druids of Great Britain who began their New Year on the 1st of November. The Druids were pagans and their New Year's celebrations involved pagan rites and superstitions. They believed that as the old year came to an end the Devil would gather up all the demons and evil in the world and take them back to Hell with him. Witches were women who had sold their souls to the Devil and, with their black cat in attendance, flew up through their chimneys on brooms. When the Roman Catholic Church came into power in 700 A.D., they changed the holiday into a religious event called 'All Saints Day,' or 'Allhallows.' The evening before, October 31, became 'Allhallow's Eve' or 'Halloween.' Today Halloween is strictly a fun time, and Halloween items are fun to collect. Pumpkin-head candy containers of papier-mache or pressed cardboard, noisemakers, post cards with black cats and witches, costumes, and decorations are only a sampling of the variety available. See also Candy Containers.

Candy container, devil emerges from pumpkin, 2½"	250.00
Candy container, goblin, clear glass, metal base, 3½", G	400.00
Candy container, jack-o'-lantern, Fleischmann's label, 4½"	75.00
Candy container, jack-o'-lantern, papier-mache, 5"	65.00
Candy container, jack-o'-lantern, pressed cb, lt wear, lg	65.00
Candy container, pumpkin man, papier-mache, mc pnt, 5"	195.00
Candy container, vegetable man, squash body/bean legs, 2¼"	195.00
Candy container, witch, papier-mache, mc pnt, 6½", EX	295.00

Candy container, pumpkin-head figure, papier-mache on plaster, 1880s, 3½", EX, $185.00.

Costume, Big Bad Wolf mask & clothes, Gund, early, 24", EX	250.00
Decoration, bat w/honeycomb, Beistle	20.00
Decoration, girl clown, celluloid w/crepe paper body, 11"	75.00
Decoration, girl holding pumpkin, bsk, Germany, EX	65.00
Decoration, house, metal, Kirchaf, USA, EX	45.00
Decoration, owl, papier-mache, blk w/orange & gold, lg	150.00
Decoration, owl, pressed paper, Germany, 1930s, EX	85.00
Decoration, pumpkin head figure, compo, Germany	95.00
Decoration, skeleton, cb, metal joints, old, 23x23", EX	95.00
Game, Halloween Pie, Stunt & Fortune, 6" dia	135.00
Jack-o'-lantern, papier-mache, w/insert, Germany, 4"	68.00
Jack-o'-lantern, papier-mache, w/insert, Germany, 6"	88.00
Jack-o'-lantern, tin, worn yel/blk pnt, w/bail, early, 6½"	650.00
Jack-o'-lantern, tin litho, med sz, EX	65.00

Jack-o'-lantern, tin/glass, battery op, M **65.00**
Lantern, owl form, glass..**45.00**
Lantern, owl form, gr crepe eyes, EX...**65.00**
Mask, man, appl hair & mustache, molded wire mesh, 1900s, 12".**85.00**
Mask, skeleton, gauze type, EX..**10.00**
Mask, witch, paper litho, Germany **85.00**
Nodder, witch, plaster wash on cb, mc pnt, Germany, 10½" **450.00**
Noisemaker, Blk musicians, metal & wood, EX..............................**15.00**
Noisemaker, clown & girl, metal & wood, USA, EX **10.00**
Noisemaker, clowns, metal & wood, Kirchaf, USA, EX................**17.50**
Noisemaker, clowns play drums, metal & wood, USA **20.00**
Noisemaker, girls in costumes, tin & wood, Barone Toy Mfg **17.50**
Noisemaker, witch & pumpkin emb, wood, 1920s, EX.................**45.00**
Roly poly, scarecrow, celluloid, 3½", NM **120.00**
Tambourine, witches/cats/goblins, plain top, EX...........................**65.00**

Hampshire

The Hampshire Pottery Company was established in 1871 in Keene, New Hampshire, by James Scollay Taft. Their earliest products were redware and stoneware utility items such as jugs, churns, crocks, and flowerpots. In 1878 they produced majolica ware which met with such success that they began to experiment with the idea of manufacturing art pottery. By 1883 they had developed a Royal Worcester type of finish which they applied to vases, tea sets, powder boxes, and cookie jars. It was also utilized for souvenir items that were decorated with transfer designs prepared from photographic plates.

Cadmon Robertson, brother-in-law of Taft, joined the company in 1904 and was responsible for developing their famous matt glazes. Colors included shades of green, brown, red, and blue. Early examples were of earthenware, but eventually the body changed to semi-porcelain. Some of his designs were marked with an M in a circle as a tribute to his wife, Emoretta. Robertson died in 1914, leaving a void impossible to fill. Taft sold the business in 1916 to George Morton, who continued to use the matt glazes that Robertson had developed. After a temporary halt in production during WWI, Morton returned to Keene and re-equipped the factory with the machinery needed to manufacture hotel china and floor tile. Because of the expense involved in transporting coal to fire the kilns, Morton found he could not compete with potteries of Ohio and New Jersey who were able to utilize locally available natural gas. He was forced to close the plant in 1923.

Chocolate pot, gr/brn/lt gr, acorn final, shell spout, 9" **80.00**
Cookie jar, Royal Worcester, gold trim, melon shape, 6" **75.00**
Cookie jar, Royal Worcester, souvenir, egg form/claw ft, 7" **125.00**
Creamer, Royal Worcester, souvenir, log hdl, 3½" **35.00**
Dish, Royal Worcester, souvenir, heart w/bow shape, 5½".............**37.50**

Ewer, ivory with holly decal, 12½", $155.00.

Ewer, gr matt, mk JST&Co, Keene NH, 6½x4" **90.00**
Lamp base, bl texture, swollen cylinder, drilled, 22" **400.00**
Pitcher, Royal Worcester, grs w/blk hdl, souvenir, 6½" **80.00**
Pitcher, Royal Worcester, HP lilacs, melon ribs, 8" **150.00**
Pitcher, Royal Worcester, souvenir, upright top, no mk, 5½" **40.00**
Plate, Royal Worcester, emb designs, souvenir, 8" **45.00**
Shell dish, souvenir, twig ftd, no mk **30.00**
Shoe, yel gloss, no mk, 4" L **30.00**
Stein, Royal Worcester, souvenir (train), holly band, 5½"............**85.00**
Tankard, gr matt, mk, 12x6" **200.00**
Tea set, demitasse; olive gr gloss w/gold, 3-pc............................**90.00**
Tea tile, Royal Worcester, souvenir, scalloped, sgn WAK, 6"........**70.00**
Teapot, brn/gr, butterfly finial, 5" **55.00**
Vase, gr matt, elephant ear leaf, leaf/stem hdls, sgn, 8" **320.00**
Vase, gr matt, gathered/tied-at-neck mold, ruffled, 11"...............**425.00**
Vase, gr matt w/exposed areas of wht clay, #54-L, 5" **135.00**
Vase, mauve mottle w/lt mauve arrowhead leaves, mk, 7x4½" **250.00**
Vase, Royal Worcester, souvenir, tree stump form, mk, 4½"..........**45.00**

Handel

Philip Handel was best known for the art glass lamps he produced at the turn of the century. His work is similar to the Tiffany lamps of the same era. Handel made gas and electric lamps with both leaded glass and reverse-painted shades. Chipped ice shades with a texture similar to overshot glass were also produced. Shades signed by artists such as Bailey, Palme, and Parlow are highly valued.

China and glassware decorated by Handel are rare and command high prices on today's market. Teroma is a term used to describe glassware decorated on the exterior with paint that has a sandy finish. Many of Handel's chinaware blanks were supplied by Limoges

Our advisor for this category is Daniel Batchelor; he is listed in the Directory under New York.

Lamps

Boudoir, rvpt 7" moon/mtn shade; hexagonal std, 14" **1,800.00**
Boudoir, rvpt 7" windmill scene shade; tree trunk std **1,400.00**
Boudoir, rvpt 7" 3-butterfly/quinces shade; bronzed std...........**1,400.00**
Boudoir, sqd/scalloped shade mk Brn-6034; strapwork std, 14"....**750.00**
Boudoir, Teroma 7" bluebird on branch dome shade; 14" **1,800.00**
Boudoir, Teroma 7" moon/trees shade; orig base, 14" **1,800.00**
Chandelier, hammered copper w/7 hanging lily shades, att **950.00**
Chandelier, ldgl, wht slag dome w/bronze came, tag, 10x18" .. **1,200.00**
Desk, cased 12½" L shade, sq brass std, 2 mks, 14" **850.00**
Desk, rvpt 8" moon/pine trees cylinder shade; base adjusts......**1,600.00**
Shade, rvpt daisies, yel/lav/pk/brn, domical, sgn/#d, 18" **8,500.00**
Shade, waterfront/courtyard, sgn Ambero T, 6x12", EX **750.00**
Table, gr glass 7" 4-sided dome shade; incised bronze std **950.00**
Table, ldgl 23" rstr floral band shade (att); rstr std, 23" **1,000.00**
Table, ldgl 24" iris drop-apron shade; petal platform std **3,500.00**
Table, rvpt 14" Arts & Crafts-style floral shade; sgn std **2,300.00**
Table, rvpt 14" floral border shade sgn GO; mk rpt base **1,600.00**
Table, rvpt 14" winter lake/trees shade sgn FU; leafy std **3,500.00**
Table, rvpt 15" ship in tropical seas shade; ribbed std..............**3,750.00**
Table, rvpt 16" sunset lagoon shade; 3-scroll std, 23½" **3,500.00**
Table, rvpt 18" butterflies & flowers shade; w/label, 24" **16,750.00**
Table, rvpt 18" floral shade w/blk border sgn M; rtcl base **5,500.00**
Table, rvpt 18" floral/scroll band shade; std w/rtcl ft...............**4,000.00**
Table, rvpt 18" jungle parrots shade sgn G; floral-emb base ...**18,000.00**
Table, rvpt 18" parrots shade sgn Bedigie; 3-leg std, 24" **23,000.00**
Table, rvpt 7" wisteria on blk shade, sgn/#6905, 13", EX.........**4,750.00**
Table, Teroma 15" forget-me-not shade; ribbed/petaled std ... **7,500.00**

Table, 6-panel slag 14" shade in emb metal fr, #979664, 22" **750.00**

Miscellaneous

Candlestick, copper, studs hold top/base to stem, 10", pr **550.00**
Candlestick, windmills, HP by Gubsich, #4213, 8½", pr **1,100.00**

Humidor, standing bear, $1,300.00.

Humidor, 5 dogs on gr & red, shield mk, 7½x6" **900.00**
Vase, landscape w/birds in trees, sgn, 11" **1,900.00**
Vase, Opal Ware, lilies, mc on aqua-bl, 11" **550.00**

Harker

The Harker Pottery was established in East Liverpool, Ohio, in 1840. Their earliest products were yellowware and Rockingham produced from local clay. After 1900 whiteware was made from imported materials. The plant eventually grew to be a large manufacturer of dinnerware and kitchenware, employing as many as three hundred people. It closed in 1972 after it was purchased by the Jeannette Glass Company. Perhaps their best-known lines were their Cameo wares, decorated with white silhouettes in a cameo effect on contrasting solid colors. Floral silhouettes are standard, but other designs were also used. Blue and pink are the most often found background hues; a few pieces are found in yellow.

Tray, $12.00; Pie lifter, $17.50, both in the Mallow pattern.

Bean pot, Deco Dahlia, ind 6.00
Bowl, Amy, deep, 9" 20.00
Bowl, berry; Pastel Tulip, sm 8.00
Bowl, Cameo Rose, deep 20.00
Bowl, Chesterton Gray, 5½" 5.00
Bowl, cream soup; Cameo Rose..14.00
Bowl, salad; Pastel Tulip, 9" 20.00
Bowl, utility; Deco Dahlia, 9" 17.50
Cake plate, Amy 15.00
Cake plate, Calico Tulip...15.00
Cake plate, Cameo Rose, sq 15.00
Cake plate, pk roses 15.00
Cake plate, Universal Tulips 15.00
Creamer, Cameo Rose 8.00
Creamer, Chesterton Gray 5.00
Creamer & sugar bowl, Orange Tulip w/Wheat 12.00
Custard, Red Apple... 6.00
Drip jar, Deco Dahlia 12.00
Jug, Cameo Rose, rnd, w/lid, 6" 35.00
Jug, high-rise; Amy 40.00
Pie plate, Cameo Rose, 10" 24.00
Pie plate, Cameo Rose, 9" 20.00
Pie server, Modern Age 12.50
Plate, Chesterton Gray, 10"... 5.00
Plate, Pastel Tulip, dinner sz.. 7.50
Plate, Pastel Tulip, salad sz 3.00
Plate, Petit Point II, 8" 6.00
Platter, Cameo Rose, oval, 12" 20.00
Platter, Cameo Rose, 14" 15.00
Platter, Chesterton Gray, 13½" 12.50
Platter, Pastel Tulip, 14" 15.00
Rolling pin, Amy 65.00
Rolling pin, Cameo Rose 85.00
Rolling pin, gold w/wht hdls...80.00
Rolling pin, Kelvinator...85.00
Rolling pin, Mallow 75.00
Rolling pin, Mexican decal...75.00
Rolling pin, Morning Glory..85.00
Rolling pin, Orange Tulip w/Wheat 75.00
Rolling pin, Pastel Tulip 80.00
Rolling pin, Petit Point 65.00
Rolling pin, Red Apple..75.00
Shakers, Deco Dahlia, pr 22.00
Spoon, Red Apple...12.00
Spoon & fork, Amy 30.00
Teapot, Cameo Rose, 6-cup 30.00
Teapot, Orange Tulip w/Wheat 20.00
Teapot, Red Apple 30.00

Harlequin

Harlequin dinnerware, produced by the Homer Laughlin China Company of Newell, West Virginia, was introduced in 1938. It was a lightweight ware made in maroon, mauve blue, and spruce green, as well as all the Fiesta colors except ivory (see Fiesta). It was marketed exclusively by the Woolworth stores, who considered it to be their all-time best seller. For this reason, they contracted with Homer Laughlin to reissue Harlequin to commemorate their 100th anniversary in 1979. Although three of the original glazes were used in the reissue, the few serving pieces that were made were restyled, and collectors found the new line to be no threat to their investments.

The Harlequin animals, including a fish, lamb, cat, penguin, duck, and donkey, were made during the early 1940s, also for the dime-store trade. Today these are very desirable to collectors of Homer Laughlin China. In the listings that follow, use the values designated 'high' for all colors other than turquoise and yellow. For medium green, double the 'high' values on all items other than flat items and small bowls.

The Story of Fiesta by Sharon and Bob Huxford contains a more thorough study of this subject. Available from Collector Books or your local bookstore.

Animals, mavericks 30.00
Animals, non-standard colors 140.00
Animals, standard colors 65.00
Ash tray, basketweave, high 42.00
Ash tray, basketweave, low 30.00
Ash tray, regular, high 40.00
Ash tray, regular, low 32.00
Bowl, '36s oatmeal; high 16.00
Bowl, '36s oatmeal; low 10.00
Bowl, '36s; high 22.00
Bowl, '36s; low 15.00
Bowl, cream soup; high 16.00
Bowl, cream soup; low 12.00
Bowl, fruit; high, 5½" 8.00
Bowl, fruit; low, 5½" 5.00
Bowl, ind salad; high 20.00
Bowl, ind salad; low 15.00
Bowl, mixing; Kitchen Kraft, mauve bl, 8" 110.00
Bowl, mixing; Kitchen Kraft, red or spruce gr, 6" 70.00
Bowl, mixing; Kitchen Kraft, yel, 10" 110.00
Bowl, nappy; high, 9" 22.00
Bowl, nappy; low, 9" 15.00
Bowl, oval baker, high 22.00
Bowl, oval baker, low 16.00
Butter dish, high, ½-lb 82.00
Butter dish, low, ½-lb 70.00
Candle holder, high, pr 180.00
Candle holder, low, pr 150.00
Casserole, w/lid, high 80.00
Casserole, w/lid, low 50.00
Creamer, high lip, any color 70.00
Creamer, ind; high 16.00
Creamer, ind; low 12.00
Creamer, novelty, high 20.00
Creamer, novelty, low 14.00
Creamer, regular, high 12.00
Creamer, regular, low 8.00
Cup, demitasse; high 40.00
Cup, demitasse; low 25.00
Cup, lg, any color 88.00
Egg cup, dbl, high 18.00
Egg cup, dbl, low 12.00
Egg cup, single, high 20.00
Egg cup, single, low 16.00
Gravy boat, high 20.00
Gravy boat, low 15.00
Marmalade, any color 100.00
Nut dish, basketweave, orig color 7.50
Perfume bottle, any color 65.00
Pitcher, service water; high 45.00
Pitcher, service water; low 35.00
Pitcher, 22-oz jug, high 42.00
Pitcher, 22-oz jug, low 24.00
Plate, deep; high 18.00
Plate, deep; low 12.00
Plate, high, 10" 22.00

Plate, high, 6" 4.50
Plate, high, 7" 6.50
Plate, high, 9" 12.00
Plate, low, 10" 13.00
Plate, low, 6" 3.50
Plate, low, 7" 4.50
Plate, low, 9" 7.00
Platter, high, 11" 16.00
Platter, high, 13" 22.00

Relish tray, mixed colors, $180.00.

Platter, low, 11" 10.00
Platter, low, 13" 15.00
Saucer/ash tray, high 42.00
Saucer/ash tray, ivory 60.00
Saucer/ash tray, low 40.00
Shakers, high, pr 15.00
Shakers, low, pr 12.00
Sugar bowl, w/lid, high 16.00
Sugar bowl, w/lid, low 12.00
Syrup, any color 160.00
Teacup, high 9.00
Teacup, low 7.50
Teapot, high 80.00
Teapot, low 55.00
Tray, relish; mixed colors 180.00
Tumbler, high 40.00
Tumbler, low 30.00

Hatpin Holders

Most hatpin holders were made from 1860 to 1920 to coincide with the period during which hatpins were popularly in vogue. The taller types were required to house the long hatpins necessary to secure the large hats that were in style from 1890 to 1914. They were usually porcelain, either decorated by hand or by transfer with florals or scenics, although some were clever figurals. Glass examples are rare, and those of slag or carnival glass are especially valuable.

If you are interested in collecting or dealing in hatpins or hatpin holders, you will find that authority Lillian Baker has several fine books available on the subject, including her most recent publication *Hatpins and Hatpin Holders,* complete with beautiful color illustrations and current market values. She is listed in the Directory under California. For information concerning the International Club for Collectors of Hatpins and Hatpin Holders, see the Clubs, Newsletters, and Catalogs section of the Directory. Our advisor for this category is Robert Larsen; he is listed in the Directory under Nebraska.

Admiral Dewey, 13 pin holes, solid bottom, RS Prussia, red mark, 3¾", $1,200.00.

Hand-crafted brass leaf-and-flower mount set with 22mm green glass plaque, 2½" on 7" pin, $150.00. (Photo courtesy Vern Gaston.)

Chocolate glass, emb florals, ca 1905, 7⅞" 350.00
Goss, City of York crest, 3½" 110.00
Limoges, Nouveau lady & peacock, gold trim, 3⅝" 250.00
Nippon, moriage butterflies, gold beading, 5⅛" 85.00
Royal Bayreuth, clover figural, bl mk, 4½" 375.00
Royal Bayreuth, Nouveau lady figural, bl mk, 4½" 475.00
Royal Doulton, hunt scene, ca 1910, 4¾" 145.00
Royal Doulton, Shakespeare's Ophelia, 5x3½" 225.00
Schafer & Vater, bl jasper, Kewpies, sgn O'Neill, 4½" 165.00
Schafer & Vater, strawberries on brick tower, 5" 185.00
Willow Art China, Jewish symbol transfer, Jerusalem, 5½"............75.00

Hatpins

A hatpin was used to securely fasten a hat to the hair and head of the wearer. Hatpins, measuring from 4" to 12" in length, were worn from approximately 1850 to 1920. During the Art Deco period, hatpins became ornaments rather than the decorative functional jewels that they had been. The hatpin period reached its zenith in 1913 just prior to World War I, which brought about a radical change in women's headdress and fashion. About that time, women began to scorn the bonnet and adopt 'the hat' as a symbol of their equality. The hatpin was made of every natural and manufactured element in a myriad of designs that challenge the imagination. They were contrived to serve every fashion need and complement the milliner's art. Collectors often concentrate on a specific type: hand-painted porcelains, sterling silver, commemoratives, sporting activities, carnival glass, Art Nouveau and/or Art Deco designs, Victorian Gothics with mounted stones, exquisite rhinestones, engraved and brass-mounted escutcheon heads, gold and gems, or simply primitive types made in the Victorian parlor. Some collectors prefer the long pin-shanks while others select only those on tremblants or nodder-type pin-shanks.

If you are interested in collecting or dealing in hatpins, see the information in the Hatpin Holders introduction concerning reference books and a national collectors' club. For further study we recommend *The Collector's Encyclopedia of Hatpins and Hatpin Holders*, available at your local bookstore. Our advisor for this category is Robert Larsen; he is listed in the Directory under Nebraska.

Key: cab — cabochon

Amethyst, faceted oval, in sterling mt, lg 55.00
Amethyst stone atop brass mt w/emb florals, 1¼x1¼"....................50.00
Baroque MOP on gold mt w/faux rubies, 1½" 80.00
Ceramic w/HP Deco motif, brass mt, ca 1913, 1½" 95.00
Concentric rings of molded plastic, brass mts, 1920s, 2" 25.00
Enameled scene on brass w/hand-set bl stones, oval........................60.00
Jet teardrop form, faceted, 2" 40.00
Mercury glass, cased, Bohemia, ca 1905, 2¼".................................85.00
Mosaic flower in metal mt w/gold-wire trim, ca 1875, 1" 75.00
Nouveau flower form, enamel on copper, ca 1900, 1" 50.00
Nouveau lady in open shell, emb sterling, 1"...................................75.00
Pearl enfolded by silver-metal calla lilies, 1½"................................60.00
Porc w/HP figures, gold overlay, ca 1890, 1¾" 155.00
Satsuma, HP birds & leaves, 1½", on 10½" steel pin........................250.00
Satsuma, HP robins, metallic mt, 1½", on 9" pin 275.00
Scorpion, brass on pearl & brass filigree, 3", EX 125.00
Sweet pea figural, sterling, 1¼", 8" pin..80.00

Haviland

The Haviland China Company was organized in 1840 by David Haviland, a New York china importer. His search for a pure white, non-porous porcelain led him to Limoges, France, where natural deposits of suitable clay had already attracted numerous china manufacturers. The fine china he produced there was translucent and meticulously decorated, with each piece fired in an individual sagger.

It has been estimated that as many as 60,000 chinaware patterns were designed, each piece marked with one of several company backstamps. 'H. & Co.' was used until 1890 when a law was enacted making it necessary to include the country of origin. Various marks have been used since that time including 'Haviland, France'; 'Haviland & Co. Limoges'; and 'Decorated by Haviland & Co.' Various associations with family members over the years have resulted in changes in management as well as company name. In 1892 Theodore Haviland left the firm to start his own business. Some of his ware was marked 'Mont Mery.' Later logos included a horseshoe, a shield, and various uses of his initials and name. In 1941 this branch moved to the United States. Wares produced here are marked 'Theodore Haviland, N.Y.' or 'Made In America.'

Though it is their dinnerware lines for which they are most famous, during the 1880s and 1890s they also made exquisite art pottery using a technique of underglaze slip decoration called Barbotine, which had been invented by Ernest Chaplet. In 1885 Haviland bought the formula and hired Chaplet to oversee its production. The technique involved mixing heavy white clay slip with pigments to produce a compound of the same consistency as oil paints. The finished product actually resembled oil paintings of the period, the texture achieved through the application of the heavy medium to the clay body in much the same manner as an artist would apply paint to his canvas. Primarily the body used with this method was a low-fired faience, though they also produced stoneware.

Authority Mary Frank Gaston has compiled a lovely book, *Haviland Collectibles and Objects of Art*, with full-color illustrations and current values; you will find her address in the Directory under Texas. Numbers in the listings below refer to pattern books by Arlene Schleiger.

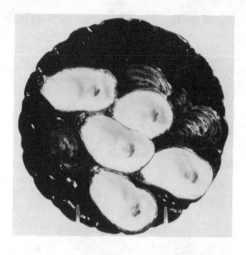

Oyster plate, 8¾", $175.00.

Berry set, HP florals, Diana form, 1876-89, 4-pc	400.00
Berry set, violets, amateur decor, 6-pc	80.00
Bonbon plate, florals on Marseille form, 1893-1930, 9"	110.00
Bowl, vegetable; Blackberry, sq, w/lid	65.00
Box, powder; gr ivy w/red berries, star blank	125.00
Box, Sandoz, crouching monkey form, yel & wht, 7"	625.00
Butter tub, floral swags, 1904-20s, 3½", +6½" plate	85.00
Cake plate, Her Majesty, Satsuma form, 8½x12"	165.00
Chamberstick, rosebuds & florals on Marseille form, 3x5½"	145.00
Chocolate pot, boat scenic, bl transfer, anchor blank	150.00
Chocolate pot, Diana form, salesman's sample, 1876-89, 9½"	125.00
Chocolate pot, florals, ribbon hdl, dbl mk, 10", +5 c/s	425.00
Chocolate pot, florals w/gold, star form, 1893-1931, 8"	175.00
Chocolate pot, HP birds/butterflies/florals, 1876-89, 9"	175.00
Chocolate pot, pk florals w/gold, emb scallops, 1890s, 5¼"	95.00
Chocolate pot, roses w/gold, Rouen form, mk	125.00
Chocolate set, Baltimore Rose, Ranson, 1893-1930, 12-pc	2,850.00
Coffeepot, floral sprays, Pompador, 1888-96, 8½"	175.00
Coffeepot, no decor, 1850s-65, rare, 10½"	435.00
Coffeepot, Sandoz, bird figural, 1904-20s, 5½"	500.00
Compote, center medallion, ormulu mtd, 1893-1930, 7x5½"	125.00
Cracker jar, cobalt w/gold, Marseille form, 1888-96, 8"	180.00
Cracker jar, HP violets, Rouen form, 1895-1903, 7¼"	160.00
Creamer, Sandoz, bird figural, 1920-36, 4½"	400.00
Cup & saucer, demi; bird & floral w/gold, 1876-1930	55.00
Cup & saucer, mustache; floral, Marseille form, 1876-89	135.00
Cup & saucer, orchids & dragonflies, salesman's sample, mk	100.00
Cup & saucer, pk floral in center, Ranson form	80.00
Cup & saucer, Rosalinde, French	35.00
Ewer, rose & daisies HP over relief, 1865-75, 8"	165.00
Game plate, wild bird on Tresse form, 1876-80, 9"	55.00
Humidor, bl ribbon bands w/pk flowers & gold, 7"	275.00
Humidor, elephant form, gold trim, 1850s-65, 8"	11,000.00
Ice cream shell, RR china, De Pew, 1893-1930, 5¼x5"	115.00
Invalid feeder, no decor, whiteware, 1893-1930, 2½x6½"	55.00
Jam jar, gold floral bands & trim, 1893-1930, 4", +6" plate	160.00
Jardiniere, gold decor on wht, Marseille form, 4x9¾"	185.00
Jardiniere, HP over transfer florals, 1876-89, 12x8"	165.00
Menu stand, florals on Marseille form, 1888-96, 6½x4"	190.00
Pitcher, milk; Norma, Ranson form, 1893-1930, 7"	145.00
Pitcher, Moss Rose, gold trim, 1850s-65	85.00
Pitcher, water; HP emb florals w/gold, 1850s-65, 10"	150.00
Plate, #24, Ranson blank, salad sz	12.00
Plate, fish center, F Bracquemond, 1876-89, 8½", pr	175.00
Plate, Greenaway-style figures, Tresse mold, 1876-80, 9½"	175.00
Plate, stag sits, doe stands, ornate border	95.00
Platter, floral, pk on wht, gold & wht bows, Limoges, 16x11"	50.00
Pudding dish, gold trim, hdld liner, 1904-20s	170.00
Sardine box, HP, fish form hdl, 1888-96, 1¼x4½"	95.00
Shaving mug, gold name & trim, 1876-78, 3¼"	100.00

Spooner, Hotel China, for J Reed Whipple, 1893, 6"	145.00
Spooner, yel & brn florals, sq vase shape	150.00
Sugar bowl, emb florals, flower finial, gold trim, 1850s-60	70.00
Teacup, gray ivy & wht berries, butterfly hdl	90.00
Teapot, bl & gold bands, anchor blank, +cr/sug	125.00
Teapot, emb florals, flower finial, gold trim, 1850s-65	85.00
Teapot, pk floral, Frank Haviland mk, 5", +cr/sug	325.00
Teapot, pk floral & gr ivy, ca 1893-1930, 5"	80.00
Tray, Drop Rose, wht, 1876-1930, 15¾x10¾"	495.00
Tureen, Napkin Fold form, shell finial/hdls, 8¼x12½"	185.00
Tureen, soup; Blackberry	150.00
Vase, birds on flowering branches on bl/gr, 1880s, 16", EX	1,800.00
Vase, cream bsk finish, Marseille form, 1876-89, 8½"	265.00
Vase, grapes, sgn, non-factory decor, hdls, 1893-1930, 12"	225.00
Vase, pottery, young fisherman (sgraffito), Chaplet mk, 11"	1,500.00
Vase, Terra Cotta, florals, sgn R, 1873-82, 5"	500.00
Vase, Terra Cotta, mc florals on brn, 3-ftd, 1873-82, 5"	475.00
Vase, Terra Cotta, sculpted florals, 12", pr	1,200.00

Vase, art pottery, gold and silver birds on green and blue mottled background, marked, late 19th century, rim chips, 16", $3,600.00 for the pair.

Hawkes

Thomas Hawkes established his factory in Corning, New York, in 1880. He developed many beautiful patterns of cut glass, two of which were awarded the Grand Prize at the Paris Exposition in 1889. By the end of the century, his company was renowned for the finest in cut glass production. The company logo was a trefoil form enclosing a hawk in each of the two bottom lobes with a fleur-de-lis in the center. Approximately one of every two pieces is marked.

Our advisors for this catgory are Jeanette and Marvin Stofft; they are listed in the Directory under Indiana.

Basket, brilliant cut, t'print hdl, flared sides, 9x7x9"	**1,500.00**
Bottle, scent; floral etch, bl enamel stopper w/cupids, 6"	400.00
Bowl, daisies/feathered leaves, scalloped base, 6x10" dia	500.00
Bowl, Gravic, low, 7"	395.00
Candelabra, 3-arm, etched floral, 15x13½", pr	500.00
Candlestick, hollow teardrop stem, star-cut base, 14", pr	600.00
Carafe, dmn/hobstar vesicas, paneled neck, 1900, sgn, 8"	175.00
Cocktail shaker, etched & gilt dragon, SP top, 8½"	275.00
Creamer & sugar bowl, hobstars, faceted knop ped, 5¾"	550.00
Cruet, etched/cut, Oil & Vinegar, orig stopper, 1900, 7½"	100.00
Decanter, Colonial, sgn	180.00
Decanter, thistle etching, sterling rim/top, monogram, 12"	150.00
Display sign, wedge form w/trademk & 'Hawkes Crystal', 4"	425.00
Ice cream set, Gravic, Poppy, 15" dia tray+12 ind	5,500.00
Lamp base, 8-sided/faceted, 6-sided cut base, 22½"	650.00
Pitcher, Hawkes bust portrait/armorial, sgn WH Morse, 15"	4,000.00
Pitcher, Navarre, +4 tumblers	850.00
Plate, St Regis, 5"	95.00
Punch bowl, plain & alternating cut panel sections, 12" H	800.00
Ring tray, Garcia etch, ca 1920, 4x3"	75.00
Toothpick holder, Gravic, mk	120.00
Tray, Late Devonshire, heavy, sgn, 13"	1,200.00
Vase, bl flashed, eng floral swags, silver trim, sgn, 8"	110.00
Vase, eng decor & silver o/l bands on bl, mk, 12¼"	225.00
Vase, eng decor & silver o/l bands on bl, mk, 8¼"	125.00
Vase, eng leaves, clear w/gr ft, 7½"	150.00
Vase, flowers eng on cobalt, 7"	125.00
Vase, Gravic, cut & etched flower garlands, mk, 11¾"	255.00
Vase, Gravic, flower garlands, mk, 11¾"	350.00
Vase, Gravic, Iris, w/presentation, cylinder, 12½"	800.00
Vase, Vernay, bulbous stem, 12½x5"	210.00

Heisey

A.H. Heisey began his long career at the King Glass Company of Pittsburgh. He later joined the Ripley Glass Company which soon became Geo. Duncan and Sons. After Duncan's death, Heisey became half-owner in partnership with his brother-in-law, James Duncan. In 1895 he built his own factory in Newark, Ohio, initiating production in 1896 and continuing until Christmas of 1957. At that time, Imperial Glass Corporation bought some of the moulds. After 1968 they removed the old 'Diamond H' from any moulds they put into use. In 1985 HCA purchased all of Imperial's Heisey molds with the exception of the Old Williamsburg line.

During their highly successful period of production, Heisey made fine hand-crafted tableware with simple, yet graceful designs. Early pieces were not marked. After November 1901, the glassware was marked either with the 'Diamond H' or a paper label. Blown ware is often marked on the stem, never on the bowl or foot. For information concerning Heisey Collectors of America, see the Clubs, Newsletters, and Catalogs section of the Directory.

Animals and Birds

Airdale	450.00
Asiatic Pheasant	325.00

Bull, sgn	1,200.00
Chick, head down	60.00
Chick, head up	60.00
Clydesdale	375.00
Clydesdale, Harvey amber	1,500.00
Colt, kicking	190.00
Colt, kicking, amber	550.00
Colt, kicking, cobalt	950.00
Colt, rearing	195.00
Colt, rearing, amber	575.00
Colt, rearing, cobalt	950.00
Colt, standing	90.00
Colt, standing, amber	550.00
Colt, standing, cobalt	900.00
Cygnet, baby swan, 2½"	185.00
Dolphin, candlestick, #110, pr	240.00
Dolphin, candlestick, moongleam, #110, pr	400.00
Donkey	235.00
Duck, ash tray	95.00
Duck, ash tray, flamingo	140.00
Duck, ash tray, marigold	195.00
Duck, flower block	130.00
Duck, flower block, hawthorne	240.00
Elephant, amber, lg	1,850.00
Elephant, amber, med	1,850.00
Elephant, amber, sm	1,600.00
Elephant, lg	350.00
Elephant, med	325.00
Elephant, sm	195.00
Fish, bookend	125.00

Fish bowl, 9", $495.00.

Fish, candlestick	140.00
Fish, match holder	140.00
Fish, Tropical	1,200.00
Flying Mare	2,200.00
Flying Mare, dk amber	3,500.00
Frog, cheese plate, #1210, flamingo	125.00
Frog, cheese plate, marigold	285.00
Frog, cheese plate, moongleam	240.00
Gazelle	1,800.00
Giraffe, head bk	175.00
Giraffe, head to side	175.00
Goose, wings down	375.00
Goose, wings half	95.00
Goose, wings up	100.00
Hen	360.00

Hen, amber.. 1,000.00
Horse head, bookend 135.00
Horse head, bookend, amber........................... 2,000.00
Horse head, cigarette box, #1489, 4½x4"..............55.00
Horse head, cocktail shaker.................................85.00
Irish Setter, ash tray...30.00
Irish Setter, ash tray, flamingo...........................45.00
Irish Setter, ash tray, moongleam 55.00
Kingfisher, flower block, flamingo.....................225.00
Kingfisher, flower block, hawthorne 300.00
Kingfisher, flower block, moongleam 250.00
Mallard, wings down..275.00
Mallard, wings half 150.00
Mallard, wings up 130.00
Piglet, sitting 75.00
Piglet, standing 75.00
Plug Horse..110.00
Plug Horse, amber..600.00
Plug Horse, cobalt 1,000.00
Pouter Pigeon 600.00
Rabbit, paperweight..145.00
Ringneck Pheasant, 11¾"..................................125.00
Rooster, amber, 5⅜".......................................2,500.00
Rooster, Fighting, 8" 150.00
Rooster, vase, 6½" 85.00
Rooster, 5⅜"..350.00
Rooster head, cocktail 50.00
Rooster head, cocktail shaker, 1-qt 95.00
Scotty..95.00
Scotty, frosted 95.00
Sea Horse, cocktail 140.00
Show Horse..800.00
Sow 440.00
Sparrow...80.00
Swan, ind nut, #1503...18.00
Swan, master nut, #1503....................................45.00
Swan, 7"...600.00
Wood Duck 500.00

Dinnerware

Adam, crystal; sherbet, #3376, 6-oz...................20.00
Adam, crystal; tumbler, #3376, ftd, 10-oz 20.00
Adam, flamingo; goblet, #3376, 11-oz................60.00
Adam, flamingo; wine, #3376, 3-oz 60.00
Admiralty, crystal; cocktail, #3424, 3-oz.............40.00
Admiralty, crystal; cordial, #3424, 1-oz 125.00
Admiralty, crystal; wine, #3424, 2-oz 75.00
African, crystal; goblet, #3370, 8-oz 30.00
African, crystal; wine, #3370, 3-oz 30.00
African, flamingo; cocktail, #3370, 4-oz..............45.00
Albemarle, crystal; cordial, #3368, 1-oz 75.00
Albemarle, flamingo; cocktail, #3368, 3-oz..........25.00
Albemarle, marigold; finger bowl, #3309 ....55.00
Albemarle, moongleam; claret, #3368, 4-oz 25.00
Albemarle, moongleam; wine, #3368, 2½" 60.00
Barbara Fritchie, crystal; claret, #3416, 3¾-oz......50.00
Barbara Fritchie, crystal; finger bowl, #3335 ....10.00
Barbara Fritchie, crystal; wine, #3416, 2½-oz 40.00
Barbara Fritchie, sahara; cordial, #3416, tall, 1-oz....400.00
Biltmore, crystal; bowl, finger; #4075 ....10.00
Biltmore, crystal; burgundy, #3316, 3-oz.............15.00
Biltmore, crystal; cocktail, #3316, 3-oz...............15.00
Carcassonne, crystal; claret, #3390, 4-oz 20.00

Carcassonne, crystal; wine, #3390, 2½-oz 30.00
Carcassonne, flamingo; finger bowl, #3390, ftd 30.00
Carcassonne, flamingo; goblet, tall, #3390, 11-oz....50.00
Carcassonne, sahara; cigarette holder, #3390 ....45.00
Carcassonne, sahara; goblet, short, #3390, 11-oz 50.00
Charter Oak, crystal; finger bowl, #3326 ....10.00
Charter Oak, flamingo; goblet, luncheon; #3326, 8-oz....40.00
Charter Oak, flamingo; jug, #3362, ½-gal............175.00
Charter Oak, moongleam; cocktail, 3-oz...............30.00
Coarse Rib, crystal; creamer, #407, ind 20.00
Coarse Rib, crystal; finger bowl 10.00
Coarse Rib, crystal; jug, ½-gal 65.00
Coarse Rib, crystal; sugar bowl, #407, ind............20.00
Coarse Rib, crystal; tumbler, str, 8-oz.................15.00
Coarse Rib, moongleam; celery tray, #407, 9" 30.00
Coarse Rib, moongleam; hotel sugar bowl, #406, w/lid....35.00
Coarse Rib, moongleam; tumbler, #406, 8-oz.........45.00
Coleport, crystal; goblet, #1486, 8-oz 40.00
Coleport, crystal; tumbler, #1486, 10-oz..............20.00
Coleport, crystal; wine, #1486, 2½-oz 40.00
Comet Leaf, crystal; goblet, #1306, 9-oz 45.00
Comet Leaf, sahara; soda, #1306, ftd, 12-oz.........55.00
Coronation, crystal; cocktail, #4054, 3-oz............20.00
Coronation, crystal; jug, #4054, ½-gal 95.00
Coventry, crystal; claret, #4090, 4½-oz................40.00
Coventry, crystal; finger bowl, #4090 ....10.00
Coventry, zircon; goblet, #4090, 10-oz...............160.00
Coventry, zircon; wine, #4090, 2½-oz.................185.00
Creole, alexandrite; finger bowl, #3381, ftd 90.00
Creole, alexandrite/crystal; cocktail, #3381, 4-oz....125.00
Creole, alexandrite/crystal; cordial, #3381, 1-oz 325.00
Creole, sahara/crystal; parfait, #3381, 5-oz...........70.00
Delaware, crystal; cocktail, #3324, 3½-oz 20.00
Delaware, crystal; goblet, luncheon; #3324, 9-oz....30.00
Delaware, flamingo; finger bowl, #3324 ....15.00
Delaware, hawthorne; goblet, #3324, 9-oz 90.00
Diamond Rose, crystal; goblet, #3386, 11-oz........50.00
Diamond Rose, flamingo; cocktail, #3386.............50.00
Diamond Rose, sahara; pilsner, #3386, 12-oz........125.00
Double Ring, crystal; goblet, #7005 ....200.00
Duquesne, crystal; cocktail, #3389, 3-oz..............25.00
Duquesne, crystal; cordial, #3389, 1-oz 65.00
Duquesne, crystal; tumbler, #3389, ftd, 10-oz.......10.00
Duquesne, sahara; parfait, #3389, 5-oz................40.00
Duquesne, sahara; wine, #3389, 2½-oz.................50.00
Empress, crystal; bowl, salad; #1401, sq, 10".......35.00
Empress, flamingo; candlestick, #1401, pr, 6".......300.00
Empress, flamingo; plate, dessert; #1401, oval, 10"....60.00
Empress, flamingo; sugar bowl, #1401, ind...........35.00
Empress, moongleam; candy box, #1401, w/lid, 6"....135.00
Empress, moongleam; plate, #1401, 8"..................20.00
Empress, moongleam; plate, #1401, 9" 20.00
Empress, moongleam; platter, #1401, oval, 14".......45.00
Empress, sahara; goblet, #1401, 9-oz...................60.00
Empress, sahara; plate, #1401½, sq, 8"................25.00
Fairacre, crystal; iced tea, #3355, ftd, hdl, 12-oz 25.00
Fairacre, crystal; wine, #3355, 2½-oz..................35.00
Fairacre, flamingo; sherbet, #3355, 6½-oz 30.00
Fairacre, moongleam; finger bowl, #4074 ....15.00
Fern, crystal; cheese, #1495, hdl 15.00
Fern, zircon; plate, torte; #1495, hdl, 13".............110.00
Galaxy, crystal; goblet, #8005............................45.00
Galaxy, moongleam; sherbet, #8005 ....40.00
Gascony, crystal; candlestick, #138, pr, 5"............100.00

Gascony, crystal; cocktail, #3397, 3-oz 35.00
Gascony, sahara; creamer, #3397 ....80.00
Gascony, sahara; tumbler, #3397, ftd, 10-oz 100.00
Gayoso, crystal; goblet, #3312, 11-oz 15.00
Gayoso, flamingo; cocktail, #3312, 9½-oz 20.00
Gayoso, marigold; wine, #3312, 2½" 100.00
Ipswich, crystal; candlestick, #1405, pr, 6" 175.00
Ipswich, flamingo; tumbler, #1405, 10-oz 45.00
Ipswich, moongleam; plate, #1405, 8" 25.00
Ipswich, sahara; plate, #1405, sq, 7" 20.00
Jamestown, crystal; wine, #3408, 2-oz 45.00
Jamestown, flamingo; goblet, #3408, 9-oz 200.00
Jamestown, sahara; claret, #3408, 4½-oz 80.00
Jamestown, sahara; finger bowl, #3309 ....35.00
Kenilworth, crystal; claret, #4092, 4½-oz 45.00
Kenilworth, crystal; finger bowl, #4092 ....20.00
Kenilworth, crystal; wine, #4092, 2-oz 85.00
Kimberly, crystal; goblet, #4091, 10-oz 40.00
Kimberly, crystal; wine, #4091, 2-oz 55.00
Kimberly, zircon; claret, #4091, 4½-oz 100.00
Kimberly, zircon; finger bowl, #3335 ....45.00
King Arthur, crystal; cocktail, #3357, 3½-oz 15.00
King Arthur, flamingo; iced tea, #3357, ftd, 12-oz 30.00
King Arthur, moongleam; cocktail, oyster; #3357, 3½-oz 30.00
King Arthur, moongleam; parfait, #3357, 5-oz 45.00
Kohinoor, crystal; finger bowl, #3335 ....10.00
Kohinoor, zircon; bowl, salad; #4085, 11" 160.00
Kohinoor, zircon; bridge ash tray, #1488 ....50.00
Kohinoor, zircon; cocktail, #4085, 3-oz 45.00
Kohinoor, zircon; hors d'oeuvres, #1488, 17" 175.00
Kohinoor, zircon; wine, #4085, 2½-oz 130.00
Marriette, crystal; bowl, finger; #3335 ....10.00
Marriette, crystal; claret, #3414, 3¾-oz 40.00
Marriette, crystal; cordial, #3414, 1-oz 100.00
Marriette, crystal; wine, #3414, 2½-oz 75.00
Monte Cristo, crystal; claret, #3411, 4-oz 30.00
Monte Cristo, crystal; finger bowl, #3309 ....10.00
Monte Cristo, crystal; tumbler, #3411, ftd, 9-oz 15.00
Monte Cristo, sahara; sherbet, #3411, 6-oz 80.00
Monte Cristo, sahara; wine, #3411, 2½-oz 200.00
Narrow Flute w/Rim, crystal; plate, #473, oval, 6" 15.00
Narrow Flute w/Rim, flamingo; tray, pickle; #473, 6" 20.00
New Era, cobalt; cordial, clear stem, #4044, 1-oz 300.00
New Era, cobalt; goblet, clear stem, #4044, 10-oz 200.00
New Era, crystal; celery tray, #4044, 13" 35.00
New Era, crystal; sherbet, #4044, 6-oz 25.00
Octagon, crystal; ice tub, #500 ....35.00
Octagon, flamingo; plate, sandwich; #1229, 10" or 12" 25.00
Octagon, flamingo; sugar bowl, #500 ....25.00
Octagon, marigold; bowl, bonbon; #1229, 6" 40.00
Octagon, moongleam; dessert dish, #1229, oval, 8" 35.00
Octagon, moongleam; tray, #500, oblong, 6" 22.00
Octagon, sahara; hors d'oeuvres, #1229, 13" 40.00
Old Dominion, alexandrite; comport, #3380, 7" 275.00
Old Dominion, crystal; cordial, #3380, 1-oz 70.00
Old Dominion, crystal; finger bowl, #4075 ....10.00
Old Dominion, flamingo; sherbet, #3380, 6-oz 35.00
Old Dominion, moongleam; cocktail, oyster; #3380, 4-oz 25.00
Old Glory, crystal; finger bowl, #3309 ....10.00
Old Glory, crystal; wine, #3333, 2-oz 45.00
Old Glory, hawthorne; burgundy, #3333, 3-oz 75.00
Old Glory, hawthorne; goblet, #3333, 9-oz 80.00
Old Sandwich, crystal; creamer, #1404, 12-oz 30.00
Old Sandwich, crystal; shakers, #1404, pr 35.00

Old Sandwich, flamingo; cocktail, #1404, 3-oz 35.00
Old Sandwich, flamingo; sugar bowl, #1404, oval 35.00
Old Sandwich, moongleam; goblet, #1404, ftd, 10-oz 45.00
Old Sandwich, moongleam; mug, beer; #1404, 12-oz 310.00
Old Sandwich, moongleam; plate, #1404, sq, 7" 20.00
Old Sandwich, sahara; cigarette holder, #1404 ....200.00
Old Sandwich, sahara; plate, #1404, sq, 6" 20.00

**Orchid pattern scent bottle,
8", $175.00.**

Park Lane, crystal; cocktail, #4055, 3-oz 25.00
Park Lane, crystal; finger bowl, #4080 ....10.00
Penn Charter, crystal; finger bowl, #3309 ....10.00
Penn Charter, crystal; goblet, #3360, 10-oz 25.00
Penn Charter, crystal; soda, #3360, 12-oz 20.00
Penn Charter, flamingo; cocktail, #3360, 3-oz 40.00
Penn Charter, hawthorne; goblet, #3360, 8½-oz 75.00
Plateau, crystal; cocktail, #3359, 3-oz 12.00
Plateau, crystal; rose bowl, #3359, 6" 35.00
Plateau, flamingo; finger bowl, #3359 ....20.00
Plateau, marigold; soda, #3359, 8-oz 40.00
Pleat & Panel, flamingo; goblet, luncheon; #1170, 7½-oz 30.00
Pleat & Panel, moongleam; bowl, cereal; #1170, 6½" 20.00
Pleat & Panel, moongleam; platter, #1170, oval, 12" 30.00
Plymouth, sahara; cocktail, oyster; #3409, 3-oz 35.00
Plymouth, sahara; finger bowl, #3335 ....80.00
Portsmouth, crystal; cocktail, #3340, 3½-oz 15.00
Quaker, crystal; nappy, #1463, 8" 25.00
Quaker, crystal; plate, #1463, 9" 25.00
Quator, crystal; sanitary syrup, #355, 24-oz 80.00
Quator, moongleam; creamer, #355, ftd 35.00
Queen Guinevere, crystal; goblet, #8045 ....100.00
Rampul, crystal; cocktail, oyster; #3325, 4½-oz 15.00
Rampul, hawthorne; cocktail, #3325, 3-oz 65.00
Ramshorn, crystal; fruit salad, #3365, 5" 15.00
Ramshorn, flamingo; cocktail, #3365, 3-oz 40.00
Rib in Ring, moongleam; cocktail, #8021 ....350.00
Ribbed Octagon, flamingo; bowl, grapefruit; #1231, 6½" 20.00
Ribbed Octagon, flamingo; vegetable dish, #1231, 9" 22.00
Ribbed Octagon, moongleam; candlestick, #1231, 3", pr 70.00
Ribbed Octagon, moongleam; plate, #1231, 8" 15.00
Ridgeleigh, amber; shakers, #1469½ 350.00
Ridgeleigh, crystal; comport, #1469, low ftd, w/lid, 6" 45.00
Ridgeleigh, crystal; decanter, #1469, w/stopper, 1-pt 95.00
Ridgeleigh, crystal; marmalade w/lid, #1469 ....55.00

Ridgeleigh, crystal; nappy, #1469, 4½" 15.00
Ridgeleigh, crystal; plate, #1469, sq, 8" 30.00
Ridgeleigh, crystal; plate, #1469, 6" 15.00
Ridgeleigh, crystal; plate, sandwich; #1469, 13½" 35.00
Ridgeleigh, crystal; plate, torte; #1469, 13" 45.00
Ridgeleigh, crystal; tray, celery & olive; #1469, 12" 25.00
Ridgeleigh, sahara; cigarette holder, #1469, rnd............60.00
Ridgeleigh, zircon; ash tray, #1469, sq...........................55.00
Ridgeleigh, zircon; vase, #1469½, 8".............................185.00
Rococo, crystal; cigarette box, #1447, w/lid...................70.00
Rococo, crystal; comport, #1447, 6"................................55.00
Rococo, crystal; plate, #1447, 7" 25.00
Rococo, sahara; celery tray, #1447, 12".........................60.00
Rococo, sahara; plate, cheese & cracker; #1447, ftd......175.00
Rococo, sahara; tray, roll; #1447 ....75.00
Saturn, crystal; bowl, salad; #1485, 11" 35.00
Saturn, crystal; cocktail, #1485, 3-oz 15.00
Saturn, crystal; plate, #1485, 8" 10.00
Saturn, crystal; sugar bowl, #1485 ....25.00
Saturn, crystal; tumbler, luncheon; #1485, 10-oz..........60.00
Saturn, zircon; baked apple dish, #1485.........................75.00
Saturn, zircon; candleblock, #1485, 2-lite, pr 400.00
Saturn, zircon; finger bowl, #1485..................................50.00
Saturn, zircon; plate, #1485, 7".......................................45.00
Saturn, zircon; plate, torte; #1485, 15"...........................75.00
Saturn, zircon; tumbler, #1485, 10-oz.............................60.00
Saturn, zircon; vase, violet; #1485.................................125.00
Savoy Plaza, crystal; claret, #3418, 4-oz 30.00
Savoy Plaza, crystal; cocktail, #3418, 3½-oz..................30.00
Savoy Plaza, crystal; finger bowl, #4080 ....10.00
Savoy Plaza, crystal; sherry, #3418, 1½-oz 90.00
Saxony, crystal; goblet, #3394, short, 12-oz 35.00
Saxony, crystal; vase, #3394, ftd, 9" 60.00
Saxony, sahara; cordial, #3394, 1-oz 140.00
Saxony, sahara; finger bowl, #4074.................................20.00
Saxony, sahara; goblet, #3394, tall, 12-oz 80.00
Spanish, cobalt; comport, #3404, 6"...............................300.00
Spanish, crystal; claret, #3404, 4-oz 40.00
Spanish, crystal; wine, #3404, 2½-oz 60.00
Stanhope, crystal; ash tray, #1469, ind...........................20.00
Stanhope, crystal; bowl, salad; #1483, 11" 40.00
Stanhope, crystal; claret, #4083, 4-oz.............................30.00
Stanhope, crystal; creamer, #1483, 1-hdl 25.00
Stanhope, crystal; plate, #1483, 7"..................................15.00
Stanhope, crystal; vase, #1483, ball form, 7"..................50.00
Stanhope, crystal; wine, #4083, 2½" 35.00
Sussex, flamingo; goblet, #419, 10-oz 70.00
Sussex, moongleam; finger bowl, #419............................25.00
Trojan, crystal; goblet, #3366, 8-oz.................................25.00
Trojan, flamingo; cordial, #3366, 1-oz...........................110.00
Trojan, hawthorne; sherbet, #3366, 5-oz 50.00
Trojan, moongleam; cocktail, #3366, 3-oz.......................30.00
Tudor, crystal; bowl, nut; 4½" 25.00
Tudor, crystal; finger bowl, #411 ....12.00
Tudor, crystal; finger bowl, #412 ....10.00
Tudor, crystal; fruit dish, 10" 35.00
Tudor, crystal; punch bowl, #411, ftd 200.00
Tudor, crystal; shakers, #411, pr......................................35.00
Tudor, crystal; sherbet, #412, 5-oz...................................15.00
Tudor, crystal; tray, pickle; 7"..20.00
Tudor, crystal; tumbler, #412, 8-oz..................................12.00
Tudor, crystal; tumbler, juice; #411, 4½-oz.....................10.00
Tudor, flamingo; cigarette box, #412, w/lid 80.00
Tudor, hawthorne; bowl, bonbon; #411, hdls 35.00

Tudor, hawthorne; cigarette jar & ash tray, #411...........150.00
Tudor, moongleam; goblet, luncheon; #411, 7-oz............45.00
Tudor, moongleam; sugar bowl, #411, hdld, hotel sz 35.00
Twentieth Century, crystal; soda, #1415, ftd, 5-oz 20.00
Twentieth Century, flamingo; bowl, cereal; #1415, w/7" plate 60.00
Twist, crystal; creamer, #1252 ....20.00
Twist, crystal; sugar bowl, #1252, ind.............................20.00
Twist, flamingo; platter, #1252, oval, 12" 35.00
Twist, flamingo; tray, pickle; #1252, 7"............................25.00
Twist, marigold; goblet, luncheon; #1252, 9-oz 50.00
Twist, marigold; ice tub, #1252......................................130.00
Twist, marigold; plate, #1252, 12"...................................60.00
Twist, marigold; plate, #1252, 9".....................................30.00
Twist, marigold; relish, #1252, 3-part, 13" 40.00
Twist, moongleam; candlestick, #1252, pr, 2"..................80.00
Twist, moongleam; plate, muffin; #1252, hdls, 12" 40.00
Twist, moongleam; tumbler, #1252, 8-oz..........................25.00
Universal, crystal; champagne, #3304, 6½" 15.00
Universal, crystal; finger bowl, #3304 ....10.00
Universal, crystal; sherbet, #3304, 5½-oz 15.00
Velvedere, crystal; cocktail, #3311, 3½-oz 15.00
Velvedere, crystal; cordial, #3311, 1-oz...........................35.00
Velvedere, crystal; goblet, #3311, 10-oz 20.00
Velvedere, crystal; wine, #3311, 2-oz 20.00
Victorian, cobalt; bowl, floral; #1425, 10½" 275.00
Victorian, cobalt; candlestick, #1425, 3-lite, pr 600.00
Victorian, cobalt; shakers, #1425, pr..............................200.00
Victorian, crystal; plate, #1425, 7" 12.00
Victorian, crystal; plate, buffet; #1425, 21" 70.00
Victorian, crystal; vase, #1425, ftd, 9" 50.00
Victorian, sahara; plate, cracker; #1425, 12" 65.00
Victorian, sahara; shakers, #1425, pr..............................200.00
Victorian, sahara; tray, celery; #1425, 12" 60.00
Wabash, crystal; cocktail, #3350, 3-oz 15.00
Wabash, crystal; comport, #3350, ftd, w/lid, 6" 55.00
Wabash, crystal; parfait, #3350, 5-oz 25.00
Wabash, flamingo; tumbler, #3350, ftd, 10-oz 25.00
Wabash, hawthorne; parfait, #3350, 5-oz.........................75.00
Wabash, moongleam; sherbet, #3350, 6-oz 20.00
Wabash, moongleam; wine, #3350, 2½-oz 45.00
Waldorf, crystal; claret, #3318, 4-oz 25.00
Waldorf, crystal; cocktail, #3318, 3½" 15.00
Waldorf, crystal; cordial, #3318, 1-oz..............................50.00
Waldorf, crystal; finger bowl, #4080...............................10.00
Yeoman, crystal; plate, coaster; #1184, 4½" 10.00
Yeoman, crystal; plate, grapefruit; #1184, 6½" 10.00
Yeoman, crystal; plate, sandwich; #1184, hdld, 10½"......20.00
Yeoman, flamingo; bowl, bonbon; #1184, hdld, 6½".......35.00
Yeoman, flamingo; plate, #1184, 14" 30.00
Yeoman, marigold; plate, #1184, 7" 20.00
Yeoman, marigold; vegetable dish, #1184, w/lid.............140.00
Yeoman, moongleam; cocktail, #1184, 3-oz 25.00
Yeoman, moongleam; comport, #1184, ftd, 5" 40.00
Yeoman, moongleam; plate, #1184, oval, 7" 25.00
Yeoman, moongleam; plate, grill; #1184, 9" 40.00

Heubach

Gebruder Heubach is a German porcelain company that has been in operation since the 1800s producing quality figurines and novelty items. They are perhaps most famous for their doll heads and piano babies, most of which are marked with the circular rising sun device containing an 'H' superimposed over a 'C.'

Baby, seated, w/eggshell behind, surprised look, #9743, 5" 325.00
Baby crawling in wht gown, 5½x8" 425.00
Baby in brn bear costume, crawling, #5578, 3" 295.00
Baby in wht & bl smock, lying on bk, plays w/toe, 4" 250.00
Blk boy, seated/leaning on arm, clutches ear of corn, 6" 500.00
Blond baby sits in tattered shoe, 12" 1,900.00
Bowl, gr jasper, wht Indian on horse, oval, 5¾x5" 115.00
Boy & girl play Blind Man's Bluff, roses/gold, mk, 8" 550.00
Boy & girl playing dress-up, mirror in boy's hands, 10", pr..........735.00
Boy does handstand, mk, 6" 300.00
Boy sits bkwards on wicker chair, wears eyeglasses/hat, 10" 425.00
Boy stands at water's edge w/shovel & pail (wire bail), 10" 385.00
Bull dog, muzzled, sits on haunches, blk/wht, mk, 8" L 675.00
Child in bunny costume stands before eggshell, 9" 425.00

Dark Secret, 6", $450.00.

Dog, recumbent, head lifted, gray/wht gloss, 8" L 300.00
Dog (jar), very shaggy wht fur, sits upright/begging, 5" 450.00
Dutch boy & girl kissing, hands at sides, mk, 10" 395.00
Dutch boy by sq vase, mk, 6⅜x3⅜" 295.00
Dutch boy seated, leaning on basket, lg.......................................350.00
Dutch girl holds lg eggshell in apron, #3467, 6" 235.00
Dutch girl sits between milk pails, mk, 4" 200.00
Girl (jar), nude blonde is lid, wht egg is base, 7" 400.00
Girl dances in bl dress, lace collar, mc base, 11½" 500.00
Girl holds skirt wide/dances, lace bodice/bl skirt, 6" 225.00
Girl in lg hat sits & pulls off socks, 5" 200.00
Girl lifts skirt to curtsy, blonde in bl dress, mk, 9".....................300.00
Girl sits on wicker chair, knits scarf, wears mobcap, 7" 295.00
Man w/ax, lady w/baby, 12½", pr 725.00
Oriental lady w/basket on shoulder, mk, 6" 225.00
Vase, pastoral tapestry, cylindrical, MIG, 7" 145.00

Hickman, Royal Arden

Born in Willamette, Oregon, Royal A. Hickman was a genius in all aspects of design interpretation. Mr. Hickman's expertise can be seen in the designs of the lovely Heisey figurines, Kosta crystal, Bruce Fox aluminum, Three Crowns aluminum, Vernon Kilns, and Royal Haeger Pottery (as well as hand-crafted silver, furniture, and paintings).

Because Mr. Hickman moved around during much of his lifetime, his influence has been felt in all forms of the media. Designs from his independent companies include 'Royal Hickman Pottery and Lamps' (sold through Ceramic Arts, Inc., of Chattanooga, Tennessee), 'Royal Hickman's Paris Ware,' 'Royal Hickman — Florida,' and 'California Designed by Royal Hickman.' The following listings will give examples of pieces bearing the various trademarks. Our advisor for this category is

Lee Garmon; she is listed in the directory under Illinois. See also Royal Haegar; Vernon Kilns, Melinda pattern.

Bruce Fox Aluminum

Banana leaf, mk Royal Hickman-RH 6, 22½" L 20.00
Candle snuffer, sterling silver, sgn Royal Hickman, 12" 35.00
Dish, lobster, lg 40.00
Dish, 3-point leaf, sgn Royal Hickman, 15½" L............................20.00
Platter, fish, EX detail, sgn Royal Hickman-RH 3, 13x9" 50.00

California, Designed by Royal Hickman

Bowl, red w/blk highlights, #607, 9½"...15.00
Figurine, deer, apple gr w/wht spots, appl eyes, 15" 25.00
Figurine, giraffe & young, pk w/blk spots & base, 11x7" 35.00
Swan, red w/blk highlights, #643, 17" 40.00

Miscellaneous Signatures

Sea horse vase, sgn Royal Hickman USA, #468, 8" 25.00
Vase, fish figurine, 'petty crystal glaze,' #467 ....25.00
Vase, lg heart, sgn Royal Hickman, Italy, #3774 ....35.00

Royal Hickman — Florida

Vase, horse's head, gray w/wht mane, 13¾" 75.00
Vase, pouter pigeon, blk cascade, #599, 8½".................................40.00
Vase, swan, head down, blk cascade, #624-R, 14" 60.00

Historical Glass

Glassware commemorating particularly significant historical events became popular in the late 1800s. Bread trays were the most common form; but plates, mugs, pitchers, and other items were also pressed in clear as well as colored glass. It was sold in vast amounts at the 1876 Philadelphia Centennial Exposition by various manufacturers who exhibited their wares on the grounds. It remained popular well into the twentieth century.

In the listings that follow, L numbers refer to a book by Lindsey; M numbers correspond with a book by Marsh. Both are standard guides used by many collectors.

Our advisor for this category is Darlene Yohe; she is listed in the Directory under Arkansas. See also Bread Plates; Pattern Glass.

Bottle, Granger, L-266 ....110.00
Celery, Washington Centennial, L-29..55.00
Compote, Lincoln Drape, L-281, 8" 95.00
Cup, McKinley, w/lid, L-335 ....60.00
Cup plate, Garfield, L-297..110.00
Flask, Paul Jones 20.00
Flask, Washington & Jackson, dk amber 495.00
Goblet, Centennial Drape..45.00
Goblet, Philadelphia Centennial 45.00
Goblet, Pittsburgh Centennial 95.00
Goblet, Shield, 1876 Centennial 50.00
Goblet, Washington Centennial 60.00
Hat, Uncle Sam, no pnt, L-110 ....35.00
Jar, apothecary; Statue of Liberty, 1876 Phila Expo, pr...............275.00
Jar, apothecary; Viking 75.00
Lamp, oil; Goddess of Liberty, 1876 Centennial 125.00
Mug, Bumper to the Flag, sabers & 35-star flag 235.00
Mug, Centennial 1776-1876, emb stars on sides 90.00

Mug, Independence Hall, dtd 1876...................................65.00
Mug, Liberty Bell, 2"...155.00
Mug, Martyrs, L-272...100.00
Mug, Martyrs Lincoln & Garfield 50.00
Mug, Tennessee, L-102 ....55.00
Paperweight, Buddha, Philadelphia Centennial Expo 1876, 6" ...295.00
Paperweight, clear & frosted oval, L-276....................155.00
Paperweight, Director Goshorn, 1876, Gillinder, L-449 ....155.00
Paperweight, Indian Peace, clear/frosted, NE Glass, 1850...........450.00
Paperweight, Lincoln, clear/frosted, Gillinder, 1876, L-276 ....250.00
Paperweight, Lincoln, L-275 ....175.00
Paperweight, McKinley portrait, milk glass 125.00
Paperweight, Philadelphia 1876, Memorial Hall intaglio..........245.00
Paperweight, Plymouth Rock, L-18..............................90.00
Paperweight, Reclining Lion, Gillinder 225.00
Pickle dish, Emblem, L-58 ....45.00
Pitcher, Dewey, L-400 ....55.00
Pitcher, Grindley, L-401 ....95.00
Plate, Absecon Lighthouse, 7½".................................28.00
Plate, Columbus, milk glass 35.00
Plate, Garfield Memorial, L-302 ....35.00
Plate, Garfield Monument, milk glass, L-306................45.00
Plate, George Washington, milk glass 45.00
Plate, Liberty Bell, 10"...80.00
Plate, McKinley, #333 ....30.00
Plate, Niagara Falls, milk glass...................................35.00
Plate, Old Glory...45.00
Plate, Pittsburgh Expo, egg-&-dot border, 5¼" 25.00

Plate, We Mourn Our Nation's Loss, Garfield, gold
on clear, 11", $55.00.

Platter, George Washington, L-27 ....45.00
Relish, Centennial 1776-1876, bear-paw hdls 75.00
Relish, Liberty Bell, oval, 5¼x9¼"...............................45.00
Spooner, Log Cabin, L-184 ....115.00
Statue, Benjamin Harrison, frosted 225.00
Statue, Drummer Boy w/Dog, frosted, Gillinder, dtd 1876...........125.00
Statue, Ruth the Gleaner, frosted, 1876 Phila Expo, Gillinder ...175.00
Sugar bowl, Eagle, frosted, L-479 ....175.00
Sugar bowl, Liberty Bell, L-25 ....95.00
Sugar shaker, Proclaim Liberty Throughout the Land................195.00
Tumbler, Admiral Dewey portrait in wht enamel medallion 75.00
Tumbler, America, L-48 ....25.00
Tumbler, bar; Bumper to the Flag, Civil War, L-480 ....110.00
Tumbler, Civil War, Bay State Glass, set of 3: 3", 4", 4¾" 700.00

Tumbler, Lincoln Tribute...20.00
Tumbler, Lord's Prayer...35.00
Tumbler, Louisiana Purchase, L-107 ....35.00
Tumbler, Remember the Maine, L-471.........................22.00
Tumbler, Star Spangled Banner, blown, thin walls 25.00
Tumbler, whiskey; flag w/13 stars, eagle on shield, 3¼" 135.00

Hobbs, Brockunier, & Co.

Hobbs and Brockunier's South Wheeling Glass Works was in operation during the last quarter of the 19th century. They are most famous for their peachblow, amberina, Daisy and Button, and Hobnail pattern glass. The mainstay of the operation, however, was druggist items and plain glassware — bowls, mugs, and simple footed pitchers with shell handles. See also Frances Ware.

Butter pat, Daisy & Button, amberina, set of 6.............................650.00
Cruet, Hobnail, bl opal, orig bl faceted stopper, M 225.00
Cruet, Hobnail, vaseline, orig stopper, 7¾" 335.00
Cruet, wht mottling on clear to bl w/silver mica 325.00
Pitcher, Hobnail, amber, sq mouth, bulbous, 8x6¼" 225.00
Shade, Hobnail, amber frost, scalloped/pointed rim, 9" dia 225.00
Tray, ice cream; Daisy & Button, amberina, +8 6"plates......... 1,250.00
Tumbler, Hobnail, frosted amber, 10-row, 4x2⅝" 75.00

Homer Laughlin

The Homer Laughlin China Company of Newell, West Virginia, was founded in 1871. The superior dinnerware they displayed at the Centennial Exposition in Philadelphia in 1876 won the highest award of excellence. From that time to the present, they have continued to produce quality dinnerware and kitchenware, many lines of which are becoming very popular collectibles. Most of the dinnerware is marked with the name of the pattern and occasionally with the shape name as well. The 'HLC' trademark is usually followed by a number series, the first two digits of which indicate the year of its manufacture. See also Fiesta; Harlequin; Riviera.

Laughlin Art China, Mug (either style), $38.00; Tankard, $100.00.

Amberstone, ash tray, rare...20.00
Amberstone, bowl, vegetable... 9.50
Amberstone, casserole 32.00
Amberstone, creamer.. 7.50
Amberstone, dessert dish 3.50

Amberstone, jam jar, w/lid 38.00
Amberstone, pie plate 28.00
Amberstone, sauce boat stand 21.00
Amberstone, tea server 38.00
Americana, creamer...15.00
Americana, sauce boat, w/liner 50.00
Americana, sugar bowl, w/lid 20.00
Casualstone, bowl, salad; jumbo, 10" 14.00
Casualstone, bowl, vegetable; rnd 7.50
Casualstone, coffee server 22.00
Casualstone, cup & saucer 6.50
Casualstone, mug, jumbo... 6.50
Casualstone, plate, salad 2.50
Casualstone, platter, oval, 13" 9.50
Casualstone, sauce boat 12.00
Casualstone, sugar bowl, w/lid 6.50
Conchita, bowl, fruit; 5" 7.00
Conchita, plate, deep; 8" 13.50
Conchita, platter, 11½" 17.00
Epicure, bowl, soup 8.00
Epicure, coffeepot 50.00
Epicure, creamer.. 8.00
Epicure, plate, 6½" 3.00
Epicure, shakers, pr 12.00
Epicure, teacup & saucer 12.00
Hacienda, bowl, vegetable; 8" 16.50
Hacienda, casserole, Nautilus 88.00
Hacienda, plate, 6" 4.00
Hacienda, platter, w/oval well, 13½" 22.00
Hacienda, sauce boat 18.00
Hacienda, teapot 75.00
Jubilee, bowl, fruit 4.00
Jubilee, bowl, mixing; Kitchen Kraft, 10" 95.00
Jubilee, casserole 25.00
Jubilee, cup & saucer 5.00
Jubilee, platter, 11" 4.00
Jubilee, sauce boat...12.00
Laughlin Art China, bowl, American Beauty, 10" 105.00
Laughlin Art China, jardiniere, flow blue, 10x14½" ...425.00
Laughlin Art China, pot, demitasse; Currant 175.00
Laughlin Art China, vase, Currant, 16".....................150.00
Mexicana, bowl, vegetable; 8½" 17.00
Mexicana, cup & saucer 14.00
Mexicana, egg cup, rolled edge................................26.00
Mexicana, plate, deep; 8" 14.00
Mexicana, plate, 7".. 7.00
Mexicana, platter, 10"...15.00
Mexicana, sauce boat, scarce 25.00
Priscilla, bowl, fruit; 9½" 12.00
Priscilla, creamer... 6.00
Priscilla, plate, 8".. 4.00
Priscilla, sauce boat, 8½" 10.00
Rhythm, bowl, fruit; 5½" 4.50
Rhythm, bowl, mixing; Kitchen Kraft, 6" 65.00
Rhythm, bowl, soup 9.00
Rhythm, cup & saucer 9.00
Rhythm, plate, 6"... 4.50
Rhythm, plate, 9"... 8.00
Rhythm, platter, 11½"..13.00
Rhythm, sauce boat, cobalt 18.00
Rhythm, spoon rest, gr..235.00
Rhythm, sugar bowl, w/lid 9.00
Rhythm Rose, bowl, nested, med 15.00
Rhythm Rose, casserole, Kitchen Kraft, 8½" 30.00

Rhythm Rose, creamer.. 6.00
Rhythm Rose, plate, 9"... 5.00
Rhythm Rose, platter, 13" 9.00
Rhythm Rose, sugar bowl, w/lid................................ 9.00
Serenade, bowl, nappy, 9" 9.00
Serenade, pickle dish 9.00
Serenade, plate, 10" 9.00
Serenade, shakers, pr 12.00
Serenade, sugar bowl, w/lid.....................................10.00
Serenade, teapot 45.00
Tango, bowl, nappy, 8¾" 6.00
Tango, creamer 5.00
Tango, plate, deep.. 8.00
Tango, plate, 10" 8.00
Tango, sugar bowl, w/lid 7.50
Virginia Rose, bowl, nested, sm................................15.00
Virginia Rose, bowl, vegetable; w/lid.........................45.00
Virginia Rose, bowl, vegetable; 7½"..........................10.00
Virginia Rose, butter dish, ½-lb...............................75.00
Virginia Rose, cake plate 22.00
Virginia Rose, pitcher, milk; 5".................................22.00
Virginia Rose, plate, 10½".......................................15.00
Virginia Rose, sauce boat 12.00
Wells Art Glaze, bowl, nappy, 8" 10.00
Wells Art Glaze, casserole 35.00
Wells Art Glaze, pickle dish, w/hdls 10.00
Wells Art Glaze, platter, oval, 15½" 14.00
Wells Art Glaze, sauce boat......................................10.00
Wells Art Glaze, syrup..60.00
Wells Art Glaze, teapot...45.00

Hull

The A.E. Hull Pottery was formed in 1905 in Zanesville, Ohio, and in the early years produced stoneware specialities. They expanded in 1907, adding a second plant and employing over two hundred workers. By 1920 they were manufacturing a full line of stoneware, art pottery with both airbrushed and blended glazes, florist pots, and gardenware. They also produced toilet ware and kitchen items with a white semi-porcelain body. Although these continued to be staple products, after the stock market crash of 1929, emphasis was shifted to tile production. By the mid-thirties interest in art pottery production was growing; over the next fifteen years, several lines of matt pastel floral-decorated patterns were designed, consisting of vases, planters, baskets, ewers, and bowls in various sizes.

The Red Riding Hood cookie jar, patented in 1943, proved so successful that a whole line of figural kitchenware and novelty items were added. They continued to be produced well into the fifties. Through the forties their floral artware lines flooded the market, due to the restriction of foreign imports. Although best known for their pastel matt-glazed ware, some of the lines were high gloss. Rosella, glossy coral on a pink clay body, was produced for a short time only; and Magnolia, although offered in a matt glaze, was produced in gloss as well.

The plant was destroyed in 1950 by a flood which resulted in a devastating fire when the floodwater caused the kilns to explode. The company rebuilt and equipped their new factory with the most modern machinery. It was soon apparent that the matt glaze could not be duplicated through the more modern processes, however, and soon attention was concentrated on high-gloss artware lines such as Parchment and Pine and Ebb Tide. Figural planters and novelties, piggy banks, and dinnerware were produced in abundance in the late fifties and sixties. By the mid-seventies dinnerware and florist ware were the mainstay of their business. The firm discontinued operations in 1986.

Our advisor, Brenda Roberts, has compiled a lovely book, *The Collector's Encyclopedia of Hull Pottery*, with full-color photos and current values which has been recently reprinted. You will find her address in the Directory under Missouri. Mark Supnick (see Directory under Florida) has written a book entitled *Collecting Hull Pottery's Red Riding Hood*, published by L-W Sales.

Blossom, pitcher, #22, pk floral, 64-oz..................................75.00
Blossom, pitcher, #29, yel floral, 16-oz.................................28.00
Blossom, sugar bowl, #27, yel floral, w/lid, 4½"...................22.00
Blossom Flite, creamer & sugar bowl....................................48.00
Blossomflite, bowl, console; T-10, ring hdls, 16½".............75.00
Blossomflite, ewer, T-13, rope hdl, 13½"............................115.00
Blue Bird, canister...65.00
Blue Bird, cruet..90.00
Bouquet, pitcher, #29, mc florals, yel rim, 32-oz...............35.00
Bouquet, teapot, #26, mc floral, yel rim, 42-oz.................80.00
Bow Knot, candle holder, B-17, 4".......................................55.00
Bow Knot, dbl cornucopia, B-13, 13".................................175.00
Bow Knot, ewer, B-1, 5½"..75.00
Bow Knot, flowerpot, B-6, 6½"..95.00
Bow Knot, vase, B-10, 10½"...225.00
Bow Knot, vase, B-4, 6½"...75.00
Bow Knot, vase, B-7, 8½"...145.00
Bow Knot, vase, B-8, 8½"...135.00
Bow Knot, wall pocket, B-26, pitcher form, 6" 95.00

Butterfly, three-piece tea/coffee set, $120.00.

Butterfly, cornucopia, B-12, 10½"...55.00
Butterfly, ewer, B-15, gold hdl, 13½"..................................120.00
Butterfly, pitcher, B-11, 8¾"..70.00
Butterfly, teapot, B-18...75.00
Butterfly, vase, B-10, ftd, 7"...36.00
Butterfly, window box 36.00
Calla Lily, bowl, console; #590/33, flower form, 4x13".......130.00
Calla Lily, candle holder, unmk, 2¼"...................................45.00
Calla Lily, vase, #530/33, 5"..60.00
Calla Lily, vase, #550/33, gr/brn, angle hdls, 7½".............75.00
Camellia, ewer, #105, squat, 7"..115.00
Camellia, jardiniere, #114, 8¼"..165.00
Camellia, mermaid/shell planter, #104, 10½"....................550.00
Camellia, vase, #118, swan form, 6½".................................62.00
Camellia, vase, bud; #129, 7"...65.00
Capri, basket, #48, sea gr, 12¼"...48.00
Classic, vase, #5, floral on pk, 6".......................................22.00
Continental, candle holder/planter, unmk, 4".....................22.00

Continental, ewer, #56, orange w/yel stripes, 12½".............110.00
Crab Apple, jardiniere, matt semi-porc, floral, unmk, 4".......55.00
Crab Apple, vase, buff stoneware, floral, unmk, 4".............24.00
Crab Apple, vase, buff stoneware, floral, unmk, 8¾"..........75.00
Crescent, bowl, B-1, dk gr, yel int, 5½"...............................12.00
Crescent, shaker, B-4, 3½" 9.00
Crestone, carafe, turq, w/lid 32.00
Crestone, coffee server, turq, 11".......................................45.00
Crestone, cup & deep-well saucer, mirror brn..................... 3.50
Crestone, plate, dinner; turq, 10½"..................................... 8.00
Crestone, shakers, turq, pr...12.00
Debonair, creamer & sugar bowl, #0-14-15..........................45.00
Debonair, shakers, lav & pk, blk stripe, pr 40.00
Delft, canister..65.00
Delft, cruet...90.00
Delft, jar, spice..48.00
Dogwood, bowl, #521, low style, tab hdls, 7"......................50.00
Dogwood, bowl, console; #511, 11½"..................................210.00
Dogwood, cornucopia, #522, 3¾"...40.00
Dogwood, ewer, #516, florals on pk to bl, 11½".................245.00
Dogwood, vase, #504, orig label, 8½"..................................99.00
Dogwood, vase, #517, 4¾"...39.00
Double Border, cruet...70.00
Double Border, salt box...135.00
Early Art, flowerpot, w/saucer, 6½".....................................45.00
Early Art, jardiniere, semi-porc, emb trees, #546, 7" 75.00
Early Art, jardiniere, stoneware, blended matt, 6½"............50.00
Early Art, vase, semi-porc, turq, 4½"...................................44.00
Early Art, vase, stoneware, #39, 8".....................................72.00
Early Utility, American Legion Stein, #498, H in circle, 6½"........60.00
Early Utility, bowl, #100, H in circle, gr on tan, 8"..............32.00
Early Utility, pitcher, #107, H in circle, brn on tan, 4¾" 38.00
Early Utility, salt box, #111, gr, wooden lid, 6" 95.00
Early Utility, spice jar, block H in dmn, gr, 3½"...................46.00
Ebb Tide, bowl, console; E-12, 15".......................................90.00
Ebb Tide, candle holder, E-13, 2¾".....................................18.00
Ebb Tide, creamer, E-15, shell form, 4"...............................36.00
Ebb Tide, pitcher, E-10, 14"..120.00
Fiesta, basket, #51, 12½"..55.00
Fiesta, flowerpot, #40, blk, scalloped rim, 4¼".....................20.00
Floral, bowl, mixing; #40, yel on wht, brn band, 9"............38.00
Floral, jar, grease; #43, yel on wht, 5¾"..............................28.00
Grecian Border, canister..65.00
Grecian Border, cruet 70.00
Grecian Border, jar, spice...42.00
Heartland, bowl, brn on cream, nested set, 6", 8", 10" 24.00
Heartland, cookie jar, #423, brn on cream, 8".....................18.00
Heartland, pitcher & bowl set, brn on cream 46.00
Heartland, plate, dinner; brn on cream, 10¼"..................... 5.00
Heritage Ware, cookie jar, #0-18, 9¼".................................46.00
Heritage Ware, pitcher, A-6, 7"...26.00
House 'N Garden, butter dish, avocodo gr, ¼-lb, 7¾"...........15.00
House 'N Garden, casserole, covered hen, mirror brn, 2-qt..........38.00
House 'N Garden, cookie jar, #523, mirror brn, 9"...............22.00
House 'N Garden, cookie jar, gingerbread man, mirror brn, 12" ...65.00
House 'N Garden, mug, mirror brn, 16-oz............................. 4.00
House 'N Garden, plate, dinner; mirror brn, 10½" 5.00
House 'N Garden, spoon rest, mirror brn, 6¾"....................12.00
House 'N Garden, teapot, gr agate, 6¾"..............................16.00
House 'N Garden, water jug, mirror brn, 5-pt.......................22.00
Imperial, basket, F-38, gr, 6¾"..24.00
Imperial, Madonna, F-7, 7"...22.00
Imperial, urn vase, #454, 5" 8.00
Iris, basket, #408, pk rim & hdl, bl base, 7" 170.00

Iris, ewer, #401, mc florals on ivory, 5" 42.00
Iris, vase, bud; #410, hdls, 7½" 76.00
Lustreware, candle holder, 3" 60.00
Lustreware, pitcher, 4" 48.00
Lustreware, vase, bud; 8" 95.00
Magnolia, glossy; bowl, console; H-23, pk floral w/gold, 13"...78.00
Magnolia, glossy; dbl cornucopia, H-15, pk floral, 12" 95.00
Magnolia, glossy; teapot, H-20, pk floral, 6½" 85.00
Magnolia, glossy; vase, gold trim, H-13, 10½" 74.00
Magnolia, matt; cornucopia, #19, 8½" 72.00
Magnolia, matt; dbl cornucopia, #6, 12" 110.00
Magnolia, matt; teapot, #23, 6½" 90.00
Magnolia, matt; vase, #13, 4¾" 28.00
Magnolia, matt; vase, #17, 12¼" 170.00
Magnolia, matt; vase, #20, side hdls, 15" 285.00
Magnolia, matt; vase, #21, open hdls, 12½" 170.00
Magnolia, matt; vase, #7, 8½" 74.00
Marcrest, ash tray, dk gr, 8½x4½" 22.00
Mardi Gras, bowl, mixing; unmk, 10¼" 32.00
Mardi Gras, ewer, #31, Shafer gold trim, sgn Grany, 10" 165.00
Mardi Gras, vase, #49, ivory, 9" 34.00
Novelty, baby planter, #92, 5½" 18.00
Novelty, Bandana Duck, #76, 3½x3½" 16.00
Novelty, Corky Pig bank, mirror brn, 5" 22.00
Novelty, goose, wall pocket, #67, 6½" 30.00
Novelty, kitten planter, #61, 7½" 34.00
Novelty, lamb planter, #965, 8" 34.00
Novelty, musician, 5¾" 60.00
Novelty, Old Spice after shave bottle, orig closure, 5" 100.00
Novelty, Old Spice shaving mug, 3" 22.00
Novelty, owl bank, 3¾" 75.00
Novelty, pheasant planter, #61, 6x8" 26.00
Novelty, pig bank, emb decor, satin, 3½" 42.00
Novelty, poodle planter, #114, pk & gr, 8" 26.00
Novelty, rabbit, hole at tail for cotton ball, 5½" 18.00
Novelty, Siamese cats, #63, pk/gr, 5¾x13" 62.00
Orchid, bookends, #316, 7", pr.....................................480.00
Orchid, vase, #304, 10¼"1 ....284.00
Parchment & Pine, bowl, console; S-9................................76.00
Parchment & Pine, candle holder, unmk, 5" 20.00
Parchment & Pine, creamer, S-12....................................26.00
Plaidware, bowl, cereal; #60, red/yel on wht, 5" 20.00
Plaidware, cookie jar, #66, red/yel on wht, 8¾" 140.00
Plaidware, creamer, #67, red/yel on wht, tab hdls, 3½" 35.00
Plaidware, sugar bowl, #68, red/yel on wht, w/lid, 3½" 35.00
Poppy, vase, #607, angle hdls, ftd, 8½" 96.00
Poppy, wall pocket, #609, florals on pk to bl, 9" 140.00
Rainbow, leaf dish, tangerine, 12¼" 24.00
Red Riding Hood, canister, cereal 300.00
Red Riding Hood, canister, tea, coffee, sugar, or flour; ea 260.00
Red Riding Hood, canister, tidbits 600.00
Red Riding Hood, casserole, red hdls, extremely rare 2,000.00
Red Riding Hood, cookie jar, open-end basket, 13" 150.00
Red Riding Hood, cookie jar, rnd basket, 13" 120.00
Red Riding Hood, creamer & sugar bowl, head pour, w/lid.......200.00
Red Riding Hood, creamer & sugar bowl, side pour 70.00
Red Riding Hood, feeding dish, 3-compartment 2,000.00
Red Riding Hood, jar, cracker; skirt held wide, 8½"..............195.00
Red Riding Hood, jar, dresser; w/bow, 9"..........................175.00
Red Riding Hood, jar, spice (any) 285.00
Red Riding Hood, jar, wolf (any)....................................300.00
Red Riding Hood, matchbox, wall hanging........................300.00
Red Riding Hood, mug, chocolate 400.00
Red Riding Hood, pitcher, batter....................................120.00

Little Red Riding
Hood flour canister,
$260.00.

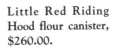

Red Riding Hood, pitcher, milk; ruffled skirt 1,500.00
Red Riding Hood, pitcher, milk; standing, 8" 95.00
Red Riding Hood, planter, standing................................. 1,200.00
Red Riding Hood, shakers, sitting, 5½", pr 300.00
Red Riding Hood, shakers, standing, 3¼", pr......................25.00
Red Riding Hood, shakers, standing, 5¼", pr......................45.00
Red Riding Hood, string holder, wall mt 350.00
Red Riding Hood, teapot or hot chocolate pot, ea 135.00
Rosella, lamp base, L-3, 11"..240.00
Rosella, vase, R-15, low hdls, ftd, 8½" 65.00
Rosella, vase, R-5, 6½" 32.00
Rosella, vase, R-8, heart form, ftd, 6½" 70.00
Serenade, ash tray, S-23, 13x10½" 65.00
Serenade, basket, S-14, 12x11½" 230.00
Serenade, pitcher, beverage; S-21, 10½" 90.00
Sueno Tulip, ewer, #109, 8" 120.00
Sueno Tulip, ewer, #109-33, 12" 265.00
Sueno Tulip, flowerpot, #116-33, 6" 85.00
Sueno Tulip, jardiniere, #115-33, 7" 165.00
Sun Glow, flowerpot, #98, 7½" 36.00
Sun Glow, wall pocket, unmk, iron form, 6"........................46.00
Thistle, vase, #53, floral on bl, hdls, 6½" 42.00
Tile, decorated border, 2⅞x6" 52.00
Tile, dolphin decor, faience mk, 2⅞x2⅞" 75.00
Tile, plain, 4¼x4¼" 20.00
Tokay, leaf dish, #19 ....34.00
Tuscany, creamer, #17, gold hdl....................................25.00
Tuscany, ewer, #13, gold hdl, 12" 135.00
Utility, bowl, unmk, rust, 8"...22.00
Vegetable, bowl, batter; #21, yel, w/lip, 9".......................140.00
Vegetable, cookie jar, #28, coral, 8¾" 165.00
Water Lily, candle holder, L-22, 4½" 34.00
Water Lily, ewer, L-17, 13½" 240.00
Water Lily, lamp base, glossy, unmk, 7½" 110.00
Water Lily, vase, L-A, ftd flower form, low hdls, 8½" 120.00
Water Lily, vase, L-13, 10½" 145.00
Water Lily, vase, L-2, gold trim, 5½" 35.00
Wildflower, basket, W-16, 10½" 165.00
Wildflower, candle holder, unmk....................................25.00
Wildflower, cornucopia, #58, 6¼" 42.00
Wildflower, cornucopia, W-10, 8½" 70.00
Wildflower, cornucopia, W-7, 7½" 45.00
Wildflower, ewer, #55, 13½" 280.00
Wildflower, ewer, W-11, 8½" 95.00
Wildflower, ewer, W-19, 13½".......................................240.00

Wildflower, teapot, #72, 8" 260.00
Wildflower, vase, #52, 5¼" 42.00
Wildflower, vase, W-1, 5½" 28.00
Wildflower, vase, W-12, 9½" 100.00
Wildflower, vase, W-18, 12½" 170.00
Wildflower, vase, W-3, 5½" 35.00
Wildflower, vase, W-5, 6½" 45.00
Wildflower, vase, W-8, 7½" 50.00

Wildflower vase,
W-6, 6½", $45.00.

Woodland, glossy; cornucopia, W-10, 11" 45.00
Woodland, glossy; ewer, W-3, 5½" 38.00
Woodland, glossy; jardiniere, W-7, 5½" 50.00
Woodland, glossy; vase, W-4, 6½" 35.00
Woodland, matt; basket, W-22, gr twig hdl, 10½" 380.00
Woodland, matt; bowl, console; W-29, 14" 230.00

Hummel

Hummel figurines were created through the artistry of Berta Hummel, a Franciscan nun called Sister M. Innocentia. The first figures were made about 1935 by Franz Goebel of Goebel Art Inc., Rodental, West Germany. Plates, plaques, and candy dishes are also produced; and the older, discontinued editions are highly-sought collectibles. Generally speaking, an issue can be dated by the trademark. The first Hummels, from 1934-1950, were either incised or stamped with the 'Crown WG' mark. The 'full bee in V' mark was employed with minor variations until 1959. At that time the bee was stylized and represented by a solid disk with angled symmetrical wings completely contained within the confines of the 'V.' The three-line mark, 1964-1972, utilized the stylized bee and included a three-line arrangement, 'c by W. Goebel, W. Germany.' Another change in 1970 saw the 'stylized bee in V' suspended between the vertical bars of the 'b' and 'l' of a printed 'Goebel, West Germany.' Collectors refer to this mark as the 'last bee' or 'Goebel bee.' The current mark in use since 1979 omits the 'bee in V.' For a more thorough study of the subject we recommend *Hummel Figurines and Plates, A Collector's Identification and Value Guide*, by Carl Luckey, available at your local book dealer. Idiosyncrasies in the numerical order of the following listings are due to computer sorting. See also Limited Edition Plates.

Key:
ce — closed edition	GB — Goebel bee
CM — crown mark	SB — stylized bee
FB — full bee	LB — last bee

#III/53, Joyful, candy box, FB, 6¼" 350.00
#III/57, Chick Girl, candy box, 3-line mk, 5¼" 145.00
#III/58, Playmates, candy box, SB, 5¼" 295.00
#III/69, Happy Pastime, candy box, 3-line mk, 6" 145.00
#1, Puppy Love, 3-line mk, 5" 125.00
#10/I, Flower Madonna, color, SB, 8¼" 220.00
#109/II, Happy Traveler, 3-line mk, 8" 330.00
#11/2/0, Merry Wanderer, 3-line mk, 4¼" 95.00
#110/I, Let's Sing, FB, 3⅞" 180.00
#111/I, Wayside Harmony, SB, 5" 160.00
#111/110, Let's Sing, candy box, SB, 6" 295.00
#111/3/0, Wayside Harmony, 3-line mk, 3¾" 95.00
#112/3/0, Just Resting, FB, 3¾" 140.00
#114, Let's Sing, ash tray, 3-line mk, 3½x6¾" 115.00
#118, Little Thrifty, SB, 5" 175.00
#119, Postman, 3-line mk, 5¼" 145.00
#12/I, Chimmey Sweep, 3-line mk, 5½" 125.00
#123, Max & Moritz, LB, 5¼" 125.00
#124/I, Hello, SB, 7" 165.00
#125, Vacation Time, plaque, 3-line mk, 4x4¾" 175.00
#127, Doctor, LB, 4¾" 120.00
#128, Baker, 3-line mk, 4¾" 120.00
#129, Band Leader, 3-line mk, 5¼" 150.00
#13/V, Meditation, FB, 13¾" 5,000.00
#13/2/0, Meditation, SB, 4¼" 125.00
#130, Duet, SB, 5¼" 180.00
#131, Street Singer, LB, 5" 110.00
#133, Mother's Helper, 3-line mk, 5" 150.00
#134, Quartet, plaque, SB, 6x6" 250.00
#135, Soloist, FB, 4¾" 140.00
#137/B, Child-in-Bed, plaque, rnd, 3-line mk, 2¾x2¾" 55.00
#139, Flitting Butterfly, LB, 2½x2½" 55.00
#140, The Mail Is Here (Mail Coach), plaque, SB, 4½x6¼" 215.00
#141/3/0, Apple Tree Girl, SB, 4" 95.00
#142/3/0, Apple Tree Boy, 3-line mk, 4" 95.00
#143/0, Boots, FB, 5¼" 180.00
#144, Angelic Song, SB, 4¼" 110.00
#146, Angel Duet, font, 3-line mk, 2x4¾" 35.00
#147, Devotion (Angel Shrine), font, FB, 3x5" 60.00
#15/I, Hear Ye Hear Ye, CM, 6" 600.00
#152/A/0, Umbrella Boy, SB, 5" 450.00
#152/B/0, Umbrella Girl, LB, 4¾" 450.00
#153/0, Auf Widersehen, 3-line mk, 5¼" 160.00
#16/I, Little Hiker, FB, 5½" 195.00
#163, Whitsuntide, 3-line mk, 7¼" 215.00
#164, Worship, font, SB, 2¾x4¾" 45.00
#166, Boy w/Bird, ash tray, 3-line mk, 3¼x6¼" 130.00
#167, Angel w/Bird, font, FB, 3¼x4¼" 60.00
#168, Standing Boy, plaque, SB, 4⅛x5½" 135.00
#169, Bird Duet, 3-line mk, 4" 115.00
#17/2 or #17/II, Congratulations, FB, 8¼" 5,000.00
#170/I, School Boys, 3-line mk, 7½" 900.00
#171, Little Sweeper, SB, 4½" 95.00
#172/0, Festival Harmony, angel w/mandolin, 3-line mk, 8" 195.00
#173/0, Festival Harmony, angel w/flute, 3-line mk, 8" 195.00
#174, She Loves Me, She Loves Me Not; 3-line mk, 4¼" 125.00
#176/I, Happy Birthday, SB, 6" 240.00
#177/I, School Girls, 3-line mk, 7½" 900.00
#178, The Photographer, 3-line mk, 4¾" 180.00
#18, Christ Child, LB, 2x6" 70.00
#180, Tuneful Goodnight, plaque, 3-line mk, 4x4¾" 250.00
#182, Good Friends, 3-line mk, 4" 145.00
#183, Forest Shrine, SB, 7x9" 550.00
#184, Latest News, SB, 5¼" 145.00

#185, Accordion Boy, 3-line mk, 5¼".................125.00
#186, Sweet Music, SB, 5¼" 125.00
#188, Celestial Musician, SB, 7" 195.00
#192, Candlelight, candle holder, long candle, SB, 6¾" 350.00
#193, Angel Duet, candle holder, SB, 5" 145.00
#195/2/0, Barnyard Hero, SB, 4" 125.00
#2, Little Fiddler, SB, 7½" 300.00
#20, Prayer Before Battle, SB, 4¼" 125.00
#21/0, Heavenly Angel, SB, 4¼" 75.00

Boy with Toothache, #217, full bee mark, 5½", $200.00.

#22/0, Angel w/Birds, font, FB, 2¾x3½" 40.00
#23/I, Adoration, 3-line mk, 6¼" 235.00
#24/III, Lullaby, candle holder, SB, 6x8" 400.00
#26/0, Child Jesus, font, 3-line mk, 1½x5" 30.00
#27/III, Joyous News, SB, 4¼x4¾" 750.00
#28/III, Wayside Devotion, 3-line mk, 8½" 375.00
#29, Guardian Angel, font, SB, 2½x5⅜" 2,000.00
#3/III, Bookworm, SB, 9½" 1,200.00
#30/0A&B, Ba-Bee Rings, plaques, LB, 5" dia, pr 150.00

Little Bookkeeper, #306, 3-line mark, 4½", $195.00.

#32/1, Little Gabriel, SB, 5" 95.00
#34, Singing Lesson, ash tray, 3-line mk, 3½x6¼" 140.00
#35/I, The Good Shepherd, font, SB, 2¾x5¾"..............150.00

#36/I, Child w/Flowers, font, CM, 3½x4½" 350.00
#37, Herald Angels, candle holder, 3-line mk, 2¼x4"......140.00
#4, Littler Fiddler, FB, 4¾" 180.00
#42/0, Good Shepherd, 3-line mk, 6¼".....................115.00
#43, March Winds, SB, 5"..................................95.00
#44/B, Out of Danger, table lamp, CM, 9½"................450.00
#45/III, Madonna w/Halo, 3-line mk, 16¼".................145.00
#46/III, Madonna w/out Halo, 3-line mk, 16"..............145.00
#46/0, Madonna w/out Halo, 3-line mk, 10¼"...............65.00
#47/III, Goose Girl, 3-line mk, 7½"......................335.00
#47/3/0, Goose Girl, LB, 4".............................115.00
#48/0, Madonna, plaque, 3-line mk, 3x4"..................90.00
#49/0, To Market, 3-line mk, 5½".........................195.00
#5, Sensitive Hunter, 3-line mk, 4¾".....................120.00
#5, Strolling Along, 3-line mk, 4¾"......................120.00
#50/I, Volunteers, SB, 6½"...............................345.00
#51/3/0, Village Boy, SB, 4".............................70.00
#52/0, Going to Grandma's, 3-line mk, 4¾"................175.00
#53, Joyful, FB, 4"......................................125.00
#55, St George, LB, 6¾"..................................250.00
#56/A, Culprits, SB, 6¼".................................180.00
#56/B, Out of Danger, LB, 6¼"............................180.00
#58/0, Playmates, 3-line mk, 4"..........................115.00
#59, Skier, 3-line mk, 5¼"...............................150.00
#6/I, Sensitive Hunter, SB, 5½"..........................150.00
#62, Happy Pastime, ash tray, SB, 3½x6¼"................130.00
#63, Singing Lesson, FB, 2¾"............................140.00
#64, Shepherd's Boy, LB, 5½".............................145.00
#65, Farewell, 3-line mk, 4¾"............................190.00
#66, Farm Boy, 3-line mk, 5¼"............................150.00
#67, Doll Mother, 3-line mk, 4¾".........................160.00
#68/0, Lost Sheep, 3-line mk, 5½"........................130.00
#69, Happy Pastime, 3-line mk, 3¼".......................112.00
#7/I, Merry Wanderer, 3-line mk, 7"......................300.00
#70, The Holy Child, SB, 6¾".............................110.00
#72, Spring Cheer, SB, 5"................................110.00
#73, Little Helper, 3-line mk, 4¼".......................95.00
#74, Little Gardener, 3-line mk, 4¼".....................90.00
#75, White Angel Font, 3-line, 1¾x3½"....................32.00
#78/I, Infant of Krumbad, 3-line mk, 2½".................35.00
#78/VIII, Infant Of Krumbad, 3-line mk, 13½".............250.00
#79, Globe Trotter, 3-line mk, 5" 125.00
#8½/0, School Girl, FB, 4¼"..............................140.00
#82/0, School Boy, 3-line mk, 5½"........................125.00
#83, Angel Serenade, w/lamb, 3-line mk, 5"...............145.00
#84/0, Worship, 3-line mk, 5"............................115.00
#85/0, Serenade, SB, 4¾".................................95.00
#88/I, Heavenly Protector, SB, 6¾".......................290.00
#89/II, Little Cellist, LB, 8"...........................330.00
#9, Begging His Share, LB, 5½"...........................130.00
#91/A&B, Eventide & Adoration, bookends, CM, 2x4¾", pr 225.00
#92, Merry Wanderer, plaque, FB, 4¾x5⅛" 170.00
#94/I, Surprise, FB, 5½".................................235.00
#95, Brother, SB, 5½"....................................115.00
#96, Little Shopper, SB, 4¾".............................115.00
#98/0, Sister, 3-line mk, 5¾"............................115.00
#98/2/0, Sister, FB, 4¾".................................140.00
#99, Eventide, FB, 4¾"...................................300.00

Hutschenreuther

Sources do not agree as to when the Carl Hutschenreuther factory was initially established in the Bavarian district of Germany. Most indicate a year near the middle of the 19th century. Carl's sons, Christian and Lorenz, later formed their own companies and operated independently until 1969. At that time Carl and Lorenz merged; and that firm is still in business today producing limited edition plates, figurines, dinnerware, and other fine china.

Our advisor for this category is Jack Gunsaulus; he is listed in the Directory under Michigan.

Bowl, 6 mc floral panels on lt bl w/silver, 3 ft, lid, 8x8" 90.00
Figurine, cat holding ball, sgn Achtziger, 6" 165.00
Figurine, dachshund stands on bk legs, wht, 7" 165.00

Dancer, white glaze, 13", $425.00.

Figurine, finch on branch, 6½" 75.00
Figurine, nude w/gold ball, Werner, 10" 295.00
Figurine, 2 geese, 14" 250.00
Flower frog, Cupid standing, wht on gold bowl, 7½" 275.00
Plate, Music Lesson, after Lancret, bl/gilt border, 10" 280.00

Imari

Imari is a generic term which covers a broad family of wares. It was made in more than a dozen Japanese villages, but the name is that of the port from whence it was shipped to Europe. There are several types of Imari. The most common features a design with panels of birds, florals, or people surrounding a central basket of flowers. The colors used in this type are underglaze blue with overglaze red, gold, and green enamels. The Chinese also made Imari wares which differ from the Japanese type in several ways — the absence of spur marks, a thinner-type body, and a more consistent control of the blue. Imari-type wares were copied on the continent by Meissen and by English potters, among them Worcester, Derby, and Bow.

Bowl, allover vines/flowers, pomegranate finial, hdls, 11"...........275.00
Bowl, bl/wht central medallion & 8 geisha, shallow, 12" 135.00
Bowl, carp on bl, gold accents, 1880s, 12x11" 850.00
Bowl, dragon/phoenix/ship cartouch, mk, 1880s, 8½", EX 200.00
Bowl, florals, florals/geometrics w/in, 1880s, 10" 225.00
Chamber set, 1800s, 14" pitcher+4 pcs, EX 1,300.00
Charger, children/mtns, scalloped, 1880s, 17" 300.00
Charger, floral, floral rim panels, 1880s, 12", EX, pr 350.00
Charger, floral w/flower & geometric rim, scalloped, 12".............325.00
Charger, florals & diapering, mc w/cobalt, mk, 13⅝"..................375.00
Dish, fish form, figural scene reserve, 1880s, 14" L, NM 500.00
Fish set, carp shape, 1800s, 10" platter+6 servers.................... 1,700.00
Plate, floral medallion, cobalt rim w/fan-shape panels, 12" 90.00

Vase, flowering branches, 1880s, 7", pr...450.00
Vase, lg floral panels on floral ground, 1880s, 15", EX 575.00

Vase, gold scrolls on dark blue with cartouches containing birds and flowers, signed, 1800s, 12", $375.00.

Imperial Glass Company

The Imperial Glass Company was organized in 1901 in Bellaire, Ohio, and started manufacturing glassware in 1904. Their early products were jelly glasses, hotel tumblers, etc., but by 1910 they were making a name for themselves by pressing quantities of Carnival Glass, the iridescent glassware that was popular during that time. in 1914, NuCut was introduced to imitate cut glass. The line was so popular that it was made in crystal and colors and was reintroduced as Collector's Crystal in the 1950s. From 1916 to 1920, they used the lustre process to make a line called Imperial Jewels, now referred to as stretch glass. Free-Hand ware, art glass made entirely by hand using no molds, was made from 1922 to 1928.

The company entered bankruptcy in 1931 but was able to continue operations and reorganize as the Imperial Glass Corporation. In 1936 Imperial introduced the Candlewick line, for which it is best known. In the late thirties, the Vintage Grape Milk Glass line was added, and in 1950 a major ad campaign was launched making Imperial one of the leading milk glass manufacturers.

In 1940 Imperial bought the molds and assets of the Central Glass Works of Wheeling, West Virginia; in 1958 they acquired the molds of the Heisey Company and in 1960 the molds of the Cambridge Glass Company of Cambridge, Ohio. Imperial used these molds, but since 1950 they have marked their new glassware with an 'I' superimposed over the 'G' trademark. The company became a subsidiary of Lenox in 1973; subsequently an 'L' was added to the 'IG' mark. In 1981 Lenox sold Imperial to Arthur Lorch, a private investor (who modified the L by adding a line at the top angled to the left). He in turn sold the company to Robert F. Stahl, Jr., in 1982. Mr. Stahl filed for Chapter 11 to reorganize, but in mid-1984 liquidation was ordered, and all assets were sold. The few items that had been made in '84 were marked with an 'N' superimposed over the 'I' for 'New Imperial.' See also Candlewick; Carnival Glass; Stretch Glass.

Animals and Birds

Asiatic pheasant, amber 325.00
Champ Terrier, caramel slag, 5¾" 95.00
Chick, head down, milk glass 5.00
Chick, head up, milk glass 5.00

Clydesdale, amber 300.00
Clydesdale, salmon 295.00
Clydesdale, Verde Gr...150.00
Colt, balking, aqua, dtd 1979 ....70.00
Colt, balking, Ultra Bl..25.00
Colt, kicking, Ultra Bl...25.00
Colt, standing, caramel slag 30.00
Colt, standing, milk glass 75.00
Cygnet, blk...45.00
Cygnet, lt bl 20.00
Doe head, bookend, scarce 600.00
Dog, Airedale, caramel slag 125.00
Dog, Airedale, Ultra B satin 80.00
Dog, Airedale, Ultra Bl..45.00
Donkey, caramel slag 35.00
Donkey, Meadow Gr Carnival 95.00
Elephant, caramel slag, med 35.00
Elephant, Meadow Gr Carnival #674, med...................60.00
Elephant, pk satin, sm...60.00
Filly, head bkward, Verde Gr 145.00
Filly, head forward, satin...65.00
Fish, candle holder, Sunshine Yel 27.50
Fish, match holder, Sunshine Yel satin........................15.00
Gazelle, Ultra Bl 150.00
Horse head, bookend, pk, rare 300.00
Mallard, wings down, caramel slag 200.00
Mallard, wings down, lt bl satin................................22.50
Mallard, wings half, caramel slag 28.00
Mallard, wings half, lt bl satin..................................20.00
Mallard, wings up, caramel slag 28.00
Mallard, wings up, lt bl satin....................................22.00
Owl, hootless, milk glass, doeskin 50.00
Piglet, sitting...20.00
Piglet, standing, ruby, hole between legs 80.00
Piglet, standing, Ultra Bl..30.00
Plug Horse, pk, HCA, 1978 ....40.00
Rabbit, paperweight, milk glass 22.50
Rooster, amber..390.00
Rooster, fighting, pk 185.00
Sow, amber 325.00
Swan, nut dish, dtd 35.00
Tiger, paperweight, blk...55.00
Tiger, paperweight, jade 85.00
Wood duck, caramel slag 35.00
Wood duck, Sunshine Yel satin 30.00
Wood duck, Ultra Bl satin 50.00
Wood duckling, floating, Sunshine Yel satin..................12.00
Wood duckling, standing, Sunshine Yel 12.00
Wood duckling, standing, Sunshine Yel satin.................12.00

Cathay Crystal

Cathay Crystal was conceived and designed by Virginia B. Evans in 1949. Representative of China's history, this line consisted of thirty-eight designs which were produced in a satin/frosted combination. Except for items too small to accomodate it, each piece bears the script signature of its designer. The line was lavishly introduced at the National China and Glass Show in Pittsburgh in 1949. Items from the line were presented in boxes lined with green suede and lettered in gold, each piece having its own number. But as was often true for unusual art glass lines, Cathay Crystal did not meet sales expectations, and the line was manufactured for only two years; sales halted in 1957. For a short time and in limited amounts, some designs were produced in color; but the Evan's name was removed from the molds.

Cathay Crystal, Concubine bookends, $450.00 for the pair.

#5001, pagoda 550.00
#5002, Shang candy jar 250.00
#5004, Yan & Yin ash tray 175.00
#5006, butterfly ash tray 25.00
#5007, plum blossom ash tray....................................25.00
#5008, peach blossom mint or nut set 20.00
#5009, dragon candle holders, pr 400.00
#5010, junk flower bowl 250.00
#5011, Wu Ling ash tray 125.00
#5012, Ku ribbon vase 750.00
#5013, pillow candle base 50.00
#5014, bamboo urn 400.00
#5016, Fu wedding vase 200.00
#5017, egrette 300.00
#5018, pillow cigarette set, 3-pc 550.00
#5019, Ming jar..80.00
#5020, Shen console set 300.00
#5022, fan sweetmeat box 175.00
#5024, Scolding Bird 175.00
#5026, Phoenix bowl 175.00
#5027, wedding lamp..200.00
#5029, Empress book stop, pr 250.00
#5030, Lu-Tunb book holder, pr 350.00
#5033/34, candle servants, pr 350.00
#5038, Celestial centerpc 350.00
#5085, Pavillion tray 350.00

Basket, caramel slag satin 35.00
Bottle, bitters; Cape Cod 40.00
Bottle, hot sauce; Cape Cod, #160/224 ....45.00
Bowl, baked apple; Cape Cod....................................10.00
Bowl, banana; milk glass, glossy, ftd, 12".....................30.00
Bowl, Cape Cod, oval, 11" 85.00
Box, Atterbury Lion, milk glass, w/lid...........................45.00
Cake stand, Cape Cod, pattern top, 11".........................75.00
Cake stand, Cape Cod, plain top, 11"............................85.00
Cake stand, Vintage Grape, milk glass, glossy 40.00
Candy jar, owl form, purple slag satin 55.00
Creamer & sugar bowl, Nucut....................................25.00
Creamer & sugar bowl, owl form, jade slag, glossy, pr 35.00
Cup & saucer, coffee; Cape Cod, #37 ....11.50
Martini mixer, Big Shot Series, red..............................100.00
Mug, Tom & Jerry; Cape Cod 32.50
Multi-server, Cape Cod, #93, 12"................................95.00

Nest, 4" bunny, milk glass, doeskin 25.00
Pitcher, Cape Cod, ice lip, ftd, #24 ....85.00
Plate, Cape Cod, 10" 33.00
Plate, Cape Cod, 4½" 5.00
Plate, Vintage Grape, milk glass, 9½" 15.00
Punch set, Cape Cod, 15-pc, #160/20 ....175.00
Relish, Cape Cod, 5-compartment, #160/102, 11" 50.00
Salt & peppermill, Cape Cod, #160/236/23, 4½", on tray 63.00
Sherbet, Cape Cod, red, ftd 25.00
Sign, advertising; frosted..95.00
Spoon rest coaster, Cape Cod, #160/76 .... 6.00
Tumbler, Big Shot Series, red, 12-oz 12.50
Tumbler, Big Shot Series, red, 16-oz 15.00
Tumbler, iced tea; Cape Cod, ftd, #1600, 12-oz..........20.00

Cape Cod tumbler, 12-oz., $12.00.

Vase, 'Genie,' Steigel Gr, 4½" 23.00
Vase, Dancing Nudes, ruby slag satin...........................95.00
Vase, Free-Hand, bl w/orange hearts & vines, att, 11" 300.00
Vase, Free-Hand, dk bl & orange w/wht hearts & vines, 7".........250.00
Vase, Loganberry, milk glass, doeskin, 10" 30.00
Vase, Peachblow satin, 8" 175.00

Imperial Porcelain

The Blue Ridge Mountain Boys were created by cartoonist Paul Webb and translated into three-dimension by the Imperial Porcelain Corporation of Zanesville, Ohio, in 1947. These figurines decorated ash trays, vases, mugs, bowls, pitchers, planters, and other items. The Mountain Boys series were numbered 92 through 108, each with a different and amusing portrayal of mountain life. Imperial also produced American Folklore miniatures, twenty-three tiny animals one inch or less in size, and the Al Capp Dogpatch series. Because of financial difficulties, the company closed in 1960.

American Folklore Miniatures

Cat, 1½" 40.00
Cow, 1¾" 35.00
Hound dogs...35.00
Plaque, store ad, Am Folklore Porcelain Miniatures, 4½" 300.00
Sow...30.00

Blue Ridge Mountain Boys by Paul Webb

Ash tray, #101, man w/jug & snake 75.00

Ash tray, #103, hillbilly & skunk 75.00
Ash tray, #105, baby, hound dog, & frog 110.00
Ash tray, #106, Barrel of Wishes, w/hound 75.00
Ash tray, #92, 2 men by tree stump, for pipes 125.00
Box, cigarette; #98, dog atop, baby at door, sq............115.00
Decanter, #100, outhouse, man, & bird 75.00
Decanter, #104, Ma leaning over stump, w/baby & skunk 95.00
Decanter, man, jug, snake, & tree stump, Hispch Inc, 1946 ....75.00

Figurine, #101, hillbilly on open stump, 4" x 5", $90.00.

Figurine, man on hands & knees, 3" 95.00
Figurine, man sitting, 3½" 95.00
Figurine, man sitting w/chicken on knee, 3"..................95.00
Jug, #101, Willie & snake 75.00
Mug, #94, Bearing Down, 6" 95.00
Mug, #94, dbl baby hdl, 4¼" 95.00
Mug, #94, man w/bl pants hdl, 4¼" 95.00
Mug, #94, man w/yel beard & red pants hdl, 4¼" 95.00
Mug, #99, Target Practice, boy on goat, farmer, 5¾".....95.00
Pitcher, lemonade 200.00
Plack, store ad, Handcrafted Paul Webb Mtn Boys, rare, 9" 500.00
Planter, #100, outhouse, man, & bird 75.00
Planter, #105, man w/chicken on knee, washtub 110.00
Planter, #110, man, w/jug & snake, 4½" 65.00
Planter, #81, man drinking from jug, sitting by washtub 75.00
Shakers, Ma & Old Doc, pr 95.00

Miscellaneous

Items in this section that are designated 'IP' are miscellaneous novelties made by Imperial Porcelain; the remainder are of interest to Paul Webb collectors, though made by an unknown manufacturer. Prints on calendars and playing cards are signed 'Paul Webb.'

Calendar, 1954, 12 sgn scenes, Brown & Bigelow, complete 35.00
Figurine, cat in high-heeled shoe, 5½" L......................40.00
Hot pad, Dutch boy w/tulips, rnd, IP.............................30.00
Ink blotters, sgn scenes, ea... 8.00
Mug, #29, man hdl, sgn Paul Webb, 4¾" 25.00
Planter, #106, dog sitting by tub, IP 75.00
Planter, #26, man & tree stump, sgn Paul Webb, bl 25.00
Planter, #27, man, jug, & barrel, sgn Paul Webb...........25.00
Playing cards, ad: Rafe Oiling Gun, Brown & Bigelow, MIB 45.00
Shakers, pigs, 5", pr 95.00
Shakers, standing pigs, IP, 8", pr 95.00

Indian Tree

Indian Tree was a popular dinnerware pattern produced by various potteries since the early 1800s to recent times. Although backgrounds and borders vary, the Oriental theme is carried out with the gnarled, brown branch of a pink-blossomed tree. Among the manufacturers marks, you may find represented such notable firms as Coalport, S. Hancock and Sons, Soho Pottery, and John Maddock and Sons.

Bowl, vegetable; Johnson Bros, w/lid	35.00
Bowl, vegetable; oval, Johnson Bros	20.00
Bowl, vegetable; rnd, Johnson Bros	18.00

Oval vegetable bowl, Maddux, 9", $22.50.

Coffeepot, Johnson Bros	50.00
Creamer & sugar bowl, Johnson Bros	30.00
Cup & saucer, Meakin	22.00
Gravy boat, Johnson Bros	25.00
Plate, Maddock, 10"	12.00
Platter, John Bros, 13½"	30.00
Platter, Johnson Bros, 12"	25.00
Platter, Johnson Bros, 16"	35.00
Platter, pickle; Johnson Bros	10.00
Teapot, Johnson Bros, lg	45.00

Inkwells and Inkstands

Receptacles for various writing fluids have been used since ancient times. Through the years they have been made from countless materials — glass, metal, porcelain, pottery, wood, and even papier-mache. During the 18th century, gold or silver inkstands were presented to royalty; the well-known silver inkstand by Philip Syng, Jr., was used for the signing of the Declaration of Independence, and impressive brass inkstands with wells and a pounce pot (sander) were proud possessions of men of letters. When literacy vastly increased in the 19th century, the dip pen replaced the quill pen; and inkwells and inkstands were widely used and produced in a broad range of sizes in functional and decorative forms — from ornate Victorian to flowing Art Nouveau and stylized Art Deco designs. However, the acceptance of the ballpoint pen literally put inkstands and inkwells 'out of business.' But their historical significance and intriguing diversity of form and styling fascinate today's collectors.

Brass, ornate Victorian style, 2 wells w/pen rack	185.00
Cut glass, amber, pyramid shape, 3"	245.00
Cut glass, Birmingham sterling & turq lid, 3"	295.00
Cut glass, bl, hinged bl octagonal lid, 3" dia	275.00
Cut glass, sterling lid, 2" sq	225.00
Daum Nancy, sgn, brass lid, 3½" sq	950.00
French Faience, loose lid, 3¼" sq	155.00

Hand-carved and painted wood, sled lifts to reveal well, 4½", $350.00.

Glass, bl opaque, hinged metal lid, 3" dia	165.00
Glass, Ma & Pa Carter, Germany, pr	125.00
Glass, Thousand Eye, amber, loose lid, 2" sq	145.00
Mt Washington, bl swirl, hinged lid, 2" sq	275.00
Nippon, Egyptian decor, loose lid, gr mk	225.00
Pairpoint glass, controlled bubbles, sterling lid, 5"	700.00
Pietra dura base w/cut glass well	325.00
Porc, bird decor, hinged lid, sq	75.00
Porc, Deco clown figural, head is lid	150.00
Quimper, heart shape, 3¼" W	295.00
Roycroft, hinged lid, G patina, 3" sq	115.00
Silliman, orig label, 3½" dia	165.00
Silver overlay, hinged lid, rnd, 3½" H	850.00
Sterling, flat hinged lid, London, 4½" dia	395.00
Traveler, gutta percha, threaded lid, 2" sq	65.00

Insulators

The telegraph was invented in 1844. The devices developed to hold the electrical transmission wires to the poles were called insulators. The telephone, invented in 1876, intensified their usefullness; and, by the turn of the century, thousands of varieties were being produced in pottery, wood, and glass of various colors. Many are embossed with patent dates.

Of the more than 3,000 types known to exist, today's collectors evaluate their worth by age and rarity of color. Aqua and green are the most common colors in glass, dark brown the most common in ceramic. Threadless insulators (CD #737) made between 1850 and 1870, bring prices well into the hundreds.

In the listings that follow, the CD numbers are from an identification system developed in the late 1960s by N.R. Woodward.

Those seeking additional information about insulators are encouraged to contact the National Insulator Association, whose address may be found in the Directory under Clubs, Newsletters, and Catalogs.

Key:
CB — corrugated base	SDP — sharp drip points
CD — Consolidated Design	RB — rough base
SB — smooth base	RDP — round drip points

CD #122.4, Pyrex, SB, lemon	4.00

C.C. G. Co. (Australian), lavender, tall skirt, $45.00.

CD 100, Surge, RDP, clear 2.00
CD 1000, no name (Glass Block), lt gr 500.00
CD 102, BGM Co, SB, purple 18.00
CD 102, California, SB, bl...15.00
CD 102.2, Westinghouse, SB, bl.............................130.00
CD 104, Brookfield, SB, aqua.................................... 5.00
CD 106, Ericson, RDP, clear, foreign.......................10.00
CD 106, Star, SB, olive gr 8.00
CD 109.5, Harloe's, SB, aqua.................................700.00
CD 112, California, SB, smoke 6.00
CD 112, New England Telegraph & Telephone, SB, gr 80.00
CD 1130, California, purple.....................................150.00
CD 115, Hemingray, CB, clear.................................... 1.00
CD 121, Diamond, SB, purple, foreign 15.00
CD 121, Maydwell, SDP, straw 14.00
CD 122, McLaughlin, RDP, apple gr 6.00
CD 123, EC&M Co SF, SB, aqua w/olive streaks..........80.00
CD 124.6, Agee, SB, emerald gr, foreign 50.00
CD 128, Hemingray E-14-B, SB, opal.......................50.00
CD 130, Cal Elec Works, SB, gr 160.00
CD 130.7, AGM, SB, aqua, foreign 10.00
CD 134, KCGW, SB, gr...20.00
CD 138, Kerr, SB, clear 4.00
CD 140, Jumbo, SB, bl 150.00
CD 141, no name (Hot Cross Bun,) SB, emerald gr......... 9.00
CD 143, Canadian Pacific, SB, royal purple, foreign..........15.00
CD 143, CNR, SB, aqua 10.00
CD 145, Brookfield, SB, aqua.................................... 1.00
CD 145, Hemingray, SDP, bl 1.00
CD 150, Brookfield, SB, aqua...................................50.00
CD 150.2, Telefonos Ericson, SB, lt gr, foreign 30.00
CD 151, HG Co, SB, Peacock 110.00
CD 152, Hemingray, SB or DP, aqua 1.00
CD 155, Armstrong's DPL, SB, clear 1.00
CD 162, Hemingray, DP, dk cobalt bl 125.00
CD 162, SS&Co, SB, lime gr 75.00
CD 168, Hemingray, SB, carnival..............................25.00
CD 185, Jeffery, SB, aqua 60.00
CD 190/191, Am Telegraph & Telephone, SB, jade gr, 2-pc..........35.00
CD 190/191, AT&T, SB, aqua 8.00
CD 201, California, SB, gr 600.00
CD 203.2, Armstrong, SB, near clear 160.00
CD 211, Brookfield, SB, aqua.................................180.00
CD 235, Pyrex, SB, carnival......................................18.00
CD 252, M&E, SB, aqua 40.00

CD 257, Hemingray, DP, clear...................................... 4.00
CD 263, Hemingray, SB, bl 80.00
CD 267, NEGM, SB, yel-gr...220.00
CD 270, no name, SB, gr..150.00
CD 282, Knowles, SB, aqua 50.00
CD 292.5, Boston, SB, dk gr...95.00
CD 303/310, Hemingray, RDP, lt gr 45.00
CD 316, Brookfield, SB, aqua 100.00
CD 317, Chambers, SB, lime gr 150.00
CD 320, Pyrex, SB, clear 9.00
CD 679, L'Electro Verre, SB, dk aqua.........................125.00
CD 700, no name (threadless egg), bl..........................195.00
CD 724, Chester, SB, dk cobalt, threadless 600.00
CD 728, Boston Bottle Works, SB, lt aqua, threadless...........60.00
CD 731, McKee, SB, aqua, threadless........................130.00
CD 733, Brookfield, SB, aqua, threadless 200.00
CD 743, no name, SB, deep amber 400.00
CD 843, Verlica, SB, aqua 20.00

Irons

Iron collections represent centuries of civilization and history through the diversity of these implements used to smooth and press clothing. Terra cotta irons were used during the period of the Roman Empire. The Hong Kong Museum of Arts has a pan iron from the Han Dynasty. Excavations reveal mysterious primitive glass irons in Viking graves. More recent history is rich with cast iron, charcoal, box, and fuel irons.

Joining an iron-collectors' club where you can see and handle old irons is a wonderful way to gain the knowledge and experience you need to become a wise iron collector. A novice must learn to avoid the temptation to buy cheap irons; experienced collectors avow they never overpay by buying quality. Condition is of the utmost importance. Common irons should grade very good or better. Only for scarce items should the condition be relaxed. Remember that it is the top-level pieces whose values tend toward rapid appreciation. Because good old irons have been passed down through several generations, by now it is unusual to find a 'sleeper'; and, as the ranks of iron collectors continue to swell, supplies diminish and values increase. Buy fine workmanship, design, style, and quality; a well-chosen iron collection could be one of today's best investments.

In the listings that follow, prices are given for examples in very good to excellent condition. Damage, repairs, excessive wear, rust, and missing parts can dramatically reduce value. Our advisor for this category is The Iron Lady (Carol and Jimmy Walker), whose address is listed in the Directory under Texas. See also Appliances.

Boxed set: Enterprise, 5 assorted bases, 3 handles, trivet, and rest, EX, $550.00.

Alcohol, Austrian, mk w/fish in circle on cap, 5⅝", VG 260.00
Art Deco, wht porc, copper sole, Germany, 7½", EX 375.00
Box, Belgium, handmade, 18th C, w/slug, 4", VG......................290.00
Box, Portuguese, brass, 'D'uprights/swing gate/hook latch, EX 375.00
Box, Salamander, porc knob, slug, EX 150.00
Box, Tailor, no slug, 11¼", VG 150.00
Charcoal, Dalli, Germany, 8", G.......................................50.00
Charcoal, Indonesian, brass, roll top, dragon sides, 8", EX..........275.00
Detachable hdl, Ober, Pat 1895, rare, EX.............................190.00
Detachable hdl, Sensible #25, Pottstown PA, 6½", VG.................55.00
Detachable hdl, Sensible #3, sq bk, 6¼", VG.........................55.00
Detachable hdl, Sensible #4, 5¼", VG................................40.00
Detachable hdl, Sensible #6, NRS & Co, 3⅞", VG 120.00
Electric, Pelouze, 1st electric w/heat control, 6", VG...............125.00
Flower, used to make silk flowers for hats, VG 145.00
Fluter, Hand, Erie, detachable hdl, VG 225.00
Fluter, Machine, Crown, March 23, 1880, EX 125.00
Gasoline, Am Gas Machine Co #68, lt gr porc, 6¾", G 75.00
Gasoline, Coleman #3, nickel w/bl enamel hdl, 7¾", VG..............55.00
Gasoline, Montgomery Ward, brass triangle tank, 7¼", VG 55.00
Gasoline, Royal Self Heating Iron Co, Art Deco style, 7¼", G......90.00
Goffer, jellyfish on base, 2½x3x½", VG................................150.00
Goffer, Kenrick 'S'upright, orig heater, VG............................155.00
Hatter's, Brim, 2-groove, 3⅜", VG....................................125.00
Leaf w/cutter, used to make silk leaves for hats, mini, VG...........190.00
Natural gas, OK Made in England, 5½", VG............................95.00
Polisher, Enterprise Star, ventilated hdl, 5¼", EX 80.00
Polisher, French bubble sole, 6¼", EX 595.00
Sad iron, Chattanooga #8, mk on face, 6⅝", G 50.00
Sensible #25, Pottstown PA, 6½", VG.................................55.00
Sensible #3, sq bk, 6¼", VG..55.00
Sensible #4, 5¼", VG...40.00
Sensible #6, NRS & Co, detachable hdl, 3⅞", VG 120.00
Shirt, for machine presser, Troy on face, 4¼", VG 90.00
Sleeve, Sensible #5, 8", VG...60.00

Ironstone

During the last quarter of the 18th century, English potters began experimenting with a new type of body that contained calcinated flint and a higher china clay content, intent on producing a fine durable whiteware — heavy, yet with a texture that would resemble porcelain. To remove the last trace of yellow, a minute amount of cobalt was added, often resulting in a bluish-white tone. Wm. and John Turner of Caughley, and Josiah Spode II were the first to manufacture the ware successfully. Others, such as Davenport, Hicks and Meigh, and Ralph and Josiah Wedgwood, followed with their own versions. The latter coined the name 'Pearl' to refer to his product and incorporated the term into his trademark. In 1813 a 14-year patent was issued to Charles James Mason, who called his ware Patented Ironstone. Francis Morley, G.L. Asworth, T.J. Mayer, and other Staffordshire potters continued to produce ironstone until the end of the century. While some of these patterns are simple to the extreme, many are decorated with in-mold designs of fruit, grain, and foliage on ribbed or scalloped shapes. In the 1830s transfer-printed designs in blue, mulberry, pink, green, and black became popular; and polychrome versions of Oriental wares were manufactured to compete with the Chinese trade. See also Mason's Ironstone.

Our advise for this category comes from Home Place Antiques, whose address is listed in the Directory under Illinois.

Baker, Gothic, 8-sided, rectangular, Edwards..............................45.00
Bowl, vegetable; Hebe, open, Alcock......................................40.00

Bowl, vegetable; Ivy Wreath, oval, w/lid, Meir & Son, 6¼" 70.00
Bowl, vegetable; Prairie, open, oval, Clementson......................22.00
Bowl, vegetable; 1851 Octagon, w/lid, T&R Boote, 7⅜" 85.00
Butter pat, plain, rnd, unmk, 2½x2⅝" 3.00
Chamberpot, Corn & Oats, w/lid...120.00
Compote, Gothic, hdls, ped ft, 10-sided, Meir & Son, 7½" 95.00
Creamer, Cable & Ring, bulbous, Burgess, 5½"........................35.00
Cup & saucer, handleless; Ceres, Elsmore & Forster 45.00
Cup & saucer, handleless; floral, sgn Wedgwood.......................55.00
Cup & saucer, handleless; Grape & Medallion, Challinor...............35.00
Cup & saucer, Wheat 25.00
Cup plate, plain, 4¼" dia 9.50
Cup plate, Prairie, Clementson, 4¾" dia...............................18.00
Gravy boat, Ceres, Elsmore & Forster, 5¼"...........................55.00
Gravy boat, Fuchsia, bulbous, 1860s, 5¼" 25.00
Gravy boat, Wheat & Blackberry, unmk, 5" 40.00
Ladle, sauce; Cable & Ring, 6⅞"......................................45.00
Mold, pineapple, graduated sides, 3½x7x6"............................35.00
Nappy, Grape & Medallion, Challinor, 5"...............................8.00
Nappy, Nacho (Little Palm), T&R Boote, 5" 8.00
Pitcher, milk; Ceres, Elsmore & Forster, 8½".........................60.00
Pitcher, Panelled Columbia, 5" 60.00
Plate, dessert; Prairie, Clementson, 6⅝"...............................10.00
Plate, dessert; Sydenham, T&R Boote, 7¼".............................17.00
Plate, dinner; Bellflower, Edwards, 9¾"...............................18.00
Plate, dinner; Fluted Pearl, 20-sided, Wedgewood, 9½" 18.00
Platter, Sydenham, oval, T&R Boote, 16x11¾"..........................55.00
Sauce, Baltic, oval, w/lid, Hulme 85.00
Sauce, Columbia, rnd, hdls, w/lid & underplate, Goodwin..........110.00
Saucer, Wheat w/Flowers, scalloped rim, Johnson Bros, 5¾" 4.00
Shaving mug, Wheat & Poppy, Forster.................................58.00
Soup plate, Ceres, Elsmore & Forster, 9⅝"...........................25.00
Soup plate, Fig, 10-sided, Davenport, 9½".............................25.00
Soup plate, Sydenham, rnd, 10-sided, T&R Boote, 8⅜" 12.00
Sugar bowl, Ceres, w/lid, Elsmore & Forster, 7¼"...................65.00
Sugar bowl, Ceres, w/lid, Tunstal, 7¼", EX...........................65.00
Teapot, Ceres, Turner, Goddard & Co, 10"...........................235.00
Teapot, Columbia, pk band, apple finial, Challinor...................195.00
Toothbrush holder, Cable, Meakin.....................................30.00
Toothbrush holder, Cornered, Edwards.................................50.00
Toothbrush holder, Diana, Meakin, 4½" 35.00
Toothbrush holder, Tonquin, Malcolm.................................75.00
Toothbrush holder, Wheat & Blackberry, oval, w/lid, unmk.........70.00
Tureen, vegetable; acorn finial, lg....................................65.00
Tureen, vegetable; 1851 Octagon, T&R Boote, w/lid, 8¾" 85.00
Wash bowl & ewer, Hyacinth, bulbous, Hope & Carter, 12".........95.00

Ivory

Technically, true ivory is the substance composing the tusk of the elephant; the finest type comes from those of Africa. However, tusks and teeth of other animals — the walrus, the hippopotamus, and the sperm whale, for instance — are similar in composition and appearance and have also been used for carving. The Chinese have used this substance for centuries, preferring it over bone because of the natural oil contained in its pores, which not only renders it easier to carve but also imparts a soft sheen to the finished product. Aged ivory usually takes on a soft caramel patina, but unscrupulous dealers sometimes treat new ivory to a tea bath to 'antique' it! A bill passed in 1978 reinforced a ban on the importation of whale and walrus ivory. All examples listed here are Oriental in origin unless noted otherwise.

Apple corer, ca 1820...300.00

Buddha, 1"...**22.50**
Buddha on lotus ped w/2-step rnd plinth, cvd wood base, 10" **200.00**
Cigarette holder, bird claw form.....................................**30.00**
Elephant, trunk down, 2x2½".......................................**70.00**
Farmer w/rooster & basket of chickens, sgn, 10" **1,500.00**
Fisherman w/basket of shellfish, sgn, Japanese, 4⅝" **200.00**
Fisherman w/fish basket, boy w/tortoise, 1880s, 4¼" **250.00**
Lady in kimono holds figural fan, Japanese, 6¾" **275.00**
Lion, 1½x1½" **30.00**
Maid holds palm leaf, teakwood stand, 2½" **35.00**
Male (& female) in elaborate dress, 1900, 10", pr **1,100.00**
Man carries pack of mums on head, holds single mum, 13"..... **2,300.00**
Man on base of tree trunk w/axe & conch shell, EX cvg, 12".. **2,500.00**
Man sits on wood bundle holds cabbage, leaf & basket, 5"...... **1,500.00**
Man w/axe & bunch of grapes, wrapped wood on bk, sgn, 8".. **1,200.00**
Man w/ft on bbl, monkey w/fan, 2nd at his ft, mk, 13" **2,500.00**
Man w/sheaf of wheat on head, teakwood stand, 1½" **35.00**
Monk w/flowing robe holds ball aloft, birds on branch, 13".........**700.00**
Mtns/village w/figures emerge from mussel shell, mk, 14"...........**400.00**
Musician w/samisen & conch shell, umbrella at ft, sgn, 12" **2,000.00**
Pheasant, life-like colors, on teakwood base, 2x3½" **100.00**
Ship of Good Fortune, rooster figurehead, 7 gods, 9x16", EX .. **1,200.00**
Shrine, 2 doors, seated ivory Buddha w/in, ivory stand, 12" **1,000.00**
Squash, polychrome, window reveals cvd int scene, 2½" **150.00**

Chinese covered vases, flattened cylinder form with ring handles, ca 1900, minor repair, 18½", $950.00 for the pair.

Vase, figural scenes, hdls, foo dog finial, 1880s, 16", pr **1,200.00**
Vase, women/children by tree, ring hdls, w/lid, 19", pr............ **1,100.00**

Jack-in-the-Pulpit Vases

Popular novelties at the turn of the century, jack-in-the-pulpit vases were made in every type of art glass produced. Some were simple, others elaborately appliqued and enameled. They were shaped to resemble the lily for which they were named.

Amberina w/amber 3-legged base & trim, HP florals, 12"...........**440.00**
Apple gr opaque, ruffled Hobnail maroon rim, 7¼x6¾" **110.00**
Bl opal w/yel enameling, 8-petal top, 13½".........................**255.00**
Bl opaque w/maroon ruffled rim, 6⅞x6½" **120.00**
Bl opaque w/ruffled Hobnail maroon border, 7x6⅝" **118.00**
Frosted w/rose satin int, frosted rigaree, ruffled rim, 6".................**170.00**

Gr shaded, clear petal ft, 6⅞x5" **88.00**
Gr shaded overlay, Hobnail rim, 7⅛x7¼"................................**110.00**
Maroon shaded, ruffled, 6x6" **110.00**
Opaline, maroon pleated ruffle, gr Hobnail int, 7" **125.00**

Opaline with ruby edge, diamond quilted base, 7", $135.00.

Pk overlay, ruffled, 6½x6½" **110.00**
Wht, cranberry-to-wht face, 7½x6" **98.00**

Jackfield

Jackfield has come to be a generic term used to refer to wares with a red clay body and a high-gloss black glaze. It originated at Jackfield, in Stropshire, England; however, it was also produced in the Stafford-shire district as well. While some pieces are decorated with relief motifs or painted-on florals and gilding, many are unadorned. Teapots produced in the eighteenth century were known locally as 'black decanters.' These pots and figural dogs and roosters are the items most often found.

Coffee cup, emb figures, gilt trim, 3¼"..**265.00**
Coffeepot, elongated ovoid w/dome lid, long spout, 11", NM **850.00**
Creamer, cow figural, emb base..**85.00**
Pitcher, S-hdl, 6" **145.00**

Japanese Lustreware

Imported from Japan during the 1920s, novelty tableware items, vases, ash trays, etc. — often in blue, tan, and mother-of-pearl lustre glazes — were sold through five-and-dime stores or given as premiums for selling magazine subscriptions.

Plunger-type ash tray, 4½" diameter, $30.00.

Bowl, mc flowers on bl, mk, 1930s, 10½" 25.00
Cake plate, trees & flowers band on orange, 10-sided 22.50
Shakers, gold lustre w/bl lustre top, squat, pr 18.00
Shakers, mc floral band on orange lustre, pr 20.00
Shakers, tulips on tan lustre, tall slim form, pr 20.00
Shakers, vining florals on bl lustre, cylindrical form, pr 22.00
Toothpick holder, sm fish w/lg open mouth, orange 15.00
Vase, bird on wide wht band, ca 1935, 7½" 30.00
Vase, mc flowers on bl & wht lustre, fan form, '30s, 6½" 27.50

Jewelry

Jewelry as objects of adornment has always been regarded with special affection. Whether it be a trinket or a costly ornament of gold, silver, or enameled work, jewelry has personal significance to the wearer. The art of the jeweler is valued as is any art object, and the names of Lalique or Faberge on collectible pieces bring prices demanded by the signed works of Picasso. Once the province of kings and noblemen, jewelry now is a legacy of all strata of society. The creativity reflected in the jeweler's art has resulted in a myriad of decorative adornments for men and women, and the modern usage of 'lesser' gems and base metals has elevated the value and increased the demand for artistic merit, so that now it is considered by collectors to be on a par with intrinsic value. Luxuriously appointed pieces of Victorian splendor and Edwardian grandeur now compete with the unique, imaginative renditions of jewelry produced in the exciting Art Nouveau period as well as the adventurous translation of jewelry executed in man-made materials versus natural elements. Today prices for gems and gemstones crafted into antique and collectible jewelry are based on artistic merit, personal appeal, pure sentimentality, and intrinsic value. Note: Diamond prices vary greatly depending on color, clarity, etc. Values given here are for diamond jewelry with a standard commercial grade of diamonds that are most likely to be encountered.

Our advisor for this category is Rebecca Dodds; her address may be found in the Directory under Florida. If you are interested in collecting or dealing in jewelry, you will find that authority Lillian Baker has several fine books available on the subject — 100 Years of Collectible Jewelry: 1850-1950; Art Nouveau and Art Deco Jewelry; and Fifty Years of Collectible Fashion Jewelry: 1925-1975. These books are complete with beautiful full-color illustrations and current market values. Mrs. Baker is listed in the Directory under California. See also Plastics.

Key:
A/C — Arts and Crafts	gf — gold filled
AD — Art Deco	grad — graduated
AN — Art Nouveau	gp — gold plated
cab — cabochon	gw — gold washed
cl — clear	k — karat
comp — complementary	plat — platinum
ct — carat	r'stn — rhinestone
dmn — diamond	rdm — rhodium
dwt — penny weight	stn — stone
g'el-plt — gold electroplate	tw — total weight
g-stn — gemstone	wg — white gold
g-t — gold toned	yg — yellow gold

Bar pin, JH Winn, 12k w/1 lg+2 sm sapphires+2 pearls, 2" **1,100.00**
Bar pin, w/yg, 15 dmn+11 bl synthetic & natural sapphires 300.00
Bar pin, 14k openwork leaves w/oval blister pearl, A/C...............250.00
Bracelet, G Jensen, plaques w/chrysoprase or amber alternate 550.00
Bracelet, G Jensen, sterling, wide linear links, Denmark 450.00
Bracelet, G Jensen, 3 bird plaques+3 w/labadorites 650.00
Bracelet, Lebont, 14k chains join 5 cab turq in leafy fr............ **2,000.00**

Bracelet, sterling w/3 rows of rhinestones, 1930s, ½" W 90.00
Bracelet, 18k wg, 10 1.5mm+3 2mm dmns, Deco style 440.00

Brooch, attributed to Margaret Vant (Boston), pink tourmaline in gold filigree, ca 1925, 2" wide, $850.00.

Buckle, Huber/Fahrner, silver w/6 chrysoprase cabs, A/C........ **2,100.00**
Clips, silver, pierced w/gr glass cabs & bl-gr enamel, AN 225.00
Earrings, Eisenberg, 2" long drop w/3-leaf clovers, pr 65.00
Earrings, sterling w/marcasites, AD, 1⅛", pr 55.00
Locket, 14k yg & enamel, 3 seed pearls in floral mt, 1½" 550.00
Necklace, G Jensen, floral plaques joined w/dbl chain links........900.00
Necklace, G Jensen, flowers alternate w/labradorite buds **2,700.00**
Necklace, Kalo, floral plaques ea w/oval centers, +earrings 950.00
Necklace, sterling w/bl stones, 3 plaques on chain, A/C..............250.00
Necklace & bracelet, G Jensen, plain & floriform plaques 800.00
Pearls, cultured, blk, 3-strand, 6-6½mm, dmn clasp **1,500.00**
Pearls, cultured, 7-7½mm, 72" continous strand **1,600.00**
Pendant, FG Hale, 14k, A/C scrolls w/lg blister pearl, 3" **1,900.00**
Pendant, G Jensen, 3 sterling flowers w/lapis drops & cabs **1,400.00**
Pendant, Murrle-Bennett, sterling, enamel lines/florals, 1" 250.00
Pendant, Plantagenet, sterling teardrop w/peridots, w/chain 225.00
Pendant, THS, sterling, sq w/lg coral cab & drop, A/C 600.00
Pendant, 14k drop w/6 sm sapphires & freshwater pearls, A/C... **1,600.00**
Pin, brass, floral w/bl rhinestones, oval, Edwardian, lg 40.00
Pin, cameo, blk on clear Bakelite, 2" 22.00
Pin, copper frwork about pottery plaque, att Ruskin, 2½" 100.00
Pin, G Jensen, sterling, openwork flowers in oval, 1¾" 200.00
Pin, G Jensen, sterling, openwork/florals/insects, 1910, 2" 425.00
Pin, G Jensen, stylized entwining bellflowers, sgn CI, 1¾" 400.00

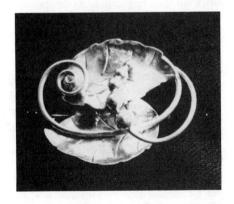

Pin, Georg Jensen (mk USA), 1½" x 2", $175.00.

Pin, kilt; silver, beads atop lapis on stem, A/C, 4½" 110.00
Pin, Mary Gage, sterling mum w/quartz cab, sgn, 3¼" dia...........450.00
Pin, sterling, bl oval cab in open leaf fr, England, 1½" 175.00
Pin, sterling, fantailed goldfish, 2" 50.00
Pin, sterling, lg amethyst+2 Baroque pearls, A/C, 2½".................450.00
Pin, sterling leaf/branch, w/4-color glass stones, A/C, 2½" 100.00
Pin, yg ram's head w/opal eye, 1" L 250.00

Pin, 14k, lg fire opal drop w/3 appl sm opals+2 in bar, A/C.........475.00
Pin+earrings, G Jensen, oval w/in wirework & floral fr, 2" 375.00
Ring, G Jensen, sterling w/3 moonstones, beading, 1910, #d.......200.00
Ring, wg, 4 dmn tw .20+bl sapphire about .10ct, rtcl mt 300.00
Ring, wht/yel gold w/lg star sapphire cab, A/C leafy mt 550.00
Ring, yg, 4 full-cut dmn tw .35ct 500.00

Costume Jewelry

Bracelet, Carnegie, g-t leaf links w/lg pearls & tiny turq 35.00
Bracelet, Florenza, g-t dmn-in-ring links, sm pearls/turq 18.00
Bracelet, H-links set w/sm r'stns & rectangular red stns................36.00
Bracelet, Haskell, 12 lg bl oval cabs w/flower clasp 50.00
Bracelet, Kreisler, 5 silver & g-t openwork floral plaques..............24.00
Bracelet, wide coiled copper links, +earrings 28.00
Bracelet, 6 floral-cvd gr glass plaques on g-t links........................22.00
Bracelet, 7 copper 3-leaf components, 1½" W 18.00
Earrings, Coro, g-t compote w/mc stn fruit, 1" 10.00
Earrings, HAR, cluster of lg turq cabs & sm r'stns, 1¼"................12.00
Earrings, spray of 4 sm cvd 'coral' flowers+lg flower, 1½" 6.00
Fur clip, cluster of 7 lg bl glass 'moonstones,' 2" 18.00
Fur clip, Mazer, g-t w/lg sq gr stns & sm r'stns, 3" L....................50.00
Fur clip, Monet, g-t plumes, 1¼", pr...24.00
Fur clip, Rosenstein, sterling filigree bell w/clapper, 1½" 60.00
Fur clip, silver metal leaf set w/tiny r'stns, 1¾" 12.00
Hat pin, 1" celluloid sq w/r'stns, pin w/screw-on end 14.00
Necklace, can-shaped wooden beads in gr & natural, 54".............15.00
Necklace, chain w/lucite fish bowl, fish w/in 18.00
Necklace, Coro, A/C cab-set 2½" plaque w/5 kite-form drops 18.00
Necklace, Coro, 5 flower forms w/pearls on g-t chain 16.00
Necklace, Haskell, chain w/g-t disks & oval stns, +earrings..........45.00
Necklace, Ora, r'stn, 1½" 3-flower center w/drop, 16" 28.00
Necklace, Renoir, 2-strand chain w/lg copper leaf, +earrings 32.00
Necklace, Sarah Coventry, leaf drop w/5 gr stns on g-t chain......... 8.00
Necklace, Trifari, 2 wide g-t link-jointed peapod sections 30.00
Necklace, wooden beads w/9 assembled mc wooden drops............30.00
Pendant, Matisse, 1½" enamel button on chain, +earrings 40.00
Pin, Alice Caviness, grape cluster w/lg leaf...................................22.00
Pin, Bell, copper scrollwork, 2¼"...16.00
Pin, Bogoff, r'stn encrusted scrollwork, many lg stns, 3½".............35.00
Pin, Capri, g-t crescent w/lg & sm gr stn cabs, 1¾" 15.00
Pin, Carnegie, g-t fly, sm r'stns on head/upper wings, 2" 35.00
Pin, Castlecliff, enamel disk in ring of marquise stns, 2"................28.00
Pin, copper poodle, 2¼x1½"..12.00
Pin, Coro, flower form w/6 faceted red stns, +drop earrings...........22.00
Pin, Coro, g-t bow holds 3 pk stn-set 'flowers,' 3".......................16.00
Pin, Coro, g-t leaf w/10 pearls, 2¾x1¼" 5.00
Pin, Coro, sterling bird & flowers w/in open ring, 1¾" 28.00
Pin, Corocraft, leavy silver 'dangle' type w/lg bl stns, 3" 25.00
Pin, Danecraft, sterling, openwork ring of sm hearts, 1¾".............24.00
Pin, Eisenberg, mushroom w/bl & gr enamel, 2¼" 38.00
Pin, elephant's head, pewter color w/turq & gr stns, 3" 50.00
Pin, Florenza, coiled snake in g-t w/wht enamel scales, 2¼" 25.00
Pin, g-t fish w/pk glass fins, 1½" 12.00
Pin, g-t key w/sm mc stns, 2¾" 16.00
Pin, g-t Siamese dancer set w/sm mc stns, 2½" 28.00
Pin, g-t sword w/r'stn hilt & gold chain 30.00
Pin, g-t w/cluster of mc cvd glass flowers & r'stns, 2" 38.00
Pin, HAR, g-t butterfly w/sm turq beads, 2"...............................25.00
Pin, HAR, starfish w/sm coral stns & wht enamel, 2" 15.00
Pin, Haskell, brass, ring of cloverleaves w/Baroque pearls 45.00
Pin, Haskell, g-t 2" flower, coral/crystal beads, +earrings 65.00
Pin, Haskell, sm gr stns+1 lg in ea of 3 lobes, 1½", pr..................70.00
Pin, Jomaz, g-t leafy cluster w/pearl in r'stn petals, 2¼" 40.00

Pin, Kim, matt copper stylized cat w/pierced eyes, 2½" 18.00
Pin, Korda, Thief of Bagdad figural, g-t, 3" 38.00
Pin, ladybug, pewter-color, 1½"...10.00
Pin, Lang, sterling lamppost, 2¼"...22.00
Pin, lg faux tiger eye in leafy stn-set outer ring, 1¾"....................32.00
Pin, Matisse, Art Moderne copper form w/mottled enamel, 3" 28.00
Pin, Matisse, lg copper leaf w/gold & wht enamel, +earrings 45.00
Pin, Mexican silver, triangular w/inlaid MOP flowers, 2" 16.00
Pin, Owl, allover r'stns, lg faceted eyes, enameling, 2" 18.00
Pin, peacock w/curled tail set w/lg & sm mc stns, 3½" 35.00
Pin, polished/faceted lucite containing flower, 1½"...................... 8.00
Pin, r'stn, Art Moderne, 2¼"...18.00
Pin, r'stn, open ring of flowers & leaves, 1¾" 18.00
Pin, Siam sterling, lg kneeling temple dancer on 1¼" sq...............24.00
Pin, Siam sterling fan w/Oriental characters, rtcl edge, 2" 22.00
Pin, silver, V-form w/5 delicate blossoms & dangles, 1½".............15.00
Pin, sterling, flower form, 2½"...16.00
Pin, sterling, Mexican in cart pulled by donkey, 2" 18.00
Pin, sunfish w/tiny allover r'stns & red cab eye, 2¼" 22.00
Pin, Trifari, bl enamel r'stn-tip leaf w/lady bug, +earrings..............36.00
Pin, Trifari, g-t ring of 3 ribbed comma forms w/pearls, 2" 14.00
Pin, Trifari, leafy flower form of shaped yel glass pcs, 3".................35.00
Pin, Trifari, silver-finish sitting sheltie dog, 1½" 8.00
Pin, Trifari, 2" wht enamel kite w/tail dangle 18.00
Pin, Trifari, 2 wht cvd glass flowers w/beads, +earrings 55.00
Pin, Usner, g-t w/9 aurora borealis stns, 1¾x1¾" 6.00
Pin, Weiss, leaf form w/marquis r'stns 30.00
Pin, 2 wooden hearts dangle from 2½" arrow 18.00
Pin, 2-blossom stem set w/mc lg sq stns & sm r'stns, 4"...............22.00
Pin, 3 wooden acorns dangle from 3" wooden leaf........................18.00

Judaica

The items listed below are representative of objects used in both the secular and religious life of the Jewish people. They are evident of a culture where silversmiths, painters, engravers, writers, and metal workers were highly gifted and skilled in their art. Most of the treasures shown in recently-displayed exhibits of Judaica were confiscated by the Germans during the late 1930s up to 1945; by then eight Jewish synagogues and fifty warehouses had been filled with Hitler's plunder.

Bible, Bezalel silver bound, etched symbols, 1940s, 5" 600.00
Charity box, German silver, cylindrical, 3" 495.00
Ethrog box, Continental silver, rnd, ftd, 1800s, 6" 1,000.00

Polish silverplated brass Hanukkah lamp, 1880s, $825.00.

Hanukkah lamp, African brass, floral bkplate, 1800s, 9" 495.00
Hanukkah lamp, Continental bronze, riveted, ca 1800, 5" 195.00
Hanukkah lamp, Dutch brass, Star of David form, 1800s, 11". 1,760.00
Hanukkah lamp, N African brass, geometrics, 1800s, 14" 550.00
Hanukkah lamp, Polish brass, lion surmounts, 1780s, 10" 1,100.00
Hanukkah spinning top, brass, mk Bezalel-Jerusalem, 1920, 1" ...358.00
Kiddush beaker, Polish silver, eng florals, 1800s, 2½" 330.00
Lap desk, olive wood, typical form, 1880s, 14" L..................... 1,100.00
Matzah tool, Continental brass, serrated end, 1800s, 5"...............330.00
Megillah, Russian silver, emb floral/inscribed, 1893, 3-pc...........400.00
Megillah, silver, rtcl cylinder/semiprecious stones, 18" 850.00
Mortar & pestle, N African brass, eng florals, 1800s, 4½"...........410.00
Mug fr, filigree, rosettes/foliage, 1900s, 6 w/+25" L tray........... 1,600.00
Napkin ring, Bezalel SP, inscr, 1920s, 2" 195.00
Necklace, Yemenite silver amulet, filigree chains, 1900s.............300.00
New year sampler, German, mc needlepoint, 1904, 9x11" 275.00
Passover plate, German pewter, eng scene, 1800s, 9"..................220.00
Passover plate, German silver, pierced rim, 3-ftd, 1800s, 9".........465.00
Pendant, Polish silver, eng Star of David, 1917, 1¾x2" 300.00
Sabbath candlestick, English silver, florals, 1880s, 13", pr...........880.00
Sabbath candlestick, Russian silver, 1900, 13", pr.....................500.00
Sabbath lamp, Continental brass, typical form, 1780s, 30" 385.00
Sabbath lamp, Continental brass, 4-holder/8-font, 1800s, 37"... 1,200.00
Spice tower, German silver, filigree, pennant top, 1800s, 10" 660.00
Spice tower, Russian silver, eagles at sides, 1890s, 70" 715.00
Torah ark curtain, Continental, red velvet, 1860s, 145x152" . 1,100.00
Torah binder, German linen, detailed pnt, metal fr, 1895 ....495.00
Torah binder, German linen, pnt inscriptions, 1897....................195.00
Torah pointer, Russian silver, eng/2 knobs, 1880s, 11½"............950.00
Tzadaka, silver, bud shape w/emb foliate, rpr, 7" 1,900.00

Jugtown

The Jugtown Pottery was started about 1920 by Juliana and Jacques Busbee, in Moore County, North Carolina. Ben Owen, a young descendant of a Staffordshire potter, was hired in 1923. He was the master potter, while the Busbees experimented with perfecting glazes and supervising design and modeling. Preferred shapes were those reminiscent of traditional country wares and classic Oriental forms. Glazes were various: natural-clay oranges, buffs, 'tobacco-spit' brown, mirror black, white, 'frog-skin' green, a lovely turquoise called Chinese blue, and the traditional cobalt-decorated salt glaze. The pottery gained national recognition; and, as a result of their success, several other local potteries were established. Jugtown is still in operation, however they no longer use their original glaze colors which are now so collectible.

Bowl, Chinese bl, spherical, ftd, 4½x6" 200.00
Inkwell, Chinese bl w/much red..90.00
Pitcher, brn speckled, incised decor, 8½".......................................58.00
Vase, Chinese bl/red flambe, 7½x4¾"...300.00
Vase, frogskin gr semi-gloss, sm rim, 7x4½"................................125.00
Vase, khaki semi-gloss/gold, incurvate, 6x4" 125.00
Vase, red/bl on gray stoneware, bulbous bottle form, 9½" 350.00
Vase, sprayed gold/khaki, bulbous, incurvate, 6½x5½" 140.00
Vase, tobacco-spit brn, jug form, 4½" 50.00

K. P. M. Porcelain

Under the tutelage of Frederick the Great, King of Prussia, porcelain manufacture was instituted in Berlin in 1751 by William K. Wegeley. In jealous competition with Meissen, hard-paste porcelain was produced — dinnerware, figurines, vases, etc. — some of which were

undecorated while other pieces were hand painted in Watteau scenes, landscapes, or florals. It soon became evident that the factory was unable to offer serious competition. The King withdrew his support, and the factory failed in 1757. In 1761 Johann Ernst Gotzkowsky bought the rights and attempted a similar operation which soon failed due to financial difficulties. Still determined to gain the same recognition enjoyed by Meissen, the King bought the plant in 1763 and ruled the operation with an iron hand, often assuring his success by taking advantage of his position. The King died in 1786, but production has continued and quality tableware and decorative porcelains are still being made on a commercial basis. Earliest marks were simply 'G' or 'W,' followed by the sceptre mark. After 1830 'K.P.M.' with an orb or eagle was adopted.

Our advisor for this category is Don Williams; he is listed in the Directory under Missouri.

Bowl, appl flowers/bird panels, rtcl basket form, 12", pr 400.00
Bowl, florals/butterflies, shaped, oblong, #4270, 17" 250.00
Ewer, appl swan on front, bl w/gold ped, 12", NM 750.00
Figurine, boy, Colonial dress, by basket of grapes, 4"..................350.00
Figurine, Napoleonic-style man (& lady), 1800s, 9", EX, pr.... 2,000.00
Figurine, polar bear, wht, 10" L...350.00
Inkwell, sphinx-head lid, #4333, 11¾" L 440.00
Plaque, angel, seated in profile, w/butterfly, sgn AR, 9x6" 3,500.00
Plaque, bust profile of girl in striped scarves, fr, 5½" 1,000.00
Plaque, Christ Child in temple among elders, 7½x10" 3,000.00
Plaque, Darling, after Coomans, 1880s, 9x6½" 4,000.00
Plaque, Duet, 2 maids w/songbook, sgn Dittrich, 11x9" 6,000.00
Plaque, Esther, R Dittrich, 13x8" 6,500.00
Plaque, Farewell, group in interior, W Sturm, 12x13" 6,500.00
Plaque, girl-angel on rocks, artist sgn, 5x7" 4,500.00
Plaque, gypsy girl, oval, in elaborate cvd fr, 9" 3,500.00
Plaque, gypsy girl by wall holds tambourine, oval, 7" 2,500.00
Plaque, Holy Margaret, after CT Lippold, 11x9" 2,800.00
Plaque, Le Fete du Jour, sgn, 7½x11½"................................... 7,000.00
Plaque, maid in rose robe stands on rock, C Cock, 13x8"........ 4,500.00

Porcelain plaque of lady in peach-colored dress, KPM and sceptre mark, late 1800s, plaque: 6¼" x 8¾", $4,000.00.

Plaque, monk in wine cellar, sgn/dtd 1865, 6x7¾" 2,750.00
Plaque, Ruth, standing/holding wheat, after Landelle, 9x6".... 3,000.00
Plaque, Vestal Virgin in interior, oval, 1800s, 9" 2,500.00

Kayserzinn Pewter

J.P. Kayser Sohn produced pewter decorated with relief-molded Art Nouveau motifs in Germany during the late 1800s and into the twentieth century. Examples are marked with 'Kayserzinn' and the mold number within an elongated oval reserve. Items with dimensional animals, insects, and birds, etc. are valued much higher than bowls, plates, and trays with simple embossed florals. Floral pieces are usually priced at $100.00 to about $200.00, depending on size.

Basket, oval w/emb sprigs, branching hdl, #18-452, 18" L....... 1,600.00
Bonbon, shell form w/Art Nouveau nude, sgn/#4136, 8x6¾" 175.00
Bowl, butterflies, cucumbers & vines, lg 350.00
Candelabrum, 2-arm, T-form std, #4531, 10½" 1,100.00
Dish, leaf form, #4065...95.00
Inkwell, sphinx's head finial, #4333, 11¾" L 440.00
Sauce boat, #4387, 7", +underplate..95.00
Sugar bowl, Dragon Ship form, open, 8" L....................................150.00
Tray, lilies relief, 3-D dragonfly ea end, #4188, 18½" 700.00
Water can, fish relief, snail finial, leaf hdl, #7-4203, 11"........ 1,300.00

Vase, embossed vintage, #49, 12", $195.00.

Keen Kutter

Keen Kutter was a brand name of E.C. Simmons Hardware, used from about 1870 until the mid-1930s. In 1923 Winchester merged with Simmons but continued to produce Keen Kutter marked knives and tools. The merger dissolved, and in 1940 the Simmons Company was purchased by Shapleigh Hardware. Older items are very collectible. For further study, we recommend *Keen Kutter*, an illustrated price guide by Jerry and Elaine Heuring, available at your favorite bookstore or public library. Our advisor for this category is Jim Calison; he is listed in the Directory under New York.

Apple peeler...100.00
Auger bit set, KK #16, 9-pc 70.00
Axe, Crown pattern, KK #153 ....35.00
Axe, KK #67 ....45.00
Axe, scout; KK #10 ....15.00
Bevel, sliding T; KK #1256, 6", EX 20.00
Bit, screwdriver; KK #102 .... 7.50
Bit brace, KK #8, 8" 12.00
Bottle, oil 30.00
Box label 10.00
Brace, ratchet; hand held 70.00
Bush hook 40.00
Butt chisel set, KK #5, 5-pc 80.00
Can opener, CI, dtd 1895, EX 30.00
Compass, 8" 22.50
Corkscrew 20.00

Cutter, glass; KK #25, EX 40.00
Drill, breast; KK #40, 16"..55.00
Drill, post; KK #1902 ....100.00
Drill set, KK #109 ....45.00
Envelope, advertising 15.00
Food grinder, KK #21..25.00
Food grinder, KK #22..10.00
Gauge, butt; KK #85...125.00
Gauge, shingle; KK #5, M..28.00
Hack saw, KK #48, EX 20.00
Hammer, brick; KK #35, 24-oz 35.00
Hammer, nail; KK #411, 20-oz 18.00
Letter opener, old logo, salesman's award, rare 195.00
Level, iron, KK #69, 9" 65.00
Level, torpedo 50.00
Level, wood, KK #104, 12" 40.00
Mallet, KK #216, EX...23.00
Mule shears 15.00
Paper roll holder 100.00
Pencil, mechanical..20.00
Plane, rabbet; KK #190...95.00
Plane, smooth; KK #4, 9"..30.00
Pliers, flat nose; KK #15, M 28.00
Pliers, long nose; KK #76, EX 15.00
Plumb bob 60.00
Pocket protector..30.00
Razor strop, KK #600, NM in box 40.00
Razor strop, KK #77, EX 20.00
Router, KK #171½, 7½", EX...48.00
Rule, steel, KK #306, 6", NM 25.00
Rule, zigzag; KK #503, 36" 40.00
Saw, compass; KK #93, M...22.00
Saw, dehorning 45.00
Saw, electric power; KK #70..65.00
Saw, keyhole 18.00
Scissors, buttonhole 10.00
Scraper, cabinet; KK #90, 11" 38.00
Spoke shave, K #91, EX 22.00
Square, carpenter's, steel, KK #18, EX 22.00
Staple puller, KK #700, EX 20.00
Tape, measuring; pocket sz, KK #45, 60", M................................28.00

Wagon, Keen Kutter Jet, red, 34" long, $200.00.

Wire cutter.. 8.00
Wrench, adjustable; KK #404, 4", M...80.00
Wrench, monkey; KK #6, 6", M..50.00

Wrench, monkey; used, 10" **18.00**
Wrench, monkey; used, 14" **20.00**

Kelva

Kelva was a trademark of the C.F. Monroe Company of Meriden, Connecticut; it was produced for only a few years after the turn of the century. It is distinguished from the Wave Crest and Nakara lines by its unique Batik-like background, probably achieved through the use of a cloth or sponge to apply the color. Large florals are hand painted on the opaque milk glass; and ormolu and brass mounts were used for the boxes, vases, and trays. Most pieces are signed. For more information we recommend *Wave Crest, The Glass of C.F. Monroe* by Wilfred R. Cohen, available at your local bookstore or from Collector Books.

Box, blown-out rose on lid, hexagonal, 2½" dia **475.00**
Box, floral on lt bl-gray, brass hdw, hinged, 6½" L **595.00**
Box, floral/beading on gr, unemb, 5" dia.................................**400.00**
Box, floral/beading on gr, unemb, 8" dia.................................**900.00**

Box, florals, 3¾", $350.00.

Box, metal filigree, glass lid w/floral, 3x3¼" **425.00**
Box, petunias, pk & wht on gr, 8" dia **650.00**
Ferner, floral on pk, ogee sides, 7½" dia **550.00**
Humidor, floral/'Cigars' on gr, cylindrical, 4¾" **550.00**
Match holder, floral, hexagonal, ormolu hdls/rim, 2½x1½".........**500.00**
Napkin ring, floral on waisted hexagonal form, rare....................**425.00**
Shakers, floral on gr, shaped wide base, 3", pr **350.00**
Tray, Crown, floral on gr, 6" dia **275.00**
Tray, floral on gr, unemb bowl form, ormolu bail, 3" dia.............**275.00**
Vase, floral on gr, emb frilly ribbon at base, ormolu, 19"............**900.00**
Vase, floral on gr, ogee form w/ornate ormolu hdls, 7¾".........**475.00**
Vase, floral on red, emb wht ribbons wrap base, ftd, 8x3" **575.00**
Whisk broom holder, floral on red, ornate ormolu bkplate.........**800.00**

Kenton Hills

Kenton Hills Porcelain was established in 1940 in Erlanger, Kentucky, by Harold Boop, former Rookwood superintendent, and David Seyler, noted artist and sculptor. Native clay was used; glazes were very similar to Rookwood's of the same period. The work was of high quality; but because of the restrictions imposed on needed material due to the onset of the war, the operation failed in 1942. Much of the ware is artist signed and marked with the Kenton Hill name or cipher and shape number.

Bowl, butterflies incised on bl, sgn Harold Bopp, 3x6"................**165.00**

Bowl, oxblood aventurine, 8"...**250.00**
Flowerpot, lotus relief, bl matt, sgn AC/mk HB, 3½x5".............**150.00**
Vase, bl gloss w/blk drip at neck, #167, 3½" **70.00**
Vase, floral, pk/brn/gr on peach, now drilled, 13".....................**275.00**
Vase, floral/leaf emb, gr aventurine, sgn W Hentschel, 7" **185.00**
Vase, lady's head figural, pk gloss, 6½", EX............................**275.00**
Vase, lg leaves, mc on lt ground, pear form, drilled, 10x5"...........**175.00**
Vase, oxblood gloss, #105, 4" **150.00**

Kentucky Derby Glasses

Since the 1940s, souvenir glasses have commemorated the famous Kentucky Derby; recently these have become popular collectibles, especially among race fans. Among the most valuable is the plastic Beetleware tumbler from the forties, the shorter version made in 1945, and the 1950 tumbler which is now valued at around $175.00. On the Gold Cup glass from 1952, current winners are shown along with those from the previous year. There were two from 1958 — one was the Gold Bar tumbler and the other was called the Iron Liege; both were simply leftover '57 glasses with the 1958 winners added at the top.

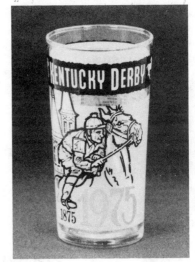

1975, $7.00.

1940s, aluminum **165.00**
1940s, plastic Beetleware **300.00**
1945, short **400.00**
1945, tall **175.00**
1948 ....**65.00**
1949, He Has Seen Them All **65.00**
1950 ....**175.00**
1951 ....**150.00**
1952, Gold Cup **65.00**
1953 ....**50.00**
1954 ....**45.00**
1955 ....**40.00**
1956 ....**40.00**
1957 ....**35.00**
1958, Gold Bar...**33.00**
1958, Iron Liege **50.00**
1959-60, ea. **30.00**
1961 ....**25.00**
1962-65 ....**22.00**
1966 ....**18.00**
1967-68, ea. **16.00**
1969 ....**15.00**
1970 ....**14.00**
1971-72 ....**12.00**

1973 ....10.00
1974 ....8.00
1975 ....7.00
1976 ....6.00
1977-78, ea 5.00
1979-80, ea 5.00
1981-82, ea 4.00
1983 ....3.00
1984-86, ea 3.00
1987-88, ea 3.00

Kew Blas

Kew Blas was a trade name used by the Union Glass Company of Summerville, Massachusetts, for their iridescent, lustered art glass produced from 1893 until about 1920. The glass was made in imitation of Tiffany and achieved notable success. Some items were decorated with pulled leaf and feather designs, while others had a monochrome lustre surface. The mark was an engraved 'Kew-Blas' in an arching arrangement.

Bowl, amber w/gold irid, spittoon form, sgn, 2½x5¾" 275.00
Candlestick, mc irid, wide flat ft, sgn, 8x5", pr 650.00
Compote, amber irid, folded-edge base, 4x5¾" 550.00
Goblet, amber irid, raised rim, 5" 100.00

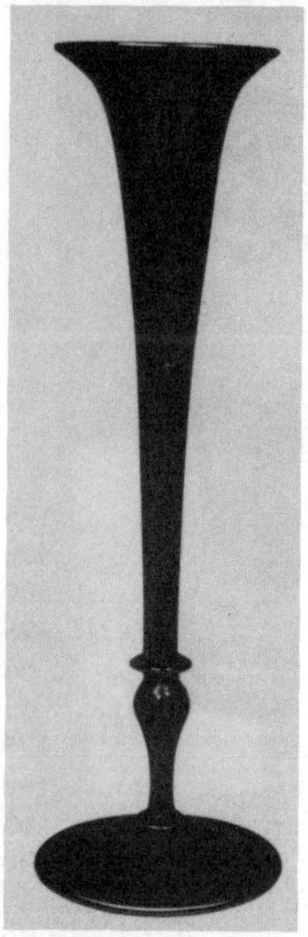

Gold lustre trumpet vase, signed, 12", $1,000.00.

Vase, feathers, gold/gr on ruby, purple int, 8½" 700.00
Vase, feathers, gr/gold on wht, gold int, spherical, 6" 1,500.00
Vase, feathers on gold, 5" 500.00
Vase, feathers on wht, gold int, waisted, 8x4" 1,250.00
Vase, gold feathers on ivory, gold rim, sgn, 4" 265.00
Vase, gold irid w/gr 'snakeskin,' scalloped, 4½" 650.00

King's Rose

King's Rose is a soft-paste ware that was made in Staffordshire, England, from about 1820 to 1830. It is closely related to Gaudy Dutch in body type as well as the colors used in its decoration. The pattern consists of a full-blown, orange-red rose with green, pink, and yellow leaves and accents. When the rose is in pink, the ware is often referred to as Queen's Rose.

Our advisor for this category is Richard Marden; he is listed in the Directory under New Hampshire.

Coffeepot, dome lid, minor wear, 11¾" 950.00
Creamer, emb shell & vine border, minor wear, 4¼" 350.00
Creamer, solid border, minor wear, 4½" 450.00
Cup & saucer, solid border, M 250.00
Cup & saucer, vine border, minor wear 200.00
Cup plate, vine border, 3½", EX 200.00

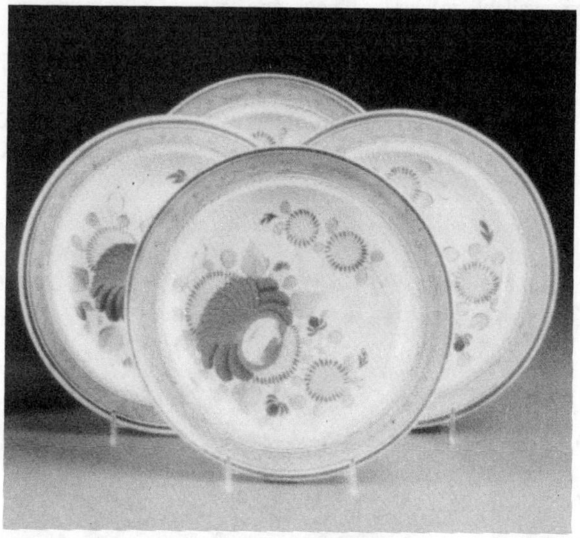

Group of four 9¾" plates, solid border, EX, $600.00.

Plate, Queen's, 8½", NM 95.00
Plate, sectional border, lt wear, 9¾" 150.00
Plate, solid border, 10", NM 225.00
Plate, soup; solid border, 9⅞" 225.00
Plate, 7½", M 175.00
Sugar bowl, emb shell & solid border, finial rpr, 5⅝" 200.00
Teapot, sectional border, lt wear, 5⅞" 400.00
Waste bowl, solid border, minor wear, 2¾x5⅝" 175.00

Kitchen Collectibles

During the last half of the 1850s, mass-produced kitchen gadgets were patented at an astonishing rate. Most were ingeniously efficient. Apple peelers, egg beaters, cherry pitters, food choppers, and such were only the most common of hundreds of kitchen tools well designed to perform only specific tasks. Today all are very collectible.

Our advisor for Cast Iron Bakers and Kettles is Denise Harned, who is the author of *Griswold Cast Collectibles*. She is listed in the Directory under Connecticut. See also Appliances; Molds; Primitives; Tinware; Wooden Ware.

Cast Kitchen Ware

Bowl, Scotch; Griswold #3, 4-qt 60.00
Broiler/grid iron, Griswold, 10½" 115.00
Brownie pan, Griswold #9 ....75.00
Cake mold, lamb, Griswold 125.00
Casserole, Griswold, lg emblem, w/lid, 9⅜x7⅜" 40.00

Cast iron corn stick pan, unmarked, 13" long, $58.00.

Cornstick pan, Griswold #262, mini, M 95.00
Cornstick pan, Griswold #273, 13¼" 115.00
Deep fryer, Griswold, 2½-qt 60.00
Dutch oven, Griswold #10, Tite Top, w/trivet 90.00
Dutch oven, Griswold #9, Erie, deep..........................95.00
French roll pan, Griswold #11 ....55.00
French roll pan, Griswold #17, Erie, 7½x6" 68.00
Gem pan, Griswold #8, lg emblem, 12¾x6¾"............75.00
Griddle, Griswold #10, oval, 22¼x10¼".....................75.00
Griddle, Griswold #18, Erie, sm emblem, 16¾x10".....50.00
Griddle, Griswold #6, Erie, 7¼" dia............................50.00
Griddle, Griswold #9, oval, 20½x10¼".......................60.00
Grill, barbeque; Griswold #10, lg emblem, 12¼" 100.00
Kettle, Griswold #12, Erie, 7½x12⅜".......................100.00
Kettle, Griswold #3, lg emblem, 4½x8".......................58.00
Kettle, Griswold #8, Erie, lg emblem, flat bottom, 7-qt...60.00
Kettle, Griswold #8, Erie, Maslin shape, 6-qt 50.00
Kettle, Wagner #0, 3" 50.00
Patty mold, Griswold, MIB 55.00
Platter, Griswold, oval, 'tree style,' 14½x8½".............45.00
Popover pan, Griswold #10, Erie, 10½x7½"................60.00
Popover pan, Griswold #18, Erie, 9½x5½" 75.00
Roaster, Griswold #5, oval, 6½-qt 55.00
Sauce pan, Griswold, Erie, 2-qt 50.00
Skillet, Griswold #11, lg emblem, w/smoke ring.........110.00
Skillet, Griswold #14, lg emblem 125.00
Skillet, Griswold #14, sm emblem 35.00
Skillet, Griswold #34, 7-egg......................................60.00
Skillet, Griswold #4, sm emblem, no smoke ring 20.00
Skillet, Griswold #5, lg emblem, no smoke ring...........42.50
Skillet, Griswold #6, Erie..45.00
Skillet, Griswold #7, Erie, w/smoke ring 55.00
Skillet, Griswold #9, Erie, w/smoke ring 60.00
Skillet, snack; Griswold #42, Erie, 7½" 68.00
Skillet, Wagner #3 ....22.00
Swedish pancake pan, Griswold #34, sm emblem.........50.00
Teakettle, Droege #6, Covington KY...........................50.00
Teakettle, Griswold #6, Erie, 4-qt..............................65.00
Teakettle, Wagner #0, 3½" 125.00
Waffle iron, French; Griswold #7, wood hdls 150.00
Waffle iron, Griswold #12, Erie, 9⅜x4" 115.00
Waffle iron, Griswold #19, Heart & Star pattern.........130.00
Wheat stick pan, Griswold #280, Erie, 13½" 115.00

Glassware

Ash tray, delphite, McKee or Pyrex 12.00
Ash tray, gr clambroth...4.00
Bottle, water; cobalt, ribbed, Hazel Atlas, 10⅝" 45.00

Bottle, water; dk amber, emb design............................45.00
Bottle, water; forest gr, long neck, Duraglas 20.00
Bottle, water; gr, raised panels, Hocking, 32-oz 16.00
Bowl, batter; gr, spout, hdl, panels, Hocking 25.00
Bowl, batter; yel, slick hdl, US Glass 30.00
Bowl, beater; Chalaine bl, w/spout, 4" 30.00
Bowl, Chalaine bl, 6" 25.00
Bowl, delphite, ribbed, Jeannette, 5½" 25.00
Bowl, gr, ribbed, Jeannette, 7¾"................................10.00
Bowl, gr, rnd, Tufglas, 4" 8.00
Bowl, gr clambroth, twist design, 4¾" 10.00
Bowl, lt jadite, ribbed, Jeannette, 7" 10.00
Bowl, mixing; amber dk, US Glass, 7" 17.50
Bowl, mixing; delphite, 9"...30.00
Bowl, mixing; pk, Hex Optic, flat rim, 9".....................20.00
Bowl, mixing; pk, ruffled edge, Hex Optic, 8¼"............18.00
Bowl, mixing; yel, Rest-Well, Hazel Atlas, 8¾".............22.00
Bowl, pk, mk Cambridge, 9¾"....................................20.00
Bowl, wht, flower decal, McKee, 9".............................20.00
Butter dish, red w/crystal top 95.00
Cake plate, pk, snowflake design in center, Hazel Atlas.....15.00
Canister, crystal, Dutch decal, Hocking.......................15.00
Canister, gr, labels, glass lid, Hocking, 47-oz..............37.50
Canister, gr, ribbed, Hazel Atlas 40.00
Canister, pk, plain, Hocking, 8-oz..............................25.00
Canister, sugar; bl checkerboard on clear, blk lid 18.00
Canister, wht, lettered, McKee, 48-oz 40.00
Casserole, clambroth, oval, w/lid, Pyrex......................75.00
Casserole, heart shape, w/lid, McKee 55.00
Cigarette jar, gr, ash tray atop, Hocking 14.00
Cookie jar, gr, barrel form, Jeannette 40.00
Cookie jar, gr frosted, 'Cookie' 40.00
Crock, gr, rnd, w/lid, 5" 18.00
Cruet, gr, w/stopper..15.00
Cruet, gr, w/stopper, Jeannette...................................75.00
Cruet, yel, Mayfair, Fostoria 75.00
Decanter, gr, ribbed, Hocking 35.00
Decanter, Peacock bl, pointed finial, Imperial...............25.00
Decanter, red, shot glass stopper 75.00
Flask, gr, metal stopper 35.00
Flour shaker, gr, emb 28.00
Gravy boat, pk, 2-spout, Cambridge............................24.00
Ice bucket, dk amber, etched grapes, hdl, Cambridge.....35.00
Ice bucket, dk red, Hocking..30.00
Ice bucket, pk, sterling bear scene 40.00
Ice bucket, yel, Fostoria 30.00
Jar, fired-on blk, oval, w/lid, 7".................................15.00

Jar, tulips on milk glass, red lid, small, $18.00.

Knife, crystal, pnt flowers, Westmoreland 24.00
Ladle, pk, Cambridge...18.00
Match holder, delphite, lettered, Jeannette 40.00
Measuring cup, amber, hdl, Federal..35.00
Measuring cup, crystal, advertising, w/lid, Westmoreland............65.00
Measuring cup, crystal, no hdl, 4-cup 30.00
Measuring cup, gr, hdl, Jeannette 25.00
Measuring cup, gr, 3-spout, hdl, Federal 32.50
Mug, gr, ftd, Priscilla, Fostoria 12.50
Mug, pk, ftd, Adam's Rib..15.00
Napkin holder, gr clambroth, emb Serv-All 100.00
Napkin holder, pk, Paramount, US Glass..................................250.00
Pitcher, amber, pointed finial, Chesterfield 65.00
Pitcher, milk; cobalt, Hazel Atlas...50.00
Refrigerator dish, Chalaine bl, 4x5" 35.00
Refrigerator dish, cobalt, rnd, w/lid, 5¾" 50.00
Refrigerator dish, gr, sq, paneled, Hocking, 8x8" 20.00
Refrigerator dish, gr clambroth, oval, w/lid, 6" 15.00
Refrigerator dish, gr clambroth, wedge shape, w/lid....................15.00
Refrigerator dish, jadite, 4x4" 11.00
Refrigerator dish, pk, rnd, hdl...25.00
Refrigerator dish, yel opaque, sq, no lid, McKee, 7¼".................30.00
Refrigerator dish, yel opaque, w/lid, Hocking, 6x6" 18.00
Refrigerator jar, fired-on red, clear lid, 3½x4¾"..........................4.00
Refrigerator jar, gr, oval, Hocking, 6" 16.00
Salt box, gr, rnd, emb Salt on lid, Jeannette, 6" 150.00
Salt box, w/glass lid, Flintext...80.00
Shakers, Chalaine bl, ea 30.00
Shakers, crystal, Dutch scene w/letters, 12-oz, ea 8.00
Shakers, gr, Zipper, pr..30.00
Shakers, milk glass, emb letters, McKee, pr 10.00
Shakers, milk glass, Roman arched side panel, McKee, ea 10.00
Shakers, red, Wheaton Nuline, pr...40.00
Shakers, wht, Bl or Red Circle, Hocking, ea.................................7.50
Shakers, wht, Blk Circle, Hocking, ea 6.00
Sugar shaker, gr, no pattern 12.00
Syrup, gr, w/liner, Paden City...40.00
Tray, clambroth, sq, 10⅝"..15.00
Tray, red, rectangular, hdls 45.00
Tumbler, gr, Hazel Atlas..8.00
Tumbler, gr, 9-oz 8.00
Tumbler, lt jadite, Jeannette, 12-oz...10.00
Vase, jadite, ribbed, Jeannette 8.00

Miscellaneous

Apple corer, A&P Eng Co, stainless, gr wood hdl 5.00
Apple peeler, Hudson, CI, Pat 1882, EX.....................................75.00
Apple peeler, Lockley-Howland, CI, dtd 1856 ....85.00
Apple peeler, Mt Goodell, wht, 1940s, MIB 25.00
Apple peeler, Sargeant & Foster, Pat 1856 ....95.00
Apple peeler, Wht Mountain, Goodell Co, CI, EX.........................45.00
Apple peeler, wood, pewter fittings, mtd on board, ca 1800 ....350.00
Baster, glass tube w/bl rubber squeeze ball..................................4.00
Bean slicer, Germany, CI, crank hdl, clamps to table, EX..............55.00
Biscuit cutter, tin w/wood hdl, early, EX 4.00
Bread maker, Universal #4, pail type, w/instructions.....................40.00
Butter cutter, Presto, cast aluminum & wire 3.00
Can opener, Edlund Jr, Pat 1925, steel w/wood knob 10.00
Canister, tin, Currants in blk on dk gilt, hasp closure, 7½"............50.00
Canister, tin, Flour & floral stenciling, hasp closure, 18" 85.00
Chopper, brass ferrule, half-rnd w/wood hdl 49.00
Chopper, Everbright, single blade, CI hdl 5.00
Chopper, Franklin, single blade, iron hdl 8.00

Apple peeler, R.P. Scott & Co., Patented 1879, $85.00.

Chopper, Magic Marmalade Cutter, CI, wood hdl, brass ferrule 70.00
Churn, Dazey, dtd, #20, 2-qt..150.00
Churn, Dazey, floor type, blued tin w/CI works, orig stencil........175.00
Churn, Dazey, older high top, 1-qt...850.00
Churn, Dazey, 6-qt, EX..125.00
Churn, Dazey #40, Pat Feb 14 1922, sq style, 4-qt, EX 85.00
Churn, Elgin, label on glass base, metal lid, wood paddles, VG 45.00
Churn, glass, unmk, 1-qt..210.00
Churn, Presto, 1-qt...120.00
Churn, Union Churn, wooden floor type, Pat Dec 20 1864, EX..275.00
Cookie board, springerle, fish/fruit/flowers/etc, 3½x6½" 130.00
Dutch oven/steamer, Griswold #8, cast aluminum, 5-qt...............55.00
Egg beater, A&J, wire, fits stoneware beater jar, dtd 1923 ....20.00
Egg beater, AJ Spinnit, Super Center Drive, EX 10.00
Egg beater, Cassady-Fairbank, tin/wood, 9¾" 35.00
Egg beater, Dover..., Pat May 6 1863..., CI, 12"........................40.00
Egg beater, Ekco/A&J, red & wht wood hdl, wire knob 5.00
Egg beater, Light Running, Pat Nov 24 '08, Taplin..., 12" 36.00
Egg beater, Taplin, CI, 1908...35.00
Flour sifter, Androck, triple screen, ivory w/red stripes 15.00
Flour sifter, Bromwell 'radio' sifter, strap hdl, blk knob..................10.00
Flour sifter, Savory #500, maple hdl, trn knob, EX 8.00
Flour sifter, Shaker Sifter, Barber's Pat 1870-85, tin....................35.00
French fry cutter, Ecko, Holland, EX 10.00
French fry cutter, sled-like form, red wood hdl 12.50
Fruit jar opener, Triumph, dtd 1903..9.00
Fruit press, Griswold, CI, 4-qt..85.00
Garlic press, Made in Italy, cast aluminum 3.50
Gas range lighter, Larson's Shoot-A-Light, pistol type...................6.00
Grater, cheese; Made in Germany, iron/tin/wood, 3-legged..........28.00
Grater, nutmeg; Edgar, Pat Aug 19 1891, Nov 18 1896, tin..........70.00
Grater, nutmeg; Everett, EX 75.00
Grater, nutmeg; French, red hdl 12.00
Grater, Vitex Safety..., plastic, NM in orig box 3.00
Griddle, Griswold #8, aluminum, rectangular, 19x8½" 140.00
Grinder, food; Enterprise #4..28.00
Grinder, food; Enterprise No-Clamp, wht enameled bottom 12.50
Grinder, food; Foley, red hdl..12.50
Grinder, food; Griswold #10, CI, ca 1915 ....48.00
Grinder, herb; CI, crescent-shaped mortar, roller pestle 575.00
Grinder, meat; Griswold #2, CI, EX...25.00
Grinder, Rollman #11, sm..55.00
Ice crusher, Jiffy Ice Crax Deluxe, spring action 10.00
Icebox, golden oak, brass hardware, rstr, lg...............................600.00
Juicer, Jiffy, ceramic, maroon..65.00

Juicer, Juice King Model JK-30, chrome gears, lever style 10.00
Juicer, Juice-O-Mat, chrome top & hdl, red base...........................16.00
Knife, bread; cvd 'Bread' on wood hdl, Sheffield blade, 13" 50.00
Kraut cutter, Indianapolis Sanitary..., 3-blade, 1905 ....40.00
Lemon squeezer, Griswold #1, nickeled CI, 7½"........................45.00
Lemon squeezer, iron, fluted bowl, 2-pc, hinged, 8" 25.00
Measure, tin, reinforced hdl, ½-gal, EX 27.00
Measure, tin, wrap-around lip, 1-qt...25.00
Measure, tin, 1-cup 10.00
Meat/juice press, Landers, Frairy & Clark, iron, rnd base, EX 45.00
Noodle roller & cutter, wood & CI, metal cog wheels, 14" 125.00
Pastry marker, brass, Victorian 35.00
Pie crimper, brass, tamper end...45.00
Pie crimper, brass w/trn curly maple hdl, 7" 75.00
Pie crimper, ivory, crimped wheel, trn hdl, 3-tine fork, 8" 165.00
Raisin seeder, Enterprise 55.00
Raisin seeder, EZY, iron, table clamp, pump hdl, 1895 ....225.00
Raisin seeder, Lightning 65.00
Raisin seeder, The Crown, CI, clamp type, ca 1895, 6½" 80.00
Reel, indoor clothesline; Acme, 1930s, NM in orig box 95.00
Ricer, CI/tin, japanned hdls 10.00
Roaster, coffee bean; tin w/wood hdls, cylindrical, 1700s, 35" 350.00
Rolling pin, cvd, 2-hdld, Conger's, ca 1800, 11" 295.00
Rolling pin, glass w/screw-on cap 12.00
Rolling pin, maple hdls, grooved iron center, 10¾" 50.00
Sausage stuffer, Simmons Hdw, complete 60.00
Scoop, Heart of Value emblem..15.00
Sharpener, knife; Dazey, CI, EX 25.00
Sifter, Bromwell, 5-cup 5.00
Sifter, Calumet Baking Powder, tin, 2-cup, EX 15.00
Sifter, Foley, orig paper label, 1-cup, NM 9.00
Sifter, Gem Sifter...JL Clark, tin, 1910s, G...............................30.00
Slicer, vegetable & fruit; CI, Eagle Mfg, dtd 1918 ....50.00
Spoon, slotted, wire hdl, bottle-opener end................................12.00
Strawberry huller, Boston Huller, Pat Oct 30 '94, EX 9.00
Tea strainer, SP, side hdl, Tetley Tea 20.00
Wax ladle, Griswold, Erie, 8" 30.00

Knives

Knife collecting as a hobby began in earnest during the 1960s when government regulations required for the first time that knife companies mark their product with the country of origin. The few collectors and dealers cognizant of this change at once began stockpiling the older knives made before this law was enacted. Another impetus to the growing interest in this area came with the Gun Control Act of 1968, which severely restricted gun trading. Frustrated gun dealers transferred their attention to knives. Today there are collectors clubs in many of the states.

The most sought-after pocket knives are those made before WWII. However, Case, Schrade, and Primble knives of a more recent manufacture are also collected. Most collectors prefer knives 'as found.' Do not attempt to clean, sharpen, or in any way 'improve' on an old knife.

The prices quoted here are for knives in mint condition (except for those in the Miscellaneous section). If a knife has been used, sharpened, or blemished in any way, its value decreases — the newer the knife, the greater the reduction in value.

Our advisor for this category is Charles D. Stapp; he is listed in the Directory under Indiana.

Key:
bd — blade   p/b — push button
Cut — Cutlery

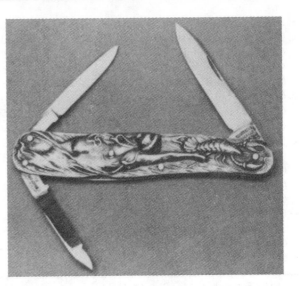

Case, figural, sterling silver, 3¾", $300.00.

Case, B100, Christmas tree hdl, 1-bd, tested XX, 1930s, M 225.00
Case, B1048, faux onyx hdl, 1-bd, tested XX, 4⅛", M...................265.00
Case, B445R, faux onyx hdl, 4-bd, tested XX, 3¾", M..................255.00
Case, C61050, SAB red bone hdl, 1-bd, XX, 5⅜", NM...................175.00
Case, GS1094, goldstone hdl, 1-bd, 4¼", M.................................365.00
Case, HA 1050, High Art hdl, push-out, tested XX, 5⅛", M......600.00
Case, M-101, metal hdl, 1-bd, tested XX, 2⅞", M.......................125.00
Case, M1218K, metal hdl, 1-bd, tested XX, 1930s, 3", M 135.00
Case, M3102RSS, metal hdl, 3-bd, USA, 1965-69, 2¾", M 37.50
Case, M345, Navy, metal hdl, 3-bd, XX, 1940-64, 3⅝", M 125.00
Case, P10051LSSP, pakkawood hdl, 1-bd, brass bolsters, 3¾", M..32.00
Case, P158LSSP, pakkawood hdl, 1-bd, Dots, 4¼", M 27.50
Case, R1093, candy stripe hdl, 1-bd, tested XX, 5", M 300.00
Case, R318HP, wht compo hdl, 3-bd, XX, 3½", M.........................55.00
Case, Texas Longhorn, faux ivory hdl, 2-bd, 4½", M 45.00
Case, 11011, walnut hdl, 1-bd, tested XX, 1930s, 4", M 110.00
Case, 11031SH, walnut hdl, 1-bd, tested XX, 1930s, 3", M 100.00
Case, 1139, walnut hdl, banana knife, 1-bd, Case XX, 4½", M..135.00
Case, 1199SHRSS, Navy, walnut hdl, XX, 1940-64, 4⅛", M 32.00
Case, 12031L, electrician's, walnut hdl, 2-bd, XX, 3¾", M............30.00
Case, 2109, slick blk hdl, 1-bd, XX, 3¼", M 95.00
Case, 2137, Sod Buster Jr, blk compo hdl, 1-bd, 7 Dot, M 12.50
Case, 2212L, slick blk hdl, 2-bd, tested XX, 3⅝", M 140.00
Case, 3 Bkspring Whittler, bone hdl, 3-bd, tested XX, 3⅜", M....365.00
Case, 31048, yel compo hdl, 1-bd, USA, 1965-69, 4⅛", M 24.00
Case, 31093, toothpick, yel hdl, 1-bd, tested XX, 5", M 200.00
Case, 31100, yel compo hdl, 1-bd, tested XX, 4½" 450.00
Case, 3111½, yel compo hdl, 1-bd, tested XX, 4⅜", M 425.00
Case, 3172, yel compo hdl, 1-bd, tested XX, 1920-40, 5½", M 800.00
Case, 3185, doctor's, yel compo hdl, 1-bd, tested XX, 3⅝", M.....180.00
Case, 3224½, yel compo hdl, 2-bd, tested XX, 1930s, 3", M........125.00
Case, 4100SS, wht compo hdl, 1-bd, XX, 5½", M 48.00
Case, 4200SS, citrus, wht compo hdl, 2-bd, USA, 5½", M 65.00
Case, 4200SS, melon tester, wht compo hdl, 2-bd, XX, 5½", M..200.00
Case, 5165, stag hdl, 1 flat bd, XX, 1940-55, M 275.00
Case, 5172, stag hdl, 1-bd, USA, 1965, 5½", M 200.00
Case, 5205, stag hdl, 2-bd, tested XX, 1920-40, 3¾", M 250.00
Case, 5347SHSP, yel compo hdl, 3-bd, XX, 3⅞", M......................45.00
Case, 551, stag hdl, 1-bd, tested XX, w/sheath, M 550.00
Case, 61048SSP, bone stag hdl, etched bd, USA, 4⅛", M 65.00
Case, 61093, bone hdl, 1-bd, 10 Dot, 1970, 5", M.......................65.00
Case, 61095, gr bone hdl, 1-bd, tested XX, 1920-40, 5", M 265.00
Case, 6111½, bone hdl, long pull, 1-bd, '30s, tested XX, M 450.00

Case, 6116½, gr bone hdl, 1-bd, tested XX, 3½", NM 85.00
Case, 61213, gr bone hdl, 1-bd, tested XX, 5⅜", M 435.00
Case, 6124½, gr bone hdl, 1-bd, 1930s, tested XX, 3", NM...........95.00
Case, 6143, gr bone hdl, 1-bd, XX, 1940-55, 5", M 160.00
Case, 6151L, gr bone hdl, 1-bd, tested XX, 5¼", M....................585.00
Case, 6165, bone hdl, 1 flat bd, tested XX, 5¼", M 465.00
Case, 6171L, gr bone hdl, 1-bd, tested XX, 1920-40, 5½", M . 1,150.00
Case, 62009, gr bone hdl, 2-bd, tested XX, 3¼", M 195.00
Case, 6202, gr bone hdl, 2-bd, tested XX, 1920-40, 3⅜", M 120.00
Case, 62024½, bone hdl, 2-bd, USA, 1960s, 3", M 32.00
Case, 6205RAZ, bone hdl, 2-bd, USA, 1965-69, 3¾", M 50.00
Case, 6206½, rough blk hdl, 2-bd, XX, 1940s, 2⅝", M 135.00
Case, 6208, bone hdl, 2-bd, USA, 1965-69, 3¼", M 22.50
Case, 6214, Delrin hdl, 2-bd, 10 Dot, 3⅜", M 20.00
Case, 6217, laminated wood hdl, 2-bd, 10 Dot, 1970, 4", M........55.00
Case, 6220, peanut, gr bone hdl, 2-bd, XX, 1940-55, 2¾", M 175.00
Case, 640045R, brn plastic hdl, 4-bd, USA, 1960s, 3¾", M...........22.50
Case, 7103SP, tortoise hdl, 1-bd, tested XX, 3¼", M 300.00
Case, 7197LSSP, curly maple hdl, 1-bd, 5", M 100.00
Case, 92009½, cracked ice hdl, 2-bd, tested XX, 3¼", M 250.00
Case, 9201, faux pearl hdl, 2-bd, tested XX, 2⅝", NM 75.00
Case, 92027, faux pearl hdl, 2-bd, tested XX, 1930s, 2¾", M......125.00
Case, 93109, cracked ice hdl, 3-bd, tested XX, 3⅝", M...............365.00
Primble, Belknap, stockman's, Rogers bone hdl, 3-bd, 3¼", M 50.00
Primble, Belknap, 4861, equal-end jack, 2-bd, 3¾", M 45.00
Primble, Belknap, 4923, dog-leg jack, bone hdl, 2-bd, 2⅞", M 35.00
Primble, Belknap, 5100, equal-end jack, bone hdl, 2-bd, 3", M 35.00
Primble, Belknap, 5511, Congress, bone hdl, 4-bd, 3¾", M 50.00
Primble, Belknap, 5517, faux bone hdl, 4-bd, 4⅛", M...................25.00
Primble, Belknap, 7002, whittler, stag hdl, 3-bd, 4½", M 350.00
Primble, Belknap, 708, faux pearl hdl, 3-bd, 2⅞", M....................20.00
Primble, Belknap, 900, peachseed bone hdl, 2-bd, 3", M 35.00
Primble, Belknap, 903, faux peachseed bone, pen w/file, 2⅞", M .20.00
Primble, 5727, equal-end cigar, bone hdl, 2-bd, 4¼", M..............88.00
Queen, 11EO, winterbottom bone hdl, 1-bd, easy open, 4", M......28.00
Queen, 14, winterbottom bone hdl, 2-bd, 2¾", M 28.00
Queen, 19, fisherman's, Rogers bone hdl, 2-bd, 5", M...................95.00
Queen, 8150, hunter's, stag hdl, 2-bd, rare, 5¼" 65.00
Queen, 8470, bone hdl, 1-bd, easy open, 4⅛", M 32.00
Queen, 9, stockman's, winterbottom bone hdl, 3-bd, 4", M...........50.00
Queen Stainless, #35, rough blk hdl, 3-bd, 2⅝", M 30.00
Queen Stainless, 47, winterbottom bone hdl, 2-bd, 3½", M 42.50
Queen Steel, 19, winterbottom bone hdl, 2-bd, 4⅛", M 90.00
Queen Steel, 24, trapper's, winterbottom bone hdl, 2-bd, 4", M....50.00
Queen Steel, 38, winterbottom bone hdl, 2-bd, 3", M 80.00
Remington, R1002, jack, blk hdl, 2-bd, 3⅝", M..........................125.00
Remington, R1143, bone hdl, 2-bd, 4⅜", M................................165.00

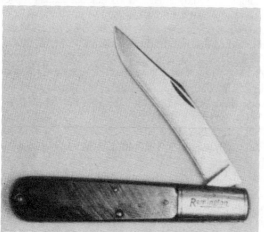

Remington, R1240, brown bone handle, 5", $250.00.

Remington, R1285, tortoise shell hdl, 2-bd, 3", M 135.00
Remington, R1483, bone hdl, 1-bd, lockbk, 3½", M 150.00
Remington, R181, jack, redwood hdl, 2-bd, M............................165.00
Remington, R1915, candy stripe hdl, 2-bd, long pull, 3⅜", M 165.00
Remington, R213, jack, bone hdl, 2-bd, easy open, 3⅝", M 175.00
Remington, R3059, stockman's, metal hdl, 3-bd, 4", M..............265.00
Remington, R3273, cattleman's, brn bone hdl, 3-bd, 3¾", M......245.00
Remington, R3333, scout's, brn bone hdl, 4-bd, 3¾", M 250.00
Remington, R3843, utility, brn bone hdl, 3⅝", M.......................275.00
Remington, R3942, sleeveboard, ebony hdl, 2-bd, 3⅝", M 150.00
Remington, R403, equal-end jack, bone hdl, 2-bd, M..................195.00
Remington, R4113, bone hdl, 3-bd, 3⅞", M.................................215.00
Remington, R4283, sowbelly, brn bone hdl, 5-bd, 3¾", M 1,850.00
Remington, R6133, whittler, brn bone, 3-bd, 3½", M.................295.00
Remington, R6195, equal end, brn mottled hdl, 2-bd, 3¼", M ...115.00
Remington, R63, Barlow, bone hdl, 2-bd, M 165.00
Remington, R6559, metal hdl, 3-bd, 3", M.................................115.00
Remington, R6644, sleeveboard, pearl hdl, 2-bd, 3⅛", M 145.00
Remington, R7833, brn bone hdl, 2-bd, pinch bolsters, 4½", M..565.00
Remington, R95, lobster, pyremite hdl, 3-bd, 3¼", M.................165.00
Shrade Cut, C2152¾, ebony hdl, 2-bd, 3⅜", M 65.00
Shrade Cut, G155, orange compo hdl, 1-bd, 4¼", M 215.00
Shrade Cut, M7936, nickel silver hdl w/o shackle, 2-bd, 2½", M .42.50
Shrade Cut, R7973, bone hdl, 2-bd, 4½", M 265.00
Shrade Cut, SD9463, bone hdl, 4-bd, 3⅝", NM..........................110.00
Shrade Cut, SS102, faux ivory hdl, 2-bd, 4¾", M..........................30.00
Shrade Cut, SS1564W, ivory celluloid hdl, 1-bd, 3⅜", M............40.00
Shrade Cut, SS2213, bone hdl, 2-bd, 3½", NM............................68.00
Shrade Cut, SS70991, smooth metal hdl, 2-bd, 3", M...................30.00
Shrade Cut, 1084J, red/wht/amber pyralin hdl, 1-bd, 5", M 160.00
Shrade Cut, 114, Grandaddy Barlow, gr bone hdl, 1-bd, 5", M....155.00
Shrade Cut, 1514V, blk & wht celluloid hdl, 1-bd, 4", M 145.00
Shrade Cut, 176, grafting, faux ivory hdl, 2-bd, 3¾", M..............42.00
Shrade Cut, 196, pruning, faux ivory hdl, 1-bd, 3⅞", M 25.00
Shrade Cut, 1974½W, wht celluloid hdl, 1-hdl, 4¼", M...............38.00
Shrade Cut, 2033¾, bone hdl, 2-bd, 3⅜", M 68.00
Shrade Cut, 204S, electrician's, walnut hdl, 2-bd, 3¾", M............60.00
Shrade Cut, 2226, MOP hdl, 2-bd, 3½", M.................................135.00
Shrade Cut, 225, hunter's, jigged bone hdl, 2-bd, 5¼", M 165.00
Shrade Cut, 272, peachseed bone hdl, 2-bd, 2⅞", M....................45.00
Shrade Cut, 7114, horn T-pyralin hdl, 2-bd, 3⅜", M 48.00
Shrade Cut, 7404GP, gold pearl celluloid hdl, 2-bd, 3⅜", M 165.00
Shrade Cut, 7426, MOP hdl, 2-bd, 3⅛", M...................................55.00
Shrade Cut, 7483T, bone hdl, 2-bd, 3¼", M.................................45.00
Shrade Cut, 7706T, MOP hdl, 2-bd, 2⅞", M.................................48.00
Shrade Cut, 787, Improved Muskrat, stag hdl, 3-bd, 4", M 225.00
Shrade Cut, 805, cocobolo hdl, 3-bd, 2¾", M...............................45.00
Shrade Cut, 881Y, yel compo hdl, 3-bd, 4", M.............................27.50
Shrade Cut, 894, stag hdl, 3-bd, 3¾", M.....................................115.00
Shrade Cut, 974, brn jigged Delrin hdl, 4-bd, 3⅛", M..................35.00
Winchester, 1201, jack, nickel silver hdl, 1-bd, 3⅜", M 175.00
Winchester, 1978, doctor's, stag hdl, 2-bd, 3⅜", M 335.00
Winchester, 2039, jack, celluloid hdl, 1-bd, 3", M 110.00
Winchester, 2302, Senator, pearl hdl w/bail, 2-bd, 2¼", M...........95.00
Winchester, 2331, Congress, pearl hdl, 2-bd, 3¼", M.................165.00
Winchester, 2613, sleeveboard, ebony hdl, 2-bd, 3⅜", M 115.00
Winchester, 2845, jack, stag hdl, 2-bd, 3¾", NM........................220.00
Winchester, 2866, Senator, stag hdl, 2-bd, 2⅞", M......................88.00
Winchester, 2992, stag hdl, 2-bd, 3⅝", M...................................145.00
Winchester, 3345, whittler, pearl hdl, 3-bd, 3¼", M...................235.00
Winchester, 3939, Senator, stag hdl, 3-bd, 3⅜", M....................215.00
Winchester, 4301, lobster, pearl hdl, 3-bd, 2¾", M 235.00
Winchester, 4950, scout's, bone hdl, 4-bd, 3⅝", M 325.00
Winchester, 4951, utility, stag hdl, 3⅝", M 250.00

Miscellaneous

Bowie, etched bd, Wilson Hawksworth Ellison, Sheffield, 14" **375.00**
Bowie, Manson, Sheffield blade, bone hdls, 1860s, 12", EX **250.00**
Bowie, nickel hilt w/eagle & shield, Leon NY, 6" blade **220.00**
Case XX, bowie style, brass guard, plastic hdl, 9⅜", EX **80.00**

Kosta

Kosta glassware has been made in Sweden since 1742. Today they are one of that country's leading producers of quality art glass. Two of their most important designers were Elis Bergh (1929-1950) and Vicke Lindstrand, artistic director from 1950 to 1973. Lindstrand brought to the company knowledge of important techniques such as Graal, fine figural engraving, Ariel, etc. He influenced new artists to experiment with these techniques and inspired them to create new and innovative designs. Today's collectors are most interested in pieces made during the 1950s and '60s.

Our advisor for this category is Abby Malowanczyk; she is listed in the Directory under Texas.

Bowl, bright pk w/wht int network, ftd, 3½x5" dia **125.00**
Bowl, cameo birds/trees/stars, cl w/bl o/l, B Vallien, 6" **500.00**
Compote, wht int swirls, Lindstrand, 7x7" **375.00**
Sculpture, free-form w/face, etched elk, Lindstrand, 7" **400.00**

Vase, blue crystal with cut and etched birds and pine boughs, thick walls, Kosta label, 7¾", $110.00 for the pair.

Vase, nude eng, sgn, 12½" **1,200.00**
Vase, twisted, int blk line decor, att Lindstrand, 1955, 13" **600.00**

Kutani

Kutani, named for the Japanese village where it originated, was first produced in the seventeenth century. The early ware, Ko Kutani, was produced for only about thirty years. Several types were produced before 1800, but these are rarely encountered. In the nineteenth century, kilns located in several different villages began to copy the old Kutani wares. This later, more familiar type has large areas of red with gold designs on a white ground decorated with warriors, birds, and flowers in controlled colors of red, gold, and black.

Bowl, Kaga Ware, figural/floral/animals/dragons on red, 10" **400.00**
Figurine, begger w/staff on rockwork, sgn, ca 1920, 7¼" **295.00**

Double-gourd vase with lid, panels with peacocks in flower gardens, dragons among clouds, 1800s, 18", $1,000.00; Incense burner, panels of birds in garden settings, firing lines, 9", $800.00.

Plate, mandarins/floral reserve, 1875, 9½", set of 6 ....**475.00**
Tazza, gardens/birds on rust, 1880s, 8¾" dia, pr **300.00**
Teapot, figures in scene, cobalt & gold, ftd, squat, mk, 8" **595.00**
Vase, peacocks/flowers in reserve, 3-toed gourd form, 18" **1,000.00**

L. E. Smith

Perhaps best known for their line of black glass vases and novelty items, this twentieth-century American glass company also made several patterns of colored depression-type dinnerware.

Animals and Birds

Elephant, ash tray, pk **45.00**

Queen fish aquarium, 15" long, $150.00.

Horse, amber, pr **75.00**
Horse, blk, pr **110.00**

Horse, cobalt 40.00
Horse, gr, pr 75.00
Horse, pr 40.00
Horse, rearing, bl..35.00
Rooster, #208 ....65.00
Swan, cobalt, lg 65.00
Swan, milk glass, lg 45.00

Bonbon, cobalt, ftd, hdl 14.00
Bonbon, gr, #81 .... 7.00
Bowl, flower; Hobnail, blk, 6½" 25.00
Bowl, Mt Pleasant, blk, ftd, #515 ....20.00
Bowl, salad; Do-Si-Do, blk, #410, 8½" 25.00
Candle holder, dbl; Double Shield, blk, #600 ....30.00
Cookie jar, blk, w/lid 110.00
Fern bowl, cobalt, Greek Key decor, 3-ftd 9.00
Flower block, pk, #1012...18.00
Shakers, Snake Dance, blk, 3½", pr 25.00
Tray, cocktail; blk 28.00
Tray, cordial; gr or pk, #381 ....10.00
Urn, cobalt, #800/4, w/lid, 11" 100.00
Vase, blk, #102-4, 6½" 11.00
Vase, blk, #432/5 ....45.00
Vase, blk, #433, 7" 18.00
Vase, blk, #49, 6" 13.00
Vase, blk, flared top, low hdls, ftd, #1900, 7¼" 25.00
Vase, cobalt, #711, 5½" 7.00
Vase, cobalt, stippled t'print, 5¾" 7.50
Vase, silver leaf band on blk, #711, 6" 12.00
Vase, Snake Dance, blk, crimped top, hdls, ftd, #433....25.00
Window box, blk, #405/10 ....65.00
Window box, cobalt, oval, 6⅜" 9.00
Window box, milk glass, Pan & dancing girls, 6¼" 9.00

Labels

Before the advent of the cardboard box, wooden crates were used for transporting products. Paper labels were attached to the crates to identify the contents and the packer. These labels often had colorful lithographed illustrations covering a broad range of subjects. Eventually the cardboard box replaced the crate, and the artwork was imprinted directly onto the carton. Today these paper labels are becoming collectible — primarily for the art but also for their advertising appeal. Our advisor for this category is Cerebro; their address is listed in the Directory under Pennsylvania.

Apple, Best Strike, baseball player, 1920s......................45.00
Apple, Deep Blue Sea, ocean liner in open seas, 1920s 12.00
Apple, Falls, wht waterfall, 1930s................................. 3.50
Apple, Lake Chelan, 2 red apples, lake, mtns, 1940 .... 2.00
Apple, State Seal, Geo Washington, 1920s 4.50
Asparagus, Coin, gold & silver coins, 1940s 5.00
Asparagus, High Goal, polo player hitting ball, 1940s 5.00
Asparagus, King of Hearts, half of card above heart, 1940s 4.00
Asparagus, Pride of the River, Mississippi riverboat, 1930s 6.50
Cigar, Camel, camel rider in desert, 1920s, 7x9" 9.00
Cigar, Favorite, lady's portrait in reserve, 1910s, 6x8½" 9.00
Cigar, Irish Singer, man in gr, 1920s, 4½x4½" 5.00
Cigar, Judge Best, bearded man in blk robe, 1910s, 7x9"................14.00
Cigar, Leo Grande, recumbent lion, 1880s, 6x8⅛" 8.00
Cigar, Susquehanna, 3 Indians & sunrise, 1920s, 4½x4⅜" 6.00
Citrus, Aunty, smiling Blk lady, FL................................28.00

Citrus, Blue Lake, nude Indian lady in canoe, FL.........................16.00
Citrus, Crown Jewel, crown on top of oranges, 1930s, FL 2.00
Citrus, King Andy, Andrew Jackson w/quill in hand, FL 20.00
Citrus, Pepper, male runner, 1940s, FL 2.00
Citrus, Sonny, boy fills red wagon w/oranges, FL.........................55.00
Citrus, Wise Bird, owl in forest, 1930s, FL.................... 4.50
Cotton spool, Camel Brand, camel on axle & wheel, flowers 3.00
Cotton spool, Tiger, tiger in the jungle......................... 3.00
Cranberry, Capital Brand, Capital building 6.00
Cranberry, Holiday Brand, child w/toys under Xmas tree.............15.00
Lemon, El Primo, 4 lemons & orchard, 1930s, CA............ 5.00
Lemon, Exposition, diploma, Alaska-Yukon-Pacific Expo, 1920s 3.00
Lemon, Helena, triangle & 2 lemons, 1930s 2.50
Lemon, Parade, 5 drummers & band leader, 1930s, CA 3.00
Lemon, Southern Cross, San Fernando Mission/stars, '30s, CA 50.00

Albion Valencias, ca 1910, $24.00.

Orange, Altissimo, pk mtns, 1920s, CA 3.00
Orange, Golden Eagle, eagle perched on oranges, 1920s, CA 3.00
Orange, Navajo, Indian portrait, 1930s, CA....................10.00
Orange, Splendid, orange, grove, & mtns, 1920s, CA..................... 2.50
Orange, Venice Cove, rooster, 1930s, CA........................ 3.00
Pear, Bellboy, bellhop in red serving pear, 1930s 4.00
Pear, Covered Wagon, scout points way, oxen & wagon, 1930s 3.00
Pear, Golden Bough, apricots & branch 4.50
Pear, Lake County, pear fr in dmn, 1930s 2.00
Pear, Snow Crest, orchard & ranch house, 1940s............. 2.00
Vegetable, Cheerio, man in blk top hat, 1930s 3.00
Vegetable, Conestoga, wagon in prairie, 1940s 3.00
Vegetable, His Nibs, cartoon: boy & monkey in red car, 1940........ 3.00
Vegetable, Mustang, bucking wht horse, 1950s 1.00
Vegetable, Safe Hit, baseball player at bat, 1940s, sm 2.00
Yam, Jack Rabbit, lg rabbit in triangle, 1923 .... 3.00
Yam, Pure Winner, 5-card royal flush of hearts 3.00
Yam, Smoky Jim's, Blk man w/crate of yams 37.50
Yam, Sweet Lue, girl in field w/yam 2.00
Yam, Treasure, treasure chest, tropical scene 2.00

Labino

Dominick Labino was a glass blower who until mid-1985 worked in his studio in Ohio, blowing and sculpting various items which he signed and dated. A ceramic engineer by trade, he was instrumental in developing the heat-resistant tiles used in space flights. His glassmaking shows his versatility in the art. While some of his designs are free-form and futuristic, others are reminiscent of the products of older glasshouses. Because of problems with his health, Mr. Labino became unable to blow glass himself; he died January, 10, 1987. Work coming from his studio after mid-1985 will be signed 'Labino Studios, Baker,' indicating ware made by his protegee, E. Baker O'Brien. In addition to her own compositions, she continues to use many of the colors developed by Labino.

Paperweight, clear, orange & blk design, irid flakes, 1971 ....**475.00**
Paperweight, gr, controlled bubbles, 1970 ....**275.00**

Paperweight, cobalt and yellow cushion in crystal, signed and dated 1981, 2⅞", $850.00.

Sculpture, bird, gr, 1976, mini **175.00**
Sculpture, clear, yel & orange festoons, 1975, 5½" **1,150.00**
Sculpture, clear over pk/gold, bubbles, 1976, 4½" **1,000.00**
Sculpture, crystal w/bl center, controlled bubbles, '85, 3" .. **1,150.00**
Sculpture, Emergence, bl w/int gold veiling, '73, 7½" **3,800.00**
Sculpture, Emergence, bubble forms & veils, sgn/12-1974, 7". **2,200.00**
Sculpture, Emergence, bubble/3 dichroic veils, #8-1980, 9½" ..**11,000.00**
Sculpture, gold aurene w/bubbles, 1972, 5" **1,300.00**
Sculpture, gr shaded, yel/red/cobalt over base, '71, 4½" **1,050.00**
Sculpture, Harlequin, sgn, #10-1982, 7" **2,090.00**
Sculpture, Lava, bl w/controlled folds on sides, 1979, 4" **1,150.00**
Sculpture, Lava, burgundy, controlled folds, 1979, 7½" **1,400.00**
Sculpture, sea kingdom style, bl w/yel design, 1973, 6½"......... **1,100.00**
Vessel form, bl, blown & appl, sgn/1965, 8¾" **1,650.00**

Lace, Linens, and Needlework

It has been recorded that lace was found in the tombs of ancient Egypt. Lace has always been a symbol of wealth and fashion. Italian laces are regarded as the finest ever produced, but the differences between them and the laces of France are nearly indistinguishable. Needlework was revived during the 18th century and became the favorite of feminine pastimes. Examples of many forms are readily available today — tatting, embroidery, needlepoint, and crochet — and, though fragile in appearance, have withstood the ravages of time with remarkable durability.

Key:
embr — embroidered   ms — machine sewn
hs — hand sewn

Bedspread, Battenburg net, 86x10", M **225.00**
Bedspread, chenille, pk w/florals, dbl, EX **185.00**
Bedspread, crochet, Star & Popcorn, full sz, M...................**250.00**
Bedspread, needle lace, handmade w/linen thread, 144x108" **650.00**
Bedspread, Victorian lace, 3 matching scarves, EX **425.00**
Bedspread, voile, embr bird & flowers, 74x96", EX **350.00**

Blanket, homespun wool, brn/pk/wht plaid, 2-pc, 72x98"............**125.00**
Curtain, crochet, Dutch children, 33x34" **65.00**
Curtains, lacy net, 63", pr...**135.00**
Doily, Battenburg, 12" dia **55.00**
Doily, Battenburg grapes & leaves, 10" dia **65.00**
Doily, crochet, butterfly, 21x11" **50.00**
Doily, crochet, Geo Washington w/eagle, star corners, 25x21"......**65.00**
Doily, crochet, God Bless Our Home, ecru, 12x20" **65.00**
Doily, crochet, initial in center, 10x17" **35.00**
Doily, crochet, pineapple, 14" dia **25.00**
Doily, crochet, star, 14" dia **35.00**
Doily, crochet, Statue of Liberty & flag, 18x22½".......................**125.00**
Dresser scarf, pk crochet edge...**12.00**
Material, bl/wht checked, hand-hemmed, 40x75", VG **75.00**
Material, brn/wht homespun, patched/worn, 40x76" **85.00**
Napkin, linen, embr flower basket corners, crochet edge **12.00**
Panel, crochet, 2 deer in forest, 27x27"..**40.00**
Panel, lady w/in oval wreath, silk on silk, 11x14".......................**325.00**
Piano scarf, ecru flax w/tatted inserts & border, 22x60" **35.00**
Pillowcase, crochet edge, pr...**14.00**
Pillowcase, embr edge, hemstitching... **3.00**
Runner, Battenburg, drawnwork center sqs, 15x32", EX **95.00**
Runner, Battenburg, 17x54"...**125.00**
Runner, crochet, Bread in center, 4½x11".....................................**35.00**
Runner, linen, Deco embr, hand-tied fringe, ecru, 58x17".............**45.00**
Sheet, homespun, hs hems, 2-pc, 78x80".......................................**35.00**
Show towel, homespun, line of red/bl embr, name/1850, EX.......**135.00**
Show towel, homespun, red embr flowers/alphabet/1839, EX......**135.00**
Show towel, homespun, red/bl embr, name/1844, 54x20", VG....**135.00**

Stumpwork wall hanging, English, early 1700s, in original frame, minor tears or losses, 12" diameter, $300.00.

Tablecloth, Battenburg trim, 40x40", EX **125.00**
Tablecloth, Battenburg 17" vintage border, 65" dia **475.00**
Tablecloth, homespun, gold/wht plaid, hs, 70x76".......................**225.00**
Tablecloth, homespun linen, wht-on-wht stripes, hs, 44x62" **85.00**
Tablecloth, Italian cut/embr linen, 84x62", +8 16" napkins........**150.00**
Tablecloth, linen w/filet crochet, picot edge, 64x51" **135.00**
Throw, chenille, flowers, red on tan, Victorian, 40" sq **95.00**
Towel, embr flowers on linen..**65.00**
Towel, finger; linen, embr children at play, hemstitched...............**15.00**

Lacy Glassware

Lacy glass became popular in the late 1820s after the development of the pressing machine. It was decorated with allover patterns — hearts, lyres, sheaves of wheat, etc. — and backgrounds were completely stippled. The designs were intricate and delicate, hence the term 'lacy.' Although Sandwich produced this type of glassware in abundance, it was also made by other eastern glassworks as well as in the midwest. By 1840, its popularity on the wane and a depressed economy forcing manufacturers to seek less expensive modes of production, lacy glass began to be phased out in favor of pressed pattern glassware. When no condition is indicated, the items listed below are assumed to be without obvious damage; minor roughness is normal. See also Sandwich Glass.

Bowl, Hairpin, 6", EX 90.00
Bowl, Rayed Peacock Eye, 11" L, VG 90.00
Bowl, Roman Rosette, 6½", VG.................................50.00
Bowl, Strawberry Dmn-type pattern, deep, 9" L, VG 80.00
Bowl, Tulip & Acanthus Leaf, deep bl, 6", EX 275.00
Bowl, Tulip & Acanthus Leaf, L-131-2, 9½", EX 40.00
Compote, Bull's Eye & Nectarine, 5x8", VG 200.00
Compote, Heart & Shield, NE Glass, 4x6½", EX 750.00
Dish, sapphire bl, leaf pattern, edge chips, 5⅝" 335.00

Vegetable dish, chain border, Sandwich, riveted repair to one handle, 12" long, $2,000.00; Bowl, unrecorded, NM, 11", $2,600.00.

Plate, Basket of Flowers, RB Curling & Sons, 7", EX...................300.00
Plate, octagonal, L 169-2, 7", EX 75.00
Plate, Scotch Plaid, vaseline, 9", EX 175.00

Lalique

Beginning his lengthy career as a designer and maker of fine jewelry, Rene Lalique at first only dabbled in glass, making small panels of pate-de-verre (paste-on-paste) and cire perdue (wax casting) to use in his jewelry. He also made small flacons of gold and silver with his glass inlays, which attracted the attention of M.F. Coty, who commissioned Lalique to design bottles for his perfume company. The success of this venture resulted in the opening of his own glassworks at Combs-la-Ville in 1909. In 1921 a larger factory was established at Wingen-sur-Moder in Alsace-Lorraine. By the thirties Lalique was world renown as the most important designer of his time.

Lalique glass is lead based, either mold blown or pressed. Favored motifs during the Art Nouveau period were dancing nymphs, fish, dragonflies, and foliage. Characteristically the glass is crystal in combination with acid-etched relief. Later, some items were made in as many as ten colors — red, amber, and green among them — and were occasionally accented with enameling. These colored pieces, especially those in black, are rare and highly prized by advanced collectors.

During the twenties and thirties, Lalique designed several vases and bowls reminiscent of American Indian art. He also developed a line in the Art Deco style decorated with stylized birds, florals, and geometrics. In addition to vases, clocks, automobile mascots, stemware, and bottles, many other useful objects were produced. Items made before his death in 1945 were marked 'R. Lalique'; later the 'R' was deleted even though some of the original molds were still used. Numbers found on the bases of some pieces are catalog numbers.

Our advisor for this category is John Danis; he is listed in the Directory under Illinois.

Key:
cl/fr — clear and frosted   RL — signed R. Lalique
L — signed Lalique   RLF — signed R. Lalique, France

Sculpture, Motif Tete de Cheval, ca 1960, 15", $5,800.00.

Atomizer, emb stylized Egyptians, cinnamon wash, RLF, 2½" 250.00
Atomizer, flowerheads, fr w/gr enamel, gilt mts, RL/MIF, 3" 450.00
Atomizer, for Le Provencal, nudes w/garlands, RL/MIF, 3¾".......245.00
Bottle, scent; Ambre D'Orsay, cl/fr, sqd cylinder, RL, 5" 1,800.00
Bottle, scent; Epines, emb briars, gr wash, RLF/RL, 3½" 500.00
Bottle, scent; Fleurettes, gray wash, RL, 6", 5", 5",set...................900.00
Bottle, scent; 5 ladies in low relief, amber wash, RL, 6¾" 850.00
Bowl, Nemours, flowers w/blk enamel centers, cl/fr, LF, 10"........600.00
Bowl, Phalenes, moths/flowers, bl, shallow, RLF, 15" 5,000.00
Box, angel faces/wings, fr w/amber wash, RLF, 2x3" dia..............600.00
Box, Coquilles, stylized shells, opal, RLF, 3" dia......................300.00
Box, powder; Dans la Nuit, stars, bl enamel, spherical, 5" 3,300.00
Box, powder; Emilane, floral-emb lid, cl/fr, RLF, 4" dia 300.00
Box, Tokio, opal, RL/lid: L, 7" dia 700.00
Box, 2 Sirenes, nymphs, opal on cl base, RLF, 10" dia 1,400.00
Box lid, 3 Dahlias, opal, RL, 8½", on satin-covered box 800.00
Chandelier, Dahlias, cl/fr, hemispherical, RLF/RL, 12" 3,800.00
Charger, Martigues, opal, RL/F, 14" 2,900.00
Collector plate, 1965 .... 1,000.00
Collector plate, 1966 ....325.00
Collector plate, 1967 ....200.00
Collector plate, 1968 ....100.00
Collector plate, 1969 ....100.00
Collector plate, 1970 ....80.00
Collector plate, 1971 ....80.00
Collector plate, 1972 ....75.00
Collector plate, 1973 ....100.00
Collector plate, 1974 ....100.00
Collector plate, 1975 ....100.00
Collector plate, 1976 ....150.00
Lampe Hygenique Berger, artichoke form, yel, RL/MIF, 4½" .. 1,200.00

Luminaire, Charmille, leaves, fr, spherical, RL, 13" dia.......... **3,800.00**
Luminaire, Gros Poisson Algues, fish, cl, RLF, 12" **8,500.00**
Mascot, Faucon, cl/fr, RL, eng France/#1124, 6", EX **650.00**
Orangeade set, Bahia, leaves/fruit, RLF, jug/tray/6 tumblers.... **1,800.00**
Paperweight, buffalo, fr, LF, 4x4¾" L **1,200.00**
Pendant, floral, bl/gray patina, triangular, RL, 1⅞" **1,100.00**
Perfume burner, Sirenes, 10 mermaids, fr, dome lid, 6¾" **1,500.00**
Sculpture, Joueuse de Flute, maid, floral surround, RLF, 15"..**15,000.00**
Sculpture, nude, left arm by face, right to lips, L, 17" **7,750.00**
Statuette, Sirene, crouching mermaid, opal, RLF, 4" **2,600.00**
Statuette, Suzanne, amber fr, RL, 8½x7½", NM **7,500.00**
Statuette, Suzanne Au Bain, nude, fr, RL, 8¾" **7,500.00**
Vase, Acanthus, allover leaves, red fr, bulbous, RL, 11" **28,500.00**
Vase, Actina, opal, RL, 8½" **2,200.00**
Vase, Archers, cl/fr, RLF/#893, 10" **2,900.00**
Vase, Avallon, birds/branches cvg, cl & fr w/amber, RLF, 6".. **1,500.00**
Vase, band of satyrs & ivy, cl & fr w/bl traces, RLF, 7" **1,100.00**
Vase, Boulouris, ribbed, w/band of birds, opal, RLF, 6" **1,700.00**
Vase, Burned, palm leaves/birds, red enamel, RLF, 9½" **6,000.00**
Vase, Camaret, fr, eng RLF/#1010, 5½" **700.00**
Vase, Camargue, horses on 'cloud' plaques, brn wash, RL, 11". **7,000.00**
Vase, Ceylan, parakeets, opal, cylindrical, RL, 10" **4,000.00**
Vase, Ceylan, parakeets, yel fr, cylindrical, RLF/#905, 10" **6,000.00**
Vase, Champagne, conical bosses, cl, RLF, 6½" **800.00**
Vase, Champagne, conical bosses, gr, RLF/10004, 6¾" **3,300.00**
Vase, Chardons, cased yel over opal, RLF, 7½"...................... **2,800.00**
Vase, Chardons, cl/fr, RLF/#929, 7½" **1,700.00**
Vase, Coquilles, bl wash, RL, 7½".. **800.00**

Vase, Courges, amethyst with matt textured and polished gourd shapes, 7½", $8,000.00.

Vase, Dahlias, enameled, RL, 5" **2,500.00**
Vase, Dampierre, birds/floral panels, cl/fr, LF, 5".......................... **300.00**
Vase, Dentele, gray, RLF/#943, 7½" **1,100.00**
Vase, Druides, mistletoe, bl wash, RL, 7" **900.00**
Vase, Druides, mistletoe, cased opal, bulbous, RL, 7" **1,300.00**
Vase, Ecailles, stylized scales, amber, ovoid, RLF, 10" **5,700.00**
Vase, Formose, fish, cl/fr, RL, 6¾" **1,300.00**
Vase, Gui, mistletoe/berries, cased yel, RL, 6¾"...................... **2,200.00**
Vase, Lagamar, cvd bands, fr w/blk enamel, U-form, RL, 7" ..**26,000.00**
Vase, Languedoc, stylized leaves, amber, spherical, RLF, 9" ...**15,000.00**
Vase, Malines, opal, later silver rim, RLF/#957, 5"...................... **400.00**
Vase, Meander, cl/fr, RLF, ca 1935, 6" **1,000.00**
Vase, Monnaie Du Pape, cl & fr w/amber wash, RLF, 9" **1,700.00**
Vase, Mossi, allover hemispherical bosses, RLF, 7", EX........... **1,800.00**

Vase, Ormeaux, elm leaves, cl/fr, RLF/#984, 6½" **385.00**
Vase, Ormeaux, elm leaves, gr opal, bulbous, RLF/#984, 6½" . **6,300.00**
Vase, Palmes, palm leaves, amber, spherical, RL, 4½" **3,500.00**
Vase, Perruches, parakeets, gr fr, L, 3"................................**17,500.00**
Vase, Ronces, briars, red, baluster w/sm neck, RL/F, 9" **7,000.00**
Vase, Saint-Francois, high-relief birds, opal, RLF, 7"............... **7,500.00**
Vase, Serpent, coiled snake, amber, RL, bulbous, 9¾"............**16,500.00**
Vase, Tournesol, cl/fr, RFL/#1007, 4¾" **600.00**
Vase, Tournesols, sunflowers, opal, ovoid, RLF, 4½" **1,300.00**
Vase, Tristan, cl/fr, RLF, 8" **3,100.00**

Lamps

The earliest lamps were simple dish containers with a wick that hung over the edge or was supported by a channel or tube. Grease and oil from animal or vegetable sources were the first fuels used. Ancient pottery lamps, crusie, and Betty lamps are examples of these early types. In 1784 Swiss inventor Ami Argand introduced the first major improvement in lamps. His lamp featured a tubular wick and a glass chimney. During the first half of the 19th century, whale oil, burning fluid (a highly explosive mixture of turpentine and alcohol), and lard were the most common fuels used in North America. Many lamps were patented for specific use with these fuels.

Kerosene was the first major breakthrough in lighting fuels. It was demonstrated by Canadian geologist Dr. Abraham Gesner in 1846. The discovery and drilling of petroleum in the late 1850s provided an abundant and inexpensive supply of kerosene. It became the main source of light for homes during the balance of the 19th century and for remote locations until the 1950s.

Although Thomas A. Edison invented the electric lamp in 1879, it was not until two or three decades later that electric lamps replaced kerosene household lamps. Millions of kerosene lamps were made for every purpose and pocketbook. They ranged in size from tiny night or miniature lamps to tall stand or piano lamps. Hanging varieties for homes commonly had one or two fonts (oil containers), but chandeliers for churches and public buildings often had six or more. Wall or bracket lamps usually had silvered reflectors. Student lamps, parlor lamps (now called Gone-with-the-Wind lamps), and patterned glass lamps were designed to compliment the popular furnishing trends of the day. From about 1910, Aladdin lamps with a mantle became the mainstay of rural America, providing light that compared favorably with the electric light bulb. Gaslight, introduced in the early 19th century, was used mainly in homes of the wealthy and public places until the early 20th century. Most fixtures were wall or ceiling mounted, although some table models were also used.

Few of the ordinary early electric lamps have survived. Many lamp manufacturers made the same or similar styles for either kerosene or electricity, sometimes for gas. Top-of-the-line lamps were made by Pairpoint, Phoenix, Tiffany, Bradley and Hubbard, and Handel. See also these specific sections.

Currently values of peg lamps are up by about 30% to 40%, and pattern glass lamps in some of the standard lines have jumped from 25% to 100%. When buying lamps that have been converted to electricity, inspect them very carefully for any damage that may have resulted from the alterations; such damage is very common, and when it does occur, the lamp's value may be lessened by as much as 50%.

For those seeking additional information on Aladdin Lamps, we recommend *Aladdin — The Magic Name in Lamps*; *Aladdin Electric Lamps*; and *A Collector's Manual and Price Guide*, all written by our advisor for Aladdins, J. W. Courter; he is listed in the Directory under Illinois.

Another of our lamp advisors is Ruth Osborne; she is listed under Ohio. See also specific manufacturers.

Aladdin Lamps

Bed, #2036-SS, whip-o-lite shade, NM.............................40.00
Bedroom, M-70, metal & ceramic, electric, NM.................20.00
Bedroom, P-52, ceramic, electric, NM............................30.00
Beehive, B-81, gr crystal, VG 60.00
Boudoir, G-19, opalique, EX.......................................40.00
Boudoir, G-36, alacite floral base, electric, 1946, NM.............60.00
Boudoir, G-50, alacite, electric, 1952, EX......................30.00
Boudoir, G-50, powder dish base, electric, w/shade, NM...........325.00
Boudoir, M-91, metal, NM..40.00
Bridge, #2063, NM 195.00
Bridge, #7016, swing arm, reflector, NM..........................185.00
Bridge, #7091, combination table lamp, EX.......................175.00
Caboose, Model B, complete w/shade, EX...........................100.00
Cathedral, B-107, clear crystal, VG..............................65.00
Cathedral, B-110, wht moonstone, NM.............................205.00
Colonial, B-104, table lamp, clear...............................75.00
Colonial, B-106, amber crystal, NM..............................135.00
Contemporary, M-446, metal w/ceramic pyramid, NM.................22.50
Contemporary, M-495, brass, NM...................................20.00
Corinthian, B-105, clear font, gr ft, NM.........................65.00
Corinthian, B-126, wht moonstone font, rose moonstone ft, EX.135.00
Crystal Vase, #1242, Bengal red, 12", NM........................225.00
Crystal Vase, #1248, Ebony Venetian Art Craft, 12", EX 90.00
Figural, G-375, Dancing Ladies Urn, NM..........................700.00
Figural, G-77, Susie, moonstone, electric, EX 850.00
Floor, #1250, w/shade, kerosene, EX.............................175.00
Floor, #3334, reflector, electric, EX 125.00
Floor, #3451-B, electric, NM....................................120.00
Floor, #3601, reflector, candle arms, electric, NM..............165.00
Floor, #3905, alacite ring, arms, night light, electric, NM.........225.00
Floor, J-134, Junior style, electric, NM........................120.00
Glass Urn, G-379, alacite tall ribbed urn w/top, electric, EX 75.00
Hanging, #5, w/#215 shade, EX 285.00
Hanging, Model B, w/parchment shade, outside chain, NM.......225.00
Majestic, B-120, wht moonstone, EX..............................175.00
Majestic, B-122, gr moonstone, VG 90.00
Orientale, B-133, silver, NM....................................140.00
Orientale, B-134, bronze, EX.....................................75.00
Pin-up, P-57, Gun 'n Holster, ceramic, electric, NM..............85.00
Practicus, parlour lamp, complete, NM...........................400.00
Queen, B-95, wht moonstone, EX..................................235.00
Queen, B-97, gr moonstone, G.....................................70.00
Quilt, B-86, gr moonstone, NM 115.00
Quilt, B-91, wht moonstone font, rose moonstone ft, EX 175.00
Short Lincoln Drape, B-60, alacite, EX..........................300.00
Short Lincoln Drape, B-62, ruby crystal, M......................410.00
Simplicity, B-30, wht, EX..75.00
Simplicity, B-76-A, alacite, plain, EX...........................95.00
Smoking stand, #7548, EX..100.00
Solitare, B-70, wht moonstone, EX 1,000.00
Table, #2, kerosene, NM...400.00
Table, #23, complete w/shade, kerosene, EX.......................50.00
Table, #8, kerosene, VG...150.00
Table, G-177, ruby, electric, EX................................200.00
Table, G-219, alacite, electric, NM..............................50.00
Table, G-84, Velvex, electric, NM 400.00
Table, M-4, metal, electric, EX..................................50.00
Table, P-409, ceramic, electric, NM..............................30.00
Table, P-435, ceramic, electric.................................30.00
Table, Vogue Pedestal, E-200, gr, electric, NM..................300.00
Table, W-503, wood & ceramic, electric, NM.......................35.00
Tall Lincoln Drape, B-75, alacite, recent, M 40.00

Tall Lincoln Drape, B-76, cobalt, plain ft, old, NM..............500.00
Touch, MT-507, ceramic base, M..................................200.00
Treasure, B-136, chromium, EX 105.00
Treasure, B-138, nickel, EX......................................85.00
TV, #385, ceramic, NM..50.00
TV, #426, metal w/foil shade, EX.................................10.00
Venetian, A-101, gr, NM..85.00
Venetian, A-103, rose, VG..65.00
Vertique, B-88, yel moonstone, NM...............................475.00
Vertique, B-93, wht moonstone, EX 500.00
Washington Drape, B-40, gr crystal, rnd base, EX.................75.00
Washington Drape, B-49, amber crystal, bell stem, M 210.00
Washington Drape, B-53, clear crystal, NM 50.00

Chandeliers

Brass, frosted mushroom shade, early electric, 8x15", EX.............165.00
Brass w/crimped pan, 4 sockets, hanging loop, dk patina, EX 205.00
Crystal, 4 rows of prisms w/brass mts, 19x13", EX 395.00
Gilt metal, 6-light, Renaissance style, 34"........................ 2,200.00
Meriden Malleable, CI, 4 cut/frosted bracket lamps, 42x33" ... 2,400.00
O/l (bl cut to clear), 6-arm, gilt bronze mts, 1800s 3,700.00

Decorated Kerosene Lamps

Blown font w/cut florals, wht base, brass connector, 12".............150.00
Dot Optic, cranberry, 26½" 595.00
Frosted w/fired-on Greek Key band, wht stem/ft, 9", EX.............145.00
Milk glass w/mc florals, flame spreader mk WYS Pat '89, 16" 150.00
O/l (cobalt), cut printie, onion font, brass stem/base, 9" 250.00
O/l (pk/wht/clear), flowers, marble base, Sandwich 850.00
O/l (red), 4 flowers/reeding/ovals, att Sandwich, 11" 400.00

Cut overlay font, pink to white to clear, brass fluted
stem, bronze base, 12", $1,400.00; Thumbprint cut
crystal font, white cut to clear overlay stem,
$300.00.

O/l (wht) w/cut ovals, tulip-form font, brass stem, #1, 11" 375.00
Opaque gr acanthus font, fire-gilt std, marble base, 12" 150.00
Ruby stained, frosted floral-decor band, brass stem, 8¾".............125.00
Vaseline w/opal swirls, finger lamp 335.00

Fairy Lamps

Bl satin, ruffled/cased, in matching base, 5½", NM 170.00

Bl satin swirl, plain stemmed holder, appl clear petals, 12" 400.00
Bl verre moire, ruffled base, Clarke cup, 7½" 785.00
Bl verre moire, wht loopings, clear Clarke base, 4¾x3¾" 165.00
Burmese, dome shade, Webb, clear Clarke base, 3¾x3" 165.00
Burmese, florals, sq folded-in base, Clarke cup, 6x6" 1,250.00
Burmese, gold prunus on base & shade, Webb, Clarke cup, 5". 1,250.00
Burmese, ivy decor, on Tunncliffe pottery base, 4" 500.00
Burmese, pyramid-sz shade, on tall clear Hobstar base, 8" 150.00
Burmese, w/matching ruffled bowl base, 5¼" 395.00
Burmese, Webb, clear mk Clarke base, 5x3¾" 225.00
Cranberry verre moire, fluted base, Clarke cup, 5½" 495.00
Cranberry verre moire, wht loopings, Clarke base, 3⅛" 435.00
Dia Quilt, gr, emb ribs on clear Clarke base, 4¾" 145.00
Hobnail shade, sapphire bl Hobnail base, 6" 40.00
Kitten's head, bsk, gr eyes/bl collar 385.00
Nailsea, bl w/wht loops, 6" 400.00
Nailsea, cranberry w/wht loops, ruffled bowl, 6¾", NM 245.00
Owl, wht bsk, amber & blk eyes, 3¼" 700.00
Peachblow, florals, Clarke cup, 5¾" 1,115.00
Pekingese pup, bsk, amber eyes/bl collar, 4" 285.00
Pk Swirl MOP satin, 5x5½" 525.00
Plique-a-jour mc-on-bl shade, lacquered wood base, 8½" 125.00
Red verre moire, clear mk Clarke base 245.00
Stars & Rays, ruby to clear, 4" 80.00

Gone-with-the-Wind and Banquet

Bl satin, emb motif, 20" 375.00
Emb classical scenes in panels of cherubs, wine/gr, 24" 350.00
Floral reserve on gr, rtcl brass base w/lion mask hdls, 24".............300.00
Florals, wine on beige & brn, 24" 325.00
Grapes, purple w/rust leaves, scenic panels, 24" 500.00
Hollyhock, red satin, 26" 725.00
Jewelling on font, floral globe, rtcl base, Juno, 26" 250.00
Lilies, mc on brn & lav, 31" 400.00
Lion's heads/desert scenes relief, gr/yel, 23" 450.00
Moss Rose, wired, 28" 300.00
Pansies, pk/yel/lav on brn & yel, 28" 550.00
Pigeon blood cased in bl, swirled/emb flowers, 19".....................425.00
Roses, pk/wht on shaded pk, 27" 400.00
Roses on shade & base, top/bottom of which are rust, 24" 375.00
Stag & doe scenes, emb motif, wine/yel, 21" 400.00
Sunflowers HP on pk & gr, 23" 350.00

Hanging Lamps

Amber ball shade w/optic honeycomb, miniature, 8½" 175.00
Cranberry T'print 14" shade, ruby Hobnail font, mc prisms ... 1,500.00
Dbl angle, emb brass w/clear elbows, rpl wht shades, EX.............300.00
Dbl angle, NP tin font, clear elbows, rpl wht shades, EX 300.00
Hall, ribbed/paneled cranbery opal, brass fr, EX....................300.00
Juno, store type, emb metal font, tin shade, 39", NM 425.00
Rvpt 12x5" cylinder w/scene, wht metal frwork 700.00
Senour, tin w/reflectors, used in public bldgs, 53x24" ... 2,400.00
Shaded pk Hobnail 14" shade/font, prisms, jeweled brass fr 1,500.00
Wht shade & font w/mc birds & flowers, working trolley, EX 350.00

Lanterns

Brass, clear globe, Pat Apr 11 1871/May 2 1871, 11", EX 70.00
Darkroom, tin, w/burner, 1860s, rpt, 8¾" 25.00
Dietz Tubular Jr, EX..79.00
Rayo #50 ....90.00
Rayo Pony #15 ....90.00

Skater's, brass, clear globe, bail hdl, 7", EX....................65.00
Tin, clear glass globe, candle-burning, ring hdl, 10" 85.00
Tin, pierced tin, open 1 side, bail hdl, 17".........................220.00

Lard Oil/Grease

Betty, blk iron, 4x3¼" 75.00
Betty, iron, adjustable ratchet arm w/3 teeth, 1800s, 7".............275.00
Betty, tin, ca 1850, 5", +hanger...................................95.00
Betty, tin, Ipswich, horizontal disk on stem std, 11" 150.00
Betty, wrought iron, w/hanger & pick, EX lid, 4¼" 125.00
Kettle, brass/copper/wrought iron/NP, Peter Derr/1843, 11" ... 2,400.00
Loom, wrought iron, ca 1800, 16" 195.00
Rush light, iron, counterbalance, twist stem, tripod, 14" 300.00
Rush light, iron, w/hogscraper base, pitted, 5" 135.00
Tin w/iron base, gold finish, label: SN&HC Ufford, 14", NM.....450.00

Miniature Lamps, Kerosene

Artichoke, amber satin, nutmeg burner, 8" 1,100.00
Beaded Drape, red satin, nutmeg burner, 9" 250.00
Beauty Night Lamp, nickel plated, wht beehive shade, 4½" 90.00
Bl MOP Raindrop, spherical shade, squat base, 7¾", NM 1,200.00
Brady's Night Lamp, emb wht opaque satin, nutmeg burner, 7½"..425.00
Bundling Lamp, emb milk glass, Imperial, 7½" 45.00
Buttercup, cobalt, finger lamp 85.00
Butterscotch satin 'umbrella' shade/base, LG Wright, 7" 125.00
Cranberry Beaded Swirl, 8¾" 125.00
Cranberry Optic, bell-shaped shade, canister base, 8" 200.00
Daisy & Button, 7¾" 210.00
Delft, bl/gray on paneled wht, Pairpoint, 8½" 800.00
Emerald gr, puffy Rococo-style shade & base, 6" 550.00
Florals, wht w/gold on bl, complete, 5¼" 880.00
Frosted w/emb scrolls & flowers, nutmeg burner, VG gilt, 8" 370.00
Girl in bonnet by hive, bsk figural, gr shade, 8½" 515.00
Gr satin w/silver holly, tall slim std, 13¾" 800.00
Lincoln Drape, textured glossy base, gold satin shade, 5½" 65.00
Little Buttercup, dk bl, acorn burner, rpl chimney, 2¾"..............100.00
Loop pattern font on milk glass stem/ft, rpl shade, 6", NM 150.00
Milk glass, emb 'fans' w/fired-on burgundy, 7¾", EX 200.00
Milk glass w/emb plain & beaded panels, pyriform, 8½" 100.00
Nelly Bly, clear w/frosted decor, hornet burner, 8" 125.00
Nelly Bly, pk base & shade, 9" 145.00
Netted Apple Blossom, orig base/shade/burner, NM..................195.00
Nutmeg, cobalt, nutmeg burner, finger lamp, 2⅝" 90.00
Owl figural, head is globe, mc on wht opaque, overall: 8" 1,600.00
Pineapple in a Basket, milk glass w/fired-on gr pnt, 7" 150.00
Pressed ribbed font, swirled bl opal paneled base, EX 100.00
Raindrop, yel to wht, clear appl hdl, finger lamp 145.00
Sandwich Loop, Sandwich, orig burner 120.00
Snow owl w/glass eyes bsk base, cased peachblow shade, 13" .. 1,500.00
Spatter, vertical beading, pear shade, shouldered base, 9"............650.00
Spatter Beaded Swirl, 8", EX 600.00
Stein base, ball shade, transfers of 3 men, 12" 1,000.00
Time lamp, wht beehive shade, Pride of Am/Grand Val, 6¾" 175.00
Wht satin w/emb ribbing, 3-color fired-on pnt, 7½", EX 150.00
Yel cased w/gold florals, canister base, 8" 1,250.00

Pattern Glass Lamps

Acanthus Leaf, stepped clambroth base/jade font, 12", EX...... 1,900.00
Acanthus Leaf, wht translucent, marble base, Sandwich, 12".....375.00
Arboresque, cranberry w/gold florals, tulip shade, 19" 650.00
Atterbury Icicle, hand lamp, Pat 1868, 3¼" 150.00

Atterbury Loop, 8½"..100.00
Beads, Bars & Flutes, 6"...100.00
Bull's Eye, stand lamp, 10¾"..125.00
Bull's Eye, vaseline opal, #40 base.................................225.00
Cabbage Rose, milk glass, decor big-bulge chimney, 9¾"............140.00
Cable, hand lamp, 1900, 3⅝"..110.00
Cable, yel-gr, hand lamp, 3⅝"..250.00
Chicago, amber, US Glass, 11"...275.00
Columbian Coin, milk glass, #2 burner, 10", EX.............300.00
Coolidge Drape, cobalt, #1 burner, 8½", EX, pr..........400.00
Daisy & Fern, cobalt opal, 16½"......................................395.00
Daisy & Fern, cranberry opal, 26½".................................595.00
Dominion Panel, 7", EX..95.00
Empress, emerald gr, #1, 8½"..125.00
Erin Fan, emerald, #1 burner, swirl chimney, MacBeth, 10"......125.00
Filley, hand lamp, 2⅞"...95.00
Fringed Curtain, finger lamp...95.00
Grant, 6½"...95.00
Grape Band, 1870s, 9"..175.00
Greek Key, finger lamp...100.00
Heavy Bull's Eye Band, 1900, 13"...................................170.00
Horn of Plenty, hexagonal base, baluster std, flint, 10"......150.00
Huber, baluster stem, sq base, flint, 8¾", EX................100.00
Inverted Leaf Panel, brass stem, marble base, 8½"............170.00
Janice, lt gr, #1 Socony burner, ftd finger lamp, 5½", EX..........125.00
Lomax Utah, Union Glass, 8¼"......................................100.00
Loop, canary yel, stepped base, 8½", NM, pr..............550.00
Loop, high hexagonal ped ft, flint, 10", EX..................100.00
Lyre, appl hdl, finger lamp, 4"..95.00
Marriage, bl, 2 fonts w/match holder between, Ripley, 13½"......695.00
Moon & Star base, partial frost/fluted amber font, 11"......275.00
Mtn Laurel font, Oval Band base, Central Glass Co, 7"......125.00
New England Centennial, finger lamp.............................140.00
Oval Window, yel-gr, 9"...225.00
Owl & Shield, brass stem, marble base, 7½", NM.........150.00
Patrician, 1870s, 11", NM...115.00
Peacock Feather, amber, #2 Venus burner, 11".............150.00
Peacock Feather, hand lamp, 6"...95.00
Peacock Feather, stand lamp, 10".....................................95.00
Periwinkle, brass stem, slate ft, #1 collar, 9"...............100.00
Plain Rib & Band, hand lamp, 3⅛"................................125.00
Pleat & Panel, Armour font, 1870s, 9½"......................110.00
Pressed Circle & Ellipse, camphene burner, Sandwich, 11"......200.00
Prince Edward, emerald gr, 10½", NM..........................275.00
Prince Edward, emerald gr, 8½", EX.............................175.00
Princess Feather, aqua, #2 burner, torch/wreath chimney, 10"......200.00
Princess Feather, finger lamp..120.00
Princess Feather, torch/wreath big-bulge chimney, 9½"......95.00
Quartered Block, stand lamp, 8½"...................................95.00
Rib Band, 7⅜"..95.00
Ring Punty, brass stem, marble base, 8¼"...................125.00
Riverside Panel, gr font...135.00
Riverside Plain, 8½"..55.00
Sandwich Blackberry, brass stem, marble base, 8¾"......325.00
Sawtooth, baluster std, hexagonal ft, flint, 12", EX......150.00
Sheldon Swirl, vaseline opal font, clear base, oil burner......225.00
Shield & Star, brass stem, marble base, 7".....................150.00
Shield & Star, finger lamp, 2¾".......................................135.00
Snail, nickel connector, stand lamp, 11¼"....................125.00
Snowdon, ftd hand lamp, 1880, 4½".................................85.00
St Louis, amber font, milk glass base, 8¾"...................375.00
Star & Punty, fluted brass stem, marble base, 9"........125.00
Teardrop & Eyewinker w/Plume, Findlay, 9".................125.00
Triple Flute w/Bar, wht opaque.......................................125.00

US Coin, quarters/half dollars, 8½".................................225.00
Waffle & Thumbprint, flint, 10½", EX............................100.00
Wave, stand lamp, metal connector, 9½".......................125.00
Wheat in Shield, finger lamp..80.00
Wheat in Shield, 9"..150.00
Wild Rose & Bow Knot, #2 burner, 8"..............................95.00
Wild Rose & Bow Knot, 10"..135.00

Peg Lamps

Bl Dia Quilt MOP, bulbous ruffled shade, brass base, 11½".......1,020.00
Cranberry, HP florals, ruffled shade, brass candlestick, 14"......325.00
Cranberry w/optic Herringbone, SP holder, rpl burner, 6½"......200.00
Heads of Blks on base, ceramic, English, 1800s, 5", EX, pr......600.00
Pk Dia Quilt, brass holder, complete, 14½"................700.00
Rubena frost w/eng ferns & florals, brass base, 15", pr......950.00

Reverse Painted Lamps

Mums on 18" shade sgn Moe Bridges; harp std on 4 paw ft......4,500.00
Palm trees/plants 14" dome shade; metal std, Pittsburgh......850.00

Reverse-painted textured glass 18" shade with double moonlit scenes with boats and waterfront cottage, 24", $1,100.00.

Scenic 14" fabric-textured bell shade; gilt metal vase std............700.00
Scenic 16" shade sgn Jefferson #2366; 2-lite metal std, 22"......1,200.00
Summer scene 15" sgn Moe Bridges shade; gilt metal base......2,000.00
Tree scene on textured 19" dome shade; wht-pnt metal std......500.00
Waterfront/sailboats 16" conical shade; Nouveau-emb std......750.00
Woods/road 18" sgn Moe Bridges shade; metal baluster std......2,000.00

Student Lamps, Kerosene

Brass, dbl, elaborate appl cable decor, rpl shades, 29"......1,800.00
Brass, dbl, opaque wht shades, rpr, incomplete burners, 24"......225.00
Brass, vertical canister font, orig wht shade, 12"........425.00
Brass, 10" gr cased shade, German Student Lamp Co, 22"......600.00
Brass, 10" gr cased shade, Manhattan Brass Co 1883, 23", EX......350.00
Brass w/opaque wht cone shade, pat dtd/CA Kleemann, 21"......200.00

Whale Oil/Burning Fluid

Bl opaque tulip font, brass stem, marble base, 13", pr, EX......550.00
Blown font w/'petals,' stepped base w/corner columns, 12"......275.00
Brass, hinged snuffer cover, knob-trn stem, 8"............100.00
Brass w/EX copper appliques, free-standing or wall mt, 12"......150.00

Acanthus Leaf oil lamps, sand finish on clambroth, attributed to Sandwich, 12", $1,500.00 for the pair.

Canary, 3 printie block, 8-side baluster std, sq base, 11" 750.00
Circle/flute facets, hollow stem, quatrefoil base, 12", pr................325.00
Clambroth, tulip form, early, 12", NM 400.00
Clear inverted bell form w/hdl, dbl-tube burner, 3¾" 125.00
Cut honeycomb font, pressed sq ft w/rosettes, 8", EX, pr 300.00
Cut/pressed, conical font, NE Glass, 11", NM...........................300.00
Free-blown teardrop font, 8-side stepped base, 9", EX 110.00
Loop, dk amethyst, brass burner, pewter collar/cap, 10", EX........550.00
Loop, dk amethyst, 8-sided octagonal std, NE, 12", NM 1,200.00
Loop, sapphire, plated burner, pewter collar/cap, 10", EX 700.00
Loop font, med bl, octagonal baluster std/sq base, 10", EX 1,100.00
O/l (cranberry), molded glass quatrefoil base, VG 450.00
Ram's head base, blown conical font, early, 7½", NM 275.00
Sparking, bell form w/appl hdl, brass burner, 4¾"..........................85.00
Sparking, blown font on std w/disk connector, 3⅝" 525.00
Sparking, blown/pressed, lacy base, 4⅜", NM.............................250.00
Sparking, rnd font, stepped scalloped pressed base, 3", pr 250.00
Sparking, rnd font w/hdl, cup plate base, tin burner, 4" 850.00
Tin, cylinder font, tubular hdl, 5-burner lid, 7" L..........................200.00
Wht opaque, rnd font on sq base w/emb, NE Glass, 9", EX 400.00
3-Printie, amethyst tint, dbl brass burners, pewter cap, 8" 1,250.00
6-petal font, 6-side stem/ft, flint, pewter collar, 8½" 135.00

Miscellaneous

Argon, tin, 1800s, 7" w/6½" saucer 250.00
Bronze crane, snake about neck, mouse on lid, lamp on chain 160.00

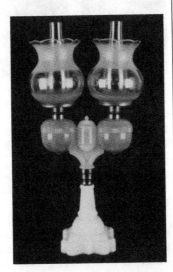

Ripley & Co. marriage lamp, double fonts, light opaque blue with clambroth match safe and pressed Baroque base and standard, pristine condition, 22½", $2,200.00.

Cigar lighter, bronzed female bust base, ruby shade, 12" 350.00
French's, finger lamp, tin base, Pat 1870 in glass font, 3" 60.00
Lacemaker's, cranberry Invt T'print, brass base, 16x10"..............425.00
Miner's, Dew-Lite, brass, swing hdl, Pat 1913 & 1926, 9½"..........90.00
Night light, church dome, alabaster, 5½" 350.00
Pottery w/metal base, sgn Hinks, 14" 175.00
Torchier, hinged base for wall mt, cranberry shade, 19"..............645.00

Le Verre Francais

Le Verre Francais was produced during the 1920s by Schneider at Epinay-sur-Seine in France. It was a commercial art glass in the cameo style composed of layered glass with the designs engraved by acid. Favored motifs were stylized leaves and flowers or geometric patterns. It was marked with the name in script or with an inlaid filigrane.

Our advisor for this category is Don Williams; he is listed in the Directory under Missouri.

Cameo

Bowl, flower buds, brn on mottled gray, ped ft, sgn, 11½"............650.00
Bowl, stemmed pods, red on yel & orange mottle, 5½x11" 865.00
Lamp, bellflowers on yel, on 10" mushroom shade/base, 17½" .. 4,000.00
Lamp, starburst shade/base, purple on pk & wht stripes, 15" ... 5,700.00
Night light, cats, brn on yel to red shade, iron base, 7" 2,300.00
Night light, floral, orange to bl on yel/orange, conial, 8".........1,100.00

Vase, irises, burgundy to orange on yellow, 20", $1,900.00; Vase, floral, red on orange to yellow mottle, 24", $1,400.00; Vase, vines and thistle-like flowers, red on orange mottle, 22", $1,900.00.

Vase, berry vines, purple on cream/rust mottle, bun ft, 17½" .. 1,300.00
Vase, butterflies, red/bl mottle on wht to turq, 9x9" 5,700.00
Vase, floral, purple/mauve on mottled gray, wide body, 5" ... 1,100.00
Vase, floral panels, orange/brn on rust, ftd, Charder, 23" 2,400.00
Vase, floral stems/clusters, wine to red on orange, 17"............. 2,300.00
Vase, foliage/stylized floral, brn to orange on yel, 6x8" 700.00
Vase, foxglove, wine to orange on pk mottle, knop ft, 20" 1,700.00
Vase, grapes, purple on amber, ovoid w/bun base, 21" 2,600.00
Vase, leaves/rosettes, lav on pk mottle, blk ft, 10" 1,500.00
Vase, orchids, orange to purple on yel, slim/ftd, 22" 2,800.00
Vase, pomegranates, orange to bl on yel, ftd trumpet, 12½" ... 1,700.00

Vase, stripes/sqs, rust on wht, hexagonal/ftd, Charder, 15"...... 1,700.00
Vase, stylized floral, bl to orange on yel, bun ft, 18" 1,400.00
Vase, stylized floral, gr to purple on yel/orange, 20" 2,800.00
Vase, stylized hydrangea, blk to pk on yel, shouldered, 19" 3,500.00
Vase, stylized orchids, wine to red on yel, wide ft, 24" 2,700.00
Vase, stylized poppies, burgundy to red on yel, bun ft, 11" 600.00
Vase, sunflowers, brn to orange on yel, ftd cylinder, 11" 2,200.00
Vase, swans/willows, brn/purple on mottle, stick neck, 18" 6,000.00
Vase, swans/willows, turquoise/purple on yel mottle, 12" 1,700.00
Vase, thorny floral limbs, wine/lav mottle, Charder, 17"......... 1,700.00

Leeds, Leeds Type

The Leeds Pottery was established in 1758 in Yorkshire and under varied management produced fine creamware, often highly reticulated and transfer printed, shiny black-glazed Jackfield wares, polychromed pearlware, and figurines similar to those made in the Staffordshire area. Little of the early wares were marked; after 1775 the impressed 'Leeds Pottery' mark was used. From 1781 to 1820, the name 'Hartley Greens & Co.' was added. The pottery closed in 1898.

Today the term 'Leeds' has become generic and is used to encompass all polychromed pearlware and creamware — wherever its origin. Thus similar wares of other potters — Wood for instance — is often incorrectly called 'Leeds.' Unless a piece is marked or can be definitely attributed to Leeds by confirming the pattern to be authentic, 'Leeds-Type' would be a more accurate nomenclature.

Key:
hl — hairline   sp — soft paste
rtcl — reticulated

Bowl, creamware, flower finial, hdls, mk Leeds, 5½", EX 180.00
Bowl, floral urn, bl feather rim, pearlware, 1800, 14"............... 1,300.00
Bowl, floral w/floral border, creamware, 1775, hl, 11".................475.00
Bowl, gaudy 5-color floral, sp, prof rpr, 4½x10" dia, EX........... 1,575.00
Charger, floral, bl feather rim, pearlware, 1775, hl, 14" 400.00
Charger, floral spray, bl feather rim, 1875, 14" 400.00
Dish, floral spray in bl & ochre, feather edge, 1800, 12" 425.00
Pitcher, gaudy 5-color floral, sp, 8", EX 700.00
Plate, eagle, 5-color, gr feather edge, sp, 10", NM.....................450.00
Plate, floral bouquet, gr feather edge, 7" 250.00
Plate, floral spray, floral-rtcl bl-swag border, 1775, 8" 250.00
Platter, floral spray in bl, bl feather rim, 15" L........................900.00
Platter, floral urn in center, bl feather rim, 16" L.................. 1,000.00
Platter, florals in ochre & bl, bl feather rim, 1800, 15" 900.00
Sauce tureen, bl feather edge, creamware, 6" L, +ladle................300.00
Sugar bowl, gaudy bl/wht floral, lion head hdls, sp, EX...............135.00
Teacup, foliate motif, bl swag border w/in, yel w/out, EX 110.00
Vase, floral sprays, bl feather rim, 5-finger, 11", EX 300.00
Warming dish, central rtcl floral, shell hdls, 10", pr...................950.00

Legras

Legras and Cie was founded in St. Denis, France, in 1864. Production continued until about 1914. In addition to their enameled wares, they made cameo art glass decorated with outdoor scenes and florals executed by acid cuttings through two to six layers of glass. Their work is signed 'Legras' in relief. Our advisor for this category is Don Williams; he is listed in the Directory under Missouri.

Cameo

Vase, autumn trees on bl & gr, baluster, 5½"...........................950.00

Vase, ivy on pk frost, 3-prong opening, 16½"............................ 2,300.00
Vase, orchids, cut/enamel on frost, baluster, 12½" 1,200.00
Vase, thistles, amber/enamel on beige cased to amber, 14" 1,700.00
Vase, trees/river, wht/lime & dk gr on pk, ftd U-form, 7" 1,000.00
Vase, vines & berries, 3-color, 4¼"......................................675.00

Miscellaneous

Bowl, water lilies, gold/bl enamel on tan, amber int, 9½"...........275.00
Vase, cherries, semi-martele frost, trumpet form, 10" 495.00
Vase, leaves, maroon enamel on acid-cut crystal, 11¾" 815.00
Vase, stylized palms/fans etched on taupe, spherical, 9"..............600.00
Vase, woodland scene, mc enamel on clear, 10" 325.00
Vase, yel/gr/wht/brn striations between clear layers, 10" 650.00

Lenox

Walter Scott Lenox, former art director at Ott and Brewer, and Jonathan Coxon founded The Ceramic Art Company of Trenton, New Jersey, in 1889. By 1906 Cox had left the company and to reflect the change in ownership, the name was changed to Lenox, Inc. Until 1930 when the production of American-made Belleek came to an end, they continued to produce the same type of high-quality ornamental wares that Lenox and Coxon had learned to master while in the employ of Ott and Brewer. Their superior dinnerware made the company famous, and since 1917 Lenox has been chosen the official White House China.

Our advisor for this category is Mary Frank Gaston; she is listed in the Directory under Texas. See also Ceramic Art Company.

Figurine, ballerina, 6½", $200.00.

Atomizer, Scottie dog begging, yel.......................................250.00
Bowl, centerpc; roses, gold hdls, Belleek mk, 4½x9½" 190.00
Bowl, Lotus Leaf, wht, shape #37...95.00
Bowl, purple clematis w/gold, sq, Belleek mk, 5" 65.00
Bowl, salad; Lace Point..15.00
Bowl, wht ware, dragon hdls, Belleek mk, 13" dia 140.00
Box, cigarette; Lenox Rose, +3 ash trays..................................58.00
Cake stand, Ming, low ped 65.00
Candlestick, wht ware, raised scalloped base, Belleek mk, pr.....165.00
Chocolate pot, roses & gold paste, sgn, palette mk, 7".................275.00
Chocolate pot, silver overlay, Belleek mk, 5¼" 195.00
Coffeepot, floral garlands, silver overlay, Belleek mk, 11" 660.00

Coffeepot, Lace Point	100.00
Creamer & sugar bowl, Lace Point	75.00
Creamer & sugar bowl, Lenox Rose	100.00
Cup & saucer, Biltmore	40.00
Cup & saucer, Country Garden	35.00
Cup & saucer, Montclair, old style	40.00
Cup & saucer, Mystic	35.00
Cup & saucer, Wyndcrest	35.00
Figurine, First Waltz, ltd ed, 1984	125.00
Figurine, flapper's head, 4"	87.00
Figurine, Floradora, no decor	265.00
Figurine, seal on ledge, ivory, 6x4"	150.00
Figurine, semi-nude lady w/greyhound, ivory, 13"	190.00
Figurine vase, blue jay in tree, 5-color, ink stamp	300.00
Gravy boat, Wyndcrest	95.00
Jam jar, florals w/gold (non-factory), Belleek mk, 4"	110.00
Lamp, boudoir; Deco lady w/hoop skirt & fan forms shade, 9"	265.00
Mug, bl florals w/gold, lily pads at rim/base, gold hdl	55.00
Mug, commemorative; girl canoeing, parian, Belleek mk, 6½"	220.00
Mug, HP berries & leaves, sgn, Belleek mk, 4½"	110.00
Mug, monk scene on brn	90.00
Pitcher, Patriots, wht w/bl garlands & emb figures, 9"	150.00
Pitcher, silver overlay w/floral cameo, palette mk, 8"	500.00
Plate, bread & butter; Repertoire	12.50
Plate, dinner; Amethyst	38.00
Plate, dinner; Mystic	30.00
Plate, dinner; Tuxedo	30.00
Plate, fuchsia border w/heavy silver overlay border, 10"	135.00
Plate, salad; Caribee	20.00
Plate, salad; Montclair	12.00
Plate, salad; Wyndcrest	25.00
Platter, Empress, lg	150.00
Salt cellar, gold rim, sterling holder, Belleek mk, 1½"	55.00
Saucer, Repertoire	12.50
Shaker, talcum; HP roses (non-factory), Belleek mk, 6"	140.00
Shakers, Orchard, pr	30.00
Shell, gold rim, bl mk, 9"	40.00
Swan, bl mk, 8½"	75.00
Swan, gold mk, 2"	25.00
Swan, gold mk, 5"	50.00
Swan, wht ware, open, Belleek wreath mk, 1¾x2"	35.00
Tea set, Flying Geese, silver overlay trim, Belleek mk, 3-pc	660.00
Tea set, Virginian, gold hdls, 11" pot, 3-pc	350.00
Teapot, Waldorf Astoria, pk w/silver bands, silver top, 1937	95.00
Underplate, silver overlay, Belleek palette mk, 10½"	195.00
Vase, bride & maiden, sgn, gold ring hdls, Belleek mk, 10"	660.00
Vase, bud; multiflorals on porc, 6"	35.00
Vase, Deco peacocks HP, cylindrical, Belleek mk, 13"	385.00
Vase, Empire, swan hdls, gr wreath mk, 10½"	65.00
Vase, floral cameos, silver overlay, Belleek mk, 10"	550.00
Vase, foliage (non-factory) HP, long neck, Belleek mk, 6½"	65.00
Vase, poppies, sgn Wilcox, baluster, Belleek mk, 16"	440.00
Vase, portrait reserve, allover silver overlay, ftd, 9"	1,700.00
Vase, shepherdess & sheep, classic form, Belleek mk, 8¼"	550.00
Vase, springer spaniel, sgn Baker, Belleek wreath mk, 8¼"	600.00
Vase, swan on lake on gr, gr palette mk, 12x9"	575.00

Letter Openers

Made in a wide variety of materials and designs, letter openers make for an interesting collection that is easy to display and easy on the budget as well. Our advisor for this category is Ron Damaska; he is listed in the Directory under Pennsylvania.

Abalone, 5¼"	5.00
Bone, scrimshaw leaves, red/blk stain, cut-out hearts, 5¼"	78.00
Brass, folding 2½" knife in hdl, 5" ruler on blade, 8¾"	16.00
Brass, sm Oriental idol on hdl stamped Siam, 7", w/box	8.00
Brass, Van Houten's Cocoas, running Dutch boy, 7¾"	15.00
Brass dagger, 9½", in red leather scabbard	15.00
Brass w/copper blade, snake-wrapped sword-shaped hdl, 6½"	10.00
Bronze, Prudential Has Strength of Gibralter, 1878-1948, 6"	15.00
Celluloid, Biltrite Rubber Heels & Nuron Shoes, 7½"	9.00
Celluloid, Railway Express Acency on hdl, 9", EX	5.00
Celluloid, relief violets & leaves w/some color, 10"	15.00
Copper, Western Employer's Service, SF/Oakland, w/rule, 6"	12.00
Ebony wood, tribal chieftain in headdress figural, 12"	7.50
Metal, Barrett Bros, International Trucks, Albany OR	10.00
Metal, Gulf Oil	10.00
Metal, Nabisco Uneeda Biscuits	80.00
Metal w/copper blade, state seal of CA, emb hdl, 7"	12.50
Plastic, Fuller Brush man figural, pk	8.00
Pot metal w/brass blade, cowboy on rearing horse, bk pnt, 8"	10.00
SP, Protective Fire Ins, Seward NB, EX	25.00
SP, Reed & Barton, cherubs in grape arbor hdl, ornate	35.00
Whalebone, sword form, 4¼", EX	50.00
Whalebone w/rosewood hdl, 7", EX	75.00

Libbey

The New England Glass Company was established in 1818 in Boston, Massachusetts. In 1892 it became known as the Libbey Glass Company. At Chicago's Columbian Expo in 1893, Libbey set up a ten-pot furnace and made glass souvenirs. The display brought them worldwide fame. Between 1878 and 1918, Libbey made exquisite cut and faceted glass, considered today to be the best from the brilliant period. The company is credited for several innovations — the Owens bottle machine that made mass-production possible and the Westlake machine which turned out both electric light bulbs and tumblers automatically. They developed a machine to polish the rims of their tumblers in such a way that chipping was unlikely to occur. Their glassware carried the patented Safedge guarantee.

Libbey also made glassware in numerous colors — cobalt, ruby, pink, green, and amber. In 1935 it was bought by Owens-Illinois and remains a division of that company. See also Amberina and other specific types.

Bonbon, amberina, 6-point rim, sgn/#3029, 7" dia	585.00
Bowl, amberina, folded-over rim, #3027, 2½x10"	525.00
Bowl, centerpc; Optic, red threading on clear, mk, 5x11"	325.00
Bowl, cut, hobstars/fan/dmn panels, sgn, 8½"	240.00
Bowl, cut, Kimberly, no mk, 1-corner, 10"	425.00
Butter dish, cut, Ozella	395.00
Celery tray, cut, Stratford, no mk	200.00
Cocktail, kangaroo stem	100.00
Compote, crystal bowl on opal elephant figural stem, 8x11"	550.00
Creamer, amberina	900.00
Ewer, Invt T'print, bl, amber hdl, sgn, 10¼"	125.00
Maize, bowl, gr husks	175.00
Maize, celery vase, clear w/amber irid, bl husks, 6½"	200.00
Maize, celery vase, wht w/bl husks, 6½"	165.00
Maize, cruet, clear w/lt bl husks, maize stopper, rare	350.00
Maize, pickle castor, gr husks, SP fr	500.00
Maize, pitcher, clear w/amber irid, bl husks, clear hdl, 9"	585.00
Maize, pitcher, wht w/gr husks, strap hdl, 8½x5½"	450.00
Maize, shakers, bl husks, pr	350.00
Maize, sugar shaker, gr husks, 5½"	235.00

Maize, syrup, gr husks, scarce, 6" 350.00
Maize, toothpick holder, gold-traced gr husks, scarce 400.00
Maize, tumbler, 4½" 175.00
Pitcher, tankard; cut, Corinthian, sgn, 8½" 385.00
Plate, amberina, blown, 7", pr 325.00
Plate, cut, Kimberly, no mk, 7" 190.00
Ring holder, kangaroo stem..125.00

Stemware with cut diamond band and florals. Goblet, $40.00; Sherbet, $30.00.

Vase, amberina, #3003, 12" 585.00
Vase, amberina, bowl rests on long hollow stem, #3002, 11¼" .. 1,000.00
Vase, amberina, paneled, folded-over rim, sgn, 6¾" 700.00
Vase, amberina, paneled trumpet form, label, 6" 350.00
Vase, dmn molded, pk threads, unsgn, 8½" 185.00

Limited Edition Plates

Currently, values of some limited edition plates have risen dramatically while others have drastically fallen. Prices charged by plate dealers in the secondary market vary greatly; we have tried to suggest an average.

Bing and Grondahl

1895, Behind the Frozen Window 5,800.00
1896, New Moon 1,800.00
1897, Christmas Meal of Sparrows 1,050.00
1898, Roses & Star 650.00
1899, Crows Enjoying Christmas.. 1,200.00
1900, Church Bells Chiming 1,000.00
1901, 3 Wise Men 400.00
1902, Gothic Church Interior...350.00
1903, Expectant Children 330.00
1904, View of Copenhagen From Fredericksberg Hill 130.00
1905, Christmas Night 130.00
1906, Sleighing to Church 80.00
1907, Little Match Girl 95.00
1908, St Petri Church 60.00
1909, Yule Tree...75.00
1910, Old Organist 70.00
1911, Angels & Shepherds 65.00
1912, Going to Church 65.00
1913, Bringing Home the Tree...70.00
1914, Amalienborg Castle 65.00
1915, Dog on Chain Outside Window 105.00
1916, Prayer of the Sparrows 60.00

1917, Christmas Boat...60.00
1918, Fishing Boat 60.00
1919, Outside the Lighted Window 55.00
1920, Hare in the Snow..55.00
1921, Pigeons 45.00
1922, Star of Bethlehem...45.00
1923, Hermitage 50.00
1924, Lighthouse 50.00
1925, Child's Christmas..50.00
1926, Churchgoers 50.00
1927, Skating Couple 70.00
1928, Eskimos 45.00
1929, Fox Outside Farm...55.00
1930, Christmas Train 70.00
1931, Tree in Town Hall Square 65.00
1932, Lifeboat at Work...65.00
1933, Korsor-Nyborg Ferry 50.00
1934, Church Bell in Tower 50.00
1935, Lillebelt Bridge...50.00
1936, Royal Guard 50.00
1937, Arrival of Christmas Guests 60.00
1938, Lighting the Candles 120.00
1939, Old Lock-Eye, The Sandman 115.00
1940, Delivering Christmas Letters..125.00
1941, Horses Enjoying Meal...190.00
1942, Danish Farm on Christmas Night 135.00
1943, Ribe Cathedral...135.00
1944, Sorgenfri Castle 70.00
1945, Old Water Mill 90.00
1946, Commemoration Cross 50.00
1947, Dybbol Mill 70.00
1948, Watchman 55.00
1949, Landsoldaten...55.00
1950, Kronborg Castle at Elsinore 85.00
1951, Jens Bang...70.00
1952, Old Copenhagen Canals & Thorsvaldsen Museum 60.00
1953, Snowman 55.00
1954, Royal Boat..65.00
1955, Kaulundorg Church 70.00
1956, Christmas in Copenhagen 90.00
1957, Christmas Candles..105.00
1958, Santa Claus 75.00
1959, Christmas Eve 95.00
1960, Village Church 125.00
1961, Winter Harmony 90.00
1962, Winter Night 50.00
1963, Christmas Elf...85.00
1964, Fir Tree & Hare 35.00
1965, Bringing Home the Tree...35.00
1966, Home for Christmas..30.00
1967, Sharing the Joy 30.00
1968, Christmas in Church 25.00
1969, Arrival of Guests...20.00
1970, Pheasants in Snow..17.00

M. I. Hummel

1972, Hear Ye, Hear Ye 50.00
1973, Glober Trotter 95.00
1974, Goose Girl...50.00
1975, Ride Into Christmas 50.00
1976, Apple Tree Girl 50.00
1977, Apple Tree Boy..60.00
1978, Happy Pastime 45.00

M.I. Hummel, Heavenly
Angel, 1971, $525.00.

1979, Singing Lesson 30.00
1980, School Girl 45.00

Royal Copenhagen

1908, Madonna & Child 2,900.00
1909, Danish Landscape................................125.00
1910, Magi 100.00
1911, Danish Landscape................................125.00
1912, Christmas Tree...................................125.00
1913, Frederik Church Spire...........................105.00
1915, Danish Landscape................................115.00
1916, Shepherd at Christmas............................80.00
1917, Our Savior Church...............................70.00
1918, Sheep & Shepherds...............................70.00
1919, In the Park 75.00
1920, Mary & Child Jesus...............................75.00
1921, Aabenraa Marketplace............................70.00
1922, 3 Singing Angels................................60.00
1923, Danish Landscape................................60.00
1924, Sailing Ship 85.00

1914 Royal Copenhagen, Holy Spirit Church, 1914, $115.00;
1925, Christianshavn, $75.00.

1926, Christianshavn Canal.............................70.00
1927, Ship's Boy at Tiller............................115.00
1928, Vicar's Family...................................70.00
1929, Grundtvig Church.................................70.00
1930, Fishing Boats....................................85.00
1931, Mother & Child...................................85.00
1932, Frederiksberg Gardens............................80.00
1933, Ferry & Great Belt..............................130.00
1934, Hermitage Castle................................105.00
1935, Kronborg Castle 160.00
1936, Roskilde Cathedral..............................140.00
1937, Main Street of Copenhagen.......................155.00

1938, Round Church of Osterlars.......................235.00
1939, Greenland Pack Ice..............................255.00
1940, Good Shepherd...................................350.00
1941, Danish Village Church...........................270.00
1942, Bell Tower 315.00
1943, Flight Into Egypt...............................410.00
1944, Danish Village Scene............................185.00
1945, Peaceful Scene..................................320.00
1946, Zealand Village Church..........................140.00
1947, Good Shepherd...................................195.00
1948, Nodebo Church...................................175.00
1949, Our Lady's Cathedral............................175.00
1950, Boeslunde Church................................160.00
1951, Christmas Angel 275.00
1952, Christmas in Forest.............................100.00
1953, Frederiksberg Castle............................100.00
1954, Amalienborg Palace..............................100.00
1955, Fano Girl 160.00
1956, Rosenborg Castle 134.00
1957, Good Shepherd....................................75.00
1958, Sunshine Over Greenland 110.00
1959, Christmas Night..................................80.00
1960, Stag..105.00
1961, Training Ship 125.00
1962, Little Mermaid..................................150.00
1963, Hojsager Mill....................................65.00
1964, Fetching the Tree................................45.00
1965, Little Skaters...................................50.00
1966, Blackbird..24.00
1967, Royal Oak..25.00
1968, Last Umiak.......................................24.00
1969, Old Farmyard.....................................25.00
1970, Christmas Rose & Cat.............................27.00

Limoges

From the mid-eighteenth century, Limoges was the center of the porcelain industry of France, where at one time more than forty companies utilized the local kaolin to make a superior quality china, much of which was exported to the United States. Various marks were used; some included the name of the American export company (rather than the manufacturer) and 'Limoges.' After 1891 'France' was added. Pieces signed by factory artists are more valuable than those decorated outside the factory by amateurs. For a more thorough study of the subject, we recommend you refer to *The Collector's Encyclopedia of Limoges Porcelain* by our advisor Mary Frank Gaston, who is listed in the Directory under Texas. Her book has beautiful color illustrations and current market values.

Butter dish, florals w/gold, sm.......................95.00
Candlestick, pastel Art Deco motif w/gold, hdl, 5", pr 95.00
Chocolate pot, floral bands, Coronet, 11", +4 c/s 325.00
Chocolate pot, floral/gilt on melon ribs, wine top/hdl, 10" 175.00
Chocolate pot, poppy panels on gr leaf ground, sgn CPG, 10".....250.00
Chocolate pot, roses ea side, melon ribs, H&Co, 9" 175.00
Figurine, 3 girls, arms joined, hold book/purse mk T&V, 25" 450.00
Jardiniere, roses & flowers, 4 Baroque ft, mk, 5x9"......................250.00
Plaque, landscape w/bldg, gold Rococo rim, sgn/unmk, 13" 200.00
Plaque, portrait of girl in feathered hat, sgn Dussou, 15"............650.00
Plaque, roses, red on gr & yel, T&V, 16" dia 450.00
Plate, floral, sgn Stafford, 9" 40.00
Plate, game birds, gold Rococo border, facing pr, 10½" 350.00
Plate, service of Wm Henry Harrison, eagle/stars/etc, 8½" 850.00

Plaques, exotic birds, gold Rococo border, 13½", $500.00 for the pair.

Platter, game birds, artist sgn, gold rim/hdls, 14" L, pr 425.00
Punch bowl, birds/grapes, wide gold band, sgn Sagar, 12½" 350.00
Punch bowl, grapes & leaves, T&V, 1880s, 16½" 450.00
Tray, dresser; roses on lt gr, artist sgn, mk, 11x7" 110.00
Tray, gold florals, scalloped rim, mk, 9½" dia 45.00
Vase, angels/roses on bl, gold hdls, sgn E Ryland, 10x9" 350.00
Vase, 2 exotic birds, 4-ftd, sgn, 6⅛" 145.00

Lithophanes

Lithophanes are porcelain panels with relief designs of varying degrees of thickness and density. Transmitted light brings out the pattern in graduated shadings — lighter where the procelain is thin and shaded in the heavy areas. They were cast from wax models prepared by artists and depict views of life from the 1800s, religious themes, or scenes of historical significance. First made in Berlin about 1803, they were used as lampshade panels, window plaques, or candle shields. Later, steins, mugs, and cups were made with lithophanes in their bases. Japanese wares were sometimes made with dragons or geisha lithophanes. See also Dragon Ware; Steins.

Candle lamp, girl & dog by mtns, mk PPM #1198, 10x8"............450.00
Fairy lamp, 3-scene mc shade w/gold trim, 4⅝" 700.00
Panel, Christ holds orb w/cross, Inri/Die incised, 6½x8"..............185.00
Panel, girl carries child & leads lamb, sgn, KPM, 4¾x6"...............150.00
Panel, Heidelberg scene, bl glass fr w/red flowers, PPM, 6x7" 450.00
Panel, man talks to lady on bridge, brass mt, French, 4x4½".........95.00
Panel, Niagara Falls, trapezoid, 5x3¼x5¼" 150.00
Tea set, Geisha girl, Kutani, 18-pc...50.00
Tea warmer, 4 mc scenic panels, ea 2¼x3", plated fr, 6" 525.00

Liverpool

In the late 1700s, Liverpool potters produced a creamy ivory ware, sometimes called Queen's Ware, which they decorated by means of the newly-perfected transfer print. Made specifically for the American market, patriotic inscriptions, political portraits, or other States themes were applied in black with colors sometimes added by hand. (Obviously their loyalty to the crown did not inhibit the progress of business!) Before it lost favor in about 1825, other English potters made a similar product. Today Liverpool is a generic term used to refer to all ware of this type.

Our advisor for this category is Richard Marden; he is listed in the Directory under New Hampshire.

Bowl, Am flag vessel, floral sprays on shoulder, 13" L, M **1,700.00**

Bowl, Sailor's Farewell/Return, Triumph of Neptune, 9", EX 300.00
Jug, Am ship/Peace Plenty.../eagle & shield, rstr, 8½" **2,650.00**
Jug, Apotheosis of WA/Am flag vessel, 8", NM...................... **3,000.00**
Jug, Comm OH Perry/Capt Jones of Macedonian, 7", NM...... **1,300.00**
Jug, East View of Liverpool lighthouse/ship, 7", VG 850.00
Jug, Independence verse/flag/US coast/US seal, 10", EX **2,950.00**
Jug, Jack in His Element/Matrimony/2 portraits, 9", EX 300.00
Jug, Masonic symbols/verse, 7¾", VG...250.00
Jug, matrimony/courtship verses, farm scene, 6½", VG 225.00
Jug, Poll & my partner Joe/British ship, 10", VG 300.00
Jug, Union of 2 Great Republics, mc, sgn Boardman, 9", EX .. **4,700.00**
Jug, Virtue & Valor/WA & chain of states, 9½", M **4,400.00**

Jug, Washington portrait surrounded by names of states, Washington standing with Liberty and viewing a map of the United States, American Eagle (titled) under 'Herculaneum Pottery' below spout, damages, 9", $1,300.00.

Mug, 3 gents/lady at table, verse below, 6", EX 300.00
Plate, Aurora of Newport John Cahoone, mc, rstr, 9¾"..............325.00
Platter, Liberty/WA tomb medallion, Herculaneum, 14½" **4,300.00**

Lladro

Lladro porcelains are currently being produced in Labernes Blanques, Spain. Their retired and limited edition figurines are popular collectibles.

Afghan, #1069, 11"..450.00
Artistic Endeavor, #5234, 11" 265.00
At Attention 215.00
Ballerina, #2075...145.00
Ballerina, seated, #68-3, 8"...135.00
Bird group, #4667, 7" 280.00
Bloodhound, #1067, 3½" 440.00
Boy w/Cape, #896, 9"..65.00
Bucephalus Bust, #2010, 10" 120.00
Bullfighter, #5115 ....130.00
Chess set 3,000.00
Chicken, #1041, 5" 65.00
Chinese Emperor & Empress, 13", pr...750.00
Columbine, plaque, wood fr, 19x25"..450.00
El Greco, w/palette, #4626, 13"..325.00
Flag Bearer 215.00
Flamenco Dancers, 19" 325.00
Flower Song 500.00
French Poodle & 4 Puppies, 5½x5½"..120.00
German Shepherd & Pup, 8x8½" 185.00
Girl Selling Vegetables, #1087, 5½" 375.00
Girl w/Deer, 9"..175.00

Girl w/Goat, #4812, 9"	375.00
Girl w/lamb	155.00
Girl w/Puppies	295.00
Goose, #4553, 6"	45.00
Gossip, #4984, 12"	200.00
Guarda Civil, #4889	150.00
Jugs for Sale, girl w/parasol sells pottery, 12"	275.00
Lady from Majorca, w/jug, #5240, 12"	135.00
Little League, Exercising	195.00
Little Pals, MIB	2,000.00
Little Traveler	950.00
Man w/Wine Bottle, #5165	150.00
Mother, child & teddy bear, #1353, 13"	200.00

Motorcyclist with sidecar, 18", MIB, $1,900.00.

My Little Pet, lady w/dog, #4994, 12"	135.00
Nuns, matt finish	165.00
Old Cellist, #4651, 12½"	950.00
Othello & Desdemona, L Ruiz, limited ed, 19x15"	850.00
Peasant Child w/Oxen, #1182, 9"	120.00
Pekinese Dog, 6x7"	65.00
Pierot, plaque, wood fr, 19x25"	450.00
Sewing a Trousseau	215.00
Soccer Player, #4809	125.00
Spanish Lady, V Marinus, limited ed, 22"	525.00
Spring Bouquets	550.00
Swan, #4829, 6"	55.00
Teasing the Dog, #5078, 10"	225.00
Toreador, #5115, 10"	100.00
Travelling Artist w/Case, 14"	135.00
Unicorn, 9"	65.00
You & Me, #4830, 10¾"	975.00
4 Dogs in Box, #1121, 8½"	750.00

Lobmeyer

J. and L. Lobmeyer, contemporaries of Moser, worked in Vienna, Austria, during the last quadrant of the 1800s. Most of the work attributed to them is decorated with distinctive enameling; favored motifs are people in eighteenth-century garb.

Bottle, scent; courting scene/florals/gilt, 4¾x2½x1½"	385.00

Bowl, couple in mc enamel, quatrefoil, 4", +underplate	950.00
Tumbler, colonial man w/cane & binoculars, faceted, sgn	385.00
Tumbler, eng cherub & 2 sheep, by Powolny, 3½"	850.00
Tumbler, lady & florals, 12-panel, sgn	385.00
Vase, gr patina w/gold & mc enameling, sgn, 1890, 8"	700.00

Locke Art

Joseph Locke already had proven himself many times over as a master glass maker, working in leading English glasshouses for more than seventeen years. He came to America and he joined the New England Glass Company. There he invented processes for the manufacture of several types of art glass — amberina, peachblow, pomona, and agata among them. In 1898 he established the Locke Art Glassware Co. in Mt. Oliver, Pittsburgh, Pennsylvania. Locke Art Glass was produced using an acid-etching process by which the most delicate designs were produced on crystal blanks. Most examples are signed simply 'Locke Art,' often placed unobtrusively near a leaf or a stem. Other items are signed 'Jo Locke,' some are dated, and some are unsigned. Most of the work was done by hand. The business continued into the 1920s.

For further study we recommend *American Art Glass* by John Shuman, available at your local bookstore. See the Locke Art Glass listing in the Directory under Pennsylvania.

Cordial, Poppy, sgn, 3"	120.00
Creamer, flowers/swirling lines/etc, ray base, sgn, 3½"	200.00
Creamer & sugar bowl, Vintage, sgn, 3½", 2⅞"	350.00
Fruit cup, Poppy, saucer ft, sgn, 3x3½"	120.00
Fruit cup, Vintage, ftd, sgn, 4½x5"	125.00
Goblet, ivy leaves, optic ribs, sgn, 6½"	110.00
Goblet, Poppy, sgn, 6", +6" underplate	265.00
Honey dish, berries/leaves, ftd, sgn, 1⅜x3"	115.00
Honey dish, chrysanthemum in center, 4 at top, sgn, ftd	100.00
Pitcher, Poinsettia, sgn, 8½"	695.00
Plate, 3 types of fruit, sgn, 6"	145.00
Sherbet, ivy leaves, saucer ft, sgn, 3x3⅝"	135.00
Tumbler, lemonade; Oriental mtn/boats, ftd/hdl, 5"	165.00
Tumbler, Poinsettia, sgn, 4⅜"	125.00
Tumbler, Poppy, optic ribs, sgn, 4½"	110.00
Tumbler, Roses, hdl, sgn, 4"	125.00
Tumbler, Vintage, vertical lines, optic ribs, sgn, 5"	125.00
Vase, allover floral, optic ribs, hdls, ray base, sgn, 6x4½"	750.00
Vase, butterflies/sheaves of wheat, sgn, ftd/ruffled, 6x5"	500.00
Whiskey glass, wheat sheaves, optic ribs, sgn, 2⅝"	125.00

Locks

The earliest type of lock in recorded history was the wooden cross bar used by ancient Egyptians and their contemporaries. The early Romans are credited with making the first key-operated mechanical lock. The ward lock was invented during the Middle Ages by the Etruscans of Northern Italy; the lever tumbler and combination locks followed at various stages of history with varying degrees of effectiveness. In the 18th century, the first precision lock was constructed. It was a device that utilized a lever-tumbler mechanism. Two of the best-known of the early 19th century American lock manufacturers are Yale and Sargent, and today's collectors value Winchester and Keen Kutter locks very highly. Factors to consider are rarity, condition, and construction. Brass and bronze locks are generally priced higher than those of steel or iron.

Our advisor for this section is Joe Tanner; he is listed in the Directory under Montana.

Key:
bbl — barrel   st — stamped

Brass Lever Tumbler

Ames Sword Co, Perfection stamped on shackle, 2¾" 50.00
Bingham's Best Brand, BBB emb on front, 3¼" 150.00
Cleveland 4 Way, Cleveland 4 Way emb on front, 3⅝" 90.00
Crusader, shield, swords emb on body, 2¾" 40.00
Eagle Lock Co, word Eagle emb on front, scrolled, 3" 60.00
Jackson's, stamped Jackson's on front, 2½" 25.00
Keen Kutter, shape of KK emblem, KK emb on front, 4¾" 115.00
Mercury, Mercury emb on body, 2¾" 25.00
Motor, Motor emb on body, 3¼" 35.00
Our Very Best, OVB emb on body, 2⅞" 150.00
Roeyonoc, Roeyonoc stamped on body, 3¼" 40.00
Romer & Co, Romer & Co stamped on dust cover, 3" 50.00
Ruby, Ruby emb in scroll on front, 2¾" 25.00
Safe, Safe emb in scroll on front, 2⅜" 20.00
Siberian, Siberian emb on shackle, 2½" 80.00
Sphinx, sphinx & pharaoh head emb on front, 2¾" 35.00
W Bohannan & Co, SW emb in scroll on front, 2⅜" 30.00
Winchester, Winchester emb on front, 3" 160.00

Combinations

Chicago Combination Lock Co, stamped on front, brass, 2¾" 80.00
Corbin Sesamee 4-Dial Brass Lock, stamped Sesamee, 2¾" 12.00
Edwards Mfg Co No-Key, stamped on lock, brass, 2¾" 60.00
Junkunc Bros Mfrs, all stamped on bk, brass, 1⅞" 25.00
Karco stamped on body, 2½" 50.00
Number or letter disk type (4 disks), brass, 2¾" 120.00
Sq lock case of steel, stamped Pat Germany, 4-wheel, 3¼" 110.00
Sutton Lock Co stamped on body, 3" 200.00
Your Own stamped on body, 3⅞" 325.00

Eight-Lever Type

Armory, brass, Armory 8-Lever stamped on front 20.00
Electric, steel, Electric stamped on front 20.00
Goliath, steel, Goliath 8-Lever stamped on front 20.00
Miller, steel, Miller 8-Lever stamped on front 15.00
Samson, brass, 8-Lever stamped on front 18.00

Iron Lever Tumbler

Bull, word Bull emb on front, 2⅝" 20.00
Bulldog, word Bulldog & face of dog emb on front, 2¾" 15.00
Dan Patch, Dan Patch emb on front, horseshoe on bk, 2¾" 130.00
Dragon, word Dragon & dragon emb on front, 2⅞" 25.00
Eagle, word Eagle emb on body, 4⅜" 40.00
Indian Head, Indian head emb on front, 3" 80.00
Jupiter, word Jupiter/star & moon emb on front, 3¼" 18.00
Karo, word Karo emb on front, CI, 3⅛" 25.00
King Korn, words King Korn emb on body, 2⅞" 20.00
Nineteen O Three, 1903 emb on front, iron, 3⅞" 90.00
Red Chief, words Red Chief emb on body, 3¾" 60.00
Rugby, football emb on body, 3" 20.00
Unique, word Unique emb on front, 3¼" 80.00
Yale & Towne, lion face emb on front, shackle mk Y&T, 3" ...100.00

Lever Push Key

Champion, emb Champion 6-Lever, brass push-key type, 2¼" 25.00

Climax, emb Climax 6-Lever, iron push-key type, 2¼" 35.00
Columbia, emb Columbia 6-Lever, brass push-key type, 2¼" 35.00
Dash, emb Dash 6-Lever, iron push-key type, 2¼" 25.00
Excelsior, emb Excelsior 6-Lever, brass push-key type, 2¼" 25.00
Harvard, emb Harvard 4-Lever, brass push-key type, 2" 60.00
IXL, emb IXL on body, 2¼" 50.00
Keystone, emb Keystone 6-Lever, brass push-key type, 2¼" 40.00
McIntosh, emb McIntosh on body, 2¼" 90.00
SB Co, emb SB Co on body, 3¼" 40.00
Smith & Egge Mfg Co, Smith & Egge stamped on front, 3" 75.00
Ten Star, emb Ten Star 6-Lever, 2¼" 45.00

Logo-Special Made

Brass pancake push key emb US Internal Revenue, 2¼" 185.00
Heart-shape brass lever type emb Shults Co, bbl key, 2¾" 45.00
Heart-shape brass lever type st Board Education, bbl key, 3½" 50.00
Sq brass pin-tumbler case st Regd US Mail, int counter, 2¾" 120.00
Sq Yale-type brass pin tumbler, emb w/Texaco & star, 3" 25.00
Sq Yale-type brass pin tumbler, st Shell Oil Co on body, 3⅛" 15.00
Sq Yale-type brass pin tumbler, st US/A/tree/Forest Svc, 2⅞" 125.00

Pin-Tumbler Type

Corbin, brass, Corbin in oval stamped on body, 3⅝" 30.00
Eagle, brass, Eagle stamped on body, 2⅞" 20.00
Fulton, emb Fulton on body, 2⅝" 30.00
Hope, brass, emb Hope on body, 2½" 18.00

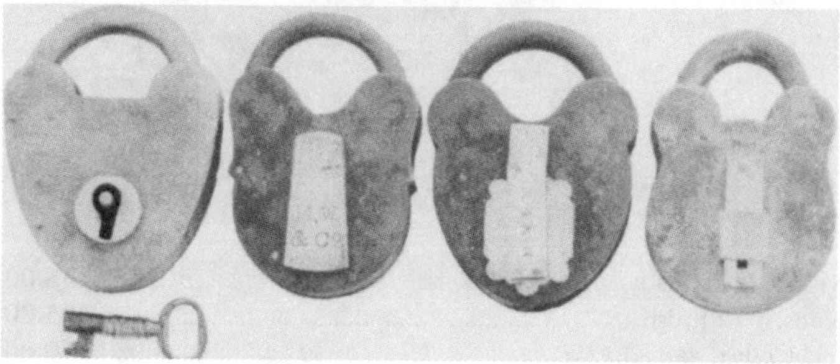

Wrought iron ward locks, center examples marked M.W. & Co., $25.00 each.

Il-A-Noy, emb Il-A-Noy on body, 2½" 40.00
Pearl, brass, emb Pearl on body, 2⅛" 16.00
Sargent, brass, emb Sargent on body, 3" 15.00
Segal, iron, emb Segal on shackle, 3¾" 40.00
Shapleigh, emb Shapleigh on body, 2⅝" 35.00
Yale, brass, emb Yale on body, Made in England on shackle, 3" ...50.00
Yale, brass, emb Yale on body, Yale & Towne on shackle, 2⅝" 25.00

Scandinavian (Jail House) Type

JHW Climax Co, iron, 2⅞" 50.00
Star, emb line on bottom, iron, 3¾" 80.00
Star, iron, 2½" 70.00
99 Miller, emb 99, brass, 1¾" 80.00
999 Miller, emb 999, brass, 2½" 70.00

Six-Lever Type

Eagle, brass, Eagle Six Lever stamped on body 15.00
Edwards, iron, Edwards stamped on body 15.00
Safe, brass, Safe stamped on body 18.00

Yale, brass, Yale emb on front 12.00

Story and Commemorative

AYPEX Seattle (Alaska Yukon Pacific Expo), emb tin/iron, 3" ..200.00
Canteen, US emb on lock, lock: canteen shape, 2"......................500.00
CI, emb ornate scroll motif throughout body of lock, 3½" 170.00
CI, emb skull/X-bones w/florals, NH Co on bk, 3¼" 250.00
CQD/sinking ship Titanic & SOS waves emb on brass, 2¾" 120.00
Eagle/stars/shield & stars, emb CI, Eagle Liberty, 2½" 300.00
Mail Pouch, emb on lock, lock in shape of a mail pouch, 3⅛".....200.00
1901 Pan Am Expo, brass, emb w/buffalo, 2⅝"............................150.00

Warded Type

Army, iron pancake ward key, emb letters, 2½"............................30.00
Globe, iron sq lock case, emb US on bk, 2⅜" 20.00
Hex, iron, sq lock case, emb US on bk, 2⅛" 95.00
Navy, iron pancake ward key, bk: scrolled emb letters, 2½" 25.00
Red Cross, brass sq case, emb letters, 2" 10.00
Rex, steel case, emb letters, 2⅝".....................................18.00
Safe, brass sq case, emb letters, 1⅞".................................. 8.00
Safety First, brass pancake type, emb letters, 2¾" 15.00
Secure, iron pancake type, emb letters, 2⅝"...........................20.00
Sprocket, brass oval shape, emb letters, 2⅛".........................55.00
Try Me, iron pancake type, emb letters, 2½"...........................25.00
Winchester, brass sq case, stamped letters, 2¾"......................110.00

Wrought Iron Lever Type (Smokehouse Type)

DM&Co, bbl key, 4¼"..15.00
MW&Co, bbl key, 2⅝"...10.00
MW&Co, flat key, 3½" 20.00
S&Co, bbl key, 3" 8.00

Loetz

The Loetz Glassworks was established in Klostermule, Austria, in 1840. After Loetz's death the firm was purchased by his grandson, Johann Loetz Witwe. Until WWII the operation continued to produce fine artware, some of which made in the early 1900s bears a striking resemblance to Tiffany's, with whom Loetz was associated at one time. In addition to the iridescent Tiffany-style glass, he also produced threaded glass and some cameo.

Our advisor for this category is Don Williams; he is listed in the Directory under Missouri.

Key:
att — attributed   o/l — overlay

Bottle, scent; bl oil spots, brass pineapple finial, 6½" 895.00
Bowl, gold w/gr irid swirls, pinched rim, att, 7" 400.00
Bowl, lime w/oil spots, pinched sides, shaped rim, deep, 6"..........650.00
Bowl vase, pk irid, 6 clear loop hdls, 3x6" 2,200.00
Bowl vase, silver/emerald layered w/crystal, opal int, 4x6" 1,700.00
Candlestick, cobalt w/oil spots, drip pan, 15½", pr 1,900.00
Compote, fuchsia w/gold-gr base, scalloped, metal ft, 9x7" 265.00
Compote, silver base w/glass scarabs, ruffled, 10" 600.00
Cornucopia, gr irid, flower ped ft, SP base, 10x8" 325.00
Sea shell, opal w/threading on gr coral branch base, 4x7" 250.00
Urn, red w/mold-blown Nouveau thistles, bronze mt, 11" 525.00
Vase, amber irid, rim & 3 rim-to-width hdls in cobalt, 6¾" ... 3,000.00
Vase, amber w/gold & gr feathers, sgn, 4¼" 1,000.00

Vase, amber w/gold feathers, cylindrical w/irreg flare, 10" 3,300.00
Vase, amber w/gold-spotted butterfly wings, shouldered, 5½" 325.00
Vase, amber w/oil spots & trailings, crimped rim, 8x8" 1,100.00
Vase, amber w/strings of bl irid, ogee sides, 4½" 550.00
Vase, amber w/zigzag threading, trumpet form, ruffled, 29"..........700.00
Vase, amethyst/gr/silver between clear layers, cylinder, 8" 1,900.00
Vase, bl striations/oil spots, rim forms 3 long hdls, 12" 2,700.00
Vase, bl-gr irid, bulbous w/lobed flaring rim, att, 5" 300.00
Vase, cameo dogwood, red on wht frost, dbl gourd, 11½" 1,100.00
Vase, clear w/striations & oil spots, ruffled rim, 11" 700.00
Vase, cobalt w/gold & irid undulations, slim, 8" 850.00
Vase, cobalt w/irid zigzags, 3 trailing prunts, 8" 5,500.00
Vase, gold, dimpled bulbous body w/trefoil rim, att, 5½" 600.00
Vase, gold w/oil spots & irid leaves, baluster, 7" 3,800.00
Vase, gold w/pulled 'waves,' high shoulder, flaring rim, 11" 1,200.00
Vase, gold w/red pulled 'swirls,' pinched sides, att, 8½"...............850.00
Vase, gold w/silver florals, dbl-gourd form, 9½" 1,400.00
Vase, gr irid frost, 5-pinch top, bulbous shoulder, 5x6" 175.00
Vase, gr irid w/purple network threading, pinched top, 10½" 365.00

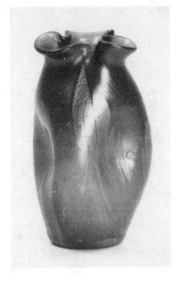

Vase, iridescent green, pink, and blue on gold, 4", $1,250.00.

Vase, gr w/striated irid, slim ftd cylinder, 8" 400.00
Vase, jack-in-the-pulpit; amethyst w/threads, 13" 485.00
Vase, lime w/lg spots, 4 lg pulled loop hdls, 10" 6,500.00
Vase, mustard w/feathers & irid dots, 4"................................... 2,200.00
Vase, silver o/l carnations on irid, bulbous, 2¾" 800.00
Vase, silver o/l female faces, silver-bl spots on gr, 4½" 600.00
Vase, silver o/l iris & curvilinears on yel w/bl waves, 7" 2,500.00
Vase, silver o/l lily pad on gold w/bl waves, twisted, 7" 2,300.00
Vase, silver o/l vines on gold irid w/spots, twisted, 9½" 1,100.00
Vase, turq irid w/oil spots, pinched oviform, 6" 950.00
Vase, violet w/gold feathers, sq w/sqd & folded rim, 6½" 600.00
Vase, wht w/lg mc tulips & dogs, chalice form, 8" 2,750.00

Lomonosov Porcelain

Founded in 1744, the Lomonosov porcelain factory produced exquisite porcelain miniatures for the Czar and other Russian nobility. One of the first factories of its kind, Lomonosov pieces consisted largely of vases and delicate sculptures. In the 1800s Lomonosov became closely involved with the Russian Academy of Fine Arts, a connection which has continued to this day, as the company continues to supply the world with these fine artistic treasures.

Figurine, bear, standing...14.00

Figurine, camel (young offspring) 24.50
Figurine, cat 36.50
Figurine, collie 22.50
Figurine, doe 90.00
Figurine, fawn, mini 10.00
Figurine, foal, brn..28.00
Figurine, gazelle 9.00
Figurine, leopard cub 15.00
Figurine, mongrel dog, mini.................................... 3.00
Figurine, moose 98.00
Figurine, panda, sm...14.00
Figurine, raccoon 11.50
Figurine, Rock Partridge #1 ....10.00
Figurine, seal 17.50
Figurine, snowbird...12.00
Figurine, snowbird chick, mini 6.00
Figurine, terrier 22.50
Figurine, tiger cub 27.50
Figurine, tiger cub, mini 12.50
Figurine, wild boar (young offspring) 12.00
Figurine, Yakut woman w/fish 62.00

Longwy

The Longwy workshops were founded in 1798 and continue today to produce pottery in the north of France near the Luxembourg-Belgian border. The ware for which they are best known was produced during the Art Deco period, decorated in bold colors and designs. Earlier wares made during the first quarter of the nineteenth century reflected the popularity of Oriental art, cloisonne enamels in particular. The designs were executed by impressing the pattern into the moist clay and filling in the depressions with enamels. Examples are marked 'Longwy,' either impressed or painted under glaze.

Bowl, cobalt w/mc floral medallion, mk, 11" 240.00
Candlestick, florals, brass mts, 8½", pr..110.00
Candlestick, mc florals on bl, brass std, prisms, 9¾", pr................185.00
Charger, fawn in abstract landscape, Primavera, 1925, 14" 1,400.00

Charger, jungle scene with two elephants, one ridden by a nude, designed by Catteau, 15", $2,500.00.

Tile, bird on floral branch on bl, 6x6" in pewter fr.......................125.00

Vase, allover tropical landscape, mc/gilt, spherical, 15" 10,000.00
Vase, incised mask ea side, gr on cream, Primavera, 11½" 495.00

Lonhuda

William Long was a druggist by trade who combined his knowledge of chemistry with his artistic ability in an attempt to produce a type of brown-glazed slip-decorated artware similar to that made by the Rookwood Pottery. He achieved his goal in 1889 after years of long and dedicated study. Three years later he founded his firm, the Lonhuda Pottery Company. The name was coined from the first few letters of the last name of each of his partners, W.H. Hunter and Alfred Day. Laura Fry, formerly of the Rookwood company, joined the firm in 1892, bringing with her a license for Long to use her patented airbrush-blending process. Other artists of note, Sarah McLaughlin, Helen Harper, and Jessie Spaulding, joined the firm and decorated the ware with nature studies, animals, and portraits, often signing their work with their initials. Three types of marks were used on the Steubenville Lonhuda ware. The first was a linear composite of the letters 'LPCO' with the name 'Lonhuda' impressed above it. The second, adopted in 1893, was a die-stamp representing the solid profile of an Indian, used on ware patterned after pottery made by the American Indians. This mark was later replaced with an impressed outline of the Indian head with 'Lonhuda' arching above it. Although the ware was successful, the business floundered due to poor management. In 1895 Long became a partner of Sam Weller and moved to Zanesville where the manufacture of the Lonhuda line continued. Less than a year later, Long left the Weller company. He was associated with J.B. Owens until 1899, at which time he moved to Denver, Colorado, where he established the Denver China and Pottery Company in 1901. His efforts to produce Lonhuda utilizing local clay were highly successful. Examples of the Denver Lonhuda are sometimes marked with the LF (Lonhuda Faience) cipher contained within a canted diamond form.

Bowl, floral, 3-ftd, sgn Jessie Spaulding, mk/1899, 7" 250.00
Ewer, branches/berries, sgn AH, #315, 3½" 165.00
Jug, bull portrait, EX art, #806, 5" 500.00
Planter, floral, half-moon w/loop hdls ea end, ftd, 10" L 325.00
Vase, floral, cylinder neck, sgn Wm Long, 11" 425.00
Vase, floral, gr to creamy yel, integral hdls, 3¼x5" 200.00
Vase, gr leaves, bulbous w/long neck, sgn STR, 8¾" 170.00
Vase, herd of steers, pillow form, shield mk, 12" 4,000.00
Vase, lg fish/waves, integral hdls, 5x8½".......................................525.00
Vase, thistles/leaves, bk: flower, mk Denver-Lonhuda, 7½".........230.00

Lotton

Charles Lotton is a contemporary glass artist, living and working in Lansing, Illinois. Examples of his glass are much in demand and are on display in many major museums and other collections of distinction, among them the Smithsonian, The Art Institute of Chicago, The Corning Museum of Glass, and the Chrysler Museum.

For further information concerning this subject, we recommend the recently released *Lotton Art Glass,* co-authored by Charles Lotton and Tom O'Conner; see the Directory under Illinois.

Bottle, scent; crystal 500.00
Bottle, scent; gold ruby, multi-flora, any sz 700.00
Bottle, scent; multi-flora, any sz..600.00
Bottle, scent; sunset 500.00
Bowl, leaf & vine, cased, 10-12", ea, up to 800.00
Bowl, leaf & vine, cased, 6"..450.00

Paperweight, floral	150.00
Paperweight, floral, cased, David Lotton, lg	300.00
Paperweight, King Tut	75.00
Paperweight, web design, David Lotton	75.00
Persian water sprinkler (swan-neck vase), old or new	600.00
Vase, dbl multi-flora, cased, 6-7", ea	2,800.00
Vase, dbl multi-flora, cased, 8x12", ea, up to	3,600.00
Vase, floral, cased, 8-12", ea, up to	2,000.00
Vase, floral, 6-7", ea	900.00
Vase, floral, 6-7", ea	500.00
Vase, floral, 8-12", ea, up to	700.00
Vase, leaf & vine, 4"	200.00
Vase, leaf & vine, 8"	250.00
Vase, web design, 4"	200.00
Vase, web design, 8"	350.00

Lotus Ware

Isaac Knowles and Issac Harvey operated a pottery in East Liverpool, Ohio, in 1853 where they produced both yellowware and Rockingham. In 1870 Knowles brought Harvey's interests and took as partners John Taylor and Homer Knowles. Their principal product was ironstone china, but Knowles was confident that American potters could produce as fine a ware as the Europeans. To prove his point, he hired Joshua Poole, an artist from the Belleek Works in Ireland. Poole quickly perfected a Belleek-type china, but fire destroyed this portion of the company. Before it could function again, their hotel china business had grown to the point that it required their full attention in order to meet market demands. By 1891 they were able to try again. They developed a bone china, as fine and thin as before, which they called Lotus. Henry Schmidt from the Meissen factory in Germany decorated the ware, often with lacy filigree applications or hand-formed leaves and flowers to which he added further decoration with liquid slip applied by means of a squeeze bag. Due to high production costs resulting from so much of the fragile ware being damaged in firing and because of changes in tastes and styles of decoration, the Lotus Ware line was dropped in 1896. Some of the early ware was marked 'KT&K China'; later marks have a star and a crescent with 'Lotus Ware' added. For further study, we recommend *American Belleek* by our advisor, Mary Frank Gaston. She is listed in the Directory under Texas.

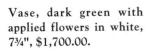

Vase, dark green with applied flowers in white, 7¾", $1,700.00.

Bowl, molded prunus flowers, beaded top, 4½"	300.00
Bowl, openwork on ends, oval, 4¼x6x4¾"	655.00
Bowl, rtcl gadrooned scrolls, beaded, ruffled, 4½" H	300.00
Creamer, fishnet, 3"	250.00

Dish, allover gold enameling & monogram, shell form, 5"	125.00
Ewer, HP leafy sprigs w/gold, 9½"	350.00
Ewer, HP/emb leafy scrolls, bulbous, 6"	300.00
Ewer, pk florals, gold-speckled twig hdl, 6½"	350.00
Pitcher, HP flowers & fishnet w/gold trim, 3½"	395.00
Pitcher, wild roses, dk gr spout, gold bamboo hdl, squat	170.00
Relish tray, textured leaf body, twig ft, 6½"	60.00
Teapot, fishnet/flowers/gilt, 4", +4" sugar/3" creamer	550.00
Vase, appl chains, ruffled bowl form, 7½"	1,000.00
Vase, jewel medallions & swags, ruffled rim, 10¼"	5,200.00
Vase, mc ferns w/gold filigree, rtcl rim, 4½x5½"	595.00
Vase, Psyche HP in oval, baluster, hdls, 14½"	2,400.00

Lu Ray Pastels

Lu Ray Pastels dinnerware was introduced in the early 1940s by Taylor, Smith, and Taylor of East Liverpool, Ohio. It was offered in assorted colors — Persian Cream, Sharon Pink, Surf Green, Windsor Blue, and Gray — in complete place settings as well as many service pieces. It was a successful line in its day and is once again finding favor with collectors of American dinnerware.

Bowl, berry; sm	6.00
Bowl, cream soup	24.00
Bowl, fruit; 5½"	4.50
Bowl, mixing; lg	45.00
Bowl, salad; lg	30.00
Bowl, soup; 9"	8.50
Bowl, tab hdl, 6"	10.00
Bowl, vegetable; oval	10.00
Bowl, vegetable; 9"	8.50
Butter dish, w/lid, ¼-lb	22.50
Casserole, w/lid	55.00
Coffeepot, demitasse; ovoid, w/lid	50.00
Coffeepot, demitasse; str sides, w/lid	85.00
Creamer	5.00
Creamer, demitasse; str sides	40.00
Cup & saucer	7.50
Cup & saucer, demitasse	16.00
Egg cup	12.00
Egg cup, Chatham Gray, rare color	15.00
Epergne	50.00
Muffin cover, w/8" underplate	65.00
Nut dish	22.50
Pitcher, bulbous w/flat bottom	35.00
Pitcher, ftd	40.00
Pitcher, juice; ovoid	75.00
Pitcher, syrup	40.00
Plate, cake	25.00
Plate, Chatham Gray, rare color, 7"	6.00
Plate, chop; 14"	16.00
Plate, grill	12.50
Plate, serving; tab hdl	25.00
Plate, very rare, 8"	15.00
Plate, 10"	10.00
Plate, 6"	2.00
Plate, 7"	3.00
Plate, 9"	5.00
Platter, #1040, 9½"	6.00
Platter, oval, 11½"	8.00
Platter, oval, 12"	9.00
Platter, oval, 13"	10.00
Sauce boat, fast-stand	15.00

Sauce pitcher 15.00
Saucer, cream soup...12.50
Shakers, pr.. 8.50

Demitasse creamer and sugar bowl, $40.00.

Sugar bowl, w/lid 9.00
Sugar bowl, w/lid, demitasse; str sides......................40.00
Teapot, w/lid, curved spout 35.00
Teapot, w/lid, flat-top spout 45.00
Tidbit, 2-tier 18.00
Tray, pickle 12.00
Tumbler, juice...12.00
Tumbler, water..37.50

Lunch Boxes

Early twentieth-century tobacco companies such as Union Leader, Tiger, and Dixie sold their products in square, steel containers with flat, metal carrying handles. These were specifically engineered to be used as lunch boxes when they became empty. (See Advertising, specific companies.) By 1930 oval lunch pails with colorful lithographed decorations on tin were being manufactured to appeal directly to children. These were made by Ohio Art, Decoware, and a few other companies. In 1950 Aladdin Industries produced the first 'real' character lunch box — a Hopalong Cassidy decal-decorated steel container now considered the beginning of the kids' lunch box industry. The other big lunch box manufacturer, American Thermos (later King Seely Thermos Company) brought out its 'blockbuster' Roy Rogers box in 1953, the first fully-lithographed steel lunch box and matching bottle.

Other companies — ADCO Liberty; Landers, Frary & Clark; Ardee Industries; Okay Industries; Universal; Tindco; Cheinco — also produced character pails. With the publication of the book *Official Price Guide to Lunch Box Collectibles* by Scott Bruce in 1988, the hobby has skyrocketed. Today's collectors often tend to specialize in those boxes dealing with a particular subject. Western, space, TV series, Disney movies, and cartoon characters are the most popular. There are well over five hundred different lunch boxes available to the astute collector.

Our advisor for this category is Alan Smith; he is listed in the Directory under Texas.

A Team, w/thermos, M..50.00
Adam Ant, EX..115.00
Batman, VG...90.00
Bedknobs & Broomsticks, Walt Disney, 1972, EX 32.00
Bionic Woman, stepping out of car, c Universal, M 27.50
Buccaneer, dome top, 1957, NM 235.00
Campbell Soup, w/plastic thermos, Aladdin, NM 50.00

Central Station, dome-top fire station, 1955, VG 50.00
Circus Wagon, dome top, EX.................................165.00
Dr Seuss, VG...75.00
Evel Knievel, w/thermos, 1974, EX..........................35.00
Fall Guy, w/thermos, 1981, NM 20.00
Hector Heathcote, NM..120.00
Hee Haw, EX..55.00

Hogan's Heroes, no thermos, $140.00.

Howdy Doody, NM 450.00
Jet Patrol, NM 230.00
Jetsons, NM 1,200.00
Knight Rider, VG 15.00
Laugh In, riding tricycle, EX 78.00
Peanuts, vinyl, w/thermos, 1977, NM......................68.00
Smokey the Bear, NM..135.00
Snoopy's Doghouse, dome top, 1969-72, VG............40.00
Space Explorer Ed McCauley, Aladdin, 1960, EX 325.00
Superman, 1954, EX..175.00
Trigger, VG...65.00
US Mail, dome top, w/thermos, EX..........................60.00
Wagon Train..85.00

Lutz

From 1869 to 1888, Nicholas Lutz worked for the Boston and Sandwich Glass Company where he produced the threaded and striped art glass that was popular during that era. His works were not marked; and, since many other glassmakers of the day made similar wares, the term Lutz has come to refer not only to his original works but to any of this type.

Bowl, clear w/wht threads, yel/gold stripes, rolled rim, 5" 75.00
Cup & saucer, bl/opal latticinio swirls 75.00
Finger bowl, caramel/wht latticinio swirl, +6¾" plate..................100.00
Lamp, wht threads on clear pear font, bl opaque ft, 10", NM 700.00
Tumbler, lemonade; etched/clear, pk-threaded bottom half........100.00
Vase, pk/wht spiral latticinio, scalloped rim, 13"..........................875.00
Wine, bl/wht opaque/clear swirl, att 120.00

Maastricht

Maastricht, Holland, was the site of the De Sphinx Pottery,

founded in 1836 by Petrus Regout. They made earthenware decorated with transfer prints as well as dinnerware with gaudy hand-painted designs. Potteries are still working in this area today.

Bowl, Oriental scene, 8" **40.00**
Bowl, stick spatter, gaudy floral, 8" **40.00**
Bowl, waste; mc marbleized decor, 3½x5" **38.00**
Pitcher, milk; Canton, mc Oriental motif........................**55.00**
Plate, Abbey, 8" **25.00**
Plate, Abe Lincoln, Petrus Regout, 9" **35.00**
Plate, parakeets, bl transfer, Petrus Regout, 8" **35.00**
Plate, stick spatter, gaudy floral, mk, 9" **32.50**
Plate, stick spatter, gaudy floral, 11" **60.00**
Plate, stick spatter, gaudy floral, 7½" **20.00**
Tea bowl & saucer, Tea Drinkers, soft paste, mk, M **70.00**

Maddux of California

One of the California-made ceramics now so popular with collectors, Maddux was founded in the late 1930s and during the years that followed produced novelty items, TV lamps, figurines, planters, and tableware accessories.

Cockatiel, on branch w/appl flower, 11" **25.00**
Deer & doe, stylized, elongated, 12", pr **35.00**
Flamingo, #400 & #401, pr **35.00**
Geese, stylized, very long necks, #968, pr......................**25.00**
Planter, flamingo, pk, #515, 10½" **25.00**
Rooster, elongated, #932, tall **25.00**
Siamese cat, Art Deco, blk, 12¼" H, facing pr...............**40.00**
TV lamp, flying mallard, #839, 11½" **35.00**
TV lamp, Malibu shell, Pearltone, 10" **25.00**
TV lamp, mare & colt, Porcelain Wht, 11" **35.00**
Vase, horse's head top, str-sided body, aqua, #225, 12" ...**18.00**

Magazines

Magazines are collected for their cover prints and for the information pertaining to defunct companies and their products that can be gleaned from the old advertisements. In the listings that follow, items are assumed to be in very good condition unless noted otherwise. See also Movie Memorabilia; Parrish, Maxfield.

Key:
M — mint condition, in original wrapper
EX — excellent condition, spine intact, edges of pages
    clean and straight
VG — very good condition, the average as-found condition

Boxing Annual, 1953, Marciano cover, EX **30.00**
Collier's, 1902, Apr 26, baseball cover, VG....................**10.00**
Collier's, 1906, June 30, JW Smith mother & child cover, VG **15.00**
Collier's, 1928, May 12, VG.. **2.50**
Cosmopolitan, 1893, World's Fair features, EX **35.00**
Cosmopolitan, 1956, Special Movie Issue, EX................**25.00**
Country Life, 1930, Mar, loose cover, G......................... **2.50**
Fortune, 1930, Oct, movie studios article, VG **20.00**
Gentleman's, 1761, Pembroke shipwreck, London, VG ...**10.00**
Harper's Bazaar, 1868, Mar 21, Opening Day in NY, VG ...**25.00**
Harper's Weekly, 1864, Oct 22, battle scenes, VG.........**12.00**
Ladies' Home Journal, 1893, May, Gibson Girl cover, EX ...**22.00**
Ladies' Home Journal, 1902, July, ladies' tennis cover, EX...**12.00**

Ladies' Home Journal, 1902, Sept, EX **15.00**
Ladies' Home Journal, 1930, June, Parrish Water Skier cover ...**40.00**
Life, 1939, Nov 27, Toscanini cover, EX **7.50**
Life, 1939, Sept 11, Mussolini cover, EX **10.00**
Life, 1940, Apr 15, Camp Roosevelt girl........................ **6.00**
Life, 1940, Jan 1, Great Britain's Queen, EX **8.00**
Life, 1940, June 3, Statue of Liberty, EX **10.00**
Life, 1941, Feb 10, new British Ambassador cover **6.00**
Life, 1947, July 14, Elizabeth Taylor cover, EX **7.50**
Life, 1953, Dec 28, Wizard of Oz article, EX.................**12.00**
Life, 1954, May 3, postage stamp pictorial essay, EX **10.00**
Life, 1962, Marilyn Monroe cover, EX............................**36.00**
Life, 1965, Nov 5, Kennedy memorial edition **10.00**
Literary Digest, 1909, Mar 6, Mucha cover, EX **45.00**
Literary Digest, 1910, July, Mucha cover, VG.................**25.00**
Literary Digest, 1918, WWI cover, EX............................ **5.00**
Look, 1950, Aug 29, Hopalong Cassidy cover **8.50**
McCall's, 1926, Apr, paper dolls, EX..............................**30.00**
Newsweek, 1956, June 25, Mickey Mantle cover, VG.......... **6.00**
Newsweek, 1957, July 1, Stan Musial cover, EX **7.50**
Playboy, 1955, Sept, Marilyn Monroe on pk elephant, EX ...**25.00**
Playboy, 1957, Feb, Jayne Mansfield, EX **35.00**
Playboy, 1957, May, Lil Abner's Gals **25.00**
Sport, 1952, June, Kiner cover, EX **8.00**
Sport, 1955, Mar, Marciano cover, EX **8.00**
Sport, 1956, June, Mays cover, EX **8.00**
Sports Illustrated, 1943, Aug 16, 1st issue, EX...............**175.00**
Sports Illustrated, 1955, Aug 1, Ted Williams cover, EX **20.00**
Sports Illustrated, 1973, golf-related cover, EX...............**12.50**
Sports Stars, 1952, Nov, Mantle & Campanella, EX........**25.00**
Time, 1938, Adolf Hitler Man of the Year cover, EX........**60.00**
Time, 1938, Bette Davis (Jezebel) cover, NM **30.00**
Time, 1938, Einstein cover, EX.......................................**25.00**
Time, 1938, Frank Lloyd Wright cover, EX......................**22.00**
Time, 1938, Picasso cover, EX..**30.00**
Time, 1939, Vivien Leigh as Scarlet O'Hara cover, EX **35.00**
Time, 1940, Hermann Goring cover, EX..........................**35.00**
Time, 1940, Stokowski cover, Fantasia feature, EX **30.00**
Time, 1941, Champion Joe Louis cover, EX....................**15.00**
Time, 1941, Dec, MacArthur cover, EX...........................**32.00**
Time, 1942, Hayworth cover by Petty, EX.......................**30.00**
Time, 1948, Jo DiMaggio cover, EX **50.00**
Time, 1950, Apr 10, Ted Williams cover, Coke ad bk, EX **8.50**
Time, 1953, June 15, Mickey Mantle cover, EX **7.50**
Time, 1954, July 26, Willie Mays cover, EX **7.50**
Time, 1955, Aug 8, Roy Campanella cover, EX **7.50**
True Story, 1951, Nov, Marilyn Monroe, EX **18.00**
TV Guide, 1954, Mar, Jackie Gleason, EX **15.00**
TV Guide, 1954, Nov, Geo Burns & Gracy Allen cover, EX **18.00**
TV Guide, 1955, Nov, Richard Boone cover, EX..............**10.00**
TV Guide, 1956, Jan, Loretta Young cover, EX................**18.00**
Who's Who in Sports, 1952, M..**30.00**
Woman's Home Companion, 1911, Sept, fashions, EX.............**20.00**
Woman's Home Companion, 1912, Feb, Kewpies, valentines, EX...**25.00**
Woman's Home Companion, 1921, May, VG **3.50**

Majolica

Majolica is a type of heavy earthenware, design-molded and decorated in vivid colors with either a lead or tin type of glaze. It reached its height of popularity in the Victorian era; examples from this period are found in only the lead glazes. Nearly every potter of note, both here and abroad, produced large majolica jardinieres, umbrella stands, pitchers with animal themes, leaf shapes, vegetable forms, and nearly any other design from nature that came to mind. Few, however, marked their ware. Among those who did were Minton, Wedgwood, and George Jones in England; Griffin, Smith and Hill (Etruscan) in Phoenixville, Pennsylvania; and Chesapeake Pottery (Avalon and Clifton) in Baltimore.

Our advisor for this category is Hardy Hudson; he is listed in the Directory under Florida.

Bowl, Basketweave & Grape Leaf on dk bl, Wedgwood, 12" L 325.00
Bowl, flower; lilies mold, boat shape, English, 5½x10" 225.00
Bowl, holly/mistletoe, bird on rim, English mk, 4x8" 600.00
Bowl, lattice band, lg ribbon/floral garland, Wedgwood, 12" 600.00
Bowl, leaf w/florals, twig legs/hdls, registry mk, 3x10" L 400.00
Bowl, Luggage Strap, Cabbage Leaf & Floral, 12" L 385.00
Bowl, open shell on shell-shaped ft, Holdcroft, 9" 195.00
Bowl, Pond Lily, ftd, Holdcroft, 8" 195.00
Bowl, Shell & Seaweed, 8-shell rim, Etruscan, 5" 195.00
Butter dish, Classical Urn, floral panels, Wedgwood, 8" L 550.00
Butter dish, Oriental, floral sprigs, Wedgwood, 9" L 400.00
Butter dish, poppy band, acorn/oak leaf lid................................400.00
Butter dish, Shell & Seaweed, Etruscan................................550.00
Butter pat, overlapping leaves 60.00
Butter pat, Shell & Seaweed, Etruscan 110.00
Cheese keeper, blkberries on bark, cobalt, Holdcroft..............2,100.00
Cheese keeper, Dogwood, G Jones 1,800.00
Cheese keeper, Oak Leaf, twig hdl, Wedgwood, 8x11½" dia... 1,400.00
Cheese keeper, Pond Lily, bud finial, Holdcroft, 9" H 1,000.00
Cheese keeper, Rose & Picket Fence, G Jones, 7x10" 1,800.00
Cheese keeper, strawberry blossoms on fence, Geo Jones........ 2,000.00
Cigarette urn, brn bear, basket on bk, pail between legs.......... 1,300.00
Compote, fruit; florals on bl, short ped, Zells, 3½x9" 150.00
Compote, lily pad upheld by putto riding dolphin, 12x12" 750.00
Compote, lily pads upheld by bullrushes, 3 cranes, 9x10" 400.00
Compote, Morning-Glory, mc on wht, Etruscan, 8" dia.............400.00
Compote, overlapping begonia leaves, Etruscan, tall 275.00
Compote, shell supported by 3 dolphins, 4x9" 425.00
Compote, 2 cherubs uphold bowl, vintage base, G Jones, 6" L 500.00
Creamer, Blkberry, yel hdl/rim, English, 3½" 75.00
Creamer, Butterfly & Bamboo, bamboo hdl, bulbous, 3" 100.00
Creamer, ear of corn figural, 4½" 85.00
Creamer & sugar bowl, cottage figural, rose finial, 4", 3" 200.00
Cup & saucer, Cottage, earth tones, unmk 60.00
Cup & saucer, Dogwood, picket fence frieze, G Jones.................195.00
Cup & saucer, Pineapple, lav int, 5½" 175.00
Dessert dish, Bow & Floral, daisy/wheat, 6", set of 6 ....360.00
Dessert set, Fan & Dragonfly, fan form, 1 lg+6 sm dishes.............850.00
Dish, Fan & Prunus, w/insects, Wedgwood, 6½" 150.00
Figurine, bird on leafy perch, mc, French, 12¼" 195.00
Game dish, pigeon lying on lid, Geo Jones 2,000.00
Game dish, vintage swags, rabbit on lid, Wedgwood, 7" L....... 1,800.00
Jardiniere, classical frieze/portraits, Minton, 8x12" 475.00
Jardiniere, grotesque masks on intersecting bands, 8" 400.00
Lamp, oil; Victorian man holds font, 22" 2,250.00
Lobster dish, lobster/seaweed on lid, shell border, 4x7½" L 950.00
Match box, acorns/leaves on ea pc, G Jones, oval, 4" L...............285.00
Match holder, dwarf on crate w/barrel figural, Germany, 6" 145.00
Mug, cattail band, scalloped fence top/base, Etruscan, 3½" 200.00
Mug, hummingbird/leaves/flowers, cylindrical, 4¼" 150.00
Mustache cup & saucer, Bamboo & Fern, Wardle 285.00
Mustache cup & saucer, Bow & Floral, mc on ivory, English 275.00
Mustache cup & saucer, Shell & Seaweed, Etruscan, 8" saucer ...400.00
Nut tray, acorns/leaves, squirrel figure in center, G Jones 1,400.00
Oyster dish, Shell & Seaweed, 7-shell, Minton, 9" 600.00

Oyster plate, 6 bl/pk/blk shells on med bl, 9".................................175.00
Pickle dish, Begonia Leaf, Griffin/Smith & Hill, 8" 125.00
Pitcher, Bamboo, 4¾" 95.00
Pitcher, bear figural, mouth-pouring, spoon hdl, 9"........................300.00
Pitcher, bird in nest, bark body/hdl, rpr, 9½" 300.00
Pitcher, bird pr feeds hatchlings on turq, tankard form, 7" 225.00
Pitcher, cherubs/satyr masks, mermaid hdl, 1870, 8" 950.00
Pitcher, chickens w/wheat sheaf figural, 7" 285.00
Pitcher, ea side formed as fish, eel hdl, 8-10", set of 3 .... 1,000.00
Pitcher, florals, 6-sided, Baroque base, Germany, 14".....................150.00
Pitcher, geranium stalk w/leaves, wht on dk bl U-form, 8" 150.00
Pitcher, ivy on tree bark, gr on brn, U-form, English, 8" 130.00
Pitcher, monkey figural, legs Xd, arms behind bk, 9" 360.00
Pitcher, parrot figural, att Geo Morley, 9"..................................225.00
Pitcher, parrot figural, mc, St Clement, 12"................................150.00
Pitcher, revelers by stone wall, jester finial, Minton, 13" 575.00
Pitcher, shell figural, waves at base, wht/bl, Fielding, 8" 335.00
Pitcher, 2 fish ea side, bamboo hdl, Holdcroft, 8" 650.00
Plaque, birds amid flowers, openwork, French, 13", pr 600.00
Plate, Bow on Basketweave, gr on turq, 6" 65.00
Plate, Cauliflower, bright colors, Etruscan, 9" 165.00
Plate, crane on rocks in water, rtcl edge, Wedgwood, 9".............200.00
Plate, Dogwood, simple branches at rim, Holdcroft, 8" 150.00
Plate, Geranium Leaf on basketweave, Wedgwood, 8".................130.00

Plate, lady on bicycle, 7½", $250.00.

Plate, leaf/ferns/flowers, rtcl border, mc on turq, 8" 95.00
Plate, Morning-Glory, red/gr on med bl, shaped rim, 9" 100.00
Plate, Pond Lily, mc flowers w/brn leaves, 9" 120.00
Plate, Shell, Wedgwood, 8½" 150.00
Plate, Sunflower, Wedgwood, 8½" 150.00
Plate, Water Lily, Minton, 9" 150.00
Platter, allover shells, Wedgwood, 21" 1,250.00
Platter, Banana Leaf, 12" dia 195.00
Platter, Barrel Staves & Floral, hdls, dmn form, 10" 150.00
Platter, basketweave, bl, swans w/wings wide as hdls, 13" 210.00
Platter, Begonia Leaf on wht basketweave, 13" 195.00
Platter, Dog & Doghouse, mc on cream, 11" dia 150.00
Platter, Lilac, wht on bl, 2 str/2 rnd sides, 13" L.......................195.00
Platter, rose on basketweave, turq w/dk bl rim, hdls, 13" 195.00
Platter, 2 fish/Xd ears of corn, mc on cobalt, 14" L 300.00
Punch bowl, trailing vines, twig base, 17", +plate 750.00
Sardine box, shell motif, lg shell finial, sq, 7" W 495.00
Sardine box, 2 lg Xd fish on lid, Etruscan, 6" W.........................650.00
Smoke set, Blk boy w/melon figural, 6x6x6"...............................400.00

Spill vase, boot on pillow w/2 kittens, Brn/Westfield/Moore **700.00**
Strawberry server, blossoms, 2 side wells, 2 3-D birds, 15" **800.00**
Strawberry server, Strawberry Blossom, G Jones, 15"............... **1,000.00**
Strawberry server, Strawberry Leaf on napkin, G Jones, 15"........**800.00**
Sugar bowl, Leaf & Bow on bl basketweave, 4" **150.00**
Sweetmeat, boy & girl holding basket, Minton........................ **2,800.00**
Sweetmeat centerpc, dk-skin boy w/bowl stands on rocks, 20". **1,000.00**
Syrup pitcher, Coral, Etruscan, 7"..**310.00**
Syrup pitcher, Dogwood, str sides, Holdcroft, 4" **150.00**
Syrup pitcher, grape leaf, gr on brn, bulbous, 4" **125.00**
Syrup pitcher, Sunflower & Classical Urn, Samuel Lear, 8" **300.00**
Syrup pitcher, sunflower on cobalt, Etruscan, 8" **300.00**
Tea-for-2 set, Pineapple, 10-pc... **1,700.00**
Teapot, Cauliflower, Griffin/Smith & Hill, 5½" **325.00**
Teapot, flatiron w/mouse, mouse finial, cat hdl, Minton, 8" ... **4,750.00**
Teapot, Floral & Basketweave, pastels on bl, squat, 5" **175.00**
Teapot, Holly & Berries on bl lattice, bark spout/hdl, 6" **180.00**
Teapot, monkey holding lg squash figural, Minton, 7"...............**750.00**
Tobacco box, Blk boy eating melon lies on lg trunk, 6" L...........**400.00**
Tray, bread; Wheat & Basketweave, inscription, 13½"...............**300.00**
Tray, bread; woven bl/brn mat on yel tray, Wedgwood, 12" L.....**300.00**
Tray, Geranium, lav on wht, att Chesapeake, oval, 8" L...............**95.00**
Tray, Onion & Pickle Relish, Wedgwood, dmn form, 8" L **195.00**
Tray, Water Lily, 3 lg+3 sm leaves w/center bud, Minton, 9"......**350.00**
Tray, 3 lg leaves w/dogwood, center twig hdl, G Jones, 12" **400.00**
Tureen, blkberries on brn, 4x10" L, ...**400.00**
Tureen, fish on bed of ferns, basket base, att Jones, 15" **1,300.00**
Umbrella holder, Nouveau flowers, 22x10", M **600.00**
Vase, bird on tree branch figural, 7" **175.00**
Vase, floral, yel/brn stems on sanded ground, hdls, 7x8½" **95.00**
Vase, half-figure of lady before harp, hair forms rim, 6" **150.00**
Vase, ram's head relief, Thomas Shirley, 6" **250.00**
Wall bracket, maid sits, holds birds/nest, Royal Worcester **500.00**
Wine cooler, Bacchanalian scene on wht, hdls, 10" **360.00**

Malachite

Malachite is a type of art glass that exhibits strata-like layerings in shades of green, similar to the mineral in its natural form.

Bottle, scent; leaf mold, Nouveau style, 14" **450.00**
Box, berries & bows, ca 1920, 3½"...**195.00**
Buddha, seated on lotus base, draped robe, headdress, 8"............**110.00**
Fish dish, Deco figural, Moser **135.00**
Toothpick holder, dmn point mold, bulbous **25.00**

Vase, nudes and trees, 5", $235.00.

Vase, draped nude at ea of 4 corners, ribbed panels, 10x7" **750.00**
Vase, nude/vintage, flared/tapering, faceted base, 9½" **295.00**
Vase, 6 standing nudes/trees in relief, att Moser, '20s, 5" **265.00**

Mantel Lustres

Mantel lustres are decorative vases or candle holders made from all types of glass, often highly decorated, and usually hung with one or more rows of prisms. In the listings that follow, values are given for a pair.

Bristol, bl w/wht scalloped rim, gilt florals, prisms, 10" **300.00**
Bristol, sapphire bl w/gold, prisms, 7½"......................................**245.00**
Cut glass, X-cuts, 1 row prisms, Anglo-Irish, 10", EX **1,150.00**

Cut glass and gilt bronze Regency lustres, 10", EX, $750.00 for the pair.

Gr w/florals & gold, 2 rows of prisms, 12¼x6½" **450.00**
Mary Gregory, gr w/wht children, prisms, 14" **600.00**
O/l, rose/wht/clear, crenelated top, prisms, 12" **500.00**
O/l, wht cut to cobalt w/HP florals & gilt, prisms, 9" **250.00**
O/l, wht cut w/panels, heavy gilt, prisms, Bohemian, 12" **460.00**
O/l, wht cut w/panels, mc flowers, prisms, 1900, 13"...................**375.00**
O/l, wht to cranberry, castellated rim, prisms, 10".......................**300.00**
Ruby w/gold decor, castellated top, prisms....................................**425.00**

Mantua

A glasshouse was established in Mantua Township, Ohio, in 1821 for the purpose of manufacturing bottle-glass. Two years later, the proprietor David Ladd, left Mantua, re-establishing and enlarging his glasshouse in Kent, Ohio. Besides bottle-glass, flint glass items such as bowls, pitchers, decanters, etc. were also blown in green, aquamarine, amber, and amethyst shades — some with decorative devices that were seldom attempted outside the area. Though plain ware was common, several patterns were used as well — 16-rib, 32-rib, broken rib, swirled, corrugated, and 15-diamond.

Our advisor for this category is Mark Vuono; he is listed in the Directory under Connecticut.

Bottle, aqua, 16 melon ribs w/slight swirl, club form, 7½" **280.00**
Bottle, gr-aqua, 16-rib, club form, EX imp, kick-up, 8" **200.00**
Bottle, lt gr, 16-rib right swirl, flattened club form, 9" **400.00**
Bottle, olive-yel, 16 vertical ribs, globular, 5", NM **225.00**
Chestnut flask, aqua, 16 vertical ribs, sheared mouth, 6" **110.00**
Chestnut flask, lt to med gr, 16 vertical ribs, att, 6½" **375.00**

Pitkin, dark green, 16-rib broken swirl to the right, 5⅞", $850.00.

Pitkin, gr, 36-rib broken left swirl, 6¾" 550.00
Pitkin, yel-gr, Type-1, 16-rib right swirl, att, 6" 650.00

Maps and Atlases

Maps are highly collectible, not only for historical value but also for their sometimes elaborate artwork, legendary information, or data that since they were printed has been proven erroneous. There are many types of maps including geographical, military, celestial, road, and railroad. The most valuable are those made before the mid-1800s.

Key:
hc — hand colored   p — publisher

Atlases

Atlas of World, Rand McNally, 1904, G 35.00
Australia, Collins & Sons, color, 1873, 9x11¾", EX 12.50
CA, pictorial, color, Boston Journal, 1891, 9x12", EX 12.00
Colton's Advertising..., 62+ maps, ads w/illus, 1857, VG........ 3,800.00
Cornell's Companion...to High School Geography, 1857, 8-pg.....45.00
Frye's Complete Geography, Ginn & Co, Boston, 1897, 201-pg ...35.00
Harper's Introductory Geography, Harper & Bros, NY, 1884, EX..22.00
Indiana, color, Bradley's Atlas, 1886, dbl folio, 22x15", EX...........15.00
Insulae Britannicae, Ginn's Classical, Edinburgh, 1886, 12x9" 10.00
Johnson's New Illustrated Family...World, NY, 1867, VG...........400.00
Kankakee County IL, w/history, 1883, EX....................................265.00
Kansas, color, Rand McNally, 1891, 18x20", EX 15.00
Mitchell's Ancient..., Am Book, NY, 1844, 12-pg, VG 15.00
Mitchell's New General, Bradley, leather bound, 1832, EX.........165.00
New Ency...& Gazetter of New World, Collier, 1917, 264-pg, EX ..35.00
New Universal, Mitchell, set of 26 maps, 1849, EX 200.00
Smith's Atlas, 12 colored maps of US, NY, 1850, EX....................50.00
Warren's . . . School Geography, Cowperthwait, 1872, 108-pg.....32.00

Maps

Australia, color, Malte Brun, Philadelphia, 1828, 8x10½", EX 65.00
Australia & E Indies, hc, fancy border, 1867, 17x28", EX..............15.00
Battle of Bull Run, survey, 1878, 9x23", EX 12.00
Battleground Near Richmond, hc, 1860s, 16x27", EX 22.00
CA Gold Fields, topographical, uncolored, 1848, 10x18", EX 35.00
Constellations of N Hemisphere, Huntington, 1856, 14x17", EX .22.50
Europe, hc, w/Russia/Middle East, Asher/Adams, 1872, 17x28" 15.00

Exploration of WY/MT Area, routes shown, 1853, 23x55", EX 45.00
GA, 50 railroads/villages/etc, printed, 1892, 19x26", EX 10.00
Global World, hc, wide border, Mitchell, 1838, 13x17", EX 22.50
Indian Territory/CO on bk, hc, Bradley, 1887, 12x15", EX 15.00
Indians of NM, Indian territories, 1856, 23x33", EX....................25.00
LA & MS, hc, Indian sites, dtd 1833, 13x16", EX..........................45.00
Mid-South, Memphis at center, Indian camps shown, 13x16".......35.00
Military Map of US, forts & bases, NY, 1864, 17x23", EX 20.00
N America, hc, printed, Germany, 1890s, 15x18", EX 15.00
N America, w/Mexico in control of West, Black, 1845, 18x11" 22.50
N CA & NV, hc, Pacific RR, Asher/Adams, 1872, 17x24", EX 18.50
New Brunswick & Newfoundland, Colton, 1855, 13x15", EX.......12.50
New Orleans, hc, streets/river, wide margins, 1867, 13x15"...........16.00
New York, Civil War, hc, Johnson, 1864, 26x18", VG 20.00
NJ, DE, & MD, hand tinted, Johnson, ca 1868, 26x28", EX..........18.00
North America, color, Gotha, 1870, 13x15½", EX 125.00
Ohio, hc, canals, roads, railroads, 1850, 13x17", EX 23.50
OR & WA, hc, forts/Indians/trails, 1865, 12x15", EX...................18.00
PA & NJ, townships & RRs, hc, Black, 1879, 12x17", EX 18.00
Pennsylvania, hc, insets, Mitchell, ca 1872, 23x15", EX...............25.00

Pennsylvania, Nova Jersey, et Nova York, engraved double-page map with hand coloring, Tobias C. Lotter, ca 1700, 24" x 21", $1,300.00.

San Francisco, hc, details of city, 1891, 20x26", EX 15.00
Sioux District & IL, hc, dtd 1833, 13x16", EX 35.00
South Dakota, from land office, 1901, 13x18", EX 12.00
Texas, counties in east, ca 1860s, 17x24½", EX 68.00
US, LA Territory shown, Indians/landmarks, 1784, 9x10", EX......55.00
US, unexplored West shown, 1797, 9x9", VG 25.00
US w/Territories, gold fields/Indians/etc, 1849, 11x16", EX 24.00
VA, 25 railroads shown, 1892, 19x26", EX....................................10.00
WA Territory, Dept of Interior, 1879, 15x21", EX........................12.00
Western Hemisphere, Philip, Liverpool, ca 1850s, 22" dia 165.00
Western states, hc, RRs/towns as far as MO/TN, 1849, 13x17" 20.00
Yorktown, plans for siege, dtd 1862, 18x29", EX 25.00
Yosemite Valley, hc, recommended changes, 1904, 23x25", EX 10.00

Marblehead

What began as therapy for patients in a sanitarium in Marblehead,

Massachusetts, has become recognized as an important part of the Arts and Crafts movement in America. Results of the early experiments under the guidance of Arthur E. Baggs in 1904 met with such success that by 1908 the pottery had been converted to a solely commercial venture. Simple vase shapes were often incised with stylized animal and floral motifs or sailing ships. Some were decorated in low relief; many were plain. Simple matt glazes in soft yellow, gray, wisteria, rose, tobacco brown, and their most popular, Marblehead blue, were used alone or in combination. The Marblehead logo is distinctive — a boat with full sail and the letters 'M' and 'P.' The pottery closed in 1936.

Bowl, floral band, orange/gr/brn on lt yel, sgn HT, 7½", EX.... 1,100.00
Bowl, gray-bl, sky-bl int, hand thrown, 3½x14" 525.00
Bowl, poppy pods, bl on gr-gray speckled, sgn HT, 3x5" 700.00
Bowl, trees w/many sm petals, dk bl/gray on lt bl, 10", EX....... 3,000.00
Bowl vase, floral clusters, bl/gray, bl rim, sgn EB/T, 4" 500.00
Tile, lg oak+6 sm trees, dk gr, 6", EX...475.00
Tile, marsh scene w/reflected oaks, tan/brn/gr/yel, 6" 3,000.00
Tile, schooner, wht on bl w/wht fr, kiln line, 9½" 375.00
Tile, ships/clouds, gr/bl, paper label, 5¾"....................................425.00
Vase, bl gloss, trumpet form, 6x5½"...275.00

Vase, brown and green trees on light yellow, signed Arthur Baggs, 4½", $2,700.00; Vase, charcoal gray trees on gray-blue, initialed HT for Hannah Tutt, 7", $2,200.00.

Vase, cvd flowers, gr on dk bl, wide body, 3½" 700.00
Vase, dk bl, straight cylinder, 4½"..195.00
Vase, dk bl, swollen cylinder, 5½" 225.00
Vase, dogwood band, dk gr on bl, tapered cylinder, 5" 600.00
Vase, floral, gray on speckled gray-gr, sgn W, 7" 1,600.00
Vase, gr, bulbous w/short flared neck, 9" 325.00
Vase, gr, cylindrical, 5" 300.00
Vase, Greek Key band, dk gray on gray-gr, cylindrical, 5¾" 650.00
Vase, long-stem floral, yel/gr/bl on gray, Hennesey II, 5" 650.00
Vase, lt gr mottle, ovoid w/wide mouth, no mk, 9x5" 450.00
Vase, pea-gr, 3½x4¼" 300.00
Vase, repeating branches, bl/brn/tan on lt slate, HT, 4½"............800.00
Vase, sqs at rim, 3-line panels, brn on gr, 5¾"..........................1,600.00
Vase, stylized floral, slate/bl on speckled gray-gr, BT, 5" 650.00
Vase, stylized waves, gray on cream, sgn AEB/1924, 7x5½".........850.00
Vase, trees, brn/gr on yel, sgn A Baggs, dtd 1913, 4½x3½"...... 2,700.00
Vase, trees, dk gray on gray-bl, sgn HT, 7" 1,700.00
Vase, vine/berry band, bl-gr/red on dk bl, 5⅜" 550.00

Vase, 7 groups of 2 trees, tan/gr/brn on yel, sgn BI, 4" **3,850.00**

Marbles

Marbles have been popular with children since the mid-1800s. They've been made in many types from a variety of materials. Among some of the first glass items to be produced, the earliest marbles were made from a solid glass rod broken into sections of the proper length which were placed in a tray of sand and charcoal and returned to the fire. As they were reheated, the trays were constantly agitated until the marbles were completely round. Other marbles were made of china, pottery, steel, and natural stones.

Below is a listing of the various types, along with a brief description of each. When size is not otherwise indicated, prices are listed for mint condition marbles of average size, ½" to 1".

Agates: stone marbles of many different colors — bands of color alternating with white usually encircle the marble; most are translucent.

Ballot Box: handmade (with pontils), opaque white or black, used in lodge elections.

Bloodstone: green chalcedony with red spots, a type of quartz.

China: with or without glaze, in a variety of hand-painted designs — parallel bands or bull's-eye designs most common.

Clambroth: opaque glass with outer evenly spaced swirls of one or alternating colors.

Clay: one of the most common older types; some are painted while others are not.

Comic Strip: a series of twelve machine-made marbles with faces of comic strip characters, Peltier Glass Factory, Illinois.

Crockery: sometimes referred to as Benningtons; most are either blue or brown, although some are speckled. The clay is shaped into a sphere, then coated with glaze and fired.

End of the Day: single-pontil glass marbles — the colored part often appears as a multicolored blob or mushroom cloud.

Goldstone: clear glass completely filled with copper flakes that have turned gold-colored from the heat of the manufacturing process.

Indian Swirls: usually black glass with a colored swirl appearing on the outside next to the surface, often irregular.

Latticinio Core Swirls: double-pontil marble with an inner area with net-like effects of swirls coming up around the center.

Lutz Type: glass with colored or clear bands alternating with bands which contain copper flecks.

Micas: clear or colored glass with mica flecks which reflect as silver dots when marble is turned. Red is rare.

Onionskin: spiral type which are solidly colored instead of having individual ribbons or threads, multicolored.

Peppermint Swirls: made of white opaque glass with alternating blue and red outer swirls.

Ribbon Core Swirls: double-pontil marble — center shaped like a ribbon with swirls that come up around the middle.

Rose Quartz: stone marble, usually pink in color, often with fractures inside and on outer surface.

Solid Core Swirls: double-pontil marble — middle is solid with swirls coming up around the core.

Steelies: hollow steel spheres marked with a cross where the steel was bent together to form the ball.

Sulfides: generally made of clear glass with figures inside. Rarer types have colored figures or colored glass.

Tiger Eye: stone marble of golden quartz with inclusions of asbestos, dark brown with gold highlights.

Vaseline: machine-made of yellowish-green glass with small bubbles.

For a more thorough study of the subject, we recommend *Antique and Collectible Marbles, Revised Second Edition*, an identification and value guide by Everett Grist; you will find his address in the Directory under Illinois.

Agate, contemporary, carnelian, 1¾" 175.00
Banded Opaque, gr & wht, 2" 375.00
Banded Opaque, red & wht, ¾" 75.00

Banded Opaque with pontil, 1¾", $500.00.

Banded Transparent Swirl, bl, ¾" 40.00
Banded Transparent Swirl, lt gr, 1¾" 300.00
Bennington, bl, 1¾" 15.00
Bennington, bl, ¾" 1.00
Bennington, brn, 1¾" 10.00
Bennington, fancy, 1¾" 20.00
Bennington, fancy, ¾" 2.00
China, decorated, glazed, apple, 1¾" 350.00
China, decorated, glazed, rose, 1¾" 400.00
China, decorated, glazed, wht w/geometrics, 1¾" 65.00
China, decorated, unglazed, geometrics & flowers, ¾" 250.00
Clambroth, opaque, bl & wht, 1¾" 800.00
Clambroth, opaque, bl & wht, ¾" 150.00
Clambroth Swirl, red/wht, Germany, 1900, ⅞" 275.00
Clear Swirl Lutz-type, clear w/wht & gold swirls, 1¾" 375.00
Clear Swirl Lutz-type, clear w/wht & gold swirls, ¾" 85.00
Cloud, w/mica, red & wht, 1¼" 450.00
Cloud, yel, rare, 1¾" 500.00
Comic, Cotes Bakery, advertising 250.00
Comic, Kayo, rare 85.00
Comic, Little Orphan Annie...55.00
Comic, Moon Mullins 65.00
Comic, set of 12...750.00
Comic, Skeezix...55.00
Cork Screw, machine-made...3.00
End of Day, bl & wht, 1¾" 400.00
End of Day, mc bits swirled in clear, lt wear, 2" 750.00
Goldstone, ¾" 35.00
Indian Swirl, 1¾" 700.00
Indian Swirl Lutz-type, gold flakes, ¾" 300.00
Line Crockery, clay, wht w/zigzag gr & bl lines, ¾" 25.00
Mica, bl, ¾" 25.00
Mica, gr, 1¾" 200.00
Onionskin, w/mica, 1¾" 500.00
Onionskin, w/mica, ¾" 75.00
Onionskin, 16-lobe, unusual, 2" 700.00
Onionskin, 2" 400.00
Onionskin, ¾" 50.00
Onionskin, 4-lobe, 1¼" 175.00
Onionskin Lutz-type, gold flakes, 1¾" 800.00

Opaque Swirl, gr, ¾" 35.00
Opaque Swirl Lutz-type, bl, yel, gr, or vaseline, ¾" 225.00
Peppermint Swirl, opaque, red, wht, & bl, 1¾" 450.00
Peppermint Swirl, opaque, red, wht, & bl, ¾" 85.00
Pottery, tan w/purple lines, 1¾" 35.00
Ribbon Core Lutz-type, red, 1¾" 800.00
Slag, machine-made, sm 1.00
Slag, machine-made, 1½" 35.00
Solid Opaque, bl, ¾" 75.00
Solid Opaque, gr, 1¾" 300.00
Sulfide, aardvark, 1⅜" 100.00
Sulfide, alligator, 1¾" 160.00
Sulfide, baboon, 2⅛", NM 230.00
Sulfide, bear, sitting, 1⅝", EX 80.00
Sulfide, bear, standing, 1¾", M 140.00
Sulfide, bear, standing, 2¼" 250.00
Sulfide, bear, walking, 1", M 110.00
Sulfide, bird, flying, surface wear, 2 int bubbles, 1¼" 80.00
Sulfide, bird w/long feathers, 1½", M 150.00
Sulfide, bust of Geo Washington, 2⅜", NM 650.00
Sulfide, camel, 2" 250.00
Sulfide, cat, 1¼" 75.00
Sulfide, cat reclining, many bubbles, 1½", EX 60.00
Sulfide, child, seated, 1½", NM 260.00
Sulfide, child w/ball & mallet, 1¼" 250.00
Sulfide, child w/sailboat, 1¾" 650.00
Sulfide, coin w/number 7, 2" 350.00
Sulfide, cow, grazing, 2⅛", NM 225.00
Sulfide, cow, 1⅛" 100.00
Sulfide, dbl eagle, very rare, 1¾" 675.00
Sulfide, dog, begging, 2", NM 160.00

Sulfide, dog with bird in mouth, 1¼", $250.00.

Sulfide, dog, long haired, 1¼", NM 135.00
Sulfide, donkey, 1⅝", NM 125.00
Sulfide, dove, 1⅝", M 160.00
Sulfide, dove on post, 1⅛" 175.00
Sulfide, eagle, 1⅝" 185.00
Sulfide, eagle on post, 2", EX 285.00
Sulfide, elephant, 1⅝", M 160.00
Sulfide, fish, 2", NM 150.00
Sulfide, fish, 2⅛", M 200.00
Sulfide, fox, 1½", EX 130.00
Sulfide, goat, 1¾", M 190.00
Sulfide, goat, 2", M 225.00
Sulfide, hen, 1⅛" 65.00
Sulfide, hen on nest, 1½", M 120.00
Sulfide, horse, rearing, 2", NM 175.00
Sulfide, jackal, 1", EX 150.00
Sulfide, Jenny Lind bust (pnt), 1⅜" 1,600.00

Sulfide, lady in dress (pnt), 1¼", M 900.00
Sulfide, lamb, 1¼", EX 100.00
Sulfide, lamb, 1¾", M 140.00
Sulfide, lion, 1⅝", NM 85.00
Sulfide, lion, 2", NM 175.00
Sulfide, man & lady, 2⅜", NM 1,500.00
Sulfide, monkey, 1⅛" 95.00
Sulfide, otter, 1½" 135.00
Sulfide, papoose, 1⅝" 300.00
Sulfide, papoose, 2" 450.00
Sulfide, pelican, 1¼" 275.00
Sulfide, pig, 1¼" 90.00
Sulfide, pig, 1⅝", NM 120.00
Sulfide, pig, 2", M 180.00
Sulfide, rabbit, running, 2" 180.00
Sulfide, rabbit, 1¼" 80.00
Sulfide, raccoon, 2" 200.00
Sulfide, ram, 2" 175.00
Sulfide, rooster, lt yel glass, 1¾" 375.00
Sulfide, rooster, 2", M 180.00
Sulfide, Santa Claus, 2" 350.00
Sulfide, squirrel on bk legs, 1½", EX 75.00
Sulfide, squirrel w/nut, 1½", M..................................125.00
Sulfide, squirrel w/nut, 2", EX 200.00
Sulfide, steer, 1⅝", M 125.00

Marine Collectibles

See also Steamship Collectibles, Scrimshaw, and Tools.

Binnacle, Beck Lee...Chicago, US Navy...1942, 8½" dia 150.00
Binnacle, brass hood, wood base, floor standing, 54", EX 1,550.00
Binnacle, ES Ritchie & Sons #99406, teak base, 19x16", EX 900.00
Binnacle, Solver & Svarreriverc, Weilbach & Co, brass, 14" 235.00
Binnacle, Steering Gear....1893, brass dome top w/compass, 12".150.00
Bolt, keel; bronze, 31", EX 20.00
Cane, shark vertebrae w/ebony & horn separators, 35" 70.00
Case, gr sharkskin, for drawing instruments, 1880s, EX 400.00
Chronometer, Glashutter Uhrenbetriebe #8087, brass mts, EX...600.00
Chronometer, Hamilton, dbl-cased, 56-hour, EX 550.00
Clock, Pat Apr 16 1878 Ship Bells..., Seth Thomas, 11", EX 500.00
Clock, Seth Thomas, brass, VG 110.00
Compass, English, azimuth type, ca 1800, 17x12x12", EX 750.00
Gauge, Marine Speed Indicator, brass, 3¼" dia.........................35.00
Gauge, Nurnberg Instruments, water temperature, brass, EX 30.00
Inclinometer, pendulum type on mahog bkplate, EX 75.00
Lamp, diver's; Ceag, Barnsley Yorks, England, brass, 9", EX 110.00
Lavatory, porc, scalloped bowl, Sands & Son NY, VG 400.00
Mast head truck w/pully, early 1800s, 11" 50.00
Meter, Palmer, solid brass, nonlinear scale, VG.........................45.00
Model, 2-masted schooner, cloth sails, wire rigging, 34" 200.00
Octant, Spencer & Co, Longon-NY, ebony/brass/ivory, 23½".....950.00
Octant, Spencer Browning...London, ebony/brass/ivory, 1850s...450.00
Pen, whalebone hdl w/hand holding heart at top, 7½" 150.00
Porthole, polished brass, 15" dia 90.00
Quadrant, gunner's; Honeywell #2074, 1942, EX, +leather case....50.00
Sextant, Brandis & Sons, US Navy #2842, brass, VG 340.00
Sextant, H Hughes & Son, London, cased brass, ca 1947, EX 250.00
Sextant, Heath & Co New Eltham London, brass, EX.................275.00
Sextant, Lafayette Inst NY NY, EX in orig dvtl case...................175.00
Sextant, W Desilva...Liverpool, brass & silver, EX in case 585.00
Sight, Pelorus, drift type, wood stand, EX 50.00
Stadimeter, US Maritime Commission Schick, VG in case 150.00

Navigational octant, mid-19th century, ebony, ivory, and brass, $450.00.

Martin Bros.

The Martin Bros. were studio potters who worked from 1873 until 1914, first at Fulham and later at London and Southall. There were four brothers, each of whom excelled in their particular area. Robert, known as Wallace, was an experienced stonecarver. He modeled a series of grotesque bird and animal figural caricatures. Walter was the potter, responsible for throwing the larger vases on the wheel, firing the kiln, and mixing the clay. Edwin, an artist of stature, preferred more naturalistic forms of decoration. His work was often incised or had relief designs of seaweed, florals, fish, and birds. The fourth brother, Charles, was their business manager. Their work was incised with their names, place of production, and letters and numbers indicating month and year.

Beast, squatting frog w/humanoid head, sgn/dtd, 10", EX.......25,000.00
Bird, dtd 1887, 10½" 9,000.00
Bird, dtd 1899, 14" 17,000.00
Bird jar, deep-set eyes, wings behind, tan/brn, 13½", EX......... 4,600.00
Bird jar, scolding, in ruffled nightcap, sgn/dtd, 12" 26,000.00
Figure of dead parakeet, Latin inscription, sgn/dtd, 12" L........ 1,900.00
Jug, bearded face under spout, fans at base, sgn/dtd, 8" 3,000.00
Jug, head of smiling man, dbl sided, sgn/dtd, 6" 3,000.00
Jug, leaf cvg, brn on cream, bulbous, 7¾x5½" 425.00
Lovebirds, he w/wing around smiling mate, sgn/dtd, 11" 17,500.00
Spoon warmer, smiling animal, lg ears/eyes, sgn/dtd, 5½" 9,000.00
Vase, brn lines/yel protrusions, gourd form, sgn/dtd, 9x6"............750.00
Vase, cvd creatures, cream/brn on dk bl, sgn/dtd, 10x7" 1,200.00
Vase, cvd lizards/beatles/snails, lt bl/brn, 11x5½" 1,500.00
Vase, cvd winged dragons, brn/ivory, sgn/dtd, drilled, 10"....... 2,200.00
Walley Bird jar, beak points downward, heavy body, 11", EX ..10,000.00
Walley Bird jar, bl/gr/gray, sgn/dtd, rstr, 13½"......................... 6,000.00
Walley Bird jar, smile/plump, bl/brn/blk, sgn/dtd, rpr, 12" 9,500.00
Walley Bird jar, tan/gr/bl w/ochre beak & ft, sgn/dtd, 11"....... 6,400.00

Mary Gregory

Mary Gregory glass, for reasons that remain obscure, is the namesake of a Boston and Sandwich Glass Company employee who worked for the company for only two years in the mid-1800s. Although no evidence actually exists to indicate that glass of this type was even produced there, the fine colored or crystal ware decorated with figures of children in white enamel is commonly referred to as Mary Gregory. The glass, in fact, originated in Europe and was imported into this country where it was copied by several eastern glasshouses. It was popular from the mid-1800s until the turn of the century. It is generally accepted that examples with all-white figures were made in the U.S.A., while gold-trimmed items and those with children having tinted faces or a small amount of color on their clothing are European. Though amethyst is rare, examples in cranberry command the higher prices. Blue ranks next; and green, amber, and clear items are worth the least.

Bottle, atomizer; cobalt, boy by lake w/ducks, 5½" 225.00
Bottle, barber; cobalt, girl plays tennis, w/gold, 8x4"...................375.00

Bottle, boy with balloon in white on medium blue, decorated on 4 sides, tulip stopper, 8½", $345.00.

Bottle, barber; gr, boy & flowers, ribbed, 7⅞" 325.00
Bottle, scent; clear, boy/butterfly, sq, Sandwich, 2½" 185.00
Bottle, scent; sapphire bl, girl w/flowers, 9" 375.00
Bottle, scent; teal, boy w/kite, sq, tulip-form stopper, 5½" 400.00
Box, cranberry, boy w/bouquet on lid, brass fr, 4¼" dia................625.00
Box, dk amethyst, girl, brass mts, sq, 3" H 325.00
Box, jewel; bl, girl w/basket, 5" dia 350.00
Box, jewel; cranberry, boy & girl, ormolu mts, 4½x6"..................700.00
Box, patch; amber, girl on lid, 1⅞" dia......................................165.00
Box, peach to wht, girl w/angel wings, 3½x2¾" 195.00
Butter dish, cranberry satin, boy w/pnt detail on tricycle.............575.00
Cruet, amber, boy, 3-petal top, amber hdl & stopper, 9½"...........265.00
Cruet, clear, boy holds flower, 8" 125.00
Cruet, cranberry, drummer boy, clear hdl, hollow stopper, 8"......350.00
Cruet, gr, boy, 8¼" 325.00
Decanter, cranberry, lady by swan, clear stopper, 9½"................385.00
Decanter, gr, boy, clear stopper, 9" 250.00
Decanter, gr, seated girl, clear stopper, w/hdl, 9½".....................300.00
Fairy lamp, rose frost, boy, pyramid, 3¾x3"..............................325.00
Jar, cranberry, girl walking, basketweave at base, hdl, 6".............345.00
Lamp, blk amethyst, girl w/parrot, 7".......................................315.00
Mantel lustre, gr, children, prisms, 14", pr................................600.00
Night light, amethyst, boy w/flag, ormolu rim/ft, 9x3"..................395.00
Pitcher, bl, girl & trees, ribbed, 11"..325.00
Pitcher, cranberry, boy w/fishing pole, 7" 225.00
Pitcher, tankard; bl, tinted figure, pewter lid, 14½".....................275.00
Pitcher, tankard; gr, boy w/staff, 10" 285.00
Rose bowl, cranberry, girl, gold rim on collared base, 2" 225.00
Shot glass, lt amber, boy, 2x1⅞"...65.00
Stein, amber, boy w/stick, pewter lid, 5" 335.00
Stein, sapphire bl, Invt T'print, boy, pewter lid/insert, 7"...........385.00

Toothpick holder, clear, boy, 2½" 85.00
Tumbler, bl, girl in forest, 3¾" 85.00
Tumbler, cranberry, boy w/flower, juice sz 95.00
Tumbler, gr, girl, 3½" 75.00
Vase, amethyst, girl w/grapes, gold hdls, 15", pr 1,575.00
Vase, bl, girl stands by boy on ladder, ormolu, hdls, 10" 1,000.00
Vase, bl, herons in flight, rare, 11", pr 475.00
Vase, blk amethyst, child, facing pr, 11x4½"............................450.00
Vase, cobalt, cherubs/florals, gold/wht, ormolu, 9½", pr.............365.00
Vase, cobalt, girl, ruffled rim on baluster, 7"...........................150.00
Vase, cobalt, girl w/flower, bulbous, 5" 135.00
Vase, cobalt, lady by fence, tulip-shape top, ftd, 14", pr.............575.00
Vase, cranberry, child in forest, ruffled, English, 11", pr 450.00
Vase, cranberry, girl in garden, mini, 3" 145.00
Vase, cranberry, girl w/flower, w/lid, 15½"..............................675.00
Vase, cranberry, girl w/umbrella, boy w/oars, 9⅛", pr................495.00
Vase, cranberry, 2 children w/butterfly, 13x5".........................585.00
Vase, dk gr, boy w/flower & trees, fan form, 6" 285.00
Vase, emerald gr, girl blowing horn, cylindrical, 8" 135.00
Vase, gr, girl dancing, stick neck, 6¾" 130.00
Vase, lime gr, girl at shore, sailboat, snail hdls, 11⅝" 285.00
Vase, lime gr satin, lady, pyramidal form, 7".............................165.00
Vase, pk over clear, shepherdess, pillow form, 5" 195.00
Vase, sapphire bl, boy, dbl-ring mold, Mt WA, 8x2½" 225.00

Mason's Ironstone

In 1813 Charles J. Mason was granted a patent for a process said to 'improve the quality of English porcelain.' The new type of ware was in fact ironstone which Mason decorated with colorful florals and scenics, some of which reflected the Oriental taste. Although his business failed for a short time in the late 1840s, Mason re-established himself and continued to produce dinnerware, tea services, and ornamental pieces until about 1852 at which time the pottery was sold to Francis Morley. Ten years later, Geo. L. and Taylor Ashworth became owners. Both Morley and the Ashworths not only used Mason's molds and patterns but often his mark as well. Because the quality and the workmanship of the later wares do not compare with Mason's earlier product, collectors should take care to distinguish one from the other. Consult a good book on marks to be sure.

Partial dinnerware set, Mason's Japan pattern, 19 pieces for $1,200.00.

Jug, Bandana, orange & wht, mk, 1860, 5¼" 200.00
Jug, Chinese Urn & Emblems, mk, 1860, 6¾".............................145.00
Jug, Chrysanthemum, bl & orange, unmk, 1820s, 3⅝"................165.00
Jug, Mandarin, mk, 1840, 6½"...225.00

Jug, Mandarin, mk, 1860, 7¾"..255.00
Jug, Mazareen, bl chrysanthemums, unmk, 1820s, 7" 285.00
Jug, Mazareen, gold floral, unmk, 1820s, 4¼" 245.00
Jug, Mazareen, gold/wht/bl, mk, 1820s, 4⅝" 265.00
Jug, Twigg Peacock, mk, 1820s, 8" 225.00
Tureen, Canton pattern, bl/wht, boar head hdls, 13"..................450.00
Wash bowl & pitcher, bl dragon transfer, 11", 16", EX 325.00

Massier

Clement Massier was a French artist-potter who in 1881 established a workshop in Golfe Juan, France, where he experimented with metallic lustre glazes. (one of his pupils was Jacques Sicardo, who brought the knowledge he gained through his association with Massier to the Weller Pottery Company in Zanesville, Ohio.) The lustre lines developed by Massier incorporated nature themes with allover decorations of foliage or flowers on shapes modeled in the Art Nouveau style. The ware was usually incised with the Massier name, his initials, or the location of the pottery. Massier died in 1917.

Jardiniere, high relief waves w/nude figure, irid, 10x16" **2,900.00**
Medallion, profile of bearded man, irid, MCM, 1901, 6" dia **500.00**
Vase, fish, brn w/gilt on gr & brn texture, 3-sided lip, 7" **600.00**
Vase, floral, maroon on gray mottled irid, 5¾" **225.00**

Match Holders

Before the invention of the safety match in 1855, matches were kept in matchboxes and carried in pocket-size match safes because they ignited so easily. John Walker, an English chemist, invented the match more than one hundred years ago — quite by accident. Walker was working with a mixture of potash and antimony, hoping to make a combustible that could be used to fire guns. The mixture adhered to the end of the wooden stick he had used for stirring. As he tried to remove it by scraping the stick on the stone floor, it burst into flames. The invention of the match was only a step away! From that time to the present, match holders have been made in amusing figural forms as well as simple utilitarian styles and in a wide range of materials. Most were wall-hanging; a few were table-top models — all designed to keep matches conveniently at hand. Our advisor for this category is Ron Damaska; he is listed in the Directory under Pennsylvania. See also Advertising.

Cast iron, reticulated backplate, 2-compartment, 7", $65.00.

Bacchus head, CI, open pocket w/grapes & leaves, hanging 85.00
Chambestick w/matchbox holder, Dresden 95.00

Girl in bonnet, bsk, Germany, EX..25.00
Hatchet, NP iron, wall hanging, 1908 ....36.00
Miss Liberty's head, clear glass, 4½", EX......................................80.00
Rifles & game, bag forms safes, CI, 10x6" 65.00
Tinware, 2-part, rtcl 'Matches' on 1, 'Good' on other, 4½" 90.00
Turtle form, CI, urn on bk, 1850s, 3⅜" L 110.00
Urn form w/hdls, on sq saucer base, CI, 1870s, 3" 140.00

Match Safes

Match safes, aptly-named cases used to carry matches in the days before cigarette lighters, were used during the last half of the 19th century until about 1920. Some incorporated added features — hidden compartments, cigar cutters, etc. — some were figural, and others were used by retail companies as advertising giveaways. They were made from every type of material, but silverplated styles abound. See also Advertising.

Our advisor for this category is Ron Damaska; he is listed in the Directory under Pennsylvania. See also Advertising.

Advertising, AE Sonnedecker Coal, tin, EX 69.00
Advertising, Arm & Hammer, gutta percha 50.00
Advertising, Barthomey's Brewing, SP, 2½", VG............................110.00
Advertising, Flint's Cigar Store, tin, EX 25.00
Advertising, Gimball Printing, nickel, celluloid insets, NM..........45.00
Blatz Trademark, nickel/brass, worn..55.00
Deco geometric in relief, SP 45.00

Sterling with embossed Flat Iron Building, NY, 2¼", $85.00.

Golfer enameled on brass, sm...55.00
Indian chief eng, MOP & brass 85.00
Liberty head in relief, sterling 105.00
Lion w/floral border, silveroin, EX 45.00
Nouveau florals in relief, sterling, inscribed/dtd 1898 ....65.00
Nouveau lady ea side, 14k gold-plated brass 95.00
Nouveau lady w/flowing hair ea side, German silver 65.00
Nouveau nude & 2 stallions in relief, Bristol Silver 145.00
Repousse florals & scrolls ea side, sterling....................................75.00
Shepherd & florals, sterling, sm..65.00
Shoe figural, lift top, lacquer...125.00
Winged nude on diagonal stripes, German silver, 2½" 70.00

McCoy

The third generation McCoy potter in the Roseville, Ohio, area was Nelson, who with the aid of his father, J.W., established the Nelson

McCoy Sanitary Stoneware Company in 1910. They manufactured churns, jars, jugs, poultry fountains, and foot warmers. By 1925 they had expanded their wares to include majolica jardinieres and pedestals, umbrella stands and cuspidors, and an embossed line of vases and small jardinieres in a blended brown and green matt glaze. From the late twenties through the mid-forties, a utilitarian stoneware was produced, some of which was glazed in the soft blue and white so popular with collectors today. They also used a dark brown mahogany color and a medium to dark green — both in a high gloss. In 1933 the firm became known as the Nelson McCoy Pottery Company. They expanded their facilities in 1940 and began to make the novelty artware, cookie jars, and dinnerware that today are synonomous with 'McCoy.' To date, more than two hundred cookie jars of every theme and description have been produced. Some are very common. Mammy, the Clown, and the Bear (although very old) are easy to find, while the Dalmations, Christmas Tree, and Kangaroo, for instance, (though not so old) are harder to locate. The Indian and the Tepee, both made in the fifties, are two of the most popular and some of the most expensive!

More than a dozen different marks have been used by the company; nearly all incorporate the name 'McCoy,' although some of the older items were marked 'NM USA.' For further information, consult *The Collector's Encyclopedia of McCoy Pottery* by Sharon and Bob Huxford, available at your local bookstore or public library.

Our McCoy cookie jar advisor is Judy Posner; she is listed in the Directory under Pennsylvania.

Dalmations in Rocking Chair, $200.00.

Cookie Jars

Animal Crackers	85.00
Apollo Age	250.00
Apple, 1950-64	30.00
Apple on Basketweave	35.00
Bananas	55.00
Barnum's Animals	150.00
Bear, cookie in vest	45.00
Betsy Baker	125.00
Black Kettle, w/immovable bail, HP flowers	25.00
Bobby Baker	45.00
Caboose	115.00
Chef	85.00
Chiffoniere, Early American Chest	50.00
Chinese Lantern	45.00
Chipmunk	75.00
Christmas Tree, from	300.00
Circus Horse	125.00
Clown Bust	45.00
Clown in Barrel	75.00
Clyde Dog	85.00
Coalby Cat	110.00
Coffee Grinder	30.00
Coffee Mug	30.00
Colonial Fireplace	85.00
Cookie Barrel	25.00
Cookie Boy	115.00
Cookie Cabin	55.00
Cookie Jug, dbl loop	20.00
Cookie Jug, single loop, 2-tone gr rope	18.00
Cookie Jug, w/cork stopper, brn & wht	15.00
Cookie Log	30.00
Cookie Safe	55.00
Cookstove	30.00
Corn	80.00
Covered Wagon	45.00
Cylinder, w/red flowers	22.00

Dog on Basketweave	50.00
Drum	55.00
Duck on Basketweave	45.00
Dutch Boy	35.00
Dutch Girl, boy on reverse, rare	125.00
Dutch Treat Barn	50.00
Elephant	105.00
Elephant w/Split Trunk, rare, from	250.00
Engine, blk	110.00
Forbidden Fruit	55.00
Friendship	75.00
Frontier Family	40.00
Fruit in Bushel Basket	45.00
Gingerbread Boy	30.00
Globe	150.00
Grandfather Clock	50.00
Granny	55.00
Hamm's Bear	125.00
Happy Face	30.00
Hen on Nest	75.00
Hillbilly Bear, rare, from	350.00
Hobby Horse	95.00
Honey Bear	55.00
Indian	195.00
Jack-O'-Lantern	225.00
Kangaroo, bl	195.00
Kettle, jumbo sz	25.00
Kissing Penguins	55.00
Kitten on Basketweave	50.00
Kittens on Ball of Yarn	75.00
Kookie Kettle, blk	25.00
Lamb on Basketweave	45.00
Leprechaun, from	400.00
Liberty Bell	40.00
Little Clown	65.00
Lollipop	45.00
Mac Dog	55.00
Mammy	125.00
Mammy w/Cauliflower, G pnt, from	350.00
Modern	25.00
Monk	35.00
Mother Goose	85.00
Mr & Mrs Owl	75.00
Oaken Bucket	25.00
Old Churn	25.00
Pears on Basketweave	35.00

Pelican 90.00
Pepper, yel..22.00
Picnic Basket 55.00
Pineapple 45.00
Pineapple, Modern 35.00
Pirates Chest 55.00
Pot Belly Stove, blk 30.00
Puppy, w/sign 75.00
Quaker Oats, from 200.00
Red Barn, cow in door, rare 175.00
Rooster, 1955-57 ....85.00
Rooster, 1970-74 ....45.00
Round w/HP Leaves 30.00
Sad Clown 45.00
Snoopy on Doghouse..125.00
Snow Bear 45.00
Strawberry, 1955-57 ....35.00
Strawberry, 1971-75 ....30.00
Teapot..25.00
Tepee 195.00
Tilt Pitcher, blk w/roses 26.00
Tomato...25.00
Touring Car 55.00
Tudor Cookie House..85.00
Tulip on Flowerpot 50.00
Turkey..125.00
Upside Down Bear, panda 45.00
WC Fields 125.00
Wedding Jar 65.00
Windmill..65.00
Wishing Well..35.00
Woodsy Owl...125.00
Wren House..75.00
Yosemite Sam 150.00

Miscellaneous

Basket, oak leaf & acorn decor 25.00
Bean pot, Suburbia Ware, mk, 1964, 2-qt............10.00
Beverage jug, Sunburst Gold, w/lid 40.00
Bookend/planter, violin, pr................................22.00
Bowl, shoulder; bl, ringed, rectangular base, 9"....22.00
Coffee server & warmer, El Rancho Bar-B-Que 50.00
Coffeepot, Grecian, gr & gold, w/creamer & sugar bowl 55.00
Creamer, dog figural, 1950s...............................22.50
Creamer, stick hdl, 1945..................................... 4.00
Decanter, Jupiter 60, train set, 4-pc 200.00
Decanter, 1932 Pierce Arrow Sport Phantom 30.00
Dripolator, hexagonal shape, 1943 ....17.50
Elephant, Victory Depends on You, WWII era 20.00
Ice tub, El Rancho Bar-B-Que............................30.00
Lamp, cowboy boots form, orig shade, lg..............50.00
Lamp base, blk panther figural, 1950s 20.00
Lamp base, mermaid w/seashell figural 50.00
Mug, Campbell kids, mk USA, recent 2.00
Pitcher, chicken figural, unmk, 1943 ....14.00
Pitcher, curved top, flattened sides, 1950s............10.00
Pitcher, elephant figural, wht, 1940s, NM 20.00
Pitcher, water lily emb on gr, fish hdl, 1935 ....20.00
Planter, cat figural, bow at neck, 1953 .... 8.00
Planter, conch shell figural, unmk, 1954...............10.00
Planter, cradle, unmk 6.00
Planter, Grecian, rectangular, 1958 ....22.50
Planter, Liberty Bell 60.00

Planter, rolling pin w/Boy Blue 18.00
Planter, stork beside basket, 1956........................12.00
Planter, turtle figural, 1955 ....15.00
Planter, Village Smithy 14.00
Shakers, cabbage figural, 1954, pr 20.00
Spoon rest, penguin figural, 1953 ....35.00
Tea set, Two-Tone Green, 3-pc 50.00
Teapot, cat figural, paw spout, head forms lid 35.00
Teapot, Grecian, 1958 ....40.00
Teapot, Sunburst Gold, mk, 1957 ....32.00
Vase, feather shape, unmk, 1950s........................ 8.00

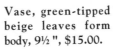
Vase, green-tipped beige leaves form body, 9½", $15.00.

Wall pocket, Blossomtime 16.00
Wall pocket, clock figural 16.00
Wall pocket, pear figural 16.00
Wall pocket, Sunburst Gold 16.00
Wall pocket, violin figural...................................15.00

McCoy, J.W.

The J.W. McCoy Pottery Company was incorporated in 1899. It operated under that name in Roseville, Ohio, until 1911 when McCoy entered into a partnership with George Brush, forming the Brush-McCoy Company. During the early years, McCoy produced kitchenware, majolica jardinieres and pedestals, umbrella stands, and cuspidors. By 1903 they had begun to experiment in the field of art pottery and, though never involved to the extent of some of their contemporaries, nevertheless produced several art lines of merit. Their first line was Mt. Pelee, examples of which are very rare today. Two types of glazes were used, matt green and an iridescent charcoal gray. Though the line was primarily mold formed, some pieces evidence the fact that while the clay remained wet and pliable it was pulled and pinched with the fingers to form crests and peaks in a style not unlike George Ohr.

The company rebuilt in 1904 after being destroyed by fire, and other artware was designed. Loy-Nel Art and Renaissance were standard brown lines, hand decorated under the glaze with colored slip. Shapes and artwork were usually simple but effective. Olympia and Rosewood were relief-molded brown-glaze lines decorated in natural colors with wreaths of leaves and berries or simple floral sprays. Although much of this ware was not marked, you will find examples with the die-stamped 'Loy-Nel Art, McCoy' or an incised line identification.

Florastone, vase, unmk, 1923 ....165.00
Grape, cuspidor, 1½" 45.00

Loy-Nel-Art, jardiniere, 1905, 6" 100.00
Loy-Nel-Art, lamp base, irises, 8½" 120.00
Loy-Nel-Art, spittoon, wild roses, flared rim 85.00
Loy-Nel-Art, vase, unmk, 1905, 8" 115.00

Olympia tankard, 16", $300.00; Mug, $120.00.

Olympia, vase, ears of corn, cylindrical, 11" 185.00
Rosewood, vase, pre-1903, unmk, 3" 30.00

McKee

McKee Glass was founded in 1853 in Pittsburgh, Pennsylvania. Among their early products were tableware of both the flint and non-flint variety. In 1888 the company relocated to avail themselves of a source of natural gas, thereby founding the town of Jeannette, Pennsylvania. One of their most famous colored dinnerware lines, Rock Crystal, was manufactured in the 1920s. During the thirties and forties, colored opaque dinnerware, Sunkist reamers, and 'bottoms up' cocktail tumblers were produced as well as a line of black glass vases, bowls, and novelty items. All are popular items with today's collectors. The company was purchased in 1916 by Jeannette Glass, under which name it continues to operate. See also Animal Dishes with Covers; Depression Glass; Kitchen Collectibles; Reamers.

Tambour mantel clock, 14" long, in vaseline: $450.00; in black: $1,100.00; in amber or pink: $300.00.

Bottoms Up, caramel w/crystal 70.00
Bottoms Up, clear frost w/blk 95.00

Bottoms Up, jade w/crystal......................................60.00
Bottoms Up, jade w/gr frost.....................................60.00
Bottoms Up, jadite, w/coaster 95.00
Bowl, drippings; Red Dot, w/lid.................................12.50
Bowl, mixing; Red Ships, 6" 14.00
Bowl, Red Dot, 7½" 6.00
Bowl, Red Dot, 8½" 7.50
Butter dish, Red Ships 35.00
Canister, Red Ships, 3½" 15.00
Canister, Red Ships, 5" 25.00
Coaster, gr flashed...12.00
Plate, Ray, flint, 1860s, rough rim............................25.00
Refrigerator dish, Red Ships, w/lid, 4x5" 18.00
Shakers, Red Ships, 3¼", pr.....................................20.00

Medical Collectibles

The field of medical-related items encompasses a wide area from the primitive bleeding bowl to the X-ray machines of the early 1900s. Other closely related collectibles include apothecary and dental items. Many tools that were originally intended for the pharmacist found their way to the doctor's office, and dentists often used surgical tools when no suitable dental instrument was available. A trend in the late 1700s toward self-medication brought a whole new wave of home-care manuals and 'patent' medical machines for home use. Commonly referred to as 'quack' medical gimmicks, these machines were usually ineffective and occasionally dangerous.

Our advisor for this category is Jim Calison; he is listed in the Directory under New York.

Bag, doctor's; leather, w/orig tools & bottles, ca 1900, EX..........165.00
Bleeder, brass w/2 iron blades, Castle, 1830s, EX 55.00
Bleeder, wooden w/1 single blade, Hawcroft, 1860s, EX 15.00
Bleeding cup, glass, bell shape, ca 1810s, NM 22.00

Blood centrifuge, brass wells, ca 1890, $150.00.

Book, Doctor Looks at Love & Life, c 1926, 280-pg, EX 17.50
Book, Physician & Surgeon, p Hendricks, dtd 1887, 50+ pgs 6.00
Booklet, Laws of Life, health information, NY, 1876, 30-pg........... 6.00
Bottle, pharmaceutical; amber, w/stopper, 1900s, 3½" 20.00
Bottle, pharmaceutical; blown, glass label: TR Kino, 7".................40.00
Bottle, pharmaceutical; blown, w/stopper, ca 1900, 8" 35.00
Breast pump, brass plunger, Weiss & Son, 1880s, 2-pc, EX.........285.00
Catheter, urinary; sterling, dtd 1852, extends to 6¼"....................115.00
Chair, dentist's, Ridder, hydraulic, EX upholstery, 1920 .... 3,750.00
Dose glass, Dr Harters (in half-moon, bottle), 3" 25.00

Dose glass, Enjoy Life Bismarck Bitters Once a Day, 2½" 160.00
Dose glass, Hopkins Union Bitters, etched, gold rim, 2¼" 75.00
Dose glass, Union Bitters, etched, gold trim, 2⅝" 90.00
Drill, dental, foot treadle, ca 1895, EX...345.00
Ear scoop, silver w/ebony hdl, dtd 1804 ....250.00
Ear trumpet, gutta percha, 2-pc, collapsible...................................195.00
Ear trumpet, tortoise w/attached lorgnette, 1890s, EX 500.00
Eye cup, bl glass 30.00
Eye cup, gr glass, Made in England, W on base 30.00
Eyelid retractor, ivory hdl, Hills King St Borough, 1850s 115.00
Fleam, horn, 3-blade, ca 1830, EX..195.00
Fleam, steel, 3-blade, folding, mk Gregory, in bone case................75.00
Infuser, porc, mk Berlin Germany 25.00
Inhaler, pottery, Dr Nelson's Improved, ca 1890s, EX...................55.00
Inhaler, tin, Simplex Lamp Co, 1890s, 7", EX 17.50
Jar, label under glass: Cotton, 8", EX 25.00
Kit, stereo visual aids, viewer+130 cards of illnesses, 1910s 300.00
Magazine, Medical Gazette, articles/news, NY, 1882, 16-pg 5.00
Nipple shield, glass, 1860s, EX 50.00
Quack device, Advance 1¢ Electricity, 14½x6½" base, EX...........65.00
Spoon, pewter, C Gibson Inventor, ca 1837 ....350.00
Surgical kit, 16 instruments in wooden box, 1840s, EX 325.00
Syringe, glass, w/orig wooden case, 1860s, EX 32.50
Syringe, glass w/cotton string-wound plunger, 1860s....................27.50
Syringe, irrigation; brass, Reynolds & Branson, 1890s, 8" 130.00
Tongue depressor, brass, folding, ca 1860, EX 175.00
Tooth key, ebony X-hatched hdl, Weiss London, 1850s..............380.00
Trocar, silver, w/4 canulae, ca 1840 ....355.00

Meissen

The Royal Saxon Porcelain Works was established in 1710 in Meissen, Saxony. Under the direction of Johann Freidrick Bottger, who in 1708 had developed the formula for the first true porcelain body, fine ceramic figurines with exquisite detail and tableware of the highest quality were produced. Although every effort was made to insure the secrecy of Bottger's discovery, others soon began to copy his ware; and in 1731 Meissen adopted the famous crossed sword trademark to identify their own work. The term 'Dresden ware' is often used to refer to Meissen porcelain, since Bottger's discovery and first potting efforts were in nearby Dresden. See also Onion Pattern.

Box, snuff; lady's leg form, pk shoe/wht stocking, 2½" 500.00
Candlestick, appl/HP flowers on Rococo vase stem, 9½", pr........600.00
Candlestick, child w/baskets, appl flowers, 8", EX, pr 1,200.00
Candlestick, gold-traced bl florals, 6-side top/base, 6"..................150.00
Coffeepot, birds/prunus/rocks in bl, loop band, 1750s, 7½" 450.00
Coffeepot, floral sprigs, pear form, angle hdl, 1700s, 9" 180.00
Compote, floral-emb/beaded center, floral-emb edge, 7x12" 550.00
Cup & saucer, flowers in quatrefoils on yel, 1700s 300.00
Desk set, harbor view/gilt, 1880s, 7x11" tray, bell, +2 pcs...........900.00
Figurine, cherub holds fish & baskets, mk CGS, 4", EX 400.00
Figurine, draped lady w/appl flowers in arms, bsk, 6", NM 325.00
Figurine, falconer on plinth, Xd swords mk, 8"............................250.00
Figurine, girl w/basket of flowers, 1880s, 4¾", EX 250.00
Figurine, he w/flute, she in floral/lav robe, 1880s, 8" 450.00
Figurine, lad holds grapes, hat draped w/vines, 1760, 8" 675.00
Figurine, lad w/baton, pk jerkin/bl pants, scroll base, 5½" 225.00
Figurine, maid w/harp, bl coat/floral skirt, 1880s, 5¾"................225.00
Figurine, Rape of Prosperpina, abducted by Pluto 1880, 9" 375.00
Figurine, sea gull on stump, rocky base, 1880, 8" 225.00
Figurine, seated female monarch/standing attendant, 11x12" . 2,600.00
Figurine, Venus in bird-drawn chariot, putto aside, 7", EX..........600.00

Figure of a woman eating fruit, monkey and child in attendance, 12", $900.00.

Jar, scenic, gilt metal mts, rtcl metal lid, 1730s, rpr, 4" 900.00
Medallion, Madonna del Sedia in panel, after Raphael, 2¾" 220.00
Plaque, penitent Magdalene, after Batoni, metal fr, 7" W............450.00
Teacup, Orientals by fence pat dog, gilt metal hdl/ft, 1730..........450.00
Teapot, wht w/emerald gr & gold, Rococo emb, +cr/sug...............490.00
Tray, bouquets in puce, brn-lined rim, 1750s, mk, 6¾" 125.00
Vase, HP fruit, snake hdls, fluted/gilt rim, 1880, 11", pr 450.00
Vase, snowball style w/appl birds & fruit, bird finial, 18" 1,200.00
Vase, 2 reserves: lovers/birds on bl, emb leaves, rtcl, 12" 450.00

Mercury Glass

Mercury glass was popular during the 1850s and enjoyed a short revival at the turn of the century. It was made with two thin layers, either blown with a double wall or joined in sections, with the space between the walls of the vessel filled with a mixture of tin, lead, bismuth, and mercury. The opening was sealed to prevent air from dulling the bright color. Though most examples are silver, blue and gold can be found on occasion. Remember that the value of this type of glass hinges greatly upon condition of the mercury lining. In the listings that follow, all examples are silver unless noted another color.

Bottle, vintage eng, amber-flashed cut neck, bulbous, 7½" 175.00
Bowl, 3 clear appl ft, 4¾x9½"..80.00
Candlestick, bl, 14", pr..100.00
Candlestick, gold, dome base, 6", pr..75.00
Compote, gold, knop stem, 8¼"...100.00
Goblet, gold, wht enamel floral band, 5" 35.00
Mug, clear hdl, 3"...25.00
Rolling pin 75.00
Salt, master; gold int, initials on plug, 2½" 85.00
Spooner, HP floral 40.00
Vase, HP deer & foliage, bulbous, 7"...35.00
Vase, HP floral sprays in panel, 10", pr 200.00
Vase, lt wear on base, 9¼", pr 65.00
Witch ball, 18", +stand 150.00

Merrimac

Founded in 1897 in Newburyport, Massachusetts, the Merrimac

Pottery Company primarily produced tile and gardenware. In 1901, however, they introduced a line of artware that is now attracting the interest of collectors. Marked examples carry an impressed die-stamp or a paper label, each with the firm name and the outline of a sturgeon, the Indian word for which was Merrimac.

Chamberstick, gr mottle, cylindrical neck, loop hdl, 6"	325.00
Mug, dk gr matt, frog w/in, 4½"	275.00
Mug, gr mottle, flared rim, 6¾", EX	125.00
Mug, gr/charcoal mottle, unsgn, 4", NM	70.00
Vase, Arts & Crafts floral, blk to purple, AA/1915, 16x8"	650.00
Vase, dk gr matt w/lt gr textured highlights, 24"	750.00
Vase, gr feathered matt, ogee sides, unmk (early), 4½x3½"	150.00
Vase, gr matt, tapered cylinder, paper label, rpr, 12x5"	350.00
Vase, gr matt w/feathering, bulbous w/collar rim, 10x10"	750.00
Vase, pitted gr, stamp mk w/fish, 7x5"	600.00
Vase, thick irregular gr matt, wide shoulder, 6x5¼"	100.00
Vase, yel matt, short neck, wide shoulder, dtd 1906, 8x6"	550.00

Metlox

The Metlox Manufacturing Company was founded in 1927 in Manhattan Beach, California. Before 1934 when they began producing the ceramic housewares for which they have become famous, they made ceramic and neon outdoor advertising signs. The company went out of business in 1989.

Well-known sculptor Carl Romanelli designed artware in the late 1930s and early 1940s (and again briefly in the 1950s). His work is especially sought after today.

Aztec, bowl, divided vegetable; 11½"	25.00
Aztec, carafe, w/lid, 18"	65.00
Aztec, creamer & sugar bowl w/lid	15.00
Aztec, cup	7.50
Aztec, gravy boat	15.00
Aztec, pitcher, water; 14½"	50.00
Aztec, plate, 10½"	7.50
Aztec, platter, oval, 9½"	10.00
Aztec, tumbler, 13-oz	12.50
California Ivy, bowl, cereal	8.00
California Ivy, bowl, fruit; 5¼"	6.00
California Ivy, bowl, 9¼"	15.00
California Ivy, butter dish	25.00
California Ivy, casserole, w/lid	25.00
California Ivy, chop plate, 13"	25.00
California Ivy, coaster	5.00
California Ivy, creamer	6.00
California Ivy, cup & saucer	8.00
California Ivy, gravy boat	15.00
California Ivy, gravy boat, w/underplate	27.50
California Ivy, pepper mill	12.50
California Ivy, pitcher, water; ice lip	30.00
California Ivy, plate, salad; 8"	5.00
California Ivy, plate, 10¼"	10.00
California Ivy, platter, oval, 13"	20.00
California Ivy, sugar bowl	10.00
California Ivy, teapot	30.00
California Provincial, bowl, fruit; 6"	7.50
California Provincial, plate, 10"	10.00
California Provincial, plate, 7"	5.00
California Provincial, plate, 9"	8.00
California Provincial, soup, flat	10.00
California Provincial, water can	25.00

Homestead Provincial, bowl, cereal	3.50
Homestead Provincial, bread tray	25.00
Homestead Provincial, coaster	4.00
Homestead Provincial, creamer	6.00
Homestead Provincial, cup & saucer	10.00
Homestead Provincial, match holder, wall hanging	30.00

Homestead Provincial, Jug, $16.00; Plate, 10", $7.50; Mug, $15.00.

Homestead Provincial, plate, 6"	4.00
Homestead Provincial, platter, 13"	20.00
Homestead Provincial, server, 3-part	25.00
Homestead Provincial, shakers, hdl, pr	8.00
Provincial Fruit, bowl, vegetable; rnd	15.00
Provincial Fruit, coffeepot	38.00
Provincial Fruit, nappy, hdls, 5"	9.00
Provincial Fruit, pitcher, 7"	25.00
Provincial Fruit, platter, med	18.00
Provincial Fruit, platter, sm	14.00
Provincial Fruit, shakers, pr	12.00
Provincial Fruit, tankard	12.00
Provincial Fruit, tumbler	12.00
Red Rooster, bowl, vegetable; 10"	25.00
Red Rooster, bowl, vegetable; 2-part, hdls	30.00
Red Rooster, bread tray	25.00
Red Rooster, casserole, rooster figural, w/lid	45.00
Red Rooster, coffeepot	27.50
Red Rooster, cup & saucer	10.00
Red Rooster, lug soup	4.00
Red Rooster, plate, 10"	10.00
Red Rooster, plate, 7½"	5.00
Red Rooster, platter, 11"	15.00
Red Rooster, platter, 13½"	20.00
Red Rooster, shakers, pr	12.00
Red Rooster, stein	35.00
Red Rooster, teapot	27.50
Red Rooster, tureen, soup	110.00
Romanelli Artware, bookends, nude w/dogs, mc, pr	100.00
Romanelli Artware, deer, wht matt, Poppy Trail, Deco, 7½"	45.00
Romanelli Artware, semi-nude cowgirl, mc, 9½"	85.00
Romanelli Artware, swordfish vase, bl matt, 9"	65.00
Sculptured Daisy, bowl, divided vegetable; hdls, 8"	22.50
Sculptured Daisy, bowl, vegetable; hdls, 7"	17.50
Sculptured Daisy, bowl, vegetable; hdls, 8"	20.00
Sculptured Daisy, bowl, w/lid, 8"	40.00

Sculptured Daisy, bowl, w/lid, 9" 40.00
Sculptured Daisy, coffeepot 45.00
Sculptured Daisy, creamer 4.00
Sculptured Daisy, cup & saucer 7.50
Sculptured Daisy, mug, coffee 12.00
Sculptured Daisy, pitcher, milk; 6" 30.00
Sculptured Daisy, pitcher, 9" 45.00
Sculptured Daisy, platter, 14" 27.50
Sculptured Daisy, shakers, pr 12.50
Sculptured Daisy, tumbler, 5¼" 12.50
Sculptured Grape, bowl, vegetable; 9¼" 24.00
Sculptured Grape, butter dish 24.00
Sculptured Grape, casserole, w/lid..............................38.00
Sculptured Grape, cup & saucer 10.00
Sculptured Grape, plate, dinner 12.00
Sculptured Grape, shakers, pr 12.00

Cookie Jars

Barrel of Apples 48.00
Basket of Fruit 50.00
Bear, roller skates 60.00
Bear, sombrero 60.00
Bear, sweater & cookie 38.00
Beau Bear 40.00
Clown 65.00
Cow, crier in lid 195.00
Drum, bsk, mk 30.00
Dutch Boy 80.00
Fido 65.00
Frog 68.00
Humpty Dumpty 70.00
Lamb's Head...70.00
Mammy 155.00
Owl 65.00
Puddles Duck 65.00
Rose 120.00
Squirrel on Pine Cone 55.00
Uncle Sam Bear..250.00

Mettlach

In 1836 Nicholas Villeroy and Eugene Francis Boch, both of
whom were already involved in the potting industry, formed a partnership and established a stoneware factory in an old restored abbey in
Mettlach, Germany. Decorative stoneware with in-mold relief was their
specialty, steins in particular. Through constant experimentation, they
developed innovative methods of decoration. One process, called chro-
molith, involved inlaying colorful mosaic designs into the body of the
ware. Later, underglaze printing from copper plates was used. Their
stoneware was of high quality, and their steins won many medals at the
St. Louis Expo and early world's fairs. Most examples are marked with
an incised castle and the name 'Mettlach.' The numbering system indicates size, date, stock number, and decorator. Production was halted by
a fire in 1921 — the factory was not rebuilt.

Our advisor for this category is Ron Fox; he is listed in the Directory under New York.

Key:
L — liter   PUG — print under glaze
POG — print over glaze   tl — thumb lift

#1005, stein, relief: tavern scenes, inlay lid, 1-L, M 300.00

#1028, stein, relief: couple at harvest, inlay lid, ½-L, M 160.00
#1037, stein, relief: tavern scenes, inlay lid, 1886, ½-L 120.00
#1044, plaque, HP: lady/bird/flowers, 17", EX 375.00
#1044/167-B, plaque, PUG: castle, 15", M 225.00
#1044/190, plaque, PUG: Schlossplatz in Stuttgart, 12", M 250.00
#1044/217, plaque, PUG: Schlosshof Heidelberg, 12", M 155.00
#1044/95, plaque, PUG: Burg Eitz, sm chip, 12" 160.00
#1055/2271, stein, PUG: cavaliers & monkeys, ½-L, M 255.00
#1076/1526, stein, PUG: Schuzenfest, eagle tl, ½-L, NM 235.00
#1077/1526, stein, PUG: elder musician, gnome tl, ½-L, M 185.00
#109½ 368, beaker, PUG: waiter serves wine, ¼-L, M 75.00
#1093/2368, beaker, PUG: guitar player, 1 of 6, ¼-L, M.............65.00
#1108/1526, stein, PUG: Bock Beer, Munich Maid tl, ½-L, M....315.00
#1134/2327, beaker, PUG: couple at fest, sm flake, ¼-L 100.00
#1135/2327, beaker, PUG: Alpine couple, ¼-L, NM 110.00
#1143/1526, stein, PUG: tavern scene, crack, 1-L 220.00
#1145/1526, stein, PUG: man w/pipe & beer, ½-L, M 150.00
#1179/2327, beaker, PUG: Gesang, 1 of 6, ¼-L, M 80.00
#1233/2327, beaker, PUG: boy w/dog & stein, ¼-L, M 140.00
#1395, stein, etched: cards, inlay lid, card tl, ½-L, M 450.00
#1409, vase, mc tapestry, dragon hdls, 11¼"........................450.00
#1431, stein, enameled: Gabelsberger..., pewter lid, 1-L, M 1,040.00
#1475, stein, etched: gnomes, grape inlay lid, ½-L, M 635.00
#1513, pitcher, couples dancing, Warth, 6¼" 305.00
#1526, stein, appl relief: Yale banner, flag tl, ½-L, M 155.00
#1526, stein, enameled: Kochelbrau..., .3-L, M 285.00
#1526, stein, HP on POG: early guard, pewter lid, ½-L, EX 175.00
#1526, stein, incised, Bamberger Franken, pewter lid, .3-L, M ...200.00
#1526, stein, incised, wht int, pewter lid, .3-L, M 180.00
#1526, stein, POG: Brewer's Convention, pewter lid, ½-L, NM ..145.00
#1526, stein, POG: comic map, pewter lid, ½-L, M 260.00
#1526, stein, PUG, courting scene, pewter top, dtd 1919, 6".......195.00
#1526, stein, PUG & enamel: Frankfurter Burgerbrau, .3-L, M...140.00
#1526, stein, PUG & enamel: Frankfurter Burgerbrau, 1-L, M....215.00
#1527, stein, etched: cavalier & knights, inlay lid, ½-L, M 535.00
#1533, stein, tapestry: man drinking, pewter lid, chip, 1-L 260.00
#1566, stein, etched: high-wheel cyclist, brass lid, ½-L, M 965.00
#1607, plaque, Autumn Season, sgn Warth, dtd 1885, mk, 11"...525.00
#1675, stein, etched: Heidelberg, inlay lid, ½-L, M 475.00
#1733, stein, etched: jockey, cap inlay lid, ½-L, M 825.00
#1734, stein, etched: couple, jewel base, inlay lid, 1½-L, EX 900.00
#1740, stein, relief: hops buds & vines, flakes, ¼-L 115.00
#1744, stein, threaded relief: Munich Maid in star, ½-L, M.........215.00
#1909, stein, PUG: Germania, pewter lid, .4-L, NM 145.00
#1995, stein, etched: tuba player, rim line, ½-L 260.00
#1997, stein, etched/PUG: 6-pointed star, Ehret, ½ -L, NM 315.00
#2001C, stein, book w/owl tl, castle mk, ½-L, 7" 495.00
#2002, stein, etched: Munich, brewer's vat inlay lid, ½-L, M 450.00
#2024, stein, etched/glazed: Berlin, prof rpr, ½-L 260.00
#2035, stein, etched: Bacchus scene, inlay lid, .3-L, M 235.00
#2035, stein, etched: Bacchus scene, inlay lid, 1-L, M 560.00
#2035, stein, etched: Bacchus scene, inlay lid, ½-L, M 400.00
#2052, stein, etched: Munich Maid, cherub inlay lid, ¼-L, M 365.00
#2057, stein, etched: peasants dancing, inlay lid, ½-L, M............450.00
#2077, stein, relief: coat of arms, inlay lid, .3-L, M 100.00
#2080, plaque, etched: 4 Kurassiers, sgn Stocke, 15", NM....... 1,250.00
#2090, stein, etched: club, sgn H Schlitt, inlay lid, 1-L, M..........650.00
#2100, stein, etched: Prosit, Schlitt, inlay lid, ½-L, M 900.00
#2123, stein, etched: knight, H Schlitt, inlay lid, .3-L, EX 500.00
#2134, stein, etched: gnome in nest, gnome tl, ½-L, M........... 1,600.00
#2140, stein, enameled transfer: crest, 1901, rprs, ½-L............125.00
#2189, coaster, etched: drinking/smoking, bk flake, 4½" 105.00
#2194, stein, relief: In Blk Whale in Ascalon, 3¼-L, EX 695.00
#2211, stein, relief: bowling scene, sgn HF, .3-L, M................235.00

#2226/1062, punch bowl, PUG: tavern scenes, lines, 2-L............250.00
#2235, stein, etched: barmaid & archers, eagle tl, ½-L, M.........675.00
#225/2184, stein, PUG/relief: mtn scenes, gnome tl, ½-L, M 350.00
#2278, stein, relief: Turnfest scenes, pewter lid, ½-L, M 310.00
#2280/1005, punch bowl, PUG: gnomes at wine press, 2-L, EX ..335.00
#2286, stein, etched: cavaliers & maid, inlay lid, 2½-L, M 675.00
#2324, stein, etched: early football game, inlay lid, ½-L, M 1,500.00
#2358, stein, relief: dance scene, corn inlay lid, ½-L, M 200.00
#2373, stein, etched: St Augustine, alligator hdl/tl, ½ -L, M 555.00
#2382 , stein, etched: knight, Schlitt, tower lid, ½-L, M 835.00
#2388, stein, glazed character: stack of pretzels, ½-L, M 360.00
#2391, stein, etched: Lohengrin's wedding, inlay lid, ½-L, M......675.00
#2394, stein, etched: Siegfried, sm rpr on inlay lid, ½-L 390.00
#2442, plaque, Grecian soldiers in boat, sgn/dtd 1899, 18" 1,250.00
#2501, stein, etched: outdoor scene, Quidenus, ½-L, M...............600.00
#2524, stein, etched: Dekannenburg, prof rpr, 4¼-L, EX 1,110.00
#2623, plaque, etched: water w/wine, sgn Quidenus, 7½"...........135.00
#2626, plaque, etched: man drinking, Quidennus, 7½", M.........135.00
#2632, stein, etched: bowling, pin tl, inlay lid, ½-L, M................410.00
#2715, stein, cameo: dancing (3 panels), pewter lid, ½-L, M 525.00
#2765, stein, etched: knight on horse, knight tl, ½-L, M 2,400.00
#2776, stein, etched: keeper of cellar, inlay lid, ½-L, M..............895.00
#2796, stein, etched: Heidelberg scene, inlay lid, 3-L, M 1,600.00
#2800, stein, etched: Nouveau hops, inlay lid, 1903, ½-L, M 365.00
#2815, beaker, cameo: dancers, ¼-L, M...................................290.00
#2818, coaster, etched: smoker toasting, 4½", M.........................215.00
#2833, stein, etched: man by tree, inlay lid, ½-L, M 500.00
#2833, stein, etched: students drinking, inlay lid, ½-L, M 555.00
#2872, stein, etched: Cornell, owl tl, inlay lid, ½-L, M................615.00
#2880, stein, etched: tavern scene, sgn Q, inlay lid, ½-L, M........600.00
#2935, stein, etched: hops & barley, inlay lid, rpr, ½-L................215.00
#2960, plate, etched: Nouveau flower, rpr, 15"...........................80.00
#2997, plaque, etched: autumn, 17½", NM............................. 1,870.00
#3024, relief: cavalier smoking, inlay lid, 3-L, 12¼"....................340.00
#3089, stein, etched: Diogenes, Socrates inlay lid, ½-L, NM 800.00
#3142, stein, etched: Bavarian dancers, inlay lid, ½-L, M............625.00

Stein, #2382, etched, knight and tavern keeper, tower lid, ½-liter, $835.00.

#330/1000, convention character stein, Abby Tower, '78, 12", M.105.00
#3358, vase, Art Nouveau feathers, shouldered, 12", M 225.00
#5013/965, stein, faience/PUG: In Arte Libertas, ½-L, M 495.00
#5022, stein, faience: boat cartouch, 1-L, M 1,180.00
#5024, stein, faience: floral, pewter mts, hairline, 1-L.................845.00
#675, stein, relief: keg, pewter lid: Prosit emb, ½-L, NM 90.00

#702/1909, stein, PUG: Gambrinus leads parade, ½-L, M 245.00
#727/1909, stein, PUG: gnomes bowling, pewter lid, .3-L, M......270.00
#727/1909, stein, PUG: gnomes bowling, pewter lid, ½-L, M.....340.00
#90½ 221, stein, PUG: Murttemburg commemorative, ½-L, M . 1,040.00
#958/2181, stein, PUG: musician/hares, Munich Maid tl, ¼-L, M..250.00
#960/2177, stein, PUG: jester, Munich Maid tl, ¼-L, M 205.00
#96½ 179, stein, PUG: gnome w/pitcher/Prosit, ¼-L, M 200.00
#967/2184, stein, PUG/relief: gnomes/radishes, ½-L, NM 250.00
#983/1909, stein, PUG: Fallstaff, pewter lid, ½-L, M 315.00

Militaria

Because of the wide and varied scope of items available to collectors of militaria, most tend to concentrate mainly on the area or areas that interest them most or that they can afford to buy. Some items represent a major investment and because of their value have been reproduced. Extreme caution should be used when purchasing Nazi items. Every badge, medal, cap, uniform, dagger, and sword that Nazi Germany issued is being reproduced today. Some repros are crude and easily identified as fakes, while others are very well done and difficult to recognize as reproductions. Purchases from WWII veterans are usually your safest buys. Reputable dealers or collectors will normally offer a money-back guarantee on Nazi items purchased from them. There are a number of excellent Third Reich reference books available in bookstores at very reasonable prices. Study them to avoid losing a much larger sum spent on a reproduction.

Our advisor for this category is Ron Willis; he is listed in the Directory under Oklahoma.

Imperial German

Badge, Afrika Colonial, elephant center, silvered metal, EX.......200.00
Badge, Bavarian Aviation Observer, 800 silver, 3-pc....................500.00
Badge, sleeve; Artillery Shooting Prize, Juncker, 1907.................125.00
Badge, wound; WWI, blk, hollow, stamped type, EX pnt..............15.00
Badge, wound; WWI, Kriegsmarine, gold, hollow, stamped...........80.00
Badge, WWI, Army Standard Bearer, embr w/Xd flags, EX 150.00
Bayonet knot, WWI, Infantry NCO, wht strap w/blk/bl/yel, EX ...35.00
Belt, WWI, brn leather, field-gray pnt buckle, EX 38.00
Book, Kriegs Erinnernungen, maps & drawings, 1895, EX 18.00
Buckle, Gott Mit Uns, Prussian Crown, brass & nickel, EX..........22.50
Buckle, WWI, crown w/Cott Mit UNS motto, brass, 2-pc.............25.00
Buckle, WWI, stamped steel w/field-gray pnt, 1-pc 18.00
Cap, visor; WWI, Army officer, crush style, bl w/band, EX 85.00
Certificate of service, WWI, notes decorations/etc, 10x13".........12.00
Cocard, WWI, Feldmutz, red/wht/blk on metal.............................15.00
Document, award for Kaiser Jubilee medal, dtd 1898, EX 18.00
Document, award of Landwehr Reserve Medal 2nd Class, 1882 ...25.00
Document, WWI, Army NCO becomes sergeant, 1918, 8x12" 27.50
Dog tag, WWI, name & regiment, EX 27.50
Drum hanger, brass crowned eagle w/hooks for drum, EX 95.00
Epaulettes, pre-WWI, red w/brass trim, silver/blk piping, pr 60.00
Helmet, spike; Baden Guard Grenadier, silver trim, EX 465.00
Helmet, spike; field-gr felt, VG 80.00
Helmet, WWI, blk leather w/brass, spike & frontplate, EX 265.00
Knife, trench; WWI, Polish hdl & blade, mk Eikhorn, EX 38.00
Medal, Bavaria Napoleonic Wars 1913-14 Campaign Cross, EX ..40.00
Medal, Chino 1900 Combat, Boxer Rebellion, bronze 80.00
Medal, Franco-Prussian War, gilt bronze, w/ribbon 20.00
Medal, Prussia Officer's XXV Long Service Cross, gilt, type 2 ......38.00
Medal, War Merit Cross w/Xd swords, enameled silver w/ribbon ..88.00
Medal, WWI, Iron Cross 2nd Class, w/ribbon & hallmk ring........32.00
Medal, WWI, 1914 Iron Cross 2nd Class, w/ribbon, EX 40.00

Medallion, WWI, gold donation, kneeling lady, 1916, EX **12.50**
Post card, group photo of 8 soldiers, letter on bk, 1917 ....**5.00**
Post card, photo of village ruins, soldiers beyond, 1918.................**6.50**
Post card, WWI, photo: Immelmann Air Ace w/decorations, EX..**27.50**
Post card, WWI, photo: soldier w/sweetheart, EX **5.00**
Ring, WWI, Flying officer, skull w/pilot's helmet/goggles **235.00**
Shoulderboards, Lieutenant, silver w/blk, slip-on, pr **30.00**
Shoulderboards, Medical Staff, silver w/blk, slip-on, pr.................**35.00**
Shoulderboards, WWI, field grey, sew-on, pr, VG.........................**22.50**
Stickpin, WWI, Army Pilot badge miniature, wht metal, EX........**32.00**
Sword, Baden Infantry officer, 38", w/blued steel scabbard **185.00**
Sword, Navy, w/leather scabbard **400.00**
Tunic, WWI, Air Service, field gray, concealed buttons, EX.......**475.00**

Third Reich

Armband, Deutscher Volkssturm Wehrmacht, printed, EX...........**15.00**
Armband, political leader, swastika on red wool, EX.....................**48.00**
Badge, Genear's Assault, solid type, needle pin, EX **42.50**
Badge, Infantry Assault, silver, solid type, hallmk, EX **42.50**
Badge, Kriegsmarine U-Boat, brass, swastika, early, EX **135.00**
Badge, Luftwaffe Observer, wreath/eagle/swastika, 2-pc, EX........**215.00**
Badge, pre-WWII, Hitler Youth Potsdam, SP, solid type, 1932 .....**60.00**
Badge, wound; brass, hollow type, worn pnt, early, VG **15.00**
Badge, wound; WWII, gold-washed, solid type, EX.......................**18.00**
Badge, WWII, General Assault, hollow stamped-out type, EX **40.00**
Badge, WWII, Kriegsmarine Destroyer, brass, early, EX **75.00**
Badge, WWII, Kriegsmarine U-Boat officer, gold bullion embr.....**55.00**
Badge, WWII, Luftwaffe Ground Combat, late war, 1-pc, EX **60.00**
Badge, WWII, Tank Assault, silver, solid type, SA hallmk............**40.00**
Band, sleeve; Afrikakorps, tan w/gr, bevo-type embr, EX..............**60.00**
Book, Der Kampf im Westen, 3-D book w/viewer, EX **150.00**
Book, Der Sieg in Polen, combat pictures, 1939, 174-pg, EX.........**50.00**
Book, Hitler at My Side, Bauer, English translation, 1986 ....**20.00**
Book, Hitler Jugend, Hitler Youth, p 1942, 315-pg, EX................**90.00**
Breeches, riding; WWII, NSKK, blk wool, EX **125.00**
Canteen, Afrikakorps officer, early felt cover/web strap **30.00**
Cap, M-43 type, waffen camo, field made, reversible, EX..............**85.00**
Cap, overseas; Army, field-gray wool, w/eagle & cocard, EX **88.00**
Cap, overseas; WWII, Labor Corps, silk lining, EX **145.00**
Cap, overseas; WWII, Nazi Army, wht infantry piping, VG..........**88.00**
Cap, visor; Army Administrative officer, gr/field gray, EX............**200.00**
Cap, visor; WWII, Kyffhauserbund, swastikas/eagle, EX **85.00**
Cap, WWII, Luftwaffe, bl-gray w/gold beads, blk visor, EX **125.00**
Collar tabs, Army Infantry officer, wht piping on dk gr, pr............**32.00**
Cuff links, WWII, Dutch SS, blk enamel on silver, EX **135.00**
Flag, WWII, SS District, for auto, eagle/etc in metal fr.................**735.00**
Flagpole top, WWII, eagle w/wings wide, swastika in wreath **195.00**
Gloves, WWII, Wermacht Motorcycle Driver, leather & cotton ..**55.00**
Hand grenade, WWII, missing ceramic bead, no mks.................**145.00**
Hat, visor; WWII, Luftwaffe, yel piping, VG................................**235.00**
Hat, visor; WWII, SS Concentration Camp Officer, NM **1,750.00**
Helmet, Waffen SS, M-42, steel, EX...**465.00**
Helmet, WWII, Luftwaffe, single decal, EX **235.00**
Helmet, WWII, M-39 pattern, steel, rpt, VG................................**120.00**
Helmet, WWII, Nazi SS, dbl decals, rolled rim, complete, EX **525.00**
Medal, Mother's Cross, bl/wht enamel on bronze, w/ribbon, EX....**34.00**
Medal, War Merit Cross 1st Class, w/swords, SP, wide, mk............**45.00**
Medal, War Merit Cross 2nd Class, w/issue packet, NM **22.50**
Medal, WWII, German Cross, Afrikakorps, cloth version, EX ...**200.00**
Medal, WWII, German Social Welfare, wht metal, w/ribbon, EX.**55.00**
Medal, WWII, Lurtschutz 2nd class, lt aluminum, w/ribbon..........**38.00**
Medal, WWII, War Merit Cross 2nd Class, w/swords/ribbon, NM .**32.00**
Overcoat, WWII, officer's general dress, red lapels, EX **1,750.00**

**Photograph of Hitler,
7" x 5", $25.00.**

Pants, WWII, Afrikakorps, short tropical style, EX......................**165.00**
Shield, Demjansk, stamped metal, curved, w/bkplate, EX.............**48.00**
Shield, Demjansk, w/Luftwaffe clothbking, complete, EX.............**88.00**
Shield, sleeve; Turkistan Volunteer, bevo-type embr, EX..............**37.50**
Shield, sleeve; WWII, Waffen SS Danish Volunteer, blk wool **40.00**
Shoulderboards, Army Cavalry, gray w/gold, slip-on, pr................**27.50**
Shoulderboards, Army Gen Staff Major, crimson, slip-on, pr **42.50**
Stickpin, blk enameled swastika, EX...**14.00**
Stickpin, WWII, German Lifesaver, gold washed, w/ribbon **37.50**
Stickpin, WWII, Nazi flag design, EX...**55.00**
Stickpin, WWII, Nazi Party banner, enameled, for lapel **60.00**
Tunic, Army Panzer, blk wraparound, w/insignias, +pants, EX....**800.00**
Tunic, WWII, Afrikakorps Panzer Lieutenant, 3rd pattern, EX ..**355.00**
Tunic, WWII, Army Parade NCO, w/insignias/badges/tabs, EX .**375.00**

Japanese

Badge, breast; WWII, Fire Police, wht metal, oval, wide, EX..........**35.00**
Badge, WWII, Railway Police, silver w/red enamel, EX **45.00**
Book, WWII, Army soldier's ID, EX **22.00**
Bottle, saki; WWII, Army star & rising sun emblem **40.00**
Cap ribbon, WWII, Navy, yel characters on blk, EX **30.00**
Chevrons, WWII, Police, bevo-type embr mum on yel, pr **10.00**
Collar tabs, WWII, Army private, olive-drab wool, pr...................**10.00**
Flag, WWII, 'Meatball' symbol, silk, 27x40", EX..........................**45.00**
Generator switch, WWII, 4 wire connectors, w/3x4" ID plate.......**12.00**
Grenade, WWII, type #97, inert, w/fuse assembly, EX **40.00**
Gun sight, WWII, 7x86 power, field use, w/wood case, EX..........**285.00**
Hat cover, visor; WWII, khaki w/metal vent holes, EX **15.00**
Helmet, post-WWII, Self Defense Forces, steel, US liner **40.00**
Manual, WWII, Army, olive-drab canvas cover, rice paper, EX **18.00**
Medal, pre-WWII, member of military band, bronze w/lion, M.....**15.00**
Medallion, pre-WWII, KEIO School graduate, silver/gilt, M **22.00**
Mortar shell, WWII, type #89, inert, w/fuse assembly, EX.............**38.00**
Neck flap, WWII, cotton, for tropical hat, NM **18.00**
Packet, first aid; WWII, olive-drab cotton, unused, 2½x3"............**32.00**
Shirt, WWII, tropical, collarless, 2-pocket, EX **18.00**
Tunic & pants, model 1930, officer's tropical, 4-pocket, VG.........**90.00**

United States

Badge, WWII, Army Recruiter, wht metal, clutch-bk, NM **15.00**
Badge, WWII, Marine Corps Marksman, clutch-bk, NM **15.00**
Bag, grenade; WWII, canvas, w/shoulderstrap, EX **20.00**
Bayonet, Civil War, triangular socket, TN, much rust **50.00**

Belt, cartridge; WWII, M-1910 style, 10-pouch, Mills, EX 32.00
Binoculars, Civil War, Paris, VG 50.00
Book, Civil War Illustrated, 1886, 255-pg, 17x12", VG 155.00
Boots, Vietnam, jungle type, leather w/gr canvas, M................45.00
Box, Civil War, tin, soldered seams, 4x5", EX 8.00
Bracelet, Vietnam War, Missing in Action, M 5.00
Breastplate, Civil War, Union Eagle emb, VG 38.00
Bugle, Indian War, Phila/Chicago, tongue & groove seam 95.00
Button, Civil War, hard rubber, Maltese Cross, Pat 1851 ....6.00
Button, Civil War, NY Militia, eagle/shield/etc, cuff type 12.50
Button, lapel; Civil War, Grand Army...1861-66, bronze 35.00
Canteen, Civil War, bull's-eye type, no cover, mk Phila, EX........28.00
Canteen, Revolutionary War, wooden barrel style, 1750s, EX.....115.00
Canteen, WWII, Marine Corps, banana flap cover, w/cup 22.50
Cartridge box, Civil War, leather w/brass tacks, EX................95.00
Chest, saddler's; folding, for battery wagon, 1917, EX..............400.00
Chevrons, WWII, Army Master Sergeant, silver-gray on blk, pr 5.00
Compass, WWI, US Army, all brass, dtd 1918, EX 25.00
Doubletrees, iron, US Army, EX..65.00
Flight suit, WWII, Army/Air Force, summer, EX 95.00
Gas mask, WWII, Navy, Mark III type, +hoses/canister/bag.........28.00
Hat, overseas; WWII, Army Air Corps, olive-drab cotton, EX 7.50
Hat, visor; pre-WWII, Marine, dress gr, brn bill, NM 40.00
Hat, visor; WWII, Army officer, olive-drab wool, EX 38.00
Helmet, WWI, Marine, steel, mustard pnt, EX........................55.00
Helmet, WWII, Army officer, steel, standard issue, EX 25.00
Horse collar, Army, iron w/blk pnt, 20".................................150.00
Inkwell, Civil War, rosewood, traveling style, EX 50.00
Jacket, fatigue; Indian Wars, 5-button, VG 175.00
Jacket, field; WWII, olive drab, 4-pocket, M-1943 style, EX 35.00
Jacket, WWII, Marine Corps, herringbone, 3-pocket, flapless 35.00
Jacket, WWII, Navy G-1 flight, leather, unissued, NM................250.00
Lanyard, pistol; Military Police, wht nylon, modern, M...............5.00
Leggings, WWI, Marine Corps, tan canvas, brass eyelets.............15.00
Manual, WWII, Browning machine gun, illus, 54-pg, EX 6.00
Medal, Civil War, Bronze Star, on silk flag & eagle pin, EX..........45.00
Medal, WWII, Navy Good Conduct, named, +2nd bar/ribbon 60.00
Medal, WWII, Victory, w/ribbon & post-WWII brooch, NM 12.00
Medical case, Revolutionary War, leather saddle-bag type, EX......75.00
Mess kit, WWI, aluminum, mk & dtd, EX 5.00
Mirror, emergency signal; WWII, Aviator, ESM/type #1, EX........12.50
Newspaper, Stars & Stripes, War Ends edition, Aug 15, 1945, EX . 8.00
Overalls, WWII, Army Tankers, olive drab, bib style, EX 15.00
Overcoat, Korean War, Marine Corps, gr, wartime buttons, EX....15.00

Patch, pocket; Navy P-3 Orion Flight Engineer, oval.....................5.00
Razor strap, US Cavalry, leather w/brass, 1860s, 21", VG.............35.00
Saddle, US Cavalry, hooded stirrups/hair girth, 11½", EX..........325.00
Sea bag, WWII, Marine Corps, tan canvas, brass fittings, EX........35.00
Sextant, WWII, Army Air Force, A-12 type, w/case, NM 90.00
Shoulder patch, WWII, 1st Cavalry Division, machine embr.........5.00
Soap container, Civil War, wooden, for shaving, EX 27.50
Spurs, US Cavalry, ca 1900, pr...32.00
Stirrup, Grimsley, brass, pr...165.00
Stove, camp; Civil War, tin & brass, fluid burner, 9x7", EX...........65.00
Telescope, Civil War, brass/leather, 4-section, 15", EX 88.00
Tunic, WWII, Navy Pilot, w/stripes & wings, EX.......................80.00
Valise, Cavalry officer, canvas roll-up, dtd Jan 12, 1904 ....65.00
Wing, WWII, Ground Observer, wht metal, pin-bk, 1¼"..............12.00
Yoke, neck; Army, iron..35.00

Other Types

Britain, WWII, medical officer, tin, oversz, w/tin cup, EX 24.00
British, WWII, battle jacket, olive-drab wool, dtd 1943, EX 30.00
Egypt, wings, King Farouk period, Pilot's, silvered wreath, M 60.00
France, badge, baret; Foreign Legion, wht metal, NM..................12.50
France, medal, Dardanelles Expedition, bronzed, w/ribbon, M 24.00
France, WWII, gas mask, civilian, complete, EX...........................18.00
Ivory Coast, badge, Paratroopers, wht metal, Drago, Paris, EX 22.50
Lybia, wing, Air Force Navigator, wht metal globe & wings 20.00
Nepal, wing, Parachutist, blk metal, bl plastic bk.........................14.00
Poland, beret, Marine officer, royal bl w/eagle, modern, M...........65.00
Portugal, badge, Reserve Parachutist, gilt wing/silver chute...........14.00
USSR, badge, Submariner's, wht metal w/red enamel, modern 55.00
USSR, pack, Army, canvas w/brn web straps, for RPG-7, EX........85.00
USSR, WWI era, Adrian cap star, dbl-loop bk, 2", EX...................55.00
West Germany, Wing, Army Para Jumpers NCO, post-1966 ....12.00

Milk Glass

Milk glass is the current collector's name for milk-white opaque glass. The early glassmaker's term was Opal Ware. Originally attempted in England in the 18th century with the intention of imitating china, milk glass was not commercially successful until the mid-1800s. Pieces produced in the U.S.A., England, and France during the 1870-1900 period are highly prized for their intricate detail and fiery, opalescent edges.

Our advisor for this category is Rod Dockery; he is listed in the Directory under Texas. In our listings, B stands for Belknap, F for Ferson, L for Lindsey, M for Millard, and W for Warman, all standard reference books. See also Animal Dishes with Covers; Bread Plates; Historical Glass; Westmoreland.

Bowl, Daisy & Tree of Life, hexagonal, B-106C 55.00
Bowl, Lattice Edge, B-106B, 2x9½" 45.00
Butter dish, Daisy & Tree of Life 95.00
Butter dish, Sawtooth, flint, B-197C 125.00
Candy box, heart shape, 3-compartment, 1950s...........................45.00
Compote, Atlas, lacy edge, Atterbury, B-104, 8x9" 100.00
Compote, Jenny Lind, tall, 7½" 100.00
Compote, Lattice Edge, pnt center, repro, M-116A 25.00
Covered dish, Battleship Oregon, F-39 ....60.00
Covered dish, Covered Wagon, L-128, F-409, 6" 80.00
Covered dish, Football..60.00
Creamer, Coreopsis, gr band...80.00
Creamer, openwork border, repro, M-134B 10.00
Creamer, owl form w/glass eyes, F-587, sm...............................35.00

Nutrition pamphlet, King comics characters, ca 1942, NM, $70.00.

Pail, US Lyon & Coulson, canvas, 1943, 11x11" 25.00

Creamer, Panelled Wheat, F-255 ....47.00
Creamer & sugar bowl, Blackberry, dtd, F-250, F-251 ....97.00
Creamer & sugar bowl, Flat Diamond, F-195, mini 25.00
Egg cup, Melon w/Leaf, dtd 25.00
Figurine, dog on wheat base, EC Flaccus, Wheeling, F-36 ....280.00
Lamp, Goddess of Liberty, w/milk glass shade, F-329, 20" 335.00
Match holder, Indian head figural, B-204A, 5" 85.00
Match holder, pipe form, F-532 ....25.00
Mustard, bull's head, dtd, F-53, w/ladle 175.00
Mustard, bull's head, Pat Appl For, dtd, F-53, no ladle 90.00
Novelty, Scottie dog, sitting, solid, lg 60.00
Novelty, swan, closed neck, basketweave base, B-155B 65.00
Pitcher, owl form, B-80, 7¼" 195.00
Plaque, Lincoln, nutmeg stain, F-529, M 400.00
Plate, Angel & Harp 32.00
Plate, Apple Blossom, lattice edge, 10½" 25.00
Plate, Battleship Maine, L-463 ....25.00
Plate, Bryan, F-565, 7" 75.00
Plate, California Bear, F-543 ....100.00
Plate, Contrary Mule 32.00
Plate, Cupid & Psyche, EX pnt 30.00
Plate, Easter Bunny & Egg, B-3C, 7¼" 60.00
Plate, Easter Lay, W-6½, 6½" 70.00
Plate, Easter Opening, B-70, 7½" 65.00
Plate, Easter Rabbits, B-3F, 7¼" 35.00
Plate, Emerging Chick, B-24F, 6¼" 45.00
Plate, Flag, Eagle & Fleur-de-lis, openwork border, M-32B, 7" 25.00
Plate, Indian, lacy edge, B-4F, 7¼" 65.00
Plate, Little Red Hen, B-21A 45.00
Plate, Owl Lovers, B-7B, 7" 50.00
Plate, Rooster & Hens, F-30, 7¼" 35.00
Plate, Sailboat, old, B-13A 25.00
Plate, Sunken Rabbit, B-6E, 7½" 35.00
Plate, Three Kittens, rare sz, 6¼" 40.00
Plate, Three Owls, dtd 1901, F-500 ....35.00
Plate, Three Puppies, EX gold pnt, B-2C 95.00
Plate, Yacht & Anchor, orig pnt, B-15F 35.00
Platter, Retriever, after bird, lily pad border, B-53 ....85.00
Platter, Rock of Ages, F-569 ....155.00

Shaker, John Bull, Atterbury, F-340, 1873, $80.00.

Spooner, Ceres 65.00
Sugar bowl, Blackberry, w/lid, dtd, F-250 ....55.00
Toothpick holder, owl, wings up, 3" 25.00

Tray, Child & Shell, B-47 ....90.00
Tray, oval center, Pat USA, Jan 22 1908, 14x11" 45.00

Millefiori

Millefiori was a type of art glass produced during the late 1800s. Literally, the term means 'thousand flowers,' an accurate description of its appearance. Canes, fused bundles of multicolored glass threads such as are often used in paperweights, were cut into small cross sections, arranged in the desired pattern, refired, and shaped into articles such as cruets, lamps, and novelty items. It is still being produced, and many examples found on the market today are of fairly recent manufacture. See also Paperweights.

Bottle, scent; paperweight type, 5½" 175.00
Box, domed w/ormolu hinge, 4⅞x5⅜" 250.00

Cup and saucer, 2¼", $100.00.

Dish, swan form, gold flecks, appl eyes, 6x5" 65.00
Lamp, mc canes, early electric porc fittings, 12½" 300.00
Lamp base, bl/gr, orig seals, dtd 1910, mini 195.00
Paperweight, teapot form, solid, 3x5" 135.00
Pitcher, tricorner, 2¾" 135.00
Toothpick holder, hat form 45.00
Tumbler, bl ground, 4" 125.00
Vase, mc canes w/clear opal windows, 5" 150.00

Miniatures

There is some confusion as to what should be included in a listing of miniature collectibles. Some feel the only true miniature is the salesman's sample; other collectors consider certain small-scale children's toys to be appropriately referred to as miniatures, while yet others believe a miniature to be any small-scale item that gives evidence to the craftsmanship of its creator. For salesman's samples, see specific category; other types are listed below. See also Dollhouses and Furnishings; Children's Things.

Ranking at the top of today's leading collectibles, scaled 1:12" miniatures represent the work of hundreds of artisans who supply local shops with highly prized one-of-a-kind articles and specialties, all scaled one inch to the foot. Many leading producers and distributors of collectibles have entered the field as well. Clubs for miniature enthusiasts have sprung up throughout the United States, Canada, and abroad.

Authority Lillian Baker has compiled a lovely book, *Creative and Collectible Miniatures*, with many full-color photos; you will find her address in the Directory under California.

Armchair, 2 arched slats, splint seat, red rpt, 15½", EX 225.00
Blanket chest, mahog, lift top, dvtl, rfn, 7x15" 200.00
Blanket chest, pine w/old pnt, 3 drws w/cvg, 14" L 450.00
Book, snap-lock scrolls front & bk, 3 leaves, dtd 1896, 1x⅞"........28.00
Bureau, Louis XVI-style fruitwood/marquetry, 1800s, 10x13"......400.00
Candelabrum, 3-light, crystal 20.00
Chamberstick, opal glass, ornate hdl, Sandwich, 2" 110.00
Chest, chestnut, 3-drw, sq nails, 16½"+simple crest....................200.00
Chest, mahog Sheraton bow-front, inlay, twist pilasters, 13" .. 1,100.00
Chest of drw, poplar w/blk pnt, sq nails, primitive, 15".............150.00
Cupboard, hanging; oak, molded base/cornice, 1890s, 19".........375.00
Dough box, poplar w/red flame grpt, sq nails, 8½" L, EX 225.00
Pot, tole, worn red pnt, loose hinge, 2⅜" 150.00

Austrian enamel and gilt metal salon group, 6 pieces, canape: 3" long, $700.00.

Secretary, grpt, 5-drw, 2-drw bonnet top, ogee base, 16" 275.00
Tea table, figured walnut Chpndl, 10" rnd top w/cvd edge 800.00
Tea table, mahog w/line inlay, Mersman label, 5" dia....................70.00
Teakettle, copper, gooseneck, brass lid/hdl, handmade, 4" 95.00
Wash set, florals w/gold on lt pk, 7-pc 195.00

Minton

Thomas Minton established his firm in 1793 at Stoke on Trent and within a few years began producing earthenware with blue-printed patterns similar to the ware he had learned to decorate while employed by the Caughley Porcelain Factory. The Willow pattern was one of his most popular. Neither this nor the porcelain made from 1798 to 1805 was marked (except for an occasional number series), making identification often impossible.

After 1805 until about 1816, fine tea services, beehive-shaped honey pots, trays, etc. were hand decorated with florals, landscapes, Imari-type designs, and Neoclassic devices. These were often marked with crossed 'L's. From 1816 until 1823, no porcelain was made. Through the twenties and thirties, the ornamental wares with colorful decoration of applied fruits and florals and figurines in both bisque and enamel were usually left unmarked. As a result, they have been erroneously attributed to other potters. Some of the ware that was marked

bears a deliberate imitation of Meissen's crossed swords. From the late twenties through the forties, Minton made a molded stoneware line — mugs, jugs, teapots, etc. — with florals or figures in high relief. These were marked with an embossed scroll with an 'M' in the bottom curve. Fine parian ware was made in the late 1840s, and in the fifties Minton perfected and produced a line of quality majolica for which they gained widespread recognition. During the Victorian era, M.L. Solon decorated pieces in the pate-sur-pate style, often signing his work; these examples are considered to be the finest of their type. After 1862 all wares were marked 'Minton' or 'Mintons,' with an impressed year cipher. See also Majolica; Pate-Sur-Pate.

Bowl, pate-sur-pate, gladiators, 3-color/gilt, 3¼" H.....................300.00
Figurine, Chelsea Pensioner, seated, table aside, 1845, 6"............150.00
Plate, eagle grasping rabbit, acid-etched on brn, 1875, 10"..........250.00
Plate, fan/2 exotic birds in landscape on yel, 1881, 9½"...............250.00

Miniature pate-sur-pate screen, parian body tinted terra cotta, signed H. Hollins, black and gilt pattern on sides, 6¾", $1,800.00.

Soup tureen, Hawthorne, bl transfer, 12" 150.00
Vase, birds/florals on turq, cylindrical w/4 ft, 1880s, 7"...............500.00

Mirrors

The first mirrors were made in England in the 13th century of very thin glass backed with lead. Reverse-painted glass mirrors were made in this country as early as the late 1700s and remained popular throughout the next century. The simple hand-painted panel was separated from the mirrored section by a narrow slat, and the frame was either the dark-finished Federal style or the more elegant, often-gilded Sheraton.

Mirrors changed with the style of other furnishings; but whatever type you purchase, as long as the glass sections remain solid, even broken or flaking mirrors are more valued than replaced glass. Careful resilvering is acceptable if excessive deterioration has taken place.

Key:
Emp — Empire   QA — Queen Anne
Fed — Federal

Chpndl giltwood/mahog, cvd/rtcl/shaped, eagle finial, 61" 6,000.00
Chpndl mahog scroll, country style, inlay, 28x16", EX 825.00
Chpndl mahog scroll, minor damage/old rprs & glass, 20x12" 375.00
Chpndl mahog scroll, molded fr, rpr/rpl, 18x11" 225.00

Chpndl mahog-on-pine scroll, molded fr, rprs, 44x22" **1,700.00**
Chpndl scroll, molded fr, gilt liner/feather crest, 27x15" **450.00**
Chpndl-style mahog scroll, rpr, 1800s, 16x10" **225.00**
Courting, pine, appl moldings/sm pcs rvpt glass, 17x12", VG......**600.00**
Emp giltwood w/gesso, rope pilasters, emb vintage, 33x21" **350.00**
Emp 2-part, trn columns/brass corner rosettes, rstr, 28" **300.00**
Emp 2-part architectural fr, worn rvpt, 40x22"............................**200.00**
Emp 2-part w/rvpt knight, fr w/gold rpt, 25x12", EX...................**200.00**

Adam style Federal mirror in mahogany frame, broken arch and eagle pediment, gilded detail, 55", $500.00.

Fed convex gilt/cvd wood/gesso, sea horse/dolphin atop, 35" .. **2,900.00**
Fed giltwood, rvpt floral urn, spiral-molded fr, 1820s, 41" **2,400.00**
Fed mahog architectural, acorn drops, rvpt, reed sides, 32"..........**300.00**
Gilded architectural, rvpt child, discoloration, 40x23" **450.00**
Giltwood convex w/eagle, leafy appendage, 1830s, 26" dia **2,000.00**
Hplwht mahog veneer w/inlaid banding/scroll, rpr/rpl, 40" **550.00**
Louis XVI-style giltwood, cvd ovolos/swags, urn atop, 76" **465.00**
Oak, att Limbert, pointed/stepped crest rail, hooks, 41x22" **550.00**
Oak architectural, orig 3-color varnish, easel bk, 8½x12"............**400.00**
Overmantel, Victorian giltwood, 3-part, cvgs/columns, 33x54" ..**450.00**
Pier, giltwood, acorn drops/rtcl frieze/twist-cvd fr, 58" **2,000.00**
Pier, giltwood, cornice w/acorn drops, cvd shell, 1820, 45" **1,900.00**
Pine 2-part, fluted pilasters/corner blocks, rvpt, 12x21" **400.00**
QA pine, country style, crest w/traces of decor, 25x14" **725.00**
QA walnut-faced, fancy crest, orig beveled glass, 27" **1,050.00**
QA walnut-faced, molded fr/scrolled crest, rpl/rpr, 16x9" **450.00**
Rococo, 2 oval mirrors w/in ornate gilt-pnt cvd fr, 61x39" **375.00**
Shaving, Hplwht mahog w/line inlay, dvtl drw, rfn/rpr, 14" **225.00**
Shaving, mahog Emp, flame grain veneer/line inlay, 30x26" **300.00**
Sheraton mahog 2-part, 7 drop acorns in cornice, rvpt, 22" **240.00**
SP, Nouveau cherubs, heart shape, Dominick & Haff, 17½".... **1,650.00**
Venetian Rococo, bl glass w/rope border, glass leaves, 43"...........**500.00**
Victorian giltwood, cvd panel over 3-part glass, 40x70" **200.00**

Mocha

Mocha Ware is utilitarian pottery made principally in England (and to a lesser extent in France) between 1780 and 1840 on the then prevalent creamware and pearlware bodies. Initially, only those pieces decorated in the seaweed pattern were called 'Mocha,' while geometrically-decorated pieces were referred to as 'Banded Creamware.' Other types of decorations were called 'Dipped Ware.' During the last thirty

to forty years the term 'Mocha' has been applied to the entire realm of 'Industrialized Slipware' — pottery decorated by the turner on his lathe using coggle wheels and slip cups.

Mocha was made in numerous patterns — Tree, Seaweed or Dandelion, Rope (also called Worm or Loop), Cat's-eye, Tobacco Leaf, Lollypop or Balloon, Marbled, Marbled and Combed, Twig, Geometric or Checkered, Banded, and slip decorations of rings, dots, flags, tulips, wavy lines, etc. It came into its own as a collectible in the latter half of the 1940s and has become increasingly popular as more and more people are exposed to the rich colorings and artistic appeal of its varied forms of abstract decoration.

The collector should take care not to confuse the early pearlware and creamware Mocha with the later kitchen yellowware, graniteware, and ironstone sporting mocha-type decoration that was produced in America by such potters as J. Vodrey, George S. Harker, Edwin Bennett, and John Bell. This type was also produced in Scotland and Wales and was marketed well into the twentieth century.

Bowl, bl, emb wht rib band, blk/wht sqs in rim, ftd, 4", EX..........**425.00**
Bowl, brn/bl/tan agate, engine-trn border, 9½", M **1,600.00**
Bowl, waste; earthworm on gray band, blk rim, 2½x4½", EX.......**325.00**
Bowl, waste; 3-color daubs on rust, blk/wht rim, 5½", EX............**700.00**
Creamer, earthworm on bl, emb gr band/leaf hdl, 3⅜", EX..........**550.00**
Humidor, checkerbrd in blk/tan/wht, acorn finial, 7", EX....... **2,500.00**
Jug, earthworm/cat's eye/twig, dbl w/center hdl, 10x15" **8,000.00**
Mug, banded geometrics, bl/gold/dk brn, 5½", NM **1,000.00**
Mug, banded/wavy lines on dk brn, 5¾", NM **650.00**
Mug, bl/wht/brn agate, engine-trn rim decor, 4¼" **1,000.00**
Mug, earthworm, gold/brn/bl, bl/brn banding, 6" **800.00**
Mug, marbleized, 3-color, blk/wht checked rim, 6", EX **900.00**
Mug, marbleized, 5-color, emb gr bands, 5⅞", EX **925.00**
Mug, marbleized bl/brn/gold, incised gr Leeds border, 4½" **950.00**
Mug, marbleized orange, emb gr rim, leaf hdl, 3¾", NM.............**600.00**
Mug, marbleized orange, EX color, bl band, leaf hdl, 4", EX........**775.00**
Mug, repeated twigs, bl/brn/mustard, matching banding, 4½" **850.00**
Mug, repeated twigs, blk/bl on lt gr, bl/brn bands, 6", NM **1,000.00**
Mug, rows of sm linked ovals in wide band, bl/brn, 4½", NM .. **1,050.00**
Mug, seaweed, blk on gr-brn, wide bl top band, 5¾", NM **500.00**
Mug, seaweed on gray, blk stripes, emb leaf hdl, 3⅝", NM.........**250.00**
Mug, seaweed on yel band, brn stripes, 2½", NM **200.00**
Mug, vertical earthworm patterns, Leeds gr rim, 5¾", NM...... **1,500.00**
Mug, vibrant combing in blk/wht, gold bands, 5½" **2,200.00**
Mug, wavy lines on lt bl, blk bands/bl waves, 6"..........................**600.00**
Pepper pot, earthworm, EX **425.00**
Pepper pot, earthworm & cat's eye, 3-color, edge flakes, 5" **700.00**
Pepper pot, engine-trn geometrics, brn/blk/cream, 4", NM..........**650.00**
Pepper pot, incised geometrics, bl/brn, 4¾", NM **700.00**
Pepper pot, scroddled, lt bl/brn/yel on wht, 3½", EX...................**525.00**

Pitcher, double earthworm on medium blue, crosshatched and geometric bands, leaf-end handle, 8½", NM, $3,500.00.

Pitcher, cat's eye/earthworm, bl/brn, bl/brn bands, 7", EX 650.00
Pitcher, cat's eye/earthworm, brn/bl/gold, 8" 1,300.00
Pitcher, dots in brn/wht, gr incised loop band, 6½", EX.............800.00
Pitcher, earthworm, bl/brn on cream w/wht trim, 8", EX............350.00
Pitcher, earthworm, bl/brn/wht on gray-gr, 7", EX 500.00
Pitcher, earthworm & cat's eye, bands of 3 colors, 7", EX 900.00
Pitcher, earthworm bands, polka dot bands, 7", EX 800.00
Pitcher, earthworm in 3 colors, purple-rimmed band, 6", EX.......650.00
Pitcher, incised gr Leeds band/combed bands, leaf spout, 6½" 800.00
Pitcher, repeated twigs, tobacco/dk brn/tan, 7", NM..................700.00
Pitcher, seaweed on lt gr band, emb rim, 5", EX........................375.00
Tea caddy, marbleized brn/wht, 4¼", NM 1,600.00
Teapot, marbleized brn/wht, gr Leeds rim, 4½", EX................ 2,000.00

Molds

Food molds have become a popular collectible — not only for their value as antiques, but because they also revive childhood memories of elaborate ice cream Santas with candy trim, or barley sugar figurals adorning a Christmas tree. Ice cream molds were made of pewter and came in a wide variety of shapes and styles. Chocolate molds were made in fewer shapes but were more detailed. They were usually made of tin, copper, and occasionally of pewter. Hard candy molds were usually metal, although primitive maple sugar molds (usually simple hearts, rabbits, and other animals) were carved from wood. (Unless otherwise indicated, those in our listings are cast aluminum or stainless steel.) Cake molds were made of cast iron or cast aluminum and were most common in the shape of a lamb, a rabbit, or Santa Claus.

Our advisors for this category are Dale and Ruth Van Kuren; they are listed in the Directory under New York.

Chocolate Molds

Arab on horse, 6x4½" 60.00
Boy w/horn, 2 rows of 5 in tray, 7x5¼" 50.00
Bulldog, 4½x3½" 40.00
Bunny w/basket, ½-mold 35.00
Champagne bottle, 2-part, #84, 5½x3" 25.00
Chick in top hat, much detail, 2-pc, 4¾x2½" 75.00
Children, 6 different in tray, 9¼x3½" 80.00
Christmas tree, ½-mold 65.00

Clown with concertina, #15262, 2-piece, 9", $150.00.

Cradle, Vormenfabiek, 4½x5½" 25.00
Donkey, 4½x5" 50.00

Dutch girl, 2-part, Hamburg, 4½x3" 40.00
Elephant, 2x4½" 45.00
Father Christmas, 2-part, #143, 7x3½" 80.00
Girl in early clothing, 2-pc, 3x2¼" 50.00
Girl singing & holding book, 4¼" 60.00
Girl stands in profile, 7½x4"..65.00
Girl w/finger in mouth, Riecher & Co, 5" 60.00
Hen on basket, 2-part, 5x3" 40.00
Hen on basket, 2-part, 6x6¼" 45.00
Hens (2) facing ea other, 2-part, #63, 2½x5¾" 42.00
Jack climbing up tree, 2-part, 9x5½" 65.00
Jester, 2-part, 11x5" 75.00
Kewpie, 5½" 42.00
Kitten, ½-mold 40.00
Kris Kringle riding mule, 2-part, 6x5½" 145.00
Kris Kringle riding mule, 3x3" 115.00
Lady rabbit doing laundry, 2-part, 6x4".......................................75.00
Lion, 2-part, 3x6½" 70.00
Mail box, Germany, #213, 4¼x4" 25.00
Pig, smiling, 2½x3½" 50.00
Rabbit, sitting, 2-part, 4x3" 25.00
Rabbit face w/bow tie, 8 in 2 rows in 11¼x12½" fr 65.00
Rabbit standing w/basket on bk, 16x5½" hinged fr 110.00
Rabbit w/cracked egg cart, 4 in 11½x6x3" hinged fr 85.00
Rabbit w/egg on bk, 4 in fr 150.00
Rooster, 2 rows of 6..60.00
Santa, pointed hat, 2-part, Hamburg, 6x4¼" 125.00
Santa, 2-part, 5x3" 80.00
Santa on motorcycle, 2-part, 4½x3½" 70.00
Santa's boot, 2-part, 4½x3¾" 48.00
Scottie, side view, 4½x6½" 30.00
Scottie, 2-part, 6x4¾" 58.00
Snowman, 2-part, Holland, #15276, 4¾x2¾" 40.00
Soccer player, 2-part, 7¾x5" 68.00
St Nicholas w/children, 2-part, 10¼x6" 155.00
St Nicholas w/staff in bishop's robes, 2-part, 4x2¼" 70.00
Stork, 2-part, 7x4" 70.00
Stork w/chick on bk, 3¼x2¼" 50.00
Swiss man, 2-part, 4x2¼" 38.00
Train, 2-part, 3x6¾" 75.00
Turkey, ½-mold 45.00
Wolf, 2-part, 5x4" 45.00

Hard Candy Molds

Elephant, TM-138, groove for stick, 1¾x1¼" 60.00
Lamb, recumbent, CI, 2-pc, groove for stick.................................45.00
Lion, 3-part, TM-40, groove for stick, 4x5" 115.00
Lion w/cubs, TM-248, groove for stick, 2x2" 68.00
Locomotive, 3-part, TM-14, 3½x6" 125.00
Rabbit, upright, TM-231, groove for stick, 2¾x1" 50.00
Steamboat w/paddle wheel, groove for stick, 1¼x2¼" 88.00
Teddy bear, walnut, rectangular, 2-part, makes 6, 1½x12"..........130.00

Ice Cream Molds

Apple, E-239 ....22.50
Apple, E-240 ....25.00
Asparagus bunch #333, 3" 35.00
Aster, #926, 3" 22.50
Auto, #1080, 3" 65.00
Ball, E-936 ....16.00
Basket, octagon, E-1013 ....35.00
Basket, 3-part, oval, E-305...35.00

Beehive, old dome style, #302, 3" 37.50
Bell, #605 ....32.00
Bonnet w/face, E-968 ....125.00
Bunch of grapes, #159 ....28.00
Bunch of grapes, E-278 ....30.00
Calla lily, 3-part, #210 ....35.00
Card, Ace of Clubs, #919, 4" 20.00
Carnation w/stem, E-361 ....35.00
Cat w/arched bk, E-644 ....35.00
Cherries, 4 in mold, E-240 ....30.00
Chick in egg, horizontal, #599, 3" 35.00
Chick in egg, vertical, #600, 4" 35.00
Chrysanthemum, #313 ....30.00
Chrysanthemum, E-344 ....30.00
Couple 25.00
Cucumber, E-226 ....25.00
Cupid in rose, E-959 ....50.00
Cupid standing on cloud, #492, 5" 38.00
Dahlia, #299, 3" 18.00
Dutch shoe, #978, 5" 32.00
Eagle, E&Co, #655 ....150.00
Easter lily, 3-part 55.00
Egg, #906, 3" 25.00
Egg, #908, lg 25.00
Egg, E-907 ....20.00
Engagement ring, #376 ....30.00
Football, 3-part, #381 ....30.00
Goose egg, #298 ....25.00
Gourd, 4" 18.00
Harlequin, ruffled collar, 5" 60.00
Kiwanis club emblem, E-1111 ....28.00
Lion, side view, #618, 4" 32.00
Log, E-987 ....25.00
Maltese Cross, #296 ....35.00
Masonic emblem, #323 ....35.00
Masonic emblem, Shrine, E-1081 ....35.00
Melon, E-204 ....15.00
Morning-glory, 2 in mold, #251 ....20.00
Orange, #155...22.00
Orange, #307, 3".....................................25.00
Orange, #357...20.00
Orange blossoms, E-360 ....35.00
Peach, #152..22.50
Peach, #234, 2"......................................28.00
Peach, E-233 ....25.00
Peach half w/stone, #160 ....25.00
Pears, 3 in mold, #942, 4" 25.00
Pears, 3 in mold, E-284 ....30.00
Petunia, 3"..22.00
Playing card, Ace of Dmns, E-901 ....24.00
Pond lily, E-318 ....30.00
Potato, #245, sm 25.00
Pumpkin, E-309 ....25.00
Rose, E-295 ....35.00
Rose, open, 3 in mold, #939, 4" 25.00
Rotary Club emblem, E-1110 ....27.50
Santa Claus, E-991 ....48.00
Slipper, 3-part, #570 ....30.00
Slipper, 3-part, E-899-A 38.00
Stork 35.00
Strawberry, E-1021 ....30.00
Strawberry, E-316 ....32.00
Tomato, #208, 3" 40.00
Tomato medallion, #326, 3" 25.00

Shield shape with stars and stripes, S & Co. #281, 3½", $58.00.

Tulip, E-352 ....32.00
Turkey, E-650 ....38.00
Turkey, roasted, #364, 4" 38.00
Victorian girl, #286, 5" 50.00
Washington bust, #1084, 4" 60.00
Wedding bell w/cupid, E-1019 ....40.00

Miscellaneous

Copper, fish, sculped details, 1890s, 10x11", EX.....50.00
Copper, turtle, 3x8" 175.00
Tin, corn 30.00
Tin, fish, w/loop hanger, 3x12½x10"..................45.00
Tin, heart shape w/lifter ea side for cake, 2¾x12x12" 100.00
Tin/copper, eagle relief, oval, 5¾", EX..............100.00
Tin/copper, grapes, 4½x6½"...........................145.00
Tin/copper, wheat design, 4½x5½x7"...................140.00

Monmouth

The Monmouth Pottery Company was established in 1892 in Monmouth, Illinois. Their primary products were salt-glazed stoneware crocks, churns, and jugs, Bristol, spongeware, and brown glaze. In 1906 they were absorbed by a conglomerate called the Western Stoneware Company. Monmouth became their #1 plant and until 1930 continued to produce stoneware marked with their maple leaf logo. Items marked 'Monmouth Pottery Co.,' were made before 1906; after the merger, 'Co.' was dropped and 'Ill.' was substituted.

Strawberry jar, black gloss, 8½", $50.00.

Cookie jar, Cookie Jug, w/cork.......................................20.00
Jug, beehive; 5-gal...125.00
Pig, brn, emb pottery label, 7½" L, NM 400.00
Pitcher, brn, shell pattern at base, 6" 22.00
Pitcher, tan, horizontal ribs, 5½" 7.50
Vase, brn speckled, hdls, 8½" 12.00
Vase, gr matt, 8" 8.50
Vase, rust, 8" 10.00

Mont Joye

Mont Joye was a type of acid-cut French cameo glass produced by Cristallerie de Pantin in Paris around the turn of the century. It is accented by enamels.

Our advisor for this category is Don Williams; he is listed in the Directory under Missouri.

Bowl, floral w/gold on gr, 8½" L 75.00
Bowl, poppies on red, 12", +pr matching 12" vases 2,700.00

Vase, gold and silver cameo acorns and oak leaves on emerald green, 13", $2,500.00.

Vase, daisies, wht on gr w/gold band, 14½" 1,500.00
Vase, floral, gold & silver on amber, 10" 1,000.00
Vase, iris, pk on dk gr satin, 7½" 500.00
Vase, irises, mc w/gold spike leaves on textured frost, 20" 2,500.00
Vase, irises, mc/gold on crystal, 6" 700.00
Vase, lilies of valley, wht w/gold on Nile gr, 5½" 375.00
Vase, snapdragons, pk/yel/gilt on lt gr, twig hdls, 10" 1,000.00
Vase, violet bouquet front & bk, mc/gold on gr, ruffled, 7"..........425.00
Vase, violets, purple w/gold on clear, 10" 350.00

Moorcroft

William Moorcroft was an English potter who worked for MacIntyre Potteries from 1897 to 1913, signing his pieces with his last name or 'W. M.' In 1913 he established a workshop in Burslem, England, where he produced tablewares and a line of fine Art Nouveau vases, bowls, etc., which until 1913 were marked with the impressed mark 'Burslem,' either with or without his initials or signature. After 1916 an impressed 'England' was added, and from 1918 to 1929 the mark was 'Moorcroft' and 'Made in England,' with or without initials or signature. For the period from 1928 until 1945, the impressed mark read

'Moorcroft — Potter to HM the Queen,' with or without initials or signature; it was sometimes accompanied by a paper label. A second version of this mark was used from 1945 until 1949. At that time 'Moorcroft' and 'Made in England' was reinitiated and is the mark still in use today; a paper label (Potter to the Late Queen Mary) was added from 1953 until 1979. The latest variation may contain the initials of William's son, Walter, or Walter's signature. Note: Except for pieces with a salmon-pink background, all of William's work was signed. Those he refused to sign because he personally did not like them.

William Moorcroft died in 1945, and Walter continued in the business. Walter soon created his own designs, but he signed only the larger examples. Today W. Moorcroft Ltd. continues to use many of the same methods of hand-applied, slip-trailed decoration that William developed. Walter recently retired, and his brother William John is presently in charge of the company. He is developing his own designs that are introducing a new look to the Moorcroft line.

Our advisor for this category is Bob Haynes. He is listed in the Directory under Washington.

Key:
#1 — Potter to Her Majesty the Queen, Made in England
#2 — MacIntyre
#3 — W. Moorcroft
#4 — Burslem England
#5 — Florian (brown)
#6 — WM Moorcroft, Des

Bowl, Florian, tulips, lt/dk gr, #5/#6, 8" 1,400.00
Bowl, pomegranates, pk/purple/gr on bl, #3, 8" 495.00
Bowl, poppies, yel/gr on dk bl & yel, bl exterior, #3, 13" 900.00
Bowl, poppies, 5-color on bl/gr mottle, ca 1925, 11", NM 795.00
Bowl, salad; Florian, silver stand, 2 Florian servers, #3 .... 1,600.00
Box, Flamminian, foliate roundels, rust on gr mottle, 6" L............495.00
Candlestick, pomegranates, #3", pr 675.00
Charger, poppies, rose/orange/gr on bl, #3, 14" 750.00
Creamer & sugar bowl, fruit/leaves, mc on dk bl, #3/MIE, 3" 395.00
Jar, ginger; forget-me-nots, bl on wht, #3/#4, 8" 1,000.00
Jar, pomegranates, 5-color on bl mottle, lid, 1920s, 10¾" 800.00
Jug, Gesso Faience, pewter mts, ca 1898, 5¾"...............................595.00
Lamp, grapes on gr/purple mottle, drilled, #3, 16" 950.00
Lamp, orchids, mc on dk bl to wht, #3/#1, 12" 900.00
Lamp, pomegranates, #3/paper label, drilled, 12" 850.00
Lamp base, orchids, 3-color on flambe, drilled, 1928, 19" 1,600.00
Lamp base, orchids, 4-color on gr, #3/paper label, 9½" 675.00
Mug, cockerel, blk on cream, blk/yel bands, dtd '56, 5" 390.00
Mug, King George VI commemorative, gr top/base bands, 1937 .350.00
Tea set, Aurelian Ware, mc, #2/#6, rpr pot, 3-pc 795.00

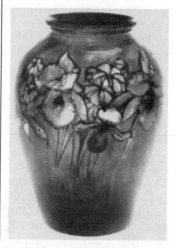

Vase, Flambe Orchid in red, yellow, purple, red flambe, signed W. Moorcroft in blue and dated 1939, 16", $2,000.00.

Vase, clematis, mc on dk bl, flambe over, MIE, 5" 225.00
Vase, cornflowers, dk & lt bl w/yel piping on bl, 1928, 15" 1,400.00
Vase, Florian, florals, lt bl/wht on dk bl, #5/#6, 13" 1,400.00
Vase, Florian, flowers/leaves, lt/dk bl, #3, rstr rim, 5¾" 700.00
Vase, Florian, irises, bl on wht, #2, 7" 925.00
Vase, Florian, poppies, lt/dk bl, #5/#6, 9¾" 1,100.00
Vase, fruit/leaves, 6-color on bl/flambe over, #1, 13" 950.00
Vase, fruit/leaves, 6-color on brn mottle, rstr, 1930s, 9" 700.00
Vase, Hazeldene, Moonlit Bl, #3/MIE, 3¾" 350.00
Vase, Hazeldene, Moonlit Bl, #3/MIE, 7" 825.00
Vase, hills/trees, red/gr/brn/bl, 1920s, 8", EX 950.00
Vase, pansies, mc on dk bl, hdls, #3/MIE, 8" 925.00
Vase, pansies, mc/flambe over, #3/MIE, 12¼" 1,250.00
Vase, plums, mc on dk bl, MIE, 1920s, 2½" 225.00
Vase, plums, mc on dk bl, MIE, 1920s, 4" 200.00
Vase, pomegranates, pk/purple/gr on dk bl, hdls, #3, 11" 1,195.00
Vase, pomegranates, pk/purple/tan/gr on dk bl, #4, 12½" 1,200.00
Vase, pomegranates, red/purple on gr, ftd/flaring, #3, 12" 1,295.00
Vase, pomegranates, 3-color on deep bl, 9" 995.00
Vase, pomegranates frieze/flowerhead borders, 1930s, 4" 700.00
Vase, pomegranates on flambe, ca 1930, 6" 700.00
Vase, poppies, red on dk bl, #3/MIE, 9" 895.00
Vase, stylized florals w/in 3 narrow bands, #3, 8" 1,400.00
Vase, wheat stalks, bl/gr matt, ca 1930s, 6" 600.00
Vase, wisteria, Phyllis, mc on wht, 1920s, #3, 19¾" 1,950.00
Vase, wisteria, 5-color on purple/bl mottle, ca 1930s, 9" 1,100.00
Vase, wisteria, 5-color on purple/bl mottle, 1930s, 4" 625.00
Vase, wisteria, 6-color on bl mottle, ca 1930, 6" 695.00

Moravian Pottery & Tile Works

Dr. Henry Chapman Mercer was an author, anthropologist, historian, collector, and artist. One of his diversified interests was pottery. In 1898 he established the Moravian Pottery and Tile Works in Doylestown, Pennsylvania, the name inspired by his study and collection of decorative stove plates made by the early Moravians. Because the red clay he used there proved unfit for tableware, he turned to the production of handmade tile which he himself designed. Though never allowing it to become more than a studio operation, the tile works was nevertheless responsible for some important commercial installations, one of which was in the capitol building at Harrisburg.

Mercer died in 1930. Business continued in the established vein under the supervision of Mercer's assistant, Frank Swain, until his death in 1954. Since 1968 the studio has been operated by The Bucks County Commission, and tiles are still fashioned in the handmade tradition. They are marked 'Mercer' and are dated.

Tile, Doctor, from Canterbury Tales, bl/wht, 4" 75.00
Tile, grapes & leaves on bl, 2¾" 14.00
Tile, medieval musician, mc gloss, 6½", set of 12..................... 1,200.00

Morgan, Matt

From 1883 to 1885, the Matt Morgan Art Pottery of Cincinnati, Ohio, produced fine artware, some of which resembled the pottery of the Moors with intense colors and gold accents. Some of the later wares were very similar to those of Rookwood, due to the fact that several Rookwood artists were also associated with the Morgan pottery. Some examples were marked with a paper label, others with either a two- or three-line impression: 'Matt Morgan Art Pottery Co.,' with 'Cin. O.' sometimes added.

Honey jug, birds in flight, Limoges style, sgn Hirshfield 350.00

Umbrella stand, florals in relief, bl w/gold, rtcl, 20½" 500.00
Vase, Spanish Moresque relief, 'wing' hdls, red clay, 11" 550.00
Vase, textured gr w/gold, floral cvg exposes red clay, 5" 180.00

Moriage

The term 'moriage' refers to certain Japanese wares decorated with applied slipwork designs. There are several methods used to achieve the characteristic relief effect. The decorative devices may be designed separately and applied to the vessel, piped on in narrow ribbons of clay (slip-trailed), or built up by brushing on successive layers of liquified slip. See also Dragon Ware; Nippon.

Box, floral reserves, 2x4" dia 110.00
Cup & saucer, demitasse; mc florals w/gold, Oriental mk..............48.00
Ewer, grape clusters over orchids on dk brn, 8", NM...................245.00
Pitcher, slip-trail florals, mc lotus in panels, 8x8¼" 325.00

Planter, enameled and moriage florals, 8¼" wide, $225.00.

Planter, HP poppies, brn moriage trim, ruffled, ftd, 5" 80.00
Plaque, fronds & pods, ornate border, 8½" 185.00
Sugar shaker, roses, barrel shape 80.00
Vase, mc floral panels, 3 gr hdls w/dots, 5½x7" 240.00

Mortar and Pestle

Mortars are bowl-shaped vessels used for centuries for the purpose of grinding drugs to a powder or grain into meal. The masher or grinding device is called a pestle.

Birch wood, grooved rings, trn, ca 1900, 6", +pestle.......................20.00
Brass, diagonal zigzags, sq hdls, 4x4½", +7¾" pestle 70.00
Brass, flared side, ped base, 5x8", +7½" trn pestle 175.00
Brass, heavy, polished, ca 1800, 4x4", +pestle, EX.........................85.00
Burl, dk patina, minor age cracks, 5¼" 95.00
Burl, trn ped base, orig dk gr pnt, 1700s, 6x6½" 350.00
Burl, wear/edge damage, 4¾", +trn poplar pestle...........................160.00
Burl, 6", +trn poplar pestle 205.00
Porc, pharmacist's display, blk w/gold details, sm, EX....................25.00
Porc, wht w/gold decor, Owens IL, 7", +pestle, 7" 20.00
Stoneware, mk Standard Trenton, +glass pestle, mk #4................45.00
Wood, heavy, no cracks, solid, ca 1860s, 8x5", +pestle.................55.00

Mortens Studio

Oscar Mortens was already established as a fine sculptural artist when he left his native Sweden to take up residency in Arizona. During the 1940s he developed a line of detailed animal figures which were distributed through the Mortens Studios, a firm he co-founded with Gunnar Thelin. Thelin hired and trained artists to produce Mortens' line, which he called Royal Designs. More than two hundred dogs were modeled and over one hundred horses. Cats and wild animals such as elephants, panthers, deer, and elk were made, but on a much smaller-scale. Bookends with sculptured dog heads were shown in their catalogs, and collectors report finding wall plaques on rare occasions. The material they used was a plaster-type composition with wires embedded to support the weight. Examples were marked 'Copyright by the Mortens Studio' either in ink or decal. Watch for flaking, cracks, and separations — crazing seems to be present in some degree in many examples. When no condition is indicated, the items listed below are assumed to be in near-mint condition, allowing for minor crazing.

Afgan, tan & charcoal, standing, 7x7", M 85.00
Airedale, tan, blk detail, standing, 5¼x5¼" 55.00
Beagle, ivory/tan/blk, standing, paper label, 6x6", M 65.00
Bedlington Terrier, ivory & gray, standing, 6½x4¾", M 75.00

Bookends, recumbent lions, $110.00 for the pair.

Borzoi, ivory & tan, reclining, 3½x7½", M.........................85.00
Boxer, brn/ivory w/blk detail, 5½x5½", M..........................55.00
Boxer, standing, 7"..85.00
Cocker Spaniel pup, sitting 35.00
Collie, tan & ivory, standing, 6x7" 75.00
Dachshund, standing, lg 70.00
Dalmation, lg spots, standing, 7½x5½" 75.00
Doberman, blk & tan, standing, paper label, 7½x8", M 85.00
Doberman, standing, 6"..65.00
French Poodle, ivory, blk features, standing, 5x5", M 70.00
Horse, rearing, 9"...70.00
Irish Setter, rust, standing, paper label, 6x7", M.............75.00
Mexican Chihuahua, tan, blk detail, sitting, 3x3½", M....55.00
Pekingese, tan & blk, standing, 4½x3½", M.......................70.00
Pointer, ivory w/blk spots, sitting, 4x4¾", M....................60.00
Samoyed, ivory w/blk eyes & nose, sitting, 4x4½", M......65.00
Scottie, sitting, blk, 4½" 55.00
Spaniel puppy, ivory w/blk spots, 3¾x3" 35.00
St Bernard, standing, 6½x8½"..95.00

Morton Pottery

Six potteries operated in Morton, Illinois, at various times from 1877 to 1976. Each traced its origin to six brothers who immigrated to America to avoid military service in Germany. The Rapp brothers established their first pottery near clay deposits on the south side of

town where they made field tile and bricks. Within a few years, they branched out to include utility wares such as jugs, bowls, jars, pitchers, etc. During the ninety-nine years of pottery operations in Morton, the original factory was expanded by some of the sons and nephews of the Rapps. Other family members started their own potteries where artware, gift-store items, and special-order goods were produced. The Cliftwood Art Pottery and the Morton Pottery Company had showrooms in Chicago and New York City during the 1930s. All of Morton's potteries were relatively short-lived operations with the Morton Pottery Company being the last to shut down on September 8, 1976. For a more thorough study of the subject, we recommend *Morton's Potteries: 99 Years* by Doris and Burdell Hall; their address can be found in the Directory under Illinois.

Morton Pottery Works — Morton Earthenware Co. (1877-1917)

Bowl, rice nappy, brn Rockingham, fluted, 10" 55.00
Bowl, rice nappy, yellowware, fluted, 8"......................................65.00
Coffeepot, dripolator, brn Rockingham, lg infuser, 8-cup 50.00
Coffeepot, dripolator, brn Rockingham, sm infuser, 10-cup 70.00
Cuspidor, brn Rockingham, urn shape, 7" 45.00
Cuspidor, cobalt, urn shape, 7"..55.00
Miniature, coffee dripolator, brn Rockingham, 3" 40.00
Miniature, creamer, brn Rockingham, 1¾" 25.00
Miniature, creamer, jade gr, 1¾" 30.00
Miniature, milk jug, cobalt, 4¼"..50.00
Stein, yellowware, 2 bl slip stripes top & bottom 40.00
Tea pot, Rebecca in shield, brn Rockingham, bulbous, 2½-pt 40.00
Teapot, brn Rockingham, +cr/sug & ftd spooner 125.00

Cliftwood Art Potteries, Inc. (1920-1940)

Bookends, elephant, bl/mulberry, 3¼", pr.....................................85.00
Clock, octagonal, chocolate drip, 2 inkwells & tray on base........150.00
Dresser set, apple gr, tray+jar+powder box+2 candle holders.........65.00

Cliftwood Art Potteries, lioness figure, turquoise, $30.00. (In any drip glaze, $55.00.)

Flower bowl insert, water lily pad #1, rose glaze, 2x4" 12.00
Flower bowl insert, water lily pad #2, med bl, 2x6" 18.00
Lamp, boudoir; melon shape, orchid/pk drip, 7½" 30.00
Lamp, bulb w/emb lovebirds, jade gr, w/harp, 20"........................50.00
Lamp, bulb w/matching Blenheim parchment shade, 20" 75.00
Lamp, fluted bulb/hdls, bl/mulberry, Art Deco #31, 10⅝"..............48.00
Lamp, fluted pillar, bulbous, hdls, bl/mulberry, 10⅝" 48.00
Lamp, pillar base, star-emb globe, wht, Art Deco #23, 8½"............30.00

Vase, bulbous, ftd, chocolate drip, 7" 35.00
Vase, rectangular w/simulated palm fronds, turq matt, 14" 30.00

Midwest Potteries, Inc. (1940-1944)

Candle holder, Jack-be-nimble type, hdl, lime gr, 7" 15.00
Candle holder, Liberty arm w/torch, wht, 7" 25.00
Figurine, canaries, 2 on stump, yel w/gold, 4" 22.00
Figurine, hen & rooster, cold pnt comb & ft, 5", 7", pr 50.00
Figurine, Irish setter, brn drip, gr base, 4½" 35.00
Figurine, pony, wht, 3½" 12.00
Pitcher, cow, tail is hdl, wht w/gold, 4½" 20.00
Pitcher, duck, cattail hdl, yel/gr drip, 9½" 36.00
Pitcher, fish, jade gr, 9½" 34.00
Planter, dog w/bow tie, brn matt, 4½" 6.50
Planter, elephant, bl/yel drip, 4" 7.00
Planter, fox, wht, 4" 5.50

Morton Pottery Company (1922-1976)

Ash tray, Meuhlebach Hotel, Kansas City, burgundy 12.00
Bank, cat, wht w/pk bow & bell, 9" 20.00
Bank, scottie dog, blk, 7" 22.00
Bank, shoe house, yel w/red roof, 9" 30.00
Bowl, mixing; yellowware, wht slip bands, Hohulin . . ., Ill..........50.00
Easter item, chick on decorated egg 12.00
Easter item, rabbit, creeping, brn spray glaze, 5" 12.00
Easter item, rabbit in bonnet, bl egg at side, 9½" 15.00
Easter item, rabbit in top hat, yel egg at side, 9½" 15.00
Easter item, rabbit pushing cart, brn & wht, 7" 18.00
Figurine, Colonials, he w/bouquet, she w/2 baskets, 7", pr 35.00
Flower bowl, log shape 2/8-hole insert, Woodland glaze, 12" 50.00
Honey jug, underglaze flowers & bee, Herm's Honey 15.00
Humidor, bbl shape, pipe finial on lid, brn 22.00
Jug, ice box; Woodland glaze, w/lid, 4" 100.00

Lamp, Irish Setter and pheasant base, 10" x 8", $50.00.

Lamp, TV; gondola, gray w/blk, removable planters, 18" L 45.00
Lamp, TV; horse's head, brn, 18" 35.00
Lapel stud, stein, brn Rockingham, We Want Beer, std hdl, 1" 35.00
Lapel stud, stein, brn Rockingham, We Want..., donkey hdl, 1" ..45.00
Pie bird, rooster, wht w/pk comb & base, scarce, 5" 37.00
Planter, covered wagon, Compliments of Weidman's Store...........20.00

Shakers, loaf of bread, Miller Bakery...1909-1959, pr 15.00
Stein, bbl form, brn Rockingham, Blatz emb on side......................18.00
Stein, bbl form, brn Rockingham, Budweiser emb on side 18.00
Stein, bbl form, brn Rockingham, Goldenglow emb on side.............18.00
Stein, bbl form, brn Rockingham, Sweeney emb on side 18.00
Stein, cylindrical, brn Rockingham, Old Heidelberg emb..............20.00
Stein, cylindrical, brn Rockingham, Old Milwaukee emb 20.00
Tumbler, ear of corn, Travelers Protective Agency..., 1951 ....15.00
Vase, spherical, Woodland glaze, rare, 10½x32" 200.00
Wall pocket, harp, wht w/underglaze florals 15.00
Wall pocket, lady gardener w/hoe, ring pot on front 10.00
Wall pocket, lady gardener w/watering can, ringed pot 10.00
Weiner warmer, electric, Woodland glaze, rare, 8x7x3¾" 125.00

American Art Potteries (1947-1961)

Creamer, bird figural, tail forms hdl, spray glaze, 4" 15.00
Doll parts, head, arms, & legs, HP, rare, 1¾", 3½" dia.................55.00
Doll parts, head, arms, & legs, HP, 3½" H, 6" dia.....................60.00
Doll parts, head, arms, & legs, HP, 7½" H, 12" dia 90.00
Lamp, TV; 2 Afghan hounds, blk, 15" 50.00
Planter, bird on leaf w/stump planter, bl, 6½" 12.00
Planter, fish, mauve/pk spray glaze, 4"...............................12.00
Vase, pitcher form, wht w/rust spackling, 14" 20.00
Vase, tubular w/ruffled top, yel spray over wht, 9" 16.00
Vase, 6-sided, pk w/bl int, 10" 18.00
Wall pocket, elongated flower, mauve petals/gr leaves, 8½" 15.00

Mosaic Tile Co.

The Mosaic Tile Company was organized in 1894, in Zanesville, Ohio, by Herman Mueller and Karl Langenbeck, both of whom had years of previous experience in the industry. They developed a faster, less-costly method of potting decorative tile, utilizing paper patterns rather than copper molds. By 1901 the company had grown and expanded with offices in many major cities. Faience tile was introduced in 1918, greatly increasing their volume of sales. They also made novelty ash trays, figural boxes, bookends, etc., though not to any large extent. Until they closed during the 1960s, Mosaic used various marks that included the company name or their initials — 'MT' superimposed over 'Co.' in a circle.

Figurine, bear, blk, 5¾x10" 130.00
Figurine, German shepherd, recumbent, tan, 6x10½" 130.00
Paperweight, Wm Penn, dtd 30.00
Tile, crystalline, olive-gr on bl, 6x3".............................60.00

Tile, Currier and Ives, $25.00.

Tile, Lincoln bust, wht on bl, hexagonal, 3"...................50.00

Tile, PA Dutch floral, in CI trivet, 4½" 10.00
Tile, pond lily, 4-color, 4¼x2¼" 70.00

Moser

Ludwig Moser began his career as a struggling glass artist, catering to the rich who visited the famous Austrian health spas. His talent and popularity grew and in 1857 the first of his three studios opened in Karlsbad, Czechoslovakia. The styles developed there were entirely his own; no copies of other artists have ever been found. Some of his original designs include grapes with trailing vines, acorns and oak leaves, and richly enameled, deeply cut or carved floral pieces. Sometimes jewels were applied to the glass as well. Moser's animal scenes reflect his careful attention to detail. Famed for his birds in flight, he also designed stalking tigers — even elephants — all created in fine enameling.

Moser died in 1916, but the business was contined by his two sons who had been personally and carefully trained by their father. They merged with Meyer's Nephews Glassworks in 1921, and continued to produce quality glass until the Nazi invasion in 1938 when these fine Jewish artists were all placed in concentration camps.

When identifying Moser, look for great clarity in the glass; deeply carved, continuous engravings; perfect coloration; finely applied enameling (often covered with thin gold leaf); and well-polished pontils.

Our advisor for this category is Don Williams; he is listed in the Directory under Missouri. Items described below are enameled unless noted otherwise.

Basket, cranberry, fluted, clear/ribbed hdl, sgn, 6x6" 285.00
Bowl, alexandrite, gilt/bl arabesque medallions, +7" plate 975.00
Box, amethyst, appl amber salamanders, HP florals, 4½" 610.00
Box, cranberry w/florals, 3 ormolu ft, sgn, 5½x5½" dia 350.00
Cologne, cranberry, portrait on wht/gilt, sgn, 10", +plate 375.00
Compote, alexandrite, cut decor, sgn, 7" 425.00
Compote, amber w/bl rim & applications, cherries/leaves, 4" 645.00
Cruet, amber w/florals, clear stopper, bell form, sgn, 9" 110.00
Cruet, amber w/mc design, matching stopper, sgn, 6½" 125.00
Cruet, bl w/mc florals, clear hdl/ped/faceted top, sgn, 8" 185.00
Decanter, amber crackle w/mc seaweed & fish, lobed, sgn, 8" 350.00
Decanter, cranberry, gold/silver scene, mk, 10½", +6 shots 550.00
Decanter, cranberry w/overall oak leaves, slim form, 17" 1,200.00
Decanter, sapphire bl w/floral, 9½", pr, +condiment, sgn 365.00
Nut dish, cranberry to clear, gold band w/florals, +plate 585.00
Pitcher, amberina w/wht florals, bulbous, sgn, 8" 400.00
Pitcher, cameo florals/pine cones, gold on frost, 11x6" 950.00
Pitcher, gr w/allover florals, sgn, 8½" 165.00
Shot glass, gr, mc oak leaves w/gold leaves & branches 150.00
Tumbler, juice; sapphire bl w/jeweled medallions, sgn, 4" 435.00
Vase, amber, appl gr salamander/rigaree, ftd, sgn, 12", pr............685.00
Vase, amber, gold reserve w/florals & bee, sgn, 8", pr...................225.00
Vase, bl, 6 crystal ft/rim points, mc florals, sgn, 11", pr 750.00
Vase, Button & Star cutting, sq stepped base, 10" 150.00
Vase, cameo bird scenic, bright gr to wht, 2 mks, 3½x5" 400.00
Vase, cameo flower, dk gr/orange on emerald to clear, 7" 1,900.00
Vase, cameo irises, amethyst on wht, 2 mks, 3x6" dia 875.00
Vase, clear to cranberry w/florals, 4 ft, sgn, 16" 325.00
Vase, clear to gr, intaglio florals, sgn, 15x4½" 225.00
Vase, cobalt w/eng frieze of warriors, 10-panel, heavy, 8" 425.00
Vase, cranberry, allover gold florals, cone form, sgn, 14" 225.00
Vase, cranberry, allover gold/enamel, pointed rim, sgn, 9" 800.00
Vase, cranberry, allover mc paisley & gold, bulbous, 12" 1,000.00
Vase, cranberry, gold encrusted/wht enamel, sgn, 10" 800.00
Vase, cranberry, gold flowers/butterfly/hdls, 6⅝" 265.00

Vase, coralene peacock with flowers, blue feet, gold trim, 8½", $3,000.00.

Vase, cranberry w/coralene lilies, 3 lg clear ft, sgn, 11" 480.00
Vase, gr, HP fish & 4 appl pickerels (2 as hdls), 11" 675.00
Vase, gr opal to clear w/poppies & gold leaves, ribbed, 11"..........600.00
Vase, gr opaque w/wht portrait reserve, ped ft, sgn, 10" 225.00
Vase, gr w/gold, ribbed bbl form w/3 lg hdls, sgn, 7½" 500.00
Vase, gray, apple blossoms w/gold, pointed rim, hdls, 11" 285.00
Vase, jack-in-pulpit; amethyst w/gold, ribbed/scalloped, 12" 210.00
Vase, purple w/mc enameling, 4-ftd, flared neck, 8"....................325.00
Vase, rubena verde, mc/gilt leaves & acorns, prunts, 11"......... 2,300.00
Vase, sapphire bl w/birds, lg ped ft, sgn, 8" 600.00
Vase, wht over cranberry cut w/ovals, slim form, sgn, 11" 275.00

Moss Rose

Moss Rose was a favorite dinnerware pattern of many Staffordshire and American potters from the mid-1800s. In America the Wheeling Pottery of West Virginia produced the ware in large quantities, and it became one of their best sellers, remaining popular well into the nineties.

Bone dish, unmk, gold edge...30.00
Bowl, vegetable; rnd..35.00
Butter pat, sq, Meakin, EX...15.00
Chamber set, 7-pc...450.00
Coffeepot, Haviland, lg..70.00
Creamer..35.00
Cup & saucer, Meakin..35.00
Egg cup, unmk, set of 6, MIB..28.00
Gravy boat, Meakin..35.00
Mug, unmk, 3" 10.00
Plate, dinner; Haviland...25.00
Plate, sandwich; unmk, 9½" 15.00
Platter, CFH, 15½x10½" 35.00
Platter, rectangular, Meakin, 14x10" 40.00
Tea set, demitasse; fancy hdls & ft, American, 15-pc.....................150.00
Tea set, Japan, 16-pc+lids..60.00
Tray, mk JM, 11x7½" 22.50
Tureen, ftd, rpr lid, H&L Co, 12½x12½x7½" 85.00
Wash set, unmk, 11" pitcher+13½" bowl 295.00

Mother-of-Pearl Glass

Mother-of-Pearl glass was a type of mold-blown satin art glass popular during the last half of the 19th century. A patent for its manufacture was issued in 1886 to Frederick S. Shirley, and one of the companies who produced it was the Mt. Washington Glass Company of New Bedford, Massachusetts. Another was the English firm of Stevens and Williams. Its delicate patterns were developed by blowing the gather into a mold with inside projections that left an intaglio design on the surface of the glass, then sealing the first layer with a second, trapping air in the recesses. Most common are the Diamond Quilted, Raindrop, and Herringbone patterns. It was made in several soft colors, the most rare and valuable is rainbow — a blend of rose, light blue, yellow, and white. Occasionally it may be decorated with coralene, enameling, or gilt.

Our advisors for this category are Betty and Clarence Maier; they are listed in the Directory under Pennsylvania.

Basket, Dia Quilt, gold, melon ribs, sq top, Mt WA, 8" 785.00
Basket, Herringbone, pk, appl amber hdl, ruffled, 8½x4½"..........375.00
Basket, Herringbone, pk, mini, 4½x3½" 435.00
Basket, Herringbone, pk, wishbone hdls, 5½" 320.00
Biscuit jar, Dia Quilt, bl, SP ftd base/dome lid, 8¾" 735.00
Biscuit jar, Dia Quilt, bl, wht florals & decor, 9½" 615.00
Bottle, scent; Dia Quilt, bl, satin stopper, 5" 355.00
Bowl, centerpc; Drape, gold to peach, pleated, SP fr, 11" 365.00
Bowl, Dia Quilt, bl, ruffled, tricorn, 2½x6⅞" 250.00
Bowl, Dia Quilt, bl w/mc birds, brass base, 8¾x7½" 995.00
Bowl, Dia Quilt, pk, 9-crimp, ftd, mk Patent, 4⅝x8" 650.00
Bowl, Dia Quilt, rainbow, tricorn, mk Patent, 4⅝x5"............. 1,100.00
Bowl, Dia Quilt, rose to pk to wht, 8 box pleats, Webb, 10"........750.00
Bowl, Ribbon, pk shaded, crimped rim, 2¾x4½" 295.00
Ewer, Herringbone, apricot shaded, frosted hdl, 7¼x4¼".............225.00
Finger bowl, Dia Quilt, rainbow, mk Patent, w/underplate 1,100.00
Lamp, Dia Quilt, bl, melon ribbed base, brass font, 14½" 1,140.00
Mustard, Raindrop, bl, pewter lid, 3" 375.00
Pitcher, Dia Quilt, dk pk shaded, sq mouth, 5½x5¾"..................175.00
Pitcher, Herringbone, rose to wht, hexagonal top, 9x5" 565.00
Plate, Dia Quilt, rainbow, ruffled, mk Patent, 6" 395.00
Rose bowl, Herringbone, bl to lt bl, 8-crimp, 4" W 225.00
Rose bowl, Herringbone, rose shaded, 6-crimp, 3¾x5" 325.00
Rose bowl, Peacock Eye, red, wht int, 3" dia 900.00
Rose bowl, Ribbon, gold-tan, English, 2x3"................................265.00
Rose bowl, Ribbon, rose, 8-crimp, 2¾x3¾" 245.00
Sweetmeat jar, Dia Quilt, pk, stationary hdl, 7½x4¼" 485.00
Tumbler, Dia Quilt, pk w/cornflowers 335.00
Tumbler, Dia Quilt, yel & wht stripes, mk Patent, 3½" 255.00
Tumbler, Herringbone, bl to wht...150.00
Tumbler, Herringbone, rose pk, 3¾x2¾" 125.00
Vase, bud; Ribbon, bl shaded, metal holder, 8¼" 235.00
Vase, Coin Spot, bl, 4-petal top, 7¼x4" 195.00
Vase, Coin Spot, rose to pk, camphor ruffle, Mt WA, 9x4".........400.00
Vase, Dia Quilt, apricot, bulbous, ruffled top, 9" 425.00
Vase, Dia Quilt, bl, frosted rim, 7x4" 195.00
Vase, Dia Quilt, bl, 4-petal top, 6x3¾" 165.00
Vase, Dia Quilt, butterscotch, ribbed ovoid, ruffled, 9"...............550.00
Vase, Dia Quilt, pk, frosted thorn hdls, 4-petal top, 7½" 275.00
Vase, Dia Quilt, pk, 10¼x4½"..185.00
Vase, Dia Quilt, rainbow, appl ft, mk Patent, 6" 885.00
Vase, Dia Quilt, rainbow, tulip-shaped top, 6½" 845.00
Vase, Dia Quilt, yel shaded, ruffled, 6¼x3¾" 165.00
Vase, Drape, pk, ruffled top, 6x3½" 225.00
Vase, Federzeichnung, brn w/gold, 10x5" 1,695.00
Vase, Herringbone, bl, ruffled, 5⅞x3⅛".....................................155.00
Vase, Hobnail, rose shaded, sqd 4-fold top, 6x4".........................550.00
Vase, Peacock Eye, yel w/red feathers, bl int, 10½"................. 2,530.00
Vase, Peacock Eye, yel w/red feathers, bl int, 5¼" 1,500.00

Vase, Rainbow, honey-beige, Webb, 4" 190.00
Vase, Raindrop, bl, oval top, 5⅛x2½", pr 295.00
Vase, Raindrop, bl, 6-sided, scalloped, bulbous, 8x5" 210.00
Vase, Ribbon, pk, mc florals, appl hdl, 6" 960.00
Vase, Swirl, pk shaded, reeded hdls, ruffled top, 11½" 355.00
Vase, Swirl, reverse amberina w/gold florals, 9½" 1,320.00
Vase, Zipper, pk, ruffled top, Mt WA, 9½"..................................410.00
Water set, Dia Quilt, rose to pk, 9½" tankard+6 tumblers....... 1,500.00

Vase, melon-striped green with etched and gold-enamel ribbons, bows, and floral medallions, 10", $800.00.

Mountainside

John Kovacs operated a ceramic studio from the late 1920s until about 1939 in Mountainside, New Jersey, where through extensive experimentation he produced stoneware and earthenware items glazed with colors of his own formulation.

Planter, red/gr curdled glaze, corners form ft, 2½x9x6" 45.00
Vase, dk bl drip over med bl, 3 swirled hdls, 7x6½".......................50.00

Mourning Collectibles

During the 18th and early 19th centuries, ladies made needlework pictures, samplers, paintings on ivory plaques, watercolor drawings, etc. to commemorate the death of a loved one. Elements contained in nearly all examples are the tomb, mourners, a weeping willow tree, and data relating to the deceased. Often plaits of hair were included. Today these are recognized and valued as a valid form of folk art.

Our advisor for this category is Steve DeGenaro; he is listed in the Directory under Ohio.

Brooch, ivory, etched scene, inscr bk, 1860s, EX..........................400.00
Coffin, child's, pine or soft wood, viewing hole, 1870s, G 200.00
Handkerchief, blk silk, 1880s, EX 50.00
Locket on chain, containing hair pc, gold mts, 1860-80 ....150.00
Needlework picture, mourning theme, ca 1840s, 10x28", G ... 1,600.00
Photograph, lady/tomb/willow/etc, inscribed/1802, 18x13"..... 1,000.00
Photograph, post-mortem, cabinet card, 1880s-90s, EX 20.00

Movie Memorabilia

Movie memorabilia covers a broad range of collectibles, from books and magazines dealing with the industry in general to the various promotional materials which were distributed to arouse interest in a particular film. Many collectors specialize in a specific area — posters, pressbooks, stills, lobby cards, or souvenir programs (also referred to as premier booklets). In the listings below, a one-sheet poster measures approximately 27" x 41", three-sheet: 41" x 81", and six-sheet: 81" x 81". See also Autographs; Cartoon Art; Personalities.

Book, souvenir; Laurence Olivier Henry V film, 1940s, EX 30.00
Book, souvenir; Song of Bernadette, Rockwell cover, 1944 ....50.00
Display card, Betrayed, Mitchum, 1948, 22x28" 20.00
Display card, Capture, Lew Ayres, 1950, 22x28" 25.00
Display card, Condemned of Altona, Loren, 1963, 22x28" 15.00
Display card, One Night in Lisbon, MacMurray, 22x28" 35.00
Display card, Over My Dead Body, M Berle, 22x28" 40.00
Display card, Patton, Geo Scott, 1970, 22x28" 20.00
Display card, Run for Cover, J Cagney, 1955, 22x28" 20.00
Display card, Seventh Cross, Spencer Tracy, 1944, 22x28" 50.00
Display card, Southern Yankee, Red Skelton, 1948, 22x28" 30.00
Display card, Virgin Queen, B Davis, 1955, 22x28" 25.00
Insert card, Anna & King of Siam, Irene Dunn, 1946, 14x36" 30.00
Insert card, Casbah, Yvonne DeCarlo, 1948, 14x36" 30.00
Insert card, Dial M for Murder, 1954, 14x36" 85.00
Insert card, Fireball, Mickey Rooney, 1950, 14x36" 20.00
Insert card, Great Imposter, Tony Curtis, 1961, 14x36" 15.00
Insert card, Honeymoon Machine, McQueen, 1961, 14x36" 15.00
Insert card, My Favorite Spy, Bob Hope, 1951, 14x36" 30.00
Insert card, The Fly, Vincent Price, 1958, 14x36" 40.00
Insert card, Thief of Baghdad, Steve Reeves, 1961, 14x36" 15.00
Insert card, You Belong to Me, Stanwyck, 1941, 14x36" 40.00
Lobby card, Animal Crackers, Harpo Marx, 1930, oversz 400.00
Lobby card, Big Land, Virginia Mayo, 1957, 11x14" 7.00
Lobby card, Cattle Queen of Montana, R Reagan, 1954, 11x14" ... 7.00
Lobby card, Down Laredo Way, Slim Pickens, 1953, 11x14".......... 7.00
Lobby card, For Whom the Bell Tolls, 1943, 11x14", EX 35.00
Lobby card, Half Breed, R Young, 1952, 11x14" 5.00
Lobby card, Last of the Mohicans, R Scott, 11x14" 3.00
Lobby card, Maverick, Bill Elliott, 1953, 11x14" 5.00
Lobby card, Mr Deeds Goes to Town, J Coogan, 1936, 11x14" ..150.00
Lobby card, Painted Veil, Greta Garbo, 1934, 11x14", EX 450.00
Lobby card, Pony Express, Charlton Heston, 1952, 11x14" 19.52
Lobby card, Rebel in Town, Ben Johnson, 1956, 11x14" 7.50
Lobby card, Rio Bravo, John Wayne, 1959, 11x14" 10.00
Lobby card, Roberta, Astaire, 1935, 11x14" 150.00
Lobby card, Strange Cargo, Gable/Crawford, 1940, 11x14" 60.00
Lobby card, Sunnybrook Farm, Shirley Temple, 1-sided, 1939 ....400.00
Lobby card, Two-Faced Woman, Greta Garbo, 1941, 11x14" 350.00
Lobby card, Under Mexicali Stars, Buddy Edsen, 1950, 11x14"...... 7.50
Lobby card, Valley of Fire, Gene Autry, 1951, 11x14" 10.00
Lobby card, Wyoming Outlaw, J Wayne, 1939, 11x14", EX 400.00
Magazine, Film Careers, Judy Garland, 1964, EX 35.00
Magazine, Modern Screen, Fisher/Reynolds cover, 1955, EX.........20.00
Magazine, Motion Picture, Gable cover, Feb 1943, EX 25.00
Magazine, Movie Classic, July 1932, EX 10.00
Magazine, Movie Classic, Kay Francis cover, Dec 1931, EX 20.00
Magazine, Photoplay, Betty Davis cover, June 1939, EX 30.00
Magazine, Radio Mirror, Fred Astaire cover, 1936 ....30.00
Magazine, Screen Book, Lombard cover, Nov 1939, EX 35.00
Magazine, Screen Guide, Blondell cover, Aug 1940, EX................20.00
Magazine, Screen Legends, Monroe/Newman, 1965, EX 30.00
Magazine, Screen Stories, Williams/Kelly cover, 1949, EX............20.00
Magazine, Silver Screen, Lucille Ball cover, Sept 1943, EX...........25.00
Poster, Action in N Atlantic, USA, 2-sheet, EX 190.00
Poster, Airport, Lancaster, 1970, 1-sheet 15.00

Poster, Anastasia, Ingrid Bergman, 1956, 1-sheet...........................25.00
Poster, Apocalypse Now, M Brando, 1979, 1-sheet 20.00
Poster, Big Mouth, J Lewis, 1967, 1-sheet 20.00
Poster, Blues Brothers, John Belushi, 1980, 45x60" 25.00
Poster, Bombers B-52, Natalie Wood, 1957, 1-sheet 25.00
Poster, Brain That Wouldn't Die, 1940s, 1-sheet 50.00
Poster, Buccaneer, Yul Brynner, 1958, 1-sheet 30.00
Poster, Chain Lightning, H Bogart, 1949, 6-sheet.......................125.00
Poster, Dallas, Gary Cooper, 27x41", EX 60.00
Poster, Dark Delusion, L Barrymore, 1947, 1-sheet 40.00
Poster, East of Eden, James Dean, 1955, 1-sheet 150.00
Poster, Farewell to Arms, R Hudson, 1958, 1-sheet 20.00
Poster, Flamingo Road, J Crain, 1949, 1-sheet 60.00
Poster, Flash Gordon Conquers Universe, B Crabbe, '40, 1-sheet..200.00
Poster, Frankie & Johnny, Elvis Presley, 1966, 3-sheet 35.00
Poster, Gambit, Michael Caine, 1967, 1-sheet...............................15.00
Poster, Hang 'Em High, C Eastwood, 1968, 1-sheet 35.00
Poster, High & the Mighty, John Wayne, 1-sheet.........................175.00
Poster, In the Heat of the Night, S Poitier, 1967, 1-sheet.............10.00
Poster, Man Betrayed, John Wayne, 1941, 6-sheet 175.00
Poster, Moulin Rouge, Ferrer/Gabor, 63x47", EX.........................155.00
Poster, Movie Struck, Laurel & Hardy, 1-sheet 75.00
Poster, Nero's Mistress, B Bardot, 1956, 1-sheet 20.00
Poster, Odd Couple, Jack Lemmon, 1968, 1-sheet.........................15.00
Poster, Operation Petticoat, Cary Grant, 1959, 1-sheet 25.00
Poster, Paradise Alley, Stallone, 1978, 1-sheet 15.00
Poster, Secret Passion, Montgomery Cliff, 1963, 1-sheet 25.00
Poster, Sorcerers, Boris Karloff, 1967, 1-sheet..............................25.00
Poster, Spy Who Loved Me, James Bond, 1977, 1-sheet 20.00
Poster, State Fair, Ann Margret, 1962, 1-sheet..............................20.00
Poster, The Robe, R Burton, 1963, 1-sheet 15.00
Poster, Three Caballeros, Disney, 1-sheet 20.00
Poster, Thrill of It All, Doris Day, 1963, 1-sheet 15.00
Poster, Zombies of Stratosphere, 1-sheet......................................50.00
Poster, Zorro's Fighting Legion, linen mtd, 1-sheet, rare 650.00
Pressbook, Anatomy of a Murder, Stewart, 1959, 10-pg................15.00
Pressbook, Dirty Dozen, 1957, 16-pg...10.00
Pressbook, Sabrina/Breakfast at Tiffany's, 1965, 10-pg.................20.00
Pressbook, What's Up Doc?, B Streisand, 1972, 12-pg 10.00
Still, Francis Joins the WACS, D O'Conner, blk & wht, 8x10" 2.00
Still, Girl Most Likely, Jane Powell, 1957, blk & wht, 8x10".......... 1.50
Still, Towering Inferno, Steve McQueen, 1974, 8x10" 3.00

Theatre program for *Ten Commandments*, 1956, EX, $27.50.

Window card, Hard Day's Night, Beatles, 1964, 14x22" 60.00
Window card, Rack, Paul Newman, 1956, 14x22" 20.00

Window card, River of No Return, M Monroe, 1954, 14x22" **45.00**
Window card, Road to Singapore, Bing Crosby, 1940, 14x22" ...**100.00**

Mt. Washington

The Mt. Washington Glass Works was founded in 1837 in South Boston, Massachusetts, but moved to New Bedford in 1869 after purchasing the facilities of the New Bedford Glass Company. Frederick S. Shirley became associated with the firm in 1874. Two years later the company reorganized and became known as the Mt. Washington Glass Company. In 1894 it merged with the Pairpoint Manufacturing Company, a small Brittania works nearby, but continued to conduct business under its own title until after the turn of the century. The combined plants were equipped with the most modern and varied machinery available and boasted a working force with experience and expertise rival to none in the art of blowing and cutting glass. In addition to their fine cut glass, they are recognized as the first American company to make cameo glass, an effect they achieved through acid-cutting methods. In 1885 Shirley was issued a patent to make Burmese, pale yellow glassware tinged with a delicate pink blush. Another patent issued in 1886 allowed them the rights to produce Rose Amber, or amberina, a transparent ware shading from ruby to amber. Pearl Satin Ware and Peachblow, so named for its resemblance to a rosy peach skin, were patented the same year. One of their most famous lines, Crown Milano, was introduced in 1893. It was an opal glass either free-blown or pattern-molded, tinted a delicate color and decorated with enameling and gilt. Royal Flemish was patented in 1894 and is considered the rarest of the Mt. Washington art glass lines. It was decorated with raised, gold-enameled lines dividing the surface of the ware in much the same way as lead lines divide a stained glass window. The sections were filled in with one or several transparent colors and further decorated in gold enamel with florals, foliage, beading, and medallions.

Our advisors for this category are Betty and Clarence Maier; they are listed in the Directory under Pennsylvania. See also Cranberry; Salt Shakers; Burmese; Crown Milano; Royal Flemish; etc.

Basket, cameo florals/ladies, pk on wht, Pairpoint holder **975.00**
Bellows bottle whimsey, pk on yel, appl rigaree, 11½" **1,800.00**
Biscuit jar, clear w/gold floral scrolling, emb base edge **725.00**
Bottle, scent; lustreless wht satin, mushroom form, 7" **185.00**
Bowl, bl/yel stripes on wht satin, frosted edge, 3x8" **500.00**
Box, lid: emb roses/bows, rose medallion on gr w/gilt, 4x7½" .. **1,250.00**
Box, monk w/wine glass, gr-tinted opal, sgn, 3x4½" dia **500.00**
Box, pastel pansies/gold on lustreless wht, 4½x6" dia..................**550.00**
Cream ball, floral, beige on wht, rare...**250.00**
Creamer, Lava, mc chips (many sizes) w/wht edges on blk, 2".. **1,750.00**
Creamer & sugar bowl, florals/gold scrolls on wht, 4½" **1,800.00**
Flower frog, mushroom, forget-me-nots, mc **255.00**
Lamp shade, cameo bird/foliage/urns, maroon/wht, 10x9"....... **1,100.00**
Lamp shade, cameo birds/foliage, pk/wht, 8¾" dia, NM...............**350.00**
Pitcher, Verona, fish/sea plants, gold trim, 5x5" **950.00**
Pitcher, Verona, mc/gold mums, 6x5½"..**425.00**
Rose jar, Albertine, apple blossoms on yel to wht, 5x4"..............**650.00**
Salt cellar, robin's egg bl overlay, scalloped, 3¼"........................**125.00**
Sugar shaker, mums, gr/brn on pnt Burmese, Mt WA..................**275.00**
Sugar shaker, pansies on clear frost, egg form, 4x3¼".................**485.00**
Sweetmeat, Albertine, gold leaves/red berries, SP trim.....:.........**750.00**
Syrup, mc forget-me-nots w/gr leaves **1,200.00**
Vase, Easter lilies, lt ribbing, 7"...**325.00**
Vase, Lava, mc chips w/gold enhancements, loop hdls, 8" **1,750.00**
Vase, Lava, mc chips w/wht outlines, 3¾"................................ **1,750.00**
Vase, Lave, mc chips, 3½" **1,850.00**
Vase, Napoli, frog/bulrushes, vertical ribs, 8½x5" **950.00**

Vases, Lava, gold enhancements, 8", $3,500.00 for the pair.

Vase, sm floral on cream, sm cup-like top, mk, 9½" **165.00**
Violet bowl, florals on pk opaline, 3x3½".....................................**275.00**

Mulberry China

Mulberry china was made by many of the Staffordshire area potters from about 1830 until the 1850s. It is a transfer-printed earthenware or ironstone named for the color of its decorations, a purplish-brown resembling the juice of the mulberry. Shades vary; some pieces look almost gray with only a hint of purple. Some of the patterns — Corean, Jeddo, Pelew, and Formosa, for instance — were also produced in Flow Blue ware. Others seem to have been used exclusively with the mulberry color.

Our advisor for this category is Mary Frank Gaston; she is listed in the Directory under Texas.

Athens, cup plate, Adams **45.00**
Athens, gravy boat, Meigh, 1840 ....**75.00**
Athens, plate, 10"..**40.00**
Beauties of China, bowl, sauce; w/lid, Mellor & Venables...........**150.00**
Bleeding Heart, creamer **85.00**
Bochara, wash bowl, 14"...**100.00**
Bryonia, sauce dish, 5" **10.00**
Calcutta, cup & saucer, handleless...**150.00**
Calcutta, plate, 8½"...**47.00**
Chusan, cup & saucer, handleless **55.00**
Chusan, plate, Podmore Walker, 8¼"...**25.00**
Chusan, platter, PH&Co, 17"...**185.00**
Corea, plate, 12-sided, Clementson, 9½" **60.00**
Corea, teapot, Clementson **295.00**
Corean, plate, 9¾"...**60.00**
Corean, platter, 8-sided, Clementson, 15¾x12⅛" **180.00**
Corean, sugar bowl, lion hdls **125.00**
Corean, teapot, Podmore Walker, 8"...**275.00**
Corean, waste bowl, Podmore Walker, lg......................................**75.00**
Cyprus, plate, Davenport, 9"...**66.00**
Cyprus, teapot, Cyprus, Davenport **350.00**
Cyprus, tureen, vegetable; w/lid **175.00**
Delhi, relish dish, 5½x8½" **65.00**
Flora, plate, H&B, 8¾"..**40.00**
Flora, soap dish, Walker, 3-pc **150.00**
Foliage, cup & saucer, handleless; Walley **65.00**
Foliage, plate, 9" **24.00**
Heath's Flower, soup, 10½" **65.00**
Hong, plate, 5"..**35.00**
Hyson, sugar bowl **150.00**

Jeddo, bowl, vegetable; w/lid, Adams, ca 1845 ....210.00
Jeddo, pitcher, Adams & Son, ca 1845, 8" 135.00
Jeddo, pitcher, milk; 1-pt...90.00
Jeddo, teapot...275.00
Lozere, cup & saucer, handleless..45.00
Madras, plate, 10"...125.00
Neva, pitcher, 9"...200.00
Neva, plate, Challinor, 9"..60.00
Ning Po, cup plate 35.00
Pelew, cup & saucer, handleless 65.00
Peruvian, plate, Wedgwood, 7½"...30.00
Peruvian, teapot...225.00
Rhone Scenery, creamer, hexagonal, Mayer, 5¼" 110.00
Rhone Scenery, plate, luncheon; TJ&J Mayer, 8⅝" 30.00
Rhone Scenery, plate, 7¼"...30.00
Rhone Scenery, relish dish, TJ&J Mayer 20.00
Rhone Scenery, sauce tureen, w/underplate 225.00
Rhone Scenery, soup tureen..295.00
Rhone Scenery, tureen, 8-sided, w/lid, TJ&J Mayer, 10x8" 300.00
Rose, cup & saucer, handleless...55.00
Scinde, cup & saucer, handleless..55.00
Scinde, platter, Walker, 15½" 175.00

Shannon, plate, 8¼", $20.00.

Shapoo, waste bowl 90.00
Susa, cup & saucer, Meigh 55.00
Temple, plate, Podmore Walker, ca 1850, 8¾"...........................40.00
Temple, plate, Podmore Walker, 7¾" 35.00
Temple, plate, 10"...55.00
Temple, platter, 14x10½"...160.00
Temple, tea tile, Podmore Walker 75.00
Tonquin, cup & saucer, Heath..75.00
Tonquin, plate, 9½"..45.00
Tonquin, sugar bowl, w/lid, Heath 165.00
Venus, plate, Podmore Walker, 8"...48.00
Vincennes, plate, Alcock, 9½"...55.00
Vincennes, platter, 15½"...175.00
Vincennes, sauce tureen, w/ladle & tray, Alcock 395.00
Washington Vase, bowl, vegetable; 8"...95.00
Washington Vase, creamer...175.00
Washington Vase, cup & saucer, handleless 65.00
Washington Vase, pitcher, water; Podmore Walker, 8½" 250.00
Washington Vase, plate, 9"...50.00
Washington Vase, platter, 16x12" 180.00
Washington Vase, relish..85.00
Washington Vase, sauce tureen 125.00

Washington Vase, sugar bowl, w/lid, Podmore Walker, 9½"........255.00
Wreath, cup & saucer, handleless 55.00

Muller Freres

Henri Muller established a factory in 1900 at Croismare, France. He produced fine cameo art glass decorated with florals, birds, and insects in the Art Nouveau style. The work was accomplished by acid engraving and hand finishing. Usual marks were 'Muller,' 'Muller Croismare,' or 'Croismare, Nancy.' In 1910 Henri and his brother Deseri formed a glassworks at Luneville. The cameo art glass made there was nearly all produced by acid cuttings of up to four layers with motifs similar to those favored at Croismare. A good range of colors was used, and some pieces were gold flecked. Handles and decorative devices were sometimes applied by hand. In addition to the cameo glass, they also produced an acid-finished glass of bold mottled colors in the Deco style. Examples were signed 'Muller Freres' or 'Luneville.'

Our advisor for this category is Don Williams; he is listed in the Directory under Missouri.

Cameo

Bowl, Dutch landscape, purple on lt bl & purple, 6¾" 1,200.00
Lamp, prs of birds, red on wht/yel 13" shade & rnd base 23,000.00
Lamp, trees/mtns, brn/umber/orange 12" shade/rnd base........13,000.00

Cameo glass and wrought-iron table lamp, leaves and berry vines in brown on mottled orange, 15", $3,850.00.

Vase, anemone, brn on yel mottle, rnd/flattened, 9" 3,000.00
Vase, cockatoos, wht/bl on yel w/bl & gr splashes, 14½" 5,000.00
Vase, magnolia limbs, dbl overlay, baluster, 17½" 12,000.00
Vase, magnolias, pk/bl on cream, bulbous/ftd, 13" 7,500.00
Vase, panthers, acid-etched clear on turq w/foil, 10" 2,700.00
Vase, polar bears, dbl overlay on amber, bulbous, 14½" 27,500.00
Vase, river/boats/bldgs fr by trees, wine on rose/gray, 9" 4,000.00
Vase, roses, yel/red on peach frost, spherical, 8"...................... 3,500.00
Vase, tiger lilies, red on wht/yel mottle, bulbous, 10½............. 3,800.00
Vase, trees/lake on bl & wht, pnt detail, slim form, 7½".............875.00
Vase, trees/mtns, brn on orange, rim extends to hdls, 14" 3,500.00

Miscellaneous

Chandelier, cream/lav mottle, gilt floral mts, 14" dia.................800.00

Lamp, floor; mottled bowl form in wrought leafy std, 70" **3,000.00**
Plant stand, mottled lily form in wrought leafy std, 24" **800.00**
Vase, artichoke leaves relief on opal, ovoid, 6" **130.00**
Vase, dk bl, gold foil/yel & brn streaks, clear cased, 11".............**600.00**

Muncie

Muncie Pottery, established in Muncie, Indiana, by Charles O. Grafton, was produced from 1922 until about 1935. It is made of a heavier clay than most of its contemporaries; the styles are sturdy and simple. Early glazes were bright and colorful. In fact, Muncie was advertised as the 'rainbow pottery.' Later, most of the ware was finished in a matt glaze. The more collectible examples are those modeled after Phoenix Glass vases — sculptured with lovebirds, grasshoppers, and goldfish. Their line of Art Deco-style vases bear a remarkable resemblance to the Consolidated Glass Company's Ruba Rombic line. Vases, candlesticks, bookends, ash trays, bowls, lamp bases, and luncheon sets were made. A line of garden pottery was manufactured for a short time. Items were frequently impressed with MUNCIE in block letters. Letters such as A, K, E, or D and the numbers 1, 2, 3, 4, or 5 often found scratched into the base are finishers' marks.

Canoe/insert, lt gr gloss, 11½" **115.00**
Chamberstick, gr/bl drip, glossy, 4" **42.50**
Lamp base, dk gr matt, 12x5" **75.00**
Vase, blk matt, gourd shape, 6½" **60.00**
Vase, lav/gr drip, matt, hand turned, ruffled top, 4" **25.00**
Vase, mirror blk, Deco, star form, 4" **75.00**
Vase, orange/blk drip, glossy, stick form, 8" **45.00**
Vase, rose/bl airbrush, matt, stick form, 8" **35.00**

Vase, rose and green drip glaze, 12", $145.00.

Vase, rose/gr airbrush, matt, 9" **52.50**
Vase, tan/gr drip, matt, gourd shape, 6½"..**40.00**
Wall pocket, brn gloss, emb vines, rectangular, 9" **65.00**

Musical Instruments

The field of automatic musical instruments covers many different categories ranging from tiny dolls and trinkets concealing musical movements to huge organs and orchestrions which weigh many tons. Music boxes, first made in the late 18th century by Swiss watchmakers, were produced in both disk and cylinder models. The latter type employs a cylinder studded with tiny projections. As the cylinder turns,

these projections lift the tuned teeth in the 'music comb,' and the melody results. The value of the instrument depends upon the length of the cylinder and the quality of workmanship, though other factors must also be considered. Those in ornate cabinets or with extra features such as bells, mechanical birds, etc. often sell for much more. Units built into matching tables sell for about twice the amount they would bring otherwise. While small and medium size units are still being made today, most of the larger ones date from the 19th century. Disk-type music boxes utilize interchangeable steel disks with projecting studs, which by means of an intervening 'star wheel' cause a music comb to play. There are many different variations and mechanisms. Most were made in Germany, but some were produced in the United States. Among the most popular makes are Polyphon, Symphonion, and Regina. The latter was made in Rahway, New Jersey, from about 1894 through 1917.

Player pianos were made in a wide variety of styles. Early varieties consisted of a mechanism which pushed up to a piano and played on the keyboard by means of felt-tipped fingers. These use sixty-five note rolls. Later models have the playing mechanisms built in. At first these also used sixty-five note rolls, but those produced from about 1908 until 1940 use eighty-eight note rolls.

Coin-operated electric pianos are deluxe versions of player pianos. These incorporate expression mechanisms so that by using special-made rolls they can play the hand-recorded rolls of famous pianists. Popular makes include Ampico, Duo-Art, and Welte. Roll-operated organs were made in many forms, ranging from table-top models to large foot-pumped versions. Of the latter, the Aeolian Orchestrelle is considered to be one of the best.

Unless noted, prices given are for instruments in fine condition, playing properly, with cabinets or cases in well-preserved or refinished condition. In all instances, unrestored instruments sell for much less, as do pieces with broken parts, damaged cases, and the like. On the other hand, particularly superb examples in especially ornate case designs and pieces which have been particularly well restored often will command more.

Key:
c — cylinder   d — disk

Mechanical

Box, Capital Cuff Box A, EX orig... **3,500.00**
Box, Capital Cuff Box B, mahog, EX orig **5,000.00**
Box, Criterion, 12" d, cherry case, EX **1,400.00**
Box, Criterion, 14" dbl comb, mahog, 11x20x18", +21 disks . **2,100.00**
Box, Criterion, 15½" d, oak case, 84", M rstr **4,000.00**
Box, Criterion, 20½" d, oak floor model, 78", EX orig............. **8,000.00**
Box, Dawkins, 6-tune 11" c, burled walnut case, EX orig **2,800.00**
Box, Euphonia, 20½" d, w/matching oak base, +20 disks **6,800.00**
Box, Kalliope, 20½" d, dbl comb, 12 bells, EX **4,200.00**
Box, Mermond Sublime Harmonie, 11" interchangeable d **2,250.00**
Box, Polyphon, upright style w/16 bells, 22½", EX **7,250.00**
Box, Polyphon, 15½" d, rosewood/walnut, 12-drw base, 34" ... **3,500.00**
Box, PVF, 6-tune, rstr movement, 8¼" c, EX **1,400.00**
Box, Regina, 15½" d, dbl comb, cvd case, EX orig................... **3,750.00**
Box, Regina, 15½" d, dbl comb, oak case, coin op **4,500.00**
Box, Regina, 15½" d, single comb, mahog case, +6 disks **3,000.00**
Box, Regina, 20½" d, dbl comb, cupola top, rstr **5,800.00**
Box, Regina, 8¼" d, mahog case, EX orig................................. **1,000.00**
Box, Regina #11A, 15½" d, mahog case, EX **4,750.00**
Box, Regina #2, 15½" d, dbl comb, mahog, EX orig............... **4,000.00**
Box, Regina #20, 11" d, single comb, rough case, EX **750.00**
Box, Regina #34, 27" changer, EX orig **15,000.00**
Box, Regina #40, 15½" d changer, rosewood, art case, NM..... **6,800.00**

Box, Regina #8A, 27" d, dbl comb, cvd case, EX orig.............16,000.00
Box, Stella, 17" d, dbl comb, mahog, 1900, 28x21" 4,000.00
Calliope, Tangley #43, hand or roll plate, EX orig.................8,000.00
Concertina, Tanzbar, 11x9x11", EX orig, +3 rolls 1,150.00
Harmonica, Norcross, red plastic, M, +3 rolls 45.00
Nickelodeon, Coinola, keyboard, 3 windows, rail, oak, EX 4,750.00
Nickelodeon, Empress Electric, stained glass front, oak, EX....3,600.00
Nickelodeon, Peerless D, rstr 6,500.00
Nickelodeon, Seeburg C, orig stained glass, VG 3,000.00
Nickelodeon, Western Electric Mascot, rstr.............................7,500.00
Nickelodeon, Wurlitzer A, early, w/pipes, rstr 20,000.00
Orchestrelle, Aeolian V, oak, rfn/rstr...................................7,000.00
Orchestrion, Coinola Midget, 8 instruments, rstr 18,000.00
Orchestrion, Cremona K, upright, ca 1908, EX orig 30,000.00
Orchestrion, Linc C, art glass panels, 1917, EX orig.............15,000.00
Orchestrion, Seeburg KT Special Replica, NM 14,800.00
Orchestrion, Wurlitzer CX, automatic roll changer, NM 27,000.00
Organ, band; Artisan C-1, EX orig.....................................18,000.00
Organ, band; Wurlitzer #125, no vacuum pump, VG orig......16,500.00
Organ, band; Wurlitzer #145, w/bells & dual tracker, rstr 20,000.00
Organ, band; Wurlitzer #146B, dbl tracker, EX 21,000.00
Organ, barrel; Molinari, 35-key, 98 pipes, 45" 7,500.00
Organ, barrel; Reimer, 61-key, 184 pipes, 66", EX orig............9,500.00
Organ, bench; Aeolian Hammond, late '30s, EX, +100 rolls ..3,200.00
Organ, dance; Mortier, Deco, 84-key/350 pipes, 180" W 35,000.00
Organ, grand; Aeolian #1500, rstr 5,000.00
Organ, monkey; reed type, VG...3,800.00
Organ, monkey; Shinek, 26-key, 63 pipes, 4 ranks, EX............4,500.00
Organ, pipe; Aeolian Duo-Art, walnut console, EX orig 3,250.00
Organ, reed; Estey, gallery top, rstr 1,000.00
Piano, grand; Apollo, cvd mahog art case, rstr, +bench...........5,300.00
Piano, grand; Chickering Ampico A, mahog, 1927, 78", VG..7,200.00
Piano, grand; Ellington (Baldwin), 1912, 69", EX orig 3,500.00
Piano, grand; Geo Steck Duo-Art, 1929, mahog, 63", EX orig ..3,800.00
Piano, grand; Henry F Miller, walnut case, 1896, 70", EX.......3,400.00
Piano, grand; Kimball Welte, EX orig 1,500.00
Piano, grand; Knabe Ampico A, Italianate art case, EX orig..37,500.00
Piano, grand; Knabe Ampico A, mahog, 1920s, 68", EX orig..3,600.00
Piano, grand; Knabe Ampico B, mahog, 1934, 64", EX orig....6,800.00
Piano, grand; Mason & Hamlin 1973, 68", M 5,000.00
Piano, grand; Schiller Welte, art case, EX orig.......................2,600.00
Piano, grand; Steinway Duo-Art AR, walnut case, 82", EX ...26,500.00
Piano, grand; Steinway Duo-Art XR, mahog, 1920, 73", rstr ..14,500.00
Piano, grand; Stroud Duo-Art, EX orig 2,200.00
Piano, grand; Stroud Duo-Art, late, NM.................................2,300.00
Piano, grand; Weber Duo-Art, ebony, mid-1920s, 68", EX 5,800.00
Piano, grand; Weber Duo-Art F, mahog, 1920, 72", VG 4,200.00
Piano, Griggs, fancy oak case, +850 rolls 3,000.00
Piano, spinet; Geo Steck Ampico, EX orig.............................3,800.00
Piano, upright; Geo Steck Duo Art, 2-tone veneer, 68", EX ..2,400.00
Piano, upright; Kimball Welte, 67", EX orig 1,400.00
Piano, upright; Steinway Duo-Art, 1916, rstr 14,000.00
Piano, upright; Weber Duo-Art, mahog, VG...........................4,500.00
Piano, upright; Wheelock Duo-Art, VG orig 1,500.00
Pianocorder, upright; Mason-Hamlin, EX orig.......................6,000.00
Pianola, upright; Weber, foot pump, 1910, rstr 7,500.00
Pianolodeon, Chein, 1960s, maroon plastic, +7 rolls, EX 225.00
Rolamonica, w/4 rolls, EX orig...175.00
Violano, Mills Virtuoso, VG 15,000.00

Non-Mechanical

Accordion, Trafficanty, MOP inlay, Italy, EX.........................125.00
Accordion, 10-key, Monarch, 1880s, in damaged box 100.00

Banjo, 5-string; Gibson, w/resonator, EX................................165.00
Castanets, gold dancers on blk lacquer......................................4.50
Clarinet, Paul Duzarion, France, Elbert, EX............................95.00
Cornet, all brass, sheperd's crook design, ca 1870, VG...............45.00
Cornet, Frank Holton & Co, silver metal, Pat 1911 mouthpc 36.00
Dulcimer, handmade, 37x8", EX 40.00
Fife, Cosby, rosewood, silver ends, EX.....................................60.00
Fife, metal, hard rubber mouthpc, EX 35.00
Harmonica, Echo Harp, 96-hole, EX in orig box 22.50
Harmonica, Hohner Blues Harp, EX.......................................10.00

Lyon and Healy giltwood and maple harp, original case, 1880s, 71", $6,000.00.

Harpsichord, Chickering & Sons, bird's-eye mahog, '08, EX ..10,000.00
Mandolin, Stella, label, inlaid butterfly, early, VG........................35.00
Piano, grand; Chickering, rosewood, Boston, 1830, NM 3,500.00
Piano, grand; Columbia, ribbon mahog/rosewood, '05, rstr ...12,000.00
Piano, grand; Ivers & Pond, 1897, 72" 10,000.00
Piccolo, blk wood, 6-key, Austria, ca 1900, EX 40.00
Saxophone, alto; Silver Supertone Bandmaster, EX.....................35.00
Ukulele, marquetry inlay border, Lyra label, EX in bag.................20.00
Violin, Carlo Ferdinando Landolfi Milano, 2-pc bk, 15", VG........45.00
Violin, Francois Richard, Paris, 14", EX 50.00
Violin, Joseph Gagliona, 1-pc bk, EX grain, 14", EX.................95.00
Violin, Vittorio Bellarose Napoli 1939 label, 14" 295.00

Mustache Cups

Mustache cups were popular items during the late Victorian period, designed specifically for the man with the mustache! They were made in silverplate as well as china and ironstone. Decorations ranged from simple transfers to elaborately applied and gilded florals. To properly position the 'mustache bar,' special cups were designed for the 'lefties' — these are the rare ones!

Florals, artist sgn, left-handed, France...................................65.00
Florals, mc on wht, china, 3x3¼"...32.00
Knight & angels, gold trim, Royal Bavaria, w/saucer.................60.00
Lady w/flowers transfer, lg..35.00
Pk lustre with floral band, Germany, 4½" 35.00
Purple scenic medallion, unmk 45.00
SP, cut/beaded decor, Eureka Silver, 1901, +saucer 110.00
SP, floral eng, Barbour, EX..75.00

Nailsea

Nailsea is a term referring to clear or colored glass decorated in contrasting spatters, swirls, or loops. These are usually white but may also be pink or blue. It was first produced in Nailsea, England, during the late 1700s but was made in other parts of Britain and Scotland as well. During the mid 1800s a similar type of glass was produced in this country. Originally used for decorative novelties only, by that time tumblers and other practical items were being made from Nailsea-type glass. See also Lamps.

Bottle, bellows; cranberry w/wht loopings, rigaree, ftd, 11"..........**400.00**
Flask, perfume; pk w/wht swirls, blown, 1800s, 5¼" **200.00**
Flask, wht w/pk & bl loopings, pontil, lt wear, 7½" **175.00**
Pipe whimsey, wht w/red loopings, att Sandwich, 13½"..............**300.00**
Powder horn, clear-cased wht w/cranberry loopings, ftd, 12".......**220.00**
Rolling pin whimsey, aqua w/wht loopings, open ends, 17".........**150.00**
Vase, clear w/opal loopings, clear appl base/stem, 13½"..............**325.00**
Vase, yel-gr w/wht loopings, squat, 5"...**60.00**

Nakara

Nakara was a line of decorated opaque milk glass produced by the C.F. Monroe Company of Meriden, Connecticut, for a few years after the turn of the century. It differs from their Wave Crest line in several ways — the shapes were simpler; pastel colors were deeper and covered more of the surface; more beading was present; flowers were larger; and large transfer prints of figures, Victorian ladies, cherubs, etc. were used. Ormolu and brass collars and mounts complemented these opulent pieces. Most items were signed, however this is not important since the ware was never reproduced. For more information we recommend *Wave Crest: The Glass of C. F. Monroe* by Wilfred R. Cohen, available from Collector Books or your local bookstore.

Ash tray, astors on gr, ormolu rim, octagonal, 6" dia **300.00**
Ash tray, floral on bl, octagonal bowl form, 3 rests **250.00**
Biscuit jar, Indian portrait on gr, 6x5" **750.00**
Bonbon tray, irregular yel panels on bl w/florals, 6½" dia **400.00**
Box, appl tiny pk flowers, octagonal, med **550.00**
Box, Bishop's Hat, floral on bl, ormolu ft, 4¼" dia **400.00**
Box, Bishop's Hat, portrait transfer, 4½" **500.00**
Box, blown-out pansy on lid, 3¾" dia **500.00**
Box, cherub transfer on unemb form, 3¾" dia **375.00**
Box, cherubs transfer/beading on bl, unemb, 8" dia **1,000.00**
Box, courting couple/beading/flowers, unemb, 6" dia..................**800.00**
Box, Crown, floral on dk gr, 8½" dia...**800.00**
Box, Crown, panels w/sailing scenes, ftd, 6½" dia.................. **1,200.00**
Box, emb scrolls, portrait transfer/flowers, 8" dia **1,100.00**
Box, floral panels w/beading, octagonal, 6" dia............................**500.00**
Box, Gibson girl transfer/'Collars & Cuffs' on bl **1,000.00**
Box, Greenaway-style girls at tea on bl, 3x4½x4½"......................**600.00**
Box, lady's portrait/beading, unemb, mirror w/in, 4½" dia **575.00**
Box, ring; lady's portrait in wht on rose, unemb, 2x2¼" **550.00**
Box, Spindrift, florals on bl, 8" dia **900.00**
Card holder, emb scrolls w/flowers...**375.00**
Cigar holder, floral/beadwork, ormolu base & rim, 3x2¼" **500.00**
Cracker jar, emb scroll panels, floral/'Crackers' on red.................**500.00**
Ferner, emb scrolls, wht daisies on pk, ormolu ft/rim **525.00**
Hair receiver, astors on gr unemb bowl form, ormolu top **425.00**
Hair receiver, autumn leaves on bl, sq form, 4¼" **485.00**
Humidor, floral/'Cigars' on bl, 5½x4" **675.00**
Humidor, florals/'Tobacco' banner on bl, ogee sides, 7½"............**375.00**
Humidor, owl on tree transfer, 5½x4" **1,200.00**

Box, cherubs transfer, 6" diameter, $750.00.

Match holder, tiny beaded flowers on gr, ormolu rim, 2" dia **325.00**
Pin receiver, floral on sm bowl form, beaded rim, 1x2½" **275.00**
Pin tray, floral on octagonal bowl form, ormolu rim.....................**225.00**
Tray, floral/beading, rnd mirror atop, 3¾" dia **525.00**
Tray, florals, pk on gr w/mirror, sq, 5x4½"....................................**595.00**
Tray, Puffy, florals, rectangular **375.00**
Umbrella stand, emb scrolls/flowers, Indian portrait, 20½" **2,000.00**
Vase, floral/beading on yel to bl, wide bottom, ftd, 8".................**425.00**

Napkin Rings

Napkin rings became popular during the late 1800s. They were made from various materials. Among the most popular and collectible today are the large group of varied silverplated figurals made by American manufacturers.

When no condition is indicated, the items listed below are assumed to be all original and in very good to excellent condition. A timely warning: inexperienced buyers should be aware of excellent reproductions on the market, especially the wheeled pieces. However, these do not have the fine detail and patina of the originals and tend to have a more consistent, soft pewter-like finish. Recently the larger figurals in excellent condition have appreciated considerably. Only those with a blackened finish, corrosion, or broken and/or missing parts have maintained their earlier price levels.

Key:
gw — gold washed   SH&M — Simpson, Hall, & Miller
R&B — Reed & Barton

Arab kneels, holds torch, oblong base, Tufts #1583 ....**225.00**
Bear on haunches holds ring, scalloped base, Middletown #68....**195.00**
Bird peers into nest, rnd base, Webster #178................................**125.00**
Bird perched on top of ring, ornate ped base, Meriden #186..........**95.00**
Bird w/long tail perched on stem, leaf base, Meriden #202 ....**150.00**
Boy dancing, hand on hip, octagonal base, SH&M #022.............**295.00**
Boy sits X-legged/reads book, ring at bk, rfn, SH&M **250.00**
Boy w/sleeves rolled pushes ring, Meriden #161 ....**195.00**
Bud vase on top of ring, tubular arches form base, R&B #1257 ...**125.00**
Camel on oval ftd base, Meriden #269 ....**265.00**
Cat, lg, seated on oval ball ftd base, sgn.......................................**300.00**
Cat w/glass eyes, ring on bk, Meriden #235, EX **235.00**
Cherries & leaves on side of ring, leafy base, Standard #732 ....**125.00**

Cherub holds vase by ring, circular base, Rockford #178 ....250.00
Cherub in clown hat sits on bench reading to dog 295.00
Cherub in top hat kneels on rnd base, Meriden #222 ....175.00
Cherub plays w/bird under ring, octagonal base, Wilcox #4302 ..115.00
Cherub sits on ring, ped base, Meriden #131 ....95.00
Chick pulls cart holding ring, lg, Wilcox #4304.....................295.00
Chick sits on wishbone, circular base, Meriden #552 ....95.00
Cockatoo perched on ring, ornate base, R Smith #255, rstr 195.00
Conquistador leans on rifle, ftd base, Toronto #1337..................245.00
Cupid, lg, w/ring on bk, octagonal base, SH&M #016 ....295.00
Cupid blowing horn, floral rectangular base, SH&M #051 ....185.00
Cupid on carpet w/dog & basket, Meriden #170 ....245.00
Deer harnessed to ring resting on filigree sled, Toronto #11 ....165.00
Dog chases bird up ring, octagonal base.................................175.00
Dog howls w/head up, lg oval floral base, Barbour #49 ....285.00
Dog on haunches, carries ring on bk, Meriden #275 ....235.00
Dog pulls cart, collar is chained to ring 295.00
Dog pulls sled that carries ring, Meriden #285.........................195.00
Dog w/glass eyes, sits, ring forms body, Wilcox #4311 ....300.00
Eagle holds shield, sits on rectangular base 115.00
Fan forms base for 2 butterflies holding ring 95.00
Fawn peers over fence that juts from ring, Meriden #0282 ....235.00
Flintlock rifles Xd on ea side of filigree ring, Meriden #355 ....175.00
Fox climbs up tree base, bird atop ring, Meriden #123 ....225.00
Foxes on ea side of ring, detailed base, Middletown #119 ....195.00
Frog stands on lily leaf, beats drum-shaped ring, R&B #1475 ......350.00
Giraffe nibbles vine tied to ring, Manhattan #239 ....285.00
Girl w/basket of eggs stands on oval base, R&B #1492 ....295.00
Grapes & leaves around ring, leafy base, Standard #701 ....85.00
Greenaway baby w/bonnet on chair, Middletown #98.................265.00
Greenaway boy crawls w/ring on bk, no base, R&B #480 ....125.00
Greenaway boy on horse, flat irregular base, SH&M #225 ....425.00
Greenaway boy on sled w/ring at bk, Tufts #1655 ....400.00
Greenaway boy on swing by 6-sided ring 450.00
Greenaway boy stands by dog, rectangular base, Cromwell #175..240.00
Greenaway girl & boy on seesaw, Tufts 450.00
Greenaway girl on stomach, ring on bk, Wilcox #01548 ....300.00
Greenaway girl pulls wheeled ring, SH&M #030 ....395.00
Greenaway girl w/dog beside ring, Middletown..........................295.00

Greenaway girl with drum, Simpson, Hall, and Miller, 3", $425.00.

Greenaway girl w/fawn, arm on ring, oval base, Meriden............425.00
Greenaway girl w/parasol, boy, ring is hoop, Tufts 450.00
Horse stands by fence attached to ring, Meriden #0284 ....295.00
Hummingbird on branch, leaf base, Toronto #1142....................115.00

Knight, arm raised w/torch, rnd base, Barbour #59 ....150.00
Ladderbk chair (rustic wood) holds ring in fr 125.00
Leaves & logs ea sided of bbl-form ring, R&B #625, EX 95.00
Lion lies on rectangular base, ring on bk 195.00
Little Red Riding Hood w/basket, Pelton Bros #99 ....275.00
Monkey dressed, w/cane & tricorner hat, Middletown #72 ....350.00
Owl & violin, scrolled ring, ball-ftd base................................195.00
Owl on perch in front of ring, no base 125.00
Parakeet on branch, leafy base, Toronto #1108 ....100.00
Peacock on ring, tail steadies ring, no base, Meriden #151 ....110.00
Pheasant leans on branch, flat octagonal base, Meriden #246 .....150.00
Pig chases mouse over ring 175.00
Rabbit crouches against leaves & berries that cover ring 195.00
Rat on haunches beside ring, rectangular base 195.00
Roses & leaves on oval ring, Rogers #4 ....45.00
Scabbards & horns hold ring ea side, Meriden #288 ....150.00
Soldier in tunic stands before ring, Middletown #340.................125.00
Squirrel reads book, glass eyes, Meriden #282 ....250.00
Squirrel under leafy arch, ring on top, R&B #1497 ....175.00
Stork pulls rope attached to ring, oval base, R&B #1126............115.00
Thistles on base hold ring, Meriden #664 ....65.00
Turtle w/ring on bk, rectangular ball-ftd base, Derby #642 ....125.00
Wheelbarrow holds ring, shield-shaped base, Tufts #1537...........150.00

Nash

A. Douglas Nash founded the Corona Art Glass Company in Long Island, New York. He produced tableware, vases, flasks, etc. using delicate artistic shapes and forms. After 1933 he worked for the Libbey Glass Company.

Bowl, gold irid, everted rim, sgn/#562, 6" 200.00
Candlestick, Chintz, dk red w/gray, ball stem, 4", pr 4,150.00
Decanter, Chintz, aqua, bl/gr swags, steeple stopper, 16" 375.00
Finger bowl, Chintz, gr/amethyst/clear.....................................70.00
Pitcher, gr loops on clear, 8½" 375.00
Tumbler, Chintz, dk bl/gr, clear ped & ball stem, 6¼" 110.00
Vase, gold, leaf relief above rnd ft, slender, #568, 8" 300.00
Vase, gold w/bl irid, knopped trumpet form, ftd, #529, 9½" 600.00

Natzler, Gertrude and Otto

The Natzlers came to the United States from Vienna in the late 1930s. They settled in Los Angeles where they continued their work in ceramics, for which they were already internationally recognized. Gertrude created the forms; Otto formulated a variety of interesting glazes — among them volcanic, crystalline, and lustre.

Bottle, dk bl crystalline, bulbous, narrow neck, 9" 3,600.00
Bowl, bl/purple mottled gloss, thin-walled, bulbous, 3x4½" 950.00
Bowl, brn/bl-gr drip, conical on ft, w/label, 6" 7,100.00
Bowl, cobalt crystalline, low ft, shallow, 12" 1,300.00
Bowl, frothy wht matt on red clay, mk/#546, 2¼x4¾" 475.00
Bowl, irregular turq drip crystalline, rnd/ftd, 3x5⅜", NM............650.00
Bowl, orange/brn, heavily pitted, pnt sgn, label, 4¾"...............1,300.00
Bowl, orange/rust drip, thin walled, sgn in ink, K112, 6" 2,400.00
Bowl, salmon/wht veined, pnt sgn, 4½".....................................900.00
Bowl, sepia-red/salmon mottle, pnt sgn, 6" 1,800.00
Bowl, thick wht over dk brn, hemispherical, pnt sgn, 5½" 2,000.00
Bowl, thin robin's egg bl drip, narrow ft, flared, 8½" 1,400.00
Bowl, yel over terra cotta clay, rnd base, label: K741, 6½".........700.00
Bowl, yel w/gray to brn streaks, oval rim, flared/ftd, 8" 2,200.00

Bowl vase, volcanic pk/bl drip over sand, spherical, 7½" **9,600.00**
Vase, dk bl/blk crystalline, wide cylinder/sm cone neck, 4" **3,500.00**

New Martinsville

The New Martinsville Glass Company took its name from the town in West Virginia where it began operations in 1901. In the beginning years, pressed tablewares were made in crystal as well as colored and opalescent glass. Considered an innovator, the company was known for their imaginative applications of the medium in creating lamps made entirely of glass, vanity sets, figural decanters, and models of animals and birds. In 1944 the company was purchased by Viking Glass, who continued to use many of the old molds — the animals molds included. They marked their wares 'Viking' or 'Rainbow Art.' Viking recently ceased operations and has been purchased by Kenneth Dalzell, President of the Fostoria Company. They, too, are making the bird and animal models. Although at first they were not marked, future productions are to be marked with an acid stamp. Dalzell/Viking animals are in the $50.00 to $60.00 range. See also Depression Glass.

Animals and Birds

Bear, baby, head turned or head straight 40.00
Bear, mama 195.00
Bear, papa 225.00
Chick 20.00
Crow, cocktail..15.00
Duck, dk teal, Viking 28.00
Duck, fighting, head up 35.00
Elephant, bookend 95.00
Gazelle...65.00
German Shepherd...65.00
Hen 65.00
Horse, head up 95.00
Nautilus shell 35.00
Piglet, standing 150.00
Pony, long-legged, bl, Viking 65.00
Porpoise, orig 450.00
Rooster, lg 85.00
Seal, candlestick, lg, pr 150.00
Seal w/ball, bookends, lg, pr 130.00
Seal w/ball, candle holder, sm, ea..55.00
Seal w/ball, sm, ea 45.00
Ship, bookends, pr 95.00
Squirrel, flat or on base 35.00
Starfish, ea...65.00
Tiger 175.00
Tiger, head down..195.00
Wolfhound 65.00
Woodsman 95.00

Bookends, lady's head, pr 195.00
Bowl, console; Prelude..23.00
Bowl, nut; Florentine, clear center hdl, 11" 20.00
Bowl, Prelude, ruffled, lg...35.00
Bowl, Prelude, 3-ftd, 6" 10.00
Bowl, punch; Radiance, +4 cups 55.00
Cake salver, Mardi Gras, 10" 65.00
Cake stand, Gerlude, ftd..48.00
Candlestick, Prelude, 5" 24.00
Champagne, Prelude..20.00
Cocktail, Prelude 15.00

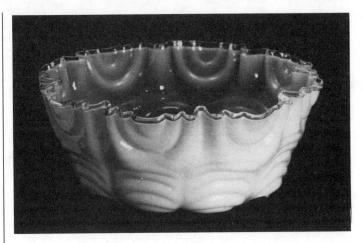

Cased peachblow bowl, ca 1940s, $295.00.

Cordial, Moondrops, red...15.00
Cordial, Prelude 24.00
Cruet, Prelude, w/stopper, 4-oz..38.00
Cup & saucer, Janice, lt bl 12.50
Cup & saucer, Prelude 15.00
Decanter, Mardi Gras, 12-oz, +6 cordials....................................185.00
Goblet, Mt Vernon, ruby, golf-ball stem, 6" 7.50
Goblet, ruby w/platinum trim, #1000, 4" 5.00
Goblet, water or wine; Prelude, ea 18.00
Mayonnaise, Prelude, 3-pc 35.00
Old Fashioned, Prelude, 3¼" 20.00
Pitcher, Oscar, amber, +2 tumblers 35.00
Plate, Janice, red, 8½"..17.00
Plate, sandwich; Prelude, 14" 42.00
Plate, torte; Prelude 55.00
Powder jar, Queen Ann, Ritz Bl..30.00
Punch cup, Mardi Gras 7.00
Punch cup, Radiance, ice bl..12.00
Relish, Flower Basket 12.00
Sherbet, Mt Vernon, ruby, golf-ball stem....................................... 7.50
Sherbet, Prelude, tall 14.00
Tumbler, iced tea; Prelude, ftd 22.50
Tumbler, Oscar, amber, platinum trim.. 4.00
Tumbler, Oscar, red, ftd, 4½"...10.00

Newcomb

The Newcomb College of New Orleans, Louisiana, established a pottery in 1895 to provide the students with first-hand experience in the fields of art and ceramics. Using locally dug clays — red and buff in the early years, white-burning by the turn of the century — potters were employed to throw the ware which the ladies of the college decorated. Until about 1910, a glossy glaze was used on ware decorated by slip painting or incising. After that a matt glaze was favored. Soft blues and greens were used almost exclusively, and decorative themes were chosen to reflect the beauty of the South. 1930 marked the end of the matt-glaze period and the art-pottery era.

Various marks used by the pottery include an 'N' within a 'C,' sometimes with 'HB' added to indicate a 'hand-built' piece. The potter often incised his initials into the ware, and the artists were encouraged to sign their work. Among the most well-known artists were Sadie Irvine, Henrietta Bailey, and Fannie Simpson.

Newcomb pottery is evaluated to a large extent by two factors: design and condition. In the following listings, items are assumed matt unless noted otherwise.

Our advisor for this category is Dave Rago; he is listed in the Directory under New Jersey.

Bowl, floral band, bl/gr/wht gloss, sgn JM/AM, 3x8" dia, EX 700.00
Bowl, floral band, Sadie Irvine, 1915, 3x8½" 635.00
Bowl, trees in meadow, gr/bl, AFS/ED-4, 3x8½", NM 700.00
Bowl vase, mock orange rim band, AF Simpson, 1918, 8" dia 750.00
Bud vase, crocus buds, glossy, M LeBlanc, ca 1900, 6" 2,500.00
Candle holder, allover heart forms, glossy, Irvine, hdl, 4"............400.00
Candlestick, long-stem daisies, wht on bl, ML Dunn, 9" 1,500.00
Candlestick, morning-glory, bl/yel on bl-gr, H Bailey, 7x5".........550.00
Creamer & sugar (open), jasmine rim band, AF Simpson, 1927..500.00
Flower frog, 3 bullfrogs, rnd 325.00
Inkwell, cvd florals, H Bailey, 1906, sm lid chip, 4¼" 1,100.00
Inkwell, depicting skulls, MT Ryan, ca 1900, no lid, 4" dia..... 1,700.00
Lamp, horizontal rings relief, glossy, S Irvine, 15", pr.............. 1,000.00
Loving cup, bleeding hearts/motto, glossy, M Ryan, '03, 6"....4,750.00
Mug, German text/holly bands, bl/gr gloss, Scudder, '07, 4" 700.00
Mug, goldfish, glossy, ca 1940s, 3¼" 200.00
Mug, Nouveau 'vines,' glossy, G Roberts Smith, ca 1900 .... 1,200.00
Pitcher, grapes/vines, glossy, Roberta Kennon, 1904, 8" 3,400.00
Pitcher, stylized flowers, gr/bl gloss, JM/EE24, 8x6", NM 3,700.00
Pitcher, trees cvg, bl/glossy, M LeBlanc, 6" 2,300.00
Plate, peacock feather band, artist unknown, 1915, 8" 1,900.00
Teapot, florals, EX cvg, glossy, A Lonnegan, 1906, sm chip.... 1,900.00
Tile, day lily, AF Simpson, 1912..375.00
Tile, Meyer at potter's wheel, L Nicholson, no date 3,600.00
Tile, tall pine trees, M LeBlanc, 1908..550.00

Vase, clematis vines in green and pink on blue ground, signed Henrietta Bailey, 1922, 5", $1,200.00.

Vase, Deco roses, A Mason, 1912, 10" 1,000.00
Vase, elephants ear leaves/freesia, glossy, att Drennan, 6"....... 4,400.00
Vase, evening sky/moss/oaks, high relief, S Irvine, '28, 5"....... 1,350.00
Vase, floral, wht/yel/gr on bl, sgn HB, wide shoulder, 7" 1,300.00
Vase, floral shoulder band, S Irvine, 1927, orig label, 7".............900.00
Vase, gr matt, mk JM, 7¾x3¾" 325.00
Vase, grapes/leaves, bl/gr gloss, SB Levy, 1904, 4¾x5" 3,700.00
Vase, hollyhock, EX cvg, H Bailey, 1919, 8½" 1,200.00
Vase, lilies, blk/yel/gr on cream gloss, S Gregory, 10", NM 4,000.00
Vase, lilies, gold/gr on cream gloss, SB Gregory, 10x4", NM ... 1,600.00
Vase, moon/moss/cypress trees, H Bailey, 1933, 6¾" 1,300.00
Vase, moon/moss/cypress trees, S Irvine, 1922, 12" 3,000.00
Vase, moon/moss/oak/house, S Irvine, 1929, 10½" 3,400.00
Vase, moon/moss/oaks, Aurelia Arbo, ca 1935, 8" 1,400.00
Vase, moon/moss/oaks, S Irvine, 1930, 5½" 1,100.00
Vase, moon/moss/trees, EX cvg/detail, AF Simpson, 6x5"....... 1,600.00
Vase, narcissus, AF Simpson, incurvate/slender, 1920, 7½".........850.00
Vase, narcissus, upright stalks, M Sheerer, 1909, 10" 3,400.00
Vase, pine cones swirl from inverted rim, H Bailey, 4x5" 775.00
Vase, shaded olive gloss w/incising, hdls, J Mauras, 17½"........ 2,600.00
Vase, stylized leaves, Corinne Chalaron, 1920, 3½" 325.00
Vase, stylized peonies, H Bailey, 1904, 6½x8½"....................... 3,000.00

Vase, thistles, glossy, E LeBlanc, ca 1900, rim rpr, 6" 1,300.00
Vase, yucca plants, glossy, M LeBlanc, 1901, mfg defect, 8".... 1,800.00

Newspapers

In addition to historic content, there are other factors that can add or take away from the value of an old newspaper. These factors are: whether or not the account is a 'first report' (the first time that the news appeared — a 'later-report' is a subsequent reporting); location of articles on the event (those with front-page articles are more highly valued); displayability (size of headlines, presence of photos or graphics to illustrate the event, etc.); whether the paper is from a small or large town; a daily or weekly; and charisma of the paper or event. Prices listed here are for a typical mid-sized town paper with front-page coverage and medium-size headlines.

Papers that do not cover a specific event are called 'atmosphere' newspapers. While these are not as valuable, they offer interesting insight into a particular era through ads for runaway slaves, ships' schedules, jobs wanted, etc. Many have interesting articles on topics such as mermaids, hangings, sea voyages, and a host of other topics.

For a more complete price guide and information on how to determine values as well as how to grade historic newspapers, detect reprints, where to buy and sell originals, and much more, the Newspaper Collectors Society of America offers a *Free Mini-Course About Historic Newspapers*. To obtain your copy of the 32-page primer and extensive price guide, send $1.50 to NCSA, Box 19134-S, Lansing, MI 48901. From it you will learn, for instance, how to recognize the original April 15, 1865, New York Herald version of the report of Lincoln's assassination from among the thousands of reprints which abound today. This booklet could save collectors from making bad investments and prevent dealers from loosing their honest reputation.

Our advisor for this category is Rick Brown; his name, address, and phone number are listed in the Directory under Michigan.

Key:
lr — letter   pub — publisher

An original Benjamin Franklin newspaper, *The Pennsylvania Gazette*, printed on his press in Philadelphia, June 3, 1762, $1,250.00.

1784-1799, Atmosphere papers...20.00
1800-1859, Atmosphere papers 5.00
1861, Civil War opens, first reports 150.00
1861, Civil War opens, later reports 85.00
1861-1865, Atmosphere papers, Confederate 60.00

1861-1865, Atmosphere papers, Union	4.00
1861-1865, Major battles of Civil War, Confederate titles	185.00
1861-1865, Major battles of Civil War, first reports	115.00
1861-1865, Major battles of Civil War, later reports	60.00
1862, Emancipation Proclamation	125.00
1863, Battle of Gettysburg, first reports	150.00
1863, Battle of Gettysburg, later reports	115.00
1863, Gettysburg address	165.00
1865, Capture & death of J Wilkes Booth	75.00
1865, End of Civil War, first reports	160.00
1865, End of Civil War, later reports	60.00
1865, Fall of Richmond	75.00
1865, Harper's Weekly, Apr 29 edition	165.00
1865, Leslie's Illustrated Newspaper, Apr 29 edition	200.00
1865, Lincoln assassination, NY Herald, Apr 15, 10 AM ed	1,500.00
1865, Lincoln assassination, NY Herald, Apr 15, 2 AM ed	600.00
1865, Lincoln assassination, NY Herald, Apr 15, 3 AM ed	500.00
1865, Lincoln assassination, other titles, first reports	165.00
1865, Lincoln assassination, other titles, later reports	85.00
1866-1900, Atmosphere papers	3.00
1871, Chicago fire, Chicago paper, 1st reports	400.00
1871, Chicago fire, later reports	50.00
1871, Chicago fire, other first reports	75.00
1872, Grant elected 2nd term	12.00
1876, Custer's Last Stand, first reports	170.00
1876, Custer's Last Stand, later reports	125.00
1876, Tilden defeats Hayes, lg graphics	115.00
1876, Tilden defeats Hayes, no graphics	35.00
1877, Hayes declared president	17.00
1880, Garfield elected	18.00
1881, Billy the Kid killed	215.00
1881, Garfield assassinated	30.00
1881, Gunfight at OK Corral	240.00
1882, Jesse James killed, first reports	240.00
1882, Jesse James killed, later reports	115.00
1884, Grover Cleveland elected	12.00
1885, Ulysses S Grant dies	40.00
1889, Johnstown flood	30.00
1892, Grover Cleveland re-elected 2nd term	17.00
1892, Lizzie Borden crime & trial	15.00
1898, Sinking of Maine, NY Journal or World	250.00
1898, Sinking of Maine, other titles	50.00
1898, Spanish American War begins	35.00
1898, Spanish American War ends	35.00
1900, James Jeffries defeats Jack Corbett to retain title	12.00
1900, McKinley elected 2nd term	17.00
1900-1945, Atmosphere papers	1.00
1901, McKinley assassinated	28.00
1903, Wright Brother's flight	550.00
1904, Teddy Roosevelt elected	17.00
1906, San Francisco earthquake, other titles	50.00
1906, San Francisco earthquake, San Francisco paper	185.00
1908, Taft elected	10.00
1912, Sinking of Titanic, first reports	215.00
1912, Sinking of Titanic, later reports	100.00
1912, Wilson elected	15.00
1914, WWI begins	30.00
1915, Lusitania sunk, first reports	85.00
1916, Woodrow Wilson elected	12.00
1917, US declares war	27.00
1918, November 11 Armistice	25.00
1920, Harding elected	12.00
1920, Prohibition takes effect	22.00
1920, Women's Suffrage, 19th amendment	22.00
1924, Coolidge elected	12.00
1925, Scopes 'Monkey' trial verdict	22.00
1926, Tunney defeats Jack Dempsey	25.00
1927, Babe Ruth hits 60th home run	175.00
1927, Lindbergh in Paris, first reports	65.00
1927, Lindbergh in Paris, later reports	25.00
1928, Hoover elected	12.00
1929, Byrd flies to South Pole	15.00
1929, St Valentine's Day Massacre	115.00
1929, Stock Market crash	85.00
1931, Al Capone found guilty	45.00
1932, FDR elected 1st term	12.00
1932, Lindbergh baby found dead	20.00
1933, Prohibition repealed	18.00
1934, Bonnie & Clyde killed	65.00
1934, Dillinger killed, Chicago title	185.00
1934, Dillinger killed, other titles	95.00
1936, FDR elected 2nd term	10.00
1936, King Edward renounces crown	13.00
1937, Amelia Earhart vanishes	15.00
1937, Hindenbergh explodes, first reports	65.00
1937, Hindenbergh explodes, later reports	35.00
1939, Gone w/Wind, Atlanta Constitution/Journal, Dec 15-16	75.00
1939, Gone w/the Wind, either Atlanta title, Dec 17-19	17.00
1939-1945, Major battles in the war	18.00
1940, FDR elected 3rd term	12.00
1941, Pearl Harber attacked, Honolulu Star-Bulletin	600.00
1941, Pearl Harbor attacked, Dec 8 issues, first reports	25.00
1941, Pearl Harbor attacked, other titles w/lg headlines	40.00
1944, D-Day	20.00
1944, FDR elected 4th term	12.00
1945, FDR dies	12.00
1945, First atomic bomb dropped	25.00
1945, Japan surrenders	25.00
1945, VE-Day or VJ-Day	30.00
1948, Babe Ruth's death	100.00
1948, Dewey Defeats Truman, Chicago Daily Tribune	500.00
1950, US enters Korean War	12.00
1953, Truce signed to end Korean War	17.00
1956, Eisenhower elected 2nd term	8.00
1957, Soviets launch Sputnik	15.00
1958, Alaska joins Union, Alaska title	35.00
1959, Hawaii joins Union, Honolulu title	35.00
1960, JFK elected	8.00
1961, Alan Shepard, 1st American in space	12.00
1961, Roger Maris hits 61st home run, breaks Ruth's record	85.00
1962, Death of Marilyn Monroe	20.00
1962, John Glenn orbits the earth	12.00
1963, JFK assassination, Nov 22, Dallas title	50.00
1963, JFK assassination, Nov 22, other titles	10.00
1963, JFK assassination, papers dtd Nov 23 to Nov 26	3.00
1964, LBJ elected	7.00
1967, Superbowl I	12.00
1968, Bobby Kennedy assassination	12.00
1968, Martin Luther King assassination	15.00
1968, Nixon elected 1st term	5.00
1969, Moon landing	17.00
1973, Vietnam peace pacts signed	7.00
1974, Nixon resigns	12.00
1976, Carter elected	3.00
1977, Death of Elvis, Memphis paper	40.00
1977, Death of Elvis, other titles	7.00
1980, Chicago Sun-Times error: It's Reagan & Ford	2.00
1980, Death of John Lennon, NY title	12.00

1986, Challenger explodes **7.00**

Niloak

Benton, Arkansas, was an area rich with natural clay, high in quality and easily accessible. During the last half of the 1800s, a dozen potteries flourished there; but by 1898 the only one remaining was owned by Charles Dean Hyten. In 1909 he began to experiment, trying to preserve in his finished ware the many colors of the native clay. By 1912 he had perfected a method that produced the desired effect. He obtained a U.S. patent for his handcrafted Niloak Mission pottery, characterized by swirling layers of browns, blues, red, and buff clays. Only a few early pieces were glazed both inside and out; these are extremely rare. After the process was perfected, only the interior was glazed. The ware was marked 'Niloak,' the backward spelling of Kaolin, a type of fine porcelain clay. No sooner had production began than the pottery burned, but Hyten rebuilt and added a stoneware line called Eagle Pottery. Hywood, an inexpensive novelty ware, was introduced in 1929 in an attempt to boost sales during the onset of the depression years. Until 1934 when the management changed hands, the line was marked 'Hywood-Niloak.' After that, 'Hywood' no longer appeared on the ware. Hyten left the pottery in 1941; in 1946 the operation closed.

Our advisors for this category are Lila and Fred Schrader; they are listed in the Directory under California.

Ash tray, Mission Ware, pierced metal insert **85.00**
Bookends, Mission Ware, resembles stacked books, pr **235.00**
Bowl, bl, scalloped rim, 3½x7½" **32.00**
Bowl, Mission Ware, flat w/str sides, 2x9" **110.00**
Bowl, Mission Ware, rolled rim, 9½" **72.00**
Box, Mission Ware, w/lid, 2x3x4" **110.00**
Candle holder, Mission Ware, w/finger ring, 6½" **145.00**
Candlestick, Mission Ware, 8" **125.00**
Chamberstick, Mission Ware, finger grip, orig label **85.00**
Creamer, stylized florals in relief, lt bl, 3½" **12.50**
Creamer & sugar bowl, maroon, open **25.00**
Ewer, brn gloss, 6½" **12.00**
Ewer, maroon w/gr tint overglaze, 8¼" **20.00**
Ewer, pk/gr, emb wing & star decor, 10" **16.00**
Figurine, doe, stylized, maroon, 8" **18.00**

Donkey figure, maroon, ca 1935, 3½" high, $35.00.

Figurine, piglet, bbl shaped, 2½" **21.00**
Figurine, razorbk hog w/ or w/o Arkansas emblem, maroon **75.00**
Inkwell, Mission Ware, w/lid & insert, 3" **170.00**
Jug, bl hi-gloss, 7" **35.00**
Lamp base, Mission Ware, cylindrical, metal ped, 13½" **200.00**
Lamp base, Mission Ware, slightly boulbous, 9" **195.00**

Mug, pk gloss, 3½" **8.00**
Pitcher, maroon, 4 flat sides, 4" **21.00**
Pitcher, Mission Ware, lemonade style, 8½" **225.00**
Pitcher, Mission Ware, squat, 5½" **110.00**
Pitcher, tan-ivory, bulbous, 5" **10.00**
Planter, bird w/very lg beak, dk yel, 4" **45.00**
Planter, bunny, wht, 3¾" **35.00**
Planter, camel, wht matt, 5x5½" **25.00**
Planter, kangaroo w/boxing gloves at front, 5½" **20.00**
Planter, parrot, yel & dk orange, 4" **35.00**
Planter, pelican, wht & orange, 5" **35.00**
Planter, pk/gr, shoe form, 5" L **8.00**
Planter, squirrel, maroon, 5½" **35.00**
Shakers, penguin, orig label, pr **35.00**
Toothpick holder, Mission Ware, 1¾" **55.00**
Umbrella stand, Mission Ware, w/flared ft, 15" **275.00**
Vase, amphora-like, maroon, orig label, 7" **28.50**
Vase, Hywood, ear-of-corn shape, orange to gr, 6" **29.00**
Vase, maroon, hdls, 7" **16.00**
Vase, Mission Ware, baluster, 10" **145.00**
Vase, Mission Ware, bbl form, dk brn, deep reds, 4½" **65.00**
Vase, Mission Ware, brn/pk/wine, cylindrical, 8x3¾" **110.00**
Vase, Mission Ware, bulbous base, corset top, 8" **125.00**
Vase, Mission Ware, bulbous w/flared top, 9" **110.00**
Vase, Mission Ware, cylindrical w/sm holes at top, 9" **120.00**
Vase, Mission Ware, flared base & top, brn & bl, 4½" **55.00**
Vase, Mission Ware, hourglass shape, 6" **60.00**
Vase, Mission Ware, oval, cylindrical, 6" **65.00**
Vase, Mission Ware, red/wine/beige, angle shoulder, 11x4" **175.00**
Vase, ringed neck w/hdls & melon base, chartreuse, 6½" **24.00**
Vase, rose, hdls, 6x3½" **10.00**
Vase, ruffled top, molded cord around neck, 7" **28.00**
Vase/flower arranger, Mission Ware, sgn/dtd, 5x5" **125.00**
Wall pocket, Mission Ware, inverted V shape, 7½x3½" **125.00**
Wall pocket, stylized florals in relief, dusty rose **35.00**
Wall pocket, stylized lg flower, pk matt **28.00**

Nippon

Nippon generally refers to Japanese wares made during the period from 1891 to 1921, although the Nippon mark was also used to a limited extent on later wares (accompanied by 'Japan'). Nippon, meaning Japan, identified the country of origin to comply with American importation restrictions. After 1921 'Japan' was the acceptable alternative. The term does not imply a specific type of product and may be found on items other than porcelains.

Authority Joan Van Patten has recently released the third volume of her lovely series *The Collector's Encyclopedia of Nippon Porcelain*, with many full-color photos and current prices; you will find her address in the Directory under New York. In the following listings, items are assumed hand painted unless noted otherwise. Numbers included in the descriptions refer to these specific marks:

Key:
#1 — China E-OH   #5 — Rising Sun
#2 — M in Wreath   #6 — Royal Kinran
#3 — Cherry Blossom   #7 — Maple Leaf
#4 — Double T Diamond in   #8 — Royal Nippon, Nishiki
    Circle   #9 — Royal Moriye Nippon

Ash tray, dog in relief, matchbox holder at side, #2, 5¼" **500.00**
Ash tray, Indian chief in relief, w/match holder, #2, 8" **800.00**
Ash tray, landscape, red fox figure on rim, #2, 6" **500.00**

Bottle, scent; river scene, cobalt rim, gr #2, 5" 175.00
Bowl, floral & gold scalloped hdl, HP mk, 7¾" 75.00
Bowl, floral medallions, 8-scallop rim, bl #7, 7½" 85.00
Bowl, lg roses, yel on wht, upright sq hdls, #27, 7½" 175.00
Bowl, mc florals, gold & cobalt rim, sq, #2, 8½" 140.00
Bowl, mc roses, ornate gold scalloped rim, bl #7, 11" 240.00
Bowl, nut; nuts in relief, sq w/upright hdls, #2, 5¾" 140.00
Bowl, pk & yel roses, cobalt & gold scalloped rim, #7, 9¾" 200.00
Box, cigarette; camel rider in desert, gr #2, 4½" L 250.00
Box, cigarette; river scene, much gold, bl #2, 4½" 225.00
Box, pin; Washington Capitol Building, bl #7, 1¼x2" 65.00
Box, powder; landscape, earth tones, 4-ftd, gr #2, 4¼" 80.00
Box, powder; portrait on lid, gold overlay, #7, 5¼" 200.00
Box, trinket; scenic reserve, heart form, #7 ....85.00
Cake plate, floral swags on wht, gold rim, mk, 10½" 75.00
Cake plate, roses w/ornate gold & floral rim, #7, 11½" 250.00
Cake plate, wide floral band w/gold, scalloped, hdls, #7, 11¼" ...250.00
Candlestick, florals, many gold beads, bl #7, 10¾" 280.00
Candlestick, moriage landscape, triangular, #2, 8¼" 275.00
Candlestick, Nouveau florals on cobalt w/gold, #2, 8", pr 340.00
Candlestick, Wedgwood, cream on bl, #2, 7½", pr...............550.00
Candlestick lamp, mc mums, gold beads, sq base, #7, 13" 325.00
Candy dish, hunt scene rim, 4-ftd, bl #7, 12" 225.00
Celery dish, lg florals on wht, hdls, oval, #2, 12" 75.00
Charger, desert horsemen in relief, gr #2, 13½" 1,900.00
Charger, floral tapestry, gold rim, bl #7, 11¾".................1,000.00
Charger, palms at sunset, narrow gold rim, gr #2, 14" 250.00
Cheese & cracker dish, sampan scene, earth tones, #7, 8½" 135.00
Cheese dish, Wedgwood, cream on bl, slant top, #2, 7¾" 425.00
Chocolate pot, gold & florals w/cobalt, #7, 10", +2 c/s 700.00
Chocolate pot, roses w/gold, slim form, mk, 11½", +4 c/s 550.00
Chocolate pot, silver overlay/cobalt on wht, mk, 11", +4 c/s.......400.00
Cigar holder & tray, sampan scene, earth tones, oval, #2 ....150.00
Cinnamon stick holder, river scene, gold base & top, #7, 4½" 200.00
Coffeepot, florals on wht, stick hdl, mk, ind, 5¾" 70.00
Compote, woodland scene, scalloped rim, #2, 3½x6½" 175.00
Condensed milk container, floral reserves, #7, 6" 155.00
Cookie jar, floral on tan, cobalt rim & ft, unmk, 9½" dia 200.00
Cookie jar, gold bands on wht, w/underplate, gr mk, 8" 325.00
Cookie jar, gold florals on wht, bl #7, 8½" 240.00
Cookie jar, moriage dragon on brn, ftd, #2, 7" 325.00
Cracker jar, florals, bl on wht w/gold, gr #2, 9½" 200.00
Creamer & sugar bowl, Egyptian sailboats & palms, #2.............85.00
Creamer & sugar bowl, geese at water, geometric rim band, mk..150.00
Creamer & sugar bowl, gold overlay on wht, mk 60.00
Cup, bouillon; roses & gold swags on wht, ftd, mk, 3¾" 20.00
Cup & saucer, demitasse; birds on branches w/lustre, mk............30.00
Cup & saucer, floral swags, pk on wht w/gold, mk.................40.00
Cup & saucer, lacy gold on cobalt, unmk 80.00
Egg cup, sampan scene, earth tones, bl mk, 2½" 55.00
Ferner, camel rider at oasis scene, ftd, gr #2, 5¾x10½" 400.00
Ferner, floral w/gold, 3-ftd, hdls, gr #2, 10½" dia.................325.00
Ferner, moriage dragon on brn, ftd, ornate rim, #7, 7½" 325.00
Ferner, river reserve, gold overlay, hdls, #2, 5¾x10½" 425.00
Ferner, roses, yel on gr, gold scalloped rim, ftd, #7, 7¼" 200.00
Ferner, roses w/gold rim & ft, sq, bl #7, 5¾" 150.00
Ferner, sampan scene, triangular, gr #2, 8" 200.00
Ferner, Wedgwood, cream on bl, relief-molded hdls, #2, 8½" 600.00
Hair receiver, floral reserves, much gold, unmk, 4½" dia................80.00
Hair receiver, florals on wht, gold rim & ft, sq, #2, 4¾" 75.00
Hatpin holder, gold on cobalt & wht, undertray, #7, 4¾"............110.00
Humidor, bridge scene, bl water & earth tones, #2, 5½" 450.00
Humidor, buffalo reserve, gr #2, 6"...............................550.00
Humidor, Egyptian figures & writing in relief, #2, 6½" 1,300.00

Humidor, Egyptian reserve ea side, sq lid, gr #2, 4" 375.00
Humidor, elk at sunset, earth tones, gr #2, 5½" 350.00
Humidor, elk runs in landscape, geometric bands, #2, 5½" 525.00
Humidor, fisherman at shore in relief, geometrics, #2, 7" 1,600.00
Humidor, fox hunters in landscape, gr at base, #7, 6½" 550.00
Humidor, gold pine cones, gold squirrel finial, #7, 8".............600.00
Humidor, Greek scene in relief, vintage top, #2, 7½" 1,300.00
Humidor, horse & wagon w/driver, geometric band, #7, 5½" 550.00
Humidor, horses in relief, 3-ftd, gr #2, 7½" 950.00
Humidor, hunt scene, floral bands, bl #2, 7¼" 600.00
Humidor, Indian on running horse in relief, #2, 6" 900.00
Humidor, lion w/kill in relief, brn tones, #2, 6¾" 1,000.00
Humidor, moriage owl on earth-tone tapestry, #7, 6½" 1,000.00
Humidor, pipe & pouch in relief, ftd, gr #2, 6½" 800.00

Humidor decorated in playing cards, 6½", $550.00.

Humidor, rose reserve, gold trim, hdls, bl #7, 6½" 425.00
Incense burner, East Indian woman figural, mk, 8" 300.00
Jar, pastoral band on gr w/gold, shouldered, #2, 6½" 125.00
Jar, potpourri; florals on wht, cobalt rim, #2, 5½" 140.00
Jar, potpourri; Wedgwood, cream on bl, #2, 5½" 400.00
Lamp, river scene reserves, much gold, gr #7, 16" 280.00
Mug, camel rider in desert, moriage trim, gr #2, 4¾".............250.00
Mug, mc grapes w/gold, angular hdl, #7, 4¾" 200.00
Mustard jar, river scene, earth tones, angle hdls, mk, 3½" 50.00
Night light, owl figural, gr #2, 6¼" 1,400.00
Pancake server, floral band on wht, gold trim, #2, 8¾" 125.00
Pitcher, floral reserve on beaded gold, cylindrical, mk, 4"............150.00
Pitcher, lemonade; pk roses, mk, +4 tumblers 135.00
Pitcher, moriage floral on gr, scalloped, Dowsie mk, 6½".............250.00
Pitcher, rose medallion on blk w/gold beads, #7, 13¾".............450.00
Pitcher, roses, mc on wht, 6-sided rim & base, mk, 7" 200.00
Pitcher, wide floral band, gold overlay on cobalt, #7, 7½" 450.00
Plaque, bulldog in relief, gr #2, 10" 1,150.00
Plaque, bulldog reserve, geometric border, gr #2, 10" 450.00
Plaque, exotic bird amid grapes, bl #7, 11" 275.00
Plaque, florals, woods & mtns in relief, gr #2, 10½" 1,250.00
Plaque, gull & surf, wide gold swag border, bl #7, 11½" 325.00
Plaque, Indian w/bird on bk in relief, #2, 10½" 900.00
Plaque, moriage owl on branch, gr #7, 9½".....................375.00
Plaque, portrait reserve, gold overlay (heavy), #7, 10"................350.00
Plaque, river landscape, earth tones, bl #7, 7¾" 250.00
Plaque, sampan scene, gold geometric rim, #7, 10" 250.00
Plaque, squirrel w/nut in relief, earth tones, #2, 10½" 900.00
Plaque, stag in landscape in relief, earth tones, #2, 10½" 700.00

Plaque, horse heads in relief, 10¾", $1,150.00.

Plate, man in boat scene, floral & cobalt border, #2, 10" 220.00
Plate, river scene, narrow gold band at rim, #2, 8½" 110.00
Punch bowl, mc grapes on brn w/gold, ftd, hdls, #2, 13" 900.00
Relish, river scene at sunset, oval, #2, 8½" 145.00
Rose bowl, grapes in relief, gr #2, 3½" H 325.00
Shaving mug, roses, yel on wht w/gold, gr #2, 3¾" 140.00
Spoon holder, floral medallions on wht w/gold, #7, 7¾" 100.00
Stein, dogs in relief, leash twisted around hdl, #2, 7" 850.00
Stein, landscape, earth tones, bands at top & base, #7, 7" 500.00
Stein, man w/pipe, grapes at top & base, gr #2, 7" 550.00
Stein, monk w/stein, grape border, gr #2, 7" 500.00
Tankard, moriage florals on gr, gold hdl, #7, 14¼" 600.00
Tankard, moriage gulls, mk, 15¾" 650.00
Tea strainer, floral reserves w/gold, bl #7, 6" L top pc 135.00
Teapot, gold overlay swags on wht, bl #2, 5¼", +cr/sug 150.00
Teapot, river scene w/pyramids, bl #7, +cr/sug 200.00
Tray, 1700s couple, floral medallions, gold moriage, mk, 11".........90.00
Urn, draped lady reserve on turq w/gold, w/lid, #7, 14" 1,000.00
Urn, moriage florals, ornate gold hdls, w/lid, #7, 14½" 700.00
Urn, peach tapestry, w/lid, bl #7, 10½" 950.00
Urn, portrait reserve, gold overlay on red & wht, #7, 12" 900.00
Urn, river reserve w/gold, hdls, gr #2, 13¾" 550.00
Urn, river scene, gold overlay on cobalt, w/lid, mk, 13¾"............900.00
Urn, river scene band, 3-ftd, ring hdls, w/lid, unmk, 9¼" 450.00
Vase, bird on moriage branch, ftd, hdls, #7, 9¼" 350.00
Vase, camel rider in desert, angle hdls, ftd, gr #2, 9" 300.00
Vase, camel rider in desert, urn form, angle hdls, #2, 6" 850.00
Vase, exotic birds reserves, bottle form, sm hdls, #2, 14" 400.00
Vase, floral, flared cylinder, scalloped rim, #7, 9" 275.00
Vase, floral, mc on gr, heavy gold beads, hdls, #7, 7½" 375.00
Vase, floral reserve band on cobalt, gold overlay, #2, 7½" 475.00
Vase, gold overlay florals on cobalt, sm hdls, #7, 10" 500.00
Vase, gold overlay on cobalt, urn form, angle hdls, #7, 12½".......550.00
Vase, grapes on brn shaded, bottle form, #7, 10¼" 200.00
Vase, landscape scene, gold overlay on cobalt, #7, 9" 375.00
Vase, lg pk roses, landscape beyond, cylindrical, #7, 12" 375.00
Vase, lg pk stemmed roses on tan w/gold, sm ft, #7, 8½" 180.00
Vase, long-stemmed flowers, shouldered, ftd, bl #7, 9" 185.00
Vase, man at shore in relief, earth tones, hdls, gr #2, 10" 1,700.00
Vase, mc mums, gold beads, bulbous, hdls, ftd, #7, 9¼" 350.00
Vase, mixed florals, cylindrical, angle hdls, gr #2, 10¾" 300.00
Vase, moriage butterflies w/jewels, sm hdls, #7, 9" 350.00
Vase, moriage dragon, 3-ftd, angle hdls, gr #7, 6" 150.00
Vase, moriage florals, ftd, hdls, bl #9, 9" 325.00
Vase, moriage grapes, swan scenic band, hdls, mk, 10" 425.00
Vase, moriage landscape, earth tones, bulbous, hdls, #7, 9" 400.00

Vase, moriage landscape, 4-lobe incurvate form, #2, 10" 400.00
Vase, moriage trees, landscape in relief, #2, 6" 550.00
Vase, moriage trees, landscape in relief, #2, 9½" 600.00
Vase, ostrich reserve, gold overlay on cobalt, hdls, #2, 13" 500.00
Vase, pastoral scene, Wedgwood (cream on bl) trim, #2, 11" 500.00
Vase, pastoral scene on cobalt, ftd baluster, #7, 9" 350.00
Vase, poppies w/gold on lav shaded, Royal mk, 12x5½" 125.00
Vase, portrait in banded reserve, gold/cobalt, hdls, #7, 7"...........425.00
Vase, river reserve, gold overlay on cobalt, #2, 12" 400.00
Vase, river scenic tapestry w/gold, cylindrical, gr #7, 9" 625.00
Vase, river tapestry, basket form, ftd, bl #7, 8¾" 950.00
Vase, river/mtn scene, gold on cobalt rim & base, #7, 14" 550.00
Vase, rose tapestry, bottle form, #7, 8½" 575.00
Vase, rose tapestry w/gold, bulbous, bl #7, 6" 525.00
Vase, roses, pk on tan mottle, slim pitcher form, mk, 11" 240.00
Vase, roses on bl shaded, gourd form, ornate hdls, #6, 8¾" 225.00
Vase, roses on tan, basket form, integral hdls, #7, 10" 275.00
Vase, roses reserve, gold overlay on gr, hdls, #7, 10¼" 350.00
Vase, roses w/gold, squat, sm ruffled rim, hdls, #7, 5¼" 150.00
Vase, scenic reserve band on cobalt, integral hdls, #2, 8" 300.00
Vase, swan reserve, gold overlay on cobalt, bl #7, 9½" 500.00
Vase, swan tapestry reserve, sm hdls, bl #7, 8" 550.00
Vase, Wedgwood, cream on bl, angle hdls, #2, 7¼" 475.00
Vase, Wedgwood, cream on bl, classic form, hdls, gr #2, 8" 500.00
Vase, windmill scene, earth tones, loving cup form, #2, 5½" 100.00
Wall pocket, florals, rainbow lustre w/gold, '30s, mk, 8" 35.00
Whiskey jug, coaching scene, gr #2, 7½" 525.00
Whiskey jug, pine branches & cones, angle hdl, #2, 7½" 450.00
Wine jug, autumn landscape, slim form, bl #7, 11" 675.00
Wine jug, desert scene, gold hdl, gr #2, 9½" 650.00
Wine jug, English coach scene reserve on gr, #7, 9½" 650.00
Wine jug, moriage roses, ornate hdl, #7, 8" 650.00

Nodders

So called because of the nodding action of their heads and hands, nodders originated in China where they were used in temple rituals to represent deity. Early in the 18th century, the idea was adopted by Meissen and by French manufacturers who produced not only china nodders but bisque as well. Most nodders are individual — couples are unusual. The idea remained popular until the end of the 19th century and was used during the Victorian era by toy manufacturers.

Andy Gump, bsk, Germany, 4" 100.00
Bank, Eskimo w/polar bear, papier-mache 45.00
Beachcomber, 3-way nodder, bsk, Occupied Japan 135.00
Blk child seated w/slate, bsk, 6" 235.00
Chubby Chauncy, bsk, Germany 100.00
Crocodile, porc 80.00
Daddy Warbucks, bsk, Germany 100.00
Dog w/ear cocked, metal 95.00
Girl in pk removing sock, bsk, 4" 145.00
Girl w/skirt up, legs swing, porc, Japan..95.00
Goose, celluloid, Germany 25.00
Indian girl, bsk Germany..100.00
Jockey seated on chair, metal 115.00
Kayo, bsk, Germany, 2½" 85.00
Little Orphan Annie, bsk, Germany, 3½" 110.00
Man w/glasses, papier-mache on wooden base, 5", EX 325.00
Monk w/wine, brn habit, bsk, 5¼" 145.00
Moon Mullins, bsk, Germany, 4" 100.00
Old man removing nightshirt, bsk, 7"..145.00
Oriental lady w/water baskets, porc, 5" 95.00

Oriental, seated, hands/head/tongue nod, porc, 7", pr 525.00
Oriental lady holding book, pottery, 3" 80.00
Oriental man w/open fan behind head, bsk, Victorian................265.00

Boxed set of 'Our Gang' nodders, copyright 1930 by Hal Roach Studios, each in the 2" to 3½" range, $1,100.00.

Rachel, bsk, Germany 100.00
Tilda, bsk, Germany 100.00
Uncle Bim, bsk, Germany 100.00
Willie Mays, bsk, MIB 275.00
Woodpecker, picks up matches, w/strikers, 3¾x4½" 100.00

Noritake

The Noritake Company was first registered in 1904 as Nippon Gomei Kaisha. In 1917 the name became Nippon Toki Kabushiki Toki. The 'M' in wreath mark is that of the Morimura Brothers, distributors with offices in New York. It was used until 1941. The tree crest mark is the crest of the Morimura family.

The Noritake Company has produced fine porcelain dinnerware sets and occasional pieces decorated in the delicate manner for which the Japanese are noted. Their Azalea pattern was produced exclusively for the Larkin Company, who gave the lovely ware away as premiums to club members and their home agents. From 1916 through the thirties, Larkin distributed fine china which was decorated in pink Azaleas on white with gold tracing along edges and handles. Early in the thirties, six pieces of crystal hand painted with the same design were offered: candle holders, a compote, a tray with handles, a scalloped fruit bowl, a cheese and cracker set, and a cake plate. All in all, seventy different pieces of Azalea were produced. Some, such as the fifteen-piece child's set, bulbous vase, china ash tray, and the pancake jug, are quite rare. Marks varied over the years; the earliest was the blue rising sun Nippon mark, followed by the Noritake M in wreath with variations. Later the ware was marked 'Noritake, Azalea, hand painted, Japan.'

Authority Joan Van Patten has compiled a lovely book, *The Collector's Encyclopedia of Noritake*, with many full-color photos and current prices; you will find her address in the Directory under New York. In the following listings, examples are hand painted unless noted otherwise. Numbers refer to these specific marks:

#1 — Komaru   #2 — M in Wreath
#3 — N in Wreath

Azalea

Basket, mint; Dolly Varden, #193 ....145.00
Bonbon, #184, 6¼" 45.00
Bowl, #12, 10" 32.00

Bowl, deep, #310..50.00
Bowl, fruit; shell form, #188, 7¾" 325.00
Bowl, oatmeal; #55, 5½" 18.00
Bowl, vegetable; divided, #439, 9½" 235.00
Bowl, vegetable; oval, #101, 10½" 40.00
Butter chip, #312, 3¼" 40.00
Butter tub, w/insert, #54 ....44.00
Cake plate, #10, 9¾" 50.00
Candy jar, #313 ....525.00
Casserole, gold finial, w/lid, #371......................................420.00
Casserole, gold finial, w/lid, #372......................................450.00
Casserole, w/lid, #16..85.00
Celery tray, closed hdls, #444, 10" 240.00
Celery/roll tray, #99, 12" 50.00
Child's set, #253, 15-pc.. 1,500.00
Coffeepot, AD; #182..500.00
Compote, #170 ....70.00
Condiment set, #14, 5-pc 60.00
Creamer & sugar bowl, #122...115.00
Creamer & sugar bowl, #401...110.00
Creamer & sugar bowl, #449, ind..130.00
Creamer & sugar bowl, #7...50.00
Creamer & sugar bowl, AD; open, #123...............................100.00
Cruet, #190..175.00
Cup & saucer, #2..17.50
Cup & saucer, AD; #183 ....25.00
Cup & saucer, bouillon; #124, 3½" 20.00
Egg cup, #120 ....40.00

Azalea jam jar, #125, 3-piece, $130.00.

Mayonnaise set, scalloped, #453, 3-pc 440.00
Mustard jar, #191 ....47.50
Pitcher, milk jug; #100, 1-qt 175.00
Plate, #4, 7½" 10.00
Plate, bread & butter; #8, 6½" 10.00
Plate, breakfast; #99, 8½" 17.50
Plate, cream soup; #363 ....65.00
Plate, dinner; #13, 9¾" 20.00
Plate, grill; 3-compartment, #338, 10¼" 95.00
Plate, soup; #19, 7⅛" 18.00
Plate, sq, #315, 7⅝" 45.00
Platter, #17, 14" 55.00
Platter, #186, 16" 325.00
Platter, #311, 10¼" 180.00
Platter, #56, 12" 38.00
Refreshment set, #39, 2-pc 42.00
Relish, #194, 7⅛" 70.00
Relish, loop hdl, 2-part, #450..300.00

Relish, oval, #18, 8½" 17.50
Relish, 4-part, #119, 10" 110.00
Saucer, fruit; #9, 5¼" 10.00
Shakers, #126, ind, pr 32.00
Shakers, bell form, #11, pr 27.50
Shakers, bulbous, #89, pr 25.00
Snack set, #39, 2-pc 35.00
Spoon holder, #189, 8" 75.00
Spoon holder, 339, 2-pc 35.00
Syrup, #97, w/underplate 95.00
Tea tile, #169, 6" 45.00
Teapot, #15 ....80.00
Teapot, gold finial, #400 ....420.00
Toothpick holder, #192 ....90.00
Vase, bulbous, #452 ....925.00
Vase, fan form, ftd, #187 ....150.00
Whipped cream set, #3, 3-pc 135.00

Ash tray, Deco lady & whippet on cream, #2, 3½"........45.00
Ash tray, Deco lady holds skirt wide, lustre rim, #2, 4¼"........120.00
Ash tray, Egyptian portrait, gr #2, 5" 90.00
Ash tray, Indian portrait, geometric rim, gr #2, 6½" 125.00
Asparagus set, asparagus on cream, bl & gold rim, #2, 7-pc 175.00
Basket, fruit & basketweave in relief, gr #2, 6" L 100.00
Basket, Tree in Meadow, Dolly Varden, rare 75.00
Bottle, scent; flower basket on cream, bulbous, #2, 6"........145.00
Bowl, exotic bird, chinoiserie at rim, gr mk, 7¼" 40.00
Bowl, floral & gold lustre panels form rim, 3-hdl, mk,6" 35.00
Bowl, floral medallion, orange & bl lustre, hdls, mk, 9¼" 55.00
Bowl, floral reserve, orange lustre, 1-hdl, mk, 5¾"........35.00
Bowl, floral reserves on lt bl, 4-scallop rim, gr #2, 8" 40.00
Bowl, flower form, arched hdl, ftd, red #2, 6¼" 80.00
Bowl, iris, bl lustre band w/gold, hdls, gr mk, 10½" 55.00
Bowl, leaves on bl, bluebird figural on rim, #3, 7½" L 110.00
Bowl, nut; squirrel in relief on side, #2, 6½" L 185.00
Bowl, parakeets, gold lustre rim, hdls, gr mk, 7" 40.00
Bowl, salad; orange w/florals on wht int, #2, +plate/servers 120.00
Bowl, salad; yel w/vegetables on wht int, scalloped, #2, 10"........60.00
Bowl, winter scene, 3 sm gold hdls, red #2, 6½" 50.00
Box, cigarette; cupid medallion on wht w/gold, #2, 6" 125.00
Box, elephant w/howdah figural, red #2, 6½" 240.00
Box, puff; Deco style, red & gold w/flower finial, #2, 3¾" 145.00
Box, trinket; Deco lady & whippet on lid, gr #2, 3" 55.00
Cake plate, exotic birds, pk rim w/gold, hdls, #2, 8¼" 40.00
Cake plate, river scene, geometric border, hdls, #2, 11"........40.00
Cake plate, Tree in Meadow 35.00
Candlestick, bird on leafy branch on bl, rnd ft, #2, 8¼"........95.00
Candlestick, bl butterfly at orange lustre base, #2, 5½" 75.00
Candy dish, florals, wht int, center ring hdl, mk, 6" 30.00
Celery set, river scene, #2, 12½" tray+6 3¾" salts 95.00
Celery tray, roses, pk on wht, gold rim, oval, #2, 11"........35.00
Celery tray, Tree in Meadow 40.00
Chamberstick, floral band, orange lustre, rnd hdls, #2, 4¾"........80.00
Cheese dish, sampan scene, earth tones, slant lid, mk, 6¼"........85.00
Chocolate set, exotic bird w/orange lustre & gold, #2, 13-pc........245.00
Chocolate set, florals on wht w/silver trim, #2, 9-pc 200.00
Cigarette holder, Deco couple smoking, bird finial, #2, 5"........160.00
Coaster, sailboat, orange & bl lustre, #2, 4" 12.50
Creamer, florals on cream w/orange lustre, gold hdl, #2, 5¾"........30.00
Creamer & sugar bowl, florals & orange lustre, child's, #2 ....32.00
Cup & saucer, Tree in Meadow.....................................15.00
Demitasse set, windmill scene, #2, 7" pot+11¾" tray+6 c/s........285.00
Dish, river scene, 2-tier, gr #2, 8¾" 75.00

Chip and dip set, windmill on banks of river, 9¾", $75.00.

Egg cup, windmill scenic, gold rim, gr #2, 3½" 25.00
Fish set, trout in water, lacy gold rim, 16" platter+8 pcs 750.00
Humidor, Deco couple smoking, gr #2, 6¾" 350.00
Humidor, floral reserve on red, gr #2, 4¼" 200.00
Humidor, floral tapestry reserve on bl, #2, 6" 185.00
Humidor, playing cards, dog finial, gr #2, 5¼" 365.00
Inkwell, boy in pointed hat figural, #2, 4" 265.00
Jam dish, Tree in Meadow 85.00
Jam jar, strawberries, rose finial, gr #2, 5½", +plate 55.00
Jar, potpourri; florals, mc on bl, rose finial, #2, 6½".......80.00
Lemon dish, lemons, orange & bl lustre, 1-hdl, #2, 5¾"........25.00
Match holder, horses on tan, bell form, #2, 3½" 110.00
Match holder, trees in yel band on red, bell form, #2, 3½" 105.00
Mustard jar, florals, pk & yel on wht, gr #2, 3" 30.00
Napkin ring, roses, pk & yel on cream, #2, 2¼" W.......40.00
Night light, lady figural, orange lustre dress, #2, 9¾" 925.00
Plaque, hunting dog at river, ornate rim, gr #2, 7½" 155.00
Plaque, 3 dogs in relief, earth tones, #2, 10½" 775.00
Plate, dinner; Tree in Meadow 22.50
Plate, florals (stylized), mc on dk bl, #2, 7½" 20.00
Plate, Tree in Meadow, 6½" 8.00
Platter, Tree in Meadow, 12" 40.00
Sauce dish, flower form, mc flowers at rim, #2, 5", +plate........65.00
Shaving mug, river scene, gold hdl, gr #2, 3¾" 95.00
Shell dish, Tree in Meadow..230.00
Smoking set, Deco florals on red w/blk trim, #2, 3-pc 265.00
Spooner, house by river, gold trim, red #2, 8"...............40.00
Sugar bowl, parrots on red, gold trim, #2, 3¼" 25.00
Sugar bowl, river & bridge scene, angle hdls, #2, 3½" 20.00
Sugar shaker & creamer, Tree in Meadow 75.00
Sweetmeat set, Deco fruit w/red & blk, 7-compartment, #2 ....100.00
Syrup, river scenic, earth tones, w/underplate, #2, 4¼" 60.00
Tea set, rose medallions on wht w/much gold, mk, 9-pc 265.00
Tea set, snow scene w/gold trim, #2, 4¾" pot+20 pcs........220.00
Tea tile, river scene, earth tones, canted corners, #2, 5" 40.00
Teapot, Tree in Meadow 60.00
Tray, Deco fruit at rim, gold hdls, red #2, 11"...............90.00
Tray, river reserves, much gold, canted corners, #1, 13" 65.00
Vase, birds on perch on yel w/gold, basket form, #2, 7½"........120.00
Vase, Deco lady in wht on red, slim form, #3, 8½" 185.00
Vase, open roses on cream w/gold, sm hdls, #2, 11¼" 165.00
Vase, peacock feathers on tan, ruffled rim, mk, 8".......110.00
Vase, river reserve on bl w/gold, scrolled hdls, #2, 7¼"........325.00
Vase, river scene, yel int, jack-in-pulpit form, #2, 7¾"........145.00
Vase, river scene in leafy fr, orange lustre, hdls, #1, 6"........145.00

Vase, roses, mc on wht, gold at top, upright hdls, #2, 8½" 110.00
Vase, Tree in Meadow, fan form, 7" 125.00
Vase, tulip figural, lav & gr, red #2, 5½" 195.00
Vase, Wedgwood, cream on bl, sq hdls, #1, 9½" 325.00
Vase, wide floral band on gr, ftd fan form, #2, 6½" 90.00
Waffle set, Tree in Meadow, sugar shaker & syrup 85.00
Wall pocket, butterflies on orange lustre, #2, 9" 120.00
Wall pocket, florals, mc on cream, gold trim, #2, 8½" 90.00
Wall pocket, swan scenic band, orange lustre, #3, 8" 90.00

North Dakota School of Mines

The School of Mines of the University of North Dakota was established in 1890; but due to a lack of funding it was not until 1898 that Earle J. Babcock was appointed as Director, and efforts were made to produce ware from the native clay he had discovered several years earlier. The first pieces were made by firms in the east from the clay Babcock sent them. Some of the ware was decorated by the manufacturer; some was shipped back to North Dakota to be decorated by native artists. By 1909 students at the University of North Dakota were producing utilitarian items — tile, brick, shingles, etc. — in conjunction with a ceramic course offered through the Chemistry Department. By 1910 a ceramic department had been established, supervised by Margaret Kelly Cable. Under her leadership, fine artware was produced. Native flowers, grains, buffalo, cowboys, and other subjects indigenous to the state were incorporated into the decorations. Some pieces have an Art Nouveau — Art Deco style easily attributed to her association with Frederick H. Rhead, with whom she studied in 1911. During the twenties the pottery was marketed on a limited scale through gift and jewelry stores in the state. From 1927 until 1949 when Miss Cable announced her retirement, a more widespread distribution was maintained with sales branching out into other states. The ware was marked in cobalt with the official seal — 'Made at School of Mines, N.D. Clay, University of North Dakota, Grand Forks, N.D.' in a circle. Very early ware was sometimes marked 'U.N.D.' in cobalt by hand.

Ash tray, Flossie the Fish, sgn M Cable 165.00
Bowl, Bentonite w/roadrunners, sgn J Mattson 450.00
Bowl, cvd leaf frieze, gr w/brn band, sgn Tobiason, 4x7" 300.00
Bowl, fruit, sgn Miller, dtd 3-20-'41, 8" 650.00
Cookie jar, Blk lady, 2-tone brn, M Cable, 9½x7" 1,250.00
Paperweight, Rebecca, gr gloss, sgn EL Harriman 70.00
Pitcher, milk; bl/gray tulips, sgn Huck, 5" 475.00
Trivet, emb florals, 3-color, 6½" 225.00
Vase, bl to violet to gr, sgn Hall, 1942, 4" 165.00

Vase, stylized flowers in vivid colors on high gloss glaze, signed HPD (unknown student), 7", $1,500.00.

Vase, crazed chrome yel, sgn FLH-463, 4½" 140.00
Vase, gr, ribbed, hand thrown, 5" 98.00
Vase, gr to ivory, sgn Hall, 1942, 4" 125.00
Vase, lotus, bl on lt bl gloss, mk Huck/Ottem/#4100, 3x6" 500.00
Vase, ND Rodeo, cvd/titled on brn, Huck/#208, 8x5" 1,000.00
Vase, Pasque Flower, cvd/titled on red-brn, C Huck/#53, 4" 225.00
Vase, pines cvd in gr/brn on gr, Thorne/Huckfield/#d, 12x6" . 1,500.00
Vase, stoneware, cobalt, sgn UND, early, 5" 200.00
Vase, wagon train in cvd shoulder band, brn, M Cable, 6x8" 500.00

North State

In 1924 the North State Pottery of Sanford, North Carolina, began small-scale production, the result of the extreme fondness Mrs. Rebecca Copper had for potting. With the help of her husband and the abundance of suitable local clay, the pottery flourished and became well known for lovely shapes and beautiful glazes. They were in business for thirty-five years; most of the ware was sold in gift and craft shops throughout North Carolina.

Ash tray, burnt orange/gr, imp mk, 1¾" H, NM 25.00

Ewer, blue over red clay, 8½", $95.00; Puzzle jug, blue over red clay, 4½", $18.00.

Jug vase, Chinese red, sm 35.00
Pitcher, copper lustre, slender form, 6½" 25.00
Sugar bowl, yel, imp 1920s-30s mk, 3" H 30.00
Vase, beige, fan form, 3¾" 25.00

Northwood

The Northwood Company was founded in 1896 in Indiana, Pennsylvania, by Harry Northwood, whose father, John, was the art director for Stevens and Williams, an English glassworks. Northwood joined the National Glass Company in 1899 but in 1901 again became an independent contractor and formed the Harry Northwood Glass Company of Wheeling, West Virginia. He marketed his first carnival glass in 1908, and it became his most popular product. His company was also famous for its custard, goofus, and pressed glass. Northwood died in 1923, and the company closed. See also Carnival; Custard; Goofus; Opalescent; Pattern Glass.

Bowl, berry; Leaf Umbrella, mauve, master+6 ind 415.00
Bowl, berry; Memphis, gr w/gold, master+6 sm 150.00
Butter dish, Peach, gr w/gold, 6x7¾" 125.00
Butter dish, Royal Oak, frosted 150.00
Butter dish, Royal Oak, rubena frost 200.00

Creamer, Dbl Loop, cobalt 65.00
Creamer, Leaf Medallion, cobalt w/gold 90.00
Creamer, Peach, clear w/ruby stain & gold 40.00
Creamer, Peach, gr..45.00
Cruet, Leaf Umbrella, cranberry, orig faceted stopper 395.00
Cruet, Royal Ivy, pk crackle, 6" 375.00
Cruet, Royal Oak, rubena, cut faceted stopper 375.00
Mug, Mum & Acorn, purple w/gold..75.00
Pitcher, Leaf Umbrella, cased yel satin, frosted hdl..................425.00
Pitcher, Regent, gr w/gold, water sz......................................110.00
Pitcher, Royal Ivy, cased spatter, water sz.............................245.00
Pitcher, Royal Oak, clear/frosted 110.00
Shakers, Leaf Mold, bl opaque, pr 135.00
Shakers, Leaf Mold, cased spatter, pr 175.00
Shakers, S Repeat, gr, pr 75.00
Shakers, Snail, gr, pr...50.00
Spooner, Royal Oak, rubena..95.00
Sugar bowl, Peach, clear w/ruby stain & gold 60.00
Sugar shaker, Leaf Mold, cased spatter w/gold flecks...................145.00
Sugar shaker, Leaf Umbrella, lav opaque 275.00
Sweetmeat, Grape & Cable, amethyst 315.00
Syrup, Leaf Mold, milk glass, rare.....................................255.00
Syrup, Royal Ivy, clear/frosted..150.00
Toothpick holder, Leaf Mold, cased spatter.............................175.00
Toothpick holder, Leaf Umbrella, cranberry 165.00
Toothpick holder, Royal Ivy, rubena 95.00
Toothpick holder, Royal Oak, rubena frost 165.00
Tumbler, Flute, orange 35.00
Tumbler, Leaf Umbrella, bl satin 65.00
Tumbler, Memphis, gr w/gold..30.00
Tumbler, Peach, gr w/gold 35.00
Tumbler, Regency, emerald gr w/gold....................................75.00
Vase, pull-up, brn on yel, flared, scalloped, 4½x4⅜" 695.00
Vase, pull-up, emb Herringbone, gold to red, pk int, 6x4" 1,750.00
Vase, pull-up, rose/pk/lime on wht, cream int, 8x4"....................550.00

Regent, green with gold, 5-piece water set, $300.00.

Water set, Grape & Cable, amethyst, 7-pc.............................450.00
Water set, Peach, gr w/EX gold, mk, 7-pc.............................355.00
Water set, Plum & Cherry, gold & red trim, 5-pc 250.00
Water set, Royal Ivy, rubena frost, 7-pc.............................595.00

Nutcrackers

The nutcracker, though a strictly functional tool, is a good exam-

ple of one to which man has applied ingenuity, imagination, and engineering skills. Though all were designed to accomplish the same end, hundreds of types exist in almost every material sturdy enough to withstand sufficient pressure to crack the nut. Figurals are popular collectibles, as are those with unusual design and construction. Patented examples are also desirable.

Our advisor for this cateogry is Early MacSorley; he is listed in the Directory under Connecticut.

Alligator, brass, early 1900s, 12½" 85.00
Bird form, all wood, worn brn finish, 7".......................................100.00
Cat, NP brass, 4½" 45.00

Dog, cast metal, 12" long, $50.00.

Eagle, brass..25.00
Elephant, CI, red/blk/ivory pnt, Art Deco, 1920s, 4x9" 90.00
Fagan & Bill Sikes, brass 35.00
Lady's legs, brass, worn pnt...25.00
Lady's legs, CI, orig pnt 25.00
Lion, brass, 4¾"...35.00
Pliers, CI, mk Torrington 6.50
Santa Claus' head, wood, mouth holds nut, EX pnt, 7½".............250.00
Squirrel on branch, bronze 25.00
St Bernard, brass, 8¾" 60.00

Occupied Japan

Items marked 'Occupied Japan' have become popular collectibles in the last few years. They were produced during the period from the end of World War II until April 18, 1952, when the occupation ended. By no means was all of the ware exported during that time marked 'Occupied Japan' — some was marked 'Japan' or 'Made In Japan.' It is thought that because of the natural resentment felt by the Japanese toward the occupation, only a fraction of these wares carried the 'Occupied' mark. Even though you may find identical 'Japan'-marked items, because of its limited use, only those with the 'Occupied Japan' mark are being collected to any great extent. Values vary considerably, based on the quality of workmanship. Generally, bisque figures command much higher prices than porcelain, since on the whole they are of a finer quality.

For those wanting more information, we recommend *The Collector's Encyclopedia of Occupied Japan Collectibles* by Gene Florence; he is listed in the Directory under Kentucky.

Our advisor for this category is Florence Archambault; she is listed in the Directory under Rhode Island. She represents the Occupied Japan Club, whose mailing address may be found in the Directory under

Clubs, Newsletters, and Catalogs. All items in the listings that follow are assumed ceramic unless noted otherwise.

Ash tray, curled leaf, lt & dk gr	3.00
Ash tray, face, looks like mug w/no hdl	8.00
Ash tray, fielder's glove, metal, emb mk	10.00
Ash tray, nude Blk baby by clothesline, 2½"	26.00
Bottle, scent; emb pk glass, w/dauber, 3½"	20.00
Bottle, scent; emb pressed glass, 3½"	20.00
Candle holder, seated Colonials holding flowers, 3½", pr	35.00
Candy dish, floral hdl, sq w/rnd corners, 5½ x5½"	10.00
Cigarette box, appl pk roses on lid	22.50
Cigarette box set, moriage dragon, bsk	48.00
Cigarette lighter, alligator on metal, 1¼x¾"	13.00
Creamer, cottage, 3"	15.00
Cup & saucer, demitasse; tulips on red	12.50
Cup & saucer, flower, wht on blk, yel int, Trimont China	18.00
Cup & saucer, gr w/ornate gold rim	10.00
Doll, celluloid, boy, jtd limbs, 5"	22.50
Doll, celluloid, football player, jtd arms, 6"	15.00
Egg cup, Bl Willow, 3¾x2½"	15.00
Figurine, angel on butterfly, bsk, 3⅜x3"	30.00
Figurine, angel w/horn sits by vase, 3"	10.00
Figurine, ballerina, arm & leg extended, rose base, 3¾"	77.00
Figurine, baseball player w/catcher's mitt, 3¼"	17.00
Figurine, boy & girl on fence, 4"	16.00
Figurine, boy seated on stump playing horn, chick on ground, 2¾"	7.00
Figurine, boy w/guitar & dog, 4½"	17.00
Figurine, bride & groom, bsk, 4"	20.00

Busts of cherubs, one with harp, the other with scroll, 3" x 4½", $50.00 for the pair.

Figurine, Colonial couple, gray hair, 4½", pr	15.00
Figurine, Colonial farmer, arms full of grapes, 8"	25.00
Figurine, cowboy & cowgirl, bsk, 6½", pr	36.00
Figurine, cowboy w/gun belt, shotgun at side, 5"	15.00
Figurine, cowgirl, Annie Oakley type, 5"	15.00
Figurine, dancer, ruffled dress, Delft style, 5⅜"	20.00
Figurine, doctor w/bald head, carries brn bag, 6"	27.00
Figurine, Dutch girl, Delft style, 4½"	20.00
Figurine, elf on butterfly, 3½"	20.00
Figurine, elf on snail, 4½x4"	25.00
Figurine, female peasant w/lamb, rnd object in hand, 5"	15.00
Figurine, girl hiker, backpack & umbrella, 5½"	18.00
Figurine, Indian Chief, 6"	20.00
Figurine, lady playing violin, 3-D flower on base, 7"	25.00
Figurine, lady w/lute, seated, bsk, 6"	20.00
Figurine, lady wears aqua hat & scarf, 10"	20.00
Figurine, man holding cup, 5¾"	20.00
Figurine, man w/hands in pockets, bsk, 2½"	7.00

Figurine, Mexican w/guitar, red & wht sombrero, 6⅞"	25.00
Figurine, Oriental boy, mc clothes, bsk, 4⅝"	14.00
Figurine, Oriental coolie, red hat, shoulder yoke, 4"	12.00
Figurine, Oriental dancer w/gr headdress, holds fan, 6¼"	18.00
Figurine, Oriental girl kneels in gr kimono, holds fan, 4"	12.00
Figurine, Oriental girl lies on stomach, 3¼x3¾"	12.00
Figurine, Oriental lady dressed in wht, 6¼"	15.00
Figurine, piano, brn w/blk & wht keys & music, 2¼x2"	7.00
Figurine, pixie playing drum w/cymbals, 3½"	12.00
Figurine, schoolgirl, hood, books, lunch box, bsk, 4¾"	12.00
Figurine, seaman, Delft style, 5"	20.00
Figurine, windmill w/mobile blades, Delft style, 4"	25.00
Lamp, Colonial figures, pk & purple shade, 10"	30.00
Lamp, parrot/tree trunk, pnt parrot on shade, 10"	28.00
Match holder, bald fat man w/fly on upper lip, 3⅜"	25.00
Mug, stagecoach scene w/floral base, bunny hdl, 5"	26.00
Planter, bird at birdhouse, thatched roof, 3½x3½"	12.00
Planter, cat, lt gr w/red lines on side, 5¾"	15.00
Planter, clown couple, log fence, 4x2½x3"	14.00
Planter, duck w/top hat, 6¾x5"	15.00
Planter, elephant w/trunk up, mc garland surround, 3"	7.00
Planter, Oriental man w/big hat & wht suit, 5⅛"	8.00
Planter, pixie seated at front, 4¾x3¾"	25.00
Planter, shoe house, bird on toe, 4⅜x5"	10.00
Planter, shoe house, red roof, bl shoestring, 4¼x5"	10.00
Planter, wheelbarrow filled w/flowers, 3½"	10.00
Plate, banana & plums center, sgn Parry	20.00
Plate, flower, pk on wht, lattice rim, 6"	22.50
Plate, ladies, lacy rim, 5"	20.00
Salt cellar, swan, 1¾x1¾"	7.00
Shakers, apples in basket, 2⅝x4", pr	15.00
Shakers, cabbage form, 3¼x4⅛", pr.	15.00
Shakers, Indian head bust, 3", pr	16.00
Shakers, mc florals w/gold top, 5½", pr	20.00
Shakers, pig, blk & gray spotted, pr	15.00
Shelf sitter, ballerina, pk costume, right hand on head, 6⅛"	25.00
Shelf sitter, boy fishing, barefooted, matt, 4¼"	17.00
Sugar bowl, cottage form, w/lid, 4½"	16.00
Sugar bowl, florals, ornate hdls, w/lid	9.00
Tea set, floral pattern, 11-pc, mini	40.00
Toby mug, devil bust, 2"	25.00
Toby mug, figure sitting w/book, 5¼"	50.00
Tray, mc plaid, 6x2⅛"	5.00
Vase, bird & florals HP on tan lustre, 2½"	7.50
Vase, cornucopia; tea roses, red on wht w/gold, 2½"	7.00
Vase, florals on gr, maroon trim, 2¾"	7.00
Vase, fluted, scalloped lip, hdls, metal, 5¾"	7.00
Vase, Satsuma style, 3¾"	7.00

Ohr, George

George Ohr established his pottery around 1893 in Biloxi, Mississippi. The unusual style of the ware he produced and his flamboyant personality earned him the dubious title of 'the mad potter of Biloxi.' Though acclaimed by some of the critics of his day to be perhaps the most accomplished thrower in the history of the industry, others overlooked the eggshell-thin walls of his vessels, each a different shape and contortion, and saw only that their 'tortured' appearance contradicted their own sedate preferences.

Ohr worked alone. His work was typically pinched and pulled, pleated, crumpled, dented, and folded. Lizards and worms were often applied to the ware, each with detailed, expressive features. He was well recognized, however, for his glazes, especially those with a metallic patina. The ware was marked with his name, alone or with 'Biloxi' added. Ohr died in 1918.

Our advisors for this category are Fer-Duc, Inc.; they are listed in the Directory under New York.

Bank, baked potato form, brn w/yel 'butter,' mk, 5½" 550.00
Bank, bsk, pinched/folded, 2½x3" 125.00
Bowl, lapis mottle, bulbous, ea side w/pinch & pleat, 4" 5,000.00
Bowl, lav/gr/bl, brn/bl specks, boldly folded/pinched, 3½" 13,000.00
Creamer+sugar, gr w/gun-metal drip, in-body twist/pleats.......2,600.00
Dish, orange/gr, trough-like w/cone-like ends, 2x7" 425.00
Inkwell, log cabin form, metallic blk, block mk, 2½x2½" 275.00
Pitcher, brn/tan bsk, folded side forms hdl, dimpled, 4x6".......2,700.00
Pitcher, gr w/rose & yel streaks, dbl C-hdl w/top loop, 8" 3,250.00
Pitcher, lav/bl/gr gloss, 4-section, dimpled, bent hdl, 8" 4,750.00
Pitcher, lt/brn bsk, in-body twist, ornate scroll hdl, 9" 1,700.00
Pitcher, red & wht bsk, trefoil spout, orig tag, 12x6" 750.00
Pitcher, wht bsk, appl snake, deep in-body twist, 5x8" 2,000.00
Pitcher, wht/rust bsk, twisted neck/hdl, dimpled body, 4½" ...1,200.00
Plate, gr translucent, ruffled, no mk, 4¼" 125.00
Puzzle jug, dk gr metallic, 8x5" 400.00
Puzzle mug, brn metallic, tooled hdl, 3¾x5" 275.00
Teapot, blk metallic, flat lid, snake-like curving spout, 4".......1,500.00
Teapot, rose/brn/gray-gr feathering, long spout, rpr, 7x8"........3,500.00
Vase, blk metallic, bulbous w/crimped & ruffled rim, 8x6" 2,500.00
Vase, blk metallic/mahog flambe, collar neck w/twist, 4½".....2,700.00
Vase, brn bsk, fluted top/crimped middle, 4x5" 950.00
Vase, brn gun metal, pinched/ruffled rim, base rpr, 3¾"...............350.00
Vase, cobalt mottle, lateral dimples/rim fold on 1 side, 4" 4,000.00
Vase, gr metallic to rust flambe, 'peachblow' form, rpr, 7".......1,800.00
Vase, gr-brn to mahog, deep rim twist, 4¾x4", NM.................1,300.00
Vase, gun metal, depressed/twisted shoulder, shaped rim, 3" ...1,900.00
Vase, hematite lustre, crimped rim, twist at neck, 13"...........22,000.00
Vase, khaki gr, baluster form w/cup-like top, 5x3" 475.00
Vase, lav/gr/bl mottle, dimpled, folded everted rim, 3x4" 2,800.00
Vase, lt bsk, trefoil shape, 3x5" 325.00
Vase, med bl w/rust int, pinched in ea side & at rim, 4x4" 1,800.00
Vase, moss gr on swirled/scroddled clay, sm rim break, 2x4"........400.00
Vase, mustard w/4-color 'trails,' bulbous w/flared rim, 4".........2,200.00
Vase, mustard/brn dapple, cylinder neck w/crimped rim, 5¾" . 2,600.00
Vase, mustard/mossy metallic mottle, twist at neck, ftd, 7" 5,500.00
Vase, ochre w/brn specks, manipulated rim (minor rpr), 4x5" 950.00
Vase, olive/brn dapple, folded pendant rim, ovoid, 4¾" 6,000.00
Vase, orange w/gun-metal specks, ruffled, rpr rim, 5x3½" 425.00

Vase, rich pink with blue, red, and green spots, bulbous with deep, in-body twists, block mark, firing line in base, 4" x 4¾", $6,500.00.

Vase, pk bsk, ruffled/mid-twist, tells source of clay, 3x4" 900.00
Vase, pk/red/cobalt dapple, ruffled neck, 7" 11,000.00

Vase, pk/wht bsk, open wing-like hdls, dbl opening, 4½" 900.00
Vase, red/brn bsk, pinched/folded rim & body, 4½x5", NM.... 1,800.00
Vase, royal bl w/pk traces, long hdls w/looped tops, 7x4½" 1,700.00
Vase, rust gloss w/gr specks, bulbous w/can neck, 4½ x3½"......600.00
Vase, silver on gr, can neck, crimped/jagged rim, 4", NM 1,200.00
Vase, speckled chartreuse, very lg flared neck, 3½x2½" 325.00
Vase, wht/red bsk, 'handkerchief' style, tooled, 3x3" 900.00
Vase, yel/gr spatter, rnd/compressed, extreme rim fold, 3½" 8,000.00

Old Ivory

Old Ivory dinnerware was produced during the late 1800s by Herman Ohme, of Lower Salzbrunn in Selesia. The patterns are referred to by the numbers stamped on the bottom of each piece. The mark sometimes includes a crown and the name 'Selesia.' Patterns #16 and #84 are the easiest to find and come in a wide variety of table items. Values are about the same for both patterns. Other floral designs include pink, yellow, and orange roses; holly; and lavender flowers — all on the same soft ivory background.

The ware was not widely distributed; its two main distribution points were in Maine and, to a lesser extent, Chicago. Our prices are intended to represent a nationwide average, though you may have to pay a little more on the west coast.

Bowl, #11, 5⅜" 20.00
Bowl, #15, 5½ " 25.00
Bowl, #16 or #84, 5" 22.50
Bowl, #16 or #84, 6¼" 40.00
Bowl, #16 or #84, 9½" 125.00
Bowl, #200, 9"...125.00
Bowl, #32, 5½" 20.00
Bowl, #73, 10" 85.00
Bowl, #75, 9½" 85.00
Bowl, oyster; #16 or #84, fluted...175.00
Bowl, pk roses, unnumbered, 9½" 175.00
Butter pat, #28...50.00
Cake plate, #15, 10", +8 dessert plates.....................................295.00
Cake plate, #16 or #84, hdls, 10" or 11"...................................125.00
Cake plate, #22, Holly Berry, 9½", +6 6½" ind 600.00
Celery tray, #16 or #84, 11½"..115.00
Chocolate pot, #11 ....450.00
Chocolate pot, #16 or #84 ....400.00
Chocolate set, #11, 13-pc...600.00
Chocolate set, #15, 13-pc...750.00
Chocolate set, #16 or #84, 13-pc..800.00
Chop plate, #15 ....185.00
Chop plate, #16 or #84..185.00
Cracker jar or biscuit jar, #16 or #84...350.00
Creamer, #11 ....45.00
Creamer, #22, Holly..165.00
Creamer, unnumbered, 3"...55.00
Creamer & sugar bowl, #16 or #84...175.00
Cup, coffee; #15 ....40.00
Cup & saucer, chocolate; #11 ....60.00
Cup & saucer, chocolate; #33 ....65.00
Cup & saucer, coffee; #15 ....60.00
Cup & saucer, tea; #11 ....60.00
Cup & saucer, tea; #16 or #84, ftd..55.00
Cup & saucer, tea; #33 ....60.00
Mayonnaise, #28, w/underplate 95.00
Mustard pot, #16 or #84..195.00
Plate, #11, 7½"...45.00
Plate, #15, 6"..25.00

Demitasse cup and saucer, #16, $75.00.

Plate, #15, 7½"	45.00
Plate, #16 or #84, 6"	25.00
Plate, #16 or #84, 6¾"	30.00
Plate, #16 or #84, 7½"	45.00
Plate, #16 or #84, 8½"	65.00
Plate, #28, rnd rim, 9¾"	125.00
Plate, #28, 8½"	65.00
Plate, #32, 6"	20.00
Plate, #33, 7½"	45.00
Platter, #16 or #84, 11¾"	150.00
Platter, #16 or #84, 16"	275.00
Platter, #30, 12"	125.00
Relish tray, #16 or #84, hdls, 6" dia	60.00
Relish tray, #16 or #84, 8½"	60.00
Relish tray, #200, hdls	95.00
Rose bowl, #16 or #84, fluted	175.00
Saucer, #16 or #84, 4½"	10.00
Saucer, #16 or #84, 5½"	10.00
Saucer, #28, 5½"	10.00
Saucer, #32, 4½"	5.00
Saucer, #40, 6"	10.00
Shakers, #16 or #84, pr	145.00
Shakers, #40, pr	125.00
Shakers, unnumbered, pr	100.00
Sugar bowl, #11	75.00
Sugar shaker, #16 or #84	395.00
Tray, dresser; #28, worn gold, 12"	175.00
Tray, dresser; #73, 12"	175.00
Tureen, soup; #16 or #84, oval	695.00

Old Paris

Old Paris porcelains were made from the mid-18th century until about 1900. Seldom marked, the term refers to the area of manufacture rather than a specific company. In general, the ware was of high quality; characterized by classic shapes, colorful decoration, and gold application.

Cake stand, Honore style, rare gr border, pr	325.00
Clock, lyre form, figures ea side of dial, stippled, 12", NM	350.00
Coffee service, Anneau d'Or, 15-pc	1,100.00
Figurine, Napoleon, standing, 1 arm behind/1 in shirt, 19"	600.00
Plate, dinner; floral on melon ground, set of 6	160.00
Plate, maid kneels in woods, 4 cherubs on hay bale, 9"	375.00
Spill holder, neoclassical, cylindrical	375.00
Tray, armorial for Sultan of Jahor, 'jewelling,' hdls, 17"	150.00
Tureen, soup; flowers on melon ground, 8-sided, +platter	750.00
Vase, children/goat on gr w/HP florals, ormolu mt, lid, 18"	500.00

Vase, floral fan form w/appl leaves & mc florals, 13x11"	350.00
Vase, floral/fruit, 4 appl snails, ca 1860s, 15"	600.00
Vase, florals/gilt sprigwork, scrolled borders, 7¾", NM, pr	250.00
Vase, fruit/florals, thick scroll hdls at base, 13"	325.00
Vase, leaf body, peach w/bl side panels, HP florals, 13"	150.00
Vase, long bellflower stem as hdl, lovers reserve, 18", EX	150.00
Vase, man (or lady), leafy top/emb flowers, 18", pr, EX	225.00
Vase, mc tulips in vertical panel, fan shape, 9x14"	350.00

Urns, landscapes and romantic scenes each side, figural handles, 16", $5,000.00 for the pair.

Old Sleepy Eye

Old Sleepy Eye was a Sioux Indian chief who was born in Minnesota in 1780. His name was used for the name of a town as well as a flour mill. The Sleepy Eye Milling Company of Sleepy Eye, Minnesota, contracted the Weir Pottery Company of Monmouth, Illinois, to make steins, vases, salt crocks, and butter tubs which the company gave away to their customers in each bag of their flour. A bust profile of the old Indian and his name decorated each piece of the blue and gray stoneware. In addition to these four items, the Minnesota Stoneware Company of Red Wing made a mug with a verse which is very scarce today.

In 1906 Weir Pottery merged with six others to form the Western Stoneware Company in Monmouth. They produced a line of blue and white ware using a lighter body, but these pieces were never given as flour premiums. This line consisted of pitchers (five sizes), steins, mugs, sugar bowls, vases, trivets, and mustache cups. These pieces turn up only rarely in other colors and are highly sought by advanced collectors.

Advertising items such as trade cards, pillow tops, thermometers, paperweights, letter openers, post cards, cookbooks, and thimbles are considered very valuable.

The original ware was made sporadically until 1937. Brown steins and mugs were produced in 1952.

Barrel, flour; orig paper label, 1920s	750.00
Barrel, grapevine-effect banding	1,200.00
Butter crock, Flemish	500.00
Calendar, 1904	350.00
Cookbook, Indian on cover, Sleepy Eye Milling Co, 4¾x4"	55.00
Cookbook, loaf of bread shape, NM	250.00
Coupon, for ordering cookbook	60.00
Dough scraper, tin/wood, To Be Sure, EX	350.00
Fan, Indian chief, die-cut cb, 1900	175.00
Flour sack, cloth, mc Indian, red letters	275.00
Flour sack, paper, Indian in blk, blk lettering, NM	100.00
Ink blotter	100.00
Label, barrel end; mc Indian portrait, 16", NM	125.00

Label, egg crate; Indian chief in color, 1930s, 9x11" 25.00
Label, egg crate; unused...18.00
Letter opener, bronze 850.00
Match holder, pnt 1,500.00
Match holder, wht 850.00
Milk carton 18.00
Mirror, advertising, 1935 ....35.00
Mug, bl & wht, 4¼" 175.00
Mug, verse, Redwing, EX 1,300.00
Paperweight, bronzed company trademk............................450.00
Pillow cover, Sleepy Eye & tribe meet Pres Monroe 600.00
Pillow cover, trademk center w/various scenes, 22", NM...........600.00
Pitcher, #1 ....150.00
Pitcher, #2 ....200.00
Pitcher, #3, rare 250.00
Pitcher, #3, w/bl rim 1,100.00
Pitcher, #4 ....325.00
Pitcher, #5 ....350.00
Pitcher, bl on cream, 8", M 275.00
Pitcher, bl/gray, 5" 190.00
Pitcher, gold & brn, 1981 ....125.00
Pitcher, standing Indian, good color, #5 size 1,250.00
Post card 90.00
Post card, colorful trademk, 1904 Expo Winner 150.00
Ruler, wooden 400.00
Salt crock, Flemish 450.00
Sign, self-fr tin, Old Sleepy Eye Flour, 20x24" 2,000.00
Sign, tin, Sleepy Eye Flour & Cereal Products 3,500.00
Spoon, demitasse; emb roses in bowl, Unity SP 85.00
Spoon, Indian-head hdl...100.00

Stein, brown glaze, 1952, $350.00.

Stein, bl & wht, 7¾" 500.00
Stein, brn & yel, Western Stoneware 900.00
Stein, cobalt 800.00
Stein, Flemish...475.00
Stein, ltd edition, 1979-84, ea..100.00
Sugar bowl, bl & wht, 3" 600.00
Tumbler, etched, 1979 commemorative 25.00
Vase, bl & wht, good color, 9" 425.00
Vase, brn on yel, rare color..800.00
Vase, Indian & cattails, Flemish, 8½" 375.00
Watch fob, Sleepy Eye Mills, Indian, M 50.00

O'Neill, Rose

Rose O'Neill's Kewpies were introduced in 1909 when they were

used to conclude a story in the December issue of *Ladies' Home Journal*. They were an immediate success, and soon Kewpie dolls were being produced worldwide. German manufacturers were among the earliest and also used the Kewpie motif to decorate chinaware as well as other items. The Kewpie is still popular today and can be found on products ranging from Christmas cards and cake ornaments to fabrics and wallpaper.

In the following listings, 'sgn' indicates that the item is signed Rose O'Neill. Unsigned items are of little interest to collectors. Items marked 'Germany' are sometimes reproductions.

6" Kewpie in original box, $295.00; 8½" Kewpie, $425.00; Each is marked on its foot and is jointed at shoulders only. Sitting Kewpie has ladybug on extended fingers, $425.00. Kewpie Huggers, $225.00.

Bell, Kewpie figural hdl, brass...65.00
Book, For Love of Mary Ellen, O'Neill illus, 1912, EX 35.00
Bottle, scent; Kewpie figural, bsk, 3½" 475.00
Box, handkerchief; Kewpies on bl, sgn/dtd 50.00
Cookbook, Jell-O, O'Neill illus 15.00
Ink well, metal w/glass insert, O'Neill.....................................250.00
Kewpie, bsk, jtd arms, 1-pc body, w/sticker, 2½" 115.00
Kewpie, bsk, jtd arms, 2-pc body, w/sticker, 1½" 95.00
Kewpie, bsk, jtd hips & arms, w/sticker, 4" 465.00
Kewpie, bsk, jtd hips & arms, w/sticker, 9" 850.00
Kewpie, bsk, 1-pc body, jtd arms, w/sticker, 12".................. 1,300.00
Kewpie, bsk, 1-pc body, jtd arms, w/sticker, 4" to 5", ea 145.00
Kewpie, bsk, 1-pc body, jtd arms, w/sticker, 6" 185.00
Kewpie, bsk head, jtd limbs, chubby toddler, sgn, 10" 4,000.00
Kewpie, bsk head, jtd limbs, chubby toddler, sgn, 12" 4,500.00
Kewpie, bsk head, pnt eyes, cloth body, 12"......................... 2,200.00
Kewpie, bsk shoulder head, cloth body, sgn, 6" 600.00
Kewpie, celluloid, jtd arms, w/sticker, 12" 250.00
Kewpie, celluloid, jtd arms, w/sticker, 16" 500.00
Kewpie, celluloid, jtd arms, w/sticker, 22" 700.00
Kewpie, celluloid, jtd arms, w/sticker, 3" 60.00
Kewpie, celluloid, jtd arms, w/sticker, 5" 95.00
Kewpie, celluloid, w/sticker, 2" 40.00
Kewpie, celluloid, w/sticker, 5" 85.00
Kewpie, cloth, mask face, Kreuger, 20", M 475.00
Kewpie Bride & Groom, bsk, sgn, 4", pr 465.00
Kewpie Confederate Soldier, bsk, molded-on details, sgn, 6".......775.00
Kewpie in basket w/flowers, bsk, w/sticker, 3½" 600.00
Kewpie on stomach, bsk, w/sticker, 4" 425.00

Kewpie Soldier, bsk, w/sticker, 4½" 500.00
Kewpie w/broom, bsk, w/sticker, 4" 465.00
Kewpie w/dog Doodle, bsk, w/sticker, 3½" 1,500.00
Kewpie w/outhouse, bsk, w/sticker, 2½" 1,100.00
Kewpie w/teddy bear, bsk, w/sticker, 4" 750.00
Kewpie w/turkey, bsk, w/sticker, 2" 350.00
Pitcher, 4 Kewpies, c Rose O'Neill Wilson, Royal Rudolstadt.....180.00
Plate, action Kewpies (including Prussian Soldier), sgn 80.00
Plate, Kewpie, Being Loved, sgn O'Neill, ltd ed 30.00
Post card, Kewpies, sgn Rose O'Neill, Gibson, unused...................30.00
Santa, cb, sgn O'Neill, 1913, M 45.00
Shakers, Kewpie figural, c O'Neill, Sheffield, pr 150.00
Talcum container, Kewpie figural, tin or celluloid, 7" or 8".........195.00
Tea rest, Germany 105.00
Tea set, Kewpie eating ice cream, china, serves 4 ....25.00
Tray, 11 action Kewpies, c R O'Neill, mk Rudolstadt, 9¾" 100.00
Vase, bud; Kewpie sweeper stands beside 100.00

Onion Pattern

The familiar pattern known to collectors as Onion acquired its name through a case of mistaken identity. Designed in the early 1700s by Johann Haroldt of the Meissen factory in Germany, the pattern was a mixture from earlier Oriental designs. One of its components was a stylized peach, which was mistaken for an onion; as a result, the pattern became known by that name. Usually found in blue, an occasional piece may also be found in pink and red. The pattern is commonly associated with Meissen, but it has been reproduced by many others including Villeroy and Boch and Royal Copenhagen.

Blue Danube is a modern line of Onion-patterned dinnerware produced in Japan and distributed by Lipper International of Wallingford, Connecticut. 125 items are available in porcelain; it is sold in most large stores with china departments.

Partial dinnerware set marked with the Meissen crossed swords indication, $1,500.00. (See listings for individual prices.)

Basket, rtcl, rustic hdls form ft, oval, 10" L..........................325.00
Bowl, berry; X-swords, 5¼" 40.00
Bowl, Cauldon, 9" 48.00
Bowl, fruit; hdls, mk Meissen 125.00
Bowl, Meissen in oval, 8½" 100.00
Bowl, notched corners, X-swords, sq, 9" 275.00
Bowl, scalloped, floral finial, X-swords, 5¾x5" dia 200.00
Bowl, sq, Meissen in oval, #19, 8½", pr 200.00
Bowl, vegetable; quatrefoil rim w/rtcl corners, X-swords.............250.00
Bowl, X-swords, 4½" dia, set of 4 ....100.00
Butter chip 25.00
Cache pot, gilt borders, Meissen, 1890s, 5½"..........................225.00
Canister, Zucker, stenciled, ped base 65.00

Canister set, unmk Germany, 4-pc......................................325.00
Coffeepot, 1800s, 9½" 375.00
Compote, X-swords, 15" 425.00
Creamer, X-swords 75.00
Cruet, Meissen, 5½", pr 300.00
Cup, chocolate; Meissen in oval, set of 6 ....200.00
Dish, shell shape, Meissen, 1900, 7¾", pr 220.00
Funnel, loop hdl, unmk Germany 95.00
Ladle, wood hdl, unmk Germany 125.00
Leaf dish, hdl, Meissen, 7½" 135.00
Leaf dish, w/hdl, X-swords, 3½" 75.00
Meat tenderizer, heavy porc, wood hdl, old, unmk Germany.......142.50
Mustard pot, flower finial, X-swords, 4", +6" undertray...............120.00
Plate, Meissen, 8¼" 45.00
Plate, Villeroy & Boch, 6", set of 4 ....120.00
Plate, w/hot water warmer, dbl hdl, Meissen, 10" 165.00
Plate, X-swords, 9¾" 45.00
Platter, oval, X-swords, 19th C, 21" 435.00
Platter, oval w/tab hdls, Meissen, 20" 400.00
Platter, X-swords, 1850s, 15½", pr 475.00
Reamer, Made in Japan, 2-pc 100.00
Reamer, red, old, unmk Germany 100.00
Rolling pin, fish mark, Made in USA, 17"...............................35.00
Rolling pin, heavy porc, unmk Germany, 17" 220.00
Rolling pin, heavy porc, unmk Germany, 18" 270.00
Rolling pin, unmk Germany, 13".......................................185.00
Salt box, fish mark, Made in USA 35.00
Salt box, rnd, wood lid, hangs, Made in Japan, 7" H 95.00
Salt cellar, X-swords 75.00
Sauce boat, oval w/cup hdl ea side, X-swords 200.00
Sauce boat, w/attached undertray, X-swords, 3½x4⅞x8" 190.00
Service for 6, w/teapot & candlesticks, X-swords, 65-pc.......... 3,000.00
Spice set, fish mk, Made in USA, 8-pc 40.00
Sugar bowl, w/lid, mk Thurn, Kloesterle, Meissen-Form, 3" 100.00
Teapot, X-swords, late, 10" 325.00
Tureen, leaf finial & hdls, Meissen, w/lid, 13½" 600.00
Utensil holder, hanging, 15-slot, lg...................................150.00
Vase, ftd, X-swords, 5" 125.00

Opalescent Glass

First made in England in 1870, opalescent glass became popular in America around the turn of the century. Its name comes from the milky-white opalescent trim that defines the lines of the pattern. It was produced in table sets, novelties, toothpick holders, vases, and lamps.

Alaska, banana boat, bl 250.00
Alaska, berry set, bl, 7-pc 275.00
Alaska, bowl, bl, sq, 8"..95.00
Alaska, butter dish, bl or vaseline 260.00
Alaska, butter dish, bl w/HP floral 250.00
Alaska, celery tray, bl 155.00
Alaska, celery tray, vaseline 145.00
Alaska, creamer, bl 70.00
Alaska, creamer, vaseline 60.00
Alaska, creamer, vaseline w/HP floral 70.00
Alaska, cruet, bl, w/stopper 265.00
Alaska, cruet, vaseline 250.00
Alaska, cruet, vaseline w/HP floral 265.00
Alaska, pitcher, water; bl 325.00
Alaska, pitcher, water; bl w/HP floral 400.00
Alaska, pitcher, water; clear 225.00
Alaska, pitcher, water; vaseline......................................350.00

Alaska, sauce, bl 25.00
Alaska, sauce, gr w/HP floral 30.00
Alaska, shakers, bl or vaseline, pr................65.00
Alaska, spooner, bl..65.00
Alaska, spooner, vaseline 45.00
Alaska, sugar bowl, bl, w/lid........................150.00
Alaska, sugar bowl, vaseline, w/lid..............130.00

Alaska table set in blue, $495.00.

Alaska, tumbler, vaseline 60.00
Arabian Nights, pitcher, water; cranberry 600.00
Arabian Nights, tumbler, bl.............................60.00
Arabian Nights, tumbler, cranberry 95.00
Argonaut Shell, berry set, clear, 7-pc..........275.00
Argonaut Shell, butter dish, bl.....................275.00
Argonaut Shell, compote, jelly; vaseline........75.00
Argonaut Shell, creamer, bl............................75.00
Argonaut Shell, cruet, bl 275.00
Argonaut Shell, pitcher, water; bl................350.00
Argonaut Shell, spooner, bl..........................150.00
Argonaut Shell, sugar bowl, bl, w/lid 200.00
Argonaut Shell, tumbler, vaseline 100.00
Astro, bride's bowl, bl, ruffled, 8" 35.00
Beaded Ovals in Sand, butter dish, gr 250.00
Beaded Ovals in Sand, creamer, bl 70.00
Beatty Rib, creamer, ind; clear 20.00
Beatty Rib, sugar bowl, bl, w/lid 125.00
Beatty Rib, table set, bl, 4-pc 265.00
Beatty Rib, toothpick holder, clear 24.00
Beatty Swirl, butter dish, bl 150.00
Beatty Swirl, celery vase, bl 75.00
Beatty Swirl, pitcher, water; bl.....................130.00
Beatty Swirl, syrup, bl, rare 200.00
Beatty Swirl, tray, water; vaseline 75.00
Bubble Lattice, pitcher, water; cranberry 325.00
Bubble Lattice, sugar bowl, bl, w/lid 160.00
Buttons & Braids, pitcher, water; bl..............165.00
Buttons & Braids, pitcher, water; cranberry.....350.00
Buttons & Braids, tumbler, bl 35.00
Buttons & Braids, tumbler, cranberry.............85.00
Chrysanthemum Base Reverse Swirl, mustard, bl 135.00
Chrysanthemum Base Reverse Swirl, sugar shaker, cranberry 245.00
Chrysanthemum Base Swirl, butter dish, cranberry......300.00
Chrysanthemum Base Swirl, spooner, bl 75.00
Chrysanthemum Base Swirl, syrup, bl............175.00
Chrysanthemum Base Swirl, toothpick holder, cranberry 125.00
Chrysanthemum Base Swirl, tumbler, cranberry......85.00
Circled Scroll, butter dish, bl 295.00
Circled Scroll, compote, gr............................125.00
Circled Scroll, cruet, bl 350.00

Circled Scroll, shakers, bl, pr......................190.00
Circled Scroll, sugar bowl, bl, w/lid 225.00
Circled Scroll, tumbler, gr..............................70.00
Coin Spot, celery vase, cranberry 150.00
Coin Spot, compote, peach 35.00
Coin Spot, creamer, bl....................................50.00
Coin Spot, pitcher, water; bl, 9" 120.00
Coin Spot, pitcher, water; clear......................85.00
Coin Spot, pitcher, water; cranberry 250.00
Coin Spot, sugar shaker, bl, bulbous base......85.00
Coin Spot, sugar shaker, cranberry, ring neck 120.00
Coin Spot, tumble-up, cranberry...................250.00
Coin Spot, tumbler, cranberry 45.00
Contessa, basket, amber, 4¼x7" 100.00
Criss Cross, finger bowl, cranberry 95.00
Daisy & Fern, cruet, Netted Blossom mold, bl.....110.00
Daisy & Fern, pitcher, water; bl....................165.00
Daisy & Fern, pitcher, water; clear..................95.00
Daisy & Fern, pitcher, water; cranberry, solid hdl 225.00
Daisy & Fern, syrup, bl 120.00
Daisy & Fern, tumbler, cranberry 45.00
Daisy in Criss Cross, pitcher, water; bl.........275.00
Daisy in Criss Cross, syrup, bl......................245.00
Daisy in Criss Cross, syrup, cranberry 400.00
Diamond Spearhead, butter dish, gr..............225.00
Diamond Spearhead, butter dish, vaseline.....195.00
Diamond Spearhead, celery vase, bl..............110.00
Diamond Spearhead, compote, bl.....................95.00
Diamond Spearhead, compote, jelly; vaseline, rare 75.00
Diamond Spearhead, creamer, cobalt 125.00
Diamond Spearhead, cup, cobalt......................75.00
Diamond Spearhead, goblet, bl 125.00
Diamond Spearhead, mug, bl...........................75.00
Diamond Spearhead, pitcher, water; cobalt 450.00
Diamond Spearhead, pitcher, water; gr 325.00
Diamond Spearhead, sugar bowl, cobalt, w/lid 175.00
Diamond Spearhead, sugar bowl, gr, w/lid......150.00
Diamond Spearhead, syrup, cobalt.................450.00
Diamond Spearhead, tumbler, vaseline.............45.00
Dolly Madison, butter dish, bl......................290.00
Dolly Madison, creamer, bl..............................75.00
Dolly Madison, pitcher, water; gr 350.00
Dolly Madison, spooner, gr...............................75.00
Dolly Madison, sugar bowl, gr, w/lid..............125.00
Dolly Madison, tumbler, bl...............................75.00
Double Greek Key, butter dish, bl.................300.00
Double Greek Key, celery vase, bl 115.00
Double Greek Key, creamer, bl.........................65.00
Double Greek Key, shakers, bl, pr.................250.00
Double Greek Key, spooner, bl.........................70.00
Double Greek Key, sugar bowl, bl, w/lid 150.00
Double Greek Key, toothpick holder, bl 300.00
Double Greek Key, tumbler, bl 65.00
Drapery, pitcher, water; bl.............................165.00
Drapery, rose bowl, aqua 75.00
Drapery, rose bowl, bl......................................65.00
Drapery, water set, bl, 7-pc...........................375.00
Drapery, water set, clear, 7-pc.......................200.00
Everglades, butter dish, bl w/gold.................225.00
Everglades, butter dish, vaseline 275.00
Everglades, compote, jelly; bl w/gold 85.00
Everglades, compote, jelly; vaseline 110.00
Everglades, creamer, bl....................................80.00
Everglades, cruet, vaseline.............................350.00

Everglades, pitcher, water; bl	350.00
Everglades, pitcher, water; vaseline	325.00
Everglades, spooner, vaseline	85.00
Everglades, sugar bowl, bl w/gold	150.00
Everglades, sugar bowl, vaseline, w/lid	150.00
Everglades, tumbler, bl	65.00
Everglades, tumbler, bl w/gold	75.00
Fern, shaker, cranberry	50.00
Fern, spooner, cranberry	120.00
Flora, bowl, master berry; vaseline	75.00
Flora, butter dish, bl	245.00
Flora, butter dish, vaseline	175.00
Flora, butter dish, vaseline w/gold	210.00
Flora, celery vase, bl	110.00
Flora, compote, jelly; bl, rare	135.00
Flora, creamer, vaseline	80.00
Flora, cruet, vaseline	375.00
Flora, pitcher, water; vaseline	400.00
Flora, shakers, bl, pr	350.00
Flora, shakers, vaseline, pr	300.00
Flora, spooner, vaseline	70.00
Flora, sugar bowl, vaseline, w/lid	110.00
Flora, toothpick holder, bl	400.00
Flora, toothpick holder, vaseline	375.00
Flora, tumbler, vaseline	75.00
Fluted Scrolls, bowl, master berry; bl	65.00
Fluted Scrolls, butter dish, bl w/HP decor	215.00
Fluted Scrolls, butter dish, vaseline	165.00
Fluted Scrolls, creamer, bl	55.00
Fluted Scrolls, creamer, vaseline	60.00
Fluted Scrolls, cruet, vaseline, orig stopper	175.00
Fluted Scrolls, dresser jar, vaseline, w/lid	55.00
Fluted Scrolls, pitcher, water; bl	225.00
Fluted Scrolls, pitcher, water; vaseline	195.00
Fluted Scrolls, puff box, bl	55.00
Fluted Scrolls, puff box, vaseline	50.00
Fluted Scrolls, spooner, bl	50.00
Fluted Scrolls, sugar bowl, vaseline, w/lid	88.00
Fluted Scrolls, water set, clear, 5-pc	225.00
Frosted-Leaf & Basketweave, butter dish, bl	250.00
Frosted-Leaf & Basketweave, creamer, bl	135.00
Frosted-Leaf & Basketweave, sugar bowl, bl, w/lid	165.00
Frosted-Leaf & Basketweave, sugar bowl, vaseline, w/lid	145.00
Hobnail, bowl, bl, scalloped, 11"	95.00
Hobnail, box, vaseline, Hobnail finial, 5x5" dia	90.00
Hobnail, creamer, vaseline, bulbous, 4"	225.00
Hobnail, pitcher, bl, bl hdl, bulbous w/ruffled rim, 8x8"	250.00
Hobnail, pitcher, bl, clear threaded hdl, 5½"	75.00
Hobnail, pitcher, cranberry, sq mouth, lg	185.00
Hobnail, pitcher, rubena, clear hdl, +6 tumblers	750.00
Hobnail, pitcher, vaseline, clear reeded hdl, milk sz	115.00
Hobnail, pitcher, yel, 7"	225.00
Honeycomb & Clover, butter dish, bl	300.00
Honeycomb & Clover, pitcher, water; bl	300.00
Honeycomb & Clover, sugar bowl, bl, w/lid	200.00
Honeycomb & Clover, tumbler, bl	85.00
Horse Chestnut, bowl, vaseline, twisted stem, 4½x5½"	230.00
Idyll, butter dish, bl	325.00
Idyll, butter dish, gr	350.00
Idyll, creamer, clear	36.00
Idyll, creamer, gr	85.00
Idyll, spooner, gr, 4½x3½"	70.00
Idyll, sugar bowl, bl, w/lid	200.00
Idyll, toothpick holder, bl	230.00

Idyll, tumbler, bl	90.00
Intaglio, bowl, master berry; bl	100.00
Intaglio, butter dish, bl	350.00
Intaglio, compote, jelly; bl	30.00
Intaglio, compote, jelly; vaseline	39.00
Intaglio, creamer, bl w/HP decor	55.00
Intaglio, creamer, clear	20.00
Intaglio, creamer, vaseline	45.00
Intaglio, cruet, bl, w/bl stopper	135.00
Intaglio, pitcher, water; bl	200.00
Intaglio, sugar bowl, vaseline, w/lid	90.00
Intaglio, tumbler, bl	100.00
Inverted Fan & Feather, creamer, bl	135.00
Inverted Fan & Feather, pitcher, water; bl	495.00
Inverted Fan & Feather, sugar bowl, bl, w/lid	200.00
Inverted Fan & Feather, tumbler, bl	75.00
Iris w/Meander, berry set, vaseline, 6-pc	220.00
Iris w/Meander, bowl, bl, 8½"	85.00
Iris w/Meander, bowl, master berry; bl, 10"	90.00
Iris w/Meander, butter dish, bl	265.00
Iris w/Meander, compote, jelly; bl	45.00
Iris w/Meander, creamer, vaseline	75.00
Iris w/Meander, cruet, vaseline	350.00
Iris w/Meander, pitcher, water; bl	375.00
Iris w/Meander, pitcher, water; vaseline	300.00
Iris w/Meander, plate, bl, 7"	40.00
Iris w/Meander, shakers, bl, pr	200.00
Iris w/Meander, spooner, bl	75.00
Iris w/Meander, sugar bowl, bl, w/lid	150.00
Iris w/Meander, sugar bowl, gr, w/lid	125.00
Iris w/Meander, toothpick holder, clear	45.00
Iris w/Meander, toothpick holder, gr	55.00
Iris w/Meander, toothpick holder, vaseline	75.00
Iris w/Meander, tumbler, bl	75.00
Jackson, butter dish, bl	250.00
Jackson, butter dish, vaseline	225.00
Jackson, cruet, clear	95.00
Jackson, cruet, vaseline	165.00
Jackson, pitcher, water; vaseline	450.00
Jackson, powder box, bl	55.00
Jackson, shakers, vaseline, pr	175.00
Jackson, spooner, vaseline	60.00
Jackson, sugar bowl, bl, w/lid	110.00
Jackson, tumbler, vaseline	80.00
Jewel & Flower, butter dish, clear	95.00
Jewel & Flower, butter dish, vaseline	225.00
Jewel & Flower, creamer, vaseline	85.00
Jewel & Flower, cruet, bl	300.00
Jewel & Flower, pitcher, water; bl	450.00
Jewel & Flower, shakers, vaseline, pr	180.00
Jewel & Flower, sugar bowl, vaseline, w/lid	145.00
Jewel & Flower, tumbler, bl	80.00
Jeweled Heart, compote, bl	125.00
Jeweled Heart, cruet, bl	350.00
Jeweled Heart, nappy, clear, ruffled, 6"	22.00
Jeweled Heart, spooner, bl	110.00
Jeweled Heart, sugar bowl, bl, w/lid	175.00
Jeweled Heart, toothpick holder, bl	250.00
Jeweled Heart, water set, bl, 7-pc	625.00
Leaf Chalice, rose bowl, gr, ped ft	45.00
Leaf Chalice, sugar bowl, gr, ped ft, w/lid	55.00
Lustre Flute, butter dish, bl	280.00
Lustre Flute, creamer, bl	85.00
Lustre Flute, pitcher, water; bl	325.00

Lustre Flute, spooner, bl 85.00
Lustre Flute, sugar bowl, bl, w/lid 175.00
Lustre Flute, tumbler, bl 65.00
Palm Beach, butter dish, bl.....275.00
Palm Beach, compote, vaseline 175.00
Palm Beach, creamer & sugar bowl, bl, w/lid.....195.00
Palm Beach, pitcher, water; bl.....385.00
Palm Beach, pitcher, water; vaseline.....350.00
Palm Beach, sauce, bl 25.00
Palm Beach, spooner, bl.....85.00
Palm Beach, tumbler, bl.....85.00
Paneled Holly, berry set, bl opal, 6-pc.....350.00
Paneled Holly, butter dish, bl.....300.00
Paneled Holly, creamer, bl.....75.00
Paneled Holly, pitcher, water; bl w/gold.....500.00
Paneled Holly, sauce bowl, bl w/gold.....45.00
Paneled Holly, spooner, bl.....65.00
Paneled Holly, sugar bowl, bl, w/lid.....225.00
Paneled Holly, tumbler, bl.....75.00
Paneled Sprig, toothpick holder, clear 45.00
Poinsettia, bowl, clear, ruffled, 3-ftd.....40.00
Poinsettia, pitcher, water; bl, tankard form.....275.00
Poinsettia, sugar shaker, bl 150.00
Poinsettia, syrup, bl 300.00
Poinsettia, tumbler, bl.....50.00
Queen's Crown, creamer, yel, 5" 80.00
Regal, butter dish, clear 95.00
Regal, butter dish, gr w/gold 200.00
Regal, celery vase, bl.....125.00
Regal, cruet, bl.....400.00
Regal, pitcher, water; bl 250.00
Regal, pitcher, water; clear 95.00
Regal, spooner, gr.....55.00
Regal, sugar bowl, bl, w/lid.....145.00
Reverse Swirl, butter dish, bl opal.....125.00
Reverse Swirl, creamer, bl 125.00
Reverse Swirl, pitcher, water tankard; cranberry.....425.00
Reverse Swirl, shakers, cranberry, cylindrical, ring neck, pr 250.00
Reverse Swirl, spooner, bl.....95.00
Reverse Swirl, spooner, cranberry 110.00
Reverse Swirl, sugar bowl, bl, w/lid.....175.00
Reverse Swirl, syrup, vaseline.....135.00
Ribbed Spiral, butter dish, bl.....350.00
Ribbed Spiral, compote, bl.....47.00
Ribbed Spiral, creamer, bl 65.00
Ribbed Spiral, plate, vaseline 35.00
Ribbed Spiral, shakers, vaseline, pr.....185.00
Ribbed Spiral, sugar bowl, bl, w/lid.....225.00
Ribbed Spiral, tumbler, bl.....75.00
Scottish Moor, pitcher, water; cranberry 375.00
Scottish Moor, tumbler, cranberry 125.00
Scroll w/Acanthus, butter dish, bl.....350.00
Scroll w/Acanthus, creamer, bl 60.00
Scroll w/Acanthus, cruet, bl, w/clear stopper 190.00
Scroll w/Acanthus, cruet, vaseline.....350.00
Scroll w/Acanthus, pitcher, water; vaseline.....350.00
Scroll w/Acanthus, spooner, bl.....65.00
Scroll w/Acanthus, sugar bowl, vaseline, w/lid.....125.00
Scroll w/Acanthus, tumbler, bl.....75.00
Seaweed, cruet, bl.....245.00
Seaweed, rose bowl, vaseline, lg 95.00
Shell, butter dish, bl.....450.00
Shell, compote, bl.....110.00
Shell, cruet, bl.....425.00

Shell, pitcher, water; bl 500.00
Shell, sauce, clear, 6 for.....150.00
Shell, spooner, bl.....95.00
Shell, toothpick holder, bl.....400.00
Shell, tumbler, bl.....75.00
Spanish Lace, pitcher, water; bl 195.00
Spanish Lace, pitcher, water; clear.....95.00

Spanish Lace in cranberry, 8½" pitcher, $425.00; 4" tumbler, $75.00.

Spanish Lace, rose bowl, clear.....35.00
Spanish Lace, shakers, cranberry, pr 175.00
Spanish Lace, sugar bowl, bl, w/lid.....175.00
Spanish Lace, sugar shaker, bl.....135.00
Spanish Lace, sweetmeat, cranberry, SP rim/lid/hdl, M 375.00
Squirrel & Acorn, compote, gr.....95.00
Stippled Leaf & Basketweave, spooner, bl 75.00
Sunburst on Shield, creamer, bl 125.00
Sunburst on Shield, cruet, vaseline.....650.00
Sunburst on Shield, pitcher, water; bl.....500.00
Sunburst on Shield, spooner, vaseline.....85.00
Sunburst on Shield, sugar bowl, clear, w/lid 135.00
Sunburst on Shield, sugar bowl, vaseline, w/lid.....175.00
Sunburst on Shield, tumbler, bl.....100.00
Swag w/Brackets, berry set, gr, 7-pc 200.00
Swag w/Brackets, butter dish, gr.....135.00
Swag w/Brackets, compote, gr 30.00
Swag w/Brackets, pitcher, water; vaseline 250.00
Swag w/Brackets, sauce, vaseline.....25.00
Swag w/Brackets, shakers, bl, pr 190.00
Swag w/Brackets, spooner, gr.....45.00
Swag w/Brackets, sugar bowl, gr, w/lid 75.00
Swag w/Brackets, toothpick holder, bl 300.00
Swag w/Brackets, tumbler, bl.....60.00
Swag w/Brackets, tumbler, clear 30.00
Swag w/Brackets, water set, vaseline, 7-pc.....495.00
Swirl, hat, clear, lg 75.00
Swirl, pitcher, water; bl 125.00
Swirl, pitcher, water; clear.....60.00
Swirl, sugar shaker, cranberry 150.00
Swirl, toothpick holder, cranberry, scarce tumbler shape.....65.00
Tokyo, compote, gr.....33.00
Tokyo, creamer, bl.....65.00
Tokyo, cruet, bl, w/clear stopper 175.00
Tokyo, pitcher, water; bl, rare 300.00
Tokyo, shakers, bl, pr.....180.00
Tokyo, sugar bowl, clear, w/lid 50.00
Tokyo, water set, gr, 7-pc.....675.00
War of Roses, boat dish, vaseline, 3x7½x2½" 50.00

Water Lily & Cattails, bowl, gr, 9"...50.00
Water Lily & Cattails, bowl, master berry; clear, ruffled 35.00
Water Lily & Cattails, butter dish, bl....................................375.00
Water Lily & Cattails, creamer, bl..45.00
Water Lily & Cattails, pitcher, water; bl 395.00
Water Lily & Cattails, sugar bowl, bl, w/lid.............................175.00
Water Lily & Cattails, tumbler, bl..50.00
Wild Bouquet, berry set, clear, 6-pc.....................................145.00
Wild Bouquet, butter dish, bl...400.00
Wild Bouquet, compote, jelly; bl...125.00
Wild Bouquet, compote, jelly; clear..45.00
Wild Bouquet, cruet, bl..325.00
Wild Bouquet, cruet, clear..175.00
Wild Bouquet, pitcher, water; bl...250.00
Wild Bouquet, sugar bowl, bl, w/lid......................................200.00
Wild Bouquet, toothpick holder, bl..300.00
Wild Bouquet, tumbler, bl...100.00
Wild Bouquet, tumbler, gr..60.00
Wreath & Shell, bowl, master berry; bl....................................85.00
Wreath & Shell; butter dish, bl...225.00
Wreath & Shell, celery vase, bl...165.00
Wreath & Shell, cracker jar, bl...695.00
Wreath & Shell, creamer, bl...110.00
Wreath & Shell, creamer, vaseline 75.00
Wreath & Shell, pitcher, water; bl...350.00
Wreath & Shell, rose bowl, bl 75.00
Wreath & Shell, salt dip, bl...135.00
Wreath & Shell, sauce, vaseline..18.00
Wreath & Shell, spittoon, lady's, vaseline 90.00
Wreath & Shell, spooner, bl..75.00
Wreath & Shell, spooner, vaseline 65.00
Wreath & Shell, sugar bowl, vaseline, w/lid..............................130.00
Wreath & Shell, toothpick holder, bl......................................225.00
Wreath & Shell, toothpick holder, vaseline w/decor 250.00
Wreath & Shell, tumbler, bl..70.00

Opaline

A type of semi-opaque opal glass, opaline was made in white as well as pastel shades and was often enameled. It is similar in appearance to English bristol glass, though its enamel or gilt decorative devices tend to exhibit a French influence.

Bottle, scent; bl, gold & wht allover decor, 5" 65.00
Bottle, scent; pk, gold filigree scrolls, 2¾x1½" 110.00
Box, bl w/gold prunus, not hinged, 1½x1½" 50.00

Cameo portraits on blue with gold trim; Powder jar, 4", $135.00; Cologne, 8", $175.00.

Ring tree, gold & wht decor on bl, 2½" 48.00
Vase, pk, exotic bird among flowers, mk, 1880s, 10½" 225.00
Vase, pk w/floral, elongated U-form in SP base w/flower mt........150.00

Optical Items

Collectors of Americana are beginning to appreciate the charm of antique optical items, and those involved in the related trade find them particularly fascinating. Anyone, however, can appreciate the evolution of technology apparent when viewing a collection of old eye wear and at the same time admire the primitive ingenuity involved in its construction.

Binoculars, military, mts on tripod, 26x29", +metal case 365.00
Magnifier, brass mt, mahog hdl, 1850s, 5", in case 275.00
Microscope, Aronsberg...Manchester, brass, +dvtl mahog case ...315.00
Microscope, brass, free standing, 1900, 5", EX 75.00
Microscope, Spencer, 3 lens w/adjustable mechanism, VG..........100.00
Opera glasses, Gualdoni of Paris, MOP, leather case 60.00
Opera glasses, LeMaire Paris, MOP & brass, 1890s 85.00
Opera glasses, Theodore B Starr, MOP, NY, EX in case.................75.00
Opera glasses, 14k gold, rnd retractable lens, 4¼" 395.00
Spectacles, granny style, 12k gold filled, octagonal 5.00
Spectacles, handmade, iron frames, rnd lenses, 1700s, EX 32.50
Spectacles, silver wire, J Owen, Phila, 1820s, EX 225.00
Spectacles, wire rims, Franklin style, ca 1850s, EX 25.00

Orientalia

The art of the Orient is an area of collecting currently enjoying strong collector interest, not only in those examples that are truly 'antique' but in the 20th-century items as well. Because of the many aspects involved in a study of Orientalia, we can only try through brief comments to acquaint the reader with some of the more readily-available examples. We suggest specialized reference sources for detailed information.

Our advisor for this category is Clarence Bodine; he is listed in the Directory under Pennsylvania.

Blanc de Chine

Figurine, Amida Buddha, 1800s, 13½".....................................675.00
Figurine, Guanyin on throne, Dehua, 1800s, 10" 950.00
Jar, prunus relief, mask hdls, spherical, 5" dia, pr.........................250.00

Blue and White Porcelain

Lotus dish, medallion with Buddhist characters, Wanli mark and period, hairline, 8", $3,500.00.

Bowl, deer in landscape reserve, low, 1850s, 15" 1,100.00
Bowl, lotus blooms, circle enclosing a bee, 14" 350.00
Plate, figures in garden, butterfly rim, 6-sided, 1850s, 7" 175.00
Plate, flower basket, rtcl butterfly border, 1700s, 9" 400.00
Plate, Nanking, Oriental scene, 9½", EX 175.00
Platter, coastal village, lattice border, 1800s, 20" 850.00
Platter, village scene, Nanking, 1820s, 16" 450.00
Platter, village scene, Nanking, 1820s, 18½" 850.00
Punch bowl, scenic, lattice/spearhead border, Nanking, 11" ... 1,100.00
Salt cellar, E, crane/garden, floral/butterfly base, 1800 .... 200.00
Salt cellar, scene, diaper border, ftd oval bowl, 3½" L 90.00
Tureen, lake scene, boar's head hdls, fruit finial, 13" 750.00
Urn, Ko, foo dragon pursuing flaming pearl, 14" 325.00
Vase, floral & lappet bands, shouldered, Ming, 1600s, 18" 2,000.00

Bronze

Asian elephant, Jp, ivory tusks, mk, 1880s, 4½x8" 350.00
Bowl, lattice/leaf motif, Warring States period, ftd, 7½" 800.00
Bowl, stylized dragon band, 3 shaped legs, hdls, 12" 300.00
Buddha, Thai, stepped throne, gilt patina, 15" 275.00
Buddha Amitayus, Nepalese, on lotus throne, gilt patina, 13" 350.00
Candlestick, Jp, globular ends, gr-brn patina, 14", pr 275.00
Charger, flowers on cerulean, scalloped, 1880s, 14" 175.00
Hand of Buddha, Thai, gilt traces, 1700s, 12" 300.00
Hoti, seated, lacquered, gilt, 1850s, hardwood stand, 8" 325.00
Incense burner, archaic style, rtcl lid w/foo dog, 16" 200.00
Lantern, Jp, pagoda top, rtcl body, animals in relief, 18" 200.00
Planter, cut-out coins around rim, cut-out hdls, 1880s, 8" 475.00
Scholar, seated, gilt patina, 1800s, cvd hardwood stand, 9½" 850.00
Sitatara, Nepalese, lotus throne, 10" 175.00
Siva, Thai, 10-armed, holding attributes, on bull, 17" 425.00
Vajrapani on lotus throne, Qianlong mk, gilt, 1700s, 6½" 950.00
Vase, Jp, appl leaves/vines/tendrils, curved gourd form, 8" 250.00
Vase, Jp, birds & florals in relief, ca 1920, 12" 595.00

Celadon

    Celadon, introduced during the Ching Dynasty, is a green-glazed ware developed in an attempt to imitate the color of jade. Designs are often incised or painted on over the glaze in heavy enamel applications. Chinese export ware was designed to appeal to Western tastes and was often made to order. During the 18th century, vast amounts were shipped to Europe and on westward. Many of these lines of dinnerware were given specific pattern names — Rose Mandarin, Fitzhugh, Armorial, Rose Medallion, and Canton are but a few of the more familiar. See also Canton; Champleve; Cloisonne; Coralene, Oriental; Dragon Ware; Geisha Girl; Imari; Ivory; Kutani; Moriage; Nippon; Noritake; Peking Glass; Rose Medallion; Satsuma; Soapstone.

Key:
Ch — Chinese	FV — Famille Verte
ctp — contemporary	E — export
cvg — carving	hdwd — hardwood
do — door	Jp — Japan
drw — drawer	Ko — Korean
Dy — Dynasty	lcq — lacquer
FJ — Famille Juane	rswd — rosewood
FN — Famille Noire	tkwd — teakwood
FR — Famille Rose	

Bowl, cvd long-life character, rim w/waves, red ft, 10" 600.00
Censer, rnd w/3 legs, Lonquan, wood cover, 1600s, 5¾", EX 200.00
Jar, burnt red mouth/ft rim, flat lid w/cvd medallion, 2½" 260.00

Rock crystal carvings: Guanyin holding child, 19th century, 9", $1,900.00; Tiger, reticulated tail curled to side, 19th century, 9½" long, $4,750.00.

Plate, cvd long-life medallion, heavy rim, Ming, 10" 600.00
Vase, mc florals, cylinder neck, now lamp, 13", pr 1,250.00
Vase, 8 trigrams in low relief, cong form, 1800s, 13" 400.00

Furniture

Armchair, Ch, ebonized, rtcl/cvd dragons, cabriole legs 350.00
Armchair, Ch, hdwd, marble seat/medallion in bk, MOP inlay .. 450.00
Cabinet, Ch, red lacquer, palace/garden scenes w/in, 62x35" 475.00
Cabinet, Jp, 4 cloisonne doors w/birds & wisteria, 48x25" 1,400.00
Stand, Ch, hdwd, rtcl/cvd, claw/ball ft, marble top, 32x16" 175.00
Table, Ch, hdwd/marble, cvd dragon ped, claw ft, 32" dia 850.00
Table, Ch, 15" inset marble top, cvd florals, ball/claw ft 150.00
Wedding bed, Ch, canopy, mirror-door cabinet, on cvd legs 650.00

Hardstones

Agate, owl, inset glass eyes, attached metal ft, 2⅛" 150.00
Agate, owl, inset glass eyes, metal ft & branch, 3" 300.00
Amethyst, crow & foliage, 1⅞" 200.00
Amethyst, vase, floral cvg, peony lid, 11x9" 450.00
Carnelian, rabbits, graduated set of 4, largest: 3¾" 300.00
Coral, red; girl in fancy kimono, hand to ear, 2½" 175.00
Coral, red; laughing Buddha, standing, flowers in hand, 2" 150.00
Jade, burmese; Kwan Yin w/bottle, w/red skin, 9" 325.00
Jade, gr w/wht; vase, floral panels, loose ring hdls, 6" 250.00
Jade, med gr w/gray; magpie on limb, beak open, 4½x3½" 250.00
Jade, nephrite; archer's ring, wht w/honey yel skin, 1½" 120.00
Jade, nephrite; immortal & phoenix, 1700s, 5" 1,100.00
Jade, nephrite; mtn, relief cvd w/sage & attendant, 5x3" 2,700.00
Jade, spinach; incense burner, Tao-Tieh maks, 3 ft, 7x5" 295.00
Lapis lazuli, owl, pnt details, 2⅜" 125.00
Quartz, smoky; owl, inset glass eyes, 2⅛" 200.00
Rock crystal, owl, inset glass eyes, 2¼" 100.00
Tigereye, duck (box), standing, cvd base, 5½" L, pr 650.00
Tigereye, Tang Horse, front ft raised, 5" L 150.00

Lacquer

    Lacquerware is found in several colors, but the one most likely to be encountered is cinnabar. It is often intricately carved, sometimes involving hundreds of layers built one at a time on a metal or wooden base. Later pieces remain red, while older examples tend to darken.

Box, cinnabar, swastikas/peonies, dragon on lid, 13" L 500.00
Box, Jp, iris, gold/bronze on keiran-nuri ground, 1800s, 3½" 175.00
Mask, Jp, lion head w/articulated jaw & ears, red/blk, 8" 250.00
Sewing box, gilt on blk, paw ft, fitted int, w/ivory tools 1,575.00
Tea caddy, battle scenes in gold on blk, 4x9x6", EX 275.00
Tray, cinnabar, pagoda/house/bridge/people, 12x14" 90.00
Vase, dragon/clouds on blk, 1880s, 10", pr 1,300.00

Vase, allover scenery and flowers, on teakwood stand, 10", $155.00.

Mud Figures

Elder holding bundle, 3½" 25.00
Elder seated w/pnt brush in hand, brn robe, 5" 50.00
Elder w/blk beard, gr & bl robe, bl hat, mk China, 9¾" 175.00
Elder w/fish, cobalt, 6" 65.00
Lady seated, holds flower, wht robe, 4" 60.00

Netsukes

A netsuke is a miniature Japanese carving made with a hole called a Himitoshi, either channeled or within the carved design, that allows it to be threaded onto a waist cord and worn with the kimono. Because the kimono had no pockets, the Japanese man hung his tools, pipe, tobacco pouch, and other daily necessities from his sash. The netsuke was the toggle that secured them all. Although most are of ivory, others were made of bone, wood, metal, porcelain, or semi-precious stones. Some were inlaid or lacquered. They are found in many forms, but figurals are the most common and desirable. They range in size from 1" up to 3", which was the maxium size allowed by law. Most netsukes represented the religion, mythology, and the habits of the average person. There was no written word, hence carvers depicted the daily life of their people.

Careful study is required to recognize the quality of the netsuke. Many have been made in Hong Kong in recent years; and even though some are very well carved, these are considered copies and avoided by the serious collector. There are many books that will help you learn to recognize quality netsukes, and most reputable dealers are glad to assist you. Use your magnifying glass to check for repairs. In the listings that follow, netsukes are ivory unless noted otherwise; 'stained' indicates a color wash.

Boy w/monkey, horn inlay, 19th C, 1½" 550.00
Chokaro's mule emerges from gourd, wood, Sosai, 19th C, 1½" ..500.00

Figure Fukurokuju, wood, sgn, 19th C, 2" 500.00
Group Noh masks, stained details, Togyokusai, 19th C, 1⅜" 715.00
Ryusa Manju, walrus ivory, 19th C, 1½" 385.00
2 Manzai dancers, stained details, sgn Ryoji, 19th C, 1½" 990.00
2 Shishi, sgn Masatomo, 19th C, 1⅞" 400.00

Porcelain

Basin, E, figures/scenic reserves on red, 1800s, rstr, 14"...............400.00
Bowl, bamboo sprays, gr on yel, lotus form, Tongzhi, 6" 160.00
Bowl, dragons/flaming pearl, iron red, 1880s, 11" 200.00
Bowl, E, armorials/florals, lobed rim, 1850s, 9" 2,600.00
Bowl, E, eagle in mc/gold, geometric bands, w/lid, 2x3" dia........950.00
Bowl, E, FR, florals, 1825, 7½", pr 1,500.00
Bowl, FN, florals/butterfly, mk China, ca 1900, 6½x8½ " 80.00
Bowl, FR, rockwork/mums/pedestal, 6½" 100.00
Bowl, FV, bird/floral reserve on floral ground, 1915, 7½" 500.00
Bowl, FV, continuous frieze of phoenix birds & dragons, 6" 165.00
Bowl, Imperial yel, Kangxi mk, hairline, 4¾" 320.00
Box, brush; Bl Fitzhugh, butterflies/etc, 1820s, 7" L 750.00
Charger, E/FR, floral, gold/gr floral bands on rim, 15", EX..........750.00
Charger, FR, peonies, scalloped rim, 15" 100.00
Charger, FR & yel, mandarin & attendants, 1880s, 16"................250.00
Charger, long-life characters, bl on yel, Tongzhi, 11" 525.00
Cream jug, E, mandarin in courtyard, w/lid, 1780s, 5½", EX 275.00
Cup & saucer, E, Am eagle, scalloped bl border w/stars, NM 750.00
Cup & saucer, E, State Arms of NY, mc/gold, NM 750.00
Dish, peachbloom, ogee sides, Kangxi, Ming Xuande mk, 6¾"....500.00
Figurine, court lady, bl kimono/red floral coat, w/goat, 16"..........350.00
Figurine, dragon, gr w/red nose, head, & spine, 18" L 250.00
Figurine, FR, Guanyin on lotus pad above waves, 10"..................325.00
Figurine, multi-arm goddess on pk & gr throne, 16" 350.00
Figurine, Siamese god, seated, w/bl vase & jacket, 10x7"............125.00
Ginger jar, children, teak cover, Kangxi, 7⅜" 325.00
Jardiniere, FV, floral disks, gilt-metal leaf-cvd base, 13" 1,700.00
Jostick, elephant, birds/floral trappings, 1830, 5¾", pr.............. 4,250.00
Mug, E, Imari pattern, 1775, 6½ " 950.00
Mug, floral sprays, orange/gilt diaper border, twist hdl 400.00
Pitcher, E, Bl Fitzhugh, sheep w/banner, ovoid, 7" 1,500.00
Plate, E, armorials/florals, shaped rim, 1850s, 9", pr.................. 4,500.00
Plate, E, Chief of Seattle, gilt & bl blorders, 1800, 6"............... 1,300.00
Plate, E, floral in puce, bl scene, shaped rim, 1850, 9" 110.00
Plate, E, man in temple, scroll/floral border, 8-sided, 9".............250.00
Plate, Fitzhugh, red-orange, eagle/banner w/'BLP,' 16" 850.00
Plate, FR, armorials/lion & bear, scalloped, 9", set of 3 ....350.00
Plate, marriage; E, armorials, spearhead/gilt border, 9".................700.00
Platter, E, Bl Fitzhugh, 4 floral panels, lattice border, 16" 750.00
Platter, E, Bl Fitzhugh border, river scene, 1850s, 12" 400.00
Platter, E, florals in mc, octagonal, 11" & smaller, pr...................200.00
Platter, E, Gr Fitzhugh, spread eagle in brn, 10½" 4,000.00
Platter, E, Sepia Fitzhugh, insect/trellis rim, 1810, 13" 1,500.00
Punch bowl, E, Masonic, star border, armorials, rstr, 13" 1,900.00
Punch bowl, E/FR, fruit/flower/gilt band, 1780s, 10¾".............800.00
Sauce boat, E, FR floral garland, armorial, leaf form, 8" 250.00
Teapot, E, diaper border, gilt sprays, dome lid, 1825, 5" 200.00
Teapot, E, floral sprays, puce scaled/gilt border, 1850, 6" 600.00
Teapot, mandarin figural, gr/orange, 1874, 7x5" 175.00
Umbrella stand, FV, florals/2 bird & tree panels, 18" 140.00
Vase, butterfly motif & shape, 8x9", pr 50.00
Vase, E, florals, underglaze bl/gilt/mc, 1700s, 12", pr 1,700.00
Vase, FR, butterflies/florals on 4 bands & at neck, 18" 800.00
Vase, FR, 2 figural panels on gilt, foo dog finial, 15"............... 1,320.00
Vase, God of Longevity/Kwan Yin, calligraphy, ca 1861, 23" 450.00
Vase, mirror blk w/gilt birds, Kangxi mk, 17" 2,500.00

Pottery

Amphora vase, wht-glazed stoneware, Tang style, 1600s, 13" **700.00**
Bowl, gr crackle w/bl cast, cvd flower, Qingbai/Song Dy, 7" **800.00**
Bowl, Jp, lt bl/maroon/blk/wht mottle, 8-sided, 1700s, 9" **250.00**
Bowl, lt gr crackle, lotus form, fish reserve, Song Dy, 7" **450.00**
Bowl, Yingqin, cvd floral on gr-bl, Song Dy, 8", NM **150.00**
Figurine, camel w/grotesque mask saddlebags, Tang style, 9" **275.00**
Figurine, caparisoned horse, N Wei style, pnt, 9", EX **200.00**
Figurine, chicken, gray w/wht slip & red pnt, Han Dy, 5½"........**325.00**
Figurine, equestrienne, red w/wht slip, Tang style, 11" **275.00**
Figurine, falconer, gray, wht slip/pnt, Tang Dy, rprs, 12" **1,700.00**
Figurine, lady, Sancia glaze, rpt face, 10" **650.00**
Figurine, lady w/lotus handwarmer, red clay, Tang Dy, 9" **8,500.00**
Figurine, man w/bird, red w/wht slip, Tang Dy, 5" **250.00**
Figurine, Money Boy, yoke on shoulders, holds money pc, 8x8"...**40.00**
Figurine, official in long-sleeve robe, Tang Dy, rstr, 18" **1,200.00**
Head of a lady, bound coiffure, blk w/some pnt, 200 BC, 11" **260.00**
Horse head, red/wht pnt on gray, Han, 200 BC, 6" **2,500.00**
Jar, E, genre reserves w/scholars, figured ground, 1900, 7"...........**700.00**
Jar, emb animals/geometrics, mtns on lid, Han style, 9" **1,500.00**
Jar, geometric/shell bands, Neolithic, Banshan phase, 5"............**300.00**
Jar, gr mottle w/blk streaks, 8-lobe body, Tang Dy, 6" dia...........**850.00**
Jar, Ko, stoneware, rnd on rnd openwork ft, ash glaze **300.00**
Pillow, recumbent lion form, cvd florals, rstr, 12" L **200.00**
Roof tile, mtd rider, robe over armor, 3-color glaze, 14" **950.00**
Saucer, yel-bl w/dk streaks, copper rim, Jun, Song Dy, 3¾" **200.00**
Tea bowl, hare's fur glaze, copper rim, Song Dy, rpr, 4" **400.00**
Vase, dk brn, conical w/narrow mouth, 4 hdls, stoneware, 9" **300.00**
Vase, flambe, strawberry w/bl streaks, 1800s, 7", pr **250.00**
Vase, gr irid w/horizontal bands, Hu shape, Han, 5¾" **750.00**
Vase, Jp, HP flowers on lattice, rnd-top cylinder, 20" **300.00**
Vase, sang-de-boeuf, crackled, bl edges, ovoid, 12½" **200.00**
Vase, sang-de-boeuf, cream rim, bottle form, 1800s, 5"................**100.00**
Vase, splash-glazed strawberry & olive, 1800s, 13" **500.00**
Vase, streaky copper red, high shouldered ovoid, 1990, 15".........**260.00**

Snuff Bottles

The Chinese were introduced to snuff in the 17th century, and their carved and painted snuff bottles typify their exquisite taste and workmanship. These small bottles, seldom measuring over 2½", were made of amber, jade, ivory, and cinnabar; tiny spoons were often attached to their stoppers. By the 18th century, some were being made of porcelain, others were of glass with delicate designs tediously reverse painted with minuscule brushes sometimes containing a single hair. Copper and brass were used but to no great extent.

Cloisonne, peacock & flowers on bl, fine brass wires, 3" **150.00**
Crackliture, molded mask & rings, quartz stopper, 2⅝" **1,850.00**
Glass, bl, prunus blossom form, 1800s, 2½", EX **600.00**
Glass, children, red enamel on camphor, 2¼" **400.00**
Glass, red, geometric relief, greenstone top, 1900s, 3" **200.00**
Glass, red overlay ft on vaseline, carnelian/jade stopper, 3" **525.00**
Glass, rvpt birds/branches, quartz stopper, 2¾"........................**125.00**
Glass, rvpt mtn scene/poem, greenstone stopper, 2⅛"................**150.00**
Glass, yel, 8-rib, coral/greenstone stopper, 1900s, 3" **250.00**
Graystone, pebble form, metal stopper, 1900s, 2¼".....................**120.00**
Ivory, man figural, mc pnt, head stopper, drilled, 2¼" **100.00**
Ivory, pirate & ship cvgs, sgn, 1900s, 2¼" **100.00**
Jade, cvd leaves on oval form, gr frog stopper, 2⅜".....................**450.00**
Jade, cvd prunus blossom, wht, lav quartz stopper, 2⅜" **1,150.00**
Jade, nephrite; cvd dragon on shoulder, gray-wht, 3" **140.00**
Jade, nephrite; God of Longevity & crane, lt gr, 3½" **120.00**

Jade, nephrite; tiger & bat cvg, gray-gr w/brn, 3"..........................**80.00**
Milk glass, appl florals, red plastic stopper, 1900s, 2" **100.00**
Milk glass, red foliage overlay, w/stopper, 1900s, 2½" **1,350.00**
Overlay glass, florals, 5-color, greenstone stopper, 3⅝".............**1,200.00**
Peking glass, animals & plants, wht on red, 1800s, 2½" **550.00**
Peking glass, emb florals, red w/greenstone stopper, 2⅜"............**850.00**
Peking glass, fruit & animals, bl on wht, 2⅜", EX **275.00**
Peking glass, gardener & foliage, brn on bl, 1800s, 2¾"..............**750.00**
Peking glass, pagoda & foliage, yel on amber, 2½".....................**650.00**
Porc, ear of corn w/praying mantis on leaf form, 3⅝"................**125.00**
Porc, pnt scholar & pupil, cylindrical, graystone stopper, 3" **100.00**
Porc, repousse fruit & vines, 1800s, 3⅛"..................................**900.00**
Rvpt, blk/wht bird on rock, bk: mtns, amethyst cap, 3¾" **280.00**
Rvpt, bugs/rocks/fish, gr glass stopper, sgn Leyuan, 2¾" **400.00**
Rvpt, houses/trees, cvd faces ea side, 2¼" **120.00**
Rvpt, 3 men at table, bk: lady/boat, sgn Ye Zhongsan, 3" **225.00**
Silver, rtcl, inset stones, screw top, Mongolia, 2¾" **200.00**
Tigereye, fantail fish/foo lion cvg ea side, 3"............................**120.00**
Wood, pnt Tibetan characters & florals, 3" **200.00**

Sumida

Brush pot, Poo Ware, appl monkeys, sgn, 4" **89.00**
Brush pot, 2 appl monkeys, seal signature, 4" **130.00**
Figurine, monk gathers celadon robe about him, 5" **335.00**
Mug, boy after nest of eggs, imp mks, 4⅝x3⅛".............................**88.00**
Teapot, lady/flowers, Art Deco shape **265.00**
Vase, lg floral branch, bl/wht leaves on red texture, 18" **265.00**
Water pot, Gama Sennin seated on toad, 6¾" L **275.00**

Bowl, two characters climbing on side, hut within, 7" diameter, $350.00.

Textiles

Kimono, blk silk w/family crest, 1940s, EX **90.00**
Obi, narrow, bl stripe w/red & wht embr **25.00**
Obi, wide, orange & cream **35.00**
Robe, dragon w/flaming pearl embr on bl silk, ca 1880, 53" **1,760.00**
Robe, embr/woven silk gauze, 1800s, long style...........................**300.00**
Robe, silk gauze brocade, mc dragons & clouds, 1800s.................**325.00**
Vest, purple padded silk w/yel ribbon borders, 1800s, 28" **880.00**
Wall hanging, embr silk, blk birds/plum trees, 60x34" **200.00**
Wall hanging, embr silk, cranes/pines, mc on blk, 76x55"...........**325.00**

Woodblock Prints, Japanese

Actor Asao Sojuro in Character, Shunei, 1800s, chuban **950.00**
Actor Ichikawa Yaozo, Toyokuni, 1800s, oban......................**4,400.00**
Actor Iwai Hanshiro in Character, Toyokuni, ca 1800, oban **500.00**
Actor Segawa Kikunojo, Sunsho, hosoban.............................**1,650.00**

Beauty Holding Samurai Fan, Shinsui, 20th C, dai-oban **2,640.00**
Beauties...Famous Places Edo, Kuniyoshi, 1850s, triptych **15,400.00**
Boys Fishing & Playing at the Seashore, Kuniyasu, 1820, oban...**275.00**
Courtesan Parading on New Year, Utamaro, oban **3,080.00**
Evening Shower at Tadasu Embankment, Hiroshige, oban yoko-e.**550.00**
Genji Entertained by Beauty, Shigenaga, 1740s, yoko-e **2,400.00**
Ishibe, from Gojusantsugi Meisho Zue, Hiroshige, 1855, oban **550.00**
Little Temple Gate, Yoshida, oban tate-e, 15x10" **300.00**
Memorial Portrait of Hiroshige, Kunisada, 1850s, oban **880.00**
Minamoto Yorimitsu (portrait), Kuniyoshi, 13½x9", EX **450.00**
Moon at Magome, Kawase Hasui, 1930, oban **700.00**
Motomachi Detour, Totsuka, Hiroshige, 1840s, oban **2,420.00**
Yodo River in Moonlight, Hokusai, 1820s, oban **6,600.00**

Miscellaneous

Bonsai tree, wood w/coral blossoms, in gr jade planter, 11" **475.00**
Brazier, Ch, brass, sq w/ftd cylinder support, 1800s, 25" **800.00**
Screen, coramandel, 4-panel, cvd birds/palace, 1900s, 72x64" **400.00**
Tsuba, Jp, copper, sleeping Hotei/butterflies, 2¾" dia **500.00**
Tsuba, Jp, iron, bearded hiker watched by oni on tree, 2¾" **400.00**
Tsuba, Jp, iron, cvd sukashi lily, openwork, 2¾" dia **250.00**
Tsuba, Jp, iron, dragon cavorts among waves, 3" dia....................**475.00**
Tsuba, Jp, iron, samurai motif, lobed, 2⅞" dia **400.00**
Watercolor on silk, wht parrot/insect, 33x15" **225.00**

Orrefors

Orrefors Glassworks was founded in 1742 in the Swedish province of Smaaland. Utilizing the expertise of designers such as Simon Gate, Edward Hald, Vicke Lindstrand, and Edwin Ohrstrom, it produced art glass of the highest quality. Various techniques were used in achieving the decoration; some were wheel engraved, others were blown through a unique process that formed controlled bubbles or air pockets resulting in unusual patterns and shapes.

Our advisor for this category is Abby Malowanczyk; she is listed in the Directory under Texas.

Ash tray, etched/frosted nude, 6-sided, sgn Palmqvist, 7½" **150.00**
Candle holder, Eden, #8700, pr...**48.00**
Cordial set, etched/floral, 8" decanter w/nude, 12 wines..............**500.00**
Decanter, nude picks flowers, Landberg/#2475-1-LB-3, 10" **500.00**
Goblet, etched spurs, sgn Palmqvist #3397, 8" **275.00**
Goblet, etched/frosted spurs, Sven Palmqvist, #3396, 8" **475.00**
Ice bucket, dk sapphire, pulled/appl hdl openings, 8x9½"...........**120.00**

Ariel glass vase, amorphic figures, thick walls, signed E. Ohrstrom, 1938, 9", $6,500.00.

Vase, Ariel, bubble leaves, bl on lime cased, Alberius, 7½".........**700.00**

Vase, Ariel, Profiles, 4 abstract faces, I Lundin, '79, 7" **2,500.00**
Vase, Ariel, red bands alternate w/bubbles, sgn Edvin, 6"...........**800.00**
Vase, Ariel, red int decor, E Ohrstrom, M 92F, bulbous, 4".........**700.00**
Vase, Ariel, wht/clear int lines, shouldered, sgn Edvin, 6"............**650.00**
Vase, bl/clear fishnet, bl neck, Sven Palmqvist Kraka **750.00**
Vase, etched dancers, flared, Palmqvist #2941, '44, 10½x5" **500.00**
Vase, Graal, fish/seaweed, E Hald, Nr 160, spherical, 6".............**600.00**
Vase, mc threads & int bubbles, Lundin, Expo 2Y22, 4½" **500.00**
Vase, nude, arms lifted, etched, Lindstrand, 1935, 14" **1,400.00**
Vase, Selena smoke, sgn P Palmqvist, #3090-5, 7" **85.00**
Vase, Shark Killer, Lindstrand/#1753B8EL, 14x9" **11,000.00**
Vase, St Francis/flying birds etching, Lindstrand, 8" **200.00**
Vase, 2 deep oval t'prints, teardrop shape, DU #3322, 11" **150.00**
Vase, 4-layered, heavy, sgn/#H-Z-48, 5½" **175.00**

Ott and Brewer

The partnership of Ott and Brewer began in 1865 in Trenton, New Jersey. By 1876 they were making decorated graniteware, parian, and 'ivory porcelain' — similar to Irish belleek though not as fine and of different composition. In 1883, however, experiments toward that end had reached a successful conclusion, and a true belleek body was introduced. It came to be regarded as the finest china ever produced by an American firm. The ware was decorated by various means — hand painting, transfer printing, gilding, and lustre glazing. The company closed in 1893, one of many that failed during that depression. In the listings below, the ware is belleek unless noted otherwise.

Our advisor for this category is Mary Frank Gaston; she is listed in the Directory under Texas.

Basket, floral, appl blossoms on cactus hdl, 7½x9" **1,000.00**
Bowl, dessert; bl int, shell ft, rare, 2x4".....................................**195.00**
Bowl, gold florals & leaves, scalloped, 2 mks, 2x4¾" **440.00**
Chocolate pot, floral, bl on wht, ca 1866 mk **185.00**
Creamer, gold florals, branch hdl, 4" **200.00**
Cup & saucer, cream & gold, ca 1865-79 ....**250.00**
Cup & saucer, gold-paste florals, 2½", 5½" dia **220.00**
Ewer, gold stylized leaves, cactus hdl, 8½"................................ **1,000.00**
Ewer, gold-paste florals, curved body, 5¼" **550.00**
Pitcher, gold thistles, emb body w/much gold, 8" **715.00**
Plate, pk lustre w/gold rim, 6¾" **110.00**
Ram's horn, pk lustre w/gold at rim, 5½" W **2,200.00**
Salt cellar, mc leaves & cattails, 3-ftd, ind **140.00**
Shell dish, purple lustre int, ftd, 2½x5¼" **220.00**
Shoe, appl bow, sponged gold, 7½" **660.00**
Sugar bowl, Tridacna, gold-paste florals, unmk, 4" **275.00**
Teapot, florals, bark at top, branch hdl, 8½" **725.00**
Teapot, Tridacna w/gold florals, unmk, 4½" **495.00**
Tray, gold paste orchid, sq, ruffled rim, 8¼" **395.00**
Tray, wild duck scene, scalloped, ftd, 8" sq **770.00**
Vase, floral, gold paste on matt, short ped, 6½"..........................**550.00**
Vase, floral w/gold-paste leaves on matt, bulbous, 10" **770.00**
Vase, leaves & butterfly, gold paste on matt, hdls, 5½"................**550.00**

Overbeck

The Overbeck Studio was established in 1911 in Cambridge City, Indiana, by four Overbeck sisters. It survived until the last sister died in 1955. Early wares were often decorated with carved designs of stylized animals, birds, or florals with the designs colored to contrast with the background. Others had tooled designs filled in with various colors for a mosaic effect. After 1937, Mary Frances, the last remaining sister, favored handmade figurines with somewhat bizarre features in fanciful combinations of color. Overbeck ware is signed 'OBK.' Large vases from 8" to 12" usually command prices from $1,000 to $3,000 on today's market.

Figurine, gentleman in hat, w/cane, imp mk, 5", NM 155.00
Figurine, girl in pk bonnet, w/lg duck, grassy mound, 4" 375.00
Figurine, turtle, mc, 1½x2½" 350.00

Model of a blue jay, 7" long, $425.00.

Vase, circular motifs cvd in panels, bl/gr, sgn EF, rpr, 6" 800.00
Vase, dk mauve, 3 vertical emb Oriental style bands, 4x5" 475.00
Vase, girls/cats/spirals, ochre on lt bl, sgn, OBKEF, 11x8"....... 1,700.00
Vase, stylized sea horses/flora, yel texture w/gr, rstr, 7" 465.00
Vase, stylized wht deer on turq, 6" 1,500.00

Overshot

Overshot glass is characterized by the beaded or craggy appearance of its surface. Earlier ware was irregularly textured, while 20th-century examples tend to be more uniform.

Biscuit jar, appl gr threading 135.00
Bowl, lime gr, wafer base, oval, 3½x10½" 145.00
Bowl, rubena, clear ruffle, brass ft, 6¾x8¾" 95.00

Pitcher, light blue with red-amber handle, 7", $100.00.

Pitcher, cranberry, clear ft & hdl, bulbous, 9¼x5¼" 240.00
Pitcher, cranberry, emb swirls, clear reeded hdl, 9x5½" 225.00
Pitcher, cranberry, quatrefoil top, clear reeded hdl, 9½" 250.00
Pitcher, tankard; cranberry, clear hdl, metal top, 9" 175.00
Shade, sapphire bl to clear, 5¼x7⅞" 125.00
Vase, pk w/opal, fluted body, clear gauffered rim, 8" 100.00

Owens Pottery

J.B. Owens founded his company in Zanesville, Ohio, in 1891, and until 1907, when the company decided to exert most of its energies in the area of tile production, made several quality lines of art pottery. His first line, Utopian, was a standard brown ware with underglaze slip decoration of nature studies, animals, and portraits. A similar line, Lotus, utilized lighter background colors. Henri Deux, introduced in 1900, featured incised Art Nouveau forms inlaid with color. (Be aware that the Brush McCoy Pottery acquired many of Owens' molds and reproduced a line similar to Henri Deux, which they called Navarre.) Other important lines were Opalesce, Rustic, Feroza, Cyrano, and Mission, examples of which are rare today.

The factory burned in 1928, and the company closed shortly thereafter. Values vary according to the quality of the artwork and subject matter. Examples signed by the artist bring higher prices than those that are not signed.

Aborigine, pitcher, Indian motif, red/beige/blk, 7½"....................150.00
Aqua Verde, vase, pine cones/needles emb, bulbous, 6½" 150.00
Cyrano, vase, brn & bl, bulbous, long neck, unmk, 8¼" 250.00
Feroza, bowl base, metallic w/pk & gr, hdls, 3½x10" 75.00
Henri Deux, vase, lady's profile, grn w/gold, hdls, 7x9"...............295.00
Lotus, jardiniere, butterflies at rim, 11" dia.................................425.00
Lotus, vase, thistles on bl shaded to cream, #1257, 12" 350.00
Matt Gr, loving cup, tree stump w/lizard, #234, 5" 200.00
Matt Gr, mug, orange tree emb, no mk, 4½" 35.00
Mission, vase, bulbous w/tiny opening, no mk, 16½x7½" 775.00
Opalesce, vase, floral, slim neck, 8" 350.00
Soudanese, vase, Nouveau florals, gold on blk, slim neck, 10" 350.00

Plaque, cloisonne-type cottage and trees, 6-color, 12" x 17", $1,100.00.

Utopian, ewer, pansies, sgn Steele, #1056, 6" 165.00
Utopian, tankard, Indian portrait, 17" 2,350.00
Utopian, vase, leaves, sm top opening, rnd shoulder, 15" 295.00
Utopian, vase, silver overlay w/ornate florals, 5" 1,500.00
Utopian, vase, tiger portrait, sgn Leffler, 6x4"........................... 1,600.00
Utopian, vase, trumpet flowers, #215, 15" 275.00
Utopian, vase, wild roses, artist sgn, #1060, ovoid, 10" 275.00

Pacific Clay Products

The Pacific Clay Products Company got its start in the 1920s as a consolidation of several smaller southern California potteries. The main Los Angeles plant had been founded in 1890 to make kitchen stoneware, ollas, and similar items. Terra cotta and brick were later produced.

In 1932 Hostess Ware, a vividly-colored line of dinnerware, was introduced to compete with Bauer's Ring Ware. Coralitos, a lighter-weight, pastel-hued dinnerware line was first marketed in 1937, and a similar but less expensive line called Arcadia soon followed. Art ware including vases, figurines, candlesticks, etc. was produced from 1932 to 1942, at which time the company went into war-related work and pottery manufacture ceased. A limited amount of hand-decorated dinnerware was also made.

Bowl, Ring-style, 8½" 18.00
Casserole, Ring, orange, w/lid, in metal rack 45.00
Chop plate, Ring-style, 12" 30.00
Coaster, Ring-style...6.50
Coffee cup, Ring-style, lg.......................................15.00
Coffeepot, demitasse; Ring-style, wht 65.00
Creamer, demitasse; Ring, gr 10.00
Cup & saucer, demitasse; Ring-style 12.50
Figurine, nude holds feather, 15½" 45.00
Figurine, Spanish dancers, Valencia Oranges, rare 100.00
Platter, emb fish, orange, oval 35.00
Shakers, Ring-style, dk bl 10.00
Sugar bowl, demitasse; Ring, yel...............................10.00
Teapot, Ring-style, turq, ftd, lg 65.00
Tumbler, Plain, orange 15.00
Tumbler, Ring-style 15.00
Vase, Art Deco, bl, 7"...25.00
Vase, gr, #417, 4"...15.00

Paden City

The Paden City Glass Company began operations in 1916 in Paden City, West Virginia. The company's early lines consisted largely of the usual pressed tablewares, but by the 1920s production had expanded to include colored wares in translucent as well as opaque glass in a variety of patterns and styles. The company maintained its high standards of handmade perfection until 1949, when under new management much of the work formerly done by hand was replaced by automation. The Paden City Glass Company closed in 1951; and its earlier wares, the colored patterns in particular, are becoming very collectible. See also Depression Glass.

Animals and Birds

American eagle head, bookends, crystal, 7½", pr................250.00
Bunny, cotton-ball dispenser, ears bk, bl frosted 90.00
Bunny, cotton-ball dispenser, ears bk, milk glass 95.00
Bunny, cotton-ball dispenser, ears bk, pk frosted 70.00
Bunny, cotton-ball dispenser, ears up, pk frosted 150.00
Goose, bl, 5"..95.00
Pheasant, head turned, 12" L..................................90.00
Pheasant (Chinese), 13¾".......................................85.00
Pony, 12"...90.00
Pouter pigeon, bookends, 6½", ea..............................75.00
Rooster, head down, 8¾".......................................75.00
Rooster (Barn Yard), 8¾"......................................80.00
Rooster (Chanticleer), 9¼"....................................85.00
Rooster (Elegant), 11".......................................125.00
Squirrel on curved log, 5¾"...................................65.00
Swan (Dragon), 9¾" L...125.00

Bottle, scent; Penny Line, gr 20.00
Bowl, Peacock & Roses, gr, 13"................................75.00

Crow's Foot bowl in ruby, 8", $25.00.

Bowl, Vermillion, 9"...15.00
Cake stand, Gothic Garden, pk, 9¼" 55.00
Candy dish, Crow's Foot, amber, sq, w/lid 35.00
Candy dish, Springtime, red w/silver trim 85.00
Compote, #444 Line, red, w/lid, 7" 75.00
Compote, blk, etched 28.00
Cream soup, Crow's Foot, red, w/liner 20.00
Creamer, Wotta Line 5.00
Cup & saucer, Bees Knees 7.50
Cup & saucer, Crow's Foot, red...............................15.00
Ice bucket, Party Line, amber 25.00
Mayonnaise, #300 Line, gr, w/ladle...........................33.00
Mayonnaise, Vermillion, w/undertray & spoon 25.00
Napkin holder, Party Line, gr 75.00
Plate, Bees Knees, 7½" 5.00
Plate, Bees Knees, 9" 10.00
Plate, Crow's Foot, amber, 6" 3.50
Plate, Crow's Foot, red, 8" 8.00
Plate, Watta Line, 9½".......................................8.00
Saucer, Watta Line 2.50
Server, Gazebo, lt bl, center hdl 35.00
Server, Gazebo, swan center hdl..............................48.00
Sundae, Party Line, tulip shape..............................25.00
Tumbler, Ardith, amber, flat, 5⅛"............................25.00
Tumbler, Party Line, amber, 14-oz 8.00
Tumbler, Rena, gr 8.00
Vase, Crow's Foot, red, 11½".................................50.00

Paintings on Ivory

Miniature works of art executed on ivory from the 1800s are assessed by the finesse of the artist, as is any fine painting. Signed examples and portraits with an identifiable subject are usually preferred.

Child sits on fur throw on lady's lap, sgn Bravour, 5x6" 1,750.00
Dr & wife, identified, in shadow box fr, 2½x3", pr 400.00
Lady in wht dress w/pk sash, gilt metal fr, ca 1790s........475.00
Lola Montez, sgn Steiler, boulle fr, 3½x2½" 175.00
Officer in red/wht uniform, w/lock of hair, ca 1800, 2" 495.00
Semi-nude in bath, servants, dog, mtd in 8x10" fr 650.00
1920s gentleman, sgn Wms, in tooled gold fr, 3½x2¾" 275.00

Pairpoint

The Pairpoint Manufacturing Company was built in 1880 in New

Bedford, Massachusetts. It was primarily a metalworks whose chief product was coffin fittings. Next door, the Mt. Washington Glassworks made quality glasswares of many varieties. (See Mt. Washington for more information concerning their artware lines.) By 1894 it became apparent to both companies that a merger would be to their best interest.

From the late 1890s until the 1930s, lamps and lamp accessories were an important part of Pairpoint's production. There were three main types of shades, all of which were blown: puffy — blown-out reverse-painted shades (usually floral designs); ribbed — also reverse painted; and scenic — reverse painted with scenes of land or seascapes (usually executed on smooth surfaces, although ribbed scenics may be found occasionally). Cut glass lamps and those with metal overlay panels were also made. Scenic shades were sometimes artist signed; and, although many are unmarked, some are stamped 'Pairpoint Corp.' Blown-out shades may be marked 'Pat July 9, 1907.' Bases were made from bronze, copper, brass, silver, or wood and are always signed. Because they produced only fancy, handmade artware, the company's sales lagged seriously during the depression; and, as time and tastes changed, their style of product was less in demand. As a result, they never fully recovered; consequently part of the buildings and equipment was sold in 1938. The company reorganized in 1939 under the direction of Robert Gunderson and again specialized in quality hand-blown glassware. Isaac Babbit regained possession of the silver departments, and together they established Gunderson Glassworks, Inc. After WWII, because of a sharp decline in sales, it again became necessary to reorganize. The Gunderson-Pairpoint Glassworks was formed, and the old line of cut, engraved artware was reintroduced. The company moved to East Wareham, Massachusetts, in 1957. But business continued to suffer, and the firm closed only one year later. In 1970, however, new facilities were constructed in Sagamore under the direction of Robert Bryden, sales manager for the company since the 1950s.

In 1974 the company began to produce lead glass cup plates which were made on commission as fund raisers for various churches and organizations. These are signed with a 'P' in diamond and are becoming quite collectible.

Our advisor for Pairpoint lamps is Daniel Batchelor; he is listed in the Directory under New York. See also Napkin Rings.

Key: pwt — paperweight

Glass

Biscuit jar, lg florals on gr, sgn metal lid, 6x7½" 425.00
Bottle, scent; bubble ball w/stopper 145.00

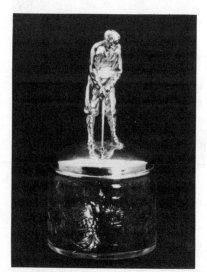

Marmalade, silver-plated golfer on lid, cut glass base, $265.00.

Bottle, scent; floral eng by OC Banks, rose pwt stopper, 7" 750.00
Bowl, blk w/bubble ball ft & silver o/l, 11", +pr sticks 475.00
Bowl, cobalt, flattened rim, ped ft, 5¾x14" 275.00
Bowl, console; apple gr, eng vintage, bubble bottom, 12" 155.00
Box, aqua, wild roses & scrolls w/gold, mk, 4x6¾x4¼" 660.00
Box, jewel; bl wash on opal w/rose medallions, metal bottom......325.00
Compote, eng Gainsborough, 7½x8½" 135.00
Creamer, Delft, windmill/ships, emb scrolls, SP mts, #7906 ....325.00
Ice bucket, polar bear eng, SP rim & drain, 5½" 175.00
Ice pail, vintage eng, SP rim & drain, 7½x6" 150.00
Lustre, canary, vintage eng, bubble ball, 10 prisms, 11" 200.00
Smoking set, Delft, 3 bowls mtd on brass/wood shield base 500.00
Vase, cornucopia; ruby, bubble-ball base, pr...............................250.00

Lamps

Boudoir, puffy 9" roses/pansies on lattice shade (EX), 15" **2,800.00**
Peg, font & 8" shade pnt w/water lilies, SP uptrn base, 15" **2,000.00**
Puffy 12" nautilus shell shade; 4-lobe rtcl std, 19" **9,000.00**
Puffy 14" butterfly/flower shade; sgn base w/flowers, NM **7,800.00**
Puffy 18" 4-panel lilac & trellis shade; trumpet std **5,500.00**
Puffy 8" floral on blk shade, sgn/dtd, 14", EX **4,000.00**
Puffy 8" peaked shade w/tulips in ea corner; sgn std, 14" **3,900.00**
Rvpt 14" Venetian harbor ribbed 4-sided shade; sgn std, 20" . **11,250.00**
Rvpt 16" Directorie shade: garden scene; bubble-ball std **2,500.00**

Table lamp, 15½" reverse-painted 'Directorie' shade with clipper ships signed C. Durand, bronzed triple-dolphin signed base, 22½", $3,600.00.

Rvpt 16" shaped sqd shade w/butterfly at ea corner; mk std **4,000.00**
Rvpt 16" 3-man rowboat shade; 3-dolphin std **3,250.00**
Rvpt 18" Berkeley dogwood tree shade; gr glass base, NM....... **4,250.00**
Rvpt 18" Directorie pastoral scene shade; cut-glass knop **3,600.00**
Rvpt 18" Exeter shade: Persian florals; sgn 3-ftd std, 23" **1,500.00**
Rvpt 20" shade & base w/gulls & ships, sgn Rae, 25", NM..... **10,000.00**
Rvpt 8" ocean w/ships shade; dolphin std/marble base, 14½" . **1,600.00**

Silverplate

Cake stand, cut-out hearts, geometrics, raised rim, 9½" 110.00
Orange bowl, cut florals, Rococo, scalloped, ftd, 6½x10½" 85.00

Pairpoint Limoges

Limoges china blanks were imported from France in strict accordance with Pairpoint specifications. They were decorated by Pairpoint in designs that ranged from simple to elaborate florals and scenics. These are easily identified — look for the Pairpoint name over a crown with the Limoges name below. You may also find similar ware marked 'Pairpoint Minton.'

Gravy boat, Dresden-type mc flowers, New Bedford's, +tray 175.00
Plate, mums, gold scroll borders, 10" 145.00
Tureen, mums foliage, fish finial, 8x6½x6" 465.00
Vase, gladiolus, cherub w/peonies, w/gilt, cobalt hdls, 15" 1,200.00
Vase, mums on cream, rtcl foliate hdls & rim, 5x9" 375.00

Paper Dolls

No one knows quite how or when paper dolls originated. One belief is that they began in Europe as 'pantins' (jumping jacks) and were frequently worn as part of the costume. By the late 1790s, they were being mass-produced. During the 19th century, most paper dolls portrayed famous dancers and opera stars such as Fanny Elssler and Jenny Lind. In the late 1800s, the Raphael Tuck Publishers of England produced many series of beautiful paper dolls; retail companies used them as advertisements to further the sale of their products. Around the turn of the century, many popular women's magazines began featuring a page of paper dolls.

Most familiar to today's collectors are the books with dolls on cardboard covers and clothes on the inside pages. These made their appearance in the late 1920s and early thirties. The most collectible (and the most valuable) are those representing celebrities, movie stars, and comic-strip characters of the thirties and forties.

Authority Mary Young has compiled an informative book, *Collector's Guide to Paper Dolls*, with current prices; you will find her address in the Directory under Ohio. When no condition is indicated, the dolls listed below are assumed to be in mint, uncut, original condition. Cut sets will be worth about half price if all dolls and outfits are included and pieces are in very good condition. If dolls were produced in die-cut form, these prices reflect such a set in mint condition with all costumes and accessories.

American Beauties, Reuben Lilja & Co, #917, ca 1942, VG 12.00
American Family, Grinnell, #C1002, EX 55.00
Army Nurse & Doctor, Merrill, #3425, 1942, EX 25.00
Baby Sitter, Lowe, #945, EX...25.00
Belle of the Ball, Saalfield, #2702, 1948, EX 35.00
Betsy McCall Around the World, ca 1962, VG................................10.00
Bette Davis, Merrill, 1942, VG 20.00
Betty Grable, Merrill, #1558, 1951, VG..77.00
Blue Bonnet, Merrill, #3444, 1942, EX 40.00
Bob Hope & Dorothy Lamour, Whitman, #976, 1942, M 215.00
Brenda Lee, DeJournette, #4360, 1964, VG....................................17.00
Buffy (Family Affair), Whitman, #1955, 1968, M 20.00
Charming Paper Dolls, Saalfield, #1357, ca 1960, EX 4.00
Chitty Chitty Bang Bang, Whitman, #1952, 1968, NM 22.50
Circus, Saalfield, #2610, 1952, VG.. 7.00
College Style, Merrill, #3400, 1941, M...80.00
Debbie Reynolds, Whitman, #1948, 1962, NM 42.50
Debbie Reynolds, Whitman, w/clothes, 1957, VG 15.00
Donna Reed, Saalfield/Artcraft, #5197, 1960, EX 40.00
Double Wedding, Merrill, #3472, 1939, EX.....................................77.00
Dress-Up, Reuben Lilja & Co, 1947, VG 10.00
Eve Arden, Saalfield, #158510, 1953, M..47.00
Family Princess, Merrill, #1548, 1958, EX 17.00
Four Sisters, Saalfield, #269, VG 7.00
Gigi Perreau, Saalfield, #1542, 1951, EX 38.00

Dollies To Paint, Cut Out, and Dress, **printed by Saalfield, no date, 13" x 8½", $60.00.**

Gilda Radner, book style, Avon Books, 1979, M 12.50
Gloria Jean, Saalfield, 1940, NM 50.00
Gone With the Wind, Merrill, 1940, NM 150.00
Hayley Mills, from Moon-Spinners, Disney, Whitman, 1964, M...32.00
Jane Powell Paper Dolls Book, 1952, VG..15.00
Janet Leigh, Abbott #1805, uncut, 1958, EX 40.00
Julia, Saalfield #6855-150, 1970, uncut, NM.................................22.50
June Allyson, Whitman, #1173, 1953, VG.......................................22.00
Kewpies, Saalfield #4461, 1968, M 27.50
Lucille Ball, Saalfield, 1945, VG 20.00
Martha Hyer, Saalfield, #4423, 1958, M...42.00
Mickey & Minnie, 2 10" figures w/clothes, 1930s, VG..................87.00
Modern Miss, Saalfield, #2397, 1942, M...43.00
Movie Starlets, Stephens Publishing, #178, 1949, EX 21.00
Mrs Beasley, Whitman, #1973, 1970, EX 7.00
Munster's Paper Dolls, Whitman, 1966, NM...................................15.00
Our Soldier Jim, Whitman, #3980, 1943, 10½", M 28.00
Paper Dolls of All Nations, Saalfield, #227, 1939, VG 27.50
Partridge Family, Artcraft, #5137, 1971, VG.................................11.00
Pat Boone, Whitman, #1968, 1959, EX 27.00
Patti Page, 1958, EX 49.00
Pebbles & Bamm-Bamm, Whitman, #1983, 1964, NM 38.00
Pinocchio Paper Dolls Book, Whitman, 1939, lg format, VG.......25.00
Prince & Princess, Saalfield, #2706, 1949, EX 21.00
Raggedy Ann & Andy, Saalfield, #2719, 1953, EX 21.00
Ricky Nelson, 1959, M 42.00
Rita Hayworth in Carmen, Saalfield, 1948, NM 35.00
Robin Hood & Maid Marian, Saalfield, #1761, 1950s, EX 17.00
Rosemary Clooney, Samuel Lowe, #2487, 1958, VG 21.00
Sleeping Beauty, Disney, Whitman, 1959, VG................................10.00
Snow White & 7 Dwarfs, Whitman, #1998, ca 1970, EX 14.00
Square Dance, Lowe, #968-10, 1950, EX 14.00
Style Shop, Saalfield, #1516, 1943, M 32.00
Susan Dey as Laurie, Artcraft, 1972, VG 7.00
Tarzan of the Apes, 1933 figure set, M..57.00
Tiny Chatty Twins, Whitman, #1985, 1963, VG.............................12.00
Tricia Nixon, Saalfield, 1970, M..14.00
Twiggy, Whitman, #1999, 1967, EX 21.00
Wedding Paper Dolls, Whitman, #1970, 1970, VG 10.00
Ziegfeld Girl, Merrill, #3466, 1941, EX...17.00

Paperweights

The term 'paperweight' technically refers to any small, heavy object used to hold down loose papers. They have been made from a broad range of materials; many have been sold as souvenirs or given away by retail companies as advertising premiums. But today those attracting the most interest are the antique and contemporary artists' glass weights.

During the mid-1800s, the French factories of St. Louis, Baccarat, and Clichy incorporated millefiori and lampwork into glass domes which were called paperweights. This was done commercially and was probably the result of earlier efforts by Pierre Bigaglia of Venice. These 'baubles' were eagerly snapped up. Weights from the French factories that originally sold for a mere $2.00 to $3.00 are today commanding prices of $500.00 and up, depending on condition and craftsmanship. Many have been damaged but are restored or restorable. Interest waned in the late 1860s, and production nearly came to a halt. Clichy closed in the late 1800s. Baccarat is known to have made weights until about 1910 and again in the 1920s and 1930s. In the early 1950s, a revival of interest in paperweights resulted in renewed production at both Baccarat and St. Louis.

In the United States, production started in the 1850s, a little later than in France; and paperweights continued to be in vogue a little longer. The New England and Sandwich factories along with Millville, New Jersey, are the best-known manufacturers of weights made in the 1920s and 1930s. Today several well-known glass artists such as Ayotte, Tarsitano, Trabucco, Rosenfield, Grube, G. Smith, and Stankard are making weights with floral motifs as well as other designs.

Paperweight collecting began with the 19th-century weights, but much knowledge and interest was lost during the period when production drastically declined. During the 1920s, collector-interest began to pick up and by 1950 had intensified to the point that books and articles on the subject began to be published. The Paperweight Collectors' Association was formed in 1953. It has bi-annual conventions, and there are several state and regional associations. Interest in weight collecting shows continuous growth.

Note: Prices do not reflect the usual 10% buyer's fee charged by most auction houses. Furthermore, there are many factors which determine value, particularly of antique weights. Auction-realized prices of contemporary weights are usually other than issue price; 'list price' may be for weights issued earlier and reduced for clearance or influenced by market demand and other factors. The dimension given at the end of the description is diameter.

Key:

A — antique	latt — latticinio
cl — clear	mill — millefiori
con — concentric	o/l — overlay
fct — faceted	pm — pastry mold
gar — garland	pwt — paperweight
grd — ground	sil — silhouette
jsp — jasper	

Ayotte, Rick

Chrysanthemums, ltd ed 25, 1990, 3¾" 900.00
Fall Bouquet, pine cones/acorns/berries, ltd ed 50, 3¾"............700.00
Goldfinch, 5/1 fct, sgn, dtd 1979, 2¼" 200.00
Hummingbird & orange-yel bellflowers, sgn, 69/75, '85, 3" 450.00
Lg yel moon/Snow Owl on pine branch, blk grd, ltd ed.............550.00
Robin on flowering dogwood, 1⅞".......................225.00
Wren on cherry branch, compound structure, sgn/1981, 3".........400.00

Baccarat, Antique

Butterfly on wht clematis+4 leaves, star base, 3", EX 2,400.00
Butterfly w/marbled wings w/in gar of gr & wht canes, 3" 2,400.00

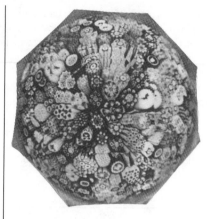

Baccarat dated (1848) close millefiori weight with allover geometric faceting and three animal silhouette canes, 3¼", $1,450.00.

Close mill, pk/bl/wht canes, 1¾"...................................800.00
Close mill w/latt pcs+5 animal sil & 'B 1848' cane, 3" 1,800.00
Close mill w/4 animal sil & '1849' cane, 2½"..........................1,500.00
Con mill, 3 rows about pk/wht star, red/turq outer row, 2½" 600.00
Dbl o/l mushroom, bl & wht cut w/window+6 printies, 3" 4,000.00
Ducks on pond, 'seaweed,' extended base, fct, 3" 8,000.00
Patterned mill, 7-row, arrowhead canes, fct, 3" 600.00
Red/wht primrose (yel honeycomb center)+8 leaves, 2¾".......1,100.00
Scattered mill, 8 animal sil+'B 1848' cane, gauze bed, 2¾" 1,600.00
Snake, red/blk, coiled on buff rocks w/gr & silver grd, 3" 9,300.00
Wild strawberry flower+2 berries+4 leaves, 2¾" 1,600.00
2 entwined trefoil gar on close pack wht star canes, 3" 6,000.00
2 entwined trefoils w/6 animal sil, bl flashed, fct, 3" 3,000.00
3 strawberries+leaves, star base, 2⅞" 5,500.00
7 rings ea w/arrowhead cane, ruby flashed, 1/6 fct, 2⅞" 3,300.00

Baccarat, Modern

Sulfide, dbl o/l A Lincoln on cl dmn-cut grd, 3" 450.00
Sulfide, dbl o/l Will Rodgers on cl cut grd, swirled, 3" 180.00
Sulfide, Virgo on cobalt, 1/6 ftc, sgn, 2¾" 150.00
Tan snail on gr sea bed, purple/wht florals, pebbles, 3" 400.00
Triple-cut o/l (lav/wht/cl), pansies, #68 ltd ed, 1970, 3½" 750.00
Wht flower+leaves, sgn/#377 ltd ed, 2⅞" 300.00
Wht lotus+sm blossom+2 leaves, #64 of 250, sgn, 1977, 3".........750.00
2 bl flowers, red/wht center, bl bud & ladybug on amber, 3"........350.00

Banford, Bob

Bl/blk/wht B cane mtd w/purple flower+2 buds+bee, fct, 2½" 400.00
Pansy, purple/yel, columnar, top+top-to-bottom fcts, 2¾"..........600.00
Striped snake on pebbly gr w/branch, 'B' cane, 3" 600.00
12-petal yel/brn wheat flower+bud in star-cut cl grd, 3" 500.00

Banford, Ray

Bouquet in basket, cut to resemble basket, 3" 900.00
Pk/wht iris on purple aventurine, sgn, 2⅞" 400.00
Roses in basket, red/wht o/l on cl, dmn-cut base, 3¼" 1,200.00
Triple-cut o/l (gr/wht/cl) pk Weymouth rose/fruit w/in, 2½".......450.00
2 pk-striped iris/leaves on opaque mauve, fct, 'B' cane, 2½" 350.00
2 purple flowers+bud, sunburst fct, 'B' cane, 3" 500.00
2 roses on purple aventurine+2 gold bees, fct, 1976, 2½".............300.00

Clichy, Antique

Chequered con mill w/latt pcs, cable bed, fct, 2½" 800.00
Chequered mill, 2 rows canes about pm & latt pcs, 2¾" 1,100.00
Chequered mill, 2 rows lg canes, latt pcs, cable bed, 3" 1,200.00

Close mill w/3 pk roses & 'C' cane, 3" 1,500.00
Con close mill, 6-row, in basket of wht spiral staves, 2¾" 1,800.00
Con mill w/rose, 3 outer rows of canes, fct, 2⅜" 900.00
Con mill w/stars in center & outer ring on opaque red, 2½" .. 1,000.00

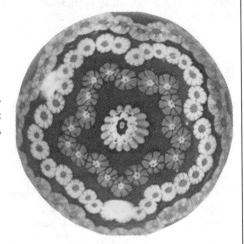

Clichy pentagon pattern millefiori weight on blue ground, 3⅛", $1,100.00.

Patterned con mill w/rose, 6 lg pk/wht canes, fct, 2⅝" 825.00
Scattered mill w/pk & wht rose cane in clear, 2⅞", EX...............600.00
Spaced con mill w/2 pk roses on muslin grd, cable bed, 3" 1,870.00
Swirl, pk staves alternate w/wht, bl/wht cane center, 3⅛" 1,500.00
3-row star-patterned con mill on opaque rose grd, 3⅛" 2,400.00

Kaziun, Charles

Blk/wht cameo lady+6 gr/wht/pk floral canes on pk, fct, 1⅜" 600.00
Button, 3 roses (red/yel/bl) on gr swirls w/goldstone, ⅞" 250.00
Gold lady sil+6 bl/wht flower canes on amethyst, fct, 1⅜"...........550.00
Purple crocus+3 leaves, sgn cane, ped, 2⅞" H, NM.....................800.00
Red rose+gold bee+3 pastel canes on wht latt on bl, ped, 1¼" 550.00
Red rose+6 leaves+bud, sgn cane, ped, 3½x2½" 850.00
Red/wht tiger lily on rare yel grd, ped ft, sgn, 1⅞" 400.00
Yel rose+3 leaves+3 star canes on wht, ftc, ped, 1¾" H 400.00
Yel/pk rose+4 leaves, sgn cane, ped, 3¼x2⅛", NM 700.00
6-petal yel flower+3 leaves, bl/wht 'K' cane, 1/6 fct, 1½".............600.00

Lundberg Studios

Daniel Salazar, pk/bl hydrangias, 1990..225.00
Daniel Salazar, Sterling rose, miniature, 1990 ....195.00
James Lundberg, pk chrysanthemum, 1990.....................................290.00
James Lundberg, pk jonquils, 1990 ....260.00

New England Glass

Apple, gr-yel to orange, lying on rnd pad base, 3¼" 900.00
Apple, orange-red to yel, lying on rnd pad base, 3¼" 800.00
Apple, pk to yel, lying on rnd pad base, 3½" 850.00
Apple, pk-yel tint, lying on rnd pad base, 2½" 700.00
Mill cane nosegay w/4 lt gr leaves on cl, 1¾" 325.00
Pear, pk to yel, lying on rnd pad base, 2¾" 900.00
Scramble, tight-packed canes, top fct+honeycomb sides, 2¾" 100.00
3 florettes+4 gr leaves in cane gar on latt cushion, 2½" 500.00

Perthshire

Bouquet of flowers on blk swirled grd, 1988, 3⅛" 185.00
Con mill on blk, 1⅝" 45.00
Gr/wht crown spiral enclosing cane w/robin, Xmas/1974, 2¾" ...120.00

Mill close pack on dk bl, 1973, 2⅞" 100.00
Orange/yel pansy w/in gar on wht upset muslin, 1/8 fct, 2¾" 250.00
Pattern mill, cluster of 5+1 w/in gar on dk gr, '75, 2⅞" 65.00
Royal Wedding Feathers on wht upset muslin grd, 1981, 2" 140.00
Scrambled canes on cl, sgn/dtd canes w/in, 2¾" 85.00
Setup canes w/latt twists in sq on cobalt, fct, 1979, 3¼" 150.00
Sunflower in leafy gar w/in perimeter gar on rust, 1979, 3".........130.00
Triple-cut o/l (gr/wht/cl), butterfly w/in, #92, 1976, 2" 150.00
Triple-cut o/l (tan/wht/cl) mill mushroom w/in, 2⅞"....................225.00
Triple-cut o/l (teal/wht/cl), rose on wht platform w/in, 3"...........300.00
18-petal pk/wht flower on 2 tiers of leaves, 1/12 fct, 3⅛"............210.00
5 pk mill loops tied at center on bl, w/label, 2½" 30.00
7 sil: flowers/animals/birds+lav & pk canes on yel & bl, 3"..........100.00

St. Louis, Antique

Bouquet w/in leafy gar, window+3 rows fct, 3⅛" 1,600.00
Close con mill, 5-row, 1 w/cruciforms & 'SL' cane, 3⅛" 2,800.00
Close con mill, 5-row, 2¾" 2,400.00
Con mill mushroom, 5 cane rows w/cruciform center, fct, 2" 900.00
Crown, twisted red/gr ribbons alternate w/latt, 2¾", NM........ 2,600.00
Flowers+5 leaves in gar of pk/gr canes on muslin grd, 3⅞"...........900.00
Pk clematis w/10 ribbed petals+3 leaves, gr jsp grd, 2⅛"..............770.00
Vine w/grapes & leaves, 1/7/6 fcts, 2¾" 3,800.00
5 lg canes ea w/sil, gr crimped tube cane grd, 2⅜" 6,000.00
5 mc flowers w/leaves, honeycomb-cut top+8 fct, 3⅛"..............660.00

St. Louis, Modern

Bl/wht lg bouquet (yel centers) on latt swirl, dtd, 2¾" 425.00
Carpet grd (purple/gr/wht/red) w/6 mill clusters, '72, 3" 300.00
Dbl Clematis, red w/6 latt petals on dk bl, 1/6 fct, 3"..................375.00
Dbl o/l 6-row con mill mushroom, 1/5 fct, 1970, 3"....................500.00
Orange pear+3 red cherries+4 leaves on wht latt swirls, 2".........185.00
Piedouche, con mill dome on wht latt ped, 1953, 3x3⅛".............900.00
Sulfide, King St Louis w/in cane gar, 1/5 fcts, 1967, 2½" 130.00
Triple-cut o/l (wine/wht/cl) mill mushroom w/in, 3".................500.00

Stankard, Paul

Botanical Interpretation, floral, eng title, 1978, 3" 1,200.00
Bouquet of purple/wht violets, 1/6 fct, sgn/1978, 2¾" 1,200.00
Lady Slipper+2 buds w/root system, 1982 ....850.00
Multi-layered bouquet, sgn, H-153, dtd 1982, 3⅛" 1,900.00
Nature's Splendor, mixed bouquet, sgn, A-210, 1978, 3" 1,800.00
Orange/gr Indian gourds+2 lg leaves & blossoms on cl, 3¼" ... 1,100.00
Showy Lady Slipper, 2 pk+wht flowers w/roots on dk bl, 3" ... 1,100.00
St Anthony's Fire, red floral on lt bl, 1/6 fct, 1978, 3" 850.00
Trilaflora, 2 blkberries/blossom, sgn, 6/6 15876, 3" 1,900.00
2 wht orchids+5 buds w/roots on cobalt, B-567, sgn/1982, 3" . 1,000.00
3 tiger orchids+floating seed pod+roots, ltd ed, 1978, 2⅝" 950.00

Tarsitano, Debbie

Opening Night Bouquet, 3 lg red flowers+3 wht sprigs, 2¾"........450.00
Yel basket w/pk & purple flowers, 1/6 fct, 3¼" 600.00
10-petal pk flower w/bee inside, 2¼"..500.00
21-petal zinnia, purple w/yel stamen, bud/4 leaves, 2¾".............700.00
3 mc flowers in wht-hdld yel basket, star base, sgn, 3¼".............550.00
4 5-petal flowers in yel & orange+9 leaves, sgn, 2¾" 550.00

Tarsitano, Delmo

Bee atop honeycomb+red flower, 1/8/8 fct, 3¼"............................850.00

Dbl strawberry+wht blossom & leaves, 2¾".........................**600.00**
Earth Life, snake+3 flowers on sandy grd, 3⅞"......................... **1,100.00**
Earth Life, spider on web, sandy grd, 3⅜" **650.00**
Lg peach on brn branch w/8 leaves, sgn, 3" **750.00**
Spider on leaf+yel flower, web eng by Erlacher, 3½"...................**750.00**
2 peaches hang from branch, star-cut base, 3" **750.00**

Whitefriars

Con mill, pastels, 2⅞" **100.00**
Con mill, 8-point star center, ftd, 3½"...............................**150.00**
Pattern mill, Am flag in center, 1/5 fct, sgn/1976, 3⅛"..............**245.00**
Pattern mill, 3 Wisemen in center, 1/5 fct, sgn/1976, 3⅛"..........**235.00**
5 butterfly canes, bl/wht, 1/5 ftc, dtd 1975, 3" **200.00**

Whittemore, Francis D.

Bleeding heart+2 buds & 4 leaves on gr flash grd, 2⅜" **350.00**
Bottle, scent; lav crocus in stopper & base, sgn cane, 4" **400.00**
Hummingbird on stalk w/bluebell on claret grd, 2½".................**350.00**
Pk cyclamen+bud on translucent gr grd **300.00**
15-petal rose+4 gr leaves, upright on ped ft, sgn, 2½" **375.00**
2 yel pears on pk jsp, 2 gr leaves/stems, cane sgn, 2⅛"..................**250.00**

Ysart, Paul

Bl fish w/gold & orange fins on tan & pk w/2 shells, 3" **495.00**
Bouquet w/4 flowers (pk/yel/bl) in bl/wht & purple/wht gar........**550.00**

Paul Ysart, flat bouquet weight on transparent green, 3", $550.00.

Copper aventurine snake w/rust spots on gr w/wht rocks, 3" **525.00**
Flat 2-flower bouquet on gr w/in 2 rows canes, unsgn, 3" **400.00**
Gr aventurine fish+pk fish on pastel sea bed w/shells, 3" **375.00**
Gr/wht cane w/in 4 con mill rings, pastels, sgn, 2⅞" **300.00**
Gr/wht cane w/in 5 mc florets, outer row of mc canes, unsgn **100.00**
Pattern mill, lg central setup/mc perimeter on pk, sgn, 2⅞".........**275.00**
Pattern mill, star-shaped design, on orange, unsgn, 2⅞" **150.00**
Purple flower+bud+leaves on wht latt basket, airtraps, 2¾" **400.00**
12-petal dk bl flower w/red/wht center on latt basket, 3" **450.00**

Miscellaneous

Bohemian, A, con mill, red/wht canes w/in+4 circles, 1¾", NM.**120.00**
Bohemian, A, scattered mill, dancing devil sil center, 2⅝" **450.00**
Gillinder, A, red flower+bud & leaves on latt cushion, 2⅞" **935.00**
Hacker, Harold; gr salamander on flecked gray-gr, 2¾"...............**350.00**
Hansen, Ron; lg pk rose+4 leaves in cl, 'H' cane, 1⅞" **140.00**
Hansen, Ron; 3 yel pears on bright bl, 1/6 ftc, sgn, 2¼" **85.00**
J-Glass, 4 wht 5-petal flowers+4 buds in cl, 1/10 fct, 3⅛" **130.00**
Mt WA, A, full-blown pk rose w/central wht & gr cane, 4".... **3,850.00**
Orient & Flume, bl fish/sea urchins/aquatic plants, 3" **100.00**

Orient & Flume, Marbrie looping in bl/wht, red center, 3" **45.00**
Pairpoint, pk rose/foliage, extensively cut/fct, 2¾" **200.00**
Rosenfeld, K; Flower Bed, 10 5-petal flowers on cl, sgn, 3" **350.00**
Rosenfeld, K; 3-pc bouquet on cl star-cut grd, 1984, 2⅝" **200.00**
Sandwich, poinsettia, pk, 10-petal/3-leaf, latt cushion, 3" **600.00**
Sandwich, 2 cherries+4 leaves, fct, 2⅞", EX................................**660.00**
Triple-cut o/l, upright bouquet w/in, 1/6 fct, 3" **375.00**

Papier-Mache

The art of papier-mache was mainly European. It originated in Paris around the middle of the 18th century and became popular in America during Victorian times. Small items such as boxes, trays, inkwells, frames, etc. as well as extensive ceiling moldings and larger articles of furniture were made. The process involved building layer upon layer of paper soaked in glue, then coaxed into shape over a wood or wire form. When dry it was painted or decorated with gilt or inlays. Inexpensive 20th-century 'notions' were machine processed and mold pressed. See also Christmas; Candy Containers.

Apple, red w/brn stem & gr cloth leaves, 1900s, 10x8" dia **65.00**
Box, patch; Joys of Angling reserve, English, 3" dia **200.00**
Dog, pull chain, mechanism activates mouth, French, 8" L.........**300.00**
Lamb, on wood fr, wooly coat, 2⅝" L.......................................**65.00**
Owl on stump, w/mortarboard cap, HP, ca 1900, 22x12x10", EX ...**250.00**

Rabbit, 4" long, $95.00.

Parian Ware

Parian is hard-paste unglazed porcelain made to resemble marble. First made in the mid-1800s by Staffordshire potters, it was soon after produced in the United States by the U.S. Pottery at Bennington, Vermont. Busts and statuary were favored, but plaques, vases, mugs, and pitchers were also made.

Adriane, nude riding panther, Minton, 14", EX **700.00**
Beatrice, hand to heart, mk Copeland, 1850s, 21", EX **400.00**
Bust, Alexandra, Art Union of London, Copeland, 15"...............**800.00**
Bust, Schiller, Germany, 9½" **175.00**
Clorinda in armour, mk J Bell/1848/Minton, 13" **500.00**
Death, dog & stag, 10½", EX..**150.00**
Dying nude gladiator, Bates Brn-Westhead, 14", EX **500.00**
Lady w/dove & urn, 10½"...**95.00**
Maiden Hood, classical standing maid, Copeland, 22", NM.......**500.00**
Nude seated on cloth, fish below, Copeland, 12" **500.00**
Pitcher, classical lady w/cherub & angels overhead, 6½" **115.00**
Queen Victoria, English, 1837, rpr hand, 5¾"..............................**400.00**

Flower Vendor, minor chips, 15½", $275.00; Female extracting thorn from lion's paw, titled 'Lion in Love,' NM, 15", $800.00.

Parrish, Maxfield

Maxfield Parrish was a painter and illustrator who began his career in the last decade of the 19th century. His work remained prominent until the early 1940s. His most famous painting, *Daybreak*, was published in print form and sold nearly two thousand copies between 1910 and 1930. All prices are for framed prints except for those from the 1960s.

Ad, Djer Kiss, girl on swing, LHJ, 1921, 14x10" 100.00
Ad, Ferry Seed, Peter, Peter Pumpkin Eater, 1919, 16x10½" 125.00
Ad, Hires, gnomes at cauldron, 1921, fr, 7½x10" 75.00
Ad, Jell-O, King & Queen Might Eat Thereof, 1921, 9½x6" 55.00
Ad, Royal Baking Powder, maid w/cake, Dec 1895 ....80.00
Ad, Swift's Ham, Jack Sprat..., 1921, fr 125.00
Book, Arabian Nights, Scribner, orig dust jacket 200.00
Book, Dream Days, 1902, EX 195.00
Book, Poems of Childhood, orig 175.00
Book, Tanglewood Tales, Hawthorne, 10 illus, 1923, EX 185.00
Booklet, Polly, Jell-O recipes, 1924, EX 50.00
Calendar, Contentment, ca 1959, full pad, 11x7" 150.00
Calendar, Contentment, Edison/Mazda, full pad, fr, lg 425.00
Calendar, Enchantment, Edison/Mazda, cropped, 1926, fr, lg......550.00
Calendar, Evening Shadows, 1953, lg, EX 250.00
Calendar, Old Glen Mill, Brn/Bigelow, 1954, fr, lg......................275.00
Calendar, Peaceful Valley, Brn/Bigelow, 1936, fr, lg 250.00
Calendar, Thy Templed Hills, Brn/Bigelow, 1942, lg, NM..........275.00
Calendar, Venetian Lamplighter, Edison/Mazda, 1924, M 200.00
Calendar, Waterfall, Edison/Mazda, complete, 1931, sm 175.00
Card, Christmas; Afterglow, Brn/Bigelow, 1947, 8¼x6" 15.00
Card, Christmas; Silent Night, Brn/Bigelow..................................15.00
Card, Christmas; Twilight Hour, Hilltop Farm, ca 1951 ....15.00
Card, greeting; Mill Pond, 1940s..12.00
Figure, Drum Major, jtd compo/wood, Parrish design, 18", EX 150.00
Figure, GE Bandi, jtd wood, rare 850.00
Figure, Radiotrons, jtd compo/wood, Parrish design, 16" 275.00
Magazine, Life, Easter cover, Apr 6, 1922, EX 60.00
Magazine cover, Collier's, Christmas Shepherds, Dec 1904...........55.00
Magazine cover, Collier's, Mama Ox, Mar 1906, 14½x10½" 55.00
Magazine cover, Collier's, Music Hath Charms, Mar 1907 ....55.00

Magazine cover, LHJ, Sweet Nothings, Apr 1921 ....55.00
Magazine cover, LHJ, Wht Birch, Mar 1930, 14x10" 65.00
Magazine cover, Life, masked figure in costume, Oct 1922 ....60.00
Magazine cover, Life, self-portrait, Jan 31, 1924 ....65.00
Magazine cover, New Hampshire Troubador, ca 1940, 6x4⅜".......24.00
Magazine cover, Scribner's, Nativity scene, Dec 1900 ....50.00
Playing cards, Dawn, 1918, rare, EX 275.00
Playing cards, Enchantment, Edison/Mazda, complete.................215.00
Playing cards, In the Mountains, Brn/Bigelow, unopened............165.00
Playing cards, Waterfall, 1931, VG in box 225.00
Poster, New Hampshire Winter Paradise, EX 450.00
Print, Afterglow, Brn/Bigelow, 1949, orig fr, 7x9" 65.00
Print, Atlas, nude giant holds up sky, 1909, fr, 11x13½" 145.00
Print, Bl & Yel Hose, comic chefs, 1925, orig fr, 12x14"...............65.00
Print, By Rocks & Rills, lg..225.00
Print, Canyon, bright colors, 1924, 13x16" 200.00
Print, Chef Serving Tarts, 1925, orig fr, 12x14" 95.00
Print, Circe's Palace, Maiden, 1908, 15½x12½" 110.00
Print, Cleopatra, w/label, fr, med, 16x14" 575.00
Print, Cleopatra, 1917, fr, 24½x28", EX 750.00
Print, Contentment, cropped, fr, sm 95.00
Print, Daybreak, orig fr, 13½x16½" 150.00
Print, Daybreak, orig gesso fr, 6x10" 125.00
Print, Dream Castles, nude youth/castle, 1912, fr, 7½x10", EX ...125.00
Print, Dreaming, 1928, orig fr, 12½x14½" 275.00
Print, Ecstasy, Edison/Mazda, sm..165.00
Print, Enchantment, cropped, sm...175.00
Print, Evening Shadows #2, Brn/Bigelow, fr, 17½x22½" 225.00
Print, Garden of Allah, orig sticker, 16x30" 200.00
Print, Garden of Allah, 18x33"..275.00
Print, Harvest, farmer on grassy knoll, fr, 1911, 8x10" 50.00
Print, Hilltop, fr, 34x23", EX 500.00

The Century, lithograph in colors, 20" x 13½", $950.00.

Print, Interlude, 1924, fr, 11x14", M 225.00
Print, Land of Make Believe, fr, 11x8½" 70.00
Print, Lute Players, 3 maidens w/lutes, 1924, fr, 18x30" 525.00
Print, Moonlight, fr, 12x15" 200.00
Print, New Hampshire, fr, 19x24" 95.00
Print, Old Glen Mill, 1954, orig fr, 14x18" 275.00
Print, Path to Home, Brn/Bigelow, orig fr, 1950, 11x13" 115.00
Print, Pied Piper, plays flute, orig fr, 1909, 10x24" 450.00
Print, Pierrot's Serenade, 9x11", EX 165.00

Print, Pool of the Villa Este, fr, 15x13"	65.00
Print, Primitive Man, Edison/Mazda, 1929, fr, 9½x14"	225.00
Print, Prince, House of Arts, ca 1925, fr, 12x10"	150.00
Print, Queen Gulnare, ca 1907, 16½x12"	95.00
Print, Quiet Solitude, Brn/Bigelow, 1961, 19x16"	135.00
Print, Reveries, ladies at fountain, 1938, 6x10", NM	85.00
Print, Sandman, gnome w/sack, 1905, orig fr, 6½x8½"	50.00
Print, Sheltering Oaks, 1960, orig fr, 12½x20"	245.00
Print, Solitude, Edison/Mazda, 11x14", M	290.00
Print, Spirit of Transportation, fr, ca 1923, 20x16"	395.00
Print, Sugar Plum Tree, ca 1902, fr, 15x10"	125.00
Print, Sunrise, 16x22"	225.00
Print, To Autumn, 1904, orig fr, 10x13"	75.00
Print, Twilight, 1935, orig fr, 30x12½"	195.00
Print, Wild Geese, ca 1924, fr, 15x12"	185.00
Puzzle, Queen's Page, 1925, EX in orig 9½x12" box	95.00
Puzzle, The Prince, 1925, NM in box	90.00
Sign, 2 knaves, Edison/Mazda Lamps, tin, 1924, 12x20", EX	575.00
Tape measure, 2 knaves, Edison/Mazda, scarce, NM	75.00

Pate-De-Verre

Simply translated, pate-de-verre means paste of glass. In the manufacturing process, lead glass is first ground, then mixed with sodium silicate solution to form a paste which can be molded and refired. Some of the most prominent artisans to use this procedure were Almaric Walter, Daum, Argy-Rousseau, and Decorchemont.

Bowl, upright leaves, streaky sapphire bl, Decorchemont, 5"	3,800.00
Bust of a satyr, amethyst, mk Despret/#1099, 6½"	1,000.00
Figure of seated woman, Cubist, wht w/lt opal, no mk, 6½"	600.00
Sculpture, woman's head, yel, sgn Despret, 4" L	525.00

Pate-Sur-Pate

Pate-sur-pate, literally paste-on-paste, is a technique whereby relief decorations are built up on a ceramic body by layering several applications of slip, one on the other, until the desired result is achieved. Usually only two colors are used, and the value of a piece is greatly enhanced as more color is added. See also Walter, A.

Box, lady w/flute sits on branch, mk JG&Cie/Limoges, 5½"	200.00
Plaque, dancer, wht/dk bl, sgn A Barriere, Limoges, 6x5"	150.00

Vase, blue and white, signed Limoges, Orcelain de Paris, 10", $800.00; Vase, pink, blue, and white with gilt, marked with a superimposed HI beneath a star, 9½", $900.00.

Plaque, Queen Elizabeth, lav w/teal border, 6" dia	165.00
Screen, pr of winged figures, wht/red/gilt, Mintons, 7"	1,800.00
Vase, cupid chases butterfly, wht on blk, Geo Jones, 6"	650.00
Vase, lady w/basket over head, wht on gr, 8½"	375.00
Vase, 2 figures in garden, wht on dk gr, sgn Schenk, #5639	1,250.00

Pattern Glass

Pattern Glass was the first mass-produced fancy tableware in America and was much prized by our ancestors. From the 1840s to the Civil War, it contained a high lead content and is known as 'Flint Glass.' It is exceptionally clear and resonant. Later glass was made with soda lime and is known as non-flint. By the 1890s pattern glass was produced in great volume in thousands of patterns, and colored glass came into vogue. Today the highest prices are often paid for these later patterns flashed with rose, amber, canary, and vaseline; stained ruby; or made in colors of cobalt, green, yellow, amethyst, etc. Demand for pattern glass declined by 1915, and glass fanciers were collecting it by 1930. No other field of antiques offers more diversity in patterns, prices, or pieces than this unique and historical glass that represents the Victorian era in America.

Our advisor for this category is Darlene Yohe; she is listed in the Directory under Arkansas. For a more thorough study on the subject, we recommend *The Collector's Encyclopedia of Pattern Glass*, by Mollie Helen McCain, available from Collector Books. See also Bread Plates; Cruets; Historical Glass; Salt and Pepper Shakers; Salts, Open; Sugar Shakers; Syrups; specific manufacturers such as Northwood.

Note: Values are given for open sugar bowls and compotes unless noted 'w/lid.'

Actress, bottle, scent; 11"	48.00
Actress, bowl, 9½"	68.00
Actress, bread tray, Miss Neilson, 13"	70.00
Actress, celery vase, Pinafore scene	165.00
Actress, creamer	75.00
Actress, goblet	70.00
Actress, shakers, orig tops, pr	90.00
Actress, sugar bowl, w/lid	100.00
Admiral Dewey, see Dewey; See also Greentown, Dewey	
Alabama, butter dish, ruby stained	150.00
Alabama, creamer, ruby stained	55.00
Alabama, spooner	37.50
Almond Thumbprint, compote, high std, flint, 10½"	70.00
Almond Thumbprint, egg cup, flint	24.00
Almond Thumbprint, tumbler, ftd, flint	32.00
Amazon, banana stand	68.00
Amazon, butter dish	55.00
Amazon, pitcher, water	55.00
Amazon, wine, etched	24.00
Amberette, see Klondike	
Anthemion, marmalade	38.00
Anthemion, pitcher, water; 8¼"	45.00
Apollo, bowl, 8"	20.00
Apollo, butter dish, etched	58.00
Apollo, sugar bowl, w/lid	48.00
Apollo, tumbler, frosted	37.50
Arabesque, goblet	25.00
Argus, bottle, bitters	65.00
Argus, bowl, 5½"	45.00
Argus, celery vase, plain base	85.00
Argus, champagne	55.00
Argus, egg cup	25.00
Argus, mug, appl hdl	65.00

Argus, tumbler, ale; ftd, 5" 32.00
Art, biscuit jar, ruby stained 200.00
Art, compote, w/lid, 7" 50.00
Art, compote, w/lid, 9x9½" 50.00
Ashburton, bottle, water; tumble up, flint 100.00
Ashburton, egg cup, dbl, flint 57.00

Ashburton

Ashburton, goblet, flint 35.00
Ashburton, tumbler, bar; flint, 6½" 65.00
Atlas, celery vase 30.00
Atlas, salt cellar, ind 15.00
Atlas, sugar bowl, w/lid 40.00
Atlas, whiskey, ruby stained 45.00
Aurora, goblet, ruby stained 40.00
Aurora, waste bowl 27.50
Aurora, wine, ruby stained 40.00
Austrian, rose bowl 48.00
Austrian, sugar bowl 35.00
Austrian, tumbler 22.00
Austrian, wine...32.00
Baby Thumbprint, see Dakota
Balder, see Pennsylvania
Baltimore Pear, bread plate, 12½" 65.00
Baltimore Pear, cake stand, high std 50.00
Baltimore Pear, celery vase 55.00
Baltimore Pear, goblet 35.00
Banded Portland, candlestick, pr.......................................85.00
Banded Portland, relish, oval, 8½" 17.50
Banded Portland, toothpick holder 25.00
Bar & Diamond, cup & saucer 30.00
Bar & Diamond, shakers, orig tops, pr 48.00
Bar & Diamond, sugar bowl, w/lid....................................50.00
Bar & Diamond, water set, ruby stained 265.00
Bar & Diamond, wine 30.00
Barberry, butter dish, shell finial 65.00
Barberry, sauce dish, ftd 15.00
Barberry, tumbler, ftd...22.00
Barberry, wine 30.00
Barley, bowl, vegetable; oval, 10" 17.50
Barley, celery vase 25.00
Barley, cordial 48.00
Barley, spooner..22.00
Barred Forget-Me-Not, goblet 40.00
Barred Forget-Me-Not, sugar bowl, w/lid 40.00
Barrel Huber, see Huber
Basket Weave, mug, 3" 15.00
Basket Weave, pitcher, milk; gr..70.00
Basket Weave, plate, sq, 8" 32.00
Beaded Band, pickle dish, w/lid...40.00
Beaded Band, spooner...25.00
Beaded Band, wine 22.50
Beaded Grape, cake stand, 6x9" 62.50
Beaded Grape, sauce dish, hdls..15.00
Beaded Grape, tumbler, water; clear w/gold......................22.00
Beaded Medallion, bottle castor, orig stopper 26.00

Beaded Medallion, butter dish 42.50
Beaded Medallion, compote, low std, w/lid, 8¼" 85.00
Beaded Medallion, egg cup 22.50
Beaded Mirror, see Beaded Medallion
Beaded Panel, bowl, 8¼" 75.00
Beaded Rosette, goblet..40.00
Beaded Tulip, creamer 88.00
Beaded Tulip, plate, 6" 22.00
Beaded Tulip, tray, water 48.00
Bearded Head, see Viking
Bellflower, bottle, cologne; yel-gr opaque, rpl stopper, 9" 525.00
Bellflower, celery vase 145.00
Bellflower, champagne, bbl form, single vine 100.00
Bellflower, creamer, fine rib, single vine 145.00
Bellflower, decanter, dbl vine, w/orig stopper, pt............235.00
Bellflower, egg cup, single vine..40.00
Bellflower, goblet, bbl form, single vine 38.00
Bellflower, honey dish, 3"..25.00
Bellflower, pitcher, milk; 7¾" 325.00
Bellflower, pitcher, water; dbl vine 300.00
Bellflower, plate, fine rib, single vine, 6" 95.00
Bellflower, syrup, appl hdl, David Baker Pat lid..............500.00
Bellflower, tumbler, bar; fine rib, single vine 85.00
Bellflower, tumbler, water; dbl vine 100.00
Bellflower, wine, bbl form, knop stem, flint.....................100.00
Bent Buckle, see New Hampshire
Bevelled Diamond & Star, pitcher, milk; 7"......................30.00
Bevelled Diamond & Star, shakers, pr 17.50
Bigler, celery vase..90.00
Bigler, champagne 95.00
Bigler, decanter, bar lip, 1-pt 60.00
Bigler, tumbler, short stem...57.00
Bird & Fern, see Hummingbird
Bird & Strawberry, bowl, 5½" 32.00
Bird & Strawberry, butter dish 115.00
Bird & Strawberry, sugar bowl, w/lid.................................75.00
Bird & Strawberry, tumbler 50.00
Birds in Swamp, goblet 70.00
Blaze, creamer, molded hdl...48.00
Bleeding Heart, bowl, 8"..37.50
Bleeding Heart, cake stand, 9¼" 70.00
Bleeding Heart, pitcher, water; appl hdl 150.00
Bleeding Heart, wine, knob stem 165.00
Block, celery, ruby stained 18.00
Block, tumbler, ruby stained...35.00
Block & Fan, bowl, berry; ftd, 8" 22.50
Block & Fan, cookie jar 68.00
Block & Fan, finger bowl...30.00
Block & Fan, goblet, ruby stained 98.00
Block & Star Spearpoint, goblet 17.50
Block w/Thumbprint, goblet 18.00
Blue Jay, see Cardinal Bird
Bosworth, butter dish 27.50
Bouquet, pitcher, water...40.00
Bouquet, sugar bowl, w/lid...32.00
Bow Tie, butter dish 75.00
Bow Tie, cake stand, 9" 60.00
Bow Tie, pitcher, 5½" 45.00
Bow Tie, salt cellar, master...40.00
Bradford Blackberry, goblet, flint 67.50
Broken Column, banana stand...115.00
Broken Column, claret 68.00
Broken Column, compote, w/lid, ruby stained, 10" 345.00
Broken Column, relish, oval, 11x5"....................................25.00

Broken Column, spooner..32.50
Broken Column, spooner, ruby stained................................120.00
Buckle, champagne, flint...65.00
Buckle, creamer..32.00
Buckle, goblet, flint 40.00
Buckle, lamp, brass/iron base 175.00
Buckle, sugar bowl, w/lid 45.00
Buckle, wine..45.00
Buckle w/Star, creamer 35.00
Buckle w/Star, mug 55.00
Buckle w/Star, sauce dish, ftd 10.00
Buckle w/Star, tumbler, bar 60.00
Bull's Eye, spill holder...35.00
Bull's Eye, spooner 42.00
Bull's Eye, sugar bowl, w/lid 125.00
Bull's Eye & Daisy, creamer 24.00
Bull's Eye & Daisy, shaker 18.00
Bull's Eye & Daisy, tumbler, water; clear w/gold...............17.50
Bull's Eye & Daisy, wine, ruby stained 44.00
Bull's Eye & Fan, creamer, 3¼" 15.00
Bull's Eye & Fan, pitcher, lemonade; ftd............................50.00
Bull's Eye & Fan, pitcher, water; tankard form 42.50
Bull's Eye & Spearhead, compote, Findlay, 7½" 55.00
Bull's Eye Band, see Reverse Torpedo
Bull's Eye in Heart, see Heart w/Thumbprint
Bull's Eye w/Diamond Point, bottle, scent 85.00

Bull's Eye w/Diamond Point

Bull's Eye w/Diamond Point, celery 160.00
Bull's Eye w/Diamond Point, sauce 22.00
Bull's Eye w/Fleur-de-Lis, ale glass, rare 195.00
Bull's Eye w/Fleur-de-Lis, butter dish 100.00
Bull's Eye w/Fleur-de-Lis, goblet 80.00
Bull's Eye w/Fleur-de-Lis, sugar bowl, w/lid 115.00
Button Arches, mug, ruby stained 27.50
Button Arches, punch cup..12.50
Button Arches, toothpick holder 22.50
Button Arches, wine, ruby stained, vintage etched 35.00
Cabbage Rose, champagne 45.00
Cabbage Rose, compote, w/lid, 7½" 90.00
Cabbage Rose, egg cup 30.00
Cabbage Rose, pitcher, 3-pt 150.00
Cabbage Rose, spooner 25.00
Cable, butter dish...95.00
Cable, champagne 215.00
Cable, honey dish 18.00
Cable, spooner 38.00
California, see Beaded Grape
Canadian, bowl, 4½x7"...65.00
Canadian, celery vase..50.00
Canadian, spooner 48.00
Cane, goblet, bl...37.50
Cane, goblet, vaseline..40.00
Cane, pitcher, water...48.00

Cane, relish, oval, 5½x8"...15.00
Cane, wine 22.50
Cardinal Bird, butter dish 85.00
Cardinal Bird, goblet 33.00
Cardinal Bird, honey dish 22.50
Cathedral, bowl, amethyst, 8" 68.00
Cathedral, cake stand, bl, 4½x10"..55.00
Cathedral, goblet, ruby stained..72.50
Cathedral, relish tray, fish shape, vaseline 50.00
Cathedral, spooner, vaseline 45.00
Centennial, see Liberty Bell
Chain, bread plate 28.00
Chain, goblet 22.50
Chain, spooner..27.50
Chain w/Diamonds, see Washington Centennial
Chain w/Star, creamer 25.00
Chain w/Star, pitcher, water 65.00
Chain w/Star, plate, 7"...22.00
Champion, goblet, amber stained...67.50
Champion, pitcher, water 65.00
Champion, tumbler 18.00
Chandelier, butter dish, etched 90.00
Chandelier, creamer 32.00
Chandelier, goblet, etched 60.00
Chandelier, tumbler, water; etched.......................................38.00
Checkerboard, compote, 8" 27.50
Checkerboard, punch cup...8.00
Cherry & Cable, pitcher, water...82.00
Chrysanthemum Leaf, vase, bulbous w/flutes, Sandwich, 7"........125.00
Classic, butter dish, log ft 195.00
Classic, pitcher, water; collared style 225.00
Classic, plate, 10"...180.00
Classic, sauce dish, ftd 30.00
Coin, see US Coin
Colorado, cake stand 65.00
Colorado, celery vase..45.00
Colorado, shaker..32.00
Colorado, vase, 12"..42.50
Columbian Coin, butter dish, frosted coins 165.00
Columbian Coin, creamer, gold coins.................................140.00
Columbian Coin, spooner, frosted coins 60.00
Columbian Coin, spooner, gold coins 65.00
Comet, pitcher, water 525.00
Comet, tumbler, water 115.00
Comet, tumbler, whiskey; hdld 225.00
Compact, see Snail
Connecticut, celery vase...25.00
Connecticut, pitcher, water..48.00
Coral Gables, wine...50.00
Cord & Tassel, egg cup...37.50
Cord & Tassel, spooner 30.00
Cord & Tassel, sugar bowl 50.00
Cord Drapery, creamer, 5" 55.00
Cord Drapery, mug 38.00
Cottage, champagne, ruby stained..78.00
Cottage, creamer..32.00
Croesus, bowl, gr w/gold, 8"...115.00
Croesus, butter dish, purple w/gold 220.00
Croesus, creamer, regular, purple w/gold............................140.00
Croesus, toothpick holder, purple w/gold...........................110.00
Croesus, tumbler, water; gr w/gold.......................................50.00
Crow's Foot, see Yale
Crown Jewels, see Chandelier
Cryptic, see Zippered Block

Crystal Wedding, compote, high std, 7x13" 115.00
Crystal Wedding, creamer, etched 56.00
Crystal Wedding, plate, ruby stained, 10" 47.50
Crystal Wedding, vase, twisted, ftd 27.50
Cube w/Fan, see Pineapple & Fan
Cupid & Venus, compote, w/lid, high std, 8" 95.00
Cupid & Venus, cruet 80.00
Cupid & Venus, marmalade jar 80.00
Cupid & Venus, wine 90.00
Currant, cordial 48.00
Currant, egg cup 18.00
Currant, goblet, buttermilk 35.00
Currant, wine 37.50
Currier & Ives, bottle, bitters 35.00
Currier & Ives, plate, 10" 18.00
Currier & Ives, shaker 15.00
Currier & Ives, waste bowl 40.00
Curtain, butter dish 55.00
Curtain, celery vase 30.00
Curtain, creamer 28.00
Curtain Tie-Back, goblet, flat base 25.00
Curtain Tie-Back, relish 12.50
Cut Log, compote, high std, 8¼x6½" 50.00
Cut Log, compote, w/lid, 7½x5½" 48.00
Cut Log, vase, 16" 37.50
Cut Log, wine 25.00
Dahlia, butter dish 50.00
Dahlia, egg cup, dbl 58.00
Dahlia, mug, sm 32.00
Dahlia, pitcher, water; vaseline 90.00
Dahlia, spooner 30.00
Daisy & Button, bottle, cologne; orig stopper 25.00
Daisy & Button, celery vase 32.00
Daisy & Button, creamer, ruby stained 40.00
Daisy & Button, dish, fan shape, 7x10½" 20.00
Daisy & Button, tumbler, water; amber 24.00
Daisy & Button w/Crossbar, celery vase, vaseline 52.00
Daisy & Button w/Crossbar, compote, 8½" 30.00
Daisy & Button w/Crossbar, goblet, bl 40.00
Daisy & Button w/Thumbprint, butter dish 80.00
Daisy & Button w/V Ornament, finger bowl 25.00
Daisy & Button w/V Ornament, pitcher, water; amber 95.00
Daisy & Button w/V Ornament, sauce dish, flat 15.00
Dakota, celery vase, ped ft 27.50
Dakota, compote, 9x8" 58.00
Dakota, condiment tray, metal hdls 78.00
Dakota, spooner, ped ft, etched 37.50
Dakota, waste bowl 60.00
Dakota, wine 28.00
Dart, creamer 32.00
Dart, goblet 25.00
Dart, tumbler 15.00
Deer & Dog, marmalade jar 95.00
Deer & Dog, spooner 60.00
Deer & Dog, wine 75.00
Deer & Oak Tree, pitcher, water 155.00
Deer & Pine Tree, creamer, apple gr 90.00
Deer & Pine Tree, mug, bl, lg 50.00
Deer & Pine Tree, platter, 13x8" 55.00
Delaware, butter dish, rose w/gold 145.00
Delaware, creamer, rose w/gold 70.00
Delaware, jug, claret; tankard shape 120.00
Dew & Raindrop, bowl, berry; 8" 40.00
Dew & Raindrop, pitcher, water 45.00

Dew & Raindrop, punch cup 7.50
Dewdrop, egg cup, dbl 22.00
Dewdrop, mug, appl hdl 27.50
Dewdrop, relish 15.00
Dewdrop Band, goblet 12.50
Dewdrop w/Star, creamer, appl hdl 34.00
Dewey, mug 35.00
Dewey, plate, ftd 17.50
Dewey, see also Greentown, Dewey
Dewey, sugar bowl, w/lid 35.00
Dewey, tumbler 48.00
Diagonal Band, cake stand 28.00
Diagonal Band, goblet 27.50
Diagonal Band, goblet, gr 45.00
Diagonal Band, wine 25.00
Diagonal Band w/Fan, butter dish 40.00
Diagonal Band w/Fan, compote, 7½" 27.50
Diagonal Band w/Fan, plate, 8" 12.50
Diamond & Sunburst, spooner 20.00
Diamond & Sunburst, sugar shaker 24.00
Diamond Cut w/Leaf, creamer 23.00
Diamond Horseshoe, see Aurora
Diamond Medallion, see Grand
Diamond Point, celery, flint 75.00
Diamond Point, decanter, flint, 1-qt 175.00
Diamond Point, goblet 40.00
Diamond Point, pitcher, water; tankard form, flint, qt 175.00
Diamond Point, sugar bowl, w/lid, flint 75.00
Diamond Quilted, champagne 20.00
Diamond Quilted, compote, low std, amber, 5½" dia 15.00
Diamond Quilted, pitcher, water; bl 95.00
Diamond Quilted, tumbler, bl 44.00
Diamond Thumbprint, cake stand, 3x8⅜" 190.00
Diamond Thumbprint, cordial 300.00
Diamond Thumbprint, spooner 85.00
Diamond Thumbprint, tumbler, bar 135.00
Dinner Bell, see Cottage
Doric, see Feather
Double Leaf & Dart, see Leaf & Dart
Drapery, compote, low std 60.00
Drapery, plate, 6" 32.00
Drapery, spooner 30.00
Drapery, tumbler 28.00
Drum, creamer 50.00
Egg in Sand, dish, swan center 45.00
Egg in Sand, tray, water 38.00

Egg in Sand

Egg in Sand, tumbler 35.00
Egg in Sand, wine 32.00
Egyptian, celery vase 80.00
Egyptian, pickle dish, oval 27.50
Egyptian, pitcher, water 195.00
Egyptian, sugar bowl, w/lid 70.00

Elephant, see Jumbo
Emerald Green Herringbone, see Florida
Empress, butter dish 55.00
Empress, sugar bowl, gr w/gold, w/lid 115.00
Empress, tumbler, gr w/gold 50.00
English Hobnail Cross, see Klondike
Esther, compote, jelly; gr w/gold 60.00
Esther, cruet, orig stopper, gr w/gold 225.00
Esther, ice cream tray, gr w/gold 150.00
Esther, jelly compote, gr w/gold 50.00
Esther, sauce bowl, ftd, gr w/gold 17.50
Esther, sugar bowl, w/lid 45.00
Etched Dakota, see Dakota
Eureka, compote, jelly 50.00
Eureka, cordial 40.00
Eureka, salt cellar, ftd 37.50
Eureka, wine 30.00
Excelsior, champagne, flint 65.00
Excelsior, cordial, flint 45.00
Excelsior, creamer, flint 85.00
Excelsior, sugar bowl, w/lid, flint 85.00
Eyewinker, banana stand, high std 150.00
Eyewinker, sauce dish, flat, sq, 3¾" 15.00
Eyewinker, tumbler 30.00
Fairfax Strawberry, see Strawberry
Fan w/Crossbars, see Champion
Fan w/Diamond, pitcher, water 55.00
Fan w/Diamond, spooner 20.00
Feather, goblet 58.00
Feather, tumbler, water 50.00
Festoon, creamer 45.00
Festoon, relish dish, 9x5½" 36.00
Festoon, waste bowl 35.00
Fine Cut, plate, 10" 20.00
Fine Cut, tray, water 30.00
Fine Cut, tumbler, water 17.50
Fine Cut & Block, butter dish, ftd 78.00
Fine Cut & Block, goblet, pk blocks 45.00
Fine Cut & Block, pitcher, water; amber 88.00
Fine Cut & Block, tumbler, bl 32.00
Fine Cut & Diamond, see Grand
Fine Cut & Feather, see Feather
Fine Cut & Panel, celery vase 32.00
Fine Cut & Panel, plate, bl, 7" 30.00
Fine Cut & Panel, tumbler, vaseline 40.00
Fine Rib, butter dish, flint 75.00
Fine Rib, cordial, flint 90.00
Fine Rib, honey dish, flint, 3½" dia 20.00
Fine Rib, salt cellar, ind; flint 30.00
Fine Rib w/Cut Ovals, goblet, flint 235.00
Fingerprint, see Almond Thumbprint
Fishscale, cake stand, 10½" 35.00
Fishscale, plate, sq, 9" 30.00
Fishscale, relish tray, teardrop shape 20.00
Flamingo Habitat, champagne 40.00
Flamingo Habitat, sugar bowl, w/lid 48.00
Flamingo Habitat, tumbler 32.00
Flat Diamond & Panel, tumbler, bar; flint 75.00
Florida, butter dish, gr 80.00
Florida, mustard pot 20.00
Florida, plate, 7½" 12.00
Florida, tumbler, water; gr 28.00
Flower Pot, goblet 38.00
Flower Pot, pitcher, milk 45.00

Flower Pot, sugar bowl 40.00
Flute, celery vase 75.00
Flute, goblet 30.00
Flute, tumbler, ale 48.00
Frosted Circle, cake stand, 8" 35.00
Frosted Circle, punch cup 18.00
Frosted Circle, tumbler 25.00
Frosted Circle, wine 40.00
Frosted Flower Band, sauce dish, ftd, 3⅜" 15.00
Frosted Leaf, compote, w/lid 265.00
Frosted Leaf, spooner 100.00
Frosted Leaf, tumbler, ftd 100.00
Frosted Leaf, wine 175.00
Frosted Lion, see Lion
Frosted Roman Key, butter dish 48.00
Frosted Roman Key, cordial 40.00
Frosted Roman Key, goblet 45.00
Frosted Stork, jam jar, w/lid 115.00
Frosted Stork, spooner 45.00
Frosted Stork, waste bowl 42.00
Galloway, carafe 78.00
Galloway, goblet 75.00
Galloway, pitcher, ruby stained, water sz 175.00
Galloway, punch bowl, 14" dia 140.00
Galloway, shakers, orig tops, clear w/gold, 3", pr ...32.00
Galloway, tumbler, ruby stained 55.00
Garden Fruits, sugar bowl, w/lid 27.50
Garfield Drape, goblet 32.00
Garfield Drape, pitcher, milk 60.00
Garfield Drape, spooner 28.00
Garfield Drape, sugar bowl, w/lid 65.00
Gem, see Nailhead
Good Luck, see Horseshoe
Gothic, celery vase 85.00
Gothic, goblet 55.00
Gothic, wine, 3¾" 125.00
Grand, bread plate, 10" 30.00
Grand, celery vase, ftd 25.00
Grand, cordial 58.00
Grand, waste bowl 32.00
Grape & Festoon w/Shield, compote, 10½" 62.50
Grape & Festoon w/Shield, creamer 35.00

Grape & Festoon w/Shield

Grape & Festoon w/Shield, relish, 4¼x7" 15.00
Grape & Festoon w/Shield, spooner 25.00
Grape & Festoon w/Stippled Leaf, creamer 48.00
Grape & Festoon w/Stippled Leaf, plate, 6" 18.00
Grape & Festoon w/Stippled Leaf, sugar bowl, w/lid ...60.00
Grape Band, tumbler, flint 37.50
Grape Band, wine, flint 37.50

Grasshopper, butter dish, amber 95.00
Grasshopper, pickle dish..22.50
Grasshopper, salt cellar..45.00
Grasshopper, sugar bowl, w/lid 44.00
Guardian Angel, see Cupid & Venus
Hairpin, celery vase..35.00
Hairpin, compote, high std, w/lid 235.00
Hairpin, goblet..42.50
Hairpin, pitcher, 8"..180.00
Halley's Comet, butter dish 75.00
Halley's Comet, creamer..38.00
Halley's Comet, salt cellar..22.00
Halley's Comet, tumbler..32.00
Halley's Comet, wine..28.00
Hamilton, cake stand..150.00
Hamilton, goblet..40.00
Hamilton, spooner..35.00
Hamilton, tumbler, water 75.00
Hamilton w/Leaf, goblet, clear leaf..45.00
Hamilton w/Leaf, tumbler 50.00
Hamilton w/Leaf, whiskey, hdl, clear leaf 95.00
Hand, cordial, 3½"..85.00
Hand, goblet 45.00
Hartley, creamer, vaseline 42.50
Hartley, sauce dish, ftd, amber, 4" 15.00
Hartley, tumbler..27.50
Hawaiian Lei, cake stand, 9¼" 30.00

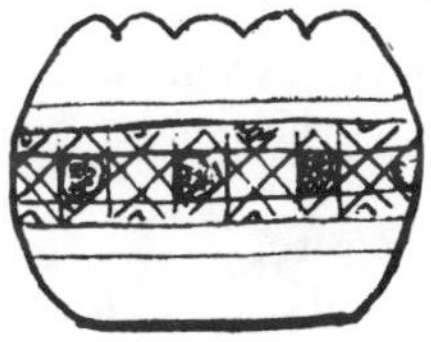

Hawaiian Lei

Hawaiian Lei, cup & saucer 38.00
Heart w/Thumbprint, creamer..40.00
Heart w/Thumbprint, cruet 80.00
Heart w/Thumbprint, goblet..55.00
Heart w/Thumbprint, vase, 10" 68.00
Hearts & Spades, see Medallion
Heavy Panelled Finecut, creamer, 6" 22.00
Heavy Panelled Finecut, goblet, vaseline 32.00
Heavy Panelled Finecut, salt cellar, ind 10.00
Herringbone Band, see Ripple
Herringbone Buttress, see Greentown, Herringbone Buttress
Hexagon Block, sauce dish, flat, etched, amber stained, 4¼" 12.50
Hickman, butter dish, gr..65.00
Hickman, compote, 5½x8"..20.00
Hickman, creamer, gr..35.00
Hickman, goblet 40.00
Hickman, nappy, 5"..12.00
Hidalgo, celery vase, flat base, amber stained 40.00
Hidalgo, compote, w/lid, 7"..45.00
Hidalgo, pickle dish, boat shape, amber stained 22.50
Hidalgo, pitcher, water 55.00
Hidalgo, tumbler..27.50
Hinoto, egg cup..38.00
Hinoto, salt cellar..38.00
Hinoto, tumbler, ftd..40.00
Hinoto, wine..65.00
Holly, creamer 135.00
Holly, goblet 95.00
Holly, sauce dish, flat..22.50
Holly, spooner..55.00

Holly Amber, see Greentown Holly Amber
Honeycomb, cake stand, 10½" 32.00
Honeycomb, compote, flint, 7"..50.00
Honeycomb, pitcher, water; flint, 9"..150.00
Honeycomb w/Flower Rim, bowl, berry; gr..46.00
Hops & Barley, see Wheat & Barley
Horn of Plenty, bowl, oval, flint, 6¼x9"..135.00
Horn of Plenty, celery, flint..180.00
Horn of Plenty, compote, flint, 6x8"..110.00
Horn of Plenty, creamer, flint, 7"..145.00
Horn of Plenty, goblet, flint 70.00
Horn of Plenty, spooner, flint..42.00
Horn of Plenty, tumbler, whiskey; hdl, flint 245.00
Horseshoe, butter dish..95.00
Horseshoe, doughnut stand 85.00
Horseshoe, plate, 10"..48.00
Horseshoe, salt cellar, ind..20.00
Horseshoe, sauce dish, ftd, 4"..16.00
Huber, decanter, bar lip, flint, 1-qt..88.00
Huber, salt cellar, ftd, flint..32.00
Huber, tumbler, lemonade; flint..27.50
Huber, tumbler, water; flint..22.50
Hummingbird, pitcher, milk..45.00
Hummingbird, pitcher, water; bl..126.00
Hummingbird, tumbler, amber..48.00
Hummingbird, waste bowl, 5¼"..37.50
Icicle w/Star, pitcher, water 25.00
Idaho, see Snail
Illinois, butter dish, sq, 7"..50.00
Illinois, olive dish 15.00
Illinois, sauce dish..12.50
Illinois, sugar bowl, w/lid 50.00
Illinois, toothpick holder 30.00
Inverted Fern, butter dish..110.00
Inverted Fern, honey dish 17.50
Inverted Fern, salt cellar, master..30.00
Inverted Fern, spooner..48.00
Inverted Fern, sugar bowl, w/lid..80.00
Invincible, sugar bowl, w/lid..55.00
Iris Column, see Broken Column
Iris w/Meander, see Opalescent Glass
Iris w/Meander, sugar bowl, w/lid, clear w/gold..55.00
Iris w/Meander, vase, clear w/gold, 11"..25.00
Ivy in Snow, creamer..17.50
Ivy in Snow, mug, ruby stained 47.50
Ivy in Snow, pitcher, milk; ruby stained 235.00
Ivy in Snow, wine 30.00
Jacob's Ladder, castor bottle 22.50
Jacob's Ladder, compote, high std, 10"..47.50
Jacob's Ladder, compote, 7x6"..30.00
Jacob's Ladder, goblet, water; amber 40.00
Jacob's Ladder, mug..115.00
Jacob's Ladder, pitcher, water..145.00
Jacob's Ladder, sauce dish, ftd, 4½"..15.00
Jacob's Ladder, wine..32.00
Jersey Swirl, butter dish, bl..65.00
Jersey Swirl, goblet, buttermilk..32.00
Jersey Swirl, salt cellar, ind, canary 20.00
Jersey Swirl, spooner, canary 17.50
Jersey Swirl, wine..18.00
Jewel Band, celery vase..38.00
Jewel Band, goblet 35.00
Jewel Band, pitcher, milk..42.00
Jewel Band, sauce dish, ftd..15.00

Jewel w/Dewdrop, wine, rare 65.00
Jewel w/Moondrop, cake plate 48.00
Jewel w/Moondrop, mug 48.00
Jewel w/Moondrop, pitcher, water 60.00
Jewel w/Moondrop, tumbler 42.50
Jewelled Moon & Star, carafe................................40.00
Jewelled Moon & Star, goblet 20.00
Jewelled Moon & Star, platter 45.00
Jewelled Moon & Star, sugar bowl, w/lid 60.00
Jewelled Moon & Star, tumbler, water; clear w/gold 30.00
Job's Tears, see Art
Jumbo, creamer 235.00
Jumbo, goblet 425.00
Jumbo, salt cellar..80.00
Jumbo, spoon rack 500.00
Jumbo, sugar bowl, w/lid 425.00
Kentucky, cup, gr 22.00
Kentucky, shakers, pr 60.00
Kentucky, toothpick holder 28.00
Kentucky, wine 30.00
Kentucky, wine, gr 37.50
King's Crown, cake stand 70.00
King's Crown, claret, ruby stained.........................55.00
King's Crown, compote, ruby stained, w/lid, 7" 185.00
King's Crown, cordial 40.00
King's Crown, pitcher, water tankard, 13" 125.00
King's Crown, plate, 7" 17.50
King's Crown, tumbler, ruby stained 35.00
King's Crown, wine 20.00
Klondike, butter dish, frosted w/amber stain.............385.00
Klondike, goblet, frosted w/amber stain 225.00
Klondike, relish, frosted w/amber stain, boat shape, 9x4" ...125.00
Klondike, shaker, clear w/amber stain, orig top 65.00
Klondike, sugar bowl, frosted w/amber stain 178.00
La Clede, see Hickman
Lace, see Drapery
Ladder w/Diamonds, creamer, ind; clear w/gold 15.00
Ladder w/Diamonds, shakers, pr 25.00
Lady Hamilton, butter dish.................................35.00
Lady Hamilton, egg cup, saucer base 22.00

Lady Hamilton

Lady Hamilton, sauce dish, flat, 4" 6.00
Lady Hamilton, tumbler, bar 36.00
Lawrence, see Bull's Eye
Leaf, see Maple Leaf
Leaf & Dart, butter dish...................................90.00
Leaf & Dart, pitcher, water................................85.00
Leaf & Dart, relish 17.50
Leaf & Dart, wine 34.00
Leaf Bracket, see Greentown, Leaf Bracket
Leaf Medallion, see Northwood, Leaf Medallion
Liberty Bell, creamer, appl reeded hdl.....................95.00
Liberty Bell, goblet.......................................40.00
Liberty Bell, pitcher, water..............................750.00
Liberty Bell, spooner......................................65.00
Liberty Bell, sugar bowl, w/lid............................95.00

Lily of the Valley, egg cup 45.00
Lily of the Valley, goblet 50.00
Lily of the Valley, honey dish 15.00
Lily of the Valley, sugar bowl, w/lid 80.00
Lincoln Drape, compote, med std, 8" 100.00
Lincoln Drape, creamer 150.00
Lincoln Drape, spill 45.00
Lincoln Drape w/Tassel, salt cellar, master 120.00
Lion, bowl, oval, frosted, 8" 70.00
Lion, champagne, frosted 165.00
Lion, compote, low std, frosted, 5x7¾" dia 65.00
Lion, egg cup, frosted 65.00
Lion, goblet...55.00
Lion, pickle dish 50.00
Lion, pitcher, water; 9"..................................250.00
Log Cabin, butter dish....................................265.00
Log Cabin, compote, 10½".................................285.00
Log Cabin, spooner..125.00
Log Cabin, sugar bowl, w/lid 275.00
Long Spear, see Grasshopper
Loop, egg cup, flint 32.50
Loop, goblet 18.00
Loop, salt cellar, master; flint 25.00
Loop, tumbler, water; flint................................22.00
Loop, wine, flint 32.00
Loop & Dart, cake stand, 10" 47.50
Loop & Dart, goblet..35.00
Loop & Dart, pitcher, water 75.00
Loop & Dart w/Diamond Ornament, celery vase 34.00
Loop & Dart w/Diamond Ornament, tumbler, ftd...............42.00
Loop & Dart w/Round Ornament, creamer 38.00
Loop & Dart w/Round Ornament, goblet 30.00
Loop & Dart w/Round Ornament, relish 20.00
Loop & Moose Eye, egg cup, flint...........................30.00
Loop w/Stippled Panels, see Texas
Louisianna, wine 35.00
Magnet & Grape, champagne, frosted leaf 150.00
Magnet & Grape, cordial, frosted leaf, 4" 145.00
Magnet & Grape, decanter, clear leaf, 1-qt.................90.00
Magnet & Grape, sugar bowl, w/lid, clear leaf 75.00
Magnet & Grape, whiskey, frosted leaf 135.00
Maine, compote, jelly; gr 70.00
Maine, sugar bowl, w/lid 48.00
Maine, wine, gr 70.00
Manhattan, creamer, ind 20.00
Manhattan, goblet, gold trim...............................22.50
Manhattan, vase, 7".......................................15.00
Maple Leaf, compote, jelly; amber, 9" 58.00
Maple Leaf, goblet, vaseline..............................100.00
Maple Leaf, sugar bowl, w/lid 75.00
Maryland, goblet, clear w/gold 30.00
Maryland, goblet, ruby stained 55.00
Maryland, plate, clear w/gold, 7" 22.50
Mascotte, compote, etched, 7x5"............................30.00
Mascotte, goblet...30.00
Mascotte, sugar bowl, w/lid................................45.00
Mascotte, tumbler, etched 32.00
Massachusetts, cordial.....................................55.00
Massachusetts, relish, 8½" 28.00
Massachusetts, tumbler, juice 22.00
Massachusetts, vase, trumpet form, 6½" 25.00
Medallion, cake stand 28.00
Medallion, celery vase, amber 32.00
Medallion, pitcher, water; bl 75.00

Medallion, sugar bowl, w/lid 32.50
Melrose, plate, 8" 12.00
Michigan, finger bowl 12.50
Michigan, pickle dish 10.00
Michigan, shakers, HP decor, orig tops, pr........50.00
Michigan, shakers, pr 40.00
Minerva, butter dish 95.00
Minerva, creamer..40.00
Minerva, spooner..42.00
Minnesota, carafe 40.00
Minnesota, creamer, ind....................................22.00
Minnesota, hair receiver....................................32.00
Minnesota, tumbler, water 20.00
Minor Block, see Mascotte
Mirror, see Galloway
Missouri, celery vase 30.00
Missouri, spooner..24.00
Monkey, butter dish..225.00
Monkey, spooner..85.00
Moon & Star, creamer 50.00
Moon & Star, egg cup..28.00
Moon & Star, goblet..40.00
Moon & Star, tray, water....................................75.00
Morning Glory, egg cup, Sandwich....................90.00
Nail, bowl, flat, ruby stained, etched, 6" 47.50
Nail, decanter 35.00
Nail, pitcher, water..80.00

Nail

Nail, sauce dish, ftd, 3½" 12.00
Nail, tumbler, ruby stained 65.00
Nail, wine, ruby stained....................................55.00
Nailhead, butter dish 45.00
Nailhead, pitcher, water; 9½" 45.00
Nailhead, plate, 9" 18.00
Nailhead, tumbler 40.00
New England Pineapple, champagne................185.00
New England Pineapple, creamer......................70.00
New England Pineapple, pitcher, water 310.00
New England Pineapple, sauce dish, flint 18.00
New England Pineapple, sugar bowl, w/lid, flint......125.00
New England Pineapple, tumbler, gr................38.00
New Hampshire, bowl, clear w/gold, 8" 16.00
New Hampshire, tumbler, clear w/gold............20.00
New Hampshire, vase, clear w/gold..................22.00
New Jersey, olive dish, clear w/gold................22.50
New Jersey, sauce dish, flat, clear w/gold, 4½"......12.50
New Jersey, wine, str sides, ruby stained 75.00
Notched Rib, see Broken Column
O'Hara Diamond, pitcher, water tankard..........40.00
Oak Leaf Band, butter dish................................45.00
Oak Leaf Band, pitcher, 6"................................35.00
Oak Leaf Band, relish 12.00
Oaken Bucket, see Wooden Pail
One Hundred & One, goblet 50.00

One Hundred & One, sauce dish 18.00
One Hundred & One, spooner............................40.00
One Hundred & One, sugar bowl, w/lid............45.00
One-O-One, see One Hundred & One
Open Rose, egg cup..28.00
Open Rose, pitcher, water 175.00
Open Rose, sugar bowl, w/lid 42.50
Oregon #1, creamer, ftd....................................38.00
Oregon #1, spooner, ftd....................................25.00
Oregon #1, tumbler, water................................28.00
Oregon #1, wine..45.00
Orion, see Cathedral
Ostrich Looking at Moon, goblet....................125.00
Palmette, cake stand..68.00
Palmette, cup plate..45.00
Palmette, pitcher, water 127.50
Palmette, spooner..32.00
Panelled Daisy, bowl, oval, 5¾x8¼"..................18.00
Panelled Daisy, goblet..27.50
Panelled Daisy, mug..28.00
Panelled Daisy, plate, sq, 9"..............................28.00
Panelled Dewdrop, pitcher, milk......................40.00
Panelled Dewdrop, sugar bowl, w/lid..............40.00
Panelled Dewdrop, wine....................................22.50
Panelled Forget-Me-Not, butter dish 45.00
Panelled Forget-Me-Not, creamer....................32.00
Panelled Forget-Me-Not, goblet........................28.00
Panelled Forget-Me-Not, sugar bowl, w/lid 42.00
Panelled Herringbone, see Florida
Panelled Nightshade, goblet, bl........................68.00
Panelled Nightshade, wine 20.00
Panelled Star & Button, compote, high std, 8½"......42.00
Panelled Star & Button, creamer......................35.00
Panelled Star & Button, pitcher, water............50.00
Panelled Star & Button, relish dish..................15.00
Panelled Star & Button, spooner......................25.00
Panelled Star & Button, wine............................20.00
Panelled Thistle, candy dish, ftd, sq, 6¼x5"......35.00
Panelled Thistle, goblet......................................38.00
Panelled Thistle, punch cup..............................27.50
Panelled Thistle, sugar bowl, w/lid..................30.00
Pavonia, compote, 7"..45.00
Pavonia, finger bowl, 7"....................................35.00
Pavonia, salt cellar, master 25.00
Pavonia, sugar bowl, w/lid 60.00
Pavonia, tumbler..35.00
Peerless, see Lady Hamilton
Pennsylvania, butter dish, clear w/gold..........60.00
Pennsylvania, cruet, gr......................................50.00
Pennsylvania, decanter, clear w/gold 125.00
Pennsylvania, sauce dish, flat, clear w/gold, 5¼"......10.00
Pennsylvania, shot glass, clear w/gold............14.00
Pennsylvania, tumbler, gr................................42.00
Pennsylvania, tumbler, water; clear w/gold....25.00
Pillow Encircled, pitcher, water; tankard form......45.00
Pillow Encircled, tumbler 25.00
Pineapple & Fan, celery tray............................32.00
Pineapple & Fan, pitcher, water......................75.00
Pineapple & Fan, tumbler, water; gr................50.00
Pineapple & Fan, vase, trumpet form, 10"........32.00
Pineapple & Fan, wine......................................10.00
Pineapple Stem, see Pavonia
Pioneer, see Westward Ho
Pioneer's Victoria, tumbler, water; ruby stained 25.00

Pittsburgh Daisy, wine 20.00
Pleat & Panel, butter dish, ftd 50.00
Pleat & Panel, goblet 25.00
Pleat & Panel, pitcher, milk 25.00
Pleat & Panel, sugar bowl 25.00
Plume, compote, w/lid, 6½x12" 88.00
Plume, relish 27.50
Plume, sugar bowl 20.00
Pointed Jewel, goblet 28.00
Pointed Jewel, sugar bowl, w/lid 30.00
Polar Bear, goblet 110.00
Polar Bear, pitcher, water; frosted 265.00
Polar Bear, tray, water; frosted, 16" 200.00
Polar Bear, waste bowl, frosted 100.00
Popcorn, butter dish 50.00
Popcorn, pickle dish, oval 15.00
Popcorn, sugar bowl, w/lid, w/ears 50.00
Popcorn, wine 32.00
Portland, celery tray, clear w/gold 20.00
Portland, spooner, clear w/gold 37.50
Portland, syrup, clear w/gold 85.00
Portland, tumbler, clear w/gold 22.00
Powder & Shot, creamer, flint 98.00
Powder & Shot, egg cup, flint 55.00
Powder & Shot, salt cellar, master; flint 40.00
Powder & Shot, sugar bowl, w/lid 88.00
Prayer Rug, see Horseshoe
Pressed Leaf, cordial 18.00
Pressed Leaf, spooner 20.00
Pressed Leaf, sugar bowl, w/lid 40.00
Pressed Leaf, wine 35.00
Primrose, creamer 30.00
Primrose, goblet 30.00
Primrose, plate, bl, 7" 20.00
Primrose, wine 20.00
Princess Feather, butter dish 50.00
Princess Feather, egg cup 35.00
Princess Feather, goblet 35.00
Princess Feather, nappy 25.00
Princess Feather, sauce dish, bl, flint 30.00
Priscilla, creamer 40.00
Priscilla, goblet 38.00
Priscilla, rose bowl, 3¾" 32.00
Priscilla, tumbler 26.00
Prism, tumbler, buttermilk 38.00
Prism w/Diamond Points, cruet 90.00
Prism w/Diamond Points, tumbler 40.00
Prism w/Diamond Points, wine 48.00
Pygmy, see Torpedo
Raindrop, creamer, bl 35.00
Raindrop, syrup 32.50
Recessed Pillared Red Top, see Nail
Red Block, creamer, lg 60.00
Red Block, mug 35.00
Red Block, salt cellar, ind 58.00
Red Block, tumbler, water 35.00
Red Block, wine 38.00
Red Top, see Button Arches
Regal Block, goblet 16.00
Regal Block, wine 18.00
Reverse Torpedo, celery vase 110.00
Reverse Torpedo, goblet 60.00
Reverse Torpedo, honey dish 165.00
Reverse Torpedo, pitcher, water; 10" 155.00

Reverse Torpedo, tumbler 40.00
Ribbed Ivy, butter dish 88.00
Ribbed Ivy, egg cup 30.00
Ribbed Ivy, goblet 40.00
Ribbed Ivy, spooner 40.00
Ribbed Ivy, tumbler, bar 95.00
Ribbed Palm, pitcher, water; 9" 245.00
Ribbed Palm, plate, 6" 50.00
Ribbed Palm, spooner 35.00
Ribbed Palm, sugar bowl, w/lid 65.00
Ribbon, cake stand, frosted, 8½" 47.50
Ribbon, creamer, frosted 40.00

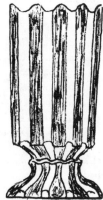

Ribbon

Ribbon, shaker, frosted 45.00
Ribbon, waste bowl, frosted 40.00
Ribbon Candy, claret 45.00
Ribbon Candy, cordial 42.50
Ribbon Candy, mug 24.00
Ribbon Candy, pitcher, milk 37.50
Ribbon Candy, plate, 11" 40.00
Ripple, goblet 20.00
Ripple, ice tub 50.00
Ripple, sugar bowl 15.00
Ripple, wine 18.00
Ripple Band, see Ripple
Rising Sun, cake plate, 10½" 28.00
Rising Sun, cruet 48.00
Rising Sun, goblet, purple trim 25.00
Rising Sun, tumbler, gr trim 32.00
Rising Sun, wine 18.00
Rochelle, see Princess Feather
Roman Key, champagne, frosted 75.00
Roman Key, egg cup, frosted 40.00
Roman Key, goblet, frosted 50.00
Roman Key, sugar bowl, frosted, w/lid 80.00
Roman Key, wine, frosted 65.00
Roman Rosette, bowl, 6" 14.00
Roman Rosette, celery vase 32.00
Roman Rosette, cordial 48.00
Roman Rosette, shakers, pr 30.00
Roman Rosette, tumbler, lemonade 34.00
Rope Bands, creamer 25.00
Rope Bands, tumbler 17.50
Rose in Snow, butter dish, bl 145.00
Rose in Snow, creamer, sq 55.00
Rose in Snow, goblet, bl 45.00
Rose in Snow, pitcher, water 135.00
Rose in Snow, platter, oval 135.00
Rose in Snow, sauce dish, flat, 4" 8.00
Rose in Snow, tumbler, bar 65.00

Rose in Snow, tumbler, bar, amber 65.00
Rose Sprig, bowl, 9" 20.00
Rose Sprig, creamer, yel 38.00

Rose Sprig

Rose Sprig, goblet 30.00
Rose Sprig, pitcher, water 47.50
Rose Sprig, sauce dish, ftd, bl 18.00
Rosette, cake stand, 7" 30.00
Rosette, goblet 32.00
Rosette, pickle dish 15.00
Rosette, plate, hdls, 9" 15.00
Rosette, tumbler, 5" 20.00
Rosette, waste bowl 27.50
Rosette & Palms, plate, 10" 18.00
Rosette & Palms, sugar bowl, w/lid 40.00
Royal Ivy, see Northwood, Royal Ivy
Royal Oak, see Northwood, Royal Oak
Ruby Thumbprint, see King's Crown
Sandwich Star, butter dish 175.00
Sandwich Star, compote, low std, 8½" 58.00
Sandwich Star, decanter, bar lip, 1-pt 65.00
Sandwich Star, spill holder 60.00
Sandwich Star, spill holder, clambroth 435.00
Sawtooth, creamer, flint 85.00
Sawtooth, creamer, pressed hdl 35.00
Sawtooth, salt cellar, flint 32.00
Sawtooth, spooner 25.00
Sawtooth, tumbler, bar; flint 60.00
Sawtooth, wine, flint 36.00
Sawtooth Band, see Amazon
Scalloped Daisy Red Top, see Button Arches
Scroll, celery vase 30.00
Scroll, pitcher, water 88.00
Scroll, wine 38.00
Scroll w/Flowers, cordial 38.00
Scroll w/Flowers, mustard jar 45.00
Scroll w/Flowers, pickle dish, hdls 22.50
Scroll w/Flowers, spooner 25.00
Scroll w/Flowers, sugar bowl, w/lid 55.00
Sedan, see Panelled Star & Button
Seneca Loop, see Loop
Sequoia, see Heavy Panelled Finecut
Shell & Jewel, creamer 32.00
Shell & Jewel, pitcher, water 35.00
Shell & Jewel, relish dish, oblong 20.00
Shell & Jewel, sauce dish 7.50
Shell & Jewel, tumbler 20.00
Shell & Jewel, tumbler, amber 30.00
Shell & Tassel, butter dish, dog finial 110.00

Shell & Tassel, goblet, knop stem 32.00
Shell & Tassel, spooner, rnd 35.00
Shell & Tassel, sugar bowl, sq 27.50
Sheraton, goblet, bl 40.00
Sheraton, plate, sq, 8½" 12.00
Sheraton, relish, hdld, bl 20.00
Sheraton, spooner, amber 32.00
Sheraton, wine 20.00
Shoshone, carafe 35.00
Shoshone, celery vase, ruby stained 78.00
Shoshone, creamer, gr 45.00
Shoshone, relish dish, 7½" 12.50
Shoshone, toothpick holder, clear w/gold 32.00
Shoshone, wine 42.00
Shovel, compote, jelly 18.00
Shovel, tumbler 15.00
Shrine, pickle dish 18.00
Shuttle, cordial 38.00
Shuttle, mug 25.00
Shuttle, see also Greentown, Shuttle
Shuttle, shaker 55.00
Shuttle, spooner 30.00
Skilton, creamer, ruby stained 35.00
Skilton, pitcher, water 45.00
Skilton, relish 15.00
Skilton, shakers, pr 48.00
Skilton, tray, water 50.00
Skilton, wine 30.00
Smocking, butter dish 80.00
Smocking, creamer, ind 110.00
Smocking, goblet 40.00
Smocking, sugar bowl, w/lid 125.00
Smocking, wine 55.00
Snail, basket, ruby stained, 8" 55.00
Snail, creamer 70.00
Snail, plate, 5" 40.00
Snail, rose bowl, 5" 55.00
Snail, salt cellar, master, ruby stained 90.00
Snail, shakers, pr 65.00
Snail, shakers, ruby stained, pr 98.00
Snakeskin & Dot, celery vase 32.00
Snakeskin & Dot, creamer 35.00
Snakeskin & Dot, goblet 32.00
Snakeskin & Dot, plate, amber, 4½" 10.00
Snakeskin & Dot, sugar bowl, w/lid 38.00
Spades, see Medallion
Spirea Band, bowl, bl, 8" 48.00
Spirea Band, cordial, amber 40.00
Spirea Band, platter, bl, 10¾x8½" 40.00
Spirea Band, platter, vaseline, 10½" 38.00
Spirea Band, wine 25.00
Spirea Band, wine, vaseline 32.00
Sprig, cake stand 40.00
Sprig, goblet 32.00
Sprig, pitcher, water 50.00
Sprig, sugar bowl, w/lid 50.00
Squirrel, creamer, rare 85.00
Squirrel, sugar bowl 55.00
Star Rosetted, butter dish 45.00
Star Rosetted, creamer 36.00
Star Rosetted, spooner 22.00
Star Rosetted, sugar bowl, w/lid 45.00
Stars & Stripes, cordial 18.00
Stars & Stripes, creamer 22.00

Stars & Stripes, shaker...15.00
Stars & Stripes, wine 15.00
States, cocktail, flared, clear w/gold 24.00
States, nappy, hdls, clear w/gold 25.00
States, punch bowl, clear w/gold, 5½x13".......75.00
States, toothpick holder, clear w/gold 40.00
States, tumbler, clear w/gold 22.00
States, wine, clear w/gold..28.00
Stedman, champagne..38.00
Stedman, egg cup...22.00
Stedman, goblet..30.00
Stedman, sauce dish, flat, 4"......................................15.00
Stedman, spooner 15.00
Stedman, syrup, 8¼"...98.00
Stepped Flute, champagne, flint 37.50
Stippled Chain, cake stand...48.00
Stippled Chain, egg cup...28.00
Stippled Chain, goblet..22.50
Stippled Chain, spooner 25.00
Stippled Chain, sugar bowl, w/lid 38.00
Stippled Double Loop, butter dish 45.00
Stippled Double Loop, creamer 32.00
Stippled Double Loop, sugar bowl, w/lid.................35.00
Stippled Double Loop, tumbler 25.00
Stippled Forget-Me-Not, butter dish........................45.00
Stippled Forget-Me-Not, pitcher, milk 38.00

Stippled Forget-Me-Not

Stippled Forget-Me-Not, sugar bowl, w/lid 36.00
Stippled Forget-Me-Not, tray, water............................70.00
Stippled Grape & Festoon, creamer 45.00
Stippled Grape & Festoon, goblet...............................30.00
Stippled Grape & Festoon, salt cellar, master 25.00
Stippled Grape & Festoon, sugar bowl, w/lid...........55.00
Stippled Grape & Festoon, wine 40.00
Stippled Ivy, egg cup 25.00
Stippled Ivy, sauce dish, flat 10.00
Stippled Ivy, spooner 28.00
Stippled Ivy, sugar bowl, w/lid....................................36.00
Stippled Panelled Flower, see Maine
Stippled Scroll, see Scroll
Stork, celery vase, frosted 65.00
Straight Banded Worchester, tumbler, ftd 40.00
Strawberry, spooner 35.00
Strawberry, wine 98.00
Strawberry & Currant, butter dish 48.00
Strawberry & Currant, mug 36.00
Strawberry & Currant, pitcher, milk..........................42.00
Strigil, celery tray 15.00
Strigil, goblet...42.50
Strigil, punch cup...12.50
Strigil, wine 25.00
Sunburst, plate, 7"..9.00
Sunk Honeycomb, cup & saucer, ruby stained.......32.00
Sunk Honeycomb, punch cup 7.50
Sunk Honeycomb, shakers, pr 14.00

Sunk Honeycomb, shakers, ruby stained, pr 40.00
Sunk Honeycomb, tumbler, eng................................25.00
Sunk Honeycomb, wine, ruby stained....................35.00
Sunken Primrose, see Florida
Swan, celery vase...55.00
Swan, creamer...45.00
Swan, mug...30.00
Swan, mustard jar, amber..78.00
Swan, spooner...48.00
Swan, sugar bowl, w/lid...125.00
Tape Measure, goblet..20.00
Teardrop, tumbler, water; etched...............................22.50
Teardrop & Diamond Block, see Art
Teardrop & Tassel, butter dish, emerald gr.............175.00
Teardrop & Tassel, celery vase 40.00
Teardrop & Tassel, goblet, cobalt 130.00
Teardrop & Tassel, pitcher, water 70.00
Teardrop & Tassel, sauce dish 13.00
Texas, butter dish, rose stained 125.00
Texas, goblet, clear w/gold...65.00
Texas, pitcher, water; clear w/gold..........................120.00
Texas, plate, rose stained 65.00
Texas, toothpick holder, rose stained 90.00
Texas, wine, rose stained 98.00
Theatrical, see Actress
Thousand Eye, cake stand, 3-knob stem, gr 60.00
Thousand Eye, egg cup, gr 88.00
Three Face, biscuit jar 900.00
Three Face, butter dish...145.00
Three Face, celery vase 125.00
Three Face, champagne, saucer type.........................150.00
Three Face, claret 125.00
Three Face, compote, 7½x6" 75.00
Three Face, creamer 125.00
Three Face, marmalade jar 225.00
Three Face, pitcher, water...325.00
Three Face, spooner...80.00
Three Face, sugar bowl, w/lid 120.00
Three Panel, bowl, amber, 7".......................................25.00
Three Panel, creamer..25.00
Three Panel, goblet, vaseline 40.00
Three Panel, mug..24.00
Three Panel, tumbler..12.50
Thumbprint, see Argus
Thumbprint Band, see Dakota
Thunderbird, see Hummingbird
Torpedo, bowl, flat, 8½x2¾"..18.00
Torpedo, butter dish..88.00
Torpedo, cup & saucer 60.00
Torpedo, spooner 45.00
Torpedo, sugar bowl...32.00
Torpedo, tumbler, water; ruby stained 45.00
Torpedo, wine 88.00
Tree of Life, compote, w/lid, 6x8" 75.00
Tree of Life, salt cellar, ftd, gr opaque 98.00
Triangular Prism, goblet 18.00
Triple Triangle, mug, ruby stained 35.00
Triple Triangle, wine, ruby stained 48.00
Truncated Cube, butter dish, ruby stained 85.00
Truncated Cube, decanter, 12" 60.00
Truncated Cube, salt cellar, ruby stained 20.00
Truncated Cube, spooner, ruby stained 48.00
Truncated Cube, tumbler, ruby stained 38.00
Tulip w/Ribs, tumbler, whiskey; hdld, flint..............45.00

Tulip w/Sawtooth, bottle, bar; flint 75.00
Tulip w/Sawtooth, creamer, flint 85.00
Tulip w/Sawtooth, spooner, flint 38.00
Tulip w/Sawtooth, tumbler, flint 32.00
Two Panel, creamer 30.00
Two Panel, marmalade 35.00
Two Panel, pitcher, water; gr 60.00
Two Panel, salt cellar, amber, master 22.50
Two Panel, sauce dish, ftd, oval, amber 15.00
Two Panel, spooner, amber 36.00
US Coin, bowl, frosted, 9" 325.00
US Coin, champagne, frosted 365.00
US Coin, compote, frosted, 6½x8½" 235.00
US Coin, compote, w/lid, high std, frosted, 8" 450.00
US Coin, creamer 325.00
US Coin, creamer, frosted 350.00
US Coin, spooner 225.00
US Coin, sugar bowl, w/lid, frosted 365.00
US Coin, tumbler, clear 145.00
US Coin, tumbler, frosted 225.00
Valencia Waffle, butter dish, amber 65.00
Valencia Waffle, creamer 40.00
Valencia Waffle, pitcher, water 42.00
Valencia Waffle, salt cellar, master 24.00
Valencia Waffle, tumbler, ruby stained 32.00
Vermont, basket, clear w/gold 32.00
Vermont, creamer, gr w/gold, 4" 50.00
Vermont, goblet, clear w/gold 42.00
Vermont, pitcher, water; gr w/gold 120.00
Vermont, see also Custard Glass
Vermont, tumbler, clear w/gold 18.00
Vermont, tumbler, gr w/gold 40.00
Viking, butter dish 68.00
Viking, creamer 55.00
Viking, mug 60.00
Viking, shaving mug, milk glass 65.00
Viking, sugar bowl, w/lid 65.00
Waffle, salt cellar, master 30.00
Waffle, tumbler, bar 70.00
Waffle & Thumbprint, champagne 95.00
Waffle & Thumbprint, goblet, knop stem 62.00
Waffle & Thumbprint, salt cellar, master 42.00
Waffle & Thumbprint, tumbler, whiskey 90.00
Waffle & Thumbprint, whiskey 90.00
Waffle & Thumbprint, wine 70.00
Washington, celery vase 90.00
Washington, claret 140.00
Washington, egg cup 60.00
Washington, pitcher, water 275.00
Washington, salt cellar, master; rnd 30.00
Washington Centennial, cake stand 88.00
Washington Centennial, creamer, appl hdl 75.00
Washington Centennial, pitcher, milk 90.00
Washington Centennial, salt cellar, master 35.00
Washington Centennial, toothpick holder 55.00
Washington Centennial, tumbler, bar 60.00
Wedding Bells, goblet 45.00
Wedding Bells, spooner 38.00
Wedding Bells, sugar bowl, w/lid 50.00
Wedding Bells, wine 25.00
Wedding Ring, butter dish 78.00
Wedding Ring, goblet 45.00
Wedding Ring, pitcher, milk 88.00
Wedding Ring, sugar bowl, w/lid 75.00

Wedding Ring, syrup 97.50
Wedding Ring, tumbler 80.00
Westward Ho, celery vase 115.00
Westward Ho, compote, low std, 6" dia 95.00
Westward Ho, compote, w/lid, 8" dia 275.00
Westward Ho, creamer 100.00
Westward Ho, goblet 75.00
Westward Ho, pitcher, water 245.00
Westward Ho, platter, 13x9" 170.00
Westward Ho, spooner 80.00
Westward Ho, sugar bowl, w/lid, 4½" 170.00
Wheat & Barley, butter dish, amber 45.00
Wheat & Barley, mug 22.50
Wheat & Barley, plate, hdls, amber, 9" 25.00
Wheat & Barley, plate, 7" 20.00
Wheat & Barley, salt cellar, bl 37.50
Wheat & Barley, spooner 20.00
Wheat & Barley, tumbler 22.00
Wildflower, cake stand 48.00
Wildflower, creamer 40.00
Wildflower, pitcher, water 50.00
Wildflower, pitcher, water; amber 70.00
Wildflower, relish 20.00
Wildflower, shaker 20.00
Willow Oak, bowl, w/lid, 7" 40.00
Willow Oak, butter dish 45.00
Willow Oak, mug, amber, 3¾" 40.00
Willow Oak, shaker, amber 32.00
Willow Oak, sugar bowl, w/lid 40.00
Willow Oak, waste bowl 32.00
Windflower, creamer 32.00
Windflower, sauce dish 12.00
Windflower, sugar bowl, w/lid 50.00
Windflower, tumbler, bar 38.00
Windflower, wine 30.00
Wisconsin, banana stand 75.00
Wisconsin, celery tray 42.00

Wisconsin

Wisconsin, shakers, pr 45.00
Wisconsin, spooner 35.00
Wisconsin, toothpick holder 40.00
Wooden Pail, butter dish 60.00
Wooden Pail, pitcher, water 55.00
Wooden Pail, spooner, amber 42.00
Wooden Pail, sugar bowl, amethyst, mini 24.00
Wooden Pail, tumbler 18.00
X-Ray, butter dish, gr 70.00
X-Ray, creamer, ind 18.00
X-Ray, goblet 22.00
X-Ray, toothpick holder 30.00
X-Ray, tumbler, gr 27.50
X-Ray, water set, pitcher+6 tumblers, gr 235.00

Yale, butter dish 42.00
Yale, goblet 32.00
Yale, spooner 25.00
Yale, sugar bowl, w/lid 40.00
Yale, tumbler 18.00
Zipper, cheese dish..48.00
Zipper, compote, w/lid, 8" 42.00
Zipper, pitcher, water...42.50
Zipper, sugar bowl, w/lid 40.00
Zipper, wine 20.00
Zipper Slash, champagne 30.00
Zippered Block, pickle dish, ruby stained 45.00
Zippered Block, pitcher, water 125.00
Zippered Block, sugar bowl, w/lid, ruby stained................100.00
Zippered Block, tumbler 35.00

Paul Revere Pottery

The Saturday Evening Girls was a social group of young Boston ladies who met to pursue various activities, among them pottery making. Their first kiln was bought in 1906, and within a few years it became necessary to move to a larger location. Because their new quarters were near the historical Old North Church, they chose the name Paul Revere Pottery. With very little training, the girls produced only simple ware. Until 1915 the pottery operated at a deficit; then a new building with four kilns was constructed on Nottingham Road. Vases, miniature jugs, children's tea sets, tiles, dinnerware, and lamps were produced, usually in soft matt glazes often decorated with incised, hand-painted designs from nature. Occasional examples in a dark high gloss may also be found.

Several marks were used: 'P.R.P.'; 'S.E.G.'; or the circular device, 'Boston, Paul Revere Pottery' with the horse and rider.

The pottery continued to operate; and, even though their product sold well, the high production costs of the handmade ware caused the pottery to fail in 1946.

Bookends, owl on tree branch, SEG, 4x5x2½" 250.00
Bowl, bl w/band, tree band w/in, SEG/SG/29-12, 11".................950.00
Bowl, floral band on yel, SEG/FL/4-16, rim rpr, 8½"....................275.00
Bowl, stylized lotus band, bl on wht, PRP/11-26, 10½" 200.00
Compote, gun metal, shallow, PRP, 12½" dia 110.00
Cup, chick/mtns, yel/gr/bl on turq, sgn EM, PRP, 3", +plate 375.00
Mug, lg roosters/motto, 5-color on teal, SEG label, 5", EX 550.00
Paperweight, Paul Revere on horsebk, SEG, 1x3" dia 200.00
Pitcher, landscape, bl/gr on bl, SEG/IMD/10-19, 4", NM 150.00
Pitcher & bowl, goose center on bl, PRP, 5½" 400.00

Pitcher, three repeats of Viking ships on brown and green bands, signed FL for Fanny Levine, 9½", $4,900.00.

Plaque, house/trees, 3-color on tan, SEG/10-16, 6", EX..............125.00
Tile, galleon on turq, SEG/E Brown, 11-23, w/label, 6" dia 175.00
Tray, pen; galleon band, SEG/AM/4-14, 8" L 800.00
Tumbler, lotus band, wht on yel, SEG/FL/3-14, 3¾"......................175.00
Tumbler, rabbit border on cream, SEG/IG/10-13, 3¾" 150.00
Vase, flower trellis, brn & gr on mustard, hdls, SEG, 6½"............275.00
Vase, key motif, bl/brn on gr, SEG, sgn, 4" 200.00
Vase, sea bl, swollen cylinder w/wide mouth, SEG, 10", NM 250.00

Pauline Pottery

Pauline Pottery was made from 1883 to 1888 in Chicago, Illinois, from clay imported from the Ohio area. Its founder was Mrs. Pauline Jacobus, who had learned the trade at the Rookwood Pottery. Mrs. Jacobus moved to Edgerton, Wisconsin, to be near a source of suitable clay, thus eliminating shipping expenses. Until 1905 she produced high-quality wares, able to imitate with ease designs and styles of such masters as Wedgwood and Meissen. Her products were sold through leading department stores, and the names of some of these firms may appear on the ware. Not all were marked; and, unless signed by a noted local artist, positive identification is often impossible. Marked examples carry a variety of stamps and signatures: 'Trade Mark' with a crown, 'Pauline Pottery,' and 'Edgerton Art Pottery' are but a few.

Bowl, dogwood on dusty red, trefoil w/3 loop hdls, 9½", EX 150.00
Jug, bamboo reeds, gold on cobalt, 2-spout, 9x9" 180.00
Teapot, floral, gold trim, EX 265.00

Pitcher, Limoges-type floral branches on brown, 5", $550.00.

Tray, berries & vines, gold traced, EX art, 10", M.......................600.00
Vase, ivory w/blue & gold arabesque motif, 5" 295.00

Peachblow

Peachblow, made to imitate the colors of the Chinese Peachbloom porcelain, was made by several glasshouses in the late 1800s. Among them were New England Glass; Mt. Washington; Webb; and Hobbs, Brockunier, and Company. Its pink shading was achieved through action of the heat on the gold content of the glass. While New England's peachblow shades from pink to cool white, Mt. Washington's tends to shade from peach to ivory. Although usually glossy, a satin (or acid) finish was also produced, and many pieces were enameled and gilded. In the 1950s, Gunderson-Pairpoint Glassworks initiated the reproduction of Mt. Washington peachblow using an exact duplication of the original formula. Though of recent manufacture, this glass is very collectible. In the listings that follow, the finish is glossy unless noted acid.

Our advisors for this category are Betty and Clarence Maier; they are listed in the Directory under Pennsylvania.

Bottle, scent; florals/butterfly, gold-tone top, Webb, 6x5" 750.00
Compote, Gunderson, ca 1953, 5x6" 435.00
Creamer, amber hdl, bulbous, Wheeling, rare sz, 3½" 1,100.00
Creamer, sq top, thin walled, Wheeling, 4½" 965.00
Creamer, violets w/gold, bulbous, ribbed, NE Glass, 3" 500.00
Creamer & sugar bowl, narrow panels, reeded hdls, Gunderson ..485.00
Cruet, acid, Wheeling 1,350.00
Cup, punch; bbl shape, peachblow hdl, NE Glass, 2½" 465.00
Cup, punch; ring hdl, Wheeling, 2½x2⅝" 300.00
Cup, punch; wht hdl, NE Glass, 2¾" 385.00
Cup & saucer, ftd, wht reeded hdl, Gunderson, cup: 2¾" 265.00
Decanter, wine; EX color, ftd/bulbous, Gunderson, 10x5" 775.00
Ewer, amber rigaree, amber reeded hdl, Wheeling, 10½" 2,000.00
Finger bowl, acid, ruffled, NE Glass, 5" 425.00
Finger bowl, Drape, Wheeling...150.00
Goblet, acid, Gunderson, lg 275.00
Jam dish, gold flowers/butterfly, Webb, SP fr, 5½x5¾" 515.00
Mustard jar, ovoid, SP lid, Wheeling, 4½" 375.00
Pear, NE Glass, 4¾x3" 165.00
Pear, red/amber, wht int, 1¾" stem, Wheeling, 6¾" 750.00
Pitcher, appl clear hdl, bulbous, 3½x2⅜" 295.00
Pitcher, crimped top, NE Glass, 6¼" 1,185.00
Pitcher, sq top, Wheeling, 4½" 850.00

Wheeling pitcher, acid finish, minor inside staining, 7", $1,200.00; Wheeling Morgan vase in acid-finish stand (having minor chips), 9¾", $1,800.00.

Rose bowl, acid, 1893 World's Fair, 8-crimp, att NE Glass 650.00
Rose bowl, NE Glass, 4x4" 485.00
Rose bowl, 7-crimp, NE Glass, 2⅜x2¾".................................295.00
Shaker, Mt WA 1,185.00
Sherbet, Gunderson...150.00
Spooner, ruffled top, NE Glass, 1880s, 5x3¼" 725.00
Sugar bowl, baluster std, Gunderson, 3½"..............................275.00
Toothpick holder, acid, NE Glass 450.00
Toothpick holder, tricorner, Mt WA, 2½" dia 900.00
Toothpick holder, yel coralene seaweed, sq top, 3" 1,500.00
Tumbler, acid, Wheeling..485.00
Tumbler, NE Glass, 3¾" 445.00
Tumbler, Wheeling, 3¾x2¾" 325.00
Vase, acid, gold floral/prunus/butterfly, Webb, 8½x5½" 785.00
Vase, box-pleat top, NE Glass, 5½" 350.00
Vase, gold floral/bird/top & bottom bands, Webb, 8½" 675.00
Vase, gold leaves & branches, silver berries, Webb, 10"...............450.00
Vase, gold prunus & bee, Webb, 6¼x3½".................................450.00
Vase, gold prunus & bee, Webb, 9½x4¾"................................495.00
Vase, lily; Mt WA, 8¾" 1,300.00

Vase, lily; NE Glass, 12" 985.00
Vase, lily; 3-point top, NE Glass, 6" 850.00
Vase, pk shoulder band, Gunderson, 6½x3¾" 145.00

Peking Glass

The first glasshouse was established in Peking in 1680. It produced glassware made in imitation of porcelain, a more desirable medium to the Chinese. By 1725 multi-layered carving that resulted in a cameo effect lead to the manufacture of a wider range of shapes and colors. The factory was closed from 1736 to 1795, but glass made in Po-shan and shipped to Peking for finishing continued to be called Peking glass. In addition to the cameo ware, other types were made as well.

Our advisor for this category is Donald Penrose; he is listed in the Directory under Ohio. See also Orientalia.

Bowl, lotus, emerald gr on wht, on stand, 6", pr 500.00
Jar, lotus, emerald gr on wht, wood stand, 9" 350.00

Vases, yellow with molded flowers, ca 1900, 7", $900.00 for the pair.

Vase, cranes/peonies, gr on wht, Ching mk, 14", pr................. 1,150.00
Vase, dragons/flaming pearls, turq on wht, 12", pr.................. 1,500.00
Vase, ducks/lotus, red on wht, dbl-ring neck, 8½", pr 550.00
Vase, leaves, gr on wht, 3½", on wood base 125.00
Vase, prunus branches/narcissus, red to wht, 9", pr 450.00
Vase, tropical fish, red on wht, ca 1900, 13" 850.00

Peloton

Peloton glass was first made by Wilhelm Kralik in Bohemia in 1880. This unusual art glass was produced by rolling colored threads onto the transparent or opaque glass gather as it was removed from the furnace. Usually more than one color of threading was used, and some items were further decorated with enameling. It was made with both shiny and acid finishes.

Pitcher, blue-green threads on clear with enameled flowering branch, 5", $225.00.

Rose bowl, pk cased, mc strings, clear wishbone ft, 2x2¾"..........225.00
Rose bowl, pk overshot, mc strings, 7½x3½".........................225.00
Rose bowl, wht opaque, mc strings, clear ft, 4⅛x3½"..............195.00
Sweetmeat, mc strings on rose satin, SP lid & hdl, 5½"............565.00
Vase, clear, wht strings, 3⅛"...130.00
Vase, lav to wht opaque cased in crystal w/mc threads, 6"..........450.00
Vase, mauve cased, mc strings, corset shaped, 6x4½"................450.00
Vase, pastel strings on wht, triangular 3-fold top, 4x5"............295.00
Vase, ribbed/frosted, mc strings, V-form, floral-emb ft, 4"..........280.00
Vase, wht w/pastel strings, ribbed, 5 ft, ruffled, 6½x4".............450.00

Pennsbury

Established in the 1950s in Morrisville, Pennsylvania, by Henry Below, the Pennsbury Pottery produced dinnerware and novelty items, much of which was sold in gift shops along the Pennsylvania Turnpike. Henry and his wife, Lee, worked for years at the Stangl Pottery before striking out on their own. Lee and her daughter were the artists responsible for many of the early pieces, the bird figures among them. Pennsbury pottery was hand painted, some in blue on white, some in multicolor on caramel. Pennsylvania Dutch motifs, Amish couples, and barber shop singers were among their most popular decorative themes. Sgraffito, or hand incising, was used extensively. The company marked their wares 'Pennsbury Pottery' or 'Pennsbury Pottery, Morrisville, PA.'

In October of 1969 the company closed. Contents of the pottery were sold in December of the following year; and, in April of 1971, the buildings burned to the ground. Items marked Pennsbury Glenview or Stumar pottery (or these marks in combination) were made by Glenview after 1969. Pieces manufactured after 1976 were made by the Pennington Pottery. Several of the old molds still exist, and the original Pennsbury Caramel process is still being used on novelty items, some of which are produced by Lewis Brothers, NJ. Production of Pennsbury dinnerware was not resumed after the closing. For those wishing to learn more, we recommend *Pennsbury Pottery Video Book 1* and accompanying 1987-88 price guide offered by our advisor Shirley Graff and BA Wellman. He is listed in the Directory under Massachusetts; Mrs. Graff is in Ohio.

Ash tray, Folkart, rnd..17.00
Ash tray, It Wonders Me, 5"..20.00
Bank, Bryn Mawr, Main Line RR, 7½".................................55.00
Bowl, Dutch figures & sayings, 11¼"...................................40.00
Bowl, gray, Fidelity Mutual, 7"..40.00
Bowl, Hex, 11"...30.00

Bowl, pretzel; Barber Shop Quartet......................................45.00
Bowl, Revere, ftd, 7"...25.00
Bowl, soup; Folkart, deep...25.00
Butter dish, Lovebirds..25.00
Cake stand, Amish..75.00
Candlestick, hummingbird on flower, 5", pr..........................145.00
Canister, Hex, wood lid, 6½"...60.00
Casserole, Hex, w/lid, 9"..35.00
Cheese & cracker set, Red or Blk Rooster, 3½x11"....................45.00
Cigarette box, Rotary Internat'l..20.00
Coffeepot, Folkart, 6-cup, 8½"...45.00
Coffeepot, Red Rooster, 2-cup, 6½".....................................40.00
Cookie jar, Folkart, Harvest or Hex, ea.................................75.00
Creamer, Amish, regular..25.00
Creamer, Rooster, regular..25.00
Creamer & sugar bowl, Folkart, 4".......................................30.00
Cruet, Gay Nineties, pr...150.00
Cruet, Red Rooster...50.00
Cup & saucer, Rooster...22.00
Desk basket, Eagle...25.00
Egg cup, Folkart..10.00
Figurine, Sparrow, 3x3½"..45.00
Hot plate, Red Rooster, 6x6" tile in metal fr, electric.................75.00
Mug, beer; Here's Looking at You...25.00
Mug, coffee; Eagle, Folkart, Gay Nineties or Hex, 3¼"................15.00
Mug, pretzel; Amish, 5"...22.00
Mug, Red Barn, 4½"..18.00
Pitcher, Folkart, 1-pt, 5"...25.00
Pitcher, Hex, 1-qt, 6¼"...45.00
Pitcher, Red Rooster, 9¾"..55.00
Plaque, Amish couple..25.00
Plaque, Central Pacific RR, CP Huntington..............................45.00
Plaque, Outen Light..30.00
Plaque, Papa's Half...27.00
Plaque, Pennsylvania RR 1856 Tiger, EX color..........................45.00
Plaque, Solebury, New Hope, 5" dia......................................25.00
Plate, Folkart or Hex, 10"...25.00
Plate, Red Rooster, in factory fr, 11".....................................45.00
Platter, Red Rooster, 11x8"...25.00
Silent butler, Eagle, bellows shape, w/lid................................30.00
Sugar bowl, Hex..20.00
Tile, any 3 mtd on wood...100.00
Tile, Eagle, sq, 6"..30.00
Tray, horse, 5x3"...25.00
Tureen, Hex, w/ladle hook & ladle.......................................150.00
Wall pocket, sailboat, 6½x6½"...45.00

Pens and Pencils

The first metallic writing pen was patented in 1809, and soon machine-produced pens with steel nibs gradually began replacing the quill. The first fountain pen was invented in 1830; but, due to the fact that a suitable metal for the tips had not yet been developed, they were not manufactured commercially until the 1880s. The first successful commercial producers were Waterman in 1884 and Parker with the Lucky Curve in 1888.

The self-filling pen of 1890 featured the soft, interior sack which filled with ink as the metal bar on the outside of the pen was raised and lowered. Variations of the pumping mechanism were tried until 1932 when Parker introduced the Vacumatic, a sackless pen with an internal pump.

Our advisors for this category are Judy and Cliff Lawrence; they are listed in the Directory under Florida. For those seeking additional

Pretzel bowl, Amish and red barn, 12", $65.00.

information, a magazine is published monthly by the Pen Fancier's Club, whose address can be found in the Directory under Clubs, Newsletters, and Catalogs. In the listings that follow, all pens are lever-filled unless otherwise noted.

Key :
AF — aeromatic filler
BF —button filler
CF — cartridge filler
CPT — chrome-plated trim
ED — eyedropper filler
GFM — gold-filled metal
GPT — gold-plated trim

HR— hard rubber
LF — lever filler
NPT — nickel-plated trim
PF — plunger filler
TD — touchdown filler
VF — vacumatic filler

Ballpoint Pens

Eberhard Faber, 1946, brn/GF cap, EX............65.00
Eversharp, CA, 1946, bl/GF cap, M 95.00
Eversharp, CA, 1947, GFM, EX.......................125.00
Eversharp, Skyline, CA, 1944, maroon w/striped cap, EX.............50.00
Eversharp, Skyline, CA, 1948, brn/gold striped cap, M 50.00
Reynolds, Internat'l, 1945, aluminum, GF clip, EX 125.00
Sheaffer, Stratowriter, 1946, GFM, M 95.00

Fountain Pens

Blue Diamond Major Vacumatic 39, silver pearl stripe, EX 150.00
Blue Diamond 51, 1941, blk, GFM cap & trim, VF, EX..............125.00
Blue Diamond 51, 1943, blk, sterling cap, GFM trim, VF, EX.....149.00
Blue Diamond 51, 1945, blk w/GFM cap & trim, VF, EX 95.00
Blue Diamond 51, 1946, bl, Lustraloy cap, GFM trim, VF, EX.....59.00
Conklin, 1925, blk chased HR, GFM trim, LF, EX 99.00
Conklin #20 Crescent, 1920, blk chased HR, GFM trim, G........159.00
Eclipse, 1927, GFM & trim, LF, G.....................85.00
Golden Rule, 1926, blk w/GFM trim, LF, M 125.00
Grieshaber, 1902, blk chased HR, GFM trim, ED, EX 250.00
Hub #31 Jointless, 1910, blk chased HR, ED, EX....................125.00
Inkograph Stylographic, 1925, blk HR, GFM trim, LF, EX..........225.00
Mont Blanc, 1975, blk, GFM trim, twist filler, G...................125.00
Moore, 1934, blk, GFM trim, LF, EX 95.00
Moore Non-Leakable, 1908, blk chased HR, ED, EX..................165.00
Parker, Challenger, 1937, emerald pearl, GFM trim, BF, G 69.00
Parker, Duofold, 1940, gold/gr/blk stripes, GFM trim, VF, EX.......89.00
Parker, Duofold, 1941, pk/silver/blk stripes, GFM trim, VF, EX 80.00
Parker, Duofold Jr, 1924, red HR, GFM trim, BF, EX 149.00
Parker, Duofold Jr, 1927, blk, GFM trim, BF, G.....................115.00
Parker, Duofold Jr, 1928, red, 2 cap bands, GFM trim, BF, EX 150.00
Parker, Duofold Sr, 1925, red, GF trim, BF, EX......................325.00
Parker, Jack Knife Safety #20, 1918, blk HR, NPT, BF, EX.........175.00
Parker, Lucky Curve, 1920, blk chased HR, GF trim, BF, NM ...125.00
Parker, Vacumatic, 1938, blk, GFM trim, VF, EX 89.00
Parker, Vacumatic, 1942, bl pearl stripe, GFM trim, VF, EX 85.00
Parker, Vacumatic Oversz, 1935, gold pearl stripes, VF, EX........595.00
Parker 45 Flighter, 1960, stainless, GFM trim, AF, EX 89.00
Parker 50P, 1971, blk matt, CPT, AF, M................................89.00
Parker 51, 1955, bl, Lustraloy cap, CPT, AF, EX......................59.00
Parker 51 Demi, bl, Lustraloy cap, CPT, VF, EX.......................69.00
Parker 51 Demi, 1947, bl, GFM cap & trim, VF, EX....................99.00
Parker 51 Special, 1950, blk w/chrome cap, CPT, AF, EX.............59.00
Parker 51 Special, 1955, gray, chrome cap, CPT, AF, M 79.00
Sheaffer, Lifetime, 1925, blk, GFM trim, LF, EX.....................295.00
Sheaffer, Lifetime, 1928, gr jade marble, GFM trim, LF, EX........295.00
Sheaffer, Lifetime, 1934, blk, GFM trim, LF, EX.....................350.00
Sheaffer, Lifetime 875, 1941, golden pearl stripe, LF, EX 95.00

Sheaffer, Triumph Lifetime, 1942, golden pearl, PF, EX.............125.00
Sheaffer, Triumph Lifetime #1250, '46, blk, GFM trim, PF, EX ..250.00
Sheaffer, Triumph Tuckaway Lifetime, '46, red stripes, PF, EX 89.00
Sheaffer, Tuckaway, 1947, brn, GFM trim, PF, EX....................49.00
Sheaffer, Vigilant #875 Lifetime, 1941, blk, GFM trim, LF, EX ..89.00
Sheaffer, Wht Dot Triumph Snorkel, 1957, blk, TD, M 79.00
Waterman Ideal, 1929, pearl gr marble, GFM trim, LF, EX 250.00
Waterman Ideal 42½V Safety, 1922, blk HR, ED, EX 149.00
Waterman Ideal 52, 1922, blk chased HR, NPT, LF, G 59.00

Mechanical Pencils

Eversharp, Coronet, 1936, blk, GFM top, pyralin insets, EX..........95.00
Eversharp, Skyline Repeater, 1946, maroon, gold trim, EX............20.00
Eversharp, Ventura Repeater, 1953, sterling, M 89.00
Parker, Duofold Sr, 1932, burgundy & blk marble, EX................175.00
Parker, Duofold Sr Deluxe, 1932, modern gr & pearl, EX.............159.00
Parker, Lady Duofold, 1932, lapis bl marble, NM.....................125.00
Parker, Vacumatic, 1942, pearl, NPT, EX..............................35.00
Parker, Vacumatic, 1946, silver pearl stripe, NPT, EX..................42.00
Parker, Vacumatic Oversz, 1935, silver pearl stripes, EX.............295.00
Parker, 1962, metallic violet, GFM trim, M............................29.00
Parker, 51, 1943, gray w/GFM top & trim, EX..........................69.00
Parker, 51 Demi Repeater, 1948, gray, GFM top, EX 29.00
Parker, 51 Repeater, 1948, bl w/Lustraloy top, CPT, M 35.00
Parker, 51 Repeater, 1951, bl w/Lustraloy top, CPT, M 35.00
Sheaffer, Lifetime, 1924, gr jade marble, GFM trim, NM 169.00
Sheaffer, Lifetime, 1925, NP w/NPT, EX................................19.00
Sheaffer, Lifetime, 1926, gr jade marble, EX...........................159.00
Sheaffer, Lifetime, 1926, pearl & blk marble, G 99.00
Sheaffer, Tuckaway, 1946, golden pearl stripe, GFM trim, EX.......35.00
Sheaffer, 1955, bl, M...12.00
Swan, Fyne Point, 1920, GFM, EX......................................65.00
Wahl, Oxford, 1936, silver marble, EX 25.00
Wahl-Eversharp, 1920, sterling, EX......................................45.00
Wahl-Eversharp, 1920, triple-plated silver, EX...........................35.00
Wahl-Eversharp, 1922, blk chased HR, EX 49.00
Wahl-Eversharp, 1925, red chased HR, EX...............................115.00
Wahl-Eversharp, 1928, blk chased HR, EX 52.00

Sets

Eversharp, 1954, gray, GFM caps & trim, AF, EX........................125.00
Eversharp, 64, 1946, maroon, 14k caps & trim, LF, EX................395.00

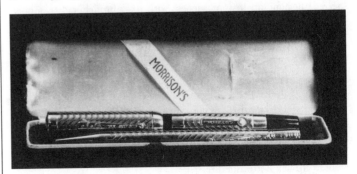

Morrison gold-filled pen and pencil set, ca 1920s, $375.00.

Parker, 21 Special, 1954, red, chrome caps, CPT, AF, M..............29.00
Sheaffer, #3, golden pearl stripe, GFM trim, LF, EX....................69.00
Sheaffer, #3, 1934, silver pearl marble, CPT, LF, EX....................59.00
Sheaffer, #375, 1941, golden pearl stripe, GFT, LF, EX.................89.00
Sheaffer, Lifetime, 1932, emerald pearl marble, EX......................95.00
Sheaffer, Sentinel Triumph, 1950, maroon, gold trim, TD, M 150.00

WS Hicks & Sons, 1925, sterling, EX...**195.00**

Personalities, Fact and Fiction

One of the largest and most popular areas of collecting today, if trade-paper ads and articles be any indication, is character-related memorabilia. Everyone has favorites, whether they be comic-strip personalities or true-life heroes. The earliest comic strip dealt with the adventures of the Yellow Kid, the smiling, bald-headed Oriental boy always in a nightshirt. He was introduced in 1895, a product of the imagination of Richard Fenton Outcault. Today, though very hard to come by, items relating to the Yellow Kid bring premium prices.

In 1902 Buster Brown and Tige, his dog and constant companion (more of Outcault's progenies), made it big in the comics as well as in the world of advertising. Shoe stores appealed to the younger set through merchandising displays that featured them both. Today, items from their earlier years are very collectible.

Though her 1923 introduction was unobtrusively made through only one newspaper, New York's *Daily News*, *Little Orphan Annie*, the vacant-eyed redhead in the inevitable red dress, was quickly adopted by hordes of readers nationwide; and, before the demise of her creator, Harold Gray, in 1968, she had starred in her own radio show. She made two feature films, and in 1977 'Annie' was launched on Broadway.

Other early comic figures were Moon Mullins, created in 1923 by Frank Willard; Buck Rogers by Philip Nowlan in 1928; and Betty Boop, the round-faced, innocent-eyed, chubby-cheeked Boop-Boop-a-Doop girl of the early 1930s. Bimbo was her dog and KoKo her clown friend.

Popeye made his debut in 1929 as the spinach-eating sailor with the spindly-limbed girlfriend, Olive Oyl, in the comic strip *Thimble Theatre*, created by Elzie Segar. He became a film star in 1933 and had his own radio show that during 1936 played three times a week on CBS. He obligingly modeled for scores of toys, dolls, and figurines, and especially those from the thirties are very collectible.

Tarzan, created around 1930 by Edgar Rice Burroughs, and Captain Midnight, by Robert Burtt and Willfred G. Moore, are popular heroes with today's collectors. During the days of radio, Sky King of the Flying Crown Ranch (also created by Burtt and Moore) thrilled boys and girls of the mid-1940s. Hopalong Cassidy, Red Rider, Tom Mix, and the Lone Ranger were only a few of the other 'good guys' always on the side of law and order.

But of all the fictional heroes and comic characters collected today, probably the best loved and most well known is Mickey Mouse. Created in the late 1920s by Walt Disney, Micky (as his name was first spelled) became an instant success with his film debut, Steamboat Willie. His popularity was parlayed through wind-up toys, watches, figurines, cookie jars, puppets, clothing, and numerous other products. Items from the 1930s are usually copyrighted 'Walt Disney Enterprises'; thereafter, 'Walt Disney Productions' was used. For those interested in Disneyanna, we recommend *Stern's Guide to Disney Collectibles*, available from Collector Books.

Our advisors for this category are Cathy and Norm Vigue; they are listed in the Directory under Massachusetts. See also Autographs; Banks; Big Little Books; Cartoon Books; Children's Books; Comic Books; Cookie Jars; Dolls; Lunch Boxes; Movie Memorabilia; Paper Dolls; Pin-Back Buttons; Posters; Toys.

A Team, board game, Mr T on cover, ca 1984, MIB.....................**10.00**
Addams Family, Mystery jigsaw puzzle, Milton Bradley.................**45.00**
Agent Zero M, weapons set/attache case, MIB...........................**58.00**
Alfred Hitchcock, Why game, M...**20.00**
Alice in Wonderland, paint book, Whitman, WD, 1950, NM **8.00**
Alice in Wonderland, phonograph, Disney, 1950s, EX..................**48.00**
Alice in Wonderland, wristwatch, 1955, NM **75.00**

Alvin & Chipmunks, soap dispenser, MIB **15.00**
Andy Gump, face mask, Listerine premium, 1930s, EX.................**25.00**
Annette Funicello, color book, WDP, 1950s, NM **17.50**
Atom Ant, push puppet, Hanna Barbera, no label, EX.................**12.50**
Baba Looey, color book, 1960, M...**35.00**

Bambi multiplane painting by Courvoisier, C-WDP #5, in box, $250.00.

Bambi, picture book, paper cover, 1940s, EX..............................**25.00**
Bambi, plate, ceramic, Shaw, 1947, M.......................................**35.00**
Barnie Google, book, Saalfield, 1935, EX **25.00**
Barnie Google, doll, cloth, 1920-30, 12", EX..............................**80.00**
Bat Masterson, figure, Hartland, 7½", MIB.............................**165.00**
Batman, Batmobile, w/figures, Worchester, 1966, 9"..................**65.00**
Batman, chair, inflatable vinyl, 1978, MIB................................**55.00**
Batman, color book, 1966, unused, M.......................................**22.00**
Batman, costume, Ben Cooper, 1966, MIB................................**45.00**
Batman, Escape Gun, 1966, NM on card....................................**78.00**
Batman, Fun Poncho w/mask & hood, Cooper, 1975, NM...........**22.50**
Batman, mug, ceramic, blk transfer on wht, 1966.......................**15.00**
Batman, Paint by Numbers set, Hasbro, 1981, NM **17.50**
Batman, roller skates, 1966, M..**55.00**
Batman, sticker book, Whitman, 1966, M..................................**28.00**
Batman, wristwatch, Gilbert, 1966 ....**295.00**
Battlestar Galactica, Colorforms, 1978, MIB.............................**15.00**
Beany & Cecil, Cecil's disguise kit, 1962, NM in box...................**65.00**
Beany & Cecil, Leakin' Lena boat, 1961, 14", NM in box..........**225.00**
Beatles, book, All About Us, paperback, 30-pg, EX **15.00**
Beatles, book, Beatles on Broadway, Leach, 1964, EX..................**20.00**
Beatles, book, Hard Day's Night, paperback, 1964, EX................**15.00**
Beatles, Ringo's photo album, 1964, 48-pg **20.00**
Beatles, song book, Golden Beatles, piano music, 1964 ....**22.50**
Beatles, wig, 1960s, M in pkg **42.50**
Betty Boop, ash tray, lustre ware, 1930s, NM **95.00**
Betty Boop, doll blanket, Max Fleischer, 1930s, VG...................**45.00**
Betty Boop, wall pocket, glazed ceramic, 6", NM **85.00**
Betty Boop & Bimbo, score pad, 1930s, 4", EX...........................**25.00**
Betty Grable, color book, 1951, EX...**35.00**
Beverly Hillbillies, card game, EX in box **16.50**
Bewitched, card game, EX...**15.00**
Big Bad Wolf, alarm clock, animated, red case, 1930s, MIB **750.00**
Big Bird, lamp, figural, w/orig shade, 1960s, 24", EX **20.00**
Bing Crosby, board game, 1947, EX **55.00**
Blondie, baby carriage, 1949, NM..**275.00**
Blondie, paint set, tin box, 1952, used, EX................................**12.00**
Bobby Benson, H-Bar-O Ranch pin, M in orig mailer **23.00**
Bonzo, pencil tablet, Dog's Life, 1930s, VG...............................**25.00**
Bonzo, post card, British, 1930s, EX...**20.00**

Buck Jones, Big Big Book, BJ & the Night Riders, 1937, EX 38.00
Buck Rogers, pop gun, blk grip, Dorsey, 1920s, EX 165.00
Buck Rogers, pop gun, Daisy, 1920s, EX 165.00
Buck Rogers, Rocket Ranger Club card, premium, 1930s, rare 245.00
Buck Rogers, Shaker Maker, 1979, MIB 15.00
Buck Rogers, Solar Scout pin-bk, brass, 1½", VG 45.00
Buck Rogers, Sonic Ray gun, plastic, 1952, NM in orig box 75.00
Bugs Bunny, bank, chalkware, early, VG.....................................120.00
Bugs Bunny, mug, plastic figural, F&F Mold & Die Works, EX 12.50
Bugs Bunny, soap, Warner Bros, 1930s, NM in box 40.00
Bullwinkle, Electric Quiz game, 1971, M on card..........................20.00
Bullwinkle, stamp set, 1969, M on card 16.50
Bullwinkle, target game, PAT Productions, 1961, NM...................50.00
Buster Brown, paint book, diecut, 1915, EX..................................55.00
Buster Brown, Pin the Tail on Tige game, paper, 1900s, EX 120.00
Buster Brown, playing cards, early, EX in box 60.00
Campbell Kids, puzzle, Jamar, MIB 22.00
Captain Action, Phantom outfit, MIB...250.00
Captain Marvel, booklet, Fawcett, 1940s, sm, EX 15.00
Captain Marvel, key chain, 1944, NM..60.00
Captain Marvel, Shazam game, 1944, M in envelope 30.00
Captain Midnight, mug, Ovaltine, red plastic, NM........................35.00
Captain Midnight, Whistling Code-O-Graph, 1947 ....46.00
Captain Video, board game, NM in box 65.00
Captain Video, rocket launcher, 1950s, unused boxed set 65.00
Casper the Ghost, board game, Milton Bradley, 1959, EX 15.00
Casper the Ghost, record, 1962, 78 rpm..5.00
Casper the Ghost & Wendy, Halloween containers, 1960s, pr 35.00
Charlie Chan, card game, Whitman, 1939, EX in box 35.00
Charlie Chaplin, book, Up in the Air, Donahue, 1917, EX...........75.00
Charlie Chaplin, figure, pnt lead, 1930s, 2½", EX.......................30.00
Charlie McCarthy, paint book, Whitman, 1938, 13x11", VG.......35.00
Charlie McCarthy, picture puzzles, 2 in set, 1938, EX in box 55.00
Charlie McCarthy, Rummy game, 1939, NM in box 40.00
Charlie McCarthy, spoon, SP, ca 1930, EX 12.00
Charlie the Tuna, beach towel, VG 18.00
Charlie the Tuna, lamp, figural, VG..65.00
Charlie the Tuna, tie clasp, M...15.00
Charlie's Angels, board game, NM...12.00
Charlie's Angels, Cosmetic Beauty Kit, 1977, EX in box.............12.50
Chuck Conners, Branded game, Milton Bradley, 1966, M............40.00
Cinderella, sweeper, tin w/brush, 1950s, EX 30.00
Cinderella, wristwatch, Milton Bradley, MIB...............................35.00
Cinderella, wristwatch, w/slipper, MIB.......................................400.00
Cisco Kid, comic album, 1953, EX 20.00
Cleveland Indians, bank, ceramic Indian w/feather, '50s, EX 60.00
Cleveland Indians, nodder doll, gold base, 1950s, EX 50.00
Daffy Duck, pull toy, paper litho on wood, Brice, '50s, NM..........68.00
Daisy Mae, scrap book, 1954, M..12.50
Daisy Mae, slide puzzle, 1950s, M on card 14.00
Dale Evans, cowgirl outfit, MIB...185.00
Dale Evans, Lucky Horseshoe pendant necklace, M on card..........15.00
Dale Evans, wristwatch, w/jewelry, EX in box 250.00
Daniel Boone, flintlock rifle, cap shooter, EX...............................35.00
Daniel Boone/Fess Parker, activity book, M 12.50
Dark Shadows, book, Ace paperbk, 1970, NM 10.00
Dark Shadows, game, w/teeth game pcs, EX 35.00
Darth Vader, figural telephone, MIB 125.00
Davy Crockett, badge, Alamo type, 1950s, M on card 15.00
Davy Crockett, bandana, EX...22.50
Davy Crockett, bank, metal, 1950s, 5¼", M 20.00
Davy Crockett, cap rifle, Cohn, 1950s, 33", in cb case.................55.00
Davy Crockett, card game, 1950s, EX in box 12.00
Davy Crockett, color book, WDP, 1950s, NM 28.00

Davy Crockett, coon skin cap, Halco, EX....................................35.00
Davy Crockett, doll, w/pin, early, 32", NM..................................100.00
Davy Crockett, flintlock pistol, Irwin, 1950s, EX 15.00
Davy Crockett, Indian craft set, WD, unused 48.00
Davy Crockett, lamp, ceramic figural, orig shade, 1950s, NM 85.00
Davy Crockett, lamp shade, 1950s, NM......................................40.00
Davy Crockett, movie stamp book, 1958, complete 22.00
Davy Crockett, powder horn, vinyl w/fringe, 1950s, NM 12.50
Davy Crockett, powder pouch, TV show related, 1950s, EX..........15.00
Davy Crockett, T-shirt, 1950s, child's sz, NM 12.00
Davy Crockett, tool kit, Liberty Steel, complete, EX 70.00
Davy Crockett, vest, ca 1950s, EX 30.00
Davy Crockett, wall plaque, mc, 1955, 8", EX..............................45.00
Davy Crockett, 3-ring binder, 1950s, EX 33.00
Deanna Durbin, song book, 1939, 61-pg, EX...............................20.00
Debbie Reynolds, color book, 1953, EX 20.00
Dennis the Menace, hand puppet, cloth & vinyl, 1950s, NM 15.00
Dennis the Menace, Stuff 'N Lace doll, 1960sMIB 40.00
Deputy Dawg, 8mm movie, 1953, NM 9.00
Dick Tracy, candy bar wrapper, mc 20.00
Dick Tracy, car, tin litho, EX...135.00
Dick Tracy, color book, Saalfield, 1945, M..................................38.00
Dick Tracy, Crimestoppers game, 1963, MIB 85.00
Dick Tracy, Detective lapel pin...25.00
Dick Tracy, Master Detective game, 1961, MIB...........................40.00
Dick Tracy, paint book, 1935, lg, EX...40.00
Dick Tracy, Secret Code Maker, 1930s, EX.................................40.00
Dick Tracy, Secret Service Patrol Sergeant badge, EX 35.00
Dick Tracy, walkie-talkies, 1973, NM in pkg 12.00
Dino the Dinosaur, bath puppet, 1980, M in pkg 8.00
Dino the Dinosaur, figure, vinyl, Hanna Barbera, 1960 ....15.00
Dionne Quints, fan, cb, N Haledon Bus Lines, 1935, VG 27.50
Doc, lamp, plaster/compo, La Mode Studios, w/shade, '30s, EX...175.00
Doc Savage, membership pin, bronze...100.00
Donald Duck, bank, compo, WDE, 1938, NM 325.00
Donald Duck, bread wrapper, Purity Maid, 1950s.........................12.50
Donald Duck, bubble duck, 1950s, EX in box..............................20.00
Donald Duck, card game, Disney, 1949, EX in box 14.00
Donald Duck, color book, 1938, VG 20.00
Donald Duck, figure, bsk, long-billed, 1930s, 4½", NM................325.00
Donald Duck, figure, bsk, on gr scooter, WD, 3"..........................55.00
Donald Duck, lamp, ceramic figural, Leeds, 1940s, EX................35.00
Donald Duck, Little Golden Book, DD's Safety Book, 1950s, NM. 5.00
Donald Duck, music box, wood, 1950s, EX 160.00
Donald Duck, napkin ring, amber Bakelite w/decal, 1930s, EX 55.00
Donald Duck, party game, Parker Bros, 1938, MIB 45.00
Donald Duck, roly poly, hard plastic, 1970s, 4", NM 15.00
Donald Duck, scissors, electric, Royal American Corp, MIB 55.00
Donald Duck, stool, 3-leg, WDP, NM 22.50
Donald Duck, wristwatch, Milton Bradley, MIB 40.00
Dopey, ceramic figurine, 1940s...40.00
Dopey, pencil sharpener, Bakelite, WDE, 1930s, NM 35.00
Dr Doolittle, Fun Gum, plastic animal kit, Remco, 1967, EX........12.50
Dracula, I Want To Bite Your Finger game, Hasbro, 1981, NM 15.00
Dracula, poseable figure, Universal, 1986, 8", M on card 7.00
Dumbo, bank, ceramic figural, Leeds, 1940s, M 38.00
Elizabeth Taylor, color book, Whitman, 1950, VG.......................15.00
Elsie, dexterity puzzle, Borden's, 1941 ....38.00
Elvis Presley, bracelet, dog-tag style, 1960s, EX.........................10.00
ET, book bag, M in pkg... 8.00
Fat Albert & the Cosby Kids, game, Milton Bradley, 1973, EX.....12.00
Felix the Cat, bead game under glass, 3", EX...............................30.00
Felix the Cat, board game, Milton Bradley, 1960, EX in box........17.50
Felix the Cat, figure, pnt lead, 1920s, 2", EX...............................60.00

Felix the Cat child's dish, in lustre with chromed hot water reservoir, $85.00.

Felix the Cat, pencil box, 1938, VG 55.00
Felix the Cat, walking figure, celluloid, 1920x, 2", EX 75.00
Ferdinand the Bull, doll, compo, 1930s, VG 120.00
Ferdinand the Bull, game, no instructions, 1938, EX 38.00
Ferdinand the Bull, hand puppet, WDE, 1938 ....45.00
Figaro the Cat, mask, paper, Gilette premium, 1938, EX 15.00
Flash Gordon, Champion Jet-Propelled kite, paper, '40s, EX in box ..45.00
Flash Gordon, pencil box, Eagle pencils, 1951, EX 22.50
Flash Gordon, pop-up book, 1934, EX 200.00
Flash Gordon, ring, Post Toasties, 1949, M in wrapper 40.00
Flash Gordon, slide puzzle, 1981, M on card 5.00
Flash Gordon, Sparkling Ray Gun, 1976, NM 6.00
Flash Gordon, wrist compass, 1950s, M on card 45.00
Flintstones, Bamm Bamm wristwatch, NM in box 150.00
Flintstones, Barney & Betty Rubble puzzle, 1975, NM in box 10.00
Flintstones, Fred costume, Ben Cooper, 1961, EX 28.00
Flintstones, Fred costume, Ben Cooper, 1973, MIB...................17.50
Flintstones, Fred night light, vinyl figure, 1961, 11", EX...............40.00
Flintstones, Fred plastic wind-up walker, 1971, 3" 28.50
Flintstones, Jell-O mold set, M in pkg... 6.50
Flintstones, Pebbles & Bamm Bamm punch-out sticker book, '74, M..16.00
Flintstones, Pebbles push puppet, Hanna Barbera, no label, EX ...11.00
Flintstones, Transogram game, 1961, NM 25.00
Flipper, frame-tray puzzle, 1966, set of 4, MIB 32.00
Frankenstein, pencil sharpener, gray plastic, 1960s, NM...............12.50
Frankenstein, tumbler, glass, Universal Pictures, 1960s 22.00
Frankenstein Jr, slide puzzle, Hanna Barbera, '60s, M on card 20.00
Garfield, Rookie roller skates, 1978, MIB 35.00
Gene Autry, color book, 1949, lg, NM 30.00
Gene Autry, guitar, Emenee, MIB...85.00
Gene Autry, pin-bk button, Sunbeam Bread premium, EX............12.00
Gene Autry, wristwatch, gun moves, EX 325.00
Gene Autry, writing tablet, 1950s, unused, EX 12.50
Gentle Ben, 3-D Animal Hunt game, 1967, M 28.00
GI Joe, wristwatch, MIB...15.00
Goofy, ball action toy, 1950s, MIB...35.00
Great Grape Ape, felt picture kit, 1976, M....................................18.00
Green Hornet, playing cards, 1966, NM in box..............................12.00
Green Hornet, spoon & fork set, 1966, M on card 40.00
Green Hornet, View Master reels (3) & book, M in envelope 75.00
Green Hornet, walkie-talkies, Remco, 1966, EX in box..............120.00
Groucho Marx, wristwatch, 1950s, NM...55.00
Happy Hooligan, pencil holder, pnt bsk, 8½", EX 100.00

Happy Hooligan, roly poly, compo, 4", NM 100.00
Herman & Katnip, frame-tray puzzle, EX....................................10.00
Herman & Katnip, kite, M in pkg...15.00
Herman the Mouse, Halloween costume, EX 24.00
Homer Pigeon, planter, ceramic, Walter Lantz, 1958, EX.............20.00
Hong Kong Phooey, bath puppet, Hanna Barbera, '74, M in pkg ..13.00
Hopalong Cassidy, bath rug, 1950s, EX..35.00
Hopalong Cassidy, binoculars, 1950s, EX.....................................35.00
Hopalong Cassidy, board game, Milton Bradley, 1950, EX 45.00
Hopalong Cassidy, color book, 1951, 13x11", M 26.00
Hopalong Cassidy, costume, 1950s, MIB.......................................85.00
Hopalong Cassidy, cut-out color book, 1950, EX 12.50
Hopalong Cassidy, dart board, metal, w/guns & darts, MIB.........100.00
Hopalong Cassidy, figure, pnt lead, rare.....................................125.00
Hopalong Cassidy, hat, felt, Official, 1950s, EX 30.00
Hopalong Cassidy, hat, paper, Bond Bread, 1950s, EX.................15.00
Hopalong Cassidy, holster set, 2 guns, M in orange box 135.00
Hopalong Cassidy, night light, revolves, NM............................225.00
Hopalong Cassidy, puzzle, set of 3, complete 30.00
Hopalong Cassidy, rocking horse, 1950, EX 175.00
Hopalong Cassidy, Savings Club Teller button, 1950s, NM 18.00
Hopalong Cassidy, scrapbook, faux leather cover, '50s, 14", EX 55.00
Hopalong Cassidy, Singing Bandit record set 35.00
Hopalong Cassidy, T-shirt decal, 1950s, NM............................... 9.00
Hopalong Cassidy, Tenderfoot pin.. 6.00
Hopalong Cassidy, wallet, leather, illus ea side, NM 18.50
Hopalong Cassidy, wristwatch, lg, 1950, NM in NM box...........275.00
Howdy Doody, bowling game, Parker Bros, 1949, VG 45.00
Howdy Doody, color book, Whitman, 1950s, EX 12.00
Howdy Doody, Dot-to-Dot book, 1951, VG 10.00
Howdy Doody, figure, plastic, movable jaw, 1950, 4", MIB...........36.00
Howdy Doody, frame-tray puzzle 15.00
Howdy Doody, ice cream spoon, M in pkg....................................12.50
Howdy Doody, push puppet, wood, Kohner, EX 55.00
Howdy Doody, shakers, plastic figural, Kagran, 1950s, MIB 95.00
Howdy Doody, shoe polish, Kagran, 1950s, EX in mc box 12.00
Howdy Doody, TruVue stereo card, 1955, pr 20.00
Howdy Doody, ukelele, Emenee, unused, 1950s, +VG case 85.00
Howdy Doody, wristwatch, girl's, 1950s, working, EX.................225.00
Howdy Doody, 3-pc child's set, mug, bowl & plate, ceramic 65.00
Huckleberry Hound, cowboy gloves, paper litho tag, 1959, NM....23.00
Huckleberry Hound, Huck-A-Chuck carnival game, 1960, MIB...55.00
Huckleberry Hound, Jungle Roll game, 1960, EX 40.00
Hulk, sun glasses, 1978, EX... 5.00
Hulk, wallet, 1978, M on card 7.50
Ignatz Mouse, figure, jtd wood, early, VG 75.00
Indiana Jones, Desert Convoy truck, MIB 28.00
Inspector Gadget, wristwatch, Milton Bradley, MIB 35.00
Jack Armstrong, Big Ten Football game, NM 30.00
Jack Armstrong, Hike-O-Meter, NM...30.00
Jack Armstrong, telescope, EX 30.00
Jack Westaway, Membership badge...25.00
Jackie Gleason, Away We Go game, complete, 1956, EX..............70.00
Jackie Gleason/Ralph Kramden, wristwatch, Showtime, EX.........48.00
James Bond 007, Goldfinger puzzle, United Kingdom, MIB...........30.00
James Bond 007, scuba accessory pack, complete, NM...................32.00
James Bond 007, Secret Service game, United Kingdom, EX.........65.00
James Bond 007, Secret Service walkie-talkie, 1984, M 7.50
James Bond 007, Thunderball puzzle, Milton Bradley, MIB...........30.00
James Bond 007, wristwatch, Gilbert, 1964, NM in worn box 195.00
Jane Mansfield, figural bottle..35.00
Jetsons, mini puzzle, MIB 30.00
Jetsons, Official Bubble Blaster gun, 1975, M in pkg.....................12.50
Jetsons, space ship, Wendy's premium, set of 6.............................18.00

Jiminy Cricket, figure, American Pottery, 1940s, 6" 100.00
Jiminy Cricket, lamp, Disney, old shade, EX 300.00
John Travolta, doll, 1970s, M 18.00
JR (from Dallas), wristwatch, MIB 35.00
Kermit the Frog, wristwatch, Timex, MIB 25.00
King Kong, bank, figural, 1977, 13", EX 13.50
King Kong, promo brochure, mc, from 1933 movie, NM............125.00
Knight Rider, radio, Kit car form, MIB 27.50
Kojak, game, Milton Bradley, 1975, MIB 10.00
Kukla & Ollie, game, Parker Bros, 1962, MIB 25.00
Lady & Tramp, frame-tray puzzle, EX 15.00
Land of the Lost, color book, unused, EX..................................12.50
Lassie, color book set, Whitman, complete, EX 25.00
Laurel & Hardy, shakers, heads on tray w/bow ties, Beswick..........65.00
Laurel & Hardy, Super-Flex figures, Lakeside, '67, MIB................40.00
Leave It to Beaver, Rocket to the Moon board game, M................46.00
Lil Abner, birthday card, unused, w/envelope 11.50
Little Lulu, bank, vinyl figure, 1950s, 8", NM 28.00
Little Lulu, doll, cloth, yarn hair, Gund, 1972, EX in box..............30.00
Little Orphan Annie, book, LOA at Happy Home, 1930s, EX 15.00
Little Orphan Annie, ironing board set, Goshen, 1930s, VG 75.00

Little Orphan Annie and Sandy key-wind figures, marked Harold Gray, 5", 4", $675.00 for the set.

Little Orphan Annie, mask, paper, Ovaltine, 1933.......................18.00
Little Orphan Annie, pin-bk code pin, brass, 1935, 1¼" 22.50
Little Orphan Annie, pop-up book, Pleasure Books, 1935, EX....175.00
Little Orphan Annie, Sunburst decoder, 1937, EX.........................25.00
Little Orphan Annie, Treasure Hunt game board, 1930s................25.00
Little Orphan Annie, wristwatch, 7-jewel, Pecco, MIB 32.00
Little Orphan Annie & Sandy, pull toy, wood, 1930s, 9", EX 115.00
Little Red Riding Hood, doll, cloth, WD, w/hood & cape, EX....125.00
Lone Ranger, Atom Bomb ring, Kix premium, EX......................35.00
Lone Ranger, bendable figure, Lakeside, 1967, 6", NM................12.50
Lone Ranger, blotter, Bond Bread premium, EX..........................12.00
Lone Ranger, bread card, EX color, 1938 .... 7.50
Lone Ranger, cap pistol, tin, sm, EX 55.00
Lone Ranger, color book, 1953, NM 30.00
Lone Ranger, compass, bullet shape, EX 35.00
Lone Ranger, hairbrush, wooden hdl, 1939, EX 23.00
Lone Ranger, Hi-Yo Silver game, Parker Bros, 1938, NM 35.00
Lone Ranger, Hidden Rattler Adventure play set, 1973, NM........16.00
Lone Ranger, Official Deputy kit, 1980 premium, M in mailer......20.00
Lone Ranger, paint book, Whitman, 1941, EX............................20.00

Lone Ranger, pedometer, EX..20.00
Lone Ranger, post card, General Mills, 1951 ....17.50
Lone Ranger, Safety Scout badge, M..25.00
Lone Ranger, scrapbook, Whitman, 1950s, EX...........................35.00
Lone Ranger, Silver Bullet board game, 1956, EX......................25.00
Lone Ranger, target board, 1939, EX in box.............................175.00
Loopy de Loop, paint book, 1960, M 35.00
Ludwig Von Drake, mug, WDP, 1961...45.00
Maggie, figure, chalkware, 12", EX...45.00
Magilla Gorilla, bank, plastic book form, Ideal, 1964, EX 35.00
Mandrake the Magician, magic kit, 1949, NM in case................100.00
Margaret O'Brien, Book of Games & Fun, 1948, EX..................35.00
Margaret O'Brien, color book, 1930s, EX..................................20.00
Marilyn Monroe, statue, Royal Orleans, 1983, MIB...................65.00
Mary Marvel, wristwatch, EX in box..400.00
Mary Poppins, paint & crayon set, Disney, 1964, MIB................30.00
Mary Poppins, wallet, Aristocratic Leather, 1960s, NM 18.00
MASH, Hawkeye action figure, Tristar, 3¾", M on card 7.00
Melvin Purvis, Secret Operator's manual....................................25.00
Michael Jackson, radio, MIB..25.00
Mickey Mouse, acrobat string toy, wood, WDP, 1930s, EX............85.00
Mickey Mouse, alarm clock, Ingersoll, 1940s, NM in box............100.00
Mickey Mouse, bank, hard vinyl, 1950s, 4", NM 12.00
Mickey Mouse, bank, pnt compo treasure chest, 6¼", G.............135.00
Mickey Mouse, blackboard, Strathmore, 1940s, NM in box 50.00
Mickey Mouse, Bondex applique, 1946.....................................25.00
Mickey Mouse, book, ABC Book, Whitman, hardcover, '30s, EX 65.00
Mickey Mouse, book, ABC Storybook, Whitman, 1936, 7", G 30.00
Mickey Mouse, book, Bedtime Stories, 1930s, NM 50.00
Mickey Mouse, book, MM in Pigmy Land, paperbk, WD, '30s, VG....45.00
Mickey Mouse, bottle opener, brass figural 10.00
Mickey Mouse, clothes brush, 1930s, NM 66.00
Mickey Mouse, crayon set, Transogram, WDP, 1946, EX 28.00
Mickey Mouse, doll, velvet, Charlotte Clark, 1930s, 15", EX......950.00
Mickey Mouse, figure, bsk, w/walking stick, 1930s, 4½" 65.00
Mickey Mouse, figure, pnt cast lead, w/umbrella, 4", EX.............165.00
Mickey Mouse, gumball machine, plastic, Hasbro/WDP, 1968, M...25.00
Mickey Mouse, handkerchief, MM flying kite, 1930s, NM 20.00
Mickey Mouse, Magic Milk pump, Disney, 1950s, EX in box 15.00
Mickey Mouse, mask, starched cotton, pie-eyed, 1930s, VG..........50.00
Mickey Mouse, Movie Jecktor, electric, lt rust, 10", VG.............110.00
Mickey Mouse, paint box, metal, Transogram, 1950s, unused 20.00
Mickey Mouse, party game, WDE, EX in box............................135.00
Mickey Mouse, pencil box, cb diecut, Dixon, 1930s, EX 100.00
Mickey Mouse, pillow cover, pie-eyed, Vogue, 1931, M 115.00
Mickey Mouse, planter, sitting on ABC blocks, WDP 195.00
Mickey Mouse, plate, Bavarian china, WD, 1930s, 7", M 125.00
Mickey Mouse, pull toy, upright MM, NN Hill Brass, '30s, EX......85.00
Mickey Mouse, radio, 1950s, EX 130.00
Mickey Mouse, Rolatoy rattle, celluloid, WD, 1930s, 3", EX.........65.00
Mickey Mouse, saxophone, Czechoslovakia, 1930s, 16", EX 145.00
Mickey Mouse, Scuffy shoe polish, MIB 16.00
Mickey Mouse, sheet music, Wedding Party, Bagar, 1930s, VG 25.00
Mickey Mouse, Slugaroo game, 1950s, MIB...............................30.00
Mickey Mouse, spoon, premium, 1940s, NM in box....................40.00
Mickey Mouse, spoon, SP, Wm Rogers & Son, 1930s, NM 17.50
Mickey Mouse, Stardust paint-by-number kit, M 16.00
Mickey Mouse, Sunshine straws, EX in box 7.50
Mickey Mouse, teapot, brn lustre ware, 1930s, EX 25.00
Mickey Mouse, top, many characters, 1930s, 10", EX 60.00
Mickey Mouse, Touch of Velvet paint set, 1960s, M 16.00
Mickey Mouse, toy chest, cb, Odora, 1939, EX 85.00
Mickey Mouse, wristwatch, w/plastic statue, 1958, EX 140.00
Mickey Mouse & Beanstalk, shakers, ceramic, pr, MIB................12.50

Mickey Mouse watch with chain-link band, Ingersoll, late 1930s, $300.00. (Photo courtesy Hake's Americana, York, PA)

Mickey Mouse & Friends, globe, Rand McNally, 1940s, EX 65.00
Mighty Mouse, color book, 1953, EX..15.00
Mighty Mouse, fashion watch, wide band, Bradley, 1970s, M 30.00
Milton the Monster, game, Milton Bradley, 1975, EX 20.00
Minnie Mouse, cup, Patriot China, 1930s, 2"..............................35.00
Minnie Mouse, Fun-E-Flex figure, jtd wood, 1930s, 4", EX...........85.00
Minnie Mouse, pop-up book, 1933, M...300.00
Minnie Mouse, toothbrush holder, pnt bsk, decal, 5", VG...........275.00
Mission Impossible, View Master set, 1968, NM 38.00
Monkees, Hey-Hey Monkee puzzle, MIB.......................................38.00
Monkees, song book, w/photos throughout, 1967, EX 10.00
Mork, radio, eggship form, MIB...22.50
Mork & Mindy, card game, Milton Bradley, 1978, NM 7.50
Mother Goose, game, cb, 1914, EX in 7" sq box 135.00
Mr Spock, costume, 1976, MIB...25.00
Mr T, activity/color book, NM 5.00
Mummy, bendable figure, Universal, 1986, 8", M on card 16.00
Munsters, card game, EX..22.00
Mutt & Jeff, bank, AC Williams, 1915, 5¼", EX 145.00
Mutt & Jeff, cigar box, wood, paper labels, 1920s, EX 55.00
Our Gang, nodders, Hal Roach Studios, set of 6, EX in box 650.00
Our Gang, pencil box, Dixon, 1930s, VG......................................25.00
Pancho, mask, paper, Tip Top Bread premium 15.00
Partridge Family, color book, Saalfield, 1972, M 12.00
Patty Duke, game, Milton Bradley, 1963, EX................................20.00
Penelope Pitstop, jewelry kit, Hanna Barbera, '71, M on card 10.00
Peter Pan, color book, Whitman, 1950s, EX 12.00
Peter Pan, tie clasp, M..15.00
Pinky Lee, xylophone, Emenee, EX in orig box............................125.00
Pinocchio, alarm clock, metal case, Bayard/Fr, 1960s, M............185.00
Pinocchio, doll, cloth, 1950s, 14", EX..10.00
Pinocchio, doll, jtd wood, Made in Poland, 7½", M.....................35.00
Pinocchio, doll, plaster, 1960s, VG..40.00
Pinocchio, paint book, paper cover, Whitman, 1939, lg, EX 35.00
Pinocchio, school tablet, w/Stromboli, 1940, M...........................30.00
Pinocchio, scrapbook, Whitman, 1939, X-lg, VG.........................32.00
Pinocchio, squeeze toy, 1930s, VG 70.00
Pinocchio, valentine, Gepetto on raft, Disney, 1940, EX.............25.00
Planet of the Apes, battering ram, Mego, 1967, MIB...................18.50
Planet of the Apes, board game, MIB...15.00
Planet of the Apes, target game, NM on card..............................14.00
Pluto, color book, Whitman, WD, 1960s, NM 8.00
Popeye, ash tray, Schavoior Rubber, 1935, 3", EX.......................125.00
Popeye, Bingo game, tin litho, 1929, EX......................................48.00
Popeye, Colorforms, Popeye's Birthday Party, 1961, NM 28.00
Popeye, crayon set, King Features, 1932, EX................................35.00

Popeye, magic putty, 1950s, M on card 8.00
Popeye, modeling clay, American Crayon, 1936, EX 35.00
Popeye, pencil box, Eagle Pencils, 1929, EX................................30.00
Popeye, Pipe Toss game, EX in orig box......................................110.00
Popeye, popcorn sack, burlap, EX graphics, '50s, 100-lb sz 55.00
Popeye, post card, mc, 1973, M, set of 12 ....20.00
Popeye, ramp walker, compo figure, 1930s, EX...........................125.00
Popeye, scrapbook, 1929, VG..25.00
Popeye, Where's Me Pipe game, 1937, EX in box 200.00
Popeye & the Pirates, book, Duenewald, 1945, 9", G..................75.00
Porky Pig, planter, ceramic, 1940s, NM.......................................20.00
Prince Valiant, color book, 1954, 14x11", M...............................35.00
Quickdraw McGraw, game, 1970s, NM 12.50
Ramar of the Jungle, color book, unused, M................................22.00
Ramar of the Jungle, puzzle, 1955, set of 4, NM in box 30.00
Red Ryder, holster, leather, no gun, EX.......................................15.00
Red Ryder, lucky coin, Penney's...12.00
Rin-Tin-Tin, ring, gr plastic, premium, 1950s, M.........................18.00
Road Runner, costume, Ben Cooper, 1979, MIB...........................15.00
Road Runner, puzzle, Whitman, 1968, M 12.50
Road Runner, thermos, 1971, NM..28.50
Robin Hood, 3-D Adventure game, unused, 1955.........................40.00
Ronald Reagan, mug, ceramic, M...15.00
Roy Rogers, bank, metal boot form, Almar, 1950s, NM................30.00
Roy Rogers, March of Comics, Sears ad premium, EX 15.00
Roy Rogers, photo post card, Quaker Oats premium 10.00
Roy Rogers, pin, boot form, cereal premium, M 12.50
Roy Rogers, pin-bk button, Happy Trails, EX................................ 7.50
Roy Rogers, playing cards, 1950s, EX in box.................................20.00
Roy Rogers, souvenir book, 1950, M..40.00
Roy Rogers, wristwatch, w/jewelry..275.00
Roy Rogers & Trigger, camera, 1950s, NM...................................45.00
Roy Rogers & Trigger, rocking horse, EX 150.00
Roy Rogers & Trigger, Signal Siren flashlite, VG in box..............65.00
Roy Rogers' dog Bullet, figure, Hartland, 1950s, sm, EX 35.00
Sal Mineo, Fan Club button, tin litho, 1950s, 3", NM 5.00

Schmoo nesting figures in celluloid, largest: 5½", $75.00 for six.

Schmoo, planter, United Features, Hanzako's Ceramic, 1943 ......50.00
Scoobie-Doo, stuffed dog, 4", NM..20.00
Secret Agent, board game, MIB 25.00
Secret Squirrel, costume, 1965, NM in box 35.00
Sergeant Preston of Yukon, premium card, 1956, NM, 10 for 12.50
Shadow, bookmark, 1940s, 3", VG..18.00

Shirley Temple, barrette & bow set, 1930s, EX 30.00
Shirley Temple, book, Captain January, movie illus, EX.............20.00
Shirley Temple, book, Heidi, Saalfield, 1937, NM......................30.00
Shirley Temple, bowl, cereal; cobalt glass, 1930s 35.00
Shirley Temple, Christmas card, Hallmark, 1935, NM 27.50
Shirley Temple, color book, Saalfield, 1936, EX 30.00
Shirley Temple, creamer, cobalt glass, 4½" 38.00
Shirley Temple, mug, cobalt glass, 3¾" 40.00
Shirley Temple, print, Drink Milk Daily, 1938, fr, 8x10".............30.00
Shirley Temple, school tablet, 1930s, unused, NM 30.00
Shirley Temple, scrapbook, Saalfield, 1937, EX 35.00
Six Million Dollar Man, puzzle, 200-pc, NM 10.00
Sleeping Beauty, Colorforms dress designer, WD 20.00
Sleeping Beauty, game, Parker Bros, WD, VG...........................27.50
Sleeping Beauty, Magic Paint book, Whitman, NM 25.00
Sleepy, figure, bsk, Japan/WD, 3" 20.00
Smilin' Jack, color book, Saalfield, 1946, M 20.00
Smitty, color book, McLoughlin, 1932, 24-pg, VG 37.50
Smokey Bear, beach ball, M 15.00
Smokey Bear, clock, electric, VG...27.50
Smurf, alarm clock, plastic figural, talking, NM 25.00
Sniffles, bank, pnt pot metal, EX 35.00
Snoopy, humidifier, w/instructions, NM..................................48.00
Snoopy, wristwatch, 1958, NM 35.00
Snow White, bedspread, Bates, twin sz, NM 175.00
Snow White, flour sack, common, 1950s, EX 7.50
Snow White, handkerchief, pk, 1930s, M................................20.00
Snow White, lamp, rpl shade, 1938, EX 125.00
Snow White, night light, La Mode Studios, 1930s, NM 100.00
Snow White, satchel, vinyl, 1940s, EX 75.00
Snow White, sink, Wolverine, 1960s, NM................................18.00
Snow White, valentine, mechanical cottage, 1938, lg, EX 20.00
Snow White, wristwatch, w/ceramic statue, 1958, NM in box ...185.00
Snow White & Dopey, telephone, NN Hill Brass, 1930s, NM....125.00
Snow White & 7 Dwarfs, cut-out book, Whitman, 1938, EX 85.00
Snow White & 7 Dwarfs, drawing tablet, paper, 1937, NM...........35.00
Space Girl, costume, Ben Cooper, 1950s, EX in box 18.50
Space Patrol, Hydrogen Ray Gun ring.....................................145.00
Space Patrol, rocket gun w/darts, NM in box 175.00
Space 1999, Colorforms, 1976, M 12.50
Space 1999, friction Moon car, 1976, M on card......................30.00
Space 1999, Stun Ray gun, 1976, M on card 20.00
Speedy Gonzales, decanter, ceramic figural, 1960s, 11", NM.........40.00
Spider Woman, sunglasses, 1979, M on card 7.00
Spiderman, mask, rubber, Ben Cooper, 1978, NM 8.00
Spiderman, Secret War figure, 1st issue, Mattel, M on card..........12.00
Spiro Agnew, wristwatch, MIB 65.00
Star Trek, Colorforms, 1975, MIB..20.00
Star Trek, Klingon Cruiser, die-cast metal, Dinky, 1979, M 22.00
Star Trek, motion picture gum card set, M 8.50
Star Trek, napkins, Paramount, 1976, set of 20, M in pkg 32.00
Star Trek, Phaser Ray gun, 1976, M on card...........................20.00
Star Wars, blueprints, M in pkg.. 7.50
Starsky & Hutch, game, Milton Bradley, 1977, MIB.................... 6.00
Starsky & Hutch, Gyro-Powered car, Fleetwood, 1975, M 20.00
Steve Canyon, color book, 1952, lg, NM.................................18.00
Steve Canyon, space goggles, plastic & rubber, 1940s, VG.........15.00
Straight Arrow, bandana 22.00
Straight Arrow, cereal bowl..22.00
Superman, Action Comics pin, 1st issue.................................100.00
Superman, ballpoint pen, plastic, 1978, NM 5.00
Superman, book, Official Quiz, paperbk, 1978, EX..................... 5.00
Superman, Calling Superman game, 1954, NM 65.00
Superman, Colorforms, 1964, NM 36.00

Superman, gum wrapper, 1966, EX 10.00
Superman, horseshoe set, 1950s, VG in orig box........................130.00
Superman, pencil case, w/contents, 1940s, M..........................88.00
Superman, Superman of America pin-bk button, 1940s, EX........28.00
Superman, wristwatch, all orig, ca 1940, NM..........................265.00
Tarzan, pin-bk button, Foster art on yel, 1974, 3", M 10.00
Tarzan, popsicle coin, EX 8.00
Tarzan, radio giveaway figures, Tarzan/chimp & baby/2 lions........45.00
Tom & Jerry, hand puppet, cloth & vinyl, 1952, NM.................25.00
Tom & Jerry, talking hand puppet, silent, Mattel, 1965, EX..........30.00
Tom Corbett, binoculars, w/complete decals, NM 30.00
Tom Corbett, folder for goggles, Kellogg's, 4-pg......................23.00
Tom Corbett, punch-out book, EX 35.00
Tom Mix, Arrowhead compass, plastic, EX..............................32.00
Tom Mix, Championship belt buckle 65.00
Tom Mix, color book, 1936, EX...35.00
Tom Mix, decoder pin-bk, set of 5 ....50.00
Tom Mix, glow medal & ribbon 50.00
Tom Mix, Good Luck spinner 35.00
Tom Mix, gun, wood, 1939, EX 95.00
Tom Mix, ID bracelet, premium, 1947, NM 40.00
Tom Mix, knife, Ralston Straight Shooters, NM 28.50
Tom Mix, manual, 1941, lt foxing on cover 35.00
Tom Mix, Paint & Draw book, Whitman, 1935, 96-pg, EX..........38.00
Tom Mix, periscope, Ralston Straight Shooters premium, NM 50.00
Tom Mix, Rodeo rope, Mordt, 1930s, EX 70.00
Tom Mix, signal arrow, Lucite, EX 30.00
Tom Mix, sliding whistle ring 60.00
Tom Mix, wristwatch, NM..295.00
Tom Mix & Tony, pocketknife, EX 75.00
Tony the Tiger, radio, figural, NM..25.00
Top Cat, costume, 1962, NM in box 30.00
Twiggy, game, Milton Bradley, 1967, VG in split box.................18.00
Uncle Scrooge, bank, ceramic, 1961, M 18.00
Underdog, puzzle, 1971, EX in box 12.50
Wagon Train, color book, M 20.00
Welcome Back Kotter, color book, Whitman, 1975, M 10.00
Wild Bill Hickok, color book, 1962, NM..................................22.50
Wild Bill Hickok & Jingles, bunkhouse kit, M in envelope..........28.00
Wimpy, walking figure, compo, from Thimble Theatre set, EX 75.00
Wolfman, bendable figure, Universal, 1986, 8", M on card............ 7.50
Wonder Woman, signature stamp set, Craft, 1984, M on card 7.50
Woody Woodpecker, Learn To Draw book, unused.....................12.50
Wyatt Earp, board game, 1958, EX in box 25.00
Wyatt Earp, mug, milk glass, 1950s, M 10.00
Yellow Kid, Adams gum card #1 ....17.50
Yellow Kid, Alphabet booklet, color, EX..................................55.00
Yellow Kid, cap bomb, CI, Ives, EX.......................................165.00
Yellow Kid, checkerboard #3 puzzle 60.00
Yellow Kid, cvd wood figure, 1940s.......................................125.00
Yellow Kid, ice cream mold..190.00
Yellow Kid, newspaper panel, Visit to NJ, 1897, full pg.............280.00
Yellow Kid, newspaper panel, 1897, fr, ½-pg 230.00
Yellow Kid, pack gum 150.00
Yellow Kid, paperweight, CI, early, VG...................................125.00
Yellow Kid, poster, NY Journal, mc 775.00
Yellow Kid, rocking chair, imprint on bk, 30", EX 700.00
Yellow Kid, stick pin, full body 100.00
Yellow Kid, store receipt, Brucker 15.00
Yogi Bear, costume, 1963, NM in box....................................25.00
Yogi Bear, Little Golden Book, 1960, M.................................... 8.00
Yogi Bear, night light, ceramic figural, 1980, MIB 30.00
Yogi Bear, Paint By Number set, Craftmaster, 1979, NM 12.00
Yogi Bear, Stuff 'N Lace doll kit, 1959, M 40.00

Zorro, gauntlets, Wells Lamont, mk WDP, pr 65.00
Zorro, gloves, cotton, portrait on bl, NM 20.00
Zorro, Secret Signet mask, M in orig display pkg........................22.50
Zorro, whip set, Shimmel, 1950s, M on card..............................45.00

Peters and Reed

John Peters and Adam Reed founded their pottery in Zanesville, Ohio, just before the turn of the century, using the local red clay to produce a variety of wares. Moss Aztec, introduced about 1912, has an unglazed exterior with designs molded in high relief and the recesses highlighted with a green wash. Only the interior is glazed to hold water. Pereco (named for Peters, Reed and Company) is glazed in semi-matt blue, maroon, or cream. Orange was also used very early, but such examples are rare. Shapes are simple with in-mold decoration sometimes borrowed from the Moss Aztec line. Wilse Blue is a line of high-gloss medium blue with dark specks on simple shapes. Landsun, characterized by its soft matt multicolor or blue and gray combinations, is decorated either by dripping or by hand brushing in an effect sometimes called Flame or Herringbone. Chromal, in much the same colors as Landsun, may be decorated with a realistic scenic, or the swirling application of colors may merely suggest one. (Brush-McCoy made a very similar line called Chromart. Neither will be marked; and, due to the lack of documented background material available, it may be impossible make a positive identification. Collectors nearly always attribute this type of decoration to Peters and Reed.) Shadow Ware is a glossy, multicolor drip over a harmonious base color. When the base is black, the effect is often iridescent.

Perhaps the most familiar line is the brown high-glaze artware with the 'sprigged'-type designs. Although research has uncovered no positive proof, it is generally accepted as having been made by Peters and Reed. It is interesting to note that many of the artistic shapes in this line are recognizable as those made by Weller, Roseville, and other Zanesville area companies. Other lines include Mirror Black, Persian, and an unidentified line which collectors call Mottled Colors. In this high-gloss line, the red clay body often shows through the splashed-on multicolors.

In 1922 the company became known as the Zane Pottery. Peters and Reed retired, and Harry McClelland became president. Charles Chilcote designed new lines, and production of many of the old lines continued. The body of the ware after 1922 was light in color. Marks include the impressed logo or ink stamp 'Zaneware' in a rectangle.

Ash tray, Landsun, bl/gr/brn, 3½" 35.00
Bookends, Pereco, section of fluted column w/leaves, 5"................70.00
Bowl, Landsun, bl/wht, 6"...35.00
Bowl, Moss Aztec, dragonflies, 2x4"..................................35.00
Bowl, Moss Aztec, emb fans, #402, 4".................................30.00
Bowl, Moss Aztec, pine cones/needles, #404, 7" W.....................45.00
Bowl, Pereco, emb twigs, flared, 3x8"................................35.00
Candlestick, Zaneware, yel, twisted, 9", pr..........................85.00
Ewer, Brn Ware, garlands, 3 sm ft, 5x5½".............................50.00
Ewer, Brn Ware, grape sprigs, 11"...................................100.00
Flower frog, Landsun, lily pad form, 6½" W...........................35.00
Flower frog, Zaneware, turtle figure, 3" W...........................85.00
Flowerpot, Moss Aztec, pine cones/needles, 6x5".....................45.00
Ginger jar, Landsun, gr/bl swirls, #1, w/lid........................125.00
Hanging basket, Moss Aztec, grapevines, sgn Ferrell, 9"..............95.00
Jardiniere, Egyptian Ware, matt gr, fine detail, 10"................450.00
Jardiniere, Moss Aztec, floral border relief, 7½"...................85.00
Jardiniere & pedestal, Moss Aztec, floral band, 32"................450.00
Jug, Brn Ware, sprigged-on cavalier ea side, 5½".....................95.00
Letter holder, Brn Ware, floral sprigs, 8" L.........................65.00

Loving cup, Brn Ware, lyre & leaf sprigs, 3-hdl, 6".................125.00
Mug, Brn Ware, leafy sprigs ea side, ornate hld, 5"..................65.00
Mug, Brn Ware, sprigged-on cavalier, incurvate sides, 5½"...........75.00
Tankard, Brn Ware, grapes/leafy garlands, ornate hdl, 14"..........175.00
Tankard, Brn Ware, sprigs of grapes/leaves, scalloped, 18".........245.00
Umbrella stand, Marbleized, 22"....................................425.00
Vase, Brn Ware, appl lion's heads, sm neck, 15"....................165.00
Vase, Brn Ware, floral garlands, rim-to-shoulder hdls, 11".........125.00
Vase, Brn Ware, floral garlands, 5x4"...............................45.00
Vase, Brn Ware, floral sprigs, hdls, 12"...........................140.00
Vase, Brn Ware, garlands appl on doughnut form w/hdls, 11".........150.00
Vase, Brn Ware, grapevine sprigs, bulbous bottom, 18"..............250.00
Vase, bud; Landsun, swirled colors, 10".............................55.00
Vase, bud; Marbleized, petticoat base, 6½"..........................50.00
Vase, Chromal, house/fence/trees (realistic), bulbous, 7"..........395.00
Vase, Chromal, mtn scene w/trees (realistic), #6, 8"...............350.00
Vase, Landsun, bl/beige/brn, flared, #336, 4".......................35.00
Vase, Landsun, gr/bl/brn 'flames,' 5"...............................50.00

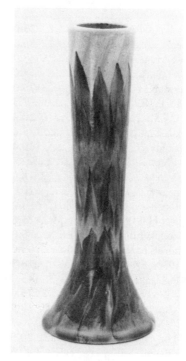

Vase, Landsun, 12", $65.00.

Vase, Landsun, gr/bl/brn swirls, #40D, 14"..........................95.00
Vase, Marbleized, tan/gr swirls on yel, 9"..........................70.00
Vase, Mirror Ware, blk irid w/gr drips, 4"..........................75.00
Vase, Moss Aztec, pine cone relief, flared rim, #173, 8"............65.00
Vase, Shadow Ware, tan w/bl & yel runs, bulbous, 8".................85.00
Vase, Wilse Blue, bulbous top & base, 5½"...........................40.00
Vase, Wilse Blue, waisted cylinder, 7"..............................35.00
Wall pocket, Egyptian Ware, Pharoah profile on gr matt, 8".........125.00
Wall pocket, Marbleized, bl/yel/blk/brn, 7".........................75.00
Wall pocket, Moss Aztec, wide floral/leaf band, Ferrell, 10".......90.00
Wall pocket, Zaneware, yel, 10½"....................................55.00
Window box, Moss Aztec, Grecian females, 13" L....................135.00

Pewabic

The Pewabic Pottery was formally established in Detroit, Michigan, in 1907 by Mary Chase Perry Stratton and Horace James Caulkins. The two had worked together since 1903, firing their ware in a small kiln Caulkins had designed especially for use by the dental trade.

Always a small operation which relied upon basic equipment and the skill of the workers, they took pride in being commissioned for several important architectural tile installations.

Some of the early artware was glazed a simple matt green; occasionally other colors were added, sometimes in combination, one over the other in a drip effect. Later Stratton developed a lustrous crystalline glaze. The body of the ware was highly fired and extremely hard. Shapes were basic, and decorative modeling, if used at all, was in low relief. Mary Stratton kept the pottery open until her death in 1961. In 1968 it was purchased and reopened by Michigan State University.

Several marks were used over the years: a triangle with 'Revelation Pottery' (for a short time only); 'Pewabic' with five maple leaves; and the impressed circle mark.

Ash tray, burgundy lustre, paper label, 4" dia 130.00
Ash tray, pk/gr, triangular 100.00
Bowl, crazed gold/gr, grooved lines at top, mk/label, 2" H 385.00
Bowl, gr, rolled rim, ftd, imp mk, 5x9½" 195.00
Bowl, purple/bl/tan irid, shallow/flared/ftd, mk/label, 10" **1,600.00**
Bowl vase, mauve/gr/bl metallic, shouldered, short ft, 5" **1,300.00**
Box, gr/beige, outline of deer on lid, imp mk, 5x4", pr 650.00
Box, moss/burgundy, stylized bird cvg on lid, 5x4" 300.00
Candle holder, moss gr, flower form, 4" dia, set of 4 ....220.00
Charger, turq/gray/gr flambe, EX irid, 14½" 800.00
Lamp, orange matt, thrown, scrolled metal base, 1910, 29" 800.00
Lamp base, globby gray-brn/lt purple, pear form, 12x8" 850.00
Tile, geometric Mayan bird, 6" 125.00
Vase, beige matt w/lustrous gr drip at rim, cup form, 4" 435.00
Vase, bl drips at top on irid, 2½" 295.00

Vase, blue-green and umber, hand turned, 10", $1,760.00.

Vase, bl/gr/purple irid, bulbous body, flaring neck, 6" **2,400.00**
Vase, cvd sqs in band at shoulder, royal bl matt, 9x4" 400.00
Vase, gr/gray/bl mottle, baluster, 2½" 250.00
Vase, irid purple feathering on gold-tan, label, 4x3½" 650.00
Vase, lustrous aqua/rose, cylindrical w/flared rim, 4½" 650.00
Vase, purple metallic/sand-color, waves at base, WBS, 8" **2,800.00**
Vase, purple/bl metallic, gourd form, paper label, 4¾" **1,100.00**
Vase, speckled orange, rolled rim, firing chip, 5x4½" 175.00
Vase, trefoils in high relief on gr matt, gourd form, 6x4½" **1,000.00**
Vase, yel-gr drip w/copper irid, ogee sides, rnd mk, 5x3" 275.00

Pewter

Pewter is a metal alloy of tin, copper, very small parts of bismuth and/or antimony, and sometimes lead. Very little American pewter contained lead, however, because much of the ware was designed to be used as tableware, and makers were aware that the use of lead could

result in poisoning. (Pieces that do contain lead are usually darker in color and heavier than those that have no lead.) Most of the fine examples of American pewter date from 1700 to the 1840s. Many pieces were melted down and recast into bullets during the American Revolution in 1775; this accounts to some extent why examples from this period are quite difficult to find. The pieces that did survive may include buttons, buckles, and writing equipment as well as the tableware we generally think of.

After the Revolution, makers began using antimony as the major alloy with the tin in an effort to regain the popularity of pewter, which glassware and china was beginning to replace in the home. The resulting product, known as britannia, had a lustrous silver-like appearance and was far more durable. While closely related, britannia is a collectible in its own right and should not be confused with pewter.

Key: tm — touch mark

Basin, Boardman & Co NY, minor wear, 8¼" 275.00
Basin, English, faint tm, battering/wear, 3x12" 145.00
Basin, Geo Lightner, pitting/dents/1 rpr, 7½" 175.00
Basin, Joseph Danforth, minor wear/dents, 8" 425.00
Basin, Joseph Danforth Jr, EX tm, 12" 2,200.00
Basin, Nathaniel Austin, eagle tm, minor wear/dents, 2x8" 600.00
Basin, Samuel Danforth, partial tm, 6½" 500.00
Basin, Thos D Boardman, minor wear, 1¾x7" 300.00
Basin, Thos Danforth, EX tm, 8", NM..475.00
Basin, unmk, minor battering/sm soldered rpr, 1¾x6⅝" 100.00
Basin, Wm & Samuel Yale, partial tm, 6½", EX...........................500.00
Beaker, Boardman & Hart, EX tm, 5", NM..................................250.00
Beaker, unmk Am, tapered, sm base dent, 2¾" 50.00
Beaker, Yale & Co, Britannia mk, minor dents, 3" 100.00
Candlestick, Fuller & Smith, EX tm, minor dents, 8½", pr..........500.00
Candlestick, Rufus Dunham, line tm, 6" EX, pr 600.00
Candlestick, unmk, 20", pr..500.00
Candlestick, unmk, 8", pr..290.00
Chalice, communion; James Dixon & Son, pr 250.00
Chalice, communion; Reed & Barton, 7" 125.00
Chalice, unmk Am, 6½", EX..75.00
Charger, Chas White Leigh, wear/scratches, 15"..........................300.00
Charger, Cornhill, wear/scratches, 16½" 300.00
Charger, Nathaniel Austin, minor wear/rprs, 13½".....................450.00
Charger, Richard Austin, booge rpr, polished, 13" 200.00
Charger, Richard King, 16½" 375.00
Charger, Samuel Hamlin, minor wear/scratches 13½" 600.00
Charger, Samuel Hamlin, sm rim split/minor wear, 13½" 525.00
Charger, Semper Eadem, partial tm, 13½", NM 800.00
Charger, Thos Badger, eagle tm, minor wear/scratches, 13½" 650.00
Charger, Thos Badger, partial tm, numerous knife mks, 12" 400.00
Charger, Townsend & Griffin, very worn/scratched, 13" 100.00
Charger, Wm J Ellsworth, faint tm, pitted areas, 13" 500.00

Coffeepot, Allen Porter, Westbrook, Maine, 1830-40, 12", $600.00.

Coffeepot, Roswell Gleason, EX tm, 11" 250.00
Communion flagon, Taunton Britannia, 11", VG.....................175.00
Cuspidor, Eben Smith, line tm, 6" dia, EX 225.00
Cuspidor, unmk, vase form w/flaring rim, 5"........................400.00
Dish, deep; Samuel Pierce, EX tm, minor pitting/mks, 13½" 750.00
Flagon, communion; James Dixon & Son, EX detail, 12¾" 375.00
Flagon, Eben Smith, minor dents, 10½"...............................375.00
Flagon, Thos Danforth Boardman, EX tm, 11" NM 900.00
Flagon, Wm Calder, line tm, 11", NM.................................650.00
Inkwell, Fenn Gaius & Jason, worn tm, 1½x1¾", EX 200.00
Lamp, camphene; Henry Hopper, floral band, saucer base, 10" ...400.00
Lamp, Capen & Molineux, rpl brass collar, 10" 150.00
Lamp, fluid; Endicott & Summer, snuffer caps gone, 6½" 400.00
Lamp, hand; Capen & Molineux, 5½", VG...........................150.00
Lamp, hand; Wm H Starr, 2¾", VG..................................125.00
Lamp, whale oil; Capen & Molineux, period burner, 12", EX 300.00
Lamp, whale oil; F Porter, saucer base, ring hdl, 6" 275.00
Lamp, whale oil; Roswell Gleason, period burner, 7¾", EX 200.00
Lamp, whale oil; S Rust's Pat, polished/battered, no burner, 8" ...400.00
Lamp, whale oil; single spout burner, simple tooled band, 4".........85.00
Lamp, whale oil; unmk Am, minor pitting, orig burner, 2⅛".......150.00
Lamp, whale oil; Wm H Starr, keg-shape font, 10", EX 400.00
Mug, Geo Richardson, VG tm, side pouring, 1-pt, NM 600.00
Mug, Nathaniel Austin, EX tm, rprs, 1-qt, EX 1,400.00
Mug, Thos Danforth III, strong tm, minor marring, 1-pt.........1,100.00
Mug, Thos Danforth III, 2 tm, minor dents, 1-qt, EX.............1,000.00
Pitcher, Boardman & Hart, wear & minor damage w/rpr, 8" 325.00
Pitcher, Rufus Dunham, w/lid, minor rprs, 2-qt, VG..................150.00
Pitcher, syrup; Homan & Co, EX tm, w/lid, minor dents, 7½" ...125.00
Pitcher, unmk Am, minor pitting, 2-qt 150.00
Plate, Badger tm, initials on rim, wear/scratches, 8" 300.00
Plate, Ben & Joseph Harbeson, EX tm, normal wear, 5⅞" 400.00
Plate, eagle tm, att R Palethorp Jr, Phila, 1820s, 8" 100.00
Plate, Edward Danforth, wear/pitting, soldered split, 8" 225.00
Plate, Frederick Bassett, EX tm, 8¼", VG...........................300.00
Plate, Henry Will, hammered booge, 9", EX 500.00
Plate, Jacob Whitmore, dbl tm, normal wear, 8" 225.00
Plate, John Danforth, partial tm, very worn/corroded, 8½".........135.00
Plate, John Skinner, smooth brim, normal mks, 9" 600.00
Plate, Love tm, minor wear/sm plugged hole, 8⅜" 250.00
Plate, Made in Newport by D Melville, battered/rpr, 8".............250.00
Plate, Nathaniel Austin, eagle tm, wear/rpr, 8" 250.00
Plate, Richard Austin, wear/minor battering, 8" 200.00
Plate, Richard Lee, EX tm, pitted areas, 8" 200.00
Plate, Samuel Danforth tm, 7⅞" 325.00
Plate, Samuel Havelin, good rpr, 8" 375.00
Plate, Samuel Pierce, EX dbl tm, normal knife wear, 8" 400.00
Plate, Thos & Townsend Compton, minor wear, 7⅝" 125.00
Plate, Thos Badger, Boston, ca 1790s, 14¾" 500.00
Plate, Thos Danforth Boardman, EX dbl tm, 8¼", NM.............300.00
Plate, unmk Am, dent, 8"..150.00
Plate, unmk Am, normal wear, rare sz, 4¾" 225.00
Porringer, att Richard Lee, emb hdl, rare, 2¼" 150.00
Porringer, cast flowered hdl, 5" dia 250.00
Porringer, cast Lee-type hdl, sm rim rpr, 5" dia......................275.00
Porringer, mk NA, att Nathaniel Austin, crown hdl, 4½" 600.00
Porringer, Samuel Hamlin Sr, EX tm, rpr/minor dent, 4¾" 550.00
Porringer, Thos Danforth Boardman, crown hdl, 5", NM...........350.00
Spigot, unmk, 4¼", EX 30.00
Spoon, eagle tm, 8"...40.00
Sugar bowl, unmk Am, 8" 275.00
Sugar bowl, unmk English, 3¾"..225.00
Sundial, IH tm, 4½", EX..200.00
Tall pot, A Porter, minor split/lip damage, 12" 425.00

Tall pot, Benham Best Britannia, minor dents/rpr, 13½" 250.00
Tall pot, G Richardson Warranted, minor wear/battering, 11"....525.00
Tankard, J Moyes-Edinborough, hinged lid, '½ Pint,' EX............125.00
Teapot, Henry H Graves, line tm, 8", EX.............................100.00
Teapot, Thos D & Samuel Boardman, TD & SB tm, 7", EX 500.00
Teapot, unmk Am, battered hdl, minor bottom damage, 7¾" 165.00
Tumbler, ummk, wear/battered, 2½"....................................60.00

Phoenix Bird

Blue and white Phoenix Bird china has been produced by various Japanese potteries from the early 1900s. With slight variations, the design features the Japanese bird of paradise and scroll-like vines of Kara-Kusa, or Chinese grass. Although some of their earlier ware is unmarked, the majority is marked in some fashion. More than one hundred different stamps have been reported, with 'Made in Japan' the one most often found, and Morimura's wreath or crossed stems (both having the letter 'M' within) coming in second. The cloverleaf with 'Japan' below very often indicates an item having a high-quality transfer print design. Newer items, if marked at all, carry a paper label. Compared to the older ware, the coloring of the new is whiter and the blue more harsh; the design is sparse with more ground area showing. Although collectors buy even 'new' pieces, the older is of course more highly prized and valued. For further information we recommend *Phoenix Bird Chinaware, Books I — IV*, written and privately published by our advisor, Joan Oates; her address is in the Directory under Michigan. Join Phoenix Bird Collectors of America (PBCA) and receive the *Discoveries* newsletter, an informative publication that will further your appreciation of this chinaware.

Bowl, bouillon; w/underplate...17.50
Bowl, cereal; 6" 12.50
Bowl, scalloped, 5½" 18.00
Butter dish, w/patterned insert 75.00
Cake tray, rnd 65.00
Chocolate pot 135.00
Cracker jar, 5½" 45.00
Creamer & sugar bowl, loop hdl..35.00
Cup, inverted bell, 2¾"..18.00
Cup & saucer, coffee; 2"...10.00
Custard cup, no inside border 15.00
Egg cup, single...10.00
Gravy boat, attached underplate, 7".......................................65.00
Hair receiver 45.00
Pitcher, lemonade; bulbous, 6"...125.00
Platter, 17"..135.00
Sauce boat, leaf shape, w/underplate, 6¼" 65.00
Shaker, dome top, 2¾", pr...20.00
Tea tile, 6⅛" 35.00

Child's 3-piece tea set (#2), $95.00.

Teapot, loop hdl, 8¼" W 45.00
Tureen, oval, 11" 125.00

Phoenix Glass

Founded in 1880 in Monaca, Pennsylvania, the Phoenix Glass Company became one of the country's foremost manufacturers of lighting glass by the early 1900s. They also produced a wide variety of utilitarian and decorative glassware, including art glass by Joseph Webb, colored cut glass, Gone-with-the-Wind style oil lamps, hotel and bar ware, and pharmaceutical glassware. Today, however, collectors are primarily interested in the 'Sculptured Artware' produced in the 1930s and 1940s. These beautiful pressed and mold-blown pieces are most often found in white milk glass or crystal with various color treatments or a satin finish.

Phoenix did not mark their 'Sculptured Artware' line on the glass; instead, a silver and black or gold and black foil label in the shape of the mythical phoenix bird was used.

Quite often glassware made by the Consolidated Lamp and Glass Company of nearby Coraopolis, Pennsylvania, is mistaken for Phoenix' 'Sculptured Artware.' Though the style of the glass is very similar, one distinguishing characteristic is that perhaps 80% of the time Phoenix applied color to the background leaving the raised design plain in contrast, while Consolidated generally applied color to the raised design and left the background plain. Also, for the most part, the patterns and colors used by Phoenix were distinctively different from those used by Consolidated. The glassware of both firms is of equal quality and comparable value.

In 1970 Phoenix Glass became a division of Anchor Hocking which in turn was acquired by the Newell Group in 1987. Phoenix has the distinction of being one of the oldest continuously operating glass factories in the United States. For more information, see the section on Consolidated Glass.

Key:
MG — milk glass

Lighting

Oil lamp, GWTW, MG, bl & pk flowers, filigree base.................**300.00**
Shade, crystal w/acid-etched design, 2" fitter, 5" H.......................**18.00**

Reuben Line

Catalonian, sugar bowl, dk bl on crystal, triangular.........................**30.00**
Catalonian, vase, amber on crystal, cylindrical, label, 7"..............**60.00**
Catalonian, vase, fan, dk bl on crystal, 7".....................................**50.00**
Philodendron, vase, Reuben line bl on opal, 11".........................**150.00**
Wild Geese, vase, amber on crystal, satin pattern, label..............**200.00**

Sculptured Artware

Ash tray, coral bkground/MOP flowers on MG, 5½" L..................**65.00**
Ash tray, slate gray bkground/MOP flowers on MG, 3" L.............**35.00**
Aster, vase, cadet bl bkground on satin MG, 7"............................**90.00**
Bachelor Button, vase, gr bkground on satin MG, 7"...................**150.00**
Bluebell, vase, taupe bkground on satin MG, 7"..........................**115.00**
Candy box, lt bl bkground, wht violets on crystal, 6½" dia.........**150.00**
Cigarette box/lid, wht satin bkground, bl flowers/gr leaves..........**100.00**
Cosmos, vase, aqua bkground, wht flowers on crystal, 7½".........**125.00**
Daisy, vase, bl bkground on MG, glossy figures, 9¼" dia.............**190.00**
Dancing Girl, vase, gr bkground on MG, satin figures, 12".........**350.00**
Diving Girl, bowl, pk bkground/wht figures on crystal, oval........**200.00**
Fern, vase, pk ferns, gr grass, pale bl bkground on MG, 7".............**90.00**
Freesia vase, cedar rose bkground on crystal, 8".........................**140.00**
Jewel, vase, lt bl bkground, MOP pattern on MG, 5".....................**65.00**

Diving Girl bowl, pink on crystal, 13" long, $200.00.

Jonquil, platter, lt bl bkground on crystal satin, 14" dia...............**250.00**
Lily, vase, sea gr bkground on crystal satin, tri-crimp, 8".............**120.00**
Madonna, vase, burgundy bkground on MG, MOP figure, 10"....**175.00**
Philodendron, vase, amber, 1960s...**40.00**
Pine Cone, vase, no cones, aqua on crystal satin, 6½".................**200.00**
Primrose, vase, cedar rose on crystal, 8¾"..................................**275.00**
Strawberry, bowl, 3-part, tan on MG, 10½".................................**375.00**
Strawberry, candle holders, tan on MG, 4¼", pr..........................**130.00**
Thistle, vase, orchid bkground on crystal, wht pattern, 18".........**375.00**
Tiger Lily, bowl, wht bkground, crystal satin flowers, 11½".........**200.00**
Water Lily, bowl, gr bkground on crystal, satin pattern, 14"........**300.00**
Water Lily, candle holders, gr on crystal, 4¾", pr.......................**115.00**
Wild Geese, vase, flint opal, satin finish, 9¼"............................**200.00**
Wild Rose, vase, taupe bkground on MG, shaded pattern, 10½".**150.00**

Miscellaneous

Anniversary, vase, 1880-1980, crystal sprayed ivory......................**40.00**
Bicentennial, vase, crystal w/red, wht, & bl pattern......................**40.00**
Blackberry, creamer & sugar bowl, pearl lustre on MG, w/lid........**50.00**
Blackberry, goblet, caramel lustre on MG, 7-oz............................**20.00**
Ivy & Snow, bowl, crystal, oval, 9"..**15.00**
Ivy & Snow, celery, crystal, 7¾"..**25.00**
Lace Dew Drop, bowl, pk on MG, 8" q...**35.00**
Lace Dew Drop, jam jar, caramel lustre on MG, w/lid, 4½"...........**20.00**
Lace Dew Drop, server, bl on MG, ftd, 11".................................**45.00**
Moon & Star, comport, pearl lustre on MG, lg, 8" dia...................**40.00**
Queen Anne, Jell-O mold, crystal, star shaped..............................**2.50**

Phonographs

The phonograph, invented by Thomas Edison in 1877, was the first practical instrument for recording and reproducing sound. Sound wave vibrations were recorded on a tinfoil-covered cylinder and played back with a needle that ran along the grooves made from the recording, thus reproducing the sound. Other companies further improved Edison's invention, and by 1900 three phonograph companies were in business.

Early models had morning-glory horns; these are especially desirable. The early cylinder players are all of special interest, because after 1910 nearly all models were made to play disk records. By 1925 the hand-cranked players were discontinued and were replaced by electric phonographs.

Our advisor for this category is Steve Oliphant; he is listed in the Directory under California.

Brunswick, floor model, mahog, EX...**125.00**
Brunswick Panatrope, expotential model #15-8...........................**350.00**

Busy Bee, disk records, 8-petal red horn w/decal, EX 300.00
Busy Bee, key wind, cylinder, EX 225.00
Columbia AH Graphophone, NM...850.00
Columbia AK, oak case, 16" brass bell horn, EX 750.00
Columbia AQ, 2-min, key wind, sm horn, EX...........................325.00
Columbia AT Graphophone, 2-min, 12" horn, oak case, 1901 ...375.00
Columbia AU, 78 rpm, w/horn, EX...400.00
Columbia BF Graphophone Peerless, oak, 6" mandrell, 14" horn ..525.00
Columbia BI, oak case, red rear-mt horn 750.00
Columbia BK Graphophone, 2-min reproducer, brass horn, '06 ..400.00
Edison, diamond disk, Chippendale cabinet, EX 400.00
Edison D Red Gem, 2/4-min, K reproducer, 2-part horn, VG......825.00
Edison Fireside, 2/4-min, K reproducer, cygnet metal horn 600.00
Edison Home, C reproducer, 14" brass bell horn 400.00
Edison Maroon Gem, orig finish, EX...................................... 1,000.00
Edison Standard, N reproducer, oak, cygnet metal horn 600.00
Edison Triumph, C reproducer, ribbon decal, 14" brass horn.......500.00
Edison Triumph, 2/4-min, oak case, cygnet oak horn.............. 2,300.00
Lyre type, 2 min, 12" horn w/attached reproducer, Germany 375.00
Marx, 78 rpm turntable, child's model #3650, 1940s, EX.............40.00
Reginaphone #139, serpentine, 20¾" 5,000.00
Silvertone, table-top, internal horn, Sears, 1914 ....200.00
Sonora, oak case, table-top style, internal horn, EX...................200.00
Victor E, exhibition reproducer, rear mt, brass bell horn 700.00

Victor E, wind-up, oak case with columns, black-painted brass 16" horn, early, NM, $625.00; Victor II, oak with decal, 14" x 14", NM, $1,600.00.

Victor II, oak horn w/decal, NM 1,600.00
Victor II, 23" metal horn 700.00
Victor IV, disk player, mahog case, 20" brass bell horn, EX 1,000.00
Victor Junior, oak case, front mt, blk horn, EX decal, 1910.........900.00
Victor Orthophonic #10-50, rstr 1,000.00
Victor Orthophonic #4-40 ....350.00
Victor Orthophonic Granada..250.00
Victor P, oak case, exhibition reproducer, 18" brass horn 800.00
Victor VI, gold-plate tone arm, mahog case/horn, 1906, EX ... 3,500.00
Victor Victrola #100, mahog, NP trim, EX orig 100.00
Victor Victrola VI 150.00
Victor Z, exhibition reproducer, front mt, brass bell horn 1,100.00
Yankee Prince, rear mt, w/horn, G label, ca 1904 ....375.00
Zonophone A, oak case, glass sides, brass horn, NM............... 2,150.00
Zonophone C, V sound box reproducer, 16" brass horn, EX 850.00
Zonophone Grand Opera, reproducer, brass horn, EX 1,050.00

Photographica

Photographic collectibles include not only the cameras and equip-

ment used to 'freeze' special moments in time, but also the photographic images produced by a great variety of processes that have evolved since the daguerrean era of the mid-1800s.

Among the earliest cameras was the sliding box-on-a-box camera. It was focused by sliding one box in and out of the other, thus adjusting the distance of the lens to the ground glass. This was replaced on later models with leather bellows. These were the forerunners of the multilens cameras developed in the late 1870s, which were capable of recording many small portraits on a single plate. Double-lens cameras produced stereo images which, when viewed through a device called a stereoscope, achieved a 3-dimensional effect. In 1888 George Eastmann introduced his box camera, the first to utilize roll film. This greatly simplified the process, making it possible for the amateur to enjoy photography as a hobby. Detective cameras, those disguised as books, handbags, etc., are among the most sought after by today's collectors.

Many processes have been used to produce photographic images: daguerreotypes — the most-valued examples being the full-plate which measures 6½" x 8½"; ambrotypes, produced by an early wet-plate process whereby a faint negative image on glass is seen as positive when held against a dark background; and tintypes, contemporaries of ambrotype but produced on japanned iron and not as easily damaged.

Other collectible images include carte de visites, known as CDVs, which are portraits printed on paper and produced in quantity. The CDV fad of the 1800s enticed the famous and the unknown alike to pose for these cards, which were circulated among the public to the extent that they became known as 'publics.' When the popularity of CDVs began to wane, a new fascination developed for the cabinet photo, a larger version measuring about 4½" x 6½". Note: A common portrait CDV is worth only about 50¢ unless it carries a revenue stamp on the back; those that do are valued at about $1.00 each.

Stereo cards, photos viewed through a device called a stereoscope, are another popular collectible. The glass stereo plates of the mid-1800s and photo prints produced in the darkroom are among the most valuable. In evaluating stereo views, the date and condition are all-important. Some views were printed over a thirty- to forty-year period — 'first generation' prices are far higher than later copies. Right now, quality stereo views are at a premium.

For the most part, good quality images have either maintained or increased in value. Poor quality examples (regardless of rarity) are not selling well. Interest in cameras and stereo equipment is down, and dealers report that often average-priced items that were moving well are often completely overlooked. Though rare items always have a market, collectors seem to be buying only if they are bargain priced.

Our advisor for this category is John Hess; he is listed in the Directory under Massachusetts. For more information on the market values of collectible photographs, we recommend *Huxford's Fine Art Value Guide*, available at your local bookstore or from Collector Books. See also Gutta Percha.

Ambrotypes

4th plate, drummer boy w/mother & sister, +case 140.00
4th plate, Flag Grade officer & daughter, milk glass, +case..........100.00
6th plate, Blk lady, well dressed, 1860s, +full case......................200.00
6th plate, man w/dog on chair beside him, ca 1855, EX 20.00
6th plate, post mortem, baby in wht, 1855, +case 35.00
6th plate, Rebel w/carbine & pistol, soft campaign hat, EX.........250.00
6th plate, Rebel w/gold buttons & sleeve stripes, EX 220.00
6th plate, Rebel w/homespun jacket w/velvet collar, EX................60.00
6th plate, seated couple, in mat, EX...45.00
6th plate, soldier, seated in uniform, some color, +case................45.00
6th plate, twin sisters, in 2-tone leather case, EX 27.50
6th plate, Union soldier w/beard seated by wife, EX, +case............75.00
9th plate, Albert Edward, Prince of Wales, Clark, 1860, EX........285.00

9th plate, boy & girl w/dog on her lap, EX.............................24.00
9th plate, dk-skinned lady, tinted cheeks/lips, VG.............18.00
9th plate, gentleman's portrait in profile, from painting, EX.........12.00
9th plate, girl w/long curls, wht mat, EX..............................20.00
9th plate, lace & button salesman w/case, +case...............35.00
9th plate, man & wife, dbl in full case, ca 1850s, EX..........22.00
9th plate, Rebel soldier in gray uniform, EX, +case............90.00
9th plate, sheriff w/5-pointed star badge in rnd disk, EX.....20.00
9th plate, soldier in full uniform w/epaulets, +leather case............45.00
9th plate, Union officer w/sabre to chest, EX, +case...........85.00

Cabinet Photos

Allan E Doncette, Centre Rush Harvard Varsity, 1894-95, EX.....22.00
Annie Oakley, stands w/4 guns & medals, Gilbert & Bacon, EX.425.00
Col Ruth Goshon Age 43 Yrs, 620 lbs, 7'11", Bogardus.................20.00
Custer, standing in dress uniform, by Mora, NY, 1870s, EX.........200.00
JA Garfield, Harroun & Bierstadt NY, sgn, EX.............................400.00
Lady taking aim w/single-shot rifle, dog at ft, EX.....................48.00
Major Atom, Age 18 Years, midget in tux, Eisenmann, EX...........10.00
Man w/mustache playing 5-string banjo, EX.............................30.00
Overview of Hot Springs NY, stream shown, 1875, EX.................25.00
Sailor from USS San Francisco, Spanish-Am War era, VG...........15.00
US Consulate, Cadiz Spain, view of sq, ca 1897, EX.....................7.50
Wild West cowboy w/hand on revolver, Eisenmann, NY, EX........65.00

Cameras

Argus Argoflex 75, w/flash & box...15.00
Brownie #2A, box type, blk...10.00

No. 2 Beau Brownie, designed by WD Teague, brown vinyl case with chromed-metal geometrics, Kodak label inside, 5" x 5", $1,300.00.

Brownie Bullet, w/box...6.00
Brownie Viligant Jr...17.50
Kodak Brownie Target, NM...12.00
Kodak Rainbow Hawk-Eye #2C, box style, EX.........................7.50
Minetta, 2¼" W, in orig pigskin case, EX...............................16.00
Poloroid Land Camera Speedliner #941, MIB...........................20.00
Revere-8 Cine, +lenses/filters/exposure meter, in case.............17.50

Carte De Visites

Admiral Dot, 14 Yrs Old, 25" High, 16 Lbs, Anthony, VG..........10.00
An Ambush, foot soldiers face cavalry, dtd 1865, EX.................10.00
Artillery soldiers (2) clasping hands, Brown, Providence RI.........30.00
Calamity Jane w/rifle, Dunshee, Boston, 1883, EX....................45.00

Camp of Salem Lt Infantry, barracks view, EX...............................50.00
Capt CB Newton, campaign hat & sword, Salem MA, EX............35.00
Capt Theophilus H Barr standing w/sword, Schleier, TN, EX.....50.00
Che-Mah, Chinese Dwarf, Eisenmann, VG..................................20.00
Civil War veteran w/GAR medal, sepia, 1870s, VG....................17.50
Coach before tavern-hotel, Burnham, Norwich VG, 1866, EX.....20.00
Columbia College Law School, front view, G Stacy, 1863, EX......15.00
Corporal Moulton, 11th Mass Battery, seated by table, VG...........30.00
Custer, bust portrait, unmk/from Brady negative, 1860s, EX.......150.00
Custer, seated, copy of Brady photo by JS Brown, VG.................130.00
Custer, vignette profile, by Brady, 1863, EX.............................250.00
Edwin Booth, profile portrait, VG..55.00
Fireman in uniform w/helmet, belt, & trumpet, 1865.................40.00
Gen Banks, seated, sword on lap, Anthony, Brady Studios...........15.00
Gen Burnside, Manchester Bros, RI, EX.....................................15.00
Gen Gilmore, ¾-standing pose, w/sword, Broadway, VG..............24.00
Gen Grant, seated w/4 stars on uniform, EX.............................15.00
Gen Hancock, seated in uniform, Anthony, Brady Studios...........15.00
Gen Speed S Fry, vignette portrait, Anthony, EX.......................30.00
Gen Winfield Scott, ¾-view, Anthony, Brady Studios, EX...........15.00
Girl w/china head doll, dressed alike, VG..................................10.00
Girls (3) seated around table w/stereoviewer, EX.......................30.00
Horace Greely, oval bust portrait, EX.......................................12.50
House of Representatives...Impeachment of...Johnson, Brady.....175.00
Illustration of camp life, barracks & tent, Brady, EX.................50.00
Imperial German officer in full uniform, Prumm, Berlin.............10.00
John G Nicolay, Lincoln's secretary, rare, EX............................300.00
Libby Prison, Richmond VA, outdoor scene, EX.........................15.00
Lt John Avery in frock coat w/epaulets, Bunker, Hudson WI.......30.00
Midget Dudly Foster, 4 Yrs, Weight 5 Lbs, Eisenmann, EX...........18.00
Miss Grace Sutherland, 72" long hair, LM Baker, Columbus OH..14.00
Mrs John C Fremont, Anthony, Brady Gallery, EX.....................10.00
Robert Fulton, taken from period engraving, EX........................12.50
Royal family in 5 separate portraits, EX....................................95.00
Sergeant Boston Corbet, documentary stamp on bk, rare, EX....195.00
Signal Corps soldier w/map, Zanesville OH, EX.........................115.00
Tom Thumb & His Wife in Later Years, VG..................................8.00
Union officer w/mustache, vignette, EX....................................15.00
Washington Irving, from engraving, EX.......................................8.00
Wm Lloyd Garrison, seated, in glasses, Warren Bros, VG............14.00

Daguerreotypes

Half plate, lady in blk w/book on lap, lace bonnet, +case.............88.00
Half plate, mason w/apron & neck devices, gold tint, +case........650.00
Half plate, New England minister in robes, EX, +case...............475.00

Half-plate daguerreotype of a man in full dress uniform with sword, $650.00.

Half plate, 3 musicians w/instruments, ca 1850s, EX, +case **2,000.00**
Half plate, 3 seated men, lady in bonnet stands, 1850s, EX...........**98.00**
Half plate, 4 seated men (2 bearded), EX **125.00**
Whole plate, well-dressed man, ¾-length, Appleby, NY, EX.......**950.00**
4th plate, fine lady, 1850s, EX, +full case **100.00**
4th plate, lady w/child & book by table, +full case.........................**45.00**
4th plate, lg Phila house, in case mk Richards, NM **600.00**
4th plate, man's portrait, gr paper mat, ogee wood fr, EX **155.00**
4th plate, mother & daughter in bonnets, +full case **80.00**
4th plate, well-dressed young couple, matted, 1840s, EX **60.00**
4th plate, 2 girls w/flowers & doll, 1850s, EX................................**120.00**
6th plate, blind girl, +full case, EX **27.50**
6th plate, boy in balloon pants stands on couch, EX **37.50**
6th plate, boy in fancy hat by table, 1850s, +full case **22.00**
6th plate, carpenter w/plane, ca 1848, early mat, EX....................**325.00**
6th plate, child in fur hat & fur-trimmed coat, EX, +case **18.00**
6th plate, girl w/wicker handbag, toddler in highchair, EX...........**85.00**
6th plate, hunter w/percussion rifle & sword, ca 1847, +case **300.00**
6th plate, lady w/arm on books, holds open dag case, early **40.00**
6th plate, man in stove-pipe hat, early image, +full case **65.00**
6th plate, man's portrait, Agustus Washington, ca 1852..............**100.00**
6th plate, mother & daughter, 1840s, MOP case, EX **120.00**
6th plate, Odd Fellow seated in fraternal costume, EX **95.00**
6th plate, old lady knitting, blk dress, wht bonnet, VG **30.00**
6th plate, paper hanger w/tools & paper, +case, scratched **130.00**
6th plate, post mortem, baby in wht gown, NM, +full case............**85.00**
6th plate, sisters (2) in wht dresses w/red-tinted necklaces **50.00**
6th plate, sisters w/doll, +full case **50.00**
6th plate, sm boy in dress, 1840s, EX **35.00**
6th plate, sm girl stands by table, EX..**48.00**
6th plate, soldier w/epaulets & tall hat w/pompon, EX **350.00**
6th plate, well-dressed man, Langenhelm, 1840s, +full case **100.00**
6th plate, 2 seated ladies w/man standing behind, EX, +case.........**18.00**
9th plate, girl w/earrings & brooch, 1850s, EX **20.00**
9th plate, lady & 3 children, ca 1850, +half-case, EX **55.00**
9th plate, well-dressed boy, SD Carleton, +case **15.00**

Photos

Albumen, African man, scarred face/tasseled hat, 1869, EX **45.00**
Albumen, fire pumper w/4 horses & hose carriage, 1880s, 10x13".**55.00**
Albumen, Great Falls of Yellowstone, tinted, 17x21", EX **165.00**
Albumen, Lincoln, HF Warren, Mar 6, 1865, 13½x10½", EX....**400.00**
Albumen, member of US Lifesaving Service, 1900s, 7½x5¼" **28.00**
Albumen, Niagara Falls closeup, 16x19", in orig fr **100.00**
Albumen, Palace of St Telmo, Seville Spain, 8x10", EX **12.50**
Albumen, Robert E Lee on horse Traveler, M Miley, 1868, EX ..**200.00**
Albumen, Union Colonel, hand colored, whole plate, oval fr.....**200.00**
Albumen, Union soldiers (2) w/regimental flags, 3x2¾", EX.........**75.00**
Glazed salt print, A Lincoln, A Hesler, 1857, EX **3,700.00**

Edward S. Curtis orotone, Maid of Dreams, signed, original frame, 13½" x 10½" (sight), $3,000.00.

Orotone, Canyon de Chelley, ES Curtis, fr, 11x14" **1,870.00**
Orotone, Prayer to Great Mystery, ES Curtis, VG fr, 14x10".. **3,100.00**
Photogravure, Eva Watson-Schutze, 1905, 8x5½" **100.00**
Photogravure, Vanishing Race, Indians on path, Curtis, 6x8".....**200.00**
Photogravure, Wm M Chase, Steichen, 1906, 8½x6⅜" **150.00**
Platinum, Chief of Desert, Indian portrait, Curtis, 1909.............**450.00**
Silverprint, Indian Profile, 1916, ES Curtis, 16x12" **3,000.00**
Silverprint, Post's Pool, landscape, 5½x2¾" **85.00**
Silverprint, Standing Brave, ES Curtis, early 1900s, 7x5" **440.00**
Union Pacific Dbl Track, train/mtns, fr, EX/foxing, 24x36" **190.00**

Stereoscopic Views

Aboard Ship, NY Harbor, Kilburn #6511, 1891, VG **27.50**
American Falls, Anthony, 1859, EX **22.50**

Stereoscopic view, Abraham Lincoln by Anthony and Co., tax stamp and dealer's label on back, $1,500.00.

Boston Harbor From Bunker Hill, EX..**15.00**
Canada scenery, Wm Center Port, 2 for **20.00**
Cosmopoliton Hotel, Tucson AZ, Buehman #75, 1875, scarce **30.00**
Deserted, empty homestead, Campbell #903, 1896, VG **15.00**
French field hospital, use of X-ray, Keystone, G **10.00**
Idols of Alaska Indians, totem poles, 1870s, EX...........................**10.00**
Independence Hall interior, 1875, EX.. **8.00**
Louisiana Purchase Expo, 1904, 6 for...**25.00**
Market House, steamships in foreground, 1880s, EX **12.50**
Martha's Vinyard, Shute & Woodword, 12 for.............................**75.00**
Miracle of Lucy, church ruins, Keystone, EX **10.00**
NY Cityscape, Church St, ca 1902, VG..**12.00**
Pennsylvania landscape, TH Johnson, ivory mt, 6 for..................**75.00**
Pueblo Indians, lg group, Gillinghams, 1870, EX........................**70.00**
San Francisco Earthquake, Keystone #13263, VG **20.00**
Summit of Gray's Peak, man w/mules, dtd 1899, VG....................**12.50**
T Wharf, Boston, ships & schooners, men on wharf, Kilburn **15.00**
Temple, Salt Lake City UT, Underwood, 1901, EX.....................**10.00**
Terrapin Tower, Niagara Falls, Anthony, 1859, EX **27.50**
Union Meeting, Anthony #909, 1861, EX **15.00**
Upstate NY, Staddard, Baker, & Record, set of 9 ....**65.00**
US Massachusetts in War Paint, Graves #5002, 1899, VG **10.00**
Yel Vs Princeton, football game, 1893, VG **14.00**
Zepplin Wrecked & Burned Ruins, EX.......................................**10.00**

Tintypes

Full plate, soldier w/rifle, blk/gold fr, EX......................................**130.00**
Half plate, cavalry soldier w/musket, standing, +full case **200.00**
Half plate, soldiers (8), pnt bkground, case w/emb fruit................**200.00**
Half plate, Union soldier, standing, flag at bk, EX **225.00**
4th plate, Federal soldier w/corps badge, half pose, EX.................**45.00**
4th plate, Union engineer, standing, lt tinting, EX.........................**65.00**

4th plate, Union soldier w/many weapons, EX 125.00
6th plate, Army musician w/English horn, +case, EX....................65.00
6th plate, baseball player w/bat & ball, EX......................................250.00
6th plate, boy w/drum, holds sticks as if to play, EX 30.00
6th plate, carpenter in overalls w/saw, VG 35.00
6th plate, child on rocking horse, 1870s, EX, +half case 55.00
6th plate, Confederate w/pistol, full beard, VG 60.00
6th plate, Federal Cavalry trooper w/sabre, EX.............................70.00
6th plate, Union artillery soldier standing, EX................................30.00
6th plate, Union captain w/high crown McDowell fatigue kepi.....40.00
6th plate, Union corporal w/musket across chest, EX...................100.00
9th plate, Blk lady portrait, oval gold-bordered mat, VG.............10.00
9th plate, CA gold miners by sluice way, +case...........................140.00
9th plate, fireman w/leather fire belt, brimmed hat, EX.................35.00
9th plate, Old veteran seated w/draped US flag, EX......................30.00
9th plate, uniformed ball team, stamped, 1870s, EX.....................300.00
9th plate, Union officer w/Phil Sheridan hat, sword at side...........75.00
9th plate, Union soldier w/canteen in fatigue coat, VG.................32.00

Viewers and Slides

Alex Becker's, Pats 1866, 1870, table top, EX 375.00
Keystone, 2 Bausch & Lomb-lens bellows, 1904 ....350.00
Pervecscope, Pat 1895, EX 35.00
Slides, Muybridge View of Pacific Coast & CA, 11 for................160.00
Slides, Pacific Coast Views, Watkins, 10 for..................................200.00

Miscellaneous

Stanhope, binoculars, ea lens w/scene, brass fittings, EX 35.00
Stanhope, binoculars, ivory, 4 scenic views 35.00
Stanhope, cross, ivory, Immaculate Conception 40.00
Stanhope, cross, ivory w/rosary beads, Mary Washing Christ.........60.00
Stanhope, pen, ivory, Crystal Palace, Sydenham............................75.00

Piano Babies

A familiar sight in Victorian parlors, piano babies languished atop shawl-covered pianos in a variety of poses: crawling, sitting, on their tummies, or on their backs playing with their toes. Some babies were nude, and some wore gowns. Sizes ranged from about 3" up to 12". The most famous manufacturer of these bisque darlings was the Heubach Brothers of Germany, who nearly always marked their product; see Heubach for more listings. Watch for reproductions.

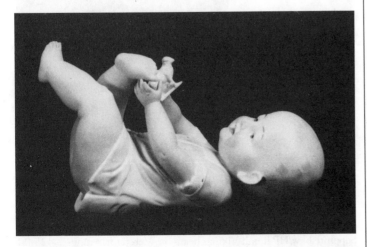

Baby on back playing with toy sheep, marked Germany #11290, excellent quality, 6" x 10", $550.00.

Blk, on tummy & elbows, w/top hat, terra cotta..........................565.00
Crawling boy, hands on book, floral gown, #5540, 16", NM........625.00
Girl, umbrella in left hand, skirt in right, fancy hat, 17" 175.00
Half reclining, holding foot, 11" 165.00
On side, rabbit under arm, cat on bk, lt bl floral gown, 9" 175.00
On stomach, str arms raise chest, cat on bk/under arm, 9" 230.00
On stomach, thumb raised to mouth, ft raised, Germany, 9x7" ...250.00
On tummy, knee bent as if to crawl, pk roses on dress, 10" 250.00
On tummy holding puppy, 8" 145.00
Seated, dog in crook of right arm, floral gown, bonnet, 8" 250.00

Picasso Art Pottery

Pablo Picasso created some distinctive pottery during the 1940s, marking the ware with his signature.

Bowl, blk, int w/lady's profile imp on red bsk, '55, 7" 1,000.00
Jug, Woman's Head Crowned w/Flowers, Madoura, 1954, 9".22,000.00
Pitcher, Face Tankard, Madoura, 1959, 8⅞" 4,950.00
Pitcher, Face w/Points, Madoura, 1969, 11¼" 8,800.00
Plaque, Flute Player & Goat, Madoura, 1956, 11¼" dia 2,860.00
Plaque, 3 Figures on Trampoline, blk slip on wht, mk, 8¼"..... 1,760.00
Plate, Bunch w/Apple, floral, Madoura, 1956, 10¼" dia..........4,400.00
Plate, Face #59, Madoura, 1963, 9⅞" dia 3,850.00
Plate, Face w/Herringbone Patterned Mask, 10½" dia 1,760.00
Plate, Motifs #66, Madoura, 1963, 10" dia, fr 3,080.00
Plate, Picador & Bull, blk/rust slip on wht, mk, 1959, 10½".... 5,280.00
Plate, Square-Eyed Face, Madoura, 1959, 10½" dia 8,800.00
Platter, face, bl on yel, Madoura, 1947, 15¼x12½".................. 8,250.00
Platter, fish, bl & yel on wht, Madoura, 1952, 16½"............... 9,350.00
Platter, Jacqueline at the Easel, Madoura, 1956, 16½" dia....... 8,800.00
Platter, Tormented Faun's Face, Madoura, 1956, 16" dia 4,400.00
Tankard, face, brn & bl slip on wht, Madoura, 1959, 8⅞" 4,950.00

Vase with female form, #63/100, 14", $4,500.00.

Vase, Face & Owl, blk pnt/rust & gray slip, mk, 1958, 9¾" ...22,000.00
Vase, face in profile, earthenware, 1953, Madoura, 10¼".......22,000.00

Pickard

Founded in 1897 in Chicago, Illinois, the Pickard China Company was originally a decorating studio, importing china blanks from European manufacturers. Some of these early pieces bear the name of those companies as well as Pickard's. Trained artists decorated the wares with hand-painted studies of fruit, florals, birds, and scenics and often signed their work. In 1915 Pickard introduced a line of 23k gold over a dainty floral-etched ground design. In the 1930s, they began to experiment with the idea of making their own ware and by 1938 had succeeded in developing a formula for fine translucent china. Since 1976 they have issued an annual limited edition Christmas plate. They are now located in Antioch, Illinois.

The company has used various marks: 'Pickard' with double circles; the crown mark; 'Pickard' on a gold maple leaf; and the current mark, the lion and shield. Work signed by Challinor, Marker, and Yeschek is especially valued by today's collectors.

Our advisors for this category are Lois and Milt Steinfeld; they are listed in the Directory under New Jersey.

Bonbon, Wildwood, C Marker, 7½" **145.00**
Bowl, poinsettias w/gold, ped ft, 4⅝x9" **165.00**
Cake plate, stylized florals w/gold, ca 1905-10, 11" **155.00**
Candy dish, 4 medallions, cobalt w/wht daisies, 5½x6".....**70.00**
Coffeepot, Aura Argenta Linear, Richter, 10¾", +cr/sug **755.00**
Compote, lemon trees w/gold, Tolpin, hexagonal, 1910 mk, 6" ..**145.00**
Creamer & sugar bowl, mc florals w/gold, TV Limoges blanks.......**85.00**
Jardiniere, leaves, pk on gr w/gold, Hessler, ca 1900 mk, 5½" **275.00**
Marmalade, strawberries, 1910 mk, w/lid...............................**135.00**
Marmalade, tulips w/gold trim, 1910 mk, w/underplate **210.00**

Pitcher, black band with fruit on gold, with lid, 9½", $295.00.

Pitcher, etched gold w/band of water lilies, 6-sided, 8" **315.00**
Pitcher, tankard; roses allover, gold trim, T&V, 11" **425.00**
Plate, carnations w/gold, 9" **110.00**
Plate, irises, sgn Lind, ca 1895-98, 8½"...**125.00**
Plate, walnuts, artist sgn, 1905-10 mk, 9" **110.00**
Plate, waterfall scene w/gold, artist sgn, mk, 8" **135.00**
Shaker, lemon trees, heavy gold, sgn Tolpin, 1905 mk **35.00**
Vase, birds & butterflies, mc on wht w/gold, mk, 8½".................**325.00**
Vase, pines w/moonlight, mc matt w/gold, Challinor, 8" **455.00**
Vase, trees/mtn/lake, sgn Haley, gold top & hdls, mk, 7" **210.00**
Vase, violets, sgn, Rosenthal blank, 1905 mk, 10" **250.00**

Pickle Castors

Pickle castors, which were both functional and decorative, became popular after the Civil War, reaching their peak about 1885. By 1900 they had virtually disappeared from factory catalogs. Numerous styles were available. They consisted of a decorated, silverplated frame that held either a fancy clear pressed-glass insert or one of decorated art glass — the latter being popular in the more affluent Victorian households and more desirable with collectors today.

In the listings below, the description prior to the semi-colon refers to the jar (insert), and the remainder of the line describes the frame. Where no condition is indicated, the silverplate is assumed to be in very good to excellent condition; glass jars are assumed mint.

Amberina, diagonal ribs; cherub-ftd fr **395.00**
Amberina, swirled ribs, Libbey; ftd Meriden fr **450.00**
Amberina w/lg hobs; SP stand, fan finial, 11½", +tongs **400.00**
Baby T'print, mc flowers; 6" cherub pulls cart, Wilcox **850.00**
Bead & Drape, red satin; ftd SP frame, +tongs **300.00**
Beaded Dart; orig SP ftd fr, +tongs..**250.00**
Beatty Rib, bl opal; resilvered fr, 10½", +tongs..........................**335.00**
Bl, rows of dmn prisms/faceted blocks; fr w/emb birds etc **165.00**
Broken Column; orig ornate SP fr...**250.00**
Burmese w/HP florals; sq Middletown fr **595.00**
Clear textured, raised scenes in 3 medallions; fretwork, fancy fr..**225.00**
Cone, pk satin cased; rstr Tufts fr..**395.00**
Coreopsis, red satin, HP florals; orig ornate ftd fr **365.00**
Cranberry, HP florals on raised band; ornate Derby fr **550.00**
Crane etched ea side; ornate lid & fr, 12½", +tongs....................**195.00**
Crown Milano, cream satin w/gilt florals; emb skirt, Aurora fr....**850.00**
Cupid & Venus; Derby fr w/3 owls at top **250.00**
Daisy & Button, canary; orig SP fr & tongs **185.00**
Daisy & Button, sapphire bl; orig ftd SP fr...................................**295.00**
Daisy & Button, topaz; ornate fr w/side ornaments, +tongs **165.00**
Daisy & Fern in Apple Blossom mold, bl opal; ornate SP fr **450.00**
Dbl, clear/frosted barrel shape; dbl ftd, R&B fr w/leaves **450.00**
Dia Quilt, pk shaded, Mt WA; orig SP ftd fr, 12½"......................**500.00**
Dia Quilt, rubena w/mc coralene florals; Tufts fr, EX **495.00**
Fine Cut, vaseline; SP fr, +tongs **185.00**
Florette, pk; rstr Tufts fr..**250.00**
Hobnail, amberina, egg form; greyhound at base of fr, NM..........**650.00**
Hobnail, cranberry opal; rstr Meriden SP fr..................................**550.00**
Invt T'print, amberina w/HP bird on branch; SP fr, 10¼" **885.00**
Invt T'print, bl w/HP florals; orig ftd fr, 11½" **485.00**
Invt T'print, cranberry, HP flowers/birds; 12½" fr w/cupid **650.00**
Invt T'print, cranberry; Rockford fr, +tongs, 10½" **260.00**
Invt T'print, cranberry; SP fr, 9¾x4½", EX **325.00**
Little River; rstr Monarch fr **150.00**
Nailsea, ribbed; rstr Reed & Barton fr..**300.00**

Royal Ivy, cranberry/vaseline spatter, unmarked holder, 7½", $450.00.

Rubena, HP florals; rstr SP fr **395.00**
Sapphire bl, egg shape, HP decor; Tufts fr **595.00**
Sapphire bl w/HP floral; Vikings heads on Webster fr, +tongs **425.00**
Star & Block, dbl; Rogers fr...**90.00**
Torquay, pigeon blood **295.00**

Yel satin quilt, cased, HP decor; orig ornate SP fr, EX 750.00

Pie Birds

Pie birds (also known as pie vents and pie funnels) have been in use since late Victorian times. Placed in the middle of a pie, they serve the dual purpose of supporting the pastry and allowing steam to escape from the pie so that it does not boil over. They come in various, interesting forms.

Our advisor for this category is Alan Pedel; he is listed in the Directory under England.

Benny the Baker, wht w/pk, Cardinal China, 1940s-50s, 5¼" **45.00**
Bird baby, mc, mk Yellowstone Park, 3½" **25.00**
Black Chef, James Barry Products, bl or yel clothes, 4½" **50.00**
Black Chef, James Barry Products, brn face, yel clothes, 4½".........**70.00**
Black Chef, James Barry Products, gr clothes, 4½" **65.00**
Black chef holding pie, vents from mouth **35.00**
Black circus clown, vents from pointed hat **35.00**
Black mermaid sitting on rock **35.00**
Black monk, praying, vents from bald pate **35.00**
Bluebird, speckled, blk wings & tip of tail, heavy, 4½" **25.00**
Bluebird w/babies on nest, circled C mk, 1950, rare, 5" **50.00**
Canary singing, pk or gr mc, 4½" **45.00**
Chick, long neck, Pillsbury premium, common, 5" **15.00**
Dragon's head, vents from between horns...................................**35.00**
Duckling, long neck, bl, pk, yel, or mc, 1950s, 5" **18.00**
Eggman (similar to Humpty Dumpty) **35.00**
Elephant on drum, mk CCC (Cardinal China Co), 1940s-50s, 4" ...**45.00**
Elephant on stand, vents from mouth **35.00**
Funnel with Four & Twenty Blackbirds nursery rhyme illus **35.00**
Gnome sits on red-spotted toadstool...**35.00**
Irish funnel, mythological figure emb on side **35.00**
Jackie Sammond (Utah), odd shape, fish mk, 3" **25.00**
Mallard duck...**35.00**
Pelican perched on rock **35.00**
Ralphie or Patrick Rooster, Cleminson **20.00**

Rooster, $35.00.

Rooster, Bl Willow **20.00**
Rooster, Pearle China, East Liverpool OH, 5" **35.00**
Teddy bear in chef's hat, vents from hat....................................**35.00**

Pierce, Howard

Howard Pierce opened a studio in Claremont, California, in the mid-1940s where he produced small ceramic models of birds and animals, figurines, and vases, making his molds and decorating his ware with no outside help except for his wife and more recently his daughter. He is best known for his skill at sculpting his models, which he decorates entirely with the airbrush. Early items were incised 'Howard Pierce, Claremont, California' or stamped 'Howard Pierce Porcelain.' Not all of his ware is marked, however, and some pieces carry only his initials.

Dealer sign, recent **35.00**
Figurine, African head, 1950s **45.00**
Figurine, bear, brn, 5¾" **20.00**
Figurine, bull, brn, 1950s, lg **25.00**
Figurine, bulldog, USMC, brn, recent, sm **20.00**
Figurine, ducks (decoy type), speckled gr on wht, '50s, 3-pc **45.00**
Figurine, elephant, pk, recent..**18.00**
Figurine, heron, wht **25.00**
Figurine, hippo, 'volcanic' brn glaze, recent, 6" **18.00**
Figurine, partridge, stylized, brn, 1950s, lg **25.00**

Quail family, $50.00 for the four pieces.

Figurine, roadrunner, blk, recent, lg **22.00**
Figurine, robin, blk/gr, 3"...**20.00**
Figurine, turtle, speckled brn on wht, 1950s, 5"..........................**25.00**
Figurine, unicorn, recent, sm **18.00**
Flower frog, quail w/2 young, 6½" **35.00**
Vase, Deco girl w/in circular cutout, creche style, gr, sq...............**45.00**
Vase, wht deer/tree at side, creche style, gr, Claremont, 8"............**35.00**

Pietra-Dura

From the Italian Renaissance period, Pietra-Dura is a type of mosaic work used for plaques, table tops, frames, etc. that includes small pieces of gemstones, mother-of-pearl, and the like.

Brooch, detailed, oval, sterling mts...**115.00**
Plaque, coral rose bud on blk marble mosaic, 2¾x4" **195.00**

Pigeon Blood

Pigeon blood glass, produced in the late 1800s, may be distinguished from other dark red glass by its distinctive orange tint.

Cracker jar, Torquay, SP lid, bail & hdl 295.00
Creamer, clear appl hdl, Torquay.................................125.00
Decanter, Bulging Loops, 8" 48.00
Goblet, lovers in pastoral scene, ca 1900, Germany.....................195.00
Pickle castor, Torquay 295.00
Pitcher, HP florals, clear hdl, 11½", +4 tumblers 150.00
Shakers, Flower Band, pr..135.00
Syrup, Scroll & Net w/Cosmos, satin, frosted hdl, orig lid..........575.00
Water set, Venecia, w/Wild Rose HP decor 650.00

Pillin

Polia Pillin was born in Poland in 1909; many of her family were artisans and craftsmen. Except for a few weeks of formal instruction at the Hull House in Chicago, Pillin is self-taught in the arts. Her work has been shown in many exhibits, and she has received awards from the Los Angeles County Art Institute, Syracuse Museum, Los Angeles County Fair, and the California State Fair. First interested in oils and watercolors, she has carried the same Byzantine quality over to her pottery. All of her work is signed 'Pillin' or 'W&P Pillin,' both with the loop of the P extended in an arc over the remaining letters of her name.

Bowl, bust portraits & birds on bl, 5½x10½" 350.00
Bowl, bust portraits on blk, 6½x5½" 300.00
Bowl, red abstract, 3¾x5½" 150.00
Charcoal, Southwest scene, fr, 19x12" 475.00
Painting, abstract, paper, fr, 15x11" 750.00
Pendant, horse on bl, 2" 40.00
Plaque, HP scene, 11x10"...950.00
Plate, children w/balloons on yel, 7½" 100.00
Plate, frolicking horses on gr, 7½"................................110.00

Tray, children on brown background, 8", $200.00; Vase, girl with cat on green background, 7", $250.00.

Vase, birds on gr w/pastels, 5¼" 150.00
Vase, birds on yel, 1½"..50.00
Vase, bust portraits on blk, bulbous, 9½" 350.00
Vase, bust portraits on gr, bulbous, 8½" 275.00
Vase, fish, pk & gr, squat, 2"..75.00
Vase, gr/pastel, bottle form, 11½" 140.00
Vase, horses on pastels, 5¾" 195.00
Vase, 3 nudes on bl, 9¼" 375.00
Vase, 3 nudes on pastels, 4½"..195.00

Pin-Back Buttons

Most of the advertising buttons made until the 1920s were top-quality, full-color, celluloid-covered buttons termed 'cellos.' Many were issued in sets on related topics featuring historical people and events, animals and birds, and other themes. Several cigarette, gum, and candy companies used buttons as inserts in their products. Usually the name of the company or product was printed on a paper placed in the back of the button and held securely by the pin. Most of the back papers are still in place today, aiding in the identification of the button. Beginning in the 1920s, a large number of buttons were lithographed (printed on metal); these buttons are referred to as 'lithos.' Nearly all advertising buttons are collected today with perhaps these exceptions: common buttons picturing flags of various nations, general labor union buttons denoting the payment of dues, and similar buttons with clever sayings.

Following is a listing of some of the most popular non-political buttons. Values reflect buttons which have designs centered, colors aligned, no fading or yellowing, no spots or stains, and no cracks, splits, or dents. See also Personalities; Political.

Brotherhood of Railroad Trainmen, celluloid, 1¼", EX 15.00
Bunker Hill Breweries, NM 35.00
Case, eagle, celluloid, EX..20.00
Darkies' Dream, watermelon & knife, mc, 1890s, ⅞" 22.50
Fisher's Blend Flour, celluloid, 1½" 15.00
Golden Guernsey Milk, salesman's..30.00
Hamilton Watch, locomotive, blk/wht, 1900, 1¾", EX 75.00
Happy Farmer, tractor, celluloid, EX.............................45.00
Hoover, potato digger, celluloid, EX 30.00
John Alden Flour, lady at wheel, mc, 1906, ⅞", EX 30.00
Kellogg's Cornflakes, celluloid, 1½", EX 32.00
Kick 'Em in the Axis, cartoon, mc, 1940s, 1¼", EX 15.00
Mrs Tom Thumb in wedding dress, EX........................22.50
Old Dutch Cleanser, 1", EX 17.00
Old Dutch Cocoa, couple drinking, mc, 1906, 1¼", NM 40.00
Reddy Kilowatt, early version, mc, 1930s, 1", EX 28.00
Shoot Peter's Shells, celluloid, red & gold, ⅞", EX 28.00
St Louis Auto Show Exhibitor, 1929, NM.....................12.00
Stay Over Here w/Me, Uncle Sam, 1930s, EX 25.00
Wilbur's Cocoa, cherub stirs cup, mc, 1890s, ⅞", EX 32.00
Yellow Kid w/top hat & cane, EX 35.00

Pink Lustre Ware

Pink lustre was produced by nearly every potter in the Staffordshire district in the 18th and 19th centuries. The application of gold lustre on white or light-colored backgrounds produced pinks, while the same over dark colors developed copper. The wares ranged from hand-painted plaques to transfer-printed dinnerware.

Bowl, blk transfer: lady/chicks/deer, ftd, w/lid, 5½".....................125.00
Bowl w/saucer & lid, bands/blk & orange stripes, hdls, 5" 75.00
Creamer, blk transfer scenes w/mc, floral rim, 4¼", NM 135.00
Creamer, cow figural, pk spots, gr base, wear, 5" 130.00
Crocus pot, houses, gr trim, ftd semicircular, 8½" W, VG...........650.00
Cup & saucer, handleless; House 40.00
Cup & saucer, handleless; purple transfer of children, mini..........40.00
Dish, blk transfer: King Henry, quatrefoil, wear, 8x10".................275.00
Figurine, couple, silver lustre/mc enamel, minor wear, 4½" 425.00
Figurine, recumbent greyhound, solid pk, rare, 5" L 450.00
Flowerpot, emb pastoral scenes on clay-color band, 5½x6½".......145.00
Pitcher, coach, blk transfer w/mc, pk resist top, 6", VG...............400.00
Pitcher, emb hunt scenes w/mc enamel, 5", EX.....................275.00
Pitcher, House, 6" 95.00
Pitcher, landscape, purple transfer, 5⅝", EX 95.00
Pitcher, Prince Leopold/Princess Charlotte, emb/mc, 8", VG......200.00

Pitcher, House pattern, pink and blue lustre, 5", $150.00.

Pitcher, Queen Victoria/Drunkard, blk transfer, 5½" 200.00
Pitcher, Queen Victoria/Prince Albert on bl, 7", EX 200.00
Pitcher, Tidings of Peace/Come Britons, purple transfer, 5" 250.00
Pitcher, Volunteer..., soldiers/trees, emb/mc, gun hdl, 8" 185.00
Pitcher, wide vintage band, wear/hairlines, 8" 350.00
Pitcher, woman/child, brn transfer w/mc, urn form, 6⅜" 150.00
Plaque, bust of Queen Caroline emb, mk QC, 4½x5½", EX 325.00
Punch bowl, House, floral band, mk Fell, 6½x11", VG................200.00
Taperstick, human form, silver/mc enamel, 4" 380.00
Teapot, emb cherubs, mc on pk lustre & bl bands, 4½", EX 175.00
Teapot, gr band/mc florals, ftd, chips, 5"..................................55.00

Pink Pigs

Pink Pigs on cabbage green were made in Germany around the turn of the century. They were sold as souvenirs in train depots, amusement parks, and gift shops. 'Action pigs' (those involved in some amusing activity) are the most valuable, and prices increase with the number of pigs. Though a similar type of figurine was made in white bisque, most serious collectors prefer only the pink ones. They are marked in two ways: 'Germany' in incised letters and a black ink stamped 'Made in Germany' in a circle.

1 beside gr drum, wall-mt match holder.................................60.00
1 beside stump, camera around neck, toothpick holder.................95.00
1 coming out of cup 65.00
1 coming out of suitcase...85.00
1 coming through gr fence, post at sides, open for flowers............95.00
1 in case looking through binoculars...................................85.00
1 in gr Dutch shoe...50.00
1 in gr suitcase bank, head 1 side, bk other, gold trim 75.00
1 in Japanese submarine, Japan imp on both sides......................125.00
1 in money sack bank 85.00
1 lg pig sitting behind 3" trough 75.00
1 on binoculars, gold trim...95.00
1 on gr trinket dish, leg caught in lobster claw 65.00
1 on horseshoe-shaped dish w/raised 4-leaf clover 75.00
1 on shoulder of gr ink bottle 75.00
1 reclining on horseshoe ash tray 70.00
1 riding train, 4½" 125.00
1 sits, holds orange Boston Baked Beans pot match holder...........65.00
1 sitting in bathtub...95.00
1 sitting on log, mk Germany...80.00
1 standing in gr tub 95.00
1 w/attached toothpick holder 65.00
1 w/front ft in 3-part dish containing 3 dice, 1 ft on dice...........75.00
1 wearing chef's costume, holds frypan, w/basket......................95.00
2, mother & baby in bl blanket in tub, rabbit on board atop..........85.00
2, mother in tub gives baby a bottle, lamb looks on, 4x3½" 85.00
2 behind trough, unmk 65.00

Pig sitting beside boot, $70.00.

2 by eggshell 80.00
2 dancing, in top hat, tux & cane 95.00
2 holding hands in roadster, 4½" L 125.00
2 in bed, Good Night on footboard, 4x3x2½" 145.00
2 in carriage 95.00
2 in love sit on lg log, 2 openings on tree stump, 7" L 75.00
2 in purse 75.00
2 on basket, head raising lid, plaque on front........................80.00
2 on binoculars, gold trim..115.00
2 on cotton bale, 1 peers from hole, 1 over top.......................90.00
2 on gr tray 50.00
2 on seesaw on top of pouch bank......................................75.00
2 on top hat..95.00
2 on tray hugging, 3x4½"..65.00
3, 1 on lg slipper playing banjo, 2 dancing on side 125.00
3 dressed up on edge of dish..80.00
3 sm pigs behind oval trough, mk, 2¾x2½x1¾" 90.00
3 w/baby carriage, father & 2 babies, Wheeling His Own 75.00
3 w/carriage, mother & 2 babies, Germany.............................85.00

Pisgah Forest

The Pisgah Forest Pottery was established in 1920 near Mount Pisgah in Arden, North Carolina, by Walter B. Stephen, who had worked in previous years at other locations in the state — Nonconnah and Skyland (the latter from 1913 until 1916). Stephen, who was born in the mountain region near Asheville, was known for his work in the Southern tradition. He produced skillfully executed wares exhibiting an amazing variety of techniques. He operated his business with only two helpers. Recognized today as his most outstanding accomplishment, his Cameo line was decorated by hand in the pate-sur-pate style (similar to Wedgwood Jasper) in such designs as Fiddler and Dog, Spinning Wheel, Covered Wagon, Buffalo Hunt, Mountain Cabin, Square Dancers, Indian Campfire, and Plowman. Stephen is known for other types of wares as well. His crystalline glaze is highly regarded by today's collectors.

At least nine different stamps mark his wares, several of which contain the outline of the potter at the wheel and 'Pisgah Forest.' Stephen died in 1961, but the work was continued by his associates.

Cookie jar, wine crackle, 7½"...50.00
Creamer, Cameo, hunting scene 395.00
Creamer & sugar bowl, turq, 1942, 2¼" 25.00
Jug, wine & turq, dtd 1940, 5"...38.00
Pitcher, eggplant glaze, dtd 1951, 3½".................................30.00

Pitcher, Nonconnah in blk slip, Nellie CR Stephen, 6½" 200.00
Pitcher, tankard, wine glaze, dtd 1948, 6" 40.00
Pitcher, turq crackle, 8" 85.00
Teapot, Cameo, wagon train on bl, sgn Stephen, 1949, 5" 125.00
Vase, bl & purple, 1938, 9"...70.00
Vase, bl crackle, 6½" 125.00
Vase, Cameo, harvest & sowing scene, wht on gr slip, 18" 500.00
Vase, Cameo, sq dancers & fiddler, wht on brn matt, 13"............350.00
Vase, Cameo, wagon train at collar, med gr body, 1930, 9" 600.00
Vase, Cameo, wht figures on brn neck, gr body, sgn/dtd, 8".........450.00
Vase, crystalline, bl, 7¾" 150.00
Vase, crystalline, wht on cream, baluster form, 1942, 7" 300.00
Vase, Nonconnah, brn, Trade Nonconnah mk, 7½"....................200.00
Vase, pk w/gr int, 3¼" 75.00

Pittsburgh Glass

As early as 1797, utility window glass and hollowware were being produced in the Pittsburgh area. Coal had been found in abundance, and it was there that it was first used instead of wood to fuel the glass furnaces. Because of this, as many as 150 glass companies operated there at one time. However, most failed due to the economically disastrous effects of the War of 1812. By the mid-1850s, those that remained were producing a wide range of flint glass items including pattern-molded and free-blown glass, cut and engraved wares, and pressed tableware patterns.

Our advisor for this cagegory is Mark Vuno; he is listed in the Directory under Connecticut.

Bottle, water; Pillar, 10-rib 150.00
Canister, appl bl rings, appl finial on mismatch lid, 12" 235.00
Creamer, 16-rib right swirl, thin, folded rim, att, 3" 70.00

Pillar Mold creamer, cobalt blue, open pontil, 3⅞", $1,200.00.

Cruet, bright aqua, ribbed, hollow hdl/stopper, 8" 300.00
Hummingbird feeder, cobalt finial, 5¼" 95.00
Jigger, sapphire bl, Gothic arches, 2½", NM..................................80.00
Pitcher, appl hdl w/rnd base ornament, tooled lip, 8", NM 150.00
Pitcher, cranberry w/clear-cased cranberry blown hdl, 9½" 8,800.00
Pitcher, flared rim, solid hdl w/crimped end, 5"............................100.00
Pitcher, leaf attachment under hdl, 12-petal base edge, 4½" 175.00
Pitcher, 8-rib w/heavy medial rib, crimping at base, 5¾" 290.00
Salt cellar, 22 str ribs, dome ft, att, 2¾", NM.................................40.00
Sugar bowl, dk sapphire, gallery rim, dome lid, high ft.................220.00
Vase, dk amethyst w/wht ridges around 8 panels, ftd, 11"........ 4,000.00

Plastics

The term 'collectible plastics' is defined as those types produced

between 1868 (when synthetic plastics were invented) and the period immediately following WWII. There are several, and we shall mention each one and attempt briefly to acquaint you with their characteristics:

1) Pyroxylin (Celluloid, Loalin, French Ivory, Pyralin). Chemical name: cellulose nitrate. Earliest form, invented in 1868 by John Wesley Hyatt; highly flammable; yellows with age; much used in toiletry articles. Fairly lightweight, many articles of pyroxylin were made by heating and molding thin sheets.

2) Cellulose Acetate (Tenite, Similoid). Made in attempt to produce a product similar to cellulose nitrate but without the flammability. Had limited use in the costume jewelry trade; most often encountered as car knobs and handles of the thirties and forties. Surfaces tend to crack with age and exposure to light. Always molded, never cast. Colors varied; imitation horn and marble were most popular.

3) Casein Plastics (Ameroid, Galalith, Dorcasine, Casolith). Invented in 1904 using milk proteins. Use limited to buttons and buckles due to warping and lengthy curing time. Made in a wide range of colors; very easy to laminate or to carve from stock rods or sheets, but never molded.

4) Phenol Formaldehyde (Bakelite, Catalin, Marblette, Agatine, Gemstone, Durite, Durez, Prystal). Invented by L.H. Baekland in 1908; used extensively in the thirties. There are two major types: cast and molded. Molded types include Durez and Bakelite, dark-toned, wood-flour filled plastics that were used extensively for early telephones (still used when non-conductivity of heat and electricity is vital). The most popular name in cast phenolics was Catalin, trade name of the American Catalin Corporation of New York. Made in a wide range of colors; widely used for costume jewelry, cutlery handles, decorative boxes, lamps, desk sets, etc. Heavyweight material with a slightly 'greasy' feel; very hard but can be carved with files, grinding tools, and abrasive cutters. Buffs to high, durable polish. Cast phenolics were used primarily from 1930 to around 1950 when they proved too labor-intensive to be economical.

5) Urea Formaldehyde (Beetleware, Plaskon, Duroware, Hemocoware, Uralite). Invented around 1929, this was lighter in color than phenol formaldehyde, thus used for injection-molded products in pastel colors. Lightweight, not strong; shiny rather than glossy. It cannot be carved and was used mainly for cheap radio and clock cases, never for jewelry.

The period between the two World Wars produced acrylic resins such as Lucite and vinyl. Polystryene made its appearance then, and furfural-phenols were in use in industrial applications. Though a great future was predicted for ethyl cellulose, by the late thirties it was still in the experimental phase. For most purposes, the field of decorative plastics from the first half of the century can be narrowed down to the five major types listed above. Of these, cellulose acetate is rarely encountered. Casein is limited to button and belt buckle manufacture; urea is easily identifiable as a cheap, brittle material. Pyroxylin is the celluloid of which so many vanity sets were made. Molded phenolics such as Bakelite were dark in color and used for utilitarian objects; cast phenolics such as Catalin were used most notably for jewelry (please don't call it Bakelite), cutlery handles, desk sets, and novelties.

Dealers and collectors should be aware of '70s reproduction Marblette animal napkin rings (they have no eye rods and no age patina) and molded acrylic bracelets in imitation of carved Catalin ones (look for a seam line or lack of definition in 'carved areas'). As prices rise, copies become more common. 1986 saw the mass-production of inlaid polka-dot bracelets using old-stock findings but without the precision fit (or patina) of the originals.

In 1988 and continuing to the present, a large number of 'collage' pieces appeared in vintage clothing and antique stores on the West and East Coasts. These are over-sized, glued-together assemblages of old Catalin stock parts including buttons with the shanks filed off, poker chips, etc. made into brooches or pendants, sometimes hung on necklaces of re-strung Catalin beads. They can be recognized by their aesthetically jumbled, 'put-together' look; and although some may claim they are 'old,' they are not.

Our advisor for this category is Catherine Yronwode, who also publishes an informative newsletter, *The Collectible Plastics*; she is listed in the Directory under California.

Bakelite

Cigarette box, half-cylinder, rotates open, dk brn 40.00
Clock, electric, alarm, Deco design, blk..60.00
Clock, mantel, wind-up alarm, Deco design, dk brn 50.00
Inkwell, streamlined, blk, w/lid 20.00
Penholder, streamlined, blk..15.00
Radio, Majestic #55, dk brn, 1939...200.00
Radio, Silvertone Compact, Sears, dk brn, 1936-1937................200.00
Radio, Stewart Warner Varsity College, dk brn, 1938-1939........150.00
Roulette wheel, dk brn, 1930s 80.00
Roulette wheel, mc Catalin chips, wood rack, w/box, 1930s 200.00
Watch, lady's handbag; Westclox, blk, 2¾" dia.............................60.00

Catalin

Ash tray, marbleized lt gr, sq, 4½" 30.00
Barometer, Taylor, amber & dk gr, rectangular, 4" 40.00
Bottle opener, chrome plate, red, gr, or amber hdl 6.00
Bracelet, bangle; apple-juice clear, figural bk-cvg........................175.00
Bracelet, bangle; apple-juice clear, floral bk-cvg 150.00
Bracelet, bangle; apple-juice clear, geometric bk-cvg 130.00
Bracelet, bangle; deep cvg, w/rhinestones 70.00
Bracelet, bangle; elaborate floral cvg, narrow 30.00
Bracelet, bangle; elaborate floral cvg, wide 52.00
Bracelet, bangle; lt geometric cvg, narrow 24.00
Bracelet, bangle; lt geometric cvg, wide 34.00
Bracelet, bangle; novelty, mc, figural or animal cvg.....................250.00
Bracelet, bangle; scratch cvd, narrow 15.00
Bracelet, bangle; scratch cvd, w/rhinestones...................................25.00
Bracelet, bangle; scratch cvd, wide 22.00
Bracelet, bangle; stylized floral cvg, narrow 22.00
Bracelet, bangle; stylized floral cvg, wide 34.00
Bracelet, bangle; uncvd, narrow 4.00
Bracelet, bangle; uncvd, wide 9.00
Bracelet, bangle; 12 inlaid polka dots, wide.................................130.00
Bracelet, bangle; 2-color stripes 60.00
Bracelet, bangle; 3-color stripes 80.00
Bracelet, bangle; 4-color (or more) stripes....................................100.00
Bracelet, bangle; 6 inlaid polka dots, narrow 130.00
Bracelet, cellulose acetate chain, 7 cvd figural charms.................125.00
Bracelet, clamper; figural, animal, or novelty applique 225.00
Bracelet, clamper; inlaid geometric designs 120.00
Bracelet, clamper; stylized floral cvg..48.00
Bracelet, clamper; w/inlaid rhinestones..32.00
Bracelet, curved/flat links, deeply cvd..60.00
Bracelet, curved/flat links, uncvd 40.00
Bracelet, stretch; orig elastic, Catalin & metal 42.00
Bracelet, stretch; orig elastic, deeply cvd 60.00
Bracelet, stretch; orig elastic, mc, uncvd..40.00
Buckle, latch type, mc, novelty or figural applique........................40.00
Buckle, latch type, mc, stylized floral or geometric, cvd 40.00
Buckle, latch type, mc, uncvd..25.00
Buckle, latch type, 1-color, novelty or figural applique 20.00
Buckle, latch type, 1-color, stylized floral or geometric 10.00
Buckle, latch type, 1-color, uncvd... 5.00
Buckle, latch type, 1-color w/rhinestones, Deco.............................20.00

Buckle, slide type, mc, stylized floral or geometric, cvd 30.00
Buckle, slide type, mc, uncvd 10.00
Buckle, slide type, 1-color, stylized floral or geometric, cvd 5.00
Buckle, slide type, 1-color, uncvd... 3.00
Butter mold, gr/amber/brn, floral cvg, 2½" 32.00
Buttons, card of 6, red or blk laminated, 1½" rod 18.00
Buttons, card of 6, scotty, fruit, or cvd floral figural.....................28.00
Buttons, card of 6, uncvd octagonal, amber, 1" dia........................10.00
Cake breaker, CJ Schneider, red, gr, or amber hdl 2.00
Carving set, knife, fork, steel...30.00
Carving set, 3-pc w/wood wall rack...40.00
Checkers, red & blk, full set, in box 32.00
Cheese slicer, scotty hdl, wood & chrome base 10.00
Chess set, hand cvd, red & blk, leather box 200.00
Chopsticks, ivory, pr 3.00
Cigarette box, chrome inserts, cylindrical, 4½" 35.00
Cigarette box, lt gr, wood bottom, rectangular, 5½x3¾" 30.00
Cigarette holder, imitation amber, sterling tip, orig case...............25.00
Cigarette holder, long, mc or w/rhinestones 25.00
Cigarette lighter, Arco-Lite devil's head, red or blk 150.00
Cigarette lighter, mc stripes or inlay 30.00
Clock, New Haven, wind-up alarm, amber, Deco, 3⅝" 50.00
Clock, Sessions, electric alarm, scalloped case, 4¼" dia.................50.00
Clock, Seth Thomas, wind-up alarm, maroon case, 3½" 40.00
Clock, Westclox, Moonbeam, electric flashing light alarm..............60.00
Clothesline, Jigger, red anchors, 10 pins, metal box 10.00
Cocktail recipes, Ben Hur, mtd on drunk, red w/blk base 40.00
Cocktail recipes, Ben Hur, mtd on fighting roosters......................40.00
Cork, Ben Hur, w/red fighting roosters, blk base 20.00
Corkscrew, chrome, red, gr, or amber hdl 10.00
Corn holder, Kob Knobs, diamond shape or lathe trn, 8 +box.......30.00
Crib toy, Tykie Toy, boy, girl, clown, kitten, etc, ea...................100.00

Tykie Toy, Cannibal Mother, 5½", $100.00.

Crib toy, Tykie Toy, clown or elephant, loalin head/body 60.00
Crib toy, Tykie Toy, 11 mc spools on string, 1940s......................50.00
Crib toy, Tykie Toy, 12 1½" rings on 2⅞" ring, 1940s..................50.00
Crib toy, Tykie Toy catalogue, 1946...25.00
Crib toy, Tykie Toy Tales (book about these toys), 1946...............35.00
Dice, ivory or red, 2½", pr...15.00
Dice, ivory or red, ¾", pr... 2.00
Dice cage, metal/red Catalin, blk Lucite base, w/dice 75.00
Dice cup, leather or cork lined 30.00
Dominoes, ivory or blk, full set, w/wood box 25.00
Dominoes, red or gr, full set, w/wood box 40.00
Drawer pull, 1-color, w/pnt inlay stripe...2.00
Drawer pull, 2-color, octagon, w/inlaid dot..................................... 3.00

Dress clip, mc inlaid Deco design 20.00
Dress clip, novelty, figural, animal, or vegetable.....................50.00
Dress clip, scratch cvd..12.00
Dress clip, stylized floral cvg.....................................20.00
Dress clip, 1-color, w/rhinestones, Deco design 18.00
Earrings, lg drop style, pr 8.00
Earrings, novelty, figural, animal, or vegetable, pr.....................30.00
Earrings, stylized floral cvg, pr 10.00
Earrings, uncvd disks, pr 4.00
Egg beater, red, gr, or amber hdl 12.00
Flatware, chrome plate, 1-color hdl 1.00
Flatware, chrome plate, 3-pc matched place setting 5.00
Flatware, stainless, 1-color hdl.................................... 1.50
Flatware, stainless, 1-color hdl, leatherette box, 36-pc..................50.00
Flatware, stainless, 1-color hdl, 3-pc matched place setting 6.00
Flatware, stainless, 2-color hdl.................................... 3.00
Flatware, stainless, 2-color hdl, wood box, 36-pc 200.00
Flatware, stainless, 2-color hdl, 3-pc matched place setting 10.00
Gavel, lathe turned, ivory..18.00
Gavel, lathe turned, red, blk, & ivory 25.00
Gavel, lathe turned, red, w/presentation box, dtd 1946 ....28.00
Ice cream scoop, stainless, red hdl 18.00
Inkwell, Carvacraft Great Britain, amber, dbl well......................75.00
Inkwell, Carvacraft Great Britain, amber, single well 50.00
Knife, cvd red, gr, or amber hdl 4.00
Lamp base, brass & amber, Deco design, 10" 30.00
Lamp base, red, amber, & blk, Deco design, 8" 44.00
Letter opener, blk & amber stripes, Deco design 20.00
Letter opener, chrome/Catalin, Deco design 12.00
Letter opener, marbleized gr, dagger shape 16.00
Mah-Jong set, tiles, rails, 6-color, complete, w/box 40.00
Manicure set, tube holder, pnt floral design 35.00
Manicure set, 4-mini tools in tube, Germany 22.00
Memo pad, Carvacraft Great Britain, amber 25.00
Nail brush, Ducky, duck shape, translucent eye rod 30.00
Nail brush, marbleized lt gr, 2½x1½" 8.00
Nail brush, Masso, amber octagon, 2" dia 8.00
Nail brush, turtle shape, dark amber, 3½" 16.00
Napkin ring, amber, red, or gr, 2" dia band......................... 3.00
Napkin ring, animal or bird, no inlaid eye or ball on head............20.00
Napkin ring, elephant w/ball on head...............................30.00
Napkin ring, lathe turned, amber, red, or gr, 1¾" dia 4.00
Napkin ring, Mickey Mouse or Donald Duck shape w/decal............58.00
Napkin ring, rabbit w/inlaid eye rod...............................30.00
Napkin ring, rocking horse or camel w/inlaid eye rod 66.00
Napkin ring, scotty, w/inlaid eye rod 38.00
Napkin ring set, 6-colors, 2" band, orig box........................30.00
Necklace, cellulose acetate chain, animal figurals....................150.00
Necklace, cellulose acetate chain, Deco dangling pcs 75.00
Necklace, cvd red & amber beads, 18"...............................60.00
Necklace, uncvd gr beads, 20".......................................40.00
Ozone generator, Air-Clear, dk amber, streamlined case 60.00
Pencil sharpener, Disney character decal, silhouette shape............38.00
Pencil sharpener, gun, tank, or plane shape w/decal....................24.00
Pencil sharpener, orange, no decal, ¾x1"............................ 5.00
Pencil sharpener, red, Mickey Mouse decal, ¾x1" 24.00
Pencil sharpener, scotty, red, cvd details, blk base.....................24.00
Pencil sharpener, scotty, yel, silhouette shape 10.00
Pencil sharpener, Trylon & Perisphere, 1939 World's Fair 40.00
Penholder, amber & blk striped, Deco design.........................35.00
Penholder, marbleized amber, Deco design...........................20.00
Penholder, scotty, red w/blk base 42.00
Picture frame, amber & red Deco design, 6x7" 45.00
Picture frame, red, gr, or amber, sq, 6"............................25.00

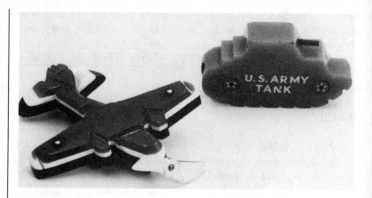

Catalin, red, white, and blue airplane pin, 2½", $170.00; Catalin, US Army tank pencil sharpener, Ace Plastic Novelties, Brooklyn, NY, 2" long, $24.00.

Pin, animal, resin wash w/glass eye, lg...............................80.00
Pin, animal, resin wash w/glass eye, sm 60.00
Pin, animal or vegetable, inlaid or appl in several colors, lg.........150.00
Pin, animal or vegetable, inlaid or appl in several colors, sm 80.00
Pin, animal or vegetable, 1-color, lg..............................70.00
Pin, animal or vegetable, 1-color, sm 50.00
Pin, mc Deco design, lg...50.00
Pin, mc Deco design, sm 35.00
Pin, novelty or patriotic figural, resin wash/inlay/appl, lg 170.00
Pin, novelty or patriotic figural, resin wash/inlay/appl, sm 90.00
Pin, novelty or patriotic figural, 1-color, lg......................85.00
Pin, novelty or patriotic figural, 1-color, sm 55.00
Pin, stylized floral cvg, lg.......................................34.00
Pin, stylized floral cvg, sm.......................................28.00
Pin, w/danglers, animal or vegetable, resin wash/inlay/appl.........160.00
Pin, w/danglers, animal or vegetable, 1-color 95.00
Pin, w/danglers, geometric form, mc 55.00
Pin, w/danglers, geometric form, 1-color...........................40.00
Pin, w/danglers, novelty or patriotic, resin wash/inlay/appl 200.00
Pin, w/danglers, novelty or patriotic, 1-color.....................100.00
Pipe, amber & gr, bowl lined w/clay................................28.00
Pitcher, glass, red, gr, or amber hdl, syrup size 15.00
Pocket watch, Debonaire, yel Deco case, 1⅞" dia....................60.00
Poker chip rack, cylindrical, w/50 chips, 2½" 50.00
Poker chip rack, rectangular, w/200 chips, 4" 90.00
Powder box, amber & blk fluted cylinder, 2½" 42.00
Powder box, amber & gr fluted cylinder, 4" 54.00
Radio, Emerson College model, amber or gr, 1938....................450.00
Radio, Emerson College model, red, 1938...........................475.00
Radio, Fada Streamliner, amber, amber knobs/bezel, 1941 ....500.00
Radio, Fada Streamliner, amber, red knobs/bezel 525.00
Radio, Fada Streamliner, red, amber knobs/bezel, 1941 ....550.00
Radio, Kadette Klockette, amber, gr, or maroon, 1937 ....400.00
Radio, Kadette Klockette, red, 1937 ....425.00
Ring, inlaid Deco stripe design, 2-color 35.00
Ring, stylized floral cvg, 1-color 30.00
Ring, uncvd, 1-color 8.00
Ring, uncvd, 2-color..18.00
Ring case, hinged-lid style, amber or maroon 100.00
Ring case, open-top style, amber, red, or blk, Deco design............75.00
Safety razor, Schick Injector, amber hdl 10.00
Safety razor, Schick Injector, extra blades, orig box, 1939 ....35.00
Salad servers, Chase chrome, ivory, blk, or brn, pr 30.00
Salad servers, chrome, red, gr, or amber hdls, pr 10.00
Shakers, ball shape or half-cylinder shape, 1½", pr...................23.00
Shakers, glass, in 3⅛" Catalin holder, pr.........................18.00
Shakers, mushroom shape, amber & ivory, 1⅞", pr 25.00

Shakers, stepped cylinder shape, 3½", pr...................................**23.00**
Shakers, Washington Monument, 3¼", pr...................................**22.00**
Shaving brush, red, gr, or amber..**20.00**
Shaving brush, red, gr, or amber, w/holder...............................**30.00**
Spatula, stainless, red, gr, or amber hdl 3.00
Spoon, iced tea, chrome, w/Catalin knob, 6-pc set **12.00**
Spoon, slotted, stainless, red, gr, or amber hdl................................ 4.00
Steering knob, chrome clamp...**12.00**
Stirrer, iced tea; Chase, chrome ball/mint leaf, 6-pc set **20.00**
Stirrer, iced tea; shovel blade, Catalin hdl, 6-pc set **24.00**
Strainer, red, gr, or amber hdl, 2¾" dia 4.00
Strainer, red, gr, or amber hdl, 5" dia 6.00
Swizzle stick, baseball-bat shape, amber or red............................. 4.00
Swizzle stick holder, amber or red, Rheingold Lager decal **70.00**
Thermometer, BT Co, amber & blk, 2¾" dia...............................**36.00**
Thermometer, Taylor, amber & dk gr, rectangular, 4" **45.00**
Writing set, blk, amber, or gr marble, Deco, 5-pc, orig box..........**150.00**

Celluloid

Bracelet, imitation tortoise w/inlaid rhinestones **36.00**
Bracelet, snake w/inlaid rhinestones **46.00**
Bridge marker, pnt ivoroid animal or figure, France **20.00**
Bridge pencil holder, animal, pearlescent ivory on blk..................**60.00**
Buttons, ivoroid or pearlescent, ¾" dia, card of 6........................ 8.00
Carving set, ivoroid, knife/fork/steel, eng blade **30.00**
Clock, Greek temple facade, wind-up alarm, ivoroid **45.00**
Dresser set, amberoid & gr marbleized, 7-pc.................................**70.00**
Dresser set, ivoroid, 10-pc, w/9" bevel glass mirror......................**100.00**
Dresser set, ivory pearlescent or amberoid, 5-pc **50.00**
Flatware, gr pearl on blk hdl, 3-pc set.. 9.00
Flatware, ivoroid hdl, table knife, fork, or spoon, ea...................... 1.00
Hair receiver, ivoroid, pearlescent or amberoid, w/2-part lid **10.00**
Manicure set, ivoroid, pearlescent or amberoid, 10-pc, +case........**30.00**
Manicure set, ivoroid, 18-pc, roll-up leather case **25.00**
Mirror, dresser; ivoroid, cut-out hdl, bevel glass, 8" **18.00**
Mirror, dresser; ivoroid, oval bevel glass, 13" **28.00**
Mirror, dresser; pearlescent or amberoid, bevel glass, 12" **20.00**
Picture frame, easel bk, ivoroid, 2" dia **12.00**
Powder box, ivoroid, pearlescent or amberoid **10.00**
Shaving stand, ivoroid, 5-pc, w/razor **75.00**

Lucite

Bottle, perfume; w/atomizer, rose inclusion.................................**10.00**
Bracelet, stretch, orig elastic, clear, bk-cvd..................................**25.00**
Picture frame, Deco, clear, sq, 6"...**14.00**
Purse, box style, clear or tortoise **32.00**
Shakers, translucent red, 4", pr.. 9.00

Playing Cards

Playing cards can be an enjoyable way to trace the course of history. Knowledge of the art, literature, and politics of an era can be gleaned from a study of its playing cards. When royalty lost favor with the people, Kings and Queens were replaced by common people. During the periods of war, generals, officers, and soldiers were favored. In the United States, early examples had portraits of Washington and Adams as opposed to Kings, Indian chiefs instead of Jacks, and goddesses for Queens.

Tarot cards were used in Europe during the 1300s as a game of chance, but in the 18th century they were used to predict the future and were regarded with great reverence.

The backs of cards were of no particular consequence until the 1890s. The marble design used by the French during the late 1800s and the colored wood-cut patterns of the Italians in the 19th century are among the first attempts at decoration. Later the English used cards printed with portraits of royalty. Eventually cards were decorated with a broad range of subjects from reproductions of fine art to advertising.

Although playing cards are becoming popular collectibles, prices are still relatively low. Complete decks of cards printed earlier than the first postage stamp can still be purchased for less than $100. Periodic auction catalogs are available from 'Full House' Antique Playing Cards and Gambling Memorabilia. See the Directory under Clubs, Newsletters and Catalogs for the address.

Key:
C — complete   OB — original box
cts — courts   sz — size
hc — hand colored   XC — extra card
J — joker

Advertising

Canby, Aura Roberts, 1938, 68+instructions, OB, M **10.00**
Chatfield & Woods, gold edges, 52+JJ, M 8.00
Clavecin, Catel & Farcey, ca 1960, 52+J, OB, M...........................**15.00**
Clismic Table Water, special aces & photo Js, 52+J, OB, VG **18.00**
Frank's Kutlery Kuts, wide, USPC, ca 1900, 52+J+2XC, OB, M ...**30.00**
French Standards, Darax Fabricant, 1815, 32C, M in wrapper **225.00**
Moore & Calvin, tobacco inserts, 52+J, VG to M, rare **250.00**
Palmafina, animal cts/J, Mesmaekers, 1956, 52+J+blank, OB, M ..**25.00**
Royal Lancer Cigars, ads on aces, pinochle, 48C, VG in box **25.00**
Washburn Cigars, colorful aces & Js, 52+J+XC, VG in box **50.00**

France and Belgium

Aluette, silver corners, Grimaud, 1950s, 46/48, EX.......................**25.00**
Cassandre, for Hermes by Draeger Freres, '50, 52+J+XC, MIB **40.00**
Classique, Draeger Freres, 52+J, 1964, MIB................................**22.00**
De Gaulle, caricature cts, Sine, 1965, 52 no J, OB, M **25.00**
Guerre Mondiale I, allied leaders cts, Brepols, 1919, 36+J, M **110.00**
Jeu de Copains, singing cts, Triboulet, 1965, 52+JJ+XC, MIB.......**12.00**
Jeu Louis XV #1502, gold edges, Grimaud, 1890s, 52, MIB **100.00**
Palmafina, animal cts/J, Mesmaekers, 1956, 52+J+blank, OB, M ..**25.00**

Games, No Suit Signs

American, Christensen, 1933, 52+flag card+rules, M **20.00**
Bible Game #1124, Fireside, 1899, 52+XC+rules, VG in box........**15.00**
Big Funeral, Claude Souci, complete, orig cb case, EX **10.00**
Canby, Aura Roberts, 1938, 68+instructions, OB, M **10.00**
In Dixieland #1118, slave scenes, Fireside, 1897, 52+2, VG..........**60.00**
Komponisten-Quartet, Scholz, Mainz, 1930s, 48+rules, EX, OB ...**15.00**
Lexicon, Waddington, 1933, 52+2 booklets, EX in box................**10.00**
Multiplication & Division, Cincinnati, 1903, NM **12.00**
Quien Sabe, cowboy game, Parker Bros, '06, 120+rules, VG, OB .**25.00**
Victory Rummy, Hitler/Mussolini/etc photos, 1942, 63C, MIB.....**25.00**

Germany, Austria, and Czechoslovakia

Arnold Schoenberg, Piatnik, 1981, 52C, +booklet, MIB...............**45.00**
Dondorf #150, chromolitho, 1890s, no indices, VG......................**22.00**
Dondorf #162, ca 1895, 52+J, OB, VG **40.00**
John Peter Burgers, stenciled cts, Cologne, 1800s, 52C, M **200.00**
Leipsig Fair, ASS, 1897, 32C, VG..**85.00**
Piquet #54, French suits, Wust, ca 1800, 32C, M in wrapper.........**50.00**

Seasons Pattern #86, Piatnik, ca 1950, 33C, MIB **10.00**
Tarock Politische, caricature, Hartung, 1975, 36+XC, OB, M **10.00**
Wust, fantasy cts, scenic aces, ca 1870, 50/52, EX......................**200.00**

Great Britain

Edward VIII, sepia bust, Universal PCC, 1936, 52+J+XC, M........**35.00**
Falstaff & Jester, narrow named, gold border, 52+J, EX................**10.00**
Royal Wedding (Charles & Diana), Worshipful, 1981, dbl, M......**50.00**
Stag Glamour Pack #11, blk/wht nudes, 1945, 52+JJ, OB, M **15.00**
Winston Churchill, bl border, Worshipful, 1955, 52+J+XC, M **30.00**

Italy, Spain, and Latin America

Cuauhtemoc, Aztecs, Jacques, 1950, 52+J+XC+booklet, MIB **25.00**
Czechov, play characters, Massenghini, 52+JJ+XC, MIB..............**15.00**
Jover y Serra, Igualada, ca 1810, 48C, M **100.00**
Madriguera, historic cts, ca 1895, 33/48, rare, G **55.00**
Military Uniforms, Il Meneghello, '76, 40+4J+title card, MIB **30.00**
Naipe Centauro, Columbia, Colina, 1979, 40C, MIB....................**15.00**

Miniatures and Patience

Dondorf #1320, ca 1900, 52C, 39x22mm, VG **25.00**
Dondorf #189, Swiss costumes, 52+J, MIB..................................**18.00**
Grimauld #536, Hollandaise cts, 1890 stamp, 52+J, EX in box......**25.00**
Liliput, standard faces, Fourn, 1954, 52+J (photo), M **5.00**
Little Duke, USPC, ca 1920, 52C, 31x44mm, OB, EX **10.00**
Piatnik #119, luxury pack, 1930s, 52+JJ, M.................................**12.00**
Suisse Historique #94, Muller, ca 1925, 52+J, MIB **22.00**

Souvenir and Expositions

Bermuda, scenic linen finish bk, 1930s, 52, MIB.........................**12.00**
California, wide scenic, gold edges, 1907, 52+J, OB, M **40.00**
Chicago World's Fair, gold edges, 1934, 52+XC, EX **10.00**
De Laurence, Chicago, ca 1929, 78C, OB, M **35.00**
Florentine Minchiate, ca 1700s, 2 tax stamps, 97C, EX **1,000.00**
Minnesota, narrow scenic, dbl, ea: 52+JJ (state seal), MIB...........**16.00**
New England, scenic, 1950s, dbl, ea: 52+J, MIB..........................**15.00**
New Zeland, sepia photos, 52+JJ, worn, soiled **5.00**

Tarot and Fortune Telling

Church of Light, 1964, 78+XC, MIB **25.00**
Dondorf #2, German rhymes, 1890s, 36C, VG **10.00**
Dondorf Cego Tarock #246, rnd corners, EX in box....................**200.00**
Florentine Minchiate, ca 1700s, 2 tax stamps, 97C, EX **1,000.00**
Let's Tell Fortunes, Spring Valley NY, 1941, 48C+rules, OB, M ..**20.00**
Princess Yvonne, Deco-style, Phila, 1929, 52+rules, OB, VG........**22.00**
Ravensburg Tardock, woodblock, tax stamp, ca 1870, 54C, M ...**500.00**
Wiener Veduten, Piatnik '74 repro of 1870 deck, 78+booklet, M ...**40.00**
Zodiac, w/lucky numbers, 30C+instructions, 1940s, EX in box **10.00**

Transformations

Cartoonist's Pack, Carta Mundi, 1890, 52+4 Js, OB, M.................**25.00**
Hand drawn pen & ink pip cards, Congress, 52+J, EX **75.00**
Tiffany Harlequin, gold edges, gr bks, 1878, 51/52, EX..............**375.00**
Vanity Fair #41, USPC, 51+J, ½ OB, EX **225.00**

Transportation: Airline, Steamship, Railroad

Atlantic Coast Line, Engine #525, 1958, sealed, M **35.00**

Chessie, Sleep Like a Kitten, dbl deck, sealed, M **25.00**
Cotton Belt Route, watermelon girl bks, 1903, 52+J+XC, VG ...**185.00**
Green Club, Hanzel, 1923, 52+J, OB, M **65.00**
Lockhead C-58, plane on bks, Taiwan, 52+JJ, OB, M **6.00**
Monarch Airlines, 757 in flight to left, sealed, M.........................**8.00**
Norgulf Lines, wheel on yel, ca 1950, M, sealed **8.00**
Pittsburgh & Lake Erie RR, red/bl dbl deck, sealed, M **20.00**
Squeezers #220, NYCC, ca 1800, 52+Best Bower, OB, M **50.00**
TransAmerica Air Lines, DC-10 flying, 102, M, sealed **16.00**

United States

American Steamboats #99, APCC, ca 1895, 52+photo J, OB, EX...**75.00**
Bicycle, New Fan, bl, ca 1895, 52, no J, VG **8.00**

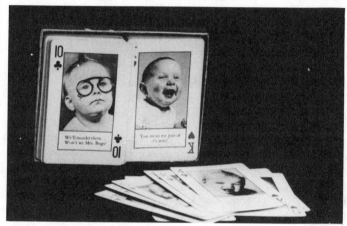

Constance Bannester's Babies, double deck, 1940s, $50.00.

Columbia Whist, Nat'l Card Co, ca 1900, 52 no J, EX **7.00**
Golden Dmn, 4 color suits, Hanzel, 1923, 52+J, M **60.00**
High Stepper Brand, Gibson, 52+J, VG..**8.00**
Mast Mail #44, railroad bks, Standard, 52+J, soiled, OB...............**15.00**
Pacific-Union Club, San Francisco, 1920s, 52+J, OB, M **15.00**
Poppy, narrow named, gr border w/gold, 52, OB, EX **15.00**
Shirley Temple, photo silhouette, bl border, 52, no J, VG **30.00**
United China Relief, dbl, ARRCO, WWII, OB, M......................**20.00**

Political

The most valuable political items are those from any period which relate to a political figure whose term was especially significant or marked by an important event or one whose personality was particularly colorful. Posters, ribbons, badges, photographs, and pin-back buttons are but a few examples of the items popular with collectors of political memorabilia.

Political campaign pin-back buttons were first mass-produced and widely distributed in 1896 for the president-to-be William McKinley and for the first of three unsuccessful attempts by William Jennings Bryan. Pin-back buttons have been used during each presidential campaign ever since and are collected by many people. The most scarce are those used in the presidential campaigns of James Davis in 1924 and James Cox in 1920.

Our advisor for this category is Paul Longo; he is listed in the Directory under Massachusetts. See also Autographs; Broadsides; Historical Glass; Watch Fobs.

Announcement, funeral, w/JF Kennedy photo **50.00**
Banner, Smith for President, cloth, lt wear at top.......................**350.00**

Bas relief, Lincoln, metal w/bronze patina, OJ Willard, 21".........140.00
Book, Republican Nat'l Convention, 1960, 176-pg, EX................12.00
Bottle, Nixon/Agnew, gr glass, Wheaton, 1968...........................15.00
Broadside, Last Rally!, Kennett Sq, 1852, 13x10", EX 400.00
Broadside, WJ Bryan, The Issue, 1900..., scenes/Bryan, VG 950.00
Broadside, Wm McKinley, Prosperity, J Morgan litho, 1900s 500.00
Bust, Teddy Roosevelt, metal, 1921, 4"..................................40.00
Button, Goldwater, red/wht/bl trim, 7", NM 7.00
Button, Gov James F Curley of US Senate, 1", EX........................30.00
Button, Italians for Ford, red & wht litho, 1½"......................... 4.00
Card, Christmas; Hallmark, sgn by Jackie Kennedy 90.00
Card, library; sgn by JF Kennedy...250.00
Cuff links, Nixon/Agnew, 1973 Inaugural Ball, MIB 30.00
Election ticket, Liberty vignette, candidates listed, 1877 ....15.00

Flag, For President John Bell, For Vice President Edward Everett, 1860 campaign, 8" x 11½", $1,500.00.

Flowerpot, WH Taft/Sherman, mc transfer, 3x4" 135.00
Game, Who Can Beat Nixon?, Harrison/Blaine, 1970, NM..........25.00
Handkerchief, Hoover portrait, silk, 1928, 14x16", NM 40.00
Hat, I Like Ike, paper, 1956, EX...20.00
Letter opener, Kennedy Will Win, CA campaign, NM.................10.00
Ornament, radiator; Al Smith's head figural, 1928 ....125.00
Pendant, Wallace/Lemay jugate, portrait photos, EX....................10.00
Pin-bk, Cleveland/Stevenson jugate, lithos, 1888, 1" 125.00

Pin-back Grant and Colfax jugate ferrotype, ⅝", $175.00.

Pin-bk, Hoover, emb bust, 1932, EX.....................................15.00
Pin-bk, Scranton for President, lg 10.00
Pin-bk, We Don't Want Eleanor Either, EX............................ 7.00
Pin-bk, Win w/Wilson, portrait, NM.....................................25.00
Place mat, Landon, paper, portrait in sunflower, 1936, EX 15.00
Plaque, Lincoln, bronze, by D Brenner, Klaker Co, 1907, 9" 250.00
Post card, Roosevelt/Bryan, Presidential Fight, 1908.....................14.00
Post card, Vote for JFK, color print, M....................................20.00
Poster, Hoover for President, 18x12", VG 35.00

Poster, Wm McKinley, 1900, 21x28", EX 65.00
Sheet music, Keep Cool & Keep Coolidge, 1924, VG 25.00
Ticket, Phila Democratic Nat'l Convention, 1936, EX................10.00
Ticket, Republican Nat'l Convention, 1892, VG 25.00
Toby, Al Smith, ceramic, 7"...85.00
Tray, metal, emb Republican convention, Phila, 1900, 5".............35.00
Tumbler, Blaine portrait on bottom......................................80.00
Tumbler, Dewey photo transfer w/gold trim 50.00
Window decal, MacArthur for President, 7¼x3½"....................12.00

Pomona

Pomona glass was patented in 1885 by the New England Glass Works. Its characteristics are an etched background of crystal lead glass often decorated with simple designs painted with metallic stains of amber or blue. The etching was first achieved by hand cutting through an acid resist. This method, called first grind, resulted in an uneven feather-like frost effect. Later, to cut production costs, the hand-cut process was discontinued in favor of an acid bath which effected an even frosting. This method is called second grind.

Our advisors for this category are Betty and Clarence Maier; they are listed in the Directory under Pennsylvania.

Bowl, 2nd grind, Rivulet w/bl stain, fluted, 2⅝x5" 80.00
Creamer, 2nd grind, cornflowers, crimped base, ruffled, 3" 225.00
Creamer & sugar, 1st grind, ruffled 585.00
Creamer & sugar bowl, 1st grind, mini, 3" 425.00
Cruet, 1st grind, rpl stopper 150.00
Cruet, 2nd grind, pansy/butterfly (no stain), 7"..........................365.00
Finger bowl, 2nd grind, Rivulet w/bl stain, fluted, 2½x6" 145.00

First grind nappy with blue cornflowers, 5¼", $125.00; First grind lemonade, leaf design, $150.00.

Pickle castor, 2nd grind, bl cornflowers, all orig...........................495.00
Punch cup, 1st grind, amber leaves 35.00
Punch cup, 1st grind, bl cornflowers 60.00
Punch cup, 2nd grind, cornflowers 40.00
Spooner, 2nd grind, Invt T'print, blueberries, crimped base 125.00
Tumbler, 1st grind, pansies, bk: butterfly, 3¾" 135.00
Tumbler, 2nd grind, cornflowers, amber stain, 3¾x2½"...............145.00
Vase, lily; 2nd grind, optic dmns, 5" 335.00
Vase, 1st grind, ribs/panels of flowers alternate, ftd, 6"................775.00
Vase, 2nd grind, blueberries, crimped base, ruffled, 5x2¾" 550.00

Post Cards

A German by the name of Emmanuel Herrman is credited for

inventing the post card, first printed in Austria in 1869. They were eagerly accepted by the Continentals and the English alike, who saw them as a more economical way to send written messages.

Post cards, first sold here in the 1880s, were made to order by private firms in Germany. The first to be printed in the United States were on U.S. government postals. The Columbian Exposition of 1892-1893 served as the spark that ignited the post card phenomenon. Souvenir cards by the thousands were sent to folks back home — expo scenes, transportation themes, animals, birds, and advertising messages became popular. There were patriotic themes, Black themes, and cards for every occasion and holiday. Scenics, cards with small-town railroad depots, and views of U.S. towns (especially photos) are very sought-after.

Some of the earliest post card publishers were Raphael Tuck, Nister and Gabriel. Early 20th-century illustrators such as Frances Brundage, Rose O'Neill, and Ellen Clapsaddle designed cards that are especially sought after today.

Although the post card rage waned at the onset of WWI, they rank today among the most sought-after paper collectibles, second only to stamps.

Even though post cards may be sixty to ninety years old, they must be in excellent condition. As a worth-accessing factor, condition is second only to subject matter. When no condition is indicated, the items listed below are assumed to be in excellent condition whether used or unused.

Our advisor for this category is Mrs. Sally Carver; she is listed in the Directory under Massachusetts.

Key:
p/ — publisher   s/ — signed

Advertising, Cracker Jack Bear #13, flying over factory, 1907, G..**18.00**
Advertising, Cracker Jack Bear #9, in peanut field, VG.................**20.00**
Alligator border, Grand Canal, FL, p/Langsdorf, VG **35.00**
Alligator border, Picking Cotton, p/Langsdorf, EX......................**30.00**
Animals, Animal School, Jungle Animals, p/Nister, VG...............**15.00**
Animals, camel, rnd corners, G..**12.00**
Animals, cat hanging socks on line, p/Nister, EX.......................**12.00**
Animals, frog blows bubbles for 1907 New Year, US, VG **18.00**
Animals, On Duty, fire-bears in hats, etc, p/A Hahn, VG **12.00**
Animals, pig makes toast, #2845, p/Salmon, VG **8.00**
Animals, Zebra, p/Tuck, VG...**15.00**
Animals, 2 Wise Old Owls..., 4-line poem, p/Valentine, VG **10.00**
Aviation, Defiants & Junkers 88K's, p/Salmon, VG......................**8.00**
Bergman, gr-suited Santa w/sack by fireplace, #3125, VG.............**15.00**
Boileau, Queenliness, Watercolor Series #374, VG......................**25.00**
Brundage, Proposal, man proposing to shy woman, p/Tuck, VG....**28.00**
Carter, Reg; girl & golliwog swing, 2 golliwogs watch, VG **22.00**
Christmas, Santa in red robe w/angel & boys, p/PFB, VG.............**28.00**

F. Earl Christy, ladies in silk dresses, primary colors, $25.00 each.

Christy, Cornell, #2625, p/Tuck, VG.......................................**20.00**
Christy, Love, Here Is My Heart, Watercolor Series #945, VG **14.00**
Clapsaddle, boy pours candy in toy house, Xmas, p/Wolf, VG.......**10.00**
Clapsaddle, Halloween mechanical, girl moves arm, #1236, VG...**65.00**
Clapsaddle, St Valentine Greeting, boy w/2 girls, VG **9.00**
Clapsaddle, Wearing of the Gr, boy in gr suit & top hat, VG........**10.00**
Clark, Rose; Roosevelt Bears #18, bears/boys/fireworks, VG..........**25.00**
Clarkston, GT; female pilot, Ruth Law, oilette, VG **18.00**
Clarkston, GT; Horace Farman, biplane, oilette, p/Tuck, VG.......**20.00**
Coins, USSR, 18 coins, p/Walter Erhard, VG.............................**18.00**
Coins, 10 Swiss coins w/insert picture of Luzern, p/HSM, VG.......**25.00**
Coins, 12 US coins, actual sz, p/Max Heimbrecht, rare, VG **35.00**
College Women, Vassar, lady in red, p/Langsdorf, EX...................**20.00**
Cowboys & Indians, Bear-Heart & Wife photo, p/J Weiner, VG..**18.00**
Cowboys & Indians, Indians on horsebk photo, p/J Weiner, VG ..**17.00**
Dwig, Horseshoe, woman w/horsehoe, #2140, 1908, VG...............**10.00**
Ebner, Wedding Breakfast, couple served outside by dolls, EX.......**15.00**
Fantasy, Dr Cook, face made of Eskimos/dog/US Flag, '09, VG.....**75.00**
Fisher, Harrison; A Lucky Beggar, woman feeding dog, EX...........**20.00**
Fisher, Harrison; Dreaming of You, woman asleep, VG **16.00**
Gibson, Dana; ...There Are Mermaids, woman by rocks, VG........**12.00**
Gibson, Dana; Love Song, woman sings w/cherubs, VG **12.00**
Golliwog, heavy, emb, p/Opf, VG...**25.00**
Golliwog & girl, Birthday Greetings, p/Valentine, VG.................**20.00**
Halloween, Don't I Look Like a Regular Witch?, p/Tuck, VG **12.00**
Halloween, Guess I Must be a Real Artist, p/Tuck, VG...............**12.00**
Halloween, Josephine Is You a Witch-Cat, p/Tuck, VG...............**12.00**
Halloween, Pooh-Pooh, It's Halloween, p/Gibson, VG................**10.00**
Halloween, vegetable people in field, p/Valentine, EX.................**15.00**
Harre, TE; Behold the Woman, book advertising, VG.................**10.00**
Hold-to-light, Board Walk, Atlantic City, p/Koehler, EX............**30.00**
Hold-to-light, Garfield Park, Chicago, p/Koehler, VG................**28.00**
Hold-to-light, Malick, Christmas winter scene, VG **22.00**
Hold-to-light, Mississippi River Steamer, p/Cupples, VG............**30.00**
Hold-to-light, New State House, Boston, p/Koehler, VG **28.00**
Hold-to-light, Public Library & New S Church, p/Koehler, VG ...**28.00**
King, Hamilton; Atlantic City Girl, VG....................................**9.00**
Mechanical, Hooligans Again, c Am Journal Examiner, 1906.......**15.00**
Novelty, mechanical kaleidescope, p/ASB, VG **25.00**
Novelty, mechanical kaleidoscope, p/Internat'l Art, EX................**30.00**
O'Neill, Rose; valentine, Kewpie eats from jam jar, EX **35.00**
Oren, Boer War, General Botha, blk/wht line drawing, EX...........**30.00**
Outcault, Buster Brown & Mary Jane kiss Tige, p/Tuck, VG........**15.00**
Patriotic, Gen Joseph E Johnson, p/Tuck, VG...........................**15.00**
Payne, H; Defenders of Empire, #8761 oilette, p/Tuck, VG..........**17.00**
Photo, 4 fire engines, Knox Co, Springfield MA, 1910, EX...........**10.00**
Political, 1908 campaign card, Hello Bill, p/BB London, VG........**25.00**
Political, 3 Great Leaders, Stalin, Churchill, FDR, VG................**12.00**
Real hair, lady in bl cloche, orange ornaments, p/PFB, VG **18.00**
Real hair, woman w/purple silk cloche, p/PFB, EX **18.00**
Rockwell, Norman; Oculist, boy getting glasses, 1956, EX...........**35.00**
Royalty, Czar & Family, all aboard ship, p/Rotary, VG **20.00**
Royalty, Italy, King Victor Emannuel & family, vignettes, EX......**10.00**
Royalty, Norway, King, Queen, & child, p/Fredrickson, VG **9.00**
Royalty, Queen Victoria, jewels on gown, p/Bamforth, VG..........**30.00**
Royalty, Queen Victoria & family, blk/wht, p/Beagles, VG...........**25.00**
Russell, Charles; Indian Dog Team, muted colors, VG **20.00**
Russell, Charles; Last of the Buffalo, Indians in tent, VG.............**25.00**
Silk, Martyr Ypres, town on fire, p/E Duffrene, WWI, VG...........**35.00**
Silk, Nancy La Cathedral, church afire, p/E Duffrene, EX **35.00**
Silk, RMS Cedric, couple holds hands, Stevens, VG **40.00**
Silk, SS California, ship faces left, Stevens, VG **55.00**
Silk, Theodore Roosevelt, violet tie, p/ED Paris, VG...................**75.00**
Sowerby, Flower Children Series, blond girl in flowers, VG **12.00**

Sports, '36 Olympics, blk/wht torchbearer photo, p/US, VG 20.00
Sports, Wrestling, George Hackenschmidt, p/Rotary, VG 12.00
Sports, 1948 Boston Braves Baseball, roster, p/Tichnor, EX...........14.00
Stamps, Chile, 15 stamps, p/Ottmar-Zieher, EX 12.00
Stamps, Greece, 19 stamps, p/Ottmar-Zieher, EX 12.00
Stamps, 2 men (made of stamps) running, p/Stampcards, '30s, EX...18.00
Thiele, You Ought To See the Other Guy, cat w/bandage, VG.....14.00
Wain, Louis; Blind Man's Bluff, 6 cats, VG 32.00
Wain, Louis; Knut's Mascot, dressed dog, VG 28.00
Wain, Louis; Wash & Brush Up, 3 cats washing, VG 27.00
Wall, B; This Little Bear Went..., p/Ullman, 1907, EX 12.00
Winsch, boy kisses girl under mistletoe, 1910, VG 14.00
Winsch, mechanical valentine, My Heart's Gift, 1912, EX 35.00
Winsch, valentine, Loving Thought, 1914, VG 8.00
WWII, House Painter, Hitler paints outhouse, blk/wht, VG 10.00
WWII, Let's Go Forward Together, p/Tichnor, 1941, EX.............. 8.00
WWII, Strive for Victory, p/Tichnor, 1941, EX 8.00

Posters

Advertising posters by such French artists as Cheret and Toulouse-Lautrec were used as early as the mid-1800s. Color lithography spurred their popularity. Circus posters by the Strobridge Lithograph Co. are considered to be the finest in their field, though Gibson and Co. Litho, Erie Litho, and Enquirer Job Printing Co. printed fine examples as well. Posters by noted artists such as Mucha, Parrish, and Hohlwein bring high prices. Other considerations are good color, interesting subject matter, and of course, condition. The WWII posters listed below are among the more expensive examples — 80% of those on the market bring less than $50.00. See also Movie Memorabilia; Political; Rockwell, Norman.

Advertising

Barker's Powder, Running from the Bull, 19½x14½", EX 525.00
Colchester Tennis Shoes, Brett Litho, fr, 28x22", VG 5,500.00
County Fair, Donaldson, girl w/corn, 30x20", NM.....................100.00
Cycles Perfecta, Mucha, linen bk, 59x41½" 6,300.00
Dixon's Carburet...Stove Polish, lady w/net, 28x13", VG...........550.00
Granite Iron Ware, girl w/milk pail, 1884, 28x12", EX 1,500.00
Greenway's Brewing & Malting, NY brewery, fr, 25x36", VG.. 3,200.00
Hannis Distilling, factory, Wells & Hope, fr, 20x18", EX...........450.00
J&P Coats Cotton Thread, Crusoe, fr, 18x22", G 425.00
Job, Mucha, Champenois, Paris, fr, 21x16" 6,500.00
Nat'l Air & Space Museum, Smithsonian, Nesbitt, '33, 40x30"..150.00
Readville Racetrack, trotters, 1905, 20x26", EX.........................425.00
Renault, linen bk, French, 20th C, 36¼x45", EX 950.00
Runkel Bros Breakfast Cocoa, family scene, fr, 24x18", EX 1,300.00
Uneeda Bakers, fruit cake, Nat'l Biscuit, 42x28", EX 120.00
Where Pure Schlitz..., factory, 1903, fr, 24x36", EX 1,300.00

Travel

Austria Vias Harwich, landscape, Gorbatcheff, '20s, 50x40" 900.00
Blackpool, beach scene, tower beyond, Matania, '20s, 50x40" .. 2,500.00
Castle Above the Sea, Russian, 20th C, 40x24½", NM 350.00
Isle of Man, beach scene, Pears, 1940s, 50x40", EX 850.00
Lowestoft, sailor & flags, Cooper, 1930s, 50x40"..........................750.00
Mountains of France, Nathan, 20th C, 30½x21", EX....................75.00
Scarborough, Yorkshire, aerial view, Pervis, '20s, 25x40" 600.00

War

America's Immortals, WWI, John Kelly, 1918, 20x27", EX...........25.00

Americans All, WWI, HC Christy, 1919, 40x26½", EX.............250.00
Aviation in Itself..., plane over sea, 1944, 17x18", EX................25.00
Don't Burn Waste Paper..., WWII, 17x21", EX.........................25.00
Don't Wait for the Draft..., WWI, Guenther, 27x40", EX 75.00
Enlist...Nurse Corps, WWII, cadet, Edmundson, 20x26", EX 50.00
Fight, WWI, HC Christy, 30x10" 165.00
First in Fight,...Faithful...Marine, WWI, Flagg, 27x40", EX.........150.00
Have You a Red Cross...Flag, WWI, JW Smith, 1918, 28x22" 50.00
Hug the Ground & Live longer, WWII, 1943, 14x18", EX...........15.00
Hun or Home, WWI, mother/child/soldier, 19x29", EX.............100.00
I'm Counting on You, WWII, Uncle Sam, 1943, 8x11", EX 30.00
John Paul Jones Said: I..., color, 1942, 12x18", EX...................30.00
L'Italia Ha Bosigno Carne..., WWI, 2 generals, 1918, 19x28" 15.00
Red Cross Roll Call, WWI, Haskel Coffin, 40x29", EX.............125.00
Seeds of Victory..., WWI, JM Flagg, 1918, 33x22", EX.............275.00
Serve Those..., WWII, nurse/man in wheelchair, '46, 20x26" 40.00
Serve w/Women's Reserve..., WWII, girl in uniform, 10x15", EX ..25.00
Sure! We'll Finish the Job, WWI, Beneker, 37x25½" 55.00
They Shall Not Perish, WWI, Volk, 1918, 40x28", EX 200.00
To Win Our Freedom We Cross Oceans..., WWII, 12x18", EX 25.00

Miscellaneous

Brush, King of Wizards, Goes Litho, ca 1910, 31x24", NM 425.00
C Chaplin, Himalaya Film Presente..., he w/couple, 60x48" 300.00

Charlie Chaplin, in The Bank, Essanay Film Co., Central Litho, Ohio, taped repair, 42" x 28", $8,500.00.

Cacao Lhara, Cheret, linen bk, 98x35", EX 1,500.00
Charbook, Wm H Bradley, fr, 21x14" 2,000.00
Circus, RB B&B, 4 giraffes, sgn Bill Baily, c 1944, 28x21", M 245.00
Engine Is Wheeled, men build train, Cuneo, '40s,50x40", G.......800.00
George the Supreme Master..., 1930s, 27x41", EX 150.00
Ragtime Show, Blk in top hat, cb, 1940s, 14x22", EX...................45.00
Return of Nat-U-Ritch, man carring Indian lady, 1906, 27x20"....70.00
Salvation Army, A Man May Be Down, Duncan, 1919, 40x30" .300.00
Vient de Paraitre, Mucha, linen bk, 30x18", EX...................... 2,000.00
150 Years of Am Independence, ca 1936, 17x26", EX 50.00

Pot Lids

Pot lids were pottery covers for containers that were used for hair dressing, potted meats, etc. The most desirable were decorated with colorful transfer prints under the glaze in a variety of themes, animal and scenic. The first and probably the largest company to manufacture these lids was F & R Pratt of Fenton, Staffordshire, established in the early 1800s. The name or initials of Jesse Austin, their designer, may sometimes be found on exceptional designs. Although few pot lids were made after the 1880s, the firm continued into the 20th century.

American pot lids are very rare. Most have been dug up by collectors searching through sites of early gold rush mining towns in California. Minor rim chips are expected and normally do not detract from listed values.

American

Amandine...Chapped Hands, blk transfer, Hauel, 2¾", M..........240.00
Bear, blk transfer, Bears Grease, Hauel Perfumer, 2⅞", EX..........400.00
Brazin's...Premium Shaving Cream, blk transfer, 3", M 80.00
Burdell's Tooth Powder, mc transfer, Wakelee, rare, 3" 135.00
Bust of Franklin, purple transfer, Hauel Perfumer, 2⅝" 280.00
Cold Cream, mc transfer, HP Waklee, 3⅛", NM 240.00
Compound for Shaving by Glenn & Co, blk transfer, 3¾", NM .400.00
Eugene Rousell Odontine..., blk transfer, early, 2¾", M..........210.00
Grand Internat'l Bldg of 1851, blk transfer, Hauel, 3⅜", EX......200.00
HP&WC Taylor's...Shaving Compound, blk transfer, 3¾", NM...70.00
Improved Cold Cream of Roses, blk transfer, X Bazin, 2¼", EX ..130.00
Man shaving, bl transfer, Taylors Compound, 3¾", M 220.00
Man shaving, blk transfer, Wrights...Shaving Compound, 3½" ..600.00
Odonto Oak Bark...Tooth Paste, purple transfer, Choate, 3", M ..450.00
Purified Charcoal Tooth Paste, X Bazin, in blk, 3¼x2½".............230.00
Roussel's...Shaving Cream, blk transfer, 3", EX............................170.00
Steer, bl transfer, Beef Marrow, X Bazin, 2⅝", w/base, EX..........600.00
Superior Rose Tooth Paste, red transfer, X Bazin, 2¼", EX..........220.00
Williams Swiss Violet Shaving Cream, mc transfer, 3⅝", EX......250.00
2 Cows, blk transfer, Liston's Extract of Beef, 2⅝", M 55.00
7 Highest Premiums...World's Fair 1851, HP&WC Taylor, 3½" .120.00

English

Albert Memorial, 3¾" 150.00
Ambrosial Shaving Cream, John Gosnell, blk transfer, 3½" 95.00
Anne Hathaway's Cottage, 3¾"..150.00
Battle of the Nile, minor crazing, 3¾" 200.00
Cavalier, 3¾"..125.00
Cherry Tooth Paste, Cleansing/Preserving, blk transfer, 3"............70.00
Circus bear, +jar 215.00
Dutch Battle Scene..125.00
England's Pride 125.00
Enthusiast, old man fishing in tub, Pratt, 4" 200.00
Fish Peddler, shaped rectangle, minor crazing, 5¾" 125.00
Girls on a Swing, minor crazing, 3¾"..250.00
Hamlet & His Father's Ghost, 3¾" 200.00
Holburn Village, minor crazing, 3¾" 135.00
Master of the Hounds, 4"..185.00
New Blackfriars Bridge, minor crazing, 3¾" 135.00
On Guard, 3¾"..125.00
Pair, card player, minor crazing, 3¾"..250.00
Pegwell Bay, minor crazing, 3¾"..135.00
Pegwell Bay, 3¾", M 195.00
Preparing for the Ride, 3¾"...125.00
Pretty Kettle of Fish 165.00
Rimmel (cherries) Cherry Tooth Paste, yel/brn transfer, 3"..........70.00
Rivals, minor crazing, 3¾"...150.00
Rivals, 3¾", M 200.00
Room in Which Shakespeare Was Born, minor crazing, 3¾" 350.00
Shakespeare's House, 3¾"..335.00
Spaonaceous Tooth Powder, Dr Bowditch, blk transfer, 3⅜".........45.00
Swintons...Tooth Paste, bl transfer w/primrose, 2½", EX.............175.00
Thames Embankment, minor crazing, 3¾" 150.00
Trafalgar Square, minor crazing, 3¾"..150.00
Trooper, 3¾"...200.00

Uncle Toby, fr 195.00
Vinolia Co Ltd...Shaving Soap, brn transfer, 3⅛" 80.00
Wolf & the Lamb, 3¾"..200.00

Potschappel

In the town of Potschappel in 1872, Carl Thieme began a porcelain factory called the Saxonian Porcelain Factory. His work was of excellent quality and consisted of figures, vases, urns, lamp bases, birds, bowls, and animals, the work being similar to Dresden-Meissen and Sitzendorf. After World War II the company was incorporated and became Saxonian Porcelain Factory Dresden. There are four or five marks assigned to his work.

Our advisor for this category is Donald Penrose; he is listed in the Directory under Ohio.

Figurine, birds of paradise, 15x9½", pr...................................... 1,150.00

Dame de la Courde Francois I, red dress, 8", $350.00.

Figurine, flower couple w/baskets, 9½" 650.00
Figurine, Lady Marquise de Vereuil, bl gown, 8" 350.00
Figurine, monkey seated w/apple, tan & wht, 16" 750.00
Figurine, pug dogs, tan & wht, male & female, 7x7", pr................570.00
Pillow perfumer, cherubs & flowers, umbrella cork, 4½x4½" 80.00
Tea set, molded heads & flowers, 15-pc.......................................450.00
Urn, appl flowers, bird finial, w/lid, 19".................................... 2,750.00
Urn, appl roses/garden scene, sq base, Thieme, 18", EX, pr..... 1,950.00
Vase, figures in garden reserve, floral panels, 1880s, 12" 450.00

Powder Horns and Shot Flasks

Though powder horns had already been in use for hundreds of years, collectors usually focus on those made after the expansion of the United States westward in the very early 1800s. While some are basic and very simple, others were scrimshawed and highly polished. Especially nice carvings can quickly escalate the value of a horn that has survived intact to as high as $400.00. Those with detailed maps, historical scenes, etc. bring even higher prices.

Metal flasks were introduced in the 1830s; by the middle of the century they were produced in quantity and at prices low enough that they became a viable alternative to the powder horn. Today's collector regards the smaller flasks as the more desirable and valuable, and those made for specific companies bring premium prices.

Flask, brass, Colt's Pat, flags/cannon/anchors/etc, 7", EX **500.00**
Flask, brass, hunting scenes/1775, sporting sz, VG.........................**80.00**

Copper and brass powder flask with embossed horses, measures 8½ to 3¼ drams, 8½", $185.00.

Jug, Sailor's Farewell and Sailor's Return, restored, 5", $250.00.

Pipe, snake w/bowl in open mouth, dbl-loop stem, 10", NM... **2,600.00**
Pitcher, canary lustre, emb satyr heads in mc, 5", VG **150.00**
Tea caddy, Chinaman sits on ea side, 5½", EX...........................**275.00**
Teapot, emb fruit panels/leaves, seated boy finial, 10" W **450.00**

Precious Moments

Known as 'America's Hummels,' Precious Moments are a line of well-known collectibles created by Samuel J. Butcher and produced by Enesco, Inc. These pieces have endeared themselves to many because of the inspirational messages they portray. The collection is approximately twelve years old and is produced in bisque porcelain in Taiwan. Each piece is produced with a different mark each year. This mark, not the date, is usually the link to the value of the piece. Most mold changes result in increased values; and, when a piece is retired or suspended, its price increases as well. As an example, 'God Loveth a Cheerful Giver' retailed for $9.50 in 1980; it was retired in 1981 and has a secondary market price now of $650.00.

Rosie Wells Enterprises, Inc., our advisor for this category, has published the Precious Moments collector magazine, *Precious Collectibles*, as well as a secondary market price guide. Her address is in the Directory under Clubs, Newsletters, and Catalogs. Items listed below are assumed to be in mint condition with the original box.

Flask, copper, dots/stars ea side, EX orig lacquer, 4" **125.00**
Flask, copper, open game bag, sitting dogs, Hawksley, 8" **325.00**
Flask, copper, scrolls ea side, brass top mk Hawksley, 8" **60.00**
Flask, glass, linear relief w/beads, screw tip, 9" **40.00**
Flask, leather covered, brass top, blued spring, 5" **50.00**
Horn, brass mts, 8"..**75.00**
Horn, coat of arms/birds/animals/hunters cvgs, provenance **170.00**
Horn, eagle/sailing ship/flag cvgs, dtd 1813, 15", EX **825.00**
Horn, Hartford, 1762..., military scene eng, 13¼", EX **5,000.00**
Horn, J Elliot 1775..., soldiers/ships/stars, 14½", EX **7,000.00**
Horn, sailing scenes cvgs, silver mts, 8", EX **400.00**
Horn, ship cvgs, wood cap, 1811, 14" **400.00**

Pratt

Prattware is a type of relief-molded earthenware with polychrome decoration. Scenic motifs with figures were popular; sometimes captions were added. Jugs are most common; but teapots, tableware, even figurines were made. The term 'Pratt' refers to Wm. Pratt of Lane Delph, who is credited with making the first of this type, though similar wares were made later by other Staffordshire potters.

Creamer, cow w/milkmaid figural, mc/pearlware, glued rpr..........**675.00**
Creamer, emb foliage, sailor's farewell/return, 4-color, VG..........**250.00**
Dessert set, figures/gardens, brn/gilt borders, 1890, 15-pc **700.00**
Figurine, Autumn (& Spring), sq base, att, 9", pr **750.00**
Figurine, cow faces right, dog on base, att, 1800, 6", VG **750.00**
Figurine, lad in bl jacket/brn pants by cow & calf, 6" **1,350.00**
Figurine, maid in bl hat/yel apron, cow/recumbent calf, 6" **1,500.00**
Jug, equestrian, bk: martial trophies, leaf band, 1815, 5"...............**225.00**
Jug, hunting scenes emb, mc, 1795, 6" **225.00**
Jug, Mischievous Sport/Sportive Innocence emb panels, 8" **450.00**
Jug, rabbit hunting scenes emb, fluted band, 1795, 6" **180.00**
Mug, hearts/playful figures, leaves at the base, 1795, 6" **600.00**
Pipe, Admiral Nelson in tall hat bowl, loop stem, 8", EX........ **1,300.00**
Pipe, coiled snake w/bowl in mouth stem, 1800, 8½", NM **750.00**
Pipe, coiled snake w/head of man in turban, 1800s, 7½" **1,600.00**
Pipe, coiled/twisted, w/bowl as head of lady, 1800, 8", NM..... **1,400.00**

Bride 'n Groom Dolls, E-7267G/E-7267B, unmk, pr................ **1,000.00**
Come Let Us Adore Him, E-2800, unmk **145.00**
Fishing for Friends, BC861, Birthday Club pc, dove mk **75.00**
God Loveth a Cheerful Giver, E-1378, retired, no mk.................**650.00**
Hello, Lord, It's Me Again, PM-811, Club pc, triangle mk..........**350.00**
I'll Play My Drum for Him, E-2357, plate, 1983, unmk...................**65.00**
I'll Play My Drum for Him, E-2359, ornament, '82, hourglass mk..**80.00**
Jesus Loves Me, 104531, Easter Seals Figurine, cedar tree mk . **1,600.00**
Let Heaven & Nature Sing, E-2346, hourglass mk, suspended ...**110.00**
Let the Heavens Rejoice, E-5629, ornament, dtd 1981, unmk ...**175.00**
Lord Bless You & Keep You, E-3114, unmk......................................**80.00**
Love One Another, E-1376, unmk **100.00**
Make a Joyful Noise, E-1374G, triangle mk **95.00**
Peace on Earth, 523062, ball ornament, bow 'n arrow mk, '89 ......**55.00**
Reindeer, 102466, ornament, Birthday Series, olive branch mk **80.00**
Thee I Love, E-3116, unmk **95.00**
Voice of Spring, 12068, cross mk, ltd ed.......................................**250.00**

Primitives

Like the mouse that ate the grindstone, so has collectible interest in primitives increased, a little bit at a time, until demand is taking bites instead of nibbles into their availability. Although the term 'primitives' once referred to those survival essentials contrived by our American settlers, it has recently been expanded to include objects needed or desired by succeeding generations — items representing the cabin-n'-cornpatch existence as well as examples of life on larger farms and in towns. Through popular usage, it also respectfully covers what are actually 'country collectibles.'

From the 1600s into the latter 1800s, factories employed carvers, blacksmiths, and other artisans whose handwork contributed to turning out quality items. When buying, 'touchmarks' — a company's name and/or location and maker's or owner's initials — are exciting discoveries.

Primitives are uniquely individual. Following identical forms, results more often than not show typically personal ideas. Using this as a guide (combined with circumstances of age, condition, desire to own, etc.) should lead to a reasonably accurate evaluation. For items not listed, consult comparable examples. Authority Kathryn McNerney has compiled several lovely books on primitives and related topics: *Primitives, Our American Heritage; Collectible Blue and White Stoneware;* and *Antique Tools, Our American Heritage.* You will find her address in the Directory under Florida. See also Butter Molds and Stamps; Boxes; Copper; Farm Collectibles; Fireplace Implements; Kitchen Collectibles; Molds; Tinware; Weaving; Woodenware; and Wrought Iron.

Apple parer, cvd, knob hdl, hand held, ca 1800, 9" 150.00
Bed warmer, brass, eng WH/1820, geometric border, grpt hdl 350.00

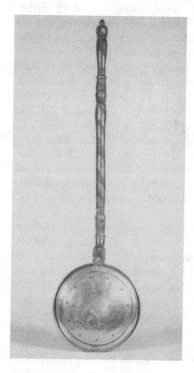

Brass bed warmer with folded rim and punched decoration of a peafowl and scrolls, turned and painted handle, 43" long, $495.00.

Bed warmer, copper, floral emb, 42", EX 250.00
Bed warmer, copper, pinwheel eng, trn hdl, 40" 150.00
Biscuit pricker, wooden w/metal spikes, early, 1¾" dia 70.00
Bullet mold, Colt Pat on cutter, 36-cal, EX 35.00
Candle box, dvtl pine, old red, strap hinges, 1780s, 6x7x9".........450.00
Candle mold, 1-tube, tin, pewter nipple, 22½x1½".....................120.00
Candle mold, 12-tube, tin, 11"....................100.00
Candle mold, 24-tube, tole tin hdls ea side, ca 1840s, 11" 265.00
Candle mold, 34-tube, tin, orig pine fr, EX.............................1,100.00
Candle mold, 36-tube, tin, 1800s, 13x10½x5", EX 350.00
Candle mold, 6-tube, oblong top & base, dk gray tin, EX 80.00
Candle mold, 9-tube, tin, free-standing tray type, 36x36" 260.00
Chopper, wrought iron, wood hdl, 1820s, 5x7", EX....................35.00
Chopper, wrought iron w/tiger maple hdl, mtd on 6x11" board.....75.00

Churn, tin, can shape, JP Lynott's Pat Triumph, 1912, 12½" 125.00
Churn, tin w/wooden dasher, 19½x8½" dia, VG 275.00
Churn, wood, staved drum shape, tin bands, 15x13", EX 125.00
Churn, wood w/red stencil, Hall Bros Improved #0, 13½", NM .190.00
Coals carrier, sheet iron w/wrought fittings, trn hdl, 19"............45.00
Cup, cvd horn w/glass bottom, 1840s, EX patina, lg.....................22.50
Curtain stretcher, pine, lg, EX....................25.00
Darner, sock; tiger maple, EX patina.....................125.00
Doll, cvd wood, no arms, flat base, cotton clothes, 3½" 45.00
Fireboard, geometrics, center: star in circle, mc, 23x36" 2,000.00
Foot warmer, pierced tin, trn posts, mortised fr, 17" L 250.00
Foot warmer, pierced tin, trn wooden posts, wire hdl, G.............225.00
Kraut cutter, walnut, tombstone crest, 21x8"....................40.00
Lard squeezer, pine, paddle shape, leather hinged, 1870s, 14" 65.00
Lard squeezer, wood, folds out to V shape, ca 1900, EX 135.00
Mold, bronze, for making pewter spoons, 8¾" 150.00
Pie lifter, 2-tine, iron, brass ferrule, wood hdl w/ring.....................55.00
Quilting fr, sawbuck base, 32x56" 175.00
Rack, candle dipping/drying; mortised/pinned, 12x24", EX.........295.00
Rack, candle dipping/drying; wood, 2 Xd arms, 1850s, 30" H......265.00
Rug beater, bentwood, Goodenough's Improved..., 42".................45.00
Scraper, for candle-mold tray; cvd maple, 1-pc, 4x8" 50.00
Smoothing board, cvd horse hdl, 1700s, 5x29" w/4x7" hdl..........350.00
Smoothing board, cvd wood, 1-pc, 5" hdl, 21½" L 75.00
Smoothing board, wood, corrugations/chamfered edge, 1850s, 24" ..75.00
Sugar hammer, wrought iron, blade 1 end, 1700s, 6½" 130.00
Tallow skimmer, wrought iron hdl, tin dipper, early, EX.............85.00
Wagon jack, wood/wrought iron, simple details, CG/1758, VG..150.00
Washboard, cvd, corrugated, 1-pc, 1700s, 25x8", EX....................75.00
Washboard, grooved wood & tin surfaces, EX 65.00
Washboard, wood, 15 rnd movable rollers, sq nails, 23x13" 175.00
Water gourd, horn embedded as spout, 1830s, 9" 32.50
Wick trimmer, brass, scissors style, 6", on cast tray 65.00
Wick trimmer, wrought iron, scissors style, 1700s, EX 35.00
Wig stand, maple, trn, on sq base, 11" 45.00

Prints

The term 'print' may be defined today as almost any image printed on paper by any available method. Examples of collectible old 'prints' are Norman Rockwell magazine covers and Maxfield Parrish posters and calendars. 'Original print' refers to one achieved through the efforts of the artist or under his direct supervision. A 'reproduction' is a print produced by an accomplished print maker who reproduces another artist's print or original work. Thorough study is required on the part of the collector to recognize and appreciate the many variable factors to be considered in evaluating a print. Prices vary from one area of the country to another and are dependent upon new findings regarding the scarcity or abundance of prints as such information may arise. Although each collector of old prints may have their own varying criteria by which to judge condition, for those who deal only rarely in this area or newer collectors, a few guidelines may prove helpful. Staining, though unquestionably detrimental, is nearly always present in some degree and should be weighed against the rarity of the print. Professional cleaning should improve its appearance and at the same time help preserve it. Avoid tears that affect the image; minor margin tears are another matter, especially if the print is a rare one. Moderate 'foxing' (brown spots caused by mold or the fermentation of the rag content of old paper) and light stains from the old frames are not serious unless present in excess. Margin trimming was a common practice; but look for at least ½" to 1½" margins, depending on print size.

For further study, see *Huxford's Fine Art Value Guide,* available from your local bookstore or Collector Books. When no condition is indicated, the items listed below are assumed to be in very good to excellent condition. See also Parrish, Maxfield; Rockwell, Norman.

Audubon, John J.

Audubon is the best known of American and European wildlife artists. His first series of prints, 'Birds of America,' was produced by Robert Havell of London. They were printed on Whitman watermarked paper bearing dates of 1826 to 1838. The Octavo Edition of the same series was printed in seven editions, the first by J.T. Bowen under Audubon's direction. There were seven volumes of text and prints, each 10" x 7", the first five bearing the J.J. Audubon and J.B. Chevalier mark, the last two, J.J. Audubon. They were produced from 1840 through 1871. The Bien Edition prints were full size, made under the direction of Audubon's sons' late 1850s. Due to the onset of the Civil War, only 105 plates were finished. These are considered to be the most valuable of the reprints of the 'Birds of America Series.'

In 1971 the complete set was reprinted by Johnson Reprint Corp. of New York and Theaturm Orbis Terrarum of Amsterdam. Examples of the latter bear the watermark G. Schut and Zonen. In 1985 a second reprint was done by Abbeville Press for the National Audubon Society.

Although Audubon is best known for his portrayal of birds, one of his less-familiar series, 'Vivaparous Quadrupeds of North America,' portrayed various species of animals. Assembled in corroboration with John Bachman from 1839 until 1851, these prints are 28" x 22" in size. Several octavo editions were published in the 1850s. Our advisor for this category is Ed Kenney; he is listed in the Directory under Virginia.

American Coot, #305, Bowen, 1850s, 6½x10" 125.00
American Crow, #225, Bien, ca 1858-60, 39x26" 2,000.00
American Magpie, #357, Havell, ca 1826-38, 37x25" 6,000.00
American White Egret, #386, Ariel Press, 1972, 26x38" 195.00
Baltimore Oriole, #12, Havell, ca 1826-38, 37¾x25" 10,000.00
Baltimore Oriole, #217, Bien, 1858-60, 39x26" 3,000.00

Barred Owl, from Birds of North America, Amsterdam Edition, 1971, 39" x 26", $600.00.

Bonaparte's Gull, #442, Bowen, 1850s, 6½x10" 125.00
Booby, #207, Amsterdam Edition, 39x26" 400.00
Brown Finch, #187, Bowen, 1850s, 6½x10" 75.00
Canada Flycatcher, #72, Bowen, 1st edition, 6½x10" 125.00
Canada Lynx, #16, Bowen, 1st edition, 7x10" 150.00
Carbonated Swamp Warbler, #109, Bowen, 1850s, 6½x10" 100.00
Cardinal, #203, Bowen, 1st edition, 6½x10" 350.00

Carolina Wren, #78, Havell, ca 1826-38, 37½x15" 4,500.00
Common Puffin, #454, Bien, fr 600.00
Cowpen Bird, #99, Havell, ca 1826-38, 37¾x25" 1,450.00
Downy Squirrel, #25, Bowen, 1st edition, 21x27" 655.00
Duck Hawk, #16, Amsterdam Edition, 39x26" 500.00
Fish Crow, #226, Bowen, 1850s, 6½x10" 120.00
Franklin's Marmot, #84, Bowen, 1st edition, 21x27" 500.00
Golden-Eye Duck, #342, Amsterdam Edition, 39x26" 425.00
Golden-Winged Woodpecker, #273, Bowen, 1850s, 6½x10" 125.00
Great Horned Owl, #39, Bowen, 1st edition, 6½x10" 250.00
Greenshank, #269, Havell, ca 1826-38, 18x25" 1,200.00
Ivory Gull, #445, Bowen, 1850s, 6½x10" 80.00
Least Flycatcher, #491, Bowen, 1st edition, 6½x10" 185.00
Least Tern, #319, Amsterdam Edition, 39x26" 250.00
Lewis's Marmot, #107, Bowen, 1850s, 7x10" 45.00
Lincoln's Finch, #277, Bien, 18x25" 365.00
Louisiana Heron, #373, Bowen, 1st edition, 6½x10" 450.00
Mountain Mockingbird, #139, Bowen, 1850s, 6½x10" 65.00
Muskrat, #13, Bowen, 1st edition, 21x27" 475.00
Night Heron, #236, Amsterdam Edition, 39x26" 585.00
Osprey, 381, Amsterdam Edition, 39x26" 2,000.00
Red Texan Wolf, #82, Bowen, 1850s, 7x10" 195.00
Red-Shouldered Hawk, #56, Ariel Press, 1972, 26x38" 155.00
Robin, #131, Amsterdam Edition, 39x26" 725.00
Rose Grosbeak, #127, Ariel Press, 1972, 26x38" 80.00
Rusty Grackle, #222, Bien, ca 1858-60, 39x26" 465.00
Savannah Bunting, #160, Bowen, 1850s, 6½x10" 100.00
Shoveller Duck, #394, Bowen, 1st edition, 6½x10" 400.00
Sooty Tern, #235, Havell, ca 1826-38, 37¾x25" 2,250.00
Swamp Hare, #37, Bowen, 1850s, 7x10" 150.00
Turnstone, #323, Bowen, 1850s, 6½x10" 115.00
Virginian O'possum, #55, Bowen, 1850s, 7x10" 120.00
Washington Sea Eagle, #13, Bowen, 1850s, 6½x10" 150.00
White-Crowned Pigeon, #280, Bien, ca 1858-60, 39x26" 2,500.00

Currier and Ives

Nathaniel Currier was in business by himself until the late 1850s when he formed a partnership with James Merrit Ives. Currier is given credit for being the first to use the medium to portray newsworthy subjects, and the Currier and Ives views of 19th-century American culture are familiar to us all. Values are given for prints in very good condition; all are colored unless indicated black and white. Unless noted 'NC' (Nathaniel Currier), all prints are published by Currier and Ives.

Abraham Lincoln, 16th President of US, sm folio 225.00
Agnes, NC, sm folio..95.00
American Brook Trout, sm folio 350.00
American Country Life, Pleasures of Winter, NC, lg folio 3,000.00
American Farm Yard, Evening, lg folio 2,750.00
American Game Fish, lg folio... 2,200.00
American Homestead, Autumn, sm folio 400.00
American Scenery, Palenville NY, sm folio 295.00
American Winter Scenes, Morning, NC, lg folio 7,500.00
Arguing the Point, NC, lg folio 5,000.00
Autumn in New England, Cider Making, lg folio 13,500.00
Autumn on Lake George, sm folio..295.00
Battery, NY by Moonlight, NC, sm folio......................................650.00
Battle of Buene Vista, NC, sm folio...125.00
Battle of Cerro Gordo, NC, sm folio..125.00
Battle of Fredericksburg VA, sm folio 175.00
Battle of Pea Ridge, March 8th, 1862, sm folio..........................175.00
Battle of Spottsylvania VA, sm folio..175.00
Beautiful Empress, sm folio 50.00

Benjamin Franklin, Statesman & Philosher, NC, sm folio 600.00
Between Two Fires, sm folio..250.00
Black Duck Shooting, sm folio..250.00
Blackberry Dell, med folio...400.00
Bombardment of Island #10 in Mississippi River, sm folio..........300.00
Boss of the Road, sm folio...250.00
Bound To Smash, sm folio..250.00
Brave Wife, sm folio 85.00
Brer Thuldy's Statue, sm folio 250.00
Bridge at the Outlet, sm folio..275.00
Brush for the Lead, NY Flyers on the Snow, lg folio 4,500.00
Buffalo & Chicago Steam Packet Empire State, NC, sm folio 375.00
Burning of the Henry Clay Near Yonkers, NC, sm folio.............350.00
Butt of the Jokers, sm folio...250.00
California Scenery, Seal Rocks, sm folio................................395.00
Canal Scene, Moonlight, sm folio..300.00
Cares of a Family, sm folio..500.00
Celebrated Horse GM Patchen, Champion of Turf, lg folio....2,000.00
Central Park Winter, Skating Carnival, sm folio.....................1,800.00
Champion Stallion Directum by Director, sm folio...................300.00
Chicago in Flames, sm folio...525.00
Children's Picnic, sm folio 125.00
City of Mexico From..., Vista de Mexico, NC, sm folio 195.00
City of New York From Jersey City, NC, sm folio 500.00
Clearing on the American Frontier, sm folio...........................295.00
Clipper Ship Great Republic, sm folio 500.00
Col Frank P Blair Jr, sm folio..125.00
Constitution & Java, NC, sm folio 450.00
Cork River, sm folio...95.00
Creating a Sensation, sm folio..250.00
Cross Matched Team, sm folio..250.00
Darktown Bowling Club, Bowled Out, sm folio.......................250.00
Darktown Fire Brigade, Prize Squirt, sm folio 250.00
Darktown Tournament, Close Quarters, sm folio 250.00
Deacon's Mare, sm folio 250.00
Dead Game, Quail, sm folio 225.00
Death of Washington, NC, sm folio 95.00
Death Shot, sm folio...225.00
Dexter, Ethan Allen, & Mate, sm folio.................................300.00
Distanced, sm folio...250.00
Don Juan, Plate 1, NC, sm folio 45.00
Drive Through the Highlands, med folio................................500.00
Easter Flowers, sm folio..55.00
Eliza, NC, sm folio...95.00
Emeline, NC, sm folio 95.00
English Winter Scene, sm folio..450.00
Evacuation of Richmond VA by the Gov..., sm folio 200.00
Evening Star, sm folio...75.00
Fall of Richmond VA, sm folio 200.00
Falls of the Ottawa River, Canada, sm folio 250.00
Family Register, NC, sm folio...45.00
Feast of Roses, sm folio...150.00
Feeding the Swans, sm folio...175.00
First Ride, NC, sm folio..95.00
First Trot of the Season, lg folio 2,500.00
Fort Sumter, Charleston Hanbon SC, sm folio........................295.00
Fourth of July, sm folio...350.00
From Shore to Shore, sm folio...75.00
Frontier Lake, sm folio..295.00
Fruits of the Season, sm folio...150.00
Game Dog, sm folio..250.00
Gen Andrew Jackson, Hero of New Orleans, NC, sm folio 150.00
Gen George McClellan & Staff, sm folio 125.00
Gen John C Breckenridge, sm folio 125.00

Gen Shields at Battle of Winchester VA, sm folio....................125.00
Gen Tom Thumb & Wife, sm folio 225.00
Gen US Grant, med folio...125.00
Geo Washington, First President of US, NC, sm folio.................195.00
Giants Causeway, Country Antrim, Ireland, sm folio.................95.00
God Bless Our School, sm folio...295.00
Good Little Sisters, sm folio 95.00
Got 'Em Both, sm folio..250.00
Grand Nat'l Am Banner, Fillmore/Donnelson, NC, sm folio 275.00
Grand Pacer Flying Jib, sm folio...300.00
Great Bartholdi Statue, Liberty Enlightening..., lg folio 600.00
Great Eastern, sm folio..325.00
Great Fight Between Merrimac & Monitor, sm folio..................650.00
Great Mississippi Steamboat Race, sm folio............................800.00
Great West, sm folio 1,350.00
Grottoes of the Sea, sm folio...65.00
Harbor for the Night, sm folio..350.00
Harvest Dance, NC, sm folio..125.00
Hewitt's Quick Step, NC, sm folio 95.00
Hiawatha's Wooing, lg folio...425.00
High Water in the Mississippi, lg folio 7,250.00
Home in the Country, med folio...600.00
Home in the Wilderness, sm folio...800.00
Home of Washington, Mt Vernon VA, med folio......................295.00
Home on the Mississippi, sm folio 450.00
Homeward Bound, NC, sm folio...700.00
Horse Shed Stakes Free for All, sm folio................................250.00
Household Treasures, sm folio..95.00
Hug Me Closer George..., sm folio 275.00
Hung Up w/the Starch Out, sm folio.....................................250.00
Husking, lg folio 10,000.00
Ice Cream Racket, Thawing Out, sm folio..............................250.00
Idlewild, On the Hudson, sm folio 225.00
In the Springtime, sm folio..125.00
Infant St John, sm folio...35.00
Inundation, NC, sm folio...125.00
Ivy Bridge, sm folio...150.00
James K Polk, 11th President of US, NC, sm folio....................150.00
James Monroe, 5th President of US, NC, sm folio....................150.00
Jay Eye See by Dictator, sm folio 300.00
John J Dwyer, Champion of America, med folio 250.00
John L Sullivan, Champion Pugilist of the World, med folio 250.00
Jolly Jumper, sm folio...175.00
Kilkenny Castle, Ireland, sm folio 95.00
Kiss Me Quick, sm folio..125.00
Lake Memphremagog, Owl's Head, sm folio...........................250.00
Lake Winnepiseogee from Center Harbor NH, lg folio 5,000.00
Last Ditch of Chivalry, med folio 150.00
Last Shot, lg folio 3,500.00
Lexington of 1861, sm folio..225.00
Life & Age of Man, NC, sm folio...225.00
Life of a Fireman, The Race, NC, lg folio 3,500.00
Life of Sportsman, Camping in Woods, sm folio 600.00
Light of the Dwelling, sm folio..95.00
Lincoln Family, sm folio..95.00
Little Daisy, sm folio..95.00
Little White Kitties Fishing, sm folio....................................150.00
Looking Down the Yo-Semite, sm folio..................................400.00
Loss of Steamship Arctic Off Cape Race, NC, sm folio 350.00
Magic Lake, med folio...125.00
Maj Gen Ambrose E Burnside, sm folio.................................125.00
Maj Gen Henry Halleck, Gen-in-Chief US Army, sm folio 125.00
Mambrino, sm folio..300.00
Maple Sugaring, Early Spring in Northern Woods, sm folio....1,500.00

Marriage, NC, sm folio	125.00
Martin Van Buren, 8th President of US, NC, sm folio	150.00
Midnight Race on the Mississippi, lg folio	5,500.00
Midnight Race on the Mississippi, sm folio	1,000.00
Mill-Stream, med folio	425.00
Miniature Ship Red, White, & Blue, sm folio	350.00
Mixed at the Finish, sm folio	250.00
Moosehead Lake, sm folio	295.00
More Free Than Welcome, sm folio	195.00
Morning in the Woods, lf folio	2,000.00
Moss Roses & Buds, sm folio	150.00
Mother's Dream, med folio	95.00
Mt Holyoke Female Seminary, NC, sm folio	500.00
My Boyhood's Home, sm folio	295.00
My Sweetheart, sm folio	95.00
National Washington Monument, NC, sm folio	400.00
Natural Bridge, sm folio	295.00
Naval Heroes of the US, NC, sm folio	600.00
Neck & Neck to the Wire, lg folio	1,000.00
New England Winter Scene, lg folio	10,000.00
New Jersey Fox Hunt, Taking Breath, sm folio	250.00
Niagara Falls From Goat Island, med folio	295.00
Niagara Falls From the Canada Side, sm folio	225.00
Night, sm folio	75.00
Nip & Tuck, sm folio	250.00
Noah's Ark, NC, sm folio	250.00
Nova Scotia Scenery, med folio	375.00
Old Bull Dog on Right Track, med folio	250.00
Old Farm Gate, lg folio	1,200.00
Old Oaken Bucket, sm folio	250.00
Old Plantation Home, sm folio	600.00
On a Point, NC, med folio	650.00
On the St Lawrence, Indian Encampment, sm folio	295.00
Outlet of Niagara River, sm folio	295.00
Pacing King Robert J, sm folio	300.00
Part of the Battle of Shilo, sm folio	175.00
Partridge Shooting, NC, med folio	1,500.00
Patriot of 1776 Defending His Homestead, sm folio	250.00
Phebe, NC, med folio	95.00
Pic-Nic Party, lg folio	495.00
Pickerel, sm folio	250.00
Pioneer Cabin of the Yosemite Valley, sm folio	650.00
Point of the Joke, sm folio	250.00
Poultry Show on a Bust, sm folio	250.00
Power of Music, NC, sm folio	125.00
Prairie Hens, sm folio	400.00
Presidential Reception in 1789, sm folio	295.00
Pride of the Garden, sm folio	150.00
Quail or Virginia Partridge, sm folio	295.00
Rabbit Catching, Trap Sprung, sm folio	750.00
Rail Shooting, NC, lg folio	8,000.00
Reconciliation, NC, sm folio	125.00
Return From the Woods, med folio	1,000.00
Roadside Mill, sm folio	295.00
Roses of May, sm folio	150.00
Rural Lake, med folio	400.00
Saratoga Springs, sm folio	295.00
Scenery on Upper Mississippi, Indian Village, sm folio	395.00
Season of Joy, sm folio	175.00
Shooting on the Beach, sm folio	1,200.00
Sisters, NC, sm folio	125.00
Snipe Shooting, NC, lg folio	5,000.00
Snow Storm, med folio	2,500.00
Soldier's Return, NC, sm folio	125.00

Sorry Dog, sm folio	175.00
South Sea Whale Fishery, NC, sm folio	1,500.00
Spaniel, NC, sm folio	250.00
Spirit of the Union, sm folio	195.00
Sports Who Lost Their Tin, sm folio	250.00
Steamer Messenger No 2, NC, sm folio	350.00
Steeple Chase Cracks, sm folio	195.00
Still Hunting on Susquehana, med folio	700.00
Straw-Yard Winter, med folio	750.00
Summer Flowers, sm folio	150.00
Summer Fruits, med folio	395.00
Summer Morning, sm folio	295.00
Summer Ramble, med folio	375.00
Surrender of Cornwallis at Yorktown VA, NC, lg folio	4,000.00
Sussex Vale, New Bruswick, sm folio	195.00
Swell Sport Stampeded, sm folio	250.00
Through to the Pacific, sm folio	1,250.00
Tomb & Shade of Napoleon, NC, sm folio	125.00
Tomb of Gen WH Harrison, NC, sm folio	95.00
Tomb of Washington, med folio	250.00
Tree of Temperance, sm folio	125.00
Trotters on Snow, sm folio	1,000.00
Trotting Gelding Frank w/Jo Nay, lg folio	1,500.00
Trotting Stallion Smuggler, sm folio	300.00
Tumbled to It, sm folio	250.00
Two To Go, sm folio	250.00
Uncle Tom & Little Eva, NC, sm folio	150.00
United States Capitol, sm folio	350.00
Up the Hudson, sm folio	295.00
US Frigate Constitution, NC, sm folio	450.00
Valley Falls, VA, sm folio	295.00
View of Bunker Hill & Monument, NC, sm folio	295.00
View of Park Fountain/City Hall, NY, NC, sm folio	600.00
View on Hudson From Ruggles House, Newburgh, sm folio	295.00
View on Long Island NY, lg folio	2,500.00
Virginia Home in the Olden Time, sm folio	295.00
Washington, First in War..., NC, sm folio	125.00
Washington's Reception by the Ladies, NC, sm folio	125.00
We've Had a Healthy Time, sm folio	250.00
Western Farmer's Home, sm folio	495.00
Who Will Love Me?, sm folio	95.00
Wild Duck Shooting, Good Day's Sport, NC, lg folio	3,500.00
Wild West in Darktown, sm folio	250.00
William R King, VP of US, NC, sm folio	95.00
Willie & Mary, sm folio	95.00

Winter in the Country, Old Grist Mill, after G.H. Durrie, 18½" x 27", $12,000.00.

Winter Morning, med folio	2,400.00
Won by a Foot, sm folio	250.00
Won by a Neck, Lady T Goldsmith Maid/Am Girl, lg folio	1,800.00
Woodcock Shooting, lg folio	2,500.00
Woodland Gate, NC, med folio	395.00
Word & the Sign, sm folio	50.00
Wreck of the Atlantic, sm folio	295.00
Yo-Semite Falls CA, sm folio	295.00
Young America, The Child of Liberty, sm folio	175.00

Erte (Romain de Tirtoff)

A, From the Alphabet, sgn, Circle Fine Art, 1976, 16x11"	600.00
Aladdin & His Bride, sgn, Sevenarts Ltd, 1984, 31x37"	650.00
Autumn Song From Twenties Remembered, sgn, 1977, 25x22"	650.00
Broadway's in Fashion, sgn, 1978, Circle Fine Art, 24x17"	650.00
Clasp, sgn, 1982, 42x36"	2,200.00
Coquette, sgn, Circle Fine Art, 1981, 24x19"	775.00
End of Romance, sgn, Circle Fine Art, 1981, 30x23"	1,650.00
Fantasia, sgn, 1982, 33x25"	1,100.00
Giulietta, Sevenarts Ltd, 1983, 30x22"	715.00
Helen of Troy, sgn, 1985, 36x31"	1,200.00
Lafayette, sgn, Circle Fine Art, 1979, 32x24"	715.00
Melisande, From At the Theatre, sgn, Kane Fine Art, 30x22"	825.00
Mystique, backstamp, wide margins, 32x20"	1,000.00
Printemps, sgn, Circle Fine Art, 1975, 29x23"	500.00
Rain, sgn, Circle Fine Art, 1980, 10x20"	825.00
Salome, sgn, Circle Fine Art, 1981, 17x23"	1,200.00
Stolen Kisses, sgn, 1982, 29x24"	500.00
Summer Breeze, sgn, Circle Fine Art, 1978, 31x23"	1,650.00
Three Graces, sgn, 1985, 33x25"	2,300.00
Winter, sgn, Circle Fine Art, 1975, 20x14"	440.00
Y, From the Alphabet, sgn, Circle Fine Art, 1977, 16x11"	385.00

Fox, R. Atkinson

Aces All, 1929, 10x8"	245.00
Artist Supreme, 10x8"	225.00
At the Foothills of Pikes Peak, 9x7"	90.00
Day Dreams, 10x14"	155.00
Dreamy Paradise, 9x7"	75.00
Golden West, 1934, 13x15"	130.00
In New York Bay, calendar top, 6x4"	115.00
Old Mill, 9x7"	90.00
Prize Winners, 8x10"	90.00
Ready for All Comers, 12x10"	245.00
Seeking Protection, 9½x8"	195.00

Gutmann, Bessie Pease

Delicately tinted prints of appealing children sometimes accompanied by their pets, sometimes asleep, often captured at some childhood activity are typical of the work of Gutmann; she painted lovely ladies as well and was a successful illustrator of children's books. Her career spanned the earlier decades of this century. Our advisor for this category is Earl MacSorley; he is listed in the Directory under Connecticut.

Buddies, child w/puppy on bench, #779, 17½x13½"	525.00
Chuckles, 1937, #216, 11x14", EX	50.00
Contentment, 1929, oval, #781, 4½x8"	90.00
Daddy's Coming, 1915, #644, 9½x12½"	190.00
Double Blessing, 1915, sepia, #232, 15x10½"	225.00
Excuse My Back, 1911, oval, 8x4", VG	40.00
Feeling, baby w/toy lamb, 1909, #19, 11½x8¾"	100.00

Always, #774, 18" x 14", $950.00.

Great Love, 1919, #678, 17x13"	325.00
Harmony, 1940, #802, 13x10"	110.00
Home Builders, matted, #655, 19x15"	100.00
In Disgrace, 1935, #792, 10¼x13¾"	100.00
In Port of Dreams, 1937, #214, 10¾x13¾"	75.00
Little Boy Blue, 1930, #206, 11x14"	70.00
Little Mother, 1940, #803, 12x9½"	120.00
Love's Blossom, 1927, #223, 13½x10½"	60.00
May We Come In?, 1943, #808, 14x10½"	120.00
Message of the Roses, 1915, #641, 15¼x11"	250.00
Mighty Like a Rose, 1915, #642, 10½x15"	80.00
Mischief, 1924, #122, 10½" dia	150.00
New Love, 1907, #107, 9½x13½"	130.00
On Dreamland's Border, 1921, #692, 13¾x16½"	100.00
On the Up & Up, 1938, #796, 10½x14"	75.00
Reward, 1936, #794, 13¼x10¼"	100.00
Secret, fr, 10x17"	125.00
Seeing, #211, 11x14", EX	50.00
Sunbeam, 1924, #730, 10½" dia	150.00
Tasting, child w/cup, 1909, sepia, #21, 11½x8½"	100.00
Thank You God, full color, #822, 21x14", EX	65.00
To Love & To Cherish, 1911, #615, 13x8¼"	150.00
Tommy, sepia, #788, 14x21", EX	75.00
Winged Aureole, 1921, #700, 10¼x14"	150.00

Icart, Louis

Louis Icart was a Parisian artist who immortalized the woman of France through his etchings, which were widely produced in the 1920s. During the '30s and '40s, his popularity waned, and etchings from this period are harder to find. He also produced a few lithographs and about four hundred oils. Most etchings made after 1925 have Icart's embossed 'windmill' seal at the lower left. Be skeptical of watercolors and etchings that look similar in subject to one of the etchings. Our Icart advisor is William Holland; he is listed in the Directory under Pennsylvania.

Apple Girl, bare bosom, litho, ca 1928, 18x14"	245.00
Belle Rose, 1933, 17x21"	2,500.00
Bird of Prey, ca 1918, 19x13"	1,200.00
Blue Buddha, 1924, 16x21"	1,000.00
Don Juan, ca 1928, 21x14"	1,400.00
Faust, 1928, 21x13"	1,100.00
Gust of Wind, copy w/blindstamp, 1986, 22x18"	200.00
Gust of Wind, 1925, no blindstamp, 22x18"	2,400.00

Hydrangeas, oval, 17x21" 2,000.00
Jitterbug, La Ronde des Danses, 1938, 7x6" 825.00
Lady of the Camelias, sgn, 1927, 17x21" 2,090.00
Lilies, sgn, ca 1934, 28x19" 5,500.00
Louise, blindstamp, 1927, 21x14" 2,100.00

L'Orchides, L. Icart Society,
1937, 28" x 20", $6,600.00.

Mardi Gras, 1936, 19x19" 8,000.00
Miss America (lady draped in flag/doves), 1927, fr, 21x16"..... 2,600.00
Monte Carlo, poster, sgn in plate, 28x43" 2,500.00
Orchids, sgn/blindstamp, ca 1937, 27x19" 6,600.00
Puppies, sgn, 1925, 17x21" 1,700.00
Seville, sgn, 1928, 20x14" 1,100.00
Sleeping Beauty, sgn, 1927, 15x19" 2,000.00
Speed, trimmed margins, 1933, 15x25" 2,200.00
Summer, later print, 9x6" 175.00
Sweet Mystery, sgn/blindstamp, 21x16" 2,700.00
Symphony in Blue, sgn/blindstamp, 1936, 23x19" 2,800.00
Thais, sgn/blindstamp, 1927, 16x21" 2,200.00
Tosca, sgn/blindstamp, ca 1928, 13x21" 1,950.00
Venus in the Waves, fr, ltd ed, ca 1983....................65.00
Volupte, sgn, 1935, 17x15" 3,000.00
Winsome, sgn/blindstamp, 1935, 17x15" 2,400.00
Woman w/Doves, sgn, 1926, 19x11" 1,800.00
Zest, sgn/blindstamp, 1928, 20x15" 4,000.00

Kellogg

Christian Family Altar, fr, 12x17"..........................65.00
James Madison, 13x17" 85.00
John Tyler, 1841, 11x14" 220.00
Lieutenant-General Ulysses S Grant, 16x12" 45.00
Lincoln at Home, 10x14" 275.00
Nellie, 13x17" 50.00
Stephen A Douglas, 10x14" 85.00
Storming of Fort Donelson, Feb 16, 1862, 10x13"..........125.00
Three Friends, 14x10" 65.00

Kurz and Allison

Louis Kurz founded the Chicago Lithograph Company in 1833. Among his most notable works were a series of thirty-six Civil War scenes and one hundred illustrations of Chicago architecture. His company was destroyed in the Great Fire of 1871, and in 1880 Kurz formed a partnership with Alexander Allison, an engraver. Until both retired in 1903, they produced hundreds of lithographs in color as well as black and white.

Assault on Fort Sanders, lg folio 145.00
Battle of Champion Hills MS, lg folio 190.00
Battle of Corinth MS, Rosecrans Vs Van Dorn, lg folio 200.00
Battle of Fort Donelson TN, Grant & Buckner, lg folio 190.00
Battle of Franklin NT, Schofield Vs Hood, lg folio 200.00
Battle of Gettysburg, lg folio 195.00
Choncape, Oto Chief, Greenough, 1838, 14x20" 170.00
David Vann, Cherokee Chief, Rice & Clark, 1842, 14x20" 195.00
Die Harmann's Schlacht, lg folio, 25x38".................200.00
Execution of Robert Emmett, Hanged...1803, lg folio.................175.00
Flags of the Union, Kugler, lg folio 175.00
General Geo B McClellan, blk/wht bust view, lg folio.................90.00
Katawabeda, Chippewa Chief, Bowen, 1841, 14x20"..............195.00
Little Crow, Sioux Chief, Greenough, 1838, 14x20" 160.00
Major Ridge, Cherokee Chief, Greenough, 1838, 14x20"..............200.00
Me Na Wa, Creek Chief, Greenough, 1838, 14x20" 110.00
Pashenine, Chippewa Chief, Rice & Clark, 1843, 14x20" 180.00
Siege of Vicksburg, Grant & Porter Combine...Forces, lg folio ...200.00
Stamanu, Flathead Boy, Greenough, 1838, 14x20" 150.00
Storming Stony Point, blk/wht, med folio, 14x21"..........50.00
Tish Co Han, Delaware Chief, Biddle, 1837, 14x20" 175.00
Waapashaw, Sioux Chief, Biddle, 1836, 14x20"..............180.00
Washington Entering Trenton...Inauguration, blk/wht, 16x22"....70.00
Weshcubb or Sweet, Chippewa Chief, Biddle, 1837, 14x20".......160.00
Wm Penn Treating w/Indians, lg folio.....................265.00
Yoholo Micco, Creek Chief, Greenough, 1838, 14x20" 80.00

Nutting, Wallace

Born in 1862, Nutting pursued many careers. His hand-tinted photographs of landscapes and interior scenes are prized by collectors today. He was also a writer, minister, farmer, and a furniture maker, designing reproductions of early American pieces. Collectors of his prints should be aware of rosy-hued, inconsistently bright or dark examples — especially large prints of *An Elaborate Dinner* and *A Chair for John*; these have been reproduced. Prices for large interior prints have recently been on the increase. Those with animals have risen at least 50% in the past few years, and prints with men are commanding extremely high prices. Those with babies and/or adolescent children bring very high prices as well.

Our advisor for this category is Milt Steinfeld; he is listed in the Directory under New Jersey.

Almost Ready 235.00
Angel Garden, 12x20"....................................335.00
August Garden, 10x16" 275.00
Chair for John, 11x17" 215.00
China Closet, 5x9½", EX..................................95.00
Clustered at the Well, trimmed, 9¼x7½", VG 100.00
Comfort & the Cat, 13x16" 435.00
Coming Out of Rosa, lt foxing 140.00
Corner Cupboard..190.00
Good Man Is Coming, 4½x6½", VG..........................75.00
Great Wayside Oak, 11x14" 130.00
Honeymoon Drive, 11x14"................................90.00
In Wales, 11x14" 185.00
Lingering Water, 14x17" 115.00
Little Killarney Lake, 20x24" 335.00
Lorna Doone Brook, 11x14" 135.00
May Countryside, 1910, 9½x7½" in 18x15" fr, EX.........135.00
May Drive, 10x16" 100.00
Mossy Logs, 18x22" 375.00
Natural Bridge, 16x13" 115.00
New England Road in May, 14x17"........................155.00

October Splendors, 18x22"	175.00
Orchard Shadows, 6x9"	85.00
Over the Canal, 11x17"	110.00
Pine Landing, 10x12"	75.00
Plymouth Curves, 11x17"	135.00
Polishing the Silver, 4x6", EX	75.00
Portsmouth Belles, 10x12"	160.00
Ready for Callers, 11x14"	175.00
Rural Sweetness, orig fr, 18x15"	75.00
Seascape, 1909, 3x7", EX	100.00
Sip of Tea, 7½x9½"	185.00
Southern Puritan, 13x16"	335.00
Spring Bower, 10x12"	88.00
Tail Race & Bridge, 14x17"	130.00
Uncle Sam, 13x16"	375.00
Vermont Valley, 11x14"	110.00
Warm Spring Day, orig fr, 16½x23½"	300.00
Where Grandma Was Wed	175.00

Prang, Louis

Andersonville Stockade, AJ Klapp, 15x21½"	130.00
Battle of Antietam, Prang's Am Litho Co, 15x21½"	98.00
Battle of Chattanooga, L Prang & Co, 15x21½"	275.00
Battle of Kenesaw Mtn, Prang's Am Litho Co, 15x21½"	98.00
Battle of Manila, Muller & Luchsinger, 1898, 16x20"	120.00
Battle of Port Hudson, Prang's Am Litho Co, 15x21½"	150.00
Cycles Perfecta, poster paper, 59x42"	6,300.00
Exposition Universelle...de St Louis, 1903, 41x30"	3,200.00
Fruits, sgn, 22x14"	825.00
Gismonda, sgn, 1894, 85x29"	3,850.00
Job, sgn in block, 1896, fr, 64x44"	1,870.00
Lorenzaccio, linen bk, 1896, 41x15"	1,750.00
Salome, poster paper, 16x13"	350.00
Sarah Bernhardt, Am Tour, 1895, 78x30"	4,400.00
Sheridan's Charge at Winchester, Prang's Am Litho, 15x21½"	130.00
Vient de Paraitre, poster paper, linen bk, 30x18"	600.00
Vin des Incas, poster paper, linen bk, 33x81"	7,500.00

Yard Long

Values for yard-longs are given for examples in very good to excellent condition, full length, nicely framed, and with the original glass. To learn more about this popular area of collector interest, we recommend *Those Wonderful Yard-Long Prints and More,* by our advisors W.D. and M.J. Keagy, and C.G. and J.M. Rhoden. They are listed in the Directory under Indiana and Illinois respectively. A word of caution: watch for reproductions; know your dealer.

A Shower of Sweet Peas	125.00
A Yard of Roses	125.00
Pabst, American Girl, dtd 1914	200.00
Pabst, American Girl, info on bk, no date	190.00
Pabst, info on bk, dtd 1916	185.00
Pabst, lady in yel dress, info on bk, dtd 1917	175.00
Pabst, sgn Alfred Everitt Orr, dtd 1914	185.00
Pompeian, Absence Cannot Hearts Divide, sgn M Clark, 1921	225.00
Pompeian, Beauty Gained Is Love Retained, dtd 1925	145.00
Pompeian, Forbes, sgn Mary Pickford, dtd 1918	250.00
Pompeian, Honeymooning in the Alps, sgn G Pressler, 1923	125.00
Pompeian, info on bk, dtd 1915	160.00
Pompeian, info on bk, dtd 1916	185.00
Pompeian, sgn Gene Pressler, dtd 1926	150.00
Pompeian, Sweetest Story Ever Told, dtd 1920	175.00

Selz Good Shoes, lovely lady w/opera glasses	225.00
Selz Good Shoes, lovely lady w/walking stick, dtd 1925	225.00
Unknown, Lady in pk gown, sgn Haskell Coffin	200.00
Walk-Over Shoe Co, A Walk-Over Girl, dtd 1909	150.00

Purinton

Founded in 1936 in Wellsville, Ohio, Purinton Pottery relocated in 1941 in Shippenville, Pennsylvania, and began producing hand-painted wares that are today attracting the interest of collectors of 'country-type' dinnerware. Using bold brush strokes of vivid color, simple yet attractive patterns such as Apple, Fruits, Tea Rose, and Pennsylvania Dutch were manufactured in tableware sets as well as in many accessory pieces. The pottery closed in 1959.

Our advisor for this category is Pat Dole; she is listed in the Directory under Alabama. Pat is the editor of *The Glaze;* see Clubs, Newsletters, and Catalogs.

Bowl, Apple, 5½"	5.00
Bowl, Normandy Plaid, clover shape	15.00
Bowl, vegetable; Plaid	20.00
Casserole, Apple, w/lid	30.00
Chop plate, Plaid, 12"	30.00
Cookie jar, Apple & Pear	30.00
Creamer & sugar bowl, Apple, w/lid	15.00
Creamer & sugar bowl, Plaid	15.00
Cruet, oil or vinegar; Apple	25.00
Cup & saucer, Apple	7.50
Cup & saucer, Plaid	12.00
Jug, Apple, Kent	15.00
Pitcher, Apple, water sz	30.00
Platter, meat; Plaid	15.00
Relish, Apple, 3-section, center hdl	20.00
Shakers, Apple, jug form, pr	6.00
Shakers, Apple, lg, pr	22.50
Shakers, Apple & Pear, pr	10.00
Shakers, Normandy Plaid, jug form, sm, pr	10.00
Shakers, Palm Tree, pr	35.00
Snack plate, Apple	5.00
Sugar bowl, Apple, w/lid	10.00
Teapot, Apple, lg	30.00
Teapot, Apple, 2-cup	15.00
Teapot, Apple & Pear, 2-cup	10.00
Tumbler, Apple, 12-oz, 4¾"	12.00
Tumbler, Apple & Pear, 2¾"	6.00
Tumbler, Apple & Pear, 4¾"	10.00

Purses

Beaded purses and bags represent an area of collecting interest that is very popular today. Purses from the early 1800s are often decorated with small, brightly-colored glass beads. Cut steel beads were popular in the 1840s and remained stylish until about 1930. Mesh purses are also popular. In the 1820s, mesh was woven. Chain-link mesh came into usage in the 1890s, followed by the enamel mesh bags carried by the flappers in the 1920s. Purses are divided into several categories by (a) construction techniques — whether beaded, embroidered, or a type of needlework; (b) material — fabric or metal; and (c) design and style. Condition is very important. Watch for dry, brittle leather or fragile material. For those interested in learning more, we recommend *Antique Purses, A History, Identification, and Value Guide, Second Edition,* by Richard Holiner, available at your library or local bookstore.

Beaded, amber, clutch style w/beaded strap 35.00
Beaded, amber, dbl beaded fringe, lg, EX 60.00
Beaded, amber carnival, curved fr, ornate fringe, 15" L 115.00
Beaded, bl & wht w/gold, drawstring, tassles, EX 80.00
Beaded, bl carnival, 3-layer fringe, beaded tassle, EX 100.00
Beaded, blk & silver floral, zip closure, wrist band, VG 20.00
Beaded, blk all over, metal fr, Belgium, sm, VG 25.00
Beaded, floral tapestry, ornate SP fr w/roses, 8x13", EX 145.00
Beaded, gold, heavy clutch type w/chain, EX 45.00
Beaded, gold & silver, gold fringed, chain strap, EX 80.00
Beaded, gold metal, mesh drawstring, Whiting & Davis, EX 45.00
Beaded, gray hearts, clutch type, Germany, VG 40.00
Beaded, jet florals on blk satin, beaded fringe, lg, EX 35.00
Beaded, mc florals, Belgium, sm, VG 25.00
Beaded, mc peacock pattern, bl stone clasp, EX 95.00

White beads surround needlework flowers, gilt clasp with jewels and enameling, 6", $75.00.

Beaded petit point, Victorian lady in metal fr, EX 295.00
Beadwork w/floral embr, drawstring, VG 35.00
Crochet, drawstring w/pk beaded cloth tassels 45.00
Mesh, silver, heavy fr, link chain & strap, EX 55.00
Mesh, silver, heavy fr, silver fringe drops, Germany 75.00
Petit point (floral), ornate brass fr w/chain, EX 85.00
Rhinestones, hand set, Czechoslovakia, sm 55.00
Rhinestones allover, Tiffany clasp, EX 65.00
Suede clutch w/sterling & chrysoprase accents, Spaulding 250.00
Tapestry (floral), gold chain & clasp, France, EX 45.00

Quezal

The Quezal Art Glass and Decorating Company of Brooklyn, New York, was founded in 1901 by Martin Bach. A former Tiffany employee, Bach's glass closely resembled that of his former employer. Most pieces were signed 'Quezal,' a name taken from a Central American bird. After Bach's death in 1920, his son-in-law, Conrad Vohlsing, continued to produce a Quezal-type glass in Elmhurst, New York, which he marked 'Lustre Art Glass.' See also that particular category. Examples listed here are signed unless noted otherwise.

Candlestick, King Tut, opal w/orange & gr, 10", pr 950.00
Lamp, 8" amber w/gr & gold feathers shade, 10½" 650.00
Salt cellar, swirled optic panels, master 225.00
Shade, amber irid, 10-rib bell form, sgn, 5" 100.00
Shade, feathers, bl on wht w/gold, 5x2¼", set of 5 .... 1,200.00

Shade, gold, ribbed, bell form, 5" 150.00
Shade, wht w/gr & gold feathers, egg form, 11x4" 575.00
Vase, bud; gold, slim cylinder, rnd base, 12" 425.00
Vase, gold, sgn, 4" 325.00
Vase, gold, very slim floriform, sgn, 6" 650.00
Vase, gold w/bl & pk highlights, 4 dimples, 4¼" 350.00
Vase, gr & opal w/feathers, shouldered/flared rim, 4½" 2,500.00
Vase, gr & opal w/hooked feathers, bulb w/slim neck, 4½" 2,500.00
Vase, opal w/gold swirls on gr, ribbed, long neck, 6½" 2,200.00
Vase, opal w/gr & gold feathers, gold int, conical, 9½" 1,200.00
Vase, opal w/gr & gold feathers, trumpet w/trefoil rim, 6" 600.00
Vase, opal w/gr feathers, gold int, conical, 7¾" 850.00
Vase, opal w/random gold linears, gold int, ftd, 8" 1,100.00

Vase, orange feathering above striated green on opalescent ground, signed, 9", $900.00; Vase, green feathering with opalescent ruffled edge, signed, 7", $750.00.

Vase, silver o/l long-stem carnations on amber irid, 8½" 2,200.00
Vase, wht w/gr & gold feathers, gold int, 6" 650.00

Quilts

Quilts, while made of necessity, nevertheless represent an art form which expresses the character and the personality of the designer. During the 17th and 18th centuries, quilts were considered a necessary part of a bride's hope chest — the traditional number required to be properly endowed for marriage was a 'baker's dozen'! Quilts were used not only for bed coverings but for curtains, extra insulation, and mattresses as well. The early quilts were made from pieces salvaged from cloth items that had outlived their original usefulness and from bits left over from sewing projects. Regardless of shape, these scraps were fitted together following no organized lines. The resulting hodge-podge design was called a crazy quilt.

In 1793 Eli Whitney developed the cotton gin; as a result, textile production in America became industrialized. Soon inexpensive fabrics were readily available, and ladies were able to choose from colorful prints and solids to add contrast to their work. Both pieced and appliqued work became popular — pieced quilts were considered utilitarian, while appliqued work was shown with pride of accomplishment at the fair. Today many collectors prize pieced quilts and their intricate geometric patterns above all other types. Many of these designs were given names: Daisy and Oak Leaf, Grandmother's Flower Garden, Log Cabin, and Ocean Wave are only a few. Appliqued quilts involved stitching one piece — carefully cut into a specific form such as a leaf, a flower, or a stylized device — onto either a large one-piece ground fabric or an individual block. Often the background fabric was quilted in a decorative pattern.

Amish women scorned printed calicos as 'worldly' and instead used colorful blocks set with black fabrics to produce a stunning pieced effect. During the Victorian era, the crazy quilt was revived, but the ladies of the 1870s used plush velvets, brocades, silks, and linen patches and embroidered along the seams with feather or chain stitches.

Another type of quilting, highly prized and rare today, is trapunto. These quilts were made by first stitching the outline of the design onto a solid sheet of fabric which was backed with a second having a much looser weave. White was often favored, but color was sometimes used for accent. The design (grapes, flowers, leaves, etc.) was padded through openings made by separating the loose weave of the underneath fabric; a backing was added and the three layers quilted as one.

Besides condition, value is judged on intricacy of pattern, color effect, and craftsmanship. In the listings that follow, examples rated excellent have minor defects.

Key:
dmn — diamond   ms — machine sewn
embr — embroidered   X — cross
hs — hand sewn

Appliqued eagle quilt, Pennsylvania, ca 1880, 78" x 76", $1,900.00.

Amish

Bar, maroon & bl w/maroon border, 1900, rprs, 35x27".............700.00
Blk rectangle in borders of purple & blk, purple binding.............600.00
Bow Tie, ea w/embr initials, blk sateen ground, IN, 1925.......1,100.00
Bow Tie, mc, gr/purple edge stripes, 65x70", EX.........................700.00
Bow Tie, vivid colors, ms binding, EX quilting, 72x88", EX....1,600.00
Broken Star, mc on blk, rope-twist quilting, '30, 86x86", M...2,650.00
Carpenter's Wheel, 4-color, contemporary, 80x94", M................650.00
Checkerboard, blk/maroon, fraying & wear, 85x87", G..............165.00
Crazy, all cotton, diagonal quilting, 1925, 58x70", EX...........1,000.00
Detailed feather heart & star, contemporary.................................495.00
Dmn Sq, teal dmn on raspberry sq, forest gr bars, PA, 1910....5,400.00
Dmn-in-Sq, pk on teal, 2 borders, wools, 1900, lg, EX...........7,150.00
Feathered wreath stitching ea side, A Rabert, OH, 1930s.......1,500.00
Fence Row Vt, band border, sawtooth edge, '10, 82x64", EX.1,000.00
Flower baskets, pk/gr/lav, chain/floral quilting, OH, 1940.......1,900.00
Log Cabin, coronet/heart quilting, PA, 1890, 66x77"............2,500.00
Pointed Star, 30 mc stars on blk sateen, OH, 1900.................2,000.00
Sawtooth Dmn, gr/royal bl, feather/dmn quilting, PA, 1900..2,400.00
Spring Star, 12 8-point stars on teal, pk border, OH, 1920......2,600.00
Star center, blk on orange, contemporary, 78x94", M.................700.00
Stepped Cross blocks, blk/pk, 8-point star quilting, 1920s.........850.00
Strips around central rectangle, wreath stitching, 1930s.............850.00
Young Man's Fancy, wool, chain/dmn quilting, IA, 1915.......4,800.00
9-Patch, 24 blocks, vine/diagonal stitching, IN, 1900.................600.00

Appliqued

Acorn & Leaf, 12 mc blocks, gr border, ltweight, 98x80", EX.....450.00
Album, 39 pictorals, floral border, 1850s, 85x95", NM..........6,000.00
Broiderie perse florals, grapevine border, 1815, 98x98", EX....3,500.00
Carolina Lily, red/gr on wht, sgn, 92x101"..............................1,125.00
Central snowflake w/foliage, pineapple corners, '30, 86x86"...1,650.00
Cherry trees w/hatchet by ea, EX quilting, 1850s, 76x67".......3,950.00
English Flower Pot, pk/yel/gr on wht, summer weight, 74x76"...375.00
Fleur-de-lis, primitive, pencil pattern intact, 80x80", VG..........350.00
Floral medallions, 4 repeats, floral border, 82x100", EX..............850.00
Folk art birds & flowers w/in sqs, 67x78", EX.........................4,700.00
Grandmother's Garden in 3 rings, stuffed, 1830, 104x96", EX..3,520.00
Poppies, mc w/blk embr details, 1950s, 72x88", EX.....................350.00
Princess Feather in 4 pinwheels, quilted pineapple, 1850........4,600.00
Rose of Sharon, mc calico on wht, 1850s, 82x80", EX................845.00
Rose Wreath, red/pks/gr cotton, much embr, 94x77", NM.........450.00
Snowflake medallions, 9 repeats, red on wht, 72x74", EX...........350.00
Whig Rose in 4 lg blocks, floral swagged border, 1850s.............900.00

Pieced

Barn Raising, blk embr w/appl lace, 1890s, 65x64", EX.............990.00
Bear Paw, mc prints, red binding, sawtooth border, 70x86"........350.00
Checkerboard w/appl & embr ABC blocks, 1932, 60x76", EX....350.00
Crazy, pnt story characters, embr, 1900, 68x70", EX...............1,750.00
Crown of Thorns, dk bl/ivory, 3 borders, hs, old, 92x84", NM....500.00
Dbl Irish Chain, indigo on wht, 1890s, full sz, NM.....................515.00
Dbl Irish Chain, lt bl on wht, ca 1920s, full sz, NM....................400.00
Dbl Irish Chain, olive/red, dmn quilting, 1890s, 74x92".............850.00
Dbl Wedding Ring, pk/bl, EX quilting, hs, 1920s, 90x72", NM...400.00
Diagonal 9 Patch, mc calico, EX quilting, old, 72x84"................350.00
Dresden Plate, mc percale on wht, hs, 1930s, 76x66", NM..........450.00
Flower Garden, pastel yel, ca 1910, rebound, lg, EX....................350.00
Flower Garden, pastels, scalloped border, hs, '30s, 78x83", EX....450.00
Four Leaf Clover, mc w/orange border, 80x88", VG....................235.00
Friendship Star, mc, 1950s, 72x82", VG....................................250.00
Friendship Star, teal/wht cotton, EX quilting, 62x75", EX..........240.00
Geometric circles, yel/wht, 88x96", EX.....................................275.00
Golden Dbl Wedding Ring, mc cottons, 1930s, 91x76", NM......265.00
Grandmother's Flower Garden, mc prints, 1930s, 86x74", EX....350.00
Hands All Around, gr/indigo, 1870s, full sz, EX.........................325.00
Hearts & Gizzards, mc, 72x74", EX...350.00
Hexagons w/in Hexagon, mc calicos, ca 1900, 90x77", EX..........275.00
Indian Wedding Ring, mc, 1940s, 58x77", EX.............................450.00
Irish Chain, bl & wht, EX quilting, 75x77", EX...........................325.00
Jacob's Ladder, gold on wht, 1930s, lg, EX................................410.00
Joseph's Coat, mc stripes, EX quilting, 1900, 78x80", EX........5,775.00
Lemoyne Star, reds/yels, 62x74", EX...500.00
Log Cabin, mc prints, 66x78", EX...400.00
Lone Star, mc prints/solids, hs, 1930s, 69x81", EX.....................300.00
Lone Star, red/wht/bl, 80x82", EX...250.00
Mosaic, mc pastels, ltweight, 70x94", NM..................................325.00
Ocean Waves, mc prints on pk, homespun bk, ms, 78x78".........800.00
Ohio Star, red/wht/bl, close quilting, 1930s, 70x85", EX............375.00
Pieced Star, mc prints, floral border, 1930s, 90x75", EX............250.00
Rising Star, mc on bl, diapered quilting, 1850s, 95x85", EX........500.00
Rose of Sharon, pks/grs, 74x82", EX...450.00
Schoolhouse, mc on tan, all cotton, 72x78", EX......................2,200.00
Simple Pleasures, gingham & calicos w/gr, 1875, 61x74", NM....425.00
Smoothing Iron, pumpkin/reds, 60x76", EX..............................240.00
Square in Square, mc w/blk, 70x80", VG....................................250.00
Star & Block, bl/wht, 76x76", EX..885.00

Pieced Star on field with cable and diagonal line quilting, early 20th century, 80" x 84", $500.00.

Star of N Carolina, red/wht/gr, 1880s, full sz, NM......................400.00
Stars in sq gridwork, mc on navy, 78x80", EX 700.00
Sunflower, bright colors, hs, 1938, full sz 425.00
Touching Stars, mc calicos/ginghams, 1920s, 60x76", EX............350.00
Wedding Ring, bright mc prints, 82x82", EX 345.00
Wedding Ring, mc, 74x76", EX 325.00
Wild Goose Chase, gold/lav, 1930s, twin sz, VG 425.00
Yo-Yo, bright colors, yel border, 1930s, lg, unused 325.00
8-Patch Variation, blk/beige, 1890s, lg, EX................................275.00
9-Patch, Irish Chain border, mc, 88x88", 1910, EX 350.00
9-Patch, mc prints & solids, ms bking & binding, 74x80", EX 225.00

Trapunto

Bride's, vines & flowers in urns, 1820s, 88x90" 2,400.00
Federal urn, wht on wht, swag border, sgn/1821, 100x100" 13,200.00
Wht on wht, vintage/meandering feathers, lt wear, 68x72" 1,100.00
16 sqs w/tulips alternate w/blocks of appl flowers, 1850s 3,800.00
9 floral designs, appl florals, sgn/1850, rebound, 82x86" 3,300.00

Quimper

Quimper is a type of pottery produced in Quimper, France. A tin enamel-glazed earthenware pottery with hand-painted decoration, it was first produced in the 1600s by the Bousquet and Caussy Factories. Little of this early ware was marked. By the late 1700s, three factories were operating in the area, all manufacturing the same type of pottery. The Grande Maison de HB, a company formed as a result of a marriage joining the Hubaudiere and Bousquet families, was a major producer of Quimper pottery. They marked their wares with various forms of the 'HB' logo; but of the pottery they produced, collectors value examples marked with the 'HB' within a triangle most highly.

Francois Eloury established another pottery in Quimper in the late 1700s. Under the direction of Charles Porquier, the ware was marked simply 'P.' Adolph Porquier replaced Charles in the 1850s, marking the ware produced during that period with an 'AP' logo.

Jule HenRiot began operations in 1886, using molds he had purchased from Porquier. His mark was 'HR,' and until the twentieth century he was in competition with The Grande Maison de HB. In 1926 he began to mark his wares 'HenRiot Quimper.' In 1968 the two factories merged. They are still in operation under the name Les Faenceries de Quimper. The factory sold in the fall of 1983 to Sarah and Paul Janssens from the United States, making it the first time the owners were not French.

For those interested in learning more about Quimper, we recommend *Quimper Pottery: A French Folk Art Faience*, by Sandra V. Bondhus, our advisor for this category, whose address can be found in the Directory under Connecticut.

Beaker, man/lady, decor ordinaire, HQF, 6½", pr........................120.00
Bell, man w/cane figural, sgn AG, HQF, 4⅞x3⅛"..........................120.00
Bell, peasant figure, 1930s, 5"...60.00
Bookend, man pushes against support, Sevellec/HQ, 5½", pr.....375.00
Bowl, Breton lady, scalloped rim, hdl, HBQF, 5x13½x8½".........150.00
Bowl, Breton lady, 3-stripe band, shallow, HQF, 4x10½" 140.00
Bowl, Breton man, handkerchief shape, HBQ, 6x5" 180.00
Bowl, peasant man, 6-sided, HB Quimper, 7½" 85.00
Bridge set, Breton men & ladies, 4 shapes, HBQF, 1920s 100.00
Bust, baby, sgn B Savigny, HB Quimper, 5x4" 160.00
Butter dish, Breton man, floral borders/geometrics, HBQ, 7½" ...230.00
Butter pat, Eskimos, scalloped rim, gr ground, HenRiot 15.00
Candle holder, Deco figure w/polka dots & stripes, HBQF, 8¾"....90.00
Charger, classical scene, Celtic border, HBQ, 1800s, 11¾" 400.00
Charger, man/lady, la touche border, HBQ, 11½" 375.00
Cigarette holder, camel in desert, HQF, 1920s, 2½x3½" 210.00
Cruet, lady & florals, peach-shaped finial, HBQ, 6½" 95.00
Cup & saucer, berry & sponge border, HenRiot Quimper..............30.00

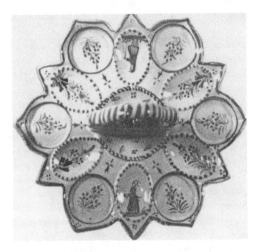

Egg server, signed HQF, 5½" high, 10½" diameter, NM, $350.00.

Figurine, Breton man/lady, sgn Micheau-Vernez, HQ, 13" 175.00
Figurine, peasant couple, HenRiot Quimper, pr 400.00
Figurine, St Ann & child, HB Quimper, 13½" 350.00
Inkwell, florals, heart shape, HBQ, 3¼x5x5"..............................150.00
Olive jar, Breton couple/'Olives,' HQF, recent, 6½x7½" 85.00
Pitcher, Breton figural hdl, HQF, 1920s, 9x8" 375.00
Pitcher, Deco man pours cider, apples, HQF, 6x7½"....................195.00
Pitcher, Deco-style lady's portrait, HBQ, 8x7" 55.00
Pitcher, man w/cane, floral sprays, HenRiot Quimper, 8½" 150.00
Plate, Breton man or lady, canted corners, 9⅞" 55.00
Plate, florals, rose-colored sponge border, 8", 6 for 275.00
Platter, Breton lady, oval, recent, HBQF, 23x11½" 160.00
Platter, 5 peasants at well scene, decor riche, HBQ, 18" 800.00
Porringer, lady, HenRiot Quimper, 7"...25.00
Salt cellar, dbl; man/lady, swan form, HQF, 3½x3½" 45.00
Shakers, Breton couple, HBQF, 1930s, 3½", pr 85.00
Snuff bottle, rooster, book shape, unmk, 3" 150.00
Tile, Breton lady, leafy sprays, HBQ, 8¾" dia.............................125.00
Tile, lady, bl border, HQF, 4¾"..60.00
Tray, peasant girl, yel trim, fluted, HB, 9¾" 115.00
Umbrella stand, peacocks/florals, HB Quimper, rstr, 10x9½" 200.00
Vase, Breton man, ivoire corbeille variant, bulbous, HQ, 8" 130.00
Vase, dancing couple, dragon figural hdls, HQ, 14¼" 650.00
Vase, Deco-style lady, jug form, HBQ, 6½x6" 100.00

Vase, genre scenes/fleur-de-lis, flared, HB, sm rpr, 10"................100.00
Wall pocket, Breton lady, slipper shape, HB, 7¾x2¾" 325.00
Wall pocket, man/boy at wheel, Briec PB, 19th C, 13" 1,100.00
Wall pocket, peasant, cone shape, HB Quimper, 1960s, 5½"........80.00

Radford

The Jasperware listed below was made in Zanesville, Ohio, at the A. Radford Pottery Company incorporated there in 1903. This type of ware was first designed and produced in 1896 when Albert Radford worked in Tiffin, Ohio. The Zanesville Jasper, in contrast to the original line, was decorated with Wedgwood-type cameos in relief that were not applied but were formed within the general mold. The only mark found on the ware is a two-digit shape number. The Tiffin Jasper, though not always marked, is sometimes impressed 'Radford Jasper.'

After only a few months Radford sold the plant to Arc-En-Ciel and moved his works to West Virginia. In addition to the regular line of utility wares, several artware lines were also produced there. Among them were Ruko, a standard brown underglaze decorated line; Thera, matt glazed with slip decoration; and Radura, usually done in matt green glazes.

Jasper

Letter holder, lady w/bow & target scene, bark trim, #61 ....375.00
Mug, floral relief, lt bl, 4½ " 150.00
Pitcher, grapes, Old Man Winter on hdl, #17, 9" 285.00
Vase, angels in relief, bl & blk, 7" 250.00
Vase, bust of Washington, reverse: eagle, bark trim, #12, 7"........265.00
Vase, cupids w/instruments, column 1 side, bark trim, 14", 7" 285.00
Vase, lady sits, trees & dog, bark trim, #22, 9"............................475.00
Vase, lady under grape arch, #58, 5½ " 225.00
Vase, lady w/dog, bk: Roman kneels, bark trim, #18, 7"..............275.00
Vase, lady w/flowers, bk: grapes, #59, 4" 175.00
Vase, man's head ea side, twisted form, 3" 125.00
Vase, 2 children & lion, wht/lt brn, #15, 7" 225.00
Vase, 3 horses in clouds pull chariot, bark trim, #16, 7" 295.00

Miscellaneous

Candle holder, Ruko, floral, sgn/mk, rare, 7" 175.00
Jardiniere, Ruko, tulips, brn glaze, 8½ x9" 250.00
Jardiniere & ped, winged creatures/foliage, streaky gr, 34"..........500.00

Radura vase, matt green, 10", $275.00.

Vase, Radura, gr, Nouveau form, 4 long in-mold hdls, rare, 9" ...350.00
Vase, Thera, floral, red on gr matt, rare, 12"...............................450.00

Radios

Vintage radios are becoming very collectible. There were thousands of styles and types produced, the most popular of which today are the breadboard and the cathedral. Consoles are usually considered less saleable, since their size makes them hard to display and store.

For those wishing to learn more about antique radios, we recommend *The Collectors' Guide to Antique Radios,* by Sue and Marty Bunis, available from your local library or bookstore.

Addison, Bakelite, maroon w/amber inset U-form speaker, 9".....600.00
Admiral, Am clock radio, Bakelite, 1940s, EX 55.00
Airline #15-GHM-107A, portable..20.00
All-American Mohawk Lyric 35.00
American Bosch #38, w/headphones 125.00
Arvin #440-T..30.00
Atwater Kent #217, beehive, 1933 ....225.00
Atwater Kent #30, in writing desk 100.00
Atwater Kent #37...35.00
Atwater Kent #555, table model, hinged lid, unusual 180.00
Atwater Kent #60, metal case 50.00
Bendix, end-table model..50.00
Commemorative Thomas, cathedral, AM/FM...............................75.00
Coronado #908, wood..40.00
Crosley, Model 25-AW, 3-band shortwave, M 75.00
Crosley #148, cathedral 85.00
Crosley #51, Harko, museum quality w/tubes 400.00
Crosley #51-P, portable 150.00
Crosley #56-TNL, wood case..15.00
Crosley RFL-90 ....50.00
Crosley Super 5, shortwave, police band, 1930s, EX.....................65.00
Crosley Super 6, AM shortwave, police band, 1930s, EX 65.00
DeWald #802, tombstone, 8-tube, 4-band, EX 125.00
Emerson, red Bakelite, portable transistor, 1950s, EX 55.00
Emerson #543, blk Bakelite, metal grill, moon-type dial, VG........30.00
Emerson #652, wht 20.00
ERLA, cathedral w/clock, 2 knobs, rare..250.00
Fada, Bakelite, caramel yel w/red accents, rnded ends, 11" 550.00
FADA #160-A...75.00
Flash-A-Call Intercom, 1930s, wood cabinet, EX........................45.00
General Electric #81, tombstone, 1934 ....110.00
General Radio BC-14-A, crystal set, dtd 1918 ....450.00
Grebe CR-13 ....800.00
Grebe CR-18, w/4 coils 450.00
Grebe CR-9 ....300.00
Hallicrafters S-38B, 4-band 25.00
Lincoln Electric, Bakelite, cathedral, EX 35.00
Motorola, swivel hdl, portable...15.00
National HRO-50-T, metallic gray, w/speaker, 5 coil sets 200.00
Philco, AM shortwave, 1920s, EX...125.00
Philco, 95th Anniversary cathedral, replica of 1930s 89.00
Philco #20-A, mini-console 125.00
Philco #37-620, 1937 ....110.00
Philco #38-12, wraparound grill, wood table model, EX 30.00
Philco #48-141, brn Bakelite...25.00
Philco #48-460...25.00
Philco #50, cathedral 125.00
Philco #90, cathedral 290.00
RCA #16..75.00
RCA #18, radiola...75.00
RCA #8, portable..125.00
RCA #9-X-510, radio-phono, brn Bakelite, table top 50.00
RCA #9-X-571 ....20.00

Philco cathedral radio
with illuminated dial,
all original cabinet,
17", EX, $85.00.

RCA ACR-136, shortwave receiver 250.00
RCA D-22-1, record recorder, shortwave, 5-band, 1937, rare......500.00
RCA Radiola #16 ....40.00
RCA Victor 9-X-561, brn Bakelite 20.00
Sentinel #10356, plastic 25.00
Silvertone #101.801, wood cabinet 30.00
Silvertone #7036, shortwave 40.00
Stromberg-Carlson, radio-phono console, 1941 ....50.00
Tofunk, table model, shortwave, AM, Germany 30.00
Westinghouse, Deco jukebox style, 1940s, EX......................65.00
Zenith, gr plastic w/clock, '50s style, VG 20.00
Zenith #16EP 250.00
Zenith #4-B-413, 6-volt, brn Bakelite, VG 35.00
Zenith #7-F-04, AM/FM, brn 20.00
Zenith B-835-E, blond cabinet 20.00
Zenith R-723, AM/FM 25.00

Novelty

Blabber Puppy, MIB...25.00
Blabbermouth, NM in box 25.00
Cadillac 1960s Convertible, MIB...35.00
Getty Gas Pump, MIB 30.00
Heinz Catsup, MIB 45.00
Knight Rider car, MIB 25.00
Mississippi Fire Pumper, NM 35.00
Raisin Man, MIB 30.00
Seagram, Wine Cooler, MIB 25.00
Tony Tiger, NM 35.00

Railroadiana

Collecting railroad-related memorabilia has become one of America's most popular hobbies. The range of collectible items available is almost endless, considering the fact that more than 175 different railroad lines are represented. Some collectors prefer to specialize in only one, while others attempt to collect at least one item from every railway line known to have existed. For the advanced collector, there is the challenge of locating rarities from short-lived railroads; for the novice, there are abundant keys, buttons, passes, and playing cards. Among the most popular specializations are dining-car collectibles — flatware, glassware, dinnerware, etc., in a wide variety of patterns and styles.

For a more thorough study, we recommend *Railroad Collectibles,*

Third Revised Edition, by Stanley L. Baker, available at your local library or bookstore. Some of our listings were provided by Shrader's Antiques (see Directory, California).

Key:
BL — bottom logo   SM — side marked
BS — bottom stamped   TL — top logo
SL — side logo   TM — top marked

Dinnerware

Ash tray, C&O, Geo Washington, 3x7" 85.00
Ash tray, GN, Mountains & Flowers, 4½" 75.00
Ash tray, N&W, Dogwood, 3¾" 45.00
Bowl, ATSF, California Poppy, 8" 150.00
Bowl, cereal; ACL, BS, 6" 78.00
Bowl, cereal; ATSF, Adobe, 6" 45.00
Bowl, cereal; B&O, Capitol, 6" 47.00
Bowl, cereal; B&O, Centenary, BS, 6" 50.00
Bowl, cereal; CB&Q, Violets & Daisies, 6½" 40.00
Bowl, cereal; CMStP&P, Peacock, 6" 28.00
Bowl, cereal; GN, Glory of the West, 6½" 35.00
Bowl, cereal; N&W, Dogwood, 6½" 25.00
Bowl, cereal; SP, Prairie-Mountain Wildflowers, BS, 6" 55.00
Bowl, cereal; SP, Prairie-Mountain Wildflowers, 6" 35.00
Bowl, cereal; UP, Blue & Gold, 6½" 18.00
Bowl, cereal; UP, Portland Rose, BS, 6½" 185.00
Bowl, NYNH&H, Platinum Blue, BS, 6½" sq 100.00
Bowl, soup; ATSF, California Poppy, 8½" 75.00
Bowl, soup; B&O, Centenary, BS, 9" 80.00
Bowl, soup; D&RGW, Prospector, 7" 42.00
Bowl, soup; MStP&SStM, Logan, BS, 9" 137.00
Bowl, soup; N&W, Cavalier, 9" 65.00
Bowl, soup; NYC, Hyde Park, 8½" 82.00
Bowl, soup; PRR, Keystone, 9" 45.00
Bowl, soup; UP, Harriman Blue, BS, 9" 65.00
Bowl, SP, Prairie-Mountain Wildflowers, 9¼" 285.00
Bowl, SRR, Peach Blossom, 7¼" sq....................................155.00
Butter pat, ACL, Flora of the South, BS...............................95.00
Butter pat, ATSF, Black Chain 22.00
Butter pat, ATSF, California Poppy......................................26.00
Butter pat, ATSF, Mimbreno, BS 52.00
Butter pat, B&O, Capitol...100.00
Butter pat, B&O, Centenary 38.00
Butter pat, B&O, Centenary, BS...55.00
Butter pat, C&NW, Flambeau 22.00
Butter pat, C&O, Train Ferry..30.00
Butter pat, CB&Q, Spider Mums, BS 125.00
Butter pat, CB&Q, Violets & Daisies 30.00
Butter pat, CMStP&P, Peacock 45.00
Butter pat, CN, Windsor, BS...29.00
Butter pat, FEC, Mistic 27.00
Butter pat, Fred Harvey, Encanto...28.00
Butter pat, NYC, Platinum Blue, BS 95.00
Butter pat, PRR, Keystone 48.00
Butter pat, PRR, Purple Laurel...26.00
Butter pat, Pullman, Calumet..65.00
Butter pat, Pullman, Indian Tree 75.00
Butter pat, SP, Prairie-Mountain Wildflowers, BS 85.00
Butter pat, SP, Sunset..85.00
Butter pat, UP, Blue & Gold...18.00
Butter pat, UP, Columbine 250.00
Butter pat, UP, Harriman Blue 24.50
Butter pat, UP, Winged Streamliner......................................26.00

Compote, PRR, Purple Laurel, ped ft, BS	110.00
Creamer, ATSF, Mimbreno, BS, ind	185.00
Creamer, CP, Empress, BS, ind	55.00
Creamer, KCS, Roxbury, w/hdl, ind	35.00
Creamer, PRR, Keystone, ind	75.00
Creamer, StL&SF, Denmark, w/hdl, ind	38.00
Cup, bouillon; CB&Q, Violets & Daisies	28.00
Cup, bouillon; CI&L, Monon	150.00
Cup, bouillon; UP, Harriman Blue	28.00
Cup & saucer, ACL, Flora of the South, BS	145.00
Cup & saucer, ATSF, Adobe	75.00
Cup & saucer, ATSF, Mimbreno	135.00
Cup & saucer, B&O, Capitol	200.00
Cup & saucer, C&O, Centenary	150.00
Cup & saucer, C&O, Chessie	145.00
Cup & saucer, CB&Q, Violets & Daisies	55.00
Cup & saucer, CM&StP, Olympian	95.00
Cup & saucer, CMStP&P, Galatea	125.00
Cup & saucer, CN, Queen Elizabeth	75.00
Cup & saucer, CP, Empress, BS	90.00
Cup & saucer, demitasse; C&O, Centenary, BS	75.00
Cup & saucer, demitasse; C&O, Silhouette	110.00
Cup & saucer, demitasse; CMStP&P, Peacock	65.00
Cup & saucer, demitasse; CMStP&P, Traveler	75.00
Cup & saucer, demitasse; CP, York	25.00
Cup & saucer, demitasse; GN, Mountains & Flowers	190.00
Cup & saucer, demitasse; SP&S, Red Leaves	32.00
Cup & saucer, demitasse; UP, Winged Streamliner	38.00
Cup & saucer, Fred Harvey	12.00
Cup & saucer, GN, Mountains & Flowers	95.00
Cup & saucer, KCS, Roxbury	45.00
Cup & saucer, L&N, Regent	225.00
Cup & saucer, N&W, Coach & Four	125.00
Cup & saucer, N&W, Dogwood	45.00
Cup & saucer, NYC, Mercury, BS	81.00
Cup & saucer, NYC, Platinum Blue, BS	175.00
Cup & saucer, NYC, Vanderbilt, BS	260.00
Cup & saucer, PRR, Broadway, BS	88.00
Cup & saucer, PRR, Mountain Laurel	45.00
Cup & saucer, Pullman, Indian Tree	225.00
Cup & saucer, SP, Prairie-Mountain Wildflowers, BS	85.00
Egg cup, ATSF, California Poppy	45.00
Egg cup, CMStP&P, Traveler	75.00
Egg cup, dbl; GN, Oriental	75.00
Egg cup, dbl; MStP&SStM, Logan	95.00
Egg cup, dbl; UP, Desert Flower	65.00
Egg cup, GN, Mountains & Flowers, BS	75.00
Egg cup, UP, Desert Flower	45.00
Gravy boat, ACL, Carolina, BS	85.00
Gravy boat, ATSF, Mimbreno	150.00
Gravy boat, C&O, Train Ferry	35.00
Gravy boat, NYC, Platinum Blue, BS	100.00
Hot food cover, ATSF, California Poppy	145.00
Ice cream shell, ATSF, Mimbreno, BS	81.00
Ice cream shell, CN, Bonaventure	36.00
Ice cream shell, NYC, DeWitt Clinton, BS	75.00
Ice cream shell, PRR, Purple Laurel, BS	65.00
Ice cream shell, UP, Winged Streamliner	35.00
Mustard, C&NM, Coach & Four, lid slotted for spoon	145.00
Mustard, D&RGW, Blue Adam, lid slotted for spoon	40.00
Pitcher, SP, Imperial, BS, 7"	250.00
Pitcher, UP, Winged Streamliner, 6½"	85.00
Plate, ACL, Flora of the South, BS, 7¾"	85.00
Plate, ACL, Flora of the South, BS, 9"	175.00
Plate, ATSF, California Poppy, BS, 9¾"	140.00
Plate, ATSF, California Poppy, 7½"	32.00
Plate, ATSF, Mimbreno, BS, 9½"	100.00
Plate, B&A, Berkshire, 7"	95.00
Plate, B&O, Capitol, 9"	90.00
Plate, B&O, Centenary, 10½"	85.00
Plate, C&NW, Wild Rose, 7¼"	36.00
Plate, C&O, Geo Washington, 10½"	500.00
Plate, D&H, Adirondack, 10½"	135.00
Plate, Fred Harvey, Encanto, 5½"	8.00
Plate, GN, Hill, 9"	145.00
Plate, GN, Mountains & Flowers, BS, 9½"	98.00
Plate, GN, Oriental, 8"	82.00
Plate, MP, Eagle, BS, 9"	110.00
Plate, MP, State Capitols, BS, 10½"	305.00
Plate, MP, State Flowers, BS, 10½"	185.00
Plate, N&W, Coach & Four, 9½"	95.00
Plate, NP, Monad, 7½"	45.00
Plate, NP, Stampede, 5½"	90.00
Plate, NYC, Commodore, 8"	26.00
Plate, NYC, DeWitt Clinton, 7¾"	35.00
Plate, NYC, Mercury, BS, 6½"	20.00
Plate, NYNH&H, Platinum Blue, BS, 7"	75.00
Plate, Pullman, Indian Tree, 7½"	79.00
Plate, Pullman, Indian Tree, 9"	110.00
Plate, SAL, Palm Beach, 6½"	55.00
Plate, SL&SF, Denmark, 9"	50.00
Plate, SP, Harriman, TL, 10½"	135.00
Plate, SP, Prairie-Mountain Wildflowers, 5½"	35.00
Plate, SP, Prairie-Mountain Wildflowers, 9½"	85.00
Plate, SP, Sunset, BS, 7¼"	110.00
Plate, UP, Challenger, 9½"	45.00
Plate, UP, Columbine, 7½"	120.00
Plate, UP, Desert Flower, 10½"	75.00
Plate, UP, Historical, BS, 7¼"	85.00
Plate, UP, Winged Streamliner, 6½"	30.00
Plate, UP, Zion, 8"	190.00
Platter, ACL, Flora of the South, BS, 9½ x6½"	200.00
Platter, ATSF, Black Chain, BS, 7x5½"	95.00
Platter, ATSF, California Poppy, 10½ x7"	75.00
Platter, B&O, Capitol, 8x5½"	65.00
Platter, C&NW, Depot Ornaments, 11½ x8"	55.00
Platter, CB&Q, Violets & Daisies, BS, 12x8½"	110.00
Platter, Centenary, BS, 13x9½"	310.00
Platter, CMStP&P, Galatea, 10x7"	100.00
Platter, CMStP&P, Peacock, 8x6"	45.00
Platter, CMStP&P, Traveler, 8x6"	45.00
Platter, D&H, Canterbury, 8½ x5½"	145.00
Platter, GN, Mountain & Flowers, BS, 9x7"	75.00
Platter, KCS, Roxbury, 11x9¼"	35.00
Platter, L&N, Regent, 8x5½"	100.00
Platter, NP, Garnet, 10½x7"	300.00
Platter, NYC, DeWitt Clinton, BS, 9½ x6½"	45.00
Platter, NYC, Hyde Park, BS, 11x7"	110.00
Platter, PRR, Keystone, 11x8"	100.00
Platter, PRR, Purple Laurel, BS, 9x6"	45.00
Platter, Pullman, Calumet, 8x5½"	85.00
Platter, Pullman, Indian Tree, 10½x7"	90.00
Platter, SOO, Logan, BS, 8x5½"	40.00
Platter, SP, Harriman Blue, TL, 10x7"	175.00
Platter, SP, Prairie-Mountain Wildflowers, BS, 12½x8"	150.00
Platter, SP, Sunset, 12x8½"	185.00
Platter, UP, Blue & Gold, 8½x6"	30.00
Platter, UP, Desert Flower, BS, 11x9"	75.00

Platter, UP, Harriman Blue, 12½x9" **45.00**
Platter, UP, Winged Streamliner, 8x6½" **38.00**
Relish, B&O, Capitol, 11¾x5½" **110.00**
Relish, B&O, Centenary, BS, 11½x5½" **185.00**
Relish, CMStP&P, Galatea, 7x3½" **72.00**
Relish, CMStP&P, Traveler, 9½x4½" **42.00**
Relish, N&W, Yellowbird, 9½x4½" **72.00**
Relish, NP, Monad, 7½x3½" **225.00**
Relish, NYC, DePew, 10x5½" **150.00**
Relish, NYC, DeWitt Clinton, BS, 9x4½" **68.00**
Relish, PRR, Keystone, 12x6" **135.00**
Relish, SRR, Piedmont, BS, 7x3½" **21.00**
Relish, UP, Blue & Gold, 10½ x5" **28.00**
Relish, UP, Historical, BS, 7½ x3½" **200.00**
Sherbet, ATSF, California Poppy **75.00**
Sherbet, CN, Bonaventure, BS **55.00**
Sherbet, UP, Winged Streamliner.......................................**48.00**
Sugar bowl, CMStP&P, Galatea, w/lid **165.00**
Teapot, ATSF, California Poppy..**95.00**
Teapot, CRI&P, LaSalle, BS...**235.00**
Teapot, UP, Winged Streamliner **135.00**
Toothpick holder, MKT, Katy Ornaments **75.00**

Glassware

Ash tray, Erie in bl & wht w/in dmn logo, 3½" **15.00**
Ash tray, N&W, gr w/red logo, 4¼" dia **13.50**
Bottle, milk; MP, buzz saw logo, ½-pt **14.00**
Cordial, AT&SF, script logo **15.00**
Cruet, GN, older frosted goat logo....................................**150.00**
Shot glass, UP, modern shield, frosted, 1½-oz, NM **8.00**
Tumbler, ACL, purple logo **4.00**
Tumbler, Burlington Rte, 4½" **4.00**
Tumbler, C&O, bl Chessie cat logo, 4½" **5.00**
Tumbler, Long Island, train & track in tunnel, 3¼" **8.00**
Tumbler, MP, eagle logo, 4¼" **8.00**
Tumbler, Santa Fe, bl cross logo, 4½" **4.00**
Wine, IC, dmn logo, stemmed...**17.50**

Lamps

Caboose bunk, UP, steel/brass, pebbled top globe **38.00**
Inspector's, Star Headlight & Lantern Co, ornate, NM **58.00**
Semaphore, GN, Adlake, oil, clear lens, w/fuel pot, EX **135.00**
Semaphore, UP, Adlake, aqua lens, cylindrical, EX **75.00**
Switch, Adlake, red/wht lenses, unissued, M.....................**115.00**
Switch, BR, Adlake Non-Sweating, 2 red/2 gr lenses, TM ...**130.00**
Switch, C&O, Handlan, snow hoods, glass lenses, rstr **125.00**
Switch, PRR, Adlake, SM PRR Keystone, 1909, EX **150.00**
Switch, WRR, cast steel, all glass lenses, electric, EX.........**70.00**

Lanterns

B&O, Adlake, Capitol Dome logo globe, Pat 1913, EX.......**115.00**
BR, Adlake Kero, 1959-P, clear unmk 3¼" globe, EX **48.00**
Buffalo St RY, Adlake Reliable, tall red globe, TM, EX **95.00**
C&A, Adlake Reliable, clear etched tall globe, TM, EX **145.00**
CCC&StL, Handlan, insert font, clear Corning globe, EX.....**65.00**
CTA, Adlake Kero, red unmk globe, dtd 2-37, EX.............**35.00**
HV RY, Keystone, ST wire base, mk red cast globe, EX.....**150.00**
Interstate, Adlake Kero, red unmk globe, dtd 1936 ....**65.00**
KCS, Adlake Reliable, amber mk globe, bell bottom, EX **145.00**
KCS RY, Adlake Kero, short clear mk globe, M.................**40.00**
L&N, Armspear, tall clear mk globe, dtd 1895, TM, complete....**145.00**

LS&MS, Adlake Reliable, tall clear mk globe, complete, VG **115.00**
MC, Armspear, clear mk globe, Pat 1889, VG **125.00**
N&W, Adlake Kero, short amber globe, dtd 1936, NM **48.00**
NYC, Handlan, short red mk globe, G **35.00**
NYNH&H, Adlake 1913 Reliable, red Dietz unmk globe, EX.......**65.00**
NYO&W, Adlake 1913 Reliable, mk 6" globe, bell bottom **175.00**
Pere Marquette, Adlake Reliable, tall clear mk globe, M....**175.00**
PRR, Adams, amber mk globe, Pat 1897, EX **165.00**
Rock Island, brakeman's, clear mk 3½" globe, EX **32.00**
Santa Fe, Adlake, pot insert, tall clear mk globe, Pat 1895.........**115.00**
StL&SW, short clear mk globe, complete, rpt **35.00**
T&OC, Adlake 1913 Reliable, mk globe, bell bottom, EX **195.00**
TTRR, Adlake 1923 Reliable, tall red mk globe, single guard **135.00**

Linens

Blanket, CA Zephyr, brn w/logo, sm rpr **65.00**
Blanket, NP, cinnamon & tan, private car, EX **150.00**
Blanket, NP, lt tan w/brn letters, North Star wool, EX.......**150.00**
Blanket, Pullman, interwoven stars, EX.............................**65.00**
Headrest cover, Denver Zephyr, interwoven logo, 15x18" **20.00**
Headrest cover, RI, Golden State Rte, orange letters..........**17.50**
Headrest cover, SR, brn w/gr circle logo, button-down **15.00**
Headrest cover, UP, yel w/red Streamliner logo, button-down **17.50**
Napkin, Burlington Rte, wht-on-wht logo, 20x20" **8.00**
Napkin, GN, old logo, 20" sq, NM....................................**14.00**
Napkin, GN, wht-on-wht leaf design, gr script, 20x20" **8.00**
Napkin, IC, interwoven logo in center, 20x20", NM **15.00**
Napkin, NP, wht-on-wht leaf design, 20x20", EX **12.00**
Napkin, NRPC, tan, 18x18", M...**5.00**
Napkin, Rio Grande, wht w/wht embr script logo, EX **6.00**
Napkin, Santa Fe, wht-on-wht interwoven logo, 15x15" **8.00**
Napkin, Santa Fe, wht-on-wht leaf motif, 18x20" **10.00**
Napkin, SP, Forty Niner, wht-on-wht floral, 21x21", NM **15.00**
Napkin, UP, wht-on-wht, sewn logo, 18x18" **8.00**
Napkin, UP, yel w/interwoven Winged Streamliner logo, 16x18".. **7.50**
Pillowcase, Amtrax, stamped letters, NM **4.00**
Pillowcase, CA Zephyr, stamped logo, regular sz, EX.........**5.00**
Sheet, BN, stamped gr letters, twin sz **8.00**
Sheet, D&RG, sleeping car, w/logo, twin sz, EX **14.00**
Sheet, GN, wht, twin sz, NM...**14.00**
Sheet, Pullman, stamped logo, dtd 1924, twin sz, EX **12.50**
Sheet, RG Mainline, wht, stamped logo, twin sz **7.50**
Sheet, UP, stamped shield logo, twin sz, EX **10.00**
Tablecloth, CA Zephyr, wht-on-wht logo, 48" dia **12.00**
Tablecloth, CN, maple leaf logo, 44x48", EX **10.00**
Tablecloth, GN, wht-on-wht center logo, lg **25.00**
Tablecloth, GN, wht-on-wht leaf design, gr script, 44" sq **32.50**
Tablecloth, Santa Fe, wht-on-wht leaf design, 52x60"...........**24.00**
Towel, BN, sewn-on gr letters, 20x22", M **7.50**
Towel, CA Zephyr, red stripe on wht, EX............................**5.00**
Towel, CN, bl stripe on wht, interwoven logo **5.00**
Towel, GN, wht-on-wht Puritan Dundee, red stripe, VG **10.00**
Towel, Pullman, Property of..., wht letters on bl stripe, M **7.50**
Towel, SR, wht letters on gr stripe, EX **8.00**
Towel, UP, bl stripe on wht, interwoven logo **10.00**
Towel, UP, orange stripe on wht, EX **8.00**

Locks

Service, B&S, brass, incised mk, heart shape w/chain............**48.00**
Switch, BT, Bohannon, brass heart shape, 1885, VG **45.00**
Switch, D&RGW, steel, w/mk brass key.............................**27.50**
Switch, IOC, Slaymaker, brass heart shape, no chain, EX **45.00**

Brass Raco signal lock, B&O RR, white metal, $25.00.

Switch, SP, brass, serifs, incised bk panel, 1890, EX 65.00
Switch, VGN, Yale, heart shape, steel hasp dtd 1903 ....95.00

Silverplate

Bowl, NP, Yellowstone Park logo, BS/TM, 1930, 6½" 75.00
Butter pat, UP, fancy rim, BS, dtd 1917, 3½" dia 27.50
Butter pat, UP, sq, BS, Reed & Barton, 3⅛" 22.50
Cocktail strainer, GN, pierced star design, BS, 3" dia 88.00
Coffeepot, Fred Harvey, Deco style, mushroom finial 70.00
Coffeepot, GN, intertwined logo, SM, dtd 1946, 14-oz................55.00
Coffeepot, NP, Monad logo, old style, Reed & Barton, 7-oz 88.00
Coffeepot, NP, pagoda finial, BS, 20-oz 70.00
Cover, hot food; GN, intertwined logo, BS, 6" 32.00
Cover, shrimp; NP, Yellowstone Park logo, TM, lg, EX 45.00
Crumber, GN, Silhouette, ca 1947, 12" L....................................45.00
Crumber, UP, Westfield, Overland logo, fancy, worn...................65.00
Finger bowl, GN, pierced sides, BS, ca 1946................................24.00
Finger bowl, Rio Grande, basket type 40.00
Fork, pickle; Fred Harvey, Albany 17.50
Fork, RI, Lexington, TM, Meriden, Pat 1905 ....22.50
Holder, menu; GN, Art Deco design, BS, 1948............................70.00
Knife, Fred Harvey, Cromwell, TM.. 7.50
Knife, NP, Embassy, TM, VG 12.00
Knife, Pere Marquette 17.50

Syrup pitcher and tray, GN, 1963, $125.00.

Mayonnaise holder, UP, w/attached tray, 1947 ....65.00
Plate, hot cake; GN, BS/TM, 6½"...60.00
Sherbet, GN, intertwined logo, BS/SM, ca 1946, 3¼" 36.00

Sherbet, GN, old interwoven medallion, BS, 3¼ " 60.00
Spoon, demitasse; UP, Savoy 14.00
Spoon, Fred Harvey, Priscell, Meriden, M 14.00
Spoon, iced tea; Soo Line, Sussex, Internat'l, TM logo.................24.00
Spoon, serving; NP, Alden TM, VG..14.00
Sugar bowl, Atlantic Coast Line, BS, w/lid.................................90.00
Sugar bowl, B&M, Meriden, BM, w/lid, 6-oz 100.00
Sugar bowl, GN, ball finial, BS/SM, 1948, 8-oz 90.00
Sugar tongs, T&P, TM..32.00
Syrup, CA Zephyr, acorn finial, hinged lid, BS, w/tray 100.00
Teaspoon, CGW, Clarendon, Reed & Barton, TM.......................38.00
Tray, bread; CB&Q, BS, 11¼x5¾"..68.00
Tray, GN, TM, 10x6", EX 65.00
Vase, bud; GN, BS, ca 1947, 7"..75.00

Wax Sealers and Accessories

Adams Express, brass toadstool hdl, rnd matrix, EX 85.00
American Express, Durant IA 75.00
AT&SF, Agent, Gauge OK, tall iron hdl 110.00
KCS, freight station, Joplin, wood hdl..100.00
Public, El Centro CA 25.00
PW&B, toadstool hdl 95.00
Railway Express, Corona CA 45.00
Wells Fargo, Zeeland ND 95.00
Wells Fargo Express, Steele MO, brass 150.00

Miscellaneous

Apron, bartender's, UP, Overland logo in waist, 11x15" 17.50
Ash tray, Pullman, emb logo on tin, 4" dia 5.00
Badge, breast; C&A Special Police, star form, 3½" 85.00
Badge, breast; D&H Police Patrolman, shield, 2¼x2½" 135.00
Badge, hat; Brakeman, silver color, 3" L, M...............................32.00
Badge, hat; CB&Q Brakeman, pk enamel on silver, 4" L, G........55.00
Badge, hat; Rio Grande Conductor, brass, mc logo, 2x4", M 65.00
Badge, hat; Santa Fe Brakeman, bl logo on silver, VG 55.00
Badge, hat; Santa Fe Porter, bl logo on silver, 3½x1½", M 55.00
Badge, Milwaukee Waiter, NP pin-bk, 1½x1¾" 17.50
Blotter, MP, Missourian, 4-digit phone number, 4x9", EX 7.50
Blotter, NP, potato shape, 4x8½" 15.00
Book, Book of Rules, Delaware & Hudson RR, 1914, EX 15.00
Book, conductor's train record; Santa Fe, 4x8", VG 2.50
Book, dining car report; WP, lists inventory, 21-pg, 5x9" 5.00
Book, freight conductor's car report; TX Zephyr, 4x12", EX 5.00
Book, MP, lists stations, 1978, 114-pg, 4x6½", NM 4.00
Book, Rio Grande Western, Crossing Rockies, 1896, 42-pg...........35.00
Book, rule; RI, Rules of Operations Dept, blk cover, 1904 .... 6.00
Book, rule; UP, Time Service, 1946, EX 4.00
Box, cigar; PRR, wood, streamliner on curve, 2x9¼x6" 22.50
Brochure, Pullman, Here's What You Get..., 1950, 3x5" 4.00
Brochure, SP, Great Salt Lake Cutoff, 1920, 4x6", 29-pg............17.50
Builder's plate, AM Locomotive Co, brass, 1912, 7x14" 165.00
Calendar, C&O, Chessie, 1960, 10x12½", VG 15.00
Calendar, desk; MKT, slanted wood base, plastic top, 1972 .... 5.00
Calendar, UP, May, 1974, NM.. 4.00
Calender, perpetual; Mopac, diesel engine pictured, M 150.00
Cap, KCS Brakeman, pillbox style, twill top, VG 65.00
Cap, Milwaukee, pillbox style, Carlson, VG................................65.00
Card, breakfast call; C&O, heavy stock, unused............................ 1.00
Coaster, Santa Fe, bl plastic, gold logo, set of 4 .... 4.00
Cookbook, Meals by Fred Harvey, soft cover, 63-pg, EX 8.00
Cuff protector, B&O, Chessie System, Safety First, pr 5.00
Cuspidor, Pullman, nickeled brass, BS, 7x3"................................75.00

Hat, child's, NP, heavy paper, gray & wht, lg 4" logo, M 2.50
Key, caboose; ACL, Adlake, long solid bbl, EX 17.50
Key, oil box; UP, Bohannan, ringed shank, EX 16.00
Key, switch; B&O, JHW Climax Co, Newark NJ 20.00
Key, switch; Burlington Rte, Adams & Westlake, steel, EX 24.00
Key, switch; CM&StP, Loefelholz & Co, lt wear 22.00
Key, switch; CNS&M, Adlake, lt wear 12.00
Key, switch; NYCS, Adlake 20.00
Key, switch; NYNH&H, steel, EX 10.00
Key, switch; UP, Adlake, NM 15.00
Key, switch; UP, JHW Climax Co, Newark NJ 25.00
Knife, pocket; C&NW, stainless steel, Zippo, EX 10.00
Ladder, berth; Pullman, 4-step, metal top hooks, 55" 55.00
Ledger, accounts payable; 148 filled pgs, 1911, VG 25.00
Letterhead, WP, wht w/Feather River logo, 9x12" sheet 1.00
Luggage tag, Burlington Rte 100th Anniversary 5.00
Magazine, RR Telegrapher, May 1927, EX 4.50
Map, MP, Union RY Industrial...of Memphis, 1935, 32x40", EX .. 10.00
Map, WP System, San Jose to Pit River, 9x15", EX 4.00
Matchbook, T&P, bl, Fast Freight, diesel logo, M 2.00
Medallion, Santa Fe, 2nd Century of Progress, 1868-2068, 1½" 5.00
Menu, B&O, Maple Sugar Excursion, single card, 1966, 6x9" 4.00
Menu, Fred Harvey, Los Angeles Union Station, 1955, 8x11" 12.00
Menu, Pullman, beverages, ca 1915, 3x8" 6.00
Pants, CA Zephyr waiter's, wht w/purple stripe on legs, EX 4.00
Paperweight, PC, silver metal, Metroliner shape, 4½" 7.50
Paperweight, PRR, CI, w/mushroom & button top knob 18.00
Pass, annual; D&RG, scenic line logo, 1936 .... 5.00
Pass, annual; NYC, center logo, 1934, VG 4.00
Pass, annual; UP, emb Overland color logo, 1926 .... 4.50
Pass, monthly; LS&MS employee, 1881, EX 6.00
Pass, N&W, emb blk letters, 1914, VG 10.00
Pass, New England RR, red stamped: Sample, VG 5.00
Pencil, mechanical; C&NW, gr & yel, Redipoint, EX 8.00
Pencil, Railway Express Agency, brn, NM 1.25
Pin, lapel; Burlington Rte Veterans Association, ½" dia 12.50
Place mat, Fred Harvey, paper, map & illus, 11x20", M 3.50
Playing cards, Amtrak, red/wht/bl, single, EX 5.00
Playing cards, BN, gr & wht, dbl, MIB 15.00
Playing cards, C&O, Chessie/Peake, dbl, unopened, M 20.00
Playing cards, CA Zephyr, logo on bl w/silver, 1957, EX 20.00
Playing cards, PC, logo, dbl, EX in box 12.50
Playing cards, Rio Grande, Main Line logo, bridge, M 22.00
Playing cards, Soo Line, fall foliage, single, NM 15.00
Playing cards, UP, shield in right corner, single, EX 12.50
Post card, CM, Glenwood Springs, 1905, EX 4.00
Post card, Milwaukee, mc scenes, folding, early, EX 7.50
Post card, NP, blk/wht of Minnetonka at '49 Chicago Fair, M 2.00
Poster, UP, WWII, Giving Them a Helping Hand, 1-sheet, EX ... 20.00
Rack, baggage; brass, horizontal rods w/coat hooks, 36" 95.00
Receipt, Boston, Hartford & Erie, 1860x, 3x7" 5.00
Ruler, KCS, Port Arthur Rte, wood, bk: map, 1903, 15" 38.00
Score pad, GN, bl, goat logo, 4x6", NM 2.00
Sheet music, I've Been Working..., Calumet Music, 1935, EX 10.00
Stamper, Govt Freight US 10.00
Stamper, ST&SFCL, Orange CA, agent dates at edge 10.00
Stationery, B&O, Chessie, 1 full packet, NM 4.00
Stool, Canadian Nat'l, metal, pnt logo, 14x14", VG 65.00
Stool, Chessie, C&O emb on side, 13x16", EX 195.00
Stool, MP, silver pnt, Morton nameplate, older sz, 9½x14" 150.00
Stool, Wabash, metal w/rubber ft, Morton nameplate, 16x14" 185.00
Tag, baggage; WP, heavy stock, unused, 2½x5" 1.00
Ticket punch, PRR, L punch mk, Pat Dec 23, 1884 .... 25.00
Timetable, MP, buzz saw logo, red & bl, 1966 .... 3.50

Timetable, Oregon Short Line, blk & wht, 1919, EX 17.50
Timetable, public; T&P, pk cover, 1936 .... 8.00
Timetable, Santa Fe, Indian scenes, bl & wht, 1923 .... 6.00
Torch, Soo Line, teapot style, 9" hdl, 4½" 22.00
Whistle, steam locomotive; 4-chime, brass chambers 150.00
Wrench, monkey; GN, metal, TRIMO, 11" 17.50

Razors

As straight razors gain in popularity, prices increase. And with the lure of investment appreciation, the novice or the speculator sometimes find themselves making purchases that later prove to be unwise. It is important to be able to recognize the material of which the handle is made. This has a great bearing on value, and imitations abound. Learn to distinguish between celluloid and genuine ivory. Razors with plain celluloid handles are practically worthless unless the blade carries a desirable trademark. Those with decorations of scrollwork, leaves and vines, or decorative metal on each end fall into the $8 to $12 price range. Even plain ivory-handled razors are not especially valuable unless the blade is well marked and from a good manufacturer. On a more positive note, celluloid-handled razors with designs such as castles, windmills, nudes, deer, alligators, automobiles, horses, cowboys, peacocks, and various kinds of birds, etc., are very desirable — some more than others — and are usually worth from $25 to $50 to collectors. Those with a figural handle such as a fish, shotgun, eagle, or a barber pole might be worth in excess of $100 for an especially nice example. Ivory, on the other hand, is rarely found; if the carvings are well done, clean, undamaged specimens should start at about $100 and escalate according to the intricacy of the design.

Buffalo horn is sometimes mistakenly called bone. It is usually black, translucent tan, or gray. Though plain handles are worth very little, the early heat-molded examples with a motif such as mentioned above often sell for more than $100. In the same range are mother-of-pearl and stag (deer horn) handles; very elaborate designs go even higher, but watch for imitations.

There is one imitation, however, that is highly desirable. That is jigged bone made to look like stag. This material is rough textured and dyed a handsome tan or brown; usually examples with these handles sell in the $40 to $75 range. Razors with wooden handles are very rare, but even those from the 1800s are worth only about $35, since they are usually very plain. 20th-century examples are only valued at around $15. Don't be fooled by buffalo horn colored in imitation of tortoise — and you'll find celluloid imitations, too. Genuine tortoise handles are worth from $25 to $100 depending on age, condition, and workmanship. Sterling razors are valued at $75 and up, but make sure they are marked 'sterling.' Even if you were to mistake aluminum for silver, those with relief-cast designs are worth $50 to $75 — only $20 or so if the design is incised.

Corn razors were made to pare troublesome corns on the feet. They are a bit smaller and if plain worth a little more than full-size razors. Fancy examples are generally not worth as much as their full-size couterparts.

The older blades are wedge-shaped (flat-sided) in cross-section; hollow-ground blades (made after 1880) are concave. Generally speaking, those etched with words are only worth a little more than a plain, common blade. Try to find those with people, places, and things — the more famous, the better.

Key:
cell — celluloid   gw — gold washed
bd — blade

A Arnold 614 Piccadilly, etched bd: ...Surgical...Lancet 25.00

Alison's Celebrated, crude wood hdl, wedge bd, 1850s, VG **12.00**
Assy Shareen MIG, etched bd: Liberty Bell, cell hdl: lady **35.00**
Blue Steel Special, blk faux stag hdl, EX **20.00**
Case Bros Tested XX, faux ivory hdl, rpl tang, EX **25.00**
Cast Steel Warranted, pressed horn hdl: Sheaf Works, 1815, EX .**40.00**
Challenge...Conn, faux ivory hdl: beads & scrolls, NM **27.50**
Columbia Cutlery, blk cell hdl w/MOP inlay, VG **30.00**
Damascus, etched bd: 2 snakes, aluminum hdl, mk tang **75.00**
E Rhodes, wedge bd: steeplechase scene, horn hdl, 1810, NM.......**65.00**
Ern, faux ivory gunstock hdl, hollow ground bd, NM......................**35.00**
Ern, faux ivory hdl: gr flower & ribbon, etched bd, EX **40.00**
Flack Demon, ivory hdl w/inlaid German silver devil, EX **30.00**
Frederick Reynolds Sheffield, mottled horn hdl, EX **12.50**
G Wostenholm, mottled horn hdl, wedge bd, ca 1815, EX **20.00**
Genco, faux ivory hdl: nude on lily pad, clean bd, EX **35.00**
Geneva Cutlery, blk cell hdl, etched bd: Improved Eagle, EX **20.00**
Gilbert Brothers Eclipse, German silver pin covers, 1830s **25.00**
Griffon, MOP tang, ivory hdl, M bd, NM.....................................**35.00**
H Boker & Co, etched bd: Ea Bd Fully Warranted..., EX **30.00**
H Hobson Warranted, bone hdl w/German silver inlay, 1860s **25.00**

Celluloid handles, top, with horses and riders etched on blade: $65.00; bottom, fancy scrollwork, Clauss etched on blade: $30.00.

J Elliot Silver Steel, horn hdl, wedge bd w/thumb grip, EX............**20.00**
Jackson Fremont, faux ivory hdl w/scrolled ends, EX **25.00**
Johan Engstrom Eskilstuna, Sweden, framebk, etch bd: JE 1874....**25.00**
John Bert, cell hdl: stag horn & leaf, etched bd: Wizard, EX **30.00**
Joseph Rogers & Sons Sheffield, mottled horn hdl, etched bd.......**15.00**
Jr Torrey, Worcester MA, blk celluloid hdl, EX **20.00**
JR Torrey..., etch bd: Our Beauty, faux ivory hdl, EX **20.00**
Landers, Frary, & Clark Universal, framebk, faux ivory hdl...........**25.00**
Levering, NY, faux ivory hdl, etched advertising on bd, EX...........**40.00**
Manhattan Cutlery Sheffield, horn hdl w/gold: Old English, EX ..**27.50**
Parex Safety Corn Knife, gutta percha hdl, guard on bd, EX.........**25.00**
Premier 510 on tang, faux tortoise shell w/German inlay................**25.00**
Rashid Bohakel on tang, tan cell hdl w/German silver inlay..........**40.00**
Refined Steel etched on bd, mottled horn hdl, ca 1820, EX **20.00**
Robeson Shuredge, yel cell hdl: fishscale, cell tang, EX **40.00**
Schermack, rnd head, pearl hdl, w/blades & booklet, EX...............**30.00**
SH Zacour & Bros, cell hdl: clipper & flag, etched bd, EX **115.00**
Shake Sharp Razor, blk cell hdl, NM in box...................................**25.00**
Simplified Schick Automatic Magazine, gold-plated, NM in box..**25.00**
Star Safety, gutta percha hdl, corn knife, EX **25.00**
Taylor Bros Hamilton Canada, faux ivory hdl w/silver caps **28.00**
Unmk, hdl: chief w/tomahawk at head, tang: peace pipe, EX **65.00**
Wade & Butcher, blk horn hdl, rpl pin, barber's style **25.00**
Wade & Butcher, horn hdl, etched bd: Clean Shaver, 1870s **40.00**
Wadsword XLNT, faux ivory hdl: nude on lily pad, NM...............**95.00**
Warner Hudnut Reelshave, red cell hdl, ribbon cartridge..............**25.00**

Weck Safety, faux ivory hdl, Pat July 27 '09, corn razor.................**35.00**
Weinhaus-Cerf, faux ivory hdl: nude w/flowers, EX bd **50.00**
Whitte's A-1 Corn Razor on etched bd, EX....................................**36.00**
Wm Greaves & Sons Sheaf . . . Sheffield, horn hdl, 1820s, VG **20.00**
Wm Greaves Warranted, pressed horn hdl: fox hunt, 1810s, EX.**295.00**

Reamers

Reamers have been made in hundreds of styles and colors and by as many manufacturers. Their purpose is to extract the juices from lemons, oranges, and grapefruits. The largest producer of glass reamers was McKee, who pressed their products from many types of glass — custard; delphite and Chalaine blue; opaque white; Skokie green; black; caramel and white opalescent; Seville yellow; and transparent pink, green, and clear. Among these, the black and the caramel opalescents are the most valuable.

The Fry Glass Company also made reamers that are today very collectible. The Hazel Atlas Crisscross orange reamer in pink often brings in excess of $225; the same in blue, $200. Hocking produced a light blue orange reamer and, in the same soft hue, a two-piece reamer and measuring cup combination. Both are considered rare and very valuable with currently-quoted estimates at $400 and up for the former and $500 and up for the latter. In addition to the colors mentioned, red glass examples — transparent or slag — are rare and costly.

Among the most valuable ceramic reamers are those made by American potteries. The Spongeband reamer by Red Wing is valued in excess of $350; Coorsite reamers with gold or silver trim are worth $200 and up. Figurals are popular — Mickey Mouse and John Bull may bring $300 to $400. Others range from $45 to $150. Fine china one- and two-piece reamers are also very desirable and command very respectable prices.

A word about reproductions: A series of limited edition reamers is being made by Edna Barnes of Uniontown, Ohio. These are all marked with a 'B' in a circle. Other repoductions have been made from old molds. The most important of these are: Anchor Hocking 2-piece 2-cup measure and top, Gillespie 1-cup measure with reamer top, Westmoreland N-365 with flattened handle, Westmoreland 4-cup measure embossed with orange and lemons, Duboe, Easley's diamonds 1-piece, and spiral 1-piece #202.

Our advisor for this category is Dee Long; she is listed in the Directory under Illinois. For more information concerning reamers and reproductions, contact our advisor or the National Reamer Collectors Association (see Clubs, Newsletters, and Catalogs). Be sure to include SASE when requesting information.

Reference numbers in the ceramic reamer listings correspond with *200 Years of Reamers* by Mary Walker, available at your local library or from the National Reamer Collectors Association.

Ceramic

Clown figural, purple/bl/wht, C-65, 6" **35.00**
Pail w/hdl form, tan & yel, Japan, P-73, 7¾" **60.00**
Pear figural, yel w/wht florals, Japan, L-40, 4¾"............................**35.00**
Pitcher form, mc floral w/blk trim, Germany, E-27, 3½" **48.00**
Pitcher form, mc florals, Austria, E-42, 3¼" **45.00**
Pitcher form, purple flowers, bl trim, loop hdl, D-37 ....**25.00**
Pitcher form, rust leaves, navy trim, D-55, 3½" **35.00**
Pitcher form, wht, France, D-85, recent, 3¼" **10.00**
Pitcher form, yel fruit w/tan & gr, E-54, 3¼" **55.00**

Glass

Cambridge, crystal, tab hdl...**14.00**

Clambroth, wht, boat-shaped, ribbed, loop hdl	170.00
Federal, crystal, horizontal hdl	12.00
Federal, gr, panelled, loop hdl	24.00
Federal, gr, pointed cone, tab hdl	14.00
Federal, gr, ribbed, seed dam, tab hdl	13.00
Federal, pk, ribbed, loop hdl	23.00
Fleur-de-Lis, red/orange slag, flattened loop hdl	375.00
Hazel Atlas, gr, pitcher form, stippled	32.00
Hazel Atlas, pk, pitcher & reamer	115.00
Hazel Atlas, wht w/gr leaves, yel trim, tab hdl	32.00
Hazel Atlas, wht w/red trim, pitcher form, 4-cup	34.00
Hazel Atlas Crisscross, crystal, loop hdl	6.00
Hazel Atlas Crisscross, pk, tab hdl	250.00
Hocking, fired-on blk, tab hdl	20.00
Hocking, gr, pitcher form, 16-oz	21.00
Jeannette, crystal, loop hdl, lg	9.00
Jeannette, gr, tab hdl	14.00
Jeannette, lt jadite, pitcher & reamer, 2-cup	25.00
Jenkins, gr, flattened loop hdl, child's sz	105.00
McKee, gr, unemb, flattened loop hdl	225.00
McKee, olive-gr opaque, emb SUNKIST	550.00
McKee, pk, emb SUNKIST, flattened loop hdl	45.00
Paden City, gr, pitcher form	225.00
Paden City, Party Line, blk, pitcher form	475.00
Sunkist, jadite, loop hdl	30.00
Sunkist, Skokie gr, pointed cone, loop hdl	53.00
US Glass, gr, slick hdl	32.00
US Glass, Handy Andy, gr	45.00
US Glass, pk, pitcher & reamer, 3-pc	235.00
US Glass, pk, tub & reamer	175.00

Valencia, pink, $175.00.

Valencia, wht, emb letters, flattened loop hdl	95.00
Westmoreland, frosted crystal, child's sz	55.00
Westmoreland, frosted pk, tab hdl, baby's sz	115.00
Westmoreland, gr, pitcher form, emb orange/lemon, 2-pc	135.00

Miscellaneous

Cast aluminum, skillet shape	15.00
Silverplate, PM-24, 2-pc	125.00
Sterling, fancy, 1-pc	200.00
Sunkist Junior, electrical	25.00

Records

Records of interest to collectors are generally not the million-sell-ing hits by 'superstars.' Very few records by Bing Crosby, for example, are of any more than nominal value, and those that are valuable usually don't even have his name on the label! Collectors today are most interested in records that were made in limited quantities, early works of a performer who later became famous, and those issued in special series or aimed at a limited market. Because by late 1991 most all of the major manufacturers will have completely stopped production of records, record collecting may well become the sleeper investment of the '90s. Rare records have already doubled and tripled in value since 1989.

Condition plays a critical factor in establishing values for records. In the listings that follow, values in these subcategories: LPs, EPs, and 45s are for records in mint condition. LPs must be in their original jackets; EPs (each has four songs, play at 45 rpm) are priced with their covers which must be free of defects such as writing, stickers, etc.; values for 45s do not include any picture sleeves that may accompany the record. Prices for records in all other subcategories are suggested for examples in excellent condition — the record has been played but displays no obvious defects and retains some of the original shine. If you plan to sell your records, don't expect a dealer to pay retail prices, and expect him to critically inspect them before he makes you an offer; it is very difficult for a novice with an untrained eye to recognize the faults that detract from a record's value. Right now, the best collectibles are Rock and Roll from the '50s, early Rhythm and Blues, and early Country.

Our advisor for this category is L.R. Docks, author of *American Premium Record Guide,* which lists 50,000 records by over 6,000 artists. Some of our listings were provided by Mark Phillips, associate editor for the international record collectors' magazine, *DISCoveries,* part-owner of Sunrise Records in Beaumont, Texas, and a member of the board of advisors for the *Rockin' Records* price guide for used and collectible records. You will find both listed in the Directory under Texas.

Key:
Bru — Brunswick   Para — Paramount
Ch — Champion   Orch — Orchestra
Col — Columbia   Vi — Victor
Edi — Edison   Vo — Vocalion

Blues, Rhythm and Blues, Rock 'N Roll, Rockabilly

Amy, Curtis; Sleepin' Blues, Gold Star 618, 78 rpm	25.00
Armstrong, May; Joe Boy Blues, Vo 1129, 78 rpm	35.00
Bill & Slim, Papa's Gettin' Hot, Ch 16015, 78 rpm	75.00
Brown, Freddie; Whip to a Jelly, Para 12910, 78 rpm	75.00
Clarke, Jim; Fat Fanny Stomp, Vo 1536, 78 rpm	100.00
Cole, Kid; Sixth Street Moon, Vo 1186, 78 rpm	50.00
Crawford, James; Flood & Thunder, Gennett 6536, 78 rpm	50.00
Davis, Genevieve; I've Got Something, Vi 20648, 78 rpm	75.00
Davis, Walter; Blue Seas Blues, Vi 23250, 78 rpm	100.00
Delaney, Tom; Georgia Stockade Blues, Col 14082-D, 78 rpm	12.00
Erby, John; Lonesome Jimmy Blues, Col 14151-D, 78 rpm	20.00
Five Breezes, Sweet Louise, Bluebird 8590, 78 rpm	15.00
Foster, Rudy; Corn Trimmer Blues, Para 12981, 78 rpm	175.00
Franklin, Buck; Crooked World Blues, Vi 23310, 78 rpm	175.00
Glen, Emery; Two Ways to Texas, Col 14283-D, 78 rpm	40.00
Harlem Stars, All Right Baby, E&W 100, 78 rpm	15.00
Hicks, Edna; Hard Luck Blues, Para 12023, 78 rpm	20.00
Jammin' Jim, Shake Boogie, Savoy 1106, 78 rpm	10.00
Johnson, Fannie; Slow Up Papa, Cameo 1144, 78 rpm	15.00
Kansas Katie, Deep Sea Diver, Bluebird 8944, 78 rpm	12.00
Kyle, Charlie; Kyle's Worried Blues, Vi 21707, 78 rpm	100.00
Lillie Mae, Mama Don't Want It, Okeh 8920, 78 rpm	40.00
Louisiana Johnny, Policy Blues, Vo 02980, 78 rpm	20.00
Miles, Josie; Sweet Man Joe, Edi 51476, 78 rpm	50.00

Moore, Alice; Black & Evil Blues, Para 12819, 78 rpm.................100.00
Nelson, Red; Gambling Man, Decca 7256, 78 rpm 15.00
Nixon, Elmore; Playboy Blues, Mercury 70061, 45 rpm 7.00
Noble, Georgia; New Milk Cow Blues, Vo 02905, 78 rpm...........150.00
Page, Star; Georgia Blues, Para 12684, 78 rpm 50.00
Paul, Ruby; Red Letter Blues, Para 12592, 78 rpm......................80.00
Poor Boy Lofton, Poor Boy Blues, Decca 7010, 78 rpm...............75.00
Poor Jab, Poor Jab Blues, Ch 16483, 78 rpm............................200.00
Quattlebaum, Doug; Lizzie Lou, Gotham 519, 45 rpm 20.00
Quillan, Rufus & Ben; Keep It Clean, Col 14560-D, 78 rpm.........25.00
Richard, Seth; Lonely Seth Blues, Col 14325-D, 78 rpm 35.00
Ridley, Ethel; Get It Fixed, Ajax 17126, 78 rpm 25.00
Rose, Lucy; Papa You're Too Slow, Ch 15471, 78 rpm.................50.00
Sanders, Bessie; It Must Be Hard, Ch 15101, 78 rpm 30.00
Sluefoot Joe, House Top Blues, QRS 7080, 78 rpm.....................150.00
Smith, Ruby; Back Water Blues, Vo 04903, 78 rpm.....................15.00
Stone, Joe; Back Door Blues, Bluebird 5169, 78 rpm...................75.00
Strange, Jimmy; No Limit Blues, Vi 23317, 78 rpm 130.00
Tate, Rose; My Man Left Me Blues, Ch 15302, 78 rpm 80.00
Teardrops, Come Back to Me, Sampson 634, 78 rpm....................20.00
Tom, Georgia; Levee Bound Love, Decca 7362, 78 rpm 8.00
Two of Spades, Meddlin' w/the Blues, Col 14072-D, 78 rpm.........20.00
Umbrian Glee Club, Swing Along, Vo 1012, 78 rpm.....................12.00
Uncle Skipper, Cutting My ABCs, Decca 7353, 78 rpm.................20.00
Vigal, John; Fowler Twist, Blk Swan 14115, 78 rpm 20.00
Virgial, Otto; Bad Notion Blues, Bluebird 6213, 78 rpm..............25.00
Walker, William; I'll Remember You, Gennett 7100, 78 rpm.........20.00
Walton, Lorraine; If You're a Viper, Vo 03989, 78 rpm 12.00
Wilson & Reed, France Blues, Ch 15264, 78 rpm 75.00
Yas Yas Girl, Worried Heat Blues, Okeh 05870, 78 rpm 8.00

Country and Western

Armstrong & Ashley, No More Dying, Para 3291, 78 rpm 25.00
Autry, Gene; Bear Cat Papa, Vi 23530, 78 rpm 100.00
Britton, Maynard; Drunkard's Hell, Ch 16543, 78 rpm................50.00
Burke Brothers, Lonesome & Lonely, Vi 40294, 78 rpm...............12.00
Butcher, Dwight; Lonesome Cowboy, Vi 23772, 78 rpm...............50.00
Cook, Herb; Arkansas Sweetheart, Col 15729-D, 78 rpm............20.00
Cox, Richard; Sleeping Lulu, Ch 16475, 78 rpm 40.00
Denmon, Morgan; Naomi Wise, Okeh 45075, 78 rpm..................10.00
Elm City Quartet, Tree Song, Ch 16827, 78 rpm 10.00
Evans, John B; Mother's Grave, Supertone 2051, 78 rpm 10.00
Ford & Grace, Kiss Me Cindy, Okeh 45157, 78 rpm....................10.00
Freeman & Ashcraft, Alabama Rag, Col 15442-D, 78 rpm............30.00
Gass, Aubrey; KC Boogie, Capitol 1427, 78 rpm 8.00
Giggers, Grinnell; Duck Shoes Rag, Vi 23511, 78 rpm.................35.00
Graves & Tanner, Bum's Rush, Vo 5342, 78 rpm.........................12.00
Hail, Ewen; Cowboy's Lament, Vo 5146, 78 rpm......................... 8.00
Hinton, WA; Leather Breeches, Vi 23555, 78 rpm.......................50.00
Homonica Jim, Prisoner's Radio, Superior 2789, 78 rpm 20.00
Irby, Jerry; Almost Every Time, Cireco 101, 78 rpm..................... 7.00
Irwin, Harvey; Blind Child, Okeh 45014, 78 rpm........................ 8.00
Isabell, Wallie & Tex; Sugar Cain Gal, Eddie's 1219, 78 rpm........ 8.00
Jennings Bros, Cripple Creek, Ch 15148, 78 rpm........................ 8.00
Kentucky Girls, Old & Only in the Way, Col 15364-D, 78 rpm ...10.00
Kincaid, Bradley; Ain't We Crazy, Decca 5025, 78 rpm............... 8.00
Larkan/Larkin, Bob; Kansas City Reel, Okeh 45205, 78 rpm.........20.00
Locke, Rusty; Milk Cow Blues, TNT 1012, 78 rpm...................... 8.00
Lunsford, Ted; Hobo's Return, Ch 16287, 78 rpm.......................30.00
Major, Jack; Tennessee Mountain Blues, Bru 252, 78 rpm............15.00
Moore, Lattie; Juke Joint Johnny, Speed 101, 78 rpm..................10.00
New, Jim; Wreck of Six Wheeler, Timely Tunes 1564, 78 rpm 15.00
Norris, Land; Groundhog, Okeh 40096, 78 rpm...........................12.00

Norris, Lymon; Lonely Trail, Ch 16431, 78 rpm 20.00
Northlanders, Over the Waves, Vo 5274, 78 rpm 10.00
Oak Mountain Four, Medley, Ch 15874, 78 rpm..........................10.00
Owens, EB; Sweet Carlyle, Col 15414-D, 78 rpm.........................15.00
Parker, Charlie; Rabbit Chase, Col 15154-D, 78 rpm....................12.00
Pavey, Phil; Broncho Bustin' Blues, Okeh 45308, 78 rpm.............12.00
Pine Ridge Boys, Convict & the Rose, Bluebird 8360, 78 rpm 8.00
Quadrillers, Drunk Man Blues, Para 3008, 78 rpm......................30.00
Record Boys, Harmonica Jim, Vo 5136, 78 rpm...........................12.00
Reeves, Jim; Teardrops of Regret, Macy's 115, 78 rpm.................50.00
Richards, Fred; Danville Blues, Col 15483-D, 78 rpm..................15.00
Rogers, Roy; When a Cowboy Sings a Song, Vo 04050, 78 rpm 8.00
Rolling Stones, Down by Old Rio Grande, Vi 40316, 78 rpm.......12.00
Sloan & Threadgill, Clover Blossom, Bru 284, 78 rpm.................12.00
Stoneman, Willie; Katy Lee, Gennett 6565, 78 rpm 16.00
Toombs, Jack; 2 Cheaters in Love, Excello 2033, 45 rpm 8.00
Uncle Bud & Plowboys, 5 Cent Cotton, Oriole 8170, 78 rpm....... 8.00
Underwood, Charles; Blk Snake Moan, Ch 16144, 78 rpm...........30.00
Underwood, Marion; Coal Creek March, Gennett 6240, 78 rpm .20.00
Val & Pete, Yodel Blues, Okeh 45224, 78 rpm............................. 8.00
Vest, Billy; Billy's Blue Yodel, Col 15692-D, 78 rpm...................15.00
Walter Family, Too Young To Get Married, Ch 16595, 78 rpm ...40.00
White, Clyde; Beside a Lonely River, Ch 16318, 78 rpm 20.00
Williams, Marc; Roy Bean, Decca 5010, 78 rpm..........................10.00
Wingate, F; Sleep Baby Sleep, Supertone 9121, 78 rpm............... 8.00
Wyoming Cowboy, Utah Carroll, Ch 16724, 78 rpm....................18.00
Yellow Jackets, Heel to Toe Polka, Ch 16070, 78 rpm.................12.00
Yodeling Twins, Mountain Rangers Lullaby, Ch 16723, 78 rpm ...25.00
Young, Clarence; Lonely Village Churchyard, Ch 15550, 78 rpm.15.00
Zack & Glen, Gambler's Lament, Okeh 45212, 78 rpm 7.00

Extended Play

Ace, Johnny; Memorial Album, Duke 80 ....75.00
Ames Brothers, Tammy, RCA 4096 .... 8.00
Annette, Annette, Buena Vista 3301 ....75.00
Beach Boys, Best of the Beach Boys, Capitol 2545 ....25.00
Boone, Pat; Tenderly, Dot 1082 ....10.00
Bowen, Jimmy; Jimmy Bowen, Roulette 1-302 ....100.00
Brewer, Teresa; & Dixieland Band, Coral 81176.........................15.00
Cline, Patsy; Crazy, Decca 2707 ....25.00
Clooney, Rosemary; Whoop-Up, MGM 1651 ....15.00
Cole, Nat King; Unforgettable, Capitol 357 .... 8.00
Connor, Chris; Chris, Bethlehem 114 ....25.00
Crickets, Baby My Heart, Coral 81992 ....100.00
Del-Vikings, Come Go w/Us, Dot 1058 ....150.00
Domino, Fats; I'm Walkin', London 1079 ....45.00
Fireballs, The Fireballs, Top Rank 1000 ....50.00
Fisher, Eddie; This Is Eddie Fisher, RCA 2786 ....20.00
Ford, Frankie; Best of Frankie Ford, Ace 105 ....40.00
Four Aces, Amor, Decca 2324...10.00
Four Freshmen, Lost Love, Capitol 1189 .... 8.00
Four Tunes, The Four Tunes, RCA 586......................................75.00
Gaylords, Tops in Pops, Mercury 4010......................................10.00
Grant, Earl; Just One More Time, Decca 34284 .... 8.00
Haley, Bill; Shake Rattle & Roll, Decca 2168.............................50.00
Hirt, Al; Best of Al Hirt, RCA 3309.. 8.00
Ink Spots, For Sentimental Reasons, Waldorf 173 ....10.00
James, Sonny; You're the Only..., Capitol SXA-2209 ....10.00
Kingston Trio, Last Month of the Year, Capitol 3-1466 ....15.00
Leadbelly, Classics in Jazz, Capitol 2-369..................................50.00
Lee, Brenda; By Request, Decca 74509 ....10.00
Lee, Peggy; That Was Then, Capitol 2388 ....12.00
March, Little Peggy; I Wish I Were a Princess, RCA 3476............50.00

Price, Ray; Ray Price, Columbia 8556..15.00
Robbins, Marty; A White Sport Coat, Columbia 2134 ....45.00
Sinatra, Frank; Only the Lonely, Capitol 1053 ....10.00
4 Knights, Sing, Capitol 4-414..50.00

Jazz, Dance Bands, Personalities

Abrams, Irwin; & Orch, Magnolia, Okeh, 40846, 78 rpm.............10.00
Alabama Jug Band, My Gal Sal, Decca 7000, 78 rpm 12.00
Alabama Serenaders, Alabama Stomp, Ch 15140, 78 rpm 15.00
Arcadian Serenaders, Co-ed, Okeh 40503, 78 rpm......................25.00
Armstrong, Louis; Cuban Pete, Decca 1353 ....8.00
Armstrong, Louis; Dinah, Okeh 8800, 78 rpm................................25.00
Armstrong, Louis; Home, Vo 3125, 78 rpm 8.00
Armstrong, Louis; Honey Do!, Bluebird 7787, 78 rpm 8.00
Armstrong, Louis; Laughin' Louie, Bluebird 5363, 78 rpm.............10.00
Arnheim, Gus; & Orch, Evening, Vi 24061, 78 rpm.......................8.00
Astaire, Fred; Cheek to Cheek, Brunswick 7486, 78 rpm 8.00
Astaire, Fred; They All Laughed, Columbia 3165-D, 78 rpm..........8.00
Atlanta Merrymakers, Sweet Little Sis, Madison 50024, 78 rpm....10.00
Atlanta Syncopators, Step on It, Madison 50009, 78 rpm 12.00
Auburn, Frank; & Orch, Rockin' Chair, Clarion 5273-C 10.00
Austin, Gene; Marie, Decca 1578, 78 rpm....................................8.00
Bailey, William; Squeeze Me, Banner 1563, 78 rpm.....................25.00
Baird, Maynard; & Orch, Sorry, Vo 15834, 78 rpm 100.00
Banks, Billy; & Orch, Scat Song, Vi 24027, 78 rpm 12.00
Barbary Coast Orch, Weary Blues, Personal Record 94-P, 78 rpm ..25.00
Barnet, Charlie; & Orch, Growlin', Bluebird 5816, 78 rpm 8.00
Barnet, Charlie; & Orch, Surrealism, Variety 633, 78 rpm............10.00
Baxter, Phil; & Orch, Honey Child, Vi V-40204, 78 rpm 40.00
Beasley, Irene; Missin' My Pal, Vi 21639, 78 rpm.........................10.00
Beiderbecke, Bix; In a Mist, Okeh 40916, 78 rpm 30.00
Belasco, Leon; & Orch, Jammin', Vo 7863, 78 rpm......................25.00
Berton, Vic; & Orch, Dardanella, Vo 2915, 78 rpm......................15.00
Bestor, Don; & Orch, 42nd Street, Vi 24253, 78 rpm...................10.00
Blythe's Blue Boys, Oriental Man, Ch 15676, 78 rpm..................150.00
Boots & His Buddies, Jealous, Bluebird 6862, 78 rpm..................12.00
Boots & His Buddies, Riffs, Bluebird 6081, 78 rpm......................10.00
Britt, Mart; & Orch, Learning, Vi 22933, 78 rpm 12.00
Broadway Dance Orch, Eliza, Edi 51420, 78 rpm 12.00
Brown, Henry; Blues Stomp, Para 12934, 78 rpm.......................100.00
Brown, Les; & Orch, Lazy River, Decca 1323, 78 rpm 8.00
Brown, Russell; & Orch, Little Sunshine, PNY-34130, 78 rpm 15.00
Bryant, Laura; Dentist Chair Blues, QRS 7055, 78 rpm...............125.00
Buffalodians, Wouldja?, Col 723-D, 78 rpm 10.00
Casa Loma Orch, Overnight, Okeh 41477, 78 rpm 10.00
Cline's Collegians, Peruna, Bru 4162, 78 rpm................................20.00
Connie's Inn Orch, You Rascal You, Crown 3180, 78 rpm 25.00
Cooper, Al; Looney, Decca 7549, 78 rpm 8.00
Corrol, Roy; & Orch, Chances Are, Harmony 1403-H, 78 rpm 15.00
Count Basie & Orch, Louisanna, Col 35448, 78 rpm 7.00
Count Basie & Orch, Pennies From Heaven, Decca 1121, 78 rpm..10.00
Crawford, Jack; & Orch, Beautiful, Ch 15422, 78 rpm..................20.00
Crosby, Bing; Paradise, Bru 6285, 78 rpm 10.00
Crosby, Bing; Star Dust, Bru 6169, 78 rpm 10.00
Crosby, Bing; Temptation, Bru 6695, 78 rpm 8.00
Deppe, Louis; Southland, Gennett 20021, 78 rpm 16.00
Elgar's Creole Orch, Cafe Capers, Vo 15477, 78 rpm...................60.00
Ellington, Duke; It's Glory, Vi 22791, 78 rpm 15.00
Ford & Ford, I'm Three Times Seven, Para 12244, 78 rpm............40.00
Fuller, Bob; Crossword Puzzle Blues, Ajax 17099, 78 rpm.............15.00
Goofus Five, Oh! Mabel, Okeh 40261, 78 rpm 8.00
Grey, Glen; & Orch, Zig-Zag, Decca 1312, 78 rpm.......................8.00
Harvey, Georgia; Castaway, Blk Swan 14119, 78 rpm 15.00

Ideal Serenaders, Dawning, Col 1131-D, 78 rpm 8.00
Ink Spots, Your Feet's Too Big, Vi 24851 ....25.00
Kemp, Hal; & Orch, Brown Sugar, Bru 3486, 78 rpm 8.00
King, Frances; She's Got It, Okeh 40854, 78 rpm 10.00
Lawrence, Sara; Don't Love Me, Oriole 894, 78 rpm 10.00
Lee, Ruth; Maybe Someday, Sunshine 3002, 78 rpm 200.00
Mitchell, Eddie; & Orch, Pleasure Mad, Gennett 5612 ....20.00
Naylor's Seven Aces, Sweet Georgia Brown, Vi 19688, 78 rpm......8.00
Nicholson, Nick; & Band, True Blue, Ch 15699, 78 rpm...............15.00
Pope, Bob; & Orch, Early Bird, Bluebird 6283, 78 rpm................10.00
Preer, Evelyn; Sunday, Banner 1895, 78 rpm...............................12.00
QRS Boys, Wiggle Yo' Toes, QRS 7062, 78 rpm...........................50.00
Questal, Mae; Sweet Betty, Vi 24261, 78 rpm 15.00
Red Caps, Niagara Falls, Vi 23382, 78 rpm 40.00
Schepp, Rex; Russian Rag, Autograph 630, 78 rpm......................20.00
Seven Blue Babies, That's Her Now!, Edi 52495, 78 rpm 20.00
Thomas, Hociel; Fish Tail Dance, Okeh 8222, 78 rpm..................25.00
Thurston, Bud; My Senorita, Ch 15489, 78 rpm..........................50.00
University Sexette, Mean Blues, Lincoln 2168, 78 rpm 8.00
Vagabonds, Ukelele Lady, Gennett 3100, 78 rpm.........................12.00
Vallee, Rudy; & Yankees, Maori, Col 2700-D, 78 rpm..................10.00
Wallace, Trixie; Copenhagen, Claxtonola 40393, 78 rpm 30.00
Woods, Babe; & Pals, Let's Misbehave, Ch 15468, 78 rpm...........20.00
Yale Collegians, Blue Again, Okeh 41474, 78 rpm 20.00
Zutty & Band, Look Over Yonder, Decca 431, 78 rpm 8.00

Long Playing

Adderly, Cannonball; Poll Winners, Riverside RLP 9355 ....20.00
Alabama, Alabama Band, Alabama Records 78901......................350.00
Anka, Paul; My Heart Sings, ABC 296...25.00
Annette, Beach Party, Vista 3316 ....35.00
Badfinger, Straight Up, Apple 33887..150.00
Baker, Chet; Chet Baker Big Band, Pacific Jazz PJ-1229 ....30.00
Baker, Lavern; Saved, Atlantic 8050 ....30.00
Beach Boys, Greatest Hits, Wand WDS-688................................10.00
Beatles, Abby Road, MFSL 023..30.00
Berry, Chuck; Twists, Chess 1465 ....35.00
Big Bopper, Chantilly Lace, Mercury (blk label) 20402 ....200.00
Brennon, Walter; The President, Everest 1123 ....15.00
Brown, James; Cold Sweat, King 1030...25.00
Cannon, Freddy; The Explosive, Swan 502 ....50.00
Casinos, Then You Can Tell, Fraternity 1019 ....25.00
Charles, Ray; Genius of Ray Charles, Imperial 12281 ....30.00
Clark, Petula; Uptown w/Petula Clark, Imperial 12281 ....15.00
Coltrane, John; Lush Life, Prestige 7188......................................20.00
Cooke, Sam; Songs By Sam Cooke, Keen 2001 ....50.00
Crawford, Johnny; Rumors, DelFi 1224 ....25.00
Dinning, Mark; Teen Angel, MGM 3828 ....100.00
Fred, Alan; Rock & Roll Show, Bru 54043....................................75.00
Griffith, Andy; Andy Griffith Show, Capitol 1611........................35.00
Harpo, Slim; Raining in My Heart, Excello 8003..........................150.00
Howlin' Wolf, More Folk Blues, Chess 1512 ....25.00
Isley Brothers, This Old Heart of Mine, Tamla 269 ....20.00
Jade Warrior, Last Autumn Dream, Vertigo 1012 ....25.00
James, Elmore; Blues After Hours, Crown 5168 ....200.00
Jan & Dean, Golden Hits, Liberty 3248 ....15.00
King, BB; Spirituals, Crown 5119 ....20.00
Kinks, Kinks-Size, Reprise 6158..15.00
Liggins, Joe; Honey Dripper, Mercury 60731 ....25.00
Marcels, Blue Moon, Coplix (gold label) 416...............................75.00
March, Little Peggy; I Will Follow Him, RCA Victor 2732 ....100.00
Memphis Slim, In Paris, Battle 96122..30.00
Miller, Ned; From a Jack to a King, Fabor (blk label) 1001...........20.00

Moody Blues, Days of Future Passed, Deram 820006 .... 6.00
Mullican, Moon; Moon Over Mullican, Coral 57235 ....150.00
Nelson, Rick; Garden Party, Decca 75391 ....15.00
Nesmith, Michael; Nevada Fighter, RCA LSP-4497.....................50.00
Noland, Terry; Terry Noland, Brunswick 54041 ....175.00
O'Jays, Back on Top (stereo), Bell, 6014 ....50.00
Olympics, Party Time, Arvee 429 ....75.00
Oswald, Lee Harvey; Portrait in Red, INCA 20.00
Perkins, Carl; Dance Album, Sun 1225 ....300.00
Renay, Diane; Navy Blue, 20th Century 3133 ....30.00
Sam & Dave, Best of Sam & Dave, Atlantic 8218 ....15.00
Stafford, Terry; Suspicion, Crusader 1001 ....30.00
Teddy Bears, Sing, Imperial 7067...250.00
Tymes, Sound of Wonderful Tears, Parkway 7038 ....25.00
Waters, Muddy; Best of Muddy Waters, Chess 1427 ....45.00
Wells, Mary; On Stage, Motown 611...30.00
Willis, Chuck; King of Stroll, Atlantic 8018 ....75.00
Yuro, Timi; Best of..., Liberty LST-7286......................................25.00

45 rpm

Adams, Billy; You Gotta Have a Ducktail, NavVoo 802 ....75.00
Adams, Faith; Johnny Lee, Imperial 5456.....................................30.00
Adams, Jo Jo; Call My Baby, Parrot 788 ....45.00
Adams, Johnny; Closer to You, Ric 976 ....10.00
Admarils, Oh Yes, King 4772 ....75.00
Alimo, Steve; I Want You To Love Me, Marlin 6064...................12.00
Allen, Rex; Knock Knock Rattle, Decca 30651 ....15.00
Andrews, Lee; White Cliffs, Rainbow (yel label) 256...................350.00
Annette, Something Borrowed, Buena Vista 438.........................30.00
Apollos, I Love You Darling, Harvard 803 ....175.00
Bartholomew, Dave; The Monkey, Imperial 5438........................50.00
Bartholomew, Dave; My Ding A Ling, King 4544........................70.00
Beach Boys, Surfin', Candix 331 ....50.00
Bell-Tones, I Love You Darling, Scatt 1610 ....600.00
Big Bill, Little City Woman, Chess 1546.......................................100.00
Big Bopper, Chantilly Lace, D 1006...50.00
Big Walter, Hard-Hearted Woman, States 145 ....60.00
Bland, Bobby; IOU Blues, Duke 105 ....50.00
Blenders, Never in a Million Years, Decca 28241 ....125.00
Bo, Eddie; If It's Good to You, Scram 119 ....20.00
Bob & Sheri, Surfer Moon, Safari 101 ....550.00
Boone, Pat; Beach Girl, Dot 16658 .... 5.00
Brooks, Dusty; Heaven of Fire, Sun 183 ....130.00
Brostic, Earl; I Got Loaded, King 4491 ....25.00
Brown, Roy; Travelin' Man, King 4682 ....50.00
Brown, Ruth; Teardrops, Atlantic 919 ....200.00
Cameos, He, Gigi 100...25.00
Cardinals, The; You Are My Only Love, Atlantic 995 ....30.00
Cavaliers, Charm Bracelet, NRC 28 ....30.00
Cobras, Cindy, Modern 964 ....150.00
CoCoas, Flip Your Daddy, Chesterfield 364 ....200.00
Dee, Ronnie; Action Packed, Backbeat 522 ....70.00
Doctor Ross, Juke Box Boogie, Sun 212 ....175.00
Domino, Fats; Walking to New Orleans, Imperial 5675................. 8.00
Downbeats, Midnight Express, Amp 792 ....25.00
El Dorados, My Loving Baby, red plastic, Vee Jay 115 ....200.00
El Rays, The; Darling I Know, Checker 794 ....100.00
Fairlanes, Writing This Letter, Continental 100..........................300.00
Five Keys, Deep in My Heart, Aladdin 3245 ....200.00
Five Royales, With All Your Heart, Apollo 467 ....20.00
Four Buddies, Delores, Club 51105 ....400.00
Four Tops, Could It Be You, Chess 1623 ....25.00
Gaddie, Grover; High Stepping Daddy, Blue Angel 2007.............40.00

Gordon, Big Mike; Walkin', Slippin', & Slidin', Baton 219 ....15.00
Greer, Big John; Bottle It Up & Go, Groove 0002.........................25.00
Griffin Brothers, Weepin' and Cryin', Dot 1071 ....100.00
Hall, Getri; Mr Blues, RAI 101 ....40.00
Harptones, Shrine of St Cecelia, Rama 221 ....75.00
Hawkins, Jay; When I Tried, Wing 90005 ....40.00
Henry, Robert; Miss Anna B, King 4624 ....150.00
Holly, Buddy; Blue Days-Black Nights, Decca 29854 ....60.00
Hooker, John Lee; High Priced Woman, Chess 1505 ....100.00
Hopkins, Lightning; Santa Fe Blues, RPM 398.............................75.00
Houston, David; Sugar Sweet, RCA Victor 6611..........................15.00
Howlin' Wolf, My Last Affair, Chess 1528 ....75.00
Jackson, George; Uh Huh, Atlantic 1024......................................15.00
Jackson, Michael; Someone in the Dark, MCA 1786 (promo)....250.00
James, Elmore; Can't Stop Lovin', Flair 1014 ....50.00
James, Elmore; She Just Won't Do Right, Checker 777 ....100.00
Johnson, Rev A; God Don't Like It, Glory 4011 ....25.00
Johnson, Stan; Baby Baby Doll, Ruby 550 ....100.00
King, Charles; Bop Cat, Folk Star 1131 ....100.00
Kittrell, Christine; Evil-Eyed Woman, Republic 7055 ....60.00
Knight, Curtis; Hornet's Nest, RSVP 1124...................................50.00
Lewis, Smiley; Come On, Imperial 5372 ....40.00
Liggins, Jimmy; I Ain't Drunk, Aladdin 3250...............................100.00
Limelighters, My Sweet Norma, Joz 795 ....75.00
Little Esther, Stop Cryin', Decca 48305..50.00
Lynn, Barbara; Oh Baby, Jamie 1277 ....10.00
Mack, Bill; Cat Just Got in Town, Starday 252 ....35.00
Mae, Lonnie; Record Hop Dream, Fine 601120 ....55.00
Martin, Billy; If It's Lovin' That You Want, Lucky 0009 ....20.00
Meters, Chican Strut, Josie 1018... 4.00
Moroccos, Somewhere Over the Rainbow, United 193 ....40.00
Muddy Waters, She's All Right, Chess 1537 ....100.00
Noland, Terry; Hypnotized, Brunswick 55017...............................15.00
Perkins, Carl; Gone Gone Gone, Sun 224 ....75.00
Presley, Elvis; Milkcow Blue's Boogie, Sun 215..........................350.00
Prisonaires, Softly & Tenderly, Sun 189.......................................100.00
Riley, Bill; Red Hot, Sun 277 ....25.00
Scott, Jack; Flakey John, Groove 0049 ....15.00
Skelton, Eddie; That's Love, Starday 315 ....15.00
Sloan, Earl; Bullfrog Boogie, Ring 1219..125.00
Smith, LC; Let the Big Times Roll, Wango 202............................75.00
Spaniels, Let's Make Up, red plastic, Vee Jay 116 ....200.00
Starlighters, Hotlicks, Wheel 1004 ....40.00
Vernon, Ray; I'm Counting on You, Cameo 115...........................75.00
Wells, Junior; Tomorrow Night, States 143 ....300.00
Wood, Tommy; Can't Play Hookey, D 1000 ....200.00

Red Wing

The Red Red Wing Stoneware Company, founded in 1878, took its name from its location in Red Wing, Minnesota. In 1906 the name was changed to the Red Wing Union Stoneware Company after a merger with several of the other local potteries. For the most part they produced utilitarian wares such as flowerpots, crocks, and jugs. Their early 1930s catalogs offered a line of art pottery vases in colored glazes, some of which featured handles modeled after swan's necks, snakes, or female nudes. Other examples were quite simple, often with classic styling. After the addition of their dinnerware lines in the 1935, 'Stoneware' was dropped from the name, and the company became known as Red Wing Potteries, Inc. They closed in 1967. For further study we recommend *Red Wing Stoneware, An Identification and Value Guide,* and *Red Wing Collectibles* by Dan and Gail DePasquale and Larry Peterson, available at your local library or bookstore.

Key:
MN — Minnesota RW — Red Wing
NS — North Star   RWUS — Red Wing Union
         Stoneware

Cookie Jars

Bob White	65.00
Bunch of Bananas, bl	38.00
Carousel	210.00
Crock, wht	25.00
Dutch girl, yel w/brn trim	55.00
French Baker, tan & brn, mk	60.00
Grapes	50.00
Jack Frost	250.00
King of Tarts, no mk	210.00
Monk, yel w/brn trim	65.00
Pineapple, yel	38.00

Dinnerware

Bob White, bowl, cereal; 6½"	10.50
Bob White, bowl, divided vegetable; hdls	25.00
Bob White, casserole, w/lid, 4-qt, in warming stand	65.00
Bob White, cookie jar	100.00
Bob White, creamer	15.00
Bob White, cup & saucer	14.00

Bob White, gravy boat with lid, $47.50.

Bob White, hors d'oeuvre bird	38.00
Bob White, plate, 10"	10.00
Bob White, plate, 6½"	4.00
Bob White, shaker	11.00
Bob White, teapot	55.00
Capistrano, platter, 13½"	13.00
Capistrano, platter, 15"	15.00
Lexington, cup & saucer	6.50
Lexington, pitcher, water	20.00
Lexington, teapot	20.00
Lotus, bowl, divided vegetable	17.50
Lotus, creamer	8.00
Lotus, cup & saucer	8.00
Lotus, gravy boat, w/attached plate	18.00
Lotus, plate, dinner; 10½"	7.50
Lotus, plate, 7½"	6.50
Lotus, platter, 13"	17.50
Lotus, shakers, pr	18.00

Pitcher, Hearthside, 7½", $17.50.

Lute Song, bowl, berry; 5"	6.50
Lute Song, bowl, cereal; 6¾"	7.50
Lute Song, bowl, 8¼"	15.00
Lute Song, creamer & sugar bowl, w/lid	18.00
Lute Song, cup & saucer	8.50
Lute Song, plate, dinner; 10¼"	8.50
Lute Song, plate, 7¼"	6.50
Lute Song, platter, 13"	20.00
Magnolia, chop plate, 13"	17.50
Magnolia, cup & saucer	10.00
Morning Glory, bowl, 6"	4.00
Morning Glory, celery tray, 11"	6.00
Morning Glory, creamer & sugar bowl	7.50
Morning Glory, cup & saucer	6.00
Morning Glory, plate, 10"	7.50
Morning Glory, plate, 7"	3.00
Morning Glory, platter, 13"	15.00
Pepe, plate, 6½"	3.00
Plum Blossom, bowl, 5½"	4.00
Plum Blossom, cup	4.00
Plum Blossom, plate, 10"	6.00
Plum Blossom, sugar bowl, w/lid	7.50
Provincial Oomphware, bowl, 11½"	45.00
Provincial Ware, bean pot, 3-qt	25.00
Random Harvest, casserole, w/lid	25.00
Random Harvest, celery	10.00
Random Harvest, plate, 10"	6.00
Random Harvest, plate, 8½"	4.00
Random Harvest, platter, 13"	12.50
Round Up, beverage mug	125.00
Round Up, beverage server, w/lid	300.00
Round Up, bowl, cereal	36.00
Round Up, bowl, divided vegetable	55.00
Round Up, butter dish, w/lid	110.00
Round Up, plate, dinner; 10½"	26.00
Round Up, relish, 3-part	65.00
Round Up, teapot	150.00
Tampico, bowl, cereal	10.00
Tampico, cup & saucer	12.00
Tampico, plate, dinner; 10½"	10.00
Tampico, platter, 13¼"	18.00
Two Step, creamer	3.00
Two Step, plate, 10"	4.50

Miscellaneous

Ash receiver, cat figural w/open mouth	32.00

Ash receiver, donkey figural w/open mouth, bl 32.00
Ash tray, maroon/gr, scalloped shell shape, 3-ftd, 7" 6.00
Ash tray, red wing form, Anniversary 40.00
Ash tray, red wing form, emb Indian maiden 165.00
Bottle, pig figural, Albany slip, rare 350.00
Bowl, console; long feathery leaves, tan wash on cream, 16" 20.00
Bowl, floral relief on gun-metal brn, lime int, 13½" 25.00
Bowl, leaves/berries/bows relief on wht, #866, 6¾" 7.50
Bowl, oak leaves & acorns on gr & tan, dk gr int, 5½" 7.50
Bowl, 2-cherub ped ft, gr & ivory, 7x9" 30.00
Bust, President McKinley, sgn bk 275.00
Candlestick, magnolia, wht, #1226, pr 28.00
Cornucopia, gr, yel int, leaf base, #1356, 5½x7½" 10.00
Figurine, bulldog, brn 365.00
Figurine, cow w/nursing calf on base, brn 455.00
Figurine, pig, brn, 5" L 235.00

Pitcher, high gloss Brushware type, 8½", $160.00.

Planter, geometrics, Brushware 32.00
Planter, glossy speckled gold, fluted, #1561, 12" L........................12.00
Planter, hat form, bl, #670.. 6.00
Planter, pk speckled, #5020, 6½ x12½" L 8.00
Reamer/juice pitcher, yel, #256...125.00
Sewer pipe, advertising, pottery..35.00
Urn, Grecian motif, #159, 9"..45.00
Vase, acanthus panel relief, lt gr, cream int, fan form, 9" 20.00
Vase, cherub, Brushware, 1931, tall 75.00
Vase, cherub, RWUS..85.00
Vase, copper-oxide gr, gourd shape w/tall slim neck, 12½" 14.00
Vase, elephant-head hdls, mustard gloss, 6x6" 20.00
Vase, exotic flower relief, chartreuse w/gr int, 8x7x3¾"..................16.00
Vase, fish figural, open mouth, bl, #879 ....38.00
Vase, gr, pk int, base hdls, #505, 7½ " 12.00
Vase, leaf relief, wht w/turq int, #1082, pitcher form, 9" 15.00
Vase, lt gr semi-gloss, ribbed flared top, bulb bottom, 6" 7.50
Vase, piped-on lines/dmn bands/people, gr-brn, M3013, 14x5" ...350.00

Stoneware

Bean pot, Boston style, Albany slip, RW, 1-gal.............................165.00
Bean pot, brn/wht, bail hdl, RWU, 1-qt....................................70.00
Bowl, grapes emb on saffron, geometric rim, RWUS.....................90.00
Bowl, mc sponging, paneled, unmk, 11".....................................120.00
Bowl, red & bl sponging on saffron, narrow ribs 60.00
Bowl, shouldered; Albany slip, RW, 1-qt....................................60.00
Bowl, shouldered; red & bl sponging on wht 70.00
Canteen, Red Wing Minnesota on salt glaze 425.00
Casserole, allover sponging, w/lid, lg.....................................225.00
Chamber pot, Albany slip, fancy hdl, RWUS 85.00

Churn, dbl leaf/#8 on wht, unsgn, 8-gal....................................300.00
Churn, leaf/#5 on salt glaze, unsgn, 5-gal.................................225.00
Churn, red wing/#2 on salt glaze, RWUS, 2-gal 165.00
Combinette, emb floral swags on bl to wht, unmk 185.00
Combinette, emb lily/bl bands on salt glaze, unmk 185.00
Cooler, birch leaf/#3/Ice Water on wht, MN, 3-gal........................300.00
Cooler, butterfly/#6 on salt glaze, RWUS, 6-gal 1,500.00
Cooler, drop 8 motif/#5 on salt glaze, unmk, 5-gal........................225.00
Cooler, red wing/#3/Ice Water on wht, RWUS, 3-gal.......................300.00
Cooler, red wing/bl bands on salt glaze, 8-gal 350.00
Crock, birch leaves/#40 on salt glaze, unmk, 40-gal......................275.00
Crock, butter; Albany slip, low, MN, 2-lb 35.00
Crock, butter; salt glaze, low style, RW, 10-lg 70.00
Crock, butter; wht, low, MN, 10-lb 35.00
Crock, butterfly/#20 on salt glaze, RWUS, 20-gal 335.00
Crock, dbl 'P'/#4 on salt glaze, MN, 4-gal................................275.00
Crock, dbl birch leaves stamped/#10 on wht, 10-gal 185.00
Crock, lily/#30 on salt glaze, stenciled RWUS mk, 30-gal..........950.00
Crock, red wing/#12 on wht, RWUS, 12-gal...............................75.00
Crock, 2 elephant ear leaves/#8 on wht, MN, 8-gal 55.00
Cuspidor, molded seam, bl & wht sponging, unmk, 10" dia........325.00
Cuspidor, molded seam, brn & wht, unmk 90.00
Jar, packing; wht, bailed, MN, 3-lb..75.00
Jar, preserve; Albany slip, RW, 1-gal 325.00
Jar, preserve; Albany slip, str sides, NS, 1-gal...........................165.00
Jar, preserve; Albany slip, str sides, RW, 4-gal..........................140.00
Jar, wax sealer, Albany slip, RW, 1-qt.....................................50.00
Jug, bailed, wht, RWUS, ca 1895, 1-gal...................................135.00
Jug, bailed, wht, wide mouth, MN, 1-gal 120.00
Jug, beehive; #5 etched on Albany slip, RW, 5-gal.......................575.00
Jug, beehive; birch leaf/#5 on salt glaze, RW, 5-gal................ 1,200.00
Jug, beehive; birch leaves/#3 on wht, RWUS, 3-gal 155.00
Jug, beehive; birch leaves/#5 on wht, RWUS, 5-gal 155.00
Jug, beehive; red wing/#3 on wht, RWUS, 3-gal 165.00
Jug, common, wht, MN, ½-gal 55.00
Jug, common, wht, RW, ½-gal 45.00
Jug, fancy, brn/wht, RWUS, 1-qt...85.00
Jug, fancy, brn/wht, RWUS, 2-gal..225.00
Jug, fancy, red wing on wht, brn top, 2-gal 385.00
Jug, molded seam, Albany slip, bird mk/RW, 1-gal......................120.00
Jug, shoulder; Albany slip, cone top, RW, 2-gal 425.00
Jug, shoulder; birch leaves/#5, standard top, RWUS, 5-gal 120.00
Jug, shoulder; bl bands on wht, cone top, RWUS, 1-gal 425.00
Jug, shoulder; brn & salt glaze, funnel top, MN, 2-gal.................125.00
Jug, shoulder; brn & salt glaze, wide mouth, NS, 1-gal...............300.00
Jug, shoulder; red wing on wht, brn funnel top, 2-gal 285.00
Jug, shoulder; turkey eye drips on salt glaze, NS, 2-gal 550.00
Jug, shoulder; wht, cone top, RW, 1-gal..................................55.00
Jug, shoulder; wht, standard top, MN, 2-gal 45.00
Jug, shoulder; wht, standard top, RW, 2-gal 45.00
Jug, shoulder; wht, standard top, short, MN, 1-qt 135.00
Jug, standard; brn & salt glaze, RW, 1-gal...............................125.00
Jug, syrup; wht, pour spout, MN, ½-gal 55.00
Pan, milk; Albany slip, NS...80.00
Pitcher, Albany slip, barrel form, RWUS 120.00
Pitcher, Albany slip, barrel form, unmk 45.00
Pitcher, Dutch boy & girl on bl & wht, RWUS, sm....................450.00
Pitcher, emb geometric band on Albany slip, MN 325.00
Pitcher, iris emb on Albany slip, RWUS 80.00
Pitcher, mustard; Albany slip, NS 200.00
Pitcher, mustard; salt glaze, MN..75.00
Pitcher, Russian milk; Albany slip, unmk, ½-gal 65.00
Pitcher, Spongeband & saffron, RWUS 135.00
Spittoon, German type, 'cvg'/bl bands on salt glaze, unmk 285.00

Spittoon, German type, 'cvg'/bl bands on wht, unmk 225.00
Spittoon, salt glaze, RWUS side stamp 550.00
Umbrella stand, bl & wht sponging, ca 1906..............................625.00

Water cooler, transitional style, 8-gallon, $375.00.

Redware

The term redware refers to a type of simple earthenware produced by the Colonists as early as the 1600s. The red clay used in its production was abundant throughout the country, and during the 18th and 19th centuries redware was made in great quantities. Intended for utilitarian purposes such as everyday tableware or use in the dairy, redware was simple in design and decoration. Glazes of various colors were used, and a liquid clay referred to as 'slip' was sometimes applied in patterns such as zigzag lines, daisies, or stars. In the following listings, EX (excellent condition) indicates only minor damage.

Our advisor for this category is Barbara Rosen; she is listed in the Directory under New Jersey.

Basket, hanging, 6x5½" dia 500.00
Basket, yel w/appl brn foliage, tooled, braided hdl, 7", EX 200.00
Bottle, beige speckled, pinched neck, Maine, early, 7½"..............260.00
Bowl, coggled rim, 3x5½" 50.00
Bowl, yel slip waves, 1850s, 2x9" 300.00
Bowl, 2-line yel slip waves, 7½", EX 240.00
Bucket, grapevine hdl, 7½x8½ " 300.00
Charger, yel slip script-like flourish, coggled, 12", EX.................300.00
Flask, dk brn, initials on front, 6"..400.00
Flask, rust w/blk splotches, 1800s, 5", 7", & 8", set of 3.............220.00
Flowerpot, rust/gr, flared, Bloomfield NY, 5½x7".......................150.00
Flowerpot, wht slip w/brn mottle, saucer base, 6", EX 225.00
Inkwell, tapered sides, 2"...160.00
Jar, amber w/orange spots, wear/sm flakes, 9¾" 95.00
Jar, brn splotches, ribbed hdl, tooled lines, 5½ ", EX..................200.00
Jar, clear w/EX color, ovoid, appl hdls, tiered finial, 12", EX 450.00
Jar, dk brn w/gr-amber spots, ovoid, 6¾ " 90.00
Jug, Albany slip, stencil: ST Suit...Whiskey, 1869-80, 7" 350.00
Jug, dk brn, ribbed strap hdl, ovoid, minor flakes, 8"..................100.00
Jug, dk gr, ribbed strap hdl, ovoid, 10" 110.00
Jug, gr, air hole in hdl, ovoid, 12", EX...95.00
Jug, gray-gr, 7"..200.00
Jug, red w/blk splotches, ribbed strap hdl, ovoid, 7", EX 225.00
Jug, red-brn, squat, 3½" 295.00
Jug, ribbed strap hdl, 6" 50.00
Loaf pan, 3-line yel slip waves, coggled, wear/rpr, 15" L 475.00
Loaf pan, 4-line yel slip band center & sides, oval, 14" 900.00
Mold, butter; pineapple, NM 400.00

Mold, clear w/brn spots, bundt type w/tooled line, 7½" 95.00
Mold, Turk's head, blk glaze, med 45.00
Mold, Turk's head, sm 35.00
Pie plate, 3-line yel waves, coggled, wear/minor chips, 8"...........350.00

Plate, yellow and green stylized tulip on red-brown ground, minor chips and flakes, 11½", $500.00.

Platter, 3-line yel slip waves, yel/dk gr splotches, 20" 2,800.00
Pounce sander, mustard glaze, cylindrical, gallery rim, EX...........285.00
Tankard, sgraffito floral/words/1717, pewter lid, 11", EX 4,600.00
Vase, incised loops, ruffled rim, hdls, att Schofield, 4½" 175.00

Regal China

Located in Antioch, Illinois, the Regal China Company has been in business since 1938. Products of interest to collectors are James Beam decanters, cookie jars, salt and pepper shakers, and similar novelty items. The Old MacDonald Farm series listed below are becoming especially collectible. See also Cookie Jars.

Old McDonald's Farm

Butter dish, cow's head 75.00
Canister, flour; med 95.00
Canister, pretzels, peanuts, popcorn, chips, tidbits, lg, ea............175.00

Spice canisters, $55.00 each.

Cookie jar, barn figural..125.00
Creamer, rooster 50.00
Jar, grease; pig figural...100.00
Pitcher, milk; cow's head, gold bell, tankard form...................200.00
Shakers, churn, pr...25.00
Shakers, feed sacks w/sheep's head, pr.................................100.00
Shakers, son & daughter, pr...35.00
Sugar bowl, rooster, lg...95.00
Teapot, duck's head..150.00

Restraints

Since the beginning of time, many things from animals to treasures have been held in bondage by hemp, bamboo, chests, chains, shackles, and other constructed devices. Many of these devices were used to hold captives who awaited further torture, as if the restraint wasn't torturous enough. The study and collecting of restraints enables one to learn much about the advancement of civilization in the country or region from which they originated. Such devices at various times in history were made of very heavy metals — so heavy that the wearer could scarcely move about. It has only been in the last sixty years that vast improvements have been made in design and construction that afford the captive some degree of comfort.

Our advisor for this category is Joseph Tanner; he is listed in the Directory under Montana.

Key:
bbl — barrel	lc — lock case
d-lb — double lock button	NST — non-swing through
K — key	ST — swing through
Kd — keyed	stp — stamped

Foreign Handcuffs

Adams, teardrop lc, bbl Kd, NST, usually not stp 170.00
Australian, Saf Lock, ST, takes pin-tumbler K in side, stp...........110.00
Chubb, NST, English hi-security 10-slider lock mechanism........220.00
Deutsche Polizei, ST, middle hinge, folds, takes bbl-bit K 105.00
French Lapegy, ST, aluminum alloys, takes flat bitted K................65.00
German Clejuso, oval design, ST, dbl-cuff weight, 22-oz.............100.00
German Clejuso, sq lc, adjusts/NST, d-lb on side, bbl K................95.00
German Darby, adjusts, well finished, sm 120.00
German Hamburg 8, non-adjust NST, center bar/post w/K-way ..250.00
Hiatt, English Darby, like US CW Darby, stp Hiatt & #d 65.00
Hiatt, solid state, 2 separate cuffs joined bk to bk, stp/#d.............125.00
Hiatt English non-adjust screw K Darby style, uses screw K.........100.00
Hiatt Figure 8, swings open to insert/withdraw wrists 125.00
Italian, stp New Police, modern Peerless type, ST, sm bbl K.........30.00
Plug 8, remove plug before inserting external threaded K............200.00
Spanish, stp Alcyon/Star, modern Peerless type, ST, flat K 65.00
Spanish, stp Alcyon/Star, modern Peerless type, ST, sm bbl K......45.00

Foreign Leg Shackles

German Clejuso, sq lc, adjusts/NST, d-bl on side, bbl K.............125.00
German Clejuso Darby type, adjusts/NST/plated, uses screw K...140.00
Hiatt English combo manacles, handcuff/leg irons w/chain 200.00
Hiatt English non-adjust screw K Darby style, uses screw K.........100.00
Hiatt Plug leg irons, same K-ing as Plug-8 cuffs, w/chain 225.00

U.S. Handcuffs

American Munitions, modern/rnd, sm bbl Kd, ST bow, stp...........45.00

Bean Patrolman, kidney-bean form, d-lb on lc, NST, stp T 90.00
Bean-Cobb, sm rnd lc, removable cylinder, d-lb, NST, 1899 ....80.00
Civil War padlocking type, various designs w/loop for lock.........120.00
Colt, modern ST bow, sm bbl Kd, stp w/Colt & co name 90.00
H&R Super, NST, shaft-hinge connector takes hollow titted K....75.00
Harvard, takes sm bbl K, ST, stp Harvard Lock Co 65.00
Judd, NST, used rnd/internally triangular K, stp Mattatuck 100.00
Marlin Daley, NST, bottle-neck form, neck stp, dbl-titted K 150.00
Mattatuck, NST, propeller-like K-way, stp Mattatuck/etc 85.00
Peerless, ST, takes sm bbl K, stp Mfg'ered by Peerless Co 40.00
Peerless, ST, takes sm bbl K, stp Mfg'ered by S&W Co 75.00
Phelps, NST, twist chain between cuffs, Tower look-alike 200.00
Pratt combo, 1 cuff connects w/nipper/claw, ST, mk Pratt 225.00
Romer, NST, takes flat K, resembles padlock, stp Romer Co 200.00
S&W 94 Maximum Security, ST, takes Ace-type K, stp S&W 65.00
Strauss, ST, takes lg solid bitted K, stp Strauss Eng Co 85.00
Tower, NST, bottom K, solid/flat fitted K goes in cuff edge.........100.00
Tower bar cuffs, cuffs separate by 10-12" steel bar 120.00
Tower Dbl Lock, NST, takes bbl-bitted K, usually stp Tower........50.00
Tower Detective Pinkerton, NST, sq lc, bbl-bitted K, no stp 110.00
Tower Single Lock, NST, bbl-bit K, K-way slanted on lc, sm........70.00
Tower-Bean, NST, sm rnd lc, takes tiny bbl-bitted K, stp..............70.00
Walden 'Lady Cuff,' NST, takes sm bbl K, lightweight, stp 200.00

U.S. Leg Shackles

American Munitions, as handcuffs..55.00
Civil War or prison ball & chain, padlocking or rivet type..........225.00
H&R Supers, as handcuffs...200.00
Harvard, as handcuffs 75.00
Judd, as handcuffs...110.00
Oregon boot, break-apart shackle on above ankle support..........400.00
Strauss, as handcuffs 90.00
Tower, bottom K, as handcuffs 90.00
Tower ball & chain, leg iron w/chain & 6-lb to 50-lb ball 200.00
Tower Dbl-Lock, as handcuffs 75.00
Tower Detective, as handcuffs 135.00

Various Other Restraining Devices

African slave Darby-style cuffs, heavy iron/chain, handmade........95.00
African slave Darby-style leg shackles, heavy/hand forged 150.00
African slave padlocking or riveted forged iron shackles 125.00
Darby neck collar, rnd steel loop opens w/screw K 150.00
English Figure-8 nipper, claws open by lifting top lock tab 65.00
German Nipper, twist hdl opens/closes cuff, stp Germany/etc 75.00

Reverse Painting on Glass

Verre eglomise is the technique of painting on the underside of glass. Dating back to the early 1700s, this art became popular in the 19th century when German immigrants chose historical figures and beautiful women as subjects for their reverse glass paintings. Advertising mirrors of this type came into vogue at the turn of the century.

Flower basket, on tinsel, mc on wht, gilt fr, 5½x7" 200.00
Flowers in vase, on tinsel, mc on blk, grpt fr, 12x17".................325.00
Girl holds cat (or dog), Chinese, 1800s, 19x14", pr............... 1,300.00
Lady in wht dress, bl cloak, Chinese, 1800s, 20x14", EX 200.00
Landscape w/crane & deer, Chinese, 1800s, 18x25" 300.00
Napoleon, ¾-portrait, 12x9" 100.00
St Peter's Basilica, Rome, Victorian, 16x20" 200.00
3 Wise Men, German inscription, orig pine fr, 9x12" 350.00

Richard

Richard, who at one time worked for Galle, made cameo art glass in France during the 1920s. His work was often multi-layered and acid cut with florals and scenics in lovely colors. The ware was marked with his name in relief.

Our advisor for this category is Don Williams; he is listed in the Directory under Missouri.

Cameo

Atomizer, leaves, raspberry/pk, wafer ft, sgn, 7"	750.00
Lamp, mtns/lake/trees on 8" shade & baluster base, 14"	4,700.00
Vase, floral, brn on orange, 6x1¾"	500.00
Vase, mtns/house/river, ped ft, 8"	700.00
Vase, trees/cottage/mtns/lake, yel to lav, 13¾"	1,500.00
Vase, vintage, frosted/mahog/yel, sgn, 8½"	875.00

Ridgway

As early as 1792, the Ridgway brothers, Job and George, produced fine quality earthenwares in Shelton, Staffordshire, marking their products 'Ridgway, Smith, & Ridgway,' and later, 'Job & George Ridgway.' Around 1800 the brothers split, and each had his own firm, both in Shelton. They were joined in the business by various members of the Ridgway family, and in fact their descendants still operate there today.

The two firms created by the split were the Bell Works and the Cauldon Pottery. Bell produced stone china and earthenware decorated with blue transfer printing. Their mark was 'J. & W. Ridgway' or 'J. & W.R.' (John and William) until 1848 when 'William Ridgway' was used. The Cauldon Pottery made earthenware, stone china, and high-quality porcelains fine enough to win them the distinction of being appointed potters to the Queen. From 1830 their wares attest to this fact, bearing the Royal Arms mark with 'J.R.' within the crest. In 1840 '& Co.' was added. Most examples of Ridgway's wares found today are transfer-printed historical scenes. See also Staffordshire, Historical; and Flow Blue.

Biscuit jar, Coaching Days, rattan hdl, 6½"	230.00
Mug, Coaching Days, silver lustre trim, 2-hdl, mk, 3⅞"	40.00
Mustard pot, Coaching Days, 3½"	125.00
Pitcher, Coaching Days, silver lustre trim, 4⅛"	45.00
Pitcher, Coaching Days, silver lustre trim, 4¾"	55.00
Pitcher, tankard; Coaching Days, 12⅝x6⅛"	150.00
Plaque, Coaching Days, In a Snow Drift, 12" dia	130.00
Plaque, Coaching Days, Taking Up the Mails, 12" dia	130.00
Plate, Coaching Days, 9"	40.00
Tea caddy, Coaching Days, sq, 5¾x4¼"	150.00

Platter, Giraffe, medium blue transfer, marked Published Aug. 30, 1836, internal hairline, 15", $210.00.

Tray, Coaching Days, Christmas Visitor, 12½" dia	125.00
Wine cooler, smear-glaze stoneware, twig hdls/grape finial	400.00

Riviera

Riviera was a line of dinnerware introduced by the Homer Laughlin China Company in 1938. It was sold exclusively by the Murphy Company through their nationwide chain of dime stores. Riviera was unmarked, lightweight, and inexpensive. It was discontinued sometime prior to 1950. Colors are mauve blue, red, yellow, light green, and ivory. On rare occasions, dark blue pieces are found, but this was not a standard color.

Batter set, complete	185.00
Batter set, ivory, w/decals	135.00

Various bowls, see listings for specific descriptions and values.

Bowl, baker; 9"	16.00
Bowl, cream soup; w/liner, ivory	40.00
Bowl, fruit; 5½"	8.00
Bowl, nappy, 9¼"	14.00
Bowl, oatmeal; 6"	14.00
Butter dish, cobalt, ¼-lb	190.00
Butter dish, colors other than cobalt & turq, ¼-lb	85.00
Butter dish, turq, ¼-lb	175.00
Butter dish, ½-lb	75.00
Casserole	65.00
Creamer	7.50
Cup & saucer, demitasse; ivory	45.00
Jug, w/lid	85.00
Pitcher, juice; mauve bl	125.00
Pitcher, juice; yel	60.00
Plate, 10"	20.00
Plate, 6"	5.50
Plate, 9"	12.00
Platter, cobalt, 12"	12.00
Platter, w/closed hdls, 11¼"	15.00
Platter, 11½"	12.00
Sauce boat	15.00
Saucer	3.00
Shakers, pr	12.00
Sugar bowl, w/lid	12.00
Syrup, w/lid	85.00
Teacup	8.50
Teapot	75.00
Tumbler, hdld	50.00
Tumbler, juice	38.00

Robertson

Fred H. Robertson, clay expert for the Los Angeles Brick Company and son of Alexander Robertson of the Roblin Pottery, experimented with crystalline glazes as early as 1906. In 1934 Fred and his son George established their own works in Los Angeles, but by 1943 they had moved operations to Hollywood. Though most of their early wares were turned by hand, some were also molded in low relief. Fine crackle glazes and crystallines were developed. The ware was marked with 'Robertson,' 'F.H.R.,' or 'R.,' with the particular location of its manufacture noted. The small pottery closed in 1952.

Bowl, bl drip over wht crackle, 4" 45.00
Tile, children & goose, blk on wht, 4x4" 85.00
Vase, crystalline, bl flakes on gold-yel, Los Angeles, 5" 1,300.00
Vase, gr gloss, mk FHRLA, 7/08, 4x3" 225.00

Robineau

After short-term training in ceramics in 1903, Adelaide Robineau (with the help of her husband Samuel) built a small pottery studio at her home in Syracuse, New York. She was adept at mixing the clay and throwing the ware, which she often decorated by incising designs into the unfired clay. Samuel developed many of the glazes and took charge of the firing process. In 1910 she joined the staff of the American Women's League Pottery at St. Louis, where she designed the famous Scarab Vase. After this pottery failed, she served on the faculty of Syracuse University. Her work was and is today highly acclaimed for the high standards of excellence to which she aspired.

Bowl, 5 frogs on rim, frogs in center pond, mfg flaw, 13" 35,000.00
Lozenge, cvd scarab, 'Scarab Vase 8900,' rectangular, 3" L...... 1,900.00

Robj Bottles

Robj was the name of a retail store that operated in Paris for only a few years, from about 1925 to 1931. Robj solicited designs from the best French artisans of the period to produce decorative objects for the home. These objects were produced mostly in porcelain but also in glass and earthenware. The most well known are the figural bottles which were particularly popular in the United States. However, Robj also produced tea sets, perfume lamps, chess sets, ash trays, bookends, humidors, powder jars, cigarette boxes, figurines, lamps, and milk pitchers. Robj objects tend to be whimsical, and all embody the Art Deco style.

Our advice for this category comes from Cocktails and Laughter Antiques (Randall Monsen and Rod Baer), whose address is listed in the Directory under Virginia.

Decanters, Girl in a Bonnet and Professor, 10", $400.00 each.

Decanter, Blk Mammy, gold trim, Limoges France, 10" 600.00
Decanter, French priest, hat stopper, blk/wht, 10" 335.00
Decanter, Napoleon, hat stopper, mk, 10" 335.00
Decanter, Scotsman, 11" 335.00
Veilleuse, formed as flower-filled gold & wht urn, 5" 1,300.00
Veilleuse, red mottled shade, 3-arm foliate arm base, 5" 500.00

Roblin

In the late 1800s, Alexander W. Robertson and Linna Irelan established a pottery in San Francisco, combining parts of their respective names to coin the name Roblin. Robertson was responsible for potting and firing the ware, which often reflected his taste for classic styling. Mrs. Irelan did much of the decorating, utilizing almost every method but favoring relief modeling. Mushrooms and lizards were her favorite subjects. Vases were a large part of their production, all of which was made from native California red, buff, and white clays. The ware was well marked with the firm name or the outline of a bear. Roblin Pottery was destroyed in the earthquake of 1906.

Shaker, wht bsk, hand thrown/tooled, AW Robertson, 1906, 5".100.00
Vase, beaded band/cvd leaves on wht bsk, mk RAPC/A3, 4" 350.00
Vase, cvd flowers/butterflies on bsk, hdls, sgn LI/98, 6x4" 750.00

Rock 'N Roll Memorabilia

Memorabilia from the early days of Rock and Roll recalls that era of history that many of us experienced firsthand; these listings are offered to demonstrate the many and various aspects of this area of collecting. Values are for mint condition examples. Some are one-of-a-kind items that have sold at specialty auctions and are included as a reference guide to demonstrate price range and rarity. Our advisor for this category is Mark Phillips; he is listed in the Directory under Texas.

Alpert, Herb; autograph on blk/wht photo 15.00
Apple Records, dart board, apple logo in center, 18" 760.00
Astley, Rick; autograph on 8x10" blk/wht photo...........................20.00
Bandy, Moe; autograph on 8x10" blk/wht photo 15.00
Beatles, A Hard Days' Night lobby cards set (8)............................300.00
Beatles, apron, cartoon portrait on cotton..................................100.00
Beatles, bobbin' head dolls, 1964, 8", set of 4 ....640.00
Beatles, curtains, group picture, musical notes.............................360.00
Beatles, radio, TV shape, 4" 340.00
Beatles, Yel Submarine lobby cards set (8) 425.00
Bee Gees, World Tour jacket, RSR on front, 1979..........................85.00
Benatar, Pat; autograph on 8x10" color photo.............................35.00
Benton, Brook; autograph on 8x10" blk/wht photo.....................35.00
Berry, Chuck; autograph on 8x10" blk/wht photo.........................50.00
Black, Clint; autograph on 8x10" blk/wht photo...........................25.00
Blondie, tour book, 1979, 20-pg 20.00
Bon Jovi, autograph on 8x10" blk/wht photo of band 50.00
Boon, Pat; autograph on 8x10" color photo 20.00
Boston, Cherry Blossom tour book, Japan, 1990, 20-pg.................45.00
Bowie, David; autograph on blk/wht photo 320.00
Bowie, David; promotional mirror for Let's Dance 75.00
Brown, James; concert poster, Apollo Theater, 1966 ....300.00
Bush, Kate; sheet music, Man w/Child, United Kingdom 30.00
Cash, Johnny; autograph on 8x10" blk/wht photo........................20.00
Cash, Roseanne; autograph on 8x10" blk/wht photo.....................25.00
Chicago, Chicago XI cast metal promotional paperweight 20.00
Clapton, Eric; autograph on blk/wht photo 440.00
Cochran, Eddie; autograph on blk/wht photo..............................990.00

Cooke, Sam; autograph on plain paper 375.00
Cooper, Alice; autograph on 8x10" blk/wht photo 25.00
Dane, Taylor; autograph on 8x10" color photo 20.00
Dave Clark 5, sheet music, Fab Favorites, 1694, 6-pg 35.00
Denver, John; autograph on 8x10" blk/wht photo 15.00
Diamond, Neil; autograph on 8x10" color photo 50.00
Diamond, Neil; tour book, 1988, 20-pg 15.00
Domino, Fats; autograph on 8x10" blk/wht photo 225.00
Duran Duran, Into the Arena board game, Milton Bradley, 1985..40.00
Dylan, Bob; autograph on songbook 520.00
Fleetwood Mac, Tusk tour book, Japan, 32-pg 60.00
Ford, Lita; autograph on 8x10" blk/wht photo 20.00
Gabriel, Peter; autograph on 8x10" blk/wht photo 35.00
Garcia, Jerry (Grateful Dead); autograph on 8x10" color photo ...95.00
Gibson, Debbie; autograph on 8x10" blk/wht photo 25.00
Haley, Bill; stage suit, ca 1957 ....1,100.00
Holiday, Billy; autographed record 500.00
Holly, Buddy; check, sgn Charles Holly, 1959 ....3,300.00
Holly, Buddy; handkerchief 250.00
Holly, Buddy; handwritten letter 1,210.00
Holly, Buddy; personal trademk eyeglasses 45,100.00
Holly, Buddy; shoes sold w/verification letter 900.00
Holly, Buddy; social security card 4,675.00
Jackson, Michael; autograph on 8x10" blk/wht photo 125.00
Jennings, Waylon; autograph on 8x10" blk/wht photo 25.00
Jet, Joan; autograph on 8x10" blk/wht photo 30.00
John, Elton; autograph on 8x10" color photo 45.00
John, Elton; concert book, IN University, Oct 7, 1973 ......40.00
Jones, Brian (Rolling Stones); handwritten letter 1,200.00
Joplin, Janis; autograph on 8x10" blk/wht photo 760.00
Kiss, autograph on 8x10" blk/wht photo of band 60.00
Kiss, bubble gum cards, NM in full box 75.00
Kiss, bubble gum cards, single pack, unopened 3.00
Kiss, comic book, Marvel #5 ....30.00
Kiss, jigsaw puzzle, Love Gun, cover photo 50.00
Kiss, radio, 1977, NM in box 75.00
Kiss, transistor radio 40.00
Led Zepplin, Earls Court tour book, 1975, 12-pg 50.00
Led Zepplin, Knebworth tour book, 1979, 22-pg 45.00
Led Zepplin, promotional blow-up blimp 100.00
Lewis, Jerry Lee; autograph on 8x10" color photo 45.00
Love, Mike; autograph on 8x10" blk/wht photo 50.00
Madonna, autograph on album cover 640.00
Madonna, Breathless Mahoney doll, Disney, 9", +yel stand.....25.00
McCartney, Paul; handwritten letter, ca 1963 ....1,760.00
McCartney, Paul; tour book, Japan, 1989, 40-pg 40.00
Monkees, hand mirror 10.00
Monkees, hand puppet, no box 85.00
Monkees, looseleaf binder 150.00
Moody Blues, neon sign 495.00
Morrison, Jim; autograph on plain paper 1,540.00
Nelson, Willie; autograph on magazine cover 35.00
New Kids on the Block, tour jacket 95.00
Nicks, Stevie; Rock a Little tour book 20.00
Orbison, Roy; handwritten lyrics to Coming Home 750.00
Pink Floyd, tour book, United Kingdom, 1989, 22-pg 15.00
Presley, Elvis; 'TCB' 14k necklace 1,000.00
Presley, Elvis; doll, complete, 1957, 18", in box 750.00
Presley, Elvis; game, Elvis P Enterprises, 1956 ....750.00
Presley, Elvis; turq & silver concho belt 11,000.00
Prince, Parade tour book, United Kingdom, 1988, 20-pg 15.00
Prince, Purple Rain LP promotional poster 25.00
Proby, PJ; autographed letter 180.00
Queen, autographed 'bicycle' poster 260.00

Queen, Sheer Heart Attack tour book, Japan, 22-pg 60.00
Raitt, Bonnie; autograph on 8x10" blk/wht photo 25.00
Rolling Stones, autographs, ca 1966, 5 members 1,870.00
Rolling Stones, toy guitar, Electra 400.00
Ross, Diana; autograph on 45 record sleeve 30.00
Runaways, Japan tour book, 1977, 28-pg 85.00
Rush, Power; Windows tour book, 28-pg 12.00
Seger, Bob; tour jacket, 1986-87 ....100.00
Shannon, Del; autograph on 8x10" blk/wht photo 100.00
Sonny & Cher, concert poster, Atlanta, 1971 ....50.00
Springsteen, Bruce; harmonica, ca 1984-85 ....750.00
Starr, Ringo; drum kit, complete w/box 1,200.00
Stevens, Cat; Bamboo 26 tour book, 1974 ....35.00
Waters, Roger; Berlin Wall jacket, blk denim, 1990 ....100.00
Who, Fugs concert poster, Russo 'Lectric Theatre, 1968.....125.00
Who, Kids Are All Right tour jacket, 1989 ....250.00
Woodstock, orig handbill/flier, 1969 ....275.00
Young, Neil; Harvest song book, 62-pg 15.00

Rockingham

In the early part of the 19th century, American potters began to favor brown- and buff-burning clays over red because of their durability. The glaze favored by many was Rockingham, which varied from a dark brown mottle to a sponged effect sometimes called tortoise shell. It consisted in part of manganese and various metallic salts and was used by many potters until well into the 20th century. Over the past two years, demand and prices have risen sharply, especially in the East. See also Bennington.

Bottle, Coachman, ca 1870s, 10⅜" 250.00
Bottle, old lady w/guitar figural, chipped, 5" 55.00
Bowl, mixing; minor wear, 12½" 225.00
Bowl, mixing; minor wear/hairline, 13¾" 175.00
Bowl, mixing; 9" 95.00
Bowl, oval, minor wear, 7x9½" 95.00
Bowl, oval, 11" 95.00
Bowl, oval, 8¼" 95.00
Bowl, shallow, 11" 85.00
Bowl, 4x9½" dia 85.00
Creamer, ribbed strap hdl, sm flake on spout, 4" 175.00
Dish, shaped emb rim, shallow, sqd, 9x9", EX 75.00
Dog, free-standing front legs, EX detail, 10½", EX 450.00
Flowerpot, emb tulips, 2-part w/removable base, 8¾", VG.........250.00
Frame, ornately emb design, shaped perimeter, 10x11" 550.00

Martha Gunn toby jug, 8", $285.00.

Jar, crazing/hairline in lid, 5x5½" 85.00
Jar, paneled, emb hdls, hairline, minor chips on lid, 9x10" 175.00
Mug, emb beaded bands, minor wear/hairline, 3¼" 75.00
Mug, ribbed strap hdl, 4", EX 100.00
Pie plate, 11" 135.00
Pie plate, 7¾" 125.00
Pie plate, 9¾" 125.00
Pitcher, bust form, Wellington, w/death date, 7½x4¾ " 265.00
Pitcher, emb berries, 8½" 150.00
Pitcher, emb bust of Washington in wreath, 8", EX 145.00
Pitcher, emb flutes, str flaring sides, sm flakes, 5½" 200.00
Pitcher, emb hanging game, 10", EX..225.00
Pitcher, emb hunt scene/vintage, hound hdl, JB Caire, 10", EX .750.00
Pitcher, leaf-like panels, str sides widen at base, 10" 125.00
Plate, bear's paw mottle, emb leaf border, sq, 8x9" 80.00
Plate, emb rim, octagonal, 8" 235.00
Platter, 13" 200.00
Spaniel, seated on shaped plinth, mfg flaws, 10½" 400.00
Teapot, paneled, emb leaves, chips, 5" 125.00

Rockwell, Norman

Norman Rockwell began his career in 1911 at the age of seventeen doing illustrations for a children's book entitled *Tell Me Why Stories*. Within a few years he had produced the Saturday Evening Post cover that made him one of America's most-beloved artists. Though not well accepted by the professional critics of his day who did not consider his work to be art but 'merely' commercial illustration, Rockwell's popularity grew to the extent that today there is an overwhelming abundance of examples of his work or those related to the theme of one of his illustrations.

Ad, Look, Cinderfella, 1966...10.00
Bell, Butter Girl 25.00
Bell, Dr & Doll, 7" 45.00
Bell, Young Love, 9" 50.00
Figurine, Lazy Bones...350.00
Figurine, Springtime 65.00
Ingot, Fondest Memories, Fun on the Hill, 1976..........................300.00
Lithograph, After Chistmas, #4/35 AP, 36x20" 1,100.00
Lithograph, After the Prom, artist proof, 21x38" 3,500.00
Lithograph, Problem We All Live With, artist proof, 24x38" . 1,300.00
Lithograph, Sports Portfolio, 18½x16", set of 4 ....3,500.00
Magazine cover, Family Circle, Santa, Dec 1970............................12.00
Magazine cover, Sat Evening Post, Shuffleton's Barber Shop, '50.85.00
Plate, Coin Toss, Gorham 28.00
Plate, Grandma's Courting Dress, Knowles, 1984...........................25.00
Plate, Horse Trader, 1979 ....40.00
Plate, Leapfrog, 1979 ....55.00
Plate, The Secret, 1979 ....50.00
Plate, Traveling Salesman, 1977 ....40.00
Plate, Young Love, 1972..195.00
Sheet music, Over There, Rockwell cover...25.00
Stein, Fishin' Pals 75.00
Toby mug, Merrie Christmas...40.00

Rogers, John

John Rogers (1829-1904) was a machinist from Manchester, New Hampshire, who turned his hobby of sculpting into a financially-successful venture. From the originals he meticulously fashioned of red clay, he had bronze master molds made from which plaster copies were

cast. He specialized in five different categories: theatrical, Shakespeare, Civil War, everyday life, and horses. His large detailed groupings portrayed the life and times of the period between 1859 and 1892. When no condition is indicated, examples are assumed to be in very good to excellent condition.

Our advisor for this category is George Humphrey; he is listed in the Directory under Maryland.

Bath 2,000.00
Bubbles..700.00
Bushwacker.. 2,000.00
Charity Patient..650.00
Checkers Players, sm... 1,500.00
Chess...825.00
Coming to the Parson, Pat Aug 9, 1870, 21" 425.00
Country Post Office 750.00
Fairy's Whisper, ca 1881 .... 1,400.00
Fetching the Doctor 750.00
Fighting Bob, ca 1889 .... 1,100.00
Football, inscribed, 16x11" 1,000.00
Frolic at the Ol' Homestead, 1887, 22½"......................................800.00
Going for the Cows 450.00
Home Guard 800.00
Madam Your Mother Craves a Word..700.00

Neighboring Pews, $475.00.

One More Shot 550.00
Parting Promise...475.00
Peddler at the Fair 825.00
Pickett Guard 750.00
Playing Doctor 700.00
Politics 700.00
Rip Van Winkle at Home, 18½"...425.00
Rip Van Winkle on the Mountain, Pat July 25, 1871, 21".........450.00
Rip Van Winkle Returned 550.00
School Days 600.00
Slave Auction 2,000.00
Speak for Yourself John 600.00
Taking the Oath & Drawing Rations, sgn, 23"............................525.00
Tap on the Window 525.00
Traveling Magician, ca 1877 ....750.00
Village Schoolmaster..850.00
Washington..1,250.00
Watch for the Santa Maria 700.00
Weighing the Baby, Pat 1875, 21" 600.00
Wounded Scout, ca 1864 ....750.00
Wrestler...1,250.00

Rookwood

The Rookwood Pottery Company was established in 1879 in Cincinnati, Ohio. Its founder was Maria Longworth Nichols Storer, daughter of a wealthy family who provided the backing necessary to make such an enterprise possible. Mrs. Storer hired competent ceramic workers who through constant experimentation developed many lines of superior art pottery. While in her employ, Laura Fry invented the airbrush-blending process for which she was issued a patent in 1884. From this, several lines were designed that utilized blended backgrounds.

One of their earlier lines, Standard, was a brown ware decorated with underglaze slip-painted nature studies, animals, portraits, etc. Iris and Sea Green were introduced in 1894 and Vellum, a transparent mat-glaze line, in 1904. Other lines followed: Ombroso in 1910 and Soft Porcelain in 1915. Many of the early artware lines were signed by the artist. Soon after the turn of the twentieth century, Rookwood manufactured 'production' pieces that relied mainly on molded designs and forms rather than freehand decoration for their esthetic appeal.

The Depression brought on financial difficulties from which the pottery never recovered. Though it continued to operate, the quality of the ware deteriorated, and the pottery was forced to close in 1967.

Unmarked Rookwood is only rarely encountered. Many marks may be found, but the most familiar is the reverse 'RP' monogram. First used in 1886, a flame point was added above it for each succeeding year until 1900. After that, a Roman numeral added below indicated the year of manufacture. Impressed letters that related to the type of clay utilized for the body were also used — G for ginger, O for olive, R for red, S for sage green, W for white, and Y for yellow.

Artware must be judged on an individual basis. Quality of the artwork is a prime factor to consider. Portraits, animals, and birds are worth more than florals; and pieces signed by a particularly renowned artist are highly prized.

Our advisors for this category are Fer-Duc, Inc.; they are listed in the Directory under New York.

Iris

Pitcher, berries/branches, tricorn top, S Sax, #259E, 4⅛" **475.00**
Vase, cabbage roses, pk/wht on gr to wht, E Diers, '04, 10" **1,500.00**
Vase, clover blossoms on pk to gr, C Steinle, 1911, 6x2½" **600.00**
Vase, floral on bl to wht, C Baker, sm neck, 10", Xd/M **1,500.00**
Vase, grapes/leaves at shoulder, Asbury, 1906, 9", NM **850.00**
Vase, irises, bl/sepia on shaded gray, C Baker, 1895, 7"...............**750.00**
Vase, leaves/flower buds on pk shaded, S Sax, 1907, 8x3¾" **900.00**
Vase, lg floral, wht on dk bl to gr, E Diers, crazed, 9" **750.00**
Vase, mistletoe branches on gr to brn, L Asbury, 1909, 9x4" .. **2,100.00**
Vase, mums, purple on lav to gr, F Rothenbusch, 10", Xd/M . **1,600.00**
Vase, poppies, peach on lt pk to gr, SE Coyne, 1908, 7x6" **1,300.00**
Vase, poppies, wht on bl-gray, EX art, L Ashbury, 1907, 10" .. **2,800.00**
Vase, roses, pk on pk to gr, F Rothenbusch, 1909, 10x4"......... **1,800.00**
Vase, tulips, peach on gray to gr, sgn LA, 1905, 10".....................**800.00**
Vase, winter scene, Rothenbusch, 1909, minor crazing, 8x5".. **1,600.00**
Vase, wisteria, purple on gray to pk, L Asbury, '04, 10x5" **1,500.00**
Vase, 3 crows on bl to pk, ET Hurley, 1906, uncrazed, 8x3".... **1,700.00**

Jewel Porcelain

Jar, repeating triangles/stylized flowers, dome lid, SC, 6" **650.00**
Vase, berries/flowers on peach to bl, A Conant, 1919, 4" **500.00**
Vase, deer/mtns, ivory/bl, J Jensen, 1948, 16x7" **2,750.00**
Vase, flowering stems, wht on dk bl, pk int, S Coyne, 14" **1,700.00**
Vase, wrens/clematis, J Jensen, #6930, 1949, 13x7" **950.00**
Vase, 3 panels w/bird in bamboo tree, S Sax, 1927, 6½x3½"... **2,250.00**

Mat

Bowl vase, stylized floral cvg at shoulder, E Lincoln, 5" **350.00**

Pitcher+4 mugs, cvd ears of corn on brick matt, JD Wareham .. **1,000.00**
Ring tray, Loie Fuller figural, lime, AM Valentien, '01, 8" **1,300.00**
Vase, abstract flowers, cvd/mottled, C Todd, 1917, 8x4" **400.00**
Vase, bleeding heart cvg in 3 colors, AR Valentien, 9x6½" ... **1,600.00**
Vase, butterfly cvg, gr/red, W Hentschel, #1660A, 1912, 16"......**725.00**
Vase, crocus, wht on gr, S Toohey, #120D, Z glaze, '01, 5" **500.00**
Vase, cvg, bl/gr on red, A Pons, #654D, 1906, 4½" **600.00**
Vase, cvg, red on gr-brn, WE Hentschel, #1659D, 9", Xd/M **300.00**
Vase, cvg at shoulder, olive/brn, SC Todd, #973, 1915, 4½" **300.00**
Vase, drippings in red/bl on yel/red, SC Todd, #1278E, 9" **375.00**
Vase, floral, mc on bl-gray, L Asbury, 1926, 13x7" **1,300.00**
Vase, floral, rose/dk bl on shaded lav, S Sax, 1918, 9" **750.00**
Vase, floral (repeating), 3-color on yel, S Sax, 1918, 9" **700.00**
Vase, floral clusters hang from rim, OG Reed, 1906, 11x4" **1,600.00**
Vase, floral/vine cvg, 3-color on dk gr, CS Todd, 1915, 11" **450.00**
Vase, fruit/leaves, red/gr on bl, C Steinle, 1918, 7x3" **325.00**
Vase, horses/flowers emb on lt bl/wht, W Rehm, 1945, 12" **600.00**
Vase, leaf/berry cvg, bl, SC Todd, #670C, 1918, 9".....................**600.00**
Vase, lg irises, violet on shaded gr, A Valentien, '01, 15"........ **2,600.00**
Vase, line cvg/floral emb, brn on gr, Hentschel, '27, 10" **400.00**
Vase, pine cones emb on brn, Arts & Crafts, 1911, 7x3" **200.00**
Vase, poppies emb on sky bl, 1929, 11x7" **200.00**
Vase, repeating floral, 3-color on yel, S Sax, 1918, 8¾" **700.00**
Vase, sections of circles & lines, blk on turq, W Rehm, 8" **550.00**
Vase, stylized leaves, brn on gray-brn, Barrett, 7", Xd/M **450.00**
Wall vase, cvg, bl/gr, #1389, 1920, 8" **240.00**
Wall vase, fly form, yel w/gr, 1915, 8½" L **325.00**
Wall vase, peacock feather cvg, bl w/some yel, 1922, 12..............**140.00**

Porcelain

Vase, abstract floral on yel, rust int, L Epply, 1923, 6" **200.00**
Vase, bluebird on floral branch, WE Hentschel, 1922, 5½" **400.00**

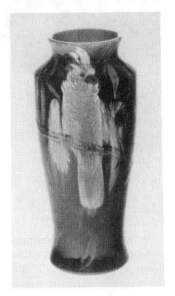

Porcelain vase, cockatoos on dark blue, dark rose interior, signed Shirayamadani, 1924, 11", $5,000.00.

Vase, gazelles, red-lined gray on salmon, Toohey, '46, 7½" **600.00**
Vase, irises, pk/peach, J Jensen, 1914, 6½x5" **550.00**
Vase, robin in tree, Key Ley, flared rim, 1946, 6x5¼" **300.00**
Vase, unicorn/circles, gray on cream, W Hentschel, 1931, 6"......**425.00**

Sea Green

Ewer, 4 fish, ET Hurley, #818G, 1900, 7" **1,400.00**
Vase, fish/seaweed, gr/coral/purple, ET Hurley, 1904, 7x3½" .. **1,300.00**
Vase, lotus leaf & bud cvg, MA Daly, 1898, 7½" **1,100.00**

Vase, salamander at shoulder, MA Daly, 1896, 6" **1,700.00**
Vase, wisteria on dk bl-gr, AR Valentien, hairline, 12" **1,300.00**

Standard

Bowl, wild roses, red clay body, M Daly, #181, 1887, 4x8" **425.00**
Candle holder, daffodils, C Steinle, w/hdl, #710, 1894, 3" **245.00**
Ewer, bittersweet, ST, #611C, 1896, 9½" **500.00**
Ewer, crocus, AM Valentien, fluted top, #468C, 1892, 9" **500.00**
Ewer, daisies, EC Lawrence, #777, 1902, 6" **300.00**
Ewer, floral on yel to brn, AB Sprague, 1890, 13" **1,400.00**
Jug, corn on brn to orange, L Asbury, #676, 1897, 6" **550.00**
Lamp base, leaves/berries, brass base w/4 gargoyle ft, 23" **375.00**
Mug, collie dog, ET Hurley, 1901, 6" **1,000.00**
Pitcher, holly, S Coyne, 1900, 5x6½" **150.00**
Pitcher, leafy spray, AR Valentien, 1891, 12x6" **1,200.00**
Pitcher, lilies, 3-spout, AD Sehon, 1898, 5x6" **350.00**
Vase, berries, Edith Felton, quatrelobed, #551, 1900, 6" **475.00**
Vase, blueberries, E Noonan, #942E, 1906, 4" **325.00**
Vase, branches of leaves, Shirayamadani, 1896, rstr, 7x7" **475.00**
Vase, dogwood, M Foglesong, narrow neck, 1899, 7x3½" **375.00**
Vase, floral, H Strafer, #20F, 1902, 6" **325.00**
Vase, floral, Jeanette Swing, #935E, 1902, 6" **450.00**
Vase, floral, R Flechheimer, hdls, 1899, 8x4" **350.00**
Vase, floral, S Toohey, #933D, 1902, 7" **450.00**
Vase, floral, SE Coyne, #583F, 1893, minor scratches, 5" **325.00**
Vase, floral, yel int, unsgn, #517D, 1901, 5" **150.00**

Standard vase with Indian portrait entitled Buffalo Hunter Shoshone, signed O.G. Reed, 1899, 10", $7,000.00.

Vase, lg gold fish, AM Valentien, flare-rim cylinder, 7" **1,400.00**
Vase, poppies, E Lincoln, #926C, 1901, hdls, 9" **600.00**
Vase, poppies in orange, 'TJM' cvd at neck, AB Sprague, 12". **1,700.00**
Vase, poppies on curving stems, SE Coyne, sm hdls, 6" **450.00**
Vase, Rembrandt portrait, MA Daly, 1897, 9" **1,100.00**
Vase, roses, Caroline Steinle, #871B, 1899, 4½x6½" **375.00**
Vase, sunflowers, C Lindeman, 1905, 9x4½" **750.00**
Vase, wild roses, J Zettel, swirl mold, #612F, 1892, 4" **400.00**

Tiger Eye

Ewer, grapes, amber on burnt orange, sgn ARV, 12" **1,900.00**
Vase, blossoms, gold on mahog, red clay, AR Valentien, 12" **900.00**
Vase, dragon coils at shoulder, MAD, squat w/long neck, 6".. **1,900.00**
Vase, flying dragon, AM Valentien, flare-mouth cylinder, 7"......**900.00**

Vase, turtle pr, AR Valentien, sq-base cylinder, 1898, 5" **800.00**

Vellum

Candlestick, cvg, bl/gr on gr, Sara Sax, mk GV, 1907, 8" **325.00**
Plaque, Bleak December, ET Hurley, orig fr, 9x15" **4,000.00**
Plaque, canal/boats, trees/ladies/bldgs, E Diers, 8x10", M **6,500.00**
Plaque, lg trees/stream, F Rothenbusch, 1917, 9x11" **3,750.00**
Plaque, Quiet Evening, trees/field/mtns, Asbury, 10x10", Xd.. **1,650.00**
Plaque, Quiet Stream, C Schmidt, 1916, orig fr, 10x7" **2,700.00**

Scenic Vellum plaque with pastoral lake scene, signed McDermott, ca 1917, 7" x 9½", $2,800.00.

Plaque, ships in harbor, C Schmidt, 1920, crazed, 8x6" **2,640.00**
Plaque, tall trees, L Asbury, in EX fr, uncrazed, 9x13" **5,250.00**
Plaque, trees/lake/mtns, L Asbury, 5x9" in 8x12" in fr............. **1,200.00**
Plaque, woodland river scene, Rothenbusch, 1922, 8x6" **2,640.00**
Vase, apple blossoms on lt gr, L Asbury, #925D, 1904, 8"........... **425.00**
Vase, berries, orange on lt yel w/dk aqua, P Conant, 9" **475.00**
Vase, birch trees by river, ET Hurley, 1940, 7x3½" **1,500.00**
Vase, cherry blossoms, SE Coyne, jard/ped shape, 12", Xd/M **550.00**
Vase, daffodils on pk, SC, 1912, 8¾" **400.00**
Vase, daisies on yel to pk, E Noonan, #950E, 1906, 8" **375.00**
Vase, fish, gray on shaded pk, ET Hurley, 1906, 10" **1,200.00**
Vase, floral, pk/bl/blk on ivory, A Conant, 1916, 10" **370.00**
Vase, floral band, L Asbury, #890E, 1924, 3½x3½" **375.00**
Vase, floral band on dk bl crackle, Steinle, 1917, 7" **450.00**
Vase, floral branch band on bl, wine int, LE, bulbous, 9" **800.00**
Vase, floral branches on pk, L Asbury, #1927, 1926, 4" **325.00**
Vase, geese on pk to gr, dtd/inscribed, ET Hurley, '06, 6" **850.00**
Vase, landscape band, pastels, Shirayamadani, 1912, 9" **1,400.00**
Vase, landscape w/barn in distance, Ed Diers, 1912, 9" **750.00**
Vase, lg iris (EX art), Ed Diers, 1931, uncrazed, 9" **2,900.00**
Vase, mistletoe on dk bl w/wht top, L Asbury, 1918, 6"............. **325.00**
Vase, nasturtium (detailed), Ed Diers, 1931, uncrazed, 9x6" ... **1,400.00**
Vase, night landscape, ET Hurley, #1356D, 1913, 9" **950.00**
Vase, peacock feathers, AMV, #904C, 1904, 12x4½" **4,000.00**
Vase, poppies, pk on gr-gray, LNL, #900D, 1907, 7" **375.00**
Vase, poppies, wht on aqua, L Asbury, #943C, 1915, 10½" **475.00**
Vase, roses at shoulder, bl to pk, Ed Diers, 1926, 6", NM **240.00**
Vase, sailboats/mtns, bl/gr/pk, S Sax, #1124D, '09, 9", NM **800.00**
Vase, sailboats/trees, gr/blk on charcoal-bl, SE Coyne, 8" **1,500.00**
Vase, snow/mtns/trees, EF McDermott, 1918, 8½" **900.00**
Vase, tree scene, bl/gr on peach, E Diers, 1910, 7", Xd/M **325.00**
Vase, tree scene, EX pastels, SE Coyne, 1921, 5½" **600.00**

Vase, tree scene, F Rothenbusch, 1928, uncrazed, 11x6" **1,800.00**
Vase, tree scene, pea gr/purple on lt bl, MG Denzler, 7" **500.00**
Vase, tree scene, yel on bl & cream, E Diers, 1924, 6x3" **1,000.00**
Vase, trees/mtns (some strong colors), Rothenbusch, 1921, 8" **950.00**
Vase, trees/river/house, pastels, F Rothenbusch, '23, 8x3" **1,000.00**
Vase, trees/snow, Shirayamadani, #917D, 1911, 7", Xd/M **950.00**
Vase, trees/stream, SE Coyne, #654C, 1922, 5½" **700.00**
Vase, trees/water, gray-bl on yel to peach, ETH, 1913, 14" **2,000.00**
Vase, village/trees, sketchy style, J Jensen, 1945, 14" **4,000.00**
Vase, water lilies, F Rothenbusch, 1906, 9x5" **1,200.00**
Vase, water lily, L Asbury, #394C, 1904, 11½" **3,250.00**
Vase, wild roses, raspberry/cream, F Rothenbusch, 1915, 7" **375.00**

Wax Mat

Match holder, bat, striker lines on front, pk/gr, rpr chip **260.00**
Vase, abstract roses on pk, E Abel, 1927, 7½x5", Xd/M **375.00**
Vase, band of pods at shoulder, CS Todd, 1920, 10x3½" **325.00**
Vase, berries on lime to dk gr, MH McDonald, 1927, 8" **400.00**
Vase, cherries in orange/lt tan, CCL, #915C, 1902, 7" **375.00**
Vase, cherry blossoms on bl/pk/wht, yel int, K Jones, 7" **275.00**
Vase, crocus, Shirayamadani, 1934, 5" **600.00**
Vase, daffodils on dk bl, SE Coyne, #2545, 1926, 11" **750.00**
Vase, dogwood, pk on pk, Shirayamadani, 1932, 5¾x5" **450.00**
Vase, floral, bl on shaded bl, L Abel, #927F, 1926, 6" **325.00**
Vase, floral, bl-lined pk on gr & bl, SE Coyne, 1928, 8" **275.00**
Vase, floral, Shirayamadani, #80C, 1904, 7", Xd/M **600.00**
Vase, floral, yel/red on bl/red, E Lincoln, #324, 1922, 17" **650.00**
Vase, floral (EX art), SE Coyne, #2078, 1928, 5" **425.00**
Vase, floral cvg on dk red w/yel, L Abel, #950C, 1920, 11" **375.00**
Vase, floral on bl-gr, MH McDonald, #951E, 1929, 7½" **375.00**
Vase, floral on bright yel, K Jones, 1925, 8x4" **350.00**
Vase, floral on shaded pk, SE Coyne, #614D, 1929, 11½" **650.00**
Vase, gr/red/yel drip decor, V Tischler, #2785, 1924, 14" **600.00**
Vase, grapes on pk shaded, sgn ENL, 1930, bulbous, 6" **450.00**
Vase, hibiscus, red/gr on yel shaded, E Lincoln, 1925, 13" **600.00**
Vase, iris on gr to brn, MH McDonald, minor pitting, 13" **650.00**

Wax Mat vase, llamas and deer in white on dark orange and brown, signed Hentschel, 1929, 7", $1,000.00.

Vase, lg dogwood blossoms, bl/gr on bl, sgn, 1929, 12" **300.00**
Vase, lg mum, dk red on shaded bl, E Barrett, 1924, 14" **600.00**
Vase, narcissus, bl/yel on shaded mc, Shirayamdani, '36, 10" **950.00**
Vase, nasturtiums on pk to gr, M McDonald, 1939, rpr, 6x4" **300.00**
Vase, pineapple cvg, mc on rose & gr, CS Todd, 1918, 18" **775.00**

Vase, tulips, vivid colors, Shirayamadani, 1942, 6½x5" **650.00**
Vase, water lilies/pads, purple/bl, 1926, 7x4" **300.00**

Miscellaneous

Bookends, 1917, rook, olive over bl mat, #2275 ....**300.00**
Bookends, 1921, seated woman w/book, gr mat, #2184, 7x7" **275.00**
Bookends, 1928, lion, bl-gr mat, L Abel, #6019, 6½" **275.00**
Bookends, 1944, puppy, wht mat, #2998, 5x5" **250.00**
Bud vase, 1951, incised, wht on bl crystalline, Holtkamp **400.00**
Figurine, 1924, lion sitting on base, bl mat, #2747, 4" **260.00**
Figurine, 1928, collie (standing), orange mat, #2778, 6x6" **250.00**
Figurine, 1928, seated nude, wht mat, L Abel, #2826, 4" **225.00**
Figurine, 1929, swan, 3-color mat, ST, #6021, 3¾" **350.00**
Figurine, 1930, rook, dk bl/gray mat w/brn, #1623, 3" **275.00**
Figurine, 1933, dog, brn/bl mat, #2777, 5" **275.00**
Figurine, 1934, sailing ship, wht mat, #2792, 3½" **125.00**
Figurine, 1945, donkey, wht mat, #6241, 6x4½" **160.00**
Flower frog, 1928, pelican, orange mat, #2801, 7½" **175.00**
Inkwell & pen tray, 1920, figure of sphinx, LA, no lid.................**250.00**
Jar, intricately emb w/rabbits, pk gloss, Conant, w/lid, 15" **1,300.00**
Jar, 1950, oxblood gloss, Ed Abel, 5½x6" **275.00**
Tile, lakeside mtns/trees, cloisonne technique, 11¾" **1,500.00**
Vase, 1924, violets on 'Chinese plum,' HE Wilcox, #2782, 10" ..**375.00**
Vase, 1927, floral (EX art), wht on 'Chinese plum,' HEW, 7" **800.00**
Vase, 1930, geometrics, mc on pk, S Sax, 5-sided, 6", EX **550.00**
Vase, 1932, bl gr crystalline drip over gray, #2587E, 5" **120.00**
Vase, 1932, brn/tan crystalline, #6303, 4" **110.00**
Vase, 1932, feathered brn gloss, teal gloss int, mk S, 7" **190.00**
Vase, 1932, gray w/bl crystalline neck, bulbous, #6318C, 5" **275.00**
Vase, 1932, gray/orange drip over brn, #630F, 3" **300.00**
Vase, 1932, lt gr drip over brn, lt gr int, mk S, 6" **475.00**
Vase, 1932, red goldstone, gray-brn top, #6318F, 3" **220.00**
Vase, 1932, tan drip over pk gloss, #6303, 7" **190.00**
Vase, 1933, thick red-brn & bl, mk S, 5" **300.00**
Vase, 1943, turq crystalline drip over pk, #6303, 4" **80.00**
Vase, 1945, flowers/foliage, bl, orig label, 8½x7" **75.00**
Vase, 1946, deer/grass, brn on tan, J Jensen, #6940, 10" **1,000.00**
Vase, 1948, wavy line/dot bands, J Jensen, 7½" **375.00**
Vase, 1953, olive to bl gloss, lt gr int, RE Menzel, 7" **250.00**

Rose Mandarin

Similar in design to Rose Medallion, this Chinese Export porcelain features the pattern of a robed mandarin, often separated by florals, ladies, genre scenes, or butterflies in polychrome enamels, often having gold trim. Elaborate in decoration, this pattern was popular from the late 1700s until the early 1840s.

Bowl, vegetable; bamboo lid hdl, rectangular, 1840s, 8x10" **1,200.00**
Dish, shaped rim, 1830, rstr, 12", pr **950.00**
Fruit basket, rtcl sides & rim, 1830, rstr hdls, 8", +tray............ **1,300.00**
Hot water platter, acorn finial, oval, w/lid, 1840, 11x14" **2,400.00**
Jardiniere, hexagonal, 1830s, 6¾", +undertray **750.00**
Platter, early 1800s, 17" L **1,300.00**
Shrimp dish, wide border, 1830, 10" W **750.00**
Soup plate, armorial crests, 1810, 9¾", set of 6 .... **2,800.00**
Vase, 4-lobed neck & rims, baluster body, 1830, rstr, 12" **250.00**

Rose Medallion

Rose Medallion is one of the patterns of Chinese export porcelain produced from before 1850 until the second decade of the 20th century. It is decorated in rose colors with panels of florals, birds, and butterflies that form reserves containing Chinese figures. Pre-1850s ware is unmarked and is characterized by quality workmanship and gold trim. From about 1850 until circa 1860, the kilns in Canton did not operate, and no Rose Medallion was made. Post-1860 examples (still unmarked) can often be recognized by the poor quality of the gold trim or its absence. In the 1890s, the ware was often marked 'China'; 'Made in China' was used from 1910 through the 1930s.

Basin, Quin Export, 1800s, 15¾" dia 750.00
Bowl, soup; mk China, w/lid & saucer, 1880s....................85.00
Bowl, vegetable; shaped oval, acorn finial, 1880s, 12", NM........450.00
Brush box, rectangular, 1880, 7" L 350.00
Candlestick, mk China, 1900, rim chip, 9", pr 750.00
Canister, sqd, dome lid, 1880s, 3" to 5¾", set of 5, EX............ 2,100.00

Jar, late 18th century, 15", EX, $650.00.

Platter, fruit; shaped rim, gilt, ftd, 1850s, 15" L 600.00
Platter, mk China, 1900s, 10x8" 125.00
Platter, 14½" 325.00
Platter, 1850s, 19", on mahog wood stand............................... 1,300.00
Punch bowl, stabilized hairline, rim chip, 16" 900.00
Punch bowl, 1880s, 16", on ormolu stand 1,700.00
Shrimp dish, shaped rim, 1850s, 10", NM 550.00
Tea cup & saucer, 1880s...55.00
Tea set, in orig wicker basket, pre-1900s, 3-pc 450.00
Teapot, 1860s, 5" 275.00
Teapot, 1860s, 6" 295.00
Umbrella stand, cylindrical, 1880s, 24", EX 850.00
Vase, bat border, lizard hdls & trim, long neck, 9", EX, pr..........550.00
Vase, bird & flower panels, cylindrical, 9"..................................150.00
Vase, bottle form, 1850s, now lamp, 15", EX..............................600.00
Vase, dragons/sun relief at neck, baluster, 1850s, 14"................850.00
Vase, foo dog hdls, 2 lizards, gilt, 1880s, 17½" 700.00

Rosemeade

Rosemeade was the name chosen by Wahpeton Pottery Company of Wahpeton, North Dakota, to represent their product. The founders of the company were Laura Meade Taylor and R.J. Hughes, who organized the firm in 1940. It is most noted for small bird and animal figurals, either in high gloss or a Van Briggle-like matt glaze. The ware was marked 'Rosemeade' with an ink stamp or carried a 'Prairie Rose' sticker. The pottery closed in 1961.

Ash tray, Indian head 42.50
Ash tray, N Dakota shape..30.00
Ash tray, pheasant 35.00
Bank, hippo form 40.00
Basket, navy matt, plain, sm..12.50
Bell, flower form 32.00
Candle holder, aqua, sq, 1½x3¼" 12.00
Candle holder, bird form, pr 25.00
Figurine, elephant, seated, mini 16.00
Figurine, goose, 2", pr 20.00
Figurine, Indian God of Peace, 9" 80.00
Figurine, pheasant, 11" 125.00
Figurine, prairie dog, 1¾", pr 22.50
Figurine, seal, lg 30.00
Figurine, wolfhound, bl & gr 75.00
Flower frog, fish 27.50
Flower frog, heron, med bl on blk base...................................32.00
Jug, blk & bronze, hdl, 7½" 20.00
Lamp, TV; dog running 395.00
Pitcher, aqua, ball form, 4" 20.00
Pitcher, blk, 7½" 30.00
Pitcher, bronze, 7½" 35.00
Planter, bird on log 25.00
Planter, elephant, bl & gr 40.00
Planter, pk, hanging, 3" 20.00
Planter, pony, bronze 40.00
Rose bowl, tulip form, rose, 3" 17.50
Shakers, blk bear w/tan face, lg, pr..40.00
Shakers, blk bear w/tan face, walking, sm, pr 32.00
Shakers, bloodhound, brn, pr 32.00
Shakers, donkey head, grayish-brn, pr 35.00
Shakers, elephant, pr 45.00
Shakers, English bulldog, pr...22.00
Shakers, fish, gr, pr 25.00
Shakers, mule, brn, pr 36.00
Shakers, Palomino head, pr 30.00
Shakers, pekingese, pr..25.00
Shakers, pheasant, pr 20.00
Shakers, prairie dog, pr 28.00
Shakers, raccoon, tan w/blk & wht, pr 32.00
Shakers, rooster & hen, rose, pr 22.50
Shakers, skunk, pr...25.00
Shakers, turkey, pr 45.00
Spoon rest, rooster & hen, 4-color 38.00
Sugar bowl, corn cob, shiny..17.50

Tray with teddy bear, inscribed Teddy Roosevelt Memorial Park, $50.00.

Tidbit tray, rooster 45.00
Vase, bud; 2 parrots..25.00
Vase, lovebird, cream/aqua matt 17.50
Vase, pk, squat, 5" W..20.00
Vase/planter, Dutch shoe, gr, lg......................................17.50

Rosenthal

In 1879 Phillip Rosenthal established the Rosenthal Porcelain Factory in Selb, Bavaria. Its earliest products were figurines and fine tablewares. The company has continued to operate to the present decade, manufacturing limited edition plates.

Card tray, gold leaves on wht, sgn, 5x7" 85.00
Coaster, roses w/sterling rim 15.00
Coffeepot, ironstone, 10" 85.00
Creamer & sugar bowl, pate-sur-pate bl cherries 85.00
Ewer, swags/curving florals overall, mk w/stork, 11" 600.00

Dancer with swirling skirt, bare midriff, 10", $225.00.

Figurine, Egyptian woman, snake charmer, mk, 8" 325.00
Figurine, nude w/drape on silver base w/gr knop, Wenck, 12" 400.00
Figurine, princess & frog, pastels w/gold, mk, 11" 350.00
Figurine, Prinzessin, sgn Schliepstein, 1827, 18" 1,900.00
Plate, Delft type w/windmill, 6¾" 30.00
Tray, florals, mk Sevres Style, Madeline, 12x9"..............40.00
Vase, girl w/flower basket by bush, gold trim, 13½"........250.00
Vase, silver overlay on orange & gray-bl, ewer form, mk, 6" 275.00
Vase, Studio Line, stylized bird/flowers, 6".....................45.00

Roseville

The Roseville Pottery Company was established in 1892 by George F. Young in Roseville, Ohio. Finding their facilities inadequate, the company moved to Zanesville in 1898, erected a new building, and installed the most modern equipment available. By 1900 Young felt ready to enter into the stiffly competitive art pottery market.

Roseville's first art line was called Rozane. Similar to Rookwood's Standard, Rozane featured dark blended backgrounds with slip-painted underglaze artwork of nature studies, portraits, birds, and animals. Azurean, developed in 1902, was a blue and white underglaze art line on a blue blended background. Egypto (1904) featured a matt glaze in a soft shade of old green and was modeled in low relief after examples of ancient Egyptian pottery. Mongol (1904) was a high-gloss oxblood red line after the fashion of the Chinese Sang de Boeuf. Mara (1904), an

iridescent lustre line of magenta and rose with intricate patterns developed on the surface or in low relief, successfully duplicated Sicardo's work. These early lines were followed by many others of highest quality: Fudjiyama and Woodland (1905-06) reflected an Oriental theme; Crystalis (1906) was covered with beautiful frost-like crystals. Della Robbia, their most famous line (introduced in 1906), was decorated with designs ranging from florals, animals, and birds to scenes of Viking warriors and Roman gladiators. These designs were accomplished by sgraffito with slip-painted details. Very limited but of great importance to collectors today, Rozane Olympic (1905) was decorated with scenes of Greek mythology on a red ground. Pauleo (1914) was the last of the artware lines. It was varied — over two hundred glazes were recorded — and some pieces were decorated by hand, usually with florals.

During the second decade of the century until the plant closed forty years later, new lines were continually added. Some of the more popular of the middle-period lines were Donatello, 1915; Futura, 1928; Pine Cone, 1931; and Blackberry, 1933. The floral lines of the later years have become highly collectible. Pottery from every era of Roseville production — even its utility ware — attest to an unwavering dedication to quality and artistic merit.

Examples of the fine art pottery lines present the greatest challenge to evaluate. Scarcity is a prime consideration. The quality of artwork varied from one artist to another. Some pieces show fine detail and good color, and naturally this influences their values. Studies of animals and portraits bring higher prices than the floral designs. An artist's signature often increases the value of any item, especially if the artist is one who is well recognized. For further information, consult *The Collector's Encyclopedia of Roseville Pottery, First and Second Series,* by Sharon and Bob Huxford, available at your local library or bookstore.

Our advisors for this category are Jeanette and Marvin Stofft; they are listed in the Directory under Indiana.

Apple Blossom, bowl vase, hdls, #342, 6" 65.00
Apple Blossom, vase, hdls, #388, 10" 125.00
Artcraft, jardiniere & pedestal, 24½"............................550.00
Artcraft, planter, 4 buttresses on angle shoulder, 8x12" 200.00
Artwood, planter, #1054, 6½x8½" 35.00
Autumn, jardiniere, 9½" 600.00
Autumn, pitcher, 8½" 400.00
Aztec, vase, cylinder w/wider shoulder, 11½".................375.00
Aztec, vase, simple decor, slim ovoid w/long neck, 9½" 225.00
Azurean, mug, cloverleaves, scroll hdl 450.00
Azurean, vase, floral spray, Leffler, slim, 15½" 1,000.00
Baneda, bowl vase, hdls, 5" H..200.00
Baneda, candle holder, hdls, 5½" 125.00
Baneda, vase, hdls, 4" 100.00
Baneda, wall pocket, 8" 525.00
Bank, beehive, yel sponged, 3" 200.00
Bank, buffalo, 6½" L...150.00
Bank, cat's head, 4" 175.00
Bank, eagle's head, 2½" 175.00
Bank, Uncle Sam, no mk, 4" 125.00
Bittersweet, basket, #807, 8½" 60.00
Bittersweet, dbl vase, 4" H..40.00
Bittersweet, planter, #828, 10½" L 40.00
Blackberry, hanging basket, 4½" 500.00
Blackberry, jardiniere, hdls, 7" H...................................250.00
Blackberry, jardiniere & pedestal, 28" 4,000.00
Blackberry, vase, rim hdls, 6" 175.00
Blackberry, wall pocket, 8½"..325.00
Bleeding Heart, candlestick, 5" 45.00
Bleeding Heart, hanging basket, 8" 125.00
Bleeding Heart, vase, hdls, 8" 55.00
Bleeding Heart, wall pocket, 8½"....................................150.00

Borden's Elsie the Cow plate, 7½", $150.00.

Bushberry, bud vase, 7½"	50.00
Bushberry, cider pitcher, 8½"	200.00
Bushberry, dbl cornucopia, 6"	45.00
Bushberry, hanging basket, 7"	350.00
Bushberry, vase, hdls, #34, 8"	75.00
Bushberry, wall pocket, 8"	150.00
Capri, basket, 9"	75.00
Carnelian I, bowl w/hdls, flower frog, 8½" L	35.00
Carnelian I, vase, fluted fan form, hdls, 8"	40.00
Carnelian I, wall pocket, 9½"	75.00
Carnelian II, bowl vase, hdls, 5"	40.00
Carnelian II, ewer, 12½"	125.00
Carnelian II, wall pocket, 8"	100.00
Ceramic Design, wall pocket, 11"	200.00
Cherry Blossom, jardiniere & pedestal, 25½"	1,500.00
Cherry Blossom, wall pocket, 8"	400.00
Chloron, vase, bullet form in base w/3 lg ft, 12"	350.00
Chocolate pot, floral, artist sgn, #936, 9½"	400.00
Clemana, bowl, #281, 4½x6½"	65.00
Clemana, vase, bulbous, #754, 8½"	150.00
Clematis, console bowl, 14" L	50.00
Clematis, vase, hdls, #102, 6½"	30.00
Clematis, wall pocket, 8½"	60.00
Columbine, bookend/planter, 5"	50.00
Columbine, vase, hdls, 7½"	50.00
Corinthian, jardiniere, 7"	85.00
Corinthian, vase, 8½"	70.00
Corinthian, wall pocket, 8"	75.00
Cosmos, console bowl, #374, 15½" L	100.00
Cosmos, hanging basket, 7"	200.00
Cosmos, vase, hdls, #905, 8"	75.00
Cremona, vase, angle body, 4"	40.00
Cremona, vase, flat rim, slim ftd baluster form, 12"	100.00
Crystalis, candle holder, gr, 9"	900.00
Crystalis, vase, orange, 5½"	900.00
Dahlrose, hanging basket	100.00
Dahlrose, jardiniere & pedestal, 30½"	750.00
Dahlrose, vase, hdls, 6"	55.00
Dahlrose, vase, rim hdls, 8"	100.00
Dahlrose, wall pocket, 10"	125.00
Dawn, vase, 12"	100.00
Decorated Landscape, jardiniere & pedestal, 44"	2,500.00
Della Robbia, letter holder, stylized irid, no mk, 3½"	650.00
Della Robbia, teapot, stylized flowers, sgn GB, 8½"	1,200.00
Della Robbia, teapot, stylized roses, cream/bl, rpr, 6x8"	700.00
Della Robbia, vase, swans, sgn FB, 11½"	4,200.00
Della Robbia, vase, trees, buff on tan, 4-sided cone, 11"	1,200.00

Dogwood I, bowl, shallow, 2½" H	45.00
Dogwood I, hanging basket, 7" W	110.00
Dogwood I, jardiniere & pedestal, 30"	600.00
Dogwood I, vase, ovoid, 7"	100.00
Dogwood II, dbl bud vase, 8"	70.00
Dogwood II, tub, 4x7"	60.00
Dogwood II, wall pocket, 9"	90.00
Donatello, ash tray, 3" H	75.00
Donatello, basket, 7½"	125.00
Donatello, bowl, shallow, 6"	40.00
Donatello, cuspidor, 5½"	165.00
Donatello, hanging basket, 7"	125.00
Donatello, jardiniere & pedestal, 34"	1,200.00
Dutch, humidor, Compliments of..., 6"	200.00
Dutch, soap dish w/lid	150.00
Dutch, tankard, 11½"	150.00
Earlam, bowl vase, hdls, 4"	45.00
Earlam, vase, hdls, 6"	60.00
Earlam, wall pocket, 6½"	200.00
Early Pitcher, Bridge, 6"	55.00
Early Pitcher, Cow, head down, 7½"	175.00
Early Pitcher, Cow, rare, 6½"	200.00
Early Pitcher, Iris, 7"	175.00
Early Pitcher, Landscape, 7½"	55.00
Early Pitcher, Poppy, 9"	100.00
Early Pitcher, Tulip, 7½"	55.00
Egypto, pitcher vase, geometrics, 11"	225.00
Falline, bowl vase, hdls, 6" H	200.00
Falline, vase, slim ftd U-form, hdls, 7½"	200.00
Ferella, vase, hdls, 4"	125.00
Ferella, vase, wide body, 6"	175.00
Florentine, candlestick, 10½"	80.00
Florentine, dbl bud vase, 4½"	40.00
Florentine, hanging basket	110.00
Florentine, wall pocket, 7"	50.00
Foxglove, hanging basket, 6½"	135.00
Foxglove, jardiniere & pedestal, 30½"	750.00
Foxglove, tray, 8½"	50.00
Foxglove, vase, #52, 12½"	200.00
Foxglove, vase, hdls, #47, 8½"	125.00
Freesia, basket, #390, 7"	60.00
Freesia, flowerpot & saucer, 5½"	60.00
Freesia, vase, hdls, #121, 8"	60.00
Fuchsia, candlestick, 2"	35.00
Fuchsia, vase, hdls, #892, 6"	75.00
Futura, jardiniere, leaves, angle hdls, 6" H	125.00
Futura, vase, acorn form in 4-buttress base, bl, 7"	550.00
Futura, vase, ball on flat quatrelateral, leaf panels, 7½"	450.00
Futura, vase, upright rectangle w/stepped top, hdls, 8", NM	375.00
Futura, wall pocket, 8"	200.00
Futura, window box, 15½" L	350.00

Luffa vase, 9", $150.00.

Gardenia, hanging basket, 6" 135.00
Gardenia, vase, #683, 8" 45.00
Gardenia, wall pocket, 9½" 125.00
Holland, mug, no mk, 4" 45.00
Holland, pitcher, #1, 6½" 135.00
Holland, powder jar, 3" H 95.00
Holland, tankard, #2, 9½" 125.00
Imperial I, basket, #8, 10" 80.00
Imperial I, comport, 6½" H 80.00
Imperial I, vase, hdls, 10" 80.00
Imperial II, bowl, yel drip on med bl, flared, 12½" L 125.00
Imperial II, vase, rose w/ring-cvd neck, 7" 150.00
Imperial II, vase, yel top on aqua body, 5" 70.00
Iris, vase, #917, 6½" 70.00
Iris, vase, pillow form, #922, 8½" 90.00
Ivory Florentine, wall pocket, 8½" 95.00
Ivory II, cornucopia, 5½" 35.00
Ivory II, vase, stepped base, hdls, 7" 45.00
Ixia, console bowl, shallow, 3½" H 25.00
Ixia, hanging basket 150.00
Jonquil, bowl vase, lg loop hdls, 3" H 60.00
Jonquil, bowl vase, 4" 50.00
Jonquil, jardiniere & pedestal, 29" 1,500.00
Jonquil, vase, hdls, 8" 100.00
Juvenile, Duck, cup & saucer 95.00
Juvenile, Duck, mug, 3½" 85.00
Juvenile, Fancy Cat, divided plate, 8½" 300.00
Juvenile, Fancy Cat, mug, 3" 125.00
Juvenile, Nursery Rhyme, sugar bowl, 3" 125.00
Juvenile, Santa Claus, cup & saucer 150.00
Juvenile, Sitting Rabbit, baby's plate, 8" 150.00
Juvenile, Sitting Rabbit, custard cup, 2½" 60.00
Juvenile, Sitting Rabbit, egg cup, single, 3" 125.00
La Rose, vase, 6" 40.00
La Rose, wall pocket, 9" 90.00
Landscape, wall pocket, 2½" 200.00
Laurel, bowl vase, sm rim hdls, 6½" H 100.00
Laurel, vase, ftd V-form, 10" 125.00
Lombardy, wall pocket, 8" 175.00
Lotus, planter, sq, #L9, 3½" 60.00
Luffa, candlestick, 5" 80.00
Luffa, jardiniere & pedestal, 24½" 750.00
Luffa, vase, hdls, 10" 150.00
Luffa, vase, hdls, 8" 110.00

Luffa, wall pocket, 8½" 225.00
Magnolia, ash tray, 7" 45.00
Magnolia, candlestick, 5" 20.00
Magnolia, vase, #88, 6" 30.00
Mara, vase, lobed pear form w/shoulder hdls, #13, 5½" 1,650.00
Matt Green, gate, 5x8" 35.00
Mayfair, pitcher, 5" 35.00
Mayfair, planter, sq/ftd, #90, 4½" 30.00
Ming Tree, hanging basket, 6" 150.00
Ming Tree, vase, #572, 6½" 65.00
Ming Tree, vase, #584, 12½" 100.00
Ming Tree, wall pocket, 8½" 175.00
Mock Orange, vase, 1-hdl, #973, 8½" 45.00
Mock Orange, window box, #956, 8½" L 35.00
Moderne, candle holder, triple, 6" 100.00
Moderne, vase, hdls, 6½" 50.00
Mongol, vase, cylindrical, 16" 900.00
Montacello, basket, 6½" 175.00
Montacello, vase, hdls, 5" 65.00
Montacello, vase, low hdls, 10½" 175.00
Morning Glory, candlestick, 5" 125.00
Morning Glory, vase, pillow form, 7" 225.00
Morning Glory, vase, wht, hdls, 10", NM 220.00
Morning Glory, wall pocket, 8½" 425.00
Moss, bowl vase, low hdls, #209, 6" 70.00
Moss, vase, hdls, #781, pillow form, 8" 80.00
Mostique, bowl, hdls, shallow, 9" 55.00
Mostique, vase, concave cylinder w/hdls, 12" 100.00
Mostique, vase, 10" 85.00
Mostique, wall pocket, 9½" 125.00
Normandy, sand jar, 14" 350.00
Normandy, umbrella stand, 20" 550.00
Novelty Stein, ea 225.00
Olympic, vase, Juno Commanding the Sun To Set, 20" 4,500.00
Orian, vase, ftd/hdls, 10½" 110.00
Pasadena, ash tray, sq, 8½" 30.00
Pauleo, vase, lg iris on wht to lav, 19" 1,200.00
Pauleo, vase, wine to maroon, 19" 900.00
Peony, conch shell, 9½" 45.00
Peony, dbl candle holder, 5" 35.00
Peony, mug, 3½" 45.00
Peony, vase, #68, 14" 125.00
Peony, wall pocket, 8" 75.00
Persian, wall pocket, 11" 250.00
Pine Cone, basket, #353, 11" 250.00
Pine Cone, boat dish, #427-8, 8" 125.00
Pine Cone, console bowl, 11" L 175.00
Pine Cone, vase, #121, 7" 125.00
Pine Cone, vase, #907, 7" 75.00
Pine Cone, vase, bl, branch hdls, pillow form, 8" 200.00
Poppy, basket, 12½" 270.00
Poppy, bowl vase, hdls, 6½" 75.00
Poppy, ewer, 18½" 270.00
Poppy, vase, low hdls, 6" 55.00
Primrose, vase, hdls, 6½" 70.00
Raymor, bowl, vegetable; 9" 12.00
Raymor, butter dish w/lid, 7½" 30.00
Raymor, casserole, ind; 7½" 18.00
Raymor, gravy bowl, 9½" 12.00
Raymor, water pitcher 75.00
Rosecraft Hexagon, candlestick, 8" 100.00
Rosecraft Hexagon, vase, 8" 150.00
Rosecraft Hexagon, wall pocket, 8½" 125.00
Rosecraft Panel, vase, pendant flowers, 10" 150.00

Gardenia vase, #685, 10", $125.00.

Rosecraft Panel, vase, 6" 50.00
Rosecraft Vintage, jardiniere & pedestal, 30½" 550.00
Rosecraft Vintage, vase, 12" 175.00
Rosecraft Vintage, window box, 11½" L 125.00
Rozane, vase, berries, artist sgn, squat hdld bottle form, 7" 250.00
Rozane, vase, bulldog, ruffled/hdld pillow form, #882, 9" 2,000.00
Rozane, vase, cat portrait, sgn HS, collared ovoid, 9½" 2,000.00
Rozane, vase, cherries, Myers, ovoid w/shoulder hdls, 12" 350.00
Rozane, vase, dog w/pheasant in mouth, pillow form, 8½" 1,800.00
Rozane, vase, floral, ruffled/hdld pillow form, no mk, 7" 200.00
Rozane, vase, floral, Walter Myers, flared cylinder, 15" 325.00
Rozane, vase, pansies, C Neff, cylinder expands to 3 ft, 9½"........125.00
Rozane, vase, 4-sided funnel w/bun base, gr/bl, 10" 400.00
Rozane Light, mug, berries, M Timberlake, 5" 250.00
Rozane Light, sugar bowl, sm florals, lg hdls, 4½" 200.00
Rozane Light, tankard, corn, J Imlay, 10" 400.00
Rozane Light, tankard, grapes, C Mitchell, 11" 450.00
Rozane Light, tankard, lg plums, L Mitchell, 16" 600.00
Rozane Light, teapot, birds on lt bl, ornate hdl, Rhead, 8" 1,200.00
Rozane Light, vase, floral, W Myers, expanded cylinder, 8½".....300.00
Rozane Light, vase, lilies of the valley, J Imlay, 10½"...................275.00
Rozane Light, vase, long-stem clover, H Pillsbury, slim, 11".......275.00
Rozane Light, vase, narcissus, J Imlay, tiny neck, 8" 300.00
Rozane Pattern, vase, #10, 12" 45.00
Rozane 1917, basket, 11" 90.00
Rozane 1917, bowl, incurvate, 3" H 45.00
Rozane 1917, compote, 8" 65.00
Rozane 1917, jardiniere & pedestal, 28½" 475.00
Russco, triple cornucopia, 12½" L 70.00
Russco, vase, ftd, hdls, crystalline, 8" 95.00
Savona, candlestick, 10"...125.00
Savona, window box, 9" L 35.00
Silhouette, box, 4½" 40.00
Silhouette, ewer, 6½" 40.00
Silhouette, vase, #781, 6" 25.00
Silhouette, vase, #787, 10" 125.00
Snowberry, basket, 12½" 75.00
Snowberry, candlestick, 4½" 20.00
Snowberry, ewer, 16" 150.00
Snowberry, jardiniere & pedestal, 25" 450.00
Snowberry, vase, hdls, #V-6, 6" 25.00

Juvenile baby plate, Sunbonnet girl, $100.00.

Sunflower, bowl vase, sm rim hdls, 4" 150.00
Sunflower, jardiniere & pedestal, 20½" 1,200.00
Sunflower, vase, sm hdls, 5" 200.00
Sunflower, vase, sm rim hdls, 10" 450.00
Teasel, vase, ftd, 12" 55.00

Thornapple, dbl bud vase, 5½" 35.00
Thornapple, vase, hdls, 8½" 45.00
Topeo, bowl, bl, 11½"...45.00
Topeo, vase, red, 7" 125.00
Tourist, umbrella stand, 22½" 2,000.00
Tourist, window box, 19" L 1,100.00
Tourmaline, cornucopia, 7"...45.00
Tourmaline, vase, bl, hdld pillow form, 6" 50.00
Tourmaline, vase, gold, hdls, 5½" 70.00
Tuscany, vase, ftd V-form, 4" 35.00
Tuscany, vase, hdls, 12" 95.00
Tuscany, wall pocket, 7" 50.00
Velmoss, vase, 14½" 140.00
Velmoss, vase, 8" 55.00
Velmoss Scroll, vase, 5" 70.00
Velmoss Scroll, wall pocket, 11½" 115.00
Victorian Art Pottery, jar w/lid, berry band, 8" 350.00
Victorian Art Pottery, vase, beetle band, 8x6".........................150.00
Vista, basket, 12"...200.00
Vista, jardiniere & pedestal, 28" 750.00
Vista, vase, cylindrical w/bulbous top, hdls, 12" 260.00
Vista, vase, spreading ft, 10"...225.00
Water Lily, flower frog, 4½" 20.00
Water Lily, vase, hdls, #78, 9" 100.00
White Rose, candlestick, 4½" 25.00
White Rose, dbl bud vase, 4½" 40.00
White Rose, vase, hdls, #979, 6" 55.00
White Rose, wall pocket, 6½" 75.00
Wincraft, bookends, 6½" 50.00
Wincraft, cornucopia, 5x9" 40.00
Wincraft, mug, plain, 4½" 60.00
Wincraft, vase, #274, 7" 50.00
Wincraft, wall pocket, 5" 90.00
Windsor, bowl, hdls, 10½" L 90.00
Windsor, vase, hdls, 6" 90.00
Wisteria, hanging basket 450.00
Wisteria, jardiniere & pedestal, 24½".................................. 1,500.00
Wisteria, vase, hdls, 10" 400.00
Wisteria, vase, hdls, 8½" 275.00
Woodland, vase, floral, elongated dbl gourd form, 11" 700.00
Woodland, vase, floral, 6" 525.00
Woodland, vase, long-stem floral, 19" 1,750.00
Woodland, vase, 3 spider flowers in gold/brn, 6x2½", NM 300.00
Zephyr Lily, bud vase, 7½" 30.00
Zephyr Lily, candlestick, 2" 20.00
Zephyr Lily, cornucopia, 8½" 40.00
Zephyr Lily, hanging basket, 7½" 125.00
Zephyr Lily, wall pocket, 8" 75.00

Rowland and Marsellus

Though the impressive back stamp seems to suggest otherwise, Rowland and Marsellus were not Staffordshire potters but American importers who commissioned various English companies to supply them with the transfer-printed historical ware that had been a popular import item since the early 1800s. Plates (both flat and with a rolled edge), cups and saucers, pitchers, and platters were sold as souvenirs from 1890 through the 1930s. Though other importers — Bawo & Dotter, and A. C. Bosselman & Co., both of New York City — commissioned the manufacture of similar souvenir items, by far the largest volume carries the R. & M. mark, and Rowland and Marsellus has become a generic term that covers all 20th century souvenir china of this type. Their mark may be in full or 'R. & M.' in a diamond. Though primarily made with blue transfers on white, other colors may occasionally be found as well.

Our advisor for this category is David Ringering; he is listed in the Directory under California.

Key:
r/e — rolled edge   v/o — view of
s/o — souvenir of

Cup & saucer, Albany NY	65.00
Cup & saucer, Lewis & Clark Expo	85.00
Cup & saucer, Panama Pacific Expo	85.00
Plate, Altoona PA, s/o, Horseshoe Curve, r/e, 10"	50.00
Plate, Bermuda, Aliss Somers Island, 1609-1909, r/e	50.00
Plate, Bridgeport CT, s/o, Soldiers Monument, r/e, 10"	50.00
Plate, Butte MT, s/o, Bronco Busting, r/e, 10"	60.00
Plate, Chicago, s/o, State Street, r/e, 10"	50.00
Plate, Columbus OH, s/o, OH State Capital, r/e, 10"	55.00
Plate, coupe; Early Missions of California, bl, 6½"	30.00
Plate, coupe; Early Missions of California, gr, 6½"	20.00
Plate, coupe; Vancouver BC, 6½"	35.00
Plate, Detroit (MI), s/o, Log Cabin..., r/e, 10"	50.00
Plate, Golden Rule Co, ...Store, r/e, 10"	55.00
Plate, Hot Springs VA, s/o, Homestead, r/e, 10"	50.00
Plate, Jackson MS, s/o, New Capital Building, r/e, 10"	55.00
Plate, Kansas City, s/o, Convention Hall, r/e, 10"	45.00
Plate, Memphis TN, r/e, 10"	50.00
Plate, Memphis TN, s/o, Skyscraper District, r/e, 10"	50.00
Plate, Porfirio Diaz, Mexican General, r/e, 10"	55.00
Plate, Spokane WA, r/e, 10"	50.00

Platter, marked R&M, A.S. Burbank, 17" x 12", $300.00.

Tumbler, Niagara Falls, s/o	65.00
Tumbler, Thousand Islands, v/o	65.00

Royal Bayreuth

Founded in 1794 in Tettau, Bavaria, the Royal Bayreuth firm originally manufactured fine dinnerwares of superior quality. Their figural items, produced from before the turn of the century until the onset of WWI, are highly sought after by today's collectors. Perhaps the most abundantly produced and easily recognized of these are the tomato and lobster pieces. Fruits, flowers, people, animals, birds, and vegetables shapes were also made. Aside from figural items, pitchers, toothpick holders, cups and saucers, humidors and the like were decorated in florals and scenic motifs. Some, such as the very popular Rose Tapestry line, utilized a cloth-like tapestry background. Transfer prints were used as well. Two of the most popular are Sunbonnet Babies and Nursery Rhymes (in particular, those decorated with the complete verse).

Caution: Many pieces were not marked; some were marked 'Deponiert' or 'Registered' only. While marked pieces are the most valued, unmarked items are still very worthwhile.

Our advisors for this category are Larry Brenner from New Hampshire and Dee Hooks from Illinois; they are listed in the Directory under their home states.

Figurals

Ash tray, lettuce leaf w/lobster hdl, bl mk	48.00
Ash tray, murex shell, bl mk	65.00
Bowl, Art Nouveau, bl mk, 2 figures, 5¾"	1,500.00
Bowl, oak leaf, MOP, bl mk, lg	285.00
Candle holder, dachshund, bl mk, 4½"	255.00
Candlestick, Art Nouveau, bl mk, tall	1,495.00
Candy dish, Devil & Cards, bl mk	195.00
Candy dish, murex shell, bl mk	85.00
Compote, poppy w/gr leaf stem, bl mk, 5¾x3½"	300.00
Creamer & sugar bowl, strawberry, bl mk	225.00
Cup & saucer, coffee; tomato, bl mk	85.00
Cup & saucer, demitasse; apple, bl mk	135.00
Dish, leaf, bl mk, loop hdl, 4⅛"	30.00

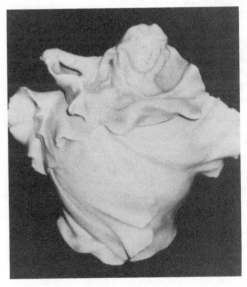

Humidor, Art Nouveau, blue mark, 7", $1,560.00.

Humidor, bellringer, bl mk, rare	785.00
Humidor, Devil & Cards, bl mk	525.00
Inkwell, elk, bl mk, 2x5"	200.00
Match holder, Devil & Cards, bl mk, wall hanging	375.00
Match holder, elk, bl mk, wall hanging	295.00
Match holder, mountain goat, bl mk, wall hanging	575.00
Match holder, poppy, bl mk, wall hanging	200.00
Mustard, grapes, pk MOP, Tettau mk	95.00
Mustard, grapes, yel, bl mk	120.00
Mustard, lobster, red, unmk	45.00
Mustard, orange, bl mk	145.00
Mustard, poppy, pk MOP, bl mk	95.00
Mustard, poppy, red, Deponiert & bl mk	95.00
Mustard, poppy, red, Deponiert & gr mk, w/spoon	110.00
Mustard, rose, bl mk	300.00
Pin dish, crab lid, unmk, 1¾x4x3¾"	60.00
Pitcher, alligator, gr, bl mk, cream sz	285.00
Pitcher, apple, bl mk, cream sz	135.00
Pitcher, apple, bl mk, milk sz	200.00

Pitcher, apple, unmk, cream sz 60.00
Pitcher, apple, unmk, water sz 325.00
Pitcher, Art Nouveau, bl mk, cream sz 650.00
Pitcher, Art Nouveau, deep pk coloring, bl mk, cream sz...........750.00
Pitcher, bear, bl mk, cream sz 850.00
Pitcher, bull, blk, unmk, cream sz 150.00
Pitcher, bull, brn & wht, bl mk, cream sz 160.00
Pitcher, bull, dk to lt gray, bl mk, cream sz 165.00
Pitcher, butterfly, bl mk, closed wings, milk sz 450.00
Pitcher, butterfly, bl mk, open wings, milk sz 355.00
Pitcher, cat, blk, bl mk, cream sz 135.00
Pitcher, chrysanthemum, bl mk, cream sz 375.00
Pitcher, clown, red, bl mk, cream sz 195.00
Pitcher, clown, yel, bl mk, cream sz 165.00
Pitcher, coachman, bl mk, milk sz 325.00
Pitcher, coachman, red, bl mk, water sz 435.00
Pitcher, coachman, unmk, cream sz 165.00
Pitcher, conch shell, MOP, bl mk, cream sz 55.00
Pitcher, crow, blk, bl mk, cream sz 155.00
Pitcher, dachshund, bl mk, cream sz 175.00
Pitcher, dachshund, unmk, water sz 425.00
Pitcher, duck, bl mk, water sz 365.00
Pitcher, duck, Deponiert mk, cream sz 145.00
Pitcher, eagle, bl mk, cream sz 195.00
Pitcher, eagle, bl mk, water sz 445.00
Pitcher, elk, bl mk, milk sz 220.00
Pitcher, elk, unmk, cream sz 65.00
Pitcher, fish head, bl mk, milk sz 240.00
Pitcher, fox, bl mk, cream sz 750.00
Pitcher, frog, bl mk, cream sz 185.00
Pitcher, geranium, bl mk, cream sz 300.00
Pitcher, girl w/candle, bl mk, milk sz 130.00
Pitcher, girl w/pitcher, bl mk, cream sz 395.00
Pitcher, girl w/sq basket on bk, bl mk, cream sz 395.00
Pitcher, grapes, MOP, bl mk, cream sz 100.00
Pitcher, kangaroo, bl mk, cream sz...............................1,000.00
Pitcher, ladybug, bl mk, cream sz 295.00
Pitcher, lamplighter, bl mk, cream sz 245.00
Pitcher, lemon, bl mk, cream sz 145.00
Pitcher, lemon, bl mk, lemonade sz, rare 500.00
Pitcher, lemon, bl mk, milk sz 225.00
Pitcher, lettuce leaf, bl mk, yel flowers, ring hdl, 7" 45.00
Pitcher, lettuce leaf w/lobster hdl, bl mk, cream sz 85.00
Pitcher, lobster, bl mk, cream sz 80.00
Pitcher, lobster, bl mk, water sz 365.00
Pitcher, maple leaf, bl mk, cream sz 210.00
Pitcher, melon, bl mk, cream sz...............................245.00
Pitcher, milkmaid, bl mk, milk sz 295.00
Pitcher, monk, brn & tan, bl mk, cream sz 800.00
Pitcher, monkey, bl mk, water sz...............................600.00
Pitcher, monkey, gr, bl mk, milk sz 275.00
Pitcher, mountain goat, bl mk, cream sz 250.00
Pitcher, mouse, bl mk, cream sz...............................900.00
Pitcher, murex shell, unmk, low, cream sz 50.00
Pitcher, oak leaf, bl mk, cream sz 135.00
Pitcher, oak leaf, MOP, bl mk, cream sz 185.00
Pitcher, Old Man of the Mountain, bl mk, cream sz 95.00
Pitcher, orange, bl mk, cream sz 125.00
Pitcher, orange, bl mk, water sz 450.00
Pitcher, owl, bl mk, milk sz...............................275.00
Pitcher, oyster & pearl, bl mk, cream sz 145.00
Pitcher, pansy, bl mk, cream sz...............................195.00
Pitcher, parakeet, bl mk, cream sz 225.00
Pitcher, parrot, gr, bl mk, cream sz 235.00

Pitcher, pear, bl mk, water sz...............................600.00
Pitcher, poodle, bl mk, cream sz...............................200.00
Pitcher, rabbit, bl mk, cream sz, rare 900.00
Pitcher, robin, bl mk, cream sz 160.00
Pitcher, rooster, red top, bl mk, cream sz 325.00
Pitcher, sea horse hdl, bl mk, cream sz 140.00
Pitcher, seal, pk & gray, bl mk, cream sz 280.00
Pitcher, shell, brn & wht MOP, Tettau mk, low, cream sz...........45.00
Pitcher, shell, MOP, bl mk, cream sz 125.00
Pitcher, shell, Tettau mk, milk sz 75.00
Pitcher, shell w/coral hdl, unmk, cream sz 50.00
Pitcher, St Bernard, bl mk, water sz 425.00
Pitcher, St Bernard, unmk, cream sz 220.00
Pitcher, strawberry, twist hdl, unmk, cream sz 85.00
Pitcher, tomato, bl mk, cream sz...............................65.00
Pitcher, tomato, bl mk, water sz 400.00
Pitcher, turtle, bl mk, cream sz, 2½" 325.00
Pitcher, water buffalo, blk, bl mk, cream sz...............................165.00
Pitcher, watermelon, bl mk, water sz...............................485.00
Plate, lettuce leaf, bl mk, sm...............................20.00
Plate, tomato & lettuce, unmk, 7½" 35.00
Relish, grapes, wht MOP w/lav, unmk 80.00
Shakers, chili peppers, bl mk, pr...............................95.00
Shakers, conch shell, MOP, bl mk, pr...............................45.00
Shakers, elk, bl mk, ea...............................70.00
Shakers, tomato, bl mk, pr...............................75.00
Shakers, tomato, unmk, pr...............................40.00
Shaving mug, elk, bl mk...............................475.00
Sherbet, shell, unmk...............................70.00
Shoes, man's high top, bl mk, 2-tone brn, eyelets, tab bk 385.00
Stein, elk, bl mk 395.00
String holder, rooster, bl mk, wall hanging...............................225.00
Sugar bowl, grapes, purple, bl mk 135.00
Sugar bowl, oyster & pearl, bl mk 125.00
Sugar bowl, poppy, red w/gr vine hdls, bl mk, w/lid...............................145.00
Sugar bowl, tomato, unmk, w/lid...............................45.00
Teapot, grapes, bl mk 275.00
Teapot, poppy, lt purple satin lustre, bl mk 525.00
Toothpick holder, murex shell, unmk...............................75.00
Wall pocket, Art Nouveau, bl mk 1,200.00
Wall pocket, grapes, yel, bl mk...............................175.00

Scenics

Ash tray, goose girl, bl mk, spade shape 55.00
Ash tray, lawyers scene, sgn Dixon, bl mk 165.00
Ash tray, man playing lyre, bl mk, heart shape, 5¼"...............................55.00
Bell, Dutch children playing, orig clapper, mk 225.00

Bowl, Arabs on camels, 5½", $185.00.

Bowl, boy in barnyard, much gold, bl mk, 11" 230.00
Box, Jack Horner, fan shape, bl mk, 5¼" 80.00
Cake plate, Ring Around the Rosie, bl mk, 10½" 160.00
Candlestick, Beach Babies, bl mk, 4½" 110.00
Chamberstick, pansies & roses, unmk, shield bk 75.00
Cheese dish, children playing, slant top, 2x2¾x2x2" 225.00
Cheese dish, farmer w/turkeys, slant top, bl mk, 2x2¾x2" 110.00
Chocolate pot, Beach Babies, tankard form, bl mk 375.00
Creamer, Jack & Jill, bl mk, 3¾x3" 95.00
Cup & saucer, Beach Babies, unmk, 2½", 4½" 100.00
Cup & saucer, Corinthian, bl mk, blk & wht figures 25.00
Cup & saucer, demitasse; cattle, unmk 70.00
Flowerpot, Brittany Women, bl mk, w/orig insert 110.00
Hatpin holder, swans in lake at sunset, bl mk 245.00
Humidor, sailing ship & windmills, bl mk, hdls, 6¾" 275.00
Nappy, Ring Around the Rosie, 4 children, bl mk, 4½x4" 85.00
Pipe holder, girl w/ducks, gold trim, bl mk, rare 195.00
Pitcher, Beach Babies, unmk, 3" 85.00
Pitcher, cows in sunset, bl mk, milk sz 85.00
Pitcher, Dutch children in boat, bl mk, 2¾x2½" 50.00
Pitcher, English coaching scene, bl mk, 5¼x2½" 65.00
Pitcher, farmer w/turkeys, bl mk, milk sz 135.00
Pitcher, lady holding candle, bl mk, cream sz 75.00
Pitcher, lady w/basket, sailboat, bl mk, cream sz 65.00
Pitcher, Little Jack Horner, bl mk, cream sz 150.00
Pitcher, Ring Around the Rosie, bl mk, 3½" 150.00
Pitcher, sailboat, gray matt, bl mk, milk sz 165.00
Pitcher, Snowbabies, sledding, bl mk, 3" 125.00
Pitcher, 2 musketeers at table, bl mk, cream sz 65.00
Plate, Beach Babies, bl mk, 7½" 60.00
Plate, Jack & the Beanstalk, bl mk, 6½" 90.00
Shoe, Dutch people, roses & pansies, bl mk 250.00
Toothpick holder, hunter on horse & dogs, ftd, unmk 110.00
Toothpick holder, pastoral scene, scuttle shape, bl mk 175.00
Vase, donkey & boy, bl mk, 4¼" 95.00
Vase, Dutch people, bl mk, 3⅝x2⅜" 45.00
Vase, lady w/basket, boats beyond, bl mk, 3¼x2¼" 48.00
Vase, musicians, hdls, SP trim, bl mk, 3¼x2⅞" 45.00

Sunbonnet Babies

Ash tray, babies fishing, bl mk, club shape 220.00
Ash tray, babies washing, bl mk, heart shape 220.00
Bowl, babies ironing, unmk, 2½x8½" 150.00
Bowl, cereal; babies washing/ironing, bl mk, 6¼" 150.00
Box, stamp; babies washing, bl mk, 2½x2x1½" 195.00
Cake plate, babies washing, bl mk, 10½" 235.00
Candlestick, babies cleaning, bl mk, tall 180.00
Chamberstick, babies fishing, bl mk, shield bk 435.00
Chamberstick, babies sweeping, bl mk, shield bk 550.00
Creamer & sugar bowl, bl mk, 4½x3½" 325.00
Flowerpot, babies ironing, bl mk, w/insert, 4" 500.00
Hatpin holder, babies sweeping, bl mk 425.00
Inkwell, babies running, bl mk, w/insert, rare 425.00
Mug, babies washing, bl mk 215.00
Pitcher, babies cleaning, bl mk, 3¼" 200.00
Pitcher, babies cleaning, bl mk, 4½" 250.00
Pitcher, babies fishing, bl mk, tall, milk sz 265.00
Pitcher, babies fishing, bl mk, 4½" 230.00
Pitcher, babies ironing, bl mk, 3¼" 125.00
Pitcher, babies sweeping, bl mk, cream sz 325.00
Pitcher, babies washing, bl mk, cream sz 265.00
Plate, babies fishing, bl mk, 6½" 175.00
Plate, babies hanging clothes, bl mk, 7⅝" 125.00

Plate, babies sweeping, bl mk, 5" 175.00
Plate, babies sweeping, 7½" 190.00
Relish, babies sweeping, bl mk 325.00
Salt cellar, babies, bl mk, ped ft, master 325.00
Sauce dish, babies sewing, bl mk 175.00
Sugar bowl, babies washing, bl mk, 3½" 195.00
Tea tile, babies washing, bl mk, 5" 200.00
Tray, babies washing & ironing, bl mk, 10x7" 325.00
Vase, babies cleaning, bl mk, cylindrical, 4" 400.00

Tapestries

Basket, Rose Tapestry, gold trim, rope hdl, bl mk 345.00
Basket, Rose Tapestry, gr mk, 3¼" 400.00
Basket, Violet Tapestry, bl mk 200.00
Bottle, scent; floral tapestry, bl mk, sterling cap, 1" dia 275.00
Bowl, floral tapestry w/gold, bl mk, 10½" 135.00
Box, powder; Lady & Prince Tapestry, bl mk, 2½" dia 275.00
Box, trinket; Christmas Cactus Tapestry, bl mk, 3½" dia 325.00
Box, trinket; Rose Tapestry, 3-color, bl mk, 3½" dia 345.00
Cake plate, Rose Tapestry, pierced hdls, bl mk, 10" 245.00
Chocolate pot, Rose Tapestry, 3-color, bl mk 1,300.00
Hair receiver, floral tapestry, bl mk 200.00
Hair receiver, Lady & Prince Tapestry, bl mk 275.00
Hair receiver, turkeys on tapestry, bl mk 200.00
Hatpin holder, Rose Tapestry, 3-color, bl mk 385.00
Match holder, cavalier tapestry, unmk, 3¼x2½" 90.00
Match holder, lady tapestry, bl mk, wall hanging 395.00
Nappy, Arab & horse scenic tapestry, bl mk 175.00
Nappy, Rose Tapestry, bl mk, ring hdl 245.00
Nut dish, Rose Tapestry, bl mk, ind 225.00
Pitcher, goats tapestry, bl mk, bulbous, cream sz 95.00
Pitcher, musicians tapestry, bl mk, dbl hdls, cream sz 165.00
Pitcher, Rose Tapestry, bl mk, pinched spout, cream sz 275.00
Pitcher, Rose Tapestry, bl mk, pinched spout, milk sz, 4½" 325.00
Pitcher, Rose Tapestry, corset shape, w/platinum, bl mk, 4" 900.00
Planter, Rose Tapestry, bl mk, orig liner 365.00
Plaque, lady w/veil by horse on tapestry, bl mk, 9½" 525.00
Rose bowl, Rose Tapestry, 3-color, bl mk 350.00
Shakers, Rose Tapestry, bl mk, pr 235.00
Shoe, lady's, Rose Tapestry, bl mk, w/laces, pr 770.00
Shoe, lady's slipper, Rose Tapestry, bl mk, 5" 335.00
Toothpick holder, pastoral tapestry, bl mk, bl mk 245.00
Tray, dresser; Christmas Cactus Tapestry, bl mk 455.00
Tray, dresser; Rose Tapestry, bl mk, rectangular, 7¾x4¼" 325.00
Vase, cows tapestry, bl mk, 2½x2¼" 50.00
Vase, goats tapestry, bl mk, 5½" 85.00
Vase, hunt scene tapestry, bl mk, 4¾" 65.00
Vase, peacock tapestry, bl mk, slim neck, 5" 295.00
Vase, polar bear tapestry, bl mk, gold hdls, 4½" 255.00
Vase, rooster & turkey tapestry, bl mk, 5¼" 265.00

Royal Bonn

Royal Bonn is a fine-paste porcelain, ornately decorated with scenes, portraits, or florals. The factory was established in the mid-1800s in Bonn, Germany; however, most pieces found today are from the latter part of the century.

Biscuit jar, mc florals, SP top/rim/hdl, mk, 7x5½" 110.00
Clock, mc florals, mk, 6¼x5½x2¾" 165.00
Vase, bust of lady, sgn Digendorf, scalloped/hdls, 9", pr 700.00
Vase, exotic flowers on blk matt, 12¼" 450.00

Vase, portrait of a lady, signed Beerbohm, 13", $700.00.

Vase, gnarled trees & tulips, mk Old Dutch #247, 19" 700.00
Vase, gold-traced flowers on ivory, ovoid, 12" 135.00
Vase, iris w/gold, 8", pr 225.00
Vase, maid in garden, sgn Artiz, gilt trim, 1860s, 7", pr 400.00
Vase, maid's portrait on yel to gr w/gold, EX art, 9x4½" 375.00
Vase, man looking out to sea, sgn, mk, 8⅞x7¼" 450.00
Vase, roses, ogre-head & loop hdls, F Mehlen, 1890, 14" 350.00

Royal Copenhagen

The Royal Copenhagen Manufactory was established in Denmark in about 1775 by Frantz Henrich Muller. When bankruptcy threatened in 1779, the Crown took charge. The fine dinnerware and objects of art produced after that time carries the familiar logo, the crown over three wavy lines. See also Limited Edition Plates.

Figurine, barn owl, #273, 8½" 375.00
Figurine, bear, brn, #21433...85.00
Figurine, boy in carnival attire, #4794..155.00
Figurine, children reading, #1567 ....140.00
Figurine, drummer, #3647..145.00
Figurine, duck pr, after K Kylhn, stoneware w/brn & gr, 7" 360.00

Figure of an eagle after a model by Vilhelm Theodor Fischer, dated 1919, 21", $1,000.00.

Figurine, elephant, #22741, wht, sm, 2¼" 75.00

Figurine, girl dancing, #2444 ....300.00
Figurine, girl in long dress, #5605...45.00
Figurine, girl w/doll, #3539, 5¾" 230.00
Figurine, goose girl, #527, 9½" 225.00
Figurine, hunter & dog, #1087, 8½" 550.00
Figurine, Little Mermaid, #4431 ....815.00
Figurine, monkey, #1444, 5"..900.00
Figurine, nude sitting on rock, #4027, 5¾" 175.00
Figurine, Pan on goat, #1228...175.00
Figurine, Pan w/lizard, #433 ....285.00
Figurine, polar bear, #502, 13" 275.00
Figurine, poodle, #4368 ....195.00
Figurine, Red Wing, #1235 ....150.00
Figurine, seal, #1441 ....135.00
Figurine, soldier w/witch, #1112 ....545.00
Figurine, Victorian couple, #1593 ....925.00
Vase, bellflower pendants, bl/gray, Jenny Meyer/1917, 18" 1,600.00
Vase, florals on bl, #2778, 8" 95.00
Vase, lg peonies, shades of bl/gray/sand, J Meyer, 29" 2,000.00
Vase, stems of hollyhocks before river, C Zernichow, 29" 1,600.00

Royal Copley

Royal Copley is a decorative type of pottery made by the Spaulding China Company in Sebring, Ohio, from 1942 to 1957. They also produced two other major lines — Royal Windsor and Spaulding. Royal Copley was primarily marketed through five-and-ten cent stores; Royal Windsor and Spaulding were sold through department stores, gift shops, and jobbers.

Items trimmed in gold are worth 25% to 50% more than the same item with no gold trim. Our advisor for this category is Joe Devine; he is listed in the Directory under Iowa.

Ash tray, lily pad w/bird, 5" 6.00
Bank, pig, bl, hands at sides, tall...20.00
Bowl, blossom form, aqua, pk bird at rim, 4"................................10.00
Creamer, duck, pk hat, bl wings, 4½"...12.00
Figurine, cockatoo, 8¼"...22.50
Figurine, hen, #1, 5½"...15.00
Figurine, kinglet, 5"..15.00
Figurine, kitten w/yel yarn..25.00
Figurine, lark, paper label, 6½"..15.00
Figurine, Oriental boy, 7½" 10.00
Figurine, parrot, 5"...12.50
Figurine, pheasant, Spaulding 18.00
Figurine, spaniel, brn, 5"...15.00

Swallow on Double Stump (one of a matching pair), 7½", $18.00.

Figurine, tanager, 6¼" 15.00
Figurine, titmouse, paper label, 8" 15.00
Figurine, vireo, 4½" 12.00
Figurine, warbler, 5" 10.00
Figurine, wren, paper label, 6¼" 12.50
Pitcher, Daffodil, yel & pk, 8" 25.00
Planter, Balinese girl, 8½" 15.00
Planter, bear cub clinging to stump, 8¼" 25.00
Planter, bird in flight, bl, 7¼" 20.00
Planter, blackamoor, yel turban, 8", pr 40.00
Planter, blk cat & tub 18.00
Planter, blossom, bl & rose, 3" 7.50
Planter, boy leaning on barrel, 6" 15.00
Planter, bunting, 5" 15.00
Planter, coach figural, plum, 3¼x6" 15.00
Planter, cocker spaniel's head, 5" 12.00
Planter, Colonial man & lady, 8", pr 45.00
Planter, deer w/fawn, 9" 20.00
Planter, dog pulling wagon, 5¾" 22.50
Planter, duck & wheelbarrow, paper label, 3¾" 15.00
Planter, duck eating grass, 5" 12.00
Planter, finch beside lg apple, paper label, 5½" 15.00
Planter, finch on tree stump, 7½" 37.50
Planter, Harmony, 6½" 10.00
Planter, kitten & boot, 7½" 28.00
Planter, kitten & moccasin, 8" 25.00
Planter, kitten w/yarn 18.00
Planter, mallard, 7¾" 14.00
Planter, Oriental lantern boy 15.00
Planter, pouter pigeon, paper label, 5¾" 15.00
Planter, pup in basket, brn & turq, 7" 18.00
Planter, rooster, 7¼" 15.00
Planter, salt box, yel & gr, 5½" 20.00
Planter, 3-section, 2½x6¼" 10.00
Plaque/planter, fruit plate, 6¼" 15.00
Plaque/planter, hen, 6¾" 18.00
Vase, bamboo, cylindrical, 8" 15.00
Vase, Carol's Corsage, aqua, 7" 10.00
Vase, fish, half-circle, 5" 15.00
Vase, floral decal, cornucopia form, 8½" 18.00
Vase, floral decal, floral hdls, gold stamp, 6¼" 8.00
Vase, Floral Elegance, cobalt, 8" 20.00
Vase, Ivy, dk gr on ivory, ftd pillow form, 6¼" 12.00
Vase, mare & foal, 8½" 22.50
Vase, nuthatch, 5½" 12.50
Vase/planter, deer, paper label, 7½" 22.00
Vase/planter, fish, paper label, 5¾" 18.00
Wall pocket, bonnet w/flowers 18.00
Wall pocket, dancing lady 40.00
Wall pocket, Tony, pirate's head................................25.00
Wall vase, girl in gray hat, 7" 18.00

Royal Crown Derby

In the latter 1870s, a new firm, the Derby Crown Porcelain Company Ltd., began operations in Derby, England. Since 1890 when they were appointed Manufacturers of Porcelain to Her Majesty, their fine porcelain wares have been known as Royal Crown Derby. Their earliest wares were marked with a crown over 'Derby'; often a complicated dating code indicated the year of manufacture. After 1890 the 'Royal Crown Derby, England' mark was employed; in 1921 'Made In England' was substituted in the wording. 'Bone China' was added after 1945. See also Derby.

Bowl, fruit; Gold Aves, birds/etc, 10½", +pr 11" sticks 400.00
Bowl, Imari, w/lid, oval, 11" 100.00
Creamer, Imari 150.00
Cup & saucer, Imari, MIE, 1937...65.00
Cup & saucer, Imari, 1907 ....95.00
Cup & saucer, Imari, 1910, mini 150.00
Ewer, florals & arabesques, gold on Chinese red, 1880s, 7½" 225.00
Jar, emb/HP gilt-decor flowers, w/lid, 6" 400.00
Plate, Imari, 7" 50.00
Sugar bowl, Imari 150.00
Tray, Imari, shaped oval, 20th C, 18" 350.00
Urn, gold butterflies on yel, w/lid, 1887, 5" 295.00

Urn, insects, hummingbirds, flowers, and lily pads, reticulated dome lid, reattached finial, 15", $600.00.

Vase, bird panels, mc w/gold on wht, mk, 1922, 7", pr 495.00
Vase, chinoiserie, red/gr/gilt/underglaze bl, 1914, 1¼" 180.00
Vase, florals/butterflies, gold on yel, floral hdls, 9" 250.00
Vase, gold decor on yel, 1887, 7" 295.00

Royal Doulton, Doulton

The range of wares produced by the Doulton Company since its inception in 1815 has been vast and varied. The earliest wares produced in the tiny pottery in Lambeth, England, were salt-glazed pitchers, plain and fancy figural bottles — all utility-type stoneware geared to the practical needs of everyday living. The original partners, John Doulton and John Watts, saw the potential for success in the manufacture of drain and sewage pipes and during the 1840s concentrated on these highly lucrative types of commercial wares. Watts retired from the company in 1854, and Doulton began experimenting with a more decorative style of product. As time went by, many glazes and decorative effects were developed, among them Faience, Impasto, Silicon, Carrara, Marqueterie, Chine, and Rouge Flambe. Tiles and architectural terra cotta were an important part of their manufacture. Late in the nineteenth century at the original Lambeth location, fine artware was decorated by such notable artists as Hannah and Arthur Barlow, George Tinworth, and J.H. McLennan. Stoneware vases with incised animal drawings, gracefully shaped urns with painted scenes, and cleverly modeled figurines rivaled the best of any competitor.

In 1882 a second factory was built in Burslem which continues even yet to produce the famous figurines, character jugs, series ware, and table services so popular with collectors today. Their Kingsware line, made from 1899 to 1946, featured flasks and flagons with drinking scenes, usually on a brown-glazed ground. Some were limited editions, while others were commemorative and advertising items. The Gibson Girl series, twenty-four plates in all, was introduced in 1901. It was drawn by Charles Dana Gibson and is recognized by its blue and white borders and central illustrations, each scene depicting a humorous or poignant episode in the life of 'The Widow and Her Friends.' Dickensware, produced from 1911 through the early 1940s, featured illustrations by Charles Dickens, with many of his famous characters. The Robin Hood series was introduced in 1914; the Shakespeare series #1, portraying scenes from the Bard's plays, was made from 1914 until World War II. The Shakespeare series #2 ran from 1906 until 1974 and was decorated with featured characters. Nursery Rhymes was a series that was first produced in earthenware in 1930 and later in bone china. In 1933 a line of decorated children's ware, the Bunnykins series, was introduced; it continues to be made to the present day. About 150 'bunny' scenes have been devised, the earliest and most desirable being those signed by the artist Barbara Vernon.

Factors contributing to the value of a figurine are age, color, and detail. Those with a limited production run and those signed by the artist or marked 'Potted' (indicating a pre-1939 origin) are also more valuable. After 1920 wares were marked with a lion — with or without a crown — over a circular 'Royal Doulton.'

Our advisor for this category is Nicki Budin; she is listed in the Directory under Ohio.

Animals and Birds

Dog, Airedale, K5	175.00
Dog, Alsatian, #1117, 4¼"	150.00
Dog, Boxer, #2643, 6½"	145.00
Dog, Bulldog, #1047, sm	150.00
Dog, Bulldog, K1, 2¼"	70.00
Dog, Bulldog pup, K2, 1¾"	70.00
Dog, Cairn, #1033, lg	500.00
Dog, Cairn, #1034, med	165.00
Dog, Cairn, sitting, K11, 2½"	45.00
Dog, Cocker Spaniel, #1020, 5"	125.00
Dog, Cocker Spaniel, #1104, lg	165.00
Dog, Cocker Spaniel, #1187, 5"	95.00
Dog, Cocker Spaniel in basket, #2585, 2"	50.00
Dog, Cocker Spaniel in basket, #2586, 2½"	50.00
Dog, Cocker Spaniel w/pheasant, #1029, 3¾"	165.00
Dog, Cocker Spaniel w/pheasant, #1062, 3¾"	145.00
Dog, Collie, #2958, med	175.00
Dog, Dachshund, #1127, lg	500.00
Dog, Dachshund, #1128, 4"	145.00
Dog, Dalmation, #1113, 5¾"	125.00
Dog, English Setter, #1049, 8"	375.00
Dog, English Setter, #1051, 3¾"	125.00
Dog, Foxhound, K7, 2½"	50.00
Dog, Greyhound, #1077, sm	300.00
Dog, Irish Setter, #1056, 3¾"	135.00
Dog, Pekingese, #1011, med	475.00
Dog, Scottish Terrier, #1015, med	250.00
Dog, Sealyham, #2508, sm	110.00
Dog, Springer Spaniel, #2517, sm	115.00
Dog, St Bernard, recumbent, K19, 1¾"	40.00
Dog, Terrier pup in basket, #2587, 3"	45.00
Dog, Terrier pups (3) in basket, #2588, 3¼"	45.00
Dog, Welsh Corgi, #2559, 3⅝"	95.00
Dog, Welsh Corgi, K16, 2¼"	50.00
Dog chewing clipper, #2654, 3¼"	45.00
Dog running after ball, #1092	45.00
Dog w/bone, #1159, 3¾"	45.00

Dog w/sugar cube on nose, rare, 8½"	1,500.00
Elephant, #2644, 5½"	95.00
Kitten, crouching, #2584	45.00
Kitten, Lucky, K12, 2¾"	95.00
Kitten, sleeping, #2581, 1½"	45.00
Nyala Antelope, Chatcull, #2664, 5⅝"	175.00
Penguin, K21, 2"	125.00
Penguins, #133, dbl, 6"	395.00
Pig, recumbent, head up, #2648, 1¾"	135.00
Pig, sitting, #2652, 2"	135.00
Polar Bear, #119	145.00
Sea Gull, #2574, sm	135.00
Winter Wren, #3505, 4¾"	3,500.00
Wren, #144	110.00

Character Jugs

Apothecary, D6567, lg	95.00
Aramis, D6508, mini	45.00
Ard of 'Earring, D6588, lg	1,100.00
Arriet, D6256, tiny	210.00
Arry, D6249, mini	75.00
Artful Dodger, tiny	40.00
Auld Mac, D5823, lg	85.00
Auld Mac, D5824, sm	50.00
Auld Mac, D6253, mini, A	45.00
Bacchus, D6521, mini	45.00
Beefeater, D6233, GR hdl, sm, A	78.00
Blacksmith, D6571, lg	95.00
Bootmaker, D6586, mini	50.00
Cap'n Cuttle, D5842, sm, A	95.00
Captain Ahab, D6522, mini	45.00
Captain Hook, D6597, lg	425.00
Cardinal, D5614, lg	155.00
Cardinal, D6258, tiny	230.00
Catherine of Aragon, D6657, sm	50.00
Cavalier, D6614, lg, A	160.00
Clown, D6322, wht hair, lg, A	950.00
Dick Turpin, D5618, gun hdl, sm	70.00
Dick Turpin, D6485, gun hdl, lg	145.00
Dick Turpin, D6528, horse hdl, lg	110.00
Dick Turpin, D6542, horse hdl, mini	50.00
Don Quixote, D6455, lg	100.00
Falstaff, D6287, lg	100.00
Farmer John, D5788, lg	165.00
Fat Boy, D6139, mini	75.00
Fat Boy, D6142, tiny	95.00
Friar Tuck, D6321, lg	450.00
Gaoler, D6570, lg	95.00
Gardener, D6634, sm	75.00
George Washington, D6669, lg	95.00
Gladiator, D6553, sm	350.00
Gladiator, D6556, mini	350.00
Gondolier, D6589, lg	575.00
Gone Away, D6545, mini	50.00
Granny, D5521, toothless, lg	795.00
Granny, D6384, sm	45.00
Gulliver, D6560, lg	595.00
Gulliver, D6563, sm	335.00
Gunsmith, D6587, mini	50.00
Henry Morgan, D6469, sm	50.00
Isaac Walton, D6404, lg	95.00
Jane Seymour, D6646, lg	95.00
Jarge, D6295, sm	175.00

John Barleycorn, D5327, lg, A 165.00
John Doulton, 1980, sm 60.00
John Peel, D6130, mini, A 50.00
Johnny Appleseed, D6372, lg........................350.00
Lumberjack, D6610, lg..................................110.00
Lumberjack, D6613, sm 65.00
Mad Hatter, D6606, mini................................50.00
Mae West, D6688, lg......................................100.00
Mine Host, D6507, sm 50.00
Mr Bumble, tiny..40.00
Mr Micawber, D6138, mini..............................50.00
Mr Pickwick, D6060, lg, A 165.00
Mr Pickwick, D6260, tiny 235.00
Neptune, D6548, lg..95.00
Night Watchman, D6583, mini 50.00
Old Charley, D6046, mini..............................45.00
Paddy, D5753, lg, A......................................160.00
Paddy, D5768, sm 65.00
Paddy, D6042, mini 45.00
Parson Brown, D5529, sm, A..........................65.00
Pied Piper, D6403, lg 100.00
Porthos, D6516, mini......................................45.00
Regency Beau, D6565, mini 650.00
Robin Hood, D6205, bow hdl, lg....................95.00
Robin Hood, D6205, feather hdl, lg..............165.00
Robinson Crusoe, D6532, lg............................95.00
Robinson Crusoe, D6539, sm 50.00
Romeo, D6670, lg..95.00
Sairey Gamp, D5451, lg..................................95.00
Sairey Gamp, D5528, sm..................................50.00
Sairey Gamp, D6045, mini..............................45.00
Sairey Gamp, D6147, tiny................................95.00
Sam Weller, D6064, lg, A 160.00
Sam Weller, D6147, tiny..................................95.00
Santa Claus, D6690, stocking hdl, lg............110.00
Scaramouche, D6561, sm 425.00
Scrooge, tiny 40.00
Simon the Cellerar, D5504, lg, A 145.00

S m u g g l e r,
#6616, discon-
tinued in 1980,
7½", $95.00.

Tam O' Shanter, D6636, sm 50.00
Tam O' Shanter, D6640, mini..........................45.00
Toby Philpots, D5736, lg..................................95.00
Toby Philpots, D6043, mini 50.00
Tony Weller, D5530, sm..................................55.00
Tony Weller, D5531, lg..................................145.00
Tony Weller, D6044, mini................................45.00
Tony Weller, X-lg..195.00

Town Crier, D6544, mini................................135.00
Trapper, D6609, lg..110.00
Trapper, D6612, sm..50.00
Ugly Duchess, D6603, sm..............................300.00
Veteran Motorist, D6633, lg..........................110.00
Vicar of Bray, D5615, lg................................195.00
Walrus & Carpenter, D6600, lg 145.00
Walrus & Carpenter, D6608, mini..................50.00

Figurines

A Courting, HN2004 ....395.00
Abdullah, HN2104..475.00
Adrienne, HN2152 ....145.00
Affection, HN2236 ....125.00
Afternoon Tea, HN1747 ....295.00
Alchemist, HN1259, red hat 1,500.00
Alexandra, HN2398..135.00
Alice, HN2158 ....130.00
Alison, HN2336 ....175.00
All Aboard, HN2940......................................150.00
Angela, HN2389, wht dress, tiara 95.00
Antoinette, HN2326 ....125.00
Apple Maid, HN2160......................................335.00
As Good As New, HN2971 ....85.00
At Ease, HN2473..195.00
Autumn Breezes, HN1911..............................225.00
Autumn Breezes, HN1934, red dress 175.00
Baba, HN1244 ....750.00
Baby Bunting, HN2108 ....295.00
Bachelor, HN2319..225.00
Ballerina, HN2116 ....295.00
Balloon Man, HN1954....................................295.00
Bather, HN687 ....750.00
Beachcomber, HN2487..................................150.00
Beat You to It, HN2871..................................325.00
Bedtime, HN1978..95.00
Bedtime Story, HN2059..................................325.00
Bess, HN2002 ....295.00
Biddy, HN1445, 6" 180.00
Biddy, HN1513 ....165.00
Biddy Penny Farthing, HN1843....................295.00
Blacksmith of Williamsburg, HN2240 ....195.00
Blithe Morning, HN2021................................195.00
Blithe Morning, HN2065................................195.00
Bride, HN2166 ....185.00
Bridesmaid, HN2196......................................115.00
Bridget, HN2070..325.00
Buddies, HN2546 ....185.00
Bunny, HN2214 ....150.00
Buttercup, HN2309..175.00
Carolyn, HN2974, gr dress 125.00
Carpet Seller, HN1464 ....275.00
Cassim, HN1231..750.00
Cavalier, HN2716 ....195.00
Celeste, HN2237 ....225.00
Cellist, HN2226 ....350.00
Centurion, HN2726..150.00
Chloe, HN1765 ....285.00
Choir Boy, HN2141 ....95.00
Christine, HN2792 ....295.00
Christmas Morn, HN1992..............................230.00
Christmas Parcels, HN2851 ....275.00
Christmas Time, HN2110 ....350.00

Clare, HN2793	150.00
Clarinda, HN2724	175.00
Cobbler, HN1706	275.00
Country Lass, HN1991A	115.00
Cradle Song, HN2246, gr dress	400.00
Cup of Tea, HN2322	165.00
Daffy Down Dilly, HN1712	325.00
Dancer of the World, Philippines, HN2439	700.00
Darling, HN1985	95.00
Delight, HN1772	160.00
Detective, HN2359	195.00
Diana, HN1986, red dress	125.00
Doctor, HN2858	350.00
Dorcas, HN1558	320.00
Dreamweaver, HN2283	175.00
Dulcie, HN2305	150.00
Elegance, HN2264	150.00
Eliza, HN2543	185.00
Ermine Coat, HN1981	225.00
Esmeralda, HN2168	395.00
Fair Lady, HN2193	250.00
Fair Maiden, HN2211	170.00
Falstaff, HN2054	250.00
Fiddler, HN2171	750.00
Fiona, HN2694	140.00
First Dance, HN2803	280.00
First Waltz, HN2682	195.00
Fleur, HN2368	195.00
Fleurette, HN1587	475.00
Flower Seller's Children, HN1342	650.00
Foaming Quart, HN2162	280.00
Fortune Teller, HN2159	450.00
Forty Winks, HN1974	195.00
Francine, HN2422	95.00
Gay Morning, HN2135	250.00
Genevieve, HN1962	225.00
Gentleman from Williamsburg, HN2227	190.00
Geraldine, HN2348	125.00
Giselle, HN2139	350.00
Gollum, HN2913	95.00
Good Morning, HN2671	175.00
Goody Two Shoes, HN1905	360.00
Goody Two Shoes, HN2037	125.00
Grace, HN2318	165.00
Grand Manner, HN2723	175.00
Granny's Heritage, HN2031	395.00
Grief, HN595	995.00
Gypsy Dance, HN2230	295.00
Helmsman, HN2499	250.00
Her Ladyship, HN1977	295.00
Hilary, HN2355	150.00
Honey, HN1909	325.00
Hostess of Williamsburg, HN2209	185.00
Huckleberry Finn, HN2927	95.00
Huntsman, HN2492	185.00
Innocence, HN2842	135.00
Invitation, HN2170	145.00
Irishman, HN1307, gr jacket	2,000.00
Ivy, HN1768	95.00
Jack, HN2060	145.00
Jane, HN2806	135.00
Janet, HN1537, current	195.00
Jill, HN2061	145.00
Jovial Monk, HN2144	195.00
Judge, HN2443, matt	200.00
Judith, HN2089	295.00
Julia, HN2705	155.00
Kate Hardcastle, HN1719	525.00
Kirsty, HN2381, orange dress	295.00
Lady Musican Cymbals, HN2699	495.00
Lambing Time, HN1890	195.00
Laurianne, HN2719	175.00
Lavinia, HN1955	95.00
Legolas, HN2917	95.00
Leisure Hour, HN2055	400.00
Lights Out, HN2262	195.00
Lily, HN1798	155.00
Linda, HN2106	145.00
Lisa, HN2310, matt	150.00
Little Boy Blue, HN2062	125.00
Little Bridesmaid, HN1433	145.00
Little Lady Make Believe, HN1870	445.00
Little Nell, M-51	55.00
Lobster Man, HN2317	280.00
Loretta, HN2377	135.00
Lorna, HN2311	150.00
Love Letter, HN2149	325.00
Lunchtime, HN2485	150.00
Lydia, HN1908	195.00
Lyric, HN2757	175.00
Make Believe, HN2225	150.00
Mary Jane, HN1990	375.00
Mary Mary, HN2044	145.00
Masque, HN2554	195.00
Masquerade, HN2259	250.00
Master, HN2325	200.00
Master Sweep, HN2205, 8⅝"	495.00
Meditation, HN2330	295.00
Melanie, HN2271	135.00
Melody, HN2202	225.00
Memories, HN2030	350.00
Mendicant, HN1365	250.00
Midinette, HN2090	275.00
Milkmaid, HN2057A	145.00
Minuet, HN2019	275.00
Miss Demure, HN1402	195.00
Miss Demure, HN1560	525.00
Miss Muffet, HN1936	165.00
Monica, HN1467	170.00
Mother's Help, HN2151	195.00
Mr Micawber, HN1895	295.00
Mr Pickwick, HN1894	295.00
Musicale, HN2756	75.00
My Teddy, HN2177	495.00
Negligee, HN1219, bl hairband	995.00
Nelson, HN2928, ship's head, ltd edition	800.00
Newsboy, HN2244	475.00
Nicola, HN2839	425.00
Nina, HN2347	175.00
Officer of Line, HN2733	175.00
Old Balloon Seller, HN1315	295.00
Old King, HN358	1,200.00
Old Mother Hubbard, HN2314	295.00
Olga, HN2463	175.00
Omar Khayyam, HN2247	165.00
Once Upon a Time, HN2047	450.00
One That Got Away, HN2153	295.00
Orange Lady, HN1759	195.00

Orange Lady, HN1953	195.00
Owd Willum, HN2042	225.00
Paisley Shawl, HN1914	275.00
Paisley Shawl, HN1988	165.00
Pantalettes, M31, bl suit	395.00
Parisian, HN2445	150.00
Past Glory, HN2484	165.00
Patricia, HN2715	150.00
Paula, HN2906	160.00
Peggy, HN2038	110.00
Penelope, HN1901	295.00
Phyllis, HN1486	575.00
Pied Piper, HN2102	225.00
Pierrette, HN644	625.00
Polka, HN2156	275.00
Polly Peachum, HN549	375.00
Pollyanna, HN2965	95.00
Potter, HN1493	535.00
Premiere, HN2343	175.00
Pretty Lady, HN565	875.00
Pretty Polly, HN2768	150.00
Professor, HN2281	150.00
Punch & Judy Man, HN2765	295.00
Puppet Maker, HN2253	400.00
Queen of Ice, HN2435	195.00
Rachel, HN2919	175.00
Rag Doll, HN2142	95.00
Regal Lady, HN2709	145.00
Repose, HN2272	215.00
Rest Awhile, HN2728	175.00
Reverie, HN2306	225.00
Romany Sue, HN1757, gr dress	965.00
Rosabell, HN1620	675.00
Rose, HN1368	95.00
Roseanna, HN1926	325.00
Rosina, HN1556	700.00
Royal Governor's Cook, HN2233	350.00
Sabbath Morn, HN1982	295.00
School Marm, HN2223	225.00
Sea Harvest, HN2257	185.00
Secret Thoughts, HN2382	210.00
Shore Leave, HN2254	175.00
Sibell, HN1735	475.00
Silversmith of Williamsburg, HN2208	175.00
Sir Thomas, HN2372	350.00
Skater, HN2117	325.00
Solitude, HN2810	215.00
Sonata, Enchantment series, HN2438	85.00
Southern Belle, HN2229	335.00
Spring Flowers, HN1807	300.00
Spring Morning, HN1923	195.00
Stitch in Time, HN2352	150.00
Stop Press, HN2683	160.00
Summer, HN2086	350.00
Summer's Day, HN2181	265.00
Sunday Best, HN2206	195.00
Suzette, HN2026	295.00
Sweet & Twenty, HN1298	275.00
Sweeting, HN1935	125.00
Taking Things Easy, HN2677	150.00
Tall Story, HN2248	195.00
Tea Time, HN2255	195.00
Thank You, HN2732	115.00
This Little Pig, HN1793	125.00

Tinkle Bell, HN1677	95.00
Tom, HN2864	125.00
Tootles, HN1680	115.00
Town Crier, HN2119	295.00

Top o' the Hill, #1849, $250.00.

Toymaker, HN2250	325.00
Treasure Island, HN2243	135.00
Tuppence a Bag, HN2320	280.00
Twilight, HN2256	175.00
Uncle Ned, HN2094	355.00
Uriah Heep, HN1892	295.00
Valerie, HN2107	170.00
Veneta, HN2722	125.00
Viking, HN2375	295.00
Votes for Women, HN2016	195.00
Wayfarer, HN2362	175.00
Wigmaker of Williamsburg, HN2239	175.00
Wistful, HN2396	325.00
Wizard, HN2877	350.00
Young Master, HN2872	250.00

Flambe

Cat, #2259, 11½"	195.00
Cat, #9, 5"	125.00
Drake, #137, 6¼"	95.00
Duck, #112, 1½"	95.00
Duck, #395, 2½"	125.00
Elephant, #489A, 5½"	250.00
Fox, recumbent, #29B, 1x6"	75.00
Fox, sitting, head up, #14, 4"	65.00
King Penguin, #84, 6"	125.00
Owl, #2249	195.00
Owl, Great Horned; on limb, gr/red mottle on body, PD, 12"	750.00
Rabbit, ear up, #113	65.00
Rabbit, recumbent, 656A, 3¼"	110.00
Rhinoceros, half seated, head & horn up, rouge, 9x17"	850.00
Tiger, #809	450.00
Vase, Sung, mc veining/mottling, sgn Noke/FM, 1930, 7"	550.00

Series Ware

Ash tray, Dutch People, mk, 3⅝" dia	35.00

Ash tray, Welsh Ladies, sgn Noke, mk, 3⅝" dia 40.00
Ash tray, witches at cauldron on tan, mk, 3½" 40.00
Biscuit jar, Dutch People, SP top/rim/hdl, mk, 6¼x4⅞" 225.00
Biscuit jar, Royal Mail Coach, 8" 160.00
Box, Nursery Series, girl by seashore 50.00
Box, Robin Hood, rectangular, mk, 2x4½x3⅝" 98.00
Coffeepot, Dickensware, Tony Weller, 7¼x3¾" 185.00
Coffeepot, Moorish Gate, mk, 6¾x3¾" 145.00
Cup & saucer, demitasse; Dickensware, mk, 2¼"................75.00
Flask, Kingsware, Dewars, Bonnie Prince Charlie 200.00
Flask, Kingsware, Scotsman..........................250.00
Jardiniere, Shakespeare Ware, Ophelia & Hamlet, 9x10" 325.00
Match holder, Monks, profile on front, 2½" 70.00
Mug, shaving; Kingsware, sterling rim 550.00
Pitcher, Dickensware, Alfred Jingle, sq, mk, 7⅜" 125.00
Pitcher, Dickensware, Curiosity Shop, sq 165.00
Pitcher, hot water; Shakespeare Ware, w/Orlando, mk, 7x4" 145.00
Pitcher, Old Sea Dogs, Jack's the Boy for Play, 6" 125.00
Plate, Airships, men in varied craft, sgn, 10½" 195.00
Plate, Automobile Series, Deaf, scarce, 10⅜" 350.00
Plate, Babes in Woods, mk, 10" 435.00
Plate, Babes in Woods, mother & child w/basket, mk, 8¾" 395.00
Plate, Gibson Girl, 1904, 10½" 125.00

Plate, The Gypsies, 10", $95.00.

Plate, Old English Inns, King's Head, Chigwell, 10" 75.00
Plate, Old English Proverbs, Fine Feather 75.00
Plate, Shakespeare, As You Like It, 10" 90.00
Plate, Windsor Castle, 10½"..........................50.00
Sugar shaker, Jackdaw of Rheims, SP lid, mk, 6¾x2½" 175.00
Teapot, Robin Hood, Little John, & Friar Tuck, 5½" 195.00
Toothpick holder, sunset scene, 2-hdl 85.00
Tray, sandwich; Cecil Alden's Dogs, mk, 11x5" 135.00
Tray, sandwich; Zunday Zmocks, Noke, mk, 11x5"...................85.00
Tray, Shakespeare, Katharine, 15½" 95.00
Vase, Babes in Woods, 2 girls/pixie, gold trim hdls, 8x3½" 350.00
Vase, cows in pastoral scene, mk, 4⅝" 100.00
Vase, Dickensware, Sydney Carton, hdls, 7" 175.00
Vase, Dunolly Castle, sgn Hughes, mk, 4⅜x2¾" 165.00
Vase, Shakespeare, Romeo & Juliet, mk, 11⅞x3⅛", pr.................425.00
Vase, Welsh Ladies, ladies & children on path to house, 7" 165.00

Stoneware

Biscuit jar, ferns, Silicon, Lambeth, 7¼x5½"...........................280.00
Humidor, hunting figures in relief, mk, 5x4⅛" 150.00

Jug, emb Cupids & vintage, Good Is Not..., Lambeth, 7¼" 175.00
Jug, Sea Shanty, sailor & girl, mk, 6⅝x4¾" 80.00

Jug, Silicon Ware, 3¾", $85.00.

Jug, 4 scenes in relief, SP rim, Lambeth, 7x7½" 350.00
Vase, emb flowers, bl on bl-gr mottle, Lambeth, 6½" 80.00
Vase, geese in scroll-border reserves, F Barlow, 9½" 900.00
Vase, horses, scrolled leaves, H Barlow, Lambeth, 11" 1,100.00

Toby Jugs

Best Is None Too Good, D6107, 4½" 275.00
Cap'n Cuttle, D6266, 4½"..........................185.00
Charrington, One Toby Leads to Another 345.00
Cliff Cornell, tan, 9".........................425.00
Double XX D6088, 6½" 300.00
Falstaff, 8½" 135.00
Fat Boy, D6264, 4½".........................225.00
George Roby............................ 2,750.00
Happy John, D6070, 5½" 85.00
Honest Measure, D6108, 4½" 80.00
Huntsman, D6320, 7½" 135.00
Jolly Toby, D6109, 6½" 85.00
Mr Furrow, D6701, 4" 45.00
Reverend Cassock, D6702 ....45.00
Sairey Gamp, D6263 ....195.00
Sam Weller, D6265, 4½"..........................185.00
Sir Francis Drake, D6660, 9" 135.00
Sir Winston Churchill, D6172, 5½" 70.00

Miscellaneous

Biscuit jar, florals, SP rim/lid/hdl, mk, 7½x6" 125.00
Ewer, bl crocus, cobalt & gold trim, Burslem, 6¾" 150.00
Pitcher, bl body w/snowflakes & leafy band, Lambeth, 8½".........200.00
Plate, daisies w/gold tracery, openwork rim, Burslem, 9¼"...........170.00
Vase, mc flowers w/gold trim & hdls, Burslem, 11½" 235.00
Vase, stylized palmette trees, squeezebag, dk bl/brn, 11" 300.00

Royal Dux

The Duxer Porzellan Manufactur was established by E. Eichler in 1860. Located in what is now Duchcov, Czechoslovakia, the area was known as Dux, Bohemia, until WWI. The war brought about changes in both the style of the ware as well as the mark. Pre-war pieces were modeled in the Art Nouveau or Greek Classical manner and marked with 'Bohemia' and a pink triangle containing the letter 'E.' They were usually matt glazed in green, brown, and gold. Better pieces were made of porcelain, while the larger items were of pottery. After the war, the ware was marked with the small pink triangle but without the Bohemia designation; 'Made in Czechoslovakia' was added. The style became Art Deco, with cobalt blue a dominant color.

Bust, Caesar, gold shirt w/pk toga, laurel wreath, mk, 9" 350.00
Bust, Deco-style girl, sgn, triangle mk, 6½" 300.00
Bust, lady, eyes right, orchids in hair/on bodice, 21"................ 3,800.00
Centerpc, maid+2 cherubs support shell, girl beside, 20x15"... 1,150.00
Ewer, leaves & fruits on gr shaded, mk, 4½x5½" 185.00
Figurine, Ben Hur in chariot pulled by 2 horses, 18" L.................750.00
Figurine, cockatoos, 15" 325.00
Figurine, Deco couple, lt bl & gold dress, on ped, 16" 750.00
Figurine, elephant w/trunk up, celluloid tusks, mk, 8x12" 185.00
Figurine, girl w/urn on shoulder, lamb at ft, pk mk, 10" 175.00
Figurine, Goose Girl, earth tones, purple mk, 10x9" 500.00
Figurine, he (& she) before stone wall & tree, mk, 14", pr 875.00
Figurine, he w/basket on shoulder, she w/jug, 15", pr 850.00
Figurine, he w/sickle, she has wheat in apron, 21", pr 850.00
Figurine, lad, stick over shoulder, dog beside, 14x10" 225.00
Figurine, lovers, Grecian attire, earth tones, 19" 750.00
Figurine, maid sits on high rocks, cream w/gilt, 16" 475.00
Figurine, male water carrier, triangle mk, 20" 975.00
Figurine, man seated, working on pottery jugs, 7½"" 415.00

Man with basket and water jug, 14½", $750.00.

Figurine, mother holds child, pk triangle mk, 8½" 375.00
Figurine, Mountain Boy, basket at shoulder/lg 1 beside, 20"........225.00
Figurine, Rebecca at Well, flower-form vase at rear, 17x9"..........950.00
Figurine, Spanish dancer lady, cobalt/gold, sgn, 15"....................450.00
Figurine, Wheat Girl, earth tones, incised mk/#d, 19" 225.00
Figurine, wolf chasing deer..110.00
Figurine, 2 boys in boat, pk triangle mk, 6x8" 175.00
Figurine, 2 children w/basket, pk triangle mk, 8½" 385.00
Lamp, perfume; Deco lady in cobalt leans over urn, 10" 650.00
Powder jar, lady on lid, cobalt & gold, pk triangle mk, 6½".........600.00
Vase, Oriental figures on tan w/gold, triangle mk, 7¼", pr 245.00
Vase, vintage emb, gold female masks, dolphin hdls, 13".............500.00

Royal Flemish

Royal Flemish was introduced in the late 1880s and was patented in 1894 by the Mt. Washington Glass Company. Transparent glass was enameled with one or several colors and the surface divided by a network of raised lines suggesting leaded glass work. Some pieces were further decorated with enameled florals, birds, or Roman coins.

Our advisors for this category are Betty and Clarence Maier; they are listed in the Directory under Pennsylvania.

Biscuit jar, frosted w/gold lines & pastel roses, 8" 1,200.00
Biscuit jar, gilt-edged disks of various szs w/mums, 7½" 1,400.00
Bowl, water lilies/mc leaves, emb gold, brn/gold collar, 4" 2,000.00
Ewer, gold lines/heraldic shield, 12" 1,500.00

Humidor, gold coins and lines on brown tones, 8", $2,500.00.

Pickle castor, pansies HP on frost w/gold; ped fr, 9½" 1,270.00
Rose bowl, asters, wht/bl on lt brn to frost, 8-crimp, lg 1,285.00
Vase, fall leaves/jeweled berries, cut-out rim w/hdls, 9" 1,400.00
Vase, frosted w/roses, stick neck w/snake wrap, no mk, 11"..... 1,800.00
Vase, Roman coins, w/dome lid & hdls, 6½" 2,350.00
Vase, 3 butterflies on bkground of purple asters, 5x4".............. 1,850.00

Royal Haeger, Haeger

In 1871 David Henry Haeger, a young son of German immigrants, purchased a brick factory at Dundee, Illinois, and began an association with the ceramic industry that his descendants have pursued to the present time. Soon their production was expanded to include drainage tile. By 1914 they had ventured into the field of commerical artware. Vases, figurines, lamp bases, and gift items in a pastel matt glaze carried the logo of the company name written over the bar of an 'H.' From 1929 to 1933, they produced a line of dinnerware in solid colors — blue, rose, green, and yellow — which they marketed through Marshall Fields. Royal Haeger, their premium line designed in 1938 by Royal Hickman, and the Flower Ware line (1954 to 1963, marked 'RG' for Royal Garden) are especially desirable with collectors today. Ware produced before the mid-thirties sometimes is found with a paper label; these are also of special interest. A stylized script mark, 'Royal Haeger' in raised lettering, was used during the thirties and forties; later a paper label in the shape of a crown was used. The Macomb plant, built in 1939, primarily made ware for the florist trade. A second plant, built there in 1969, produces lamp bases.

Note: the Earth Graphic Wrap series, two examples of which are listed here, was produced from 1973 until approximately 1975. Characteristic of the line is the applied free-forms representative of Earth on a background of marigold, white, or fern brown. It was made in both glossy and matt finishes.

For those interested in learning more about the subject, we recommend *Collecting Royal Haeger*, by our advisors, Lee Garmon and Doris Frizzell; both are listed in the Directory under Illinois.

Ash tray, gr/rust gloss, hexagonal, #138, 8½x4¾" 5.00
Ash tray, w/sitting leopard, R-632, 9" 20.00
Candle holder, Pei Tung dragon, R-570, 15½" 25.00
Electric fountain, bow w/watering can, #8030, 12" dia 75.00
Elephant w/rider, trunk down, R-563, 10½" 25.00

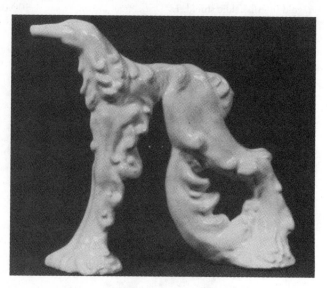

Figure of a wolfhound, R-319, 7", $50.00.

Giraffe head & neck, sq base, R-305, 19" 95.00
Hen Pheasant, R-847, 9" 30.00
Lamp, TV; girl w/fawn, 'Diana,' #6199 ....30.00
Lamp, TV; sitting poodle, #6356, 10½" 30.00
Planter, colt w/head down, R-875, 14" L 50.00
Planter, Earth Graphic Wrap, loop hdls, hanging, #8207-H 20.00
Planter, elephant w/trunk up, #509, 9" 15.00
Planter, Madonna w/bowed head, RG-17, 11¼" 15.00
Planter, Madonna w/lilies, RG-132, 12" 15.00
Plate, turq, grape leaf, Royal Hickman, #126, 15" 20.00
Ship sailing, R-775, 12" 30.00
Vase, Earth Graphic Wrap, #4170, 13" 15.00
Vase, mustard mottle over gr, sculptured leaves, 11" 9.00
Vase, Pie Tung, sq, R-551, 15½" 20.00
Vase, running deer figural, ivory, 9" 15.00
Vase, 3 sea gulls, R-208, 16" 60.00
3 horses w/lightning, 'Thunder & Lightning figurine,' #6234 ....75.00

Royal Rudolstadt

The hard-paste porcelain that has come to be known as Royal Rudolstadt was produced in Thuringia, Germany, in the early 18th century. Various names and marks have been associated with this pottery — one of the earliest was a hay fork symbol associated with Johann Frederich von Schwarzburg-Rudolstadt, one of the first founders. Variations, some that included an 'R,' were also used. In 1854 Earnst Bohne produced wares that were marked with an anchor and the letters 'EB.'

Wares commonly found today are those made during the late 1800s and early twentieth century. These are usually marked with an 'RW' within a shield under a crown and the words 'Crown Rudolstadt.' Items marked 'Germany' were made after 1890.

Berry set, wht roses w/gold, 9½" master+6 5" bowls 185.00
Bust, Grecian man, 7" 38.00
Bust, Indian Chief 175.00
Creamer, Kewpies play leap frog, sgn O'Neill, 4x2", EX 100.00
Ewer, fruit reserve on gr w/gilt florals, sgn, ornate, 14"...............300.00
Figurine, girl & boy on bench, gold trim, bsk, mk 195.00
Figurine, lady on bench embraced by man, sgn, 8½"..................175.00

Lamp, Delft, windmill painted on globe, 23", $700.00.

Vase, floral panels, 2 maidens as hdls, 14x9" 550.00
Vase, florals w/gold on tan, branch hdls, mk, 11½" 165.00
Vase, florals w/raised gold, mk, 6½" 140.00

Royal Vienna

In 1719 Claude Innocentius de Paquier established a hard-paste porcelain factory in Vienna where he made highly ornamental wares similar to the type produced at Meissen. Early wares were usually unmarked; but after 1744, when the factory was purchased by the Empress, the Austrian shield (often called 'beehive') was stamped on under the glaze. In the following listings, values are for hand-painted items unless noted otherwise. Decal-decorated items would be considerably lower.

Note: An influx of Japanese reproductions on the market have influenced values to decline on genuine old Royal Vienna. Buyer beware! On new items, the beehive mark is over the glaze, the weight of the porcelain is heavier, and the decoration is obviously decaled.

Our advisor for this category is Madeleine France; she is listed in the Directory under Florida.

Box, allegorical on bl, wht floral base band, 2½" dia 100.00
Box, lady on couch, 3 attendants (1 w/mirror), 5x6½" dia...........350.00
Cup & saucer, putti in reserve, 1770, rstr, pr 600.00
Dish, 3 nymphs on rock: Sirenen, sgn Knoeller, 1880s, 14" ... 2,400.00
Plaque, mythological scene w/couple, chariots in rim, 9½".........700.00
Plaque, Paris & Venus, after Kauffman, fr, 1890s, 4½x7" 500.00

Charger, Allegorie, after Titian, underglaze blue beehive mark and #7, 24", $8,400.00.

Plaque, 18th-C lady, sgn Groner, dk bl border w/gold, 13½" .. **1,200.00**
Plate, Faustina, girl in 'jeweled' reserve, E Tobt, 9¾" **225.00**
Plate, floral, purple scale-like border w/gilt, 1700s, 9½" **280.00**
Plate, floral+3 kidney-form floral panels, rtcl rim, 9½" **300.00**
Plate, Madonna Della Ledia, sgn Geuer, gold decor rim, 9" **350.00**
Plate, maid plays lute to children by river, gilt, 9½" **550.00**
Plate, Napoleon on dk bl w/gilt, sgn Seller, 1880s, 14" **450.00**
Plate, Psyche & sisters on cobalt, putti in border, 12" **950.00**
Tureen, floral, basketwork border, vegetable finial, 12" H....... **1,100.00**
Vase, Comtesse du Barry, by Wagner, gilt/jewels, 1910, 10" **740.00**
Vase, lady's portrait on maroon, ornate hdls, mk, 7¼" **950.00**
Vase, lady's portrait w/much gold, mk, 7½x3½" **365.00**
Vase, maids reserve, bk: cupids, 1880s, 22½", EX **5,000.00**
Vase, portrait in gold reserve on burgundy, sgn/#d, 9½"..............**850.00**
Vase, portrait/flowers/gold on wht, sqd shoulder hdls, 8" **365.00**

Royal Worcester, Worcester

The Worcester Porcelain Company was deeded in 1751. During the first or Dr. Wall period (so called for one of its proprietors), porcelain with an Oriental influence was decorated in underglaze blue. Useful tablewares represented the largest portion of production, but figurines and decorative items were also made. Very little of the earliest wares were marked and can only be identified by a study of forms, glazes, and the porcelain body, which tends to transmit a greenish cast when held to light. Late in the fifties, a crescent mark was in general use, and rare examples bare a facsimile of the Meissen crossed swords. The first period ended in 1783, and the company went through several changes in ownership during the next eighty years. The years from 1783-1792 are referred to as the Flight period. Marks were a small crescent, a crown with 'Royal,' or an impressed 'Flight.' From 1792-1807, the company was known as Flight and Barr and used the trademark 'F&B' or 'B,' with or without a small cross. From 1807-1813, the company was under the Barr, Flight, and Barr management; this era is recognized as having produced porcelain of the highest quality of artistic decoration. Their mark was 'B.F.B.' From 1813-1840, many marks were used, but the most usual was 'F.B.B.' under a crown to indicate Flight, Barr, and Barr. In 1840 the firm merged with Chamberlain, and in 1852 they were succeeded by Kerr and Binns. The firm became known as Royal Worcester in 1862. Since 1930 Royal Worcester has been considered one of the leaders in the field of limited edition plates and figurines.

Biscuit jar, leaves, cobalt on wht bamboo, 7x5¾" 350.00
Bottle, bl pine cone transfer, neck w/knop, 1765, 10" 600.00
Bottle, chinoiserie landscape, bl transfer, 1765, 10" 1,300.00
Bowl, chinoiserie landscape, bl transfer, 1770, 6".......................200.00
Bowl, fruit; Oriental-style geese/moon on bl, 1924, 15"............425.00
Bowl, Gold Chantilly, hdls, 11" 65.00
Bowl, junket; floral int, bl transfer, 1750s, mk, 7" dia 375.00
Bowl, sauce; bl floral transfer, rtcl dome lid, 1700, 5" H 400.00
Bowl, waste; Cannonball, islands/trees/houses, 1770, 6" 200.00
Box, leafy base, rtcl lid w/gold, dome top, sgn, 3½x2¼" 145.00
Box, pin; sgn Granger, rtcl dome lid, 2¼x3¼" 195.00
Butter dish, bl floral transfer, floral finial, 1770, 5" dia 550.00
Cake plate, Gold Chantilly, 12", MIB..65.00
Candle snuffer, lady in winter wraps, purple mk, 3" 60.00
Candle snuffer, witch, purple mk, #610726, 3½".........................90.00
Coffeepot, Bat, bats/terraced gardens, 1780, 9¾", NM................500.00
Coffeepot, Gold Chantilly...95.00
Coffeepot, Mansfield, bl floral on wht, dome lid, 1770, 9" 2,300.00
Creamer, floral/gilt on peach, tapered w/horn hdl, 1900, 7" 160.00
Creamer, wren in leaves, twig stem, mk, 2⅞x2½" 35.00
Cup & saucer, floral, mc on beige, mk, 2½x3⅜", 5⅝" 95.00
Cup & saucer, Gold Chantilly...30.00
Dish, floral, lattice rim on yel, leaf hdls, 1775, 13", NM......... 2,700.00
Dish, shell form, florals/gold on peach to yel, hdl, 4½" 100.00
Ewer, blanc de chine, coiled dragon hdl, 1890, 7" 100.00
Ewer, roses, sgn Shuck, dragon hdl, 1909, 4" 200.00
Ewer, thistles/wild flowers on peach, ftd, 1900, 9".......................165.00
Ewer vase, butterfly/floral on ivory, lizard as hdl, 12" 300.00
Figurine, Anne Boleyn, #2652, 8¾"..150.00
Figurine, Arab Stallion, D Linder, 9¾" 600.00
Figurine, Blue Tit & Pussywillow, Cock & Hen, Doughty, pr 450.00
Figurine, boy holds wide basket at waist level, #960, 9" 450.00
Figurine, Brigideen Indians, #1243, pr...750.00
Figurine, Cairo Water Carrier, male, #1250 ....295.00
Figurine, Eastern Water Carriers, after Hadley, 17", pr, VG 850.00
Figurine, girl in frilly dress & bonnet holds basket, 6½"..............300.00
Figurine, Grandmother's Dress, yel 135.00
Figurine, Grey Wagtail & Celandine, D Doughty, 6" 240.00
Figurine, June, gr, lg...210.00
Figurine, June, pk, sm...110.00
Figurine, Kingfisher & Autumn Beech, D Doughty, 13", NM 600.00
Figurine, Lesser Whitethroat & Wild Rose, Doughty, 11", pr......550.00
Figurine, Mallard Male & Female, van Ruyckevelt, 13", pr..... 1,400.00
Figurine, monk, blk mk, 6"...100.00
Figurine, November...100.00
Figurine, Parakeet, red..140.00
Figurine, Sisters 275.00
Figurine, Wren & Burnet Rose, Cock & Hen, Doughty, 7", pr ...500.00
Gravy boat, Gold Chantilly, w/underplate......................................85.00
Inkwell, exotic bird cartouch, 1820s, 4" dia, +9" tray..................600.00
Inkwell & stand, chinoiserie, florals/gilt, #240, 1810, 2".............380.00
Loving cup, leaves/gilt on ivory, 3 horn-shape hdls, #1421..........425.00
Mug, chinoiserie figures in garden, bl transfer, 1770, 3½" 1,100.00
Mug, chinoiserie figures in garden, bl transfer, 1770, 4½" 1,600.00
Mug, floral, mc on yel to apricot, 1903, 3¼"................................135.00
Mug, gnarled tree, bl transfer, 1770, 5½"......................................750.00
Mug, parrot/fruit/insects, bl transfer, 1770, 5½" 600.00
Pitcher, floral clusters/butterfly, bl transfer, 1770, 4½" 150.00
Pitcher, floral on cream w/gold, bulbous bottom, 10x5½"............250.00
Pitcher, horn hdl, #1116, ca 1886, 10" 300.00
Pitcher, leaf molded, gold-dusted apricot/gr, leaf hdl, 7" 180.00
Plate, armorial, shaped gr border, 1820, 10", set of 6 .... 1,500.00
Plate, birds, by Telford after Audubon, 1970, 9", set of 12.........500.00
Plate, floral sprays on yel & apricot, gilt rim, 1903, 8½" 135.00

Incense burner with spreadwing bird support, 8", $750.00.

Plate, florals, rtcl rim, 3-ftd, Granger, 10½" 755.00
Plate, Gold Chantilly, 6" 15.00
Plate, Silver Chantilly, dinner sz..25.00
Platter, eagle crest & motto, floral band, 1820, rstr, 22" 750.00
Soup plate, sprig, bl transfer, basketweave border, 1780s 100.00
Tea caddy, exotic birds/trees, fluted ovoid, 1770, 6" 600.00
Teapot, Oriental scene, bl transfer, Dr Wall, 6", NM 300.00
Urn, florals w/gold bands, mask hdls, 1889 mk, 8¼" 225.00
Vase, bud; florals, rtcl hdls, mk, 6" 225.00
Vase, butterflies/gilt leaves, moon flask w/hdls & ft, 6" 500.00
Vase, florals, molded/gilt lower body & neck, sgn Shuck, 10" 500.00
Vase, florals on shaded yel, 3 apertures, fan form, #2488 ....135.00
Vase, florals w/gold, pilgrim flask form, ftd 125.00
Vase, florals w/gold, salamander hdl, mk, 9x4¾" 425.00
Vase, florals/butterfly on gr, long neck/steeple hdls, 12" 550.00
Vase, florals/gilt on ivory, dolphin hdls, #1578, 7½" 225.00
Vase, forest scene, mc w/lustre & gold, 4¼".................................200.00
Vase, formed as a bag w/gilt tasseled cord, 1883, 4", pr 170.00
Vase, funerary; floral/emb gold on gr, rtcl dome lid, 12" 800.00
Vase, nautilus shell on coral-branch dome ft, 8½x5" 450.00
Vase, pheasants, sgn Stinton, #G-1047, 8¾" 475.00
Vase, rose sprays on ivory, gr fluted rim, #158, 3¾"......................135.00
Vase, roses on cream w/gold, sgn Hood, dtd 1900, 5x5½" 265.00
Vase, shell/seaweed panels on gr, ped ft, hdls, 1905, 5"................400.00

Covered vase, reticulated neck and lid, ca 1887, 27", $3,800.00.

Wall pocket, nest on branch, cobalt & gold trim, mk, 8" 165.00
Wall pocket, prunus/insects in bl, cornucopia form, 11", pr 6,000.00

Roycroft

Near the turn of the century, Elbert Hubbard established the Roycroft Printing Shop in East Aurora, New York. Named in honor of two 17th-century printer-bookbinders, the print shop was just the beginning of a community called Roycroft, which came to be known worldwide. Hubbard became a popular personality of the early 1900s, known for his talents in a variety of areas from writing and lecturing to manufacturing. The Roycroft community became a meeting place for people of various capabilities and included shops for the production of furniture, copper, leather items, and a multitude of other wares which were marked with the Roycroft symbol, an 'R' within a circle below a stylized cross. Hubbard lost his life on the Lusitania in 1915; production in the community continued until the Depression.

Interest is escalating in the field of Arts and Crafts in general, and Roycroft items in particular (along with Stickley, Rolfs, etc.) are rapidly appreciating in value. Copper items are evaluated to a large extent by the condition of the original patina that remains.

Book, Elbert Hubbard's Notebook, c 1927, EX 15.00
Book, Maud, Tennyson, 1 of 40 on Whatman, leather bound, M..500.00
Book, Virginius Puerisque, Stevenson, hand-illumined, vellum ..775.00
Book, Wht Hyacinths, Hubbard, 3-color print, suede bound.......175.00
Bookends, brass half-rnds w/etched flowers & rivets, 3½"...........150.00
Bookends, brass washed, ship at sea on rnd leather pc, mk 325.00
Bookends, brass-washed copper, leather insets w/elephants 250.00
Bookends, copper, lg emb poppy, riveted, orig patina, 5½".........400.00
Bookends, copper, medallion w/emb floral, 8x6" 200.00
Bookends, copper, tooled floral, NM dk brn patina, 3½x2" 200.00
Bookends, hammered copper, open fr w/cvd flowers, 8½x6"........150.00
Bookends, stylized owl w/in rectangle, logo, 4x6" 150.00
Bowl, copper w/brass spikes from base to rim, conical, 12" 300.00
Bowl, etched geometrics, flared/ftd, orig patina, 4½x12" 275.00
Bowl, hammered copper, rolled rim, 3-ftd, orb mk, 10" 1,400.00
Bowl, SP copper, band of grapes, ftd, sgn KK, 4x9" dia 550.00
Box, mahog, hammered brass hinges, logo on lid, 9x23x12"........400.00
Bust, E Hubbard, terra cotta, by Connor, dtd 1899, 12x9" 1,800.00
Cabinet, printer's; 8 drw by panel door, mk, rfn, 52x47" 3,750.00
Candelabra, silver, 3 slim scrolled stems on twist std, 20"...........600.00
Candlestick, brass/copper, cut-out dish base, logo, 9", pr 500.00
Candlestick, Princess, design by K Kipp, sgn, 8x4", pr 375.00
Ceiling light, hammered copper 17" dia cone on chain, pr 14,850.00
Chair, ladderbk side; sgn, M orig leather seat, NM finish 275.00
Chamberstick, brass, curved strap hdl, orig patina, 1x5"............100.00
Creamer & sugar bowl w/lid, geometrics & logo, Buffalo, EX......350.00
Lamp, copper, shade w/leaves & parchment panels, #902, 15".. 3,000.00
Lamp, copper, shade w/mica inserts, sq base, #903, 14x8" 1,600.00
Lamp, ldgl fruit panels in 10" copper shade; str std, 17" 2,300.00
Lamp, tan Egyptian-border helmet shade, strapwork std, 15" .. 4,600.00
Magazine stand, #078, 3-shelf/arched gallery, mk, rfn, 38" 850.00
Plate, red/gr geometrics & logo, Buffalo Pottery, 9½" 150.00
Sconce, copper, orig dk brn patina, 9x2½", pr.............................325.00
Sconce, hammered copper, rectangular bk, no mk, 10x3", pr 300.00
Table, dressing; #1001, lg mirror, 37x39" 900.00
Tray, #826, octagonal w/sq loop hdls, logo, 10"...........................175.00
Vase, Am Beauty, #201, old cleaning, 19" 900.00
Vase, Am Beauty, brass (rare), bulbous w/flared neck, 19" 1,200.00
Vase, Am Beauty, riveted band, flared, orig patina, mk, 22" .. 2,300.00
Vase, Am Beauty, riveted strapwork, squat angled body, 19" .. 2,000.00
Vase, copper tube w/4 silver sqs, 4 open triangle hdls, 8" 1,300.00

Vase, American Beauty, hammered copper, marked, 12", $1,000.00.

Vase, emb floral frieze, sgn, orig patina, 10x3" 550.00
Walking stick, leather thong, imp logo, dtd 1903, 35" ...275.00

Rozenburg

Some of the most innovative and original Art Nouveau ceramics were created by the Rozenberg factory at The Hague in The Netherlands between 1885 and 1916. Some pieces are similar to Gouda. Rozenburg also made highly-prized eggshell ware, so called because of its very thin walls; this is eagerly sought after by collectors. T.A.C. Colenbrander was their artistic leader, with Samuel Schellink and J. Kok designing many of the eggshell pieces.

Bowl, tulips amid curling/dotted border, free-form, 11" 240.00
Cup & saucer, Nouveau floral, octagonal, Van Rossum 500.00
Jug, Nouveau butterflies/florals, sgn VW, #614, mks, 7" 500.00
Plaque, Dutch windmill in landscape, JG Vogel, 3x6" 100.00
Vase, eggshell, florals, lav on wht & yel, ribbed, 6" 600.00
Vase, Nouveau pomegranates, bulbous, sgn KE, #1025, 4¾" 200.00
Vase, pansies, orange on bl, blk-dotted yel neck/hdls, 10" 695.00

Rubena

Rubena glass was made by several firms in the late 1800s. It is a blown art glass that shades from clear to red. See also Art Glass Baskets; Cruets; Sugar Shakers; Salts; specific manufacturers.

Bottle, scent; T'print, HP daisies, faceted stopper, 7x3" 165.00
Pitcher, tankard; florals w/gold tracery, 13", +6 tumblers..........890.00
Shot glass, threaded, Northwood.......................................65.00
Tumbler, Hobnail, 10-row, 4x3" 110.00
Vase, enamel & gold w/threaded base, 4-lobed top, 10½" 225.00
Vase, frosted, etched floral, int ribs, bell-shape top, 6".............275.00

Rubena Verde

Rubena Verde glass was introduced in the late 1800s by Hobbs, Brockunier, and Company of Wheeling, West Virginia. Its transparent colors shade from red to green. See also Art Glass Baskets; Cruets; Sugar Shakers; Salts.

Bottle, scent; Invt T'print, faceted stopper, 6"...................215.00

Pitcher, Hobnail, water sz..350.00
Syrup, Invt T'print, tapered form 395.00
Tumbler, Hobnail...115.00
Tumbler, Hobnail, 10-row, 4x2¾" 165.00
Vase, appl clear spirals & rim, 10¼" 190.00
Vase, mc floral/bl ribbon, ruffled w/str ribbed sides, 11"......175.00

Ruby Glass

Produced for over one hundred years by every glasshouse of note in this country, ruby glass has been used to create decorative items such as one might find in gift shops, utilitarian bottles and kitchenware, figurines, and dinnerware lines such as were popular in the depression era. For further information and study, we recommend *Ruby Glass of the 20th Century* by our advisor, Naomi Over; she is listed in the Directory under Colorado.

Bowl, Oyster & Pearl, Anchor Hocking, 1938-40, 6½" 15.00
Cake salver, American Sweetheart, Macbeth-Evans, 1930s, 12" .200.00
Console set, Tiara's Sunset Leaf, Indiana, bowl+2 5" sticks...........45.00
Cup, American Sweetheart, Macbeth-Evans, 1930s, rare 100.00
Cup & saucer, Anchor Hocking, ca 1940s 8.00
Cup & saucer, sq form, Anchor Hocking, 1940s.......................4.00
Figure, elephant, Swedish Glass, ca 1980, 5" 15.00
Goblet, wine; chrome stem, unknown maker 8.00
Paperweight, apple, Viking, 3¾" 20.00
Pie pan, Pyrex, 9½"..50.00
Pitcher, Blenko, #3750, 16-oz......................................20.00
Punch set, Royal Ruby, Anchor Hocking, bowl+stand+6 cups......75.00
Sherbet, plain stem, Anchor Hocking, ca 1942 ....6.00
Swan, Summit Art Glass (Cambridge Mold), 1986, 13" 80.00
Tumbler, Georgian, Anchor Hocking, 1940s, 9-oz.....................6.00
Vase, Blenko, #404M, 11x8¼" 55.00
Vase, Harding, Anchor Hocking, 1940s, 6¾" 8.00

Ruby-Stained Souvenirs

Ruby-flashed or ruby-stained glass was made through the application of a thin layer of color over clear. It was used in the manufacture of some early pressed tableware and from the Victorian era well into the 20th century for souvenir items which were often engraved on the spot with the date, location, and buyer's name.

Hatchet, Alaska Yukon Pacific Expo 1909, 6", $85.00.

Bell, St Louis, 7" 75.00
Box, trinket; heart shape, Niagara Falls 25.00
Creamer, Arched Ovals, 1908, mini 24.00
Creamer, Block & Star 35.00

Creamer, Gettysburg PA, 1863	25.00
Creamer, Heart Band	25.00
Creamer, Scalloped Daisy	25.00
Mug, Heart Band, 3"	24.00
Paperweight, calendar, 1912	45.00
Spooner, Buttons & Arches	28.00
Toothpick holder, Shamrock	72.00
Toothpick holder, Witch's Kettle, w/hdl	22.00
Tumbler, Clarence, Ocean Grove 1896	25.00
Tumbler, Diamond Peg	30.00
Tumbler, Pavonia	48.00

Rugs

Hooked

Hooked rugs are treasured today for their folk-art appeal. It was a craft that was introduced to this country in about 1830 and flourished its best in the New England states. The prime consideration is not age but artistic appeal. Scenes with animals, buildings, and people; patriotic designs; or whimsical themes are preferred. Condition is, of course, also a factor. Marked examples bearing the stamps of 'Frost and Co.,' 'Abenakee,' 'C.R.,' and 'Ouia' are highly prized. Note: the rugs listed here are rag unless noted otherwise.

Allover mc leaves on bl-gray stripes, unused, 112x79"	2,600.00
Cat, gray on 5-color stripes, damage/rpr needed, 47x25"	275.00
Compass star, minor wear & fading, 39" dia	400.00

Confronting horses, one black, the other white, ca 1890, 26" x 43", $650.00.

Dog, wht/blk w/purple ribbon on lt bl, dk border, 35x23"	125.00
Floral, mc in lt reserve on dk rectangle, 38x26"	90.00
Floral, mc in tan reserve, hearts in spandrels, 38x23", M	250.00
Floral, mc on bl oval w/in 4-color border, 32x20"	125.00
Floral medallion, floral border, wear/rpr, 58x33"	275.00
Floral on gray oval on khaki rectangle w/gr leaves, 46x30"	90.00
Foliage, soft colors, blk border, 91x118"	325.00
Grenfell, 2 Eskimos/sled/dog team, 6-color, 21x31"	400.00
Grenfell-type stag pulling sled w/2 children, trees, 38x28"	450.00
Horse & buggy, blk/wht, 2 shades of gr/mc flowers, 36x23"	100.00
Horse & buggy/dog/goose shapes, dk/lt bl, brn border, 66"	500.00
Penny design, mc on gray, striped border, unused, 72x27"	1,175.00
Roses, red/gr on varigated gr stripes, mc border, 24x14"	55.00
Stripes of mc in alternate blocks, blk separators, 68x32"	175.00
Tulips around gray center on bl, blk border, 35x23"	125.00
Welcome, w/flowers & blk cat, semicircular, 19x34"	125.00
2 bl parrots in mc floral on tan, some yarn, 31x46", EX	500.00
2 brn pups on grass by yel picket fence, mc border, 37x20"	225.00

2 stylized blk chickens on gray, red border, 40x23", VG	150.00

Oriental

The Oriental and Eastern rug market has enjoyed a renewal of interest in recent years as collectors have become aware of the fact that some of the semi-antique rugs (those sixty to one hundred years old) may be had at a price within the range of the average buyer.

Key:
comp — complimentary	mdl — medallion
dmn — diamond	s/a — semi-antique
gb — guard border	

Anatolian prayer, cotton, lamp/columns on wine, 72x50"	550.00
Chinese, floral-spray corners, birds/etc, 1950s, 144x99"	1,300.00
Fereghan, gold/coral med on bl, peach gb, 80x53"	1,700.00
Hamadan, hooked mdl on dk bl, multiple gb, 69x47"	700.00
Hamadan, ivory mdl on dk bl Herati-filled cartouch, 96x60"	900.00
Hamadan, lg floral mdl on rust, palmette gb, 79x46", EX	425.00
Hamadan, rose Herati-filled cartouch on bl, wear, 78x52"	900.00
Heriz, bl/coral sq mdl on rust w/floral, 1920s, 160x125", VG	1,800.00
Heriz, center mdl, 3-color on navy, tightly woven, 32x65"	300.00
Heriz, flowerheads on red, dk bl meander border, 100x85"	13,000.00
Karabagh, dmn pole mdl on wine, floral gb, 150x130", EX	3,750.00
Kashan, allover florals on ivory, palmette border, 180x130"	2,000.00
Kashan, dmn mdl, ivory on rust cartouch w/florals, 81x52"	2,000.00
Kashan, multi-facted mdl on red cartouch on bl, 150x100"	6,500.00
Kashan, sm mdl/florals on peach, dk bl floral border, 74x53"	500.00
Kashan, sm red mdl on lg mc mdls, bl gb, 140x99", EX	5,500.00
Kasvin, floral mdl on red floral field, 3 gb, 120x150"	6,500.00

Kazak, blue and green hooked open medallions on brick red, gold and royal blue reciprocal trefoil guard, wear/repair, 8 ft x 4½ ft, $750.00.

Kerman, bl/rose/ivory mdl on cream cartouch, 1880s, 76x51"	850.00
Kerman, cobalt mdl on cartouch, ivory gb, 96x50", NM	1,800.00
Khotan, 1 lg+2 sm med on dk bl, 5 gb, 1900, 150x78", EX	2,000.00
Luri, mdl on wine cartouch on ivory, 1880s, 79x52", EX	1,200.00
Oushak, allover geometrics, gr/wine/bl on red, 134x160"	2,000.00
Sarouk, dmn mdl/floral sprays on coral, 1950s, 210x120"	3,000.00
Sarouk, floral in bl, geometric yel fringe, 1930s, 234x136"	4,250.00
Sarouk, floral mdl/flowers on lt rose, 75x50", VG	1,000.00
Sarouk, floral spray center/florals on dk bl, 79x53", EX	1,250.00
Sarouk, floral sprays on raspberry, 1920s, 79x50", EX	1,300.00
Sarouk, sm mdl/floral sprays on dk bl, palmette gb, 130x96"	3,600.00

Senneh, 2 ivory/1 dk bl mdl on red, 1900s, 74x52", EX **1,500.00**
Tibetan, dragon/clouds on bl, borderless, 1900s, 64x24" **500.00**
Ushak, floral mdl, turtle gb, gold w/bl & mc, 160x120", EX.... **4,250.00**
Yomud Ensi, garden plan on 4-part rust field, 66x48", EX **500.00**

Miscellaneous

Penny, wool, dk shades on ivory cotton, star shaped, 58" **400.00**
Rag, carpet, unused, Zoar OH, 13x33"...**300.00**
Rag carpet, gray w/mc stripes, 3 sewn strips, PA, 106x144" **450.00**

Rumrill

George Rumrill designed and marketed his pottery from 1933 until the early 1940s. During this period at least three different companies produced his works. Today the most popular lines are those made in the 1930s by Red Wing Stoneware and later Red Wing Potteries such as Trumpet Flower, Classica, Manhattan, and of course the Nudes. Rumrill pottery is often recognizable simply by the glaze. A number of two-toned glazes were produced, and these are being avidly sought by today's collectors. It's interesting to note that many Rumrill designs can be found with the Red Wing mark. Our advisors for this category are Wendy and Leo Frese; they are listed in the Directory under Texas.

Basket, Classic, Egg Shell, #285, 8" **30.00**
Candle holder, nude, Egg Shell, #576, 9½".......................**80.00**
Creamer & sugar bowl, Shell, Seashell, 4" **25.00**
Lamp, nude, jade, #570, 10" **225.00**
Planter, nude, yel, #567, 8½"..**60.00**
Planter, swan, charcoal, #259, 6" **15.00**
Vase, aqua, #J-24, not mfg by Red Wing, 11½" **20.00**
Vase, bl, #H-52, not mfg by Red Wing, 9½" **25.00**

Vase, lilies on base, curdled green glaze, 7", $45.00.

Vase, Fluted, Dutch bl, #320, 5½"....................................**20.00**
Vase, Fluted, Goldenrod, #301, 11" **65.00**
Vase, Grecian, Egg Shell, #302, 6".....................................**15.00**

Rushmore

Ivan Houser studied sculpture and fine arts at the University of Oregon. He gained valuable experience in the potting field, first from the work he did in producing terra cotta architectural sculptures and later through the work he did with the carvers on Mt. Rushmore. In 1933 he purchased a tract of land near Mt. Rushmore where he built

his own pottery. Using the especially adaptable clay he found there, he produced a line of decorative items until 1941, after which he went into the teaching field. His wares are characterized by the natural shading of the clay which he allowed to show through the glazes.

Pitcher, gr, water sz **47.50**
Vase, bsk, 3" **25.00**
Vase, burnt orange, 1940s, 4" **28.00**
Vase, red, 5½" **30.00**

Ruskin

John Ruskin was an English author, painter, architect, ceramist, and social reformer who lived from 1819 until 1900. Today his art pottery is especially interesting to collectors and is finding its way into some of the major pottery auctions in this country.

Vase, aquamarine/royal bl crystalline, 8x5½" **600.00**
Vase, dots/squiggles on streaky bl, dtd 1908, 8", EX **180.00**
Vase, gray dappled/mauve lustre, gourd form, 7" **175.00**
Vase, orange irid, bulbous shoulder, collared, 7½x5¾"................**125.00**
Vase, orange irid, collared, 7x4½" **80.00**
Vase, orange irid, 3½x2½" **50.00**
Vase, red-brn w/cream & lt bl speckles, drilled, 10½" **230.00**

Russel Wright Dinnerware

Russel Wright, one of America's foremost industrial designers, also designed several lines of ceramic dinnerware, glassware, and aluminum ware that are now highly sought-after collectibles.

His most popular dinnerware then and with today's collectors, American Modern, was manufactured by the Steubenville Pottery Company from 1939 until 1959. It was produced in a variety of solid colors in assortments chosen to stay attune with the times.

Casual (his first line sturdy enough to be guaranteed against breakage for ten years from date of purchase) is relatively easy to find today — simply because it has held up so well. During the years of its production, the Casual line was constantly being restyled, some items as many as five times. Early examples were heavily mottled, while later pieces were smoothly glazed and patterned. The ware was marked with Wright's signature and 'China by Iroquois.' It was marketed in fine department stores throughout the country. After 1950 the line was marked 'Iroquois China by Russel Wright.'

To calculate values for items in American Modern, add 100% to the suggested prices in the following listings for examples in these colors: White, Bean Brown, Cantaloupe, and Glacier Blue. In Casual, Brick Red and Aqua items go for around 200% more than any other color, while those in Avocado Yellow are priced lower than suggested values.

For those wanting to learn more about the subject, we recommend *The Collector's Encyclopedia of Russel Wright,* by our advisor, Ann Kerr. She is listed in the Directory under Ohio.

American Modern

Bowl, child's **27.50**
Bowl, divided vegetable..**65.00**
Bowl, salad **62.50**
Bowl, vegetable; coral...**15.00**
Butter dish, gray **135.00**
Carafe, bean brn **185.00**
Casserole, w/lid, 12" **42.50**

American Modern, see listings for specific values.

Celery, glacier	35.00
Celery dish, gray	22.50
Chop plate	24.00
Coaster/ash tray	12.50
Coffee cup cover	55.00
Coffeepot, demitasse	65.00
Coffeepot, 8x8½"	75.00
Creamer	9.00
Cup & saucer	10.00
Cup & saucer, demitasse	20.00
Gravy boat, 10½"	17.50
Ice box jar	125.00
Mug	37.50
Pitcher, water; gray	75.00
Pitcher, water; wht	125.00
Plate, child's	35.00
Plate, dinner; seafoam, 10"	7.00
Plate, salad; 8"	9.00
Relish, divided	95.00
Salad fork & spoon	75.00
Sauce boat, chutney, 8¾"	15.00
Shakers, pr	12.50
Soup, lug; seafoam	11.00
Sugar bowl, w/lid	10.00
Teapot, 6x10"	65.00

Casual

Bowl, fruit; restyled, 5¾"	5.00
Bowl, salad; 10"	25.00
Bowl, vegetable; 36-oz, 8⅛"	17.50
Butter dish, charcoal, ¼-lb	85.00
Butter dish, pk, ½-lb	55.00
Carafe, wine/coffee	95.00
Casserole, deep, w/lid, 4-qt, 8"	45.00
Casserole, 2-qt, 8"	22.00
Chop plate, 13⅞"	22.50
Coffeepot, demitasse; 4½"	65.00
Creamer, family sz, lg	15.00
Cup & saucer, demitasse	67.50
Cup & saucer, restyled	10.00
Dutch oven	75.00
Fry pan, w/lid	70.00
Gravy bowl, restyled, lid becomes stand	75.00
Gravy bowl, 12-oz, 5¼"	8.00

Gumbo (flat soup), 21-oz	18.00
Mug, restyled, 9-oz	65.00
Mug, 13-oz	55.00
Pepper mill	75.00
Percolator	110.00
Pitcher, water; 1½ -qt, 5¼"	45.00
Plate, party; w/cup	37.50
Plate, 10"	8.00
Plate, 7½"	6.00
Plate, 9½"	5.00
Platter, oval, 12¾"	18.00
Shaker, restyled	75.00
Shakers, stacking, pr	10.00
Soup, restyled, 18-oz	8.00
Soup, 11½ -oz	10.00
Sugar bowl, restyled	10.00
Teapot, restyled	67.50

Glassware

American Modern, cocktail, coral, 3-oz, 2½"	25.00
American Modern, cocktail, smoke, 3-oz, 2½"	22.00
American Modern, cordial, chartreuse	35.00
American Modern, cordial, coral	40.00
American Modern, goblet, crystal, 10-oz, 4"	25.00
American Modern, sherbet, chartreuse, 5-oz, 2½"	24.00
American Modern, tumbler, iced tea; coral, 13-oz	22.00
American Modern, tumbler, juice; smoke, 7-oz, 4"	15.00
American Modern, tumbler, pilsner, crystal, 7"	40.00
American Modern, tumbler, water; coral, 11-oz	45.00
American Modern, wine, smoke, 4-oz, 3"	22.00
Flair, tumbler, iced tea; 14-oz	50.00
Flair, tumbler, juice; 6-oz	50.00
Flair, tumbler, water; 11-oz	50.00
Pinch, tumbler, iced tea; 14-oz	30.00
Pinch, tumbler, juice; 6-oz	28.00
Pinch, tumbler, water; 11-oz	30.00

Highlight

Bowl, salad; rnd	40.00
Bowl, snow glass, rnd	100.00
Bowl, vegetable; oval	40.00
Creamer	20.00
Cup	16.00
Fruit/sherbet, snow glass	55.00
Lid for vegetable bowl, later 1953 addition	35.00
Mug	35.00
Plate, bread & butter	8.00
Plate, dinner	15.00
Platter, rnd, sm	40.00
Saucer, later 1953 addition	8.00
Shakers, lg or sm, pr	35.00
Sugar bowl	20.00
Sugar bowl, snow glass, w/lid & tray	45.00
Tumbler, snow glass, 10-oz	100.00

Spun Aluminum

Russel Wright's aluminum ware may not have been especially well accepted in its day — it tended to damage easily and seems to have had only limited market appeal — but today's collectors feel quite differently about it, as is apparent in the suggested values noted in the following listings.

Bain Marie server 400.00
Candelabrum, rare, 18x14" 175.00
Casserole 50.00
Cheese board..40.00
Flower ring 110.00
Gravy boat 125.00
Hot relish server 175.00
Humidor, sandwich 150.00
Humidor, tobacco; 12" 100.00
Ice bucket..50.00
Muffin warmer, wire insert, w/lid 90.00
Old fashioned set, 20-pc 400.00
Peanut scoop 40.00
Pitcher, sherry..225.00
Portable bar/serving cart 1,750.00
Punch set 1,500.00
Relish rosette, sm 75.00
Smoking stand 300.00
Spaghetti set, 3-pc 325.00
Tea set, 4-pc 400.00
Vase, 12" 65.00
Vase or flowerpot, sm, ea 50.00
Waste basket..100.00

Sterling

Ash tray..55.00
Bowl, fruit; 5" 5.00
Bowl, 7½" 10.00
Coffee bottle 65.00
Cup, demitasse; 3½-oz 25.00
Pitcher, water; restyled 45.00
Plate, Shun Lee, dinner sz 20.00
Plate, 10¼" 7.50
Plate, 11½" 8.00
Plate, 9" 6.00
Platter, oval, 13⅝" 16.00
Platter, oval, 7½" 10.00
Sauce boat, 9-oz 15.00
Sugar bowl, w/lid, 10-oz 12.50
Teapot, 10-oz 45.00

Miscellaneous

Bartlett Collins Eclipse, tumbler, water sz.............15.00
Bauer, ash tray, sm...175.00
Bauer, bowl, centerpc 650.00
Bauer, vase, pillow form...................................500.00
Chase, corn set, chrome, 4-pc 550.00
Chase, ice bucket w/tongs 65.00
Harker Wht Clover, bowl, fruit............................ 7.50
Harker Wht Clover, chop plate, 11" 15.00
Harker Wht Clover, gravy boat 15.00
Harker Wht Clover, sugar bowl, w/lid, ind 15.00
Harker Wht Clover, teacup 8.00
Highlight, fork, stainless steel............................55.00
Highlight, knife, stainless steel 75.00
Ideal, coffeepot, plastic, child's.........................15.00
Knowles, cup & saucer, 7½-oz 10.00
Knowles, Grass, pitcher, water sz 55.00
Knowles, platter, oval, 16" 25.00
Knowles, Seeds, compote, deep 65.00
Knowles, shakers, pr..17.50
Knowles, teapot..75.00

Meladur, plate, plastic, 8" 8.00
Oak, bowl, frosted..75.00
Oceana, bowl, centerpc 350.00
Oceana, snail relish, wood, lg 350.00
Residential, plate, plastic, dinner sz...................... 5.00
Residential, tumbler, plastic 15.00
Salad fork & spoon, wood.................................75.00
Theme Formal, coffeepot..................................500.00
Theme Formal, tumbler 110.00

Russian Art

    Before the Revolution in 1917, many jewelers and craftsmen created exquisite marvels of their arts, distinctive in the extravagant detail of their enamel work, jeweled inlays, and use of precious metals. These treasures aptly symbolized the glitter and the romance of the glorious days under the reign of the Tsars of Imperial Russia.

    The most famous of these master jewelers was Peter Carl Faberge. Following the tradition of his father, he took over the Faberge workshop in 1870 at the age of twenty-four. His specialties were enamel work, clockwork automated figures, carved animal and human figures of precious or semiprecious stone and his best-known creations, the Imperial Easter Eggs — each of an entirely different design. By the turn of the century, his influence had spread to other countries, and his work was revered by royalty and the very wealthy. The onset of the war marked the end of the era.

Icon to Our Lady of Joy to Those Who Suffer, initialed I.D., silver and cloisonne enamel, 12" x 10", $1,100.00.

Beaker, niello silver gilt, tapered, 1842, 3¼" 950.00
Beaker, silver, repousse/eagles, gilt int, ftd, 1769, 2½" 950.00
Bowl, cloisonne blossoms, octagonal, sgn, dtd 1899-1908, 3" 550.00
Box, malachite, rectangular, metal hinge, 1800s, 2½" L 240.00
Candlestick, silver, repousse/chased florals, 1873, 15", pr........ 2,600.00
Charka, silver, scrolls above fluted base, ca 1770, 2⅝" 560.00
Cigarette case, emb Napoleon on horse, sgn/ca 1910, 4½" L 745.00
Cigarette case, Samorodok, wht metal w/gr stone, 1900s, 4" 500.00
Figurine, bear & cub, gilt/bronze/malachite, 1800s, 6" L 2,975.00
Figurine, dancing man holds hat aloft, porc, Popov, 8" 800.00
Icon, Virgin Vladimirskaya on red, giltwood fr, 13x10" 1,400.00
Jug, milk; silver, gadrooning, Empire style, 1834, 5½" 465.00
Jug, milk; silver, plain, oval, scroll hdl, 1880s, 2¾" 700.00
Match-case holder, papier-mache/lacquer, peasant lady, 1800s ...450.00
Napkin ring, wht metal, repousse/chased bogatyrs, 1911 ....375.00

Snuff box, niello silver gilt, equestrian on lid, 1830, 2¼" **925.00**
Spoon, basting; silver, fiddle pattern, mk MK/1889, 4½ -oz.........**220.00**
Tazza, silver-mtd cut glass, pierced stem, 1880s, 7¾" **925.00**
Teapot, silver, pear shape, scrolls, MOP knob, 1890s, 4¼" **1,000.00**

Sabino

Sabino art glass was produced by Marius-Ernest Sabino in France during the 1920s and '30s. It was made in opalescent, frosted, and colored glass and was designed to reflect the Art Deco style of that era. In 1960 using molds he modeled by hand, Sabino once again began to produce art glass using a special formula he himself developed that was characterized by a golden opalescence. Although the family continued to produce glassware for export after his death in 1971, they were never able to duplicate Sabino's formula.

Ash tray, shell form, 3½x5½" **24.00**
Ash tray, thistle, 4" dia **24.00**
Bottle, scent; Frivolites, ladies & swans, 4¼" **48.00**
Bottle, scent; Frivolites, ladies & swans, 6¼" **65.00**
Box, powder; Petalia, med **90.00**
Figurine, Art Deco lady, draped armed extended, opal, 8" **450.00**
Figurine, bird, nesting, 2x1¼" **20.00**
Figurine, bird, resting, 3" L **27.50**
Figurine, bird, wings down, 2½" **48.00**
Figurine, butterfly, lg **165.00**
Figurine, butterfly, wings closed, 2¾" **18.00**
Figurine, cherub...**24.00**
Figurine, dragonfly..**120.00**
Figurine, draped nude **355.00**
Figurine, elephant..**24.00**
Figurine, fish, 2x2" **20.00**
Figurine, fox **25.00**
Figurine, gazelle, 4x6" **60.00**
Figurine, heron, 7½" **100.00**
Figurine, Hesitation..**450.00**
Figurine, Isadora Duncan...**785.00**
Figurine, L'Idole, seated nude, opal/frosted, 6½" **3,800.00**
Figurine, Madonna, sq base, med.....................................**75.00**
Figurine, Madonna, 3" **24.00**
Figurine, mouse...**50.00**

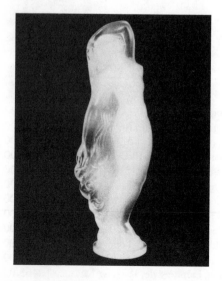

Figure of a nude, 7",
$195.00.

Figurine, panther group **500.00**
Figurine, pekingese dog, lg...**70.00**
Figurine, polar bear..**115.00**

Figurine, rooster, sm **32.00**
Figurine, Scotty dog...**65.00**
Figurine, snail...**30.00**
Figurine, Venus de Milo, sm **30.00**
Knife rest, duck form **25.00**
Knife rest, frog form **22.00**
Lamp, fan panels/triangles, 3-tier shade, frosted, 8" **800.00**
Luminaire, fish form, on ftd chrome base, 8" **550.00**
Mask, Triton **2,300.00**
Plate, fish form, lg...**200.00**
Tray, swallow form, lg..**110.00**
Tray, swallow form, med...**40.00**
Vase, Colombes **525.00**
Vase, La Danse...**990.00**
Vase, La Danse & Colombes **650.00**
Vase, Manta Ray..**255.00**
Vase, Ovals & Pearls **225.00**
Vase, Paradis **675.00**

Salesman's Samples and Patent Models

Salesman's samples and patent models are often mistaken for toys or homemade folk art pieces. They are instead actual working models made by very skilled craftsmen who worked as model-makers. Patent models were made until the early 1900s. After that, the patent office no longer required a model to grant a patent. The name of the inventor or the model-maker and the date it was built is sometimes noted on the patent model. Salesman's samples were occasionally made by model-makers, but often they were assembled by an employee of the company. These usually carried advertising messages to boost the sale of the product. Though they are still in use today, the most desirable examples date from the 1800s to about 1945.

Many small stoves are incorrectly termed a 'salesman's sample'; remember that no matter how detailed one may be, it must be considered a toy unless accompanied by a carrying case — the indisputable mark of a salesman's sample.

Bathtub, SM Co, CI...**65.00**
Burial vault, Monarch Vaults, CI, cutaway view, 8x16x8", EX....**175.00**
Case, w/180 blown glass miniatures, documentation, 1940s **695.00**
Cement block maker, Samson, brass, 7½", EX in box **325.00**
Chest, oak, 3-drw, swivel mirror, orig pulls, 12x19x5" **150.00**
Clothes dryer, Whitesville, folding **45.00**
Clothes ringer, Anchor Brand #5, Lovell Mfg Co, Erie PA...........**50.00**
Clothes ringer, Horseshoe Brand #2, Gem Ringer.......................**50.00**
Clothesline, NuWay, Elgin IL, folding **10.00**
Collar, Arrow, in box, 2½x2½" **15.00**
Corn-planting head, dbl, Powell Bros **20.00**
Egg box, Star brand, w/wooden eggs, 1½x4½x3½", EX **160.00**
Food chopper, Rollman #75 ....**40.00**

Food grinder, Patented '06, '14, '15, 7" long, $40.00.

Food grinder, mk AG...30.00
Furnace, Andes, Seneca Parin Works 55.00
Furnace, Titan, CI..60.00
Girdle, Nu Vogue Maternity, w/compo display 125.00
Gumball machine, Ford, w/carrying case 250.00
Hat, Stetson, M in EX orig box...25.00
Hay knife, old & orig 150.00
Hog trough, Lion's Perfect, wood, red pnt, 1902, 4½x6½", M 195.00
Horse collar, leather, 3½" 65.00
Ice cream freezer, Peerless, 6", M 125.00
Ice cream freezer, Shepard's...400.00
Icebox, oak, 13x8x5", EX 200.00
Icebox, wood/glass, Gordonair LaPorte, '25, 15", VG, w/case 800.00
Pitcher & bowl, wht graniteware w/bl trim, mk Sweden 70.00
Radiator, Richmond, floor standing 25.00
Radio, Westinghouse, floor model, ca 1920 ....350.00
Revelation shotgun shells, 5 stages of manufacture, EX 135.00
Roasting pan, Reed, lt bl graniteware, w/lid 280.00
Shirt, Yale, in box, 5x9" 70.00
Silo, pyramid top w/tin finial, w/ladder, EX......................295.00
Sink, Lenox, porc 25.00
Stove, Jenco, wood burner, cylindrical w/pipe 80.00
Stove, space heater, w/pipe & collar, 1903, NM 450.00
Tombstone, granite w/emb brass plaque, w/case 65.00
Top hat, Henry Heath, beaver, w/case...............................160.00
Wash boiler, tin w/lid, EX 85.00
Wash pan, Royal Granite Steelware, gray, 6" 75.00
Washboard, glass, mk USA, 11x5", NM...............................40.00
Washing machine, wooden w/metal bands, Tinley Park IL 320.00

Salt Glaze

As early as the 1600s, potters used common salt to glaze their stoneware. This was accomplished by heating the salt and introducing it into the kiln at maximum temperature. The resulting gray-white glaze was a thin, pitted surface that resembles the peel of an orange.

Crock, figures/armorial relief, English, 1800s, 9" 200.00
Dish, scrolls/basketwork, rtcl trellis rim, 1760, 12½", EX 275.00

Footed leaf dish, relief bird on branch, ca 1750s, NM, 7" x 9½", $3,000.00.

Jug, Tam O' Shanter on horse in relief, Ridgway, 8x5" 175.00
Pitcher, neoclassical frieze, brn-glaze neck, Adams, 11"...............450.00
Plate, emb scalloped rim, 12" 450.00

Teapot, Fred Prussia Rex panel on ermine fields, 4⅜", EX 1,300.00

Salt Shakers

The screw-top salt shaker was invented by John Mason in 1858. In 1871 when salt became more refined, some ceramic shakers were molded with pierced tops. 'Christmas' shakers, so called because of their December 25, 1877, patent date, were fitted with a rotary agitator designed to break up any lumps in the salt. There are four types: Christmas Barrel (rare in cranberry and amethyst); Christmas Panel (rare in colors); Christmas Pearl (opaque, pearly white with painted decor); and Octagon Waffle (clear, thick glass made in three sizes with a rotary agitator, usually having undated tops). The dated top and patented agitator for the Christmas Barrel and Christmas Panel salt shakers were produced by Dana K. Alden of Boston; most of the glass bodies were made by the Boston and Sandwich Glass Co. in the late 1870s and 1880s. Identical shakers which have no agitator or dated top are the companion peppers; these fetch about 30% less than the salts on today's markets.

Today much of the interest in collecting is concentrated on art glass, Wave Crest, and custard glass examples. (See also specific categories.) If you would like to learn more about salt shakers, we recommend *The World of Salt Shakers II* by Mildred and Ralph Lechner; their address may be found in the Directory under Virginia. Those interested in novelty shakers will enjoy *Salt and Pepper Shakers*, an illustrated price guide by Helene Guarnaccia, and *The Collector's Encyclopedia of Salt and Pepper Shakers, Figural and Novelty*, by Melva Davern. Both are available at your local library or bookstore. In the following listing, prices are for single shakers unless noted 'pair.' Values are for old, original shakers. Some of these have been reproduced, and this will be noted in the description.

Acorn, pk to wht, Hobbs, ca 1890, pr.............................70.00
Annie 45.00
Apple Blossom, milk glass, M pnt..65.00
Apricot Band, brn enamel w/8 apricots around base, pr 45.00
Artichoke (Valencia), Fostoria Glass, 1891.......................33.00
Aster & Leaf, bl, pr...125.00
Atterbury Twin, milk glass, combination S&P, Pat 1873 ....85.00
Ball fruit jar (reproduced), pr, MIB.....................................20.00
Barrel, Excelsior, emb Excelsior, Pat 1886, rare...............65.00
Basket, milk glass, HP decor..25.00
Beaded Dahlia, gr opaque, pr..32.50
Bevelled Diamond & Star 25.00
Boot on Fan 20.00
Broken Column 35.00
Bulging Loops, pigeon blood, pr..110.00
Bulging Petal, bl...25.00
Bull's Eye & Daisy Variant, gr eyes 24.00
Burmese, ribbed barrel, no decor, Mt WA, pr...................400.00
Chick head, HP roses on wht, SP head, Mt WA................335.00
Chick head, mums & leaves on lime, SP head, Mt WA 375.00
Christmas Barrel, amber, lid dtd, w/agitator, Dana K Alden........100.00
Christmas Barrel, apple gr, orig agitator 110.00
Christmas Barrel, cobalt, orig agitator, +pepper, pr 200.00
Christmas Barrel, cranberry, orig lid & agitator...............290.00
Christmas Barrel, cranberry, salt w/agitator, +pepper, pr 450.00
Christmas Barrel, dk amethyst, orig lid & agitator 100.00
Christmas Barrel, gr, orig lid & agitator, pr 225.00
Christmas Barrel, peacock bl, salt w/agitator, +pepper, pr 250.00
Christmas Panel, amethyst, w/lid & agitator 225.00
Christmas Panel, cranberry, w/lid & agitator....................300.00
Christmas Panel, dk amethyst, w/lid & agitator 275.00

Christmas Panel, sapphire bl, w/lid & agitator 225.00
Circled Scroll, opal colors, gr or bl, ca 1903 ....80.00
Cone, gr opaque, Consolidated 30.00
Cord & Tassel, gr 20.00
Creased Bale, bl opaque..35.00
Creased Waist, opaque Muranese, New Martinsville, pr 90.00
Croesus, gr w/VG gold, pr 150.00
Crossroads, amber, pr 35.00
Currier & Ives, bl or vaseline, rare 55.00
Diamond w/Peg, custard, pr 85.00
Dice, orig lids, rare, pr 130.00
Double Leaf, pk 30.00
Egg in Blossom, Mt WA 95.00
Eureka, ruby stained, pr 48.00
Fig, violets, wht on cranberry, Mt WA, orig lid............................185.00
Fine Cut, yel, pr 50.00
Fleur-de-lis in wreath, pigeon blood satin, orig top......................58.00
Flower Band, pigeon blood, pr 110.00
Flower Band, pk cased, pr 85.00
Footed Ten Panel, opaline gr or bl, rare..60.00
Forget-Me-Not, tall, gr, Challinor...25.00
Forget-Me-Not, tall, milk glass, pr 45.00
Geneva, gr w/gold, orig lid, McKee 65.00
Georgia Gem, custard, souvenir, pr..80.00

Iris with Meander, light green with gold, Jefferson Glass Co., rare, $68.00; **Globule**, red satin, Lancaster Glass Works, very scarce, $60.00.

Guttate, milk glass...25.00
Guttate, pk cased (reproduced), pr..75.00
Half Cone, satin, Consolidated Lamp & Glass, 1890s...................60.00
Hand w/Fishscale, frosted (reproduced), pr...................................75.00
Heart, milk glass, pr 40.00
Heart, pk opaque, pr 90.00
Herringbone MOP, pk, pewter top...290.00
Honeycomb, amberina..95.00
Honeycomb, rubena verde..110.00
Horseshoe, amber, lg, pr 35.00
Ingalio, emerald gr w/gold, Northwood, rare, pr..........................325.00
Invt Fan & Feather, pk slag, Northwood, 1900s, rare, pr 800.00
Invt T'print, bl w/HP florals, pr...75.00
Jefferson Optic, amethyst, HP, pr...65.00
Jewel & Flower, bl opal w/gold...95.00
King's Crown 22.00
Leaf & Spear, HP opalware, Wave Crest, pr 165.00
Leaf Bracket, opaque caramel slag, Indiana Tumbler Co, rare 175.00

Leaf Mold, cranberry cased, silver flecks, pr 175.00
Leaf Mold, vaseline spatter, pr 140.00
Leaf Overlapping, bl, pr..60.00
Lobe Four, shiny Crown Milano w/florals & gilt, pr....................225.00
Lobe Four, wht/bl floral on yel, 6-lobed, Mt WA, pr...................185.00
Many Petals (Periwinkle), New Martinsville.................................35.00
Nail, etched, red flashed, orig top..40.00
National's Eureka, ruby stained, pr...65.00
Nestor, amethyst, gold & enamel, pr...55.00
Nestor, bl, no enamel 35.00
Optic, Hobb's, rubena w/florals, pr..190.00
Overlapping Shell, pk 40.00
Owl's head, milk glass, orig top 150.00
Panelled Scroll, gr..20.00
Panelled Shell, pk cased 48.00
Panelled Sprig, milk glass w/gr decor, pr 40.00
Peachblow, acid finish, orig SP top, NE Glass, 3¾".....................525.00
Peachblow, bulbous, Wheeling 300.00
Pillar, Ribbed, satinized burmese, HP florals, Mt WA, rare, pr 900.00
Raindrop, bl MOP, rare, pr..410.00
Reverse Swirl, clear opal 48.00
Reverse Swirl, cranberry opal, pr 95.00
Rubena, HP butterflies & plants, pr..145.00
Rubena verde, HP floral 105.00
Scroll, gr opaque, ftd..23.00
Sequoia, bl, in stand, pr 85.00
Spider Web (Alba), pk opaque, Dithridge, pr 70.00
States, glass lid, pr 35.00
Sunset, milk glass...20.00
Swag w/Brackets, amethyst w/gold, pr..110.00
Thousand Eye, amber...18.00
Three Face (reproduced) 150.00
Tokyo, clear opal 48.00
Torch & Wreath, custard, Dithridge, pr 85.00
Wildflower, vaseline (reproduced) 45.00
Woven Neck, Wave Crest, kitten in grass decor 110.00
Wreath 12-Panel, pk roses, Mt WA, Pairpoint, pr 97.00
X-Ray, gr w/gold, Riverside Glass, ca 1896-99, pr 125.00

Novelty

Collie head, ceramic, Japan, 1950s-60s, pr....................................10.00
Cow, comic, yel flower on side, ceramic, Japan, pr 7.50
Cow bride & groom, tails curled over bk, ceramic, Japan, pr 10.00

Van Tellingen Huggers, Black boy and his dog, $55.00.

Dog & fire hydrant, ceramic, unmk, pr 10.00
Dog w/bone, ceramic, Japan, nesting pr 12.00
Frog & toadstool, ceramic, Japan, nesting pr 12.00

Frog w/bow tie & hat, frog in pk dress w/fan, ceramic, pr 10.00
Hugger, Love Bug, sm, pr..65.00
Hugger, Mary & lamb, Van Tellingen, pr 35.00
Hugger, mermaid & sailor, Van Tellingen, pr..............................85.00
Kitten in boot, ceramic, Japan, 1950s-60s, pr 8.00
Kitten w/real ball of yarn, ceramic, Japan, pr.............................. 8.00
Panda bears, smiling faces, ceramic, Taiwan, mid-1970s, pr..........10.00
Pig playing flute, ceramic, sticker, Japan, pr.............................. 7.50
Poodles, blk & wht, 1 up on haunches, 1 recumbent, ceramic, pr... 9.00
Siamese cats, tall slim form, ceramic, Japan...............................10.00
Turtle in vest & hat, comic, ceramic, Japan, pr 12.00

Salts, Open

Before salt became refined, processed, and free-flowing as we know it today, it was necessary to serve it in a salt cellar. An innovation of the early 1800s, the master salt was placed by the host and passed from person to person. Smaller individual salts were a part of each place setting. A small silver spoon was used to sprinkle it onto the food. If you would like to learn more about the subject of salts, we recommend *5,000 Open Salts*, written by William Heacock and our advisor for this category, Patricia Johnson, with many full-color illustrations and current values; you will find Patricia Johnson's address in the Directory under California.

In the listings below, the numbers refer to *Open Salts* by Johnson and Heacock, and *Pressed Glass Salt Dishes* by L.W. and D.B. Neal. Lines with 'repro' within the description reflect values for reproduced salts.

Key: EPNS — electroplated nickel silver   HM — hallmarked

Art Glass

Bristol, w/enameling, bucket form w/silver rim & hdl 80.00
Cranberry, vaseline rigaree, ruffled, in EPNS holder....................165.00
Daum, cameo, autumn scene, oval...950.00
Daum, enameled windmills, tub shape...450.00
English, bl ruffled glass w/threading, EPNS holder.......................250.00
English, pk & wht wide stripes, EPNS holder................................275.00
Moser type, HP florals on clear, tazza shape.................................85.00
Spatterware, wht cased, clear rigaree, appl ft 195.00
Steuben, gold Aurene, low ruffled edge, salt or nut cup 250.00
Steuben, Jade Gr w/Alabaster ped ft, H&J-2041 ....190.00
Tiffany, Favrile, panelled design, 1¾" H.......................................250.00
Vaseline opal, ruffled edge, EPNS holder 295.00
Venetian, gold flecked, ped ft, 2 dolphin hdls 40.00
Venetian, ribbon glass, very lightweight..30.00
Wave Crest, tulip molded sides, enamel decor, rnd, H&J-47 ......175.00

Cut Glass

Anglo-Irish, boat, oval, ped ft, H&J-3698 ....90.00
Buzz Star, H&J-3127..20.00
Canoe shape, cane cutting, 3" L..55.00
Diamond Points, gr to clear, ped ft...85.00
Hawkes, cut lower section, top eng, rnd, sgn, H&J-3083 ....50.00
Notched Prism, H&J-3727 ....15.00
Russian pattern, heavy, rnd, H&J-3708, master 55.00
Tub w/tab hdls, eng, H&J-3318 ....20.00

Doubles

Art Nouveau, SP, 6" woman between 2 salts 225.00

Austrian, porc, floral, ring hdl, H&J-1149 ....40.00
Cranberry glass shells on ped w/silver holder, H&J-2061.............200.00
Faience (French), shell-shaped bowls, HP, H&J-1800.................125.00
Glass, ribbed bowls, knob hdl 15.00
Imari style, w/pepper 75.00
Intaglio, in brass holder w/stones, H&J-4652 ....95.00
Meissen, girl sitting on 2 baskets, Bl Onion................................550.00
Quimper, 2 swans, HP peasant designs..95.00
Silver, 2 sterling bowls w/fancy ring hdl, Europe, H&J-4233 ....85.00

Lacy Glass

Neal BF-1F, opal, Basket of Flowers, NM 125.00
Neal BT-5, med bl, Lafayette boat 850.00
Neal BT-9, opal, boat shape, EX 150.00
Neal CT-1, silvery opaque bl, chariot, EX 600.00
Neal EE-8A, eagle w/ships, rnd, NM 125.00
Neal HL-1A, Washington & Lafayette busts, 3x2x2⅛", EX, pr...550.00
Neal HN-13, med bl, Greek Key around bottom, NM 225.00
Neal NE-1, fiery opal, mk NE Glass Co, NM 200.00
Neal OG-4, Pittsburgh area 75.00
Neal OL-11, citron, NM 275.00
Neal OL-12, NM 30.00
Neal OL-17, med amethyst, NM...450.00
Neal OO-2, oval 60.00
Neal OP-12, aqua opaque, NM 400.00
Neal OP-20, EX 70.00
Neal RP-3, silvery bl opaque 700.00
Neal WN-1A, wagon, VG 120.00

Pottery and Porcelain

Austrian, HP, ruffled edge, rnd...15.00
Belleek, star shaped, 3rd blk mk 55.00
Celery salt, HP, oval platter 12.00
Chinese Export, bl & wht, trencher, 18th C 350.00

Doulton Lambeth, reticulated base with birds, signed Fanny Clark, ca 1870s, 3½", $400.00.

Haviland, H&J-1613 ....35.00
Lenox, Belleek, HP, rnd, HJ-1290, sm 28.00
Meissen, oval w/scrolling ft, H&J-1812 ....125.00
Nippon, HP, rnd, 3 sm ft, simple style..15.00
Nippon, HP w/gold trim, ped ft 25.00
Pepper & salt, non-factory decor on blank 22.00
Quimper, HP shoe, Breton figures 50.00
Royal Bayreuth, poppy figural, H&J-1790 ....95.00
Royal Doulton, pottery w/gold swirls, bl int 65.00
Royal Worcester, snail-type shell, ivory stained 95.00

Satsuma, delicate facial features, much gold, H&J-1905 ....95.00
Torquay motto ware, 'Be aisy w/tha salt' 45.00
Wedgwood, gr jasper, ped ft, H&J-1846, 1956 ....110.00
Yellowware, mocha decor in band, ped ft, ca 1850......................300.00

Pressed Glass, Clear

Bevelled Buttons, Duncan, H&J-2782...15.00
Blackberry, Hobbs, H&J-3557, 2¾" 35.00
Candlewick, Imperial, H&J-2641, 2½" dia 12.00
Chippendale style, H&J-3546..22.00
Faceted, in SP leaf-shape fr, H&J-3838......................................25.00
Frog, new 8.00
Frog, old 60.00
Gold-pnt etching on rnd clear salt, H&J-172 ....30.00
Lalique, rows of beading, sgn R Lalique, ind, H&J-4641............110.00
Late Buckle, H&J-3622, master...30.00
Leaf & Dart, ftd, w/lid, H&J-3525, master 110.00
Pillows, Heisey, H&J-2697 ....40.00
Pineapple & Fan, H&J-2670 ....12.00
Rayed base, plain, rectangular 6.00
Silver overlay, rnd, H&J-3912 ....18.00
Sleigh, Fostoria, H&J-3735, 3" 50.00
T'print & Hobnail, ped ft, master 35.00

Pressed Glass, Colored

Amber, triangular, H&J-524 ....15.00
Blk amethyst, honeycomb, H&J-2047 ....25.00
Bohemian, clear w/red flashing..35.00
Boyd, hen on nest, various colors 6.00
Degenhart, purple slag, sgn, H&J-890, 3⅛" dia 35.00
Intaglio, polo players, gr, H&J-224 ....18.00
Milk glass, crossed logs, H&J-4473...50.00
Sowerby's #1350, custard glass, rnd w/sq hdls, H&J-4629 ....87.00
Swan, Cambridge, pk, sgn...35.00
Swan, Crown Tuscan, unsgn 50.00
Swan, Mosser (1970s) or other repro 10.00
Wreath & Shell, bl opal 110.00

Silverplate

Fluted, ped ft, H&J-4022 ....25.00
Heart shaped, rim decor...25.00

Dog pulling open salt, marked Hall and Elton, Walkingford Connecticut, $375.00.

Meriden, egg w/chick's head, on wishbone, H&J-4284 ....45.00
Pairpoint, dolphin supporting shell 75.00

Reed & Barton, Roman Key, H&J-4132......................................27.00

Sterling, Continental Silver, and Enamel

Cloisonne, Chinese, w/pepper..65.00
English, rectangular, Birmingham 1911 ....65.00
English, trencher, 1892, H&J-4161 ....80.00
French, oval w/4 hdls, glass liner, H&J-3979............................125.00
Gorham, Oriental-style etching, ped ft 60.00
Gorham, rnd bowl supported by 3 griffins.................................175.00
Jensen, Georg; acorn design, bl enameling, w/spoon 175.00
Mexico, simple rnd shape, H&J-4125..20.00
Pierced holder, w/garlands, ftd, cobalt liner 120.00
Plique-a-jour filigree rim, enamel bowl, Scandinavia 650.00
Russian enamel, pastel shaded florals, ca 1900 ....850.00
Sheffield, boxed presentation set of 4, matching spoons 250.00
Shreve & Co holder, Lenox insert, H&J-3856 ....45.00
Sleigh on runners, glass insert, H&J-4315 ....375.00
Swan, all silver, Germany 80.00

Miscellaneous

Children's set, berry bowl, H&J-2679 ....15.00
MOP, real shell, on base 18.00
Novelty, bandmaster's cap, US Glass, H&J-A5013......................75.00
Onyx, on metal base 55.00
Pewter, rnd, ftd, European 35.00
Treen, turned wood 35.00

Samplers

American samplers were made as early as the the colonial days; even earlier examples from 17th-century England still exist today. Changes in style and decorative motif are evident down through the years. Verses were not added until the late 17th century. By the 18th century, samplers were used not only for sewing experience but also as an educational tool. Young ladies, who often signed and dated their work, embroidered numbers and letters of the alphabet and practiced fancy stitches as well. Fruits and flowers were added for borders; birds, animals, and Adam and Eve were popular subjects. Later, houses and other buildings were included. By the 19th century, the American Eagle and the little red schoolhouse had made their appearances.

Adam & Eve, house/church/windmill, linen, sgn/dtd, 18x15" 900.00
Alphabet/verse/flower baskets, sgn/dtd 1820, 12x17", EX...........575.00
Alphabets, red/bl/pk lettering, sgn, ca 1840, 6x10", VG.............325.00
Alphabets, sgn/dtd 1829, 10x13", VG 325.00
Alphabets, 2-line verse, sgn/dtd 1827, 9x12", VG......................225.00
Alphabets (3 styles), sgn/dtd 1847, 10x9", VG 450.00
Alphabets (4 styles), sawtooth border, sgn/1820, 11x16", EX......525.00
Alphabets (4 styles)/verse, sgn/dtd 1834, 14x17", EX 650.00
Alphabets/birds/people/crowns, data, fine homespun, 16x13½" ..400.00
Alphabets/birds/urns/hearts, sgn/dtd 1809, 10x21", EX 975.00
Alphabets/dogs/florals/verse, sgn/1782, fr, 10x18", EX...............675.00
Alphabets/strawberry border/flowers/verse, sgn/1803, 14x17" . 1,100.00
Alphabets/stripes, bl-gr homespun, wear/holes, 9x8" 150.00
Alphabets/verse/couple/sheep/trees/birds, sgn/1765, 10x12" ... 6,000.00
Alphabets/verse/floral border, sgn/dtd 1813, 25x28", EX......... 1,350.00
Alphabets/verse/name/1803, homespun, gilt fr, 19x14" 1,325.00
Alphanumerics, ornate border, sgn/1877, fr, 12½x12½" 350.00
Alphanumerics/house/animals/birds, sgn, ca 1840, 10x19", EX ...575.00
Alphanumerics/strawberries/peacocks, sgn/1848, 10x16", EX 995.00
Alphanumerics/berry border/name/1831, homespun, 18x12" 775.00

Four lines of verse, alphabet repeated five times, gives maker's birthdate as January 28, 1795, signed 'Sally Cook, Age 14 years,' 15" x 13", $650.00.

Alphanumerics/verse/fruit baskets, sgn/1821, 7x19", EX..............785.00
Bldgs/trees/verse/name/1845, homespun, stains/holes, 18x15".....700.00
Deer/birds/bldgs/verse, sgn/1850, wear/faded, 23x20"..................700.00
Family registry, corn plant border, sgn/dtd 1825, 12x12", EX......850.00
Family registry, sgn/dtd 1828, 16x14", VG 500.00
Garden of God verse, mc embr, sgn/1826, 15x19", EX................725.00
Verse/flower baskets, sgn/1816, 12x15", EX..................................875.00
Verses/birds/flowers/buildings/trees, sgn/1810, fr, 23x23" 1,400.00
Verses/deer/buildings, sgn/dtd Oct 1798, 14x17", EX 1,650.00
2-Story house/trees/verse, sgn/1819, sewn at Lymans, 22x26" . 4,750.00

Sandwich Glass

The Boston and Sandwich Glass Company was founded in 1820 by Deming Jarves in Sandwich, Massachusetts. Their first products were simple cruets, salts, half-pint jugs, and lamps. They were attributed as being one of the first to perfect a method for pressing glass, a step toward the manufacture of the 'lacy' glass which they made until about 1840. Many other types of glass were made there — cut, colored, snakeskin, hobnail, and opalescent among them.

After the Civil War, profits began to dwindle due to the keen competition of the Western factories which were situated in areas rich in natural gas and easily accessible sand and coal deposits. The end came with an unreconcilable wage dispute between the workers and the company, and the factory closed in 1888.

Our advisor for this category is Richard Marden; he is listed in the Directory under New Hampshire. See also Cup Plates; Salts, Open; specific types of glass.

Bottle, scent; sea horse, clear w/opal stripes & bl rigaree 295.00
Bottle, scent; violin shape, wht opaque, pewter lid 115.00
Bottle, scent; wht satin w/HP florals & scrolls, 9", pr..................175.00
Candlestick, Acanthus Leaf, opaque bl/wht, 10", VG.................400.00
Candlestick, canary, petal & loop base, ftd, 6¾", VG, pr............400.00
Candlestick, dolphin, bl opaque, sq base, 10", NM, pr 3,800.00
Candlestick, dolphin, clambroth, 2-step base, 10", EX, pr 800.00
Candlestick, dolphin, dolphins & shells on socket, 9", NM ... 1,600.00
Candlestick, dolphin, translucent wht, assembled pr, 10" 1,400.00
Samdlestick, dolphin, 2-step base, 10", NM, pr 150.00
Candlestick, hexagonal, bl opaque, annealing check, 7".............175.00
Candlestick, hexagonal, purple opaque, petal/hoop base, 6½".....250.00
Candlestick, L 83-1 & 2, 1½", EX, pr......................................50.00

Chalice, cranberry cut to clear, airtrap in stem, mk, 8" 600.00
Goblet, Chilson 200.00
Iron, amethyst, mini, NM..400.00
Lamp, Acanthus Leaf, bl translucent, brass 4-burner, 11" 1,400.00
Lamp, Acanthus Leaf, jade gr/wht, rpl brass 4-burner, 11½" .. 1,600.00
Lamp, banquet, cut o/l font & std (cobalt), marble base.......... 9,000.00
Lamp, fluid; clambroth onion font, brass & marble base, 7"..........80.00
Lamp, Moon & Star, triple-cut o/l (red), marble base, 13" 200.00
Lamp, o/l (pk/wht), wht base/std, 13" 1,200.00
Lamp, Sandwich Star, dbl brass burner/pewter caps, 10", NM.....175.00
Lamp, Sweetheart, eng brass stem, marble base, 12" 100.00
Lamp, Tulip, clambroth, 13", NM, pr...................................... 1,500.00

Overshot pitcher, gold with iridescent blue handle, 7", $295.00.

Plate, Peacock Feather & Thistle, 8", EX 70.00
Plate, Roman Rosette, dk amethyst, 5¼", EX 275.00
Plate, Shield & Cornucopia, 8-sided, deep, 8", VG 50.00
Pomade, blk amethyst, bear figural, 3¾"......................................250.00
Spill holder, Excelsior Plus, canary, att, 5¾" 250.00
Spill holder, Sandwich Star, electric bl, 5", EX 800.00
Spill holder, Sandwich Star, peacock bl, att, 5" 900.00
Tray, Hairpin, 10" L, NM...375.00
Tumbler, lemonade; wht w/HP heron in rushes, 4" 30.00
Vase, hyacinth; dk bl, tooled lip, pontil, lt stain, 9" 200.00
Vase, Sawtooth, jade gr/wht, gauffered rim, ftd, att, 9" 1,250.00
Vase, tulip; Barred Oval & Ellipse, dk gold-amber, 5" 1,950.00
Vase, tulip; canary, ftd, 10", EX 400.00
Vase, tulip; fiery opal, wafer on ped ft, 10", M 3,600.00
Whiskey taster, lacy, clambroth, L-150-5 & 7, NM 100.00
Wine, mushroom cane paperweight base in bowl, rare...............495.00

Sarreguemines

Sarreguemines, France, is the location of Utzschneider and Company, founded in 1770, producers of majolica, transfer-printed dinnerware, figurines, and novelties which are usually marked 'Sarreguemines.'

Character jug, bl knotted band around head, rosy cheeks, 7".......135.00
Character jug, man w/lg brows & rosy cheeks, mk, 5½"...............120.00
Cup & saucer, breakfast; cherries 35.00
Jardiniere, putti reserve, bow/garlands, leaf hdls, 7" 600.00
Plate, fruits & leaves, 7¾" 28.00
Plate, La Militarie, military scenes, 10", set of 6...........................125.00
Plate, oyster; 6 gray & coral wells, mk, 9½" 155.00

Ewer, gold enameling on royal blue, 8½", $125.00.

Platter, fruit on gold leaves, 10" 55.00
Platter, fruit on gold leaves, 12" 70.00
Vase, potpourri; pk lustre, emb satyr head hdls, 8½" 350.00

Satin Glass

Satin glass is simply glassware with a velvety matt finish achieved through the application of an acid bath. This procedure has been used by many companies since the 20th century, both here and abroad, on many types of colored and art glass. See also Mother-of-Pearl.

Bowl, ivory w/gold roses & leaves, crimped/fluted, 10½" 175.00
Bowl, pk swirl, box-pleated rim, 10", in SP stand w/birds 350.00
Ewer, bl shaded, HP daisies w/gold leaves, 8⅛x4" 120.00
Ewer, bl shaded, HP florals w/gold, 9¾x4" 225.00
Ewer, rainbow swirl, appl rim & hdl, 8½" 580.00
Pitcher, bl, emb swirls, frosted hdl, 5x4½" 175.00
Rose bowl, bl shaded w/appl pk flowers & frosted stems, 5½" 150.00
Rose bowl, gr to wht, blown-out floral & leaf 275.00
Rose bowl, pk overlay, HP florals, ftd egg form, 5½x3½" 135.00
Rose bowl, pk overlay, HP flowers w/gold, 8-crimp, 3x3⅝" 125.00
Rose bowl, pk shaded, emb florals, 8-crimp, 3¼x3⅜" 135.00
Rose bowl, pk shaded, Shell & Seaweed, 8-crimp, 3¾x4" 125.00
Rose bowl, pk shaded overlay, HP bird & flowers, 6x4" 145.00

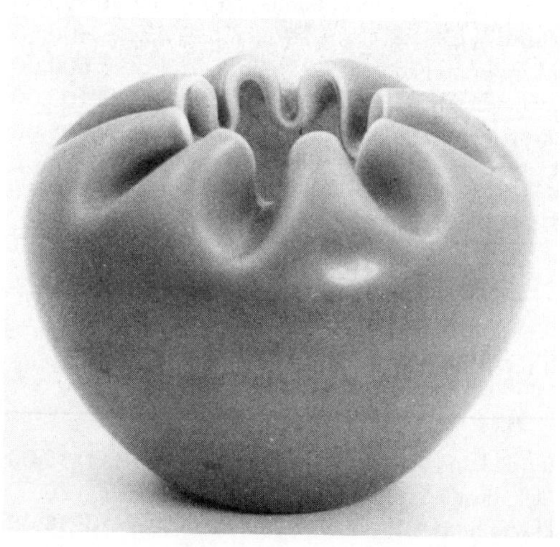

Rose bowl, rose cased, English, 3½", $65.00.

Rose bowl, yel, HP florals & coralene, egg form, 4½x4" 125.00
Vase, bl, HP violets, frosted hdls, 7⅜x4", pr 195.00
Vase, bl overlay, HP flowers, gold scrolls, ruffled, 12" 265.00
Vase, bl shaded w/floral, fluted str body, frosted hdls, 12" 265.00
Vase, brn to gold, cased, gold seaweed, 6" neck, Mt WA, 11" 500.00
Vase, jack-in-pulpit; rose to wht satin cased, Mt WA, 10" 475.00
Vase, lt bl cased, HP florals/butterfly, #d, 12" 750.00
Vase, pk, swirled ribs, frosted rim, bulbous, 7" 225.00
Vase, pk shaded, HP berries/leaves, ribbed ewer form, 12" 210.00
Vase, pk shaded overlay, HP florals, ewer form, 8¼" 120.00
Vase, pk w/mc floral, melon ribs, ruffled, 5 satin ft, 9" 150.00
Vase, tan w/thorn overlay, pk liner, camphor base, 15" 225.00

Satsuma

Satsuma is a type of fine cream crackle-glaze pottery or earthenware made in Japan as early as the 17th century. The earliest wares, made at the original kiln in the Satsuma province, were enameled with only simple florals. By the late 18th century, a floral brocade (or nishikide design) was favored, and similar wares were being made at other kilns under the direction of the Lord of Satsuma. In the early part of the 19th century, a diaper pattern was added to the florals. Gold and silver enamels were used for accents by the latter years of the century.

During the 1850s, as the quality of goods made for export to the western world increased and the style of decoration began to evolve toward becoming more appealing to the Westerners, human forms such as Arhats, Kannon, geisha girls, and Samurai warriors were added.

Today the most valuable pieces are those marked 'Kinkozan,' 'Shuzan,' 'Ryuzan,' and 'Kozan.' The genuine Satsuma 'mon' or mark is a cross within a circle — usually in gold on the body or on the lid, or in red on the base of the ware. Character marks may be included.

Caution: Much of what is termed 'Satsuma' comes from the Showa Period (1926 to the present); it is not true Satsuma but a simulated type, a cheaper pottery with heavy enamel.

Our advisor for this category is Donald Penrose; he is listed in the Directory under Ohio.

Bowl, butterflies on ivory, ca 1900, 6½" 250.00
Bowl, ceremonial scene/florals, 1800s, 7" 650.00
Bowl, floral in autumn tones w/gilt, scalloped blk rim, 4" 100.00
Bowl, 1000 Face on blk, hexagonal, EX detail, sgn, 5¾" 350.00
Box, pill; floral, sgn, 2" dia 25.00
Cookie jar, Kwannon & Arhat on brn, gold foo dog hdls, 9" 175.00
Ewer, mums, wht on orange to yel, ca 1870, 5½" 75.00
Jar, allover figures, foo dog hdl/finial, 3-ftd, 14" 450.00
Koro, Arhats ea side, tiger hdls, foo lion finial, mk, 11" 500.00
Koro, elephant hdls, scholar finial, hiking scene, 7", EX 800.00
Planter, emb florals, figural scenes w/in, 1800s, 11" L, EX 275.00
Tea set, tropical bird, Shizan, 6¾" pot, cr/sug, 6 c/s 1,500.00

Tea set with dragon handles, finials, and spouts, Teapot, 5"; Creamer, 3⅛"; Sugar bowl, 4¼"; $1,450.00 for 3-piece set.

Vase, Arhats/dragons, sqd, Shimazu, 1880s, 6" 450.00
Vase, Arhats/2 dragons/seated Kannon, mk Kinkozan, '10, 17". **3,500.00**
Vase, birds/iris, 1800s, 12" 450.00
Vase, female genre scenes, sqd, Kinkozan School, 8¾" 600.00
Vase, figural reserves, gold/mc on blk, now lamp, 1890, 12" 300.00
Vase, floral, bl w/gold on rust, panelled, 1800s, 5" 200.00
Vase, genre scenes, cobalt rims, gilt, 1900, 12", pr 800.00
Vase, genre scenes, dragon about neck, EX work, sgn, 4½".........200.00
Vase, ladies in kimonos in garden w/pagoda shrines, 6" 300.00
Vase, Lohans/scholars & children, ring/tassel hdls, 12", EX........600.00
Vase, numerous figures/mtns/pagodas, gilt, 1840, 10".................500.00
Vase, Radan & Kannon on blk w/gilt dragons relief, 5" 275.00
Water pail, panels w/scholar & Arhats, 1880s, 15" 650.00

Scales

In today's world of pre-measured and pre-packaged goods, it is difficult to imagine the days when such products as sugar, flour, soap, and candy first had to be weighed by the grocer. The variety of scales used at the turn of the century was highly diverse; at the Philadelphia Exposition in 1876, one company alone displayed over three hundred different weighing devices. Among those found today, brass and iron models are the most common. Those seeking additional information concerning antique scales are encouraged to contact the International Society of Antique Scale Collectors, whose address can be found in the Directory under Clubs, Newsletters, and Catalogs.

Key:
bal — balance   lb — pound
g — gram   NP — nickel plated

Army, gold weighing, brass beam/pans/weights, 1840s, in box.......**75.00**
Balance, heavy wrought iron, very well made, EX detail, 35" **150.00**

Balance type with three brass weights, 9½" long, $165.00.

Browning & Sharp, gold weighing, CI, stenciled base, EX...........135.00
Burrough, Stewart, & Kline, CI bal, NP pan, 10x14", EX.............65.00
Butter, wood, old red pnt, beam: 34½", EX................................225.00
Chatillon's, star w/figure, Pat Dec 10, 1867, 0-24 lb 55.00
Christian Becker, jeweler's bal, glass/wood case+accessories........110.00
Detecto-Gram, bal type, CI, EX..75.00
EJ Hoadley, florals on brass, 0-1 lb, EX 145.00
Eureka, CI w/red pnt, brass pan, 0-16 lb, 18", EX 350.00
Fairbanks, bal, wht porc platters, 5½x14", EX 40.00
Fairbanks, bullion, iron/brass/wood, 1880s, 36x40x13", EX **1,700.00**
Fairbanks, oak case, red pnt w/gold, brass pans, 12", M.............330.00
Forschner, brass, spring type, hanging, 0-100 lb........................65.00

Frary Improved, brass, 16" L 65.00
Jasco, CI, measurements read w/mirror, lbs & stones, EX 165.00
Kohlbusch, NY, brass, table-top bal, 1870s, 15x9x16", EX.............85.00
Landers, Frary, & Clark, postal, up to 4 lbs, EX..........................40.00
Landers Improved, circular spring, brass face, 0-60 lb.................60.00
Pelouze Victor, postal, brass & steel, 1898, 4½x4½" 25.00
Phila Scoop & Scale Co, produce, porc base, EX 95.00
Salter's Improved Family, CI base, enamel face, 0-14 lb...............85.00
Toledo Confectionery, 5-lb capacity scoop, all orig 145.00
Torsion, prescription, glass & metal fr, box type, 1891, EX 145.00
Triner, candy store, wht enamel, 0-1 lb 38.00
Troemner, brass/steel pan bal, w/compartment for 5 weights.......135.00
Troemner, oak based bal beam, brass pans, 3x11x5½", ...90.00
Troemner's Apothecary, oak box, traveling type, EX...................62.00
Volano & Sons, walnut, bal beam, 1913, M................................275.00

Schafer and Vater

Schafer and Vater operated in Volkstadt, Germany, from the last decade of the 1800s until about 1920. They produced novelties such as figural bottles, flasks, vases, etc., marked with an 'R' within a star device.

Ash holder, bald man w/open mouth, Keep Your Hair On 150.00
Ash holder, nude cherub, 3x3½" 100.00
Ash tray, open-mouthed tiger, red int, 4x5" 95.00
Basket, pk jasper w/wht cameo bust, 4½x2" 55.00
Figurine, Everybody's Doing It, boy & girl/doves/rabbits, 4" 70.00
Figurine, fat man on bench, googly eyes, 4½" 180.00
Figurine, girl holds 2 lg slippers, mk, 4⅜x3⅜"............................110.00
Hatpin holder, cameo on jasper, wall hanging............................125.00
Hatpin holder, ladies in medallions, jasper, 5" 165.00
Hatpin holder, lady w/fan, lav & gr jasper w/gold, 4½" 145.00

Jewelry box, Jasperware, cameo with profiles of two ladies, 5½" long, $145.00.

Match striker, Scratch...on My Patch, boy/fat man, mk, 3½" 95.00
Pitcher, billy goat w/orange coat, gr pants, mk, 5½"....................125.00
Pitcher, Dutch girl w/basket on bk & keys, mk, 3¾" 70.00
Pitcher, goat w/boutonniere, mk, 5½"...85.00
Pitcher, goose in bonnet, cream sz 100.00

Scheier

The Scheiers began their ceramics careers in the late 1930s and soon thereafter began to teach their craft at the University of New Hampshire. After WWII they cooperated with the Puerto Rican government in establishing a native ceramic industry, an involvement which would continue to influence their designs. In the fifties they retired and moved to Mexico; they currently reside in Arizona.

Bowl, wht/tan matt on red clay, speckled int, thin, 6" 195.00
Jardiniere, stylized figures in fish shapes, blk/turq, 11" 1,700.00

Jardiniere, figures and masks, blue, charcoal, and gold, 15", $2,300.00.

Mug, ea w/different animal, blk on ivory, 6½", 6 for 325.00
Pitcher, leaves, gr on tan 75.00

Schiebe-Alsbach

Founded in Thuringia in the 1840s and still in production today, the Schiebe-Alsbach factory was the first in the area to make porcelain figures on a large scale. Their earliest were devotional Madonnas, though Rococo figures were soon included in their line as well. In 1890 they added groups such as female dancers and dancing couples. By 1894 they were producing Meissen-style figures, lace figures, and historical figures and groups. Now nationalized and incorporated into a larger firm, the factory is Europe's largest manufacturer of this type of ware. Their mark is an 'S' with superimposed crossed lines, today slightly modified from the original.

Our advisor for this category is Donald Penrose; he is listed in the Directory under Ohio.

Pully on Horse, green coat, red trousers, 11" x 9", $450.00.

Bust of Napoleon, gr tunic w/medals, blk hat, 10½" 225.00
Children's Tea Party, 4 children, parian, AF Kister, 10x7"..........350.00
Dancing Couple, boy in tan trousers, girl in red skirt, 6" 160.00
Marshal DeBeauharnais, in uniform, 10½" 175.00
Marshal Dumoriez, wht pants, long bl coat, 10" 175.00
Marshal Kellerman, bl coat jacket, wht cockade in hat, 10" 175.00
Marshal Lepic, bl military jacket w/gold epaulets, 10" 175.00
Marshal Murat, long gr fur-trimmed coat, 10" 175.00
Marshal Murat, on prancing horse, 9x11"....................................450.00
Napoleon, wht uniform, gr jacket, long gray coat, 10" 175.00
Napoleon Coronation Preparation, 3 figures at table, 9x12" 950.00
Napoleon Crossing Alps, gr coat/red cloak, on horse, 11" 325.00
Napoleon Crossing Berezina, rides horse over bridge, 11"...........475.00
News Vendor, bl coat/brn hat, papers in left arm, 5½".................125.00
Othello, on balcony before man & lady, 10x15" 1,350.00
Othello, seated girl w/lute, & man w/book on stand, 11x15" .. 1,350.00

Schlegelmilch Porcelain

Authority Mary Frank Gaston, who is our advisor, has completed two volumes of *The Collector's Encyclopedia of R.S. Prussia* with full-color illustrations and current values. Mold numbers appearing in some of the listings refer to these books. You will find Mrs. Gaston's address in the Directory under Texas.

Key:
BM — blue mark   SM — steeple mark
GM — green mark   RM — red mark

E.S. Germany

Fine chinaware marked 'E.S. Germany' or 'E.S. Prov. Saxe' was produced by E.S. Schlegelmilch at his Suhl factory in the Thuringia region of Prussia from the turn of the century until about 1925.

Basket, lady & child, pearl lustre w/gold hdl 125.00
Bowl, boat scene, diamond shape, hdls, mk, 6½x6½"....................50.00
Bowl, fox hunt scene, mk, 9⅝"...75.00
Bowl, Indian/peace pipe/war club, ornate mold, mk, 12" 265.00
Candy dish, roses, dbl-oval form, gold hdl & rim, 2 mks..............45.00
Cup, Indian portrait on gr irid..85.00
Cup & saucer, demitasse; lady w/daisy crown, mk 75.00

E.S. Germany cup and saucer, 2", $40.00.

Pin dish, roses, gold stenciled rim, oval, scalloped, mk..................30.00

Pitcher, maiden w/cupid, raised florals w/gold, 7½"......................180.00
Plate, lady's portrait, Kauffmann, open hdls, mk, 10¼" 175.00
Plate, roses & lily of the valley, mk, 9½" 30.00
Tea strainer, floral, gold rim..155.00
Tray, dresser; pansies, carnation mold, unmk 100.00
Tray, tidbit; berries & flowers, center hdl, mk, 6½"........................40.00
Vase, lady w/peacock portrait, maroon & gold, mk, 8" 400.00
Vase, man & 2 ladies in portrait, curled hdls, mk, 7½" 200.00
Vase, portrait, cylindrical, mk, 8"...100.00
Vase, portrait, gold medallions, wht/purple, gold hdls, 9¼" 275.00

R.S. Germany

In 1869 Reinhold Schlegelmilch began to manufacture porcelain in Tillowitz in upper Silesia. He had formerly worked with his brother, Erdmann, in his factory in Suhl in the German province of Thuringia. Both areas were rich in resources necessary for the production of hard-paste porcelain. Wares marked with the name 'Tillowitz' and the accompanying 'R.S. Germany' phrase are attributed to Reinhold. The most common mark is a wreath and star in a solid color under the glaze. Items marked 'R.S. Germany' are usually more simply decorated than R.S. Prussia. Some reflect the Art Deco trend of the 1920s. Certain hand-painted floral decorations and themes such as 'Sheepherder,' 'Man with Horses,' and 'Cottage' are especially valued by collectors — those with a high-gloss finish or on Art Deco shapes in particular. Not all hand-painted items were painted at the factory. Those with an artist's signature but no 'Hand Painted' mark indicate that the blank was decorated outside the factory.

Bonbon, carnations, pk on gray w/gold, side hdl, mk, 7¾" 45.00
Bowl, berry; pk magnolias, lustre finish, 10", +6 5" bowls 255.00
Bowl, dogwood on pearly lustre, BM, 5"..20.00
Bowl, pheasants, 2-color on wooded bkground, 10"........................195.00
Bowl, pk & wht florals w/gold, rose border, RM, 9½"...................115.00
Bowl, roses, mc on cream shaded, gold bands, sq, mk, 9¼" 65.00
Bowl, tiger lilies w/much gold, mk, 10"..65.00
Cake & ice cream set, azaleas, wht on gr, BM, 9-pc.....................100.00
Cake plate, roses spill from wicker basket, mk, 9⅞"........................60.00
Cheese & cracker dish, pk orchids, 2-tier, mk, 8½" 125.00
Cheese & cracker set, yel roses w/wide gold band, BM, 7-pc 165.00
Chocolate pot, wht lilacs on satin...125.00
Chocolate pot, wht lilies, RM, +4 c/s 175.00
Condensed milk holder, floral w/gold, mk, 5" +underplate..........145.00
Cookie jar, tulip spray, gold rim, BM 85.00
Creamer & sugar bowl, iris, purple on wht, mk, 2½" 48.00
Cup & saucer, floral, ftd, mk 40.00
Mayonnaise, hydrangeas, wreath mk, 3-pc.......................................75.00
Nappy, hydrangeas on gr w/gold hdls, triangular, BM 40.00
Pitcher, clown figural, wht pearlized, mk, 6" 95.00
Pitcher, tankard; poppies & berries, RM, 11" 185.00
Plate, coconut tree, gold trim, mk, 8½"..75.00
Plate, dogwood, Rococo rim, 2 sm hdls, mk, 9½" 60.00
Plate, scenic, sgn Klette, mk, 6" 75.00
Plate, yel & red florals w/gold, hdls, RM, 9⅝" 90.00
Shaving mug, floral, divided int, mk 55.00
Syrup, lilies of the valley, BM, +underplate.....................................75.00
Teapot, wht azaleas, BM, ind 175.00
Toothbrush holder, floral, 5-slot, mk 125.00
Tray, dresser; sheepherder & mill scene, hdls, 11½x7¼".............275.00
Tray, floral, open hdls, mk, 11¾"..85.00
Tray, florals w/gold, floral relief rim, steeple mk, 11x7" 145.00
Tray, mc floral w/gold tracery, RM, 11½x7½" 105.00
Vase, Nightwatch scene, deep red w/gold, GM, 6½" 450.00
Vase, Nouveau decor, gold on wht, 3"...28.00

R.S. Germany plate, 8", $350.00.

R.S. Poland

'R.S. Poland' is a mark attributed to Reinhold Schlegelmilch's factory in Tillowitz, Silesia.

Candlestick, roses, pk & peach w/brn trim, mk, 6¼", pr 195.00
Candlestick, tulips w/gold, mk, 6¼", pr 195.00
Candlestick, violets & lilies of the valley, 6"................................115.00
Dresser set, pk florals, tray/hair receiver/box, mk 345.00
Planter, pk floral band w/gold, ped ft, 6¾x6½".............................230.00
Plate, dogwood & pine, 8" 85.00
Relish bowl, dogwood & pine, open hdl, RM 65.00
Urn, roses, pk & wht on brn, hdls, w/lid, RM, 11½" 800.00
Vase, crowned crane, RS Poland, 3½"..800.00
Vase, Nightwatch scene on bl to gr, salesman's sample, mk, 4" ..300.00
Vase, roses, mc on gr w/gold, scalloped, mk, 10¼", pr 365.00
Vase, roses, wht/beige on brn & gold, mk, 8¾x4½" 148.00
Vase, roses on brn shaded, 4¼" 105.00

R.S. Prussia

Art porcelain bearing the mark 'R.S. Prussia' was manufactured by Erdmann and Reinhold Schlegelmilch from the late 1870s to the early 1900s in a Germanic area known until the end of WWI as Prussia. The vast array of mold shapes in combination with a wide variety of decorations is the basis for R.S. Prussia's appeal. Themes can be categorized as figural (usually based on a famous artist's work), birds, florals, portraits, scenics, and animals.

Basket, floral, wht on gr w/gold, mk, 2⅝x7"....................................75.00
Bowl, florals & buds reflect on water, gold rim, RM, 11" 265.00
Bowl, mc roses, blown-out florals, unmk, 12" 125.00
Bowl, pansies, mc on cream w/gold, RM, 10⅞" 265.00
Bowl, pastel roses, nut mold, 10" dia 345.00
Bowl, poppies, pk on gr shaded, iris mold, RM, 10½"...................300.00
Bowl, roses, cabbage mold, RM, lg 350.00
Bowl, roses, pk on pearl w/gold, mk, 10¼" 400.00
Bowl, swallows, medallion mold, 3-ftd, RM, 6" 250.00
Bowl, yel roses, RM, 10½"...195.00
Bowl, 5 rose medallions, ftd, RM, 4¼x10½" 435.00
Box, sheepherder w/gold, 6-sided, mk, 4⅛" 285.00
Butter pat, dogwood on pearly lustre, mk 35.00
Cake plate, birds & lilies, swag & tassel mold, 10½" 200.00
Cake plate, lilies of the valley, open hdls, RM, 12" 250.00

R.S. Prussia bowl, portrait, red mark, 10", $895.00.

Cake plate, Man in the Mountain, medallion mold, RM, 10½" ..695.00
Cake plate, rose baskets, lustre, medallion mold, mk, 10½" 275.00
Cake plate, rose chains w/gold, 6-point/clover mold, RM, 11" 255.00
Cake plate, yel roses w/cherries, open hdls, unmk, 11"...................75.00
Celery dish, sheepherder scene on bl to gr, RM, 12" 550.00
Celery tray, Melon Boys, brn, RM 650.00
Celery tray, roses, pk border, gold trim, mk 195.00
Celery tray, roses on yel, RM 175.00
Chocolate pot, florals, iris mold at top, unmk, 9½".....................275.00
Chocolate pot, irises, iris mold, 4-ftd, bulbous top, mk 375.00
Chocolate pot, roses, pk on gr, RM, 11" 125.00
Chocolate pot, roses w/pearlized lustre, RM, +5 c/s....................395.00
Chocolate pot, swan & pines, mk, +6 c/s 2,450.00
Coffeepot, demitasse; Melon Boys, jeweled, RM 800.00
Cracker jar, roses on quilted MOP, mk, 9¼" W 385.00
Creamer & sugar bowl, cottage & castle scenes, RM 650.00
Creamer & sugar bowl, lilies w/gold, unmk 100.00
Creamer & sugar bowl, mill scene, RM...................................300.00
Creamer & sugar bowl, ostrich, RM 2,200.00
Cup, demitasse; roses w/Tiffany band at top, RM 55.00
Cup & saucer, coffee; violets, lily of valley mold, RM...................95.00
Cup & saucer, demitasse; red roses w/gold branches, RM...............98.00
Cup & saucer, lilacs, ped base cup, RM 125.00
Cup & saucer, swans w/pine trees, RM 195.00
Hair receiver, pk florals, RM 175.00
Hatpin holder, basket of roses, mk, 4½"..................................185.00
Hatpin holder, floral w/gold, ftd, RM 145.00
Hatpin holder, sheepherder, RM..350.00
Mustard pot, floral on gr, RM, orig ladle 165.00
Pitcher, flowers in bowl of water, Wheelock mk, water sz............325.00
Pitcher, milk; florals w/gold, scalloped, unmk...........................250.00
Pitcher, tankard, Dice Players, jeweled, RM 4,800.00
Pitcher, tankard; Melon Boys, jeweled, RM 4,800.00
Plaque, mill scene, lav & yel border, unmk, 11¼" dia.................700.00
Plaque, mill scene tapestry, RM, 8¾".....................................650.00
Plate, Dice Players, RM, 9"..395.00
Plate, fruit & leaves, scalloped rim, RM, 10¾" 295.00
Plate, Melon Boys, jewel & ribbon mold, mk, 6"........................525.00
Plate, Melon Boys, keyhole mold, RM, 6" 450.00
Plate, roses & mc florals w/gold, RM, 9½".............................250.00
Plate, roses w/gold tracery, scalloped rim, RM, 7"......................70.00
Plate, sailboat & mtn cove, icicle mold, RM, 9¾" 550.00
Plate, Spring Season, RM, 9"... 1,250.00
Plate, sunflower w/gold hdls, RM, 9⅝".................................260.00
Plate, swans & gazebo, petal mold, RM, 8¾"...........................215.00
Relish, irises w/gold, iris mold, mk, 9½x4½".............................125.00

Relish, snowballs & tulips, jewels, RM, 9½" 95.00
Shaving mug, roses & gold on gr, mirror, right-handed, RM 500.00
Sugar bowl, mc roses w/gold, ftd, 2 hdls, mk 55.00
Sugar shaker, calla lily, skirted base, 4¾".................................235.00
Teapot, surrealistic dogwood blossoms w/gold, mk, +cr/sug 350.00
Tray, dresser; floral, carnation mold, pearlized, RM 450.00
Tray, dresser; pk roses w/gold branches, open hdls, RM, 11x7" ...195.00
Vase, cottage & mill scene, cobalt top, bulbous, RM, 5½"...........525.00
Vase, florals, gold on bl to cream, RM, sm...............................265.00
Vase, golden pheasant, unmk, 4" 300.00
Vase, Melon Boys, gr, ped ft, ornate hdls, RM, 9½" 500.00
Vase, Winter, portrait medallion, w/gold & lustre, RM, 11" ... 1,250.00

R.S. Suhl, E.S. Suhl

Porcelains marked with this designation are attributed to Schlegelmilch's Suhl factory.

Box, floral, w/beveled mirror, mk 200.00
Cup & saucer, Colonial couple w/gold, mk, 2⅛", 4¾" 135.00
Cup & saucer, Nightwatch, brn shaded 60.00
Jar, tapestry, w/lid, 7"..140.00
Vase, lady & girls on bench, cobalt w/gold trim, mk, 8¾"...........275.00
Vase, Melon Boys, mk, 9"..815.00
Vase, Napoleon scene, mk, 5"..275.00
Vase, Nightwatch, brn shades, sgn Rembrandt, 7½" 750.00
Vase, women feeding chickens & winding flax, hdls, mk, 6½" ...500.00
Wall plaque, daisies, 10½" 60.00

R.S. Tillowitz

R.S. Tillowitz-marked porcelains are attributed to Reinhold Schlegelmilch's factory in Tillowitz, Silesia.

Ash tray, pine cones & evergreen branches on lustre, mk 125.00
Bowl, berry; dogwood on gr, sm, set of 6 ....100.00
Bowl, lilacs w/bl & gold tracing, 10x8" 55.00
Charger, roses, mk, 12" 55.00
Chocolate pot, lovers in garden, Kauffmann, gold rim, 9½" 150.00
Creamer & sugar bowl, lilies, wht on gr shaded...........................175.00
Nut dish, peonies & snowballs on cream, openwork, mk, 6".........90.00
Plate, roses, peach on cream to brn, mk, 8" 45.00
Tray, floral, bl on gr, heavy gold trim, pierced hdls, 4x8"............40.00
Tray, floral, hdls, 7¼x9½" 35.00
Tray, magnolias, w/gold, mk, 8¼x4".....................................45.00
Tray, sm floral, bl on gr, heavy gold, pierced hdls, 4x8" 35.00

Schneider

The Schneider Glass Company was founded in 1914 at Epinay-sur-seine, France. They made many types of art glass, some of which sandwiched designs between layers. Other decorative devices were applique and carved work. These were marked 'Charder,' or 'Schneider.' During the twenties, commercial artware was produced with Deco motifs cut by acid through two or three layers and signed 'LeVerre Francais' in script or with a section of inlaid filigrane. See also Le Verre Francais.

Bowl, gr w/blk rim & stem, 6x9" 225.00
Charger, concave center: brn/orange mottle, Ovington, 16" 200.00
Compote, amber w/red-amber glass balls, metal base, 6x8"..........895.00
Compote, amethyst base & stem, peach bowl, bl rim, 7½x6¼" ...380.00
Ewer, yel/pk mottle, purple triangular bosses/hdl, 14" 900.00

Novelty, Christmas tree, solid, sgn, 8" 50.00
Vase, brn w/air bubbles, frosted floral-emb appliques, 11" **8,000.00**
Vase, bubbly clear/orange, 3 bosses/etch sqs, wine ft, 14" **1,900.00**
Vase, burgundy & red w/purple hdls, rnd w/can neck, 12" **800.00**
Vase, flared U-form in bl-streaked clear coiled in yel, 10" **1,400.00**
Vase, fruit etched on clear to orange, sq red hdls, 14" **2,000.00**
Vase, gray, etched, w/2 vertical glass drips, 11" **275.00**
Vase, impressionistic floral in clear, purple ft, sqd, 24" **800.00**
Vase, jade w/bubbles, 4 appl crimped strips, ftd pear, 17" **1,500.00**
Vase, palms, bl on wht, bun ft, Charder, 16" **2,900.00**
Vase, tangerine to lime, trumpet form w/folded rim, 16" **1,200.00**
Vase, thick glass w/bubbles, cylindrical on bun ft, 6" **165.00**

Schoolhouse Collectibles

Schoolhouse collectibles bring to mind memories of a bygone era when the teacher rang her bell to call the youngsters to class in a one-room schoolhouse — where often both the 'hickory stick' and an apple occupied a prominent position on her desk.

Bell, brass, trn wood hdl, 7½" 25.00
Book, Analytical Orthography (English), 1842, EX 38.00
Book, Barnes Elementary Geography, 1895, 93-pg, VG 6.00
Book, Before We Read, Dick & Jane, softcover, EX 10.00
Book, McGuffey's New Eclectic Speaker, 1858 .... 5.00
Book, Murray's Grammar, 1818, no cover 50.00
Book, Palmer Method Writing, 1936, EX 12.00
Book, Young People's Natural History, 1900, EX 8.00
Booklet, Board of Education, Brooklyn, 1860, 107-pg, EX 25.00
Booklet, NY State Teachers' Assn, 1897 ....10.00
Desk, teacher's, Chautauqua, EX 185.00
Dictionary, Webster, leather bk, 1841, VG 45.00
Pencil box, dvtl wood, sliding top, 2½" W 22.50
Puzzle, Holbrook Arithmetic, 1957, EX 7.50

Schoop, Hedi

Swiss-born Hedi Schoop started her ceramics business in North Hollywood in 1940. With a talented crew of about twenty decorators, she produced figurines, figure-vases, console sets, TV lamps, and other decorative housewares — much of which was accented with gold or platinum trim. Schoop's pottery closed after a fire destroyed the building in 1958. Marks are impressed or printed.

Bowl, formed by lady's skirt, #418, 13" dia......................................65.00

Conchita, 12½", $45.00.

Cookie jar, King, rare 175.00
Cookie jar, Queen, rare 175.00
Figurine, '50s dancing lady w/fan & flower basket, 12" 45.00
Figurine, Bali dancer lady holds fans for flowers, 12½", pr 125.00
Figurine, ballerina, dk gr dress & shoes, 11½" 35.00
Figurine, Chinese boy & girl on base hold flowers, 8½" 45.00
Figurine, Dutch boy w/water buckets, wht/gr/yel, 11" 35.00
Figurine, flower girl w/appl flowers, 9" 24.00
Figurine, hobby horse holds flowers, 5" 24.00
Figurine, hula dancer, 11"..45.00
Figurine, lady w/basket leads lg poodle, 10" 35.00
Figurine, Oriental man in blk & wht jacket, tall 35.00
Figurine, peasant lady dances/holds bowl up, 13" 35.00
Flower holder, peasant woman, 12" 35.00
Flower holder, 2 girls, hands joined, rare, 8" 85.00
Lamp, TV; skyscrapers (modern city), 1950s, rare......................165.00
Planter, geisha w/umbrella, bl, #223....................................30.00
Vase, fan form, gold trim, 10" 24.00

Scouting Collectibles

Scouting was founded in England in 1907 by a retired Major General, Lord Robert Baden-Powell. Its purpose is the same today as it was then — to help develop physically strong, mentally alert boys and to teach them basic fundamentals of survival and leadership. The movement soon spread to the United States, and in 1910 a Chicago publisher, William Boyce, set out to establish Scouting in America. The first World Scout Jamboree was held in 1911 in England. Baden-Powell was honored as the Chief Scout of the World. In 1926 he was awarded the Silver Buffalo Award in the United States. He was knighted in 1929 for distinguished military service and for his scouting efforts. Baden-Powell died in 1941. For further reading on the subject, we recommend *Scouting Collectibles* by R.J. Sayers; you will find his address in the Directory under North Carolina.

Badge, Eagle, TH Foley type, w/BSA, bronze metal, 1913 era **400.00**
Badge, Eagle, type 1, BSA on tan khaki sq cloth, 1920 ....**50.00**
Badge, Eagle, type 3, no BSA in coffin box, 1930........................**50.00**
Badge, First Aid contest, wht cross, 3-color ribbon, 1920 ....**40.00**
Badge, First Class, Asst Scoutmaster, metal, red, 1920..................**50.00**
Badge, First Class, for Scoutmaster, metal, gr, 1920.....................**40.00**
Badge, Scoutmaster, tan sq cloth w/gr emblem, 1920.....................**40.00**
Book, Cave, Boy Scout Hike Book, Rockwell illus, 1913 ....**17.50**
Book, Cub Scout, Wolf, Bear & Lion, 1931 series, ea **10.00**
Book, Handbook for Patrol Leaders, 1st ed, gr cover, 1929 ....**15.00**
Book, Handbook for Scoutmasters, 1st ed, 1913-14 ....**20.00**
Book, Official Boy Scout Diary, illus, 1920................................**12.00**
Book, Official Boy Scout Handbook, 1st ed, gr cover, 1911 ....**90.00**
Book, Official Silver Jubilee Handbook for Boys, 1935 ....**100.00**
Calendar, Rockwell cover, sm type, 1930-40s..............................**12.50**
Game, Game of Scouting, cards, M Bradley, 1912 ....**20.00**
Game, Scout Ten Pins, action game, 1920 ....**20.00**
Game, The Scout Trail, board game, M Bradley, 1916 ....**22.00**
Hat, broad brim, Yogi-Bear type, logo, 1920-60 era, VG................**12.50**
Jamboree, flag patch w/#s 1-5000, World Jamboree 1924 .... **1,000.00**
Jamboree, neckerchief, Nat'l Staff, purple, sq, 1937....................**400.00**
Jamboree, neckerchief, red or bl, full sq, 1937 ....**40.00**
Jamboree, patch, Capitol on felt, 1935, 3" **50.00**
Jamboree, patch, Geo Washington on twill, 1950, 3", M **25.00**
Jamboree, patch (sub-camps), World Jamboree 1947, 20+ types.**300.00**
Jamboree, Washington Monument on wht felt, 1937, 3", M **50.00**
Knife, hunting; Remington, RS34, 1930s **60.00**
Knife, utility, Ulster, 6 types w/varied logos on hdl, ea **15.00**

Knife, utility; NY Knife Co, 4-blade, w/logo, 1920s.......................75.00
Knife, utility; Official Remington, RS-3333, 4-blade 50.00
Medal, Air Scouts Ace, plane w/4 props, ribbon, VG 300.00
Medal, Explorer Ranger, powder horn, gr ribbon, 1940s 200.00
Medal, Sea Scout Quartermaster, sterling, enamel tips, 1950s.......25.00
Membership card, plastic, 4-page type, dtd 1915 ....10.00
Pennant, BSA, bl felt, lg, VG 10.00
Pennant, 1937 National Jamboree, lg, VG 30.00
Pin, Eagle Scout hat, type 1, BSA on sterling w/mc enamel 50.00
Statue, Scout Presentation, scout w/hat, pot metal, 1930s 25.00
Uniform, BSA WWI type, bellows pockets, metal buttons, 1915..35.00
Uniform, shirt, breeches, hat, socks, & belt, 1930, all for 40.00
Watch, pocket; 1937 Jamboree w/Jamboree logo, runs...................50.00
Watch, 1st issue, 1950 Times, w/BSA logo, band, runs.................15.00

Scrimshaw

The most desirable examples of the art of scrimshaw can be traced back to the first half of the 19th century to the heyday of the whaling industry. Some voyages lasted for several years, and conditions on board were often dismal. Sailors filled the long hours by carving or engraving designs in whale or walrus ivory. Using the tools of their trade, they created animal figures, boxes, pie crimpers, etc., often emphasizing the lines of their carvings with ink or berry stain. Eskimos also made scrimshaw, sometimes borrowing designs from the sailors who traded with them. See also Powder Horns.

Blackfish jaw bone, lady's portrait, lady/girls, 22", EX 950.00
Bodkin, trn from 1 pc whalebone, 5½" 100.00
Busk, eagle/ship/poem, 7", EX 175.00
Busk, hearts/compass roses/ship, 15" 250.00
Busk, ship/Xd flags/monument/etc, 1875, 15", EX 400.00
Busk, 6 panels: sunburst/lady/birds/hearts/etc, 13½" 350.00
Candlestand, top: geometric inlay bone/shell/wood, 28" 900.00
Cane, L-hdl, whale ivory w/3 wood rings, bone shaft, 1850s........300.00
Cane, whale ivory knob & separators, coconut wood shaft..........350.00
Cane, whalebone shaft, trn ivory knob, 34", EX...........................200.00

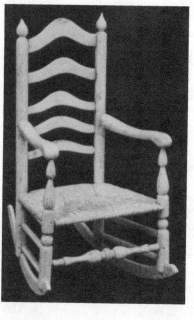

Miniature ladderback rocking chair, whalebone with seat carved to represent rush, 20th century, 7½", $850.00.

Cvg, sperm whale, blk pnt, 23", EX 125.00
Domino set, prisoner-of-war, bone box w/cribbage brd top..........325.00
Fid, geometric cvgs, EX..75.00

Fid, trn hdl w/hole for sling strap, 8"...100.00
Fid, whalebone, simple cvg, 9½"..150.00
Footstool, ivory/wood geometric inlay, 11½" L, EX.....................300.00
Hook, steel w/2-pc whalebone hdls, 3¼", EX.................................20.00
Jagging wheel, ebony & shell inlay, rope-cvd section, 8½" 700.00
Jagging wheel, ice tong-shape hdl w/3 overbars, 6".....................650.00
Jagging wheel, slim str hdl, simple, 1825, 6½" 225.00
Jagging wheel, trn hdl w/medial wood ring, Nantucket, 6"...........275.00
Knife, dbl-edged, florals in relief on hdl, 7¼", VG.........................55.00
Knife, steel blade, lead & cvd whalebone hdl, 9"...........................35.00
Nutcracker, bust of Blk man in shirt & jacket, jaw opens............800.00
Ostrich egg, eng ships, on mahog stand, 1800s, 5½" 900.00
Pin, belaying; overall cvg, 8½", G...100.00
Pipe, made of 2 whale's teeth, sailing ship cvg, 5", VG...............145.00
Plaque, sailing ship mtd on wood panel, 4½"................................35.00
Plaque, sailing ship under full sail, 3¾x1½".................................50.00
Rolling pin, whale ivory w/ironwood sections, 14", EX 1,200.00
Seam rubber, trn whalebone w/red wax lines, 4¾", EX 450.00
Shoe horn, whalebone, scalloped hdl, early, 5¼" 65.00
Swift, whale ivory clamp & cup, 1850s, 17", NM 1,300.00
Tooth, boy on hobby horse, 1850s, 4¾"..350.00
Tooth, full-figure portrait 'John Geo Ellison,' 1850s, 6" 1,200.00
Tooth, lady in ballgown, 1850s, 5"...550.00
Tooth, lg eagle/flags/arms, man/cabin, ship/lighthouse, 6" 2,300.00
Tooth, Man o' War w/British flag, detailed cvg, 6½", EX 350.00
Tooth, panoramic whaling scene, 1850s, 5¾", EX 550.00
Tooth, ship in storm/Cleopatra in barge, 1825, 5" 400.00
Tooth, ship trapped in ice, dtd 1871, 7½", EX.............................235.00
Tooth, sperm whale & long boat w/crew, 6⅞"...............................275.00
Tooth, standing woman, Am eagle, ship Neptune, 1850, 6"........750.00
Tooth, tropical bird, some mc, EX eng, 1850s, 3½".......................250.00
Tooth, Victorian figures, 3½", EX..75.00
Tooth, whaler heading for flukes of whale, 5", EX 150.00
Tooth, yachting scene, dtd 1851, 5¼"..65.00
Tooth, 3-masted ship, star border, 6", EX 250.00
Tooth, 3-masted ship w/caption, dtd 1840, 4", EX.........................75.00
Yardstick, whalebone w/tortoise shell divisions, 1850s.................400.00

Sebastians

Sebastian miniatures were first produced in 1938 by Prescott W. Baston in Marblehead, Massachusetts. Since then more than four hundred have been modeled. These figurines have been sold through gift shops all over the country, primarily in the New England states. In 1976 Baston withdrew his Sebastians from production. Under an agreement with the Lance Corporation of Hudson, Massachusetts, one hundred designs were selected to be produced by that company under Baston's supervision. Those remaining were discontinued. In the short time since then, the older figurines have become very collectible. Price is determined by two factors: 1) in production/out of production; 2) labels — color of oval label, i.e. red, blue, green, etc.; Marblehead label, a green and silver palette-shaped label used until 1977; or no label. If there is no label and the varnish coat is quite yellowed, then it is considered to be of the Marblehead era. Dates are merely copyright dates and have no particular significance in regard to value. (Signed) 'P.W. Baston' should only have impact on price when the signature is an actual autograph — most pieces are manufactured with an imprinted 'P.W. Baston' on the base.

Abraham Lincoln, Marblehead label 60.00
Adams, pewter 75.00
Becky Thatcher, gr label..40.00
Betsy Ross, Marblehead label 55.00

Betsy Ross, red label 25.00
Boy Scout Plaque 200.00
Building Days, pr 69.00
Cleopatra, Marblehead era 225.00
Clown, bl label..95.00
Colonial Blacksmith, bl label 38.00
David Copperfield & Wife, Marblehead label.....250.00
Evangeline, Marblehead label 125.00
Family Picnic 50.00
Geo & Martha Washington, Marblehead era, pr.....60.00
Grandma at Cookstove, gr label 35.00
Grocery Store, Marblehead label 60.00
In the Candy Store (Necco) 180.00
James & Elizabeth Monroe, pr 195.00
John & Priscilla Alden, ea....................................95.00
John Smith & Pocahontas, Marblehead era, pr ...215.00
Madonna, chair, gr label 40.00
Mark Anthony...200.00
Micawber, 1946..65.00
Mr Beacon Hill 200.00
Olivea 200.00

Oliver Twist and the Beadle, 1949, $30.00.

Outboard Fishers, bl label.....................................25.00
Parade Rest, Marblehead label 55.00
Plaque, Marblehead label 200.00
Rip Van Winkle, Collector Club issue, MIB 50.00
Shaker Man & Woman, Marblehead era, pr 130.00
St Theresa..125.00
Swan Boat, Boston Public Garden, Marblehead era, 2¼x3x5" 160.00
Toll House, Pilgrims 200.00
Victorian Couple, Marblehead label....................200.00
Washington w/Cannon, bl label 20.00
Weaver & Loom, Marblehead label 55.00

Sevres

Fine-quality porcelains have been made in Sevres, France, since the early 1700s. Rich ground colors were often hand painted with portraits, scenics, and florals. Some pieces were decorated with transfer prints and decalcomania; many were embellished with heavy gold. These wares are the most respected of all French porcelains. Their style and designs have been widely copied, and some of the items listed below are Sevres-type wares.

Box, mc florals, oblong, mk, 2¼" L 150.00
Box, red enamel decor w/gilt, rectangular, mk, 3" L..............275.00

Centerpc, portrait plate, 14", in ftd/hdld ormolu fr, 6x18" **1,400.00**
Cup & saucer, floral garlands, mottled brn band, gilt rim 375.00
Figurine, Deco lady clasps flowers to breast, G Privat, 20" 500.00
Plaque, figures by river/4 shaped panels, 1890s, 18", pr 750.00
Plaque, portrait of girl on bl, gilt metal fr, 1880s, 6" 450.00
Plate, Chateau de Tulieries, figural reserves, gold rim, 9½"............75.00
Plate, figures in woodland, sgn Shultz, 1910, 9", pr 240.00
Plate, panel of figures in interior, sgn Dumas, 9½", pr.................400.00
Plate, portrait, sgn Morin, 3 floral panels in rim, 9½" 140.00
Plate, roses/bl ribbons, turq/gilt border, 1800, 9¾" 300.00

Urn, cartouch with landscape and 18th-century figures on azure, signed Poiteuin, 21", $1,400.00.

Urn, cottage on lt bl, ormolu mts/ftd base, 1880s, 11", pr 400.00
Urn, courting couple on cobalt, sgn Pascot, ormolu mts, 23" .. **4,000.00**
Urn, lady/putto/stream, sgn Lheri, cobalt lid/ft, 29", EX **2,300.00**
Urn, lady's portrait on gr, sgn, ormolu mts, mk, 8" 295.00
Urn, 2 reserves on cobalt, ormolu mts, 1800s, 32" **9,000.00**
Vase, pate-sur-pate, 1924 Olympics commemorative, 13" **1,700.00**
Wine cooler, floral sprigs, bl/gilt ribbons, 1800s, 6" 300.00

Sewer Tile

Whimsies, advertising novelties, and other ornamental items were sometimes made in potteries where the primary product was simply tile.

Ash tray, frog w/open mouth on lily pad, Dickey Clay, 5x4½x3" ..85.00
Birdhouse, cone-shaped roof, limb-like perch at hole, 5x6½" 100.00
Birdhouse, VG tooled detail, edge flakes, 8" 175.00
Bookends, gorilla, tooled coat/open mouth, mk Superior, 15" 700.00

Figure of a dog, 7½", EX, $75.00.

Dog, brn mottled, simple tooling, old base chips, 8" 170.00
Dog, EX tooled details, unglazed, 11½" 1,000.00
Dog, smoked 2-tone tan, curled tail/pug nose, 7", EX 275.00
Frog, stamped Superior, 7½" 175.00
Frog (naughty), What Cheer...75.00
Lion, tiered rectangle base w/tooling, minor flakes, 7" L 350.00
Lion on oval base, tooled details, 14" L 375.00
Paperweight, frog on rnd base, incised features, 2¼x4¼" 80.00
Planter, stump form, What Cheer, 5x7½" 65.00
Tile, lion, recumbent, brn 125.00

Sewing Items

Sewing collectibles continue to intrigue collectors, and fine 19th-century and earlier pieces are commanding higher prices due to increased demand and scarcity. Complete needlework boxes and chatelaines in original condition are rare. But even though they may be incomplete, as long as boxes contain fittings of the period, and the chains of the chatelaine are intact and contemporary with the style and the individual holders original and matching the brooch, they should be considered prime additions to any collection. As 19th-century items become harder to find, new trends in collecting develop. Among them are needlebooks, many of which were decorated with horses, children, beautiful ladies, etc. Some were giveaways printed with advertisements of products and businesses. Even early pins are collectible; the earliest were made in two parts with the round head attached separately. Pin disks, pin cubes, and other pin holders make interesting additions to a sewing collection as well.

Tape measures are now popular — Victorian figurals command premium prices. Early wooden examples of transfer ware and Tunbridge ware have gained in popularity as have figurals of vegetable ivory, celluloid, and other early plastics. From the 20th-century, tatting shuttles made of plastics as well as bone, brass, sterling, and wood decorated with Art Nouveau, Deco, and more modern designs are in demand . . . so are darning eggs, stillettos, and thimbles. Because of the decline in the popularity of needlework after the 1920s (due to increased production of machine-made items), many novelty-type items were made in an attempt to regain consumer interest, and many collectors today find them appealing.

Watch for reproductions! Sterling thimbles are being made in Holland and in the U.S. and are available in many designs from the Victorian era. But the originals are usually plainly marked — either in the inside apex or outside on the band. Avoid testing gold and silver thimbles for content — this often destroys the inside marks. Instead, research the manufacturer's mark; this will often denote the material as well. Even though the reproductions are well finished, they do not have the manufacturers' marks. Many thimbles are being made specificaly for the collectible market; reproductions of porcelain thimbles are also found. Prices should reflect the age and availability of these thimbles.

Our advisor for this cateogry is Marjorie Geddes; she is listed in the Directory under Oregon.

Awl, sterling 25.00
Basket, mc sweetgrass, early, sm, EX 25.00
Basket, woven reed, glass beads, Chinese coins, 7½" 25.00
Bodkin, sterling, Deco emb, flat, ¾" W, VG...........................38.00
Bodkin, whalebone, scrimshaw decor, 2¾" 50.00
Book, Art of Dressmaking, 1st ed, 1927, G 25.00
Book, Dressmaking Made Easy, Balt, 1904, NM 5.00
Box, thread; cb, child litho, orig thread, Hemingway, EX.............20.00
Buttonhole cutter, wrought steel, 4" L 35.00
Chatelaine, silvered metal, old, 5-pc................................800.00
Clamp, japanning on CI, open scroll swing arm, 4½" 145.00

Crochet hook, ivory hdl, Milward, for fine thread, 4½" 5.00
Darner, bl glass, foot shape, molded, 5"............................75.00
Darner, ebony w/sterling repousse hdl, lg..........................65.00
Darner, end of day, sheared end, 6¾".............................250.00
Darner, glove; sterling repousse, mk, Victorian, 4"...............125.00

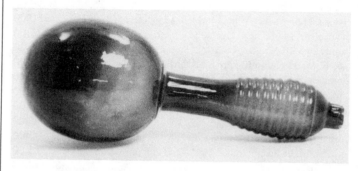

Darner, mold blown with ribbed handle, cobalt, 7" long, $175.00.

Darner, oak, elongated & narrow, 6", EX 15.00
Darner, peachblow, rnd w/hdl, ca 1890 ....295.00
Darning egg, lt wood, natural patina, 6"........................ 4.00
Dressmaker's form, ¾-figure, adjustable, early, EX.............125.00
Emery, strawberry, pk, sterling top, 1⅛"......................75.00
Hem gauge, sterling, ornate, dtd Oct 2, '94...................95.00
Kit, Calvert's, yel enamel, w/thimble & thread, 2"............15.00
Kit, chrome, rnd, cushion top, orig thimble & thread, NM 20.00
Kit, Lydia Pinkham, 9x6", EX 25.00
Kit, red Bakelite w/thimble cap, NM 40.00
Knitting guard, blk celluloid hoof form w/fur, pr, M..........75.00
Knitting sheath, wood, geometric cvg, brass at opening, 7¾" ...145.00
Measure, Blk man's head, cigarette in mouth is tab...........145.00
Measure, brass, straw hat figural, ...We Cover the Feet, EX ...145.00
Measure, celluloid, cloth tape, Mead Johnson 5.00
Measure, celluloid, duck form, VG 45.00
Measure, celluloid, fish form, EX 35.00
Measure, celluloid, John Deere advertising, EX 22.50
Measure, celluloid, Lydia Pinkham, portrait front, EX 80.00
Measure, celluloid, man in tux on red 10.00
Measure, celluloid, owl figural.............................65.00
Measure, celluloid, pig, This Little Pig Came..., Japan......65.00
Measure, celluloid, pig figural in red shoe 45.00
Measure, celluloid, policeman figural, Japan................40.00
Measure, cloth, Indian figural w/blanket around her, EX.......30.00
Measure, John Deere, celluloid, M 25.00
Measure, metal, grist mill w/wheel that turns, EX 195.00
Measure, metal, owl figural.................................45.00
Measure, plastic, apple, M 50.00
Measure, plastic, Liberty Bell..............................50.00
Measure, porc, Deco lady's head, tape in mouth, EX..........110.00
Measure, tin, clock w/moving hands, 1¼"....................95.00
Measure, tin, hoover vacuum figural, 1950s..................30.00
Needle case, Bakelite, w/thimble cap, Deco trim, tassle 45.00
Needle case, celluloid, umbrella figural, 4" 75.00
Needle case, gold-washed sterling, French, 2¼" 250.00
Needle case, ivory, cvd couple amid flowers, 5¼", EX.......165.00
Needle case, ivory, cvd florals, age checks, 3¼"...........85.00
Needle case, silver, ribbed, 2½"...........................125.00
Needle case, sterling, w/hook for hanging 185.00
Needle case, whalebone, rolling pin form, hdls remove, 3¾"...120.00
Needle case, wood, tubular, 4", +long heavy needles.......... 7.50
Needle case, wood, Tyrolean, ornate, 1870s..................125.00
Needle holder, Tunbridge, mosaic book form, 1½x2" 85.00
Pincushion, brass, lady's shoe, 3½"........................20.00

Pincushion, bsk, dog figural in man's shoe w/cushion, Japan 32.00
Pincushion, celluloid, high-heeled red shoe, EX.....................22.50
Pincushion, celluloid, lady's high-heeled shoe, opens 27.50
Pincushion, ceramic, elephant w/fabric howdah, 2¼x3½" 17.50
Pincushion, cross-stitch bolster shape, gr & wht, 1819 ....75.00
Pincushion, lustreware, cat, Deco style, Japan 15.00
Pincushion, lustreware, slipper, Japan, 1930s, 4" 10.00
Pincushion, spelter, man's shoe, 3½" 25.00
Pincushion, Wilcox SP box w/cushion top 65.00
Punch, eyelet; bone hdl, 5¾" 14.00
Ribbon threader, NP, Prudential.....................................10.00
Scissors, buttonhole; Sheffield, steel, ¼" 45.00
Scissors, celluloid hdls & shanks, folding, 2", EX.....................55.00
Scissors, embroidery; EM Oakes, steel, ca 1880, EX 45.00
Scissors, MOP hdls, folding, Germany................................145.00
Scissors, sterling, cupids emb, EX 145.00
Scissors, sterling, folding, advertising, pre-1900 ....95.00
Seam/buttonhole cutter, wrought iron, 1700s, 3¾" 75.00
Sewing aid, cast bronze, w/table clamp, 3½" 65.00
Sewing bird, brass, dbl-dtd Feb 15, 1853.............................250.00
Sewing bird, brass, mid-1800s, 4x5½" 220.00
Sewing bird, steel, clamp-on, ca 1800, EX 220.00
Sewing bird, tin, dbl pincushion 225.00
Silk winder, bone, snowflake shape..................................45.00
Spool caddy, mahog, 3-tier, trn center post/3 ft, 12" 65.00
Spool caddy, oak, 2-tier w/pincushion, Victorian, 9¼" 125.00
Spool caddy, trn hardwood w/ebonized trim, 9½" 90.00
Tatting shuttle, Bakelite, 1920s, VG.................................20.00
Tatting shuttle, celluloid 10.00
Tatting shuttle, celluloid, Lydia Pinkham, portrait top, M 100.00
Tatting shuttle, MOP, EX 125.00
Tatting shuttle, sterling, plain.....................................75.00
Thimble, aluminum, Prudential 12.50

Silver thimble with cupids, Pat Nov 21-105, $135.00. (Watch for reproductions — patent number (date) is often faint.)

Thimble, sterling, eng country scene band, Simons 38.00
Thimble, sterling, stars in band......................................32.00
Thimble, sterling, wide gold band, Simons 75.00
Thimble holder, milk glass, blown, 6" 75.00
Thimble holder, vegetable ivory, acorn figural, Victorian, 3" 85.00
Thimble holder, vegetable ivory, floral cvgs, +thimble.............135.00
Thread case, red Bakelite thimble atop, EX..........................22.50
Thread waxer, sterling, repousse pierced cap, unmk, 2" 75.00
Threader, brass, Threadmaster Automatic, M in pkg 18.00

Sewing Machines

Child's, Artcraft, worn pnt..27.50
Child's, Betsy Ross, VG...30.00
Child's, Casige, blk, mc decals, British Zone, EX in box..............65.00

Child's, Casige, lt gr, all metal, British Zone, lg, VG....................55.00
Child's, Gateway, red metal, orig needle & thread 55.00
Child's, Jay-Mar, red/wht, battery op, Japan, EX 22.00
Child's, Kay-An-Ee Sew Master, tan, sm head, low base, VG 25.00
Child's, Little Mother, red, 7½x4x8", EX 58.00
Child's, Sew-E-Z, battery op..20.00
Child's, Sew-O-Matic, blk, heavy metal head & arm, EX 60.00
Child's, Singer, tan, electric, 6x11x5½", in case......................75.00
Child's, Stitch Mistress, EX orig 25.00
Child's, US Zone Germany, w/eagle, MIG, VG 75.00
Child's, Vulcan, plastic-clad steel 30.00
Favorite, child's, Germany, ca 1900, sm, +instructions...............110.00
Simmons Hardware #28919, VG 300.00
Singer Featherweight #221, w/bobbins & attachments, +case 225.00

Shaker Items

The Shaker community was founded in America in 1776 at Niskeyuna, New York, by a small group of English 'Shaking Quakers.' The name referred to a group dance which was part of their religious rites. Their leader was Mother Ann Lee. By 1815 their membership had grown to more than one thousand in eighteen communities as far west as Indiana and Kentucky. But in less than a decade, their numbers began to decline until today only a handful remain.

Their furniture is prized for its originality, simplicity, workmanship, and practicality. Few pieces were signed. Some were carefully finished to enhance the natural wood; a few were painted.

Although other methods were used earlier, most Shaker boxes were of oval construction with overlapping 'fingers' at the seams to prevent buckling as the wood aged. Boxes with original paint fetch double the price of an unpainted box; number of fingers and size should also be considered.

Although the Shakers were responsible for weaving a great number of baskets, their methods are not easily distinguished from those of their outside neighbors, and it is nearly impossible without first-hand knowledge to positively attribute a specific example to their manufacture. They were involved in various commercial efforts other than woodworking — among them sheep and dairy farming, sawmilling, and pipe and brick making. They were the first to raise crops specifically for seed and to market their product commercially. They perfected a method to recycle paper and were able to produce wrinkle-free fabrics. Prices realized for Shaker artifacts at today's large auctions are very erratic.

Standard two-letter state abbreviations have been used throughout the following listings.

Key:
bj — bootjack   PH — Pleasant Hill
CB — Canterbury   ML — Mt. Lebanon
EF — Enfield   SDL — Sabbathday Lake
NL — New Lebanon   WV — Watervliet

Apple peeler, cherry, pegged/mortised, ME, 1840s, 26" 450.00
Basket, ash, hoop hdl, open-weave bottom, 10x14½" 325.00
Basket, berry; tin rims w/wood bottom, sgn/1859, 4x4½" 125.00
Basket, blk ash, open-weave bottom, cvd hdls, 7½x14x11" 250.00
Basket, blk ash/leather, swing hdl, NL, 17x13¾" 1,950.00
Basket, cheese; blk ash/maple, NL, 20" dia 1,000.00
Basket, cutlery; ash, dk varnish, cvd hdl, 5½x17x8½" 1,100.00
Basket, gathering; ash, EX patina, swing +side hdls, 14x18" ... 1,200.00
Basket, maple, lt patina, 2-hdl, dbl-wrapped rim, EF, 6x7½" 550.00
Basket, maple/ash, cvd hdls, dbl-wrapped rim, 6½x15x9" 750.00
Basket, maple/ash, flared top, EF, 1850s, 29x17" sq top...........1,400.00

Flax-gathering basket, ash and maple, Enfield NH, ca 1835, 48" long, $1,400.00.

Basket, oak, natural, swing hdl, SDL, 1840s, 16x14" dia..............500.00
Basket, pie; ash, gr stain, dbl swing hdls, lid, 6x12½" 1,000.00
Basket, sewing; maple, dk finish, side hdls, 7½x15" sq 450.00
Basket, storage; ash, oval rim, NL, 1860s, 13x36x26" 350.00
Bed, maple/pine, orig wheels, pinned, 33x79x46", pr 3,500.00
Bench, pine, bj ends, dvtl braces, 1840s, 19x39x10"................ 4,000.00
Bench, yel pine, worn finish, plank seat, WV, 1850s, 56" L 350.00
Box, bureau; cherry, varnish, dvtl, divided, MA, 22x36x9" 800.00
Box, desk; chestnut/cherry/pine, 4-part int, 1850s, 5x16x12" 700.00
Box, document; pine, bl pnt, nailed, wire hinges, SDL, 5x12"....550.00
Box, dough; maple, red pnt, dvtl, cut-out hdls, WV, 32" L 1,700.00
Box, maple/pine, red pnt, 3-finger, oval, PH, 3x6" 650.00
Box, maple/pine, 4-finger, ship scene on lid, 2⅝x6⅜" 450.00
Box, natural w/EX patina, 3-finger base, 1 on lid, rpr, 12" 400.00
Box, pine, bl pnt, 5-finger, EF, 1840s, 4¼x11¼" 3,750.00
Box, pine/ash, brn pnt, 4-finger, ME, 3x7¼" 1,550.00
Box, pine/ash, gray pnt over gr, 7-finger, SDL, 3¾x8¼" 450.00
Box, pine/birch, orig wht pnt, 5-finger, 1840s, 5x12½" 1,100.00
Box, pine/maple, red pnt, floral decal, 4-finger, 4¾x11¼" 1,100.00
Box, pine/maple, varnish, 3-finger, SDL, 1850s, 1¼x3¼" 600.00
Box, seed; pine, orig red pnt, ML, 3½x23½x11¾" 1,300.00
Box, spit; maple/pine, varnish over pnt, ML, 1850s, 3¾x18" 950.00
Box, spit; maple/pine, yel stain, 2-finger, CB, 1840s, 2x11" 900.00
Box, storage; mahog, dvtl, MA, 1840s, 7½x19x11" 1,100.00
Box, storage; maple burl/poplar, dvtl, 1850s, 8¼x16x9" 1,200.00
Box, storage; pine, stain, dvtl, appl molding, WV, 12x25x13"... 1,600.00
Box, storage; poplar, brn pnt, dvtl, WV, 1840s, 7½x15½" 900.00
Box, storage; poplar, red stain, nailed, CB, 15x31x15" 1,300.00
Box, wood; pine, orange stain, dvtl, NL, 1850s, 23x24x16" ... 6,600.00
Box, 2-finger, wood pins/copper fasteners, 1x2½x3½", EX 330.00
Bucket, lunch; pine/ash, swing hdl, CB, 1830s, 8½x7¾" 400.00

Four oval Shaker boxes, graduated, with three or four tapering fingers, original finish, from 5½" long to 12" long, $3,100.00.

Bucket, pine, bl pnt, w/lid, ML, 1850s, 15x9¾" 800.00
Bucket, pine, ochre pnt, red top, MA, 1850s, 13x10" 1,400.00
Candlestand, cherry, snake leg, rfn, NL, 1840s, 23½x16"........ 2,600.00
Cape, sister's, beige wool, MOP buttons, 32"..............................225.00
Carrier, pine/maple, pnt traces, 3-finger, swing hdl, 10x11" 750.00
Carrier, poplar/maple, orig gr pnt, swing hdl, 11x9" dia..............500.00
Carrier, sewing, pine, dvtl, canted sides, 1798, 9x12¾" 1,600.00
Chair, arm #3; maple, varnish, tape seat, ML, 1870s, 34" 400.00
Chair, arm #7; maple, varnish, rush seat, ML, 1870s, 41" 1,800.00
Chair, dressing; birch, rush seat, dbl dowel bk, ML, 28" 1,000.00
Chair, revolver; hickory/pine/maple/oak, 8-spindle, NL, 27" .. 5,250.00
Chair, rocker #3; armless, maple, stain, tape seat, ML, 33" 475.00
Chair, rocker #3; w/arms, stenciled label, rpl seat, ML 1,000.00
Chair, rocker #4; maple, shawl bar, tape seat, ML, 37" 650.00
Chair, rocker #5; maple, tape seat, ML, 39½".............................900.00
Chair, rocker #7; armless, cherry, oak bar, tape seat, 42" 900.00
Chair, rocker #7; maple, ebony finish, tape seat, NL, 42" 1,250.00
Chair, rocker #7; maple, shawl bar, tape seat, ML, 42" 1,400.00
Chair, rocker #7; maple, varnish, tape seat, ML, 1900, 42"..........900.00
Chair, rocker; armless, maple, shawl bar, tape seat, ML, 41" ... 1,150.00
Chair, rocker; tiger maple, taped seat, WV, 1830s, 40" 1,000.00
Chair, side #3; cherry, split reed seat, tilters, 33½"....................900.00
Chair, side #3; maple, dk stain, tape seat, ML, 1870, 34" 600.00
Chair, side; birch, orig varnish, cane seat, EF, 1840s, 42"........ 5,500.00
Chair, side; birch, rfn, rush seat, EF, 1840s, 41" 1,100.00
Chair, side; bird's-eye maple, tape seat, EF, 1840s, 37".........10,000.00
Chair, side; cherry, natural, tape seat, EF, 41".......................... 1,100.00
Chair, side; maple, cane seat, tilters, NL, 1850s, 41" 1,900.00
Chair, side; maple, lt varnish, cane seat, tilters, CB, 41" 6,000.00
Chair, side; maple, yel pnt, taped seat, AF, 1830s, 42"...............900.00
Chair, side; maple/birch, 2-slat, tape seat, NL, 1820s, 25" 1,900.00
Chest, blanket; pine, varnish, 1-drw, bj ends, CB, 36x43x18".. 2,500.00
Chest, blanket; poplar, bl pnt, 2-drw, WV, 1840s, 43x41x17"... 5,500.00
Chest, candle; maple/poplar/pine, 6-drw, SDL, 36x33x18" 1,000.00
Chest, pine, 3 grad dvtl drws, WV, rfn, 1850s, 34x34x17"..........800.00
Chest, poplar, red stain, dvtl, WV, 1850s, 15x28x11½" 900.00
Chest, spice; walnut, natural, dvtl, 13-drw, WV, 17x17x7" 800.00
Cloak, sister's, bl wool, purple satin, EF, 56" 300.00
Clock, pine/cherry, paper dial, dtd 1835, 80x17x11"...............25,000.00
Cupboard, pine, orig stain, dmn escutcheon, WV, 27x21x11" . 6,000.00
Cupboard, pine, red pnt, 2-door, brass pulls, 80x48x19".......... 3,250.00
Cupboard, pine, red stain, 2-door, rpl pegs, 87x44x22" 1,750.00
Cupboard, pine, 4 panel doors, 4 shelves, 1860s, 66x44x19".... 1,000.00
Cutter, herb; pine, stain, dvtl, wrought blade, WV, 8x29x23".....650.00
Desk, sewing; pine, varnish, 5-drw, CB, 1830s, 33x23x19" 3,250.00
Desk, trustee's, pine, 3-shelf/4-drw, slant lid, 82x24x19"......... 4,000.00
Dipper, ash, orig yel pnt, 1-pc, curved hdl, 4" dia, 6½" 550.00
Hanger, pine/hickory, CB, 1850s, 3 for...................................... 250.00
Mirror, hand; birch, dmn shaped, copper nails, EF, 5x2¾" 175.00
Mirror holder, cherry/maple, tapered bk, brass hangers, 17x9" ...400.00
Pie lifter, wire w/wooden hdl, 13½" 55.00
Rack, drying; chestnut, tapered sides, NL, 1840s, 38x24" 400.00
Rack, drying; pine, red pnt, arched base, WV, 1850s, 55" 1,000.00
Rack, pine w/5 mushroom-ended pegs, EX patina, 43" 260.00
Rail, dbl peg; pine, 14 cherry pegs, NY, 52".................................600.00
Rail, peg; pine, birch pegs, 50", 67", 78", 3 for 650.00
Rug, silk, mc central field, blk border, cotton bk, 24x40" 150.00
Rug, silk/wool, mc field, striped border, fr, 18x58"................... 1,700.00
Screen, infirmary; pine, 3-panel, 3-peg, NL, 81x70" 900.00
Sheet music, Little Shaking Quakers, Bristow, EX......................500.00
Shovel, birch, varnish, cvd, 1-pc, EF, 1850s, 36" 900.00
Sieve, maple & horsehair, NL, 10", 7", 4½", set of 3....................150.00
Stand, birch/pine, dvtl drw/brass pull, EF, 1830s, 26x27x21".17,000.00
Stand, cherry, dvtl drw, CB, 1840s, 27½x17x23" 1,700.00

Stand, cherry/poplar, dvtl drw, EF, 1840s, 28x18x17" **3,100.00**
Stand, chestnut/pine, 1-drw, CB, 1850s, rprs, 26x26x19"........ **2,500.00**
Stand, sewing; cherry, red stain, dvtl drw, MA, 29x22x18" **1,000.00**
Stand, sewing; maple/chestnut, dvtl drw, CB, 1840s, 25x16x24" . **3,500.00**
Stand, sorting; birch, tray top, dvtl drw, EF, 32x15x21" **1,000.00**
Stand, work; pine/birch, 3-drw, SDL, 1840s, 27x32x21" **3,500.00**
Stick, tailoring; cherry, dk varnish, ML, 1840s, 36" **1,200.00**
Stool, birch, brn stain, adjustable bk, EF, 1850s, 38" **4,400.00**
Stool, maple, orig tape seat, ML, 1880s, 9½x10x13", pr **800.00**
Stove, CI, canted sides, str legs, NL, 1840s, 19x29" **600.00**
Swift, table-mt style w/cup top, sgn, Hancock MA **600.00**
Table, chair; pine/birch, dvtl drw, CB, 1840s, 27x74x40" **4,000.00**
Table, sorting; oak, tray top, dvtl drw, NL, 29x76x21" **2,200.00**
Table, sorting; poplar/oak, stain, MA, 1860s, 29x18x33" **600.00**
Table, tilt top; cherry, pegged/mortised, PH, 35x23" dia..............**800.00**
Table, wash; pine, orig pnt, drying rack, SDL, 33x29x20" **2,900.00**
Table, work; birch/pine, dvtl drw, CB, 1830s, 28x45x28" **3,500.00**
Table, work; pine, gr over red pnt, dvtl drw, 25x24x31".......... **1,000.00**
Table, work; pine/maple, dvtl drw, PH, 1840s, 29x27x40" **2,250.00**
Table, work; pine/oak, red stain, 1 drw, SDL, 28x21x36" **350.00**
Washstand, pine, dvtl drw/cup holders, rfn, CB, 39x19x15" **950.00**
Washstand, pine, pnt traces, 2 paneled doors, EF, 35x33x16". **3,250.00**
Washstand, walnut/poplar, dvtl drw, NL, 1850s, 32x28x18"... **7,000.00**
Wheel, flax; oak/maple, Alfred ME, w/distaff..............................**300.00**
Wheel, wool; maple/ash, SDL, 1830s..**350.00**

Shaving Mugs

In the 1860s it became a popular practice for every man who shaved to have his own special shaving mug. Mugs belonging to men who frequented the barber shop for their tonsorial services were often personalized with their owner's name and kept on display on the barber's shelf. Occupational shaving mugs became the high point of individualism during this period. China mugs, mostly made in France, Germany, and Austria, were imported by American barber-supply companies where artists hand painted the occupation or the fraternal or sports affiliation of its customer on the mug. Often his name was added in gold. Because of sanitary rules and restrictions imposed around 1915, these personalized mugs were eventually taken off the barbers' shelves. Today, occupational shaving mugs are the most valuable. Although some are valued by the excellence of the artist, most are priced by the rarity of the subject matter.

Gibson girl portrait, marked Bavaria, 4¾", $55.00.

Fraternal, BF of L, gold trim, lt wear **36.00**
Fraternal, BF of L, mc symbols w/gold, Herold Bros, EX.................**95.00**
Fraternal, Eagles Lodge, Liberty, Truth, Justice..., NM **135.00**

Fraternal, Elks, elk scene, gold letters, VG................................**30.00**
Fraternal, Jr Order United Am Machinists, tools, gold trim **165.00**
Fraternal, Masonic, bl symbols w/gold & name **95.00**
Fraternal, Moose, moose scene, T&V Limoges, EX.......................**67.50**
Fraternal, Odd Fellows, symbols, name in gold, Royal China, EX..**45.00**
Fraternal, Odd Fellows, 3-link chain, gold script **85.00**
Jasper ware, Grecian scenes, scuttle style, EX..............................**95.00**
Lithophane, courting couple, celluloid hdl, w/orig brush **75.00**
Occupational, artist, palette & brushes, gold trim........................**210.00**
Occupational, artist, palette & brushes, name in gold, EX **250.00**
Occupational, bartender, man behind detailed bar, Haviland **650.00**
Occupational, butcher, steer w/Xd knife & bone, EX....................**90.00**
Occupational, butcher, steer's head & tools, name in gold **185.00**
Occupational, conductor, trolly car & passengers, gold trim........**235.00**

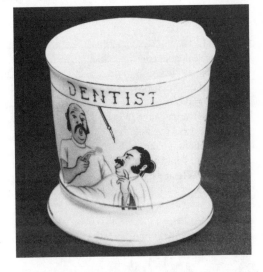

Occupational, Dentist, numbered, 20th century, $90.00.

Occupational, farmer, man w/team in field, gold trim, VG..........**115.00**
Occupational, fireman, helmet, gold trim, Austria, EX **175.00**
Occupational, fireman, pumper decal, USA, EX **30.00**
Occupational, horseman, horse's head, gold trim, EX **165.00**
Occupational, lamplighter, transfer scene, EX **450.00**
Occupational, mayor, name & town, dtd 1864, EX.......................**175.00**
Occupational, pharmacist, RX & medical symbol, gold trim **35.00**
Occupational, RR, stationary steam engine, name in gold...........**190.00**
Occupational, sportsman, hunting scene, T&V Limoges.............**125.00**
Occupational, tinsmith, tools, floral border w/gold, EX.................**90.00**
Occupational, trainman, locomotive, Buckey Supply, EX **165.00**
Occupational, trolly car operator, Meriden Electric RR, EX........**650.00**
Souvenir, Erie PA, florals, harbor scene, milk glass **20.00**
Veteran's Victory Metal, dtd 1861-66, name in gold, EX.............**395.00**

Shawnee

The Shawnee Pottery Company operated in Zanesville, Ohio, from 1937 to 1961. They produced inexpensive novelty ware — vases, flowerpots, and figurines — as well as a very successful line of figural cookie jars. Their first dinnerware line was called Valencia; it was designed by Louise Bauer in 1937 for Sears & Roebuck. A starter set was given away with the purchase of one of their refrigerators.

You'll find three versions of Shawnee's Corn line. Their first attempt, produced in 1940, was not a particularly good seller. You'll recognize this line by the white-glazed corn kernels. In 1946, they changed the white glaze to a more realistic yellow and called this line King Corn. The third variation, produced in 1954, was Queen Corn; the corn was the same yellow color, but the shucks were of a darker green than King Corn's. The white line was rather limited; it consisted of the pitcher, creamer, sugar bowl, large and small shakers, 30-oz teapot, and sugar shaker. The line expanded in '46, but the sugar shaker was never made in either of the yellow corn lines — you'll find it only in white. The utility jar doubled as a sugar bowl, the small jug as a creamer. A three-piece range set combination comprised of a pair of shakers and the utility jar (used in this instance as a drip jar) was available as well. In the listings that follow, gold trim may add from 50% to 100% on small items.

For further study, we recommend these books: *Collecting Shawnee Pottery, A Pictorial Reference and Price Guide* by Mark Supnick (planters, vases, cookie jars — see Directory under Florida); and *The Collectors Guide to Shawnee Pottery* by our advisors, Janice and Duane Vanderbilt (kitchenware and cookie jars); they are listed in the Directory under Indiana.

Cookie Jars

Clown, #12	150.00
Clown w/Seal, gold trim	300.00
Cottage House, USA #6	300.00
Dutch Girl or Dutch Boy, #1025 or #1026, Great Northern	175.00
Elephant, #60	75.00
Jug, Pennsylvania Dutch, #75	125.00
Little Chef, USA	50.00
Lucky Elephant, gold trim, USA	200.00
Mugsey, gold trim & decals, USA	300.00
Octagon w/Wheat, USA	300.00

Cookie jar, owl, hand painted and gold trimmed, $150.00.

Puss-N-Boots	125.00
Sailor, gold trim	300.00
Sailor Boy, USA	85.00
Smiley the Pig	125.00
Winnie the Pig, gold trim	200.00

Corn Line

Bowl, fruit; 6"	25.00
Bowl, mixing; 5"	22.00
Bowl, mixing; 6½"	25.00
Bowl, mixing; 8"	35.00
Bowl, soup/cereal	30.00
Bowl, vegetable; #95, 9"	35.00
Butter dish	45.00
Casserole, ind	50.00
Casserole, 1½-qt	30.00

Cookie jar	130.00
Creamer	20.00
Cup	30.00
Jug, 1-qt	50.00
Mug, 8-oz	40.00
Plate, salad; 8"	28.00
Plate, 10"	30.00
Platter, 12"	45.00
Range set, 3-pc	40.00
Relish tray	17.00
Saucer	10.00
Shaker, 3½", pr	12.00
Shaker, 5½", pr	20.00
Sugar bowl	20.00
Teapot, 10-oz	125.00
Teapot, 30-oz	50.00

Miscellaneous

Clock, Grandfather	80.00
Clock, pyramid	100.00
Clock, trellis	50.00
Creamer, elephant, w/gold & decals	135.00
Creamer, Smiley w/clover bud	55.00
Creamer, sunflower	40.00
Lamp, deer	65.00
Lamp, Spanish dancer, pr	35.00
Lamp, Victorian, pr	30.00
Lobster, casserole, Kenwood, #904	35.00
Lobster, shakers, claw form, pr	17.00
Lobster, spoon holder	100.00
Lobster, sugar bowl, Kenwood, #907	22.00
Pitcher, Charlie Chicken, Pat Chanticleer	45.00
Pitcher, Pennsylvania Dutch, ball jug, USA	90.00
Pitcher, Smiley, Pat Smiley	80.00

Valencia pitcher with lid (from waffle set), 9", $20.00.

Planter, bird on perch, #502	50.00
Planter, canopy bed, #734	60.00
Planter, cat on highchair, #727	65.00
Planter, frog on lily pad	25.00
Planter, frog playing guitar	15.00
Planter, gazelle w/baby, #840	45.00
Planter, red pony, #506	30.00
Planter, trailer, #681	35.00

Planter, truck, #680 ....35.00
Shakers, duck, pr 32.00
Shakers, Dutch boy & girl, gold & decals, pr.....................80.00
Shakers, farmer pig, pr 20.00
Shakers, Mugsey, sm, pr...30.00
Shakers, Mugsey, w/gold, lg, pr....................................80.00
Shakers, Puss 'N Boots, pr..30.00
Shakers, Smiley & Winnie, sm, pr...................................35.00
Teapot, elephant...80.00
Teapot, Granny Anne...135.00
Teapot, Pennsylvania Dutch, #10....................................65.00
Teapot, Tom the Piper's Son..55.00
Valencia, chop plate, 13" 10.00
Valencia, cup 7.00
Valencia, pitcher, ball jug..17.00
Valencia, pitcher, water; mk Valencia, w/lid.......................20.00
Valencia, plate, 10" 7.00
Valencia, shakers, pr 5.00
Vase, Cameo, 32512 ....25.00
Vase, Elegance, #1402 ....25.00
Vase, Touche, #1007 ....20.00
Wall pocket, telephone, USA #529...................................20.00

Shearwater

Since 1928 generations of the Peter, Walter, and James McConnell Anderson families have been producing figurines and artwares in their studio at Ocean Springs, Mississippi. Their work is difficult to date. Figures from the twenties and thirties won critical acclaim and have continued to be made to the present time. Early marks include a die-stamped 'Shearwater' in a dime-sized circle, a similar ink stamp, and a half-circle mark. Any older item may still be ordered in the same glazes as it was originally produced, so many pieces on the market today may be relatively new. However, the older marks are not currently in use. Retail sales are available at the pottery or by mail order.

Black figures and pirates are usually valued at $35.00 to $50.00.

Figurine, crow, gr metallic glaze 65.00
Figurine, fox, mk 35.00

Figure of a pirate, 6", $50.00.

Pitcher, lt bl gloss, 5" 25.00
Pitcher, ochre, bird hdl, sm lid, 6"...............................50.00

Teapot, dusty gr, hand trn, appl hdl & spout, imp mk, 6" 60.00
Vase, aquatic scene, sgn Anderson, ca 1930, 11" 1,900.00
Vase, cvd fish on bl gloss, sgn Anderson, 1930, rim crack, 9" 800.00

Sheet Music

Sheet music is often collected more for the colorful lithographed covers rather than for the music itself. Transportation songs which have pictures or illustrations of trains, ships, and planes; ragtime tunes which feature popular entertainers such as Al Jolson; or those with Disney characters are among the most valuable. Much of the sheet music on the market today is valued at under $5.00; some of the better examples are listed here.

Our advisor for this category is Jeannie Peters; she is listed in the Directory under Ohio.

Battle Cry of Freedom, 1st ed, 2-sheet, 1862, VG 55.00
Battle of Waterloo, Wm Hall & Son, ca 1830, 6-pg, VG.............20.00
Beautiful Dreamer, Stephen Foster, 1st ed, 1864, EX.............18.50
Columbia Is Free, patriotic cover, Diston, 1865, 6-pg, VG 22.50
Columbia the Gem of the Ocean, flags cover, 1843, VG 22.50
Cotton States Rag, Blk cover, 1910 ....20.00

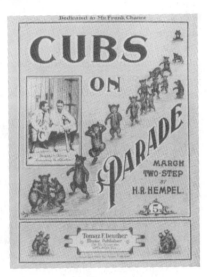

Cubs on Parade, Frank Chance on cover, copyright 1907, EX, $350.00.

Darkie's Dream, Lancing, printed cover, 1889, 5-pg, EX.............10.00
Doncha' Think It's Time?, Elvis cover, EX 30.00
Drummer Boy of Shiloh, Faulds, KY, 1864, scarce, EX..............35.00
Field of Monterey, Diston, Boston, 1846, 4-pg, VG 20.00
General Pope's Grand March, portrait cover, 1862, 8-pg, VG.......40.00
Gentlemen Prefer Blondes, Monroe cover, NM 30.00
Good Ship Lollipop, Temple cover, 1934, VG 25.00
Hard Times, comic cover, NY, 1850, VG 17.50
Hero's Quickstep, soldier cover, Thayer, 1836, 4-pg, VG 30.00
I Want My Mammy, Cantor (in Blk face) cover, 1921, EX 15.00
I Will Be No Submissive Wife, Chandler cover, 1838, 5-pg 6.00
Just Before the Battle Mother, Chicago, 1863, 6-pg, EX 25.00
Last Parting, Bufford, 1847, VG 35.00
Love's Fascination Waltz, Prang repro cover, ET Paull, 1920 ....90.00
Man the Life Boat, Russell, ship cover, 10-pg, G 15.00
Massa's in De Cold Ground, Stephen Foster, 1852, EX............12.50
My Own Chosen Bride, T Birch, blk/wht cover, 1840s, VG.........22.50
Nelly Was a Lady, Steven Foster, 1849, 4-pg, VG.................20.00
On to Charleston, Marsh, Phila, 1853, EX 37.50
Red Rover, pirates cover, 1820s, VG 17.50
Rifle Quickstep, fancy cover, 1860s, VG 30.00

Round Hill Quick Step, camp scene cover, 1840, VG 27.50
Santa Baby, Eartha Kitt cover, 1953 .... 5.00
Soldier's Welcome Home, 3 men on cover, 1820s, EX 35.00
Tiger Quick Step, 1834, EX...42.50
Walking Down Broadway, Lingard, p Pond, NY, 1868, VG..........35.00
Who Will Care for Mother Now, Brooklyn NY, 1863, VG 17.50
Willie My Brave, Stephen Foster, 1851, 6-pg, G 25.00
Your Lips Are No Man's Land But Mine, 1918 .... 5.00

Shelley

In 1872 Joseph Shelley became partners with James Wileman, owner of Foley China Works, thus creating Wileman & Co., in Stoke-on-Trent. Twelve years later James Wileman withdrew from the company, though the firm continued to use his name until 1925 when it became known as Shelley Potteries Ltd. Like many successful 19th-century English potteries, this firm continued to produce useful household wares as well as dinnerware of considerable note. In 1896 the beautiful Dainty White shape was introduced, and it is regarded by many as synonymous with the name Shelley. In addition to the original Dainty 6-Flute design, other lovely shapes were produced: 12-Flute, 14-Flute, Leaf, Shell, Queen Anne, and the more modern shapes of Vogue, Regent, and Eve.

Though often overlooked, striking earthenware was produced under the direction of Frederick Rhead and later Walter Slater and his son Eric. Many notable artists contributed their talents in designing unusual, attractive wares: Rowland Morris, Mabel Lucie Attwell, and Hilda Cowham, to name but a few.

In 1966 Allied English Potteries acquired control of the Shelley Company, and by 1967 the last of the exquisite Shelley China had been produced to honor remaining overseas orders. In 1971 Allied English Potteries merged with the Doulton group. The name Shelley China Ltd. still exists, and it has been reported that Royal Doulton has produced trial wares bearing the Shelley backstamp.

Our advisors for this category are Lila and Fred Shrader; they are listed in the Directory under California.

Ash tray, Bridal Rose, 3½" dia 22.00
Ash tray, Dainty Pink, 5" dia 31.00
Ash tray, Maytime, 3" dia 29.00
Bowl, cereal; Bl Rock, 6 flutes, 6½".............................35.00
Bowl, cereal; Dainty Pink, 6 flutes, 6½".........................35.00
Bowl, cereal; Harebell, Oleander shape, 6½".....................35.00
Bowl, child's, Mabel Lucie Attwell, 6½"..........................65.00
Bowl, cream soup; Regency, w/underplate 50.00
Bowl, cream soup; Rose Pansy Forget-Me-Not, 6 flutes, w/plate ...55.00
Bowl, sauce; Blue Rock, 6 flutes, 5½"............................30.00
Bowl, sauce; Bridal Rose, Oleander shape, 5½" 30.00
Bowl, sauce; Lily of the Valley, 14 flutes, 5½" 35.00
Bowl, vegetable; Blue Rock, 6 flutes, oval, 10½" 75.00
Bowl, vegetable; Dainty Blue, 6 flutes, oval, 10½" 75.00
Bowl, vegetable; Dainty White, 6 flutes, w/lid, 9" 75.00
Bowl, vegetable; Daisy, Queen Anne shape, w/lid, 9" 85.00
Bowl, vegetable; Heavenly Blue, 6 flutes, oval, 10½".............85.00
Butter dish, Blue Rocks, 6 flutes, oblong 85.00
Butter dish, Bridal Rose, Oleander shape, oblong.................95.00
Butter dish, Regency, 6 flutes, rnd..............................95.00
Butter pat, Bridal Rose, 6 flutes 38.00
Butter pat, Dainty Blue..35.00
Butter pat, floral w/pin striping 32.00
Butter pat, gr dots on Dainty White..............................38.50
Butter pat, Rose, Pansy, Forget-Me-Not, 6 flutes.................38.50
Butter pat, Victorian couple scene 30.00

Cake plate, Begonia, ped ft, 6 flutes, 8" 110.00
Cake plate, Garland of Flowers, Queen Anne shape, tab hdls 55.00
Cake plate, Heavenly Pink, ped ft, 6 flutes, 8" 125.00
Cake plate, Regency, ped ft, 6 flutes, 8" 110.00
Cake plate, Violets, 6 flutes, tab hdls..........................75.00
Candle holder, Dainty White, 2½", pr.............................50.00
Candle holder, Harmony, 2½", pr.................................110.00
Candle holder, Primrose, 6 flutes (6" plate w/metal insert)......45.00
Candlestick, Cloisonne, 6".......................................55.00
Candy dish, Blue Rock, 6 flutes, rnd, 5".........................26.00
Candy dish, Dainty Blue, scalloped, oval, 6" 35.00
Candy dish, Indian Peony, squarish, 5"...........................28.00
Candy dish, pk dots on Dainty White, 5"..........................38.00
Chamber set, blk w/decor, bowl+candlestick+7 pcs................450.00
Cheese dish, Bridal Rose, 6 flutes..............................135.00
Chocolate pot, Blue Rock, 6 flutes, 6" 120.00
Chocolate pot, Dainty Pink, 6 flutes, 8" 135.00
Chocolate pot, Regency, 6 flutes, 6" 100.00
Chocolate pot, Stocks, 6 flutes, 6".............................125.00
Cigarette holder, Begonia, 6 flutes..............................29.00
Cigarette holder, Campanula, 6 flutes 32.00
Cigarette holder, Regency, 6 flutes..............................27.00
Coffeepot, Archway of Roses, Queen Anne shape, 9" 110.00
Coffeepot, Dainty Blue, 6 flutes, 6½"...........................165.00
Coffeepot, Dainty White, 6 flutes, 8" 125.00
Coffeepot, Indian Peony, 8-cup..................................110.00
Coffeepot, Primrose, 6 flutes, 8" 165.00
Coffeepot, Serenity, 7"...110.00
Comport, Intarsio, w/ped & 3 curved supports, 8"................375.00
Creamer & sugar bowl, Dainty Blue, 6 flutes 55.00
Creamer & sugar bowl, Dainty White, w/lid & tray 75.00
Creamer & sugar bowl, Harebell, Oleander shape 60.00
Creamer & sugar bowl, Primrose, 6 flutes, +tray..................78.00
Creamer & sugar bowl, Regency, 6 flutes, +tray 70.00
Creamer & sugar bowl, Sheraton, w/lid 55.00
Creamer & sugar bowl, yel dots on Dainty White 75.00
Cup & saucer, Archway of Roses, Queen Anne shape.................52.00
Cup & saucer, Begonia, 6 flutes..................................52.00
Cup & saucer, Begonia, 6 flutes, farmer sz 59.00
Cup & saucer, Blue Daisy, gold ped 49.50
Cup & saucer, Bridal Rose, Oleander shape 54.00
Cup & saucer, Dainty Blue, 6 flutes..............................52.00
Cup & saucer, Dainty White, 6 flutes 42.00
Cup & saucer, Daisy, Eve shape 54.00
Cup & saucer, Daisy, Queen Anne shape 52.00
Cup & saucer, demitasse; Begonia, 6 flutes 52.00
Cup & saucer, demitasse; Dainty Blue, 6 flutes...................52.00
Cup & saucer, demitasse; Dainty White, 6 flutes..................42.00
Cup & saucer, demitasse; Lily of the Valley, 6 flutes 52.00
Cup & saucer, DuBarry, Gainsborough shape 48.00
Cup & saucer, Georgian, Gainsborough shape 48.00
Cup & saucer, Georgian, Mocha shape..............................45.00
Cup & saucer, gr w/Celandine int, Oleander shape.................54.00
Cup & saucer, Harebell, Oleander shape 52.00
Cup & saucer, Heavenly Mauve, 6 flutes 65.00
Cup & saucer, Hedgerow, Gainsborough shape 45.00
Cup & saucer, Indian Peony, Mocha shape 45.00
Cup & saucer, Iris, 6 flutes.....................................55.00
Cup & saucer, lav w/Thistle int, Oleander shape..................54.00
Cup & saucer, Lilac, 14 flutes...................................52.00
Cup & saucer, Morning-Glory, 6 flutes 55.00
Cup & saucer, pk w/Stocks int, Oleander shape 54.00
Cup & saucer, Rock Garden, Henley shape..........................48.00
Cup & saucer, scenics, 6 flutes..................................49.00

Mayfair cup and saucer, $49.00.

Cup & saucer, Shamrock, 6 flutes	50.00
Cup & saucer, Violets, 14 flutes	52.00
Cup & saucer, Wildflowers, 6 flutes	52.00
Cup & saucer, Wisteria, Regent shape	45.00
Egg cup, child's, Mabel Lucie Attwell, sm	49.50
Egg cup, Dainty Blue, 6 flutes, lg	55.00
Egg cup, Dainty Blue, 6 flutes, sm	49.50
Egg cup set, Regency, 4 sm cups on indented tray	185.00
Egg cup set, Violets, 4 sm cups on indented tray	210.00
Gravy boat, Begonia, 6 flutes, w/underplate	110.00
Gravy boat, Heavenly Blue, 6 flutes, w/underplate	165.00
Gravy boat, Regency, 6 flutes, attached underplate	85.00
Horseradish container, Blue Rock, w/lid & underplate	75.00
Jam container, Primrose, w/lid & underplate	75.00
Jam container, Sheraton, w/lid	35.00
Lamp base, Indian Peony, 11"	65.00
Lamp base, Kingfisher decor, 14"	85.00
Mug, Blue Daisy, 5"	32.00
Mug, Blue Rock, 6 flutes, 5"	45.00
Mug, Celandine, 6 flutes, 5"	45.00
Mug, child's, Mabel Lucie Attwell, 4½"	55.00
Mustard, Celandine, 6 flutes, w/lid	55.00
Mustard, Dainty Blue, 6 flutes, w/lid	55.00
Mustard, Harebell, Oleander shape, w/lid & underplate	75.00
Napkin ring, Rosebud	45.00
Napkin ring, Stocks	45.00
Pitcher, Dainty Blue, 6 flutes, 1-qt	95.00
Pitcher, Harmony, 9"	110.00
Plate, Archway of Roses, Queen·Anne shape, 8"	31.00
Plate, Begonia, 6 flutes, 8"	32.00
Plate, Blue Daisy, 7"	24.00
Plate, Blue Iris, Queen Anne shape, 7½"	32.00
Plate, Blue Rock, 6 flutes, 10¾"	65.00
Plate, Celandine, 6 flutes, 8"	35.00
Plate, Dainty Blue, 6 flutes, 6"	25.00
Plate, Green Daisy, 10½"	35.00
Plate, Harebell, Oleander shape, 10¾"	75.00
Plate, Heather, 8"	35.00
Plate, Heraldic ware: Coronation of Edward III, 6 flutes, 10"	75.00
Plate, Indian Peony, 8"	30.00
Plate, Lilac, 6 flutes, 8"	35.00
Plate, Lily of the Valley, 6 flutes, 8"	35.00
Plate, Maytime, 8"	32.00
Plate, Morning-Glory, 6 flutes, 10¾"	95.00
Plate, Morning-Glory, 6 flutes, 8"	35.00
Plate, Old Sevres, in ¾" sterling fr, 10½"	175.00

Plate, Pansy, 6 flutes, 8"	35.00
Plate, pk dots on Dainty White, 6 flutes, 8"	45.00
Plate, Primrose Chintz, sq, 7"	28.00
Plate, Regency, 6 flutes, 10¾"	55.00
Plate, Regency, 6 flutes, 6"	20.00
Plate, Rock Garden, 8"	32.00
Plate, Rose, Pansy, Forget-Me-Not, 6 flutes, 10½"	65.00
Plate, Rosebud, 6 flutes, 8"	35.00
Plate, Sheraton, 10½"	35.00
Plate, Sunray, sq, 7"	31.00
Plate, Swirls, 8"	28.00
Platter, Dainty Blue, 6 flutes, oval, 12"	125.00
Platter, Heavenly Blue, 6 flutes, oval, 12"	135.00
Platter, Old Sevres, rnd, 12"	85.00
Platter, Regency, 6 flutes, oval, 14"	110.00
Platter, Violets, 6 flutes, rnd, 12"	135.00
Pudding mold, geometric shape, 7"	45.00
Pudding mold, star shape, 5"	40.00
Shakers, Bridal Rose, pear shape, 3½", pr	65.00
Shakers, Dainty Blue, cylindrical, 3½", pr	65.00
Shakers, Forget-Me-Not, pear shape, 3½", pr	65.00
Snack set, Blue Rock, 6-flute cup+indented 8" dia plate	65.00
Snack set, Dainty White, 6-flute cup+indented 8" sq plate	45.00
Snack set, pk, 6-flute cup+indented 8" sq plate	65.00
Snack set, pk w/gold, 6-flute cup+indented 8" dia plate	75.00
Soup plate, Blue Rock, 6 flutes, 8½"	48.00
Soup plate, Bridal Rose, Oleander shape, 8½"	52.00
Soup plate, Regency, 6 flutes, 8½"	40.00
Soup plate, Swirls, 8"	35.00
Tea & toast set, bl w/gold, 6 flutes, w/6x9" tray	55.00
Tea & toast set, Dainty Blue, w/6x9" tray	65.00
Tea & toast set, Rosebud, 6 flutes, w/6x9" tray	55.00
Teapot, Blue Rock, 6 flutes, 6"	160.00
Teapot, Bridal Rose, 6 flutes, 5"	155.00
Teapot, Dainty White, 6"	110.00
Teapot, Harebell, Oleander shape, 7"	155.00
Teapot, pk dots on Dainty White, 6 flutes, 5"	165.00
Teapot, Rosebud, 6 flutes, 4"	150.00
Teapot, Thistle, 6 flutes, 6"	175.00
Toast rack, Blue Rock, 6 flutes	65.00
Toast rack, Campanula, 6 flutes	65.00
Toast rack, Primrose, 6 flutes	67.50
Toothpick holder, Celandine, 6 flutes	45.00
Toothpick holder, Wild Anemone, 6 flutes	55.00

Silhouettes

Silhouette portraits were made by positioning the subject between a bright light and a sheet of white drawing paper. The resulting shadow was then traced and cut out, the paper mounted over a contrasting color and framed. The hollow-cut process was simplified by an invention called the Physiognotrace, a device that allowed tracing and cutting to be done in one operation. Experienced silhouette artists could do full-length figures, scenics, ships, or trains freehand. Some of the most famous of these artists were Charles Peale Polk, Charles Wilson Peale, William Bache, Doyle, Edouart, Chamberlain, Brown, and William King. Though not often seen, some silhouettes were drawn or executed in wax. Examples listed here are hollow-cut unless noted.

Key:
bk — backing   p — profile
c/p — cut and pasted   wc — watercolor
fl — full length

Composite pr, p, emb Peale's label, rvpt glass, 13x17", VG 375.00
Couple, p, in rnd blk fr, 5" dia, pr 300.00
John Blake Jr, pnt lapel/collar, name label, silk bk, 4x2½" 600.00
Lady, p, ink w/gilt detail, mk Hubbard, gilt fr, 5x6" 195.00
Lady, p, label: Cut w/...scissors by Seville, English, 5x6" 200.00
Lady in bonnet, p, pencil detail, name/1829, paper bk, 6x5" 225.00
Man, fl, ink w/gold highlights, wc wash, 12x7½" 350.00
Man, fl, on litho ground, att Eduoart, 14x11" 250.00
Man, p, gilt highlights, blk lacquered fr, 5½x4⅝" 165.00
Man, tailcoat/eyeglasses, wc/ink library bk, c/p, 10x8" 200.00
Man in chair, ink ground, name/1838, att Eduoart, 10x14" 200.00

Porter family, free cut and pasted against a painted ink landscape above name inscriptions, signed Edouart, Saratoga NY, 1842, 12" x 15", $1,760.00.

Wm Henry Harrison, mtd on litho of room, by Mr Brn, 14x11" .300.00
3 youths/toys/cat/dog, named, c/p, wc bk, Edouart, 7x14" 2,100.00

Silver

Our advise for this category comes from the Sterling Shop, whose address is in the Directory under Oregon.

Coin Silver

The mark 'Coin Silver' was used after the 1830s to indicate items made with 900 parts of silver to every 1000 parts of content.

A Bancker, NY NY; teaspoon, ca 1760 ....175.00
A Dubois, NJ & PA; tablespoon, ca 1790 ....175.00
A Pitts, Phila; tablespoon 70.00
Aracanian Topu, spoon 68.00
Bigelow Bros & Kennard, Boston; master butter knife, Olive 38.00
C Beal, Hingham, Boston & Pittsfield MA; teaspoon, 1760s 175.00
C Brewer & Co, CT & NY City; teaspoon, Sheaf of Wheat, 1825 ..75.00
G Haversticker, PA; tablespoon, 1805, 6 for 925.00
G&H, mug, eng monogram, 3" 275.00
Gorham & Co, Persian, sardine fork 35.00
Haddock, Lincoln & Foss, Boston; breakfast knife, Olive 30.00
Haddock, Lincoln & Foss, Boston; pastry server, Olive 175.00
Hall & Hewson, Albany NY; crumber, ca 1819 ....135.00
J Clarke, Newport & Providence; tablespoon, rattail, 1730 ....395.00
J Cluett, Kingston, & Fonda, NY; tablespoon, ca 1750 ....350.00
J Edwards, Boston; tablespoon, rattail, 1720s, lt wear..................725.00
J Gibbs, Providence RI; tablespoon, ca 1760 ....325.00
J Letellier, DE & PA; tablespoon, bird bk, 1790s 175.00

Ewer, Hyde & Goodrich, New Orleans, ca 1850, 16", $5,750.00.

J Musgrave, Phila; tablespoon, ca 1790 ....175.00
J Owen, Phila; tablespoon 40.00
J Sayre, NY; tablespoon, ca 1790 ....175.00
J Trott Jr, Norwich & New Haven CT; tablespoon, ca 1780 ....175.00
J Watts, Phila; tablespoon, Fiddle Thread, 1840s, 6 for...............295.00
J&N Richardson, Phila; teaspoon, ca 1785 ....75.00
JA Fog, Salem MA; soup ladle, chased hdl, 1840s, 10½" 225.00
JC Farr, Boston; sauce ladle, sm..35.00
Jones, Lows & Ball, Boston MA; porringer, ca 1835 ....975.00
Krider & Biddle, Phila; salt cellar w/underplate, 1860s 60.00
Krider & Biddle, Phila; sugar tongs, 1828-50, 5" 60.00
Lincoln & Reed, Boston MA; porringer, 1840s, child's sz............475.00
Lydia Moulton, Newburyport MA; teaspoon, coffin top, 1880s...125.00
P Jones, Wilmington DE; teaspoon, ca 1840 ....40.00
P Vergereau, NY City; tablespoon, ca 1740 ....295.00
R Dunlevy, Phila; teaspoon, 6 for 135.00
R Fairchild, NY & CT; teaspoon, ca 1760....................................175.00
R Humphreys, DE & PA; tablespoon, 1765..................................375.00
R&W Wilson, Phila; mustard ladle, 5" 35.00
Stevens Lakeman, Salem; tablespoon, 1825 ....32.00
T Richards, tea service, griffin spout, fruit finials, 3-pc............ 1,200.00
W Haverstick, Lancaster PA; teaspoon, bird-bk, ca 1790 ....85.00
W Homes, Boston; tablespoon, ca 1750..325.00
W Tenney, NY NY; 5 o'clock spoon, Fiddle Thread, 1850 ....22.00
Wm Pittman, New Bedford; tablespoon, 1835 ....30.00

Flatware

Silver flatware is being collected today either to replace missing pieces of heirloom sets or, in lieu of buying new patterns, by those who admire and appreciate the style and quality of the older ware. Prices vary from dealer to dealer; some pieces are harder to find and are therefore more expensive. Items such as olive spoons, cream ladles, lemon forks, etc., once thought a necessary part of a silver service, may today be slow to sell; as a result, dealers may price them low and make up the difference on items that sell more readily. Many factors enter into evaluation. Popular patterns may be high due to demand though easily found, while scarce patterns may be passed over by collectors who find them difficult to reassemble. See also Tiffany, Silver.

Key:
FH — flat handle   HH — hollow handle

Angelique, salad fork, Internat'l 23.00
Antique Hammered, berry spoon, Shreve 85.00
Antique Hammered, dinner knife, Shreve....................25.00
Antique Hammered, gravy ladle, Shreve 72.00
Antique Hammered, ice cream fork, Shreve................25.00
Antique Hammered, tablespoon, Shreve......................60.00
Atlantis, chicken tongs, Tiffany................................495.00
Avalon, berry spoon, Internat'l................................175.00
Avalon, gravy ladle, Internat'l.................................125.00
Avalon, jelly spoon, Internat'l...................................65.00
Avalon, meat fork, Internat'l 112.00
Carmel, bouillon, Wallace 30.00
Carmel, dinner fork, Wallace 50.00
Carmel, dinner knife, Wallace 45.00
Carmel, salad fork, Wallace..35.00
Carmel, 5 o'clock spoon, Wallace 20.00
Celeste, fork, Gorham, 7½"..24.00
Celeste, knife, Gorham, 9¼".......................................22.00
Charlemagne, cold meat fork, Towle 75.00
Charlemagne, gravy ladle, Towle 75.00
Charlemagne, place spoon, Towle...............................40.00
Charlemagne, salad fork, Towle 40.00
Charlemagne, tablespoon, Towle 75.00
Chrysanthemum, beef fork, Imperial, sm 75.00
Chrysanthemum, berry scoop, Imperial 350.00
Chrysanthemum, cocktail fork, Imperial.....................30.00
Classic Rose, gravy spoon, Reed & Barton..................57.00
Classic Rose, place spoon, Reed & Barton...................30.00
Classic Rose, sauce ladle, Reed & Barton 49.00
Classic Rose, teaspoon, Reed & Barton 14.00
Classic Rose, tomato server, Reed & Barton................79.00
Cloeta, bouillon, Internat'l..30.00
Cloeta, butter knife, Internat'l 45.00
Cloeta, coffee spoon, Internat'l 25.00
Cloeta, dessert spoon, Internat'l 50.00
Cloeta, dinner fork, Internat'l 75.00
Cloeta, dinner knife, Internat'l....................................75.00
Cloeta, gumbo soup spoon, Internat'l.........................50.00
Cloeta, luncheon fork, Internat'l 50.00
Cloeta, luncheon knife, Internat'l................................50.00
Cloeta, pickle fork, Internat'l 65.00
Cloeta, sugar tongs, Internat'l 75.00
Cloeta, teaspoon, Internat'l...35.00
Cluny, grapefruit spoon, Gorham................................35.00
Cluny, gravy ladle, Gorham 250.00
Contour, cold meat fork, Towle 72.00
Contour, gravy ladle, Towle 72.00
Contour, master butter spreader, Towle.......................20.00
Contour, sugar spoon, Towle.......................................21.00
Contour, tablespoon, Towle...48.00
Edgewood, butter spreader, FH, Simpson, Hall, & Miller 35.00
Edgewood, cream ladle, Simpson, Hall, & Miller 65.00
Edgewood, dinner fork, Simpson, Hall, & Miller..........45.00
Edgewood, dinner knife, Simpson, Hall, & Miller.........40.00
Edgewood, rnd soup spoon, Simpson, Hall, & Miller ...40.00
Edgewood, sugar spoon, Simpson, Hall, & Miller.........35.00
Edgewood, tablespoon, Simpson, Hall, & Miller 50.00
Edgewood, teaspoon, Simpson, Hall, & Miller 30.00
El Grandee, iced teaspoon, Towle 30.00
El Grandee, knife, Towle, 8¾"......................................28.00
El Grandee, teaspoon, Towle.......................................19.00
English Gadroon, butter spreader, FH, Gorham 16.00
English Gadroon, carving set, Gorham, 2-pc, lg.........129.00
English Gadroon, cream soup spoon, Gorham.............28.00

English Gadroon, tablespoon, Gorham........................49.00
English King, asparagus tongs, Tiffany......................650.00
English King, gravy spoon, Tiffany............................195.00
English King, olive spoon, Tiffany.............................150.00
English King, pickle fork, Tiffany................................37.50
English King, pie server, Tiffany, 1-pc 495.00
Etruscan, butter spreader, FH, Gorham 17.50
Fontainebleau, pickle fork, Gorham............................47.50
Fontainebleau, teaspoon, Gorham 20.00
French Renaissance, iced teaspoon, Reed & Barton.....24.00
George & Martha, master butter spreader, FH, Westmoreland 16.00
George & Martha, tablespoon, Westmoreland 34.00
Georgian, beef fork, Towle, sm 125.00
Georgian, butter spreader, FH, Towle..........................35.00
Georgian, cocktail fork, Towle.....................................30.00
Georgian, demitasse spoon, Towle...............................25.00
Georgian, salad fork, Towle...50.00
Georgian, sugar spoon, Towle 35.00
Georgian, tablespoon, Towle 55.00
Henry II, pie server, Gorham 150.00
Hunt Club, bonbon, Gorham 35.00
Hunt Club, butter spreader, FH, Gorham 25.00
Hunt Club, cocktail fork, Gorham...............................18.50
Hunt Club, cold meat fork, Gorham............................55.00
Hunt Club, cream ladle, Gorham.................................35.00
Hunt Club, gumbo soup spoon, Gorham......................35.00
Hunt Club, jelly spoon, Gorham..................................35.00
Hunt Club, pickle fork, Gorham...................................30.00
Hunt Club, sugar spoon, Gorham.................................30.00
Hunt Club, sugar tongs, Gorham..................................35.00
Hunt Club, tablespoon, Gorham 55.00
Hunt Club, tomato server, Gorham..............................75.00
Iris, grapefruit spoon, Durgin......................................50.00
Lansdowne, pickle fork, Gorham..................................30.00
Lansdowne, tablespoon, Gorham 60.00
Lansdowne, tomato server, Gorham.............................90.00
Les Six Fleurs, beef fork, Reed & Barton, sm.............125.00
Les Six Fleurs, cream ladle, Reed & Barton...............125.00
Les Six Fleurs, 5 o'clock spoon, Reed & Barton...........30.00
Lily, demitasse spoon, Whiting 20.00
Lily, lettuce fork, Whiting..150.00
Lily, sugar tongs, Whiting..85.00
Louis XIV, salad fork, Towle..26.00
Luxembourg, punch ladle, Gorham...........................275.00
Luxembourg, vegetable spoon, Gorham.......................85.00

Mary II by Lunt, 132-piece set, total weight 127 oz., $1,200.00.

Marlborough, cold meat fork, Reed & Barton 65.00
Marlborough, gravy spoon, Reed & Barton..............64.00
Marlborough, jelly spoon, Reed & Barton 28.00
Marlborough, tablespoon, Reed & Barton..............47.00
Mary Chilton, asparagus server, Towle 250.00
Mary Chilton, bonbon, Towle 30.00
Mary Chilton, cream ladle, Towle 30.00
Mary Chilton, demitasse spoon, Towle 10.00
Mary Chilton, iced teaspoon, Towle..............30.00
Mary Chilton, jelly server, Towle 25.00
Mary Chilton, lemon fork, Towle 27.50
Mary Chilton, sardine server, Towle..............50.00
Mary Chilton, toast fork, Towle..............55.00
Mary Chilton, tomato server, Towle 85.00
Mayflower, butter spreader, Kirk 25.00
Mayflower, cream soup spoon, Kirk 30.00
Mayflower, gravy ladle, Kirk..............50.00
Melrose, knife, Gorham, 9"..............29.00
Mille Fleurs, butter knife, Simpson, Hall, & Miller 40.00
Mille Fleurs, cocktail fork, Simpson, Hall, & Miller..............22.00
Mille Fleurs, ice cream spoon, Simpson, Hall, & Miller..............47.50
Mille Fleurs, 5 o'clock spoon, Simpson, Hall, & Miller..............20.00
Old Colonial, dessert spoon, Towle 50.00
Old Colonial, dinner fork, Towle..............50.00
Old Colonial, ice cream server, Towle 425.00
Old Colonial, ice cream spoon, Towle 55.00
Old Colonial, orange spoon, Towle 50.00
Old Colonial, seafood fork, Towle 35.00
Old Colonial, soup ladle, Towle..............550.00
Old Colony, bouillon spoon, Towle 30.00
Old Colony, cream ladle, Towle..............60.00
Paul Revere, dessert spoon, Towle 30.00
Paul Revere, dinner fork, Towle..............35.00
Paul Revere, dinner knife, Towle 35.00
Paul Revere, gumbo soup spoon, Towle 30.00
Paul Revere, lemonade spoon, Towle..............25.00
Paul Revere, luncheon fork, Towle 30.00
Paul Revere, salad fork, Towle 35.00
Paul Revere, tablespoon, Towle 30.00
Paul Revere, teaspoon, Towle 18.00
Repousse, bonbon, Kirk 30.00
Repousse, dinner fork, Kirk 40.00
Repousse, dinner knife, Kirk..............40.00
Rose, cocktail fork, Kirk 25.00
Rose Tiara, butter spreader, HH, Gorham 18.00
Rose Tiara, pickle fork, Gorham 23.00
Rose Tiara, sugar shell, Gorham..............19.00
Rose Tiara, tablespoon, Gorham..............49.00
Spring Glory, butter spreader, FH, Internat'l 18.00
Spring Glory, cream soup spoon, Internat'l..............24.00
Spring Glory, place spoon, Internat'l 28.00
Spring Glory, tablespoon, Internat'l..............49.00
Spring Serenade, butter spreader, HH, Lunt..............17.00
Spring Serenade, meat fork, Lunt..............48.00
Spring Serenade, place spoon, Lunt 21.00
Spring Serenade, sugar shell, Lunt 17.00
Spring Serenade, tablespoon, Lunt 42.00
Spring Serenade, teaspoon, Lunt..............11.00
Virginian, cream soup spoon, Onda 18.00
Virginian, dinner fork, Onda..............19.00
Virginian, knife, Onda..............17.00
Virginian, salad fork, Onda 18.00
Virginian, teaspoon, Onda 11.00
Wave Edge, ice cream spoon, Tiffany 68.00

Wave Edge, sugar sifter, Tiffany..............185.00
Wave Edge, sugar spoon, Tiffany..............80.00
Wave Edge, waffle server, Tiffany 385.00

Hollow Ware

Until the middle of the 19th century, the silverware produced in America was custom made on order of the buyer directly from the silversmith. With the rise of industrialization, factories sprung up that manufactured silverware for retailers who often added their trademark to the ware. Silver ore was mined in abundance, and demand spurred production. Changes in style occurred at the whim of fashion. Repousse decoration (relief work) became popular about 1885, reflecting the ostentatious taste of the Victorian era. Later in the century, Greek, Etruscan, and several classic styles found favor. Today the Art Deco styles of this century are very popular with collectors. In the listings that follow, manufacturer's name or trademark is noted first; in lieu of that information, listings are by item. Weight is given in troy ounces. See also Tiffany, Silver.

Abraham Dubois, cream jug, scalloped rim, scroll hdl, 4" 800.00
AE Warner, pitcher, reeded banding, hook-end hdl, 8" 8,000.00
American, bowl, serpentine rim w/rtcl roses, 12½" L 600.00
Andred Fogelberg, creamer, chased, helmet form, 5-oz 300.00
Andrew E Warner, beaker, flaring cylinder, 3½" 700.00
Arthur Stone, bowl, Colonial style, 7"..............275.00
Arthur Stone, bowl, deep/ftd, sgn T, dtd, 4x10"..............425.00
Arthur Stone, bowl, rim pinched into 5 sections, sgn U, 9½" 400.00
Arthur Stone, plate, wide rim/appl edge, sgn C, 7" 150.00
Arthur Stone, shaker, urn form w/dome lid, 4", set of 4..............425.00
Arthur Stone, tray, dbl dolphin hdls, sgn T, 19"..............4,000.00
Austrian, foliate border w/shells, inscriptions, 1800s, 21" 550.00
Ball-Blk Co, tea/coffee, profile medallions, 5-pc 3,300.00
Ball-Tompkins-Blk, tea set, paneled, kettle on stand+5 pcs 4,900.00
Bigelow-Kennard, tray, wide rtcl scroll/foliage rim, 16" 950.00
Blk-Starr-Frost, fruit bowl, shaped decor rim, 12¾" 450.00
Blk-Starr-Frost, punch bowl, classic revival, 7x11"..............1,000.00
Bunde, pitcher, modernistic, bone hdl, 9½" 1,000.00
Chinese Export, cake basket, allover rtcl, swing hdl, 12" 1,000.00
Christian Wiltberger, sugar urn, monogram, 10" 1,300.00
Comyns-Sons, vase, trumpet form w/emb florals, 1900, 12"..............450.00
D&R, English, master salt, Georgian, oval, set of 4, 8-oz 250.00
David Darling, creamer, Georgian, 6-oz..............230.00
David-Galt, pitcher, allover emb flowers, 7¾" 650.00
Dominick-Haff, kettle/lamp stand, hammered/lotus pads, 12".. 4,600.00
Dominick-Haff, tea set, plain, sq hdls, 9½" pot+2 pcs..............500.00
Dorothy Mills, creamer, repousse, rprs, 4-oz 150.00
Dutch, biscuit box, 18th-C genre scenes, mk O/77, 7" L 1,200.00
Edwin Stebbins, pitcher, ornate hdl, leaf bands, 14"..............1,000.00
Fenton-Cresnick, candlestick, ornate base, 12½", 4 for 4,000.00
Fisher, tray, gadroon hdls, inscription, 1930s, 24" L 600.00
Frank Whiting, platter, scroll rim, 14½"..............300.00
Franklin Porter, bowl, hand hammered, scalloped, sgn, 2x8"..............500.00
Garrett Eoff, teapot, serpent spout, ivory mts, 9"..............600.00
Geo Fox, teapot, 12-sided, trifid ft, Victorian, 6" 250.00
Geo Hunter, caster, repousse/chased, 6-oz 150.00
Geo Shreve-Co, bottle vase, hammered/appl flowers, 8½" 1,500.00
Georg Jensen, candelabra, 3 strap arms, Pedersen, 6½", pr..............5,000.00
Georg Jensen, candlestick, 2-lite, beaded foliage, 13", pr..............9,000.00
Georg Jensen, cocktail shaker, grape finial, 9½" 1,300.00
Georg Jensen, cocktail shaker, hammered, rim hdls, 10½" 2,600.00
Georg Jensen, compote, grapevines, spiral stem, 7½", pr..............6,500.00
Georg Jensen, tazza, appl grape clusters, 12x12½"..............9,000.00
Georg Jensen, tea set, #984, simple styling, Denmark, 45-oz 900.00

Georg Jensen, water pitcher, fluted rosewood hdl, 7" 1,600.00
Gorham, bowl, dome lid w/appliques, by Magnussen, 9" 1,200.00
Gorham, bowl, ribbed/fluted, ftd, 1941, 12" 425.00
Gorham, bowl, rtcl/eng foliage swags, shaped oval, 6" H 450.00
Gorham, bride's basket, tall rtcl hdl, eng florals, 41-oz 1,400.00
Gorham, compote, foliate scroll hdls/appl masks, 14" W 700.00
Gorham, compote, upswept hdl: fox/grapevines, gilt, 13"........ 6,000.00
Gorham, dish, 2 mice on rim, raised sides, scroll hdls, 7"............900.00
Gorham, loving cup, appl/eng grapevines, very lg hdls, 20" 7,000.00
Gorham, Martele, card tray, emb buttercup/dandelion, 6¾"........350.00
Gorham, Martele, inkstand, emb flowers, raised well, 10" 200.00
Gorham, Martele, tray, undulating rim w/flowers, 18" 5,750.00
Gorham, pepper caster & open salt, bbl-staved, 4-oz+ 400.00
Gorham, pitcher, leaf-end hdl, inscription cartouch, 11" 1,100.00
Gorham, pitcher, repousse/eng cartouch, serpentine rim, 9"........600.00
Gorham, serving dish, eng florals, oval, 1900, 7" L 1,500.00
Gorham, tazza, female busts on hdls, 1870, 7", EX 500.00
Gorham, tureen, scroll/floral detail, oval, w/lid, 15" L 1,000.00
Gorham, waiter, folded napkin relief, eng birds, ftd, 6" 1,400.00
Haddock-Lincoln-Foss, pitcher, acanthus rim/hdl/spout, 10" 900.00
Henry Birks-Sons, salver, pie-crust rim, 4 sm ft, sq, 13" 450.00
Henry Birks-Sons, tea/coffee, eng scroll/floral band, 4-pc 850.00
Henry Birks-Sons, waiter, shaped pie-crust rim, 10", pr 640.00
Herbert Taylor/Stone Associates, punch bowl, fluted, 16" 9,000.00
Howard & Co, cup, emb spiral flutes/scrolls, dome lid, 16" 1,800.00
Indian, plate, repousse/chased hunting scenes, 12" 100.00
International, candelabra, Prelude, 3-arm, rpr, 17", pr.................650.00
James Wooley, bowl, fluted, imp JW, 2x5½" 325.00

John Cameron & Son, Glascow, presentation wine cooler, with dates of 1901, 1902, and 1903, on ebonized socle stand, 16", $2,500.00.

Paul Storr, condiment, crest on lid, cut crystal liner 300.00
Peter & Ann Bateman, creamer & sugar, Geo III, ea 4½" 325.00
Porter Blanchard, tray, scalloped, logo, 11" 250.00
Redlich, punch bowl, eng floral rocaille at intervals, 8" 2,100.00
Richard Dimes, bowl, rtcl flat hdls, Art Deco, 3" H....................400.00
Richard Dimes, vase, molded rim, spreading ft, 12" 300.00
Robert Jones/John Schofield, salver, Georgian, 7-oz 325.00
Roseph Richardson Jr, sugar urn, dtd 1780, 9½" 2,800.00
Samuel Crosby, tea caddy, Chinaman finial, florals, 5½"............600.00
Samuel Kirk, bowl, emb flowers, elk finial, leaf hdls, 13" 5,000.00
Samuel Kirk, coffeepot, grapevine bands/griffin spout, 12"....... 3,900.00
Samuel Kirk, salver, brite cut, emb floral rim, ftd, 9" sq 385.00
Samuel Kirk, tureen, emb flowers, pineapple finial, 10x11" 2,200.00
Schroth, tea tray, rnded corners, molded rim, 13" L 200.00
Shepherd-Boyd, beaker, bbl shaped, eng name, 3½" 450.00
Steiff, butter dish, repousse, w/liner 350.00
Theo Starr, compote, rtcl foliate rim, 10½", pr 1,200.00
Theo Starr, plate, reeded rim/chased flowers, 10" 350.00
Theo Starr, tea/coffee, fluted/ovoid, eng monogram, 6-pc....... 3,250.00
W Bogert, napkin ring, profile of Roman warrior, 2¼" 400.00
Whiting, ice cream set, parcel gilt, 14-pc, in box 800.00
Wm A Williams, beaker, eng crest, cylindrical, 3½" 1,600.00
Wm B Kerr, bowl, fluted, undulating rim w/flowers, 11" L...........300.00
Wm Forbes, ewer, flowers/scrolls, ftd, tall scroll hdl, 18" 2,800.00
Wm Simmons, teapot, oval cylinder, wood hdl/finial, 5½" 275.00
Wm Thompson, pap boat, scroll hdl, 6½" L 400.00
Wm Waldo Dodge Jr, fruit bowl+tray, striated/hammered, 14" . 1,200.00

Silver Lustre Ware

Much of the ware known as silver lustre was produced in the early 1800s in Staffordshire, England. This type of earthenware was entirely covered with the metallic silver glaze. It was most popular prior to 1840 when the technique of electroplating was developed and silverplated wares came into vogue. Later in the century, artisans used silver lustre to develop designs on vases and other decorative ware.

Candlestick, 8", pr 300.00
Figurine, lad in period costume, worn, 7½" 125.00

Jay McKay, Edinburgh, pitcher, armorial crest, ca 1822, 9½", $2,100.00.

John Burt Lyng, beaker, eng border/monogram/1788, 4½" 7,000.00
John Emes, chamberstick, oval w/reed rim, snuffer, 2½" 700.00
John Germon, sugar tongs, openwork arms, shell tops, 5½" 1,200.00
John Langlands, coffeepot, foliate finial, 1796, 28-oz 1,100.00
Joseph Heinrich, hammered, rolled rim, die mk, 3x10" 100.00
Joseph Richardson, mug, eng monogram, dbl-scroll hdl, 5"..... 2,000.00
Joseph Richardson, mug, eng monogram, dbl-scroll hdl, 5"..... 2,000.00
Julius Randahl, bowl, 4-petal form w/openwork leaf ft, 6" 300.00
Kalo, bowl, 4-petal form, monograms, set of 4, lg: 10" 3,000.00
Kalo, tray, rtcl/emb hdls w/berry vines, rnd, 15½" 1,650.00
Kirk, bowl, fruit; repousse, low form w/ped ft, 9" 1,250.00
Kirk, sauce boat, emb florals, 8½" L 400.00
Matthias Lamar, sugar tongs, brite cut/roulette work, 6" 150.00
Newell Harding, pitcher, rustic hdl/grapevine spout, 13" 1,600.00

Jugs from early 19th century: With peafowl and flowers, 5½", $150.00; With black scenic transfers, 5½", $100.00.

Figurine, woman, child, & dolphin, 6¾", NM 85.00
Lion, front ft on ball, 12" L, VG 250.00
Pitcher, emb harlequin pattern, make-do tin hdl & lip, 14" 400.00
Pitcher, Faith, Hope, Charity transfer, silver rim, 5½", EX 95.00
Pitcher, Oriental motif, blk transfer w/mc, base chips, 6" 175.00
Pitcher, ribbed body w/floral medallion, mc floral rim, 6".........185.00
Pitcher, seated man figural, base hairlines, 9"..........................375.00
Pitcher, toby, worn, 5" 95.00
Plaque, May They Ever Be United, blk transfer/mc, 8x9" 250.00
Puzzle jug, rtcl bust in disk body, ftd, 11", G 400.00
Shaker, toby figural, minor wear, 5" 85.00
Vase, wear/scratches, urn form, 12" 225.00

Silver Overlay

The silver overlay glass made during the 1800s was decorated with a cut-out pattern of sterling silver applied to the surface of the ware.

Bottle, scent; gr, floral/scrolls o/l, spherical, 6" 900.00
Bowl, silver forms fr for HP floral, 3-sided, Steiff, 10" 675.00
Decanter, vintage o/l, twist stopper, heavy, 14"...........................850.00
Ice bucket, flowers & leaves o/l, 6x5½"......................................65.00
Loving cup, cranberry, Nouveau o/l, 3-hdl, lg 495.00
Pitcher, scrolling foliage o/l, tapered cylinder, 10" 200.00
Vase, gr, long-stem tulip o/l, baluster, 11½"...............................850.00
Vase, gr, scrolling o/l, baluster, 12" 275.00

Silverplate

Silverplated hollowware is fast becoming the focus of attention for many of today's collectors.

Our advise for this category comes from the Sterling Shop, whose address is in the Directory under Oregon. See also Pairpoint, Silverplate; Railroadiana, Silverplate.

Key: gw — gold wash

Hollow Ware

Basket, bird/flowers on hdl, stag on base, Wilcox, 13x12" 200.00
Bowl, Chippendale style, scalloped, shaped, 10"...........................30.00
Cake basket, rtcl hdl/base, Japanese style, hammered, Derby.......600.00
Candelabra, Rococo shells/scrolls, 4-arm, 1800s, 13", pr.............400.00
Casserole holder, rtcl, ftd, hdls, 18" L 60.00
Centerpc, shell-shape bowl w/cherub & 2 swans, 21" L 800.00
Coffee set, Persian Ataba, emb warriors, Rogers, 3-pc+tray 150.00
Creamer & sugar bowl, shell motif, ftd...25.00
Dish, scroll/leaf/floral motif, 1x8x11"..40.00
Entree dish, 3-part, w/lid, 12" dia 60.00
Goblet, Vintage, 7", pr 30.00

Ice bucket, dbl hdls, thermal, sq ft..65.00
Ice bucket, gadroon border, w/lid, 7" 75.00
Ice bucket, gadrooned, lion's mask hdls, ped ft, Poole, 8½"...........70.00
Ice bucket, staved w/faux screws, liner, Wilcox, 5½" dia.............240.00
Pitcher, appl insects/emb foliage, hammered, Reed/Barton 1,800.00
Pitcher, eng crest w/'1876 & 1901,' porc liner, lid, 11" 75.00
Pitcher, hammered, eng dragonfly/water lilies, Meriden, 10" .. 1,100.00
Platter, narrow floral border, gadrooned, ftd, 16", pr 75.00
Sauce boat, berry hdls...40.00
Sauce boat, gadrooned, crescent form, 8" L 18.00
Tazza, frog on fluted rim, stem support, Derby, 5¾x7" 200.00
Tea service, Japanese style, eng birds, sqd, Tufts, 3-pc.............2,400.00
Tea/coffee, brite cut/emb floral, cylindrical, Racine, 5-pc...........300.00
Tray, chased, shell corners, ftd, 25" L 150.00
Tray, gypsy dancer panel, Assyrian-head border, Meriden, 11"....350.00
Tray, hand chased, scroll border, ftd, 27" L 200.00
Tray, scrolled edge, wood inset center, Rogers, 18" 50.00

Trinket holder with monkey, Tufts, Boston, 3", $250.00.

Waiter, eng fish/sea grass, hammered, Meriden, 12" sq 600.00

Sheffield

Basket, ped base, 8-sided, swing hdl, 1800s, 9" L 100.00
Bowl, leafy fan-scalloped border, oval, 12", pr 75.00
Bun warmer, shell form, wreaths & floral emb, 10" 200.00
Candelabra, emb/chased foliage, Victorian, 19", pr......................350.00
Candelabrum, 5 reeded arms, leaf/scroll border, 1930, 16" 300.00
Candlestick, fluted w/stepped sq base, HE&Co, 12", pr 600.00
Casserole, Brandon Hall, w/lid, Wilcox, 12" W 60.00
Dish, rtcl liner, hot water base, leaf ft, dome lid, 14" 300.00
Dish, shell form, crystal insert, Celtic, 5" L..................................15.00
Entree dish, gadroon border, detachable hdl, w/lid, 10" L 80.00
Ice bucket, lion mask/ring hdls, gadrooned edge, 10x10"............500.00
Punch bowl, shell/scroll band, +19" tray/ladle/12 ftd cups 500.00
Sauce dish, Queen Anne style, Wilkinson, ftd, 3" dia....................20.00
Shell dish, crystal insert, Celtic, 5" L...25.00
Tray, armorial crest, threaded hdls/rim, ftd, Geo III, 25" 475.00
Tray, beaded edge, hand eng, rtcl border, mk, 14" 75.00
Tray, gadrooned w/shells & plumes, etched motif, 17" 100.00
Tray, scroll border, leaf ft, 1900, 16" 125.00

Silver Resist

The process for decorating pottery with the silver-resist method involved first coating the design or that portion of the pattern that was to be left unsilvered with a water-soluble solution. The lustre was applied to the entire surface of the vessel and allowed to dry. Before the final firing, the surface was washed, removing only the silver from the coated areas. This type of ware was produced early in the 1800s by many English potteries, Wedgwood included.

Bough pot, mc reserve w/fisherman, semicircular, 8½", EX..........300.00
Goblet, wide vintage band, wear/stains, 4½" 85.00
Pitcher, allover lg florals, minor wear, 7⅜" 450.00
Pitcher, birds/flowers/name/1811, 5⅜", EX.................................175.00
Pitcher, floral band, emb vintage, minor wear, 6½" 120.00
Pitcher, floral on putty color, wht int, wear/hairlines, 6" 225.00
Vase, 3-neck, allover florals, prof rpr, 6½", EX 350.00

Sinclaire

In 1904 H.P. Sinclaire and Company was founded in Corning, New York. For the first sixteen years of production, Sinclaire used blanks from other glassworks for his cut and engraved designs. In 1920 he established his own glass-blowing factory in Bath, New York. His most popular designs utilize fruits, flowers, and other forms from nature. Most of Sinclaire's glass is unmarked; items that are carry his logo: an 'S' within a wreath with two shields.

Candlestick, gr, eng florals, mushroom top, sgn, 4¾", pr..............125.00
Clock, mantel; dome case w/ribbed silver threading etc, 12"... 3,700.00
Pitcher, step-cut bands, floral bands, notched hdl, ped ft.............650.00
Teapot, carnation intaglio, sgn..2,200.00
Tray, Greek Key & Laurel, 14" 175.00
Tray, Plaid & Thistle, cut/eng, sgn, 14½" 4,200.00
Vase, amber, eng grapes & leaves, ring hdls, 8" 275.00
Vase, Honeycomb & Hobstar, 14" 350.00

Sitzendorf

The Sitzendorf factory began operations in East Germany in the mid 1800s, adopting the name of the city as the name of their company. They produced fine porcelain groups, figurines, etc. in much the same style and quality as Meissen and the Dresden factories. Much of their ware was marked with a crown over the letter 'S.'

Box, fairy w/Nouveau hairdo, pk wings, gold trim, mk, 4¼" 125.00
Candlestick, cherubs stands w/arm around std, 15x7" 350.00
Figurine, girl in floral dress on sofa, man w/violin, 9" L 750.00
Figurine, man on ladder picks apples, girl/dog below, 10" 650.00
Figurine, man w/watering can, lady w/flower basket, 9", pr..........325.00
Figurine, Monkey Band, 6", set of 9 ....850.00
Figurine, slave trader/3 females/seated Roman/2 dogs, 9x17" .. 1,250.00
Figurine, 2 dogs, lady seated on couch, man stands, 9x10" 850.00
Plaque, girl & goat emb on cream, Voigt, 1885, 12" dia 500.00

Slag Glass

Slag glass is a marbleized opaque glassware made by several companies from about 1870 until the turn of the century. It is usually found in purple or caramel (see Chocolate Glass), though other colors were also made. Pink is rare and very expensive.

Pink, Invt Fan & Feather, butter dish 800.00
Pink, Invt Fan & Feather, creamer 450.00

Pink, Invt Fan & Feather, cruet, orig stopper 1,200.00
Pink, Invt Fan & Feather, jelly compote 400.00
Pink, Invt Fan & Feather, pitcher, water 1,450.00
Pink, Invt Fan & Feather, punch cup 265.00
Pink, Invt Fan & Feather, sauce dish, ftd, 4½" 265.00
Pink, Invt Fan & Feather, shakers, pr 800.00
Pink, Invt Fan & Feather, sugar bowl, w/lid 650.00
Pink, Invt Fan & Feather, toothpick holder.................................575.00
Pink, Invt Fan & Feather, tumbler 450.00
Purple, celery, fluted..115.00
Purple, compote, lacy edge, 8x8" 65.00

Purple, lattice-edge plate, 10", $27.50.

Purple, Flower Panel, spooner 60.00
Purple, Paneled Grape, butter dish...65.00
Purple, Sandwich Star, spill...60.00

Smith Bros.

Alfred and Harry Smith founded their glassmaking firm in New Bedford, Massachusetts. They had been formerly associated with the Mt. Washington Glass Works, working there from 1871 to 1875 to aid in establishing a decorating department. Smith glass is valued for its excellent enameled decoration on satin or opalescent glass. Pieces were often marked with a lion in a red shield.

Our advisors for this category are Betty and Clarence Maier; they are listed in the Directory under Pennsylvania.

Atomizer, carnations w/gold, melon shaped, lion mk...................600.00
Biscuit jar, mums/gold floral on cream, melon ribs, SP mts..........800.00
Bowl, emb floral w/gold scrolls, melon ribs, beaded rim, 9"..........325.00
Bowl, oak leaves/acorns in heavy gold, metal rim, mk, 4x8¾" 550.00
Box, gold iris on melon ribs w/much gold trim, 3¼x4" dia...........335.00
Creamer & sugar bowl, mc flowers, SP trim, mk, 2¾", 3½" 415.00
Pitcher, florals around rim, melon ribbed, SP mts, mk, 5" 585.00
Rose bowl, lg pansies on cream, mk, 4¼".....................................310.00
Rose bowl, sm florals, yel on bl, ribbed, 4"...................................275.00
Sugar shaker, pk floral neck band, melon ribbed, no mk, 4¾" 325.00
Sweetmeat, bl florals, ribbed lid, mk, 5¼".....................................635.00
Syrup, daisy swags, melon ribs, metal lid, 5¼" 485.00
Vase, daisies/bouquets on cream, swirled ribs, mk, 7x4" 750.00

Vase, daisies on brn to gold, swirled, gourd form, 7x5".................850.00
Vase, florals & gilt on bl, swirled, lion mk, 6¾" 525.00
Vase, pansies, gold tracery, beaded rim, mk, 6x4" 450.00
Vase, roses, 9" 350.00
Vase, wisteria, purple on cream w/gold, canteen form, 8½"..... **1,250.00**

Snow Babies

During the last quarter of the 19th century, snow babies — little figurals in white snowsuits — originated in Germany. They were made of sugar candy and were often used as decorations for Christmas trees. Later on, they were made of marzipan, a confection of crushed almonds, sugar, and egg whites. Eventually porcelain manufacturers began making them in bisque. They were popular until WWII. These tiny china figures range in size from just over 1" to the very rare jointed babies sometimes nearly 7" tall. Any example brings a very respectable price on the market today. Beware of reproductions.

Angel, sitting, arms outstretched, 1¾" 200.00
Babies, 2 on sled, Germany 150.00

Three babies on sled, Germany, 2½" long, $150.00.

Babies slide down brick wall, #6602, 1⅝x2½" 125.00
Baby, hanging on brass ribbon 40.00
Baby, jtd, good pnt, impish features, 4½".....................................250.00
Baby, lying flat on sled, Germany, 1½" 55.00
Baby, pulling sled, Germany, 2" 65.00
Baby, riding bear, Japan, 2¾" 38.00
Baby, riding snow bear, Germany, 3" 165.00
Baby, sitting, arms outstretched, Germany, 1" 45.00
Baby, sitting, Germany, 2"..95.00
Baby, sitting, Japan, 1"...20.00
Baby, sitting, ⅞"...35.00
Baby, sitting on yel sled, Germany, 1½"...55.00
Baby, standing, Germany, 2½" 75.00
Baby in shell, lg 25.00
Baby on bench, 1½" 55.00
Baby on ice skates, Germany, #3116, 1¾" 150.00
Baby on red airplane, Germany, 2¼" 175.00
Baby on sled pulled by 2 dogs, #7153, 1⅜x3"................................75.00
Baby on snowball, Japan, 2" 40.00
Baby on stomach, googly-eyed, Hertivig & Co, 1915, 2¾" 175.00
Baby plays tuba, mk Germany, 1½"...75.00
Baby standing w/pr of skis, 2" 75.00
Bear, Germany, 1½" 40.00
Bear, Germany, 2⅜" 65.00
Bunny, paw raised, Germany, 2" 95.00
Carollers, 3 stand in snow, lantern above, Germany, 2¼".............100.00

Girl on sled, Germany, #8448, 1¾"...100.00
Igloo, baby inside, Santa on roof, Germany.................................125.00
Man skating on 1 leg..48.00
Penguin, Germany, 4"...65.00
Santa climbs down chimney, 3" 90.00
Seal w/ball, 2" 35.00
Snowman, 1½" 50.00
Twins, joined 75.00

Snuff Boxes

As early as the 17th century, the Chinese began using snuff. By the early 19th century, the practice had spread to Europe and America. It was used by both the gentlemen and the ladies alike, and expensive snuff boxes and bottles were the earmark of the genteel. Some were of silver or gold set with precious stones or pearls, while others contained music boxes. In the following listings, the dimension noted is length. See also Orientalia, Snuff Bottles.

Brass, heart form, 3-compartment, hinged, 1800s, 2x2½" 85.00
Burl, 2¾x3⅜"..150.00
Enamel, figures on landscape, 1700s, 2⅜" 400.00
Papier-mache, lady pnt on blk lacquer lid, 3⅜", EX 95.00
Porc, figural arm, blk lace glove, holds grapes, 1700s, 3".............425.00
Silver, eng foliage, shaped rectangle, Birmingham, 1897, 2"........300.00
Silver, gilt int, jasper stone on lid, eng hunt motif, 2½" 500.00

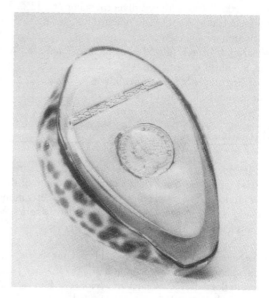

Silver-mounted cowrie-shell snuff box, George II silver sixpence coin dated 1757 set in lid, engraved hinge, signed inside cover, repaired, 3¾" long, $800.00.

Tigereye, front/bk relief-cvd goldfish & foo lion, 3" 90.00
Tortoise shell, inlaid w/gold & silver, English, 3" L 275.00

Soapstone

Soapstone is a soft talc in rock form with a smooth, greasy feel from whence comes its name. In colonial times, it was extracted from out-croppings in large sections with hand saws, carted by oxen to mills, and fashioned into useful domestic articles such as footwarmers, cooking utensils, inkwells, etc. During the early 1800s, it was used to make heating stoves and kitchen sinks. Most familiar today are the carved vases, bookends, and boxes made in China during the Victorian era.

Bookend, jardinere w/trailing plants, China, 3x4", pr 42.50
Candle holder, gray, trapezoidal, 1½x2½x2½" 110.00
Cvg, foo dog, 8" 40.00
Cvg, foo lion, in clouds & flames, cvd base, 9x8½" 80.00
Cvg, foo lions, female w/pup, male w/ball, 6½" L, pr..................90.00
Cvg, Guan Yin, seated, teak stand, 1800s, 5⅜", EX 450.00
Cvg, horse, pk, 6½x6", on teakwood base....................................95.00
Cvg, lady in flowing robes holds incense burner, gr/blk, 8" 125.00
Cvg, Oriental girl, arms over head, holds fruit tray, 13" 125.00
Cvg, pig & piglets, on wooden stand..40.00
Cvg, 2 elephants & palm tree, gr, on teakwood base, 9" L 65.00
Incense burner, foo dogs flank body, 11".....................................50.00
Lamp, urn w/florals & birds cvgs, brass base, 10", +shade 400.00
Plaque, birds & trees, 9½x5½", on soapstone stand......................115.00
Screen, goggle-eye goldfish/seaweed, blk/pk/gr, 7½x5½" 50.00

Double vase with monkeys and bats, 6", $95.00.

Vase, dbl; peonies/vines/birds, 3-color, 9x7" 140.00
Vase, triple; cvd flowers, 9½x6", EX..80.00

Soda Fountain Collectibles

As the neighborhood ice cream parlor becomes a thing of the past, soda fountain memorabilia from fancy backbars to ice cream advertising is becoming a popular field of collecting. One area of interest is the glassware used to serve the more elaborate ice cream concoctions. A sundae glass is familiar to us all, but there was also a 'lucky mondae' glass, narrow at the bottom and flaring to a top dimension equal to one scoop. There are footed banana split dishes and soda pop glasses with the name or logo of the beverage company painted on them.

Syrup dispensers, especially those from the teens, today command high prices. These had spherical or urn-shaped dispensers and carried names such as Jersey Creme, Buckeye, Cherry Smash, etc.

It is estimated that ice cream dippers may be found in approximately two hundred different styles — some bowl shaped or cylindrical, some for making ice cream sandwiches, and even a very rare heart-shaped dipper. (This one was used along with matching heart-shaped ice cream dishes.)

Glass straw holders are very collectible. Clear is the most common color, but they are also found in green and pink; some are made of frosted glass. Early examples were pattern molded; some had matching glass lids — these are the most desirable.

Our advisors for this category are Joyce and Harold Screen; they are listed in the Directory under Maryland. See also Advertising.

Book, recipe; pre-1900, per pg 50
Book, recipe; 1900-20, per pg 25
Bottle, syrup; Fowler's Cherry Smash, label under glass, 12" 200.00
Bowl, glass, crushed fruit, hollow finial 175.00
Bowl, glass, crushed fruit, metal lid 25.00
Catalog, equipment & supply, per illus pg, pre-1900 ....1.00
Catalog, equipment & supply, per illus pg, 1900-20........................75
Catalog, equipment & supply, per illus pg, 1921-35........................50
Change receiver, Abbotts, china...60.00
Container, Borden's Malted Milk, emb polished chrome, pr 450.00
Container, Bowey's Chocolate, porc w/Blk lady, metal lid 550.00
Container, Kraft Malted Milk, aluminum.....................................70.00
Cup, Armour's Bouillon Cubes, china...25.00
Cup, Cudahy's Rexsoma, china...25.00
Dipper, banana split; United, 12", EX 650.00
Dipper, Bohlig...700.00
Dipper, Delmonico, N&Co, key type 75.00
Dipper, Dover #10, nickeled brass, 11", EX..................................75.00
Dipper, Gem, 1895 ....60.00
Dipper, Gilchrist #30, sizes 6 & 30..50.00
Dipper, Gilchrist #30, szs 8 to 24...35.00
Dipper, Gilchrist #31, szs 6, 60, & 40...75.00
Dipper, Gilchrist #31, szs 8 to 24...30.00
Dipper, Gilchrist #33, szs 6 & 20..125.00
Dipper, Gilchrist #33, szs 8 to 24...65.00
Dipper, Hamilton Beach, chrome plated, 10", M 35.00
Dipper, Hamilton Beach, No-Pak...90.00
Dipper, Indestructo #3..45.00
Dipper, Mosteller, bowl flips over..700.00
Dipper, NP brass, cone shape, key release 80.00
Dipper, sandwich; Mayer, curved...300.00
Dipper, sandwich; Mayer, flat..250.00
Dipper, sandwich; Polar-Pak..350.00
Dipper, sandwich; Rainbow Cake Cone Co 350.00
Dipper, tin, cone shape, key release 15.00
Dipper, Zeroll, metal, non-mechanical 15.00
Dish, sundae; clear glass 5.00
Dish, sundae; dbl dip, scalloped edge 30.00
Dish, sundae; pk glass...25.00

Dispenser, Buckeye Root Beer with dancing satyrs, porcelain, replaced pump, rare, 11½" x 7½", EX, $1,400.00.

Dispenser, Birchola, w/orig pump 1,500.00
Dispenser, Cardinal Cherry, w/orig pump 1,500.00
Dispenser, Cherry Chic, w/orig pump.................... 1,500.00
Dispenser, Coca-Cola, urn style............................. 3,000.00
Dispenser, Dr Pepper, urn style.............................. 6,000.00
Dispenser, Fowler's Cherry Smash, cluster only, orig pump 1,200.00
Dispenser, Fowler's Cherry Smash, orig pump........ 1,200.00
Dispenser, fudge; Thompson's, bl crockery 150.00
Dispenser, Grape Ola, bowl top, w/lid, M 1,800.00
Dispenser, Grape Ola, urn top, w/lid, M................ 2,000.00
Dispenser, Green River, clear glass, pnt metal base, 10", EX 225.00
Dispenser, Hires, hourglass style, w/orig pump........500.00
Dispenser, Hires, hourglass type, w/spigot & orig pump........... 1,400.00
Dispenser, Hires, Muni-Maker, salesman's sample.................10,000.00
Dispenser, Howell's Cherry Julep, w/orig pump 1,000.00
Dispenser, Hypo, milk glass base, clear top.............225.00
Dispenser, Lime Crush, orig ball pump, M 1,200.00
Dispenser, Mission, fruit juice, gr 195.00
Dispenser, Mission, orange w/blk amethyst base, pk top, NM......250.00
Dispenser, Root Beer, bbl, wooden 150.00
Fan, soda pop, cb 15.00
Fountain glass, Allen's Red Tame Cherry....................40.00
Fountain glass, banana split; amber, flat 10.00
Fountain glass, banana split; gr, flat 15.00
Fountain glass, banana split; Heisey, flat...................20.00
Fountain glass, goblet, Hayner's Florida Orange emb 20.00
Fountain glass, Howell's Root Beer emb, ribbed, sm......................25.00
Fountain glass, ice cream soda; 'soda fountain' pattern, gr 15.00
Fountain glass, ice cream soda; Ginger-Mint Julep, w/logo 20.00
Fountain glass, ice cream soda; Tea Room, pk.........30.00
Fountain glass, ice cream soda; 7-Up, gr 15.00
Fountain glass, Mondae sundae glass........................30.00
Fountain glass, Nesbitt's, frosted, tall......................10.00
Fountain glass, Richardson's Liberty Root Beer emb, bbl 30.00
Fountain glass, TJ Clement Chambrose Orange Juice, hourglass ...30.00
Ice chipper, Gilchrist #50 ....10.00
Ice cream cone holder, glass, Heisey, ind 40.00
Jug, stoneware, S&H Root Beer Syrup, 12", EX 70.00
Milk shake mixer, Albert Pick & Co, marble base, early, EX 125.00
Milk shake mixer, Gilchrist #22, as found 50.00
Milk shake mixer, Gilchrist #22, polished 100.00
Milk shake mixer, Hamilton Beach, marbled base, as found..........75.00
Milk shake mixer, Hamilton Beach, porc base, 1920s, NM............55.00
Milk shake mixer, Hamilton Beach, repolished to brass 250.00
Milk shake mixer, hand-cranked counter model 400.00
Milk shake mixer, hand-cranked floor model 600.00
Milk shake mixer, Hire's, hand crank 500.00
Milk shake mixer, Horlick's, dbl ped, friction drive motor...........300.00
Milk shake mixer, Minute Made-Rite Mfg, gr pnt, 1930s, VG 75.00
Mug, Berry's Famous Root Beer, bl glaze....................90.00
Mug, Buckeye Root Beer, dbl bl bands, pottery 30.00
Mug, Dr Seett's, cameo high-relief style 200.00
Mug, Hires, fat, Mettlach 80.00
Mug, Richardson's Liberty Root Beer emb, glass, heavy 30.00
Mug, Schuester's of Cleveland Root Beer, glass, bl bands 45.00
Plate, ice cream; product name on china 35.00
Plate, ice cream; product name on waxed cb 15.00
Post card, soda fountain, interior view, blk/wht, post-1920............. 5.00
Post card, soda fountain, interior view, blk/wht, pre-1920.............15.00
Post card, soda fountain, interior view, color, post-1920 .... 5.00
Post card, soda fountain, interior view, color, pre-1920 ....20.00
Sheet music, I Scream, You Scream, We All Scream for..., EX......25.00
Sheet music, Oh, My Eskimo Pie 25.00
Sign, Cherry Blossom, bottle display, cb 60.00

Sign, Cherry Smash, emb cb, 11x6" 125.00
Sign, Grape Ola, tin, 20x13", M 100.00
Sign, ice cream flavors, cb 25.00
Sign, ice cream flavors, rvpt 125.00
Sign, ice cream flavors, tin 50.00
Sign, Sonny Sugar Cones, paper, 19x8", M 35.00
Soda fountain, marble, box style, Tufts, 1880s, very rare 3,500.00
Soda fountain, marble, doghouse style, ND Robbins 2,500.00
Soda fountain, marble cottage 'oracle,' RM Green Co, gr 4,000.00
Soda fountain, Matthews, w/top, rstr 5,000.00
Soda fountain, w/top, Matthews, 1880s, rstr, very rare 5,000.00
Straw dispenser, Hires, M 800.00
Straw dispenser, Sani Server, rnd 200.00
Straw holder, Aztec, gr, sq, w/lid 400.00
Straw holder, Aztec, sq, w/lid.................................300.00
Straw holder, common, w/lid & insert, 10" 100.00
Straw holder, glass, flared base, EX 225.00
Straw holder, gr, nickeled lid, 11", NM 350.00
Straw holder, gr, standard style, 10" 275.00
Straw holder, gr pressed glass w/metal base................325.00
Straw holder, Heisey, Colonial pattern, w/lid 250.00
Straw holder, orig Gilchrist rubber bumper at base 150.00
Straw holder, Prize pattern, w/lid............................300.00
Straw holder, wide mouth, lift lid & straws rise, 11", NM 200.00
Trade card, ice cream freezer 10.00
Trade card, ice cream freezer, mechanical 50.00
Trade card, ice cream related 5.00
Trade card, soda water flavors, EX............................ 3.00
Tray, Arctic Ice Cream, rnd 300.00
Tray, Decoursey's, Kewpie, rectangle 350.00
Tray, Meyer's Ice cream, mother/children, rectangular, M 775.00
Tray, Meyer's Ice Cream, mother/children, rectangular, EX........525.00
Tray, Yuengling's Ice Cream, boy & girl, rnd, M.........................400.00
Tray, Zipp's Cherri-O, rnd, M 500.00

Soft Paste

Soft paste is a low-fired, granular type of porcelain that must be glazed to retain water.

Coffeepot, floral on yel band w/brn lines, dome top, 5½", EX 300.00
Coffeepot, scenes w/ruins, blk transfer, dome top, 9¾", VG 200.00

Pitcher, Nautilus pattern, 6½", $145.00.

Pitcher, Oriental scene, blk transfer w/mc, 5¾", VG 100.00
Plate, Bl Willow, rtcl basketweave rim, 8½"................................125.00
Tea bowl & saucer, Tea Drinkers, Petrous Regout, M....................70.00

Teapot, emb designs w/mc enamel, rpr/damage, 5⅝", VG 650.00
Teapot, granite-like bl, wht & emb blk/wht bands, 7¾", EX 700.00

South Jersey Glass

As early as 1739, Caspar Wistar established a factory in Salem County, taking advantage of the large beds of sand suitable for glass blowing and the abundant forests available for fueling his furnaces. Scores of glassworks followed, many of which were short-lived. It is generally conceded that aside from the early works of Wistar and the Harmony Glass Works, which emerged from the Glassboro factory originally founded by the Strangers, the finest quality glassware was blown after 1800. In the 1850s coal was substituted for the wood as fuel. Though a more efficient source of heat, the added cost of transporting the coal inland proved to be the downfall of many of the smaller factories, and soon many had failed.

Glassware can be attributed to this area through the study of colors, shapes, and decorative devices that were favored there; but because techniques were passed down through generations of South Jersey glass blowers, without documentation it is usually impossible to identify the specific factory that produced it.

Our advisor for this category is Mark Vuono; he is listed in the Directory under Connecticut.

Bottle, cranberry bands & wht loops, powder horn form, 12" 225.00
Bowl, clear w/wht loopings, ftd, 5¾" H 175.00
Bowl, sapphire, folded-over lip, thickly made, ftd, 5x6" 300.00
Creamer, aqua, flaring lip w/pouring spout, crude hdl, 3¾" 250.00
Creamer, dk bl, arched lip, crimped ear hdl, solid ft, 4" 500.00
Jug, aqua, ribbed/globular, appl ft, crude hdl, 4½", NM 800.00
Jug, bright aqua, globular w/thick hdl, crimped ft, 6½" 550.00
Mug, cobalt, str sides, tooled lip, folded hdl end, 3" 250.00
Pitcher, aqua, lily pads, curled-end hdl, appl base, 8x6" 2,200.00
Pitcher, bl-gr, nearly str neck, crimped ft, ear hdl, 4¾" 550.00
Pitcher, dk aqua, flared threaded lip, solid ft, lg hdl, 6" 850.00
Pitcher, dk sapphire, type-1 lily pads, 7", NM 2,400.00
Pitcher, lt gr, 4 lily-pad pulls, threaded lip, 6" 800.00

Free-blown pitcher, medium green, tooled lip, pontil scar, 4¾", $3,500.00.

Salt, aqua, dbl ogee, threaded lip, 2", +witch ball cover 650.00
Sugar bowl, grass gr, w/witch ball cover, total H: 5¼" 2,600.00
Vase, aqua w/wht loopings, 3 appl rings on stem, 6⅝" 500.00

Southern Folk Pottery

Southern Folk Pottery is vernacular ware produced by a small group of Southern potters, many of whom are descendents of 19th-century potters. Rich alkaline glazes (lustrous greens and browns) are typical, and occasionally shards of glass are applied to the surface of the ware which during firing melts to produce opalescent 'glass runs' over the alkaline. In some locations, clay deposits contain elements that result in areas of fluorescent blue or rutile; another varation is swirled or striped ware, reminescent of 18th-century agateware from Staffordshire. The most recognizable form of Southern folk pottery is the face jug. Collector demand for these unique one-of-a-kind jugs is at an all-time high and is still escalating. Choice examples made by Burlon B. Craig and Lanier Meaders often bring over $1,000 on the secondary market. If you're interested in learning more about this type of folk pottery, contact the Southern Folk Pottery Collectors Society; their address is in the Directory under Clubs, Newsletters, and Catalogs. Our advisor for this category is the club's founder, Roy Thompson; he is listed in the Directory under Connecticut.

Face jugs: by Burlon B. Craig, 12", $385.00; by Lanier Meaders, quartz teeth, 11", $3,520.00.

Face jug, alkaline w/glass runs, hdls, mk C Lisk, 3-gal.................495.00
Face jug, bl/wht/brn swirl, C Lisk, 2-gal, 13" 528.00
Face jug, cigar in mouth, brn, sgn Brown's Pottery, 8" 176.00
Face jug, devil w/snake, alkaline, hdls, sgn BR Hussy, 21" 330.00
Face jug, typical glaze, Javan Brown, stamped mk, 1930, 6" 2,200.00
Figure, pig, brn/dk brn, sgn Marie Rogers, 7" L.........................121.00
Figure, rooster w/snake, sgn E Meaders, 16"...............................412.50
Figure, Watermelon Eater, polychromed, sgn BR Hussy, 8" 412.50
Wig stand, face w/porc teeth, alkaline, sgn C Hewell, 10" 220.00

Spangle Glass

Spangle glass, also known as Vasa Murrhina, is cased art glass characterized by the metallic flakes embedded in its top layer. It was made both abroad and in the United States during the latter years of the 19th century, and it was reproduced in the 1960s by the Fenton Art Glass Company.

Vasa Murrhina was a New England distributor who sold glassware of this type manufactured by a Dr. Flower of Sandwich, Massachusetts. Flower had purchased the defunct Cape Cod Glassworks in 1885 and used the facilities to operate his own company. Since none of the ware was marked, it is very difficult to attribute specific examples to his manufacture. See also Art Glass Baskets; Fenton.

Basket, mc w/silver mica, appl branch hdl, ruffled, 4x5" 65.00
Basket, wht, int: pk to wht w/mica, melon ribbed, Mt WA, 6"....235.00
Bowl, mc spatter w/silver mica, 8-crimp, 5x5" 85.00

Cruet, clear to bl, silver mica, Hobbs & Brockunier......................275.00
Pitcher, salmon pk to lt gold w/mica, amber hdl, 6".....................125.00
Rose bowl, bl & wht spatter w/mica, 8-crimp, 3x3½" 88.00
Rose bowl, bl shaded w/mica, 3¾"..95.00
Rose bowl, pk w/coral-like mica, 8-crimp, 3⅜x3½".....................110.00
Tumbler, amber & bl w/silver flecks, MN...................................70.00
Vase, brn w/mica, cranberry int, swirled, bulbous, 10x5" 145.00
Vase, pk & gr swirl, wht cased, 8" 160.00
Vase, pk overlay w/silver mica, vaseline hdls, 9⅞"......................95.00
Vase, pk w/gold mica & applied cherries, ruffled, 8½", pr............550.00
Vase, pk w/silver mica, clear hdl & rim, ewer form, 9⅜".............135.00
Vase, pk w/silver mica, clear ruffled rim, 8⅞" 85.00

Vase, red-cased tortoise shell with gold mica, 7", $150.00.

Vase, red w/silver mica, bulbous/ruffled, 7½x4½"........................175.00
Vase, yel w/allover silver mica, crystal edge, wht int, 4"................65.00

Spatter Glass

Spatter glass, characterized by its multicolor 'spatters,' has been made from the late 19th century to the present by American glass houses as well as those abroad. Although it was once thought to have been made entirely by workers at the 'end of the day' from bits and pieces of leftover scrap, it is now known that it was a standard line of production. See also Art Glass Baskets.

Basket, gold/pk/wht, crimped, clear thorn hdl, 6x5½x6" 165.00
Box, mc, appl clear petal, fruit finial, 5x5½" 75.00
Cruet, bl/wht, clear hdl, lapidary stopper, Mt WA, 8" 225.00
Cruet, pk & gr w/opaque lining, clear hdl & stopper, 6" 65.00
Cruet, yel & wht, amber hdl, cut amber stopper, 5½" 135.00
Muffineer, Ribbed Pillar, cranberry & wht 98.00
Pitcher, gr/wht/bl, gr hdl, 10x5½"..95.00
Pitcher, Invt T'print, maroon/wht, rnd mouth, bulbous, 8¼" 125.00
Pitcher, mc swirl w/8 glass rings at base, clear hdl, 6"...................85.00
Pitcher, rust/bl/wht, swirled ribs, clear hdl, 9" 80.00
Salt cellar, cranberry cased in crystal, SP rim, 1⅜x2⅜" 70.00
Salt cellar, maroon/pk/wht, cylindrical, clear ft/hdl, 3" L............120.00
Tumbler, maroon/pk/wht/yel/gr swirl, 3¾x2¾" 50.00
Tumbler, pk/yel/wht swirl, 3¾x2¾" 45.00
Vase, mc swirl, cased, cupped neck, 10", pr 250.00

Spatterware

Spatterware is a general term referring to a type of decoration used

by English potters beginning in the late 1700s. Using a brush or a stick, brightly-colored paint was dabbed onto the soft-paste earthenware items, achieving a spattered effect which was often used as a border. Because much of this type of ware was made for export to the United States, some of the subjects in the central design — the schoolhouse and the eagle patterns, for instance — reflect American tastes. Yellow, green, and black spatterware is scarce and highly valued by collectors.

In the descriptions that follow, the color listed after the item indicates the color of the spatter. The central design is identified next, and the color description that follows that refers to the design.

Bowl, waste; red, peafowl, 4-color, 3x6" dia, EX........................375.00
Child's set, purple, Staffordshire, 5" pot, cr/sug, 4 c/s 300.00
Coffeepot, bl, rose, red, sm rpr, 9" 370.00
Creamer, brn, rose, pk/gr, 3½" 375.00
Creamer, rainbow, red/bl, stains/chips, 5½".............................265.00
Creamer, red, peafowl, 3-color, 4", EX....................................350.00
Mug, purple, 2¾", EX 225.00
Pitcher, rainbow, 5-color stripes, short hairlines, 8¾" 750.00
Plate, bl, house in yel, 9½", M 1,200.00
Plate, bl, peafowl, 4-color, 9½" 450.00
Plate, bl, pomegranate, 3-color, 9½" 550.00
Plate, marbleized bl/gr, wear/sm rim flakes, 8½" 50.00
Plate, marbleized bl/gr, 6"...65.00
Plate, purple, floral transfer, T Walker, 10", NM 75.00
Plate, rainbow, bl/gr/red, glued hairline/sm chips, 7"..................75.00
Plate, rainbow, bl/purple, wear/stains, 9½"..............................125.00
Platter, bl, rose, 3-color, 13½", EX...550.00
Saucer, red, parrot, 5⅝"..250.00
Saucer, red, peafowl on bar, 4-color, 5¾"................................350.00
Sugar bowl, bl, windmill, 3-color, w/lid, 4"..............................600.00
Tea bowl, handleless; bl, mini, EX 45.00
Tea bowl, marbleized bl/gr..55.00
Tea bowl & saucer, bl, rooster, 4-color, NM............................725.00
Tea bowl & saucer, red/bl border 275.00
Teapot, bl, dove, 3-color, rnd ft, 6¼" 900.00
Teapot, bl/purple mottle, rpr/sm chips, 10" 175.00
Teapot, red/yel, thistle, red/gr, rpr lid, 9", EX 1,000.00

Spelter

Spelter figurines are cast from commercial zinc and coated with a metallic patina. The result is a product very similar to bronze in appearance, yet much less expensive.

Bookends, Gothic Bldg style, 1930, pr 20.00
Box, semi-nude seated on Oriental rug atop, Austria, 4x6x4" 200.00
Bust, Geo Washington, Fabrications Francais, gilt, 8½" 200.00
Bust, Nouveau lady w/floral garlands in hair, Coudray, 17"..... 1,200.00
Ewer, allover repousse, 1800s, 16" 75.00
Figurine, Cavalier, drawn sword, shell/scroll plinth, 14" 250.00
Figurine, German Shepherd, onyx plinth, 5"...............................75.00
Figurine, Joan D'Arc, after Gomeux, marble base, 1900, 13".......600.00
Figurine, seated young hunter w/gold, gilt trim, 1800s, 8"...........225.00
Figurine, 3 putti wrestle goat, after Rancoulet, gilt, 10" 300.00
Lamp, 12" seated Buddha, 1920s, 27", pr....................................200.00
Mirror, child plays w/crescent Man in the Moon, 12" dia............200.00
Torchiere, cupid figural, 3-light, 27"..150.00

Spode-Copeland

The Spode Works was established in 1770 and continued to operate under that title until 1843. Their earliest products were typical underglaze blue-printed patterns, though basalt was also made. After 1790 a translucent porcelain body was the basis for a line of fine enamel-decorated dinnerware. Stone china was introduced in 1805, often in patterns reflecting an Oriental influence.

In 1833 Wm. Taylor Copeland purchased the company, continuing business in much the same tradition. During the last half of the 19th century, Copeland produced excellent parian figures and groups with such success that many other companies attempted to reproduce his work. He employed famous painters to decorate plaques, vases, and tablewares, many examples of which were signed by the artist. Most of the Copeland wares are marked with one of several variations that incorporate the firm name. Today the company is owned by Royal Worcester Ltd. and operates under the name of Royal Worcester Spode Ltd.

Bottle, scent; birds/flowers, pear form, 4", VG 80.00
Bowl, floral cluster transfer, 14" 170.00
Bowl, fruit; Billingsley Rose 18.00
Bowl, fruit; Patricia 22.00
Bowl, fruit; Rosebud Chintz 12.00
Bowl, vegetable; Patricia, oval 75.00
Butter pat, Billingsley Rose 12.50
Coffee can & saucer, Kakiemon, 1820, 5" dia 180.00
Coffeepot, Camilla, pk 150.00
Cream soup, Rosebud Chintz, w/liner 60.00
Creamer, Billingsley Rose 35.00
Creamer & sugar bowl, Camilla, pk 75.00
Creamer & sugar bowl, Patricia, w/lid 85.00
Cup & saucer, Billingsley Rose 25.00
Cup & saucer, Camilla, pk 35.00
Cup & saucer, demitasse; Billingsley 20.00
Cup & saucer, demitasse; Buttercup 15.00
Cup & saucer, demitasse; Raeburn 14.50
Cup & saucer, demitasse; Tower, red 17.50
Cup & saucer, Fairy Dell 18.00
Cup & saucer, Patricia 39.00
Cup & saucer, Royal Windsor, gr 29.00
Cup & saucer, Wickerdale 29.00

Copeland dessert service, each piece titled and signed Birbeck, 8 comports, 12 plates, late 1800s, $5,000.00.

Flowerpot, rural view, dolphin hdls, gilt, +stand, 6½" 750.00
Mug, Christmas Tree, 2-hdl, child's sz 18.00
Pitcher, Drabware, Golfing, cream on dk gr, 1900, 4¾" 425.00
Pitcher, milk; bl & wht figures, Copeland 60.00
Plate, Billingsley Rose, dinner sz 20.00
Plate, Billingsley Rose, luncheon sz 18.00
Plate, chop; Tower, Spode, 12" 45.00
Plate, Death of the Bear, bl transfer, 1805, 9¾" 150.00

Plate, Fairy Dell, 6" 15.00
Plate, Fairy Dell, 10½" 29.00
Plate, Fairy Dell, 8" 25.00
Plate, Patricia, dinner sz 35.00
Plate, Reynolds, dinner sz 29.00
Plate, Rosebud Chintz, dinner sz 30.00
Plate, Tower, pink, Spode, 5¼" 15.00
Platter, Cowslip, Spode, 13" 65.00
Platter, Rosebud Chintz 45.00
Platter, Willis, Stone China, #2147, 1820, 14½" 200.00
Soup, Tower, bl, rimmed, Spode 20.00
Teapot, bands of leaves, gilt on lt bl, oval, 1815, 8" W 125.00
Teapot, Rose Briar, +4 demi c/s 85.00
Vase, Fitzhugh, iron red, cylindrical, 1875, 11", pr 200.00
Vase, florals, stoneware, baluster, 10", pr 325.00

Spongeware

Spongeware is a type of factory-made earthenware that was popular during the last quarter of the 19th century. It was decorated by dabbing color onto the drying ware with a sponge, leaving a splotched design at random or in simple patterns. Sometimes a solid band of color was added. The vessel was then covered with a clear glaze and fired at a high temperature. Blue on white is the most preferred combination, but green on ivory, orange on white, or those colors in combination may also occasionally be found.

Bowl, bl on yellowware, rim spout, wire bail, 3½x5½" 80.00
Bowl, bl/wht, pattern sponging, scalloped hdls, 9" 300.00
Bowl, bl/wht, scalloped, minor edge chips, 9" L 125.00
Bowl, bl/wht, w/lid, mini, 3⅛" dia, EX 95.00
Bowl, bl/wht, wht band, 6x13", EX 275.00
Bowl, bl/wht, 2x4½", NM 200.00
Bowl, bl/wht, 4¾x9¾", VG 65.00
Bowl, orange/bl on grayish ground, minor wear, 5x8½" dia 235.00
Cup & saucer, bl/wht, heavy sponging 225.00
Cuspidor, bl/wht, bl stripes, 5x7½" dia 175.00

Pitcher, American Beauty Rose, heavy blue sponging on white, 9", M, $485.00.

Pitcher, bl/wht, can neck, bulbous bottom, 9½" 425.00
Pitcher, bl/wht, str sides, 9", VG 275.00
Pitcher, bl/wht, tankard form, hairlines, 9" 325.00
Pitcher, gr/cream, 7", NM 45.00
Plate, bl/wht, mfg flaw, 9¼" 85.00
Platter, bl/wht, Trenton NJ, 12x8" 325.00

Platter, bl/wht, 12¾" **325.00**
Sauce boat, bl/wht, lion & unicorn mk, 7" L **300.00**
Teapot, bl/wht, minor edge flakes, 7" **950.00**
Tray, bl/wht, scalloped, 11¼" L **225.00**

Spoons

Souvenir spoons have been popular remembrances since the 1890s. The early hand-wrought examples of the silversmith's art are especially sought and appreciated for their fine craftsmanship. Commemorative, personality-related, advertising, and those with Indian busts or floral designs are only a few of the many types of collectible spoons. Our advise for this cagegory comes from the Sterling Shop, whose address is in the Directory under Oregon. In the following listing, spoons are entered by city, character, or occasion.

Key:
B — bowl   FF — full figure
BR — bowl reverse   GW — gold wash
emb — embossed   H — handle
eng — engraved   HR — handle reverse

Admiral Dewey finial H; US Asiatic Squadron in B; Alvin **30.00**
Alligator FF H; Govt House Brinidad view emb in B **42.50**
Atlantic City NJ eng in B; golfer emb on H **27.50**
Baby in scales emb on H; plain B; Watson.................................**34.00**
Boston & pot of beans emb on H; State House view emb in B **15.00**
Boston & seal on H; State House on HR; plain B; Wallace..........**35.00**
Bromley's Sanitarium Sonora CA eng in B; stork FF H................**55.00**
Brooklyn Bridge emb in B; state seal finial H; Gorham **35.00**
Brooklyn Bridge view emb on H; Oct 18, '02 on HR; plain B **78.00**
Bunker Hill Monument FF H; Bunker Hill emb in B **42.00**
Catalina, harbor view in B; tuna forms shaft of H; 5" **48.00**
Catalina Island eng in B; lg fish finial H...................................**27.50**
Chicago cutout w/bird finial H; plain B; Watson **32.00**
Christmas bells w/gr pnt holly on H; plain B; Gorham...............**27.50**
Daniel Boone emb on H; plain B; Frank Smith **20.00**
Danville IL emb on H; Soldiers Home/Court House emb in B **48.00**
Easter egg finial H: emb Easter in B...**25.00**
Easter/flowers/cross eng in GW B; cherub finial H; Watson **22.50**
Empire State & Capitol buildings on H; Brooklyn Bridge in B......**25.00**
Fish finial H; Norris eng in B; Tammer......................................**45.00**
Flathead CO High School, Kalispell MT, globe finial H **32.00**
Floral emb H; Delaware Water Gap eng in GW B; Shiebler..........**25.00**
French Market New Orleans emb in B; alligator FF H; Watson ...**65.00**
Ft Monroe entrance emb in B; fish finial H **20.00**
Galveston TX, sailboat emb in GW B; fish emb on H **45.00**
Golden State Bridge view emb in B; bear & redwood H; Watson .**20.00**
Goldenrod finial H: verse eng in B...**32.00**
Grover Cleveland emb on H; White House view in B...................**20.00**
Honolulu/pineapple/state seal emb on H; plain B; Meyer Bros **57.50**
Indian chief finial H; Arch Rock view in GW B; Alvin **22.50**
Indian emb on H; Milwaukee, lady w/mugs on beer bbl eng in B ..**32.00**
Indian finial H; monument view in B..**22.00**
Indian head finial H w/mc enamel; Niagara Falls view in B **48.00**
Indianapolis & race cars emb on H; race scene in B..................**62.50**
Indianapolis 500, race car/balloons/biplane in B; 1915 on H.......**100.00**
Jacksonville FL emb in B; alligator FF H....................................**65.00**
Jacksonville FL in GW B; 1892 eng on H; Pat 1889, demi **34.00**
Jacksonville on H w/alligator finial; plain B **17.50**
Jamestown Expo, Pocahontas saves Capt Smith emb in B **85.00**
Kansas, sunflower on H; capitol building in B **30.00**
Knights of Columbus & pnt cross on H; plain B; Watson **30.00**

Lake Placid NY eng in heart-shaped B; cherub finial H; Watson .**32.00**
Library Park Ogdensburg NY mc view in B; scroll H; 1907 on HR ..**80.00**
Little Red Riding Hood hdl, 1895..**30.00**
McKinley & eagle emb on H; plain B; dtd HR............................**55.00**
Miles Standish emb on H; plain B; Durgin **18.00**
Mission Delores San Francisco CA emb in B; rose finial H **27.50**
Mount Vernon scenes emb on H & HR; scenes emb in B.............**20.00**
Mt Hood view eng in B; salmon FF H...**32.00**
Mt Hood/Portland OR in B; chinook salmon forms shaft of H **45.00**
Mt Rainier & Seattle emb on H; plain B; Meyer & Co.................**42.50**
Music Hall, Cincinnati in B; Indian emb H; Indians emb HR **225.00**
N Carolina & emb scene on H; Asheville eng in B; Watson.........**25.00**
New Jersey w/state seal finial H: eng monument in B; Gorham.....**27.50**
New Orleans, cotton & crescent emb on H; plain B; Gorham........**30.00**
New Orleans, pelican & cotton bale on H; plain B; Durgin...........**22.00**
New Orleans & Andrew Jackson on H; monument emb in B........**32.00**
New Orleans on H; Jackson monument on HR; plain B **35.00**
New Orleans w/pelican on nest finial H; Mother eng in B............**27.50**
New York 1647 w/emb figure finial H; Brooklyn Bridge eng in B ...**55.00**
Niagara Falls emb in B; Indian FF H; Ellis, 5¾" **135.00**
North Dakota & crest emb on H; plain B; Gorham **20.00**
Obelisk on H; pyramid & sphinx emb in GW B; Gorham.............**78.00**
Old Point Comfort scenes on H & HR; emb view in B; Shepard ..**25.00**
Old South Church Boston emb in B; Boston & hub on H.............**20.00**
Oswego NY & building on H; harbor view & 1755 in B; Gorham..**48.00**
Pagoda finial H; GW in plain B; Oriental mk **24.00**
Pikes Peak & tram on H; Signal Station view emb in GW B.........**20.00**
Pope Leo XIII emb on hdl, view in B; Dominic & Haff **37.50**
Poughkeepsie NY eng in B; holly emb on H; Whiting **22.50**
Priest FF H; Riverside CA & mission bell emb in B **24.00**
Princeton University, tiger & cannon on H; view in B; Durgin.....**48.00**
Rocky Mountains & miners emb on H; miners emb in B.............**38.00**
Royal Poinciana, Palm Beach FL in B; Blk Boy bust emb on H.....**50.00**
Rubenstein finial H; plain B; Watson **30.00**

Salem Witch, $75.00.

San Antonio emb on H; Alamo view emb in B **25.00**
San Francisco/crest/shovel emb on H; plain GW B; Durgin **22.50**
San Miguel Church Santa Fe 1580 eng in B; scroll H; Gorham.....**32.00**
Santa Rosa & enameled grapes on H; plain B; demi.....................**22.50**
Saratoga & Indian emb on H: plain B; Durgin **22.50**
Seattle WA eng in B; totem pole FF H..**20.00**
South Bend IN, Court House scene in B; scenes on H; Watson **32.00**
St Louis, bridge emb in B; crowned man's bust finial H **85.00**
St Maries eng in B; waterfall & state seal emb on H **18.00**
Statue of Liberty FF H; GW B; Tiffany, 6" **135.00**
Stork FF H; birth data in B; Reed & Barton, 6"...........................**22.50**
Sumter SC eng in B; cut-out holly on H; Alvin **25.00**
Tacoma & Old Bell Tower emb on H; Mt Hood eng in B; Smith ..**42.00**
Totem pole w/Chief cut-out finial H; Olympic view in B.............**24.00**
Uncle Sam FF H; Capitol scene emb in B...................................**88.00**
Washington Monument w/enameled shield on H; Watson **48.00**

Westerly RI & man's head finial H; plain B; Howard, demi...........18.00
Wm Penn FF H; Liberty Bell emb in B 92.50
Wm Penn FF H; plain B; allover GW, Caldwell, demi 37.50
Wolfs Tavern...Chicago 1835 on HR; University of Chicago in B ..38.00
Yellowstone Park, elk/bear on H; Old Faithful Inn emb in B.........38.00
Zodiac, November, Sagitarius on H; plain B; Gorham 27.50

Sporting Goods

Our advisor for this category is Paul Longo; he is listed in the Directory under Massachusetts. See also Target Balls.

Badge, MN Football, football form, NM 9.00
Banner, Our Nat'l Game (football), Giants/Bears, 1948 ....35.00
Baseball, sgn Babe Ruth in bold signature 2,500.00
Baseball, sgn by Ted Williams, EX 60.00
Bat, sgn by Johnny Bench, NM...200.00
Bicycle lamp, H&W Columbia, carbide, lens missing, EX 50.00
Book, Base Ball, AG Spaulding, illus, 1911, 542-pg, VG 50.00
Book, How To Play Your Best Golf..., Armour, 1953, EX 10.00
Booklet, Milwaukee Braves Baseball Instruction, Ford, 1960s 10.00
Bowl, ceramic, red sports figures on wht, Wheaties, 1930s 45.00
Cup, collapsible; brass & chrome, Cyclist Cup on lid, 3" 50.00

Gillette flip movie book with Paul Richards, 1957, $15.00.

Jackie Robinson Baseball Game, 1950s, EX, in VG box, $500.00.

St. Clair

The St. Clair Glass Company began as a small family-oriented operation in Elwood, Indiana, in 1941. Most famous for their lamps, the family made numerous small items of carnival, pink and caramel slag, and custard glass as well. Later, paperweights became popular production pieces; many command considerably high prices on today's market. Weights are stamped and usually dated, while small production pieces are often unmarked.

Bell, Bicentennial; carnival glass, Joe St Clair................................12.00
Bottle, mc pulled ribbon w/matching stopper, Joe St Clair 95.00
Marble, bl & wht swirl, polished pontil, Joseph Rice, 2" 50.00
Paperweight, owl stands in center, Joe St Clair, 1½".....................78.00
Paperweight, wht Lincoln head on cobalt, sgn Joe St Clair 45.00
Plate, Bicentennial, gr carnival, Joe St Clair, 5½" 30.00
Salt cellar, basket on wheelbarrow, caramel slag 18.00
Toothpick holder, Cactus, golden agate, early 95.00
Toothpick holder, Cherry Wreath, cobalt, mk 25.00
Toothpick holder, Grand Opening 71, marigold.............................35.00
Toothpick holder, Indian Chief, chocolate slag, Joe St Clair.........25.00
Toothpick holder, Invt Fan & Feather, ice gr.................................25.00
Toothpick holder, Sheaf of Wheat, red 35.00
Toothpick holder, Witch, cobalt..45.00
Tumbler, Grape & Cable, caramel slag, Joe St Clair.......................85.00

Staffordshire

Scores of potteries sprang up in England's Staffordshire district in the early 18th century; several remain to the present time. (See also specific companies.) Figurines and groups were made in great numbers; dogs were favorite subjects. Often they were made in pairs, each a mirror image of the other. They varied in heights from 3" or 4" to the largest, measuring 16" to 18". From 1840 until about 1900, portrait figures were produced to represent specific characters, both real and fictional. As a rule, these were never marked.

The Historical Ware listed here was made throughout the district; some collectors refer to it as Staffordshire Blue Ware. It was produced

Golfer's pal, eng wristwatch-type counter, NM 15.00
Helmet, football; Philadelphia Eagles, Rawlings.............................50.00
Jacket, warm-up; Herschel Walker, NJ General, NM 250.00
Manual, American Racing, 1965, NM 15.00
Manual, golf caddy, 1928, EX...25.00
Pennant, Brooklyn Dodgers, 1950, EX...75.00
Pin-bk button, Waldorf Homecoming, 1928, EX............................ 8.00
Program, Indianapolis 500, 1958, 96-pg, EX..................................25.00
Program, Nat'l Hockey League Allstar Game, 1971, M..................30.00
Schedule, Chicago Daily News, Major League Baseball, 1960 ......10.00
Schedule, St Paul Saints, 1949, pocket sz, EX 15.00
Shoes, Joe Dimaggio Baseball Shoes, in photo cover box, EX......300.00
Sign, Nat'l League Baseball Schedule 1912, cb, fr, 16x11", EX ...700.00
Soccer ball, sgn by Pele, M...200.00
Ticket, phantom; Cardinal's 1949 World Series, w/apology...........65.00
Ticket, Super Bowl XIV, 1980, M...40.00
Tintype, baseball team, stamped on bk, 1870s, 9th plate 300.00

as early as 1820; and, because much was exported to America, it was very often decorated with transfers depicting scenic views of well-known American landmarks. Early examples were printed in a deep cobalt. By 1830 a softer blue was favored, and within the next decade black, pink, red, and green prints were used. Although sometimes careless about adding their trademark, many companies used their own border designs that were as individual as their names.

Our advisor for the Historical Blue Ware is Richard Marden; he is listed in the Directory under New Hampshire. See also specific manufacturers.

Key:
blk — black   l/b — light blue
gr — green   m/b — medium blue
d/b — dark blue   m-d/b — medium dark blue

Historical

Basket, Battle of Bunker Hill, d/b, Stevenson, rtcl, 10" W	7,700.00
Bowl, Fairmount Near Philadelphia, d/b, beaded rim, 3x13"	5,100.00
Bowl, Fulham Church Middlesex, d/b, shallow, 11", NM	235.00
Bowl, Hindu Temple, d/b, wht emb border, Rogers, 10"	175.00
Bowl, Pains Hill, Surrey, d/b, beaded rim, Hall, 12", EX	475.00
Bowl, vegetable; Lake George, d/b, Wood, w/lid, 12" L	850.00
Bowl, vegetable; Quebec, d/b, sq, w/lid, Wood, 9½"	1,500.00
Bowl, waste; Mt Vernon, Seat of Late Gen WA, d/b, 5¾"	875.00
Bowl, Wild Rose, m/b, w/lid, 10"	275.00

Coffeepot, Lafayette at Franklin's Tomb on obverse and reverse, 12", EX, $1,900.00.

Compote, English Scenery, d/b, emb scrolls, rstr, 4x10"	400.00
Creamer, Am & Independence, d/b, Clews, 5"	1,500.00
Cup & saucer, Lafayette at Franklin's Tomb, Wood	325.00
Cup & saucer, Virginia Church, d/b, scalloped rim	275.00
Cup plate, Am & Independence, full border, d/b, Clews, 4½"	400.00
Cup plate, Arms of S Carolina, d/b, Mayer, 4"	850.00
Cup plate, Asian Scenery, m/b, Adams, 4"	30.00
Cup plate, Batahal Portugal, d/b, 3⅞", NM	125.00
Cup plate, Castle Garden Battery NY, d/b, Wood, 3⅞"	375.00
Cup plate, Columbus Georgia, m-l/b, Wood Celtic China, 3⅞"	1,000.00
Cup plate, Constitution Grievances, l/b, 4"	450.00

Cup plate, Coronation, d/b, Adams, 3⅞"	65.00
Cup plate, English Country House, m/b, Enoch Wood, 3¾"	95.00
Cup plate, Entrance to Blaize Castle, l/b, 2¾"	95.00
Cup plate, Fr View, Stone Bridge (1 arch), d/b, 3½", NM	95.00
Cup plate, Landing of Lafayette, d/b, Clews, 4¾"	375.00
Cup plate, Man & Dog in Woods, d/b, Wood, 3⅝"	160.00
Cup plate, Quebec, d/b, Clews, Cities Series, 3⅞"	1,200.00
Cup plate, Scudder's Am Museum, d/b, Stevenson, 4"	1,600.00
Cup plate, Vase w/Flowers, d/b, partial transfer, 3½"	65.00
Cup plate, View Near Conway NY, pk, Jackson, 4⅛"	235.00
Cup plate, 3-Story House, d/b, Wood, no border, 3⅝"	120.00
Fruit basket, canal scene/ext: wild roses, d/b, 12", +tray	600.00
Gravy boat, Sussex Place, Regents Park, d/b, Wood, 4", EX	225.00
Gravy ladle, 4 Men in a Boat, d/b, Wood, shell border, rstr	425.00
Leaf dish, Cokethorpe Oxfordshire, d/b, Hall, EX	275.00
Mug, English Manor House, d/b, str sides, Riley, 4½"	400.00
Pitcher, Erie Canal View of Aqueduct Bridge..., d/b, 6½"	1,250.00
Pitcher, Hudson River Near Fort Miller, red, 7¾"	325.00
Pitcher, Seal of US, d/b, EX/sharp, melon form, 6½", EX	6,400.00
Pitcher, Welcome Lafayette, Nations Guest, d/b, Clews, 8", EX	950.00
Plate, Am & Independence, d/b, Clews, 8"	250.00
Plate, B&O RR (incline), d/b, Wood, circular center, 9"	600.00
Plate, B&O RR (level), d/b, Wood, 10"	650.00
Plate, Beach at Brighton, d/b, E Wood & Sons, 10", EX	450.00
Plate, Boston State House, m-d/b, Wood, 6½", NM	80.00
Plate, British Views, d/b, fruit & flower border, 8¼"	100.00
Plate, Cadmus, d/b, Wood, shell border, 10"	650.00
Plate, Capital Washington DC, d/b, Stevenson & Wms, 10"	475.00
Plate, City Hall NY, brn, Jackson, 10½"	70.00
Plate, City Hall NY, m/b, Ridgway, Beauties of Am, 9¾"	225.00
Plate, Columbia College NY, d/b, Stevenson, 7½"	400.00
Plate, Commodore MacDonnough's Victory, d/b, shell rim, 8¾"	350.00
Plate, Commodore MacDonnough's Victory, d/b, Wood, 10"	475.00
Plate, Cupid & Psyche, d/b, Adams, 8"	150.00
Plate, East View of LaGrange Residence..., d/b, E Wood, 9"	150.00
Plate, Erie Canal Views, d/b, rare, 5⅝"	575.00
Plate, Exchange Baltimore, d/b, Henshall Wmson & Co, 10"	500.00
Plate, Fairmount Near Philadelphia, d/b, Stubbs, 10"	325.00
Plate, Fall of Montmorenci Near Quebec, d/b, Wood, 9"	300.00
Plate, Fort Montgomery, Hudson River, l/b, Clews, 5¾"	95.00
Plate, Harvard College, d/b, Stevenson, 8½", NM	275.00
Plate, Harvard College, sepia, Enoch Wood, 10½"	135.00
Plate, Hobart Town NY, d/b, Clews Cities Series, 9"	275.00
Plate, House w/Fountain in Foreground, Springvale, d/b, 4¾"	110.00
Plate, Insane Hospital Boston, c/s, 7", EX	275.00
Plate, Kosciusco's Tomb, l/b, Ridgway's Catskill Moss, 10½"	85.00
Plate, Landing of Gen Lafayette, d/b, Clews, 9"	225.00
Plate, Landing of the Fathers, m/b, Wood, 10"	150.00
Plate, Landing of the Fathers, m/b, Wood, 8½"	125.00
Plate, Mitchell & Freeman's China Warehouse, d/b, Adams, 8"	575.00
Plate, Narrows From Fort Hamilton, l/b, Ridgway, 7"	125.00
Plate, Narrows From Fort Hamilton, m/b, Goodwin, 10¾"	125.00
Plate, Narrows From Fort Hamilton, pk, Mellor Venables, 9½"	150.00
Plate, Near Fishkill, d/b, Clews Cities Series, 7¾"	325.00
Plate, Near Sandy Hill Hudson River, l/b, Clews, 7¾"	95.00
Plate, Niagara (sheep sheering), d/b, Stevenson, 10"	275.00
Plate, NY, pk, Adams, 6", NM	55.00
Plate, NY Battery (Flagstaff Pavilion), d/b, Stevenson, 7"	425.00
Plate, Park Theatre NY (4 portraits)/Aqueduct Bridge, 10"	3,400.00
Plate, Pass in Catskill Mtns, m/b, Wood, Celtic China, 6¾"	165.00
Plate, Residence of Late Richard Jordan NJ, l/b, 9", EX	175.00
Plate, Shannondale Springs VA, red, Adams, 7¾", EX	65.00
Plate, Ship Under Half Sail, d/b, Wood, shell border, 5¾"	350.00
Plate, States...Bldg, Sheep on Lawn, d/b, Clews, 8¾", NM	350.00

Plate, Steamboat, d/b, diorama border, 10¼" 375.00
Plate, Table Rock Niagara, d/b, Wood, glaze wear, 10" 225.00
Plate, Texian Campaign, gr, 9½" 175.00
Plate, toddy; Conway, purple, Jackson, 5" 235.00
Plate, toddy; Residence of...Richard Jordan, dk brn, 5¾" 275.00
Plate, Union Line, d/b, Wood, shell border, 10" 400.00
Plate, Univ Bldg (6 chimneys/2 people/8 sheep), d/b, 8¾" 250.00
Plate, View From Ruggles House, l/b, Ridgway, 10¾" 95.00
Plate, View Near Conway, pk, Adams, 9" 85.00
Plate, View of Liverpool, d/b, Wood, shell border, 10" 300.00
Plate, Vue Prise en Savoie, d/b, Enoch Wood, 7½" 135.00
Plate, Washington's Tomb, d/b, Wood, 10" 550.00
Plate, West Point, Hudson River, l/b, Clews, 7⅞" 125.00
Plate, Winter View of Pittsfield MA, d/b, Clews, 10½" 325.00
Plate, Wm Penn's Treaty, l/b, 9½" 125.00
Platter, Albany, l/b, Meigh, cut corners, 13½" 275.00
Platter, Albany, sepia, Meigh's Am Cities & Scenery, 13½" 275.00
Platter, All Souls College, l/b, Ridgway, 21" 400.00
Platter, All Souls College, m/b, well & tree, 21" 950.00
Platter, Alms House NY, d/b, Ridgway, Beauties of Am, 17" . 1,500.00
Platter, Arms of Delaware, d/b, Mayer, Arms of States, 17" 2,900.00
Platter, Boston State House, d/b, Rogers, 12", M 1,450.00
Platter, Christianburg...Gold Coast, d/b, Wood, 18½" 3,100.00
Platter, Church of St Charles/Polytechnic..., d/b, Hall, 19"..........525.00
Platter, Columbus OH, d/b, Clews Cities Series, 14½" 3,800.00
Platter, Detroit, d/b, Clews, rim rpr, rare, 18½" 2,800.00
Platter, From Fishkill Hudson River, sepia, Clews, 15½" 275.00
Platter, Hudson, l/b, Ridgway, Catskill Moss, 17" 325.00
Platter, Hunters Shooting Ducks, d/b, 13¼" 650.00
Platter, Lake George NY, d/b, Wood, shell border, 16½" 1,200.00
Platter, Moose & Hunters, d/b, Hall's Quadruped Series, 15" . 1,300.00
Platter, Near Weehawken, l/b Ridgway's Catskill Moss, 15" 325.00
Platter, Newburgh, mulberry, Jackson, 18" 450.00
Platter, NY from Heights 'Nr' Brooklyn, m-d/b, 16", NM 2,200.00
Platter, Port Putman Hudson River, blk, Ridgway, 15½" 275.00
Platter, Sheltered Peasants, d/b, Hall, 19" 550.00
Platter, St Woolston's Kildare Ireland, d/b, Hall, 14½" 525.00
Platter, States Variant, d/b, Clews, States border, 15" 1,600.00
Platter, SW View of LaGrange...Lafayette, d/b, Wood, 20½" 950.00

Sauce boat, Boston State House, d/b, Ridgway, lg, M 575.00
Shell dish . . . MacDonnough's Victory, d/b, Wood, 6" 5,100.00
Soup, B&O RR, d/b, Wood, 10" 550.00
Soup, Columbus (& men landing), purple, Adams, 10½" 75.00
Soup, Priory, l/b, Alcock, 8½" 23.00
Soup, Residence of Late Richard Jordan, red, 9", EX 150.00
Soup, State House Boston, pk, Jackson, 10" 165.00
Soup plate, Dilston Towers..., d/b, Adams, 10", NM 150.00
Soup plate, Oriental Scenery, d/b, Adams, sm flakes, 10½" 50.00
Soup plate, Table Rock Niagara, d/b, Wood's shell border, 10" ..450.00
Teapot, Boston Harbor, d/b, att Rogers, 10", EX 600.00
Tray, Battle of Bunker Hill, d/b, Stevenson, rtcl, 11" L 8,600.00
Tureen, Almshouse Boston, d/b, w/lid & undertray, 13" W 3,800.00
Tureen, Castle Garden Battery NY, d/b, Wood, +ladle/tray.... 3,000.00
Tureen, gravy; Quadrupeds, d/b, Hall, +lid/undertray, EX 500.00
Tureen, Landing of Gen Lafayette at Castle Garden, d/b, 15".. 3,700.00
Tureen, Landing of Lafayette, d/b, Clews, 8½" L 650.00
Tureen, sauce; Neptune (ship/lighthouse), l/b, +ladle/tray 225.00
Tureen, soup; Batahal Portugal, d/b, leaf hdls, +lid/tray 2,500.00
Undertray, Hyena, d/b, Wood's Zoological series, 8"..................300.00
Undertray, Landing of Lafayette, d/b, hdls, Clews, 10" L 425.00
Wash bowl, Entrance of Erie Canal Into Hudson..., d/b, 12" 850.00

Miscellaneous

Bowl, Franklin Flying Kite, oval, 4⅛" L 40.00
Castle, elephant helps man escape clock tower, 6" 400.00
Covered dish, bull's head, wht w/yel & brn, 1850s, 8x11" 385.00
Covered dish, hen on nest, mc, 10" L 285.00
Creamer, cow, blk/brn sponging, seated milkmaid, 1800, 6" L.....450.00
Creamer, cow, yel/blk splashed, milkmaid, 1800, 6½" L 900.00
Cup & saucer, Temperance, red transfer w/pk lustre band 35.00
Dog, copper lustre spots/etc, facing pr, 12½" 775.00
Dog, red, mc flower basket in mouth, 7½", pr, EX....................800.00
Dog, rust spots/gold collars, 1850s, facing pr, 7" 450.00
Dog, spaniel, blk spots, gilt chain/collar, 12", EX, pr 475.00
Dog, whippet, reclining, 3¼" L, pr 225.00
Figurine, Abraham offers Isaac, bocage/lamb, Sherratt, 11" 650.00
Figurine, Autumn, nymph in yel/floral robe, 1785, 8½" 300.00
Figurine, boy & girl drape flowers about neck of sheep, 6"...........300.00
Figurine, Britannia w/lion, silver lustre trim, 9½", EX................500.00
Figurine, buck, recumbent, Sherratt-type base, 6", NM 325.00
Figurine, Burns & Mary, seated w/in bower, ca 1860, 12" 250.00
Figurine, Christ's Agony (group), bocage, Sherratt, 9½"..............475.00
Figurine, cloaked lady holds sm coffin, dog on pillow, 9" 725.00
Figurine, colt, orange/brn/gr, 1785, 3" 1,000.00
Figurine, Country Pastimes, 2 shepherds, herd/dog, 1780, 10".....750.00
Figurine, couple, she in plaid skirt/bucket on head, 10" 275.00
Figurine, couple by well, she w/ewer, he w/wheat, 10" 265.00
Figurine, dancing couple on base w/clock face, 11" 300.00
Figurine, David Garrick as Richard III, under canopy, 10" 325.00
Figurine, death of Lion Queen Ellen Bright, tiger/lion, 12" 475.00
Figurine, dog, hound on rocky base, Walton style, 1850, 7" 150.00
Figurine, Elephant of Siam, figure in window of castle, 6" 300.00
Figurine, Friendship, 2 boys/dog, mk Walton, 8", NM............. 1,300.00
Figurine, giraffe seated by palm tree, 1850, 8" 650.00
Figurine, giraffe seated by palm tree, 5½", pr 650.00
Figurine, girl w/animal, 4-leaf bocage, Walton, 6", NM..............275.00
Figurine, girl/basket of flowers, gr/brn splashed, 1780, 4" 225.00
Figurine, Good Shepherd, rocky base w/sq plinth, Neal, 9" 325.00
Figurine, Grandfather's clock, red w/marbled blk base, 6" 600.00
Figurine, Grecian & Daughter, cottage/bocage, Sherratt, 10".......650.00
Figurine, greyhound w/game, rocky base, 1850, rstr, 7½" 100.00
Figurine, Highlander w/bagpipes, recumbent hound, 1850, 11"...150.00

Platter, View of Clarence Terrace Regent's Park, marked Wood, 13", $350.00.

Platter, Wadham College Oxford, d/b, Ridgway, 17" 875.00
Salt cellar, Landing of Lafayette, d/b, ftd, Clews, 2x3¼" 2,900.00

Figurine, huntsman by stump spill vase, dog/dead bird, 12" 210.00
Figurine, lady seated w/cat, 3½" 325.00
Figurine, lady seated w/mandolin, 6½" 245.00
Figurine, lion, glass eyes, facing pr, 1910, 14" L.......................225.00
Figurine, lovers, branches arching overhead, 9¾", NM...............250.00
Figurine, monkey holding gr branch, ca 1880, 3½" 95.00
Figurine, mother w/child & basket, pk lustre trim, 6⅜" 200.00
Figurine, Neptune, w/dolphin fountain head, Sherratt, 11" 400.00
Figurine, Prince Albert w/kilt, dog, & game, 1850, 15" 700.00
Figurine, Prince Albert w/unicorn & lion, 6¾" 300.00
Figurine, Prodigal's Return, 14"...300.00
Figurine, pugilist Molineaux stands by pillar, 1815, 9" 450.00
Figurine, Queen Victoria, 11" 275.00
Figurine, Queen Victoria seated w/book, 1840, 7" 225.00
Figurine, ram entwined w/snake, rocky ground, 1840, 7½" 250.00
Figurine, recumbent ewe faces left, lamb to side, wht, 4" 300.00
Figurine, Robbie Burns & Highland Mary, 14" 325.00
Figurine, Roman Charity (group), rocky ground, R Wood, 8" 500.00
Figurine, Shakespeare & Milton, 1 elbow on ped, 10¾", pr.........425.00
Figurine, shepherdess kneels by ram, att Parr, 1850, 5½" 180.00
Figurine, Soldier's Dream, 1-legged sleeping soldier, 10" 425.00
Figurine, St Geo on prancing horse slays dragon, 1770, 11" 1,200.00
Figurine, Tithe Pig, couple/parson, bocage rprs, 1815, 6" 400.00
Figurine, Uncle Tom & Eva, ca 1860s, 8", pr 450.00
Figurine, Victoria & Albert seated w/in vine bower, 14" 425.00
Figurine, Widow, lady/child/bocage, R Wood the Younger, 10"..450.00
Figurine, Winter, woman in cloak, mk, ca 1780, 9", EX 350.00
Figurine, Wm Tell, boy standing to side, 1855, 10"......................180.00
Figurine, Wm Tell holds apple & bow, 1855, 13½" 150.00
Figurine, zebra, rocky ground, 8" 325.00
Figurine, 2 girls & dog under lg clock face, 9½" 340.00
Flask, ½-figure of man w/pipe & cup emb ea side, 8", EX 325.00
Gravy boat, Franklin Flying Kite, bl transfer, 3⅛" L...................185.00
Inkwell, whippet recumbent on bl base, minor wear, 5", pr 400.00
Jug, pearlware, Paul Pry figural, dk bl/red/yel, 1830, 6" 150.00
Jug, pearlware, Success to Lord Rodney, head mold, 1785, 5"......350.00
Jug, satyr mask w/HP portraits of Brougham & Denman, 6¾" 180.00
Mold, jelly; sheaf of corn impression, 1830, 8" W 150.00
Mug, head of Bacchus in deep relief, gr/yel/brn, 1800, 4" 150.00
Plate, Boston Mails, Gentleman's Cabin, sepia, 7".......................145.00
Plate, creamware, exotic birds in iron red, shaped, 9" 150.00
Plate, Franklin Flying Kite, bl transfer, 3¼" 50.00
Platter, Franklin Flying Kite, bl transfer, 5½" L............................60.00
Soup, Peace on Earth, lav transfer, 10" 150.00

Spill vase, leaping stag/running dog before tree, 11", pr 925.00
Spill vase, leopard/cubs on rocks w/tree & serpent, 9" 600.00
Spill vase, Return From Egypt (group), Walton, 1820, 8"...........750.00
Spill vase, stag & tiger on rocky ground, 1830, 8½" 350.00
Spill vase, tree w/stag & hunting hound, 1850, 8", EX 225.00
Teapot, gaudy red/gr polka-dot flowers, 7".................................125.00
Teapot, redware, sprigged w/Oriental figures & animals, 8"........225.00
Vase, lion cubs play by snake-coiled tree trunks, 11", EX 800.00
Watch stand, castle form, turrets/stair steps, 12" 385.00
Watch stand, 3 Scottish girls support watch fr, 1850, 11" 300.00

Stained Glass

There are many factors to consider in evaluating a window or panel of stained glass art. Besides the obvious factor of condition, intricacy, jeweling, beveling, and the amount of selenium (red, orange, and yellow) present should all be taken into account. Remember, repair work is itself an art and can be very expensive.

Our advisor for this category is Carl Heck; he is listed in the Directory under Colorado.

Lamps

Floral dome shade, 10"; slim std, 1915, EX 750.00
Geometric 19" sunburst shade; Duffner-Kimberly, 23" 3,750.00
Shade, oranges/gr leaves, dome shape, 11x20" dia 1,200.00
Shade, pk flowers w/brn leaves on gr dome, 24" dia, EX 600.00
3 repeating scroll/floral segments, 19"; Duffner-Kimberly 5,500.00

Windows

Allegorical lady w/instrument, columns, 69x23", pr 2,500.00
Arts & Crafts flowerheads in clear, 43x14", 4 for 500.00
Arts & Crafts geometrics, mc/clear, 34x22½"..............................300.00
Crane panel, HP w/jeweled arch, Eastlake, 40x18"................... 1,600.00
Lady seated playing harp, arched top, fr, 33x47"...................... 2,500.00

Prairie School leaded glass window, 38" x 20", $550.00.

Spill vase, cow and calf by tree, 10½", $750.00.

Stanford

The Stanford Company produced a Corn Line, similar to that of the Shawnee Company, that is today becoming very collectible. Most examples are marked, so there should be no difficulty in distinguishing one from the other.

Corn Line, butter dish 45.00

Cookie jar, $80.00.

Corn Line, creamer & sugar bowl 45.00
Corn Line, shakers, pr..25.00
Corn Line, teapot 50.00

Stangl

In 1910 Johann Martin Stangl joined the Fulper Pottery Company, working there as ceramic chemist and superintendent of the plant. After a brief absence from 1914 until 1919 when he was employed by the Haeger Pottery, Stangl returned to Fulper. He developed glazes for a new line of cigarette boxes, ash trays, vases, figurines, etc. In 1926 J.M. Stangl became president of the company, and by 1946 he and a partner gained total ownership. The Stangl name first appeared on solid-color dinnerware and novelties in 1926. By 1942 a higher grade of hand-decorated and hand-colored dinnerware was made — Fruit, Yellow Tulip, etc. — which was sold in great abundance. During the war years (1940-1946), bird figures were in great demand, since imports were restricted at that time. Stangl created its famous line of birds; these are very collectible today. Stangl ware continued to be produced after J.M. Stangl died in 1972; soon after 1978 the factory closed. Reference: *The Collector's Handbook of Stangl Pottery* by Norma Rehl, published in 1979.

Our advisors for this category are Robert and Nancy Perzel; they are listed in the Directory under New Jersey.

Birds

#3250, Duck, preening	85.00
#3276, Bluebird, 5"	85.00
#3276D, Bluebirds, 8½"	150.00
#3400, Lovebird, 4"	60.00
#3401, Wren, 3½"	60.00
#3401D, Wrens, bl, 8"	100.00
#3402, Oriole, 3¼"	60.00
#3402D, Orioles	95.00
#3404D, Lovebirds, 5½"	95.00

#3405, Cockatoo, 6"	55.00
#3405D, Cockatoos	115.00
#3406, Kingfisher, 3½"	80.00
#3406D, Kingfishers, 5"	150.00
#3408, Bird of Paradise, dtd 5/9/41, 5½"	95.00
#3432, Duck, running	325.00
#3443, Duck, flying, grey, 9"	320.00
#3444, Cardinal, lt red, 6½"	80.00
#3445, Rooster, gray, 9"	185.00
#3446, Hen, yel, 7"	165.00
#3448, Blue-Headed Vireo, 4¼"	75.00
#3454, Key West Quail Dove, 9"	255.00
#3456, Cerulean Warbler, 4¼"	75.00
#3490D, Redstarts	185.00
#3491, Hen Pheasant, blk	240.00
#3492, Cock Pheasant, 6¼x11"	240.00
#3581D, Chickadees, gr, 5½x8½"	200.00
#3582D, Parakeets, 7"	200.00
#3583, Parula Warbler, 4¾"	50.00
#3584, Cockatoo, 11½"	260.00
#3585, Rufous Hummingbird, 3"	65.00
#3591, Brewer's Blackbird	80.00
#3592, Titmouse, 2½"	65.00
#3593, Nuthatch	50.00
#3594, Red-Faced Warbler, 3"	70.00
#3595, Bobolink, 4¾"	125.00
#3596, Grey Cardinal, 4¾"	75.00
#3597, Wilson Warbler, blk, rare color	80.00
#3597, Wilson Warbler, yel, 3½"	45.00
#3598, Kentucky Warbler, 3"	50.00

#3599D Hummingbirds, $275.00.

#3624, Allen Hummingbird	65.00
#3627, Rivoli Hummingbird	115.00
#3628, Rieffer's Hummingbird, 4½"	125.00
#3629, Broadbill Hummingbird	115.00
#3635D, Goldfinches, 4x11½"	200.00
#3715, Blue Jay, w/peanut	575.00
#3749, Scarlet Tanager	125.00
#3750D, Western Tanagers, 8"	350.00
#3751, Red-Headed Woodpecker, 6¼"	200.00
#3754D, White-Wing Crossbills	300.00

#3776, Bluebird...80.00
#3811, Chestnut-Backed Chickadee, 5" 85.00
#3813, Evening Grosbeak.......................................120.00
#3815, Western Bluebird, 7" 250.00
#3848, Golden Crown Kinglet, 4" 110.00
#3851, Red-Breasted Nuthatch, 3¾"..........................70.00
#3853D, Golden-Crowned Kinglets, 5½x5" 375.00
#3911, Chestnut-Backed Chickadee 85.00
#3923, Vermillion Flycatcher, 5¾"...........................650.00

Advertising plaque, Town & Country 80.00
Ash tray, Antique Gold, sq, #3915, 9" 10.00
Ash tray, Colonial Silver, #5174..................................10.00
Bowl, Antique Gold, shell shape, #4019 ....20.00
Bowl, berry; Thistle, sm 8.00
Bowl, cereal; Country Garden, 5½" 12.00
Bowl, cereal; Town & Country, yel, deep, 5½" 10.00
Bowl, flower; Colonial, #3410-7.................................15.00
Bowl, Fruit, 5½" 10.00
Bowl, gravy; Fruit..20.00
Bowl, Rhythmic Yel, #2092, 7" 20.00
Bowl, salad; Colonial, 9" 25.00
Bowl, Star Flower, 8" 20.00
Bowl, tulip; Artware, #1878 ....25.00
Bowl, vegetable; Town & Country, brn, 10" 30.00
Candle holder, Town & Country, gr, pr 65.00
Candlestick, Antique Gold, #5138, pr.........................20.00
Candlestick, Terra Rose, pr 20.00
Candy, Granada Gold, #5180, w/lid 25.00
Casserole, Town & Country, bl, w/lid, lg.....................85.00
Chop plate, Magnolia, 12½" 20.00
Cigarette box, Terra Rose, w/lid.................................25.00
Coaster, jeweled Christmas tree 10.00
Coffeepot, Blueberry..40.00
Coffeepot, Orchard Song..30.00
Coffeepot, Town & Country, bl 60.00
Compote, Antique Gold, #4021..................................15.00
Creamer, Fruit... 9.00
Creamer, Star Flower 7.50
Creamer, Terra Rose, yel tulip.................................... 9.00
Creamer, Town & Country, bl 20.00
Creamer & sugar bowl, Thistle, w/lid.........................20.00
Cup, Bittersweet.. 7.00
Cup, Thistle 7.00
Cup & saucer, Fruit..12.00
Cup & saucer, Golden Harvest.................................... 9.00
Cup & saucer, Thistle 10.00
Flowerpot, Town & Country, honey, 4½" 10.00
Flowerpot, w/yel tulip, mini, 2¼" 15.00
Lamp, Rembrandt, Antique Gold 75.00
Mug, 'D' of ABCs, child's 15.00
Nut dish, Spun Gold, hdld 5.00
Pitcher, Antique Gold, #4055, 12" 20.00
Pitcher, bl, ball form, #3311 ....25.00
Pitcher, Bl Daisy, 6-oz.. 8.00
Pitcher, Colonial, red, 5½" 15.00
Pitcher, Garden Flower, 1-qt, 5½" 20.00
Pitcher, gr, #1583, 3" 9.00
Pitcher, Terra Rose, yel, 4½".......................................15.00
Pitcher, Town & Country, yel, 1½-pt 30.00
Pitcher, Town & Country, yel, 2½-pt...........................40.00
Plate, Apple Delight, bread & butter 4.00
Plate, Apple Delight, 8".. 8.00

Plate, Bl Daisy, 10" 10.00
Plate, Bl Daisy, 6" 6.00
Plate, Blueberry, 10" 12.00
Plate, Festival, 6" 6.00
Plate, Fruit, 10" 12.00
Plate, Golden Harvest, 8" 8.00
Plate, Magnolia, 6"... 6.00
Plate, Maple Whirl, 10"..10.00
Plate, Mt Laurel, 5" 5.00
Plate, Orchard Song, 10" 10.00
Plate, Orchard Song, 5" 5.00
Plate, Prelude, 6" 4.00
Plate, Prelude, 8".. 8.00
Plate, Provincial, 6" 4.50
Plate, Rooster, 9¾"...12.00
Plate, Star Flower, 6" 5.00
Plate, Thistle, 5" 2.50
Platter, Thistle 30.00
Platter, Town & Country, bl, oval, 15" 45.00
Relish tray, Magnolia 15.00
Serving dish, Apple, Terra Rose, gr, #3785..................10.00
Shakers, Golden Harvest, pr..11.00
Shakers, Magnolia, pr 15.00
Shakers, Town & Country, bl, hdld, lg, pr...................30.00
Shakers, Town & Country, sm, pr................................20.00
Spoon rest, Town & Country, yel 25.00
Sugar bowl, Blueberry, w/lid......................................12.00
Sugar bowl, Colonial, w/lid.. 8.00
Sugar bowl, Terra Rose, Bl Tulip, w/lid.......................10.00
Sugar bowl, Town & Country, gr, w/lid 20.00
Toothbrush holder, Town & Country, yel......................35.00
Tray, yel, 7½x7½" 5.00
Tumbler, bathroom; Town & Country 20.00
Vase, Artware, gr, #2043, 9" 20.00
Vase, Artware, Granada Gold, #2067, 7" 12.00
Vase, Artware, red, twisted, #2047, 4½" 18.00
Vase, Artware, wht satin, hdls, #3140 ....20.00

Statue of Liberty

Long before she began greeting immigrants in 1886, the Statue of Liberty was being honored by craftsmen both here and abroad. Her likeness was etched on blades of the finest straight razors from England, captured in finely detailed busts sold as souvenirs to Paris fairgoers in 1878, and presented on colorfully lithographed trade cards, usually satirical, to American shoppers. Perhaps no other object has been represented in more forms or with such frequency as the universal symbol of America.

Liberty's keepsakes are also universally accessible. Delightful souvenir models created in 1885 to raise funds for Liberty's pedestal are frequently found at flea markets, while earlier French bronze and terra cotta Liberties have been auctioned for over $100,000. Some collectors hunt for the countless forms of 19th-century Liberty memorabilia, while many collections were begun in anticipation of the 1986 Centennial with concentration on modern depictions.

Our advisor for this category is Mike Brooks; he is listed in the Directory under California.

Billhead, Liberty Chemical Company, 1903 ....10.00
Biscuit tin, Wiles Biscuit Co, pictorial, octagonal........110.00
Booklet, Our Gift From France, Travelers Ins, 1886 ......60.00
Bookmark, Paris Internat'l Expo, BB Tilt, silk, 1878......90.00
Bottle, Liberty Milk Co, Buffalo NY, 1-qt 15.00

Bust, Souvenir de la Exposition Internat'l, 1878, 5"	400.00
Candle holder, frosted glass, 9"	125.00
Candy container, glass ped w/metal statue top, 6"	60.00
Clock, mantel; Liberty on glass, Elias Ingraham	250.00
Dominoes, Liberty emb, set	25.00
Flyer, Liberty Excursions on Iron Steamers..., ca 1895	20.00
Handkerchief, w/presidents, silk, WWI era	50.00
Label, cigar box; Victory Day (WWI), Celestino Fernandez & Co	8.00
Label, Statue, California Bartletts	7.00
Letter, handwritten, sgn Auguste Bartholdi, Paris, 1891	350.00
Lithograph, Root & Tinker, 1883, 31x12½"	350.00
Lithograph, souvenir Aux Subscripteurs..., Fr, 1880s, 18x14"	375.00
Medal, American Legion, 1947	10.00
Medal, Bartholdi bust/statue, w/ribbon, 1886, 38 mm	75.00
Medal, Union Franco Americaine, Fr, bronze, 1886, 101 mm, pr	330.00
Model, American Committee, 12"	1,000.00
Model, American Committee, 1885, 6"	100.00
Needle book, Air Mail	15.00
Paperweight, brass, Gen Silk Importing NY, Whitehead & Hoag	45.00
Paperweight, glass, Bartholdi statue, Gift of French...to Am	125.00
Penny pipe, clay, emb, ca 1885	65.00
Pin-bk, Liberty flower	20.00
Pin-bk, Liberty Loan of 1917	7.00
Plaque, wood, Lord & Taylor merchant handout, 4x3"	30.00
Plate, royal bl, Staffordshire, Rowland & Marsellus, 1913	125.00
Pocket knife, Liberty/Woolworth building, Germany	30.00
Post card, hold-to-light, Germany, 1906	55.00
Program, unveiling of Statue, Oct 28, 1886	325.00
Razor, Liberty etched on blade, J Allen & Sons, Sheffield	80.00
Spoon, Statue figural, sterling, Charles Casper	80.00
Stanhope viewer, ivory, ⅝"	75.00
Stereo card, Collosal Hand & Torch, Liberty, 1876	125.00
Ticket, Columbia Expo, Manhattan Day, Oct 21, 1893	15.00
Tin, Brights Kidney Beans	75.00
Trade card, Bartholdi Central Draft Burner	15.00
Trade card, mechanical, Eagle Pencil Co	70.00
View Book, ...Enlightening the World, Am Committee, 1891	75.00
View Book, ...Enlightening the World, Wittemann, NY, 1885	45.00

Steamship Collectibles

For centuries, ocean-going vessels with their venturesome officers and crews were the catalyst that changed the unknown aspects of our world to the known. Changing economic conditions, unfortunately, have now placed the North American shipping industry in the same jeopardy as the American passenger train. They are becoming a memory. The surge of interest in railroad collectibles and the railroad-related steamship lines has lead collectors to examine the whole spectrum of steamship collectibles.

Our advisors for this category are Lila and Fred Shrader; they are listed in the Directory under California.

Ash tray, Queen Elizabeth II, brass, portrait, 6½"	30.00
Ash tray, Queen Elizabeth II, compass center, triangular	18.00
Booklet/timetable, Bergen, 1947, 14-pg, NM	8.00
Bowl, American Mail Line, SP, side logo, dtd 1929, 6¼"	48.00
Button, uniform; Cunard, brass	6.50
Button, uniform; Grace Line, aluminum	2.00
Coaster, United States, ship's portrait, paper, M	1.50
Cup & saucer, Alaskan Steamship, demitasse	45.00
Cup & saucer, SS Hudson	18.00
Cup & saucer, White Star	45.00
Deck plan, Aquitania, tissue, Mar 1929, opens to: 27x31"	35.00

Deck plan, Oriente, 1939-40, opens to: 27x33"	24.00
Deck plan, Queen Elizabeth I, cabin class, blk/wht, 1952	10.00
Envelope, Cunard, legal sz, M	2.00
Magazine, France III, France via French Line, 1961, NM	12.00
Map, Arctic Ocean, routes shown, ca 1900, 15x14", EX	40.00
Menu, Cunard Line, RMS Mauretania, Mar 1934, EX	24.00
Menu, Il de France, breakfast, ca 1950s	2.50
Napkin, United States Line, linen, woven logo, lg, M	5.00
Needle case, SS United States, complete, 1952, 4½x6½"	5.00
Pamphlet, Pacific Coast Steamship Co, 1911	12.50
Passenger list, Adriatic, 1st class, 1907, EX	28.00
Passenger list, America, cabin class, 1950, EX	5.00
Passenger list, Amerika, NY to Hamburg, 1906	14.00
Passenger list, Constitution, 1965	5.00
Passenger list, Leonardo da Vinci, portrait cover, 1970s, M	7.50
Passenger list, President Cleveland, much gold leaf, M	12.50
Pen knife, France II, portrait emb ea side, 3¼", EX	40.00
Pin-bk button, Queen Elizabeth I, blk/wht	7.50
Playing cards, Princess Cruises, logo on bks, VG in box	5.00
Program, Independency, daily type	1.50
Puzzle, Canadian Pacific, Empress portrait on wood, 9-pc, M	12.00
Schedule, NY & Liverpool US Mail Steamers, 1853, EX	30.00
Songbook, Constitution, Cushing pilgrimage voyage, 1958	5.00
Stationery, Michelangelo, portrait, 1 sheet	2.50
Stationery, Queen Elizabeth II, portrait, 1 sheet	2.50
Stationery, Queen Mary, portrait on gr, 1 sheet	6.00
Sticker, baggage; France III, portrait on crest shape	9.00
Swizzle stick, Cunard, lucite, oar shape, eng name	2.00
Tie bar, Queen Mary, portrait on brass	12.50
Timetable, Niagara to Sea, Canada, 1917	12.50
Tip tray, San Francisco, mc, NM	68.00

Steins

Steins have been made from pottery, pewter, glass, stoneware, and porcelain, from very small up to the four-liter size. They are decorated by etching, in-mold relief, decals, and occasionally they may be hand painted. Some porcelain steins have lithophane bases. Collectors often specialize in a particular type — faience, regimental, or figural — while others limit themselves to the products of only one manufacturer.

Our advisor for this category is Ron Fox; he is listed in the Directory under New York. See also Mettlach.

Key:
L — liter	PUG — print under glaze
litho — lithophane	tl — thumb lift
POG — print over glaze	

Character, artillery shell w/1914 Iron Cross, pewter, ½-L	420.00
Character, barbells, pottery relief, #1227, 1-L, M	315.00
Character, Bismark in retirement, porc, Schierholz, ½-L, NM	950.00
Character, Bismark Radish, porc, Schierholz, prof rpr, ½-L	400.00
Character, boar, porc, Schierholz, ½-L, M	4,400.00
Character, cat w/hangover, porc, Musterschutz, ½-L, M	435.00
Character, Dooley cartoon figure, pottery, Webco, ½-L, NM	62.00
Character, egg, pottery, R Hanky, ca 1893, prof rpr, ½-L	215.00
Character, elephant, lid: ash tray, porc, Schierholz, ½-L, NM	645.00
Character, Fredrich III, pottery, Merlelbach & Wick, ½-L, M	440.00
Character, Happy Radish, porc, Schierholz, sm rpr, ½-L	350.00
Character, man w/pipe, pottery, verse, pewter lid, ½-L, NM	270.00
Character, monk, porc, monk & lady lithophane, ½-L, M	205.00
Character, monk grinning, stoneware, #112, ½-L, M	285.00
Character, Mother-in-Law, pottery, ½-L, M	360.00

Character, Munich Maid, pottery, rpl hinge, ½-L 135.00
Character, newspaper lady, porc, Schierholz, ½-L, M 3,225.00
Character, nun w/hands at belt, pottery, mk, ½-L, M 210.00
Character, Nurnberg Tower, stoneware, mk TW, ½-L, M 265.00
Character, owl, pottery, Hanky #999, flakes, ½-L 155.00
Character, owl w/bird & rodent, stoneware, R Hanke, ½-L, M 440.00
Character, pillow fight (on lid), pewter, dtd 1871, ½-L, NM 840.00
Character, pixie, porc, Schierholz, ½-L, M................................895.00
Character, pottery, relief: bowling pin, gold 9, 1½-L, EX............140.00
Character, Russian soldier, stoneware, mk LB&C, flakes, ½-L ...630.00
Character, Sad Radish, pewter mts, Schierholz, 6½" 325.00
Character, skull, porc, E Bohne, ¼-L, M 260.00
Character, stag, porc, Schierholz, sm rpr, ½-L 2,365.00
Character, student, porc, ca 1950s, ½-L, NM 125.00
Character, Von Moltke, porc, Schierholz, ½-L, M 1,100.00
Character, Zugspitz mtn, HP stoneware, pewter lid, ½-L, M........890.00
Character, 10 bowling pins, pottery, #1663, ½-L, M...................210.00

Ceramic steins: 2½-L with decorative panels,
$150.00; 3-L with 6 figures in a landscape, $200.00;
4-L with figures and castles, $250.00.

Copper, HP: boy & girl, inlay lid, glaze flakes, 3⅝" 150.00
Earthenware, yel/orange glazes, Wetterau, 1750s, 1-L, EX....... 4,155.00
Faience, lion & trees, Thuringen, wear/rprs, 1750s, 1-L..............335.00
Faience, pewter lid & base ring, Salzburg, 1840s, .6-L, VG..........270.00
Filigreed silver, florals, gold wash, ca 1870, .3-L, G 3,225.00
Gerz #020, stoneware, golfers, pewter lid, ca 1900, 2-L, M...... 2,965.00
Glass, blown, amber, HP florals, Zum Hohl, pewter lid, ½-L, M..145.00
Glass, blown, amber, pnt Munich Maid, pewter lid, ½-L, M........210.00
Glass, blown, bl, HP florals/Andenkan An Karisbad, ¼-L, NM ..145.00
Glass, blown, clear over cranberry, metal lid, 1850s, ½-L, EX....470.00
Glass, blown, cobalt, Biedermeier 'wedding,' 1860, 1-L, NM.......935.00
Glass, blown, enameled State Crest of Saxony, ½-L, M...............230.00
Glass, blown, HP birds & florals, metal lid, 2¾", M.....................48.00
Glass, blown, HP scene, pewter lid w/porc insert, ½-L, EX..........200.00
Glass, blown, HP strawberries, pewter lid, 1907, ½-L, M 155.00
Glass, blown, ped base, prism in pewter lid, .3-L, M.....................95.00
Glass, blown, porc lid inlay: King Gambrinus, 1850s, ½-L...........125.00
Glass, Mary Gregory boy on bl, bl insert lid, rpr tl, ¼-L..............215.00
Glass, mold blown, amber, checked ovals, pewter lid, .3-L, M.....140.00
Glass, mold blown, bl, HP florals, pk insert in lid, ¼-L, M 145.00
Glass, mold blown, cranberry, encased in pewter, ped base, M....245.00
Glass, mold blown, Mary Gregory man on gr, int ovals, .4-L, NM.200.00
Glass, mold blown, red jewel top insert in pewter lid, ½-L, M 78.00
Glass, mold blown: Mary Gregory girl on bl, circles, ¼-L, M 225.00

Glass, pewter lid w/cvd crest from stag antler base, ½-L, M 315.00
Glass, pressed, HP Edelweiss, Saxony, 1930s, ½-L, M 145.00
Glass, pressed, hunter & lady porc lid insert, .3-L, M.................95.00
Glass, pressed, pewter lid, ped base, Saxony, ½-L, M..................65.00
Glass, star-cut base, insert in pewter lid, 1850s, ½-L, M.............68.00
Ivory, gold-washed silver mts, mythological cvgs, 13½", EX ... 4,000.00
Military, German coats of arms of 4 kingdoms, pottery, ½-L 275.00
Military, Kaiser Franz Josef I transfer, porc, ½-L, M 340.00
Military, Ungonnen battles transfer, porc, ½-L, EX 245.00
Nazi, Preisschiesen 1937..., motorcycle, stoneware, ½-L, M 835.00
Nazi, 17 Kemp IR 63 Eichstatt, flag, stoneware, ½-L, M.............650.00
Occupational, brewer, porc w/transfer, pewter lid, ½-L, EX........235.00
Occupational, machinist, ped base, porc w/transfer, ½-L, NM ...350.00
Occupational, shoemaker, porc w/transfer, ½-L, M....................365.00
Pewter, relief: girl, boy & 9 pins on lid, ½-L, M........................100.00
Pewter, relief: Imperial Eagle w/crest, eng lid, .3-L, M 130.00
Pewter, relief: Nouveau hops & malt, dtd 1905, ½-L, NM..........115.00
Pewter, simplistic style, 1½-L, NM 190.00
Pewter, 16th C-style repro, ca 1900, .4-L, NM 210.00
Porc, Cornflower, hunter inlay lid, ¼-L, M 225.00
Porc, Cornflower, porc Alpine couple inlay lid, ½-L, M 260.00
Porc, HP: monk w/pig, O'Hara Dial Co, Am, 1900s, .3-L, NM ..260.00
Porc, Royal Vienna type, mythological scene, ½-L, M 1,250.00
Porc, transfer: gnomes & flowers, flakes/wear, ½-L....................165.00
Porc, transfer: hunters eating, girl lithophane, ⅛-L, M................55.00
Pottery, appl relief: portraits, Franconia, 1680s, ¾-L, VG............695.00
Pottery, Capo-di-Monte style, majolica, 1750s, ¾-L, G 495.00
Pottery, etched: Bock Bier, 2 goats, pewter lid, .8-L, M..............155.00
Pottery, etched: card game, ceramic inlay, 3-L, 16", M...............415.00
Pottery, etched: knights & wine keeper, ceramic lid, 1-L, NM....190.00
Pottery, etched: outdoor scene, Remy #1218, ½-L, EX 155.00
Pottery, etched: Rizzi Brau..., gold logo/pewter lid, .4-L, M 200.00
Pottery, etched: tavern scene, Grimshied #768, ½-L, M 160.00
Pottery, HP transfer: Munich Maid, SP lid, 1-L, EX...................150.00
Pottery, POG: Hacher Brau, pewter lid: axes relief, .4-L, M 270.00
Pottery, relief: couple & house, postwar, 2-L, 15½", M................75.00
Pottery, relief: dancer in tavern, molded lid, ½-L, NM 135.00
Pottery, relief: keg w/bands, Blatz, brn glaze, Am, ½-L................28.00
Pottery, relief: lion logo, Merkelbach & Wick, ½-L, NM 100.00
Pottery, relief: man on high wheeler, pewter lid, ½-L, M.............415.00
Pottery, relief: souvenir of NY, pewter lid, ⅛-L, M 30.00
Pottery, transfer: ...Rad Fahrer Bund, bicycle, ½-L, EX 745.00
Regimental, Bayr Inf Lelb...1910-12, screw-off lid, porc, EX........825.00
Regimental, Kaiser Alex Garde Gren...1906-08, porc, rprs.............650.00
Regimental, Naval, SMS Schlesien 1908-11, pottery, 15", NM ..990.00
Regimental, 1st Bayr Ulan...1905-08, porc, 11½", EX..................300.00
Regimental, 1st Gaude Feld Art...1906-08, porc, tang rpr 365.00
Regimental, 11th Feld Art...1908-10, cannon finial, 12¼", M 365.00
Regimental, 133rd Inf Zwickau, stanhope glass eye, 12", EX 365.00
Regimental, 15th Bayr Inf...Neuburg 1897-99, porc, EX 215.00
Regimental, 15th Bayr Inf...Neuburg 1904-06, stoneware, rpr.....270.00
Regimental, 19th Ulan...1898-1901, porc, music box, 12", EX....625.00
Regimental, 22nd Bayr Inf...1907-09, lion tl, 13", M 365.00
Regimental, 29th Feld Art...1905-07, rider finial, porc, M 415.00
Regimental, 3rd Inf Rgt Augsburg 1897-99, pottery, rprs.............160.00
Regimental, 32nd Inf...1906-08, soldier finial, porc, M...............460.00
Regimental, 39th Feld Art...1912-14, rider tl, 13½", EX..............415.00
Regimental, 5th Bayr Inf...Bamberg 1911-13, porc, 12¼", EX 295.00
Stoneware, enameled POG: happy man w/2 steins, 1-L, M 185.00
Stoneware, enameled POG: tavern scenes, 1930s, ½-L, M 70.00
Stoneware, enameled: Munich Maid, pewter lid, 1-L, NM...........315.00
Stoneware, incised/relief: Schutzenfest, 1897, 1-L, M 225.00
Stoneware, incised: bird, Westerwald, 1750s, 1-L, G 365.00
Stoneware, POG: Dusseldorf & shield, pewter lid, ½-L, M 80.00

Stoneware, POG: Lemp's..., w/logo, pewter lid, ½-L, M..............725.00
Stoneware, POG: Lowenbrau, pewter lid: lion relief, 1-L, M.......105.00
Stoneware, POG: Lowenbrau, pewter lid: lion relief, 2-L, M.......170.00
Stoneware, POG: sun/moon/stars, Nouveau pewter lid, ½-L, M..275.00
Stoneware, relief: Art Nouveau tree, pewter lid, 1-L, M.............145.00
Stoneware, relief: Art Nouveau tree, pewter lid, ½-L, M.............125.00
Stoneware, relief: cavalier, pewter lid, 3", M.............................45.00
Stoneware, relief: hunter/dogs/stag, metal lid, 1-L, M.................115.00
Stoneware, relief: knight & lady, pewter lid, 2", M.....................36.00
Stoneware, relief: lovers kiss, molded lid, 3-L, 17½", M.............195.00
Stoneware, relief: musical angels, Regensburg, 1850s, ½-L, EX..135.00
Stoneware, relief: stag/turkey/rabbit, metal lid, ½-L, M.............70.00
Stoneware, stencil & enamel: Spaten-Brau, pewter lid, 1-L, M...140.00

Steuben

The Steuben Glass Works of Corning, New York, was founded in 1903 by Frederick Carder and Thomas Hawkes. They made art glass of high quality similar to some of Tiffany's. One of their earliest types was Aurene, a lustrous metallic gold or blue. They also made Verre de Soie, Rosaline, and Silverene as well as other unique types of art glass. In 1918 Steuben became a branch of Corning Glass Works.

In the listings that follow, examples are signed unless noted otherwise. See also Aurene; Cluthra.

Key: ACB — acid cut back

Basket, Pomona Gr, open basketweave, appl prunts, 4x8"...........175.00
Basket, Verre de Soie, 1¾"...465.00
Bonbon, llama head finial, conical, 6½x5"................................200.00
Bottle, scent; Cintra, blk & wht w/faceted casing, bubbles......6,000.00
Bowl, ACB, floral swag border, Jade Gr on Alabaster, 2x8".......550.00
Bowl, amber Aurene, amethyst neck, goblet form, unsgn, 7"......850.00
Bowl, appl ped w/4 scrolling ft, 4x10½"..................................125.00

Bowl, blue Aurene on Alabaster, acid cut back, Compton pattern, very rare, 8", $7,500.00.

Bowl, centerpc; rose & gr, #6046, mk, 9½".............................400.00
Bowl, clear w/cerice florals & threads, #3584, 13"....................450.00
Bowl, gold Aurene on Calcite, flaring rim, unsgn, 10"................300.00
Bowl, gold Aurene on Calcite, heavy, low disk ft, 2x8".............225.00
Bowl, gold Aurene on Calcite, ring ft, 2¾x9¾".......................275.00
Bowl, gold Aurene on Calcite, rtcl sterling holder, 3" dia...........200.00
Bowl, gold Aurene on Calcite, 4x10"......................................350.00
Bowl, Ivorene, Grotesque, 7x11½"..450.00

Bowl, Jade Gr, wafered low ped ft, incurvate, 5x9¾"................225.00
Bowl, Jade Gr on Alabaster base, sgn, 12" dia..........................425.00
Bowl, Jade Yel, shallow, 1½x10"...600.00
Candle holder, gold Aurene on Calcite, flat bobeche, 6", pr.......850.00
Candlestick, appl amber twist on clear, #3354, 10", pr..............425.00
Candlestick, 3-ring shaft w/trapped bubble, 4½", 3 for.............325.00
Compote, bl, optic ribs, yel/rose/gr pear & leaf finial, 9".........900.00
Compote, Rosalene, Alabaster stem & ft, 4½x10" dia................325.00
Creamer & sugar bowl, Bristol Yel w/blk threads, #6771...........375.00
Finger bowl, Celeste Bl, #1820, +underplate.............................200.00
Goblet, bl, clear base & swirled stem, 8"...................................90.00
Ice bucket, Jade Gr w/Alabaster threading, #6676, 6¼"............325.00
Lamp, ACB, stylized leaves/pods, Aurene on blk, 12" base.....1,500.00
Nappy, Rosaline w/Alabaster hdl, #205, 4½x5½".....................325.00
Newel post ornament, Rosalene on wht, roundels, 7½".............500.00
Plate, amber w/aquamarine folded edge, 8¾", set of 9.............275.00
Salt cellar, gr w/topaz ft...150.00
Sculpture, angel fish, hand polished, 10x10"............................800.00
Sculpture, fish, perched on tail, 6"..350.00
Shade, opal w/gr & gold feathers, gilt int, lily form, 6"............200.00
Sherbet, gold Aurene on Calcite, w/underplate..........................235.00
Sherbet, Jade Gr over Alabaster, eng festoons, +7" plate...........450.00
Tazza, amber, swirled top, blown stem, 8x6".............................135.00
Torchere, gold amber plaque, iron std w/vintage sgn Griest...1,500.00
Vase, ACB, Chinese pattern/scrollwork, Plum Jade, 8x10".....3,100.00
Vase, ACB, flowers, Rose Quartz, int crackle, hdls, 11½".......5,000.00
Vase, ACB, hunter/trees, bl Aurene/Pomona Gr, 6-sided, 10"..2,300.00
Vase, ACB, medieval motif on blk, #2694, 9".........................3,000.00
Vase, ACB, pagoda in shaped reserve, 3-layer, 12", NM........2,200.00
Vase, amethyst Silverina, #938, mk, 9"...................................850.00
Vase, bl Aurene on Calcite, flared/conical, on disk ft, 6"...........900.00
Vase, Bristol Yel, fan form, mk, 9"...225.00
Vase, gold Aurene on Calcite, everted hat form, 3½", pr...........400.00
Vase, gold Aurene on Calcite, ruffled trumpet form, 6x5".........310.00
Vase, Ivorene, classic form, thick walled, no mk, 10½"............500.00
Vase, Ivorene, cornucopia, #7579, 7".....................................325.00
Vase, Jade Gr, flared ftd U-form, shaped rim, 8½"..................475.00
Vase, Jade Gr, spiraling U-form body, 6¾x7".........................200.00
Vase, Pomona Gr, tree stump, #2743, mk................................275.00
Vase, Rosalene, Alabaster dome ft, ovoid, 7", pr......................850.00
Vase, Selenium Red, trumpet form, 3-ring wafer base, 24".......700.00
Vase, topaz w/Celeste Bl knop-stem ped ft, ribbed fan, 8½"......350.00

Stevengraph

A Stevengraph is a small picture made of woven silk resembling an elaborate ribbon, created by Thomas Stevens in England in the latter half of the 1800s. They were matted and framed by Stevens, usually with his name appearing on the mat or, more commonly, the trade announcement on the back of the mat. He also produced silk post cards and bookmarks, all of which have 'Stevens' woven in silk on one of the mitered corners.

Anyone wishing to learn more about Stevengraphs is encouraged to contact the Stevengraph Collectors' Association, whose address can be found in the Directory under Clubs, Newsletters, and Catalogs.

Banner, Am flag, eagle shield, Lincoln, & lines of speech..........200.00
Bookmark, Happy Birthday...50.00
Bookmark, Merry Christmas/Happy New Year, robins..................65.00
Bookmark, Prayer to a Bridal Couple.......................................100.00
Called to the Rescue..150.00
Death of Nelson, fr..300.00
Declaration of Independence, woven at Columbian Exhibition..225.00

Edward VII and Alexandra, $165.00.

Good Old Days, fr 200.00
Kaiser Franz Joseph I & Kaiserine Elizabeth, pr in fr 100.00
Lady Godiva Procession 225.00
Panels, coach, locomotive, & portrait of Fulton Past, 1-pc 400.00
Present Time...150.00
Robert Burns, both sides complete 135.00
The Meet, orig matt, old fr...250.00
Washington Centennial 80.00
Wellington & Blugher..300.00

Stevens and Williams

Stevens and Williams glass was produced at the Brierly Hill Glassworks in Stourbridge, England, for nearly a century, beginning in the 1830s. They were credited with being among the first to develop a method of manufacturing a more affordable type of cameo glass. Other lines were also made — silver deposit, alexandrite, and engraved rock crystal, to name but a few.

Our advisor for this category is Don Williams; he is listed in the Directory under Missouri.

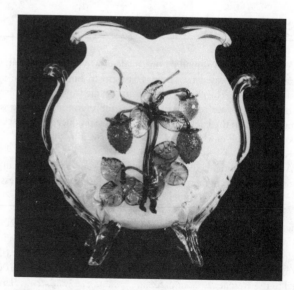

Vase, applied red strawberries and green leaves on opal, amber feet and rim, 12" x 12", $3,000.00.

Basket, bl w/amber hdls & crimped rim, HP florals, 6x9" 225.00
Basket, pk, floral intaglio, on saucer base, 8¾" 965.00
Biscuit jar, bl/wht/clear swirls, metal lid & hdl, 8" 420.00
Bottle, scent; bl w/HP berries & gilt, swirled, 13" 325.00
Bowl, amber to aqua Swirl MOP, bl int, ruffled, 3¾x7⅜" 895.00
Bowl vase, pk/yel/bl swirls, gilt traces, 4½x6" 645.00
Finger bowl, bl to clear, fruit intaglio, 6⅛", +8" plate 295.00
Pitcher, bl/wht diagonal stripes on clear, bulbous, 5½" 125.00
Pitcher, peachblow, amber hdl/rigaree, appl florals, 12" 550.00
Pitcher, Rainbow, pk/yel stripes, ribbed, reeded hdl, 6" 375.00
Sherbet, royal bl cut w/fruit, clear cut stem, +7" plate 325.00
Vase, cabinet; honey amber cut w/water lilies, sgn, 6" 100.00
Vase, clear w/pk casing, lt gr appl florals, ped ft, 8½" 75.00
Vase, cranberry, 6 clear appl florals/leaves, hdls, 7" 275.00
Vase, cream, pk int, appl leaves, amber ruffle, 7½x4½" 225.00
Vase, Rainbow Swirl, trefoil crimped top, 6¾" 485.00
Vase, wht, pk int, amber rigaree, 8-flute top, 11x5" 275.00
Vase, wht, pk int, amber/red rigaree, lg appl fruit, 13" 475.00
Vase, wht w/cranberry & amber appl florals+2" acorn, 13x7" 485.00
Vase, yel opaque, appl gr floral/rigaree/rim/ft, 9½" 235.00

Cameo

Rose bowl, coral branches, pk on custard, yel int 600.00
Vase, apple blossoms/medial & rim borders, wht on yel, 12" ... 2,200.00
Vase, blackberries/medial border/insect, wht on rust, 12" 4,300.00
Vase, ferns/thistles, wht on bright bl, bbl form, 4" 1,200.00
Vase, floral/tendrils, wht on rust, bulbous bottom, 7" 1,800.00
Vase, foxglove, wht on yel, conical, 12" 2,000.00
Vase, morning-glories, wht on wht over amber to bl-gr, 9" 3,600.00
Vase, nasturtiums/beetle, wht on amethyst, 6" 3,200.00
Vase, wildflowers, red on wht, broad body, 7½" 3,300.00

Stickley

Among the leading proponents of the Arts and Crafts Movement, the Stickley brothers — Gustav, Leopold, Charles, Albert, and John George — were at various times and locations involved in designing and producing furniture as well as decorative items for the home. (See Arts and Crafts for further information.)

The oldest of the five Stickley brothers was Gustav; his work is the most highly regarded of all. He developed the style of furniture refered to as Mission. It was strongly influenced by the type of furnishings found in the Spanish missions of California — utilitarian, squarely built, and simple. It was made most often of oak, and decoration was very limited or non-existent. The work of his brothers display adaptations of many of Gustav's ideas and designs. His factory, the Craftsman Shops, operated in Eastwood, New York, from the late 1890s until 1915, when he was forced out of business by larger companies who copied his work and sold it at much lower prices. Among his shopmarks are the early red decal containing a joiner's compass and the words 'Als Ik Kan,' the branded mark with the very similar components, and paper labels.

The firm known as Stickley Brothers was located first in Binghampton, New York, and then Grand Rapids, Michigan. Albert and John made the move to Michigan, leaving Charles in Binghamton (where he and an uncle continued the operation under a different name). After several years, John George left the company to rejoin Leopold in New York. (These two later formed their own firm called L. & J.G. Stickley.) The Stickley Brothers Company under Albert's sole direction produced furniture that featured fine inlay work, decorative cutouts, and leaned strongly toward a style of Arts and Crafts with an English influence. It was tagged with a paper label 'Made by Stickley

Brothers, Grand Rapids' or with a brass plate or decal with the words 'Quaint Furniture,' an English term he chose to refer to his product. In addition to his furniture, he made metal furnishings as well.

The workshops of the L. & J.G. Stickley Company operated under the name 'Onandaga Shops.' Located in Fayetteville, New York, their designs were often all but copies of Gustav's work. Their products were well made and marketed, and their business was very successful. Their decaled labels contained all or a combination of the words 'Handcraft' or 'Onandaga Shops,' along with the brothers' initials and last name. The firm continues in business today.

Our advisor for this category is Bruce Austin; he is listed in the Directory under New York. Note: When only one dimension is given for tables, it is length.

Gustav Stickley

Book rack, #74, V top shelf+flat 2nd tier, unmk, rfn, 31" 550.00
Book rack, #90, 4-compartment, revolves, label/decal, 9x12"......600.00
Bookcase, #715, 16-pane door, gallery, decal/label, 56x35"..... 3,500.00
Bookcase, #716, gallery top/2 8-pane doors, label, rfn, 56" 2,500.00
Bookcase, #717, 2 8-pane doors, brand, EX orig finish, 56" 4,250.00
Catalog, 1902, Things Wrought by United Crafts, w/prices 800.00
Chair, arm; #314, H-bk, slip seat, red decal, 35", pr 1,200.00
Chair, child's; #344, 3-slat bk, unmk, new leather/finish 150.00
Chair, dining; #1304, 2 wide bk slats, leather seat, decal 665.00
Chair, dining; #308, H bk slat, slip seat, decal, 40", M.................400.00
Chair, flat arm; #324, fixed bk, 5-slat sides, sgn, rstr................ 1,300.00
Chair, Morris; #332, 5-slat bk/sides, rope seat fr, unsgn 4,100.00
Chair, Morris; #367, spindle-sided, bk adjusts, branded...........8,000.00
Chair, Morris; #369, drop-arm, 5-slat sides, unmk, rstr............ 3,400.00
Chair, office; #361½, unmk, re-tacked/leathered, rfn...................750.00
Chamberstick, hammered copper, cylindrical std, mk, 9", pr .. 1,100.00
China cabinet, 9-pane door over 2 in base, unmk, 67x38", M.. 9,000.00
Clock, tall case; #3, brass/copper dial, sgn, 71", VG 7,500.00
Costumer, dbl; #53, unsgn, 66x22" 1,700.00
Day bed, #216, 5-slat bk, cane seat, red decal, 30x80" 3,300.00
Desk, #706, drop front w/inset panels, label, rfn, 44x30" 2,750.00
Desk, #729, drop front, 2 short drw/3 long drw, label, EX 2,700.00
Desk, #731, drop front over 2½-drw over 1, label, rstr 600.00
Desk, #732, drop front, 2 sm drw over 2, branded, 44x32" 1,600.00
Desk, chalet; drop front, key tenons, decal, 46x22" 1,700.00
Desk, child's; 3-drw cabinet to side, unmk, 26x32x19", EX 275.00
Desk, partner's; 1 side mirrored, sgn in red/label, 60", EX........ 7,000.00
Footstool, #320, leather top, decal/label, 12" dia, EX...................425.00

Gustav Stickley hanging lantern, copper with heart-shaped cutouts, yellow glass liner, 13" x 6" diameter, $1,600.00.

Mirror, #68, 3-part, peaked crest, decal, rfn, 28x48" 1,400.00
Rocker, arm; #323, 4-slat bk/5-slat sides, sgn, VG re-uphl....... 1,700.00
Rocker, sewing; #303, 4-slat bk, canvas seat, sgn, 33" 375.00
Rug, drugget w/dk bl & camel geometrics on neutral, 96x76" . 1,100.00
Sconce, #400, yel opal bell shade hangs from copper mt, 6" 750.00
Sconce, copper/hammered glass 4-side lantern on hook, 9x8".. 1,000.00
Screen, 3 curved-top oak & linen panels, unmk/att, 66x66" 750.00
Settee, #286, tall spindle bk, flat arms, unmk, rfn, 49x48" 3,500.00
Settle, #165, even-arm, flared bk splats form arch, mk, 60"....12,000.00
Settle, #208, str rail/9-slat bk, caned seat missing, unsgn......... 9,250.00
Sideboard, #817, 4-drw/2-door, strap hinges, decal, 70" L 7,000.00
Table, #446, X-stretchers, through tenons, rnd, decal 2,200.00
Table, #624, 6-sided, 6-spoke base/sq legs, label, rpl top.......... 3,000.00
Table, dining; #632, 5-leg, decal, nicks/roughness, 48" dia...... 1,900.00
Table, library; #619, 3-drw, oval iron hdw, label, 67", EX 4,300.00

Gustav Stickley trestle-base table, #404, unsigned, 36" wide, $2,500.00.

Tabouret, #601, arched X-stretchers, box decal, rfn top 475.00
Tabouret, #601, arched X-stretchers, 14" dia, unmk 350.00
Tabouret, #603, arched X-stretchers, unmk, 20" dia, EX 475.00
Telephone stand, #605, branded, rfn, 30x14" sq 900.00
Tray, hammered copper, #355, new patina, mk Als Ik Kan, 23"..700.00
Umbrella stand, #54, 4-post/boxed shelf, sgn, no pan, 33" 400.00

L. & J.G. Stickley

Bookcase, #326½, 1-door, tenon/key built, unmk, 55x30", M .. 3,500.00
Bookcase, #674, 3 12-pane doors, unmk, 70" L, EX 5,500.00
Catalog, Fayetteville NY, Art Press, 1914, 9½x7", VG...............100.00
Chair, arm; 3-slat bk, horsehair seat, unmk, rfn, 47" 650.00
Chair, dining; #1340, 3-slat bk, unsgn, set of 10 .... 1,100.00
Chair, dining; #1350, 3-slat bk, orig leather, sgn, 4 for 700.00
Chair, dining; #800, 3-slat bk, branded, arm+5 side, 6 for....... 2,100.00
Chair, Morris, #471, 6-slat sides w/corbels, unmk, NM 2,100.00
Chair, Morris, #406, bow arms, 4-slat sides, label, 44" 9,750.00
Chair, Morris, #471, 6-slat side, spring seat, sgn, EX................ 1,200.00
Chair, Morris, #770, flat arms, dbl side rail, label, EX 950.00
Chair, open arm; #816, 6 vertical bk slats, sgn, 35" 375.00
Chair, open arm; #816, 6-slat bk, spring seat, sgn, EX.................250.00
China closet, #646, 2-door, sm ldgl panes top/sides, unmk 2,700.00
China closet, #746, 2 glass doors, ea w/6 sm panes at top 3,500.00
China closet, 2 8-pane doors, glass sides, branded, 57x36" 3,500.00
Clock, mantel; #85, wide beveled top/base, decal, 22", EX ...10,000.00

Davenport bed, #285, seat rail opens/cushion unfolds, unmk .. 2,700.00
Day bed, #291, 5-slat ends, slanted head, sgn, 26x70" 1,200.00
Day bed, #293, recessed panel ends, re-uphl, decal, 80" 3,750.00
Desk, #601, 1-drw form w/lower shelf, sgn, minor stain, 34" 550.00
Desk, #612, 8-drw superstructure, kneehole, unsgn, 48", VG .. 1,400.00
Drink stand, #22, 4 splay legs, X-stretcher, decal, 28x18" 1,300.00
Drink stand, #574, cut corners, shelf, branded, 29x18", EX 550.00
Footstool, #391, leather top, Handcraft decal, 18x19x14" 300.00
Footstool, #394, leather top, arched sides, unmk, 16x19x15" 375.00
Footstool, #394, leather top/arched rails, decal, 19" W, EX 550.00
Magazine stand, #46, 4-shelf, 3-slat sides, unmk, rfn, 42" 1,100.00
Rocker, #809, 5-slat bk, spring seat, unmk, cleaned, 34" 75.00
Settle, #220, 2 corbels ea arm/6 in bk, branded, rfn, 85" ...18,000.00
Settle, #232, even-arm, 5 broad bk slats/1 ea side, mk, 72" 3,500.00
Sideboard, #738, plate rail, door ea side 2 center drw, EX 1,900.00
Table, #558, 8-sided, legs mortised through top, unmk, 17" 850.00
Table, book; #516, sides alternate w/shelf & slats, stains 3,250.00
Table, library; #530, 1-drw, shelf, decal, top wear, 36" 750.00
Table, library; ½-drw ea side, decal, rstr top, 54" L.....................800.00
Table, ped base w/4 corbels, branded, stained, 48" dia............. 2,000.00
Table, trestle; #593, shelf/key tenons, unsgn, rfn, 28x48" 600.00
Table, trestle; #594, shelf, dbl supports, unsgn, rfn, 72" 1,700.00
Table, trestle; #594, well-shaped shoe ft base, unsgn, 72" 3,700.00
Tabouret, #558, 6-sided, unsgn, some stains, 20x18" 500.00
Tabouret, #559, 8-sided, legs mortised through top, decal 1,100.00
Wastebasket, cut-out hdls, arched aprons, unmk/stripped, 15" 125.00

Stickley Bros.

Chair, Morris; att, slanted arms, rfn, unsgn, 39x27x36"........... 1,800.00
China closet, 2 glaze doors, mirror int, branded, 62x46" 8,500.00
Costumer, #175, 1-post, X-base, exposed key, unsgn, 72" 300.00
Desk, #6500, drop front, 2½-drw over 1, cut-out sides, EX 950.00
Magazine ped, shaped sides widen toward base, 4-shelf, 46" 850.00
Magazine rack, #4602, mahog, 4-shelf, slat sides, 47x15x12" 800.00
Magazine stand, #4602, 5-shelf, shaped gallery, tag, 47" 900.00
Plant stand, #5873, 4 posts, dbl stretchers, 18x15".....................550.00
Rocker, Morris; #322, shaped open arms, spring seat, tag.............250.00
Sconce, dbl; copper w/Nouveau lines, #342, new patina, 15" 475.00
Sideboard, #8609, 2-door top over 2 in base+3 drws, #d, 62".......950.00
Table, lamp; 3-slat sides, shelf, label, rfn, 30x18", EX 400.00
Table, library; #184, medial shelf, unmk, rfn, 36".......................300.00
Table, occasional; #2503, 8-sided/2-tier, unmk, 26x30", NM 850.00
Table, trestle; #639, child's, unsgn, toe missing, 36" 475.00

Stiegel

Baron Henry Stiegel produced glassware in Pennsylvania as early as 1760, very similar to glass being made concurrently in Germany and England. Without substantiating evidence, it is impossible to positively attribute a specific article to his manufacture. Although he made other types of glass, today the term Stiegel generally refers to any very early ware made in shapes and colors similar to those he is known to have produced — especially that with etched or enameled decoration. It is generally conceded, however, that most glass of this type is of European origin.

Our advisor for this category is Mark Vuono; he is listed in the Directory under Connecticut.

Bottle, eng floral, sq w/rnded shoulder, 9" 130.00
Bottle, med red-amethyst, dmn-daisy variant, thin, 5½", NM .. 3,300.00
Flask, dk amethyst, 20 dmn on honeycomb, flattened, 5½"..... 3,700.00
Flip, floral eng, tooled lip, pontil, 8", pr.....................................400.00

Mug, elaborate eng, strap hdl, 6" 250.00
Salt cellar, sapphire, 12-Honeycomb Over Dmns, dbl ogee, 3"....150.00

Stocks and Bonds

Scripophily (scrip-awfully), the collecting of 'worthless' old stocks and bonds, gained recognition as an area of serious interest around the mid-1970s. Today there are an estimated 5,000 collectors in the United States and 15,000 worldwide. Collectors who come from numerous business fields mainly enjoy its hobby aspect, though there are those who consider scripophily an investment. Some collectors like the historical significance that certain certificates have. Others prefer the beauty of older stocks and bonds that were printed in various colors with fancy artwork and ornate engravings. Even autograph collectors are found in this field, on the lookout for signed certificates.

Many factors help determine the collector value: autograph value, age of the certificate, the industry represented, whether it is issued or not, its attractiveness, condition, and collector demand. Certificates from the mining, energy, and railroad industries are the most popular with collectors. Other industries or special collecting fields include banking, automobiles, aircraft, and territorials. Serious collectors usually prefer only issued certificates that date from before 1930. Unissued certificates are usually worth one-fourth to one-eighth the value of one that has been issued. Inexpensive issued common stocks and bonds dated between the 1940s and 1980s usually retail between $1.00 to $10.00. Those dating between 1890 and 1930 usually sell for $10.00 to $50.00. Those over one hundred years old retail between $25.00 and $100.00 or more, depending on the quantity found. Autographed stocks normally sell anywhere from $100.00 to $1,000.00. A formal collecting organization for scripophilists is known as The Bond & Share Society with an American chapter located in New York City.

In many of the following listings, two-letter state abbreviations immediately follow company name. All are in near-mint condition unless noted otherwise.

Our advisor for this category is Warren Anderson; he is listed in the Directory under Utah.

Key:
cp — coupon   U — unissued
I/C — issued/cancelled   vgn — vignette
I/U — issued/uncancelled

Atchison, Topeka & Santa Fe RR, KS/1886, 3 vgns, I/C..............45.00
AZ Belmont Mining, AZ/1913, 3/vgns, gold seal, I/U...................20.00
Bank of United States of America, PA/1837, eagle/ship, I/U 400.00
Blackfoot Mining & Milling, MT/1880s, 3 vgns, U.......................20.00
Bull Run Petroleum Co, PA/1866, early oil scene........................125.00
Butte Copper Exploration, MT/1905, miners in tunnel vgn, I/U...20.00
Cedar Hollow Line, PA/1856, train/smelters vgn, I/C...................50.00
Copper Belt Mines, WY/1909, eagle vgn, seal, I/U.......................25.00
Deming, Sierra Madre & Pacific RR, 1889, $1000, I/U................65.00
Edison Portland Cement, NJ/1899, issued to & sgn by T Edison.750.00
El Dorado Grand Mining, NV/1923, miners vgn, I/U 25.00
Eureka Hamilton Mines, NV/1921, miners vgn, seal, I/U 15.00
Florence-Goldfield Mining, SD/1908, miners vgn, I/U 30.00
Florence-Jumbo Lease, NV/1908, goddess vgn, seal, I/U 25.00
Gold Reef Divide Mining, NV/1919, 3 vgns/seal, I/U 20.00
Golden Dream Montezuma Mining, AZ/1907, 3 vgns, I/U............25.00
Golden Streak Mining & Milling Co, Nevada/1868, miners.......150.00
Goldfield Canadian Mining, AZ/1907, vgn, seal, I/U 25.00
Good Hope Mining & Milling, British Columbia/1898, vgn, I/U..25.00
Grand Republic Gold Mining, CO/1906, miners vgn/border, I/U .25.00
Jefferson Co, Radarsburg/1872, red on gr, bond, 5x11" 75.00

Keystone Tire & Rubber, NY/1927, car/angels vgn, ABNCo, I/U ..20.00
Little Joe Gold Mining of Manhattan, AZ/1906, vgns, I/U 25.00
Little Pittsburgh Mining, UT/1907, goddess vgn, I/U 25.00
MO, KS & TX Railway Co, 1880, cattle scene, sgn Jay Gould ...450.00

1902 New Mexico Territory RR (trolly) bond, $125.00 at auction.

New Viola Co Ltd, England/Idaho/1890, ornate print, I/U 30.00
Northern RR, NH/1902, train vgn, red seal, I/C 20.00
Possum Oil, OK/1915, train/oilfield vgn, I/U.................................20.00
Red Cloud. . .Mines, AZ/1918, eagle vgn, ABNCo, I/U 15.00
Rugby Oil Co, WY/1917, oilfield vgn/scenes in border, I/U 15.00
SE KY Oil & Gas, DE/1902, oilwagon vgn, stamp/seal, I/U 20.00
Sierra Consolidated Gold Mining, WV/1906, gold title, I/U 30.00
Sierra Consolidated Gold Mining, WV/1906, 20 coupons, I/U 40.00
Silver King Mines, AZ/1924, oval miners vgn, I/U 15.00
Springville Co-Op Mercantile Institution, UT/1870s, vgn, U.......60.00
Steinmetz Electric Motor Car Co, MD/1922, eagle......................100.00
Summit Gold Mining, CO/1902, lion vgn, gr on blk, I/U 25.00
Tamarack Gold Mining & Milling, AZ/1906, train vgn, I/U.........30.00
Treasury Dept, Stonewall Jackson Issue, dtd Mar 1863, EX 28.50
Two Bros Consolidated Mines, CA/1914, 3 vgns, I/U 20.00
Union Passenger Railway, portraits, ABNCo, 1874, I/C, EX 10.00
United Verde Mining, NV/1907, eagle vgn, gr seal, I/C 20.00
Utah & Pleasant Valley RR, UT Territory/1878, $1000 bond 150.00
Vella Vista Oil, AZ/1900, derrick vgn, gold eagle, I/U...................25.00
West Morning Glory Mining, UT/1901, miners vgn, I/U 25.00
Western Plains Oil, CO/1917, steer vgn, orange border, I/U 15.00
Yel Pine Mines & Reduction, CO/1916, miners/tunnel vgn, I/U ..20.00
1st Nat'l Bank of Bend, OR/1926, eagle vgn, 20 shares, I/U 30.00
13th & 15th Streets Passenger Railway of Phila, 1912, I/C 10.00

Stoneware

There are three broad periods of time that collectors of American pottery can look to in evaluating and dating the stoneware and earthenware in their collections. Among the first permanent settlers in America were English and German potters who found a great demand for their individually-turned wares. The early pottery was produced from red and yellow clays scraped from the ground at surface levels. The earthenware made in these potteries was fragile and coated with lead glazes that periodically created health problems for the people who ate or drank from it. There was little stoneware available for sale until the early 1800s, because the clays used in its production were not readily available in many areas and transportation was prohibitively expensive.

The opening of the Erie Canal and improved roads brought about a dramatic increase in the accessibility of stoneware clay, and many new potteries began to open in New York and New England.

Collectors have difficulty today locating earthenware and stoneware jugs produced prior to 1840, because few have survived intact. These ovoid or pear-shaped jugs were designed to be used on a daily basis. When cracked or severely chipped, they were quickly discarded.

The value of hand-crafted pottery is often determined by the cobalt decoration it carries. Pieces with elaborate scenes (a chicken pecking corn, a bluebird on a branch, a stag standing near a pine tree, a sailing ship, or people) may easily bring $1,000 to $12,000 at auction.

After the Civil War, there was a need and a national demand for stoneware jugs, crocks, canning jars, churns, spittoons, and a wide variety of other pottery items. The competition among the many potteries reached the point where only the largest could survive. To cut costs, most potteries did away with all but the simplest kinds of decoration on their wares. Time-consuming brush-painted birds or flowers quickly gave way to more simply-executed swirls or numbers and stenciled designs. The coming of home refrigeration and Prohibition in 1919 effectively destroyed the American stoneware industry.

Investment possibilities: 1) Early 19th-century stoneware with elaborate decorations and a potter's mark is expensive and will continue to rise in price. 2) Late 19th century hand-thrown stoneware with simple cobalt swirls or numbers is still reasonably priced and a good investment. 3) Mass-produced stoneware (ca. 1890-1920) is available in large quantities, inexpensive, and has been slowly increasing in price over the last ten years.

Skillfully repaired pieces often surface; their prices should reflect their condition. Look for a slight change in color and texture. The use of a black light is also useful in exposing some repairs. Buyer beware! Hint: Buy only from reputable dealers who will guarantee their merchandise.

In the following listings, 'c/s' means 'cobalt on salt glaze'; all decoration described before this abbreviation is in cobalt. See also Bennington, Stoneware.

Bottle, band/label highlight, c/s, D Bacon, 9", EX........................150.00
Bowl, floral/#2, c/s, brn int, appl hdls, 12", EX 300.00
Bowl, milk; foliage, brushed, c/s, rim spout/appl hdls, 12"...........425.00
Bowl, milk; foliage, brushed, c/s, str sides, 4x9" dia.....................300.00
Bowl, stripes, brushed, c/s, 4x7" dia 125.00
Butter crock, floral, brushed, c/s, appl hdls, lid, 11" dia...............725.00
Canteen, emb: Utica Commandery/X/1900, c/s, Whites, 2¾" 500.00
Churn, deer (EX art/detail), c/s, Wm A Lewis, 6-gal, EX 3,700.00
Churn, foliage/#6, brushed, c/s, wear/flakes, 20" 175.00

Crock, rose in cobalt, Ottman Brothers, Fort Edward, NY, applied handles, 12", $350.00.

Crock, bird on branch/#1½, c/s, minor flakes, 8" 250.00
Crock, bird w/topknot looks bk, c/s, brn int, Burger, 10" 1,850.00
Crock, brushwork, c/s, sm chips, 7½" 55.00
Crock, elaborate vintage, blk on salt glaze, L Lehman, 9" 480.00
Crock, floral band, brushed, c/s, 7" 175.00
Crock, pecking chicken, quilled, c/s, brn int, 13", NM..............600.00
Crock, tulip, brushed, c/s, Evan...Pittston PA, 7", EX 145.00
Crock, tulip, brushed, c/s, minor edge flakes, 8" 150.00
Crock, 1839/line in sepia on stoneware, Lyman & Clark, 14" 850.00
Crock, 2 birds (stylized)/#2, c/s, S Hart, 8¾", EX 1,500.00
Inkwell, zigzags, c/s, conical, 2⅜" 350.00
Jar, Albany slip, incised #3, 14" 30.00
Jar, bird (stylized/polka dotted), c/s, S Hart, 9¾", EX................550.00
Jar, bird on branch, c/s, w/lid, 10" 350.00
Jar, brushed designs all around, c/s, ovoid, 5½" 400.00
Jar, brushwork, c/s, 7⅝" 200.00
Jar, canning; commas (lg to sm), brushed, c/s, 6" 400.00
Jar, canning; flourish, quilled, c/s, 7⅜" 375.00
Jar, canning; fruit, brushed, c/s, 10", EX 200.00
Jar, canning; stencil: Jas Hamilton, c/s, wear/hairlines, 6" 250.00
Jar, canning; stripes, brushed, c/s, 6½" 175.00
Jar, canning; swan (primitive)/1890, brushed, c/s, 8" 550.00
Jar, canning; 7 horizontal stripes, brushed, c/s, 6¾"..................300.00
Jar, floral, brushed, c/s, brn highlights, ovoid, hdls, 16" 250.00
Jar, floral, brushed, c/s, gold highlights, red int, 11" 300.00
Jar, floral, brushed, c/s, N Clark, ovoid, hdls, 13", EX 250.00
Jar, floral, brushed, c/s, 6½", EX 150.00
Jar, floral (bold/allover)/Five, c/s, ovoid, 16", EX 600.00
Jar, floral (EX color/detail), brushed, c/s, 8" 400.00
Jar, floral (simple), brushed, c/s, N Tracy, 1864, 17", EX 625.00
Jar, floral ea side, brushed, c/s, ovoid, hdls, 12", EX...................350.00
Jar, floral/#2, brushed, c/s, Lyons, appl hdls, 12", EX 325.00
Jar, floral/daubs, bk: 'One,' c/s, ovoid, hdls, 11", NM 450.00
Jar, foliage/#4, c/s, John Burger, stains, 20" 350.00
Jar, red clay w/salt glaze, spots unglazed, #4, ovoid, 14" 40.00
Jar, stencil: Hamilton & Jones, c/s, 12½", EX.............................125.00
Jug, bird (long neck/polka dotted) on twig, c/s, White, 14" 825.00
Jug, bird (long tail) on twig, quilled, c/s, NY Co, 16", EX...........600.00
Jug, bird (polka dotted) on branch, c/s, West & Gregg, 14" 850.00
Jug, bird (polka dotted) on vintage branch, Edmonds, 16" 1,800.00
Jug, bird (polka dotted)/#3, c/s, N Clark, ovoid, 17", EX 700.00
Jug, bird on flowering branch, quilled, c/s, W Roberts, 12"..........850.00
Jug, brushwork/#2, c/s, hairlines, 13" 85.00
Jug, brushwork/dashes/1840, c/s, ovoid, firing chips, 12" 300.00
Jug, floral, brushed, c/s, ovoid, 15" 200.00
Jug, floral, c/s, Ballard & Bros, firing flaw, 15¾"........................525.00
Jug, floral, quilled, c/s, 13¾"...375.00
Jug, floral (bold), c/s, Cowden & Wilcox, 16", NM 350.00
Jug, floral (EX detail/color), quilled, c/s, J Burger, 14" 1,750.00
Jug, floral (lg)/#2, c/s, Geddes, 14" 475.00
Jug, floral (lg/EX color) quilled, c/s, WH Farrar, 14"...............1,300.00
Jug, floral (2/lg), brushed, c/s, ovoid w/ear hdls, 17" 450.00
Jug, floral/#2, brushed, c/s, brn highlights, 12", EX 225.00
Jug, floral/#2, quilled, c/s, Burger & Lang, ovoid, 14½"..............300.00
Jug, floral/stencil & brushed label, c/s, Vidvard, 11", EX 500.00
Jug, flourish/#2, brushed, c/s, N Clark & Co, ovoid, 13"............325.00
Jug, foliage, brushed, c/s, 11" 175.00
Jug, harvest; floral, c/s, Cowden & Wilcox, tin lid, 8", NM.........475.00
Jug, imp: Geo McKnight...Wholesale Dealing, c/s, ovoid, 7".......190.00
Jug, imp: JV Machett/hdl/lip, c/s, ribbed hdl, ovoid, 12" 350.00
Jug, leaf/#2, brushed, c/s, N Clark, ovoid, 13", EX.....................250.00
Jug, lovebirds (poor color), quilled, c/s, S Pepson, 12", EX 550.00
Jug, pecking chicken, c/s, West Troy, minor flakes, 11" 1,550.00
Jug, pumpkin-head man/leaves, brushed, c/s, 14", EX 900.00

Jug, smoked gray salt glaze, minor flakes, 6" 75.00
Jug, sunflower (dbl/dotted), quilled, c/s, JD McCarthy, 18" 650.00
Jug, tooled lines/lip trim/X, c/s, ovoid, 4"..................................150.00
Jug, wreath/#2, quilled, c/s, F Stetzenmeyer, ovoid, 12" 600.00

Pitcher, leaves and berries in cobalt, minor rim chips, 11", $900.00. Co., dated 1902, $1,200.00.

Pitcher, floral, brushed, c/s, gray w/brn mottle, ovoid, 9" 55.00
Pitcher, floral frieze at shoulder & tooled neck, c/s, 13" 1,200.00
Pitcher, leaves/#2, hdl stripes, brushed, c/s, 13"........................375.00
Rolling pin, gray w/bl bands, wood hdls, 14½" 295.00
Salt cellar, brushwork, c/s, 2½" dia, NM 85.00

Store

   Perhaps more more than any other yester-year establishment, the country store evokes the most nostalgic feelings for folks old enough to remember its charms — barrels for coffee, crackers, and big green pickles; candy in a jar for the grocer to weigh on shiny brass scales; beheaded chickens in the meat case outwardly devoid of nothing but feathers. Today, mementos from this segment of Americana are being collected by those who 'lived it' as well as those less fortunate!

   Our advisor for this category is Charles Reynolds; he is listed in the Directory under Virginia. See also Advertising.

Broom holder, Merkle's Blu-J, metal, 1910s, 28x17x13", EX 250.00
Cabinet, oak w/glass doors, 96x72", EX 750.00
Candy hammer, metal, Dimling's emb on hdl, 1930s, 4" 15.00
Cash drawer, Bell's Mechanical, under counter, Pat 1870 ....65.00
Ceiling fan, Emerson Electric, brass castings, 25" blades, M 250.00
Ceiling fan, iron w/4 wood blades, 52" span, EX 125.00

Cigar showcase, beveled glass top, louvered shelf, 48" long, $175.00.

Display doll, celluloid, toddler, 22" 175.00
Hammer, sugar; wrought iron, flared blade/hammer, 1700s, 6" ...130.00
Holder, wrapping paper; countertop style, 20" 15.00
Holder, wrapping paper; countertop style, 31" 20.00
Lamp, The Pittsburgh, brass, 1880s, 36x16½", EX 300.00
Manequin, man in chair, Stensgard, 11x10x5", EX.....................365.00
Manequin, wooden, countertop, Stensgard, 1945, 15", EX 250.00
Marking machine, Monarch, type in tray, orig cover, EX 75.00
Necklace holder, all brass, revolving counter type.........................60.00
Paper dispenser, Columbia, CI, 29" L, NM 25.00
Printing set, Easy Sign Maker, Pat 1894, lg, EX..........................110.00
String holder, gazebo shape, CI, NM 85.00
String holder, SSS for the Blood, CI caldron, 7x5", EX..............150.00

Stoves

Antique stoves' desirability is based on two criteria: their utility and their decorative value. It's the latter that adds an 'antique' premium to the basic functional value that could be served just as well by a modern stove. Sheer age is usually irrelevant. Decorative features that enhance desirability include fancy, embossed ornamentation, nickel-plated trim, mica windows, ceramic tiles, and (in cooking stoves) water reservoirs and high warming closets rather than mere high shelves. The less sheet metal and the more cast iron, the better. Look for crisp, sharp designs in preference to those made from worn or damaged and repaired foundry patterns. Stoves with pastel porcelain finish can be very attractive; blue is a favorite, white is least desirable. Chrome trim, rather than nickel, is the mark of a stove too recent to be interesting. Among stove types, base burners (with self-feeding coal magazines) are the most desirable. Then come the upright, cylindrical 'oak' stoves, kitchen ranges, and wood parlors. Potbellies approach the margin of undesirability; laundries and gasoline stoves plunge through it.

In judging condition, look out for deep rust pits, warped or burnt-out parts, unsound firebricks, poorly-fitting parts, poor repairs, and empty mounting holes indicating missing trim. Search meticulously for cracks in the cast iron. Our listings reflect auction prices of completely restored, safe, and functional stoves, unless indicated otherwise.

There's a thin but continuing stream of desirable antique stoves going to the high-priced Pacific Coast market. Interest in antique stoves is least in the Deep South. Demand for wood/coal stoves is strongest in areas where firewood is affordable and storage of it is practical. Demand for antique gas ranges has recently surged, especially in metropolitan markets.

The market for antique stoves is so thin and the variety so bewildering that a consensus on a going price can hardly emerge. They are only worth something to the right individual, and prices realized depend very greatly on who happens to be in the auction crowd. Even an expert's appraisal will usually miss the realized price by a substantial percent.

Base Burners

Acme Sunburst #112, Wehrle Co, Newark OH, M **2,900.00**
Art Amherst #15, NP trim, tiles, 11" urn, 50x25x28" **1,500.00**
Burdett, Smith & Co #44, Chicago, swivel top, tiles, 38"...........950.00
Detroit Emerald Jewel #14, mica doors, NP trim, 69", EX....... **2,500.00**
Favorite #30, Piqua OH, ornate chrome/mica windows, 52" ... **1,600.00**
Waverly #12, Thos Caffney & Co, Boston MA, 40x20x22" ... **1,350.00**
Weir Glennwood #5, NP trim, mica windows, 1909, 68" 700.00

Box Stoves

A Belanger Barge No 14, scrollwork, CI, 1906, sm 300.00

BF&M Co #1, front load, early 1800s, 17x24"............................**100.00**
E Eaton No 24, Amherst NH, CI schoolhouse type, 24x38x16" .**350.00**
Shaker, 1-pc cast body, wrought latch, 1800s, 21x35x14" 275.00
Unknown, parlor type, reeded column sides, 1830s, 25x32x17" ..**400.00**

Franklin Stoves

Acme #18 Orient 1890, 6 tiles, mica window, fancy **300.00**
Atlanta Franklin #8M, CI, 2-burner, coal/wood, EX **100.00**
Barstow #137 Orient 1886, CI fireplace, coal, 37"+6" urn...........**900.00**
C Newcomb & Co Worcester, fireplace, ca 1800, 38x24x30". **1,250.00**
Home Franklin #2, fireplace, dtd 1852, 31x26x36" **150.00**
IA Sheppard Open Franklin #6, fireplace, 1860s, 37x21x26" **500.00**
Magee Ideal #3, CI fireplace, 2 side trivets, 1892, 32x28".........**150.00**
Muzzy & Co Villa Franklin, fancy CI fireplace, 20x29x19" **150.00**
SH Ransom Ben Franklin Air Tight, Pat 1850, 33x22x34" **225.00**
Sunny Hearth #2, CI fireplace, 1850s, 11x18x18" **850.00**
Sunny Hearth #2, coal burning, water urn at top, 1850s, 35" **250.00**
Unknown, #13, Abendroth NY, fireplace, 3-leg, dtd 1874 ....**75.00**
Walker/Pratt Berkeley #3, fancy CI fireplace, 42" **700.00**

Parlor

AJ Coffin #4, 4 Corinthian columns, 1840s, 47"+10" urn....... **1,200.00**
Albany NY, 4 Corinthian-style columns, 1820s, 42"+15" urn . **1,300.00**
Anthony Davy & Co Lady Washington, Pat 1848, 26"+7" urn...**225.00**
Barstow Gem #3, Pat June 3, 1892, CI, 2 doors, 30x21x27" **275.00**
Beckwith Air Tight #18, NP trim & rail, 1880s, 48x23x21".......**275.00**
Burdett, Smith & Co #44, CI, mica windows, 38"+8" urn **275.00**
C&EL Granger #1, 2-column, sheet metal top, 1830s, 26" **300.00**
Cooperative Cycle #12, 6-panel mica door, 1890s, 46"+10" urn .**400.00**
Cooperative Foundry Sylvan Red Cross #45, Pat 1899, 52".........**200.00**
Fuller, Warren, & Morrison Floral #2, 1853, 45x22x27" **1,000.00**
GH Ransom Parlor #3 Gem, Pat 1855, ornate CI, 32"+6" urn **550.00**
GW Eddy Forest #3, Pat 1854, ornate CI, 28"+6" urn **225.00**
Ilion #3, CI, rnd body w/claw ft, 1853, 27x11" urn **500.00**
Ilion #5, ornate CI, rnd body, ca 1853, 33"+13" 2-pc urn...........**400.00**
J Petree Excelsior #5, ornate CI, side door, 27"+12" urn.............**200.00**
Low & Hicks #4, Revere Air-Tight, cathedral front, 29"+urn.....**275.00**
Low & Hicks Gothic #4, CI, 4 front doors, 1840s, 36"+6" urn **350.00**

Oak Pennsular #216, coal burner,
48" with 11" urn, $775.00.

Perry Dandy #12 Albany NY 1889, mica door, 46"+7" urn **300.00**
Pratt/Wentworth Peerless, CI w/sheet iron, 1850s, 37x19x25" **90.00**

Rathbone/Sard Floral Acorn #38, NP trim ca 1894, 37"+9" urn .600.00
SH Ranson, Albany, Pat 1848, Victorian CI, 31"+13" urn..........225.00
Somerset Oak #18, Pat 1894, NP trim on CI, 61½" 200.00
Sylvan Red Cross #31, Pat 1888-89, tiles, 37"+6" urn.................225.00
Tropic Crawford #114, mica windows/NP trim, 1890s, 60" 150.00
Tyson Furnace #1, 2 sheet-metal columns, fancy, 36x17x25" 250.00
Union Airtight, Pat 1851, Victorian styling, 26x18x24" 200.00
Weir Glenwood #25, oven in top, NP trim, 1880s, 64x24x26" ..700.00
Wood/Bishop Royal Clarion #14, oven in top/mica window, 50"..150.00
Wood/Bishop Sunrise-Sunshine #23, 1870s, 28"+10" dome/urn ..275.00

Ranges

Atlantic Grand, Portland, ornate bk shelf, 12x20x18", EX 1,700.00
Detroit Jewel, cabinet, gas, glass door, 1916, VG 400.00
Lakeside Eastern Windsor, warming oven/reservoir, 1908, lg 400.00
Monitor #20, Cleveland 1887, oil burning, 29x21x23"................100.00
Noyes/Nutter Star Kineo #8-20, CI, high closet, ca 1910 ....700.00
Queen Atlantic, Portland, 1-shelf, simple style, 1930s.................500.00
Taunton Quaker Standard #8-20, nickel trivets/trim, 1880s 700.00
Walker & Pratt Village Crawford Royal, chrome trim, 1910s 600.00
Weir Modern Glenwood Home Grand #280, NP trim, 1910, lg..600.00
Wood/Bishop Imperial Clarion #8, 2-shelf, ornate CI, 1897 ....850.00

Miscellaneous

Atlantic #214, potbelly, NP on CI, dtd 1901, 56x19x19", EX.....160.00
Fireplace, Laconia, CI w/NP trim/tin cover, 1860s, 35x31x23" ...100.00
Griswold, space heater, sheet steel, iron base & top, 27" 88.00
Laundry, Stamford Laundry #20, 4-ring lid, 21½x21x26" 150.00
Laundry, Walker/Pratt #14, Pat 1874, dtd 1883, 25x24x24" 400.00
Standard Globe Incandescent, kerosene burner, 1900s, 29"..........75.00
Unknown, fancy CI, corner style w/3 legs, 1890s, 33x22x24" 100.00

Stove Manufacturers' Toy Stoves

Buck's Jr range, St Louis MO, new body/pnt/recast parts, 26".....850.00
Charter Oak #503, GF Filley, St Louis MO, 14x12x25", EX ... 2,050.00
Dainty, Reading Stove Works, PA, 7x13x8", VG 150.00
Great Majestic Jr, Majestic Mfg, 31x16x23", M 5,650.00
Karr Range, Belleville IL, bl porc, old model, 21½x9x13" 3,100.00
Little Eva, T Southard, NYC, 8½x14x11", G.............................350.00
Little Fanny, CI, minor rust, EX..300.00
Little Willie, CI, EX 75.00
Qualified, bl porc w/nickel, Karr, Belleville IL, 1925, EX........ 2,500.00
Qualified, bl porc w/nickel, 1960s repro, EX 2,500.00
Royal American, Bridgeford, Louisville KY, 14x12x20", G 950.00

Toy Manufacturers' Toy Stoves

Eagle, Hubley, Lancaster PA, nickeled, recast parts 450.00
Eclipse, CI, EX...175.00
Little Giant, unmk/unidentified, 7½x8½x11", EX orig 675.00
Novelty, Kenton Hdwe, bl pnt/nickel trim, rfn, 13x6½x8½".......600.00
Pet, The; Young Bros, Albany NY, 10½x6x8½".........................165.00
Queen, The; unmk/unidentified, copper o/l, 23½", M 2,400.00
Rival, J&E Stevens, Cromwell CT, 14x8½x16", M, +2 kettles . 1,350.00
Rival, J&E Stevens, Cromwell CT, 1895, 13x7½x18½", G.........240.00
Triumph, Kenton Hdwe, OH, 14x8½x19", G 195.00

Strawberry Soft Paste and Lustre Ware

Strawberry lustre is a general term for pearlware and semi-porce-

lain decorated with hand-painted strawberries, vines, tendrils, and pink lustre trim. Strawberry soft paste is decorated creamware without the pink lustre trim. Both were made by many manufactures in England in the 19th century, most of whom never marked their ware.

Sugar bowl, vine border, 6⅝", $350.00; Coffeepot, vine border, repaired, chips, 10½", $650.00; Creamer, vine border, 3½", $300.00.

Bowl, soft paste, rstr, 6" 325.00
Coffeepot, dome lid, soft paste, 12", NM...................................... 1,750.00
Cup & saucer, handleless; early, lustre, NM 200.00
Cup & saucer, soft paste, EX 200.00
Plate, soft paste, Davenport, ca 1810, 6½" 175.00
Plate, Wood, lustre, 9"...135.00
Platter, lustre, 11" 200.00
Sauce boat, lustre, 6"...165.00
Sauce boat, soft paste, 5", EX 250.00
Sugar bowl, lustre, w/lid, early...225.00
Teapot, soft paste, rstr, 11" 525.00
Teapot, squat, 1820s, 6", VG...500.00
Teapot, vine border, ftd, 11", NM 575.00

Stretch Glass

Stretch glass, produced from 1916 until after 1930, was made in an effort to emulate the fine art glass of Tiffany and Carder. The glassware was sprayed with a special finish while still hot, and a reheating process caused the coating to contract, leaving a striated, crepe-like iridescence. Northwood, Imperial, Fenton, Diamond, Lancaster, and the United States Glass Company were the largest manufacturers of this type of glass. See also specific companies.

Bowl, bl, w/flower frog, Fenton, sm 25.00
Bowl, bl, Fenton, 3x10" 35.00
Bowl, bl w/blk rim, ftd, US Glass, 2¼x4¾" 25.00
Bowl, vaseline, rolled rim, Fenton, 1½x8¾" 35.00
Compote, bl, Colonial, Fenton or Northwood, 4x5½" 25.00
Pitcher, lemonade; Celeste Bl, cobalt hdl...195.00
Plate, vaseline, octagonal, 6" 12.50
Sherbet, bl, ribbed, Colonial, Imperial..22.00
Vase, pk, dolphin hdls, fan form, Fenton, 6".....................................60.00
Vase, Ribbed Optic, HP florals, Lancaster, 6"...................................45.00

String Holders

Today, if you want to wrap and secure a package, you have a variety of products to choose from: cellophane tape, staples, etc. But in the 1800s, string was about the only available binder; thus the string holder, either the hanging or counter type, was a common and practical item found in most homes and businesses. Chalkware and ceramic figurals from the 1930s and 1940s contrast with the cast and wrought iron examples from the 1800s to make for an interesting collection. Our advisor for this category is Charles Reynolds; he is listed in the Directory under Virginia.

Apple, tin litho figural, 2-part, 4x4", EX 75.00
Apple & berries, chalkware 20.00
Ball type, CI, hinged, ca 1910, EX 110.00
Beehive, CI, blk pnt, 5x6½" dia, EX 45.00
Brass, 2-part sphere on stand, traces of nickel plate, 7½" 55.00
Caldron shape, SSS for the Blood, CI, 7x5" 150.00
Cat, Hold, 1958 ....22.50
Chef's face, ceramic 35.00
Court jester, plaster 40.00
Gazebo shape, CI, NM..85.00
Heart, You'll Always Have a Pull w/Me, mc, ceramic 35.00
Old lady in rocker, chalkware 32.00
Pear, ceramic 26.00
Sailor, eyes to side, w/pipe, chalkware.............................35.00
Sensible, CI, countertop, upright, 1885 ....32.00

Varnished wood sphere with ivory eyelets, 5½", $90.00.

Strawberry face, ceramic...27.50
Tabby, CI, mc pnt, 1880s, 5⅝"....................................900.00

Sugar Shakers

Sugar shakers (or muffineers, as they were also called) were used during the Victorian era to sprinkle sugar and spice onto breakfast muffins, toast, etc. They were made of art glass, in pressed patterns, and in china. See also specific types and manufacturers.

Acorn, peachbloom w/gold florals....................................145.00
Acorn, pk shaded opaque 155.00
Acorn, sapphire bl...165.00
Baby T'print, amberina...235.00
Beatty Honeycomb, wht opal 125.00
Brass, boy on dolphin atop, England, 8½"...........................85.00
Bubble Lattice, cranberry satin, rare 450.00

China, floral spray, pk/wht on wht, no mk 42.00
Chrysanthemum Base Swirl, cranberry opal 95.00
Cone, gr opaque..295.00
Cone, pk cased, tall form 135.00
Corn, turq opaque..110.00
Cranberry, molded panels, SP lid, English, 5¾x2⅜".....................95.00
Jewelled Heart, bl, scarce..195.00
Jumbo & Barnum...145.00

Leaf Umbrella, blue cased, $275.00.

Melligo, bl opaque 95.00
Parian Swirl, wht opaque, HP roses, Northwood, EX 95.00
Quilted Phlox, bl opaque 145.00
Rubena, cut panels, SP top, 5½x2¼" 115.00
Windows Swirled, wht opal 135.00

Sunderland Lustre

Sunderland lustre was made by various potters in the Sunderland district of England during the 18th and 19th centuries. It is characterized by a splashed-on application of the pink lustre, which results in an effect sometimes referred to as the 'cloud' pattern. Some pieces are transfer printed with scenes, ships, florals, or portraits.

Punch bowl, hunting scenes, 12", M, $700.00.

Bowl, Sailor's Farwell/Mason's Arms, blk transfer/mc, 10" 600.00

Bust, Shakespeare, pearlware w/pk lustre base, 8½", EX 325.00
Chamber pot, verse 'Marriage'/other blk transfers w/mc, EX 550.00
Cow creamer, splotched lustre, gr molded base, lid, 6", EX..........265.00
Creamer, copper lustre trim, bl band: emb/mc florals, 3⅝" 135.00
Cup & saucer, cloud pattern, pk lustre, 2¼x4½" 85.00
Cup & saucer, handleless; mini, EX..45.00
Figurine, Seasons, allegorical, Dixon-Austin, 9", set of 4 .... 3,000.00
Jug, Decator/Brown portraits, blk on wht reserves, rare, 6"...... 4,500.00
Jug, puzzle; Gaudy Welsh-type floral, prof rpr, 7" 300.00
Jug, Sunderland Bridge/verse, transfer on wht, 7", EX 375.00
Jug, West View of Iron Bridge/nautical verses, 9½", EX 475.00
Mug, cloud pattern, wear, 6" 175.00
Mug, Sailor's Farewell, blk transfer/mc, frog inside, 5", EX 225.00
Plaque, Gladstone portrait, gr & gold lustre rim, 8¼x7¼"..............80.00
Plaque, Thou God Seest..., blk transfer, wear, 6" dia...................175.00
Salt cellar, master; cloud pattern, pk lustre, ftd.............................55.00
Tea caddy, blk transfer of 4 seasons, late, 4¾" 35.00
Tumbler, cloud pattern, pk lustre 45.00
Wine, wht band w/mc florals, copper lustre trim, wear, 4" 110.00

Surveying Instruments

The practice of surveying offers a wide variety of precision instruments primarily for field use, most of which are associated with the recording of distance and angular measurements. These instruments were primarily made from brass; the larger examples were fitted with tripods and protective cases. These cases also held accessories for the instruments, and these can sometimes play a key part in their evaluation. Instruments in complete condition and showing little use will have much greater values than those that appear to have had moderate or heavy use. Instruments were never polished during use, and those that have been polished as decorator pieces are of little interest to most avid collectors.

Abney level, K&E, ca 1910, w/case 75.00
Abney level, K&E, w/top compass & case......................................125.00
Alidade, folding sight vanes, leather case 45.00
Alidade, telescopic, exploration type, 10" 350.00
Alidade, telescopic, w/post, ca 1910 ....250.00
Barometer, pocket-watch type, 1½" dia, w/case 60.00
Barometer, surveyor's aneroid, w/magnifier, 4" dia......................150.00
Chain, Chesterman Sheffield, 100-ft 100.00
Chain, Chesterman Sheffield, 4-pole, 66-ft....................................120.00
Chain, Grumann's patent..250.00
Chain, Gurley, 4-pole, 66-ft...175.00
Chain, K&E, convertible type, 50- to 100-ft 150.00
Circumferentor, 4 vanes, ca 1810..1,250.00
Clinometer, ca 1890, leather case 75.00
Compass, brass housing, France, 5" 75.00
Compass, geologist's, w/inclinometer needle, 4" sq 100.00
Compass, HM Poole, ca 1850...550.00
Compass, plain, B Pike & Son 450.00
Compass, plain, Chandlee, ca 1810 ....1,200.00
Compass, pocket type, wooden housing, 3" 55.00
Compass, prismatic, ca 1900, leather case......................................95.00
Compass, Railroad type, Wm J Young No 3001.............................700.00
Compass, Solar, W&LE Gurley, ca 1890, w/case & tripod 2,250.00
Compass, staff, folding sight vanes...125.00
Compass, telescopic vernier, Randolf 600.00
Compass, vernier, B Platt, ca 1870 ....550.00
Compass, vernier, W&LE Gurley, ca 1880, 15" 450.00
Compass, wooden, ca 1810, 12" 750.00
Cross staff head, simple type w/4 slits, case 100.00

Cross staff head, w/top-mtd compass...150.00
Drawing instruments, K&E, wooden case, 12x8" tray 150.00
Drawing instruments, leatherette roll, 10" 25.00
Drawing instruments, 8 items in wooden case, 5x8" 75.00
Jacobs staff, oak w/steel tip, octagonal..75.00
Level, Bostrom, unused, w/case & tripod......................................120.00
Level, dumpy, Brunson, blk pnt 175.00
Level, dumpy, K&E, 18"...200.00
Level, farmer's drainage type, simple, 10", w/box & tripod 120.00
Level, hand, peep, 5" long w/bubble, w/leather case......................35.00
Level, wye, architect's convertible, 12"...250.00
Level, wye, builder's, 12" telescope 125.00
Level, wye, CG King, ca 1855, 14"...600.00
Level, wye, Gurley, ca 1880, 18" 350.00
Level, wye, Gurley #18345, 22" 350.00
Level, wye, Phelps & Gurley, 24" 1,100.00
Level, wye, Spencer, London, w/compass 750.00
Level, wye, Stackpole Bros, ca 1870, 16" 500.00
Plumb-bob, mining type w/wick & gimbals, in box.......................350.00
Plumb-bob, w/internal reel 110.00
Pocket transit, Brunton, Wm Ainsworth, 1893..............................110.00
Semi-circumferentor, Am, all brass, ca 1800............................. 1,650.00
Semi-circumferentor, Am, wooden w/brass sights.................... 1,100.00
Theodolite, Buff & Buff, 8" horizontal circle 1,250.00
Theodolite, English, 18th C 1,000.00
Theodolite, Fauth & Co, 16" horizontal circle 2,250.00
Theodolite, Wm Wurdemann #2 — , 12" telescope............... 1,050.00
Transit, blk pnt, ca 1930 ....225.00
Transit, builder's type, Bostrom, K&E, Leitz, ca 1930 ....120.00
Transit, convertible, solar-mining, complete 1,850.00

Surveyor's transit, E. & G.W. Blunt, NY, mid-19th century, VG, $595.00.

Transit, exploration type, ca 1890, 8" 450.00
Transit, K&E, bent-standard design, ca 1910 ....500.00
Transit, lt mountain, ca 1900 ....450.00
Transit, mining, dbl telescope...900.00
Transit, W&LE Gurley, Troy NY, #1235 ....450.00
Transit, W&LE Gurley, Troy NY, ca 1860......................................600.00
Transit, w/Burt solar attachment 1,200.00
Transit, w/side mtd solar attachment, ca 1910 ....850.00
Transit, w/top mtd solar attachment, ca 1900 ....950.00
Transit, Wm J Young Maker Phila...700.00
Transit, Young & Sons #9405 ....450.00
Tripod, compass type, 1-pc legs...75.00

Tripod, transit type, telescopic legs	45.00
Tripod, transit type, 1-pc legs	75.00
Tripod, w/alidade table	150.00

Swastika Keramos

Swastika Keramos was a line of artware made by the Owens China Co., of Minerva, Ohio, around 1902-1904. It is characterized either by a coralene type of decoration (similar to the Opalesce line made by the J.B. Owens Pottery Company of Zanesville) or by the application of metallic lustres, usually in simple designs. Shapes are often plain and handles squarish and rather thick, suggestive of the Arts and Crafts style.

Pitcher, flowers/leaves, red/gr on gold, sm mouth, 11"	170.00
Vase, iris, purple-lined red & gold on metallic, 12"	450.00
Vase, landscape, mc, 9"	550.00
Vase, Nouveau florals, red on gold lustre, 3-hdl, 6x6"	185.00
Vase, Nouveau florals on copper, 6½"	125.00
Vase, tree trunks, bronzed/gold against red horizon, 10"	600.00
Vase, trees, gray & rose, squat, 6"	250.00
Vase, 3-color La Sa type, bowling pin form, flared top, 14½"	225.00

Syracuse

Syracuse was a line of fine dinnerware which was made for nearly a century by the Onondaga Pottery Company of Syracuse, New York. Collectors of American dinnerware are focusing their attention on reassembling some of their many lovely patterns. In 1966 the firm became officially known as the Syracuse China Company in order to better identify with the name of their popular chinaware. By 1971 dinnerware geared for use in the home was discontinued, and the company turned to the manufacture of hotel, restaurant, and other types of commercial tableware.

Arcadia, bowl, vegetable; oval	45.00
Arcadia, cup & saucer	25.00
Arcadia, plate, cake	50.00
Arcadia, platter, 14"	55.00
Arlington, coffeepot	75.00
Arlington, creamer	20.00
Arlington, cup, demitasse	15.00
Arlington, platter, 14"	60.00
Arlington, rimmed soup	15.00
Arlington, shakers, pr	12.00
Beverly, bowl, vegetable; oval	30.00
Beverly, cup & saucer	27.50
Beverly, plate, bread & butter	15.00
Beverly, plate, dinner	25.00
Beverly, plate, salad	16.00
Beverly, platter, 12"	25.00
Beverly, sauce bowl	10.00
Beverly, sugar bowl, w/lid	25.00
Bracelet, cup & saucer	30.00
Jefferson, coffeepot	95.00
Jefferson, gravy boat	65.00
Jefferson, soup, rimmed	20.00
Jefferson, sugar bowl	35.00
Melrose, cup & saucer	12.00
Melrose, relish	15.00
Suzanne, gravy boat	65.00
Suzanne, plate, dinner	20.00

Suzanne, platter, 14"	60.00
Victoria, bowl, vegetable; oval	35.00
Victoria, cup & saucer	22.00
Victoria, gravy boat	50.00
Victoria, plate, bread & butter	9.00
Victoria, plate, dinner	18.00
Victoria, plate, salad	12.00
Victoria, platter, lg	65.00

Syrups

Values are for old, original syrups. Beware of reproductions! See also various manufacturers and specific types of glass.

Alabama	125.00
Banded Portland	75.00
Banded Portland, rose flashed, very scarce	325.00
Beaded Swag, ruby stained, etched scrolls, Heisey	195.00
Beauty, ruby stained	350.00
Block Band, George Duncan, 1880s	135.00
Bulging Midriff, vaseline	165.00
Button Arches, orig pewter lid, 7"	75.00
Challinor's Forget-Me-not, chartreuse	135.00
Chrysanthemum Base Swirl, wht speckled	165.00
Coin Spot, bl opal	165.00
Columbian Coin, EX gold, orig lid	225.00
Cone, pk cased, squatty, orig lid	175.00
Cord & Tassel	125.00
Cordova	45.00
Coreopsis, EX decor	145.00
Daisy & Fern, cranberry swirled, Northwood, rare	450.00
Dewdrop, Findley, scarce	85.00
Diamonds, emb pk opal w/appl opal hdl	225.00
Emerald Green Herringbone (Florida)	185.00
Eyewinker	120.00
Fishnet & Poppies, milk glass	125.00
French Primrose, milk glass	65.00
Frosted Lion, orig dtd pewter lid	300.00

Gonterman's Swirl, very rare, 7½", $495.00.

Grape & Leaf, bl opaque	250.00
Guttate, pk cased, metal lid	295.00
Heart w/T'print, pewter lid	75.00

Hexagon Block, amber flashed, frosted florals 245.00
Hexagon Block, ruby stained 195.00
Hobnail, cranberry opal, pewter lid, 6½" 400.00
Lattice, cranberry opal, w/SP spring lid, Pat 81 & 82, rare...........575.00
Leaf Mold, vaseline spatter, rare 425.00
Leaf Umbrella, mauve cased, pewter lid, rare 635.00
Locket on Chain, ruby stained 1,350.00
Medallion Sprig, rubena.............375.00
Millard, etched, ruby stained.............225.00
Millard, plain, ruby stained 175.00
Moon & Star, orig tin lid, rare 125.00
Netted Oak, milk glass, w/gold.............115.00
Notched Panel 50.00
Optic, rubena, Hobbs.............175.00
Optic Rib, vaseline 125.00
Parian Swirl, cranberry, rare 335.00
Patee Cross.............50.00
Pk & wht spatter, Hobbs' Coloratura series.............150.00
Priscilla 110.00
Prize 150.00
Prize, ruby flashed.............235.00
Ring Band, custard w/EX gold 350.00
Rope & T'print, Hobbs, Pat Jan 29 '84 on lid, EX.............65.00
Rubena to clear, ribbed, clear hdl, 6".............145.00
Shoshone, yel stained.............275.00
Snail (Idaho) 65.00
Spanish Lace, vaseline opal.............225.00
Sunburst & Block 50.00
Sunk Honeycomb.............165.00
Swan/Wading Heron, milk glass, pewter lid, dtd June 22, 1869...185.00
Thousand Eye, amber 135.00
Torpedo.............65.00
Torquay, milk glass w/yel stripes 135.00
Truncated Cube, ruby, rare, 7½".............235.00
Utah, tin lid 75.00
Valencia Waffle, bl.............135.00
Venetia, cranberry.............295.00
Venetian Diamond, vaseline & wht spatter, rare 185.00
Wisconsin 85.00

Target Balls

Prior to 1880 when the clay pigeon was invented, blown glass target balls were used extensively for shotgun competitions. Approximately 2¾" in diameter, these balls were hand-blown into a three-piece mold. All have a ragged hole where the blowpipe was twisted free. Target balls date from approximately 1840 (English) to World War I, although they were most widely used in the 1870-1880 period. Common examples are unmarked except for the blower's code — dots, crude numerals, etc. Some balls are embossed in a dot or diamond pattern so they were more likely to shatter when struck by shot, and some have names and/or patent dates. When evaluating condition, bubbles and other minor manufacturing imperfections are acceptable; cracks are not. The prices below are for mint condition examples.

Black Pitch, CTB Co.............250.00
Bogardus' Glass Ball Pat'd April 10 1877, amber.............250.00
Bogardus' Glass Ball Pat'd April 10 1877, other than amber.......800.00
Emb ribs, amber.............150.00
English, shooter emb in 2 rnd panels, clear.............300.00
English, shooter emb in 2 rnd panels, gr.............300.00
English, shooter emb in 2 rnd panels, purple.............300.00
For Hockey's Patent Trap, gr.............500.00

Great Western Gun Works, amber.............900.00
Gurd & Son, London, Ontario, amber.............400.00
Ira Paine's Filled Ball Pat Oct 23 1877, amber.............250.00
Ira Paine's Filled Ball Pat Oct 23 1877, amber, set of 10 ....950.00
Ira Paine's Filled Ball Pat Oct 23 1877, other than amber.........800.00
NB Glass Works Perth, other than pale gr.............300.00
NB Glass Works Perth, pale gr, almost clear.............200.00
Plain, amber.............65.00
Plain, clear, w/mold marks............. 1,000.00
Plain, cobalt.............150.00
Plain, purple.............150.00
WW Greener St Mary's Works Brim/68 Haymarket London 250.00

Related Memorabilia

Clay birds, Winchester, Pat May 29 1917, 1 flight in box.............100.00
Pitch bird, blk, DUVROCK 1.00
Shell, dummy, w/single window, any brand 25.00
Shell, dummy shotgun, Winchester, window w/powder, 6".........100.00
Shell set, dummy, Gamble Stores, 2 window shells, 3 cut out......125.00

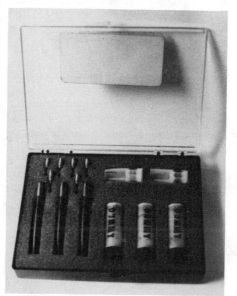

Remington functional dummy shell set $50.00.

Shell set, dummy, Winchester, 5 window shells.............125.00
Shell set, dummy shotgun, Peters, 6 window shells+full box 125.00
Shotshell loader, rosewood/brass, Parker Bros, Pat 1884 ....50.00
Target, Am sheet metal, rod ends mk Pat Feb 8 '21, set.............25.00
Target, blk japanned sheet metal, Bussy Patentee, London.............50.00
Target, BUST-O, blk or wht breakable wafer 20.00
Trap, DUVROCK, w/blk pitch birds 150.00
Trap, MO-SKEET-O, w/birds 150.00

Tea Caddies

Because tea was once regarded as a precious commodity, special boxes called caddies were used to store the tea leaves. They were made from various materials: porcelain, carved and inlaid woods, and metals ranging from painted tin or tole to engraved silver. Our advisor for this category is Tina Carter; she is listed in the Directory under California.

Bird's eye maple w/inlay, Federal, brass ft, 6x10x5".............400.00
Gilt & lacquer w/figures in landscape, Chinese, 1800s, 4" 300.00
Mahog, blown/etched Stiegle-type container w/in, trn ft 1,000.00
Mahog & satinwood, flower inlay in top, 1810, 4½".............300.00

Federal mahogany tea caddy, early 19th century, 5" x 9" x 5", $200.00.

Pearwood, pear form, Geo III, 1780s, 5½", EX **1,500.00**
Pearwood w/mahog banding, cvd flower, dmn form, 1700s, 5" ...**500.00**
Tortoise shell veneer, basketweave panels, 5x4x3", EX **800.00**

Tea Leaf Ironstone

Tea Leaf Ironstone became popular in the 1880s when middle-class American housewives became bored with the plain white stone china that English potters had been exporting to this country for nearly a century. The original design has been credited to Anthony Shaw of Longport, who decorated the plain ironstone with a hand-painted copper lustre design of bands and leaves. Originally known as Lustre Band and Sprig, the pattern has since come to be known as Tea Leaf Lustre. It was produced with minor variations by many different firms both in England and the United States. By the early 1900s, it had become so commonplace that it had lost much of its appeal.

Our advice for this category comes from Home Place Antiques, whose address is listed in the Directory under Illinois.

Bone dish, Crescent, Meakin, 9⅝x3⅛" **65.00**
Bone dish, Crescent, Wilkinson, 6¼x3" **65.00**
Bowl, fruit; low ped, Meakin **435.00**
Bowl, fruit; tall ped, Wilkinson **475.00**
Bowl, pie crust edge, 2½x7½" **65.00**
Bowl, vegetable; Bamboo, w/lid, Meakin **115.00**
Bowl, vegetable; Ribbed, w/lid, Wedgewood **65.00**
Bowl, vegetable; Sunburst, w/lid, 6-sided, Shaw...........................**175.00**
Butter pat, sq, Meakin, 2⅝" **12.00**
Butter pat, unmk, English, 2⅞" **12.00**
Cake plate, Bamboo, sq, hdls, Meakin **55.00**
Coffeepot, Fish Hook, Meakin, 8¾"..**175.00**
Compote, Mellor-Taylor, 4¾x8" **335.00**
Creamer, Bamboo, Meakin, 5⅛" **115.00**
Creamer, Fish Hook, Meakin **120.00**
Creamer, Teaberry Vt, sq, Clementson, 5¼" **195.00**
Cup & saucer, handleless; Lily of the Valley, Shaw........................**65.00**
Cup & Saucer, handleless; pre-Tea Leaf, Niagara shape, Walley ..**85.00**
Cup & saucer, Morning-Glory Vt, Portland, Elsmore & Forster....**85.00**
Cup & saucer, str-sided, Meakin **75.00**
Cup plate, English, 3⅝" **40.00**

Gravy boat, Bamboo, w/tray, Meakin...................................**75.00**
Gravy boat, Fish Hook, Meakin, 3¼" **45.00**
Mug, Chinese, Shaw..**165.00**
Nappie, rectangular, Wilkinson, 5⅝x3⅞".............................**22.00**
Pitcher, Acanthus Leaf, bulbous, Wilkinson, 8" **250.00**
Pitcher, Bamboo, Grindley, 7¼" **185.00**
Pitcher, Sq Ridged, Wedgwood, 7¾"..................................**140.00**
Plate, Grindley, 9" **22.00**
Plate, Meakin, 8" **12.00**
Plate, Wedgwood, 8¼"..**14.00**
Plate, Wilkinson, 6¾"..**10.00**
Platter, oval, Shaw, lg..**40.00**
Platter, rectangular, Meakin, 12x8½" **55.00**
Relish tray, Meakin..**35.00**
Sauce dish, Wedgwood, 5"..**20.00**
Shaving mug, Bamboo, ca 1880s, Grindley **225.00**
Soup plate, Wedgwood, 8⅞"..**24.00**
Sugar bowl, Bamboo, w/lid, Meakin, 6¾" **65.00**
Sugar bowl, Pomegranate Vt, w/lid, Walley, 6¾" **115.00**
Sugar bowl, w/lid, Meakin **75.00**

Sugar bowl, 7", $125.00.

Teapot, Fish Hook, Meakin **150.00**
Teapot, Red Cliff **75.00**
Toothbrush holder, Meakin **145.00**
Waste bowl, Meakin..**60.00**

Teapots

The custom of drinking tea has resulted in the production of many tea-related collectibles; the most popular is the teapot. The first teapots were manufactured in the Chinese village of Vi-Hsing during the late 16th century and were no bigger than the tiny cups previously used for tea drinking. Amazingly, these same tiny teapots are still being used today.

A wide range of teapots can be found by the avid searcher; those most readily available today were produced from about 1870 to the present. Several books have been written solely devoted to teapots, although most are out of print. *An Anthology of British Teapots* by Philip Miller and Michael Berthoud is an extensive work with over 2,000 photographs; it is currently available from Micawber Publications, The Lawns, Church Street, Brosely, Stropshire TF12 5DG for L. 24.95.

Another is titled *The Eccentric Teapot*; it is written by Garth Clark and is available at your local bookstore.

Almost every pottery and porcelain manufacturer in Europe as well as in America have produced teapots. Some are purely functional, others decorative and whimsical. Refer to various manufacturers' names for further listings.

Our advisor for this category is Tina Carter; she is listed in the Directory under California.

Austria Victoria Carlsbad, floral on china 30.00

Automobile, green glaze, no mark, 8" long, $300.00; Tank, green with silver details, Made in England, 8½" long, $200.00.

Dbl spout, earthenware, slip decor, ca 1890........................80.00
DM mk, coralene dragon, Japanese, 6-cup........................22.00
Ellgreave, Wood & Sons, England, ironstone w/floral....................35.00
Flow blue, man sits w/legs outstretched, conical hat, 8x9" 60.00
Germany, Royal Hanover, gr luster, HP, 6½" 75.00
Germany, Royal Hanover, gr lustre, HP, 6½", +cr/sug................140.00
Grimwades, Royal Winton, England, cozy set, floral hdls 55.00
H&K England, Old English Sampler, 6-cup, EX..........................45.00
HW&Co Wreath, England, ca 1895-1902................................98.00
Japan, Tea for Two, man in tux hdl, girl in gown forms pot..........45.00
Ming Tea Co, made in Japan, w/label, 1½ -cup 18.00
Monterey, made in CA, pk spatter, lg....................................25.00
Noritake, mk M, HP Japan, yel w/flowers, tall, 2-cup....................25.00
Pyrex mk, blown glass, etched flowers, 6-cup............................45.00
S Derbyshire, England, barge, brn, emb mk, lg 75.00
Sadler, pk w/sm flowers, oval, mk, 6-cup................................35.00
Spode's Tower, England, bl/wht transfer, London shape, VG 45.00
Sutherland, England, silver lustre, mk, 6-cup 60.00
SYP, 'Simple Yet Perfect,' brn earthenware, ca 1905....................95.00
SYP, Wedgwood, bone china, bl/wht/gold, ca 1905-06................110.00
Wade, Scotty, mk, 1953-55, 9"...45.00
Wales CM, Charles & Diana, brn pottery, 2½"............................78.00
Walt Disney Productions, Snow White w/Dwarfs, musical 50.00
Wedgwood, Jasperware, bl/wht, ca 1784, 2-cup.........................210.00
WS George, yel w/gold, rnd, mk, 6-cup, EX 20.00

Teco

Teco artware was made by the American Terra Cotta and Ceramic Company, located near Chicago, Illinois. The firm was established in 1886 and until 1901 produced only brick, sewer tile, and other redware. Their early glaze was inspired by the matt green made popular by Grueby. 'Teco Green' was made for nearly ten years. It was similar to Grueby's yet with a subtle silver-gray cast. The company was one of the first in the United States to perfect a true crystalline glaze. The only decoration used was through the modeling and glazing techniques; no hand painting was attempted. Favored motifs were naturalistic leaves and flowers.

The company broadened their lines to include garden pottery and faience tiles and panels. New matt glazes (browns, yellows, blue, and

rose) were added to the green in 1910. By 1922 the artware lines were discontinued; the company was sold in 1930.

Values are dictated by size and color of glaze, with examples in colors other than green bringing the higher prices. High-gloss glaze is seldom seen and expensive.

Teco is usually marked with a vertical impressed device comprised of a large 'T' to the left of the remaining three letters.

Bookends, Rebecca at the Well, 2-color, 5¼x6¾"......................550.00
Bowl, berries emb, gr matt, designed by F Albert, #136, 8" 325.00
Bowl, gr w/wht int, cone form in 4-leg frwork, #400, 6" H 4,600.00
Bowl vase, gr, frieze of sqs/lines about shoulder, #75, 7½" 1,650.00
Pitcher, gr w/blk trails, long wishbone hdl, 2 mks, 9x5".............600.00
Vase, bright yel, #403, 8x6"..950.00
Vase, gr, amphora w/buttresses forming str hdls, 7", EX 500.00
Vase, gr, bulbous w/short neck, flared/wavy rim, mk, 5x4" 350.00
Vase, gr, bullet form supported by 4 V-form ft, 8⅝"................2,500.00
Vase, gr, Chinese shape, #165, 8" 800.00
Vase, gr, cylindrical, 4 cutaway bars at neck, 11x3".................1,900.00
Vase, gr, cylindrical w/buttressed ea side, 5½".........................425.00
Vase, gr, dbl gourd w/flaring rim & 4 buttresses, #287, 13"......7,000.00
Vase, gr, emb cattails, cylindrical, 3 mks, 12" 7,000.00
Vase, gr, emb tulips frieze, basketweave neck, #154, 10" 1,600.00
Vase, gr, floral emb, 4 in-mold hdls at rtcl top, 7x6"...............2,400.00
Vase, gr, leaves swirl to form openwork base, #310, 17" 28,600.00
Vase, gr, lg looping integral hdls, 2 mks, 5½x8½".....................650.00
Vase, gr, long neck w/rim-to-width hdls, 10x5"..........................600.00
Vase, gr, mk, 5½"...350.00
Vase, gr, ovoid form w/flared rim in 4-buttress frwork, 10"......4,000.00
Vase, gr, tall/cylindrical on bun base, mk, 13½x5½"..................850.00
Vase, gr, upright lotus form w/in 4 buttresses, #423, 12" 5,500.00
Vase, gr, 2 lg integral loop hdls, bulbous, 6x9" 600.00
Vase, gr, 6-lobe squash blossom form, #197, 10x7", EX 1,500.00

Vase, green matt with black traces, marked, 11½" x 10", $2,500.00.

Vase, gr w/some blk, 4 long S-curve hdls, 3 mks, 12x5"...........1,700.00
Vase, gr w/some gun metal, cylinder w/emb ribs, mk, 7x3"..........750.00
Vase, gr/gun metal, swollen cylinder, #60D, 18x9" 2,000.00
Vase, gray high gloss experimental glaze, 11" 350.00
Wall pocket, gr matt, leaves emb, 15x7".................................700.00

Teddy Bear Collectibles

The story of Teddy Roosevelt's encounter with the bear cub has been oft recounted with varying degrees of accuracy, so it will suffice to say that it was as a result of this incident in 1902 that the teddy bear got his name. These appealing little creatures are enjoying renewed popularity with collectors today. To one who has not yet succumbed to their obvious charms, one bear seems to look very much like another. How to tell the older ones? Look for long snouts, jointed limbs, large feet and felt paws, long curving arms, and glass or shoe-button eyes. Most old bears have a humped back and are made of mohair stuffed with straw or excelsior. Cute expressions, original clothes, a nice personality, and, of course, good condition add to their value. Some Steiff bears in mint condition may go as high as $100 per inch. These are easily recognized by the trademark button within the ear. See also Toys, Steiff.

Key: jtd — jointed

Bears

Brn mohair, swivel head, orig pads, soft stuffed, 18", VG 65.00
Brn wool, button eyes, straw stuffed, 1900s, 11", VG 250.00
Bruin, gold mohair, pull toy w/bell, 15", VG 225.00
Clown, jtd, mohair, glass eyes, orig clothes, 8", EX 425.00
England, mohair, fully jtd, canvas pads, 14", EX 250.00
Fully jtd, gold curly mohair, felt pads, '30s, 18", EX 275.00
Fully jtd, gold mohair, glass eyes, worn pads, 10½", G 135.00
Fully jtd, gold mohair, glass eyes, worn pads, 16", G 185.00
Fully jtd, gold mohair, swivel head, 1920s, 14", VG.....................135.00
Fully jtd, mohair, hump, straw filled, button eyes, 24", VG 300.00
Fully jtd, tan mohair, glass eyes, early, 9", VG............................200.00
Fully jtd, wood open mouth w/4 wood teeth, squeaker, 19" 900.00
Fully jtd, yel mohair, hump, button eyes, ca 1900, 24", VG.........500.00
Fully jtd, yel plush, glass eyes, 1940s, 19", EX............................150.00
Fully jtd, yel plush mohair, glass eyes, 1915, 24", EX..................350.00
Germany, jtd, mohair, glass eyes, hump, early, 17", EX...............550.00
Germany, mohair, glass eyes, on all 4s, '30s, 9x13", EX 225.00
Gold mohair, straw stuffed, glass eyes, 1920s, 25", EX.................375.00
Gold mohair, swivel head, button eyes, 1920s, 20", G 275.00
Hermann, yes/no, yel mohair, jtd, 1925, 15", EX 375.00
Ideal, gold mohair, 11½" 325.00

Schoenhut skating bear with cane, mohair with glass eyes, key wind, marked Made in US Zone Germany DBGM, 8", $1,500.00.

Schuco, lt tan, straw stuffed, glass eyes, 1940s, VG.....................425.00
Steiff, blond mohair, button eyes, early, 9½" 900.00
Steiff, brn cub on all 4s, chest tag, no button, '70s, NM 90.00

Steiff, fully jtd, yel mohair, hump, button, '10, 13", VG 600.00
Steiff, ltd edition of 5000, based on 1903 model, 16", EX 425.00
Steiff, mohair, button eyes, embr nose, early, 18", VG.................650.00
Steiff, tan mohair, glass eyes, tags/button, late, 9", EX 45.00
Tan mohair, glass eyes, swivel head, 1920s, 19", VG 195.00
Tan mohair (long), swivel head, soft stuffed, '20s, 24", VG 65.00
Tan plush, glass eyes, swivel head, 1940s, 23", VG......................75.00
Wht mohair (long), straw stuffed, rpl pads, early, 26", G 300.00
Wool, fully jtd, glass eyes, hump, straw stuffed, 14", VG 250.00
Wool, fully jtd, glass eyes, straw stuffed, '30s, 22", VG 195.00

Telephones

Since Alexander Graham Bell's first successful telephone communication, the phone itself has undergone a complete evolution in style as well as efficiency. Early models, especially those wall types with ornately carved oak boxes, are of special interest to collectors. Also of value are the candlestick phones from the early part of the century and any related memorabilia.

Am Electric, oak dbl box, swivel mouthpc, 31x12", NM 695.00
Cradle style, Federal, brass & Bakelite, 1905, 8x10x5", EX............75.00
Crank style, wood, wall hanging, unmk, EX 180.00
Dbl box, oak, 7" outside terminal receiver, SC, NM 500.00
Kellogg, candlestick, dial, blk finish, 12", NM 155.00
Kellogg, candlestick & box, no dial...135.00
Pay type, blk, 1940s, rstr...225.00
Schmidt & Bruckner, candlestick, NP brass, 1890s, 10", EX .. 2,400.00
Stromberg Carlson, candlestick, early, orig, complete 575.00
Swedish American, wood, wall hanging, EX 255.00
Viaduct, counter, oak/NP brass, 18x6x29", EX............................700.00

Wall phone in oak cabinet, Kellogg mouthpiece, 26", $250.00.

Western Electric, operator's phone, candlestick 85.00
Western Electric #302, desk style, metal, ca 1938, rstr..................50.00
Williams-Abbot, candlestick, oil-can type, EX 495.00

Blue Bell Paperweights

First issued in the early 1900s, these bell-shaped glass weights were used by telephone company employees to prevent stacks of papers from blowing off their desks in the days of overhead fans. Over the years, they have all but vanished — some carried off by retiring employees, others broken. The weights came to be widely used as advertising by individual telephone companies; and, as the smaller companies merged to form larger companies, more and more new weights were created. They were widely distributed with the opening of the first trans-continental telephone line in 1915. For further study we recommend *Blue Bell Paperweights* by Jacqueline Linscott; she is listed in the Directory under Florida.

Bell System C&P Telephone Co & Assoc Companies, ice bl......**225.00**
Bell System NY Telephone Co, peacock **95.00**
Bell Telephone Company, cobalt...**150.00**
Missouri & Kansas Telephone Company, peacock.....................**100.00**

Blue Bell Paperweight, peacock blue, $325.00.

No embossing, cobalt...**50.00**
No embossing, ice bl...**45.00**
Southwestern Bell Telephone Company, peacock **175.00**

Related Memorabilia

Directory, Jonesburg MO, 1913, EX **20.00**
Directory, St Louis MO, 1911, EX **35.00**
Padlock, Bell System, Yale, EX..**18.00**
Phone booth, dbl wall, 1-pc door, EX.................................... **2,500.00**
Pin, Long Lines, Bell, mk 10k **22.00**
Shade, milk glass, Bell System, hanging, 4x11½", EX **500.00**
Shade, milk glass, Independent Telephone, hanging, 4x8", EX...**350.00**
Sign, brass, emb letters, 4x30", EX **85.00**
Sign, porc, Bell System, bl & wht, 16x16", NM **75.00**
Sign, porc, Bell System, New England T&T, flanged, 16x16" **150.00**
Sign, porc, Bell System, Telephone Payments, 20x14", VG **225.00**
Sign, stained glass, Telephone, 1915, 7x19", EX **350.00**
Sign, tin, Bell System, Public..., flanged, 18 dia, EX...................**150.00**
Sign, wooden arrow figural, old pnt, 2-sided, 8x52", VG **175.00**
Switchboard, Western Electric, oak, desk type, 1930s..................**150.00**

Telescopes

Old telescopes are still appreciated for the quality of the workmanship and materials that went into their production. Some of the more elaborate styles were covered in leather or ebony and the 'draws' or extensions were often brass.

Brass, 4-draw, clear optics, 37", EX **150.00**

Brass & leather, allover NP, 4-draw, 41", EX **150.00**
Brass & leather, 3-draw, clear optics, 29", EX............................**100.00**
Brass & leather, 4-draw, clear optics, 27", EX..............................**90.00**
Brass w/wooden bbl, 3-draw, ca 1850s, 34", EX **150.00**
Clarkson, London 1908, brass/German silver, 1-draw, 24", EX......**95.00**
France, brass, 2-draw, tripod, 29", EX **175.00**
J Watson London, reflecting table-top tripod, early, 27" **1,150.00**
JJ Messer London, brass, 1-draw, 1850s, EX...............................**150.00**
S&B Solomons London, rack/pinion adjust, tripod, EX in case...**650.00**
Selsi Evion Paris, terrestrial/celestial, brass, 5 lens **1,500.00**

Televisions

Collectible TV's are becoming popular. Those made prior to WWII (circa 1925-1940) often sell for up to $4,000.00 and more! Unusual wood and Bakelite sets from the '40s are worth $20.00 to $300.00; metal sets and those with square cabinets usually sell for under $100.00. Large screen TV's (over 14") are still poor sellers in most markets.

Our advisor for this category is Harry Poster; he is listed in the Directory under New Jersey.

Admiral #19A1, 7" wooden table top **100.00**
Air King #A-1000, 10" table top..**75.00**
Andrea #T-VK12, 12" table top **100.00**
Ansley #701, 10" table top **75.00**
Automatic #TV-PA90, 7" portable, w/magnifier.........................**235.00**
Belmont #10DX21, pull-out tube console..................................**125.00**
Belmont #21A21, 7" table top...**175.00**
Bendix #325, 10" push-button combo..**50.00**
CBS-Columbia #205, 19" color console **175.00**
Cleervue Regency, 15" console w/doors **85.00**
Crosley #EU30, 30" console..**300.00**
Crosley #9-425, 7" portable table top **135.00**
DeWald #CT-102, 10" table top **100.00**
DuMont #RA-103, 12" Chatman table top **135.00**
DuMont #RA-119-A, Royal Sovereign, 30".................................**300.00**
Emerson #600, 7" cloth-covered portable..................................**125.00**
Emerson #639, 7" wooden table top **112.00**
Fada #930, 12" table top..**85.00**
Garod #1000TV, 12" **150.00**
General Electric #803, 10" table top w/top speaker.....................**125.00**
General Electric #901, lg projection **175.00**
Hallicrafters #514, 7" portable **150.00**

Philco Predicta, metal housing, 1961, 48", tube size: 19", $550.00.

RCA #630-TCS, 10" console, rare..................................600.00
Sony #8-301W, transistor, Japanese, 1961....................115.00
Zenith #28T925, Mayflower, porthole table top 115.00

Teplitz

Teplitz, in Bohemia, was an active art pottery center at the turn of the century. The Amphora Pottery Works was only one of the firms that operated there. (See Amphora.) Art Nouveau and Art Deco styles were favored, and much of the ware was hand decorated with the primary emphasis on vases and figurines. Items listed here are marked 'Teplitz' or 'Turn,' a nearby city.

Our advisor for this category is Jack Gunsaulus; he is listed in the Directory under Michigan.

Figural group, Arabs and camels, early 20th century, minor damage, 18" x 19", $700.00.

Pitcher, Arab on horse, Stellmacher, mk, 4" 85.00
Vase, autumn leaves, branch neck, mc/gilt on ivory, 12" 200.00
Vase, clover emb band on bl-gr panels, Stellmacher, rpr, 8" 175.00
Vase, cylinder caged in 4 uprights, flower rim, gr-brn, 13" 800.00
Vase, emb clover band, gr/bl mottle, beehive form, 8" 400.00
Vase, florals in relief, wht on cobalt w/gold, mk, 17" 625.00
Vase, gold florals, serpent hdls, mk, 12" 350.00
Vase, modernistic, panels w/men, geometrics, 2 pr hdls, 11" 325.00
Vase, sketchy florals on ivory & gr, ornate hdls, RS&K, 12"... 1,400.00

Terra Cotta

Terra cotta is a type of earthenware or clay used for statuary, architectural facings, or domestic articles. It is unglazed, baked to durable hardness, and characterized by the color of the body which may range from brick red to buff.

Bust of young woman, Chas Eugene Breton, 1916, 22", EX 650.00
Bust of 18th-century child, mk Le Brun, socle base, 13½" 350.00
Nude seated on rectangular plinth, M Fernandez, 19" 600.00
Plaque, Victorian lady w/lute, artist sgn, Athens 1870.................350.00
Teapot, Oriental scenes, unglazed, 3⅝", EX 1,200.00

Sculpture, dogs attacking wolf, fine detail, 18" x 12", $500.00.

Tray, HP Arabic scene: pilgrims resting on gilt, 1920, 9x7"..........75.00

Thermometers

Though the collecting of advertising thermometers has been popular for years, only recently have decorative thermometers come into their own as bona fide items of interest and value. Indoor and outdoor decorative models have been manufactured for hundreds of years, yet their relative scarcity enhances their value and interest for the collector. Most American thermometers manufactured early in the 20th century were produced by Taylor (Tycos), and today their thermometers remain the most plentiful on the market. They also serve as the price standards for most historical thermometers.

Insofar as sheer beauty, uniqueness, and scientific accuracy, decorative thermometers are far superior to the ordinary and inexpensive versions which carry advertising. Decorative thermometers run the gamut from plain tin household varieties to the highly ornate creations of Tiffany and Bradley and Hubbard. They have been manufactured from nearly every conceivable material — oak, sterling, brass, and glass being the favorites — and have tested the artistry and technical skills of some of America's finest craftsmen. Ornamental models can be found in free-hanging, wall-mounted, or desk/mantel versions.

Thermometer prices are based on age, ornateness, and whether mercury or alcohol is used as the filler in the tube. Thermometers with damaged, missing, or substitute parts bring greatly reduced prices. Paper scales indicate either replacement of a broken metal scale or a device of lower quality.

Virtually all American-made thermometers available today as collectors' items were made between 1875 and 1940. The Golden Age of decoratives ended in the early 1940s as modern manufacturing processes and materials robbed them of their natural distinctiveness. European thermometers, while of comparable beauty and craftsmanship, have not yet migrated to this country in any great numbers; those produced in America still dominate the buy/sell market.

Our advisor for this category is Warren Harris; he is listed in the Directory under California.

Key:
br — brass	pmc — permacolor
F & C — Fahrenheit and Celsius	sc — scales
F & R — Fahrenheit & Reamer	stl — stainless
mrc — mercury	

Adam Kilt, desk; br portico/scallop roof, F&R sc/mrc, 4½"...........42.00
Alexandre, folding; F&R sc, mrc, 1850s 85.00
Anonymous, desk; picture fr w/glass, mrc, 1902, 7" 85.00

Bargess Reversible Box, br sc, oak case, mrc, 5½" 30.00
Bearskin Ltd, desk; fluted base, brass, brass sc, 6" 150.00
Bearskin Ltd, wall; metal clip, rnd mcr, 1930, 3x4" 240.00
Bertrand Mumser, desk; cast/cathedral, months rotate/mrc, 12" .930.00
BLT-Luce, desk; figural, flared base, br w/br sc, mrc, 6" 75.00
Bradley & Hubbard, desk; br/ornate lion, br sc/mrc, 9", VG 70.00
Bradley & Hubbard, scroll bk, steel/cb, Mensh, mrc, 8" 190.00
Brown Penzance, desk; brn marble, ivory sc, mrc, 6" 70.00
C Wilder Co, bear & billboard br figural, mrc, 6½" 65.00
Casella London, wall; maxi/minimum, 2 units, wood, plastic sc .235.00
CE Lange, kitchen; The Modern Thermometer, tin, pmc 150.00
Chester, desk; stl sc, sterling bezel, mrc, 2x6" 95.00
Clark, desk; ivory ped, crown, mrc, 1904, 7" 145.00
Cloister, inkwell, stl bk & base w/angels at side, 1901 ....975.00
Creswel, travel; ivory case/mirror, removable sc, mrc, 2½" 2,400.00
Desk, cvd walrus tusk, 2-tier disk base, inlay sc, 1860, 9" 220.00
Dr Dan'l Draper's Self-Recording, metal/glass, 1887, 20" 25.00
E Berman Co, desk; br/filigree/top scrollwork, mrc, 8" 110.00
Freeborn, desk; bronze w/lead decor/br sc, mrc, 8" 39.00
G Barnes, oak fold-out box, plastic sc, mrc, 2½" 90.00
G Cooper, desk; bell shape w/cupola, sterling, dial, 2x3" 50.00
Gloucester Scientific, stl case, glass front, pmc, 42" 1,050.00
Golub, hanging; mahog/br bulb cap, lg sc/red spirit, 9x2" 65.00
H Lauramark, hanging; gold stipple on boxwood, 0-120, mrc 60.00
Harriman, P, desk; br ped on griffin, mrc, 9" 90.00
Hiergelsell Bros, indoor; cabinet/oak bk, bl liquid, #159 ......65.00
Hohmann Maurer Co, steel F&C sc & bk, mrc, 12" 27.00
Honeywell, desk; Bakelite bell base, dial sc, 1935, 3" dia 95.00
J Needle, desk; figural, calendar, br w/porc sc, mrc, 6" 95.00
Jed Sirrah, hanging; silver, umbrella, mrc, 8" 70.00
Jedseth Ltd, desk; Mercury figure w/base filigree, mrc, 7" 90.00
Jockomo IN, desk; sterling face/br sc, mrc, 1904, 6" 65.00
Koizumisan, desk; w/br candelabra, rnd mrc tube, 1875, 10" ... 4,000.00

Mother cat knits in rocking chair by stove which houses thermometer, bronze, 6½", $225.00.

Nova Products, desk; glass cover over bronze sc, 4" 35.00
Nova Products, desk; rnd, glass encased, dial sc, Pat 1923...........75.00
Orchard, iron case, br face, w/glass intact, 14" 75.00
Pairpoint, desk; sterling picture fr, mrc, 1907, 5" 220.00
Pairpoint, mantel; br, w/angel, sterling sc/mrc, 1904 ....325.00
Phila Therm Co, hygrometer; br sc, rotating bezel, 1928 ....40.00
Reau, desk; ornate blk bronze, wood F&C sc, mrc 57.00
Reau, desk; sq incline base, floral top, mrc, 1895 ....180.00
S Mitzutani, alabaster ped, candle figural atop, mrc, 15" 80.00
Short & Mason, recording drum; copper case, 1910..............75.00
Slouche, desk; alabaster ped, paper sc inset, mrc, 8x2½" 75.00

Standard, for Fairbanks & Co, rnd, br case, 1886, 7" 90.00
Standard, hanging; rnd, br rim, -40 to 150, dial................40.00
Standard, wall; br case, dial counterbalance, 1885, 9" 110.00
Taylor, hanging; ornate wood bk, br sc, 10x7" 50.00
Taylor, hanging; pnt wood, red spirit, 6x24"..................50.00
Taylor, lady's profile, cvd wood, emb Art Deco, 20½", EX 195.00
Taylor, wall; blk enameled case, F&R sc on stl, mrc, 12" 35.00
Taylor, wall; octagonal wood fr/metal sc, red liquid, 5" 45.00
Tiffany, desk; horoscope, bronze, mrc, 1907, 4x7" 86.00
Tycos, incubator hygrometer; glass reservoir, 4x4" 16.00
Tycos, maxi/minimum, japanned tin/br, mrc, T-5452, 8" 85.00
Tycos-Taylor, outdoor wall; wood fr, red liquid, 27x5".........55.00
Vogue, desk; Victorian, dial, gr, 1931 ....25.00
W Pratt, desk; wood inlays, ivory sc, mrc, 1900, 6" 90.00
Warren Foundries, wall; umbrella w/dragon hdl, br sc, mrc, 12" ..220.00
Wise, desk; Tunbridge, twin columns, mrc, 1870, 5" 1,250.00
Zeradatha, desk; cast metal, dial w/rotate sc, 1926, 7" 43.00

Tiffany

Louis Comfort Tiffany was born in 1848 to Charles Lewis and Harriet Young Tiffany of New York. By the time he was eighteen, his father's small dry goods and stationery store had grown and developed into the world-renowned Tiffany and Company.

Preferring the study of art to joining his father in the family business, Louis spent the next six years under the tutelage of noted artists. He returned to America in 1870 and until 1875 painted canvases that focused on European and North African scenes. Deciding the more lucrative approach was in the application of industrial arts and crafts, he opened a decorating studio called Louis C. Tiffany and Co., Associated Artists. He began seriously experimenting with glass; and, eschewing traditionally painted-on details, he instead learned to produce glass with qualities that could suggest natural textures and effects. His experiments broadened, and he soon concentrated his efforts on vases, bowls, etc. that came to be considered the highest achievements of the art. Peacock feathers, leaves and vines, flowers and abstracts were developed within the plane of the glass as it was blown. Opalescent and metallic lustres were combined with transparent color to produce stunning effects. Tiffany called his glass Favrile, meaning handmade.

In 1900 he established Tiffany Studios and turned his attention full time to producing art glass, leaded-glass lamp shades, and household wares with metal components. He also designed a complete line of jewelry which was sold through his father's store. He became proficiently accomplished in silverwork and produced such articles as hand mirrors embellished with peacock feather designs set with gems and candlesticks with Favrile glass inserts.

Tiffany's work exemplified the Art Nouveau style of design and decoration, and through his own flamboyant personality and business acumen he perpetrated his tastes onto the American market to the extent that his name became a household word. Tiffany Studios continued to prosper until the second decade of this century when due to changing tastes his influence began to diminish. By 1920 the company had closed.

Serial numbers were assigned to much of Tiffany's work, and letter prefixes indicated the year of manufacture: A-N for 1896-1900, P-Z for 1901-1905. After that, the letter followed the numbers with A-N in use from 1906-1912; P-Z from 1913-1920. O-marked pieces were made especially for friends of relatives; X indicated pieces not made for sale.

Our listings are primarily from the auction houses in the East where Tiffany sells at a premium; we have been advised that at present the Tiffany market is slightly uncertain, due to the economy.

Our advisor for Tiffany lamps is Carl Heck; he is listed in the Directory under Colorado.

Glass

Bowl, amber irid, 8-rib, flared rim, 2½x6", +underplate 225.00
Bowl, bl irid, foliate form on ftd base, 1920s, 5¾" 800.00
Bowl, bl irid, wide flaring rim, #1925, 10" 900.00
Bowl, fruit; gold, swirled prunts, 4½", +undertray 350.00
Bowl, gold, pinched/scalloped rim, 4½" 275.00
Bowl, gold, pulled swirled knobs, 3x6", +knobby tray 375.00
Bowl, gold, stretched/paneled rim, 3½x12" 950.00
Bowl, gold, 10-rib, scalloped, 2¾x4¾", +undertray 300.00
Box, powder; pk marbleized, bronze lid w/enameling, 4½" .. 1,375.00
Candle holder, gold, twisted/ribbed, flared bobeche, 5" 275.00
Compote, floriform; amber irid, flared/ruffled, 4¾x5½" 400.00
Compote, floriform; gold, flared/scalloped/stretched, 5x6¾"........700.00
Compote, gold, stretched/flared rim, 2½x7¾" 450.00
Compote, gold, stretched/ruffled, low ft, 4x6½" 375.00
Compote, gold, 3½", set of 6 .... 1,100.00
Compote, pastel gr opal, #1702, 5¾" H 425.00
Compote, pastel mint gr w/wht radiating stripes, 2¼" 385.00
Cup & saucer, gold w/free-form zigzag band, curled hdl 850.00
Finger bowl & underplate, gold, lily pad forms, 4½", 6" 650.00
Goblet, clear/wht-to-amethyst cup, wht/clear stem, 8½" 350.00
Goblet, cobalt irid, baluster stem, 7" 425.00
Goblet, gold, ped ft, 5¼" 350.00
Humidor, gold w/leafy gr vine, bronze inner cover/lid, 10" 1,400.00
Jar, gold, sterling rim/bail/monogrammed lid, cylinder, 4" 450.00
Liquor glass, lt gr w/gold int, gr/gold stem................................195.00
Loving cup, gold, 3-hdl, 5¾" 375.00
Salt cellar, bl-purple w/gold tones, bean pot form, 1⅛x2¼" 375.00
Salt cellar, gold, crimped/ruffled, 2½" dia 190.00
Salt cellar, gold, floriform, X271-5, 3" dia 350.00
Salt cellar, gold, lobed urn form, short ft, 2¼", set of 6 ....650.00
Shade, gold, floriform, 2½x3", pr 550.00
Tazza, gr opal to lt gr, clear std, flower form, 6x6½" 1,000.00
Toothpick holder, bl-gold, w/snail prunts, #1003, 2" 495.00
Vase, amber cased to opal w/gold feathers, cylindrical, 9" 700.00
Vase, bl irid, trumpet form w/long str neck, 12" 850.00
Vase, bud; gold w/gr feathers, slim/ftd, 8" 1,000.00
Vase, bud; ruby translucent, gold int, mfg bubble, 5½" 3,250.00
Vase, cobalt irid, elongated dbl-gourd form, 12" 2,200.00
Vase, cobalt irid, 10-rib, pinched panels, X89, 4½" 2,300.00
Vase, cobalt irid w/5 pulled knobs, classic form, 3¼" 850.00
Vase, cream, gold/gr feathers, bronze pineapple-knop ft, 12"... 1,300.00

Vase, dk amber cased to opal w/gold leaves, long neck, 14" 4,500.00
Vase, floriform; amber/opal, 10-rib, scalloped, 10"................. 1,000.00
Vase, floriform; gold irid, scalloped, 10-rib, 12" 1,200.00
Vase, floriform; gold w/gr leaves, conical/upright, 11¾" 2,800.00
Vase, floriform; opal w/gr feathers, 5-lobe rim on cup, 5"...........750.00
Vase, floriform; pastel pk/wht stripes, yel knop stem, 14" 1,650.00
Vase, floriform; wht opal w/gr stems, amber bulb base, 15" 4,700.00
Vase, floriform; wht w/gr pulled feathers, bronze base, 13" 3,000.00
Vase, floriform; wht w/gr stem & feathers, gold int/ft, 15" 8,200.00
Vase, gold, deeply ruffled rim, rnd body, 4 pulled ft, 4" 400.00
Vase, gold, ruffled rim, ped ft, sgn, 11" 1,875.00
Vase, gold, slim trumpet form, orig label, 3½" 325.00
Vase, gold, urn form, rnd ft, 1¾" 165.00
Vase, gold, 10-rib, squat, 3¼" 500.00
Vase, gold, 10-rib ftd trumpet form, 8½" 650.00
Vase, gold cylinder in bronze Artichoke holder, 16"....................850.00
Vase, gold flared cylinder in mc enamel ped-ft holder, 13"..........800.00
Vase, gold w/bl irid, flared, ped ft, 10x6" 965.00
Vase, gold w/gr irid feathers, Y4190, 4" 2,400.00
Vase, gr, blk/gold feather-stripes, intaglio at sq rim, 7½" 2,700.00
Vase, gr cased to opal w/gold feathers, long neck, 10" 3,100.00
Vase, jack-in-pulpit; gold irid on wht opal, stretched, 14"....... 5,500.00
Vase, morning-glory paperweight frieze, exhibit pc, 6"...........14,000.00
Vase, pastel gr w/gr & gold feathers, raised rim, ovoid, 5" 1,300.00
Vase, turq cased to wht creates optic ribs, Expo vase, 7" 3,500.00
Wine, gold irid, thin stem, 5½"..325.00

Lamps

Base, bronze, harp std/fluted rnd base/5 ball ft, unmk, 12"....... 1,000.00
Base, bronze, 3-arm std, 4 paw ft on rnd base, #427, 12" 700.00
Base, floor lamp; bell harp, accessory holders on std, 57".........3,250.00
Base, gilt-bronze, floriform w/harp std, 8 petal ft, #470 .... 1,000.00
Base, gilt-bronze, harp std, fluted rnd base, #419, 13" 600.00
Base, ribbed/ringed shaft, leaf-border base, #638, 31", pr......... 1,500.00
Bridge, gr damascene 10" shade w/intaglio butterflies, 55" 7,000.00
Candle, feathered shade, glass-lined cup, 3-part std, 16" 1,000.00
Candle, fringed metallic lace shade, bl irid swirl std, 14" 850.00
Candle, gold stretched/ruffled dome shade & twist base, 13" .. 1,100.00
Candle, metal lace shade; gold rib std, Gorham insert, 12".........800.00
Candle, opal shade w/feathers, slag blown into cup, 16" 850.00
Chandelier, ldgl acorn-band dome shade, 16" dia................... 4,500.00
Chandelier, ldgl brickwork dome shade w/15 bull's eyes, 13" .. 6,600.00
Chandelier, ldgl brickwork dome shade w/16 bull's eyes, 21" .. 8,000.00
Chandelier, ldgl w/iris, leaf-cast 6-sided frwork, 22x13" 9,900.00
Chandelier, ldgl w/turtle-bk tile band, strapwork mt, 31" 11,000.00
Desk, gold 7" dome shade hangs w/in bell harp, #419, EX....... 1,700.00
Desk, ldgl 12" 12-panel shade; Zodiac std #1587, 16½" 2,200.00
Desk, 3 10-rib gold bell shades; stepped-base std #309............. 3,750.00
Floor, bell form gold shade; dbl-arm counterbalance, rstr 750.00
Floor, damascene 10" dome shade; counterbalance, #609, 58" .. 6,500.00
Floor, ldgl 22½" dragonfly shade; leaf-emb std #379 ....77,000.00
Floor, ldgl 24" geometric dome shade; #376 petal-mold std ...29,000.00
Floor, student; ldgl 12" acorn-band shade; std #423, 58" 10,000.00
Floor, 10" amber zipper-panel dome shade; counterbalance 5,500.00
Hall, gr/opal 10½" teardrop shade w/feathers, on chains 1,600.00
Lily, 18-light, amber irid shades (1 cracked), #383 std 44,000.00
Lily, 3-light, 3 rpl modern gold shades sgn Zephyr, 13" 1,650.00
Nautilus, ldgl shell-form shade; shell-molded base, 15" 6,500.00
Shade, ldgl Blk-Eyed Susan dome shade, 16" 9,000.00
Table, ldgl 12" apple blossom dome shade; tripod std #433 ...18,000.00
Table, ldgl 12" leaf-band shade; 4-sided 'Chinese' std #535 .... 7,000.00
Table, ldgl 14" pomegranate shade; Grueby base sgn WP 24,000.00
Table, ldgl 15" web shade w/spider finial; std #337, 19" 15,000.00

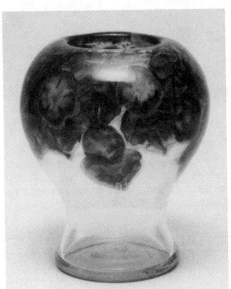

Paperweight exhibition vase, blue and red morning-glories with green leaves, 6", $14,000.00.

Ten-Lily lamp, lily pad base, all original, $15,000.00.

Table, ldgl 16" acorn-band shade; urn w/4 legs std, unsgn **5,000.00**
Table, ldgl 16" bellflower shade; paneled std #585, 22" **19,000.00**
Table, ldgl 16" crocus shade; emb bun-base std w/6 ft, 22" **16,000.00**
Table, ldgl 16" gridwork shade; bulbous/ftd base #1324..........**12,000.00**
Table, ldgl 17" sqs w/triangular border shade; bronze std **7,500.00**
Table, ldgl 18" swirling leaf shade; Grueby base, 22½" **17,600.00**
Table, ldgl 18" tulip shade; leaf-emb #357 std, 24" **30,000.00**
Table, ldgl 20" filigree poppy shade; figural maid std, 32".......**37,000.00**
Table, ldgl 20" poppy shade; paneled std #532, 27" **46,000.00**
Table, ldgl 22½" brickwork shade; ceramic base, 30"..............**12,100.00**
Table, linenfold 20" 12-panel shade; std #634, 22½".............**17,500.00**

Metal Work

Ash stand, rnd lotus base, #1695, 32" **1,100.00**
Bookends, sq w/geometrics in gr enamel, #365 ....**325.00**
Bookends, Venetian, ermine border, gold patina w/mc decor **375.00**
Bowl, brass, LC Tiffany Furnaces, Favrile, #315A, 1¼x5" **120.00**
Bowl, gilt patina, #1708, 9" **175.00**
Bowl, 4 lion's head medallions at rim, 2½x5" **175.00**
Box, Pine Cone over slag, gilt patina, 2¾x7¾" sq, EX **225.00**
Box, Zodiac, #816, 5" L **275.00**
Calendar fr, Grapevine, gr slag glass, #940, 6½x7½" **700.00**
Candelabra, 2-arm, stem w/bud atop, fluted ft, #1230, 9", pr.......**800.00**
Candle holder, cup in tripod sling, pencil std, #1213, 17" **1,100.00**
Candle holder, cup w/jewels, cobra form std, leaf base, 8" **1,500.00**
Candle holder, 7-jewel glass-lined cup, 3 4-toe ft, 12", pr **3,000.00**
Candlestick, Wild Carrot, slag inserts, #30055, 20", pr **8,000.00**
Clock, mantel; octagonal w/emb chains on long base, 9½" **3,000.00**
Coffee spoons, gold, foliate terminals, 12 in box, +tongs **2,600.00**
Desk clock, Venetian, beehive form, gilt patina, 5¾" **1,100.00**
Desk set, Abalone, letter file/blotter ends/inkwell/tray............. **1,300.00**
Desk set, Pine Needle, letter holder/inkwell/calendar+4 pcs... **1,200.00**
Desk set, Venetian, letter rack/pen tray/paper clip+4 pcs **800.00**
Earrings, 14k leaf & beaded spray, mk **125.00**
Inkwell, Venetian, chest type, gilt patina, 5" L **600.00**
Ladle, copper w/appl gold butterflies, pierced bowl, 8½" **4,400.00**
Letter opener, crab design, #1096 ....**80.00**
Loving cup, silver/copper, gilt int, 3 appl shells, 5⅜" **300.00**
Mirror, 60+ bl irid turtlebk tiles in fr, 68x44x17", EX **5,700.00**
Paperweight, reclining lion, bronze-gr patina, 5" L **500.00**
Paperweight, reclining lion, red-bronze patina, 5" L **550.00**
Paperweight, turtle-bk tile w/in bronze fr, no mk, 4" L **450.00**

Smoking stand, tray/undertray on Artichoke std, 27" **500.00**
Tray, Abalone, gold patina, 14" dia **950.00**

Pottery

Bowl, tulips/leaves emb, gr wash glaze, incurvate, 8" **6,300.00**
Bowl vase, apple branches emb/cvd on buff bsk, gr int, 5" **4,000.00**
Pitcher, cattails emb on cream w/dk detail, rpr, 12x5" **750.00**
Pitcher, cattails eng on wht bsk, gr int, tankard form, 13" **1,200.00**
Vase, apple branches on bark texture, gr, 8" **2,000.00**
Vase, bl/blk, molded w/incurling foliate fronds at rim, 7" **1,430.00**
Vase, brn/gr/tan mottle, dbl sphere joined by 6 hdls, 5" **2,000.00**
Vase, dogwood frieze relief, copper clad, bulbous top, 6x7" **2,700.00**
Vase, flowing gr/brn, 4 hdls rest on low shoulder, rstr, 8½".........**700.00**
Vase, leaves emb at neck on bsk, olive int, 4½", EX **500.00**
Vase, poppies/leaves emb, silvered bronze, mk Bronze, 9½" **2,000.00**
Vase, rtcl w/inverted teardrops on ribbed bottom, bsk, 9" **1,500.00**
Vase, stemmed tulips emb on bsk, gr-bl int, str sides, 6½" **1,900.00**
Vase, tomato form w/emb tomato vines, bsk, gr int, 8x14"...... **2,000.00**
Vase, 2 lilies emb on mint & olive, hourglass form, 13" **1,200.00**

Silver

Bowl, Clover, rtcl flower rim, minor dents, 9", pr **1,100.00**
Bowl, ribbed rim, swollen hexagonal form, 2½x8½" **400.00**
Cake basket, eng/appl scrolls & leaves, rtcl hdl, 9x12" **2,000.00**
Coffeepot, AD; ribbed band, monogram, ca 1920s, 11" **650.00**
Coffeepot, panels w/mask cartouch on basketweave, 10" **2,750.00**
Compote, emb/eng foliage, key fret band, gilt int, 5" H **650.00**
Demitasse service, etched Persian motif/monogram, 3-pc **2,800.00**
Dish, coiled as an Indian basket, gilded, flat, 5¾" dia **1,300.00**
Flask, etched scenes of Brownies, 8x4½" **8,000.00**
Inkwell, repousse sides, 4½" dia **450.00**
Kettle on stand & teapot, emb central band, 1880s, 85+ oz ... **1,800.00**

Pitcher, repousse and chased with flowers, monogram on base, dated 1886, 8", $7,000.00.

Pitcher, hdl cast w/leafage & classical mask, matt, 8½" **3,500.00**
Soup ladle, Olympian, oval bowl, 13" **700.00**

Tiffin Glass

The Tiffin Glass Company was founded in 1887 in Tiffin, Ohio, one of the many factories composing the U.S. Glass Company. Its early wares consisted of tablewares and decorative items such as lamps and globes. Among the most popular of all Tiffin products was the black satin glass produced there during the 1920s. In 1959 U.S. Glass was sold, and in 1962 the factories closed. The plant was re-opened in 1963 as the Tiffin Art Glass Company. Products from this period were tableware, hand-blown stemware, and other decorative items.

Those interested in learning more about Tiffin glass are encouraged to contact the Tiffin Glass Collectors' Club, whose address can be found in the Directory under Clubs, Newsletters, and Catalogs. See also Black Glass.

Basket, blk satin, 11x6½"	95.00
Bowl, centerpiece; Canterbury, flame & crystal, 7⅝"	150.00
Bowl, Cherokee Rose, 12½"	45.00
Bowl, console; Flanders, pk, 12"	38.00

Governor's bowl, Clyde King cutting, Da Vinci feet, ca 1950-1970, 6¾" x 8", $275.00.

Bowl, Moderne Wisteria, oval, 11x9"	85.00
Box, puff; Flower Garden & Butterflies, low, ftd	75.00
Candlesticks, blk satin, twisted, #66, 8", pr	75.00
Candy dish, Julia, crystal & amber, ½-lb	95.00
Champagne, Byzantine	18.00
Champagne, Empire, pk	23.00
Champagne, Flanders, yel	22.00
Champagne, Fontaine, gr	30.00
Champagne, Fontaine, pk	32.00
Champagne, Forever Yours	12.50
Champagne, Fuchsia	22.00
Champagne, June Night, reeded stem	20.00
Champagne, Spiral Optic, clear w/gr stem	20.00
Cheese & cracker set, Flanders, pk	145.00
Cheese compote, Flanders, pk	35.00
Cheese compote, Sylvan, gr	15.00
Claret, Cherokee Rose, #17403, 4-oz	25.00
Claret, Persian Pheasant, 6⅜"	32.00
Claret, pk, #024	22.50
Cocktail, Classic	35.00
Cocktail, June Night, 5¼"	20.00
Cocktail, Persian Pheasant	25.00
Cocktail, Spiral Optic, clear w/gr stem, 3½-oz	20.00
Cordial, Flanders, pk	75.00
Cordial, June Night	20.00
Cordial, Kelly Gr, crystal stem, #17662, 5½"	20.00
Cordial, Persian Pheasant	40.00

Cordial, Princess	22.00
Cordial, Twilight stem, #17507	50.00
Creamer, Fuchsia, flat, beaded hdl	40.00
Creamer & sugar bowl, Cerise	50.00
Creamer & sugar bowl, Le Fleur, yel, ftd	125.00
Cup & saucer, Byzantine, yel	40.00
Cup & saucer, Flanders, ftd	35.00
Cup & saucer, Flanders, pk	40.00
Cup & saucer, Rosalind, yel, blown	35.00
Figurine, swan, citron, 10½"	65.00
Goblet, water; Byzantine	25.00
Goblet, water; Camelot	10.00
Goblet, water; Cerise, 8"	24.00
Goblet, water; Classic, #185	24.00
Goblet, water; Dbl Columbine, amber stem	15.00
Goblet, water; Empire, pk	24.00
Goblet, water; Flanders	17.50
Goblet, water; Flanders, yel	25.00
Goblet, water; Huntington	10.00
Goblet, water; June Night, #17418	25.00
Goblet, water; Persian Pheasant, stemmed, 8½"	32.50
Goblet, water; Picadilly	12.50
Goblet, water; Rambling Rose, 9-oz	23.00
Goblet, water; Rosalind, Mandarin Yel, 7½"	20.00
Goblet, water; Southern Star	14.00
Goblet, water; Wheat	24.00
Lamp shade, Fuchsia, 12"	150.00
Oyster cocktail, Flanders, pk	40.00
Parfait, Coronet, pk	22.00
Parfait, Flanders	22.00
Pitcher, Byzantine, yel, 64-oz	185.00
Plate, Flanders, pk, 6"	12.50
Plate, Flanders, yel, 10½"	35.00
Plate, Flanders, 10½"	35.00
Plate, Flower Garden & Butterflies, pk, 10¼"	70.00
Plate, Fontaine, gr, 8"	15.00
Plate, Fontaine, pk, 8"	15.00
Plate, Fuchsia, 8½"	12.50
Plate, Rambling Rose, 8"	6.00
Plate, Rosalind, yel, 10½"	35.00
Rose bowl, bl w/crystal ft, #525, 6"	77.00
Sherbet, Camelot	7.50
Sherbet, Carillon	17.50
Sherbet, Cherokee Rose, tall	20.00
Sherbet, Dbl Columbine, amber stem	12.50
Sherbet, Flying Nun, gr, low	25.00
Sherbet, Fuchsia, low std	18.00
Sherbet, June Night, reeded stem	20.00
Sherbet, Lyndley	8.00
Sherbet, Picadilly	9.00
Sherbet, Rambling Rose, low	16.00
Sherbet, Wheat, tall	20.00
Sugar bowl, Flying Nun, gr	65.00
Sugar bowl, Fuchsia, flat, beaded hdl	40.00
Sundae, Fontaine, gr	25.00
Tumbler, iced tea; Cherokee Rose, ftd, 10½-oz	20.00
Tumbler, iced tea; Flanders	17.50
Tumbler, iced tea; June Night, ftd, 6⅝"	22.00
Tumbler, iced tea; Picadilly	12.50
Tumbler, iced tea; Southern Star	15.00
Tumbler, iced tea; Wheat	24.00
Tumbler, juice; Fontaine, gr	30.00
Vase, blk satin w/emb poppies, 5x7"	35.00
Vase, bud; Cherokee Rose, #14185, 10½"	42.00

Vase, bud; Cherokee Rose, #14185, 8" 32.00
Vase, Empress, smoke & crystal, 11¾" 150.00
Vase, Flanders, pk, 8" 195.00
Vase, florals, blk satin, no beads, #16264, 10½" 95.00
Vase, Lily of the Valley etched, #17350, 9", pr........................125.00
Vase, Twilight, teardrop shape, 8½"........................95.00
Vase, Twilight & smoke, flared, 8" 295.00
Whiskey, Flanders, pk 65.00
Wine, Carillon........................24.00
Wine, Cherokee Rose........................24.00
Wine, Cordelia, #072 ....17.50
Wine, Flanders, pk, 6⅛" 45.00
Wine, Flanders, yel, 6⅜" 38.00
Wine, Forever Yours........................15.00
Wine, Huntington........................10.00
Wine, June Night........................22.50
Wine, Persian Pheasant, 6"........................34.00
Wine, Psyche, gr........................50.00
Wine, Rambling Rose........................22.00
Wine, Rosalind, topaz, 6" 22.00

Tiles

Though originally strictly functional, tiles were being produced in various colors and used as architectural highlights as early as the Ancient Roman Empire. By the 18th century, Dutch tiles were decorated with polychrome landscapes and figures. During the 19th century, there were over a hundred companies in England involved in the manufacture of tile. By the Victorian era, the use of decorative tiles had reached its peak. Special souvenir editions, campaign and portrait tiles, and Art Nouveau motifs with lovely ladies and stylized examples from nature were popular. Today all of these are very collectible. See also specific manufacturers.

Alexander Mortis, Greek lady, Victorian, 1894 ....45.00
CA Art, courtyard, mc on red, architectural form, 14x4" 175.00
Cambridge, portrait, high glaze, 4" 65.00
Claycraft, mtns/trees/water, brn/gr/bl tones, 8x12", EX........................150.00
Claycraft, waterfall/mtn/rocks/trees, brn/gr/bl, 8x16" 450.00

Claycraft, 24-tile landscape frieze, mounted, repair to corner, 35" x 24", $600.00.

Craven Dunnill & Co, stylized floral, ruby lustre on cream 50.00
Empire, gr crystalline glaze, 4¼"........................110.00
Harris Strong, cityscape, 6", in wood & linen fr 95.00
Issac Broome; cows go to barn, cvd on brn, sgn, 12x20" 2,000.00

Low, Greek profile, celadon border, pr........................150.00
Low, leaves in relief, gr irid, 1880s, 4"........................45.00
Low, monks in monastery emb, pine gr gloss, sgn AO, 14x9" . 1,800.00
Provincial by Broome, hunter, tan, 6", set of 3 ....300.00
Robertson, trees, 4"........................50.00
Ruth Leonard, landscape w/house, 3-color, mk, 4¾x4½"........................125.00
Trent, florals on brn, 4-pc........................80.00
Unmk, faience, mc fruit compote, Grueby style, 6" 150.00
Walrich, floral, mc, 4⅝" 195.00
Wheeling, mc ship, 4" 30.00
Wm de Morgan, stylized flowerhead on ruby lustre, 1890s, 6" 55.00

Tinware

In the American household of the 17th and 18th centuries, tinware items could be found in abundance, from food containers to foot warmers and mirror frames. Although the first settlers brought much of their tinware with them from Europe, by 1798 sheets of tin plate were being imported from England for use by the growing number of American tinsmiths. Tinwares were often decorated either by piercing or painted designs which were both freehand and stenciled. (See Toleware.) By the early 1900s, many homes had replaced their old tinware with the more attractive aluminum and graniteware.

In the 19th century, tenth wedding anniversaries were traditionally celebrated by gifts of tin. Couples gave big parties, dressed in their wedding clothes, and reaffirmed their vows before their friends and family who arrived bearing (and often wearing) tin gifts, most of which were quite humorous. Anniversary tin items may include hats, cradles, slippers and shoes, rolling pins, etc. See also Primitives and Kitchen Collectibles.

Apple corer, rnd wooden knob hdl, ca 1877, EX 15.00
Bread raiser, side wire hdls, w/lid, 14" dia 55.00

Candle lantern, outstanding piercing, red paint, all original, early 19th century, 15", $350.00.

Chamber lamp, whale oil; 1800s, 11", pr........................375.00
Chamberstick, deep saucer base & push-up, 5"........................95.00
Chamberstick, saucer base, push-up, conical snuffer, 8x5" 175.00
Dipper, walnut hdl........................38.00
Dredger, brn japanning, cylindrical, pierced top, hdld 25.00
Dutch oven, iron spit, lt rust, 19"........................245.00
Egg poacher, oval, 4-ftd, wire stem, loop hdl, 7" 25.00

Egg poacher, 2-egg, wire hdl at bk, EX 27.00
Egg separater, rnd bowl shape w/slot at side, sm 20.00
Hand warmer, bl & gold litho, pierced, 1x4⅝x2¾" 55.00
Ladyfinger pan, 5 fluted oval cups w/tin strips, soldered 45.00
Lamp, wide saucer base, font w/lid, copper wick support, 8" 175.00
Mug, emb decor, child's sz 40.00
Sconce, crimped edge on pan/reflector, pitted/rpt, 8½" 200.00
Sconce, crimped oval bk, 1800s, 15x9" 200.00
Sconce, rectangular w/simple hood extension, rpr, 9¾", pr 210.00
Sconce, simple crimped circle top, 10½" 100.00
Sconce, tooled w/hammered 'dimples,' ribbed crest, 9½", pr 900.00
Scoop, flour; rnd stick hdl, mk Dover, lg 35.00
Soap grater, curved front, rolled edges, 5½x13" 48.00

Tobacciana

Tobacciana is the generally accepted term used to cover a field of collecting that includes smoking pipes, cigar molds, cigarette lighters, humidors — in short, any article having to do with the practice of using tobacco in any form.

Perhaps the most valuable variety of pipes is the meerschaum — hand carved from hydrous magnesium, an opaque white-gray or cream-colored mineral of the soapstone family. (Much of this is today mined in Turkey which has the largest meerschaum deposit in the world, though there are other deposits of lesser significance around the globe.) These figural bowls often portray an elaborately carved mythological character, an animal, or a historical scene. Amber is sometimes used for the stem. Other collectible pipes are corn cob (Missouri Meerschaum) and Indian peace pipes of clay or catlinite. (See American Indian Art.)

Chosen because it was the Indians who first introduced the white man to smoking, the cigar store Indian was a symbol used to identify tobacco stores in the 19th century. The majority of them were hand carved between 1830 and 1900 and are today recognized as some of the finest examples of early wood sculptures. When found they command very high prices.

Our advisor for this category is Chuck Thompson; he is listed in the Directory under Texas. See also Advertising; Snuff Boxes.

Box, cigar; Old Virginia Cheroots, Blk trademk, 1883, lg 50.00
Case, cigarette; wooden, w/sliding top, souvenir 32.00

Cigar lighter with clock, white metal, iron, brass and glass, ca 1800s, replaced shade, 14", $450.00; Gemelo cigar cutter and lighter, cast iron and tin, ca 1895, 14", EX, $700.00.

Cigarette holder, whalebone, cvd lady's face, 3¼", EX 40.00

Cigarette/cigar holder set, cherry amber glass, Czech, 3", MIB 45.00
Cutter, cigar; Gemelo, CI/tin, ca 1895, w/bird lighter, EX 700.00
Cutter, cigar; Harvard, key wind, EX 300.00
Cutter, cigar; Keystone, key wind 185.00
Cutter, cigar; McNeil & Co, NP, key wind, countertop, EX 165.00
Cutter, cigar; mechanical, key wind, figure on top, 10½", G 200.00
Cutter, cigar; meerschaum, St George & Dragon, in case, 6" 450.00
Cutter, cigar; spring-operated blade, 4x7½" 40.00
Cutter, plug; Brown & Williamson, CI, orig pnt 70.00
Cutter, plug; Champion Knife Improved..., pnt CI, 19", EX 50.00
Cutter, plug; Chew Climax Plug, NP CI, 17", VG 80.00
Cutter, plug; Drummond, Good Luck/cloverleaf on CI, 17", G 50.00
Cutter, plug; Griswold Erie #I, CI, 21" 125.00
Cutter, plug; John Finzer & Bros, CI, 18", VG 75.00
Cutter, plug; Larillard 55.00
Cutter, plug; Reading Hardware Standard, pnt CI, 17", EX 55.00
Cutter, plug; Spear Head, PJ Sorg, pnt CI, 16½" 150.00
Dispenser, cigarette; wood w/inlay, bird dispenser on top 50.00
Holder, cigar; meerschaum, cvd lady w/fan, +leather case 65.00
Holder, cigar; meerschaum, girl/spinning wheel, cased, 6" 550.00
Holder, cigar; meerschaum, head of agitated horse, cased, 7" 475.00
Holder, cigar; meerschaum, tavern scene, in case, 7" 425.00
Holder, cigarette; ivory w/'Solid Gold' ferrule, 5½" 45.00
Humidor, Arab w/pipe & camel's head in relief, Austria 250.00
Humidor, hen figural, majolica-type trim, pottery, 10" 88.00
Humidor, hen figural, mc pnt, pottery, 10" 75.00
Humidor, Imperial Cube Cut, w/lid, 8", M 75.00
Humidor, Indian's head w/headdress, ceramic, mk Germany 95.00
Humidor, monkey w/pipe in mouth, pnt bsk, Germany, sm 95.00
Humidor, tree stump w/branch hdl, pottery, 1920s, 8x7¼" 125.00
Lighter, cigar; Aladdin's lamp, cast brass, 6" L 175.00
Lighter, cigar; gargoyle form, brass, 3-ftd, 4" 125.00
Lighter, cigarette; golfer scene, Lenox 150.00
Lighter, gold heart shape, hangs from chain, Japan, 1½" 15.00
Lighter, Gretchen Cigars, Bruhnoff Mfg, sheet metal arm, 8" 350.00
Lighter, metal, hand grenade shape, 4½" 25.00
Opener, cigar box; Napoleon Cigars, Oneida NY 10.00
Opener, cigar box; Pennant Cigars, NY, EX 3.00
Opener, cigar box; Zeussanitt Bros, Pittsburgh PA, EX 3.00
Pipe, briar, copper deer, amber stem, Zurich 20.00
Pipe, briar, sterling filigree on bowl & shank 50.00
Pipe, china, flower on wht, Germany 65.00
Pipe, cvd wood w/mc relief figures, 1700s, 6¾" 200.00
Pipe, meerschaum, Amazon & soldier battle, horse, 4½x6" 800.00
Pipe, meerschaum, bearded Arab's head, in case, 4½", EX 150.00
Pipe, meerschaum, bird/Venus/Cupid around rose, rpr, 11" 550.00
Pipe, meerschaum, boxer dogs cvg, rpl stem, EX 50.00
Pipe, meerschaum, bull head, amber horns/stem, 8½", EX 750.00
Pipe, meerschaum, cottage & horse, dtd 1816 ....175.00
Pipe, meerschaum, cvd dog, mini, in case 65.00
Pipe, meerschaum, eagle in eagle claw, 1880s, in case, 6¾" 400.00
Pipe, meerschaum, Gibson girl, amber stem, 4½", EX 75.00
Pipe, meerschaum, group revels about floral-drape vase, 7x9" . 6,000.00
Pipe, meerschaum, head of Pan, in case, 6⅝" 375.00
Pipe, meerschaum, head of soldier/map, set w/turq, 6x8" 2,600.00
Pipe, meerschaum, Indian head, ferrule mk Shreve & Co, 8" 650.00
Pipe, meerschaum, maids/wolf chase stag around rose, 10½" ... 1,300.00
Pipe, meerschaum, Man in Moon (lady in pantomime), 9", EX .700.00
Pipe, meerschaum, prospector/dog, in case, 4⅝", VG 500.00
Pipe, meerschaum, relief horses against flower, 8", EX 100.00
Pipe, meerschaum, stag & doe scene cvg, amber stem, VG 50.00
Pipe, meerschaum, 2 clowns/dog, tulip bowl, 9", VG 400.00
Pipe, wood, cvd stag, tin lid, German, 1800s 150.00
Pipe, wood, fox head cvd at bowl, red glass eyes, mk JKM 150.00

Spittoon, brn scrolls, mk Medalta	35.00
Spittoon, Lucy Locket, bird form, porc	135.00
Spittoon, red & bl flowers on wht porc	75.00
Spittoon, wht-enameled iron, traditional form	50.00
Tamp, bone, overall scrimshaw, 2¾", EX	28.00
Tamp, whalebone, geometric cvg, EX	40.00

Toby Jugs

The delightful jug known as the Toby dates back to the 18th century, when factories in England produced them for export to the American colonies. Named for the character Toby Philpots in the song *The Little Brown Jug,* the Toby was fashioned in the form of a jolly fellow, usually holding a jug of beer and a glass. The earlier examples were made with strict attention to details such as fingernails and teeth. Originally representing only a non-entity, a trend developed to portray well-known individuals such as George II, Napoleon, and Ben Franklin. Among the most-valued Tobies are those produced by Ralph Wood I in the late 1700s. By the mid-1830s, Tobies were being made in America. See also Doulton, Lenox, and Occupied Japan.

Judy, sitting position, hat stopper, 1850, 10"	160.00
Man seated w/jug, mc clothes, 1780s, 9¾", EX	1,000.00
Man w/bottle & cup sits on barrel, creamware, 10½", VG	200.00
Man w/jug on left knee, pearlware, manganese/gr, rpr, 10"	600.00
Pearlware, gr/brn high-temp colors, 1775, 9", EX	400.00
Pearlware, sponged/striped base, att Yorkshire, 1800, 4½"	1,000.00
Portobello, man w/jug, mc sponging, ca 1840, rstr, 9½"	200.00
Pratt type, brn/ochre/blk high-temp colors, 1780s, 10"	1,200.00
Pratt type, man seated w/jug/pipe, mc sponging, 1800s, 10"	500.00
Ralph Wood, Rodney's Sailor, 1770s, no lid, 12"	5,700.00
Ralph wood (att), bl-sponged jacket/lav-speckled vest, 9"	1,900.00
Ralph Wood type, man seated w/jug, goblet in hand, 9¾"	1,500.00
Ralph Wood type, w/jug lifts drink to lips, 1780, 10", NM	1,500.00
Sailor on sea chest w/emb ship, stump hdl, no lid, 12", EX	200.00
Sailor seated, beaker to lips, holds jug, 1800, rstr, 11"	800.00

Staffordshire Toby, ca 1820s, 8", $395.00.

Walton, man seated w/jug, spots on face, ca 1820, 10½", EX 600.00

Toleware

The term 'toleware' originally came from a French term meaning 'sheet iron.' Today it is used to refer to paint-decorated tin items. The earliest toleware was hand painted; by the 1820s, much of it was deco-rated by means of a stencil. Among the most collectible today are those items painted by the Pennsylvania Dutch in the 1800s. This type of toleware has a very distinctive look. The surface is dull and unvarnished; background colors range from black to cream. Geometrics are quite common, but florals and fruits were also popular motifs. Often gold-stenciled borders were added.

American toleware is usually found in practical, everyday forms — trays, pails, jugs, boxes, and tankards, for instance — while French examples might include candlesticks, wine coolers, jardinieres, etc. Be sure to note color, design, and condition when determining date and value. In the listings that follow, the dimension given for boxes and trays indicates length.

Box, document; faded floral stencil on orig brn, mini, 4"	90.00
Box, document; floral, mc on blk, late, 6¾"	85.00
Box, document; floral, mc on brn, ring hdl, 8¾", EX	650.00
Box, document; floral, red & gold on blk, late, 10"	165.00
Box, document; flowers/berries in yel & red, 6" L	525.00
Box, document; yel stripes/wht band w/red & gr commas, 4½"	250.00
Box, sugar; berries, red/gr on yel, wire hdls, rstr, lg	600.00
Bread basket, gr/yel/blk bands on red, sloped sides, 13"	300.00
Candle snuffer, floral stencil, matching 9½x4" tray	55.00
Canister, tea; HP sharpshooter w/rifle, gold stencil, 8"	425.00
Chamberstick, red w/gold lip, rpr hdl, mini, 2⅜" dia	125.00
Coal bin, marine motif, tapered rectangle, Victorian, 19"	1,400.00
Coal hod, landscape on red, worn, 19"	500.00
Food warmer, gold floral on brn, dbl-boiler w/burner, 8"	225.00
Lantern, pnt traces, collapses into shape of book, 6"	220.00
Pitcher, stenciled floral/Molasses Cup on gr, lid, 4½"	175.00
Screen, cranes/water lily/tree on blk, late, 28x23"	175.00
Tea caddy, japanned tin, apple blossoms, blk domed lid, 8x4½"	55.00
Tea caddy, pnt bands, sarcophagus shape, paw ft, 5x5"	285.00
Tea caddy, roses, 4-color on bl, worn, 4⅝"	85.00
Teapot, floral, 4-color on red, str sides, minor wear, 5"	2,300.00
Tray, border stencil, gold on blk, 16x12"	45.00
Tray, bun; brush strokes, gold on blk, 9x5⅝"	100.00
Tray, flowers/peacocks, mc on blk w/gold, wear, 20x26"	365.00
Tray, freehand decor, gold on blk, 18x13½"	80.00
Tray, hunter/dog/tree, stenciled & freehand, 1800s, 26"	950.00
Tray, prancing pony w/flowers & ferns, 10x7½", EX	650.00
Tray, stenciled/freehand floral, mc on blk, 12"	100.00

Tools

Before the Civil War, tools for the most part were handmade. Some were primitive to the point of crudeness, while others reflected the skill of those who took pride in their trade. Increasing demand for quality tools and the dawning of the age of industrialization resulted in tools that were mass-produced.

Factors important in evaluating antique tools are scarcity, usefulness, and portability. Those with a manufacturer's mark are worth more than unmarked items. When no condition is indicated, the items listed here are assumed to be in excellent condition. See also Winchester and Keen Kutter. Our advisor for this category is Jim Calison; he is listed in the Directory under New York.

Adze, polled lip, curved 25" hdl, EX	75.00
Axe, mortising; smithy made, early 1800s, 16" hdl	150.00
Back saw, H Disston & Sons, mk Langdon Miter Box Co, 29"	20.00
Beader, Windsor, mahog, brass tips/hardware, EX	120.00
Brace, electrician's, Millers Falls Co, 12", EX	15.00
Brace, Sheffield style, brass plated, mk W Round	75.00
Brace, W Marples & Son, brass-plated beech, M	260.00

Cabinet, tool; Stanley, oak roll front, EX 170.00
Calipers, wrought iron & brass, old red pnt, 18", EX........65.00
Carrier, carpenter's, wood, center cut-out hdl, 4x14x8" 60.00
Chisel, Samson, flat-edge, ornate hdl, 1¾" 14.00
Clapboard slick, wrought iron w/side hdl, 32" 150.00
Combination wrench, Lowentraut, Pat 1909........................100.00
Cranberry picker, wooden teeth, 10x21x24" 295.00
Draw knife, coach maker's, wood hdls, brass ferrules, 7" 35.00
Drill, CI w/wood crank hdl, unmk, old, 7½", EX 75.00
Hammer, Sawyer's, orig hdl, 5½" head........................55.00
Hand drill, Millers Falls #2, rosewood hdl, 15" 18.00
Level, Davis Co Pat 1867, CI w/pierced foliage, 24" 65.00
Level, LS Starrett Co, 24", EX........................40.00
Level, Stanley, CI w/brass front, dtd 1896, EX 25.00
Level, torpedo; Diamond Edge........................50.00
Level, W Marples, brass top/wood base, 9" 28.00
Level & plumb, Stanley #98, brass/rosewood, rare, 9" 185.00
Log caliper, Fabian, wood/brass, unmk, 48x20" 85.00
Lumber scale, cane-style, octagonal 45.00
Marking gauge, Stanley #77, rosewood, EX 33.00
Marking gauge, Stanley #93 ....50.00
Mortise gauge, rosewood face/brass bar, EX....................75.00
Plane, Elegant Millers Falls #714, Art Deco style, rare.........110.00
Plane, Gage Tool Co #4, steel plate, rare, 10" 65.00
Plane, plow; Stanley #46, w/11 blades 100.00
Plane, rabbet fillister; Stanley #278 ....135.00
Plane, Stanley #101, 1910-19, toy sz........................20.00
Plane, Stanley #8C........................50.00
Rule, Stanley #5, folding, EX 25.00
Rule, Stanley #94, boxwood/brass, 4-fold, rare 85.00
Scraper, Stanley #80, Pat 1914, EX........................22.00
Scraper, veneer; Stanley #12, G........................55.00
Screwdriver, Stanley, brass ferrule/beech hdl, 14" 12.00
Scribe, Stanley #90, metal, EX........................20.00
Spoke shave, brass, compass bottom, 3½" 28.00
Spoke shave, Stanley #68, brass plate, unmk, 11"................17.00
Spoke shave, Stanley #68, steel rabbet, rare 38.00
Spoon mold, bronze, 8" 250.00
Tack hammer, rosewood hdl, mk CS Osborne & Co, 11"............25.00
Wrench, alligator; Diamond Edge, adjustable, Pat 2-26-03..........125.00
Wrench, Wullweber's #464, dbl-sided, 4" 25.00

Toothpick Holders

Once common on every table, the toothpick holder was relegated to the china cabinet near the turn of the century. Fortunately, this contributed to their survival; as a result, many are available to collectors today. Because they are small and easily displayed, they are a very popular collectible; and they come in a wide range of prices to fit every budget. The rare ones have been reproduced and, unfortunately, are being offered for sale right along with the originals. (These 'repros' should be priced in the $10.00 to $15.00 range.) So unless you're sure of what you're buying, choose a reputable dealer.

In addition to pattern glass, you'll find examples in china, bisque, art glass, and silverplate. In the listings that follow, items are glass unless noted otherwise. Those that have been reproduced are designated with a (+), however values are for the originals.

Amberina, 3-cornered top, Mt WA, lg........................365.00
Atlas, etched leaf & berry........................30.00
Baby T'print, reverse amberina, hexagonal 225.00
Box-in-Box, gr w/gold 30.00
Box-in-Box, ruby stained........................48.00

Two roosters and basket, amber glass, 3", $135.00.

Bristol, hat shape w/turned-over brim, bl w/gold florals..............125.00
British Barrel, Optic Paneled in honey amber w/bl ft.................145.00
Bubble Lattice, canary satin, tricorner rim 225.00
Bubble Lattice, wht opal........................115.00
Buffalo figural, cobalt, emb Pan Am Expo, Buffalo 1901 ....195.00
Button Arches, ruby stained (+) 18.00
California 50.00
Champion 28.00
Champion, clear w/gold 35.00
Chrysanthemum Base Swirl, bl opal 150.00
Chrysanthemum Leaf Swirl, clear w/gold........................95.00
Chute & Ladders........................22.00
Colorado, gr w/gold........................45.00
Cordova, gr........................27.50
Cordova, ruby stained 85.00
Cranberry, mc forget-me-nots w/gold, ruffled 175.00
Creased Bale, pk........................50.00
Daisy & Button, amberina, 3"........................200.00
Daisy & Button w/V Ornament, bl 45.00
Delaware, clear w/gold........................65.00
Delaware, gr w/gold........................90.00
Delaware, milk glass, pk flowers, bl decor ft & rim................55.00
Diamond Lil, rare........................45.00
Diamond Spearhead, vaseline opal........................66.00
Dolphin, amber........................90.00
Double Ring Panel, apple gr, rare 45.00
Double Ring Panel, rose 40.00
Empress, gr w/gold........................210.00
Esther, gr w/gold 85.00
Falcon Strawberry 30.00
Feather, Cambridge........................60.00
Florette, gr........................50.00
Florette, pk cased........................140.00
Framed Ovals, raised base, scalloped rim, flint........................85.00
Frazier, cranberry w/HP decor 78.00
Gaelic, no gold........................24.00
Gaelic, clear w/gold 32.00
Geneva, custard 135.00
Georgia Gem........................22.00
Holly 125.00
Holly Amber, sm 375.00
Horseshoe & Clover, milk glass........................20.00
Invt T'print, ruby w/etching 42.50
Iris w/Meander, bl opal 75.00
Iris w/Meander, gr opal 45.00
Ivanhoe........................45.00

Jefferson Optic, bl, souvenir	55.00
Jefferson Optic, gr, souvenir	42.50
Kentucky, gr w/gold	150.00
Kitten on Pillow, amber	65.00
Ladders w/Diamonds	30.00
Manhattan, clear w/gold	32.00
Mardi Gras	45.00
Michigan	32.00
Millefiori	85.00
Minnesota	32.00
Oregon	88.00
Palm Leaf, gr opaque	95.00
Peachblow w/tricorner rim, NE Glass	295.00
Pineapple & Fan, Heisey	75.00
Pleating, ruby stained	30.00
Pretty Maid	55.00
Priscilla	40.00
Punty Band, custard, souvenir	45.00
Queen's Necklace, no gold	50.00
Reverse Swirl, vaseline opal	75.00
Ribbed Spiral	44.00
Royal Ivy, rubena, glossy	75.00
Ruby T'rint, Scranton souvenir	30.00
Scalloped Panel, gr	35.00
Scroll w/Cane Band	37.50
Scroll w/Cane Band, amber	60.00
Scroll w/Cane Band, ruby stained	85.00
Serrated Prism, clear w/EX gold	40.00
Shoshone, clear w/gold	20.00
Shoshone, ruby stained	115.00
States	45.00
Stippled Sand Burr	50.00
Sunset, bl opaque	72.00
Swag w/Bracket, amethyst, EX gold	75.00
Swirl & Panel	32.50
Sylvan, clear w/gold	35.00
Tennessee	65.00
Texas, clear w/gold	25.00
Texas Star	55.00
Thumbnail	30.00
Tiny T'print, custard	55.00
US Regal	24.00
Vermont, gr w/EX gold	50.00
West Virginia Optic, gr	35.00
Wheeling Block	45.00
Windows, cranberry opal	195.00
Winged Scroll, emerald gr w/EX gold, Heisey	225.00
Wisconsin, pk opal	55.00
Wreath & Shell, bl opal	295.00
Wreath & Shell, vaseline opal	200.00
X-Ray, gr w/gold	45.00
Zippered Swirl	20.00

Torquay 'Devon Motto' Ware

Torquay is a unique type of pottery made in the South Devon area of England as early as 1867. At the height of productivity, at least a dozen companies flourished there, producing simple folk pottery from the area's natural red clay. The ware was both wheel-turned and molded and decorated under the glaze with heavy slip resulting in low-relief nature subjects or simple scrollwork.

Three of the best-known of these potteries were: Watcombe (1867-1962); Aller Vale (in operation from the mid-1800s, producing domestic ware and architectural products); and Longpark (1890 until 1957). Watcombe and Aller Vale merged in 1901 and operated until 1962 under the name of Royal Aller Vale and Watcombe Art Pottery.

Perhaps the most famous type of ware potted in this area was Motto Ware, so called because of the verses, proverbs, and quotations that decorated it. This decor was achieved by the sgraffito technique — scratching the letters through the slip to expose the red clay underneath. The most popular decorative devices were cottages, black cockerel, multi-cockerel, and a scrollwork pattern called Scandy. Other popular patterns were Kerswell Daisy, ships, kingfishers, and many other birds on blue ground.

Aller Vale ware may sometimes be found marked 'H.H. and Company,' a firm who assumed ownership from 1897 to 1901. 'Watcombe Torquay' was an impressed mark used from 1884 to 1927.

Our advisors for this category are Jerry and Gerry Kline; they are listed in the Directory under Ohio. If you're interested in joining a Torquay club, there are two: The Torquay Pottery Collectors' Society and The North America Torquay Society. Both are listed under Clubs, Newsletters, and Catalogs.

Ash tray, Cottage, rnd, flat, unmk, sm	25.00
Ash tray, Cottage, Watcombe, 'Who burnt the...,' 4" dia	28.00
Biscuit barrel, Cottage, Watcombe, 'Do the work...,' 6½"	150.00
Bottle, scent; Cornish Lavender, crown stopper, 3¾"	40.00
Bowl, Cottage, MIE, 'We live in deeds...,' 2¼x4"	50.00
Cache pot, Scandy, 'One good turn...,' unmk, 3x4"	48.00
Candlestick, ship, Longpark, 'Many are called...,' 5½"	90.00
Chamberstick, Blk Cockerel, 'Hear all...,' 5½x5" dia	78.00
Coffeepot, Cottage, Watcombe, 'Happiness in the...,' 6½"	115.00
Coffeepot, Watcombe, 'May the hinges of friendship...,' 7"	115.00
Compote, Watcombe, 'Kind words are the music...,' 7½" dia	225.00
Condiment holder, shakers, egg cup & mustard, 3½"	125.00
Creamer, Blk Cockerel, Longpark, 'From Rothbury...,' 3"	55.00
Creamer, Cottage, 'Fresh from the dairy,' 2½"	37.00
Creamer, Scandy, Longpark, 'Elp yerzel to craim,' 2½"	35.00
Creamer, Scandy, Longpark, ped ft, 'Fresh from the diary'	38.00
Cruet, vinegar; Cottage, Watcombe, 'Lynmouth,' 7½"	60.00
Cup & saucer, Cottage, 'Speak little, speak well'	35.00
Cup & saucer, Cottage, 'There's a time for all things'	37.50
Cup & saucer, Cottage, Watcombe, 'Take a cup of tea'	32.00
Cup & saucer, demitasse; Cottage, Watcome, 'Have a cup...,'	30.00
Dish, Scandy, Longpark, 'There more in the kitchen,' 7" dia	88.00
Ewer, Peacock, Royal Torquay, 9¾"	100.00
Figurine, classical, Watcombe, terra cotta, 11½"	350.00

Hatpin holder, sailboats, marked Helecrose, 5", $65.00.

Honey pot, Cottage, Watcombe, 'Have some honey...,' 4"	55.00

Hot water pot, Cottage, Watcombe, 'Gude thing be scarce...,' 85.00
Inkwell, Scandy, Aller Vale, 'Us be always glad tu...,' 2" 50.00
Jar, jam; Cockington Forge, Watcombe, 'Actions speak...,' 5" 50.00
Jar, jam; Darthmouth Cottage, 'Elp yerzel...,' heart shape 30.00
Jar, jam; Scandy, 'Elp yerzel tu jam,' unmk, 1½x5¼" 40.00
Jardiniere, Orchids, on gr, 9x7½" 300.00
Jug, milk; Cottage, Watcombe, 'Help yourself,' 3½" 42.00
Jug, puzzle; Scandy, Allervale, 'I'll hold a wager...,' 3½" 80.00
Match holder, Longpark, motto, w/striker 60.00
Match holder/striker, Blk Cockerel, 'A match for...,' 3x3⅝" 98.00
Mug, Cottage, 'Here's to me & my wife's...,' unmk, 3¼" 38.00
Mug, shaving; Multi-Cockerel, 4x5½" from hdl to spout 125.00
Mustard pot, Scandy, 'Be canny wi the mustard,' unmk 35.00
Pitcher, Cottage, Watcombe, 'Fresh from the dairy,' 2½" 35.00
Pitcher, Cottage, Watcombe, 'Nothing can be sweeter,' 5½".........65.00
Pitcher, ship, 'Gold & lands may be lost...,' 8" 100.00
Plate, Cottage, Watcombe, 'Better wait on the cook...,' 5" 35.00
Plate, Cottage, Watcombe, 'Enough's as good as...,' 7½" 48.00
Plate, Cottage, Watcombe, 'Fairest gems lie deepest,' 5" 40.00
Plate, Cottage, Watcombe, 'Heaven send thee...,' 6½" 45.00
Plate, Cottage, Watcombe, 10" 85.00
Plate, gold w/cherries at rim, 'He who hesitates...,' 7" 55.00
Shakers, Watcombe, 'Take a little...,' 3", pr 55.00
Sugar bowl, Blk Cockerel, Longpark, 'Elp yerzel...,' 2" 42.00
Sugar bowl, Cottage, 'Elp yerzel...,' 1½" 40.00
Sugar bowl, Cottage, Watcombe, 'Takee a little...,' 1½x4" 40.00
Sugar bowl, Scandy, ped ft, 'Sweeten to your liking,' unmk 38.00
Teapot, Cottage, Watcombe, 'Ave a cup,' 5x9½" hdl to spout ...138.00
Toast rack, Forget-Me-Not, Watcombe, 'Help yourself...,'...........130.00
Tray, dresser; Kingfisher, Watcombe, 10½x7½" 140.00
Tray, lunch; Blk Cockerel, Longpark, 'Be Aisy...,' 7" dia 94.00
Tumbler, Blk Cockerel, Longpark, 'Every blade...,' 3½" 55.00
Tumbler, Scandy, Longpark, 'Few words are best,' 3¾" 50.00

Tortoise Shell Glass

By combining several shades of glass — brown, clear, and yellow — glass manufacturers of the 19th century were able to produce an art glass that closely resembled the shell of the tortoise. Some of this type of glassware was manufactured in Germany. In America it was made by several firms, the most prominent of which was the Boston and Sandwich Glass Works.

Biscuit jar, ornate SP rim, lid, & hdl..110.00
Bowl, 3-ftd, 4" 100.00
Butter dish 175.00
Pitcher, water; crimped rim, clear appl hdl, 9x8" 125.00
Vase, pinched rim, polished pontil, 8" 95.00
Vase, random fluted top, 10" 125.00

Toys

Toy collecting has grown tremendously in the past few years; toy shows and auctions are common, and the market has broadened. Now, toys from the fifties and sixties are as eagerly sought as 19th-century toys. It is important for collectors to become familiar with their areas of interest — seek out dealers with experience; take advantage of the many fine toy books that are available. These are some of the most helpful: *American Toy Cars and Trucks* by Lillian Gottschalk; *Toy Autos 1890-1939*, the Peter Ottenheimer Collection; *Collecting the Tin Toy Car, 1950-1970*, by Dale Kelley; *Arcade Toys*, by Al Aune; *The Art of the Tin Toy*, by David Pressland; *Lehmann Toys*, by Cieslik, *The History*

of *Martin Mechanical Toys*, by Marchand; *Mechanical Toys*, by Spilhaus; *American Antique Toys*, by Barenholtz, Mc Clintock, and Holland; *American Clockwork Toys*, by Whitton; *The George Brown Sketchbook*, by Edith Barenholtz; *Toy Dreams*, by Kitahara; and *Collecting Toys*, by O'Brien. *The Dictionary of Toys Sold in America Vol. I & II*, by Earnest and Ida Long are good for identification and dating.

In the listings that follow, toys are listed by manufacturer's name if possible, otherwise by type. Condition is given when known, since it is one of the major factors in establishing the price of any toy. Measurements are given when appropriate and available; if only one dimension is noted, it is the greater one — height if the toy is vertical, length if it is horizontal. Values given here result from monitoring auctions and checking known retail sales; to some extent, they have been taken from sale lists. In tracking prices realized at auctions, it was found that 42% of the time items were knocked down within the estimated range. 54% sold below estimate, and the remaining 28% exceeded the auctioneer's range. See also Children's Things; Personalities. For toy stoves, see Stoves.

Key:
b/o — battery operated   NP — nickel plated
jtd — jointed   w/up — wind-up

Cast Iron

Cast iron toys were made from shortly before the Civil War until the beginning of the 20th century. They are evaluated to a large extent by scarcity, complexity, design, and detail. See next section for examples of cast iron toys listed by company name.

American Stove, 1920s, 8½", VG 75.00
Coach w/2 horses, pnt traces, 11x4", VG....................................85.00
Coast-to-Coast bus, red rpt, 8", EX..150.00
Coupe, pnt rstr, 5", G..80.00
Dray w/driver, 1889, 19", VG...700.00
Elephant-drawn 2-wheeled cart w/Brownie driver, G pnt, 6½" ..750.00
Express wagon w/2 horses, 1890s, 17½", EX............................1,000.00
Fire Co hook & ladder truck, 1889, 24", VG 1,000.00
Fire engine, worn pnt, rubber tires, 5", VG.................................100.00
Girl w/doll on sled, bell ringer, Daisy, 1892, EX 2,250.00
Horse & sulky, w/rider, worn pnt, 1-pc, 5½" 30.00
Horse-drawn fire patrol wagon, w/5 riders, 16", EX....................350.00
Horse-drawn fire pump wagon, w/firemen, rpt, 15", EX 260.00
Horse-drawn ladder wagon, w/riders, G pnt, 15" 120.00
Horseless carriage, no driver, orig pnt, early type, 4", VG............100.00
Horses pull bells on 4 wheels, worn pnt, 6¾x12" 155.00
Hose reel, worn/chipped pnt, 10¾", G......................................120.00
Jonah & Whale, pull toy, G pnt, lt rust, 1850s, 6" 500.00
Ladder truck, chipped pnt, rpt on tires, 5½", G............................85.00
Mack Oil truck, 1920s, 10", VG...400.00
Monkey on wheels, bell toy, worn paint, 6x5", VG......................375.00
Roadster, VG pnt, 8" 300.00
Rough Rider, dbl wells on 2-wheel fr, 1905, 8¾", EX..................600.00
Santa & sleigh, 1880s, 17", EX 1,500.00
Side-wheeler, VG cream pnt w/red trim, 1910s, 5⅝" 175.00
Sled, scroll runners, 'Santa Claus' emb on top, 5½", VG 100.00
Touring auto, top down, couple seated, rpt, 9½", VG 200.00
Truck, old red pnt, steel wheels, 5", EX......................................55.00
Truck, open type w/delivery bk, no pnt, 4¼", G...........................30.00
Yel Kid goat cart, worn pnt, 7", VG...175.00

Company or Country of Manufacturer

Alps, Cadillac, tin, friction, MIB...220.00

Alps, Daisy Drumming Duck, plush, b/o, 8", NM in box...............95.00
Alps, Fighting Bull, plush, b/o, 12", EX...............................38.00
Alps, Happy Santa, b/o, 9", NM 145.00
Alps, Pressmobile Car, tin w/up, 6", MIB..............................65.00
Alps, Teddy Drummer, plush/tin, b/o, 11", NM 55.00
Althof/Bergman, Boy on Cart, clockwork, EX 18,500.00
America, Columbia Side-wheeler, pnt tin, 12", VG............3,900.00
Arcade, Buick, CI, metal wheels, 1920s, 8", NM 950.00
Arcade, Chevrolet, wht tires, 1928, 8", EX.........................125.00
Arcade, Chevrolet Coupe, CI, worn pnt, 1927, 9¼", EX........2,200.00
Arcade, Fageol Bus, CI, rpt, lt rust, 8", G 110.00
Arcade, Internat'l Harvester Dump Truck, CI, 10", VG.......250.00
Arcade, kitchen set, pnt CI, 8-pc, VG.................................175.00
Arcade, Model-A Coupe, CI, metal wheels, EX...................650.00
Arcade, Model-T Ford Coupe, CI, spoke wheels, '22, 6½", EX ...300.00
Arcade, Sedan, CI, NP driver, 6½", EX.................................525.00
Arcade, Tow Truck, CI, orig stenciling/pnt, 10½", EX..........500.00
Arnold, Airboat, tin litho, lg bk propeller, 8½", EX............715.00
Arnold, Clown & Pig, pnt tin, clockwork, 1914, 8", VG......450.00
Arnold, Mac Motorcycle, tin litho w/up, 8", EX..................440.00
Aviva, Snoopy's Airplane, yel biplane, diecast, 1977, 5" 35.00
Bandai, Cycling Daddy, cloth over tin w/vinyl, b/o, 10", MIB.......75.00
Bandai, Fiat 600, tin, friction, cloth sun roof, 7", NM..........60.00
Bandai, Jaguar Convertible, tin, friction, 10", M 65.00
Bandai, Mercedes 219, MIB...650.00
Bandai, Mercedez Benz 250 SL, tin, friction, 10", NM.........120.00
Bandai, 1959 Cadillac, tin, friction, EX details, 11", EX 165.00
Bandi, Mercedes 220 S/SE, M in box 1,250.00
Bing, Battleship, tin litho w/up, 3-stack, 14", EX.............2,860.00
Bing, Destroyer, pnt tin, clockwork, 4-stack, 22", VG 2,600.00
Bing, Jumping Frog, w/up, 1900s, moth damage, 8¾".........325.00
Bing, Limousine, tin litho w/up, rpl fenders, 9½", EX.........660.00
Bing, Model-T Ford Sedan, tin litho w/up, 1930s, 6½", VG......400.00
Bing, Open Door Sedan, tin w/up, 1930, 6", VG.................265.00
Bing, Open Tourer Auto, tin clockwork w/up, 1928, 8½", M......600.00
Bing, Roadster, tin litho, clockwork, ca 1900, 9", EX 5,500.00
Bing, Steamer, pnt steel, clockwork, 4-stack, 11", VG 400.00
Bing, Submarine, pnt tin, clockwork, 9½", G......................275.00
Bing, Torpedo Boat, tin, steam driven, 1910s, 27¾", EX ...1,800.00
Bliss, Trolley Car, paper on wood, 2 horses, 28", VG 1,100.00
Borgfeldt, Mickey & Minnie on Seesaw, celluloid, 9½", EX ...1,100.00
Borgfeldt, Mickey & Minnie on Seesaw, celluloid/tin, 7", EX.....880.00
Browers, Automatic Dancer, compo/wood, clockwork, 9", G..1,000.00
Browers, Automatic Dancer, compo/wood, clockwork, 9", VG. 2,500.00
Buddy L, Army truck & transport, steel, 1940s, EX 125.00
Buddy L, coupe, pnt steel, 11", EX....................................800.00
Buddy L, dump truck, pnt steel, open cab, 1930s, 11", EX......475.00
Buddy L, Railroad Express truck, pnt steel, 1920s, 25", VG......350.00
Buddy L, sand & gravel truck, pressed steel, 1940s, 14", VG.....35.00
Buddy L, tanker truck, pnt steel, lt rust, 24½".....................800.00
Buddy L, 1927 Model-T car, 1930s, minor dents, EX 925.00
Carpenter, Fire Pumper, CI, gold/blk/red pnt, 1890s, 18½" 550.00
Chad Valley, stove, tin, w/orig cookware, EX.....................175.00
Chein, Barnacle Bill, tin litho w/up, ca 1930, 6½", NM 155.00
Chein, Boxing Popeye, tin/celluloid w/up, 7½", VG............800.00
Chein, Broadway Trolly, tin litho, 8¼", EX 165.00
Chein, Clown in Barrel, tin w/up, 1920s, 8", NM 190.00
Chein, Happy Hooligan, tin litho w/up walker, 6", EX........330.00
Chein, Hercules Ferris Wheel, tin litho w/up, 16½", VG.....160.00
Chein, Ignatz Mouse, jtd wood, on scooter, '32, 8½", VG 495.00
Chein, Popeye in Barrel, tin w/up walker, 7", EX................350.00
Chein, Popeye Puncher, tin litho w/up, 7½", VG 900.00
Chein, Popeye Walker, tin litho w/up, 6", EX.....................165.00
Chein, Roadster, tin litho, 1920s, 8½", VG 40.00

Chein, Popeye Overhead Punching Bag, rare, 10", $2,000.00.

Chein, Seaplane, tin litho w/up, 1935, 8" wing span, VG..............45.00
China, Ice Cream Vendor, tin litho w/up, 4½", MIB 50.00
China, Panda Drummer, rubber head, clockwork, 4½", MIB 35.00
China, Spank Tank, gyro action, b/o, 10", MIB.........................25.00
Cragston, Scottie Spaniel, b/o, 8½", MIB.................................75.00
Daisy, Target BB Rifle, EX in box...135.00
Dent, La Salle tow truck, EX..425.00
Dent, Tanker Truck, CI, wht rubber tires, 10", VG 875.00
Dinky, Chrysler Airflow Saloon, 1930s, 4", NM 75.00
Dinky, Halftrack, diecast, mesh treads, 1950, NM....................20.00
Doepke, bulldozer, VG..365.00
Doepke, Jaquar, EX...435.00
Doepke, ladder truck, EX...345.00
Fischer, Limousine, tin litho w/up, early, 13", G 800.00
Fisher-Price, Barky Buddy, 1934-36, EX.................................250.00
Fisher-Price, Barky Puppy, pull toy, 1931, VG..........................30.00
Fisher-Price, Bucky Burro, 1955-58, NM................................100.00
Fisher-Price, Chubby Chief, 1932, EX....................................275.00
Fisher-Price, Corn Popper, 1957-63, EX...................................35.00
Fisher-Price, Donald & Donna Duck, 1937, NM 300.00
Fisher-Price, Donald Duck Cart, 1954-58, EX.........................100.00
Fisher-Price, Go 'N Back Bruno, 1932, EX...............................245.00
Fisher-Price, Jumbo Jitterbug, 1940, NM................................115.00
Fisher-Price, Kicking Donkey, 1937-39, EX.............................165.00
Fisher-Price, Looky Push Car, 1962-66, NM 30.00
Fisher-Price, Pinky Pig, litho eyes, 1958, EX.............................35.00
Fisher-Price, Playland Express, 1962, M...................................48.00
Fisher-Price, Pluto paddle toy, 1940s, EX.................................75.00
Fisher-Price, Roller Chime, 1953-61, NM.................................25.00
Fisher-Price, Sleepy Sue Turtle, 1962-64, M.............................25.00
Fisher-Price, Streamline Express, 1935, EX.............................265.00
Fisher-Price, Talk-Back Telephone, 1961, NM...........................45.00
Fisher-Price, Teddy Choo-Choo, 1937, VG................................75.00
Fisher-Price, Tiny Teddy, #635, 1962, VG.................................20.00
Fleishmann, Live Steam Roller, pnt steel, 12", EX in box 275.00
Fleishmann, Ocean Liner, tin litho w/up, 2-stack, 12½", EX 425.00
Fleishmann, Tug Boat, tin litho w/up, 7", VG...........................170.00
France, Balloon Dirigible, tin w/up, 1900, 10", EX in box 825.00
France, Bicycle Race, HP riders, felt track, 1910, 18", EX........4,180.00
Germany, Airship Los Angeles, tin litho w/up, 9", EX................900.00
Germany, Airship Tower, tin litho w/up, lt rust, 5½", G........52,500.70
Germany, Arab & Camel, tin litho w/up, 6", EX in box..............170.00
Germany, Armored Car, tin litho w/up, 6½", VG.......................750.00

Germany, Auto w/Driver, tin litho w/up, ca 1900, 11", EX 2,700.00
Germany, Auto w/Monkey Driver, tin w/up, 1900, 6¼", VG 500.00
Germany, Birds Fighting Over Worm, tin key wind, 1920s, 9" 220.00
Germany, Buckingham Palace w/Guards, tin w/up, 8½", EX 385.00
Germany, Chaplin, tin litho w/up, 8½", NM 1,430.00
Germany, Chaplin w/Cymbals, tin push/pull toy, 7", EX 1,430.00
Germany, Chimney Sweep Sparkler, tin litho, 5", VG 95.00
Germany, Delivery Van, tin litho w/up, 1890s, 9⅛", EX 400.00
Germany, Donkey Walker, tin w/up, HP, 1900, 8¾", EX 600.00
Germany, Ferris Wheel, pnt int, steam driven, 15", VG 1,000.00
Germany, Ferris Wheel, tin w/up, HP, ca 1910, 15½", VG 1,200.00
Germany, Fishing Fred, tin litho w/up, 6", EX in box 360.00
Germany, Folding Village, pnt tin, 1850s, 12x10", VG 325.00
Germany, Fox Chasing Goose, tin, clockwork, 1890s, 10", VG .. 600.00
Germany, Happy Hooligan, roly-poly, HP, 6", EX 200.00
Germany, Horse on Platform, felt on papier-mache, 9", VG 175.00
Germany, Jousting Boxers, tin litho w/up, 7", EX 495.00
Germany, Kentucky Paddle-Wheeler, steel, clockwork, 14" ... 2,100.00
Germany, Lady w/Fan, HP tin, clockwork, 7½", G 450.00
Germany, Limousine w/Chauffeur, tin w/up, 1900s, 13", EX ... 2,000.00
Germany, Mickey Mouse w/Umbrella, lead, ca 1935, 4¾", EX .. 1,870.00
Germany, Native, tin litho, pull string, 2½", G 60.00
Germany, Noah's Ark, pnt wood, 30 compo animals, 16", VG ... 425.00
Germany, Ocean Liner, tin litho w/up, 2-stack, 9", VG 100.00
Germany, Peacock, tin litho, clockwork, 1914, 9¾", EX 400.00
Germany, Picture Block Puzzle, farm animals, G in box 170.00
Germany, Pool Player, tin litho w/up, 1910s, 6⅛", VG 150.00
Germany, Saloon Car, tin litho w/up, 1912, 11½", EX 4,000.00
Germany, Steamliner, tin, clockwork, 3-stack, '12, 12", G 1,000.00
Germany, Toonerville Trolley, tin litho, clockwork, 5", G 350.00
Germany, Twin Monkeys, tin w/up seesaw, 1920, 11", EX 300.00
Germany, Zeppelin, HP tin w/up, ca 1910, 17", EX 2,850.00
Gibbs, Horse Cart, paper-on-wood horse, wood cart, 14", VG 170.00
Gilbert, erector set #7½, w/2 motors, NM in box 175.00
Gilbert, Illya Kuryakin hand puppet, vinyl, 1965, NM 110.00
Gong Bell, Ranch Phone, tin litho, crank, '55, 13", EX in box 35.00
Gong Bell, Tub Boat Pete, pull toy, dbl action, 1930s 125.00
Guntherman, Blk Lady, HP tin w/up walker, 6½", EX 990.00
Guntherman, Gardener Lady w/Rake, EX 1,100.00
Guntherman, zylophone, dbl figure, EX 2,800.00
Guntherman, 2-Man Band, tin w/up, ca 1895, 9", EX 2,850.00
Hasbro, Bubble Jet Plane, shoots bubbles, MIB 38.00
Hess, Hessmobile, tin litho w/flywheel, 7", G 225.00
Hubley, Army Truck, 15" 1,650.00
Hubley, Bell Telephone Truck, 5½", EX 300.00
Hubley, Blk & Wht Cab, VG 950.00
Hubley, Dump Truck, wht metal, lever action, 9½", MIB 55.00
Hubley, Five-Ton Truck, CI, yel pnt, 16", VG 775.00
Hubley, Hook & Ladder Firetruck, tin litho w/up, MIB 95.00
Hubley, Navy Fighter Bomber, wht metal, 11½", NM 95.00
Hubley, Race Car #2241, 1930s, 7", VG 30.00
Hubley, Racer, metal body, rubber wheels, 7", MIB 135.00
Irwin, Dancing Cinderella & Prince, tin litho w/up, MIB 250.00
Issmayer, Bird in Chest, tin w/up, ca 1910, 4½", VG 525.00
Ives, Bear, brn fur, glass eyes, clockwork, 1890s, 9", EX 300.00
Ives, Butter Churner, clockwork, G 4,500.00
Ives, Circus Rider, clockwork, EX 22,000.00
Ives, Dancin' Blk Man, pnt metal, clockwork, 11", EX 2,000.00
Ives, Fast Mail Wagon w/Horse, pnt CI, 17", VG 750.00
Ives, General Butler, pnt tin & cloth, clockwork, 10", EX 2,860.00
Ives, General Grant (smoker), clockwork 25,000.00
Ives, Preacher, clockwork, EX in box 9,200.00
Ives, Preacher at Pulpit, tin/cloth w/up, 10", NM 4,400.00
Ives, Rowboat, clockwork, EX 11,000.00

Ives, Seesaw, clockwork, EX 8,500.00
Japan, Basketball Player, tin, lever action, 7", EX 65.00
Japan, Blacksmith Bear, plush w/tin base, b/o, 10", NM 115.00
Japan, Bubble Musician, tin litho, b/o, 10", MIB 95.00
Japan, Chick Merry-Go-Round, celluloid w/up, 7", EX in box 20.00
Japan, Chicken & Man, tin litho w/up, rpl pan, 7¼", VG 500.00
Japan, Dancing Merry Chimp, plush, b/o, 12", MIB 80.00
Japan, Dentist Bear, tin w/plush head, b/o, 10", EX in box 195.00
Japan, Dilly Duck, tin w/up, 4½", MIB 50.00
Japan, Donald Duck & Nephews Ring Toss game, 1950s, EX 45.00
Japan, Donald Duck Carousel, celluloid/metal, 7", NM 935.00
Japan, Donald Duck on Trapeze, celluloid w/up, 8½", VG 440.00
Japan, Donald Duck Riding Pluto, celluloid w/up, 1937, EX .. 6,750.00
Japan, Elephant, celluloid, w/up, mc, working, 8", VG 250.00
Japan, Fighting Robot, tin, b/o, 10", NM in EX box 60.00

Japan, Fire Car, friction, MIB, $185.00.

Japan, Fire Patrol Boat, tin litho, b/o, 12", EX in box 100.00
Japan, Gorilla, plush/celluloid, b/o, albino, 10", NM 175.00
Japan, Greyhound Bus, tin litho, friction, 1950s, 11", NM 60.00
Japan, Grumpy Doll, cloth w/plastic hands, 7" 10.00
Japan, Henry the Acrobat, celluloid w/up, 8", VG 385.00
Japan, Henry the Riding Elephant, celluloid, prewar, 8" 1,100.00
Japan, Herbie Volkswagen #53, tin b/o, M 50.00
Japan, Highway Patrol Car, b/o remote, 1950s, 10½", MIB 85.00
Japan, Lincoln Convertible, tin litho, remote b/o, 11", VG 150.00
Japan, Mad Russian Drummer, tin w/up, 7", MIB 100.00
Japan, Mercedes Benz, tin litho, friction, 8", G 80.00
Japan, Mercury Car, tin, friction, 1950s, 8", MIB 60.00
Japan, Mickey Mouse Carousel, celluloid w/up, 7", EX 1,500.00
Japan, Mickey Mouse on Tricycle, tin w/up, 7", EX 1,100.00
Japan, Minnie Mouse, celluloid, jtd arms, 6", EX 525.00
Japan, Old Fashioned Car, tin, 9½", MIB 95.00
Japan, Oldsmobile, tin litho, friction, 12", G 230.00
Japan, Playful Cat, celluloid & tin w/up, 5½", MIB 95.00
Japan, Policeman on Motorcycle, tin litho, b/o, 11½", EX 300.00
Japan, Racer #301, tin litho, b/o, 17½", EX 155.00
Japan, Road Roller, tin litho, friction, 7", NM 45.00
Japan, Sam the Shaving Man, tin/cloth, b/o, 12", MIB 150.00
Japan, School Bus, tin, b/o, noise at bk, lights, 13", EX 65.00
Japan, Shell Gas Truck w/trailer, 1950s, 9", VG 15.00
Japan, Skirted Robot, tin, crank action, 7", EX 115.00
Japan, Space Cruiser, tin, b/o, MIB 150.00
Japan, Sparkling Super Robot, tin w/up, 6½", MIB 120.00
Japan, Speed Boat, wood w/chrome, 1950s, 14", MIB 85.00

Japan, Trumpet Player, tin litho w/up, 10", EX 220.00
Jaymar, Mickey Mouse Magic Adder, 1950s, EX in box 35.00
Kellerman, Airplane Round-A-Bout, tin litho w/up, 9", G 225.00
Kenner, Big Burger Grill, 1950s, MIB 78.00
Kenton, Bunny Cart, pnt CI, 1929, 5⅛", EX 325.00
Kenton, Pickwick Nite Coach, 9¾", EX 3,100.00
Kenton, Racing Sulky, pnt CI, NP wheels, 7", VG 130.00
Keystone, Hydraulic-Lift Dump Truck, pnt steel, 1920s, VG 300.00
Kingsbury, Golden Arrow Racer, tin litho w/up, 19½", VG 400.00
Knickerbocker, Huckleberry Hound bank, plastic, 1960s, 10" 18.00
Knickerbocker, Pinocchio Doll, wood/compo, 1939, 14", NM 225.00
Knickerbocker, Raggedy Ann, 2-face, 40", EX 265.00
Kretzschimer, Picture Puzzle Blocks, paper on wood, VG 550.00
LaBelle, Original Anchor Blocks, NM in EX 13" wood box 350.00
Lehmann, Alabama Coon Jigger, tin litho w/up, 10", G 500.00
Lehmann, Balky Mule, tin litho w/up, 7", VG 195.00
Lehmann, Beetle, tin litho w/up, 1900, 3⅝", VG 100.00
Lehmann, Bird & Fly, tin w/up, VG pnt, 1890s, 8¼" 75.00
Lehmann, Dare Devil, Zebra & Wagon, tin w/up, 7", EX 275.00
Lehmann, Duo, tin litho w/up, 7", EX 1,150.00
Lehmann, Echo Motorcycle, tin litho w/up, 8½", EX 2,300.00
Lehmann, Going to the Fair, tin, friction, 1890s, 6", VG 1,300.00
Lehmann, Going to the Fair, tin, friction, 6", NM in box 4,180.00
Lehmann, Mars Sailor, tin litho w/up, 7½", EX 770.00
Lehmann, Na-Ob Horse-Drawn Wagon #680, tin w/up, 6", VG .245.00
Lehmann, Oh-My Jigger #685, tin litho w/up, 10", EX 440.00
Lehmann, Paddy & the Pig #500, tin litho w/up, 5½", EX 1,200.00
Lehmann, Quack-Quack, tin litho w/up, 7½", VG 260.00
Lehmann, Tut-Tut & Horse, pull toy, lt rust, 6⅝", 12" 200.00
Lehmann, Tut-Tut Auto, tin litho w/up, 6½", EX 1,650.00
Lehmann, Tyras the Walking Dog #432, tin w/up, 7", NM 935.00
Lehmann, Uhu Land/Sea Racer, tin litho w/up, 9½", NM 2,420.00
Lehmann, Walking Down Broadway, tin w/up, 1890s, 6", G .. 2,000.00
Lindstrom, Dancing Dutch Boy, tin w/up, 8", NM in box 125.00
Lindstrom, Dancing Lassie, tin litho w/up, 1930s, EX 85.00
Lindstrom, Miss America Speed Boat, tin w/up, 7", NM 125.00
Linemar, Cabin Cruiser w/Outboard Motor, tin, b/o, '55, 13", EX.95.00
Linemar, Casper the Ghost Turnover Tank, tin w/up, 3¾", EX .220.00
Linemar, Climbing Fireman, tin litho, b/o, 13", VG 165.00
Linemar, Cocoa Puffs Train, tin litho w/up, 1960s, NM 78.00
Linemar, Crawling Baby, celluloid/fabric, 10", EX 55.00
Linemar, Donald Duck Tricycle, celluloid w/up, 4", VG 85.00
Linemar, Flower the Skunk, tin, friction, 3", EX 38.00
Linemar, Henry Eating Ice Cream Cone, tin w/up, 6", VG 135.00
Linemar, Hungry Cat, plush/tin, b/o, 9", NM in box 195.00
Linemar, Mickey Mouse Roller Skater, tin w/up, 6½", NM 1,760.00
Linemar, Minnie Mouse in Rocker, tin litho w/up, 7", EX 300.00
Linemar, Mobile Gas Truck, tin, friction, 1950s, 11", NM 55.00
Linemar, Pony Express Wagon, tin litho, friction, 5½", EX 55.00
Linemar, Popeye & Olive Ball Toss, tin litho w/up, 19", EX... 1,000.00
Linemar, Popeye in Airplane, tin litho w/up, 6¼", EX 3,850.00
Linemar, Popeye on High-wheel Bicycle, tin w/up, 6¾", NM . 1,550.00
Linemar, Popeye Skater, tin litho w/up, 6½", EX 485.00
Linemar, Slinky Pluto, tin litho w/up, 8", VG 200.00
Linemar, Thumper, tin litho friction figure, 1950s, VG 55.00
Lionel, Lionel City RR Station, pnt metal, '20s, 13½", EX 100.00
Lionel, Mickey Mouse Handcar #1100, metal, '30s, EX in box....850.00
Lionel, Peter Rabbit Chick-Mobile, tin w/up, 10½", VG 330.00
Martin, Advocate, HP tin w/up walker, 9", EX 1,320.00
Martin, Auto-Transport, tin litho w/up, side dump, 8", VG 650.00
Martin, Man Climbing Ladder, tin w/up, 1890s, 14¾", EX 1,100.00
Marusan, Sidecar Cycle, MIB 2,750.00
Marx, Amos 'N Andy Fresh Air Taxi, tin w/up, 5x7½", NM 850.00
Marx, Atomic Cape Canaveral Missile Base set, '61, NM in box ..235.00
Marx, Auto Mac, w/figure, EX in VG box 200.00
Marx, BO Plenty, tin litho w/up walker, 8½", VG 135.00
Marx, Buck Rogers Roller Skates, 11", NM in box 4,180.00
Marx, Busy Bridge, tin litho w/up, pnt soiled/worn, 24" 95.00
Marx, Busy Parking Station, tin litho w/up, 1935, 17", EX 115.00
Marx, Cat Pushing Ball, w/up, 1930s, EX 65.00
Marx, Caterpillar Tractor, tin litho w/up, 1930s, 9½", G 95.00
Marx, Charlie McCarthy Benzine Buggy, tin w/up, 8", EX 825.00
Marx, Cowboy Rider, tin w/up, 1930s, 8", EX 135.00
Marx, Dick Tracy Squad Car, tin litho w/up, 11", G 70.00
Marx, Dino the Dinosaur, tin & cloth, b/o, 1962, 18", VG 300.00
Marx, Donald Duck & Goofy Duet, tin litho w/up, 10", NM.. 1,100.00
Marx, Dopey, tin litho walker, Disney, 8", EX 175.00
Marx, Dumbo, tin w/up, Disney Productions, 1949, NM 225.00
Marx, Ferdinand the Bull, tin litho w/up, 1938, VG 145.00
Marx, Fire Engine, sheet iron, ca 1920, 9", VG 45.00
Marx, Fireman, tin litho w/up, 2-part ladder, 1935, 22", VG 150.00
Marx, G-Man Car, tin litho, minor pnt chips, 1930s, 4⅝" 300.00
Marx, Great Garloo, plastic monster, b/o, EX in orig box 455.00

Marx, Harold Lloyd walking figure, tin, 10", $300.00.

Marx, Hi-Way Express Truck, tin w/tin tires, 1940s, 16", EX 65.00
Marx, Honeymoon Express, tin litho w/up, 9½", EX in box 200.00
Marx, Joe Pennar & Duck Goo-Goo, tin w/up, 1934, 8¼", VG ..550.00
Marx, Leopard, tin/cloth, roars & walks, 9", EX 125.00
Marx, Merry Music Makers, tin litho w/up, 9½", EX 600.00
Marx, Modern Farm Set #3939, sealed, M 235.00
Marx, Moon Mullins & Kayo Handcar, tin litho w/up, 6½", EX ...500.00
Marx, Mortimer Snerd Eccentric Car, tin w/up, 7½", EX 300.00
Marx, Officer 666, tin w/up walker, 10¾", EX 2,860.00
Marx, Old Jalopy, tin litho w/up, no passenger, 7", G 90.00
Marx, Pecos Bill, tin w/up, Disney, 1950s, MIB 400.00
Marx, Pinocchio, tin litho walker, moving eyes, 8½", VG 135.00
Marx, Popeye the Pilot, tin litho w/up, 8½", EX 440.00
Marx, Porky Pig, tin litho w/up, w/umbrella, 1939, EX 300.00
Marx, Range Rider, tin litho w/up, ca 1935, EX in box 185.00
Marx, Rin Tin Tin Fort Apache, 1958, EX in box 300.00
Marx, Ring-A-Ling Circus Roundabout, tin w/up, 8", EX 440.00
Marx, Rookie Pilot, EX 800.00
Marx, Roy Rogers Rodeo Ranch, EX in box 145.00
Marx, Royal Oil Mack Truck, tin litho w/up, 1925, 9", EX 495.00
Marx, Sanitation Truck, pnt steel, lt rust, 13", VG 140.00
Marx, Skyhawk Tower Aeroplane, tin w/up, 1930s, 8", EX 115.00
Marx, Son of Garloo, tin w/up, 6", EX 265.00
Marx, Sparkling Tank #2, tin litho w/up, MIB 200.00
Marx, Speedway Racer, tin litho w/up, 1948, 4", NM 40.00

Marx, Superman Rollover Tank, tin litho w/up, 10", VG 285.00
Marx, Tricky Action Tiger, tin w/up, MIB...................................110.00
Marx, Tricky Taxi, tin litho w/up, blk/wht, 1935, 4½", EX............55.00
Marx, Wilma Flintstone on Tricycle, celluloid w/up, 4", NM........75.00
Mattel, Beany Doll, cloth/vinyl, talking, 15½", EX 115.00
Mattel, Cecil Sea Serpent, stuffed, 1962, 20", EX in box.............110.00
Mattel, Chitty Chitty Bang Bang car, w/figures, 1968, M 48.00
McLoughlin Bros, Building Blocks, wood, 9½", EX in box 750.00
McLoughlin Bros, Magic Mirror, w/24 cards, 1890s, EX in box...450.00
McLoughlin Bros, Pretty Village Boat House Set, G in 12" box 70.00
McLoughlin Bros, Santa Cube Puzzle, wood, EX in box 4,000.00
Metalcraft, Heinz delivery truck, pnt steel, 12", VG 325.00
Metalcraft, Sunshine Biscuits truck, pnt steel, 12", G 300.00
Metalcraft, tow truck, pnt steel, 11½", VG 275.00
Milton Bradley, Animal Tenpins, paper/wood, 1890, EX in box ..440.00
National, Ragtime Rastus, jtd dancer, 1900s, 5½" 175.00
Nifty, Battling Maggie & Jiggs, tin litho w/up, 7", EX 1,320.00
Nifty, Powerful Katrinka w/Wheelbarrow, tin w/up, 6¾", NM.. 2,200.00
Ohio Art, Doodle Lite Glow Worm, 1975, MIB 15.00
Ohio Art, Hot Job Seaplane, tin litho w/up, M in VG box............45.00
Ohio Art, Mickey & Minnie Mouse Washing Machine, '30s, EX .120.00
Ohio Art, tea set, metal, Disney characters, MIB........................145.00
Orkincraft, Cabin Cruiser, pnt metal w/up, 33", VG 1,450.00
Parker Bros, Toy Town Garage, tin litho, w/box, 10½", VG .. 1,350.00
Parker Bros, Toy Town RR, tin w/cb buildings, 16", VG 1,300.00
Patterson, Andy Gump Racing Car #348, cvd resin, 14½" 1,550.00
Payton, Panzer Tank, 1960s, EX in orig box 40.00
Reed, Rover boat, tin litho, 18" L, EX 525.00
Remco, Daniel Boone Trailblazer Canteen, 1964, NM 20.00
Remco, Frogman, missing bayonette, 1961, VG in orig box 100.00
Remco, Mighty Mike, motorized truck, b/o, 1967, MIB.................30.00
Remco, Mr Brain, plastic, b/o, 13", NM.....................................85.00
Remco, Mummy action doll, 1980, MIB......................................22.00
Remkel, Smilin' Ed's Froggy Gremlin, 1950s, 9", EX in box 90.00
Schoenhut, see Toys, Schoenhut
Schuco, Auto & Garage, tin litho w/up, 6", VG 180.00
Schuco, Blk-face Drummer, tin litho & felt w/up, 4½", EX 300.00
Schuco, Clown w/Mouse, w/up, 4½", NM..................................100.00
Schuco, Mirakomot 1012 Cycle, tin litho w/up, NM in box........200.00
Schuco, Motodrill 1005, tin litho w/up, w/driver, 5¼", NM 195.00
Secor, Banjo Player, clockwork, EX.....................................25,000.00
Shuco, car, 1913 Mercer type, 9x4", M in orig box 160.00

Strauss, Alabama Coon Jigger, EX...625.00
Strauss, Boob McNutt, tin w/up, 1920s, 9", EX 500.00
Strauss, Interstate Bus, tin w/up, dbl-decker, 10", VG.................200.00
Strauss, Scout Flyer Airplane, orig pnt, 9½", VG.........................60.00
Strauss, Tombo Dancer, tin litho w/up, 9½", EX 330.00
Structo, farm truck, steel w/plastic animals, 20", NM 85.00
Structo, steam shovel, orig pnt, 1930s, EX.................................120.00
Sun Rubber, Donald Duck squeak toy, 1949, EX..........................12.00
Sun Rubber, truck, rubber, yel & bl, 5", NM 22.50
Taiwan, Super Astronaut, metal/plastic, 13", MIB........................65.00
Tonka, car carrier, yel, EX...135.00
Tonka, dump truck, 1960s, VG...95.00
Tonka, pickup truck #2360, metal, M in box................................45.00
Tonka, trencher, #534, EX in box...95.00
Tootsietoy, Buick coupe, running boards, 1926, 3", EX.................32.00
Tootsietoy, Cadillac roadster, rumble seat, 1926, 3", NM 38.00
Tootsietoy, Chevrolet coupe, iron wheels, EX pnt, 3" 25.00
Tootsietoy, Dairy truck w/tandem dual tanks, 9", EX..................115.00
Tootsietoy, Ford sedan w/house trailer, 5½", VG 55.00
Tootsietoy, Graham ambulance, rpl tires, pnt loss, 1⅞" 45.00
Tootsietoy, Graham wrecker, rpl tires, EX pnt, 3⅞" 85.00
Tootsietoy, Graham 5-wheel sedan, EX pnt, 4" 55.00
Tootsietoy, LaSalle coupe, rpl tires, EX pnt, 4" 145.00
Tootsietoy, Mack oil truck, gr & yel, 1925, 3¼", NM 32.00
Tootsietoy, Moon Mullins Police Car, 1930s, VG.......................100.00
Tootsietoy, Overland bus, metal tires, EX pnt, 3⅞".......................45.00
Tootsietoy, US Navy plane, rubber tires, EX pnt, 3⅞"...................65.00
Unique Art, Dogpatch Band, tin litho w/up, 12" 250.00
Unique Art, L'il Abner Dogpatch Band, tin w/up, 9½", EX 425.00
US Zone Germany, Technofix Motorcycle, tin w/up, 7", NM.....175.00
US Zone Germany, Wonder Teddy, tin litho w/up, 4½", NM 75.00

US Zone Germany, Boxers, wind-up, MIB, $175.00.

W Germany, motorcycle, tin, friction, Dunlop tires, 6½", VG 30.00
Wolverine, stove, Snow White, tin, 11½", EX 65.00
Wolverine, Sunny Andy Kiddie Kampers, tin w/up, 1930s, EX ..785.00
Wolverine, Zilotone, tin w/up w/4 inserts, 7½", EX 715.00
Woolsey, Kicker 21, pnt CI, mechanical, 7", VG........................250.00
Wyandotte, Ambulance, steel, wood tires 1930s, 11", EX..............60.00
Wyandotte, Humphrey Mobile, tin litho w/up, 9", EX.................330.00
Wyandotte, Mac Dump Truck, orange, 1930s, 13", M.................100.00
Wyandotte, Speed King Scooter, tin litho w/up, 6", EX 220.00

Farm Toys

Combine, Allis Chalmers, Ertl, EX 20.00
Combine, John Deere Turbo, Ertl, 11x14", EX.............................55.00
Combine, Massey Harris Self-Propelled, metal/wood, 10", VG ...425.00
Corn planter, rubber wheels, Arcade 27.50
Dump truck, Internat'l Harvester, ca 1929, Arcade 150.00

S.A. Smith Mfg. Co. pull cart, cat in shoe, 14" high, $600.00.

Steiff, see Toys, Steiff

Baler, marked SLIK, 1952, 10", $130.00.

Hay rake, McCormick-Deering, Arcade, 7x10", NM 175.00
Hay wagon, metal w/wire, horse-drawn style, orig pnt, 13x4" 40.00
Manure spreader, John Deere, VG 38.00
Manure spreader, McCormick-Deering...650.00
Mower, Arcade 22.50
Plow, Internat'l Harvester, Ertl, EX..20.00
Plow, 2-gang, Arcade, M 25.00
Rake, metal w/wire, horse-drawn style, orig pnt, 9x7", EX 35.00
Thresher, John Deere, Vindex, 1935, M 1,150.00
Tractor, Allis Chalmers, Model AC-6, decal, Arcade.................175.00
Tractor, Allis Chalmers, Model C, ca 1950, EX 120.00
Tractor, Caterpillar, #269, Arcade, M 400.00
Tractor, Caterpillar, diesel, steel tracks, Arcade, 8", NM.............265.00
Tractor, CI, Fordson, 6" 135.00
Tractor, Cochshutt #540, MIB..500.00
Tractor, Farmall M, plastic, w/trailer, EX 110.00
Tractor, Internat'l, Ertl, 1960s, M...40.00
Tractor, Internat'l Harvester #966...100.00
Tractor, John Deere #3020, steel bk wheels.................................125.00
Tractor, John Deere #820, EX..25.00
Tractor, Massey Harris #44, w/driver, EX.......................................35.00
Tractor, Minneapolis-Moline, w/butane tank..................................45.00
Tractor, Monarch, Hubley, 5½" 125.00
Tractor, Oliver, w/driver, 8½", w/7" drill....................................265.00
Tractor, Oliver #60, CI, Arcade, sm..65.00
Tractor, plastic, Ideal, 1948, 4", NM..22.50
Tractor, Select-O-Speed, Hubley, NM in box...............................135.00
Tractor/loader/backhoe, Internat'l Harvester #478, MIB...............55.00
Tractor/trailer, Allis Chalmers, Arcade, 1927, 12", G 65.00
Truck, all metal, Structo, lg, EX 85.00
Truck, pickup; Internat'l Harvester, plastic & metal....................100.00
Wagon, Arcade, 3½" 37.00

Guns and Cap Bombs

Though toy guns were patented as early as the 1850s, the cap pistol was not invented until 1870, when paper caps that were primarily developed to detonate muzzleloaders became available. Some of the earlier models were very ornate and were occasionally decorated with figural heads. Most are marked with the name of their manufacturer — Ace, Daisy, Bulldog, Victor, and Excelsior are the most common.

Automatic Disintegrator, cap pistol, Hubley, VG 45.00
Bang-O Repeater, cap pistol, Stevens, 1950s, MIB 135.00
Big Chief, 1930s, 3½", EX..35.00
Bob, cap pistol, CI, 1930, Kilgore, 5", NM...................................32.50
Bronco, disk cap pistol, ornate, EX in box 95.00
Buc-A-Roo, single shot cap pistol, Kilgore, 1950s, MIB.............130.00
Bunker Hill, cap pistol, CI, Nat'l, 1925, 5¼", EX..........................37.50

Colt 45, diecast, Hubley, M..32.00
Coyote Civil War, diecast 20.00
Dagger derringer, Hubley, 7", M 130.00
Deputy, repeating cap pistol, Hubley, 1950s, MIB.......................115.00
Dixie, cap pistol, CI, 1935, Kenton, 6¼", EX.................................40.00
Echo 6-Shooter, CI, Stevens, 1920, 4¼", EX.................................27.50
Fanner, diecast, Mattel, 1950s, EX...40.00
Golden Eagle, BB gun, Daisy, 1936, 50-yr commemorative, NM...75.00
Johnny Ringo Quickdraw set, Marx, 1960, 12", M on card.........165.00
Kentucky Long Rifle, Marx, 1974, 12", M 38.00
Lone Eagle, cap pistol, CI, Kilgore, 1929, 5¼", NM......................55.00
Monkey w/coconut, Ives or Stevens, late 1800s, 4¼", EX 375.00
Peacemaker, cap pistol, CI, Stevens, 1940, 8½", EX 45.00
Polo, Ives, 1878, 5", NM...60.00
Red Ranger Jr, stallion hdls, Wyandotte, 8", NM...........................55.00
Scout, Stevens, EX...75.00
Scout #75, BB gun, plastic stock, 1950s, Daisy, NM......................28.00
Scout Jr, cap pistol, CI, Stevens, 1935, 6", NM..............................37.50
Shoo Fly, cap pistol, CI, EX...135.00
Shootin' Shell, snub-nose 38, Mattel, NM....................................115.00
Signal Siren, pistol, Marx, 1950s, EX in orig box 48.00
Smoking Tex, cap pistol, longhorn hdls, Hubley, 8", NM...............25.00
Sparkling Electric Burp Gun, Marx, NM in box............................65.00
Stallion 32 6-Shooter, cap pistol, Nichols, 1950s, MIB 100.00
Stallion 38 6-Shooter, cap cartridge, Nichols, 9½", M..................48.00
Stevens 25 Jr, MIB...85.00
Texan Jr, cap pistol, NP hammer, Hubley, 8", EX 25.00
Wilderness Scout, Marx, 12", NM...60.00
Zip, cap pistol, CI, Hubley, 1938, 6", VG.......................................25.00
Zorro Flintlock, Marx, 12", EX...45.00

Pedal Cars and Ride-On Toys

AMF Sports GT, pedal, M 150.00
Auto Racer, sheet metal/wood, orig pnt & leather, 56", VG .. 1,900.00
BMW Special Racer, sheet metal, orig red pnt, 18x38x16", G 230.00
Caterpillar tractor, electrical, rpt, 22x35x20", G........................550.00
Charger, car, orig red/wht/bl pnt, 32½", G 50.00
Essex Roadster, Toledo Metal Wheel Co, G pnt,'20s, 24x34". 1,800.00
Irish Mail, wood/metal, CI gears, orig pnt, 34x16", VG 325.00
Keystone, wood/sheet metal, orig gr pnt, ride-on, 35", VG 800.00
Murry Racer, w/windshield, orig pnt, 24x32x18", EX 475.00
Packard Roadster, electric, Gendron, rare, 31x68x24", G 26,000.00
Pioneer, pnt wood, wire wheels, ride-on, 20x35x14" 2,100.00
Pioneer Line, pedal, pnt pressed steel on wood fr, 36", VG 1,700.00

Pedal car 'Racer,' painted pressed steel, green, minor rust, partial rubber tires, 30" long, VG, $210.00.

Sherwood Roadster, sheet metal, 3-wheeler, 16x42x18½", G......250.00
Speedboat, sheet metal, rpt, 19x39x17", G 120.00
Steelcraft, Chevy, 1936, rstr 2,500.00
US Army Airplane, orig gray pnt w/red & bl trim, 47" L, G .. 1,000.00

Penny Toys

Ambulance, tin litho, 4½", G 350.00
Baby in convertible highchair, tin litho, Meier, 3¾" 175.00
Beetle, gr w/gold trim, blk wheels, 1¼", EX 60.00
Bird in cage, tin litho, Germany 140.00
Butterfly, paper litho on tin w/CI wheels, push toy, 1900s...........275.00
Carriage w/dbl team & driver, ca 1900, 5⅛", EX 250.00
Cow w/horns & bell, wheeled base, Germany 175.00
Ferris wheel/horn, tin, France, 1914, EX............................125.00
Goat, bucking, Germany 150.00
Goose, tin litho, pull toy, early 1900s, 3½"........................275.00
Hay wagon, tin litho, Germany, 4½", VG 230.00
Irish Mail cart, tin w/bsk doll, 1900s, 2⅝", EX 200.00
Man plays pool at end of table, tin, Germany, 4", EX 185.00
Run-A-Bout, tin litho, Germany, 3", VG 260.00
Touring car w/driver, top down, EX 135.00
Train, engine #100 w/3 cars, tin, 4⅛", EX in box 250.00
Train, engine #905 w/6 cars & tender, Germany, 1900s, EX 450.00
Trolly, litho passengers, Germany, EX 250.00

Pipsqueaks

Pipsqueak toys were popular among the Pennsylvania Germans. The earliest had bellows made from sheepskin. Later, cloth replaced the sheepskin, and finally paper bellows were used.

Baboon, papier-mache, flocked natural coat, silent, 6½" 220.00
Bird feeds young, animated wings, papier-mache/mc, 5", EX 325.00
Blk boy in striped cloth costume, glass eyes, silent, 12" 950.00
Boy w/horn, goat w/tin horns, wooly sheep, silent, 5" 500.00
Cat, papier-mache w/mc pnt & flocking, silent, 5", VG 85.00
Cat w/2 kittens, striped flocking, animated mouth, 7", VG 425.00
Duck/2 ducklings, papier-mache/mc pnt, animated, 6", VG 275.00
Ducks, 1 on nest (wings move), 1 w/spring legs, 9" L, VG 450.00
Elephant, gray flocking, paper blanket, silent, 3¼", VG 125.00
Goose on spring legs, squeaks, glued rprs, 7" 160.00
Hen on nest, papier-mache/mc pnt, faint squeak, 5", EX 150.00
Husky dog, wht w/gr pnt, rpr/touchup, silent, 7" 225.00
Lion, papier-mache, orig pnt, minor wear, silent, 5⅜" 200.00
Parrot on stump, orange on gr base, faint squeak, 4", EX 175.00
Rabbit, animated ears, flocked pnt, silent, 5¼" L, EX 225.00
Rabbit, haircloth, animated ears, glass eyes, silent, 9" 375.00
Rooster, papier-mache, mc pnt, silent, 6", EX 175.00

Pull Toys

Boy w/dog, tin, 4 wheels, ca 1900, 7", EX 300.00
Cow, hide covered, metal wheels, Germany, 1800s, 20" 275.00
Cow, hide covered, metal wheels, 1890s, 11", VG 150.00
Cow, wood/compo, hide coat, voice box, 16" L, VG 450.00
Cow, wood/compo, hide coat, voice box, 14", EX 185.00
Dog, tin, on platform, bell on bk, 14", EX 200.00
Dump cart w/horse, tin litho, 1886, 12", VG 200.00
Elephant, cloth, embr features, cloth tusks, glass eyes, 10" 75.00
Elephant, HP wood, on 8" platform w/wheels, 1924, EX.............300.00
Fran-Zell the Cute Bow-Wow, barks, wooden, 1924, NM 185.00
Girl w/dog on sled, bell ringer, Daisy, 1892, EX 1,600.00
Goat, rabbit fur, glass eyes, CI wheels, Germany, 11", VG 225.00
Horse, pnt tin, lt wear, 1880s, 7", EX.............................350.00
Horse, wood/compo/haircloth, harness/saddle, 8½", EX.............250.00
Horse (cloth) on platform pulls coal wagon, 1912, 16", VG 350.00
Horse & carriage, tin, 12", VG....................................115.00
Horse on wheeled platform, papier-mache, 1914, 10", EX..........300.00
Horses (pr), mohair covered, on CI wheels, orig harness, 11"......175.00

Elephant on platform, tin, very worn, 9" long, $165.00.

Lamb, lambskin/felt, glass eyes, wooden wheels, 1900s, 25" 1,900.00
Polo player on horse, tin, 4 wheels, 4½", EX 65.00
Pug dog, plush, on casters, 1889, VG.............................200.00
Rooster, pnt tin, much wear, late 1800s, 4⅝", VG 225.00
Sheep, wood/compo, wooly coat/glass eyes, voice box, 13" L.......850.00

Schoenhut

African, compo head, rpl clothes, 8", VG..........................800.00
African, compo head, 8", VG................................... 1,100.00
Boob McNutt, HP wood & cloth, jtd limbs, 8½", EX 1,200.00
Bulldog, glass eyes, regular.....................................575.00
Camel, glass eyes, 1 hump, 8½" L, VG 250.00

Schoenhut Barney Google, 7", $350.00.

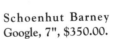

Camel, glass eyes, 2 humps, pnt rstr, 7", VG 425.00
Camel, pnt eyes, 2 humps, regular, EX 275.00
Circus, 22 pcs, 1900, regular, EX 1,300.00
Clown, compo head, orig clothes, 8", VG..........................80.00
Clown, pnt eyes, regular, EX 115.00
Donkey, glass eyes, blk pnt, 7", VG 130.00
Donkey, pnt eyes, regular, EX 110.00
Elephant, glass eyes, gray pnt, no tail, 9" L, VG 75.00
Farmer, compo head, rpl ft, 8", G................................200.00
Felix the Cat, blk/wht pnt, 8", EX...............................220.00
Felix the Cat, wood jtd, leather ears, paper label, 4", NM 225.00
Giraffe, glass eyes, ears shortened, rpt, 8½", G...................125.00
Giraffe, glass eyes, regular, EX 260.00
Hippo, glass eyes, pnt rstr, 9½", VG.............................450.00
Hippo, pnt eyes, regular, EX 310.00
Hobo, compo head, rpl clothes, 7½", G 110.00
Hobo, compo head, rpl ft/clothes, 8", G..........................70.00
Horse, brn, pnt eyes, regular 160.00
Horse, wht, pnt eyes, regular, EX 185.00

Humpty Dumpty Circus Band, sm rprs, 45" L, VG 11,500.00
Humpty Dumpty Circus Wagon, chips/rprs, 26" L, VG 2,200.00
Lady acrobat, bsk head, orig clothes, sm rpr, 8", VG...................250.00
Leopard, glass eyes, yel/brn pnt, minor scuffs, 7", G 225.00
Lion, glass eyes, regular, EX 350.00
Lion tamer, bsk head, brn hair, rpl hat, 8½", VG........................325.00
Ostrich, spring-jtd body, lg webbed ft, 9¼", EX...........................165.00
Piano, baby grand; 3 trn legs, 10x15½x15", EX 95.00
Piano, wood & plastic, wht, pnt, 5¼x12½", VG 135.00
Polar bear, glass eyes, scuffed, 8", G 700.00
Poodle, glass eyes, 7", VG..200.00
Reindeer, glass eyes, leather ears, 7", VG......................................600.00
Reindeer, glass eyes, regular, EX 550.00
Rhinoceros, glass eyes, missing ear, 9", VG 475.00
Sea lion, glass eyes, regular 600.00
Teddy Roosevelt, compo head, missing hat, 8", VG.................950.00
Tiger, pnt eyes, regular, EX 275.00
Zebra, glass eyes, 1 short ear, 8½", VG..125.00

Steiff

Margaret Steiff began making her felt stuffed toys in Germany in the late 1800s. The animals she made were tagged with an elephant in a circle. Her first teddy bear, made in 1903, became such a popular seller that she changed her tag to a bear. Felt stuffing was replaced with excelsior and wool; when it became available, foam was used. In addition to the tag, look for the 'Steiff' ribbon and the button inside the ear. For further information we recommend *Teddy Bears and Steiff Animals*, a full-color identification and value guide by Margaret Fox Mandel, available at your local bookstore or public library. See also Teddy Bears.

Bear, gold mohair, chest tag, 1940s, 8", EX 350.00
Bear, Kellie, curly mohair, button eyes, 1905, 23", EX 3,200.00
Bear, Lully, button & chest tag, 1970s, 8", M 140.00
Bear, mohair, jtd, glass eyes, embr nose, 1950s, 11", EX..............400.00
Bear, Otto, gold mohair, button eyes, floss mouth, 1904, 12" 900.00
Bear, Tyler, cinnamon mohair, button eyes, ca 1903, 16" 1,500.00
Bear on wheels, brn mohair, glass eyes, button, '20s, 11", VG 350.00
Beaver, Naggy, mohair, jtd head, glass eyes, w/tag, 6½", EX 75.00
Camel, tan mohair, velvet legs/face, w/button, 1950s, 5½" 75.00
Cat, Puss 'N Boots, long mohair, fully jtd, 1910, 11½" 300.00
Chimp, tan mohair/felt, glass eyes, jtd, 1930s, 11", VG 125.00
Chimp on wheels, glass eyes, felt ears, button, 10", EX 170.00
Clown, Clownie, molded vinyl head, pnt features, 1950s, 7½" 65.00
Cow, Bessy Bell, orig tag, 13", NM 225.00
Deer, doe, mohair, glass eyes, w/button, 1960, 6½", EX 65.00
Dog, Tessie, mohair, jtd head, w/tag & button, 5", M 60.00
Donkey (ride-on), mohair, glass eyes, '30s, 33", VG 400.00
Fox, Xorry, mohair, w/button, ca 1955, 6½", EX.............................55.00
Gendarme, felt face, button eyes, w/button, 1913, 11½" 1,500.00
Girl, Lizzie, center seam, mostly orig clothes, button, 14"...........850.00
Horse, mohair, button eyes, wooden wheels, '25, 11x12", EX......200.00
Lamb, curly mohair & felt, pull toy, button, 1913, 13" 400.00
Max & Moritz, polyvinyl chloride, bendable, 1960, 3½", pr 250.00
Mickey Mouse, appl features, button/tag, gr pants, 9½", VG .. 3,000.00
Mickey Mouse, appl/embr features, red pnts, 12", VG 3,200.00
Mickey Mouse, appl/pnt features, gr pants, 6½", VG 1,800.00
Moorish man, compo head w/beard, button/tag, 1930s, 22" 2,800.00
Neander man, tooth necklace, w/tag & button, 8"........................150.00
Pig, blond mohair, straw stuffed, swivel head, 1920s, 14" 300.00
Pigeon, mohair, not jtd, w/tag & button, 8½", M..........................85.00
Polar bear, mohair, internal hinged joints, ca 1908, 13" 700.00
Pup, mohair, seated, jtd neck, button/tag, 3½" 110.00

Squirrel, Perri, mohair, w/tag & button, ca 1958, 4½", M.............60.00
Terrier, Skye, long mohair, w/button, ca 1930, 5½" H, M 225.00
Turtle, Slo, mohair, rubber shell, ca 1958, 5½", M 40.00
Witch, button eyes, mohair hair, fingers, 1912, 17", EX.......... 2,800.00

Steiff, zebra riding toy, 21", $900.00.

Zebra, cotton plush, airbrushed mks, ca 1938, 10", M 70.00

Toy Soldiers

Toy soldiers were popular playthings with children of the 19th century. They were made by many European manufacturers in various sizes until 1848 when a standard size of approximately 1⅓" was established. The most collectible of all toy soldiers were made in England by Britains Ltd. from 1893 to 1966. In America some of the important manufacturers were Barclay, Manoil, Grey, and All-Nu.

Auburn, doctor, NM..22.50
Auburn, farmer's wife, EX 5.00
Auburn, signalman, EX 10.00
Auburn, soldier marching, VG..9.00
Barclay, aviator, M...8.00
Barclay, Boy Scout hiking, EX 17.50
Barclay, cycle officer, VG 5.00
Barclay, doughboy w/rifle, NM..14.00
Barclay, officer w/pistol, VG 6.00
Barclay, pilot w/parachute, NM...10.00
Barclay, soldier peeling potatoes, EX 15.00
Barclay, soldier running, w/rifle & tin helmet, NM.....................15.00
Barclay, Tommy Gunner soldier, NM 12.00

Britains, set #211, Colour Party of the Black Watch, with Queen's and regimental colour bearers and escort of four sergeants, ca 1950s, MIB, $750.00.

Britains, Ambulance #1512, 3 figures, prewar, EX in box 375.00
Britains, Anti-aircraft Gun #1787, prewar, G in box 275.00
Britains, Cameroon Highlanders, 1901, 8-pc set, EX in box 200.00
Britains, Centurian Tank #2150, postwar, EX in box..................550.00
Britains, Coldstream Guard bugler, EX 14.00
Britains, Coldstream Guard on horse, 1939, NM 37.50
Britains, farmer's wife w/basket, NM..7.50
Britains, French Dragoon officer, EX 65.00
Britains, infantry officer w/gas mask, postwar, NM.....................10.00
Britains, King's Royal Rifle Corps trooper, postwar, VG............12.50
Britains, man w/wheelbarrow, EX.. 8.00
Britains, Motor Machine Gun Corps #199, 3-pc, EX in box........425.00
Britains, shepherd w/lamb, NM 10.00
Britains, soldier w/gun to shoulder, NM......................................12.50
Britains, soldier w/gun to shoulder, NM......................................15.00
Elastolin, artillery man, VG...10.00
Elastolin, rifleman, prewar Germany, 3¾", NM 10.00
Elastolin, soldiers w/mortar & machinegunners, 20-pc set, EX 165.00
Elastolin, swordsmen, prewar Germany, 4", set of 3, EX............40.00
Grey Iron, cowboy on horse, early, EX 20.00
Grey Iron, nurse & wounded soldier, 1-pc, VG..........................150.00
Grey Iron, Royal Canadian Police, early, VG...............................7.50
Grey Iron, traffic cop, EX 12.50
Ideal, bugler, hollow-cast lead, EX 6.50
Ideal, Indian, arm raised, hollow-cast lead, NM 5.00
Ideal, infantryman w/rifle, hollow-cast lead, VG 5.00
Lineol, flag bearer, charging, NM 95.00
Lineol, Nazi soldier marching, VG 20.00
Manoil, bomb thrower, grenades in pouch, NM...........................16.00
Manoil, lineman & telephone pole on oval base, NM 50.00
Manoil, observer w/binoculars, VG 10.00
Manoil, schoolteacher, EX 25.00
Manoil, soldier kneeling & firing gun, M......................................12.50
Marx, Navy signalman, EX 3.50
Marx, US Army training center #3146, EX in orig box.................65.00

Trains

Electric trains were produced as early as the late 19th century.
Names to look for are Lionel, Ives, and American Flyer.

The following listings were prepared by Bruce C. Greenberg and
are taken from his comprehensive publications on Lionel, American
Flyer, and Ives trains. The prices presented are for the most common
versions of each item. In many cases, there are several other variations
often having a substantially higher value. Identification numbers given
in the listings below actually appear on the item. Mr. Greenberg is
listed in the Directory under Maryland.

Key: Std Gauge — Standard Gauge

American Flyer 283, S Gauge engine w/tender, EX........................55.00
American Flyer 332DC, S Gauge engine w/tender, EX 350.00
American Flyer 332DC, S Gauge engine w/tender, G 100.00
American Flyer 360, 361 S Gauge diesels, EX 200.00
American Flyer 360, 361 S Gauge diesels, G 100.00
Ives 11, 0 Gauge steam engine w/tender, EX.............................135.00
Ives 11, 0 Gauge steam engine w/tender, G.................................75.00
Ives 1118, 0 Gauge steam engine w/tender, EX 135.00
Ives 1118, 0 Gauge steam engine w/tender, G.............................65.00
Ives 1132, Wide Gauge steam engine w/tender, 1921-26, EX.....850.00
Ives 1132, Wide Gauge steam engine w/tender, 1921-26, G........325.00
Ives 3240, 1 Gauge electric engine, 1912-20, EX 950.00
Ives 3240, 1 Gauge electric engine, 1912-20, G 350.00
Ives 3241, Wide Gauge electric engine, 1921-25, EX 225.00
Ives 3241, Wide Gauge electric engine, 1921-25, G 85.00

Ives 3243, Wide Gauge electric engine, 1921-28, EX 550.00
Ives 3243, Wide Gauge electric engine, 1921-28, G 200.00
Lionel 1668, 0 Gauge steam engine w/tender, 1937-41, EX.........100.00
Lionel 1668, 0 Gauge steam engine w/tender, 1937-41, G............60.00
Lionel 2037, 0 Gauge steam engine/tender, 1954-55, 57-58, EX .100.00
Lionel 2037, 0 Gauge steam engine/tender, 1954-55, 57-58, G 50.00
Lionel 224, 0 Gauge steam engine w/tender, 1938-42, EX.........150.00
Lionel 224, 0 Gauge steam engine w/tender, 1938-42, G............75.00
Lionel 2343, 0 Gauge diesels, 2 units, EX 650.00
Lionel 2343, 0 Gauge diesels, 2 units, G 200.00
Lionel 252, 0 Gauge electric engine, 1926-32, EX 125.00
Lionel 252, 0 Gauge electric engine, 1926-32, G 75.00
Lionel 380, Std Gauge electric engine, 1923-27, EX 400.00
Lionel 380, Std Gauge electric engine, 1923-27, G 250.00
Lionel 400E, Std Gauge steam engine, 1931-40, EX..............2,000.00
Lionel 400E, Std Gauge steam engine, 1931-40, G 950.00
Lionel 408E, Std Gauge electric engine, 1927-36, EX 1,200.00
Lionel 408E, Std Gauge electric engine, 1927-36, G 600.00
Lionel 42, Std Gauge electric engine, 1913-23, rnd hood, EX 450.00
Lionel 42, Std Gauge electric engine, 1913-23, rnd hood, G.......200.00
Lionel 50, 027 Gauge gang car, 1955-64, EX...............................55.00
Lionel 50, 027 Gauge gang car, 1955-64, G 15.00
Lionel 58, 027 Gauge rotary snowplow, 1959-61, EX 400.00
Lionel 58, 027 Gauge rotary snowplow, 1959-61, G 160.00
Lionel 60, 0 Gauge trolly, 1955-58, EX.....................................275.00
Lionel 60, 0 Gauge trolly, 1955-58, G 100.00
Lionel 675, 0 Gauge steam engine w/tender, 1947, EX 115.00
Lionel 700E, 0 Gauge steam engine w/tender, 1937-42, G......1,700.00
Lionel 726, 0 Gauge steam engine w/tender, 1946-49, EX.........375.00
Lionel 726, 0 Gauge steam engine w/tender, 1946-49, G 200.00
Lionel 773, 0 Gauge steam engine w/tender, 1950, EX...........1,100.00
Lionel 773, 0 Gauge steam engine w/tender, 1950, G 400.00
Lionel 8, Std Gauge electric engine, 1925-32, EX.....................160.00
Lionel 8, Std Gauge electric engine, 1925-32, G.........................80.00

Miscellaneous

Rocking horse, brn mohair/leather, glass eyes, 1890s, 40" 325.00
Rocking horse, cvd w/hide cover, EX pnt, 1890s, 24x43", EX 475.00
Rocking horse, horsehide on wood & sawdust body, 1850s..........500.00
Rocking horse, mohair covered, straw stuffed, 39", VG 575.00

Trade Signs

Trade signs were popular during the 1800s. They were usually
made in an easily recognizable shape that one could mentally associate
with the particular type of business it was to represent, especially appropriate in the days when many customers could not read!

Apothecary, sheet tin/gold leaf, pestle w/Am eagle atop, 30".. 2,900.00
Blacksmith, wood horseshoe, blk letters on wht, 45x36x2" 750.00
Boot form, CI w/orange & blk pnt, mk Sol Levin Co, 11" 375.00
Dr HA Stribley, pnt wood, dbl-sided, 12x27" on wrought fr 425.00
Fish form, cast zinc, gold pnt, Am, 1800s, 9x37" 750.00
Gunsmith, dbl-sided, wood w/illus ea side, 20x27", VG 2,800.00
Horse Shoeing, Todd's Garage, wood w/pnt letters, 15x61" 100.00
Locksmith, key, steel, EX 400.00
Mae's Lunch, welded chain forms fish, letters above, 31" L 165.00
Monarch Bicycles, wooden, blk w/gold letters, 5x42", EX 350.00
Mortar & pestle, eagle surmount, cast zinc, gold pnt, 30" 1,300.00
Optician, eyeglasses frames, wood, EX pnt, 36".......................1,500.00
Padlock, sheet tin, Hardware/Stoves, 50" 2,700.00
Razor, wooden, realistically cvd, dtd 1895, 17" L 115.00

Painted cast iron top hat, red and white paint, 7", $2,200.00.

Top hat, sheet tin, 3-D, w/band & feather, pnt, 1800s, 8" **1,100.00**
TW Donahue Wines..., wooden, scalloped shape, 29x51", VG...**425.00**
We Sell & Repair, wooden shoe form, 2-sided, 16x31", EX **9,000.00**

Tramp Art

Today considered a type of American folk art, tramp art was made from the late 1800s until after the turn of the century. Often produced by 'tramps' and 'hobos' from wooden materials which could be scavenged (crates and cigar boxes, for instance), articles such as jewelry boxes and picture frames were usually decorated by chip carving and then stained.

Box, tiered, pyramidal legs, sliding top, gold pnt, 10x7x7" **125.00**
Chest, 3-drw, scalloped crest, gr trim, rpr, 6x10x12" **160.00**
Frame, chip-cvd hearts/diamonds/florals, 19x16½" **165.00**

Picture frame, Texas Star pattern, 10", $245.00.

Frame, chip-cvd pyramids, red & silver pnt, 14x12", 1¾" W **85.00**
Frame, EX detail, ornate, brn pnt, 7½x8½" **115.00**
Match box holder/ash tray, chip cvd, gold pnt, '20s, 9½x3x3".......**65.00**

Traps

Though of interest to collectors for many years, trap collecting has gained in popularity over the past ten years in particular, causing prices to appreciate rapidly. Traps are usually marked on the pan as to manufacturer, and the condition of these trademarks are important when determining their value. Grading is as follows:

Good: one-half of pan legible.
Very Good: legible in entirety, but light.
Fine: legible in entirety, with strong lettering.
Mint: in like-new, shiny condition.

Our advisor for this category is Boyd Nedry; he is listed in the Directory under Michigan. Prices listed here are for traps in fine condition.

Adirondak, wire trip 240.00
Alexander, sz A 200.00
Alligator #1, w/teeth 135.00
Bell Spring, #1¼, single long spring...175.00
Blake & Lamb #1, long spring 3.00
Bullock, #1...250.00
Cabella's Professional #2, dbl coil spring..8.00
Catchemalive, wood & tin, mousetrap...45.00
Chasse, 3-hole choker, mousetrap..35.00
Dahlgren Killer, 7½"...15.00
Diamond, #11, coil spring 8.00
Elgin, metal, mousetrap 12.00
Escape Proof, 7-hole pan..22.00
Fut Set, metal, rattrap..18.00
Gabriel, fish & game trap 135.00
Gibbs, hawk trap...125.00
Good Luck #1, Swastika cut in pan, single long spring 45.00
Hawley & Norton #3, dbl long spring...30.00
Hercules #1½, dogless single long spring......................................70.00
Herters, Kodiak bear trap 400.00
Hotchkiss & Sons #4, dbl long spring..135.00
Imbra, English killer 15.00
Jackson Otter Dog, #1½, single long spring 90.00
Ketchem #1, runway trap...25.00
Klip Trap, metal, mousetrap 15.00
Kompakt #0, jump trap 15.00
Last Word, wood snap, mousetrap..8.00
Lomar #3, dbl coil spring 20.00
Michigan Wire Goods, spear-type mole trap 8.00
Montgomery Digger, #1½, dbl coil spring......................................20.00
Newhouse #0...35.00
Newhouse #114, Animal Trap Co 125.00
Newhouse #150, bear trap..325.00
NFMS Works #1, clincher, long spring...70.00
Niagara Special #1, single long spring..35.00
Oberto #200, dbl coil spring 20.00
Onieda Victor #1, jump..4.00
Prott #1½, single long spring 20.00
PS Mfg Co #2, dbl long spring 30.00
PS&W #1, cast pan, single long spring 12.00

Wire ware rattrap, 17" long, $28.00.

Rittenhouse, spear type, mole trap...15.00

Runway, mousetrap 18.00
Sabo killer, cast jaws 75.00
Schyler, folding killer, mousetrap 20.00
Trailsend #5, dbl long spring 300.00
Triumph, #415X, triple clutch, dbl long spring 225.00
Triumph #115X Triple, clutch, single long spring 20.00
U-Neek, glass, poison feeding station 35.00
Victor, #4, dbl long spring 20.00
Victor #11, single long spring 22.00
Watkins #4, hand forged, dbl long spring 125.00
Wee Stinky, fruit jar fly trap 10.00
Zip, metal, snap mousetrap 8.00

Trenton

Trenton, New Jersey, was an area that supported several pottery companies from the mid-1800s until the late 1960s. A consolidation of several smaller companies that occurred in the 1890s was called Trenton Potteries Company. Each company produced their own type of wares independent of the others.

Bowl, ivory, vertical ribs, ftd, attached flower frog, 11" 8.50

Bowl, turquoise semi-gloss, 10", $45.00.

Planter, iris emb, turq gloss, circle mk, 13" L 20.00
Vase, concentric rings, bl, bulbous, sm...............................22.50
Vase, cream, hdls, 7⅝x6" 22.00
Vase, raspberry semi-gloss, 16x7½" 75.00
Vase, turq, Deco shape, flat pillow form..............................20.00

Trivets

Although strictly a decorative item today, the original purpose of the trivet was much more practical. They were used to protect table tops from hot serving dishes, and irons heated on the kitchen range were placed on trivets during use to protect work surfaces. The first patent date was 1869; many of the earliest trivets bore portraits of famous people or patriotic designs. Florals, birds, animals, and fruit were other favored motifs.

Watch for remakes of early original designs. Some of these are marked Wilton, Emig, Wright, and Iron Art.

Brass

Geometric designs, 4-leg, EX patina, 4x5½x10½", EX 45.00
Heart form w/greyhound cutout, 3 cutouts in hdl, 9" 85.00
Iron form, fox & tree cutouts, 8" 165.00
Outer ring contains lg star, 6"...80.00
Tilt-top tea table form, 6 heart cutouts in center, 12"..................350.00
6-point star in hexagon, 3-ftd, 8½" 65.00

Cast Iron

Lacy flowers & geometrics, Ober...Ohio, sq, 4½"..................55.00
Scalloped rnd form w/7 open concentric hearts, 7½" 125.00

Cast iron trivets, footed, 5", $20.00; Heart motif, $27.50.

Turtle, openwork design, ca 1900, 1½x7½x6½", EX 85.00
5-way, fluter/lid lifter/candle holder/kettle lifter/trivet..................85.00

Wrought Iron

Heart shape, flat, fits in Dutch oven kettle, 5" 85.00
Heart shape, penny ftd, wood hdl, 1700s, 11½" 220.00
Heart shape, primitive, scrolled ft, 11" 200.00
Heart shape w/S-scrolls ea side of point & w/in, 11" 275.00
Rnd, 3 penny ft, 2¼x4½" dia 55.00

Trolls

The modern-day version of the troll was designed in 1952 by Helena and Marti Kuuskoski of Tampere, Finland. Those made by Dam and those marked with a horseshoe are among the most valuable, since both are made from the original Kuuskoski design. Many copies have been produced, the best of which are the Wishniks, made by the Uneeda Doll Company. These were first marketed in 1979 and are currently still available. Troll animals are scarce, and values are rising. New Dam animals are easily distinguished from the old ones; and, though they are popular sellers, it's the old issues that hold their value and collectors' interest.

Bank, boy w/yel hair, purple & wht clothes, 8" 25.00
Bank, girl w/yel hair, purple dress, med.................................25.00

Santa bank, by Dam, 9", $65.00.

Batman, gr hair w/blk tips, orig clothes, Wishnik, 5½" 40.00
Bobo the Clown, pk hair, Dam, lg...75.00
Boy, long orange hair, bl overalls w/patches, Dam, 12" 75.00
Bride, brn hair, orig dress, Wishnik, 5½" 20.00
Cheerleader, molded red & wht body, wht hair, Dam, 3" 17.50
Cow, sm 20.00
Creature w/tail 75.00
Devil, brn hair & horns, red & yel clothes, Reisler JM, 4½" 15.00
Dog, bl hair, rare 60.00
Donkey, 9" 85.00
Elephant, sm 20.00
Giraffe, wht hair, Dam, 12" 75.00
Girl w/yel hair, bl raincoat, Dam, 7½" 20.00
Gorilla..25.00
Halloween mask & costume, Wishnik, 1965 ....32.00
House, vinyl, Ideal 15.00
Leprechaun, sitting 50.00
Lion, lg 95.00
Nude, 12" 45.00
Orange hair, gr suit, Dam, 1968, 6" 20.00
Pattern, McCall's, uncut..10.00
Pirate, long red hair, orig clothes, 8" 40.00
Sailor, silver hair, orig clothes, Dam 75.00

Trunks

In the the days of steamboat voyages, stagecoach journeys, and railroad travel, trunks were used to transport clothing and personal belongings. Some, called 'dome top' or 'turtle backs,' were rounded on top to better accommodate milady's finery. Today, some of the more interesting examples are used in various ways in home decorating. For instance, a flat-topped trunk may become a coffee table, while a smaller dome style may be 'home' for antique dolls or a teddy bear collection.

Chinese export, pnt leather/camphorwood, 1850s, 36" L, EX 350.00
Dome top, leather-bound, 1811 Boston newspaper lined, 12" 150.00
Dome top, pnt swags/feathers, NE, 1820s, 20" 1,400.00
Dome top, tooled leather, wrought hdls, Spanish, 1700s, 41"......500.00
Leather covered, gr/tan w/brass-tack trim, 15½" L 350.00
Pine, leather trim w/brass tacks, 17½x9½x8½" 95.00

Tuthill

The Tuthill Glass Company operated in Middletown, New York, from 1902 to 1923.

Bowl, Rosemere, nailhead band, 3-ftd, 7½" 225.00
Bowl, Vintage, ped ft, incurvate, mk, 5x9¾" 595.00
Celery, brilliant cuttings, sgn, 8" 100.00
Compote, intaglio & geometric, 7½" dia 300.00
Compote, vintage intaglio, rolled rim, 8½" dia 400.00
Nappy, Primrose & Hobstars, 6" 145.00
Pitcher, water; poppy intaglio, split vesicas, +6 tumblers......... 1,100.00
Tray, intaglio vintage, hobstar border, 10" dia 850.00
Vase, sweet pea; Wood Lily, deep intaglio, heavy, 4x5½"............325.00

Typewriters

The first commercially successful typewriter was the Sholes and Glidden, introduced in 1874. By 1882 other models appeared, and by the 1890s dozens were on the market. At the time of the First World War, the ranks of typewriter-makers thinned, and by the 1920s only a few survived.

Collectors informally divide typewriter history into the pioneering period, up to about 1890; the classic period, from 1890 to 1920; and the modern period, since 1920. There are two broad classifications of early typewriters: (1) Keyboard machines, in which depression of a key prints a character and via a shift key prints up to three different characters per key. (2) Index machines, in which a chart of all the characters appears on the typewriter; the character is selected by a pointer or dial and is printed by operation of a lever or other device. Even though index typewriters were simpler and more primitive than keyboard machines, they were none-the-less a later development, designed to provide a cheaper alternative to the standard keyboard models that were selling for upwards of $100. Eventually second-hand keyboard typewriters supplied the low-price customer, and index typewriters vanished except as toys. Both classes of typewriters appeared in a great many designs.

It is difficult, if not impossible, to assign standard market prices to early typewriters. Unlike collectors of postage stamps, carnival glass, etc., few people collect typewriters — so there is no active marketplace from which to establish prices. Also, condition is a very important factor, and typewriters can vary infinitely in condition. A third factor to consider is that an early typewriter achieves its value mainly through the skill, effort, and patience of the collector who restores it to its original condition, in which case its purchase price is insignificant. Some unusual-looking early typewriters are not at all rare or valuable, while some very ordinary-looking ones are scarce and could be quite valuable. No general rules apply. When no condition is indicated, the items listed below are assumed to be in excellent, unrestored condition.

Our advisor for this category is Mike Brooks; he is listed in the Directory under California.

American, indicator type, M 85.00
Automatic 500.00
Berwin, tin, 1950s, MIB..15.00
Bing #2, 1926, EX 125.00
Blickensderfer #5, EX 110.00
Blickensderfer #5, w/case 140.00
Blickensderfer #6, VG 45.00
Blickensderfer #8 ....50.00
Blickensderfer Electric 3,000.00
Brooks 500.00
Caligraph 175.00
Coffman, index 175.00
Columbia, index 500.00
Corona, folding 20.00
Crandall.. 1,000.00
Crown, index 300.00
Densmore...300.00
Edison, index 750.00
Fitch 425.00
Ford..500.00
Geniatus Indicator..250.00
Hall, index 150.00
Jackson..600.00
Keystone 350.00
McCool..300.00
Monarch, portable 35.00
O'Dell #4, orig box 275.00
Oliver #9, EX 50.00
Pearl, index 500.00
Remington-Rand #5, portable...35.00
Royal #10, 1922, EX 45.00
Simplex, on orig wooden stand, 6½" dial......................................25.00
Smith Corona, folding 45.00

Sholes and Glidden, decorated, $2,500.00; Including table, $3,500.00.

Smith Premier #1	245.00
Underwood #5, EX	15.00
Underwood Standard, gr, portable, in orig case, EX	45.00
Victor, index	350.00
World, last Pat date 1886, orig case	200.00
Underwood Standard, gr, portable, in orig case, EX	45.00
Victor, index	350.00
World, last Pat date 1886, orig case	200.00

Uhl Pottery

Founded in Evansville, Indiana, in 1849 by German immigrants, the Uhl Pottery was moved to Huntingburg, Indiana, in 1908 because of the more suitable clay available there. They produced stoneware — Acorn Ware jugs, crocks, and bowls — which were marked with the acorn logo and 'Uhl Pottery.' They also made mugs, pitchers, and vases in simple shapes and solid glazes marked with a circular ink stamp containing the name of the pottery and 'Huntingburg, Indiana.' The pottery closed in the mid-1940s. Those seeking additional information about Uhl pottery are encouraged to contact the Uhl Collectors' Society, whose address is listed in the Directory under Clubs, Newsletters, and Catalogs.

Ash tray, acorn, brn, mk	80.00
Ash tray, Shell Oil, brn	65.00
Bowl, batter; bl, mk, 8"	100.00
Bowl, bulb, pond lily, brn, 7"	60.00
Bowl, chili; bl, mk, 12-oz	35.00
Bowl, mixing; basketweave, brn, 8"	55.00
Bowl, mixing; bl, 4" to 12", set of 9	360.00
Bowl, salad; pk, mk, 11"	80.00
Candle holder, gr, hand trn, w/hdl, mk, 6"	85.00
Casserole, pk, w/lid, mk, 3-pt	43.00
Churn, Acorn Ware, w/bail, 2-gal	85.00
Churn, Evansville, mk, 3-gal	100.00
Cookie jar, brn, #522, mk	65.00
Cookie jar, globe, bl	120.00
Cookie jar, globe, bl, mini	135.00
Dispenser, ice water; Acorn Ware, 5-gal	165.00
Jug, Acorn Ware, harvest, stone hdl, 1-gal	155.00
Jug, Acorn Ware, 1-pt	110.00
Jug, Acorn Ware, ½-gal	65.00
Jug, Acorn Ware, 5-gal	50.00
Jug, brn/wht, mk, 1"	90.00
Jug, canteen, Believe-it-or-not	250.00
Jug, canteen, pk, mini	55.00

Jug, cat, bl	75.00
Jug, Egyptian, pk, #133, 12-oz	62.00
Jug, elephant, pk	50.00
Jug, football, brn, 4"	40.00
Jug, horse head, wht	90.00
Jug, Merry Christmas, 1941	220.00
Jug, polar bear, bl, ½-gal, 10"	375.00
Jug, prunella, brn/wht, 8-oz	55.00
Jug, refrigerator; flat, bl, w/stopper, #190	60.00
Jug, softball, wht, 3½"	210.00
Jug, tan, mk, 14-oz	12.00

Acorn jug, 5", $40.00.

Mug, coffee; pk, mk	50.00
Mug, grape, bl, 12-oz	85.00
Pitcher, bbl, bl, mk, 1-qt	110.00
Pitcher, flagon, pk, mk, 5-qt	90.00
Pitcher, grape, bulbous, bl, #182	95.00
Pitcher, grape, str sides, bl, mk, 6-pt	120.00
Pitcher, Lincoln, bl, mk, 1-pt, 6"	240.00
Pitcher, Lincoln, bl, mk, 2-qt, 10"	300.00
Shoe, baby, pk, mk	45.00
Shoe, Dutch, bl, #2	50.00
Shoe, Dutch, bl, #6	65.00
Teapot, bl, mk, #132	130.00
Teapot, bl, mk, #143	275.00
Vase, bl, #152, 5"	50.00

Unger Brothers

The Art Nouveau silver produced by Unger Brothers, who operated in Newark, New Jersey, from the early 1880s until 1909, is fast becoming very popular with today's collectors. In addition to tableware, they also made brushes, mirrors, powder boxes, and the like for milady's dressing table as well as jewelry and small personal accessories such as match safes and flasks. They often marked their products with a circle seal containing an intertwined 'UB' and '925 fine sterling.' In addition to sterling, a very limited amount of gold was also used. Note: This company made no pewter items; Unger designs may occasionally be found in pewter, but these are copies. Items dated in the mark or signed 'Birmingham' are English (not Unger).

Ash tray, man-in-moon, Nouveau lady formed by pipe smoke	700.00
Cigarette case, Egyptian/scarab motif, monogram, 4x3½"	250.00
Locket, cupid kissing lady, heart form	275.00
Sardine, Douvaine	150.00
Sauce, Douvaine	95.00
Sewing notion, cloth strawberry emory w/sgn sterling cap	125.00
Sifter, Douvaine, sm	110.00

Universal

Universal Potteries Incorporated operated in Cambridge, Ohio, from 1934 to 1956. Many lines of dinnerware and kitchen items were produced in both earthenware and semi-porcelain. In 1956 the emphasis was shifted to the manufacture of floor and wall tiles, and the name was changed to the Oxford Tile Company, Division of Universal Potteries. The plant closed in 1976. Our advisor for this category is Ted Haun; he is listed in the Directory under Indiana.

Ballerina, bowl, 9"	8.00
Ballerina, cup	5.00
Ballerina, gravy boat, gray	7.50
Ballerina, plate, hdls, 10½"	7.50
Ballerina, shakers, pr	8.00
Calico Fruit, plate, 7"	3.50
Calico Fruit, soup, flat	7.00
Canister set, floral, 1940s, 4-pc+refrigerator jug	45.00
Cattail, bowl, berry; sm	5.00
Cattail, cup & saucer	10.00
Cattail, jar, sm	10.00
Cattail, plate, 6"	4.00
Cattail, platter, lg	10.00
Cattail, soup, flat	10.00
Cattail, tray, utility; 11½"	15.00

Pitcher with reamer top in the Iris pattern, $150.00.

Garden Gate, refrigerator jar, 4"	10.00
Iris, soup, tab hdl	4.00

University City

Located in University City, Missouri, this pottery operated for only five years (1910-1915), but because of the outstanding potters associated with it, produced notable artware. The company's founder was Edward Gardner Lewis, and among the well-known artists he employed were Adelaide Robineau, Frederick Rhead, Taxile Doat, and Julian Zolnay.

Vase, dk bl/buff/umber speckled, angular shoulder, 7½"	1,000.00
Vase, ivory crystalline, str sides, oval rim & body, 3⅝"	600.00
Vase, pk to gray gloss, bl UC mk, 1910, 3"	400.00

Val St. Lambert

Since its inception in Belgium at the turn of the 19th century, the

Val St. Lambert Cristalleries has been involved in the production of high quality glass, specializing in cameo.

Our advisor for this category is Don Williams; he is listed in the Directory under Missouri.

Candlestick, frosted, reeded, on ftd 4-eagle base, 11", pr	200.00
Candlestick, hexagonal knop & ft, 11", set of 4	250.00
Compote, red, on clear knopped stem, flat base, 6x8½"	125.00
Vase, cameo leaves, lt/bright pk on frost, stick neck, 10"	500.00
Vase, red o/l on clear, molded/faceted, flared, 11"	350.00

Valentines

Pagan ritual once held that on Valentine's Day the birds of the air elected to choose their mates; and, as this premise was eagerly adopted by the homo sapien species, romantic poems became a familiar expression of one's intentions. By the mid-1800s, comical hand-colored lithographic and wood-block prints were mass-produced both here and abroad. At the turn of the century, the more romantic, often mechanical German imports forced many American companies out of business. Today's collectors often specialize — comics, post cards, mechanicals, Victorian, Kewpies, Greenaway characters, or those signed by a specific artist are among many well-established categories.

If you're interested in learning more about valentines, we recommend *Tokens of Love* by Roberta Etter, available at bookstores.

Folding diecut, Cupid on bike, Victorian	25.00
Folding diecut, Cupid plays mandolin, Cupid w/message, 7"	15.00
Folding diecut, Zeppelin, Germany, 7x9½"	75.00

Fold-out diecut, ca 1917, $12.00.

Handmade, folding, brn ink w/verses & decor, 1825, EX	150.00
Handmade, Sailor's Lament type, HP, 1830s	45.00
Lacy w/ribbon, 1920s, 3x5"	5.00
Mechanical, boy & girl pump-up heart, 1920s, 5"	7.50
Mechanical, boy & girl theme, Germany, 5"	6.00
Mechanical, I Want To Make a Hit..., boy w/hammer, '20s, 5"	5.00
Mechanical, messenger boy & girl w/golliwog, 1920s, 5"	12.00
Open cut, To My Valentine, pk/red roses on bl w/gold, 8x12"	18.00
Sheet, Edwardian cherubs/children, Germany, ca 1918, 14x10"	5.00
Stand-up, You Are 1-4 Me, 1920s, 5"	5.00

Van Briggle

The Van Briggle Pottery of Colorado Springs, Colorado, was

established in 1901 by Artus Van Briggle, whose early career had been shaped by such notables as Karl Langenbeck and Maria Nichols Storer. His quest for several years had been to perfect a completely flat matt glaze; and, upon accomplishing his goal, he opened his pottery. His wife, Anne, worked with him, and they, along with George Young, were responsible for the modeling of the wares. Their work typified the flow and form of the Art Nouveau movement, and the shapes they designed played as important a part in their success as their glazes. Some of their most famous pieces were Despondency, Lorelei, and Toast Cup.

Increasing demand for their work soon made it necessary to add to their quarters as well as their staff. Although much of the ware was eventually made from molds, each piece was carefully trimmed and refined before the glaze was sprayed on. Their most popular colors were Persian Rose, Ming Blue, and Mustard Yellow.

Van Briggle died in 1904, but the work was continued by his wife. New facilities were built; and by 1908, in addition to their artware, tiles, gardenware, and commercial lines were added. By the twenties, the emphasis had shifted from art pottery to novelties and commercial wares. As late as 1970, reproductions of some of the early designs continued to be made. Until about 1920, most pieces were marked with the date and shape number; after that the AA mark was used.

Bookends, dog, Persian Rose, AA mk only **145.00**
Bowl, bl-gr, shell form, 14" L, +8" mermaid flower frog **750.00**
Bowl, dragonflies, Persian Rose/bl, #837, 3x4¼" dia **65.00**
Bowl, dragonfly, turq, #903D, 8½", +3-frog flower frog **235.00**
Bowl, floral at closed rim, pk/gr on gray-gr, dtd 1902, 8" **900.00**
Bowl, heart-shaped leaves, Persian Rose/bl, #858, USA, 6" **85.00**
Bowl, leathery purple/lt bl, dtd 1905, 2½x4¾" **200.00**
Bowl, leaves at rim, bl to turq, #776, 2¼x6½" **70.00**
Bowl, leaves extend to base, turq/bl, #510, USA, 4½x7½" **95.00**

Bowl with mermaid on rim and fish inside, with flower frog, mulberry, 15" long, $750.00.

Bowl, pansies, turq, #19, 3½x3¾" **65.00**
Bowl, stylized leaves, dk/lt bl, #776, dtd 1920, 2½x6" **150.00**
Bowl, tulips/leaves, turq, 4-lobed oval, pre-1919, 8" L **135.00**
Bowl, turq, boat shape, scalloped, 5" L **50.00**
Bowl vase, acorns/oak leaves, lt gr, #670, ca 1908, 4x5½" **300.00**
Bowl vase, leaves, Persian Rose, #733, 3¾x6" **85.00**
Bowl vase, 8 floral panels, Persian Rose, hdls, 3⅝x4½" **75.00**
Conch shell, Ming Bl, 9" **35.00**
Creamer, turq, hexagonal, 2" **15.00**
Cup, turq, 6 incised panel lines, 1917, 3½" dia **45.00**
Figurine, donkey, turq, 3¾" **50.00**
Figurine, elephant, turq, trunk raised, 4¼x3¼" **65.00**
Figurine, elephant, wht, 4½x8" **55.00**

Figurine, kneeling Indian girl grinds corn, Persian Rose **125.00**
Figurine, nude seated w/legs Xd holds lg shell, lt bl, 7" **115.00**
Flower frog, 3-frog figural, turq, 5¼" **35.00**
Lamp, nude, right arm overhead, drape behind, bl, '20s, 17" **325.00**
Mug, bsk, buff clay, 1908-11, 4¾" **150.00**
Paperweight, sombrero, turq, 2½x5¼x4⅜" **60.00**
Plate, lg poppies & leaves, apple gr, #20, 1903, 8½" **775.00**
Shakers, wild roses, Persian Rose, 2⅝", pr **45.00**
Sugar bowl, Persian Rose, hexagonal, 2x2¼" **15.00**
Tile, trees/hills/grass, 6-color, sgn VB Co/B-107, 6" **650.00**
Vase, apple gr w/rose blush, spherical, dtd 1903, 6" **500.00**
Vase, aqua, collared rim, mk FVX/#343, dtd 1905, 4½x2" **225.00**
Vase, clover at bottle neck, bl-gr crystalline, dtd '03, 7" **950.00**
Vase, clover at rim, robin's egg bl, #821, ca '10, 7" **475.00**
Vase, daisies, lt bl w/gr on maroon, hdls, dtd 1903, 4x4½" **1,100.00**
Vase, dragonflies, Persian Rose, #688, 1908-11, 12" **585.00**
Vase, elongated roots/2 flowers, gr, #30, 1903, 16" **1,900.00**
Vase, flowers, red/gr on lime, #140/III, dtd 1903, 14x6" **6,000.00**
Vase, flowers & roots (3 ea side), Persian Rose/bl, 5x4" **95.00**
Vase, flowers at sm neck w/3 open hdls, pk-red, 1904, 10" **1,600.00**
Vase, flowers on oxblood, #132/III, dtd 1903, 6½x2¾" **2,200.00**
Vase, flowers on squatty base, Persian Rose/bl, flared, 4" **65.00**
Vase, forest gr, collar neck, #301, dtd 1905, 4½x4" **275.00**
Vase, geese heads frieze, gr-blk, dtd 1902, 6" **3,300.00**
Vase, leaves (6 at rim), turq, #847, 4½x4¾" **55.00**
Vase, leaves swirled around top, Persian Rose/dk bl, 4½" **60.00**
Vase, leaves w/panels, Mtn Craig Brn/gr, #820, 12½" **350.00**
Vase, lt/dk bl w/exposed clay, 7-sided, mk AA/116, 7x3½" **160.00**
Vase, luna moths, Persian Rose/bl, #684, 2¾" **45.00**
Vase, morning-gories, copper clad, #591, ca 1910, 8" **1,500.00**
Vase, ochre, sm mouth, bulbous shoulder, #349, dtd 1907, 4" **350.00**
Vase, overall leaves/thistles, mauve, #137, dtd 1905, 8½" **2,000.00**
Vase, plum, dtd 1920, 6" **160.00**
Vase, poppy buds w/diagonal stems, gr matt, dtd 1902, 4x4" ... **1,400.00**
Vase, robin's egg bl, classic form, #313, dtd 1918, 8x4" **195.00**
Vase, spiderwort, raspberry w/gr details, #727, ca 1908, 5" **375.00**
Vase, stylized leaves, bl/gr, #389, ca 1908, 5x4½" **325.00**
Vase, swirling leaves, purple to magenta, ca 1919, 8x3", NM **175.00**
Vase, tulips/leaves, bl matt crystalline, ca '07, 14x4" **1,100.00**
Vase, upright arrow leaves, dk bl on lt bl, ca 1920, 10x6" **250.00**
Vase, violets & leaves, dk turq, #645, 4½" **80.00**
Vase, yucca leaves, gr/brn, #747, 4" **125.00**
Vase, 3 Indian heads, gr/brn, ca 1920, 12" **450.00**

Vance Avon

Although pottery had been made in Tiltonville, Ohio, since about 1880, the ware manufactured there was of little significance until after the turn of the century when the Vance Faience Company was organized for the purpose of producing quality artware. By 1902 the name had been changed to the Avon Faience Company, and late in the same year it and three other West Virginia potteries incorporated to form the Wheeling Potteries Company. The Avon branch operated in Tiltonville until 1905 when production was moved to Wheeling. Art pottery was discontinued.

From the beginning, only skilled craftsmen and trained engineers were hired. Wm. P. Jervis and Frederick Hurten Rhead were among the notable artists responsible for designing some of the early artware. Some of the ware was slip decorated under glaze, while other pieces were molded with high-relief designs. Examples with squeeze-bag decoration by Rhead are obviously forerunners of the Jap Birdimal line he later developed for Weller. Ware was marked 'Vance F. Co.'; 'Avon F. Co., Tiltonville'; or 'Avon W. Pts. Co.'

Flower holder, rust/gr/brn gloss, organic form w/hdl, 7x7½"..........60.00
Jardiniere, stylized trees, yel/gr on rust, 10x14", EX.....................400.00

Pitcher, squeeze-bag decoration, 5", EX, $75.00.

Pitcher, hound hdl, emb hunt scene, bl on yel, 12½"...................250.00
Vase, mermaid in high relief, gr/yel/brn gloss, 12"........................375.00

Vaseline

Vaseline, a greenish-yellow colored glass produced by adding uranium oxide to the batch, was made in large quantities during the Victorian era. It was used for pressed glass tablewares, vases, and souvenir items.

Bottle, scent; octagonal, 2 neck rings, steeple stopper, 8"...........195.00
Bowl, fruit; Rose Sprig..75.00
Box, pin; floral emb, heart shape, 3¼x3½"......................................45.00
Butter dish, Daisy & Button, faceted knob, 5x6½"........................125.00
Butter pat, Daisy & Button...45.00
Celery vase, Riverside's Petticoat, EX gold.....................................225.00
Celery vase, Two Panel...45.00
Compote, basketweave, swirl ped ft, Pat June 20th 1874, 8".......140.00
Compote, Dia Quilt, 9x6½"...38.00
Compote, dolphin, ribbed base, Bakewell/Pears, +7" sticks........425.00
Cornucopia, twisted w/wide mouth, 2 vaseline block ft, 14".......225.00
Creamer, Daisy & Button w/Crossbars...48.00
Creamer, Maple Leaf...70.00
Marmalade jar, Daisy & Button, faceted finial, 5"........................125.00
Mustard, bird w/berry figural, acorn finial, flint...........................195.00
Pitcher, Basketweave...95.00
Pitcher, Daisy & Button..125.00
Pitcher, Fine Cut..125.00
Shakers, Fine Cut, pr..48.00
Shakers, Sunken Buttons, orig pewter lids, pr..................................85.00

Venetian Glass

Venetian glass is a thin, fragile ware usually made in colors, often with internal gold or silver flecks. It was produced on the island of Murano, near Venice, from the 13th century to the early 1900s. 20th-century glassware is always heavier and thicker than the older ware.

Bottle, scent; embedded glass bits & portrait of man, 2⅝"..........350.00
Bottle, scent; pk- & gold-flecked panels, flower top, 10"..............85.00
Bowl, gr, blown, scrolled sides, flared lip, 3x6" dia.......................60.00
Bowl, latticinio bands, gr/gold ribbon motif, w/lid, 6x6½".........180.00
Candlestick, blk opaque, wafer ft, 3-knob stem, sgn, 4".............125.00
Candlestick, seated female by ovoid cup, 1950, 6½", pr........ 1,600.00

Bowls with undertrays, Crosshatched pink, gold, and white stripes on clear, 5", 6", $65.00; Twisted ribbon stripes in pink, yellow, and green on clear, 5", 7", $65.00.

Figurine, Blackamore, gold w/pk & gr florals, 10".......................250.00
Fish, wht opal w/appl rigaree fins, 5½" L..35.00
Vase, gilt, enamel overlay HP w/florals, 16"................................500.00
Vase, glass snake entwines millefiori cornucopia, ftd, 9".............145.00

Venini Glass

Fine contemporary art glass signed Venini (sometimes with Murano added) has been commanding high prices in some of the Eastern auction galleries. Art Deco items and those from the fifties are the most sought after.

Decanter, bl, lav/clear casings, fine incising, Venini, 14"............900.00
Figurine, musician, long gown, opal, 1950, 9", 4 for............... 1,300.00
Vase, aqua w/wht 'net' inclusions, Venini Murano, 13"......... 6,000.00
Vase, gr/gray/clear striped, pear form, Venini Italia, 9"..............385.00
Vase, handkerchief; wht cased in clear, Venini Murano, 6".......350.00
Vase, wht flecks, appl leaves, 10"...50.00

Verlys

Verlys art glass, produced in France after 1931 by the Holophane Company of Verlys, was made in crystal with acid-finished relief work in the Art Deco style. Colored and opalescent glass was also used. In 1935 an American branch was opened in Newark, Ohio, where very similar wares were produced.

French Verlys was signed with one of three mold-impressed script signatures, all containing the company name and country of origin. The American-made glassware was signed 'Verlys' only, either scratched with a diamond-tipped pen or impressed in the mold. There is very little if any difference in value between items produced in France and America. Though some seem to feel that the French should be the higher priced (assuming it to be scarce), many prefer the American-made product.

In June of 1955, about sixteen Verlys molds were leased to the A.H. Heisey Company. Heisey's versions were not signed with the Verlys name; so if an item is unsigned, it is almost certainly a Heisey piece. The molds were returned to Verlys of America in July 1957.

Our advisor for this category is Don Frost; he is listed in the Directory under Oregon.

Ash tray, Swallow, crystal etched, 4¾"..60.00
Bonbon, floral, smoked or amber, 7½"..185.00
Bowl, Crysanthemums, 10"..125.00
Bowl, Pine Cone, bl, mk, 6"...95.00
Bowl, Poppies, clear/frosted, 13½"..120.00

Box, mum on lid, topaz, 2-pc, 5½" dia 325.00
Vase, Alpine Thistle, dk olive gr, shouldered, 9" 900.00
Vase, Alpine Thistle, opal, shouldered, 9" 600.00

Vase, Alpine Thistle, topaz with frosted blossoms and leaves, 9", 600.00.

Vase, Gem, w/flower frog, ca 1930s........................245.00
Vase, Lovebirds, dusty rose, 4¼x6½x2¾" 500.00
Vase, Mandarin, crystal etched, 9½" 250.00
Vase, Mermaid, shouldered, Directoire bl, 1 of 2 forms, 11" 1,320.00

Vernon Kilns

Vernon Potteries Ltd. was established by Faye G. Bennison in Vernon, California, in 1931. The name was later changed to Vernon Kilns; until it closed in 1958, dinnerware and figurines were their primary products. Among its wares most sought after by collectors today are items designed by such famous artists as Rockwell Kent, Walt Disney, and Don Blanding.

Our advisor for this category is Maxine Nelson; she is listed in the Directory under California.

Barkwood, cup 3.00
Barkwood, gravy boat........................ 8.00
Brown-Eyed Susan, creamer & sugar bowl, w/lid 17.50
Brown-Eyed Susan, shakers, regular, pr........................10.00
Calico, pitcher, 11"........................22.50
Chatelaine Jade, cup & saucer, ped ft 18.00
Chatelaine Jade, plate, 6½" 5.00
Chatelaine Jade, saucer........................ 3.00
Chintz, bowl, 5½" 2.50
Chintz, creamer........................ 5.00
Chintz, plate, 10" 7.50
Chintz, plate, 7½" 3.00
Chintz, platter, 14"........................15.00
Coral Reef, bowl........................45.00
Delores, plate, salad; 7½" 8.00
Delores, shaker........................ 8.00
Early California, bowl, vegetable; 8½" 10.00
Early California, coffee carafe, maroon 25.00
Early California, cup & saucer, pk........................12.00
Early California, platter, yel, 12"........................12.50
Early California, shakers, dk bl, pr........................16.00
Fantasia, Baby Weems........................200.00
Fantasia, Ballet Elephant, #27........................400.00
Fantasia, bowl, Mushroom, aqua & wht, #120........................150.00
Fantasia, Dumbo, #40........................90.00
Fantasia, Dumbo, #41........................125.00
Fantasia, Hyacinth Hippo 450.00

Fantasia, Mr Stork 800.00
Fantasia, Ostrich Ballerina, bowing, 5", M 715.00
Fantasia, Pegasus, blk & wht, 4¼" L, NM........................165.00
Fantasia, shakers, Milk Weed, pr........................40.00
Fantasia, shakers, Mushroom, 3½", pr........................100.00

Frontier Days (originally Winchester, name changed due to legal conflict with Winchester Arms Co.) plate, signed Paul Davidson, made only four years, 6½", $12.00.

Gingham, bowl, salad; ind 8.00
Gingham, casserole, stick hdl 10.00
Gingham, pitcher, 2-qt........................25.00
Gingham, pitcher, 5"........................15.00
Gingham, plate, 6"........................ 3.00
Hawaiian Flowers, shakers, bl, pr........................20.00
Homespun, mug 10.00
Homespun, pitcher, ice lip, lg........................20.00
Lei Lani, creamer & sugar bowl, w/lid........................30.00
Lei Lani, cup, demitasse........................20.00
Lei Lani, shakers, gourd, pr........................15.00
Lei Lani, tumbler 18.00
Mayflower, plate, bread & butter; 6½" 5.00
Mayflower, platter, oval, 14" 22.50
Mayflower, shakers, pr........................15.00
Monterey, bowl, chowder 5.00
Monterey, pitcher, 2-qt........................25.00
Native Californian, bowl, vegetable; rnd........................10.00
Native Californian, creamer & sugar bowl, w/lid........................15.00
Native Californian, cup & saucer, pk........................12.00
Native Californian, plate, salad........................ 5.00
Organdie, bowl, divided vegetable; oval, 11½"........................12.00
Organdie, bowl, 5½"........................ 3.00
Organdie, chop plate 10.00
Organdie, coffee carafe 22.50
Organdie, cup & saucer 6.00
Organdie, pitcher, lg........................25.00
Organdie, pitcher, sm 15.00
Organdie, plate, 6"........................ 2.00
Organdie, plate, 9½"........................ 6.00
Organdie, platter, 12¾"........................12.50
Organdie, shakers, pr 8.00
Organdie, sugar bowl, w/lid........................10.00
Organdie, tumbler, 5½"........................10.00
Plate, Baker's Chocolate, 10"........................45.00
Plate, Honolulu, 10½"........................15.00
Plate, New England, The Cove........................22.00
Plate, San Juan Capistrano, 10½" 15.00
Plate, Southwest, Baking Bread........................22.00
Plate, Yosemite Nat'l Park, 10½"........................15.00
Salamina, cup & saucer 50.00

Salamina, plate, 14" 150.00
Salamina, plate, 9½" 95.00
Salamina, sugar bowl, w/lid, regular 35.00
Sherwood, creamer 5.00
Sherwood, sugar bowl, w/lid 7.00
Tam-O'-Shanter, cup & saucer 7.50
Tam-O'-Shanter, plate, dinner; 10½" 8.00
Tam-O'-Shanter, plate, 6" 3.00
Tam-O'-Shanter, platter, 14" 12.00
Tam-O'-Shanter, shakers, pr 10.00
Tweed, teapot, scarce 35.00
Ultra California, bowl, 5¾" 3.00
Ultra California, creamer 8.00
Ultra California, cup & saucer, maroon......................12.00
Ultra California, plate, chop; ivory, 17" 35.00
Ultra California, plate, chop; pk, 12½" 17.50
Ultra California, plate, 7½" 5.00

Villeroy and Boch

The firm of Villeroy and Boch, located in Mettlach, Germany, was brought into being by the 1841 merger of three German factories — the Wallerfangen factory, founded by Nicholas Villeroy in 1787; the Mettlach factory, founded by Jean Francis Boch in 1809; and Boch's father's factory in Septfontaines, established in 1767. Villeroy and Boch produced many varieties of wares, including earthenware with printed under-glaze designs which carried the well-known castle mark with the name 'Mettlach.' See also Mettlach.

Beaker, Dresden, bowler, mk 55.00

Cake plate with fruit motif, 12", $50.00.

Candlestick, geometrics, red/tan on cream, 8" 175.00
Ewer, cupid figure under spout, scroll hdl, 13"............185.00
Plaque, #1532, Mercury mk w/Wallerfangen boats, 10¼" 60.00
Plaque, Germania w/crown, eagle & angel, sgn RF&C, 20x14" .450.00
Tile, windmill scene, bl/wht..50.00

Vistosa

Vistosa was produced from about 1938 through the early forties. It was Taylor, Smith, and Taylor's answer to the very successful Fiesta line of their nearby competitor, Homer Laughlin. Vistosa was made in four solid colors — mango red, cobalt blue, light green, and deep yellow. 'Pie crust' edges and a dainty five-petal flower molded into handles and lid finials made for a very attractive yet nevertheless commercially unsuccessful product.

Our advisor for this category is Ted Haun; he is listed in the Directory under Indiana.

Bowl, salad 95.00
Creamer & sugar bowl, w/lid 30.00
Cup & saucer 15.00
Egg cup, 3" 22.50
Gravy boat 75.00
Pitcher, red...50.00
Plate, gr, 6" 4.00
Plate, serving, yel, 11"..25.00
Plate, 9" 8.00
Shakers, pr..18.00

Teapot, $75.00.

Volkmar

Charles Volkmar established a workshop in Tremont, New York, in 1882. He produced artware decorated under the glaze in the manner of the early barbotine work done at the Haviland factory in Limoges, France. He relocated in 1888 in Menlo Park, New Jersey, and together with J.T. Smith established the Menlo Park Ceramic Company for the production of art tile. The partnership was dissolved in 1893. From 1895 until 1902, Volkmar located in Corona, New York, first under the name Volkmar Ceramic Company, later as Volkmar and Cory, and for the final six years as Crown Point. During the latter period he made art tile, blue under-glaze Delft-type wares, colorful polychrome vases, etc. The Volkmar Kilns were established in 1903 in Metuchen, New Jersey, by Volkmar and his son. Wares were marked with various devices consisting of the Volkmar name, initials, or 'Crown Point Ware.'

Vase, coppertone, w/flower frog, sm.............................125.00
Vase, dk gr matt, mk V, 3x4¼" 250.00
Vase, dogwood, wht/teal on brn shaded, fluted rim, 6½" 350.00

Volkstadt

The Volkstadt Porcelain Factory was established in Thuringia, Germany, about 1760. They continue to operate to the present, often marking their wares with the 'crossed hayfork' device used since the late 1700s.

Figurine, artist & seated lady in lace dress w/fan, 8x9" 650.00
Figurine, ballerina, wht lace dress w/appl flowers, 6x4" 160.00
Figurine, boy & girl stand by rail/watch 2 swans, 9" 550.00
Figurine, Chess Game, couple at table, 6x9" 900.00
Figurine, girl in floral gown w/goose, after Canova, 6" 150.00

Figurine, girl w/torch & lamp, after Canova, 6" 140.00
Figurine, kneeling man offers flowers to girl on bench, 7" 450.00
Figurine, musical trio, 2 ladies/1 man, 9½x9" 1,050.00
Figurine, seated lady w/lute, man w/music book beside, 9x9" .. 1,050.00
Figurine, veiled lady w/hat & fan, ca 1910, 9½" 110.00
Plaque, Jasper, 3 dancing cupids, wht on gr, 1874, 9x11" 450.00
Vase, floriform w/HP maid, 3-D nymph on base, 1910, 18" 275.00

Wade

The Wade Group of Potteries originated in 1810 with a small, single-oven pottery near Chesterton, just west of Burslem, England. This pottery, first owned by a Henry Hallen, was eventually taken over by George Wade who had opened his own pottery (also in Burslem) in 1867. Both the Hallen pottery and the original Wade pottery specialized in ceramic and pottery items for the textile industry, then booming in northern England. By the early 20th century, the two potteries were merged, taking the name of George Wade Pottery, which in 1919 became George Wade & Son Ltd.

George Wade's brother, Albert, had interests in two potteries, A.J. Wade Ltd. and Wade Heath & Co. Ltd. which manufactured decorative tiles, teapots, and other related dinnerware. In 1938 Wade Heath took over the Royal Victoria Pottery, also in Burslem, and began producing a wide range of figurines and other decorative items. In 1947 a new pottery was opened in Portadown, Northern Ireland, to produce both industrial ceramics and Irish porcelain giftware. In 1958 all the Wade potteries were amalgamated, becoming the Wade group of Potteries. The most recent addition to the group is Wade (PDM) Limited, a marketing arm for the advertising ware made by Wade Heath at the Royal Victoria Pottery. Wade (PDM) Limited was incorporated in 1969. In 1989 the Wade Group of Potteries was bought out by Beauford Engineering. With this takeover, Wade Heath and George Wade & Son Ltd. were combined to form Wade Ceramics. Wade (Ireland) Ltd. and Wade (PDM) Ltd. became subsidiaries of Wade Ceramics. In 1990 Wade (Ireland) Ltd. changed its name to Seagoe Ceramics Limited.

For those interested in learning more about Wade pottery, we recommend *The World of Wade* by Ian Warner and Mike Posgay; Mr. Warner is listed in the Directory under Canada.

Aqua dishes, 1958-66, set 1 (boxed) 20.00
Aqua dishes, 1960, set 2 (boxed)..............................25.00
Baa Baa Blk Sheep, Red Rose Tea, 1971-79 ....20.00
Beagle, Whimsies set 5, 1956 ....30.00
Bramble teapot, ca 1950 ....45.00
Candy box, IP92 (Wade Ireland), ca mid-1960s..............35.00
Cat & Fiddle, Red Rose Tea, 1971-79 ....15.00
Cockatoo, Whimsies set 9, 1958 ....65.00
Corgi, Whimsies set 7, 1957....................................32.00
Crocodile, Whimsies set 4, 1955 ....30.00

Gilbey's wine barrel, ca 1953, sm 22.00
Irish Song figure, Wida Cafferty, 1962-86 ....95.00
Lady, 'blow-up' Disney figurine, 1961-65................200.00
Lady, Disney miniature figurine, 1956-65.................20.00
Lamb, Whimsies set 2, 1954................................32.00
Lucky Leprechaun, ca 1956-86..............................15.00
Man in a Boat, 1978-84......................................45.00
Paddy Maginty, Irish Character figurine, 1970s-86 ....25.00
Pegasus posy bowl, 1958-59................................75.00
Polar Bear, Whimsies set 6, 1956..........................35.00
Poodle, Whimsies set 1, 1953...............................25.00
Regency coffee set, mid-1950s-61..........................150.00
Sea Lion corkscrew, ca 1960 ....160.00
Shetland Pony, Whimsies set 3, 1955......................32.00
Shire Horse, Whimsies set 10, 1959........................150.00
Snow White & the Seven Dwarfs, 1981-86, set of 8 ....650.00
Snowy Owl, Whimsies set 9, 1958 ....65.00
Tankard, Festival pattern, ca 1954.........................35.00
Tankard, Veteran Car, ca 1960 ....15.00
Tony Weller, Guinness promotional figurine, ca 1968.........95.00
TT tray, 1959-60 ....200.00
Wagon Train dishes (wall plaques), ca 1960, set of 2...........110.00
Yachts (wall plaques), 1955, set of 3 ....250.00
Zoo Lights (mini candle holders), 1959, ea................25.00

Walley

The Walley Pottery operated in West Sterling, Massachusetts, from 1898 to 1919. Never more than a one-man operation, Walley himself hand crafted all his wares from local clay. The majority of his pottery was simple and unadorned and usually glazed in matt green. On occasion, however, you may find high- and semi-gloss green, as well as matt glazes in blue, cream, brown, and red. The rarest and most desirable examples of his work are those with applied or relief-carved decorations. Some pieces are marked 'WJW.'

Vase, brick-red striated semi-matt, waisted, 5½x3" 150.00
Vase, brn/khaki flambe, ½-hdls, no mk, 8x6" 150.00
Vase, cobalt, flambe int, bulbous, sgn/dtd 1914, 4x4¾" 100.00
Vase, gr matt, 2 lg emb trout, sm shoulder hdls, WJW, 12" 2,300.00
Vase, gr matt w/brn at long slim neck, 5¾" 200.00
Vase, leathery gr matt, incised initials, 3x3½"......................175.00
Vase, tan-gr semi-gloss, 3 lg appl rim-to-width hdls, 10" 800.00

Walrath

Frederick Walrath was a studio potter who worked from around the turn of the century until his death in 1920. He was located in Rochester, New York, until 1918 when he became associated with the Newcomb Pottery in New Orleans, Louisiana.

Bowl w/figural kneeling nude, gr matt, 5¾x6¾" 250.00
Flower holder, nude kneels w/arm extended, wht, 5x5" 375.00
Paperweight, scarab form, brn-gr, 3½" 200.00
Pitcher, stylized flowers, 3-color, loop hdl, 11", NM 350.00
Vase, repeating floral stalk, 3-color, spherical, 3½x4" 800.00

Walter, A.

Almaric Walter was employed from 1904 through 1914 at Verreries Artistiques des Freres Daum in Nancy, France. After 1919 he

Duck teapot, ca 1938, $85.00.

opened his own business where he continued to make the same type of quality objects d'art in pate-de-verre glass as he had earlier. His pieces are signed A. Walter, Nancy H. Berge Sc.

Ash tray, mustard w/gr-spotted lizard ea side, 4½" dia 3,000.00
Box, kneeling nude w/bird & snake on lid, lemon yel, 7" H ... 7,000.00
Cat, grooming himself, butterscotch/yel, 4" L 2,700.00
Loie Fuller, standing/right leg forward, lemon yel, 8½" 2,700.00
Mermaid, kneeling/head bk, ochre/gr/turq, 5" 2,700.00
Paperweight, baby bird stands on leafy base, bl mottle, 4" 2,700.00
Paperweight, beetle atop rock, brn/mustard, 3½" 2,000.00
Paperweight, field mouse nibbles nut, Henri Berge, 3½" 3,500.00
Paperweight, scarab atop domed rnd base, Henri Berge, 2" 1,500.00
Paperweight, 2 lizards on rocky base, Henri Berge, 3½" 4,000.00
Pendant, scarab on oval plaque, tan on gr & bl, 2" L 900.00
Sea nymph, kneeling/holding lg snail, yel tones, sgn JM, 5" 1,600.00
Tray, bumblebee at end, boat form, Henri Berge, 4" L............. 2,900.00
Tray, bumblebee ea end of long narrow form, H Berge, 9" 7,000.00
Tray, lizard crouching on side, leaf-strewn/lobed, 6½" 9,000.00
Tray, 2 interlocking fish on side, 5¾" L................................. 5,700.00
Vase, apple pickers/geometrics, wht/amber/brn/blk, 9½" 30,500.00
Vase, lions/vegetation, brn/yel, tumbler form, 9" 33,000.00

Warwick

The Warwick China Company operated in Wheeling, West Virginia, from 1887 until 1951. They produced both hand-painted and decaled plates, vases, teapots, coffeepots, pitchers, bowls, and jardinieres featuring lovely florals or portraits of beautiful ladies done in luscious colors. Backgrounds were usually blendings of brown and beige, but ivory was also used (and on rare occasion, pink).

Various marks were employed, all of which incorporate the Warwick name. For a more thorough study of the subject, we recommend *Warwick, A to W*, a supplement to *Why Not Warwick* by our advisor, Donald C. Hoffmann; his address can be found in the Directory under Illinois.

Dinnerware

Bowl, cereal; #AB-1000.. 4.00
Bowl, cereal; #C-9275 .... 5.00
Bowl, cereal; #C-9336 .... 3.00
Bowl, cereal; #9071 .... 6.00
Creamer & sugar bowl, #A-9354 ....12.00
Creamer & sugar bowl, #C-9406 ....14.00
Creamer & sugar bowl, #7231 ....10.50
Creamer & sugar bowl, #9103 .... 9.00
Cup & saucer, #P-9566 .... 8.00
Cup & saucer, #3455 .... 6.50
Cup & saucer, #9588 .... 7.00
Cup & saucer, #9596 .... 7.50
Plate, #AB-9501, 10" 3.00
Plate, #C-502, 10".. 1.50
Plate, #D-2107, 10".. 2.50
Plate, #L-855, 10" 2.25
Platter, #A-9417, oval, lg... 9.25
Platter, #AB-1000, oval, lg.. 7.50
Platter, #AB-9361, oval, lg.. 8.00

Spirit Jugs

Brn, Dickens-type character w/guitar, 6" 185.00
Brn, Dickens-type character w/top hat, 6" 180.00

Brn, friar w/wine glass, 6" 185.00
Brn, gypsy portrait, 6" 230.00
Brn, Indian w/braid, 6" 300.00
Brn, monk w/red cap, 6" 190.00
Brn, Negro boy w/banjo, 6" 285.00

Unique Items

Candle holder, wht w/bl striping, 3" 70.00
Cane stand, brn w/floral, 29" 365.00
Humidor, cigar; brn w/bulldog, w/lid, 6¼".........................210.00
Humidor, cigar; brn w/monk, w/lid, 6¼"............................170.00
Humidor, cigar; Flow Blue type, crackle pattern, 8"..............245.00
Humidor, tobacco; brn w/bulldog, w/lid, 6¼"......................200.00
Humidor, tobacco; brn w/eagle/FOE, w/lid, 6¼"..................160.00
Humidor, tobacco; brn w/elk/BPOE, w/lid, 6¼"...................170.00
Humidor, tobacco; brn w/monk in red cap, w/lid, 6¼"...........150.00
Humidor, tobacco; brn w/monk in red cap, w/lid, 7"..............235.00
Humidor, tobacco; brn w/rose hips, pouch type, 7¼".............185.00
Humidor, tobacco; pk to wht w/floral, pouch type, 7¼"..........215.00
Jardiniere, bl to wht w/floral, 9" 100.00
Jardiniere, bl w/floral, 14" 95.00
Jardiniere, brn w/rose hips, 10" 90.00

Plate, hand-painted hunting dogs, signed R.K. Beck, 10", $150.00.

Spittoon, brn, emb, 8" 155.00
Spittoon, pk to wht w/floral, hole hdl, 5" 135.00
Spittoon, pk to wht w/floral, 5" 125.00
Tankard, brn, Indian w/full headdress, ring hdl, 13" 200.00
Tankard, brn w/BPOE, sq hdl, 10½" 175.00
Tankard, brn w/bulldog Champion Ambassador, sq hdl, 10" 225.00
Tankard, brn w/bulldog Champion Rodney Stone, sq hdl, 10" ...215.00
Tankard, brn w/Chief Joseph, ring hdl, 13" 220.00
Tankard, brn w/Dickens-type character, sq hdl, 10½"..............195.00
Tankard, brn w/fisherman, sq hdl, 10" 215.00
Tankard, brn w/FOE, 10½" 175.00
Tankard, brn w/friars, sq hdl, 10½" 195.00
Tankard, brn w/mermaids, ring hdl, 15" 250.00
Tankard, brn w/monk in red cap, ring hdl, 13" 195.00
Tankard, brn w/monk in red cap, sq hdl w/support bar, 13" 175.00
Tankard, charcoal w/bulldog Champion Bromley Crib, 10" 230.00
Tankard, pk to gr w/monk in red cap, sq hdl w/bar, 13" 225.00

Vase, A Beauty, tan matt w/flowers, 15".............................235.00
Vase, A Beauty, wht w/roses, 15" 250.00
Vase, Bouquet #1, brn w/lady in pearls, 11½" 245.00
Vase, Bouquet #1, brn w/Madame Le Brun, 11½" 270.00
Vase, Bouquet #2, brn, Gypsy in red turban/long hair, 10½" 225.00

Vase, Bouquet #2, brn w/countess A Patocka, 10½" 220.00
Vase, Bouquet #2, brn w/floral, 10½" 200.00
Vase, Bouquet #2, brn w/gypsy in bl turban, 10½" 215.00
Vase, Bouquet #2, brn w/lady, medallion in hair, 10½" 215.00
Vase, Bouquet #2, brn w/lady in pillbox hat, 10½" 265.00
Vase, Bouquet #2, brn w/Madame Le Brun as adult, 10½" 210.00
Vase, Bouquet #2, brn w/Madame Le Brun as child, 10½" 210.00
Vase, Bouquet #2, brn w/nude, sgn Carreno, 10½" 300.00
Vase, Bouquet #2, brn w/redheaded lady, 10½" 315.00
Vase, Bouquet #2, brn w/redheaded lady w/roses, 10½" 225.00
Vase, Bouquet #2, brn w/redheaded lady w/scarf, 10½" 285.00
Vase, Bouquet #2, red w/Countess Potocka, 10½" 275.00
Vase, Bouquet #2, red w/gypsy in bl turban, 10½" 280.00
Vase, Bouquet #2, red w/lady in red cap, 10½" 275.00
Vase, Bouquet #2, red w/Madame Le Brun as adult, 10½" 285.00
Vase, Bouquet #2, red w/Madame Re Camier, 10½" 290.00
Vase, Chicago, brn floral, 8" 325.00
Vase, Chicago, pk w/portrait, 8" 390.00
Vase, Chrys, brn w/floral, 13" 175.00
Vase, Chrys, brn w/portrait, 15" 180.00
Vase, Chrys, red w/floral, 13" 170.00
Vase, Chrys, red w/portrait, 13" 190.00
Vase, Chrys, yel to gr, 15" 295.00
Vase, Clematis, brn w/portrait of Madame Le Brun, 10½" 325.00
Vase, Clematis, red w/portrait of Countess A Potocka, 10½" 340.00
Vase, Clematis, wht w/egrets, 10½" 330.00
Vase, Cloverleaf, brn w/pine cones, 7½" 315.00
Vase, Cloverleaf, red w/floral, 7½" 320.00
Vase, Cuba, brn w/sm roses, 7¼" 300.00
Vase, Cuba, tan matt w/portrait, 7¼" 350.00
Vase, Dahlia, brn w/portrait, 8½" 280.00
Vase, Egyptian, brn w/floral, 11¾" 350.00
Vase, Favorite, pk w/portrait, 10½" 320.00
Vase, Favorite, tan matt w/floral, 10½" 280.00
Vase, Flower, brn w/floral, 12" 160.00
Vase, Flower, pk w/floral, 10" 210.00
Vase, Flower, pk w/portrait, 10" 250.00
Vase, Gem, brn w/floral, 12" 215.00
Vase, Gem, matt (gr to tan) w/floral, 12" 220.00
Vase, Geran, charcoal w/floral, 11" 215.00
Vase, Grecian, brn w/florals, 8" 160.00
Vase, Grecian, brn w/portraits, 8" 200.00
Vase, Helene, brn w/floral, 12" 215.00
Vase, Henrietta, brn w/florals, 10" 220.00
Vase, Henrietta, pk w/portrait, 10" 290.00
Vase, Hyacinth, brn w/floral, 11" 230.00
Vase, Hyacinth, brn w/portrait, 11" 250.00
Vase, Hyacinth, red w/portrait, 11" 250.00
Vase, Iris, brn w/floral, 9¾" 135.00
Vase, Iris, charcoal w/floral, 9¾" 150.00
Vase, Iris, red w/floral, 9¾" 150.00
Vase, Lily, brn w/peonies, 9½" 185.00
Vase, Lily, charcoal w/floral, 9½" 190.00
Vase, Lily, red w/floral, 9½" 185.00
Vase, Lily, red w/portrait, 9½" 200.00
Vase, Magnolia, brn w/portrait, 10½" 190.00
Vase, Magnolia, red w/portrait, 10½" 210.00
Vase, Magnolia, wht w/birds, 10½" 220.00
Vase, Maria, brn w/floral, 10½" 185.00
Vase, Maria, pk w/portrait (Hilda type), 10½" 290.00
Vase, Monroe, brn w/floral, 10½" 220.00
Vase, Monroe, brn w/portrait, 10½" 235.00
Vase, Monroe, red w/portrait, 10½" 245.00
Vase, Oriental, brn w/floral, 11" 245.00

Vase, Oriental, red w/floral, 11" 250.00
Vase, Pansy, brn w/floral, 4" 45.00
Vase, Parisian, brn w/floral, 4" 210.00
Vase, Parisian, charcoal w/portrait, 4" 245.00
Vase, Parisian, pk w/portrait, 4" 285.00
Vase, Poppy, brn w/floral, 10½" 295.00
Vase, Poppy, charcoal w/floral, 10½" 310.00
Vase, Roberta, red w/fisherman, 10" 310.00
Vase, Tobio Jug #1, brn w/monk in red cap, 7¾" 140.00
Vase, Tobio Jug #1, brn w/portrait, 7¾" 150.00
Vase, Tobio Jug #2, brn w/Indian, 7" 160.00
Vase, Tobio Jug #2, brn w/monk, 7" 145.00
Vase, Tobio Jug #2, charcoal w/floral, 7" 170.00
Vase, Violet, brn w/floral, 4" 85.00
Vase, Violet, charcoal w/floral, 4" 100.00
Vase, Violet, red w/floral, 4" 110.00
Vase, Windsor, pk w/portrait, 9" 240.00

Wash Sets

Before the days of running water, bedrooms were standardly equipped with a wash bowl and pitcher as a matter of necessity. A 'toilet set' was comprised of the pitcher and bowl, toothbrush holder, covered commode, soap dish, shaving dish, and mug. Some sets were even more elaborate. Through everyday usage, the smaller items were often broken, and today it is unusual to find a complete set.

Porcelain sets decorated with florals, fruits, or scenics were produced abroad by Limoges in France; some were imported from Germany and England. During the last quarter of the 1800s and until after the turn of the century, American-made toilet sets were manufactured in abundance. Tin and graniteware sets were also made.

Alhambra, flow bl, Meakin, pitcher/bowl/soap dish/pot 975.00
Bl dragon transfer, Mason's Ironstone, 16" pitcher+bowl, EX......325.00
Bl Willow, Myott, 9½" pitcher+bowl+chamber pot 600.00
Bl Willow, Wedgwood, ca 1800, 12" pitcher+bowl, NM 800.00
Cintra, bl/wht, Staffordshire, 12" pitcher+13" bowl...............400.00
Empire, bl/wht windmills, 12" pitcher+bowl+chamber pot..........300.00
English, bl-gr florals, pitcher+bowl+toothbrush holder+pot........350.00

Floral decal and gold trim in white, marked Record England, $225.00.

Homer Laughlin, pk & yel roses on bl, gold trim, 2-pc 160.00
Imari style, foliage, gilt/orange/bl, 13" pitcher+18" bowl 700.00
Ironstone, wht w/gold trim, pitcher+bowl 265.00
Knowles-Taylor-Knowles, child's, wht w/gold, bowl+pitcher 50.00

Medcina, bl transfer, Staffordshire, pitcher+bowl, rpr..............175.00
Mercer Pottery, Trenton NJ, wht w/gold trim, 5-pc, EX 375.00
Minton, child's, gr ivy on cream, 7" pitcher+9½" bowl..............225.00
Old Paris, floral & scrollwork panels on wht, pitcher+bowl 550.00
Rosetti, Royal Doulton, pitcher+bowl 210.00

Watch Fobs

Watch fobs have been popular since the last quarter of the 19th century. They were often made by retail companies to advertise their products. Souvenir, commemorative, and political fobs were also produced. All are popular collectibles today. Beware of modern restrikes and reproductions.

Bryan & Kern, 1908...30.00
Case Centennial, tractor & plow 75.00
Dr Pepper w/billiken..75.00
Football, brn metal.. 4.00
Ford, porc 65.00
Golden Nugget Gambling Hall, Las Vegas, chain type 25.00

Holt Mfg. Co. Combines, $400.00; Dead Shot Powder, $185.00; Le Tourneau Certified Operator, worn, $150.00.

Horse's head, cvd MOP 25.00
Hupmobile, bl & wht porc..75.00
Internat'l Harvester, brass w/strap, NM 28.00
Jamestown 1907 Expo...40.00
Jersey Cream, The Perfect Drink..40.00
John Deere, bl porc, oval 160.00
KC Southern Golden Spike Anniversary, 1897-1947 ....48.00
Luther League of Pennsylvania, pewter, dtd 1929.................... 7.50
Mack Truck, bronze 12.00
Maine, emb eagle, Spanish-Am War 17.50
Massey Harris Farm Equipment..70.00
Peters Weatherbird Shoes, EX...80.00
Pierce Arrow..100.00
Sharples Cream Separator, Indians 100.00
Taft & Sherman, 1909..30.00
Terratrac, JI Case 30.00
Veterans of Foreign Wars, symbols, bronze, NM 10.00
Wallis, tractor 75.00
Wisconsin #127 Nat'l Guard..60.00
Wm Jennings Bryan, leather & celluloid................................125.00
13-star flag, Salute the Flag, brass..20.00

Watch Stands

Watch stands were decorative articles designed with a hook from which to hang a watch. Some displayed the watch as the face of a grandfather clock or as part of an interior scene with figures in period costumes and contemporary furnishings. They were popular products of Staffordshire potters and silver companies as well.

Brass, easel type 40.00
Grandfather clock, cvd from 1 pc, ivory pull, primitive 100.00
Grandfather clock, cvd/pnt, 'Time/JST/1808,' 10", EX 3,250.00
Ivory w/brass trim, for lapel watch...45.00

Inlaid mahogany set with watercolor portraits, ca 1800, 18" x 12" x 4", $495.00.

Silver lustre, classical form w/emb dots & tassels, 8", VG............300.00

Watches

First made in the 1500s in Germany, early watches were actually small clocks, suspended from the wrist or belt. By 1700 they had become the approximate shape and size we know today. The first watches produced in America were made in 1810. The well-known Waltham Watch Company was established in 1850. Later, Waterbury produced inexpensive watches which they sold by the thousands.

Open-face and hunting-case watches of the 1890s were solid gold or gold-filled and were often elaborately decorated in several colors of gold. Gold watches became a status symbol in this decade and were worn by both men and women on chains with fobs or jeweled slides. Ladies sometimes fastened them to their clothing with pins often set with jewels. The chatelaine watch was worn at the waist, only one of several items such as scissors, coin purses, or needle cases, each attached by small chains.

Most turn-of-the-century watch cases were gold-filled; these are plentiful today. Sterling cases, though interest in them is on the increase, are not in great demand.

Our advisor for this category is Miles Sandler (Maundy International Watches), an Antiquarian Horologist, collector, dealer, price consultant, and researcher for many watch reference guides and books on Horology. His firm is one of the world's largest mail-order dealers in antique watches of all varieties. He is listed in the Directory under Kansas. For character-related watches, see Personalities.

Key:
adj — adjusted   brg — bridge plate design

d/s — double sunk dial
fbd — finger bridge design
gf — gold-filled
g/j/s — gold jewel setting
h/c — hunter case
j — jewel
k — karat
k/s — key set
k/w — key wind
l/s — lever set

mvt — movement
o/f — open face
p/s — pendant set
r/g/p — rolled gold plate
s — size
s/s — single sunk dial
s/w — stem wind
w/g/f — white gold-filled
y/g/f — yellow gold-filled

Am Watch Co, 10s, 15j, 20-yr, y/g/f, h/c, s/s 110.00
Am Watch Co, 12s, 15j, #1894, 14k, h/c...325.00
Am Watch Co, 14s, 13j, #1884, 14k, h/c...450.00
Am Watch Co, 16s, 11-15j, #1872, p/s, silver h/c, Park Road 250.00
Am Watch Co, 16s, 15-16j, #1899, y/g/f, h/c 175.00
Am Watch Co, 16s, 15j, #1883, y/g/f, 2-tone, Railroad King.......325.00
Am Watch Co, 16s, 15j, #1899, silveroid, s/w...............................70.00
Am Watch Co, 16s, 16j, #1884, 5-min, coin silver, Repeater . 3,200.00
Am Watch Co, 16s, 17j, #1888, Railroader, rare, NM.................725.00
Am Watch Co, 16s, 19j, #1872, Am Watch Co, h/c.............. 1,450.00
Am Watch Co, 16s, 19j, #1872, 14k, ¾-mvt, rare 2,250.00
Am Watch Co, 16s, 21j, #1888, o/f, 14k, Riverside Maximus 975.00
Am Watch Co, 16s, 21j, #1899, y/g/f, l/s, o/f, Crescent St...........165.00
Am Watch Co, 16s, 23j, #1908, y/g/f, o/f, adj, RR, Vanguard......225.00
Am Watch Co, 16s, 23j, #1908, y/g/f, o/f, Vanguard Up/Down...425.00
Am Watch Co, 18s, #1857, k/w, silver h/c, Howard/Rice, M.. 1,700.00
Am Watch Co, 18s, #1877, k/w, silver h/c, Excelsior...................150.00
Am Watch Co, 18s, 11j, #1857, k/w, 1st run, PS Barlett 625.00
Am Watch Co, 18s, 11j, #1857, silver h/c, k/w, s/s, Ellery, EX 175.00
Am Watch Co, 18s, 15j, #1877, k/w, RE Robbins 275.00
Am Watch Co, 18s, 17j, #1883, y/g/f, o/f, Crescent Street 85.00
Am Watch Co, 18s, 17j, #1892, HC, Canadian Railway.............450.00
Am Watch Co, 18s, 17j, #1892, y/g/f, o/f, Railroader, rare 850.00
Am Watch Co, 18s, 17j, #1892, y/g/f, o/f, s/w, AT&Co................90.00
Am Watch Co, 18s, 17j, #1892, y/g/f, s/w, h/c, PS Bartlett..........150.00
Am Watch Co, 18s, 17j, 25-yr, y/g/f, o/f, s/s, PS Bartlett.............95.00
Am Watch Co, 18s, 7j, #1857, k/w, CT Parker, scarce 1,400.00
Auburndale Watch Co, 18s, 7j, k/w, l/s, Lincoln........................600.00
Aurora Watch Co, 18s, 11j, o/f, k/w, h/c....................................350.00
Aurora Watch Co, 18s, 15 ruby j, k/w, h/c 725.00
Ball (Elgin), 18s, 16j, o/f, silver, Official Standard 275.00
Ball (Hamilton), 16s, 21j, #999, g/f, o/f, l/s...............................225.00
Ball (Hampden), 18s, 17j, o/f, adj, RR, Superior Grade........... 1,350.00
Ball (Seth Thomas), 18s, 17j, #3, o/f, l/s, g/j/s, scarce 1,350.00
Ball (Waltham), 16s, 21j, o/f, Offical Standard 190.00
Ball (Waltham), 19j, 16s, o/f, up/down indicator.................... 2,500.00
Columbus Watch Co, 18s, 11j, o/f, silveroid case........................100.00
Columbus Watch Co, 18s, 15j, o/f, l/s 160.00
Columbus Watch Co, 18s, 15j, y/g/f, o/f, Jay Gould 300.00
Columbus Watch Co, 18s, 15j, 18k, k/w, k/s.............................950.00
Columbus Watch Co, 6s, 15j, 18k, g/j/s, nickel plate..................575.00
Cornell, 18s, 15j, s/w, CM Cady 450.00
Dudley, 12s, #1, 14k, o/f, display case, Masonic 2,500.00
Elgin, 10s, h/c, k/w, k/s, s/s, Gail Borden.................................550.00
Elgin, 10s, 14k, h/c, mc case 570.00
Elgin, 12s, 15j, 14k, h/c 375.00
Elgin, 12s, 17j, g/f, h/c, Lord Elgin 90.00
Elgin, 12s, 17j, 14k, h/c, GM Wheeler 350.00
Elgin, 12s, 21j, g/f, h/c, Lord Elgin 175.00
Elgin, 16s, 15j, doctor's, 4th model, 14k, 2nd sweep hand 1,275.00
Elgin, 16s, 15j, 14k, h/c...550.00
Elgin, 16s, 21j, g/f, 3 fbd, grade #72-91, scarce 975.00
Elgin, 16s, 21j, y/g/f, g/j/s, o/f, BW Raymond...........................125.00

Elgin, 16s, 21j, y/g/f, g/j/s, 3 fbd 285.00
Elgin, 16s, 21j, y/g/f, o/f, l/s, RR, Father Time 165.00
Elgin, 16s, 23j, up/down indicator, BW Raymond......................525.00
Elgin, 17s, 7j, k/w, orig silver case, Leader 165.00
Elgin, 18s, 15j, o/f, d/s, k/w, silveroid, RR, BW Raymond 175.00
Elgin, 18s, 15j, y/g/f, l/s, s/w, box hinge case 340.00
Elgin, 18s, 15j, 14k, k/w, k/s, h/c, HL Culver...........................850.00
Elgin, 18s, 17j, silveroid, BW Raymond...................................125.00
Elgin, 18s, 21j, g/f, h/c, l/s, s/w 240.00
Elgin, 18s, 21j, y/g/f, o/f, Father Time 225.00
Elgin, 6s, 11j, 14k, h/c 275.00
Elgin, 6s, 15j, 20-yr, y/g/f, h/c, s/s 85.00
Hamilton, #3992B, 16s, 22j, o/f, steel case 175.00
Hamilton, #904, 12s, 21j, y/g/f, g/j/s, o/f, brg.............................60.00
Hamilton, #910, 12s, 17j, 20-yr, y/g/f, o/f, s/s 55.00
Hamilton, #918, presentation, 14k w/20 diamonds, orig box 925.00
Hamilton, #920, 12s, 23j, o/f, w/g/f 225.00
Hamilton, #922MP, 12s, 18k case, Masterpiece (sgn)..................800.00
Hamilton, #925, 18s, 17j, y/g/f, h/c, s/s, l/s................................125.00
Hamilton, #928, 18s, 15j, y/g/f, o/f, s/s 65.00
Hamilton, #933, 18s, 16j, h/c, nickel plate 825.00
Hamilton, #940, 18s, 21j, nickel plate, coin silver, o/f 160.00
Hamilton, #946, 18s, 23j, y/g/f, o/f, g/j/s, EX...........................425.00
Hamilton, #947, 18s, 23j, h/c, orig/sgn, EX 5,500.00
Hamilton, #950, 16s, 23j, y/g/f, o/f, l/s, sgn d/s.........................400.00
Hamilton, #965, 16s, 17j, 14k, p/s, h/c, brg, scarce 825.00
Hamilton, #972, 16s, 17j, y/g/f, o/f, g/j/s, d/s, l/s, adj 95.00
Hamilton, #992, 16s, 21j, y/g/f, o/f, adj, d/s, dbl roller 185.00
Hamilton, #992B, 16s, 21j, l/s, o/f, ¾-mvt 225.00
Hampden, 12s, 17j, w/g/f, o/f, thin model, Aviator.......................70.00
Hampden, 12s, 7j, g/f, o/f, s/w..40.00
Hampden, 16s, 17j, o/f, adj 65.00
Hampden, 16s, 17j, y/g/f, h/c, s/w 125.00
Hampden, 16s, 21j, o/f, adj, dbl roller, Special Railway 150.00
Hampden, 16s, 7j, gilded, nickel plate, ¾-mvt............................55.00
Hampden, 18s, 15j, k/w, mk on mvt, Railway 675.00
Hampden, 18s, 15j, s/w, gilded, JC Perry 100.00
Hampden, 18s, 15j, silver, k/w, h/c, Hayward...........................175.00
Hampden, 18s, 16j, y/g/f, gilded, damaskeened, h/c, Dueber.......125.00
Hampden, 18s, 17j, g/j/s, y/g/f, h/c, adj, Dueber 150.00
Hampden, 18s, 21j, g/j/s, y/g/f, h/c, New Railway 250.00
Hampden, 18s, 21j, y/g/f, o/f, d/s, l/s, N Am Railway 200.00
Hampden, 18s, 23j, y/g/f, d/s, adj, New Railway 300.00
Hampden, 18s, 23j, 14k, h/c, Special Railway 775.00
Hampden, 18s, 7-11j, k/w, gilded, Springfield............................95.00
Howard, 12s, 23j, 14k, h/c, brg, Series 8 ....625.00
Howard, 18s, 17j, 25-yr, y/g/f, o/f, orig case..............................250.00
Illinois, 0s, 7j, 14k, l/s, h/c..275.00
Illinois, 12s, 17j, y/g/f, o/f, d/s dial 65.00
Illinois, 16s, 17j, silver, h/c, RR King 475.00
Illinois, 16s, 17j, y/g/f, o/f, d/s, Bunn, EX 175.00
Illinois, 16s, 19j, y/g/f, o/f, d/s, 60-hr, Sangamo Special 775.00
Illinois, 16s, 21j, h/c, Sangamo Special 1,500.00
Illinois, 16s, 21j, o/f, d/s, Santa Fe Special 185.00
Illinois, 16s, 21j, y/g/f, o/f, s/s, Bunn Special 225.00
Illinois, 16s, 23j, y/g/f, o/f, d/s, RR, Bunn Special 490.00
Illinois, 18s, 11j, #1, silver, k/w, Alleghany 185.00
Illinois, 18s, 11j, Forest City..150.00
Illinois, 18s, 15j, #1, adj, k/w, k/s, Stuart 1,200.00
Illinois, 18s, 15j, #1, y/g/f, k/w, h/c, gilt, Bunn.........................950.00
Illinois, 18s, 15j, s/w, silveroid..70.00
Illinois, 18s, 17j, g/j/s, adj, B&O RR Special 800.00
Illinois, 18s, 17j, o/f, d/s, adj, silveroid case, Lakeshore 185.00
Illinois, 18s, 17j, o/f, s/w, 5th pinion, Miller 350.00

Illinois, 18s, 17j, s/w, nickel plate, coin silver, Bunn...................240.00
Illinois, 18s, 21j, g/j/s, adj, B&O RR Special.............................. 1,000.00
Illinois, 18s, 21j, g/j/s, g/f, o/f, A Lincoln 265.00
Illinois, 18s, 21j, g/j/s, h/c, Ben Franklin USA 2,200.00
Illinois, 18s, 23j, g/j/s, Bunn Special 375.00
Illinois, 18s, 24j, g/j/s, adj, Chesapeake & Ohio Special 2,400.00
Illinois, 18s, 24j, g/j/s, Bunn Special 475.00
Illinois, 18s, 26j, Penn Special, orig case 6,250.00
Illinois, 18s, 7j, #3, silveroid, America 125.00
Illinois, 18s, 9-11j, o/f, k/w, s/s, silveroid case, Hoyt 150.00
Illinois, 8s, 13j, ¾-mvt, Rose LeLand, scarce 325.00
Ingersoll, 16s, 7j, wht base metal, Reliance...............................55.00
Lancaster, 18s, 7j, o/f, k/w, k/s, eng case 250.00
Marion US, 18s, h/c, k/w, k/s, ¾-plate, Asa Fuller 425.00
Marion US, 18s, 15j, nickel plate, h/c, s/w, Henry Randel 525.00
Melrose Watch Co, 18s, 7j, k/w, k/s...470.00
New York Watch Co, 18s, 7j, silver, h/c, k/w, Geo Sam Rice......300.00
New York Watch Co, 19j, low sz #, wolf's teeth wind 2,275.00
Patek Philippe, 12s, 18j, 18k, o/f 1,650.00
Patek Philippe, 16s, 20j, 18k, h/c 2,500.00
Rockford, 16s, 17j, y/g/f, h/c, brg, dbl roller 175.00
Rockford, 16s, 21j, #515, y/g/f 375.00
Rockford, 16s, 21j, o/f, g/j/s, grade #537, rare 1,450.00
Rockford, 16s, 23j, o/f, mk Doll on dial & mvt, rare................. 1,250.00
Rockford, 18s, 15j, o/f, k/w, silver case 150.00
Rockford, 18s, 17j, silveroid w/mc dial, fancy mvt/hands.............225.00
Rockford, 18s, 17j, y/g/f, o/f, Winnebago......................................225.00
Rockford, 18s, 21j, o/f, King Edward 350.00
Seth Thomas, 18s, 17j, #2, g/j/s, adj, Henry Molineux 800.00
Seth Thomas, 18s, 17j, Edgemere 125.00
Seth Thomas, 18s, 25j, g/j/s, of, Maiden Lane 2,400.00
Seth Thomas, 18s, 7j, ¾-mvt, bk: eagle/Liberty model................175.00
South Bend, 12s, 21j, dbl roller, grade #431 ....110.00
South Bend, 12s, 21j, orig o/f, d/s, Studebaker.............................250.00
South Bend, 18s, 21j, g/j/s, h/c, full plate, grade #328 ....450.00
South Bend, 18s, 21j, 14k, h/c 750.00
Swiss, 18k, h/c, 5-min, Repeater, Hish grade 2,450.00

Waterford

The The Waterford Glass Company operated in Ireland from the late 1700s until 1851 when the factory closed. One hundred years later (in 1951) another Waterford glassworks was instituted that produced glass similar to the 18th century wares — crystal glass, usually with cut decoration. Today, Waterford is a generic term referring to the type of glass first produced there.

Biscuit jar, dmns & flutes, star base, SP trim, heavy 125.00
Bowl, centerpc; dmn cuttings, 9" 125.00
Bowl, centerpc; Lismore, 8"...100.00
Bowl, dmn band cutting, 11" dia..150.00
Bowl, dmn bands, lobed/fan-cut rim, ftd, 20th C, 5", pr..............300.00
Champagne, Colleen, oval/dmn designs, set of 8 ....200.00
Chandelier, 10-lite, 2-tier, faceted arms, rope prisms, 28" 2,000.00
Coasters, star center, set of 6 ....80.00
Cruet, t'prints & fans..175.00
Iced tea tumbler, Alana, 6½", set of 6 ....280.00
Napkin ring, Alana, set of 4 ....50.00
Perfume caddy, egg form w/4 sm int vials & stoppers, 8"..............330.00
Pitcher, Lismore, 6½" 120.00
Vase, dmn/leaf cuttings, ped ft, no mk, 13" 300.00
Vase, X-banding, dmn cuttings, 4x5"..80.00
Wine, Royal Tara, 6½", set of 8 ....300.00

Watt Pottery

The Watt Pottery Company was incorporated on July 5, 1922, in Perry County, Crooksville, Ohio. Their products were stoneware jars, jugs, milk pans, Dutch pots, mixing bowls (white with blue bands), churns, preserve jars, and chicken waterers, all marked in cobalt with their trademark, 'Acorn.' In 1935 these items were discontinued, and the company began to make free-hand decorated kitchen and ovenware items such as 'Banded' and 'Decorated' mixing bowls, 'spaghetti' bowls, canister sets, covered casseroles, nappies, cookie jars, ice buckets, pitchers, handled French casseroles, bean pots, salad sets, and dog dishes. Bold brush strokes of red and green contrasted with the natural buff color of the glazed body. Several patterns were produced: 'Red Apple,' 'Star Flower,' 'Rooster,' 'Autumn Foliage,' 'Morning Glory,' and 'Tulip.' Other lines were 'Basket Weave' (made in solid colors), 'Wood Grain' (a brown-glazed line), and 'Royal Danish' dinnerware.

Fire destroyed the entire manufacturing plant on October 4, 1965.

Because of the country flavor of the hand-decorated yellowware pieces, Watt Pottery is fast becoming a favorite collectible. Much of the ware was made for advertising premiums and is often found stenciled with the name of a retail company.

Bean cup, Bleeding Heart, #75 ....15.00
Bean pot, Bleeding Heart 45.00
Bowl, Apple, #60, porridge, w/advertising 30.00
Bowl, Apple, #73, salad 45.00
Bowl, Autumn Foliage, #65, mixing 30.00
Bowl, Autumn Foliage, #94, cereal 25.00
Bowl, Autumn Foliage, mixing set of 4 ....65.00
Bowl, Autumn Leaf, #65..50.00
Bowl, Bleeding Heart, #63 ....25.00
Bowl, Pansy, #39, spaghetti 45.00
Bowl, Starflower, deep, 7½"...35.00
Bowl, Starflower, salad, #55...40.00
Casserole, Apple, #600, w/lid...65.00
Casserole, Apple, #601, w/lid...75.00
Casserole, Apple, #96, w/lid...55.00
Casserole, French; Apple...110.00
Casserole, Poinsettia, #52 ....68.00
Casserole, Starflower, #67..55.00
Custard, Pennsylvania Dutch Days commemorative, sm...............35.00
Drip jar, Apple, #01 ....75.00
Ice bucket, Apple, w/lid...95.00
Ice bucket, Poinsettia..75.00
Mug, Apple, #121 ....95.00
Mug, Poinsettia, lg 80.00
Pie plate, Apple 100.00
Pie plate, Apple, w/advertising...115.00
Pie plate, plain w/gr band..35.00
Pitcher, Apple, #15..40.00
Pitcher, Apple, #15, w/advertising 45.00
Pitcher, Apple, #16, milk sz 55.00
Pitcher, Apple, #17, no ice lip 135.00
Pitcher, Apple, #62, cream sz 40.00
Pitcher, Apple, #62, w/advertising, cream sz 75.00
Pitcher, Bleeding Heart, #15 ....35.00
Pitcher, Starflower, #15..28.00
Pitcher, Starflower, #16..40.00
Pitcher, Tulip, #16...65.00
Pitcher, Tulip, #62, cream sz 55.00
Plate, snack; Pansy..40.00
Plate, Starflower, cupped edge, 15½"..75.00
Platter, Apple, #49, 12"..150.00

Rooster pitcher, 8",
$125.00.

Platter, Pansy 45.00
Ramekin, Apple 125.00
Roaster, Pansy, w/lid, lg 110.00
Shaker, Apple 100.00
Shakers, Starflower, pr...75.00
Sugar bowl, Apple, hdls, w/advertising 115.00

Wave Crest

Wave Crest is a line of decorated opal ware (milk glass) patented in 1892 by the C.F. Monroe Co. of Meriden, Connecticut. They made a full line of items for every room of the house, but they are probably best known for their boxes and vases. Most items were hand painted in various levels of decoration, but more transfers were used in the later years prior to the company's demise in 1916. Floral themes are common; items with the scenics and portraits are rarer and more highly prized. Many pieces have ornately scrolled ormolu and brass handles, feet, and rims attached. Early pieces were often signed with a black mark; later a red banner mark was used, and occasionally a paper label may be found. However, the glass is quite distinctive and has not been reproduced, so even unmarked items are easy to recognize.

Our advisors for this category are Dolli and Wilfred Cohen; they are listed in the Directory under California.

Ash receiver/jewel tray, emb scrolls w/flowers, ormolu mts..........225.00
Biscuit jar, HP/transfer floral, SP hdl/lid..............................275.00
Biscuit jar, Swirl, florals in beaded reserves on pastel...................550.00
Blotter, floral on rectangular form, ormolu sides/knob 950.00
Bonbon, emb scrolls/flowers, metal bail & rim, 5" W...................300.00
Box, apple blossoms w/pk lustre & gold, banner mk, 6x6½" 650.00
Box, blown-out shell on lid & base, florals, 4" dia.......................350.00
Box, crystal w/9 storks on lid, 7" dia 1,500.00
Box, emb scrolled panels w/florals, 3½" sq 300.00
Box, glove; emb/HP flowers on cobalt & wht, ftd, 10" 650.00
Box, Puffy, lady in wht, overall wht beading, 6½" sq 1,600.00
Box, Rococo, daisies, 10" L 750.00
Box, Rococo, florals, 5" dia 400.00
Box, Rococo, Venetian boat scene, 3¾" dia 500.00
Candlestick, emb scrolls w/floral sprays, ormolu top/ft, 7" 675.00
Card holder, Puffy, florals, ornate rim, 4x3x6" 385.00
Creamer & sugar, Swirl, flower buds on yel & wht, SP mts 475.00
Ferner, ferns, ormolu rim, str sides, rnd 450.00
Humidor, cobalt w/'Cigarettes' in wht panel, blown-out lid 500.00
Humidor, scrolled wht panel w/'Cigarettes' on gr, sm 500.00
Jardiniere, floral spray on smooth unemb surface, 7"...................450.00
Paperweight, floral on hemisphere, ormolu cherub atop, ftd........550.00
Pitcher, water; wild roses on unemb wht ogee form, bl hdl 700.00

Plate, emb scrolled oval w/sailboat scene, 11½" L....................950.00
Shakers, Erie Twist, bl asters on wht/tan swirls, 2¾", pr...............185.00
Shakers, Tulip, HP flowers, pr...100.00
Syrup pitcher, long emb leaves at waisted neck, florals................300.00
Tray, floral on shallow bowl form, ormolu ft/rim.......................275.00
Tray, jewel; emb scrolls, flowers, 3½" dia 125.00
Vase, emb scrolls w/EX florals, ornate ormolu hdls/ft, 10" 600.00
Vase, floral sprays on unemb form w/bun base, 4½x4" 450.00
Vase, lady/cherubs in wht panel on gr, ormolu mts, 12x9" 1,400.00
Vase, orchids, 18".. 1,950.00
Vase, Rococo panels w/flowers, ornate ormolu hdls/ft, 6" 550.00
Vase, scrolls emb at base & rim, florals, ormolu ft, 6" 250.00
Whisk broom holder, floral cartouch on yel, ornate ormolu 800.00

Weapons

Among the varied areas of specialization within the broad category of weapons, guns are by far the most popular. Muskets are among the earliest firearms; they were large-bore shoulder arms, usually firing black powder with separate loading of powder and shot. Some ignited the charge by flintlock or caplock, while later types used a firing pin with a metallic cartridge. Side arms, referred to as such because they were worn at the side, include pistols and revolvers. Pistols range from early single-shot and multiple barrels to modern types with cartridges held in the handle. Revolvers were supplied with a cylinder that turned to feed a fresh round in front of the barrel breech. Other firearms include shotguns, which fired round or conical bullets and had a smooth inner barrel surface, and rifles, so named because the interior of the barrel contained spiral grooves (rifling) which increased accuracy.

For further study, we recommend *Modern Guns, Eighth Edition*, by Russell Quertermous and Steve Quertermous, available at your local bookstore.

Our advisor for this cateogory is Steve Howard; he is listed in the Directory under California. See also Militaria.

Key:
bbl — barrel   hdw — hardware
cal — caliber   h/s — half stock
conv — conversion   mag — magazine
cyl — cylinder   oct — octagon
f/l — flintlock   p/b — patch box
f/s — full stock   perc — percussion
ga — gauge

Carbine

Eastern, 55-cal, serpent head muzzle, 14" bbl, 23¾" 200.00
Marlin 1936, 30/30-cal, pistol grip stock, 20" rnd bbl, EX 600.00
Peiper, 32-cal, revolving 9-shot cyl, for Mexican Army, EX........450.00
Rugar, 44 magnum cal, pistol grip stock, 18" bbl, EX 275.00
Savage 1899, 38/55-cal, saddle ring, 20" bbl, VG.......................575.00
Smith's Pat, 54-cal, 21½" oct bbl, Civil War era, G....................225.00
Winchester 1885, 32-cal, low-wall single shot, 26" bbl, EX.........675.00
Winchester 53, take-down, 44/40-cal, 22" ltweight bbl, EX 600.00

Musket

European military f/l, 70-cal, unmk, 41½" bbl, G........................550.00
European military f/l, 72-cal, 39½", G 550.00
European military perc, 70-cal, brass mts, 39½" bbl, VG 250.00
European Swiss Army perc, 70-cal, 42½" bbl, VG 650.00
Mid-Eastern f/l, 60-cal, gold inlay, 32¼" bbl, G 450.00
Winchester Hotchkiss, 45/70-cal, bolt action, 28" bbl, VG 450.00

Pistol

AH Waters military f/l, 54-cal, iron mts, 1844, 8½" bbl	375.00
Allen & Thurber perc, 34-cal, single shot, oct bbl, VG	125.00
Allen's Pat perc, 34-cal, 3" dbl bbls, twin hammers, G	225.00
Argentina 1927, semi-auto, 45-cal, plastic grips, 5" bbl, EX	250.00
Astra 1921, 9-cal, hard rubber grips, 6" bbl, G	125.00
Baretta, semi-auto, 32-cal, rubber grips, 1944, VG	300.00
Belgium military f/l, 70-cal, brass trigger guard, 9" bbl, G	135.00
Colt 1905, semi-auto, 45-cal, walnut grips, 5" bbl, G	575.00
Colt 1908 pocket, semi-auto, 380-cal, 3¾" bbl, EX	295.00
Colt 1911 WWI Army, 45-cal, wood grips, 5" bbl, G	300.00
European f/l, 45-cal, brass sight, 4⅝" ribbed bbl, G	225.00
French officer's perc, 69-cal, 8" rnd bbl, 1833, pr	1,250.00
H Nock reconverted f/l, 60-cal, 9½" bbl, G	200.00
Johnson perc, 54-cal, brass mts, swivel ramrod, 1842, G	275.00
Lugar Am Eagle, 30-cal, wood grips, 3¾" bbl, VG	1,550.00
Lugar Am Eagle, 9-cal, wood grips, 3¾" bbl, VG	800.00
Lugar 1906 Navy, 9-cal, wood grips, 6" bbl, EX	1,750.00
Lugar 1917, 9-cal, wood grips, 3¾" bbl, rfn, EX	450.00
Mauser 1930, 30-cal, broom-hdl style, 5½" bbl, EX	1,400.00
North 1816 conv f/l, 54-cal, wood stock, 9" bbl, G	400.00
North 1819 military f/l, 54-cal, iron mts, 10" bbl, G	325.00
Norwegian 1914, semi-auto, 45-cal, wood grips, 5" bbl, VG	425.00
Pritchard muff perc, 36-cal, over/under swivel bbl, VG	200.00
Remington Rand 1911-A1, semi-auto, 45-cal, 5" bbl, VG	600.00
Remington UMC 1911 Army, 45-cal, walnut grips, 5" bbl, G	425.00
Remington vest pocket derringer, 32-cal, 4" bbl, VG	500.00
Salmon & Co f/l muff, 45-cal, walnut hdl, 1⅝" bbl, VG	150.00
Savage, semi-auto, Pat Nov 21, 1905, 3¾" bbl, EX	200.00
Sharps, derringer, 22-cal, 4-bbl, gutta percha grips, G	250.00
Sharps, derringer, 32-cal, 4-bbl, brass fr, G	250.00
Smith & Wesson, 22-cal, 3rd model, single shot, 10" bbl, EX	450.00
Springfield Armory 1911 Army, 45-cal, wood grips, 5" bbl, G	725.00
Tower perc, 58 cal, 6" iron bbl w/swivel ramrod, 1855, VG	200.00
Turkish military f/l, 70-cal, brass mts, 9" rnd bbl, G	275.00
W Ketland f/l, 65-cal, all orig, 7⅝" brass bbl, VG	525.00
W Ketland f/l muff, 45-cal, all brass, 3⅜" bbl, G	300.00
W Waters martial f/l, 54-cal, iron mts, 8½" bbl, VG	375.00
Williamson derringer, 41-cal, single shot, 2½" bbl, G	300.00

Revolver

Allen's Pat (JG Bolen, NY), 32-cal, 6-shot pepperbox, VG	400.00
Colt, 45-cal, single action, horn grips, 7½" bbl, G	750.00
Colt Bisley, 44/40-cal, single action, pearl grips, 5" bbl, G	550.00
Colt Bisley target, 32-cal (Smith & Wesson), 7½" bbl, G	3,000.00
Colt Courier, 32-cal, walnut grips, aluminum fr, 3" bbl, EX	175.00
Colt Detective Special, 32-cal, plastic grips, 2" bbl, EX	250.00
Colt Lightning (Thunderer) 1877, 41-cal, 4½" bbl, G	200.00
Colt New Service, 45-cal, rubber grips, 7½" bbl, EX	375.00
Colt Official Police, 38-cal, walnut grips, 5" bbl, EX	300.00
Colt Richards conv of 1860 Army, 44-cal, 8" rnd bbl, G	500.00
Colt 1849 pocket, 31-cal, 5-shot cyl, 4" bbl, VG	650.00
Colt 1860 Army, 44-cal, cut for shoulder stock, 8" bbl, G	500.00
Colt 1860 Army perc, 44-cal, 8" rnd bbl, G	500.00
Colt 2nd Generation, 44-cal, single action, 7½" bbl, VG	800.00
Cooper Firearms perc, 31-cal, 5-shot, 6" bbl, G	300.00
English Tranter perc, 40-cal, 5¾" oct bbl, G	150.00
Holland & Holland, 32-cal, walnut grip, tip-up, 3" bbl, EX	875.00
Hopkins derringer perc, 54-cal, 4⅜" oct bbl, G	225.00
James Reid, 32-cal, 6" oct bbl w/ejector rod, 7-shot, VG	250.00
Manhattan Arms, 36-cal, brass guard, 6½" oct bbl, G	225.00
Marlin XX Standard, 22-cal, rosewood grips, 3" bbl, G	125.00

Colt single action revolver, 45 long caliber, 5½" barrel, rare cylinder made without flutes, in original box with label, Colt Custom Gun Shop, Horsepistol Special Edition, new condition, $600.00.

Remington Army perc, 44-cal, rpl grips, 8" oct bbl, G	225.00
Remington New Model Army, cavalry mks, walnut grips, G	1,400.00
Rogers & Spencer Army perc, 44-cal, walnut grips, 7½" bbl, VG	975.00
Smith & Wesson Victory, 38-cal, walnut grips, 4" bbl, M	300.00
Smith & Wesson 1, 22-cal, 3rd issue, pearl grips, VG	400.00
Smith & Wesson 1, 22-cal, 6th type, brass fr, 3¼" bbl, G	250.00
Smith & Wesson 1½, 32-cal, 1st issue, 2-tone, VG	350.00
Smith & Wesson 2, 32-cal, rosewood grips, 6" bbl, G	350.00
Smith & Wesson 25, 125th Anniversary, 45-cal, 6½" bbl, M	400.00
Smith & Wesson 29 Class A, 44 magnum cal, 8⅜" bbl, M	825.00

Rifle

Ball & Williams (Ballard), 38-cal, single shot, 26" bbl, G	525.00
Belgium Browning, semi-auto, 22-cal, 19" bbl, M	500.00
Colt Lightning, slide action, 32/20-cal, 26" rnd bbl, VG	425.00
Colt Lightning, 38/40-cal, str stock, 26" oct bbl, G	400.00
Emil R Martin, 219 zipper cal, single shot, 24" bbl, VG	650.00
Frank Wesson, 32-cal, single shot tip-up, 26" bbl, G	275.00
Japanese Army, 7.7 M/M cal, bolt action, single shot, G	100.00
KY perc, 45-cal, maple stock, dbl triggers, 32" rpl bbl, VG	250.00
Marlin #9, lever action, 22-cal, 24" oct bbl, EX	450.00
Remington 03A3 Army, 30/06-cal, 24" bbl, NM	300.00
Remington 12, 22-cal, pump action, 24" oct bbl, EX	275.00
Remington 16, semi-auto, 22 cal, 22" bbl, EX	450.00
Savage 99, 250/300-cal, take-down, 22" bbl, EX	475.00
Sharps, 3-cal, pistol grip stock, 25" bbl, G	1,400.00
Swiss military trap door conv, 45-cal, 36½" bbl, EX	1,000.00
Winchester 1886, 40/82-cal, 26" oct bbl, VG	1,200.00
Winchester 1890, 22-cal, pump action, 24" oct bbl, G	250.00
Winchester 1894, take-down, 32/40-cal, 26" oct bbl, G	500.00
Winchester 1903 semi-auto, 22-cal, 20" rnd bbl, EX	450.00
Winchester 1907, 351-cal, self-loading, 20" rnd bbl, EX	385.00
Winchester 52 Sport, 22-cal, ramp front sight, 24" bbl, EX	1,200.00
Winchester 52A target, 22-cal, 28" heavy bbl, VG	600.00
Winchester 52B target, 22-cal, 28" bbl, EX	450.00
Winchester 61, 22-cal, pump action, rear sites, VG	350.00
Winchester 63, 22-cal, semi-auto, 23" rnd bbl, EX	350.00
Winchester 63, 22-cal, 20" cut bbl, Weaver D4 scope, G	175.00
Winchester 64, 30/30 cal, 24" rnd bbl, EX	375.00
Winchester 70, 22 hornet cal, 24" rnd bbl, early, G	750.00
Winchester 90, 22-cal, pump action, 24" oct bbl, G	125.00
Wm Lawrence, 45-70-cal, single shot tip-up, 28" bbl, VG	900.00

Shotgun

Ansley H Fox A Grade, 12-ga, pistol grip stock, 28" bbls, G	700.00
Bermond Geneve conv perc, 16-ga, 35" dbl-bbl, G	200.00
Browning A-5 semi-auto, 12-ga, 28" bbl, VG	275.00

Coufax f/l conv to perc, 20-ga, 33" dbl-bbl, G.............**150.00**
Edward Kettner, 16-ga/72-cal, over-under 27" bbls, G.............**950.00**
Ithaca Field Grade, 12-ga, pistol grip, 30" db- bbl, EX.............**300.00**
LC Smith Field Grade, 30" Damascus dbl-bbl, G.............**300.00**
LC Smith Specialty Grade Deluxe, 12-ga, 26" dbl-bbl, VG.............**975.00**
Parker, 12-ga, lever action, stub twist bbl, EX.............**700.00**
Parker Deluxe DH, 16-ga, 26" dbl-bbl, 1930s, NM.............**5,500.00**
Parker VH, 12-ga, #2 fr, str grip stock, 20" dbl-bbl, G.............**450.00**
Parker VH, 20-ga, single O fr, dbl triggers, 28" bbl, VG.............**1,300.00**
Remington 1889, Wells Fargo Express, 12-ga, 20" bbls, VG.............**1,000.00**
Westley Richards, 20-ga, 27½" over/under bbls, EX.............**3,600.00**
Winchester 12, 12-ga, pigeon grade, 25" bbl, G.............**500.00**
Winchester 12 Blk Diamond Trap, 12-ga, 30" vent rib bbl, EX.............**500.00**
Winchester 12 Deluxe, 12-ga, 30" vent rib bbl, VG.............**500.00**
Winchester 1901, 10-ga, lever action, 32" bbl, VG.............**250.00**
Winchester 42, 410-ga, pump action, 26" bbl, EX.............**650.00**
Winchester 42, 410-ga, pump action, 28" full choke bbl, EX.............**775.00**

Sword

Engineers officer, Horstmann & Sons, steel scabbard, 41".............**350.00**
Heissen, Civil War type, metal scabbard, 37", VG.............**250.00**
Medical staff officer, etched blade, silver hdl, 1860s, 36".............**425.00**
N Starr, leather-covered hdl, metal scabbard, 37", VG.............**300.00**
Non-commissioned officer, Ames Mfg, 1849, 39", EX.............**150.00**
Officer's, str blade, brass eagle guard, 36", EX.............**325.00**
Saber, brass guard, wood hdl, Revolutionary War era, 32".............**800.00**
Staff & Field officer, Horstmann & Sons, 1850s, 37", EX.............**325.00**
Staff & Field officer's presentation, silver hilt, 1850s, 37".............**850.00**
US Cavalry, N Starr, 1912, steel scabbard, 39", VG.............**300.00**
US Navy, Ames, 1861, leather scabbard, 32", EX.............**600.00**
US officer, curved blade, grooved wood hdl, 1800s, 30", EX.............**250.00**

Weathervanes

The earliest weathervanes were of handmade wrought iron and were generally simple angular silhouettes with a small hole suggesting an eye. Later, copper, zinc, and polychromed wood were fashioned into more realistic forms with features in relief. Ships, horses, fish, Indians, roosters, and angels were popular motifs. In the 19th century, silhouettes were often made from sheet metal. Wooden figures became highly carved and were painted in vivid colors. E.G. Washburne and Company in New York was one of the most prominent manufacturers of weathervanes during the last half of the century.

Two-dimensional sheet metal weathervanes are increasing in value due to the already heady prices of the full-bodied variety. Originality, strength of line, and patination help to determine value. When no condition is indicated, the items listed below are assumed to be in excellent condition.

Key:
fb — full-bodied   f/fb — flattened full-bodied

Cow, f/fb, copper w/weathered gilt, att Cushing & Wht, 33"..**4,600.00**
Cow, galvanized sheet tin, ca 1900, 26x19".............**300.00**
Cow, sheet iron, 22" L, on stand.............**400.00**
Cow w/lg udder, tinned sheet iron, on wooden base, 13x18½"...**350.00**
Dolphin, f/fb, copper w/appl fins, scaly, 30" L.............**7,000.00**
Eagle, 3-D copper w/gilt, minor wear, shot scars, 40" W.............**500.00**
Fish, wooden, orig wht pnt, ca 1920s, 7x9", EX.............**95.00**
Galleon, copper/sheet metal, 1910, bullet holes/etc, 32x29".............**800.00**
Horse, running, Col Patchen, copper/zinc, EX finish, 43".............**4,000.00**
Horse, running, copper body, zinc head, Fiske, 1890s, 28".............**1,750.00**

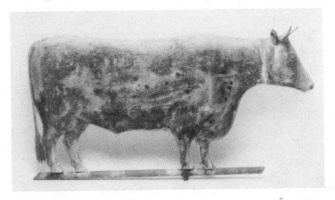

Cow, flattened full-bodied, sheet copper ears, zinc horns, traces of gold leaf, attributed to Cushing & White, crack at head/dents, 12" x 25", $3,250.00.

Horse, running, f/fb copper w/gilt traces, rpr, 1800s, 32".............**3,000.00**
Horse, running, Smuggler, molded copper, att Harris, 31".............**1,500.00**
Horse, trotting, tin, no pnt, 9x8x1½", on 21" CI arrow.............**135.00**
Indian on horse, sheet metal w/pnt traces, 1800s, 23" L.............**2,700.00**
Indian w/pulled bow, sheet iron, ca 1900, 16".............**2,400.00**
Pig, fb gilt copper w/zinc tail & appl ears, 1800s, 26" L.............**8,000.00**
Rooster, sheet copper, cut-out feathers, gr patina, 12".............**1,000.00**
Rooster, sheet iron, blksmith riveted, EX detail, 16".............**375.00**
Rooster, sheet tin, handmade, worn mc pnt, 1900s, 29x21".............**250.00**
Rooster on arrow, copper w/VG pnt, att Cushing, 38", EX.............**1,500.00**
Setter dog, f/fb, copper w/verdigris, Washburne, 31", EX.............**5,200.00**
Stag, running, fb copper, mtd on rod, 32" L.............**700.00**

Weaving

Early Americans used a variety of tools and a great amount of time to produce the material from which their clothing was made. Soaked and dried flax was broken on a flax brake to remove waste material. It was then tapped and stroked with a scutching knife. Hackles further removed waste and separated the short fibers from the longer ones. Unspun fibers were placed on the distaff of the spinning wheel for processing into yarn. The yarn was then wound around a reel for measuring. Three tools used for this purpose were the niddy-noddy, the reel yarn winder, and the click reel. After it was washed and dyed, the yarn was transferred to a barrel-cage or squirrel-cage swift and fed onto a bobbin winder.

Today, flax wheels are more plentiful than the large wool wheels, since they were small and could be more easily stored and preserved. The distaff, an often-discarded or misplaced part of the wheel, is very scarce. French spinners from the Quebec area painted their wheels. Many have been stripped and refinished by those unaware of this fact. Wheels may be very simple or have a great amount of detail, depending upon the owner's ethnic background and the maker's skill.

Hatchel, mtd on brass-covered block & wood brd, 5x14".............**85.00**
Niddy-noddy, birch, mortised & pinned, NH, 1820s, EX.............**60.00**
Niddy-noddy, half-skein, short, 9".............**150.00**
Niddy-noddy, trn shaft/chamfered ends, bentwood braces, 19".............**45.00**
Spinning wheel, wooden, w/flax holder, mini, 11½".............**135.00**
Swift, gr-pnt Windsor, Am, 1800s, 39x24", EX.............**300.00**
Wheel, spinning; oak w/EX trn detail, 38"+distaff.............**325.00**
Winder, clock reel; hickory, cvd swivels on post.............**55.00**
Yarn winder, hardwood, blk/wht clock faces/red lines, 31".............**300.00**
Yarn winder, metal, adjustable, dtd 1867.............**75.00**
Yarn winder, oak, handmade wood gears/pegs/counter, early.............**450.00**
Yarn winder, oak, spoked wheel/counter, trn legs, 34x33".............**200.00**

Webb

Thomas Webb and Sons have been making fine art glass in Stourbridge, England, since 1837. Besides their fine cameo glass, they have also made enameled ware and pieces heavily decorated with applied glass ornaments. The butterfly is a motif that has been so often featured that it tends to suggest Webb as the manufacturer.

Our advisor for this category is Don Williams; he is listed in the Directory under Missouri. See also specific types of glass such as Alexandrite, Burmese, Mother-of-Pearl, and Peachblow.

Bowl, florals on tan, folded rim, 12", on 7" metal ft 185.00
Bowl, lime gr satin to wht, frosted hdls, ruffled, 9½" L...............200.00
Bowl, pk to cream, bamboo/floral intaglio, 3¾x5¾".....................695.00
Bowl, wht to opaque fuchsia, bl int, 9-point rim, 10" 265.00
Compote, bl satin, fluted/scalloped; metal ped base, 6x9" 175.00
Ewer, gold branch w/3 apples on gr to wht satin, 9x4"................425.00
Perfume, Flower & Acorn MOP, gr w/gold prunus, clear top .. 1,450.00
Rose bowl, rainbow MOP, quilted, lobed rim, 2½x5"...................700.00
Rose bowl, yel to cream satin, wht int, box pleated, 5x6" 325.00
Sweetmeat, Flower & Acorn MOP, bl w/berries, SP mts.........1,100.00
Tumble up, allover florals/gilt/bugs on cranberry, 4" 450.00
Vase, allover gold branches/florals, red w/wht int, 9x4"..............350.00
Vase, bird/prunus/butterfly, yel on shaded bl satin, 8x6" 425.00
Vase, florals, mc on gr satin, fluted/scalloped/lobed, 10" 160.00
Vase, florals, mc on pk shaded w/gold, ca 1884, 6½".................350.00
Vase, gold florals on coral o/l, unmk, 5x2¾"..............................225.00
Vase, gold florals on pk o/l, clear ft, mk, 7⅜x2¾"........................325.00
Vase, gold prunus on apricot, pk int, ormolu fr, 7¼x4½" 525.00
Vase, gold prunus/butterfly on yel shaded, mk, 6½" 325.00
Vase, gold/silver/jewels, red w/wht int, ovoid, 4½".....................300.00
Vase, Honeycomb MOP, bl w/wht int, 10x5".............................650.00
Vase, mc enameling on tan opaque, 9½x5" 185.00
Vase, pk w/appl clear drippings, clear ft, 5x5⅝"..........................210.00
Vase, pk/wht satin stripes, ruffled, bulbous bottom, 8x4" 400.00
Vase, raised gilt on tan to butterscotch opaque, hdls, 10" 210.00
Vase, yel shaded satin, wht int, gourd form, 10½".......................285.00
Vase, 2 brn serpents w/gold trim on yel satin, 11" 550.00

Cameo

Bottle, scent; ferns, wht on red-cased clear, lay-down, 4" 750.00
Bottle, scent; floral, 3-color, sea horse/etc on lid, 4"................ 2,900.00
Bottle, scent; floral/butterfly, red/wht on frost, rnd, 6" 1,500.00
Bottle, scent; roses/butterfly, wht on yel, lay-down, 9" 1,500.00
Bowl, apple blossoms/floral band, wht on gr, ruffled, 6" 1,800.00
Bowl, apple branches, bk: fruit, wht on lt bl, 2¾x5".....................850.00
Bowl, fruit; florals, crystal on royal bl, 3½x7¾"...........................395.00
Cane knob, 3 repeating floral motifs, wht on yel, 1½" dia 400.00
Creamer & sugar bowl, fish scales, ivy w/gold, 1¾", 3½" 900.00
Cup & saucer, chinoiserie garden, pk on wht frost 1,900.00
Custard cup, foliage/butterfly, bl on crystal moire, +plate...........600.00
Inkwell, wildflowers/lappet border, wht on brn, att, 4¾" 2,000.00
Vase, apple blossoms, wht on lt bl, spherical, 3¼" 1,000.00
Vase, apple blossoms/butterfly, wht on clear-cased red, 9"....... 1,900.00
Vase, asters/wildflowers/3 butterflies, wht on teal, 12"............ 4,500.00
Vase, berry branches, wht on yel, bulb w/long neck, 13½" 4,250.00
Vase, bird on apple branch, wht on red-cased clear, 4x4".........4,250.00
Vase, birds/flowers, wht on lt bl, 3-ftd, att, 4" 4,000.00
Vase, cluster floral/leaves, ribbon rim band, 3-color, 10" 6,500.00
Vase, floral branch/linear borders, wht on teal, 6" 1,400.00
Vase, floral/fern/butterfly, wht on apple gr, Gem mk, 7" 3,900.00
Vase, fuchsia/butterfly, med bl/wht on frost, dbl gourd, 7" 3,400.00

Vase, geraniums, wht & red on yel frost, bottle form, 9" 2,500.00
Vase, honeysuckle/arrow neck band, wht on cased red, 15" 5,500.00
Vase, Ivory, brocading/6 phoenix medallions, no mk, 9".........2,800.00
Vase, Ivory, flowers/feathers, brn stain, crimp top, 4x3" 1,200.00
Vase, Ivory, swags/ornate bands, collar neck, 4" 1,400.00
Vase, lilies/butterflies, wht on yel, ovoid, 6" 2,200.00
Vase, mums/insects/linear borders, wht on bl, ovoid, 6" 2,000.00

Vase, opal on clear with gold and bronze trees and gold blossoms and berries, signed 'Gem,' 7¾", $4,500.00.

Vase, poppies/butterflies, wht on bl, cone neck, att, 8½" 2,250.00
Vase, roses/insect, clear cased to wht & red, wht o/l, 2x3"..........800.00
Vase, Serpentina, wht on wine-brn, Geo Woodall, 7½".........25,000.00
Vase, thorny branches/butterfly, wht on teal, ovoid, 3¾"........ 1,500.00
Vase, vines/berries, EX detail, wht on lt bl, ftd, 6½" 4,000.00

Wedgwood

Josiah Wedgwood established his pottery in Burslem, England, in 1759. He produced only molded utilitarian earthenwares until 1770 when new facilities were opened at Etruria. It was there he introduced his famous Basalt and Jasperware. Jasperware, an unglazed fine stoneware decorated with classic figures in white relief, was usually produced in blues; but it was also made in ground colors of green, lilac, yellow, black, or white. Occasionally, three or more colors were used in combination. It has been in continuous production to the present day and is the most easily recognized of all the Wedgwood lines. (Jasper is a body of solid color; the term 'Jasper-Dip' refers to ware with a white body that has been dipped in an overlay color. This type, introduced in the late 1700s, is the type most often encountered on today's market.)

Though Wedgwood's Jasperware was highly acclaimed, on a more practical basis his creamware was his greatest success. Due to the ease with which it could be potted and because its lighter weight significantly reduced transportation expenses, Wedgwood was able to offer 'chinaware' at affordable prices. Queen Charlotte was so pleased with the ware that she allowed it to be called 'Queen's Ware.' Most creamware was marked simply 'Wedgwood.' ('Wedgwood & Co.' and 'Wedgewood' are marks of other potters.) From 1769 to 1780, Wedgwood was in partnership with Thomas Bently; artwares of the highest quality bear the mark indicating this partnership.

Moonlight Lustre, an allover splashed-on effect of pink intermingling with gray, brown, or yellow, was made from 1805 to 1815. Porcelain was made, though not to any great extent, from 1812 to 1822. Both of these types of wares were marked 'Wedgwood.' Stone china and

Pearlware were made from about 1820 to 1875. Examples of either may be found with a mark to indicate their body type. During the late 1800s, Wedgwood produced some fine parian and majolica. Creamware, hand painted by Emile Lessore, was sold from about 1860 to 1875. From the 20th century, several lines of lustre wares — Butterfly, Dragon, and Fairyland (the latter designed by Miss Makeig-Jones) — have attracted the collector and, as their prices suggest, are highly sought-after and admired.

Nearly all of Wedgwood's wares are clearly marked. 'Wedgwood' was used before 1891, after which time 'England' was added. Most examples marked 'Made In England' were made after 1921. A detailed study of all marks is recommended for accurate dating. See also Majolica.

Key:
WW — Wedgwood   WWE — Wedgwood England

Ash tray, Jasper, terra cotta/wht, WWE, ca 1958, 3½" dia 70.00
Basin, Pearlware, feather/berry border, bl/wht, 1800, 17" 850.00
Basket, silver & pk lustre w/appl wht vintage, WW, 3⅜" 185.00
Biscuit jar, bone china, bl/wht, SP rim & hdl, WW, 3x4½" 165.00
Biscuit jar, Jasper, dk bl, SP top/rim/hdl, WWE, 6x5¼" 150.00
Biscuit jar, Jasper, yel, acorn finial, WWE, 6" 575.00
Biscuit jar, Jasper, yel & blk, WW, 5½" 725.00
Bottle, barber; Jasper, 3-color, WWE, 10" 2,250.00
Bowl, Basalt, WW, 2¾x12¾" 300.00
Bowl, Chinese Animals Lustre, octagonal, 4" 285.00
Bowl, Dragon Lustre, bl w/gold, 8½" 550.00
Bowl, Dragon Lustre, orange/red, WWE, 6½" 400.00
Bowl, Fairyland Lustre, fairy in lg hat, WW, Z-4968, 3x7" ... 1,895.00
Bowl, Fairyland Lustre, orange/bl w/gold, 9¼" 1,100.00
Bowl, Fairyland Lustre, Smoke Ribbons int, WW, 4x8½" 2,710.00
Bowl, Jasper, blk, Imperial shape, 8" 355.00
Bowl, Jasper, dk bl, WW, 2¾x5" 110.00
Bowl, Jasper, lt bl, WWE, 2x4¾" 80.00
Bowl, Jasper, med bl, WW, 2¾x4½" 95.00
Bowl, Ningpo, peonies/etc, octagonal, 9½", +12" underplate 250.00
Box, Basalt, cherubs/servants, acanthus lid, 3½x4" 75.00
Box, Jasper, dk bl, WWE, 3¾x4¾" 95.00
Box, Jasper, lilac, heart form, WWE, 1981 ....115.00
Box, Jasper, lilac, WWE, 4" sq 130.00
Box, Jasper, olive gr, heart shape, WWE, 2x3½x4½" 165.00
Box, Stoneware, olive gr, heart form, 2x3½x4½" 190.00
Bust, Basalt, Mercury, WW, 17" 1,100.00
Butter tub, Jasper, dk bl, WW, 4½" 265.00
Candlestick, Basalt, Triton, WW, late 1700s, 11", pr 3,000.00
Cigarette lighter, Jasper, lt gr, Caesar, WWE 55.00
Clock, Jasper, lav/gr/wht, seated figures, Tempus Fugit, WW.. 1,475.00
Console set, Jasper, primrose/terra cotta, WWE, 1976, 3-pc........300.00
Creamer, Drabware, lt brn, WW, ca 1830, 2½x5" 180.00
Creamer, Jasper, lt bl, St Louis shape, WWE, 2¼x3½" 85.00
Creamer, Jasper, lt bl, WWE, 2" 80.00
Creamer & sugar bowl, Jasper, purple, WWE, 4", 3¾" 650.00
Cup, Basalt, foliage & arabesques, WW, ca 1800, 4¼"...............465.00
Cup & saucer, Basalt, cameo, WWE 48.00
Cup & saucer, Basalt, husk & berry decor, WW......................95.00
Cup & saucer, Caneware, blk, vintage, WW, ca 1810 ....435.00
Cup & saucer, Jasper, lilac, WWE 120.00
Cup & saucer, Jasper, lt bl, WWE 65.00
Ferner, Jasper, buff/blk, WW, 2¾x4½" 465.00
Ferner, Jasper, buff/blk, 3-ftd, WWE, ca 1929 ....300.00
Figurine, Basalt, cupid, WW, ca 1830, 8" 950.00
Flower frog, Creamware, tree trunk form, WWE, ca 1919, 6" dia .78.00
Flowerpot, Basalt, attached saucer, WW, ca 1820.......................745.00

Fork & spoon, salad; Jasper, dk bl, WW 135.00
Inkwell, Jasper, lt bl, dolphins, brass top, WW, 6" 500.00
Jardiniere, Stoneware, olive gr, flared top, 7½" 435.00
Loving cup, Jasper, lt bl, 3-hdl, WWE, 4½" 120.00
Matchbox holder, Jasper, lt bl, WW, 3¾x6" 120.00
Medallion, Jasper, Elizabeth & Phillip, WWE, '53, 4¼x3¼", pr ..325.00
Muffineer, Creamware, vintage band, WW, ca 1912, 6½" 155.00
Pitcher, Basalt, Victoria BC, WWE, 3½" 125.00
Pitcher, Capriware, terra cotta/enamel, WW, 8½" 700.00
Pitcher, Drabware, WWE, 7½" 400.00
Pitcher, Jasper, bl, bulbous, WW, ca 1850, 4½" 210.00
Pitcher, Jasper, dk bl, classical figures, WW, mini, 2x1¾" 165.00
Pitcher, Jasper, lt bl, WW, milk sz, 6" 150.00
Pitcher, tankard; Jasper, bl, WWE, 7¾x3½" 175.00
Pitcher, tankard; Jasper, dk bl, WW, 5½" 120.00
Pitcher, tankard; Jasper, dk bl, WWE, 4" 80.00
Pitcher, tankard; Jasper, dk bl, WWE, 6⅜x3¾" 145.00

Basalt 'Egyptian' plaque, 1974, 8" x 8½", $425.00.

Plaque, Jasper, bl, Flower Girl, WW, 10x7"................................265.00
Plaque, Jasper, bl, Sacrifice of Iphigenia, WW, fr, 3½x8" 500.00
Plaque, Jasper, blk, Sympathy, WW, 5¼x7⅛" 525.00
Plaque, Jasper, gr, Achilles...Hector..., WW, 1790, 7x21" 1,250.00
Plaque, Jasper, lt bl, 7 Graces, WW, 13½x6" 495.00
Plate, Creamware, Bl Willow, WWE 130.00
Plate, Creamware, Buns! Buns! Buns!, E Lessore, WW, 9", NM .600.00
Plate, Creamware, Knave of Hearts, WWE, ca 1905.....................140.00
Plate, Creamware, shell edge, WW, ca 1800, 8" sq........................95.00
Plate, Drabware, sunflower relief, WW, 1860s, 8⅝" 120.00
Plate, Jasper, lilac, coupe shape, WWE, 6" 65.00
Potpourri, Pearlware, gr/bl, WW, ca 1840.......................... 1,850.00
Ring tree, Jasper, lt gr, WW, ca 1880 ....165.00
Salt cellar, Jasper, bl, WWE, 2x2½" 98.00
Shakers, Jasper, lt gr, WWE, ca 1955, 4", pr 130.00
Sugar bowl, Drabware, w/lid, WW, 1810 ....245.00
Sugar bowl, Jasper, dk bl, w/lid, WWE 105.00
Syrup, Jasper, red, WW, 6¼" 900.00
Tea caddy, Jasper, dk bl, WWE 295.00
Tea caddy, Jasper, 3-color, WWE, 5¼" 1,395.00
Tea set, Egyptianware, terra cotta/blk, crocodile, WW, 3-pc .. 3,000.00
Tea set, Stoneware, platinum over copper, WWE, 3-pc..............775.00
Teapot, Caneware, Rosso decor, WW, ca 1805, lg........................525.00
Teapot, Drabware, gold trim, parapet shape, WW.....................265.00
Teapot, Jasper, dk bl, WWE, 4½x6¼" 110.00
Tile, 1903 calendar, NM 75.00
Toothpick holder, Jasper, dk bl, WWE, 1⅞x1¾" 135.00
Tray, Jasper, blk, WWE, ca 1967, 3x5¾" 80.00
Tray, Jasper, primrose, WWE, 3" dia....................................25.00

Creamware tureen and underdish, green and puce enamel, early 19th century, NM, 16", $2,300.00.

Urn, Jasper, dk bl, ped base, w/lid, WWE, 8¼x5" 395.00
Urn, Jasper, lav, classic figures, w/lid, WW, 9¼" 1,190.00
Urn, Jasper, lt gr, 4 medallions, w/lid, WW, 8¼" 695.00
Vase, Basalt, cherubs in cat-driven chariot, hdls, WW, 10" 750.00
Vase, Butterfly Lustre, 9½" 425.00
Vase, Dragon Lustre, bl mottled, Portland mk/MIE, 13" 975.00
Vase, Jasper, bl, Portland shape, WW, 5x4" 265.00
Vase, jasper, blk, Geo III/Caesar commemorative, WW, 5½" 325.00
Vase, Jasper, dk bl, classical figures, WWE, 3x2" 88.00
Vase, Jasper, lilac, WWE, ca 1960, 3⅜" 55.00
Vase, Jasper, lt bl, Dancing Hours, WW, 1830, 8" 395.00
Vase, Jeweled Tree Lustre, flame, 8" 2,250.00
Water set, Creamware, dog hdls, gilt, WW, 3-pc+tray................900.00

Weil Ware

Max Weil came to the United States in the 1940s, settling in California. There he began manufacturing dinnerware, figurines, cookie jars, and wall pockets. American clays were used, and the dinnerware was all hand decorated. Weil died in 1954; the company closed two years later. The last backstamp to be used was the outline of a burro with the words 'Weil Ware — Made in California.'

Ash tray, Bamboo, 5" 5.00
Coffee server, Bamboo 20.00
Compote, floral, ftd...14.00
Dish, Dogwood, divided, sq, 10½" 7.50
Figurine, boy w/wheelbarrow, #4005 ....15.00

Girl by bud base, 10½", $45.00.

Figurine, Dee Lee, girl, 7" 15.00
Plate, Bamboo, dinner sz... 5.00
Shelf sitter, Oriental boy, pr..40.00
Vase, bud; Ming Tree, w/coralene, #946, 6" 22.00
Wall pocket, Oriental girl, #4046 ....22.50

Weller

The Weller Pottery Company was established in Zanesville, Ohio, in 1882, the outgrowth of a small one-kiln log cabin works Sam Weller had operated in Fultonham. Through an association with Wm. Long, he entered the art pottery field in 1895, producing the Lonhuda Ware Long had perfected in Steubenville six years earlier. His famous Louwelsa line was merely a continuation of Lonhuda and was made in at least five hundred different shapes until 1924.

Many fine lines of artware followed under the direction of Charles Babcock Upjohn, Art Director from 1895 to 1904: Dickens Ware (1st Line), under-glaze slip decorations on dark backgrounds; Turada, featuring applied ivory bands of delicate openwork on solid dark brown backgrounds; and Aurelian, similar to Louwelsa, but with a brushed-on rather than blended ground.

One of their most famous lines was 2nd Line Dickens, introduced in 1900. Backgrounds, characteristically caramel shading to turquoise matt, were decorated by sgraffito with animals, golfers, monks, Indians, and scenes from Dickens' novels. The work is often artist signed. Sicardo, 1903, was a metallic lustre line in tones of rose, blue, green, or purple with flowing Art Nouveau patterns developed within the glaze.

Frederick Hurten Rhead, who worked for Weller in 1903 to 1904, created the prestigious Jap Birdimal line decorated with geisha girls, landscapes, storks, etc., accomplished through application of heavy slip forced through the tiny nozzle of a squeeze bag. Other lines to his credit are L'Art Nouveau, produced both in high-gloss brown and matt pastels, and 3rd Line Dickens, often decorated with Cruikshank's illustrations in relief.

Other early artware lines were Eocean, Floretta, Hunter, Perfecto, Dresden, Etched Matt, and Etna.

In 1920 John Lessel was hired as Art Director, and under his supervision several new lines were created. LaSa, LaMar, Marengo, and Besline attest to his expertise with metallic lustres.

The last of the artware lines and one of the most sought-after by collectors today is Hudson, first made during the early 1920s. Hudson, a semi-matt glazed ware, was beautifully artist decorated on shaded backgrounds with florals, animals, birds, and scenics. Notable artists often signed their work, among them Hester Pillsbury, Dorothy England Laughead, Ruth Axline, Claude Leffler, Sarah Reid McLaughlin, E.L. Pickens, and Mae Timberlake.

During the thirties, Weller produced a line of gardenware and naturalistic life-sized figures of dogs, cats, swans, geese, and playful gnomes.

The depression brought a slow, steady decline in sales, and by 1948 the pottery was closed. For a more thorough study, we recommend *The Collector's Encyclopedia of Weller Pottery* by Sharon and Bob Huxford, available at your local library or bookstore.

Alvin, bud vase, dbl; no mk, 6" 55.00
Alvin, vase, tree trunk form, no mk, 8½"..35.00
Arcadia, bud vase, wht, 7½" 20.00
Arcola, planter, floral, scalloped rim, hdls, 5x9" 50.00
Arcola, vase, grape cluster, baluster, hdls, 5½" 50.00
Ardsley, bud vase, floral, 7½" 30.00
Ardsley, corner vase, iris, ftd triangular form, 7"...........................90.00
Ardsley, wall pocket, dbl; floral, 11½" 85.00
Athens, vase, flared cylinder, 15"...350.00
Atlas, bowl, star-shaped rim, #C-3, 4"..45.00

Ardsley console bowl and kingfisher flower frog, $265.00.

Atlas, candle holder, #C-12, pr 45.00
Aurelian, tankard, corn, 12½" 750.00
Aurelian, tankard, lion portrait, sgn AKEL, crazed, 17" 1,000.00
Aurelian, vase, floral, no mk, 9" 250.00
Aurelian, vase, floral, sgn Fouts, ring hdls, 18" 2,300.00
Aurelian, vase, floral, sgn HM, silver overlay top, 11½" 1,700.00
Aurelian, vase, irises, EX art, Hattie M Ross, 11" 850.00
Baldin, vase, apples, squat/bulbous, 9½" 130.00
Baldin, vase, apples, 7" 55.00
Barcelona, candle holder, 2x5", pr 50.00
Barcelona, ewer, 9½" 100.00
Bedford Matt, umbrella stand, 20" 160.00
Besline, candlestick, ea 70.00
Besline, vase, classic form, 11" 150.00
Blossom, vase, slim neck, hdls, 9½" 25.00
Blossom, wall vase, floral, 7½" 50.00
Blue Drapery, jardiniere, no mk, 5½" 40.00
Blue Drapery, jardiniere & pedestal, no mk, 33½" 300.00
Blue Drapery, vase, slim form, 8" 30.00
Blue Ware, jardiniere, 4 angels, 9" 200.00
Blue Ware, lamp base, 9" 65.00
Blue Ware, vase, tapered cylinder, 8½" 110.00
Bonito, candle holder, upturned ring hdls, 3½" 50.00
Bonito, vase, floral, hdls, sgn HP, 11" 140.00
Bonito, vase, floral, hdls, 7½" 80.00
Bouquet, bowl, #B-8, 4" 15.00
Bouquet, vase, tapered cylinder, 12" 30.00
Breton, bowl, 2-tone, 4" 35.00
Breton, vase, brn, 7" 35.00
Brighton, bluebird, #6, 5" 200.00
Brighton, kingfisher, 6½" 250.00
Brighton, parakeets, 9" 500.00
Brighton, parrot, 13½" 650.00
Brighton, pheasant, 5" 200.00
Brighton, swan flower frog, 4½" 175.00
Brighton, wall bud vase, triple; bird/grape cluster, 15" 300.00
Brighton, wall vase, bird on perch, 9½" 85.00
Burntwood, plaque, 12" 150.00
Burntwood, urn vase, 6½" 75.00
Burntwood, vase, 3½" 50.00
Camelot, vase, 8" 160.00
Cameo, flower arranger, floral, 3" 25.00
Cameo, vase, floral, urn form, hdls, 13" 55.00
Cameo Jewell, vase, cvd fish/bubbles, 10" 375.00
Candis, candle holder, 1½", pr 20.00
Candis, ewer, 11" 25.00
Chase, vase, hunt scene, fan form, 8½" 200.00
Chase, vase, hunt scene, glossy, no mk, 7½" 500.00
Chengtu, urn vase, 5½" 40.00

Chengtu, vase, classic form, 6" 45.00
Clarmont, candlestick, brn, 10" 60.00
Classic, vase, gr, ftd, 6½" 15.00
Claywood, bowl, 2" 30.00
Claywood, mug, 5" 50.00
Claywood, vase, cylindrical, 5½" 35.00
Coppertone, candle holder, 2", pr 30.00
Coppertone, floor vase, no mk, 26½" 450.00
Coppertone, flowerpot w/saucer, 5" 50.00
Coppertone, vase, bulbous, hdls, 8" 300.00
Coppertone, vase, fan form, 8" 300.00
Copra, basket, floral, ftd, 11" 125.00
Copra, vase, floral, ring hdls, 10" 100.00
Cornish, candle holder, paper label, 3½", pr 40.00
Creamware, comport, no mk, 6" 90.00
Creamware, match holder, emb pattern, no mk, 6½" 55.00
Creamware, planter, Coat of Arms pattern, w/liner, 3½" 40.00
Cretone, vase, gazelles, brn on tan, H Pillsbury, 8" 325.00
Crystalline, vase, leaves, flared cylinder, 10" 30.00
Darsie, flowerpot, ivory, 5½" 30.00
Decorated Creamware, mug, decalcomania, 5" 50.00
Decorated Creamware, mug, HP, 5" 55.00
Decorated Creamware, teapot, decalcomania, 5½" 125.00
Delsa, vase, floral, high ft, hdls, 6" 30.00
Dickens I, jardiniere, floral, 8½" 200.00
Dickens I, loving cup, floral, sgn, 3-hdld, 5½" 400.00
Dickens I, oil lamp, floral on navy, wrought legs, 30" 500.00
Dickens I, vase, floral, baluster, 11" 275.00
Dickens II, advertising plate, Dickens...SA Weller, 12½" 1,750.00
Dickens II, ewer, mermaid amid waves, no mk, 10½" 500.00
Dickens II, jug, Indian 'Blue Hawk,' #330, 6½x5" 400.00
Dickens II, jug, Mt Vernon Bridge, 6" 375.00
Dickens II, tankard, Chief Blackbear, sgn AD, 12" 1,100.00
Dickens II, vase, Chief Hollowhorn Bear, sgn AD, 13" 950.00
Dickens II, vase, Dombey & Son, men at table, 8" 600.00
Dickens II, vase, God Bless Me..., men, baluster, 10" 700.00
Dickens II, vase, Irishman, sgn RD, no mk, 6½" 500.00
Dickens II, vase, kitten, baluster, 9" 1,100.00
Dickens II, vase, men play chess, glossy, bulbous, 5" 240.00
Dickens II, vase, monk, bulbous, sgn UJ, 6½" 500.00
Dickens II, vase, sleigh scene, glossy, 13½" 1,600.00
Dickens III, vase, Mr Weller Sr, #15, 8" 750.00
Dickens III, vase, portrait, sm angular hdls, 6" 325.00
Dog, Pop-eyed, 4" 300.00
Dog, Terrier, 10½x16" 1,100.00
Dorland, vase, hdls, #D-14, 7½" 20.00
Dresden, vase, figure in landscape, flared cylinder, 8½" 500.00
Dupont, bowl, flower basket panels, no mk, 2½" 30.00
Dupont, vase, flower basket panels, 10" 90.00
Dynasty, vase, ring hdls, 4" 30.00
Elberta, nut dish, 3" 25.00
Elberta, vase, classic form, 5" 25.00
Eocean, basket, floral, ftd, no mk, 6½" 300.00
Eocean, Late Line; vase, floral, ftd baluster, no mk, 8½" 90.00
Eocean, vase, dog, sgn L Blake, flask form, 7½" 1,000.00
Eocean, vase, floral, flared cylinder, 7½" 300.00
Eocean, vase, floral, sgn MS, tub hdls, 6" 250.00
Eocean, vase, lg pk lilies on lav to bl, A Haubrich, 17" 650.00
Eocean, vase, poppies on blk to gr, 11" 200.00
Etched Matt, vase, lady's profile, 11" 150.00
Ethel, vase, creamware, fan form, 6" 40.00
Etna, jardiniere, florals at rim, 9½" 135.00
Etna, vase, floral, baluster, 7" 100.00
Etna, vase, floral, bulbous, hdls, 9" 140.00

Etna, vase, frog & snake relief, 6½" 200.00
Evergreen, console bowl, ftd, scalloped rim, 5" 20.00
Evergreen, vase, classic form, hdls, 10" 40.00
Fairfield, bowl, 4½" 30.00
Fairfield, vase, cylindrical, 9½" 50.00
Flask, Never Dry, 6" 60.00
Flask, Old Kentuck, 5" 60.00
Flemish, jardiniere, floral, no mk, 7½" 110.00
Flemish, tub, floral, hdls, no mk, 4" 60.00
Flemish, umbrella stand, floral, 21½" 325.00
Fleron, vase, flared rim, 4½" 15.00
Floral, console bowl, #F-9, 4½x10", +2 2" candle holders 50.00
Floral, vase, squat, #F-2, 4½" 20.00
Florala, candlestick, no mk, 11" 35.00
Florenzo, pillow vase, 4" 30.00
Floretta, Matt; tankard, fruit on branch, 10½" 280.00
Floretta, vase, floral, hdls, 7½" 75.00
Floretta, vase, grape cluster, baluster, 13½" 175.00
Forest, jardiniere & pedestal, woodland scene, 26" 550.00
Forest, vase, woodland scene, flared cylinder, no mk, 12" 125.00
Fruitone, vase, baluster, 8" 40.00
Fruitone, wall pocket, 5½" 45.00
Garden ornament, crow, 14x15" 700.00
Garden ornament, Pan, 16½" 1,600.00
Glendale, console set, bowl+frog+2 5½" candle holders 350.00
Glendale, vase, birds among plants, 5" 145.00
Glendale, vase, nesting bird, tapered cylinder, 12" 325.00
Gloria, vase, ftd, twig hdls, #G-14, 6½" 40.00
Gloria, vase, iris, cylindrical, 12½" 60.00
Goldenglow, candle holder, triple; 3½" 40.00
Goldenglow, flower arranger, 4x16½" 25.00
Greenbriar, ewer, 11½" 90.00
Greenbriar, vase, 8½" 70.00
Greoria, strawberry vase, no mk, 5" 70.00
Greoria, vase, cylindrical, flared rim, 11½" 70.00
Hobart, girl w/flowers, bl, no mk, 8½" 65.00
Hobart, wall vase, girl figural, turq, 8" 135.00
Hudson, vase, dogwood, C Leffler, 7" 200.00
Hudson, vase, iris in pk, sgn Hunter, cylindrical, 9" 325.00
Hudson, vase, lg iris, wht on bl, sgn LBM, 9½" 475.00
Hudson, vase, lily of the valley, hdls, 7x6" 150.00
Hudson, vase, morning-glories on bl to wht, 9" 300.00
Hudson, vase, sailboat w/billowing sail, Pillsbury, 8½" 1,100.00
Hudson, vase, trees/snow-capped mtn/lake, Pillsbury, 10" 950.00
Hudson Perfecto, vase, acorns/leaves, bulbous, sgn HP, 4½" 100.00
Hudson Perfecto, vase, pine cones/needles, C Leffler, 10x8" 600.00
Hunter, vase, birds in flight, sgn UJ, baluster, 7½" 450.00
Hunter, vase, duck, ewer form, 7" 550.00
Ivoris, basket, 5" 30.00
Ivoris, powder box, pointed finial, 4" 30.00
Ivory, jardiniere, no mk, 6½" 40.00
Ivory, planter, figures in landscape, sq, 5" 45.00
Ivory, vase, flared cylinder, 15" 70.00
Ivory, vase, pillow form, 5" 15.00
Ivory, wall pocket, ram, 10½" 225.00
Jap Birdimal, oil pitcher, sampan border, sgn HMR, 10½" 700.00
Jap Birdimal, vase, fish, bulbous, no mk, 4½" 350.00
Jap Birdimal, vase, trees, 9" 300.00
Jewell, mug, cameo portrait, 6½" 125.00
Juneau, bud base, 6" 40.00
Kenova, vase, floral, waisted, hdls, 6½" 85.00
Kenova, vase, vining floral, squat, 5½" 75.00
Klyro, bowl, floral, 3½" 40.00
Klyro, circle vase, floral, ftd, 8" 85.00

Klyro, planter, floral, sq form, 4" 40.00
Knifewood, humidor, dog pointing, no mk, 7" 375.00
Knifewood, urn vase, florals, no mk, 8" 125.00
L'Art Nouveau, mug, floral, 5" 100.00
L'Art Nouveau, sunflower bank, 2x4" 150.00
L'Art Nouveau, umbrella stand, glossy, no mk, 26" 500.00
L'Art Nouveau, wall pocket, no mk, 6½" 125.00
LaMar, lamp, 16" 300.00
LaMar, vase, 11½" 275.00
LaSa, lamp base, scenic, wood base, glass finial, 24" total 475.00
LaSa, vase, landscape, golds/pk, 9" 400.00
Lebanon, vase, bulbous, hdls, 9" 325.00
Lido, planter, cornucopia form, 5" 25.00
Lido, vase, flower form, yel & wht, #11, 8" 30.00
Lonhuda, floral, sgn AH, bulbous, integral hdls, 4½" 200.00
Lorbeek, candle holder, 2½", pr 45.00
Lorbeek, console bowl, 3x14", +5" flower frog 80.00
Lorber, vase, satyrs, sgn DE, glossy, 13" 750.00
Loru, vase, ftd cylinder, 11" 25.00
Loru, vase, slim form, 8½" 20.00
Louella, hair receiver, 3" 40.00
Louella, powder jar, 4" 40.00
Louwelsa, Blue; vase, floral, bulbous, 1 hdl, 3" 450.00
Louwelsa, Blue; vase, floral, sgn LM, slim form, 10" 750.00
Louwelsa, Blue; vase, nasturtiums, concave sides, 6" 325.00
Louwelsa, candle holder, floral, sgn MH, 4½" 145.00
Louwelsa, ewer, silver overlay floral, 9" 1,800.00
Louwelsa, jardiniere, mums, spherical w/3 ft, 10x13" 250.00
Louwelsa, jardiniere & pedestal, floral, sgn, 33" 700.00
Louwelsa, Matt; pitcher, iris on lt gr, 12" 350.00
Louwelsa, Matt; vase, corn, A Haubrich, 12½" 425.00
Louwelsa, mug, floral, 4½" 140.00
Louwelsa, tankard, Indian portrait, EX art, E Sulfer, 12" 950.00
Louwelsa, vase, floral, integral hdls, 3-ftd, 6½" 160.00
Louwelsa, vase, floral, sgn WH, baluster, 14½" 500.00
Louwelsa, vase, Indian lady/child seated, Dunlavy, 15½" 1,300.00
Louwelsa, vase, Rubens portrait, LJ Burgess, 16" 2,500.00
Lustre, basket, 6½" 45.00
Lustre, bud vase, no mk, 5½" 25.00
Lustre, Cloudburst vase, no mk, 4½" 60.00
Malvern, candle holder, buds & leaves, pr 40.00
Malvern, circle vase, buds & leaves, 8" 55.00
Manhattan, pitcher, floral, cylindrical, 10" 60.00
Marbleized, jardiniere, 10" 150.00
Marbleized, vase, shouldered, 9½" 100.00
Marbleized, vase, squat, 4½" 50.00
Marengo, wall pocket, 8½" 100.00
Marvo, console bowl, +flower frog 60.00
Marvo, pitcher, 8" 100.00
Marvo, wall vase, 8½" 40.00
Matt Gr, vase, floral emb, 4 buttresses, 12" 600.00
Melrose, console bowl, scalloped rim, hdls, 5x8½" 70.00
Mi-Flo, vase, floral, angle hdls, 9½" 80.00
Minerva, vase, emb running horse, 8½" 450.00
Mirror Black, strawberry jar, no mk, 6½" 65.00
Monochrome, bowl, pk, 1½x8" 20.00
Monochrome, bud vase, triple; 7" 40.00
Montego, vase, hdls, 8" 50.00
Muskota, bowl, goose perched at side of rim, 4½" 200.00
Muskota, fish bowl base, kingfisher, 13½" 265.00
Muskota, girl on knees, no mk, 4" 100.00
Muskota, girl on stump, 8½" 225.00
Muskota, nude kneeling, no mk, 3" 80.00
Muskota, powder jar, lady figural, no mk, 7" 150.00

Neiska, vase, hdls, 6" 30.00
Noval, candle holder, 9½", pr.....................................80.00
Noval, vase, ftd, hdls, no mk, 6" 45.00
Novelty, bumble bee, 2¼" 50.00
Novelty, butterfly, 2" 40.00
Novelty, dragonfly, 3¼" 65.00
Novelty, kangaroo w/lg open pouch, 5½" 85.00
Novelty, name card w/blk bird, no mk, 2x3" 100.00
Novelty, wall vase, teapot..65.00
Oak Leaf, basket vase, brn, 9½" 40.00
Oak Leaf, ewer, slim form, 8½" 25.00
Orris, wall pocket, brn, no mk, 9" 35.00
Panella, wall pocket, floral, 8" 45.00
Paragon, candle holder, 2", pr 30.00
Parian, vase, no mk, 13" 100.00
Pastel, ewer, 10" 30.00
Pastel, planter, ftd, #P-5, 4x8" 30.00
Patra, nut dish, shape #2, 3" 35.00
Patra, vase, 5" 35.00
Patricia, bowl, ducks' heads along rim, 13" 80.00
Patricia, planter, swan form, wht, 3½" 40.00
Pearl, basket, no mk, 6½" 130.00
Pearl, bowl, 3" 40.00
Pearl, vase, flared cylinder, sm hdls, 9" 200.00
Perfecto, ewer, corn, sgn A Haubrich, no mk, 12" ...500.00
Perfecto, vase, horse, sgn H Pillsbury, pillow form, 10½" 3,000.00
Pierre, creamer, 2"..15.00
Pumila, bowl, lotus form, 4" 35.00
Pumila, candle holder, lotus form, 3", pr 50.00
Ragenda, urn, draped swag, 6½" 30.00
Ragenda, vase, draped swag, bowl form, 9" 40.00
Raydance, vase, hdls, 7"..35.00
Roba, wall pocket, floral, 10".....................................40.00
Rochelle, vase, floral, baluster, 6" 170.00
Rochelle, vase, floral on brn, 10" 250.00
Roma, bud vase, triple; 8" 35.00
Roma, candelabrum, 8" 55.00
Roma, letter pocket, floral, 4½x7½" 125.00
Roma, planter, log form, 3x10½" 40.00
Rosella, vase, dbl; floral, 5" 45.00
Rosemont, jardiniere, bird on floral branch, 6½" 200.00
Rosemont, vase, bird on floral branch, 10" 300.00
Rudlor, console bowl, 4½x17½" 15.00
Rudlor, vase, cylindrical, 6½" 30.00
Sabrinian, bowl, paper label, 2½x9"...........................40.00
Sabrinian, vase, sea horse hdls, 12" 125.00
Sabrinian, wall vase, 8½"..55.00
Scandia, bowl, no mk, 3" 30.00
Senic, planter, ftd, #S-17, 5½" 20.00
Senic, vase, bulbous, #S-14, 10" 30.00
Sicardo, bowl, geometrics, 4 buttresses become ft, 4½x9" 450.00
Sicardo, box, mums, gold on irid, mk lid, 7x8½" ... 1,100.00
Sicardo, vase, clover, purple/red/gr/bl lustre, twisted, 5" 375.00
Sicardo, vase, floral, bl/purple, 4-lobe bulbous top, 11½" 1,800.00
Sicardo, vase, flowers/insects, shades of purple, 5½" 400.00
Sicardo, vase, lilies, purple/gr irid, cylindrical, 14" 1,650.00
Sicardo, vase, thistles, gr on dk purple & gr irid, 8" 800.00
Silvertone, basket, floral, 13" 225.00
Silvertone, candle holder, 3", pr 60.00
Softone, bud vase, dbl; pk, 9" 28.00
Softone, hanging basket...55.00
Souevo, humidor, 6" 200.00
Souevo, urn, 6½x8" 80.00
Sydonia, candle holder, 7", pr 50.00

Tivoli, vase, ftd cylinder, no mk, 8½" 90.00
Trellis, wall shelf, turq, no mk, 10½" 55.00
Turada, lamp base, 8" 600.00
Turkis, vase, angle hdls, 5½" 50.00
Turkis, vase, flared rim, 8" 40.00
Tutone, vase, floral, incurvate rim, ftd, 6" 30.00
Underglaze Blue Ware, bowl, bl, 1½x6", +frog 25.00
Utility ware, bean pot, 5½" 20.00
Utility ware, casserole, w/lid, 6x9½", +holder 25.00
Utility ware, pitcher, 5½" 20.00
Velva, bowl, brn, 3½x12½" 20.00
Velva, vase, brn, baluster, hdls, 9½" 25.00
Velvetone, pitcher, mk Hand Made, 10" 60.00
Velvetone, strawberry pot, 10" 25.00
Voile, jardiniere, floral, 6" 60.00
Warwick, basket, 7" 80.00
Warwick, planter, silver & blk foil label/paper label, 3½" 40.00
Wild Rose, console bowl, 6x18" 20.00
Wild Rose, vase, dbl; 6" 15.00
Woodcraft, bowl, cherries, 3" 45.00
Woodcraft, jardiniere, woodpecker & squirrel, 9½" ..250.00
Woodcraft, tankard, no mk, 12½" 350.00
Woodcraft, wall pocket, owl, 10" 150.00
Woodrose, vase, floral, tub hdls, 4" 35.00
Woodrose, wall pocket, floral on wht, no mk, 6" 65.00
Xenia, vase, Nouveau flowers, red/wht on bl matt, 11" 280.00
Zona, bowl, Juvenile line, rabbit/bird on branch, 5½" 30.00
Zona, pitcher, milk; rabbit/bird on branch, 3½" 50.00
Zona, platter, no mk, 12" 35.00
Zona, tea set, fruit, 6" pot+3" sugar bowl+4" creamer 220.00
Zona, umbrella stand, ladies w/garlands, 20½" 850.00

Western Americana

The collecting of Western Americana encompases a broad spectrum of memorabilia and collectibles. Examples of various areas within the main stream would include the following fields: weapons, bottles, photographs, mining/railroad artifacts, cowboy paraphernalia, farm and ranch implements, maps, barbed wire, tokens, Indian relics, saloon/gambling items, and branding irons. Some of these areas have their own separate listings in this book.

Western Americana is not only a collecting field but is also a collecting *era* with specific boundries. Depending upon which field the collector decides to specialize in, prices can start at a few dollars and run into the thousands.

Our advisor for this category is Bill Mackin, author of *Cowboy and Gunfighter Collectibles* (order from the author); he is listed in the Directory under Colorado.

Bit, driving; Imperial...27.50
Bit, nude lady, chased silver overlay 175.00
Book, Cowboy & His Horse, tack info, Fletcher, 1951, EX...........25.00
Branding iron, eyelet hdl, 45".....................................35.00
Brush, horse; US Calvary, Herbert Mfg, 1917 ....21.00
Chaps, wooly angora, mk Clark, Portland OR, 1910...........800.00
Cinch, horsehair, Whitman-Melbach, 1917..................85.00
Coat, horse hide, long, EX..180.00
Gauntlets, studded star pattern, pr............................150.00
Hat, Stetson, rolled 3½" brim, 6" crown, 1920s, EX ...115.00
Hitching post, CI, horse head, late 1800s, 10x7½x3" ...135.00
Neckerchief, red silk, 31" sq, EX 25.00
Saddle, lady's 'astride'; hand tooled/stitched, 1890, rare 250.00
Saddle, lady's side; tooled leather, silk stitching, 1880 ....300.00

Saddle, tooled leather, silver medallion w/horse head, Wht 650.00
Saddle, Western Saddle Co, 1920......................................300.00
Saddle pockets, leather, floral tooling, EX 125.00
Skull, Texas longhorn, 72" wide horns 175.00
Speculum, Tevero & Bro, Pat 1891, EX................................88.00
Spurs, Buermann, silver inlay, long shank, w/leathers, pr 275.00
Spurs, Buermann, str shank, 1¼" rowel, pr 75.00
Spurs, eng silver conchos, leather straps mk JS Collins............275.00
Spurs, Eureka, 1½" rowel, dbl button, pr............................90.00
Spurs, OK's, dbl button, pr 85.00
Vest, bl wool, silk bk, 4-pocket, EX 25.00
Whip, bull snake; leather wrapped, EX 85.00

Westmoreland

Originally titled the Specialty Glass Company, Westmoreland began operations in East Liverpool, Ohio, producing utility items as well as tableware in milk glass and crystal. When the company moved to Grapeville, PA, in 1890, lamps, vases, covered animal dishes, and decorative plates were introduced. Prior to the 1920s, Westmoreland was a major manufacturer of carnival glass and soon thereafter added a line of lovely reproduction art glass items. High-quality milk glass became their speciality, accounting for about 90% of their production. Black glass was introduced in the 1940s, and later in the decade ruby-stained pieces and items decorated in the Mary Gregory style became fashionable. By the 1960s, colored glassware was being produced, examples of which are very popular with collectors today.

Early pieces were marked with a paper label; by the 1960s the ware was embossed with a superimposed 'WG.' The last mark was a circle containing 'Westmoreland' around the perimeter and a large 'W' in the center. The company closed in 1985. See also Animal Dishes with Covers; Carnival Glass.

Ash tray, English Hobnail, gr, 4½" dia 12.00
Basket, Panelled Grape, milk glass, oval, 6½" 25.00
Bowl, Beaded Grape, milk glass, sq, w/lid, 4" 18.00
Bowl, Lattice, milk glass, low, flared, 11" 24.00
Bowl, Panelled Grape, milk glass, lipped, 9½" 42.00
Bowl, Panelled Grape, milk glass, ped ft, 9" 50.00
Box, Beaded Edge, milk glass, w/lid, 4" sq 18.00
Box, cigarette; Beaded Grape, milk glass............................35.00
Butter dish, English Hobnail, ruby, rectangular 25.00
Butter dish, Panelled Grape, milk glass, ¼-lb.......................35.00
Cake plate, Ring & Petal, milk glass 35.00
Cake stand, Panelled Grape, milk glass, skirted....................60.00
Candelabrum, English Hobnail, 2-light, crystal......................45.00
Candlestick, Dolphin, milk glass, 9", pr 65.00
Candy dish, Della Robbia, purple marble, scalloped, ftd 65.00
Candy dish, Dolphin, milk glass, 3-ftd 35.00
Candy dish, English Hobnail, milk glass, 3-ftd 25.00
Cheese dish, Old Quilt, milk glass, rnd 45.00
Compote, English Hobnail, milk glass, ftd, 6" 12.50
Compote, Panelled Grape, milk glass, ruffled, 4½" 20.00
Compote, Sawtooth, ruby, tall ped, w/lid.............................60.00
Cordial, Wakefield, HP w/ruby accent................................22.00
Creamer, Panelled Grape, milk glass, lg..............................14.00
Creamer & sugar bowl, Beaded Grape, milk glass, #1884, sq 30.00
Creamer & sugar bowl, Old Quilt, milk glass, lg.....................45.00
Cruet, Old Quilt, milk glass..30.00
Cup, Fruit, strawberry, milk glass....................................10.00
Cup, punch; Panelled Grape, milk glass..............................10.00
Cup & saucer, Della Robbia, crystal..................................20.00

Cup & saucer, Panelled Grape, milk glass............................13.00
Goblet, water; Wakefield, HP w/ruby accent.........................30.00
Goblet, wine; Princess Feather 12.00

Della Robbia (with flashed color), Goblet, $35.00; Champagne, $22.50.

Honey dish, Beaded Grape, milk glass, #1884, 5" 30.00
Ice bucket, Doreen, gr..45.00
Ivy ball, Panelled Grape, milk glass.................................35.00
Jardiniere, Panelled Grape, milk glass, 6½".........................25.00
Mayonnaise, Panelled Grape, milk glass, ftd.........................15.00
Mustard, English Hobnail, milk glass, ftd 12.00
Nappy, English Hobnail, milk glass, 1-hdl, crystal...................15.00
Pitcher, Old Quilt, milk glass, 3-qt..................................40.00
Pitcher, Panelled Grape, milk glass, 1-pt 35.00
Planter, Panelled Grape, milk glass, oblong, 8½" 30.00
Plate, Beaded Edge, HP fruit, milk glass, 7½".......................10.00
Plate, bl satin, Mary Gregory style, lacy rim, dtd 1975 ....60.00
Plate, Della Robbia, crystal, 10½" 15.00
Plate, 3 kittens, milk glass...28.00
Rose bowl, Doric border, milk glass, 6½".............................28.00
Saucer, Fruit, grape, milk glass....................................... 7.00
Shakers, English Hobnail, milk glass, ftd, pr 15.00
Shakers, Panelled Grape, milk glass, sm, pr 20.00
Sherbet, Della Robbia, milk glass, 3½" 15.00
Sherbet, Old Quilt, milk glass 12.50
Sugar bowl, Panelled Grape, milk glass, w/lid, 4½" 20.00
Toothpick holder, milk glass, 3 swan hdls 12.00
Trinket dish, leaf, bl opaque 7.50
Tumbler, Beaded Edge, milk glass, ftd, 10-oz 8.00
Tumbler, iced tea; Della Robbia, flashed color 23.00
Tumbler, iced tea; Old Quilt, milk glass, flat.......................15.00
Vase, bl satin, Mary Gregory style, dtd 1974, 7" 85.00
Vase, Panelled Grape, milk glass, ftd, 11½"..........................45.00
Water set, Panelled Grape, turq, 7-pc 200.00

Wheatley, T. J.

In 1880 after a brief association with the Coultry Works, Thomas J. Wheatley opened his own studio in Cincinnati, Ohio, claiming to have been the first to discover the secret of under-glaze slip decoration on an unbaked clay vessel. He applied for and was granted a patent for his process. Demand for his ware increased to the point that several artists were hired to decorate the ware. The company incorporated in 1880 as the Cincinnati Art Pottery, but until 1882 it continued to operate under Wheatley's name. Ware from this period is marked 'T.J. Wheatley' or 'T.J.W. and Co.,' and it may be dated.

Lamp, emb leaves on gr, 12½"; 18" ldgl shade w/florals 825.00

Lamp base, floral spray, Limoges style, dtd 1880, 9½", NM..........325.00
Vase, appl blossoms/leaves on gr, No 53 Pat Sept 1880, 18"........825.00
Vase, dogwood in slip relief, pk on gr, sq form, 9x7x3½" 150.00
Vase, emb leaves/bud on gr, slim neck, imp mk, 8x5" 300.00

Vase, relief leafage, green matt, no mark, 13", $1,750.00.

Footstool, enclosed tightly woven sides, uphl top, 20" L.............175.00
Lamp, natural, mushroom shape, 30", EX....................................295.00
Platform rocker, rolled ogee fr w/center panel, Ordway 650.00

Child's rocker, early 20th century, 20", EX, $250.00.

Rocker, loose-weave bk, rolled arms, 37", EX.............................180.00
Rocker, rnd bk, loosely woven w/tiny balls added, cane seat........385.00
Rocker, solid arms & posts, wht pnt, child's, 28", EX 60.00
Rocker, tightly woven w/Deco motif, arms, slip seat 250.00
Table, ornate apron, medial shelf w/gallery, pnt, 27" 650.00
Table, wicker top & medial shelf, 1930s, 16x30" L 135.00
Table, wood top, ogee apron, ornate stretchers, H-W, 30" 700.00
Table, 2-tier, woven top w/braided edge, medial shelf, 36" 225.00

Whieldon

Thomas Whieldon was regarded as the finest of the Staffordshire potters of the mid-1700s. He produced marbled and black Egyptian wares as well as tortoise shell, a mottled brown-glazed earthenware accented with touches of blue and yellow. In 1754 he became a partner of Josiah Wedgwood. Other potters produced similar wares, and today the term Whieldon is used generically.

Bowl, tortoise shell, brn w/bl & gr, emb rim, 5¾", EX..................275.00
Creamer, streaky rose/gr/cream, floral-cap hdl, lid, 6", EX 700.00
Creamer, yel/gr alternating melon stripes, dimpled, 4", NM.... 1,300.00
Plate, brn tortoise shell, ribbed rim, 1760, 9" 600.00
Plate, tortoise-shell sponging, feather rim, 8", EX 220.00
Saucer, brn/gr splashed glazes, 5" 120.00
Tea caddy, emb fruit panels/basketweave, streaky glaze, 4½" 375.00
Teapot, molded/pnt cauliflower, discolored, 4¼" 800.00

Wicker

Wicker is the basket-like material used in many types of furniture and accessories. It may be made from bamboo cane, rattan, reed, or artificial fibers. It is airy, lightweight, and very popular in hot regions.

Imported from the Orient in the 18th century, it was first manufactured in the United States in about 1850. The elaborate, closely-woven Victorian designs belong to the mid-to-late 1800s, and the simple styles with coarse reedings usually indicate a post-1900 production. Art Deco styles followed in the twenties and thirties.

The most important consideration in buying wicker is condition — it can be restored, but only by a professional. Age is an important factor, but be aware that 'Victorian-style' furniture is being manufactured today.

Key:
HB — Heywood Brothers   H-W — Heywood-Wakefield
WR — Wakefield Rattan Co.

Armchair, tufted headrest/seat, curlicues, HB #6001 C 2,200.00
Baby buggy, iron wheels w/rubber, trn wood knobs, 37x34".........600.00
Chair, elaborate bkrest w/woven panel, caned seat, pnt.............160.00
Chair, gossip; beaded curlicues/braiding, pnt, H-W #6520 ....250.00
Chair, ornate bkrest w/beadwork, caned seat, ornate apron 250.00
Day bed, scroll headrest, trn support, gr pnt, 74" 250.00

Willets

The Willets Manufacturing Company of Trenton, New Jersey, produced a type of belleek porcelain during the late 1880s and 1890s. Examples were often marked with a coiled snake that formed a 'W' with 'Willets' below and 'Belleek' above.

Not all Willet's is factory decorated. Items painted by amateurs outside the factory are worth considerably less. In the listings below, all items are belleek unless noted otherwise. For more information, we recommend *American Belleek* with full-color photos and current market values, by Mary Frank Gaston. You will find her address in the Directory under Texas.

Bowl, floral medallions, gold swags, ftd, mk, 2x6" 110.00
Bowl, scalloped rim, no decor, unmk, 2¾x9" 60.00
Chalice, monk smokes cigar on brn, sgn AHP, mk, 11½".................660.00
Chamberstick, appl flowers & spaghetti-type work, att, 5" 385.00
Clock, gold scrolls & leaves, sm pk florals, mk, 13½"....................825.00
Creamer, gold-paste florals, rope hdl, scalloped top, 3¾" 195.00
Creamer, wht ware, no decor, rope hdl, mk, 3¾" 45.00
Creamer & sugar bowl, silver overlay, w/lid.................................110.00
Egg cup, flower form, gold trim, mk, 2¾" 220.00
Figurine, swan, gold breast neck & head, 2⅝" L 50.00
Hatpin holder, mc florals in relief w/gold, mk/1911, 5¼"..............150.00
Loving cup, angels, gold scrolling & hdls, ped ft, mk, 8" 495.00
Muffineer, emb scrolls, no decor, snake mk, 4½"...........................88.00
Mug, lady's & cherub's portrait, sgn, much gold, mk, 5¾"....... 1,100.00
Mug, scenic on dk gr, 7" 95.00
Pitcher, Cane, lav w/gold sponging, snake mk, 7" 220.00
Pitcher, floral, scalloped top, gold dragon hdl, mk, 13" 440.00
Pitcher, pk & gold floral, body indents, branch hdl, 5¼" 195.00
Plate, floral center, raised gold on rim, mk, 10½" 275.00

Salt, scalloped heart shape, no decor, snake mk, 1¾" H 17.50
Teapot, bamboo w/mc flowers on gold, 4", +cr/sug 495.00
Vase, birds on branch, cylindrical, snake mk, 17" 550.00
Vase, child's portrait, sgn Nosek, much gold, mk, 18½" 1,650.00
Vase, florals & berries (non-factory), tapered/ftd, mk, 10½"........195.00
Vase, gold & rust violets, mk, 5" 395.00
Vase, HP & openwork florals, gold trim, ftd, hdls, 12" 1,100.00
Vase, Nouveau nude blows bubbles, sgn, snake mk, 15½" 1,100.00
Vase, roses, gold hdls, urn form, snake mk, 14" 770.00
Vase, tree trunk form, no decor, att, 5" 195.00
Vase, violets, gold/rust on oyster wht, 5" 395.00

Willow Ware

Willow Ware, inspired no doubt by the numerous patterns of the blue and white Nanking imports, has been popular since the late 18th century and has been made in as many variations as there were manufacturers. English transfer wares by such notable firms as Allerton and Ridgway are the most sought-after and the most expensive. Japanese potters have been producing Willow-patterned dinnerware since the late 1800s, and American manufacturers have followed suit. Although blue is the color most commonly used, mauve, black, and even multicolor Willow Ware may be found. Complementary glassware, tinware, and linens have also been made.

In addition to 'Allerton' and 'Ridgway,' both companies used the possessive forms of their names in marking their wares (i.e. Allerton's, Ridgway's). For further study, we recommend the book *Blue Willow*, with full-color photos and current prices, by Mary Frank Gaston. You will find her address in the Directory under Texas. In the following listings, if no manufacturer is noted, the ware is unmarked.

Ash tray, unmk, whale form 22.00
Bowl, cereal; Ridgway 8.00
Bowl, divided vegetable; Allerton, 7¼" L 70.00
Bowl, England, 5" 6.00
Bowl, Homer Laughlin, 8½" 7.00
Bowl, Japan, 5¾" 4.50
Bowl, John Tams Ltd, ped ft, 5x9¼" 110.00
Bowl, Johnson Bros, 8¼" 25.00
Bowl, mixing; Moriyama, 3-pc set...500.00
Bowl, Royal China, 5½" 3.50
Bowl, soup; England, 9" 20.00
Bowl, soup; Homer Laughlin, flat... 8.00
Bowl, soup; Japan, 7⅝" 12.00
Bowl, soup; Ridgway, flat 16.00
Bowl, soup; Royal China 10.00
Bowl, unmk, deep, tab hdls, 5" 9.00
Bowl, vegetable; Buffalo, oval...75.00
Bowl, vegetable; Buffalo, rectangular, w/lid................................150.00
Bowl, vegetable; Japan, oval, 10" 25.00
Butter dish, Buffalo..150.00
Butter dish, unidentified English mk, 3x8" 75.00
Cake plate, Royal China, tab hdls, 11¾" 12.50
Canister, coffee; unmk, rnd, w/lid, 4½" 55.00
Canister, tea; unmk, sq, w/lid 70.00
Canister, unmk, graduated set of 4..250.00
Carafe & warmer, unmk 100.00
Casserole, England, w/lid, ca 1935 ....70.00
Clock, wall; Seth Thomas, rare 500.00
Coffeepot, graniteware, unmk, 6"..75.00
Creamer, Buffalo...30.00
Creamer, Shenango China, hotel ware, 2½".............................20.00
Creamer & sugar bowl, Japan, oval 15.00

Creamer & sugar bowl, Johnson Bros.......................................50.00
Creamer & sugar bowl, Ridgway, w/lid 75.00
Cruet, Japan, pr..45.00
Cruet set, unmk, 4 pcs on wire rack 95.00
Cup & saucer, handleless; unmk, pk 60.00
Cup & saucer, Homer Laughlin...10.00
Cup & saucer, Japan 8.50
Cup & saucer, Johnson Bros 8.00
Egg cup, dbl, Occupied Japan 25.00
Fork & spoon, salad; unmk 25.00
Gravy boat, Buffalo, lg...75.00
Hot pot, Japan, borderless, 6" 25.00
Mug, unmk, lg 15.00
Pitcher, Doulton, Deco style 275.00
Pitcher, Royal Worcester, pk...260.00
Plate, Allerton, 9¾"..18.00
Plate, bread & butter; Royal China 5.00
Plate, cup; unmk, purple lustre rim, 4", EX 75.00
Plate, England, 6¼".. 4.00
Plate, grill; Grimwades..35.00
Plate, grill; Occupied Japan 30.00
Plate, Homer Laughlin, 10" 10.00
Plate, Japan, 6⅛".. 5.50
Plate, Johnson Bros, 8" 8.00
Plate, Maastricht, 9" 10.00
Plate, Ridgway, 10½" 17.50
Plate, Royal China, 10" 10.00
Platter, England, 14x11"...60.00
Platter, Homer Laughlin, 13½" 20.00
Platter, Japan, red, 12½"...35.00
Platter, Johnson Bros, 12"..60.00
Platter, unmk, 12"...65.00
Platter, Woods, 11¾"..50.00
Reamer, pitcher form, unmk 175.00
Salt box, unmk, wood cover, hanging 75.00
Shakers, Wood, pr...12.00
Sugar bowl, Buffalo...35.00
Tea set, England, chrome w/blk Bakelite lid & trim, 5-pc 125.00
Teacup & saucer, unmk, child's, brn, 1½", 3¼".........................20.00
Teapot, creamer & sugar bowl, unmk, 3-pc stacking set 60.00
Teapot, demitasse; Japan 40.00
Teapot, Royal China 30.00
Toby mug, unmk, allover pattern...485.00
Tumbler, juice; unmk, glass, 5"...12.00
Tumbler, juice; unmk Japan, ceramic.......................................20.00

Winchester

The Winchester Repeating Arms Company lost their important government contract after WWI and of necessity turned to the manufacture of sporting goods, hardware items, tools, etc. to augment their gun production. Between 1920 and 1931, over 7,500 different items, each marked 'Winchester Trademark U.S.A.,' were offered for sale by thousands of Winchester Hardware stores throughout the country. After 1931 the firm became Winchester-Western. See also Knives.

Our advisor for this category is James Anderson; he is listed in the Directory under Minnesota.

Badge, Jr Rifle Corps Marksman...35.00
Baseball glove, fielder's 45.00
Belt buckle, man on horse, brass 5.00
Brochure, bicycles, 1897 ....20.00
Catalog, bicycles, 1928 ....35.00

Catalog, Guns & Ammo, 1930s, 32-pg, EX 35.00
Catalog, pocket; tools, 1923, EX 30.00
Catalog, Western Cartridge Co, 1938, M 60.00
Catalog, 1925, M 85.00
Chisel, metal 7.50
Chopper, food; #12 ....12.50
Diploma, Jr Rifle Corp, 1919 ....45.00
Envelope, 2 men w/gun, 4x6", NM 20.00
Fan, electric, 7½" 175.00
Flashlight, 3-cel, MIB 35.00
Fountain pen, NM 85.00
Golf putter, metal hdl 145.00
Golf putter, wood, EX 135.00
Hammer, machinist's 25.00
Hoe 45.00
Ice pick, store; M 25.00
Knife, butcher 30.00
Knife, paring; #4203 ....20.00
Knife, pocket 40.00
Level, #9825, 28" 50.00
Nippers 7.50
Paperweight, 1910 (beware of repros) 55.00
Pencil, bullet form 75.00
Pin-bk button, Going Great Guns... 4.00
Pistol, air; #363, M 145.00
Plane, #3025 ....75.00
Plane, #3045, wooden bottom...50.00
Plane, block; #3093 ....50.00
Plane, block; W-130, dbl end 80.00
Pliers, #3117 ....45.00
Poster, hunters at camp, buck beyond, standup, 1954, 19x26".......65.00
Poster, Junior Rifle Corps, man & boys, 36x18", NM 575.00
Reel, #2345 ....48.00
Scale, grain; brass, w/orig bucket..190.00
Scissors, #9014 ....17.50
Skate pads 10.00
Store bag 15.00
Wrench, monkey; #1063, wood hdl 20.00
Wrench, open end; #1152 ....60.00
Wrench, pipe; 10" 20.00

Windmill Weights

Windmill weights were used to protect the windmill's plunger rod from damage during high winds by adding weight that slowed down the speed of the blades.

Fairbury bull, 22½", $695.00.

Bob-tailed horse, Dempster, no pnt, worn, 13-lb, 16⅝x17" 275.00
Bull, Fairbury, CI, bl pnt, early 1900s, 38-lb, 24½x18x1" 900.00
Bull, Fairbury NE, no pnt, 58-lb, 18¼x24½x1⅛" 650.00

Crescent moon, Fairbanks, Morse & Co, Eclipse, no pnt, 22-lb ..165.00
Rooster, CI, no pnt, 19" 525.00
Rooster, Elgin, CI w/traces of red & wht pnt, 19" 1,200.00
Rooster, Hummer #184, CI, orig pnt, 11" 485.00
W form, Althouse Wheeler, CI, worn brn-red pnt, 24-lb 335.00

Wire Ware

Two thousand years B.C. wire was made by cutting sheet metal into strips which were shaped with mallet and file. By the late 13th century, craftsmen in Europe had developed a method of pulling these strips through progressively smaller holes until the desired gauge was obtained. During the Industrial Revolution of the late 1800s, machinery was developed that could produce wire cheaply and easily; and it became a popular commercial commodity. It was used to produce large items such as garden benches and fencing as well as innumerable small pieces for use in the kitchen or on the farm. Beware of reproductions.

Our advisor for this category is Rosella Tinsley; she is listed in the Directory under Kansas.

Basket, coiled/wrapped iron hdls, 14x24", EX 110.00
Basket, egg gathering; hexagonal, wire in circles, top hdl 50.00
Basket, egg gathering; ribbed pattern, 3-hdl, 8½x7" 55.00
Basket, fruit; oval, braided rim, hdls, 2¾x11x6¾" 30.00
Basket, onion; like potato boiler, no ft or hdl 95.00
Basket, picnic; oval wire, dbl lidded, w/hdl, lg...........................125.00
Basket, potato boiling; twisted wire, bail hdl, 5x6" 125.00
Basket, twisted wire, screen wire base, looped sides, 6½x12".........60.00
Bench, garden; mesh weave, rpt, 37" 95.00
Broom holder, 24 looped pcs for 24 brooms, wall mt.....................95.00
Buggy whip holder, twisted wire & tin, scalloped indents 75.00
Card holder, twisted wire, 12 loops for cards, 12" 50.00
Clam lifter, net for draining, spring action, long twist hdl 25.00
Dish drainer, looped wire & ft, oblong, 19x18" 38.00

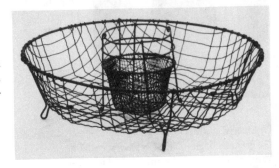

Dish rack, ca 1890-1920, 16" diameter, $45.00.

Floral armature, anchor form, ca 1900, 18x12x1½".......................50.00
Ladle, ornate, lamp chimney cleaner at hdl end 25.00
Napkin ring, twisted wire, ornate, rare, set of 4 ....195.00
Pie lifter, 2-prong, wooden Shaker-style hdl.................................40.00
Pie rack, heavy, holds 6 pies, hdl at top 75.00
Plant stand, 2-tier, on castors, 33x33x21".....................................85.00
Rack, skewer; 6 skewers in 3 szs, ca 1860 ....195.00
Soap dish, spiral bk, twisted wire..65.00
Sponge holder, twisted wire, EX..75.00
Tote, milk bottle; twisted wire fr, carries 4 ....12.50
Trivet, triangular shape, ftd, 6½" 30.00
Vegetable washer, oval wire, 2-pc, EX 55.00

Wisecarver, Rick

Rick Wisecarver is a contemporary ceramic artist from Ohio who is well known not only for his renderings of Indian portraits on brown-glaze ware reminiscent of those made by earlier Ohio potteries but for his figural cookie jars as well, most of which have a Black theme.

Cookie jar, Cookstove Mammy, 1988 ....110.00
Cookie jar, Mammy w/Child, 1989..110.00
Cookie jar, Young Blk Woman, 1989 ....110.00
Mug, Indian Chief, standard brn glaze 45.00
Vase, chief in headdress, flat ovoid, sgn, 10x10" 175.00
Vase, Indian girl w/turq earrings on bl/wht mottle, 9x7"..............225.00
Vase, Indian in headdress & necklace on brn, flat ovoid, 8"........125.00
Vase, Indian warrior w/sheath of arrows on wht, 8x8" 150.00
Vase, mill & stream w/fox chasing pheasant on bl, 14x7"............325.00
Vase, rainbow trout on bl, 9x7"...225.00
Vase, spaniel dog on bl matt, short ped base, 10x7" 225.00

Witch Balls

Witch balls were a Victorian fad touted to be meritorious toward ridding the house of evil spirits, thus warding off sickness and bad luck. Folklore would have it that by wiping the dust and soot from the ball, the spirits were exorcised. It is much more probable, however, considering the fact that such beautiful art glass was used in their making, that the ostentatious Victorians perpetrated the myth rather tongue-in-cheek while enjoying them as lovely decorations for their homes.

Aqua w/wht loopings, cotton/herbs inside, 5", pr 175.00
Aqua w/wht loopings, New England, 1850s, 6¾", pr....................475.00

Clear with opaque white loopings, with stands, South Jersey, 13½", $2,000.00 for the pair.

Cranberry w/wht loopings, 5"..200.00
Dk gr-aqua, 5", in matching vase w/6" dia lip, att S Jersey...........900.00
Wht, pk-red/gr loops evenly spaced into 4 sections, 3", pr...........425.00
Wht w/pk & red loopings, crudely made, att Sandwich, 4¼".......175.00

Wood Carvings

Wood sculptures represent an important section of American folk art. Wood carvings were made not only by skilled woodworkers such as cabinetmakers, carpenters, etc. but by amateur 'whittlers' as well. They take the form of circus-wagon figures, carousel animals, decoys, busts, figurines, and cigar store Indians. Oriental artists show themselves to have been as proficient with the medium of wood as they were with ivory or hardstone. See also Carousel Animals; Decoys; Tobacciana.

Ball-in-cage whimsey, blk pnt, 2¾" 65.00
Bird on branch mtd on shield-shape bk, mc pnt, 3⅜" 95.00
Cat, full body, sitting, butternut wood, 1910, 16" 850.00
Chicken, EX patina, ca 1900, 3½x3x1", EX 15.00

Doll, cvd face w/fur hair, 3-joint legs/2 in arms, 13"...................400.00
Eagle, cherry wood, cvd from 1 pc, sgn D James, 15"..................550.00
Eagle, cvd from natural tree growth, 16", EX.............................700.00
Eagle w/shield, pine w/gold rpt, sgn PL, 1910, rpr, 31"..............375.00
Girl's head & face, walnut, sculpted hair & curls, 4x4½"............130.00
Hand, artist's model, pine, Am, ca 1860, life sz..........................260.00
Horse, mahog, EX cvg, slightly stylized, 8" L.............................200.00
Man, articulated/detail/mc pnt, on trn ped, Wm Bennett, 12" 325.00
Man in tailcoat/waistcoat/trousers, mc pnt, 1800s, 12" 600.00
Marble game, spiral tower, king's-head finial, mc pnt, 9" 300.00
Parrot, standing/grasping base, mc pnt, Wm Schimmel, 10" ... 7,000.00

Model of a physicist, German inscription, 6", $95.00.

Puppet head, animated mouth, lever at bk of neck, 1800s, 8" 475.00
Sow, piglets, & boar, unpnt pine, Loren Skaggs, 8¾" L 250.00
Tree, w/cat, caterpillar, & 3 birds, 14" 230.00

Woodenware

Woodenware (or treenware, as it is sometimes called) generally refers to those wooden items such as spoons, bowls, food molds, etc. that were used in the preparation of food. Common during the 18th and 19th centuries, these wares were designed from a strictly functional viewpoint and were used on a day-to-day basis. With the advent of the Industrial Revolution which brought with it new materials and products, many of the old woodenwares were simply discarded. Today, original hand-crafted American woodenwares are extremely difficult to find.

Biscuit pricker, cross pattern, trn post w/mushroom hdl, 3" 220.00
Bowl, almond shaped, natural patina, 5½x16x24" 200.00
Bowl, ash burl, 1700s, EX patina, 2x6¼" 475.00
Bowl, burl, EX figure, protruding rim hdls, EX patina, 13"...........925.00
Bowl, burl, minor age crack, 1½x4½" dia 275.00
Bowl, burl, VG color & patina, rpr minor age crack, 3½x12" 650.00
Bowl, burl, worn, 1⅜x2⅝" dia...250.00
Bowl, burl w/EX figure, branded initials, 15" 1,650.00
Bowl, butter; striped tiger maple, 4x14½", EX............................395.00
Bowl, chopping; strong figuring, 15½" 750.00
Bowl, dough; hewn, rectangular, sloped sides, 1800s, 23x13x6" .110.00
Bowl, hewn, oval, 2" cvd-out hdls ea end, 6x42x14½".................235.00
Bowl, maple, mustard pnt, 10" dia 135.00
Bowl, maple, trn w/incised concentric circles outside, 22" 350.00
Bowl, shallow, 1700s, shallow, 9" 110.00
Bowl, trn, blk finish, 9½"..210.00
Bowl, trn, EX detail, blk pnt, str sides, 8½" 180.00
Bowl, trn from 1 pc poplar, red pnt traces, cracks, 24"................250.00
Bucket, pickle; tin bands, bail hdl, 13x12" dia 125.00
Bucket, sap; lap banded, gr pnt, 10¼x10½", EX 65.00

Bucket, staved, metal bands, wire bail, worn grpt, 6" 85.00
Bucket, sugar; copper tacked laps, old brn pnt, 10" 135.00
Bucket, sugar; staved, wood bands, bentwood hdl, 8x12" 325.00
Busk, hearts/pinwheel cvg, natural, 12" 150.00
Butter paddle, burl, EX figure & patina, 10" 500.00
Butter paddle, burl, rpr break in hdl, 8¾" 125.00
Butter paddle, maple, bowl-rim hook on hdl, rfn, 9" 45.00
Butter tamper, cvd cherry, right-hand hdl, 1700s, EX 220.00
Candlestick, ped ft, red pnt, tin top, 1860s, 17", pr 175.00
Canteen, staved, lap banding, orig red pnt, 1800s, 8½" dia 350.00
Charger, trn, early, 20" 325.00
Cheese drainer, pine, ½-rnd, rnd spindles, 1850s, 13x9" 225.00
Cheese drainer, staved, urn shape, ped base, 9" 110.00
Cheese hoop, bentwood, 4½x12" dia 40.00
Cheese ladder, mortised & wood-pinned crossbars, 26x10" 90.00
Cheese mold, staved, interlocking wood bands, wht pnt, 12" 85.00
Churn, staved, worn red pnt, 19" 250.00
Cookie brd, floral/birds/etc, 1 cvg on front/2 on bk, 4x9" 210.00
Cookie brd, foliate reserve: mtd soldier, sgn Watkins, 11" 800.00
Cookie brd, lady/horse+2 figural reserves, sgn/1835, 24x13" ... 2,250.00
Cookie brd, springerle, 6 sq designs, 3⅞x6", VG 95.00
Cookie brd, 2 hearts, bk: heart, worm holes, 8½x20" 485.00
Curd breaker, sq slant-sided hopper, dk red pnt, 1850s 235.00
Cutting brd, shaped crest, drilled holes at sides, 11x18" 65.00
Dipper, maple, well shaped, curved hdl, rpr pot hook, 11" 55.00
Doughnut cutter, elongated knob hdl, sgn/Mar 26, 1905 ....130.00
Doughnut cutter, rnd w/trn hdl 60.00
Fork, kraut; 3 wide tines, 1-pc, 4" hdl, 7½" 40.00
Funnel, hand cvd, 1-pc, 8¼x6" dia, EX 75.00
Garlic press, cvd cherry, hinged, 2 hdls, 10", EX 85.00
Jar, poplar w/traces of orig red sponging, rpr lid, 9½" 275.00
Jar, trn, natural varnish finish, Pease, 3¾" 150.00
Lemon squeezer, hand cvd, hinged, long hdl, ca 1858, 20" 95.00
Lemon squeezer, 2-part, hinged, EX 50.00
Noggin, maple, 1-pc, 1850s, 7½x4" 125.00
Noggin, 5⅝" 175.00
Paddle, butter, maple, mid-1800s, EX 23.00
Paddle, stirring; trn hdl, EX patina & color, 13½" 50.00
Paddle, stirring, cvd w/S-shape hdl, ca 1800, 8" L 75.00
Pastry wheel, cvd w/S-shape hdl, ca 1800, 8" L 85.00
Peel, pine w/beveled edges, paddle end, 1820s, 21" 90.00
Pie lifter, 2-tine, brass ferrule, trn hdl, 1700s 130.00
Pounce sander, maple, trn, mustard pnt, 1810s, EX 175.00
Rolling pin, curly maple, 20" 26.00
Rolling pin, maple, 1-pc 26.00
Scoop, bird's head hdl, low/flat, wear, 6¾" 200.00
Scoop, cranberry; cvd wooden teeth, box-like bottom, 18" 225.00
Skimmer, cream; shell form w/3 pierced holes, tab hdl, 4x7½" 150.00
Skimmer, speckled ash burl, worn tab hdl, 4x6" +2½" hdl 295.00
Spoon, maple, broad bowl, curved hdl, 1-pc, 16", EX 125.00
Tray, knife; dvtl w/arched center, open cvd hdl, old pnt 250.00
Trencher, hand scorped, old dk gr pnt, 3½x17x9¼" 185.00
Trencher, wear/worm holes, 9" 100.00
Wine, trn, 4½" 35.00

Woodworking Machinery

Vintage cast iron woodworking machines are monuments to the highly skilled engineers, foundrymen, and machinists who devised them, thus making possible the mass production of items ranging from clothespins, boxes, and barrels to decorative moldings and furniture. Though attractive from a nostalgic viewpoint, many of these machines are bought by the hobbyist and professional alike, to be put into actual use — at far less cost than new equipment. Many worth-assessing fac-

tors must be considered; but as a general rule, a machine in good condition is worth about 65¢ a pound (excluding motors). A machine needing a lot of restoration is not worth more than 35¢ a pound, while one professionally rebuilt and with a warranty can be calculated at $1.10 a pound. Modern, new machinery averages over $3.00 a pound.

Two of the best sources of information on purchasing or selling such machines are *Vintage Machines — Searching for the Cast Iron Classics* by Tom Howell, and *Used Machines and Abused Buyers* by Chuck Seidel from *Fine Woodworking*, November/December 1984. The address for The Woodworking Power Tool Association is listed in the Directory under Clubs, Newsletters, and Catalogs.

American Saw Mill Machinery Company, 1890s

Band saw, tilting table, 36" 850.00
Planer, Jewel, 20" 500.00
Planer/matcher/moulder, Triumph, dbl surface, 24" 1,700.00

Boice-Crane Power Tools, 1937

Band saw, #800, 14" 100.00
Belt sander, #1136, hand stroke 125.00
Jointer, #1400, 6" 100.00
Lathe, #1100, gap bed 50.00
Scroll saw, #900, 24" 75.00
Spindle sander, #560 ....100.00
Table saw, #1500, tilting arbor, 10" 10.00

Crescent Machine Company, 1921

Band saw, 36" 975.00
Jointer, #83, 8" 525.00
Mortiser, hollow chisel 525.00
Planer, #118, 18" 825.00
Table saw, cut off; 16" 550.00

G.N. Goodspeed Company, 1876

Boring machine, upright 225.00
Rod, pin & dowel machine 600.00
Table saw, 12" 200.00

Ober Manufacturing Company, 1889

Saw, rip; self feed, 14" 725.00
Saw, swing cut off; 18" 275.00
Shaper, saw & jointer combination 400.00

Oliver Machinery Company, 1912

Band saw, #17, 30" 925.00
Jointer, #12, 16" 1,950.00
Jointer, #14, 12" 1,100.00
Lathe, #24, dbl end, 8-ft bed, 16" 1,175.00
Lathe, #54, 4-ft bed, 12" 295.00
Planer, #61, 24" 2,550.00
Sander, vertical & disk, #34, 24" 1,475.00
Saw, swing cut off; #36, 18" 650.00
Shaper, #483, high speed, dbl spindle 1,300.00
Table saw, #32, Variety, 12" 500.00

Parks Ball Bearing Machine Company, 1925

Band saw, H-58, Rex, 18" 200.00

Band saw, H-66, Century, 30" 450.00
Jointer, H-133, Ideal, 12" 400.00
Planer, H-117, Endurance, 20" 950.00
Sander, H-139, Peerless, flexible belt......................................650.00
Saw, swing cut off; H-97, Alert, 12".......................................225.00

P.B. Yates Machine Company, 1917

Jointer, #199, 12" 1,235.00
Planer, #160, dbl surface, 20" 5,000.00
Sander, #430, flexible belt..780.00
Saw, rip; #255, self feed, circular, 20" 1,235.00
Saw, swing cut off; #235, 36" 500.00
Saw, tilting ship; Type V-40 .... 5,200.00
Scroll/band saw, #50, 30"..700.00
Shaper, N-1 .... 2,150.00

S.A. Woods Machine Company, 1876

Circular re-sawing machine, Joslin's Improved, 50" 2,275.00
Moulding, planing & matching machine, #1, 4-roll, 10" 1,950.00
Planer, panel; Improved, 20" 520.00

Sprunger Power Tools, 1950s

Band saw, 14" 60.00
Jointer, 4½" 30.00
Lathe, gap bed, 10" 50.00
Table saw, tilt arbor, 10¼" 75.00

Miscellaneous

De Loach Mfg, planer, Paragon, varied friction feed, 20".............650.00
Defiance Machine Works, planer, #1 Improved, 1892, 24" 1,950.00
JD Wallace Co, jigsaw, Work Ace, 1930s, 18" 35.00
Rockwell Mfg, table saw, #34-160, Delta Homecraft, 1930s, 8".....50.00

World's Fairs and Expos

Since 1851 and the Crystal Palace Exhibition in London, World's
Fairs and Expositions have taken place at a steady pace. Many of them
commemorate historical events. The 1904 Louisiana Purchase Exposition, commonly known as the St. Louis World's Fair, celebrated the
100th anniversary of the Louisiana Purchase agreement between
Thomas Jefferson and Napoleon in 1803. The 1893 Columbian Exposition, known as The Chicago World's Fair, commemorated the 400th
anniversary of the discovery of America by Columbus in 1492. (Both of
these fairs were held one year later than originally scheduled.) The
multitude of souvenirs from these and similar events have become a
growing area of interest to collectors in recent years. Many items have a
'crossover' interest into other fields: i.e., collectors of post cards and
souvenir spoons eagerly search for those from various fairs and expositions.

For additional information, collectors may contact World's Fairs
Collectors Society (WFCS), whose address is in the Directory under
Clubs, Newsletters, and Catalogs; or our advisor, D.D. Woollard, Jr. His
address is listed in the Directory under Missouri.

Key: T&P — Trylon & Perisphere

1876 Centennial, Philadelphia

Belt Buckle, brass medallion, Art Gallery, 3½" 40.00

Book, Frank Leslie's Historical Register, EX 125.00
Flag, mini, lt stain, 3x4½"..50.00
Medal, gilt brass, Independence Hall, 1776-1876 .... 6.00
Paperweight, glass, Memorial Hall, Gillinder 40.00
Puzzle set, 5 buildings, orig box 500.00
Trade card, Memorial Hall, Geo Young Baker & Confectioner 9.00

1893 Columbian, Chicago

Album, photographic views, Rand & McNally, EX 55.00
Ax, solid glass, George Washington eng...................................150.00
Bank, CI, Administration Building figural 450.00
Book, Magic City, hardcover, lg, EX...25.00

1893 Columbian Expo: Ticket, M, $12.50; Sterling napkin ring,
$35.00; Box, metal, Chicago Fisheries on lid, Made in Germany,
1¼" diameter, $45.00.

Cup & saucer, flower figural, frosted, Libbey 85.00
Medal, aluminum, fair scene, 2" 17.00
Mug, Columbus & Washington busts, 1893 WF 60.00
Paperweight, Columbus head atop coins form, 1".........................48.00
Pitcher, etched flags & flowers, 10" 295.00
Plaque, pewter standup, w/color photo of Ferris wheel...................80.00
Plate, Columbus emb on clear glass, 9" 60.00
Playing cards, by Clark, complete, NM 100.00
Portfolio, 24 photographic prints, Jones......................................65.00
Post card, Goldsmith series, 8 different for 150.00
Spoon, sterling, 4" Mrs Palmer, Children's Building 45.00
Stevengraph, Landing of Columbus, orig matt 400.00
Straight razor, Expo buildings etched on blade 85.00
Thimble, gold-washed sterling, wide band, mk.............................50.00
Token, brass, Machinery Hall, EX...22.00
Watch case opener, German silver, watch shape, EX 16.00

1898 Trans-Mississippi

Badge, pin-bk; brass, Government Building, 2-part 30.00
Match safe, NP, female figure, Expo buildings 45.00
Medallion, brass, Nebraska Building, heart shape.........................22.50
Penny, Good Luck Souvenir, 1901, encased 17.50
Spoon, SP, Government Building in bowl.....................................22.50

1901 Pan American

Bucket, wood w/wood bail hdl, mini...20.00
Letter opener, buffalo figural hdl..45.00
Stein, bl & gr, White's Pottery, Utica NY, M 400.00

1904 St. Louis

Magazine, Cosmopolitan, World Fair's edition, 104-pg, EX...........25.00

Pin-bk button, Missouri Day, state seal, 1¼", EX 25.00
Pocket knife, aluminum case, Germany, 3" 65.00
Post card, hold-to-light building w/62 windows, EX 30.00
Sword, Jefferson Guard, rare 250.00
Tip tray, Am Can Co, EX 45.00
Token, silvered brass, Jefferson, ring at top, 1¼" dia 32.00
Tray, brass, Transportation Building, 6" dia, EX 40.00
View book, Sights, Scenes, & Wonders, 5x7", 200-pg, EX 25.00

1905 Lewis and Clark

Plate, china, Miss Liberty, Lewis & Clark, Staffordshire 60.00
Poster stamps, sheet of 12 ....15.00
Token, Louis & Clark, map of Louisiana, EX 22.50

1907 Jamestown

Book, Art of the Expo, hardcover, 92-pg, 5½x8½" 15.00
Pin, mc enamel on sterling, EX 65.00
Post card, John Smith, EX 10.00
Purse, leather, 9" 60.00
Statue, bsk, John Smith, 5½" 70.00
Tray, views on copper plated wht metal, 7" dia 12.50

1915 Panama Pacific

Book, Official View; miniature 15.00
Cent, elongated, Administration Building, 1¼", VG 10.00
Colortypes of PPIE, Reid, 32-pg 17.50
Napkin ring, faux ivory, Tower of Jewels, 2x2" 20.00
Photos, Art of the Exposition, tipped in, Neuhaus 35.00
Pin-bk, celluloid w/ribbon, Closing Day 45.00
Post card, ship scene, opens to sz of 4, NM 8.00
Tray, metal, 5" dia 30.00

1926 Sesquicentennial

Ash tray, metal, emb Liberty Bell 15.00
Case, pencil; leather, Liberty Bell design 30.00
Medallion, brass, Washington/Liberty Bell, 1½" dia 10.00
Paperweight, metal, Liberty Bell figural 25.00
View book, Official Souvenir 15.00

1933 Chicago

Ash tray, copper kettle on stand..30.00
Bank, tin, Am Can 20.00
Pillow cover, mc scene, M 22.50
Pinball game, mk souvenir of Century of..., 11½x17½" 180.00
Plate, china, Carillion Tower, Pickard, 8¼" 40.00
Tapestry, bird's-eye view, mc, 25x40", EX 75.00
Vase, blk glass, etched World's Fair 1934, 9¼" 35.00
Wallet, leather, Hall of Science, unused...40.00

1935 California Pacific

Book, Official Guide, dancers on cover, 84-pg, EX 35.00
Bowl, Mammoth Outdoor Organ, gold washed, scalloped, 5" 40.00
Hat, felt, yel letters on navy, folds, EX 30.00
Post card, House of Charm reflects in pool, unused, NM 3.00

1939 New York

Bank, tin, Libbey's Treasure Ship, can form, EX color 25.00

Bottle, milk glass, emb glove, Trylon neck 17.50
Bracelet, metal links, medallion, turq beads, EX 15.00
Coasters, wood w/scenic decals, set of 6, MIB 12.50
Matchbook holder, brass, Washington bust, T&P 20.00
Mug, pottery, Martha Washington..40.00
Pencil, Westinghouse NY, 3½", M 5.00
Pillow cover, T&P, bl & gray fringe, EX 25.00
Pin, chrome & enamel, T&P, ¾", on orig card 15.00
Powder/music box, plays Happy Birthday, NM...............................95.00
Program, China Day, single sheet.. 5.00
Rabbit's foot 10.00
Relish tray, 5 emb buildings on frosted glass, 10" 95.00
Spoon, SP, T&P, Food Building 12.50
Spoon, SP, Vatican Pavilion, demitasse.. 6.50

1939 San Francisco

Ash tray, celluloid, emb fair scenes 20.00
Book, Official Guide, arch on cover, foldout map, 96-pg, EX 25.00
Horseshoe, copper-plated metal, medallion center, 2¼x2".............. 5.00
Pennant, bridge & plane on felt, 25", EX..23.00

1964 New York

Apron, colorful graphics, M..15.00
Bank, ceramic, Unisphere, children w/balloons 30.00
Bowl, papier-mache, Unisphere in center, EX 8.00
Rain bonnet 3.00

Wrought Iron

Until the middle of the 19th century, almost all the metal hand forged in America was made from a material called wrought iron. When wrought iron rusts it appears grainy, while the mild steel that was used later shows no grain but pits to an orange-peel surface. This is an important aid in determining the age of an ironwork piece.

Bark spud, hook end, 1700s, 26" L 39.00
Bowl, fruit; ped ft, 6½x9½" 15.00
Candlestand, tripod base w/scroll ft, scroll on shaft, 28" 750.00
Door strap, ornate scrolling foliage, old pnt, 33", pr 70.00
Fireplace crane, twisted support, 14x18" 65.00
Food chopper, lg hourglass blade, curly maple hdl, 9" 400.00
Fork, tooled/twisted hdl, 18½" 200.00
Hook, w/spike, scrollwork & bird atop, 8½" 275.00
Latch, gate; twisted style.. 5.00
Meat hook, 5 prongs in 2 tiers, primitive, 13½"..............................95.00
Peel, 44" 125.00
Pipe tong, incising near tamp end, ca 1790, very rare 450.00
Rack, utensil; 7-hook/2-tier, stylized floral detail, 26" 300.00
Reins holder, open heart form, ca 1800s, 3½x7½" 220.00
Skewer, flat & tapered w/twisted rattail hdl, 8¼" 57.00
Skimmer, smithy made, lg bowl, long hdl, ca 1830s, EX patina 50.00
Spear, ice fishing; sgn, late 1890s, 24x4"..40.00
Sugar nippers, EX detail, mk Timmins & Sons, 9" 275.00
Sugar nippers, primitive, 11" 150.00
Teakettle, gooseneck spout, ftd, ball form, 1700s, 8x10"..............260.00
Toaster, primitive, 11x15" 105.00
Toaster, sawtooth, 13" 65.00
Toaster, swivel, 1800, 5x13"..400.00
Trammel, heart cutout in crest/tooled vines, 47", VG 1,750.00
Trammel, sawtooth, twisted rod, star at ratchet, 47".....................125.00
Trammel, sawtooth, very primitive, pitted, 21" 250.00

Yellowware

Yellowware is most often a plain type of earthenware, so called because of the color of the clay used in its manufacture. Pieces may vary from buff to yellow to nearly brown; the glaze itself is clear. Some yellowware was decorated with blue, white, brown, or black bands; only seldom was it relief molded. Yellowware was made to a large extent in East Liverpool, Ohio, but other Ohio potteries as well as some in Pennsylvania, New Jersey, and Vermont also produced it. Because it was not often marked, it is almost impossible to identify the manufacturer. English yellowware has a harder body composition. There is a growing interest in this type of pottery, and consequently prices are continually increasing.

Bottle, emb bands, imp label: D Colver, minor wear, 8" 125.00
Bowl, batter; bl sponging, bail hdl, hairline, 4x7" dia....................85.00
Bowl, bl/brn sponging, emb ribs, minor wear, 3½x6¾" 125.00
Bowl, label: Brunts Derbyshire Ironstone Warranted, 2½x10" 75.00
Bowl, mixing; seaweed on wht, East Liverpool, 4x8" 250.00
Bowl, seaweed on wht, str sides w/hdls, E Liverpool, 6x9" 300.00
Bowl, wht rib-emb band/brn stripes, stains/crazed, 4x9" dia...........65.00
Butter crock, dk bl stripes, ribbed bottom 95.00
Cat, seated, free-standing front legs, streaky brn/bl, 12" 2,000.00
Colander, bowl form w/holes in star pattern, 5x9½", EX 175.00
Creamer, bl sponging, tankard form, chips on spout, 4" 40.00
Custard cup, 3 bl bands, early 1900s, 3¼x3⅛" 25.00
Desk set, emb shell & lion head between well & sander, NM 200.00
Dog w/keg, crazed heavy amber glaze, chips/wear, 7½" 175.00
Jar, canning; flared w/scalloped cvg at top, 1870s, 6¼x5" 65.00
Jar, canning; w/lid, 5", NM 145.00
Jar, seaweed on wht band, mismatched lid/rpr, 4" dia 250.00
Jug, bald man w/beer mug in medallion, Gesundheit, 8½" 90.00
Lion, recumbent on oval base, brn running glaze, 15" L, VG .. 1,300.00
Mold, ear of corn, 6" 75.00
Mold, geometric w/bunch of grapes, octagonal, 5½x8" 100.00
Mold, heart, mini 85.00
Mold, pineapple, 5x7" 145.00
Mold, pinwheel..95.00
Mold, rabbit, 4¾x8"..150.00
Mug, blk stripes, emb hdl, 3⅜" 95.00
Mug, brn stripes, emb hdl, 3", VG 75.00
Mug, emb leaf hdl, flared lip, 3" 105.00
Mug, marbleized wht/brn band, emb rib hdl, prof rpr, 3", EX......200.00
Mug, seaweed band, bl on wht w/brn stripes, 3" 275.00
Mug, seaweed band in bl, brn band border, 3x4" 350.00
Mug, wht band w/tan stripes, emb hdl, 2⅞", NM 75.00
Pepper pot, bl & wht bands, 4½", EX 250.00
Pig bank, blk & brn sponging on amber, 3¾", EX 100.00
Pitcher, brn sponging, minor wear, 5⅝" 55.00
Pitcher, seaweed, gr/brn on wht band, 9", M 600.00
Rolling pin, trn wood hdl, 16"...350.00
Tobacco stand, eagle 240.00

Zanesville Art Pottery

Prior to 1900, this company was known as The Zanes Roofing Tile Company; then it was reorganized, and production shifted to the manufacture of art pottery. Their most familiar line, La Mora, was made in the standard brown glaze as well as in a matte version very similar to Owens' Matt Utopia.

Loving cup, La Moro, autumn leaves, sgn KH, 5¾" 150.00

Vase, La Moro, cloverleaves, hdls, 7" 100.00
Vase, La Moro, woman in bl drape, semi-gloss, 14½" 1,900.00
Vase, La Moro, 18th-C gentleman, 10".................................. 1,250.00

Zanesville Glass

Glassware was produced in Zanesville, Ohio, from as early as 1815 until 1851. Two companies produced clear and colored hollowware pieces in five characteristic patterns: 1) diamond faceted, 2) broken swirls, 3) vertical swirls, 4) perpendicular fluting, 5) plain, with scalloped or fluted rims and strap handles. The most readily-identified product is perhaps the whiskey bottles made in the vertical swirl pattern, often called globular swirls because of their full, round body. Their necks vary in width; some have a ringed rim and some are collared. They were made in several colors — amber, light green, and light aquamarine are the most common.

Our advisor for this category is Mark Vuono; he is listed in the Directory under Connecticut.

Bottle, globular, amber, 24 swirled ribs, 7¾", EX........................300.00
Bottle, globular, aqua, 24 swirled ribs, wear/sickness, 8" 425.00
Bottle, globular, aqua, 24 swirled ribs, 9½", EX.........................700.00
Bottle, globular, aqua, 24-rib left swirl, 9½" 425.00
Bottle, globular, citron, 24 swirled ribs, 7½", EX........................800.00
Flask, chestnut, med gold-amber, 10-dmn, EX mold, 5¾" 2,700.00
Flask, chestnut, red-amber, 24-rib left swirl, 5½" 275.00
Snuff bottle, lt gr-aqua w/brn swirl, 24-rib, sq, 5⅞"..................2,800.00

Zsolnay

Zsolnay pottery has been made at Pecs in Hungary since the mid-1800s. The factory received international attention in 1878 by winning the Grand Prix gold medal at the Paris World Exhibition for their technological innovations and high artistic level. Zsolnay used lead-free high-temperature glazes on his unique 'porcelain-faience' material. The Hungarian, Persian, Turkish, Japanese, and Renaissance motifs were applied with colored glazes which after firing resulted in rich ornamentation almost in relief. In the 1890s Zsolnay introduced iridescent 'eosine' glazes in nearly every color and subsequently adopted the Art Nouveau style. The unique eosine glazes and special application techniques allowed striking artistic designs which brought the factory worldwide fame and recognition. Presently the factory produces porcelain wares and various decorative items such as the red or green iridescent-glazed figurines that are frequently seen on the market today.

Bowl, lizards relief, bl-gr irid on gold, #657523, 8" 900.00
Figurine, abstract woman w/harp, irid lustre, 12½" 800.00
Figurine, chickadees, HP, gr Hungary ink stamp, 4½" 85.00
Figurine, owl clutching fish on rock base, gold irid, 13½" 1,900.00
Jug, 3-D centaur sits/female stands by spout, gold-gr, 18" 2,600.00
Pitcher, puzzle; florals, 5 rtcl medallions, sgn, 8" 365.00
Plate, floral, mc on yel, rtcl rim w/gold, 12"...............................225.00
Tray, 3 bears on edge of dished Arctic pool, gold, 13" dia............700.00
Vase, allover birds/flowers, mc/gold on red, 16" 1,700.00
Vase, figural upright fish w/wavy base, pearl/lav irid, 16" 4,000.00
Vase, landscape fr by fruit trees, mc lustre, cylinder, 9" 3,000.00
Vase, marbleized gold, panel indentions, dbl hdls, ftd, 13" 900.00
Vase, peacocks, mc lustre on floral ground, shouldered, 13".... 2,400.00
Vase, rtcl florals, upright hdls, 4 claw ft, tower mk, 9½" 435.00
Vase, tree scenic, mc irid, slim w/triangular lip, 13" 4,600.00
Vase, 3 frogs/underwater bubbles, slim ogee form, 1900, 12" ... 5,000.00
Vase, 6 rim-to-width straps divide leaf tips, mc lustre, 7½" ... 3,500.00

The editors and staff take this opportunity to express our sincere gratitude and appreciation to each person who has in any way contributed to the preparation of this guide. We believe the credibility of our book is greatly enhanced through their efforts. See each advisor's Directory listing for information concerning their specific areas of expertise.

You will notice that at the conclusion of some of the narratives the advisor's name is given. This is optional and up to the discretion of each individual. Simply because no name is mentioned does not indicate that we have no advisor for that subject. Our board grows with each issue and now numbers over 300; if you care to correspond with any of them or anyone listed in our Directory, you must send a SASE with your letter. If you are seeking an appraisal, first ask about their fee, since many of these people are professionals who must naturally charge for their services.

Charles & Barbara Adams
Middleboro, Massachusetts

Geneva D. Addy
Winterset, Iowa

James Anderson
New Brighton, Minnesota

Tim Anderson
Provo, Utah

Warren R. Anderson
Cedar City, Utah

John Apple
Racine, Wisconsin

Dick & Ellie Archer
St. Augustine, Florida

Una Arnbal
Ames, Iowa

Bruce Austin
Fairport, New York

Rod Baer
Arlington, Virginia

Mrs. Lillian Baker, Fellow IBA
Cambridge, England
Gardena, California

Roger Baker
Woodside, California

Robert Banks
Brookeville, Maryland

Jim A. Barker
Hawley, Pennsylvania

Kit Barry
Brattleboro, Vermont

Daniel J. Batchelor
Oswego, New York

D.R. Beeks
Coeur d'Alene, Idaho

Scott Benjamin
Lancaster, California

Phyllis & Tom Bess
Tulsa, Oklahoma

Robert Bettinger
Mt. Dora, Florida

John E. Bilane
Union, New Jersey

Clarence H. Bodine, Jr.
New Hope, Pennsylvania

Sandra V. Bondhus
Unionville, Connecticut

Clifford Boram
Monticello, Indiana

Dick & Waunita Bosworth
Kansas City, Missouri

Jeff Bradfield
Dayton, Virginia

Larry Brenner
Manchester, New Hampshire

William J. Brinkley
McLeansboro, Illinois

Mike Brooks
Oakland, California

Jim Broom
Effingham, Illinois

Rick Brown
Newspaper Collector's Society of America
Lansing, Michigan

Nicki Budin
Worthington, Ohio

Jim Calison
Wallkill, New York

Donald Calkins
Lakewood, Ohio

Tod Carley
V.P., International Society of Antique
Scale Collectors
Arlington Heights, Illinois

Carol & Jim Carlton
Englewood, Colorado

Fran Carter
Coos Bay, Oregon

Tina M. Carter
El Cajon, California

Sally S. Carver
Chestnut Hill, Massachusetts

Cerebro
Lancaster, Pennsylvania

Jackie Chamberlain
La Canada, California

Jack Chipman
Redondo Beach, California

John Cobabe
Redondo Beach, California

Bea Cohen
Easton, Pennsylvania

Wilfred & Dolli Cohen
Santa Ana, California

Lillian M. Cole
Flemington, New Jersey

J.W. Courter
Simpson, Illinois

Jim Cummings
Terre Haute, Indiana

Ron Damaska
New Brighton, Pennsylvania

John Danis
Rockford, Illinois

Patricia M. Davis
Wilmington, Delaware

Gael deCourtivron
Sarasota, Florida

Steve DeGenaro
Youngstown, Ohio

Richard Degenhardt
Hendersonville, North Carolina

Joe Devine
Council Bluffs, Iowa

Ginny Distel
Tiffin, Ohio

DLK Nostalgia & Collectibles
Johnstown, Pennsylvania

Rod Dockery
Ft. Worth, Texas

L.R. 'Les' Docks
San Antonio, Texas

Rebecca Dodds
Ft. Lauderdale, Florida

Pat Dole
Birmingham, Alabama

Ron Donnelly
Panama City Beach, Florida

Robert A. Doyle, CAI, ISA
Fishkill, New York

Louise Dumont
Coventry, Rhode Island

Ken & Jackie Durham
Washington, DC

William Durham
Belvidere, Illinois

Rita & John Ebner
Columbus, Ohio

Bill Edwards
Rushville, Indiana

J. David Ehrhard
Los Angeles, California

Delleen Enge
Ojai, California

Maurice Feinblatt
Wilmette, Illinois

Joseph Ferrara
Newburgh, New York

Steven Fishler
New York, New York

Vicki Flanigan
Winchester, Virginia

Gene Florence
Lexington, Kentucky

Ruth Forsythe
Galena, Ohio

Daniel Fortney
Milwaukee, Wisconsin

Fostoria Glass Society of America, Inc.
Moundsville, West Virginia

Ron Fox
North Babylon, New York

Madeleine France
Plantation, Florida

James Fred
Cutler, Indiana

Leo & Wendy Frese
Dallas, Texas

Terry Friend
Galax, Virginia

Donald M. Frost
Roseburg, Oregon

William Galaway
Belvidere, Illinois

Lee Garmon
Springfield, Illinois

Sandi & Jerry Garrett
Kokomo, Indiana

Mary Frank Gaston
Bryan, Texas

Marjorie Geddes
Beaverton, Oregon

Tony George
Mill Creek, Washington

Walter Glenn
Atlanta, Georgia

George Goehring
Baltimore, Maryland

Shirley Graff
Brunswick, Ohio

Bruce C. Greenberg, Ph. D.
Sykesville, Maryland

Helen Greguire
Hilton, New York

Woody Griffith
Crystal Lake, Illinois

Everett Grist
Charleston, Illinois

Tom Guenin
Chardon, Ohio

Jack Gunsaulus
Plymouth, Michigan

Dr. Laszlo Gyugyi
Pittsburgh, Pennsylvania

Norman Haas
Quincy, Michigan

Don Haase
Mukilteo, Washington

Doris & Burdell Hall
Morton, Illinois

Denise Harned
Elmwood, Connecticut

Warren D. Harris
Carmichael, California

John Hathaway
Bryant Pond, Maine

Ted Haun
Kokomo, Indiana

Fred & Lila Shrader
Crescent City, California

Allan Smith
Sherman, Texas

Pat Smith
Independence, Missouri

Dick Spencer
O'Fallon, Illinois

Charles D. Stapp
Georgetown, Indiana

Nancy Steinbock
Albany, New York

Lois & Milt Steinfeld
Westfield, New Jersey

Stella's Collectibles
Harbor City, California

The Sterling Shop
Silverton, Oregon

Marvin & Jeanette Stofft
Tell City, Indiana

Dick Strickfaden
Pekin, Illinois

Joseph & Pamela Tanner
Great Falls, Montana

Bruce Thalberg
Weston, Connecticut

Chuck Thompson
Houston, Texas

Roy M. Thompson Jr.
Glastonbury, Connecticut

Barry Thomsen
Westchester, Illinois

Rosella Tinsley
Osawatomie, Kansas

Marlena Toohey
Sherwood, Arkansas

Dan Tucker
Toledo, Ohio

Richard & Valerie Tucker
Argyle, Texas

Robert Tuggle
New York, New York

Ruth & Dale Van Kuren
Clarence, New York

Joan F. Van Patten
Rexford, New York

Duane & Janice Vanderbilt
Indianapolis, Indiana

Norm & Cathy Vigue
Stoughton, Massachusetts

Mark Vuono
Stamford, Connecticut

Mary Jo Walczak
Toledo, Ohio

Carol & Jimmy Walker
Waelder, Texas

Ian Warner
Brampton, Ontario, Canada

Pastor Frederick S. Weiser
New Oxford, Pennsylvania

BA Wellman
Southboro, Massachusetts

Rosie J. Wells
Canton, Illinois

Douglass White
Orlando, Florida

Margaret & Kenn Whitmyer
Gahanna, Ohio

Doug Wiesehan
St. Charles, Missouri

Juanita Wilkins
Lima, Ohio

Don Williams
Kirksville, Missouri

Ron L. Willis
Moore, Oklahoma

Roy M. Willis
Lebanon Junction, Kentucky

Jo Ellen Winther
Arvada, Colorado

D.D. Woollard, Jr.
Bridgeton, Missouri

Veryl Marie Worth
Oakridge, Oregon

Darlene Yohe
Stuttgart, Arkansas

Art & Penny Young
Little Falls, New Jersey

Catherine Yronwode
Forestville, California

Audrey Zeder
Long Beach, California

Auction Houses

We wish to thank the following auction houses whose catalogs have been used as sources for pricing information. Many also granted us permission to reproduce their photographs.

A-1 Auction Service
P.O. Box 540672, Orlando, Florida 32854;
407-841-6681. Specializing in American
antique sales

America West Archives
Anderson, Warren
P.O. Box 100, Cedar City, Utah 84721
26-page illustrated catalog issued quarterly
includes an auction section featuring scarce
and historical early western documents, letters, autographs, stock certificates, and
other important ephemera. 1-year subscription: $10.00

Arman Absentee Auctions
P.O. Box 174, Woodstock, CT 06281; 203-
928-5838. Specializing in American glass,
Historical Staffordshire, English soft paste,
paperweights

Barrett/Bertoia Auctions & Appraisals
1217 Glenwood Dr., Vineland, NJ 18630;
609-692-4092. Specializing in antique toys
and collectibles

Brian Riba
Riba Auctions Inc.
P.O. Box 53, Main St., S. Glastonbury, CT
06073; 203-633-3076

C.E. Guarino
Box 49, Denmark, ME 04022

Charles E. Kirtley
P.O. Box 2273, Elizabeth City, North Carolina 27096; 919-335-1262. Specializing in
World's Fair, Civil War, Political, Advertising, and other American collectibles

Col. Doug Allard
P.O. Box 460, St. Ignatius, MT 59865

David Rago
P.O. Box 3592, Station E, Trenton, NJ
08629; 609-397-9374

Gallery: 17 S. Main St., Lambertville, NJ
08530. Specializing in American art pottery and Arts & Crafts

Doyle, Auctioneers & Appraisers
R.D. 3, Box 137, Osborne Hill Road,
Fishkill, NY 12524; 914-896-9492. Thousands of collectibles offered: call for free
calendar of upcoming events

Du Mouchelles
409 Jefferson Ave., Detroit, MI 48226

Early Auction Co.
123 Main St., Milford, OH 45150

Garth's Auctions Inc.
2690 Stratford Rd., Box 369, Delaware, OH
43015; 614-362-4771

Greenberg Auctions
7566 Main St.
Sykesville, MD 21784. Specializing in
trains: Lionel, American Flyer, Ives, Marx,
Ho

Guernsey's
136 E. 73rd St., New York, NY 10021;
212-794-2280. Specializing in carousel figures

Gunther's International Auction Gallery
P.O. Box 235, 24 S. Virginia Ave.,
Brunswick, MD 21716; 301-834-7101 or
800-274-8779. Specializing in political,
Oriental rugs, art, bronzes, antiques, the
unusual

Hake's Americana & Collectibles
Specializing in character and personality
collectibles along with all artifacts of popular culture for over 20 years. To receive a
catalog for their next 3,000-item
mail/phone bid auction, send $3.00 to
Hake's Americana, P.O. Box 1444M, York,
PA 17405

Jack Sellner
Sellner Marketing of California
P.O. Box 308, Fremont, CA 94536; 415-
745-9463

James D. Julia
P.O. Box 210, Showhegan Rd., Fairfield,
ME 04937

L.R. 'Les' Docks
Box 691035, San Antonio, TX 78269-
1035. Providing occasional mail-order
record auctions, rarely consigned; the only
consignments considered are exceptionally
scarce and unusual records

Lloyd Ralston Toys
447 Stratford Rd., Fairfield, CT 06432

Manion's International Auction House,
Inc.
P.O. Box 12214, Kansas City, KS 66112

Maritime Auctions
R.R. 2, Box 45A, York, ME 03909; 207-
363-4247

Milwaukee Auction Galleries, Ltd.
4747 W. Bradley Rd., Milwaukee, WI
53223; 414-355-5054

Noel Barrett Antiques & Auctions
P.O. Box 1001, Carversville, PA 18913;
215-297-5109

Nostalgia Co.
21 S. Lake Dr., Hackensack, NJ 07601;
201-488-4536

Nostalgia Galleries
657 Meacham Ave., Elmont, NY 11003;
516-326-9595. Auctioning items from
almost every area of the collectible field,
catalogs available

Phillips
406 E. 79th St., New York City, NY 10021

Rex Stark Auctions
49 Wethersfield Rd., Bellingham, MA
02019

Richard A. Bourne Co. Inc.
Estate Auctioneers & Appraisers
Box 141, Hyannis Port, MA 02647; 617-
775-0797

Roan Inc.
Box 118, R.D. 3, Cogan Station, PA 17728

Robert W. Skinner Inc.
Auctioneers & Appraisers
Rt. 117, Bolton, MA 01740; 617-779-5528

Sally S. Carver Postcard Mail Auctions
179 South St., Chestnut Hill, MA 02167;
617-469-9175. Specializing in all better
quality pre-1930 postcards; SASE with correspondence, no consignments accepted

Sotheby Parke Bernet Inc.
980 Madison Ave., New York City, NY
10021

TSACO (The Stein Auction Company)
East
Ron Fox
416 Throop St., N. Babylon, NY 11704.
Telephone and Fax: 516-669-7232

Weschler's, Adam A. Weschler & Son
905 E. St. N.W., Washington, DC 20004

Willis Henry Auctions
22 Main St., Marshfield, MA 02050

Alabama

Dole, Pat
Editor of *The Glaze*
P.O. Box 4782 Birmingham, 35206; 205-833-9853. Specializing in Purinton pottery

Luckey, Carl
Carl F. Luckey Communications
R.R. 4, Box 301, Lingerlost Tr., Killen, 35645. Freelance writer specializing in art, antiques, and collectibles

Arizona

Kielsmeier, Wayne B.
Covington Fine Arts Gallery, Inc.
4951 E. Grant, Rd. 107, Tucson, 85712; 602-326-6111. Specializing in 19th and 20th Century American and European art pottery, paintings, prints, watercolors

Arkansas

Hall, Doris & Burdell
B&B Antiques
P.O. Box 1501, Fairfield Bay, 72088 or 210 W. Sassafras Dr., Morton, IL 61550. Authors of *Morton's Potteries: 99 Years*. Specializing in Morton pottery, American dinnerware, early American pattern glass, historical items, small primitives

Musgrave, Marge
Look Nook Antiques
R.R. 3, Box 352, Mountain Home, 72653; 501-499-5283. Specializing in art glass and colored Victorian glass

Toohey, Marlena
405 Beaconfield, Sherwood, 72116; 501-834-1033. Specializing in black glass

Yohe, Darlene
Timberview Antiques
P.O. Box 343, Stuttgart, 72160; 501-673-3437. Specializing in American pattern glass, historical glass, Victorian pattern glass, carnival glass, and custard glass

California

Baker, Mrs. Lillian
15237 Chanera Ave., Gardena, 90249; 213-329-2619. Author Collector Books on antique, collectible, and high-fashion costume jewelry, hatpins and hatpin holders, miniatures

Baker, Roger
Baker's Lady Luck Emporium
Box 620417, Woodside, 94062; 415-851-7188. Specializing in Saloon Americana — advertising, gambling, bar bottles, cigar lighters, match safes, bowie knives, dirks, daggers, cowboy hats, spurs, chaps, saddles, barber items: bottles, shaving mugs, razors

Benjamin, Scott
2616 Via Madalena, Lancaster, 93535; 805-946-0075. Specializing in gasoline pump globes

Brooks, Mike
7335 Skyline, Oakland, 94611; 415-339-1751. Specializing in typewriters, early televisions

Carter, Tina M.
882 S. Mollison, El Cajon, 92020; 619-440-5043. Specializing in teapots, tea-related items, tea tins, children's and toy tea sets, coffeepots, etc.

Chamberlain, Jackie
P.O. Box 594, La Canada, 91012-0594; 18-790-5416. Specializing in holiday collectibles, antique reference books, teddy bears, pewter ice cream molds

Chipman, Jack
California Spectrum
Box 1429, Redondo Beach, 90278. Specializing in California and other American ceramics

Cobabe, John
John Cobabe Antiques
1874 S. Pacific Coast Hwy. #225, Redondo Beach, 90277; 213-373-9956. Specializing in Europe an glass and pottery

Cohen, Wilfred & Dolli
Antiques & Art Glass
P.O. Box 27151, Santa Ana, 92799; 714-545-5673. Specializing in Wave Crest (C.F. Monroe), Victorian Era art and pattern glass, shakers, toothpick holders, Moorcroft pottery, art and pattern glass biscuit jars, burmese glass

Ehrhard, J. David
Psycho-Ceramic Restorations
1336 Sutherland St., Los Angeles, 90026; 213-481-3956. Specializing in restoration of ceramics, collects Susie Cooper and British pottery

Enge, Delleen
Franciscan Dinnerware Matching Service
323 E. Matilija, Ste. 112, Ojai, 93023

Harris, Warren D.
6130 Rampart Dr., Carmichael, 95608; 916-966-3490. Specializing in decorative (non-advertising) thermometers

Howard, Steve
101 1st St., Suite 404, Los Altos, 94022; 415-484-4488. Specializing in antique American firearms, Bowie knives, Western Americana, old advertising and vintage gambling items

Johnson, Patricia A.
Box 1221, Torrance, 90505. Specializing in open salts

Long, Earnest & Ida
Long's Americana
P.O. Box 90, Mokelumne Hill, 95245; 209-286-1348. Specializing in children's items: toys, banks, games, etc.; publishers of *Dictionary of Toys, Vol. I & II*; *Dictionary of Still Banks*; and *Penny Lane*, a history of antique mechanical toy banks

Maurer, Oveda L.
Oveda Maurer Antiques
137 Tunstead Ave., San Anselmo, 94960; 415-454-6439. Specializing in 18th-century and early 19th-century American furniture, lighting, pewter, and hearthware

Muller, Jerry
Museum Graphics
P.O. Box 10743; 714-540-0808. Specializing in original comic strips, magazine cartoons, and animation art

Nelson, Maxine
873 Marigold Ct., Carlsbad, 92009. Specializing in Vernon Kilns

Oliphant, Steve
5255 Allott Ave., Van Nuys, 91401; 818-789-2339. Specializing in phonographs

Pardini, Dick
3107 N. El Dorado St., Dept. SAPG, Stockton, 95204; 209-466-5550. Specializing in California Perfume Company items: buyer and information center. Not interested in items that have Avon or Anniversary Keepsake markings. Inquiries require LSASE; not necessary if offering items for sale

Ringering, David
Belle Ringer Antiques
1509 Wilson Terrace, Glendale, 91206; 818-241-8469. Specializing in Rowland & Marsellus, Royal Fenton, Bawo & Dotter, A.C. Bosselman & Co., souvenir china. Feel free to contact David if you have any questions about Rowland & Marsellus china. He will be happy to answer any questions about souvenir china as well

Shrader, Fred & Lila
Shrader Antiques
2025 Hwy. 199, Crescent City, 95531; 707-458-3525. Specializing in railroad, steamship and other transportation memorabilia; Shelley and select Americana

Stella's Collectibles
Memory Lanes Antique Mall
2451 Frampton St., Harbor City, 90710; 213-316-7198. Also at Westchester Fair Mall & Farmer's Market Showcase Gallery in Los Angeles. Specializing in quality glass and china, paperweights, figurines, plates, jewelry

Yronwode, Catherine
6632 Covey Rd., Forestville, 95436; 707-887-2424. Specializing in pre-1950 collectible plastic

Zeder, Audrey
6755 Coralite St. S, Long Beach, 90808. (By appointment only). Specializing in British Royal Commemorative Souvenirs (mail-order catalog available). Author of *British Royal Commemoratives* (Wallace Homestead)

Canada

Melis, Mirko
Marcelle Antiques
416-820-8066. Specializing in American and European art glass, Russian works of art (enamels, porcelains, silver, etc.), English & Continental glass and china

Warner, Ian
P.O. Box 44, Brampton, Ontario, L6V 2K7. Specializing in Wade porcelain and Swankyswigs, author of *The World of Wade*, Co-author: Mike Posgay

Colorado

Carlton, Carol & Jim
8115 S. Syracuse St., Englewood, 80112; 303-773-8616. Specializing in Broadmore and Coors pottery

Heck, Carl
Carl Heck Antiques
Box 8416, Aspen, 81612; 303-925-8011. Specializing in antique stained, beveled glass, and Tiffany windows; leaded and reverse-painted lamps, Tiffany and French Cameo lamps

Mackin, Bill
Author of *Cowboy and Gunfighter Collectibles*. Available directly from author: P.O. Box 70, Meeker, 81641, clothbound: $29.95, paperback: $19.95; 303-878-4525. Specializing in old and fine spurs, guns, gun leather, western Americana

Over, Naomi L.
8909 Sharon Lane, Arvada, 80002; 303-424-5922. Specializing in ruby glassware

Winther, Jo Ellen
8449 W. 75th Way, Arvada, 80005; 800-872-2345 or 303-421-2371. Specializing in Coors

Connecticut

Bondhus, Sandra V.
Box 100, Unionville, 06085; 203-678-1808. Author of *Quimper Pottery: A French Folk Art Faience*. Specializing in Quimper pottery

Harned, Denise
P.O. Box 10373, Elmwood, 06133. Author of *Griswold Cast Collectibles*. Specializing in Griswold cast iron and aluminum

Kilbride, Richard J.
81 Willard Terrace, Stamford, 06903; 203-322-0568. Author of *Art Deco Chrome, The Chase Era*, and *Art Deco Chrome, Book 2, A Collector's Guide, Industrial Design in the Chase Era* .

MacSorley, Earl
823 Indian Hill Road, Orange, 06477; 203-387-1793. Specializing in nutcrackers, Bessie Pease Gutmann prints, figural spittoons

Mayer, Fran
Mechanical Music Center
21 Albert Square, Bridgeport, 06604; 203-332-7815. Specializing in mechanical musical instruments; illustrated catalogs of items for sale, $5 annual subscription.

Rivera, Ted
Box 163, Torrington, 06790; 203-489-4325. Specializing in inkwells and inkstands; co-author of *Inkstands and Inkwells: a Collector's Guide*

Southern Folk Pottery Collectors' Society
Thompson, Roy M. Jr., Founder
1224 Main St, Glastonbury, 06033; 203-659-3695

Thalberg, Bruce
Mountain View Dr., Weston, 06883; 203-227-8175. Specializing in canes and walking sticks: novelty, carved, and Black

Vuono, Mark
306 Mill Rd., Stamford, 06903; 203-329-8744. Specializing in historical flasks, blown-3-mold glass, blown American glass

Delaware

Davis, Patricia M.
700 Greenhill Ave. Wilmington, 19805; 302-658-2992

District of Columbia

Durham, Ken & Jackie
By appointment
909 26 St. N.W., Washington, DC 20037; 202-338-1342. Specializing in countertop arcade machines, trade stimulators, and vending machines; publish *Coin-Op Newsletter*, 16-page illustrated list: $2

England

Pedel, Alan
Collectibles from England
Marwood Lee, Barnstaple, Devon, EX31 4EB; 011-44-271-75166 (anytime). Specializing in pie birds, open salts, cat post cards, most other collectibles

Florida

Archer, Dick & Ellie
Artiques
419 Sevilla Dr., St. Augustine, 32086; 904-797-4678. Specializing in Victorian silverplate: figurals, fancy hollowware, and collectibles

Bettinger, Robert
P.O. Box 333, Mt. Dora, 32757; 904-343-1393. Specializing in American art pottery

deCourtivron, Gael
Cocaholics
4811 Remington Dr., Sarasota, 34234; 813-351-1560. Specializing in Coca-Cola memorabilia. Cocaholics hot line: 813-355-COLA

Dodds, Rebecca
Silver Flute
Box 39644, Ft. Lauderdale, 33339. Specializing in jewelry

Donnelly, Ron
Saturday Matinee
Box 7047, Panama City Beach, 32413. Specializing in Big Little Books, movie posters, premiums, western heroes, character collectibles

France, Madeleine
P.O. Box 15555, Plantation, 33318; 305-584-0009. Specializing in top-quality perfume bottles: Rene Lalique, Steuben, Czechoslovakian, DeVilbiss, Baccarat, Commercials

Hochman, Gene
Full House
9320 Laurel Green Dr., Boynton Beach, 33437; 407-734-8690. Mail auctions; specializing in antique playing cards, gambling memorabilia

Hudson, Hardy
108 Green Leaf Lane, Altamonte Springs, 32714. Specializing in majolica, American art pottery

Lawrence, Judy & Cliff
1169 Overcash Dr., Dunedin, 34698; 813-734-4742. Specializing in fountain pens and mechanical pencils

Linscott, Jacqueline
3557 Nicklaus Dr., Titusville, 32780. Specializing in Blue Bell paperweights. Author of *Blue Bell Paperweights*, complete with history, illustrations, and price guide. Available from author for $7 (including postage and handling)

Linscott, Len
Line Jewels
3557 Nicklaus Dr., Titusville, 32780. Specializing in glass insulators, Blue Bell paperweights and other telephone items, rare Ball fruit jars and Ball items. SASE required

McNerney, Kathryn
502 Kettering Way, Orange Park, 32073. Author Collector Books on blue and white stoneware, primitives, tools

Supnick, Mark
8524 N.W. 2 St., Coral Springs, 33065; 305-755-3448. Author of *Collecting Hull Pottery's Little Red Riding Hood*. Specializing in American pottery

White, Douglass
Classic Interiors & Antiques
2144 Edgewater Dr., Orlando, 32804; 407-841-6681. Specializing in Fulper, other American art pottery

Georgia

Glenn, Walter
Geode Ltd.
3393 Peachtree Rd., Atlanta, 30326; 404-261-9346. Specializing in Frankart

Joiner, John R.
245 Ashland Trail, Tyrone, 30290; 404-487-3732. Specializing in commercial aviation collectibles

Idaho

Beeks, D.R.
P.O. Box 2515, Coeur d'Alene 83814; 208-667-0830. Specializing in instruments of early science, technology, and medicine. Also surveying instruments, microscopes

Illinois

Brinkley, Wm. J.
Brinkley Interiors & Galleries
401 S. Washington Ave., McLeansboro, 62859. Specializing in Meissen, Dresden, European porcelains, American porcelains (Cybis)

Broom, Jim
Box 65, Effingham, 62401. Specializing in opalescent pattern glassware

Carley, Tod
Vice President — International Society of Antique Scale Collectors
811 E. Central Rd., Apt. 304, Arlington Heights, 60005. Specializing in scales

Courter, J.W.
R.R. 1, Simpson, 62985; 618-949-3884. Specializing in Aladdin lamps. Author of *Aladdin — The Magic Name in Lamps,* softbound, 180 pages; and *Aladdin Electric Lamps,* hardbound, 154 pages

Danis, John
11028 Raleigh Ct., Rockford, 61111; 815-963-0757, Fax: 815-877-6042. Specializing in R. Lalique

Feinblatt, Maurice
Wilmette Porcelain Shop
3207 Lake Ave., Wilmette, 60091; 708-251-1170. Specializing in Lladro (since 1973), finer American and European porcelain figurines, western and Art Nouveau bronze recasts

Frizzell, Doris
Doris' Dishes
16 Oakdale Dr., Springfield, 62707; 217-529-3873. Specializing in Royal Haeger, American china and pottery, Depression Glass

Garmon, Lee
1529 Whittier St., Springfield, 62704; 217-789-9574. Specializing in Royal Haeger, Royal Hickman, glass animals

Griffith, Woody
4107 White Ash Rd., Crystal Lake, 60014; 815-459-7808. Specializing in Jewel Tea, Noritake, Hall

Grist, Everett
734 12th St., Charleston, 61920. Specializing in marbles

Hall, Doris & Burdell
B&B Antiques
210 W. Sassafras Dr., Morton, 61550 or P.O. Box 1501, Fairfield Bay, Arkansas 72088. Authors of *Morton's Potteries: 99 Years.* Specializing in Morton pottery, American dinnerware, early American pattern glass, historical items, small primitives

Haussmann, Richard A., Past President, Aurora Historical Society
Aurora, 60507

Hilst, Randy
1221 Florence #4, Pekin, 61554; 309-346-2710. Specializing in old fishing tackle, duck and goose calls

Hoffmann, Pat & Don, Sr.
1291 N. Elmwood Dr., Aurora, 60506; 312-859-3435. Authors of *Warwick, A to W,* a supplement to *Why Not Warwick? China Collector's Guide.* Specializing in Warwick china

The Home Place Antiques
Durham, William; Galaway, William
615 S. State St., Belvidere, 61008; 815-544-0577. Specializing in Tea Leaf ironstone, and white ironstone

Hooks, Dee
Dee's China Shop
Box 142, Lawrenceville, 62439. Specializing in R.S. Prussia, Royal Bayreuth, Haviland, other fine china

Lambrich, Charles
P.O. Box 105
Alton, 62002. Specializing in art glass, porcelain, carnival

Long, Dee
112 S. Center, Lacon, 61540. Specializing in reamers

Lotton, Charles
Specializing in Lotton art glass. Co-author of *Lotton Art Glass,* a comprehensive study with 96 color pages and current values. Available from Antique Publications, P.O. Box 553, Marietta, OH, 45750

Miller, Larry; and Strickfaden, Dick
218 Devron Circle, E. Peoria, 61611. Specializing in German and Czechoslovakian Erphila

Owen, Larry & Sally
Specializing in Morten Studio dogs, etc.

Rhoden, Joan & Charles
Memories/Rhoden's Antiques
605 N. Main, Georgetown, 61846; 217-662-8046. Specializing in Heisey and other Elegant Glassware, general line antiques. Co-authors of *Those Wonderful Yard-Long Prints and More,* an illustrated value guide

Spencer, Dick
Glass and More (shows only)
1203 N. Yale, O'Fallon, 62269; 618-632-9067. Specializing in Cambridge, Fenton, Fostoria, Heisey, etc.

Stevenson, Tom & Mary
TMS Glassware
61 Carla Dr., Granite City, 62040; 618-797-6313. Specializing in glassware and American art pottery

The Home Place Antiques
Durham, William; Galaway, William
9633 Beaver Valley Rd., Belvidere, 61008; 815-547-5128. Specializing in Tea Leaf and white ironstone

Thomsen, Barry
P.O. Box 7066, Westchester, 60154; 708-409-0909. Specializing in cookie jars

Twin's Antiques and Collectibles
Hefley, Phyllis; and McClanahan, Doris
Rt. 242 South, Wayne City, 62895; 618-895-2582 or 618-895-2456. Specializing in pottery, glassware

Weldi, Frank John
1736 W. Farragut Ave., Chicago, 60640; 312-728-7750. Specializing in American and European art pottery, fine glass, designer collectibles

Weldi-Skinner, Mary
1656 W. Farragut Ave., Chicago, 60640 Specializing in American and European art pottery, designer collectibles

Wells, Rosalie J. 'Rosie'
R.R. 1S, Canton, 61520; 1-800-445-8745. Publishes magazines and annual price guides for Precious Moments Collectibles, Hallmark Ornament Collectibles, Lowell Davis Collectibles, and others! She has hosted the International Convention for Precious Moments Collectors each year since 1984 and hosts the Annual Midwest Collectibles Fest. Write for free literature.

Yester-Daze Glass
Illinois Antique Mall, Booth #28, 100 Walnut St., Peoria, 61554. Specializing in Depression Glass, Heisey, Fostoria, and American pottery

Indiana

Boram, Clifford
Antique Stove Information Clearinghouse
417 N. Main St., Monticello, 47960. Inquiries should be accompanied by SASE and marked 'Urgent' in red

Conrad, Beth
Beth's Antiques
P.O. Box 654, N. Lakeshore Dr., Monticello 47960

Cummings, Jim
2822 Mariposa, Terre Haute, 47803

Edwards, Bill
423 N. Main, Rushville, 46173. Author Collector Books on Carnival Glass

Fred, James A.
Antique Radio Labs
R.R. 1, Box 41, Cutler, 46920; 317-268-2214. Specializing in radios made from 1922 to 1950

Garrett, Jerry & Sandi
Jerry's Antiques (shows only)
1807 W. Madison St., Kokomo, 46901; 317-457-5256. Specializing in Greentown glass, old post cards

Haun, Ted
2426 N. 700 East, Kokomo, 46901; 317-628-3640. Specializing in American pottery and china, '50s items, Russel Wright designs

Heiss, Virginia
7777 N. Alton Ave., Indianapolis, 46268; 317-875-6797. Specializing in Muncie, AMACO, Brandt Steele, Marblehead, Kenton Hills

Keagy, William & June
P.O. Box 106, Bloomfield 47424; 812-384-3471. Co-authors of *Those Wonderful Yard-Long Prints and More*, an illustrated value guide

Miller, Susan
606 E. Wabash Ave., Crawfordsville, 47933; 317-362-0352. Specializing in trolls

Old Storefront Antiques
P.O. Box 357, Dublin, 47335; 317-478-4809. Specializing in country store items, tins, primitives, pharmaceuticals, advertising, etc. Active in mail order with catalogs available. Information requires LSASE

Scowden, Virgil
303 Lincoln, Williamsport, 47993; 317-762-3408 or 317-762-3178. Antiques museum, general line, tours

Stapp, Charles Dennis
7037 Haynes Rd., Georgetown, 47122. Specializing in knives, straight razors, safety razors

Stofft, Marvin & Jeanette
Marnette Antiques
Tell City, 47586; 812-547-5707. Specializing in Ohio art pottery, cut glass, R.S. Prussia, buy and sell

Vanderbilt, Duane
4040 West Over Dr., Indianapolis, 46268; 317-875-8932. Author of *Collectors Guide to Shawnee Pottery*

Iowa

Addy, Geneva D.
Winterset, 50273; 515-462-3027

Arnbal, Una
Woodland Antiques
236 Trail Ridge Rd., Ames, 50010; 515-292-1005 Specializing in china, glass, Lomonosov figurines

Bennington Antiques
1372 8th Ave., Marion, 52302; 319-377-2427

Brenner, Paul & Paula
The Mansion
1215 Grand Ave., Spencer, 51301; 712-262-4113. Specializing in Arts & Crafts period art pottery, toys, holiday items

DeGood, Hal & Meredith
The Baggage Car
513 Elm St., West Des Moines, 50265; 515-225-3070. Specializing in Hallmark collectibles; publishers of Hallmark newsletter

Devine, Dennis; Norman; and Joe
D&D Antique Mall, 1411 3rd St., Council Bluffs, 51503; 712-323-5233 or 712-328-7305. Specializing in furniture, phonographs, collectibles, general line. Joe Devine: Royal Copley collector

Gordy, Jerry & Linda
Gordy's Depression Glass
6015 Main St., Davenport, 52802; 319-386-4484. Specializing in Depression Glass

Jaarsma, Ralph
De Pelikaan Antieks
812 Washington St. c/o Red Ribbon Antique Mall, Pella 50219. Specializing in Dutch antiques

Laitinen, Jerry
Jerry's Antiques (shows only)
#3 Thode Court, Davenport, 52802; 319-324-9238. Specializing in Heisey

Nichols, Harold J.
632 Abb, Ames 50010; 515-292-9167. Specializing in Roseville, Weller, McCoy

Picek, Louis
Main Street Antiques
110 W. Main St., Box 340, West Branch, 52358. Specializing in folk art, country Americana, the unusual

Kansas

McCormick, John & Marilyn
8005 Perry, Apt. 103, Overland Park, 66204; 913-649-6947. Specializing in Gonder pottery

Robison, Joleen A.
502 Lindley Dr., Lawrence, 66044. Collector Books author on advertising dolls

Sandler, Miles
Maundy International Watches
P.O. Box 13028-SA, Overland Park, 66212; 1-800-235-2866. Specializing in watches — antique pocket and vintage wristwatches

Tinsley, Rosella
105 15th St., Osawatomie, 66064. Specializing in primitives, kitchen, farm, woodenware, misc.

Kentucky

Florence, Gene
Box 7186H, Lexington, 40522. Author Collector Books on Depression Glass, Occupied Japan

Johnson, Wes
1725 Dixie Hwy., Box 169001, Louisville, 40256-0001. Specializing in Cracker Jack: toys, point of sale, packages, etc.; Checkers Confection, Schoenhut toys, Victor Toy Oats, Universal Theatre (Chicago), toys

Willis, Roy M.
Heartland of Kentucky Decanters and Steins
P.O. Box 428, Lebanon Jct., 40150; 502-833-2827. Specializing in most brands of decanters, domestic beer steins, and advertising. Open showroom

Louisiana

Decker, Dorothy B. & Wade N.
Dottie's Antiques (shows only)
P.O. Box 1141, St. Francisville, 70775; 504-635-3284. Specializing in Elegant and Depression Glass

Wood, Jerry L.
The Wood Post
808 W. 4th, De Quincy, 70633; 318-786-2540. Specializing in pressed and pattern glass

Maine

Hathaway, John
Hathaway's Antiques
Upper Main St., Bryant Pond, 04219; 207-665-2124. Specializing in fruit jars — mail order a specialty

Maryland

Banks, Robert
18901 Gold Mine Court, Brookeville, 20833. Specializing in American flags of historical significance and exceptional design

Dennis & George Collectibles
O'Brien, Dennis; and Goehring, George
3407 Lake Montebello Dr., Baltimore, 21218; 301-889-3964. Specializing in upright pocket tobacco tins, advertising items, character collectibles, unusual items

Greenberg, Bruce C., Ph. D.
Greenberg Publishing Company, Inc.
7566 Main St., Sykesville, 21784. Specializing in toy trains; author and publisher of comprehensive publications on Lionel, American Flyer, and Ives trains

Gunther's International Auction Gallery
P.O. Box 235, 24 S. Virginia Ave., Brunswick, 21716; 301-834-7101 or 800-274-8779. Specializing in political, Oriental rugs, bronzes, art, antiques, and the unusual

Humphrey, George C.
4932 Prince George Ave., Beltsville, 20705; 301-937-7899. Specializing in John Rogers groups

Screen, Harold & Joyce
2804 Munster Rd., Baltimore, 21234; 301-661-6765. Specializing in soda fountain 'tools of the trade' and paper: catalogs, soda fountain magazines, etc.

Massachusetts

Adams, Charles & Barbara
Middleboro, 02346; 508-947-7277. Specializing in Bennington (brown only)

Carver, Mrs. Sally S.
179 South St., Chestnut Hill, 02167; 617-469-9175. Author of *The American Postcard Guide to Tuck*; columnist for *Hobbies*; *Collector's News*; *Postcard Collector*; *Antique Trader Price Guide*. Specializing in all better-quality antique pre-1930 postcards; yearly postcard mail auctions with illustrated catalogs, does not accept consignment material; SASE required with all correspondence

Hess, John A.
Fine Photographic Americana
P.O. Box 3062, Andover, 01810; 508-470-0327. Specializing in 19th-Century photography

Longo, Paul J.
Paul Longo Americana
Box 490, Chatham Rd., South Orleans, Cape Cod, 02662; 508-255-5482. Specializing in political pins, ribbons, banners, autographs, old stocks and bonds, baseball and sports memorabilia of all types

Morin, Albert
668 Robbins Ave. #23
Dracut, 01826; 508-454-7907. Specializing in miscellaneous Akro Agate and Westite

Owings, K.C., Jr.
Antiques Americana
Box 19, N. Abington 02351; 617-857-1655. Specializing in Civil War, Revolutionary War, autographs, documents, books, antiques

Rudisill, John & Barbara
Rudisill's Alt Print Haus
3 Lakewood, Medfield, 02052; 508-359-2261. Specializing in Currier and Ives

Vigue, Norm & Cathy
62 Bailey St., Stoughton, 02072; 617-344-5441. Buying and selling comic character, TV and western character collectibles

Wellman, BA
#9 Cottage St., Southboro, 01772. Specializing in Ceramic Arts Studio and Pennsbury pottery: price guide and video-tape identification guides available

Michigan

Brown, Rick
Newspaper Collectors Society of America
Box 9134-S, Lansing, 48901; 517-372-8381; Fax: 517-485-9115. Specializing in newspapers

Gunsaulus, Jack
Gray's Gallery
583 W. Ann Arbor Trail, Plymouth, 48170; 313-455-2373. Specializing in porcelain, glass, jewelry, books

Haas, Norman
264 Clizbe Rd., Quincy, 49082; 517-639-8537. Specializing in American art pottery

Nedry, Boyd W.
728 Buth Dr., Comstock Park, 49321; 616-784-1513. Specializing in traps and trap-related items

Newbound, Betty
4567 Chadsworth, Union Lake, 48387. Author Collector Books on Blue Ridge dinnerware. Specializing in collectible china and glass

Nickel, Mike
A Nickel's Worth
P.O. Box 456, Portland, 48875; 517-647-7646. Specializing in Roseville, Weller, Rookwood and other important American art pottery, Louis Icart etchings, Maxfield Parrish prints

Oates, Joan
5912 Kingsfield, West Bloomfield, 48322; 313-661-2335. Specializing in Phoenix Bird chinaware

Minnesota

Anderson, James
Box 12704, New Brighton, 55112; 612-484-3198. Specializing in old fishing lures and reels, also tackle catalogs, posters, calendars

Ketcham, Steve
Steve Ketcham Antiques (shows and mail order only)
Box 24114, Edina, 55424; 612-920-4205. Specializing in early American bottles, stoneware, advertising

Lee, Richard J.
St. Paul, 612-771-2357. Specializing in American art pottery, Arts and Crafts, world's fair and expo memorabilia

Nelson, Cheryl L.
Box 222, Spring Park, 55384; 612-473-5625. Specializing in ABC plates, relief-moulded jugs, Gaudy Welsh

Podpeskar, Doug
624 Jones St., Eveleth, 55734-1631; 218-744-4854. Specializing in Red Wing dinnerware

Schoneck, Steve
P.O. Box 56, Newport, 55055; 612-459-2980. Specializing in American art pottery, Arts & Crafts, Handicraft Guild Minneapolis

Missouri

Allen, Helen (shows and mail order only)
629 E. 65th Terrace Kansas City, 64131. Specializing in Depression Glass

Bine, John & Judy
32 San Carlos Dr., St. Charles, 63303; 314-724-1568. Specializing in Cambridge, Fostoria, Heisey, and Depression Glass

Bosworth, Dick & Waunita
Kansas City Trade Winds
7307 N.W. 75th St., Kansas City, 64152. Specializing in American art pottery, Parrish prints, art glass

Hankins, Doris
5311 N. Walrond, Kansas City, 64119; 816-452-1738. Specializing in pottery

Miller, Elma L.
R.R. #2, Box 127A, DeSoto, 63020; 314-586-6914. Specializing in pottery, cookie jars, Depression Glass

Old World Antiques
1715 Summit, Kansas City, 64108
Branch Location: 4436 State Line Rd., Kansas City 66103. Specializing in 18th-and 19th-Century furniture, paintings, accessories, clocks, medical and scientific instruments, chandeliers, sconces, Sabino, and much more

Rhoades, Evelyn
7818 N.E. 54th St., Kansas City, 64119; 816-453-7169. Specializing in Jewel Tea 'Autumn Leaf,' Franciscan dinnerware

Roberts, Brenda
Country Side Antiques
R.R. 2, Marshall, 65340. Specializing in Hull pottery and general line. Author Collector Books on Hull pottery; SASE required

Scott, John and Peggy
Scotty's Antiques
4650 S. Leroy, Springfield, 65810; 417-887-2191. Specializing in Depression-era glassware and pottery

Smith, Pat
Independence
Author Collector Books doll book series

Stratton, Bill
Blue Buds Antiques
Box 8711, Springfield; 417-862-4212. Specializing in Akro, pottery, etc.

Wiesehan, Doug
D&R Farm Antiques
4535 Hwy. H, St. Charles, 63301. Specializing in salesman's samples and patent models, antique toys, farm toys, metal farm signs

Williams, Don
Kirksville 63501. Specializing in art glass

Woollard, D.D., Jr.
11614 Old St. Charles Rd., Bridgeton, 63044. Specializing in world's fair & exposition memorabilia

Montana

Tanner, Joseph & Pamela
Wheeler-Tanner Escapes
P.O. Box 349, Great Falls, 59403; 406-453-4961. Specializing in handcuffs, leg shackles, balls and chains, restraints and padlocks of all kinds (including railroad), locking and non-locking devices

Nebraska

Larsen, Robert V.
3214 19th St., Columbus, 68601. Specializing in old hatpins and hatpin holders

Nevada

Sakach, Gary L.
S. & S.
316 California Ave., Suite #675, Reno, 89509; 702-825-4840. Specializing in fine American pottery and tiles

New Hampshire

Brenner, Larry
L. Brenner Antiques
1005 Chestnut St., Manchester, 03104; 603-625-8203. Specializing in Royal Bayreuth

Marden, Richard G.
Box 524, Elm St., Wolfeboro, 03894; 603-569-3209

New Jersey

Bilane, John E.
(mail order only, no shop) 2065 Morris Ave., Apt. 109, Union, 07083. Specializing in antique glass cup plates

Cole, Lillian M.
Editor of *Piebirds Unlimited* newsletter
14 Harmony School Rd., Flemington, 08822; 908-782-3198. Specializing in pie birds, pie funnels, pie vents

Perzel, Robert & Nancy
Popkorn
4 Mine St. (near Main St.), P.O. Box 1057, Flemington, 08822; 201-782-9631. Specializing in Stangl dinnerware, birds, and artware; Depression Glass

Poster, Harry
Vintage TVs
Box 1883, S. Hackensack, 07606; 201-794-9606. Specializing in vintage TVs, unusual radios, 1950s items, view master

Rago, David
Box 3592, Station E, Trenton, 08629; 609-397-9374. Specializing in Arts & Crafts, American art pottery

Rosen, Barbara
6 Shoshone Trail, Wayne, 07470. Specializing in figural bottle openers and antique dollhouses

Sight Sound Style
Box 2224, S. Hackensack, 07606. Specializing in vintage TVs, collectible radios; publishes price guide

Steinfeld, Lois & Milt
633 Westfield Ave., Box 457, Westfield, 07091. Specializing in collectible glass and china, Victorian silverplate, and other small collectibles

Young, Art & Penni
P.O. Box 81, Little Falls, 07424; 201-785-8115. Specializing in Stevengraphs, police and fire badges, police collectibles, photographs

New York

Austin, Bruce A.
40 Selborne Chase, Fairport 14450; 716-223-0711 (evenings); 716-475-2879 (days). Specializing in clocks

Batchelor, Daniel J.
R.D. 3, Box 10, Oswego, 13126; 315-342-1511. Specializing in Pairpoint, Handel, Bradley and Hubbard lamps

Calison, Jim
Tools of Distinction
Wallkill, 12589; 914-895-8035. Specializing in antique and collectible tools, buying and selling

Doyle, Robert A.
Doyle Auctioneers & Appraisers
R.D. 3, Box 137, Osborne Hill Rd., Fishkill, 12524. Thousands of collectibles offered: call for free calendar of upcoming auctions

Fer-Duc Inc.
Ferrara, Joseph; Leduc, Gerard
Box 1303, Newburgh, 12550; 914-565-5990. Specializing in American art pottery (Ohr, Rookwood, Zanesville), 19th- and 20th-Century American paintings

Fishler, Stephen
Metropolis Comics
7 W. 18th St., New York, 10011; 212-627-9691. Specializing in comic books, comic strip original art, and animation art

Fox, Ron
TSACO (The Stein Auction Company) East
416 Throop St., N. Babylon, 11704; Telephone and Fax: 516-669-7232. Specializing in steins; auctions with illustrated catalogs and video tapes

Greguire, Helen
Helen's Antiques
103 Trimmer Rd., Hilton, 14468; 716-392-2704. Specializing in graniteware (any color), carnival glass lamps and shades, carnival glass lighting of all kinds. Author of *The Collector's Encyclopedia of Graniteware, Colors, Shapes & Values* , available from author for $27.95 (including postage and handling)

Jordan, Ruth E.
Meridale, 13806; 607-746-2082. Specializing in cut glass, American Brilliant period

Laun, H. Thomas & Patricia
Little Century
215 Paul Ave., Syracuse, 13206; 315-437-4156
Summer residence: Box 69-A, Cape Vincent, 13618; 315-654-3244. Specializing in firefighting collectibles

Meisel, Louis K. & Susan P.; Bonanno, Joann
Susan P. Meisel Decorative Arts Gallery
133 Prince St., New York City, 10012. Specializing in Clarice Cliff and 20th-Century designs in jewelry, watches, toys, unusual vintage bicycles, and quirky folk art objects

Owens, Lowell
Owens' Collectibles
12 Bonnie Ave., New Hartford, 13413. Specializing in beer advertising

Pisello, Faye
577 Lake St., Wilson, 14172. Specializing in Brownies by Palmer Cox

Rifken, Blume J.
Author of *Silhouettes in America — 1790-1840 — a Collector's Guide*. Specializing in American antique silhouettes from 1790 to 1840

Scanlin, Terry
Scanlin Enterprises
1504 Monroe St., Endicott, 13760; 607-785-5123. Specializing in pottery

Schleifman, Roselle
Ed's Collectibles
16 Vincent Rd., Spring Valley, 10977; 914-356-2121. Specializing in Duncan & Miller

Steinbock, Nancy
Nancy Steinbock Posters & Prints
518-438-1577. Specializing in posters: travel, war, literary, advertising

Tuggle, Robert
105 W. St., New York City, 10023; 212-595-0514. Specializing in John Bennett, Anglo-Japanese china

Van Kuren, Ruth & Dale
Ruth & Dale Van Kuren Antiques
9060 Main St., Clarence, 14031; 716-741-2606. Specializing in Buffalo pottery, general line

Van Patten, Joan F.
Box 102, Rexford, 12148. Author Collector Books on Nippon and Noritake

North Carolina

Degenhardt, Richard K.
Sugar Hollow Farm, 124 Cypress Point, Hendersonville, 28739; 704-696-9750. Author of *Belleek, The Complete Collectors' Guide and Illustrated Reference*. Specializing in Belleek (The only Belleek is the Irish. Established by legal action in 1929)

Kirtley, Charles E.
P.O. Box 2273, Elizabeth City, 27096; 919-335-1262. Specializing in monthly auctions and bid sales dealing with World's Fair, Civil War, Political, Advertising, and other American collectibles

Ricketts, Bill
Pepper's Deli
126 Cherry St., Black Mountain, 28711. Specializing in items advertising Dr. Pepper

Sayers, R.J.
Southeastern Antiques & Appraisals
P.O. Box 629, Brevard, 28712. Specializing in Boy Scout collectibles, Pisgah Forest pottery, primitive American furniture

Ohio

Baker, Shirley & John Ned
Shirley's Collectibles
673 W. Twp Rd. #118, Tiffin, 419-447-9875. Specializing in Tiffin glass

Batory, Mr. Dana H.
402 E. Bucyrus St., Crestline, 44827. Specializing in antique woodworking machinery

Blair, Betty
Golden Apple Antiques
216 Bridge St., Jackson, 45640; 614-286-4817. Specializing in art pottery, Watt, cookie jars, chocolate molds, general line

Budin, Nicki
Gourmet Antiques Inc.
679 High St., Worthington, 43085; 614-885-1986 and (800)-331-8543. Specializing in Royal Doulton

Calkins, Donald
Calkins Antiques Company
17893 Captain's Cove, Lakewood, 44107; 216-226-0752. Interested in buying Cowan and Clewell

Deason, Betty
Tiffin, 44883; 414-447-4482

DeGenaro, Steve
P.O. Box 5662, Youngstown, 44505; 216-759-7151. Specializing in post-mortem photos, mourning collectibles

Distel, Ginny
Distel's Antiques
4041 S.C.R. 22, Tiffin, 44883; 419-447-5832. Specializing in Tiffin glass

Ebner, Rita & John
Cracker Barrel Antiques
P.O. Box 328866, Columbus, 43232. Specializing in door knockers, cast iron bottle openers, doorstops, toy tractors, general line

Ferguson, Maxine
Wayside Antiques
2290 E. Pike, Zanesville, 43701. General line, furniture, dolls, pottery, glass

Forsythe, Ruth A.
Box 327, Galena, 43021. Author of *Made in Czechoslovakia*

Graff, Shirley
4515 Grafton Rd., Brunswick, 44212. Specializing in Pennsbury pottery

Guenin, Tom
Box 454, Chardon, 44024. Specializing in antique telephones and antique telephone restoration

Hermes, Dianne
5664 W. Harbor Rd., Port Clinton, 43452; 419-635-2495. Specializing in glass, pottery, general line

Hothem, Lar
Hothem House
Box 458, Lancaster, 43130. Specializing in books about Indians and artifacts

Huffman, Mary (Shows only)
3143 S. State Rd. 53, Tiffin, 44883; 419-447-5938. Specializing in glass, kitchen items, general line

Kao, Fern
Lustre Pitcher Antiques
Box 312, Bowling Green, 43402; 419-352-5928. Specializing in Shelley china, small antiques

Kerr, Ann
P.O. 437, Sidney, 45365; 513-492-6369. Author of *Collector's Encyclopedia of Russel Wright Designs*. Specializing in work of Wright, interested in 20th-Century decorative arts

Klender, James & Grace
Town & Country Antiques & Collectibles
P.O. Box 447, Pioneer, 43554; 419-737-2880. Specializing in Depression Glass, and general line

Kline, Mr. & Mrs. Jerry & Gerry
Members of Torquay Pottery Collectors' Society and North America Torquay Society
604 Orchard View Dr., Maumee, 43537; 419-893-1226. Specializing in collecting Torquay pottery

Krick, Bryan
Jeffrey's Antique Gallery
Rt. 75, Findlay, 419-423-7500. Specializing in quilts, glass canes

Loucks, Walter L.
The Carousel News & Trader
87 Parke Ave. W., Suite 206, Mansfield, 44902. A monthly magazine for the carousel enthusiast. Subscription: $22 per year, sample $3

McLaughlin, Joyce
1403 N. Union St., Fostoria, 44830; 419-435-1262. Specializing in general line

Moore, Carolyn
445 N. Prospect, Bowling Green, 43402. Specializing in primitives, yellowware, graniteware

National Cambridge Collectors Inc.
Box 416, Cambridge, 43725
Specializing in Cambridge glass

National Heisey Glass Museum
Heisey Collectors of America Inc.
6th & Church Sts., P.O. Box 4367, Newark, 43055; 614-345-2932

Nelson, Norman
449 N. Town St., Fostoria, 44830; 419-435-6446. Specializing in jukeboxes

Osborne, Ruth
Box 85, Higginsport, 45131. Specializing in vintage clothing, lamps, jewelry

Penrose, Donald M. (mail order only)
6351 Garber Rd., Dayton, 45415; 513-890-3728. Specializing in continental porcelains and art glass

Peters, Jeannie L.
Mt. Washington Antiques
3742 Kellogg, Cincinnati, 45226; 513-231-6584. Specializing in sheet music

Pierce, David
27544 Black Road, P.O. Box 248, Danville, 43014 Specializing in Glidden pottery

Radel, Erle & Janice
Rapids Renovations & Antiques
Grand Rapids. Specializing in furniture and fine jewelry, (collectors only) Labino art glass

Rees, Debbie & Bill
Zanesville. Specializing in Watt, blue and white stoneware, Steiff, cookie jars, Roseville pottery

Rodgers, Joanne
Stretch Glass Society
P.O. Box 770643, Lakewood, 44107. Specializing in stretch glass

Roscoe, Michael
Days Gone By
3351 Lagrange, Toledo, 43608; 419-244-6935. Specializing in quality glass, pottery, old toys, and coin-operated machines

Stoma, James E.
Latcham House Antiques
Waterville, 419-878-0657. Specializing in early lighting, prints, photos, framing

Tucker, Dan; Kitchen, Lorrie
Toledo, 43612; 419-478-3815. Specializing in Depression-era glass, Hall china, Fiesta, Blue Ridge, Shawnee

Walczak, Mary Jo
Toledo, 43611. Specializing in dolls and snow babies

Walker, Bunny
Box 502, Bucyrus, 44820; 419-562-8355. Specializing in Steiff teddy bears, penny toys, pottery

Whitmyer, Margaret & Kenn
Box 30806, Gahanna, 43230. Author Collector Books on children's dishes. Specializing in Depression-era collectibles

Wilkins, Juanita
The Bird of Paradise
Lima, 419-227-2163. Specializing in R.S. China, Old Ivory, colored pattern glass, lamps, jewelry

Willey, Harold & Mildred
Willey's Antiques
11110 Cannon Rd., Frazeysburg, 43822; 614-828-2557. Specializing in Heisey

Young, Mary
1040 Greenridge Dr., Kettering, 45429. Author Collector Books *Collector's Guide to Paper Dolls*

Oklahoma

Bess, Phyllis & Tom
Authors of *Frankoma Treasures* 14535 E. 13th St., Tulsa, 74108; 918-437-7776. Specializing in Frankoma pottery

Cox, David; & Gunter, A.W.
Colonial Antiques
1329 E. 15th St., Tulsa, 74120; 918-582-5645. Specializing in 18th- & 19th-Century country and formal furniture and accessories, oil paintings, orientals

Moore, Art & Shirley
2161 S. Owasso Place, Tulsa, 74114; 918-747-4164. Specializing in Lu Ray Pastels, Depression Glass

Willis, Ron L.
2110 Fox Ave., Moore, 73160. Specializing in militaria

Oregon

Bartsch, Henry
Antique Registers
2050 N. Hwy. 101, Rockaway Beach, 97136; 503-355-2932. Specializing in antique cash registers, co-author of *Antique Cash Registers 1880-1920*

Carter, Fran (appointment only)
Box 3220, Coos Bay, 97420; 503-888-5780. Specializing in estate sales

Coe, Debbie
Coe's Mercantile
748 3rd (Hwy. 99W), Lafayette, 97127; 503-864-2120. Specializing in Victorian and elegant glassware

Collins, Harriett & Hank
Harriett's Antiques (shows and by appointment only) 192 Janney Lane, Medford, 97501; 503-776-0727. Specializing in children's things

Crapo, Lynda
P.O. Box 1013, Medford, 97501; 503-779-6483. Specializing in Metlox, Carnival, Jell-O, Nippon, R.S. Prussia, art glass, toys

Frost, Donald M.
Country Estate Antiques
690 Lower Cleveland Rapids Rd., Roseburg, 97470; 503-672-7613. Specializing in fine glass and porcelain

Geddes, Marjorie
Beaverton, 503-649-1041. Specializing in sewing items, butter pats, egg cups, miscellaneous small and elegant collectibles

Miller, Don & Robby
P.O. Box 508, Talent, 97504; 503-535-1231

Morris, Thomas G.
Prize Publishers
P.O. Box 8307, Medford, 97504; 503-779-3164. Author of *The Carnival Chalk Prize*, a pictorial price guide on carnival chalkware figures with brief histories and values for each

Schroeder, George
Schroeder & Sons Antiques
23305 S. Pacific Hwy., #43, Medford, 97501; 535-2670. Specializing in sports memorabilia

The Sterling Shop
Box 595, Silverton, 97381; 503-873-6315. Specializing in silver

Worth, Veryl Marie (25 years in mail order)
76248 Gale St., P.O. Box 601, Oakridge, 97463; 503-782-2703. Specializing in Blue and White China, Blue Onion, Willow, Liberty Blue, Flow Blue

Pennsylvania

Atkinson, Phil & Karol
903 Apache Trail, Mercer, 16137; 412-475-2490. Specializing in antique advertising, country store collectibles

Barker, Jim
Toastermaster Antique Appliances
P.O. Box 592, Hawley, 18428; 717-253-1951. Specializing in electric toasters and appliances

Barrett, Noel
Rosebud Antiques
P.O. Box 1001, Carversville, 18913; 215-297-5109. Specializing in toys

Bodine, Clarence H., Jr., Proprietor
East/West Gallery
41B Ferry St., New Hope, 18938; 908-782-3430. Specializing in antique Japanese woodblock prints, netsuke, inro, tsuba

Cerebro
P.O. Box 1221, Lancaster, 17603; 717-656-7875 or 800-69-LABEL. Specializing in antique advertising labels, especially cigar box labels, cigar bands, food labels

Cohen, Bea
Box 825, Easton, 18044-0825; 215-252-1098. Specializing in spatterware, Gaudy Dutch, mocha, chalkware, Dedham, spongeware, Canton, textiles

Damaska, Ron
738 9th Ave, New Brighton, 15066; 412-843-1393. Specializing in match holders

DLK Nostalgia & Collectibles
P.O. Box 5112, Johnstown, 15904. Specializing in corkscrews and openers, Art Deco, clocks, toys, breweriana, miscellaneous

Gyugyi, Dr. Laszlo
P.O. Box 17329, Pittsburgh, 15235. Specializing in Zsolnay art pottery

Holland, William
William Holland Fine Arts
1708 E. Lancaster Ave., Suite 133, Paoli, 19301; 215-648-0369; FAX: 215-647-4448. Specializing in Louis Icart etchings and oils, Art Nouveau and Art Deco items. Author: Louis Icart: The Complete Etchings

Kamm, George
George Kamm Paperweights
508 Lafayette St., Lancaster 17603; 717-299-1169. Specializing in paperweights — color brochure published 4-5 times a year; $5 1-time charge

Kelly, Kathy
The Kelly Collection
1621 Princess Ave., Pittsburgh, 15216; 412-561-3379. Buying Phoenix glass and related items, glass company catalogs, trade journals, Monaca PA post cards

Krause, Gail
994 Jefferson Ave., Washington, 15301. Author book on Duncan glass

Lindsay, Ralph
P.O. Box 21, New Holland, 17557. Specializing in target balls

Locke, Ken & Phyllis
Locke Art Glass
825 6th St., Patt. Heights, Beaver Falls, 15010; 412-846-4393. Specializing in Locke art glass

Maier, Clarence & Betty
Mail order: The Burmese Cruet
Box 432, Montgomeryville, 18936; 215-855-5388. Specializing in Victorian art glass. SASE required with correspondence

Posner, Judy
R.D.1, Box 273, Effort, 18330; 717-629-6583. Specializing in figural pottery, cookie jars, salt and peppers, Black memorabilia, Disneyana

Rosso, Philip J. & Philip Jr.
Wholesale Glass Dealers
1815 Trimble Avenue, Port Vue, 15133; 412-678-7352. Specializing in Westmoreland glass

Weiser, Pastor Frederick S.
55 Kohler School Rd., New Oxford, 17350; 717-624-4106. Specializing in frakturs

Rhode Island

Dumont, Louise
579 Old Main St., Coventry, 02816; 401-828-2799. Specializing in cookie jars, pottery: Hull and Shawnee

The Occupied Japan Club
c/o Florence Archambault
29 Freeborn St., Newport, 02840. Publishes monthly newsletter, The Upside Down World of an O.J. Collector. SASE required when requesting information

Tennessee

Price, Gene
Railroad Antiques
Box 278, Erwin, 37650. Specializing in railroadiana

Texas

Dockery, Rod
4600 Kemble St., Ft. Worth, 76103; 817-536-2168. Specializing in milk glass; SASE required with correspondence

Docks, L.R.'Les'
Shellac Shack; Discollector
Box 691035, San Antonio, 78269-1035. Author of American Premium Record Guide. Specializing in vintage records

Frese, Leo & Wendy
Three Rivers Collectibles
Box 551542, Dallas, 75355; 214-341-5165. Specializing in Rumrill pottery, Red Wing pottery and stoneware, Hull pottery

Gaston, Mary Frank
Box 342, Bryan, 77806. Author Collector Books on china and metals

Malowanczyk, Abby & Wlodek
Collage
4130 Proton Dr., #45D, Dallas, 75244; 214-233-1523. Specializing in Art Deco and mid-century classic furniture; Scandinavian and Italian art glass

Norris, Kenn
Schoolmaster Auctions
P.O. Box 4830, 208 Kerr St., Sanderson, 79848; 915-345-2640. Specializing in school-related items and barbed wire

Phillips, Mark
Sunshine Records
2425 S. 11th St. Beaumont, 77701; 409-835-4438. Specializing in records and Rock 'n Roll memorabilia

Sack, Gordon
10914 Shawnbrook, Houston, 77071; 713-995-6577. Specializing in cartoon books (not comics)

Smith, Allan
1806 Shields Dr., Sherman, 75090; 903-893-3626. Specializing in children's lunch boxes and all types of advertising, especially Coca-Cola, Dr. Pepper, Pepsi Cola, RC Cola, Red Goose, Buster Brown Shoes, character tin wind-up toys, and western stars' items

Thompson, Chuck
Chuck Thompson & Associates
P.O. Box 11652, Houston, 77293. Specializing in food-related items of the Old West. Speaks and writes on the subject

Tucker, Richard & Valerie
Argyle Antiques
P.O. Box 262, Argyle, 76226; 817-464-3752. Specializing in windmill weights, shooting gallery targets, and other figural cast iron

Walker, Jimmy & Carol
The Iron Lady
501 N. 5th, Waelder, 78959; 512-665-7166. Specializing in pressing irons

Wood, Anita
Anita's End
1412 Alamosa, Odessa, 79763; 915-337-1297. Specializing in Depression Glass

Utah

Anderson, Tim
Box 461, Provo, 84603; 801-226-1787. Specializing in autographs: buys single items or collections — historical, movie stars, Mormons, sports figures, etc.

Anderson, Warren R.
America West Archives
P.O. Box 100, Cedar City, 84721. Specializing in old stock certificates and bonds, western documents and books, financial ephemera, autographs, maps, prints

Vermont

Barry, Kit
143 Main St., Brattleboro, 05301. Author of The Advertising Trade Card. Specializing in advertising trade cards and ephemera in general

Virginia

Bradfield, Jeff
Jeff's Antiques
Corner of Rt. 42 & Rt. 257, Dayton, 22821; 703-879-9961. Also located in Rocky's Antique Mall (I-81), Exit 60, Weyers Cove. Specializing in post cards, candy containers, toys, pottery, furniture, lamps, and advertising items

Flanigan, Vicki
Flanigan's Antiques
P.O. Box 1662, Winchester, 22601. Specializing in antique dolls and hand fans

Friend, Terry
R.R. 4, Box 152-D, Galax, 24333; 703-236-9027 after 9:30 p.m. EST. Specializing in coffee mills. SASE required

Kenney, Ed
Audubon Prints & Books
9720 Spring Ridge Lane, Vienna, 22182; 703-759-5567. Specializing in Audubon and other natural history antique prints

Lechner, Mildred & Ralph
Box 554, Mechanicsville, 23111; 804-737-3347. Author Collector Books on glass salt shakers. Specializing in art and pattern glass salt shakers circa 1870-1940. Directors of Antique and Art Glass Salt Shakers Society Club, 1991-92

Monsen, Randall; Baer, Rod
Cocktails & Laughter Antiques
P.O. Box 1503, Arlington, 22210; 703-938-2129. Specializing in perfume bottles, Roseville pottery, Art Deco

Reynolds, Charles
Reynolds Toys
2836 Monroe St., Falls Church, 22042; 703-533-1322. Specializing in limited edition mechanical and still banks, figural bottle openers

Washington

George, Tony
16212 Bothell Way S.E. #F215, Mill Creek, 98012; 206-483-6074. Specializing in watch fobs

Haase, Don (Mr. Spode)
D&D Antiques
P.O. Box 818, Mukilteo, 92875; 206-348-7443. Specializing in Spode china

Haynes, Bob
House of Haynes Antiques
P.O. Box 6842, Bellevue, 98008; 206-641-5198 or 800-321-5198. Specializing in Royal Doulton and Moorcroft

Rothe, Linda
P.O. Box 27374, Seattle, 98125-1874. Specializing in Black Americana

West Virginia

Fostoria Glass Society of America Inc.
Box 826, Moundsville, 26041. Specializing in Fostoria glass

Wisconsin

Apple, John
John Apple Antiques
1720 College Ave., Racine, 53403; 414-633-308. Specializing in brass cash registers and parts

Fortney, Daniel
Suite 713 Chalet at the River, 823 N. 2nd St., Milwaukee, 53203. Specializing in china and glass

Goldmine Magazine
700 E. State St., Iola, 54990; 715-445-2214. Specializing in collectible records

Matzke, Gene
Gene's Badges & Emblems
2345 S. 28th St., Milwaukee, 53215; 414-383-8995. Specializing in police badges, leg irons, old police photos, fire badges (old), patches, and memorabilia

Rice, Ferill J.
302 Pheasant Run, Kaukauna, 54130. Specializing in Fenton art glass

America West Archives
Anderson, Warren
P.O. Box 100, Cedar City, Utah, 84721. 26-page illustrated catalogs issued quarterly. Has both fixed-price and auction sections offering early western documents, letters, stock certificates, autographs, and other important ephemera. 1-year subscription: $10.00

Antique & Art Glass Salt Shaker Collectors' Society (AAGSSCS)
2832 Rapidan Trail, Maitland, FL 32751

Antique & Art Glass Salt Shaker Collectors' Society, c/o Albert Mills, Secretary/Treasurer, 348 N. Hamilton St., Painted Post, NY 14870

Antique Radio Club of America
81 Steeplechase Rd., Devon, PA 19333

Antique Souvenir Collectors' News
Gary Leveille, Editor
P.O. Box 562, Great Barrington, MA 01230

Antique Stove Association
Clifford Boram, Secretary
417 N. Main St., Monticello, IN 47960. Inquiries should be accompanied by SASE and marked 'Urgent' in red

Antique Wireless Association
Ormiston Rd., Breesport, NY 14816

Antique Woodworking Power Tool Assn.
Walt Vinoski, Editor/Publisher
P.O. Box 1027, Connellville, PA 15425. Information requires SASE

Arts & Crafts Quarterly
P.O. Box 3592, Station E
Trenton, NJ 08629
1-800-541-5787

Avon Collectors' Club
Western World
c/o Floyd or Ellen Busby
P.O. Box 23785, Dept P
Pleasant Hill, CA 94523. Information requires LSASE

Avon Times
c/o Dwight or Vera Young
P.O. Box 9868, Dept. P
Kansas City, MO 64134. Information requires LSASE

Black Memorabilia Catalog
Judy Posner
R.D. 1, Box 273 SC, Effort, PA 18830.
Send $1 and LSASE

British Royal Commemorative Souvenirs
Mail Order Catalog
Audrey Zeder
6755 Coralite St. S, Long Beach, CA 90808

Butter Pat Collectors' Notebook
c/o 5955 S.W. 179th Ave, Beaverton, OR 97007.
Send LSASE for subscription information

California Perfume Company
For information contact Dick Pardini
3107 North El Dorado St., Dept. SAPG, Stockton, CA 95204. Information requires LSASE; not necessary when offering items for sale

Candy Container Collectors of America
P.O. Box 1088
Washington, PA 15301

The Cane Collector's Chronicle
Linda Beeman
15 Second St. N.E., Washington, D.C. 20002; $30 for 4 issues

The Carousel News & Trader
87 Parke Ave., W., Suite 206, Mansfield, OH 44902. A monthly magazine for the carousel enthusiast. Subscription: $22 per year, sample $3

Central Florida Insulator Collectors
3557 Nicklaus Dr., Titusville, FL 32780

Character Collectibles Catalog
Judy Posner
R.D. #1, Box 273 SC, Effort, PA 18330.
Send $1 and LSASE

Chicagoland Antique Advertizing
Slot Machine & Jukebox Gazette
Ken Durham, Editor
P.O. Box 2426, Dept. S, Rockville, MD 20852. 20-page newspaper published twice a year. Subscription: 4 issues for $10; sample $5

Coin-Op Newsletter
Ken Durham, Publisher
909 26th St. NW, Washington, DC 20037
Subscription (10 issues) $24, sample issue $5

The Cola Clan
Alice Fisher, Treasurer
2084 Continental Drive N.E., Atlanta, GA 30345

Cookie Jar Catalog
Judy Posner
R.D. #1, Box 273 SC, Effort, PA 18330.
Send $1 and LSASE

Cookie Jarrin' with Joyce: The Cookie Jar Newsletter
R.R. #2, Box 504, Walterboro, SC 29488

Cutting Edge
Adrienne S. Escoe, Editor
P.O. Box 342, Los Alamitos, CA 90720. Newsletter of glass knife collectors, published quarterly. Subscription: $2.50 per year, 50¢ for sample

Depression Glass Daze
12135 N. State St., Otisville, MI 48463

DISCoveries Magazine
P.O. Box 255, Port Townsend, WA 98368-2923 Specializing in collectible records, international distribution

Disneyana Catalog
Judy Posner
R.D. #1, Box 273 SC, Effort, PA 18330.
Send $1 and LSASE

Docks, L.R. 'Les'
Shellac Shack
Box 691035, San Antonio, TX, 78269-1035. Send $2 for a 72-page catalog of thousands of 78s that Docks wants to buy, the prices he will pay, and shipping instructions

Doyle Auctioneers & Appraisers
Doyle, Robert A.
R.D. 3, Box 137, Osborne Hill Rd., Fishkill, NY 12524; 914-896-9492. Thousands of collectibles offered; call for free calendar of upcoming auctions

Fenton Art Glass Collectors of America Inc.
Williamstown, WV 26187

Figural Bottle Opener Collectors
c/o Barbara Rosen
6 Shoshone Trail, Wayne, NJ 07470

Fostoria Glass Society of America Inc.
P.O. Box 826, Moundsville, WV 26041

Full House Antique Playing Cards & Gambling Memorabilia
9320 Laurel Green Dr., Boynton Beach, FL, 33437; 407-734-8690. Mail auction catalogs; will date and price cards — include SASE

George Kamm Paperweights
508 Lafayette St., Lancaster, 17603; 717-299-1169. Specializing in paperweights — color brochure published 4 to 5 times a year. $5 one-time charge

The Glaze, Pottery Collectors' Newsletter
P.O. Box 4782, Birmingham, AL 35706

Gonder Pottery Collectors' Newsletter
c/o John & Marilyn McCormick
8005 Perry, Apt #103, Overland Park, KS 66204

Hake's Americana & Collectibles
Specializing in character and personality collectibles along with artifacts of popular culture for over 20 years. To receive a catalog for their next 3,000-item mail/phone bid auction, send $3.00 to Hake's Americana, P.O. Box 1444M, York, PA, 17405

Heisey Collectors of America Inc.
National Heisey Glass Museum
169 W. Church St., Newark, OH 43055; 614-345-2932

Ice Screamer
c/o Ed Marks, Publisher
P.O. Box 5387, Lancaster, PA 17601. Published bimonthly, $15 for 1 year's dues; annual convention late June

Indiana Historical Radio Society
245 N. Oakland Ave., Indianapolis, IN 46201

International Club for Collectors of Hatpins & Hatpin Holders (ICC of H&HH)
Lillian Baker, Founder
15237 Chanera Ave., Gardena, CA 90249; 213-329-2619. Monthly *Points* newsletter and *Pictorial Journal*

International Society of Antique Scale Collectors
Bob Stein, President
111 N. Canal St., Suite 380, Chicago, IL 60606. Publishes quarterly magazine

Loose Change Magazine
Jackie Durham, Agent
909 26th St. NW, Washington, DC, 20037. Subscription: 10 issues for $39 (payable to Jackie Durham)

Mechanical Music Center
Mayer, Fran
Bridgeport, CT 203-332-7815. Illustrated catalogs of mechanical musical instruments for sale, $5 annual subscription

Metropolis Quarterly Catalog (comics)
7 W. 18th St., New York, NY 10011. $4 annual subscription

Mystic Lights of the Aladdin Knights newsletter, bimonthly
c/o J.W. Courter
R.R. 1, Simpson, IL 62985; 618-949-3883. Information requires LSASE

National Association of Avon Collectors
c/o Bill Armstrong
P.O. Box 68, Dept. P
West Newton, IN 46183. Information requires LSASE

National Association of Miniature Enthusiasts (N.A.M.E.)
Box 2621, Anaheim, CA 92804-0621; (714) 871-NAME

National Autumn Leaf Collectors' Club
c/o Woody Griffith
4107 White Ash Rd., Crystal Lake, IL 60014; 815-459-7808

National Blue Ridge Newsletter
Norma Lilly
144 Highland Dr., Blountville, TN 37617. $12 per year (6 issues)

National Cambridge Collectors Inc.
P.O. Box 416, Cambridge, OH 43725

National Graniteware Society
P.O. Box 10013, Cedar Rapids, IA 52410

National Greentown Glass Association
1807 W. Madison, Kokomo, IN 46901

National Imperial Glass Collectors' Society
P.O. Box 534, Bellaire, OH 43906

National Insulator Association #256
3557 Nicklaus Dr., Titusville, FL 32780

National Milk Glass Collectors' Society and Quarterly Newsletter
c/o Arlene Johnson, Treasurer
1113 Birchwood Dr., Garland, TX 75043. Please include SASE

National Reamer Association
c/o Larry Branstad, R.R. 3, Box 67, Frederic, WI 54837

National Toothpick Holder Collectors' Society
c/o Joyce Ender, Box 246, Sawyer, Michigan, 49125. Annual dues are $10 for single or $15 per couple which includes monthly *Toothpick Bulletin*. Annual convention held in August

New England Society of Open Salt Collectors
Mrs. Ruth Arch, Treasurer
Stoneridge Estates, 9 Casey Circle, Waltham, MA 02154. Dues $5

Newspaper Collectors' Society of America
Rick Brown
Box 19134-S, Lansing, MI 48901; 517-372-8381; FAX: 517-485-9115

North America Torquay Society
Beth Pulsipher, Co-ordinator
P.O. Box 373, Schoolcraft, MI 49087-0373; 616-679-4195

North American Trap Collectors' Association
c/o Tom Parr
P.O. Box 94, Galloway, OH 43119-0094. Dues: $7.50 per year. Newsletter published 6 times a year

The Occupied Japan Club
c/o Florence Archambault
29 Freeborn St., Newport, RI 02840
Publishes *The Upside Down World of an O.J. Collector*, a monthly newsletter. Information requires SASE

Old Storefront Antiques
P.O. Box 357, Dublin, IN 47335; 317-478-4809. Publishes catalogs on store items, primitives, advertising, profession-related, etc. Each is available for $1.50 or all 17 for $17 postpaid. Include LSASE

Open Salt Collectors of the Atlantic Regions (O.S.C.A.R.)
Lee Anne Gommer, 56 Northview Dr., Lancaster, PA 17601. Dues $5

Open Salt Seekers of the West, Northern California Chapter
Verna Boller, 1552 Bicardy, Stockton, CA 95203. Dues $5

Open Salt Seekers of the West, Southern California Chapter
Marie Smith, Treasurer, 4208 Country Club Dr., Bakersville, CA 93306. Dues $5

Our McCoy Matters
Kathy Lynch, Editor
12704 Lockleven Lane, Woodbridge, VA 22192; 703-590-0274. Subscription: $19 for 6 issues, sample copy: $4

Paperweight Collectors' Association
P.O. Box 468, Garden City Park, NY 11040; 516-741-3090. Membership: $15 per person, $25 per couple; 6 newsletters per year; bi-annual conventions. To promote and study paperweights

Pen Fancier's Club
1169 Overcash Dr., Dunedin, FL 34698. Publishes monthly magazine of pens and mechanical pencils. Yearly subscription rate: $45, sample copy: $4

Perfume & Scent Bottle Collectors
Jeane Parris
2022 E. Charleston Blvd., Las Vegas, NV 89104; 702-385-6059. Membership of $15 USA ($30 Foreign) includes an informative quarterly newsletter. Information requires SASE

Phoenix Bird Collectors of America (PBCA) Dues payable to Joan Oates
5912 Kingsfield, MI 48322; 313-661-2335. $10 a year includes a newsletter, *Phoenix Bird Discoveries* , 3 times a year

Pie Birds Unlimited newsletter
Lillian M. Cole, 14 Harmony School Rd., Flemington, NJ 08822; 908-782-3198. Specializing in pie birds, pie funnels, pie vents

Postcard Mail Auctions
Run by Mrs. Sally S. Carver, 179 South St., Chestnut Hill, MA 02167; 617-469-9175. Specializing in all better quality pre-1930 postcards; large illustrated auction published yearly. $5 charge for auction, no consignment accepted. No new subscribers accepted at this time

Precious Collectibles magazine for Precious Moments figurine collectors, *The Ornament Collector* magazine for Hallmark ornaments and other ornaments, and the *Collectors' Bulletin* magazine for all Limited Edition collectibles. Rosie Wells Enterprises, Inc. R.R. 1S, Canton, IL 61520. Write for free literature on *The Secondary Market Price Guide for Precious Moments Collectibles, The Secondary Price Guide for Hallmark Ornaments* , and *The Secondary Market Price Guide for Enesco Treasury of Christmas Ornaments*. Rosie also has an informational secondary market price guide for Lowell Davis collectors

R. Lalique — listings of items for sale
John Danis
11028 Raleigh Ct., Rockford, IL 61111; 815-963-0757; FAX: 815-877-6042

Roseville's of the Past newsletter
Jack Bomm, Editor
P.O. Box 1018, Apopka, FL 32704-1018. $19.95 per year for 6 to 12 newsletters

Salt & Pepper Catalog
Judy Posner
R.D. #1, Box 273 SC, Effort, PA 18330. Send $1 and LSASE (2 stamps)

Shawnee Pottery Collectors' Club
1100 3rd Ave, New Smyrna Beach, FL 32169. Membership is $19.95 per year (including monthly newsletter). Please send SASE when requesting package for membership. Optional: send $3 and SASE to Pamela Curran in care of above address for sample of current newsletter

Stretch Glass Society
P.O. Box 770643, Lakewood, OH 44107. Annual dues: $8; quarterly newsletter, annual convention

Susie Cooper Catalogs
J. David Ehrhard
Psycho-Ceramic Restorations
1336 Sutherland St., Los Angeles, CA 90026; 213-481-3956

Southern Folk Pottery Collectors Society
Roy M. Thompson, Jr., Founder
1224 Main Street, Glastonbury, CT 06033; 203-659-3965.

Surveyors Historical Society Identification Committee
D.R. Beeks
P.O. Box 2515, Coeur d'Alene, ID, 83814; 208-667-0830

Table Toppers
1340 West Irving Park Rd., P.O. Box 161, Chicago, 60613; 312-769-3184. Individual membership is $18 per year, which includes *Table Topics*, a bi-monthly newsletter for those who appreciate and enjoy spreading information about table-top collectibles and the multiple ways in which they can be used and enjoyed

Tea Leaf Club International
P.O. Box 904, Mt. Prospect, IL 60056. Publishes *Tea Leaf Reading* newsletter, sent to all members as part of membership fee. $20 for single membership, $25 for double membership per year

Tea Talk
Tina M. Carter, teapot columnist
Diana Rosen & Lucy Roman, Editors
419 N. Larchmont Blvd., Los Angeles, CA 90004; 213-652-9306. Annual subscription rate: $17.95; sample: $2

Thermometer Collectors' Club of America
Warren D. Harris, President
6130 Rampart Dr., Carmichael, CA 95608; 916-966-3490

Thimble Collectors International
6411 Montego Rd.
Louisville, KY 40228

Three Rivers Depression Era Glass Society
Meetings held 1st Monday of each month in Pittsburgh, PA; for more information contact Nancy Zamborsky, 4038 Willett Rd., Pittsburgh, PA 15227; 412-882-1989

Tiffin Glass Collectors
P.O. Box 554, Tiffin, OH 44883
Meetings at Seneca Cty. Museum on 2nd Tuesday of each month

Tops & Bottoms Club (Rene Lalique perfumes only)
c/o Madeleine France
P.O. Box 15555, Plantation, FL 33318

Torquay Pottery Collectors' Society
Jerry & Gerry Kline, members
604 Orchard View Dr., Maumee, OH 43537

Toy Gun Collectors of America
Jim Buskirk, Secretary and Editor of newsletter
430-B N. Lakeview, Suite 704, Anaheim, CA 92807

The Trade Card Journal
Kit Barry
86 High St., Brattleboro, VT 05301. A quarterly publication on the social and historical use of trade cards

UHL Collectors' Society
Roger Shelton, President
607 Willow Dr., Shelbyville, IN 46176. For membership or newsletter information contact Sue Uhl Maynard, 3570 Candlewood, Corona, CA 91719. Information requires SASE

Vernon Views newsletter
P.O. Box 945, Scottsdale, AZ 85252. Published quarterly beginning with the spring issue, $6 per year

Walking Stick Notes
Cecil Curtis, Editor
4051 E. Olive Rd., Pensacola, FL 32514. Quarterly publication with limited distribution

Wheeler-Tanner Escapes
P.O. Box 349, Great Falls, Montana 59403. 40-page catalog of magician/escape artist equipment from trick and regulation handcuffs, padlocks, leg shackles, straight jackets to picks, and pick sets. Books on all of the above and much more. Catalog: $3

The Whimsey Club
c/o Christopher Davis
522 Woodhill, Newark, NY 14513. *Whimsical Notions* newsletter published quarterly, dues: $5 per year. Annual meeting in Rochester, NY, in April during Genessee Valley Bottle Collectors' Show

World's Fair Collectors' Society, Inc.
P.O. Box 20806, Sarasota, FL 34238; 813-923-2590. Publishes monthly *Fair News* newsletter. Michael R. Pender, Editor. Dues: (including subscription to *Fair News*) $12 per year in U.S.A., $13 in Canada, and $20 for overseas members

Books on Antiques and Collectibles

Most of the following books are available from your local book seller or antique dealer, or on loan from your public library. If you are unable to locate certain titles in your area you may order by mail from COLLECTOR BOOKS, P.O. Box 3009, Paducah, KY 42002-3009. Add $2.00 for postage for the first book ordered and $.30 for each additional book. Include item number, title and price when ordering. Allow 14 to 21 days for delivery. All books are well illustrated and contain current values.

Books on Glass and Pottery

1810	American Art Glass, Shuman	$29.95
2016	Bedroom & Bathroom Glassware of the Depression Years	$19.95
1312	Blue & White Stoneware, McNerney	$9.95
1959	Blue Willow, 2nd Ed., Gaston	$14.95
1627	Children's Glass Dishes, China & Furniture II, Lechler	$19.95
1892	Collecting Royal Haeger, Garmon	$19.95
1373	Collector's Ency of American Dinnerware, Cunningham	$24.95
2133	Collector's Ency. of Cookie Jars, Roerig	$24.95
2017	Collector's Ency. of Depression Glass, 9th Ed., Florence	$19.95
2209	Collector's Ency. of Fiesta, 7th Ed., Huxford	$19.95
1439	Collector's Ency. of Flow Blue China, Gaston	$19.95
1961	Collector's Ency. of Fry Glass, Fry Glass Society	$24.95
2086	Collector's Ency. of Gaudy Dutch & Welsh, Schuman	$14.95
1813	Collector's Ency. of Geisha Girl Porcelain, Litts	$19.95
1915	Collector's Ency. of Hall China, 2nd Ed., Whitmyer	$19.95
1358	Collector's Ency. of McCoy Pottery, Huxford	$19.95
1039	Collector's Ency. of Nippon Porcelain I, Van Patten	$19.95
2089	Collector's Ency. of Nippon Porcelain II, Van Patten	$24.95
1665	Collector's Ency. of Nippon Porcelain III, Van Patten	$24.95
1447	Collector's Ency. of Noritake, Van Patten	$19.95
1037	Collector's Ency. of Occupied Japan I, Florence	$14.95
1038	Collector's Ency. of Occupied Japan II, Florence	$14.95
1719	Collector's Ency. of Occupied Japan III, Florence	$14.95
2019	Collector's Ency. of Occupied Japan IV, Florence	$14.95
1715	Collector's Ency. of R.S. Prussia II, Gaston	$24.95
1034	Collector's Ency. of Roseville Pottery, Huxford	$19.95
1035	Collector's Ency. of Roseville Pottery, 2nd Ed., Huxford	$19.95
1623	Coll. Guide to Country Stoneware & Pottery, Raycraft	$9.95
2077	Coll. Guide Country Stone. & Pottery, 2nd Ed., Raycraft	$14.95
1523	Colors in Cambridge, National Cambridge Society	$19.95
1425	Cookie Jars, Westfall	$9.95
1843	Covered Animal Dishes, Grist	$14.95
1844	Elegant Glassware of the Depression Era, 4th Ed., Florence	$19.95
2024	Kitchen Glassware of the Depression Years, 4th Ed., Florence	$19.95
1465	Haviland Collectibles & Art Objects, Gaston	$19.95
1917	Head Vases Id & Value Guide, Cole	$14.95
1392	Majolica Pottery, Katz-Marks	$9.95
1669	Majolica Pottery, 2nd Series, Katz-Marks	$9.95
1919	Pocket Guide to Depression Glass, 7th Ed., Florence	$9.95
1438	Oil Lamps II, Thuro	$19.95
1670	Red Wing Collectibles, DePasquale	$9.95
1440	Red Wing Stoneware, DePasquale	$9.95
1958	So. Potteries Blue Ridge Dinnerware, 3rd Ed., Newbound	$14.95
2221	Standard Carnival Glass, 3rd Ed., Edwards	$24.95
2222	Standard Carnival Glass Price Guide, 1991, 8th Ed., Edwards	$7.95
1814	Wave Crest, Glass of C.F. Monroe, Cohen	$29.95
1848	Very Rare Glassware of the Depression Years, Florence	$24.95
2140	Very Rare Glassware of the Depression Years, Second Series	$24.95

Books on Dolls & Toys

1887	American Rag Dolls, Patino	$14.95
2079	Barbie Fashion, Vol. 1, 1959-1967, Eames	$24.95
1514	Character Toys & Collectibles 1st Series, Longest	$19.95
1750	Character Toys & Collectibles, 2nd Series, Longest	$19.95
2021	Collectible Male Action Figures, Manos	$14.95
1529	Collector's Ency. of Barbie Dolls, DeWein	$19.95
1066	Collector's Ency. of Half Dolls, Marion	$29.95
2151	Collector's Guide to Tootsietoys, Richter	$14.95
2082	Collector's Guide to Magazine Paper Dolls, Young	$14.95
1891	French Dolls in Color, 3rd Series, Smith	$14.95
1631	German Dolls, Smith	$9.95
1635	Horsman Dolls, Gibbs	$19.95
1067	Madame Alexander Collector's Dolls, Smith	$19.95
2025	Madame Alexander Price Guide #16, Smith	$7.95
2185	Modern Collector's Dolls, Vol. I, Smith, 1991 Values	$17.95
2186	Modern Collector's Dolls, Vol. II, Smith, 1991 Values	$17.95
2187	Modern Collector's Dolls, Vol. III, Smith, 1991 Values	$17.95
2188	Modern Collector's Dolls, Vol. IV, Smith, 1991 Values	$17.95
2189	Modern Collector's Dolls Vol. V, Smith, 1991 Values	$17.95
1540	Modern Toys, 1930-1980, Baker	$19.95

2218	Patricia Smith Doll Values, Antique to Modern, 7th Ed.	$12.95
1886	Stern's Guide to Disney	$14.95
2139	Stern's Guide to Disney, 2nd Series	$14.95
1513	Teddy Bears & Steiff Animals, Mandel	$9.95
1817	Teddy Bears & Steiff Animals, 2nd, Mandel	$19.95
2084	Teddy Bears, Annalees & Steiff Animals, 3rd, Mandel	$19.95
2028	Toys, Antique & Collectible, Longest	$14.95
1648	World of Alexander-Kins, Smith	$19.95
1808	Wonder of Barbie, Manos	$9.95
1430	World of Barbie Dolls, Manos	$9.95

Other Collectibles

1457	American Oak Furniture, McNerney	$9.95
1846	Antique & Collectible Marbles, Grist, 2nd Ed.	$9.95
1712	Antique & Collectible Thimbles, Mathis	$19.95
1880	Antique Iron, McNerney	$9.95
1748	Antique Purses, Holiner	$19.95
1868	Antique Tools, Our American Heritage, McNerney	$9.95
2015	Archaic Indian Points & Knives, Edler	$14.95
1426	Arrowheads & Projectile Points, Hothem	$7.95
1278	Art Nouveau & Art Deco Jewelry, Baker	$9.95
1714	Black Collectibles, Gibbs	$19.95
1666	Book of Country, Raycraft	$19.95
1960	Book of Country Vol II, Raycraft	$19.95
1811	Book of Moxie, Potter	$29.95
1128	Bottle Pricing Guide, 3rd Ed., Cleveland	$7.95
1751	Christmas Collectibles, Whitmyer	$19.95
1752	Christmas Ornaments, Johnston	$19.95
1713	Collecting Barber Bottles, Holiner	$24.95
2132	Collector's Ency. of American Furniture, Vol. I, Swedberg	$24.95
2018	Collector's Ency. of Graniteware, Greguire	$24.95
2083	Collector's Ency. of Russel Wright Designs, Kerr	$19.95
1634	Coll. Ency. of Salt & Pepper Shakers, Davern	$19.95
2020	Collector's Ency. of Salt & Pepper Shakers II, Davern	$19.95
2134	Collector's Guide to Antique Radios, Bunis	$16.95
1916	Collector's Guide to Art Deco, Gaston	$14.95
1537	Collector's Guide to Country Baskets, Raycraft	$9.95
1437	Collector's Guide to Country Furniture, Raycraft	$9.95
1842	Collector's Guide to Country Furniture II, Raycraft	$14.95
1962	Collector's Guide to Decoys, Huxford	$14.95
1441	Collector's Guide to Post Cards, Wood	$9.95
1629	Doorstops, Id & Values, Betoria	$9.95
1716	Fifty Years of Fashion Jewelry, Baker	$19.95
2213	Flea Market Trader, 7th Ed., Huxford	$9.95
1668	Flint Blades & Proj. Points of the No. Am. Indian, Tully	$24.95
1755	Furniture of the Depression Era, Swedberg	$19.95
2081	Guide to Collecting Cookbooks, Allen	$14.95
1424	Hatpins & Hatpin Holders, Baker	$9.95
1964	Indian Axes & Related Stone Artifacts, Hothem	$14.95
2023	Keen Kutter Collectibles, 2nd Ed., Heuring	$14.95
2216	Kitchen Antiques - 1750-1940, McNerney	$14.95
1181	100 Years of Collectible Jewelry, Baker	$9.95
2137	Modern Guns, Identification & Value Guide, Quertermous	$12.95
1965	Pine Furniture, Our Am. Heritage, McNerney	$14.95
2080	Price Guide to Cookbooks & Recipe Leaflets, Dickinson	$9.95
2164	Primitives, Our American Heritage, McNerney	$9.95
1759	Primitives, Our American Heritage, 2nd Series, McNerney	$14.95
2026	Railroad Collectibles, 4th Ed., Baker	$14.95
1632	Salt & Pepper Shakers, Guarnaccia	$9.95
1888	Salt & Pepper Shakers II, Guarnaccia	$14.95
2220	Salt & Pepper Shakers III, Guarnaccia	$14.95
2141	Schroeder's Antiques Price Guide, 10th Ed.	$12.95
2096	Silverplated Flatware, 4th Ed., Hagan	$14.95
2027	Standard Baseball Card Pr. Gd., Florence	$9.95
1922	Standard Bottle Pr. Gd., Sellari	$14.95
1966	Standard Fine Art Value Guide, Huxford	$29.95
2085	Standard Fine Art Value Guide Vol. 2, Huxford	$29.95
2078	The Old Book Value Guide, 2nd Ed	$19.95
1923	Wanted to Buy	$9.95
1885	Victorian Furniture, McNerney	$9.95